PETERSON'S
GRADUATE PROGRAMS
IN THE
BIOLOGICAL SCIENCES

2011

PETERSON'S
Publishing

About Peterson's Publishing
To succeed on your lifelong educational journey, you will need accurate, dependable, and practical tools and resources. That is why Peterson's is everywhere education happens. Because whenever and however you need education content delivered, you can rely on Peterson's to provide the information, know-how, and guidance to help you reach your goals. Tools to match the right students with the right school. It's here. Personalized resources and expert guidance. It's here. Comprehensive and dependable education content—delivered whenever and however you need it. It's all here.

For more information, contact Peterson's, 2000 Lenox Drive, Lawrenceville, NJ 08648; 800-338-3282 Ext. 54229; or find us online at www.petersonspublishing.com.

Stephen Clemente, Managing Director, Publishing and Institutional Research; Bernadette Webster, Director of Publishing; Jill C. Schwartz, Editor; Ken Britschge, Research Project Manager; Courtney Foust, Amy L. Weber, Research Associates; Phyllis Johnson, Programmer; Ray Golaszewski, Manufacturing Manager; Linda M. Williams, Composition Manager; Karen Mount, Danielle Vreeland, Shannon White, Client Relations Representatives

ISSN 1088-9434
ISBN-13: 978-0-7689-2854-9
ISBN-10: 0-7689-2854-0

Printed in the United States of America

10 9 8 7 6 5 4 3 2 1   13 12 11

Forty-fifth Edition

By producing this book on recycled paper (40% post consumer waste) 77 trees were saved.

CONTENTS

A Note from the Peterson's Editors

The six volumes of Peterson's *Graduate and Professional Programs*, the only annually updated reference work of its kind, provide wide-ranging information on the graduate and professional programs offered by accredited colleges and universities in the United States, U.S. territories, and Canada and by those institutions outside the United States that are accredited by U.S. accrediting bodies. More than 44,000 individual academic and professional programs at more than 2,200 institutions are listed. Peterson's *Graduate and Professional Programs* have been used for more than forty years by prospective graduate and professional students, placement counselors, faculty advisers, and all others interested in postbaccalaureate education.

Graduate & Professional Programs: An Overview contains information on institutions as a whole, while the other books in the series are devoted to specific academic and professional fields:

> *Graduate Programs in the Humanities, Arts & Social Sciences*
> *Graduate Programs in the Biological Sciences*
> *Graduate Programs in the Physical Sciences, Mathematics, Agricultural Sciences, the Environment & Natural Resources*
> *Graduate Programs in Engineering & Applied Sciences*
> *Graduate Programs in Business, Education, Health, Information Studies, Law & Social Work*

The books may be used individually or as a set. For example, if you have chosen a field of study but do not know what institution you want to attend or if you have a college or university in mind but have not chosen an academic field of study, it is best to begin with the Overview guide.

Graduate & Professional Programs: An Overview presents several directories to help you identify programs of study that might interest you; you can then research those programs further in the other books in the series by using the Directory of Graduate and Professional Programs by Field, which lists 500 fields and gives the names of those institutions that offer graduate degree programs in each.

For geographical or financial reasons, you may be interested in attending a particular institution and will want to know what it has to offer. You should turn to the Directory of Institutions and Their Offerings, which lists the degree programs available at each institution. As in the Directory of Graduate and Professional Programs by Field, the level of degrees offered is also indicated.

All books in the series include advice on graduate education, including topics such as admissions tests, financial aid, and accreditation. **The Graduate Adviser** includes two essays and information about accreditation. The first essay, "The Admissions Process," discusses general admission requirements, admission tests, factors to consider when selecting a graduate school or program, when and how to apply, and how admission decisions are made. Special information for international students and tips for minority students are also included. The second essay, "Financial Support," is an overview of the broad range of support available at the graduate level. Fellowships, scholarships, and grants; assistantships and internships; federal and private loan programs, as well as Federal Work-Study; and the GI bill are detailed. This essay concludes with advice on applying for need-based financial aid. "Accreditation and Accrediting Agencies" gives information on accreditation and its purpose and lists institutional accrediting agencies first and then specialized accrediting agencies relevant to each volume's specific fields of study.

With information on more than 44,000 graduate programs in 500 disciplines, Peterson's *Graduate and Professional Programs* give you all the information you need about the programs that are of interest to you in three formats: **Profiles** (capsule summaries of basic information), **Displays** (information that an institution or program wants to emphasize), and **Close-Ups** (written by administrators, with more expansive information than the **Profiles**, emphasizing different aspects of the programs). By using these various formats of program information, coupled with **Appendixes** and **Indexes** covering directories and subject areas for all six books, you will find that these guides provide the most comprehensive, accurate, and up-to-date graduate study information available.

Find Us on Facebook® and Follow Us on Twitter™

Join the grad school conversation on Facebook® and Twitter™ at www.facebook.com/usgradschools and www.twitter.com/usgradschools. Peterson's expert resources are available to help you as you search for the right graduate program for you.

Peterson's publishes a full line of resources with information you need to guide you through the graduate admissions process. Peterson's publications can be found at college libraries and career centers and your local bookstore or library—or visit us on the Web at www.petersonspublishing.com. Peterson's books are now also available as eBooks.

Colleges and universities will be pleased to know that Peterson's helped you in your selection. Admissions staff members are more than happy to answer questions, address specific problems, and help in any way they can. The editors at Peterson's wish you great success in your graduate program search!

THE GRADUATE ADVISER

The Admissions Process

Generalizations about graduate admissions practices are not always helpful because each institution has its own set of guidelines and procedures. Nevertheless, some broad statements can be made about the admissions process that may help you plan your strategy.

Factors Involved in Selecting a Graduate School or Program

Selecting a graduate school and a specific program of study is a complex matter. Quality of the faculty; program and course offerings; the nature, size, and location of the institution; admission requirements; cost; and the availability of financial assistance are among the many factors that affect one's choice of institution. Other considerations are job placement and achievements of the program's graduates and the institution's resources, such as libraries, laboratories, and computer facilities. If you are to make the best possible choice, you need to learn as much as you can about the schools and programs you are considering before you apply.

The following steps may help you narrow your choices.

- Talk to alumni of the programs or institutions you are considering to get their impressions of how well they were prepared for work in their fields of study.
- Remember that graduate school requirements change, so be sure to get the most up-to-date information possible.
- Talk to department faculty members and the graduate adviser at your undergraduate institution. They often have information about programs of study at other institutions.
- Visit the Web sites of the graduate schools in which you are interested to request a graduate catalog. Contact the department chair in your chosen field of study for additional information about the department and the field.
- Visit as many campuses as possible. Call ahead for an appointment with the graduate adviser in your field of interest and be sure to check out the facilities and talk to students.

General Requirements

Graduate schools and departments have requirements that applicants for admission must meet. Typically, these requirements include undergraduate transcripts (which provide information about undergraduate grade point average and course work applied toward a major), admission test scores, and letters of recommendation. Most graduate programs also ask for an essay or personal statement that describes your personal reasons for seeking graduate study. In some fields, such as art and music, portfolios or auditions may be required in addition to other evidence of talent. Some institutions require that the applicant have an undergraduate degree in the same subject as the intended graduate major.

Most institutions evaluate each applicant on the basis of the applicant's total record, and the weight accorded any given factor varies widely from institution to institution and from program to program.

The Application Process

You should begin the application process at least one year before you expect to begin your graduate study. Find out the application deadline for each institution (many are provided in the **Profile** section of this guide). Go to the institution's Web site and find out if you can apply online. If not, request a paper application form. Fill out this form thoroughly and neatly. Assume that the school needs all the information it is requesting and that the admissions officer will be sensitive to the neatness and overall quality of what you submit. Do not supply more information than the school requires.

The institution may ask at least one question that will require a three- or four-paragraph answer. Compose your response on the assumption that the admissions officer is interested in both what you think and how you express yourself. Keep your statement brief and to the point, but, at the same time, include all pertinent information about your past experiences and your educational goals. Individual statements vary greatly in style and content, which helps admissions officers differentiate among applicants. Many graduate departments give considerable weight to the statement in making their admissions decisions, so be sure to take the time to prepare a thoughtful and concise statement.

If recommendations are a part of the admissions requirements, carefully choose the individuals you ask to write them. It is generally best to ask current or former professors to write the recommendations, provided they are able to attest to your intellectual ability and motivation for doing the work required of a graduate student. It is advisable to provide stamped, preaddressed envelopes to people being asked to submit recommendations on your behalf.

Completed applications, including references, transcripts, and admission test scores, should be received at the institution by the specified date.

Be advised that institutions do not usually make admissions decisions until all materials have been received. Enclose a self-addressed postcard with your application, requesting confirmation of receipt. Allow at least ten days for the return of the postcard before making further inquiries.

If you plan to apply for financial support, it is imperative that you file your application early.

ADMISSION TESTS

The major testing program used in graduate admissions is the Graduate Record Examinations (GRE) testing program, sponsored by the GRE Board and administered by Educational Testing Service, Princeton, New Jersey.

The Graduate Record Examinations testing program consists of a General Test and eight Subject Tests. The General Test measures critical thinking, verbal reasoning, quantitative reasoning, and analytical writing skills. It is offered as an Internet-based test (iBT) in the United States, Canada, and many other countries.

The typical computer-based General Test consists of one 30-minute verbal reasoning section, one 45-minute quantitative reasoning sections, one 45-minute issue analysis (writing) section, and one 30-minute argument analysis (writing) section. In addition, an unidentified verbal or quantitative section that doesn't count toward a score may be included and an identified research section that is not scored may also be included.

The Subject Tests measure achievement and assume undergraduate majors or extensive background in the following eight disciplines:

- Biochemistry, Cell and Molecular Biology
- Biology
- Chemistry
- Computer Science
- Literature in English
- Mathematics
- Physics
- Psychology

The Subject Tests are available three times per year as paper-based administrations around the world. Testing time is approximately 2 hours and 50 minutes. You can obtain more information about the GRE by visiting the ETS Web site at www.ets.org or consulting the *GRE Information and Registration Bulletin*. The *Bulletin* can be obtained at many undergraduate colleges. You can also download it from the ETS Web site or obtain it by contacting Graduate Record Examinations, Educational Testing Service, P.O. Box 6000, Princeton, NJ 08541-6000; phone: 609-771-7670.

If you expect to apply for admission to a program that requires any of the GRE tests, you should select a test date well in advance of the application deadline. Scores on the computer-based General Test are reported within ten to fifteen days; scores on the paper-based Subject Tests are reported within six weeks.

Another testing program, the Miller Analogies Test (MAT), is administered at more than 500 Controlled Testing Centers, licensed by Harcourt Assessment, Inc., in the United States, Canada, and other countries. The MAT computer-based test is now available. Testing time is 60 minutes. The test consists of 120 partial analogies. You can obtain the *Candidate Information Booklet,* which contains a list of test centers and instructions for taking the test, from http://www.milleranalogies.com or by calling 800-622-3231 (toll-free).

Check the specific requirements of the programs to which you are applying.

How Admission Decisions Are Made

The program you apply to is directly involved in the admissions process. Although the final decision is usually made by the graduate dean (or an associate) or the faculty admissions committee, recommendations from faculty members in your intended field are important. At some institutions, an interview is incorporated into the decision process.

A Special Note for International Students

In addition to the steps already described, there are some special considerations for international students who intend to apply for graduate study in the United States. All graduate schools require an indication of competence in English. The purpose of the Test of English as a Foreign Language (TOEFL) is to evaluate the English proficiency of people who are nonnative speakers of English and want to study at colleges and universities where English is the language of instruction. The TOEFL is administered by Educational Testing Service (ETS) under the general direction of a policy board established by the College Board and the Graduate Record Examinations Board.

The TOEFL iBT assesses the four basic language skills: listening, reading, writing, and speaking. It was administered for the first time in September 2005, and ETS continues to introduce the TOEFL iBT in selected cities. The Internet-based test is administered at secure, official test centers. The testing time is approximately 4 hours. Because the TOEFL iBT includes a speaking section, the Test of Spoken English (TSE) is no longer needed.

The TOEFL is also offered in the paper-based format in areas of the world where Internet-based testing is not available. The paper-based TOEFL consists of three sections—listening comprehension, structure and written expression, and reading comprehension. The testing time is approximately 3 hours. The Test of Written English (TWE) is also given. The TWE is a 30-minute essay that measures the examinee's ability to compose in English. Examinees receive a TWE score separate from their TOEFL score. The *Information Bulletin* contains information on local fees and registration procedures.

Additional information and registration materials are available from TOEFL Services, Educational Testing Service, P.O. Box 6151, Princeton, New Jersey 08541-6151. Phone: 609-771-7100. Web site: www.toefl.org.

International students should apply especially early because of the number of steps required to complete the admissions process. Furthermore, many United States graduate schools have a limited number of spaces for international students, and many more students apply than the schools can accommodate.

International students may find financial assistance from institutions very limited. The U.S. government requires international applicants to submit a certification of support, which is a statement attesting to the applicant's financial resources. In addition, international students *must* have health insurance coverage.

Tips for Minority Students

Indicators of a university's values in terms of diversity are found both in its recruitment programs and its resources directed to student success. Important questions: Does the institution vigorously recruit minorities for its graduate programs? Is there funding available to help with the costs associated with visiting the school? Are minorities represented in the institution's brochures or Web site or on their faculty rolls? What campus-based resources or services (including assistance in locating housing or career counseling and placement) are available? Is funding available to members of underrepresented groups?

At the program level, it is particularly important for minority students to investigate the "climate" of a program under consideration. How many minority students are enrolled and how many have graduated? What opportunities are there to work with diverse faculty and mentors whose research interests match yours? How are conflicts resolved or concerns addressed? How interested are faculty in building strong and supportive relations with students? "Climate" concerns should be addressed by posing questions to various individuals, including faculty members, current students, and alumni.

Information is also available through various organizations, such as the Hispanic Association of Colleges & Universities (HACU), and publications such as *Diverse Issues in Higher Education* and *Hispanic Outlook* magazine. There are also books devoted to this topic, such as *The Multicultural Student's Guide to Colleges* by Robert Mitchell.

Financial Support

The range of financial support at the graduate level is very broad. The following descriptions will give you a general idea of what you might expect and what will be expected of you as a financial support recipient.

Fellowships, Scholarships, and Grants

These are usually outright awards of a few hundred to many thousands of dollars with no service to the institution required in return. Fellowships and scholarships are usually awarded on the basis of merit and are highly competitive. Grants are made on the basis of financial need or special talent in a field of study. Many fellowships, scholarships, and grants not only cover tuition, fees, and supplies but also include stipends for living expenses with allowances for dependents. However, the terms of each should be examined because some do not permit recipients to supplement their income with outside work. Fellowships, scholarships, and grants may vary in the number of years for which they are awarded.

In addition to the availability of these funds at the university or program level, many excellent fellowship programs are available at the national level and may be applied for before and during enrollment in a graduate program. A listing of many of these programs can be found at the Council of Graduate Schools' Web site: http://www.cgsnet.org. There is a wealth of information in the "Programs" and "Awards" sections.

Assistantships and Internships

Many graduate students receive financial support through assistantships, particularly involving teaching or research duties. It is important to recognize that such appointments should not be viewed simply as employment relationships but rather should constitute an integral and important part of a student's graduate education. As such, the appointments should be accompanied by strong faculty mentoring and increasingly responsible apprenticeship experiences. The specific nature of these appointments in a given program should be considered in selecting that graduate program.

TEACHING ASSISTANTSHIPS

These usually provide a salary and full or partial tuition remission and may also provide health benefits. Unlike fellowships, scholarships, and grants, which require no service to the institution, teaching assistantships require recipients to provide the institution with a specific amount of undergraduate teaching, ideally related to the student's field of study. Some teaching assistants are limited to grading papers, compiling bibliographies, taking notes, or monitoring laboratories. At some graduate schools, teaching assistants must carry lighter course loads than regular full-time students.

RESEARCH ASSISTANTSHIPS

These are very similar to teaching assistantships in the manner in which financial assistance is provided. The difference is that recipients are given basic research assignments in their disciplines rather than teaching responsibilities. The work required is normally related to the student's field of study; in most instances, the assistantship supports the student's thesis or dissertation research.

ADMINISTRATIVE INTERNSHIPS

These are similar to assistantships in application of financial assistance funds, but the student is given an assignment on a part-time basis, usually as a special assistant with one of the university's administrative offices. The assignment may not necessarily be directly related to the recipient's discipline.

RESIDENCE HALL AND COUNSELING ASSISTANTSHIPS

These assistantships are frequently assigned to graduate students in psychology, counseling, and social work, but they may be offered to students in other disciplines, especially if the student has worked in this capacity during his or her undergraduate years. Duties can vary from being available in a dean's office for a specific number of hours for consultation with undergraduates to living in campus residences and being responsible for both counseling and administrative tasks or advising student activity groups. Residence hall assistantships often include a room and board allowance and, in some cases, tuition assistance and stipends. Contact the Housing and Student Life Office for more information.

Health Insurance

The availability and affordability of health insurance is an important issue and one that should be considered in an applicant's choice of institution and program. While often included with assistantships and fellowships, this is not always the case and, even if provided, the benefits may be limited. It is important to note that the U.S. government requires international students to have health insurance.

The GI Bill

This provides financial assistance for students who are veterans of the United States armed forces. If you are a veteran, contact your local Veterans Administration office to determine your eligibility and to get full details about benefits. There are a number of programs that offer educational benefits to current military enlistees. Some states have tuition assistance programs for members of the National Guard. Contact the VA office at the college for more information.

Federal Work-Study Program (FWS)

Employment is another way some students finance their graduate studies. The federally funded Federal Work-Study Program provides eligible students with employment opportunities, usually in public and private nonprofit organizations. Federal funds pay up to 75 percent of the wages, with the remainder paid by the employing agency. FWS is available to graduate students who demonstrate financial need. Not all schools have these funds, and some only award them to undergraduates. Each school sets its application deadline and work-study earnings limits. Wages vary and are related to the type of work done. You must file the Free Application for Federal Student Aid (FAFSA) to be eligible for this program.

Loans

Many graduate students borrow to finance their graduate programs when other sources of assistance (which do not have to be repaid) prove insufficient. You should always read and understand the terms of any loan program before submitting your application.

FEDERAL DIRECT LOANS

Federal Direct Stafford Loans. The Federal Direct Stafford Loan Program offers low-interest loans to students with the Department of Education acting as the lender.

There are two components of the Federal Stafford Loan program. Under the *subsidized* component of the program, the federal government pays the interest on the loan while you are enrolled in graduate school on at least a half-time basis, during the six-month grace period after you drop below half-time enrollment, as well as during any period of deferment. Under the *unsubsidized* component of the program, you pay the interest on the loan from the day proceeds are issued. Eligibility for the federal subsidy is based on demonstrated financial need as determined by the financial aid office from the information you provide on the FAFSA. A cosigner is not required, since the loan is not based on creditworthiness.

Although *unsubsidized* Federal Direct Stafford Loans may not be as desirable as *subsidized* Federal Direct Stafford Loans from the student's perspective, they are a useful source of support for those who may not qualify for the subsidized loans or who need additional financial assistance.

Graduate students may borrow up to $20,500 per year through the Direct Stafford Loan Program, up to a cumulative maximum of $138,500, including undergraduate borrowing. This may include up to $8500 in *subsidized* Direct Stafford Loans annually, depending on eligibility, up to a cumulative maximum of $65,500, including undergraduate borrowing. The amount of the loan borrowed through the *unsubsidized* Direct Stafford Loan Program equals the total amount of the loan (as much as $20,500) minus your eligibility for a *subsidized* Direct Loan (as much as $8500). You may borrow up to the cost of attendance at the school in which you are enrolled or will attend, minus estimated financial assistance from other federal, state, and private sources, up to a maximum of $20,500.

Direct Stafford Loans made on or after July 1, 2006, carry a fixed interest rate of 6.8% both for in-school and in-repayment borrowers.

A fee is deducted from the loan proceeds upon disbursement. Loans with a first disbursement on or after July 1, 2010 have a borrower origination fee of 1 percent. The Department of Education offers a 0.5 percent origination fee rebate incentive. Borrowers must make their first twelve payments on time in order to retain the rebate.

Under the *subsidized* Federal Direct Stafford Loan Program, repayment begins six months after your last date of enrollment on at least a half-time basis. Under the *unsubsidized* program, repayment of interest begins within thirty days from disbursement of the loan proceeds, and repayment of the principal begins six months after your last enrollment on at least a half-time basis. Some borrowers may choose to defer interest payments while they are in school. The accrued interest is added to the loan balance when the borrower begins repayment. There are several repayment options.

Federal Perkins Loans. The Federal Perkins Loan is available to students demonstrating financial need and is administered directly by the school. Not all schools have these funds, and some may award them to undergraduates only. Eligibility is determined from the information you provide on the FAFSA. The school will notify you of your eligibility.

Eligible graduate students may borrow up to $6000 per year, up to a maximum of $40,000, including undergraduate borrowing (even if your previous Perkins Loans have been repaid). The interest rate for Federal Perkins Loans is 5 percent, and no interest accrues while you remain in school at least half-time. There are no guarantee, loan, or disbursement fees. Repayment begins nine months after your last date of enrollment on at least a half-time basis and may extend over a maximum of ten years with no prepayment penalty.

Federal Direct Graduate PLUS Loans. Effective July 1, 2006, graduate and professional students are eligible for Graduate PLUS loans. This program allows students to borrow up to the cost of attendance, less any other aid received. These loans have a fixed interest rate of 7.9 percent, and interest begins to accrue at the time of disbursement. The PLUS loans do involve a credit check; a PLUS borrower may obtain a loan with a cosigner if his or her credit is not good enough. Grad PLUS loans may be deferred while a student in school and for the six months following a drop below half-time enrollment. For more information, contact your college financial aid office.

Deferring Your Federal Loan Repayments. If you borrowed under the Federal Direct Stafford Loan Program, Federal Direct Loan Program, or the Federal Perkins Loan Program for previous undergraduate or graduate study, your repayments may be deferred when you return to graduate school, depending on when you borrowed and under which program.

There are other deferment options available if you are temporarily unable to repay your loan. Information about these deferments is provided at your entrance and exit interviews. If you believe you are eligible for a deferment of your loan repayments, you must contact your lender or loan servicer to request a deferment form. The deferment must be filed prior to the time your repayment is due, and it must be refiled when it expires if you remain eligible for deferment at that time.

SUPPLEMENTAL (PRIVATE) LOANS

Many lending institutions offer supplemental loan programs and other financing plans, such as the ones described here, to students seeking additional assistance in meeting their education expenses. Some loan programs target all types of graduate students; others are designed specifically for business, law, or medical students. In addition, you can use private loans not specifically designed for education to help finance your graduate degree.

If you are considering borrowing through a supplemental or private loan program, you should carefully consider the terms and be sure to "read the fine print." Check with the program sponsor for the most current terms that will be applicable to the amounts you intend to borrow for graduate study. Most supplemental loan programs for graduate study offer unsubsidized, credit-based loans. In general, a credit-ready borrower is one who has a satisfactory credit history or no credit history at all. A creditworthy borrower generally must pass a credit test to be eligible to borrow or act as a cosigner for the loan funds.

Many supplemental loan programs have minimum and maximum annual loan limits. Some offer amounts equal to the cost of attendance minus any other aid you will receive for graduate study. If you are planning to borrow for several years of graduate study, consider whether there is a cumulative or aggregate limit on the amount you may borrow. Often this cumulative or aggregate limit will include any amounts you borrowed and have not repaid for undergraduate or previous graduate study.

The combination of the annual interest rate, loan fees, and the repayment terms you choose will determine how much you will repay over time. Compare these features in combination before you decide which loan program to use. Some loans offer interest rates that are adjusted monthly, some quarterly, some annually. Some offer interest rates that are lower during the in-school, grace, and deferment periods and then increase when you begin repayment. Some programs include a loan "origination" fee, which is usually deducted from the principal amount you receive when the loan is disbursed and must be repaid along with the interest and other principal when you graduate, withdraw from school, or drop below half-time study. Sometimes the loan fees are reduced if you borrow with a qualified cosigner. Some programs allow you to defer interest and/or principal payments while you are enrolled in graduate school. Many programs allow you to capitalize your interest payments; the interest due on your loan is added to the outstanding balance of your loan, so you don't have to repay immediately, but this increases the amount you owe. Other programs allow you to pay the interest as you go, which reduces the amount you later have to repay. The private loan market is very competitive, and your financial aid office can help you evaluate these programs.

Applying for Need-Based Financial Aid

Schools that award federal and institutional financial assistance based on need will require you to complete the FAFSA and, in some cases, an institutional financial aid application.

If you are applying for federal student assistance, you **must** complete the FAFSA. A service of the U.S. Department of Education, the FAFSA is free to all applicants. Most applicants apply online at www.fafsa.ed.gov. Paper applications are available at the financial aid office of your local college.

After your FAFSA information has been processed, you will receive a Student Aid Report (SAR). If you provided an e-mail address on the FAFSA, this will be sent to you electronically; otherwise, it will be mailed to your home address.

Follow the instructions on the SAR if you need to correct information reported on your original application. If your situation changes after you file your FAFSA, contact your financial aid officer to discuss amending your information. You can also appeal your financial aid award if you have extenuating circumstances.

If you would like more information on federal student financial aid, visit the FAFSA Web site or download the most recent version of *Funding Education Beyond High School: The Guide to Federal Student Aid* at http://studentaid.ed.gov/students/publications/student_guide/index.html. This guide is also available in Spanish.

The U.S. Department of Education also has a toll-free number for questions concerning federal student aid programs. The number is 1-800-4-FED AID (1-800-433-3243). If you are hearing impaired, call toll-free, 1-800-730-8913.

Summary

Remember that these are generalized statements about financial assistance at the graduate level. Because each institution allots its aid differently, you should communicate directly with the school and the specific department of interest to you. It is not unusual, for example, to find that an endowment vested within a specific department supports one or more fellowships. You may fit its requirements and specifications precisely.

Accreditation and Accrediting Agencies

Colleges and universities in the United States, and their individual academic and professional programs, are accredited by nongovernmental agencies concerned with monitoring the quality of education in this country. Agencies with both regional and national jurisdictions grant accreditation to institutions as a whole, while specialized bodies acting on a nationwide basis—often national professional associations—grant accreditation to departments and programs in specific fields.

Institutional and specialized accrediting agencies share the same basic concerns: the purpose an academic unit—whether university or program—has set for itself and how well it fulfills that purpose, the adequacy of its financial and other resources, the quality of its academic offerings, and the level of services it provides. Agencies that grant institutional accreditation take a broader view, of course, and examine university-wide or college-wide services with which a specialized agency may not concern itself.

Both types of agencies follow the same general procedures when considering an application for accreditation. The academic unit prepares a self-evaluation, focusing on the concerns mentioned above and usually including an assessment of both its strengths and weaknesses; a team of representatives of the accrediting body reviews this evaluation, visits the campus, and makes its own report; and finally, the accrediting body makes a decision on the application. Often, even when accreditation is granted, the agency makes a recommendation regarding how the institution or program can improve. All institutions and programs are also reviewed every few years to determine whether they continue to meet established standards; if they do not, they may lose their accreditation.

Accrediting agencies themselves are reviewed and evaluated periodically by the U.S. Department of Education and the Council for Higher Education Accreditation (CHEA). Recognized agencies adhere to certain standards and practices, and their authority in matters of accreditation is widely accepted in the educational community.

This does not mean, however, that accreditation is a simple matter, either for schools wishing to become accredited or for students deciding where to apply. Indeed, in certain fields the very meaning and methods of accreditation are the subject of a good deal of debate. For their part, those applying to graduate school should be aware of the safeguards provided by regional accreditation, especially in terms of degree acceptance and institutional longevity. Beyond this, applicants should understand the role that specialized accreditation plays in their field, as this varies considerably from one discipline to another. In certain professional fields, it is necessary to have graduated from a program that is accredited in order to be eligible for a license to practice, and in some fields the federal government also makes this a hiring requirement. In other disciplines, however, accreditation is not as essential, and there can be excellent programs that are not accredited. In fact, some programs choose not to seek accreditation, although most do.

Institutions and programs that present themselves for accreditation are sometimes granted the status of candidate for accreditation, or what is known as "preaccreditation." This may happen, for example, when an academic unit is too new to have met all the requirements for accreditation. Such status signifies initial recognition and indicates that the school or program in question is working to fulfill all requirements; it does not, however, guarantee that accreditation will be granted.

Institutional Accrediting Agencies—Regional

MIDDLE STATES ASSOCIATION OF COLLEGES AND SCHOOLS
Accredits institutions in Delaware, District of Columbia, Maryland, New Jersey, New York, Pennsylvania, Puerto Rico, and the Virgin Islands.
Dr. Elizabeth Sibolski, Acting President
Middle States Commission on Higher Education
3624 Market Street, Second Floor West
Philadelphia, Pennsylvania 19104
Phone: 267-284-5000
Fax: 215-662-5501
E-mail: info@msche.org
Web: www.msche.org

NEW ENGLAND ASSOCIATION OF SCHOOLS AND COLLEGES
Accredits institutions in Connecticut, Maine, Massachusetts, New Hampshire, Rhode Island, and Vermont.
Barbara E. Brittingham, Director
Commission on Institutions of Higher Education
209 Burlington Road, Suite 201
Bedford, Massachusetts 01730-1433
Phone: 781-271-0022
Fax: 781-271-0950
E-mail: CIHE@neasc.org
Web: www.neasc.org

NORTH CENTRAL ASSOCIATION OF COLLEGES AND SCHOOLS
Accredits institutions in Arizona, Arkansas, Colorado, Illinois, Indiana, Iowa, Kansas, Michigan, Minnesota, Missouri, Nebraska, New Mexico, North Dakota, Ohio, Oklahoma, South Dakota, West Virginia, Wisconsin, and Wyoming.
Dr. Sylvia Manning, President
The Higher Learning Commission
230 South LaSalle Street, Suite 7-500
Chicago, Illinois 60604-1413
Phone: 312-263-0456
Fax: 312-263-7462
E-mail: smanning@hlcommission.org
Web: www.ncahigherlearningcommission.org

NORTHWEST COMMISSION ON COLLEGES AND UNIVERSITIES
Accredits institutions in Alaska, Idaho, Montana, Nevada, Oregon, Utah, and Washington.
Dr. Sandra E. Elman, President
8060 165th Avenue, NE, Suite 100
Redmond, Washington 98052
Phone: 425-558-4224
Fax: 425-376-0596
E-mail: selman@nwccu.org
Web: www.nwccu.org

SOUTHERN ASSOCIATION OF COLLEGES AND SCHOOLS
Accredits institutions in Alabama, Florida, Georgia, Kentucky, Louisiana, Mississippi, North Carolina, South Carolina, Tennessee, Texas, and Virginia.
Belle S. Wheelan, President
Commission on Colleges
1866 Southern Lane
Decatur, Georgia 30033-4097
Phone: 404-679-4500
Fax: 404-679-4558
E-mail: questions@sacscoc.org
Web: www.sacsoc.org

WESTERN ASSOCIATION OF SCHOOLS AND COLLEGES
Accredits institutions in California, Guam, and Hawaii.
Ralph A. Wolff, President and Executive Director
Accrediting Commission for Senior Colleges and Universities
985 Atlantic Avenue, Suite 100
Alameda, California 94501
Phone: 510-748-9001
Fax: 510-748-9797
E-mail: www.wascsenior.org
Web: www.wascweb.org/contact

Institutional Accrediting Agencies—Other

ACCREDITING COUNCIL FOR INDEPENDENT COLLEGES AND SCHOOLS
Albert C. Gray, Ph.D., Executive Director and CEO
750 First Street, NE, Suite 980
Washington, DC 20002-4241
Phone: 202-336-6780
Fax: 202-842-2593
E-mail: info@acics.org
Web: www.acics.org

DISTANCE EDUCATION AND TRAINING COUNCIL (DETC)
Accrediting Commission
Michael P. Lambert, Executive Director
1601 18th Street, NW, Suite 2
Washington, DC 20009
Phone: 202-234-5100
Fax: 202-332-1386
E-mail: detc@detc.org
Web: www.detc.org

Specialized Accrediting Agencies

[Only *Graduate & Professional Programs: An Overview* of *Peterson's Graduate and Professional Programs* Series includes the complete list of specialized accrediting groups recognized by the U.S. Department of Education and the Council on Higher Education Accreditation (CHEA). The list in this book is abridged.]

DIETETICS
Ulric K. Chung, Ph.D., Executive Director
American Dietetic Association
Commission on Accreditation for Dietetics Education (CADE-ADA)
120 South Riverside Plaza, Suite 2000
Chicago, Illinois 60606-6995
Phone: 800-877-1600
Fax: 312-899-4817
E-mail: cade@eatright.org
Web: www.eatright.org/cade

How to Use These Guides

As you identify the particular programs and institutions that interest you, you can use both the *Graduate & Professional Programs: An Overview* volume and the specialized volumes in the series to obtain detailed information.

- *Graduate Programs in the Physical Sciences, Mathematics, Agricultural Sciences, the Environment & Natural Resources*
- *Graduate Programs in Engineering & Applied Sciences*
- *Graduate Programs the Humanities, Arts & Social Sciences*
- *Graduate Programs in the Biological Sciences*
- *Graduate Programs in Business, Education, Health, Information Studies, Law & Social Work*

Each of the specialized volumes in the series is divided into sections that contain one or more directories devoted to programs in a particular field. If you do not find a directory devoted to your field of interest in a specific volume, consult "Directories and Subject Areas" (located at the end of each volume). After you have identified the correct volume, consult the "Directories and Subject Areas in This Book" index, which shows (as does the more general directory) what directories cover subjects not specifically named in a directory or section title.

Each of the specialized volumes in the series has a number of general directories. These directories have entries for the largest unit at an institution granting graduate degrees in that field. For example, the general Engineering and Applied Sciences directory in the *Graduate Programs in Engineering & Applied Sciences* volume consists of **Profiles** for colleges, schools, and departments of engineering and applied sciences.

General directories are followed by other directories, or sections, that give more detailed information about programs in particular areas of the general field that has been covered. The general Engineering and Applied Sciences directory, in the previous example, is followed by nineteen sections with directories in specific areas of engineering, such as Chemical Engineering, Industrial/Management Engineering, and Mechanical Engineering.

Because of the broad nature of many fields, any system of organization is bound to involve a certain amount of overlap. Environmental studies, for example, is a field whose various aspects are studied in several types of departments and schools. Readers interested in such studies will find information on relevant programs in the *Graduate Programs in the Biological Sciences* volume under Ecology and Environmental Biology; in the *Graduate Programs in the Physical Sciences, Mathematics, Agricultural Sciences, the Environment & Natural Resources* volume under Environmental Management and Policy and Natural Resources; in the *Graduate Programs in Engineering & Applied Sciences* volume under Energy Management and Policy and Environmental Engineering; and in the *Graduate Programs in Business, Education, Health, Information Studies, Law & Social Work* volume under Environmental and Occupational Health. To help you find all of the programs of interest to you, the introduction to each section within the specialized volumes includes, if applicable, a paragraph suggesting other sections and directories with information on related areas of study.

Directory of Institutions with Programs in the Biological Sciences

This directory lists institutions in alphabetical order and includes beneath each name the academic fields in which each institution offers graduate programs. The degree level in each field is also indicated, provided that the institution has supplied that information in response to Peterson's Annual Survey of Graduate and Professional Institutions. An M indicates that a master's degree program is offered; a D indicates that a doctoral degree program is offered; a P indicates that the first professional degree is offered; an O signifies that other advanced degrees (e.g., certificates or specialist degrees) are offered; and an * (asterisk) indicates that a **Close-Up** and/or **Display** is located in this volume. See the index, "Close-Ups and Displays," for the specific page number.

Profiles of Academic and Professional Programs in the Specialized Volumes

Each section of **Profiles** has a table of contents that lists the Program Directories, **Displays**, and **Close-Ups**. Program Directories consist of the **Profiles** of programs in the relevant fields, with **Displays** following if programs have chosen to include them. **Close-Ups**, which are more individualized statements, again if programs have chosen to submit them, are also listed.

The **Profiles** found in the 500 directories in the specialized volumes provide basic data about the graduate units in capsule form for quick reference. To make these directories as useful as possible, **Profiles** are generally listed for an institution's smallest academic unit within a subject area. In other words, if an institution has a College of Liberal Arts that administers many related programs, the **Profile** for the individual program (e.g., Program in History), not the entire College, appears in the directory.

There are some programs that do not fit into any current directory and are not given individual **Profiles**. The directory structure is reviewed annually in order to keep this number to a minimum and to accommodate major trends in graduate education.

The following outline describes the **Profile** information found in the guides and explains how best to use that information. Any item that does not apply to or was not provided by a graduate unit is omitted from its listing. The format of the **Profiles** is constant, making it easy to compare one institution with another and one program with another.

Identifying Information. The institution's name, in boldface type, is followed by a complete listing of the administrative structure for that field of study. (For example, University of Akron, Buchtel College of Arts and Sciences, Department of Theoretical and Applied Mathematics, Program in Mathematics.) The last unit listed is the one to which all information in the **Profile** pertains. The institution's city, state, and zip code follow.

Offerings. Each field of study offered by the unit is listed with all postbaccalaureate degrees awarded. Degrees that are not preceded by a specific concentration are awarded in the general field listed in the unit name. Frequently, fields of study are broken down into subspecializations, and those appear following the degrees awarded; for example, "Offerings in secondary education (M.Ed.), including English education, mathematics education, science education." Students enrolled in the M.Ed. program would be able to specialize in any of the three fields mentioned.

Professional Accreditation. Some **Profiles** indicate whether a program is professionally accredited. Because it is possible for a program to receive or lose professional accreditation at any time, students entering fields in which accreditation is important to a career should verify the status of programs by contacting either the chairperson or the appropriate accrediting association.

Jointly Offered Degrees. Explanatory statements concerning programs that are offered in cooperation with other institutions are included in the list of degrees offered. This occurs most commonly on a regional basis (for example, two state universities offering a cooperative Ph.D. in special education) or where the specialized nature of the institutions encourages joint efforts (a J.D./M.B.A. offered by a law school at an institution with no formal business programs and an institution with a business school but lacking a law school). Only programs that are truly cooperative are listed; those involving only limited course work at another institution are not. Interested students should contact the heads of such units for further information.

Part-Time and Evening/Weekend Programs. When information regarding the availability of part-time or evening/weekend study appears in the **Profile**, it means that students are able to earn a degree exclusively through such study.

Postbaccalaureate Distance Learning Degrees. A postbaccalaureate distance learning degree program signifies that course requirements can be fulfilled with minimal or no on-campus study.

Faculty. Figures on the number of faculty members actively involved with graduate students through teaching or research are separated into full-and part-time as well as men and women whenever the information has been supplied.

Students. Figures for the number of students enrolled in graduate and professional programs pertain to the semester of highest enrollment from the 2009–10 academic year. These figures are broken down into full-and part-time and men and women whenever the data have been supplied. Information on the number of matriculated students enrolled in the unit who are members of a minority group or are international students appears here. The average age of the matriculated students is followed by the number of applicants, the percentage accepted, and the number enrolled for fall 2009.

Degrees Awarded. The number of degrees awarded in the calendar year is listed. Many doctoral programs offer a terminal master's degree if students leave the program after completing only part of the requirements for a doctoral degree; that is indicated here. All degrees are classified into one of four types: master's, doctoral, first professional, and other advanced degrees. A unit may award one or several degrees at a given level; however, the data are only collected by type and may therefore represent several different degree programs.

Degree Requirements. The information in this section is also broken down by type of degree, and all information for a degree level pertains to all degrees of that type unless otherwise specified. Degree requirements are collected in a simplified form to provide some very basic information on the nature of the program and on foreign language, thesis or dissertation, comprehensive exam, and registration requirements. Many units also provide a short list of additional requirements, such as fieldwork or an internship. For complete information on graduation requirements, contact the graduate school or program directly.

Entrance Requirements. Entrance requirements are broken down into the four degree levels of master's, doctoral, first professional, and other advanced degrees. Within each level, information may be provided in two basic categories: entrance exams and other requirements. The entrance exams are identified by the standard acronyms used by the testing agencies, unless they are not well known. Other entrance requirements are quite varied, but they often contain an undergraduate or graduate grade point average (GPA). Unless otherwise stated, the GPA is calculated on a 4.0 scale and is listed as a minimum required for admission. Additional exam requirements/recommendations for international students may be listed here. Application deadlines for domestic and international students, the application fee, and whether electronic applications are accepted may be listed here. Note that the deadline should be used for reference only; these dates are subject to change, and students interested in applying should always contact the graduate unit directly about application procedures and deadlines.

Expenses. The typical cost of study for the 2009–10 academic year is given in two basic categories: tuition and fees. Cost of study may be quite complex at a graduate institution. There are often sliding scales for part-time study, a different cost for first-year students, and other variables that make it impossible to completely cover the cost of study for each graduate program. To provide the most usable information, figures are given for full-time study for a full year where available and for part-time study in terms of a per-unit rate (per credit, per semester hour, etc.). Occasionally, variances may be noted in tuition and fees for reasons such as the type of program, whether courses are taken during the day or evening, whether courses are at the master's or doctoral level, or other institution-specific reasons. Expenses are usually subject to change; for exact costs at any given time, contact your chosen schools and programs directly. Keep in mind that the tuition of Canadian institutions is usually given in Canadian dollars.

Financial Support. This section contains data on the number of awards administered by the institution and given to graduate students during the 2009–10 academic year. The first figure given represents the total number of students receiving financial support enrolled in that unit. If the unit has provided information on graduate appoint-

ments, these are broken down into three major categories: fellowships give money to graduate students to cover the cost of study and living expenses and are not based on a work obligation or research commitment, research assistantships provide stipends to graduate students for assistance in a formal research project with a faculty member, and teaching assistantships provide stipends to graduate students for teaching or for assisting faculty members in teaching undergraduate classes. Within each category, figures are given for the total number of awards, the average yearly amount per award, and whether full or partial tuition reimbursements are awarded. In addition to graduate appointments, the availability of several other financial aid sources is covered in this section. Tuition waivers are routinely part of a graduate appointment, but units sometimes waive part or all of a student's tuition even if a graduate appointment is not available. Federal Work-Study is made available to students who demonstrate need and meet the federal guidelines; this form of aid normally includes 10 or more hours of work per week in an office of the institution. Institutionally sponsored loans are low-interest loans available to graduate students to cover both educational and living expenses. Career-related internships or fieldwork offer money to students who are participating in a formal off-campus research project or practicum. Grants, scholarships, traineeships, unspecified assistantships, and other awards may also be noted. The availability of financial support to part-time students is also indicated here.

Some programs list the financial aid application deadline and the forms that need to be completed for students to be eligible for financial awards. There are two forms: FAFSA, the Free Application for Federal Student Aid, which is required for federal aid, and the CSS PROFILE®.

Faculty Research. Each unit has the opportunity to list several keyword phrases describing the current research involving faculty members and graduate students. Space limitations prevent the unit from listing complete information on all research programs. The total expenditure for funded research from the previous academic year may also be included.

Unit Head and Application Contact. The head of the graduate program for each unit is listed with academic title and telephone and fax numbers and e-mail address if available. In addition to the unit head, many graduate programs list a separate contact for application and admission information, which follows the listing for the unit head. If no unit head or application contact is given, you should contact the overall institution for information on graduate admissions.

Displays and Close-Ups

The **Displays** and **Close-Ups** are supplementary insertions submitted by deans, chairs, and other administrators who wish to offer an additional, more individualized statement to readers. A number of graduate school and program administrators have attached a **Display** ad near the **Profile** listing. Here you will find information that an institution or program wants to emphasize. The **Close-Ups** are by their very nature more expansive and flexible than the **Profiles**, and the administrators who have written them may emphasize different aspects of their programs. All of the **Close-Ups** are organized in the same way (with the exception of a few that describe research and training opportunities instead of degree programs), and in each one you will find information on the same basic topics, such as programs of study, research facilities, tuition and fees, financial aid, and application procedures. If an institution or program has submitted a **Close-Up**, a boldface cross-reference appears below its **Profile**. As with the **Displays**, all of the **Close-Ups** in the guides have been submitted by choice; the absence of a **Display** or **Close-Up** does not reflect any type of editorial judgment on the part of Peterson's, and their presence in the guides should not be taken as an indication of status, quality, or approval. Statements regarding a university's objectives and accomplishments are a reflection of its own beliefs and are not the opinions of the Peterson's editors.

Appendixes

This section contains two appendixes. The first, "Institutional Changes Since the 2010 Edition," lists institutions that have closed, merged, or changed their name or status since the last edition of the guides. The second, "Abbreviations Used in the Guides," gives abbreviations of degree names, along with what those abbreviations stand for. These appendixes are identical in all six volumes of *Peterson's Graduate and Professional Programs*.

Indexes

There are three indexes presented here. The first index, "Close-Ups and Displays," gives page references for all programs that have chosen to place **Close-Ups** and **Displays** in this volume. It is arranged alphabetically by institution; within institutions, the arrangement is alphabetical by subject area. It is not an index to all programs in the book's directories of **Profiles**; readers must refer to the directories themselves for **Profile** information on programs that have not submitted the additional, more individualized statements. The second index, "Directories and Subject Areas in Other Books in This Series", gives book references for the directories in the specialized volumes and also includes cross-references for subject area names not used in the directory structure, for example, "Computing Technology (see Computer Science)." The third index, "Directories and Subject Areas in This Book," gives page references for the directories in this volume and cross-references for subject area names not used in this volume's directory structure.

Data Collection Procedures

The information published in the directories and **Profiles** of all the books is collected through Peterson's Annual Survey of Graduate and Professional Institutions. The survey is sent each spring to more than 2,200 institutions offering postbaccalaureate degree programs, including accredited institutions in the United States, U.S. territories, and Canada and those institutions outside the United States that are accredited by U.S. accrediting bodies. Deans and other administrators complete these surveys, providing information on programs in the 500 academic and professional fields covered in the guides as well as overall institutional information. While every effort has been made to ensure the accuracy and completeness of the data, information is sometimes unavailable or changes occur after publication deadlines. All usable information received in time for publication has been included. The omission of any particular item from a directory or **Profile** signifies either that the item is not applicable to the institution or program or that information was not available. **Profiles** of programs scheduled to begin during the 2010–11 academic year cannot, obviously, include statistics on enrollment or, in many cases, the number of faculty members. If no usable data were submitted by an institution, its name, address, and program name appear in order to indicate the availability of graduate work.

Criteria for Inclusion in This Guide

To be included in this guide, an institution must have full accreditation or be a candidate for accreditation (preaccreditation) status by an institutional or specialized accrediting body recognized by the U.S. Department of Education or the Council for Higher Education Accreditation (CHEA). Institutional accrediting bodies, which review each institution as a whole, include the six regional associations of schools and colleges (Middle States, New England, North Central, Northwest, Southern, and Western), each of which is responsible for a specified portion of the United States and its territories. Other institutional accrediting bodies are national in scope and accredit specific kinds of institutions (e.g., Bible colleges, independent colleges, and rabbinical and Talmudic schools). Program registration by the New York State Board of Regents is considered to be the equivalent of institutional accreditation, since the board requires that all programs offered by an institution meet its standards before recognition is granted. A Canadian institution must be chartered and authorized to grant degrees by the provincial government, affiliated with a chartered institution, or accredited by a recognized U.S. accrediting body. This guide also includes institutions outside the United States that are accredited by these U.S. accrediting bodies. There are recognized specialized or professional accrediting bodies in more than fifty different fields, each of which is authorized to accredit institutions or specific programs in its particular field. For specialized institutions that offer programs in one field only, we designate this to be the equivalent of institutional accreditation. A full explanation of the accrediting process and complete information on recognized institutional (regional and national) and specialized accrediting bodies can be found online at www.chea.org or at www.ed.gov/admins/finaid/accred/index.html.

DIRECTORY OF INSTITUTIONS WITH PROGRAMS IN THE BIOLOGICAL SCIENCES

ACADIA UNIVERSITY

Biological and Biomedical Sciences—General	M

ADELPHI UNIVERSITY

Biological and Biomedical Sciences—General	M

ALABAMA AGRICULTURAL AND MECHANICAL UNIVERSITY

Biological and Biomedical Sciences—General	M

ALABAMA STATE UNIVERSITY

Biological and Biomedical Sciences—General	M

ALBANY MEDICAL COLLEGE

Cardiovascular Sciences	M,D
Cell Biology	M,D
Immunology	M,D
Microbiology	M,D
Molecular Biology	M,D
Neuroscience	M,D
Pharmacology	M,D

ALBERT EINSTEIN COLLEGE OF MEDICINE

Anatomy	D
Biochemistry	D
Biological and Biomedical Sciences—General	D
Biophysics	D
Cell Biology	D
Developmental Biology	D
Genetics	D
Genomic Sciences	D
Immunology	D
Microbiology	D
Molecular Biology	D
Molecular Genetics	D
Molecular Pharmacology	D
Neurobiology	D
Pathology	D
Physiology	D

ALCORN STATE UNIVERSITY

Biological and Biomedical Sciences—General	M

ALLIANT INTERNATIONAL UNIVERSITY–SAN FRANCISCO

Pharmacology	M

AMERICAN UNIVERSITY

Biological and Biomedical Sciences—General	M
Biopsychology	M
Neuroscience	D
Toxicology	M,O

THE AMERICAN UNIVERSITY OF ATHENS

Biological and Biomedical Sciences—General	M

AMERICAN UNIVERSITY OF BEIRUT

Biochemistry	P,M
Biological and Biomedical Sciences—General	M
Microbiology	P,M
Neuroscience	P,M
Nutrition	M
Pharmacology	P,M
Physiology	P,M

ANDREWS UNIVERSITY

Biological and Biomedical Sciences—General	M
Nutrition	M

ANGELO STATE UNIVERSITY

Biological and Biomedical Sciences—General	M

ANTIOCH UNIVERSITY NEW ENGLAND

Conservation Biology	M

APPALACHIAN STATE UNIVERSITY

Biological and Biomedical Sciences—General	M
Cell Biology	M
Molecular Biology	M
Nutrition	M

ARGOSY UNIVERSITY, ATLANTA

Biopsychology	M,D,O

ARGOSY UNIVERSITY, CHICAGO

Neuroscience	D

ARGOSY UNIVERSITY, HAWAI'I

Pharmacology	M,O

ARGOSY UNIVERSITY, PHOENIX

Neuroscience	M,D

ARGOSY UNIVERSITY, SCHAUMBURG

Neuroscience	M,D,O

ARGOSY UNIVERSITY, TAMPA

Neuroscience	M,D

ARGOSY UNIVERSITY, TWIN CITIES

Biopsychology	M,D,O

ARIZONA STATE UNIVERSITY

Biochemistry	M,D
Biological and Biomedical Sciences—General	M,D
Cell Biology	M,D
Computational Biology	M
Microbiology	M,D
Molecular Biology	M,D
Neuroscience	M,D
Nutrition	M
Plant Biology	M,D

ARKANSAS STATE UNIVERSITY—JONESBORO

Biological and Biomedical Sciences—General	M,O
Molecular Biology	D

A.T. STILL UNIVERSITY OF HEALTH SCIENCES

Biological and Biomedical Sciences—General	P,M

AUBURN UNIVERSITY

Anatomy	M,D
Biochemistry	M,D
Biological and Biomedical Sciences—General	M,D
Botany	M,D

Cell Biology (continued)

Cell Biology	M,D
Entomology	M,D
Microbiology	M,D
Molecular Biology	M,D
Nutrition	M,D
Pathobiology	M,D
Pharmacology	M,D
Plant Pathology	M,D
Radiation Biology	M,D
Zoology	M,D

AUSTIN PEAY STATE UNIVERSITY

Biological and Biomedical Sciences—General	M
Radiation Biology	M

BALL STATE UNIVERSITY

Biological and Biomedical Sciences—General	M,D
Physiology	M

BARRY UNIVERSITY

Anatomy	M
Biological and Biomedical Sciences—General	M

BASTYR UNIVERSITY

Nutrition	M*

BAYLOR COLLEGE OF MEDICINE

Biochemistry	D
Biological and Biomedical Sciences—General	M,D
Biophysics	D*
Cancer Biology/Oncology	D
Cardiovascular Sciences	D
Cell Biology	D*
Computational Biology	D*
Developmental Biology	D*
Genetics	D*
Human Genetics	D
Immunology	D
Microbiology	D
Molecular Biology	D*
Molecular Biophysics	D
Molecular Medicine	D
Molecular Physiology	D
Neuroscience	D
Pathology	D
Pharmacology	D
Structural Biology	D*
Translational Biology	D*
Virology	D

BAYLOR UNIVERSITY

Biological and Biomedical Sciences—General	M,D
Ecology	D
Environmental Biology	M,D
Nutrition	M,D

BEMIDJI STATE UNIVERSITY

Biological and Biomedical Sciences—General	M

BENEDICTINE UNIVERSITY

Nutrition	M

BLACK HILLS STATE UNIVERSITY

Genomic Sciences	M

BLOOMSBURG UNIVERSITY OF PENNSYLVANIA

Biological and Biomedical Sciences—General	M

BOISE STATE UNIVERSITY

Biological and Biomedical Sciences—General	M

BOSTON COLLEGE

Biochemistry	D
Biological and Biomedical Sciences—General	D*

BOSTON UNIVERSITY

Anatomy	M,D
Biochemistry	M,D
Biological and Biomedical Sciences—General	M,D
Biophysics	D
Cell Biology	M,D
Immunology	M,D
Microbiology	M,D
Molecular Biology	M,D
Molecular Medicine	D
Neuroscience	M,D
Nutrition	M
Pharmacology	M,D
Physiology	M,D

BOWLING GREEN STATE UNIVERSITY

Biological and Biomedical Sciences—General	M,D*
Nutrition	M

BRADLEY UNIVERSITY

Biological and Biomedical Sciences—General	M

BRANDEIS UNIVERSITY

Biochemistry	M,D
Biological and Biomedical Sciences—General	O
Biophysics	M,D
Cell Biology	M,D
Genetics	M,D
Microbiology	M,D
Molecular Biology	M,D
Neurobiology	M,D
Neuroscience	M,D
Structural Biology	M,D

BRIGHAM YOUNG UNIVERSITY

Biochemistry	M,D
Biological and Biomedical Sciences—General	M,D
Developmental Biology	M,D
Microbiology	M,D
Molecular Biology	M,D
Neuroscience	M,D
Nutrition	M
Physiology	M,D

BROCK UNIVERSITY

Biological and Biomedical Sciences—General	M,D
Neuroscience	M,D

BROOKLYN COLLEGE OF THE CITY UNIVERSITY OF NEW YORK

Biological and Biomedical Sciences—General	M,D
Nutrition	M

BROWN UNIVERSITY

Biochemistry	M,D
Biological and Biomedical Sciences—General	M,D
Biopsychology	D
Cancer Biology/Oncology	M,D
Cell Biology	M,D

Developmental Biology	M,D
Ecology	D
Evolutionary Biology	D
Immunology	M,D
Microbiology	M,D
Molecular Biology	M,D
Molecular Pharmacology	M,D
Neuroscience	D
Pathobiology	M,D
Pathology	M,D
Physiology	M,D
Toxicology	M,D

BUCKNELL UNIVERSITY

Animal Behavior	M
Biological and Biomedical Sciences—General	M

BUFFALO STATE COLLEGE, STATE UNIVERSITY OF NEW YORK

Biological and Biomedical Sciences—General	M

CALIFORNIA INSTITUTE OF TECHNOLOGY

Biochemistry	M,D
Biological and Biomedical Sciences—General	D*
Biophysics	D
Cell Biology	D
Developmental Biology	D
Genetics	D
Immunology	D
Molecular Biology	D
Molecular Biophysics	M,D
Neurobiology	D
Neuroscience	M,D

CALIFORNIA POLYTECHNIC STATE UNIVERSITY, SAN LUIS OBISPO

Biochemistry	M
Biological and Biomedical Sciences—General	M

CALIFORNIA STATE POLYTECHNIC UNIVERSITY, POMONA

Biological and Biomedical Sciences—General	M

CALIFORNIA STATE UNIVERSITY, BAKERSFIELD

Biological and Biomedical Sciences—General	M

CALIFORNIA STATE UNIVERSITY, CHICO

Biological and Biomedical Sciences—General	M
Botany	M
Nutrition	M

CALIFORNIA STATE UNIVERSITY, DOMINGUEZ HILLS

Biological and Biomedical Sciences—General	M

CALIFORNIA STATE UNIVERSITY, EAST BAY

Biochemistry	M
Biological and Biomedical Sciences—General	M

CALIFORNIA STATE UNIVERSITY, FRESNO

Biological and Biomedical Sciences—General	M

CALIFORNIA STATE UNIVERSITY, FULLERTON

Biological and Biomedical Sciences—General	M

CALIFORNIA STATE UNIVERSITY, LONG BEACH

Biochemistry	M
Biological and Biomedical Sciences—General	M
Microbiology	M
Nutrition	M

CALIFORNIA STATE UNIVERSITY, LOS ANGELES

Biochemistry	M
Biological and Biomedical Sciences—General	M
Nutrition	M

CALIFORNIA STATE UNIVERSITY, NORTHRIDGE

Biochemistry	M
Biological and Biomedical Sciences—General	M

CALIFORNIA STATE UNIVERSITY, SACRAMENTO

Biological and Biomedical Sciences—General	M

CALIFORNIA STATE UNIVERSITY, SAN BERNARDINO

Biological and Biomedical Sciences—General	M

CALIFORNIA STATE UNIVERSITY, SAN MARCOS

Biological and Biomedical Sciences—General	M

CALIFORNIA STATE UNIVERSITY, STANISLAUS

Biological and Biomedical Sciences—General	M
Ecology	M

CARLETON UNIVERSITY

Biological and Biomedical Sciences—General	M,D
Neuroscience	M,D

CARNEGIE MELLON UNIVERSITY

Biochemistry	M,D
Biological and Biomedical Sciences—General	M,D
Biophysics	M,D
Biopsychology	D
Cell Biology	M,D
Computational Biology	M,D
Developmental Biology	M,D
Genetics	M,D
Molecular Biology	M,D
Molecular Biophysics	D
Neurobiology	M,D
Neuroscience	M,D
Structural Biology	D

CASE WESTERN RESERVE UNIVERSITY

Anatomy	M
Biochemistry	M,D
Biological and Biomedical Sciences—General	M,D
Biophysics	M,D
Cancer Biology/Oncology	D
Cell Biology	M,D
Genetics	D
Genomic Sciences	D
Human Genetics	D
Immunology	M,D
Microbiology	D
Molecular Biology	D
Molecular Medicine	D
Molecular Physiology	M,D
Neurobiology	D
Neuroscience	D
Nutrition	M,D*
Pathology	M,D
Pharmacology	D
Physiology	M,D*
Virology	D

THE CATHOLIC UNIVERSITY OF AMERICA

Biological and Biomedical Sciences—General	M,D
Cell Biology	M,D
Microbiology	M,D

CEDARS-SINAI MEDICAL CENTER

Biological and Biomedical Sciences—General	D
Translational Biology	D

CENTRAL CONNECTICUT STATE UNIVERSITY

Biochemistry	M,O
Biological and Biomedical Sciences—General	M,O
Molecular Biology	M

CENTRAL MICHIGAN UNIVERSITY

Biological and Biomedical Sciences—General	M
Conservation Biology	M
Neuroscience	M,D
Nutrition	M,O

CENTRAL WASHINGTON UNIVERSITY

Biological and Biomedical Sciences—General	M
Nutrition	M

CHAPMAN UNIVERSITY

Nutrition	M

CHATHAM UNIVERSITY

Biological and Biomedical Sciences—General	M
Environmental Biology	M

CHICAGO STATE UNIVERSITY

Biological and Biomedical Sciences—General	M

THE CITADEL, THE MILITARY COLLEGE OF SOUTH CAROLINA

Biological and Biomedical Sciences—General	M

CITY COLLEGE OF THE CITY UNIVERSITY OF NEW YORK

Biochemistry	M,D
Biological and Biomedical Sciences—General	M,D

CITY OF HOPE NATIONAL MEDICAL CENTER/BECKMAN RESEARCH INSTITUTE

Biological and Biomedical Sciences—General	D*

CLAREMONT GRADUATE UNIVERSITY

Botany	M,D
Computational Biology	M,D

CLARION UNIVERSITY OF PENNSYLVANIA

Biological and Biomedical Sciences—General	M

CLARK ATLANTA UNIVERSITY

Biological and Biomedical Sciences—General	M,D

CLARK UNIVERSITY

Biological and Biomedical Sciences—General	M,D

CLEMSON UNIVERSITY

Biochemistry	D
Biological and Biomedical Sciences—General	M,D
Biophysics	M,D
Ecology	M,D
Entomology	M,D
Evolutionary Biology	M,D
Genetics	M,D
Microbiology	M,D
Molecular Biology	D
Nutrition	M
Plant Biology	M,D

CLEVELAND STATE UNIVERSITY

Biological and Biomedical Sciences—General	M,D
Molecular Medicine	M,D

COLD SPRING HARBOR LABORATORY, WATSON SCHOOL OF BIOLOGICAL SCIENCES

Biological and Biomedical Sciences—General	D*

THE COLLEGE AT BROCKPORT, STATE UNIVERSITY OF NEW YORK

Biological and Biomedical Sciences—General	M

COLLEGE OF CHARLESTON

Marine Biology	M

COLLEGE OF SAINT ELIZABETH

Nutrition	M,O

COLLEGE OF STATEN ISLAND OF THE CITY UNIVERSITY OF NEW YORK

Biological and Biomedical Sciences—General	M
Neuroscience	M

---

*M—master's degree; P—first professional degree; D—doctorate; O—other advanced degree; *—Close-Up and/or Display*

THE COLLEGE OF WILLIAM AND MARY

Biological and Biomedical Sciences—General	M

COLORADO STATE UNIVERSITY

Biochemistry	M,D
Biological and Biomedical Sciences—General	M,D
Botany	M,D
Cell Biology	M,D
Conservation Biology	M,D
Ecology	M,D
Entomology	M,D
Immunology	M,D
Microbiology	M,D
Molecular Biology	M,D
Neuroscience	D
Nutrition	M,D
Pathology	M,D
Plant Pathology	M,D
Radiation Biology	M,D
Zoology	M,D

COLORADO STATE UNIVERSITY–PUEBLO

Biochemistry	M
Biological and Biomedical Sciences—General	M

COLUMBIA UNIVERSITY

Anatomy	M,D
Biochemistry	M,D
Biological and Biomedical Sciences—General	P,M,D,O*
Biophysics	M,D
Biopsychology	M,D
Cell Biology	M,D
Conservation Biology	M,D,O*
Developmental Biology	M,D
Ecology	D,O
Evolutionary Biology	D,O
Genetics	M,D
Microbiology	M,D
Molecular Biology	M,D
Neurobiology	D
Nutrition	M,D*
Pathobiology	M,D
Pathology	M,D
Pharmacology	M,D
Physiology	M,D
Toxicology	M,D

CONCORDIA UNIVERSITY (CANADA)

Biological and Biomedical Sciences—General	M,D,O
Genomic Sciences	M,D,O

CONNECTICUT COLLEGE

Botany	M

CORNELL UNIVERSITY

Anatomy	M,D
Animal Behavior	D
Biochemistry	D
Biological and Biomedical Sciences—General	M,D
Biophysics	D
Biopsychology	D
Cell Biology	M,D
Computational Biology	D
Developmental Biology	M,D
Ecology	M,D
Entomology	M,D
Evolutionary Biology	D
Genetics	D
Immunology	M,D
Infectious Diseases	M,D

Microbiology	D
Molecular Biology	D
Molecular Medicine	M,D
Neurobiology	D
Nutrition	M,D
Pharmacology	M,D
Physiology	M,D
Plant Biology	M,D
Plant Molecular Biology	M,D
Plant Pathology	M,D
Plant Physiology	M,D
Reproductive Biology	M,D
Structural Biology	M,D
Toxicology	M,D
Zoology	M,D

CORNELL UNIVERSITY, JOAN AND SANFORD I. WEILL MEDICAL COLLEGE AND GRADUATE SCHOOL OF MEDICAL SCIENCES

Biochemistry	M,D
Biological and Biomedical Sciences—General	M,D
Biophysics	M,D
Cell Biology	M,D
Computational Biology	D
Immunology	M,D
Molecular Biology	M,D
Neuroscience	M,D
Pharmacology	M,D
Physiology	M,D
Structural Biology	M,D
Systems Biology	M,D

CREIGHTON UNIVERSITY

Anatomy	M
Biological and Biomedical Sciences—General	M,D
Immunology	M,D
Medical Microbiology	M,D
Pharmacology	M,D

DALHOUSIE UNIVERSITY

Anatomy	M,D
Biochemistry	M,D
Biological and Biomedical Sciences—General	M,D
Biophysics	M,D
Immunology	M,D
Microbiology	M,D
Neurobiology	M,D
Neuroscience	M,D
Pathology	M,D
Pharmacology	M,D
Physiology	M,D

DARTMOUTH COLLEGE

Biochemistry	D
Biological and Biomedical Sciences—General	D*
Cancer Biology/Oncology	D
Cardiovascular Sciences	D
Cell Biology	D
Ecology	D
Evolutionary Biology	D
Genetics	D
Immunology	D
Microbiology	D
Molecular Biology	D
Molecular Medicine	D
Molecular Pathogenesis	D
Molecular Pharmacology	D
Neuroscience	D
Pharmacology	D
Physiology	D
Systems Biology	D
Toxicology	D

DELAWARE STATE UNIVERSITY

Biological and Biomedical Sciences—General	M
Neuroscience	M,D

DELTA STATE UNIVERSITY

Biological and Biomedical Sciences—General	M

DEPAUL UNIVERSITY

Biochemistry	M
Biological and Biomedical Sciences—General	M

DOMINICAN UNIVERSITY OF CALIFORNIA

Biological and Biomedical Sciences—General	M

DREW UNIVERSITY

Biological and Biomedical Sciences—General	M

DREXEL UNIVERSITY

Biochemistry	M,D
Biological and Biomedical Sciences—General	M,D,O*
Biopsychology	M,D
Cell Biology	M,D
Genetics	M,D
Immunology	M,D
Microbiology	M,D
Molecular Biology	M,D
Molecular Medicine	M
Neuroscience	M,D
Nutrition	M
Pathobiology	M,D
Pharmacology	M,D

DUKE UNIVERSITY

Anatomy	D
Biochemistry	D
Biological and Biomedical Sciences—General	D
Biopsychology	D
Cancer Biology/Oncology	D
Cell Biology	D,O
Developmental Biology	D,O
Ecology	M,D,O
Genetics	D
Immunology	D
Microbiology	D
Molecular Biology	D,O
Molecular Biophysics	O
Molecular Genetics	D
Neurobiology	D
Neuroscience	D,O
Pathology	M,D*
Pharmacology	D
Structural Biology	O
Toxicology	D,O

DUQUESNE UNIVERSITY

Biochemistry	M,D
Biological and Biomedical Sciences—General	M,D
Pharmacology	M,D

D'YOUVILLE COLLEGE

Nutrition	M

EAST CAROLINA UNIVERSITY

Anatomy	D
Biochemistry	D
Biological and Biomedical Sciences—General	M,D
Biophysics	M,D

Cell Biology	D
Immunology	D
Microbiology	D
Molecular Biology	M,D
Nutrition	M
Pathology	D
Pharmacology	D
Physiology	D

EASTERN ILLINOIS UNIVERSITY

Biological and Biomedical Sciences—General	M
Nutrition	M

EASTERN KENTUCKY UNIVERSITY

Biological and Biomedical Sciences—General	M
Ecology	M
Nutrition	M

EASTERN MICHIGAN UNIVERSITY

Biological and Biomedical Sciences—General	M
Cell Biology	M
Ecology	M
Molecular Biology	M
Nutrition	M
Physiology	M

EASTERN NEW MEXICO UNIVERSITY

Biological and Biomedical Sciences—General	M

EASTERN VIRGINIA MEDICAL SCHOOL

Biological and Biomedical Sciences—General	M,D
Reproductive Biology	M

EASTERN WASHINGTON UNIVERSITY

Biological and Biomedical Sciences—General	M

EAST STROUDSBURG UNIVERSITY OF PENNSYLVANIA

Biological and Biomedical Sciences—General	M

EAST TENNESSEE STATE UNIVERSITY

Anatomy	M,D
Biochemistry	M,D
Biological and Biomedical Sciences—General	M,D
Biophysics	M,D
Microbiology	M,D
Nutrition	M
Pharmacology	M,D
Physiology	M,D

EDINBORO UNIVERSITY OF PENNSYLVANIA

Biological and Biomedical Sciences—General	M

ELIZABETH CITY STATE UNIVERSITY

Biological and Biomedical Sciences—General	M

EMORY UNIVERSITY

Animal Behavior	D
Biochemistry	D

Biological and Biomedical
  Sciences—General D
Biophysics D
Cancer Biology/Oncology D
Cell Biology D
Developmental Biology D
Ecology D
Evolutionary Biology D
Genetics D
Immunology D
Microbiology D
Molecular Biology D
Molecular Genetics D
Molecular Pathogenesis D
Neuroscience D
Nutrition M,D
Pharmacology D

EMPORIA STATE UNIVERSITY

Biological and Biomedical
  Sciences—General M
Botany M
Cell Biology M
Environmental Biology M
Microbiology M
Zoology M

**FAIRLEIGH DICKINSON
UNIVERSITY, COLLEGE AT
FLORHAM**

Biological and Biomedical
  Sciences—General M
Pharmacology M,O

**FAIRLEIGH DICKINSON
UNIVERSITY, METROPOLITAN
CAMPUS**

Biological and Biomedical
  Sciences—General M

**FAYETTEVILLE STATE
UNIVERSITY**

Biological and Biomedical
  Sciences—General M

FISK UNIVERSITY

Biological and Biomedical
  Sciences—General M

FITCHBURG STATE UNIVERSITY

Biological and Biomedical
  Sciences—General M,O

**FLORIDA AGRICULTURAL AND
MECHANICAL UNIVERSITY**

Biological and Biomedical
  Sciences—General M
Entomology M
Pharmacology M,D
Toxicology M,D

FLORIDA ATLANTIC UNIVERSITY

Biological and Biomedical
  Sciences—General M,D
Neuroscience D

**FLORIDA INSTITUTE OF
TECHNOLOGY**

Biological and Biomedical
  Sciences—General M,D
Cell Biology M,D*
Ecology M
Marine Biology M*
Molecular Biology M,D

**FLORIDA INTERNATIONAL
UNIVERSITY**

Biological and Biomedical
  Sciences—General M,D
Nutrition M,D

FLORIDA STATE UNIVERSITY

Biochemistry M,D
Biological and Biomedical
  Sciences—General M,D*
Cell Biology M,D
Computational Biology D
Ecology M,D
Evolutionary Biology M,D
Genetics M,D
Molecular Biology M,D
Molecular Biophysics D
Neuroscience M,D
Nutrition M,D
Structural Biology D

FORDHAM UNIVERSITY

Biological and Biomedical
  Sciences—General M,D

FORT HAYS STATE UNIVERSITY

Biological and Biomedical
  Sciences—General M

FRAMINGHAM STATE UNIVERSITY

Nutrition M

FROSTBURG STATE UNIVERSITY

Biological and Biomedical
  Sciences—General M
Conservation Biology M
Ecology M

GENEVA COLLEGE

Cardiovascular Sciences M

GEORGE MASON UNIVERSITY

Biological and Biomedical
  Sciences—General M,D,O
Cell Biology M,D,O
Computational Biology M,D,O
Evolutionary Biology M,D,O
Microbiology M,D,O
Molecular Biology M,D,O
Neuroscience M,D,O
Nutrition M,O

GEORGETOWN UNIVERSITY

Biochemistry M,D
Biological and Biomedical
  Sciences—General M,D
Biophysics M,D
Cell Biology D
Immunology M,D
Infectious Diseases M,D
Microbiology M,D
Molecular Biology M,D
Neuroscience D
Pathology M,D
Pharmacology M,D
Physiology M,D
Radiation Biology M

**THE GEORGE WASHINGTON
UNIVERSITY**

Biochemistry M,D
Biological and Biomedical
  Sciences—General M,D
Genetics D
Genomic Sciences M

Immunology D
Infectious Diseases M
Microbiology M,D,O
Molecular Biology M,D
Molecular Genetics D
Molecular Medicine D
Toxicology M

**GEORGIA CAMPUS—
PHILADELPHIA COLLEGE OF
OSTEOPATHIC MEDICINE**

Biological and Biomedical
  Sciences—General M,O

**GEORGIA COLLEGE & STATE
UNIVERSITY**

Biological and Biomedical
  Sciences—General M

**GEORGIA INSTITUTE OF
TECHNOLOGY**

Biochemistry M,D
Biological and Biomedical
  Sciences—General M,D
Physiology M

GEORGIAN COURT UNIVERSITY

Biological and Biomedical
  Sciences—General M,O

GEORGIA SOUTHERN UNIVERSITY

Biological and Biomedical
  Sciences—General M

GEORGIA STATE UNIVERSITY

Biochemistry M,D
Biological and Biomedical
  Sciences—General M,D
Cell Biology M,D
Environmental Biology M,D
Microbiology M,D
Molecular Biology M,D
Molecular Genetics M,D
Neurobiology M,D
Nutrition M
Physiology M,D

**GERSTNER SLOAN-KETTERING
GRADUATE SCHOOL OF
BIOMEDICAL SCIENCES**

Biological and Biomedical
  Sciences—General D
Cancer Biology/Oncology D*

GOUCHER COLLEGE

Biological and Biomedical
  Sciences—General O

GOVERNORS STATE UNIVERSITY

Environmental Biology M

**GRADUATE SCHOOL AND
UNIVERSITY CENTER OF THE CITY
UNIVERSITY OF NEW YORK**

Biochemistry D
Biological and Biomedical
  Sciences—General D
Biopsychology D
Neuroscience D

**GRAND VALLEY STATE
UNIVERSITY**

Biological and Biomedical
  Sciences—General M

Cell Biology M
Molecular Biology M

HAMPTON UNIVERSITY

Biological and Biomedical
  Sciences—General M
Environmental Biology M

HARVARD UNIVERSITY

Biochemistry D
Biological and Biomedical
  Sciences—General M,D,O
Biophysics D*
Biopsychology D
Cell Biology D
Evolutionary Biology D
Genetics D
Genomic Sciences D
Immunology D
Infectious Diseases D
Microbiology D
Molecular Biology D
Molecular Genetics D
Molecular Pharmacology D
Neurobiology D
Neuroscience D
Nutrition D
Pathology D
Physiology M,D
Structural Biology D
Systems Biology D

HERITAGE UNIVERSITY

Biological and Biomedical
  Sciences—General M

HOFSTRA UNIVERSITY

Biological and Biomedical
  Sciences—General M

HOOD COLLEGE

Biological and Biomedical
  Sciences—General M,O
Environmental Biology M
Immunology M,O
Microbiology M,O
Molecular Biology M,O

HOWARD UNIVERSITY

Anatomy M,D
Biochemistry M,D
Biological and Biomedical
  Sciences—General M,D
Biophysics D
Biopsychology M,D
Microbiology D
Molecular Biology M,D
Nutrition M,D
Pharmacology M,D
Physiology D

HUMBOLDT STATE UNIVERSITY

Biological and Biomedical
  Sciences—General M

**HUNTER COLLEGE OF THE CITY
UNIVERSITY OF NEW YORK**

Biochemistry M,D
Biological and Biomedical
  Sciences—General M,D
Biopsychology M
Nutrition M

**HUNTINGTON COLLEGE OF
HEALTH SCIENCES**

Nutrition M

*M—master's degree; P—first professional degree; D—doctorate; O—other advanced degree; *—Close-Up and/or Display*

ICR GRADUATE SCHOOL

Biological and Biomedical Sciences—General	M

IDAHO STATE UNIVERSITY

Biological and Biomedical Sciences—General	M,D
Medical Microbiology	M,D
Microbiology	M,D
Nutrition	M,O
Pharmacology	M,D

ILLINOIS INSTITUTE OF TECHNOLOGY

Biological and Biomedical Sciences—General	M,D
Molecular Biology	M,D
Molecular Biophysics	M,D

ILLINOIS STATE UNIVERSITY

Animal Behavior	M,D
Bacteriology	M,D
Biochemistry	M,D
Biological and Biomedical Sciences—General	M,D
Biophysics	M,D
Botany	M,D
Cell Biology	M,D
Conservation Biology	M,D
Developmental Biology	M,D
Ecology	M,D
Entomology	M,D
Evolutionary Biology	M,D
Genetics	M,D
Immunology	M,D
Microbiology	M,D
Molecular Biology	M,D
Molecular Genetics	M,D
Neurobiology	M,D
Neuroscience	M,D
Parasitology	M,D
Physiology	M,D
Plant Biology	M,D
Plant Molecular Biology	M,D
Structural Biology	M,D
Zoology	M,D

IMMACULATA UNIVERSITY

Nutrition	M

INDIANA STATE UNIVERSITY

Biological and Biomedical Sciences—General	M,D
Ecology	M,D
Microbiology	M,D
Nutrition	M
Physiology	M,D

INDIANA UNIVERSITY BLOOMINGTON

Biochemistry	M,D
Biological and Biomedical Sciences—General	M,D
Cell Biology	M,D
Ecology	M,D
Evolutionary Biology	M,D
Genetics	M,D
Microbiology	M,D
Molecular Biology	M,D
Neuroscience	D
Nutrition	M,D
Plant Biology	M,D
Zoology	M,D

INDIANA UNIVERSITY OF PENNSYLVANIA

Biological and Biomedical Sciences—General	M
Nutrition	M

INDIANA UNIVERSITY–PURDUE UNIVERSITY FORT WAYNE

Biological and Biomedical Sciences—General	M

INDIANA UNIVERSITY–PURDUE UNIVERSITY INDIANAPOLIS

Anatomy	M,D
Biochemistry	D
Biological and Biomedical Sciences—General	M,D
Biopsychology	M,D
Cell Biology	M,D
Immunology	M,D
Microbiology	M,D
Molecular Biology	D
Molecular Genetics	M,D
Nutrition	M,D
Pathology	M,D
Pharmacology	M,D
Toxicology	M,D

INTER AMERICAN UNIVERSITY OF PUERTO RICO, BAYAMÓN CAMPUS

Ecology	M

INTER AMERICAN UNIVERSITY OF PUERTO RICO, METROPOLITAN CAMPUS

Microbiology	M
Molecular Biology	M

INTER AMERICAN UNIVERSITY OF PUERTO RICO, SAN GERMÁN CAMPUS

Environmental Biology	M

IOWA STATE UNIVERSITY OF SCIENCE AND TECHNOLOGY

Biochemistry	M,D*
Biological and Biomedical Sciences—General	M,D
Biophysics	M,D
Cell Biology	M,D
Computational Biology	M,D
Developmental Biology	M,D
Ecology	M,D
Entomology	M,D
Evolutionary Biology	M,D
Genetics	M,D
Immunology	M,D
Microbiology	M,D
Molecular Biology	M,D
Neuroscience	M,D
Nutrition	M,D
Pathology	M,D
Plant Biology	M,D
Plant Pathology	M,D
Structural Biology	M,D
Toxicology	M,D

JACKSON STATE UNIVERSITY

Biological and Biomedical Sciences—General	M,D

JACKSONVILLE STATE UNIVERSITY

Biological and Biomedical Sciences—General	M

JAMES MADISON UNIVERSITY

Biological and Biomedical Sciences—General	M

JOHN CARROLL UNIVERSITY

Biological and Biomedical Sciences—General	M

THE JOHNS HOPKINS UNIVERSITY

Anatomy	D
Biochemistry	M,D
Biological and Biomedical Sciences—General	M,D
Biophysics	D
Cell Biology	D
Developmental Biology	D
Evolutionary Biology	D
Genetics	M,D
Human Genetics	D
Immunology	M,D
Infectious Diseases	M,D
Microbiology	M,D
Molecular Biology	M,D
Molecular Biophysics	M,D
Molecular Medicine	D
Neuroscience	D
Nutrition	M,D
Pathobiology	D
Pathology	D
Pharmacology	D*
Physiology	M,D
Toxicology	M,D

KANSAS CITY UNIVERSITY OF MEDICINE AND BIOSCIENCES

Biological and Biomedical Sciences—General	M

KANSAS STATE UNIVERSITY

Biochemistry	M,D
Biological and Biomedical Sciences—General	M,D
Entomology	M,D
Genetics	M,D
Microbiology	M,D
Nutrition	M,D
Pathobiology	M,D
Physiology	D
Plant Pathology	M,D

KECK GRADUATE INSTITUTE OF APPLIED LIFE SCIENCES

Biological and Biomedical Sciences—General	M,D,O
Computational Biology	M,D,O

KENT STATE UNIVERSITY

Biochemistry	M,D
Biological and Biomedical Sciences—General	M,D
Cell Biology	M,D
Ecology	M,D
Molecular Biology	M,D
Neuroscience	M,D
Nutrition	M
Pharmacology	M,D
Physiology	M,D

LAKE ERIE COLLEGE OF OSTEOPATHIC MEDICINE

Biological and Biomedical Sciences—General	P,M,O

LAKEHEAD UNIVERSITY

Biological and Biomedical Sciences—General	M

LAMAR UNIVERSITY

Biological and Biomedical Sciences—General	M

LAURENTIAN UNIVERSITY

Biochemistry	M
Biological and Biomedical Sciences—General	M,D
Ecology	M,D

LEHIGH UNIVERSITY

Biochemistry	M,D
Biological and Biomedical Sciences—General	M,D
Molecular Biology	M,D
Neuroscience	M,D

LEHMAN COLLEGE OF THE CITY UNIVERSITY OF NEW YORK

Biological and Biomedical Sciences—General	M
Nutrition	M

LESLEY UNIVERSITY

Ecology	M,D,O

LOMA LINDA UNIVERSITY

Anatomy	M,D
Biochemistry	M,D
Biological and Biomedical Sciences—General	M,D
Microbiology	M,D
Nutrition	M,D
Pathology	M,D
Pharmacology	M,D
Physiology	M,D

LONG ISLAND UNIVERSITY, BROOKLYN CAMPUS

Biological and Biomedical Sciences—General	M
Pharmacology	M,D
Toxicology	M,D

LONG ISLAND UNIVERSITY, C.W. POST CAMPUS

Biological and Biomedical Sciences—General	M
Cardiovascular Sciences	M
Immunology	M
Microbiology	M
Nutrition	M,O

LOUISIANA STATE UNIVERSITY AND AGRICULTURAL AND MECHANICAL COLLEGE

Biochemistry	M,D
Biological and Biomedical Sciences—General	M,D
Biopsychology	M,D
Entomology	M,D
Plant Pathology	M,D
Toxicology	M

LOUISIANA STATE UNIVERSITY HEALTH SCIENCES CENTER

Anatomy	M,D
Biological and Biomedical Sciences—General	M,D
Cell Biology	M,D
Developmental Biology	M,D
Human Genetics	M,D
Immunology	M,D
Microbiology	M,D
Neurobiology	M,D
Neuroscience	M,D
Parasitology	M,D

Pathology	M,D
Pharmacology	M,D
Physiology	M,D

LOUISIANA STATE UNIVERSITY HEALTH SCIENCES CENTER AT SHREVEPORT

Anatomy	M,D
Biochemistry	M,D
Biological and Biomedical Sciences—General	M,D
Cell Biology	M,D
Immunology	M,D
Microbiology	M,D
Molecular Biology	M,D
Pharmacology	D
Physiology	M,D

LOUISIANA TECH UNIVERSITY

Biological and Biomedical Sciences—General	M
Nutrition	M

LOYOLA UNIVERSITY CHICAGO

Anatomy	M,D
Biochemistry	M,D
Biological and Biomedical Sciences—General	M
Cardiovascular Sciences	M,O
Cell Biology	M,D
Immunology	M,D
Infectious Diseases	M,O
Microbiology	M,D
Molecular Biology	M,D
Molecular Physiology	M,D*
Neurobiology	M,D
Neuroscience	M,D
Nutrition	M,O
Pharmacology	M,D

MARQUETTE UNIVERSITY

Biological and Biomedical Sciences—General	M,D
Cell Biology	M,D
Developmental Biology	M,D
Ecology	M,D
Evolutionary Biology	M,D
Genetics	M,D
Microbiology	M,D
Molecular Biology	M,D
Neurobiology	M,D
Physiology	M,D

MARSHALL UNIVERSITY

Biological and Biomedical Sciences—General	M,D
Nutrition	M

MARYWOOD UNIVERSITY

Nutrition	M,O

MASSACHUSETTS COLLEGE OF PHARMACY AND HEALTH SCIENCES

Pharmacology	M,D

MASSACHUSETTS INSTITUTE OF TECHNOLOGY

Biochemistry	D
Biological and Biomedical Sciences—General	P,M,D
Cell Biology	D
Computational Biology	D
Developmental Biology	D
Environmental Biology	M,D,O

Genetics	D
Immunology	D
Microbiology	D
Molecular Biology	D
Molecular Toxicology	D
Neurobiology	D
Neuroscience	D
Structural Biology	D
Systems Biology	D
Toxicology	M,D

MAYO GRADUATE SCHOOL

Biochemistry	D
Biological and Biomedical Sciences—General	D
Cancer Biology/Oncology	D
Cell Biology	D
Genetics	D
Immunology	D
Molecular Biology	D
Molecular Pharmacology	D
Neuroscience	D
Structural Biology	D
Virology	D

MCGILL UNIVERSITY

Anatomy	M,D
Biochemistry	M,D
Biological and Biomedical Sciences—General	M,D
Cell Biology	M,D
Entomology	M,D
Human Genetics	M,D
Immunology	M,D
Microbiology	M,D
Neuroscience	M,D
Nutrition	M,D,O
Parasitology	M,D,O
Pathology	M,D
Pharmacology	M,D
Physiology	M,D

MCMASTER UNIVERSITY

Biochemistry	M,D
Biological and Biomedical Sciences—General	M,D
Cancer Biology/Oncology	M,D
Cardiovascular Sciences	M,D
Cell Biology	M,D
Genetics	M,D
Immunology	M,D
Molecular Biology	M,D
Neuroscience	M,D
Nutrition	M,D
Pharmacology	M,D
Physiology	M,D
Virology	M,D

MCNEESE STATE UNIVERSITY

Nutrition	M

MEDICAL COLLEGE OF GEORGIA

Anatomy	D
Biochemistry	D
Biological and Biomedical Sciences—General	M,D,O
Cardiovascular Sciences	D
Cell Biology	D
Genomic Sciences	D
Molecular Biology	D
Molecular Medicine	D
Neuroscience	D
Pharmacology	D
Physiology	D

MEDICAL COLLEGE OF WISCONSIN

Biochemistry	D
Biological and Biomedical Sciences—General	M,D,O
Biophysics	D
Cell Biology	D
Developmental Biology	D
Microbiology	M,D
Molecular Genetics	M,D
Neuroscience	D
Pharmacology	D
Physiology	D
Toxicology	D

MEDICAL UNIVERSITY OF SOUTH CAROLINA

Biochemistry	M,D
Biological and Biomedical Sciences—General	M,D
Cancer Biology/Oncology	D
Cardiovascular Sciences	D
Cell Biology	D
Developmental Biology	D
Genetics	D
Immunology	M,D
Microbiology	M,D
Molecular Biology	M,D
Molecular Pharmacology	M,D
Neuroscience	M,D
Pathobiology	D
Pathology	M,D
Toxicology	D

MEHARRY MEDICAL COLLEGE

Biological and Biomedical Sciences—General	D
Cancer Biology/Oncology	D
Immunology	D
Microbiology	D
Neuroscience	D
Pharmacology	D

MEMORIAL UNIVERSITY OF NEWFOUNDLAND

Biochemistry	M,D
Biological and Biomedical Sciences—General	M,D,O
Biopsychology	M,D
Cancer Biology/Oncology	M,D
Cardiovascular Sciences	M,D
Human Genetics	M,D
Immunology	M,D
Marine Biology	M,D
Neuroscience	M,D

MEREDITH COLLEGE

Nutrition	M,O

MIAMI UNIVERSITY

Biochemistry	M,D
Botany	M,D
Microbiology	M,D
Plant Biology	M,D
Zoology	M,D*

MICHIGAN STATE UNIVERSITY

Biochemistry	M,D
Biological and Biomedical Sciences—General	M,D
Cell Biology	M,D
Ecology	D
Entomology	M,D
Evolutionary Biology	D
Genetics	M,D
Microbiology	M,D

Molecular Biology	M,D
Molecular Genetics	M,D
Neuroscience	M,D
Nutrition	M,D
Pathobiology	M,D
Pathology	M,D
Pharmacology	M,D
Physiology	M,D
Plant Biology	M,D
Plant Pathology	M,D
Structural Biology	D
Systems Biology	D
Toxicology	M,D
Zoology	M,D

MICHIGAN TECHNOLOGICAL UNIVERSITY

Biological and Biomedical Sciences—General	M,D
Ecology	M
Plant Molecular Biology	M,D

MIDDLE TENNESSEE STATE UNIVERSITY

Biological and Biomedical Sciences—General	M
Nutrition	M

MIDWESTERN STATE UNIVERSITY

Biological and Biomedical Sciences—General	M

MIDWESTERN UNIVERSITY, DOWNERS GROVE CAMPUS

Biological and Biomedical Sciences—General	M

MIDWESTERN UNIVERSITY, GLENDALE CAMPUS

Biological and Biomedical Sciences—General	M
Cardiovascular Sciences	M

MILLERSVILLE UNIVERSITY OF PENNSYLVANIA

Biological and Biomedical Sciences—General	M

MILLS COLLEGE

Biological and Biomedical Sciences—General	O

MILWAUKEE SCHOOL OF ENGINEERING

Cardiovascular Sciences	M

MINNESOTA STATE UNIVERSITY MANKATO

Biological and Biomedical Sciences—General	M

MISSISSIPPI COLLEGE

Biochemistry	M
Biological and Biomedical Sciences—General	M

MISSISSIPPI STATE UNIVERSITY

Biochemistry	M,D
Biological and Biomedical Sciences—General	M,D
Entomology	M,D
Genetics	M,D

---

*M—master's degree; P—first professional degree; D—doctorate; O—other advanced degree; *—Close-Up and/or Display*

Molecular Biology — M,D
Nutrition — M,D
Plant Pathology — M,D

MISSOURI STATE UNIVERSITY

Biological and Biomedical
 Sciences—General — M
Cell Biology — M
Molecular Biology — M

MISSOURI UNIVERSITY OF SCIENCE AND TECHNOLOGY

Biological and Biomedical
 Sciences—General — M
Environmental Biology — M

MONTANA STATE UNIVERSITY

Biochemistry — M,D
Biological and Biomedical
 Sciences—General — M,D
Ecology — M,D
Microbiology — M,D
Molecular Biology — M,D
Neuroscience — M,D
Nutrition — M
Plant Pathology — M,D
Zoology — M,D

MONTCLAIR STATE UNIVERSITY

Biochemistry — M
Biological and Biomedical
 Sciences—General — M,O
Molecular Biology — M,O
Nutrition — M,O

MOREHEAD STATE UNIVERSITY

Biological and Biomedical
 Sciences—General — M

MOREHOUSE SCHOOL OF MEDICINE

Biological and Biomedical
 Sciences—General — M,D*

MORGAN STATE UNIVERSITY

Biological and Biomedical
 Sciences—General — M,D
Environmental Biology — D

MOUNT ALLISON UNIVERSITY

Biological and Biomedical
 Sciences—General — M

MOUNT MARY COLLEGE

Nutrition — M

MOUNT SAINT VINCENT UNIVERSITY

Nutrition — M

MOUNT SINAI SCHOOL OF MEDICINE OF NEW YORK UNIVERSITY

Biological and Biomedical
 Sciences—General — M,D
Neuroscience — M,D

MURRAY STATE UNIVERSITY

Biological and Biomedical
 Sciences—General — M,D

NEW JERSEY INSTITUTE OF TECHNOLOGY

Biological and Biomedical
 Sciences—General — M,D
Computational Biology — M

NEW MEXICO INSTITUTE OF MINING AND TECHNOLOGY

Biochemistry — M,D
Biological and Biomedical
 Sciences—General — M

NEW MEXICO STATE UNIVERSITY

Biochemistry — M,D
Biological and Biomedical
 Sciences—General — M,D
Entomology — M
Molecular Biology — M,D
Plant Pathology — M

NEW YORK CHIROPRACTIC COLLEGE

Anatomy — M
Nutrition — M

NEW YORK INSTITUTE OF TECHNOLOGY

Nutrition — M

NEW YORK MEDICAL COLLEGE

Anatomy — M,D
Biochemistry — M,D
Biological and Biomedical
 Sciences—General — M,D*
Cell Biology — M,D
Immunology — M,D
Microbiology — M,D
Molecular Biology — M,D
Neuroscience — M,D
Pathology — M,D
Pharmacology — M,D
Physiology — M,D

NEW YORK UNIVERSITY

Biological and Biomedical
 Sciences—General — M,D*
Cancer Biology/Oncology — P,M,D
Cell Biology — P,M,D
Computational Biology — D
Developmental Biology — M,D
Genetics — M,D
Immunology — P,M,D
Microbiology — P,M,D
Molecular Biology — P,M,D
Molecular Genetics — M,D
Molecular Pharmacology — D
Molecular Toxicology — M,D
Neurobiology — M,D
Neuroscience — P,M,D
Nutrition — M,D
Parasitology — P,M,D
Pathobiology — P,M,D
Pharmacology — P,M,D
Physiology — P,M,D
Plant Biology — M,D
Structural Biology — P,M,D
Toxicology — M,D

NICHOLLS STATE UNIVERSITY

Environmental Biology — M
Marine Biology — M

NORTH CAROLINA AGRICULTURAL AND TECHNICAL STATE UNIVERSITY

Biological and Biomedical
 Sciences—General — M
Nutrition — M

NORTH CAROLINA CENTRAL UNIVERSITY

Biological and Biomedical
 Sciences—General — M

NORTH CAROLINA STATE UNIVERSITY

Biochemistry — D
Biological and Biomedical
 Sciences—General — M,D,O
Botany — M,D
Cell Biology — M,D
Entomology — M,D
Genetics — M,D
Genomic Sciences — M,D
Immunology — M,D
Infectious Diseases — M,D
Microbiology — M,D
Molecular Toxicology — M,D
Nutrition — M,D
Pathology — M,D
Pharmacology — M,D
Physiology — M,D
Plant Biology — M,D
Plant Pathology — M,D
Toxicology — M,D
Zoology — M,D

NORTH DAKOTA STATE UNIVERSITY

Biochemistry — M,D
Biological and Biomedical
 Sciences—General — M,D
Botany — M,D
Cell Biology — M,D
Conservation Biology — M,D
Ecology — M,D
Entomology — M,D
Genomic Sciences — M,D
Microbiology — M,D
Molecular Biology — M,D
Molecular Pathogenesis — M,D
Nutrition — M
Pathology — M,D
Plant Pathology — M,D
Zoology — M,D

NORTHEASTERN ILLINOIS UNIVERSITY

Biological and Biomedical
 Sciences—General — M

NORTHEASTERN UNIVERSITY

Biochemistry — M,D
Biological and Biomedical
 Sciences—General — M,D
Marine Biology — M,D

NORTHERN ARIZONA UNIVERSITY

Biological and Biomedical
 Sciences—General — M,D

NORTHERN ILLINOIS UNIVERSITY

Biological and Biomedical
 Sciences—General — M,D
Nutrition — M

NORTHERN MICHIGAN UNIVERSITY

Biological and Biomedical
 Sciences—General — M

NORTH SHORE–LIJ GRADUATE SCHOOL OF MOLECULAR MEDICINE

Molecular Medicine — D

NORTHWESTERN UNIVERSITY

Biochemistry — D
Biological and Biomedical
 Sciences—General — D
Biophysics — D
Biopsychology — D
Cancer Biology/Oncology — D
Cell Biology — D
Computational Biology — M
Developmental Biology — D
Evolutionary Biology — D
Genetics — D
Immunology — D
Microbiology — D
Molecular Biology — D
Neurobiology — M,D
Neuroscience — D
Pharmacology — D
Physiology — M
Reproductive Biology — D
Structural Biology — D
Toxicology — D

NORTHWEST MISSOURI STATE UNIVERSITY

Biological and Biomedical
 Sciences—General — M

NOTRE DAME DE NAMUR UNIVERSITY

Biological and Biomedical
 Sciences—General — O

NOVA SCOTIA AGRICULTURAL COLLEGE

Botany — M
Ecology — M
Environmental Biology — M
Physiology — M
Plant Pathology — M
Plant Physiology — M

NOVA SOUTHEASTERN UNIVERSITY

Biological and Biomedical
 Sciences—General — M
Marine Biology — M,D
Pharmacology — M

OAKLAND UNIVERSITY

Biological and Biomedical
 Sciences—General — M,D

OCCIDENTAL COLLEGE

Biological and Biomedical
 Sciences—General — M

OGI SCHOOL OF SCIENCE & ENGINEERING AT OREGON HEALTH & SCIENCE UNIVERSITY

Biochemistry — M,D
Molecular Biology — M,D

THE OHIO STATE UNIVERSITY

Anatomy	M,D
Biochemistry	M,D
Biological and Biomedical Sciences—General	M,D
Biophysics	M,D
Cardiovascular Sciences	M
Cell Biology	M,D
Developmental Biology	M,D
Ecology	M,D
Entomology	M,D
Evolutionary Biology	M,D
Genetics	M,D
Immunology	M,D
Microbiology	M,D
Molecular Biology	M,D
Molecular Genetics	M,D
Neuroscience	M,D
Nutrition	M,D
Pathobiology	M,D
Pathology	M
Pharmacology	M,D
Physiology	M,D
Plant Biology	M,D
Plant Pathology	M,D
Toxicology	M,D
Virology	M,D

OHIO UNIVERSITY

Biochemistry	M,D
Biological and Biomedical Sciences—General	M,D
Cell Biology	M,D
Ecology	M,D
Environmental Biology	M,D
Evolutionary Biology	M,D
Microbiology	M,D
Molecular Biology	M,D
Neuroscience	M,D
Nutrition	M
Physiology	M,D
Plant Biology	M,D

OKLAHOMA STATE UNIVERSITY

Biochemistry	M,D
Botany	M,D
Entomology	M,D
Microbiology	M,D
Molecular Biology	M,D
Molecular Genetics	M,D
Nutrition	M,D
Plant Pathology	M,D
Zoology	M,D

OKLAHOMA STATE UNIVERSITY CENTER FOR HEALTH SCIENCES

Biological and Biomedical Sciences—General	M,D
Molecular Biology	M,O
Toxicology	M,O

OLD DOMINION UNIVERSITY

Biochemistry	M,D
Biological and Biomedical Sciences—General	M,D
Ecology	D

OREGON HEALTH & SCIENCE UNIVERSITY

Biochemistry	M,D
Biological and Biomedical Sciences—General	M,D,O
Biopsychology	M,D
Cell Biology	D
Developmental Biology	D
Genetics	D
Immunology	D

Microbiology	D
Molecular Biology	M,D
Neuroscience	M,D*
Nutrition	M
Pharmacology	D
Physiology	D

OREGON STATE UNIVERSITY

Biochemistry	M,D
Biophysics	M,D
Botany	M,D
Cell Biology	M,D
Genetics	M,D
Microbiology	M,D
Molecular Biology	M,D
Molecular Toxicology	M,D
Nutrition	M,D
Plant Pathology	M,D
Plant Physiology	M,D
Toxicology	M,D
Zoology	M,D

PALMER COLLEGE OF CHIROPRACTIC

Anatomy	M

PALO ALTO UNIVERSITY

Biopsychology	D

PENN STATE HERSHEY MEDICAL CENTER

Anatomy	M,D
Biochemistry	M,D
Biological and Biomedical Sciences—General	M,D
Cell Biology	M,D
Genetics	M,D
Immunology	M,D
Microbiology	M,D
Molecular Biology	M,D
Molecular Medicine	M,D
Molecular Toxicology	M,D
Neuroscience	M,D
Pharmacology	M,D
Physiology	M,D
Virology	M,D

PENN STATE UNIVERSITY PARK

Biochemistry	M,D
Biological and Biomedical Sciences—General	M,D
Biopsychology	D
Cell Biology	M,D
Developmental Biology	M,D
Ecology	M,D
Entomology	M,D
Genetics	M,D
Immunology	M,D
Microbiology	M,D
Molecular Biology	M,D
Nutrition	M,D
Pathobiology	D
Physiology	M,D
Plant Pathology	M,D
Plant Physiology	M,D

PHILADELPHIA COLLEGE OF OSTEOPATHIC MEDICINE

Biological and Biomedical Sciences—General	M,O

PITTSBURG STATE UNIVERSITY

Biological and Biomedical Sciences—General	M

POINT LOMA NAZARENE UNIVERSITY

Biological and Biomedical Sciences—General	M

PONCE SCHOOL OF MEDICINE

Biological and Biomedical Sciences—General	D

PONTIFICAL CATHOLIC UNIVERSITY OF PUERTO RICO

Biological and Biomedical Sciences—General	M

PORTLAND STATE UNIVERSITY

Biological and Biomedical Sciences—General	M,D

PRAIRIE VIEW A&M UNIVERSITY

Biological and Biomedical Sciences—General	M
Toxicology	M

PRINCETON UNIVERSITY

Computational Biology	D
Ecology	D
Evolutionary Biology	D
Marine Biology	D
Molecular Biology	D
Neuroscience	D

PURDUE UNIVERSITY

Anatomy	M,D
Biochemistry	M,D
Biological and Biomedical Sciences—General	M,D
Biophysics	M,D
Botany	M,D
Cell Biology	M,D
Developmental Biology	M,D
Ecology	M,D
Entomology	M,D
Evolutionary Biology	M,D
Genetics	M,D
Immunology	M,D
Microbiology	M,D
Molecular Biology	M,D
Molecular Pharmacology	M,D
Neurobiology	M,D
Nutrition	M,D
Pathobiology	M,D
Pathology	M,D
Pharmacology	M,D
Physiology	M,D
Plant Pathology	M,D
Plant Physiology	M,D
Toxicology	M,D
Virology	M,D

PURDUE UNIVERSITY CALUMET

Biological and Biomedical Sciences—General	M

QUEENS COLLEGE OF THE CITY UNIVERSITY OF NEW YORK

Biochemistry	M
Biological and Biomedical Sciences—General	M

QUEEN'S UNIVERSITY AT KINGSTON

Anatomy	M,D
Biochemistry	M,D

Biological and Biomedical Sciences—General	M,D
Cancer Biology/Oncology	M,D
Cardiovascular Sciences	M,D
Cell Biology	M,D
Immunology	M,D
Microbiology	M,D
Molecular Biology	M,D
Molecular Medicine	M,D
Neurobiology	M,D
Neuroscience	M,D
Pathology	M,D
Pharmacology	M,D
Physiology	M,D
Reproductive Biology	M,D
Toxicology	M,D

QUINNIPIAC UNIVERSITY

Biological and Biomedical Sciences—General	M
Cardiovascular Sciences	M
Cell Biology	M
Microbiology	M
Molecular Biology	M
Pathology	M

RENSSELAER POLYTECHNIC INSTITUTE

Biochemistry	M,D
Biological and Biomedical Sciences—General	D
Biophysics	M,D

RHODE ISLAND COLLEGE

Biological and Biomedical Sciences—General	M

RICE UNIVERSITY

Biochemistry	M,D
Cell Biology	M,D
Ecology	M,D
Evolutionary Biology	M,D

ROCHESTER INSTITUTE OF TECHNOLOGY

Biological and Biomedical Sciences—General	M

THE ROCKEFELLER UNIVERSITY

Biological and Biomedical Sciences—General	D*

ROSALIND FRANKLIN UNIVERSITY OF MEDICINE AND SCIENCE

Anatomy	M,D
Biochemistry	M,D
Biological and Biomedical Sciences—General	M,D*
Biophysics	M,D
Cell Biology	M,D
Immunology	M,D
Microbiology	M,D
Molecular Biology	M,D
Molecular Pharmacology	M,D
Neuroscience	D
Nutrition	M
Pathology	M
Physiology	M,D

RUSH UNIVERSITY

Anatomy	M,D
Biochemistry	D
Cell Biology	M,D
Immunology	M,D
Microbiology	M,D

---

*M—master's degree; P—first professional degree; D—doctorate; O—other advanced degree; *—Close-Up and / or Display*

Neuroscience	M,D
Nutrition	M
Pharmacology	M,D
Physiology	D
Virology	M,D

RUTGERS, THE STATE UNIVERSITY OF NEW JERSEY, CAMDEN

Biological and Biomedical Sciences—General	M

RUTGERS, THE STATE UNIVERSITY OF NEW JERSEY, NEWARK

Biochemistry	M,D
Biological and Biomedical Sciences—General	M,D
Biopsychology	D
Computational Biology	M
Neuroscience	D

RUTGERS, THE STATE UNIVERSITY OF NEW JERSEY, NEW BRUNSWICK

Biochemistry	M,D
Biological and Biomedical Sciences—General	D
Biopsychology	D
Cancer Biology/Oncology	M,D
Cell Biology	M,D
Computational Biology	D
Developmental Biology	M,D
Ecology	M,D
Entomology	M,D
Environmental Biology	M,D
Evolutionary Biology	M,D
Genetics	M,D
Immunology	M,D
Marine Biology	M,D
Medical Microbiology	M,D
Microbiology	M,D
Molecular Biology	M,D
Molecular Biophysics	D
Molecular Genetics	M,D
Molecular Pharmacology	D
Molecular Physiology	M,D
Neuroscience	M,D
Nutrition	M,D
Physiology	M,D
Plant Biology	M,D
Plant Molecular Biology	M,D
Plant Pathology	M,D
Reproductive Biology	M,D
Systems Biology	D
Toxicology	M,D
Virology	M,D

SACRED HEART UNIVERSITY

Nutrition	M,D

SAGE GRADUATE SCHOOL

Nutrition	M,O

ST. CLOUD STATE UNIVERSITY

Biological and Biomedical Sciences—General	M

SAINT FRANCIS UNIVERSITY

Biological and Biomedical Sciences—General	M

ST. FRANCIS XAVIER UNIVERSITY

Biological and Biomedical Sciences—General	M

ST. JOHN'S UNIVERSITY (NY)

Biological and Biomedical Sciences—General	M,D
Toxicology	M

SAINT JOSEPH COLLEGE

Biochemistry	M
Biological and Biomedical Sciences—General	M
Nutrition	M

SAINT JOSEPH'S UNIVERSITY

Biological and Biomedical Sciences—General	M

SAINT LOUIS UNIVERSITY

Anatomy	M,D
Biochemistry	D
Biological and Biomedical Sciences—General	M,D
Immunology	D
Microbiology	D
Molecular Biology	D
Nutrition	M
Pathology	D
Pharmacology	D
Physiology	D

SALISBURY UNIVERSITY

Physiology	M

SAM HOUSTON STATE UNIVERSITY

Biological and Biomedical Sciences—General	M
Nutrition	M

SAN DIEGO STATE UNIVERSITY

Biological and Biomedical Sciences—General	M,D
Cell Biology	M,D
Ecology	M,D
Microbiology	M
Molecular Biology	M,D
Nutrition	M
Toxicology	M,D

SAN FRANCISCO STATE UNIVERSITY

Biochemistry	M
Biological and Biomedical Sciences—General	M
Cell Biology	M
Conservation Biology	M
Ecology	M
Marine Biology	M
Microbiology	M
Molecular Biology	M
Physiology	M

SAN JOSE STATE UNIVERSITY

Biological and Biomedical Sciences—General	M
Ecology	M
Microbiology	M
Molecular Biology	M
Nutrition	M
Physiology	M

SARAH LAWRENCE COLLEGE

Human Genetics	M

SAYBROOK UNIVERSITY

Nutrition	M,D,O

THE SCRIPPS RESEARCH INSTITUTE

Biological and Biomedical Sciences—General	D

SETON HALL UNIVERSITY

Biochemistry	M,D
Biological and Biomedical Sciences—General	M,D
Microbiology	M,D
Molecular Biology	M,D
Neuroscience	M,D

SHIPPENSBURG UNIVERSITY OF PENNSYLVANIA

Biological and Biomedical Sciences—General	M

SIMMONS COLLEGE

Nutrition	M,O

SIMON FRASER UNIVERSITY

Biochemistry	M,D
Biological and Biomedical Sciences—General	M,D
Biophysics	M,D
Entomology	M,D
Molecular Biology	M,D
Toxicology	M,D

SMITH COLLEGE

Biological and Biomedical Sciences—General	M

SONOMA STATE UNIVERSITY

Biological and Biomedical Sciences—General	M
Environmental Biology	M

SOUTH CAROLINA STATE UNIVERSITY

Nutrition	M

SOUTH DAKOTA STATE UNIVERSITY

Biological and Biomedical Sciences—General	M,D
Microbiology	M,D
Nutrition	M,D

SOUTHEASTERN LOUISIANA UNIVERSITY

Biological and Biomedical Sciences—General	M

SOUTHEAST MISSOURI STATE UNIVERSITY

Biological and Biomedical Sciences—General	M
Nutrition	M

SOUTHERN CONNECTICUT STATE UNIVERSITY

Biological and Biomedical Sciences—General	M

SOUTHERN ILLINOIS UNIVERSITY CARBONDALE

Biochemistry	M,D
Biological and Biomedical Sciences—General	M,D
Microbiology	M,D
Molecular Biology	M,D
Nutrition	M
Pharmacology	M,D

Physiology	M,D
Plant Biology	M,D
Zoology	M,D

SOUTHERN ILLINOIS UNIVERSITY EDWARDSVILLE

Biological and Biomedical Sciences—General	M

SOUTHERN METHODIST UNIVERSITY

Biological and Biomedical Sciences—General	M,D

SOUTHERN UNIVERSITY AND AGRICULTURAL AND MECHANICAL COLLEGE

Biochemistry	M
Biological and Biomedical Sciences—General	M

SOUTHWESTERN OKLAHOMA STATE UNIVERSITY

Microbiology	M

STANFORD UNIVERSITY

Biochemistry	D
Biological and Biomedical Sciences—General	M,D
Biophysics	D
Cancer Biology/Oncology	D
Developmental Biology	D
Genetics	D
Immunology	D
Microbiology	D
Molecular Pharmacology	D
Neuroscience	D
Physiology	D
Structural Biology	D

STATE UNIVERSITY OF NEW YORK AT BINGHAMTON

Biological and Biomedical Sciences—General	M,D
Biopsychology	M,D

STATE UNIVERSITY OF NEW YORK AT FREDONIA

Biological and Biomedical Sciences—General	M

STATE UNIVERSITY OF NEW YORK AT NEW PALTZ

Biological and Biomedical Sciences—General	M

STATE UNIVERSITY OF NEW YORK COLLEGE AT ONEONTA

Biological and Biomedical Sciences—General	M
Nutrition	M

STATE UNIVERSITY OF NEW YORK COLLEGE OF ENVIRONMENTAL SCIENCE AND FORESTRY

Biochemistry	M,D
Conservation Biology	M,D
Ecology	M,D
Entomology	M,D
Environmental Biology	M,D
Plant Pathology	M,D

STATE UNIVERSITY OF NEW YORK DOWNSTATE MEDICAL CENTER

Biological and Biomedical Sciences—General	M,D

Cell Biology — D
Molecular Biology — D
Neuroscience — D

STATE UNIVERSITY OF NEW YORK UPSTATE MEDICAL UNIVERSITY

Anatomy — M,D
Biochemistry — M,D*
Biological and Biomedical
  Sciences—General — M,D*
Cancer Biology/Oncology
Cardiovascular Sciences
Cell Biology — M,D*
Immunology — M,D
Infectious Diseases
Microbiology — M,D*
Molecular Biology — M,D
Neuroscience — D*
Pharmacology — D*
Physiology — M,D

STEPHEN F. AUSTIN STATE UNIVERSITY

Biological and Biomedical
  Sciences—General — M

STEVENS INSTITUTE OF TECHNOLOGY

Biochemistry — M,D,O

STONY BROOK UNIVERSITY, STATE UNIVERSITY OF NEW YORK

Anatomy — D
Biochemistry — D
Biological and Biomedical
  Sciences—General — D
Biophysics — D
Biopsychology — D
Cell Biology — M,D
Developmental Biology — M,D
Ecology — M,D
Evolutionary Biology — M,D
Genetics — D
Immunology — M,D
Microbiology — D
Molecular Biology — M,D
Molecular Genetics — D
Molecular Physiology — D
Neuroscience — D
Pathology — M,D
Pharmacology — D
Physiology — D
Structural Biology — D

SUL ROSS STATE UNIVERSITY

Biological and Biomedical
  Sciences—General — M

SYRACUSE UNIVERSITY

Biochemistry — D
Biological and Biomedical
  Sciences—General — M,D
Biophysics — D
Nutrition — M
Structural Biology — D

TARLETON STATE UNIVERSITY

Biological and Biomedical
  Sciences—General — M

TEACHERS COLLEGE, COLUMBIA UNIVERSITY

Neuroscience — M,D
Nutrition — M,D
Physiology — M,D

TEMPLE UNIVERSITY

Anatomy — M,D
Biochemistry — M,D
Biological and Biomedical
  Sciences—General — M,D
Cell Biology — M,D
Genetics — D
Immunology — M,D
Microbiology — M,D
Molecular Biology — D
Neuroscience — M,D
Pathology — D
Pharmacology — M,D
Physiology — D

TENNESSEE STATE UNIVERSITY

Biological and Biomedical
  Sciences—General — M,D

TENNESSEE TECHNOLOGICAL UNIVERSITY

Biological and Biomedical
  Sciences—General — M,D

TEXAS A&M HEALTH SCIENCE CENTER

Biological and Biomedical
  Sciences—General — M,D
Cell Biology — D
Immunology — D
Microbiology — D
Molecular Biology — D
Molecular Medicine — D
Molecular Pathogenesis — D
Neuroscience — D
Systems Biology — D
Translational Biology — D
Virology — D

TEXAS A&M INTERNATIONAL UNIVERSITY

Biological and Biomedical
  Sciences—General — M

TEXAS A&M UNIVERSITY

Anatomy — M,D
Biochemistry — M,D
Biological and Biomedical
  Sciences—General — M,D
Biophysics — M,D
Biopsychology — M,D
Botany — M,D
Cell Biology — M,D
Entomology — M,D
Genetics — M,D
Microbiology — M,D
Neuroscience — M,D
Parasitology — M,D
Pathobiology — M,D
Pathology — M,D
Physiology — M,D
Plant Biology — M,D
Plant Pathology — M,D
Toxicology — M,D
Zoology — M,D

TEXAS A&M UNIVERSITY AT GALVESTON

Marine Biology — M,D

TEXAS A&M UNIVERSITY–COMMERCE

Biological and Biomedical
  Sciences—General — M

TEXAS A&M UNIVERSITY–CORPUS CHRISTI

Biological and Biomedical
  Sciences—General — M

TEXAS A&M UNIVERSITY–KINGSVILLE

Biological and Biomedical
  Sciences—General — M

TEXAS CHRISTIAN UNIVERSITY

Biological and Biomedical
  Sciences—General — M
Neuroscience — M,D

TEXAS SOUTHERN UNIVERSITY

Biological and Biomedical
  Sciences—General — M
Toxicology — M,D

TEXAS STATE UNIVERSITY–SAN MARCOS

Biochemistry — M
Biological and Biomedical
  Sciences—General — M
Conservation Biology — M
Marine Biology — M,D
Nutrition — M

TEXAS TECH UNIVERSITY

Biological and Biomedical
  Sciences—General — M,D
Entomology — M,D
Genomic Sciences — M
Microbiology — M,D
Nutrition — M,D
Toxicology — M,D
Zoology — M,D

TEXAS TECH UNIVERSITY HEALTH SCIENCES CENTER

Biochemistry — M,D
Biological and Biomedical
  Sciences—General — M,D
Cell Biology — M,D
Medical Microbiology — M,D
Molecular Biophysics — M,D
Molecular Genetics — M,D
Molecular Pathology — M
Molecular Physiology — M,D
Neuroscience — M,D
Pharmacology — M,D

TEXAS WOMAN'S UNIVERSITY

Biological and Biomedical
  Sciences—General — M,D
Molecular Biology — M,D
Nutrition — M,D

THOMAS JEFFERSON UNIVERSITY

Biochemistry — D*
Biological and Biomedical
  Sciences—General — M,D,O*
Biophysics — D
Cell Biology — M,D
Developmental Biology — M,D
Genetics — D*
Immunology — D*
Microbiology — M,D
Molecular Biology — D
Molecular Pharmacology — D
Molecular Physiology — D
Neuroscience — D*
Pharmacology — M*
Structural Biology — D

TOWSON UNIVERSITY

Biological and Biomedical
  Sciences—General — M

TRENT UNIVERSITY

Biological and Biomedical
  Sciences—General — M,D

TROPICAL AGRICULTURE RESEARCH AND HIGHER EDUCATION CENTER

Conservation Biology — M,D

TRUMAN STATE UNIVERSITY

Biological and Biomedical
  Sciences—General — M

TUFTS UNIVERSITY

Biochemistry — D
Biological and Biomedical
  Sciences—General — P,M,D
Cell Biology — D
Developmental Biology — D
Genetics — D
Immunology — D
Microbiology — D
Molecular Biology — D
Molecular Physiology — D
Neuroscience — D
Nutrition — M,D
Pharmacology — D
Physiology — D

TULANE UNIVERSITY

Biochemistry — M,D
Biological and Biomedical
  Sciences—General — M,D
Cell Biology — M,D
Ecology — M,D
Evolutionary Biology — M,D
Human Genetics — M,D
Immunology — M,D
Infectious Diseases — M,D,O
Microbiology — M,D
Molecular Biology — M,D
Neuroscience — M,D
Nutrition — M
Parasitology — M,D,O
Pharmacology — M,D
Physiology — M,D
Structural Biology — M,D

TUSKEGEE UNIVERSITY

Biological and Biomedical
  Sciences—General — M,D
Nutrition — M

UNIFORMED SERVICES UNIVERSITY OF THE HEALTH SCIENCES

Biological and Biomedical
  Sciences—General — M,D
Cell Biology — D
Immunology — D
Infectious Diseases — D
Molecular Biology — D
Neuroscience — D
Zoology — M,D

UNIVERSIDAD ADVENTISTA DE LAS ANTILLAS

Biological and Biomedical
  Sciences—General — M

M—master's degree; P—first professional degree; D—doctorate; O—other advanced degree; *—Close-Up and / or Display

UNIVERSIDAD CENTRAL DEL CARIBE

Anatomy	M
Biochemistry	M
Biological and Biomedical Sciences—General	M
Cell Biology	M
Immunology	M
Microbiology	M
Pharmacology	M
Physiology	M

UNIVERSIDAD DE CIENCIAS MEDICAS

Anatomy	P,M,O
Biological and Biomedical Sciences—General	P,M,O

UNIVERSIDAD DE IBEROAMERICA

Neuroscience	P,M,D

UNIVERSIDAD DEL TURABO

Environmental Biology	M,D

UNIVERSITÉ DE MONCTON

Biochemistry	M
Biological and Biomedical Sciences—General	M
Nutrition	M

UNIVERSITÉ DE MONTRÉAL

Biochemistry	M,D,O
Biological and Biomedical Sciences—General	M,D
Cancer Biology/Oncology	D
Cell Biology	M,D
Genetics	D
Immunology	M,D
Infectious Diseases	D
Microbiology	M,D
Molecular Biology	M,D
Neuroscience	M,D
Nutrition	M,D,O
Pathology	M,D
Pharmacology	M,D
Physiology	M,D
Toxicology	O
Virology	D

UNIVERSITÉ DE SHERBROOKE

Biochemistry	M,D
Biological and Biomedical Sciences—General	M,D,O
Biophysics	M,D
Cell Biology	M,D
Immunology	M,D
Microbiology	M,D
Pharmacology	M,D
Physiology	M,D
Radiation Biology	M,D

UNIVERSITÉ DU QUÉBEC À CHICOUTIMI

Genetics	M

UNIVERSITÉ DU QUÉBEC À MONTRÉAL

Biological and Biomedical Sciences—General	M,D

UNIVERSITÉ DU QUÉBEC À TROIS-RIVIÈRES

Biophysics	M,D

UNIVERSITÉ DU QUÉBEC EN ABITIBI-TÉMISCAMINGUE

Biological and Biomedical Sciences—General	M,D

UNIVERSITÉ DU QUÉBEC, INSTITUT NATIONAL DE LA RECHERCHE SCIENTIFIQUE

Biological and Biomedical Sciences—General	M,D
Immunology	M,D
Medical Microbiology	M,D
Microbiology	M,D
Virology	M,D

UNIVERSITÉ LAVAL

Anatomy	M,D,O
Biochemistry	M,D,O
Biological and Biomedical Sciences—General	M,D,O
Cancer Biology/Oncology	O
Cardiovascular Sciences	O
Cell Biology	M,D
Immunology	M,D
Infectious Diseases	O
Microbiology	M,D
Molecular Biology	M,D
Neurobiology	M,D
Nutrition	M,D
Pathology	O
Physiology	M,D
Plant Biology	M,D

UNIVERSITY AT ALBANY, STATE UNIVERSITY OF NEW YORK

Biochemistry	M,D
Biological and Biomedical Sciences—General	M,D*
Biopsychology	M,D,O
Cell Biology	M,D
Conservation Biology	M
Developmental Biology	M,D
Ecology	M,D
Evolutionary Biology	M,D
Genetics	M,D
Immunology	M,D
Molecular Biology	M,D
Molecular Pathogenesis	M,D
Neurobiology	M,D
Neuroscience	M,D
Structural Biology	M,D
Toxicology	M,D*

UNIVERSITY AT BUFFALO, THE STATE UNIVERSITY OF NEW YORK

Anatomy	M,D
Biochemistry	M,D
Biological and Biomedical Sciences—General	M,D
Biophysics	M,D
Cancer Biology/Oncology	D
Cell Biology	D
Ecology	M,D,O
Evolutionary Biology	M,D,O
Immunology	M,D
Microbiology	M,D
Molecular Biology	D
Molecular Pharmacology	D
Neuroscience	M,D
Nutrition	M,D
Pathology	M,D
Pharmacology	M,D
Physiology	M,D
Structural Biology	M,D
Toxicology	M,D

THE UNIVERSITY OF AKRON

Biological and Biomedical Sciences—General	M,D
Nutrition	M

THE UNIVERSITY OF ALABAMA

Biological and Biomedical Sciences—General	M,D
Nutrition	M

THE UNIVERSITY OF ALABAMA AT BIRMINGHAM

Biochemistry	D
Biological and Biomedical Sciences—General	M,D*
Cell Biology	D
Genetics	D
Microbiology	D
Molecular Biology	D
Molecular Genetics	D
Molecular Physiology	D
Neurobiology	D
Neuroscience	D
Nutrition	M,D
Pathology	D
Pharmacology	D

THE UNIVERSITY OF ALABAMA IN HUNTSVILLE

Biological and Biomedical Sciences—General	M

UNIVERSITY OF ALASKA ANCHORAGE

Biological and Biomedical Sciences—General	M

UNIVERSITY OF ALASKA FAIRBANKS

Biochemistry	M,D
Biological and Biomedical Sciences—General	M,D
Botany	M,D
Marine Biology	M,D
Nutrition	M,D
Zoology	M,D

UNIVERSITY OF ALBERTA

Biochemistry	M,D
Biological and Biomedical Sciences—General	P,M,D
Cancer Biology/Oncology	M,D
Cell Biology	M,D
Conservation Biology	M,D
Ecology	M,D
Environmental Biology	M,D
Evolutionary Biology	M,D
Genetics	M,D
Immunology	M,D
Medical Microbiology	M,D
Microbiology	M,D
Molecular Biology	M,D
Neuroscience	M,D
Pathology	M,D
Pharmacology	M,D
Physiology	M,D
Plant Biology	M,D

THE UNIVERSITY OF ARIZONA

Anatomy	D
Biochemistry	M,D
Biological and Biomedical Sciences—General	M,D
Cancer Biology/Oncology	D
Cell Biology	M,D
Ecology	M,D
Entomology	M,D
Evolutionary Biology	M,D
Genetics	M,D
Immunology	M,D
Microbiology	M,D
Molecular Biology	M,D
Neuroscience	D
Nutrition	M,D

THE UNIVERSITY OF ALABAMA

Pathobiology	M,D
Pharmacology	M,D
Physiology	M,D
Plant Pathology	M,D

UNIVERSITY OF ARKANSAS

Biological and Biomedical Sciences—General	M,D
Cell Biology	M,D
Entomology	M,D
Molecular Biology	M,D
Plant Pathology	M

UNIVERSITY OF ARKANSAS AT LITTLE ROCK

Biological and Biomedical Sciences—General	M

UNIVERSITY OF ARKANSAS FOR MEDICAL SCIENCES

Anatomy	M,D
Biochemistry	M,D
Biological and Biomedical Sciences—General	M,D,O
Biophysics	M,D
Immunology	M,D
Microbiology	M,D
Molecular Biology	M,D
Neurobiology	M,D
Nutrition	M
Pathology	M
Pharmacology	M,D
Physiology	M,D
Toxicology	M,D

UNIVERSITY OF BRIDGEPORT

Nutrition	M

THE UNIVERSITY OF BRITISH COLUMBIA

Anatomy	M,D
Biochemistry	M,D
Biopsychology	M,D
Botany	M,D
Cell Biology	M,D
Genetics	M,D
Immunology	M,D
Microbiology	M,D
Molecular Biology	M,D
Neuroscience	M,D
Nutrition	M,D
Pathology	M,D
Pharmacology	M,D
Physiology	M,D
Reproductive Biology	M,D
Zoology	M,D

UNIVERSITY OF CALGARY

Biochemistry	M,D
Biological and Biomedical Sciences—General	M,D
Cancer Biology/Oncology	M,D
Cardiovascular Sciences	M,D
Immunology	M,D
Infectious Diseases	M,D
Microbiology	M,D
Molecular Biology	M,D
Neuroscience	M,D

UNIVERSITY OF CALIFORNIA, BERKELEY

Biochemistry	D
Biological and Biomedical Sciences—General	D
Biophysics	D
Cell Biology	D
Immunology	D
Infectious Diseases	M,D
Microbiology	D

Molecular Biology	D
Molecular Toxicology	D
Neuroscience	D*
Nutrition	D
Physiology	M,D
Plant Biology	D

UNIVERSITY OF CALIFORNIA, DAVIS

Animal Behavior	D
Biochemistry	M,D
Biophysics	M,D
Cell Biology	M,D
Developmental Biology	M,D
Ecology	M,D
Entomology	M,D
Evolutionary Biology	D
Genetics	M,D
Immunology	M,D
Microbiology	M,D
Molecular Biology	M,D
Neuroscience	D
Nutrition	M,D
Pathology	M,D
Pharmacology	M,D
Physiology	M,D
Plant Biology	M,D
Plant Pathology	M,D
Toxicology	M,D
Zoology	M

UNIVERSITY OF CALIFORNIA, IRVINE

Anatomy	M,D
Biochemistry	M,D
Biological and Biomedical Sciences—General	M,D
Biophysics	D
Cell Biology	M,D
Developmental Biology	M,D
Ecology	M,D
Evolutionary Biology	M,D
Genetics	D
Microbiology	M,D
Molecular Biology	M,D
Molecular Genetics	M,D
Neurobiology	M,D
Pharmacology	M,D*
Physiology	D
Toxicology	M,D

UNIVERSITY OF CALIFORNIA, LOS ANGELES

Anatomy	D
Biochemistry	M,D
Biological and Biomedical Sciences—General	M,D
Cell Biology	D
Developmental Biology	D
Ecology	M,D
Evolutionary Biology	M,D
Human Genetics	M,D
Immunology	M,D
Microbiology	M,D
Molecular Biology	M,D*
Molecular Genetics	M,D
Molecular Toxicology	D
Neurobiology	D
Neuroscience	D
Pathology	M,D
Pharmacology	D
Physiology	M,D
Toxicology	D

UNIVERSITY OF CALIFORNIA, MERCED

Biological and Biomedical Sciences—General	M,D
Systems Biology	M,D

UNIVERSITY OF CALIFORNIA, RIVERSIDE

Biochemistry	M,D
Biological and Biomedical Sciences—General	M,D
Botany	M,D
Cell Biology	M,D
Developmental Biology	M,D
Entomology	M,D
Evolutionary Biology	M,D
Genetics	D
Genomic Sciences	D
Microbiology	M,D
Molecular Biology	M,D
Molecular Genetics	D
Neuroscience	D
Plant Biology	M,D
Plant Pathology	M,D
Toxicology	M,D

UNIVERSITY OF CALIFORNIA, SAN DIEGO

Biochemistry	M,D
Biological and Biomedical Sciences—General	M,D
Biophysics	M,D
Cancer Biology/Oncology	D
Cardiovascular Sciences	D
Cell Biology	D
Developmental Biology	D
Ecology	D
Evolutionary Biology	D
Genetics	D
Immunology	D
Marine Biology	M,D
Microbiology	D
Molecular Biology	D
Molecular Pathology	D
Neurobiology	D
Neuroscience	D
Pharmacology	D
Physiology	D
Plant Biology	D
Plant Molecular Biology	D
Structural Biology	D
Systems Biology	D
Virology	D

UNIVERSITY OF CALIFORNIA, SAN FRANCISCO

Anatomy	D
Biochemistry	D
Biological and Biomedical Sciences—General	D
Biophysics	D
Cell Biology	D
Developmental Biology	D
Genetics	D
Genomic Sciences	D
Immunology	D
Microbiology	D
Molecular Biology	D
Neuroscience	D
Pathology	D
Pharmacology	D
Physiology	D

UNIVERSITY OF CALIFORNIA, SANTA BARBARA

Biochemistry	M,D
Cell Biology	M,D
Developmental Biology	M,D
Ecology	M,D
Evolutionary Biology	M,D
Marine Biology	M,D
Molecular Biology	M,D

UNIVERSITY OF CALIFORNIA, SANTA CRUZ

Biochemistry	M,D
Cell Biology	M,D
Developmental Biology	M,D
Ecology	M,D
Environmental Biology	M,D
Evolutionary Biology	M,D
Molecular Biology	M,D
Toxicology	M,D

UNIVERSITY OF CENTRAL ARKANSAS

Biological and Biomedical Sciences—General	M

UNIVERSITY OF CENTRAL FLORIDA

Biological and Biomedical Sciences—General	M,D,O
Conservation Biology	M,D,O
Microbiology	M
Molecular Biology	M

UNIVERSITY OF CENTRAL MISSOURI

Biological and Biomedical Sciences—General	M,D

UNIVERSITY OF CENTRAL OKLAHOMA

Biological and Biomedical Sciences—General	M
Nutrition	M

UNIVERSITY OF CHICAGO

Anatomy	D
Biochemistry	D
Biological and Biomedical Sciences—General	D
Biophysics	D
Cancer Biology/Oncology	D
Cell Biology	D
Developmental Biology	D
Ecology	D
Evolutionary Biology	D
Genetics	D
Genomic Sciences	D
Human Genetics	D
Immunology	D
Microbiology	D
Molecular Biology	D
Molecular Medicine	D
Molecular Pathogenesis	D
Molecular Physiology	D
Neurobiology	D
Neuroscience	D
Nutrition	D
Pathology	D
Pharmacology	D
Physiology	D
Systems Biology	D
Zoology	D

UNIVERSITY OF CINCINNATI

Biochemistry	M,D
Biological and Biomedical Sciences—General	M,D
Biophysics	D
Cancer Biology/Oncology	D
Cell Biology	D
Developmental Biology	D
Genomic Sciences	M,D
Immunology	M,D
Microbiology	M,D
Molecular Biology	M,D
Molecular Genetics	M,D
Molecular Medicine	D

UNIVERSITY OF COLORADO AT BOULDER

Animal Behavior	M,D
Biochemistry	M,D
Cell Biology	M,D
Developmental Biology	M,D
Ecology	M,D
Evolutionary Biology	M,D
Genetics	M,D
Marine Biology	M,D
Microbiology	M,D
Molecular Biology	M,D
Neurobiology	M,D
Physiology	M,D

UNIVERSITY OF COLORADO AT COLORADO SPRINGS

Biological and Biomedical Sciences—General	M

UNIVERSITY OF COLORADO DENVER

Biochemistry	D
Biological and Biomedical Sciences—General	M,D
Cancer Biology/Oncology	D
Cell Biology	D
Computational Biology	D
Developmental Biology	D
Genetics	M,D
Immunology	D
Microbiology	D
Molecular Biology	D
Neuroscience	D
Pathology	D
Pharmacology	D
Physiology	D
Reproductive Biology	D
Toxicology	D

UNIVERSITY OF CONNECTICUT

Biochemistry	M,D
Biological and Biomedical Sciences—General	D
Biophysics	M,D
Biopsychology	M,D,O
Botany	M,D
Cell Biology	M,D
Developmental Biology	M,D
Ecology	M,D,O
Entomology	M,D
Genetics	M,D
Genomic Sciences	M
Microbiology	M,D
Molecular Biology	M
Neurobiology	M,D
Neuroscience	M,D,O
Nutrition	M,D
Pathobiology	M,D
Pharmacology	M,D
Physiology	M,D*
Plant Biology	M,D*
Plant Molecular Biology	M,D
Structural Biology	M,D
Toxicology	M,D
Zoology	M,D

UNIVERSITY OF CONNECTICUT HEALTH CENTER

Biochemistry	D

*M—master's degree; P—first professional degree; D—doctorate; O—other advanced degree; *—Close-Up and/or Display*

Biological and Biomedical Sciences—General	D*
Cell Biology	D*
Developmental Biology	D
Genetics	D*
Immunology	D*
Molecular Biology	D*
Neuroscience	D*

UNIVERSITY OF DAYTON

Biological and Biomedical Sciences—General	M,D

UNIVERSITY OF DELAWARE

Biochemistry	M,D
Biological and Biomedical Sciences—General	M,D
Cancer Biology/Oncology	M,D
Cell Biology	M,D
Developmental Biology	M,D
Ecology	M,D
Entomology	M,D
Evolutionary Biology	M,D
Genetics	M,D
Microbiology	M,D
Molecular Biology	M,D
Neuroscience	D
Nutrition	M
Physiology	M,D

UNIVERSITY OF DENVER

Biological and Biomedical Sciences—General	M,D

UNIVERSITY OF DETROIT MERCY

Biochemistry	M

UNIVERSITY OF FLORIDA

Biochemistry	M,D*
Biological and Biomedical Sciences—General	D
Botany	M,D
Cell Biology	M,D*
Ecology	M,D
Entomology	M,D
Genetics	D*
Genomic Sciences	D
Immunology	D*
Microbiology	M,D
Molecular Biology	M,D
Molecular Genetics	M,D
Neuroscience	M,D*
Nutrition	M,D
Pathology	D
Pharmacology	M,D
Physiology	M,D*
Plant Biology	M,D
Plant Molecular Biology	M,D
Plant Pathology	M,D
Toxicology	M,D,O
Zoology	M,D

UNIVERSITY OF GEORGIA

Anatomy	M
Biochemistry	M,D
Biological and Biomedical Sciences—General	D
Cell Biology	M,D
Ecology	M,D
Entomology	M,D
Genetics	M,D
Infectious Diseases	M,D
Microbiology	M,D*
Molecular Biology	M,D
Neuroscience	D
Nutrition	M,D
Pathology	M,D
Pharmacology	M,D
Physiology	M,D

Plant Biology	M,D
Plant Pathology	M,D
Toxicology	M,D

UNIVERSITY OF GUAM

Biological and Biomedical Sciences—General	M
Marine Biology	M

UNIVERSITY OF GUELPH

Anatomy	M,D
Biochemistry	M,D
Biological and Biomedical Sciences—General	M,D
Biophysics	M,D
Botany	M,D
Cardiovascular Sciences	M,D,O
Cell Biology	M,D
Ecology	M,D
Entomology	M,D
Environmental Biology	M,D
Evolutionary Biology	M,D
Immunology	M,D,O
Infectious Diseases	M,D,O
Microbiology	M,D
Molecular Biology	M,D
Molecular Genetics	M,D
Neuroscience	M,D,O
Nutrition	M,D
Pathology	M,D,O
Pharmacology	M,D
Physiology	M,D
Plant Pathology	M,D
Toxicology	M,D
Zoology	M,D

UNIVERSITY OF HARTFORD

Biological and Biomedical Sciences—General	M
Neuroscience	M

UNIVERSITY OF HAWAII AT HILO

Conservation Biology	M
Marine Biology	M

UNIVERSITY OF HAWAII AT MANOA

Biological and Biomedical Sciences—General	M,D
Botany	M,D
Conservation Biology	M,D
Developmental Biology	M,D
Ecology	M,D
Entomology	M,D
Evolutionary Biology	M,D
Genetics	M,D
Marine Biology	M,D
Medical Microbiology	M,D
Microbiology	M,D
Molecular Biology	M,D
Nutrition	M,D
Physiology	M,D
Plant Pathology	M,D
Reproductive Biology	M,D
Zoology	M,D

UNIVERSITY OF HOUSTON

Biochemistry	M,D
Biological and Biomedical Sciences—General	M,D
Nutrition	M,D

UNIVERSITY OF HOUSTON–CLEAR LAKE

Biological and Biomedical Sciences—General	M

Plant Biology	M,D
Plant Pathology	M,D
Toxicology	M,D

UNIVERSITY OF IDAHO

Biochemistry	M,D
Biological and Biomedical Sciences—General	M,D
Computational Biology	M,D
Entomology	M,D
Microbiology	M,D
Molecular Biology	M,D
Neuroscience	M,D

UNIVERSITY OF ILLINOIS AT CHICAGO

Anatomy	D
Biochemistry	D
Biological and Biomedical Sciences—General	M,D
Biophysics	M,D
Cell Biology	D
Genetics	D
Immunology	D
Microbiology	D
Molecular Biology	D
Molecular Genetics	D
Neurobiology	D*
Neuroscience	D
Nutrition	M,D
Pharmacology	D
Physiology	M,D

UNIVERSITY OF ILLINOIS AT SPRINGFIELD

Biological and Biomedical Sciences—General	M

UNIVERSITY OF ILLINOIS AT URBANA–CHAMPAIGN

Biochemistry	M,D
Biological and Biomedical Sciences—General	M,D
Biophysics	M,D
Cell Biology	D
Computational Biology	M,D
Conservation Biology	M,D
Developmental Biology	D
Ecology	M,D
Entomology	M,D
Evolutionary Biology	M,D
Microbiology	M,D
Molecular Physiology	M,D
Neuroscience	D
Nutrition	M,D
Pathobiology	M,D
Physiology	M,D
Plant Biology	M,D
Zoology	M,D

UNIVERSITY OF INDIANAPOLIS

Biological and Biomedical Sciences—General	M

THE UNIVERSITY OF IOWA

Anatomy	D
Bacteriology	M,D
Biochemistry	M,D
Biological and Biomedical Sciences—General	M,D
Biophysics	M,D
Cell Biology	M,D
Computational Biology	M,D,O
Evolutionary Biology	M,D
Genetics	M,D
Immunology	M,D
Microbiology	M,D
Molecular Biology	D
Neurobiology	M,D
Neuroscience	D
Pathology	M
Pharmacology	M,D
Physiology	M,D
Plant Biology	M,D

Radiation Biology	M,D
Toxicology	M,D
Translational Biology	M,D
Virology	M,D

THE UNIVERSITY OF KANSAS

Anatomy	M,D
Biochemistry	M,D
Biological and Biomedical Sciences—General	M,D*
Biophysics	M,D
Botany	M,D
Cell Biology	M,D
Developmental Biology	M,D
Ecology	M,D
Entomology	M,D
Evolutionary Biology	M,D
Immunology	D
Microbiology	M,D
Molecular Biology	M,D
Molecular Genetics	D
Neuroscience	M,D
Nutrition	M,D,O
Pathology	M,D
Pharmacology	M,D
Physiology	M,D
Toxicology	M,D

UNIVERSITY OF KENTUCKY

Anatomy	D
Biochemistry	D
Biological and Biomedical Sciences—General	M,D
Entomology	M,D
Microbiology	D
Neurobiology	D
Nutrition	M,D
Pharmacology	D
Physiology	M,D
Plant Pathology	M,D
Plant Physiology	D
Toxicology	M,D

UNIVERSITY OF LETHBRIDGE

Biochemistry	M,D
Biological and Biomedical Sciences—General	M,D
Molecular Biology	M,D
Neuroscience	M,D

UNIVERSITY OF LOUISIANA AT LAFAYETTE

Biological and Biomedical Sciences—General	M,D
Environmental Biology	M,D
Evolutionary Biology	M,D

UNIVERSITY OF LOUISIANA AT MONROE

Biological and Biomedical Sciences—General	M

UNIVERSITY OF LOUISVILLE

Anatomy	M,D
Biochemistry	M,D
Biological and Biomedical Sciences—General	M,D
Biophysics	M,D
Environmental Biology	M,D
Immunology	M,D
Microbiology	M,D
Molecular Biology	M,D
Neurobiology	M,D
Pharmacology	M,D
Physiology	M,D
Toxicology	M,D

UNIVERSITY OF MAINE

Biochemistry	M,D

Biological and Biomedical Sciences—General	D
Botany	M
Ecology	M,D
Entomology	M
Marine Biology	M,D
Microbiology	M,D
Molecular Biology	M,D
Nutrition	M,D
Plant Biology	M,D
Plant Pathology	M
Zoology	M,D

UNIVERSITY OF MANITOBA

Anatomy	M,D
Biochemistry	M,D
Biological and Biomedical Sciences—General	M,D,O
Botany	M,D
Cancer Biology/Oncology	M
Ecology	M,D
Entomology	M,D
Human Genetics	M,D
Immunology	M,D
Medical Microbiology	M,D
Microbiology	M,D
Nutrition	M,D
Pathology	M
Pharmacology	M,D
Physiology	M,D
Plant Physiology	M,D
Zoology	M,D

UNIVERSITY OF MARYLAND, BALTIMORE

Biochemistry	M,D
Biological and Biomedical Sciences—General	M,D
Cancer Biology/Oncology	M,D
Cell Biology	M,D
Genomic Sciences	M,D
Human Genetics	M,D
Immunology	D
Microbiology	D
Molecular Biology	M,D
Molecular Medicine	M,D
Neurobiology	D
Neuroscience	D
Pathology	M
Pharmacology	M,D
Toxicology	M,D

UNIVERSITY OF MARYLAND, BALTIMORE COUNTY

Biochemistry	M,D
Biological and Biomedical Sciences—General	M,D
Cell Biology	D
Molecular Biology	M,D
Neuroscience	D

UNIVERSITY OF MARYLAND, COLLEGE PARK

Biochemistry	M,D
Biological and Biomedical Sciences—General	M,D
Biophysics	D
Cell Biology	M,D
Conservation Biology	M
Ecology	M,D
Entomology	M,D
Evolutionary Biology	M,D
Molecular Biology	D
Molecular Genetics	M,D
Neuroscience	M,D
Nutrition	M,D
Plant Biology	M,D

UNIVERSITY OF MARYLAND EASTERN SHORE

Toxicology	M,D

UNIVERSITY OF MASSACHUSETTS AMHERST

Animal Behavior	M,D
Biochemistry	M,D
Biological and Biomedical Sciences—General	M,D
Cell Biology	M,D
Developmental Biology	D
Ecology	M,D
Entomology	M,D
Environmental Biology	M,D
Evolutionary Biology	M,D
Genetics	M,D
Microbiology	M,D*
Molecular Biophysics	D
Neuroscience	M,D
Nutrition	M,D
Physiology	M,D
Plant Biology	M,D
Plant Molecular Biology	M,D
Plant Physiology	M,D

UNIVERSITY OF MASSACHUSETTS BOSTON

Biological and Biomedical Sciences—General	M
Cell Biology	D
Environmental Biology	D
Molecular Biology	D

UNIVERSITY OF MASSACHUSETTS DARTMOUTH

Biological and Biomedical Sciences—General	M
Marine Biology	M

UNIVERSITY OF MASSACHUSETTS LOWELL

Biochemistry	M,D
Biological and Biomedical Sciences—General	M,D
Nutrition	M,O
Pathology	M,O

UNIVERSITY OF MASSACHUSETTS WORCESTER

Biochemistry	D
Biological and Biomedical Sciences—General	D
Cancer Biology/Oncology	D
Cell Biology	D
Immunology	D
Microbiology	D
Molecular Genetics	D
Molecular Pharmacology	D
Molecular Physiology	D
Neuroscience	D
Physiology	D
Virology	D

UNIVERSITY OF MEDICINE AND DENTISTRY OF NEW JERSEY

Biochemistry	M,D
Biological and Biomedical Sciences—General	M,D,O
Cardiovascular Sciences	M,D
Cell Biology	M,D
Developmental Biology	M,D,O
Immunology	M,D,O
Microbiology	M,D
Molecular Biology	M,D
Molecular Genetics	M,D
Molecular Medicine	D
Molecular Pathology	M,D,O

Molecular Pharmacology	M,D
Neuroscience	M,D
Nutrition	M,D,O
Pathology	D
Pharmacology	D
Physiology	M,D
Toxicology	M,D

UNIVERSITY OF MEMPHIS

Biological and Biomedical Sciences—General	M,D
Nutrition	M

UNIVERSITY OF MIAMI

Biochemistry	D
Biological and Biomedical Sciences—General	M,D
Biophysics	D
Cancer Biology/Oncology	D
Cell Biology	D
Developmental Biology	D
Evolutionary Biology	M,D
Genetics	M,D
Immunology	D
Marine Biology	M,D
Microbiology	D
Molecular Biology	D
Neuroscience	M,D
Pharmacology	D
Physiology	D

UNIVERSITY OF MICHIGAN

Biochemistry	D
Biological and Biomedical Sciences—General	M,D
Biophysics	D
Biopsychology	D
Cell Biology	M,D
Conservation Biology	M,D
Developmental Biology	M,D
Ecology	M,D
Evolutionary Biology	M,D
Human Genetics	M,D
Immunology	D
Microbiology	D
Molecular Biology	M,D
Molecular Pathology	D
Neuroscience	D
Nutrition	M,D
Pathology	D
Pharmacology	D
Physiology	D
Toxicology	M,D

UNIVERSITY OF MICHIGAN–FLINT

Biological and Biomedical Sciences—General	M

UNIVERSITY OF MINNESOTA, DULUTH

Biochemistry	M,D
Biological and Biomedical Sciences—General	M,D
Biophysics	M,D
Immunology	M,D
Medical Microbiology	M,D
Molecular Biology	M,D
Pharmacology	M,D
Physiology	M,D
Toxicology	M,D

UNIVERSITY OF MINNESOTA, TWIN CITIES CAMPUS

Animal Behavior	M,D
Biochemistry	D
Biological and Biomedical Sciences—General	M,D
Biophysics	M,D*

Biopsychology	D
Cancer Biology/Oncology	D
Cell Biology	M,D
Conservation Biology	M,D
Developmental Biology	M,D
Ecology	M,D
Entomology	M,D
Evolutionary Biology	M,D
Genetics	M,D
Immunology	D
Infectious Diseases	M,D
Microbiology	D
Molecular Biology	M,D
Neurobiology	M,D
Neuroscience	M,D
Nutrition	M,D
Pharmacology	M,D
Physiology	D
Plant Biology	M,D
Plant Pathology	M,D
Structural Biology	D
Toxicology	M,D
Virology	D

UNIVERSITY OF MISSISSIPPI

Biological and Biomedical Sciences—General	M,D
Pharmacology	M,D

UNIVERSITY OF MISSISSIPPI MEDICAL CENTER

Anatomy	M,D
Biochemistry	M,D
Biological and Biomedical Sciences—General	M,D
Biophysics	M,D
Microbiology	M,D
Pathology	M,D
Pharmacology	M,D
Physiology	M,D
Toxicology	M,D

UNIVERSITY OF MISSOURI

Anatomy	M
Biochemistry	M,D
Biological and Biomedical Sciences—General	M,D
Cell Biology	M,D
Ecology	M,D
Entomology	M,D
Evolutionary Biology	M,D
Genetics	M,D
Immunology	M,D
Microbiology	M,D
Neurobiology	M,D
Neuroscience	M,D
Nutrition	M,D
Pathobiology	M,D
Pathology	M
Pharmacology	M,D
Physiology	M,D
Plant Biology	M,D

UNIVERSITY OF MISSOURI–KANSAS CITY

Biochemistry	D
Biological and Biomedical Sciences—General	M,D
Biophysics	D
Cell Biology	D*
Molecular Biology	D*

UNIVERSITY OF MISSOURI–ST. LOUIS

Animal Behavior	M,D,O
Biochemistry	M,D,O
Biological and Biomedical Sciences—General	M,D,O
Botany	M,D,O

*M—master's degree; P—first professional degree; D—doctorate; O—other advanced degree; *—Close-Up and / or Display*

Cell Biology	M,D,O
Conservation Biology	M,D,O
Developmental Biology	M,D,O
Ecology	M,D,O
Evolutionary Biology	M,D,O
Genetics	M,D,O
Molecular Biology	M,D,O
Neuroscience	M,D,O
Physiology	M,D,O

THE UNIVERSITY OF MONTANA

Animal Behavior	M,D,O
Biochemistry	M,D
Biological and Biomedical Sciences—General	M,D
Ecology	M,D
Infectious Diseases	D
Microbiology	M,D
Neuroscience	M,D
Toxicology	M,D
Zoology	M,D

UNIVERSITY OF NEBRASKA AT KEARNEY

Biological and Biomedical Sciences—General	M

UNIVERSITY OF NEBRASKA AT OMAHA

Biological and Biomedical Sciences—General	M
Biopsychology	M,D,O

UNIVERSITY OF NEBRASKA–LINCOLN

Biochemistry	M,D
Biological and Biomedical Sciences—General	M,D
Biopsychology	M,D
Entomology	M,D
Nutrition	M,D
Toxicology	M,D

UNIVERSITY OF NEBRASKA MEDICAL CENTER

Anatomy	M,D
Biochemistry	M,D
Biological and Biomedical Sciences—General	M,D
Cancer Biology/Oncology	D
Cell Biology	M,D
Genetics	M,D
Microbiology	M,D
Molecular Biology	M,D
Neuroscience	M,D
Nutrition	Q
Pathology	M,D
Pharmacology	M,D
Physiology	M,D
Toxicology	M,D

UNIVERSITY OF NEVADA, LAS VEGAS

Biochemistry	M,D
Biological and Biomedical Sciences—General	M,D

UNIVERSITY OF NEVADA, RENO

Biochemistry	M,D
Biological and Biomedical Sciences—General	M
Cell Biology	M,D
Conservation Biology	D
Ecology	D
Evolutionary Biology	D
Molecular Biology	M,D
Molecular Pharmacology	D
Nutrition	M

Physiology	D

UNIVERSITY OF NEW BRUNSWICK FREDERICTON

Biological and Biomedical Sciences—General	M,D

UNIVERSITY OF NEW BRUNSWICK SAINT JOHN

Biological and Biomedical Sciences—General	M,D

UNIVERSITY OF NEW ENGLAND

Biological and Biomedical Sciences—General	M

UNIVERSITY OF NEW HAMPSHIRE

Biochemistry	M,D
Biological and Biomedical Sciences—General	M,D
Genetics	M,D
Microbiology	M,D
Nutrition	M,D
Plant Biology	M,D
Zoology	M,D

UNIVERSITY OF NEW HAVEN

Cell Biology	M,O
Ecology	M,O
Molecular Biology	M,O
Nutrition	M

UNIVERSITY OF NEW MEXICO

Biochemistry	M,D
Biological and Biomedical Sciences—General	M,D
Biophysics	M,D
Cell Biology	M,D
Genetics	M,D
Microbiology	M,D
Molecular Biology	M,D
Neuroscience	M,D
Nutrition	M
Pathology	M,D
Physiology	M,D
Toxicology	M,D

UNIVERSITY OF NEW ORLEANS

Biological and Biomedical Sciences—General	M,D

THE UNIVERSITY OF NORTH CAROLINA AT CHAPEL HILL

Biochemistry	M,D
Biological and Biomedical Sciences—General	M,D
Biophysics	M,D
Botany	M,D
Cell Biology	D
Developmental Biology	M,D
Ecology	M,D
Evolutionary Biology	M,D
Genetics	M,D
Immunology	M,D
Microbiology	M,D
Molecular Biology	M,D
Molecular Physiology	D
Neurobiology	D
Nutrition	M,D
Pathology	D
Pharmacology	D
Toxicology	M,D

THE UNIVERSITY OF NORTH CAROLINA AT CHARLOTTE

Biological and Biomedical Sciences—General	M,D

THE UNIVERSITY OF NORTH CAROLINA AT GREENSBORO

Biochemistry	M
Biological and Biomedical Sciences—General	M
Nutrition	M,D

THE UNIVERSITY OF NORTH CAROLINA WILMINGTON

Biological and Biomedical Sciences—General	M,D
Marine Biology	M,D

UNIVERSITY OF NORTH DAKOTA

Anatomy	M,D
Biochemistry	M,D
Biological and Biomedical Sciences—General	M,D
Botany	M,D
Ecology	M,D
Entomology	M,D
Environmental Biology	M,D
Genetics	M,D
Immunology	M,D
Microbiology	M,D
Pharmacology	M,D
Physiology	M,D
Zoology	M,D

UNIVERSITY OF NORTHERN COLORADO

Biological and Biomedical Sciences—General	M

UNIVERSITY OF NORTHERN IOWA

Biological and Biomedical Sciences—General	M

UNIVERSITY OF NORTH FLORIDA

Biological and Biomedical Sciences—General	M
Nutrition	M,O

UNIVERSITY OF NORTH TEXAS

Biochemistry	M,D
Biological and Biomedical Sciences—General	M,D
Molecular Biology	M,D

UNIVERSITY OF NORTH TEXAS HEALTH SCIENCE CENTER AT FORT WORTH

Anatomy	M,D
Biochemistry	M,D
Biological and Biomedical Sciences—General	M,D
Genetics	M,D
Immunology	M,D
Microbiology	M,D
Molecular Biology	M,D
Pharmacology	M,D
Physiology	M,D

UNIVERSITY OF NOTRE DAME

Biochemistry	M,D
Biological and Biomedical Sciences—General	M,D
Cell Biology	M,D
Ecology	M,D
Evolutionary Biology	M,D
Genetics	M,D
Molecular Biology	M,D
Parasitology	M,D
Physiology	M,D

UNIVERSITY OF OKLAHOMA

Biochemistry	M,D

Botany	M,D
Ecology	D
Evolutionary Biology	D
Microbiology	M,D
Neurobiology	D
Zoology	M,D

UNIVERSITY OF OKLAHOMA HEALTH SCIENCES CENTER

Biochemistry	M,D
Biological and Biomedical Sciences—General	M,D
Biopsychology	M,D
Cell Biology	M,D
Immunology	M,D
Microbiology	M,D
Molecular Biology	M,D
Neuroscience	M,D
Nutrition	M
Pathology	D
Physiology	M,D
Radiation Biology	M,D

UNIVERSITY OF OREGON

Biochemistry	M,D
Biological and Biomedical Sciences—General	M,D
Biopsychology	M,D
Ecology	M,D
Evolutionary Biology	M,D
Genetics	M,D
Marine Biology	M,D
Molecular Biology	M,D
Neuroscience	M,D
Physiology	M,D

UNIVERSITY OF OTTAWA

Biochemistry	M,D
Biological and Biomedical Sciences—General	M,D
Cell Biology	M,D
Immunology	M,D
Microbiology	M,D
Molecular Biology	M,D

UNIVERSITY OF PENNSYLVANIA

Biochemistry	D
Biological and Biomedical Sciences—General	M,D
Cancer Biology/Oncology	D
Cell Biology	D
Computational Biology	D
Developmental Biology	D
Genetics	D
Genomic Sciences	D
Immunology	D
Microbiology	D
Molecular Biology	D
Molecular Biophysics	D
Neuroscience	D
Parasitology	D
Pharmacology	D
Physiology	D
Virology	D

UNIVERSITY OF PITTSBURGH

Biochemistry	M,D
Biological and Biomedical Sciences—General	D
Cell Biology	M,D
Computational Biology	D
Developmental Biology	D
Ecology	D
Evolutionary Biology	D
Human Genetics	M,D,O
Immunology	M,D
Infectious Diseases	M,D,O
Microbiology	M,D,O
Molecular Biology	D
Molecular Biophysics	D

Molecular Genetics	M,D
Molecular Pathology	M,D
Molecular Pharmacology	M,D
Molecular Physiology	M,D
Neuroscience	D
Nutrition	M
Pathology	M,D
Structural Biology	D
Systems Biology	D
Virology	M,D

UNIVERSITY OF PRINCE EDWARD ISLAND

Anatomy	M,D
Bacteriology	M,D
Biological and Biomedical Sciences—General	M
Immunology	M,D
Parasitology	M,D
Pathology	M,D
Pharmacology	M,D
Physiology	M,D
Toxicology	M,D
Virology	M,D

UNIVERSITY OF PUERTO RICO, MAYAGÜEZ CAMPUS

Biological and Biomedical Sciences—General	M

UNIVERSITY OF PUERTO RICO, MEDICAL SCIENCES CAMPUS

Anatomy	M,D
Biochemistry	M,D
Biological and Biomedical Sciences—General	M,D
Microbiology	M,D
Nutrition	M,D,O
Pharmacology	M,D
Physiology	M,D
Toxicology	M,D

UNIVERSITY OF PUERTO RICO, RÍO PIEDRAS

Biological and Biomedical Sciences—General	M,D
Cell Biology	M,D
Ecology	M,D
Evolutionary Biology	M,D
Genetics	M,D
Molecular Biology	M,D
Neuroscience	M,D
Nutrition	M

UNIVERSITY OF REGINA

Biochemistry	M,D
Biological and Biomedical Sciences—General	M,D

UNIVERSITY OF RHODE ISLAND

Biochemistry	M,D
Biological and Biomedical Sciences—General	M,D
Cell Biology	M,D
Entomology	M,D
Microbiology	M,D
Molecular Biology	M,D
Molecular Genetics	M,D
Nutrition	M,D
Pharmacology	M,D
Toxicology	M,D

UNIVERSITY OF ROCHESTER

Anatomy	M,D
Biochemistry	M,D

Biological and Biomedical Sciences—General	M,D
Biophysics	M,D
Computational Biology	M,D
Genetics	M,D
Immunology	M,D
Microbiology	M,D
Neurobiology	M,D
Neuroscience	M,D
Pathology	M,D
Pharmacology	M,D
Physiology	M,D
Toxicology	M,D

UNIVERSITY OF SAN FRANCISCO

Biological and Biomedical Sciences—General	M

UNIVERSITY OF SASKATCHEWAN

Anatomy	M,D
Biochemistry	M,D
Biological and Biomedical Sciences—General	M,D
Cell Biology	M,D
Immunology	M,D
Microbiology	M,D
Pathology	M,D
Pharmacology	M,D
Physiology	M,D
Reproductive Biology	M,D
Toxicology	M,D,O

THE UNIVERSITY OF SCRANTON

Biochemistry	M

UNIVERSITY OF SOUTH ALABAMA

Biochemistry	D
Biological and Biomedical Sciences—General	M,D
Cell Biology	D
Immunology	D
Microbiology	D
Molecular Biology	D
Neuroscience	D
Pharmacology	D
Physiology	D
Toxicology	M

UNIVERSITY OF SOUTH CAROLINA

Biochemistry	M,D
Biological and Biomedical Sciences—General	M,D,O
Cell Biology	M,D
Developmental Biology	M,D
Ecology	M,D
Evolutionary Biology	M,D
Molecular Biology	M,D

THE UNIVERSITY OF SOUTH DAKOTA

Biological and Biomedical Sciences—General	M,D
Cardiovascular Sciences	M,D
Cell Biology	M,D
Immunology	M,D
Microbiology	M,D
Molecular Biology	M,D
Neuroscience	M,D
Pharmacology	M,D
Physiology	M,D

UNIVERSITY OF SOUTHERN CALIFORNIA

Biochemistry	M,D

Biological and Biomedical Sciences—General	M,D
Biophysics	M,D
Cell Biology	M,D
Computational Biology	D
Environmental Biology	M,D
Evolutionary Biology	D
Genetics	M,D
Immunology	M,D
Marine Biology	M,D
Microbiology	M,D
Molecular Biology	M,D
Molecular Pharmacology	M,D
Neurobiology	M,D
Neuroscience	D
Pathobiology	M,D
Pathology	M,D
Physiology	M,D
Systems Biology	D
Toxicology	M,D

UNIVERSITY OF SOUTHERN MAINE

Biological and Biomedical Sciences—General	M
Immunology	M
Molecular Biology	M

UNIVERSITY OF SOUTHERN MISSISSIPPI

Biochemistry	M,D
Biological and Biomedical Sciences—General	M,D
Environmental Biology	M,D
Marine Biology	M,D
Microbiology	M,D
Molecular Biology	M,D
Nutrition	M,D

UNIVERSITY OF SOUTH FLORIDA

Biochemistry	M,D
Biological and Biomedical Sciences—General	M,D
Cancer Biology/Oncology	D
Cell Biology	M,D
Conservation Biology	M,D
Marine Biology	M,D
Molecular Biology	M,D
Neuroscience	D

THE UNIVERSITY OF TENNESSEE

Anatomy	M,D
Animal Behavior	M,D
Biochemistry	M,D
Biological and Biomedical Sciences—General	M,D
Ecology	M,D
Entomology	M,D
Evolutionary Biology	M,D
Genetics	M,D
Genomic Sciences	M,D
Microbiology	M,D
Nutrition	M
Physiology	M,D
Plant Pathology	M,D
Plant Physiology	M,D

THE UNIVERSITY OF TENNESSEE AT MARTIN

Nutrition	M

THE UNIVERSITY OF TENNESSEE HEALTH SCIENCE CENTER

Anatomy	D
Biological and Biomedical Sciences—General	M,D
Neurobiology	D

THE UNIVERSITY OF TENNESSEE–OAK RIDGE NATIONAL LABORATORY GRADUATE SCHOOL OF GENOME SCIENCE AND TECHNOLOGY

Biological and Biomedical Sciences—General	M,D
Genomic Sciences	M,D

THE UNIVERSITY OF TEXAS AT ARLINGTON

Biological and Biomedical Sciences—General	M,D

THE UNIVERSITY OF TEXAS AT AUSTIN

Animal Behavior	M,D
Biochemistry	M,D
Biological and Biomedical Sciences—General	M,D
Biopsychology	D
Cell Biology	D
Ecology	M,D
Evolutionary Biology	M,D
Microbiology	D
Molecular Biology	D
Neurobiology	D
Neuroscience	D
Nutrition	M,D
Plant Biology	M,D

THE UNIVERSITY OF TEXAS AT BROWNSVILLE

Biological and Biomedical Sciences—General	M

THE UNIVERSITY OF TEXAS AT DALLAS

Biological and Biomedical Sciences—General	M,D
Cell Biology	M,D
Molecular Biology	M,D
Neuroscience	M,D

THE UNIVERSITY OF TEXAS AT EL PASO

Biological and Biomedical Sciences—General	M,D

THE UNIVERSITY OF TEXAS AT SAN ANTONIO

Biological and Biomedical Sciences—General	M,D*
Cell Biology	M,D
Molecular Biology	M,D
Neurobiology	M,D

THE UNIVERSITY OF TEXAS AT TYLER

Biological and Biomedical Sciences—General	M

THE UNIVERSITY OF TEXAS HEALTH SCIENCE CENTER AT HOUSTON

Biochemistry	M,D
Biological and Biomedical Sciences—General	M,D
Cancer Biology/Oncology	M,D
Cell Biology	M,D
Developmental Biology	M,D
Genetics	M,D
Human Genetics	M,D
Immunology	M,D
Microbiology	M,D

*M—master's degree; P—first professional degree; D—doctorate; O—other advanced degree; *—Close-Up and/or Display*

Molecular Biology	M,D
Molecular Genetics	M,D
Molecular Pathology	M,D
Neuroscience	M,D
Virology	M,D

THE UNIVERSITY OF TEXAS HEALTH SCIENCE CENTER AT SAN ANTONIO

Biochemistry	M,D
Biological and Biomedical Sciences—General	M,D
Cell Biology	M,D
Immunology	D
Microbiology	D
Molecular Medicine	M,D
Pharmacology	D
Physiology	M,D
Structural Biology	M,D

THE UNIVERSITY OF TEXAS MEDICAL BRANCH

Bacteriology	D
Biochemistry	D
Biological and Biomedical Sciences—General	M,D
Biophysics	D
Cell Biology	D
Computational Biology	D
Genetics	D
Immunology	M,D
Infectious Diseases	D
Microbiology	M,D
Molecular Biophysics	M,D
Neuroscience	D
Pathology	D
Pharmacology	M,D
Physiology	M,D
Structural Biology	D
Toxicology	M,D
Virology	D

THE UNIVERSITY OF TEXAS OF THE PERMIAN BASIN

Biological and Biomedical Sciences—General	M

THE UNIVERSITY OF TEXAS–PAN AMERICAN

Biological and Biomedical Sciences—General	M

THE UNIVERSITY OF TEXAS SOUTHWESTERN MEDICAL CENTER AT DALLAS

Biochemistry	D
Biological and Biomedical Sciences—General	M,D
Cancer Biology/Oncology	D
Cell Biology	D
Developmental Biology	D
Genetics	D
Immunology	D
Microbiology	D
Molecular Biophysics	D
Neuroscience	D
Radiation Biology	M,D

UNIVERSITY OF THE DISTRICT OF COLUMBIA

Cancer Biology/Oncology	M
Nutrition	M

UNIVERSITY OF THE INCARNATE WORD

Biological and Biomedical Sciences—General	M
Nutrition	M,O

UNIVERSITY OF THE PACIFIC

Biological and Biomedical Sciences—General	M

UNIVERSITY OF THE SCIENCES IN PHILADELPHIA

Biochemistry	M,D
Cell Biology	M,D
Molecular Biology	D
Pharmacology	M,D
Toxicology	M,D

THE UNIVERSITY OF TOLEDO

Biochemistry	M,D
Biological and Biomedical Sciences—General	M,D,O
Biopsychology	M,D
Cancer Biology/Oncology	M,D
Cardiovascular Sciences	M,D
Ecology	M,D
Genomic Sciences	M,O
Immunology	M,D
Molecular Biology	M
Neuroscience	M,D
Pathology	O
Pharmacology	M

UNIVERSITY OF TORONTO

Biochemistry	M,D
Biological and Biomedical Sciences—General	M,D
Biophysics	M,D
Cell Biology	M,D
Ecology	M,D
Evolutionary Biology	M,D
Genetics	M,D
Immunology	M,D
Nutrition	M,D
Pathobiology	M,D
Pharmacology	M,D
Physiology	M,D
Systems Biology	M,D
Toxicology	M,D

UNIVERSITY OF TULSA

Biochemistry	M
Biological and Biomedical Sciences—General	M,D

UNIVERSITY OF UTAH

Anatomy	D
Biochemistry	M,D
Biological and Biomedical Sciences—General	M,D,O
Cancer Biology/Oncology	M,D
Human Genetics	M,D
Molecular Biology	D
Neurobiology	D
Neuroscience	D
Nutrition	M
Pathology	M,D
Pharmacology	D
Physiology	D
Toxicology	D

UNIVERSITY OF VERMONT

Biochemistry	M,D
Biological and Biomedical Sciences—General	M,D
Biophysics	M,D
Cell Biology	M,D
Microbiology	M,D
Molecular Biology	M,D
Molecular Genetics	M,D
Molecular Physiology	M,D
Neuroscience	D
Nutrition	M,D
Pathology	M

Pharmacology	M,D
Plant Biology	M,D

UNIVERSITY OF VICTORIA

Biochemistry	M,D
Biological and Biomedical Sciences—General	M,D
Microbiology	M,D

UNIVERSITY OF VIRGINIA

Biochemistry	D
Biological and Biomedical Sciences—General	M,D
Biophysics	M,D
Cell Biology	D
Microbiology	D
Molecular Genetics	D
Molecular Physiology	M,D
Neuroscience	D
Pathology	D
Pharmacology	D
Physiology	D

UNIVERSITY OF WASHINGTON

Animal Behavior	D
Bacteriology	D
Biochemistry	D
Biological and Biomedical Sciences—General	M,D
Biophysics	D
Cell Biology	D*
Ecology	M,D
Genetics	M,D
Genomic Sciences	D
Immunology	M,D
Microbiology	D
Molecular Biology	D
Molecular Medicine	D
Neurobiology	D
Nutrition	M,D
Parasitology	D
Pathobiology	D
Pathology	D
Pharmacology	D
Physiology	D
Structural Biology	D
Toxicology	M,D

UNIVERSITY OF WATERLOO

Biochemistry	M,D
Biological and Biomedical Sciences—General	M,D

THE UNIVERSITY OF WESTERN ONTARIO

Anatomy	M,D
Biochemistry	M,D
Biophysics	M,D
Cell Biology	M,D
Immunology	M,D
Microbiology	M,D
Molecular Biology	M,D
Neuroscience	M,D
Pathology	M,D
Physiology	M,D
Plant Biology	M,D
Zoology	M,D

UNIVERSITY OF WEST FLORIDA

Biochemistry	M
Biological and Biomedical Sciences—General	M
Environmental Biology	M

UNIVERSITY OF WEST GEORGIA

Biological and Biomedical Sciences—General	M

UNIVERSITY OF WINDSOR

Biochemistry	M,D
Biological and Biomedical Sciences—General	M,D
Biopsychology	M,D

UNIVERSITY OF WISCONSIN–LA CROSSE

Biological and Biomedical Sciences—General	M
Cell Biology	M
Medical Microbiology	M
Microbiology	M
Molecular Biology	M
Physiology	M

UNIVERSITY OF WISCONSIN–MADISON

Bacteriology	M
Biochemistry	M,D
Biological and Biomedical Sciences—General	M,D
Biophysics	D
Biopsychology	D
Botany	M,D
Cancer Biology/Oncology	D
Cell Biology	D
Conservation Biology	M
Ecology	M
Entomology	M,D
Environmental Biology	M,D
Genetics	M,D*
Medical Microbiology	D
Microbiology	D
Molecular Biology	D
Neurobiology	D
Neuroscience	D
Nutrition	M,D
Pathology	D*
Pharmacology	D
Physiology	M,D
Plant Pathology	M,D
Toxicology	M,D
Zoology	M,D

UNIVERSITY OF WISCONSIN–MILWAUKEE

Biochemistry	M,D
Biological and Biomedical Sciences—General	M,D

UNIVERSITY OF WISCONSIN–OSHKOSH

Biological and Biomedical Sciences—General	M
Botany	M
Microbiology	M
Zoology	M

UNIVERSITY OF WISCONSIN–PARKSIDE

Molecular Biology	M

UNIVERSITY OF WISCONSIN–STEVENS POINT

Nutrition	M

UNIVERSITY OF WISCONSIN–STOUT

Nutrition	M

UNIVERSITY OF WYOMING

Botany	M,D
Cell Biology	D
Computational Biology	D
Ecology	M,D
Entomology	M,D
Genetics	D

Microbiology	D
Molecular Biology	M,D
Nutrition	M
Pathobiology	M
Physiology	M,D
Reproductive Biology	M,D
Zoology	M,D

UTAH STATE UNIVERSITY

Biochemistry	M,D
Biological and Biomedical Sciences—General	M,D
Ecology	M,D
Microbiology	M,D
Molecular Biology	M,D
Nutrition	M,D
Toxicology	M,D

VANDERBILT UNIVERSITY

Biochemistry	M,D
Biological and Biomedical Sciences—General	M,D
Biophysics	M,D
Cancer Biology/Oncology	M,D
Cell Biology	M,D
Human Genetics	D
Immunology	M,D
Microbiology	M,D
Molecular Biology	M,D
Molecular Physiology	M,D
Nutrition	M,D
Pathology	D
Pharmacology	D

VASSAR COLLEGE

Biological and Biomedical Sciences—General	M

VILLANOVA UNIVERSITY

Biological and Biomedical Sciences—General	M*

VIRGINIA COMMONWEALTH UNIVERSITY

Anatomy	D,O
Biochemistry	M,D,O
Biological and Biomedical Sciences—General	M,D,O
Genetics	M,D
Human Genetics	M,D,O
Immunology	M,D
Microbiology	M,D,O
Molecular Biology	M,D
Neurobiology	D
Neuroscience	M,D
Pathology	M,D
Pharmacology	M,D,O
Physiology	M,D,O
Systems Biology	D
Toxicology	M,D

VIRGINIA POLYTECHNIC INSTITUTE AND STATE UNIVERSITY

Biochemistry	M,D
Biological and Biomedical Sciences—General	M,D
Botany	M,D
Computational Biology	D
Developmental Biology	M,D
Ecology	M,D
Entomology	M,D
Evolutionary Biology	M,D
Genetics	M,D
Microbiology	M,D
Molecular Biology	D
Nutrition	M,D
Plant Pathology	M,D

Plant Physiology	M,D
Zoology	M,D

VIRGINIA STATE UNIVERSITY

Biological and Biomedical Sciences—General	M

WAGNER COLLEGE

Biological and Biomedical Sciences—General	M
Microbiology	M

WAKE FOREST UNIVERSITY

Anatomy	D
Biochemistry	D
Biological and Biomedical Sciences—General	M,D
Cancer Biology/Oncology	D
Genomic Sciences	D
Human Genetics	D
Immunology	D
Microbiology	D
Molecular Biology	D
Molecular Genetics	D
Molecular Medicine	M,D
Neurobiology	D
Neuroscience	D
Pathobiology	M,D
Pharmacology	D
Physiology	D

WALLA WALLA UNIVERSITY

Biological and Biomedical Sciences—General	M

WASHINGTON STATE UNIVERSITY

Biochemistry	M,D
Biological and Biomedical Sciences—General	M
Biophysics	M,D
Botany	M,D
Cell Biology	M,D
Entomology	M,D
Genetics	M,D
Microbiology	M,D
Molecular Biology	M,D
Neuroscience	M,D
Nutrition	M,D
Pharmacology	M,D
Plant Molecular Biology	M,D
Plant Pathology	M,D
Toxicology	M,D
Zoology	M,D

WASHINGTON STATE UNIVERSITY TRI-CITIES

Biological and Biomedical Sciences—General	M

WASHINGTON UNIVERSITY IN ST. LOUIS

Biochemistry	D
Biological and Biomedical Sciences—General	D
Cell Biology	D
Computational Biology	D
Developmental Biology	D
Ecology	D
Environmental Biology	D
Evolutionary Biology	D
Genetics	M,D,O
Immunology	D
Microbiology	D
Molecular Biology	D
Molecular Biophysics	D
Molecular Genetics	D
Molecular Pathogenesis	D

Neuroscience	D
Plant Biology	D

WAYNE STATE UNIVERSITY

Anatomy	M,D
Biochemistry	M,D
Biological and Biomedical Sciences—General	M,D
Biopsychology	M,D
Cancer Biology/Oncology	M,D*
Genetics	M,D
Immunology	M,D
Microbiology	M,D
Molecular Biology	M,D
Neuroscience	D
Nutrition	M,D
Pathology	M,D
Pharmacology	P,M,D
Physiology	M,D
Toxicology	M,D

WESLEYAN UNIVERSITY

Animal Behavior	D
Biochemistry	M,D
Biological and Biomedical Sciences—General	D
Cell Biology	D
Developmental Biology	D
Ecology	D
Evolutionary Biology	D
Genetics	D
Genomic Sciences	D
Molecular Biology	D
Neurobiology	D

WEST CHESTER UNIVERSITY OF PENNSYLVANIA

Biological and Biomedical Sciences—General	M,O
Nutrition	M,O

WESTERN CAROLINA UNIVERSITY

Biological and Biomedical Sciences—General	M

WESTERN CONNECTICUT STATE UNIVERSITY

Biological and Biomedical Sciences—General	M

WESTERN ILLINOIS UNIVERSITY

Biological and Biomedical Sciences—General	M,O
Marine Biology	M,O
Zoology	M,O

WESTERN KENTUCKY UNIVERSITY

Biological and Biomedical Sciences—General	M

WESTERN MICHIGAN UNIVERSITY

Biological and Biomedical Sciences—General	M,D
Physiology	M

WESTERN WASHINGTON UNIVERSITY

Biological and Biomedical Sciences—General	M

WEST TEXAS A&M UNIVERSITY

Biological and Biomedical Sciences—General	M

WEST VIRGINIA UNIVERSITY

Biochemistry	M,D
Biological and Biomedical Sciences—General	M,D
Cancer Biology/Oncology	M,D
Cell Biology	M,D
Developmental Biology	M,D
Entomology	M,D
Environmental Biology	M,D
Evolutionary Biology	M,D
Genetics	M,D
Genomic Sciences	M,D
Human Genetics	M,D
Immunology	M,D
Microbiology	M,D
Molecular Biology	M,D
Neurobiology	M,D
Neuroscience	D
Nutrition	M
Pharmacology	M,D
Physiology	M,D
Plant Pathology	M,D
Reproductive Biology	M,D
Teratology	M,D
Toxicology	M,D

WICHITA STATE UNIVERSITY

Biological and Biomedical Sciences—General	M*

WILFRID LAURIER UNIVERSITY

Biological and Biomedical Sciences—General	M

WILLIAM PATERSON UNIVERSITY OF NEW JERSEY

Biological and Biomedical Sciences—General	M

WINTHROP UNIVERSITY

Biological and Biomedical Sciences—General	M
Nutrition	M

WOODS HOLE OCEANOGRAPHIC INSTITUTION

Marine Biology	M,D,O

WORCESTER POLYTECHNIC INSTITUTE

Biochemistry	M,D
Biological and Biomedical Sciences—General	M,D

WRIGHT STATE UNIVERSITY

Anatomy	M
Biochemistry	M
Biological and Biomedical Sciences—General	M,D
Biophysics	M
Immunology	M
Microbiology	M
Molecular Biology	M
Pharmacology	M
Physiology	M
Toxicology	M

YALE UNIVERSITY

Biochemistry	D
Biological and Biomedical Sciences—General	D
Biophysics	D
Cancer Biology/Oncology	D
Cell Biology	D
Computational Biology	D
Developmental Biology	D

*M—master's degree; P—first professional degree; D—doctorate; O—other advanced degree; *—Close-Up and/or Display*

Ecology	D	Molecular Physiology	D	**YORK UNIVERSITY**	
Evolutionary Biology	D	Neurobiology	D	Biological and Biomedical	
Genetics	D	Neuroscience	D	Sciences—General	M,D
Genomic Sciences	D	Parasitology	D		
Immunology	D	Pathobiology	D	**YOUNGSTOWN STATE**	
Infectious Diseases	D	Pathology	M,D	**UNIVERSITY**	
Microbiology	D	Pharmacology	D	Anatomy	M
Molecular Biology	D	Physiology	D	Biochemistry	M
Molecular Biophysics	D	Plant Biology	D	Biological and Biomedical	
Molecular Medicine	D	Structural Biology	D	Sciences—General	M
Molecular Pathology	D	Virology	D		

Environmental Biology	M
Microbiology	M
Molecular Biology	M
Physiology	M

ACADEMIC PROGRAMS
IN THE BIOLOGICAL SCIENCES

Section 1
Biological and Biomedical Sciences

This section contains a directory of institutions offering graduate work in biological and biomedical sciences, followed by in-depth entries submitted by institutions that chose to prepare detailed program descriptions. Additional information about programs listed in the directory but not augmented by an in-depth entry may be obtained by writing directly to the dean of a graduate school or chair of a department at the address given in the directory.

Programs in fields related to the biological and biomedical sciences may be found throughout this book. In the other guides in this series:

Graduate Programs in the Humanities, Arts & Social Sciences,

See *Psychology and Counseling* and *Sociology, Anthropology, and Archaeology*

Graduate Programs in the Physical Sciences, Mathematics, Agricultural Sciences, the Environment & Natural Resources

See *Chemistry, Marine Sciences and Oceanography,* and *Mathematical Sciences*

Graduate Programs in Engineering & Applied Sciences

See *Agricultural Engineering and Bioengineering, Biomedical Engineering and Biotechnology, Civil and Environmental Engineering, Management of Engineering and Technology,* and *Ocean Engineering*

Graduate Programs in Business, Education, Health, Information Studies, Law & Social Work

See *Allied Health, Chiropractic, Dentistry and Dental Sciences, Medicine, Nursing, Optometry and Vision Sciences, Pharmacy and Pharmaceutical Sciences, Public Health,* and *Veterinary Medicine and Sciences*

CONTENTS

Program Directory

Close-Ups and Display

Biological and Biomedical Sciences—General

Acadia University, Faculty of Pure and Applied Science, Department of Biology, Wolfville, NS B4P 2R6, Canada. Offers M Sc. *Faculty:* 16 full-time (3 women), 4 part-time/adjunct (0 women). *Students:* 16 full-time (12 women), 12 part-time (8 women). 12 applicants, 58% accepted, 6 enrolled. In 2009, 5 master's awarded. *Degree requirements:* For master's, comprehensive exam, thesis. *Entrance requirements:* For master's, minimum B- average in last 2 years of major. Additional exam requirements/recommendations for international students: Required—TOEFL (minimum score 580 paper-based; 237 computer-based; 93 iBT), IELTS (minimum score 6.5). *Application deadline:* For fall admission, 2/1 for domestic and international students. Applications are processed on a rolling basis. Application fee: $50. *Financial support:* In 2009–10, research assistantships (averaging $5,000 per year), teaching assistantships (averaging $9,000 per year) were awarded; scholarships/grants and unspecified assistantships also available. Financial award application deadline: 2/1. *Faculty research:* Respiration physiology, estuaries and fisheries, limnology, plant biology, conservation biology. *Unit head:* Dr. Soren Bondrup-Nielsen, Head, 902-585-1424, E-mail: soren.bondrup-nielsen@acadiau.ca. *Application contact:* Lisa Taul, Administrative Secretary, 902-585-1344, Fax: 902-585-1059, E-mail: lisa.taul@acadiau.ca.

Adelphi University, Graduate School of Arts and Sciences, Department of Biology, Garden City, NY 11530-0701. Offers MS. Part-time and evening/weekend programs available. *Students:* 5 full-time (1 woman), 27 part-time (17 women); includes 7 minority (4 African Americans, 2 Asian Americans or Pacific Islanders, 1 Hispanic American), 11 international. Average age 26. In 2009, 14 master's awarded. *Degree requirements:* For master's, thesis or alternative. *Entrance requirements:* For master's, 3 letters of recommendation. Additional exam requirements/recommendations for international students: Required—TOEFL (minimum score 550 paper-based; 213 computer-based; 80 iBT). *Application deadline:* For fall admission, 5/1 for international students; for spring admission, 12/1 for international students. Applications are processed on a rolling basis. Application fee: $50. Electronic applications accepted. *Expenses:* Tuition: Full-time $28,340; part-time $830 per credit. Required fees: $600; $250 per credit. Full-time tuition and fees vary according to course load and program. *Financial support:* Research assistantships with full and partial tuition reimbursements, teaching assistantships, career-related internships or fieldwork, Federal Work-Study, institutionally sponsored loans, and unspecified assistantships available. Financial award application deadline: 2/15; financial award applicants required to submit FAFSA. *Faculty research:* Plant-animal interactions, physiology (plant, cornea), reproductive behavior, topics in evolution, fish biology. *Unit head:* Dr. George K. Russell, Director, 516-877-4199, E-mail: russell@adelphi.edu. *Application contact:* Christine Murphy, Director of Admissions, 516-877-3050, Fax: 516-877-3039, E-mail: graduateadmissions@adelphi.edu.

Alabama Agricultural and Mechanical University, School of Graduate Studies, School of Arts and Sciences, Department of Biology, Huntsville, AL 35811. Offers MS. Part-time and evening/weekend programs available. *Degree requirements:* For master's, comprehensive exam, thesis. *Entrance requirements:* For master's, GRE General Test. Additional exam requirements/recommendations for international students: Required—TOEFL (minimum score 500 paper-based; 173 computer-based; 61 iBT). Electronic applications accepted. *Faculty research:* Radiation and chemical mutagenesis, human cytogenetics, microbial biotechnology, microbial metabolism, environmental toxicology.

Alabama State University, School of Graduate Studies, College of Arts and Sciences, Department of Biological Sciences, Montgomery, AL 36101-0271. Offers MS. Part-time programs available. *Degree requirements:* For master's, one foreign language, comprehensive exam, thesis. *Entrance requirements:* For master's, GRE, GRE Subject Test, graduate writing competency test. Additional exam requirements/recommendations for international students: Required—TOEFL (minimum score 500 paper-based; 173 computer-based). *Faculty research:* Salmonella pseudomonas, cancer cells.

Albert Einstein College of Medicine, Medical Scientist Training Program, Bronx, NY 10461. Offers MD/PhD.

Albert Einstein College of Medicine, Sue Golding Graduate Division of Medical Sciences, Bronx, NY 10461. Offers PhD, MD/PhD. *Degree requirements:* For doctorate, thesis/dissertation. *Entrance requirements:* For doctorate, GRE General Test. Additional exam requirements/recommendations for international students: Required—TOEFL.

Alcorn State University, School of Graduate Studies, School of Arts and Sciences, Department of Biology, Alcorn State, MS 39096-7500. Offers MS.

American University, College of Arts and Sciences, Department of Biology, Program in Biology, Washington, DC 20016-8007. Offers MA, MS. Part-time programs available. *Students:* 5 full-time (2 women), 14 part-time (12 women); includes 4 minority (2 African Americans, 2 Asian Americans or Pacific Islanders), 3 international. Average age 26. 15 applicants, 60% accepted, 6 enrolled. In 2009, 6 master's awarded. *Degree requirements:* For master's, comprehensive exam, directed literature research. *Entrance requirements:* For master's, GRE General Test, GRE Subject Test, minimum GPA of 3.0. Additional exam requirements/recommendations for international students: Required—TOEFL. *Application deadline:* For fall admission, 2/1 for domestic students; for spring admission, 10/1 for domestic students. Application fee: $80. *Expenses:* Tuition: Full-time $22,266; part-time $1237 per credit hour. Required fees: $430. Tuition and fees vary according to program. *Financial support:* Fellowships, research assistantships with tuition reimbursements, teaching assistantships with tuition reimbursements, career-related internships or fieldwork, Federal Work-Study, and institutionally sponsored loans available. Financial award application deadline: 2/1.

The American University of Athens, School of Graduate Studies, Athens, Greece. Offers biomedical sciences (MS); business (MBA); business communication (MA); computer sciences (MS); engineering and applied sciences (MS); politics and policy making (MA); systems engineering (MS); telecommunications (MS). *Entrance requirements:* For master's, resume, 2 recommendation letters. Additional exam requirements/recommendations for international students: Required—TOEFL (minimum score 550 paper-based; 213 computer-based). *Faculty research:* Nanotechnology, environmental sciences, rock mechanics, human skin studies, Monte Carlo algorithms and software.

American University of Beirut, Graduate Programs, Faculty of Arts and Sciences, Beirut, Lebanon. Offers anthropology (MA); Arabic language and literature (MA); archaeology (MA); biology (MS); chemistry (MS); computer science (MS); economics (MA); education (MA); English language (MA); English literature (MA); environmental policy planning (MSES); financial economics (MAFE); geology (MS); history (MA); mathematics (MA, MS); Middle Eastern studies (MA); philosophy (MA); physics (MS); political studies (MA); psychology (MA); public administration (MA); sociology (MA); statistics (MA, MS). Part-time programs available. *Degree requirements:* For master's, one foreign language, comprehensive exam, thesis (for some programs). *Entrance requirements:* For master's, GRE, letter of recommendation. Additional exam requirements/recommendations for international students: Required—TOEFL (minimum score 600 paper-based; 250 computer-based; 100 iBT), IELTS (minimum score 7.5). *Faculty research:* String theory and supergravity; computer graphics; algebra and number theory; popular Arabic literature; marine and freshwater biology; integrating science, math and technology.

Andrews University, School of Graduate Studies, College of Arts and Sciences, Department of Biology, Berrien Springs, MI 49104. Offers MAT, MS. *Faculty:* 7 full-time (0 women). *Students:* 3 full-time (2 women), 1 (woman) part-time, 1 international. Average age 24. 8 applicants, 50% accepted, 2 enrolled. In 2009, 4 master's awarded. *Degree requirements:* For master's, comprehensive exam, thesis. *Entrance requirements:* For master's, GRE Subject Test. Additional exam requirements/recommendations for international students: Required—TOEFL (minimum score 550 paper-based). *Application deadline:* Applications are processed on a rolling basis. Application fee: $40. *Financial support:* Fellowships, research assistantships, teaching assistantships, career-related internships or fieldwork, Federal Work-Study, and institutionally sponsored loans available. Financial award application deadline: 3/15. *Unit head:* Dr. David A. Steen, Chairman, 269-471-3243. *Application contact:* Carolyn Hurst, Supervisor of Graduate Admission, 800-253-2874, Fax: 269-471-6321, E-mail: graduate@andrews.edu.

Angelo State University, College of Graduate Studies, College of Sciences, Department of Biology, San Angelo, TX 76909. Offers MS. Part-time and evening/weekend programs available. *Faculty:* 8 full-time (2 women). *Students:* 10 full-time (5 women), 5 part-time (0 women). Average age 27. 6 applicants, 100% accepted, 4 enrolled. In 2009, 4 master's awarded. *Degree requirements:* For master's, comprehensive exam, thesis optional. *Entrance requirements:* For master's, GRE General Test. Additional exam requirements/recommendations for international students: Required—TOEFL or IELTS. *Application deadline:* For fall admission, 7/15 priority date for domestic students, 6/10 for international students; for spring admission, 12/1 priority date for domestic students, 11/1 for international students. Applications are processed on a rolling basis. Application fee: $40 ($50 for international students). Electronic applications accepted. *Expenses:* Tuition, state resident: full-time $3396; part-time $142 per credit hour. Tuition, nonresident: full-time $10,152; part-time $423 per credit hour. Required fees: $1786; $36.25 per credit hour. $494 per semester. Full-time tuition and fees vary according to course load, degree level and program. *Financial support:* In 2009–10, 12 students received support, including 1 research assistantship, 2 teaching assistantships (averaging $10,251 per year); career-related internships or fieldwork, Federal Work-Study, scholarships/grants, and unspecified assistantships also available. Support available to part-time students. Financial award application deadline: 3/1. *Faculty research:* Texas poppy-mallow project, Chisos hedgehog cactus, skunks, reptiles, amphibians, rodents, seed germination, mammals. *Unit head:* Dr. Kelly McCoy, Department Head, 325-942-2189 Ext. 246, Fax: 325-942-2184, E-mail: kelly.mccoy@angelo.edu. *Application contact:* Dr. Bonnie B. Amos, Graduate Advisor, 325-942-2189 Ext. 256, Fax: 325-942-2184, E-mail: bonnie.amos@angelo.edu.

Appalachian State University, Cratis D. Williams Graduate School, Department of Biology, Boone, NC 28608. Offers cell and molecular (MS); general (MS). Part-time programs available. *Faculty:* 27 full-time (11 women). *Students:* 28 full-time (14 women), 7 part-time (3 women); includes 2 minority (both Asian Americans or Pacific Islanders). 24 applicants, 29% accepted, 7 enrolled. In 2009, 10 master's awarded. *Degree requirements:* For master's, comprehensive exam, thesis. *Entrance requirements:* For master's, GRE General Test, 3 letters of recommendation. Additional exam requirements/recommendations for international students: Required—TOEFL (minimum score 570 paper-based; 230 computer-based; 79 iBT), IELTS (minimum score 6.5). *Application deadline:* For fall admission, 7/1 for domestic students, 2/1 for international students; for spring admission, 11/1 for domestic students, 7/1 for international students. Applications are processed on a rolling basis. Application fee: $50. Electronic applications accepted. *Expenses:* Tuition, state resident: full-time $2960. Tuition, nonresident: full-time $14,051. Required fees: $2320. *Financial support:* In 2009–10, 25 teaching assistantships (averaging $9,500 per year) were awarded; fellowships, research assistantships, career-related internships or fieldwork, Federal Work-Study, scholarships/grants, and unspecified assistantships also available. Financial award application deadline: 4/1; financial award applicants required to submit FAFSA. *Faculty research:* Aquatic and terrestrial ecology, animal and plant physiology, behavior and systematics, immunology and cell biology, molecular biology and microbiology. Total annual research expenditures: $451,508. *Unit head:* Dr. Steven Seagle, Chairman, 828-262-3025, E-mail: seaglesw@appstate.edu. *Application contact:* Dr. Gary Walker, Graduate Coordinator, 828-262-3025, E-mail: walkergl@appstate.edu.

Arizona State University, Graduate College, College of Liberal Arts and Sciences, Division of Natural Sciences, School of Life Sciences, Tempe, AZ 85287. Offers biological design (PhD); biology (MNS, MS, PhD); biology and society (PhD); human and social dimensions of science and technology (PhD); microbiology (MNS, MS, PhD); molecular and cellular biology (MS, PhD); neuroscience (PhD); plant biology (MNS, MS, PhD). *Accreditation:* NAACLS. *Degree requirements:* For master's, thesis (MS); for doctorate, one foreign language, thesis/dissertation. *Entrance requirements:* For master's and doctorate, GRE.

Arizona State University, Graduate College, College of Technology and Innovation, Department of Applied Biological Sciences, Tempe, AZ 85287. Offers MS. Part-time programs available. *Degree requirements:* For master's, thesis, oral defense. *Entrance requirements:* For master's, GRE General Test or MAT, 3 letters of recommendation, resume, 18 hours of biological sciences or related courses. Additional exam requirements/recommendations for international students: Required—TOEFL (minimum score 550 paper-based; 213 computer-based; 83 iBT); Recommended—TWE. Electronic applications accepted. *Faculty research:* Ecological restoration, wildlife ecology, urban horticulture, geographic information systems, riparian ecology.

Arkansas State University—Jonesboro, Graduate School, College of Sciences and Mathematics, Department of Biological Sciences, Jonesboro, State University, AR 72467. Offers biological sciences (MA); biology (MS); biology education (MSE, SCCT). Part-time programs available. *Faculty:* 14 full-time (4 women), 1 part-time/adjunct (0 women). *Students:* 22 full-time (7 women), 14 part-time (4 women); includes 1 minority (American Indian/Alaska Native), 12 international. Average age 27. 24 applicants, 75% accepted, 12 enrolled. In 2009, 5 master's awarded. *Degree requirements:* For master's, comprehensive exam, thesis (for some programs); for SCCT, comprehensive exam. *Entrance requirements:* For master's, GRE General Test, appropriate bachelor's degree, letters of reference, interview; for SCCT, GRE General Test or MAT, interview, master's degree, letters of reference, official transcript, personal statement, immunization records. Additional exam requirements/recommendations for international students: Required—TOEFL (minimum score 550 paper-based; 213 computer-based; 79 iBT), IELTS (minimum score 6). *Application deadline:* For fall admission, 7/1 for domestic and international students; for spring admission, 11/15 for domestic students, 11/13 for international students. Applications are processed on a rolling basis. Application fee: $30 ($40 for international students). Electronic applications accepted. *Expenses:* Tuition, state resident: full-time $3744; part-time $208 per credit hour. Tuition, nonresident: full-time $9540; part-time $530 per credit hour. Required fees: $896; $47 per credit hour. $25 per term. One-time fee: $50. Tuition and fees vary according to course load and program. *Financial support:* In 2009–10, 19 students received support; research assistantships, career-related internships or fieldwork, scholarships/grants, and unspecified assistantships available. Financial award application deadline: 7/1; financial award applicants required to submit FAFSA. *Unit head:* Dr. Stanley Trauth, Interim Chair, 870-972-3082, Fax: 870-972-2638, E-mail: strauth@astate.edu. *Application contact:* Dr. Andrew Sustich, Dean of the Graduate School, 870-972-3029, Fax: 870-972-3857, E-mail: sustich@astate.edu.

A.T. Still University of Health Sciences, Kirksville College of Osteopathic Medicine, Kirksville, MO 63501. Offers biomedical sciences (MS); osteopathic medicine (DO). *Faculty:* 53 full-time (12 women), 33 part-time/adjunct (9 women). *Students:* 698 full-time (270 women), 25 part-time (11 women); includes 106 minority (12 African Americans, 6 American Indian/Alaska Native, 73 Asian Americans or Pacific Islanders, 15 Hispanic Americans), 12 international. Average age 27. 3,241 applicants, 11% accepted, 172 enrolled. In 2009, 166 first professional degrees, 7 master's awarded. *Degree requirements:* For master's, thesis; for DO, Level 1 and 2 COMLEX-PE exams. *Entrance requirements:* For DO, MCAT, bachelor's degree with minimum undergraduate GPA of 2.5 (cumulative and science) or 90 semester hours with minimum GPA of 3.5 (cumulative and science) and minimum MCAT of 28; for master's, GRE, MCAT, or DAT, minimum undergraduate GPA of 2.5 (cumulative and science). *Application deadline:* For fall admission, 2/1 for domestic and international students. Applications are processed on a rolling basis. Application fee: $60. Electronic applications accepted. *Expenses:* Contact institution. *Financial support:* In 2009–10, 630 students received support, including 12 fellowships with full tuition reimbursements available (averaging $16,000 per year); research assistantships, teaching assistantships, Federal Work-Study and scholarships/grants also available. Financial award application deadline: 5/1; financial award applicants required to submit FAFSA. *Faculty research:* Osteopathic palpatory procedures, Duchenne muscular dystrophy, gene array studies of pain remediation, thoracic lymphatic pump techniques. Total annual research expenditures: $338,806. *Unit head:* Dr. Philip C. Slocum, Dean, 660-626-2354, Fax: 660-626-2080, E-mail: pslocum@atsu.edu. *Application contact:* Donna Sparks, Associate Director for Admissions, 660-626-2237, Fax: 660-626-2969, E-mail: admissions@atsu.edu.

Auburn University, College of Veterinary Medicine and Graduate School, Graduate Programs in Veterinary Medicine, Auburn University, AL 36849. Offers biomedical sciences (MS, PhD), including anatomy, physiology and pharmacology (MS), biomedical sciences (PhD), clinical sciences (MS), large animal surgery and medicine (MS), pathobiology (MS), radiology (MS), small animal surgery and medicine (MS); DVM/MS. Part-time programs available. *Faculty:* 100 full-time (40 women), 5 part-time/adjunct (1 woman). *Students:* 17 full-time (6 women), 51 part-time (35 women); includes 8 minority (2 African Americans, 1 American Indian/Alaska Native, 3 Asian Americans or Pacific Islanders, 2 Hispanic Americans), 22 international. Average age 31. 70 applicants, 34% accepted, 10 enrolled. In 2009, 12 master's, 7 doctorates awarded. *Degree requirements:* For doctorate, thesis/dissertation. *Entrance requirements:* For master's, GRE General Test; for doctorate, GRE General Test, GRE Subject Test. *Application deadline:* For fall admission, 7/7 for domestic students; for spring admission, 11/24 for domestic students. Applications are processed on a rolling basis. Application fee: $50 ($60 for international students). Electronic applications accepted. *Expenses:* Tuition, state resident: full-time $6240. Tuition, nonresident: full-time $18,720. International tuition: $18,938 full-time. Required fees: $492. Tuition and fees vary according to course load, program and reciprocity agreements. *Financial support:* Research assistantships, teaching assistantships, Federal Work-Study available. Support available to part-time students. Financial award application deadline: 3/15; financial award applicants required to submit FAFSA. *Unit head:* Dr. Timothy R. Boosinger, Dean, 334-844-4546. *Application contact:* Dr. George Flowers, Dean of the Graduate School, 334-844-2125.

Auburn University, Graduate School, College of Sciences and Mathematics, Department of Biological Sciences, Auburn University, AL 36849. Offers botany (MS, PhD); microbiology (MS, PhD); zoology (MS, PhD). *Faculty:* 33 full-time (8 women), 1 (woman) part-time/adjunct. *Students:* 42 full-time (17 women), 60 part-time (36 women); includes 9 minority (4 African Americans, 1 American Indian/Alaska Native, 3 Asian Americans or Pacific Islanders, 1 Hispanic American), 21 international. Average age 28. 134 applicants, 20% accepted, 18 enrolled. In 2009, 22 master's, 11 doctorates awarded. *Entrance requirements:* For master's and doctorate, GRE General Test. Additional exam requirements/recommendations for international students: Required—TOEFL. *Application deadline:* For fall admission, 7/7 for domestic students; for spring admission, 11/24 for domestic students. Application fee: $50 ($60 for international students). Electronic applications accepted. *Expenses:* Tuition, state resident: full-time $6240. Tuition, nonresident: full-time $18,720. International tuition: $18,938 full-time. Required fees: $492. Tuition and fees vary according to course load, program and reciprocity agreements. *Financial support:* Research assistantships, teaching assistantships available. Financial award applicants required to submit FAFSA. *Unit head:* Dr. James M. Barbaree, Chair, 334-844-1647, Fax: 334-844-1645. *Application contact:* Dr. George Flowers, Dean of the Graduate School, 334-844-2125.

Austin Peay State University, College of Graduate Studies, College of Science and Mathematics, Department of Biology, Clarksville, TN 37044. Offers clinical laboratory science (MS); radiologic science (MS). Part-time programs available. *Faculty:* 6 full-time (1 woman). *Students:* 5 full-time (all women), 18 part-time (11 women); includes 6 minority (1 African American, 5 Hispanic Americans), 1 international. Average age 29. 19 applicants, 100% accepted, 9 enrolled. In 2009, 4 master's awarded. *Degree requirements:* For master's, comprehensive exam, thesis optional. *Entrance requirements:* For master's, GRE General Test, 3 letters of recommendation, minimum undergraduate GPA of 2.5. Additional exam requirements/recommendations for international students: Required—TOEFL (minimum score 500 paper-based; 173 computer-based). *Application deadline:* For fall admission, 7/27 priority date for domestic students; for spring admission, 12/17 priority date for domestic students. Applications are processed on a rolling basis. Application fee: $25. Electronic applications accepted. *Expenses:* Tuition, state resident: full-time $6160; part-time $608 per credit hour. Tuition, nonresident: full-time $17,080; part-time $854 per credit hour. Required fees: $1224; $61.20 per credit hour. *Financial support:* In 2009–10, 10 students received support, including 10 research assistantships with full tuition reimbursements available (averaging $5,184 per year); career-related internships or fieldwork, Federal Work-Study, institutionally sponsored loans, scholarships/grants, and unspecified assistantships also available. Support available to part-time students. Financial award application deadline: 3/1. *Faculty research:* Non-paint source pollution, amphibian biomonitoring, aquatic toxicology, biological indicators of water quality, taxonomy. *Unit head:* Dr. Don Dailey, Chair, 931-221-7781, Fax: 931-221-6323, E-mail: daileyd@apsu.edu. *Application contact:* Dr. Dixie Dennis Pinder, Dean, College of Graduate Studies, 931-221-7662, Fax: 931-221-7641, E-mail: dennisdi@apsu.edu.

Ball State University, Graduate School, College of Sciences and Humanities, Department of Biology, Muncie, IN 47306-1099. Offers biology (MA, MAE, MS); biology education (Ed D). *Degree requirements:* For doctorate, thesis/dissertation. *Entrance requirements:* For master's, GRE General Test; for doctorate, GRE General Test, minimum graduate GPA of 3.2. *Faculty research:* Aquatics and fisheries, tumors, water and air pollution, developmental biology and genetics.

Barry University, College of Health Sciences, Programs in Biology and Biomedical Sciences, Miami Shores, FL 33161-6695. Offers biology (MS); biomedical sciences (MS). Part-time and evening/weekend programs available. *Degree requirements:* For master's, comprehensive exam, thesis (for some programs). *Entrance requirements:* For master's, GRE General Test or Florida Teacher's Certification Exam (biology); GRE General Test, MCAT, or DAT (biomedical sciences). Electronic applications accepted. *Faculty research:* Genetics, immunology, anthropology.

Baylor College of Medicine, Graduate School of Biomedical Sciences, Houston, TX 77030-3498. Offers MS, PhD, MD/PhD. *Faculty:* 417 full-time (105 women). *Students:* 583 full-time (309 women), 210 international. Average age 26. 1,187 applicants, 19% accepted, 107 enrolled. In 2009, 11 master's, 74 doctorates awarded. Terminal master's awarded for partial completion of doctoral program. *Degree requirements:* For master's, thesis; for doctorate, thesis/dissertation, public defense. *Entrance requirements:* For doctorate, GRE General Test, GRE Subject Test (strongly recommended), minimum GPA of 3.0. Additional exam requirements/recommendations for international students: Required—TOEFL. *Application deadline:* For fall admission, 1/1 priority date for domestic students. Applications are processed on a rolling basis. Application fee: $30. Electronic applications accepted. *Financial support:* Fellowships, research assistantships, teaching assistantships, career-related internships or fieldwork, Federal Work-Study, institutionally sponsored loans, health care benefits, and students receive a scholarship unless there are grant funds available to pay tuition available. Financial award applicants required to submit FAFSA. *Faculty research:* Cell and molecular biology of cardiac muscle, structural biophysics, gene expression and regulation, human genomes, viruses. *Unit head:* Dr. William R. Brinkley, Dean of Graduate Sciences, 713-798-5263, Fax: 713-798-6325, E-mail: brinkley@bcm.tmc.edu. *Application contact:* Melissa Houghton, Administrator for GSBS Admissions, 713-798-4031, Fax: 713-798-6325, E-mail: melissah@bcm.edu.

Baylor University, Graduate School, College of Arts and Sciences, Department of Biology, Waco, TX 76798. Offers biology (MA, MS, PhD); environmental biology (MS); limnology (MS). Part-time programs available. *Faculty:* 13 full-time (3 women). *Students:* 34 full-time (15 women); includes 1 minority (Asian American or Pacific Islander), 10 international. In 2009, 8 master's, 4 doctorates awarded. *Degree requirements:* For master's, thesis (for some programs); for doctorate, thesis/dissertation. *Entrance requirements:* For master's and doctorate, GRE

General Test. *Application deadline:* For fall admission, 1/31 priority date for domestic students. Applications are processed on a rolling basis. Application fee: $25. *Financial support:* Teaching assistantships, career-related internships or fieldwork, Federal Work-Study, institutionally sponsored loans, and tuition waivers (full and partial) available. Support available to part-time students. Financial award application deadline: 2/28. *Faculty research:* Terrestrial ecology, aquatic ecology, genetics. *Unit head:* Dr. Myeongwoo Lee, Graduate Program Director, 254-710-2141, Fax: 254-710-2969, E-mail: myeongwoo_lee@baylor.edu. *Application contact:* Tamara Lehmann, Administrative Assistant, 254-710-2911, Fax: 254-710-2969, E-mail: tamara_lehmann@baylor.edu.

Baylor University, Graduate School, Institute of Biomedical Studies, Waco, TX 76798. Offers MS, PhD. *Students:* 26 full-time (14 women), 2 part-time (both women); includes 3 minority (2 Asian Americans or Pacific Islanders, 1 Hispanic American), 10 international. In 2009, 2 master's, 6 doctorates awarded. *Entrance requirements:* For master's and doctorate, GRE General Test. *Application deadline:* Applications are processed on a rolling basis. Application fee: $25. *Financial support:* Research assistantships, teaching assistantships available. *Unit head:* Dr. Chris Kearney, Graduate Program Director, 254-710-2131, Fax: 254-710-3878, E-mail: chris_kearney@baylor.edu. *Application contact:* Rhonda Bellert, Administrative Assistant, 254-710-2514, Fax: 254-710-3870, E-mail: rhonda_bellert@baylor.edu.

Bemidji State University, School of Graduate Studies, College of Social and Natural Sciences, Department of Biology, Bemidji, MN 56601-2699. Offers MS. Part-time programs available. *Degree requirements:* For master's, thesis or alternative, departmental qualifying exam. *Entrance requirements:* For master's, GRE General Test, letters of recommendation, letter of intent. Additional exam requirements/recommendations for international students: Required—TOEFL. Electronic applications accepted. *Faculty research:* Immunology, aquatic biology, wetlands ecology, forest regeneration, mammology.

Bloomsburg University of Pennsylvania, School of Graduate Studies, College of Science and Technology, Department of Biological and Allied Health Sciences, Program in Biology, Bloomsburg, PA 17815-1301. Offers MS. *Degree requirements:* For master's, thesis or alternative. *Entrance requirements:* For master's, minimum QPA of 3.0, 2 letters of recommendation. Additional exam requirements/recommendations for international students: Required—TOEFL (minimum score 550 paper-based; 213 computer-based; 79 iBT). Electronic applications accepted.

Boise State University, Graduate College, College of Arts and Sciences, Department of Biology, Program in Biology, Boise, ID 83725-0399. Offers MA, MS. Part-time programs available. *Degree requirements:* For master's, thesis. *Entrance requirements:* For master's, GRE General Test, minimum GPA of 3.0. Electronic applications accepted. *Expenses:* Tuition, state resident: full-time $3106; part-time $209 per credit. Tuition, nonresident: part-time $284 per credit.

Boston College, Graduate School of Arts and Sciences, Department of Biology, Chestnut Hill, MA 02467-3800. Offers PhD, MBA/MS. *Students:* 46 full-time (25 women); includes 6 minority (3 African Americans, 3 Asian Americans or Pacific Islanders), 12 international. 129 applicants, 28% accepted, 15 enrolled. In 2009, 5 doctorates awarded. *Degree requirements:* For doctorate, thesis/dissertation. *Entrance requirements:* For doctorate, GRE General Test, GRE Subject Test. Additional exam requirements/recommendations for international students: Required—TOEFL (minimum score 600 paper-based; 250 computer-based; 100 iBT). *Application deadline:* For fall admission, 1/2 priority date for domestic students, 1/2 for international students. Application fee: $70. Electronic applications accepted. *Financial support:* In 2009–10, fellowships with full tuition reimbursements (averaging $26,000 per year), research assistantships with full tuition reimbursements (averaging $26,000 per year), teaching assistantships with full tuition reimbursements (averaging $26,000 per year) were awarded; Federal Work-Study and scholarships/grants also available. Support available to part-time students. Financial award application deadline: 3/1; financial award applicants required to submit FAFSA. *Faculty research:* DNA replication in mammalian cells, control of the cell cycle, immunology, plant genetics. *Unit head:* Dr. Thomas Chiles, Chairperson, 617-552-3540, E-mail: thomas.chiles@bc.edu. *Application contact:* Dr. Charlie Hoffman, Graduate Program Director, 617-552-2779, E-mail: charles.hoffman@bc.edu.

See Close-Up on page 79.

Boston University, Graduate School of Arts and Sciences, Department of Biology, Boston, MA 02215. Offers MA, PhD. *Students:* 85 full-time (46 women); includes 13 minority (4 African Americans, 6 Asian Americans or Pacific Islanders, 3 Hispanic Americans), 8 international. Average age 28. 141 applicants, 27% accepted, 21 enrolled. In 2009, 5 master's, 20 doctorates awarded. Terminal master's awarded for partial completion of doctoral program. *Degree requirements:* For master's, one foreign language, thesis (for some programs); for doctorate, one foreign language, comprehensive exam, thesis/dissertation. *Entrance requirements:* For master's and doctorate, GRE General Test, GRE Subject Test, 3 letters of recommendation. Additional exam requirements/recommendations for international students: Required—TOEFL (minimum score 600 paper-based; 250 computer-based). *Application deadline:* For fall admission, 12/7 for domestic and international students. Application fee: $70. Electronic applications accepted. *Expenses:* Tuition: Full-time $37,910; part-time $1184 per credit hour. Required fees: $386; $40 per semester. Part-time tuition and fees vary according to class time, course level, degree level and program. *Financial support:* In 2009–10, 2 fellowships with full tuition reimbursements (averaging $18,900 per year), 46 research assistantships with full tuition reimbursements (averaging $18,400 per year), 50 teaching assistantships with full tuition reimbursements (averaging $18,400 per year) were awarded; Federal Work-Study, institutionally sponsored loans, scholarships/grants, and traineeships also available. Financial award application deadline: 12/7; financial award applicants required to submit FAFSA. *Unit head:* Geoffrey M. Cooper, Chairman, 617-353-3856, Fax: 617-353-6340, E-mail: gmcooper@bu.edu. *Application contact:* Meredith Canode, Academic Administrator, 617-353-2432, Fax: 617-353-6340, E-mail: mcanode@bu.edu.

Boston University, School of Medicine, Division of Graduate Medical Sciences, Boston, MA 02215. Offers MA, MS, PhD, MBA/MA, MD/MA, MD/PhD, MPH/MA. Part-time programs available. Terminal master's awarded for partial completion of doctoral program. *Degree requirements:* For master's, qualifying exam; for doctorate, thesis/dissertation, qualifying exam. *Entrance requirements:* Additional exam requirements/recommendations for international students: Required—TOEFL. Electronic applications accepted. *Expenses:* Contact institution.

Bowling Green State University, Graduate College, College of Arts and Sciences, Department of Biological Sciences, Bowling Green, OH 43403. Offers MAT, MS, PhD. Part-time programs available. *Degree requirements:* For master's, thesis or alternative; for doctorate, comprehensive exam, thesis/dissertation. *Entrance requirements:* For master's and doctorate, GRE General Test. Additional exam requirements/recommendations for international students: Required—TOEFL. Electronic applications accepted. *Faculty research:* Aquatic ecology, endocrinology and neurophysiology, nitrogen fixation, photosynthesis.

See Close-Up on page 81.

Bradley University, Graduate School, College of Liberal Arts and Sciences, Department of Biology, Peoria, IL 61625-0002. Offers MS. Part-time programs available. *Degree requirements:* For master's, comprehensive exam, thesis. *Entrance requirements:* For master's, GRE General Test, 2 letters of recommendation. Additional exam requirements/recommendations for international students: Required—TOEFL (minimum score 550 paper-based; 213 computer-based).

Brandeis University, Graduate School of Arts and Sciences, Post-Baccalaureate Premedical Program, Waltham, MA 02454-9110. Offers Certificate. Part-time programs available. *Students:* 5 full-time (2 women), 5 part-time (2 women). Average age 26. 98 applicants, 49% accepted, 9 enrolled. In 2009, 1 Certificate awarded. *Entrance requirements:* For degree, GRE or SAT,

Biological and Biomedical Sciences—General

Brandeis University (continued)

resume with paid and/or volunteer work relevant to field of medicine, letters of recommendation. Additional exam requirements/recommendations for international students: Required—TOEFL (minimum score 600 paper-based; 250 computer-based; 100 iBT); Recommended—IELTS (minimum score 7). *Application deadline:* For fall admission, 5/1 priority date for domestic students. Applications are processed on a rolling basis. Application fee: $75. Electronic applications accepted. *Financial support:* Applicants required to submit FAFSA. *Unit head:* Judith Hudson, Director of Health Professions Advising, 781-736-3470, Fax: 781-736-3469, E-mail: hudsonj@brandeis.edu. *Application contact:* David Cotter, Assistant Dean, Graduate School of Arts and Sciences, 781-736-3410, E-mail: gradschool@brandeis.edu.

Brigham Young University, Graduate Studies, College of Life Sciences, Department of Biology, Provo, UT 84602. Offers biological science education (MS); biology (MS, PhD). *Faculty:* 22 full-time (2 women). *Students:* 35 full-time (13 women), 3 part-time (0 women); includes 9 minority (4 Asian Americans or Pacific Islanders, 5 Hispanic Americans). Average age 30. 15 applicants, 67% accepted, 9 enrolled. In 2009, 7 master's awarded. *Degree requirements:* For master's, comprehensive exam, thesis, prospectus, defense of research, defense of thesis; for doctorate, comprehensive exam, thesis/dissertation, prospectus, defense of research, defense of dissertation. *Entrance requirements:* For master's and doctorate, GRE General Test, minimum GPA of 3.0 for last 60 credit hours of course work. Additional exam requirements/recommendations for international students: Required—TOEFL (minimum score 580 paper-based; 85 iBT). *Application deadline:* For fall admission, 1/31 for domestic and international students. Application fee: $50. Electronic applications accepted. *Expenses:* Tuition: Full-time $5580; part-time $301 per credit hour. Tuition and fees vary according to student's religious affiliation. *Financial support:* In 2009–10, 2 students received support, including 2 fellowships with full and partial tuition reimbursements available (averaging $2,607 per year); research assistantships with full and partial tuition reimbursements available, teaching assistantships with full and partial tuition reimbursements available, career-related internships or fieldwork, institutionally sponsored loans, scholarships/grants, health care benefits, tuition waivers (full and partial), and unspecified assistantships also available. Financial award application deadline: 2/1; financial award applicants required to submit FAFSA. *Faculty research:* Systematics, bioinformatics, ecology, evolution. Total annual research expenditures: $1.4 million. *Unit head:* Dr. Keith A. Crandall, Chair, 801-422-3495, Fax: 801-422-0090, E-mail: keith_crandall@byu.edu. *Application contact:* Hilary H. Oldroyd, Graduate Secretary, 801-422-2010, Fax: 801-422-0090, E-mail: hilary_oldroyd@byu.edu.

Brock University, Faculty of Graduate Studies, Faculty of Mathematics and Science, Program in Biological Sciences, St. Catharines, ON L2S 3A1, Canada. Offers M Sc, PhD. Part-time programs available. *Degree requirements:* For master's, thesis; for doctorate, thesis/dissertation. *Entrance requirements:* For master's, honors B Sc in biology, minimum undergraduate GPA of 3.0; for doctorate, M Sc. Additional exam requirements/recommendations for international students: Required—TOEFL (minimum score 550 paper-based; 213 computer-based; 80 iBT), IELTS (minimum score 6.5), TWE (minimum score 4). Electronic applications accepted. *Faculty research:* Viticulture, neurobiology, ecology, molecular biology, molecular genetics.

Brooklyn College of the City University of New York, Division of Graduate Studies, Department of Biology, Brooklyn, NY 11210-2889. Offers MA, PhD. *Students:* 2 full-time (1 woman), 15 part-time (8 women); includes 9 minority (4 African Americans, 5 Asian Americans or Pacific Islanders), 2 international. Average age 30. 23 applicants, 87% accepted, 6 enrolled. In 2009, 3 master's awarded. *Degree requirements:* For master's, one foreign language, comprehensive exam, thesis. *Entrance requirements:* For master's, minimum GPA of 3.0, 2 letters of recommendation. Additional exam requirements/recommendations for international students: Required—TOEFL (minimum score 500 paper-based; 173 computer-based; 61 iBT). *Application deadline:* For fall admission, 7/31 for domestic students, 6/30 for international students; for spring admission, 12/18 for domestic students, 11/18 for international students. Applications are processed on a rolling basis. Application fee: $125. Electronic applications accepted. *Expenses:* Tuition, state resident: full-time $7360; part-time $310 per credit hour. Tuition, nonresident: full-time $13,800; part-time $575 per credit hour. Required fees: $140.10 per semester. *Financial support:* Federal Work-Study, institutionally sponsored loans, and scholarships/grants available. Support available to part-time students. Financial award application deadline: 5/1; financial award applicants required to submit FAFSA. *Faculty research:* Evolutionary biology, molecular biology of development, cell biology, comparative endocrinology, ecology. *Unit head:* Dr. Peter Lipke, Chairperson, 718-951-5396, E-mail: plipke@brooklyn.cuny.edu. *Application contact:* Hernan Sierra, Graduate Admissions Coordinator, 718-951-4536, Fax: 718-951-4506, E-mail: grads@brooklyn.cuny.edu.

Brooklyn College of the City University of New York, Division of Graduate Studies, School of Education, Program in Middle Childhood Education (Science), Brooklyn, NY 11210-2889. Offers biology (MA); chemistry (MA); earth science (MA); general science (MA); physics (MA). Part-time and evening/weekend programs available. *Students:* 2 full-time (both women), 80 part-time (55 women); includes 34 minority (22 African Americans, 3 Asian Americans or Pacific Islanders, 9 Hispanic Americans), 4 international. Average age 31. 43 applicants, 98% accepted, 31 enrolled. In 2009, 29 master's awarded. *Entrance requirements:* For master's, LAST, interview, previous course work in education and mathematics, resume, 2 letters of recommendation, essay. Additional exam requirements/recommendations for international students: Required—TOEFL (minimum score 500 paper-based; 173 computer-based; 61 iBT). *Application deadline:* For fall admission, 7/15 priority date for domestic students, 6/1 priority date for international students; for spring admission, 11/15 priority date for domestic students, 10/1 priority date for international students. Applications are processed on a rolling basis. Application fee: $125. Electronic applications accepted. *Expenses:* Tuition, state resident: full-time $7360; part-time $310 per credit hour. Tuition, nonresident: full-time $13,800; part-time $575 per credit hour. Required fees: $140.10 per semester. *Financial support:* Federal Work-Study, institutionally sponsored loans, and scholarships/grants available. Support available to part-time students. Financial award application deadline: 5/1; financial award applicants required to submit FAFSA. *Faculty research:* Geometric thinking, mastery of basic facts, problem-solving strategies, history of mathematics. *Unit head:* Dr. Jennifer Adams, Program Head, 718-951-5214, E-mail: jadams@brooklyn.cuny.edu. *Application contact:* Hernan Sierra, Graduate Admissions Coordinator, 718-951-4536, Fax: 718-951-4506, E-mail: grads@brooklyn.cuny.edu.

Brown University, Graduate School, Division of Biology and Medicine, Providence, RI 02912. Offers M Med Sc, MA, MPH, MS, Sc M, PhD, MD/PhD. Part-time programs available. Terminal master's awarded for partial completion of doctoral program. *Degree requirements:* For doctorate, thesis/dissertation. *Entrance requirements:* For master's and doctorate, GRE General Test. Additional exam requirements/recommendations for international students: Required—TOEFL. Electronic applications accepted.

Bucknell University, Graduate Studies, College of Arts and Sciences, Department of Biology, Lewisburg, PA 17837. Offers MA, MS. Part-time programs available. *Degree requirements:* For master's, thesis. *Entrance requirements:* For master's, GRE General Test, GRE Subject Test, minimum GPA of 2.8. Additional exam requirements/recommendations for international students: Required—TOEFL.

Buffalo State College, State University of New York, The Graduate School, Faculty of Natural and Social Sciences, Department of Biology, Buffalo, NY 14222-1095. Offers biology (MA); secondary education (MS Ed), including biology. Evening/weekend programs available. *Degree requirements:* For master's, thesis (for some programs), project. *Entrance requirements:* For master's, minimum GPA of 2.75. Additional exam requirements/recommendations for international students: Required—TOEFL (minimum score 550 paper-based; 213 computer-based).

California Institute of Technology, Division of Biology, Pasadena, CA 91125-0001. Offers biochemistry and molecular biophysics (PhD); cell biology and biophysics (PhD); developmental biology (PhD); genetics (PhD); immunology (PhD); molecular biology (PhD); neurobiology (PhD). *Faculty:* 40 full-time (9 women). *Students:* 78 full-time (42 women); includes 2 African Americans, 5 Hispanic Americans. 197 applicants, 18% accepted, 18 enrolled. In 2009, 28 doctorates awarded. *Degree requirements:* For doctorate, thesis/dissertation, qualifying exam. *Entrance requirements:* For doctorate, GRE General Test. Additional exam requirements/recommendations for international students: Required—TOEFL. *Application deadline:* For fall admission, 1/1 for domestic and international students. Application fee: $80. Electronic applications accepted. *Financial support:* In 2009–10, fellowships with full tuition reimbursements (averaging $23,766 per year), teaching assistantships with full tuition reimbursements (averaging $4,782 per year) were awarded; research assistantships with full tuition reimbursements, institutionally sponsored loans, unspecified assistantships, and federal grants also available. Financial award application deadline: 1/1. *Faculty research:* Molecular genetics of differentiation and development, structure of biological macromolecules, molecular and integrative neurobiology. *Unit head:* Prof. Stephen L. Mayo, Chairman, 626-395-4951, Fax: 626-683-3343. *Application contact:* Elizabeth M. Ayala, Graduate Program Coordinator, 626-395-4497, Fax: 626-683-3343, E-mail: biograd@caltech.edu.

See Close-Up on page 83.

California Polytechnic State University, San Luis Obispo, College of Science and Mathematics, Department of Biological Sciences, San Luis Obispo, CA 93407. Offers MS. Part-time programs available. *Faculty:* 10 full-time (5 women), 1 (woman) part-time/adjunct. *Students:* 22 full-time (15 women), 16 part-time (11 women); includes 3 minority (2 Asian Americans or Pacific Islanders, 1 Hispanic American), 1 international. Average age 25. 30 applicants, 67% accepted, 15 enrolled. In 2009, 6 master's awarded. *Degree requirements:* For master's, comprehensive exam (for some programs), thesis (for some programs). *Entrance requirements:* For master's, GRE General Test, minimum GPA of 3.0 in last 90 quarter units. Additional exam requirements/recommendations for international students: Required—TOEFL (minimum score 550 paper-based; 213 computer-based) or IELTS (minimum score 6). *Application deadline:* For fall admission, 2/1 for domestic students, 11/30 for international students. Applications are processed on a rolling basis. Application fee: $55. Electronic applications accepted. *Expenses:* Tuition, nonresident: full-time $11,160; part-time $248 per unit. Required fees: $7134; $1553 per quarter. *Financial support:* Research assistantships, teaching assistantships, career-related internships or fieldwork and Federal Work-Study available. Support available to part-time students. Financial award application deadline: 3/2; financial award applicants required to submit FAFSA. *Faculty research:* Ancient fossil DNA, restoration ecology microbe biodiversity indices, biological inventories. *Unit head:* Dr. Christopher Kitts, Graduate Coordinator, 805-756-2949, Fax: 805-756-1419, E-mail: ckitts@calpoly.edu. *Application contact:* Dr. Christopher Kitts, Graduate Coordinator, 805-756-2949, Fax: 805-756-1419, E-mail: ckitts@calpoly.edu.

California State Polytechnic University, Pomona, Academic Affairs, College of Science, Program in Biological Sciences, Pomona, CA 91768-2557. Offers MS. Part-time programs available. *Students:* 32 full-time (18 women), 47 part-time (33 women); includes 29 minority (1 African American, 1 American Indian/Alaska Native, 17 Asian Americans or Pacific Islanders, 10 Hispanic Americans), 10 international. Average age 27. 53 applicants, 36% accepted, 17 enrolled. In 2009, 13 master's awarded. *Degree requirements:* For master's, thesis. *Entrance requirements:* For master's, GRE General Test. *Application deadline:* For fall admission, 5/1 priority date for domestic students; for winter admission, 10/15 priority date for domestic students; for spring admission, 1/20 priority date for domestic students. Applications are processed on a rolling basis. Application fee: $55. Electronic applications accepted. *Expenses:* Tuition, nonresident: full-time $6696; part-time $248 per credit. Required fees: $5487; $3237 per term. Tuition and fees vary according to course load, degree level and program. *Financial support:* Career-related internships or fieldwork, Federal Work-Study, and institutionally sponsored loans available. Support available to part-time students. Financial award application deadline: 3/2; financial award applicants required to submit FAFSA. *Unit head:* Dr. David Moriarty, Professor, 909-869-4055, Fax: 909-869-4078, E-mail: djmoriarty@csupomona.edu. *Application contact:* Scott J. Duncan, Director, Admissions, 909-869-3258, Fax: 909-869-4529, E-mail: sjduncan@csupomona.edu.

California State University, Bakersfield, Division of Graduate Studies, School of Natural Sciences and Mathematics, Program in Biology, Bakersfield, CA 93311. Offers MS. *Entrance requirements:* For master's, GRE, minimum undergraduate GPA of 3.0 in last 90 quarter units, 3 letters of recommendation. Additional exam requirements/recommendations for international students: Required—TOEFL.

California State University, Chico, Graduate School, College of Natural Sciences, Department of Biological Sciences, Program in Biological Sciences, Chico, CA 95929-0722. Offers MS. *Students:* 9 full-time (5 women), 12 part-time (7 women); includes 3 minority (2 Asian Americans or Pacific Islanders, 1 Hispanic American). Average age 28. 24 applicants, 71% accepted, 11 enrolled. In 2009, 7 master's awarded. *Degree requirements:* For master's, thesis, oral exam. *Entrance requirements:* For master's, GRE General Test, GRE Subject Test (biology), 2 letters of recommendation. Additional exam requirements/recommendations for international students: Required—TOEFL (minimum score 550 paper-based; 213 computer-based; 80 iBT), IELTS (minimum score 6.5). *Application deadline:* For fall admission, 3/1 priority date for domestic students, 3/1 for international students; for spring admission, 9/15 priority date for domestic students, 9/15 for international students. Applications are processed on a rolling basis. Application fee: $55. Electronic applications accepted. *Financial support:* Fellowships, research assistantships, teaching assistantships, career-related internships or fieldwork available. *Unit head:* Dr. Jonathan Day, Graduate Coordinator, 530-898-6303. *Application contact:* Larry Hanne, Graduate Coordinator, 530-898-5356.

California State University, Dominguez Hills, College of Natural and Behavioral Sciences, Department of Biology, Carson, CA 90747-0001. Offers MS. Part-time and evening/weekend programs available. *Faculty:* 7 full-time (2 women), 12 part-time/adjunct (5 women). *Students:* 10 full-time (6 women), 11 part-time (7 women); includes 11 minority (3 African Americans, 6 Asian Americans or Pacific Islanders, 2 Hispanic Americans). Average age 33. 12 applicants, 67% accepted, 6 enrolled. In 2009, 7 master's awarded. *Degree requirements:* For master's, thesis. *Entrance requirements:* For master's, minimum GPA of 2.75. Additional exam requirements/recommendations for international students: Required—TOEFL (minimum score 550 paper-based). *Application deadline:* For fall admission, 6/1 for domestic students, 5/1 for international students; for spring admission, 12/15 for domestic students, 10/1 for international students. Application fee: $55. Electronic applications accepted. *Expenses:* Tuition, nonresident: full-time $6696; part-time $372 per unit. Required fees: $5946; $1752 per semester. *Faculty research:* Cancer biology, infectious diseases, ecology of native plants, remediation, community ecology. *Unit head:* Dr. John Thomlinson, Chair, 310-243-3381, Fax: 310-243-2350, E-mail: jthomlinson@csudh.edu. *Application contact:* Dr. Getachew Kidane, Graduate Program Coordinator, 310-243-3564, Fax: 310-243-2350, E-mail: gkidane@csudh.edu.

California State University, East Bay, Graduate Programs, College of Science, Department of Biological Sciences, Hayward, CA 94542-3000. Offers biological sciences (MS); marine science (MS). Part-time programs available. *Faculty:* 10 full-time (7 women). *Students:* 29 full-time (23 women), 25 part-time (16 women); includes 13 minority (3 African Americans, 10 Asian Americans or Pacific Islanders), 15 international. Average age 29. 80 applicants, 26% accepted, 18 enrolled. In 2009, 19 master's awarded. *Degree requirements:* For master's, thesis. *Entrance requirements:* For master's, GRE General and Subject Tests, minimum GPA of 3.0 in field, 2.75 overall. Additional exam requirements/recommendations for international students: Required—TOEFL (minimum score 550 paper-based; 213 computer-based). *Application deadline:* For fall admission, 4/15 for domestic students, 5/31 for international students. Applications are processed on a rolling basis. Application fee: $55. Electronic applications accepted. *Financial support:* Fellowships, teaching assistantships, career-related internships or fieldwork, Federal Work-Study, institutionally sponsored loans, and scholarships/grants available. Support available to part-time students. Financial award application deadline: 3/1; financial award applicants required to submit FAFSA. *Unit head:* Dr. Michael Hedrick,

Chair, 510-885-3471, Fax: 510-885-4747, E-mail: michael.hedrick@csueastbay.edu. *Application contact:* Donna Wiley, Interim Associate Director, 510-885-2928, Fax: 510-885-4777, E-mail: donna.wiley@csueastbay.edu.

California State University, Fresno, Division of Graduate Studies, College of Science and Mathematics, Department of Biology, Fresno, CA 93740-8027. Offers biology (MA); biotechnology (MBT). Part-time and evening/weekend programs available. *Degree requirements:* For master's, thesis. *Entrance requirements:* For master's, GRE General Test, GRE Subject Test, minimum GPA of 2.5 in last 60 units. Additional exam requirements/recommendations for international students: Required—TOEFL. Electronic applications accepted. *Faculty research:* Genome neuroscience, ecology conflict resolution, biomechanics, cell death, vibrio cholerae.

California State University, Fullerton, Graduate Studies, College of Natural Science and Mathematics, Department of Biological Science, Fullerton, CA 92834-9480. Offers MS. Part-time programs available. *Students:* 31 full-time (24 women), 39 part-time (22 women); includes 22 minority (1 African American, 13 Asian Americans or Pacific Islanders, 8 Hispanic Americans), 8 international. Average age 28. 70 applicants, 36% accepted, 16 enrolled. In 2009, 11 master's awarded. *Degree requirements:* For master's, thesis. *Entrance requirements:* For master's, GRE General and Subject Tests, MCAT, or DAT, minimum GPA of 3.0 in biology. Application fee: $55. *Expenses:* Tuition, nonresident: full-time $11,160; part-time $373 per credit. Required fees: $1440 per term. Tuition and fees vary according to course load, degree level and program. *Financial support:* Research assistantships, teaching assistantships, career-related internships or fieldwork, Federal Work-Study, institutionally sponsored loans, and scholarships/grants available. Support available to part-time students. Financial award application deadline: 3/1; financial award applicants required to submit FAFSA. *Faculty research:* Glycosidase release and the block to polyspermy in ascidian eggs. *Unit head:* Dr. Robert Koch, Chair, 657-278-3614. *Application contact:* Admissions/Applications, 657-278-2371.

California State University, Long Beach, Graduate Studies, College of Natural Sciences and Mathematics, Department of Biological Sciences, Long Beach, CA 90840. Offers biology (MS); microbiology (MS). Part-time programs available. *Faculty:* 38 full-time (14 women), 1 part-time/adjunct (0 women). *Students:* 11 full-time (9 women), 58 part-time (32 women); includes 25 minority (1 African American, 14 Asian Americans or Pacific Islanders, 10 Hispanic Americans), 7 international. Average age 28. 70 applicants, 39% accepted, 16 enrolled. *Entrance requirements:* For master's, GRE Subject Test, minimum GPA of 3.0. *Application deadline:* For fall admission, 3/15 for domestic students. Applications are processed on a rolling basis. Application fee: $55. Electronic applications accepted. *Expenses:* Required fees: $1802 per semester. Part-time tuition and fees vary according to course load. *Financial support:* Teaching assistantships, Federal Work-Study, institutionally sponsored loans, scholarships/grants, traineeships, and unspecified assistantships available. Financial award application deadline: 3/2. *Unit head:* Dr. Brian Livingston, Chair, 562-985-4807, Fax: 562-985-8878, E-mail: blivings@csulb.edu. *Application contact:* Dr. Christopher Lowe, Graduate Advisor, 562-985-4918, Fax: 562-985-8878, E-mail: clowe@csulb.edu.

California State University, Los Angeles, Graduate Studies, College of Natural and Social Sciences, Department of Biological Sciences, Los Angeles, CA 90032-8530. Offers biology (MS). Part-time and evening/weekend programs available. *Faculty:* 3 full-time (2 women), 11 part-time/adjunct (5 women). *Students:* 28 full-time (15 women), 51 part-time (35 women); includes 46 minority (4 African Americans, 16 Asian Americans or Pacific Islanders, 26 Hispanic Americans), 10 international. Average age 27. 60 applicants, 100% accepted, 25 enrolled. In 2009, 20 master's awarded. *Degree requirements:* For master's, comprehensive exam or thesis. *Entrance requirements:* Additional exam requirements/recommendations for international students: Required—TOEFL (minimum score 500 paper-based; 173 computer-based). *Application deadline:* For fall admission, 5/1 for domestic and international students. Applications are processed on a rolling basis. Application fee: $55. *Financial support:* Federal Work-Study available. Support available to part-time students. Financial award application deadline: 3/1. *Faculty research:* Ecology, environmental biology, cell and molecular biology, physiology, medical microbiology. *Unit head:* Dr. Nancy McQueen, Chair, 323-343-2050, Fax: 323-343-6451, E-mail: nmcquee@exchange.calstatela.edu. *Application contact:* Dr. Cheryl L. Ney, Associate Vice President for Academic Affairs and Dean of Graduate Studies, 323-343-3820, Fax: 323-343-5653, E-mail: cney@cslanet.calstatela.edu.

California State University, Northridge, Graduate Studies, College of Science and Mathematics, Department of Biology, Northridge, CA 91330. Offers MS. *Faculty:* 30 full-time (11 women), 19 part-time/adjunct (8 women). *Students:* 51 full-time (38 women), 55 part-time (34 women); includes 31 minority (7 African Americans, 11 Asian Americans or Pacific Islanders, 13 Hispanic Americans), 13 international. Average age 28. 170 applicants, 55% accepted, 49 enrolled. In 2009, 25 master's awarded. *Degree requirements:* For master's, thesis, seminar. *Entrance requirements:* For master's, GRE Subject Test, GRE General Test. Additional exam requirements/recommendations for international students: Required—TOEFL. *Application deadline:* For fall admission, 3/15 priority date for domestic students; for spring admission, 10/15 priority date for domestic students. Application fee: $55. *Financial support:* Research assistantships, teaching assistantships, Federal Work-Study, institutionally sponsored loans, tuition waivers (partial), and unspecified assistantships available. Support available to part-time students. Financial award applicants required to submit FAFSA. *Faculty research:* Cell adhesion, cancer research, fishery research. *Unit head:* Dr. Randy Cohen, Chair, 818-677-3356, E-mail: randy.cohen@csun.edu. *Application contact:* Dr. David Gray, Graduate Coordinator, 818-677-7653, E-mail: dave.gray@csun.edu.

California State University, Sacramento, Graduate Studies, College of Natural Sciences and Mathematics, Department of Biological Sciences, Sacramento, CA 95819. Offers biological sciences (MA, MS); immunohematology (MS); marine science (MS). Part-time programs available. *Degree requirements:* For master's, thesis, writing proficiency exam. *Entrance requirements:* For master's, bachelor's degree in biology or equivalent, minimum GPA of 3.0 in biology, minimum overall GPA of 2.75 during last 2 years of course work. Additional exam requirements/recommendations for international students: Required—TOEFL. Electronic applications accepted.

California State University, San Bernardino, Graduate Studies, College of Natural Sciences, Department of Biology, San Bernardino, CA 92407-2397. Offers MS. Part-time programs available. *Faculty:* 5 full-time (1 woman), 1 part-time/adjunct (0 women). *Students:* 26 full-time (15 women), 30 part-time (18 women); includes 32 minority (6 African Americans, 1 American Indian/Alaska Native, 13 Asian Americans or Pacific Islanders, 12 Hispanic Americans), 2 international. Average age 30. 24 applicants, 67% accepted, 7 enrolled. In 2009, 3 master's awarded. *Degree requirements:* For master's, thesis or alternative, advancement to candidacy. *Entrance requirements:* For master's, minimum GPA of 3.0. *Application deadline:* For fall admission, 8/31 priority date for domestic students. Application fee: $55. *Financial support:* Fellowships, research assistantships, teaching assistantships, career-related internships or fieldwork available. *Faculty research:* Ecology, molecular biology, physiology, cell biology, neurobiology. *Unit head:* Dr. David M. Polcyn, Chair, 909-537-5313, Fax: 909-537-7038, E-mail: dpolcyn@csusb.edu. *Application contact:* Olivia Rosas, Director of Admissions, 909-537-7577, Fax: 909-537-7034, E-mail: orosas@csusb.edu.

California State University, San Marcos, College of Arts and Sciences, Program in Biological Sciences, San Marcos, CA 92096-0001. Offers MS. Part-time programs available. *Degree requirements:* For master's, thesis. *Entrance requirements:* For master's, GRE Subject Test, minimum GPA of 2.7 in mathematics and science or minimum GPA of 3.0 in the last 35 units of mathematics and science. *Faculty research:* Gene regulation of life states, carbon cycling, genetic markers of viral infection, neurobiology.

California State University, Stanislaus, College of Natural Sciences, Department of Biological Sciences, Turlock, CA 95382. Offers ecology and sustainability (MS); genetic counseling (MS); marine sciences (MS). Part-time programs available. *Degree requirements:* For master's, thesis. *Entrance requirements:* For master's, GRE General Test, GRE Subject Test, minimum

GPA of 3.0, 3 letters of reference. Additional exam requirements/recommendations for international students: Required—TOEFL (minimum score 550 paper-based; 213 computer-based). Electronic applications accepted. *Faculty research:* Long-term smoking and pregnancy rate, vertebrate paleobiology, terrestrial animals, benthic invertebrates of central California coastline.

Carleton University, Faculty of Graduate Studies, Faculty of Science, Department of Biology, Ottawa, ON K1S 5B6, Canada. Offers M Sc, PhD. *Degree requirements:* For master's, thesis, seminar; for doctorate, comprehensive exam, thesis/dissertation, seminar. *Entrance requirements:* For master's, honors degree in science; for doctorate, M Sc. Additional exam requirements/recommendations for international students: Required—TOEFL. *Faculty research:* Biochemical, structural, and genetic regulation in cells; behavioral ecology; insect taxonomy; physiology of cells.

Carnegie Mellon University, Mellon College of Science, Department of Biological Sciences, Pittsburgh, PA 15213-3891. Offers biochemistry (PhD); biophysics (PhD); cell biology (PhD); computational biology (MS, PhD); developmental biology (PhD); genetics (PhD); molecular biology (PhD); neuroscience (PhD). *Degree requirements:* For doctorate, comprehensive exam, thesis/dissertation. *Entrance requirements:* For doctorate, GRE General Test, GRE Subject Test, interview. Electronic applications accepted. *Faculty research:* Genetic structure, function, and regulation; protein structure and function; biological membranes; biological spectroscopy.

Case Western Reserve University, School of Graduate Studies, Department of Biology, Cleveland, OH 44106. Offers MS, PhD. Part-time programs available. *Faculty:* 20 full-time (6 women), 8 part-time/adjunct (4 women). *Students:* 61 full-time (39 women), 8 part-time (3 women); includes 3 minority (1 African American, 1 Asian American or Pacific Islander, 1 Hispanic American), 39 international. Average age 26. 137 applicants, 28% accepted, 24 enrolled. In 2009, 6 master's, 3 doctorates awarded. Terminal master's awarded for partial completion of doctoral program. *Degree requirements:* For master's, thesis or alternative; for doctorate, thesis/dissertation. *Entrance requirements:* For master's and doctorate, GRE General Test and GRE Subject Test or MCAT. Additional exam requirements/recommendations for international students: Required—TOEFL (minimum score 550 paper-based; 213 computer-based; 79 iBT). *Application deadline:* For fall admission, 1/7 priority date for domestic students. Applications are processed on a rolling basis. Application fee: $50. Electronic applications accepted. *Financial support:* Fellowships, research assistantships, teaching assistantships, career-related internships or fieldwork, Federal Work-Study, and unspecified assistantships available. Financial award application deadline: 2/15; financial award applicants required to submit FAFSA. *Faculty research:* Cellular, developmental, and molecular biology; genetics; genetic engineering; biotechnology; ecology. *Unit head:* Christopher Cullis, Chairman, 216-368-3557, Fax: 216-368-4762, E-mail: christopher.cullis@case.edu. *Application contact:* Julia Brown, Program Coordinator, 216-368-3556, Fax: 216-368-4672, E-mail: jab12@case.edu.

Case Western Reserve University, School of Medicine and School of Graduate Studies, Graduate Programs in Medicine, Biomedical Sciences Training Program, Cleveland, OH 44106. Offers PhD. *Degree requirements:* For doctorate, thesis/dissertation. *Entrance requirements:* For doctorate, GRE General Test. Additional exam requirements/recommendations for international students: Required—TOEFL. Electronic applications accepted. *Faculty research:* Biochemistry, molecular biology, immunology, genetics, neurosciences.

Case Western Reserve University, School of Medicine and School of Graduate Studies, Graduate Programs in Medicine, Department of Biochemistry, Program in RNA Biology, Cleveland, OH 44106. Offers PhD. *Degree requirements:* For doctorate, comprehensive exam, thesis/dissertation. *Entrance requirements:* For doctorate, GRE. Additional exam requirements/recommendations for international students: Required—TOEFL (minimum score 550 paper-based; 213 computer-based).

Case Western Reserve University, School of Medicine, Medical Scientist Training Program, Cleveland, OH 44106. Offers MD/PhD. Electronic applications accepted. *Faculty research:* Biomedical research.

The Catholic University of America, School of Arts and Sciences, Department of Biology, Washington, DC 20064. Offers cell and microbial biology (MS, PhD), including cell biology, microbiology; clinical laboratory science (MS, PhD); MSLS/MS. Part-time programs available. *Faculty:* 7 full-time (4 women), 2 part-time/adjunct (both women). *Students:* 3 full-time (2 women), 23 part-time (15 women); includes 8 minority (2 African Americans, 3 Asian Americans or Pacific Islanders, 3 Hispanic Americans), 8 international. Average age 29. 30 applicants, 47% accepted, 3 enrolled. In 2009, 3 doctorates awarded. *Degree requirements:* For master's, comprehensive exam, thesis or alternative; for doctorate, comprehensive exam, thesis/dissertation. *Entrance requirements:* For master's and doctorate, GRE General Test, GRE Subject Test, statement of purpose, official copies of academic transcripts, three letters of recommendation. Additional exam requirements/recommendations for international students: Required—TOEFL (minimum score 580 paper-based; 237 computer-based). *Application deadline:* For fall admission, 8/1 priority date for domestic students, 7/15 for international students; for spring admission, 12/1 priority date for domestic students, 10/15 for international students. Applications are processed on a rolling basis. Application fee: $55. Electronic applications accepted. *Expenses:* Tuition: Full-time $31,740; part-time $1245 per credit hour. One-time fee: $425 full-time. *Financial support:* Fellowships, research assistantships, teaching assistantships, Federal Work-Study, scholarships/grants, tuition waivers (full and partial), and unspecified assistantships available. Financial award application deadline: 2/1; financial award applicants required to submit FAFSA. *Faculty research:* Cell and microbiology, microbial pathogenesis, molecular biology of cell proliferation, cellular effects of electromagnetic radiation, biotechnology. Total annual research expenditures: $853,913. *Unit head:* Dr. Venigalla Rao, Chair, 202-319-5271, Fax: 202-319-5721, E-mail: rao@cua.edu. *Application contact:* Julie Schwing, Director of Graduate Admissions, 202-319-5057, Fax: 202-319-6533, E-mail: cua-admissions@cua.edu.

Cedars-Sinai Medical Center, Graduate Program in Biomedical Sciences and Translational Medicine, Los Angeles, CA 90048. Offers PhD. *Degree requirements:* For doctorate, comprehensive exam, thesis/dissertation. *Entrance requirements:* For doctorate, GRE, 3 letters of recommendation. Additional exam requirements/recommendations for international students: Required—TOEFL (minimum score 560 paper-based; 220 computer-based; 87 iBT). *Faculty research:* Immunology and infection, neuroscience, cardiovascular science, cancer, human genetics.

Central Connecticut State University, School of Graduate Studies, School of Arts and Sciences, Department of Biology, New Britain, CT 06050-4010. Offers biological sciences (MA, MS), including anesthesia (MS), ecology and environmental sciences (MA), general biology (MA), health sciences specialization (MS), professional education program (MS); biology (Certificate). Part-time and evening/weekend programs available. *Faculty:* 13 full-time (4 women), 7 part-time/adjunct (4 women). *Students:* 99 full-time (58 women), 32 part-time (25 women); includes 29 minority (11 African Americans, 12 Asian Americans or Pacific Islanders, 6 Hispanic Americans), 1 international. Average age 32. 36 applicants, 28% accepted, 7 enrolled. In 2009, 37 master's, 5 other advanced degrees awarded. *Degree requirements:* For master's, comprehensive exam, thesis or alternative; for Certificate, qualifying exam. *Entrance requirements:* For master's, minimum undergraduate GPA of 2.7. Additional exam requirements/recommendations for international students: Required—TOEFL. *Application deadline:* For fall admission, 7/1 for domestic students; for spring admission, 12/1 for domestic students. Applications are processed on a rolling basis. Application fee: $50. Electronic applications accepted. *Expenses:* Tuition, area resident: Full-time $4662; part-time $440 per credit. Tuition, state resident: full-time $6994; part-time $440 per credit. Tuition, nonresident: full-time $12,988; part-time $440 per credit. Required fees: $3606. One-time fee: $62 part-time. *Financial support:* In 2009–10, 20 students received support, including 3 research assistantships; career-related internships or fieldwork, Federal Work-Study, scholarships/grants, and unspecified

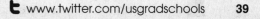

Biological and Biomedical Sciences—General

Central Connecticut State University *(continued)*
assistantships also available. Support available to part-time students. Financial award application deadline: 3/1; financial award applicants required to submit FAFSA. *Faculty research:* Environmental science, anesthesia, health sciences, zoology, animal behavior. *Unit head:* Dr. Jeremiah Jarrett, Chair, 860-832-2645. *Application contact:* Dr. Jeremiah Jarrett, Chair, 860-832-2645.

Central Michigan University, College of Graduate Studies, College of Science and Technology, Department of Biology, Mount Pleasant, MI 48859. Offers biology (MS); conservation biology (MS). Part-time programs available. *Degree requirements:* For master's, thesis or alternative. *Entrance requirements:* For master's, GRE, bachelor's degree with a major in biological science, minimum GPA of 3.0. Electronic applications accepted. *Faculty research:* Conservation biology, morphology and taxonomy of aquatic plants, molecular biology and genetics, microbials and invertebrate ecology, vertebrates.

Central Washington University, Graduate Studies and Research, College of the Sciences, Department of Biological Sciences, Ellensburg, WA 98926. Offers MS. Part-time programs available. *Faculty:* 23 full-time (8 women). *Students:* 23 full-time (10 women), 7 part-time (3 women); includes 3 minority (1 Asian American or Pacific Islander, 2 Hispanic Americans), 2 international. 26 applicants, 73% accepted, 17 enrolled. *Degree requirements:* For master's, thesis or alternative. *Entrance requirements:* For master's, GRE General Test, minimum GPA of 3.0. Additional exam requirements/recommendations for international students: Required—TOEFL (minimum score 550 paper-based; 213 computer-based; 79 iBT). *Application deadline:* For fall admission, 2/1 priority date for domestic students; for winter admission, 10/1 for domestic students; for spring admission, 1/1 for domestic students. Applications are processed on a rolling basis. Application fee: $50. *Expenses:* Tuition, state resident: full-time $7353; part-time $245 per credit. Tuition, nonresident: full-time $16,383; part-time $546 per credit. Required fees: $882. Tuition and fees vary according to degree level. *Financial support:* In 2009–10, 2 research assistantships with full and partial tuition reimbursements (averaging $9,145 per year), 10 teaching assistantships with full and partial tuition reimbursements (averaging $9,145 per year) were awarded; Federal Work-Study and health care benefits also available. Financial award application deadline: 3/1; financial award applicants required to submit FAFSA. *Unit head:* Dr. Paul James, Chair, 509-963-2731. *Application contact:* Justine Eason, Admissions Program Coordinator, 509-963-3103, Fax: 509-963-1799, E-mail: masters@cwu.edu.

Chatham University, Program in Biology, Pittsburgh, PA 15232-2826. Offers environmental biology-non-thesis track (MS); environmental biology-thesis track (MS); human biology-non-thesis track (MS); human biology-thesis track (MS). Part-time programs available. *Students:* 23 full-time (18 women). Average age 25. 30 applicants, 83% accepted, 13 enrolled. In 2009, 8 master's awarded. *Degree requirements:* For master's, thesis optional. *Entrance requirements:* For master's, 3 letters of recommendation. Additional exam requirements/recommendations for international students: Required—TOEFL (minimum score 600 paper-based; 250 computer-based; 100 iBT), IELTS (minimum score 6.5), TWE. *Application deadline:* For fall admission, 5/1 priority date for domestic and international students; for spring admission, 11/1 priority date for domestic and international students. Applications are processed on a rolling basis. Application fee: $45. Electronic applications accepted. *Financial support:* Applicants required to submit FAFSA. *Faculty research:* Molecular evolution of iron homeostasis, characteristics of soil bacterial communities, gene flow through seed movement, role of gonadotropins in spermatogonial proliferation, phosphatid/linositol metabolism in epithelial cells. *Unit head:* Dr. Lisa Lambert, Director, 412-365-1217, E-mail: lambert@chatham.edu. *Application contact:* Maureen Stokan, Assistant Director of Graduate Admissions, 412-365-2988, Fax: 412-365-1609, E-mail: gradadmissions@chatham.edu.

Chicago State University, School of Graduate and Professional Studies, College of Arts and Sciences, Department of Biological Sciences, Chicago, IL 60628. Offers MS. Part-time and evening/weekend programs available. *Degree requirements:* For master's, thesis. *Entrance requirements:* For master's, minimum GPA of 2.75, 15 credit hours in biological sciences. *Faculty research:* Molecular genetics of gene complexes, mammalian immune cell function, genetics of agriculturally important microbes, environmental toxicology, neuromuscular physiology.

The Citadel, The Military College of South Carolina, Citadel Graduate College, Department of Biology, Charleston, SC 29409. Offers MA. *Accreditation:* NCATE. Part-time and evening/weekend programs available. *Faculty:* 8 full-time (4 women). *Students:* 2 full-time (1 woman), 16 part-time (9 women); includes 4 minority (all African Americans). Average age 28. In 2009, 18 master's awarded. *Entrance requirements:* For master's, GRE (minimum score 900) or MAT (minimum score 396), minimum undergraduate GPA of 2.5. Additional exam requirements/recommendations for international students: Required—TOEFL (minimum score 550 paper-based; 213 computer-based). *Application deadline:* Applications are processed on a rolling basis. Application fee: $30. Electronic applications accepted. *Expenses:* Tuition, state resident: part-time $400 per credit hour. Tuition, nonresident: part-time $657 per credit hour. Required fees: $40 per term. *Financial support:* Health care benefits and unspecified assistantships available. Support available to part-time students. Financial award application deadline: 7/1; financial award applicants required to submit FAFSA. *Faculty research:* Genetic control of parasite-host interactions, mechanisms of development of antibiotic resistance in Pseudomonas aeruginosa, interaction of visual and vocal signals in avian mate choice and competition, effects of pollutants on salt marsh animals, structure and function of mitochondrial histone H3 protein, development of cardiac conduction tissue in tadpoles with left-right axis perturbation, evolution and ecology of barnacles and marine hosts. *Unit head:* Dr. Paul Rosenblum, Department Head, 843-953-5203, Fax: 843-953-7264, E-mail: paul.rosenblum@citadel.edu. *Application contact:* Dr. Steve A. Nida, Associate Provost, The Citadel Graduate College, 843-953-5089, Fax: 843-953-7630, E-mail: cgc@citadel.edu.

City College of the City University of New York, Graduate School, College of Liberal Arts and Science, Division of Science, Department of Biology, New York, NY 10031-9198. Offers MA, PhD. Part-time programs available. Terminal master's awarded for partial completion of doctoral program. *Degree requirements:* For master's, thesis or alternative; for doctorate, one foreign language, thesis/dissertation, teaching experience. *Entrance requirements:* For doctorate, GRE General Test. Additional exam requirements/recommendations for international students: Required—TOEFL (minimum score 500 paper-based; 61 iBT). Electronic applications accepted. *Expenses:* Tuition, state resident: part-time $310 per credit. Tuition, nonresident: part-time $575 per credit. Tuition and fees vary according to course load and program. *Faculty research:* Animal behavior, ecology, genetics, neurobiology, molecular biology.

City of Hope National Medical Center/Beckman Research Institute, Irell and Manella Graduate School of Biological Sciences, Duarte, CA 91010. Offers PhD. *Degree requirements:* For doctorate, comprehensive exam, thesis/dissertation. *Entrance requirements:* For doctorate, GRE General Test, GRE Subject Test, 2 years of course work in chemistry (general and organic); 1 year course work in each biochemistry, general biology, and general physics; 2 semesters of course work in mathematics; significant research laboratory experience. Additional exam requirements/recommendations for international students: Required—TOEFL (minimum score 595 paper-based). *Faculty research:* DNA damage and repair, protein structure, cancer biology, T cells and immunology, RNA splicing and binding.
See Display on this page and Close-Up on page 85.

Clarion University of Pennsylvania, Office of Research and Graduate Studies, College of Arts and Sciences, Department of Biology, Clarion, PA 16214. Offers MS. *Degree requirements:* For master's, thesis or alternative. *Entrance requirements:* For master's, GRE General Test, minimum QPA of 2.75. Additional exam requirements/recommendations for international students: Required—TOEFL (minimum score 600 paper-based; 250 computer-based; 100 iBT). Electronic applications accepted.

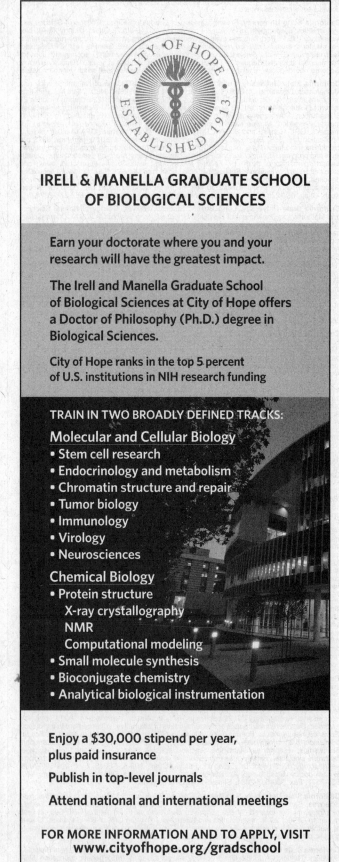

Clark Atlanta University, School of Arts and Sciences, Department of Biology, Atlanta, GA 30314. Offers MS, PhD. Part-time programs available. *Faculty:* 5 full-time (2 women). *Students:* 11 full-time (9 women), 9 part-time (6 women); includes 18 minority (16 African Americans, 2 Asian Americans or Pacific Islanders), 1 international. Average age 30. 11 applicants, 73% accepted, 5 enrolled. In 2009, 1 doctorate awarded. Terminal master's awarded for partial completion of doctoral program. *Degree requirements:* For master's, one foreign language, thesis; for doctorate, 2 foreign languages, thesis/dissertation. *Entrance requirements:* For master's, GRE General Test, minimum GPA of 2.5; for doctorate, GRE General Test, minimum graduate GPA of 3.0. Additional exam requirements/recommendations for international students: Required—TOEFL (minimum score 500 paper-based; 173 computer-based). *Application deadline:* For fall admission, 4/1 for domestic and international students; for spring admission, 11/1 for domestic and international students. Applications are processed on a rolling basis. Application fee: $40 ($55 for international students). Electronic applications accepted. *Expenses:* Tuition: Full-time $12,240; part-time $680 per credit hour. Required fees: $710; $355 per semester. *Financial support:* In 2009–10, 2 fellowships, 6 research assistantships, 5 teaching assistantships were awarded; career-related internships or fieldwork, Federal Work-Study, scholarships/grants, traineeships, and unspecified assistantships also available. Support available to part-time students. Financial award application deadline: 4/30; financial award applicants required to submit FAFSA. *Faculty research:* Regulation of amino-DNA, cellular regulations. *Unit head:* Dr. Marjorie Campbell, Chairperson, 404-880-6190, E-mail: mcampbell@cau.edu. *Application contact:* Michelle Clark-Davis, Graduate Program Admissions, 404-880-6605, E-mail: cauadmissions@cau.edu.

Clark University, Graduate School, Department of Biology, Worcester, MA 01610-1477. Offers MA, PhD. *Faculty:* 9 full-time (4 women). *Students:* 28 full-time (14 women), 1 part-time (0 women); includes 2 minority (1 African American, 1 Asian American or Pacific Islander), 7 international. Average age 28. 37 applicants, 57% accepted, 18 enrolled. In 2009, 7 master's, 3 doctorates awarded. *Degree requirements:* For master's, thesis; for doctorate, thesis/dissertation. *Entrance requirements:* For master's and doctorate, GRE General Test. Additional exam requirements/recommendations for international students: Required—TOEFL. *Application deadline:* For fall admission, 2/15 priority date for domestic students. Applications are processed on a rolling basis. Application fee: $50. Electronic applications accepted. *Expenses:* Tuition: Full-time $34,900; part-time $4362.50 per course. *Financial support:* In 2009–10, fellowships with full tuition reimbursements (averaging $19,825 per year), 4 research assistantships with full tuition reimbursements (averaging $19,825 per year), 12 teaching assistantships with full tuition reimbursements (averaging $19,825 per year) were awarded; scholarships/grants and tuition waivers (full and partial) also available. *Faculty research:* Nitrogen assimilation in marine algae, phylogenetic relationships, fungal tree of life, ancestral plasticity, drosophi genetic analysis, cytokinesis proteins. Total annual research expenditures: $1.1 million. *Unit head:* Dr. David Hibbett, Chair, 508-793-7173. *Application contact:* Bogna Sowinska, Department Secretary, 528-793-7173, Fax: 528-793-8861, E-mail: biology@clarku.edu.

Clemson University, Graduate School, College of Agriculture, Forestry and Life Sciences, Department of Biological Sciences, Program in Biological Sciences, Clemson, SC 29634. Offers MS, PhD. *Students:* 38 full-time (21 women), 2 part-time (1 woman); includes 3 minority (2 Asian Americans or Pacific Islanders, 1 Hispanic American), 11 international. Average age 28. 38 applicants, 21% accepted, 6 enrolled. In 2009, 2 master's, 4 doctorates awarded. *Degree requirements:* For master's, thesis optional; for doctorate, comprehensive exam, thesis/dissertation. *Entrance requirements:* For master's and doctorate, GRE General Test. Additional exam requirements/recommendations for international students: Required—TOEFL, IELTS. *Application deadline:* For fall admission, 1/15 for domestic students, 4/15 for international students. Applications are processed on a rolling basis. Application fee: $70 ($80 for international students). Electronic applications accepted. *Expenses:* Tuition, state resident: full-time $8684; part-time $528 per credit hour. Tuition, nonresident: full-time $15,330; part-time $1078 per credit hour. Required fees: $736; $37 per semester. Part-time tuition and fees vary according to course load and program. *Financial support:* In 2009–10, 39 students received support, including 12 fellowships with full and partial tuition reimbursements available (averaging $9,529 per year), 11 research assistantships with partial tuition reimbursements available (averaging $18,008 per year), 28 teaching assistantships with partial tuition reimbursements available (averaging $17,393 per year); career-related internships or fieldwork, institutionally sponsored loans, scholarships/grants, health care benefits, and unspecified assistantships also available. Support available to part-time students. Financial award application deadline: 3/15; financial award applicants required to submit FAFSA. *Unit head:* Dr. Alfred Wheeler, Department Chair, 864-656-1415, Fax: 864-656-0435, E-mail: wheeler@clemson.edu. *Application contact:* Jay Lyn Martin, Coordinator for Graduate Program, 864-656-3587, Fax: 864-656-0435, E-mail: gradbio@clemson.edu.

Cleveland State University, College of Graduate Studies, College of Science, Department of Biological, Geological, and Environmental Sciences, Cleveland, OH 44115. Offers biology (MS); environmental science (MS); museum studies for natural historians (MS); regulatory biology (PhD); JD/MS. Part-time programs available. Terminal master's awarded for partial completion of doctoral program. *Degree requirements:* For master's, comprehensive exam (for some programs), thesis (for some programs); for doctorate, comprehensive exam, thesis/dissertation. *Entrance requirements:* For master's, GRE General Test, 2 letters of recommendation; for doctorate, GRE General Test, 2 letters of recommendation; 1-2 page essay statement of career goals and research interests. Additional exam requirements/recommendations for international students: Required—TOEFL (minimum score 525 paper-based; 197 computer-based). Electronic applications accepted. *Faculty research:* Molecular and cell biology, immunology, urban ecology.

Cold Spring Harbor Laboratory, Watson School of Biological Sciences, Graduate Program, Cold Spring Harbor, NY 11724. Offers biological sciences (PhD). *Faculty:* 46 full-time (7 women). *Students:* 51 full-time (21 women); includes 4 minority (2 Asian Americans or Pacific Islanders, 2 Hispanic Americans), 28 international. Average age 23. 170 applicants, 16% accepted, 7 enrolled. In 2009, 5 doctorates awarded. *Degree requirements:* For doctorate, comprehensive exam, thesis/dissertation, lab rotations, teaching experience, qualifying exam, postdoctoral proposals. *Entrance requirements:* For doctorate, GRE General Test, GRE Subject Test. Additional exam requirements/recommendations for international students: Required—TOEFL. *Application deadline:* For fall admission, 12/1 for domestic and international students. Application fee: $60. Electronic applications accepted. *Financial support:* In 2009–10, 44 students received support, including 44 fellowships with full tuition reimbursements available (averaging $29,500 per year); health care benefits and tuition waivers (full) also available. Financial award application deadline: 12/1. *Faculty research:* Genetics; neurobiology; cancer, plant, molecular, cellular, quantitative and structural biology. *Unit head:* Dr. Leemor Joshua-Tor, Dean, 516-367-6890, Fax: 516-367-6919, E-mail: gradschool@cshl.edu. *Application contact:* Dawn Pologruto, Director of Admissions, Recruitment and Student Affairs, 516-367-6911, Fax: 516-367-6919, E-mail: gradschool@cshl.edu.

See Close-Up on page 87.

The College at Brockport, State University of New York, School of Science and Mathematics, Department of Biology, Brockport, NY 14420-2997. Offers biological sciences (MS), including professional science masters. Part-time programs available. *Students:* 8 full-time (6 women), 5 part-time (3 women). 12 applicants, 75% accepted, 8 enrolled. In 2009, 5 master's awarded. *Degree requirements:* For master's, comprehensive exam, thesis or alternative. *Entrance requirements:* For master's, GRE General or Subject Test (biology, biochemistry, cell and molecular biology), letters of recommendation, minimum GPA of 3.0, scientific writing sample. Additional exam requirements/recommendations for international students: Required—TOEFL (minimum score 550 paper-based; 213 computer-based; 79 iBT). *Application deadline:* For fall admission, 7/15 priority date for domestic and international students; for spring admission, 11/15 priority date for domestic and international students. Application fee: $50. Electronic applications accepted. *Expenses:* Tuition, state resident: full-time $8370; part-time $349 per credit. Tuition, nonresident: full-time $13,250; part-time $522 per credit. *Financial support:* In 2009–10, 8 teaching assistantships with full tuition reimbursements (averaging $6,000 per year) were awarded; Federal Work-Study, scholarships/grants, and unspecified assistantships also available. Support available to part-time students. Financial award application deadline: 3/15; financial award applicants required to submit FAFSA. *Faculty research:* Microbiology, molecular genetics, cellular biology developmental biology, animal physiology. *Unit head:* Dr. Rey Sia, Chairperson, 585-395-2193, Fax: 585-395-2741, E-mail: rsia@brockport.edu. *Application contact:* Dr. Adam Rich, Graduate Program Director, 585-395-5740, Fax: 585-395-2741, E-mail: arich@brockport.edu.

College of Staten Island of the City University of New York, Graduate Programs, Program in Biology, Staten Island, NY 10314-6600. Offers MS. Part-time programs available. *Faculty:* 8 full-time (1 woman), 3 part-time/adjunct (1 woman). *Students:* 1 (woman) full-time, 8 part-time (4 women); includes 2 minority (1 African American, 1 Hispanic American). Average age 27. 20 applicants, 40% accepted, 4 enrolled. In 2009, 1 master's awarded. *Degree requirements:* For master's, thesis. *Entrance requirements:* For master's, GRE General Test, GRE Subject Test (biology), minimum GPA of 3.0 in science and math, 2.75 overall; bachelor's degree in biology; 2 letters of recommendation (preferred). Additional exam requirements/recommendations for international students: Required—TOEFL (minimum score 550 paper-based; 213 computer-based; 79 iBT). *Application deadline:* Applications are processed on a rolling basis. Application fee: $125. Electronic applications accepted. *Expenses:* Tuition, state resident: full-time $7360; part-time $310 per credit. Tuition, nonresident: part-time $575 per credit. Required fees: $378; $113 per semester. *Financial support:* Career-related internships or fieldwork, Federal Work-Study, and scholarships/grants available. Support available to part-time students. Financial award applicants required to submit FAFSA. Total annual research expenditures: $148,000. *Unit head:* Dr. Frank Burbrink, Coordinator, 718-982-3961, Fax: 718-982-3852, E-mail: biologymasters@mail.csi.cuny.edu. *Application contact:* Sasha Spence, Assistant Director of Graduate Recruitment Admissions, 718-982-2699, Fax: 718-982-2500, E-mail: sasha.spence@csi.cuny.edu.

The College of William and Mary, Faculty of Arts and Sciences, Department of Biology, Williamsburg, VA 23187-8795. Offers MS. Part-time programs available. *Students:* 19 full-time (12 women), 1 part-time (0 women), 2 international. Average age 25. 35 applicants, 34% accepted, 8 enrolled. In 2009, 10 master's awarded. *Degree requirements:* For master's, comprehensive exam, thesis (for some programs). *Entrance requirements:* For master's, GRE Subject Test, GRE General Test, minimum GPA of 3.0. Additional exam requirements/recommendations for international students: Required—TOEFL. *Application deadline:* For fall admission, 2/1 priority date for domestic and international students. Application fee: $45. Electronic applications accepted. *Expenses:* Tuition, state resident: full-time $6400; part-time $315 per credit hour. Tuition, nonresident: full-time $19,720; part-time $840 per credit hour. Required fees: $4114. *Financial support:* Teaching assistantships with full tuition reimbursements, Federal Work-Study, institutionally sponsored loans, and unspecified assistantships available. Financial award application deadline: 3/1; financial award applicants required to submit FAFSA. *Faculty research:* Cellular and molecular biology, genetics, ecology, organismic biology, physiology. Total annual research expenditures: $2.5 million. *Unit head:* Dr. Lizabeth A. Allison, Chair, 757-221-2207, Fax: 757-221-6483, E-mail: laalli@wm.edu. *Application contact:* Dr. Patty Zwollo, Graduate Director, 757-221-1969, Fax: 757-221-6483, E-mail: pxzwol@wm.edu.

Colorado State University, College of Veterinary Medicine and Biomedical Sciences, Department of Biomedical Sciences, Fort Collins, CO 80523-1680. Offers MS, PhD. *Faculty:* 25 full-time (6 women), 1 part-time/adjunct (0 women). *Students:* 76 full-time (41 women), 29 part-time (19 women); includes 9 minority (1 African American, 1 American Indian/Alaska Native, 2 Asian Americans or Pacific Islanders, 5 Hispanic Americans), 5 international. Average age 26. 156 applicants, 40% accepted, 53 enrolled. In 2009, 46 master's, 5 doctorates awarded. *Degree requirements:* For master's, comprehensive exam, thesis (for some programs); for doctorate, thesis/dissertation. *Entrance requirements:* For master's, GRE General Test, GRE Subject Test, MCAT, or other standardized test or professional school entrance exam, bachelor's degree, minimum GPA of 3.0; for doctorate, GRE General Test, GRE Subject Test, bachelor's or professional degree, minimum GPA of 3.0. Additional exam requirements/recommendations for international students: Required—TOEFL (minimum score 650 paper-based; 280 computer-based). *Application deadline:* For fall admission, 4/1 priority date for domestic students, 4/1 for international students. Applications are processed on a rolling basis. Application fee: $50. Electronic applications accepted. *Expenses:* Tuition, state resident: full-time $6434; part-time $359.10 per credit. Tuition, nonresident: full-time $18,116; part-time $1006.45 per credit. Required fees: $1496; $83 per credit. *Financial support:* In 2009–10, 28 students received support, including 9 fellowships with full tuition reimbursements available (averaging $28,633 per year), 14 research assistantships with full and partial tuition reimbursements available (averaging $18,744 per year), 5 teaching assistantships with full tuition reimbursements available (averaging $7,738 per year); Federal Work-Study, scholarships/grants, traineeships, and unspecified assistantships also available. Financial award application deadline: 4/1. *Faculty research:* Integrative neuroscience, developmental neurobiology, reproductive physiology, equine reproduction, molecular signal transduction. Total annual research expenditures: $5.3 million. *Unit head:* Dr. Barbara M. Sanborn, Chair, 970-491-4263, Fax: 970-491-7569, E-mail: barbara.sanborn@colostate.edu. *Application contact:* Erin Bisenius, Graduate Education Coordinator, 970-491-6188, Fax: 970-491-7569, E-mail: erin.bisenius@colostate.edu.

Colorado State University, Graduate School, College of Natural Sciences, Department of Biology, Fort Collins, CO 80523-1878. Offers botany (MS, PhD); zoology (MS, PhD). Post-baccalaureate distance learning degree programs offered (no on-campus study). *Faculty:* 25 full-time (10 women), 1 part-time/adjunct (0 women). *Students:* 31 full-time (15 women), 20 part-time (11 women); includes 4 minority (1 American Indian/Alaska Native, 1 Asian American or Pacific Islander, 2 Hispanic Americans), 7 international. Average age 29. 38 applicants, 26% accepted, 9 enrolled. In 2009, 8 master's, 2 doctorates awarded. Terminal master's awarded for partial completion of doctoral program. *Degree requirements:* For master's, comprehensive exam (for some programs), thesis (for some programs); for doctorate, comprehensive exam, thesis/dissertation. *Entrance requirements:* For master's, GRE General Test, minimum GPA of 3.0; 3 letters of recommendation; for doctorate, GRE General Test, minimum GPA of 3.0; statement of purpose; 2 transcripts; 3 letters of recommendation. Additional exam requirements/recommendations for international students: Required—TOEFL (minimum score 550 paper-based; 213 computer-based; 80 iBT). *Application deadline:* For fall admission, 9/15 priority date for domestic students, 8/15 priority date for international students; for spring admission, 1/15 priority date for domestic and international students. Applications are processed on a rolling basis. Application fee: $50. Electronic applications accepted. *Expenses:* Tuition, state resident: full-time $6434; part-time $359.10 per credit. Tuition, nonresident: full-time $18,116; part-time $1006.45 per credit. Required fees: $1496; $83 per credit. *Financial support:* In 2009–10, 15 fellowships (averaging $26,286 per year), 26 research assistantships with full tuition reimbursements (averaging $11,410 per year), 48 teaching assistantships with full tuition reimbursements (averaging $12,007 per year) were awarded; health care benefits also available. Financial award application deadline: 1/15; financial award applicants required to submit FAFSA. *Faculty research:* Aquatic and terrestrial ecology, cell biology and genetics, plant/animal physiology, developmental biology, evolutionary biology. Total annual research expenditures: $5 million. *Unit head:* Dr. Daniel R. Bush, Chair, 970-491-7013, Fax: 970-491-0649, E-mail: dbush@colostate.edu. *Application contact:* Dorothy Ramirez, Graduate Coordinator, 970-491-1923, Fax: 970-491-0649, E-mail: dorothy.ramirez@colostate.edu.

Colorado State University–Pueblo, College of Science and Mathematics, Pueblo, CO 81001-4901. Offers applied natural science (MS), including biochemistry, biology, chemistry. Part-time and evening/weekend programs available. *Degree requirements:* For master's, comprehensive exam (for some programs), thesis (for some programs), internship report (if non-thesis). *Entrance requirements:* For master's, GRE General Test (minimum score 1000), 2 letters of reference, minimum GPA of 3.0. Additional exam requirements/recommendations for international students: Required—TOEFL (minimum score 500 paper-based; 173 computer-

Biological and Biomedical Sciences—General

Colorado State University–Pueblo (continued)
based), IELTS (minimum score 5). *Faculty research:* Fungal cell walls, molecular biology, bioactive materials synthesis, atomic force microscopy-surface chemistry, nanoscience.

Columbia University, College of Physicians and Surgeons, New York, NY 10032. Offers MD, M Phil, MA, MS, DN Sc, DPT, Ed D, PhD, Adv C, MBA/MS, MD/DDS, MD/MPH, MD/MS, MD/PhD, MPH/MS. Part-time programs available. *Entrance requirements:* For MD, MCAT; for master's and doctorate, GRE General Test. Additional exam requirements/recommendations for international students: Required—TOEFL. *Expenses:* Contact institution.

Columbia University, Graduate School of Arts and Sciences, Division of Natural Sciences, Department of Biological Sciences, New York, NY 10027. Offers M Phil, MA, PhD, MD/PhD. *Degree requirements:* For master's, teaching experience, written exam; for doctorate, thesis/dissertation. *Entrance requirements:* For master's and doctorate, GRE General Test, GRE Subject Test. Additional exam requirements/recommendations for international students: Required—TOEFL.

See Close-Up on page 89.

Concordia University, School of Graduate Studies, Faculty of Arts and Science, Department of Biology, Montréal, QC H3G 1M8, Canada. Offers biology (M Sc, PhD); biotechnology and genomics (Diploma). *Degree requirements:* For master's, thesis; for doctorate, thesis/dissertation, pedagogical training. *Entrance requirements:* For master's, honors degree in biology; for doctorate, M Sc in life science. *Faculty research:* Cell biology, animal physiology, ecology, microbiology/molecular biology, plant physiology/biochemistry and biotechnology.

Cornell University, Graduate School, Graduate Fields of Comparative Biomedical Sciences, Field of Comparative Biomedical Sciences, Ithaca, NY 14853-0001. Offers cellular and molecular medicine (MS, PhD); developmental and reproductive biology (MS, PhD); infectious diseases (MS, PhD); population medicine and epidemiology (MS, PhD); structural and functional biology (MS, PhD). *Faculty:* 106 full-time (29 women). *Students:* 41 full-time (28 women); includes 1 minority (African American), 17 international. Average age 32. 32 applicants, 31% accepted, 9 enrolled. In 2009, 1 master's, 10 doctorates awarded. *Degree requirements:* For master's, thesis; for doctorate, comprehensive exam, thesis/dissertation. *Entrance requirements:* For master's and doctorate, GRE General Test, 2 letters of recommendation. Additional exam requirements/recommendations for international students: Required—TOEFL (minimum score 550 paper-based; 213 computer-based; 77 iBT). *Application deadline:* For fall admission, 12/15 for domestic students. Application fee: $70. Electronic applications accepted. *Expenses:* Tuition: Full-time $29,500. Required fees: $70. Full-time tuition and fees vary according to degree level, program and student level. *Financial support:* In 2009–10, 4 fellowships with full tuition reimbursements, 2 research assistantships with full tuition reimbursements were awarded; teaching assistantships with full tuition reimbursements, institutionally sponsored loans, scholarships/grants, health care benefits, tuition waivers (full and partial), and unspecified assistantships also available. Financial award applicants required to submit FAFSA. *Faculty research:* Receptors and signal transduction, viral and bacterial infectious diseases, tumor metastasis, clinical sciences/nutritional disease, developmental/neurological disorders. *Unit head:* Director of Graduate Studies, 607-253-3276, Fax: 607-253-3756. *Application contact:* Graduate Field Assistant, 607-253-3276, Fax: 607-253-3756, E-mail: graduate_edcvm@cornell.edu.

Cornell University, Joan and Sanford I. Weill Medical College and Graduate School of Medical Sciences, Weill Cornell Graduate School of Medical Sciences, New York, NY 10065. Offers MS, PhD. *Faculty:* 251 full-time (69 women). *Students:* 569 full-time (362 women); includes 108 minority (21 African Americans, 55 Asian Americans or Pacific Islanders, 32 Hispanic Americans), 158 international. Average age 24. 613 applicants, 19% accepted, 40 enrolled. In 2009, 49 master's, 51 doctorates awarded. Terminal master's awarded for partial completion of doctoral program. *Degree requirements:* For master's, comprehensive exam; for doctorate, thesis/dissertation, final exam. *Entrance requirements:* For doctorate, GRE General Test. Additional exam requirements/recommendations for international students: Required—TOEFL. *Application deadline:* For fall admission, 12/1 for domestic students. Application fee: $60. Electronic applications accepted. *Expenses:* Contact institution. *Financial support:* In 2009–10, 42 fellowships (averaging $23,083 per year) were awarded; scholarships/grants, health care benefits, and stipends (given to all students) also available. *Unit head:* Dr. David P. Hajjar, Dean, 212-746-6900, E-mail: dphajjar@med.cornell.edu. *Application contact:* Dr. Randi Silver, Associate Dean, 212-746-6565, Fax: 212-746-8906, E-mail: gsms@med.cornell.edu.

Cornell University, Joan and Sanford I. Weill Medical College and Graduate School of Medical Sciences, Weill Cornell/Rockefeller/Sloan-Kettering Tri-Institutional MD-PhD Program, New York, NY 10065. Offers MD/PhD. Offered jointly with The Rockefeller University and Sloan-Kettering Institute. *Faculty:* 278 full-time (83 women). *Students:* 111 full-time (40 women); includes 37 minority (15 African Americans, 8 Asian Americans or Pacific Islanders, 14 Hispanic Americans), 1 international. 443 applicants, 9% accepted, 14 enrolled. *Application deadline:* For fall admission, 10/15 for domestic and international students. Applications are processed on a rolling basis. Application fee: $0. Electronic applications accepted. *Expenses:* Contact institution. *Financial support:* In 2009–10, 111 students received support, including 111 fellowships with full tuition reimbursements available (averaging $31,600 per year); health care benefits, tuition waivers (full), and stipends, research supplements, dental insurance also available. *Faculty research:* Neuroscience, pharmacology, immunology, structural biology, genetics. *Unit head:* Dr. Olaf S. Andersen, Director, 212-746-6023, Fax: 212-746-8678, E-mail: mdphd@med.cornell.edu. *Application contact:* Ruth Gotian, Administrative Director, 212-746-6023, Fax: 212-746-8678, E-mail: mdphd@med.cornell.edu.

Creighton University, School of Medicine and Graduate School, Graduate Programs in Medicine, Department of Biomedical Sciences, Omaha, NE 68178-0001. Offers MS, PhD, MD/PhD. Terminal master's awarded for partial completion of doctoral program. *Degree requirements:* For master's, thesis; for doctorate, thesis/dissertation. *Entrance requirements:* For master's, GRE General Test (minimum 50th percentile); for doctorate, GRE General Test (minimum score: 50th percentile). Additional exam requirements/recommendations for international students: Required—TOEFL. Electronic applications accepted. *Expenses:* Tuition: Full-time $11,700; part-time $650 per credit hour. Required fees: $126 per semester. *Faculty research:* Molecular biology and gene transfection.

Dalhousie University, Faculty of Graduate Studies and Faculty of Medicine, Graduate Programs in Medicine, Halifax, NS B3H 4R2, Canada. Offers M Sc, PhD. *Degree requirements:* For master's, thesis; for doctorate, thesis/dissertation. *Entrance requirements:* Additional exam requirements/recommendations for international students: Required—TOEFL, IELTS, 1 of the following 5 approved tests: TOEFL, IELTS, CAEL, CANTEST, Michigan English Language Assessment Battery. Electronic applications accepted. *Expenses:* Contact institution.

Dalhousie University, Faculty of Science, Department of Biology, Halifax, NS B3H 4R2, Canada. Offers M Sc, PhD. *Students:* 90 full-time (46 women), 2 part-time (1 woman). 81 applicants, 43% accepted. In 2009, 8 master's, 11 doctorates awarded. Terminal master's awarded for partial completion of doctoral program. *Degree requirements:* For master's, thesis; for doctorate, thesis/dissertation. *Entrance requirements:* Additional exam requirements/recommendations for international students: Required—TOEFL, IELTS, CANTEST, CAEL, or Michigan English Language Assessment Battery. *Application deadline:* For fall admission, 5/31 for domestic students, 1/31 for international students; for winter admission, 10/31 for domestic students, 6/30 for international students; for spring admission, 2/21 for domestic students, 10/31 for international students. Application fee: $60. Electronic applications accepted. *Financial support:* Career-related internships or fieldwork, scholarships/grants, and health care benefits available. *Faculty research:* Marine biology, ecology, animal physiology, plant physiology, microbiology (cell, molecular, genetics, development). *Unit head:* Dr. H. Whitehead, Graduate Coordinator, 902-494-3723, Fax: 902-494-3736, E-mail: biology@dal.ca. *Application contact:* Carolyn Young, Graduate Secretary, 902-494-2082, Fax: 902-494-3736, E-mail: biology@dal.ca.

Dartmouth College, Graduate Program in Molecular and Cellular Biology, Department of Biological Sciences, Hanover, NH 03755. Offers PhD, MD/PhD. *Faculty:* 17 full-time (4 women), 3 part-time/adjunct (0 women). *Students:* 29 full-time (13 women), 9 international. Average age 27. 280 applicants, 22% accepted, 25 enrolled. In 2009, 1 doctorate awarded. *Entrance requirements:* For doctorate, GRE General Test, letters of recommendation. Additional exam requirements/recommendations for international students: Required—TOEFL (minimum score 450 paper-based; 90 iBT) or IELTS (minimum score 7). *Application deadline:* For fall admission, 1/4 for domestic and international students. Applications are processed on a rolling basis. Application fee: $75. Electronic applications accepted. *Financial support:* Scholarships/grants, health care benefits, and stipends ($25,500) available. *Unit head:* Dr. Thomas Jack, Chair and Professor, 603-646-2378, E-mail: biology@dartmouth.edu. *Application contact:* Janet Cheney, Program Coordinator, 603-650-1612, Fax: 603-650-1006, E-mail: mcb@dartmouth.edu.

See Close-Up on page 91.

Delaware State University, Graduate Programs, Department of Biology, Program in Biological Sciences, Dover, DE 19901-2277. Offers MS. *Entrance requirements:* For master's, GRE, prerequisite undergraduate courses. Additional exam requirements/recommendations for international students: Required—TOEFL.

Delta State University, Graduate Programs, College of Arts and Sciences, Division of Biological and Physical Sciences, Cleveland, MS 38733-0001. Offers natural sciences (MSNS). Part-time programs available. *Degree requirements:* For master's, research project or thesis. *Entrance requirements:* For master's, GRE General Test. *Expenses:* Tuition, state resident: full-time $4450; part-time $247 per credit hour. Tuition, nonresident: full-time $11,520; part-time $640 per credit hour.

DePaul University, College of Liberal Arts and Sciences, Department of Biological Sciences, Chicago, IL 60614. Offers MA, MS. *Faculty:* 10 full-time (5 women), 5 part-time/adjunct (0 women). *Students:* 11 full-time (5 women), 3 part-time (0 women); includes 5 minority (2 African Americans, 1 Asian American or Pacific Islander, 2 Hispanic Americans). Average age 25. 39 applicants, 21% accepted, 6 enrolled. In 2009, 4 master's awarded. *Degree requirements:* For master's, comprehensive exam, thesis (for some programs). *Entrance requirements:* For master's, GRE, MCAT or DAT, minimum GPA of 3.0. Additional exam requirements/recommendations for international students: Required—TOEFL (minimum score 590 paper-based; 243 computer-based; 120 iBT). *Application deadline:* For fall admission, 2/15 priority date for domestic and international students. Applications are processed on a rolling basis. Application fee: $25. Electronic applications accepted. *Expenses:* Tuition: Full-time $37,525; part-time $620 per credit hour. *Financial support:* In 2009–10, 10 teaching assistantships with full tuition reimbursements (averaging $9,000 per year) were awarded; Federal Work-Study, institutionally sponsored loans, scholarships/grants, and tuition waivers (partial) also available. Support available to part-time students. Financial award application deadline: 4/1. *Faculty research:* Cell motility, detoxification in plant cells, molecular biology of fungi, B-lymphocyte development, physiological ecology, traumatic brain injury, bacterial pathogenicity, cancer biology, molecular evolution, Drosophila genetics. *Unit head:* Dr. Stanley Cohn, Chair, 773-325-7595, Fax: 773-325-7596, E-mail: scohn@depaul.edu. *Application contact:* Dr. Margaret Silliker, Director of Graduate Admissions, 773-325-2194, E-mail: msillike@depaul.edu.

Dominican University of California, Graduate Programs, School of Health and Natural Sciences, Program in Biology, San Rafael, CA 94901-2298. Offers MS.

Drew University, Caspersen School of Graduate Studies, Program in Education, Madison, NJ 07940-1493. Offers biology (MAT); chemistry (MAT); English (MAT); French (MAT); Italian (MAT); math (MAT); physics (MAT); social studies (MAT); Spanish (MAT); theatre arts (MAT). Part-time programs available. *Students:* 21 full-time (10 women), 6 part-time (2 women); includes 1 minority (Hispanic American). Average age 24. 40 applicants, 90% accepted, 27 enrolled. In 2009, 13 master's awarded. *Entrance requirements:* For master's, transcripts, personal statement, recommendations. Additional exam requirements/recommendations for international students: Required—TOEFL, TWE. *Application deadline:* For fall admission, 2/1 priority date for domestic students. Applications are processed on a rolling basis. Application fee: $35. *Expenses:* Contact institution. *Financial support:* In 2009–10, 22 students received support. Federal Work-Study, scholarships/grants, and tuition waivers (partial) available. Support available to part-time students. Financial award application deadline: 2/15; financial award applicants required to submit FAFSA. *Unit head:* Dr. Ross Danis. *Application contact:* Carla J. Burns, Director of Graduate Admissions, 973-408-3110, Fax: 973-408-3242, E-mail: gradm@drew.edu.

Drexel University, College of Arts and Sciences, Department of Biology, Philadelphia, PA 19104-2875. Offers biological sciences (MS, PhD); human nutrition (MS). Part-time programs available. *Degree requirements:* For doctorate, thesis/dissertation. *Entrance requirements:* For master's and doctorate, GRE General Test. Additional exam requirements/recommendations for international students: Required—TOEFL. Electronic applications accepted. *Faculty research:* Genetic engineering, physiological ecology.

Drexel University, College of Medicine, Biomedical Graduate Programs, Philadelphia, PA 19129. Offers MLAS, MMS, MS, PhD, Certificate, MD/PhD. Part-time programs available. Terminal master's awarded for partial completion of doctoral program. *Degree requirements:* For master's, comprehensive exam; for doctorate, thesis/dissertation, qualifying exam. *Entrance requirements:* For master's and doctorate, GRE General Test. Additional exam requirements/recommendations for international students: Required—TOEFL. Electronic applications accepted. *Expenses:* Contact institution.

See Close-Ups on pages 93 and 95.

Drexel University, College of Medicine, MD/PhD Program, Philadelphia, PA 19104-2875. Offers MD/PhD. Electronic applications accepted.

Drexel University, School of Biomedical Engineering, Science and Health Systems, Program in Biomedical Science, Philadelphia, PA 19104-2875. Offers MS, PhD. *Degree requirements:* For master's, thesis (for some programs); for doctorate, thesis/dissertation. Electronic applications accepted.

Duke University, Graduate School, Department of Biology, Durham, NC 27708. Offers PhD. *Faculty:* 50 full-time. *Students:* 81 full-time (43 women); includes 11 minority (8 Asian Americans or Pacific Islanders, 3 Hispanic Americans), 21 international. 100 applicants, 18% accepted, 10 enrolled. In 2009, 9 doctorates awarded. *Degree requirements:* For doctorate, one foreign language, thesis/dissertation. *Entrance requirements:* For doctorate, GRE General Test, GRE Subject Test (recommended). Additional exam requirements/recommendations for international students: Required—TOEFL (minimum score 550 paper-based; 213 computer-based; 83 iBT), IELTS (minimum score 7). *Application deadline:* For fall admission, 12/8 priority date for domestic and international students. Application fee: $75. Electronic applications accepted. *Financial support:* Fellowships, research assistantships, teaching assistantships, Federal Work-Study available. Financial award application deadline: 12/8. *Unit head:* Sonke Johnson, Associate Professor, 919-684-3649, Fax: 919-660-7293, E-mail: aslzoo@duke.edu. *Application contact:* Cynthia Robertson, Associate Dean for Enrollment Services, 919-684-3913, E-mail: grad-admissions@duke.edu.

Duquesne University, Bayer School of Natural and Environmental Sciences, Department of Biological Sciences, Pittsburgh, PA 15282-0001. Offers MS, PhD, MS/MS. Part-time programs available. *Faculty:* 15 full-time (4 women), 1 part-time/adjunct (0 women). *Students:* 32 full-time (17 women), 1 part-time (0 women); includes 6 minority (1 African American, 5 Asian Americans or Pacific Islanders), 10 international. Average age 27. 30 applicants, 50% accepted, 12 enrolled. In 2009, 5 master's, 3 doctorates awarded. Terminal master's awarded for partial completion of doctoral program. *Degree requirements:* For master's, thesis (for some programs), 32 credit hours (non-thesis); for doctorate, thesis/dissertation. *Entrance requirements:* For master's, GRE General Test, GRE Subject Test (biology, biochemistry, orcell and molecular biology), BS in biological sciences or related field, 3 letters of recommendation; for doctorate, GRE General Test, GRE Subject Test (biology or biochemistry, cell and molecular biology), MS in biological sciences or related field, 3 letters of recommendation, statement of purpose, official transcripts. Additional exam requirements/recommendations for international students: Required—TOEFL (minimum score 80 iBT). *Application deadline:* For fall admission, 2/15 for domestic and international students. Applications are processed on a rolling basis. Application fee: $0 ($40 for international students). Electronic applications accepted. *Expenses:* Contact institution. *Financial support:* In 2009–10, 31 students received support, including 1 fellowship with full tuition reimbursement available (averaging $21,300 per year), 4 research assistantships with full tuition reimbursements available (averaging $20,800 per year), 25 teaching assistantships with full tuition reimbursements available (averaging $20,800 per year); scholarships/grants, tuition waivers (partial), and unspecified assistantships also available. Financial award application deadline: 5/31. *Faculty research:* Cell and developmental biology, molecular biology and genetics, evolution, ecology, physiology and microbiology. *Unit head:* Dr. Philip E. Auron, Chair, 412-396-5657, Fax: 412-396-5907, E-mail: auronp@duq.edu. *Application contact:* Heather Costello, Graduate Academic Advisor, 412-396-6339, Fax: 412-396-4881, E-mail: costelloh@duq.edu.

East Carolina University, Brody School of Medicine, Graduate Programs in Medicine, Greenville, NC 27858-4353. Offers MPH, PhD. *Degree requirements:* For doctorate, comprehensive exam, thesis/dissertation. *Entrance requirements:* For doctorate, GRE General Test. Additional exam requirements/recommendations for international students: Required—TOEFL.

East Carolina University, Graduate School, Thomas Harriot College of Arts and Sciences, Department of Biology, Greenville, NC 27858-4353. Offers biology (MS); molecular biology/biotechnology (MS). Part-time programs available. *Degree requirements:* For master's, one foreign language, comprehensive exam, thesis. *Entrance requirements:* For master's, GRE General Test, GRE Subject Test. Additional exam requirements/recommendations for international students: Required—TOEFL. *Faculty research:* Biochemistry, microbiology, cell biology.

Eastern Illinois University, Graduate School, College of Sciences, Department of Biological Sciences, Charleston, IL 61920-3099. Offers MS. In 2009, 1 master's awarded. *Degree requirements:* For master's, exam. *Application deadline:* For fall admission, 3/31 priority date for domestic students. Applications are processed on a rolling basis. Application fee: $30. *Expenses:* Tuition, state resident: full-time $9434; part-time $239 per credit hour. Tuition, nonresident: full-time $23,774; part-time $717 per credit hour. Required fees: $802.63. *Financial support:* In 2009–10, 15 research assistantships with tuition reimbursements (averaging $8,100 per year), 5 teaching assistantships with tuition reimbursements (averaging $8,100 per year) were awarded; career-related internships or fieldwork also available. *Unit head:* Dr. Karen Gaines, Chair, 217-581-6235, Fax: 217-581-7141, E-mail: kfgaines@eiu.edu. *Application contact:* Dr. Jeff Laursen, Coordinator, 217-581-6390, E-mail: jrlaursen@eiu.edu.

Eastern Kentucky University, The Graduate School, College of Arts and Sciences, Department of Biological Sciences, Richmond, KY 40475-3102. Offers biological sciences (MS); ecology (MS). Part-time programs available. *Degree requirements:* For master's, thesis. *Entrance requirements:* For master's, GRE General Test, minimum GPA of 2.5. *Faculty research:* Systematics, ecology, and biodiversity; animal behavior; protein structure and molecular genetics; biomonitoring and aquatic toxicology; pathogenesis of microbes and parasites.

Eastern Michigan University, Graduate School, College of Arts and Sciences, Department of Biology, Ypsilanti, MI 48197. Offers cell and molecular biology (MS); community college biology teaching (MS); ecology and organismal biology (MS); general biology (MS); water resources (MS). Part-time and evening/weekend programs available. Postbaccalaureate distance learning degree programs offered (minimal on-campus study). *Faculty:* 20 full-time (5 women). *Students:* 10 full-time (8 women), 35 part-time (21 women); includes 3 minority (2 African Americans, 1 Asian American or Pacific Islander), 7 international. Average age 28. 57 applicants, 63% accepted, 20 enrolled. In 2009, 17 master's awarded. *Entrance requirements:* For master's, GRE General Test, GRE Subject Test. Additional exam requirements/recommendations for international students: Required—TOEFL. *Application deadline:* Applications are processed on a rolling basis. Application fee: $35. Tuition and fees vary according to course level. *Financial support:* In 2009–10, 22 teaching assistantships with full tuition reimbursements (averaging $8,660 per year) were awarded; fellowships, research assistantships with full tuition reimbursements, career-related internships or fieldwork, Federal Work-Study, institutionally sponsored loans, scholarships/grants, tuition waivers (partial), and unspecified assistantships also available. Support available to part-time students. Financial award applicants required to submit FAFSA. *Unit head:* Dr. Marianne Laporte, Department Head, 734-487-4242, Fax: 734-487-9235, E-mail: mlaporte@emich.edu. *Application contact:* Dr. Marianne Laporte, Department Head, 734-487-4242, Fax: 734-487-9235, E-mail: mlaporte@emich.edu.

Eastern New Mexico University, Graduate School, College of Liberal Arts and Sciences, Department of Biology, Portales, NM 88130. Offers MS. Part-time programs available. *Faculty:* 7 full-time (0 women). *Students:* 2 full-time (both women), 12 part-time (6 women); includes 4 minority (1 African American, 3 Hispanic Americans), 3 international. Average age 25. 15 applicants, 27% accepted, 4 enrolled. In 2009, 5 master's awarded. *Degree requirements:* For master's, comprehensive exam, thesis optional. *Entrance requirements:* For master's, GRE, minimum GPA of 3.0, letters of recommendation. Additional exam requirements/recommendations for international students: Required—TOEFL (minimum score 550 paper-based; 213 computer-based; 79 iBT), IELTS (minimum score 6). *Application deadline:* For fall admission, 7/20 priority date for domestic students, 6/20 priority date for international students. Applications are processed on a rolling basis. Application fee: $10. Electronic applications accepted. *Expenses:* Tuition, state resident: full-time $2922; part-time $121.75 per credit hour. Tuition, nonresident: full-time $8454; part-time $352.25 per credit hour. Required fees: $1038; $43.25 per credit hour. *Financial support:* In 2009–10, 1 research assistantship with tuition reimbursement (averaging $4,250 per year), 10 teaching assistantships with tuition reimbursements (averaging $4,250 per year) were awarded; fellowships, unspecified assistantships also available. Support available to part-time students. Financial award applicants required to submit FAFSA. *Unit head:* Dr. Darren Pollock, Graduate Coordinator, 575-562-2862, E-mail: darren.pollock@enmu.edu. *Application contact:* Dr. Darren Pollock, Graduate Coordinator, 575-562-2862, E-mail: darren.pollock@enmu.edu.

Eastern Virginia Medical School, Doctoral Program in Biomedical Sciences, Norfolk, VA 23501-1980. Offers PhD. *Students:* 26. 22 applicants, 27% accepted, 4 enrolled. In 2009, 6 doctorates awarded. *Degree requirements:* For doctorate, thesis/dissertation. *Entrance requirements:* For doctorate, GRE General Test. Additional exam requirements/recommendations for international students: Required—TOEFL. *Application deadline:* For fall admission, 2/1 for domestic students. Applications are processed on a rolling basis. Application fee: $60. Electronic applications accepted. *Expenses:* Contact institution. *Financial support:* Research assistantships with full tuition reimbursements available. *Faculty research:* Cancer, cardiovascular biology, diabetes, infectious disease, neuroscience, reproductive biology. Total annual research expenditures: $14 million. *Unit head:* Dr. Earl Godfrey, Director, 757-446-5609, Fax: 757-624-2255, E-mail: godfreew@evms.edu. *Application contact:* Leah Solomon, Administrative Support Coordinator, 757-446-5944, Fax: 757-446-6179, E-mail: solomoLJ@evms.edu.

Eastern Virginia Medical School, Master's Program in Biomedical Sciences (Clinical Embryology and Andrology), Norfolk, VA 23501-1980. Offers MS. Postbaccalaureate distance learning degree programs offered (minimal on-campus study). *Faculty:* 12 full-time, 8 part-time/adjunct. *Students:* 55 full-time (41 women); includes 6 African Americans, 8 Asian Americans or Pacific Islanders, 9 Hispanic Americans. 32 applicants, 75% accepted, 21 enrolled. In 2009, 11 master's awarded. *Entrance requirements:* Additional exam requirements/recommendations for international students: Required—TOEFL (minimum score 550 paper-based; 213 computer-based; 80 iBT). *Application deadline:* For fall admission, 1/1 for domestic and international students. Applications are processed on a rolling basis. Application fee: $60. Electronic applications accepted. *Expenses:* Contact institution. *Unit head:* Dr. Jacob Mayer, Director, 757-446-5049, Fax: 757-446-5905. *Application contact:* Nancy Garcia, Administrator, 757-446-8935, Fax: 757-446-5905, E-mail: garcianw@evms.edu.

Eastern Virginia Medical School, Master's Program in Biomedical Sciences (Medical Master's), Norfolk, VA 23501-1980. Offers MS. *Faculty:* 25. *Students:* 22 full-time (12 women); includes 9 Asian Americans or Pacific Islanders, 1 Hispanic American. 343 applicants, 12% accepted. In 2009, 23 master's awarded. *Entrance requirements:* For master's, MCAT. *Application deadline:* For fall admission, 4/1 for domestic students. Applications are processed on a rolling basis. Application fee: $60. Electronic applications accepted. *Expenses:* Contact institution. *Financial support:* Institutionally sponsored loans available. *Unit head:* Dr. Donald Meyer, Director, 757-446-5615, Fax: 757-446-6179, E-mail: meyerdc@evms.edu. *Application contact:* Leah Solomon, Administrative Support Coordinator, 757-446-5944, Fax: 757-446-6179, E-mail: solomoLJ@evms.edu.

Eastern Virginia Medical School, Master's Program in Biomedical Sciences Research, Norfolk, VA 23501-1980. Offers MS. *Faculty:* 57. *Students:* 6 full-time (all women); includes 2 minority (1 African American, 1 Hispanic American). 10 applicants, 70% accepted, 4 enrolled. In 2009, 2 master's awarded. *Degree requirements:* For master's, comprehensive exam (for some programs), thesis optional. *Entrance requirements:* For master's, GRE. Additional exam requirements/recommendations for international students: Required—TOEFL. *Application deadline:* For fall admission, 3/1 for domestic students. Applications are processed on a rolling basis. Application fee: $60. Electronic applications accepted. *Expenses:* Contact institution. *Faculty research:* Cancer, cardiovascular biology, diabetes, infectious disease, neuroscience, reproductive biology. *Unit head:* Dr. Earl Godfrey, Director, 757-446-5609, Fax: 757-624-2255, E-mail: godfreew@evms.edu. *Application contact:* Leah Solomon, Administrative Support Coordinator, 757-446-5944, Fax: 757-446-6179, E-mail: solomoLJ@evms.edu.

Eastern Washington University, Graduate Studies, College of Science, Health and Engineering, Department of Biology, Cheney, WA 99004-2431. Offers MS. *Degree requirements:* For master's, comprehensive exam, thesis. *Entrance requirements:* For master's, GRE General Test, minimum GPA of 3.0. *Expenses:* Tuition, state resident: full-time $7476; part-time $249 per quarter hour. Tuition, nonresident: full-time $18,030; part-time $601 per quarter hour. Required fees: $3.50 per quarter hour. $142 per quarter. *Faculty research:* Ecology of Eastern Washington Scablands, Columbia River fisheries, biotechnology applied to vaccines, role of mycorrhiza in plant nutrition, exercise and estrous cycles.

East Stroudsburg University of Pennsylvania, Graduate School, College of Arts and Sciences, Department of Biology, East Stroudsburg, PA 18301-2999. Offers M Ed, MS. Part-time and evening/weekend programs available. *Faculty:* 11 full-time (4 women). *Students:* 24 full-time (13 women), 28 part-time (14 women); includes 4 minority (2 African Americans, 2 Asian Americans or Pacific Islanders). Average age 29. In 2009, 25 master's awarded. *Degree requirements:* For master's, comprehensive exam, thesis or alternative. *Entrance requirements:* For master's, GRE, resume, undergraduate major in life science (or equivalent), completion of organic chemistry (minimum two semesters), 3 letters of recommendation, letter of intent. Additional exam requirements/recommendations for international students: Required—TOEFL (minimum score 560 paper-based; 220 computer-based; 83 iBT) or IELTS. *Application deadline:* For fall admission, 7/31 for domestic students, 5/1 priority date for international students; for spring admission, 11/30 for domestic students, 10/1 for international students. Applications are processed on a rolling basis. Application fee: $50. *Expenses:* Tuition, state resident: full-time $9942; part-time $387 per credit. Tuition, nonresident: full-time $14,240; part-time $619 per credit. *Financial support:* In 2009–10, 31 research assistantships with full and partial tuition reimbursements (averaging $1,654 per year) were awarded; Federal Work-Study and institutionally sponsored loans also available. Financial award application deadline: 3/1; financial award applicants required to submit FAFSA. *Unit head:* Dr. Jane Huffman, Graduate Coordinator, 570-422-3725, Fax: 570-422-3724, E-mail: jhuffman@po-box.esu.edu. *Application contact:* Kevin Quintero, Associate Provost for Enrollment Management, 570-422-3890, Fax: 570-422-3711, E-mail: kquintero@po-box.esu.edu.

East Tennessee State University, James H. Quillen College of Medicine, Biomedical Science Graduate Program, Johnson City, TN 37614. Offers anatomy (MS, PhD); biochemistry (MS, PhD); biophysics (MS, PhD); microbiology (MS, PhD); pharmacology (MS, PhD); physiology (MS, PhD). Part-time programs available. Terminal master's awarded for partial completion of doctoral program. *Degree requirements:* For master's, one foreign language, thesis, comprehensive qualifying exam; for doctorate, 2 foreign languages, thesis/dissertation. *Entrance requirements:* For master's, GRE General Test, minimum GPA of 3.0, bachelor's degree in biological or related science; for doctorate, GRE General Test, GRE Subject Test. Additional exam requirements/recommendations for international students: Required—TOEFL (minimum score 550 paper-based; 213 computer-based). *Expenses:* Contact institution.

East Tennessee State University, School of Graduate Studies, College of Arts and Sciences, Department of Biological Sciences, Johnson City, TN 37614. Offers biology (MS); microbiology (MS). *Degree requirements:* For master's, comprehensive exam, thesis or alternative. *Entrance requirements:* For master's, GRE General Test or GRE Subject Test, minimum GPA of 3.0. Additional exam requirements/recommendations for international students: Required—TOEFL (minimum score 550 paper-based; 213 computer-based). *Faculty research:* Vertebrate natural history, mutation rates in fruit flies, regulation of plant secondary metabolism, plant biochemistry, timekeeping in honeybees, gene expression in diapausing flies.

Edinboro University of Pennsylvania, School of Graduate Studies and Research, School of Science, Management and Technology, Department of Biology and Health Services, Edinboro, PA 16444. Offers biology (MS). Part-time and evening/weekend programs available. *Faculty:* 5 full-time (2 women). *Students:* 3 full-time (2 women), 3 part-time (all women); includes 1 minority (Asian American or Pacific Islander). Average age 28. *Degree requirements:* For master's, thesis or alternative, competency exam. *Entrance requirements:* For master's, GRE or MAT, minimum QPA of 2.5. *Application deadline:* Applications are processed on a rolling basis. Application fee: $30. Electronic applications accepted. *Expenses:* Tuition, state resident: full-time $6666; part-time $370 per credit. Tuition, nonresident: full-time $10,666; part-time $593 per credit. Required fees: $2206.28. One-time fee: $204 part-time. *Financial support:* In 2009–10, 2 research assistantships with full and partial tuition reimbursements (averaging $4,050 per year) were awarded; Federal Work-Study, scholarships/grants, and unspecified assistantships also available. Support available to part-time students. Financial award application deadline: 2/15; financial award applicants required to submit FAFSA. *Faculty research:* Microbiology, molecular biology, zoology, botany, ecology. *Unit head:* Dr. Peter Lindeman, Program Head, 814-732-2447, E-mail: plindeman@edinboro.edu. *Application contact:* Dr. Peter Lindeman, Program Head, 814-732-2447, E-mail: plindeman@edinboro.edu.

Elizabeth City State University, School of Mathematics, Science and Technology, Program in Biology, Elizabeth City, NC 27909-7806. Offers MS. Part-time programs available. *Degree requirements:* For master's, thesis. *Entrance requirements:* For master's, GRE. Additional exam requirements/recommendations for international students: Required—TOEFL. Electronic applications accepted. *Faculty research:* Apoptosis and cancer, plant bioengineering, development of biofuels, microbial degradation, insect cell-like discovery.

Emory University, Graduate School of Arts and Sciences, Division of Biological and Biomedical Sciences, Atlanta, GA 30322-1100. Offers PhD. *Faculty:* 312 full-time (77 women). *Students:* 443 full-time (284 women); includes 82 minority (33 African Americans, 1 American Indian/Alaska Native, 27 Asian Americans or Pacific Islanders, 21 Hispanic Americans), 71 international. Average age 27. 677 applicants, 18% accepted, 60 enrolled. In 2009, 65 doctorates awarded. *Degree requirements:* For doctorate, comprehensive exam, thesis/dissertation. *Entrance requirements:* For doctorate, GRE General Test, minimum GPA of 3.0 in science course work (recommended). Additional exam requirements/recommendations for international students:

Biological and Biomedical Sciences—General

Emory University (continued)
Required—TOEFL. *Application deadline:* For fall admission, 1/3 for domestic and international students. Application fee: $50. Electronic applications accepted. *Expenses:* Contact institution. *Financial support:* In 2009–10, 155 students received support, including 155 fellowships with full tuition reimbursements available (averaging $24,500 per year); institutionally sponsored loans, scholarships/grants, and health care benefits also available. *Faculty research:* Biochemistry and genetics, immunology and microbiology, neuroscience and pharmacology, nutrition, population biology and ecology. Total annual research expenditures: $142 million. *Unit head:* Dr. Keith Wilkinson, Director, 404-727-2545, Fax: 404-727-3322. *Application contact:* Kathy Smith, Director of Recruitment and Admissions, 404-727-2547, Fax: 404-727-3322, E-mail: kathy.smith@emory.edu.

Emporia State University, School of Graduate Studies, College of Liberal Arts and Sciences, Department of Biological Sciences, Emporia, KS 66801-5087. Offers botany (MS); environmental biology (MS); general biology (MS); microbial and cellular biology (MS); zoology (MS). Part-time programs available. *Faculty:* 13 full-time (3 women). *Students:* 9 full-time (7 women), 17 part-time (11 women); includes 1 minority (African American), 8 international. 22 applicants, 95% accepted, 18 enrolled. In 2009, 24 master's awarded. *Degree requirements:* For master's, comprehensive exam or thesis. *Entrance requirements:* For master's, GRE, appropriate undergraduate degree, interview, letters of reference. Additional exam requirements/recommendations for international students: Required—TOEFL (minimum score 520 paper-based; 133 computer-based; 68 iBT). *Application deadline:* For fall admission, 8/15 priority date for domestic students. Applications are processed on a rolling basis. Application fee: $30 ($75 for international students). Electronic applications accepted. *Expenses:* Tuition, state resident: full-time $4154; part-time $173 per credit hour. Tuition, nonresident: full-time $12,864; part-time $536 per credit hour. Required fees: $948; $58 per credit hour. Tuition and fees vary according to campus/location. *Financial support:* In 2009–10, 7 research assistantships with full tuition reimbursements (averaging $6,876 per year), 10 teaching assistantships with full tuition reimbursements (averaging $7,419 per year) were awarded; career-related internships or fieldwork, Federal Work-Study, institutionally sponsored loans, health care benefits, and unspecified assistantships also available. Financial award application deadline: 3/15; financial award applicants required to submit FAFSA. *Faculty research:* Fisheries, range, and wildlife management; aquatic, plant, grassland, vertebrate, and invertebrate ecology; mammalian and plant systematics, taxonomy, and evolution; immunology, virology, and molecular biology. *Unit head:* Dr. R. Brent Thomas, Interim Chair, 620-341-5311, Fax: 620-341-5608, E-mail: rthomas2@emporia.edu. *Application contact:* Dr. Scott Crupper, Graduate Coordinator, 620-341-5621, Fax: 620-341-5607, E-mail: scrupper@emporia.edu.

Fairleigh Dickinson University, College at Florham, Maxwell Becton College of Arts and Sciences, Department of Biological and Allied Health Sciences, Program in Biology, Madison, NJ 07940-1099. Offers MS. *Students:* 5 full-time (3 women), 19 part-time (11 women). Average age 29. 18 applicants, 83% accepted, 10 enrolled. In 2009, 3 master's awarded. *Application deadline:* Applications are processed on a rolling basis. Application fee: $40. *Unit head:* Dr. June Middleton, Chair, 973-443-8500. *Application contact:* Susan Brooman, University Director, Graduate Admissions, 973-443-8905, Fax: 973-443-8088, E-mail: grad@fdu.edu.

Fairleigh Dickinson University, Metropolitan Campus, University College: Arts, Sciences, and Professional Studies, School of Natural Sciences, Program in Biology, Teaneck, NJ 07666-1914. Offers MS. *Students:* 16 full-time (8 women), 10 part-time (6 women), 15 international. Average age 26. 35 applicants, 66% accepted, 7 enrolled. In 2009, 10 master's awarded. *Application deadline:* Applications are processed on a rolling basis. Application fee: $40. *Application contact:* Susan Brooman, University Director of Graduate Admissions, 201-692-2554, Fax: 201-692-2560, E-mail: globaleducation@fdu.edu.

Fayetteville State University, Graduate School, Department of Natural Sciences, Fayetteville, NC 28301-4298. Offers biology (MS). Part-time and evening/weekend programs available. *Faculty:* 6 full-time (1 woman). *Students:* 6 full-time (5 women), 4 part-time (2 women); includes 6 minority (3 African Americans, 1 Asian American or Pacific Islander, 2 Hispanic Americans). Average age 32. 2 applicants, 100% accepted, 2 enrolled. *Degree requirements:* For master's, comprehensive exam, thesis, internship. *Entrance requirements:* For master's, GRE General Test. *Application deadline:* For fall admission, 4/15 for domestic students; for spring admission, 10/15 for domestic students. Applications are processed on a rolling basis. Application fee: $35. Electronic applications accepted. *Faculty research:* Genomic science of selected plant species and pathological/industrial microorganisms, procedures to identify and eliminate defective spermatozoa in the epididymis, role of STAT3 to block gastric cancer cell proliferation and metastasis, genetic and biochemical pathways in PAO1. Total annual research expenditures: $353,280. *Unit head:* Dr. Ronald Johnston, Chairperson, 910-672-1691, E-mail: rjohnston@uncfsu.edu. *Application contact:* Roxie Shabazz, Associate Vice-Chancellor for Enrollment Management, 910-672-1784, Fax: 910-672-2209, E-mail: rshabazz@uncfsu.edu.

Fisk University, Division of Graduate Studies, Department of Biology, Nashville, TN 37208-3051. Offers MA. Part-time programs available. *Faculty:* 4 full-time (2 women). *Students:* 5 full-time (4 women); all minorities (all African Americans). Average age 26. 3 applicants, 33% accepted, 1 enrolled. In 2009, 3 master's awarded. *Degree requirements:* For master's, comprehensive exam, thesis. *Entrance requirements:* For master's, GRE. *Application deadline:* For fall admission, 6/1 priority date for domestic students, 6/1 for international students. Applications are processed on a rolling basis. Application fee: $50. Electronic applications accepted. *Expenses:* Tuition: Full-time $16,848; part-time $936 per credit hour. Required fees: $1510; $465 per semester. *Financial support:* In 2009–10, 1 student received support, including 1 fellowship with full tuition reimbursement available (averaging $17,115 per year); research assistantships with partial tuition reimbursements available, tuition waivers (full and partial) and unspecified assistantships also available. *Faculty research:* Cell biology, topographical imaging, serotonin receptors in rats, enzyme assays, developmental biology. *Unit head:* Dr. Justus Ike, Chair, 615-329-8796, E-mail: jike@fisk.edu. *Application contact:* Keith Chandler, Dean of Admission, 615-329-8819, Fax: 615-329-8774, E-mail: kchandler@fisk.edu.

Fitchburg State University, Division of Graduate and Continuing Education, Programs in Biology and Teaching Biology (Secondary Level), Fitchburg, MA 01420-2697. Offers MA, MAT, Certificate. *Accreditation:* NCATE. Part-time and evening/weekend programs available. *Students:* 1 full-time (0 women), 4 part-time (all women). Average age 36. 3 applicants, 100% accepted, 1 enrolled. In 2009, 5 master's awarded. *Entrance requirements:* For master's, GRE General Test, letters of recommendation, resume. Additional exam requirements/recommendations for international students: Required—TOEFL (minimum score 550 paper-based; 213 computer-based; 79 iBT). *Application deadline:* Applications are processed on a rolling basis. Application fee: $25 ($50 for international students). *Expenses:* Tuition, area resident: Part-time $150 per credit. Tuition, state resident: part-time $150 per credit. Tuition, nonresident: part-time $150 per credit. Required fees: $120 per credit. *Financial support:* In 2009–10, research assistantships with partial tuition reimbursements (averaging $5,500 per year); Federal Work-Study, scholarships/grants, and unspecified assistantships also available. Support available to part-time students. Financial award application deadline: 3/1; financial award applicants required to submit FAFSA. *Unit head:* Dr. Christopher Cratsley, Chair, 978-665-3617, Fax: 978-665-3658, E-mail: gce@fsc.edu. *Application contact:* Director of Admissions, 978-665-3144, Fax: 978-665-4540, E-mail: admissions@fsc.edu.

Florida Agricultural and Mechanical University, Division of Graduate Studies, Research, and Continuing Education, College of Arts and Sciences, Department of Biology, Tallahassee, FL 32307-3200. Offers MS. Part-time programs available. *Faculty:* 11 full-time (3 women). *Students:* 11 full-time (8 women), 2 part-time (1 woman); all minorities (all African Americans). In 2009, 3 master's awarded. *Degree requirements:* For master's, comprehensive exam, thesis. *Entrance requirements:* For master's, GRE General Test, minimum GPA of 3.0. Additional exam requirements/recommendations for international students: Required—TOEFL (minimum score 550 paper-based). *Application deadline:* For fall admission, 5/18 for domestic students, 12/18 for international students; for spring admission, 11/12 for domestic students, 5/12 for

international students. Application fee: $20. *Unit head:* Dr. Lekan Latinwo, Chairperson, 850-599-3907, Fax: 850-561-2996. *Application contact:* Dr. Chanta M. Haywood, Dean of Graduate Studies, Research, and Continuing Education, 850-599-3315, Fax: 850-599-3727.

Florida Atlantic University, Charles E. Schmidt College of Science, Department of Biological Sciences, Boca Raton, FL 33431-0991. Offers MS, MST. Part-time programs available. *Faculty:* 23 full-time (6 women), 5 part-time/adjunct (1 woman). *Students:* 102 full-time (67 women), 16 part-time (11 women); includes 22 minority (5 African Americans, 7 Asian Americans or Pacific Islanders, 10 Hispanic Americans), 20 international. Average age 30. 99 applicants, 45% accepted, 25 enrolled. In 2009, 14 master's awarded. *Degree requirements:* For master's, thesis (for some programs). *Entrance requirements:* For master's, GRE General Test, minimum GPA of 3.0. Additional exam requirements/recommendations for international students: Required—TOEFL. *Application deadline:* For fall admission, 3/15 for domestic and international students; for spring admission, 10/1 for domestic and international students. Application fee: $30. *Expenses:* Tuition, state resident: full-time $7055; part-time $293.94 per credit hour. Tuition, nonresident: full-time $22,096; part-time $920.66 per credit hour. *Financial support:* Fellowships, research assistantships, teaching assistantships with tuition reimbursements, career-related internships or fieldwork and Federal Work-Study available. *Faculty research:* Ecology of the Everglades, molecular biology and biotechnology, marine biology. *Unit head:* Dr. Rodney K. Murphey, Chair, 561-297-3320, Fax: 561-297-2749. *Application contact:* Becky Dixon, Graduate Program Assistant, 561-297-3230.

Florida Atlantic University, College of Biomedical Science, Boca Raton, FL 33431-0991. Offers biomedical science (MS); integrative biology (PhD). *Faculty:* 30 full-time (14 women), 2 part-time/adjunct (1 woman). *Students:* 33 full-time (18 women), 10 part-time (5 women); includes 13 minority (6 African Americans, 3 Asian Americans or Pacific Islanders, 4 Hispanic Americans), 5 international. Average age 26. 83 applicants, 40% accepted, 17 enrolled. In 2009, 37 master's awarded. *Degree requirements:* For master's, thesis (for some programs). *Entrance requirements:* For master's, GRE, minimum GPA of 3.0. *Application deadline:* For fall admission, 5/1 for domestic students, 3/15 for international students; for spring admission, 10/1 for domestic and international students. Application fee: $30. *Expenses:* Tuition, state resident: full-time $7055; part-time $293.94 per credit hour. Tuition, nonresident: full-time $22,096; part-time $920.66 per credit hour. *Financial support:* Research assistantships available. *Faculty research:* Protein engineering, biology of mind-body interaction, neuroendocrinology, gene expression, methodologies of correction of gynecomastia. *Unit head:* Dr. Michael L. Friedland, Dean, 561-297-4341. *Application contact:* Julie Sivigny, Academic Program Specialist for Graduate Studies, 561-297-2216, E-mail: jsivigny@fau.edu.

Florida Institute of Technology, Graduate Programs, College of Science, Department of Biological Sciences, Melbourne, FL 32901-6975. Offers biological sciences (PhD); biotechnology (MS); cell and molecular biology (MS, PhD); ecology (MS); marine biology (MS). Part-time programs available. *Faculty:* 15 full-time (1 woman). *Students:* 60 full-time (35 women), 6 part-time (4 women); includes 4 minority (all Hispanic Americans), 28 international. Average age 27. 188 applicants, 43% accepted, 20 enrolled. In 2009, 16 master's, 4 doctorates awarded. *Degree requirements:* For master's, thesis (for some programs), thesis seminar of publication quality; for doctorate, thesis/dissertation, dissertations seminar, publications. *Entrance requirements:* For master's, GRE General Test, 3 letters of recommendation, minimum GPA of 3.0, resume; for doctorate, GRE General Test, GRE Subject Test, resume, 3 letters of recommendation, minimum GPA of 3.2, statement of objectives. Additional exam requirements/recommendations for international students: Required—TOEFL (minimum score 550 paper-based; 213 computer-based; 79 iBT). *Application deadline:* For fall admission, 3/1 for domestic and international students; for spring admission, 9/1 for domestic and international students. Applications are processed on a rolling basis. Application fee: $50. Electronic applications accepted. *Expenses:* Tuition: Part-time $1015 per credit. Tuition and fees vary according to campus/location and program. *Financial support:* In 2009–10, 35 students received support, including 14 research assistantships with full and partial tuition reimbursements available (averaging $12,417 per year), 21 teaching assistantships with full and partial tuition reimbursements available (averaging $14,255 per year); career-related internships or fieldwork, institutionally sponsored loans, tuition waivers (partial), unspecified assistantships, and tuition remissions also available. Support available to part-time students. Financial award application deadline: 3/1; financial award applicants required to submit FAFSA. *Faculty research:* Initiation of protein synthesis in eukaryotic cells, fixation of radioactive carbon, changes in DNA molecule, endangered or threatened avian and mammalian species, hydroacoustics and feeding preference of the West Indian manatee. Total annual research expenditures: $1.2 million. *Unit head:* Dr. Richard B. Aronson, Department Head, 321-674-8034, Fax: 321-674-7238, E-mail: raronson@fit.edu. *Application contact:* Thomas M. Shea, Director of Graduate Admissions, 321-674-7577, Fax: 321-723-9468, E-mail: tshea@fit.edu.

Florida International University, College of Arts and Sciences, Department of Biology, Miami, FL 33199. Offers MS, PhD. Part-time programs available. *Faculty:* 34 full-time (9 women). *Students:* 72 full-time (41 women), 20 part-time (15 women); includes 23 minority (3 African Americans, 1 American Indian/Alaska Native, 3 Asian Americans or Pacific Islanders, 16 Hispanic Americans), 26 international. Average age 28. 79 applicants, 19% accepted, 15 enrolled. In 2009, 5 master's, 10 doctorates awarded. *Degree requirements:* For master's, thesis; for doctorate, comprehensive exam, thesis/dissertation. *Entrance requirements:* For master's, GRE General Test, 2 letters of recommendation, minimum GPA of 3.0, faculty sponsor; for doctorate, GRE General Test, 3 letters of recommendation, faculty sponsor with dissertation advisor status, minimum GPA of 3.0. Additional exam requirements/recommendations for international students: Required—TOEFL (minimum score 550 paper-based; 80 iBT). *Application deadline:* For fall admission, 2/1 priority date for domestic and international students; for spring admission, 8/1 priority date for domestic and international students. Applications are processed on a rolling basis. Application fee: $30. Electronic applications accepted. *Expenses:* Tuition, state resident: full-time $8008; part-time $4004 per year. Tuition, nonresident: full-time $20,104; part-time $10,052 per year. Required fees: $298; $149 per term. *Financial support:* Institutionally sponsored loans and scholarships/grants available. Financial award application deadline: 3/1; financial award applicants required to submit FAFSA. *Unit head:* Dr. Laurie Richardson, Chair, 305-348-2201, Fax: 305-348-4096, E-mail: laurie.richardson@fiu.edu. *Application contact:* Nanett Rojas, Associate Director of Graduate Admissions, 305-348-7442, Fax: 305-348-7441, E-mail: gradadm@fiu.edu.

Florida State University, The Graduate School, College of Arts and Sciences, Department of Biological Science, Tallahassee, FL 32306-4295. Offers cell and molecular biology and genetics (MS, PhD); ecology and evolutionary biology (MS, PhD); neuroscience (PhD). *Faculty:* 52 full-time (15 women). *Students:* 106 full-time (58 women); includes 14 minority (2 African Americans, 1 American Indian/Alaska Native, 4 Asian Americans or Pacific Islanders, 7 Hispanic Americans), 12 international. 268 applicants, 16% accepted, 28 enrolled. In 2009, 10 master's, 10 doctorates awarded. Terminal master's awarded for partial completion of doctoral program. *Degree requirements:* For master's, comprehensive exam, thesis, teaching experience, seminar presentations; for doctorate, comprehensive exam, thesis/dissertation, teaching experience, seminar presentations. *Entrance requirements:* For master's, GRE General Test (minimum combined score 1100, 500 verbal, 500 quantitative), minimum upper division GPA of 3.0; for doctorate, GRE General Test (minimum combined score 1100, Verbal 500, Quantitative 500), minimum upper division GPA of 3.0. Additional exam requirements/recommendations for international students: Required—TOEFL (minimum score 600 paper-based; 250 computer-based; 92 iBT). *Application deadline:* For fall admission, 12/15 for domestic and international students. Application fee: $30. Electronic applications accepted. *Expenses:* Tuition, state resident: full-time $7413. Tuition, nonresident: full-time $22,567. *Financial support:* In 2009–10, 104 students received support, including 9 fellowships with full tuition reimbursements available (averaging $22,000 per year), 28 research assistantships with full tuition reimbursements available (averaging $20,000 per year), 67 teaching assistantships with full tuition reimbursements available (averaging $18,540 per year); traineeships and unspecified assistantships also available. Financial award application deadline: 12/15; financial award applicants required to submit FAFSA. *Faculty research:* Cell and molecular biology and genetics, ecology and evolutionary biology. *Unit head:* Dr. George W. Bates, Professor and Associate Chairman, 850-644-5749, Fax: 850-644-9829, E-mail: bates@bio.fsu.edu. *Application contact:* Judy Bowers, Coordinator, Graduate Affairs, 850-644-3023, Fax: 850-644-9829, E-mail: gradinfo@bio.fsu.edu.

See Close-Up on page 97.

Florida State University, The Graduate School, College of Arts and Sciences, Department of Mathematics, Tallahassee, FL 32306-4510. Offers applied computational mathematics (MS, PhD); biomedical mathematics (MS, PhD); financial mathematics (MS, PhD); pure mathematics (MS, PhD). Part-time programs available. *Faculty:* 57 full-time (14 women). *Students:* 140 full-time (35 women), 9 part-time (2 women); includes 8 minority (2 African Americans, 2 Asian Americans or Pacific Islanders, 4 Hispanic Americans), 84 international. Average age 26. 273 applicants, 38% accepted, 34 enrolled. In 2009, 36 master's, 6 doctorates awarded. Terminal master's awarded for partial completion of doctoral program. *Degree requirements:* For master's, comprehensive exam (for some programs), thesis optional; for doctorate, comprehensive exam (for some programs), thesis/dissertation, candidacy exam. *Entrance requirements:* For master's and doctorate, GRE General Test, minimum upper-division GPA of 3.0, 4-year bachelor's degree. Additional exam requirements/recommendations for international students: Required—TOEFL (minimum score 550 paper-based; 213 computer-based; 80 iBT) or IELTS. *Application deadline:* For fall admission, 1/10 priority date for domestic students, 12/15 priority date for international students; for spring admission, 11/1 for domestic and international students. Applications are processed on a rolling basis. Application fee: $30. Electronic applications accepted. *Expenses:* Tuition, state resident: full-time $7413. Tuition, nonresident: full-time $22,567. *Financial support:* In 2009–10, 102 students received support, including 4 fellowships with full tuition reimbursements available (averaging $19,000 per year), 12 research assistantships with full tuition reimbursements available (averaging $20,000 per year), 84 teaching assistantships with full tuition reimbursements available (averaging $17,000 per year); career-related internships or fieldwork, scholarships/grants, and unspecified assistantships also available. Financial award application deadline: 4/1. *Faculty research:* Geometric topology, algebraic geometry, fluid dynamics, financial mathematics, biomedical mathematics. *Unit head:* Dr. Philip L. Bowers, Chairperson, 850-645-3338, Fax: 850-644-4053, E-mail: bowers@math.fsu.edu. *Application contact:* Dr. Bettye Anne Case, Associate Chair for Graduate Studies, 850-644-1586, Fax: 850-644-4053, E-mail: case@math.fsu.edu.

Fordham University, Graduate School of Arts and Sciences, Department of Biological Sciences, New York, NY 10458. Offers MS, PhD. Part-time and evening/weekend programs available. *Faculty:* 18 full-time (2 women). *Students:* 20 full-time (14 women), 15 part-time (13 women). Average age 27. 70 applicants, 59% accepted, 21 enrolled. In 2009, 8 master's, 5 doctorates awarded. Terminal master's awarded for partial completion of doctoral program. *Degree requirements:* For master's, one foreign language, comprehensive exam, thesis optional; for doctorate, one foreign language, comprehensive exam, thesis/dissertation. *Entrance requirements:* For master's and doctorate, GRE General Test, GRE Subject Test (recommended). Additional exam requirements/recommendations for international students: Required—TOEFL (minimum score 550 paper-based; 213 computer-based). *Application deadline:* For fall admission, 1/4 priority date for domestic students; for spring admission, 11/1 for domestic students. Application fee: $70. Electronic applications accepted. *Financial support:* In 2009–10, 28 students received support, including 3 fellowships with full and partial tuition reimbursements available (averaging $30,500 per year), 24 research assistantships with full and partial tuition reimbursements available (averaging $27,020 per year), 1 teaching assistantship with full and partial tuition reimbursement available (averaging $9,600 per year); Federal Work-Study, institutionally sponsored loans, scholarships/grants, tuition waivers (full and partial), and unspecified assistantships also available. Support available to part-time students. Financial award application deadline: 1/4; financial award applicants required to submit FAFSA. *Faculty research:* Analysis of tumor suppressor genes, chromatic biology and epigenetics, insect ecology, ecology and physiology of mycorrhizal associations, molecular biology of familial dysautonomia. Total annual research expenditures: $2.7 million. *Unit head:* Dr. William Tornhill, Chair, 718-817-3642, Fax: 718-817-3645, E-mail: tornhill@fordham.edu. *Application contact:* Charlene Dundie, Director of Graduate Admissions, 718-817-4420, Fax: 718-817-3566, E-mail: dundie@fordham.edu.

Fort Hays State University, Graduate School, College of Health and Life Sciences, Department of Biological Sciences, Program in Biology, Hays, KS 67601-4099. Offers MS. Part-time programs available. *Degree requirements:* For master's, comprehensive exam, thesis optional. *Entrance requirements:* Additional exam requirements/recommendations for international students: Required—TOEFL (minimum score 550 paper-based; 213 computer-based). Electronic applications accepted.

Frostburg State University, Graduate School, College of Liberal Arts and Sciences, Department of Biology, Frostburg, MD 21532-1099. Offers applied ecology and conservation biology (MS); fisheries and wildlife management (MS). Part-time and evening/weekend programs available. *Faculty:* 9 full-time (1 woman), 1 part-time/adjunct (0 women). *Students:* 18 full-time (12 women), 3 part-time (all women); includes 1 minority (American Indian/Alaska Native), 1 international. Average age 26. 23 applicants, 9% accepted, 1 enrolled. In 2009, 4 master's awarded. *Degree requirements:* For master's, thesis. *Entrance requirements:* For master's, GRE General Test, resume. Additional exam requirements/recommendations for international students: Required—TOEFL. *Application deadline:* For fall admission, 7/15 priority date for domestic students. Applications are processed on a rolling basis. Application fee: $30. Electronic applications accepted. *Expenses:* Tuition, state resident: full-time $5706; part-time $317 per credit hour. Tuition, nonresident: full-time $6948; part-time $386 per credit hour. Required fees: $1476; $82 per credit hour. $11 per term. One-time fee: $30 full-time. *Financial support:* In 2009–10, 15 research assistantships with full tuition reimbursements (averaging $5,000 per year) were awarded; career-related internships or fieldwork and Federal Work-Study also available. Financial award application deadline: 4/1; financial award applicants required to submit FAFSA. *Faculty research:* Molecular and morphological evolution, ecology and behavior of birds, conservation genetics of amphibians and fishes, biology of endangered species. *Unit head:* Dr. William Seddon, Coordinator, 301-687-4306, E-mail: wseddon@frostburg.edu. *Application contact:* Vickie Mazer, Director, Graduate Services, 301-687-7053, Fax: 301-687-4597, E-mail: vmmazer@frostburg.edu.

George Mason University, College of Humanities and Social Sciences, Department of Public and International Affairs, Fairfax, VA 22030. Offers association management (Certificate); biodefense (MS, PhD); critical analysis and strategic responses to terrorism (Certificate); nonprofit management (Certificate); political science (MA, PhD); public administration (MPA); public management (Certificate). *Accreditation:* NASPAA (one or more programs are accredited). *Faculty:* 37 full-time (14 women), 34 part-time/adjunct (7 women). *Students:* 115 full-time (62 women), 323 part-time (182 women); includes 60 minority (29 African Americans, 1 American Indian/Alaska Native, 18 Asian Americans or Pacific Islanders, 12 Hispanic Americans), 21 international. Average age 31. 458 applicants, 60% accepted, 129 enrolled. In 2009, 147 master's, 2 doctorates, 6 other advanced degrees awarded. *Entrance requirements:* For master's, GRE General Test, minimum GPA of 3.0 in last 60 hours of course work. Additional exam requirements/recommendations for international students: Required—TOEFL. *Application deadline:* For fall admission, 3/1 priority date for domestic students; for spring admission, 10/15 for domestic students. Application fee: $75. Electronic applications accepted. *Expenses:* Tuition, state resident: full-time $7568; part-time $315.33 per credit hour. Tuition, nonresident: full-time $21,704; part-time $904.33 per credit hour. Required fees: $2184; $91 per credit hour. *Financial support:* In 2009–10, 27 students received support, including 3 fellowships with full tuition reimbursements available (averaging $18,000 per year), 10 research assistantships with full and partial tuition reimbursements available (averaging $11,033 per year), 14 teaching assistantships with full and partial tuition reimbursements available (averaging $9,213 per year); Federal Work-Study, scholarships/grants, unspecified assistantships, and health care benefits (full-time research or teaching assistantship recipients) also available. Support available to part-time students. Financial award application deadline: 3/1; financial award applicants

required to submit FAFSA. *Faculty research:* The Rehnquist Court and economic liberties; intersection of economic development with high-tech industry, telecommunications, and entrepreneurism; political economy of development; violence, terrorism and U.S. foreign policy; international security issues. Total annual research expenditures: $429,868. *Unit head:* Dr. Robert Dudley, Chair, 703-993-1400, Fax: 703-993-1399, E-mail: rdudley@gmu.edu. *Application contact:* Peg Koback, Information Contact, 703-993-9466, E-mail: mkoback@gmu.edu.

George Mason University, College of Science, Fairfax, VA 22030. Offers biodefense (MS, PhD); bioinformatics and computational biology (MS, PhD, Certificate); biology (MS, PhD), including bioinformatics (MS), ecology, systematics and evolution (MS), interpretive biology (MS), molecular and cellular biology (MS), molecular and microbiology (PhD), organismal biology (MS); chemistry and biochemistry (MS), including chemistry; climate dynamics (PhD); computational and data sciences (MS, PhD, Certificate); computational social science (PhD); computational techniques and applications (Certificate); earth systems and geoinformation sciences (MS, PhD, Certificate); environmental science and policy (MS, PhD); geography (MS), including geographic and cartographic sciences; mathematical sciences (MS, PhD), including mathematics; nanotechnology and nanoscience (Certificate); neuroscience (PhD); physical sciences (PhD); physics and astronomy (MS), including applied and engineering physics; remote sensing and earth image processing (Certificate). Part-time and evening/weekend programs available. *Degree requirements:* For doctorate, comprehensive exam, thesis/dissertation. *Entrance requirements:* For master's and doctorate, GRE General Test, minimum GPA of 3.0 in last 60 hours. Additional exam requirements/recommendations for international students: Required—TOEFL. Electronic applications accepted. *Expenses:* Tuition, state resident: full-time $7568; part-time $315.33 per credit hour. Tuition, nonresident: full-time $21,704; part-time $904.33 per credit hour. Required fees: $2184; $91 per credit hour. *Faculty research:* Space sciences and astrophysics, fluid dynamics, materials modeling and simulation, bioinformatics, global changes and statistics.

Georgetown University, Graduate School of Arts and Sciences, Department of Biology, Washington, DC 20057. Offers MS, PhD. Terminal master's awarded for partial completion of doctoral program. *Degree requirements:* For master's, comprehensive exam, thesis; for doctorate, comprehensive exam, thesis/dissertation. *Entrance requirements:* For master's and doctorate, GRE General Test, GRE Subject Test (biology). Additional exam requirements/recommendations for international students: Required—TOEFL (minimum score 550 paper-based; 213 computer-based). Electronic applications accepted. *Faculty research:* Parasitology, ecology, evaluation and behavior, neuroscience and development, cell and molecular biology, immunology.

Georgetown University, Graduate School of Arts and Sciences, Programs in Biomedical Sciences, Washington, DC 20057. Offers MS, PhD, MD/PhD, MS/PhD. *Entrance requirements:* For doctorate, GRE General Test. Additional exam requirements/recommendations for international students: Required—TOEFL.

Georgetown University, National Institutes of Health Sponsored Programs, GU-NIH Graduate Partnership Programs in Biomedical Sciences, Washington, DC 20057. Offers MS, PhD, MD/PhD, MS/PhD. *Entrance requirements:* For doctorate, GRE General Test. Additional exam requirements/recommendations for international students: Required—TOEFL.

The George Washington University, Columbian College of Arts and Sciences, Department of Anthropology, Program in Hominid Paleobiology, Washington, DC 20052. Offers MS, PhD. Part-time and evening/weekend programs available. *Students:* 9 full-time (4 women), 8 part-time (6 women); includes 2 minority (1 African American, 1 Hispanic American), 3 international. 20 applicants, 20% accepted, 4 enrolled. In 2009, 1 doctorate awarded. Terminal master's awarded for partial completion of doctoral program. *Degree requirements:* For master's, comprehensive exam, thesis; for doctorate, thesis/dissertation, general exam. *Entrance requirements:* For master's, GRE General Test, bachelor's degree in field, minimum GPA of 3.0; for doctorate, GRE General Test, minimum GPA of 3.0. Additional exam requirements/recommendations for international students: Required—TOEFL (minimum score 550 paper-based; 213 computer-based). *Application deadline:* For fall admission, 2/1 priority date for domestic and international students; for spring admission, 10/1 priority date for domestic and international students. Applications are processed on a rolling basis. Application fee: $60. Electronic applications accepted. *Financial support:* In 2009–10, 16 students received support; fellowships with full tuition reimbursements available, teaching assistantships, tuition waivers available. Financial award application deadline: 2/1. *Unit head:* Dr. Bernard A. Wood, Director, 202-994-6077, Fax: 202-994-6097. *Application contact:* Information Contact, 202-994-6075, E-mail: anth@gwu.edu.

The George Washington University, Columbian College of Arts and Sciences, Department of Biological Sciences, Washington, DC 20052. Offers MS, PhD. Part-time and evening/weekend programs available. *Faculty:* 19 full-time (7 women), 8 part-time/adjunct (1 woman). *Students:* 13 full-time (11 women), 14 part-time (9 women); includes 2 minority (1 African American, 1 Asian American or Pacific Islander), 10 international. Average age 30. 54 applicants, 11% accepted, 4 enrolled. In 2009, 1 master's, 5 doctorates awarded. Terminal master's awarded for partial completion of doctoral program. *Degree requirements:* For master's, comprehensive exam; for doctorate, thesis/dissertation, general exam. *Entrance requirements:* For master's and doctorate, GRE General Test, minimum GPA of 3.0. Additional exam requirements/recommendations for international students: Required—TOEFL (minimum score 550 paper-based; 213 computer-based; 80 iBT). *Application deadline:* For fall admission, 1/2 priority date for domestic and international students; for spring admission, 10/1 priority date for domestic and international students. Applications are processed on a rolling basis. Application fee: $60. Electronic applications accepted. *Financial support:* In 2009–10, 25 students received support; fellowships with full tuition reimbursements available, teaching assistantships with full tuition reimbursements available, Federal Work-Study and tuition waivers available. Financial award application deadline: 1/2. *Faculty research:* Systematics, evolution, ecology, developmental biology, cell/molecular biology. Total annual research expenditures: $900,000. *Unit head:* Dr. James M. Clark, Chair, 202-994-7144, Fax: 202-994-6100, E-mail: jclark@gwu.edu. *Application contact:* Dr. John R. Burns, Professor, 202-994-7149, Fax: 202-994-6100, E-mail: jrburns@gwu.edu.

The George Washington University, Columbian College of Arts and Sciences, Institute for Biomedical Sciences, Washington, DC 20052. Offers biochemistry and molecular genetics (PhD); microbiology and immunology (PhD); molecular medicine (PhD), including molecular and cellular oncology, neurosciences, pharmacology, and physiology. Part-time and evening/weekend programs available. *Students:* 16 full-time (8 women), 32 part-time (22 women); includes 7 minority (2 African Americans, 1 American Indian/Alaska Native, 3 Asian Americans or Pacific Islanders, 1 Hispanic American), 6 international. Average age 30. In 2009, 2 doctorates awarded. *Degree requirements:* For doctorate, thesis/dissertation. *Entrance requirements:* For doctorate, GRE General Test, minimum GPA of 3.0. Additional exam requirements/recommendations for international students: Required—TOEFL (minimum score 600 paper-based; 250 computer-based; 80 iBT). *Application deadline:* For fall admission, 1/2 priority date for domestic and international students. Applications are processed on a rolling basis. Application fee: $60. Electronic applications accepted. *Financial support:* In 2009–10, 24 students received support; fellowships with full tuition reimbursements available, Federal Work-Study, institutionally sponsored loans, and tuition waivers available. *Unit head:* Dr. Linda L. Werling, Director, 202-994-2918, Fax: 202-994-0967. *Application contact:* 202-994-2179, Fax: 202-994-0967, E-mail: gwibs@gwu.edu.

Georgia Campus–Philadelphia College of Osteopathic Medicine, Program in Biomedical Sciences, Suwanee, GA 30024. Offers MS, Certificate.

Georgia College & State University, Graduate School, College of Arts and Sciences, Department of Biology, Milledgeville, GA 31061. Offers MS. Part-time programs available. *Faculty:* 21 full-time (7 women). *Students:* 27 full-time (13 women), 4 part-time (1 woman); includes 4 minority (1 African American, 1 American Indian/Alaska Native, 1 Asian American or Pacific Islander, 1 Hispanic American), 5 international. Average age 27. 17 applicants, 94%

Biological and Biomedical Sciences—General

Georgia College & State University (continued)
accepted, 12 enrolled. In 2009, 9 master's awarded. *Degree requirements:* For master's, thesis optional. *Entrance requirements:* For master's, GRE (minimum score of 800), 30 hours undergraduate course work in biological science. Additional exam requirements/recommendations for international students: Recommended—TOEFL (minimum score 550 paper-based; 213 computer-based; 79 iBT). *Application deadline:* For fall admission, 7/1 priority date for domestic students, 4/1 for international students; for spring admission, 8/1 for international students. Applications are processed on a rolling basis. Application fee: $40. Electronic applications accepted. *Expenses:* Tuition, area resident: Part-time $241 per credit hour. Tuition, state resident: full-time $4338. Tuition, nonresident: full-time $17,352; part-time $964 per credit hour. Required fees: $609 per semester. Tuition and fees vary according to course load and campus/location. *Financial support:* In 2009–10, 22 research assistantships with tuition reimbursements were awarded; career-related internships or fieldwork, Federal Work-Study, and unspecified assistantships also available. Support available to part-time students. Financial award application deadline: 3/1; financial award applicants required to submit FAFSA. *Faculty research:* Vertebrate collecting and monitoring, paleontologic expedition. *Unit head:* Dr. William Wall, Chair, 478-445-0818, E-mail: bill.wall@gcsu.edu. *Application contact:* Dr. Bill Wolfe, Graduate Coordinator, 478-445-3464, E-mail: bill.wolfe@gcsu.edu.

Georgia Institute of Technology, Graduate Studies and Research, College of Sciences, School of Biology, Atlanta, GA 30332-0001. Offers applied biology (MS, PhD); bioinformatics (MS, PhD); biology (MS). Part-time programs available. Terminal master's awarded for partial completion of doctoral program. *Degree requirements:* For master's, thesis; for doctorate, thesis/dissertation, qualifying exam. *Entrance requirements:* For master's, GRE General Test, minimum GPA of 2.9; for doctorate, GRE General Test, minimum GPA of 3.0. Additional exam requirements/recommendations for international students: Required—TOEFL. Electronic applications accepted. *Faculty research:* Microbiology, molecular and cell biology, ecology.

Georgian Court University, School of Sciences and Mathematics, Lakewood, NJ 08701-2697. Offers biology (MS); counseling psychology (MA); holistic health (Certificate); holistic health studies (MA); mathematics (MA); professional counselor (Certificate); school psychology (Certificate). Part-time and evening/weekend programs available. *Faculty:* 18 full-time (11 women), 9 part-time/adjunct (6 women). *Students:* 74 full-time (67 women), 79 part-time (67 women); includes 19 minority (8 African Americans, 1 American Indian/Alaska Native, 2 Asian Americans or Pacific Islanders, 8 Hispanic Americans), 2 international. Average age 32. 137 applicants, 50% accepted, 54 enrolled. In 2009, 27 master's, 2 other advanced degrees awarded. *Degree requirements:* For master's, comprehensive exam (for some programs), thesis (for some programs). *Entrance requirements:* For master's, GRE General Test, GRE Subject Test in biology (MS), 3 letters of recommendation. Additional exam requirements/recommendations for international students: Required—TOEFL (minimum score 550 paper-based; 213 computer-based). *Application deadline:* For fall admission, 8/1 priority date for domestic students, 4/1 for international students; for spring admission, 1/1 priority date for domestic students, 7/1 for international students. Applications are processed on a rolling basis. Application fee: $40. Electronic applications accepted. *Expenses:* Tuition: Full-time $12,510; part-time $695 per credit. Required fees: $416 per year. Tuition and fees vary according to campus/location. *Financial support:* Scholarships/grants, health care benefits, and unspecified assistantships available. Financial award application deadline: 4/15; financial award applicants required to submit FAFSA. *Unit head:* Dr. Linda James, Dean, 732-987-2617, Fax: 732-987-2007. *Application contact:* Eugene Soltys, Director of Graduate Admissions, 732-987-2770, Fax: 732-987-2084, E-mail: graduateadmissions@georgian.edu.

Georgia Southern University, Jack N. Averitt College of Graduate Studies, Allen E. Paulson College of Science and Technology, Department of Biology, Statesboro, GA 30460. Offers MS. Part-time programs available. *Students:* 35 full-time (18 women), 8 part-time (5 women); includes 5 minority (1 African American, 2 American Indian/Alaska Native, 2 Asian Americans or Pacific Islanders), 2 international. Average age 26. 33 applicants, 64% accepted, 14 enrolled. In 2009, 13 master's awarded. *Degree requirements:* For master's, comprehensive exam, thesis optional, terminal exam. *Entrance requirements:* For master's, GRE General Test, GRE Subject Test, minimum GPA of 2.8, BS in biology, 2 letters of reference. Additional exam requirements/recommendations for international students: Required—TOEFL (minimum score 550 paper-based; 216 computer-based; 80 iBT). *Application deadline:* For fall admission, 3/1 priority date for domestic and international students; for spring admission, 10/1 priority date for domestic students, 10/1 for international students. Applications are processed on a rolling basis. Application fee: $50. Electronic applications accepted. *Expenses:* Tuition, state resident: full-time $5040; part-time $210 per credit hour. Tuition, nonresident: full-time $20,136; part-time $839 per credit hour. Required fees: $1644. *Financial support:* In 2009–10, 36 students received support, including research assistantships with partial tuition reimbursements available (averaging $10,000 per year), teaching assistantships with partial tuition reimbursements available (averaging $10,000 per year); career-related internships or fieldwork, Federal Work-Study, scholarships/grants, tuition waivers (partial), and unspecified assistantships also available. Support available to part-time students. Financial award application deadline: 4/15; financial award applicants required to submit FAFSA. *Faculty research:* Evolutionary biology, ecology, behavior, genetics, physiology. Total annual research expenditures: $615,362. *Unit head:* Dr. Stephen Vives, Chair, 912-478-5487, Fax: 912-478-0845, E-mail: svives@georgiasouthern.edu. *Application contact:* Dr. Charles Ziglar, Coordinator for Graduate Student Recruitment, 912-478-5635, Fax: 912-478-0740, E-mail: gradadmissions@georgiasouthern.edu.

Georgia State University, College of Arts and Sciences, Department of Biology, Atlanta, GA 30302-3083. Offers applied and environmental microbiology (MS, PhD); cellular and molecular biology and physiology (MS, PhD); molecular genetics and biochemistry (MS, PhD); neurobiology and behavior (MS, PhD). Part-time programs available. Terminal master's awarded for partial completion of doctoral program. *Degree requirements:* For master's, thesis or alternative; for doctorate, thesis/dissertation, exam. *Entrance requirements:* For master's and doctorate, GRE General Test. Additional exam requirements/recommendations for international students: Required—TOEFL. Electronic applications accepted. *Faculty research:* Physiological biochemistry, gene expression, molecular virology, microbial ecology, integration in neural systems.

Georgia State University, College of Arts and Sciences, MD/PhD Program, Atlanta, GA 30302-3083. Offers MD/PhD.

Gerstner Sloan-Kettering Graduate School of Biomedical Sciences, Program in Cancer Biology, New York, NY 10021. Offers PhD. *Faculty research:* Biochemistry and molecular biology, biophysics/structural biology, computational biology, genetics, immunology.

See Close-Up on page 235.

Goucher College, Program in Post-Baccalaureate Premedical Studies, Baltimore, MD 21204-2794. Offers Certificate. *Expenses:* Contact institution.

Graduate School and University Center of the City University of New York, Graduate Studies, Program in Biology, New York, NY 10016-4039. Offers PhD. *Faculty:* 78 full-time (24 women). *Students:* 207 full-time (109 women); includes 30 minority (11 African Americans, 7 Asian Americans or Pacific Islanders, 12 Hispanic Americans), 54 international. Average age 32. 87 applicants, 57% accepted, 29 enrolled. In 2009, 24 doctorates awarded. *Degree requirements:* For doctorate, thesis/dissertation, teaching experience. *Entrance requirements:* For doctorate, GRE General Test. Additional exam requirements/recommendations for international students: Required—TOEFL. *Application deadline:* For fall admission, 1/1 for domestic students. Application fee: $125. Electronic applications accepted. *Financial support:* In 2009–10, 198 students received support, including 157 fellowships, 1 research assistantship, 1 teaching assistantship; career-related internships or fieldwork, Federal Work-Study, institutionally sponsored loans, and tuition waivers (full and partial) also available. Financial award application deadline: 2/1; financial award applicants required to submit FAFSA. *Unit head:* Dr. Laurel Eckhardt, Executive Officer, 212-817-8101, Fax: 212-817-1504. *Application contact:* Executive Officer, 212-817-8100, Fax: 212-817-1504, E-mail: biology@gc.cuny.edu.

Grand Valley State University, College of Liberal Arts and Sciences, Biology Department, Allendale, MI 49401-9403. Offers MS. Part-time programs available. *Faculty:* 4 full-time (1 woman), 4 part-time/adjunct (1 woman). *Students:* 19 full-time (12 women), 7 part-time (3 women); includes 3 minority (1 African American, 2 Asian Americans or Pacific Islanders). Average age 28. 19 applicants, 74% accepted, 14 enrolled. In 2009, 8 master's awarded. *Degree requirements:* For master's, comprehensive exam, thesis or alternative. *Entrance requirements:* For master's, GRE General Test, 3 letters of reference. Additional exam requirements/recommendations for international students: Required—TOEFL. *Application deadline:* For winter admission, 1/15 priority date for domestic students. Applications are processed on a rolling basis. Application fee: $30. Electronic applications accepted. *Expenses:* Tuition, state resident: part-time $471 per credit hour. Tuition, nonresident: part-time $646 per credit hour. Tuition and fees vary according to course level. *Financial support:* In 2009–10, 19 students received support, including 2 fellowships (averaging $996 per year), 18 research assistantships (averaging $8,701 per year). Financial award application deadline: 1/15. *Faculty research:* Natural resources conservation biology, aquatic sciences, terrestrial ecology, behavioral biology. *Unit head:* Dr. Shaily Menon, Director, 616-331-2470, E-mail: menons@gvsu.edu. *Application contact:* Dr. Mark Luttenton, Graduate Program Director, 616-331-2505, E-mail: luttentm@gvsu.edu.

Grand Valley State University, College of Liberal Arts and Sciences, Department of Biomedical Sciences, Allendale, MI 49401-9403. Offers MHS. Part-time programs available. *Faculty:* 4 full-time (2 women), 4 part-time/adjunct (2 women). *Students:* 6 full-time (3 women), 4 part-time (2 women). Average age 26. 9 applicants, 78% accepted, 5 enrolled. In 2009, 1 master's awarded. *Degree requirements:* For master's, thesis, qualifying exam. *Entrance requirements:* For master's, GRE General Test, minimum GPA of 3.0, 3 names of references. Additional exam requirements/recommendations for international students: Required—TOEFL. *Application deadline:* For fall admission, 2/1 priority date for domestic and international students. Applications are processed on a rolling basis. Application fee: $30. Electronic applications accepted. *Expenses:* Tuition, state resident: part-time $471 per credit hour. Tuition, nonresident: part-time $646 per credit hour. Tuition and fees vary according to course level. *Financial support:* In 2009–10, 2 students received support, including 1 fellowship (averaging $800 per year), 1 research assistantship (averaging $8,046 per year); scholarships/grants and unspecified assistantships also available. Financial award application deadline: 2/1. *Faculty research:* Cell regulation, neurobiology, parasitology, virology, microbial pathogenicity. *Unit head:* Dr. Anthony Nieuwkoop, Chair, 616-331-3318, Fax: 616-331-2090, E-mail: nieuwkot@gvsu.edu. *Application contact:* Dr. Debra Burg, Director, 616-331-3721, Fax: 616-331-2090, E-mail: burgd@gvsu.edu.

Hampton University, Graduate College, Department of Biological Sciences, Hampton, VA 23668. Offers biology (MS); environmental science (MS); medical science (MS). Part-time and evening/weekend programs available. *Degree requirements:* For master's, thesis optional. *Entrance requirements:* For master's, GRE General Test. *Faculty research:* Marine ecology, microbial and chemical pollution, pesticide problems.

Harvard University, Extension School, Cambridge, MA 02138-3722. Offers applied sciences (CAS); biotechnology (ALM); educational technologies (ALM); educational technology (CET); English for graduate and professional studies (DGP); environmental management (ALM, CEM); information technology (ALM); journalism (ALM); liberal arts (ALM); management (ALM, CM); mathematics for teaching (ALM); museum studies (ALM); premedical studies (Diploma); publication and communication (CPC). Part-time and evening/weekend programs available. *Degree requirements:* For master's, thesis. *Entrance requirements:* For master's, 3 completed graduate courses with grade of B or higher. Additional exam requirements/recommendations for international students: Required—TOEFL (minimum score 600 paper-based; 250 computer-based), TWE (minimum score 5). *Expenses:* Contact institution.

Harvard University, Graduate School of Arts and Sciences, Department of Organismic and Evolutionary Biology, Cambridge, MA 02138. Offers biology (PhD). *Degree requirements:* For doctorate, 2 foreign languages, public presentation of thesis research, exam. *Entrance requirements:* For doctorate, GRE General Test, GRE Subject Test (recommended), 7 courses in biology, chemistry, physics, mathematics, computer science, or geology. Additional exam requirements/recommendations for international students: Required—TOEFL. *Expenses:* Tuition: Full-time $33,696. Required fees: $1126. Full-time tuition and fees vary according to program.

Harvard University, Graduate School of Arts and Sciences, Division of Medical Sciences, Boston, MA 02115. Offers biological chemistry and molecular pharmacology (PhD); cell biology (PhD); genetics (PhD); microbiology and molecular genetics (PhD); pathology (PhD), including experimental pathology. *Degree requirements:* For doctorate, thesis/dissertation. *Entrance requirements:* For doctorate, GRE General Test, GRE Subject Test. Additional exam requirements/recommendations for international students: Required—TOEFL. *Expenses:* Tuition: Full-time $33,696. Required fees: $1126. Full-time tuition and fees vary according to program.

Harvard University, Harvard Medical School and Graduate School of Arts and Sciences, Division of Health Sciences and Technology, Biomedical Enterprise Program, Cambridge, MA 02138. Offers SM. *Students:* 28 full-time (15 women); includes 8 minority (1 American Indian/Alaska Native, 6 Asian Americans or Pacific Islanders, 1 Hispanic American), 5 international. Average age 30. 43 applicants, 33% accepted, 13 enrolled. In 2009, 8 master's awarded. *Degree requirements:* For master's, thesis. *Entrance requirements:* For master's, GMAT or GRE, bachelor's degree in engineering or sciences, work experience in biomedical business. Additional exam requirements/recommendations for international students: Required—TOEFL. *Application deadline:* For fall admission, 12/15 for domestic and international students. Electronic applications accepted. *Expenses:* Contact institution. *Financial support:* In 2009–10, 8 students received support, including 1 fellowship (averaging $5,000 per year), 2 research assistantships with full and partial tuition reimbursements available (averaging $34,773 per year), 6 teaching assistantships with partial tuition reimbursements available (averaging $8,637 per year); institutionally sponsored loans, health care benefits, and unspecified assistantships also available. Financial award application deadline: 12/15; financial award applicants required to submit FAFSA. *Faculty research:* Entrepreneurship, technology strategy managemen, organizational strategies and models, epidemiology and biostatistics, biomedical research from the molecular to the whole-organism level. *Unit head:* Dr. Richard Cohen, Co-Director, 617-253-7430. *Application contact:* Traci Anderson, Academic Programs Administrator, 617-253-7470, Fax: 617-253-6692, E-mail: tanderso@mit.edu.

Harvard University, School of Public Health, PhD Program in Biological Sciences in Public Health, Boston, MA 02115. Offers PhD. *Degree requirements:* For doctorate, qualifying examination and dissertation/defense. *Entrance requirements:* For doctorate, GRE General Test. Additional exam requirements/recommendations for international students: Required—TOEFL. *Expenses:* Tuition: Full-time $33,696. Required fees: $1126. Full-time tuition and fees vary according to program. *Faculty research:* Nutrition biochemistry, molecular and cellular toxicology, cardiovascular disease, cancer biology, immunology and infectious diseases, environmental health physiology.

Heritage University, Graduate Programs in Education, Program in Professional Studies, Toppenish, WA 98948-9599. Offers bilingual education/ESL (M Ed); biology (M Ed); English and literature (M Ed); reading/literacy (M Ed); special education (M Ed). Part-time and evening/weekend programs available. *Degree requirements:* For master's, comprehensive exam (for some programs), thesis (for some programs).

Hofstra University, College of Liberal Arts and Sciences, Department of Biology, Hempstead, NY 11549. Offers MA, MS. Part-time and evening/weekend programs available. *Faculty:* 11 full-time (5 women). *Students:* 9 full-time (6 women), 13 part-time (7 women); includes 4 minority (2 African Americans, 1 Asian American or Pacific Islander, 1 Hispanic American). Average age 28. 31 applicants, 68% accepted, 8 enrolled. In 2009, 13 master's awarded. *Degree requirements:* For master's, thesis. *Entrance requirements:* For master's, GRE, bachelor's degree in biology or equivalent, 2 letters of recommendation. Additional exam requirements/recommendations for international students: Required—TOEFL (minimum score 550 paper-based; 213 computer-based; 80 iBT). *Application deadline:* Applications are processed on a rolling basis. Application fee: $60. Electronic applications accepted. *Expenses:* Tuition: Full-time $16,200; part-time $900 per credit hour. Required fees: $970; $145 per term. Tuition and fees vary according to program. *Financial support:* In 2009–10, 13 students received support, including 8 fellowships with full and partial tuition reimbursements available (averaging $6,891 per year); research assistantships with full and partial tuition reimbursements available, Federal Work-Study, institutionally sponsored loans, scholarships/grants, and tuition waivers (full and partial) also available. Support available to part-time students. Financial award applicants required to submit FAFSA. *Faculty research:* Molecular basis of sex determination in turtles; molecular evaluation and biochemistry of bivalves; physiological ecology of reptiles and amphibians; population, ecology, evolution, and behavior of mammals; systematics and biology of marine polychaete worms and crustaceans. Total annual research expenditures: $180,000. *Unit head:* Dr. Peter C. Daniel, Program Director, 516-463-6718, Fax: 516-463-5112, E-mail: biopcd@hofstra.edu. *Application contact:* Carol Drummer, Dean of Graduate Admissions, 516-463-4876, Fax: 516-463-4664, E-mail: gradstudent@hofstra.edu.

Hood College, Graduate School, Program in Biomedical Science, Frederick, MD 21701-8575. Offers biomedical science (MS), including biotechnology/molecular biology, microbiology/immunology/virology, regulatory compliance; regulatory compliance (Certificate). Part-time and evening/weekend programs available. *Faculty:* 3 full-time (1 woman), 4 part-time/adjunct (2 women). *Students:* 9 full-time (2 women), 82 part-time (54 women); includes 23 minority (17 African Americans, 2 Asian Americans or Pacific Islanders, 4 Hispanic Americans), 7 international. Average age 29. 51 applicants, 67% accepted, 28 enrolled. In 2009, 11 master's, 10 other advanced degrees awarded. *Degree requirements:* For master's, comprehensive exam, thesis or alternative. *Entrance requirements:* For master's, bachelor's degree in biology; minimum GPA of 2.75; undergraduate course work in cell biology, chemistry, organic chemistry, and genetics. Additional exam requirements/recommendations for international students: Required—TOEFL (minimum score 575 paper-based; 231 computer-based; 89 iBT). *Application deadline:* For fall admission, 7/15 for domestic and international students; for spring admission, 12/15 for domestic and international students. Applications are processed on a rolling basis. Application fee: $35. Electronic applications accepted. *Expenses:* Tuition: Full-time $6480; part-time $360 per credit. Required fees: $100; $50 per term. *Financial support:* In 2009–10, 3 research assistantships with full tuition reimbursements (averaging $10,609 per year) were awarded. Financial award applicants required to submit FAFSA. *Unit head:* Dr. Oney Smith, Director, 301-696-3653, Fax: 301-696-3597, E-mail: osmith@hood.edu. *Application contact:* Dr. Allen P. Flora, Dean of Graduate School, 301-696-3811, Fax: 301-696-3597, E-mail: gofurther@hood.edu.

Howard University, Graduate School, Department of Biology, Washington, DC 20059-0002. Offers MS, PhD. Part-time programs available. *Degree requirements:* For master's, thesis, qualifying exams; for doctorate, thesis/dissertation, qualifying exams. *Entrance requirements:* For master's and doctorate, GRE General Test, minimum GPA of 3.0. Additional exam requirements/recommendations for international students: Required—TOEFL. Electronic applications accepted. *Faculty research:* Physiology, molecular biology, cell biology, microbiology, environmental biology.

Humboldt State University, Graduate Studies, College of Natural Resources and Sciences, Department of Biological Sciences, Arcata, CA 95521-8299. Offers MA. *Students:* 33 full-time (17 women), 24 part-time (17 women); includes 4 minority (1 American Indian/Alaska Native, 1 Asian American or Pacific Islander, 2 Hispanic Americans), 1 international. Average age 32. 39 applicants, 56% accepted, 16 enrolled. In 2009, 9 master's awarded. *Degree requirements:* For master's, project or thesis. *Entrance requirements:* For master's, GRE General Test, appropriate bachelor's degree, minimum GPA of 2.5, 3 letters of recommendation. Additional exam requirements/recommendations for international students: Required—TOEFL (minimum score 500 paper-based; 173 computer-based). *Application deadline:* For fall admission, 2/1 for domestic and international students. Applications are processed on a rolling basis. Application fee: $55. *Expenses:* Tuition, nonresident: full-time $8928. Required fees: $6102. Tuition and fees vary according to program. *Financial support:* Application deadline: 3/1. *Faculty research:* Plant ecology, DNA sequencing, invertebrates. *Unit head:* Dr. John Reiss, Chair, 707-826-3245, Fax: 707-826-3201, E-mail: jor1@humboldt.edu. *Application contact:* Dr. Michael Mesler, Coordinator, 707-826-3674, Fax: 707-826-3201, E-mail: mm1@humboldt.edu.

Hunter College of the City University of New York, Graduate School, School of Arts and Sciences, Department of Biological Sciences, New York, NY 10021-5085. Offers MA, PhD. Part-time programs available. *Faculty:* 13 full-time (5 women), 1 (woman) part-time/adjunct. *Students:* 10 full-time (5 women), 15 part-time (12 women); includes 9 minority (2 African Americans, 5 Asian Americans or Pacific Islanders, 2 Hispanic Americans). Average age 27. 37 applicants, 54% accepted, 8 enrolled. In 2009, 10 master's awarded. Terminal master's awarded for partial completion of doctoral program. *Degree requirements:* For master's, one foreign language, comprehensive exam or thesis. *Entrance requirements:* For master's, GRE, 1 year of course work in organic chemistry (including laboratory), college physics, calculus; undergraduate major in biology, botany, physiology, zoology, chemistry or physics. Additional exam requirements/recommendations for international students: Required—TOEFL. *Application deadline:* For fall admission, 4/1 for domestic students, 2/1 for international students; for spring admission, 11/1 for domestic students, 9/1 for international students. Application fee: $125. *Expenses:* Tuition, state resident: full-time $7360; part-time $310 per credit. Required fees: $250 per semester. *Financial support:* Fellowships, research assistantships, teaching assistantships, scholarships/grants and tuition waivers (partial) available. Support available to part-time students. *Faculty research:* Analysis of prokaryotic and eukaryotic DNA, protein structure, mammalian DNA replication, oncogene expression, neuroscience. *Unit head:* Dr. Shirley Raps, Chairperson, 212-772-5293, E-mail: raps@genectr.hunter.cuny.edu. *Application contact:* William Zlata, Director for Graduate Admissions, 212-772-4482, Fax: 212-650-3336, E-mail: admissions@hunter.cuny.edu.

ICR Graduate School, Graduate Programs, Santee, CA 92071. Offers astro/geophysics (MS); biology (MS); geology (MS); science education (MS). Part-time programs available. *Degree requirements:* For master's, comprehensive exam (for some programs), thesis (for some programs). *Entrance requirements:* For master's, minimum undergraduate GPA of 3.0, bachelor's degree in science or science education. *Faculty research:* Age of the earth, limits of variation, catastrophe, optimum methods for teaching.

Idaho State University, Office of Graduate Studies, College of Arts and Sciences, Department of Biological Sciences, Pocatello, ID 83209-8007. Offers biology (MNS, MS, DA, PhD); clinical laboratory science (MS); microbiology (MS). *Accreditation:* NAACLS. Part-time programs available. *Faculty:* 25 full-time (4 women). *Students:* 65 full-time (28 women), 24 part-time (8 women); includes 3 minority (1 American Indian/Alaska Native, 2 Hispanic Americans), 12 international. Average age 31. In 2009, 17 master's, 6 doctorates awarded. *Degree requirements:* For master's, comprehensive exam, thesis; for doctorate, comprehensive exam, thesis/dissertation, 9 credits of internship (for DA). *Entrance requirements:* For master's, GRE General Test, minimum GPA of 3.0 in all upper division classes; for doctorate, GRE General Test, GRE Subject Test (biology), diagnostic exam (DA), minimum GPA of 3.0 in all upper division classes. Additional exam requirements/recommendations for international students: Required—TOEFL (minimum score 550 paper-based; 213 computer-based; 80 iBT). *Application deadline:* For fall admission, 7/1 for domestic students, 6/1 for international students; for spring admission, 12/1 for domestic students, 11/1 for international students. Applications are processed on a rolling basis. Application fee: $55. Electronic applications accepted. *Expenses:* Tuition, state resident: full-time $3318; part-time $297 per credit hour. Tuition, nonresident: full-time $13,120; part-time $437 per credit hour. Required fees: $2530. Tuition and fees vary according to program. *Financial support:* In 2009–10, fellowships with full and partial tuition reimbursements (averaging $12,282 per year), 23 research assistantships with full and partial tuition reimbursements (averaging $12,503 per year), 27 teaching assistantships with full and partial tuition reimbursements (averaging $10,841 per year) were awarded; Federal Work-Study, institutionally sponsored loans, scholarships/grants, health care benefits, tuition waivers (full and partial), and unspecified assistantships also available. Support available to part-time students. Financial award application deadline: 1/1; financial award applicants required to submit FAFSA. *Faculty research:* Ecology, plant and animal physiology, plant and animal developmental biology, immunology, molecular biology, bioinformatics. *Unit head:* Dr. Terry Bowyer, Chair, 208-282-3765, Fax: 208-282-4570, E-mail: bowyterr@isu.edu. *Application contact:* Tami Carson, Graduate School Technical Records Specialist, 208-282-2150, Fax: 208-282-4847, E-mail: carstami@isu.edu.

Illinois Institute of Technology, Graduate College, College of Science and Letters, Department of Biological, Chemical and Physical Sciences, Biology Division, Chicago, IL 60616-3793. Offers biology (MBS, MS, PhD); molecular biochemistry and biophysics (MS, PhD). Part-time and evening/weekend programs available. Postbaccalaureate distance learning degree programs offered (no on-campus study). *Faculty:* 12 full-time (4 women), 2 part-time/adjunct (0 women). *Students:* 98 full-time (50 women), 80 part-time (45 women); includes 15 minority (6 African Americans, 6 Asian Americans or Pacific Islanders, 3 Hispanic Americans), 119 international. Average age 27. 330 applicants, 43% accepted, 57 enrolled. In 2009, 30 master's, 5 doctorates awarded. Terminal master's awarded for partial completion of doctoral program. *Degree requirements:* For master's, comprehensive exam, thesis (for some programs); for doctorate, comprehensive exam, thesis/dissertation. *Entrance requirements:* For master's and doctorate, GRE General Test, minimum undergraduate GPA of 3.0. Additional exam requirements/recommendations for international students: Required—TOEFL (minimum score 550 paper-based; 213 computer-based; 80 iBT). *Application deadline:* For fall admission, 5/1 for domestic and international students; for spring admission, 1/5 for domestic and international students. Applications are processed on a rolling basis. Application fee: $40. Electronic applications accepted. *Expenses:* Tuition: Full-time $17,550; part-time $888 per credit hour. Required fees: $850; $7.50 per credit hour. One-time fee: $50 full-time. Full-time tuition and fees vary according to program. *Financial support:* In 2009–10, 1 fellowship with full tuition reimbursement (averaging $18,000 per year), 6 research assistantships with full tuition reimbursements (averaging $15,500 per year), 11 teaching assistantships with full tuition reimbursements (averaging $15,500 per year) were awarded; career-related internships or fieldwork, Federal Work-Study, institutionally sponsored loans, scholarships/grants, traineeships, health care benefits, tuition waivers (partial), and unspecified assistantships also available. Support available to part-time students. Financial award applicants required to submit FAFSA. *Faculty research:* Structure of muscle and collagen using x-ray scattering, prostate cancer, identification and analysis of anti-cancer drugs, x-ray crystallography of proteins, developmental biology of olfaction, molecular analysis of foodbourne pathogens. Total annual research expenditures: $10.5 million. *Unit head:* Dr. Benjamin C. Stark, Professor and Associate Chair, 312-567-3488, Fax: 312-567-3494, E-mail: starkb@iit.edu. *Application contact:* Morgan Frederick, Assistant Director of Graduate Communications, 866-472-3448, Fax: 312-567-3138, E-mail: inquiry.grad@iit.edu.

Illinois State University, Graduate School, College of Arts and Sciences, Department of Biological Sciences, Normal, IL 61790-2200. Offers animal behavior (MS); bacteriology (MS); biochemistry (MS); biological sciences (MS); biology (PhD); biophysics (MS); biotechnology (MS); botany (MS, PhD); cell biology (MS); conservation biology (MS); developmental biology (MS); ecology (MS, PhD); entomology (MS); evolutionary biology (MS); genetics (MS, PhD); immunology (MS); microbiology (MS, PhD); molecular biology (MS); molecular genetics (MS); neurobiology (MS); neuroscience (MS); parasitology (MS); physiology (MS, PhD); plant biology (MS); plant molecular biology (MS); plant sciences (MS); structural biology (MS); zoology (MS, PhD). Part-time programs available. *Degree requirements:* For master's, thesis or alternative; for doctorate, variable foreign language requirement, thesis/dissertation, 2 terms of residency. *Entrance requirements:* For master's, GRE General Test, minimum GPA of 2.6 in last 60 hours of course work; for doctorate, GRE General Test. *Faculty research:* Redoc balance and drug development in schistosoma mansoni, control of the growth of listeria monocytogenes at low temperature, regulation of cell expansion and microtubule function by SPRI, CRUI: physiology and fitness consequences of different life history phenotypes.

Indiana State University, School of Graduate Studies, College of Arts and Sciences, Department of Biology, Terre Haute, IN 47809. Offers ecology (PhD); life sciences (MS); microbiology (PhD); physiology (PhD); science education (MS). *Degree requirements:* For master's, thesis (for some programs); for doctorate, comprehensive exam, thesis/dissertation. *Entrance requirements:* For master's and doctorate, GRE General Test. Electronic applications accepted.

Indiana University Bloomington, University Graduate School, College of Arts and Sciences, Department of Biology, Bloomington, IN 47405. Offers biology teaching (MAT); biotechnology (MA); evolution, ecology, and behavior (MA, PhD); genetics (PhD); microbiology (MA, PhD); molecular, cellular, and developmental biology (PhD); plant sciences (MA, PhD); zoology (MA, PhD). *Faculty:* 58 full-time (15 women), 21 part-time/adjunct (6 women). *Students:* 165 full-time (95 women); includes 14 minority (6 African Americans, 1 American Indian/Alaska Native, 7 Asian Americans or Pacific Islanders), 56 international. Average age 27. 312 applicants, 19% accepted, 24 enrolled. In 2009, 4 master's, 22 doctorates awarded. Terminal master's awarded for partial completion of doctoral program. *Degree requirements:* For master's, thesis, oral defense; for doctorate, thesis/dissertation, oral defense. *Entrance requirements:* For master's and doctorate, GRE General Test. Additional exam requirements/recommendations for international students: Required—TOEFL (minimum score 100 iBT). *Application deadline:* For fall admission, 1/5 priority date for domestic students, 12/1 priority date for international students. Application fee: $55 ($65 for international students). Electronic applications accepted. *Financial support:* In 2009–10, 165 students received support, including 62 fellowships with tuition reimbursements available (averaging $19,484 per year), 27 research assistantships with tuition reimbursements available (averaging $22,605 per year), 76 teaching assistantships with tuition reimbursements available (averaging $20,528 per year); scholarships/grants, traineeships, health care benefits, and unspecified assistantships also available. Financial award application deadline: 1/5. *Faculty research:* Evolution, ecology and behavior; microbiology; molecular biology and genetics; plant biology. *Unit head:* Dr. Roger Innes, Chair, 812-855-2219, Fax: 812-855-6082, E-mail: rinnes@indiana.edu. *Application contact:* Tracey D. Stohr, Graduate Student Recruitment Coordinator, 812-856-6303, Fax: 812-855-6082, E-mail: gradbio@indiana.edu.

Indiana University of Pennsylvania, School of Graduate Studies and Research, College of Natural Sciences and Mathematics, Department of Biology, Program in Biology, Indiana, PA 15705-1087. Offers MS. *Faculty:* 10 full-time (2 women). *Students:* 17 full-time (12 women), 5 part-time (4 women); includes 1 minority (Asian American or Pacific Islander). Average age 28. 47 applicants, 23% accepted, 7 enrolled. In 2009, 1 master's awarded. *Degree requirements:* For master's, comprehensive exam, thesis optional. *Entrance requirements:* For master's, 2 letters of recommendation. Additional exam requirements/recommendations for international students: Required—TOEFL. *Application deadline:* For fall admission, 7/1 priority date for domestic students; for spring admission, 11/1 for domestic students. Applications are processed on a rolling basis. Application fee: $40. *Expenses:* Tuition, state resident: full-time $6666; part-time $370 per credit hour. Tuition, nonresident: full-time $10,666; part-time $593 per credit hour. Required fees: $813 per semester. *Financial support:* In 2009–10, 1 fellowship (averaging $500 per year), 8 research assistantships with full and partial tuition reimbursements (averaging $5,184 per year) were awarded. Financial award application deadline: 3/15; financial award applicants required to submit FAFSA. *Unit head:* Dr. Robert Gendron, Graduate Coordinator, 724-357-2352, E-mail: robert.gendron@iup.edu. *Application contact:* Dr. Robert Hinrichsen, Graduate Coordinator, 724-357-2352, E-mail: bhinrich@iup.edu.

Indiana University–Purdue University Fort Wayne, College of Arts and Sciences, Department of Biology, Fort Wayne, IN 46805-1499. Offers MS. Part-time and evening/weekend programs available. *Faculty:* 21 full-time (2 women). *Students:* 12 full-time (7 women), 25 part-time (17 women); includes 7 minority (1 African American, 2 Asian Americans or Pacific Islanders, 4 Hispanic Americans), 2 international. Average age 27. 17 applicants, 100% accepted, 12

Biological and Biomedical Sciences—General

Indiana University–Purdue University Fort Wayne (continued)
enrolled. In 2009, 11 master's awarded. *Degree requirements:* For master's, thesis optional. *Entrance requirements:* For master's, GRE General Test, minimum GPA of 3.0, major or minor in biology, three letters of recommendation. Additional exam requirements/recommendations for international students: Required—TOEFL (minimum score 550 paper-based; 213 computer-based; 77 iBT), TWE. *Application deadline:* For fall admission, 4/15 priority date for domestic students, 2/15 priority date for international students; for spring admission, 11/15 priority date for domestic students, 9/15 priority date for international students. Applications are processed on a rolling basis. Application fee: $55 ($60 for international students). Electronic applications accepted. *Expenses:* Tuition, state resident: full-time $4595; part-time $255 per credit. Tuition, nonresident: full-time $10,963; part-time $609 per credit. Required fees: $528; $29.35 per credit. Tuition and fees vary according to course load. *Financial support:* In 2009–10, 5 research assistantships with partial tuition reimbursements (averaging $12,740 per year), 12 teaching assistantships with partial tuition reimbursements (averaging $12,740 per year) were awarded; scholarships/grants and unspecified assistantships also available. Support available to part-time students. Financial award application deadline: 3/1; financial award applicants required to submit FAFSA. *Faculty research:* Wetland reptiles, tracking tortoises, terrestrial and aerial predators, copperbelly watersnakes. Total annual research expenditures: $231,982. *Unit head:* Dr. Bruce A. Kingsbury, Chairperson, 260-481-6305, Fax: 260-481-6087, E-mail: kingsbur@ipfw.edu. *Application contact:* Dr. George S. Mourad, Graduate Program Director, 260-481-5704, Fax: 260-481-6087, E-mail: mourad@ipfw.edu.

Indiana University–Purdue University Indianapolis, School of Science, Department of Biology, Indianapolis, IN 46202-2896. Offers MS, PhD. Part-time and evening/weekend programs available. *Faculty:* 7 full-time (2 women). *Students:* 100 full-time (40 women), 12 part-time (7 women). Average age 25. In 2009, 68 master's awarded. Terminal master's awarded for partial completion of doctoral program. *Degree requirements:* For master's, thesis (for some programs); for doctorate, thesis/dissertation. *Entrance requirements:* For master's and doctorate, GRE General Test. *Application deadline:* For fall admission, 6/1 for domestic students. Application fee: $50 ($60 for international students). *Financial support:* In 2009–10, 5 fellowships with partial tuition reimbursements (averaging $9,905 per year), 8 teaching assistantships with partial tuition reimbursements (averaging $12,773 per year) were awarded; research assistantships with partial tuition reimbursements, career-related internships or fieldwork also available. Financial award application deadline: 4/1. *Faculty research:* Cell and model membranes, cell and molecular biology, immunology, oncology, developmental biology. *Unit head:* Dr. N. Douglas Lees, Chair, 317-274-0588, Fax: 317-274-2846. *Application contact:* Dr. Sherry Queener, Director, Graduate Studies and Associate Dean, 317-274-1577, Fax: 317-278-2380.

Iowa State University of Science and Technology, College of Veterinary Medicine and Graduate College, Graduate Programs in Veterinary Medicine, Department of Biomedical Sciences, Ames, IA 50011. Offers MS, PhD. *Faculty:* 22 full-time (3 women), 1 part-time/adjunct (0 women). *Students:* 30 full-time (7 women), 1 part-time (0 women); includes 3 minority (2 Asian Americans or Pacific Islanders, 1 Hispanic American), 20 international. 46 applicants, 4% accepted, 2 enrolled. In 2009, 1 master's, 1 doctorate awarded. *Degree requirements:* For master's, thesis or alternative; for doctorate, thesis/dissertation. *Entrance requirements:* For master's and doctorate, GRE General Test. Additional exam requirements/recommendations for international students: Required—TOEFL (minimum score 590 paper-based; 84 iBT) or IELTS (minimum score 6.5). *Application deadline:* For fall admission, 3/1 priority date for domestic and international students; for spring admission, 9/1 priority date for domestic and international students. Application fee: $40 ($90 for international students). Electronic applications accepted. *Expenses:* Tuition, state resident: full-time $6716. Tuition, nonresident: full-time $8908. Tuition and fees vary according to course level, course load, program and student level. *Financial support:* In 2009–10, 4 research assistantships with full and partial tuition reimbursements (averaging $15,000 per year), 5 teaching assistantships with full and partial tuition reimbursements (averaging $15,000 per year) were awarded; career-related internships or fieldwork, scholarships/grants, health care benefits, and unspecified assistantships also available. *Faculty research:* Cerebella research; endocrine physiology; memory, learning and associated diseases; ion-channels and dry resistance; glia-neuron signaling; neurobiology of pain. *Unit head:* Dr. James Bloedel, Chair, 515-294-2440, Fax: 515-294-2315, E-mail: biomedsci@iastate.edu. *Application contact:* Dr. James Bloedel, Chair, 515-294-2440, Fax: 515-294-2315, E-mail: biomedsci@iastate.edu.

Jackson State University, Graduate School, School of Science and Technology, Department of Biology, Jackson, MS 39217. Offers biology education (MST); environmental science (MS, PhD). Part-time and evening/weekend programs available. *Degree requirements:* For master's, comprehensive exam, thesis (alternative accepted for MST); for doctorate, comprehensive exam, thesis/dissertation. *Entrance requirements:* For master's, GRE General Test; for doctorate, MAT. Additional exam requirements/recommendations for international students: Required—TOEFL. *Faculty research:* Comparative studies on the carbohydrate composition of marine macroalgae, host-parasite relationship between the spruce budworm and entomepathogen fungus.

Jacksonville State University, College of Graduate Studies and Continuing Education, College of Arts and Sciences, Department of Biology, Jacksonville, AL 36265-1602. Offers MS. Part-time and evening/weekend programs available. *Faculty:* 11 full-time (0 women). *Students:* 7 full-time (5 women), 20 part-time (12 women); includes 6 minority (all African Americans), 2 international. Average age 28. 11 applicants, 55% accepted, 6 enrolled. In 2009, 14 master's awarded. *Degree requirements:* For master's, comprehensive exam, thesis (for some programs). *Entrance requirements:* For master's, GRE General Test or MAT. *Application deadline:* Applications are processed on a rolling basis. Application fee: $30. Electronic applications accepted. *Financial support:* In 2009–10, 21 students received support. Available to part-time students. Application deadline: 4/1. *Unit head:* Dr. Frank Romano, Head, 256-782-5038. *Application contact:* Dr. Jean Pugliese, Associate Dean, 256-782-8278, Fax: 256-782-5321, E-mail: pugliese@jsu.edu.

James Madison University, The Graduate School, College of Science and Mathematics, Department of Biology, Harrisonburg, VA 22807. Offers MS. Part-time programs available. *Students:* 14 full-time (9 women), 3 part-time (2 women); includes 1 minority (Asian American or Pacific Islander), 1 international. Average age 27. In 2009, 4 master's awarded. *Degree requirements:* For master's, thesis (for some programs). *Entrance requirements:* For master's, GRE General Test, GRE Subject Test, 3 letters of recommendation. Additional exam requirements/recommendations for international students: Required—TOEFL. *Application deadline:* For fall admission, 2/15 for domestic students. Applications are processed on a rolling basis. Application fee: $55. Electronic applications accepted. *Expenses:* Tuition, area resident: Part-time $305 per credit hour. Tuition, state resident: part-time $305 per credit hour. Tuition, nonresident: part-time $890 per credit hour. *Financial support:* In 2009–10, 10 students received support. Federal Work-Study available. Financial award application deadline: 3/1; financial award applicants required to submit FAFSA. *Faculty research:* Evolutionary ecology, gene regulation, microbial ecology, plant development, biomechanics. *Unit head:* Dr. Judith A. Dilts, Interim Academic Unit Head, 540-568-6225. *Application contact:* Dr. Jon Kastendiek, Interim Graduate Director, 540-568-6225.

John Carroll University, Graduate School, Department of Biology, University Heights, OH 44118-4581. Offers MA, MS. Part-time programs available. *Degree requirements:* For master's, essay or thesis, seminar. *Entrance requirements:* For master's, undergraduate major in biology, 1 semester of biochemistry, minimum 2.5 GPA. Electronic applications accepted. *Faculty research:* Algal ecology, systematics, molecular genetics, neurophysiology, behavioral ecology.

The Johns Hopkins University, National Institutes of Health Sponsored Programs, Baltimore, MD 21218-2699. Offers biology (PhD), including biochemistry, biophysics, cell biology, developmental biology, genetic biology, molecular biology; cell, molecular, and developmental biology and biophysics (PhD). *Faculty:* 25 full-time (4 women). *Students:* 126 full-time (72 women); includes 36 minority (3 African Americans, 1 American Indian/Alaska Native, 21 Asian Americans or Pacific Islanders, 11 Hispanic Americans), 19 international. 282 applicants, 26% accepted, 36 enrolled. In 2009, 15 doctorates awarded. *Degree requirements:* For doctorate, comprehensive exam, thesis/dissertation. *Entrance requirements:* For doctorate, GRE General Test. Additional exam requirements/recommendations for international students: Required—TOEFL (minimum score 600 paper-based; 250 computer-based), TWE. *Application deadline:* For fall admission, 12/15 priority date for domestic students. Application fee: $60. Electronic applications accepted. *Financial support:* In 2009–10, 24 fellowships (averaging $23,000 per year), 93 research assistantships (averaging $23,000 per year), 22 teaching assistantships (averaging $23,000 per year) were awarded; Federal Work-Study, institutionally sponsored loans, scholarships/grants, traineeships, health care benefits, tuition waivers (partial), and unspecified assistantships also available. Financial award application deadline: 4/15; financial award applicants required to submit FAFSA. *Faculty research:* Protein and nucleic acid biochemistry and biophysical chemistry, molecular biology and development. Total annual research expenditures: $11.2 million. *Unit head:* Dr. Allen Shearn, Chair, 410-516-4693, Fax: 410-516-5213, E-mail: bio_cals@jhu.edu. *Application contact:* Joan Miller, Academic Affairs Manager, 410-516-5502, Fax: 410-516-5213, E-mail: joan@jhu.edu.

The Johns Hopkins University, School of Medicine, Graduate Programs in Medicine, Baltimore, MD 21218-2699. Offers MA, MS, PhD, MD/PhD. *Faculty:* 258 full-time (77 women), 31 part-time/adjunct (12 women). *Students:* 864 full-time (447 women), 1 (woman) part-time; includes 223 minority (55 African Americans, 3 American Indian/Alaska Native, 133 Asian Americans or Pacific Islanders, 32 Hispanic Americans), 283 international. Average age 24. 1,409 applicants, 21% accepted, 147 enrolled. In 2009, 13 master's, 97 doctorates awarded. *Degree requirements:* For doctorate, thesis/dissertation. *Entrance requirements:* Additional exam requirements/recommendations for international students: Required—TOEFL. *Application deadline:* For fall admission, 1/10 priority date for domestic and international students. Applications are processed on a rolling basis. Application fee: $85. Electronic applications accepted. *Expenses:* Contact institution. *Financial support:* In 2009–10, fellowships with full tuition reimbursements (averaging $23,000 per year); research assistantships, teaching assistantships with tuition reimbursements, career-related internships or fieldwork, Federal Work-Study, institutionally sponsored loans, and tuition waivers (full) also available. Financial award applicants required to submit FAFSA. *Unit head:* Dr. Peter Maloney, Associate Dean for Graduate Programs, 410-614-3385. *Application contact:* Dr. James Weiss, Associate Dean of Admissions, 410-955-3182.

The Johns Hopkins University, Zanvyl Krieger School of Arts and Sciences, Chemistry-Biology Interface Program, Baltimore, MD 21218-2699. Offers PhD. *Faculty:* 32 full-time (6 women). *Students:* 5 full-time (all women); includes 2 minority (1 African American, 1 Hispanic American). Average age 25. 77 applicants, 23% accepted, 3 enrolled. In 2009, 8 doctorates awarded. Terminal master's awarded for partial completion of doctoral program. *Degree requirements:* For doctorate, comprehensive exam, thesis/dissertation, 8 one-semester courses, literature seminar, research proposal. *Entrance requirements:* For doctorate, GRE General Test, GRE Subject Test in biochemistry, cell and molecular biology, biology or chemistry (strongly recommended), 3 letters of recommendation, interview. *Application deadline:* For fall admission, 1/15 for domestic and international students. Applications are processed on a rolling basis. Application fee: $75. Electronic applications accepted. *Financial support:* Fellowships, teaching assistantships, Federal Work-Study, scholarships/grants, health care benefits, and unspecified assistantships available. Financial award application deadline: 4/15; financial award applicants required to submit FAFSA. *Faculty research:* Enzyme mechanisms; inhibitors, and metabolic pathways; DNA replication, damaged, and repair; using small molecules to probe signal transduction, gene regulation, angiogenesis, and other biological processes, synthetic methods and medicinal chemistry; synthetic modeling of metalloenzymes. *Unit head:* Dr. Marc Greenberg, Director, 410-516-8095, Fax: 410-516-7044, E-mail: mgreenberg@jhu.edu. *Application contact:* Lauren Riker, Academic Coordinator, 410-516-7427, Fax: 410-516-8420, E-mail: lriker@jhu.edu.

The Johns Hopkins University, Zanvyl Krieger School of Arts and Sciences, Department of Biology, Baltimore, MD 21218-2699. Offers PhD. *Faculty:* 31 full-time (11 women), 17 part-time/adjunct (5 women). *Students:* 107 full-time (59 women); includes 30 minority (1 African American, 16 Asian Americans or Pacific Islanders, 13 Hispanic Americans), 16 international. Average age 25. 210 applicants, 29% accepted, 34 enrolled. In 2009, 12 doctorates awarded. Terminal master's awarded for partial completion of doctoral program. *Degree requirements:* For doctorate, comprehensive exam, thesis/dissertation. *Entrance requirements:* For doctorate, GRE General Test. Additional exam requirements/recommendations for international students: Required—TOEFL (minimum score 600 paper-based; 250 computer-based), IELTS, TWE. *Application deadline:* For fall admission, 12/15 for domestic and international students. Application fee: $75. Electronic applications accepted. *Financial support:* In 2009–10, 95 students received support, including 4 fellowships with tuition reimbursements available (averaging $27,125 per year), 78 research assistantships with tuition reimbursements available (averaging $27,125 per year), 33 teaching assistantships with tuition reimbursements available (averaging $27,125 per year); Federal Work-Study, institutionally sponsored loans, scholarships/grants, traineeships, health care benefits, tuition waivers (full), and unspecified assistantships also available. Financial award application deadline: 4/15; financial award applicants required to submit FAFSA. *Faculty research:* Cell biology, molecular biology and development, biochemistry, developmental biology, biophysics, genetics. Total annual research expenditures: $8.3 million. *Unit head:* Dr. Beverly R. Wendland, Chair, 410-516-4693, Fax: 410-516-5213, E-mail: bwendland@jhu.edu. *Application contact:* Joan Miller, Academic Affairs Administrator, 410-516-5502, Fax: 410-516-5213, E-mail: joan@jhu.edu.

Kansas City University of Medicine and Biosciences, College of Biosciences, Kansas City, MO 64106-1453. Offers bioethics (MA); biomedical sciences (MS).

Kansas State University, College of Veterinary Medicine, Department of Diagnostic Medicine/Pathobiology, Manhattan, KS 66506. Offers biomedical science (MS); diagnostic medicine/pathobiology (PhD). *Faculty:* 22 full-time (4 women), 5 part-time/adjunct (2 women). *Students:* 23 full-time (7 women), 22 part-time (11 women), 8 international. Average age 30. Terminal master's awarded for partial completion of doctoral program. *Degree requirements:* For doctorate, thesis/dissertation. *Entrance requirements:* For master's and doctorate, interviews. Additional exam requirements/recommendations for international students: Required—TOEFL (minimum score 550 paper-based; 213 computer-based). *Application deadline:* For fall admission, 2/1 priority date for domestic and international students; for spring admission, 8/1 priority date for domestic and international students. Applications are processed on a rolling basis. Application fee: $40 ($55 for international students). Electronic applications accepted. *Financial support:* In 2009–10, 26 research assistantships (averaging $14,013 per year) were awarded; teaching assistantships, Federal Work-Study, institutionally sponsored loans, and scholarships/grants also available. Financial award application deadline: 3/1; financial award applicants required to submit FAFSA. *Faculty research:* Infectious disease of animals, food safety and security, epidemiology and public health, toxicology, and pathology. Total annual research expenditures: $2.1 million. *Unit head:* M. M. Chengappa, Head, 785-532-4403, E-mail: chengap@ksu.edu. *Application contact:* T. G. Nagaraja, Director, 785-532-1214, E-mail: tnagaraj@ksu.edu.

Kansas State University, Graduate School, College of Arts and Sciences, Division of Biology, Manhattan, KS 66506. Offers biology (MS, PhD); microbiology (PhD). *Faculty:* 40 full-time (12 women), 12 part-time/adjunct (2 women). *Students:* 49 full-time (25 women). Average age 24. 155 applicants, 6% accepted, 9 enrolled. In 2009, 5 master's, 9 doctorates awarded. Terminal master's awarded for partial completion of doctoral program. *Degree requirements:* For master's, thesis; for doctorate, thesis/dissertation. *Entrance requirements:* For master's, GRE General Test, minimum undergraduate GPA of 3.0; for doctorate, GRE General Test, minimum GPA of 3.0. Additional exam requirements/recommendations for international students: Required—TOEFL (minimum score 550 paper-based; 213 computer-based). *Application deadline:* For fall admission, 2/1 priority date for domestic and international students; for spring admission, 8/1 priority date for domestic and international students. Applications are processed on a rolling basis. Application fee: $40 ($55 for international students). Electronic applications accepted.

Financial support: In 2009–10, 18 research assistantships (averaging $22,305 per year), 30 teaching assistantships with full tuition reimbursements (averaging $14,704 per year) were awarded; institutionally sponsored loans and scholarships/grants also available. Support available to part-time students. Financial award application deadline: 3/1; financial award applicants required to submit FAFSA. *Faculty research:* Ecology, genetics, developmental biology, microbiology, cell biology. Total annual research expenditures: $7.3 million. *Unit head:* David Rintoul, Head, 785-532-6615, Fax: 785-532-6653, E-mail: drintoul@ksu.edu. *Application contact:* S. Keith Chapes, Director, 785-532-6795, Fax: 785-532-6653, E-mail: skcbiol@ksu.edu.

Keck Graduate Institute of Applied Life Sciences, Bioscience Program, Claremont, CA 91711. Offers applied life science (PhD); bioscience (MBS); bioscience management (Certificate); computational systems biology (PhD). *Degree requirements:* For master's, comprehensive exam, project. *Entrance requirements:* For master's, GRE General Test or MCAT. Additional exam requirements/recommendations for international students: Required—TOEFL. Electronic applications accepted. *Faculty research:* Computational biology, drug discovery and development, molecular and cellular biology, biomedical engineering, biomaterials and tissue engineering.

Kent State University, College of Arts and Sciences, Department of Biological Sciences, Kent, OH 44242-0001. Offers ecology (MS, PhD); physiology (MS, PhD). *Degree requirements:* For master's, thesis; for doctorate, thesis/dissertation. *Entrance requirements:* For master's, GRE General Test, minimum GPA of 3.0; for doctorate, GRE General Test, minimum GPA of 3.25. Additional exam requirements/recommendations for international students: Required—TOEFL (minimum score 600 paper-based; 257 computer-based). Electronic applications accepted.

Kent State University, School of Biomedical Sciences, Kent, OH 44242-0001. Offers MS, PhD. Terminal master's awarded for partial completion of doctoral program. *Degree requirements:* For master's, thesis; for doctorate, thesis/dissertation. *Entrance requirements:* For master's and doctorate, GRE General Test. Electronic applications accepted.

Lake Erie College of Osteopathic Medicine, Professional Programs, Erie, PA 16509-1025. Offers biomedical sciences (Postbaccalaureate Certificate); medical education (MS); osteopathic medicine (DO); pharmacy (Pharm D). *Accreditation:* ACPE; AOsA. *Degree requirements:* For first professional degree, comprehensive exam, National Osteopathic Medical Licensing Exam, Levels 1 and 2; for Postbaccalaureate Certificate, comprehensive exam, North American Pharmacist Licensure Examination (NAPLEX). *Entrance requirements:* For first professional degree, MCAT, minimum GPA of 3.2, letters of recommendation; for Postbaccalaureate Certificate, PCAT, letters of recommendation, minimum GPA of 3.5. Electronic applications accepted. *Faculty research:* Cardiac smooth and skeletal muscle mechanics, chemotherapeutics and vitamins, osteopathic manipulation.

Lakehead University, Graduate Studies, Faculty of Social Sciences and Humanities, Department of Biology, Thunder Bay, ON P7B 5E1, Canada. Offers M Sc. Part-time and evening/weekend programs available. *Degree requirements:* For master's, thesis, department seminary, oral examination. *Entrance requirements:* For master's, minimum B average. Additional exam requirements/recommendations for international students: Required—TOEFL. *Faculty research:* Systematics and biogeography, wildlife parasitology, plant physiology and biochemistry, plant ecology, fishery biology.

Lamar University, College of Graduate Studies, College of Arts and Sciences, Department of Biology, Beaumont, TX 77710. Offers MS. Part-time and evening/weekend programs available. *Faculty:* 7 full-time (1 woman). *Students:* 9 full-time (6 women), 6 part-time (4 women); includes 2 minority (both Hispanic Americans). Average age 26. 21 applicants, 43% accepted, 6 enrolled. In 2009, 4 master's awarded. *Degree requirements:* For master's, thesis. *Entrance requirements:* For master's, GRE General Test, minimum GPA of 2.5 in last 60 hours of undergraduate course work. Additional exam requirements/recommendations for international students: Required—TOEFL. *Application deadline:* For fall admission, 8/1 for domestic students; for spring admission, 12/1 for domestic students. Applications are processed on a rolling basis. Application fee: $25 ($50 for international students). *Financial support:* In 2009–10, 3 teaching assistantships (averaging $6,200 per year) were awarded. Financial award application deadline: 4/1. *Faculty research:* Microbiology, limnology, vertebrate ecology, invertebrate hemoglobin, ornithology. *Unit head:* Dr. Michael E. Warren, Chair, 409-880-8262, Fax: 409-880-1827. *Application contact:* Dr. R. C. Harrel, Graduate Adviser, 409-880-8255, Fax: 409-880-1827.

Laurentian University, School of Graduate Studies and Research, Programme in Biology, Sudbury, ON P3E 2C6, Canada. Offers biology (M Sc); boreal ecology (PhD). Part-time programs available. *Degree requirements:* For master's, thesis. *Entrance requirements:* For master's, honors degree with second class or better. *Faculty research:* Recovery of acid-stressed lakes, effects of climate change, origin and maintenance of biocomplexity, radionuclide dynamics, cytogenetic studies of plants.

Lehigh University, College of Arts and Sciences, Department of Biological Sciences, Bethlehem, PA 18015. Offers biochemistry (PhD); integrative biology and neuroscience (PhD); molecular biology (MS, PhD). Part-time programs available. Postbaccalaureate distance learning degree programs offered (no on-campus study). *Faculty:* 17 full-time (6 women), 1 (woman) part-time/adjunct. *Students:* 33 full-time (15 women), 37 part-time (25 women); includes 7 minority (1 African American, 3 Asian Americans or Pacific Islanders, 3 Hispanic Americans), 6 international. Average age 29. 45 applicants, 24% accepted, 11 enrolled. In 2009, 20 master's, 4 doctorates awarded. Terminal master's awarded for partial completion of doctoral program. *Degree requirements:* For master's, research report; for doctorate, comprehensive exam, thesis/dissertation. *Entrance requirements:* For doctorate, GRE General Test. Additional exam requirements/recommendations for international students: Required—TOEFL. *Application deadline:* For fall admission, 12/15 for domestic and international students. Applications are processed on a rolling basis. Application fee: $65. Electronic applications accepted. *Financial support:* In 2009–10, 34 students received support, including 4 fellowships with full tuition reimbursements available (averaging $23,000 per year), 6 research assistantships with full tuition reimbursements available (averaging $23,000 per year), 16 teaching assistantships with full tuition reimbursements available (averaging $23,000 per year); scholarships/grants, tuition waivers (full and partial), and unspecified assistantships also available. Financial award application deadline: 1/15. *Faculty research:* Gene expression, cytoskeleton and cell structure, cell cycle and growth regulation, neuroscience, animal behavior. Total annual research expenditures: $2 million. *Unit head:* Dr. Murray Itzkowitz, Chairperson, 610-758-3680, Fax: 610-758-4004, E-mail: mi00@lehigh.edu. *Application contact:* Dr. Jennifer M. Swann, Graduate Coordinator, 610-758-5484, Fax: 610-758-4004, E-mail: jms5@lehigh.edu.

Lehman College of the City University of New York, Division of Natural and Social Sciences, Department of Biological Sciences, Program in Biology, Bronx, NY 10468-1589. Offers MA.

Loma Linda University, School of Science and Technology, Department of Biological and Earth Sciences, Loma Linda, CA 92350. Offers MS, PhD. *Degree requirements:* For master's, comprehensive exam, thesis; for doctorate, comprehensive exam, thesis/dissertation. *Entrance requirements:* For master's, minimum GPA of 3.0. Additional exam requirements/recommendations for international students: Required—TOEFL (minimum score 550 paper-based; 213 computer-based).

Long Island University, Brooklyn Campus, Richard L. Conolly College of Liberal Arts and Sciences, Department of Biology, Brooklyn, NY 11201-8423. Offers MS. Part-time and evening/weekend programs available. *Degree requirements:* For master's, thesis or alternative. *Entrance requirements:* For master's, 2 letters of recommendation. Additional exam requirements/recommendations for international students: Required—TOEFL (minimum score 500 paper-based; 173 computer-based). Electronic applications accepted.

Long Island University, C.W. Post Campus, College of Liberal Arts and Sciences, Department of Biology, Brookville, NY 11548-1300. Offers biology (MS); biology education (MS). Part-time and evening/weekend programs available. *Degree requirements:* For master's, thesis optional. *Entrance requirements:* For master's, GRE General Test, minimum GPA of 2.75 in major. Electronic applications accepted. *Faculty research:* Immunology, molecular biology, systematics, behavioral ecology, microbiology.

Long Island University, C.W. Post Campus, School of Health Professions and Nursing, Department of Biomedical Sciences, Brookville, NY 11548-1300. Offers cardiovascular perfusion (MS); clinical laboratory management (MS); medical biology (MS), including hematology, immunology, medical biology, medical chemistry, medical microbiology. Part-time and evening/weekend programs available. Postbaccalaureate distance learning degree programs offered. *Degree requirements:* For master's, thesis. *Entrance requirements:* For master's, minimum GPA of 2.75 in major. Electronic applications accepted.

Louisiana State University and Agricultural and Mechanical College, Graduate School, College of Basic Sciences, Department of Biological Sciences, Baton Rouge, LA 70803. Offers biochemistry (MS, PhD); biological science (MS, PhD); science (MNS). Part-time programs available. *Faculty:* 65 full-time (8 women). *Students:* 135 full-time (64 women), 9 part-time (4 women); includes 14 minority (9 African Americans, 4 Asian Americans or Pacific Islanders, 1 Hispanic American), 59 international. Average age 30. 161 applicants, 16% accepted, 16 enrolled. In 2009, 3 master's, 26 doctorates awarded. Terminal master's awarded for partial completion of doctoral program. *Degree requirements:* For doctorate, thesis/dissertation. *Entrance requirements:* For master's and doctorate, GRE General Test, minimum GPA of 3.0. Additional exam requirements/recommendations for international students: Required—TOEFL (minimum score 550 paper-based; 213 computer-based; 79 iBT) or IELTS (minimum score 6.5). *Application deadline:* For fall admission, 5/15 for domestic and international students; for spring admission, 10/15 for domestic and international students. Applications are processed on a rolling basis. Application fee: $25. Electronic applications accepted. *Financial support:* In 2009–10, 138 students received support, including 16 fellowships with full and partial tuition reimbursements available (averaging $28,078 per year), 40 research assistantships with full and partial tuition reimbursements available (averaging $21,455 per year), 81 teaching assistantships with full and partial tuition reimbursements available (averaging $18,840 per year); Federal Work-Study, institutionally sponsored loans, health care benefits, and unspecified assistantships also available. Support available to part-time students. Financial award applicants required to submit FAFSA. *Faculty research:* Biochemistry and molecular biology; cell developmental and integrative biology; systematics; ecology and evolutionary biology. Total annual research expenditures: $10.5 million. *Unit head:* Dr. Marcia Newcomer, Chair, 225-578-2601, Fax: 225-578-2597. *Application contact:* Dr. Jacqueline Stephens, Associate Chairman, 225-578-1240, Fax: 225-578-7299, E-mail: biogradcoord@lsu.edu.

Louisiana State University Health Sciences Center, School of Graduate Studies in New Orleans, New Orleans, LA 70112-2223. Offers MPH, MS, PhD, MD/PhD. Part-time and evening/weekend programs available. Terminal master's awarded for partial completion of doctoral program. *Degree requirements:* For master's, comprehensive exam, thesis; for doctorate, comprehensive exam, thesis/dissertation. *Entrance requirements:* For master's and doctorate, GRE General Test. Additional exam requirements/recommendations for international students: Required—TOEFL.

Louisiana State University Health Sciences Center at Shreveport, Louisiana State University Health Sciences Center at Shreveport, Shreveport, LA 71130-3932. Offers MS, PhD, MD/PhD. *Accreditation:* SACS. Terminal master's awarded for partial completion of doctoral program. *Degree requirements:* For master's, thesis; for doctorate, thesis/dissertation. *Entrance requirements:* For master's and doctorate, GRE General Test. Additional exam requirements/recommendations for international students: Required—TOEFL.

Louisiana Tech University, Graduate School, College of Applied and Natural Sciences, School of Biological Sciences, Ruston, LA 71272. Offers MS. Part-time programs available. *Degree requirements:* For master's, thesis or alternative. *Entrance requirements:* For master's, GRE General Test, GRE Subject Test. *Faculty research:* Genetics, animal biology, plant biology, physiology biocontrol.

Loyola University Chicago, Graduate School, Department of Biology, Chicago, IL 60660. Offers MA, MS. *Faculty:* 23 full-time (5 women). *Students:* 86 full-time (35 women), 8 part-time (5 women); includes 19 minority (2 African Americans, 1 American Indian/Alaska Native, 15 Asian Americans or Pacific Islanders, 1 Hispanic American), 3 international. Average age 27. 593 applicants, 26% accepted, 62 enrolled. In 2009, 59 master's awarded. *Degree requirements:* For master's, thesis (for some programs). *Entrance requirements:* For master's, GRE General Test, 3 letters of recommendation. Additional exam requirements/recommendations for international students: Required—TOEFL. *Application deadline:* For fall admission, 6/1 for domestic and international students; for spring admission, 12/1 for domestic students. Applications are processed on a rolling basis. Application fee: $50. Electronic applications accepted. *Expenses:* Tuition: Full-time $14,220; part-time $790 per credit hour. Required fees: $60 per semester hour. Tuition and fees vary according to program. *Financial support:* In 2009–10, 7 students received support, including 7 fellowships with full tuition reimbursements available (averaging $16,000 per year); Federal Work-Study and institutionally sponsored loans also available. Financial award application deadline: 2/1; financial award applicants required to submit FAFSA. *Faculty research:* Evolution, development, aquatic biology, molecular biology and genetics, cell biology, neurobiology. Total annual research expenditures: $2.5 million. *Application contact:* Dr. Terry Grande, Graduate Program Director, 773-508-3649, Fax: 773-508-3646, E-mail: tgrande@luc.edu.

Marquette University, Graduate School, College of Arts and Sciences, Department of Biology, Milwaukee, WI 53201-1881. Offers cell biology (MS, PhD); developmental biology (MS, PhD); ecology (MS, PhD); endocrinology (MS, PhD); evolutionary biology (MS, PhD); genetics (MS, PhD); microbiology (MS, PhD); molecular biology (MS, PhD); muscle and exercise physiology (MS, PhD); neurobiology (MS, PhD); reproductive physiology (MS, PhD). *Faculty:* 23 full-time (10 women), 1 part-time/adjunct (0 women). *Students:* 23 full-time (13 women), 16 part-time (9 women); includes 1 minority (Asian American or Pacific Islander), 20 international. Average age 25. 95 applicants, 16% accepted, 10 enrolled. In 2009, 3 master's, 5 doctorates awarded. Terminal master's awarded for partial completion of doctoral program. *Degree requirements:* For master's, comprehensive exam, thesis, 1 year of teaching experience or equivalent; for doctorate, thesis/dissertation, 1 year of teaching experience or equivalent, qualifying exam. *Entrance requirements:* For master's and doctorate, GRE General Test, GRE Subject Test. Additional exam requirements/recommendations for international students: Required—TOEFL. Application fee: $40. *Financial support:* In 2009–10, 4 fellowships, 22 teaching assistantships were awarded; research assistantships, Federal Work-Study, institutionally sponsored loans, scholarships/grants, and tuition waivers (full and partial) also available. Support available to part-time students. Financial award application deadline: 2/15. *Faculty research:* Microbial and invertebrate ecology, evolution of gene function, DNA methylation, DNA arrangement. *Unit head:* Dr. Robert Fitts, Chair, 414-288-1748, Fax: 414-288-7357. *Application contact:* Debbie Weaver, Administrative Assistant, 414-288-7355, Fax: 414-288-7357.

Marshall University, Academic Affairs Division, College of Science, Department of Biological Science, Huntington, WV 25755. Offers MA, MS. *Faculty:* 25 full-time (5 women), 7 part-time/adjunct (3 women). *Students:* 41 full-time (17 women), 3 part-time (0 women); includes 8 minority (6 African Americans, 2 Asian Americans or Pacific Islanders), 1 international. Average age 26. In 2009, 15 master's awarded. *Degree requirements:* For master's, thesis (for some programs). *Entrance requirements:* For master's, GRE General Test, GRE Subject Test. Application fee: $40. *Financial support:* Career-related internships or fieldwork available. *Unit head:* Dr. Elmer Price, Chairperson, 304-696-3611, E-mail: pricee@marshall.edu. *Application contact:* Information Contact, 304-746-1900, Fax: 304-746-1902, E-mail: services@marshall.edu.

Marshall University, Joan C. Edwards School of Medicine and Academic Affairs Division, Program in Biomedical Sciences, Huntington, WV 25755. Offers MS, PhD. Terminal master's awarded for partial completion of doctoral program. *Degree requirements:* For master's,

Biological and Biomedical Sciences—General

Marshall University (continued)
comprehensive exam, thesis optional; for doctorate, thesis/dissertation, written and oral qualifying exams. *Entrance requirements:* For master's, GRE General Test or MCAT (medical science), 1 year of course work in biology, physics, chemistry, and organic chemistry and associated labs; for doctorate, GRE General Test, 1 year of course work in biology, physics, chemistry, and organic chemistry and associated labs. Additional exam requirements/recommendations for international students: Required—TOEFL (minimum score 525 paper-based; 216 computer-based). *Expenses:* Contact institution. *Faculty research:* Neurosciences, cardiopulmonary science, molecular biology, toxicology, endocrinology.

Massachusetts Institute of Technology, Harvard-MIT Division of Health Sciences and Technology, Biomedical Enterprise Program, Cambridge, MA 02139-4307. Offers SM. *Students:* 28 full-time (15 women); includes 8 minority (1 American Indian/Alaska Native, 6 Asian Americans or Pacific Islanders, 1 Hispanic American), 5 international. Average age 30. 43 applicants, 33% accepted, 13 enrolled. In 2009, 8 master's awarded. *Degree requirements:* For master's, thesis. *Entrance requirements:* For master's, GMAT or GRE, bachelor's degree in engineering or science, work experience in biomedical business. Additional exam requirements/recommendations for international students: Required—TOEFL. *Application deadline:* For fall admission, 12/15 for domestic and international students. Electronic applications accepted. *Expenses:* Contact institution. *Financial support:* In 2009–10, 8 students received support, including 1 fellowship (averaging $5,000 per year), 2 research assistantships with full and partial tuition reimbursements available (averaging $34,773 per year), 6 teaching assistantships with partial tuition reimbursements available (averaging $8,637 per year); institutionally sponsored loans, health care benefits, and unspecified assistantships also available. Financial award application deadline: 12/15; financial award applicants required to submit FAFSA. *Faculty research:* Entrepreneurship, technology strategy management, organizational strategies and models, epidemiology and biostatics, biomedical research from the molecular to the whole organism level. *Application contact:* Traci Anderson, Academic Programs Administrator, 617-258-7470, E-mail: tanderso@mit.edu.

Massachusetts Institute of Technology, Harvard-MIT Division of Health Sciences and Technology, Program in Medical Sciences, Cambridge, MA 02139-4307. Offers MD, MD/MS, MD/PhD. *Students:* 179 full-time (66 women); includes 103 minority (4 African Americans, 1 American Indian/Alaska Native, 89 Asian Americans or Pacific Islanders, 9 Hispanic Americans), 10 international. Average age 26. 683 applicants, 6% accepted, 30 enrolled. In 2009, 38 MDs awarded. *Degree requirements:* For MD, thesis/dissertation. *Entrance requirements:* MCAT. *Application deadline:* For fall admission, 10/15 for domestic students. Application fee: $85. *Expenses:* Contact institution. *Financial support:* In 2009–10, 61 students received support, including 8 fellowships with partial tuition reimbursements available (averaging $39,792 per year), 39 research assistantships with partial tuition reimbursements available (averaging $21,343 per year), 24 teaching assistantships with partial tuition reimbursements available (averaging $6,034 per year); career-related internships or fieldwork, scholarships/grants, health care benefits, and unspecified assistantships also available. Financial award application deadline: 10/15. *Unit head:* Dr. David Earl Cohen, Director, 617-726-5576. *Application contact:* Zara Smith, MD Admissions Coordinator, 617-432-7195, E-mail: zara_smith@hms.harvard.edu.

Massachusetts Institute of Technology, School of Science, Department of Biology, Cambridge, MA 02139-4307. Offers biochemistry (PhD); biological oceanography (PhD); biology (PhD); biophysical chemistry and molecular structure (PhD); cell biology (PhD); computational and systems biology (PhD); developmental biology (PhD); genetics (PhD); immunology (PhD); microbiology (PhD); molecular biology (PhD); neurobiology (PhD). *Faculty:* 54 full-time (14 women). *Students:* 237 full-time (128 women); includes 65 minority (4 African Americans, 2 American Indian/Alaska Native, 33 Asian Americans or Pacific Islanders, 26 Hispanic Americans), 25 international. Average age 26. 645 applicants, 18% accepted, 49 enrolled. In 2009, 41 doctorates awarded. *Degree requirements:* For doctorate, comprehensive exam, thesis/dissertation. *Entrance requirements:* For doctorate, GRE General Test. Additional exam requirements/recommendations for international students: Required—TOEFL (minimum score 577 paper-based; 233 computer-based), IELTS (minimum score 6.5). *Application deadline:* For fall admission, 12/1 for domestic and international students. Application fee: $75. Electronic applications accepted. *Expenses:* Tuition: Full-time $37,510; part-time $585 per unit. Required fees: $272. *Financial support:* In 2009–10, 218 students received support, including 113 fellowships with tuition reimbursements available (averaging $31,816 per year), 109 research assistantships with tuition reimbursements available (averaging $29,254 per year); teaching assistantships with tuition reimbursements available, Federal Work-Study, institutionally sponsored loans, scholarships/grants, traineeships, health care benefits, and unspecified assistantships also available. *Faculty research:* DNA recombination, transcription and gene regulation, signal transduction, cell cycle, neuronal cell fate, replication and repair. Total annual research expenditures: $114 million. *Unit head:* Prof. Chris Kaiser, Head, 617-253-4701, E-mail: mitbio@mit.edu. *Application contact:* Biology Education Office, 617-253-3717, Fax: 617-258-9329, E-mail: gradbio@mit.edu.

Mayo Graduate School, Graduate Programs in Biomedical Sciences, Rochester, MN 55905. Offers PhD, MD/PhD. *Degree requirements:* For doctorate, oral defense of dissertation, qualifying oral and written exam. *Entrance requirements:* For doctorate, GRE, 1 year of chemistry, biology, calculus, and physics. Additional exam requirements/recommendations for international students: Required—TOEFL. Electronic applications accepted.

McGill University, Faculty of Graduate and Postdoctoral Studies, Faculty of Medicine, Department of Medicine, Montréal, QC H3A 2T5, Canada. Offers experimental medicine (M Sc, PhD), including bioethics (M Sc), experimental medicine.

McGill University, Faculty of Graduate and Postdoctoral Studies, Faculty of Science, Department of Biology, Montréal, QC H3A 2T5, Canada. Offers bioinformatics (M Sc, PhD); environment (M Sc, PhD); neo-tropical environment (M Sc, PhD).

McMaster University, Faculty of Health Sciences, Department of Biochemistry and Biomedical Sciences, Hamilton, ON L8S 4M2, Canada. Offers M Sc, PhD. Terminal master's awarded for partial completion of doctoral program. *Degree requirements:* For master's, thesis; for doctorate, comprehensive exam, thesis/dissertation. *Entrance requirements:* For master's and doctorate, minimum B+ average. Additional exam requirements/recommendations for international students: Required—TOEFL (minimum score 550 paper-based; 213 computer-based). *Faculty research:* Molecular and cell biology, biomolecular structure and function, molecular pharmacology and toxicology.

McMaster University, Faculty of Health Sciences and School of Graduate Studies, Program in Medical Sciences, Hamilton, ON L8S 4M2, Canada. Offers blood and vascular (M Sc, PhD); genetics and cancer (M Sc, PhD); immunity and infection (M Sc, PhD); metabolism and nutrition (M Sc, PhD); neurosciences and behavioral sciences (M Sc, PhD); physiology/pharmacology (M Sc, PhD); MD/PhD. *Degree requirements:* For master's, thesis; for doctorate, comprehensive exam, thesis/dissertation. *Entrance requirements:* For master's, honors B Sc, B+ average in related field; for doctorate, M Sc, minimum B+ average. Additional exam requirements/recommendations for international students: Required—TOEFL (minimum score 580 paper-based; 237 computer-based; 92 iBT).

McMaster University, School of Graduate Studies, Faculty of Science, Department of Biology, Hamilton, ON L8S 4M2, Canada. Offers M Sc, PhD. Part-time programs available. *Degree requirements:* For master's, thesis; for doctorate, comprehensive exam, thesis/dissertation. *Entrance requirements:* Additional exam requirements/recommendations for international students: Required—TOEFL (minimum score 550 paper-based; 213 computer-based).

Medical College of Georgia, School of Graduate Studies, Augusta, GA 30912. Offers MCTS, MPH, MS, MSN, DNP, PhD, CCTS. Part-time programs available. Postbaccalaureate distance learning degree programs offered (no on-campus study). *Degree requirements:* For doctorate, thesis/dissertation. *Entrance requirements:* For master's and doctorate, GRE General Test. Additional exam requirements/recommendations for international students: Required—TOEFL. Electronic applications accepted. Full-time tuition and fees vary according to campus/location, program and student level. *Faculty research:* Cancer, cardiovascular biology, neurosciences, inflammation/infection, diabetes.

Medical College of Wisconsin, Graduate School of Biomedical Sciences, Milwaukee, WI 53226-0509. Offers MA, MPH, MS, PhD, Graduate Certificate, MD/PhD. MCW Programs of Interest Listed Below. Part-time and evening/weekend programs available. Postbaccalaureate distance learning degree programs offered (minimal on-campus study). *Faculty:* 115 full-time (30 women), 107 part-time/adjunct (34 women). *Students:* 248 full-time (127 women), 166 part-time (86 women); includes 33 minority (9 African Americans, 1 American Indian/Alaska Native, 16 Asian Americans or Pacific Islanders, 7 Hispanic Americans), 75 international. Average age 28. 339 applicants, 66% accepted, 131 enrolled. In 2009, 54 master's, 18 doctorates awarded. *Degree requirements:* For master's, comprehensive exam (for some programs), thesis (for some programs); for doctorate, comprehensive exam, thesis/dissertation. *Entrance requirements:* For master's and doctorate, GRE General Test. Additional exam requirements/recommendations for international students: Required—TOEFL (minimum score 100 computer-based). *Application deadline:* For fall admission, 2/15 priority date for domestic students, 1/15 for international students; for spring admission, 12/1 priority date for domestic students. Applications are processed on a rolling basis. Application fee: $50. Electronic applications accepted. *Financial support:* In 2009–10, 216 students received support, including 29 research assistantships with full tuition reimbursements available (averaging $56,265 per year); career-related internships or fieldwork, Federal Work-Study, institutionally sponsored loans, scholarships/grants, traineeships, health care benefits, unspecified assistantships, and All full time PhD seekers receive a full tuition scholarship plus cost of living stipend also available. Financial award application deadline: 2/15; financial award applicants required to submit FAFSA. *Faculty research:* Clinical and translational science, genomics and proteomics, cancer. *Unit head:* Dr. Ravindra P. Misra, Dean, 414-955-8218, Fax: 414-955-6555, E-mail: gradschool@mcw.edu. *Application contact:* Guy Berst, Recruiter, 414-955-8218, Fax: 414-955-6555, E-mail: gberst@mcw.edu.

Medical University of South Carolina, College of Graduate Studies, Charleston, SC 29425. Offers MS, PhD, DMD/PhD, MD/PhD, Pharm D/PhD. *Faculty:* 268 full-time (79 women), 20 part-time/adjunct (3 women). *Students:* 138 full-time (78 women), 21 part-time (12 women); includes 13 African Americans, 4 Asian Americans or Pacific Islanders, 5 Hispanic Americans, 23 international. Average age 29. 272 applicants, 28% accepted, 44 enrolled. In 2009, 31 master's, 47 doctorates awarded. Terminal master's awarded for partial completion of doctoral program. *Degree requirements:* For master's, thesis; for doctorate, thesis/dissertation, oral and written exams. *Entrance requirements:* For doctorate, GRE General Test, interview. Additional exam requirements/recommendations for international students: Required—TOEFL (minimum score 600 paper-based; 250 computer-based; 100 iBT). *Application deadline:* For fall admission, 1/15 priority date for domestic and international students. Applications are processed on a rolling basis. Application fee: $85 for international students. Electronic applications accepted. *Expenses:* Contact institution. *Financial support:* In 2009–10, 114 students received support, including 114 research assistantships with partial tuition reimbursements available (averaging $23,000 per year); Federal Work-Study and scholarships/grants also available. Support available to part-time students. Financial award application deadline: 3/10; financial award applicants required to submit FAFSA. *Faculty research:* Cell signaling and cancer biology, drug discovery and toxicology, biochemistry and genetics, macromolecular structure, neurosciences, microbiology and immunology. *Unit head:* Dr. Perry V. Halushka, Dean, 843-792-3012, Fax: 843-792-6590, E-mail: halushpv@musc.edu. *Application contact:* Dr. Cynthia F. Wright, Associate Dean for Career Development and Admissions, 843-792-2564, Fax: 843-792-6590, E-mail: wrightcf@musc.edu.

Meharry Medical College, School of Graduate Studies, Program in Biomedical Sciences, Nashville, TN 37208-9989. Offers cancer biology (PhD); microbiology and immunology (PhD); neuroscience (PhD); pharmacology (PhD); MD/PhD. *Degree requirements:* For doctorate, comprehensive exam, thesis/dissertation. *Entrance requirements:* For doctorate, GRE General Test, GRE Subject Test. *Faculty research:* Molecular mechanisms of biological systems and their relationship to human diseases, regulatory biological and cellular structure and function, genetic regulation of growth and cellular metabolisms.

Memorial University of Newfoundland, Faculty of Medicine and School of Graduate Studies, Graduate Programs in Medicine, St. John's, NL A1C 5S7, Canada. Offers M Sc, PhD, Diploma, MD/PhD. Part-time programs available. *Degree requirements:* For master's, thesis; for doctorate, comprehensive exam, thesis/dissertation, oral defense of thesis. *Entrance requirements:* For master's, MD or B Sc; for doctorate, MD or M Sc; for Diploma, bachelor's degree in health-related field. Additional exam requirements/recommendations for international students: Required—TOEFL (minimum score 550 paper-based; 213 computer-based). Electronic applications accepted. *Faculty research:* Human genetics, community health, clinical epidemial, cancer, immunology, cardiovascular and immol sciences, applied health services research, neuroscience.

Memorial University of Newfoundland, School of Graduate Studies, Department of Biology, St. John's, NL A1C 5S7, Canada. Offers biology (M Sc, PhD); marine biology (M Sc, PhD). Part-time programs available. *Degree requirements:* For master's, thesis; for doctorate, comprehensive exam, thesis/dissertation, oral defense of thesis. *Entrance requirements:* For master's, honors degree (minimum 2nd class standing) in related field. Electronic applications accepted. *Faculty research:* Northern flora and fauna, especially cold ocean and boreal environments.

Michigan State University, College of Human Medicine and The Graduate School, Graduate Programs in Human Medicine, East Lansing, MI 48824. Offers biochemistry and molecular biology (MS, PhD); epidemiology (MS, PhD); microbiology (MS); microbiology and molecular genetics (PhD); pharmacology and toxicology (MS, PhD); physiology (MS, PhD); public health (MPH). *Students:* 58 full-time (31 women), 31 part-time (25 women); includes 17 minority (7 African Americans, 1 American Indian/Alaska Native, 6 Asian Americans or Pacific Islanders, 3 Hispanic Americans), 22 international. Average age 30. In 2009, 8 master's, 9 doctorates awarded. *Entrance requirements:* Additional exam requirements/recommendations for international students: Required—TOEFL. *Expenses:* Tuition, state resident: part-time $478.25 per credit hour. Tuition, nonresident: part-time $966.50 per credit hour. Part-time tuition and fees vary according to program. *Financial support:* In 2009–10, 17 research assistantships with tuition reimbursements (averaging $7,053 per year), 3 teaching assistantships with tuition reimbursements (averaging $6,607 per year) were awarded. *Unit head:* Margo K. Smith, Director of Graduate Studies, 517-432-5112, E-mail: smithmk@msu.edu. *Application contact:* Margo K. Smith, Director of Graduate Studies, 517-432-5112, E-mail: smithmk@msu.edu.

Michigan State University, College of Osteopathic Medicine and The Graduate School, Graduate Studies in Osteopathic Medicine, East Lansing, MI 48824. Offers biochemistry and molecular biology (MS, PhD); microbiology (MS); microbiology and molecular genetics (PhD); pharmacology and toxicology (MS, PhD), including integrative pharmacology (MS), pharmacology and toxicology, pharmacology and toxicology-environmental toxicology (PhD); physiology (MS, PhD). *Students:* 6 full-time (1 woman), 39 part-time (22 women); includes 8 minority (2 African Americans, 2 Asian Americans or Pacific Islanders, 4 Hispanic Americans), 3 international. Average age 30. *Expenses:* Tuition, state resident: part-time $478.25 per credit hour. Tuition, nonresident: part-time $966.50 per credit hour. Part-time tuition and fees vary according to program. *Financial support:* In 2009–10, 1 research assistantship with tuition reimbursement (averaging $7,894 per year) was awarded. *Application contact:* Bethany Heinlen, Information Contact, 517-353-7785, Fax: 517-353-9004, E-mail: heinlen@msu.edu.

Michigan State University, College of Veterinary Medicine and The Graduate School, Graduate Programs in Veterinary Medicine, Program in Comparative Medicine and Integrative Biology, East Lansing, MI 48824. Offers comparative medicine and integrative biology (MS, PhD); comparative medicine and integrative biology–environmental toxicology (PhD). *Students:* 18

full-time (10 women), 8 part-time (4 women); includes 3 minority (2 African Americans, 1 Asian American or Pacific Islander), 13 international. Average age 30. 9 applicants, 33% accepted. In 2009, 2 master's, 8 doctorates awarded. *Entrance requirements:* Additional exam requirements/recommendations for international students: Required—TOEFL. Electronic applications accepted. *Expenses:* Tuition, state resident: part-time $478.25 per credit hour. Tuition, nonresident: part-time $966.50 per credit hour. Part-time tuition and fees vary according to program. *Financial support:* In 2009–10, 7 research assistantships with tuition reimbursements (averaging $8,013 per year) were awarded. *Unit head:* Dr. Vilma Yuzbasiyan-Gurkan, Program Director, 517-884-5351, Fax: 517-353-8957, E-mail: yuzbasiyan@cvm.msu.edu. *Application contact:* Dr. Victoria Hoelzer-Maddox, Administrative Assistant, 517-353-3118, Fax: 517-353-2935, E-mail: hoelzer-maddox@cvm.msu.edu.

Michigan Technological University, Graduate School, College of Sciences and Arts, Department of Biological Sciences, Houghton, MI 49931. Offers MS, PhD. Part-time programs available. Terminal master's awarded for partial completion of doctoral program. *Degree requirements:* For master's, comprehensive exam (for some programs), thesis; for doctorate, comprehensive exam, thesis/dissertation. *Entrance requirements:* For master's and doctorate, GRE. Additional exam requirements/recommendations for international students: Required—TOEFL (minimum score 550 paper-based; 213 computer-based). Electronic applications accepted. *Faculty research:* Aquatic ecology, biological control, predator-prey interactions, environmental microbiology, microbial and plant biochemistry, genomics and bioinformatics.

Middle Tennessee State University, College of Graduate Studies, College of Basic and Applied Sciences, Department of Biology, Murfreesboro, TN 37132. Offers MS. Part-time and evening/weekend programs available. Postbaccalaureate distance learning degree programs offered. *Faculty:* 23 full-time (7 women). *Students:* 2 full-time (1 woman), 74 part-time (37 women); includes 11 minority (5 African Americans, 2 American Indian/Alaska Native, 3 Asian Americans or Pacific Islanders, 1 Hispanic American). Average age 26. 43 applicants, 67% accepted, 29 enrolled. In 2009, 11 master's awarded. *Degree requirements:* For master's, one foreign language, comprehensive exam, thesis. *Entrance requirements:* For master's, GRE or MAT. Additional exam requirements/recommendations for international students: Required—TOEFL (minimum score 525 paper-based; 195 computer-based; 71 iBT) or IELTS (minimum score 6). *Application deadline:* For fall admission, 6/1 for domestic and international students. Applications are processed on a rolling basis. Application fee: $25 ($30 for international students). Electronic applications accepted. *Expenses:* Tuition, state resident: full-time $4404. Tuition, nonresident: full-time $10,956. *Financial support:* In 2009–10, 30 students received support. Institutionally sponsored loans available. Support available to part-time students. Financial award application deadline: 5/1; financial award applicants required to submit FAFSA. *Unit head:* Dr. George Murphy, Chair, 615-898-2847, E-mail: gmurphy@mtsu.edu. *Application contact:* Dr. Michael Allen, Dean and Vice Provost for Research, 615-898-2840, Fax: 615-904-8020, E-mail: mallen@mtsu.edu.

Midwestern State University, Graduate Studies, College of Science and Mathematics, Program in Biology, Wichita Falls, TX 76308. Offers MS. Part-time and evening/weekend programs available. *Degree requirements:* For master's, comprehensive exam, thesis. *Entrance requirements:* For master's, GRE General Test, MAT or GMAT. Additional exam requirements/recommendations for international students: Required—TOEFL (minimum score 550 paper-based; 213 computer-based). Electronic applications accepted. *Expenses:* Tuition, state resident: full-time $1620; part-time $90 per credit hour. Tuition, nonresident: full-time $2160; part-time $120 per credit hour. International tuition: $7506 full-time. Required fees: $3068.80; $145.60 per credit hour. $179 per semester. *Faculty research:* Ecology and systematics of spiders and mammals, plant physiology and molecular biology, Drosophila genetics.

Midwestern University, Downers Grove Campus, College of Health Sciences, Illinois Campus, Program in Biomedical Sciences, Downers Grove, IL 60515-1235. Offers MBS. Part-time programs available. *Faculty:* 1 (woman) full-time. *Students:* 47 full-time (23 women), 7 part-time (2 women); includes 4 minority (1 African American, 2 Asian Americans or Pacific Islanders, 1 Hispanic American), 1 international. Average age 24. 178 applicants, 63% accepted, 32 enrolled. In 2009, 13 master's awarded. *Entrance requirements:* For master's, GRE General Test, MCAT or PCAT, 2 letters of recommendation. *Application deadline:* Applications are processed on a rolling basis. Application fee: $50. *Unit head:* Dr. Michael Fay, Director, 630-515-6382. *Application contact:* Michael Laken, Director of Admissions, 630-515-6171, Fax: 630-971-6086, E-mail: admissil@midwestern.edu.

Midwestern University, Glendale Campus, College of Health Sciences, Arizona Campus, Program in Biomedical Sciences, Glendale, AZ 85308. Offers MBS. *Faculty:* 9 full-time (3 women). *Students:* 31 full-time (19 women), 2 part-time (both women); includes 13 minority (4 African Americans, 7 Asian Americans or Pacific Islanders, 2 Hispanic Americans). Average age 25. 232 applicants, 54% accepted. In 2009, 9 master's awarded. Application fee: $50. *Expenses:* Contact institution. *Unit head:* Dr. William P. Baker, Director, 623-572-3666. *Application contact:* James Walter, Director of Admissions, 888-247-9277, Fax: 623-572-3229, E-mail: admissaz@midwestern.edu.

Midwestern University, Glendale Campus, College of Health Sciences, Arizona Campus, Program in Biomedical Sciences, Master of Arts, Glendale, AZ 85308. Offers MA. *Faculty:* 6 full-time (2 women). *Students:* 74 full-time (35 women), 1 (woman) part-time; includes 25 minority (3 African Americans, 1 American Indian/Alaska Native, 17 Asian Americans or Pacific Islanders, 4 Hispanic Americans), 1 international. Average age 25. *Entrance requirements:* For master's, GRE General Test, MCAT, or other professional exam, bachelor's degree, minimum cumulative GPA of 2.75. *Unit head:* Leonard Bell, Program Director, 623-572-3622, Fax: 623-572-3647, E-mail: lbellx@midwestern.edu. *Application contact:* James Walter, Director of Admissions, 888-247-9277, Fax: 623-572-3229, E-mail: admissaz@midwestern.edu.

Millersville University of Pennsylvania, College of Graduate and Professional Studies, School of Science and Mathematics, Department of Biology, Millersville, PA 17551-0302. Offers MS. Part-time programs available. *Faculty:* 19 full-time (8 women), 4 part-time/adjunct (3 women). *Students:* 4 full-time (3 women), 2 part-time (both women); includes 2 minority (1 Asian American or Pacific Islander, 1 Hispanic American). Average age 27. 2 applicants, 50% accepted, 0 enrolled. In 2009, 2 master's awarded. *Degree requirements:* For master's, thesis optional. *Entrance requirements:* For master's, GRE General Test, GRE Subject Test (biology), writing sample, 3 letters of recommendation. Additional exam requirements/recommendations for international students: Required—TOEFL (minimum score 500 paper-based; 183 computer-based; 65 iBT) or IELTS (minimum score 6). *Application deadline:* For fall admission, 1/15 priority date for domestic and international students; for winter admission, 10/1 priority date for domestic and international students; for spring admission, 10/1 priority date for domestic and international students. Applications are processed on a rolling basis. Application fee: $40 ($50 for international students). Electronic applications accepted. *Expenses:* Tuition, state resident: full-time $6666; part-time $370 per credit. Tuition, nonresident: full-time $10,666; part-time $593 per credit. Required fees: $1578.50; $76.25 per credit. One-time fee: $60 part-time. Tuition and fees vary according to course load. *Financial support:* In 2009–10, 2 students received support, including 2 research assistantships with full tuition reimbursements available (averaging $5,400 per year); institutionally sponsored loans and unspecified assistantships also available. Support available to part-time students. Financial award application deadline: 3/15; financial award applicants required to submit FAFSA. *Unit head:* Dr. Daniel H. Yocom, Graduate Program Coordinator, 717-872-3338, Fax: 717-872-3905, E-mail: daniel.yocom@millersville.edu. *Application contact:* Dr. Victor S. DeSantis, Dean of Graduate and Professional Studies, 717-872-3099, Fax: 717-872-3453, E-mail: victor.desantis@millersville.edu.

Mills College, Graduate Studies, Pre-Medical Studies Program, Oakland, CA 94613-1000. Offers Certificate. Part-time programs available. *Faculty:* 11 full-time (6 women), 10 part-time/adjunct (7 women). *Students:* 61 full-time (49 women), 2 part-time (both women); includes 11 minority (9 Asian Americans or Pacific Islanders, 2 Hispanic Americans), 2 international. Average age 25. 154 applicants, 82% accepted, 41 enrolled. In 2009, 27 Certificates awarded. *Entrance requirements:* For degree, GRE General Test, bachelor's degree in a non-science

area. Additional exam requirements/recommendations for international students: Required—TOEFL. *Application deadline:* For fall admission, 2/1 for domestic and international students. Applications are processed on a rolling basis. Application fee: $50. Electronic applications accepted. *Expenses:* Tuition: Full-time $26,326; part-time $6584 per course. Required fees: $896. One-time fee: $896 part-time. Tuition and fees vary according to program. *Financial support:* In 2009–10, 40 students received support, including 21 fellowships (averaging $5,477 per year), 10 teaching assistantships with partial tuition reimbursements available (averaging $5,782 per year); institutionally sponsored loans and scholarships/grants also available. Support available to part-time students. Financial award application deadline: 2/1; financial award applicants required to submit FAFSA. *Faculty research:* Bacterial and viral genetics, microbiology, lipid biochemistry, inorganic nitrogen chemistry. *Unit head:* Dr. John Brabson, Head, 510-430-2203, Fax: 510-430-3314, E-mail: johnb@mills.edu. *Application contact:* Jessica King, Graduate Admission Specialist, 510-430-3305, Fax: 510-430-2159, E-mail: grad-studies@mills.edu.

Minnesota State University Mankato, College of Graduate Studies, College of Science, Engineering and Technology, Department of Biological Sciences, Mankato, MN 56001. Offers biology (MS); biology education (MS); environmental sciences (MS). Part-time programs available. *Students:* 9 full-time (2 women), 40 part-time (17 women). *Degree requirements:* For master's, one foreign language, comprehensive exam, thesis or alternative. *Entrance requirements:* For master's, minimum GPA of 3.0 during previous 2 years of course work. Additional exam requirements/recommendations for international students: Required—TOEFL. *Application deadline:* For fall admission, 7/1 priority date for domestic students; for spring admission, 11/1 for domestic students. Applications are processed on a rolling basis. Application fee: $40. Electronic applications accepted. *Expenses:* Tuition, state resident: full-time $5364. Tuition, nonresident: full-time $8314. *Financial support:* Fellowships, research assistantships with full tuition reimbursements, teaching assistantships with full tuition reimbursements, career-related internships or fieldwork, Federal Work-Study, institutionally sponsored loans, and unspecified assistantships available. Support available to part-time students. Financial award application deadline: 3/15; financial award applicants required to submit FAFSA. *Faculty research:* Limnology, enzyme analysis, membrane engineering, converters. *Unit head:* Dr. Penny Knoblich, Chairperson, 507-389-5736. *Application contact:* 507-389-2321, E-mail: grad@mnsu.edu.

Mississippi College, Graduate School, College of Arts and Sciences, School of Science and Mathematics, Department of Biological Sciences, Clinton, MS 39058. Offers biological science (M Ed); biology (MCS); biology-biological sciences (MS); biology-medical sciences (MS). Part-time programs available. *Faculty:* 6 full-time (1 woman), 2 part-time/adjunct (1 woman). *Students:* 113 full-time (53 women), 42 part-time (25 women); includes 64 minority (39 African Americans, 19 Asian Americans or Pacific Islanders, 6 Hispanic Americans), 11 international. Average age 25. In 2009, 72 master's awarded. *Degree requirements:* For master's, comprehensive exam, thesis optional. *Entrance requirements:* For master's, GRE General Test, minimum GPA of 2.5. Additional exam requirements/recommendations for international students: Recommended—IELTS. *Application deadline:* For fall admission, 8/15 priority date for domestic students. Applications are processed on a rolling basis. Application fee: $25. Electronic applications accepted. *Expenses:* Tuition: Part-time $452 per credit hour. Required fees: $101 per semester. Tuition and fees vary according to degree level, campus/location, program and student level. *Financial support:* Career-related internships or fieldwork, Federal Work-Study, and unspecified assistantships available. Support available to part-time students. Financial award application deadline: 4/1; financial award applicants required to submit FAFSA. *Application contact:* Elnora Lewis, Secretary, 601-925-3225, Fax: 601-925-3889, E-mail: lewis09@mc.edu.

Mississippi State University, College of Arts and Sciences, Department of Biological Sciences, Mississippi State, MS 39762. Offers biological sciences (MS, PhD); general biology (MS). Postbaccalaureate distance learning degree programs offered (minimal on-campus study). *Faculty:* 14 full-time (8 women), 1 part-time/adjunct (0 women). *Students:* 38 full-time (23 women), 131 part-time (94 women); includes 25 minority (20 African Americans, 2 American Indian/Alaska Native, 1 Asian American or Pacific Islander, 2 Hispanic Americans), 13 international. Average age 34. 150 applicants, 63% accepted, 78 enrolled. In 2009, 6 master's, 1 doctorate awarded. Terminal master's awarded for partial completion of doctoral program. *Degree requirements:* For master's, one foreign language, thesis, comprehensive oral or written exam; for doctorate, one foreign language, thesis/dissertation, comprehensive oral or written exam. *Entrance requirements:* For master's, GRE General Test, minimum GPA of 2.75 on last two years of undergraduate courses; for doctorate, GRE General Test. Additional exam requirements/recommendations for international students: Required—TOEFL (minimum score 550 paper-based; 213 computer-based; 79 iBT). *Application deadline:* For fall admission, 7/1 for domestic students, 5/1 for international students; for spring admission, 11/1 for domestic students, 9/1 for international students. Applications are processed on a rolling basis. Application fee: $40. Electronic applications accepted. *Expenses:* Tuition, state resident: full-time $2575.50; part-time $286.25 per credit hour. Tuition, nonresident: full-time $6510; part-time $723.50 per credit hour. Tuition and fees vary according to course load. *Financial support:* In 2009–10, 7 research assistantships with full and partial tuition reimbursements (averaging $12,605 per year), 29 teaching assistantships with full and partial tuition reimbursements (averaging $14,285 per year) were awarded; Federal Work-Study, institutionally sponsored loans, scholarships/grants, and unspecified assistantships also available. Financial award applicants required to submit FAFSA. *Faculty research:* Botany, zoology, microbiology, ecology. Total annual research expenditures: $5.8 million. *Unit head:* Dr. Nancy Reichert, Professor/Head, 662-325-3483, Fax: 662-325-7939, E-mail: nreichert@biology.msstate.edu. *Application contact:* Dr. Gary Ervin, Associate Dean/Graduate Coordinator, 662-325-1203, Fax: 662-325-7939, E-mail: gervin@biology.msstate.edu.

Missouri State University, Graduate College, College of Natural and Applied Sciences, Department of Biology, Springfield, MO 65897. Offers biology (MS); natural and applied science (MNAS), including biology (MNAS, MS Ed); secondary education (MS Ed), including biology (MNAS, MS Ed). *Faculty:* 18 full-time (3 women), 6 part-time/adjunct (1 woman). *Students:* 25 full-time (13 women), 22 part-time (10 women); includes 2 minority (1 American Indian/Alaska Native, 1 Asian American or Pacific Islander), 3 international. Average age 26. 17 applicants, 94% accepted, 10 enrolled. In 2009, 20 master's awarded. *Degree requirements:* For master's, comprehensive exam, thesis or alternative. *Entrance requirements:* For master's, GRE (MS, MNAS), 24 hours of course work in biology (MS); minimum GPA of 3.0 (MS, MNAS), 9-12 teacher certification (MS Ed). Additional exam requirements/recommendations for international students: Required—TOEFL (minimum score 550 paper-based; 213 computer-based; 79 iBT). *Application deadline:* For fall admission, 7/20 priority date for domestic students, 5/1 for international students; for spring admission, 12/20 priority date for domestic students, 9/1 for international students. Applications are processed on a rolling basis. Application fee: $35 ($50 for international students). Electronic applications accepted. *Expenses:* Tuition, state resident: full-time $3852; part-time $214 per credit hour. Tuition, nonresident: full-time $7524; part-time $418 per credit hour. Required fees: $696; $172 per semester. Tuition and fees vary according to course level, course load, degree level and program. *Financial support:* In 2009–10, 4 research assistantships with full tuition reimbursements (averaging $9,730 per year), 23 teaching assistantships with full tuition reimbursements (averaging $8,372 per year) were awarded; Federal Work-Study, institutionally sponsored loans, scholarships/grants, and unspecified assistantships also available. Financial award application deadline: 3/31; financial award applicants required to submit FAFSA. *Faculty research:* Hibernation physiology of bats, behavioral ecology of salamanders, mussel conservation, plant evolution and systematics, cellular/molecular mechanisms involved in migraine pathology. *Unit head:* Dr. S. Alicia Mathis, Head, 417-836-5126, Fax: 417-836-6934, E-mail: biology@missouristate.edu. *Application contact:* Dr. Eric Eckert, Coordinator of Graduate Admissions and Recruitment, 417-836-5331, Fax: 417-836-6200, E-mail: ericeckert@missouristate.edu.

Missouri University of Science and Technology, Graduate School, Department of Biological Sciences, Rolla, MO 65409. Offers applied and environmental biology (MS). *Entrance*

Biological and Biomedical Sciences—General

Missouri University of Science and Technology *(continued)*
requirements: For master's, GRE (minimum score 600 quantitative, 4 writing). Additional exam requirements/recommendations for international students: Required—TOEFL (minimum score 570 paper-based; 230 computer-based).

Montana State University, College of Graduate Studies, College of Letters and Science, Department of Cell Biology and Neuroscience, Bozeman, MT 59717. Offers biological sciences (PhD); neuroscience (MS, PhD). Part-time programs available. *Faculty:* 6 full-time (1 woman), 2 part-time/adjunct (1 woman). *Students:* 1 full-time (0 women), 4 part-time (1 woman). Average age 28. 31 applicants, 58% accepted. *Degree requirements:* For master's, comprehensive exam; for doctorate, comprehensive exam, thesis/dissertation. *Entrance requirements:* For master's and doctorate, GRE General Test. Additional exam requirements/ recommendations for international students: Required—TOEFL (minimum score 550 paper-based; 213 computer-based). *Application deadline:* For fall admission, 7/15 priority date for domestic students, 5/15 priority date for international students; for spring admission, 12/1 priority date for domestic students, 10/1 priority date for international students. Applications are processed on a rolling basis. Application fee: $30. Electronic applications accepted. *Expenses:* Tuition, state resident: full-time $5635; part-time $3492 per year. Tuition, nonresident: full-time $17,212; part-time $7865.10 per year. Required fees: $1441; $153.15 per credit. Tuition and fees vary according to course load and program. *Financial support:* In 2009–10, research assistantships with full and partial tuition reimbursements (averaging $22,000 per year), 8 teaching assistantships (averaging $10,500 per year) were awarded; health care benefits and unspecified assistantships also available. Financial award application deadline: 3/1; financial award applicants required to submit FAFSA. *Faculty research:* Development of the nervous system, neuronal mechanisms of visual perception, ion channel biophysics, mechanisms of sensory coding, neuroinformatics. Total annual research expenditures: $2.7 million. *Unit head:* Dr. Thomas Hughes, Head, 406-994-5395, Fax: 406-994-7077, E-mail: thughes@montana.edu. *Application contact:* Dr. Carl A. Fox, Vice Provost for Graduate Education, 406-994-4145, Fax: 406-994-7433, E-mail: gradstudy@montana.edu.

Montclair State University, The Graduate School, College of Science and Mathematics, Department of Biology and Molecular Biology, Montclair, NJ 07043-1624. Offers biology (MS), including biology science education, molecular biology; molecular biology (Certificate). Part-time and evening/weekend programs available. *Faculty:* 21 full-time (8 women), 27 part-time/adjunct (13 women). *Students:* 35 full-time (23 women), 57 part-time (44 women). Average age 28. 53 applicants, 64% accepted, 23 enrolled. In 2009, 26 master's, 2 other advanced degrees awarded. *Degree requirements:* For master's, comprehensive exam, thesis or alternative. *Entrance requirements:* For master's, GRE General Test, 24 credits of course work in undergraduate biology, 2 letters of recommendation, teaching certificate (biology sciences education concentration). Additional exam requirements/recommendations for international students: Required—TOEFL (minimum iBT score of 83) or IELTS. *Application deadline:* For fall admission, 6/1 for international students; for spring admission, 10/1 for international students. Applications are processed on a rolling basis. Application fee: $60. Electronic applications accepted. *Expenses:* Tuition, area resident: Part-time $486.74 per credit. Tuition, state resident: part-time $486.74 per credit. Tuition, nonresident: part-time $751.34 per credit. Tuition and fees vary according to degree level and program. *Financial support:* In 2009–10, 13 research assistantships with full tuition reimbursements (averaging $7,000 per year) were awarded; Federal Work-Study, scholarships/grants, and unspecified assistantships also available. Support available to part-time students. Financial award application deadline: 3/1; financial award applicants required to submit FAFSA. *Faculty research:* Cells, algae blooms, scallops, New Jersey bays, Barnegat Bay. *Unit head:* Dr. Quinn Vega, Chairperson, 973-655-7178. *Application contact:* Amy Aiello, Director of Graduate Admissions and Operations, 973-655-5147, Fax: 973-655-7869, E-mail: graduate.school@montclair.edu.

Morehead State University, Graduate Programs, College of Science and Technology, Department of Biology and Chemistry, Morehead, KY 40351. Offers biology (MS); biology regional analysis (MS). Part-time programs available. *Faculty:* 8 full-time (2 women). *Students:* 10 full-time (6 women), 2 part-time (both women); includes 1 minority (African American), 4 international. Average age 26. 12 applicants, 83% accepted, 7 enrolled. In 2009, 8 master's awarded. *Degree requirements:* For master's, comprehensive exam, thesis optional, oral and written final exams. *Entrance requirements:* For master's, GRE General Test, minimum GPA of 3.0 in biology, 2.5 overall; undergraduate major/minor in biology, environmental science, or equivalent. Additional exam requirements/recommendations for international students: Required—TOEFL (minimum score 525 paper-based; 173 computer-based). *Application deadline:* For fall admission, 8/1 priority date for domestic and international students; for spring admission, 12/1 priority date for domestic and international students. Applications are processed on a rolling basis. Application fee: $30. Electronic applications accepted. *Expenses:* Tuition, state resident: full-time $6318; part-time $351 per credit hour. Tuition, nonresident: full-time $15,804; part-time $878 per credit hour. *Financial support:* In 2009–10, 7 teaching assistantships (averaging $10,000 per year) were awarded; career-related internships or fieldwork, Federal Work-Study, and unspecified assistantships also available. Financial award application deadline: 3/15; financial award applicants required to submit FAFSA. *Faculty research:* Atherosclerosis, RNA evolution, cancer biology, water quality/ecology, immunoparasitology. *Unit head:* Dr. Doug Dennis, Chair, 606-783-2944, Fax: 606-783-5002, E-mail: d.dennis@ moreheadstate.edu. *Application contact:* Michelle Barber, Graduate Recruitment and Retention Assistant Director, 606-783-5127, Fax: 606-783-5061, E-mail: m.barber@moreheadstate.edu.

Morehouse School of Medicine, Graduate Programs in Biomedical Sciences, Atlanta, GA 30310-1495. Offers biomedical research (MS); biomedical sciences (PhD); biomedical technology (MS). *Faculty:* 52 full-time (17 women), 7 part-time/adjunct (2 women). *Students:* 31 full-time (19 women); includes 18 minority (all African Americans). Average age 28. 21 applicants, 38% accepted, 6 enrolled. In 2009, 3 doctorates awarded. *Degree requirements:* For master's, thesis (for some programs); for doctorate, thesis/dissertation. *Entrance requirements:* For doctorate, GRE General Test. Additional exam requirements/recommendations for international students: Required—TOEFL (minimum score 550 paper-based; 200 computer-based). *Application deadline:* For fall admission, 10/1 for domestic and international students; for spring admission, 2/1 for domestic and international students. Application fee: $50. Electronic applications accepted. *Expenses:* Contact institution. *Financial support:* Fellowships with full and partial tuition reimbursements, career-related internships or fieldwork, institutionally sponsored loans, scholarships/grants, traineeships, health care benefits, and tuition waivers (full) available. Financial award application deadline: 5/1; financial award applicants required to submit FAFSA. *Unit head:* Dr. Douglas Paulsen, Director, 404-752-1559. *Application contact:* Dr. Sterling Roaf, Director of Admissions, 404-752-1650, Fax: 404-752-1512, E-mail: phdadmissions@msm.edu.

See Close-Up on page 99.

Morgan State University, School of Graduate Studies, School of Computer, Mathematical, and Natural Sciences, Department of Biology, Baltimore, MD 21251. Offers bioenvironmental science (PhD); biology (MS). *Degree requirements:* For master's, comprehensive exam, thesis. *Entrance requirements:* For master's, minimum GPA of 3.0.

Mount Allison University, Department of Biology, Sackville, NB E4L 1E4, Canada. Offers M Sc. *Degree requirements:* For master's, thesis. *Entrance requirements:* For master's, honors degree. *Faculty research:* Ecology, evolution, physiology, behavior, biochemistry.

Mount Sinai School of Medicine of New York University, Graduate School of Biological Sciences, New York, NY 10029-6504. Offers bioethics (MS); biological sciences (PhD); clinical research (MS); community medicine (MPH); genetic counseling (MS); neurosciences (PhD); MD/PhD. Terminal master's awarded for partial completion of doctoral program. *Degree requirements:* For master's, thesis; for doctorate, comprehensive exam, thesis/dissertation. *Entrance requirements:* For master's, GRE General Test; for doctorate, GRE General Test, GRE Subject Test, 3 years of college pre-med course work. Additional exam requirements/

recommendations for international students: Required—TOEFL. Electronic applications accepted. *Faculty research:* Cancer, genetics and genomics, immunology, neuroscience, developmental and stem cell biology, translational research.

Murray State University, College of Science, Engineering and Technology, Program in Biological Sciences, Murray, KY 42071. Offers MAT, MS, PhD. Part-time programs available. *Degree requirements:* For master's, comprehensive exam, thesis optional. *Entrance requirements:* For master's, GRE General Test. Additional exam requirements/recommendations for international students: Required—TOEFL. *Faculty research:* Aquatic and terrestrial ecology, molecular systematics, micro ecology, cell biology and metabolism, palentology.

New Jersey Institute of Technology, Office of Graduate Studies, College of Science and Liberal Arts, Federated Department of Biological Sciences, Program in Biology, Newark, NJ 07102. Offers MS, PhD. Part-time and evening/weekend programs available. *Entrance requirements:* For master's, GRE General Test. Additional exam requirements/recommendations for international students: Required—TOEFL (minimum score 550 paper-based; 213 computer-based; 79 iBT). Electronic applications accepted. *Faculty research:* Realistic building codes, optimization of training programs, effect of physical and mental fatigue of training.

New Mexico Institute of Mining and Technology, Graduate Studies, Department of Biology, Socorro, NM 87801. Offers MS. Part-time programs available. *Degree requirements:* For master's, thesis. *Entrance requirements:* For master's, GRE General Test. Additional exam requirements/recommendations for international students: Required—TOEFL (minimum score 540 paper-based; 207 computer-based). Electronic applications accepted. *Faculty research:* Molecular biology, evolution and evolutionary ecology, immunology, endocrinology.

New Mexico State University, Graduate School, College of Arts and Sciences, Department of Biology, Las Cruces, NM 88003-8001. Offers MS, PhD. Part-time programs available. *Faculty:* 22 full-time (10 women). *Students:* 77 full-time (49 women), 9 part-time (6 women); includes 18 minority (4 African Americans, 1 American Indian/Alaska Native, 13 Hispanic Americans), 28 international. Average age 31. 49 applicants, 90% accepted, 18 enrolled. In 2009, 10 master's, 8 doctorates awarded. *Degree requirements:* For master's, thesis (for some programs); for doctorate, comprehensive exam, thesis/dissertation. *Entrance requirements:* Additional exam requirements/recommendations for international students: Required—TOEFL. *Application deadline:* For fall admission, 1/15 priority date for domestic students; for spring admission, 10/5 priority date for domestic students. Applications are processed on a rolling basis. Application fee: $30 ($50 for international students). Electronic applications accepted. *Expenses:* Tuition, state resident: full-time $4080; part-time $223 per credit. Tuition, nonresident: full-time $14,256; part-time $647 per credit. Required fees: $1278; $639 per semester. *Financial support:* In 2009–10, 25 research assistantships (averaging $14,338 per year), 34 teaching assistantships (averaging $15,163 per year) were awarded; fellowships, Federal Work-Study and health care benefits also available. Support available to part-time students. Financial award application deadline: 1/15. *Faculty research:* Microbiology, cell and organismal physiology, ecology and ethology, evolution, genetics, developmental biology. *Unit head:* Dr. Marvin Bernstein, Head, 575-646-3611, Fax: 575-646-5665, E-mail: mbernste@nmsu.edu. *Application contact:* Dr. Marvin Bernstein, Head, 575-646-3611, Fax: 575-646-5665, E-mail: mbernste@nmsu.edu.

New York Medical College, Graduate School of Basic Medical Sciences, Valhalla, NY 10595-1691. Offers MS, PhD, MD/PhD. Part-time and evening/weekend programs available. Terminal master's awarded for partial completion of doctoral program. *Degree requirements:* For master's, thesis; for doctorate, comprehensive exam, thesis/dissertation. *Entrance requirements:* For master's and doctorate, GRE General Test. Additional exam requirements/recommendations for international students: Required—TOEFL. *Expenses:* Tuition: Full-time $18,170; part-time $790 per credit. Required fees: $790 per credit. $20 per semester. One-time fee: $100. Tuition and fees vary according to class time, course level, course load, degree level, program, student level and student's religious affiliation.

See Close-Up on page 101.

New York University, Graduate School of Arts and Science, Department of Biology, New York, NY 10012-1019. Offers biology (PhD); biomedical journalism (MS); cancer and molecular biology (PhD); computational biology (PhD); computers in biological research (MS); developmental genetics (PhD); general biology (MS); immunology and microbiology (PhD); molecular genetics (PhD); neurobiology (PhD); oral biology (MS); plant biology (PhD); recombinant DNA technology (MS); MS/MBA. Part-time programs available. *Faculty:* 24 full-time (5 women). *Students:* 142 full-time (79 women), 44 part-time (28 women); includes 34 minority (1 African American, 25 Asian Americans or Pacific Islanders, 8 Hispanic Americans), 82 international. Average age 27. 362 applicants, 71% accepted, 72 enrolled. In 2009, 43 master's, 9 doctorates awarded. Terminal master's awarded for partial completion of doctoral program. *Degree requirements:* For master's, thesis or alternative, qualifying paper; for doctorate, comprehensive exam, thesis/dissertation. *Entrance requirements:* For master's, GRE General Test; for doctorate, GRE General Test, GRE Subject Test. Additional exam requirements/recommendations for international students: Required—TOEFL. *Application deadline:* For fall admission, 12/12 priority date for domestic students. Application fee: $90. *Expenses:* Tuition: Full-time $30,528; part-time $1272 per credit. Required fees: $2177. *Financial support:* Fellowships with tuition reimbursements, research assistantships with tuition reimbursements, teaching assistantships with tuition reimbursements, career-related internships or fieldwork, Federal Work-Study, institutionally sponsored loans, scholarships/grants, health care benefits, and unspecified assistantships available. Financial award application deadline: 12/12; financial award applicants required to submit FAFSA. *Faculty research:* Genomics, molecular and cell biology, development and molecular genetics, molecular evolution of plants and animals. *Unit head:* Gloria Coruzzi, Chair, 212-998-8200, Fax: 212-995-4015, E-mail: biology@nyu.edu. *Application contact:* Stephen Small, Director of Graduate Studies, 212-998-8200, Fax: 212-995-4015, E-mail: biology@nyu.edu.

New York University, Graduate School of Arts and Science, Department of Environmental Medicine, New York, NY 10012-1019. Offers environmental health sciences (MS, PhD), including biostatistics (PhD), environmental hygiene (MS), epidemiology (PhD), ergonomics and biomechanics (PhD), exposure assessment and health effects (PhD), molecular toxicology/carcinogenesis (PhD), toxicology. Part-time programs available. *Faculty:* 26 full-time (7 women). *Students:* 45 full-time (37 women), 15 part-time (8 women); includes 9 minority (3 African Americans, 3 Asian Americans or Pacific Islanders, 3 Hispanic Americans), 23 international. Average age 31. 60 applicants, 48% accepted, 14 enrolled. In 2009, 11 master's, 10 doctorates awarded. Terminal master's awarded for partial completion of doctoral program. *Degree requirements:* For master's, thesis or alternative; for doctorate, one foreign language, thesis/dissertation, oral and written exams. *Entrance requirements:* For master's and doctorate, GRE General Test, GRE Subject Test, minimum GPA of 3.0; bachelor's degree in biological, physical, or engineering science. Additional exam requirements/recommendations for international students: Required—TOEFL. *Application deadline:* For fall admission, 12/12 for domestic students. Application fee: $90. *Expenses:* Tuition: Full-time $30,528; part-time $1272 per credit. Required fees: $2177. *Financial support:* Fellowships with tuition reimbursements, teaching assistantships with tuition reimbursements, career-related internships or fieldwork, Federal Work-Study, institutionally sponsored loans, and health care benefits available. Financial award application deadline: 12/12; financial award applicants required to submit FAFSA. *Unit head:* Dr. Max Costa, Chair, 845-731-3661, Fax: 845-351-4510, E-mail: ehs@env.med.nyu.edu. *Application contact:* Dr. Jerome J. Solomon, Director of Graduate Studies, 845-731-3661, Fax: 845-351-4510, E-mail: ehs@env.med.nyu.edu.

See Close-Up on page 103.

New York University, School of Medicine and Graduate School of Arts and Science, Medical Scientist Training Program, New York, NY 10012-1019. Offers MD/MS, MD/PhD. Students must be accepted by both the School of Medicine and the Graduate School of Arts and Science. *Faculty:* 170 full-time (36 women). *Students:* 340 applicants, 7% accepted, 9 enrolled. *Application deadline:* For fall admission, 10/15 for domestic students. Application fee: $100.

Electronic applications accepted. *Expenses:* Contact institution. *Financial support:* In 2009–10, 29 fellowships with full tuition reimbursements (averaging $27,000 per year), 47 research assistantships with full tuition reimbursements (averaging $25,000 per year) were awarded; teaching assistantships, health care benefits and unspecified assistantships also available. *Faculty research:* Neurosciences, cell biology and molecular genetics, structural biology, microbial pathogenesis and host defense. Total annual research expenditures: $13 million. *Unit head:* Dr. Rodney E. Ulane, Director, 212-263-2149, Fax: 212-263-3766, E-mail: rodney.ulane@med.nyu.edu. *Application contact:* Cindy D. Meador, Academic Coordinator, 212-263-3767, E-mail: cindy.meador@med.nyu.edu.

North Carolina Agricultural and Technical State University, Graduate School, College of Arts and Sciences, Department of Biology, Greensboro, NC 27411. Offers biology (MS); biology education (MAT). Part-time and evening/weekend programs available. *Degree requirements:* For master's, comprehensive exam, thesis (for some programs), qualifying exam. *Entrance requirements:* For master's, GRE General Test, minimum GPA of 2.6. *Faculty research:* Physical ecology, cytochemistry, botany, parasitology, microbiology.

North Carolina Central University, Division of Academic Affairs, College of Science and Technology, Department of Biology, Durham, NC 27707-3129. Offers MS. *Degree requirements:* For master's, one foreign language, comprehensive exam, thesis. *Entrance requirements:* For master's, GRE, minimum GPA of 3.0 in major, 2.5 overall. Additional exam requirements/recommendations for international students: Required—TOEFL.

North Carolina State University, College of Veterinary Medicine, Program in Comparative Biomedical Sciences, Raleigh, NC 27695. Offers cell biology (MS, PhD); infectious disease (MS, PhD); pathology (MS, PhD); pharmacology (MS, PhD); population medicine (MS, PhD). Part-time programs available. *Degree requirements:* For master's, thesis; for doctorate, thesis/dissertation. *Entrance requirements:* For master's and doctorate, GRE General Test. Additional exam requirements/recommendations for international students: Required—TOEFL (minimum score 550 paper-based; 213 computer-based). Electronic applications accepted. *Expenses:* Contact institution. *Faculty research:* Infectious diseases, cell biology, pharmacology and toxicology, genomics, pathology and population medicine.

North Carolina State University, Graduate School, College of Agriculture and Life Sciences, Raleigh, NC 27695. Offers M Tox, MAE, MB, MBAE, MFG, MFM, MFS, MG, MMB, MN, MP, MS, MZS, Ed D, PhD, Certificate. Part-time programs available. Electronic applications accepted.

North Dakota State University, College of Graduate and Interdisciplinary Studies, College of Science and Mathematics, Department of Biological Sciences, Fargo, ND 58108. Offers biology (MS); botany (MS, PhD); cellular and molecular biology (PhD); environmental and conservation sciences (MS, PhD); genomics (PhD); natural resources management (MS, PhD); zoology (MS, PhD). *Students:* 32 full-time (21 women), 14 part-time (10 women); includes 1 Asian American or Pacific Islander, 14 international. In 2009, 12 master's, 9 doctorates awarded. *Degree requirements:* For master's, thesis; for doctorate, thesis/dissertation. *Entrance requirements:* For master's and doctorate, GRE General Test. Additional exam requirements/recommendations for international students: Required—TOEFL. *Application deadline:* For fall admission, 3/15 priority date for domestic students; for spring admission, 10/30 priority date for domestic students. Applications are processed on a rolling basis. Application fee: $45 ($60 for international students). Electronic applications accepted. *Financial support:* Fellowships with full tuition reimbursements, research assistantships with full tuition reimbursements, teaching assistantships with full tuition reimbursements, career-related internships or fieldwork, Federal Work-Study, institutionally sponsored loans, scholarships/grants, tuition waivers (full), and unspecified assistantships available. Support available to part-time students. Financial award application deadline: 4/15; financial award applicants required to submit FAFSA. *Faculty research:* Comparative endocrinology, physiology, behavioral ecology, plant cell biology, aquatic biology. Total annual research expenditures: $675,000. *Unit head:* Dr. Marinus L. Otte, Head, 701-231-7087, E-mail: marinus.otte@ndsu.edu. *Application contact:* Dr. Marinus L. Otte, Head, 701-231-7087, E-mail: marinus.otte@ndsu.edu.

Northeastern Illinois University, Graduate College, College of Arts and Sciences, Department of Biology, Program in Biology, Chicago, IL 60625-4699. Offers MS. Part-time and evening/weekend programs available. *Degree requirements:* For master's, comprehensive exam, thesis optional. *Entrance requirements:* For master's, minimum GPA of 2.75. Additional exam requirements/recommendations for international students: Required—TOEFL (minimum score 550 paper-based; 213 computer-based; 80 iBT). Electronic applications accepted. *Faculty research:* Paleoecology and freshwater biology; protein biosynthesis and targeting; microbial growth and physiology; molecular biology of antibody production; reptilian neurobiology.

Northeastern University, College of Science, Department of Biology, Boston, MA 02115-5096. Offers bioinformatics (PMS); biology (MS, PhD); biotechnology (MS); marine biology (MS). Part-time programs available. *Faculty:* 27 full-time (10 women), 5 part-time/adjunct (all women). *Students:* 111 full-time (67 women); includes 2 African Americans, 3 Asian Americans or Pacific Islanders, 3 Hispanic Americans, 39 international. 178 applicants, 28% accepted, 35 enrolled. In 2009, 31 master's, 5 doctorates awarded. Terminal master's awarded for partial completion of doctoral program. *Degree requirements:* For master's, thesis (for some programs); for doctorate, thesis/dissertation, qualifying exam. *Entrance requirements:* For master's and doctorate, GRE General Test. Additional exam requirements/recommendations for international students: Required—TOEFL (minimum score 250 computer-based). *Application deadline:* For fall admission, 1/1 priority date for domestic and international students. Applications are processed on a rolling basis. Application fee: $50. Electronic applications accepted. *Financial support:* In 2009–10, 19 research assistantships with tuition reimbursements (averaging $18,285 per year), 41 teaching assistantships with tuition reimbursements (averaging $18,285 per year) were awarded; fellowships with tuition reimbursements, career-related internships or fieldwork, Federal Work-Study, tuition waivers (full and partial), and unspecified assistantships also available. Financial award application deadline: 3/1; financial award applicants required to submit FAFSA. *Faculty research:* Biochemistry, marine sciences, molecular biology, microbiology and immunology neurobiology, cellular and molecular biology, biochemistry, marine biochemistry and ecology, microbiology, neurobiology, biotechnology. *Unit head:* Dr. Wendy Smith, Graduate Coordinator, 617-373-2260, Fax: 617-373-3724, E-mail: gradbio@neu.edu. *Application contact:* Jo-Anne Dickinson, Admissions Assistant, 617-373-5990, Fax: 617-373-7281, E-mail: gsas@neu.edu.

Northern Arizona University, Graduate College, College of Engineering, Forestry and Natural Sciences, Department of Biological Sciences, Flagstaff, AZ 86011. Offers MS, PhD. *Faculty:* 46 full-time (15 women). *Students:* 79 full-time (40 women), 16 part-time (8 women); includes 6 minority (1 American Indian/Alaska Native, 2 Asian Americans or Pacific Islanders, 3 Hispanic Americans), 4 international. Average age 30. 71 applicants, 44% accepted, 26 enrolled. In 2009, 18 master's, 8 doctorates awarded. *Degree requirements:* For master's, final exam (MAT), thesis (MS), oral exam; for doctorate, thesis/dissertation. *Entrance requirements:* For master's, GRE General Test, GRE Subject Test; for doctorate, GRE General Test. Additional exam requirements/recommendations for international students: Required—TOEFL (minimum score 550 paper-based; 213 computer-based; 80 iBT), IELTS (minimum score 7). *Application deadline:* For fall admission, 2/15 priority date for domestic students. Application fee: $65. Electronic applications accepted. *Financial support:* In 2009–10, 43 research assistantships with partial tuition reimbursements (averaging $13,164 per year), 37 teaching assistantships with partial tuition reimbursements (averaging $13,164 per year) were awarded; Federal Work-Study, traineeships, health care benefits, and tuition waivers also available. Support available to part-time students. Financial award application deadline: 3/30; financial award applicants required to submit FAFSA. *Faculty research:* Genetic levels of trophic levels, plant hybrid zones, insect biodiversity, natural history and cognition of wild jays. Total annual research expenditures: $2.2 million. *Unit head:* Dr. Maribeth Watwood, Chair, 928-523-9322, Fax: 928-523-7500, E-mail: maribeth.watwood@nau.edu. *Application contact:* Dr. Steven Hempleman, Associate Chair, 928-523-7220, Fax: 928-523-7500, E-mail: steven.hempleman@nau.edu.

Northern Illinois University, Graduate School, College of Liberal Arts and Sciences, Department of Biological Sciences, De Kalb, IL 60115-2854. Offers MS, PhD. Part-time programs available. *Faculty:* 30 full-time (6 women), 7 part-time/adjunct (1 woman). *Students:* 39 full-time (20 women), 47 part-time (30 women); includes 6 minority (1 American Indian/Alaska Native, 3 Asian Americans or Pacific Islanders, 2 Hispanic Americans), 16 international. Average age 30. 101 applicants, 42% accepted, 20 enrolled. In 2009, 15 master's, 2 doctorates awarded. Terminal master's awarded for partial completion of doctoral program. *Degree requirements:* For master's, comprehensive exam, thesis optional; for doctorate, thesis/dissertation, candidacy exam, dissertation defense. *Entrance requirements:* For master's, GRE General Test, bachelor's degree in related field, minimum GPA of 2.75; for doctorate, GRE General Test, bachelor's or master's degree in related field; minimum undergraduate GPA of 2.75, graduate 3.2. Additional exam requirements/recommendations for international students: Required—TOEFL (minimum score 550 paper-based; 213 computer-based). *Application deadline:* For fall admission, 6/1 for domestic students, 5/1 for international students; for spring admission, 11/1 for domestic students, 10/1 for international students. Applications are processed on a rolling basis. Application fee: $30. Electronic applications accepted. *Expenses:* Tuition, state resident: full-time $6576; part-time $274 per credit hour. Tuition, nonresident: full-time $13,152; part-time $548 per credit hour. Required fees: $1813; $75.53 per credit hour. Part-time tuition and fees vary according to course load. *Financial support:* In 2009–10, 3 research assistantships with full tuition reimbursements, 35 teaching assistantships with full tuition reimbursements were awarded; fellowships with full tuition reimbursements, career-related internships or fieldwork, Federal Work-Study, scholarships/grants, tuition waivers (full), and unspecified assistantships also available. Support available to part-time students. Financial award applicants required to submit FAFSA. *Faculty research:* Plant molecular biology, neurosecretory control, ethnobotany, organellar genomes, carbon metabolism. *Unit head:* Dr. Carl VanEnde, Acting Chair, 815-753-1753, Fax: 815-753-0461, E-mail: cvonende@niu.edu. *Application contact:* Dr. Carl von Ende, Director of Graduate Studies, 815-753-7826.

Northern Michigan University, College of Graduate Studies, College of Arts and Sciences, Department of Biology, Marquette, MI 49855-5301. Offers MS. Part-time programs available. Postbaccalaureate distance learning degree programs offered (minimal on-campus study). *Degree requirements:* For master's, thesis or alternative. *Entrance requirements:* For master's, GRE, minimum GPA of 3.0. *Faculty research:* Molecular genetics of sex-linked genes, biology of protozoan parasites, wildlife ecology, organochlorines in the environment, insect development.

Northwestern University, The Graduate School and Judd A. and Marjorie Weinberg College of Arts and Sciences, Interdepartmental Biological Sciences Program (IBiS), Evanston, IL 60208. Offers biochemistry, molecular biology, and cell biology (PhD), including biochemistry, cell and molecular biology, molecular biophysics, structural biology; biotechnology (PhD); cell and molecular biology (PhD); developmental biology and genetics (PhD); hormone action and signal transduction (PhD); neuroscience (PhD); structural biology, biochemistry, and biophysics (PhD). Program participants include the Departments of Biochemistry, Molecular Biology, and Cell Biology; Chemistry; Neurobiology and Physiology; Chemical Engineering; Civil Engineering; and Evanston Hospital. *Degree requirements:* For doctorate, thesis/dissertation, qualifying exam. *Entrance requirements:* For doctorate, GRE General Test. Additional exam requirements/recommendations for international students: Required—TOEFL (minimum score 600 paper-based). Electronic applications accepted. *Faculty research:* Developmental genetics, gene regulation, DNA-protein interactions, biological clocks, bioremediation.

Northwestern University, Northwestern University Feinberg School of Medicine, Combined MD/PhD Medical Scientist Training Program, Evanston, IL 60208. Offers MD/PhD. Application must be made to both The Graduate School and the Medical School. *Accreditation:* LCME/AMA. Electronic applications accepted. *Faculty research:* Cardiovascular epidemiology, cancer epidemiology, nutritional interventions for the prevention of cardiovascular disease and cancer, women's health, outcomes research.

Northwestern University, Northwestern University Feinberg School of Medicine and Interdepartmental Programs, Integrated Graduate Programs in the Life Sciences, Chicago, IL 60611. Offers cancer biology (PhD); cell biology (PhD); developmental biology (PhD); evolutionary biology (PhD); immunology and microbial pathogenesis (PhD); molecular biology and genetics (PhD); neurobiology (PhD); pharmacology and toxicology (PhD); structural biology and biochemistry (PhD). *Degree requirements:* For doctorate, comprehensive exam, thesis/dissertation, written and oral qualifying exams. *Entrance requirements:* For doctorate, GRE General Test. Additional exam requirements/recommendations for international students: Required—TOEFL (minimum score 600 paper-based; 250 computer-based). Electronic applications accepted.

Northwest Missouri State University, Graduate School, College of Arts and Sciences, Department of Biology, Maryville, MO 64468-6001. Offers MS. Part-time programs available. *Faculty:* 9 full-time (2 women). *Students:* 2 full-time (0 women), 4 part-time (3 women), 1 international. 8 applicants, 88% accepted, 4 enrolled. *Degree requirements:* For master's, comprehensive exam, thesis. *Entrance requirements:* For master's, GRE General Test, minimum GPA of 3.0 in last 60 hours or 2.75 overall, writing sample. Additional exam requirements/recommendations for international students: Required—TOEFL (minimum score 550 paper-based; 213 computer-based). *Application deadline:* For fall admission, 7/1 for domestic and international students; for spring admission, 11/15 for domestic and international students. Applications are processed on a rolling basis. Application fee: $0 ($50 for international students). *Expenses:* Tuition, state resident: part-time $296.34 per credit hour. Tuition, nonresident: part-time $510.43 per credit hour. *Financial support:* In 2009–10, 4 teaching assistantships with full tuition reimbursements (averaging $6,000 per year) were awarded; tutorial assistantships also available. Financial award application deadline: 4/1; financial award applicants required to submit FAFSA. *Unit head:* Dr. Gregg Dieringer, Chairperson, 660-562-1812. *Application contact:* Dr. Gregory Haddock, Dean of Graduate School, 660-562-1145, Fax: 660-562-1096, E-mail: gradsch@nwmissouri.edu.

Notre Dame de Namur University, Division of Academic Affairs, College of Arts and Sciences, Department of Natural Sciences, Belmont, CA 94002-1908. Offers premedical studies (Certificate). Application fee: $60. *Expenses:* Tuition: Part-time $720 per credit. Required fees: $35 per semester hour. *Financial support:* Available to part-time students. Applicants required to submit FAFSA. *Unit head:* Dr. Isabelle Haithcox, Chair, 650-508-3496, E-mail: ihaithcox@ndnu.edu. *Application contact:* Candace Hallmark, Associate Director of Admissions, 650-508-3592, Fax: 650-508-3426, E-mail: grad.admit@ndnu.edu.

Nova Southeastern University, Health Professions Division, College of Allied Health and Nursing, Department of Physician Assistant Studies, Fort Lauderdale, FL 33314-7796. Offers medical science/physician assistant (MMS). Students enter program as undergraduates. *Accreditation:* ARC-PA. *Faculty:* 15 full-time (4 women). *Students:* 449 full-time (335 women), 9 part-time (6 women); includes 102 minority (14 African Americans, 2 American Indian/Alaska Native, 30 Asian Americans or Pacific Islanders, 56 Hispanic Americans), 4 international. Average age 25. 769 applicants, 17% accepted, 87 enrolled. In 2009, 128 master's awarded. *Entrance requirements:* For master's, GRE, minimum GPA of 2.9. *Application deadline:* Applications are processed on a rolling basis. Application fee: $170. Electronic applications accepted. *Expenses:* Contact institution. *Financial support:* In 2009–10, 130 students received support. *Unit head:* Bill Marquardt, Chair and Program Director, 954-262-1252, E-mail: marquard@nsu.nova.edu. *Application contact:* Judy Dickman, Admissions Counselor, 954-262-1109, E-mail: dickman@nsu.nova.edu.

Nova Southeastern University, Health Professions Division, College of Medical Sciences, Fort Lauderdale, FL 33314-7796. Offers biomedical sciences (MBS). *Faculty:* 32 full-time (13 women), 4 part-time/adjunct (1 woman). *Students:* 30 full-time (18 women), 1 (woman) part-time; includes 14 minority (2 African Americans, 5 Asian Americans or Pacific Islanders, 7 Hispanic Americans). Average age 27. 108 applicants, 23% accepted. In 2009, 1 master's

Biological and Biomedical Sciences—General

Nova Southeastern University (continued)
awarded. *Degree requirements:* For master's, thesis. *Entrance requirements:* For master's, MCAT, DAT, minimum GPA of 2.5. *Application deadline:* For spring admission, 4/15 for domestic students. Applications are processed on a rolling basis. Application fee: $50. *Expenses:* Contact institution. *Financial support:* Applicants required to submit FAFSA. *Faculty research:* Neurophysiology, mucosal immunology, allergies involving the lungs, cardiovascular physiology parasitology. Total annual research expenditures: $125,000. *Unit head:* Dr. Harold E. Laubach, Dean, 954-262-1303, Fax: 954-262-1802, E-mail: harold@nsu.nova.edu. *Application contact:* Richard Wilson, Admissions Counselor, 954-262-1111, Fax: 954-262-1802, E-mail: rwilson@nsu.nova.edu.

Oakland University, Graduate Study and Lifelong Learning, College of Arts and Sciences, Department of Biological Sciences, Rochester, MI 48309-4401. Offers biological sciences (MA, MS); biomedical sciences: biological communications (PhD). *Degree requirements:* For master's, thesis. *Entrance requirements:* For master's, GRE Subject Test, GRE General Test, minimum GPA of 3.0 for unconditional admission. Additional exam requirements/recommendations for international students: Required—TOEFL (minimum score 550 paper-based; 213 computer-based). Electronic applications accepted. *Expenses:* Contact institution. *Faculty research:* Mechanism producing rhythmic beating in cilia and flagella, biochemical characterization of carbofuron hydroxylase, maize as a model system to study helitron-related transposable elements, genetic mapping of estrogen-induced endothelial growth factor on rat chromosomes.

Occidental College, Graduate Studies, Department of Biology, Los Angeles, CA 90041-3314. Offers MA. Part-time programs available. *Degree requirements:* For master's, thesis, final exam. *Entrance requirements:* For master's, GRE General Test, GRE Subject Test, minimum GPA of 3.0. Additional exam requirements/recommendations for international students: Required—TOEFL (minimum score 625 paper-based; 263 computer-based). *Expenses:* Contact institution.

The Ohio State University, College of Medicine, School of Biomedical Science, Integrated Biomedical Science Graduate Program, Columbus, OH 43210. Offers immunology (PhD); medical genetics (PhD); molecular virology (PhD); pharmacology (PhD). *Degree requirements:* For doctorate, thesis/dissertation. *Entrance requirements:* For doctorate, GRE, GRE Subject Test in biochemistry, cell and molecular biology (recommended for some). Additional exam requirements/recommendations for international students: Required—TOEFL (minimum score 600 paper-based; 250 computer-based). Electronic applications accepted. *Expenses:* Tuition, state resident: full-time $10,683. Tuition, nonresident: full-time $25,923. Tuition and fees vary according to course load and program.

The Ohio State University, College of Medicine, School of Biomedical Science, Program in Medical Science, Columbus, OH 43210. Offers PhD. Part-time and evening/weekend programs available. Terminal master's awarded for partial completion of doctoral program. *Degree requirements:* For doctorate, thesis/dissertation. *Entrance requirements:* For doctorate, MCAT. Electronic applications accepted. *Expenses:* Contact institution.

The Ohio State University, Graduate School, College of Biological Sciences, Columbus, OH 43210. Offers MS, PhD. Part-time programs available. *Faculty:* 429. *Students:* 191 full-time (99 women), 259 part-time (128 women); includes 34 minority (7 African Americans, 20 Asian Americans or Pacific Islanders, 7 Hispanic Americans), 220 international. Average age 27. In 2009, 26 master's, 58 doctorates awarded. *Degree requirements:* For doctorate, thesis/dissertation. *Entrance requirements:* For master's and doctorate, GRE General Test, GRE Subject Test in biology or biochemistry (recommended). Additional exam requirements/recommendations for international students: Required—TOEFL (minimum score 600 paper-based; 250 computer-based). *Application deadline:* For fall admission, 8/15 priority date for domestic students, 7/1 priority date for international students; for winter admission, 12/1 priority date for domestic students, 11/1 priority date for international students; for spring admission, 3/1 priority date for domestic students, 2/1 priority date for international students. Applications are processed on a rolling basis. Application fee: $40 ($50 for international students). Electronic applications accepted. *Expenses:* Tuition, state resident: full-time $10,683. Tuition, nonresident: full-time $25,923. Tuition and fees vary according to course load and program. *Financial support:* Fellowships, research assistantships, teaching assistantships, career-related internships or fieldwork, Federal Work-Study, and institutionally sponsored loans available. Support available to part-time students. *Unit head:* Dr. Matt Platz, Dean, 614-292-8908, Fax: 614-292-1538, E-mail: dean@biosci.ohio-state.edu. *Application contact:* 614-292-9444, Fax: 614-292-3985, E-mail: domestic.grad@osu.edu.

Ohio University, Graduate College, College of Arts and Sciences, Department of Biological Sciences, Athens, OH 45701-2979. Offers biological sciences (MS, PhD); cell biology and physiology (MS, PhD); ecology and evolutionary biology (MS, PhD); exercise physiology and muscle biology (MS, PhD); microbiology (MS, PhD); neuroscience (MS, PhD). *Faculty:* 50 full-time (14 women), 6 part-time/adjunct (1 woman). *Students:* 44 full-time (19 women), 8 part-time (3 women); includes 2 minority (1 African American, 1 Hispanic American), 21 international. 95 applicants, 24% accepted, 10 enrolled. In 2009, 4 master's, 9 doctorates awarded. Terminal master's awarded for partial completion of doctoral program. *Degree requirements:* For master's, comprehensive exam, thesis, 1 quarter of teaching experience; for doctorate, comprehensive exam, thesis/dissertation, 2 quarters of teaching experience. *Entrance requirements:* For master's, GRE General Test, names of three faculty members whose research interests most closely match the applicant's interest; for doctorate, GRE General Test, essay concerning prior training, research interest and career goals, plus names of three faculty members whose research interests most closely match the applicant's interest. Additional exam requirements/recommendations for international students: Required—TOEFL (minimum score 620 paper-based; 105 iBT) or IELTS (minimum score 7.5). *Application deadline:* For fall admission, 1/15 for domestic and international students. Application fee: $50 ($55 for international students). Electronic applications accepted. *Expenses:* Tuition, state resident: full-time $7839; part-time $323 per quarter hour. Tuition, nonresident: full-time $15,831; part-time $654 per quarter hour. Required fees: $2931. *Financial support:* In 2009–10, 1 fellowship with full tuition reimbursement (averaging $18,957 per year), 10 research assistantships with full tuition reimbursements (averaging $18,957 per year), 42 teaching assistantships with full tuition reimbursements (averaging $18,957 per year) were awarded; Federal Work-Study and institutionally sponsored loans also available. Financial award application deadline: 1/15. *Faculty research:* Ecology and evolutionary biology, exercise physiology and muscle biology, neurobiology, cell biology, physiology. Total annual research expenditures: $2.8 million. *Unit head:* Dr. Ralph DiCaprio, Chair, 740-593-2290, Fax: 740-593-0300, E-mail: dicapri@ohio.edu. *Application contact:* Dr. Donald Holzschu, Graduate Chair, 740-593-0425, Fax: 740-593-0300, E-mail: holzschu@ohio.edu.

Oklahoma State University Center for Health Sciences, Program in Biomedical Sciences, Tulsa, OK 74107-1898. Offers MS, PhD, DO/PhD. *Degree requirements:* For master's, thesis; for doctorate, thesis/dissertation, comprehensive, oral and written exam. *Entrance requirements:* For master's, GRE General Test, minimum GPA of 3.0; for doctorate, GRE General Test, MCAT, minimum GPA of 3.0. Additional exam requirements/recommendations for international students: Required—TOEFL (minimum score 213 computer-based). *Faculty research:* Neuroscience, cell biology, cell signaling, infectious disease, virology, neurotoxicology.

Old Dominion University, College of Sciences, Master of Science in Biology Program, Norfolk, VA 23529. Offers MS. Part-time programs available. *Faculty:* 22 full-time (4 women), 23 part-time/adjunct (2 women). *Students:* 19 full-time (12 women), 33 part-time (16 women); includes 3 minority (all Hispanic Americans), 3 international. Average age 27. 13 applicants, 54% accepted, 3 enrolled. In 2009, 6 master's awarded. *Degree requirements:* For master's, comprehensive exam, thesis optional. *Entrance requirements:* For master's, GRE General Test, MCAT, minimum GPA of 3.0 in major, 2.7 overall. Additional exam requirements/recommendations for international students: Required—TOEFL (minimum score 550 paper-based; 213 computer-based; 79 iBT). *Application deadline:* For fall admission, 2/1 priority date for domestic and international students; for winter admission, 6/1 priority date for domestic and international students; for spring admission, 10/1 priority date for domestic and international students. Application fee: $40. Electronic applications accepted. *Expenses:* Tuition, state resident: full-time $8112; part-time $338 per credit. Tuition, nonresident: full-time $20,256; part-time $844 per credit. Required fees: $119 per semester. One-time fee: $50. *Financial support:* In 2009–10, 2 fellowships (averaging $6,575 per year), 10 research assistantships with partial tuition reimbursements (averaging $15,000 per year), 8 teaching assistantships with partial tuition reimbursements (averaging $15,000 per year) were awarded; career-related internships or fieldwork and scholarships/grants also available. Support available to part-time students. Financial award application deadline: 2/1; financial award applicants required to submit FAFSA. *Faculty research:* Wetland ecology, systematics and ecology of vertebrates, marine biology, molecular and cellular microbiology, physiological and reproductive biology. Total annual research expenditures: $2 million. *Unit head:* Dr. Robert Ratzlaff, Graduate Program Director, 757-683-4361, Fax: 757-683-5283, E-mail: chpgpd@odu.edu. *Application contact:* Dr. Robert Ratzlaff, Graduate Program Director, 757-683-4361, Fax: 757-683-5283, E-mail: chpgpd@odu.edu.

Old Dominion University, College of Sciences, Program in Biomedical Sciences, Norfolk, VA 23529. Offers PhD. *Faculty:* 29 full-time (8 women). *Students:* 20 full-time (9 women), 13 part-time (8 women); includes 3 minority (1 African American, 1 Asian American or Pacific Islander, 1 Hispanic American), 18 international. Average age 31. 14 applicants, 71% accepted, 10 enrolled. In 2009, 3 doctorates awarded. *Degree requirements:* For doctorate, comprehensive exam, thesis/dissertation. *Entrance requirements:* For doctorate, GRE General Test, minimum GPA of 3.0. Additional exam requirements/recommendations for international students: Required—TOEFL (minimum score 213 computer-based; 79 iBT). *Application deadline:* For fall admission, 2/15 priority date for domestic and international students. Application fee: $40. Electronic applications accepted. *Expenses:* Tuition, state resident: full-time $8112; part-time $338 per credit. Tuition, nonresident: full-time $20,256; part-time $844 per credit. Required fees: $119 per semester. One-time fee: $50. *Financial support:* In 2009–10, 2 fellowships with full tuition reimbursements (averaging $18,000 per year), 2 research assistantships with full tuition reimbursements (averaging $18,000 per year), 4 teaching assistantships with full tuition reimbursements (averaging $15,000 per year) were awarded; career-related internships or fieldwork, scholarships/grants, tuition waivers (partial), and unspecified assistantships also available. Support available to part-time students. Financial award application deadline: 2/15; financial award applicants required to submit FAFSA. *Faculty research:* Systems biology and biophysics, pure and applied biomedical sciences, biological chemistry, clinical chemistry, cell biology and molecular pathogenesis. Total annual research expenditures: $3.7 million. *Unit head:* Dr. Robert Ratzlaff, Graduate Program Director, 757-683-4361, Fax: 757-683-5283, E-mail: chpgpd@odu.edu. *Application contact:* Dr. Robert Ratzlaff, Graduate Program Director, 757-683-4361, Fax: 757-683-5283, E-mail: chpgpd@odu.edu.

Oregon Health & Science University, School of Medicine, Graduate Programs in Medicine, Portland, OR 97239-3098. Offers MPH, MS, PhD, Certificate. *Students:* 273 full-time (142 women), 13 part-time (6 women); includes 35 minority (4 African Americans, 2 American Indian/Alaska Native, 17 Asian Americans or Pacific Islanders, 12 Hispanic Americans), 57 international. Average age 33. 377 applicants, 25% accepted, 83 enrolled. Terminal master's awarded for partial completion of doctoral program. *Degree requirements:* For master's, thesis, capstone experience; for doctorate, comprehensive exam, thesis/dissertation, qualifying exam. *Entrance requirements:* For master's, GRE General Test (minimum scores: 500 Verbal/600 Quantitative/4.5 Analytical), MCAT or GMAT (for some programs); for doctorate, GRE General Test (minimum scores: 500 Verbal/600 Quantitative/4.5 Analytical). Additional exam requirements/recommendations for international students: Required—TOEFL. Application fee: $65. Electronic applications accepted. *Expenses:* Contact institution. *Financial support:* Fellowships, research assistantships, teaching assistantships, PhD students have paid tuition and receive stipends available. *Unit head:* Allison Fryer, PhD, Associate Dean for Graduate Studies, 503-494-6222, Fax: 503-494-3400, E-mail: somgrad@ohsu.edu. *Application contact:* Lorie Gookin, Admissions Coordinator, 503-494-6222, Fax: 503-494-3400, E-mail: somgrad@ohsu.edu.

Penn State Hershey Medical Center, College of Medicine, Graduate School Programs in the Biomedical Sciences, Hershey, PA 17033. Offers MS, PhD, MD/PhD, PhD/MBA. *Students:* Average age 24. Terminal master's awarded for partial completion of doctoral program. *Degree requirements:* For master's, thesis or alternative; for doctorate, comprehensive exam, thesis/dissertation, oral exam. *Entrance requirements:* For master's, GRE; for doctorate, GRE, minimum GPA of 3.0. Additional exam requirements/recommendations for international students: Required—TOEFL (minimum score 560 paper-based; 220 computer-based). *Application deadline:* For fall admission, 1/31 priority date for domestic students, 2/1 priority date for international students. Applications are processed on a rolling basis. Application fee: $65. Electronic applications accepted. *Expenses:* Contact institution. *Financial support:* In 2009–10, 3 fellowships with full tuition reimbursements (averaging $26,500 per year), 37 research assistantships with full tuition reimbursements (averaging $22,250 per year) were awarded; career-related internships or fieldwork, scholarships/grants, health care benefits, tuition waivers (full), and unspecified assistantships also available. Financial award applicants required to submit FAFSA. *Unit head:* Dr. Michael F. Verderame, Associate Dean of Graduate Studies, 717-531-8892, Fax: 717-531-0786, E-mail: grad-hmc@psu.edu. *Application contact:* Kathleen M. Simon, Administrative Assistant, 717-531-8892, Fax: 717-531-0786, E-mail: grad-hmc@psu.edu.

Penn State University Park, Graduate School, Eberly College of Science, Department of Biology, State College, University Park, PA 16802-1503. Offers MS, PhD. *Unit head:* Dr. Douglas R. Cavener, Head, 814-865-4562, Fax: 814-865-9131, E-mail: drc9@psu.edu. *Application contact:* Kathryn McClintock, Graduate Programs Secretary, 814-863-7034, E-mail: biokat@psu.edu.

Penn State University Park, Graduate School, Intercollege Graduate Programs, Intercollege Graduate Program in Integrative Biosciences, State College, University Park, PA 16802-1503. Offers integrative biosciences (PhD), including biomolecular transport dynamics. *Unit head:* Dr. Peter J. Hudson, Director, 814-865-6057, Fax: 814-863-1357. *Application contact:* Dr. Peter J. Hudson, Director, 814-865-6057, Fax: 814-863-1357.

Philadelphia College of Osteopathic Medicine, Graduate and Professional Programs, Program in Biomedical Sciences, Philadelphia, PA 19131-1694. Offers MS, Certificate. *Faculty:* 28 full-time (14 women), 5 part-time/adjunct (3 women). *Students:* 181 full-time (71 women); includes 88 minority (49 African Americans, 34 Asian Americans or Pacific Islanders, 5 Hispanic Americans), 1 international. Average age 26. 553 applicants, 45% accepted, 133 enrolled. In 2009, 16 master's awarded. *Degree requirements:* For master's, thesis. *Entrance requirements:* For master's, GRE, MCAT, DAT, OAT, minimum GPA of 3.0, course work in biology, chemistry, English, physics. *Application deadline:* For fall admission, 7/15 for domestic students. Applications are processed on a rolling basis. Application fee: $50. *Faculty research:* Developmental biology, cytokines and inflammation, neurobiology of aging, pain mechanisms, cell death. Total annual research expenditures: $244,095. *Unit head:* Dr. Ruth D. Thornton, Chair, 215-871-6440, Fax: 215-871-6865, E-mail: rutht@pcom.edu. *Application contact:* Carol A. Fox, Associate Vice President for Enrollment Management, 215-871-6700, Fax: 215-871-6719, E-mail: carolf@pcom.edu.

Pittsburg State University, Graduate School, College of Arts and Sciences, Department of Biology, Pittsburg, KS 66762. Offers MS. *Degree requirements:* For master's, thesis or alternative. *Expenses:* Tuition, state resident: full-time $4212; part-time $176 per credit. Tuition, nonresident: full-time $11,530; part-time $480 per credit. Required fees: $940; $43 per credit. Tuition and fees vary according to course level, course load, degree level, campus/location, reciprocity agreements and student level.

Point Loma Nazarene University, Program in Biology, San Diego, CA 92106-2899. Offers MA, MS. Part-time programs available. *Students:* 1 (woman) full-time, 24 part-time (14 women);

includes 7 minority (1 African American, 2 Asian Americans or Pacific Islanders, 4 Hispanic Americans). Average age 40. In 2009, 7 master's awarded. *Entrance requirements:* For master's, GRE Subject Test, BA/BS in science field, letters of recommendation, writing sample, interview, minimum GPA of 3.0. Application fee: $35. *Unit head:* Dr. Darrel Falk, Co-Chair of the Department of Biology, 619-849-2272, E-mail: darrelfalk@pointloma.edu. *Application contact:* Amanda Bolton, Graduate Enrollment Counselor, 619-563-2810, E-mail: amandabolton@pointloma.edu.

Ponce School of Medicine, Program in Biomedical Sciences, Ponce, PR 00732-7004. Offers PhD. *Faculty:* 6 full-time (1 woman). *Students:* 34 full-time (25 women); includes 27 minority (all Hispanic Americans). Average age 29. 16 applicants, 38% accepted, 6 enrolled. In 2009, 3 doctorates awarded. *Degree requirements:* For doctorate, one foreign language, comprehensive exam, thesis/dissertation. *Entrance requirements:* For doctorate, GRE General Test, proficiency in Spanish and English, minimum overall GPA of 2.75, 3 letters of recommendation, minimum 35 credits in science. *Application deadline:* For fall admission, 1/15 for domestic and international students. Application fee: $100. *Expenses:* Tuition: Part-time $225 per credit hour. Part-time tuition and fees vary according to program. *Financial support:* In 2009–10, 25 students received support, including 6 fellowships with full tuition reimbursements available (averaging $19,900 per year), 13 research assistantships with full tuition reimbursements available (averaging $47,612 per year); scholarships/grants also available. Financial award application deadline: 4/30; financial award applicants required to submit FAFSA. *Unit head:* Dr. Jose Torres, Associate Dean for Graduate Studies and Research, 787-840-2158, E-mail: jtorres@psm.edu. *Application contact:* Dr. Jose Torres, Associate Dean for Graduate Studies and Research, 787-840-2158, E-mail: jtorres@psm.edu.

Pontifical Catholic University of Puerto Rico, College of Sciences, Department of Biology, Ponce, PR 00717-0777. Offers environmental sciences (MS). *Degree requirements:* For master's, thesis. *Entrance requirements:* For master's, GRE, 2 letters of recommendation, interview, minimum GPA of 2.75.

Portland State University, Graduate Studies, College of Liberal Arts and Sciences, Department of Biology, Portland, OR 97207-0751. Offers MA, MS, PhD. *Degree requirements:* For master's, one foreign language, thesis; for doctorate, thesis/dissertation. *Entrance requirements:* For master's, GRE General Test, GRE Subject Test, minimum GPA of 3.0 in upper-division course work or 2.75 overall, 2 letters of reference; for doctorate, GRE General Test, GRE Subject Test, minimum GPA of 3.5 in science. Additional exam requirements/recommendations for international students: Required—TOEFL (minimum score 550 paper-based; 213 computer-based). *Faculty research:* Genetic diversity and natural population, vertebrate temperature regulation, water balance and sensory physiology, trace elements and aquatic ecology, molecular genetics.

Prairie View A&M University, College of Arts and Sciences, Department of Biology, Prairie View, TX 77446-0519. Offers bio- environmental toxicology (MS); biology (MS). Part-time and evening/weekend programs available. *Faculty:* 5 full-time (2 women). *Students:* 4 full-time (all women), 4 part-time (2 women); all minorities (7 African Americans, 1 Hispanic American). Average age 24. 14 applicants, 86% accepted. In 2009, 8 master's awarded. *Degree requirements:* For master's, comprehensive exam, thesis optional. *Entrance requirements:* For master's, GRE General Test. Additional exam requirements/recommendations for international students: Required—TOEFL. *Application deadline:* For fall admission, 7/1 for domestic and international students; for spring admission, 11/1 for domestic and international students. Applications are processed on a rolling basis. *Expenses:* Tuition, state resident: full-time $2200. Tuition, nonresident: full-time $5600. Required fees: $1720. Tuition and fees vary according to course load. *Financial support:* Federal Work-Study and unspecified assistantships available. Financial award application deadline: 4/1; financial award applicants required to submit FAFSA. *Faculty research:* Geonomics, hypertension, control of gene express, proteins, kigands that interact with hormone receptors, prostate cancer, renin-angiotensin yeast metabolism. *Unit head:* Dr. Harriette Howard-Lee-Block, Head, 936-261-3160, Fax: 936-261-3179, E-mail: hlblock@pvamu.edu. *Application contact:* Dr. Seab A. Smith, Associate Professor, 936-261-3169, Fax: 936-261-3179, E-mail: sasmith@pvamu.edu.

Purdue University, Graduate School, College of Science, Department of Biological Sciences, West Lafayette, IN 47907. Offers biochemistry (PhD); biophysics (PhD); cell and developmental biology (PhD); ecology, evolutionary and population biology (MS, PhD), including ecology, evolutionary biology, population biology; genetics (MS, PhD); microbiology (MS, PhD); molecular biology (PhD); neurobiology (MS, PhD); plant physiology (PhD). Terminal master's awarded for partial completion of doctoral program. *Degree requirements:* For master's, thesis (for some programs); for doctorate, thesis/dissertation, seminars, teaching experience. *Entrance requirements:* For master's and doctorate, GRE General Test. Additional exam requirements/recommendations for international students: Required—TOEFL. Electronic applications accepted.

Purdue University, Graduate School, PULSe—Purdue University Life Sciences Program, West Lafayette, IN 47907. Offers PhD. *Entrance requirements:* For doctorate, GRE. Additional exam requirements/recommendations for international students: Required—TOEFL. Electronic applications accepted.

Purdue University Calumet, Graduate School, School of Engineering, Mathematics, and Science, Department of Biological Sciences, Hammond, IN 46323-2094. Offers biology (MS); biology teaching (MS); biotechnology (MS). *Entrance requirements:* For master's, GRE. Additional exam requirements/recommendations for international students: Required—TOEFL. Electronic applications accepted. *Faculty research:* Cell biology, molecular biology, genetics, microbiology, neurophysiology.

Queens College of the City University of New York, Division of Graduate Studies, Mathematics and Natural Sciences Division, Department of Biology, Flushing, NY 11367-1597. Offers MA. Part-time and evening/weekend programs available. *Faculty:* 18 full-time (6 women). *Students:* 8 full-time (5 women), 26 part-time (13 women). 50 applicants, 50% accepted, 15 enrolled. In 2009, 8 master's awarded. *Degree requirements:* For master's, comprehensive exam, thesis or alternative, qualifying exam. *Entrance requirements:* For master's, minimum GPA of 3.0. Additional exam requirements/recommendations for international students: Required—TOEFL. *Application deadline:* For fall admission, 4/1 for domestic students; for spring admission, 11/1 for domestic students. Applications are processed on a rolling basis. Application fee: $125. *Expenses:* Tuition, state resident: full-time $7360; part-time $310 per credit. Tuition, nonresident: part-time $575 per credit. One-time fee: $195 full-time; $145.25 part-time. *Financial support:* Career-related internships or fieldwork, Federal Work-Study, institutionally sponsored loans, tuition waivers (partial), and unspecified assistantships available. Support available to part-time students. Financial award application deadline: 4/1; financial award applicants required to submit FAFSA. *Faculty research:* Cell biology, evolutionary biology, environmental biology, microbiology. *Unit head:* Dr. Corrine Michels, Chairperson, 718-997-3400, E-mail: corinne_michels@qc.edu. *Application contact:* Dr. Jeanne Szalay, Graduate Adviser, 718-997-3400, E-mail: jeanne_szalay@qc.edu.

Queen's University at Kingston, School of Graduate Studies and Research, Faculty of Arts and Sciences, Department of Biology, Kingston, ON K7L 3N6, Canada. Offers M Sc, PhD. Part-time programs available. *Degree requirements:* For master's, thesis; for doctorate, comprehensive exam, thesis/dissertation. *Entrance requirements:* Additional exam requirements/recommendations for international students: Required—TOEFL. *Faculty research:* Limnology, plant morphogenesis, nitrogen fixation, cell cycle, genetics.

Quinnipiac University, School of Health Sciences, Program in Medical Laboratory Sciences, Hamden, CT 06518-1940. Offers biomedical sciences (MHS); laboratory management (MHS); microbiology (MHS). *Accreditation:* NAACLS. Part-time programs available. *Faculty:* 9 full-time (5 women), 12 part-time/adjunct (3 women). *Students:* 30 full-time (16 women), 22 part-time (13 women); includes 7 minority (3 African Americans, 1 Asian American or Pacific Islander, 3 Hispanic Americans), 13 international. Average age 28. 44 applicants, 86% accepted, 29 enrolled. In 2009, 15 master's awarded. *Degree requirements:* For master's, comprehensive exam, thesis optional. *Entrance requirements:* For master's, minimum GPA of 2.75; bachelor's degree in biological, medical, or health sciences. Additional exam requirements/recommendations for international students: Required—TOEFL (minimum score 575 paper-based; 233 computer-based; 90 iBT), IELTS (minimum score 6.5). *Application deadline:* For fall admission, 7/30 priority date for domestic students, 4/30 priority date for international students; for spring admission, 12/15 priority date for domestic students, 9/15 priority date for international students. Applications are processed on a rolling basis. Application fee: $45. Electronic applications accepted. *Expenses:* Tuition: Full-time $16,030; part-time $770 per credit. Required fees: $630; $35 per credit. *Financial support:* Federal Work-Study, tuition waivers (partial), and unspecified assistantships available. Support available to part-time students. Financial award application deadline: 4/15; financial award applicants required to submit FAFSA. *Faculty research:* Microbial physiology, fermentation technology. *Unit head:* Dr. Kenneth Kaloustian, Director, 203-582-8676, Fax: 203-582-3443, E-mail: ken.kaloustian@quinnipiac.edu. *Application contact:* Kristin Parent, Assistant Director of Graduate Health Sciences Admissions, 800-462-1944, Fax: 203-582-3443, E-mail: kristin.parent@quinnipiac.edu.

Rensselaer Polytechnic Institute, Graduate School, School of Science, Program in Biology, Troy, NY 12180-3590. Offers PhD. Part-time programs available. *Faculty:* 23 full-time (9 women). *Students:* 33 full-time (19 women), 3 part-time (all women); includes 5 Asian Americans or Pacific Islanders. Average age 23. 41 applicants, 22% accepted, 5 enrolled. In 2009, 2 degrees awarded. Terminal master's awarded for partial completion of doctoral program. *Median time to degree:* Of those who began their doctoral program in fall 2001, 100% received their degree in 8 years or less. *Degree requirements:* For doctorate, comprehensive exam, thesis/dissertation. *Entrance requirements:* For doctorate, GRE General Test. Additional exam requirements/recommendations for international students: Required—TOEFL. *Application deadline:* For fall admission, 1/15 priority date for domestic students. Applications are processed on a rolling basis. Application fee: $45. Electronic applications accepted. *Expenses:* Tuition: Full-time $38,100. *Financial support:* In 2009–10, 1 fellowship (averaging $17,500 per year), 15 research assistantships with partial tuition reimbursements (averaging $17,500 per year), 11 teaching assistantships with full tuition reimbursements (averaging $17,500 per year) were awarded; career-related internships or fieldwork, institutionally sponsored loans, and tuition waivers (partial) also available. Financial award application deadline: 2/1. *Faculty research:* Bioinformatics, molecular biology/biochemistry, cell and tissue biology, environment, ecology. Total annual research expenditures: $450,000. *Unit head:* Dr. Susan P. Gilbert, Head, 518-276-8425, Fax: 518-276-2344, E-mail: sgilbert@rpi.edu. *Application contact:* Jody Malm, Graduate Program Coordinator, 518-276-2808, Fax: 518-276-2344, E-mail: malmj@rpi.edu.

Rhode Island College, School of Graduate Studies, Faculty of Arts and Sciences, Department of Biology, Providence, RI 02908-1991. Offers MA. Part-time programs available. *Faculty:* 6 full-time (3 women). *Students:* 3 full-time (2 women), 7 part-time (2 women); includes 1 minority (African American). Average age 30. *Degree requirements:* For master's, thesis. *Entrance requirements:* For master's, GRE General and Subject Tests or MAT. Additional exam requirements/recommendations for international students: Recommended—TOEFL (minimum score 550 paper-based; 213 computer-based; 79 iBT). *Application deadline:* For fall admission, 4/1 for domestic students; for spring admission, 11/1 for domestic students. Applications are processed on a rolling basis. Application fee: $50. *Expenses:* Tuition, state resident: full-time $7440; part-time $310 per credit hour. Tuition, nonresident: full-time $14,784; part-time $616 per credit hour. Required fees: $552; $20 per credit. $70 per term. *Financial support:* In 2009–10, 2 teaching assistantships with full tuition reimbursements (averaging $4,550 per year) were awarded; career-related internships or fieldwork, Federal Work-Study, scholarships/grants, health care benefits, and unspecified assistantships also available. Support available to part-time students. Financial award application deadline: 5/15; financial award applicants required to submit FAFSA. *Unit head:* Dr. Eric Hall, Chair, 401-456-8010. *Application contact:* Graduate Studies, 401-456-8700.

Rochester Institute of Technology, Graduate Enrollment Services, College of Science, Department of Biological Sciences, Rochester, NY 14623-5603. Offers bioinformatics (MS); environmental science (MS). Part-time programs available. *Students:* 24 full-time (11 women), 9 part-time (4 women); includes 2 minority (both Asian Americans or Pacific Islanders), 9 international. Average age 26. 93 applicants, 25% accepted, 9 enrolled. In 2009, 12 master's awarded. *Degree requirements:* For master's, thesis or alternative. *Entrance requirements:* Additional exam requirements/recommendations for international students: Required—TOEFL (minimum score 570 paper-based; 230 computer-based; 88 iBT) or IELTS (minimum score 6.5). *Application deadline:* For fall admission, 2/15 priority date for domestic and international students. Application fee: $50. *Expenses:* Tuition: Full-time $31,533; part-time $876 per credit hour. Required fees: $210. *Financial support:* In 2009–10, 24 students received support; fellowships with partial tuition reimbursements available, research assistantships with partial tuition reimbursements available, teaching assistantships with partial tuition reimbursements available, career-related internships or fieldwork, scholarships/grants, and unspecified assistantships available. Support available to part-time students. Financial award applicants required to submit FAFSA. *Faculty research:* Bioinformatic software development, bioscience, biomedical research, environmental research examining the human relationship to nature and developing solutions that prevent or reverse environmental deterioration. *Unit head:* Larry Buckley, Associate Head, School of Life Sciences, 585-475-7577, Fax: 585-475-2533, E-mail: biology@rit.edu. *Application contact:* Diane Ellison, Assistant Vice President, Graduate Enrollment Services, 585-475-2229, Fax: 585-475-7164, E-mail: gradinfo@rit.edu.

The Rockefeller University, Graduate Program in Biomedical Sciences, New York, NY 10021-6399. Offers PhD, MD/PhD. *Faculty:* 100 full-time (23 women), 153 part-time/adjunct (43 women). *Students:* 215 full-time (98 women). Terminal master's awarded for partial completion of doctoral program. *Degree requirements:* For doctorate, thesis/dissertation. *Entrance requirements:* Additional exam requirements/recommendations for international students: Required—TOEFL. *Application deadline:* For winter admission, 12/6 for domestic and international students. Application fee: $80. Electronic applications accepted. *Financial support:* In 2009–10, 215 students received support, including 215 fellowships with full tuition reimbursements available (averaging $31,600 per year); institutionally sponsored loans, scholarships/grants, traineeships, and health care benefits also available. *Unit head:* Dr. Sidney Strickland, Dean of Graduate Studies, 212-327-8086, Fax: 212-327-8505, E-mail: phd@rockefeller.edu. *Application contact:* Kristen Cullen, Graduate Admissions Administrator and Registrar, 212-327-8088, Fax: 212-327-8505, E-mail: cullenk@rockefeller.edu.

See Close-Up on page 105.

Rosalind Franklin University of Medicine and Science, College of Health Professions, Department of Interprofessional Healthcare Studies, Biomedical Sciences Program, North Chicago, IL 60064-3095. Offers MS. *Faculty:* 7 full-time (0 women), 5 part-time/adjunct (all women). *Students:* 109 full-time (52 women), 1 (woman) part-time; includes 41 minority (3 African Americans, 37 Asian Americans or Pacific Islanders, 1 Hispanic American). Average age 24. 366 applicants, 62% accepted, 106 enrolled. *Entrance requirements:* For master's, MCAT, DAT, OAT, PCAT or GRE, BS in chemistry, physics, biology. Additional exam requirements/recommendations for international students: Required—TOEFL. *Application deadline:* For fall admission, 6/15 for domestic students. Applications are processed on a rolling basis. Application fee: $50. *Financial support:* In 2009–10, 50 students received support. Federal Work-Study and institutionally sponsored loans available. Support available to part-time students. Financial award applicants required to submit FAFSA. *Unit head:* Dr. Gordon Pullen, Assistant Dean and Program Director, 847-578-8603, Fax: 847-578-8778, E-mail: gordon.pullen@rosalindfranklin.edu. *Application contact:* Melissa Knox, Admissions Officer, 847-578-8772, Fax: 847-775-6559, E-mail: melissa.knoxr@rosalindfranklin.edu.

Rosalind Franklin University of Medicine and Science, School of Graduate and Post-doctoral Studies—Interdisciplinary Graduate Program in Biomedical Sciences, North Chicago, IL 60064-3095. Offers MS, PhD, MD/PhD. Terminal master's awarded for partial completion of

Biological and Biomedical Sciences—General

Rosalind Franklin University of Medicine and Science (continued)
doctoral program. *Degree requirements:* For master's, comprehensive exam, thesis; for doctorate, comprehensive exam, thesis/dissertation. *Entrance requirements:* For master's and doctorate, GRE General Test. Additional exam requirements/recommendations for international students: Required—TOEFL, TWE. *Faculty research:* Extracellular matrix, nutrition and mood, neuropsychopharmacology, membrane transport, brain metabolism.

See Close-Up on page 107.

Rutgers, The State University of New Jersey, Camden, Graduate School of Arts and Sciences, Program in Biology, Camden, NJ 08102-1401. Offers MS. Part-time and evening/weekend programs available. *Degree requirements:* For master's, comprehensive exam, thesis (for some programs). *Entrance requirements:* For master's, GRE General Test, GRE Subject Test (recommended), 3 letters of recommendation. Additional exam requirements/recommendations for international students: Required—TOEFL. Electronic applications accepted. *Faculty research:* Neurobiology, biochemistry, ecology, developmental biology, biological signaling mechanisms.

Rutgers, The State University of New Jersey, Newark, Graduate School, Program in Biology, Newark, NJ 07102. Offers MS, PhD. Part-time and evening/weekend programs available. Terminal master's awarded for partial completion of doctoral program. *Degree requirements:* For master's, comprehensive exam, thesis optional; for doctorate, thesis/dissertation, qualifying exam. *Entrance requirements:* For master's, GRE General Test, minimum undergraduate B average; for doctorate, GRE General Test, GRE Subject Test, minimum B average. Electronic applications accepted. *Faculty research:* Cell-cytoskeletal elements, development and regeneration in the nervous system, cellular trafficking, environmental stressors and their impact on development, opportunistic parasitic infections in AIDS.

Rutgers, The State University of New Jersey, Newark, Graduate School, Program in Computational Biology, Newark, NJ 07102. Offers MS. *Entrance requirements:* For master's, GRE, minimum undergraduate B average. Additional exam requirements/recommendations for international students: Required—TOEFL.

Rutgers, The State University of New Jersey, New Brunswick, Graduate School-New Brunswick, BioMaPS Institute for Quantitative Biology, Piscataway, NJ 08854-8097. Offers computational biology and molecular biophysics (PhD). *Degree requirements:* For doctorate, comprehensive exam, thesis/dissertation. *Entrance requirements:* For doctorate, GRE. Additional exam requirements/recommendations for international students: Required—TOEFL. Electronic applications accepted. *Faculty research:* Structural biology, systems biology, bioinformatics, translational medicine, genomics.

St. Cloud State University, School of Graduate Studies, College of Science and Engineering, Department of Biological Sciences, St. Cloud, MN 56301-4498. Offers MA, MS. *Faculty:* 23 full-time (7 women). *Students:* 3 full-time (2 women), 16 part-time (6 women); includes 2 minority (both Asian Americans or Pacific Islanders), 3 international. 16 applicants, 69% accepted, 0 enrolled. In 2009, 5 master's awarded. *Degree requirements:* For master's, comprehensive exam (for some programs), thesis or alternative. *Entrance requirements:* For master's, GRE General Test, minimum GPA of 2.75. Additional exam requirements/recommendations for international students: Recommended—TOEFL (minimum score 550 paper-based; 213 computer-based), IELTS (minimum score 6.5). *Application deadline:* For fall admission, 6/1 priority date for domestic students, 4/1 for international students; for spring admission, 10/1 priority date for domestic students, 8/1 for international students. Applications are processed on a rolling basis. Application fee: $35. Electronic applications accepted. *Financial support:* Federal Work-Study, scholarships/grants, and unspecified assistantships available. Financial award application deadline: 3/1. *Unit head:* Dr. Timothy Schuh, Chairperson, 320-308-2036, Fax: 320-308-4166, E-mail: tjschuh@stcloudstate.edu. *Application contact:* Linda Lou Krueger, School of Graduate Studies, 320-308-2113, Fax: 320-308-5371, E-mail: lekrueger@stcloudstate.edu.

Saint Francis University, Department of Physician Assistant Sciences, Medical Science Program, Loretto, PA 15940-0600. Offers MMS. Part-time and evening/weekend programs available. Postbaccalaureate distance learning degree programs offered (no on-campus study). *Faculty:* 1 (woman) full-time, 5 part-time/adjunct (2 women). *Students:* 124 full-time (70 women), 11 part-time (9 women); includes 47 minority (10 African Americans, 18 Asian Americans or Pacific Islanders, 19 Hispanic Americans). Average age 34. 73 applicants, 100% accepted, 73 enrolled. In 2009, 57 master's awarded. *Degree requirements:* For master's, thesis or alternative. *Entrance requirements:* For master's, minimum GPA of 2.5, 2 letters of reference. *Application deadline:* For fall admission, 8/1 for domestic students; for spring admission, 12/1 for domestic students. Applications are processed on a rolling basis. Application fee: $0. Electronic applications accepted. *Expenses:* Contact institution. *Financial support:* Available to part-time students. Applicants required to submit FAFSA. *Faculty research:* Health care policy, physician assistant practice roles, health promotion/disease prevention, public health epidemiology. *Unit head:* Deborah E. Budash, Director, 814-472-3919, Fax: 814-472-3137, E-mail: dbudash@francis.edu. *Application contact:* Cheryl Strittmatter, Office Assistant, 814-472-3136, Fax: 814-472-3137, E-mail: cstrittmatter@francis.edu.

St. Francis Xavier University, Graduate Studies, Department of Biology, Antigonish, NS B2G 2W5, Canada. Offers M Sc. *Degree requirements:* For master's, thesis. *Entrance requirements:* For master's, 2 letters of recommendation. Additional exam requirements/recommendations for international students: Required—TOEFL (minimum score 580 paper-based; 236 computer-based). *Faculty research:* Cellular, whole organism, and population levels; marine photosynthesis; biophysical mechanisms; aquatic biology.

St. John's University, St. John's College of Liberal Arts and Sciences, Department of Biological Sciences, Queens, NY 11439. Offers MS, PhD. Part-time and evening/weekend programs available. *Students:* 25 full-time (10 women), 9 part-time (6 women); includes 4 minority (2 African Americans, 1 Asian American or Pacific Islander, 1 Hispanic American), 21 international. Average age 28. 43 applicants, 51% accepted, 8 enrolled. In 2009, 7 master's, 9 doctorates awarded. *Degree requirements:* For master's, comprehensive exam, thesis optional, residency; for doctorate, comprehensive exam, thesis/dissertation, residency. *Entrance requirements:* For master's, GRE General Test, GRE Subject Test, minimum GPA of 3.0, 2 letters of recommendation; for doctorate, GRE General Test, GRE Subject Test, minimum GPA of 3.0 (undergraduate), 3.5 (graduate); 2 letters of recommendation, writing sample. Additional exam requirements/recommendations for international students: Required—TOEFL (minimum score 500 paper-based; 173 computer-based; 61 iBT), IELTS (minimum score 5.5). *Application deadline:* For fall admission, 5/1 priority date for domestic and international students; for spring admission, 11/1 priority date for domestic and international students. Applications are processed on a rolling basis. Application fee: $70. Electronic applications accepted. *Expenses:* Tuition: Full-time $16,290; part-time $905 per credit. Required fees: $300; $150 per semester. Tuition and fees vary according to program. *Financial support:* Fellowships, research assistantships, scholarships/grants available. Support available to part-time students. Financial award application deadline: 3/1; financial award applicants required to submit FAFSA. *Faculty research:* Regulation of gene transcription, molecular control of development in yeast, physiology of aging, cellular signal transduction. *Unit head:* Dr. Jay Zimmerman, Chair, 718-990-1679, E-mail: zimmermj@stjohns.edu. *Application contact:* Kathleen Davis, Director of Graduate Admission, 718-990-2790, Fax: 718-990-5686, E-mail: gradhelp@stjohns.edu.

Saint Joseph College, Department of Biology, West Hartford, CT 06117-2700. Offers biology (MS), including general biology. Program offered online only. Part-time and evening/weekend programs available. Postbaccalaureate distance learning degree programs offered (no on-campus study). *Students:* 5 full-time (4 women), 123 part-time (91 women); includes 24 minority (14 African Americans, 2 American Indian/Alaska Native, 8 Hispanic Americans). *Degree requirements:* For master's, comprehensive exam, thesis or alternative. *Entrance requirements:* For master's, 2 letters of recommendation. *Application deadline:* Applications are processed on a rolling basis. Application fee: $50. Electronic applications accepted. *Expenses:* Tuition: Part-time $595 per credit. Required fees: $30 per credit. Tuition and fees vary according to program. *Financial support:* Career-related internships or fieldwork and unspecified assistantships available. Support available to part-time students. Financial award applicants required to submit FAFSA. *Application contact:* Graduate Admissions Office, 860-231-5261, E-mail: graduate@sjc.edu.

Saint Joseph's University, College of Arts and Sciences, Department of Biology, Philadelphia, PA 19131-1395. Offers MA, MS. *Students:* 20 part-time (13 women); includes 3 minority (all Hispanic Americans), 1 international. Average age 24. In 2009, 4 master's awarded. *Entrance requirements:* For master's, GRE, 2 letters of recommendation, minimum GPA of 3.0. Additional exam requirements/recommendations for international students: Required—TOEFL (minimum score 550 paper-based; 213 computer-based; 79 iBT). *Application deadline:* For fall admission, 4/15 priority date for domestic students, 4/15 for international students; for winter admission, 1/15 for international students; for spring admission, 11/15 priority date for domestic students, 10/15 for international students. Applications are processed on a rolling basis. Application fee: $35. Electronic applications accepted. *Expenses:* Tuition: Part-time $729 per credit hour. Tuition and fees vary according to degree level and program. *Financial support:* Research assistantships with tuition reimbursements, unspecified assistantships available. *Faculty research:* Life science, undergraduate science education, confocal microscope for research and training. Total annual research expenditures: $865,347. *Unit head:* Dr. James Watrous, Director, 610-660-1829, E-mail: jwatrous@sju.edu. *Application contact:* Kate McConnell, Director, Graduate College of Arts and Sciences Admissions and Retention, 610-660-3184, Fax: 610-660-3230, E-mail: kate.mcconnell@sju.edu.

Saint Louis University, Graduate School, College of Arts and Sciences and Graduate School, Department of Biology, St. Louis, MO 63103-2097. Offers MS, MS-R, PhD. *Degree requirements:* For master's, comprehensive exam, thesis (for some programs); for doctorate, thesis/dissertation, preliminary exams. *Entrance requirements:* For master's, GRE General Test, letters of recommendation, resume; for doctorate, GRE General Test, letters of recommendation, resumé, statement, transcripts. Additional exam requirements/recommendations for international students: Required—TOEFL (minimum score 550 paper-based; 213 computer-based). Electronic applications accepted. *Faculty research:* Systematics, speciation, evolution, community ecology, conservation biology, molecular signaling.

Saint Louis University, Graduate School and School of Medicine, Graduate Program in Biomedical Sciences, St. Louis, MO 63103-2097. Offers MS-R, PhD. *Degree requirements:* For doctorate, comprehensive exam, thesis/dissertation. *Entrance requirements:* For doctorate, GRE. Additional exam requirements/recommendations for international students: Required—TOEFL. Electronic applications accepted. *Faculty research:* Biochemistry and molecular biology, physiology and pharmacology, virology, pathology, immunology.

Sam Houston State University, College of Arts and Sciences, Department of Biological Sciences, Huntsville, TX 77341. Offers biology (MA, MS). Part-time programs available. *Faculty:* 8 full-time (2 women). *Students:* 6 full-time (3 women), 30 part-time (17 women); includes 5 minority (1 African American, 4 Hispanic Americans), 1 international. Average age 27. 19 applicants, 89% accepted, 13 enrolled. In 2009, 4 master's awarded. *Degree requirements:* For master's, thesis (for some programs). *Entrance requirements:* For master's, GRE General Test. Additional exam requirements/recommendations for international students: Required—TOEFL (minimum score 550 paper-based; 213 computer-based; 79 iBT). *Application deadline:* For fall admission, 8/1 for domestic and international students; for spring admission, 12/1 for domestic and international students. Application fee: $20. *Expenses:* Tuition, state resident: full-time $3690; part-time $205 per credit hour. Tuition, nonresident: full-time $8676; part-time $482 per credit hour. Required fees: $1474. Tuition and fees vary according to course load and campus/location. *Financial support:* Research assistantships, teaching assistantships available. Financial award application deadline: 5/31; financial award applicants required to submit FAFSA. *Unit head:* Dr. Todd Primm, Chair, 936-294-1538, Fax: 936-294-3940, E-mail: tprimm@shsu.edu. *Application contact:* Dr. Anne Gaillard, Graduate Coordinator, 936-294-1549, Fax: 936-294-3940, E-mail: argaillard@shsu.edu.

San Diego State University, Graduate and Research Affairs, College of Sciences, Department of Biology, San Diego, CA 92182. Offers biology (MA, MS), including ecology (MS), molecular biology (MS), physiology (MS), systematics/evolution (MS); cell and molecular biology (PhD); ecology (MS, PhD); microbiology (MS). Terminal master's awarded for partial completion of doctoral program. *Degree requirements:* For master's, thesis; for doctorate, thesis/dissertation. *Entrance requirements:* For master's, GRE General Test, GRE Subject Test, resume or curriculum vitae, 2 letters of recommendation. Additional exam requirements/recommendations for international students: Required—TOEFL. Electronic applications accepted.

San Francisco State University, Division of Graduate Studies, College of Science and Engineering, Department of Biology, San Francisco, CA 94132-1722. Offers biomedical laboratory science (MS); cell and molecular biology (MS); conservation biology (MS); ecology and systematic biology (MS); marine biology (MS); marine science (MS); microbiology (MS); physiology and behavioral biology (MS).

San Jose State University, Graduate Studies and Research, College of Science, Department of Biological Sciences, San Jose, CA 95192-0001. Offers biological sciences (MA, MS); molecular biology and microbiology (MS); organismal biology, conservation and ecology (MS); physiology (MS). Part-time programs available. *Students:* 53 full-time (41 women), 48 part-time (30 women); includes 48 minority (2 African Americans, 1 American Indian/Alaska Native, 36 Asian Americans or Pacific Islanders, 9 Hispanic Americans), 10 international. Average age 30. 158 applicants, 28% accepted, 43 enrolled. In 2009, 36 master's awarded. *Entrance requirements:* For master's, GRE. *Application deadline:* For fall admission, 6/29 for domestic students; for spring admission, 11/30 for domestic students. Applications are processed on a rolling basis. Application fee: $59. Electronic applications accepted. *Financial support:* Teaching assistantships, Federal Work-Study available. Financial award applicants required to submit FAFSA. *Faculty research:* Systemic physiology, molecular genetics, SEM studies, toxicology, large mammal ecology. *Unit head:* Dr. John Boothby, Chair, 408-924-4850, Fax: 408-924-4840, E-mail: jboothby@email.sjsu.edu. *Application contact:* Daniel Holley, Graduate Coordinator, 408-924-4844, E-mail: dholley@email.sjsu.edu.

The Scripps Research Institute, Kellogg School of Science and Technology, La Jolla, CA 92037. Offers chemical and biological sciences (PhD). *Faculty:* 114 full-time (21 women). *Students:* 222 full-time (78 women). 494 applicants, 20% accepted, 32 enrolled. *Degree requirements:* For doctorate, thesis/dissertation. *Entrance requirements:* For doctorate, GRE General Test, GRE Subject Test, 3 letters of recommendation. Additional exam requirements/recommendations for international students: Required—TOEFL. *Application deadline:* For fall admission, 12/1 for domestic and international students. Application fee: $0. Electronic applications accepted. *Expenses:* Tuition: Full-time $5000. *Financial support:* Fellowships, institutionally sponsored loans, tuition waivers (full), and annual stipends available. *Faculty research:* Molecular structure and function, plant biology, immunology, bioorganic chemistry and molecular design, synthetic organic chemistry and natural product synthesis. *Unit head:* Dr. James R. Williamson, Dean, 858-784-8469, Fax: 858-784-2802, E-mail: gradprgm@scripps.edu. *Application contact:* Marylyn Rinaldi, Administrative Director, 858-784-8469, Fax: 858-784-2802, E-mail: mrinaldi@scripps.edu.

Seton Hall University, College of Arts and Sciences, Department of Biological Sciences, South Orange, NJ 07079-2697. Offers biology (MS); biology/business administration (MS); microbiology (MS); molecular bioscience (PhD); molecular bioscience/neuroscience (PhD). Part-time and evening/weekend programs available. *Faculty:* 17 full-time (9 women), 1 part-time/adjunct (0 women). *Students:* 19 full-time (8 women), 47 part-time (33 women); includes 13 minority (5 African Americans, 5 Asian Americans or Pacific Islanders, 3 Hispanic Americans), 5 international. Average age 29. 51 applicants, 76% accepted, 12 enrolled. In 2009, 11 master's awarded. *Degree requirements:* For master's, thesis optional; for doctorate, comprehensive exam, thesis/dissertation. *Entrance requirements:* For master's and doctorate, GRE or MS from accredited university in the U.S. Additional exam requirements/recommendations for international students: Required—TOEFL. *Application deadline:* For fall admission, 7/1 priority date for domestic and international students; for spring admission, 11/1 priority date for domestic and international students. Applications are processed on a rolling basis. Application fee: $50. Electronic applications accepted. *Financial support:* Research assistantships, teaching assistantships with full tuition reimbursements, career-related internships or fieldwork, Federal Work-Study, and unspecified assistantships available. Financial award applicants required to submit FAFSA. *Faculty research:* Neurobiology, genetics, immunology, molecular biology, cellular physiology, toxicology, microbiology, bioinformatics. *Unit head:* Dr. Carolyn Bentivegna, Chair, 973-761-9044, Fax: 973-275-2905, E-mail: bentivca@shu.edu. *Application contact:* Dr. Carroll D. Rawn, Director of Graduate Studies, 973-761-9054, Fax: 973-275-2905, E-mail: rawncarr@shu.edu.

Shippensburg University of Pennsylvania, School of Graduate Studies, College of Arts and Sciences, Department of Biology, Shippensburg, PA 17257-2299. Offers MS. Part-time and evening/weekend programs available. *Degree requirements:* For master's, thesis optional. *Entrance requirements:* For master's, 33 credits of course work in biology; minimum 4 courses/labs in chemistry including both inorganic and organic chemistry or biochemistry. Additional exam requirements/recommendations for international students: Required—TOEFL (minimum score 560 paper-based; 220 computer-based); Recommended—IELTS (minimum score 6). Electronic applications accepted.

Simon Fraser University, Graduate Studies, Faculty of Science, Department of Biological Sciences, Burnaby, BC V5A 1S6, Canada. Offers biological sciences (M Sc, PhD); environmental toxicology (MET); pest management (MPM). *Degree requirements:* For master's, thesis; for doctorate, thesis/dissertation. *Entrance requirements:* For master's, minimum GPA of 3.0; for doctorate, minimum GPA of 3.5. Additional exam requirements/recommendations for international students: Required—TOEFL or IELTS. Electronic applications accepted. *Faculty research:* Molecular biology, marine biology, ecology, wildlife biology, endocrinology.

Smith College, Graduate and Special Programs, Department of Biological Sciences, Northampton, MA 01063. Offers MAT, MS. Part-time programs available. *Faculty:* 14 full-time (5 women), 3 part-time/adjunct (1 woman). *Students:* 1 (woman) full-time, 7 part-time (6 women); includes 1 minority (Hispanic American), 2 international. Average age 25. 8 applicants, 63% accepted, 4 enrolled. In 2009, 1 master's awarded. *Degree requirements:* For master's, one foreign language, thesis (for some programs). *Entrance requirements:* For master's, GRE General Test, GRE Subject Test. Additional exam requirements/recommendations for international students: Required—TOEFL (minimum score 590 paper-based; 243 computer-based; 97 iBT). *Application deadline:* For fall admission, 1/15 for domestic and international students; for spring admission, 12/1 for domestic students. Application fee: $60. *Financial support:* In 2009–10, 8 students received support, including 3 research assistantships with full tuition reimbursements available (averaging $11,910 per year); institutionally sponsored loans and scholarships/grants also available. Support available to part-time students. Financial award application deadline: 1/15; financial award applicants required to submit CSS PROFILE or FAFSA. *Unit head:* Stephen Tilley, Chair, 413-585-3817, E-mail: stilley@smith.edu. *Application contact:* Rob P. Dorit, Graduate Student Advisor, 413-585-3638, E-mail: rdorit@smith.edu.

Sonoma State University, School of Science and Technology, Department of Biology, Rohnert Park, CA 94928. Offers environmental biology (MA); general biology (MA). Part-time programs available. *Faculty:* 8 full-time (2 women). *Students:* 19 part-time (12 women); includes 2 minority (1 American Indian/Alaska Native, 1 Hispanic American), 1 international. Average age 27. 23 applicants, 43% accepted, 6 enrolled. In 2009, 7 master's awarded. *Degree requirements:* For master's, thesis or alternative, oral exam. *Entrance requirements:* For master's, GRE General Test, GRE Subject Test, minimum GPA of 3.0. Additional exam requirements/recommendations for international students: Required—TOEFL (minimum score 500 paper-based; 173 computer-based). *Application deadline:* For fall admission, 11/30 for domestic students. Applications are processed on a rolling basis. Application fee: $55. *Expenses:* Tuition, nonresident: full-time $11,160. Required fees: $6226. Full-time tuition and fees vary according to course load. *Financial support:* In 2009–10, 5 fellowships (averaging $6,010 per year), 7 research assistantships (averaging $9,286 per year), 20 teaching assistantships (averaging $5,298 per year) were awarded; career-related internships or fieldwork, Federal Work-Study, and tuition waivers (full) also available. Financial award application deadline: 3/2; financial award applicants required to submit FAFSA. *Faculty research:* Plant physiology, comparative physiology, community ecology, restoration ecology, marine ecology, conservation genetics, primate behavior, behavioral ecology, developmental biology, plant and animal systematics. Total annual research expenditures: $238,000. *Unit head:* Dr. Dan Crocker, Chair, 707-664-2189, E-mail: james.christmann@sonoma.edu. *Application contact:* John Hopkirk, Graduate Adviser, 707-664-2180.

South Dakota State University, Graduate School, College of Agriculture and Biological Sciences, Department of Animal and Range Sciences, Brookings, SD 57007. Offers animal science (MS, PhD); biological sciences (PhD). Part-time programs available. *Degree requirements:* For master's, thesis, oral exam; for doctorate, comprehensive exam, thesis/dissertation, preliminary oral and written exams. *Entrance requirements:* Additional exam requirements/recommendations for international students: Required—TOEFL (minimum score 550 paper-based; 213 computer-based; 79 iBT). *Faculty research:* Ruminant and nonruminant nutrition, meat science, reproductive physiology, range utilization, ecology genetics, muscle biology, animal production.

South Dakota State University, Graduate School, College of Agriculture and Biological Sciences, Department of Biology and Microbiology, Brookings, SD 57007. Offers biological sciences (MS, PhD). Part-time programs available. *Degree requirements:* For master's, thesis (for some programs), oral exam; for doctorate, comprehensive exam, thesis/dissertation, oral exam. *Entrance requirements:* For master's and doctorate, GRE General Test. Additional exam requirements/recommendations for international students: Required—TOEFL (minimum score 600 paper-based; 250 computer-based; 100 iBT). *Faculty research:* Ecosystem ecology; plant, animal and microbial genomics; animal infectious disease, microbial bioproducts.

South Dakota State University, Graduate School, College of Agriculture and Biological Sciences, Department of Dairy Science, Brookings, SD 57007. Offers animal sciences (MS, PhD); biological sciences (MS, PhD). Part-time programs available. *Degree requirements:* For master's, thesis, oral exam; for doctorate, comprehensive exam, thesis/dissertation, preliminary oral and written exams. *Entrance requirements:* Additional exam requirements/recommendations for international students: Required—TOEFL (minimum score 550 paper-based; 213 computer-based). *Faculty research:* Dairy cattle nutrition, energy metabolism, food safety, dairy processing technology.

South Dakota State University, Graduate School, College of Agriculture and Biological Sciences, Department of Veterinary Science, Brookings, SD 57007. Offers biological sciences (MS, PhD). Part-time and evening/weekend programs available. *Degree requirements:* For master's, thesis (for some programs), oral exam; for doctorate, comprehensive exam, thesis/dissertation, preliminary oral and written exams. *Entrance requirements:* Additional exam requirements/recommendations for international students: Required—TOEFL (minimum score 525 paper-based; 197 computer-based; 71 iBT). *Faculty research:* Infectious disease, food animal, virology, immunology.

South Dakota State University, Graduate School, College of Engineering, Department of Agricultural and Biosystems Engineering, Brookings, SD 57007. Offers biological sciences (MS, PhD); engineering (MS). Part-time programs available. *Degree requirements:* For master's, thesis (for some programs), oral exam; for doctorate, thesis/dissertation, preliminary oral and written exams. *Entrance requirements:* For master's and doctorate, engineering degree. Additional exam requirements/recommendations for international students: Required—TOEFL (minimum score 550 paper-based; 213 computer-based; 79 iBT). *Faculty research:* Water resources, food engineering, natural resources engineering, machine design, bioprocess engineering.

South Dakota State University, Graduate School, College of Pharmacy, Department of Pharmaceutical Sciences, Brookings, SD 57007. Offers biological science (MS); pharmaceutical sciences (PhD). *Degree requirements:* For master's, thesis, oral exam; for doctorate, comprehensive exam, thesis/dissertation, oral exam. *Entrance requirements:* For master's and doctorate, GRE General Test. Additional exam requirements/recommendations for international students: Required—TOEFL (minimum score 550 paper-based; 213 computer-based). *Faculty research:* Drugs of abuse, anti-cancer drugs, sustained drug delivery, drug metabolism.

Southeastern Louisiana University, College of Science and Technology, Department of Biological Sciences, Hammond, LA 70402. Offers biology (MS). Part-time programs available. *Faculty:* 12 full-time (2 women). *Students:* 20 full-time (11 women), 11 part-time (5 women); includes 2 minority (both African Americans), 3 international. Average age 26. 12 applicants, 33% accepted, 3 enrolled. In 2009, 7 master's awarded. *Degree requirements:* For master's, comprehensive exam, thesis (for some programs), oral and written exams. *Entrance requirements:* For master's, GRE General Test (1000 or better), minimum GPA of 3.0, 30 undergraduate hours in biology, 2 letters of reference, curriculum vitae, letter of intent. Additional exam requirements/recommendations for international students: Required—TOEFL (minimum score 500 paper-based; 173 computer-based; 61 iBT). *Application deadline:* For fall admission, 7/15 priority date for domestic students, 6/1 priority date for international students; for spring admission, 12/1 priority date for domestic students, 10/1 priority date for international students. Applications are processed on a rolling basis. Application fee: $20 ($30 for international students). Electronic applications accepted. *Expenses:* Tuition, state resident: full-time $3086; part-time $225 per credit hour. Tuition, nonresident: part-time $529 per credit hour. Required fees: $1195. Tuition and fees vary according to course level and course load. *Financial support:* In 2009–10, 22 students received support, including 6 fellowships (averaging $10,800 per year), 5 research assistantships (averaging $11,700 per year), 11 teaching assistantships (averaging $9,700 per year); Federal Work-Study, institutionally sponsored loans, and administrative assistantships also available. Support available to part-time students. Financial award application deadline: 5/1; financial award applicants required to submit FAFSA. *Faculty research:* Molecular biology, microbiology, environmental biology, organismal biology, evolutionary biology. Total annual research expenditures: $836,387. *Unit head:* Dr. David Sever, Department Head, 985-549-3741, Fax: 985-549-3851, E-mail: dsever@selu.edu. *Application contact:* Sandra Meyers, Graduate Admissions Analyst, 985-549-5620, Fax: 985-549-5632, E-mail: admissions@selu.edu.

Southeast Missouri State University, School of Graduate Studies, Department of Biology, Cape Girardeau, MO 63701-4799. Offers MNS. Part-time programs available. *Faculty:* 18 full-time (8 women). *Students:* 11 full-time (5 women), 15 part-time (6 women); includes 3 minority (1 African American, 2 Hispanic Americans), 2 international. Average age 27. 16 applicants, 69% accepted. In 2009, 11 master's awarded. *Degree requirements:* For master's, comprehensive exam (for some programs), thesis (for some programs). *Entrance requirements:* For master's, GRE General Test, minimum undergraduate GPA of 2.75, minimum of 30 hours of undergraduate course work in science and mathematics, minimum C grade in upper-level biology courses, letter of intent declaring academic interest and selection of faculty sponsor. Additional exam requirements/recommendations for international students: Required—TOEFL (minimum score 550 paper-based; 213 computer-based); Recommended—IELTS (minimum score 6). *Application deadline:* For fall admission, 8/1 for domestic students, 7/1 for international students; for spring admission, 11/21 for domestic students, 11/1 for international students. Applications are processed on a rolling basis. Application fee: $25 ($100 for international students). Electronic applications accepted. *Expenses:* Tuition, state resident: full-time $4266; part-time $237 per credit hour. Tuition, nonresident: full-time $7506; part-time $417 per credit hour. Required fees: $427; $427. *Financial support:* In 2009–10, 15 students received support, including 1 research assistantship with full tuition reimbursement available (averaging $7,600 per year), 14 teaching assistantships with full tuition reimbursements available (averaging $7,600 per year); unspecified assistantships also available. Financial award applicants required to submit FAFSA. *Faculty research:* Wildlife and conservation biology, microbiology and epidemiology, ecology and animal behavior, case-based learning, plant systematics and physiology. Total annual research expenditures: $52,599. *Unit head:* Dr. William Eddleman, Chairperson, 573-651-2171, Fax: 573-651-2382, E-mail: weddleman@semo.edu. *Application contact:* Marsha L. Arant, Senior Administrative Assistant, School of Graduate Studies, 573-651-2192, Fax: 573-651-2001, E-mail: marant@semo.edu.

Southern Connecticut State University, School of Graduate Studies, School of Arts and Sciences, Department of Biology, New Haven, CT 06515-1355. Offers MS. Part-time and evening/weekend programs available. *Faculty:* 4 full-time, 2 part-time/adjunct. *Students:* 21 full-time (9 women), 74 part-time (48 women). 52 applicants, 38% accepted, 15 enrolled. In 2009, 24 master's awarded. *Degree requirements:* For master's, thesis optional. *Entrance requirements:* For master's, previous course work in biology, chemistry, and mathematics; interview. *Application deadline:* Applications are processed on a rolling basis. Application fee: $50. Electronic applications accepted. Tuition and fees vary according to program. *Financial support:* Application deadline: 4/15. *Unit head:* Dr. Dwight Smith, Chairperson, 203-392-6222, Fax: 203-392-5364, E-mail: smithd1@southernct.edu. *Application contact:* Dr. Sean Grace, Graduate Coordinator, 203-392-6216, Fax: 203-392-5364, E-mail: graces2@southernct.edu.

Southern Illinois University Carbondale, Graduate School, College of Science, Biological Sciences Program, Carbondale, IL 62901-4701. Offers MS. *Degree requirements:* For master's, thesis or alternative. *Entrance requirements:* For master's, GRE General Test, minimum GPA of 2.7. Additional exam requirements/recommendations for international students: Required—TOEFL. *Faculty research:* Molecular mechanisms of mutagenesis, reproductive endocrinology, avian energetics and nutrition, developmental plant physiology.

Southern Illinois University Carbondale, Graduate School, Graduate Program in Medicine, Carbondale, IL 62901-4701. Offers molecular, cellular and systemic physiology (MS); pharmacology (MS, PhD); physiology (MS, PhD). Terminal master's awarded for partial completion of doctoral program. *Degree requirements:* For master's, thesis; for doctorate, thesis/dissertation. *Entrance requirements:* For master's, minimum GPA of 3.0; for doctorate, minimum GPA of 3.25. Additional exam requirements/recommendations for international students: Required—TOEFL. *Faculty research:* Cardiovascular physiology, neurophysiology of hearing.

Southern Illinois University Edwardsville, Graduate Studies and Research, College of Arts and Sciences, Department of Biological Sciences, Program in Biology, Edwardsville, IL 62026-0001. Offers MA, MS. Part-time programs available. *Faculty:* 24 full-time (5 women). *Students:* 21 full-time (9 women), 34 part-time (23 women); includes 2 minority (1 African American, 1 Asian American or Pacific Islander), 2 international. Average age 26. 53 applicants, 38% accepted. In 2009, 8 master's awarded. *Degree requirements:* For master's, thesis (for some programs). *Entrance requirements:* For master's, GRE. Additional exam requirements/recommendations for international students: Required—TOEFL (minimum score 550 paper-based; 213 computer-based; 79 iBT), IELTS (minimum score 6.5). *Application deadline:* For fall admission, 7/23 for domestic students, 6/1 for international students; for spring admission, 12/11 for domestic students, 10/1 for international students. Applications are processed on a rolling basis. Application fee: $30. Electronic applications accepted. *Expenses:* Tuition, state resident: part-time $1252.50 per semester. Tuition, nonresident: part-time $3131.25 per semester. Required fees: $586.85 per semester. Tuition and fees vary according to course load. *Financial support:* In 2009–10, 1 fellowship with full tuition reimbursement, 4 research assistantships with full tuition reimbursements (averaging $8,064 per year), 31 teaching assistantships with full tuition reimbursements (averaging $8,064 per year) were awarded. Financial award application deadline: 3/1; financial award applicants required to submit FAFSA. *Unit head:* Dr. Dave Duvernell, Director, 618-650-3468, E-mail: dduvern@siue.edu. *Application contact:* Michelle

Biological and Biomedical Sciences—General

Southern Illinois University Edwardsville (continued)
Robinson, Coordinator of Graduate Recruitment, 618-650-2811 Ext. 618, Fax: 618-650-3523, E-mail: michero@siue.edu.

Southern Methodist University, Dedman College, Department of Biological Sciences, Dallas, TX 75275. Offers MA, MS, PhD. *Faculty:* 12 full-time (3 women), 1 (woman) part-time/adjunct. *Students:* 7 full-time (6 women), 6 part-time (4 women); includes 1 minority (Asian American or Pacific Islander), 9 international. Average age 27. 23 applicants, 13% accepted. In 2009, 3 master's, 3 doctorates awarded. Terminal master's awarded for partial completion of doctoral program. *Degree requirements:* For master's, thesis (MS), oral exam; for doctorate, thesis/dissertation, qualifying exam. *Entrance requirements:* For master's, GRE General Test (minimum score 1200), minimum GPA of 3.0; for doctorate, GRE General Test (minimum score: 1200), minimum GPA of 3.0. Additional exam requirements/recommendations for international students: Required—TOEFL (minimum score 550 paper-based; 217 computer-based). *Application deadline:* For fall admission, 2/1 priority date for domestic and international students; for spring admission, 11/30 priority date for domestic and international students. Applications are processed on a rolling basis. Application fee: $60. Electronic applications accepted. *Financial support:* In 2009–10, 7 research assistantships with full tuition reimbursements (averaging $20,280 per year), 7 teaching assistantships with full tuition reimbursements (averaging $20,280 per year) were awarded; Federal Work-Study, health care benefits, and tuition waivers (partial) also available. Financial award applicants required to submit FAFSA. *Faculty research:* Free radicals and aging, protein structure, chromatin structure, signal processes, retroviral pathogenesis. Total annual research expenditures: $2 million. *Unit head:* Dr. Bill Orr, Head, 214-768-4018, Fax: 214-768-3955. *Application contact:* Dr. Pia Vogel, Graduate Advisor, 214-768-1790, Fax: 214-768-3955, E-mail: pvogel@smu.edu.

Southern University and Agricultural and Mechanical College, Graduate School, College of Sciences, Department of Biology, Baton Rouge, LA 70813. Offers MS. *Degree requirements:* For master's, comprehensive exam, thesis. *Entrance requirements:* For master's, GRE General Test. Additional exam requirements/recommendations for international students: Required—TOEFL (minimum score 525 paper-based; 193 computer-based). *Faculty research:* Toxicology, neuroendocrinology, mycotoxin, virology.

Stanford University, School of Humanities and Sciences, Department of Biological Sciences, Stanford, CA 94305-9991. Offers MS, PhD. Terminal master's awarded for partial completion of doctoral program. *Degree requirements:* For doctorate, thesis/dissertation, oral exam. *Entrance requirements:* For master's, GRE General Test; for doctorate, GRE General Test, GRE Subject Test. Additional exam requirements/recommendations for international students: Required—TOEFL. Electronic applications accepted. *Expenses:* Tuition: Full-time $37,380; part-time $2760 per quarter. Required fees: $501.

Stanford University, School of Medicine, Graduate Programs in Medicine, Stanford, CA 94305-9991. Offers MS, PhD. Terminal master's awarded for partial completion of doctoral program. *Degree requirements:* For master's, thesis; for doctorate, thesis/dissertation. *Entrance requirements:* For master's, GRE General Test or MCAT. Additional exam requirements/recommendations for international students: Required—TOEFL. Electronic applications accepted. *Expenses:* Tuition: Full-time $37,380; part-time $2760 per quarter. Required fees: $501.

State University of New York at Binghamton, Graduate School, School of Arts and Sciences, Department of Biological Sciences, Binghamton, NY 13902-6000. Offers MA, PhD. *Faculty:* 23 full-time (6 women), 9 part-time/adjunct (3 women). *Students:* 57 full-time (31 women), 18 part-time (10 women); includes 7 minority (1 African American, 4 Asian Americans or Pacific Islanders, 2 Hispanic Americans), 18 international. Average age 26. 96 applicants, 48% accepted, 30 enrolled. In 2009, 11 master's, 6 doctorates awarded. Terminal master's awarded for partial completion of doctoral program. *Degree requirements:* For master's, thesis, oral exam, seminar presentation; for doctorate, comprehensive exam, thesis/dissertation. *Entrance requirements:* For master's and doctorate, GRE General Test, GRE Subject Test. Additional exam requirements/recommendations for international students: Required—TOEFL (minimum score 550 paper-based; 213 computer-based; 80 iBT). *Application deadline:* For fall admission, 1/15 priority date for domestic and international students; for spring admission, 10/15 priority date for domestic and international students. Applications are processed on a rolling basis. Application fee: $60. Electronic applications accepted. *Financial support:* In 2009–10, 42 students received support, including 1 fellowship with full tuition reimbursement available (averaging $17,500 per year), 7 research assistantships with full tuition reimbursements available (averaging $17,500 per year), 33 teaching assistantships with full tuition reimbursements available (averaging $17,500 per year); career-related internships or fieldwork, Federal Work-Study, institutionally sponsored loans, scholarships/grants, health care benefits, and unspecified assistantships also available. Financial award application deadline: 2/15; financial award applicants required to submit FAFSA. *Unit head:* Dr. Susannah Gal, Chairperson, 607-777-4448, E-mail: sgal@binghamton.edu. *Application contact:* Victoria Williams, Recruiting and Admissions Coordinator, 607-777-2151, Fax: 607-777-2501, E-mail: vwilliam@binghamton.edu.

State University of New York at Fredonia, Graduate Studies, Department of Biology, Fredonia, NY 14063-1136. Offers MS, MS Ed. Part-time and evening/weekend programs available. *Degree requirements:* For master's, thesis optional. *Expenses:* Tuition, state resident: full-time $8370; part-time $349 per credit. Tuition, nonresident: full-time $13,250; part-time $552 per credit. Required fees: $1289; $53.55 per credit.

State University of New York at New Paltz, Graduate School, School of Science and Engineering, Department of Biology, New Paltz, NY 12561. Offers MA. Part-time and evening/weekend programs available. *Faculty:* 4 full-time (1 woman). *Students:* 5 part-time (3 women). Average age 31. 9 applicants, 22% accepted, 2 enrolled. In 2009, 8 master's awarded. *Degree requirements:* For master's, comprehensive exam, thesis (for some programs). *Entrance requirements:* For master's, GRE General Test, GRE Subject Test, minimum GPA of 3.0. Additional exam requirements/recommendations for international students: Required—TOEFL (minimum score 550 paper-based; 213 computer-based; 80 iBT), IELTS (minimum score 6.5). *Application deadline:* For fall admission, 5/15 for domestic and international students; for spring admission, 11/15 for domestic and international students. Application fee: $50. Electronic applications accepted. *Financial support:* In 2009–10, 5 students received support, including 4 teaching assistantships with partial tuition reimbursements available (averaging $5,000 per year); Federal Work-Study, institutionally sponsored loans, tuition waivers (full), and unspecified assistantships also available. Financial award application deadline: 8/1; financial award applicants required to submit FAFSA. *Faculty research:* Neurohormonal regulation of feeding in insects. *Unit head:* Dr. Thomas Nolen, Chair, 845-257-3770, E-mail: nolent@newpaltz.edu. *Application contact:* Prof. Jeffrey Reinking, Coordinator, 845-257-3771, E-mail: reinkinj@newpaltz.edu.

State University of New York College at Oneonta, Graduate Education, Department of Biology, Oneonta, NY 13820-4015. Offers MA. Part-time and evening/weekend programs available. *Students:* 7 full-time (6 women). Average age 26. 2 applicants, 100% accepted, 2 enrolled. In 2009, 1 master's awarded. *Degree requirements:* For master's, comprehensive exam. *Entrance requirements:* For master's, GRE General Test, GRE Subject Test. *Application deadline:* For fall admission, 3/25 priority date for domestic students; for spring admission, 10/1 priority date for domestic students. Applications are processed on a rolling basis. Application fee: $50. *Expenses:* Tuition, state resident: part-time $349 per credit hour. Tuition, nonresident: full-time $12,870; part-time $552 per credit hour. Required fees: $1280; $15.85 per credit hour. *Unit head:* Dr. William Pietraface, Chair, 607-436-3703, Fax: 607-436-3646, E-mail: pietrawj@oneonta.edu. *Application contact:* Dean, 607-436-2523, Fax: 607-436-3084, E-mail: gradoffice@oneonta.edu.

State University of New York Downstate Medical Center, School of Graduate Studies, Brooklyn, NY 11203-2098. Offers MS, PhD, MD/PhD. *Degree requirements:* For doctorate, thesis/dissertation. *Entrance requirements:* For doctorate, GRE. Additional exam requirements/

recommendations for international students: Required—TOEFL. *Faculty research:* Cellular and molecular neurobiology, role of oncogenes in early cardiogenesis, mechanism of gene regulation, cardiovascular physiology, yeast molecular genetics.

State University of New York Upstate Medical University, College of Graduate Studies, Syracuse, NY 13210-2334. Offers MS, PhD, MD/PhD. *Faculty:* 96 full-time (17 women), 8 part-time/adjunct (1 woman). *Students:* 119 full-time (68 women), 5 part-time (4 women); includes 14 minority (2 African Americans, 9 Asian Americans or Pacific Islanders, 3 Hispanic Americans), 44 international. Average age 28. 160 applicants, 25% accepted, 20 enrolled. In 2009, 7 master's, 14 doctorates awarded. Terminal master's awarded for partial completion of doctoral program. *Degree requirements:* For master's, thesis; for doctorate, comprehensive exam, thesis/dissertation. *Entrance requirements:* For master's, GRE General Test, interview; for doctorate, GRE General Test, telephone interview. Additional exam requirements/recommendations for international students: Required—TOEFL. *Application deadline:* Applications are processed on a rolling basis. Application fee: $40. Electronic applications accepted. *Financial support:* In 2009–10, 116 students received support, including fellowships with tuition reimbursements available (averaging $21,514 per year), research assistantships with tuition reimbursements available (averaging $21,514 per year); Federal Work-Study, institutionally sponsored loans, health care benefits, and unspecified assistantships also available. Financial award application deadline: 4/15; financial award applicants required to submit FAFSA. *Faculty research:* Cancer, disorders of the nervous system, infectious diseases, diabetes/metabolic disorders/cardiovascular diseases. *Unit head:* Dr. Steven R. Goodman, Dean, College of Graduate Studies, 315-464-4538. *Application contact:* Sandra Tillotson, Coordinator of Graduate Recruitment, 315-464-7655, Fax: 315-464-4544, E-mail: tillotss@upstate.edu.

See Close-Up on page 109.

Stephen F. Austin State University, Graduate School, College of Sciences and Mathematics, Department of Biology, Nacogdoches, TX 75962. Offers MS. *Degree requirements:* For master's, comprehensive exam, thesis optional. *Entrance requirements:* For master's, GRE General Test, minimum GPA of 2.8 in last 60 hours, 2.5 overall. Additional exam requirements/recommendations for international students: Required—TOEFL.

Stony Brook University, State University of New York, Stony Brook University Medical Center, School of Medicine and Graduate School, Graduate Programs in Medicine, Stony Brook, NY 11794. Offers PhD. *Students:* 96 full-time (56 women), 29 part-time (24 women); includes 32 minority (11 African Americans, 16 Asian Americans or Pacific Islanders, 5 Hispanic Americans), 26 international. 201 applicants, 23% accepted. In 2009, 19 doctorates awarded. *Degree requirements:* For doctorate, thesis/dissertation, exam. *Entrance requirements:* For doctorate, GRE General Test. Additional exam requirements/recommendations for international students: Required—TOEFL. *Application deadline:* For fall admission, 1/15 for domestic students. Application fee: $60. Electronic applications accepted. *Expenses:* Contact institution. *Financial support:* Fellowships, research assistantships, teaching assistantships, career-related internships or fieldwork and Federal Work-Study available. Financial award application deadline: 3/15. Total annual research expenditures: $44.9 million. *Unit head:* Dr. Richard N. Fine, Dean, 631-444-2113. *Application contact:* Dr. William Jungers, Chair, 631-444-3122, Fax: 631-444-3947, E-mail: william.jungers@stonybrook.edu.

Stony Brook University, State University of New York, Stony Brook University Medical Center, School of Medicine, Medical Scientist Training Program, Stony Brook, NY 11794. Offers MD/PhD. *Application deadline:* For fall admission, 1/15 for domestic students. *Expenses:* Tuition, state resident: full-time $8370; part-time $349 per credit. Tuition, nonresident: full-time $13,250; part-time $552 per credit. Required fees: $933. *Financial support:* Tuition waivers (full) available. *Unit head:* Dr. Richard N. Fine, Dean, 631-444-2113. *Application contact:* Dr. Richard N. Fine, Dean, 631-444-2113.

Sul Ross State University, School of Arts and Sciences, Department of Biology, Alpine, TX 79832. Offers MS. Part-time programs available. *Degree requirements:* For master's, thesis optional. *Entrance requirements:* For master's, GRE General Test, minimum GPA of 2.5 in last 60 hours of undergraduate work. *Faculty research:* Plant-animal interaction, Chihuahuan desert biology, insect biological control, plant and animal systematics, wildlife biology.

Syracuse University, College of Arts and Sciences, Program in Biology, Syracuse, NY 13244. Offers MS, PhD. Part-time programs available. *Students:* 31 full-time (22 women), 4 part-time (1 woman); includes 1 minority (African American), 16 international. Average age 28. 72 applicants, 17% accepted, 7 enrolled. In 2009, 1 master's, 3 doctorates awarded. Terminal master's awarded for partial completion of doctoral program. *Degree requirements:* For master's, thesis; for doctorate, thesis/dissertation. *Entrance requirements:* For master's and doctorate, GRE General Test, GRE Subject Test (recommended). Additional exam requirements/recommendations for international students: Required—TOEFL (minimum score 100 iBT). *Application deadline:* For fall admission, 1/10 priority date for domestic and international students. Application fee: $75. Electronic applications accepted. *Expenses:* Tuition: Full-time $26,808; part-time $1117 per credit. Required fees: $1024. *Financial support:* Fellowships with full tuition reimbursements, research assistantships with full and partial tuition reimbursements, teaching assistantships with full tuition reimbursements, tuition waivers (partial) available. Financial award application deadline: 1/10; financial award applicants required to submit FAFSA. *Faculty research:* Cell signaling, plant ecosystem ecology, aquatic ecology, genetics and molecular biology of color vision, ion transport by cell membranes. *Unit head:* Dr. Scott Pitnick, Graduate Program Director, 315-443-9145, E-mail: biology@syr.edu. *Application contact:* Evelyn Lott, Information Contact, 315-443-9154, Fax: 315-443-2012, E-mail: ealott@syr.edu.

Tarleton State University, College of Graduate Studies, College of Science and Technology, Department of Biological Sciences, Stephenville, TX 76402. Offers biology (MS). Part-time and evening/weekend programs available. *Degree requirements:* For master's, comprehensive exam, thesis (for some programs). *Entrance requirements:* For master's, GRE General Test, minimum GPA of 3.0. Additional exam requirements/recommendations for international students: Required—TOEFL (minimum score 550 paper-based; 213 computer-based; 80 iBT). Electronic applications accepted.

Temple University, Graduate School, College of Science and Technology, Department of Biology, Philadelphia, PA 19122-6096. Offers MS, PhD. Terminal master's awarded for partial completion of doctoral program. *Degree requirements:* For master's, thesis; for doctorate, thesis/dissertation. *Entrance requirements:* For master's and doctorate, GRE General Test, minimum GPA of 3.0. Additional exam requirements/recommendations for international students: Required—TOEFL (minimum score 550 paper-based; 213 computer-based; 79 iBT). *Faculty research:* Membrane proteins, genetics, molecular biology, neuroscience, aquatic biology.

Temple University, Health Sciences Center, School of Medicine and Graduate School, Graduate Programs in Medicine, Philadelphia, PA 19122-6096. Offers MS, PhD, MD/PhD. Terminal master's awarded for partial completion of doctoral program. *Degree requirements:* For master's, thesis; for doctorate, thesis/dissertation, research seminars. *Entrance requirements:* For master's and doctorate, GRE General Test. Additional exam requirements/recommendations for international students: Required—TOEFL. Electronic applications accepted. *Expenses:* Contact institution. *Faculty research:* Molecular biology and biochemistry; cardiovascular, renal, and neurophysiological pharmacology; reproductive and developmental biology; immunology and microbiology; cancer research.

Tennessee State University, The School of Graduate Studies and Research, College of Arts and Sciences, Department of Biological Sciences, Nashville, TN 37209-1561. Offers MS, PhD. *Degree requirements:* For master's, thesis optional; for doctorate, thesis/dissertation. *Entrance requirements:* For master's, GRE General Test, GRE Subject Test, minimum GPA of 2.5; for doctorate, GRE General Test, GRE Subject Test. *Faculty research:* Cellular and molecular biology and agribiology.

Tennessee Technological University, Graduate School, College of Arts and Sciences, Department of Biology, Cookeville, TN 38505. Offers fish, game, and wildlife management (MS). Part-time programs available. *Faculty:* 22 full-time (2 women). *Students:* 15 full-time (4 women), 13 part-time (6 women); includes 1 minority (African American). Average age 25. 23 applicants, 52% accepted, 12 enrolled. In 2009, 14 master's awarded. *Degree requirements:* For master's, thesis. *Entrance requirements:* For master's, GRE. Additional exam requirements/recommendations for international students: Required—TOEFL (minimum score 550 paper-based; 79 iBT), IELTS (minimum score 5.5). *Application deadline:* For fall admission, 8/1 for domestic students, 5/1 for international students; for spring admission, 12/1 for domestic students, 10/1 for international students. Application fee: $25 ($30 for international students). Electronic applications accepted. *Expenses:* Tuition, state resident: full-time $7034; part-time $368 per credit hour. *Financial support:* In 2009–10, 17 research assistantships (averaging $9,000 per year), 8 teaching assistantships (averaging $7,500 per year) were awarded. Financial award application deadline: 4/1. *Faculty research:* Aquatics, environmental studies. *Unit head:* Dr. Daniel Combs, Interim Chairperson, 931-372-3134, Fax: 931-372-6257, E-mail: dcombs@tntech.edu. *Application contact:* Shelia K. Kendrick, Coordinator of Graduate Studies, 931-372-3808, Fax: 931-372-3497, E-mail: skendrick@tntech.edu.

Tennessee Technological University, Graduate School, College of Arts and Sciences, Department of Environmental Sciences, Cookeville, TN 38505. Offers biology (PhD); chemistry (PhD). *Students:* 9 full-time (5 women), 8 part-time (3 women); includes 9 minority (3 African Americans, 3 Asian Americans or Pacific Islanders, 3 Hispanic Americans). 12 applicants, 50% accepted, 3 enrolled. In 2009, 1 doctorate awarded. *Degree requirements:* For doctorate, comprehensive exam, thesis/dissertation. *Entrance requirements:* For doctorate, GRE. Additional exam requirements/recommendations for international students: Required—TOEFL (minimum score 550 paper-based; 79 iBT), IELTS (minimum score 5.5). *Application deadline:* For fall admission, 8/1 for domestic students, 5/1 for international students; for spring admission, 12/1 for domestic students, 10/2 for international students. Application fee: $25 ($30 for international students). Electronic applications accepted. *Expenses:* Tuition, state resident: full-time $7034; part-time $368 per credit hour. *Financial support:* In 2009–10, 5 research assistantships (averaging $10,000 per year), 3 teaching assistantships (averaging $10,000 per year) were awarded; fellowships also available. Financial award application deadline: 4/1. *Unit head:* Dr. Dal Ensor, Director. *Application contact:* Shelia K. Kendrick, Coordinator of Graduate Studies, 931-372-3808, Fax: 931-372-3497, E-mail: skendrick@tntech.edu.

Texas A&M Health Science Center, Baylor College of Dentistry, Graduate Division, Department of Biomedical Sciences, College Station, TX 77840. Offers MS, PhD. Part-time programs available. Terminal master's awarded for partial completion of doctoral program. *Degree requirements:* For master's, thesis; for doctorate, thesis/dissertation. *Entrance requirements:* For master's, GRE General Test; for doctorate, GRE General Test, DDS or DMD. Additional exam requirements/recommendations for international students: Required—TOEFL. *Faculty research:* Craniofacial biology, aging, neuroscience, physiology, molecular/cellular biology.

Texas A&M Health Science Center, Graduate School of Biomedical Sciences, College Station, TX 77840. Offers cell and molecular biology (PhD); microbial and molecular pathogenesis (PhD), including immunology, microbiology, molecular biology, virology; molecular and cellular medicine (PhD); neuroscience and experimental therapeutics (PhD); systems biology and translational medicine (PhD); MD/PhD. *Degree requirements:* For doctorate, thesis/dissertation. *Entrance requirements:* For doctorate, GRE General Test, minimum GPA of 3.0. Additional exam requirements/recommendations for international students: Required—TOEFL. *Faculty research:* Fetal alcohol syndrome, cardiovascular, microbial pathogenosis, cancer.

Texas A&M Health Science Center, Institute of Biosciences and Technology, Houston, TX 77030-3303. Offers medical sciences (PhD). Degree awarded by the Graduate School for Biomedical Sciences. *Degree requirements:* For doctorate, thesis/dissertation. *Entrance requirements:* For doctorate, GRE General Test. Additional exam requirements/recommendations for international students: Required—TOEFL, TWE. *Expenses:* Contact institution. *Faculty research:* Cancer biology, DNA structure, extracellular matrix biology, development, birth defects.

Texas A&M International University, Office of Graduate Studies and Research, College of Arts and Sciences, Department of Biology and Chemistry, Laredo, TX 78041-1900. Offers biology (MS). *Faculty:* 3 full-time (0 women). *Students:* 2 full-time (1 woman), 13 part-time (8 women); includes 14 minority (1 Asian American or Pacific Islander, 13 Hispanic Americans), 1 international. Average age 28. 16 applicants, 88% accepted, 6 enrolled.Application fee: $25. *Financial support:* In 2009–10, 9 students received support, including 1 fellowship, 2 teaching assistantships. *Unit head:* Dr. Daniel Mott, Chair, 956-326-2583. *Application contact:* Rosie Dickinson, Director of Admissions, 956-326-2200.

Texas A&M University, College of Science, Department of Biology, College Station, TX 77843. Offers biology (MS, PhD); botany (MS, PhD); microbiology (MS, PhD); molecular and cell biology (PhD); neuroscience (MS, PhD); zoology (MS, PhD). *Faculty:* 37. *Students:* 101 full-time (59 women), 5 part-time (3 women); includes 8 minority (1 African American, 3 Asian Americans or Pacific Islanders, 4 Hispanic Americans), 40 international. Average age 28. In 2009, 9 master's, 5 doctorates awarded. *Degree requirements:* For master's, thesis or alternative; for doctorate, comprehensive exam, thesis/dissertation. *Entrance requirements:* For master's and doctorate, GRE General Test. Additional exam requirements/recommendations for international students: Required—TOEFL. *Application deadline:* For fall admission, 1/15 for domestic students. Applications are processed on a rolling basis. Application fee: $50 ($75 for international students). Electronic applications accepted. *Expenses:* Tuition, state resident: full-time $3991; part-time $221.74 per credit hour. Tuition, nonresident: full-time $9049; part-time $502.74 per credit hour. *Financial support:* Fellowships, research assistantships, teaching assistantships available. Financial award application deadline: 4/1; financial award applicants required to submit FAFSA. *Unit head:* Dr. Jack McMahan, Department Head, 979-845-2301, E-mail: granster@mail.bio.tamu.edu. *Application contact:* Graduate Advisor, 979-845-7755.

Texas A&M University–Commerce, Graduate School, College of Arts and Sciences, Department of Biological and Earth Sciences, Commerce, TX 75429-3011. Offers M Ed, MS. *Degree requirements:* For master's, comprehensive exam, thesis (for some programs). *Entrance requirements:* For master's, GRE General Test. Electronic applications accepted. *Faculty research:* Microbiology, botany, environmental science, birds.

Texas A&M University–Corpus Christi, Graduate Studies and Research, College of Science and Technology, Program in Biology, Corpus Christi, TX 78412-5503. Offers MS.

Texas A&M University–Kingsville, College of Graduate Studies, College of Arts and Sciences, Department of Biology, Kingsville, TX 78363. Offers MS. Part-time programs available. *Degree requirements:* For master's, comprehensive exam, thesis or alternative. *Entrance requirements:* For master's, GRE General Test, minimum GPA of 3.0. Additional exam requirements/recommendations for international students: Required—TOEFL. *Faculty research:* Venom physiology, monoclonal research with venom, shore bird ecology, metabolism of foreign amino acids.

Texas Christian University, College of Science and Engineering, Department of Biology, Fort Worth, TX 76129-0002. Offers MA, MS. Part-time and evening/weekend programs available. *Degree requirements:* For master's, comprehensive exam, thesis (for some programs). *Entrance requirements:* For master's, GRE General Test. Additional exam requirements/recommendations for international students: Required—TOEFL. *Application deadline:* For fall admission, 1/15 for domestic students; for spring admission, 7/15 for domestic students. Applications are processed on a rolling basis. Application fee: $50. Electronic applications accepted. *Expenses:* Tuition: Full-time $17,640; part-time $980 per credit hour. Tuition and fees vary according to program. *Financial support:* In 2009–10, 10 teaching assistantships with full tuition reimbursements were awarded. Financial award application deadline: 1/15; financial award applicants required to submit FAFSA. *Unit head:* Dr. Ray Drenner, Chairperson, 817-257-7165, E-mail: r.drenner@TCU.edu. *Application contact:* Dr. Magnus Rittby, Associate Dean, College of Science and Engineering, 817-257-7729, E-mail: m.rittby@tcu.edu.

Texas Southern University, School of Science and Technology, Department of Biology, Houston, TX 77004-4584. Offers MS. Part-time and evening/weekend programs available. *Faculty:* 7 full-time (3 women). *Students:* 18 full-time (16 women), 16 part-time (13 women); includes 25 African Americans, 2 Asian Americans or Pacific Islanders, 1 Hispanic American, 1 international. Average age 28. 13 applicants, 92% accepted, 10 enrolled. In 2009, 2 master's awarded. *Degree requirements:* For master's, one foreign language, comprehensive exam, thesis. *Entrance requirements:* For master's, GRE General Test, minimum GPA of 2.5. Additional exam requirements/recommendations for international students: Required—TOEFL. *Application deadline:* For fall admission, 7/1 for domestic and international students; for spring admission, 11/1 for domestic and international students. Applications are processed on a rolling basis. Application fee: $50 ($75 for international students). Electronic applications accepted. *Expenses:* Tuition, state resident: full-time $1805; part-time $100 per credit hour. Tuition, nonresident: full-time $6470; part-time $343 per credit hour. Tuition and fees vary according to course level, course load and degree level. *Financial support:* In 2009–10, 9 research assistantships (averaging $4,200 per year), 4 teaching assistantships (averaging $9,600 per year) were awarded; fellowships, career-related internships or fieldwork, scholarships/grants, and unspecified assistantships also available. Financial award application deadline: 5/1. *Faculty research:* Microbiology, cell and molecular biology, biochemistry, biochemical virology, biophysics. *Unit head:* Dr. Olufisay Jejelowo, Chairman, 713-313-1032, E-mail: jejelowo_oa@tsu.edu. *Application contact:* Shirley Harris, Information Contact, 713-313-7838.

Texas State University–San Marcos, Graduate School, College of Science, Department of Biology, Program in Biology, San Marcos, TX 78666. Offers M Ed, MA, MS. *Faculty:* 7 full-time (3 women). *Students:* 27 full-time (12 women), 17 part-time (11 women); includes 12 minority (5 Asian Americans or Pacific Islanders, 7 Hispanic Americans), 3 international. Average age 29. 20 applicants, 85% accepted, 15 enrolled. In 2009, 14 master's awarded. *Degree requirements:* For master's, comprehensive exam, thesis (for some programs). *Entrance requirements:* For master's, GRE General Test (minimum score 1000 preferred), minimum GPA of 3.0 in last 60 hours of undergraduate work. Additional exam requirements/recommendations for international students: Required—TOEFL (minimum score 550 paper-based; 213 computer-based). *Application deadline:* For fall admission, 6/15 for domestic students, 6/1 for international students; for spring admission, 10/15 for domestic students, 10/1 for international students. Applications are processed on a rolling basis. Application fee: $40 ($90 for international students). Electronic applications accepted. *Expenses:* Tuition, state resident: full-time $5784; part-time $241 per credit hour. Tuition, nonresident: full-time $13,224; part-time $551 per credit hour. Required fees: $1728; $48 per credit hour. $306. Tuition and fees vary according to course load. *Financial support:* In 2009–10, 15 students received support, including 2 research assistantships (averaging $5,141 per year), 24 teaching assistantships (averaging $5,869 per year). Financial award application deadline: 4/1. *Unit head:* Dr. David Lemke, Graduate Advisor, 512-245-2178, E-mail: dl10@txstate.edu. *Application contact:* Dr. J. Michael Willoughby, Dean of the Graduate School, 512-245-2581, Fax: 512-245-8365, E-mail: jw02@swt.edu.

Texas State University–San Marcos, Graduate School, Interdisciplinary Studies Program in Biology, San Marcos, TX 78666. Offers MSIS. *Students:* 1 applicant, 0% accepted, 0 enrolled. *Degree requirements:* For master's, comprehensive exam, thesis optional. *Entrance requirements:* For master's, GRE (minimum score 1000 verbal and quantitative preferred), bachelor's degree in biology or related field, minimum GPA of 3.0 in last 60 hours of undergraduate work. Additional exam requirements/recommendations for international students: Required—TOEFL (minimum score 550 paper-based; 213 computer-based). *Application deadline:* For fall admission, 6/15 priority date for domestic students, 6/1 for international students; for spring admission, 10/15 priority date for domestic students, 10/1 for international students. Applications are processed on a rolling basis. Application fee: $40 ($90 for international students). *Expenses:* Tuition, state resident: full-time $5784; part-time $241 per credit hour. Tuition, nonresident: full-time $13,224; part-time $551 per credit hour. Required fees: $1728; $48 per credit hour. $306. Tuition and fees vary according to course load. *Financial support:* Application deadline: 4/1. *Unit head:* Dr. David Lemker, Graduate Advisor, 512-245-2178, E-mail: dl10@txstate.edu. *Application contact:* Dr. J. Michael Willoughby, Dean of Graduate School, 512-245-2581, Fax: 512-245-8365, E-mail: gradcollege@txstate.edu.

Texas Tech University, Graduate School, College of Arts and Sciences, Department of Biological Sciences, Lubbock, TX 79409. Offers biological informatics (MS); biology (MS, PhD); microbiology (MS); zoology (MS, PhD). Part-time programs available. *Faculty:* 31 full-time (6 women). *Students:* 120 full-time (59 women), 5 part-time (3 women); includes 5 minority (1 Asian American or Pacific Islander, 4 Hispanic Americans), 65 international. Average age 29. 121 applicants, 42% accepted, 24 enrolled. In 2009, 17 master's, 6 doctorates awarded. *Degree requirements:* For master's, thesis or alternative; for doctorate, thesis/dissertation. *Entrance requirements:* For master's and doctorate, GRE General Test. Additional exam requirements/recommendations for international students: Required—TOEFL (minimum score 550 paper-based; 213 computer-based). *Application deadline:* For fall admission, 3/1 priority date for international students; for spring admission, 11/1 priority date for international students. Applications are processed on a rolling basis. Application fee: $50 ($75 for international students). Electronic applications accepted. *Expenses:* Tuition, state resident: full-time $5100; part-time $213 per credit hour. Tuition, nonresident: full-time $11,748; part-time $490 per credit hour. Required fees: $2298; $50 per credit hour. $555 per semester. *Financial support:* In 2009–10, 16 research assistantships with partial tuition reimbursements (averaging $21,854 per year), 11 teaching assistantships with partial tuition reimbursements (averaging $19,985 per year) were awarded; career-related internships or fieldwork, Federal Work-Study, and institutionally sponsored loans also available. Support available to part-time students. Financial award application deadline: 4/15; financial award applicants required to submit FAFSA. *Faculty research:* Biodiversity and evolution, climate change in arid ecosystems, plant biology and biotechnology, animal communication and behavior, zoonotic and emerging diseases. Total annual research expenditures: $2.1 million. *Unit head:* Dr. Llewellyn D. Densmore, Chair, 806-742-2715, Fax: 806-742-2963, E-mail: jlou.densmore@ttu.edu. *Application contact:* Dr. Randall M. Jeter, Graduate Adviser, 806-742-2710 Ext. 223, Fax: 806-742-2963, E-mail: randall.jeter@ttu.edu.

Texas Tech University Health Sciences Center, Graduate School of Biomedical Sciences, Lubbock, TX 79430-0002. Offers MS, PhD, MD/PhD, MS/PhD. *Faculty:* 94 full-time (21 women), 10 part-time/adjunct (2 women). *Students:* 96 full-time (39 women), 1 (woman) part-time; includes 39 minority (1 African American, 1 American Indian/Alaska Native, 34 Asian Americans or Pacific Islanders, 3 Hispanic Americans), 25 international. Average age 29. 204 applicants, 22% accepted, 29 enrolled. In 2009, 8 master's, 4 doctorates awarded. Terminal master's awarded for partial completion of doctoral program. *Degree requirements:* For master's, thesis; for doctorate, thesis/dissertation. *Entrance requirements:* For master's and doctorate, GRE General Test, minimum GPA of 3.0. Additional exam requirements/recommendations for international students: Required—TOEFL (minimum score 550 paper-based; 213 computer-based). *Application deadline:* For fall admission, 5/15 priority date for domestic students, 4/15 for international students; for spring admission, 11/15 priority date for domestic students, 10/15 for international students. Applications are processed on a rolling basis. Application fee: $45. Electronic applications accepted. *Financial support:* In 2009–10, 6 fellowships with partial tuition reimbursements (averaging $21,000 per year), 43 research assistantships with full and partial tuition reimbursements (averaging $21,000 per year) were awarded; institutionally sponsored loans and scholarships/grants also available. Financial award applicants required to submit FAFSA. *Faculty research:* Genetics of neurological disorders, hemodynamics to prevent DVT, toxin A synthesis, DA neurons, peroxidases. Total annual research expenditures: $6.5 million. *Unit head:* Dr. Luis Reuss, Associate Dean, 806-743-2556, Fax: 806-743-2656, E-mail: acagsbs@ttuhsc.edu. *Application contact:* Pamela Johnson, Director of Graduate Programs, 806-743-2556, Fax: 806-743-2656, E-mail: pamela.johnson@ttuhsc.edu.

Biological and Biomedical Sciences—General

Texas Woman's University, Graduate School, College of Arts and Sciences, Department of Biology, Denton, TX 76201. Offers biology (MS); biology teaching (MS); molecular biology (PhD). Part-time programs available. *Faculty:* 12 full-time (8 women), 1 (woman) part-time/adjunct. *Students:* 25 full-time (17 women), 16 part-time (9 women); includes 6 minority (4 African Americans, 2 Hispanic Americans), 29 international. Average age 28. 29 applicants, 79% accepted, 12 enrolled. In 2009, 2 master's, 4 doctorates awarded. Terminal master's awarded for partial completion of doctoral program. *Degree requirements:* For master's, comprehensive exam, thesis (for some programs); for doctorate, comprehensive exam, thesis/dissertation, residency. *Entrance requirements:* For master's, GRE General Test (minimum score 425 verbal, 425 quantitative), 3 letters of reference; for doctorate, GRE General Test (minimum score: Verbal 425, Quantitative 425), 3 letters of reference, letter of interest. Additional exam requirements/recommendations for international students: Required—TOEFL (minimum score 550 paper-based; 213 computer-based; 79 iBT). *Application deadline:* For fall admission, 7/1 priority date for domestic students, 3/1 for international students; for spring admission, 12/1 priority date for domestic students, 7/1 for international students. Applications are processed on a rolling basis. Application fee: $50. Electronic applications accepted. *Expenses:* Tuition, state resident: full-time $3564; part-time $198 per credit hour. Tuition, nonresident: full-time $8550; part-time $475 per credit hour. Required fees: $69.26 per credit hour. Tuition and fees vary according to course load. *Financial support:* In 2009–10, 5 students received support, including 47 research assistantships (averaging $11,862 per year); career-related internships or fieldwork, Federal Work-Study, institutionally sponsored loans, scholarships/grants, traineeships, health care benefits, and unspecified assistantships also available. Support available to part-time students. Financial award application deadline: 3/1; financial award applicants required to submit FAFSA. *Faculty research:* Interacerebral effects of 8-OH-DPAT, rna purification, mechanisms in pathogenesis of gatroduodenal disorders, HHS MBRS program. *Unit head:* Dr. Sarah McIntire, Chair, 940-898-2351, Fax: 940-898-2382, E-mail: biology@twu.edu. *Application contact:* Samuel Wheeler, Assistant Director of Admissions, 940-898-3188, Fax: 940-898-3081, E-mail: wheelersr@twu.edu.

Thomas Jefferson University, Jefferson College of Graduate Studies, Philadelphia, PA 19107. Offers MS, PhD, Certificate, MD/PhD. Part-time and evening/weekend programs available. Postbaccalaureate distance learning degree programs offered (no on-campus study). *Faculty:* 181 full-time (46 women), 25 part-time/adjunct (9 women). *Students:* 142 full-time (81 women), 108 part-time (72 women); includes 48 minority (14 African Americans, 28 Asian Americans or Pacific Islanders, 6 Hispanic Americans), 34 international. Average age 29. 517 applicants, 26% accepted, 95 enrolled. In 2009, 27 master's, 21 doctorates, 5 other advanced degrees awarded. Terminal master's awarded for partial completion of doctoral program. *Degree requirements:* For master's, thesis; for doctorate, comprehensive exam, thesis/dissertation. *Entrance requirements:* For master's, GRE or MCAT; for doctorate, GRE, minimum GPA of 3.2. Additional exam requirements/recommendations for international students: Required—TOEFL (minimum score 250 computer-based; 100 iBT). *Application deadline:* For fall admission, 1/15 priority date for domestic and international students; for winter admission, 6/1 priority date for international students; for spring admission, 9/1 priority date for international students. Applications are processed on a rolling basis. Application fee: $50. Electronic applications accepted. *Expenses:* Tuition: Full-time $26,858; part-time $879 per credit. Required fees: $525. *Financial support:* In 2009–10, 160 students received support, including 125 fellowships with full tuition reimbursements available (averaging $52,883 per year); Federal Work-Study, institutionally sponsored loans, scholarships/grants, and traineeships also available. Support available to part-time students. Financial award application deadline: 5/1; financial award applicants required to submit FAFSA. *Unit head:* Dr. James H. Keen, Dean, 215-503-8982, Fax: 215-503-6690, E-mail: james.keen@jefferson.edu. *Application contact:* Marc E. Stearns, Director of Admissions, 215-503-0155, Fax: 215-503-9920, E-mail: jcgs-info@jefferson.edu.

See Close-Up on page 111.

Towson University, College of Graduate Studies and Research, Program in Biology, Towson, MD 21252-0001. Offers MS. Part-time and evening/weekend programs available. *Degree requirements:* For master's, thesis optional, exam. *Entrance requirements:* For master's, GRE General Test (for thesis students), minimum GPA of 3.0, 24 credits in related course work, 3 letters of recommendation, minimum 24 units in biology, coursework in chemistry, organic chemistry, and physics. Additional exam requirements/recommendations for international students: Required—TOEFL. Electronic applications accepted. *Faculty research:* Microbiology, molecular biology, ecology, physiology, conservation biology.

Trent University, Graduate Studies, Program in Applications of Modeling in the Natural and Social Sciences, Peterborough, ON K9J 7B8, Canada. Offers applications of modeling in the natural and social sciences (MA); biology (M Sc, PhD); chemistry (M Sc); computer studies (M Sc); geography (M Sc, PhD); physics (M Sc). Part-time programs available. *Degree requirements:* For master's, thesis. *Entrance requirements:* For master's, honours degree. *Faculty research:* Computation of heat transfer, atmospheric physics, statistical mechanics, stress and coping, evolutionary ecology.

Trent University, Graduate Studies, Program in Environmental and Life Sciences and Program in Applications of Modeling in the Natural and Social Sciences, Department of Biology, Peterborough, ON K9J 7B8, Canada. Offers M Sc, PhD. Part-time programs available. *Degree requirements:* For master's, thesis; for doctorate, thesis/dissertation. *Entrance requirements:* For master's, honours degree; for doctorate, master's degree. *Faculty research:* Aquatic and behavioral ecology, hydrology and limnology, human impact on ecosystems, behavioral ecology of birds, ecology of fish.

Truman State University, Graduate School, School of Arts and Letters, Program in Biology, Kirksville, MO 63501-4221. Offers MS. *Faculty:* 7 full-time (2 women). *Students:* 3 full-time (2 women). 3 applicants, 100% accepted, 3 enrolled. *Degree requirements:* For master's, comprehensive exam, thesis. *Entrance requirements:* For master's, GRE General Test, minimum GPA of 3.0. Additional exam requirements/recommendations for international students: Required—TOEFL (minimum score 550 paper-based; 213 computer-based). *Application deadline:* For fall admission, 6/1 priority date for domestic students, 6/1 for international students; for spring admission, 11/1 for domestic and international students. Applications are processed on a rolling basis. Application fee: $0. Electronic applications accepted. *Expenses:* Tuition, state resident: part-time $291 per credit. Tuition, nonresident: part-time $499 per credit hour. Tuition and fees vary according to course load. *Financial support:* In 2009–10, research assistantships with tuition reimbursements (averaging $8,000 per year), teaching assistantships with tuition reimbursements (averaging $8,000 per year) were awarded; career-related internships or fieldwork and Federal Work-Study also available. Financial award application deadline: 5/1; financial award applicants required to submit FAFSA. *Unit head:* Dr. Laura Fielden, Director, 660-785-4624. *Application contact:* Doris Snyder, Graduate Office Secretary, E-mail: dsnyder@truman.edu.

Tufts University, Cummings School of Veterinary Medicine, North Grafton, MA 01536. Offers comparative biomedical sciences (PhD); veterinary medicine (DVM, MS); DVM/MPH; DVM/MS. *Accreditation:* AVMA (one or more programs are accredited). *Faculty:* 85 full-time (32 women), 164 part-time/adjunct (79 women). *Students:* 355 full-time (309 women); includes 20 minority (6 African Americans, 1 American Indian/Alaska Native, 6 Asian Americans or Pacific Islanders, 7 Hispanic Americans), 6 international. Average age 25. 747 applicants, 25% accepted, 97 enrolled. In 2009, 78 first professional degrees, 13 master's, 1 doctorate awarded. *Degree requirements:* For master's, thesis (for some programs); for doctorate, comprehensive exam, thesis/dissertation; for DVM, thesis/dissertation optional. *Entrance requirements:* For DVM, master's, and doctorate, GRE General Test. Additional exam requirements/recommendations for international students: Required—TOEFL, IELTS. *Application deadline:* For fall admission, 11/1 for domestic and international students. Application fee: $70. Electronic applications accepted. *Expenses:* Contact institution. *Financial support:* In 2009–10, 69 students received support, including 6 research assistantships with full tuition reimbursements available (averaging $25,000 per year), 2 teaching assistantships (averaging $5,000 per year); career-related internships or fieldwork, Federal Work-Study, institutionally sponsored loans, scholarships/grants, and institutional aid awards also available. Financial award application deadline: 3/10; financial award applicants required to submit FAFSA. *Faculty research:* Equine sports medicine, oncology, veterinary ethics, international veterinary medicine, veterinary genomics. *Unit head:* Dr. Deborah T. Kochevar, Dean, 508-839-5302, Fax: 508-839-2953, E-mail: deborah.kochevar@tufts.edu. *Application contact:* Rebecca Russo, Director of Admissions, 508-839-7920, Fax: 508-887-4820, E-mail: rebecca.russo@tufts.edu.

Tufts University, Graduate School of Arts and Sciences, Department of Biology, Medford, MA 02155. Offers MS, PhD. Part-time programs available. *Faculty:* 23 full-time. *Students:* 44 (22 women), 11 international. Average age 27. 119 applicants, 11% accepted, 9 enrolled. In 2009, 6 master's, 4 doctorates awarded. Terminal master's awarded for partial completion of doctoral program. *Degree requirements:* For master's, thesis (for some programs); for doctorate, thesis/dissertation. *Entrance requirements:* For master's and doctorate, GRE General Test. Additional exam requirements/recommendations for international students: Required—TOEFL (minimum score 550 paper-based; 213 computer-based; 80 iBT). *Application deadline:* For fall admission, 1/15 for domestic students, 12/15 for international students; for spring admission, 10/15 for domestic students, 9/15 for international students. Applications are processed on a rolling basis. Application fee: $75. Electronic applications accepted. *Expenses:* Tuition: Full-time $38,096; part-time $3962 per credit. Required fees: $686; $40 per year. Tuition and fees vary according to course level, course load, degree level, program and student level. *Financial support:* Fellowships, research assistantships with full and partial tuition reimbursements, teaching assistantships with full and partial tuition reimbursements, Federal Work-Study, scholarships/grants, tuition waivers (partial), and unspecified assistantships available. Financial award application deadline: 1/15; financial award applicants required to submit FAFSA. *Unit head:* Dr. Juliet Fuhrman, Chair, 617-627-3195. *Application contact:* Kelly McLaughlin, Graduate Advisor, 617-627-3195.

Tufts University, Sackler School of Graduate Biomedical Sciences, Medford, MA 02155. Offers MS, PhD, DVM/PhD, MD/PhD. *Faculty:* 173 full-time (55 women). *Students:* 194 full-time (122 women), 4 part-time (all women); includes 32 minority (5 African Americans, 19 Asian Americans or Pacific Islanders, 8 Hispanic Americans), 33 international. Average age 29. 705 applicants, 10% accepted, 41 enrolled. In 2009, 18 master's, 38 doctorates awarded. Terminal master's awarded for partial completion of doctoral program. *Degree requirements:* For master's, thesis; for doctorate, thesis/dissertation. *Entrance requirements:* For doctorate, GRE General Test, 3 letters of reference. Additional exam requirements/recommendations for international students: Required—TOEFL. *Application deadline:* For fall admission, 12/15 priority date for domestic and international students. Applications are processed on a rolling basis. Application fee: $70. Electronic applications accepted. *Expenses:* Contact institution. *Financial support:* In 2009–10, 174 students received support, including 24 fellowships, 174 research assistantships with full tuition reimbursements available (averaging $28,500 per year); scholarships/grants and health care benefits also available. Financial award application deadline: 12/15. *Faculty research:* Cell biology, molecular biology, biochemistry, genetics, immunology. *Unit head:* Dr. Naomi Rosenberg, Dean, 617-636-6767, Fax: 617-636-0375, E-mail: naomi.rosenberg@tufts.edu. *Application contact:* Kellie Johnston, Associate Director of Admissions, 617-636-6767, Fax: 617-636-0375, E-mail: sackler-school@tufts.edu.

Tulane University, School of Medicine and School of Liberal Arts, Graduate Programs in Biomedical Sciences, New Orleans, LA 70118-5669. Offers MBS, MS, PhD, MD/MS, MD/PhD. *Degree requirements:* For doctorate, thesis/dissertation. *Entrance requirements:* For master's, GRE General Test, minimum B average in undergraduate course work; for doctorate, GRE General Test. Additional exam requirements/recommendations for international students: Required—TOEFL. *Expenses:* Contact institution.

Tuskegee University, Graduate Programs, College of Agricultural, Environmental and Natural Sciences, Department of Agricultural Sciences, Tuskegee, AL 36088. Offers agricultural and resource economics (MS); animal and poultry sciences (MS); environmental sciences (MS); integrative bio-science (PhD); plant and soil sciences (MS). *Faculty:* 26 full-time (12 women), 1 part-time/adjunct (0 women). *Students:* 42 full-time (23 women), 6 part-time (4 women); includes 29 African Americans, 1 Asian American or Pacific Islander, 15 international. Average age 30. In 2009, 11 master's awarded. *Degree requirements:* For master's, thesis. *Entrance requirements:* For master's, GRE General Test. Additional exam requirements/recommendations for international students: Required—TOEFL (minimum score 500 paper-based; 69 computer-based). *Application deadline:* For fall admission, 7/15 for domestic students. Applications are processed on a rolling basis. Application fee: $25 ($35 for international students). *Expenses:* Tuition: Full-time $15,630; part-time $940 per credit hour. Required fees: $650. *Financial support:* In 2009–10, 5 fellowships, 4 research assistantships were awarded. Financial award application deadline: 4/15. *Unit head:* Dr. P. K. Biswas, Head, 334-727-8446. *Application contact:* Dr. Robert L. Laney, Vice President/Director of Admissions and Enrollment Management, 334-727-8580, Fax: 334-727-5750, E-mail: planey@tuskegee.edu.

Tuskegee University, Graduate Programs, College of Agricultural, Environmental and Natural Sciences, Department of Biology, Tuskegee, AL 36088. Offers MS. *Faculty:* 12 full-time (3 women). *Students:* 11 full-time (9 women); includes 7 minority (all African Americans), 3 international. Average age 27. In 2009, 6 master's awarded. *Degree requirements:* For master's, thesis. *Entrance requirements:* For master's, GRE General Test, GRE Subject Test. Additional exam requirements/recommendations for international students: Required—TOEFL (minimum score 500 paper-based; 69 computer-based). *Application deadline:* For fall admission, 7/15 for domestic students. Applications are processed on a rolling basis. Application fee: $25 ($35 for international students). *Expenses:* Tuition: Full-time $15,630; part-time $940 per credit hour. Required fees: $650. *Financial support:* Fellowships, teaching assistantships, Federal Work-Study and institutionally sponsored loans available. Support available to part-time students. Financial award application deadline: 4/15. *Unit head:* Dr. Roberta Troy, Head, 334-727-8829. *Application contact:* Dr. Robert L. Laney, Vice President/Director of Admissions and Enrollment Management, 334-727-8580, Fax: 334-727-5750, E-mail: planey@tuskegee.edu.

Tuskegee University, Graduate Programs, College of Agricultural, Environmental and Natural Sciences, Program in Integrative Biosciences, Tuskegee, AL 36088. Offers PhD. *Faculty:* 30. *Students:* 12 full-time (7 women), 2 part-time (1 woman); includes 12 minority (11 African Americans, 1 Asian American or Pacific Islander), 1 international. Average age 31. *Degree requirements:* For doctorate, thesis/dissertation. *Entrance requirements:* For doctorate, GRE General Test, GRE Subject Test, minimum cumulative GPA of 3.0, 3.4 in upper division courses; 3 letters of recommendation; resume or curriculum vitae. Additional exam requirements/recommendations for international students: Required—TOEFL (minimum score 500 paper-based; 69 computer-based). *Application deadline:* For fall admission, 3/30 for domestic students, 3/1 for international students. Application fee: $35. Electronic applications accepted. *Expenses:* Tuition: Full-time $15,630; part-time $940 per credit hour. Required fees: $650. *Unit head:* Dr. Deloris Alexander, Associate Director, 334-552-0690, E-mail: dalexander@tuskegee.edu. *Application contact:* Dr. Robert L. Laney, Vice President/Director of Admissions and Enrollment Management, 334-727-8580, Fax: 334-727-5750, E-mail: planey@tuskegee.edu.

Uniformed Services University of the Health Sciences, School of Medicine, Graduate Programs in the Biomedical Sciences and Public Health, Bethesda, MD 20814. Offers emerging infectious diseases (PhD); medical and clinical psychology (PhD), including clinical psychology, medical and clinical psychology (clinical/dual track), medical and clinical psychology (research track); molecular and cell biology (PhD); neuroscience (PhD); preventive medicine and biometrics (MPH, MSPH, MTMH, Dr PH, PhD), including environmental health science (PhD), medical zoology (PhD), public health (MPH, MSPH, Dr PH), tropical medicine and hygiene (MTMH). *Faculty:* 372 full-time (119 women), 4,044 part-time/adjunct (908 women). *Students:* 176 full-time (96 women); includes 31 minority (6 African Americans, 4 American Indian/Alaska Native, 14 Asian Americans or Pacific Islanders, 7 Hispanic Americans), 11 international. Average age 28. 278 applicants, 20% accepted, 47 enrolled. In 2009, 36 master's, 17 doctorates awarded. Terminal master's awarded for partial completion of doctoral program. *Degree requirements:* For master's, comprehensive exam, thesis or alternative; for doctorate, comprehensive exam, thesis/dissertation, qualifying exam. *Entrance requirements:* For master's, GRE General Test; for doctorate, GRE General Test, minimum GPA of 3.0. Additional exam requirements/recommendations for international students: Required—TOEFL. *Application deadline:* For fall admission, 1/15 priority date for domestic and international students. Applications are processed on a rolling basis. Application fee: $0. Electronic applications accepted. *Financial support:* In 2009–10, fellowships with full tuition reimbursements (averaging $26,000 per year), research assistantships with full tuition reimbursements (averaging $26,000 per year) were awarded; career-related internships or fieldwork, scholarships/grants, health care benefits, and tuition waivers (full) also available. *Unit head:* Dr. Eleanor S. Metcalf, Associate Dean, 301-295-1104, E-mail: emetcalf@usuhs.mil. *Application contact:* Elena Marina Sherman, Graduate Program Coordinator, 301-295-3913, Fax: 301-295-6772, E-mail: elena.sherman@usuhs.mil.

Universidad Adventista de las Antillas, EGECED Department, Mayagüez, PR 00681-0118. Offers curriculum and instruction (MA), including secondary biology, secondary history, secondary Spanish; education (MA), including ESL (elementary school level), ESL (high school level), school administration and supervision. *Degree requirements:* For master's, comprehensive exam (for some programs), thesis (for some programs). *Entrance requirements:* For master's, EXADEP or GRE General Test, recommendations. Application fee: $175. Electronic applications accepted. *Expenses:* Tuition: Full-time $3990; part-time $190 per credit. Required fees: $570; $190 per credit. $1375 per summer. *Financial support:* Fellowships, Federal Work-Study available. *Unit head:* Dr. Zilma Sepulveda, Director, 787-834-9595 Ext. 2282, Fax: 787-834-9595, E-mail: zsantiago@uaa.edu. *Application contact:* Prof. Evelyn del Valle, Admissions Department Director, 787-834-9595 Ext. 2261, Fax: 787-834-9597, E-mail: admissions@uaa.edu.

Universidad Central del Caribe, School of Medicine, Program in Biomedical Sciences, Bayamón, PR 00960-6032. Offers anatomy and cell biology (MA, MS); biochemistry (MS); biomedical sciences (MA); microbiology and immunology (MA, MS); pharmacology (MS); physiology (MA, MS).

Universidad de Ciencias Medicas, Graduate Programs, San Jose, Costa Rica. Offers dermatology (SP); family health (MS); health service center administration (MHA); human anatomy (MS); medical and surgery (MD); occupational medicine (MS); pharmacy (Pharm D). Part-time programs available. *Degree requirements:* For master's, thesis; for first professional degree and SP, comprehensive exam. *Entrance requirements:* For first professional degree, admissions test; for master's, MD or bachelors degree; for SP, admissions test, MD degree.

Université de Moncton, Faculty of Science, Department of Biology, Moncton, NB E1A 3E9, Canada. Offers M Sc. *Degree requirements:* For master's, one foreign language, thesis. *Entrance requirements:* For master's, minimum GPA of 3.0. Electronic applications accepted. *Faculty research:* Terrestrial ecology, aquatic ecology, marine biology, aquaculture, ethology, biotechnology.

Université de Montréal, Faculty of Arts and Sciences, Department of Biological Sciences, Montréal, QC H3C 3J7, Canada. Offers M Sc, PhD. Part-time programs available. *Faculty:* 35 full-time (11 women), 7 part-time/adjunct (2 women). *Students:* 32 full-time (12 women), 52 part-time (33 women). 35 applicants, 29% accepted, 10 enrolled. In 2009, 15 master's, 9 doctorates awarded. *Degree requirements:* For master's, thesis; for doctorate, thesis/dissertation, general exam. *Entrance requirements:* For doctorate, MS in biology or related field. *Application deadline:* For fall admission, 2/1 priority date for domestic students; for winter admission, 11/1 priority date for domestic students; for spring admission, 2/1 priority date for domestic students. Application fee: $100. Electronic applications accepted. *Financial support:* Fellowships, research assistantships, teaching assistantships available. Support available to part-time students. Financial award application deadline: 9/1. *Faculty research:* Fresh water ecology, plant biotechnology, neurobiology, genetics, cell physiology. *Unit head:* Bernadette Pinel-Alloul, Director, 514-343-6878, Fax: 514-343-2293, E-mail: bernadette.pinel-alloul@umontreal.ca. *Application contact:* Jean-Fran??ois Pflieger, Professor, 514-343-6847, Fax: 514-343-2293, E-mail: jf.pflieger@umontreal.ca.

Université de Montréal, Faculty of Medicine, Programs in Biomedical Sciences, Montréal, QC H3C 3J7, Canada. Offers M Sc, PhD. *Students:* 139 full-time (72 women), 245 part-time (151 women). 110 applicants, 60% accepted, 64 enrolled. In 2009, 45 master's, 24 doctorates awarded. *Degree requirements:* For master's, thesis; for doctorate, thesis/dissertation, general exam. *Entrance requirements:* For master's and doctorate, proficiency in French, knowledge of English. *Application deadline:* For fall admission, 2/1 priority date for domestic students; for winter admission, 11/1 priority date for domestic students; for spring admission, 2/1 priority date for domestic students. Application fee: $100. Electronic applications accepted. *Unit head:* Dr. Daniel Lajeunesse, Head, 514-343-6111 Ext. 4136, Fax: 514-343-5751, E-mail: daniel.lajeunesse@umontreal.ca. *Application contact:* France Fauteux, Information Contact, 514-343-6111 Ext. 4134, Fax: 514-343-5751, E-mail: france.fauteux@umontreal.ca.

Université de Sherbrooke, Faculty of Medicine and Health Sciences, Graduate Programs in Medicine, Sherbrooke, QC J1H 5N4, Canada. Offers M Sc, PhD. Part-time programs available. Terminal master's awarded for partial completion of doctoral program. *Degree requirements:* For master's, thesis; for doctorate, thesis/dissertation. Electronic applications accepted. *Expenses:* Contact institution.

Université de Sherbrooke, Faculty of Sciences, Department of Biology, Sherbrooke, QC J1K 2R1, Canada. Offers M Sc, PhD, Diploma. *Degree requirements:* For master's, thesis; for doctorate, comprehensive exam, thesis/dissertation. *Entrance requirements:* For doctorate, master's degree. Electronic applications accepted. *Faculty research:* Microbiology, ecology, molecular biology, cell biology, biotechnology.

Université du Québec à Montréal, Graduate Programs, Program in Biology, Montréal, QC H3C 3P8, Canada. Offers M Sc, PhD. Part-time programs available. *Degree requirements:* For master's, thesis; for doctorate, thesis/dissertation. *Entrance requirements:* For master's, appropriate bachelor's degree or equivalent, proficiency in French; for doctorate, appropriate master's degree or equivalent, proficiency in French.

Université du Québec en Abitibi-Témiscamingue, Graduate Programs, Program in Environmental Sciences, Rouyn-Noranda, QC J9X 5E4, Canada. Offers biology (MS); environmental sciences (PhD); sustainable forest ecosystem management (MS).

Université du Québec, Institut National de la Recherche Scientifique, Graduate Programs, Research Center—INRS—Institut Armand-Frappier—Human Health, Québec, QC G1K 9A9, Canada. Offers applied microbiology (M Sc); biology (PhD); experimental health sciences (M Sc); virology and immunology (M Sc, PhD). Programs given in French. Part-time programs available. *Faculty:* 37. *Students:* 157 full-time (97 women), 4 part-time (all women), 41 international. Average age 30. In 2009, 14 master's, 5 doctorates awarded. *Median time to degree:* Of those who began their doctoral program in fall 2001, 67% received their degree in 8 years or less. *Degree requirements:* For doctorate, thesis/dissertation. *Entrance requirements:* For master's and doctorate, appropriate bachelor's degree, proficiency in French. *Application deadline:* For fall admission, 3/30 for domestic and international students; for winter admission, 11/1 for domestic and international students. Application fee: $30 Canadian dollars. *Financial support:* Fellowships, research assistantships, teaching assistantships available. *Faculty research:* Immunity, infection and cancer; toxicology and environmental biotechnology; molecular pharmacochemistry. *Unit head:* Alain Fournier, Director, 450-687-5010, Fax: 450-686-5501, E-mail: alain.fournier@iaf.inrs.ca. *Application contact:* Yvonne Boisvert, Registrar, 418-654-3861, Fax: 418-654-3858, E-mail: registrariat@adm.inrs.ca.

Université Laval, Faculty of Medicine, Graduate Programs in Medicine, Québec, QC G1K 7P4, Canada. Offers M Sc, PhD, Diploma. *Degree requirements:* For doctorate, comprehensive exam, thesis/dissertation. *Entrance requirements:* For doctorate, knowledge of French, comprehension of written English; for Diploma, knowledge of French. Electronic applications accepted.

Université Laval, Faculty of Sciences and Engineering, Department of Biology, Programs in Biology, Québec, QC G1K 7P4, Canada. Offers M Sc, PhD. Terminal master's awarded for partial completion of doctoral program. *Degree requirements:* For master's, thesis; for doctorate, comprehensive exam, thesis/dissertation. *Entrance requirements:* For master's and doctorate, knowledge of French and English. Electronic applications accepted.

University at Albany, State University of New York, College of Arts and Sciences, Department of Biological Sciences, Albany, NY 12222-0001. Offers biodiversity, conservation, and policy (MS); ecology, evolution, and behavior (MS, PhD); forensic molecular biology (MS); molecular, cellular, developmental, and neural biology (MS, PhD). *Degree requirements:* For master's, one foreign language; for doctorate, one foreign language, thesis/dissertation. *Entrance requirements:* For master's and doctorate, GRE General Test. Additional exam requirements/recommendations for international students: Required—TOEFL (minimum score 550 paper-based; 213 computer-based). Electronic applications accepted. *Faculty research:* Interferon, neural development, RNA self-splicing, behavioral ecology, DNA repair enzymes.

University at Albany, State University of New York, School of Public Health, Department of Biomedical Sciences, Albany, NY 12222-0001. Offers biochemistry, molecular biology, and genetics (MS, PhD); cell and molecular structure (MS, PhD); immunobiology and immunochemistry (MS, PhD); molecular pathogenesis (MS, PhD); neuroscience (MS, PhD). *Degree requirements:* For master's, thesis; for doctorate, comprehensive exam, thesis/dissertation. *Entrance requirements:* For master's and doctorate, GRE General Test, 3 letters of reference. Additional exam requirements/recommendations for international students: Required—TOEFL (minimum score 600 paper-based; 213 computer-based). Electronic applications accepted. *Faculty research:* Geno expression; RNA processing; membrane transport; immune response regulation; etiology of AIDS, Lyme disease, epilepsy.

See Close-Up on page 113.

University at Buffalo, the State University of New York, Graduate School, College of Arts and Sciences, Department of Biological Sciences, Buffalo, NY 14260. Offers MA, MS, PhD. Terminal master's awarded for partial completion of doctoral program. *Degree requirements:* For master's, thesis, research rotation, seminar; for doctorate, comprehensive exam, thesis/dissertation, oral candidacy exam, research, seminar. *Entrance requirements:* For master's and doctorate, GRE General Test, 2 semesters of course work in calculus, course work in chemistry through organic chemistry, strong biology background. Additional exam requirements/recommendations for international students: Required—TOEFL (minimum score 600 paper-based; 240 computer-based; 100 iBT). Electronic applications accepted. *Faculty research:* Biochemistry, bioinformatics, biophysics, biotechnology, botany, cell biology, developmental biology, evolutionary biology, genetics, genomics, molecular biology, microbiology, neuroscience, physiology, plant physiology, plant sciences, structural biology, virology, zoology.

University at Buffalo, the State University of New York, Graduate School, Graduate Programs in Cancer Research and Biomedical Sciences at Roswell Park Cancer Institute, Interdisciplinary Master of Science Program in Natural and Biomedical Sciences at Roswell Park Cancer Institute, Buffalo, NY 14260. Offers biomedical sciences (MS). Part-time programs available. *Faculty:* 8 full-time (3 women). *Students:* 62 full-time (39 women), 19 part-time (6 women); includes 17 minority (5 African Americans, 8 Asian Americans or Pacific Islanders, 4 Hispanic Americans), 7 international. Average age 24. 100 applicants, 40% accepted, 30 enrolled. In 2009, 24 master's awarded. *Degree requirements:* For master's, thesis, defense of thesis, research project. *Entrance requirements:* For master's, GRE General Test, MCAT, DAT, PCAT. Additional exam requirements/recommendations for international students: Required—TOEFL (minimum score 600 paper-based; 250 computer-based; 100 iBT). *Application deadline:* For fall admission, 3/1 for domestic students. Applications are processed on a rolling basis. Application fee: $50. Electronic applications accepted. *Financial support:* In 2009–10, 1 fellowship with full tuition reimbursement (averaging $8,500 per year), 1 research assistantship (averaging $8,500 per year), 1 teaching assistantship with full tuition reimbursement (averaging $8,500 per year) were awarded; Federal Work-Study and institutionally sponsored loans also available. Financial award application deadline: 2/28; financial award applicants required to submit FAFSA. *Faculty research:* Biochemistry, oncology, pathology, biophysics, pharmacology, molecular biology, cellular biology, genetics, bioinformatics, immunology, therapeutic development, epidemiology. Total annual research expenditures: $1 million. *Unit head:* Craig R. Johnson, Director of Admissions, 716-845-2339, Fax: 716-845-8178, E-mail: craig.johnson@roswellpark.org. *Application contact:* Craig R. Johnson, Director of Admissions, 716-845-2339, Fax: 716-845-8178, E-mail: craig.johnson@roswellpark.org.

University at Buffalo, the State University of New York, Graduate School, School of Medicine and Biomedical Sciences, Graduate Programs in Medicine and Biomedical Sciences, Buffalo, NY 14260. Offers MA, MS, PhD, MD/PhD. *Faculty:* 94 full-time (22 women), 30 part-time/adjunct (11 women). *Students:* 150 full-time (71 women), 16 part-time (10 women); includes 13 minority (2 African Americans, 8 Asian Americans or Pacific Islanders, 3 Hispanic Americans), 60 international. Average age 25. 584 applicants, 29% accepted. In 2009, 21 master's, 27 doctorates awarded. Terminal master's awarded for partial completion of doctoral program. *Degree requirements:* For master's, comprehensive exam (for some programs), thesis (for some programs); for doctorate, comprehensive exam, thesis/dissertation. *Entrance requirements:* For master's, GRE General Test; for doctorate, GRE General Test, 3 letters of recommendation. Additional exam requirements/recommendations for international students: Required—TOEFL (minimum score 600 paper-based; 250 computer-based; 100 iBT). *Application deadline:* For fall admission, 2/1 priority date for domestic and international students. Applications are processed on a rolling basis. Application fee: $50. Electronic applications accepted. *Expenses:* Contact institution. *Financial support:* In 2009–10, 4 fellowships with full tuition reimbursements (averaging $25,000 per year), 30 research assistantships with full tuition reimbursements (averaging $21,000 per year), 31 teaching assistantships with full tuition reimbursements (averaging $2,000 per year) were awarded; career-related internships or fieldwork, Federal Work-Study, institutionally sponsored loans, scholarships/grants, traineeships, health care benefits, and unspecified assistantships also available. Financial award application deadline: 2/1; financial award applicants required to submit FAFSA. *Faculty research:* Neuroscience; molecular, cell, and structural biology; microbial pathogenesis; cardiopulmonary physiology; biochemistry, biotechnology and clinical laboratory science. Total annual research expenditures: $117.3 million. *Unit head:* Dr. Suzanne Laychock, Senior Associate Dean for Research and Graduate Studies, 716-829-3398, Fax: 716-829-2437, E-mail: laychock@acsu.buffalo.edu. *Application contact:* Amy J. Kuzdale, Staff Associate, 716-829-3399, Fax: 716-829-2437, E-mail: akuzdale@buffalo.edu.

University at Buffalo, the State University of New York, Graduate School, School of Medicine and Biomedical Sciences, Interdisciplinary Graduate Program in Biomedical Sciences, Buffalo, NY 14260. Offers PhD. *Students:* 35 full-time (20 women), 5 part-time (1 woman); includes 6 minority (1 African American, 5 Asian Americans or Pacific Islanders), 12 international. Average age 26. 219 applicants, 22% accepted. *Degree requirements:* For doctorate, comprehensive exam, thesis/dissertation. *Entrance requirements:* For doctorate, GRE General Test, 3 letters of recommendation. Additional exam requirements/recommendations for international students: Required—TOEFL (minimum score 600 paper-based; 250 computer-based; 100 iBT). *Application deadline:* For fall admission, 2/1 priority date for domestic and international students. Applications are processed on a rolling basis. Application fee: $50. Electronic applications accepted. *Financial support:* In 2009–10, 18 students received support, including 30 fellowships with full tuition reimbursements available (averaging $25,000 per year); Federal Work-Study, scholarships/grants, traineeships, health care benefits, and unspecified assistantships also available. Financial award application deadline: 2/1; financial award applicants required to submit FAFSA. *Faculty research:* Molecular, cell and structural biology; pharmacology and toxicology; neurosciences; microbiology; pathogenesis and disease.

Biological and Biomedical Sciences—General

University at Buffalo, the State University of New York (continued)
Total annual research expenditures: $117.3 million. *Unit head:* Dr. Laurie A. Read, Director, 716-829-3398, Fax: 716-829-2437, E-mail: smbs-gradprog@buffalo.edu. *Application contact:* Amy J. Kuzdale, Staff Associate, 716-829-3399, Fax: 716-829-2437, E-mail: akuzdale@buffalo.edu.

The University of Akron, Graduate School, Buchtel College of Arts and Sciences, Department of Biology, Akron, OH 44325. Offers biology (MS); integrated bioscience (PhD). Part-time programs available. *Faculty:* 21 full-time (3 women), 1 part-time/adjunct (0 women). *Students:* 42 full-time (16 women), 3 part-time (1 woman); includes 3 minority (1 African American, 2 Asian Americans or Pacific Islanders), 6 international. Average age 28. 65 applicants, 43% accepted, 19 enrolled. In 2009, 9 master's awarded. *Degree requirements:* For master's, thesis optional, oral defense of thesis, oral exam, seminars; for doctorate, thesis/dissertation, oral defense of dissertation, seminars. *Entrance requirements:* For master's, GRE, baccalaureate degree in biology or the equivalent; minimum GPA of 3.0 overall and in biology; for doctorate, GRE, minimum overall GPA of 3.0, letters of recommendation, personal statement. Additional exam requirements/recommendations for international students: Required—TOEFL (minimum score 550 paper-based; 213 computer-based; 79 iBT). *Application deadline:* Applications are processed on a rolling basis. Application fee: $30 ($40 for international students). Electronic applications accepted. *Expenses:* Tuition, state resident: full-time $6570; part-time $365 per credit hour. Tuition, nonresident: full-time $11,250; part-time $625 per credit hour. *Financial support:* In 2009–10, 1 research assistantship with full tuition reimbursement, 17 teaching assistantships with full tuition reimbursements were awarded. *Faculty research:* Behavior/neuroscience, ecology-evolution, genetics, molecular biology, physiology. Total annual research expenditures: $1.2 million. *Unit head:* Dr. Monte Turner, Interim Chair, 330-972-7155, E-mail: meturner@uakron.edu. *Application contact:* Dr. Monte Turner, Interim Chair, 330-972-7155, E-mail: meturner@uakron.edu.

The University of Alabama, Graduate School, College of Arts and Sciences, Department of Biological Sciences, Tuscaloosa, AL 35487. Offers MS, PhD. *Faculty:* 38 full-time (13 women), 1 (woman) part-time/adjunct. *Students:* 71 full-time (30 women), 5 part-time (3 women); includes 12 minority (5 African Americans, 5 Asian Americans or Pacific Islanders, 2 Hispanic Americans), 16 international. Average age 26. 106 applicants, 18% accepted, 15 enrolled. In 2009, 11 master's, 6 doctorates awarded. Terminal master's awarded for partial completion of doctoral program. *Median time to degree:* Of those who began their doctoral program in fall 2001, 100% received their degree in 8 years or less. *Degree requirements:* For master's, thesis optional, preliminary written exam; for doctorate, thesis/dissertation, preliminary written and oral exams. *Entrance requirements:* For master's and doctorate, GRE General Test, minimum GPA of 3.0. Additional exam requirements/recommendations for international students: Required—TOEFL (minimum score 550 paper-based; 79 iBT). *Application deadline:* For fall and spring admission, 12/15 priority date for domestic and international students. Applications are processed on a rolling basis. Application fee: $50 ($60 for international students). Electronic applications accepted. *Expenses:* Tuition, state resident: full-time $7000. Tuition, nonresident: full-time $19,200. *Financial support:* In 2009–10, 13 fellowships with full tuition reimbursements (averaging $15,000 per year), 43 teaching assistantships with full tuition reimbursements (averaging $13,590 per year) were awarded; Federal Work-Study and institutionally sponsored loans also available. Support available to part-time students. Financial award application deadline: 8/14; financial award applicants required to submit FAFSA. *Faculty research:* Molecular and developmental genetics, limnology, microbiology, systematics, neurobiology. Total annual research expenditures: $2.4 million. *Unit head:* Dr. Patrica A. Sobecky, Chair, 205-348-1807, Fax: 205-348-1786, E-mail: psobecky@as.ua.edu. *Application contact:* Dr. Stevan Marcus, Graduate Program Director, 205-348-8094, Fax: 205-348-1786, E-mail: smarcus@bama.ua.edu.

The University of Alabama at Birmingham, College of Arts and Sciences, Program in Biology, Birmingham, AL 35294. Offers MS, PhD. Terminal master's awarded for partial completion of doctoral program. *Degree requirements:* For master's, thesis; for doctorate, thesis/dissertation. *Entrance requirements:* For master's and doctorate, GRE General Test, previous course work in biology, calculus, organic chemistry, and physics. Additional exam requirements/recommendations for international students: Required—TOEFL. Electronic applications accepted. *Faculty research:* Invertebrate physiology, marine biology, environmental biology, molecular biology.

See Close-Up on page 115.

The University of Alabama at Birmingham, Graduate Programs in Joint Health Sciences, Program in Basic Medical Sciences, Birmingham, AL 35294. Offers MSBMS. *Entrance requirements:* For master's, GRE. Electronic applications accepted.

The University of Alabama in Huntsville, School of Graduate Studies, College of Science, Department of Biological Sciences, Huntsville, AL 35899. Offers MS. Part-time and evening/weekend programs available. *Faculty:* 10 full-time (2 women). *Students:* 20 full-time (10 women), 7 part-time (5 women); includes 5 minority (3 African Americans, 2 Asian Americans or Pacific Islanders), 12 international. Average age 27. 37 applicants, 57% accepted, 11 enrolled. In 2009, 8 master's awarded. *Degree requirements:* For master's, comprehensive exam, thesis or alternative, oral and written exams. *Entrance requirements:* For master's, GRE General Test, previous course work in biochemistry and organic chemistry, minimum GPA of 3.0. Additional exam requirements/recommendations for international students: Required—TOEFL (minimum score 550 paper-based; 213 computer-based; 62 iBT). *Application deadline:* For fall admission, 7/15 for domestic students, 4/1 for international students; for spring admission, 11/30 for domestic students, 9/1 for international students. Applications are processed on a rolling basis. Application fee: $40 ($50 for international students). Electronic applications accepted. *Expenses:* Tuition, state resident: part-time $355.75 per credit hour. Tuition, nonresident: part-time $847.10 per credit hour. Required fees: $210.80 per semester. Tuition and fees vary according to course load and program. *Financial support:* In 2009–10, 13 students received support, including 1 research assistantship with full and partial tuition reimbursement available (averaging $9,624 per year), 13 teaching assistantships with full and partial tuition reimbursements available (averaging $9,063 per year); career-related internships or fieldwork, Federal Work-Study, institutionally sponsored loans, scholarships/grants, health care benefits, tuition waivers, and unspecified assistantships also available. Support available to part-time students. Financial award application deadline: 4/1; financial award applicants required to submit FAFSA. *Faculty research:* Physiology and developmental biology, functional genomics, biotechnology, proteomics, microbiology. Total annual research expenditures: $1.3 million. *Unit head:* Dr. Debra M. Moriarity, Interim Chair, 256-824-6045, Fax: 256-824-6305, E-mail: moriard@uah.edu. *Application contact:* Kathy Biggs, Graduate Studies Admissions Manager, 256-824-6199, Fax: 256-824-6405, E-mail: deangrad@uah.edu.

University of Alaska Anchorage, College of Arts and Sciences, Department of Biological Sciences, Anchorage, AK 99508. Offers MS. Part-time programs available. *Degree requirements:* For master's, comprehensive exam, thesis. *Entrance requirements:* For master's, GRE General Test, GRE Subject Test, bachelor's degree in biology, chemistry or equivalent science. Additional exam requirements/recommendations for international students: Required—TOEFL (minimum score 550 paper-based; 213 computer-based). *Faculty research:* Taxonomy and vegetative analysis in Alaskan ecosystems, fish environment and seafood, biochemistry, arctic ecology, vertebrate ecology.

University of Alaska Fairbanks, College of Natural Sciences and Mathematics, Department of Biology and Wildlife, Fairbanks, AK 99775-6100. Offers biological sciences (MS, PhD), including biology, botany, wildlife biology (PhD), zoology; biology (MAT, MS); wildlife biology (MS). Part-time programs available. *Faculty:* 27 full-time (9 women), 2 part-time/adjunct (0 women). *Students:* 95 full-time (61 women), 32 part-time (18 women); includes 13 minority (1 African American, 3 American Indian/Alaska Native, 4 Asian Americans or Pacific Islanders, 5 Hispanic Americans), 9 international. Average age 35. 76 applicants, 32% accepted, 24 enrolled. In 2009, 10 master's, 13 doctorates awarded. *Degree requirements:* For master's, comprehensive exam, thesis, oral exam, oral defense; for doctorate, comprehensive exam, thesis/dissertation, oral exam, oral defense. *Entrance requirements:* For master's and doctorate, GRE General Test, GRE Subject Test (biology). Additional exam requirements/recommendations for international students: Required—TOEFL (minimum score 550 paper-based; 213 computer-based; 80 iBT), TWE. *Application deadline:* For fall admission, 6/1 for domestic students, 3/1 for international students; for spring admission, 10/15 for domestic students, 9/1 for international students. Applications are processed on a rolling basis. Application fee: $60. Electronic applications accepted. *Expenses:* Tuition, state resident: full-time $7584; part-time $316 per credit. Tuition, nonresident: full-time $15,504; part-time $646 per credit. Required fees: $23 per credit. $135 per semester. Tuition and fees vary according to course level, course load and reciprocity agreements. *Financial support:* In 2009–10, 46 research assistantships (averaging $13,543 per year), 24 teaching assistantships (averaging $7,495 per year) were awarded; fellowships, career-related internships or fieldwork, Federal Work-Study, scholarships/grants, health care benefits, and unspecified assistantships also available. Support available to part-time students. Financial award application deadline: 7/1; financial award applicants required to submit FAFSA. *Faculty research:* Plant-herbivore interactions, plant metabolic defenses, insect manufacture of glycerol, ice nucleators, structure and functions of arctic and subarctic freshwater ecosystems. *Unit head:* Dr. Richard E. Boone, Chair, 907-474-7671, Fax: 907-474-6716, E-mail: fybio@uaf.edu. *Application contact:* Dr. Richard E. Boone, Chair, 907-474-7671, Fax: 907-474-6716, E-mail: fybio@uaf.edu.

University of Alberta, Faculty of Graduate Studies and Research, Department of Biological Sciences, Edmonton, AB T6G 2E1, Canada. Offers environmental biology and ecology (M Sc, PhD); microbiology and biotechnology (M Sc, PhD); molecular biology and genetics (M Sc, PhD); physiology and cell biology (M Sc, PhD); plant biology (M Sc, PhD); systematics and evolution (M Sc, PhD). *Faculty:* 72 full-time (15 women), 15 part-time/adjunct (4 women). *Students:* 238 full-time (117 women), 32 part-time (15 women), 31 international. 206 applicants, 42% accepted. In 2009, 29 master's, 31 doctorates awarded. Terminal master's awarded for partial completion of doctoral program. *Degree requirements:* For master's, thesis; for doctorate, thesis/dissertation. *Entrance requirements:* Additional exam requirements/recommendations for international students: Required—TOEFL. *Application deadline:* For fall admission, 3/1 priority date for domestic students. Applications are processed on a rolling basis. Application fee: $0. Tuition and fees charges are reported in Canadian dollars. *Expenses:* Tuition, area resident: Full-time $4626 Canadian dollars; part-time $99.72 Canadian dollars per unit. International tuition: $8216 Canadian dollars full-time. Required fees: $3590 Canadian dollars; $99.72 Canadian dollars per unit. $215 Canadian dollars per term. *Financial support:* In 2009–10, 4 research assistantships with partial tuition reimbursements (averaging $12,000 per year), 103 teaching assistantships with partial tuition reimbursements (averaging $12,300 per year) were awarded; career-related internships or fieldwork and scholarships/grants also available. *Unit head:* Laura Frost, Chair, 780-492-1904. *Application contact:* Dr. John P. Chang, Associate Chair for Graduate Studies, 780-492-1257, Fax: 780-492-9457, E-mail: bio.grad.coordinator@ualberta.ca.

University of Alberta, Faculty of Medicine and Dentistry and Faculty of Graduate Studies and Research, Graduate Programs in Medicine, Edmonton, AB T6G 2E1, Canada. Offers MD, M Sc, PhD. Part-time programs available. *Students:* 396 full-time, 97 part-time. In 2009, 53 master's, 20 doctorates awarded. Terminal master's awarded for partial completion of doctoral program. *Degree requirements:* For doctorate, thesis/dissertation. *Application deadline:* Applications are processed on a rolling basis. Application fee: $0. Tuition and fees charges are reported in Canadian dollars. *Expenses:* Tuition, area resident: Full-time $4626 Canadian dollars; part-time $99.72 Canadian dollars per unit. International tuition: $8216 Canadian dollars full-time. Required fees: $3590 Canadian dollars; $99.72 Canadian dollars per unit. $215 Canadian dollars per term. *Financial support:* Fellowships, research assistantships, teaching assistantships, career-related internships or fieldwork, institutionally sponsored loans, scholarships/grants, tuition waivers (full and partial), and tuition bursaries available. Support available to part-time students. *Faculty research:* Basic, clinical, and applied biomedicine. Total annual research expenditures: $107.8 million. *Unit head:* Kathy Megazzi. *Application contact:* Sharon Campbell, Information Contact, 780-407-3131, Fax: 780-407-3134.

The University of Arizona, College of Medicine, Graduate Programs in Medicine, Tucson, AZ 85721. Offers MPH, MS, PhD, MD/PhD. Part-time programs available. Terminal master's awarded for partial completion of doctoral program. *Degree requirements:* For doctorate, thesis/dissertation. *Entrance requirements:* For master's and doctorate, GRE General Test. *Expenses:* Contact institution.

The University of Arizona, Graduate College, College of Science, Department of Molecular and Cellular Biology and Eller College of Management, Program in Applied Biosciences, Tucson, AZ 85721. Offers PSM. Part-time programs available. *Students:* 2 full-time (1 woman), 8 part-time (5 women); includes 2 minority (both Hispanic Americans), 1 international. Average age 30. 22 applicants, 27% accepted, 4 enrolled. In 2009, 8 master's awarded. *Degree requirements:* For master's, thesis or alternative, internship, colloquium, business courses. *Entrance requirements:* For master's, 3 letters of recommendation. Additional exam requirements/recommendations for international students: Required—TOEFL (minimum score 600 paper-based; 250 computer-based; 90 iBT). *Application deadline:* For fall admission, 2/1 for domestic students, 12/1 for international students. Application fee: $75. Electronic applications accepted. *Expenses:* Tuition, state resident: full-time $9020. Tuition, nonresident: full-time $24,890. *Financial support:* Career-related internships or fieldwork, Federal Work-Study, scholarships/grants, health care benefits, and unspecified assistantships available. *Faculty research:* Biotechnology, bioinformatics, pharmaceuticals, agriculture, oncology. *Unit head:* Dr. Kathleen Dixon, Department Head, 520-621-7563, Fax: 520-621-3709, E-mail: dixonk@email.arizona.edu. *Application contact:* Marilyn Kramer, Graduate Coordinator, 520-621-1519, Fax: 520-621-3709, E-mail: mjkramer@u.arizona.edu.

University of Arkansas, Graduate School, J. William Fulbright College of Arts and Sciences, Department of Biological Sciences, Fayetteville, AR 72701-1201. Offers MA, MS, PhD. *Students:* 7 full-time (4 women), 35 part-time (15 women); includes 1 minority (Hispanic American), 7 international. In 2009, 5 master's, 5 doctorates awarded. *Degree requirements:* For doctorate, one foreign language, thesis/dissertation. *Entrance requirements:* For master's and doctorate, GRE Subject Test. Application fee: $40 ($50 for international students). *Expenses:* Tuition, state resident: full-time $7355; part-time $356.58 per hour. Tuition, nonresident: full-time $17,401; part-time $775.17 per hour. Required fees: $1203. *Financial support:* In 2009–10, 6 fellowships with tuition reimbursements, 12 research assistantships, 24 teaching assistantships were awarded; career-related internships or fieldwork and Federal Work-Study also available. Support available to part-time students. Financial award application deadline: 4/1; financial award applicants required to submit FAFSA. *Unit head:* Dr. Fred Spiegel, Department Chairperson, 479-575-3251, Fax: 479-575-4010, E-mail: fspiegel@uark.edu. *Application contact:* Dr. David McNabb, Graduate Coordinator, 479-575-3797, Fax: 479-575-4010, E-mail: dmcnabb@uark.edu.

University of Arkansas at Little Rock, Graduate School, College of Science and Mathematics, Program in Biology, Little Rock, AR 72204-1099. Offers MS.

University of Arkansas for Medical Sciences, Graduate School, Graduate Programs in Biomedical Sciences, Little Rock, AR 72205. Offers MS, PhD, Certificate, MD/PhD. *Students:* 105 full-time, 22 part-time. 181 applicants. *Degree requirements:* For doctorate, thesis/dissertation. *Entrance requirements:* For master's and doctorate, GRE General Test. Additional exam requirements/recommendations for international students: Required—TOEFL. Application fee: $0. Electronic applications accepted. *Expenses:* Contact institution. *Financial support:* In 2009–10, research assistantships with full tuition reimbursements (averaging $24,000 per year); fellowships, teaching assistantships, scholarships/grants, unspecified assistantships, and stipend and tuition for doctoral students also available. *Unit head:* Dr. Robert E. McGehee,

Dean, Graduate School, 501-686-5454. *Application contact:* Dr. Kristen Sterba, Assistant Dean, Office of Graduate Student Recruiting and Retention, 501-526-7396, E-mail: kmsterba@uams.edu.

University of Calgary, Faculty of Graduate Studies, Faculty of Science, Department of Biological Sciences, Calgary, AB T2N 1N4, Canada. Offers M Sc, PhD. Part-time programs available. *Degree requirements:* For master's, thesis; for doctorate, thesis/dissertation, candidacy exam. *Entrance requirements:* Additional exam requirements/recommendations for international students: Required—TOEFL. Electronic applications accepted. *Faculty research:* Biochemistry; cellular, molecular, and microbial biology; botany; ecology; zoology.

University of Calgary, Faculty of Medicine and Faculty of Graduate Studies, Department of Medical Science, Calgary, AB T2N 1N4, Canada. Offers cancer biology (M Sc, PhD); immunology (M Sc, PhD); joint injury and arthritis research (M Sc, PhD); medical education (M Sc, PhD); medical science (M Sc, PhD); mountain medicine and high altitude physiology (M Sc). *Degree requirements:* For master's, thesis; for doctorate, thesis/dissertation, candidacy exam. *Entrance requirements:* For master's, minimum undergraduate GPA of 3.2; for doctorate, minimum graduate GPA of 3.2. Additional exam requirements/recommendations for international students: Required—TOEFL (minimum score 600 paper-based; 250 computer-based). Electronic applications accepted. *Faculty research:* Cancer biology, immunology, joint injury and arthritis, medical education, population genomics.

University of California, Berkeley, Graduate Division, College of Letters and Science, Department of Integrative Biology, Berkeley, CA 94720-1500. Offers PhD. *Faculty:* 37 full-time, 3 part-time/adjunct. *Students:* 114 full-time (64 women). Average age 30. 171 applicants, 22 enrolled. *Degree requirements:* For doctorate, thesis/dissertation, oral qualifying exam. *Entrance requirements:* For doctorate, GRE General Test, GRE Subject Test, 3 letters of recommendation. Additional exam requirements/recommendations for international students: Required—TOEFL. *Application deadline:* For fall admission, 12/15 for domestic students. Application fee: $70 ($90 for international students). *Financial support:* Fellowships, research assistantships, teaching assistantships, Federal Work-Study, scholarships/grants, tuition waivers (full and partial), and unspecified assistantships available. Financial award applicants required to submit FAFSA. *Faculty research:* Morphology, physiology, development of plants and animals, behavior, ecology. *Unit head:* Prof. Wayne Sousa, Chair, 510-642-3281, Fax: 510-643-6264, E-mail: ibgradsao@berkeley.edu. *Application contact:* Laurie Roach, Student Affairs Officer, 510-643-7330, Fax: 510-643-6264, E-mail: ibgradsao@berkeley.edu.

University of California, Irvine, Office of Graduate Studies, School of Biological Sciences, Irvine, CA 92697. Offers MS, PhD, MD/PhD. *Students:* 418 full-time (235 women), 2 part-time (1 woman); includes 141 minority (4 African Americans, 2 American Indian/Alaska Native, 83 Asian Americans or Pacific Islanders, 52 Hispanic Americans), 42 international. Average age 27. 822 applicants, 23% accepted, 88 enrolled. In 2009, 23 master's, 55 doctorates awarded. *Degree requirements:* For doctorate, thesis/dissertation. *Entrance requirements:* For master's and doctorate, GRE General Test, GRE Subject Test, minimum GPA of 3.0. Additional exam requirements/recommendations for international students: Required—TOEFL (minimum score 550 paper-based; 213 computer-based). *Application deadline:* For fall admission, 12/15 for domestic and international students. Applications are processed on a rolling basis. Application fee: $70 ($90 for international students). Electronic applications accepted. *Financial support:* Fellowships with full tuition reimbursements, research assistantships with full tuition reimbursements, teaching assistantships with full tuition reimbursements, career-related internships or fieldwork, institutionally sponsored loans, scholarships/grants, traineeships, health care benefits, and unspecified assistantships available. Financial award application deadline: 3/1; financial award applicants required to submit FAFSA. *Faculty research:* Molecular biology and biochemistry, developmental and cell biology, physiology and biophysics, neurosciences, ecology and evolutionary biology. *Unit head:* Dr. Susan V. Bryant, Dean, 949-824-5315, E-mail: svbryant@uci.edu. *Application contact:* Kimberly McKinney, Administrator, 949-824-8145, Fax: 949-824-1965, E-mail: kamckinn@uci.edu.

University of California, Los Angeles, David Geffen School of Medicine and Graduate Division, Graduate Programs in Medicine, Los Angeles, CA 90095. Offers MS, PhD, MD/PhD. Terminal master's awarded for partial completion of doctoral program. *Degree requirements:* For doctorate, thesis/dissertation, qualifying exams. *Entrance requirements:* For master's, GRE General Test.

University of California, Los Angeles, Graduate Division, College of Letters and Science, Department of Ecology and Evolutionary Biology, Los Angeles, CA 90095. Offers MA, PhD. *Faculty:* 26 full-time (8 women), 8 part-time/adjunct (1 woman). *Students:* 64 full-time (39 women); includes 8 minority (1 African American, 1 American Indian/Alaska Native, 3 Asian Americans or Pacific Islanders, 3 Hispanic Americans), 9 international. Average age 29. 88 applicants, 19% accepted, 13 enrolled. In 2009, 5 master's, 16 doctorates awarded. Terminal master's awarded for partial completion of doctoral program. *Degree requirements:* For master's, comprehensive exam or thesis; for doctorate, thesis/dissertation, oral and written qualifying exams; teaching experience. *Entrance requirements:* For master's and doctorate, GRE General Test, GRE Subject Test (biology), minimum GPA of 3.0, 3 letters of recommendation. *Application deadline:* For fall admission, 12/1 for domestic and international students. Application fee: $70 ($90 for international students). Electronic applications accepted. *Financial support:* In 2009–10, 61 fellowships with full and partial tuition reimbursements, 18 research assistantships with full and partial tuition reimbursements, 42 teaching assistantships with full and partial tuition reimbursements were awarded; Federal Work-Study, institutionally sponsored loans, scholarships/grants, health care benefits, tuition waivers (full and partial), and unspecified assistantships also available. Financial award application deadline: 3/1; financial award applicants required to submit FAFSA. *Faculty research:* Molecular, cell, and developmental biology; interactive biology; organisms and populations. *Unit head:* Victoria Sork, Chair, 310-825-7755, Fax: 310-206-0484, E-mail: vlsork@ucla.edu. *Application contact:* Department Office, 310-825-1959, Fax: 310-206-5280, E-mail: eebgrad@eeb.ucla.edu.

University of California, Merced, Division of Graduate Studies, School of Natural Sciences, Merced, CA 95343. Offers applied mathematics (MS, PhD); biological engineering and small-scale technologies (MS, PhD); environmental systems (MS, PhD); mechanical engineering and applied mechanics (MS, PhD); physics and chemistry (PhD); quantitative and systems biology (MS, PhD). *Expenses:* Tuition, nonresident: full-time $15,102. Required fees: $10,919.

University of California, Riverside, Graduate Division, Department of Biology, Riverside, CA 92521-0102. Offers biology (MS, PhD); evolution, ecology and organismal biology (MS, PhD). Department also affiliated with following interdepartmental graduate programs: Cell, Molecular, and Developmental Biology; Evolution and Ecology; Genetics. Terminal master's awarded for partial completion of doctoral program. *Degree requirements:* For master's, oral defense of thesis; for doctorate, thesis/dissertation, 3 quarters of teaching experience, qualifying exams. *Entrance requirements:* For master's and doctorate, GRE General Test, minimum GPA of 3.2. Additional exam requirements/recommendations for international students: Required—TOEFL (minimum score 550 paper-based; 213 computer-based; 80 iBT). Electronic applications accepted. *Faculty research:* Molecular genetics, neurophysiology, evolutionary biology, physiology and organismal biology, signal transduction.

University of California, Riverside, Graduate Division, Program in Biomedical Sciences, Riverside, CA 92521-0102. Offers PhD, MD/PhD. *Faculty:* 41 full-time (14 women). *Students:* 14 full-time (11 women); includes 8 minority (1 African American, 5 Asian Americans or Pacific Islanders, 2 Hispanic Americans), 4 international. Average age 31. 48 applicants, 25% accepted, 4 enrolled. In 2009, 3 doctorates awarded. *Degree requirements:* For doctorate, thesis/dissertation, qualifying exams. *Entrance requirements:* For doctorate, GRE General Test, minimum GPA of 3.2. Additional exam requirements/recommendations for international students: Required—TOEFL (minimum score 550 paper-based; 213 computer-based; 80 iBT). *Application deadline:* For fall admission, 5/1 priority date for domestic students, 5/1 for international students. Application fee: $80 ($100 for international students). Electronic applications accepted. *Financial support:* In 2009–10, fellowships with tuition reimbursements (averaging $12,000 per year), research assistantships with tuition reimbursements (averaging $18,000 per year), teaching assistantships with tuition reimbursements (averaging $16,500 per year) were awarded; scholarships/grants also available. Financial award application deadline: 2/1; financial award applicants required to submit FAFSA. *Faculty research:* Cancer, receptor biology, developmental disorders, molecular basis of disease, neurodegeneration. *Unit head:* Dr. Craig V. Byus, Interim Dean and Program Director, 951-827-5705, Fax: 951-827-5504, E-mail: craig.byus@ucr.edu. *Application contact:* Kathy Redd, Graduate Program Assistant, 800-735-0717, Fax: 951-827-5517, E-mail: bmpasst@ucr.edu.

University of California, San Diego, Office of Graduate Studies, Division of Biological Sciences, La Jolla, CA 92093-0348. Offers biochemistry (PhD); biology (MS); cell and developmental biology (PhD); computational neurobiology (PhD); ecology, behavior, and evolution (PhD); genetics and molecular biology (PhD); immunology, virology, and cancer biology (PhD); molecular and cellular biology (PhD); neurobiology (PhD); plant molecular biology (PhD); plant systems biology (PhD); signal transduction (PhD). Offered in association with the Salk Institute. *Degree requirements:* For doctorate, thesis/dissertation, qualifying exam. *Entrance requirements:* For doctorate, GRE General Test. Additional exam requirements/recommendations for international students: Required—TOEFL. Electronic applications accepted.

University of California, San Diego, School of Medicine and Office of Graduate Studies, Graduate Studies in Biomedical Sciences, La Jolla, CA 92093-0685. Offers molecular cell biology (PhD); pharmacology (PhD); physiology (PhD); regulatory biology (PhD). *Degree requirements:* For doctorate, thesis/dissertation, qualifying exam. *Entrance requirements:* For doctorate, GRE General Test. Additional exam requirements/recommendations for international students: Required—TOEFL. Electronic applications accepted. *Faculty research:* Molecular and cellular biology, molecular and cellular pharmacology, cell and organ physiology.

University of California, San Diego, School of Medicine, Medical Scientist Training Program, La Jolla, CA 92093. Offers MD/PhD.

University of California, San Francisco, Graduate Division, Biomedical Sciences Graduate Group, San Francisco, CA 94143. Offers anatomy (PhD); endocrinology (PhD); experimental pathology (PhD); physiology (PhD). *Degree requirements:* For doctorate, thesis/dissertation. *Entrance requirements:* For doctorate, GRE General Test.

University of Central Arkansas, Graduate School, College of Natural Sciences and Math, Department of Biological Science, Conway, AR 72035-0001. Offers MS. Part-time programs available. *Faculty:* 19 full-time (6 women). *Students:* 20 full-time (8 women), 9 part-time (3 women); includes 4 minority (2 African Americans, 2 American Indian/Alaska Native), 1 international. Average age 26. 12 applicants, 92% accepted, 10 enrolled. In 2009, 7 master's awarded. *Degree requirements:* For master's, comprehensive exam, thesis optional. *Entrance requirements:* For master's, GRE General Test, minimum GPA of 2.7. Additional exam requirements/recommendations for international students: Required—TOEFL (minimum score 550 paper-based; 213 computer-based). *Application deadline:* For fall admission, 3/1 priority date for domestic students; for spring admission, 10/1 priority date for domestic students. Applications are processed on a rolling basis. Application fee: $25 ($50 for international students). *Expenses:* Tuition, state resident: full-time $5136; part-time $214 per credit hour. Required fees: $379.50; $127 per term. Tuition and fees vary according to course level, course load and campus/location. *Financial support:* In 2009–10, 4 research assistantships with partial tuition reimbursements (averaging $8,500 per year), 21 teaching assistantships with partial tuition reimbursements (averaging $8,500 per year) were awarded; unspecified assistantships also available. Financial award application deadline: 2/15; financial award applicants required to submit FAFSA. *Unit head:* Dr. Steven Runge, Chairperson, 501-450-3146, Fax: 501-450-5914, E-mail: srunge@uca.edu. *Application contact:* Brenda Herring, Admissions Assistant, 501-450-5065, Fax: 501-450-5678, E-mail: bherring@uca.edu.

University of Central Florida, College of Graduate Studies, Program in Biomedical Sciences, Orlando, FL 32816. Offers PhD. *Faculty:* 14 full-time (3 women). *Students:* 70 full-time (40 women), 1 (woman) part-time; includes 7 minority (1 African American, 2 Asian Americans or Pacific Islanders, 4 Hispanic Americans), 33 international. Average age 30. 64 applicants, 41% accepted, 14 enrolled. In 2009, 5 doctorates awarded. *Degree requirements:* For doctorate, thesis/dissertation, qualifying exam, candidacy exam. *Entrance requirements:* For doctorate, GRE General Test, letters of recommendation. Additional exam requirements/recommendations for international students: Required—TOEFL. *Application deadline:* For fall admission, 2/1 for domestic students. Electronic applications accepted. *Expenses:* Tuition, state resident: part-time $306.31 per credit hour. Tuition, nonresident: part-time $1099.01 per credit hour. Part-time tuition and fees vary according to degree level and program. *Financial support:* In 2009–10, 61 students received support, including 5 fellowships with partial tuition reimbursements available (averaging $5,800 per year), 57 research assistantships (averaging $11,000 per year), 29 teaching assistantships with partial tuition reimbursements available (averaging $7,600 per year). *Unit head:* Dr. Pappachan Kolattukudy, Director, 407-823-5932, E-mail: pk@mail.ucf.edu. *Application contact:* Dr. Pappachan Kolattukudy, Director, 407-823-5932, E-mail: pk@mail.ucf.edu.

University of Central Florida, College of Sciences, Department of Biology, Orlando, FL 32816. Offers biology (MS); conservation biology (PhD, Certificate). Part-time and evening/weekend programs available. *Faculty:* 22 full-time (5 women). *Students:* 55 full-time (36 women), 24 part-time (16 women); includes 6 minority (1 African American, 3 Asian Americans or Pacific Islanders, 2 Hispanic Americans), 6 international. 59 applicants, 47% accepted, 15 enrolled. In 2009, 17 master's, 2 doctorates awarded. *Degree requirements:* For master's, comprehensive exam, thesis or alternative, field exam. *Entrance requirements:* For master's, GRE General Test, minimum GPA of 3.0 in last 60 hours. Additional exam requirements/recommendations for international students: Required—TOEFL. *Application deadline:* For fall admission, 3/1 priority date for domestic students; for spring admission, 10/15 for domestic students. Application fee: $30. Electronic applications accepted. *Expenses:* Tuition, state resident: part-time $306.31 per credit hour. Tuition, nonresident: part-time $1099.01 per credit hour. Part-time tuition and fees vary according to degree level and program. *Financial support:* In 2009–10, 12 students received support, including 12 fellowships with partial tuition reimbursements available (averaging $5,500 per year), 8 research assistantships with partial tuition reimbursements available (averaging $8,400 per year), 37 teaching assistantships with partial tuition reimbursements available (averaging $10,600 per year); career-related internships or fieldwork, Federal Work-Study, institutionally sponsored loans, tuition waivers (partial), and unspecified assistantships also available. Financial award application deadline: 3/1; financial award applicants required to submit FAFSA. *Unit head:* Dr. Ross Hinkle, Chair, 407-823-2976, Fax: 407-823-5769, E-mail: thinkle@mail.ucf.edu. *Application contact:* Dr. Ross Hinkle, Chair, 407-823-2976, Fax: 407-823-5769, E-mail: thinkle@mail.ucf.edu.

University of Central Missouri, The Graduate School, College of Science and Technology, Warrensburg, MO 64093. Offers applied mathematics (MS); aviation safety (MS); biology (MS); computer science (MS); environmental studies (MA); industrial management (MS); mathematics (MS); technology (MS); technology management (PhD). Part-time programs available. Postbaccalaureate distance learning degree programs offered. *Faculty:* 59. *Students:* 99 full-time (31 women), 85 part-time (37 women). Average age 33. 45 applicants, 96% accepted, 42 enrolled. In 2009, 68 master's awarded. *Entrance requirements:* Additional exam requirements/recommendations for international students: Required—TOEFL (minimum score 550 paper-based; 79 computer-based). *Application deadline:* For fall admission, 6/1 priority date for domestic students, 5/1 for international students; for spring admission, 10/1 priority date for domestic students, 10/1 for international students. Applications are processed on a rolling basis. Application fee: $30 ($75 for international students). Electronic applications accepted. *Expenses:* Tuition, area resident: Part-time $245.80 per credit hour. Tuition, nonresident: part-time $491.60 per credit hour. Required fees: $24.20 per credit hour. Full-time tuition and fees vary according to course load, degree level, campus/location and reciprocity agreements. *Financial support:* In 2009–10, 15 students received support; fellowships with full

Biological and Biomedical Sciences—General

University of Central Missouri *(continued)*
and partial tuition reimbursements available, research assistantships with full and partial tuition reimbursements available, teaching assistantships with full and partial tuition reimbursements available, career-related internships or fieldwork, Federal Work-Study, scholarships/grants, and administrative and laboratory assistantships available. Support available to part-time students. Financial award application deadline: 3/1; financial award applicants required to submit FAFSA. *Unit head:* Dr. Alice Greife, Dean, 660-543-4450, Fax: 660-543-8031, E-mail: greife@ucmo.edu. *Application contact:* Laurie Delap, Admissions Coordinator, 660-543-4621, Fax: 660-543-4778, E-mail: gradinfo@ucmo.edu.

University of Central Oklahoma, College of Graduate Studies and Research, College of Mathematics and Science, Department of Biology, Edmond, OK 73034-5209. Offers MS. Part-time programs available. *Faculty:* 9 full-time (4 women), 2 part-time/adjunct (0 women). *Students:* 1 (woman) full-time, 8 part-time (4 women); includes 2 minority (1 American Indian/Alaska Native, 1 Asian American or Pacific Islander). Average age 27. 5 applicants, 80% accepted. In 2009, 3 master's awarded. *Degree requirements:* For master's, thesis. *Entrance requirements:* For master's, GRE General Test, GRE Subject Test (biology). Additional exam requirements/recommendations for international students: Required—TOEFL (minimum score 550 paper-based; 213 computer-based). *Application deadline:* For fall admission, 7/1 for international students; for spring admission, 11/1 for international students. Applications are processed on a rolling basis. Application fee: $25. Electronic applications accepted. *Expenses:* Tuition, state resident: full-time $4128; part-time $172 per credit hour. Tuition, nonresident: full-time $10,373; part-time $432.20 per credit hour. Required fees: $433.20; $18.05 per credit hour. *Financial support:* Federal Work-Study and unspecified assistantships available. Financial award application deadline: 3/31; financial award applicants required to submit FAFSA. *Faculty research:* Environmental (legionella), aquatic biology (ecological), mammalogy field studies, microbiology, genetics. *Unit head:* Dr. Jenna Hellack, Chairperson, 405-974-5773, Fax: 405-974-3824. *Application contact:* Dr. Richard Bernard, Dean, Graduate College, 405-974-3493, Fax: 405-974-3852, E-mail: gradcoll@uco.edu.

University of Chicago, Division of the Biological Sciences, The Interdisciplinary Scientist Training Program, Chicago, IL 60637-1513. Offers PhD. *Students:* 2 full-time (0 women). Average age 27. 3 applicants, 0% accepted. *Degree requirements:* For doctorate, thesis/dissertation, ethics class, 2 teaching assistantships. *Entrance requirements:* Additional exam requirements/recommendations for international students: Required—TOEFL (minimum score 600 paper-based; 250 computer-based; 104 iBT), IELTS (minimum score 7). *Application deadline:* For fall admission, 12/1 for domestic and international students. Application fee: $55. Electronic applications accepted. *Financial support:* In 2009–10, 2 students received support, including fellowships (averaging $29,781 per year), research assistantships (averaging $29,781 per year). Financial award applicants required to submit FAFSA. *Unit head:* Dr. Daniel Margoliash, Program Director, 773-702-3224, Fax: 773-702-0037. *Application contact:* Diane Hall, Student Contact, E-mail: djh8@uchicago.edu.

University of Cincinnati, Graduate School, College of Medicine, Biomedical Sciences Flex Option Program, Cincinnati, OH 45221. Offers PhD. *Degree requirements:* For doctorate, thesis/dissertation, qualifying exam. *Entrance requirements:* For doctorate, GRE, 2 letters of recommendation. Additional exam requirements/recommendations for international students: Required—TOEFL. Electronic applications accepted. *Faculty research:* Environmental health, developmental biology, cell and molecular biology, immunobiology, molecular genetics.

University of Cincinnati, Graduate School, College of Medicine, Graduate Programs in Biomedical Sciences, Cincinnati, OH 45221. Offers MS, PhD. Terminal master's awarded for partial completion of doctoral program. *Degree requirements:* For master's, thesis; for doctorate, thesis/dissertation, qualifying exam. *Entrance requirements:* For master's and doctorate, GRE General Test. Additional exam requirements/recommendations for international students: Required—TOEFL (minimum score 600 paper-based; 250 computer-based; 100 iBT). Electronic applications accepted. *Expenses:* Contact institution. *Faculty research:* Cancer, cardiovascular, metabolic disorders, neuroscience, computational medicine.

University of Cincinnati, Graduate School, College of Medicine, Physician Scientist Training Program, Cincinnati, OH 45221. Offers MD/PhD. *Entrance requirements:* Additional exam requirements/recommendations for international students: Required—TOEFL. Electronic applications accepted.

University of Cincinnati, Graduate School, McMicken College of Arts and Sciences, Department of Biological Sciences, Cincinnati, OH 45221-0006. Offers MS, PhD. Part-time programs available. Terminal master's awarded for partial completion of doctoral program. *Degree requirements:* For master's, thesis; for doctorate, comprehensive exam, thesis/dissertation. *Entrance requirements:* For master's and doctorate, GRE General Test, BS in biology, chemistry, or equivalent. Additional exam requirements/recommendations for international students: Required—TOEFL (minimum score 600 paper-based; 250 computer-based; 100 iBT). Electronic applications accepted. *Faculty research:* Physiology and development, cell and molecular, ecology and evolutionary.

University of Colorado at Colorado Springs, Graduate School, College of Letters, Arts and Sciences, Master of Sciences Program, Colorado Springs, CO 80933-7150. Offers applied science—bioscience (M Sc); applied science—physics (M Sc); biology (M Sc); chemistry (M Sc); physics (M Sc). Part-time programs available. *Faculty:* 39 full-time (14 women), 2 part-time/adjunct (0 women). *Students:* 19 full-time (6 women), 14 part-time (6 women); includes 5 minority (2 Asian Americans or Pacific Islanders, 3 Hispanic Americans). Average age 31. 29 applicants, 52% accepted, 11 enrolled. In 2009, 8 master's awarded. *Degree requirements:* For master's, thesis or alternative. *Entrance requirements:* For master's, minimum GPA of 2.75. *Application deadline:* For fall admission, 7/1 priority date for domestic students; for spring admission, 12/1 for domestic students. Application fee: $60 ($75 for international students). *Expenses:* Contact institution. *Financial support:* Fellowships, research assistantships, teaching assistantships, career-related internships or fieldwork, Federal Work-Study, and scholarships/grants available. Support available to part-time students. Financial award application deadline: 3/1; financial award applicants required to submit FAFSA. *Faculty research:* Biomechanics and physiology of elite athletic training, genetic engineering in yeast and bacteria including phage display and DNA repair, immunology and cell biology, synthetic organic chemistry. *Unit head:* Dr. Sandra Berry-Lowe, Director, 719-255-7552, Fax: 719-255-3047. *Application contact:* Michael Sanderson, Information Contact, 719-255-3417, Fax: 719-255-3037, E-mail: gradschl@uccs.edu.

University of Colorado Denver, College of Liberal Arts and Sciences, Department of Biology, Denver, CO 80217-3364. Offers MS. Part-time programs available. *Students:* 9 full-time (6 women), 16 part-time (9 women); includes 9 minority (6 Asian Americans or Pacific Islanders, 3 Hispanic Americans). 7 applicants, 57% accepted, 4 enrolled. In 2009, 5 master's awarded. *Degree requirements:* For master's, comprehensive exam, thesis or alternative. *Entrance requirements:* For master's, GRE General Test, minimum GPA of 3.0. Additional exam requirements/recommendations for international students: Required—TOEFL (minimum score 525 paper-based; 197 computer-based). *Application deadline:* For fall admission, 4/15 for domestic students; for spring admission, 10/15 for domestic students. Applications are processed on a rolling basis. Application fee: $50 ($75 for international students). Electronic applications accepted. *Financial support:* Research assistantships, teaching assistantships, Federal Work-Study available. Financial award application deadline: 4/1; financial award applicants required to submit FAFSA. *Unit head:* Dr. Leo Bruederle, Chair, 303-556-3419, Fax: 303-556-4352, E-mail: leo.bruederle@ucdenver.edu. *Application contact:* Dr. Leo Bruederle, Chair, 303-556-3419, Fax: 303-556-4352, E-mail: leo.bruederle@ucdenver.edu.

University of Colorado Denver, School of Medicine, Program in Biomedical Sciences, Denver, CO 80217-3364. Offers MS, PhD. *Students:* 11 full-time (10 women), 3 part-time (2 women); includes 4 minority (3 Asian Americans or Pacific Islanders, 1 Hispanic American). In 2009, 9

master's awarded. Terminal master's awarded for partial completion of doctoral program. *Degree requirements:* For doctorate, thesis/dissertation. *Entrance requirements:* Additional exam requirements/recommendations for international students: Required—TOEFL (minimum score 550 paper-based; 213 computer-based). Application fee: $50. *Expenses:* Contact institution. *Financial support:* Fellowships, research assistantships, teaching assistantships, career-related internships or fieldwork, Federal Work-Study, institutionally sponsored loans, and traineeships available. Support available to part-time students. Financial award applicants required to submit FAFSA. *Unit head:* Dr. Steven Anderson, Director, 303-724-3742, Fax: 303-724-3712, E-mail: steve.anderson@ucdenver.edu. *Application contact:* Gary Brown, Program Administrator, 303-724-3700, E-mail: gary.brown@ucdenver.edu.

University of Connecticut, Graduate School, University of Connecticut Health Center, Field of Biomedical Science, Storrs, CT 06269. Offers PhD. *Faculty:* 162 full-time (40 women). *Students:* 128 full-time (75 women), 28 part-time (13 women); includes 18 minority (5 African Americans, 1 American Indian/Alaska Native, 10 Asian Americans or Pacific Islanders, 2 Hispanic Americans), 62 international. Average age 28. 182 applicants, 20% accepted, 36 enrolled. In 2009, 28 doctorates awarded. *Degree requirements:* For doctorate, thesis/dissertation. *Entrance requirements:* For doctorate, GRE General Test, GRE Subject Test. Additional exam requirements/recommendations for international students: Required—TOEFL (minimum score 550 paper-based; 213 computer-based). *Application deadline:* For fall admission, 2/1 priority date for domestic and international students; for spring admission, 11/1 for domestic students, 10/1 for international students. Applications are processed on a rolling basis. Application fee: $55. Electronic applications accepted. *Expenses:* Tuition, state resident: full-time $4725; part-time $525 per credit. Tuition, nonresident: full-time $12,267; part-time $1363 per credit. Required fees: $346 per semester. Tuition and fees vary according to course load. *Financial support:* In 2009–10, 117 research assistantships with full tuition reimbursements were awarded; fellowships, Federal Work-Study, scholarships/grants, health care benefits, and unspecified assistantships also available. Financial award application deadline: 2/1; financial award applicants required to submit FAFSA. *Application contact:* Tricia Avolt, Graduate Coordinator, 860-679-2175, Fax: 860-679-1899, E-mail: robertson@nso2.uchc.edu.

University of Connecticut Health Center, Graduate School and School of Medicine, Combined Degree Program in Biomedical Sciences, Farmington, CT 06030. Offers MD/PhD. *Faculty:* 172. *Students:* 30 full-time (16 women); includes 4 minority (1 African American, 1 American Indian/Alaska Native, 2 Asian Americans or Pacific Islanders), 4 international. Average age 27. 105 applicants, 16% accepted, 5 enrolled. *Entrance requirements:* Additional exam requirements/recommendations for international students: Required—TOEFL (minimum score 600 paper-based; 250 computer-based). *Application deadline:* For fall admission, 12/31 priority date for domestic students. Applications are processed on a rolling basis. Application fee: $85. *Expenses:* Contact institution. *Financial support:* In 2009–10, 30 students received support, including 30 research assistantships with full tuition reimbursements available (averaging $27,000 per year); health care benefits and unspecified assistantships also available. *Unit head:* Dr. Barbara Kream, Director, 860-679-3849, Fax: 860-679-1258, E-mail: kream@nso1.uchc.edu. *Application contact:* Dr. Barbara Kream, Director, 860-679-3849, Fax: 860-679-1258, E-mail: kream@nso1.uchc.edu.

University of Connecticut Health Center, Graduate School, Programs in Biomedical Sciences, Farmington, CT 06030. Offers PhD, DMD/PhD, MD/PhD. *Faculty:* 156. *Students:* 164 full-time (93 women); includes 18 minority (4 African Americans, 1 American Indian/Alaska Native, 10 Asian Americans or Pacific Islanders, 3 Hispanic Americans), 61 international. Average age 29. 165 applicants, 35% accepted, 30 enrolled. In 2009, 26 doctorates awarded. *Degree requirements:* For doctorate, comprehensive exam, thesis/dissertation. *Entrance requirements:* For doctorate, GRE General Test. Additional exam requirements/recommendations for international students: Required—TOEFL (minimum score 600 paper-based; 250 computer-based). *Application deadline:* For fall admission, 12/15 for domestic students. Application fee: $55. Electronic applications accepted. *Financial support:* In 2009–10, 164 students received support, including 164 research assistantships with full tuition reimbursements available (averaging $27,000 per year); Federal Work-Study, traineeships, health care benefits, and unspecified assistantships also available. Total annual research expenditures: $88.2 million. *Application contact:* Tricia Avolt, Graduate Admissions Coordinator, 860-679-2175, Fax: 860-679-1899, E-mail: robertson@nso2.uchc.edu.

See Close-Up on page 117.

University of Connecticut Health Center, Graduate School, Programs in Biomedical Sciences—Integrated, Farmington, CT 06030. Offers PhD, DMD/PhD, MD/PhD. *Faculty:* 156. *Students:* 36 full-time (19 women); includes 2 minority (both Asian Americans or Pacific Islanders), 19 international. Average age 26. 165 applicants, 35% accepted, 30 enrolled. *Degree requirements:* For doctorate, comprehensive exam, thesis/dissertation. *Entrance requirements:* For doctorate, GRE General Test. Additional exam requirements/recommendations for international students: Required—TOEFL (minimum score 600 paper-based; 250 computer-based). *Application deadline:* For fall admission, 12/15 for domestic students. Application fee: $55. Electronic applications accepted. *Financial support:* In 2009–10, 36 students received support, including 36 research assistantships with tuition reimbursements available (averaging $27,000 per year). *Unit head:* Dr. Larry Klobutcher, Associate Dean for the Graduate School. *Application contact:* Tricia Avolt, Graduate Admissions Coordinator, 860-679-2175, Fax: 860-679-1899, E-mail: robertson@ns02.uchc.edu.

University of Dayton, Graduate School, College of Arts and Sciences, Department of Biology, Dayton, OH 45469-1300. Offers MS, PhD. *Faculty:* 19 full-time (6 women). *Students:* 16 full-time (10 women), 1 part-time (0 women), 7 international. Average age 27. 26 applicants, 15% accepted, 4 enrolled. In 2009, 2 master's, 1 doctorate awarded. Terminal master's awarded for partial completion of doctoral program. *Degree requirements:* For master's, comprehensive exam, thesis; for doctorate, comprehensive exam, thesis/dissertation. *Entrance requirements:* For master's and doctorate, GRE General Test, minimum undergraduate GPA of 3.0. Additional exam requirements/recommendations for international students: Required—TOEFL (minimum score 550 paper-based; 213 computer-based; 80 iBT). *Application deadline:* For fall admission, 3/1 priority date for domestic and international students; for winter admission, 10/15 priority date for domestic students, 7/1 priority date for international students; for spring admission, 1/1 for international students. Applications are processed on a rolling basis. Application fee: $50. Electronic applications accepted. *Expenses:* Tuition: Full-time $8412; part-time $701 per credit hour. Required fees: $325; $65 per course. $25 per semester. Tuition and fees vary according to course load, degree level and program. *Financial support:* In 2009–10, 1 research assistantship with full tuition reimbursement (averaging $21,840 per year), 14 teaching assistantships with full tuition reimbursements (averaging $13,292 per year) were awarded; institutionally sponsored loans, health care benefits, and unspecified assistantships also available. Financial award application deadline: 3/1; financial award applicants required to submit FAFSA. *Faculty research:* Tissue regeneration and developmental biology; cancer and stem cell biology; microbiology and immunology; molecular genetics, evolution and bioinformatics; environmental and restoration ecology. *Unit head:* Dr. Jayne B. Robinson, Chair, 937-229-2521, Fax: 937-229-2021. *Application contact:* Graduate Admissions, 937-229-4411, Fax: 937-229-4729, E-mail: gradadmission@udayton.edu.

University of Delaware, College of Arts and Sciences, Department of Biological Sciences, Newark, DE 19716. Offers biotechnology (MS); cancer biology (MS, PhD); cell and extracellular matrix biology (MS, PhD); cell and systems physiology (MS, PhD); developmental biology (MS, PhD); ecology and evolution (MS, PhD); microbiology (MS, PhD); molecular biology and genetics (MS, PhD). Terminal master's awarded for partial completion of doctoral program. *Degree requirements:* For master's, thesis, preliminary exam; for doctorate, comprehensive exam, thesis/dissertation, preliminary exam. *Entrance requirements:* For master's and doctorate, GRE General Test. Additional exam requirements/recommendations for international students: Required—TOEFL (minimum score 600 paper-based; 250 computer-based); Recommended—TWE. Electronic applications accepted. *Faculty research:* Microorganisms, bone, cancer metastasis, developmental biology, cell biology, DNA.

University of Denver, Faculty of Natural Sciences and Mathematics, Department of Biological Sciences, Denver, CO 80208. Offers MS, PhD. Part-time programs available. *Faculty:* 19 full-time (6 women), 2 part-time/adjunct (1 woman). *Students:* 2 full-time (0 women), 25 part-time (17 women); includes 4 minority (1 Asian American or Pacific Islander, 3 Hispanic Americans), 2 international. Average age 28. 64 applicants, 31% accepted, 16 enrolled. In 2009, 6 master's, 2 doctorates awarded. Terminal master's awarded for partial completion of doctoral program. *Degree requirements:* For master's, thesis; for doctorate, one foreign language, thesis/dissertation. *Entrance requirements:* For master's and doctorate, GRE General Test. Additional exam requirements/recommendations for international students: Required—TOEFL. *Application deadline:* Applications are processed on a rolling basis. Application fee: $50. Electronic applications accepted. *Expenses:* Tuition: Full-time $34,596; part-time $961 per quarter hour. Required fees: $4 per quarter hour. Tuition and fees vary according to course load, campus/location and program. *Financial support:* In 2009–10, 7 research assistantships with full and partial tuition reimbursements (averaging $17,000 per year), 16 teaching assistantships with full and partial tuition reimbursements (averaging $17,000 per year) were awarded; Federal Work-Study and institutionally sponsored loans also available. Support available to part-time students. Financial award application deadline: 3/1; financial award applicants required to submit FAFSA. *Faculty research:* Molecular biology, cell biology, neurobiology, ecology, molecular evolution. Total annual research expenditures: $475,000. *Unit head:* Dr. Robert Dores, Chair, 303-871-3661. *Application contact:* Information Contact, 303-871-3661.

University of Florida, College of Medicine and Graduate School, Interdisciplinary Program in Biomedical Sciences, Gainesville, FL 32611. Offers PhD, JD/MS, JD/PhD, MBA/MS, MBA/PhD, MS/M Ed. *Degree requirements:* For doctorate, thesis/dissertation. *Entrance requirements:* For doctorate, GRE General Test, minimum GPA of 3.0. Additional exam requirements/recommendations for international students: Required—TOEFL. Electronic applications accepted. *Expenses:* Contact institution.

University of Georgia, Graduate School, Biomedical and Health Sciences Institute, Athens, GA 30602. Offers neuroscience (PhD). *Entrance requirements:* For doctorate, GRE, official transcripts, 3 letters of recommendation, statement of interest. Additional exam requirements/recommendations for international students: Required—TOEFL. *Expenses:* Tuition, state resident: full-time $6000; part-time $250 per credit hour. Tuition, nonresident: full-time $20,904; part-time $871 per credit hour. Required fees: $730 per semester. *Financial support:* Unspecified assistantships available. Financial award application deadline: 12/31. *Unit head:* Dr. Gaylen Edwards, Chair, 706-542-5922, Fax: 706-542-5285, E-mail: gedwards@uga.edu. *Application contact:* Philip V. Holmes, Graduate Coordinator, 706-542-5922.

University of Guam, Office of Graduate Studies, College of Natural and Applied Sciences, Program in Biology, Mangilao, GU 96923. Offers tropical marine biology (MS). *Degree requirements:* For master's, comprehensive exam, thesis. *Entrance requirements:* For master's, GRE General Test, GRE Subject Test. Additional exam requirements/recommendations for international students: Required—TOEFL. *Faculty research:* Maintenance and ecology of coral reefs.

University of Guelph, Graduate Program Services, College of Biological Science, Guelph, ON N1G 2W1, Canada. Offers M Sc, PhD. Part-time programs available. *Degree requirements:* For master's, thesis (for some programs); for doctorate, comprehensive exam (for some programs), thesis/dissertation. *Entrance requirements:* Additional exam requirements/recommendations for international students: Required—TOEFL (minimum score 550 paper-based; 213 computer-based). Electronic applications accepted.

University of Hartford, College of Arts and Sciences, Department of Biology, West Hartford, CT 06117-1599. Offers biology (MS); neuroscience (MS). Part-time and evening/weekend programs available. *Degree requirements:* For master's, comprehensive exam, thesis optional, oral exams. *Entrance requirements:* For master's, GRE or MCAT. Additional exam requirements/recommendations for international students: Required—TOEFL (minimum score 550 paper-based; 213 computer-based). Electronic applications accepted. *Faculty research:* Neurobiology of aging, central actions of neural steroids, neuroendocrine control of reproduction, retinopathies in sharks, plasticity in the central nervous system.

University of Hawaii at Manoa, John A. Burns School of Medicine and Graduate Division, Graduate Programs in Biomedical Sciences, Honolulu, HI 96822. Offers MS, PhD. Part-time programs available. *Faculty:* 14 full-time (8 women), 2 part-time/adjunct (both women). *Students:* 9 full-time (5 women), 7 part-time (4 women); includes 9 minority (all Asian Americans or Pacific Islanders), 2 international. Average age 40. 20 applicants, 55% accepted, 9 enrolled. In 2009, 6 master's, 2 doctorates awarded. Terminal master's awarded for partial completion of doctoral program. *Degree requirements:* For master's, thesis optional; for doctorate, comprehensive exam, thesis/dissertation. *Entrance requirements:* For master's and doctorate, GRE General Test. Additional exam requirements/recommendations for international students: Required—TOEFL (minimum score 500 paper-based; 173 computer-based; 61 iBT), IELTS (minimum score 5). *Application deadline:* For fall admission, 6/1 for domestic and international students. Application fee: $60. *Expenses:* Contact institution. *Financial support:* In 2009–10, 1 fellowship (averaging $10,776 per year) was awarded; career-related internships or fieldwork, Federal Work-Study, institutionally sponsored loans, and tuition waivers (full and partial) also available. Support available to part-time students. Total annual research expenditures: $989,000. *Application contact:* Sandra Chang, Graduate Chairperson, 808-692-0909, Fax: 808-692-1979, E-mail: sandrac@hawaii.edu.

University of Houston, College of Natural Sciences and Mathematics, Department of Biology and Biochemistry, Houston, TX 77204. Offers biology (MS). *Faculty:* 28 full-time (9 women), 1 part-time/adjunct (0 women). *Students:* 82 full-time (48 women), 8 part-time (2 women); includes 10 minority (3 African Americans, 3 Asian Americans or Pacific Islanders, 4 Hispanic Americans), 59 international. Average age 28. 16 applicants, 100% accepted, 13 enrolled. In 2009, 4 master's, 11 doctorates awarded. Terminal master's awarded for partial completion of doctoral program. *Degree requirements:* For master's, comprehensive exam (for some programs), thesis optional; for doctorate, comprehensive exam (for some programs), thesis/dissertation. *Entrance requirements:* For master's and doctorate, GRE. Additional exam requirements/recommendations for international students: Required—TOEFL (minimum score 550 paper-based; 213 computer-based; 79 iBT), IELTS (minimum score 6.5). *Application deadline:* For fall admission, 4/1 for domestic and international students; for spring admission, 10/1 for domestic and international students. Application fee: $75 for international students. Electronic applications accepted. *Expenses:* Tuition, state resident: full-time $7676; part-time $320 per credit hour. Tuition, nonresident: full-time $14,324; part-time $597 per credit hour. Required fees: $3034. *Financial support:* In 2009–10, 45 fellowships with full tuition reimbursements (averaging $14,300 per year), 39 research assistantships with full tuition reimbursements (averaging $14,300 per year) were awarded; career-related internships or fieldwork, Federal Work-Study, institutionally sponsored loans, scholarships/grants, health care benefits, and unspecified assistantships also available. Support available to part-time students. Financial award application deadline: 2/1. *Faculty research:* Cell and molecular biology, ecology and evolution, biochemical and biophysical sciences, chemical biology. *Unit head:* Dr. Stuart Dryer, Chairman, 713-743-2697, E-mail: sdryer@uh.edu. *Application contact:* Amanda Paul, Academic Advisor, 713-743-2633, Fax: 713-743-2636, E-mail: biogradaffair@nsm.uh.edu.

University of Houston–Clear Lake, School of Science and Computer Engineering, Program in Biological Sciences, Houston, TX 77058-1098. Offers MS. Part-time and evening/weekend programs available. *Entrance requirements:* For master's, GRE General Test. Additional exam requirements/recommendations for international students: Required—TOEFL (minimum score 550 paper-based; 213 computer-based).

University of Idaho, College of Graduate Studies, College of Science, Department of Biological Sciences, Moscow, ID 83844-2282. Offers biology (MS, PhD). *Faculty:* 12 full-time, 4 part-time/adjunct. *Students:* 24 full-time, 3 part-time. In 2009, 3 master's, 2 doctorates awarded. *Degree requirements:* For doctorate, one foreign language, thesis/dissertation. *Entrance requirements:* For master's, GRE, minimum GPA of 2.8; for doctorate, GRE, minimum undergraduate GPA of 2.8, 3.0 graduate. *Application deadline:* For fall admission, 8/1 for domestic students; for spring admission, 12/15 for domestic students. Application fee: $55 ($60 for international students). *Expenses:* Tuition, state resident: full-time $6120. Tuition, nonresident: full-time $17,712. *Financial support:* Research assistantships, teaching assistantships available. Financial award application deadline: 2/15. *Faculty research:* Animal behavior development, germ cell development, evolutionary biology, fish reproductive biology, molecular mechanisms. *Unit head:* Joseph G. Cloud, Chair, 208-885-6280. *Application contact:* Joseph G. Cloud, Chair, 208-885-6280.

University of Illinois at Chicago, College of Medicine and Graduate College, Graduate Programs in Medicine, Chicago, IL 60607-7128. Offers MHPE, MS, PhD, MD/MS, MD/PhD. Part-time programs available. Terminal master's awarded for partial completion of doctoral program. *Degree requirements:* For master's, thesis; for doctorate, thesis/dissertation. *Entrance requirements:* For master's and doctorate, GRE General Test. *Expenses:* Contact institution.

University of Illinois at Chicago, Graduate College, College of Liberal Arts and Sciences, Department of Biological Sciences, Chicago, IL 60607-7128. Offers MS, PhD. *Degree requirements:* For master's, thesis; for doctorate, thesis/dissertation, preliminary exam. *Entrance requirements:* For master's and doctorate, GRE General Test, GRE Subject Test, previous course work in physics, calculus, and organic chemistry; minimum GPA of 2.75. Additional exam requirements/recommendations for international students: Required—TOEFL. Electronic applications accepted.

University of Illinois at Springfield, Graduate Programs, College of Liberal Arts and Sciences, Program in Biology, Springfield, IL 62703-5407. Offers MS. Part-time and evening/weekend programs available. *Faculty:* 8 full-time (3 women). *Students:* 9 full-time (6 women), 14 part-time (10 women); includes 1 minority (American Indian/Alaska Native), 3 international. Average age 30. 19 applicants, 53% accepted, 5 enrolled. In 2009, 1 master's awarded. *Degree requirements:* For master's, project or thesis. *Entrance requirements:* For master's, GRE General Test, GRE Subject Test (biology), minimum undergraduate GPA of 3.0, 3 letters of reference. Additional exam requirements/recommendations for international students: Required—TOEFL (minimum score 500 paper-based; 176 computer-based; 61 iBT). *Application deadline:* Applications are processed on a rolling basis. Application fee: $50 ($60 for international students). Electronic applications accepted. *Expenses:* Tuition, state resident: full-time $6390; part-time $266.25 per credit hour. Tuition, nonresident: full-time $14,226; part-time $592.75 per credit hour. Required fees: $2044; $14.36 per credit hour. $722.50 per term. *Financial support:* In 2009–10, research assistantships with full tuition reimbursements (averaging $8,109 per year), teaching assistantships with full tuition reimbursements (averaging $8,109 per year) were awarded; career-related internships or fieldwork, Federal Work-Study, scholarships/grants, health care benefits, and unspecified assistantships also available. Support available to part-time students. Financial award application deadline: 11/15; financial award applicants required to submit FAFSA. *Unit head:* Dr. Lucia Vazquez, Program Administrator, 217-206-7337, Fax: 217-206-6217, E-mail: vazquez.lucia@uis.edu. *Application contact:* Dr. Lynn Pardie, Office of Graduate Studies, 800-252-8533, Fax: 217-206-7623, E-mail: pardie.lynn@uis.edu.

University of Illinois at Urbana–Champaign, Graduate College, College of Liberal Arts and Sciences, School of Chemical Sciences, Champaign, IL 61820. Offers MA, MS, PhD, MS/JD, MS/MBA. *Faculty:* 50 full-time (8 women). *Students:* 423 full-time (138 women), 8 part-time (1 woman); includes 49 minority (9 African Americans, 3 American Indian/Alaska Native, 27 Asian Americans or Pacific Islanders, 10 Hispanic Americans), 132 international. 883 applicants, 16% accepted, 91 enrolled. In 2009, 20 master's, 71 doctorates awarded. *Entrance requirements:* For master's, minimum GPA of 3.0. *Application deadline:* Applications are processed on a rolling basis. Application fee: $60 ($75 for international students). Electronic applications accepted. *Expenses:* Contact institution. *Financial support:* In 2009–10, 131 fellowships, 292 research assistantships, 204 teaching assistantships were awarded; tuition waivers (full and partial) also available. *Unit head:* Andrew A. Gewirth, Director, 217-333-8329, Fax: 217-333-2685, E-mail: agewirth@illinois.edu. *Application contact:* Cheryl Kappes, Office Manager, 217-333-5070, Fax: 217-333-3120, E-mail: dambache@illinois.edu.

University of Illinois at Urbana–Champaign, Graduate College, College of Liberal Arts and Sciences, School of Integrative Biology, Champaign, IL 61820. Offers MS, MST, PhD. *Faculty:* 35 full-time (10 women). *Students:* 130 full-time (65 women), 41 part-time (26 women); includes 23 minority (6 African Americans, 1 American Indian/Alaska Native, 11 Asian Americans or Pacific Islanders, 5 Hispanic Americans), 28 international. 189 applicants, 35% accepted, 44 enrolled. In 2009, 25 master's, 17 doctorates awarded. *Application deadline:* Applications are processed on a rolling basis. Application fee: $60 ($75 for international students). Electronic applications accepted. *Financial support:* In 2009–10, 19 fellowships, 101 research assistantships, 92 teaching assistantships were awarded; tuition waivers (full and partial) also available. *Unit head:* Evan De Lucia, Director, 217-333-6177, Fax: 217-244-1224, E-mail: delucia@illinois.edu. *Application contact:* Katherine S. Jennings, Office Support Specialist, 217-333-7801, Fax: 217-244-1224, E-mail: ksjennin@illinois.edu.

University of Indianapolis, Graduate Programs, College of Arts and Sciences, Department of Biology, Indianapolis, IN 46227-3697. Offers human biology (MS). Part-time and evening/weekend programs available. *Faculty:* 5 full-time (1 woman), 1 (woman) part-time/adjunct. *Students:* 11 full-time (8 women), 7 part-time (6 women); includes 2 minority (1 Asian American or Pacific Islander, 1 Hispanic American), 2 international. Average age 25. *Degree requirements:* For master's, thesis. *Entrance requirements:* For master's, GRE General Test, 3 letters of recommendation; minimum GPA of 3.0; BA/BS in anthropology, biology, human biology or closely related field, resume. Additional exam requirements/recommendations for international students: Required—TOEFL (minimum score 550 paper-based). *Application deadline:* For fall admission, 1/15 for domestic and international students. Applications are processed on a rolling basis. Application fee: $30. *Financial support:* Federal Work-Study, scholarships/grants, and tuition waivers (full and partial) available. Support available to part-time students. Financial award application deadline: 5/1; financial award applicants required to submit FAFSA. *Unit head:* Dr. L. Mark Harrison, Chairperson, 317-788-3264, E-mail: harrison@uindy.edu. *Application contact:* Dr. Stephen P. Nawrocki, Director, Graduate Program in Human Biology, 317-788-3486, Fax: 317-788-3480, E-mail: snawrocki@uindy.edu.

The University of Iowa, Graduate College, College of Liberal Arts and Sciences, Department of Biology, Iowa City, IA 52242-1316. Offers biology (MS, PhD); cell and developmental biology (MS, PhD); evolution (MS, PhD); genetics (MS, PhD); neurobiology (MS, PhD); plant biology (MS, PhD). Terminal master's awarded for partial completion of doctoral program. *Degree requirements:* For master's, thesis optional, exam; for doctorate, comprehensive exam, thesis/dissertation. *Entrance requirements:* For master's and doctorate, GRE General Test, minimum GPA of 3.0. Additional exam requirements/recommendations for international students: Required—TOEFL (minimum score 600 paper-based; 250 computer-based; 100 iBT). Electronic applications accepted. *Faculty research:* Developmental neurobiology, evolutionary biology, signal transduction, cell motility, molecular genetics (plant and animal).

The University of Iowa, Roy J. and Lucille A. Carver College of Medicine and Graduate College, Biosciences Program, Iowa City, IA 52242-1316. Offers anatomy and biology (PhD); biochemistry (PhD); biology (PhD); biomedical engineering (PhD); chemistry (PhD); free radical and radiation biology (PhD); genetics (PhD); human toxicology (PhD); immunology (PhD); microbiology (PhD); molecular and cellular biology (PhD); molecular physiology and biophysics (PhD); neuroscience (PhD); pharmacology (PhD); physical therapy and rehabilitation science (PhD); speech and hearing (PhD). *Faculty:* 310 full-time. *Students:* 25 full-time (13 women); includes 1 African American, 2 Asian Americans or Pacific Islanders, 4 international.

Biological and Biomedical Sciences—General

The University of Iowa (continued)

225 applicants. *Degree requirements:* For doctorate, thesis/dissertation. *Entrance requirements:* For doctorate, GRE General Test, minimum GPA of 3.0. Additional exam requirements/recommendations for international students: Required—TOEFL (minimum score 600 paper-based; 250 computer-based; 100 iBT). *Application deadline:* For fall admission, 1/15 priority date for domestic and international students. Applications are processed on a rolling basis. Application fee: $60 ($100 for international students). Electronic applications accepted. *Expenses:* Contact institution. *Financial support:* In 2009–10, 25 students received support, including 25 research assistantships with full tuition reimbursements available (averaging $24,250 per year); fellowships, teaching assistantships, health care benefits also available. *Unit head:* Dr. Andrew F. Russo, Director, 319-335-7872, Fax: 319-335-7656, E-mail: andrew-russo@uiowa.edu. *Application contact:* Jodi M. Graff, Program Associate, 319-335-8305, Fax: 319-335-7656, E-mail: biosciences-admissions@uiowa.edu.

The University of Iowa, Roy J. and Lucille A. Carver College of Medicine and Graduate College, Graduate Programs in Medicine, Iowa City, IA 52242-1316. Offers MA, MPAS, MS, DPT, PhD, JD/MHA, MBA/MHA, MD/JD, MD/PhD, MHA/MA, MHA/MS, MPH/MHA, MS/MA, MS/MS. Part-time programs available. *Faculty:* 132 full-time (28 women), 86 part-time/adjunct (36 women). *Students:* 287 full-time (163 women), 9 part-time (5 women); includes 28 minority (3 African Americans, 3 American Indian/Alaska Native, 18 Asian Americans or Pacific Islanders, 4 Hispanic Americans), 33 international. 1,230 applicants, 10% accepted, 87 enrolled. In 2009, 32 master's, 29 doctorates awarded. *Degree requirements:* For doctorate, thesis/dissertation. Electronic applications accepted. *Expenses:* Contact institution. *Financial support:* In 2009–10, 158 students received support, including fellowships (averaging $24,250 per year), research assistantships (averaging $24,250 per year); teaching assistantships, career-related internships or fieldwork, Federal Work-Study, institutionally sponsored loans, health care benefits, and tuition waivers (full and partial) also available. Support available to part-time students. Financial award applicants required to submit FAFSA. *Unit head:* Dr. Paul B. Rothman, Dean, 319-384-4590, Fax: 319-335-8318, E-mail: paul-rothman@uiowa.edu. *Application contact:* Dr. Paul B. Rothman, Dean, 319-384-4590, Fax: 319-335-8318, E-mail: paul-rothman@uiowa.edu.

The University of Iowa, Roy J. and Lucille A. Carver College of Medicine and Graduate College, Medical Scientist Training Program, Iowa City, IA 52242-1316. Offers MD/PhD. *Faculty:* 137 full-time (32 women), 3 part-time/adjunct (0 women). *Students:* 61 full-time (25 women); includes 17 minority (1 American Indian/Alaska Native, 9 Asian Americans or Pacific Islanders, 7 Hispanic Americans). Average age 24. 139 applicants, 19% accepted, 9 enrolled. *Application deadline:* For fall admission, 11/15 priority date for domestic students. Applications are processed on a rolling basis. Application fee: $50. Electronic applications accepted. *Financial support:* In 2009–10, 25 students received support, including 8 fellowships with full tuition reimbursements available (averaging $20,976 per year), 25 research assistantships with full tuition reimbursements available (averaging $2,764 per year); scholarships/grants, traineeships, health care benefits, and unspecified assistantships also available. *Faculty research:* Structure and function of ion channels, molecular genetics of human disease, neurobiology of pain, viral immunology and immunopathology, epidemiology of aging and cancer, human learning and memory, structural enzymology. Total annual research expenditures: $2 million. *Unit head:* Dr. C. Michael Knudson, Director, 319-335-8147, Fax: 319-335-6634, E-mail: c-knudson@uiowa.edu. *Application contact:* Leslie Harrington, Program Associate, 319-335-8304, Fax: 319-335-6634, E-mail: mstp@uiowa.edu.

The University of Kansas, University of Kansas Medical Center, School of Medicine, Interdisciplinary Graduate Program in Biomedical Sciences (IGPBS), Kansas City, KS 66160. Offers MA, MPH, MS, PhD, MD/MPH, MD/MS, MD/PhD. Part-time and evening/weekend programs available. *Students:* 20 full-time (13 women); includes 1 minority (Asian American or Pacific Islander), 6 international. Average age 25. 160 applicants, 25% accepted, 20 enrolled. Terminal master's awarded for partial completion of doctoral program. *Degree requirements:* For master's, thesis; for doctorate, comprehensive exam, thesis/dissertation. *Entrance requirements:* For master's and doctorate, GRE. Additional exam requirements/recommendations for international students: Required—TOEFL. *Application deadline:* For fall admission, 1/15 priority date for domestic and international students. Applications are processed on a rolling basis. Application fee: $0. Electronic applications accepted. *Expenses:* Tuition, state resident: full-time $6492; part-time $270.50 per credit hour. Tuition, nonresident: full-time $15,510; part-time $646.25 per credit hour. Required fees: $847; $70.56 per credit hour. Tuition and fees vary according to course load and program. *Financial support:* In 2009–10, 20 students received support, including fellowships with full tuition reimbursements available (averaging $24,000 per year), research assistantships with full tuition reimbursements available (averaging $24,000 per year), teaching assistantships with full tuition reimbursements available (averaging $24,000 per year); Federal Work-Study also available. Support available to part-time students. Financial award application deadline: 3/30; financial award applicants required to submit FAFSA. *Faculty research:* Cardiovascular biology, neurosciences, signal transduction and cancer biology, molecular biology and genetics, developmental biology. *Unit head:* Dr. Michael J. Werle, Graduate Advisor, 913-588-7491, Fax: 913-588-2710, E-mail: mwerle@kumc.edu. *Application contact:* Miranda Olenhouse, Coordinator, 913-588-2719, Fax: 913-588-2711, E-mail: molenhouse@kumc.edu.

See Close-Up on page 119.

University of Kentucky, Graduate School, College of Arts and Sciences, Program in Biology, Lexington, KY 40506-0032. Offers MS, PhD. *Degree requirements:* For master's, comprehensive exam, thesis optional; for doctorate, comprehensive exam, thesis/dissertation. *Entrance requirements:* For master's, GRE General Test, minimum undergraduate GPA of 2.75; for doctorate, GRE General Test, minimum graduate GPA of 3.0. Additional exam requirements/recommendations for international students: Required—TOEFL (minimum score 550 paper-based; 213 computer-based). Electronic applications accepted. *Faculty research:* General biology, microbiology, *Drosophila* molecular genetics, molecular virology, multiple loci inheritance.

University of Kentucky, Graduate School, Graduate School Programs from the College of Medicine, Lexington, KY 40506-0032. Offers MS, PhD, MD/PhD. *Degree requirements:* For master's, comprehensive exam, thesis (for some programs); for doctorate, comprehensive exam, thesis/dissertation. *Entrance requirements:* For master's, GRE General Test, minimum undergraduate GPA of 2.75; for doctorate, GRE General Test, minimum undergraduate GPA of 3.0. Additional exam requirements/recommendations for international students: Required—TOEFL (minimum score 550 paper-based; 213 computer-based). Electronic applications accepted.

University of Lethbridge, School of Graduate Studies, Lethbridge, AB T1K 3M4, Canada. Offers accounting (MScM); addictions counseling (M Sc); agricultural biotechnology (M Sc); agricultural studies (M Sc, MA); anthropology (MA); archaeology (MA); art (MA, MFA); biochemistry (M Sc); biological sciences (M Sc); biomolecular science (PhD); biosystems and biodiversity (PhD); Canadian studies (MA); chemistry (M Sc); computer science (M Sc); computer science and geographical information science (M Sc); counseling psychology (M Ed); dramatic arts (MA); earth, space, and physical science (PhD); economics (MA); educational leadership (M Ed); English (MA); environmental science (M Sc); evolution and behavior (PhD); exercise science (M Sc); finance (MScM); French (MA); French/German (MA); French/Spanish (MA); general education (M Ed); general management (MScM); geography (M Sc, MA); German (MA); health science (M Sc); history (MA); human resource management and labour relations (MScM); individualized multidisciplinary (M Sc, MA); information systems (MScM); international management (MScM); kinesiology (M Sc, MA); management (M Sc, MA); marketing (MScM); mathematics (M Sc); music (M Mus, MA); Native American studies (MA); neuroscience (M Sc, PhD); new media (MA); nursing (M Sc); philosophy (MA); physics (M Sc); policy and strategy (MScM); political science (MA); psychology (M Sc, MA); religious studies (MA); social sciences (MA); sociology (MA); theatre and dramatic arts (MFA); theoretical and computational science (PhD); urban and regional studies (MA); women's studies (MA). Part-time and evening/weekend programs available. *Degree requirements:* For doctorate, comprehensive exam, thesis/dissertation. *Entrance requirements:* For master's, GMAT (M Sc in management), bachelor's degree in related field, minimum GPA of 3.0 during previous 20 graded semester courses, 2 years teaching or related experience (M Ed); for doctorate, master's degree, minimum graduate GPA of 3.5. Additional exam requirements/recommendations for international students: Required—TOEFL. *Faculty research:* Movement and brain plasticity, gibberellin physiology, photosynthesis, carbon cycling, molecular properties of main-group ring components.

University of Louisiana at Lafayette, College of Sciences, Department of Biology, Lafayette, LA 70504. Offers biology (MS); environmental and evolutionary biology (PhD). Terminal master's awarded for partial completion of doctoral program. *Degree requirements:* For master's, thesis; for doctorate, 2 foreign languages, comprehensive exam, thesis/dissertation. *Entrance requirements:* For master's, GRE General Test, minimum GPA of 2.75; for doctorate, GRE General Test, GRE Subject Test, minimum GPA of 3.0. Additional exam requirements/recommendations for international students: Required—TOEFL (minimum score 550 paper-based; 213 computer-based). Electronic applications accepted. *Faculty research:* Structure and ultrastructure, system biology, ecology, processes, environmental physiology.

University of Louisiana at Monroe, Graduate School, College of Arts and Sciences, Department of Biology, Monroe, LA 71209-0001. Offers MS. *Faculty:* 13 full-time (6 women). *Students:* 26 full-time (13 women), 3 part-time (2 women); includes 2 minority (1 African American, 1 Asian American or Pacific Islander), 3 international. Average age 25. In 2009, 4 master's awarded. *Entrance requirements:* For master's, GRE General Test, minimum GPA of 2.8 overall or 3.0 during last 21 hours of biology. Additional exam requirements/recommendations for international students: Required—TOEFL (minimum score 500 paper-based; 113 computer-based; 61 iBT). *Application deadline:* For fall admission, 8/24 priority date for domestic students, 7/1 for international students; for winter admission, 12/14 priority date for domestic students; for spring admission, 1/19 for domestic students, 11/1 for international students. Applications are processed on a rolling basis. Application fee: $20 ($30 for international students). Electronic applications accepted. *Expenses:* Tuition, state resident: part-time $159 per credit hour. Tuition, nonresident: part-time $159 per credit hour. Required fees: $1300 per year. Tuition and fees vary according to course load. *Financial support:* In 2009–10, 3 research assistantships with full tuition reimbursements (averaging $4,000 per year), 17 teaching assistantships with full tuition reimbursements (averaging $4,000 per year) were awarded; career-related internships or fieldwork, Federal Work-Study, and unspecified assistantships also available. Financial award application deadline: 4/1; financial award applicants required to submit FAFSA. *Faculty research:* Fish systematics and zoogeography, taxonomy and distribution of Louisiana plants, aquatic biology, secondary succession, microbial ecology. *Unit head:* Dr. Sushma Krishnamurthy, Department Head, 318-342-1813, Fax: 318-342-3312, E-mail: krishnamurthy@ulm.edu. *Application contact:* Dr. Kim M. Tolson, Professor, 318-342-1805, Fax: 318-342-3312, E-mail: tolson@ulm.edu.

University of Louisville, Graduate School, College of Arts and Sciences, Department of Biology, Louisville, KY 40292-0001. Offers biology (MS); environmental biology (PhD). *Students:* 38 full-time (19 women), 10 part-time (8 women); includes 1 minority (Asian American or Pacific Islander), 9 international. Average age 32. 49 applicants, 53% accepted, 9 enrolled. In 2009, 7 master's, 6 doctorates awarded. *Degree requirements:* For master's, thesis (for some programs); for doctorate, thesis/dissertation. *Entrance requirements:* For master's and doctorate, GRE General Test. *Application deadline:* Applications are processed on a rolling basis. Application fee: $50. *Unit head:* Dr. Ronald Fell, Chair, 502-852-6771, Fax: 502-852-0725, E-mail: rdfell@louisville.edu. *Application contact:* Dr. Joseph M. Steffen, Director of Graduate Studies, 502-852-6771, Fax: 502-852-0725, E-mail: joe.steffen@louisville.edu.

University of Maine, Graduate School, College of Natural Sciences, Forestry, and Agriculture, Department of Biological Sciences, Program in Biological Sciences, Orono, ME 04469. Offers PhD. *Students:* 5 full-time (3 women), 8 part-time (3 women), 3 international. Average age 33. 6 applicants, 33% accepted, 1 enrolled. In 2009, 5 doctorates awarded. *Degree requirements:* For doctorate, thesis/dissertation. *Entrance requirements:* For doctorate, GRE General Test. Additional exam requirements/recommendations for international students: Required—TOEFL. *Application deadline:* For fall admission, 2/1 priority date for domestic students. Applications are processed on a rolling basis. Application fee: $65. Electronic applications accepted. *Financial support:* Application deadline: 3/1. *Unit head:* Dr. Stellos Tavantzis, Coordinator, 207-581-2986. *Application contact:* Scott G. Delcourt, Associate Dean of the Graduate School, 207-581-3291, Fax: 207-581-3232, E-mail: graduate@maine.edu.

University of Maine, Graduate School, Program in Biomedical Sciences, Orono, ME 04469. Offers PhD. *Students:* 17 full-time (11 women), 6 part-time (3 women); includes 1 minority (American Indian/Alaska Native), 6 international. Average age 29. 28 applicants, 18% accepted, 5 enrolled. In 2009, 1 doctorate awarded. Application fee: $60. *Financial support:* In 2009–10, 8 research assistantships (averaging $25,625 per year) were awarded. *Unit head:* Dr. Carol Kim, Unit Head, 207-581-2803. *Application contact:* Dr. Carol Kim, Unit Head, 207-581-2803.

University of Manitoba, Faculty of Graduate Studies, Faculty of Science, Department of Biological Sciences, Winnipeg, MB R3T 2N2, Canada. Offers botany (M Sc, PhD); ecology (M Sc, PhD); zoology (M Sc, PhD).

University of Manitoba, Faculty of Medicine and Faculty of Graduate Studies, Graduate Programs in Medicine, Winnipeg, MB R3T 2N2, Canada. Offers M Sc, MPH, PhD, G Dip, MD/PhD. *Accreditation:* LCME/AMA. Part-time programs available. *Expenses:* Contact institution.

University of Maryland, Baltimore, Graduate School, Graduate Program in Life Sciences, Baltimore, MD 21201. Offers biochemistry and molecular biology (MS, PhD), including biochemistry; epidemiology (PhD); gerontology (PhD); molecular medicine (MS, PhD), including cancer biology (PhD), cell and molecular physiology (PhD), human genetics and genomic medicine (PhD), molecular medicine (MS), molecular toxicology and pharmacology (PhD); molecular microbiology and immunology (PhD); neuroscience (PhD); physical rehabilitation science (PhD); toxicology (MS, PhD); MD/MS; MD/PhD. *Students:* 248 full-time (148 women), 72 part-time (40 women); includes 80 minority (25 African Americans, 1 American Indian/Alaska Native, 39 Asian Americans or Pacific Islanders, 15 Hispanic Americans), 47 international. Average age 29. 719 applicants, 22% accepted, 64 enrolled. In 2009, 29 master's, 39 doctorates awarded. *Degree requirements:* For master's, comprehensive exam (for some programs), thesis (for some programs); for doctorate, comprehensive exam, thesis/dissertation. *Entrance requirements:* For master's and doctorate, GRE. Additional exam requirements/recommendations for international students: Required—TOEFL (minimum score 550 paper-based; 80 iBT); Recommended—IELTS (minimum score 7). *Application deadline:* For fall admission, 1/15 for domestic and international students. Application fee: $50. Electronic applications accepted. *Expenses:* Tuition, state resident: full-time $7290; part-time $405 per credit hour. Tuition, nonresident: full-time $12,780; part-time $710 per credit hour. Required fees: $774; $10 per credit hour. $297 per semester. Tuition and fees vary according to course load, degree level and program. *Financial support:* In 2009–10, research assistantships with partial tuition reimbursements (averaging $25,000 per year); fellowships, scholarships/grants, health care benefits, and unspecified assistantships also available. Financial award application deadline: 3/1. *Faculty research:* Cancer, reproduction, cardiovascular, immunology. *Unit head:* Dr. Margaret Merryl McCarthy, Assistant Dean for Graduate Studies, 410-706-2655, Fax: 410-706-8341, E-mail: mmccarthy@umaryland.edu. *Application contact:* Dr. Margaret Merryl McCarthy, Assistant Dean for Graduate Studies, 410-706-2655, Fax: 410-706-8341, E-mail: mmcarthy@umaryland.edu.

University of Maryland, Baltimore County, Graduate School, College of Arts, Humanities and Social Sciences, Department of Education, Program in Teaching, Baltimore, MD 21250. Offers early childhood education (MAT); elementary education (MAT); secondary education (MAT), including art, biology, chemistry, dance, earth/space science, English, foreign language, mathematics, music, physics, theatre; secondary science (MAT), including social studies. Part-time and evening/weekend programs available. *Faculty:* 24 full-time (18 women), 25 part-time/adjunct (19 women). *Students:* 52 full-time (41 women), 64 part-time (55 women);

includes 20 minority (5 African Americans, 1 American Indian/Alaska Native, 10 Asian Americans or Pacific Islanders, 4 Hispanic Americans), 3 international. Average age 31. 88 applicants, 57% accepted, 39 enrolled. In 2009, 106 master's awarded. *Degree requirements:* For master's, comprehensive exam (for some programs), thesis (for some programs). *Entrance requirements:* For master's, PRAXIS I and II, minimum GPA of 3.0. Additional exam requirements/recommendations for international students: Required—TOEFL. *Application deadline:* For fall admission, 6/1 for domestic students; for spring admission, 11/1 for domestic students. Applications are processed on a rolling basis. Application fee: $50. Electronic applications accepted. *Financial support:* In 2009–10, 6 students received support, including research assistantships with full tuition reimbursements available (averaging $12,000 per year); career-related internships or fieldwork, Federal Work-Study, scholarships/grants, tuition waivers, and unspecified assistantships also available. Financial award application deadline: 3/1. *Faculty research:* STEM teacher education, culturally sensitive pedagogy, ESOL/bilingual education, early childhood education, language, literacy and culture. *Unit head:* Dr. Susan M. Blunck, Director, 410-455-2869, Fax: 410-455-3986, E-mail: blunck@umbc.edu. *Application contact:* Dr. Susan M. Blunck, Director, 410-455-2869, Fax: 410-455-3986, E-mail: blunck@umbc.edu.

University of Maryland, Baltimore County, Graduate School, College of Natural and Mathematical Sciences, Department of Biological Sciences, Baltimore, MD 21250. Offers applied molecular biology (MS); biological sciences (MS, PhD); molecular and cell biology (PhD); neurosciences and cognitive sciences (PhD). Part-time programs available. *Faculty:* 26 full-time (10 women), 1 part-time/adjunct (0 women). *Students:* 67 full-time (43 women), 20 part-time (14 women); includes 39 minority (11 African Americans, 24 Asian Americans or Pacific Islanders, 4 Hispanic Americans). Average age 26. 138 applicants, 30% accepted, 25 enrolled. In 2009, 15 master's, 3 doctorates awarded. *Entrance requirements:* For master's and doctorate, GRE General Test, minimum GPA of 3.0. Additional exam requirements/recommendations for international students: Required—TOEFL. *Application deadline:* For fall admission, 1/15 for domestic students, 12/15 for international students. Applications are processed on a rolling basis. Application fee: $50. Electronic applications accepted. *Financial support:* In 2009–10, 67 students received support, including 7 fellowships with full tuition reimbursements available (averaging $27,500 per year), 32 research assistantships with full tuition reimbursements available (averaging $22,300 per year), 38 teaching assistantships with full tuition reimbursements available (averaging $22,300 per year); career-related internships or fieldwork and tuition waivers (partial) also available. *Faculty research:* Molecular genetics, neurobiology, metabolism. *Unit head:* Dr. Lasse Lindahl, Chairman, 410-455-2261, Fax: 410-455-3875. *Application contact:* Dr. Jeff Leips, Director, 410-455-3669, Fax: 410-455-3875, E-mail: biograd@umbc.edu.

University of Maryland, College Park, Academic Affairs, College of Chemical and Life Sciences, Department of Biology, Program in Biology, College Park, MD 20742. Offers MS, PhD. Part-time and evening/weekend programs available. *Students:* 48 full-time (29 women), 3 part-time (1 woman); includes 6 minority (4 African Americans, 2 Asian Americans or Pacific Islanders), 16 international. 82 applicants, 15% accepted, 7 enrolled. In 2009, 3 master's, 5 doctorates awarded. Terminal master's awarded for partial completion of doctoral program. *Degree requirements:* For master's, comprehensive exam, thesis optional; for doctorate, thesis/dissertation, oral exam. *Entrance requirements:* For master's and doctorate, GRE General Test, GRE Subject Test, minimum GPA of 3.0, 3 letters of recommendation. Additional exam requirements/recommendations for international students: Required—TOEFL. *Application deadline:* For fall admission, 1/6 priority date for domestic students, 1/6 for international students. Applications are processed on a rolling basis. Application fee: $60. Electronic applications accepted. *Expenses:* Tuition, area resident: Part-time $471 per credit hour. Tuition, state resident: part-time $471 per credit hour. Tuition, nonresident: part-time $1016 per credit hour. Required fees: $337.04 per term. *Financial support:* In 2009–10, 7 fellowships with full and partial tuition reimbursements (averaging $14,571 per year), 6 research assistantships with tuition reimbursements (averaging $19,329 per year), 19 teaching assistantships with tuition reimbursements (averaging $19,248 per year) were awarded. Financial award application deadline: 2/1; financial award applicants required to submit FAFSA. *Unit head:* Gerald Wilkinson, Chair, 301-405-6884, E-mail: wilkinso@umd.edu. *Application contact:* Dean of Graduate School, 301-405-0358, Fax: 301-314-9305.

University of Maryland, College Park, Academic Affairs, College of Chemical and Life Sciences, Program in Life Sciences, College Park, MD 20742. Offers MLS. *Students:* 1 (woman) full-time, 100 part-time (69 women); includes 13 minority (8 African Americans, 4 Asian Americans or Pacific Islanders, 1 Hispanic American), 1 international. 50 applicants, 98% accepted, 31 enrolled. In 2009, 36 master's awarded. *Degree requirements:* For master's, scholarly paper. *Entrance requirements:* For master's, 1 year of teaching experience, letters of recommendation. *Application deadline:* Applications are processed on a rolling basis. Application fee: $60. Electronic applications accepted. *Expenses:* Tuition, area resident: Part-time $471 per credit hour. Tuition, state resident: part-time $471 per credit hour. Tuition, nonresident: part-time $1016 per credit hour. Required fees: $337.04 per term. *Financial support:* Fellowships with tuition reimbursements, research assistantships with tuition reimbursements, teaching assistantships with tuition reimbursements, Federal Work-Study and scholarships/grants available. Support available to part-time students. Financial award applicants required to submit FAFSA. *Faculty research:* Genetic engineering, gene therapy, ecology, biocomplexity. *Unit head:* Dr. Paul Mazzocchi, Director, 301-405-8482, E-mail: pmazzocc@deans.umd.edu. *Application contact:* Dean of Graduate School, 301-405-0376, Fax: 301-314-9305.

University of Massachusetts Amherst, Graduate School, College of Natural Sciences, Department of Animal Biotechnology and Biomedical Sciences, Amherst, MA 01003. Offers MS, PhD. Part-time programs available. *Faculty:* 21 full-time (8 women). *Students:* 22 full-time (15 women); includes 2 minority (1 African American, 1 Hispanic American), 8 international. Average age 30. 41 applicants, 7% accepted, 3 enrolled. In 2009, 1 master's, 4 doctorates awarded. Terminal master's awarded for partial completion of doctoral program. *Degree requirements:* For master's, thesis or alternative; for doctorate, comprehensive exam, thesis/dissertation. *Entrance requirements:* For master's and doctorate, GRE General Test. Additional exam requirements/recommendations for international students: Required—TOEFL (minimum score 550 paper-based; 213 computer-based; 80 iBT), IELTS (minimum score 6.5). *Application deadline:* For fall admission, 2/1 for domestic and international students; for spring admission, 10/1 for domestic and international students. Applications are processed on a rolling basis. Application fee: $50 ($65 for international students). Electronic applications accepted. *Expenses:* Tuition, state resident: full-time $2640; part-time $110 per credit. Tuition, nonresident: full-time $9936; part-time $414 per credit. Tuition and fees vary according to course load. *Financial support:* In 2009–10, 42 research assistantships with full tuition reimbursements (averaging $11,650 per year), 11 teaching assistantships with full tuition reimbursements (averaging $11,217 per year) were awarded; fellowships, career-related internships or fieldwork, Federal Work-Study, scholarships/grants, traineeships, health care benefits, tuition waivers (full), and unspecified assistantships also available. Support available to part-time students. Financial award application deadline: 2/1. *Unit head:* Dr. Pablo E. Visconti, Graduate Program Director, 413-577-1193, Fax: 413-577-1150. *Application contact:* Jean M. Ames, Supervisor of Admissions, 413-545-0722, Fax: 413-577-0010, E-mail: gradadm@grad.umass.edu.

University of Massachusetts Boston, Office of Graduate Studies, College of Science and Mathematics, Program in Biology, Boston, MA 02125-3393. Offers MS. Part-time and evening/weekend programs available. *Degree requirements:* For master's, thesis, oral exams. *Entrance requirements:* For master's, GRE General Test, GRE Subject Test, minimum GPA of 2.75. *Faculty research:* Microbial ecology, population and conservation genetics energetics of insect locomotion, science education, evolution and ecology of marine invertebrates.

University of Massachusetts Boston, Office of Graduate Studies, College of Science and Mathematics, Program in Biotechnology and Biomedical Science, Boston, MA 02125-3393. Offers MS. Part-time and evening/weekend programs available. *Degree requirements:* For master's, comprehensive exam, thesis optional, oral exams. *Entrance requirements:* For master's, GRE General Test, GRE Subject Test, minimum GPA of 2.75, 3.0 in science and math. *Faculty research:* Evolutionary and molecular immunology, molecular genetics, tissue culture, computerized laboratory technology.

University of Massachusetts Dartmouth, Graduate School, College of Arts and Sciences, Department of Biology, North Dartmouth, MA 02747-2300. Offers biology (MS); marine biology (MS). Part-time programs available. *Faculty:* 17 full-time (6 women), 2 part-time/adjunct (1 woman). *Students:* 10 full-time (8 women), 7 part-time (4 women); includes 2 minority (1 Asian American or Pacific Islander, 1 Hispanic American). Average age 28. 17 applicants, 41% accepted, 6 enrolled. In 2009, 3 master's awarded. *Degree requirements:* For master's, thesis. *Entrance requirements:* For master's, GRE General Test, GRE Subject Test, 3 letters of recommendation. Additional exam requirements/recommendations for international students: Required—TOEFL (minimum score 500 paper-based). *Application deadline:* For fall admission, 3/15 for domestic students, 1/15 for international students; for spring admission, 11/15 priority date for domestic students, 9/15 priority date for international students. Application fee: $40 ($60 for international students). Electronic applications accepted. *Expenses:* Tuition, state resident: full-time $2071; part-time $86.29 per credit. Tuition, nonresident: full-time $8099; part-time $337.46 per credit. Required fees: $9446. Tuition and fees vary according to class time, course load and reciprocity agreements. *Financial support:* In 2009–10, 6 research assistantships with full tuition reimbursements (averaging $12,577 per year), 7 teaching assistantships with full tuition reimbursements (averaging $10,340 per year) were awarded; Federal Work-Study and unspecified assistantships also available. Support available to part-time students. Financial award application deadline: 3/1; financial award applicants required to submit FAFSA. *Faculty research:* Fish biology, antibody mediated protection, bottlenose dolphins, adaptations in fish via genetics evolutionary biology. Total annual research expenditures: $774,000. *Unit head:* Dr. Diego Bernal, Director, 508-999-8307, Fax: 508-999-8196, E-mail: dbernal@umassd.edu. *Application contact:* Elan Turcotte-Shamski, Graduate Admissions Officer, 508-999-8604, Fax: 508-999-8183, E-mail: graduate@umassd.edu.

University of Massachusetts Lowell, College of Arts and Sciences, Department of Biological Sciences, Lowell, MA 01854-2881. Offers biochemistry (PhD); biological sciences (MS); biotechnology (MS). Part-time programs available. *Degree requirements:* For master's, thesis; for doctorate, thesis/dissertation. *Entrance requirements:* For master's and doctorate, GRE General Test. Electronic applications accepted.

University of Massachusetts Worcester, Graduate School of Biomedical Sciences, Interdisciplinary Graduate Program in the Biomedical Sciences, Worcester, MA 01655-0115. Offers PhD. *Degree requirements:* For doctorate, comprehensive exam, thesis/dissertation. *Entrance requirements:* For doctorate, GRE General Test. Additional exam requirements/recommendations for international students: Required—TOEFL (minimum score 600 paper-based; 250 computer-based). Electronic applications accepted. *Faculty research:* Classical and molecular genetics, proteomics and genomics, x-ray crystallography and nuclear magnetic resonance, digital imaging and laser confocal microscopy of single cells and tissues.

University of Medicine and Dentistry of New Jersey, Graduate School of Biomedical Sciences, Graduate Programs in Biomedical Sciences–Newark, Newark, NJ 07107. Offers biochemistry and molecular biology (MS, PhD); biodefense (Certificate); biomedical engineering (Certificate); biomedical sciences (interdisciplinary) (PhD); cell biology and molecular medicine (PhD); integrative neuroscience (PhD); microbiology and molecular genetics (PhD); molecular pathology and immunology (PhD); neuroscience (Certificate); pharmacological sciences (Certificate); pharmacology and physiology (PhD); stem cell (Certificate); DMD/PhD; MD/PhD. *Students:* 337 full-time (191 women), 68 part-time (42 women); includes 133 minority (24 African Americans, 2 American Indian/Alaska Native, 83 Asian Americans or Pacific Islanders, 24 Hispanic Americans), 78 international. Average age 26. 576 applicants, 57% accepted, 177 enrolled. In 2009, 95 master's, 27 doctorates awarded. Terminal master's awarded for partial completion of doctoral program. *Degree requirements:* For master's, thesis (for some programs); for doctorate, thesis/dissertation, qualifying exam. *Entrance requirements:* For master's, GRE General Test, MCAT or DAT; for doctorate, GRE General Test. Additional exam requirements/recommendations for international students: Required—TOEFL. *Application deadline:* For fall admission, 1/15 for domestic students. Applications are processed on a rolling basis. Application fee: $40. Electronic applications accepted. *Financial support:* Fellowships, research assistantships, teaching assistantships, career-related internships or fieldwork, Federal Work-Study, institutionally sponsored loans, and tuition waivers (full and partial) available. Financial award application deadline: 5/1. *Unit head:* Dr. Andrew Thomas, Senior Associate Dean, 973-972-4511, Fax: 973-972-7148, E-mail: thomas@umdnj.edu. *Application contact:* Dr. B. J. Wagner, 973-972-5335, Fax: 973-972-7148, E-mail: wagner@umdnj.edu.

University of Medicine and Dentistry of New Jersey, Graduate School of Biomedical Sciences, Graduate Programs in Biomedical Sciences–Piscataway, Piscataway, NJ 08854-5635. Offers biochemistry and molecular biology (MS, PhD); biomedical engineering (MS, PhD); cellular and molecular pharmacology (MS, PhD); environmental sciences/exposure assessment (PhD); molecular genetics, microbiology and immunology (MS, PhD); neuroscience (MS, PhD); physiology and integrative biology (MS, PhD); toxicology (PhD); MD/PhD. *Students:* 397 full-time (209 women), 31 part-time (14 women); includes 109 minority (21 African Americans, 1 American Indian/Alaska Native, 58 Asian Americans or Pacific Islanders, 29 Hispanic Americans), 151 international. Average age 28. 1,030 applicants, 15% accepted, 89 enrolled. In 2009, 21 master's, 62 doctorates awarded. Terminal master's awarded for partial completion of doctoral program. *Degree requirements:* For master's, thesis, ethics training; for doctorate, comprehensive exam, thesis/dissertation, ethics training. *Entrance requirements:* For master's and doctorate, GRE General Test. Additional exam requirements/recommendations for international students: Required—TOEFL. *Application deadline:* For fall admission, 1/5 for domestic students. Applications are processed on a rolling basis. Application fee: $65. Electronic applications accepted. *Financial support:* Fellowships, research assistantships, teaching assistantships, career-related internships or fieldwork, Federal Work-Study, traineeships, health care benefits, and unspecified assistantships available. *Unit head:* Dr. Terri Goss Kinzy, Senior Associate Dean, Graduate School, 732-235-5016, Fax: 732-235-4720, E-mail: gsbspisc@umdnj.edu. *Application contact:* Johanna Sierra, University Registrar, 732-235-5016, Fax: 732-235-4720.

University of Medicine and Dentistry of New Jersey, Graduate School of Biomedical Sciences, Graduate Programs in Biomedical Sciences–Stratford, Stratford, NJ 08084-5634. Offers biomedical sciences (MBS, MS); cell and molecular biology (MS, PhD); molecular pathology and immunology (MS); DO/MS; DO/PhD; MS/MPH. *Students:* 79 full-time (43 women), 19 part-time (14 women); includes 44 minority (21 African Americans, 16 Asian Americans or Pacific Islanders, 7 Hispanic Americans), 11 international. Average age 25. 128 applicants, 74% accepted, 64 enrolled. In 2009, 36 master's, 1 doctorate awarded. Terminal master's awarded for partial completion of doctoral program. *Degree requirements:* For master's, thesis (for some programs); for doctorate, thesis/dissertation, qualifying exam. *Entrance requirements:* For master's, GRE General Test, MCAT or DAT; for doctorate, GRE General Test. Additional exam requirements/recommendations for international students: Required—TOEFL. *Application deadline:* For fall admission, 2/1 for domestic students; for spring admission, 11/1 for domestic students. Applications are processed on a rolling basis. Application fee: $40. Electronic applications accepted. *Financial support:* Fellowships, Federal Work-Study available. Financial award application deadline: 5/1. *Unit head:* Dr. Carl E. Hock, Senior Associate Dean, Graduate School, 856-566-6282, Fax: 856-566-6232, E-mail: hock@umdnj.edu. *Application contact:* University Registrar, 973-972-5338.

University of Memphis, Graduate School, College of Arts and Sciences, Department of Biology, Memphis, TN 38152. Offers MS, PhD. *Faculty:* 23 full-time (2 women). *Students:* 45 full-time (21 women), 18 part-time (9 women); includes 7 minority (3 African Americans, 3 Asian Americans or Pacific Islanders, 1 Hispanic American), 12 international. Average age 29. 23 applicants, 91% accepted, 16 enrolled. In 2009, 8 master's, 4 doctorates awarded. Terminal master's awarded for partial completion of doctoral program. *Degree requirements:* For master's, comprehensive exam, thesis (for some programs); for doctorate, one foreign language,

Biological and Biomedical Sciences—General

University of Memphis (continued)
comprehensive exam, thesis/dissertation. *Entrance requirements:* For master's, GRE General Test; for doctorate, GRE General Test, master's degree. Additional exam requirements/recommendations for international students: Required—TOEFL (minimum score 550 paper-based; 210 computer-based). *Application deadline:* For fall admission, 10/15 for domestic students, 9/15 for international students; for spring admission, 2/1 for domestic and international students. Applications are processed on a rolling basis. Application fee: $35 ($60 for international students). Electronic applications accepted. *Expenses:* Tuition, state resident: full-time $6246; part-time $347 per credit hour. Tuition, nonresident: full-time $15,894; part-time $883 per credit hour. Required fees: $1160. Full-time tuition and fees vary according to course load, degree level and program. *Financial support:* In 2009–10, 16 students received support; research assistantships with full tuition reimbursements available, teaching assistantships with full tuition reimbursements available, Federal Work-Study, scholarships/grants, and unspecified assistantships available. Financial award application deadline: 2/15; financial award applicants required to submit FAFSA. *Faculty research:* Protein trafficking and signal transduction; animal behavior and communication, neurobiology, and circadian clock function; phylogenetics, evolution, and ecology; causation and prevention of cancer; reproductive biology. *Unit head:* Dr. Randall Bayer, Chairman, 901-678-2596, Fax: 901-678-4746, E-mail: rbayer@memphis.edu. *Application contact:* Dr. Melvin Beck, Professor and Graduate Studies Coordinator, 901-678-2970, Fax: 901-678-4457, E-mail: mbeck@memphis.edu.

University of Miami, Graduate School, College of Arts and Sciences, Department of Biology, Coral Gables, FL 33124. Offers biology (MS, PhD); genetics and evolution (MS, PhD). Terminal master's awarded for partial completion of doctoral program. *Degree requirements:* For master's, comprehensive exam (for some programs), thesis (for some programs); for doctorate, thesis/dissertation, oral and written qualifying exam. *Entrance requirements:* For master's, GRE General Test, 3 letters of recommendation, research papers; for doctorate, GRE General Test, 3 letters of recommendation, research papers, sponsor letter. Additional exam requirements/recommendations for international students: Required—TOEFL (minimum score 550 paper-based; 213 computer-based; 59 iBT). Electronic applications accepted. *Faculty research:* Neuroscience to ethology; plants, vertebrates and mycorrhizae; phylogenies, life histories and species interactions; molecular biology, gene expression and populations; cells, auditory neurons and vertebrate locomotion.

University of Michigan, Horace H. Rackham School of Graduate Studies, Program in Biomedical Sciences (PIBS), Ann Arbor, MI 48109-5619. Offers MS, PhD. *Degree requirements:* For doctorate, thesis/dissertation, oral defense of dissertation, preliminary exam. *Entrance requirements:* For doctorate, GRE General Test, 3 letters of recommendation, research experience. Additional exam requirements/recommendations for international students: Required—TOEFL (minimum score 84 iBT). Electronic applications accepted. *Expenses:* Tuition, state resident: full-time $17,286; part-time $1099 per credit hour. Tuition, nonresident: full-time $34,944; part-time $2080 per credit hour. Required fees: $95 per semester. Tuition and fees vary according to course load, degree level and program. *Faculty research:* Genetics, cellular and molecular biology, microbial pathogenesis, cancer biology, neuroscience.

University of Michigan, Medical School and Horace H. Rackham School of Graduate Studies, Medical Scientist Training Program, Ann Arbor, MI 48109. Offers MD/PhD. *Accreditation:* LCME/AMA. *Students:* 88 full-time (22 women); includes 6 minority (5 African Americans, 1 Hispanic American). 222 applicants, 18% accepted, 13 enrolled. *Application deadline:* For fall admission, 10/15 for domestic students. Applications are processed on a rolling basis. Application fee: $60. Electronic applications accepted. *Expenses:* Tuition, state resident: full-time $17,286; part-time $1099 per credit hour. Tuition, nonresident: full-time $34,944; part-time $2080 per credit hour. Required fees: $95 per semester. Tuition and fees vary according to course load, degree level and program. *Financial support:* In 2009–10, 88 students received support, including 71 fellowships with full tuition reimbursements available (averaging $26,500 per year), 14 research assistantships with full tuition reimbursements available (averaging $26,500 per year), 3 teaching assistantships with full tuition reimbursements available (averaging $26,500 per year); scholarships/grants, traineeships, and health care benefits also available. *Unit head:* Dr. Ronald J. Koenig, Director, 734-764-6176, Fax: 734-764-8180, E-mail: rkoenig@umich.edu. *Application contact:* Laurie Koivupalo, Administrative Associate, 734-764-6176, Fax: 734-764-8180, E-mail: lkoivupl@umich.edu.

University of Michigan–Flint, College of Arts and Sciences, Program in Biology, Flint, MI 48502-1950. Offers MS. Part-time programs available. *Faculty:* 12 full-time (4 women), 4 part-time/adjunct (1 woman). *Students:* 5 full-time (1 woman), 16 part-time (11 women); includes 3 minority (2 African Americans, 1 Hispanic American), 5 international. Average age 31. 15 applicants, 80% accepted, 5 enrolled. In 2009, 5 master's awarded. *Degree requirements:* For master's, thesis or alternative. *Entrance requirements:* For master's, GRE, minimum undergraduate GPA of 3.0 in prerequisites. Additional exam requirements/recommendations for international students: Required—TOEFL (minimum score 560 paper-based; 220 computer-based; 84 iBT), IELTS (minimum score 6.5). *Application deadline:* For fall admission, 8/1 for domestic students, 5/1 for international students; for winter admission, 11/15 for domestic students, 9/15 for international students; for spring admission, 3/15 for domestic students, 10/15 for international students. Application fee: $55. *Expenses:* Contact institution. *Financial support:* Federal Work-Study, scholarships/grants, and unspecified assistantships available. Support available to part-time students. Financial award application deadline: 6/1; financial award applicants required to submit FAFSA. *Unit head:* Dr. Joseph Sucic, Director, 810-762-3360, Fax: 810-762-3310, E-mail: jsucic@umflint.edu. *Application contact:* Bradley T. Maki, Director of Graduate Admissions, 810-762-3171, Fax: 810-766-6789, E-mail: bmaki@umflint.edu.

University of Minnesota, Duluth, Graduate School, Swenson College of Science and Engineering, Department of Biology, Integrated Biosciences Program, Duluth, MN 55812-2496. Offers MS, PhD. *Faculty:* 62 full-time (14 women). *Students:* 41 full-time (27 women); includes 3 minority (1 American Indian/Alaska Native, 1 Asian American or Pacific Islander, 1 Hispanic American). Average age 25. 40 applicants, 50% accepted, 15 enrolled. In 2009, 13 master's awarded. Terminal master's awarded for partial completion of doctoral program. *Degree requirements:* For master's, thesis, seminar; for doctorate, comprehensive exam, thesis/dissertation, written and oral exam, seminar, written thesis. *Entrance requirements:* For master's, GRE, 1 year of biology, physics, and chemistry; 1 semester of calculus; for doctorate, GRE, 1 year each of chemistry, biology, physics, calculus, and advanced chemistry. Additional exam requirements/recommendations for international students: Required—TOEFL (minimum score 550 paper-based; 79 iBT). *Application deadline:* For fall admission, 3/31 priority date for domestic and international students. Applications are processed on a rolling basis. Application fee: $75 ($95 for international students). Electronic applications accepted. *Financial support:* In 2009–10, 15 research assistantships with full tuition reimbursements (averaging $16,505 per year), 19 teaching assistantships with full tuition reimbursements (averaging $14,305 per year) were awarded; fellowships, institutionally sponsored loans, scholarships/grants, health care benefits, and unspecified assistantships also available. *Faculty research:* Ecology, organizational and population biology; cell, molecular and physiological biology. *Unit head:* Dr. George J. Trachte, Director of Graduate Studies, 218-726-8975, Fax: 218-726-8152, E-mail: ibs@d.umn.edu. *Application contact:* Dawn C. Johnson, Director of Graduate Studies Assistant, 218-726-6898, Fax: 218-726-8152, E-mail: ibsadmit@d.umn.edu.

University of Minnesota, Twin Cities Campus, Graduate School, College of Biological Sciences, Biological Science Program, Minneapolis, MN 55455-0213. Offers MBS. Part-time and evening/weekend programs available. *Faculty:* 80 full-time (18 women). *Students:* 76 part-time (49 women); includes 2 African Americans, 16 Asian Americans or Pacific Islanders, 4 Hispanic Americans. 33 applicants, 85% accepted, 20 enrolled. In 2009, 6 master's awarded. *Entrance requirements:* For master's, 2 years of work experience. *Application deadline:* For fall admission, 6/15 priority date for domestic students; for spring admission, 10/15 priority date for domestic students. Applications are processed on a rolling basis. Application fee: $55 ($75 for international students). Electronic applications accepted. *Expenses:* Contact institution. *Unit head:* Prof. James A. Fuchs, Head, 612-624-1215, Fax: 612-624-2785, E-mail: fuchs001@umn.edu. *Application contact:* Carol Jane Gross, Program Administrator, 612-625-3133, Fax: 612-624-2785, E-mail: cgross008@umn.edu.

University of Minnesota, Twin Cities Campus, Graduate School, Stem Cell Biology Graduate Program, Minneapolis, MN 55455-0213. Offers MS, PhD. *Degree requirements:* For master's, thesis; for doctorate, thesis/dissertation. *Entrance requirements:* For master's and doctorate, BS, BA, or foreign equivalent in biological sciences or related field; minimum undergraduate GPA of 3.2. Additional exam requirements/recommendations for international students: Required—TOEFL (minimum score 580 paper-based; 237 computer-based; 92 iBT), IELTS (minimum score 6.5), TWE (minimum score 4). *Faculty research:* Stem cell and developmental biology; embryonic stem cells; iPS cells; muscle satellite cells; hematopoietic stem cells; neuronal stem cells; cardiovascular, kidney and limb development; regenerating systems.

University of Minnesota, Twin Cities Campus, Medical School and Graduate School, Graduate Programs in Medicine, Minneapolis, MN 55455-0213. Offers MA. Part-time and evening/weekend programs available. *Expenses:* Contact institution.

University of Mississippi, Graduate School, College of Liberal Arts, Department of Biology, Oxford, University, MS 38677. Offers MS, PhD. *Faculty:* 30 full-time (11 women), 3 part-time/adjunct (1 woman). *Students:* 33 full-time (14 women), 2 part-time (both women), 6 international. In 2009, 2 master's, 1 doctorate awarded. *Degree requirements:* For master's, thesis; for doctorate, thesis/dissertation. *Entrance requirements:* For master's and doctorate, GRE General Test, GRE Subject Test, minimum GPA of 3.0. Additional exam requirements/recommendations for international students: Required—TOEFL. *Application deadline:* For fall admission, 4/1 for domestic students; for spring admission, 10/1 for domestic students. Applications are processed on a rolling basis. Application fee: $25. Electronic applications accepted. *Financial support:* Research assistantships, teaching assistantships, scholarships/grants available. Financial award application deadline: 3/1; financial award applicants required to submit FAFSA. *Faculty research:* Freshwater biology, including ecology and evolutionary biology; environmental and applied biology. *Unit head:* Dr. Paul Lago, Interim Chair, 662-915-7203, Fax: 662-915-5144, E-mail: biology@olemiss.edu. *Application contact:* Dr. Christy M. Wyandt, Associate Dean, 662-915-7474, Fax: 662-915-7577, E-mail: cwyandt@olemiss.edu.

University of Mississippi Medical Center, School of Graduate Studies in the Health Sciences, Jackson, MS 39216-4505. Offers MS, MSN, PhD, MD/PhD. Terminal master's awarded for partial completion of doctoral program. *Degree requirements:* For master's, thesis; for doctorate, thesis/dissertation, first authored publication. *Faculty research:* Immunology; protein chemistry and biosynthesis; cardiovascular, renal, and endocrine physiology; rehabilitation therapy on immune system/hypothalamic/adrenal axis interaction.

University of Missouri, Graduate School, College of Arts and Sciences, Division of Biological Sciences, Columbia, MO 65211. Offers evolutionary biology and ecology (MA, PhD); genetic, cellular and developmental biology (MA, PhD); neurobiology and behavior (MA, PhD). *Faculty:* 55 full-time (15 women), 10 part-time/adjunct (4 women). *Students:* 51 full-time (30 women), 27 part-time (14 women); includes 11 minority (4 African Americans, 5 Asian Americans or Pacific Islanders, 2 Hispanic Americans), 12 international. Average age 28. 67 applicants, 22% accepted, 14 enrolled. In 2009, 3 master's, 4 doctorates awarded. Terminal master's awarded for partial completion of doctoral program. *Degree requirements:* For master's, thesis; for doctorate, comprehensive exam, thesis/dissertation. *Entrance requirements:* For master's and doctorate, GRE General Test (minimum score 1200 verbal and quantitative), minimum GPA of 3.0. Additional exam requirements/recommendations for international students: Required—TOEFL (minimum score 600 paper-based; 100 iBT). *Application deadline:* For fall admission, 1/15 priority date for domestic students. Applications are processed on a rolling basis. Application fee: $45 ($60 for international students). Electronic applications accepted. *Financial support:* In 2009–10, 34 fellowships with full tuition reimbursements, 9 research assistantships with full tuition reimbursements, 33 teaching assistantships with full tuition reimbursements were awarded; institutionally sponsored loans, traineeships, health care benefits, and unspecified assistantships also available. *Faculty research:* Evolutionary biology, ecology and behavior; genetic, cellular, molecular and developmental biology; neurobiology and behavior; and plant sciences. *Unit head:* Dr. John David, Division Director, 573-882-6659, E-mail: davidj@missouri.edu. *Application contact:* Nila Emerich, Application Contact, 800-553-5698, E-mail: emerichn@missouri.edu.

University of Missouri, School of Medicine and Graduate School, Graduate Programs in Medicine, Columbia, MO 65211. Offers MS, PhD. Part-time programs available. *Degree requirements:* For doctorate, thesis/dissertation. *Entrance requirements:* For master's and doctorate, GRE General Test, minimum GPA of 3.0. Additional exam requirements/recommendations for international students: Required—TOEFL. *Expenses:* Contact institution.

University of Missouri–Kansas City, School of Biological Sciences, Kansas City, MO 64110-2499. Offers biology (MA); cell biology and biophysics (PhD); cellular and molecular biology (MS); molecular biology and biochemistry (PhD). PhD is an interdisciplinary degree offered by the School of Graduate Studies. Part-time and evening/weekend programs available. *Faculty:* 39 full-time (10 women), 1 (woman) part-time/adjunct. *Students:* 20 full-time (13 women), 36 part-time (24 women); includes 9 minority (2 African Americans, 6 Asian Americans or Pacific Islanders, 1 Hispanic American), 2 international. Average age 32. 41 applicants, 59% accepted, 23 enrolled. In 2009, 20 master's awarded. *Degree requirements:* For doctorate, comprehensive exam, thesis/dissertation. *Entrance requirements:* For master's, GRE, minimum GPA of 3.0; for doctorate, GRE General Test. Additional exam requirements/recommendations for international students: Required—TOEFL (minimum score 550 paper-based; 213 computer-based; 80 iBT). *Application deadline:* For fall admission, 2/15 priority date for domestic and international students. Applications are processed on a rolling basis. Application fee: $45 ($50 for international students). *Expenses:* Tuition, state resident: full-time $5378; part-time $299 per credit hour. Tuition, nonresident: full-time $13,881; part-time $771 per credit hour. Required fees: $641; $71 per credit hour. Tuition and fees vary according to course load and program. *Financial support:* In 2009–10, 16 research assistantships with full tuition reimbursements (averaging $21,042 per year), 9 teaching assistantships with full tuition reimbursements (averaging $22,000 per year) were awarded; Federal Work-Study, institutionally sponsored loans, scholarships/grants, tuition waivers (full and partial), and unspecified assistantships also available. Support available to part-time students. Financial award application deadline: 3/1; financial award applicants required to submit FAFSA. *Faculty research:* Structural biology, molecular genetics. Total annual research expenditures: $3.2 million. *Unit head:* Dr. Lawrence A. Dreyfus, Dean, 816-235-5246, Fax: 816-235-5158, E-mail: dreyfusl@umkc.edu. *Application contact:* Laura Batenic, Information Contact, 816-235-2352, Fax: 816-235-5158, E-mail: batenicl@umkc.edu.

University of Missouri–St. Louis, College of Arts and Sciences, Department of Biology, St. Louis, MO 63121. Offers biology (MS, PhD), including animal behavior (MS), biochemistry, biochemistry and biotechnology (MS), biotechnology (MS), conservation biology (MS), development (MS), ecology (MS), environmental studies (PhD), evolution (MS), genetics (MS), molecular biology and biochemistry (PhD), molecular/cellular biology (MS), physiology (MS), plant systematics, population biology (MS), tropical biology (MS); biotechnology (Certificate); tropical biology and conservation (Certificate). Part-time programs available. *Faculty:* 43 full-time (13 women), 2 part-time/adjunct (1 woman). *Students:* 54 full-time (27 women), 79 part-time (43 women); includes 15 minority (6 African Americans, 7 Asian Americans or Pacific Islanders, 2 Hispanic Americans), 47 international. Average age 29. 193 applicants, 44% accepted, 44 enrolled. In 2009, 30 master's, 7 doctorates, 9 other advanced degrees awarded. *Degree requirements:* For master's, thesis or alternative; for doctorate, thesis/dissertation, 1 semester of teaching experience. *Entrance requirements:* For master's, 3 letters of recommendation; for doctorate, GRE General Test, 3 letters of recommendation. Additional exam requirements/recommendations for international students: Required—TOEFL. *Application deadline:* For fall admission, 12/1 priority date for domestic and international students; for spring admission, 10/15 priority date for domestic and international students. Applications are processed on a rolling basis. Application fee: $35 ($40 for international students). Electronic applications accepted. *Expenses:* Tuition, state resident: full-time $5377; part-time $297.70 per credit hour. Tuition, nonresident: full-time $13,882; part-time $771.20 per credit hour. Required fees: $220; $12.20 per credit hour. One-time fee: $12. Tuition and fees vary according to course level, campus/location and program. *Financial support:* In 2009–10, 22 research assistantships with full and partial tuition reimbursements (averaging $16,300 per year), 14 teaching assistantships with full and partial tuition reimbursements (averaging $16,727 per year) were awarded; fellowships with full tuition reimbursements, career-related internships or fieldwork and Federal Work-Study also available. Support available to part-time students. Financial award application deadline: 2/1. *Faculty research:* Molecular biology, microbial genetics, animal behavior, tropical ecology, plant systematics. *Unit head:* Dr. Elizabeth Kellogg, Director of Graduate Studies, 314-516-6200, Fax: 314-516-6233, E-mail: tkellogg@umsl.edu. *Application contact:* 314-516-5458, Fax: 314-516-6996, E-mail: gradadm@umsl.edu.

The University of Montana, Graduate School, College of Arts and Sciences, Division of Biological Sciences, Missoula, MT 59812-0002. Offers biochemistry and microbiology (MS, PhD), including biochemistry (MS), integrative microbiology and biochemistry (PhD), microbial ecology, microbiology (MS); organismal biology and ecology (MS, PhD). Terminal master's awarded for partial completion of doctoral program. *Degree requirements:* For master's, thesis; for doctorate, thesis/dissertation. *Entrance requirements:* For master's and doctorate, GRE General Test. Additional exam requirements/recommendations for international students: Required—TOEFL. *Faculty research:* Biochemistry/microbiology, organismal biology, ecology.

The University of Montana, Graduate School, College of Health Professions and Biomedical Sciences, Skaggs School of Pharmacy, Department of Biomedical and Pharmaceutical Sciences, Missoula, MT 59812-0002. Offers biomedical sciences (PhD); neuroscience (MS, PhD); pharmaceutical sciences (MS); toxicology (MS, PhD). *Accreditation:* ACPE. *Degree requirements:* For master's, oral defense of thesis; for doctorate, research dissertation defense. *Entrance requirements:* For master's and doctorate, GRE General Test. Additional exam requirements/recommendations for international students: Required—TOEFL (minimum score 540 paper-based; 210 computer-based). Electronic applications accepted. *Faculty research:* Cardiovascular pharmacology, medicinal chemistry, neurosciences, environmental toxicology, pharmacogenetics, cancer.

University of Nebraska at Kearney, College of Graduate Study, College of Natural and Social Sciences, Department of Biology, Kearney, NE 68849-0001. Offers biology (MS); science education (MS Ed). Part-time and evening/weekend programs available. *Degree requirements:* For master's, thesis optional. *Entrance requirements:* For master's, GRE General Test. Additional exam requirements/recommendations for international students: Required—TOEFL (minimum score 550 paper-based; 213 computer-based). Electronic applications accepted. *Faculty research:* Pollution injury, molecular biology-viral gene expression, prairie range condition modeling, evolution of symbiotic nitrogen fixation.

University of Nebraska at Omaha, Graduate Studies, College of Arts and Sciences, Department of Biology, Omaha, NE 68182. Offers MS. Part-time programs available. *Faculty:* 25 full-time (7 women). *Students:* 7 full-time (3 women), 18 part-time (6 women); includes 2 minority (1 American Indian/Alaska Native, 1 Hispanic American), 4 international. Average age 27. 33 applicants, 55% accepted, 13 enrolled. In 2009, 7 master's awarded. *Degree requirements:* For master's, comprehensive exam (for some programs), thesis (for some programs). *Entrance requirements:* For master's, GRE General Test, minimum GPA of 3.0, 24 undergraduate biology hours, 3 letters of recommendation. Additional exam requirements/recommendations for international students: Required—TOEFL (minimum score 550 paper-based; 173 computer-based; 80 iBT). *Application deadline:* For fall admission, 3/1 priority date for domestic students; for spring admission, 10/15 priority date for domestic students. Applications are processed on a rolling basis. Application fee: $45. Electronic applications accepted. *Financial support:* In 2009–10, 11 students received support; fellowships, research assistantships with tuition reimbursements available, teaching assistantships with tuition reimbursements available, Federal Work-Study, institutionally sponsored loans, scholarships/grants, tuition waivers (partial), and unspecified assistantships available. Support available to part-time students. Financial award application deadline: 3/1; financial award applicants required to submit FAFSA. *Unit head:* Dr. William Tapprich, Chairperson, 402-554-2641. *Application contact:* Dr. Alan Kolok, Student Contact, 402-554-2641.

University of Nebraska–Lincoln, Graduate College, College of Agricultural Sciences and Natural Resources, Department of Veterinary and Biomedical Sciences, Lincoln, NE 68588. Offers veterinary science (MS). Postbaccalaureate distance learning degree programs offered (minimal on-campus study). *Degree requirements:* For master's, thesis optional; for doctorate, comprehensive exam, thesis/dissertation. *Entrance requirements:* For master's, GRE General Test; for doctorate, GRE General Test, MCAT, or VCAT. Additional exam requirements/recommendations for international students: Required—TOEFL (minimum score 550 paper-based; 213 computer-based). Electronic applications accepted. *Faculty research:* Virology, immunobiology, molecular biology, mycotoxins, ocular degeneration.

University of Nebraska–Lincoln, Graduate College, College of Arts and Sciences, School of Biological Sciences, Lincoln, NE 68588. Offers MA, MS, PhD. *Degree requirements:* For master's, thesis optional; for doctorate, comprehensive exam, thesis/dissertation. *Entrance requirements:* For master's and doctorate, GRE General Test. Additional exam requirements/recommendations for international students: Required—TOEFL (minimum score 550 paper-based; 213 computer-based). Electronic applications accepted. *Faculty research:* Behavior, botany, and zoology; ecology and evolutionary biology; genetics; cellular and molecular biology; microbiology.

University of Nebraska Medical Center, Graduate Studies, Biomedical Research Training Program, Omaha, NE 68198. Offers MD/PhD. *Entrance requirements:* Additional exam requirements/recommendations for international students: Required—TOEFL (minimum score 600 paper-based; 250 computer-based). Electronic applications accepted. *Faculty research:* Neuroscience, cancer, cardiovascular immunology, genetics.

University of Nebraska Medical Center, Graduate Studies, Medical Sciences Interdepartmental Area, Omaha, NE 68198. Offers MS, PhD. Part-time programs available. Terminal master's awarded for partial completion of doctoral program. *Degree requirements:* For master's, comprehensive exam, thesis; for doctorate, comprehensive exam, thesis/dissertation. *Entrance requirements:* For master's and doctorate, GRE General Test. Additional exam requirements/recommendations for international students: Required—TOEFL (minimum score 550 paper-based; 213 computer-based). *Faculty research:* Molecular genetics, oral biology, veterinary pathology, newborn medicine, immunology.

University of Nevada, Las Vegas, Graduate College, College of Science, School of Life Sciences, Las Vegas, NV 89154-4004. Offers MS, PhD. Part-time programs available. *Faculty:* 27 full-time (5 women). *Students:* 35 full-time (18 women), 19 part-time (10 women); includes 4 minority (1 African American, 3 Asian Americans or Pacific Islanders), 6 international. Average age 33. 18 applicants, 39% accepted, 3 enrolled. In 2009, 3 master's, 5 doctorates awarded. *Degree requirements:* For master's, thesis, oral exam; for doctorate, one foreign language, comprehensive exam, thesis/dissertation. *Entrance requirements:* For master's and doctorate, GRE General Test. Additional exam requirements/recommendations for international students: Required—TOEFL (minimum score 550 paper-based; 213 computer-based; 80 iBT), IELTS (minimum score 7). *Application deadline:* For fall admission, 2/1 priority date for domestic and international students; for spring admission, 10/1 priority date for domestic and international students. Applications are processed on a rolling basis. Application fee: $60 ($95 for international students). Electronic applications accepted. *Financial support:* In 2009–10, 34 students received support, including 1 fellowship with full tuition reimbursement available (averaging $14,000 per year), 10 research assistantships with full tuition reimbursements available (averaging $14,132 per year), 23 teaching assistantships with partial tuition reimbursements available (averaging $15,275 per year); institutionally sponsored loans, scholarships/

grants, health care benefits, and unspecified assistantships also available. Financial award application deadline: 3/1. *Faculty research:* Microbiology, physiology, cell and molecular biology, ecology and evolutionary biology, immunology. *Unit head:* Dr. Dennis Bazylinski, Chair, 702-895-3399, Fax: 702-895-3956, E-mail: dennis.bazylinski@unlv.edu. *Application contact:* Graduate College Admissions Evaluator, 702-895-3320, Fax: 702-895-4180, E-mail: gradcollege@unlv.edu.

University of Nevada, Reno, Graduate School, College of Science, Department of Biology, Reno, NV 89557. Offers MS. *Degree requirements:* For master's, thesis optional. *Entrance requirements:* For master's, GRE General Test, minimum GPA of 2.75. Additional exam requirements/recommendations for international students: Required—TOEFL (minimum score 500 paper-based; 173 computer-based; 61 iBT), IELTS (minimum score 6). Electronic applications accepted. *Faculty research:* Gene expression, stress protein genes, secretory proteins, conservation biology, behavioral ecology.

University of New Brunswick Fredericton, School of Graduate Studies, Faculty of Science, Department of Biology, Fredericton, NB E3B 5A3, Canada. Offers M Sc, PhD. Part-time programs available. *Faculty:* 27 full-time (5 women), 10 part-time/adjunct (3 women). *Students:* 105 full-time (59 women), 16 part-time (7 women). In 2009, 8 master's, 4 doctorates awarded. *Degree requirements:* For master's, thesis; for doctorate, thesis/dissertation. *Entrance requirements:* For master's, minimum GPA of 3.0; undergraduate degree (preferred—BSc or equivalent); for doctorate, minimum GPA of 3.0; undergraduate and/or master's degree in related discipline. Additional exam requirements/recommendations for international students: Required—TWE (minimum score 4), TOEFL (minimum score 600 paper-based; 250 computer-based) or IELTS (minimum score 7). *Application deadline:* For fall admission, 3/1 priority date for domestic students. Applications are processed on a rolling basis. Application fee: $50 Canadian dollars. Electronic applications accepted. Tuition and fees charges are reported in Canadian dollars. *Expenses:* Tuition, area resident: Full-time $5562 Canadian dollars; part-time $2781 Canadian dollars per year. Required fees: $49.75 Canadian dollars per term. *Financial support:* In 2009–10, 33 fellowships (averaging $2,950 per year), 46 research assistantships with tuition reimbursements (averaging $20,170 per year), 40 teaching assistantships (averaging $3,376 per year) were awarded. *Faculty research:* Evolutionary biology, aquatic ecology, wildlife and conservation biology, marine biology, algae and plant biology. *Unit head:* Dr. Dion Durnford, Director of Graduate Studies, 506-452-6207, Fax: 506-453-4583, E-mail: biodogs@unb.ca. *Application contact:* Rose Comeau, Graduate Secretary, 506-452-6052, Fax: 506-453-3583, E-mail: rcomeau@unb.ca.

University of New Brunswick Saint John, Department of Biology, Saint John, NB E2L 4L5, Canada. Offers biology (M Sc, PhD). Part-time programs available. *Faculty:* 14 full-time (4 women), 22 part-time/adjunct (2 women). *Students:* 34 full-time (20 women), 7 part-time (3 women). In 2009, 6 master's, 3 doctorates awarded. *Degree requirements:* For master's, thesis; for doctorate, comprehensive exam, thesis/dissertation. *Entrance requirements:* For master's, B Sc, minimum GPA of 3.0; for doctorate, M Sc, minimum GPA of 3.0. *Application deadline:* For fall admission, 2/15 for domestic and international students. Applications are processed on a rolling basis. Application fee: $50 Canadian dollars. *Financial support:* In 2009–10, research assistantships (averaging $4,000 per year), teaching assistantships (averaging $4,000 per year) were awarded; fellowships, scholarships/grants and unspecified assistantships also available. *Faculty research:* Integrated multi-trophic aquaculture, plant community ecology, mycology, fish physiology, eco-physiology of marine invertebrates. *Unit head:* Dr. Kate Frego, Director of Graduate Studies, 506-648-5566, Fax: 506-648-5811, E-mail: frego@unbsj.ca. *Application contact:* Kim Banks, Secretary, 506-648-5605, Fax: 506-648-5811, E-mail: kbanks@unbsj.ca.

University of New England, College of Arts and Sciences, Programs in Professional Science, Biddeford, ME 04005-9526. Offers applied biosciences (MS). In 2009, 3 master's awarded. *Expenses:* Contact institution. *Unit head:* Arthur Goldstein, Chair, Department of Marine Sciences, 207-602-2371, E-mail: agoldstein@une.edu. *Application contact:* Stacy Gato, Assistant Director of Graduate Admissions, 207-221-4225, Fax: 207-221-4898, E-mail: gradadmissions@une.edu.

University of New Hampshire, Graduate School, College of Life Sciences and Agriculture, Department of Biological Sciences, Durham, NH 03824. Offers animal science (MS); plant biology (MS, PhD); zoology (PhD). Part-time programs available. *Faculty:* 31 full-time (7 women). *Students:* 31 full-time (18 women), 31 part-time (21 women); includes 1 Hispanic American, 6 international. Average age 30. 53 applicants, 25% accepted, 9 enrolled. In 2009, 13 master's, 2 doctorates awarded. *Degree requirements:* For doctorate, thesis/dissertation. *Entrance requirements:* For master's and doctorate, GRE General Test. Additional exam requirements/recommendations for international students: Required—TOEFL (minimum score 550 paper-based; 215 computer-based; 80 iBT). *Application deadline:* For fall admission, 6/1 for domestic students, 4/1 for international students; for spring admission, 12/1 for domestic students. Application fee: $65. *Expenses:* Tuition, state resident: full-time $10,380; part-time $577 per credit hour. Tuition, nonresident: full-time $24,350; part-time $1002 per credit hour. Required fees: $1550; $387.50 per semester. Tuition and fees vary according to course load and program. *Financial support:* In 2009–10, 49 students received support, including 1 fellowship, 17 research assistantships, 28 teaching assistantships. *Unit head:* Chris Neefus, Dean, 603-862-1990. *Application contact:* Dianne Lavalliere, Administrative Assistant, 603-862-2100, Fax: 603-862-0275, E-mail: grad.school@unh.edu.

University of New Mexico, Graduate School, College of Arts and Sciences, Department of Biology, Albuquerque, NM 87131-2039. Offers MS, PhD. *Faculty:* 69 full-time (24 women), 3 part-time/adjunct (0 women). *Students:* 88 full-time (51 women), 18 part-time (10 women); includes 16 minority (2 American Indian/Alaska Native, 2 Asian Americans or Pacific Islanders, 12 Hispanic Americans), 12 international. Average age 34. 61 applicants, 38% accepted, 21 enrolled. In 2009, 5 master's, 9 doctorates awarded. *Degree requirements:* For master's, comprehensive exam, thesis optional; for doctorate, comprehensive exam, thesis/dissertation. *Entrance requirements:* For master's and doctorate, GRE General Test, GRE Subject Test, minimum GPA of 3.2, letters of recommendation. Additional exam requirements/recommendations for international students: Required—TOEFL (minimum score 550 paper-based; 213 computer-based; 79 iBT). *Application deadline:* For fall admission, 1/15 for domestic and international students. Application fee: $50. Electronic applications accepted. *Expenses:* Tuition, state resident: full-time $2099; part-time $233.20 per credit hour. Tuition, nonresident: full-time $6650. Required fees: $25 per semester. Tuition and fees vary according to course load, program and reciprocity agreements. *Financial support:* In 2009–10, 28 students received support, including 7 fellowships with full tuition reimbursements available, 37 research assistantships with full tuition reimbursements available (averaging $15,673 per year), 86 teaching assistantships with full tuition reimbursements available (averaging $15,673 per year); Federal Work-Study, scholarships/grants, health care benefits, and unspecified assistantships also available. Financial award application deadline: 3/1; financial award applicants required to submit FAFSA. *Faculty research:* Aquatic ecology, behavioral ecology, botany, cell biology, comparative biology, conservation biology, developmental biology, ecology, evolutionary biology, genetics, genomics, global change biology, immunology, invertebrate biology, mathematical biology, microbiology, molecular evolution, paleobiology, parasitology, physiological ecology, plant biology, systematics, vertebrate biology. Total annual research expenditures: $10.8 million. *Unit head:* Dr. Richard Cripps, Chair, 505-277-2496, Fax: 505-277-0304, E-mail: rcripps@unm.edu. *Application contact:* Cheryl Martin, Graduate Program Coordinator, 505-277-1712, Fax: 505-277-0304, E-mail: cherylm@unm.edu.

University of New Mexico, School of Medicine, Biomedical Sciences Graduate Program, Albuquerque, NM 87131-5196. Offers biochemistry and molecular biology (MS, PhD); cell biology and physiology (MS, PhD); molecular genetics and microbiology (MS, PhD); neuroscience (MS, PhD); pathology (MS, PhD); toxicology (MS, PhD). Part-time programs available. Terminal master's awarded for partial completion of doctoral program. *Degree requirements:* For master's, thesis; for doctorate, comprehensive exam, thesis/dissertation. *Entrance*

Biological and Biomedical Sciences—General

University of New Mexico (continued)

requirements: For master's and doctorate, GRE General Test, minimum undergraduate GPA of 3.0. Additional exam requirements/recommendations for international students: Required—TOEFL. Electronic applications accepted. *Expenses:* Tuition, state resident: full-time $2099; part-time $233.20 per credit hour. Tuition, nonresident: full-time $6650. Required fees: $25 per semester. Tuition and fees vary according to course load, program and reciprocity agreements. *Faculty research:* Signal transduction, infectious disease, biology of cancer, structural biology, neuroscience.

University of New Orleans, Graduate School, College of Sciences, Department of Biological Sciences, New Orleans, LA 70148. Offers MS, PhD. *Degree requirements:* For master's, one foreign language, thesis. *Entrance requirements:* For master's, GRE General Test. Additional exam requirements/recommendations for international students: Required—TOEFL (minimum score 550 paper-based; 213 computer-based; 79 iBT). Electronic applications accepted. *Faculty research:* Biochemistry, genetics, vertebrate and invertebrate systematics and ecology, cell and mammalian physiology, morphology.

The University of North Carolina at Chapel Hill, Graduate School, College of Arts and Sciences, Department of Biology, Chapel Hill, NC 27599. Offers botany (MA, MS, PhD); cell biology, development, and physiology (MA, MS, PhD); cell motility and cytoskeleton (PhD); ecology and behavior (MA, MS, PhD); genetics and molecular biology (MA, MS, PhD); morphology, systematics, and evolution (MA, MS, PhD). Terminal master's awarded for partial completion of doctoral program. *Degree requirements:* For master's, comprehensive exam, thesis (for some programs); for doctorate, comprehensive exam, thesis/dissertation. *Entrance requirements:* For master's, GRE General Test, GRE Subject Test, 2 semesters of calculus or statistics; 2 semesters of physics, organic chemistry; 3 semesters of biology; for doctorate, GRE General Test, GRE Subject Test, 2 semesters calculus or statistics, 2 semesters physics, organic chemistry, 3 semesters of biology. Additional exam requirements/recommendations for international students: Required—TOEFL (minimum score 550 paper-based; 213 computer-based). Electronic applications accepted. *Faculty research:* Gene expression, biomechanics, yeast genetics, plant ecology, plant molecular biology.

The University of North Carolina at Chapel Hill, School of Medicine and Graduate School, Graduate Programs in Medicine, Chapel Hill, NC 27599. Offers allied health sciences (MPT, MS, Au D, DPT, PhD), including human movement science (MS, PhD), occupational science (MS, PhD), physical therapy (MPT, MS, DPT), rehabilitation counseling and psychology (MS), speech and hearing sciences (MS, Au D, PhD); biochemistry and biophysics (MS, PhD); biomedical engineering (MS, PhD); cell and developmental biology (PhD); cell and molecular physiology (PhD); genetics and molecular biology (PhD); microbiology and immunology (MS, PhD), including immunology, microbiology; neurobiology (PhD); pathology and laboratory medicine (PhD), including experimental pathology; pharmacology (PhD); MD/PhD. Post-baccalaureate distance learning degree programs offered. Terminal master's awarded for partial completion of doctoral program. *Degree requirements:* For master's, comprehensive exam; for doctorate, thesis/dissertation. Electronic applications accepted. *Expenses:* Contact institution.

The University of North Carolina at Charlotte, Graduate School, College of Arts and Sciences, Department of Biology, Charlotte, NC 28223-0001. Offers MA, MS, PhD. Part-time and evening/weekend programs available. *Faculty:* 22 full-time (9 women), 4 part-time/adjunct (0 women). *Students:* 33 full-time (17 women), 27 part-time (17 women); includes 1 Hispanic American, 14 international. Average age 28. 67 applicants, 27% accepted, 13 enrolled. In 2009, 6 master's, 8 doctorates awarded. Terminal master's awarded for partial completion of doctoral program. *Degree requirements:* For master's, thesis, 30-32 semester hours with a minimum GPA of 3.0; for doctorate, thesis/dissertation. *Entrance requirements:* For master's, GRE General Test, minimum GPA of 3.0 in undergraduate major, 2.75 overall; for doctorate, GRE General Test, minimum GPA of 3.5 in biology; 3.0 in chemistry, math, and overall. Additional exam requirements/recommendations for international students: Required—TOEFL (minimum score 557 paper-based; 220 computer-based; 83 iBT). *Application deadline:* For fall admission, 7/15 for domestic students, 5/1 for international students; for spring admission, 11/15 for domestic students, 10/1 for international students. Applications are processed on a rolling basis. Application fee: $55. Electronic applications accepted. *Financial support:* In 2009–10, 46 students received support, including 6 fellowships (averaging $36,355 per year), 8 research assistantships (averaging $7,800 per year), 31 teaching assistantships (averaging $8,086 per year); career-related internships or fieldwork, institutionally sponsored loans, scholarships/grants, and administrative assistantship also available. Support available to part-time students. Financial award application deadline: 4/1; financial award applicants required to submit FAFSA. *Faculty research:* Liver blood flow in response to stress/injury, host response to bacterial and viral infection, mechanisms of cancer development and spread, stress responses in marine organisms as a measure of environmental change. *Unit head:* Dr. Cy Knoblauch, Acting Chair, 704-687-5465, Fax: 704-687-3128, E-mail: chknobla@uncc.edu. *Application contact:* Kathy B. Giddings, Director of Graduate Admissions, 704-687-5503, Fax: 704-687-3279, E-mail: gradadm@uncc.edu.

The University of North Carolina at Greensboro, Graduate School, College of Arts and Sciences, Department of Biology, Greensboro, NC 27412-5001. Offers MS. *Degree requirements:* For master's, thesis. *Entrance requirements:* For master's, GRE General Test, GRE Subject Test. Additional exam requirements/recommendations for international students: Required—TOEFL. Electronic applications accepted. *Faculty research:* Environmental biology, biochemistry, animal ecology, vertebrate reproduction.

The University of North Carolina Wilmington, College of Arts and Sciences, Department of Biology and Marine Biology, Wilmington, NC 28403-3297. Offers biology (MS); marine biology (MS, PhD). Part-time programs available. *Degree requirements:* For master's, comprehensive exam, thesis; for doctorate, comprehensive exam, thesis/dissertation. *Entrance requirements:* For master's, GRE General Test, GRE Subject Test, minimum B average in undergraduate major; for doctorate, GRE General Test, minimum B average in undergraduate major and graduate courses. Additional exam requirements/recommendations for international students: Required—TOEFL (minimum score 550 paper-based; 217 computer-based; 79 iBT), IELTS (minimum score 6.5). Electronic applications accepted. *Faculty research:* Ecology, physiology, cell and molecular biology, systematics, biomechanics.

University of North Dakota, Graduate School, College of Arts and Sciences, Department of Biology, Grand Forks, ND 58202. Offers botany (MS, PhD); ecology (MS, PhD); entomology (MS, PhD); environmental biology (MS, PhD); fisheries/wildlife (MS, PhD); genetics (MS, PhD); zoology (MS, PhD). Terminal master's awarded for partial completion of doctoral program. *Degree requirements:* For master's, thesis, final exam; for doctorate, comprehensive exam, thesis/dissertation, final exam. *Entrance requirements:* For master's, GRE General Test, GRE Subject Test, minimum GPA of 3.0; for doctorate, GRE General Test, GRE Subject Test, minimum GPA of 3.5. Additional exam requirements/recommendations for international students: Required—TOEFL (minimum score 550 paper-based; 213 computer-based; 79 iBT), IELTS (minimum score 6.5). Electronic applications accepted. *Faculty research:* Population biology, wildlife ecology, RNA processing, hormonal control of behavior.

University of North Dakota, School of Medicine and Health Sciences and Graduate School, Graduate Programs in Medicine, Grand Forks, ND 58202. Offers MOT, MPAS, MPT, MS, DPT, PhD, MD/PhD. Postbaccalaureate distance learning degree programs offered (minimal on-campus study). *Degree requirements:* For doctorate, comprehensive exam, thesis/dissertation, final exam. *Entrance requirements:* For master's and doctorate, minimum GPA of 3.0. Additional exam requirements/recommendations for international students: Required—TOEFL (minimum score 515 paper-based; 213 computer-based; 79 iBT), IELTS (minimum score 6.5). Electronic applications accepted. *Expenses:* Contact institution.

University of Northern Colorado, Graduate School, College of Natural and Health Sciences, School of Biological Sciences, Program in Biological Sciences, Greeley, CO 80639. Offers MS. Part-time programs available. *Faculty:* 14 full-time (5 women). *Students:* 14 full-time (9 women), 3 part-time (2 women); includes 2 minority (both Hispanic Americans). Average age 27. 7 applicants, 57% accepted, 3 enrolled. In 2009, 2 master's awarded. *Degree requirements:* For master's, comprehensive exam. *Entrance requirements:* For master's, GRE General Test, 3 letters of recommendation. *Application deadline:* Applications are processed on a rolling basis. Application fee: $50 ($60 for international students). Electronic applications accepted. *Expenses:* Tuition, state resident: full-time $5770; part-time $320.55 per credit hour. Tuition, nonresident: full-time $13,847; part-time $769.27 per credit hour. Required fees: $948.78; $52.72 per credit. *Financial support:* In 2009–10, 5 research assistantships (averaging $8,507 per year), 16 teaching assistantships (averaging $11,225 per year) were awarded. Financial award application deadline: 3/1; financial award applicants required to submit FAFSA. *Unit head:* Dr. Susan Keenan, Program Coordinator, 970-351-2921, Fax: 970-951-2335. *Application contact:* Linda Sisson, Graduate Student Admission Coordinator, 970-351-1807, Fax: 970-351-2371, E-mail: linda.sisson@unco.edu.

University of Northern Iowa, Graduate College, College of Natural Sciences, Department of Biology, Cedar Falls, IA 50614. Offers MA, MS, PSM. Part-time programs available. *Students:* 31 full-time (18 women), 9 part-time (5 women); includes 1 minority (Hispanic American), 12 international. 59 applicants, 31% accepted, 16 enrolled. In 2009, 17 master's awarded. *Degree requirements:* For master's, comprehensive exam (for some programs), thesis or alternative. *Entrance requirements:* For master's, minimum GPA of 3.0; 3 letters of recommendation. Additional exam requirements/recommendations for international students: Required—TOEFL (minimum score 500 paper-based; 180 computer-based; 61 iBT). *Application deadline:* For fall admission, 8/1 priority date for domestic students. Applications are processed on a rolling basis. Application fee: $30 ($50 for international students). Electronic applications accepted. *Financial support:* Scholarships/grants available. Financial award application deadline: 2/1. *Unit head:* Dr. David Saunders, Head, 319-273-2456, Fax: 319-273-7125, E-mail: david.saunders@uni.edu. *Application contact:* Laurie S. Russell, Record Analyst, 319-273-2623, Fax: 319-273-6792, E-mail: laurie.russell@uni.edu.

University of North Florida, College of Arts and Sciences, Department of Biology, Jacksonville, FL 32224. Offers MA, MS. Part-time programs available. *Faculty:* 13 full-time (3 women). *Students:* 20 full-time (13 women), 9 part-time (6 women); includes 4 minority (1 African American, 3 Hispanic Americans), 1 international. Average age 28. 39 applicants, 49% accepted, 9 enrolled. In 2009, 10 master's awarded. *Degree requirements:* For master's, thesis (for some programs). *Entrance requirements:* For master's, GRE General Test, minimum GPA of 3.0 in last 60 hours, letters of recommendation. Additional exam requirements/recommendations for international students: Required—TOEFL (minimum score 570 paper-based; 230 computer-based). *Application deadline:* For fall admission, 3/1 for domestic students, 2/1 for international students; for spring admission, 11/1 for domestic students, 10/1 for international students. Application fee: $30. Electronic applications accepted. *Expenses:* Tuition, state resident: full-time $6649.20; part-time $277.05 per credit hour. Tuition, nonresident: full-time $22,970; part-time $957.08 per credit hour. Required fees: $985; $41.03 per credit hour. *Financial support:* In 2009–10, 13 students received support, including 1 research assistantship (averaging $6,840 per year), 15 teaching assistantships (averaging $4,435 per year). Financial award application deadline: 4/1; financial award applicants required to submit FAFSA. Total annual research expenditures: $266,776. *Unit head:* Dr. Courtney Hackney, Chair, 904-620-2830, Fax: 904-620-3885, E-mail: c.hackney@unf.edu. *Application contact:* Dr. Dale Casamatta, Graduate Coordinator, 904-620-2830, Fax: 904-620-3885, E-mail: dcasamat@unf.edu.

University of North Texas, Robert B. Toulouse School of Graduate Studies, College of Arts and Sciences, Department of Biological Sciences, Program in Biology, Denton, TX 76203. Offers MA, MS, PhD. Terminal master's awarded for partial completion of doctoral program. *Degree requirements:* For master's, variable foreign language requirement, comprehensive exam, thesis (for some programs), oral defense of thesis; for doctorate, one foreign language, comprehensive exam, thesis/dissertation, oral defense of dissertation. *Entrance requirements:* For master's, GRE General Test, admissions to Toulouse School of Graduate Studies, letters of recommendation; for doctorate, GRE General Test, admission to Toulouse School of Graduate Studies, letters of recommendation. Application fee: $50 ($75 for international students). *Expenses:* Tuition, state resident: full-time $4298; part-time $239 per contact hour. Tuition, nonresident: full-time $9878; part-time $549 per contact hour. Required fees: $265 per contact hour. *Financial support:* Fellowships, research assistantships, teaching assistantships, career-related internships or fieldwork, Federal Work-Study, and institutionally sponsored loans available. Support available to part-time students. Financial award applicants required to submit FAFSA. *Faculty research:* Animal physiology, plant science, biochemistry, environmental science. Total annual research expenditures: $2.5 million. *Unit head:* Professor and Chair. *Application contact:* Graduate Advisor, 940-565-2011, Fax: 940-565-3821.

University of North Texas Health Science Center at Fort Worth, Graduate School of Biomedical Sciences, Fort Worth, TX 76107-2699. Offers anatomy and cell biology (MS, PhD); biochemistry and molecular biology (MS, PhD); biomedical sciences (MS, PhD); biotechnology (MS); forensic genetics (MS); integrative physiology (MS, PhD); medical science (MS); microbiology and immunology (MS, PhD); pharmacology (MS, PhD); science education (MS); DO/MS; DO/PhD. Terminal master's awarded for partial completion of doctoral program. *Degree requirements:* For master's, thesis; for doctorate, thesis/dissertation. *Entrance requirements:* For master's and doctorate, GRE General Test. Additional exam requirements/recommendations for international students: Required—TOEFL. *Expenses:* Contact institution. *Faculty research:* Alzheimer's disease, aging, eye diseases, cancer, cardiovascular disease.

University of Notre Dame, Graduate School, College of Science, Department of Biological Sciences, Notre Dame, IN 46556. Offers aquatic ecology, evolution and environmental biology (MS, PhD); cellular and molecular biology (MS, PhD); genetics (MS, PhD); physiology (MS, PhD); vector biology and parasitology (MS, PhD). Terminal master's awarded for partial completion of doctoral program. *Degree requirements:* For master's, comprehensive exam, thesis; for doctorate, comprehensive exam, thesis/dissertation, candidacy exam. *Entrance requirements:* For master's and doctorate, GRE General Test. Additional exam requirements/recommendations for international students: Required—TOEFL (minimum score 600 paper-based; 250 computer-based; 80 iBT). Electronic applications accepted. *Faculty research:* Tropical disease, molecular genetics, neurobiology, evolutionary biology, aquatic biology.

University of Oklahoma Health Sciences Center, College of Medicine and Graduate College, Graduate Programs in Medicine, Oklahoma City, OK 73190. Offers biochemistry and molecular biology (MS, PhD), including biochemistry, molecular biology; cell biology (MS, PhD); medical sciences (MS); microbiology and immunology (MS, PhD), including immunology, microbiology; neuroscience (MS, PhD); pathology (PhD); physiology (MS, PhD); psychiatry and behavioral sciences (MS, PhD), including biological psychology; radiological sciences (MS, PhD), including medical radiation physics; MD/PhD. Part-time programs available. *Faculty:* 66 full-time (21 women). *Students:* 235 full-time (169 women), 108 part-time (58 women); includes 38 minority (7 African Americans, 13 American Indian/Alaska Native, 16 Asian Americans or Pacific Islanders, 2 Hispanic Americans), 47 international. Average age 27. 386 applicants, 24% accepted, 70 enrolled. In 2009, 63 master's, 28 doctorates awarded. Terminal master's awarded for partial completion of doctoral program. *Degree requirements:* For doctorate, thesis/dissertation. *Entrance requirements:* For doctorate, GRE General Test, 3 letters of recommendation. Additional exam requirements/recommendations for international students: Required—TOEFL. *Application deadline:* For fall admission, 12/15 for domestic students. Application fee: $25 ($50 for international students). *Expenses:* Contact institution. *Financial support:* In 2009–10, 74 research assistantships (averaging $18,000 per year) were awarded; fellowships, teaching assistantships, career-related internships or fieldwork, Federal Work-Study, institutionally sponsored loans, and tuition waivers (full and partial) also available. Support available to part-time students. *Faculty research:* Behavior and drugs, structure and function of endothelium, genetics and behavior, gene structure and function, action of antibiotics. *Unit head:* Dr. James

J. Tomasek, Dean of the Graduate College, 405-271-2085, Fax: 405-271-1155, E-mail: james-tomasek@ouhsc.edu. *Application contact:* Dr. James J. Tomasek, Dean of the Graduate College, 405-271-2085, Fax: 405-271-1155, E-mail: james-tomasek@ouhsc.edu.

University of Oregon, Graduate School, College of Arts and Sciences, Department of Biology, Eugene, OR 97403. Offers ecology and evolution (MA, MS, PhD); marine biology (MA, MS, PhD); molecular, cellular and genetic biology (PhD); neuroscience and development (PhD). Terminal master's awarded for partial completion of doctoral program. *Degree requirements:* For master's, thesis (for some programs); for doctorate, thesis/dissertation. *Entrance requirements:* For master's and doctorate, GRE General Test, minimum GPA of 3.2. Additional exam requirements/recommendations for international students: Required—TOEFL. *Faculty research:* Developmental neurobiology; evolution, population biology, and quantitative genetics; regulation of gene expression; biochemistry of marine organisms.

University of Ottawa, Faculty of Graduate and Postdoctoral Studies, Faculty of Science, Ottawa-Carleton Institute of Biology, Ottawa, ON K1N 6N5, Canada. Offers M Sc, PhD. Part-time programs available. *Degree requirements:* For master's, thesis, seminar; for doctorate, comprehensive exam, thesis/dissertation, seminar. *Entrance requirements:* For master's, honors B Sc degree or equivalent, minimum B average; for doctorate, honors B Sc with minimum B+ average or M Sc with minimum B+ average. Electronic applications accepted. *Faculty research:* Physiology/biochemistry, cellular and molecular biology, ecology, behavior and systematics.

University of Pennsylvania, School of Arts and Sciences, Graduate Group in Biology, Philadelphia, PA 19104. Offers PhD. *Faculty:* 47 full-time (11 women), 6 part-time/adjunct (2 women). *Students:* 61 full-time (41 women); includes 2 minority (both Asian Americans or Pacific Islanders), 37 international. 180 applicants, 13% accepted, 11 enrolled. In 2009, 6 doctorates awarded. *Degree requirements:* For doctorate, thesis/dissertation. *Entrance requirements:* For doctorate, GRE General Test, GRE Subject Test. Additional exam requirements/recommendations for international students: Required—TOEFL. *Application deadline:* For fall admission, 12/1 priority date for domestic students. Application fee: $70. Electronic applications accepted. *Expenses:* Tuition: Full-time $25,660; part-time $4758 per course. Required fees: $2152; $270 per course. Tuition and fees vary according to course load, degree level and program. *Financial support:* Fellowships, research assistantships, teaching assistantships, institutionally sponsored loans, scholarships/grants, traineeships, health care benefits, and unspecified assistantships available. Financial award application deadline: 12/15.

University of Pennsylvania, School of Medicine, Biomedical Graduate Studies, Philadelphia, PA 19104. Offers MS, PhD, MD/PhD, VMD/PhD. *Faculty:* 643. *Students:* 685 full-time (350 women); includes 176 minority (28 African Americans, 6 American Indian/Alaska Native, 102 Asian Americans or Pacific Islanders, 40 Hispanic Americans), 71 international. 1,136 applicants, 21% accepted, 100 enrolled. In 2009, 11 master's, 91 doctorates awarded. Terminal master's awarded for partial completion of doctoral program. *Degree requirements:* For master's, comprehensive exam; for doctorate, thesis/dissertation. *Entrance requirements:* For master's and doctorate, GRE General Test. Additional exam requirements/recommendations for international students: Required—TOEFL. *Application deadline:* For fall admission, 12/8 priority date for domestic and international students. Applications are processed on a rolling basis. Application fee: $70. Electronic applications accepted. *Expenses:* Contact institution. *Financial support:* In 2009–10, 685 students received support; fellowships, research assistantships, scholarships/grants, traineeships, and unspecified assistantships available. *Unit head:* Dr. Susan R. Ross, Director, 215-898-1030. *Application contact:* Sarah Gormley, Admissions Coordinator, 215-898-1030, Fax: 215-898-2671, E-mail: gormley@mail.med.upenn.edu.

University of Pittsburgh, School of Arts and Sciences, Department of Biological Sciences, Pittsburgh, PA 15260. Offers ecology and evolution (PhD); molecular, cellular, and developmental biology (PhD). *Faculty:* 30 full-time (8 women). *Students:* 66 full-time (38 women); includes 5 minority (1 African American, 2 Asian Americans or Pacific Islanders, 2 Hispanic Americans), 15 international. Average age 23. 234 applicants, 11% accepted, 13 enrolled. In 2009, 4 doctorates awarded. *Degree requirements:* For doctorate, comprehensive exam, thesis/dissertation, completion of research integrity module. *Entrance requirements:* For doctorate, GRE General Test, GRE Subject Test. Additional exam requirements/recommendations for international students: Required—TOEFL (minimum score 550 paper-based; 213 computer-based). *Application deadline:* For fall admission, 1/15 priority date for domestic students, 12/15 priority date for international students. Applications are processed on a rolling basis. Application fee: $0 ($50 for international students). Electronic applications accepted. *Expenses:* Tuition, state resident: full-time $16,402; part-time $665 per credit. Tuition, nonresident: full-time $28,694; part-time $1175 per credit. Required fees: $690; $175 per term. Tuition and fees vary according to program. *Financial support:* In 2009–10, 43 fellowships with full tuition reimbursements (averaging $27,379 per year), 110 research assistantships with full tuition reimbursements (averaging $24,608 per year), 56 teaching assistantships with full tuition reimbursements (averaging $23,398 per year) were awarded; Federal Work-Study, scholarships/grants, traineeships, and health care benefits also available. *Faculty research:* Molecular biology, cell biology, molecular biophysics, developmental biology, ecology and evolution. Total annual research expenditures: $7.6 million. *Unit head:* Dr. Graham F. Hatfull, Professor and Chair, 412-624-4350, Fax: 412-624-4759, E-mail: gfh@pitt.edu. *Application contact:* Cathleen M. Barr, Graduate Administrator, 412-624-4268, Fax: 412-624-4759, E-mail: cbarr@pitt.edu.

University of Pittsburgh, School of Medicine, Graduate Programs in Medicine, Interdisciplinary Biomedical Sciences Program, Pittsburgh, PA 15260. Offers PhD. *Faculty:* 257 full-time (58 women). *Students:* 15 full-time (5 women); includes 3 minority (1 Asian American or Pacific Islander, 2 Hispanic Americans), 5 international. Average age 27. 655 applicants, 10% accepted. In 2009, 37 doctorates awarded. *Degree requirements:* For doctorate, comprehensive exam, thesis/dissertation. *Entrance requirements:* For doctorate, GRE General Test, GRE Subject Test, minimum QPA of 3.0. Additional exam requirements/recommendations for international students: Required—TOEFL (minimum score 600 paper-based; 250 computer-based; 100 iBT), IELTS (minimum score 7). *Application deadline:* For fall admission, 12/15 priority date for domestic and international students. Application fee: $40. Electronic applications accepted. *Expenses:* Tuition, state resident: full-time $16,402; part-time $665 per credit. Tuition, nonresident: full-time $28,694; part-time $1175 per credit. Required fees: $690; $175 per term. Tuition and fees vary according to program. *Financial support:* In 2009–10, 15 research assistantships with full tuition reimbursements (averaging $24,650 per year) were awarded; teaching assistantships, institutionally sponsored loans, scholarships/grants, traineeships, and unspecified assistantships also available. *Faculty research:* Biochemistry and molecular genetics, cell biology and molecular physiology, cellular and molecular pathology, immunology, molecular pharmacology. *Unit head:* Dr. John P. Horn, Associate Dean for Graduate Studies, 412-648-8957, Fax: 412-648-1077, E-mail: gradstudies@medschool.pitt.edu. *Application contact:* Graduate Studies Administrator, 412-648-8957, Fax: 412-648-1077, E-mail: gradstudies@medschool.pitt.edu.

University of Prince Edward Island, Faculty of Science, Charlottetown, PE C1A 4P3, Canada. Offers biology (M Sc); chemistry (M Sc). *Degree requirements:* For master's, thesis. *Entrance requirements:* Additional exam requirements/recommendations for international students: Required—TOEFL (minimum score 550 paper-based; 213 computer-based; 80 iBT), Canadian Academic English Language Assessment, Michigan English Language Assessment Battery, Canadian Test of English for Scholars and Trainees. *Faculty research:* Ecology and wildlife biology, molecular, genetics and biotechnology, organametallic, bio-organic, supramolecular and synthetic organic chemistry, neurobiology and stoke materials science.

University of Puerto Rico, Mayagüez Campus, Graduate Studies, College of Arts and Sciences, Department of Biology, Mayagüez, PR 00681-9000. Offers MS. Part-time programs available. *Degree requirements:* For master's, one foreign language, comprehensive exam, thesis. *Entrance requirements:* For master's, GRE General Test, BS degree in biology or its equivalent; minimum GPA of 3.0 in biology courses. Additional exam requirements/

recommendations for international students: Required—TOEFL. *Faculty research:* Herpetology, entomology, microbiology, immunology, botany.

University of Puerto Rico, Medical Sciences Campus, School of Medicine, Division of Graduate Studies, San Juan, PR 00936-5067. Offers MS, PhD. Terminal master's awarded for partial completion of doctoral program. *Degree requirements:* For master's, one foreign language, thesis; for doctorate, one foreign language, comprehensive exam, thesis/dissertation. *Entrance requirements:* For master's and doctorate, GRE General Test, GRE Subject Test, interview, 3 letters of recommendation, minimum GPA of 3.0. Electronic applications accepted. *Expenses:* Contact institution.

University of Puerto Rico, Río Piedras, College of Natural Sciences, Department of Biology, San Juan, PR 00931-3300. Offers ecology/systematics (MS, PhD); evolution/genetics (MS, PhD); molecular/cellular biology (MS, PhD); neuroscience (MS, PhD). Part-time programs available. *Degree requirements:* For master's, one foreign language, comprehensive exam, thesis; for doctorate, one foreign language, comprehensive exam, thesis/dissertation. *Entrance requirements:* For master's, GRE Subject Test, interview, minimum GPA of 3.0, letter of recommendation; for doctorate, GRE Subject Test, interview, master's degree, minimum GPA of 3.0, letter of recommendation. *Faculty research:* Environmental, poblational and systematic biology.

University of Regina, Faculty of Graduate Studies and Research, Faculty of Science, Department of Biology, Regina, SK S4S 0A2, Canada. Offers M Sc, PhD. *Faculty:* 12 full-time (2 women), 6 part-time/adjunct (0 women). *Students:* 22 full-time (11 women), 4 part-time (all women). 17 applicants, 59% accepted. In 2009, 4 master's awarded. *Degree requirements:* For master's, thesis; for doctorate, comprehensive exam, thesis/dissertation. *Entrance requirements:* Additional exam requirements/recommendations for international students: Required—TOEFL (minimum score 580 paper-based; 237 computer-based; 80 iBT). *Application deadline:* Applications are processed on a rolling basis. Application fee: $90 ($100 for international students). *Financial support:* In 2009–10, 7 fellowships (averaging $19,000 per year), 4 research assistantships (averaging $16,910 per year), 6 teaching assistantships (averaging $6,650 per year) were awarded; scholarships/grants also available. Financial award application deadline: 6/15. *Faculty research:* Moss developmental regulation, orthopteran population genetics, microbial toxin synthesis, fish endocrinology, terrestrial ecology. *Unit head:* Dr. Mark Brigham, Head, 306-585-4145, Fax: 306-585-4894, E-mail: mark.brigham@uregina.ca. *Application contact:* Dr. Harold Weger, Graduate Program Coordinator, 306-585-4479, Fax: 306-585-4894, E-mail: harold.weger@uregina.ca.

University of Rhode Island, Graduate School, College of the Environment and Life Sciences, Department of Biological Sciences, Kingston, RI 02881. Offers MS, PhD. Part-time programs available. *Faculty:* 14 full-time (7 women), 1 part-time/adjunct (0 women). *Students:* 31 full-time (21 women), 2 part-time (1 woman); includes 2 minority (both Asian Americans or Pacific Islanders), 2 international. In 2009, 28 master's awarded. *Degree requirements:* For master's, comprehensive exam (for some programs), thesis optional; for doctorate, comprehensive exam, thesis/dissertation. *Entrance requirements:* For master's and doctorate, GRE, 2 letters of recommendation. Additional exam requirements/recommendations for international students: Required—TOEFL (minimum score 550 paper-based; 213 computer-based). *Application deadline:* For fall admission, 4/15 for domestic students, 1/15 for international students. Application fee: $65. Electronic applications accepted. *Expenses:* Tuition, state resident: full-time $8828; part-time $490 per credit hour. Tuition, nonresident: full-time $22,100; part-time $1228 per credit hour. Required fees: $1118; $57 per semester. Tuition and fees vary according to program. *Financial support:* In 2009–10, 1 research assistantship with partial tuition reimbursement (averaging $7,175 per year), 27 teaching assistantships with full and partial tuition reimbursements (averaging $11,722 per year) were awarded. Financial award application deadline: 1/15; financial award applicants required to submit FAFSA. *Faculty research:* Physiological constraints on predators in Antarctics, effects of CO2 absorption in salt water particularly as it impacts pteropods. *Unit head:* Dr. Marian Goldsmith, Chairperson, 401-874-2373, Fax: 401-874-2065, E-mail: mrgoldsmith@mail.uri.edu. *Application contact:* Dr. Marian Goldsmith, Chairperson, 401-874-2373, Fax: 401-874-2065, E-mail: mrgoldsmith@mail.uri.edu.

University of Rochester, The College, Arts and Sciences, Department of Biology, Rochester, NY 14627. Offers MS, PhD. Terminal master's awarded for partial completion of doctoral program. *Degree requirements:* For doctorate, thesis/dissertation, qualifying exam. *Entrance requirements:* For master's and doctorate, GRE General Test, GRE Subject Test (highly recommended). Additional exam requirements/recommendations for international students: Required—TOEFL.

University of Rochester, School of Medicine and Dentistry, Graduate Programs in Medicine and Dentistry, Rochester, NY 14627. Offers MA, MPH, MS, PhD, MBA/MPH, MBA/MS, MD/MPH, MD/MS, MD/PhD, MPH/MS, MPH/PhD. Part-time programs available. *Degree requirements:* For doctorate, thesis/dissertation, qualifying exam. *Entrance requirements:* For master's and doctorate, GRE General Test. Additional exam requirements/recommendations for international students: Required—TOEFL. Electronic applications accepted.

University of San Francisco, College of Arts and Sciences, Department of Biology, San Francisco, CA 94117-1080. Offers MS. *Faculty:* 4 full-time (all women). *Students:* 5 full-time (3 women), 1 part-time (0 women); includes 2 minority (both Asian Americans or Pacific Islanders). Average age 26. 42 applicants, 14% accepted, 4 enrolled. In 2009, 2 master's awarded. *Degree requirements:* For master's, thesis. *Entrance requirements:* For master's, GRE General Test, GRE Subject Test, BS in biology or the equivalent. *Application deadline:* For fall admission, 4/15 for domestic students; for spring admission, 10/15 for domestic students. Application fee: $55 ($65 for international students). *Expenses:* Tuition: Full-time $19,710; part-time $1095 per unit. Part-time tuition and fees vary according to degree level, campus/location and program. *Financial support:* In 2009–10, 6 students received support; teaching assistantships, career-related internships or fieldwork, Federal Work-Study, institutionally sponsored loans, and tuition waivers available. Financial award application deadline: 3/2; financial award applicants required to submit FAFSA. *Unit head:* Dr. Jennifer Dever, Chair, 415-422-6755, Fax: 415-422-6363. *Application contact:* Information Contact, 415-422-5135, Fax: 415-422-2217, E-mail: asgraduate@usfca.edu.

University of Saskatchewan, College of Graduate Studies and Research, College of Arts and Sciences, Department of Biology, Saskatoon, SK S7N 5A2, Canada. Offers M Sc, PhD. *Faculty:* 38. *Students:* 58. In 2009, 11 master's, 3 doctorates awarded. *Degree requirements:* For master's, thesis (for some programs); for doctorate, comprehensive exam (for some programs), thesis/dissertation. *Entrance requirements:* Additional exam requirements/recommendations for international students: Required—TOEFL (minimum score 80 iBT); Recommended—IELTS (minimum score 6.5). *Application deadline:* For fall admission, 7/1 priority date for domestic students. Applications are processed on a rolling basis. Application fee: $75. Electronic applications accepted. Tuition and fees charges are reported in Canadian dollars. *Expenses:* Tuition, area resident: Full-time $3000 Canadian dollars; part-time $500 Canadian dollars per term. Required fees: $700 Canadian dollars; $100 Canadian dollars per term. *Financial support:* Fellowships, research assistantships, teaching assistantships available. Financial award application deadline: 1/31. *Unit head:* Dr. Peta Bonham-Smith, Head, 306-966-4400, Fax: 306-966-4461, E-mail: peta.bonhamsmith@usask.ca. *Application contact:* Doug Chivers, Graduate Chair, 306-966-4400, Fax: 306-966-4461, E-mail: doug.chivers@usask.ca.

University of Saskatchewan, Western College of Veterinary Medicine and College of Graduate Studies and Research, Graduate Programs in Veterinary Medicine, Department of Veterinary Biomedical Sciences, Saskatoon, SK S7N 5A2, Canada. Offers veterinary anatomy (M Sc); veterinary biomedical sciences (M Vet Sc); veterinary physiological sciences (M Sc, PhD). *Faculty:* 25. *Students:* 35. In 2009, 5 master's awarded. *Degree requirements:* For master's, thesis; for doctorate, comprehensive exam (for some programs), thesis/dissertation. *Entrance requirements:* Additional exam requirements/recommendations for international students: Required—TOEFL (minimum score 80 iBT); Recommended—IELTS (minimum score 6.5).

Biological and Biomedical Sciences—General

University of Saskatchewan (continued)

Application fee: $75. Electronic applications accepted. Tuition and fees charges are reported in Canadian dollars. *Expenses:* Tuition, area resident: Full-time $3000 Canadian dollars; part-time $500 Canadian dollars per term. Required fees: $700 Canadian dollars; $100 Canadian dollars per term. *Faculty research:* Toxicology, animal reproduction, pharmacology, chloride channels, pulmonary pathobiology. *Unit head:* Dr. Barry Blakley, Head, 306-966-7350, Fax: 306-966-7376, E-mail: barry.blakley@usask.ca. *Application contact:* Dr. Baljit Singh, Application Contact, 306-966-7400, E-mail: baljit.singh@usask.ca.

University of South Alabama, College of Medicine and Graduate School, Program in Basic Medical Sciences, Mobile, AL 36688-0002. Offers biochemistry and molecular biology (PhD); cell biology and neuroscience (PhD); microbiology and immunology (PhD); molecular and cellular pharmacology (PhD); physiology (PhD). *Faculty:* 51 full-time (10 women), 1 part-time/adjunct (0 women). *Students:* 51 full-time (32 women), 1 (woman) part-time; includes 11 minority (5 African Americans, 2 American Indian/Alaska Native, 3 Asian Americans or Pacific Islanders, 1 Hispanic American), 12 international. Average age 29. 63 applicants, 19% accepted, 12 enrolled. In 2009, 6 doctorates awarded. *Entrance requirements:* For doctorate, GRE. Additional exam requirements/recommendations for international students: Required—TOEFL. *Application deadline:* For fall admission, 4/1 for domestic students, 6/15 for international students. Applications are processed on a rolling basis. Application fee: $35. *Expenses:* Contact institution. *Financial support:* Fellowships, research assistantships, institutionally sponsored loans available. Financial award application deadline: 4/1; financial award applicants required to submit FAFSA. *Faculty research:* Microcirculation, molecular biology, cell biology, growth control. *Unit head:* Dr. Ronald Balczon, Academic Advisor, 251-460-6153, Fax: 251-460-6071, E-mail: rbalzon@usouthal.edu. *Application contact:* Dr. B. Keith Harrison, Dean of the Graduate School, 251-460-6310, Fax: 251-461-1513, E-mail: kharriso@usouthal.edu.

University of South Alabama, Graduate School, College of Arts and Sciences, Department of Biological Sciences, Mobile, AL 36688-0002. Offers MS. Part-time programs available. *Degree requirements:* For master's, one foreign language, comprehensive exam, thesis optional. *Entrance requirements:* For master's, GRE Subject Test, minimum GPA of 3.0. *Expenses:* Tuition, state resident: part-time $218 per contact hour. Required fees: $1102 per year. *Faculty research:* Aquatic and marine biology, molecular biochemistry, plant and animal taxonomy.

University of South Carolina, The Graduate School, College of Arts and Sciences, Department of Biological Sciences, Columbia, SC 29208. Offers biology (MS, PhD); biology education (IMA, MAT); ecology, evolution and organismal biology (MS, PhD); molecular, cellular, and developmental biology (MS, PhD). IMA and MAT offered in cooperation with the College of Education. Terminal master's awarded for partial completion of doctoral program. *Degree requirements:* For master's, one foreign language, thesis (for some programs); for doctorate, one foreign language, thesis/dissertation. *Entrance requirements:* For master's and doctorate, GRE General Test, minimum GPA of 3.0 in science. Electronic applications accepted. *Faculty research:* Marine ecology, population and evolutionary biology, molecular biology and genetics, development.

University of South Carolina, School of Medicine and The Graduate School, Graduate Programs in Medicine, Columbia, SC 29208. Offers biomedical science (MBS, PhD); genetic counseling (MS); nurse anesthesia (MNA); rehabilitation counseling (MRC, Certificate), including psychiatric rehabilitation (Certificate), rehabilitation counseling (MRC). Terminal master's awarded for partial completion of doctoral program. *Degree requirements:* For master's, comprehensive exam, thesis (for some programs), practicum; for doctorate, comprehensive exam, thesis/dissertation. *Entrance requirements:* For master's, doctorate, and Certificate, GRE General Test. Electronic applications accepted. *Expenses:* Contact institution. *Faculty research:* Cardiovascular diseases, oncology, neuroscience, psychiatric rehabilitation, genetics.

University of South Carolina, School of Medicine and The Graduate School, Graduate Programs in Medicine, Graduate Program in Biomedical Science, Doctoral Program in Biomedical Science, Columbia, SC 29208. Offers PhD. *Degree requirements:* For doctorate, comprehensive exam, thesis/dissertation. *Entrance requirements:* For doctorate, GRE General Test. Electronic applications accepted. *Faculty research:* Cancer, neuroscience, cardiovascular, reproductive, immunology.

University of South Carolina, School of Medicine and The Graduate School, Graduate Programs in Medicine, Graduate Program in Biomedical Science, Master's Program in Biomedical Science, Columbia, SC 29208. Offers MBS. *Degree requirements:* For master's, comprehensive exam, thesis. *Entrance requirements:* For master's, GRE General Test. Electronic applications accepted. *Faculty research:* Cardiovascular diseases, oncology, reproductive biology, neuroscience, microbiology.

The University of South Dakota, Graduate School, College of Arts and Sciences, Department of Biology, Vermillion, SD 57069-2390. Offers MA, MNS, MS, PhD. *Degree requirements:* For master's, comprehensive exam (for some programs), thesis (for some programs); for doctorate, comprehensive exam, thesis/dissertation. *Entrance requirements:* For master's, GRE Subject Test, GRE General Test, minimum GPA of 2.7; for doctorate, GRE General Test, GRE Subject Test, minimum GPA of 2.7. Additional exam requirements/recommendations for international students: Required—TOEFL (minimum score 550 paper-based; 213 computer-based; 70 iBT). Electronic applications accepted. *Faculty research:* Evolutionary and ecological informatics, neuroscience, stress physiology.

The University of South Dakota, School of Medicine and Health Sciences and Graduate School, Biomedical Sciences Graduate Program, Vermillion, SD 57069-2390. Offers cardiovascular research (MS, PhD); cellular and molecular biology (MS, PhD); molecular microbiology and immunology (MS, PhD); neuroscience (MS, PhD); physiology and pharmacology (MS, PhD). Terminal master's awarded for partial completion of doctoral program. *Degree requirements:* For master's, thesis; for doctorate, comprehensive exam, thesis/dissertation. *Entrance requirements:* For master's and doctorate, GRE General Test, minimum GPA of 3.0. Additional exam requirements/recommendations for international students: Required—TOEFL (minimum score 550 paper-based; 213 computer-based; 80 iBT), IELTS (minimum score 6). Electronic applications accepted. *Expenses:* Contact institution. *Faculty research:* Molecular biology, microbiology, neuroscience, cellular biology, physiology.

University of Southern California, Graduate School, College of Letters, Arts and Sciences, Department of Biological Sciences, Los Angeles, CA 90089. Offers biology (MS); computational molecular biology (MS); integrative and evolutionary biology (PhD); marine biology and biological oceanography (MS, PhD), including marine and environmental biology (MS), marine biology and biological oceanography (PhD); molecular and computational biology (PhD), including biology, computational biology and bioinformatics, molecular biology; neurobiology (PhD). *Faculty:* 83 full-time (20 women), 10 part-time/adjunct (3 women). *Students:* 155 full-time (80 women), 4 part-time (1 woman); includes 28 minority (2 African Americans, 1 American Indian/Alaska Native, 17 Asian Americans or Pacific Islanders, 8 Hispanic Americans), 63 international. 216 applicants, 27% accepted, 27 enrolled. In 2009, 7 master's, 24 doctorates awarded. Terminal master's awarded for partial completion of doctoral program. *Degree requirements:* For master's, comprehensive exam (for some programs), research paper; for doctorate, thesis/dissertation, qualifying examination, dissertation defense. *Entrance requirements:* For master's, GRE, 3 letters of recommendation, personal statement, resume, minimum GPA of 3.0; for doctorate, GRE, 3 letters of recommendation, resume, minimum GPA of 3.0. Additional exam requirements/recommendations for international students: Required—TOEFL (minimum score 600 paper-based; 250 computer-based; 100 iBT). *Application deadline:* For fall admission, 12/1 priority date for domestic and international students. Application fee: $85. Electronic applications accepted. *Expenses:* Tuition: Full-time $25,980; part-time $1315 per unit. Required fees: $554. One-time fee: $35 full-time. Full-time tuition and fees vary according to degree level and program. *Financial support:* In 2009–10, 126 students received support, including 35 fellowships with full tuition reimbursements available (averaging $26,500 per year), 51 research assistantships with full tuition reimbursements available (averaging $25,066 per year), 40 teaching assistantships with full tuition reimbursements available (averaging $25,066 per year); scholarships/grants, traineeships, health care benefits, and tuition waivers also available. *Faculty research:* Microarray data analysis, microbial ecology and genetics, integrative organismal and behavioral biology and ecology, stem cell pluipotency, cancer cell biology. *Unit head:* Dr. Douglas Capone, Chair, 213-740-2772, Fax: 213-740-8123, E-mail: capone@usc.edu. *Application contact:* Adolfo dela Rosa, Student Services Advisor, 213-821-3164, Fax: 213-740-8123, E-mail: adolfode@usc.edu.

University of Southern California, Keck School of Medicine and Graduate School, Graduate Programs in Medicine, Los Angeles, CA 90089. Offers MPAP, MPH, MS, PhD, MD/PhD. *Faculty:* 254 full-time (87 women), 13 part-time/adjunct (5 women). *Students:* 737 full-time (492 women), 3 part-time (2 women); includes 322 minority (22 African Americans, 9 American Indian/Alaska Native, 217 Asian Americans or Pacific Islanders, 74 Hispanic Americans), 211 international. Average age 27. 1,513 applicants, 26% accepted, 216 enrolled. In 2009, 143 master's, 42 doctorates awarded. *Entrance requirements:* For master's, GRE General Test (minimum combined score 1150, 450 Verbal, 700 Quantitative), minimum GPA of 3.0; for doctorate, GRE General Test (minimum combined Verbal and Quantitative score of 1000), minimum GPA of 3.0. Additional exam requirements/recommendations for international students: Required—TOEFL (minimum score 600 paper-based; 250 computer-based; 100 iBT). Application fee: $85. Electronic applications accepted. *Expenses:* Tuition: Full-time $25,980; part-time $1315 per unit. Required fees: $554. One-time fee: $35 full-time. Full-time tuition and fees vary according to degree level and program. *Financial support:* In 2009–10, 53 fellowships, 243 research assistantships (averaging $27,060 per year), 34 teaching assistantships (averaging $27,060 per year) were awarded; career-related internships or fieldwork, Federal Work-Study, institutionally sponsored loans, scholarships/grants, traineeships, health care benefits, and unspecified assistantships also available. Support available to part-time students. Financial award application deadline: 5/5; financial award applicants required to submit CSS PROFILE or FAFSA. *Unit head:* Dr. Debbie Johnson, Associate Dean for Graduate Affairs, 323-442-1446, Fax: 323-442-1199, E-mail: johnsond@usc.edu. *Application contact:* Marisela Zuniga, Administrative Coordinator, 323-442-1607, Fax: 323-442-1199, E-mail: mzuniga@usc.edu.

University of Southern Maine, College of Arts and Sciences, Program in Biology, Portland, ME 04104-9300. Offers MS.

University of Southern Mississippi, Graduate School, College of Science and Technology, Department of Biological Sciences, Hattiesburg, MS 39406-0001. Offers environmental biology (MS, PhD); marine biology (MS, PhD); microbiology (MS, PhD); molecular biology (MS, PhD). *Faculty:* 27 full-time (6 women). *Students:* 55 full-time (27 women), 5 part-time (3 women); includes 7 minority (2 African Americans, 1 American Indian/Alaska Native, 2 Asian Americans or Pacific Islanders, 2 Hispanic Americans), 15 international. Average age 32. 53 applicants, 28% accepted, 10 enrolled. In 2009, 8 master's, 4 doctorates awarded. *Degree requirements:* For master's, comprehensive exam, thesis; for doctorate, comprehensive exam, thesis/dissertation. *Entrance requirements:* For master's, GRE General Test, minimum GPA of 3.0; for doctorate, GRE General Test, minimum GPA of 3.5. Additional exam requirements/recommendations for international students: Required—TOEFL. *Application deadline:* For fall admission, 3/1 priority date for domestic students, 3/1 for international students. Applications are processed on a rolling basis. Application fee: $35. *Expenses:* Tuition, state resident: full-time $5096; part-time $284 per hour. Tuition, nonresident: full-time $13,052; part-time $726 per hour. Required fees: $402. Tuition and fees vary according to course level and course load. *Financial support:* In 2009–10, 25 research assistantships with full tuition reimbursements (averaging $9,625 per year), 33 teaching assistantships with full tuition reimbursements (averaging $10,599 per year) were awarded; Federal Work-Study also available. Financial award application deadline: 3/15; financial award applicants required to submit FAFSA. *Unit head:* Dr. Frank Moore, Chair, 601-266-4748, Fax: 601-266-5797. *Application contact:* Dr. Chia Wang, Graduate Coordinator, 601-266-4748, Fax: 601-266-5797.

University of South Florida, College of Medicine and Graduate School, Graduate Programs in Medical Sciences, Tampa, FL 33620-9951. Offers MS, MSMS, PhD. *Students:* 323 full-time (168 women), 64 part-time (35 women); includes 178 minority (77 African Americans, 1 American Indian/Alaska Native, 50 Asian Americans or Pacific Islanders, 50 Hispanic Americans), 16 international. Average age 34. 532 applicants, 55% accepted, 215 enrolled. In 2009, 95 master's, 16 doctorates awarded. Terminal master's awarded for partial completion of doctoral program. *Degree requirements:* For master's, comprehensive exam, thesis; for doctorate, comprehensive exam, thesis/dissertation. *Entrance requirements:* For doctorate, GRE General Test, minimum GPA of 3.0 in last 60 hours of coursework. Additional exam requirements/recommendations for international students: Required—TOEFL (minimum score 550 paper-based; 213 computer-based). *Application deadline:* For fall admission, 2/15 for domestic students, 1/2 for international students. Application fee: $30. *Expenses:* Contact institution. *Financial support:* In 2009–10, teaching assistantships with tuition reimbursements (averaging $19,500 per year). Financial award application deadline: 4/1; financial award applicants required to submit FAFSA. *Unit head:* Michael Barber, Program Director, 813-974-9702, Fax: 813-974-4317, E-mail: mbarber@health.usf.edu.

University of South Florida, Graduate School, College of Arts and Sciences, Department of Biology, Tampa, FL 33620-9951. Offers cell biology and molecular biology (MS); coastal marine biology (MS); coastal marine biology and ecology (PhD); conservation biology (MS, PhD); molecular and cell biology (PhD). Part-time programs available. *Faculty:* 34 full-time (7 women). *Students:* 72 full-time (43 women), 18 part-time (8 women); includes 9 minority (1 African American, 2 American Indian/Alaska Native, 4 Asian Americans or Pacific Islanders, 2 Hispanic Americans), 7 international. Average age 32. 99 applicants, 20% accepted, 14 enrolled. In 2009, 8 master's, 4 doctorates awarded. *Degree requirements:* For master's, comprehensive exam, thesis (for some programs); for doctorate, comprehensive exam, thesis/dissertation. *Entrance requirements:* For master's and doctorate, GRE General Test, minimum GPA of 3.0. Additional exam requirements/recommendations for international students: Required—TOEFL (minimum score 570 paper-based; 213 computer-based). *Application deadline:* For fall admission, 2/15 priority date for domestic students, 1/2 for international students; for spring admission, 8/1 for domestic students, 6/1 for international students. Application fee: $30. Electronic applications accepted. *Financial support:* In 2009–10, teaching assistantships with tuition reimbursements (averaging $58,627 per year); unspecified assistantships also available. Financial award application deadline: 6/30; financial award applicants required to submit FAFSA. Total annual research expenditures: $1.2 million. *Unit head:* Susan Bell, Co-Chairperson, 813-974-6210, Fax: 813-974-2876, E-mail: sbell@cas.usf.edu. *Application contact:* James Garey, Graduate Advisor, 813-974-8434, Fax: 813-974-3263, E-mail: grarey@cas.usf.edu.

The University of Tennessee, Graduate School, College of Arts and Sciences, Program in Life Sciences, Knoxville, TN 37996. Offers genome science and technology (MS, PhD); plant physiology and genetics (MS, PhD). *Degree requirements:* For doctorate, one foreign language, thesis/dissertation. *Entrance requirements:* For master's and doctorate, GRE General Test, minimum GPA of 2.7. Additional exam requirements/recommendations for international students: Required—TOEFL. Electronic applications accepted. *Expenses:* Tuition, state resident: full-time $6826; part-time $380 per semester hour. Tuition, nonresident: full-time $21,844; part-time $1147 per semester hour. Tuition and fees vary according to program.

The University of Tennessee, Graduate School, Intercollegiate Programs, Program in Comparative and Experimental Medicine, Knoxville, TN 37996. Offers MS, PhD. *Degree requirements:* For master's, thesis; for doctorate, thesis/dissertation. *Entrance requirements:* For master's and doctorate, GRE General Test, minimum GPA of 2.7. Additional exam requirements/recommendations for international students: Required—TOEFL. Electronic applications accepted. *Expenses:* Tuition, state resident: full-time $6826; part-time $380 per semester hour. Tuition, nonresident: full-time $21,844; part-time $1147 per semester hour. Tuition and fees vary according to program.

The University of Tennessee Health Science Center, College of Graduate Health Sciences, Integrated Program in Biomedical Sciences, Memphis, TN 38163-0002. Offers MS, PhD. Terminal master's awarded for partial completion of doctoral program. *Degree requirements:* For master's, thesis; for doctorate, comprehensive exam, thesis/dissertation. *Entrance requirements:* For doctorate, GRE, minimum GPA of 3.0, 3 letters of recommendation. Additional exam requirements/recommendations for international students: Required—TOEFL (minimum score 600 paper-based; 213 computer-based). Electronic applications accepted. *Faculty research:* Molecular biology, physiology, pharmacology, pathology, neuroscience.

The University of Tennessee–Oak Ridge National Laboratory Graduate School of Genome Science and Technology, Graduate Program, Oak Ridge, TN 37830-8026. Offers life sciences (MS, PhD). *Degree requirements:* For master's, thesis; for doctorate, comprehensive exam, thesis/dissertation. *Entrance requirements:* For master's and doctorate, GRE General Test. Additional exam requirements/recommendations for international students: Required—TOEFL (minimum score 550 paper-based; 213 computer-based). Electronic applications accepted. *Faculty research:* Genetics/genomics, structural biology/proteomics, computational biology/bioinformatics, bioanalytical technologies.

The University of Texas at Arlington, Graduate School, College of Science, Department of Biology, Arlington, TX 76019. Offers biology (MS); quantitative biology (PhD). Part-time and evening/weekend programs available. *Faculty:* 26 full-time (7 women), 1 part-time/adjunct (0 women). *Students:* 58 full-time (31 women), 24 part-time (19 women); includes 15 minority (5 African Americans, 1 American Indian/Alaska Native, 4 Asian Americans or Pacific Islanders, 5 Hispanic Americans), 19 international. 48 applicants, 96% accepted, 12 enrolled. In 2009, 9 master's, 6 doctorates awarded. *Degree requirements:* For master's, thesis, oral defense of thesis; for doctorate, comprehensive exam, thesis/dissertation, oral defense of dissertation. *Entrance requirements:* For master's and doctorate, GRE General Test. Additional exam requirements/recommendations for international students: Required—TOEFL (minimum score 550 paper-based; 213 computer-based; 79 iBT). *Application deadline:* For fall admission, 6/15 for domestic students, 4/3 for international students; for spring admission, 10/16 for domestic students, 9/11 for international students. Applications are processed on a rolling basis. Application fee: $35 ($50 for international students). Electronic applications accepted. *Financial support:* In 2009–10, 4 fellowships (averaging $1,000 per year), 4 research assistantships (averaging $15,500 per year), 26 teaching assistantships (averaging $15,500 per year) were awarded; Federal Work-Study and institutionally sponsored loans also available. Financial award application deadline: 6/1; financial award applicants required to submit FAFSA. *Unit head:* Dr. Johnathan Campbell, Chair, 817-272-2871, Fax: 817-272-2855, E-mail: campbell@exchange.uta.edu. *Application contact:* Dr. Daniel R. Formanowicz, Graduate Adviser, 817-272-2871, Fax: 817-272-2855, E-mail: formanow@uta.edu.

The University of Texas at Austin, Graduate School, College of Natural Sciences, School of Biological Sciences, Austin, TX 78712-1111. Offers MA, PhD. *Entrance requirements:* For master's and doctorate, GRE General Test. Electronic applications accepted.

The University of Texas at Brownsville, Graduate Studies, College of Science, Mathematics and Technology, Brownsville, TX 78520-4991. Offers biological sciences (MS, MSIS); mathematics (MS); physics (MS). Part-time and evening/weekend programs available. *Degree requirements:* For master's, comprehensive exam, thesis optional. *Entrance requirements:* For master's, GRE General Test. Additional exam requirements/recommendations for international students: Required—TOEFL. *Faculty research:* Fish, insects, barrier islands, algae, curlits.

The University of Texas at Dallas, School of Natural Sciences and Mathematics, Program in Biology, Richardson, TX 75080. Offers bioinformatics and computational biology (MS); biotechnology (MS); molecular and cell biology (MS, PhD). Part-time and evening/weekend programs available. *Faculty:* 16 full-time (3 women). *Students:* 89 full-time (50 women), 16 part-time (11 women); includes 19 minority (16 Asian Americans or Pacific Islanders, 3 Hispanic Americans), 62 international. Average age 26. 313 applicants, 31% accepted, 42 enrolled. In 2009, 36 master's, 4 doctorates awarded. *Degree requirements:* For master's, thesis optional; for doctorate, thesis/dissertation, publishable paper. *Entrance requirements:* For master's and doctorate, GRE General Test. Additional exam requirements/recommendations for international students: Required—TOEFL (minimum score 550 paper-based; 213 computer-based). *Application deadline:* For fall admission, 7/15 for domestic students, 5/1 priority date for international students; for spring admission, 11/15 for domestic students, 9/1 priority date for international students. Applications are processed on a rolling basis. Application fee: $50 ($100 for international students). Electronic applications accepted. *Expenses:* Tuition, state resident: full-time $11,068; part-time $461 per credit hour. Tuition, nonresident: full-time $21,178; part-time $882 per credit hour. Tuition and fees vary according to course load. *Financial support:* In 2009–10, 15 research assistantships with full tuition reimbursements (averaging $14,347 per year), 27 teaching assistantships with full tuition reimbursements (averaging $13,511 per year) were awarded; fellowships, career-related internships or fieldwork, Federal Work-Study, institutionally sponsored loans, scholarships/grants, and unspecified assistantships also available. Support available to part-time students. Financial award application deadline: 4/30; financial award applicants required to submit FAFSA. *Faculty research:* DNA replication, regulation of gene expression, subcellular organelles, physical chemistry of macromolecules, damage and repair of cellular DNA. *Unit head:* Dr. Li Zhang, Department Head, 972-883-6032, Fax: 972-883-2502, E-mail: li.zhang@utdallas.edu. *Application contact:* Dr. Lawrence Reitzer, Graduate Advisor, 972-883-2502, Fax: 972-883-2402, E-mail: reitzer@utdallas.edu.

The University of Texas at El Paso, Graduate School, College of Science, Department of Biological Sciences, El Paso, TX 79968-0001. Offers bioinformatics (MS); biological sciences (MS, PhD). Part-time and evening/weekend programs available. *Students:* 71 (32 women); includes 39 minority (4 African Americans, 4 Asian Americans or Pacific Islanders, 31 Hispanic Americans), 17 international. Average age 34. In 2009, 16 master's, 4 doctorates awarded. *Degree requirements:* For master's, thesis; for doctorate, thesis/dissertation. *Entrance requirements:* For master's, GRE, minimum GPA of 3.0, letters of recommendation; for doctorate, GRE, statement of purpose, letters of recommendation. Additional exam requirements/recommendations for international students: Required—TOEFL; Recommended—IELTS. *Application deadline:* For fall admission, 8/1 priority date for domestic students, 3/1 for international students; for spring admission, 11/1 priority date for domestic students, 9/1 for international students. Applications are processed on a rolling basis. Application fee: $45 ($80 for international students). Electronic applications accepted. *Financial support:* In 2009–10, research assistantships with partial tuition reimbursements (averaging $22,500 per year), teaching assistantships with partial tuition reimbursements (averaging $18,000 per year) were awarded; fellowships with partial tuition reimbursements, institutionally sponsored loans, scholarships/grants, health care benefits, tuition waivers (partial), and unspecified assistantships also available. Support available to part-time students. Financial award application deadline: 3/15; financial award applicants required to submit FAFSA. *Unit head:* Dr. Robert Kirken, Chair, 915-747-5844, Fax: 915-747-5808, E-mail: rkirken@utep.edu. *Application contact:* Dr. Patricia D. Witherspoon, Dean of Graduate School, 915-747-5491, Fax: 915-747-5788, E-mail: withersp@utep.edu.

The University of Texas at San Antonio, College of Sciences, Department of Biology, San Antonio, TX 78249-0617. Offers biology (MS, PhD), including cellular and molecular biology (PhD), neurobiology (PhD); biotechnology (MS). Part-time programs available. *Faculty:* 37 full-time (6 women), 7 part-time/adjunct (1 woman). *Students:* 144 full-time (82 women), 45 part-time (28 women); includes 57 minority (6 African Americans, 13 Asian Americans or Pacific Islanders, 38 Hispanic Americans), 69 international. Average age 28. 263 applicants, 58% accepted, 72 enrolled. In 2009, 40 master's, 6 doctorates awarded. *Degree requirements:* For master's, comprehensive exam, thesis; for doctorate, comprehensive exam, thesis/dissertation. *Entrance requirements:* For master's, GRE General Test, minimum GPA of 3.0; for doctorate, GRE General Test, minimum GPA of 3.3. Additional exam requirements/recommendations for international students: Required—TOEFL (minimum score 500 paper-based; 173 computer-based; 61 iBT), IELTS (minimum score 5). *Application deadline:* For fall admission, 7/1 for domestic students, 4/1 for international students; for spring admission, 11/1 for domestic students, 9/1 for international students. Applications are processed on a rolling basis. Application fee: $45 ($80 for international students). Electronic applications accepted. *Expenses:* Tuition, state resident: full-time $3975; part-time $221 per contact hour. Tuition, nonresident: full-time $13,947; part-time $775 per contact hour. Required fees: $1853. *Financial support:* In 2009–10, 66 students received support, including 13 fellowships (averaging $31,063 per year), 87 research assistantships (averaging $15,279 per year), 66 teaching assistantships (averaging $10,368 per year); career-related internships or fieldwork, scholarships/grants, and unspecified assistantships also available. Support available to part-time students. *Faculty research:* Cell and molecular biology, neurobiology, microbiology, integrative biology, environmental science. Total annual research expenditures: $1.7 million. *Unit head:* Dr. Edwin J. Barea-Rodriguez, Interim Chair, 210-458-5481, Fax: 210-458-7498, E-mail: edwin.barea@utsa.edu. *Application contact:* Dr. Dorothy A. Flannagan, Dean of the Graduate School, 210-458-4330, Fax: 210-458-4332, E-mail: dorothy.flannagan@utsa.edu.

See Close-Up on page 121.

The University of Texas at Tyler, College of Arts and Sciences, Department of Biology, Tyler, TX 75799-0001. Offers biology (MS); interdisciplinary studies (MSIS). *Faculty:* 10 full-time (1 woman). *Students:* 11 full-time (5 women), 6 part-time (3 women); includes 1 minority (Asian American or Pacific Islander), 1 international. Average age 26. 14 applicants, 57% accepted, 7 enrolled. In 2009, 5 master's awarded. *Degree requirements:* For master's, comprehensive exam, thesis, oral qualifying exam, thesis defense. *Entrance requirements:* For master's, GRE General Test, GRE Subject Test, bachelor's degree in biology or equivalent. Additional exam requirements/recommendations for international students: Required—TOEFL (minimum score 79 computer-based). *Application deadline:* For fall admission, 8/17 priority date for domestic students, 7/1 priority date for international students; for spring admission, 12/21 priority date for domestic students, 11/1 priority date for international students. Applications are processed on a rolling basis. Application fee: $25 ($50 for international students). Electronic applications accepted. *Expenses:* Tuition, state resident: part-time $665 per semester hour. Tuition, nonresident: part-time $942 per semester hour. Part-time tuition and fees vary according to degree level and program. *Financial support:* In 2009–10, 2 research assistantships (averaging $10,000 per year), 10 teaching assistantships (averaging $10,000 per year) were awarded; scholarships/grants also available. Financial award application deadline: 7/1; financial award applicants required to submit FAFSA. *Faculty research:* Phenotypic plasticity and heritability of life history traits, invertebrate ecology and genetics, systematics and phylogenetics of reptiles, hibernation physiology in turtles, landscape ecology, host-microbe interaction, outer membrane proteins in bacteria. Total annual research expenditures: $200,000. *Unit head:* Dr. Don Killebrew, Chair, 903-566-7252, E-mail: dkillebrew@uttyler.edu. *Application contact:* Dr. Neil Ford, Program Chair, 903-566-7249, E-mail: nford@uttyler.edu.

The University of Texas Health Science Center at Houston, Graduate School of Biomedical Sciences, Houston, TX 77225-0036. Offers MS, PhD, MD/PhD. Terminal master's awarded for partial completion of doctoral program. *Degree requirements:* For master's, thesis; for doctorate, thesis/dissertation. *Entrance requirements:* For master's and doctorate, GRE General Test. Additional exam requirements/recommendations for international students: Required—TOEFL. Electronic applications accepted. *Faculty research:* Biomedical sciences.

The University of Texas Health Science Center at San Antonio, Graduate School of Biomedical Sciences, San Antonio, TX 78229-3900. Offers MS, MSN, PhD. Part-time and evening/weekend programs available. *Faculty:* 224 full-time (83 women), 54 part-time/adjunct (9 women). *Students:* 368 full-time (197 women), 243 part-time (180 women); includes 192 minority (27 African Americans, 4 American Indian/Alaska Native, 41 Asian Americans or Pacific Islanders, 120 Hispanic Americans), 144 international. Average age 33. 661 applicants, 30% accepted, 148 enrolled. In 2009, 111 master's, 42 doctorates awarded. Terminal master's awarded for partial completion of doctoral program. *Degree requirements:* For master's, comprehensive exam (for some programs), thesis; for doctorate, comprehensive exam, thesis/dissertation. *Entrance requirements:* For master's and doctorate, GRE General Test. Additional exam requirements/recommendations for international students: Required—TOEFL (minimum score 560 paper-based; 220 computer-based; 68 iBT). *Application deadline:* For fall admission, 4/1 for domestic and international students; for spring admission, 10/1 for domestic and international students. Applications are processed on a rolling basis. Application fee: $0. Electronic applications accepted. *Expenses:* Contact institution. *Financial support:* In 2009–10, 212 teaching assistantships (averaging $26,000 per year) were awarded; fellowships, research assistantships, career-related internships or fieldwork, Federal Work-Study, institutionally sponsored loans, health care benefits, and tuition waivers (full) also available. Support available to part-time students. Financial award application deadline: 4/1; financial award applicants required to submit FAFSA. *Faculty research:* Aging, cancer biology, neuroscience, protein structure, genetics. Total annual research expenditures: $50.6 million. *Unit head:* Robert L. Reddick, Interim Dean, 210-567-3709, Fax: 210-567-3719, E-mail: reddick@uthscsa.edu. *Application contact:* Nicquet Blake, Assistant Dean for Graduate Student Recruitment, 210-567-3709, Fax: 210-567-3719, E-mail: blaken@uthscsa.edu.

The University of Texas Medical Branch, Graduate School of Biomedical Sciences, Galveston, TX 77555. Offers MA, MMS, MPH, MS, PhD, MD/PhD. *Students:* 230 full-time (122 women), 63 part-time (34 women); includes 66 minority (14 African Americans, 1 American Indian/Alaska Native, 21 Asian Americans or Pacific Islanders, 30 Hispanic Americans), 70 international. Average age 32. In 2009, 21 master's, 58 doctorates awarded. Terminal master's awarded for partial completion of doctoral program. *Degree requirements:* For master's, comprehensive exam (for some programs), thesis or alternative; for doctorate, comprehensive exam, thesis/dissertation. *Entrance requirements:* For master's and doctorate, GRE General Test, 3 letters of recommendation. Additional exam requirements/recommendations for international students: Required—TOEFL (minimum score 550 paper-based; 213 computer-based; 80 iBT), IELTS (minimum score 6.5). *Application deadline:* Applications are processed on a rolling basis. Application fee: $30 ($75 for international students). Electronic applications accepted. *Expenses:* Contact institution. *Financial support:* In 2009–10, research assistantships with full tuition reimbursements (averaging $25,000 per year); career-related internships or fieldwork, Federal Work-Study, institutionally sponsored loans, scholarships/grants, traineeships, health care benefits, and unspecified assistantships also available. Support available to part-time students. Financial award applicants required to submit FAFSA. *Unit head:* Dr. Cary W. Cooper, Dean, 409-772-2665, Fax: 409-747-0772, E-mail: ccooper@utmb.edu. *Application contact:* Dr. Dorian H. Coppenhaver, Associate Dean for Student Affairs, 409-772-2665, Fax: 409-747-0772, E-mail: dcoppenh@utmb.edu.

The University of Texas of the Permian Basin, Office of Graduate Studies, College of Arts and Sciences, Department of Biology, Odessa, TX 79762-0001. Offers MS. Part-time and evening/weekend programs available. *Degree requirements:* For master's, comprehensive exam, thesis or alternative. *Entrance requirements:* For master's, GRE General Test. Additional exam requirements/recommendations for international students: Required—TOEFL (minimum score 550 paper-based; 213 computer-based).

The University of Texas–Pan American, College of Science and Engineering, Department of Biology, Edinburg, TX 78539. Offers MS. Part-time and evening/weekend programs available. *Degree requirements:* For master's, comprehensive exam. *Entrance requirements:* For master's, GRE General Test, minimum GPA of 2.75 in biology. *Expenses:* Tuition, state resident: full-time $3630.60; part-time $201.70 per credit hour. Tuition, nonresident: full-time $8617; part-time $478.70 per credit hour. Required fees: $806.50. *Faculty research:* Flora and fauna of South Padre Island, plant taxonomy of Rio Grande Valley.

The University of Texas Southwestern Medical Center at Dallas, Southwestern Graduate School of Biomedical Sciences, Division of Basic Science, Dallas, TX 75390. Offers biological chemistry (PhD); cancer biology (PhD); cell regulation (PhD); genetics and development (PhD); immunology (PhD); integrative biology (PhD); molecular biophysics (PhD); molecular

Biological and Biomedical Sciences—General

The University of Texas Southwestern Medical Center at Dallas *(continued)* microbiology (PhD); neuroscience (PhD); MD/PhD. *Faculty:* 278 full-time (70 women), 10 part-time/adjunct (0 women). *Students:* 471 full-time (227 women), 14 part-time (2 women); includes 117 minority (15 African Americans, 8 American Indian/Alaska Native, 47 Asian Americans or Pacific Islanders, 47 Hispanic Americans), 151 international. 946 applicants, 22% accepted, 87 enrolled. In 2009, 98 doctorates awarded. *Degree requirements:* For doctorate, thesis/dissertation, qualifying exam. *Entrance requirements:* For doctorate, GRE General Test, research experience. Additional exam requirements/recommendations for international students: Required—TOEFL. *Application deadline:* For fall admission, 12/15 priority date for domestic and international students. Application fee: $0. Electronic applications accepted. *Financial support:* Fellowships, research assistantships, institutionally sponsored loans and traineeships available. *Unit head:* Dr. Nancy E. Street, Associate Dean, 214-648-6708, Fax: 214-648-2102, E-mail: nancy.street@utsouthwestern.edu. *Application contact:* Dr. Nancy E. Street, Associate Dean, 214-648-6708, Fax: 214-648-2102, E-mail: nancy.street@utsouthwestern.edu.

The University of Texas Southwestern Medical Center at Dallas, Southwestern Graduate School of Biomedical Sciences, Division of Clinical Science, Clinical Science Program, Dallas, TX 75390. Offers MCS, MSCS. Part-time programs available. *Students:* 1 full-time (0 women), 83 part-time (45 women); includes 31 minority (5 African Americans, 1 American Indian/Alaska Native, 16 Asian Americans or Pacific Islanders, 9 Hispanic Americans), 7 international. Average age 26. 26 applicants, 73% accepted, 19 enrolled. In 2009, 12 master's awarded. *Degree requirements:* For master's, 1 year clinical research project. *Entrance requirements:* For master's, graduate degree in biomedical science. *Application deadline:* For fall admission, 7/15 for domestic students; for spring admission, 12/16 for domestic students. Applications are processed on a rolling basis. Electronic applications accepted. *Unit head:* Dr. Milton Packer, Chair, 214-648-0491, Fax: 214-648-6417, E-mail: milton.packer@utsouthwestern.edu. *Application contact:* Dena Wheaton, Program Coordinator, 214-648-2410, Fax: 214-648-3978, E-mail: dena.wheaton@utsouthwestern.edu.

The University of Texas Southwestern Medical Center at Dallas, Southwestern Graduate School of Biomedical Sciences, Medical Scientist Training Program, Dallas, TX 75390. Offers PhD, MD/PhD. *Faculty:* 1,464 full-time, 402 part-time/adjunct. *Students:* 18 full-time (3 women); includes 5 minority (1 African American, 3 Asian Americans or Pacific Islanders, 1 Hispanic American), 3 international. Average age 26. 29 applicants, 83% accepted, 7 enrolled. *Application deadline:* For fall admission, 11/1 for domestic students. Application fee: $0. Electronic applications accepted. *Financial support:* Application deadline: 3/1. *Unit head:* Dr. Andrew Zinn, Associate Dean, 214-648-2057, Fax: 214-648-2814, E-mail: dennis.mckearin@utsouthwestern.edu. *Application contact:* Robin Downing, Education Coordinator, 214-648-6764, Fax: 214-648-2814, E-mail: robin.downing@utsouthwestern.edu.

University of the Incarnate Word, School of Graduate Studies and Research, School of Mathematics, Science, and Engineering, Program in Biology, San Antonio, TX 78209-6397. Offers MA, MS. Part-time and evening/weekend programs available. *Students:* 7 full-time (5 women), 4 part-time (2 women); includes 3 minority (all Hispanic Americans), 4 international. Average age 27. In 2009, 7 master's awarded. *Degree requirements:* For master's, comprehensive exam (for some programs), thesis (for some programs). *Entrance requirements:* For master's, GRE Subject Test (biology), minimum GPA of 3.0 in biology or GRE (minimum combined score of 1,000 on Verbal and Quantitative sections); 8 semester hours of credit in principles of chemistry; 6 semester hours of organic chemistry; 12 upper-division hours in biology. Additional exam requirements/recommendations for international students: Required—TOEFL (minimum score 560 paper-based; 220 computer-based; 83 iBT). *Application deadline:* Applications are processed on a rolling basis. Application fee: $20. Electronic applications accepted. *Expenses:* Tuition: Full-time $12,150; part-time $675 per credit hour. Required fees: $83 per credit hour. *Financial support:* Federal Work-Study and scholarships/grants available. Financial award applicants required to submit FAFSA. *Faculty research:* Structure and function of proteins, gene expression in human leukocytes, transmission of pathogenic protozoa, environmental chemistry, professional development of educators in science. *Unit head:* Dr. David Foglesong, 210-283-5033, Fax: 210-829-3153, E-mail: davidf@uiwtx.edu. *Application contact:* Andrea Cyterski-Acosta, Dean of Enrollment, 210-829-6005, Fax: 210-829-3921, E-mail: admis@uiwtx.edu.

University of the Pacific, College of the Pacific, Department of Biological Sciences, Stockton, CA 95211-0197. Offers MS. *Faculty:* 15 full-time (5 women), 1 part-time/adjunct (0 women). *Students:* 3 full-time (2 women), 27 part-time (14 women); includes 10 minority (9 Asian Americans or Pacific Islanders, 1 Hispanic American), 2 international. Average age 25. 32 applicants, 47% accepted, 14 enrolled. In 2009, 7 master's awarded. *Degree requirements:* For master's, thesis. *Entrance requirements:* For master's, GRE General Test, GRE Subject Test. Additional exam requirements/recommendations for international students: Required—TOEFL. *Application deadline:* For fall admission, 3/1 priority date for domestic students; for spring admission, 10/1 priority date for domestic students. Applications are processed on a rolling basis. Application fee: $75. *Financial support:* In 2009–10, 22 teaching assistantships were awarded; institutionally sponsored loans also available. Support available to part-time students. Financial award application deadline: 3/1; financial award applicants required to submit FAFSA. *Unit head:* Dr. Gregg Jongeward, Chairman, 209-946-2181. *Application contact:* Information Contact, 209-946-2261.

The University of Toledo, College of Graduate Studies, College of Arts and Sciences, Department of Biological Sciences, Toledo, OH 43606-3390. Offers biology (MS, PhD). Part-time programs available. *Degree requirements:* For master's, thesis or alternative; for doctorate, 2 foreign languages, thesis/dissertation. *Entrance requirements:* For master's and doctorate, GRE General Test, GRE Subject Test. Additional exam requirements/recommendations for international students: Required—TOEFL (minimum score 550 paper-based). Electronic applications accepted. *Faculty research:* Biochemical parasitology, physiological ecology, animal physiology.

The University of Toledo, College of Graduate Studies, College of Arts and Sciences, Department of Environmental Sciences, Toledo, OH 43606-3390. Offers biology (ecology track) (MS, PhD); geology (MS), including earth surface processes, general geology. Part-time programs available. *Degree requirements:* For master's, thesis. *Entrance requirements:* For master's, GRE General Test. Additional exam requirements/recommendations for international students: Required—TOEFL. Electronic applications accepted. *Faculty research:* Environmental geochemistry, geophysics, petrology and mineralogy, paleontology, geohydrology.

The University of Toledo, College of Graduate Studies, College of Medicine, Biomedical Science Programs, Toledo, OH 43606-3390. Offers biochemistry and molecular biology (MSBS), including medical sciences; bioinformatics and proteomics/genomics (MSBS, Certificate); cancer biology (MSBS, PhD); cardiovascular and metabolic diseases (MSBS, PhD); diagnostic radiology (MSBS); gerontology (Certificate), including contemporary gerontological practice; infection, immunity and transplantation (MSBS); infection, immunology and transplantation (PhD); medical physics (MSBS); neurosciences and neurological disorders (MS, PhD); oral biology (MSBS); orthopedic science (MSBS); pathology (Certificate), including anatomic pathology, pathology; radiation oncology (MSBS), including medical physics-clinical radiation oncology; urology (MSBS); MD/MSBS; MD/PhD.

University of Toronto, School of Graduate Studies, Life Sciences Division, Toronto, ON M5S 1A1, Canada. Offers M Sc, M Sc BMC, M Sc F, MA, MFC, MH Sc, MN, PhD, MD/PhD. Part-time programs available. *Degree requirements:* For doctorate, thesis/dissertation.

University of Tulsa, Graduate School, College of Engineering and Natural Sciences, Department of Biological Sciences, Tulsa, OK 74104-3189. Offers MS, MTA, PhD, JD/MS. Part-time programs available. *Faculty:* 10 full-time (3 women). *Students:* 17 full-time (8 women), 6 part-time (5 women); includes 2 minority (1 American Indian/Alaska Native, 1 Asian American

or Pacific Islander), 6 international. Average age 29. 28 applicants, 46% accepted, 10 enrolled. In 2009, 2 master's, 1 doctorate awarded. *Degree requirements:* For master's, thesis, oral exams; for doctorate, comprehensive exam, thesis/dissertation. *Entrance requirements:* For master's and doctorate, GRE General Test. Additional exam requirements/recommendations for international students: Required—TOEFL (minimum score 550 paper-based; 213 computer-based; 80 iBT), IELTS (minimum score 6). *Application deadline:* Applications are processed on a rolling basis. Application fee: $40. Electronic applications accepted. *Expenses:* Tuition: Full-time $16,182; part-time $899 per credit hour. Required fees: $4 per credit hour. Tuition and fees vary according to course load. *Financial support:* In 2009–10, 13 students received support, including 8 fellowships with full and partial tuition reimbursements available (averaging $3,121 per year), 7 research assistantships with full and partial tuition reimbursements available (averaging $11,557 per year), 4 teaching assistantships with full and partial tuition reimbursements available (averaging $11,515 per year); career-related internships or fieldwork, Federal Work-Study, scholarships/grants, health care benefits, tuition waivers (full and partial), and unspecified assistantships also available. Support available to part-time students. Financial award application deadline: 2/1; financial award applicants required to submit FAFSA. *Faculty research:* Aerobiology, animal behavior and behavioral ecology, cell and molecular biology, ecology, developmental biology, genetics, herpetology, glycobiology, immunology, microbiology, morphology, mycology, ornithology, molecular systematic and virology. Total annual research expenditures: $3.6 million. *Unit head:* Dr. Estelle Levetin, Chairperson, 918-631-2764, Fax: 918-631-2762, E-mail: estelle-levetin@utulsa.edu. *Application contact:* Dr. Harrington Wells, Advisor, 918-631-3071, Fax: 918-631-2762, E-mail: harrington-wells@utulsa.edu.

University of Utah, Graduate School, College of Science, Department of Biology, Salt Lake City, UT 84112. Offers MS, PhD. Part-time programs available. *Faculty:* 44 full-time (7 women), 1 (woman) part-time/adjunct. *Students:* 52 full-time (23 women), 17 part-time (6 women); includes 1 minority (Hispanic American), 19 international. Average age 29. 88 applicants, 16% accepted, 14 enrolled. In 2009, 6 master's, 13 doctorates awarded. Terminal master's awarded for partial completion of doctoral program. *Degree requirements:* For master's, comprehensive exam, thesis; for doctorate, comprehensive exam, thesis/dissertation. *Entrance requirements:* For master's and doctorate, GRE General Test, minimum GPA of 3.0. Additional exam requirements/recommendations for international students: Required—TOEFL (minimum score 500 paper-based; 173 computer-based; 61 iBT). *Application deadline:* For fall admission, 1/8 for domestic and international students. Application fee: $55 ($65 for international students). *Expenses:* Tuition, state resident: full-time $4004; part-time $1674 per semester. Tuition, nonresident: full-time $14,134; part-time $5915 per semester. Required fees: $324 per semester. Tuition and fees vary according to course load, degree level and program. *Financial support:* In 2009–10, 68 students received support, including 12 fellowships with full tuition reimbursements available (averaging $25,000 per year), 26 research assistantships with full tuition reimbursements available (averaging $25,000 per year), 30 teaching assistantships with full tuition reimbursements available (averaging $16,500 per year); career-related internships or fieldwork, scholarships/grants, traineeships, and health care benefits also available. Financial award application deadline: 3/15; financial award applicants required to submit FAFSA. *Faculty research:* Ecology, evolutionary biology, cell and developmental biology, physiology and organismal biology, molecular biology, biochemistry, microbiology. Total annual research expenditures: $13.1 million. *Unit head:* Dr. Neil J. Vickers, Chair, 801-585-0622, Fax: 801-585-1930, E-mail: vickers@biology.utah.edu. *Application contact:* Shannon Nielsen, Administrative Program Coordinator, 801-581-5636, Fax: 801-581-4668, E-mail: shannon.nielsen@bioscience.utah.edu.

University of Utah, School of Medicine and Graduate School, Graduate Programs in Medicine, Salt Lake City, UT 84112-1107. Offers M Phil, M Stat, MPAS, MPH, MS, MSPH, PhD, Certificate. Part-time programs available. *Degree requirements:* For doctorate, thesis/dissertation. *Entrance requirements:* For doctorate, MCAT. Electronic applications accepted. *Expenses:* Tuition, state resident: full-time $4004; part-time $1674 per semester. Tuition, nonresident: full-time $14,134; part-time $5915 per semester. Required fees: $324 per semester. Tuition and fees vary according to course load, degree level and program. *Faculty research:* Molecular biology, biochemistry, cell biology, immunology, bioengineering.

University of Vermont, College of Medicine and Graduate College, Graduate Programs in Medicine, Burlington, VT 05405. Offers biochemistry (MS, PhD); clinical and translational science (MS, PhD); microbiology and molecular genetics (MS, PhD); molecular physiology and biophysics (MS, PhD); neuroscience (PhD); pathology (MS); pharmacology (MS, PhD); MD/MS; MD/PhD. *Students:* 78 (40 women); includes 3 minority (1 Asian American or Pacific Islander, 2 Hispanic Americans), 18 international. 139 applicants, 34% accepted, 16 enrolled. In 2009, 3 master's, 7 doctorates awarded. *Degree requirements:* For master's, thesis; for doctorate, thesis/dissertation. *Entrance requirements:* For master's and doctorate, GRE General Test. Additional exam requirements/recommendations for international students: Required—TOEFL (minimum score 550 paper-based; 213 computer-based; 80 iBT). *Application deadline:* For fall admission, 4/1 priority date for domestic students. Applications are processed on a rolling basis. Application fee: $40. Electronic applications accepted. *Expenses:* Tuition, state resident: part-time $508 per credit hour. Tuition, nonresident: part-time $1281 per credit hour. *Financial support:* Fellowships, research assistantships, teaching assistantships, traineeships and analytical assistantships available. Financial award application deadline: 3/1. *Unit head:* Dr. Frederick C. Morin, Dean, 802-656-2156. *Application contact:* Dr. Frederick C. Morin, Dean, 802-656-2156.

University of Vermont, Graduate College, College of Arts and Sciences, Department of Biology, Burlington, VT 05405. Offers biology (MS, PhD); biology education (MST). *Faculty:* 17. *Students:* 34 (18 women); includes 3 minority (1 African American, 2 Hispanic Americans), 13 international. 43 applicants, 23% accepted, 4 enrolled. In 2009, 3 doctorates awarded. *Degree requirements:* For master's, thesis; for doctorate, thesis/dissertation. *Entrance requirements:* For master's and doctorate, GRE General Test. Additional exam requirements/recommendations for international students: Required—TOEFL (minimum score 550 paper-based; 213 computer-based; 80 iBT). *Application deadline:* For fall admission, 1/15 priority date for domestic students. Applications are processed on a rolling basis. Application fee: $40. Electronic applications accepted. *Expenses:* Tuition, state resident: part-time $508 per credit hour. Tuition, nonresident: part-time $1281 per credit hour. *Financial support:* Fellowships, research assistantships, teaching assistantships available. Financial award application deadline: 3/1. *Unit head:* Dr. Jim Vigoreaux, Chairperson, 802-656-2922. *Application contact:* Dr. Judith Van Houten, Coordinator, 802-656-2922.

University of Victoria, Faculty of Graduate Studies, Faculty of Science, Department of Biology, Victoria, BC V8W 2Y2, Canada. Offers M Sc, PhD. *Degree requirements:* For master's, thesis, seminar; for doctorate, thesis/dissertation, seminar, candidacy exam. *Entrance requirements:* For master's and doctorate, GRE General Test, minimum B+ average in previous 2 years of biology course work. Additional exam requirements/recommendations for international students: Required—TOEFL (minimum score 575 paper-based; 233 computer-based), IELTS (minimum score 7). Electronic applications accepted. *Faculty research:* Neurobiology of vertebrates and invertebrates, physiology, reproduction and tissue culture of forest trees, evolution and ecology, cell and molecular biology, molecular biology of environmental health.

University of Virginia, College and Graduate School of Arts and Sciences, Department of Biology, Charlottesville, VA 22903. Offers MA, MS, PhD. *Faculty:* 36 full-time (6 women), 3 part-time/adjunct (0 women). *Students:* 53 full-time (37 women); includes 8 minority (1 African American, 4 Asian Americans or Pacific Islanders, 3 Hispanic Americans), 13 international. Average age 27. 80 applicants, 23% accepted, 11 enrolled. In 2009, 5 master's, 3 doctorates awarded. *Degree requirements:* For master's, thesis; for doctorate, thesis/dissertation. *Entrance requirements:* For master's and doctorate, GRE General Test, GRE Subject Test (recommended), 2 letters of recommendation. Additional exam requirements/recommendations for international students: Required—TOEFL (minimum score 600 paper-based; 250 computer-based; 90 iBT), IELTS (minimum score 7). *Application deadline:* For fall admission, 12/21 for domestic and international students. Applications are processed on a rolling basis. Application fee: $60. Electronic applications accepted. *Financial support:* Fellowships, research assistantships, teaching assistantships available. Financial award applicants required to submit FAFSA. *Faculty research:* Ecology and evolution, neurobiology and behavior, molecular genetics, cell, development. *Unit head:* Douglas Taylor, Chair, 434-982-5474, Fax: 434-982-5626, E-mail: drt3b@virginia.edu. *Application contact:* Rita Webb, Graduate Student Program Coordinator, 434-982-5474, Fax: 434-982-5626, E-mail: rea2d@virginia.edu.

University of Virginia, School of Medicine, Department of Molecular Physiology and Biological Physics, Program in Biological and Physical Sciences, Charlottesville, VA 22903. Offers MS. *Students:* 2 full-time (both women). Average age 27. 1 applicant, 100% accepted, 1 enrolled. In 2009, 22 master's awarded. *Entrance requirements:* For master's, GRE General Test. Additional exam requirements/recommendations for international students: Required—TOEFL. *Application deadline:* Applications are processed on a rolling basis. Application fee: $60. Electronic applications accepted. *Financial support:* Applicants required to submit FAFSA. *Unit head:* Dr. Mark Yeager, Chair, 434-924-5108, Fax: 434-982-1616, E-mail: my3r@virginia.edu. *Application contact:* Dr. Mark Yeager, Chair, 434-924-5108, Fax: 434-982-1616, E-mail: my3r@virginia.edu.

University of Washington, Graduate School, College of Arts and Sciences, Department of Biology, Seattle, WA 98195. Offers PhD.

University of Washington, Graduate School, School of Medicine and Graduate School, Graduate Programs in Medicine, Seattle, WA 98195. Offers MA, MOT, MS, DPT, PhD. Part-time programs available. *Degree requirements:* For doctorate, thesis/dissertation. *Entrance requirements:* For doctorate, GRE. Electronic applications accepted. *Expenses:* Contact institution.

University of Waterloo, Graduate Studies, Faculty of Science, Department of Biology, Waterloo, ON N2L 3G1, Canada. Offers M Sc, PhD. Part-time programs available. *Degree requirements:* For master's, thesis, seminar, proposal; for doctorate, comprehensive exam, thesis/dissertation, seminar, proposal. *Entrance requirements:* For master's, honor's degree; for doctorate, master's degree. Additional exam requirements/recommendations for international students: Required—TOEFL (minimum score 580 paper-based; 237 computer-based; 90 iBT), TWE (minimum score 4). Electronic applications accepted. *Faculty research:* Biosystematics, ecology and limnology, molecular and cellular biology, biochemistry, physiology.

University of West Florida, College of Arts and Sciences: Sciences, School of Allied Health and Life Sciences, Department of Biology, Pensacola, FL 32514-5750. Offers biological chemistry (MS); biology (MS); biology education (MST); biotechnology (MS); coastal zone studies (MS); environmental biology (MS). *Faculty:* 7 full-time (2 women), 1 (woman) part-time/adjunct. *Students:* 5 full-time (1 woman), 21 part-time (14 women); includes 2 minority (1 Asian American or Pacific Islander, 1 Hispanic American), 1 international. Average age 28. 19 applicants, 58% accepted, 7 enrolled. In 2009, 12 master's awarded. *Degree requirements:* For master's, thesis. *Entrance requirements:* For master's, GRE General Test. Additional exam requirements/recommendations for international students: Required—TOEFL (minimum score 550 paper-based; 213 computer-based). *Application deadline:* For fall admission, 6/1 for domestic students, 5/15 for international students; for spring admission, 11/1 for domestic students, 10/1 for international students. Applications are processed on a rolling basis. Application fee: $30. *Expenses:* Tuition, state resident: full-time $4982; part-time $260 per credit hour. Tuition, nonresident: full-time $20,059; part-time $919 per credit hour. Required fees: $1247; $52 per credit hour. *Financial support:* In 2009–10, 2 research assistantships with partial tuition reimbursements (averaging $8,500 per year), 10 teaching assistantships with partial tuition reimbursements (averaging $8,176 per year) were awarded; unspecified assistantships also available. Financial award application deadline: 4/15; financial award applicants required to submit FAFSA. *Unit head:* Dr. George L. Stewart, Chairperson, 850-474-2748. *Application contact:* Terry McCray, Assistant Director of Graduate Admissions, 850-473-7718, Fax: 850-473-7714, E-mail: gradadmissions@uwf.edu.

University of West Georgia, Graduate School, College of Arts and Sciences, Department of Biology, Carrollton, GA 30118. Offers MS. Part-time programs available. *Faculty:* 9 full-time (2 women). *Students:* 16 full-time (8 women), 8 part-time (4 women); includes 6 minority (5 African Americans, 1 Asian American or Pacific Islander). Average age 26. 18 applicants, 72% accepted, 2 enrolled. In 2009, 4 master's awarded. *Degree requirements:* For master's, comprehensive exam (for some programs), thesis (for some programs). *Entrance requirements:* For master's, GRE General Test, minimum GPA of 2.5, undergraduate degree in biology. Additional exam requirements/recommendations for international students: Required—TOEFL. *Application deadline:* For fall admission, 7/17 for domestic students; for spring admission, 11/20 for domestic students. Applications are processed on a rolling basis. Application fee: $30. Electronic applications accepted. *Expenses:* Tuition, state resident: full-time $2952; part-time $164 per semester hour. Tuition, nonresident: full-time $11,808; part-time $656 per semester hour. Required fees: $42.90 per semester hour. $307 per semester. Tuition and fees vary according to course load. *Financial support:* In 2009–10, 8 teaching assistantships with full tuition reimbursements (averaging $8,000 per year) were awarded; career-related internships or fieldwork, scholarships/grants, and unspecified assistantships also available. Financial award application deadline: 7/1; financial award applicants required to submit FAFSA. *Faculty research:* Molecular systematics, animal physiology, marine ecology, plant ecology. Total annual research expenditures: $200,000. *Unit head:* Dr. Henry G. Zot, Chair, 678-839-6547, Fax: 678-839-6548, E-mail: hzot@westga.edu. *Application contact:* Dr. Charles W. Clark, Dean, 678-839-6508, E-mail: cclark@westga.edu.

University of Windsor, Faculty of Graduate Studies, Faculty of Science, Department of Biological Sciences, Windsor, ON N9B 3P4, Canada. Offers M Sc, PhD. Part-time programs available. *Degree requirements:* For master's, thesis; for doctorate, comprehensive exam, thesis/dissertation. *Entrance requirements:* For master's and doctorate, minimum B average. Additional exam requirements/recommendations for international students: Required—TOEFL (minimum score 560 paper-based; 220 computer-based). Electronic applications accepted. *Faculty research:* Great Lakes Institute: aquatic ecotoxicology, regulation and development of the olfactory system, mating system evolution, signal transduction, aquatic ecology.

University of Wisconsin–La Crosse, Office of University Graduate Studies, College of Science and Health, Department of Biology, La Crosse, WI 54601-3742. Offers aquatic sciences (MS); biology (MS); cellular and molecular biology (MS); clinical microbiology (MS); microbiology (MS); nurse anesthesia (MS); physiology (MS). Part-time programs available. *Faculty:* 27 full-time (7 women). *Students:* 19 full-time (8 women), 35 part-time (20 women); includes 1 minority (Asian American or Pacific Islander), 2 international. Average age 28. 87 applicants, 32% accepted, 21 enrolled. In 2009, 18 master's awarded. *Degree requirements:* For master's, comprehensive exam, thesis. *Entrance requirements:* For master's, GRE General Test, minimum GPA of 2.85. Additional exam requirements/recommendations for international students: Required—TOEFL (minimum score 550 paper-based; 213 computer-based; 79 iBT). Application fee: $56. Electronic applications accepted. *Financial support:* In 2009–10, 19 research assistantships with partial tuition reimbursements (averaging $10,021 per year) were awarded; career-related internships or fieldwork, Federal Work-Study, health care benefits, unspecified assistantships, and grant-funded positions also available. Support available to part-time students. Financial award application deadline: 3/15; financial award applicants required to submit FAFSA. *Unit head:* Dr. David Howard, Chair, 608-785-6455, E-mail: howard.davi@uwlax.edu. *Application contact:* Kathryn Kiefer, Director of Admissions, 608-785-8939, E-mail: admissions@uwlax.edu.

University of Wisconsin–Madison, School of Medicine and Public Health and Graduate School, Graduate Programs in Medicine, Madison, WI 53705. Offers biomolecular chemistry (MS, PhD); cancer biology (PhD); genetics and medical genetics (MS, PhD), including genetics (PhD), medical genetics (MS); medical physics (MS, PhD), including health physics (MS), medical physics; microbiology (PhD); molecular and cellular pharmacology (PhD); pathology and laboratory medicine (PhD); physiology (PhD); population health sciences (MPH, MS, PhD), including clinical research (MS, PhD), epidemiology (MS, PhD), health services research (MS, PhD), population health sciences (MPH), social and behavioral health sciences (MS, PhD); DPT/MPH; DVM/MPH; MD/MPH; MD/PhD; MPA/MPH; MS/MPH; Pharm D/MPH. Part-time programs available. Postbaccalaureate distance learning degree programs offered (minimal on-campus study). Terminal master's awarded for partial completion of doctoral program. Application fee: $45. Electronic applications accepted. *Expenses:* Contact institution. *Financial support:* Fellowships with full tuition reimbursements, research assistantships with full tuition reimbursements, teaching assistantships with full tuition reimbursements, scholarships/grants, traineeships, and tuition waivers (full) available. *Unit head:* Dr. Richard L. Moss, Senior Associate Dean for Basic Research, Biotechnology and Graduate Studies, 608-265-0523, Fax: 608-265-0522, E-mail: rlmoss@wisc.edu. *Application contact:* Information Contact, 608-262-2433, Fax: 608-262-5134, E-mail: gradadmiss@mail.bascom.wisc.edu.

University of Wisconsin–Madison, School of Medicine and Public Health, Medical Scientist Training Program, Madison, WI 53705-2221. Offers MD/PhD. *Accreditation:* LCME/AMA. *Faculty:* 380 full-time (80 women). *Students:* 68 full-time (25 women); includes 13 minority (5 African Americans, 1 American Indian/Alaska Native, 7 Asian Americans or Pacific Islanders). 170 applicants, 18% accepted, 9 enrolled. *Application deadline:* For fall admission, 12/1 for domestic students. Applications are processed on a rolling basis. Application fee: $54. Electronic applications accepted. *Expenses:* Tuition, state resident: part-time $594 per credit. Tuition, nonresident: part-time $1504 per credit. Required fees: $65 per credit. Tuition and fees vary according to course load, program and reciprocity agreements. *Financial support:* In 2009–10, fellowships with full tuition reimbursements (averaging $23,500 per year), research assistantships with full tuition reimbursements (averaging $23,500 per year) were awarded; traineeships and health care benefits also available. *Unit head:* Dr. Deane Mosher, Director, 608-262-1576, Fax: 608-263-4969, E-mail: dfmosher@wisc.edu. *Application contact:* Paul Cook, Program Administrator, 608-262-6321, Fax: 608-262-4226, E-mail: pscook@wisc.edu.

University of Wisconsin–Milwaukee, Graduate School, College of Health Sciences, PhD Program in Health Sciences, Milwaukee, WI 53201-0413. Offers PhD. *Students:* 15 full-time (6 women), 5 part-time (3 women); includes 1 minority (African American), 5 international. Average age 35. 6 applicants, 83% accepted, 2 enrolled. In 2009, 1 doctorate awarded. *Degree requirements:* For doctorate, comprehensive exam, thesis/dissertation. *Entrance requirements:* For doctorate, GRE. Additional exam requirements/recommendations for international students: Required—TOEFL (minimum score 600 paper-based; 250 computer-based), IELTS (minimum score 6.5). *Expenses:* Tuition, state resident: full-time $8800. Tuition, nonresident: full-time $20,760. Tuition and fees vary according to program and reciprocity agreements. *Financial support:* Fellowships, research assistantships, teaching assistantships available. Total annual research expenditures: $7,821. *Unit head:* Roger O. Smith, Representative, 414-229-6697, E-mail: smithro@uwm.edu. *Application contact:* General Information Contact, 414-229-4982, Fax: 414-229-6967, E-mail: gradschool@uwm.edu.

University of Wisconsin–Milwaukee, Graduate School, College of Letters and Sciences, Department of Biological Sciences, Milwaukee, WI 53201-0413. Offers MS, PhD. *Faculty:* 36 full-time (10 women). *Students:* 40 full-time (19 women), 45 part-time (25 women); includes 11 minority (4 African Americans, 2 American Indian/Alaska Native, 3 Asian Americans or Pacific Islanders, 2 Hispanic Americans), 26 international. Average age 29. 105 applicants, 22% accepted, 12 enrolled. In 2009, 8 master's, 9 doctorates awarded. *Degree requirements:* For master's, thesis; for doctorate, thesis/dissertation, 1 foreign language or data analysis proficiency. *Entrance requirements:* For master's and doctorate, GRE General Test. Additional exam requirements/recommendations for international students: Required—TOEFL (minimum score 550 paper-based; 79 iBT), IELTS (minimum score 6.5). *Application deadline:* For fall admission, 3/1 priority date for domestic students. Applications are processed on a rolling basis. Application fee: $45 ($75 for international students). *Expenses:* Tuition, state resident: full-time $8800. Tuition, nonresident: full-time $20,760. Tuition and fees vary according to program and reciprocity agreements. *Financial support:* In 2009–10, 7 research assistantships, 69 teaching assistantships were awarded; career-related internships or fieldwork and unspecified assistantships also available. Support available to part-time students. Financial award application deadline: 4/15. Total annual research expenditures: $1.5 million. *Unit head:* Daad Saffarini, Representative, 414-229-2964, E-mail: daads@uwm.edu. *Application contact:* General Information Contact, 414-229-4982, Fax: 414-229-6967, E-mail: gradschool@uwm.edu.

University of Wisconsin–Oshkosh, The Office of Graduate Studies, College of Letters and Science, Department of Biology and Microbiology, Oshkosh, WI 54901. Offers biology (MS), including botany, microbiology, zoology. *Degree requirements:* For master's, comprehensive exam, thesis. *Entrance requirements:* For master's, GRE General Test, minimum GPA of 3.0, BS in biology. Additional exam requirements/recommendations for international students: Required—TOEFL (minimum score 550 paper-based; 213 computer-based; 79 iBT). Electronic applications accepted.

Utah State University, School of Graduate Studies, College of Science, Department of Biology, Logan, UT 84322. Offers biology (MS, PhD); ecology (MS, PhD). Part-time programs available. *Degree requirements:* For master's, thesis; for doctorate, thesis/dissertation. *Entrance requirements:* For master's and doctorate, GRE General Test, minimum GPA of 3.0. Additional exam requirements/recommendations for international students: Required—TOEFL (minimum score 575 paper-based). *Faculty research:* Plant, insect, microbial, and animal biology.

Vanderbilt University, Graduate School, Department of Biological Sciences, Nashville, TN 37240-1001. Offers MS, PhD, MD/PhD. *Faculty:* 30 full-time (4 women), 1 part-time/adjunct (0 women). *Students:* 56 full-time (27 women); includes 7 minority (2 African Americans, 1 Asian American or Pacific Islander, 4 Hispanic Americans), 18 international. Average age 28. 206 applicants, 3% accepted, 4 enrolled. In 2009, 1 master's, 9 doctorates awarded. Terminal master's awarded for partial completion of doctoral program. *Degree requirements:* For master's, thesis; for doctorate, thesis/dissertation, final and qualifying exams. *Entrance requirements:* For master's and doctorate, GRE General Test. Additional exam requirements/recommendations for international students: Required—TOEFL (minimum score 570 paper-based; 230 computer-based; 88 iBT). *Application deadline:* For fall admission, 1/15 for domestic and international students. Application fee: $0. Electronic applications accepted. *Financial support:* Fellowships with full and partial tuition reimbursements, research assistantships with full tuition reimbursements, teaching assistantships with full tuition reimbursements, Federal Work-Study, institutionally sponsored loans, scholarships/grants, traineeships, and health care benefits available. Financial award application deadline: 1/15; financial award applicants required to submit CSS PROFILE or FAFSA. *Faculty research:* Protein structure and function, protein transport, membrane ion channels and receptors, signal transduction, posttranscriptional control of gene expression, DNA replication and recombination, biological clocks, development, neurobiology, vector biology, insect physiology, ecology and evolution, bioinformatics. *Unit head:* Dr. Charles K. Singleton, Chair, 615-322-2008, Fax: 615-343-6707, E-mail: charles.k.singleton@vanderbilt.edu. *Application contact:* Dr. Andrzej Krezel, Director of Graduate Studies, 615-322-2008, Fax: 615-343-6707, E-mail: biosci_graduate_program@vanderbilt.edu.

Vanderbilt University, School of Medicine, Interdisciplinary Graduate Program in Biomedical and Biological Sciences, Nashville, TN 37240-1001. Offers PhD. First-year students in biomedical sciences enter the program. Degrees are awarded through participating departments of biochemistry, biological sciences, cancer biology, cell and developmental biology, human genetics, microbiology, and immunology, molecular physiology and biophysics, neuroscience, cellular and molecular pathology, and pharmacology. *Degree requirements:* For doctorate, comprehensive exam, thesis/dissertation, final and qualifying exams, dissertation defense. *Entrance requirements:* For doctorate, GRE General Test, 3 letters of recommendation, interview by invitation. Additional exam requirements/recommendations for international students: Required—TOEFL. Electronic applications accepted. *Faculty research:* Genetics; immunology; neurobiology; cell and developmental biology; signal transduction.

Vanderbilt University, School of Medicine and Graduate School, Medical Scientist Training Program, Nashville, TN 37240-1001. Offers MD/PhD. Electronic applications accepted.

Biological and Biomedical Sciences—General

Vanderbilt University (continued)

Expenses: Contact institution. *Faculty research:* Cancer biology, neurosciences, microbiology, biochemistry, metabolism/diabetics.

Vassar College, Graduate Programs, Poughkeepsie, NY 12604. Offers biology (MA, MS); chemistry (MA, MS). Applicants accepted only if enrolled in undergraduate programs at Vassar College. Part-time programs available. *Students:* 1 (woman) part-time. *Degree requirements:* For master's, thesis. *Entrance requirements:* For master's, GRE General Test, bachelor's degree in related field. *Application deadline:* Applications are processed on a rolling basis. Application fee: $60. *Expenses:* Tuition: Full-time $41,335; part-time $4890 per course. *Financial support:* Career-related internships or fieldwork available. *Unit head:* Joanne Long, Dean of Studies, 914-437-5257, E-mail: long@vassar.edu. *Application contact:* Joanne Long, Dean of Studies, 914-437-5257, E-mail: long@vassar.edu.

Villanova University, Graduate School of Liberal Arts and Sciences, Department of Biology, Villanova, PA 19085-1699. Offers MA, MS. Part-time and evening/weekend programs available. *Faculty:* 10 full-time (4 women). *Students:* 29 full-time (13 women), 32 part-time (22 women); includes 8 minority (2 African Americans, 1 American Indian/Alaska Native, 3 Asian Americans or Pacific Islanders, 2 Hispanic Americans), 5 international. Average age 27. 26 applicants, 92% accepted, 18 enrolled. In 2009, 16 master's awarded. *Degree requirements:* For master's, comprehensive exam (for some programs), thesis (for some programs). *Entrance requirements:* For master's, GRE General Test, GRE Subject Test, minimum GPA of 3.0. Additional exam requirements/recommendations for international students: Required—TOEFL. *Application deadline:* For fall admission, 2/1 priority date for domestic and international students; for spring admission, 10/15 priority date for domestic students, 11/15 priority date for international students. Applications are processed on a rolling basis. Application fee: $50. Electronic applications accepted. *Expenses:* Contact institution. *Financial support:* Research assistantships with tuition reimbursements, teaching assistantships with tuition reimbursements, Federal Work-Study and scholarships/grants available. Support available to part-time students. Financial award applicants required to submit FAFSA. *Unit head:* Dr. Russell Gardner, Chair, 610-519-4830. *Application contact:* Dr. Adele Lindenmeyr, Dean, Graduate School of Liberal Arts and Sciences, 610-519-7093, Fax: 610-519-7096.

See Close-Up on page 123.

Virginia Commonwealth University, Graduate School, College of Humanities and Sciences, Department of Biology, Richmond, VA 23284-9005. Offers MS. *Degree requirements:* For master's, thesis. *Entrance requirements:* For master's, GRE General Test, BS in biology or related field. *Faculty research:* Molecular and cellular biology, terrestrial and aquatic biology, systematics and physiology and developmental biology.

Virginia Commonwealth University, Graduate School, School of Life Sciences, Richmond, VA 23284-9005. Offers MIS, MS, PhD.

Virginia Commonwealth University, Medical College of Virginia-Professional Programs, School of Medicine, School of Medicine Graduate Programs, Richmond, VA 23284-9005. Offers MPH, MS, PhD, MD/MPH, MD/PhD. Part-time programs available. Terminal master's awarded for partial completion of doctoral program. *Degree requirements:* For doctorate, thesis/dissertation, comprehensive oral and written exams. *Entrance requirements:* For doctorate, GRE General Test, MCAT.

Virginia Commonwealth University, Program in Pre-Medical Basic Health Sciences, Richmond, VA 23284-9005. Offers anatomy (CBHS); biochemistry (CBHS); human genetics (CBHS); microbiology (CBHS); pharmacology (CBHS); physiology (CBHS). *Entrance requirements:* For degree, GRE or MCAT, course work in organic chemistry, minimum undergraduate GPA of 2.8. Additional exam requirements/recommendations for international students: Required—TOEFL (minimum score 600 paper-based).

Virginia Polytechnic Institute and State University, Graduate School, College of Science, Department of Biological Sciences, Blacksburg, VA 24061. Offers botany (MS, PhD); ecology and evolutionary biology (MS, PhD); genetics and developmental biology (MS, PhD); microbiology (MS, PhD); zoology (MS, PhD). *Faculty:* 42 full-time (11 women). *Students:* 76 full-time (45 women), 5 part-time (1 woman); includes 28 minority (23 American Indian/Alaska Native, 2 Asian Americans or Pacific Islanders, 3 Hispanic Americans). Average age 28. 117 applicants, 15% accepted, 15 enrolled. In 2009, 11 master's, 11 doctorates awarded. *Entrance requirements:* For master's and doctorate, GRE, GMAT. Additional exam requirements/recommendations for international students: Required—TOEFL (minimum score 550 paper-based; 213 computer-based). *Application deadline:* For fall admission, 5/15 for international students; for spring admission, 10/15 for international students. Applications are processed on a rolling basis. Application fee: $65. Electronic applications accepted. *Expenses:* Tuition, area resident: Full-time $10,228; part-time $459 per credit hour. Tuition, nonresident: full-time $17,892; part-time $865 per credit hour. Required fees: $1966; $451 per semester. *Financial support:* In 2009–10, 37 research assistantships with full tuition reimbursements (averaging $17,929 per year), 41 teaching assistantships with full tuition reimbursements (averaging $17,344 per year) were awarded; career-related internships or fieldwork, Federal Work-Study, scholarships/grants, and unspecified assistantships also available. Financial award application deadline: 1/15. *Faculty research:* Freshwater ecology, cell cycle regulation, behavioral ecology, motor proteins. Total annual research expenditures: $4.8 million. *Unit head:* Dr. Bob H. Jones, Dean, 540-231-9514, Fax: 540-231-9307, E-mail: rhjones@vt.edu. *Application contact:* Erik Nilsen, Information Contact, 540-231-5671, Fax: 540-231-9307, E-mail: enilsen@vt.edu.

Virginia State University, School of Graduate Studies, Research, and Outreach, School of Engineering, Science and Technology, Department of Biology, Petersburg, VA 23806-0001. Offers MS. *Degree requirements:* For master's, one foreign language, thesis. *Entrance requirements:* For master's, GRE General Test. *Faculty research:* Schwann cell cultures, selection of apios as an alternative crop, systematic botany, flowers of three species of wild ginger.

Wagner College, Division of Graduate Studies, Department of Biological Sciences, Staten Island, NY 10301-4495. Offers advanced physician assistant studies (MS); microbiology (MS). Part-time and evening/weekend programs available. *Degree requirements:* For master's, comprehensive exam or thesis. *Entrance requirements:* For master's, minimum GPA of 2.5, proficiency in statistics, undergraduate major in science. Additional exam requirements/recommendations for international students: Required—TOEFL. *Expenses:* Tuition: Full-time $15,570; part-time $865 per credit. Required fees: $2.

Wake Forest University, Graduate School of Arts and Sciences, Department of Biology, Winston-Salem, NC 27109. Offers MS, PhD. Part-time programs available. *Degree requirements:* For master's, one foreign language, thesis; for doctorate, 2 foreign languages, comprehensive exam, thesis/dissertation. *Entrance requirements:* For master's and doctorate, GRE General Test. Additional exam requirements/recommendations for international students: Required—TOEFL (minimum score 213 computer-based; 79 iBT). Electronic applications accepted. *Faculty research:* Cell biology, ecology, parasitology, immunology.

Wake Forest University, School of Medicine and Graduate School of Arts and Sciences, Graduate Programs in Medicine, Winston-Salem, NC 27109. Offers MS, PhD, MD/PhD. *Degree requirements:* For master's, thesis; for doctorate, thesis/dissertation. *Entrance requirements:* For master's and doctorate, GRE General Test. Additional exam requirements/recommendations for international students: Required—TOEFL. Electronic applications accepted. *Expenses:* Contact institution. *Faculty research:* Atherosclerosis, cardiovascular physiology, pharmacology, neuroanatomy, endocrinology.

Walla Walla University, Graduate School, Department of Biological Sciences, College Place, WA 99324-1198. Offers biology (MS). *Faculty:* 5 full-time (1 woman), 1 part-time/adjunct (0 women). *Students:* 10 full-time (5 women); includes 1 American Indian/Alaska Native, 1 Asian American or Pacific Islander. Average age 24. 9 applicants, 78% accepted, 6 enrolled. In 2009, 3 master's awarded. *Degree requirements:* For master's, thesis. *Entrance requirements:* For master's, GRE General Test, GRE Subject Test, minimum GPA of 2.75. Additional exam requirements/recommendations for international students: Required—TOEFL (minimum score 550 paper-based; 213 computer-based; 79 iBT). *Application deadline:* Applications are processed on a rolling basis. Application fee: $50. Electronic applications accepted. *Expenses:* Tuition: Full-time $19,929. *Financial support:* In 2009–10, 9 teaching assistantships with full tuition reimbursements (averaging $5,250 per year) were awarded; Federal Work-Study also available. Financial award application deadline: 4/1; financial award applicants required to submit FAFSA. *Faculty research:* Marine biology, plant development, neurobiology, animal physiology, behavior. *Unit head:* Dr. Robert A. Cushman, Chair, 509-527-2603, E-mail: bob.cushman@wallawalla.edu. *Application contact:* Dr. Joan Redd, Director of Graduate Program, 509-527-2482, E-mail: joan.redd@wallawalla.edu.

Washington State University, Graduate School, College of Sciences, School of Biological Sciences, Program in Biology, Pullman, WA 99164. Offers MS. *Faculty:* 33. *Students:* 2 full-time (1 woman), 1 (woman) part-time. 51 applicants, 8% accepted, 2 enrolled. *Degree requirements:* For master's, comprehensive exam (for some programs), thesis. *Entrance requirements:* For master's, GRE, three letters of recommendation, official transcripts from each university-level school attended. Additional exam requirements/recommendations for international students: Required—TOEFL, IELTS. *Application deadline:* For fall admission, 1/10 for domestic and international students; for spring admission, 7/1 for domestic and international students. Application fee: $50. *Financial support:* In 2009–10, 1 research assistantship with tuition reimbursement (averaging $13,917 per year), 1 teaching assistantship with tuition reimbursement (averaging $13,056 per year) were awarded. Financial award application deadline: 2/15. *Faculty research:* Inter–intra-cellular signaling in plant reproduction, biodiversity. *Unit head:* Dr. Gary Thorgaard, Director, 509-335-7438, Fax: 509-335-3184, E-mail: thorglab@wsu.edu. *Application contact:* Graduate School Admissions, 800-GRADWSU, Fax: 509-335-1949, E-mail: gradsch@wsu.edu.

Washington State University Tri-Cities, Graduate Programs, Program in Biology, Richland, WA 99354. Offers MS. *Faculty:* 17. *Students:* 1 (woman) part-time. *Degree requirements:* For master's, comprehensive exam (for some programs), thesis (for some programs), special project. *Entrance requirements:* For master's, GRE, minimum GPA of 3.0, 3 letters of recommendation. Additional exam requirements/recommendations for international students: Required—TOEFL. *Application deadline:* For fall admission, 1/10 priority date for domestic students, 1/10 for international students; for spring admission, 7/1 priority date for domestic students, 7/1 for international students. Application fee: $50. *Expenses:* Tuition, state resident: part-time $423 per credit. Tuition, nonresident: part-time $1032 per credit. *Financial support:* Application deadline: 4/1. *Unit head:* Dr. Kate McAteer, Director, 509-372-7371, E-mail: kmcateer@tricity.wsu.edu. *Application contact:* Bonnie Bates, Academic Coordinator, 509-372-7171, Fax: 509-335-1949, E-mail: bbates@tricity.wsu.edu.

Washington University in St. Louis, Graduate School of Arts and Sciences, Division of Biology and Biomedical Sciences, St. Louis, MO 63130-4899. Offers biochemistry (PhD); chemical biology (PhD); computational biology (PhD); developmental biology (PhD); evolution, ecology and population biology (PhD), including ecology, environmental biology, evolutionary biology, genetics; immunology (PhD); molecular biophysics (PhD); molecular cell biology (PhD); molecular genetics (PhD); molecular microbiology and microbial pathogenesis (PhD); neurosciences (PhD); plant biology (PhD); MD/PhD. *Degree requirements:* For doctorate, thesis/dissertation. *Entrance requirements:* For doctorate, GRE General Test, GRE Subject Test. Electronic applications accepted.

Wayne State University, College of Liberal Arts and Sciences, Department of Biological Sciences, Detroit, MI 48202. Offers biological sciences (MA, MS, PhD); molecular biotechnology (MS). Terminal master's awarded for partial completion of doctoral program. *Degree requirements:* For master's, thesis (for some programs); for doctorate, thesis/dissertation. *Entrance requirements:* For master's, GRE General Test, minimum GPA of 3.0; for doctorate, GRE General Test, GRE Subject Test, minimum GPA of 3.2. Additional exam requirements/recommendations for international students: Required—TOEFL; Recommended—TWE (minimum score 6). Electronic applications accepted. *Faculty research:* Cell and developmental biology, neurobiology, molecular biology and biotechnology, evolutionary biology, ecology.

Wesleyan University, Graduate Programs, Department of Biology, Middletown, CT 06459. Offers animal behavior (PhD); bioformatics/genomics (PhD); cell biology (PhD); developmental biology (PhD); evolution/ecology (PhD); genetics (PhD); neurobiology (PhD); population biology (PhD). *Faculty:* 13 full-time (4 women). *Students:* 23 full-time (11 women); includes 1 minority (African American), 3 international. Average age 26. 29 applicants, 10% accepted, 2 enrolled. In 2009, 3 doctorates awarded. *Degree requirements:* For doctorate, variable foreign language requirement, thesis/dissertation. *Entrance requirements:* For doctorate, GRE. Additional exam requirements/recommendations for international students: Required—TOEFL. *Application deadline:* For fall admission, 1/15 for domestic and international students. Applications are processed on a rolling basis. Application fee: $0. *Financial support:* In 2009–10, 3 research assistantships with full tuition reimbursements, 19 teaching assistantships with full tuition reimbursements were awarded; stipends also available. Financial award application deadline: 4/15; financial award applicants required to submit FAFSA. *Faculty research:* Microbial population genetics, genetic basis of evolutionary adaptation, genetic regulation of differentiation and pattern formation in *drosophila*. *Unit head:* Dr. Sonia E. Sultan, Chair/Professor, 860-685-3493, E-mail: jnaegele@wesleyan.edu. *Application contact:* Marjorie Fitzgibbons, Information Contact, 860-685-2140, E-mail: mfitzgibbons@wesleyan.edu.

West Chester University of Pennsylvania, Office of Graduate Studies, College of Arts and Sciences, Department of Biology, West Chester, PA 19383. Offers biology (MS, Teaching Certificate); biology—thesis (MS); biology–natural science (MS). Part-time and evening/weekend programs available. *Students:* 6 full-time (4 women), 30 part-time (17 women); includes 4 minority (1 African American, 2 Asian Americans or Pacific Islanders, 1 Hispanic American). Average age 29. 38 applicants, 92% accepted, 16 enrolled. In 2009, 9 master's awarded. *Degree requirements:* For master's, comprehensive exam, thesis (for some programs). *Entrance requirements:* For master's, 3 letters of reference. Additional exam requirements/recommendations for international students: Required—TOEFL (minimum score 550 paper-based; 213 computer-based; 80 iBT). *Application deadline:* For fall admission, 4/15 priority date for domestic students, 3/15 for international students; for spring admission, 10/15 for domestic students, 9/1 for international students. Applications are processed on a rolling basis. Application fee: $35. Electronic applications accepted. *Expenses:* Tuition, state resident: full-time $6666; part-time $370 per credit. Tuition, nonresident: full-time $10,666; part-time $593 per credit. Required fees: $122.56 per credit. *Financial support:* In 2009–10, 8 research assistantships with full and partial tuition reimbursements (averaging $5,000 per year) were awarded; unspecified assistantships also available. Support available to part-time students. Financial award application deadline: 2/15; financial award applicants required to submit FAFSA. *Faculty research:* Cell physiology of insect ovarian follicles, field inventory of reptiles and amphibians. *Unit head:* Dr. Jack Waber, Chair, 610-436-2319, E-mail: jwaber@wcupa.edu. *Application contact:* Dr. Judith Greenamyer, Graduate Coordinator, 610-436-1023, E-mail: jgreenamyer@wcupa.edu.

Western Carolina University, Graduate School, College of Arts and Sciences, Department of Biology, Cullowhee, NC 28723. Offers MS. Part-time and evening/weekend programs available. *Students:* 21 full-time (12 women), 7 part-time (4 women). Average age 27. 21 applicants, 71% accepted, 7 enrolled. In 2009, 4 master's awarded. *Degree requirements:* For master's, thesis. *Entrance requirements:* For master's, GRE General Test, appropriate undergraduate degree, 3 letters of recommendation. Additional exam requirements/recommendations for international students: Required—TOEFL (minimum score 550 paper-based; 270 computer-based; 79 iBT). *Application deadline:* For fall admission, 5/1 priority date for domestic students; for spring admission, 9/1 priority date for domestic students. Applications are processed on a rolling basis. Application fee: $45. *Financial support:* In 2009–10, 22 students received support, including 6 research assistantships with full and partial tuition reimbursements available (averaging $5,950 per year), 16 teaching assistantships with full and partial tuition reimbursements available (averaging $10,500 per year); fellowships, career-related internships or fieldwork, institutionally sponsored loans, scholarships/grants, and unspecified assistantships also available. Financial award application deadline: 3/31; financial award applicants required to submit FAFSA. *Faculty research:* Pathogen interactions, gene expression, plant community ecology, restoration ecology, ornithology, herpetology. *Unit head:* Dr. Malcolm Powell, Head, 828-227-7244, Fax: 828-227-7066, E-mail: mrpowell@email.wcu.edu. *Application contact:* Admission Specialist for Biology, 828-227-7398, Fax: 828-227-7480, E-mail: gradsch@email.wcu.edu.

Western Connecticut State University, Division of Graduate Studies, School of Arts and Sciences, Department of Biological and Environmental Sciences, Danbury, CT 06810-6885. Offers MA. Part-time programs available. *Faculty:* 3 full-time (1 woman), 1 part-time/adjunct (0 women). *Students:* 2 full-time (1 woman), 19 part-time (11 women); includes 2 minority (1 African American, 1 American Indian/Alaska Native). Average age 39. 15 applicants, 73% accepted, 10 enrolled. In 2009, 2 master's awarded. *Degree requirements:* For master's, comprehensive exam or thesis, completion of program in 6 years. *Entrance requirements:* For master's, minimum GPA of 2.5. Additional exam requirements/recommendations for international students: Recommended—TOEFL (minimum score 550 paper-based; 213 computer-based; 79 iBT), IELTS (minimum score 6). *Application deadline:* For fall admission, 8/5 priority date for domestic students; for spring admission, 1/5 priority date for domestic students. Applications are processed on a rolling basis. Application fee: $50. *Expenses:* Tuition, state resident: full-time $5012; part-time $278 per credit hour. Tuition, nonresident: full-time $13,962; part-time $284 per credit hour. Required fees: $3886; $139 per credit hour. Full-time tuition and fees vary according to course load and program. Part-time tuition and fees vary according to course level, degree level and program. *Financial support:* Application deadline: 5/1. *Unit head:* Dr. Richard Halliburton, Graduate Coordinator, 203-837-8233, Fax: 203-837-8525, E-mail: halliburtonr@wcsu.edu. *Application contact:* Chris Shankle, Associate Director of Graduate Studies, 203-837-9005, Fax: 203-837-8326, E-mail: shanklec@wcsu.edu.

Western Illinois University, School of Graduate Studies, College of Arts and Sciences, Department of Biological Sciences, Macomb, IL 61455-1390. Offers biological sciences (MS); environmental geographic information systems (Certificate); zoo and aquarium studies (Certificate). Part-time programs available. *Students:* 62 full-time (43 women), 28 part-time (17 women); includes 6 minority (2 African Americans, 2 Asian Americans or Pacific Islanders, 2 Hispanic Americans), 10 international. Average age 26. 53 applicants, 72% accepted. In 2009, 25 master's, 15 other advanced degrees awarded. *Degree requirements:* For master's, thesis or alternative. *Entrance requirements:* Additional exam requirements/recommendations for international students: Required—TOEFL (minimum score 550 paper-based; 213 computer-based; 80 iBT). *Application deadline:* Applications are processed on a rolling basis. Application fee: $30. Electronic applications accepted. *Expenses:* Tuition, state resident: full-time $4486; part-time $249.21 per credit hour. Tuition, nonresident: full-time $8972; part-time $498.42 per credit hour. Required fees: $72.62 per credit hour. *Financial support:* In 2009–10, 34 students received support, including 16 research assistantships with full tuition reimbursements available (averaging $7,280 per year), 18 teaching assistantships with full tuition reimbursements available (averaging $8,400 per year). Financial award applicants required to submit FAFSA. *Unit head:* Dr. Michael Romano, Chairperson, 309-298-1546. *Application contact:* Evelyn Hoing, Assistant Director of Graduate Studies, 309-298-1806, Fax: 309-298-2345, E-mail: grad-office@wiu.edu.

Western Kentucky University, Graduate Studies, Ogden College of Science and Engineering, Department of Biology, Bowling Green, KY 42101. Offers biology (MA Ed, MS). *Degree requirements:* For master's, comprehensive exam, thesis optional, research tool. *Entrance requirements:* For master's, GRE General Test, minimum GPA of 2.75. Additional exam requirements/recommendations for international students: Required—TOEFL (minimum score 555 paper-based; 213 computer-based; 79 iBT). *Expenses:* Tuition, state resident: full-time $4160; part-time $416 per credit hour. Tuition, nonresident: full-time $9550; part-time $506 per credit hour. Tuition and fees vary according to campus/location and reciprocity agreements. *Faculty research:* Phytoremediation, culturing of salt water organisms, PCR-based standards, biological monitoring (water) bioremediation, genetic diversity.

Western Michigan University, Graduate College, College of Arts and Sciences, Department of Biological Sciences, Kalamazoo, MI 49008. Offers MS, PhD. *Faculty:* 18 full-time (3 women). *Students:* 28 full-time (19 women), 20 part-time (8 women); includes 3 minority (1 African American, 1 Asian American or Pacific Islander, 1 Hispanic American), 9 international. 42 applicants, 64% accepted, 15 enrolled. In 2009, 6 master's awarded. *Degree requirements:* For master's, thesis, oral exam; for doctorate, thesis/dissertation, oral exam. *Entrance requirements:* For master's and doctorate, GRE General Test. *Application deadline:* For fall admission, 2/15 priority date for domestic students. Applications are processed on a rolling basis. Application fee: $25. *Financial support:* Fellowships, research assistantships, teaching assistantships, institutionally sponsored loans available. Financial award application deadline: 2/15; financial award applicants required to submit FAFSA. *Unit head:* Dr. David Cowan, Chair, 269-387-5600, Fax: 269-387-5609. *Application contact:* Admissions and Orientation, 269-387-2000, Fax: 269-387-2355.

Western Washington University, Graduate School, College of Sciences and Technology, Department of Biology, Bellingham, WA 98225-5996. Offers MS. Part-time programs available. *Degree requirements:* For master's, thesis. *Entrance requirements:* For master's, GRE General Test, GRE Subject Test (biology), minimum GPA of 3.0 in last 60 semester hours or last 90 quarter hours. Additional exam requirements/recommendations for international students: Required—TOEFL (minimum score 567 paper-based; 227 computer-based). Electronic applications accepted. *Faculty research:* Organismal biology, ecology and evolutionary biology, marine biology, cell and molecular biology, developmental biology, larval ecology, microzoo planton, symbiosis.

West Texas A&M University, College of Agriculture, Nursing, and Natural Sciences, Department of Life, Earth, and Environmental Sciences, Program in Biology, Canyon, TX 79016-0001. Offers MS. Part-time programs available. *Degree requirements:* For master's, comprehensive exam, thesis optional. *Entrance requirements:* For master's, GRE General Test. Additional exam requirements/recommendations for international students: Required—TOEFL (minimum score 550 paper-based). Electronic applications accepted. *Faculty research:* Aeroallergen concentration, scorpions, kangaroo mice, seed anatomy with light and scanning electron microscope.

West Virginia University, Eberly College of Arts and Sciences, Department of Biology, Morgantown, WV 26506. Offers cell and molecular biology (MS, PhD); environmental and evolutionary biology (MS, PhD); forensic biology (MS, PhD); genomic biology (MS, PhD); neurobiology (MS, PhD). Terminal master's awarded for partial completion of doctoral program. *Degree requirements:* For master's, thesis, final exam; for doctorate, thesis/dissertation, preliminary and final exams. *Entrance requirements:* For master's, GRE General Test, GRE Subject Test, minimum GPA of 3.0; for doctorate, GRE General Test, minimum GPA of 3.0. Additional exam requirements/recommendations for international students: Required—TOEFL. *Faculty research:* Environmental biology, genetic engineering, developmental biology, global change, biodiversity.

West Virginia University, School of Medicine, Graduate Programs at the Health Sciences Center, Morgantown, WV 26506. Offers MS, PhD, MD/PhD. Part-time and evening/weekend programs available. Postbaccalaureate distance learning degree programs offered (minimal on-campus study). *Expenses:* Contact institution.

Wichita State University, Graduate School, Fairmount College of Liberal Arts and Sciences, Department of Biological Sciences, Wichita, KS 67260. Offers MS. Part-time programs available. *Expenses:* Tuition, state resident: full-time $4247; part-time $235.95 per credit hour. Tuition, nonresident: full-time $11,171; part-time $620.60 per credit hour. Required fees: $34; $3.60 per credit hour. $17 per term. Tuition and fees vary according to campus/location and program. *Unit head:* Dr. William J Hendry, Chair, 316-978-3111, Fax: 316-978-3772, E-mail: william.hendry@wichita.edu. *Application contact:* Dr. William J Hendry, Chair, 316-978-3111, Fax: 316-978-3772, E-mail: william.hendry@wichita.edu.

See Close-Up on page 125.

Wilfrid Laurier University, Faculty of Graduate Studies, Faculty of Science, Department of Biology, Waterloo, ON N2L 3C5, Canada. Offers M Sc. *Degree requirements:* For master's, thesis optional. *Entrance requirements:* For master's, honours BA in last two years of undergraduate studies with a minimum B average. Additional exam requirements/recommendations for international students: Required—TOEFL (minimum score 230 computer-based; 89 iBT). Electronic applications accepted. *Faculty research:* Genetic/development, anatomy/physiology, ecology/environment, evolution.

William Paterson University of New Jersey, College of Science and Health, General Biology Program, Wayne, NJ 07470-8420. Offers MS. Part-time and evening/weekend programs available. *Degree requirements:* For master's, comprehensive exam, independent study or thesis. *Entrance requirements:* For master's, GRE General Test, minimum GPA of 2.75. *Application deadline:* Applications are processed on a rolling basis. Application fee: $50. Electronic applications accepted. *Financial support:* Research assistantships, career-related internships or fieldwork and unspecified assistantships available. Financial award application deadline: 4/1; financial award applicants required to submit FAFSA. *Unit head:* Dr. Robert Chesney, Program Director, 973-720-3455, E-mail: chesneyr@wpunj.edu. *Application contact:* Danielle Liautaud, Director, 973-720-3579, Fax: 973-720-2035, E-mail: liautaudd@wpunj.edu.

Winthrop University, College of Arts and Sciences, Department of Biology, Rock Hill, SC 29733. Offers MS. Part-time programs available. *Degree requirements:* For master's, thesis optional. *Entrance requirements:* For master's, GRE General Test. Electronic applications accepted. *Faculty research:* Anatomy of marsupials; oxygen consumption, respiratory quotient and mechanical efficiency; bioremediation with microbial mats; floristic survey.

Worcester Polytechnic Institute, Graduate Studies and Research, Department of Biology and Biotechnology, Worcester, MA 01609-2280. Offers biology and biotechnology (MS); biotechnology (PhD). *Faculty:* 7 full-time (3 women). *Students:* 17 full-time (13 women), 3 part-time (all women). 102 applicants, 8% accepted, 6 enrolled. In 2009, 4 master's awarded. Terminal master's awarded for partial completion of doctoral program. *Degree requirements:* For master's, thesis; for doctorate, comprehensive exam, thesis/dissertation, qualifying exam. *Entrance requirements:* For master's, GRE General Test, 3 letters of recommendation; for doctorate, GRE General Test, 3 letters of recommendation, statement of purpose. Additional exam requirements/recommendations for international students: Required—TOEFL (minimum score 550 paper-based; 213 computer-based; 79 iBT), IELTS (minimum score 6.5). *Application deadline:* For fall admission, 1/15 priority date for domestic and international students. Application fee: $70. Electronic applications accepted. *Financial support:* Teaching assistantships, career-related internships or fieldwork, institutionally sponsored loans, scholarships/grants, and unspecified assistantships available. *Faculty research:* Developmental/regenerative biology, plant cell biology/biotechnology, immunobiology/pathogenesis, molecular ecology/evolution, genetics, cell and molecular biology, bioprocess technology. *Unit head:* Dr. Eric Overstrom, Head, 508-831-5538, Fax: 508-831-5936, E-mail: ewo@wpi.edu. *Application contact:* Dr. Joseph Duffy, Graduate Coordinator, 508-831-5538, Fax: 508-831-5936, E-mail: jduffy@wpi.edu.

Wright State University, School of Graduate Studies, College of Science and Mathematics, Department of Biological Sciences, Dayton, OH 45435. Offers biological sciences (MS); environmental sciences (MS). *Degree requirements:* For master's, thesis optional. *Entrance requirements:* Additional exam requirements/recommendations for international students: Required—TOEFL.

Wright State University, School of Graduate Studies, College of Science and Mathematics and School of Medicine, Program in Biomedical Sciences, Dayton, OH 45435. Offers PhD. *Students:* 49 full-time, 4 part-time; includes 6 minority (2 African Americans, 4 Asian Americans or Pacific Islanders), 8 international. Average age 30. 59 applicants, 17% accepted, 10 enrolled. In 2009, 3 doctorates awarded. *Degree requirements:* For doctorate, thesis/dissertation. *Entrance requirements:* For doctorate, GRE General Test. Additional exam requirements/recommendations for international students: Required—TOEFL. *Application deadline:* For fall admission, 3/1 for domestic and international students. Application fee: $25. *Financial support:* Fellowships, Federal Work-Study, institutionally sponsored loans, unspecified assistantships, and full tuition waivers are awarded to all successful applicants, research assistantships through program or faculty grants available. Financial award applicants required to submit FAFSA. *Unit head:* Dr. Gerald M. Alter, Director, 937-775-2504, Fax: 937-775-3485, E-mail: gerald.alter@wright.edu. *Application contact:* Dr. Gerald M. Alter, Director, 937-775-2504, Fax: 937-775-3485, E-mail: gerald.alter@wright.edu.

Yale University, School of Medicine and Graduate School of Arts and Sciences, Combined Program in Biological and Biomedical Sciences (BBS), New Haven, CT 06520. Offers PhD, MD/PhD. *Faculty:* 290 full-time. *Students:* 93 full-time. 891 applicants, 27% accepted, 93 enrolled. *Degree requirements:* For doctorate, thesis/dissertation. *Entrance requirements:* For doctorate, GRE General Test. Additional exam requirements/recommendations for international students: Required—TOEFL. *Application deadline:* For fall admission, 12/6 for domestic and international students. Application fee: $95. Electronic applications accepted. *Expenses:* Contact institution. *Financial support:* In 2009–10, fellowships with full tuition reimbursements (averaging $29,600 per year), research assistantships with full tuition reimbursements (averaging $29,600 per year), teaching assistantships with full tuition reimbursements (averaging $29,600 per year) were awarded. *Unit head:* Dr. Lynn Cooley, Director, 203-785-5067, E-mail: bbs@yale.edu. *Application contact:* Bonnie Ellis, Student Services Officer, 203-785-5663, Fax: 203-785-3734, E-mail: bbs@yale.edu.

York University, Faculty of Graduate Studies, Faculty of Science and Engineering, Program in Biology, Toronto, ON M3J 1P3, Canada. Offers M Sc, PhD. Part-time and evening/weekend programs available. *Degree requirements:* For master's, thesis or alternative; for doctorate, comprehensive exam, thesis/dissertation, preliminary exam. Electronic applications accepted.

Youngstown State University, Graduate School, College of Science, Technology, Engineering and Mathematics, Department of Biological Sciences, Youngstown, OH 44555-0001. Offers environmental biology (MS); molecular biology, microbiology, and genetic (MS); physiology and anatomy (MS). Part-time programs available. *Degree requirements:* For master's, comprehensive exam, thesis, oral review. *Entrance requirements:* For master's, GRE General Test, minimum GPA of 2.7. Additional exam requirements/recommendations for international students: Required—TOEFL. *Faculty research:* Cell biology, neurophysiology, molecular biology, neurobiology, gene regulation.

BOSTON COLLEGE

Biology Department

Programs of Study	The Department offers a program of study leading to a Ph.D. degree in biology. Basic areas of study include biochemistry, cellular and developmental biology, genetics, cell cycle, vector biology, neurobiology, bioinformatics, and structural biology.
	The Ph.D. degree provides an in-depth training experience. Core course work is provided in cell biology, biochemistry, molecular biology, and genetics. Advanced electives are available in all areas of faculty expertise. Seminar courses provide students with ongoing training in critical thinking and oral presentation of scientific data. Research experience is provided by working in close cooperation with faculty members, postdoctoral fellows, and senior students in a collaborative, supportive environment. In cooperation with the School of Education, the Master of Science in Teaching (M.S.T.) degree in biology is also offered.
Research Facilities	The Biology Department, with a wing that opened in 2000, occupies more than 30,000 square feet of research space in Higgins Hall. Faculty laboratories have state-of-the-art equipment. Shared facilities include several tissue-culture rooms; common equipment rooms; TEM, fluorescence, and confocal microscopes; X-ray diffraction and a capillary DNA sequencer; machine and electronic workshops; and state-of-the-art computers for online data analysis, production of publication-quality figures, and bioinformatic research and analysis. The university science library subscribes to more than 600 scientific journals. Access to libraries of institutions in the greater Boston area is available through consortium arrangements.
Financial Aid	Graduate assistantships (teaching and research based) are available with full tuition remission. Stipends are $27,000 per calendar year.
Cost of Study	For the 2010–11 academic year, tuition and fees for a full-time student are $1206 per credit, 100 percent of which is covered by tuition remission for students receiving financial aid.
Living and Housing Costs	The Housing Office provides an extensive list of off-campus housing options, including off-campus graduate housing. Most graduate students rent rooms or apartments near Chestnut Hill; many biology students share apartments with other students in the program. Average monthly expenses (rent, food, utilities) for the academic year (nine months) are $2105 for students.
Student Group	The enrollment at Boston College is 14,500, including 4,200 students enrolled in the various graduate schools. There are 53 graduate students in the Ph.D. program. The graduate students are geographically and ethnically diverse.
Location	Boston College is located in the Chestnut Hill section of Newton, an attractive residential area about 5 miles from the heart of Boston, with easy access to the city by public transportation. The Boston area, with its numerous educational and biomedical research institutions, offers countless outstanding seminars, lectures, colloquia, and concerts throughout the year. A wide variety of cultural and recreational opportunities can be found close to the campus.
The College	Founded in Massachusetts in 1863, Boston College currently includes the Graduate School of Arts and Sciences and graduate schools of law, social work, management, nursing, and education. Its expanding campus is graced with many attractive Gothic buildings. Boston College has a strong tradition of academic excellence and service to the community.
Applying	Preference is given to completed applications received prior to January 1. Admission is granted on the basis of academic background and demonstrated aptitude in biology and related disciplines. A year of organic chemistry, physics, and mathematics and a solid background in biology are highly recommended for admission. Scores on the Graduate Record Examinations General Test and the Subject Test in biology are required.
Correspondence and Information	Professor Charles Hoffman Director, Graduate Program Biology Department Higgins Hall Boston College Chestnut Hill, Massachusetts 02467-3961 Phone: 617-552-3540 E-mail: gradbio@bc.edu Web site: http://www.bc.edu/biology

Boston College

THE GRADUATE RESEARCH FACULTY

Anthony T. Annunziato, Professor; Ph.D., Massachusetts Amherst, 1979. Biochemistry/molecular biology; DNA replication and nucleosome assembly in mammalian cells.

David R. Burgess, Professor; Ph.D., California, Davis, 1974. Spatial and temporal regulation of cytokinesis; role of the actin- and microtubule-based cytoskeletons in early development.

Hugh P. Cam, Assistant Professor; Ph.D., Harvard 2003. Epigenetic control of higher-order genome organization and chromatin structures.

Thomas C. Chiles, Professor and Chairman of Biology; Ph.D., Florida, 1988. Cell biology, signal transduction; cell-cycle control, gene regulation in mature B lymphocytes.

Jeffrey Chuang, Assistant Professor; Ph.D., MIT, 2001. Computational approaches to comparative genomics, gene regulation, and molecular evolution.

Peter G. Clote, Professor; Ph.D., Duke, 1979. Algorithms and mathematical modeling in computational biology: genomic motif detection, protein folding on lattice models, RNA secondary structure, functional genomics via gene expression profile.

Kathleen Dunn, Associate Professor; Ph.D., North Carolina at Chapel Hill, 1982. Plant molecular biology; cloning and characterization of genes induced during alfalfa nodulation.

Marc-Jan Gubbels, Assistant Professor; Ph.D., Utrecht (Netherlands), 2000. Genetics and cell biology of the apicomplexan parasite *Toxoplasma gondii.*

Laura E. Hake, Associate Professor; Ph.D., Tufts, 1992. Molecular control of early development in *Xenopus;* protein degradation; RNA-protein interactions; translational regulation during gametogenesis.

Charles Hoffman, Professor; Ph.D., Tufts, 1986. Signal transduction and transcriptional regulation in fission yeast; analysis of PKA and MAPK signal pathways in nutrient monitoring.

Daniel Kirschner, Professor; Ph.D., Harvard, 1972. Structural biochemistry of amyloids and myelin sheath; neurodegenerative diseases; peripheral demyelinating neuropathies.

Gabor T. Marth, Assistant Professor; D.Sc., Washington (St. Louis), 1994. DNA polymorphism discovery and analysis; genomic and algorithmic approaches to population genetics; long-term human demography, haplotype structure, and medical genetics.

Michelle Meyer, Assistant Professor; Ph.D., Caltech, 2006. Bioinformatic discovery and experimental characterization of RNA-based gene regulatory mechanisms.

Junona Moroianu, Associate Professor; Ph.D., Rockefeller, 1996. Cell biology; molecular mechanisms of nucleocytoplasmic transport of cellular and viral macromolecules in mammalian cells.

Marc A. T. Muskavitch, Professor and DeLuca Chair; Ph.D., Stanford, 1981. Developmental biology: intercellular signaling and cell-fate specification in *Drosophila;* host-parasite interactions in *Anopheles.*

Clare M. O'Connor, Associate Professor and Associate Chair; Ph.D., Purdue, 1977. Cellular biochemistry.

Thomas N. Seyfried, Professor; Ph.D., Illinois, 1976. Neurogenetics: use of genetics and neurochemistry in neural membrane function and developmental neurobiology.

Kenneth C. Williams, Associate Professor; Ph.D., McGill, 1993. Central nervous system macrophages; neuroAIDS; AIDS pathogenesis; monocyte/macrophage biology.

Higgins Hall, home of the Biology Department.

BOWLING GREEN STATE UNIVERSITY

Department of Biological Sciences

Programs of Study

The Department of Biological Sciences at Bowling Green State University offers graduate training for professional careers in both applied and fundamental areas of biology. Programs are available leading to the degrees of Doctor of Philosophy, Master of Science, and Master of Arts in Teaching. Major areas of specialization include ecology and conservation biology, genetics, microbiology, biochemistry and molecular biology, neuroscience and behavior, and plant science. The research interests of the individual faculty members are listed in the Faculty section of this document.

Completion of the Ph.D. program, which consists of formal and informal course work as well as dissertation research, usually takes four years after completion of the master's degree or five years after the completion of the Bachelor of Science degree. Master's programs, with both thesis and nonthesis options, take about two years to complete. The degree plan is selected by the student with the assistance of a faculty adviser and advisory committee; the program of study is flexible to allow students to pursue their individual professional goals. In addition, graduate students are expected to gain teaching experience as assistants in laboratory and lecture courses.

The Department of Biological Sciences also offers interdisciplinary research programs. Members of the Department interact with faculty members in the Departments of Chemistry, Geology, and Psychology in forming cooperative programs to meet the specialized needs and goals of graduate students.

Research Facilities

The Department of Biological Sciences is housed in the Life Sciences Building, a modern five-story, 120,000-square-foot research and teaching complex. The forty laboratories housed in the building are equipped with state-of-the-art instrumentation. Included are scanning and transmission electron microscopes, X-ray analyzers, ultracentrifuges, scanning and dual-beam spectrophotometers, PCR machines, high-performance liquid chromatography equipment, gamma and liquid scintillation counters, environmental control chambers, darkrooms, cold rooms, biochemistry and tissue-culture labs, and a biohazard work area. Other Departmental facilities include 80-acre and 100-acre forest preserves; a greenhouse complex with areas for the propagation and breeding of temperate, tropical, subtropical, and desert plants; and a herbarium containing more than 20,000 specimens. A 9,000-square-foot animal facility has thirty breeding and maintenance rooms and a P3 area.

Financial Aid

Graduate assistantship and fellowship stipends range from $10,075 to $15,231 (plus $2519 to $3808 for the summer) plus a waiver of tuition and general fees ($26,214 in state and $37,265 out of state, including the summer) for a half-time appointment during 2010–11.

Predoctoral nonservice fellowships are available to Ph.D. students, normally during the last year of study. These awards provide a stipend ($19,039 for 2010–11) and a waiver of instructional, nonresident, and general fees.

Renewal of assistantships and fellowships is contingent upon satisfactory completion of assignments and progress toward the degree. Research assistantships are also available through research grants to individual faculty members.

Cost of Study

Tuition and general fees in 2010–11 are $26,214 for Ohio residents and $37,625 for nonresidents and include the summer. Book costs are estimated at $1100 per year.

Living and Housing Costs

The University provides on-campus housing for a small number of graduate students at Founders Hall. However, there are numerous apartments and rooms for rent near the campus at costs comparable to those in other Midwestern cities of similar size.

Student Group

There were 101 graduate students (46 pursuing master's degrees and 55 pursuing Ph.D. degrees) in the Department of Biological Sciences for 2009–10. A diverse group, they were nearly equally divided between men and women and included representatives of a dozen or more states and several countries. The majority of the Department's students receive some form of financial aid from the University.

The University enrolls 21,000 students, including more than 3,000 graduate students.

Student Outcomes

Recent Ph.D. recipients have accepted postdoctoral positions at academic institutions, including Harvard, University of California at Berkeley, University of Michigan, and Yale; or have accepted positions in government, at institutions such as the Centers for Disease Control and the Environmental Protection Agency; or have accepted positions in industry. Recent master's degree recipients have gone to graduate or medical schools, such as Ohio State, Purdue, Tufts, and University of Michigan; or have accepted positions in industry with such companies as Amgen and Wyeth Laboratories.

Location

Bowling Green is a northwestern Ohio community of approximately 29,600 residents. It is located 16 miles south of Toledo; Detroit, Cleveland, and Columbus are all within a 100-mile radius. The community offers numerous recreational and social programs that supplement the activities offered by the University.

The University

Bowling Green, a state-assisted university, was founded in 1910. The attractive campus occupies 1,250 acres and has more than 100 buildings. The atmosphere is friendly, open, and reasonably informal. Graduate faculty members in the Department of Biological Sciences and throughout the University are committed to excellence in both research and teaching.

Applying

Requirements for admission include a baccalaureate degree, normally with a major in one of the sciences; GRE scores on the verbal, quantitative, and analytical portions of the General Test; favorable grade point averages in all subjects and in the major; a short research statement including a list of up to 3 faculty members who have similar research interests; and three letters of recommendation.

Applicants can apply online at https://www.applyweb.com/apply/bgsug. Applicants should correspond directly with faculty members in their areas of interest as soon as possible. Applicants are most competitive for admission and funding if complete applications are submitted by February 1. Bowling Green State University is an Equal Opportunity/Affirmative Action employer. Women and members of minorities are encouraged to apply.

Correspondence and Information

Graduate Committee Chair
Department of Biological Sciences
Bowling Green State University
Bowling Green, Ohio 43403-0212
Fax: 419-372-2024
E-mail: kvroot@bgsu.edu
Web site: http://www.bgsu.edu/departments/biology/

Bowling Green State University

THE FACULTY AND THEIR RESEARCH

Gabriela Bidart-Bouzart, Assistant Professor; Ph.D., Illinois at Urbana-Champaign. Evolutionary ecology; plant-herbivore interactions; ecology of plant defenses; ecological genomics.

Juan L. Bouzat, Associate Professor; Ph.D., Illinois at Urbana-Champaign. Molecular ecology; conservation and population genetics; molecular evolution.

George S. Bullerjahn, Professor; Ph.D., Virginia. Microbial physiology; regulation of stress-induced functions in cyanobacteria.

Sheryl L. Coombs, Professor; Ph.D., Hawaii. Mechanosensory processing by auditory and lateral line systems of aquatic vertebrates; neuroethology.

Carmen F. Fioravanti, Professor; Ph.D., UCLA. Comparative biochemistry; anaerobic energetics of the parasitic helminths; mitochondrial transhydrogenase systems; electron transport mechanisms and isoprene biosynthesis.

Michael E. Geusz, Associate Professor; Ph.D., Vanderbilt. Circadian rhythms in mammalian and molluscan neurons and control of intracellular calcium.

Carol A. Heckman, Professor and Director of Electron Microscopy Center; Ph.D., Massachusetts Amherst. Cell biology; role of ruffling in growth control; image analysis; molecular biology of transforming proteins.

Robert Huber, Professor; Ph.D., Texas Tech. Neurochemistry of aggression.

Roudabeh J. Jamasbi, Professor; Ph.D., Arkansas. Biology and immunology of digestive and respiratory tract carcinomas; generation of monoclonal antibodies against carcinomas.

Ray A. Larsen, Associate Professor; Ph.D., Montana. Bacterial membrane energetics.

R. Michael McKay, Professor; Ph.D., McGill. Aquatic microbial ecology; photoplankton-trace metal interactions; inorganic carbon acquisition and assimilation; phycotoxins.

Lee A. Meserve, Distinguished Teaching Professor; Ph.D., Rutgers. Mammalian endocrinology; altered thyroid status in development and aging.

Helen Michaels, Associate Professor; Ph.D., Illinois at Urbana-Champaign. Molecular evolution; chloroplast DNA and angiosperm phylogeny; evolution and ecology of plant mating systems; ecological genetics; molecular systematics; plant ecology.

Jeffrey G. Miner, Associate Professor; Ph.D., Ohio State. Aquatic community ecology; abiotic effects on predator-prey interactions; ecology of fishes.

Paul A. Moore, Professor; Ph.D., Boston University. Marine chemical ecology; sensory ecology; physiology and behavior of marine and aquatic organisms.

Paul F. Morris, Associate Professor; Ph.D., Queen's at Kingston. Molecular plant-microbe interactions; regulation of chemoattraction in *Phytophthora* sp.

Vipaporn Phuntumart, Assistant Professor; Ph.D., Fribourg (Switzerland). Molecular biology of plant-pathogen interactions.

Scott O. Rogers, Professor and Chair; Ph.D., Washington (Seattle). Molecular biology, evolution, introns; ancient DNA, DNA preservation, biotechnology; ancient ice, plants, microbes.

Karen V. Root, Associate Professor and Graduate Coordinator; Ph.D., Florida Tech. Conservation biology and population ecology.

Karen L. Sirum, Assistant Professor; Ph.D., Dartmouth. Biology education research and development; inquiry-based learning strategies.

Eileen M. Underwood, Associate Professor; Ph.D., Indiana. Developmental and molecular genetics of oogenesis and early embryogenesis of *Drosophila;* maternal-effect mutations.

Moira J. van Staaden, Associate Professor; Ph.D., Texas Tech. Ethology and evolution.

Daniel D. Wiegmann, Associate Professor; Ph.D., Wisconsin–Madison. Behavioral ecology; reproductive biology of fishes; animal decision making.

Ronny C. Woodruff, Distinguished Research Professor; Ph.D., Utah State. Mutagenesis and genetics of transposable DNA elements in *Drosophila;* genetics of natural populations; role of mutation in molecular evolution.

Zhaohui Xu, Assistant Professor; Ph.D., Huazhong Agricultural (China). Bacterial genetics and biotechnology; environmental microbiology.

Weidong Yang, Assistant Professor; Ph.D., Fudan (China). Single-molecule imaging and tracking; nucleocytoplasmic transport; cell cycle and nanotechnology.

Jill Zeilstra-Ryalls, Professor; Ph.D., Purdue. Gene regulation and protein structure-function relationships.

CALIFORNIA INSTITUTE OF TECHNOLOGY

Division of Biology

Program of Study	There are two principal research foci in the Division of Biology at Caltech.

The goals of research in molecular, cellular, and developmental biology and genetics are to understand the molecular mechanisms that regulate cellular proliferation, communication, and function and the mechanisms of differentiation and pattern formation that form the diverse and functionally integrated cell types in multicellular organisms. This area includes the development of the many different cell types and connections found in the nervous system.

Research in integrative neurobiology involves the analysis of the interactions of collections of neurons in behavior, both in simple insect nervous systems and in the more complex vertebrate systems. Integrative neurobiology is closely associated with computational analysis and modeling as carried out in the Computation and Neural Systems Option.

Emphasis in graduate study is on individual research under the guidance of faculty members. Normally, research is initiated during the first year of graduate study by three periods of rotation, each approximately one quarter in duration, in three different research laboratories. By the end of the first year, students will have chosen a laboratory for their thesis work. Course requirements are minimal and are limited to those that contribute to the major program of the student. Major work may be pursued in any of the seven areas: biophysics and cell biology, developmental biology, genetics, immunology, integrative neurobiology, molecular biology and biochemistry, and molecular and cellular neurobiology. Any one of these majors may be combined with biotechnology as part of a dual major. Students are admitted only for study toward the Ph.D. degree. Five to seven years are usually needed to complete the Ph.D. requirements.

Research Facilities

Caltech's Division of Biology includes the Kerckhoff, Alles, Church, Beckman, and Braun laboratories of biology; the Beckman Institute; Broad Center; and the Kerckhoff Marine Laboratory at Corona del Mar. All equipment pertinent to modern biology is available to graduate students. A complete and modern biology library is housed along with the related chemistry library in the nine-story Robert Andrews Millikan Memorial Library.

Financial Aid

Students admitted to graduate standing in biology are provided with financial support adequate to meet their normal expenses. They receive a full tuition grant and, in addition, an NIH traineeship, a fellowship, a part-time teaching assistantship, or a research assistantship. The annual stipend for 2009–10 was $28,548. There are job opportunities for spouses in the Pasadena area. Loan programs are available.

Cost of Study

Tuition costs are covered by grants, as are the fees required for participation in the health program. Funds are provided for research expenses and travel to scientific meetings.

Living and Housing Costs

A single student, or a married student whose spouse has a job, can live simply but comfortably on his or her graduate student income. University housing is available for all entering graduate students. Caltech is an informal place, and clothing costs can be kept low.

Student Group

The Division of Biology has, at any one time, approximately 90 graduate students and approximately 150 postdoctoral fellows, in addition to the 39 professors of biology. About 45 percent of the graduate students are women.

Student Outcomes

Most of the Division's graduates pursue postdoctoral research prior to joining university faculties as assistant professors. Recent examples include postdoctoral positions with the MIT Center for Genome Research and the University of California, San Francisco and a faculty position at Yonsei University in Korea.

Location

Caltech is situated in Pasadena, a city of approximately 125,000 people about 15 miles from the center of downtown Los Angeles. It is located midway between the mountains (for skiing in the winter and mountain climbing in the summer) and the sea (for swimming, surfing, and boating). Caltech offers extensive opportunities for those interested in swimming, tennis, track, and all related recreational activities. Caltech's relationship with the surrounding community is harmonious and peaceful.

The Institute

Caltech, including its Division of Biology, is an uncommon institution by virtue of its small size (about 900 undergraduate students, 1,100 graduate students, and 275 professors), its high quality, and its leadership in scientific education and research. The Division of Biology is young, having been founded in 1928, and has been able to adapt to changing circumstances in the ensuing years. Both Caltech and the Division of Biology have remarkable histories of continued important contributions in scientific research and scholarship.

Applying

To apply for admission, the applicant should write to the Dean of Graduate Studies stating an intention to apply for graduate study in biology. Application forms and related information will be mailed. There is an application fee of $80. Additional information about the research and training programs of the Division of Biology should be obtained by writing to the graduate secretary of the Division of Biology.

Applicants are normally expected to meet the following minimal requirements: mathematics through calculus and elementary differential equations; at least one year of college physics; chemistry, including organic chemistry; and elementary biology. Applications are particularly encouraged from students who have had additional course work in basic sciences and biology equivalent to the undergraduate biology option at Caltech and who have demonstrated laboratory ability and research motivation in undergraduate research projects or employment. Students may be admitted on the basis of advanced course work in psychology or other relevant subjects in lieu of some of the basic science courses normally required.

Students are usually admitted either at the beginning of the academic year in the fall or at the beginning of the summer term, July 1. Completed application materials should be received by January 1; early submission is recommended to allow ample time for a visit to the campus. Scores on the General Test of the Graduate Record Examinations should be submitted, and, if possible, the test should be taken by the November date preceding application.

Correspondence and Information

For research and training information:
Graduate Secretary
Division of Biology 156-29
California Institute of Technology
Pasadena, California 91125
Phone: 626-395-4497

For application information:
Dean of Graduate Studies 02-31
California Institute of Technology
Pasadena, California 91125

California Institute of Technology

THE FACULTY AND THEIR RESEARCH

Cellular Biology and Biophysics

Raymond J. Deshaies. Mechanisms and regulation of cell-cycle progression.
William Dunphy. Regulation of mitosis-promoting factor and the cell cycle.
Michael Elowitz. In vivo modeling: a synthetic approach to regulatory networks.
Scott E. Fraser. Developmental neurobiology; optical methods.
Alexander J. Varshavsky. Mechanics, functions, and applications of intracellular proteolysis; the ubiquitin system and the N-end rule pathway.

Molecular Biology, Biochemistry, Developmental Biology, Genetics, and Immunology

Alexei A. Aravin. Small RNAs and regulation of gene expression.
David Baltimore. Immunology and molecular biology.
Pamela J. Bjorkman. Crystal structures of cell-surface proteins involved in the immune response.
Marianne Bronner. Analysis of neural crest cell migration and differentiation in the developing nervous system using embryological, cell biological, and molecular approaches.
Judith L. Campbell. Regulation of DNA replication in the yeast cell cycle: genetic and biochemical analysis.
David C. Chan. Biochemical and structural analysis of Fzo protein.
Eric H. Davidson. Molecular biology of early development; regulation of lineage-specific gene activation in sea urchin embryos; control of gene expression in eukaryotes; DNA sequence organization and its evolution.
Bruce Hay. Molecular mechanisms of _Drosophila_ development; genetics; signal transduction; cell death.
Grant Jensen. Study of structure of large protein complexes and their arrangement within living cells by cryoelectron microscopy.
Stephen L. Mayo. Protein design; protein structure/stability correlations; protein NMR.
Sarkis Mazmanian. Mechanisms of host-bacterial symbiosis during health and disease.
Elliot M. Meyerowitz. Genetics of plant development.
Ellen Rothenberg. Development of lymphocytes; changes in gene expression during T-cell maturation; lymphocyte activation pathways.
Angelike Stathopoulos. Gene regulatory network controlling gastrulation in _Drosophila;_ control of gene expression; mechanisms of signal transduction.
Paul Sternberg. Molecular genetics of nematode development, behavior, and evolution; signal transduction; tumor suppressor genes.
Barbara Wold. Molecular genetic studies of the structure, function, and regulation of mammalian cell-surface receptors.

Neurobiology

Ralph Adolphs. Psychological and neurological investigations of human emotion and social cognition.
John M. Allman. Physiological basis of perception; organization and evolution of the primate visual system.
Richard A. Andersen. Cortical neurophysiology, visuospatial perception, and visual-motor integration.
David J. Anderson. Cell fate determination in vertebrate neurogenesis.
Michael Dickinson. Neurobiology, aerodynamic abilities, and behavior of flies; striving to build a true robotic fly.
Mary B. Kennedy. Molecular mechanisms of central nervous system synaptic plasticity.
Christof Koch. Biophysics; computational neuroscience; computational vision.
Masakazu Konishi. Neuroethology; behavioral, neurophysiological, and neuroanatomical studies of avian auditory and vocal systems.
Gilles Laurent. Olfactory and mechanosensory processing in insects; synaptic transmission in the avian brain.
Henry A. Lester. Chemical transmission at synapses and within cells; gating of membrane channels; molecular approaches.
Paul H. Patterson. Regulation of neuronal phenotype by cytokines; interactions between the nervous and immune systems; mapping of position in the mammalian nervous system.
David A. Prober. Zebrafish as a genetic model for sleep and sleep disorders.
Erin Schuman. Mechanisms of synaptic modification; role of NO as a retrograde second messenger.
Shinsuke Shimojo. Visual psychophysics and behavioral studies of sensory-motor functions.
Athanassios Siapas. Learning and memory formation across distributed networks of neurons; multitetrode electrophysiological recordings from freely behaving rodents.
Doris Y. Tsao. Dissecting the neural machinery for face processing in the macaque monkey.
Kai Zinn. Molecular genetic studies of insect nervous system development; signal transduction in vertebrate olfaction.

CITY OF HOPE NATIONAL MEDICAL CENTER/BECKMAN RESEARCH INSTITUTE

Irell & Manella Graduate School of Biological Sciences

Programs of Study	The mission of the City of Hope Graduate School of Biological Sciences is to train students to be outstanding research scientists in chemical, molecular, and cellular biology. Graduates of this program are awarded the degree of Doctor of Philosophy in biological sciences and are equipped to address fundamental questions in the life sciences and biomedicine for careers in academia, industry, and government. The time spent in the program is devoted to full-time study and research. During the first year, the student completes the core curriculum and three laboratory rotations (ten to twelve weeks each). The core curriculum contains biochemistry, molecular biology, cell biology, and biostatistics/bioinformatics. One Advanced Topics course is taken during spring of the first year. After the first year, the student prepares and orally defends a research proposal based on an original topic not related to previous work conducted by the student, and in the second year, students prepare and defend a research proposal based on their actual thesis topic. An additional Advanced Topics course is required after the first year and students are required to take a literature-based journal club every year after the first year. Students also participate in workshops on scientific communication and on the responsible conduct of research. After successfully completing the core curriculum and research proposal, students concentrate the majority of their time on their individual dissertation laboratory research project. The written thesis/dissertation must be presented by the student for examination by 4 members of the City of Hope staff and 1 qualified member from an outside institution.
Research Facilities	City of Hope is a premier medical center, one of forty National Cancer Institute–designated Comprehensive Cancer Centers. Its Beckman Research Institute launched the biotech industry by creating the first human recombinant gene products, insulin and growth hormone, which are now used by millions of people worldwide. State-of-the-art facilities include mass spectrometry, NMR, molecular modeling, cell sorting, DNA sequencing, molecular pathology, scanning and transmission electron microscopy, confocal microscopy, and molecular imaging. The Lee Graff Medical and Scientific Library allows access to the latest biomedical information via its journal and book collection, document delivery, interlibrary loans, and searches of online databases.
Financial Aid	All students in the Graduate School receive a fellowship of $30,000 per year as well as paid health and dental insurance.
Cost of Study	There are no tuition charges. A student services fee of $50 per semester ($150 per year) is the student's only financial obligation to City of Hope.
Living and Housing Costs	The School has limited, low-cost housing available. Living in student housing provides easy access to campus resources and a connection to the vibrant campus community. Additional housing is available within the immediate area at an average cost of $700 to $1000 per month.
Student Group	The Graduate School faculty consists of 82 of City of Hope's investigators. Eighty-one graduate students are working toward the Ph.D. degree in biological sciences in 2010–11.
Student Outcomes	Graduates have gone on to work as postdoctoral fellows at California Institute of Technology; Harvard University; Scripps Research Institute; Stanford University; University of California, Los Angeles; University of California, San Diego; University of California, Irvine; University of Missouri; University of Southern California; and Washington University in St. Louis. Graduates have also found positions with Wyeth-Ayerst Research; Allergan, Inc.; and the U.S. Biodefense and its subsidiary, Stem Cell Research Institute of California, Inc.
Location	City of Hope is located 25 miles northeast of downtown Los Angeles, minutes away from Pasadena and close to beaches, mountains, and many recreational and cultural activities.
The Medical Center and The Institute	City of Hope was founded in 1913, initially as a tuberculosis sanatorium. Research programs were initiated in 1951, and, in 1983, the Beckman Research Institute of City of Hope was established with support from the Arnold and Mabel Beckman Foundation. The Institute comprises basic science research groups within the Divisions of Biology, Immunology, Molecular Medicine, and Neurosciences, among others.
Applying	The deadline for application is January 1 for classes starting in August. Applying early is advisable. Candidates must submit transcripts, three letters of recommendation, and take the Graduate Record Examination (General Test required, Subject Test recommended). For further information and an application, students should contact the School at the address listed in this description.
Correspondence and Information	City of Hope Irell & Manuella Graduate School of Biological Sciences 1500 East Duarte Road Duarte, California 91010 Phone: 877-715-GRAD or 626-256-4673 Ext. 63899 Fax: 626-301-8105 E-mail: gradschool@coh.org Web site: http://www.cityofhope.org/gradschool

City of Hope National Medical Center/Beckman Research Institute

THE FACULTY AND THEIR RESEARCH

Professors

David K. Ann, Ph.D. Molecular mechanisms of maintaining genomic integrity.
Michael E. Barish, Ph.D. Imaging studies of neural progenitor and brain tumor cells.
Ravi Bhatia, M.D. Regulation of normal and malignant hematopoietic stem cell growth.
Edouard M. Cantin, Ph.D. Herpes simplex virus infections in the nervous system.
Saswati Chatterjee, Ph.D. Adeno-associated virus vector for stem-cell gene therapy.
Shiuan Chen, Ph.D. Hormones and cancer.
Yuan Chen, Ph.D., NMR spectroscopy as a tool to study biological structure.
Don J. Diamond, Ph.D. Translational research in cancer vaccines.
Richard W. Ermel, D.V.M., Ph.D. Applied animal research.
Barry Marc Forman. M.D., Ph.D. Gene regulation and drug discovery endocrinology of orphan nuclear receptors.
David Horne, Ph.D. Developing natural products as novel anticancer agents.
Richard Jove, Ph.D. Development of molecular targeted therapeutics.
Susan E. Kane, Ph.D. Drug resistance and cancer.
Theodore G. Krontiris, M.D., Ph.D. Genetic risk and disease.
Ren-Jang Lin, Ph.D. Structure and mechanisms of RNA splicing.
Chih-Pin Liu, Ph.D. Immune regulation of autoimmune disease and tumor.
Marcia M. Miller, Ph.D. Molecular immunogenetics.
Rama Natarajan, Ph.D. Diabetic vascular complications.
Susan Neuhausen, Ph.D. Genetic epidemiology of complex diseases.
Timothy R. O'Connor, Ph.D. DNA repair.
Gerd P. Pfeifer, Ph.D. Molecular mechanisms of cancer.
Arthur D. Riggs, Ph.D. Epigenetics, chromatin structure, and X chromosome inactivation.
John J. Rossi, Ph.D. The biology and applications of small RNAs.
Paul M. Salvaterra, Ph.D. Modeling Alzheimer-type neurogeneration.
Binghui Shen, Ph.D. DNA replication and repair nucleases in genome stability, cancers, and HIV life cycle.
John E. Shively, Ph.D. Structure, function, and regulation of carcinoembryonic antigen genes.
Judith Singer-Sam, Ph.D. Epigenetics and disorders of the CNS.
Steven S. Smith, Ph.D. Cancer epigenetics.
John Termini, Ph.D. Mutagenesis and carcinogenesis.
Nagarajan Vaidehi, Ph.D. Targeting G protein-coupled receptors for cancer therapy.
Jeffrey N. Weitzel, M.D. Genetic predisposition to cancer.
Jiing-Kuan Yee, Ph.D. Vectors for gene therapy.
Yun Yen, M.D., Ph.D. Novel molecular-targeted cancer therapies.
Hua Yu, Ph.D. Stat 3 and the tumor microenvironment.
John A. Zaia, M.D. Genetic and other anti-HIV therapy.

Associate and Assistant Professors

Karen S. Aboody, M.D. Neural stem cells and cancer.
Adam M. Bailis, Ph.D. Genome instability associated with aging and radiation exposure.
Wen Yong Chen, Ph.D. Epigenetics, cancer, and aging.
Warren Chow, M.D., FACP. Cell signaling and cancer.
Fong-Fong Chu, Ph.D. Role of oxidative stress in inflammatory bowel disease and cancer.
Carlotta A. Glackin, Ph.D. Understanding gene regulation from stem cells.
Wendong Huang, Ph.D. Metabolic regulation, cancer, and aging.
Janice Huss, Ph.D. Role of orphan nuclear receptors in cardiac and skeletal muscle biology.
Kazuo Ikeda, Ph.D. Synaptic transmission mechanisms.
Keiichi Itakura, Ph.D. Functions of Mrf-1 and Mrf-2.
Linda Iverson, Ph.D. Stem cells and cancer.
Jeremy Jones, Ph.D. The androgen receptor in human disease.
Markus Kalkum, Dr. rer. nat. (Ph.D.) Biodefense and emerging infectious diseases.
Mei Kong, Ph.D. Signal transduction and cancer metabolism.
Marcin Kortylewski, Ph.D. Immune cells as targets for cancer therapy.
Hsun Teresa Ku, Ph.D. Pancreatic endocrine stem cells.
Ya-Huei Kuo, Ph.D. Hematopoietic stem cell and leukemia research.
Terry D. Lee, Ph.D. Mass spectrometry of biomolecules.
Qiang Lu, Ph.D. Mechanisms that control self-renewal and differentiation of neural progenitor stem cells.
Takahiro Maeda, M.D., Ph.D. Hematological malignancies.
Edward M. Newman, Ph.D. Biochemical pharmacology of antimetabolites.
Yanhong Shi, Ph.D. Nuclear receptors in neural stem cells and adult neurogenesis.
Jeremy M. Stark, Ph.D. Pathways of chromosome break repair in mammalian cells.
Zuoming Sun, Ph.D. Signaling mechanisms that guide T cells.
Timothy W. Synold, Pharm.D. Pharmacokinetics and biomarkers of cancer.
Piroska E. Szabó, Ph.D. Mechanisms of genomic imprinting.
Toshifumi Tomoda, M.D., Ph.D. Neuronal development and degeneration.
Shizhen Emily Wang, Ph.D. Outsmarting breast cancer.
John C. Williams, Ph.D. Application of multivalency for basic science and translational medicine.
Defu Zeng, M.D. Transplantation immune tolerance.

COLD SPRING HARBOR LABORATORY

Watson School of Biological Sciences

Program of Study	The Watson School of Biological Sciences at Cold Spring Harbor Laboratory (CSHL) offers an accredited graduate training program, which leads to the Ph.D. degree, to a select group of self-motivated students of outstanding ability and intellect. The curriculum takes advantage of the unique and flexible environment of CSHL and includes the following innovative features: approximately four years from matriculation to Ph.D. degree award, broad representation of the biological sciences, a first year with course work and laboratory rotations in separate phases, emphasis on the principles of scientific reasoning and logic, continued advanced course instruction throughout the graduate curriculum, and two-tier mentoring.
	The program provides an exciting and intensive educational experience. The curriculum is designed to train self-reliant students who, under their own guidance, can acquire and assimilate the knowledge that their research or career demands require. The course work is varied, involving core courses, focused topic courses, and CSHL postgraduate courses.
	The current fields of research expertise of CSHL faculty members are behavior, bioinformatics, cellular and molecular biology, cell-cycle regulation, computational and molecular neurobiology, developmental biology, electrophysiology, genetics, genomics, imaging, plant genetics, protein chemistry, structural biology, and virology. The laboratories of all CSHL research faculty members are available to students in the program.
	Requirements for the award of the Ph.D. degree are successful completion of all course work, laboratory rotations, teaching (at the Laboratory's Dolan DNA Learning Center), the Ph.D. qualifying exam, thesis research and postdoctoral proposals, and defense of a written thesis that describes original research. The program aims to train future leaders in the biological sciences.
Research Facilities	Cold Spring Harbor Laboratory has state-of-the-art facilities for research in bioinformatics; cancer; genetics; neuroscience; and molecular, cellular, plant, and structural biology. As a National Cancer Institute–designated Cancer Center, there is an extensive set of shared resources. There are several libraries and one archive on campus. Library services, such as database searching and reference and interlibrary loan services, are available. An information technology department provides campuswide support of computing.
Financial Aid	The Watson School of Biological Sciences supports each student with an annual stipend, health benefits, affordable housing, subsidized food, and funds for tuition and research costs. To enhance their careers, students are encouraged to seek independent funding through predoctoral fellowships from federal and private sources such as the National Science Foundation.
Cost of Study	The Watson School of Biological Sciences provides full remission of all tuition fees for all accepted students. The School also supports the stipend and research costs of each student for four years.
Living and Housing Costs	The Laboratory provides affordable housing to all graduate students through a network of on-site and off-site housing. Single graduate students are offered single rooms in shared houses with house-cleaning services; married students are housed in apartments. First-year students of the Watson School are offered housing in the Townsend Knight House, a renovated house from 1810 that is located on the shore of Cold Spring Harbor opposite the Laboratory.
Student Group	The class size is approximately 10 to 15 students per year. Over the years students have come to the School from the United States, Italy, Poland, Singapore, China, England, Germany, Argentina, Mexico, Australia, Canada, India, France, and Russia. The School aims to produce graduates in the biological sciences who are likely to become ethical world leaders in science and society.
Location	The Laboratory is located on the wooded north shore of Long Island, 35 miles east of Manhattan in New York City, and offers many amenities, both cultural and recreational. Recreational activities at CSHL include a fitness room, tennis and volleyball courts, a private beach, sailboats, and many quiet back roads for running or walking. Students may also attend classical music performances and art exhibitions sponsored by the Laboratory for scientists and the neighboring community.
The Laboratory	Since its inception in 1890, CSHL has been involved in higher education and is today a world leader in biology education. The CSHL Press publishes internationally recognized books and journals. The Dolan DNA Learning Center educates students and teachers about the world of DNA. The Undergraduate Research Program, started in 1959, hosts exceptional undergraduates from around the world for a summer research experience. CSHL is also involved in education at the highest levels through a postgraduate program of twenty-five advanced courses in biology and many large and small international conferences. These meetings and courses attract 8,000 scientists annually to the Laboratory. The Laboratory has also been involved in graduate education leading to the Ph.D. degree for more than twenty-five years, particularly through shared graduate programs with Stony Brook University.
Applying	Applicants must have received a baccalaureate degree from an accredited university or college prior to matriculation. Admission is based on the perceived ability of the applicant to excel in this doctoral program, without regard to gender, race, color, ethnic origin, sexual orientation, disability, or marital status. Suitable applicants are assessed on the basis of their academic record, recommendations from their mentors, and an on-site interview. Students should ensure that the school receives all application materials (transcripts, examination scores, letters of recommendation, etc.) no later than December 1 for the following fall term. Early application is advisable. All applicants must apply online. Further information about the School and the application procedure may be requested by mail or obtained from the Web site at http://www.cshl.edu/gradschool.
Correspondence and Information	Dawn M. Pologruto Director of Admissions and Student Affairs Watson School of Biological Sciences Cold Spring Harbor Laboratory One Bungtown Road Cold Spring Harbor, New York 11724 Phone: 516-367-6911 Fax: 516-367-6919 E-mail: gradschool@cshl.edu Web site: http://www.cshl.edu/gradschool

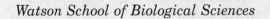 www.twitter.com/usgradschools

Cold Spring Harbor Laboratory

THE FACULTY AND THEIR RESEARCH

Research Faculty

Gurinder Singh Atwal, Assistant Professor; Ph.D., Cornell, 2002. Population genetics; bioinformatics; cancer; stochastic processes; statistical mechanics and information theory.

Anne Churchland, Assistant Professor; Ph.D., California, San Francisco, 2003. Behavior in awake animals; neuroscience and electrophysiology.

Josh Dubnau, Assistant Professor; Ph.D., Columbia, 1995. Learning; memory; genetics; behavior.

Mikala Egeblad, Assistant Professor, Ph.D., Copenhagen, 2000. Tumor microenvironment; intravital imaging; tumor-associated myeloid cells; breast cancer.

Grigori Enikolopov, Associate Professor; Ph.D., Russian Academy of Sciences (Moscow), 1978. Signal transduction in neurons; development; gene expression; nitric oxide.

Hiro Furukawa, Assistant Professor; Ph.D., Tokyo, 2001. Structural biology; neurodegenerative diseases; intramembrane proteolysis; ion channels; membrane proteins; X-ray crystallography.

Thomas Gingeras, Professor; Ph.D., NYU, 1976. Organization and regulation of eukaryotic transcription; classification and function of non–protein coding RNAs.

Chris Hammell, Assistant Professor; Ph.D., Dartmouth, 2002. MicroRNA-mediated gene regulation of *C. elegans* developmental timing; genetics; development.

Gregory Hannon, Professor; Ph.D., Case Western Reserve, 1992. Growth control in mammalian cells.

Z. Josh Huang, Professor; Ph.D., Brandeis, 1994. Neuroscience; experience-dependent development and plasticity of the neocortex; mouse genetics.

David Jackson, Professor; Ph.D., East Anglia (England), 1991. Plant development; genetics; cell-to-cell mRNA and protein trafficking.

Leemor Joshua-Tor, Professor and Dean; Ph.D., Weizmann (Israel), 1991. Structural biology; X-ray crystallography; molecular recognition; transcription; proteases.

Adam Kepecs, Assistant Professor; Ph.D., Brandeis, 2002. Decision-making; neural circuits; behavioral electrophysiology; theoretical neuroscience; neuroeconomics.

Alexei Koulakov, Associate Professor; Ph.D., Minnesota, 1998. Theoretical neurobiology; quantitative principles of cortical design.

Adrian R. Krainer, Professor; Ph.D., Harvard, 1986. Posttranscriptional regulation of gene expression; pre-mRNA splicing mechanisms; alternative splicing; RNA-protein interactions; cell-free systems.

Alexander Krasnitz, Assistant Professor; Ph.D., Tel Aviv University, 1990. High-level analysis of microarray-derived data in cancer biology; bioinformatics.

Yuri Lazebnik, Professor; Ph.D., St. Petersburg State, 1986. Apoptosis; caspases; cancer chemotherapy; proteases.

Bo Li, Assistant Professor; Ph.D., British Columbia, 2003. Neuroscience; glutamatergic synapse; synaptic plasticity; schizophrenia; depression; rodent models of psychiatric disorders.

Zachary Lippman, Assistant Professor; Ph.D., Watson School of Biological Sciences at Cold Spring Harbor Laboratory, 2004. Plant development; genetics; flowering; inflorescence architecture; sympodial growth, phase transition, heterosis; quantitative genetics.

Scott Lowe, Professor; Ph.D., MIT, 1994. Modulation of apoptosis, chemosensitivity, and senescence by oncogenes and tumor-suppressor genes.

Robert Lucito, Assistant Professor; Ph.D., NYU, 1993. Genomic analysis of cancer.

Robert Martienssen, Professor; Ph.D., Cambridge, 1986. Plant genetics; transposons; development; gene regulation; DNA methylation.

W. Richard McCombie, Professor; Ph.D., Michigan, 1982. Genome structure; DNA sequencing; computational molecular biology; Human Genome Project.

Alea A. Mills, Associate Professor; Ph.D., California, Irvine, 1997. Functional genomics; tumorigenesis; development.

Partha P. Mitra, Professor; Ph.D., Harvard, 1993. Neuroinformatics; theoretical engineering; animal communications; neural prostheses; brain imaging; developmental linguistics.

Pavel Osten, Associate Professor; M.D., Charles University (Prague), 1991; Ph.D., SUNY Downstate Medical Center, 1995. Neurobiology of autism and schizophrenia; gene expression-based mapping of brain activity; anatomical mapping of brain connectivity; high throughput microscopy.

Darryl J. Pappin, Associate Professor; Ph.D., Leeds (United Kingdom), 1984. Proteomics; mass spectrometry; protein chemistry.

Scott Powers, Associate Professor; Ph.D., Columbia, 1983. Cancer gene discovery; cancer diagnostics and therapeutics; cancer biology.

Michael C. Schatz, Assistant Professor; Ph.D., Maryland, College Park. DNA sequence data concentrating on the alignment and assembly of short reads; bioinformatics.

Stephen Shea, Assistant Professor; Ph.D., Chicago, 2004. Olfaction; audition; communication behaviors; *in vivo* electrophysiology; individual recognition.

Raffaella Sordella, Assistant Professor; Ph.D., Turin, 1998. Molecular therapeutics; signal transduction.

David L. Spector, Professor; Ph.D., Rutgers, 1980. Cell biology; nuclear structure; microscopy; pre-mRNA splicing.

Arne Stenlund, Associate Professor; Ph.D., Uppsala (Sweden), 1984. Papillomavirus; cancer; DNA replication.

Bruce Stillman, President and CEO; Ph.D., Australian National, 1979. DNA replication; chromatin assembly; biochemistry; yeast genetics; cancer; cell cycle.

Marja Timmermans, Associate Professor; Ph.D., Rutgers, 1996. Plant development; axis specification; homeobox genes; stem cell function.

Nicholas Tonks, Professor; Ph.D., Dundee (Scotland), 1985. Posttranslational modification; phosphorylation; phosphatases; signal transduction; protein structure and function.

Lloyd Trotman, Assistant Professor; Ph.D., Zurich, 2001. Molecular mechanisms of tumor suppression; cancer modeling and treatment; molecular cancer visualization; PTEN regulation.

Glenn Turner, Assistant Professor; Ph.D., Caltech, 2000. Neural coding; learning and memory; sensory processing; *Drosophila;* electrophysiology.

Linda Van Aelst, Professor; Ph.D., Leuven (Belgium), 1991. Signal transduction; Ras and Rac proteins; tumorigenesis; metastasis.

Doreen Ware, Assistant Professor; Ph.D., Ohio State, 2000. Computational biology; comparative genomics; genome evolution; diversity; gene regulation; plant biology.

Michael Wigler, Professor; Ph.D., Columbia, 1978. Cancer; genomics; oncogenes; signal transduction; Ras; yeast genetics.

Anthony Zador, Professor; M.D./Ph.D., Yale, 1994. Computational neuroscience; synaptic plasticity; auditory processing; cortical circuitry.

Hongwu Zheng, Assistant Professor; Ph.D., Boston University, 2003. Cellular renewal and differentiation in stem cells and glioma genesis; cancer development; stem cells.

Yi Zhong, Professor; Ph.D., Iowa, 1991. Neurophysiology; *Drosophila;* learning and memory; neurofibromatosis; signal transduction.

Non-Research Faculty

Alexander A. F. Gann, Editorial Director, Cold Spring Harbor Laboratory Press; Ph.D., Edinburgh, 1989.

Terri Grodzicker, Dean, Academic Affairs; Ph.D., Columbia, 1969.

John R. Inglis, Executive Director, Cold Spring Harbor Laboratory Press; Ph.D., Edinburgh, 1976.

David A. Micklos, Executive Director, DNA Learning Center; M.A., Maryland, 1982.

David J. Stewart, Director, Meetings and Courses; Ph.D., Cambridge, 1988.

Jan A. Witkowski, Executive Director, Banbury Center; Ph.D., London, 1972.

COLUMBIA UNIVERSITY

Graduate School of Arts and Sciences
Department of Biological Sciences

Program of Study	The Department offers training leading to a Ph.D. in cellular, molecular, developmental, computational, and structural biology as well as genetics, molecular biophysics, and neurobiology. The graduate program provides each student with a solid background in contemporary biology and an in-depth knowledge of one or more of the above areas. The specific nature and scheduling of courses taken during the first two graduate years are determined by the student's consultation with the graduate student adviser, taking into account the background and specific research interests of the student. During the first year, all students take an intensive core course that provides a solid background in structural biology, cell biology, genetics, molecular biology, and bioinformatics.

Beginning in the first year, graduate students attend advanced seminar courses, including the preresearch seminar, which is a forum for faculty-student research discussion. Important components of graduate education include the ability to analyze critically the contemporary research literature and to present such analyses effectively through oral and written presentations. Students acquire training in these skills through participation in advanced-level seminars and journal clubs, as well as through presentation and defense of original research proposals during the second year of graduate study.

Beginning in the first year of graduate work, students also engage in research training. Students may choose laboratories in the Department of Biological Sciences on Columbia's main Morningside Heights Campus or in about twenty-five other laboratories, including many at Columbia's Health Sciences Campus. To inform incoming students of research opportunities, faculty members discuss ongoing research projects with them in the preresearch seminar held in the autumn term of the first year. All students are required to participate in ongoing research in up to three different laboratories during the first year. The choice of a dissertation sponsor is made after consultation between the student and potential faculty advisers, and intensive research begins following the spring term of the student's first year. Each student is assigned a Ph.D. Advisory Committee made up of the student's sponsor and 2 other faculty members.

Research Facilities	The Department of Biological Sciences is located in the Sherman Fairchild Center for the Life Sciences. The building provides nearly 60,000 square feet of laboratory space for the Department's laboratories, as well as extensive shared instrument facilities, including extensive sophisticated microscopy, X-ray diffraction, fluorescence-activated cell sorting (FACS), real-time PCR analysis, mass spectrometry, infrared scanning, phosphorimaging, and microinjection, as well as housing and care of research animals, including transgenic mice.
Financial Aid	All accepted students receive generous stipends, complete tuition exemption, and medical insurance. Special fellowships with larger stipends are also available (e.g., to members of minority groups).
Cost of Study	Tuition and fees are paid for all graduate students accepted into the Department.
Living and Housing Costs	Most students live in University-owned, subsidized apartments or dormitories within easy walking distance of the laboratories. In addition, both the Morningside and Health Sciences Campuses are easily reached by public transportation from all areas of the city.
Student Group	There are about 110 graduate students and 60 postdoctoral fellows in the Department.
Location	New York is the cultural center of the country and offers unrivaled opportunities for attending concerts, operas, plays, and sporting events, for visiting outstanding museums, and for varied, affordable dining. Many excellent beaches, ski slopes, and state and national parks are within reasonable driving distance.
The University and The Department	Columbia was established as King's College in 1754 and has grown into one of the major universities of the world. The Department is located on the beautiful main campus in Morningside Heights, which combines the advantages of an urban setting and a peaceful college-town atmosphere.
Applying	Undergraduate training in one of the natural or physical sciences is recommended, although successful students have come from computer science or engineering backgrounds, as well. It is desirable for students to have had at least one year of calculus, as well as courses in organic and physical chemistry, physics, genetics, biochemistry, and cell biology. Any deficiencies may be made up while in graduate school. The Graduate Record Examinations (GRE) is required, as is the Test of English as a Foreign Language (TOEFL) for international applicants whose native language is not English and who do not hold an undergraduate degree from a U.S. college. The GRE Subject Test in biology, biochemistry, chemistry, computer science, or physics is highly recommended. Completed applications should be returned by December 1 for admission to the fall semester. Application forms and additional information can be obtained from the Department's Web site.

Columbia University is an Equal Opportunity/Affirmative Action institution.

Correspondence and Information	Graduate Student Adviser Department of Biological Sciences Columbia University 1212 Amsterdam Avenue, Mail Code 2402 Sherman Fairchild Center, Room 600 New York, New York 10027

Phone: 212-854-2313
Fax: 212-865-8246
E-mail: biology@columbia.edu
Web site: http://www.columbia.edu/cu/biology/

Columbia University

THE FACULTY AND THEIR RESEARCH

Walter J. Bock, Professor; Ph.D., Harvard, 1959. General evolutionary theory; evolutionary and functional morphology; morphology and classification of birds; history and philosophy of evolutionary biology.

J. Chloë Bulinski, Professor; Ph.D., Wisconsin, 1980. Dynamics and functions of microtubules during myogenic differentiation and cell-cycle progression.

Harmen Bussemaker, Associate Professor; Ph.D., Utrecht (Netherlands), 1995. Data-driven modeling of transcriptional and posttranscriptional networks based on biophysical principles.

Martin Chalfie, Professor; Ph.D., Harvard, 1977; Member, National Academy of Sciences and Nobel Laureate in Chemistry 2008. Developmental genetics of identified nerve cells in *Caenorhabditis elegans;* genetic analysis of cell differentiation, mechanosensory transduction, synapse specification, and aging.

Lawrence A. Chasin, Professor; Ph.D., MIT, 1967. Pre-mRNA splicing in cultured mammalian cells.

Julio Fernandez, Professor; Ph.D., Berkeley, 1982. Study of the cellular events that lead to the release of histamine or catecholamine-containing secretory granules from single, isolated mast cells or chromaffin cells; analysis of single-protein elasticity by atomic force microscopy (AFM).

Stuart Firestein, Professor; Ph.D., Berkeley, 1988. Cellular and molecular physiology of transduction; coding and neuronal regeneration in the vertebrate olfactory system.

Joachim Frank, Professor and Howard Hughes Medical Institute Investigator; Ph.D., Munich Technical, 1970; Member, National Academy of Sciences. Cryoelectron microscopy and three-dimensional reconstruction for the study of the mechanism of protein biosynthesis.

John F. Hunt, Associate Professor; Ph.D., Yale, 1993. Structural genomics and biophysical studies of the molecular mechanism of transmembrane transport.

Songtao Jia, Assistant Professor; Ph.D., UCLA, 2003. Epigenetic regulation of the genome.

Daniel D. Kalderon, Professor; Ph.D., London, 1984. Molecular mechanisms of cellular interactions mediated by cAMP-dependent protein kinase (PKA) in *Drosophila;* roles of PKA in hedgehog signaling and in generating anterior/posterior polarity in oocytes.

Darcy B. Kelley, Professor and Howard Hughes Medical Institute Professor; Ph.D., Rockefeller, 1975. Sexual differentiation of the nervous system; molecular analyses of androgen-regulated development in neurons and muscle; neuroethology of vocal communication; evolution of the nuclear receptor family.

James L. Manley, Professor; Ph.D., SUNY at Stony Brook, 1976. Regulation of mRNA synthesis in animal cells; biochemical and genetic analysis of mechanisms and control of mRNA transcription, splicing, and polyadenylation; developmental control of gene expression.

Elizabeth Miller, Assistant Professor; Ph.D., La Trobe (Australia), 1999. Protein folding, assembly, and the regulation of intracellular protein transport.

Dana Pe'er, Assistant Professor; Ph.D., Hebrew (Israel), 2003. Function and organization of molecular networks.

Robert E. Pollack, Professor; Ph.D., Brandeis, 1966. Critical analysis of issues involving molecular biology and religion.

Carol L. Prives, Professor; Ph.D., McGill, 1968; Member, National Academy of Sciences and National Institute of Medicine. Structure and function of the p53 tumor suppressor protein and p53 family members; studies on cell cycle and apoptosis; stress-activated signaling and control of proteolysis.

Ron Prywes, Professor; Ph.D., MIT, 1984. Normal and cancerous mechanisms of regulation of cellular proliferation and gene expression; signal transduction and activation of transcription factors; activation of transcription by the ER stress/unfolded protein response.

Michael P. Sheetz, Professor; Ph.D., Caltech, 1972. Motility studies of cells and microtubule motor proteins, with an emphasis on the force-dependent interactions relevant to transformed cells and neuron pathfinding, using laser tweezers.

Brent Stockwell, Associate Professor and Howard Hughes Medical Institute Investigator; Ph.D., Harvard, 1997. Diagramming disease networks with chemical and biological tools.

Liang Tong, Professor; Ph.D., Berkeley, 1989. Structural biology of proteins involved in human diseases (obesity, diabetes, cancer); structural biology of proteins involved in pre-mRNA 3'-end processing.

Alexander A. Tzagoloff, Professor of Biological Sciences; Ph.D., Columbia, 1962. Energy-coupling mechanisms; structure of membrane enzymes; biogenesis of mitochondria; genetics of mitochondria in yeast.

Jian Yang, Professor; Ph.D., Washington (Seattle), 1991. Structure and function of ion channels; molecular mechanisms of ion channel regulation and localization.

Rafael Yuste, Professor and Howard Hughes Medical Institute Investigator; M.D., Madrid, 1987; Ph.D., Rockefeller, 1992. Development and function of the cortical microcircuitry.

Additional Faculty Sponsors for Ph.D. Research

Richard Axel, Biochemistry and Molecular Biophysics/Pathology and Cell Biology; Howard Hughes Medical Institute Investigator and Nobel Laureate in Physiology or Medicine 2004; Member, National Academy of Sciences. Central and peripheral organization of the olfactory system.

Andrea Califano, Biomedical Informatics. Study of gene regulatory and signaling networks in mammalian cellular contexts using computational methods.

Virginia Cornish, Chemistry. Development of in vivo selection strategies for evolving proteins with novel catalytic properties.

Jean Gautier, Genetics and Development/Institute for Cancer Genetics. Cell cycle and cell death during early development.

Eric C. Greene, Biochemistry and Molecular Biophysics; Howard Hughes Medical Institute Investigator. Molecular mechanisms of DNA recombination and repair; single-molecule fluorescence microscopy and other biochemical approaches.

Lloyd Greene, Pathology and Cell Biology. Mechanisms of neuronal differentiation and degeneration and their regulation by external growth factors.

Iva Greenwald, Biochemistry and Molecular Biophysics; Howard Hughes Medical Institute Investigator; Member, National Academy of Sciences. Development and cell-cell interactions.

Tulle Hazelrigg, Biological Sciences. mRNA localization in *Drosophila* oocytes.

René Hen, Pharmacology. Serotonin receptors and behavior.

Wayne Hendrickson, Biochemistry and Molecular Biophysics; Howard Hughes Medical Institute Investigator; Member, National Academy of Sciences. Macromolecular structure; X-ray crystallography.

Oliver Hobert, Biochemistry and Molecular Biophysics; Howard Hughes Medical Institute Investigator. Nervous system development and function.

Thomas Jessell, Biochemistry and Molecular Biophysics; Howard Hughes Medical Institute Investigator; Member, National Academy of Sciences. Molecular mechanisms of neural differentiation.

Laura Johnston, Genetics and Development. Control of growth and cell division during development.

Eric Kandel, Physiology and Cellular Biophysics/Psychiatry/Biochemistry and Molecular Biophysics; Howard Hughes Medical Institute Investigator and Nobel Laureate in Physiology or Medicine 2000; Member, National Academy of Sciences. Cell and molecular mechanisms of associative and nonassociative learning.

Arthur Karlin, Biochemistry and Molecular Biophysics/Physiology and Cellular Biophysics/Center for Molecular Recognition; Member, National Academy of Sciences. Molecular mechanisms of receptor function.

Richard Mann, Biochemistry and Molecular Biophysics. Transcriptional control.

Ann McDermott, Chemistry/Biological Sciences/Chemical Engineering; Member, National Academy of Sciences. Solid-state NMR of enzyme active sites and model systems.

Arthur G. Palmer, Biochemistry and Molecular Biophysics. Biomolecular dynamics, structure, and function; NMR spectroscopy.

Virginia Papaioannou, Genetics and Development. Genetic control of mammalian development in the peri-implantation period.

Rodney Rothstein, Genetics and Development. Yeast genetics; mechanisms of genetic recombination; control of genome stability; functional genomics.

Christian Schindler, Microbiology/Medicine. JAK-STAT signaling and immune response.

Steve Siegelbaum, Pharmacology; Howard Hughes Medical Institute Investigator. Molecular studies of ion channel structure and function; synaptic transmission and plasticity in the mammalian brain.

Gary Struhl, Genetics and Development; Howard Hughes Medical Institute Investigator; Member, National Academy of Sciences. Developmental genetics in *Drosophila.*

Lorraine Symington, Microbiology. Homologous recombination in the yeast *Saccharomyces cerevisiae.*

Richard Vallee, Pathology and Cell Biology. Motor proteins in axonal transport, brain developmental disease, and synaptic function.

DARTMOUTH COLLEGE

Department of Biological Sciences
Graduate Program in Ecology and Evolutionary Biology
Graduate Program in Molecular and Cellular Biology

Programs of Study

The Department of Biological Sciences at Dartmouth College offers two graduate programs leading to the Ph.D. degree: the Graduate Program in Ecology and Evolutionary Biology and the Graduate Program in Molecular and Cellular Biology. Each program emphasizes independent research to prepare students for careers in academic institutions, government agencies, and industry. Five years are usually required for completion of course work and research leading to the Ph.D. In addition to offering two graduate programs, the Department also participates in the M.D./Ph.D. program, based in the Dartmouth Medical School. Many scientists located in other departments in the College as well as in the Dartmouth Medical School and in the Thayer School of Engineering interact with members of the Department of Biological Sciences, contribute to graduate teaching, and are available for consultation on graduate student research.

Faculty members and students in the Graduate Program in Ecology and Evolutionary Biology conduct basic and applied research on topics in population, community, and ecosystem ecology pertaining to aquatic and terrestrial systems. Dartmouth's location provides easy access to a great variety of natural habitats, including several extensive College-owned areas. Entering students begin thesis research in a lab of their choice and take a series of courses chosen in consultation with members of their advisory committee.

The Graduate Program in Molecular and Cellular Biology is offered in conjunction with faculty members from the Departments of Biochemistry, Chemistry, Genetics, and Microbiology and Immunology. Research by biology faculty members emphasizes model systems, with various labs pursuing studies in development (*C. elegans, Drosophila,* and *Arabidopsis*), circadian rhythms and plant nutrition (*Arabidopsis*), organelle assembly (yeast), cell motility, and the cytoskeleton (squid and sea urchins). During the first year, students attend a comprehensive two-quarter course in biochemistry and cell and molecular biology. A series of three 1-term research rotations in individual faculty members' labs trains students in research techniques and allows students to select a thesis adviser from among the program faculty members by the end of their first year.

Research Facilities

The Department occupies the Charles Gilman Life Sciences Laboratory, which is connected to the Dartmouth Medical School and Dana Biomedical Library, as well as Centerra Bio Labs in nearby Lebanon, New Hampshire. Facilities permit study at all levels of organization and include a rooftop greenhouse and controlled environment chambers. Specialized instrumentation is housed in the Rippel Electron Microscope Facility, the Robert D. Allen Video Light Microscopy Facility, and the Molecular Genetics Center (with DNA and peptide synthesis and sequencing capabilities).

Financial Aid

Research and teaching assistantships, plus federal fellowships and traineeships, provide support for most students. In 2010–11, stipends for students in the Graduate Program in Ecology and Evolutionary Biology are $23,832 for twelve months. In addition, the Department covers the cost of health insurance. For students in the Graduate Program in Molecular and Cellular Biology, stipends are $26,000 for twelve months, plus health insurance coverage.

Cost of Study

Tuition ($53,304 for the 2010–11 academic year) is paid for all graduate students by the various fellowship and assistantship awards.

Living and Housing Costs

The College assists graduate students in arranging for appropriate housing, either in College facilities or in privately owned accommodations in the Hanover area. College-owned apartments are available at various rents for married graduate students.

Student Group

There are approximately 40 students in Ph.D. programs who are working in labs in the Department of Biological Sciences. In addition, there are approximately 100 Ph.D. students in the Graduate Program in Molecular and Cellular Biology who are working in other departments. Nearly one quarter of the students are married; about one half are women.

Location

Located midway between Boston and Montreal, Hanover is the quintessential New England college town, situated in the Connecticut River Valley, which forms the border between New Hampshire and Vermont. The College supports much of the nonacademic life of the area, operating major film, music, and drama programs throughout the year, a large number of hiking trails and cabins, and facilities for cross-country and downhill skiing. It also provides the usual athletic opportunities through its swimming pools, gymnasiums, tennis courts, skating rink, and other facilities.

The College

Dartmouth College was founded as a liberal arts college in 1769 but has had students in professional degree programs since its medical school opened in 1797. Its present undergraduate population numbers 4,100. The three professional schools (medicine, engineering, and business administration) enroll approximately 800 additional students. Approximately 500 men and women are now enrolled in the arts and sciences graduate division. The smallest of the Ivy League institutions, Dartmouth has a long-standing tradition of close student-faculty ties.

Applying

Applicants should be prepared in biology, chemistry, physics, and mathematics, although some deficiencies can be made up during the first year of graduate study. Applications are encouraged from women and men of diverse backgrounds.

Applications for admission to the Graduate Program in Molecular and Cellular Biology and the Graduate Program in Ecology and Evolutionary Biology should be received by December 1 for admission in September. All applicants must submit scores from the General Test of the Graduate Record Examinations (GRE). If possible, applicants to the ecology program should submit scores from the Subject Test in biology.

It is the long-standing policy of Dartmouth College to actively support equality of opportunity for all persons regardless of race or ethnic background. No student will be denied admission or be otherwise discriminated against because of race, color, sex, religion, handicap, or national or ethnic origin.

For more information, students should visit the Department's Web site at http://www.dartmouth.edu/~biology.

Correspondence and Information

Chair, Graduate Admissions Committee
Ecology and Evolutionary Biology
Department of Biological Sciences
Dartmouth College
103 Gilman Hall
Hanover, New Hampshire 03755-3576

E-mail: ecology@mac.dartmouth.edu
Web site: http://www.dartmouth.edu/~biology

Chair, Graduate Admissions Committee
Program in Molecular and Cellular Biology at Dartmouth
7560 Remsen Building
Room 239
Dartmouth Medical School
Hanover, New Hampshire 03755-3842

E-mail: molecular.and.cellular.biology@dartmouth.edu
Web site: http://dms.dartmouth.edu/mcb/

Dartmouth College

THE FACULTY AND THEIR RESEARCH

For a complete listing of MCB Program faculty members, students should see the description under Dartmouth, Molecular and Cellular Biology.

Matthew P. Ayres, Professor; Ph.D., 1991. Terrestrial ecology; plant-herbivore interactions, nutritional ecology, plant defenses, temperature responses, population dynamics, and distribution limits.

Edward M. Berger, Professor; Ph.D., 1969. Genetics and molecular biology: ecdysterone action in *Drosophila*, mechanisms of transcriptional regulation.

Sharon E. Bickel, Associate Professor; Ph.D., 1991. Molecular and genetic analysis of chromosome behavior in *Drosophila* meiosis.

Douglas T. Bolger, Adjunct Professor; Ph.D., 1991. Conservation biology: effects of habitat fragmentation on animal populations, landscape ecology.

Ryan Calsbeek, Assistant Professor; Ph.D., 2001. Ecology and evolution: importance of ecology to natural and sexual selection in wild lizard populations.

Kathryn L. Cottingham, Associate Professor; Ph.D., 1996. Aquatic community and ecosystem ecology; quantitative ecology and biostatistics; environmental monitoring and ecological indicators.

Michael R. Dietrich, Professor; Ph.D., 1991. History and philosophy of biology.

Patrick J. Dolph, Associate Professor; Ph.D., 1989. Genetic and molecular analysis of phototransduction in *Drosophila melanogaster*.

Nathaniel J. Dominy, Adjunct Professor; Ph.D., 2001. Sensory and foraging ecology of primates; mechanical, and chemical properties of primate foods; forest canopy structure.

Albert J. Erives, Assistant Professor; Ph.D., 1999. Gene regulation in the evolution and development of metazoan systems.

Carol L. Folt, Professor; Ph.D., 1982. Aquatic ecology: competition and feeding strategies in zooplankton communities.

Andrew J. Friedland, Adjunct Professor; Ph.D., 1985. Elemental cycling in forested ecosystems: quantification of cycling rates, residence times, and elemental pools, using chemical mass balance, stable isotopes, and some micrometeorological techniques.

Tillman U. Gerngross, Adjunct Professor; Ph.D., 1992. Enzymology of microbial polymer formation; fermentation process development; development of protein expression systems; metabolic engineering of industrial microorganisms.

Amy Gladfelter, Assistant Professor; Ph.D., 2001. Cell biology and genetics: cell-cycle control in multinucleated cells, evolution of the cell cycle, morphogenesis.

Karl E. Griswold, Adjunct Assistant Professor; Ph.D., 2005. Protein engineering; directed evolution; biotherapeutics; applied biocatalysis; high throughput screening.

Robert H. Gross, Associate Professor; Ph.D., 1974. Computational molecular biology.

Mary Lou Guerinot, Professor; Ph.D., 1979. Genetics and molecular biology: genetic regulation of the nitrogen-fixing symbiosis between rhizobia and legumes; iron regulation of gene expression in plants (*Arabidopsis thaliana*) and bacteria.

Rebecca E. Irwin, Associate Professor; Ph.D., 2000. Population and community ecology; evolutionary ecology; plant-animal interactions; mutualisms; plant mating systems; invasive species.

Thomas Jack, Associate Professor; Ph.D., 1990. Molecular genetics of flower development in *Arabidopsis*.

Anne R. Kapuscinski, Adjunct Professor; Ph.D., 1984. Sustainability sciences; fisheries management; aquaculture and genetically modified fish.

Andrew D. Kern, Assistant Professor; Ph.D., 2005. Population genomics and molecular evolution.

Eric J. Lambie, Associate Professor; Ph.D., 1987. Developmental genetics of gonadal development in *Caenorhabditis elegans*.

Lee R. Lynd, Adjunct Professor; D.E., 1987. Biochemical engineering, microbiology, and molecular biology applied to conversion of plant biomass into fuels and chemicals; sustainable resource utilization.

C. Robertson McClung, Professor; Ph.D., 1986. Genetics and molecular biology of circadian rhythms in *Arabidopsis*.

Mark A. McPeek, Professor; Ph.D., 1989. Macroevolutionary ecology; evolution of community structure; phylogeography; phenotypic evolution.

David R. Peart, Professor; Ph.D., 1982. Plant ecology: plant populations, communities and succession.

Kevin J. Peterson, Associate Professor; Ph.D., 1996. Origin and early evolution of animal body plans.

G. Eric Schaller, Professor; Ph.D., 1990. Molecular, biochemical, and genetic analysis of hormone signaling pathways in *Arabidopsis thaliana*.

Roger D. Sloboda, Professor; Ph.D., 1974. Cell biology: microtubule assembly and biochemistry, mitotic apparatus assembly and function, intracellular particle motility.

Elizabeth F. Smith, Associate Professor; Ph.D., 1992. Molecular, genetic, and biochemical analysis of eukaryotic flagellar motility and assembly in *Chlamydomonas reinhardtii*.

Brad W. Taylor, Assistant Professor; Ph.D., 2006. Aquatic ecology; ecosystem ecology; nutrient cycling in rivers; tropical ecology; predator-prey interactions; invasive species.

Samuel J. Vélez, Associate Professor; Ph.D., 1974. Neurobiology: development of neuronal connections, nerve regeneration.

Ross A. Virginia, Adjunct Professor; Ph.D., 1980. Terrestrial ecosystem ecology; nutrient cycling and soil ecology, especially in deserts.

Lee A. Witters, Professor; M.D., 1969. Metabolism and enzyme regulation: hormonal and substrate regulation of protein kinases in mammalian cells; role of protein phosphorylation in cell metabolism and adaptation to cellular stress.

DREXEL UNIVERSITY

College of Medicine
Biomedical Graduate Studies

DREXEL UNIVERSITY
COLLEGE OF MEDICINE

Programs of Study

Drexel University College of Medicine (Drexel Med), formerly MCP Hahnemann University, has been educating students in biomedical sciences for more than 150 years and is committed to developing excellence in leadership, education, and training. At Drexel Med, education is the top priority, and the College is committed to preparing students for careers as academic scientists or successful professionals. The College believes that to be an effective and productive member of the scientific community, one must be trained with an extensive scientific knowledge. Drexel Med graduates leave with expertise in their own fields as well as an understanding of other disciplines—education and training that best prepares students to meet the health-care needs of today and tomorrow.

Master's and doctoral programs are offered in the following disciplines: biochemistry, microbiology and immunology, molecular and cell biology and genetics, molecular pathobiology, neuroscience, and pharmacology and physiology. A combined M.D./Ph.D. program is also available for a small pool of highly qualified applicants.

Research Facilities

Such a diverse and prolific research environment serves as an exciting backdrop for a multitude of opportunities in graduate education and research training, which have been further fortified by MCP Hahnemann's merger with Drexel University in July 2002. This merger with Drexel, a preeminent computing and engineering university, has further expanded opportunities and has culminated in the development of many new undergraduate and graduate programs interweaving medicine with biomedical engineering, robotics, computing, education, and business. Drexel Med believes that innovation is at the interface of disciplines, and this merger affords students the opportunity to discover and invent.

Financial Aid

Stipends, currently at $25,500 plus health insurance coverage, may be awarded to qualified doctoral students in each of the graduate programs. Qualified doctoral students also receive tuition remission.

Although no tuition remission or stipend waivers are currently available to students in the master's programs, the Office of University Student Financial Affairs (http://www.drexel.edu/provost/finaid/mc/pg/) strives to help all students find the financial resources they need to attend the Drexel University College of Medicine. Many work-study opportunities exist in the College, which provides substantial work experiences and financial support to qualified and deserving students. Students must complete and submit the Free Application for Federal Student Aid (FAFSA) by May 1 to determine if they are eligible to receive Federal Work-Study aid.

Cost of Study

The full-time master's student tuition rate for the 2009–10 academic year was $20,110 per year. Part-time or nonmatriculating student tuition is $1165 per credit hour. Additional fees include a $100 nonrefundable deposit, a general student fee of $150, and a student activity fee of $63 per semester. All particulars relating to tuition, fees, and financial aid are subject to change.

Living and Housing Costs

The Center City campus residence hall has been undergoing renovations. In order to help students with off-campus housing, the Office of Residential Life has prepared an apartment listing of properties in the vicinity of the University and some detailed information regarding off-campus housing options. For more information regarding off-campus housing, students should contact the Housing and Student Life Programs, at 215-762-1400, or via e-mail at studentlife.cchc@drexel.edu.

Student Group

The relatively small size of the program facilitates informal and informative exchanges between students and faculty members. Students consider the accessibility of the faculty one of the strengths of the program.

Location

Located in the vibrant city of Philadelphia, Drexel Med students have access to more than 143,000 businesses, corporations, and firms; forty-four major pharmaceutical companies; and the third-largest concentration of research institutions in the U.S. In addition to the plethora of opportunities for career growth, Philadelphia has much to offer culturally, recreationally, and historically. For avid travelers, Philadelphia is situated 1 to 3 hours from New York City, Atlantic City and other New Jersey shore points, the Pocono Mountains, and Washington, D.C.

The College

Drexel College of Medicine has three campuses within the city of Philadelphia. The main medical school campus, Queen Lane, is located in the East Falls section of Philadelphia. This is the location of all of the educational programs for the first two years of the medical school curriculum as well as the home for the Departments of Microbiology and Immunology and of Neurobiology and Anatomy.

The Center City campus is home to the Departments of Biochemistry, Pharmacology and Physiology, and Pathology. It is also the site for the premedical programs. At this location, Drexel Med also has another major teaching hospital, Hahnemann University Hospital, operated by Tenet Healthcare Corporation. The main campus, located near the 30th Street train station, is the primary home of undergraduate education at Drexel University.

Applying

The Drexel University College of Medicine has a rolling admissions policy, which means that complete applications are reviewed as they are received. Applicants are therefore advised to apply early, as decisions to accept or deny admission may be made before the official deadlines. The application deadline is March 1 for all programs except the M.D./Ph.D. program, which is November 1.

Applicants must hold a baccalaureate degree from an accredited institution and present evidence of their ability to pursue graduate work, as exemplified by high scholarship achievement, high aptitude scores, and strong recommendations. Previous research experience is highly regarded.

Satisfactory scores on the Graduate Record Examinations (GRE) General Test are required. Individual programs generally request personal interviews. Certain requirements may be waived in unusual circumstances. International applicants whose primary language is not English must demonstrate competence in English as indicated by the Test of English as a Foreign Language (TOEFL).

Correspondence and Information

Office of Biomedical Graduate and Postgraduate Studies
Drexel University College of Medicine
2900 Queen Lane, G24
Philadelphia, Pennsylvania 19129
Phone: 215-991-8570
E-mail: biograd@drexelmed.edu
Web site: http://www.drexelmed.edu/biograd

Drexel University

DIRECTORS OF GRADUATE PROGRAMS AND AREAS OF RESEARCH

Biochemistry
Under the direction of Patrick J. Loll, Ph.D., Professor of Biochemistry and Program Director, this is a challenging and broad-based graduate program of research and course work leading to the master's or doctoral degree. The aim of the biochemistry program is to train scientists to identify, address, and solve biomedical problems at the molecular level. The themes of molecular structure, molecular mechanisms, and molecular regulation are recurrent throughout the diverse research areas represented by the biochemistry faculty.

M.D./Ph.D. Program
Jane Azizkhan-Clifford, Professor and Chair of the Department of Biochemistry, is the also the Director of the M.D./Ph.D. Program. Each year, a small number of highly qualified applicants with prior research experience are accepted into the program, designed to train students for careers in academic medicine that include both research and clinical practice.

Microbiology and Immunology
The Microbiology and Immunology program, directed by Lawrence Bergman, Ph.D., Professor of Microbiology and Immunology, consists of faculty members from four different departments. The faculty members in this program have diverse research interests ranging from studying the cellular and molecular pathogenesis of infectious agents to the effect of aging on the immune function. In the first year, students spend most of their time completing required courses in the core curriculum and completing the research laboratory rotation requirements.

Molecular and Cell Biology and Genetics
Under the leadership of Michael Bouchard, Ph.D., Assistant Professor, more than 60 investigators from the various departments within the University have formed an interdisciplinary program under the broad title of Molecular and Cell Biology and Genetics. Areas of intense research focus include cancer biology, regulation of gene expression, cell-cycle regulation, cell signaling, immunobiology, and pathogenic microbiology.

Molecular Medicine
The Master of Science program in Molecular Medicine provides training in the academic, research, and entrepreneurial aspects of the biomedical sciences with an emphasis on translational research in the development of therapeutics and vaccines. It is ideally suited for enhancing the scientific credentials of industrial employees, high school biology teachers, new college graduates, college undergraduates, and premedical students.

The program is designed to accommodate students' needs. Classes are held in the late afternoon and early evening (4–7:30 p.m.) to minimize conflict with other commitments. The program offers convenient multiple-campus teaching with videoconference transmission to Drexel's Queen Lane campus in East Falls, the New College Building in Center City Philadelphia, and the Doylestown campus, so students can take classes at the facility nearest to them. The time to complete the degree is flexible. A full-time student can complete it in eighteen months, while part-time students can take up to four years.

Molecular Pathobiology
This program provides students with a comprehensive education in contemporary knowledge of pathophysiological mechanisms and prepares them for careers in research and teaching in academic and corporate institutions. Chris Sell, Ph.D., serves as the Program Director and leads the research team with topics related to neurodegeneration, tumor metastasis, angiogenesis, tumor suppressor genes, oncogenes, and mechanisms of host defense and disease.

Neuroengineering
Neuroengineering is a joint initiative between Drexel's School of Biomedical Engineering, Science, and Health Systems and the Department of Neurobiology and Anatomy. The program includes faculty members from most academic units at Drexel University, including the Colleges of Engineering, Arts and Sciences, Business, and Media Arts and Design.

The program offers four main components, designed to help students succeed. The first is courses to prepare students for the emerging field of neuroengineering. The second focuses on the development of a research rotation system that includes opportunities for laboratory experiences in clinical and industrial settings. The third component is a Journal Club and Seminar Series that reinforces what students are learning in their courses and rotations and emphasizes critical thinking within the arenas of neuroscience and engineering. The fourth is thesis research under the supervision of an adviser and a hybrid (neuroscience and engineering) dissertation committee for completion of Ph.D. requirements.

Neuroscience
Peter Baas, Ph.D., Professor of Neurobiology and Anatomy, directs the Neuroscience program. One of the few programs of its kind in the area, it gives students an opportunity to gain interdisciplinary research training. Participating faculty includes members of the Departments of Neurobiology and Anatomy, Pathology and Laboratory Medicine, Pharmacology and Physiology, and Neurology. Current research emphasizes the basic process underlying the organization and functioning of the nervous system and incorporates approaches ranging from molecular biology to systems neurobiology.

Pharmacology and Physiology
A degree in the Pharmacology and Physiology Program, directed by Janet Clark, Ph.D., requires independent research under the direction of faculty members in the department, who are engaged in highly active research programs involving molecular, cellular, and behavioral approaches to experimental pharmacology and physiology in a strongly collaborative environment. Pharmacology examines and characterizes the action of drugs in humans and animals. It emphasizes the therapeutic responses of drugs, their mechanisms of action, the fate of drugs in the body, potential adverse reactions, and drug-drug interactions. Physiology considers processes that control and regulate the functioning of systems within an intact organism. Basic physiological processes underlie all fields in biomedical science. Understanding and exploiting the specific actions of drugs can also furnish a way to probe physiological and biochemical processes in both normal and pathological circumstances.

DREXEL UNIVERSITY
COLLEGE OF MEDICINE

DREXEL UNIVERSITY

College of Medicine
Office of Professional Studies in the Health Sciences

Programs of Study

The Office of Professional Studies in the Health Sciences has been helping students gain acceptance to health professional schools for almost thirty years. Its programs are committed to developing excellence in leadership, education, and training and are dedicated to providing exceptional educational opportunities that combine rigorous academic learning, practical experience, and the use of advanced technologies. The Office of Professional Studies in the Health Sciences is committed to educating students to make an immediate contribution to their organizations and communities.

The Medical Science programs include the Interdepartmental Medical Science (IMS), Medical Science Preparatory (MSP), Veterinary Medical Science (VMS), Drexel Pathway to Medical School (DPMS), Interdisciplinary Health Science (IHS), Master of Interdisciplinary Health Science (MIHS), Master of Biological Science (MBS), Master of Medical Science (MMS), and the Evening Post-Baccalaureate Pre-Medical (PMED).

The Professional Studies programs include the Master of Clinical Research Organization and Management (CROM), Certificate of Study in Clinical Research (CSCR), Pathologists' Assistant (Path A), Master of Histotechnology (MHP), Master of Forensic Science (M.F.S.), Master of Criminalistic Science (MCS), Master of Laboratory Animal Science (M.L.A.S.), and Online Master of Laboratory Animal Science (Online M.L.A.S.).

Financial Aid

The Financial Aid Office (http://www.drexel.edu/financialaid) strives to help all students find the financial resources they need to attend the Drexel University College of Medicine programs. The programs offer many work-study opportunities that provide substantial work experiences and financial support to qualified and deserving students. Most students take out loans. For more information, students should contact the Financial Aid Office, Drexel University College of Medicine at http://ask.drexel.edu or http://www.drexel.edu/financialaid.

Cost of Study

The tuition rate for the 2010–11 academic year for full-time programs ranges from $17,000 to $25,500. All particulars relating to tuition, fees, and financial aid are subject to change.

Living and Housing Costs

In order to help students with off-campus housing, the Office of Residential Life has prepared an apartment listing of properties in the vicinity of the University and some detailed information regarding off-campus housing options. For more information regarding off-campus housing, students should contact the Housing and Student Life Programs at 215-762-1400 or via e-mail at studentlife.cchc@drexel.edu.

Student Group

In 2009–10, more than 600 students matriculated into programs within the Office of Professional Studies in the Health Sciences. The relatively small size of many of the programs facilitates informal and informative exchanges between students and faculty members. Even in the larger programs, students consider the accessibility of the faculty and staff one of the strengths of the programs.

Location

Located in the vibrant city of Philadelphia, Drexel students have accessibility to more than 143,000 businesses, corporations, and firms; forty-four major pharmaceutical companies; and the third-largest concentration of research institutions in the U.S. In addition to the plethora of opportunities for career growth, Philadelphia has much to offer culturally, recreationally, and historically. For avid travelers, Philadelphia is situated 1 to 3 hours from New York City, Atlantic City and other New Jersey shore points, the Pocono Mountains, and Washington, D.C.

The College

Drexel University College of Medicine has three campuses within the city of Philadelphia. The medical school is located in the East Falls section of Philadelphia on the Queen Lane campus.

The Office of Professional Studies in the Health Sciences is located on the Center City campus. At this location, Drexel University College of Medicine also has one of its major teaching hospitals, Hahnemann University Hospital, operated by Tenet Healthcare Corporation.

The main campus, located near the 30th Street train station, is the primary home of undergraduate education at Drexel University.

Applying

Students interested in applying to the programs may view admission eligibility requirements, admissions processes, and application procedures on Drexel's Web pages at http://www.drexelmed.edu/ims or by contacting the Office of Professional Studies in the Health Sciences at 215-762-4692.

To determine eligibility for the Federal Work-Study Program, students should complete and submit the Free Application for Federal Student Aid (FAFSA) by May 1.

Correspondence and Information

The Office of Professional Studies in the Health Sciences
Drexel University College of Medicine
245 North 15th Street, Mail Stop 344, Room 4104 NCB
Philadelphia, Pennsylvania 19102
Phone: 215-762-4692
E-mail: medicalsciences@drexelmed.edu
Web site: http://www.drexelmed.edu/ims

Drexel University

PROGRAMS AND PROGRAM DIRECTORS

MEDICAL SCIENCE PROGRAMS

Gerald Soslau, Ph.D., Professor of Biochemistry and Molecular Biology and Senior Associate Dean, is the director for the Interdepartmental Medical Science (IMS), Master of Biological Science (MBS), and Master of Medical Science (MMS) programs.

Interdepartmental Medical Science (IMS) Program

IMS is a one-year certificate graduate program in which students take six medical school courses and are graded relative to the performance of the College's first-year medical school students. This program has successfully prepared students to enhance their credentials for admission to medical schools since 1981. Students may elect to return for a second year to obtain their Master of Science degree through the Master of Medical Science program.

Medical Science Preparatory (MSP) Program

Robert McKenzie, Ph.D., is the director of the MSP Program, which is a one-year certificate graduate program with course work at the graduate and undergraduate levels. The program prepares students to improve their MCAT score if they have taken the exam previously. The MSP student may elect to return for a second year, in which they enroll in the IMS courses and work toward the Master of Science degree through the Master of Biological Science program.

Drexel Pathway to Medical School (DPMS) Program

Loretta Walker, Ph.D., is the director of the DPMS Program, which is a graduate-level early assurance program for direct entry into Drexel University College of Medicine. The DPMS Program is dedicated to disadvantaged and underrepresented minority students in the health professions. If necessary, students may return for a second year to obtain the Master of Science degree.

Evening Post-Baccalaureate Pre-Medical (PMED) Program

Laura Mangano, M.Ed., is the director of the PMED Program, which is an undergraduate-level program for career-changers who are interested in gaining admittance into a health professional school. This is a two year, part-time evening program that allows students to hold down a full-time career.

Interdisciplinary Health Sciences (IHS) Program

Directed by Nancy Minugh-Purvis, Ph.D., the IHS program is a one-year graduate certificate program designed for the student who seeks a professional career in patient care or elsewhere in the health sciences but requires additional course work in the sciences in order to become a competitive applicant to health profession programs. Students receive career counseling in the rich variety of fields available within health care while taking a program of rigorous course work specifically designed to enhance their individual needs in preparation for application to professional programs or entering the workforce.

Master of Interdisciplinary Health Sciences (MIHS) Program

The MIHS program, also under the direction of Nancy Minugh-Purvis, Ph.D., is the optional second year of the IHS program through which students may obtain the Master of Science degree. Students seeking this degree specialize in areas of concentration most beneficial to their future plans, whether targeting employment immediately following graduation or entry into a health professional school.

Veterinary Medical Science (VMS) Program

Under the leadership of Julian E. Mesina, D.V.M., Ph.D., M.P.H., Program Director, the Veterinary Medical Science (VMS) Program (the only one in the nation) is a one-year graduate-level postbaccalaureate certificate program designed to strengthen skills in the basic sciences and enhance the student's application to veterinary medical school. After successful completion of the VMS Program, students have the option to return for a second year to complete the Master of Laboratory Animal Science degree program.

PROFESSIONAL STUDIES PROGRAMS

Master of Clinical Research Organization and Management (CROM) Program

Under the direction of Sara Perkel, M.B.A., this online program was designed after extensive consultation with individuals involved in clinical research and research administration to meet the particular educational and professional needs of future leaders in the increasingly complex and highly regulated field of therapeutic product investigation. Students are selected and courses are conducted in such a manner as to maximize the opportunities for learning, both from student to student as well as from a highly experienced faculty, which includes researchers, administrators, lawyers, and scientists from academia and industry.

Pathologists' Assistant (Path A) Program

Under the direction of James W. Moore, M.H.S., and Tina Rader, M.H.S., the Pathologists' Assistant Program is a two-year, full-time program beginning in May of each year. The program is designed for students who want to pursue an advanced career as a physician extender in pathology and laboratory medicine. The first year is the didactic portion of the program, supplemented by pathology laboratory exposure. The second year is composed of several hospital-based rotations offering progressively responsible experience in autopsy and surgical pathology. These rotations are supplemented with formal classroom education. Upon completion of the degree, students are able to gain employment in community hospitals; academic centers, such as medical schools and university hospitals; private pathology laboratories; medical research centers; government hospitals; and medical examiner offices. Students receive a Master of Science degree upon successful completion of the program.

Master of Histotechnology (MHP) Program

Under the direction of Chris Migogna, M.P.H., and Tina Rader, M.H.S., the histotechnologist program is a one-year full-time program beginning in August of each year. It is comprised of two semesters of didactics, supplemented by a one-semester pathology laboratory practicum. The practicum is composed of hospital-based rotations offering progressively responsible experiences in histology laboratories supplemented with informal classroom education. Completion of the program will enable students to earn a graduate degree and prepare them to work, under the direction of a pathologist, as a highly qualified allied health professional in anatomic pathology laboratories throughout the country. Histotechnologists are employed in hospitals, for-profit laboratories, clinics, and public health facilities. Additional opportunities are available in clinical and industrial research, veterinary pathology, marine biology, and forensic pathology. Students receive a Master of Science degree upon successful completion of the program.

Master of Laboratory Animal Science (M.L.A.S.) Program

The M.L.A.S Program, directed by Julian E. Mesina, D.V.M., Ph.D., M.P.H., is a two-year full- or part-time program, designed for students who want to pursue advanced careers in laboratory animal science or laboratory animal facility management. Most classes are scheduled in late afternoon and early evening to accommodate working professionals. The M.L.A.S. degree is also a proven enhancement to the veterinary school application.

Online Master of Laboratory Animal Science (Online M.L.A.S.) Program

The Online MLAS Program, directed by Julian E. Mesina, D.V.M., Ph.D., M.P.H., is a part-time program designed for individuals who have a minimum of two years of experience working in the field of laboratory animal science and are seeking career advancement, but are unable attend the traditional program in Philadelphia. The online courses are essentially the same as those offered in the traditional program. The program can be completed in three to five years.

Master of Forensic Science (M.F.S.) Program

Detective William R. Welsh Jr., M.S.; Fredric N. Hellman, M.D., M.B.A.; and Nancy Minugh-Purvis, Ph.D., are the co-directors for the M.F.S. Program. The M.F.S. Program began in September 2005 and is designed to allow the student exposure to both the intricacies of problem solving as well as an exposure to the real-world application of the related disciplines within the field of forensic science. The curriculum is designed to provide the student with a solid foundation within the forensic sciences, while at the same time encouraging growth and leadership in new and emerging applications within the field. The students may elect to take concentrations in molecular biology, clinical sciences, or criminalistics. A collaborative network of municipal agencies, private enterprise, and allied professional programs within the University has been built to prepare professionals who can confront the forensic challenges of the new millennium.

FLORIDA STATE UNIVERSITY

Department of Biomedical Sciences

Program of Study	The Ph.D. Program in Biomedical Sciences at the Florida State University College of Medicine trains biomedical scientists in an interdisciplinary environment which takes advantage of genomics, proteomics, bioinformatics, and other contemporary approaches to address questions of developmental, cellular, and molecular biology related to human health. Students are encouraged to develop into independent researchers through a core curriculum, the choice of electives from other departments, and intellectual interaction with faculty members and fellows. The program emphasizes research in developmental biology, neuroscience, and the molecular basis of human disease.
	The curriculum strikes a balance between formal course work, research, and teaching. Students must complete at least 30 hours of course work. These include required courses in advanced molecular biology, biostatistics, bioregulation, advanced cell biology, ethics, research techniques, advanced topics in biomedical sciences, and elective courses. In addition, students enroll in a health sciences seminar each semester and participate in two semesters of teaching activities. During the first year, students begin research training through rotations in faculty research laboratories. In the second year, students select a faculty mentor and begin developing an independent research project. The program culminates in a completed research project and defense of a dissertation.
Research Facilities	Students and faculty members perform research in new state-of-the-art laboratories and have access to modern core facilities. The Cell Culture Facility accommodates the culture of mammalian cell lines and other animal cell lines used for protein expression, such as insect cells. The Flow Cytometry Laboratory contains equipment to measure the physical and/or chemical characteristics of cells or particles including DNA content. The Confocal Microscopy Laboratory allows researchers to view simultaneous images of fluorescent proteins without dichroic mirrors or filters. A new state-of-the-art live cell imaging microscope (Nikon Eclipse) was added recently to the microscopy laboratory. The Protein Biology Laboratory serves as an integral part of the school's research community, supporting and advancing faculty research and providing service, training, and/or consultation on protein identification, post-translational modification, etc. A new state-of-the-art Translational Science Laboratory with biorepository is designed to provide researchers with professional services in biomarker identification and characterization.
	The Maguire Medical Library is the first academic medical library created in the twenty-first century; over 95 percent of holdings are electronic and can be accessed by password from anywhere online.
Financial Aid	Students accepted into the Ph.D. program currently receive an annual stipend of $21,500, plus payment of all tuition and an insurance subsidy. Financial support is provided throughout the student's graduate career as long a GPA of 3.0 or better is maintained and the student is in good standing.
Cost of Study	As highlighted in the Financial Aid section, students receive financial support to cover the cost of study.
Living and Housing Costs	Students living on campus pay $355–$383 per month for a furnished one-bedroom apartment, $380–$531 for a two-bedroom apartment, or $550–$606 for a three-bedroom apartment, excluding utilities and garbage collection. Students living off campus spend between $400 and $900 per month, depending on apartment size and location.
Student Group	Currently, 5 to 7 students are accepted each year, joining a cohort of about 40 Ph.D. students in the biomedical sciences and neuroscience Ph.D. programs. Students represent a wide range of social and academic backgrounds, and they come from throughout the United States as well as from other countries, such as China, India, and Lebanon.
Student Outcomes	Graduates of the program are qualified to hold teaching positions in university biomedical departments or medical colleges, or to pursue careers as biomedical researchers in education, industry, or government.
Location	Tallahassee's designation as an "All-American City" is evidence of the balance between its small-town charm and its distinction as one of America's ten most-educated cities. Clubs and restaurants offer a wide variety of live music and cuisine from all corners of the world. The city also has museums, shops, and activities, such as the downtown Shakespeare Festival, and the Gulf Coast beaches are a short drive away. It is the capital city of Florida, a short distance from the Gulf of Mexico, and has a population of around 60,000 students most of the year.
The University	Founded in 1857, Florida State University combines traditional strength in the arts and humanities with recognized leadership in the sciences, providing unmatched opportunities for students through challenging academics, cultural discovery, and community interaction. The University's sixteen colleges offer more than 300 degree programs covering a vast array of disciplines critical to society today and enroll more than 41,000 students each year from all fifty states and 128 countries.
Applying	Prospective students must submit online the following documents: an application form, a one-page personal statement, a research statement describing the applicant's research interests, a description of relevant teaching and/or research experience, the names and addresses of the individuals providing letters of recommendation, and a listing of honors, awards, and publications. A CV should also be included as part of the application file. Official transcripts and GRE scores should be mailed to the Florida State University Office of Admissions. All other application materials, including letters of recommendation, should be submitted through the Graduate Online Application found at https://admissions.fsu.edu/gradapp/. The deadline to apply is February 1.
Correspondence and Information	Division of Research and Graduate Programs College of Medicine Florida State University 1115 West Call Street, MSB G117-C Tallahassee, Florida 32306-4300 Phone: 850-645-6420 Fax: 850-645-7153 E-mail: biomedical.admissions@med.fsu.edu Web site: http://med.fsu.edu/index.cfm?page=biomedicalSciences.home

Florida State University

THE FACULTY AND THEIR RESEARCH

Ewa Bienkiewicz, Director; Ph.D., Colorado State, 1997. Protein misfolding in disease, with the focus on Alzheimer's disease and prion-associated disorders.

Michael Blaber, Professor; Ph.D., California, Irvine, 1990. Protein structure, stability, and folding; mutational study of human fibroblast growth factor 1 for angiogenic therapy; structural biology and enzymology of human kallikrein-related peptidases.

Susanne Cappendijk, Assistant Professor; Ph.D., Rotterdam, 1995. Effects of pharmacological as well as nutritional manipulations on brain development and behavior in the zebra finch.

Akash Gunjan, Assistant Professor; Ph.D., Mississippi Medical Center, 1999. Understanding how histones and chromatin structure contribute to the maintenance of genomic stability in the presence and absence of DNA damage.

Jamila Horabin, Associate Professor; Ph.D., Duke, 1987. RNA silencing and its regulation of sex determination in *Drosophila*.

Myra Hurt, Professor and Senior Associate Dean for Research and Graduate Programs; Ph.D., Tennessee, 1981. Regulation of mammalian gene expression, cellular signaling in the cell cycle and post-translational modifications of growth regulators.

Mohamed Kabbaj, Associate Professor, Associate Chair and Director of Graduate Studies; Ph.D., Bordeaux II, 1997. Brain basis of emotional behavior.

Yoichi Kato, Assistant Professor; Ph.D., Nagoya (Japan), 1997. Role of Notch signaling pathway during development.

Sanjay Kumar, Assistant Professor; Ph.D., Pennsylvania, 1997. Cellular physiology of the neocortex in the context of determining normal neocortical function; pathophysiological mechanisms underlying certain aberrant human conditions such as epilepsy.

Choogon Lee, Assistant Professor; Ph.D., Rutgers, 1998. Molecular mechanism of mammalian circadian rhythms.

Cathy Levenson, Associate Professor; Ph.D., Chicago, 1993. Adult neurogenesis: proliferation, differentiation, and apoptosis.

Tim Megraw, Assistant Professor; Ph.D. North Carolina, 1993. Biology of centrosomes, centrioles and cilia impact in disease, using *Drosophila* and the mouse as model systems.

Richard Nowakowski, Randolph L. Rill Professor and Chair; Ph.D., Harvard, 1976. Neurogenesis and cell cycle regulation in the developing and adult brain; genetics of individual diversity in the brain.

James Olcese, Associate Professor; Ph.D., Marquette, 1979. Expression of circadian rhythmicity in the brain; neuroendocrine mechanisms.

Charles Ouimet, Professor; Ph.D., Brown, 1980. Brain mechanisms for recovery from damage and injury.

Mike Overton, Professor; Ph.D., Iowa, 1987. Neuroendocrine mechanisms by which energy homeostasis and cardiovascular function are regulated.

Johanna Paik, Assistant Professor; Ph.D., Max Planck Institute for Molecular Genetics (Berlin), 1999. Understanding how cells coordinate the synthesis of histones with the rate of ongoing DNA replication during the S-phase of the cell cycle.

Branko Stefanovic, Associate Professor; Ph.D., Florida State, 1991. Elucidating the molecular mechanisms that regulate collagen mRNA stability and translation, cloning of the specific RNA binding proteins, and discovery of novel genes involved in activation of hepatic stellate cells.

Jacob Van Landingham, Assistant Professor; Ph.D., Florida State, 2004. Role of neurosteroids in recovery following traumatic brain injury and stroke.

Yanchang Wang, Associate Professor; Ph.D., Virginia, 1997. Regulation of cell cycle and DNA damage response.

Xian-Min Yu, Associate Professor; D.Sc.H., Heidelberg, 1989. Mechanisms underlying functional plasticity of neurons associated with pathophysiological processes in the central nervous system.

Yi Zhou, Associate Professor; Ph.D., Minnesota, 1995. Function and regulation of neuronal ion channels.

MOREHOUSE SCHOOL OF MEDICINE

MOREHOUSE
SCHOOL OF MEDICINE

Graduate Education in Biomedical Sciences

Program of Study

The Graduate Education in Biomedical Sciences program encompasses four degree programs. The M.S. in Clinical Research (MSCR) develops clinical faculty members to pursue clinical research on diseases that disproportionately affect underserved populations. The M.S. in Biomedical Technology (MSBT) is a nonthesis program to enhance and document scientific background and technical expertise in the biomedical sciences in ways that improve earning power in biomedical science and technology. The M.S. in Biomedical Research (MSBR) is a thesis-based program for students seeking a terminal M.S. degree or whose future plans include pursuing a doctoral degree in research or health professions. The Ph.D. in Biomedical Sciences develops independent investigators capable of assuming leadership roles in academic, corporate, and governmental biomedical research.

Students may study with graduate faculty members from basic science or clinical departments. Areas of focus within and across disciplines include HIV/AIDS and infectious disease, cancer, cardiovascular disease, cell biology, developmental biology, immunity, microbiology, molecular biology, neuroscience, pathology, pharmacology/toxicology, physiology, stroke, and vision research. Tracks for obtaining dual degrees, including M.D./Ph.D., M.D./MSCR, and M.D./MSBR, are available for qualified medical students. An MSCR/Ph.D. track is available for qualified Ph.D. students.

All programs begin with core course work. The core sequences for each program differ but include basic biomedical sciences, statistics, and fundamentals of basic and clinical professional science. Students select advisers, complete advanced graduate (elective) courses, and begin thesis or dissertation research in their second year. The M.S. programs generally take two years to complete. At least four years of full-time study beyond the baccalaureate degree and 3½ years in residence at Morehouse School of Medicine (MSM) are required to complete the Ph.D. program.

Research Facilities

Morehouse School of Medicine currently occupies six buildings on the main campus where most biomedical research and research-related activities take place. The Gloster Basic Medical Sciences Building and the attached Medical Education Building, with its Research Wing, provide more than 105,000 square feet of research and research support space. This includes individual, shared-use, and core facilities laboratories. The 70,000-square-foot Multi-Disciplinary Research Center currently houses the Neuroscience Institute and the Clinical Research Center. The Center for Laboratory Animal Resources, located in the Gloster building, occupies an additional 8,500 square feet, and the Medical Library comprises 10,000 square feet.

Faculty investigators currently have an average of approximately 400 square feet of individual laboratory space. In addition, many core and shared-use, state-of-the-art research technology and clinical research facilities are available to all researchers. The core support facilities and individual investigator laboratories are well equipped for biomedical research. Institutional facilities include flow cytometry/FACS, monoclonal antibody preparation, nucleic acid sequencing and DNA synthesis, Affymetrix and Agilent microarray scanners and GeneNet/GeneSpring software, SELDI and mass-spectrometry proteomics instruments, protein/peptide purification (HPLC) and two-dimensional gel electrophoresis, and imaging and image analysis facilities for brightfield, fluorescence, laser-dissection, and confocal microscopy and scanning and transmission electron microscopy. Scientific imaging and graphics preparation services are provided by the Division of Information Technology Services.

Additional collaborative research opportunities are available through existing links with government agencies, biotechnology companies, and other universities.

Financial Aid

The program provides competitive stipends to help cover living expenses for all of its Ph.D. students. In subsequent years, stipends derive from a variety of funding sources. To continue stipend support, a student must maintain satisfactory progress in the program for which the stipend was awarded, must devote full time to study or research in the biomedical sciences, and must not engage in gainful employment outside the program. Students in all programs are eligible to apply for student loans through the financial aid office.

Cost of Study

Tuition waivers or reimbursements are provided for all full-time Ph.D. students in good academic standing who have not secured extramural grant support to cover these expenses. Tuition costs for MSBR and MSBT students are $16,995 per year, with fees ranging from approximately $4000 to $6000, which includes a tablet/laptop computer provided to each student.

Living and Housing Costs

University housing is not currently available. Rental units are available throughout the Atlanta metropolitan area at a reasonable cost.

Student Group

Morehouse School of Medicine is a health sciences institution comprising six postbaccalaureate programs (M.D., M.P.H., MSCR, MSBT, MSBR, and Ph.D.), with a total student population approaching 300. There are currently 40 students in the Graduate Education in Biomedical Sciences program.

Location

Morehouse School of Medicine is a member of the Atlanta University Center, a consortium of five independent institutions of higher education (Clark Atlanta University, the Interdenominational Theological Center, Morehouse College, Spelman College, and Morehouse School of Medicine). Together, the center's institutions constitute the largest predominantly black private educational complex in the world. Other major educational and research institutions in Atlanta include the Centers for Disease Control and Prevention, Emory University, Georgia Institute of Technology, and Georgia State University. In addition to being a center for higher education and biotechnology in the Southeast, Atlanta offers many cultural opportunities, including the Atlanta Symphony Orchestra, the Atlanta Ballet, the Alliance Theatre, and several smaller theater companies. Other popular destinations include the Georgia Aquarium, the World of Coke (Atlanta is the international headquarters of Coca-Cola), and the Centennial Olympic Park. The High Museum of Art is an architectural masterpiece that houses an extensive collection of its own and hosts several first-rate touring collections each year. Atlanta is also known for its world-famous centers honoring Dr. Martin Luther King Jr. and former president Jimmy Carter. Sports and entertainment facilities include the Atlanta Braves' Turner Field, the Georgia Dome, broadcasting's CNN Center, the Fox Theater, the Philips Arena, and many jazz and blues clubs. It is not surprising that many of America's best-known and most respected African American businesspeople, politicians, and professionals call Atlanta home, making this city one of the premier centers of African American culture in the country.

The School

The institution was established in 1975 to address the shortage of minority physicians and related problems in medically underserved communities. Beginning as a two-year preclinical program in 1978, Morehouse School of Medicine was approved to become a four-year medical school in 1981 and granted its first M.D. degrees in 1985. The School's accreditation by the Southern Association of Colleges and Schools was expanded in 1992 to include the Ph.D. in Biomedical Sciences, and its first graduates finished in 1998. Graduates have obtained excellent positions in academic, government, and corporate biomedical research institutions. The MSCR, MSBT, and MSBR programs are more recent additions to the School's offerings.

Applying

Applications must be submitted online. Online applications, along with accompanying photos, references, and transcripts, must be received by February 1 for consideration for admission in July. Occasionally, student slots for the Ph.D. program become available for January entry. These slots are reserved for more advanced students, such as those with thesis-based M.S. degrees and extensive research experience. Applications for January entry must be received by October 1. For the MSBR, MSBT, and Ph.D. programs, bachelor's degrees, with strong performance in science courses, are expected. GRE General Test scores are required, and scores on the Subject Test in chemistry or biology are recommended. International applicants are required to submit TOEFL scores, and third-party verification of academic records and references may be required. Application materials and information can be obtained through the Director of Admissions in the Office of Admissions and Student Affairs via phone (404-752-1650) or e-mail (phdadmissions@msm.edu).

Correspondence and Information

Office of Graduate Education in Biomedical Sciences
Morehouse School of Medicine
720 Westview Drive
Atlanta, Georgia 30310-1495
Phone: 404-752-1580
Fax: 404-756-5220

Morehouse School of Medicine

THE FACULTY AND THEIR RESEARCH

Leonard M. Anderson, Ph.D., Northwestern. Cardiovascular genomics; vascular smooth-muscle-cell fate determination from stem cells. landerson@msm.edu

Methode Bacanamwo, Ph.D., Illinois. Chromatin remodeling and epigenetic mechanisms in vascular gene expression. mbacanmwo@msm.edu

Mohamed A. Bayorh, Ph.D., Howard. Cardiovascular, neurochemical, and signaling pathways in actions of polyunsaturated fatty acids, vasoactive substances, and drugs of abuse. mbayorh@msm.edu

Morris Benveniste, Ph.D., Weizmann (Israel). NMDA channels in synaptic integration; scorpion toxin action on sodium channels. mbenveniste@msm.edu

Vincent C. Bond, Ph.D., Penn State. DNA virology; mammalian cell biology. vbond@msm.edu

L. DiAnne Bradford, Ph.D., Georgia Tech. Psychopharmacology; predicting clinical efficacy and safety. dbradford@msm.edu

Teh-Ching Chu, Ph.D., Louisville. Receptor pharmacology; medical acupuncture; herbal medicine. tchu@msm.edu

Margaret Colden-Stanfield, Ph.D., Texas Medical Branch. Cardiovascular pharmacology; membrane biophysics; cell physiology; leukocyte- and pathogen-endothelial interactions. mstanfield@msm.edu

Alec Davidson, Ph.D., Florida State. Integrative analysis of circadian systems in mammals. adavidson@msm.edu

Kamla Dutt, Ph.D., Punjab (India). Retinal cell biology; cell commitment and differentiation; tissue engineering. kdutt@msm.edu

Francis Eko, Ph.D., Vienna. Immunity and pathogenesis of *Chlamydia*, HSV-2, *Vibrio cholerae,* and related pathogens. feko@msm.edu

Byron Ford, Ph.D., Meharry. Cellular and molecular mechanisms of atherosclerosis and stroke. bford@msm.edu

Chiaki Fukuhara, Ph.D., Sophia (Japan). Diagnostic tools for mental illnesses and sleep-wake-cycle problems. cfukuhara@msm.edu

Minerva Garcia-Barrio, Ph.D., Salamanca (Spain). Molecular biology; gene expression in vascular smooth muscle. mgarcia-barrio@msm.edu

Gary Gibbons, M.D., Harvard. Regulation of vascular remodeling. ggibbons@msm.edu

Sandra A. Harris-Hooker, Ph.D., Atlanta. Endothelial cells and smooth muscle in atherosclerosis; in vitro blood vessel modeling. sharris-hooker@msm.edu

Jacqueline Hibbert, Ph.D., West Indies. Metabolic response to disease; effects on protein and energy nutritional requirements. jhibbert@msm.edu

Ward Kirlin, Ph.D., Emory. Chemical carcinogenesis and toxicology; induction pathways in carcinogen activation and detoxification. wkirlin@msm.edu

Brenda J. Klement, Ph.D., Kansas State. Endochondral bone formation and skeletal tissue changes in microgravity. bklement@msm.edu

Woo-Kuen Lo, Ph.D., Wayne State. Eye ultrastructure and cell biology; intercellular junctions; cell membrane and cytoskeleton of the lens. wlo@msm.edu

Deborah A. Lyn, Ph.D., West Indies. Genetic markers and mechanisms for susceptibility to cardiovascular and infectious diseases. dlyn@msm.edu

Peter MacLeish, Ph.D., Harvard. Functional organization of the vertebrate retina; axonal regeneration; Purkinje cell viability. pmacleish@msm.edu

David R. Mann, Ph.D., Rutgers. Reproductive endocrinology: stress and testicular steroidogenesis, sexual and behavioral differentiation in primates, postmenopausal osteoporosis; immune-endocrine interactions. dmann@msm.edu

Julian Menter, Ph.D., George Washington. Dermatology, photobiology, and photochemistry; physical organic and physical biochemistry. jmenter@msm.edu

Shobu Namura, M.D., Ph.D., Kyoto (Japan). Cerebrovascular functions and their sequelae after stroke. snamura@msm.edu

Gale Newman, Ph.D., LSU. Pathogenesis of HIV-associated nephropathy. gnewman@msm.edu

John W. Patrickson, Ph.D., Howard. Chronobiology; neural mechanisms in the generation of circadian rhythms. jpatrickson@msm.edu

Ketema Paul, Ph.D., Georgia State. Circadian and hypothalamic coordination of sleep and wakefulness. kpaul@msm.edu

Douglas F. Paulsen, Ph.D., Wake Forest. Skeletal patterning during embryogenesis; microgravity effects on the musculoskeletal system. dpaulsen@msm.edu

Michael D. Powell, Ph.D., Texas at Dallas. Role of cellular factors in the regulation of HIV-1 reverse transcription. mpowell@msm.edu

Veena N. Rao, Ph.D., Osmania (India). Molecular and functional dissection of ELK-1 and BRCA-1 tumor-suppressor genes in cancers. vrao@msm.edu

E. Shyam P. Reddy, Ph.D., Andhra (India). Functional role of ets, fusion onco-proteins, and tumor suppressors in cancer. ereddy@msm.edu

Gary L. Sanford, Ph.D., Brown. Lung growth, maturation, and function; vascular remodeling role of soluble lectins; cancer biology. gsanford@msm.edu

Qing Song, M.D., Peking; Ph.D., South Carolina. Molecular mechanisms of genetic susceptibility to cardiovascular disease, obesity, and diabetes. qsong@msm.edu

Rajagopala Sridaran, Ph.D., University of Health Sciences (Chicago). Reproductive endocrinology; gravity during pregnancy; GnRH in fertility; corpus luteum demise and parturition. rsridaran@msm.edu

Jonathan Stiles, Ph.D., Salford (England). Molecular and cell biology of *Trypanosoma-*, *Plasmodium-,* and *Trichomonas*-induced pathogenesis. jstiles@msm.edu

Myrtle Thierry-Palmer, Ph.D., Wisconsin–Madison. Vitamin D metabolism and function; calcium endocrine system; salt sensitivity; space biology. mtheirry-palmer@msm.edu

Kelwyn H. Thomas, Ph.D., California, San Diego. Gene regulation of cellular differentiation; germ-cell development in mouse testis. kthomas@msm.edu

Winston Thompson, Ph.D., Rutgers. Cell and reproductive biology; molecular mechanisms of ovarian follicle development and cyst formation. wthompson@msm.edu

Gianluca Tosini, Ph.D., Bristol (England). Interactions between retinal and hypothalamic circadian clocks. gtosini@msm.edu

Wenli Wang, M.D., Ph.D., Beijing. Notch signaling pathway components in vascular smooth-muscle-cell growth, hypertrophy, and apoptosis. wwenli@msm.edu

Evan F. Williams, Ph.D., Howard. Role of nucleoside transporters in cardiovascular function; ocular purinergic systems. ewilliams@msm.edu

Lawrence E. Wineski, Ph.D., Illinois. Neural organization of craniofacial musculature; microgravity effects on the musculoskeletal system. lwineski@msm.edu

Xuebiao Yao, Ph.D., Berkeley. Mitotic chromosome segregation; establishment and maintenance of cell polarity; biophotonics. xyao@msm.edu

Xueying Zhao, M.D., Ph.D., Suzhou Medical College (China). Epoxygenase metabolites and endothelial function. xzhao@msm.edu

NEW YORK MEDICAL COLLEGE

Graduate School of Basic Medical Sciences

Programs of Study

The Graduate School of Basic Medical Sciences (GSBMS) of New York Medical College offers programs leading to the M.S. and Ph.D. degrees in biochemistry and molecular biology, cell biology, experimental pathology, microbiology and immunology, pharmacology, and physiology plus an interdisciplinary M.S. degree in basic medical sciences. The full-time faculty of 85 basic medical scientists, with their individual and collaborative research programs, their great depth of knowledge, and their classroom experience and expertise, offer a special opportunity to those with the requisite talent and motivation. These assets are supplemented by the College's plentiful access to experts—in clinical research, the pharmaceutical and biotechnology industry, and public health—who can participate in the graduate school's research and educational activities.

Ph.D. degrees are awarded in six basic medical sciences. During the first year, students undertake an interdisciplinary core curriculum of courses and rotate through laboratories throughout the Graduate School. After this first year, students choose their major discipline and dissertation sponsor, complete the remaining didactic requirements in the chosen discipline, and begin intensive research training. Formal course work is usually substantially completed within two years, after which the student completes the qualifying exam, forms a dissertation advisory committee, presents a formal thesis proposal, and devotes his or her primary effort to the dissertation research project.

The M.S. requires completion of 30 to 32 credits, depending upon the discipline and specific track. Two M.S. degree sequences are available: (1) a research program consisting of 25 didactic and up to 5 research credits and a research thesis or (2) a program consisting of 30 of 32 didactic credits and a scholarly literature review. The M.S. degree is earned full- or part-time in evening classes. The interdisciplinary M.S. program is particularly suitable for students wishing to prepare for a career in medicine, dentistry, or other health professions. An accelerated track within this program allows completion of the degree requirements within one year for highly qualified candidates.

The Department of Cell Biology offers training in cell biology and neuroscience leading to careers in academia and industry. Ongoing research includes studies of oncogene expression and cytokines; the role of astrocytes in cerebral ischemia; modulation of neuronal and astrocytic signaling; growth control in skeletal muscle; signal transduction in a variety of tissues, including platelets, the retina, muscle cells, and the *Drosophila* nervous system; intracellular protein trafficking and degradation; cytoskeletal and receptor function; the development and regeneration of the visual system; apoptosis in glaucoma; extracellular matrices and limb development; oocyte preservation and transplantation; spinal cord injury; molecular mechanisms of neuroplasticity; learning and memory; and Alzheimer's disease.

The Department of Biochemistry and Molecular Biology provides students with a solid foundation in the concepts and applications of modern biochemistry and molecular biology. Areas of research include protein structure and function, enzyme reaction mechanisms, mechanisms of hormone action and cell signaling, enzymology, mechanisms of DNA replication and repair, cell-cycle regulation, molecular biology of cancer cells, mechanisms of nutrition and cancer prevention, molecular neurobiology and studies of neurodegenerative disorders, and the aging process.

The Department of Pathology offers a vigorous multidisciplinary milieu for training in experimental pathology. The programs focus on the comprehensive study of pathogenic mechanisms of human disease. Areas of interest in the department include apoptosis, cell signaling and gene activation in cardiovascular disease, flow cytometry and cell-cycle analysis, tumor cell biology and immunology, biochemical toxicology, carcinogenesis, tissue engineering, tuberculosis and other chronic infectious diseases, free-radical pathobiology, aging, hypersensitivity, lipid cytokine and growth factor analysis, and environmentally induced pathology.

In the Department of Microbiology and Immunology, the student acquires a broad acquaintance with microbiology, molecular biology, and immunology as well as depth in an elective field. Areas available for thesis research include molecular biology of tumor cells, cancer vaccines, the role of stem cells in cancer, bacterial genetics, pathogenesis of infectious disease, monoclonal antibody synthesis, immune function in AIDS, structure and function of influenza virus antigens, molecular virology, and the biochemistry and genetics of emerging bacterial pathogens.

The Department of Pharmacology emphasizes training in research methods for examining the mechanism of action of drugs at the systemic, cellular, and subcellular levels. Areas of research include the study of renal and corneal metabolism of arachidonic acid by cytochrome P-450 to biologically active metabolites, patch-clamp analysis of ion transport, vasoactive hormones and inflammatory cytokines in hypertension end-organ damage and cardiovascular function. Research studies center on elucidating diabetes, pathophysiologic factors in stroke, cardiac and renal disease, and pharmacological and gene-based therapy for treating these disease states.

The Department of Physiology provides students with an understanding of the function of the body's cells and organ systems and the mechanisms for regulation of these functions. Research opportunities include cellular neurophysiology, regulation of sleep and awake states, neural and endocrine control of the heart and circulation, microcirculation, the physiology of gene expression, heart failure, cardiac metabolism, and the physiological effects of oxygen metabolites.

Research Facilities

The College has an extensive laboratory complex in the basic medical and clinical sciences. The Basic Sciences Building houses the medical sciences library, which maintains 200,000 volumes, an extensive collection of print and electronic journals, and a variety of online databases and search engines. There are also a fully accredited comparative medicine facility, a well-equipped and staffed instrumentation shop, a variety of classrooms, a bookstore, a cafeteria, and student lounges.

Financial Aid

Federal and state loan programs are available for M.S. students. Ph.D. students receive a stipend and tuition remission, medical insurance, and combinations of College fellowships and research assistantships. The Office of Financial Aid should be consulted for information on federal and state loan programs.

Cost of Study

In 2010–11, tuition is $790 per credit, or $12,640 annually, for a full-time master's student taking 8 credits per semester. The Accelerated Master's Program has an annual tuition rate of $30,460. Annual Ph.D. tuition is $18,960 before candidacy (first two years) and $4000 after candidacy. Fees range between $40 and $330 per year, depending upon options chosen. Comprehensive medical insurance is available for individual ($3774 annually), student plus spouse ($7225), or family ($10,572) coverage.

Living and Housing Costs

A limited number of rooms and apartments are available for graduate students in on-campus College housing. On-campus housing costs range from $740 to $795 per month for furnished suite-style apartments and $565 to $935 for unfurnished single-student apartments. Married housing apartment costs range from $1240 for a one-bedroom apartment, $1285 to $1345 for a two-bedroom apartment and $1490 for a three-bedroom apartment (families with children). Private off-campus accommodations are also available. Students should contact the Director of Housing, Administration Building (phone: 914-594-4832 or e-mail: housing@nymc.edu), well in advance of arrival in order to make housing arrangements.

Student Group

The total College enrollment is 1,454. In fall 2010, there were 58 Ph.D. and 176 M.S. students in the Graduate School of Basic Medical Sciences.

Location

The College campus is located in the Westchester Medical Center campus, 5 miles from White Plains and 28 miles north of New York City.

The College

New York Medical College, one of the largest medical schools in the country, was established in 1860. Graduate education at the College began informally in 1910. Graduate degrees were offered as early as 1938, and a graduate division was established in 1963.

Applying

Applications for admission may be submitted from October 1 through July 1. For optimal review of credentials and consideration for financial aid and housing, however, applications for fall enrollment into Ph.D. programs should be received by February 1. International applicants to the master's program should complete their application no later than May 1. Specific program requirements are available on the College Web site at: http://www.nymc.edu/Academics/SchoolOfBasicMedicalSciences/Admissions/Requirements.htm. Students must apply online at the College Web site. M.S. and Ph.D. applicants must submit GRE General Test scores. Applicants for the Accelerated Master's Program must submit scores for the Medical College Admission Test (MCAT). International students are required to submit results of the TOEFL. Transcripts from all post-secondary institutions attended (undergraduate and graduate) and two letters of recommendation from teachers or scientists personally familiar with the applicant must be submitted directly by the school or recommenders separately.

Correspondence and Information

Francis L. Belloni, Ph.D., Dean
Graduate School of Basic Medical Sciences
Basic Sciences Building, Room A41
New York Medical College
Valhalla, New York 10595

E-mail: gsbms_apply@nymc.edu
Web site: http://www.nymc.edu/gsbms/

New York Medical College

THE GRADUATE FACULTY AND THEIR RESEARCH

Biochemistry and Molecular Biology. E. Y. C. Lee, Ph.D., Professor and Chairman: enzymology, structure-function relationships, and regulation of ser/thr protein phosphatases. A. J. L. Cooper, Ph.D., Professor: amino acid chemistry and biochemistry; biochemical mechanisms underlying neurological diseases. M. I. Horowitz, Ph.D., Professor Emeritus: interaction of glucose with histones and membrane lipids; properties and characterization of sulfotransferases; nutritional biochemistry. M. Y. W. Lee, Ph.D., Professor: DNA replication, polymerases, and repair; cell-cycle regulation. S. C. Olson, Ph.D., Associate Professor: signal transduction; regulation of phospholipase D pathway by protein kinase C and G proteins. J. T. Pinto, Ph.D., Professor: the effects of chemopreventive agents, dietary factors, and xenobiotic substances on oxidation/reduction capacity in human cells. E. L. Sabban, Ph.D., Professor: molecular neurobiology; molecular mechanisms of stress; cloning and regulation of gene expression for catecholamine-synthesizing enzymes and neuropeptides. Y. C. Tse-Dinh, Ph.D., Professor and Ph.D. Program Director: protein-DNA interactions; topoisomerase structure and function; gene regulation and DNA supercoiling. B. I. Weinstein, Ph.D., Professor Emeritus: biochemistry of steroid action; metabolism and biologic activity of cortisol; enzyme deficiencies in glaucoma. J. M. Wu, Ph.D., Professor and Master's Program Director: regulation of gene expression in leukemic and prostate cancer cells; cell-cycle control; chemoprevention by fenretinide and resveratrol. Z. Zhang, Ph.D., Assistant Professor: X-ray crystallography; stem cell factor; quinone reductase 2.

Cell Biology and Anatomy. J. D. Etlinger, Ph.D., Professor and Chairman: skeletal muscle growth and atrophy; intracellular proteolysis in erythroid and muscle cells; role of proteasomes and ubiquitin; spinal cord injury. P. Ballabh, M.D., Professor: germinal matrix hemorrhage, pericytes. A. B. Drakontides, Ph.D., Professor Emerita: pathogenesis of early and late changes at the neuromuscular junction and skeletal muscle induced by chemical irritants. V. A. Fried, Ph.D., Professor and Graduate Program Director: ubiquitin and cellular regulation; cytoskeletal structure and functions. F. Hannan, Ph.D., Assistant Professor: *Drosophila melanogaster;* neurofibromatosis; learning and memory; Res; adenylyl cyclase; expression profiles. J. Kang, M.D., Associate Professor: astrocyte-mediated modulation of inhibitory synaptic transmission; interplay between excitatory and inhibitory synapses; properties of gap junction, K+, and GABA-A channels. M. Kumarasiri, Ph.D., Assistant Professor: protein turnover, ubiquitin-conjugated enzymes. K. M. Lerea, Ph.D., Associate Professor and Interdisciplinary Program Director: mechanisms of signal transduction; role of protein ser/thr kinases and phosphatases in integrin functions and platelet activation. S. A. Newman, Ph.D., Professor: physical and molecular mechanisms of development and evolution; pattern formation in the vertebrate limb; collagen assembly. K. Oktay, M.D., Professor: preservation by freezing and transplantation of oocytes and ovarian tissues to protect these cells from damage due to radiation and chemotherapy. R. Rozental, M.D., Ph.D., Associate Professor: role of connexins in nervous system development and dysfunction in ischemia and perinatal seizures. T. Sato, M.D., Associate Professor: regulation of calcium in normal and dystrophic skeletal muscles. P. B. Sehgal, M.D., Ph.D., Professor: interleukin-6; p53; gene expression; signal transduction (STAT3). S. C. Sharma, Ph.D., Professor: genetic approaches to regeneration of adult CNS neurons. A. D. Springer, Ph.D., Professor: engineering models of retinal development; optic nerve regeneration. P. K. Stanton, Ph.D., Professor: neuronal plasticity; long-term depression and potentiation of synaptic strength; synaptic functional changes in epilepsy; mechanisms of ischemia-induced delayed neuronal death. G. Suarez, M.D., Research Associate Professor: nonenzymatic protein glycation; sorbitol pathway; cell senescence; diabetic complications; self-assembly of collagens and lens crystallins. R. J. Zeman, Ph.D., Associate Professor: β_2-adrenoceptors in musculoskeletal growth; mechanisms of spinal cord injury; regulation of intracellular calcium.

Experimental Pathology. J. T. Fallon, M.D., Ph.D., Professor and Chairman: cardiovascular pathology; ischemic heart disease; experimental vascular injury; immunopathology of human myocarditis and allograft rejection. P. M. Chander, M.B.B.S., Professor: pathogenesis of renal and vascular damage in stroke-prone spontaneously hypertensive rats; pathogenesis of HIV-associated nephropathy. Z. Darzynkiewicz, M.D., Ph.D., Professor: development of new methods of cell analysis using flow cytometry; analysis of cell-cycle specificity of antitumor drugs. H. P. Godfrey, M.D., Ph.D., Professor and Ph.D. Program Director: mechanisms of pathogenesis in tuberculosis and Lyme disease; biomedical mechanisms of delayed hypersensitivity, chronic inflammation, and infectious disease. M. I. Iatropoulos, M.D., Research Professor: comparative mechanisms of toxicity and carcinogenesis. A. M. Jeffrey, Ph.D., Research Professor: toxicology and chronic carcinogenesis. M. Jhanwar-Uniyal, Ph.D., Research Associate Professor: signal transduction, BRCA, p53, cancer, central nervous system in obesity. A. Kumar, Ph.D., Professor: role of renin-angiotensin system in hypertension and atherosclerosis. J. M. Lombardo, M.D., Ph.D., Associate Professor: immunovirology; tuberculosis; HIV. P. A. Lucas, Ph.D., Research Associate Professor: wound healing and tissue engineering. F. H. Moy, Ph.D., Associate Professor of Clinical Pathology and Master's Program Director: biostatistics and epidemiology, methodology, and applications in environmetrics and risk assessment. F. Traganos, Ph.D., Professor: mechanisms of cell-cycle progression (checkpoints) and cell death (apoptosis) in cell cultures and clinical models. G. Wang, M.D., Clinical Assistant Professor: cytokines in Lyme carditis; antibacterial properties of treated fabrics; daptomycin-nonsusceptible enterococci. J. H. Weisburger, Ph.D., M.D. (hon.), Research Professor: mechanisms of toxicity and carcinogenicity; mechanisms and role of promoters in major human cancers; role of nutrition in human carcinogenesis; rational means of prevention of cancer, coronary heart disease, and stroke. G. M. Williams, M.D., Professor: mechanisms of carcinogenesis; metabolic and genetic effects of chemical carcinogens. R. E. Zachrau, M.D., Professor: spontaneous and induced tumor-specific, cell-mediated immunity in human breast cancer and its role in development of systemic metastasis and second primary cancers of breast and nonbreast origin.

Microbiology and Immunology. I. S. Schwartz, Ph.D., Professor and Chairman: molecular pathogenesis of Lyme disease and other emerging bacterial pathogens; functional genomics. R. Banerjee, Ph.D., Assistant Professor: molecular virology and molecular oncology. D. Bessen, Ph.D., Professor: molecular pathogenesis, epidemiology, and evolutionary biology of group A *Streptococcus* (GAS); role of GAS infection in pediatric neuropsychiatric disorders. D. Bucher, Ph.D., Associate Professor: structure, function, and immunochemistry of viral antigens. F. Cabello, M.D., Professor: microbial genetics; infectious disease; recombinant DNA. R. Dattwyler, M.D., Professor. J. Geliebter, Ph.D., Professor: immunology and molecular biology of prostate cancer. C. V. Hamby, Ph.D., Associate Professor: molecular biology and immunology of human tumors. D. Mordue, Ph.D., Assistant Professor: cellular and molecular strategies used by intracellular pathogens to establish and maintain infection. M. M. Petzke, Ph.D., Assistant Professor: Lyme disease; bacterial pathogenesis; innate immunity; dendritic cells; interferons; pattern recognition receptors; functional genomics. R. K. Tiwari, Ph.D., Professor and Graduate Program Director: tumor immunology and chemoprevention; cellular immunology; immune dysregulation in disease. F. E. Wassermann, Ph.D., Professor Emeritus: virus genetics; epidemiology, bioethics.

Pharmacology. M. L. Schwartzman, Ph.D., Professor and Acting Chairwoman: cytochrome P-450 metabolism of arachidonic acid in inflammation and hypertension. M. A. Carroll, Ph.D., Professor: renal cytochrome P-450 metabolites of arachidonic acid. N. R. Ferreri, Ph.D., Professor: cytokine production and function in the kidney and vascular smooth muscle. M. S. Goligorsky, M.D., Ph.D., Professor: basic mechanisms of endothelial dysfunction, its prevention and reversal; translation of bench findings to clinical physiology and pharmacology. M. A. Inchiosa Jr., Ph.D., Professor: biochemical pharmacology of muscle. J. C. McGiff, M.D., Professor: neural and hormonal control of circulation and renal function. A. Nasjletti, M.D., Professor and Ph.D. Program Director: hormonal mediators of blood pressure regulation. C. A. Powers, Ph.D., Associate Professor: neuroendocrinology. J. Quilley, Ph.D., Professor: Interactions of vasoactive hormones and eicosanoids in vascular regulation in diabetes and hypertension. C. T. Stier, Ph.D., Associate Professor and M.S. Program Director: pharmacological protection against vascular damage and stroke. W. Wang, M.D., Professor: regulation of renal electrolytes transport.

Physiology. T. H. Hintze, Ph.D., Professor and Chairman: cardiovascular functions in chronically instrumented animals. Z. Bagi, M.D., Ph.D., Assistant Professor: coronary microcirculation in diabetes, obesity, and other cardiovascular diseases; flow-induced vasodilatation. F. L. Belloni, Ph.D., Professor: vascular and cardiac actions of adenosine; biomedical and research ethics. John G. Edwards, Ph.D., Associate Professor: physiological control of gene transcription; regulation of transcription factors; cardiac hypertrophy; exercise biochemistry and overload alterations of the myocardial phenotype. C. Eisenberg, Ph.D., Associate Professor: phenotypic potential of "adult" stem cells. L. Eisenberg, Ph.D., Professor: molecular mechanisms controlling the phenotypic direction of differentiating stem cells. A. Huang, M.D., Ph.D., Associate Professor of Physiology: role of estrogens in vascular function. G. Kaley, Ph.D., Professor: control of blood pressure and blood flow. A. Koller, M.D., Professor: regulation of blood flow in the microcirculation. C. S. Leonard, Ph.D., Professor: modulation of mesopontine cholinergic nervous and neocortical interneurons; mammalian oculomotor system in CNS. N. Levine, Ph.D., Professor and Accelerated Master's Program Director: fluid and electrolyte secretion in the male reproductive system. E. J. Messina, Ph.D., Professor: microvascular control and regulation of smooth-muscle reactivity. C. Ojaimi, Ph.D., Assistant Professor: gene array technology; functional genomics in vascular biology; gene expression of normal and diseased heart. S. S. Passo, Ph.D., Professor: neuroendocrine control of blood pressure. Fabio A. Recchia, M.D., Professor and M.D./Ph.D. Program Director: control of myocardial metabolism; nitric oxide; heart failure; cardiac mechanics and efficiency; coronary circulation. W. N. Ross, Ph.D., Professor: regional properties of neurons. J. Stewart, M.D., Ph.D., Professor: orthostatic hypotension. D. Sun, M.D., Associate Professor: role of endothelial stress on coronary arteriolar function. C. I. Thompson, Ph.D., Professor and Graduate Program Director: renal hemodynamics and GFR control. M. S. Wolin, Ph.D., Professor: vascular regulation via cyclic GMP, metabolites, and oxygen tension.

NEW YORK UNIVERSITY

Langone Medical Center and the Graduate School of Arts and Sciences
Department of Environmental Medicine
Graduate Program in Environmental Health Sciences

Programs of Study

The Department of Environmental Medicine at New York University (NYU) is a diverse and dynamic research-oriented facility that is dedicated to the study of all aspects of environmental health science, with emphasis on such major health problems as cancer, respiratory illness, and cardiovascular disease. The Department offers a strong teaching and research program leading to both the M.S. and Ph.D. degrees through the Graduate School of Arts and Sciences of NYU.

The M.S. is offered in the Graduate Program in Environmental Health Sciences, with areas of study in environmental hygiene and environmental toxicology. Areas of study toward the Ph.D. are offered in biostatistics, epidemiology, ergonomics and biomechanics, exposure assessment and health effects, molecular toxicology/carcinogenesis, and toxicology.

During the first two years, Ph.D. students devote their time to course work and to research training via laboratory rotations. Comprehensive exams are usually taken at the end of the second year or following the completion of 48 (including transfer) credits. The final two to four years are spent conducting independent research under the supervision of a thesis research mentor chosen by mutual consent of mentor and student. Weekly Departmental seminars by visiting scientists as well as student seminar groups and presentations contribute to widening the students' outlook and keeping them abreast of the advancing state of knowledge in the environmental health sciences. Because the student-faculty ratio is kept low, substantial interaction with faculty members is possible.

Research Facilities

Graduate student research is carried out in the Department's research laboratories, which are well equipped with a variety of up-to-date, specialized scientific equipment to support the approximately ninety ongoing research projects.

A specialized environmental health library is located within the Department, and the NYU Langone Medical Center provides a large resource of biomedical references. Computerized bibliographic aids are available. Computer facilities are available in-house for scientific and word processing use. Tie-ins are also available to the NYU computer network; free computer time is made available for student research.

Financial Aid

Successful Ph.D. and M.S. applicants qualify for financial aid plus tuition and fees (ergonomics and biomechanics candidates are not included). In 2010–11, Ph.D. students received a stipend of $28,000 per year; M.S. students received a stipend of $14,000 per year.

Cost of Study

Tuition for 2010–11 was $1329 per credit plus fees, but these costs are waived for students who receive financial aid.

Living and Housing Costs

The cost of living varies according to individual requirements and location. Apartments are available near the Department's labs in Tuxedo, New York, and at NYU in Manhattan.

Student Group

Because of the diversity of the program, graduate students are accepted from a variety of backgrounds, including the biological, physical, and social sciences; mathematics; and engineering. Fifty-five graduate students are enrolled in the training program. Recent doctoral graduates have taken academic (40 percent), corporate (40 percent), and government (20 percent) scientific positions. A number have received postdoctoral fellowships at leading universities.

Location

NYU is in the heart of New York City. The many cultural centers of Manhattan are only minutes away by bus or subway. The Department of Environmental Medicine has a major facility located at Sterling Forest, a 20,000-acre reserve about 45 miles north of New York City. This location offers the dual benefits of rural/suburban living and proximity to New York City. Most courses are offered in Manhattan, and transportation between locations is provided.

The University and The Department

New York University, which was founded in 1831, is a large, private university with impressive scientific, scholarly, and cultural resources. The Department of Environmental Medicine has been designated by the National Institute of Environmental Health Sciences as a university center of excellence in teaching and research. It is also supported by the National Cancer Institute as a specialized center for research on environmental cancer.

Applying

Applications and supporting documents are due by December 12 for consideration for admission and financial aid. It is necessary to submit an NYU Graduate School application form, transcripts, three letters of recommendation, and scores on the GRE General Test. International students must submit scores on the Test of English as a Foreign Language (TOEFL).

Correspondence and Information

Graduate Coordinator
Department of Environmental Medicine
New York University Langone Medical Center
57 Old Forge Road
Tuxedo, New York 10987
Phone: 845-731-3661
Fax: 845-351-2058
E-mail: ehs@env.med.nyu.edu
Web site: http://environmental-medicine.med.nyu.edu/graduate-program

New York University

THE FACULTY AND THEIR RESEARCH

Max Costa, Ph.D., Chair, Department of Environmental Medicine. Metal carcinogenesis and toxicology; DNA-protein interactions; DNA damage; histone modifications and epigenetic mechanism of carcinogenesis.

Jerome J. Solomon, Ph.D., Director of Graduate Studies. DNA-carcinogen interaction; biological consequences of DNA adducts; mass spectrometry in carcinogenesis and environmental research.

Ilana Belitskaya-Levy, Ph.D. High-dimensional data analysis; algorithms for missing data analysis; EM algorithm; cluster analysis; developing statistical methods for analyzing large data arising in genomics and molecular biology; DNA microarrays; flow cytometry; statistical design and analysis of clinical trials; data mining; teaching.

Maarten C. Bosland, D.V.Sc., Ph.D. Hormonal carcinogenesis; prostate cancer chemoprevention; prostate and breast cancer; endocrine disruption; experimental pathology.

Fredric J. Burns, Ph.D. Cancer prevention and multiple stages in radiation carcinogenesis; patched gene and DNA repair genes in cancer susceptibility; arsenic cocarcinogenesis; DNA repair and proliferation.

Marco A. Campello, Ph.D. Work retention; disability management.

Haobin Chen, Ph.D. Metal carcinogenesis and toxicology; histone modifications and epigenetic mechanisms of carcinogenesis.

Lung Chi Chen, Ph.D. Inhalation toxicology; exposure-response relationships; air pollution.

Yu Chen, Ph.D. Environmental epidemiology; epidemiology of cancer and other chronic diseases.

Beverly S. Cohen, Ph.D. Measurement of personal exposures to airborne toxicants; dosimetry of inhaled pollutant gases and aerosols; airborne radioactivity.

Mitchell D. Cohen, Ph.D. Pulmonary immunotoxicology of inhaled pollutants; effects of inhaled pollutants on lung/lung immune-cell iron homeostasis; modulation of cytokine biochemistry by metals and complex mixtures; pulmonary/immunotoxicology of World Trade Center dusts.

Mark S. Condon, Ph.D. Stromal-epithelial interactions in carcinogenesis; in vitro and animal models of prostate cancer progression and metastasis.

Wei Dai, Ph.D. Cell cycle; checkpoint control; mitosis; chromosomal instability; protein kinases; tumor suppression; oncogenesis.

Hugh L. Evans, Ph.D. Neurotoxicology.

Krystyna Frenkel, Ph.D. Carcinogenesis and chemoprevention; role of endogenous oxidative stress in cancer and aging; contribution of inflammatory cytokines to carcinogenesis; effects of radiation-, metal-, and chemical-induced free radicals and their interactions with DNA on cancer development; biomarkers of cancer risk.

George Friedman-Jiménez, M.D. Occupational and clinical epidemiology; epidemiology of radiation and cancer; epidemiology of asthma; epidemiologic methods; urban populations.

Judith D. Goldberg, D.Sc. Design and analysis of clinical trials; survival analysis; disease screening and misclassification; analysis of observational data; statistical genomics.

David Goldsheyder, M.A., M.S. Biomechanics; workplace design; workstation modification; ergonomics.

Terry Gordon, Ph.D. Genetic susceptibility of lung disease produced by environmental and occupational agents.

Albert F. Gunnison, Ph.D. Molecular mechanisms and toxicology of pulmonary inflammation; DNA microarray technology; reproductive toxicology.

Manny Halpern, Ph.D. Ergonomics; workplace intervention; injury prevention methodology; job analysis.

Naomi H. Harley, Ph.D. Dosimetry of internally deposited radionuclides; measurement of radiation and radioactivity; risk modeling of radiation carcinogenesis.

Rudi Hiebert, M.S. Epidemiology; outcome studies.

Chuanshu Huang, Ph.D. Signal transduction in tumor promotion and prevention; molecular mechanism of carcinogenesis caused by ultraviolet radiation, metal compounds, and smoking.

Xi Huang, Ph.D. Implication of iron and oxidative stress in human diseases.

Kazuhiko Ito, Ph.D. Human health effects of air pollution and risk analysis.

Rudolph J. Jaeger, Ph.D. Inhalation toxicology; aerosol science; plastics toxicology and the toxicology of their monomers; combustion products; tobacco smoke toxicology; pulmonary pathophysiology; liver toxicity and pathophysiology; effects of lead and heavy metals on the developing nervous system.

Catherine B. Klein, Ph.D., Director of the M.S. Program. Mammalian mutagenesis; epigenetic gene control; DNA methylation; oxidants; metals; estrogens; molecular cytogenetics.

Karen Koenig, Ph.D. Epidemiology of coronary heart disease and cancer; epidemiologic methods.

Morton Lippmann, Ph.D. Inhalation toxicology; aerosol science and physiology; occupational and environmental hygiene; air pollution.

Angela Lis, M.A. Occupational musculoskeletal disorders; low back pain; prevention of injury; prevention of disability; biomechanics; ergonomics.

Mengling Liu, Ph.D. Analysis of longitudinal data with informative censoring; survival analysis; semiparametric inference; analysis for quality-of-life data.

Michael Marmor, Ph.D. Epidemiology and prevention of HIV/AIDS, tuberculosis, and other infectious diseases; clinical trials of HIV vaccines and nonvaccine interventions; environmental, occupational, and ophthalmologic epidemiology.

Assieh Melikian, Ph.D. Mechanisms of environmental carcinogenesis; cancer chemoprevention; biomarkers; molecular epidemiology.

Arthur Nádas, Ph.D. Mathematical statistics; biostatistics; mathematical biology; statistical design of HIV immunotypes, with the goal of a broadly effective polyvalent vaccine for HIV; experimental design and analysis using microarrays and gene chips; statistical analysis of telemetry data; mathematical modeling of spontaneous mutagenesis; rapid multivariate diagnostic tests for tuberculosis; pattern recognition using dynamic programming, hidden Markov modeling, and neural networks.

Bhagavathi A Narayanan, Ph.D. Prostate and colon cancer chemoprevention; nonsteroidal anti-inflammatory drugs; genomic and proteomic approaches; potential molecular targets; biomarkers.

Narayanan K. Narayanan, Ph.D. Chemopreventive proteomics; Omega-3 polyunsaturated fatty acid against prostate cancer; proteomic profiling of differentiation-inducing proteins.

Margareta Nordin, Med.Dr.Sci. Occupational musculoskeletal disorders, low back pain; prevention of injury; prevention of disability; motor control; biomechanics; ergonomics.

Qingshan Qu, M.D. Pulmonary toxicology; biomarker application and risk assessment.

William N. Rom, M.D., M.P.H. Environmental and occupational lung diseases; molecular mechanisms of lung cancer; tuberculosis (TB)/AIDS; interferon-gamma therapy for TB and TB vaccine and immune response; environmental policy, wilderness preservation, and global warming.

Toby G. Rossman, Ph.D. Spontaneous mutagenesis; genotoxicity of metal compounds; mechanisms of resistance to metals; arsenic carcinogenicity.

Nirmal Roy, Ph.D. Molecular biology of the aromatic hydrocarbon receptor pathway; DNA lesions and mutations induced by xenobiotic compounds.

Ali Sheikhzadeh, Ph.D. Occupational biomechanics; biomechanical modeling and testing; electromyography; ergonomic product evaluation.

Roy E. Shore, Ph.D., Dr.P.H. Environmental and genetic epidemiology of cancer; radiation epidemiology; epidemiologic methods.

Bernard G. Steinetz, Ph.D. Environment of the newborn: possible role of milk-borne hormones in phenotypic expression of inherited hip dysplasia; role of hormones in protection against environmental carcinogen–induced breast cancer afforded by early pregnancy; role of hormones in the modulation of insulin resistance of pregnancy.

Hong Sun, Ph.D. Transcription factors; epigenetics; metal carcinogenesis; cell differentiation.

Moon-shong Tang, Ph.D. Carcinogenesis and mutagenesis; DNA damage; DNA repair.

Kam-Meng Tchou-Wong, Ph.D. p53 pathways in metal- and carcinogen-induced lung cancer; Wnt signaling pathways in lung fibrosis and cancer; chemoprevention of lung carcinogenesis; infection and ethnic disparities in diabetes risk and cardiovascular diseases.

George D. Thurston, D.Sc. Human health effects of inhaled air pollutants; asthma; aerosol science; acidic air pollution; air pollution meteorology and modeling; risk analysis.

Paolo G. Toniolo, M.D. Cancer epidemiology; role of endogenous hormones in the etiology of chronic diseases; influence of diet on endogenous hormones in health and disease; health consequences of human exposure to hormonally active agents in the environment.

Diane Trainor, Ph.D. Hazards control; occupational safety and health.

Sherri Weiser, Ph.D. Biopsychosocial models; low back pain; personality and health; occupational stress.

Isaac Wirgin, Ph.D. Molecular biology of carcinogenesis; cancer in aquatic organisms; population genetics and molecular evolution.

Judy Xiong, Ph.D. Occupational hygiene; environmental chemistry; aerosol science.

Anne Zeleniuch-Jacquotte, M.D. Cancer epidemiology; methods in epidemiology and clinical trials.

Judith T. Zelikoff, Ph.D. Immunotoxicology; development of immune biomarkers and alternative animal models for immunotoxicological studies; effects of inhaled pollutants on host resistance and pulmonary immune defense mechanisms; metal-induced immunotoxicity.

THE ROCKEFELLER UNIVERSITY

Graduate Programs

Programs of Study
Graduate education leading to the Ph.D. is offered to outstanding students regarded as potential leaders in their scientific fields. The University's research covers a wide range of biomedical and related sciences, including biochemistry, structural biology, biophysics, and chemistry; molecular, cell, and developmental biology; medical sciences and human genetics; immunology and microbiology; neurosciences; and bioinformatics, biophysics, and computational neuroscience, as summarized by the faculty list in this description. Students work closely with a faculty of active scientists and are encouraged to learn through a combination of course work, tutorial guidance, and apprenticeship in research laboratories. Graduate Fellows spend the first two years engaged in a flexible combination of courses geared toward academic qualification while conducting research in laboratories pertaining to their area of scientific interest. They choose a laboratory for thesis research by the end of the first year and devote their remaining time to pursuit of significant experimental or theoretical research, culminating in a dissertation and thesis defense. Students can spend full time in research; there are no teaching or other service obligations.

The faculties of the Rockefeller University, Weill Medical College of Cornell University, the Weill Graduate School of Medical Sciences of Cornell University, and Sloan-Kettering Institute collaborate in offering a combined M.D./Ph.D. program in the biomedical sciences to about 90 students. This program, conducted on the adjacent campuses of these three institutions in New York City, normally requires six or seven years of study and leads to an M.D. degree conferred by Cornell University and a Ph.D. degree conferred by either the Rockefeller University or the Weill Graduate School of Cornell University, depending upon the organizational affiliation of the student's adviser.

Research Facilities
The University and its affiliate Howard Hughes Medical Institute maintain a full range of laboratories and services for the research activities of the professional staff and students. Facilities include clinical and animal research centers on campus, a library, computing services, a field research center in Dutchess County, the Aaron Diamond AIDS Research Center (ADARC), as well as new centers for human genetics, studies in physics and biology, biochemistry and structural biology, immunology and immune diseases, sensory neuroscience, and Alzheimer's disease research.

Financial Aid
Each student accepted into the Ph.D. program receives a stipend ($31,600 in 2010–11) that is adequate to meet all living expenses. Students also receive an annual budget of $1500 that can be used for travel, books and journals, computer purchases, and lab supplies.

Cost of Study
The University provides full remission of all tuition and fees for all accepted students.

Living and Housing Costs
On-campus housing is available for all students at subsidized rates. The stipend is designed to cover the cost of food, housing, and other basic living expenses. Students may elect to live off campus, but rents in the vicinity are very high.

Student Group
There are 196 graduate students, of whom 167 are enrolled in the Ph.D. program and 29 in the Ph.D. phase of the combined M.D./Ph.D. program. It is the policy of the Rockefeller University to support equality of educational opportunity. No individual is denied admission to the University or otherwise discriminated against with respect to any program of the University because of creed, color, national or ethnic origin, race, sex, or disability.

Student Outcomes
Graduates of the Rockefeller University have excelled in their professions. Two graduates have been awarded the Nobel Prize, and 26 graduates are members of the National Academy of Sciences. Most Ph.D. graduates move to postdoctoral positions at academic and research centers and subsequently have careers in academics, biotechnology, and the pharmaceutical industry. A few have pursued careers in medicine, law, and business. Almost all M.D./Ph.D. graduates first complete residencies in medical specialties, and most become medical scientists at major academic and medical research centers.

Location
The University is situated between 62nd and 68th streets in Manhattan, overlooking the East River. Despite its central metropolitan location, the 15-acre campus has a distinctive nonurban character, featuring gardens, picnic areas, fountains, and a tennis court. In addition to administrative and residential buildings, there are seven large laboratory buildings and a forty-bed hospital that serves as a clinical research center. Immediate neighbors are the New York Hospital, the Weill Medical College of Cornell University, Memorial Hospital, and the Sloan-Kettering Institute for Cancer Research. The wide range of institutions in New York City affords unlimited opportunities in research specialties, library facilities, and cultural resources.

The University
The Rockefeller University is dedicated to benefiting humankind through scientific research and its application. Founded in 1901 by John D. Rockefeller as the Rockefeller Institute for Medical Research, it rapidly became a source of major scientific innovation in treating and preventing human disease. Since 1954, the institute has extended its function by offering graduate work at the doctoral level to a select group of qualified students.

Laboratories, rather than departments, are the fundamental units of the University. The absence of departmental barriers between laboratories encourages interdisciplinary, problem-oriented approaches to research and facilitates intellectual interaction and collaboration. The collegial atmosphere fosters independence and initiative in students. In addition to the 196 doctoral students, there are 350 postdoctoral associates and fellows and a faculty of 70 full, associate, and assistant professors on campus who head laboratories.

Applying
Applications for the M.D./Ph.D. program must be completed by October 15; those for the Ph.D. program must be completed by December 6. Applicants are required to submit a personal statement describing research experience and goals as well as reasons for pursuing graduate study at the Rockefeller University. Also required are official transcripts and at least three letters of recommendation. Official GRE General Test scores are required and Subject Test scores are highly recommended for admission to the Ph.D. program. MCAT scores are required for the M.D./Ph.D. program. Further information about each program and details on application procedures may be obtained from the programs' respective Web sites. This information is also available on the University Web site, from which application forms and instructions can be downloaded.

Correspondence and Information

For the Ph.D. program:
Office of Graduate Studies
The Rockefeller University
1230 York Avenue
New York, New York 10065
Phone: 212-327-8086
E-mail: phd@rockefeller.edu
Web site: http://www.rockefeller.edu

For the M.D./Ph.D. program:
Tri-Institutional M.D./Ph.D. Program
Weill Cornell/Rockefeller/Sloan-Kettering
1300 York Avenue, Room C-103
New York, New York 10065
Phone: 212-746-6023
    888-U2-MD-PHD (toll-free)
E-mail: mdphd@mail.med.cornell.edu
Web site: http://www.med.cornell.edu/mdphd

The Rockefeller University

LABORATORY HEADS AND THEIR RESEARCH

C. David Allis, Ph.D. (Histone Modifications and Chromatin Biology). Enzymology and function of covalent histone modifications; histone code and epigenetic regulation.

Cori Bargmann, Ph.D. (Neuroscience). Genetic analysis of olfactory behavior and neural development.

Günter Blobel, M.D., Ph.D. (Cell Biology). Protein translocation across membranes; macromolecular traffic into and out of the nucleus.

Sean Brady, Ph.D. (Genetically Encoded Small Molecules). Structure and function of genetically encoded small molecules.

Jan L. Breslow, M.D. (Biochemical Genetics and Metabolism). Identifying the genes that control atherosclerosis susceptibility.

Jean-Laurent Casanova, M.D., Ph.D. (Human Genetics of Infectious Diseases). Genetics of human predisposition to pediatric infectious diseases, particularly mycobacterial diseases.

Brian T. Chait, D.Phil. (Mass Spectrometry and Gaseous Ion Chemistry). Protein mass spectrometry.

Nam-Hai Chua, Ph.D. (Plant Molecular Biology). Gene regulation and signal transduction in plants.

Joel Cohen, Ph.D., Dr.P.H. (Populations). Population dynamics; ecology; epidemiology.

Barry Coller, M.D. (Clinical Hematology). Biochemistry of platelet disorders; study of heritable coagulopathies.

Frederick P. Cross, Ph.D. (Molecular Genetics). Cell-cycle control in budding yeast.

George A. M. Cross, Ph.D. (Molecular Parasitology). Regulation of gene and surface glycoprotein expression in trypanosomes.

James E. Darnell Jr., M.D. (Molecular Cell Biology). Signal transduction and gene control in mammalian differentiation.

Robert B. Darnell, M.D., Ph.D. (Molecular Neuro-Oncology). Neuro-oncology and autoimmunity; molecular neurobiology.

Seth Darst, Ph.D. (Molecular Biophysics). Protein crystallography and electron microscopy of macromolecular assemblies.

Titia de Lange, Ph.D. (Cell Biology and Genetics). Chromosome function in vertebrates.

Mitchell J. Feigenbaum, Ph.D. (Mathematical Physics).

Vincent A. Fischetti, Ph.D. (Bacterial Pathogenesis). Pathogenesis of streptococcal diseases and mucosal vaccine development.

Jeffrey M. Friedman, M.D., Ph.D. (Molecular Genetics). Genes controlling food intake and body weight; mouse genetics.

Winrich Freiwald, Ph.D. (Neural Systems). Neural processes that form object representations, as well as those that allow attention to make those representations available for cognition.

Elaine Fuchs, Ph.D. (Mammalian Cell Biology and Development). Molecular mechanisms underlying the coordination of proliferation, transcription, and cell adhesion in tissue morphogenesis and in cancer.

Hinonori Funabiki, Ph.D. (Chromosome and Cell Biology). Mechanisms controlling accurate chromosome segregation during the cell division cycle.

David C. Gadsby, Ph.D. (Cardiac and Membrane Physiology). Mechanism and function of ion pumps and channels.

Charles D. Gilbert, M.D., Ph.D. (Neurobiology). Visual spatial integration and cortical dynamics.

Konstantin A. Goulianos, Ph.D. (Experimental High-Energy Physics).

Paul Greengard, Ph.D. (Molecular and Cellular Neuroscience). Role of phosphoproteins in signal transduction in the developing and adult nervous system.

Howard C. Hang, Ph.D. (Chemical Biology and Microbial Pathogenesis). Chemical tools for studying posttranslational modifications in living cells.

Mary E. Hatten, Ph.D. (Developmental Neurobiology). Control of CNS neuronal specification and migration during vertebrate brain development.

Nathaniel Heintz, Ph.D. (Molecular Biology). Cell-cycle regulation; molecular neurobiology; mammalian neurogenetics.

Ali Hemmati-Brivanlou, Ph.D. (Molecular Embryology). Molecular embryology of vertebrates.

David D. Ho, M.D. (Dynamics of HIV/SIV Replication). Kinetics of CD4 lymphocyte turnover; determinants of disease progression; therapy of HIV infection.

A. James Hudspeth, M.D., Ph.D. (Sensory Neuroscience). Transduction and synaptic signaling by hair cells of the inner ear.

Tarun Kapoor, Ph.D. (Chemistry and Cell Biology). Small-molecule probes of cellular processes.

Bruce W. Knight Jr. (Biophysics). Neurophysiology and applied mathematics.

M. Magda Konarska, Ph.D. (Molecular Biology and Biochemistry). Splicing of mRNA precursors and replication of hepatitis delta virus.

Mary Jeanne Kreek, M.D. (Neuroscience). Neurobiology and molecular genetics of addictive diseases; endogenous opioid system.

James G. Krueger, M.D., Ph.D. (Investigative Dermatology). Cutaneous pathobiology.

Stanislas Leibler, Ph.D. (Physics and Mathematical Biology). Analysis of biological networks.

Albert J. Libchaber, Ph.D. (Experimental Condensed-Matter Physics).

Roderick MacKinnon, M.D. (Molecular Neurobiology and Biophysics). Structure and function of ion channels and associated regulatory proteins.

Marcelo Magnasco, Ph.D. (Mathematical Physics). Stochastic processes in biology systems.

Bruce S. McEwen, Ph.D. (Neuroendocrinology). Hormonal regulation of neural plasticity.

Daniel Mucida, Ph.D. (Mucosal Immunology). Mechanisms of intestinal immunity.

Tom W. Muir, Ph.D. (Synthetic Protein Chemistry). Combinatorial protein chemistry.

Fernando Nottebohm, Ph.D. (Animal Behavior). Animal communication; mechanisms of learning, memory duration, and brain repair.

Michel C. Nussenzweig, M.D., Ph.D. (Molecular Immunology). Molecular basis of B-cell development.

Michael O'Donnell, Ph.D. (DNA Replication). Underlying principles of DNA replication in the human and *E. coli* systems.

Jürg Ott, Ph.D. (Statistical Genetics). Developing, implementing, and applying statistical methods of human genetic mapping.

F. Nina Papavasiliou, Ph.D. (Molecular Immunology). Molecular mechanisms of lymphocyte diversity.

Donald W. Pfaff, Ph.D. (Neurobiology and Behavior). Gene expression in brain; hormone action; brain control of behavior.

Jeffrey V. Ravetch, M.D., Ph.D. (Molecular Genetics and Immunology). Genetics of the humoral immune response; genetic variation in malaria parasite.

George N. Reeke Jr., Ph.D. (Biological Modeling). Theoretical models of brain functions; protein structure.

Charles Rice, Ph.D. (Virology). Molecular genetics of animal RNA viruses (alphaviruses and flaviviruses, in particular hepatitis C virus); replication and pathogenesis.

Robert G. Roeder, Ph.D. (Biochemistry and Molecular Biology). Transcriptional regulatory mechanisms in animal cells.

Michael P. Rout, Ph.D. (Structural Cell Biology). Nucleocytoplasmic transport; nuclear pore complex structure, function, and assembly.

Thomas P. Sakmar, M.D. (Molecular Biology and Biochemistry). Biochemistry and molecular biology of transmembrane signal transduction and visual phototransduction.

Shai Shaham, Ph.D. (Cancer Biology). Programmed cell death in the nematode *Caenorhabditis elegans*.

Eric Siggia, Ph.D. (Theoretical Condensed-Matter Physics). Statistical physics and dynamical systems to cellular biophysics and bioinformatics.

Sanford M. Simon, Ph.D. (Cellular Biophysics). Protein biogenesis, membrane protein assembly, tumorigenesis, and drug resistance.

Agata Smogorzewska, M.D., Ph.D. (Genome Maintenance). Elucidating pathways that prevent cancer development by using Fanconi anemia as a backdrop for understanding aging and cancer.

C. Erec Stebbins, Ph.D. (Structural Microbiology). Structural studies of bacterial virulence factors and their host cell targets.

Ralph M. Steinman, Ph.D. (Cellular Physiology and Immunology). Antigen presenting cell function for initiating immune responses in health and disease, especially HIV-1 infection.

Hermann Steller, Ph.D. Molecular biology of apoptosis and cancer biology.

Sidney Strickland, Ph.D. (Neurobiology and Genetics). Genetics of neuronal function and dysfunction; genetics of early development.

Alexander Tarakhovsky, M.D., Ph.D. (Immunology). Mechanisms of the dynamic tuning of antigen receptor-mediated signaling in lymphocytes.

Sohail Tavazoie, M.D., Ph.D. (Systems Cancer Biology). Using a systems biological approach to identify and characterize key molecular regulators of metastasis.

Alexander Tomasz, Ph.D. (Microbiology). Mechanisms of antibiotic resistance and virulence in bacteria.

Thomas Tuschl, Ph.D. (Chemistry). Regulation of gene expression by double-stranded RNA in humans.

Leslie Vosshall, Ph.D. (Sensory Neuroscience). Molecular genetics of olfaction in *Drosophila melanogaster*.

Michael W. Young, Ph.D. (Genetics). Genes controlling behavior and development in *Drosophila*; molecular control of circadian rhythms.

ROSALIND FRANKLIN UNIVERSITY OF MEDICINE AND SCIENCE
School of Graduate and Postdoctoral Studies

Programs of Study	A student's decision as to what field of research to pursue is important and something that should have careful consideration. In the School of Graduate and Postdoctoral Studies (SGPS), doctoral programs lead to degrees in each of the following biomedical sciences: biochemistry and molecular biology, cell biology and anatomy, cellular and molecular pharmacology, microbiology and immunology, physiology and biophysics, and neuroscience. All students targeting these disciplines begin studies with the first-year interdisciplinary plan called Interdisciplinary Graduate Program in Biomedical Sciences (IGPBS), which allows them time to receive an education in the most current areas of the biomedical sciences before they select a laboratory in which to conduct their graduate research program.
	The School has also partnered with both Chicago Medical School and Dr. William M. Scholl College of Podiatric Medicine to create combined M.D./Ph.D. and D.P.M./Ph.D. programs in these disciplines. These programs allow individuals interested in pursuing physician/scientist careers to have a continuous balance of clinical and research training throughout all years of the their education at Rosalind Franklin University of Medicine and Science (RFUMS) and then pursue research-based residency programs fostering these unique career paths.
Research Facilities	RFUMS has invested millions of dollars in its research infrastructure and environment. These state-of-the-art facilities include fully equipped animal quarters and a spectrum of newly constructed research support laboratories, such as structural biology, cell sorting, confocal and electron microscopy, and live-cell imaging.
	At RFUMS, research is classified into three pillars of strength: Neurosciences, Structural Biology/Biochemistry, and Molecular Cellular Processes. These areas include investigations into the underlying mechanisms of protein structure and function; the molecular basis of ion transport systems; cellular and molecular mechanisms of drug dependency and neurodegenerative diseases, such as Alzheimer's and Parkinson's; and the mechanisms of viral-induced cancer. A more extensive list of areas of research emphasis can be found at http://www.rosalindfranklin.edu/research.
Financial Aid	SGPS offers stipends which are awarded on a competitive basis. As of 2010–11, stipends are awarded at $23,665 annually. Additionally, full tuition waivers are provided to all Ph.D. students. Students have access to the same health benefits as faculty members.
Cost of Study	The annual tuition for the Interdisciplinary Graduate Program in Biomedical Sciences for 2010–11 is $23,285. Tuition for the doctoral program is waived.
Living and Housing Costs	The University has moderately priced, on-campus housing facilities. The annual cost of housing in the Chicagoland area is estimated at $15,300.
Student Group	The University's 2009 fall enrollment was approximately 1,915 students in its four schools: the Chicago Medical School, the School of Graduate and Postdoctoral Studies, the undergraduate College of Health Professions, and the Dr. William M. Scholl College of Podiatric Medicine. Development of the College of Pharmacy, the newest addition to the Rosalind Franklin University family, began in early 2009.
Student Outcomes	Doctoral students at RFUMS are highly competitive and are placed in excellent postdoctoral programs. The University's combined M.D./Ph.D. and D.P.M./Ph.D. graduates continue their training by placing into residency programs and postdoctoral programs.
Location	The School of Graduate and Postdoctoral Studies is part of the Rosalind Franklin University of Medicine and Science. The University is located in North Chicago, a northern suburb in Lake County, Illinois. Situated approximately 30 miles north of downtown Chicago, it enjoys the diversity of both city sidewalks and the surrounding state forests and greenbelts. Easy access to the city is available via the Chicago Metra rail or Pace bus systems.
The School	The School of Graduate and Postdoctoral Studies was established in 1968 as a further development of the Chicago Medical School, which was founded in 1912. The graduate program is directed toward the education of students who plan careers in the biomedical sciences.
Applying	Candidates for admission must have a bachelor's degree or its equivalent from a regionally accredited college or university. Applicants are selected on the basis of previous academic work; research experience and preparation in the proposed field of graduate study, as determined by the Dean and the program's advisory board; grade point average; scores on the general Graduate Record Examination; and recommendations from persons involved in the student's previous educational and research experience. There is no application fee for the program.
	Applications are available online at the University Web site. The priority deadline for applications and all supporting documents for fall 2011 term is January 14, 2011. On-campus interviews are held in early March, and international interviews are held via telephone and videoconference throughout the application season. Early application is strongly encouraged. Stipends are awarded on a competitive basis, and recipients are selected by April 15. The application process may remain open after the priority deadline, but will be closed once the class is filled.
Correspondence and Information	Office of IGPBS Admissions Rosalind Franklin University of Medicine and Science 3333 Green Bay Road North Chicago, Illinois 60064 Phone: 847-578-8601 866-98-IGPBS (866-984-4727; toll-free) E-mail: IGPBS@rosalindfranklin.edu Web site: http://www.rosalindfranklin.edu

www.twitter.com/usgradschools   **107**

Rosalind Franklin University of Medicine and Science

ADMINISTRATORS OF GRADUATE PROGRAMS

School of Graduate and Postdoctoral Studies: Michael P. Sarras Jr., Ph.D., Dean and Vice President for Research.
Interdisciplinary Graduate Program in Biomedical Sciences: Robert Intine, Ph.D., Director and Combined Degree Program Chair.
Biochemistry and Molecular Biology: Ronald S. Kaplan, Ph.D., Chair.
Cell Biology and Anatomy: William Frost, Ph.D., Chair.
Cellular and Molecular Pharmacology: Charles Barsano, M.D./Ph.D., Acting Chair.
Microbiology and Immunology: Bala Chandran, Ph.D., Chair.
Neuroscience: Marina Wolf, Ph.D., Chair.
Physiology and Biophysics: Robert Bridges, Ph.D., Chair.

STATE UNIVERSITY OF NEW YORK
UPSTATE MEDICAL UNIVERSITY
College of Graduate Studies

Programs of Study

As one of the nation's 127 academic medical universities, SUNY Upstate Medical University in Syracuse, New York, educates students in biomedical research (master's and Ph.D.), medicine, nursing, and health professions.

At SUNY Upstate's College of Graduate Studies, Ph.D. students thrive as they participate in medically relevant research on a campus that is proud of its mentoring and multidisciplinary approach. This begins in the first year as students experience three in-depth laboratory rotations of their choice and an interdisciplinary core curriculum.

After their lab rotations, Ph.D. students select their thesis mentor and ultimate area of study. In addition to a student-faculty ratio of nearly 1:1, students have daily or near-daily interaction with their principal investigator. Students also make independent contributions to research projects, and the majority of students publish their work as "first author" in professional journals during their program. Ph.D. degrees are offered by the Departments of Cell and Developmental Biology, Biochemistry and Molecular Biology, Microbiology and Immunology, Neuroscience and Physiology, and Pharmacology. The Ph.D. program, including research, course work, and successful defense of a dissertation, is intended to be completed in four or five years.

Four Research Pillars account for 75 percent of the campus' funded activity and emphasize some of the most intriguing areas for biomedical study—cancer; infectious diseases; diabetes, metabolic disorders, and cardiovascular disease; and disorders of the nervous system. As part of a major medical center, the graduate students have an opportunity to pursue basic research with immediate clinical relevance. No matter which department students choose for their Ph.D. track, they have the opportunity to pursue research in the Pillars.

Students are trained at the Ph.D. and master's levels for research and teaching careers in the biotechnology industry, at biomedical research institutes, in government, and at academic medical centers, colleges and universities.

Research Facilities

SUNY Upstate has world-class facilities for faculty members and students. In addition to departmental resources, main core facilities on campus include the Center for Research and Evaluation, Confocal/Two Photon Imaging, Department of Laboratory Animal Resources, DNA Sequencing, Flow Cytometry, Humanized SCID Mouse and Stem Cell Processing, Imaging Research, In Vivo Computed Tomography, Microarray (SUNYMAC), MRI Research, and Proteomics.

SUNY Upstate also maintains a coalition with nearby Cornell University, the University of Rochester Medical Center, and Buffalo's Roswell Park Cancer Institute, which is dedicated to sharing cutting-edge research facilities. There are also full research-support services on campus, including laboratory-animal facilities, network access to the SeqWeb suite of software, a computer-age medical library containing more than 183,000 volumes, electronics and machine shops, and photographic and computer services.

SUNY Upstate's growth on the research side is highlighted by a $72-million expansion of its Institute for Human Performance, a high-tech facility housing shared laboratories and core facilities used in basic and clinical research. It also broke ground in 2009 for a dedicated research park facility.

Financial Aid

All accepted Ph.D. students are fully supported throughout their education by full tuition waivers and a stipend ($21,514 per year). Support comes from graduate assistantships, departmental assistantships, and NIH and NSF grants.

Cost of Study

Stipends and full tuition waivers are granted to all students accepted into the Ph.D. program. There is no teaching requirement. Student fees, which include health service, are $552 for the 2009–10 academic year. Tuition and fees for master's students for the 2009–10 academic year are $8370 for in-state students and $13,250 for out-of-state students.

Living and Housing Costs

On-campus housing is available in Clark Tower, a ten-story apartment building with attractive, fully furnished standard rooms, studio apartments, and two-bedroom suites. Costs ranged from $4127 (double occupancy) to $8618 (married/family accommodations) for 2009–10. Clark Tower also has study rooms, computer rooms, private and shared kitchens, lounges, a recreation room, laundry, and storage. Clark Tower is next door to the Campus Activities Building, which houses athletic facilities, a bookstore, and snack bar.

Many students rent nearby houses or apartments and bicycle or walk to campus. Syracuse has a low cost of living and abundant affordable housing.

Student Group

There are 124 graduate students in the biomedical sciences (58 percent women; 100 percent full-time) and approximately 600 medical students, 200 nursing students, and 200 students in the health professions enrolled at Upstate Medical University. Twenty-five percent of the graduate students come from Canada, Europe, and Asia. Syracuse University and the SUNY College of Environmental Science are located within a quarter mile of SUNY Upstate, resulting in a population of approximately 23,000 students in the immediate area.

Location

Syracuse is New York's fourth-largest city and is located in the scenic center of the state. A naturally beautiful setting, the area offers excellent hiking, biking, boating, and skiing. Nearby are the Finger Lakes region, the Adirondack and the Catskill Mountains, and Lake Ontario. Syracuse's cultural activities include a professional theater, symphony orchestra and opera company, noted author lecture series, chamber music groups, and several top-notch music festivals (classical, blues, and jazz) as well as art and history museums. The area also offers quality family life with many excellent school districts and Upstate's own day care center. Syracuse University's top-level collegiate sporting events are a major recreational activity. Syracuse is easily reached by air, rail, and car.

The University

SUNY Upstate is the only academic medical center in the central New York region and is part of the dynamic University Hill community. In addition to the College of Graduate Studies, SUNY Upstate Medical University includes three other colleges—Medicine, Nursing, and Health Professions—its own University Hospital, and a regional campus in Binghamton, New York. The University is growing with new leadership, degree programs, and further plans for expansion. SUNY Upstate Medical University is close to downtown Syracuse and is adjacent to (but not affiliated with) the campus of Syracuse University. SUNY Upstate's Campus Activities Building houses a swimming pool, sauna, gymnasium, squash courts, handball/paddleball court, weight-lifting area with a Universal Gym and a full Nautilus room, billiards, table tennis, television room, bookstore, snack bar, and lounge. Conference rooms are also available for student use.

Applying

The Admissions Committee for the College of Graduate Studies at SUNY Upstate begins reviewing applications in December prior to entry and continues until all positions are filled, which can be as early as early April. The State University of New York requires a $40 application fee. Competitive applicants must have a bachelor's degree or its equivalent, a minimum 3.0 GPA and course work that includes biology, calculus, chemistry, and physics. GRE General Test scores are required (combined score 1000 minimum), and scores from the Subject Test in chemistry or biology are recommended. International applicants must provide clear evidence of English proficiency (including speaking) by taking the Test of English as a Foreign Language (TOEFL). Candidates for admission are selected on the basis of their record and qualifications for independent scholarship in a specialized field of study. Selected applicants will be invited to campus to meet with faculty and students, and to tour lab facilities.

Correspondence and Information

Office of Graduate Studies
State University of New York Upstate Medical University
750 East Adams Street
Syracuse, New York 13210

Phone: 315-464-7655
Fax: 315-464-4544
E-mail: biosci@upstate.edu
Web site: http://www.upstate.edu/grad/

State University of New York Upstate Medical University

THE FACULTY AND THEIR RESEARCH

Jeffrey Amack, Ph.D., Assistant Professor. Genetics and cell biology of organ morphogenesis during embryonic development.

David Amberg, Ph.D., Professor. Regulation of actin dynamics and analysis of genomic influences on actin function.

Robert B. Barlow, Ph.D., Professor. Neural basis of visual behavior, computational models of neural coding, circadian and metabolic modulation of human visual sensitivity.

Edward A. Berry, Ph.D., Assistant Professor. Structure and function of membrane protein complexes from energy-transducing biological electron transfer chains.

Scott D. Blystone, Ph.D., Associate Professor. Actin cytoskeletal dynamics in the leukocyte inflammatory phenotype.

Blair Calancie, Ph.D., Professor. CNS plasticity after trauma, intraoperative electrophysiology.

Peter Calvert, Ph.D., Assistant Professor. Molecular mechanisms of protein transport and localization in retinal neurons, mechanisms of retinal degenerative diseases.

Gregory Canute, M.D., Associate Professor. Genetics and gene therapy of brain tumors.

Xin Jie Chen, Ph.D., Associate Professor. Mitochondrial biogenesis and inheritance, aging and aging-related degenerative diseases.

Richard L. Cross, Ph.D., Professor. The mechanism of mitochondrial oxidation phosphorylation, biological rotary motors.

Timothy A. Damron, M.D., Professor. Radioprotectant strategies for protecting the pediatric growth plate.

Joseph Domachowske, M.D., Adjunct Professor. Pneumovirus pathogenesis.

Dipak Dube, Ph.D., Professor. Molecular mechanism of cardiac myofibrillogenesis in vertebrates.

Thomas Duncan, Ph.D., Associate Professor, Bioenergetics, enzymology, structural biology, membrane protein function.

Russell G. Durkovic, Ph.D., Professor. Examination of processes underlying recovery from spinal cord injury in the salamander.

Timothy Endy, M.D., M.P.H., Associate Professor. Understanding the epidemiology and pathogenesis of viral hemorrhagic and encephalitic arboviruses and host-vector interactions.

Gerold Feuer, Ph.D., Associate Professor. HTLV pathogenesis and Tax function, humanized SCID mouse models of hematopoiesis, lentivirus vectors, KSHV/HHV-8 infection and pathogenesis, SCID-hu immune responses against HIV envelope.

Jeffrey C. Freedman, Ph.D., Associate Professor. Membrane physiology in normal and sickle human red blood cells, optical indicators of membrane potential and intracellular calcium, membrane biophysics.

Eileen A. Friedman, Ph.D., Adjunct Professor. Role of the serine/theonine kinase Mirk/dyrk1B in cancers of the pancreas, ovary, and colon.

Jerrie Gavalchin, Ph.D., Professor. Regulation of pathogenic antibody production in autoimmune glomerulonephritis, cell-surface receptors for retroviruses.

Stephen J. Glatt, Ph.D., Assistant Professor. Psychiatric epidemiology and genetics.

Steven Goodman, Ph.D., Professor and Dean. Proteomic assessment of sickle cell severity.

Sandra M. Hayes, Ph.D., Assistant Professor. Determining the roles of gamma/delta TCR structure and signaling potential in gamma/delta T-cell development and function.

Charles J. Hodge, M.D., Professor. Mechanisms of cortical plasticity and cortical reorganization after injury.

George G. Holz, Ph.D., Professor. Molecular pharmacology and physiology of pancreatic beta cells, drug development for the treatment of type 2 diabetes mellitus.

Huaiyu Hu, Ph.D., Professor. Molecular studies of brain malformations.

Ying Huang, M.D., Ph.D., Associate Professor. Oncogenic signaling in cellular transformation and apoptosis, tumor suppressor genes.

Ziwei Huang, Ph.D., Professor and Chair. Discovery and mechanism of action of new pharmacological agents for cancer, cardiovascular disease, neurodegeneration, infectious disease, and stem cell-based regenerative medicine.

Charles B. C. Hwang, Ph.D., Professor. DNA replication of herpes viruses.

Burk Jubelt, M.D., Professor. CNS acute and chronic polio- and entero-virus infections.

Patricia M. Kane, Ph.D., Professor and Chair. Mechanisms and regulation of cellular pH control, V-type ATPases.

Wendy Kates, Ph.D., Associate Professor. Anatomic and functional imaging investigations of neurodevelopment in individuals with genetic or psychiatric disorders.

Grant Kelley, M.D., Associate Professor. Elucidating the regulation of PLC-epsilon and its role in glucose signaling and endothelial cell function in diabetes.

William Kerr, Ph.D., Professor. Transplant immunology, stem cell biology.

Dilip Kittur, M.D., Professor. Xenotransplantation, endothelial cell dysfunction, use of herbal products in transplant biology.

Barry Knox, Ph.D., Professor. Visual transduction, gene expression, membrane proteins.

Mira Krendel, Ph.D., Assistant Professor. Physiological functions of myosin motors and their roles in diabetic kidney disease and cancer.

Andrzej Krol, Ph.D., Associate Professor. Molecular and dynamic imaging, image registration and fusion, tomographic reconstruction, ultrafast laser-based x-ray source, brain deformation quantification between mutant and normal mouse.

James Listman, M.D., Assistant Professor. Cytomegalovirus and transplantation.

Stewart N. Loh, Ph.D., Professor. Mechanism and kinetics of protein folding, structure and function of the p53 tumor suppressor, design of proteins with new or enhanced functions, protein-based molecular switches.

Michael J. Lyon, Ph.D., Associate Professor. Age-related changes in the laryngeal muscles and vocal folds.

Kenneth Mann, Ph.D., Professor. Mechanical and biological factors in total joint replacement.

Paul Massa, Ph.D., Professor. Genetic regulation of glial cell differentiation.

Russell Matthews, Ph.D., Assistant Professor. Role of glycoproteins in oncogenesis and brain development.

James S. McCasland, Ph.D., Professor. Cortical plasticity, development of somatotopic representations in cortex.

Michael E. Meguid, M.D., Adjunct Professor. Neurophysiological regulation of food intake.

Frank Middleton, Ph.D., Associate Professor. Molecular basis of cortical–basal ganglia and cortical-cerebellar circuit and dysfunction in neurological and psychiatric disease.

Michael Miller, Ph.D., Professor and Chair. Factors that regulate the proliferation, migration, and survival/death of neurons in the developing brain; models of fetal alcohol syndrome, autism, and attention-deficit hyperactivity disorder.

David R. Mitchell, Ph.D., Professor. Regulation of ciliary dynein activity and assembly, role of the central pair complex in ciliary motility regulation.

Jennifer Moffat, Ph.D., Associate Professor. Varicella zoster pathogenesis.

M. Golam Mohi, Ph.D., Assistant Professor. Molecular mechanism of leukemia, effect of oncogenic mutations in pathogenesis of leukemia, using mouse model.

Sandra Mooney, Ph.D., Assistant Professor. Cell death and survival in the developing brain, mechanisms of ethanol toxicity, models of fetal alcohol syndrome and autism.

Brad Motter, Ph.D., Research Associate Professor. Visual neurophysiology, visual attention, visual search behavior.

Nancy Nussmeier, M.D., Professor. Stroke after cardiac surgery, cerebral protection during cardiac surgery, gender-related surgical outcomes.

Eric Olson, Ph.D., Assistant Professor. Cellular and molecular mechanisms of cerebral cortex development.

Andras Perl, M.D., Ph.D., Adjunct Professor. Genes and viruses predisposing to autoimmunity, genetics, apoptosis, endogenous retroviruses, transaldolase.

Arkadii Pertsov, Ph.D., Professor. Biophysical mechanisms of cardiac arrhythmias, fluorescence imaging.

Francesa Pignoni, Ph.D., Associate Professor. Neurogenesis, retinal progenitor cells specification and proliferation, genetic control of stem cell identity and maintenance, genetic pathways in RPE formation, disease genes analysis in *Drosophila*.

Thomas J. Poole, Ph.D., Associate Professor. Vascular development and the alignment of growing nerves and blood vessels in quail and zebrafish embryos.

Dawn Post, Ph.D., Assistant Professor. Cancer treatment, using oncolytic viruses and gene therapy.

Michael F. Princiotta, Ph.D., Assistant Professor. Antigen processing and presentation, cytotoxic T-lymphocyte response to viral and bacterial infections.

David Pruyne, Ph.D., Assistant Professor. Biochemistry and cell biology of formins as actin cytoskeleton organizers using *Caenorhabditis elegans* as a model system.

Rosemary Rochford, Ph.D., Professor and Chair. Etiology of viral-associated malignancies, gammaherpesvirus pathogenesis.

Jean M. Sanger, Ph.D., Professor. Analysis of the assembly of the actin/myosin cytoskeleton in muscle and nonmuscle cells.

Joseph W. Sanger, Ph.D., Professor and Chair. Cellular analysis of the formation of myofibrils, stress fibers, and cleavage furrows in living cells.

Steven J. Scheinman, M.D., Professor. Molecular genetics of kidney stones.

Mark E. Schmitt, Ph.D., Associate Professor. Ribonucleoprotein assembly and biogenesis, mitochondrial RNA import, mRNA degradation, cell-cycle control.

M. Saeed Sheikh, M.D., Ph.D., Professor. Apoptotic signal transduction and cancer biology.

Edward J. Shillitoe, B.D.S., Ph.D., Professor. Gene therapy for cancer.

Allen E. Silverstone, Ph.D., Professor. How dioxins and estrogens and estrogenic compounds affect the immune system.

Vladimir Sirotkin, Ph.D., Assistant Professor. Mechanisms of the actin cytoskeleton assembly and role of myosin-1 during endocytosis in fission yeast.

Joseph A. Spadaro, Ph.D., Professor. Electromagnetic and mechanical regulation of bone physiology, skeletal growth and bone density.

Dennis J. Stelzner, Ph.D., Professor. CNS regeneration, spinal cord injury research, neural plasticity.

Steven M. Taffet, Ph.D., Professor. Regulation of intercellular communication in the heart, gene expression during macrophage activation.

Daniel Ts'o, Ph.D., Associate Professor. Neuronal mechanisms of visual perception, studied through physiological, anatomical, and functional imaging techniques.

Christopher E. Turner, Ph.D., Professor. Regulation of cell migration by focal adhesion adapter proteins and their role in cancer cell metastasis.

Mary Lou Vallano, Ph.D., Professor. Neuronal survival and development.

Richard D. Veenstra, Ph.D., Professor. Regulation of connexin-specific gap junctions, gap-junction channel biophysics.

Andrea Viczian, Ph.D., Assistant Professor. Mammalian retinal stem cells formation, molecular mechanism of retinal cell fate decisions, using cell replacement therapy to heal the blinded eye.

Brent Vogt, Ph.D., Professor. Structure, functions, and pathologies of cingulate cortex.

Stephan Wilkens, Ph.D., Associate Professor. Structure and mechanism of membrane-bound transport proteins.

Richard J. H. Wojcikiewicz, Ph.D., Professor. Intracellular signaling via $InsP_3$ receptors and the ubiquitin/proteasome pathway.

Steven Youngentob, Ph.D., Professor. Olfactory neural plasticity in adults, olfactory signal transduction, in-utero ethanol experience and olfactory system plasticity, peripheral and central mechanisms of odorant quality coding.

Michael Zuber, Ph.D., Assistant Professor. Molecular basis of retinal stem cell formation, regulating retinal stem/progenitor cell proliferation, using retinal stem/progenitor cells to heal the injured or degenerating retina.

THOMAS JEFFERSON UNIVERSITY

Jefferson College of Graduate Studies

Programs of Study

Jefferson College of Graduate Studies offers graduate programs leading to the degree of Doctor of Philosophy in biochemistry and molecular biology, cell and developmental biology, genetics, immunology and microbial pathogenesis, molecular pharmacology and structural biology, and neuroscience. The College also offers graduate programs leading to the degree of Master of Science in biomedical sciences, cell and developmental biology, microbiology, and pharmacology. Ph.D. students generally complete their program courses during the first two years and a comprehensive examination follows. The focus is on doctoral thesis research for the remainder of the program. Research culminates in a scholarly dissertation that is defended during a final examination.

Jefferson Medical College and Jefferson College of Graduate Studies jointly sponsor a combined M.D./Ph.D. program for students who wish to pursue a career in academic medicine and medical research. During the first two years, students complete the basic medical preclinical curriculum in Jefferson Medical College. The next four years are spent in the Graduate College in pursuit of the Ph.D. degree. The final two years involve completion of medical studies in Jefferson Medical College.

Research Facilities

The Bluemle Life Sciences Building, with 157,000 square feet of laboratory space, serves as the primary research facility for molecular biology and genetics, molecular virology, microbiology, and immunology. Other basic science departments are housed in spacious, modern facilities. Farber Institute for Neurosciences is housed in the Jefferson Hospital for Neuroscience building and Jefferson Alumni Hall. Students have access to modern research equipment for molecular analysis of gene expression and functional aspects of the immune system, sophisticated studies of cell physiology, and in-depth studies of embryonic development and all aspects of drug metabolism.

Financial Aid

Financial support is available to the majority of full-time Ph.D. students in the form of University fellowships, training grants, and research assistantships. In 2010–11, students granted full fellowship support receive funds for payment of tuition and a stipend of $26,300. Also available to students demonstrating financial need are Title IV funds, including those from the Federal Family Education Loan Programs (federally subsidized and unsubsidized Stafford student loans), Federal Perkins Loan, and Federal Work-Study programs. University loan programs are also available to qualifying students.

Cost of Study

Tuition and fees for the 2010–11 academic year are $27,798 for full-time Ph.D. students. Tuition for M.S. basic science students is $920 per credit.

Living and Housing Costs

On-campus student housing includes three residence facilities that provide apartment and dormitory accommodations with opportunity for single or shared occupancy.

Student Group

Currently, the University enrolls about 2,500 students. The College of Graduate Studies enrolls approximately 600 students, about half of whom are women.

Location

Thomas Jefferson University is centrally located in Philadelphia within walking distance of many places of cultural interest, including concert halls, theaters, museums, art galleries, and historic landmarks. There are numerous intercollegiate and professional athletic events. Convenient bus and subway lines connect the University with other local universities and colleges and with several outstanding libraries. The proximity of the New Jersey shore and the Pennsylvania mountains offers year-round recreational opportunities, and New York City and Washington, D.C., are each just two hours away.

The University

The rapidly expanding Thomas Jefferson University is an academic health center emphasizing the biological sciences. Its origin dates back to 1824, with the founding of Jefferson Medical College and includes, in addition to the Jefferson Medical College, the Jefferson College of Graduate Studies, the Jefferson School of Health Professions, the Jefferson School of Nursing, the Jefferson School of Pharmacy, the Jefferson School of Population Health, the University Hospital, and various affiliated hospitals and institutions. The Bluemle Life Sciences Building houses the Kimmel Cancer Center. The Jefferson Hospital for Neurosciences houses the Farber Institute for Neurosciences. Jefferson Alumni Hall houses, in addition to departmental laboratories, the Alcohol Research Center, the Ischemia-Shock Research Institute, and the Jefferson Institute of Molecular Medicine. Student activities offices and facilities (i.e., swimming pool, exercise rooms, gymnasium, and handball/squash court), student lounges, and JCGS administrative offices are also located in Jefferson Alumni Hall.

Applying

Applications to Ph.D. programs should be submitted by January 5 for optimal consideration for admission and fellowship support. Ph.D. applications received after this date will be evaluated at the discretion of the program faculty. Applications to M.S. programs are evaluated on a rolling basis. Graduate Record Examinations (GRE) scores, three letters of recommendation, academic transcripts, and a $50 application fee are required of all applicants. For those whose native language is not English, scores on the Test of English as a Foreign Language (TOEFL) or the IELTS are required. Campus visits and tours of respective departments are accommodated upon request.

Correspondence and Information

Office of Admissions
Jefferson College of Graduate Studies
Thomas Jefferson University
1020 Locust Street, M-60
Philadelphia, Pennsylvania 19107-6799

Phone: 215-503-4400
Fax: 215-503-9920
E-mail: jcgs-info@jefferson.edu
Web site: http://www.jefferson.edu/cgs

Thomas Jefferson University

THE FACULTY AND THEIR RESEARCH

Biochemistry and Molecular Biology–Ph.D.
Research faculty: Arthur Allen, Emad S. Alnemri, Carol L. Beck, Jeff Benovic (Department Chair), George C. Brainard, David Capuzzi, Mon-Li Chu, Edgar Davidson, John I. Farber, Barry J. Goldstein, Gerald B. Grunwald, Noreen J. Hickok, Shi-Ying Ho, Jan B. Hoek, Ya-Ming Hou, James B. Jaynes, Sergio Jimenez, Erica Johnson, Hideko Kaji, James H. Keen, Michael P. King, Jose Martinez, Alexander Mazo, W. Edward Mercer, Diane E. Merry (Program Director), Urich Rodeck, Peter Ronner, Michael Root, Barbara Schick, Matthias J. Schnell, Stephanie Schulz, Charles P. Scott, Sandor Shapiro, Thomas Tulenko, Jouni Uitto, Scott Waldman, Philip B. Wedegaertner, David A. Wenger, Eric Wickstrom, Charlene J. Williams, John C. Williams, Kevin J. Williams, Edward P. Winter, Kyonggeun Yoon, Allen R. Zeiger.

Research interests: regulation of DNA replication; RNA metabolism; mechanisms of cell synthesis; steroid and protein hormone receptors; mitochondrial DNA mutations; molecular biology of protein degradation; molecular biology–gene cloning; base sequencing of genes; gene expression in cell cultures; apoptosis and signal transduction; molecular biology of human diseases.

Cell and Developmental Biology
Research faculty: Eleni Anni, Robert Barsotti, David Birk, Alan Cahill, Ronald A. Coss, Manuel L. Covarrubias, Leonard M. Eisenman, John S. Ellingson, John L. Farber, Mark Feitelson, Bruce A. Fenderson, Giancarlo Ghiselli, Gregory E. Gonye, Fred Gorstein, Gerald B. Grunwald, Gyorgy Hajnoczky, David Herrick, Jan B. Hoek, Richard Horn, Lorraine Iacovitti, Renato Iozzo, Nathan Janes, James B. Jaynes, Suresh K. Joseph, Hideko Kaji, Boris N. Kholodenko, Devendra M. Kochhar, Edward. B. Lankford, Alexander Mazo, Peter A. McCue, A. Sue Menko, Pamela A. Norton, John G. Pastorino, Nancy J. Philp, Biddanda C. Ponnappa, Emanuel Rubin, Raphael Rubin, James D. San Antonio, Barbara P. Schick, Jay S. Schneider, James Schwaber, David S. Strayer, Christopher Stubbs, Theodore F. Taraschi (Director), Jouni J. Uitto, Elisabeth J. Van Bockstaele, Philip Wedegaertner, Edward P. Winter.

Research interests: alcohol-induced liver diseases; bioinformatics; calcium signaling; cell cycle and apoptosis; calcium metabolism; cell-cell and cell matrix adhesion; cellular differentiation; cellular effects of alcohol; cellular signaling; chemical carcinogenesis; contractility; cytoskeleton; developmental aspects of oncology; developmental neurobiology; DNA repair in malaria parasites; extracellular matrix structure and function; eye development; functional genomics; gene therapy; hepatitis virus and hepatocellular carcinoma; ion channel structure and function; mechanisms of anesthetic action; mechanisms of cell injury; membrane biology; mitochondria and cell death; neurodegeneration and pathophysiology of Parkinsonism; protein trafficking and organelle biogenesis in malaria-infected erythrocytes; regulation of cellular growth; stem cells; structure-function relationships in biological membranes; systems biology. The program also offers a concentration in tissue engineering and regenerative medicine.

Genetics–Ph.D.
Research faculty: David Abraham, Emad S. Alnemri, Raffaele Baffa, Renato Baserga, Jeffrey L. Benovic, Bruce M. Boman, Arthur M. Buchberg Bruno Calabretta, Marcella Devoto, Ya-Ming Hou, James B. Jaynes, Erica Johnson, James H. Keen, Carlisle Landel, Alexander Mazo, Steven McKenzie, W. Edward Mercer, Diane Merry, Jay L. Rothstein, Linda D. Siracusa (Program Director), Saul Surrey, Jouni J. Uitto, Scott Waldman, Ya Wang, Charlene J. Williams, Edward P. Winter.

Research interests: functional genomics; genetics of cancer susceptibility; molecular genetic analysis of normal human genome; cytogenetics of aneuploidy syndromes; genetics of immune system; molecular genetics of animal models of human disease; molecular genetics of hematopoietic neoplasias and solid tumors; genetic analysis of G-1 phase and molecular mechanisms of altered growth regulation by oncogenes and tumor suppressor genes; transcriptional regulation and control of gene expression; mechanisms of ionizing and nonionizing radiation damage to cells.

Immunology and Microbial Pathogenesis–Ph.D.
Research faculty: David Abraham, Kishore R. Alugupalli (Program Director), Melvin Bosma, Arthur M. Bunchberg, Bruno Calabretta, Catherine E. Calkins, Bernhard Dietzschold, Laurence C. Eisenlohr, Mark A Feitelson, Neal Flomenberg, Phyllis Flomenberg, Richard R. Hardy, D. Craig Hooper, Donald L. Jungkind, Tim Manser, W. Edward Mercer, Glen F. Rall, Ulrich Rodeck, Michael J. Root, Jay L. Rothstein, Matthias Schnell, Charles P. Scott, Linda D. Siracusa, Alagarsamy Srinivasan, David S. Strayer, Yuri Sykulev, Theodore F. Taraschi, John L. Wagner, Scott A. Waldman, David West, Hui Zhang, Jianke Zhang.

Research interests: antigen presentation; antiviral agents; autoimmunity; B-cell development; cancer immunology; cell biology of malaria; cell growth regulation and differentiation; cellular immunology; cell activation and signal transduction; chemical and antigenic structure of virus particles; cytokines; developmental immunology; immunochemistry; immunogenetics; immunoparasitology; immunoregulation; latent virus infections; microbial immunology and pathogenesis; molecular immunology; neuroimmunology; neurovirology; regulation of viral gene expression; reproductive immunology; transplantation immunology; viral oncogenes; viral replication; virus-cell interactions.

Molecular Pharmacology and Structural Biology
Research faculty: Emad S. Alnemri, Renato Baserga, Jeffrey L. Benovic (Program Director), Bruce Boman, George C. Brainard, John L. Farber, Barry J. Goldstein, Jan B. Hoek, Ya-Ming Hou, James H. Keen, Walter Koch, Jose Martinez, Ulrich Rodeck, Michael J. Root, Charles P. Scott, Scott A. Waldman, Philip Wedegaertner, Eric Wickstrom, John Williams, Edward P. Winter.

Research interests: biochemistry and cell, molecular, and structural biology of cell-surface and intracellular receptors; structural biology and molecular modeling of protein-protein and nucleic acid interactions; molecular mechanisms of membrane sorting and intracellular organization; neuropharmacology; signal transduction; clinical pharmacology.

Neuroscience
Research faculty: Jeffrey Benovic, George C. Brainard, Manuel Covarrubias, Leonard Eisenman, Michelle Ehrlich, Jayasri Das Sarma, Samuel Gandy (Director of Farber Institute for Neurosciences), Gregory Gonye, Gerald Grunwald, Larry Harshyne, Richard Horn, Lorraine Iacovitti, Hector Lopez, Jeffrey Mason, Sue Menko, Diane Merry, Michael Oshinsky, Michelle Page, Raymond Regan, A. M. Rostami, Jay Schneider, James Schwaber, Stephen D. Silberstein, Joseph I. Tracy, Elisabeth Van Bockstaele (Program Director), Stephen Weinstein, David A. Wenger, Ji-Fang Zhang.

Research interests: neurodegenerative disorders, neuropharmacology, neuronal signaling, protein-protein interactions, structure and function of ion channels, affective disorders, neurodevelopment, neuroopthalmology, addiction and motivated behaviors.

Basic Science M.S. Programs
Program Directors: Carol L. Beck, Dennis M. Gross, Gerald B. Grunwald.

The programs give students sound theoretical and practical foundations in four important areas of the basic biomedical sciences. Students can specialize within a discipline by selecting from the track options within each program. M.S. basic program offerings are biomedical chemistry, cell and developmental biology, microbiology, and pharmacology. In addition to the traditional laboratory-based research thesis, these programs also offer a nonthesis option that culminates in a capstone project.

Graduate Certificate Programs
Jefferson College of Graduate Studies also offers graduate certificate programs to provide industry, academic, and health professionals with skills and knowledge needed for success in today's health sciences–related environments. The two certificate programs are clinical research/trials, and infectious disease control.

UNIVERSITY AT ALBANY, STATE UNIVERSITY OF NEW YORK

School of Public Health
Department of Biomedical Sciences

UNIVERSITY AT ALBANY
State University of New York

Program of Study

The Department of Biomedical Sciences offers broadly based research training in the areas of molecular genetics, cancer biology, structural and cell biology, immunology and infectious diseases, and neuroscience. Students are admitted for study toward the Ph.D. or M.S. degree. Training is individualized, with course selection based on the area of specialization and on the background and interests of each student. During the first semester, several short projects are undertaken in the laboratories of faculty members. At the end of the laboratory rotation period, the student selects a mentor for thesis research. Emphasis is placed on informal instruction and interaction between students and faculty members in the laboratory, seminars, colloquia, and journal clubs.

Research Facilities

Faculty members are located in the Wadsworth Center, the central laboratory complex of the New York State Department of Health which has an academic relationship with the University at Albany, and in the University's newly constructed Cancer Research Center. The Wadsworth and Cancer Research Center laboratories are spacious modern facilities that are among the most technologically advanced and comprehensive laboratory complexes in the country. Faculty and student research is supported by outstanding core facilities in biochemistry, proteomics, genomics, advanced light microscopy and imaging, computational biology and statistics, mouse behavior, transgenics, immunology, X-ray crystallography, NMR, and mass spectrometry.

The Wadsworth Center and Cancer Research Center support a vibrant seminar program and provide multiple opportunities for students, post docs, and faculty to interact at the bench, in the classroom, and in conference-type environments. Students have 24/7 access to the Dickerman Library and its vast collection of scientific books and journals, most of which are available online. Including both print and online versions, the library provides access to over 2,000 medical and scientific journals.

Financial Aid

Graduate assistantships and tuition scholarships are awarded to incoming doctoral students on a competitive basis. Graduate assistantship stipends range from $24,000 to $26,000. Other forms of financial support include research assistantships from faculty research grants.

Cost of Study

Full-time tuition is $4185 per semester for New York State residents and $6625 per semester for out-of-state and international students. University fees are approximately $600 per semester.

Living and Housing Costs

In addition to student residence halls, off-campus apartments are available at rents ranging from $600 to $900 per month.

Student Group

Of the 18,000 students at the State University of New York at Albany, 4,900 are graduate students. They come from all parts of the United States and more than forty countries.

Location

Albany, the capital of the state of New York, offers a large choice of cultural attractions ranging from music, dance, and theater, to horse racing and other sports. In the nearby Adirondack and Catskill Mountains and in the Berkshires, students find an unlimited variety of outdoor activities including hiking, camping, canoeing, skiing, and climbing. Other attractions include Lake George, Saratoga Springs, Tanglewood (in Massachusetts), and the Olympic Sports Complex in Lake Placid. New York City, Boston, Montreal, Vermont, and Atlantic Ocean beaches are all within a few hours' drive. Albany has an airport, bus and train services, and an extensive public transportation system.

The University

The University at Albany is the senior campus and one of four University Centers of the sixty-four campus State University of New York system. The main campus is housed in a modern complex occupying a 400-acre site at the western edge of Albany.

Applying

College transcripts, Graduate Record Examinations scores on the General Test, three references from people who are familiar with the applicant's academic qualifications, a statement of the applicant's educational and professional aims, and a $75 application fee must be submitted to the Office of Graduate Admissions. A Subject Test in biology, biochemistry, chemistry, or physics is recommended. International applicants must submit a minimum TOEFL score of 600. Students applying for the Ph.D. program must submit their application packet to the Office of Graduate Admissions by January 1 to receive full consideration for a graduate assistantship. Students applying for the Master of Science program must submit their application through the Web site at http://www.sophas.org by April 1.

Correspondence and Information

Department of Biomedical Sciences
Wadsworth Center
University at Albany
P.O. Box 509
Albany, New York 12201-0509
Phone: 518-473-7553
Fax: 518-473-8520
E-mail: bmsdept@wadsworth.org
Web site: http://www.wadsworth.org/sph/bms

University at Albany, State University of New York

THE FACULTY AND THEIR RESEARCH

M. Joan Curcio, Chair; Ph.D., George Washington, 1987. Interplay between mobile retroelements and their hosts; formation of the retrogenome.

Janice D. Pata, Associate Chair; Ph.D., Colorado at Boulder, 1994. Structure-function studies of specialized cellular and viral polymerases.

Rajendra Kumar Agrawal, Ph.D., Banaras Hindu (India), 1993. Structure and function of macromolecular assemblies.

Nilesh Banavali, Ph.D., Maryland, 2001. Computational modeling of macromolecular machinery dynamics.

Thomas J. Begley, Ph.D., SUNY at Albany, 1999. Systems toxicology; mechanisms of DNA repair; damage signaling.

Marlene Belfort, Ph.D., California, Irvine, 1972. Gene expression; RNA splicing; intron mobility; molecular evolution; inteins in biotechnology.

Valerie Bolivar, Ph.D., Dalhousie. Genetics of complex behaviors (e.g., learning and memory, anxiety) and brain structures (corpus callosum, hippocampal commissure, mossy fibers) in the mouse; development of mouse models of autism.

April Burch, Ph.D., Arizona, 2000. Virus assembly and the host-pathogen interface.

Michele Caggana, Sc.D., Harvard, 1991. Population-based gene frequency studies; newborn screening; clinical testing; nanobiotechnology.

David Carpenter, M.D., Harvard, 1964. Study of human disease as a result of environmental exposures, especially as a result of PCBs and chlorinated pesticides; use of animal model systems to study mechanisms of toxicity.

Sudha Chaturvedi, Ph.D., Delhi (India), 1990. Fungal and parasite pathogeneses; protein transport and secretion mechanisms.

Vishnu Chaturvedi, Ph.D., Delhi (India), 1988. Unique metabolism of fungal pathogens; fungal-human phagocyte interactions.

Xiang Yang Chen, Ph.D., Hong Kong, 1990. Spinal reflex conditioning.

Richard Cole, M.S., SUNY at New Paltz, 1985. Advanced imaging and analysis technologies; LED technology; confocal multiphoton intravital imaging studying microvessel angiogenesis in skin.

Douglas S. Conklin, Ph.D., Wisconsin–Madison, 1992. Functional genomics of cancer; RNAi-based genetic technology; cell-cycle physiology.

Jan Conn, Ph.D., Toronto, 1987. Evolutionary genetics of mosquitoes that transmit infectious diseases.

Keith Derbyshire, Ph.D., Edinburgh, 1983. Molecular genetics of mycobacteria: transposition; conjugal DNA transfer; gene expression and protein secretion.

James A. Dias, Ph.D., Washington State, 1979. Structure-function relationships of pituitary glycoprotein hormones and their receptors; biochemical endocrinology; reproductive immunology.

Xinxin Ding, Ph.D., Michigan, 1988. Molecular toxicology; pharmacogenetics; gene regulation and biological function of cytochrome P-450 monooxygenases; transgenic/knockout mouse models of human diseases.

Christina Egan, Ph.D., Albany Medical College, 1997. Diagnostic assay development for the detection of biothreat agents.

Michael Fasullo, Ph.D., Stanford, 1986. DNA recombination and repair; yeast genetics; DNA damage response to environmental carcinogens.

Joachim Frank, Ph.D., Munich Technical, 1970. 3-D cryoelectron microscopy of macromolecules; mechanisms of translation.

Robert Glaser, Ph.D., Cornell, 1989. Genetics of host-arbovirus interactions; *Drosophila* genetics.

Todd Gray, Ph.D., Michigan, 1993. Epigenetics and genomic imprinting in mammals; genetics and function of the MAKORIN zinc-finger protein family.

Andrea Habura, Ph.D., Rensselaer, 1996. Molecular phylogenetics; evolution; structural biology and biogeography of protists.

Steven Hanes, Ph.D., Brown, 1988. Homeobox genes, protein-DNA interaction; prolyl isomerases, cell-cycle control.

Charles Hauer, Ph.D., Virginia, 1991. Proteomics; protein modifications; biological mass spectrometry.

Bruce J. Herron, Ph.D., SUNY at Albany, 1999. Functional analysis of the mouse genome; investigation of defects in mammalian organogenesis.

Matthew Hynd, Ph.D., Queensland, 2004. Neurotechnology research and development; implantable neural prosthetic devices for treatment of neurodegenerative diseases

Joachim Jaeger, D.Phil., Basel (Switzerland), 1991. Structure-function studies of viral replication complexes using X-ray crystallography, solution scattering, imaging techniques, mutagenesis, and kinetics.

Janet Keithly, Ph.D., Iowa State, 1984. Parasite metabolism and drug design using biochemical and molecular techniques.

Jeffrey S. Kennedy, M.D., Tufts, 1987. Clinical and experimental endocrinology and immunology.

Laura D. Kramer, Ph.D., Cornell, 1974. Virus-vector-vertebrate interactions and arboviral evolution.

Alan Laederach, Ph.D., Iowa State, 2003. RNA folding and assembly bioinformatics.

David Lawrence, Ph.D., Boston College, 1971. Biochemistry of lymphocytes; host resistance; immunotoxicology.

William Lee, Ph.D., Johns Hopkins, 1987. Cellular immunology; generation of immunologic memory; lymphocyte interactions.

David LeMaster, Ph.D., Yale, 1980. Protein structure and dynamics; enzyme catalysis; NMR spectroscopy.

Hongmin Li, Ph.D., Institute of Biophysics (Beijing), 1995. Crystal structures of scorpion neurotoxins.

Susan Madison-Antenucci, Ph.D., Duke, 1994. Molecular biology of parasites; RNA editing in pathogenic parasites.

Carmen Mannella, Ph.D., Pennsylvania, 1974. Mitochondrial structure and metabolite transport.

Nicholas Mantis, Ph.D., Cornell, 1994. Mucosal immunity and vaccine development to enteropathogenic bacteria and toxins.

Paul Masters, Ph.D., Brandeis, 1981. Molecular virology of coronaviruses; assembly of viral structural proteins and mechanism of RNA synthesis.

Joseph Mazurkiewicz, Ph.D., Colorado, 1973. Cutaneous expression of neuropeptides and their regulation; relationships of cutaneous innervation to injury and pain.

Kathleen McDonough, Ph.D., Stanford, 1990. Microbial pathogenesis; host-parasite interactions; TB and plague.

Bruce McEwen, Ph.D., Cornell, 1982. Use of cutting-edge technology in light and electron microscopy to study the structure and function of vertebrate kinetochores and axonemes.

James McSharry, Ph.D., Virginia, 1970. Pharmacodynamics and pharmacokinetics of antiviral compounds.

Anne Messer, Ph.D., Oregon, 1972. Gene therapy of brain disorders.

Randall Morse, Ph.D., Caltech, 1981. Transcription and chromatin in murine neural stem cells.

Donal Murphy, Ph.D., Michigan, 1974. Expression and function of major histocompatibility complex (MHC) genes and their products.

Kimberlee A. Musser, Ph.D., Albany Medical College, 1998. Molecular analysis of bacterial agents; bioterrorism preparedness.

Kenneth Pass, Ph.D., Medical University of South Carolina, 1976. Development of novel technologies for use in newborn screening programs.

Haydeh Payami, Ph.D., Berkeley, 1985. Genetics of aging and neurodegenerative diseases.

Robert Rej, Ph.D., Albany Medical College, 1976. New biochemical tests for disease diagnosis.

Conly L. Rieder, Ph.D., Oregon, 1977. Mitosis and the physiology of cell division; centrosome and kinetochore function.

Gerwin Schalk, Ph.D., Rensselaer, 2006. Brain-computer interface technology for communication and diagnosis.

Erasmus Schneider, Ph.D., Bern (Switzerland), 1983. Pharmacogenetics of drug effects; sensitization of tumors to chemotherapy.

Richard F. Seegal, Ph.D., Georgia, 1972. Developmental neurotoxicity of PCBs and heavy metals; neuroimmune interactions and Parkinson's disease.

Stewart Sell, M.D., Pittsburgh, 1970. Stem cells in tissue renewal and carcinogenesis; chemical hepatocarcinogenesis.

Abigail Snyder-Keller, Ph.D., Pittsburgh, 1983. Developmental neuroanatomy and neurotoxicology; effects of prenatal drug exposure.

Lawrence S. Sturman, M.D., Northwestern, 1960; Ph.D., Rockefeller, 1968. Structure and function of coronavirus glycoproteins; molecular mechanisms of viral pathogenesis; fate of viruses in soil and water.

Haixin Sui, Ph.D., Dalian (China), 1996. Structure and function of macromolecular assemblies in their cellular context.

Derek Symula, Ph.D., Wisconsin–Madison, 1995. Copy number variants and polymorphisms associated with autism; cytogenetics.

Harry Taber, Ph.D., Rochester, 1963. Bacterial gene expression and antibiotic resistance.

Norma Tavakoli, Ph.D., Bristol (England), 1994. Molecular detection and typing of viral agents; investigation of viral etiologies of central nervous system infections; diagnostic assay development.

Scott A. Tenenbaum, Ph.D., Tulane, 1994. Posttranscriptional gene expression as mediated by RNA-binding proteins; viral-host interactions; ribonomics.

Martin P. R. Tenniswood, Ph.D., Queen's at Kingston, 1979. Studies on the molecular regulation of cell survival and death in prostate and breast cancer to identify new targets for the development of adjuvant therapies for hormone-dependent and refractory cancers.

Joseph Wade, Ph.D., Birmingham (England), 2001. Regulation of gene expression in bacteria.

Terence Wagenknecht, Ph.D., Minnesota, 1977. Structure of macromolecular complexes.

JoEllen Welsh, Ph.D., Cornell, 1980. Nutrition, nuclear receptors, genomics and chronic disease; interactions between nuclear receptors and environmental factors in cancer development and aging.

David E. Wentworth, Ph.D., Wisconsin–Madison, 1996. Molecular determinants of interspecies transmission and pathogenesis of influenza and corona viruses.

Gary Winslow, Ph.D., Colorado, 1989. Immunity to intracellular bacteria.

Jonathan R. Wolpaw, M.D., Case Western Reserve, 1970. Neuronal and synaptic substrates of memory; brain-computer interfaces.

Susan J. Wong, Ph.D., Saskatchewan, 1980. Clinical laboratory immunology; vector-borne infectious diseases.

Adjunct Faculty

J. Aguirre-Ghiso; K. Bernard, Ph.D.; J. Carp, Ph.D.; S. Chittur, Ph.D.; Y. Chou., Ph.D.; J. Figge, M.D.; G. Hernandez, Ph.D.; D. Kay; R. Keller, Ph.D.; M. Kohn, Ph.D.; R. Limberger, Ph.D.; Q. Lin, Ph.D.; L. Mayerhofer, Ph.D.; D. Nag, Ph.D.; B. Parr, Ph.D.; R. Ramani, Ph.D.; I. Salkin, Ph.D.; A. Schneider, Ph.D.; N. Strominger, Ph.D.; L. Styer, Ph.D.; S.Temple, Ph.D.; R. Webster, Ph.D.; A. Willey, Ph.D.; W. Wolfgang, Ph.D.; D. Woodland, Ph.D.

THE UNIVERSITY OF ALABAMA AT BIRMINGHAM

College of Arts and Sciences
Department of Biology

Programs of Study

The Department of Biology offers programs of study leading to the M.S. and Ph.D. degrees. Graduate students may specialize in research activities at all levels of biological organization, with emphases on ecophysiology, cellular and molecular biology, endocrinology, and ecology of aquatic organisms, or on models related to human disease. The aim of the Department is to provide a broad background and a field of specialty that prepare the student for a professional career in research and/or teaching.

Two types of master's programs are available. A student may choose a research-based program that requires, in addition to a thesis, a minimum of 24 hours of committee-approved course work. The nonresearch plan requires a minimum of 30 hours of approved course work and a thesis incorporating a review and analysis of a topic of current or historical interest in biology. Either plan of study can be completed in approximately two years.

No specific number of courses is required for the Ph.D. Programs are individually designed to meet the needs of the student and to fulfill the aims of the Department. However, a dissertation embodying the results and analysis of an original experimental investigation is required.

Seminars and teaching experience are part of the training program for both the M.S. and Ph.D. degrees. To qualify for candidacy, the student in the master's program must take either a written or an oral comprehensive examination. The Ph.D. student must take both written and oral examinations. The final examination for all candidates consists of an oral defense of the research thesis or comprehensive review paper.

Research Facilities

Well-equipped research laboratories for the Department are located in Campbell Hall. Facilities are available for vertebrates and invertebrates, including marine and freshwater forms, and for botanical specimens. The University operates a farm suitable for field studies. For students interested in marine biology, the University is a member of the Marine Environmental Science Program at Dauphin Island near Mobile, Alabama. The Medical Center library and the University College library have extensive holdings in biological and related sciences.

Financial Aid

Teaching assistantships, graduate assistantships, and fellowships are available. Stipends are awarded on a yearly basis; for 2007–08, they were $15,000 for the master's program and $19,000 to $21,000 for the doctoral program. Tuition and other fees are paid for all students who are awarded stipends. Health insurance is provided for qualified individuals. Fellowships can require teaching on a regular basis, and assistantships typically require teaching a maximum of 9 contact hours per week. Students not receiving stipends may teach laboratory sections on a fee-for-service basis.

Cost of Study

Graduate tuition for in-state students was $227 per credit hour in 2009–10. Out-of-state students were charged $568 per credit hour. Tuition and fees are paid for stipend recipients.

Living and Housing Costs

The cost of living in Birmingham is slightly lower than the average for major American cities. Many reasonably priced apartments are available near campus, and some University apartments are available.

Student Group

The total enrollment at the University of Alabama at Birmingham is approximately 17,000; 11,400 are undergraduates and more than 5,700 are in graduate and professional school programs. The Department of Biology averages about 50 graduate students in M.S. or Ph.D. programs.

Student Outcomes

Recent graduates have assumed professorships in departments such as biology, zoology, immunology, or marine science at various academic institutions. Some have chosen a career in the medical or dental profession. Other positions assumed recently by graduates include staff scientists at NASA, the Army Corps of Engineers, and marine research laboratories. In addition, different environmental consulting companies and biotechnology companies have employed graduates as technicians, staff scientists, or laboratory directors.

Location

The University of Alabama at Birmingham is a comprehensive urban university situated on a campus that occupies an eighty-block area in the southern section of Birmingham. Many cultural resources are available, including the Alys Robinson Stephens Performing Arts Center, museums, the Jimmy Morgan Zoo, and the Botanical Gardens. Recreational opportunities include athletic events and a variety of outdoor activities at nearby lakes and parks or along the Gulf Coast, which is 5 hours away by car. The city has a mild climate throughout the year.

The University

The University of Alabama at Birmingham has forty-six master's and thirty-three doctoral programs. Students benefit from the active research programs that attract $600 million in research funds each year, making the University one of the highest-ranked institutions in receipt of federal research support.

Applying

Application forms, the *Bulletin of the Graduate School*, and other information can be obtained from the Dean of the Graduate School, the University of Alabama at Birmingham, UAB Station, Birmingham, Alabama 35294-1150. For admission in good standing, students should have a baccalaureate degree in biology or a related field, an overall B average in undergraduate courses, and a satisfactory score on the General Test of the Graduate Record Examinations or an equivalent test. It is also desirable that entering students have completed two years of chemistry (including a year of organic chemistry), a year of physics, and mathematics through calculus. A statement of career objectives, three letters of evaluation, and an official copy of transcripts should be included with the application.

Correspondence and Information

Dr. Stephen A. Watts, Program Director for Biology
Department of Biology
CH 375
The University of Alabama at Birmingham
1530 3rd Avenue South
Birmingham, Alabama 35294-1170
Phone: 205-934-2045
Fax: 205-975-6097
E-mail: sawatts@uab.edu
Web site: http://www.uab.edu/uabbio/

The University of Alabama at Birmingham

THE FACULTY AND THEIR RESEARCH

Charles D. Amsler, Professor; Ph.D., California, Santa Barbara. Phycology and chemical ecology.

Robert A. Angus, Professor; Ph.D., Connecticut. Aquatic ecology and toxicology.

Asim K. Bej, Professor; Ph.D., Louisville. Molecular genetics and microbial ecology.

George F. Crozier, Adjunct Professor; Ph.D., California, San Diego. Marine vertebrate physiology.

Vithal K. Ghanta, Professor; Ph.D., Southern Illinois at Carbondale. Immunology.

David T. Jenkins, Associate Professor; Ph.D., Tennessee. *Basidiomycete* taxonomy.

Daniel D. Jones, Professor Emeritus; Ph.D., Michigan State. Plant physiology; microbial ecology.

Ken R. Marion, Professor; Ph.D., Washington (St. Louis). Vertebrate ecology.

James B. McClintock, Professor; Ph.D., South Florida. Invertebrate biology; marine chemical ecology.

Timothy Nagy, Adjunct Associate Professor; Ph.D., Utah. Nutritional physiology.

Robert W. Thacker, Professor; Ph.D., Michigan. Marine and freshwater ecology.

Trygve Tollefsbol, Professor; Ph.D., North Texas; D.O., North Texas Health Science at Fort Worth. Molecular biology; telomerase and DNA methylation.

R. Douglas Watson, Professor; Ph.D., Iowa. Developmental endocrinology.

Stephen A. Watts, Professor; Ph.D., South Florida. Physiology and nutrition of aquatic invertebrates; aquaculture.

Thane Wibbels, Professor; Ph.D., Texas A&M. Comparative reproductive physiology of vertebrates.

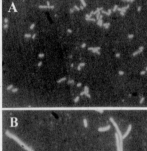

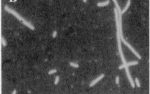

Salmonella—How expression of selected genes and their regulation enable microbes to survive in hostile environments is one area of prokaryotic research. For example, note the influence of cold temperature on morphology of *Salmonella typhimurium* LT2 grown for 78 hours at 37°C (panel A) or 10°C (panel B).

Population dynamics, reproductive ecology, and conservation of several species, including sea turtles, are studied.

Studies of marine chemical ecology are conducted in the Gulf of Mexico, the Atlantic, and, as seen here, beneath the sea ice in Antarctica.

UNIVERSITY OF CONNECTICUT HEALTH CENTER

Graduate Programs in Biomedical Sciences

Programs of Study

Work leading to the Ph.D. degree in biomedical sciences and master's degrees in dental sciences, public health, and clinical and translational research is offered through Graduate School faculty members associated with the Schools of Medicine and Dental Medicine at the University of Connecticut Health Center in Farmington. A combined-degree program with the School of Medicine offers an M.D./Ph.D. degree to qualified students interested in academic medicine and research. In addition, the Schools of Medicine and Dental Medicine, in conjunction with the Public Health Program, offer a combined program leading to the M.D./M.P.H. or D.M.D./M.P.H. The School of Dental Medicine offers a D.M.D./Ph.D. and a Combined Certificate Training Ph.D. program for students with advanced dental degrees. Ph.D. students apply to the Integrated Admissions Mode, which offers a first year of study in the basic science curriculum prior to the selection of an area of concentration in which to pursue the Ph.D. thesis work.

Research Facilities

The program offices and laboratories are part of the University of Connecticut Health Center. A wide range of general and specialized equipment and expertise in the biological, biochemical, and biophysical sciences is available. Students have access to all facilities and equipment necessary for the pursuit of their research programs. In addition, major institutional resources include central small-animal facilities and a library that contains approximately 200,000 volumes and 450 CAI programs and subscribes to more than 1,400 current periodicals.

Financial Aid

Support for doctoral students engaged in full-time degree programs at the Health Center is provided on a competitive basis. Graduate research assistantships for 2010–11 provide a stipend of $28,000 per year, which includes a waiver of tuition/University fees for the fall and spring semesters and a student health insurance plan. While financial aid is offered competitively, the Health Center makes every possible effort to address the financial needs of all doctoral students during their period of training.

Cost of Study

For 2010–11, tuition is $4455 per semester ($8910 per year) for full-time students who are Connecticut residents and $11,565 per semester ($23,130 per year) for full-time out-of-state residents. General University fees are added to the cost of tuition for students who do not receive a tuition waiver. These costs are usually met by traineeships or research assistantships for doctoral students.

Living and Housing Costs

There is a wide range of affordable housing options in the greater Hartford area within easy commuting distance of the campus, including an extensive complex that is adjacent to the Health Center. Costs range from $600 to $900 per month for a one-bedroom unit; 2 or more students sharing an apartment usually pay less. University housing is not available at the Health Center.

Student Group

Approximately 550 students in the Schools of Medicine and Dental Medicine, 400 graduate students in the Ph.D. and master's programs, and numerous postdoctoral fellows use the facilities in Farmington.

Location

The Health Center is located in the historic town of Farmington, Connecticut. Set in the beautiful New England countryside on a hill overlooking the Farmington Valley, it is close to ski areas, hiking trails, and facilities for boating, fishing, and swimming. Connecticut's capital city of Hartford, 7 miles east of Farmington, is the center of an urban region of approximately 800,000 people. The beaches of the Long Island Sound are about 50 minutes away to the south, and the beautiful Berkshires are a short drive to the northwest. New York City and Boston can be reached within 2½ hours by car. Hartford is the home of the acclaimed Hartford Stage Company, TheatreWorks, the Hartford Symphony and Chamber orchestras, two ballet companies, an opera company, the Wadsworth Athenaeum (the oldest public art museum in the nation), the Mark Twain house, the Hartford Civic Center, and many other interesting cultural and recreational facilities. The area is also home to several branches of the University of Connecticut, Trinity College, and the University of Hartford, which includes the Hartt School of Music. Bradley International Airport (about 30 minutes from campus) serves the Hartford/Springfield area with frequent airline connections to major cities in this country and abroad. Frequent bus and rail service is also available from Hartford.

The Health Center

The 200-acre Health Center campus at Farmington houses a division of the University of Connecticut Graduate School, as well as the School of Medicine and Dental Medicine. The campus also includes the John Dempsey Hospital, associated clinics, and extensive medical research facilities, all in a centralized facility with more than 1 million square feet of floor space. The Health Center's newest research addition, the Academic Research Building, was opened in 1999. This impressive eleven-story structure provides 170,000 square feet of state-of-the-art laboratory space. The faculty at the center includes more than 260 full-time members. The institution has a strong commitment to graduate study within an environment that promotes social and intellectual interaction among the various educational programs. Graduate students are represented on various administrative committees concerned with curricular affairs, and the Graduate Student Organization (GSO) represents graduate students' needs and concerns to the faculty and administration, in addition to fostering social contact among graduate students at the Health Center.

Applying

Applications for admission should be submitted on standard forms obtained from the Graduate Admissions Office or the Web site and should be filed together with transcripts, three letters of recommendation, a personal statement, and recent results from the General Test of the Graduate Record Examinations. International students must take the Test of English as a Foreign Language (TOEFL) to satisfy Graduate School requirements. The deadline for completed applications and receipt of all supplemental materials is December 15. In accordance with the laws of the state of Connecticut and of the United States, the University of Connecticut Health Center does not discriminate against any person in its educational and employment activities on the grounds of race, color, creed, national origin, sex, age, or physical disability.

Correspondence and Information

Graduate Programs in Biomedical Sciences
Graduate Admissions Office, MC 3906
University of Connecticut Health Center
Farmington, Connecticut 06030-3906

Phone: 860-679-2175
E-mail: BiomedSciAdmissions@uchc.edu
Web site: http://grad.uchc.edu

University of Connecticut Health Center

FACULTY AND RESEARCH AREAS

The Health Center's graduate faculty of more than 150 members is drawn from both the basic and clinical departments of the Schools of Medicine and Dental Medicine.

Cell Biology. This interdisciplinary program offers the student the opportunity to bring modern molecular and physical techniques to bear on problems in cell biology. Faculty members' research spans a broad range of interests in the areas of eukaryotic cell biology and related clinical aspects. The program is particularly strong in the following areas of research: angiogenesis, cancer biology, gene expression, molecular medicine, reproductive biology, signal transduction, vascular biology, optical methods, proteomics, and computer modeling of complex biological systems. Kevin Claffey, Associate Professor of Cell Biology and Program Director; Linda Shapiro, Assistant Professor of Cell Biology and Associate Program Director.

Genetics and Developmental Biology. This program emphasizes cellular and molecular bases of differentiation and development and includes opportunities in molecular human genetics. Research opportunities are available in the biology of human embryonic stem cells, mapping and cloning of genes responsible for human disease, RNA processing (including RNA editing, alternative splicing, antisense regulation, and RNA interference), the molecular mechanisms of aging, signal transduction pathways, microbial pathogenesis, developmental neurobiology, cell differentiation, musculoskeletal development, morphogenesis and pattern formation, reproductive biology, and endocrinology. James Li, Assistant Professor of Genetics and Developmental Biology and Program Director; Arthur Günzl, Associate Professor of Genetics and Developmental Biology and Associate Program Director.

Immunology. The central focus of this program is to train the student to become an independent investigator and educator who will provide research and educational contributions to basic, applied, or clinical immunology through lectures, seminars, laboratory rotations, research presentations, and a concentration on laboratory research. Research in the program is focused on the cellular and molecular aspects of immune system structure and function in animal models and in humans. Areas of emphasis include molecular immunology (mechanisms of antigen presentation, major histocompatibility complex genetics and function, cytokines and cytokine receptors, and tumor antigens), cellular immunology (biochemical mechanisms and biological aspects of signal transduction of lymphocytes and granulocytes; cellular and molecular requirements for thymic T-lymphocyte development, selection, and activation; cytokines in B- and T-cell development; regulation of antitumor immunity; immunoparasitology, including parasite genetics and immune recognition of parasite antigens; and mechanisms of inflammation), organ-based immunology (immune effector mechanisms of the intestine, lymphocyte interactions in the lung, and immune regulation of the eye), immunity to infectious agents (viruses, bacteria, and parasites, including vector-borne organisms), and autoimmunity (animal models of autoimmune disease and effector mechanisms in human autoimmunity). Adam Adler, Associate Professor of Immunology and Program Director; Carol Wu, Assistant Professor of Immunology and Associate Program Director.

Molecular Biology and Biochemistry. This program uniquely bridges modern molecular biology, microbiology, biochemistry, cell biology, and structural biology. Research in this program is directed toward explaining biological phenomena at the molecular level. The program includes four major areas of concentration and research: relation of the structure of macromolecules to their function, biosynthesis of macromolecules, biochemical genetics, and assembly of macromolecules into complex cellular structures. Stephen M. King, Professor of Biochemistry and Program Director; Chris Heinen, Assistant Professor of Medicine and Associate Program Director.

Neuroscience. This interdepartmental program offers comprehensive conceptual and experimental training in molecular, systems, and behavioral neuroscience. The faculty members of the neuroscience program engage in research that involves cellular, molecular, and developmental neurobiology; neuroanatomy; neuroimaging; neurophysiology; neurochemistry; neuroendocrinology; neuropharmacology; and neuropathology. Richard Mains, Professor of Neuroscience Program Director.

Skeletal, Craniofacial, and Oral Biology. This program offers interdisciplinary research training in the areas of skeletal, craniofacial, and oral biology, emphasizing contemporary research technologies in cell, molecular, and developmental biology; genetics; and biochemistry. Areas of research include regulation of the formation, outgrowth, and patterning of the developing limb; control of cartilage differentiation, endochondral ossification, osteogenesis, and joint formation; molecular regulation of gene expression in bone; homeobox gene regulation of osteoblast differentiation; gene therapy of bone diseases; hormonal and cytokine regulation of bone growth, formation, and remodeling; control of craniofacial skeletogenesis and tooth development; signal transduction and intracellular signaling pathways; cellular and molecular aspects of the pathogenesis of inflammatory disease; microbiology, pathogenesis, and immunology of caries and periodontal disease; neural structure and function in the gustatory system; biomaterial development for tissue engineering; bone cell–implant interactions; differentiation of human embryonic stem cells into skeletal tissues; and analysis of oral and mucosal function and disease. Mina Mina, Professor of Orthodontics, Oral and Maxillofacial Surgery, Pediatric Dentistry, and Advanced Education and Program Director; Carol Pilbeam, Professor of Medicine and Associate Program Director.

Combined M.D./Ph.D. Program. This program is designed for students interested in careers in medical research and academic medicine. It enables students to acquire competence in both the basic science and clinical aspects of their chosen fields. The program allows a student to combine the curricula of two schools in a way that meets the specific degree requirements of each, and yet it allows the completion of both in a period less than that needed if the two curricula were taken in sequence. Entry into the program is limited to a small number of unusually well qualified students who are either currently enrolled in the medical school or who have been accepted into the first-year class. Barbara Kream, Professor of Medicine and of Genetics and Developmental Biology and Program Director.

Combined D.M.D./Ph.D. Program. This program is designed for students interested in careers in dental research and academic dental medicine. It enables students to acquire competence in both the basic science and clinical aspects of their chosen fields. The program allows a student to combine the curricula of two schools in a way that meets the specific degree requirements of each, and yet it allows the completion of both in a period less than that needed if the two curricula were taken in sequence. Entry into the program is limited to a small number of unusually well qualified students who are either currently enrolled in the dental school or who have been accepted into the first-year class. Mina Mina, Professor of Orthodontics, Oral and Maxillofacial Surgery, Pediatric Dentistry, and Advanced Education and Program Director.

Combined M.D./M.P.H. or D.M.D./M.P.H. Program. A joint-degree program leading to the Master of Public Health in addition to the Doctor of Medicine or the Doctor of Dental Medicine is sponsored by the Graduate Program in Public Health and the Schools of Medicine and Dental Medicine. The joint-degree program has been developed to prepare future physicians and dentists to deal creatively with the rapidly changing environment of medicine and health care. It is possible to complete the degree requirements for both programs during the four years of medical or dental school. David Gregorio, Professor of Community Medicine and Health Care and Program Director.

Clinical and Translational Research. The Master of Science degree program in clinical and translational research is administered in the Department of Medicine and stresses clinical research methods and research practicum in order to provide practical research training in preparation for independent research. The program is offered to individuals who have a health-related terminal degree (M.D., D.M.D., or Ph.D.) or who are involved in an M.D., D.M.D., or Ph.D. program in a health-related field and are in good standing. The master's program is based on both course work and research experience, but no research thesis is required. Students are required to sit for a final examination, which may entail the oral defense of a grant application and a manuscript. Lisa Godin (godin@nso.uchc.edu).

Dental Science. The Master of Dental Science degree program is an interdepartmental program whose primary objective is to provide instruction in dental science that will enhance the student's ability to instruct and undertake research in dental schools. This program provides an opportunity for cooperative study and research between dentistry, the basic sciences, and allied health fields. Both M.Dent.Sc. and oral biology Ph.D. students may combine their work in these programs with advanced clinical training in endodontics, orthodontics, oral pathology, pedodontics, periodontics, oral medicine, oral radiology, and oral and maxillofacial surgery. Arthur Hand, Assistant Dean for Medical and Graduate Education.

Public Health. This multidisciplinary master's program, accredited by the Council for Education in Public Health, is based in the Department of Community Medicine and Health Care. It offers a core curriculum in epidemiology, biostatistics, health administration, environmental health, the sociomedical sciences, health law, and electives in these and related areas. David Gregorio, Professor of Community Medicine and Health Care and Program Director.

THE UNIVERSITY OF KANSAS MEDICAL CENTER

Interdisciplinary Graduate Program in Biomedical Sciences

Programs of Study

Presidential and congressional commissions have identified biomedicine and biotechnology as leading growth sectors of the American and world economies. Students can pursue graduate studies on the cutting edge of biomedical research at The University of Kansas Medical Center (KUMC) and place themselves in a competitive position. Students have the opportunity to develop research skills and earn a Ph.D. degree in a broad range of biomedical research areas, including neuroscience, protein structure and function, and pharmacology and toxicology, as well as viral, microbial, molecular, cellular, developmental, reproductive, immunological, renal, and physiological biology. Research also includes many clinically related studies focusing on a wide range of human diseases. The graduate program is a partnership between KUMC (http://www.kumc.edu/igpbs) and the nearby Stowers Institute for Medical Research (http://www.stowers-institute.org), and students may conduct their research at either institution.

Graduate students pursuing a Ph.D. degree in biomedical sciences are admitted through the Interdisciplinary Graduate Program in Biomedical Sciences (IGPBS). This program is responsible for the first-year curriculum and allows each student to study in the most current areas of the biomedical sciences before selecting a laboratory in which to carry out his or her research program. Each student entering the IGPBS takes a state-of-the-art, highly integrated core curriculum. In addition to courses that provide the fundamental principles essential for understanding the biomedical sciences, students receive an introduction to practical aspects of research, including biographics, bioethics, appropriate use of animals in research, laboratory safety, and procedures for human studies research. Faculty members also present their research programs to students through a research seminar series, giving students the opportunity to evaluate each research program. Following this introduction, each student selects three laboratory rotations that are completed during the first year. Laboratory rotations expose students to potential research advisers and to the principles and procedures of cutting-edge laboratory techniques, and they allow students to decide which laboratory best fits their needs. At the beginning of the second year, each student selects a research adviser, in whose laboratory her or his doctoral research project is carried out. At this time, the student also enters one of eight graduate programs.

Research Facilities

State-of-the-art technology and equipment is available through a variety of core research facilities, including DNA microarray technology, laser capture microdissection, rodent behavioral testing facilities, bioinformatics, transgenic mouse laboratories, fluorescence-activated cell sorting, molecular neurobiology, mass spectrometry, a highly automated histological and immunohistochemistry core, FT-IR microspectroscopy, electron microscopy, confocal microscopes for live cell imaging and spectral separation, noninvasive magnetic resonance spectroscopy, functional magnetic resonance imaging, and magnetoencephalography.

Financial Aid

Teaching and research assistantships are available. Students admitted into the IGPBS are awarded $24,000 in financial support and given a tuition waiver. Student travel awards are also available as pupils progress through the program.

Cost of Study

Students accepted into the IGPBS receive a tuition waiver upon meeting enrollment requirements. Students are responsible for campus and library fees, estimated at $461 per academic year. Tuition is currently estimated at $270 per credit hour for state residents and $646 per credit hour for nonresidents.

Living and Housing Costs

There is a multitude of options available to KUMC students near the campus. Current housing costs are between $450 and $800 per month.

Student Group

Twenty-five percent of the students enrolled in the IGPBS are from international locales. The age range of all students falls between 22 and 32 years.

Student Outcomes

Upon graduation from KUMC, students can expect to obtain a position in the biotechnology, academic, or governmental career fields.

Location

The University of Kansas Medical Center is located at 39th and Rainbow Boulevard in Kansas City, Kansas. It is on the border of Kansas and Missouri, with quick access to Westport, the Country Club Plaza, the Nelson-Atkins Museum of Art, and the Kansas City Art Institute.

The Graduate Program

The Interdisciplinary Graduate Program in Biomedical Sciences is an educational program within the School of Medicine at The University of Kansas Medical Center. It consists of eight degree-granting departments or programs. The IGPBS is made up of the Departments of Anatomy and Cell Biology; Biochemistry and Molecular Biology; Microbiology, Molecular Genetics and Immunology; Pathology and Laboratory Medicine; Molecular and Integrative Physiology; and Pharmacology, Toxicology and Therapeutics; the Neuroscience Graduate Program; and the Training Program in Environmental Toxicology.

Applying

Students who are interested in the IGPBS may apply online at http://www.kumc.edu/igpbs. Applications must be received by January 15, although applications received after that date are considered until the class is filled.

Correspondence and Information

Director
Interdisciplinary Graduate Program in Biomedical Sciences
5009 Wescoe, MS3025
The University of Kansas Medical Center
3901 Rainbow Boulevard
Kansas City, Kansas 66160-7836
Phone: 913-588-2719
        800-408-2039 (toll-free)
Fax: 913-588-2711
E-mail: igpbs@kumc.edu
Web site: http://www.kumc.edu/igpbs

The University of Kansas Medical Center

AREAS OF RESEARCH

Faculty members at KUMC have seventeen areas of research emphasis:

Cardiovascular biology
Cell and developmental biology
Imaging
Molecular and cellular biophysics
Molecular and cellular immunology
Molecular biology and genetics
Molecular pathogenesis of infectious diseases
Molecular toxicology and environmental health
Molecular virology
Muscle biology
Neurosciences
Pharmacological sciences
Proteomics
Renal biology
Reproductive biology
Signal transduction and cancer biology
Structural biology

UTSA.®

THE UNIVERSITY OF TEXAS AT SAN ANTONIO

Department of Biology

Programs of Study

The Department of Biology currently offers three Master of Science degree programs in biology, biotechnology, and environmental science; and the Ph.D. degree in biology, with a concentration in either neurobiology or cell and molecular biology. The M.S. in biology program allows students to pursue research in molecular and cellular neuroscience, biochemistry, molecular cell biology, enzymology, membrane biology, molecular genetics, protein and nucleic acid structure, developmental biology, tumor biology, aging, molecular virology, medical microbiology, bioremediation, endocrinology, and parasitology. The M.S. in biotechnology program is specifically designed to enable the graduate to enter the biotechnology industry. The M.S. in environmental science program gives students the opportunity to broaden their scientific background at the graduate level into the research areas of aquatic biology and chemistry, ecology, environmental quality and remediation, and environmental management. Doctoral students must obtain a minimum of 90 semester hours of graduate credit beyond the bachelor's degree and must also complete three laboratory rotations. Advancement to candidacy requires doctoral students to complete not only the University and program requirements, but also to pass written and oral qualifying examinations following the completion of course requirements. No more than two attempts to pass the qualifying examinations are allowed. Doctoral student candidates must then demonstrate their ability to conduct independent research by completing and defending an original dissertation. On average, five years of full-time study are required to complete the doctoral program, while the programs leading to the M.S. degree average two years.

Research Facilities

The Department of Biology possesses state-of-the-art laboratories (both faculty research and core laboratories) for students to pursue graduate research projects. Core equipment available to the Department includes scanning and transmission electron microscopy, confocal microscopy, fluorescence-activated cell sorting, gene chip microarray, and phosphoimagery, among many others. In addition to campuswide computing facilities, the Department has Sun Microsystems and Silicon Graphics workstations.

Financial Aid

In 2009–10, all doctoral students were supported with $21,000, which was a combination of research and teaching support. In addition to this support, all tuition and fees are paid for 21 credit hours per academic year. For qualified students, the Minority Biomedical Research Support/Research Initiative for Scientific Enhancement (MBRS/RISE) Program supports the stipend, tuition and fees, and travel to scientific meetings. Teaching and research assistantships are available to qualified M.S. students.

Cost of Study

In the 2009–10 academic year, tuition and fees for a full-time graduate degree student (9 semester hours) were approximately $3274 per semester for Texas residents and $8725 per semester for nonresidents.

Living and Housing Costs

University on-campus housing is available and includes apartment-style living at four complexes—Chisholm Hall, University Oaks, Laurel Village, and Chaparral Village. Off-campus housing is also available and includes many apartments adjacent to the University as well as a large number located within a 5-mile drive. The rate for a one-bedroom apartment is approximately $500 per month.

Student Group

In the 2010 fall semester, the University enrolled more than 30,000 students, of whom more than 3,000 were graduate students. The Department of Biology admits doctoral students in the fall semester of each academic year. Master's level students can apply for admission during the fall, spring, and summer semesters. Each year, 50–100 M.S. students are admitted each academic year. The student group is comprised of both domestic and international students.

Location

San Antonio, with a population of 1.5 million, is one of the nation's major metropolitan areas. As the home of the Alamo and numerous other missions built by the Franciscans, the city is historically and culturally diverse. The Guadalupe Cultural Arts Center, McNay Art Museum, the San Antonio Museum of Art, and the Witte Museum enrich the city. The performing arts are represented by the San Antonio Symphony, the annual Tejano Music Festival and Tejano Music Awards, and performances by opera and ballet companies. Also notable are Sea World, Six Flags Fiesta Texas, Brackenridge Park, the Botanical Gardens, and the downtown Riverwalk. The San Antonio Zoo has the third-largest collection in North America. A city landmark is the Tower of the Americas, which was built for the 1968 World's Fair. San Antonio is home to the National Basketball Association's Spurs, league champions in 2000, 2003, 2005, and 2007. Numerous nearby lakes allow almost year-round outdoor activity, and the beaches of the Texas Gulf coast are within a 2-hour drive.

The University

The University was founded in 1969 and has since become a comprehensive metropolitan institution. Its research expenditures place it in the top 25 percent of public universities in Texas. The University has entered a new building and recruitment phase with a view to greatly expand the research effort in the biosciences.

Applying

To ensure full consideration, doctoral students interested in the Ph.D. program are encouraged to submit their applications for admission along with all supporting documentation by the firm February 1 deadline for acceptance the following fall semester. Information on applying may be obtained from the Office of Graduate Studies. Applications may be done on the Internet at https://apply.embark.com/grad/utsa/36. The deadlines for the M.S. domestic application are July 1 for the fall semester, November 1 for the spring semester, and May 1 for the summer semester. International M.S. applications must be submitted by April 1 for the fall semester, September 1 for the spring semester, and March 1 for the summer semester.

Correspondence and Information

For application information:
Office of Graduate Studies
The University of Texas at San Antonio
One UTSA Circle
San Antonio, Texas 78249
Phone: 210-458-4330
Web site: http://www.utsa.edu/graduate/Admission/index.html

For program information:
Department of Biology
The University of Texas at San Antonio
One UTSA Circle
San Antonio, Texas 78249
Phone: 210-458-4459
E-mail: melinda.villarreal@utsa.edu
Web site: http://www.bio.utsa.edu

The University of Texas at San Antonio

THE FACULTY AND THEIR RESEARCH

Deborah L. Armstrong, Professor of Neurophysiology; Ph.D., Syracuse, 1982. Hippocampal synaptic modulation.

Bernard P. Arulanandam, Associate Professor of Microbiology and Immunology; Ph.D., Medical College of Ohio, 1999. Cellular immunology; mucosal immunity.

Edwin J. Barea-Rodriguez, Associate Professor of Neurobiology; Ph.D., Southern Illinois, 1992. Neurobiology; long-term potentiation.

James Bower, Professor of Neurophysiology; Ph.D., Wisconsin–Madison, 1981. Neurocomputation; structure and function in neural circuits.

Astrid Cardona, Assistant Professor of Neuroimmunology; Ph.D., Texas Health Science Center at San Antonio, 2002. Neuroimmunology; fractalkine receptor biology.

J. Aaron Cassill, Associate Professor of Cell and Molecular Biology; Ph.D., California, San Diego, 1988. Cell and molecular biology; regulation of signal transduction cascades.

James P. Chambers, Professor of Biochemistry; Ph.D., Texas Health Science Center at San Antonio, 1975. Biochemistry.

G. Jilani Chaudry, Assistant Professor of Cell and Molecular Biology; Ph.D., Texas at Dallas, 1991. Mammalian cell intoxication by anthrax toxin.

Garry Cole, Professor of Biology; Ph.D., Waterloo, 1969. Mechanisms of fungal virulence and host immunity.

Brian E. Derrick, Professor of Neurobiology; Ph.D., Berkeley, 1993. Neurobiology; cellular/molecular mechanisms of potentiation/depression.

Jurgen E. Engelberth, Assistant Professor of Plant Biochemistry; Ph.D., Ruhr (Germany). Plant biochemistry.

Thomas Forsthuber, Professor of Immunology; Ph.D., Tübingen (Germany), 1989. Cellular immunology; T-cell immunity; autoimmune diseases.

Gary O. Gaufo, Assistant Professor of Biology; Ph.D., Berkeley, 1995. Molecular and cellular approaches to neural development.

Matthew J. Gdovin, Associate Professor of Evolutionary Biology; Ph.D., Dartmouth, 1995. Developmental aspects of the neural control of respiration.

M. Neal Guentzel, Professor of Microbiology; Ph.D., Texas at Austin, 1972. Microbiology; enteric infections; bioremediation.

Luis S. Haro, Professor of Cell and Molecular Biology; Ph.D., California, Santa Cruz, 1985. Cell and molecular biology; endocrinology; growth hormone; receptors.

Hans W. Heidner, Professor of Microbiology; Ph.D., California, Davis, 1991. Virology; genetics of alphavirus replication; virus/host cell interactions.

David B. Jaffe, Professor of Neurobiology; Ph.D., Baylor College of Medicine, 1992. Hippocampal neuron synaptic integration and plasticity.

Karl Klose, Professor of Microbiology; Ph.D., Berkeley, 1993. Bacterial pathogenesis.

Richard G. LeBaron, Professor of Cell and Molecular Biology; Ph.D., Alabama at Birmingham, 1988. Cell and molecular biology; tissue engineering; extracellular matrix biology.

Jose Lopez-Ribot, Professor of Microbiology; M.D., Ph.D., Valencia (Spain), 1991. Study of the opportunistic pathogenic fungus *Candida albicans*.

Martha J. Lundell, Associate Professor of Molecular Genetics; Ph.D., UCLA, 1988. Specification of cell fate in the central nervous system.

Joe L. Martinez Jr., Professor of Neurobiology; Ph.D., Delaware, 1971. Neuroscience; neurobiology of learning and memory.

John McCarrey, Professor of Genetics; Ph.D., California, Davis, 1981. Cellular biology; cellular development and differentiation.

Paul Mueller, Assistant Professor of Cell and Developmental Biology; Ph.D., Caltech, 1990. Cell cycle regulation; developmental biology.

Carlos Paladini, Assistant Professor of Neuroscience; Ph.D., Rutgers, 1999. Dopamine neuron physiology and addiction.

George Perry, Dean and Professor of Biology; Ph.D., California, San Diego, 1979. Formation and physiological consequences of the cytopathology of Alzheimer's disease.

Clyde F. Phelix, Associate Professor of Anatomy and Neurobiology; Ph.D., Missouri, 1988. Anatomy; molecular neurobiology of cardiovascular disease.

Rama Ratnam, Assistant Professor of Computation and Neural Systems; Ph.D., Illinois, 1998. Sensory information processing; acoustic communication.

Robert R. Renthal, Professor of Biochemistry; Ph.D., Columbia, 1972. Membranes; protein biochemistry; sensory receptors.

Fidel Santamaria, Assistant Professor of Computation and Neural Systems; Ph.D., Caltech, 2000. Biophysical substrates of neuronal dendritic computation.

Stephen Saville, Assistant Professor of Genetics; Ph.D., Leicester, 1998. Yeast molecular genetics; mechanisms of fungal virulence and pathogenesis.

David M. Senseman, Associate Professor of Biology; Ph.D., Princeton, 1976. Neurophysiology; optical imaging; neural networks.

Janakiram Seshu, Assistant Professor of Microbiology; Ph.D., Washington State, 1996. Genetic analysis of *Borrelia burgdorferi* lp54 loci.

Valerie Sponsel, Associate Professor of Plant Physiology; Ph.D., Wales, 1972; D.Sc., Bristol (England), 1984. Regulation of plant growth and development by plant hormones.

Garry Sunter, Assistant Professor of Plant Pathology; Ph.D., Imperial College (London), 1985. DNA replication and plant-pathogen interactions.

Kelly J. Suter, Assistant Professor of Computational Biology; Ph.D., Pittsburgh, 1995. Sexual reproduction; GnRH pulse generator.

Judy Teale, Professor of Immunology; Ph.D., Virginia, 1976. Immunoparasitology; neuroimmunology; immune response to *Francisella tularensis*.

Todd Troyer, Assistant Professor of Neuroscience; Ph.D., Berkeley, 1993. Neural and behavioral dynamics.

Andrew T. C. Tsin, Professor of Biochemistry and Physiology; Ph.D., Alberta, 1979. Biochemistry and cell of the visual cycle; cell biology of the retina and the retinal pigment epithelium.

Oscar Van Auken, Professor of Plant Ecology; Ph.D., Utah, 1969. Plant ecology; species interactions; community composition and structure; rare species.

Yufeng Wang, Assistant Professor of Computational Biology; Ph.D., Iowa State, 2001. Bioinformatics.

Matthew J. Wayner, Professor of Neurobiology; Ph.D., Illinois, 1953. Hypothalamic-hippocampal interactions: learning and memory.

Tao Wei, Assistant Professor of Biotechnology; Ph.D., Uppsala (Sweden), 2000. Microbiology; instability of bacterial and yeast genomes during DNA replication and recombination.

Nicole Y. Wicha, Assistant Professor of Cognitive Science; Ph.D., California, San Diego, 2003. Cognitive neuroscience; human brain imaging and cognition.

Charles J. Wilson, Professor of Neurocomputation; Ph.D., Colorado at Boulder, 1979. Computational neuroscience; nonlinear dynamics of neurons and neuronal networks; neurocomputing; reinforcement learning.

Floyd Wormley, Assistant Professor of Microbiology/Immunology; Ph.D., LSU Health Sciences Center, 2001. Study of protective immune responses against *Cryptococcus neoformans* infections.

VILLANOVA UNIVERSITY

Department of Biology

Programs of Study

The Department of Biology offers a program of study that leads to the Master of Science degree in biology (with thesis) or the Master of Arts degree in biology (nonthesis). For the Master of Science degree, a minimum of 30 semester credit hours is required, up to 10 of which may be contributed as research credits. Course work is determined by the student, the research adviser, and the student's advisory committee. Thesis research may be undertaken in the areas of behavioral biology, biogeochemistry, cellular physiology, developmental biology, ecology, endocrinology, evolutionary morphology, genetics, genomics, herpetology, immunology, microbiology, molecular biology, neurophysiology, ornithology, phylogenetics, plant ecology, plant physiology, protozoology, or virology. For the Master of Arts degree, a minimum of 33 semester hours of course work is required. Certificates of Graduate Study (16 credit hours) and Advanced Graduate Study (24 credit hours) are also available in cell, molecular, and developmental biology and ecology, evolution, and organismal biology.

Research Facilities

The laboratories of the Department of Biology are well equipped for graduate instruction and research in many areas of biology. The Department maintains a research-equipped greenhouse, field vehicles, and an electron microscope facility. Available equipment and resources include: automated sequencers; liquid scintillation spectrometer and gamma counter for work with radioisotopes; still and video imaging systems; scanning and transmission electron microscopes; biomaterials testing apparatus; cabinet X-ray facility; cell-culture laboratory; and a diversity of chromatographic, electrophoretic, spectrophotometric, photographic, bioelectronic, and other instruments. Extensive computer facilities with GIS and high-end imaging capabilities are available within the Department.

Financial Aid

Teaching assistantships carrying a stipend of $13,100 and waiver of tuition were available in 2009–10, as were federally supported work-study funds and loans. A limited number of research assistantships are awarded on a competitive basis. Additional summer support is also available to qualified students.

Cost of Study

Tuition in 2009–10 was $700 per semester credit hour.

Living and Housing Costs

Privately owned rooms and apartments are available along the Main Line and in other nearby communities. Costs for rooms start at approximately $100 per week, depending on kitchen privileges. Apartments range between $550 and $900 per month, depending on their size and their location. Students who share apartments may have costs as low as $300 per month.

Student Group

The Department enrolls approximately 50 graduate students a year. Nearly 2,000 students from the United States and abroad are enrolled in various graduate programs at Villanova.

Location

Villanova University is situated in Villanova, Pennsylvania, on U.S. Route 30, 6 miles west of the Philadelphia city line. The University can be reached in half an hour from central Philadelphia by two commuter rail lines; each of these systems has a station at the University. Buses pass the campus, which is 1 mile east of I-476 and easily reached by car from I-95, I-76 (the Schuylkill), and the Mid-County exit of the Pennsylvania Turnpike.

The University

Villanova University is a Roman Catholic university, sponsored by the religious order of St. Augustine. It benefits from more than 160 years of excellent educational tradition. The University recognizes its responsibility to disseminate knowledge and to seek new knowledge through research and scholarship. It has been the University's tradition to foster close and warm relationships between its students and faculty members. Villanova is an equal opportunity employer.

With more than 220 landscaped acres in a beautiful residential section, the Villanova campus is one of the showplaces of the Philadelphia area and is a registered arboretum. The campus has facilities for a variety of athletic activities.

Applying

Graduates of accredited colleges who wish to work for their Master of Science or Master of Arts degree in biology must have completed a minimum of 24 semester hours of undergraduate work in biology and 6 to 8 hours each of calculus, physics, general chemistry, and organic chemistry. The selection of applicants is based on academic record, supporting letters, and Graduate Record Examinations (GRE) scores on the General Test. The GRE Subject Test in biology or biochemistry, cell and molecular biology is strongly recommended but not required.

Correspondence and Information

For information:
Director of the Graduate Program
Department of Biology
Villanova University
Villanova, Pennsylvania 19085
E-mail: gradbio@villanova.edu
Web site:
  http://www.villanova.edu/artsci/
  biology/

For financial aid:
Office of Financial Aid
Kennedy Hall
Villanova University
Villanova, Pennsylvania 19085
E-mail: finaid@villanova.edu

For admissions and assistantships:
Dean of Graduate Studies
Villanova University
Villanova, Pennsylvania 19085
E-mail:
  gradinformation@villanova.edu

Villanova University

THE FACULTY AND THEIR RESEARCH

Ronald A. Balsamo, Ph.D., California, Riverside, 1994. Relationship of leaf architecture and biomechanics to drought tolerance; whole plant response to environmental stress.

Anil Bamezai, Ph.D., All India Institute of Medical Sciences, 1987. Regulation of CD4+ T-lymphocyte development in the thymus and responses to protein antigens in the peripheral lymphoid tissues; focus on set of glycosylphosphatidyl-inositol (GPI)–anchored proteins housed in lipid rafts that function as signaling foci on the plasma membrane.

Aaron M. Bauer, Ph.D., Berkeley, 1986. Phylogenetic systematics of squamate reptiles, especially geckos and skinks; evolutionary morphology of reptilian integumentary and musculoskeletal systems; historical biogeography of tropical and Southern Hemisphere reptiles and amphibians; herpetology of southern Africa, islands of the southwestern Pacific, India, and Sri Lanka; eighteenth- and nineteenth-century history of herpetology.

Samantha Chapman, Ph.D., Northern Arizona, 2005. Ecosystem ecology and microbial ecology; biotic influences on ecosystem processes; impacts of plant biodiversity on carbon and nutrient cycling and microbial diversity; herbivory and chemical ecology; effects of nutrient eutrophication in mangrove ecosystems.

Robert L. Curry, Ph.D., Michigan, 1987. Vertebrate behavioral, population, and molecular ecology; ornithology; conservation biology; ecological, behavioral, and genetic aspects of hybridization in chickadees; ecology of the Florida scrub jay (collaboration at Archbold Biological Station); conservation ecology of insular Mimidae.

Mary Desmond, Ph.D., Colorado at Boulder, 1973. Developmental biology, developmental genetics, and neuroembryology; basic cellular mechanisms underlying normal development of the brain and spinal cord, using chick and mouse embryos as experimental models; findings: brain growth requires occlusion of the spinal cord and intraluminal pressure generated from cerebrospinal fluid (CSF).

Angela J. DiBenedetto, Ph.D., Cornell, 1989. Molecular and cellular biology; genetics; developmental neurobiology, especially programmed cell death.

Norman R. Dollahon, Ph.D., Nebraska–Lincoln, 1971. Parasitology, protozoology, and electron microscopy.

Russell M. Gardner, Ph.D., Indiana, 1975. Endocrinology; pharmacology; mechanisms of hormone action, development of hormone responses; hormonal control of uterine growth and differentiation.

Vikram K. Iyengar, Ph.D., Cornell, 2001. Behavioral ecology; entomology; chemical ecology; sexual selection in insects and other arthropods; how the costs and benefits of mate choice shape mating systems.

Todd Jackman, Ph.D., Berkeley, 1993. Evolutionary genetics of salamanders and lizards using DNA sequence data in combination with other data to provide a robust historical framework for examining evolutionary processes; population studies of wandering salamanders; speciation and biodiversity of the New Caledonian herpetofauna.

Janice E. Knepper, Ph.D., Brown, 1979. Molecular biology; virology; molecular mechanisms of viral oncogenesis.

John Olson, Ph.D., Michigan, 1990. Metabolic and muscle physiology; ecophysiology; functional and structural maturation of the effector tissues for thermogenesis and substrate mobilization in birds and mammals; mechanical performance of muscles during locomotion in both invertebrate and vertebrate species.

Joseph A. Orkwiszewski, Ph.D., Bryn Mawr, 1971. Regulation of plant development; control mechanisms of plant growth and development.

Michael Russell, Ph.D., Berkeley, 1990. Investigations at the intersection of marine ecology, population biology, and fisheries science; sustainable management and conservation of commercially important marine invertebrate fisheries.

Louise A. Russo, Ph.D., Penn State Hershey Medical Center, 1987. Cell biology and physiology; understanding the establishment of the uterine receptive state and fertility; hormone-induced uterine growth and remodeling, using an in vivo model system in the rat; analysis of regulated expression of specific cell-surface adhesion receptor proteins and degradative enzymes.

Philip J. Stephens, Ph.D., Aberdeen (Scotland), 1977. Physiology; use of computer technology and animations in traditional and asynchronous teaching, distance learning, animations, interactive, and student-centered learning.

R. Kelman Wieder, Ph.D., West Virginia, 1982. Ecosystem ecology and biogeochemistry, wetland ecology, constructed wetland for mine drainage or stormwater treatment; biotic and abiotic factors influencing carbon cycling and accumulation/release in boreal peatland ecosystems, including continental bogs and fens, in the discontinuous permafrost region of western Canada.

James Wilson, Ph.D., Columbia, 1998. Prokaryotic microbiology; changes of expression of genes affecting stress resistance and virulence of the facultative intracellular pathogen *Salmonella typhimurium* in response to low-fluid-shear and microgravity growth conditions.

Dennis D. Wykoff, Ph.D., Stanford, 1999. Genetics, cell biology, and molecular biology of budding and fission yeast; regulation of phosphate metabolism in Ascomycetes.

A graduate student and professor analyze the results of DNA amplification by scanning a gel on the image analyzer.

A graduate student prepares tissue sections for DNA sequencing on a field trip to Namibia, southwestern Africa.

WICHITA STATE UNIVERSITY

Department of Biological Sciences

Program of Study

The Master of Science program offered by the Department of Biological Sciences provides an advanced education with a variety of specializations in the broad areas of organismal, cell, endocrine, environmental, molecular, plant, and reproductive biology. All incoming students are assigned to a temporary graduate adviser, and typically by the end of the first year, students choose a permanent graduate adviser and committee. The advisers work with students to develop a program of studies that meets their educational goals.

All students are required to attend the Biology Seminar course each semester and must give a minimum of two oral presentations. Candidates must complete 30 credit hours of graduate work, including the presentation and oral defense of a thesis based on original research.

Research Facilities

The Department is housed primarily on 2½ floors of Hubbard Hall, which contains modern, well-equipped research laboratories. Core laboratories have been established for protein analysis, bioinformatics, and microscopic imaging. Each core facility is staffed by a faculty director. Major instrumentation is available for the sequencing and synthesis of protein, PCR-dependent procedures, digital photomicroscopy, and carbohydrate analysis, as well as state-of-the-art chromatography and electrophoresis systems. Additional facilities include isolated animal maintenance and procedure rooms, a climate-controlled greenhouse, an environmental growth chamber room, a small herbarium, and vertebrate study collections. Large areas of relatively undisturbed prairie habitats are located nearby, and a biological field station provides excellent opportunities for aquatic and field research. The library contains more than 22,190 titles of books and periodicals that cover all areas of biology.

Financial Aid

A number of graduate teaching assistantships are available to qualified students. Recipients are required to teach 8 to 10 hours per week, primarily in laboratories, receiving a stipend of $10,000 for the academic year. In addition, recipients are eligible for a tuition waiver. Nonresident graduate students who are awarded graduate teaching assistantships are assessed tuition and fees at the Kansas resident's rate. A limited number of graduate research fellowships are awarded annually, but recipients are not eligible for a tuition waiver.

Cost of Study

Information pertaining to tuition and fees for resident and nonresident students may be found at http://webs.wichita.edu/?u=tuitionfees&p=/2010/tuitionfees.

Living and Housing Costs

On-campus housing costs for the academic year may be found at http://webs.wichita.edu/?u=housing&p=/Rates10. The University is located in an urban setting, and many convenient off-campus rentals in various price ranges are available.

Student Group

As an urban institution, Wichita State University enrolls approximately 15,000 students. More than 10,000 students are employed either full-time or part-time, and nearly 1,900 are over age 30. A total of approximately 3,100 graduate students are enrolled in programs of the eight schools and colleges of the University. Currently, approximately 25 students are enrolled full-time in the graduate program of the Department of Biological Sciences.

Location

Wichita is the largest city in Kansas, with a metropolitan population of more than 400,000 residents, and is known as the "Air Capital of the World," since it is the home of Beech (now Hawker Raytheon), Boeing (now Spirit Aerosystems, Inc.), Cessna, and Learjet. It is also a regional medical center, home to energy and agricultural industries, and the industrial and educational center of Kansas. Thus, Wichita enjoys a diversified economy that provides outstanding career opportunities in a variety of fields. Wichita offers the cultural and economic advantages of a big city but maintains the friendly atmosphere of a smaller town.

The University and The Department

Wichita State University became part of the Kansas State University System in 1964 after operating as a private institution (Fairmount College) since 1895 and as a municipal university since 1895. In addition to diverse academic programs, the University provides many cultural opportunities for its students through the Ulrich Art Museum, the University Symphony, and the University Theater. As part of the Fairmount College of Liberal Arts and Sciences, the Department of Biological Sciences participates in college educational programs, such as exploring new ways to increase interdepartmental graduate contacts and cooperation, and offers basic and applied research opportunities in various biological fields.

Applying

Completed application forms and two official transcripts of all previous academic work must be submitted to the graduate school by April 1 (for international students) or June 1 (for citizens or permanent residents) for the fall semester. For the spring semester, deadlines are August 1 (for international students) or December 1 (for citizens or permanent residents). Admission as a student in full standing requires the completion of 24 semester hours in biological sciences and 15 semester hours in chemistry, an overall minimum grade point average of 2.75 on a 4.0 scale for the most recent 60 semester hours completed, a grade point average of at least 3.0 on a 4.0 scale for all undergraduate biological science courses, three letters of reference from science faculty members, receipt of satisfactory scores from the General Test and Subject Test in biology of the Graduate Record Examinations (GRE), and satisfactory TOEFL scores from students whose native language is not English. The application will not be considered complete until all requested materials are received. Current application fees may be found at the Wichita State University Graduate School Web site (http://webs.wichita.edu/?u=gradschool).

Correspondence and Information

Graduate Coordinator
Department of Biological Sciences
Wichita State University
Wichita, Kansas 67260-0026
Phone: 316-978-3111
Fax: 316-978-3772
E-mail: karen.brown@wichita.edu
Web site: http://www.webs.wichita.edu/biology/

Wichita State University

THE FACULTY AND THEIR RESEARCH

George Bousfield, Professor; Ph.D., Indiana Bloomington, 1981. Reproductive endocrinology: glycoprotein hormones; mechanism of gonadotropic action; carbohydrate biochemistry.

Karen L. Brown, Associate Professor; Ph.D., Georgia, 1982. Ecology and population genetics: genetic, behavioral, and ecological interactions involved in the regulation of animal populations; effects of environmental stress on genetic variation of populations.

Donald A. Distler, Associate Professor; Ph.D., Kansas, 1966. Aquatic biology and ecology: limnological characteristics of river basins; invertebrate distributions and life histories in river basins.

William J. Hendry III, Professor; Ph.D., Worcester Foundation for Experimental Biology/Clark, 1982. Cellular and molecular endocrinology: endocrine disruption; estrogenic control of normal and neoplastic uterine morphogenesis; mechanisms of glucocorticoid-regulated tumor cell growth and gene expression.

Gregory Houseman, Assistant Professor, Ph.D., Michigan State, 2004. Development and maintenance of ecological communities with emphasis on patterns of species diversity, invasion, and ecosystem production.

Mary Liz Jameson, Associate Professor, Ph.D., Kansas, 1997. Systematics, phylogeny, biodiversity, and biogeography of coleoptera.

Jeffrey V. May, Associate Professor; Ph.D., Rhode Island, 1979. Reproductive endocrinology and cell biology: intraovarian regulation of mammalian folliculogenesis; autocrine/paracrine regulation of ovarian function by polypeptide growth factors.

Christopher M. Rogers, Associate Professor; Ph.D., Indiana Bloomington, 1988. Avian biology; cost-benefit analysis of energy storage strategies; population biology: environmental factors affecting nest success and population trajectory; migratory behavior.

F. Leland Russell, Assistant Professor; Ph.D., Texas at Austin, 1999. Plant population and community ecology; plant-animal interaction; herbivores' effect on plant population and communities; grassland, savanna, and woodland dynamics.

Mark A. Schneegurt, Associate Professor; Ph.D., Brown, 1989. Applied and environmental microbiology: microbial ecology; bioremediation; bioprospecting; cyanobacteria.

Bin Shuai, Assistant Professor; Ph.D., California, Riverside, 2003. Molecular and cellular mechanisms underlying pollen development and function; signaling pathway mediated by pollen-specific receptor-like kinases during pollen tube growth; transcriptional regulation of pollen-specific gene expression.

Paul Wooley, Professor, Ph.D. London, 1980. Immunogenetic regulation of autoimmune diseases (particularly rheumatoid arthritis), immune response to biomaterials, gene therapy for the treatment of connective tissue disorders.

Shang-You Yang, Associate Professor; M.D., Qingdao Medical College (China); Ph.D., Thornhill University, Detroit. Biomedical engineering, orthopaedic research.

Section 2
Anatomy

This section contains a directory of institutions offering graduate work in anatomy. Additional information about programs listed in the directory may be obtained by writing directly to the dean of a graduate school or chair of a department at the address given in the directory.

For programs offering related work, see also in this book *Biological and Biomedical Sciences; Cell, Molecular, and Structural Biology; Genetics, Developmental Biology, and Reproductive Biology; Neuroscience and Neurobiology; Pathology and Pathobiology; Physiology;* and *Zoology.* In the other guides in this series:

Graduate Programs in the Humanities, Arts & Social Sciences
See *Sociology, Anthropology, and Archaeology*
Graduate Programs in Business, Education, Health, Information Studies, Law & Social Work
See *Allied Health, Dentistry and Dental Sciences,* and *Veterinary Medicine and Sciences*

CONTENTS

Anatomy

Albert Einstein College of Medicine, Sue Golding Graduate Division of Medical Sciences, Department of Anatomy and Structural Biology, Bronx, NY 10461. Offers anatomy (PhD); cell and developmental biology (PhD); MD/PhD. *Degree requirements:* For doctorate, thesis/dissertation. *Entrance requirements:* For doctorate, GRE General Test. Additional exam requirements/recommendations for international students: Required—TOEFL. Electronic applications accepted. *Faculty research:* Cell motility, cell membranes and membrane-cytoskeletal interactions as applied to processing of pancreatic hormones, mechanisms of secretion.

Auburn University, College of Veterinary Medicine and Graduate School, Graduate Programs in Veterinary Medicine, Auburn University, AL 36849. Offers biomedical sciences (MS, PhD), including anatomy, physiology and pharmacology (MS), biomedical sciences (PhD), clinical sciences (MS), large animal surgery and medicine (MS), pathobiology (MS), radiology (MS), small animal surgery and medicine (MS); DVM/MS. Part-time programs available. *Faculty:* 100 full-time (40 women), 5 part-time/adjunct (1 woman). *Students:* 17 full-time (6 women), 51 part-time (35 women); includes 8 minority (2 African Americans, 1 American Indian/Alaska Native, 3 Asian Americans or Pacific Islanders, 2 Hispanic Americans), 22 international. Average age 31. 70 applicants, 34% accepted, 10 enrolled. In 2009, 12 master's, 7 doctorates awarded. *Degree requirements:* For doctorate, thesis/dissertation. *Entrance requirements:* For master's, GRE General Test; for doctorate, GRE General Test, GRE Subject Test. *Application deadline:* For fall admission, 7/7 for domestic students; for spring admission, 11/24 for domestic students. Applications are processed on a rolling basis. Application fee: $50 ($60 for international students). Electronic applications accepted. *Expenses:* Tuition, state resident: full-time $6240. Tuition, nonresident: full-time $18,720. International tuition: $18,938 full-time. Required fees: $492. Tuition and fees vary according to course load, program and reciprocity agreements. *Financial support:* Research assistantships, teaching assistantships, Federal Work-Study available. Support available to part-time students. Financial award application deadline: 3/15; financial award applicants required to submit FAFSA. *Unit head:* Dr. Timothy R. Boosinger, Dean, 334-844-4546. *Application contact:* Dr. George Flowers, Dean of the Graduate School, 334-844-2125.

Barry University, School of Graduate Medical Sciences, Program in Anatomy, Miami Shores, FL 33161-6695. Offers MS. *Entrance requirements:* For master's, GRE.

Boston University, College of Health and Rehabilitation Sciences—Sargent College, Department of Health Sciences, Programs in Applied Anatomy and Physiology, Boston, MA 02215. Offers MS, PhD. *Faculty:* 10 full-time (9 women), 5 part-time/adjunct (2 women). *Students:* 4 full-time (2 women), 4 part-time (all women), 1 international. Average age 27. 19 applicants, 63% accepted, 6 enrolled. In 2009, 5 master's, 1 doctorate awarded. Terminal master's awarded for partial completion of doctoral program. *Degree requirements:* For master's, thesis; for doctorate, thesis/dissertation. *Entrance requirements:* For master's, GRE General Test, minimum GPA of 3.0; for doctorate, GRE General Test. Additional exam requirements/recommendations for international students: Required—TOEFL (minimum score 550 paper-based; 84 iBT). *Application deadline:* For fall admission, 1/15 priority date for domestic students; for spring admission, 10/1 for domestic students. Applications are processed on a rolling basis. Application fee: $70. Electronic applications accepted. *Expenses:* Tuition: Full-time $37,910; part-time $1184 per credit hour. Required fees: $386; $40 per semester. Part-time tuition and fees vary according to class time, course level, degree level and program. *Financial support:* In 2009–10, 1 fellowship with partial tuition reimbursement (averaging $21,000 per year), 2 research assistantships (averaging $18,000 per year) were awarded; career-related internships or fieldwork, Federal Work-Study, institutionally sponsored loans, and scholarships/grants also available. Support available to part-time students. Financial award application deadline: 4/15; financial award applicants required to submit FAFSA. *Faculty research:* Skeletal muscle, neural systems, smooth muscle, muscular dystrophy. *Unit head:* Dr. Kathleen Morgan, Chair, 617-353-2717, E-mail: kmorgan@bu.edu. *Application contact:* Sharon Sankey, Director, Student Services, 617-353-2713, Fax: 617-353-7500, E-mail: ssankey@bu.edu.

Case Western Reserve University, School of Medicine and School of Graduate Studies, Graduate Programs in Medicine, Department of Anatomy, Cleveland, OH 44106. Offers applied anatomy (MS); biological anthropology (MS); cellular biology (MS); MD/MS. Part-time programs available. *Degree requirements:* For master's, comprehensive exam, thesis (for some programs). *Entrance requirements:* For master's, GRE General Test. Additional exam requirements/recommendations for international students: Required—TOEFL. *Faculty research:* Hypoxia, cell injury, biochemical aberration occurrences in ischemic tissue, human functional morphology, evolutionary morphology.

Columbia University, College of Physicians and Surgeons, Department of Anatomy and Cell Biology, New York, NY 10032. Offers anatomy (M Phil, MA, PhD); anatomy and cell biology (PhD); MD/PhD. Only candidates for the PhD are admitted. Terminal master's awarded for partial completion of doctoral program. *Degree requirements:* For doctorate, thesis/dissertation, oral exam. *Entrance requirements:* For master's and doctorate, GRE General Test. Additional exam requirements/recommendations for international students: Required—TOEFL. *Faculty research:* Protein sorting, membrane biophysics, muscle energetics, neuroendocrinology, developmental biology, cytoskeleton, transcription factors.

Cornell University, Graduate School, Graduate Fields of Agriculture and Life Sciences, Field of Zoology, Ithaca, NY 14853-0001. Offers animal cytology (MS, PhD); comparative and functional anatomy (MS, PhD); developmental biology (MS, PhD); ecology (MS, PhD); histology (MS, PhD). *Faculty:* 24 full-time (5 women). *Students:* 4 full-time (all women); includes 1 minority (Hispanic American), 1 international. Average age 34. 7 applicants, 0% accepted, 0 enrolled. *Degree requirements:* For doctorate, comprehensive exam, thesis/dissertation, 2 semesters of teaching experience. *Entrance requirements:* For doctorate, GRE General Test, GRE Subject Test (biology), 2 letters of recommendation. Additional exam requirements/recommendations for international students: Required—TOEFL (minimum score 550 paper-based; 213 computer-based; 77 iBT). *Application deadline:* For fall admission, 2/1 priority date for domestic students. Application fee: $70. Electronic applications accepted. *Expenses:* Tuition: Full-time $29,500. Required fees: $70. Full-time tuition and fees vary according to degree level, program and student level. *Financial support:* In 2009–10, 3 students received support; fellowships with full tuition reimbursements available, research assistantships with full tuition reimbursements available, teaching assistantships with full tuition reimbursements available, institutionally sponsored loans, scholarships/grants, health care benefits, tuition waivers (full and partial), and unspecified assistantships available. Financial award applicants required to submit FAFSA. *Faculty research:* Organismal biology, functional morphology, biomechanics, comparative vertebrate anatomy, comparative invertebrate anatomy, paleontology. *Unit head:* Director of Graduate Studies, 607-253-3276, Fax: 607-253-3756. *Application contact:* Graduate Field Assistant, 607-253-3276, Fax: 607-253-3756, E-mail: graduate_edcvm@cornell.edu.

Creighton University, School of Medicine and Graduate School, Graduate Programs in Medicine, Program in Clinical Anatomy, Omaha, NE 68178-0001. Offers MS. *Degree requirements:* For master's, comprehensive exam, thesis or alternative. *Entrance requirements:* For master's, GRE, MCAT or DAT. Additional exam requirements/recommendations for international students: Required—TOEFL. Electronic applications accepted. *Expenses:* Tuition: Full-time $11,700; part-time $650 per credit hour. Required fees: $126 per semester. *Faculty research:* Neural crest cell migration; ontogenetic and phylogenetic nervous system development; skeletal biology.

Dalhousie University, Faculty of Graduate Studies and Faculty of Medicine, Graduate Programs in Medicine, Department of Anatomy and Neurobiology, Halifax, NS B3H 4R2, Canada. Offers M Sc, PhD. *Degree requirements:* For master's, thesis; for doctorate, thesis/dissertation. *Entrance requirements:* For master's and doctorate, GRE (recommended), minimum A- average. Additional exam requirements/recommendations for international students: Required—TOEFL, IELTS, 1 of the following 5 approved tests: TOEFL, IELTS, CANTEST, CAEL, Michigan English Language Assessment Battery. Electronic applications accepted. *Faculty research:* Neuroscience histology, cell biology, neuroendocrinology, evolutionary biology.

Duke University, Graduate School, Department of Biological Anthropology and Anatomy, Durham, NC 27710. Offers cellular and molecular biology (PhD); gross anatomy and physical anthropology (PhD), including comparative morphology of human and non-human primates, primate social behavior, vertebrate paleontology; neuroanatomy (PhD). *Faculty:* 8 full-time. *Students:* 14 full-time (9 women); includes 2 minority (1 African American, 1 Hispanic American), 1 international. 39 applicants, 15% accepted, 4 enrolled. In 2009, 4 doctorates awarded. *Degree requirements:* For doctorate, one foreign language, thesis/dissertation. *Entrance requirements:* For doctorate, GRE General Test. Additional exam requirements/recommendations for international students: Required—TOEFL (minimum score 550 paper-based; 213 computer-based; 83 iBT), IELTS (minimum score 7). *Application deadline:* For fall admission, 12/8 priority date for domestic and international students. Application fee: $75. Electronic applications accepted. *Financial support:* Fellowships, teaching assistantships, Federal Work-Study available. Financial award application deadline: 12/31. *Unit head:* Daniel Schmitt, Director of Graduate Studies, 919-684-5664, Fax: 919-684-4124, E-mail: mlsquire@duke.edu. *Application contact:* Cynthia Robertson, Associate Dean for Enrollment Services, 919-684-3913, E-mail: grad-admissions@duke.edu.

East Carolina University, Brody School of Medicine, Department of Anatomy and Cell Biology, Greenville, NC 27858-4353. Offers PhD. *Degree requirements:* For doctorate, comprehensive exam, thesis/dissertation. *Entrance requirements:* For doctorate, GRE General Test. Additional exam requirements/recommendations for international students: Required—TOEFL. *Faculty research:* Kinesin motors during slow matogensis, mitochondria and peroxisomes in obesity, ovarian innervation, tight junction function and regulation.

East Tennessee State University, James H. Quillen College of Medicine, Biomedical Science Graduate Program, Johnson City, TN 37614. Offers anatomy (MS, PhD); biochemistry (MS, PhD); biophysics (MS, PhD); microbiology (MS, PhD); pharmacology (MS, PhD); physiology (MS, PhD). Part-time programs available. Terminal master's awarded for partial completion of doctoral program. *Degree requirements:* For master's, one foreign language, thesis, comprehensive qualifying exam; for doctorate, 2 foreign languages, thesis/dissertation. *Entrance requirements:* For master's, GRE General Test, minimum GPA of 3.0, bachelor's degree in biological or related science; for doctorate, GRE General Test, GRE Subject Test. Additional exam requirements/recommendations for international students: Required—TOEFL (minimum score 550 paper-based; 213 computer-based). *Expenses:* Contact institution.

Howard University, Graduate School, Department of Anatomy, Washington, DC 20059-0002. Offers MS, PhD. *Degree requirements:* For master's, comprehensive exam, thesis, teaching experience; for doctorate, comprehensive exam, thesis/dissertation, teaching experience. *Entrance requirements:* For master's and doctorate, GRE General Test, minimum GPA of 3.0. Additional exam requirements/recommendations for international students: Required—TOEFL (minimum score 550 paper-based; 213 computer-based). Electronic applications accepted. *Faculty research:* Neural control of function, mammalian evolution and paleontology, cellular differentiation, cellular and neuronal communication, development, cell biology, molecular biology, anatomy.

Indiana University–Purdue University Indianapolis, Indiana University School of Medicine, Department of Anatomy and Cell Biology, Indianapolis, IN 46202-2896. Offers MS, PhD, MD/PhD. *Faculty:* 14 full-time (1 woman). *Students:* 10 full-time (5 women), 1 international. Average age 31. 21 applicants, 62% accepted, 7 enrolled. In 2009, 1 master's, 3 doctorates awarded. *Degree requirements:* For master's, thesis or alternative; for doctorate, thesis/dissertation. *Entrance requirements:* For master's and doctorate, GRE General Test. *Application deadline:* For fall admission, 1/15 priority date for domestic students. Application fee: $55 ($65 for international students). *Financial support:* In 2009–10, 1 fellowship was awarded; research assistantships, Federal Work-Study, institutionally sponsored loans, tuition waivers (partial), and stipends also available. Financial award application deadline: 2/15. *Faculty research:* Acoustic reflex control, osteoarthritis and bone disease, diabetes, kidney diseases, cellular and molecular neurobiology. *Unit head:* Dr. David B. Burr, Chairman, 317-274-7494, Fax: 317-278-2040, E-mail: dburr@indyvax.iupui.edu. *Application contact:* Dr. James Williams, Graduate Adviser, 317-274-3423, Fax: 317-278-2040, E-mail: williams@anatomy.iupui.edu.

The Johns Hopkins University, School of Medicine, Graduate Programs in Medicine, Center for Functional Anatomy and Evolution, Baltimore, MD 21218-2699. Offers PhD. *Faculty:* 5 full-time (1 woman), 2 part-time/adjunct (1 woman). *Students:* 9 full-time (6 women). Average age 25. 26 applicants, 15% accepted, 2 enrolled. In 2009, 2 doctorates awarded. *Degree requirements:* For doctorate, comprehensive exam, thesis/dissertation, oral exams. *Entrance requirements:* For doctorate, GRE. Additional exam requirements/recommendations for international students: Required—TOEFL. *Application deadline:* For fall admission, 1/10 for domestic and international students. Application fee: $85. *Financial support:* In 2009–10, 1 fellowship with partial tuition reimbursement (averaging $30,000 per year), 8 teaching assistantships with full tuition reimbursements (averaging $26,855 per year) were awarded; career-related internships or fieldwork, institutionally sponsored loans, health care benefits, and tuition waivers (full) also available. *Faculty research:* Vertebrate evolution, functional anatomy, primate evolution, vertebrate paleobiology, vertebrate morphology. *Unit head:* Dr. Kenneth D. Rose, Director, 410-955-7172, Fax: 410-614-9030, E-mail: kdrose@jhmi.edu. *Application contact:* Catherine L. Will, Coordinator, Graduate Student Affairs, 410-614-3385, E-mail: grad_study@som.adm.jhu.edu.

Loma Linda University, School of Medicine, Department of Pathology and Human Anatomy, Loma Linda, CA 92350. Offers MS, PhD. Part-time programs available. Terminal master's awarded for partial completion of doctoral program. *Degree requirements:* For master's, thesis; for doctorate, 2 foreign languages, thesis/dissertation. *Entrance requirements:* For master's and doctorate, GRE General Test. Additional exam requirements/recommendations for international students: Required—TOEFL (minimum score 550 paper-based; 213 computer-based). *Faculty research:* Neuroendocrine system, histochemistry and image analysis, effect of age and diabetes on PNS, electron microscopy, histology.

Louisiana State University Health Sciences Center, School of Graduate Studies in New Orleans, Department of Cell Biology and Anatomy, New Orleans, LA 70112-2223. Offers cell biology and anatomy (MS, PhD), including cell biology, developmental biology, neurobiology and anatomy; MD/PhD. *Degree requirements:* For master's, comprehensive exam, thesis; for doctorate, comprehensive exam, thesis/dissertation. *Entrance requirements:* For master's and doctorate, GRE General Test, GRE Subject Test, minimum undergraduate GPA of 3.0. Additional exam requirements/recommendations for international students: Required—TOEFL. *Faculty research:* Visual system organization, neural development, plasticity of sensory systems, information processing through the nervous system, visuomotor integration.

Louisiana State University Health Sciences Center at Shreveport, Department of Cellular Biology and Anatomy, Shreveport, LA 71130-3932. Offers MS, PhD, MD/PhD. Terminal master's awarded for partial completion of doctoral program. *Degree requirements:* For master's, thesis; for doctorate, thesis/dissertation. *Entrance requirements:* For master's and doctorate, GRE General Test. Additional exam requirements/recommendations for international students:

Required—TOEFL. *Faculty research:* Alcohol and immunity, neuroscience, olfactory physiology, extracellular matrix, cancer cell biology and gene therapy.

Loyola University Chicago, Graduate School, Department of Cell Biology, Neurobiology and Anatomy, Chicago, IL 60660. Offers MS, PhD. Part-time programs available. *Faculty:* 16 full-time (6 women), 9 part-time/adjunct (4 women). *Students:* 20 full-time (12 women), 1 (woman) part-time; includes 1 minority (Hispanic American), 1 international. Average age 25. 25 applicants, 40% accepted, 8 enrolled. In 2009, 1 master's, 1 doctorate awarded. Terminal master's awarded for partial completion of doctoral program. *Degree requirements:* For master's, thesis; for doctorate, comprehensive exam, thesis/dissertation. *Entrance requirements:* For master's, GRE General Test, minimum GPA of 3.0; for doctorate, GRE General Test, GRE Subject Test (biology), minimum GPA of 3.0. Additional exam requirements/recommendations for international students: Required—TOEFL (minimum score 600 paper-based; 250 computer-based). *Application deadline:* For fall admission, 5/1 priority date for domestic and international students. Applications are processed on a rolling basis. Application fee: $50. Electronic applications accepted. *Expenses:* Tuition: Full-time $14,220; part-time $790 per credit hour. Required fees: $60 per semester hour. Tuition and fees vary according to program. *Financial support:* In 2009–10, 5 fellowships with full tuition reimbursements (averaging $23,000 per year), 5 research assistantships with full tuition reimbursements (averaging $23,000 per year) were awarded; Federal Work-Study and unspecified assistantships also available. Financial award application deadline: 5/1; financial award applicants required to submit FAFSA. *Faculty research:* Brain steroids, immunology, neuroregeneration, cytokines. Total annual research expenditures: $1 million. *Unit head:* Dr. Phong Le, Head, 708-216-3603, Fax: 708-216-3913, E-mail: ple@lumc.edu. *Application contact:* Ginny Hayes, Graduate Program Secretary, 708-216-3353, Fax: 708-216-3913, E-mail: vhayes@lumc.edu.

McGill University, Faculty of Graduate and Postdoctoral Studies, Faculty of Medicine, Department of Anatomy and Cell Biology, Montréal, QC H3A 2T5, Canada. Offers M Sc, PhD.

Medical College of Georgia, School of Graduate Studies, Program in Cellular Biology and Anatomy, Augusta, GA 30912. Offers PhD. *Degree requirements:* For doctorate, comprehensive exam, thesis/dissertation. *Entrance requirements:* For doctorate, GRE General Test. Additional exam requirements/recommendations for international students: Required—TOEFL (minimum score 550 paper-based; 213 computer-based; 79 iBT). Full-time tuition and fees vary according to campus/location, program and student level. *Faculty research:* Eye disease, developmental biology, cell injury and death, stroke and neurotoxicity, diabetic complications.

New York Chiropractic College, Program in Clinical Anatomy, Seneca Falls, NY 13148-0800. Offers MS. *Faculty:* 8 full-time (4 women). *Students:* 1 (woman) full-time. 6 applicants, 0% accepted, 0 enrolled. *Degree requirements:* For master's, thesis. *Entrance requirements:* For master's, minimum GPA of 3.0, DC degree, interview. *Application deadline:* Applications are processed on a rolling basis. Application fee: $0. *Expenses:* Tuition: Full-time $18,320; part-time $426 per credit hour. Required fees: $680. Tuition and fees vary according to course load and program. *Financial support:* In 2009–10, 1 student received support, including 1 fellowship (averaging $31,000 per year). Financial award applicants required to submit FAFSA. *Faculty research:* Bone histology, biomechanics, craniofacial growth and anatomy, skeletal morphology. *Unit head:* Dr. Michael P. Zumpano, Director, 315-568-3196, E-mail: mzumpnao@nycc.edu. *Application contact:* Dr. Michael P. Zumpano, Director, 315-568-3196, E-mail: mzumpnao@nycc.edu.

New York Medical College, Graduate School of Basic Medical Sciences, Department of Cell Biology, Valhalla, NY 10595-1691. Offers cell biology and neuroscience (MS, PhD); MD/PhD. Part-time and evening/weekend programs available. Terminal master's awarded for partial completion of doctoral program. *Degree requirements:* For master's, thesis; for doctorate, comprehensive exam, thesis/dissertation. *Entrance requirements:* For master's and doctorate, GRE General Test. Additional exam requirements/recommendations for international students: Required—TOEFL. *Expenses:* Tuition: Full-time $18,170; part-time $790 per credit. Required fees: $790 per credit. $20 per semester. One-time fee: $100. Tuition and fees vary according to class time, course level, course load, degree level, program, student level and student's religious affiliation. *Faculty research:* Mechanisms of growth control in skeletal muscle, cartilage differentiation, cytoskeletal functions, signal transduction pathways, neuronal development and plasticity.

The Ohio State University, College of Medicine, School of Biomedical Science, Department of Anatomy, Columbus, OH 43210. Offers MS, PhD. Terminal master's awarded for partial completion of doctoral program. *Degree requirements:* For doctorate, thesis/dissertation. *Entrance requirements:* For master's and doctorate, GRE General Test, GRE Subject Test in biology, biochemistry, chemistry, CIS, physics, or engineering. Additional exam requirements/recommendations for international students: Required—TOEFL (paper-based 600, computer-based 250) or Michigan English Language Assessment Battery (86). Electronic applications accepted. *Expenses:* Tuition, state resident: full-time $10,683. Tuition, nonresident: full-time $25,923. Tuition and fees vary according to course load and program. *Faculty research:* Cell biology, biomechanical trauma, computer-assisted instruction.

The Ohio State University, College of Veterinary Medicine, Department of Veterinary Biosciences, Columbus, OH 43210. Offers anatomy and cellular biology (MS, PhD); pathobiology (MS, PhD); pharmacology (MS, PhD); toxicology (MS, PhD); veterinary physiology (MS, PhD). *Faculty:* 45. *Students:* 18 full-time (14 women), 20 part-time (16 women); includes 3 minority (1 African American, 1 Asian American or Pacific Islander, 1 Hispanic American), 16 international. Average age 30. In 2009, 1 master's, 9 doctorates awarded. *Entrance requirements:* For master's and doctorate, GRE General Test. Additional exam requirements/recommendations for international students: Required—TOEFL. *Application deadline:* Applications are processed on a rolling basis. Application fee: $40 ($50 for international students). Electronic applications accepted. *Expenses:* Tuition, state resident: full-time $10,683. Tuition, nonresident: full-time $25,923. Tuition and fees vary according to course load and program. *Faculty research:* Microvasculature, muscle biology, neonatal lung and bone development. *Unit head:* Dr. Michael J. Oglesbee, Graduate Studies Committee Chair, 614-292-5661, Fax: 614-292-6473, E-mail: oglesbee.1@osu.edu. *Application contact:* Graduate Admissions, 614-292-9444, Fax: 614-292-3895, E-mail: domestic.grad@osu.edu.

Palmer College of Chiropractic, Division of Graduate Studies, Davenport, IA 52803-5287. Offers clinical research (MS). *Faculty:* 133 full-time (40 women). *Students:* 8 full-time (3 women), 4 part-time (1 woman). *Degree requirements:* For master's, comprehensive exam, thesis. *Entrance requirements:* For master's, GRE General Test, minimum GPA of 2.5. Additional exam requirements/recommendations for international students: Required—TOEFL. *Application deadline:* For fall admission, 9/1 for domestic students; for spring admission, 5/28 for domestic students. Applications are processed on a rolling basis. Application fee: $50. Electronic applications accepted. *Expenses:* Contact institution. *Financial support:* In 2009–10, 5 students received support, including teaching assistantships with full and partial tuition reimbursements available (averaging $6,269 per year); research assistantships, Federal Work-Study, institutionally sponsored loans, tuition waivers (full), and stipends also available. Support available to part-time students. Financial award application deadline: 4/1; financial award applicants required to submit FAFSA. *Unit head:* Dr. Jean Murray, Administrator, 563-884-5672, Fax: 563-884-5505. *Application contact:* Dr. Brian McMaster, Assistant Dean, 563-884-5163, Fax: 563-884-5226, E-mail: brian.mcmaster@plamer.edu.

Penn State Hershey Medical Center, College of Medicine, Graduate School Programs in the Biomedical Sciences, Program in Anatomy, Hershey, PA 17033. Offers MS, PhD. *Students:* 17 applicants, 29% accepted, 4 enrolled.Terminal master's awarded for partial completion of doctoral program. *Degree requirements:* For master's, thesis or alternative; for doctorate, comprehensive exam, thesis/dissertation. *Entrance requirements:* For master's and doctorate, GRE General Test or MCAT, minimum GPA of 3.0. Additional exam requirements/recommendations for international students: Required—TOEFL (minimum score 500 paper-based; 213 computer-based). *Application deadline:* For fall admission, 1/31 priority date for domestic students, 2/1 priority date for international students. Applications are processed on a rolling basis. Application fee: $65. Electronic applications accepted. *Expenses:* Tuition, state resident: part-time $644 per credit. Tuition, nonresident: part-time $1142 per credit. Required fees: $22 per semester. *Financial support:* In 2009–10, research assistantships with full tuition reimbursements (averaging $22,260 per year); fellowships with full tuition reimbursements, scholarships/grants, health care benefits, and unspecified assistantships also available. Financial award applicants required to submit FAFSA. *Faculty research:* Developmental biology, stem cell, cancer-basic science and clinical application, wound healing, angiogenesis. *Unit head:* Dr. Patricia J. McLaughlin, Program Director, 717-531-6411, Fax: 717-531-5184, E-mail: grad-hmc@psu.edu. *Application contact:* Dee Clarke, Program Assistant, 717-531-8651, Fax: 717-531-8651, E-mail: grad-hmc@psu.edu.

Purdue University, School of Veterinary Medicine and Graduate School, Graduate Programs in Veterinary Medicine, Department of Basic Medical Sciences, West Lafayette, IN 47907. Offers anatomy (MS, PhD); pharmacology (MS, PhD); physiology (MS, PhD). Part-time programs available. *Faculty:* 23 full-time (7 women), 2 part-time/adjunct (1 woman). *Students:* 23 full-time (15 women), 1 (woman) part-time; includes 3 minority (1 African American, 2 Asian Americans or Pacific Islanders), 14 international. Average age 32. 15 applicants, 27% accepted, 4 enrolled. In 2009, 2 master's, 2 doctorates awarded. Terminal master's awarded for partial completion of doctoral program. *Degree requirements:* For master's, thesis; for doctorate, thesis/dissertation. *Entrance requirements:* For master's and doctorate, GRE General Test. Additional exam requirements/recommendations for international students: Required—TOEFL. *Application deadline:* For fall admission, 12/15 priority date for domestic students, 12/15 for international students. Application fee: $55. Electronic applications accepted. *Financial support:* In 2009–10, 14 research assistantships with partial tuition reimbursements (averaging $17,420 per year), 8 teaching assistantships with partial tuition reimbursements (averaging $15,000 per year) were awarded; fellowships with partial tuition reimbursements also available. Financial award application deadline: 3/1; financial award applicants required to submit FAFSA. *Faculty research:* Development and regeneration, tissue injury and shock, biomedical engineering, ovarian function, bone and cartilage biology, cell and molecular biology. *Unit head:* Dr. Laurie A. Jaeger, Head, 765-494-7348, Fax: 765-494-0781, E-mail: ljaeger@purdue.edu. *Application contact:* Dr. Kevin M. Hannon, Chairman, Graduate Committee, 765-494-5949, Fax: 765-494-0781, E-mail: bmsgrad@purdue.edu.

Queen's University at Kingston, School of Graduate Studies and Research, Faculty of Health Sciences, Department of Anatomy and Cell Biology, Kingston, ON K7L 3N6, Canada. Offers biology of reproduction (M Sc, PhD); cancer (M Sc, PhD); cardiovascular pathophysiology (M Sc, PhD); cell and molecular biology (M Sc, PhD); drug metabolism (M Sc, PhD); endocrinology (M Sc, PhD); motor control (M Sc, PhD); neural regeneration (M Sc, PhD); neurophysiology (M Sc, PhD). Part-time programs available. *Degree requirements:* For master's, thesis; for doctorate, one foreign language, comprehensive exam, thesis/dissertation. *Entrance requirements:* Additional exam requirements/recommendations for international students: Required—TOEFL. Electronic applications accepted. *Faculty research:* Human kinetics, neuroscience, reproductive biology, cardiovascular.

Rosalind Franklin University of Medicine and Science, School of Graduate and Postdoctoral Studies—Interdisciplinary Graduate Program in Biomedical Sciences, Department of Cell Biology and Anatomy, North Chicago, IL 60064-3095. Offers MS, PhD, MD/PhD. Terminal master's awarded for partial completion of doctoral program. *Degree requirements:* For master's, comprehensive exam, thesis, qualifying exam; for doctorate, comprehensive exam, thesis/dissertation, original research project. *Entrance requirements:* For master's and doctorate, GRE General Test, minimum GPA of 3.0. Additional exam requirements/recommendations for international students: Required—TOEFL, TWE. *Faculty research:* Neuroscience, molecular biology.

Rush University, Graduate College, Division of Anatomy and Cell Biology, Chicago, IL 60612-3832. Offers MS, PhD, MD/MS, MD/PhD. Terminal master's awarded for partial completion of doctoral program. *Degree requirements:* For master's, thesis; for doctorate, comprehensive exam, thesis/dissertation, preliminary exam, dissertation proposal. *Entrance requirements:* For master's, GRE General Test, minimum GPA of 3.0, bachelor's degree in biology or chemistry (preferred), interview; for doctorate, GRE General Test, minimum GPA of 3.0, interview. Additional exam requirements/recommendations for international students: Required—TOEFL. Electronic applications accepted. *Faculty research:* Incontinence following vaginal distension, knee replacement, biomimetric materials, injured spinal motoneurons, implant fixation.

Saint Louis University, Graduate School and School of Medicine, Graduate Program in Biomedical Sciences and Graduate School, Center for Anatomical Science and Education, St. Louis, MO 63103-2097. Offers anatomy (MS-R, PhD). *Degree requirements:* For master's, comprehensive exam, thesis; for doctorate, comprehensive exam, thesis/dissertation, departmental qualifying exams. *Entrance requirements:* For master's, GRE General Test, letters of recommendation, resume; for doctorate, GRE General Test, letters of recommendation, resumé, goal statement, transcripts. Additional exam requirements/recommendations for international students: Required—TOEFL (minimum score 525 paper-based; 194 computer-based). *Faculty research:* Neurodegenerative diseases, cerebellar cortical circuitry, neurogenesis, evolutionary anatomy.

State University of New York Upstate Medical University, College of Graduate Studies, Program in Anatomy and Cell Biology, Syracuse, NY 13210-2334. Offers anatomy (MS); anatomy and cell biology (PhD); MD/PhD. *Faculty:* 18 full-time (4 women), 1 part-time/adjunct (0 women). *Students:* 17 full-time (7 women), 1 (woman) part-time; includes 1 minority (Asian American or Pacific Islander), 6 international. In 2009, 1 master's awarded. Terminal master's awarded for partial completion of doctoral program. *Degree requirements:* For master's, thesis; for doctorate, comprehensive exam, thesis/dissertation. *Entrance requirements:* For master's, GRE General Test, interview; for doctorate, GRE General Test, telephone interview. Additional exam requirements/recommendations for international students: Required—TOEFL. *Application deadline:* Applications are processed on a rolling basis. Application fee: $40. Electronic applications accepted. *Financial support:* In 2009–10, fellowships with tuition reimbursements (averaging $21,514 per year), research assistantships with tuition reimbursements (averaging $21,514 per year) were awarded; Federal Work-Study, scholarships/grants, health care benefits, and unspecified assistantships also available. Financial award application deadline: 4/15; financial award applicants required to submit FAFSA. *Faculty research:* Cancer, disorders of the nervous system, infectious diseases, diabetes/metabolic disorders/cardiovascular diseases. *Unit head:* Dr. Joseph Sanger, Chair, 315-464-5120. *Application contact:* Sandra Tillotsson, Coordinator of Graduate Recruitment, 315-464-7655, Fax: 315-464-4544.

See Close-Up on page 237.

Stony Brook University, State University of New York, Stony Brook University Medical Center, School of Medicine and Graduate School, Graduate Programs in Medicine, Department of Anatomical Sciences, Stony Brook, NY 11794. Offers PhD. *Students:* 5 full-time (2 women). Average age 30. 9 applicants, 33% accepted. In 2009, 3 doctorates awarded. *Degree requirements:* For doctorate, comprehensive exam, thesis/dissertation. *Entrance requirements:* For doctorate, GRE General Test, GRE Subject Test, BA in life sciences, minimum GPA of 3.0. Additional exam requirements/recommendations for international students: Required—TOEFL. *Application deadline:* For fall admission, 1/15 for domestic students. Application fee: $60. *Expenses:* Tuition, state resident: full-time $8370; part-time $349 per credit. Tuition, nonresident: full-time $13,250; part-time $552 per credit. Required fees: $933. *Financial support:* Fellowships, research assistantships, teaching assistantships, Federal Work-Study available. Financial

Anatomy

Stony Brook University, State University of New York (continued)
award application deadline: 3/15. *Faculty research:* Biological membranes, biomechanics of locomotion, systematics and evolutionary history of primates. Total annual research expenditures: $366,529. *Unit head:* Dr. William Jungers, Chair, 631-444-3122, Fax: 631-444-3947, E-mail: william.jungers@stonybrook.edu. *Application contact:* Dr. William Jungers, Chair, 631-444-3122, Fax: 631-444-3947, E-mail: william.jungers@stonybrook.edu.

Temple University, Health Sciences Center, School of Medicine and Graduate School, Graduate Programs in Medicine, Department of Anatomy and Cell Biology, Philadelphia, PA 19122-6096. Offers MS, PhD. *Degree requirements:* For doctorate, thesis/dissertation, research seminars. *Entrance requirements:* For master's and doctorate, GRE General Test, GRE Subject Test, minimum GPA of 3.0. Additional exam requirements/recommendations for international students: Required—TOEFL. Electronic applications accepted. *Faculty research:* Neurobiology, reproductive biology, cardiovascular system, musculoskeletal biology, developmental biology.

Texas A&M University, College of Veterinary Medicine, Department of Veterinary Integrative Biosciences, College Station, TX 77843. Offers epidemiology (MS); food safety/toxicology (MS); veterinary anatomy (MS, PhD); veterinary public health (MS). *Faculty:* 25. *Students:* 34 full-time (22 women), 8 part-time (5 women); includes 2 minority (1 African American, 1 Asian American or Pacific Islander), 20 international. Average age 30. In 2009, 1 master's, 1 doctorate awarded. Terminal master's awarded for partial completion of doctoral program. *Degree requirements:* For master's, comprehensive exam, thesis; for doctorate, comprehensive exam, thesis/dissertation. *Entrance requirements:* For master's and doctorate, GRE General Test, minimum undergraduate GPA of 3.0. Additional exam requirements/recommendations for international students: Required—TOEFL. *Application deadline:* For fall admission, 7/15 priority date for domestic students, 4/1 priority date for international students; for spring admission, 10/1 priority date for domestic students, 9/15 priority date for international students. Applications are processed on a rolling basis. Application fee: $50 ($75 for international students). Electronic applications accepted. *Expenses:* Tuition, state resident: full-time $3991; part-time $221.74 per credit hour. Tuition, nonresident: full-time $9049; part-time $502.74 per credit hour. *Financial support:* In 2009–10, fellowships (averaging $18,000 per year), research assistantships (averaging $15,600 per year), teaching assistantships (averaging $15,600 per year) were awarded; institutionally sponsored loans, unspecified assistantships, and clinical associateships also available. Financial award application deadline: 7/15; financial award applicants required to submit FAFSA. *Faculty research:* Metal toxicology, reproductive biology, genetics of neural development, developmental biology, environmental toxicology. *Unit head:* Dr. E. Tiffany-Castiglioni, Head, 979-862-6559, E-mail: ecastiglioni@cvm.tamu.edu. *Application contact:* Dr. Jane Welsh, Chair, Fax: 979-847-8981, E-mail: jwelsh@cum.tamu.edu.

Universidad Central del Caribe, School of Medicine, Program in Biomedical Sciences, Bayamón, PR 00960-6032. Offers anatomy and cell biology (MA, MS); biochemistry (MS); biomedical sciences (MA); microbiology and immunology (MA, MS); pharmacology (MS); physiology (MA, MS).

Universidad de Ciencias Medicas, Graduate Programs, San Jose, Costa Rica. Offers dermatology (SP); family health (MS); health service center administration (MHA); human anatomy (MS); medical and surgery (MD); occupational medicine (MS); pharmacy (Pharm D). Part-time programs available. *Degree requirements:* For master's, thesis; for first professional degree and SP, comprehensive exam. *Entrance requirements:* For first professional degree, admissions test; for master's, MD or bachelors degree; for SP, admissions test, MD degree.

Université Laval, Faculty of Medicine, Department of Anatomy and Physiology, Québec, QC G1K 7P4, Canada. Offers M Sc, PhD. Terminal master's awarded for partial completion of doctoral program. *Degree requirements:* For master's, thesis (for some programs); for doctorate, comprehensive exam, thesis/dissertation. Electronic applications accepted.

Université Laval, Faculty of Medicine, Post-Professional Programs in Medical Studies, Québec, QC G1K 7P4, Canada. Offers anatomy–pathology (DESS); anesthesiology (DESS); cardiology (DESS); care of older people (Diploma); clinical research (DESS); community health (DESS); dermatology (DESS); diagnostic radiology (DESS); emergency medicine (Diploma); family medicine (DESS); general surgery (DESS); geriatrics (DESS); hematology (DESS); internal medicine (DESS); maternal and fetal medicine (Diploma); medical biochemistry (DESS); medical microbiology and infectious diseases (DESS); medical oncology (DESS); nephrology (DESS); neurology (DESS); neurosurgery (DESS); obstetrics and gynecology (DESS); ophthalmology (DESS); orthopedic surgery (DESS); oto-rhino-laryngology (DESS); palliative medicine (Diploma); pediatrics (DESS); plastic surgery (DESS); psychiatry (DESS); pulmonary medicine (DESS); radiology–oncology (DESS); thoracic surgery (DESS); urology (DESS). *Degree requirements:* For other advanced degree, comprehensive exam. *Entrance requirements:* For degree, knowledge of French. Electronic applications accepted.

University at Buffalo, the State University of New York, Graduate School, School of Medicine and Biomedical Sciences, Graduate Programs in Medicine and Biomedical Sciences, Department of Pathology and Anatomical Sciences, Buffalo, NY 14260. Offers anatomical sciences (MA, PhD); pathology (MA, PhD). *Faculty:* 13 full-time (2 women), 11 part-time/adjunct (4 women). *Students:* 8 full-time (4 women), 3 part-time (1 woman), 2 international. Average age 29. 19 applicants, 37% accepted. In 2009, 1 master's, 1 doctorate awarded. *Degree requirements:* For master's, thesis; for doctorate, comprehensive exam, thesis/dissertation. *Entrance requirements:* For master's, GRE, MCAT, or DAT, 3 letters of recommendation; for doctorate, GRE, 3 letters of recommendation. Additional exam requirements/recommendations for international students: Required—TOEFL (minimum score 600 paper-based; 250 computer-based; 100 iBT). *Application deadline:* For fall admission, 2/1 priority date for domestic and international students. Application fee: $50. *Financial support:* In 2009–10, 2 students received support, including 1 fellowship with full tuition reimbursement available (averaging $24,000 per year), 1 research assistantship with full tuition reimbursement available (averaging $22,000 per year); health care benefits also available. Financial award application deadline: 2/1. *Faculty research:* Immunopathology-immunobiology, experimental hypertension, neuromuscular disease, molecular pathology, cell motility and cytoskeleton. *Unit head:* Dr. Reid Heffner, Chairman, 716-829-2846, Fax: 716-829-2086, E-mail: rheffner@buffalo.edu. *Application contact:* Dr. Peter Nickerson, Director of Graduate Studies, 716-829-2846.

The University of Arizona, College of Medicine, Graduate Programs in Medicine, Department of Cell Biology and Anatomy, Tucson, AZ 85721. Offers PhD. *Degree requirements:* For doctorate, thesis/dissertation. *Entrance requirements:* For doctorate, GRE General Test. *Expenses:* Tuition, state resident: full-time $9028. Tuition, nonresident: full-time $24,890. *Faculty research:* Heart development, neural development, cellular toxicology and microcirculation; membrane traffic and cytoskeleton; cell-surface receptors.

University of Arkansas for Medical Sciences, Graduate School, Graduate Programs in Biomedical Sciences, Department of Neurobiology and Developmental Sciences, Little Rock, AR 72205-7199. Offers MS, PhD, MD/PhD. *Faculty:* 21 full-time (7 women), 16 part-time/adjunct (9 women). *Students:* 11 full-time, 1 part-time. In 2009, 1 doctorate awarded. *Degree requirements:* For master's, thesis; for doctorate, thesis/dissertation. *Entrance requirements:* For master's, GRE General Test; for doctorate, GRE General Test, GRE Subject Test. Additional exam requirements/recommendations for international students: Required—TOEFL. *Application deadline:* For fall admission, 2/15 for domestic and international students. Application fee: $0. *Financial support:* In 2009–10, research assistantships with full tuition reimbursements (averaging $24,000 per year); stipend and tuition for doctoral students also available. Support available to part-time students. *Faculty research:* Cellular and molecular neuroscience, translation neuroscience. *Unit head:* Dr. Gwen Childs, Chair, 501-686-5180. *Application contact:* Dr. David Davies, Graduate Coordinator, 501-686-5184, E-mail: dldavies@uams.edu.

The University of British Columbia, Faculty of Medicine, Department of Cellular and Physiological Sciences, Division of Anatomy and Cell Biology, Vancouver, BC V6T 1Z1, Canada. Offers M Sc, PhD. *Degree requirements:* For master's, thesis, oral defense; for doctorate, comprehensive exam, thesis/dissertation, oral defense. *Entrance requirements:* Additional exam requirements/recommendations for international students: Required—TOEFL (minimum score 550 paper-based; 213 computer-based), IELTS (minimum score 6.2). Electronic applications accepted. *Faculty research:* Cell and developmental biology, membrane biophysics, cellular immunology, cancer, fetal alcohol syndrome.

University of California, Irvine, School of Medicine and School of Biological Sciences, Department of Anatomy and Neurobiology, Irvine, CA 92697. Offers biological sciences (MS, PhD); MD/PhD. *Students:* 28 full-time (18 women); includes 10 minority (4 Asian Americans or Pacific Islanders, 6 Hispanic Americans), 2 international. Average age 28. In 2009, 5 doctorates awarded. *Degree requirements:* For doctorate, thesis/dissertation. *Entrance requirements:* For master's and doctorate, GRE General Test, GRE Subject Test. Additional exam requirements/recommendations for international students: Required—TOEFL (minimum score 550 paper-based; 213 computer-based). *Application deadline:* For fall admission, 1/15 priority date for domestic students, 1/15 for international students. Applications are processed on a rolling basis. Application fee: $70 ($90 for international students). Electronic applications accepted. *Financial support:* Fellowships, research assistantships with full tuition reimbursements, teaching assistantships, institutionally sponsored loans, traineeships, health care benefits, and unspecified assistantships available. Financial award application deadline: 3/1; financial award applicants required to submit FAFSA. *Faculty research:* Neurotransmitter immunocytochemistry, intracellular physiology, molecular neurobiology, forebrain organization and development, structure and function of sensory and motor systems. *Unit head:* Dr. Richard T. Robertson, Professor and Chair, 949-824-6553, Fax: 949-824-1105, E-mail: rtrobert@uci.edu. *Application contact:* Kimberly McKinney, Biological Sciences Contact, 949-824-8145, Fax: 949-824-7407, E-mail: kamckinn@uci.edu.

University of California, Los Angeles, David Geffen School of Medicine and Graduate Division, Graduate Programs in Medicine, Department of Neurobiology, Los Angeles, CA 90095. Offers anatomy and cell biology (PhD). *Degree requirements:* For doctorate, thesis/dissertation, oral and written qualifying exams. *Entrance requirements:* For doctorate, GRE General Test, GRE Subject Test, bachelor's degree in physical or biological science. *Faculty research:* Neuroendocrinology, neurophysiology.

University of California, San Francisco, Graduate Division, Biomedical Sciences Graduate Group, San Francisco, CA 94143. Offers anatomy (PhD); endocrinology (PhD); experimental pathology (PhD); physiology (PhD). *Degree requirements:* For doctorate, thesis/dissertation. *Entrance requirements:* For doctorate, GRE General Test.

University of Chicago, Division of the Biological Sciences, Darwinian Sciences Cluster: Ecological, Integrative and Evolutionary Biology, Department of Organismal Biology and Anatomy, Chicago, IL 60637-1513. Offers functional and evolutionary biology (PhD); organismal biology and anatomy (PhD). *Faculty:* 12 full-time (1 woman), 5 part-time/adjunct (3 women). *Students:* 12 full-time (6 women); includes 1 minority (Hispanic American), 1 international. Average age 27. 14 applicants, 43% accepted, 4 enrolled. In 2009, 2 doctorates awarded. *Degree requirements:* For doctorate, thesis/dissertation, ethics class, 2 teaching assistantships. *Entrance requirements:* For doctorate, GRE General Test. Additional exam requirements/recommendations for international students: Required—TOEFL (minimum score 600 paper-based; 250 computer-based; 104 iBT), IELTS (minimum score 7). *Application deadline:* For fall admission, 12/1 priority date for domestic and international students. Application fee: $55. Electronic applications accepted. *Financial support:* In 2009–10, 12 students received support, including fellowships with tuition reimbursements available (averaging $29,781 per year), research assistantships with tuition reimbursements available (averaging $29,781 per year); institutionally sponsored loans, scholarships/grants, traineeships, and health care benefits also available. Financial award applicants required to submit FAFSA. *Faculty research:* Ecological physiology, evolution of fossil reptiles, vertebrate paleontology. *Unit head:* Dr. Robert Ho, Chairman, 773-834-8423, Fax: 773-702-0037, E-mail: rkh@uchicago.edu. *Application contact:* Jeffrey Heller, Project Assistant III, 773-702-9011, Fax: 773-702-0037, E-mail: jheller@uchicago.edu.

University of Georgia, College of Veterinary Medicine and Graduate School, Graduate Programs in Veterinary Medicine, Department of Veterinary Anatomy and Radiology, Athens, GA 30602. Offers veterinary anatomy (MS). *Faculty:* 3 full-time (1 woman). *Students:* 2 applicants, 100% accepted. *Degree requirements:* For master's, thesis. *Entrance requirements:* For master's, GRE General Test. *Application deadline:* For fall admission, 7/1 priority date for domestic students; for spring admission, 11/15 for domestic students. Application fee: $50. Electronic applications accepted. *Expenses:* Tuition, state resident: full-time $6000; part-time $250 per credit hour. Tuition, nonresident: full-time $20,904; part-time $871 per credit hour. Required fees: $730 per semester. *Financial support:* Fellowships, research assistantships, teaching assistantships, unspecified assistantships available. *Unit head:* Dr. Steven D. Holliday, Head, 706-542-8309, Fax: 706-542-0051, E-mail: sdholl@.uga.edu. *Application contact:* Dr. Sharon L. Crowell-Davis, Graduate Coordinator, 706-542-8343, Fax: 706-542-0051, E-mail: scrowell@vet.uga.edu.

University of Guelph, Ontario Veterinary College and Graduate Program Services, Graduate Programs in Veterinary Sciences, Department of Biomedical Sciences, Guelph, ON N1G 2W1, Canada. Offers morphology (M Sc, DV Sc, PhD); neuroscience (M Sc, DV Sc, PhD); pharmacology (M Sc, DV Sc, PhD); physiology (M Sc, DV Sc, PhD); toxicology (M Sc, DV Sc, PhD). Part-time programs available. *Degree requirements:* For master's, thesis; for doctorate, comprehensive exam, thesis/dissertation. *Entrance requirements:* For master's, honors B Sc, minimum 75% average in last 20 courses; for doctorate, M Sc with thesis from accredited institution. Additional exam requirements/recommendations for international students: Required—TOEFL (minimum score 550 paper-based; 213 computer-based; 89 iBT). Electronic applications accepted. *Faculty research:* Cellular morphology; endocrine, vascular and reproductive physiology; clinical pharmacology; veterinary toxicology; developmental biology, neuroscience.

University of Illinois at Chicago, College of Medicine and Graduate College, Graduate Programs in Medicine, Department of Anatomy and Cell Biology, Chicago, IL 60607-7128. Offers neuroscience (PhD), including cellular and systems neuroscience and cell biology; MD/PhD. *Degree requirements:* For doctorate, preliminary oral examination, dissertation and oral defense. *Entrance requirements:* For doctorate, GRE General Test, minimum GPA of 2.75, 3 letters of recommendation, personal statement. Additional exam requirements/recommendations for international students: Required—TOEFL (minimum score 550 paper-based; 213 computer-based). Electronic applications accepted. *Faculty research:* Synapses, axonal transport, neurodegenerative diseases.

See Close-Up on page 401.

The University of Iowa, Roy J. and Lucille A. Carver College of Medicine and Graduate College, Graduate Programs in Medicine, Department of Anatomy and Cell Biology, Iowa City, IA 52242-1316. Offers PhD. *Faculty:* 19 full-time (4 women). *Students:* 12 full-time (5 women); includes 1 minority (Asian American or Pacific Islander), 1 international. Average age 28. 154 applicants, 0% accepted. In 2009, 2 doctorates awarded. *Degree requirements:* For doctorate, comprehensive exam, thesis/dissertation. *Entrance requirements:* For doctorate, GRE General Test, minimum GPA of 3.0. Additional exam requirements/recommendations for international students: Required—TOEFL (minimum score 600 paper-based; 250 computer-based; 100 iBT). *Application deadline:* For fall admission, 1/15 priority date for domestic and international students. Applications are processed on a rolling basis. Application fee: $60 ($85 for international students). Electronic applications accepted. *Financial support:* In 2009–10, 12 students received support, including 2 fellowships with full tuition reimbursements available (averaging

$23,500 per year), 7 research assistantships with full tuition reimbursements available (averaging $23,500 per year), teaching assistantships with full tuition reimbursements available (averaging $23,500 per year); institutionally sponsored loans, scholarships/grants, and health care benefits also available. Financial award application deadline: 3/1. *Faculty research:* Biology of differentiation and transformation, developmental and vascular cell biology, neurobiology. Total annual research expenditures: $5.8 million. *Unit head:* Dr. John F. Engelhardt, Professor and Head, 319-335-7744, Fax: 319-335-7198, E-mail: john-engelhardt@uiowa.edu. *Application contact:* Julie A. Stark, Program Assistant, 319-335-7744, Fax: 319-335-7198, E-mail: julie-stark@uiowa.edu.

The University of Kansas, University of Kansas Medical Center, School of Medicine, Department of Anatomy and Cell Biology, Kansas City, KS 66160. Offers MA, PhD, MD/PhD. *Faculty:* 23 full-time, 9 part-time/adjunct. *Students:* 2 full-time (1 woman), 12 part-time (10 women); includes 2 minority (both Hispanic Americans), 5 international. Average age 26. In 2009, 4 doctorates awarded. Terminal master's awarded for partial completion of doctoral program. *Degree requirements:* For master's, comprehensive oral exam, oral defense of thesis; for doctorate, comprehensive exam, thesis/dissertation. *Entrance requirements:* For master's and doctorate, GRE. Additional exam requirements/recommendations for international students: Required—TOEFL. *Application deadline:* For fall admission, 1/15 priority date for domestic students. Applications are processed on a rolling basis. Application fee: $0. Electronic applications accepted. *Expenses:* Tuition, state resident: full-time $6492; part-time $270.50 per credit hour. Tuition, nonresident: full-time $15,510; part-time $646.25 per credit hour. Required fees: $847; $70.56 per credit hour. Tuition and fees vary according to course load and program. *Financial support:* In 2009–10, 13 students received support, including 9 research assistantships with full tuition reimbursements available (averaging $21,700 per year), 4 teaching assistantships with full tuition reimbursements available (averaging $21,700 per year); fellowships, institutionally sponsored loans, health care benefits, and unspecified assistantships also available. *Faculty research:* Development of the synapse and neuromuscular junction, pain perception and diabetic neuropathies, cardiovascular and kidney development, reproductive immunology, post-fertilization signaling events. Total annual research expenditures: $9.2 million. *Unit head:* Dr. Dale R. Abrahamson, Chairman, 913-588-7000, Fax: 913-588-2710, E-mail: dabrahamson@kumc.edu. *Application contact:* Dr. Douglas Wright, Professor, 913-588-2713, Fax: 913-588-2710, E-mail: dwright@kumc.edu.

University of Kentucky, Graduate School, Graduate School Programs from the College of Medicine, Program in Anatomy and Neurobiology, Lexington, KY 40506-0032. Offers anatomy (PhD). *Degree requirements:* For doctorate, comprehensive exam, thesis/dissertation. *Entrance requirements:* For doctorate, GRE General Test, minimum undergraduate GPA of 2.75. Additional exam requirements/recommendations for international students: Required—TOEFL (minimum score 550 paper-based; 213 computer-based). Electronic applications accepted. *Faculty research:* Neuroendocrinology, developmental neurobiology, neurotrophic substances, neural plasticity and trauma, neurobiology of aging.

University of Louisville, School of Medicine, Department of Anatomical Sciences and Neurobiology, Louisville, KY 40292-0001. Offers MS, PhD, MD/PhD. *Faculty:* 20 full-time (3 women), 12 part-time/adjunct (1 woman). *Students:* 37 full-time (18 women), 2 part-time (1 woman); includes 1 minority (Hispanic American), 12 international. Average age 28. 32 applicants, 53% accepted, 12 enrolled. In 2009, 6 master's, 3 doctorates awarded. Terminal master's awarded for partial completion of doctoral program. *Degree requirements:* For master's, thesis; for doctorate, comprehensive exam, thesis/dissertation. *Entrance requirements:* For master's, GRE General Test (minimum score 1000 verbal and quantitative), minimum GPA of 3.0; for doctorate, GRE General Test (Verbal and Quantitative minimum score of 1000), minimum GPA of 3.0. Additional exam requirements/recommendations for international students: Required—TOEFL. *Application deadline:* For fall admission, 1/15 priority date for domestic students; for spring admission, 4/15 priority date for domestic and international students. Applications are processed on a rolling basis. Application fee: $50. Electronic applications accepted. *Financial support:* In 2009–10, 32 students received support, including 6 fellowships with full tuition reimbursements available (averaging $22,000 per year), 26 research assistantships with full tuition reimbursements available (averaging $22,000 per year); health care benefits and unspecified assistantships also available. Financial award application deadline: 4/15. *Faculty research:* Human adult neural stem cells, development and plasticity of the nervous system, organization of the dorsal thalamus, electrophysiology/neuroanatomy of central neurons mediating control of reproductive and pelvic organs; normal neural mechanisms and plasticity following injury and/or chronic pain, differentiation and regeneration of motor neurons and oligodendrocytes. Total annual research expenditures: $4 million. *Unit head:* Dr. Fred J. Roisen, Chair, 502-852-5165, Fax: 502-852-6228, E-mail: fjrois01@gwise.louisville.edu. *Application contact:* Dr. Charles Hubscher, Director of Graduate Studies, 502-852-3058, Fax: 502-852-6228, E-mail: chhub01@louisville.edu.

University of Manitoba, Faculty of Medicine and Faculty of Graduate Studies, Graduate Programs in Medicine, Department of Human Anatomy and Cell Science, Winnipeg, MB R3T 2N2, Canada. Offers M Sc, PhD. *Degree requirements:* For master's, thesis; for doctorate, one foreign language, thesis/dissertation.

University of Mississippi Medical Center, School of Graduate Studies in the Health Sciences, Department of Anatomy, Jackson, MS 39216-4505. Offers MS, PhD, MD/PhD. Terminal master's awarded for partial completion of doctoral program. *Degree requirements:* For master's, thesis; for doctorate, comprehensive exam, thesis/dissertation, first authored publication. *Entrance requirements:* For master's and doctorate, GRE General Test, minimum GPA of 3.0. Additional exam requirements/recommendations for international students: Required—TOEFL. *Faculty research:* Systems neuroscience with emphasis on motor and sensory, cell biology with emphasis on cell-matrix interactions, development of cardiovascular system, biology of glial cells.

University of Missouri, School of Medicine and Graduate School, Graduate Programs in Medicine, Department of Pathology and Anatomical Sciences, Columbia, MO 65211. Offers MS.

University of Nebraska Medical Center, Graduate Studies, Department of Genetics, Cell Biology and Anatomy, Omaha, NE 68198. Offers MS, PhD. Part-time programs available. Terminal master's awarded for partial completion of doctoral program. *Degree requirements:* For master's, comprehensive exam, thesis; for doctorate, comprehensive exam, thesis/dissertation. *Entrance requirements:* For master's and doctorate, GRE General Test. Additional exam requirements/recommendations for international students: Required—TOEFL (minimum score 550 paper-based; 213 computer-based). Electronic applications accepted. *Faculty research:* Hematology, immunology, developmental biology, genetics cancer biology, neuroscience.

University of North Dakota, School of Medicine and Health Sciences and Graduate School, Graduate Programs in Medicine, Department of Anatomy, Grand Forks, ND 58202. Offers MS, PhD. *Degree requirements:* For master's, thesis, final exam; for doctorate, comprehensive exam, thesis/dissertation, final exam. *Entrance requirements:* For master's and doctorate, GRE General Test, minimum GPA of 3.0. Additional exam requirements/recommendations for international students: Required—TOEFL (minimum score 550 paper-based; 213 computer-based; 79 iBT), IELTS (minimum score 6.5). Electronic applications accepted. *Faculty research:* Coronary vessel, vasculogenesis, acellular glomerular and retinal microvessel membranes, ependymal cells, cardiac muscle.

University of North Texas Health Science Center at Fort Worth, Graduate School of Biomedical Sciences, Fort Worth, TX 76107-2699. Offers anatomy and cell biology (MS, PhD); biochemistry and molecular biology (MS, PhD); biomedical sciences (MS, PhD); biotechnology (MS); forensic genetics (MS); integrative physiology (MS, PhD); medical science (MS); microbiology and immunology (MS, PhD); pharmacology (MS, PhD); science education (MS); DO/MS; DO/PhD. Terminal master's awarded for partial completion of doctoral program. *Degree requirements:* For master's, thesis; for doctorate, thesis/dissertation. *Entrance requirements:* For master's and doctorate, GRE General Test. Additional exam requirements/recommendations for international students: Required—TOEFL. *Expenses:* Contact institution. *Faculty research:* Alzheimer's disease, aging, eye diseases, cancer, cardiovascular disease.

University of Prince Edward Island, Atlantic Veterinary College, Graduate Program in Veterinary Medicine, Charlottetown, PE C1A 4P3, Canada. Offers anatomy (M Sc, PhD); bacteriology (M Sc, PhD); clinical pharmacology (M Sc, PhD); clinical sciences (M Sc, PhD); epidemiology (M Sc, PhD), including reproduction; fish health (M Sc, PhD); food animal nutrition (M Sc, PhD); immunology (M Sc, PhD); microanatomy (M Sc, PhD); parasitology (M Sc, PhD); pathology (M Sc, PhD); pharmacology (M Sc, PhD); physiology (M Sc, PhD); toxicology (M Sc, PhD); veterinary science (M Vet Sc); virology (M Sc, PhD). Part-time programs available. *Degree requirements:* For master's, thesis; for doctorate, thesis/dissertation. *Entrance requirements:* For master's, DVM, B Sc honors degree, or equivalent; for doctorate, M Sc. Additional exam requirements/recommendations for international students: Required—TOEFL (minimum score 550 paper-based; 213 computer-based; 80 iBT). *Expenses:* Contact institution. *Faculty research:* Animal health management, infectious diseases, fin fish and shellfish health, basic biomedical sciences, ecosystem health.

University of Puerto Rico, Medical Sciences Campus, School of Medicine, Division of Graduate Studies, Department of Anatomy and Neurobiology, San Juan, PR 00936-5067. Offers anatomy (MS, PhD). *Degree requirements:* For master's, one foreign language, comprehensive exam, thesis; for doctorate, one foreign language, comprehensive exam, thesis/dissertation. *Entrance requirements:* For master's and doctorate, GRE General Test, GRE Subject Test, interview, minimum GPA of 3.0, 3 letters of recommendation. Electronic applications accepted. *Faculty research:* Neurobiology, primatology, visual system, muscle structure.

University of Rochester, School of Medicine and Dentistry, Graduate Programs in Medicine and Dentistry, Department of Neurobiology and Anatomy, Program in Neurobiology and Anatomy, Rochester, NY 14627. Offers MS, PhD. *Degree requirements:* For doctorate, thesis/dissertation, qualifying exam. *Entrance requirements:* For master's and doctorate, GRE General Test.

University of Saskatchewan, College of Medicine, Department of Anatomy and Cell Biology, Saskatoon, SK S7N 5A2, Canada. Offers M Sc, PhD. *Degree requirements:* For master's, thesis; for doctorate, thesis/dissertation. *Entrance requirements:* Additional exam requirements/recommendations for international students: Required—TOEFL. Tuition and fees charges are reported in Canadian dollars. *Expenses:* Tuition, area resident: Full-time $3000 Canadian dollars; part-time $500 Canadian dollars per term. Required fees: $700 Canadian dollars; $100 Canadian dollars per term.

University of Saskatchewan, Western College of Veterinary Medicine and College of Graduate Studies and Research, Graduate Programs in Veterinary Medicine, Department of Veterinary Biomedical Sciences, Saskatoon, SK S7N 5A2, Canada. Offers veterinary anatomy (M Sc); veterinary biomedical sciences (M Vet Sc); veterinary physiological sciences (M Sc, PhD). *Faculty:* 25. *Students:* 35. In 2009, 5 master's awarded. *Degree requirements:* For master's, thesis; for doctorate, comprehensive exam (for some programs), thesis/dissertation. *Entrance requirements:* Additional exam requirements/recommendations for international students: Required—TOEFL (minimum score 80 iBT); Recommended—IELTS (minimum score 6.5). Application fee: $75. Electronic applications accepted. Tuition and fees charges are reported in Canadian dollars. *Expenses:* Tuition, area resident: Full-time $3000 Canadian dollars; part-time $500 Canadian dollars per term. Required fees: $700 Canadian dollars; $100 Canadian dollars per term. *Faculty research:* Toxicology, animal reproduction, pharmacology, chloride channels, pulmonary pathobiology. *Unit head:* Dr. Barry Blakley, Head, 306-966-7350, Fax: 306-966-7376, E-mail: barry.blakley@usask.ca. *Application contact:* Dr. Baljit Singh, Application Contact, 306-966-7400, E-mail: baljit.singh@usask.ca.

The University of Tennessee, Graduate School, College of Agricultural Sciences and Natural Resources, Department of Animal Science, Knoxville, TN 37996. Offers animal anatomy (PhD); breeding (MS, PhD); management (MS, PhD); nutrition (MS, PhD); physiology (MS, PhD). Part-time programs available. *Degree requirements:* For master's, thesis; for doctorate, thesis/dissertation. *Entrance requirements:* For master's and doctorate, GRE General Test, minimum GPA of 2.7. Additional exam requirements/recommendations for international students: Required—TOEFL. Electronic applications accepted. *Expenses:* Tuition, state resident: full-time $6826; part-time $380 per semester hour. Tuition, nonresident: full-time $21,844; part-time $1147 per semester hour. Tuition and fees vary according to program.

The University of Tennessee Health Science Center, College of Graduate Health Sciences, Department of Anatomy and Neurobiology, Memphis, TN 38163-0002. Offers PhD. *Degree requirements:* For doctorate, thesis/dissertation, oral and written preliminary and comprehensive exams. *Entrance requirements:* For doctorate, GRE General Test, minimum GPA of 3.0. Electronic applications accepted.

University of Utah, School of Medicine and Graduate School, Graduate Programs in Medicine, Department of Neurobiology and Anatomy, Salt Lake City, UT 84112-1107. Offers PhD. Part-time programs available. Terminal master's awarded for partial completion of doctoral program. *Degree requirements:* For doctorate, comprehensive exam, thesis/dissertation. *Entrance requirements:* For doctorate, GRE General Test. Additional exam requirements/recommendations for international students: Required—TOEFL. *Expenses:* Tuition, state resident: full-time $4004; part-time $1674 per semester. Tuition, nonresident: full-time $14,134; part-time $5915 per semester. Required fees: $324 per semester. Tuition and fees vary according to course load, degree level and program. *Faculty research:* Neuroscience, neuroanatomy, developmental neurobiology, neurogenetics.

The University of Western Ontario, Faculty of Graduate Studies, Biosciences Division, Department of Biology, London, ON N6A 5B8, Canada. Offers M Sc, PhD. *Degree requirements:* For master's, thesis; for doctorate, comprehensive exam, thesis/dissertation. *Entrance requirements:* For master's, honors degree or equivalent in biological sciences; for doctorate, master's degree. Additional exam requirements/recommendations for international students: Required—TOEFL. *Faculty research:* Cell and molecular biology, developmental biology, neuroscience, immunobiology and cancer.

Virginia Commonwealth University, Medical College of Virginia-Professional Programs, School of Medicine, School of Medicine Graduate Programs, Department of Anatomy and Neurobiology, Program in Anatomy and Neurobiology, Richmond, VA 23284-9005. Offers PhD. *Accreditation:* APTA. *Degree requirements:* For doctorate, thesis/dissertation. *Entrance requirements:* For doctorate, GRE General Test.

Virginia Commonwealth University, Program in Pre-Medical Basic Health Sciences, Richmond, VA 23284-9005. Offers anatomy (CBHS); biochemistry (CBHS); human genetics (CBHS); microbiology (CBHS); pharmacology (CBHS); physiology (CBHS). *Entrance requirements:* For degree, GRE or MCAT, course work in organic chemistry, minimum undergraduate GPA of 2.8. Additional exam requirements/recommendations for international students: Required—TOEFL (minimum score 600 paper-based).

Wake Forest University, School of Medicine and Graduate School of Arts and Sciences, Graduate Programs in Medicine, Department of Neurobiology and Anatomy, Winston-Salem, NC 27109. Offers PhD, MD/PhD. *Degree requirements:* For doctorate, thesis/dissertation. *Entrance requirements:* For doctorate, GRE General Test. Additional exam requirements/

Anatomy

Wake Forest University *(continued)*
recommendations for international students: Required—TOEFL. Electronic applications accepted. *Faculty research:* Sensory neurobiology, reproductive endocrinology, regulatory processes in cell biology.

Wayne State University, School of Medicine, Graduate Programs in Medicine, Department of Anatomy and Cell Biology, Detroit, MI 48202. Offers anatomy (MS, PhD); MD/PhD. *Degree requirements:* For doctorate, thesis/dissertation. *Entrance requirements:* For master's and doctorate, GRE General Test, minimum GPA of 3.0. Additional exam requirements/recommendations for international students: Required—TOEFL (minimum score 600 paper-based; 260 computer-based); Recommended—TWE (minimum score 6). Electronic applications accepted. *Faculty research:* Inflammation and inflammatory mediators, neuronal plasticity, neural connections and glia, vision and visual neurosciences, cell signaling and receptor interactions.

Wright State University, School of Graduate Studies, College of Science and Mathematics, Department of Neuroscience, Cell Biology, and Physiology, Dayton, OH 45435. Offers anatomy (MS); physiology and biophysics (MS). *Degree requirements:* For master's, thesis optional. *Entrance requirements:* Additional exam requirements/recommendations for international students: Required—TOEFL. *Faculty research:* Reproductive cell biology, neurobiology of pain, neurohistochemistry.

Youngstown State University, Graduate School, College of Science, Technology, Engineering and Mathematics, Department of Biological Sciences, Youngstown, OH 44555-0001. Offers environmental biology (MS); molecular biology, microbiology, and genetic (MS); physiology and anatomy (MS). Part-time programs available. *Degree requirements:* For master's, comprehensive exam, thesis, oral review. *Entrance requirements:* For master's, GRE General Test, minimum GPA of 2.7. Additional exam requirements/recommendations for international students: Required—TOEFL. *Faculty research:* Cell biology, neurophysiology, molecular biology, neurobiology, gene regulation.

Section 3
Biochemistry

This section contains a directory of institutions offering graduate work in biochemistry, followed by in-depth entries submitted by institutions that chose to prepare detailed program descriptions. Additional information about programs listed in the directory but not augmented by an in-depth entry may be obtained by writing directly to the dean of a graduate school or chair of a department at the address given in the directory.

For programs offering related work, see also in this book *Biological and Biomedical Sciences; Biophysics; Botany and Plant Biology; Cell, Molecular, and Structural Biology; Genetics, Developmental Biology, and Reproductive Biology; Microbiological Sciences; Neuroscience and Neurobiology; Nutrition; Pathology and Pathobiology; Pharmacology and Toxicology;* and *Physiology.* In the other guides in this series:

Graduate Programs in the Physical Sciences, Mathematics, Agricultural Sciences, the Environment & Natural Resources

See *Agricultural and Food Sciences, Chemistry,* and *Physics*

Graduate Programs in Engineering & Applied Sciences

See *Agricultural Engineering and Bioengineering, Biomedical Engineering and Biotechnology, Chemical Engineering,* and *Materials Sciences and Engineering*

Graduate Programs in Business, Education, Health, Information Studies, Law & Social Work

See *Allied Health, Pharmacy and Pharmaceutical Sciences,* and *Veterinary Medicine and Sciences*

CONTENTS

Biochemistry

Albert Einstein College of Medicine, Sue Golding Graduate Division of Medical Sciences, Department of Biochemistry, Bronx, NY 10461-1602. Offers PhD, MD/PhD. *Degree requirements:* For doctorate, thesis/dissertation. *Entrance requirements:* For doctorate, GRE General Test. Additional exam requirements/recommendations for international students: Required—TOEFL. *Faculty research:* Biochemical mechanisms, enzymology, protein chemistry, bio-organic chemistry, molecular genetics.

American University of Beirut, Graduate Programs, Faculty of Medicine, Beirut, Lebanon. Offers biochemistry (MS); human morphology (MS); medicine (MD); microbiology and immunology (MS); neuroscience (MS); pharmacology and therapeutics (MS); physiology (MS). Part-time programs available. *Degree requirements:* For master's, one foreign language, comprehensive exam, thesis (for some programs). *Entrance requirements:* For MD, MCAT, bachelor's degree; for master's, letter of recommendation. Additional exam requirements/recommendations for international students: Required—TOEFL (minimum score 600 paper-based; 250 computer-based; 100 iBT), IELTS (minimum score 7.5). *Faculty research:* Cancer research, stem cell research, genetic research, neuroscience research, bone research.

Arizona State University, Graduate College, College of Liberal Arts and Sciences, Division of Natural Sciences, Department of Chemistry and Biochemistry, Tempe, AZ 85287. Offers MS, PhD. *Degree requirements:* For master's, thesis; for doctorate, one foreign language, thesis/dissertation. *Entrance requirements:* For master's and doctorate, GRE. Additional exam requirements/recommendations for international students: Required—TOEFL.

Auburn University, Graduate School, College of Sciences and Mathematics, Department of Chemistry and Biochemistry, Auburn University, AL 36849. Offers analytical chemistry (MS, PhD); biochemistry (MS, PhD); inorganic chemistry (MS, PhD); organic chemistry (MS, PhD); physical chemistry (MS, PhD). Part-time programs available. *Faculty:* 27 full-time (6 women). *Students:* 39 full-time (20 women), 21 part-time (8 women); includes 6 minority (4 African Americans, 1 Asian American or Pacific Islander, 1 Hispanic American), 41 international. Average age 28. 54 applicants, 11% accepted, 3 enrolled. In 2009, 1 master's, 13 doctorates awarded. *Degree requirements:* For master's, thesis (for some programs); for doctorate, thesis/dissertation, oral and written exams. *Entrance requirements:* For master's and doctorate, GRE General Test. *Application deadline:* For fall admission, 7/7 for domestic students; for spring admission, 11/24 for domestic students. Applications are processed on a rolling basis. Application fee: $50 ($60 for international students). Electronic applications accepted. *Expenses:* Tuition, state resident: full-time $6240. Tuition, nonresident: full-time $18,720. International tuition: $18,938 full-time. Required fees: $492. Tuition and fees vary according to course load, program and reciprocity agreements. *Financial support:* Fellowships, research assistantships, teaching assistantships available. Financial award application deadline: 3/15; financial award applicants required to submit FAFSA. *Unit head:* Dr. J. V. Ortiz, Chair, 334-844-4043, Fax: 334-844-4043. *Application contact:* Dr. George Flowers, Dean of the Graduate School, 334-844-2125.

Baylor College of Medicine, Graduate School of Biomedical Sciences, Department of Biochemistry and Molecular Biology, Houston, TX 77030-3498. Offers PhD, MD/PhD. *Faculty:* 34 full-time (7 women). *Students:* 53 full-time (26 women); includes 7 minority (1 African American, 1 American Indian/Alaska Native, 1 Asian American or Pacific Islander, 4 Hispanic Americans), 30 international. Average age 25. In 2009, 8 doctorates awarded. *Degree requirements:* For doctorate, thesis/dissertation, public defense. *Entrance requirements:* For doctorate, GRE General Test, GRE Subject Test (strongly recommended), minimum GPA of 3.0. Additional exam requirements/recommendations for international students: Required—TOEFL. *Application deadline:* For fall admission, 1/1 priority date for domestic students. Application fee: $30. Electronic applications accepted. *Financial support:* Fellowships, research assistantships, career-related internships or fieldwork, Federal Work-Study, institutionally sponsored loans, health care benefits, and students receive a scholarship unless there are grant funds available to pay tuition available. Financial award applicants required to submit FAFSA. *Faculty research:* Mechanisms of enzyme action, nucleic acid enzymology, and mutagenesis; biochemistry of connective tissue, proteins, and polysaccharides; chemical metabolism of lipids and lipoproteins. *Unit head:* Dr. John Wilson, Director, 713-798-5760. *Application contact:* Monica Bagos, Graduate Program Administrator, 713-798-0124, Fax: 713-796-9438, E-mail: bagos@bcm.edu.

Baylor College of Medicine, Graduate School of Biomedical Sciences, Interdepartmental Program in Cell and Molecular Biology, Houston, TX 77030-3498. Offers biochemistry (PhD); cell and molecular biology (PhD); genetics (PhD); human genetics (PhD); immunology (PhD); microbiology (PhD); virology (PhD); MD/PhD. *Faculty:* 100 full-time (31 women). *Students:* 59 full-time (37 women); includes 24 minority (5 African Americans, 1 American Indian/Alaska Native, 7 Asian Americans or Pacific Islanders, 11 Hispanic Americans), 6 international. Average age 25. In 2009, 9 doctorates awarded. *Degree requirements:* For doctorate, thesis/dissertation, public defense. *Entrance requirements:* For doctorate, GRE General Test, GRE Subject Test (strongly recommended), minimum GPA of 3.0. Additional exam requirements/recommendations for international students: Required—TOEFL. *Application deadline:* For fall admission, 1/1 priority date for domestic students. Applications are processed on a rolling basis. Application fee: $0. Electronic applications accepted. *Financial support:* In 2009–10, 59 students received support; fellowships, research assistantships, teaching assistantships, Federal Work-Study, institutionally sponsored loans, health care benefits, and tuition waivers (full) available. Financial award applicants required to submit FAFSA. *Faculty research:* Gene expression and regulation, developmental biology and genetics, signal transduction and membrane biology, aging process, molecular virology. *Unit head:* Dr. Susan Marriott, Director, 713-798-6557. *Application contact:* Lourdes Fernandez, Graduate Program Administrator, 713-798-6557, Fax: 713-798-6325, E-mail: cmbprog@bcm.edu.

See Close-Up on page 231.

Boston College, Graduate School of Arts and Sciences, Department of Chemistry, Program in Biochemistry, Chestnut Hill, MA 02467-3800. Offers PhD. *Degree requirements:* For doctorate, 2 foreign languages, comprehensive exam, thesis/dissertation. *Entrance requirements:* For doctorate, GRE General Test, GRE Subject Test. *Application deadline:* For fall admission, 1/2 for domestic and international students. Application fee: $70. *Financial support:* In 2009–10, fellowships (averaging $25,000 per year), research assistantships (averaging $25,000 per year), teaching assistantships (averaging $25,000 per year) were awarded; Federal Work-Study, tuition waivers (partial), and unspecified assistantships also available. Support available to part-time students. Financial award application deadline: 3/1.

Boston University, Graduate School of Arts and Sciences, Molecular Biology, Cell Biology, and Biochemistry Program (MCBB), Boston, MA 02215. Offers MA, PhD. *Students:* 34 full-time (20 women), 1 (woman) part-time; includes 6 minority (2 African Americans, 2 Asian Americans or Pacific Islanders, 2 Hispanic Americans), 4 international. Average age 29. 77 applicants, 18% accepted, 5 enrolled. In 2009, 2 doctorates awarded. Terminal master's awarded for partial completion of doctoral program. *Degree requirements:* For master's, one foreign language, thesis (for some programs); for doctorate, one foreign language, comprehensive exam, thesis/dissertation. *Entrance requirements:* For master's and doctorate, GRE General Test, GRE Subject Test. Additional exam requirements/recommendations for international students: Required—TOEFL (minimum score 600 paper-based; 250 computer-based). *Application deadline:* For fall admission, 12/7 for domestic and international students. Application fee: $70. Electronic applications accepted. *Expenses:* Tuition: Full-time $37,910; part-time $1184 per credit hour. Required fees: $386; $40 per semester. Part-time tuition and fees vary according to class time, course level, degree level and program. *Financial support:* In 2009–10, 9 students received support, including 1 fellowship with full tuition reimbursement available (averaging $18,900 per year), 7 research assistantships with full tuition reimbursements available (averaging $14,800 per year), 1 teaching assistantship with full tuition reimbursement available (averaging $18,400 per year); Federal Work-Study, scholarships/grants, and traineeships also available. Financial award application deadline: 12/7; financial award applicants required to submit FAFSA. *Unit head:* Dr. Ulla Hansen, Director, 617-353-2432, Fax: 617-353-6340, E-mail: mccall@bu.edu. *Application contact:* Meredith Canode, Academic Administrator, 617-353-2432, Fax: 617-353-6340, E-mail: mcanode@bu.edu.

Boston University, School of Medicine, Division of Graduate Medical Sciences, Department of Biochemistry, Boston, MA 02118. Offers MA, PhD, MD/PhD. Part-time programs available. Terminal master's awarded for partial completion of doctoral program. *Degree requirements:* For master's, thesis or alternative, qualifying exam; for doctorate, thesis/dissertation, qualifying exam. *Entrance requirements:* For master's and doctorate, GRE General Test, GRE Subject Test. Additional exam requirements/recommendations for international students: Required—TOEFL. *Application deadline:* For fall admission, 1/15 priority date for domestic students; for spring admission, 10/15 priority date for domestic students. Electronic applications accepted. *Expenses:* Tuition: Full-time $37,910; part-time $1184 per credit hour. Required fees: $386; $40 per semester. Part-time tuition and fees vary according to class time, course level, degree level and program. *Financial support:* Fellowships, research assistantships, Federal Work-Study, scholarships/grants, and traineeships available. *Faculty research:* Extracellular matrix, gene expression, receptors, growth control. *Unit head:* Dr. Carl Franzblau, Associate Dean, 617-638-5120, Fax: 617-638-4842, E-mail: medsci@bu.edu. *Application contact:* Dr. Barbara Schreiber, Information Contact, 617-638-5094, Fax: 617-638-5339, E-mail: schreibe@biochem.bumc.bu.edu.

Brandeis University, Graduate School of Arts and Sciences, Department of Biochemistry, Waltham, MA 02454. Offers MS, PhD. Part-time programs available. *Faculty:* 9 full-time (2 women), 1 (woman) part-time/adjunct. *Students:* 19 full-time (6 women); includes 3 minority (2 Asian Americans or Pacific Islanders, 1 Hispanic American), 2 international. 65 applicants, 18% accepted, 4 enrolled. In 2009, 2 master's, 4 doctorates awarded. *Degree requirements:* For doctorate, thesis/dissertation, area exams. *Entrance requirements:* For doctorate, GRE General Test, resume, 3 letters of recommendation. Additional exam requirements/recommendations for international students: Required—TOEFL (minimum score 600 paper-based; 250 computer-based; 100 iBT); Recommended—IELTS (minimum score 7). *Application deadline:* For fall admission, 1/15 priority date for domestic students. Applications are processed on a rolling basis. Application fee: $75. Electronic applications accepted. *Financial support:* In 2009–10, 16 students received support, including 4 fellowships with full tuition reimbursements available (averaging $27,500 per year), 15 research assistantships with full tuition reimbursements available (averaging $27,500 per year), teaching assistantships with partial tuition reimbursements available (averaging $3,200 per year); career-related internships or fieldwork, scholarships/grants, traineeships, health care benefits, and tuition waivers (full and partial) also available. Financial award application deadline: 4/15; financial award applicants required to submit FAFSA. *Faculty research:* Enzyme mechanisms, genetics, molecular developmental biology, structural biology, neurobiology. *Unit head:* Prof. Dagmar Ringe, Director of Graduate Studies, 781-736-2301, Fax: 781-736-3107, E-mail: ringe@brandeis.edu. *Application contact:* Marcia Cabral, Department Administrator, 781-736-3100, Fax: 781-736-3107, E-mail: cabral@brandeis.edu.

Brigham Young University, Graduate Studies, College of Physical and Mathematical Sciences, Department of Chemistry and Biochemistry, Provo, UT 84602. Offers biochemistry (MS, PhD); chemistry (MS, PhD). *Faculty:* 34 full-time (3 women). *Students:* 95 full-time (33 women); includes 5 minority (4 Asian Americans or Pacific Islanders, 1 Hispanic American), 48 international. Average age 29. 101 applicants, 40% accepted, 18 enrolled. In 2009, 8 master's, 12 doctorates awarded. *Degree requirements:* For master's, thesis; for doctorate, thesis/dissertation, qualifying exam. *Entrance requirements:* For master's and doctorate, GRE General Test, minimum GPA of 3.0 in last 60 hours. Additional exam requirements/recommendations for international students: Required—TOEFL (minimum score 580 paper-based; 237 computer-based; 85 iBT); Recommended—TWE. *Application deadline:* For fall admission, 2/1 priority date for domestic and international students. Applications are processed on a rolling basis. Application fee: $50. Electronic applications accepted. *Expenses:* Tuition: Full-time $5580; part-time $301 per credit hour. Tuition and fees vary according to student's religious affiliation. *Financial support:* In 2009–10, 95 students received support, including 10 fellowships with full tuition reimbursements available (averaging $21,250 per year), 56 research assistantships with full tuition reimbursements available (averaging $21,250 per year), 29 teaching assistantships with full tuition reimbursements available (averaging $21,250 per year); institutionally sponsored loans, scholarships/grants, health care benefits, tuition waivers (full), and unspecified assistantships also available. Financial award application deadline: 2/1. *Faculty research:* Separation science, molecular recognition, organic synthesis and biomedical application, biochemistry and molecular biology, molecular spectroscopy. Total annual research expenditures: $4.4 million. *Unit head:* Dr. Paul B. Farnsworth, Chair, 801-422-6502, Fax: 801-422-0153, E-mail: paul_farnsworth@byu.edu. *Application contact:* Dr. Matthew R. Linford, Graduate Coordinator, 801-422-1699, Fax: 801-422-0153, E-mail: mrlinford@byu.edu.

Brown University, Graduate School, Department of Chemistry, Providence, RI 02912. Offers biochemistry (PhD); chemistry (AM, Sc M, PhD). *Degree requirements:* For master's, thesis; for doctorate, one foreign language, thesis/dissertation, cumulative exam.

Brown University, Graduate School, Division of Biology and Medicine, Program in Molecular Biology, Cell Biology, and Biochemistry, Providence, RI 02912. Offers biochemistry (M Med Sc, Sc M, PhD), including biochemistry (Sc M, PhD), biology (Sc M, PhD), medical science (M Med Sc, PhD); biology (MA); cell biology (M Med Sc, Sc M, PhD), including biochemistry (Sc M, PhD), biology (Sc M, PhD), medical science (M Med Sc, PhD); developmental biology (M Med Sc, Sc M, PhD), including biochemistry (Sc M, PhD), biology (Sc M, PhD), medical science (M Med Sc, PhD); immunology (M Med Sc, Sc M, PhD), including biochemistry (Sc M, PhD), biology (Sc M, PhD), medical science (M Med Sc, PhD); molecular microbiology (M Med Sc, Sc M, PhD), including biochemistry (Sc M, PhD), biology (Sc M, PhD), medical science (M Med Sc, PhD); MD/PhD. Part-time programs available. Terminal master's awarded for partial completion of doctoral program. *Degree requirements:* For master's, thesis (for some programs); for doctorate, one foreign language, thesis/dissertation, preliminary exam. *Entrance requirements:* For master's and doctorate, GRE General Test, GRE Subject Test. Additional exam requirements/recommendations for international students: Required—TOEFL. Electronic applications accepted. *Faculty research:* Molecular genetics, gene regulation.

California Institute of Technology, Division of Biology and Division of Chemistry and Chemical Engineering, Biochemistry and Molecular Biophysics Graduate Option, Pasadena, CA 91125-0001. Offers PhD. *Degree requirements:* For doctorate, thesis/dissertation, qualifying exam. *Entrance requirements:* For doctorate, GRE General Test. Additional exam requirements/recommendations for international students: Required—TOEFL. Electronic applications accepted.

California Institute of Technology, Division of Chemistry and Chemical Engineering, Program in Biochemistry and Molecular Biophysics, Pasadena, CA 91125-0001. Offers MS, PhD. Part-time and evening/weekend programs available. Postbaccalaureate distance learning degree programs offered (minimal on-campus study). *Faculty:* 16 full-time (5 women). *Students:* 51 full-time (20 women). Average age 27. 114 applicants, 23% accepted, 11 enrolled. In 2009, 1 master's, 5 doctorates awarded. Terminal master's awarded for partial completion of doctoral program. *Degree requirements:* For master's, thesis; for doctorate, thesis/dissertation. *Entrance requirements:* Additional exam requirements/recommendations for international students: Required—TOEFL; Recommended—IELTS, TWE. *Application deadline:* For fall admission, 1/1 for domestic and international students. Application fee: $80. Electronic applications accepted. *Financial support:* Fellowships, research assistantships, teaching assistantships, Federal Work-Study, institutionally sponsored loans, scholarships/grants, traineeships, health care benefits, and unspecified assistantships available. Financial award application deadline: 1/1. *Unit head:*

Prof. Jacqueline K. Barton, Chair, Chemistry and Chemical Engineering, 626-395-3646, Fax: 626-568-8824, E-mail: jkbarton@caltech.edu. *Application contact:* Alison Ross, Option Secretary, 626-395-6446, E-mail: aross@caltech.edu.

California Polytechnic State University, San Luis Obispo, College of Science and Mathematics, Department of Chemistry and Biochemistry, San Luis Obispo, CA 93407. Offers polymers and coating science (MS). Part-time programs available. *Faculty:* 3 full-time (0 women), 1 (woman) part-time/adjunct. *Students:* 2 full-time (1 woman), 2 part-time (1 woman); includes 1 minority (African American). Average age 23. 5 applicants, 80% accepted, 3 enrolled. In 2009, 5 master's awarded. *Degree requirements:* For master's, comprehensive oral exam. *Entrance requirements:* For master's, minimum GPA of 2.5 in last 90 quarter units of course work. Additional exam requirements/recommendations for international students: Required—TOEFL (minimum score 550 paper-based; 213 computer-based) or IELTS (minimum score 6). *Application deadline:* For fall admission, 7/1 for domestic students, 11/30 for international students; for winter admission, 11/1 for domestic students, 6/30 for international students; for spring admission, 2/1 for domestic students. Applications are processed on a rolling basis. Application fee: $55. Electronic applications accepted. *Expenses:* Tuition, nonresident: full-time $11,160; part-time $248 per unit. Required fees: $7134; $1553 per quarter. *Financial support:* Career-related internships or fieldwork, Federal Work-Study, and scholarships/grants available. Support available to part-time students. Financial award application deadline: 3/2; financial award applicants required to submit FAFSA. *Faculty research:* Polymer physical chemistry and analysis, polymer synthesis, coatings formulation. *Unit head:* Dr. Ray Fernando, Graduate Coordinator, 805-756-2395, Fax: 805-756-5500, E-mail: rhfernan@calpoly.edu. *Application contact:* Dr. James Maraviglia, Assistant Vice President for Admissions, Recruitment and Financial Aid, 805-756-2311, Fax: 805-756-5400, E-mail: admissions@calpoly.edu.

California State University, East Bay, Graduate Programs, College of Science, Department of Chemistry, Hayward, CA 94542-3000. Offers biochemistry (MS); chemistry (MS). *Faculty:* 5 full-time (3 women). *Students:* 16 full-time (5 women), 27 part-time (13 women); includes 22 minority (2 African Americans, 17 Asian Americans or Pacific Islanders, 3 Hispanic Americans), 11 international. Average age 28. 37 applicants, 65% accepted, 11 enrolled. In 2009, 12 master's awarded. *Degree requirements:* For master's, comprehensive exam or thesis. *Entrance requirements:* For master's, minimum GPA of 2.5 in field during previous 2 years of course work. Additional exam requirements/recommendations for international students: Required—TOEFL (minimum score 550 paper-based; 213 computer-based). *Application deadline:* For fall admission, 6/30 for domestic and international students. Application fee: $55. Electronic applications accepted. *Financial support:* Fellowships, career-related internships or fieldwork, Federal Work-Study, institutionally sponsored loans, and scholarships/grants available. Support available to part-time students. Financial award application deadline: 3/1; financial award applicants required to submit FAFSA. *Unit head:* Dr. Ann McPartland, Chair, 510-885-3452, Fax: 510-885-4675, E-mail: ann.mcpartland@csueastbay.edu. *Application contact:* Donna Wiley, Interim Associate Director, 510-885-2928, Fax: 510-885-4777, E-mail: donna.wiley@csueastbay.edu.

California State University, Long Beach, Graduate Studies, College of Natural Sciences and Mathematics, Department of Chemistry and Biochemistry, Long Beach, CA 90840. Offers biochemistry (MS); chemistry (MS). Part-time programs available. *Faculty:* 20 full-time (5 women). *Students:* 10 full-time (5 women), 21 part-time (10 women); includes 8 minority (1 African American, 3 Asian Americans or Pacific Islanders, 4 Hispanic Americans), 9 international. Average age 26. 41 applicants, 44% accepted, 7 enrolled. *Degree requirements:* For master's, thesis, departmental qualifying exam. *Application deadline:* For fall admission, 6/1 for domestic students. Applications are processed on a rolling basis. Application fee: $55. Electronic applications accepted. *Expenses:* Required fees: $1802 per semester. Part-time tuition and fees vary according to course load. *Financial support:* Research assistantships, teaching assistantships, Federal Work-Study, institutionally sponsored loans, scholarships/grants, and unspecified assistantships available. Financial award application deadline: 3/2. *Faculty research:* Enzymology, organic synthesis, molecular modeling, environmental chemistry, reaction kinetics. *Unit head:* Dr. Jeffrey Cohlberg, Chair, 562-985-4944, Fax: 562-985-8557, E-mail: cohlberg@csulb.edu. *Application contact:* Dr. Lijuan Li, Graduate Advisor, 562-985-5068, Fax: 562-985-8557, E-mail: lli@csulb.edu.

California State University, Los Angeles, Graduate Studies, College of Natural and Social Sciences, Department of Chemistry and Biochemistry, Los Angeles, CA 90032-8530. Offers analytical chemistry (MS); biochemistry (MS); chemistry (MS); inorganic chemistry (MS); organic chemistry (MS); physical chemistry (MS). Part-time and evening/weekend programs available. *Faculty:* 1 full-time (0 women), 9 part-time/adjunct (4 women). *Students:* 14 full-time (4 women), 31 part-time (15 women); includes 21 minority (5 African Americans, 9 Asian Americans or Pacific Islanders, 7 Hispanic Americans), 10 international. Average age 30. 23 applicants, 91% accepted, 13 enrolled. In 2009, 11 degrees awarded. *Degree requirements:* For master's, one foreign language, comprehensive exam or thesis. *Entrance requirements:* Additional exam requirements/recommendations for international students: Required—TOEFL. *Application deadline:* For fall admission, 5/1 for domestic and international students. Applications are processed on a rolling basis. Application fee: $55. *Financial support:* Federal Work-Study available. Support available to part-time students. Financial award application deadline: 3/1. *Faculty research:* Intercalation of heavy metal, carborane chemistry, conductive polymers and fabrics, titanium reagents, computer modeling and synthesis. *Unit head:* Dr. Scott Grover, Chair, 323-343-2300, Fax: 323-343-6490, E-mail: sgrover@calstatela.edu. *Application contact:* Dr. Cheryl L. Ney, Associate Vice President for Academic Affairs and Dean of Graduate Studies, 323-343-3820 Ext. 3827, Fax: 323-343-5653, E-mail: cney@cslanet.calstatela.edu.

California State University, Northridge, Graduate Studies, College of Science and Mathematics, Department of Chemistry and Biochemistry, Northridge, CA 91330. Offers biochemistry (MS); chemistry (MS), including chemistry, environmental chemistry. *Faculty:* 14 full-time (4 women), 12 part-time/adjunct (6 women). *Students:* 15 full-time (6 women), 29 part-time (10 women); includes 2 African Americans, 4 Asian Americans or Pacific Islanders, 6 Hispanic Americans, 11 international. Average age 29. 68 applicants, 38% accepted, 12 enrolled. In 2009, 5 master's awarded. *Degree requirements:* For master's, thesis. *Entrance requirements:* For master's, GRE General Test or minimum GPA of 3.0. Additional exam requirements/recommendations for international students: Required—TOEFL. *Application deadline:* For fall admission, 11/30 for domestic students. Application fee: $55. Electronic applications accepted. *Financial support:* Teaching assistantships available. Support available to part-time students. Financial award application deadline: 3/1. *Unit head:* Dr. Taeboem Oh, Chair, 818-677-3381, E-mail: taeboem.oh@csun.edu. *Application contact:* Dr. Taeboem Oh, Chair, 818-677-3381, E-mail: taeboem.oh@csun.edu.

Carnegie Mellon University, Mellon College of Science, Department of Biological Sciences, Pittsburgh, PA 15213-3891. Offers biochemistry (PhD); biophysics (PhD); cell biology (PhD); computational biology (MS, PhD); developmental biology (PhD); genetics (PhD); molecular biology (PhD); neuroscience (PhD). *Degree requirements:* For doctorate, comprehensive exam, thesis/dissertation. *Entrance requirements:* For doctorate, GRE General Test, GRE Subject Test, interview. Electronic applications accepted. *Faculty research:* Genetic structure, function, and regulation; protein structure and function; biological membranes; biological spectroscopy.

Case Western Reserve University, School of Medicine and School of Graduate Studies, Graduate Programs in Medicine, Department of Biochemistry, Cleveland, OH 44106. Offers biochemical research (MS); biochemistry (MS, PhD); RNA biology (PhD); MD/PhD. Part-time programs available. Terminal master's awarded for partial completion of doctoral program. *Degree requirements:* For master's, thesis (for some programs); for doctorate, thesis/dissertation. *Entrance requirements:* For master's and doctorate, GRE General Test. Additional exam requirements/recommendations for international students: Required—TOEFL. Electronic applications accepted. *Faculty research:* Regulation of metabolism, regulation of gene expression and protein synthesis, cell biology, molecular biology, structural biology.

Case Western Reserve University, School of Medicine and School of Graduate Studies, Graduate Programs in Medicine, Department of Nutrition, Cleveland, OH 44106. Offers dietetics (MS); nutrition (MS, PhD), including molecular nutrition (PhD), nutrition and biochemistry (PhD); public health nutrition (MS). Part-time programs available. Terminal master's awarded for partial completion of doctoral program. *Degree requirements:* For master's, thesis (for some programs); for doctorate, thesis/dissertation. *Entrance requirements:* For master's, GRE General Test; for doctorate, GRE General Test, GRE Subject Test. Additional exam requirements/recommendations for international students: Required—TOEFL. *Faculty research:* Fatty acid metabolism, application of gene therapy to nutritional problems, dietary intake methodology, nutrition and physical fitness, metabolism during infancy and pregnancy.

See Close-Up on page 421.

Central Connecticut State University, School of Graduate Studies, School of Arts and Sciences, Department of Chemistry and Biochemistry, New Britain, CT 06050-4010. Offers natural sciences (MS). Part-time and evening/weekend programs available. *Faculty:* 9 full-time (3 women), 5 part-time/adjunct (1 woman). *Students:* 1 (woman) part-time; minority (Hispanic American). Average age 26. *Degree requirements:* For Certificate, qualifying exam. *Entrance requirements:* Additional exam requirements/recommendations for international students: Required—TOEFL. *Application deadline:* For fall admission, 7/1 for domestic students; for spring admission, 12/1 for domestic students. Applications are processed on a rolling basis. Application fee: $50. Electronic applications accepted. *Expenses:* Tuition, area resident: Full-time $4662; part-time $440 per credit. Tuition, state resident: full-time $6994; part-time $440 per credit. Tuition, nonresident: full-time $12,988; part-time $440 per credit. Required fees: $3606. One-time fee: $62 part-time. *Financial support:* Application deadline: 3/1. *Unit head:* Dr. Thomas Burkholder, Chair, 860-832-2675. *Application contact:* Dr. Thomas Burkholder, Chair, 860-832-2675.

City College of the City University of New York, Graduate School, College of Liberal Arts and Science, Division of Science, Department of Chemistry, Program in Biochemistry, New York, NY 10031-9198. Offers MA, PhD. Terminal master's awarded for partial completion of doctoral program. *Degree requirements:* For doctorate, one foreign language, thesis/dissertation. *Entrance requirements:* For doctorate, GRE. Additional exam requirements/recommendations for international students: Required—TOEFL (minimum score 550 paper-based; 79 iBT). Electronic applications accepted. *Expenses:* Tuition, state resident: part-time $310 per credit. Tuition, nonresident: part-time $575 per credit. Tuition and fees vary according to course load and program. *Faculty research:* Fatty acid metabolism, lectins, gene structure.

Clemson University, Graduate School, College of Agriculture, Forestry and Life Sciences, Department of Genetics and Biochemistry, Program in Biochemistry and Molecular Biology, Clemson, SC 29634. Offers PhD. *Students:* 15 full-time (11 women), 8 international. Average age 27. 23 applicants, 0% accepted, 0 enrolled. *Degree requirements:* For doctorate, comprehensive exam, thesis/dissertation. *Entrance requirements:* For doctorate, GRE General Test. Additional exam requirements/recommendations for international students: Required—TOEFL. *Application deadline:* For fall admission, 1/1 for domestic students; for spring admission, 9/1 for domestic students. Applications are processed on a rolling basis. Application fee: $70 ($80 for international students). Electronic applications accepted. *Expenses:* Contact institution. *Financial support:* In 2009–10, 15 students received support, including 6 fellowships with full and partial tuition reimbursements available (averaging $6,999 per year), 5 research assistantships with partial tuition reimbursements available (averaging $16,400 per year), 10 teaching assistantships with partial tuition reimbursements available (averaging $19,600 per year); career-related internships or fieldwork, institutionally sponsored loans, scholarships/grants, health care benefits, and unspecified assistantships also available. Support available to part-time students. Financial award application deadline: 3/15; financial award applicants required to submit FAFSA. *Faculty research:* Biomembranes, protein structure, molecular biology of plants, APYA and stress response. Total annual research expenditures: $670,000. *Unit head:* Dr. Keith Murphy, Chair, 864-656-6237, Fax: 864-656-0435, E-mail: kmurph2@clemson.edu. *Application contact:* Sheryl Banks, Administrative Coordinator, 866-656-6878, E-mail: sherylb@clemson.edu.

Colorado State University, Graduate School, College of Natural Sciences, Department of Biochemistry and Molecular Biology, Fort Collins, CO 80523-1870. Offers biochemistry (MS, PhD). Postbaccalaureate distance learning degree programs offered (no on-campus study). *Faculty:* 11 full-time (5 women), 1 part-time/adjunct (0 women). *Students:* 22 full-time (15 women), 15 part-time (6 women); includes 4 minority (all Hispanic Americans), 5 international. Average age 26. 69 applicants, 17% accepted, 12 enrolled. In 2009, 5 master's, 2 doctorates awarded. Terminal master's awarded for partial completion of doctoral program. *Degree requirements:* For master's, comprehensive exam (for some programs), thesis (for some programs); for doctorate, thesis/dissertation, comprehensive oral exam at the end of second year. *Entrance requirements:* For master's, GRE General Test, minimum GPA of 3.0; 3 letters of recommendation; resume; for doctorate, GRE General Test, minimum GPA of 3.0; one year of biology, organic chemistry, physics, calculus, and biochemistry; 3 letters of recommendation; bachelor's degree. Additional exam requirements/recommendations for international students: Required—TOEFL (minimum score 550 paper-based; 213 computer-based; 80 iBT). *Application deadline:* For fall admission, 9/15 priority date for domestic and international students; for spring admission, 1/15 priority date for domestic and international students. Applications are processed on a rolling basis. Application fee: $50. Electronic applications accepted. *Expenses:* Tuition, state resident: full-time $6434; part-time $359.10 per credit. Tuition, nonresident: full-time $18,116; part-time $1006.45 per credit. Required fees: $1496; $83 per credit. *Financial support:* In 2009–10, 12 fellowships (averaging $29,153 per year), 20 research assistantships with full tuition reimbursements (averaging $21,685 per year), 7 teaching assistantships with full tuition reimbursements (averaging $18,038 per year) were awarded; health care benefits also available. Financial award application deadline: 1/15; financial award applicants required to submit FAFSA. *Faculty research:* Cellular biology, molecular gene expression, neurobiology, structural biology, yeast genetics. Total annual research expenditures: $3.4 million. *Unit head:* Dr. P. Shing Ho, Chair, 970-491-0569, Fax: 970-491-0494, E-mail: shing.ho@colostate.edu. *Application contact:* Sharon Gale, Graduate Program Assistant, 970-491-6841, Fax: 970-491-0494, E-mail: sharon.gale@colostate.edu.

Colorado State University–Pueblo, College of Science and Mathematics, Pueblo, CO 81001-4901. Offers applied natural science (MS), including biochemistry, biology, chemistry. Part-time and evening/weekend programs available. *Degree requirements:* For master's, comprehensive exam (for some programs), thesis (for some programs), internship report (if non-thesis). *Entrance requirements:* For master's, GRE General Test (minimum score 1000), 2 letters of reference, minimum GPA of 3.0. Additional exam requirements/recommendations for international students: Required—TOEFL (minimum score 500 paper-based; 173 computer-based), IELTS (minimum score 5). *Faculty research:* Fungal cell walls, molecular biology, bioactive materials synthesis, atomic force microscopy-surface chemistry, nanoscience.

Columbia University, College of Physicians and Surgeons, Department of Biochemistry and Molecular Biophysics, New York, NY 10032. Offers biochemistry and molecular biophysics (M Phil, PhD); biophysics (PhD); MD/PhD. Only candidates for the PhD are admitted. *Degree requirements:* For doctorate, one foreign language, thesis/dissertation. *Entrance requirements:* For master's and doctorate, GRE General Test. Additional exam requirements/recommendations for international students: Required—TOEFL.

Cornell University, Graduate School, Graduate Fields of Agriculture and Life Sciences, Field of Biochemistry, Molecular and Cell Biology, Ithaca, NY 14853-0001. Offers biochemistry (PhD); biophysics (PhD); cell biology (PhD); molecular and cell biology (PhD); molecular biology (PhD). *Faculty:* 64 full-time (14 women). *Students:* 91 full-time (43 women); includes 11 minority (2 African Americans, 6 Asian Americans or Pacific Islanders, 3 Hispanic Americans),

Biochemistry

Cornell University (continued)
28 international. Average age 27. 150 applicants, 11% accepted, 15 enrolled. In 2009, 17 doctorates awarded. *Degree requirements:* For doctorate, comprehensive exam, thesis/dissertation, 2 semesters of teaching experience. *Entrance requirements:* For doctorate, GRE General Test, GRE Subject Test (biology, chemistry, physics, biochemistry, cell and molecular biology), 3 letters of recommendation. Additional exam requirements/recommendations for international students: Required—TOEFL (minimum score 600 paper-based; 250 computer-based; 77 iBT). *Application deadline:* For fall admission, 1/5 for domestic students. Application fee: $70. Electronic applications accepted. *Expenses:* Tuition: Full-time $29,500. Required fees: $70. Full-time tuition and fees vary according to degree level, program and student level. *Financial support:* In 2009–10, 88 students received support, including 13 fellowships with full tuition reimbursements available, 1 research assistantship with full tuition reimbursement available; teaching assistantships with full tuition reimbursements available, institutionally sponsored loans, scholarships/grants, health care benefits, tuition waivers (full and partial), and unspecified assistantships also available. Financial award applicants required to submit FAFSA. *Faculty research:* Biophysics, structural biology. *Unit head:* Director of Graduate Studies, 607-255-2100, Fax: 607-255-2100. *Application contact:* Graduate Field Assistant, 607-255-2100, Fax: 607-255-2100, E-mail: bmcb@cornell.edu.

Cornell University, Graduate School, Graduate Fields of Arts and Sciences, Field of Chemistry and Chemical Biology, Ithaca, NY 14853-0001. Offers analytical chemistry (PhD); bio-organic chemistry (PhD); biophysical chemistry (PhD); chemical biology (PhD); chemical physics (PhD); inorganic chemistry (PhD); materials chemistry (PhD); organic chemistry (PhD); organometallic chemistry (PhD); physical chemistry (PhD); polymer chemistry (PhD); theoretical chemistry (PhD). *Faculty:* 48 full-time (3 women). *Students:* 162 full-time (67 women); includes 15 minority (1 African American, 9 Asian Americans or Pacific Islanders, 5 Hispanic Americans), 53 international. Average age 26. 359 applicants, 19% accepted, 39 enrolled. In 2009, 31 doctorates awarded. *Degree requirements:* For doctorate, comprehensive exam, thesis/dissertation. *Entrance requirements:* For doctorate, GRE General Test, GRE Subject Test (chemistry), 3 letters of recommendation. Additional exam requirements/recommendations for international students: Required—TOEFL (minimum score 600 paper-based; 250 computer-based; 77 iBT). *Application deadline:* For fall admission, 1/10 for domestic students. Application fee: $70. Electronic applications accepted. *Expenses:* Tuition: Full-time $29,500. Required fees: $70. Full-time tuition and fees vary according to degree level, program and student level. *Financial support:* In 2009–10, 1 fellowship with full tuition reimbursement, 7 research assistantships with full tuition reimbursements, 29 teaching assistantships with full tuition reimbursements were awarded; institutionally sponsored loans, scholarships/grants, health care benefits, tuition waivers (full and partial), and unspecified assistantships also available. Financial award applicants required to submit FAFSA. *Faculty research:* Analytical, organic, inorganic, physical, materials, chemical biology. *Unit head:* Director of Graduate Studies, 607-255-4139, Fax: 607-255-4137. *Application contact:* Graduate Field Assistant, 607-255-4139, Fax: 607-255-4137, E-mail: chemgrad@cornell.edu.

Cornell University, Joan and Sanford I. Weill Medical College and Graduate School of Medical Sciences, Weill Cornell Graduate School of Medical Sciences, Biochemistry, Cell and Molecular Biology Allied Program, New York, NY 10065. Offers MS, PhD. *Faculty:* 100 full-time (26 women). *Students:* 148 full-time (96 women); includes 16 minority (2 African Americans, 8 Asian Americans or Pacific Islanders, 6 Hispanic Americans), 71 international. Average age 22. 295 applicants, 16% accepted, 17 enrolled. In 2009, 19 doctorates awarded. Terminal master's awarded for partial completion of doctoral program. *Degree requirements:* For master's, comprehensive exam; for doctorate, thesis/dissertation, final exam. *Entrance requirements:* For doctorate, GRE General Test, background in genetics, molecular biology, chemistry, or biochemistry. Additional exam requirements/recommendations for international students: Required—TOEFL. *Application deadline:* For fall admission, 12/1 for domestic students. Application fee: $60. Electronic applications accepted. *Expenses:* Tuition: Full-time $44,650. Required fees: $2805. *Financial support:* In 2009–10, 12 fellowships (averaging $21,900 per year) were awarded; scholarships/grants, health care benefits, and stipends (given to all students) also available. *Faculty research:* Molecular structure determination, protein structure, gene structure, stem cell biology, control of gene expression, DNA replication, chromosome maintenance, RNA biosynthesis. *Unit head:* Dr. David Eliezer, Co-Director, 212-746-6557, Fax: 212-717-3047. *Application contact:* Linda Smith, Assistant Dean of Admissions, 212-746-6565, Fax: 212-746-8906, E-mail: lis2025@med.cornell.edu.

Cornell University, Joan and Sanford I. Weill Medical College and Graduate School of Medical Sciences, Weill Cornell Graduate School of Medical Sciences, Tri-Institutional Training Program in Chemical Biology, New York, NY 10065. Offers PhD. Offered jointly by Cornell University, Weill Graduate School of Medical Sciences, The Rockefeller University and Sloan-Kettering Institute. Students must be accepted to Cornell University Graduate Program in Chemistry. *Faculty:* 40 full-time (4 women). *Students:* 44 full-time (19 women); includes 2 minority (1 Asian American or Pacific Islander, 1 Hispanic American), 30 international. 70 applicants, 23% accepted, 7 enrolled. In 2009, 5 doctorates awarded. *Degree requirements:* For doctorate, comprehensive exam, thesis/dissertation. *Entrance requirements:* For doctorate, GRE General Test, GRE Subject Test (chemistry, biochemistry or physics), 3 letters of recommendation. Additional exam requirements/recommendations for international students: Required—TOEFL (minimum score 600 paper-based; 250 computer-based; 90 iBT). *Application deadline:* For winter admission, 1/1 for domestic and international students. Application fee: $80. Electronic applications accepted. *Expenses:* Tuition: Full-time $44,650. Required fees: $2805. *Financial support:* In 2009–10, 44 students received support, including 44 fellowships with full tuition reimbursements available (averaging $37,000 per year). *Faculty research:* Bio-organic chemistry; biological chemistry/biochemistry; biophysical chemistry; bio-analytical chemistry; computational chemistry and biology. *Unit head:* Kathleen E. Pickering, Executive Director, 212-746-6049, Fax: 212-746-8992, E-mail: tpcb@med.cornell.edu. *Application contact:* Margie Hironangan-Mendoza, Program Coordinator, 212-746-5267, Fax: 212-746-8992, E-mail: tpcb@med.cornell.edu.

Dalhousie University, Faculty of Medicine, Department of Biochemistry and Molecular Biology, Halifax, NS B3H 4R2, Canada. Offers M Sc, PhD. *Degree requirements:* For master's, thesis, demonstrating/teaching experience, oral defense, seminar; for doctorate, comprehensive exam, thesis/dissertation, demonstrating/teaching experience, oral defense, seminar, 2 short grant proposals in year 3. *Entrance requirements:* For master's and doctorate, GRE. Additional exam requirements/recommendations for international students: Required—TOEFL, IELTS, 1 of the following 5 approved tests: TOEFL, IELTS, CANTEST, CAEL, Michigan English Language Assessment Battery. Electronic applications accepted. *Expenses:* Contact institution. *Faculty research:* Gene expression and cell regulation; lipids, lipoproteins, and membranes; molecular evolution; proteins, molecular cell biology and molecular genetics; structure, function, and metabolism of biomolecules.

Dartmouth College, Graduate Program in Molecular and Cellular Biology, Department of Biochemistry, Hanover, NH 03755. Offers PhD, MD/PhD. *Faculty:* 9 full-time (0 women), 11 part-time/adjunct (4 women). *Students:* 28 full-time (12 women); includes 4 minority (2 American Indian/Alaska Native, 2 Hispanic Americans), 8 international. Average age 27. 280 applicants, 22% accepted, 25 enrolled. In 2009, 7 doctorates awarded. *Entrance requirements:* For doctorate, GRE General Test, letters of recommendation. Additional exam requirements/recommendations for international students: Required—TOEFL (minimum score 450 paper-based; 90 iBT) or IELTS (minimum score 7). *Application deadline:* For fall admission, 1/4 for domestic and international students. Applications are processed on a rolling basis. Application fee: $75. Electronic applications accepted. *Financial support:* Scholarships/grants, health care benefits, and stipends ($25,500) available. *Unit head:* Dr. Charles Barlowe, Chair and Professor, 603-650-1616, Fax: 603-650-1128, E-mail: biochemistry@dartmouth.edu. *Application contact:* Janet Cheney, Program Coordinator, 603-650-1612, Fax: 603-650-1006, E-mail: mcb@dartmouth.edu.

DePaul University, College of Liberal Arts and Sciences, Department of Chemistry, Chicago, IL 60614. Offers biochemistry (MS); chemistry (MS); polymer chemistry and coatings technology (MS). Part-time and evening/weekend programs available. *Faculty:* 13 full-time (7 women), 4 part-time/adjunct (1 woman). *Students:* 14 full-time (7 women), 9 part-time (4 women); includes 6 minority (2 African Americans, 3 Asian Americans or Pacific Islanders, 1 Hispanic American), 1 international. Average age 27. 6 applicants, 100% accepted, 4 enrolled. In 2009, 2 master's awarded. *Degree requirements:* For master's, thesis (for some programs), oral exam (for select programs). *Entrance requirements:* For master's, GRE Subject Test (chemistry), GRE General Test, BS in chemistry or equivalent. Additional exam requirements/recommendations for international students: Required—TOEFL (minimum score 590 paper-based; 243 computer-based). *Application deadline:* For fall admission, 7/15 for domestic students, 5/1 for international students; for winter admission, 11/15 for domestic students, 9/1 for international students; for spring admission, 2/15 for domestic students, 12/1 for international students. Applications are processed on a rolling basis. Application fee: $40. Electronic applications accepted. *Expenses:* Tuition: Full-time $37,525; part-time $620 per credit hour. *Financial support:* In 2009–10, 4 students received support, including 6 teaching assistantships with partial tuition reimbursements available (averaging $9,000 per year). Financial award application deadline: 6/1. *Faculty research:* Computational chemistry, organic synthesis, inorganic synthesis, polymer synthesis, biochemistry. Total annual research expenditures: $30,000. *Unit head:* Dr. Richard F. Niedziela, Chair, 773-325-7307, Fax: 773-325-7421, E-mail: rniedzie@condor.depaul.edu. *Application contact:* Dr. Matthew Dintzner, Director of Graduate Studies, 773-325-4726, Fax: 773-325-7421, E-mail: mdintzne@depaul.edu.

Drexel University, College of Medicine, Biomedical Graduate Programs, Program in Biochemistry, Philadelphia, PA 19104-2875. Offers MS, PhD, MD/PhD. Part-time programs available. Terminal master's awarded for partial completion of doctoral program. *Degree requirements:* For master's, comprehensive exam, thesis; for doctorate, thesis/dissertation, qualifying exam. *Entrance requirements:* For master's, GRE General Test, minimum GPA of 2.75; for doctorate, GRE General Test, minimum GPA of 3.0. Additional exam requirements/recommendations for international students: Required—TOEFL. Electronic applications accepted.

Duke University, Graduate School, Department of Biochemistry, Durham, NC 27710. Offers crystallography of macromolecules (PhD); enzyme mechanisms (PhD); lipid biochemistry (PhD); membrane structure and function (PhD); molecular genetics (PhD); neurochemistry (PhD); nucleic acid structure and function (PhD); protein structure and function (PhD). *Faculty:* 29 full-time. *Students:* 68 full-time (25 women); includes 6 minority (2 African Americans, 4 Asian Americans or Pacific Islanders), 21 international. 101 applicants, 23% accepted, 12 enrolled. In 2009, 8 doctorates awarded. *Degree requirements:* For doctorate, thesis/dissertation. *Entrance requirements:* For doctorate, GRE General Test, GRE Subject Test (recommended). Additional exam requirements/recommendations for international students: Required—TOEFL (minimum score 550 paper-based; 213 computer-based; 83 iBT), IELTS (minimum score 7). *Application deadline:* For fall admission, 12/8 priority date for domestic and international students. Application fee: $75. Electronic applications accepted. *Financial support:* Fellowships, research assistantships, teaching assistantships, Federal Work-Study available. Financial award application deadline: 12/8. *Unit head:* Leonard Spicer, Director of Graduate Studies, 919-681-8770, Fax: 919-684-8885, E-mail: anorfleet@biochem.duke.edu. *Application contact:* Cynthia Robertson, Associate Dean for Enrollment Services, 919-684-3913, E-mail: grad-admissions@duke.edu.

Duquesne University, Bayer School of Natural and Environmental Sciences, Department of Chemistry and Biochemistry, Pittsburgh, PA 15282-0001. Offers chemistry (MS, PhD). Part-time programs available. *Faculty:* 14 full-time (4 women), 1 part-time/adjunct (0 women). *Students:* 43 full-time (21 women), 5 part-time (0 women); includes 2 minority (both African Americans), 13 international. Average age 30. 53 applicants, 32% accepted, 8 enrolled. In 2009, 3 doctorates awarded. Terminal master's awarded for partial completion of doctoral program. *Degree requirements:* For master's, comprehensive exam (for some programs), thesis (for some programs); for doctorate, thesis/dissertation. *Entrance requirements:* For master's, GRE General Test, BS in chemistry or related field, 3 letters of recommendation; for doctorate, GRE General Test, BS in chemistry or related field, statement of purpose, official transcripts, 3 letters of recommendation with recommendation forms. Additional exam requirements/recommendations for international students: Required—TOEFL (minimum score 100 iBT). *Application deadline:* For fall admission, 2/15 priority date for domestic students, 2/15 for international students; for spring admission, 10/1 priority date for domestic students, 10/1 for international students. Applications are processed on a rolling basis. Application fee: $0 ($40 for international students). Electronic applications accepted. *Expenses:* Contact institution. *Financial support:* In 2009–10, 42 students received support, including 15 research assistantships with full tuition reimbursements available (averaging $20,800 per year), 27 teaching assistantships with full tuition reimbursements available (averaging $20,800 per year); fellowships with tuition reimbursements available, scholarships/grants and unspecified assistantships also available. Financial award application deadline: 5/31. *Faculty research:* Computational physical chemistry, bioinorganic chemistry, analytical chemistry, biophysics, synthetic organic chemistry. *Unit head:* Dr. Jeffry Madura, Chair, 412-396-6341, Fax: 412-396-5683, E-mail: madura@duq.edu. *Application contact:* Heather Costello, Graduate Academic Advisor, 412-396-6339, Fax: 412-396-4881, E-mail: costelloh@duq.edu.

East Carolina University, Brody School of Medicine, Department of Biochemistry and Molecular Biology, Greenville, NC 27858-4353. Offers PhD. *Degree requirements:* For doctorate, comprehensive exam, thesis/dissertation. *Entrance requirements:* For doctorate, GRE General Test. Additional exam requirements/recommendations for international students: Required—TOEFL. *Faculty research:* Gene regulation, development and differentiation, contractility and motility, macromolecular interactions, cancer.

East Tennessee State University, James H. Quillen College of Medicine, Biomedical Science Graduate Program, Johnson City, TN 37614. Offers anatomy (MS, PhD); biochemistry (MS, PhD); biophysics (MS, PhD); microbiology (MS, PhD); pharmacology (MS, PhD); physiology (MS, PhD). Part-time programs available. Terminal master's awarded for partial completion of doctoral program. *Degree requirements:* For master's, one foreign language, thesis, comprehensive qualifying exam; for doctorate, 2 foreign languages, thesis/dissertation. *Entrance requirements:* For master's, GRE General Test, minimum GPA of 3.0, bachelor's degree in biological or related science; for doctorate, GRE General Test, GRE Subject Test. Additional exam requirements/recommendations for international students: Required—TOEFL (minimum score 550 paper-based; 213 computer-based). *Expenses:* Contact institution.

Emory University, Graduate School of Arts and Sciences, Division of Biological and Biomedical Sciences, Program in Biochemistry, Cell and Developmental Biology, Atlanta, GA 30322-1100. Offers PhD. *Faculty:* 51 full-time (10 women). *Students:* 62 full-time (42 women); includes 9 minority (3 African Americans, 5 Asian Americans or Pacific Islanders, 1 Hispanic American), 17 international. Average age 27. 107 applicants, 12% accepted, 6 enrolled. In 2009, 10 doctorates awarded. *Degree requirements:* For doctorate, comprehensive exam, thesis/dissertation. *Entrance requirements:* For doctorate, GRE General Test, minimum GPA of 3.0 in science course work (recommended). Additional exam requirements/recommendations for international students: Required—TOEFL. *Application deadline:* For fall admission, 1/3 for domestic and international students. Application fee: $50. Electronic applications accepted. *Financial support:* In 2009–10, 24 students received support, including 24 fellowships with full tuition reimbursements available (averaging $24,500 per year); institutionally sponsored loans, scholarships/grants, and health care benefits also available. *Faculty research:* Signal transduction, molecular biology, enzymes and cofactors, receptor and ion channel function, membrane biology. *Unit head:* Richard Kahn, Director, 404-727-3561, Fax: 404-727-3746, E-mail: rkahn@emory.edu. *Application contact:* 404-727-2545, Fax: 404-727-3322, E-mail: gdbbs@emory.edu.

Florida State University, The Graduate School, College of Arts and Sciences, Department of Chemistry and Biochemistry, Specialization in Biochemistry, Tallahassee, FL 32306-4390. Offers MS, PhD. *Faculty:* 8 full-time (3 women), 1 (woman) part-time/adjunct. *Students:* 29

full-time (12 women), 1 (woman) part-time; includes 4 minority (2 African Americans, 1 Asian American or Pacific Islander, 1 Hispanic American), 13 international. Average age 25. 99 applicants, 10% accepted, 5 enrolled. In 2009, 4 master's, 2 doctorates awarded. Terminal master's awarded for partial completion of doctoral program. *Degree requirements:* For master's, comprehensive exam (for some programs), thesis (for some programs), cumulative and diagnostic exams; for doctorate, comprehensive exam (for some programs), thesis/dissertation, cumulative and diagnostic exams. *Entrance requirements:* For master's and doctorate, GRE General Test, minimum B average in undergraduate course work. Additional exam requirements/recommendations for international students: Required—TOEFL (minimum score 550 paper-based; 213 computer-based; 80 iBT). *Application deadline:* For fall admission, 12/15 for domestic and international students; for spring admission, 9/15 for domestic and international students. Applications are processed on a rolling basis. Application fee: $30. Electronic applications accepted. *Expenses:* Tuition, state resident: full-time $7413. Tuition, nonresident: full-time $22,567. *Financial support:* In 2009–10, 29 students received support, including 25 fellowships with tuition reimbursements available (averaging $19,000 per year), 25 research assistantships with tuition reimbursements available (averaging $19,000 per year), 13 teaching assistantships with tuition reimbursements available (averaging $19,000 per year); career-related internships or fieldwork, Federal Work-Study, institutionally sponsored loans, and traineeships also available. Financial award application deadline: 12/15; financial award applicants required to submit FAFSA. *Faculty research:* Metalloenzymes, gene regulation, DNA structure, NMR of synthetic membranes, secondary metabolites. Total annual research expenditures: $5.5 million. *Unit head:* Dr. Joseph Schlenoff, Interim Chairman, 850-644-5195, Fax: 850-644-8281, E-mail: schlen@chem.fsu.edu. *Application contact:* Dr. Tyler McQuade, Chair, Graduate Admissions Committee, 888-525-9281, Fax: 850-644-0465, E-mail: gradinfo@chem.fsu.edu.

Florida State University, The Graduate School, College of Arts and Sciences, Program in Molecular Biophysics, Tallahassee, FL 32306. Offers biochemistry, molecular and cell biology (PhD); computational structural biology (PhD); molecular biophysics (PhD). *Faculty:* 49 full-time (6 women). *Students:* 22 full-time (8 women); includes 6 minority (5 Asian Americans or Pacific Islanders, 1 Hispanic American). Average age 28. 30 applicants, 33% accepted, 7 enrolled. In 2009, 5 doctorates awarded. *Degree requirements:* For doctorate, comprehensive exam, thesis/dissertation, teaching 1 term in professor's major department. *Entrance requirements:* For doctorate, GRE General Test. Additional exam requirements/recommendations for international students: Required—TOEFL (minimum score 600 paper-based; 250 computer-based; 100 iBT). *Application deadline:* For fall admission, 2/15 for domestic students, 3/15 for international students; for spring admission, 11/2 for international students. Applications are processed on a rolling basis. Application fee: $30. Electronic applications accepted. *Expenses:* Tuition, state resident: full-time $7413. Tuition, nonresident: full-time $22,567. *Financial support:* In 2009–10, 21 students received support, including fellowships with partial tuition reimbursements available (averaging $21,000 per year), 18 research assistantships with partial tuition reimbursements available (averaging $21,000 per year), 4 teaching assistantships with partial tuition reimbursements available (averaging $21,000 per year); scholarships/grants, health care benefits, and unspecified assistantships also available. Financial award applicants required to submit FAFSA. *Faculty research:* Protein and nucleic acid structure and function, membrane protein structure, computational biophysics, 3-D image reconstruction. Total annual research expenditures: $1.4 million. *Unit head:* Dr. Geoffrey Strouse, Director, 850-644-0056, Fax: 850-644-7244, E-mail: strouse@chem.fsu.edu. *Application contact:* Dr. Kerry Maddox, Academic Coordinator, Graduate Programs, 850-644-1012, Fax: 850-644-7244, E-mail: bkmaddox@sb.fsu.edu.

Georgetown University, Graduate School of Arts and Sciences, Department of Chemistry, Washington, DC 20057. Offers analytical chemistry (PhD); biochemistry (PhD); computational chemistry (PhD); inorganic chemistry (PhD); materials chemistry (PhD); organic chemistry (PhD); physical chemistry (PhD); theoretical chemistry (PhD). Terminal master's awarded for partial completion of doctoral program. *Degree requirements:* For doctorate, comprehensive exam, thesis/dissertation. *Entrance requirements:* For doctorate, GRE General Test. Additional exam requirements/recommendations for international students: Required—TOEFL.

Georgetown University, Graduate School of Arts and Sciences, Programs in Biomedical Sciences, Department of Biochemistry and Molecular Biology, Washington, DC 20057. Offers MS, PhD. *Degree requirements:* For doctorate, comprehensive exam, thesis/dissertation. *Entrance requirements:* For doctorate, GRE General Test. Additional exam requirements/recommendations for international students: Required—TOEFL.

The George Washington University, Columbian College of Arts and Sciences, Institute for Biomedical Sciences, Program in Biochemistry and Molecular Genetics, Washington, DC 20052. Offers PhD. Part-time and evening/weekend programs available. *Students:* 3 full-time (all women), 4 part-time (2 women). Average age 29. 19 applicants, 68% accepted, 6 enrolled. In 2009, 1 doctorate awarded. Terminal master's awarded for partial completion of doctoral program. *Degree requirements:* For doctorate, thesis/dissertation, general exam. *Entrance requirements:* For doctorate, GRE General Test, interview, minimum GPA of 3.0. Additional exam requirements/recommendations for international students: Required—TOEFL (minimum score 600 paper-based; 250 computer-based). *Application deadline:* For fall admission, 1/2 priority date for domestic and international students; for spring admission, 10/1 priority date for domestic and international students. Applications are processed on a rolling basis. Application fee: $60. Electronic applications accepted. *Financial support:* In 2009–10, 4 students received support; fellowships, Federal Work-Study, institutionally sponsored loans, and tuition waivers available. Financial award application deadline: 2/1. *Unit head:* Valerie W. Hu, Director, 202-994-8431, E-mail: valhu@gwu.edu. *Application contact:* Information Contact, 202-994-7120, Fax: 202-994-6100, E-mail: genetics@gwu.edu.

The George Washington University, School of Medicine and Health Sciences, Department of Biochemistry and Molecular Biology, Washington, DC 20037. Offers biochemistry and molecular biology (MS); biochemistry and molecular genetics (PhD); genomics and bioinformatics (MS). *Faculty:* 20 full-time (3 women), 30 part-time/adjunct (9 women). *Students:* 20 full-time (9 women), 16 part-time (6 women); includes 2 minority (both Asian Americans or Pacific Islanders), 20 international. Average age 27. 57 applicants, 88% accepted, 15 enrolled. In 2009, 17 master's awarded. *Degree requirements:* For master's, comprehensive exam; for doctorate, thesis/dissertation, general exam. *Entrance requirements:* For master's, GRE General Test, interview, minimum GPA of 3.0; for doctorate, GRE General Test, minimum GPA of 3.0. Additional exam requirements/recommendations for international students: Required—TOEFL (minimum score 550 paper-based; 213 computer-based). *Application deadline:* For fall admission, 4/1 priority date for domestic and international students; for spring admission, 10/1 priority date for domestic and international students. Application fee: $60. *Financial support:* Fellowships available. Financial award application deadline: 2/1. *Unit head:* Dr. Allan L. Goldstein, Chair, 202-994-3171, E-mail: bcmalg@gwumc.edu. *Application contact:* Information Contact, 202-994-2179, Fax: 202-994-0967, E-mail: gwibs@gwu.edu.

Georgia Institute of Technology, Graduate Studies and Research, College of Sciences, School of Chemistry and Biochemistry, Atlanta, GA 30332-0001. Offers MS, MS Chem, PhD. Terminal master's awarded for partial completion of doctoral program. *Degree requirements:* For master's, thesis (for some programs); for doctorate, thesis/dissertation. *Entrance requirements:* For master's and doctorate, GRE General Test, GRE Subject Test, minimum GPA of 2.7. Additional exam requirements/recommendations for international students: Required—TOEFL. Electronic applications accepted. *Faculty research:* Inorganic, organic, physical, and analytical chemistry.

Georgia State University, College of Arts and Sciences, Department of Biology, Program in Molecular Genetics and Biochemistry, Atlanta, GA 30302-3083. Offers MS, PhD. Part-time programs available. Terminal master's awarded for partial completion of doctoral program. *Degree requirements:* For master's, thesis or alternative; for doctorate, thesis/dissertation, exam. *Entrance requirements:* For master's and doctorate, GRE General Test. Additional exam requirements/recommendations for international students: Required—TOEFL. Electronic applications accepted.

Graduate School and University Center of the City University of New York, Graduate Studies, Program in Biochemistry, New York, NY 10016-4039. Offers PhD. *Faculty:* 22 full-time (6 women). *Students:* 72 full-time (47 women); includes 5 minority (1 African American, 1 Asian American or Pacific Islander, 3 Hispanic Americans), 45 international. Average age 32. 59 applicants, 34% accepted, 14 enrolled. In 2009, 9 doctorates awarded. *Degree requirements:* For doctorate, thesis/dissertation, field experience. *Entrance requirements:* For doctorate, GRE General Test. Additional exam requirements/recommendations for international students: Required—TOEFL. *Application deadline:* For fall admission, 1/15 for domestic students; for spring admission, 11/15 for domestic students. Application fee: $125. Electronic applications accepted. *Financial support:* In 2009–10, 56 students received support, including 61 fellowships, 2 teaching assistantships; research assistantships, career-related internships or fieldwork, Federal Work-Study, institutionally sponsored loans, and tuition waivers (full and partial) also available. Financial award application deadline: 2/1; financial award applicants required to submit FAFSA. *Unit head:* Dr. Edward Kennely, Executive Officer, 212-817-8086, Fax: 212-817-1503. *Application contact:* Les Gribben, Director of Admissions, 212-817-7470, Fax: 212-817-1624, E-mail: lgribben@gc.cuny.edu.

Harvard University, Graduate School of Arts and Sciences, Department of Chemistry and Chemical Biology, Cambridge, MA 02138. Offers biochemical chemistry (PhD); inorganic chemistry (PhD); organic chemistry (PhD); physical chemistry (PhD). *Degree requirements:* For doctorate, thesis/dissertation, cumulative exams. *Entrance requirements:* For doctorate, GRE General Test, GRE Subject Test. Additional exam requirements/recommendations for international students: Required—TOEFL. *Expenses:* Tuition: Full-time $33,696. Required fees: $1126. Full-time tuition and fees vary according to program.

Harvard University, Graduate School of Arts and Sciences, Division of Medical Sciences, Boston, MA 02115. Offers biological chemistry and molecular pharmacology (PhD); cell biology (PhD); genetics (PhD); microbiology and molecular genetics (PhD); pathology (PhD), including experimental pathology. *Degree requirements:* For doctorate, thesis/dissertation. *Entrance requirements:* For doctorate, GRE General Test, GRE Subject Test. Additional exam requirements/recommendations for international students: Required—TOEFL. *Expenses:* Tuition: Full-time $33,696. Required fees: $1126. Full-time tuition and fees vary according to program.

Howard University, College of Medicine, Department of Biochemistry and Molecular Biology, Washington, DC 20059-0002. Offers biochemistry and molecular biology (PhD); biotechnology (MS); MD/PhD. Part-time programs available. *Degree requirements:* For master's, externship; for doctorate, comprehensive exam, thesis/dissertation. *Entrance requirements:* For master's and doctorate, GRE General Test, minimum GPA of 3.0. *Faculty research:* Cellular and molecular biology of olfaction, gene regulation and expression, enzymology, NMR spectroscopy of molecular structure, hormone regulation/metabolism.

Howard University, Graduate School, Department of Chemistry, Washington, DC 20059-0002. Offers analytical chemistry (MS, PhD); atmospheric (MS, PhD); biochemistry (MS, PhD); environmental (MS, PhD); inorganic chemistry (MS, PhD); organic chemistry (MS, PhD); physical chemistry (MS, PhD). Terminal master's awarded for partial completion of doctoral program. *Degree requirements:* For master's, comprehensive exam, thesis, teaching experience; for doctorate, comprehensive exam, thesis/dissertation, teaching experience. *Entrance requirements:* For master's, GRE General Test, minimum GPA of 2.7; for doctorate, GRE General Test, minimum GPA of 3.0. Additional exam requirements/recommendations for international students: Required—TOEFL. Electronic applications accepted. *Faculty research:* Synthetic organics, materials, natural products, mass spectrometry.

Hunter College of the City University of New York, Graduate School, School of Arts and Sciences, Department of Chemistry, Program in Biochemistry, New York, NY 10021-5085. Offers MA, PhD. Part-time programs available. *Faculty:* 1 (woman) full-time. *Students:* 2 full-time (1 woman), 9 part-time (8 women); includes 3 minority (all Asian Americans or Pacific Islanders). Average age 29. 14 applicants, 50% accepted, 3 enrolled. In 2009, 1 master's awarded. *Degree requirements:* For master's, comprehensive exam or thesis. *Entrance requirements:* For master's, GRE General Test, 1 year of course work in chemistry, quantitative analysis, organic chemistry, physical chemistry, biology, biochemistry lecture and laboratory. Additional exam requirements/recommendations for international students: Required—TOEFL. *Application deadline:* For fall admission, 4/1 for domestic students; for spring admission, 11/1 for domestic students. Application fee: $125. *Expenses:* Tuition, state resident: full-time $7360; part-time $310 per credit. Required fees: $250 per semester. *Financial support:* Teaching assistantships, Federal Work-Study, scholarships/grants, and tuition waivers (partial) available. Support available to part-time students. *Faculty research:* Protein/nucleic acid interactions, physical properties of iron-sulfur proteins, neurotransmitter receptors and ion channels Drosophila melanogaster, requirements of DNA synthesis, oncogenes. *Unit head:* Yuiia Xu, Adviser, 212-772-4310. *Application contact:* William Zlata, Director for Graduate Admissions, 212-772-4482, Fax: 212-650-3336, E-mail: admissions@hunter.cuny.edu.

Illinois State University, Graduate School, College of Arts and Sciences, Department of Biological Sciences, Normal, IL 61790-2200. Offers animal behavior (MS); bacteriology (MS); biochemistry (MS); biological sciences (MS); biology (PhD); biophysics (MS); biotechnology (MS); botany (MS, PhD); cell biology (MS); conservation biology (MS); developmental biology (MS); ecology (MS, PhD); entomology (MS); evolutionary biology (MS); genetics (MS, PhD); immunology (MS); microbiology (MS, PhD); molecular biology (MS); molecular genetics (MS); neurobiology (MS); neuroscience (MS); parasitology (MS); physiology (MS, PhD); plant biology (MS); plant molecular biology (MS); plant sciences (MS); structural biology (MS); zoology (MS, PhD). Part-time programs available. *Degree requirements:* For master's, thesis or alternative; for doctorate, variable foreign language requirement, thesis/dissertation, 2 terms of residency. *Entrance requirements:* For master's, GRE General Test, minimum GPA of 2.6 in last 60 hours of course work; for doctorate, GRE General Test. *Faculty research:* Redoc balance and drug development in schistosoma mansoni, control of the growth of listeria monocytogenes at low temperature, regulation of cell expansion and microtubule function by SPRI, CRUI: physiology and fitness consequences of different life history phenotypes.

Indiana University Bloomington, University Graduate School, College of Arts and Sciences, Department of Chemistry, Bloomington, IN 47405-7000. Offers analytical chemistry (PhD); biological chemistry (PhD); chemistry (MAT); inorganic chemistry (PhD); physical chemistry (PhD). *Faculty:* 39 full-time (3 women). *Students:* 190 full-time (67 women), 1 (woman) part-time; includes 13 minority (4 African Americans, 1 American Indian/Alaska Native, 5 Asian Americans or Pacific Islanders, 3 Hispanic Americans), 66 international. Average age 26. 207 applicants, 60% accepted, 49 enrolled. In 2009, 10 master's, 20 doctorates awarded. Terminal master's awarded for partial completion of doctoral program. *Degree requirements:* For master's, thesis; for doctorate, thesis/dissertation. *Entrance requirements:* For master's and doctorate, GRE General Test, GRE Subject Test. Additional exam requirements/recommendations for international students: Required—TOEFL. *Application deadline:* For fall admission, 1/15 priority date for domestic students, 12/15 for international students; for spring admission, 9/1 priority date for domestic students, 9/1 for international students. Applications are processed on a rolling basis. Application fee: $55 ($65 for international students). *Financial support:* Fellowships with full tuition reimbursements, research assistantships with full tuition reimbursements, teaching assistantships with full tuition reimbursements, Federal Work-Study and institutionally sponsored loans available. *Faculty research:* Synthesis of complex natural products, organic reaction mechanisms, organic electrochemistry, transitive-metal chemistry, solid-state and surface chemistry. Total annual research expenditures: $7.7 million. *Unit head:* Jim Reilly, Chairperson, 812-855-6239, E-mail: chemchair@indiana.edu. *Application contact:* Martin Jarrold, Director of Graduate Admissions, 812-855-2069, E-mail: mfj@indiana.edu.

Indiana University Bloomington, University Graduate School, College of Arts and Sciences, Interdisciplinary Biochemistry Graduate Program, Bloomington, IN 47405-7000. Offers PhD.

Biochemistry

Indiana University Bloomington (continued)

Faculty: 45 full-time (10 women). *Students:* 62 full-time (26 women), 3 part-time (1 woman); includes 6 minority (2 African Americans, 1 American Indian/Alaska Native, 3 Asian Americans or Pacific Islanders), 36 international. Average age 26. 117 applicants, 24% accepted, 13 enrolled. In 2009, 1 doctorate awarded. Terminal master's awarded for partial completion of doctoral program. *Degree requirements:* For doctorate, comprehensive exam, thesis/dissertation, Test of English Proficiency for International Associate Instructor Candidates (TEPAIC)(for international students). *Entrance requirements:* For doctorate, GRE. Additional exam requirements/recommendations for international students: Required—TOEFL (minimum score 550 paper-based; 213 computer-based; 79 iBT). *Application deadline:* For fall admission, 1/15 priority date for domestic students, 12/1 priority date for international students. Application fee: $55 ($65 for international students). Electronic applications accepted. *Financial support:* In 2009–10, 58 students received support, including 19 fellowships with full tuition reimbursements available (averaging $25,000 per year), 13 research assistantships with full tuition reimbursements available (averaging $22,000 per year), 26 teaching assistantships with full tuition reimbursements available (averaging $22,000 per year); scholarships/grants and tuition waivers (full) also available. *Faculty research:* Microbial biochemistry and virology, structural biology, chemical biology, cellular and medicinal biochemistry. *Unit head:* Dr. Carl E. Bauer, Director, 812-856-0192, Fax: 812-856-5710, E-mail: bchem@indiana.edu. *Application contact:* Suzanne Schwartz, Graduate Program Manager, 812-856-0192, Fax: 812-856-5710.

Indiana University–Purdue University Indianapolis, Indiana University School of Medicine, Department of Biochemistry and Molecular Biology, Indianapolis, IN 46202-2896. Offers PhD, MD/MS, MD/PhD. *Faculty:* 17 full-time (4 women). *Students:* 48 full-time (26 women), 16 part-time (10 women); includes 4 minority (1 African American, 3 Asian Americans or Pacific Islanders), 26 international. Average age 31. 21 applicants, 71% accepted, 15 enrolled. In 2009, 7 doctorates awarded. Terminal master's awarded for partial completion of doctoral program. *Degree requirements:* For doctorate, thesis/dissertation. *Entrance requirements:* For doctorate, GRE General Test, GRE Subject Test (recommended), previous course work in organic chemistry. *Application deadline:* For fall admission, 1/15 priority date for domestic students. Applications are processed on a rolling basis. Application fee: $55 ($65 for international students). *Financial support:* In 2009–10, 8 teaching assistantships (averaging $14,949 per year) were awarded; fellowships with tuition reimbursements, research assistantships with tuition reimbursements, Federal Work-Study, institutionally sponsored loans, scholarships/grants, and tuition waivers (partial) also available. Support available to part-time students. Financial award application deadline: 2/1. *Faculty research:* Metabolic regulation, enzymology, peptide and protein chemistry, cell biology, signal transduction. *Unit head:* Dr. Zhong-Yin Zhang, Chairman, 317-274-7151. *Application contact:* Dr. Zhong-Yin Zhang, Chairman, 317-274-7151.

Iowa State University of Science and Technology, Graduate College, College of Agriculture and College of Liberal Arts and Sciences, Department of Biochemistry, Biophysics, and Molecular Biology, Ames, IA 50011. Offers biochemistry (MS, PhD); biophysics (MS, PhD); genetics (MS, PhD); molecular, cellular, and developmental biology (MS, PhD); toxicology (MS, PhD). *Faculty:* 24 full-time (6 women), 1 (woman) part-time/adjunct. *Students:* 77 full-time (30 women), 3 part-time (2 women); includes 3 minority (1 African American, 1 Asian American or Pacific Islander, 1 Hispanic American), 56 international. 41 applicants, 32% accepted, 13 enrolled. In 2009, 2 master's, 7 doctorates awarded. *Degree requirements:* For master's, thesis; for doctorate, thesis/dissertation. *Entrance requirements:* For master's and doctorate, GRE General Test. Additional exam requirements/recommendations for international students: Required—TOEFL (minimum score 550 paper-based; 79 iBT) or IELTS (minimum score 6.5). *Application deadline:* For fall admission, 1/15 priority date for domestic and international students; for spring admission, 10/15 for domestic and international students. Application fee: $40 ($90 for international students). Electronic applications accepted. *Expenses:* Tuition, state resident: full-time $6716. Tuition, nonresident: full-time $8908. Tuition and fees vary according to course level, course load, program and student level. *Financial support:* In 2009–10, 52 research assistantships with full and partial tuition reimbursements (averaging $18,750 per year) were awarded; teaching assistantships with full and partial tuition reimbursements, scholarships/grants, health care benefits, and unspecified assistantships also available. *Unit head:* Dr. Guru Rao, Interim Chair, 515-294-6116, E-mail: biochem@iastate.edu. *Application contact:* Dr. Reuben Peters, Director of Graduate Education, 515-294-6116, E-mail: biochem@iastate.edu.

See Close-Up on page 155.

The Johns Hopkins University, Bloomberg School of Public Health, Department of Biochemistry and Molecular Biology, Baltimore, MD 21205. Offers MHS, Sc M, PhD. Part-time programs available. *Faculty:* 19 full-time (3 women), 6 part-time/adjunct (4 women). *Students:* 64 full-time (41 women), 3 part-time (1 woman); includes 13 minority (1 African American, 9 Asian Americans or Pacific Islanders, 3 Hispanic Americans), 8 international. Average age 25. 108 applicants, 47% accepted, 26 enrolled. In 2009, 27 master's, 6 doctorates awarded. *Degree requirements:* For master's, thesis; for doctorate, comprehensive exam, thesis/dissertation, oral and written exams. *Entrance requirements:* For master's, MCAT or GRE, 3 letters of recommendation, curriculum vitae; for doctorate, GRE General Test, 3 letters of recommendation, curriculum vitae. Additional exam requirements/recommendations for international students: Required—TOEFL (minimum score 600 paper-based; 250 computer-based). *Application deadline:* For fall admission, 12/22 priority date for domestic students; for winter admission, 6/1 for domestic students. Applications are processed on a rolling basis. Application fee: $45. Electronic applications accepted. *Financial support:* In 2009–10, 63 students received support, including 17 fellowships with tuition reimbursements available (averaging $26,800 per year), 19 research assistantships with tuition reimbursements available (averaging $26,800 per year), 7 teaching assistantships (averaging $1,000 per year); Federal Work-Study, institutionally sponsored loans, scholarships/grants, health care benefits, and stipends also available. Financial award application deadline: 3/15; financial award applicants required to submit FAFSA. *Faculty research:* DNA replication, repair, structure, carcinogenesis, protein structure, enzyme catalysts, reproductive biology. Total annual research expenditures: $6 million. *Unit head:* Dr. Pierre Coulombe, Chairman, 410-955-3671, Fax: 410-955-2926, E-mail: pcoulomb@jhsph.edu. *Application contact:* Sharon Warner, Senior Academic Program Coordinator, 410-955-3672, Fax: 410-955-2926, E-mail: swarner@jhsph.edu.

The Johns Hopkins University, National Institutes of Health Sponsored Programs, Baltimore, MD 21218-2699. Offers biology (PhD); including biochemistry, biophysics, cell biology, developmental biology, genetic biology, molecular biology; cell, molecular, and developmental biology and biophysics (PhD). *Faculty:* 25 full-time (4 women). *Students:* 126 full-time (72 women); includes 36 minority (3 African Americans, 1 American Indian/Alaska Native, 21 Asian Americans or Pacific Islanders, 11 Hispanic Americans), 19 international. 282 applicants, 26% accepted, 36 enrolled. In 2009, 15 doctorates awarded. *Degree requirements:* For doctorate, comprehensive exam, thesis/dissertation. *Entrance requirements:* For doctorate, GRE General Test. Additional exam requirements/recommendations for international students: Required—TOEFL (minimum score 600 paper-based; 250 computer-based), TWE. *Application deadline:* For fall admission, 12/15 priority date for domestic students. Application fee: $60. Electronic applications accepted. *Financial support:* In 2009–10, 24 fellowships (averaging $23,000 per year), 93 research assistantships (averaging $23,000 per year), 22 teaching assistantships (averaging $23,000 per year) were awarded; Federal Work-Study, institutionally sponsored loans, scholarships/grants, traineeships, health care benefits, tuition waivers (partial), and unspecified assistantships also available. Financial award application deadline: 4/15; financial award applicants required to submit FAFSA. *Faculty research:* Protein and nucleic acid biochemistry and biophysical chemistry, molecular biology and development. Total annual research expenditures: $11.2 million. *Unit head:* Dr. Allen Shearn, Chair, 410-516-4693, Fax: 410-516-5213, E-mail: bio_cals@jhu.edu. *Application contact:* Joan Miller, Academic Affairs Manager, 410-516-5502, Fax: 410-516-5213, E-mail: joan@jhu.edu.

The Johns Hopkins University, School of Medicine, Graduate Programs in Medicine, Department of Biological Chemistry, Baltimore, MD 21205. Offers PhD. *Faculty:* 16 full-time (5 women). *Students:* 22 full-time (10 women), 16 international. Average age 31. 66 applicants, 9% accepted, 3 enrolled. In 2009, 5 doctorates awarded. *Degree requirements:* For doctorate, thesis/dissertation. *Entrance requirements:* For doctorate, GRE General Test. Additional exam requirements/recommendations for international students: Required—TOEFL. *Application deadline:* For winter admission, 1/15 priority date for domestic and international students. Application fee: $75. Electronic applications accepted. *Financial support:* In 2009–10, 22 research assistantships (averaging $27,125 per year) were awarded; health care benefits and tuition waivers (full) also available. Financial award application deadline: 1/1. *Faculty research:* Cell adhesion, genetics, signal transduction and RNA metabolism, enzyme structure and function, gene expression. *Unit head:* Dr. Denise Montell, Co-Director, 410-614-2016, Fax: 410-614-8375, E-mail: dmontell@jhmi.edu. *Application contact:* Wendy Seno, Program Coordinator, 410-614-2976, Fax: 410-614-8375, E-mail: wendy@jnmi.edu.

The Johns Hopkins University, School of Medicine, Graduate Programs in Medicine, Program in Biochemistry, Cellular and Molecular Biology, Baltimore, MD 21205. Offers PhD. *Faculty:* 101 full-time (35 women). *Students:* 149 full-time (87 women); includes 33 minority (13 African Americans, 1 American Indian/Alaska Native, 17 Asian Americans or Pacific Islanders, 2 Hispanic Americans), 48 international. Average age 25. 299 applicants, 19% accepted, 18 enrolled. In 2009, 19 doctorates awarded. *Degree requirements:* For doctorate, comprehensive exam, thesis/dissertation. *Entrance requirements:* For doctorate, GRE General Test. Additional exam requirements/recommendations for international students: Required—TOEFL. *Application deadline:* For winter admission, 1/10 for domestic and international students. Applications are processed on a rolling basis. Application fee: $80. Electronic applications accepted. *Financial support:* In 2009–10, 5 fellowships with partial tuition reimbursements (averaging $32,000 per year), 144 research assistantships with full and partial tuition reimbursements (averaging $27,125 per year) were awarded; traineeships and tuition waivers (full) also available. Financial award application deadline: 12/31. *Faculty research:* Developmental biology, genomics/proteomics, protein targeting, signal transduction, structural biology. *Unit head:* Dr. Carolyn Machamer, Director, 410-955-3466, Fax: 410-614-8842, E-mail: machamer@jhmi.edu. *Application contact:* Dr. Jeff Corden, Admissions Director, 410-955-3506, Fax: 410-614-8842, E-mail: jcorden@jhmi.edu.

Kansas State University, Graduate School, College of Arts and Sciences, Department of Biochemistry, Manhattan, KS 66506. Offers MS, PhD. Part-time programs available. *Faculty:* 15 full-time (3 women), 1 part-time/adjunct (0 women). *Students:* 13 full-time (7 women); includes 3 minority (1 Asian American or Pacific Islander, 2 Hispanic Americans), 2 international. Average age 24. 38 applicants, 24% accepted. In 2009, 2 master's, 4 doctorates awarded. *Degree requirements:* For master's, thesis; for doctorate, thesis/dissertation. *Entrance requirements:* For master's, GRE General Test, minimum GPA of 3.0 for junior and senior year; for doctorate, GRE General Test, minimum undergraduate GPA of 3.0 or an excellent postgraduate record. Additional exam requirements/recommendations for international students: Required—TOEFL (minimum score 550 paper-based; 213 computer-based). *Application deadline:* For fall admission, 2/1 priority date for domestic and international students; for spring admission, 8/1 priority date for domestic and international students. Applications are processed on a rolling basis. Application fee: $40 ($55 for international students). Electronic applications accepted. *Financial support:* In 2009–10, 25 research assistantships (averaging $15,244 per year) were awarded; Federal Work-Study, institutionally sponsored loans, and scholarships/grants also available. Support available to part-time students. Financial award application deadline: 3/1; financial award applicants required to submit FAFSA. *Faculty research:* Protein structure/function, insect biochemistry, cellular signaling cascades, environmental biochemistry, biochemistry of vision. Total annual research expenditures: $1.9 million. *Unit head:* Michael Kanost, Head, 785-532-6964, Fax: 785-532-7278, E-mail: kanost@ksu.edu. *Application contact:* Michal Zolkiewski, Director, 785-532-3038, Fax: 785-532-7278, E-mail: michalz@ksu.edu.

Kansas State University, Graduate School, College of Arts and Sciences, Department of Chemistry, Manhattan, KS 66506. Offers analytical chemistry (MS); biological chemistry (MS); chemistry (PhD); inorganic chemistry (MS); materials chemistry (MS); organic chemistry (MS); physical chemistry (MS). *Faculty:* 16 full-time (2 women), 2 part-time/adjunct (0 women). *Students:* 66 full-time (22 women); includes 2 minority (1 African American, 1 Asian American or Pacific Islander), 54 international. Average age 28. 75 applicants, 23% accepted, 7 enrolled. In 2009, 3 master's, 11 doctorates awarded. Terminal master's awarded for partial completion of doctoral program. *Degree requirements:* For master's, thesis; for doctorate, thesis/dissertation. *Entrance requirements:* For master's and doctorate, GRE, minimum GPA of 3.0. Additional exam requirements/recommendations for international students: Required—TOEFL (minimum score 550 paper-based; 213 computer-based). *Application deadline:* For fall admission, 2/1 priority date for domestic and international students; for spring admission, 8/1 priority date for domestic and international students. Applications are processed on a rolling basis. Application fee: $40 ($55 for international students). Electronic applications accepted. *Financial support:* In 2009–10, 41 research assistantships (averaging $15,040 per year), 22 teaching assistantships with full tuition reimbursements (averaging $15,600 per year) were awarded; institutionally sponsored loans and scholarships/grants also available. Support available to part-time students. Financial award application deadline: 3/1; financial award applicants required to submit FAFSA. *Faculty research:* Inorganic chemistry, organic and biological chemistry, analytical chemistry, physical chemistry, materials chemistry and nanotechnology. Total annual research expenditures: $1.9 million. *Unit head:* Eric Maatta, Head, 785-532-6665, Fax: 785-532-6666, E-mail: eam@ksu.edu. *Application contact:* Christer Aakeroy, Director, 785-532-6096, Fax: 785-532-6666, E-mail: aakeroy@ksu.edu.

Kent State University, College of Arts and Sciences, Department of Chemistry, Kent, OH 44242-0001. Offers analytical chemistry (MS, PhD); biochemistry (MS, PhD); chemistry (MA, MS, PhD); inorganic chemistry (MS, PhD); organic chemistry (MS, PhD); physical chemistry (MS, PhD). Terminal master's awarded for partial completion of doctoral program. *Degree requirements:* For master's, comprehensive exam, thesis; for doctorate, comprehensive exam, thesis/dissertation. *Entrance requirements:* For master's and doctorate, placement exam, GRE General Test, GRE Subject Test (recommended), minimum GPA of 2.75. Additional exam requirements/recommendations for international students: Required—TOEFL (minimum score 575 paper-based; 230 computer-based). Electronic applications accepted. *Faculty research:* Biological chemistry, materials chemistry, molecular spectroscopy.

Laurentian University, School of Graduate Studies and Research, Programme in Chemistry and Biochemistry, Sudbury, ON P3E 2C6, Canada. Offers analytical chemistry (M Sc); biochemistry (M Sc); environmental chemistry (M Sc); organic chemistry (M Sc); physical/theoretical chemistry (M Sc). Part-time programs available. *Degree requirements:* For master's, thesis or alternative. *Entrance requirements:* For master's, honors degree with minimum second class. *Faculty research:* Cell cycle checkpoints, kinetic modeling, toxicology to metal stress, quantum chemistry, biogeochemistry metal speciation.

Lehigh University, College of Arts and Sciences, Department of Biological Sciences, Bethlehem, PA 18015. Offers biochemistry (PhD); integrative biology and neuroscience (PhD); molecular biology (MS, PhD). Part-time programs available. Postbaccalaureate distance learning degree programs offered (no on-campus study). *Faculty:* 17 full-time (6 women), 1 (woman) part-time/adjunct. *Students:* 33 full-time (15 women), 37 part-time (25 women); includes 7 minority (1 African American, 3 Asian Americans or Pacific Islanders, 3 Hispanic Americans), 6 international. Average age 29. 45 applicants, 24% accepted, 11 enrolled. In 2009, 20 master's, 4 doctorates awarded. Terminal master's awarded for partial completion of doctoral program. *Degree requirements:* For master's, research report; for doctorate, comprehensive exam, thesis/dissertation. *Entrance requirements:* For doctorate, GRE General Test. Additional exam requirements/recommendations for international students: Required—TOEFL. *Application deadline:* For fall admission, 12/15 for domestic and international students. Applications are processed on a rolling basis. Application fee: $65. Electronic applications accepted. *Financial support:* In 2009–10, 34 students received support, including 4 fellowships with full tuition reimbursements available (averaging $23,000 per year), 6 research assistantships with full tuition reimbursements available (averaging $23,000 per year), 16 teaching assistantships with full tuition reimbursements available (averaging $23,000 per year); scholarships/grants, tuition waivers (full and partial), and unspecified assistantships also available. Financial award application deadline: 1/15. *Faculty research:* Gene expression, cytoskeleton and cell structure, cell cycle and growth regulation, neuroscience, animal behavior. Total annual research expenditures: $2 million. *Unit head:* Dr. Murray Itzkowitz, Chairperson, 610-758-3680, Fax: 610-758-4004, E-mail: mi00@lehigh.edu. *Application contact:* Dr. Jennifer M. Swann, Graduate Coordinator, 610-758-5484, Fax: 610-758-4004, E-mail: jms5@lehigh.edu.

Loma Linda University, School of Medicine, Department of Biochemistry/Microbiology, Loma Linda, CA 92350. Offers MS, PhD. Part-time programs available. *Degree requirements:* For master's, thesis or alternative; for doctorate, thesis/dissertation. *Entrance requirements:* For master's and doctorate, GRE General Test. Additional exam requirements/recommendations for international students: Required—TOEFL (minimum score 550 paper-based; 213 computer-based). *Faculty research:* Physical chemistry of macromolecules, biochemistry of endocrine system, biochemical mechanism of bone volume regulation.

Louisiana State University and Agricultural and Mechanical College, Graduate School, College of Basic Sciences, Department of Biological Sciences, Baton Rouge, LA 70803. Offers biochemistry (MS, PhD); biological science (MS, PhD); science (MNS). Part-time programs available. *Faculty:* 65 full-time (8 women). *Students:* 135 full-time (64 women), 9 part-time (4 women); includes 14 minority (9 African Americans, 4 Asian Americans or Pacific Islanders, 1 Hispanic American), 59 international. Average age 30. 161 applicants, 16% accepted, 16 enrolled. In 2009, 3 master's, 26 doctorates awarded. Terminal master's awarded for partial completion of doctoral program. *Degree requirements:* For doctorate, thesis/dissertation. *Entrance requirements:* For master's and doctorate, GRE General Test, minimum GPA of 3.0. Additional exam requirements/recommendations for international students: Required—TOEFL (minimum score 550 paper-based; 213 computer-based; 79 iBT) or IELTS (minimum score 6.5). *Application deadline:* For fall admission, 5/15 for domestic and international students; for spring admission, 10/15 for domestic and international students. Applications are processed on a rolling basis. Application fee: $25. Electronic applications accepted. *Financial support:* In 2009–10, 138 students received support, including 16 fellowships with full and partial tuition reimbursements available (averaging $28,078 per year), 40 research assistantships with full and partial tuition reimbursements available (averaging $21,455 per year), 81 teaching assistantships with full and partial tuition reimbursements available (averaging $18,840 per year); Federal Work-Study, institutionally sponsored loans, health care benefits, and unspecified assistantships also available. Support available to part-time students. Financial award applicants required to submit FAFSA. *Faculty research:* Biochemistry and molecular biology; cell developmental and integrative biology; systematics; ecology and evolutionary biology. Total annual research expenditures: $10.5 million. *Unit head:* Dr. Marcia Newcomer, Chair, 225-578-2601, Fax: 225-578-2597. *Application contact:* Dr. Jacqueline Stephens, Associate Chairman, 225-578-1240, Fax: 225-578-7299, E-mail: biogradcoord@lsu.edu.

Louisiana State University Health Sciences Center at Shreveport, Department of Biochemistry and Molecular Biology, Shreveport, LA 71130-3932. Offers MS, PhD, MD/PhD. *Degree requirements:* For master's, thesis; for doctorate, thesis/dissertation. *Entrance requirements:* For master's and doctorate, GRE General Test. Additional exam requirements/recommendations for international students: Required—TOEFL. *Faculty research:* Metabolite transport, regulation of translation and transcription, prokaryotic molecular genetics, cell matrix biochemistry, yeast molecular genetics, oncogenes.

Loyola University Chicago, Graduate School, Program in Molecular and Cellular Biochemistry, Chicago, IL 60660. Offers MS, PhD, MD/PhD. *Faculty:* 23 full-time (11 women). *Students:* 16 full-time (9 women); includes 1 minority (Asian American or Pacific Islander), 6 international. Average age 27. 37 applicants, 11% accepted, 2 enrolled. In 2009, 2 doctorates awarded. *Degree requirements:* For master's, oral and written reports; for doctorate, comprehensive exam, thesis/dissertation. *Entrance requirements:* For master's and doctorate, GRE General Test. Additional exam requirements/recommendations for international students: Required—TOEFL (minimum score 600 paper-based; 250 computer-based). *Application deadline:* For fall admission, 3/30 priority date for domestic students, 3/30 for international students. Applications are processed on a rolling basis. Application fee: $50. Electronic applications accepted. *Expenses:* Tuition: Full-time $14,220; part-time $790 per credit hour. Required fees: $60 per semester hour. Tuition and fees vary according to program. *Financial support:* In 2009–10, 5 students received support, including 5 fellowships with full tuition reimbursements available, 11 research assistantships with full tuition reimbursements available; Federal Work-Study, institutionally sponsored loans, and scholarships/grants also available. Financial award application deadline: 3/30. *Faculty research:* Molecular oncology, molecular neurochemical mechanisms of brain development and alcohol addiction, biochemistry of RNA and protein synthesis and intracellular protein degradation, developmentally regulated genes, neurotransmitters and cell-cell interactions. *Unit head:* Dr. William H. Simmons, Chief, Division of Molecular and Cellular Biochemistry, 708-216-3362, Fax: 708-216-8523, E-mail: hsimmon@lumc.edu. *Application contact:* Ashyia D. Paul, Administrative Secretary, 708-216-3360, Fax: 708-216-8523, E-mail: apaul@lumc.edu.

Massachusetts Institute of Technology, School of Science, Department of Biology, Cambridge, MA 02139-4307. Offers biochemistry (PhD); biological oceanography (PhD); biology (PhD); biophysical chemistry and molecular structure (PhD); cell biology (PhD); computational and systems biology (PhD); developmental biology (PhD); genetics (PhD); immunology (PhD); microbiology (PhD); molecular biology (PhD); neurobiology (PhD). *Faculty:* 54 full-time (14 women). *Students:* 237 full-time (128 women); includes 65 minority (4 African Americans, 2 American Indian/Alaska Native, 33 Asian Americans or Pacific Islanders, 26 Hispanic Americans), 25 international. Average age 26. 645 applicants, 18% accepted, 49 enrolled. In 2009, 41 doctorates awarded. *Degree requirements:* For doctorate, comprehensive exam, thesis/dissertation. *Entrance requirements:* For doctorate, GRE General Test. Additional exam requirements/recommendations for international students: Required—TOEFL (minimum score 577 paper-based; 233 computer-based), IELTS (minimum score 6.5). *Application deadline:* For fall admission, 12/1 for domestic and international students. Application fee: $75. Electronic applications accepted. *Expenses:* Tuition: Full-time $37,510; part-time $585 per unit. Required fees: $272. *Financial support:* In 2009–10, 218 students received support, including 113 fellowships with tuition reimbursements available (averaging $31,816 per year), 109 research assistantships with tuition reimbursements available (averaging $29,254 per year); teaching assistantships with tuition reimbursements available, Federal Work-Study, institutionally sponsored loans, scholarships/grants, traineeships, health care benefits, and unspecified assistantships also available. *Faculty research:* DNA recombination, transcription and gene regulation, signal transduction, cell cycle, neuronal cell fate, replication and repair. Total annual research expenditures: $114 million. *Unit head:* Prof. Chris Kaiser, Head, 617-253-4701, E-mail: mitbio@mit.edu. *Application contact:* Biology Education Office, 617-253-3717, Fax: 617-258-9329, E-mail: gradbio@mit.edu.

Massachusetts Institute of Technology, School of Science, Department of Chemistry, Cambridge, MA 02139-4307. Offers biological chemistry (PhD, Sc D); inorganic chemistry (PhD, Sc D); organic chemistry (PhD, Sc D); physical chemistry (PhD, Sc D). *Faculty:* 29 full-time (7 women). *Students:* 219 full-time (79 women); includes 39 minority (4 African Americans, 27 Asian Americans or Pacific Islanders, 8 Hispanic Americans), 62 international. Average age 26. 548 applicants, 20% accepted, 19 enrolled. In 2009, 43 doctorates awarded. *Degree requirements:* For doctorate, comprehensive exam, thesis/dissertation, 2 terms as a teaching assistant. *Entrance requirements:* For doctorate, GRE General Test. Additional exam requirements/recommendations for international students: Required—IELTS (minimum score 7); Recommended—TOEFL (minimum score 600 paper-based; 250 computer-based). *Application deadline:* For fall admission, 12/15 for domestic and international students. Application fee: $75. Electronic applications accepted. *Expenses:* Tuition: Full-time $37,510; part-time $585 per unit. Required fees: $272. *Financial support:* In 2009–10, 219 students received support, including 57 fellowships with tuition reimbursements available (averaging $34,547 per year), 132 research assistantships with tuition reimbursements available (averaging $29,403 per year), 27 teaching assistantships with tuition reimbursements available (averaging $30,452 per year); Federal Work-Study, institutionally sponsored loans, scholarships/grants, health care benefits, and unspecified assistantships also available. *Faculty research:* Synthetic organic and inorganic chemistry, biomolecular reactions and structure, multidimensional spectroscopy and chemical dynamics, inorganic, organometallic, organic chemical catalysis, materials chemistry including nanoscience and polymers. Total annual research expenditures: $29.1 million. *Unit head:* Prof. Timothy M. Swager, Head, 617-253-1803, Fax: 617-258-7500. *Application contact:* Graduate Administrator, 617-253-1845, Fax: 617-258-0241, E-mail: chemgradeducation@mit.edu.

Mayo Graduate School, Graduate Programs in Biomedical Sciences, Programs in Biochemistry, Structural Biology, Cell Biology, and Genetics, Rochester, MN 55905. Offers biochemistry and structural biology (PhD); cell biology and genetics (PhD); molecular biology (PhD). *Degree requirements:* For doctorate, oral defense of dissertation, qualifying oral and written exam. *Entrance requirements:* For doctorate, GRE, 1 year of chemistry, biology, calculus, and physics. Additional exam requirements/recommendations for international students: Required—TOEFL. Electronic applications accepted. *Faculty research:* Gene structure and function, membranes and receptors/cytoskeleton, oncogenes and growth factors, protein structure and function, steroid hormonal action.

McGill University, Faculty of Graduate and Postdoctoral Studies, Faculty of Medicine, Department of Biochemistry, Montréal, QC H3A 2T5, Canada. Offers M Sc, PhD.

McGill University, Faculty of Graduate and Postdoctoral Studies, Faculty of Science, Department of Chemistry, Montréal, QC H3A 2T5, Canada. Offers chemical biology (M Sc, PhD); chemistry (M Sc, PhD).

McMaster University, Faculty of Health Sciences, Department of Biochemistry and Biomedical Sciences, Hamilton, ON L8S 4M2, Canada. Offers M Sc, PhD. Terminal master's awarded for partial completion of doctoral program. *Degree requirements:* For master's, thesis; for doctorate, comprehensive exam, thesis/dissertation. *Entrance requirements:* For master's and doctorate, minimum B+ average. Additional exam requirements/recommendations for international students: Required—TOEFL (minimum score 550 paper-based; 213 computer-based). *Faculty research:* Molecular and cell biology, biomolecular structure and function, molecular pharmacology and toxicology.

Medical College of Georgia, School of Graduate Studies, Program in Biochemistry and Molecular Biology, Augusta, GA 30912. Offers PhD. *Degree requirements:* For doctorate, comprehensive exam, thesis/dissertation. *Entrance requirements:* For doctorate, GRE General Test. Additional exam requirements/recommendations for international students: Required—TOEFL (minimum score 550 paper-based; 213 computer-based; 79 iBT). Electronic applications accepted. Full-time tuition and fees vary according to campus/location, program and student level. *Faculty research:* Bacterial pathogenesis, eye diseases, vitamins and amino acid transporters, transcriptional control and molecular oncology, tumor biology.

Medical College of Wisconsin, Graduate School of Biomedical Sciences, Department of Biochemistry, Milwaukee, WI 53226-0509. Offers PhD, MD/PhD. *Degree requirements:* For doctorate, comprehensive exam, thesis/dissertation. *Entrance requirements:* For doctorate, GRE General Test, GRE Subject Test. Additional exam requirements/recommendations for international students: Required—TOEFL. *Faculty research:* Enzymology, macromolecular structure and synthesis, nucleic acids, molecular and cell biology.

Medical University of South Carolina, College of Graduate Studies, Department of Biochemistry and Molecular Biology, Charleston, SC 29425. Offers MS, PhD, MD/PhD. *Faculty:* 21 full-time (3 women), 3 part-time/adjunct (1 woman). *Students:* 19 full-time (9 women), 2 part-time (0 women); includes 1 Asian American or Pacific Islander, 1 Hispanic American, 4 international. Average age 29. 9 applicants, 22% accepted, 2 enrolled. In 2009, 2 master's, 4 doctorates awarded. Terminal master's awarded for partial completion of doctoral program. *Degree requirements:* For master's, thesis; for doctorate, thesis/dissertation, oral and written exams. *Entrance requirements:* For master's, GRE General Test; for doctorate, GRE General Test, interview, minimum GPA of 3.0. Additional exam requirements/recommendations for international students: Required—TOEFL (minimum score 600 paper-based; 250 computer-based; 100 iBT). *Application deadline:* For fall admission, 1/15 priority date for domestic and international students. Applications are processed on a rolling basis. Application fee: $0 ($85 for international students). Electronic applications accepted. *Financial support:* In 2009–10, 17 research assistantships with partial tuition reimbursements (averaging $23,000 per year) were awarded; Federal Work-Study and scholarships/grants also available. Support available to part-time students. Financial award application deadline: 3/10; financial award applicants required to submit FAFSA. *Faculty research:* Lipid biochemistry, DNA replication, nucleic acids, protein structure. *Unit head:* Dr. Yusuf A. Hannun, Chairman, 843-792-9318, Fax: 843-792-6590, E-mail: hannun@musc.edu. *Application contact:* Dr. Maurizio Del Poeta, Associate Professor, 843-792-8381, Fax: 843-792-6590, E-mail: delpoeta@musc.edu.

Memorial University of Newfoundland, School of Graduate Studies, Department of Biochemistry, St. John's, NL A1C 5S7, Canada. Offers biochemistry (M Sc, PhD); food science (M Sc, PhD). Part-time programs available. *Degree requirements:* For master's, thesis; for doctorate, comprehensive exam, thesis/dissertation, oral defense of thesis. *Entrance requirements:* For master's, 2nd class degree in related field; for doctorate, M Sc. Electronic applications accepted. *Faculty research:* Toxicology, cell and molecular biology, food engineering, marine biotechnology, lipid biology.

Miami University, Graduate School, College of Arts and Science, Department of Chemistry and Biochemistry, Oxford, OH 45056. Offers MS, PhD. *Students:* 66 full-time (29 women), 2 part-time (0 women); includes 4 minority (2 African Americans, 1 Asian American or Pacific Islander, 1 Hispanic American), 30 international. *Entrance requirements:* For master's, minimum undergraduate GPA of 3.0 during previous 2 years or 2.75 overall; for doctorate, minimum undergraduate GPA of 2.75, 3.0 graduate. Additional exam requirements/recommendations for international students: Required—TOEFL. *Application deadline:* Applications are processed on a rolling basis. Application fee: $50. Electronic applications accepted. *Expenses:* Tuition, state resident: full-time $11,280. Tuition, nonresident: full-time $24,912. Required fees: $516. *Financial support:* Fellowships with full tuition reimbursements, research assistantships with full tuition reimbursements, teaching assistantships with full tuition reimbursements, Federal Work-Study, institutionally sponsored loans, tuition waivers (full), and unspecified assistantships available. Financial award application deadline: 3/1; financial award applicants required to submit FAFSA. *Unit head:* Dr. Chris Makaroff, Chair, 513-529-1659, E-mail: makaroca@muohio.edu. *Application contact:* Dr. Michael Crowder, Chair, Graduate Admissions Committee, 513-529-7274, E-mail: crowdermw@muohio.edu.

Michigan State University, College of Human Medicine and The Graduate School, Graduate Programs in Human Medicine, East Lansing, MI 48824. Offers biochemistry and molecular biology (MS, PhD); epidemiology (MS, PhD); microbiology (MS); microbiology and molecular genetics (PhD); pharmacology and toxicology (MS, PhD); physiology (MS, PhD); public health (MPH). *Students:* 58 full-time (31 women), 31 part-time (25 women); includes 17 minority (7 African Americans, 1 American Indian/Alaska Native, 6 Asian Americans or Pacific Islanders, 3 Hispanic Americans), 22 international. Average age 30. In 2009, 8 master's, 9 doctorates awarded. *Entrance requirements:* Additional exam requirements/recommendations for international students: Required—TOEFL. *Expenses:* Tuition, state resident: part-time $478.25 per credit hour. Tuition, nonresident: part-time $966.50 per credit hour. Part-time tuition and fees vary according to program. *Financial support:* In 2009–10, 17 research assistantships with tuition reimbursements (averaging $7,053 per year), 3 teaching assistantships with tuition reimbursements (averaging $6,607 per year) were awarded. *Unit head:* Margo K. Smith, Director of Graduate Studies, 517-432-5112, E-mail: smithmk@msu.edu. *Application contact:* Margo K. Smith, Director of Graduate Studies, 517-432-5112, E-mail: smithmk@msu.edu.

Biochemistry

Michigan State University, College of Osteopathic Medicine and The Graduate School, Graduate Studies in Osteopathic Medicine, East Lansing, MI 48824. Offers biochemistry and molecular biology (MS, PhD); microbiology (MS); microbiology and molecular genetics (PhD); pharmacology and toxicology (MS, PhD), including integrative pharmacology (MS), pharmacology and toxicology, pharmacology and toxicology-environmental toxicology (PhD); physiology (MS, PhD). *Students:* 6 full-time (1 woman), 39 part-time (22 women); includes 8 minority (2 African Americans, 2 Asian Americans or Pacific Islanders, 4 Hispanic Americans), 3 international. Average age 30. *Expenses:* Tuition, state resident: part-time $478.25 per credit hour. Tuition, nonresident: part-time $966.50 per credit hour. Part-time tuition and fees vary according to program. *Financial support:* In 2009–10, 1 research assistantship with tuition reimbursement (averaging $7,894 per year) was awarded. *Application contact:* Bethany Heinlen, Information Contact, 517-353-7785, Fax: 517-353-9004, E-mail: heinlen@msu.edu.

Michigan State University, The Graduate School, College of Natural Science and Graduate Programs in Human Medicine and Graduate Studies in Osteopathic Medicine, Department of Biochemistry and Molecular Biology, East Lansing, MI 48824. Offers biochemistry and molecular biology (MS, PhD); biochemistry and molecular biology/environmental toxicology (PhD). *Faculty:* 26 full-time (5 women). *Students:* 64 full-time (26 women); includes 2 minority (1 African American, 1 Asian American or Pacific Islander), 38 international. Average age 27. 111 applicants, 9% accepted. In 2009, 10 doctorates awarded. *Entrance requirements:* Additional exam requirements/recommendations for international students: Required—TOEFL. Electronic applications accepted. *Expenses:* Tuition, state resident: part-time $478.25 per credit hour. Tuition, nonresident: part-time $966.50 per credit hour. Part-time tuition and fees vary according to program. *Financial support:* In 2009–10, 48 research assistantships with tuition reimbursements (averaging $8,017 per year), 3 teaching assistantships with tuition reimbursements (averaging $8,033 per year) were awarded; scholarships/grants and unspecified assistantships also available. Total annual research expenditures: $6.4 million. *Unit head:* Dr. Thomas Sharkey, Chairperson, 517-353-0804, Fax: 517-353-9334, E-mail: tsharkey@msu.edu. *Application contact:* Jessica Lawrence, Graduate Program Secretary, 517-353-0807, Fax: 517-353-9334, E-mail: bmbgrad@cns.msu.edu.

Mississippi College, Graduate School, College of Arts and Sciences, School of Science and Mathematics, Department of Chemistry and Biochemistry, Clinton, MS 39058. Offers MCS, MS. Part-time programs available. *Faculty:* 2 full-time (0 women), 1 (woman) part-time/adjunct. *Students:* 6 full-time (1 woman), 7 part-time (3 women), 12 international. Average age 23. In 2009, 4 master's awarded. *Degree requirements:* For master's, comprehensive exam, thesis (for some programs). *Entrance requirements:* For master's, GRE. Additional exam requirements/recommendations for international students: Recommended—IELTS. *Application deadline:* For fall admission, 8/15 priority date for domestic students. Applications are processed on a rolling basis. Application fee: $30. Electronic applications accepted. *Expenses:* Tuition: Part-time $452 per credit hour. Required fees: $101 per semester. Tuition and fees vary according to degree level, campus/location, program and student level. *Financial support:* Federal Work-Study and unspecified assistantships available. Support available to part-time students. Financial award applicants required to submit FAFSA. *Unit head:* Dr. Jerry Cannon, Chair, 601-925-3425, E-mail: cannon@mc.edu. *Application contact:* Elnora Lewis, Secretary, 601-925-3225, Fax: 601-925-3889, E-mail: lewis09@mc.edu.

Mississippi State University, College of Agriculture and Life Sciences, Department of Biochemistry and Molecular Biology, Mississippi State, MS 39762. Offers agriculture life sciences (MS), including biochemistry; molecular biology (PhD). *Faculty:* 7 full-time (0 women). *Students:* 23 full-time (7 women), 4 part-time (3 women); includes 3 minority (1 African American, 1 American Indian/Alaska Native, 1 Asian American or Pacific Islander), 14 international. Average age 27. 20 applicants, 40% accepted, 2 enrolled. In 2009, 2 master's, 3 doctorates awarded. Terminal master's awarded for partial completion of doctoral program. *Degree requirements:* For master's, thesis (for some programs), comprehensive oral or written exam; for doctorate, thesis/dissertation, comprehensive oral and written exam. *Entrance requirements:* For master's, GRE General Test, minimum GPA of 2.75; for doctorate, GRE. Additional exam requirements/recommendations for international students: Required—TOEFL (minimum score 550 paper-based; 213 computer-based; 79 iBT); Recommended—IELTS (minimum score 6.5). *Application deadline:* For fall admission, 7/1 for domestic students, 5/1 for international students; for spring admission, 11/1 for domestic students, 9/1 for international students. Applications are processed on a rolling basis. Application fee: $40. Electronic applications accepted. *Expenses:* Tuition, state resident: full-time $2575.50; part-time $286.25 per credit hour. Tuition, nonresident: full-time $6510; part-time $723.50 per credit hour. Tuition and fees vary according to course load. *Financial support:* In 2009–10, 16 research assistantships with full tuition reimbursements (averaging $11,115 per year) were awarded; Federal Work-Study, institutionally sponsored loans, and unspecified assistantships also available. Financial award applicants required to submit FAFSA. *Faculty research:* Fish nutrition, plant and animal molecular biology, plant biochemistry, enzymology, lipid metabolism. *Unit head:* Dr. Scott T. Willard, Professor and Department Head, 662-325-2640, Fax: 662-325-8664, E-mail: swilliard@ads.msstate.edu. *Application contact:* Dr. Din-Pow Ma, Professor/Graduate Coordinator, 662-325-7739, Fax: 662-325-8664, E-mail: dm1@ra.msstate.edu.

Montana State University, College of Graduate Studies, College of Letters and Science, Department of Chemistry and Biochemistry, Bozeman, MT 59717. Offers biochemistry (MS, PhD); chemistry (MS, PhD). Part-time programs available. *Faculty:* 16 full-time (3 women), 11 part-time/adjunct (6 women). *Students:* 1 full-time (0 women), 68 part-time (22 women); includes 1 minority (Asian American or Pacific Islander), 12 international. Average age 27. 1 applicant, 100% accepted, 0 enrolled. In 2009, 2 master's, 4 doctorates awarded. *Degree requirements:* For master's, comprehensive exam, thesis (for some programs); for doctorate, comprehensive exam, thesis/dissertation. *Entrance requirements:* For master's, GRE General Test, letters of recommendation; for doctorate, GRE General Test, transcripts, letters of recommendation. Additional exam requirements/recommendations for international students: Required—TOEFL (minimum score 550 paper-based; 213 computer-based). *Application deadline:* For fall admission, 7/15 priority date for domestic students, 5/15 priority date for international students; for spring admission, 12/1 priority date for domestic students, 10/1 priority date for international students. Applications are processed on a rolling basis. Application fee: $30. Electronic applications accepted. *Expenses:* Tuition, state resident: full-time $5635; part-time $3492 per year. Tuition, nonresident: full-time $17,212; part-time $7865.10 per year. Required fees: $1441; $153.15 per credit. Tuition and fees vary according to course load and program. *Financial support:* In 2009–10, 68 students received support, including 5 fellowships with tuition reimbursements available (averaging $30,000 per year), 28 research assistantships with tuition reimbursements available (averaging $22,000 per year), 35 teaching assistantships with tuition reimbursements available (averaging $22,000 per year). Financial award application deadline: 3/1; financial award applicants required to submit FAFSA. *Faculty research:* Structural biology and proteomics, ultrafast optical spectroscopy and gas-surface dynamics, nanomaterials, natural products chemistry and organic synthesis, metals in biology. Total annual research expenditures: $10 million. *Unit head:* Dr. David Singel, Interim Department Head, 406-994-3960, Fax: 406-994-5407, E-mail: rchds@montana.edu. *Application contact:* Dr. Carl A. Fox, Vice Provost for Graduate Education, 406-994-4145, Fax: 406-994-7433, E-mail: gradstudy@montana.edu.

Montclair State University, The Graduate School, College of Science and Mathematics, Department of Chemistry and Biochemistry, Montclair, NJ 07043-1624. Offers chemical business (MS); chemistry (MS), including biochemistry; MS/MBA. Part-time and evening/weekend programs available. *Faculty:* 14 full-time (3 women), 3 part-time/adjunct (2 women). *Students:* 10 full-time (2 women), 23 part-time (13 women). Average age 28. 16 applicants, 56% accepted, 7 enrolled. In 2009, 8 master's awarded. *Degree requirements:* For master's, comprehensive exam. *Entrance requirements:* For master's, GRE General Test, 24 credits of course work in undergraduate chemistry, 2 letters of recommendation. Additional exam requirements/recommendations for international students: Required—TOEFL (minimum score: 83 iBT) or IELTS. *Application deadline:* For fall admission, 6/1 for international students; for spring admission, 10/1 for international students. Applications are processed on a rolling basis. Application fee: $60. Electronic applications accepted. *Expenses:* Tuition, area resident: Part-time $486.74 per credit. Tuition, state resident: part-time $486.74 per credit. Tuition, nonresident: part-time $751.34 per credit. Tuition and fees vary according to degree level and program. *Financial support:* In 2009–10, 6 research assistantships with full tuition reimbursements (averaging $7,000 per year) were awarded; Federal Work-Study, scholarships/grants, and unspecified assistantships also available. Support available to part-time students. Financial award application deadline: 3/1; financial award applicants required to submit FAFSA. *Faculty research:* Antimicrobial compounds, marine bacteria. *Unit head:* Dr. Marc Kasner, Chair, 973-655-6864. *Application contact:* Amy Aiello, Director of Graduate Admissions and Operations, 973-655-5147, E-mail: graduate.school@montclair.edu.

New Mexico Institute of Mining and Technology, Graduate Studies, Department of Chemistry, Socorro, NM 87801. Offers biochemistry (MS); chemistry (MS); environmental chemistry (PhD); explosives technology and atmospheric chemistry (PhD). Part-time programs available. *Degree requirements:* For master's, thesis; for doctorate, thesis/dissertation. *Entrance requirements:* For master's, GRE General Test; for doctorate, GRE General Test, GRE Subject Test. Additional exam requirements/recommendations for international students: Required—TOEFL (minimum score 540 paper-based; 207 computer-based). Electronic applications accepted. *Faculty research:* Organic, analytical, environmental, and explosives chemistry.

New Mexico State University, Graduate School, College of Arts and Sciences, Department of Chemistry and Biochemistry, Las Cruces, NM 88003-8001. Offers MS, PhD. Part-time programs available. *Faculty:* 16 full-time (3 women), 1 (woman) part-time/adjunct. *Students:* 47 full-time (11 women), 7 part-time (3 women); includes 9 minority (1 African American, 1 American Indian/Alaska Native, 2 Asian Americans or Pacific Islanders, 5 Hispanic Americans), 35 international. Average age 29. 99 applicants, 67% accepted, 20 enrolled. In 2009, 4 master's, 6 doctorates awarded. *Degree requirements:* For master's, comprehensive exam, thesis; for doctorate, comprehensive exam, thesis/dissertation. *Entrance requirements:* For master's and doctorate, GRE, BS in chemistry or biochemistry, minimum GPA of 3.0. Additional exam requirements/recommendations for international students: Required—TOEFL (minimum score 600 paper-based; 250 computer-based). *Application deadline:* For fall admission, 7/1 priority date for domestic students, 3/1 priority date for international students; for spring admission, 11/1 for domestic students. Applications are processed on a rolling basis. Application fee: $30 ($50 for international students). Electronic applications accepted. *Expenses:* Tuition, state resident: full-time $4080; part-time $223 per credit. Tuition, nonresident: full-time $14,256; part-time $647 per credit. Required fees: $1278; $639 per semester. *Financial support:* In 2009–10, 19 research assistantships with tuition reimbursements (averaging $12,356 per year), 27 teaching assistantships with tuition reimbursements (averaging $16,747 per year) were awarded; fellowships with tuition reimbursements, career-related internships or fieldwork, Federal Work-Study, and health care benefits also available. Support available to part-time students. Financial award application deadline: 4/1. *Faculty research:* Clays, surfaces, and water structure; electroanalytical and environmental chemistry; organometallic synthesis and organobiomimetics; molecular genetics, DNA recombination mechanisms, and NMR spectroscopy of protein interactions; spectroscopy and reaction kinetics. *Unit head:* Dr. Glenn D. Kuehn, Head, 575-646-5877, Fax: 575-646-2649, E-mail: gkuehn@nmsu.edu. *Application contact:* Dr. Cynthia Zoski, Associate Professor, Chemistry, 575-646-5292, Fax: 575-646-2649, E-mail: czoski@nmsu.edu.

New York Medical College, Graduate School of Basic Medical Sciences, Program in Biochemistry and Molecular Biology, Valhalla, NY 10595-1691. Offers MS, PhD, MD/PhD. Part-time and evening/weekend programs available. Terminal master's awarded for partial completion of doctoral program. *Degree requirements:* For master's, thesis; for doctorate, comprehensive exam, thesis/dissertation. *Entrance requirements:* For master's and doctorate, GRE General Test. Additional exam requirements/recommendations for international students: Required—TOEFL. *Expenses:* Tuition: Full-time $18,170; part-time $790 per credit. Required fees: $790 per credit. $20 per semester. One-time fee: $100. Tuition and fees vary according to class time, course level, course load, degree level, program, student level and student's religious affiliation. *Faculty research:* Mechanisms of control of blood coagulation, molecular neurobiology, molecular probes for infectious disease, protein-DNA interactions, molecular biology and biochemistry of double-stranded RNA-dependent enzymes.

North Carolina State University, Graduate School, College of Agriculture and Life Sciences, Department of Biochemistry, Raleigh, NC 27695. Offers PhD. *Degree requirements:* For doctorate, thesis/dissertation. *Entrance requirements:* For doctorate, GRE General Test. Additional exam requirements/recommendations for international students: Required—TOEFL. Electronic applications accepted. *Faculty research:* Regulation of gene expression, structure and function of proteins and nucleic acids, molecular biology, high-field NMR, bioinorganic chemistry.

North Dakota State University, College of Graduate and Interdisciplinary Studies, College of Science and Mathematics, Department of Biochemistry and Molecular Biology, Program in Biochemistry, Fargo, ND 58108. Offers MS, PhD. Part-time programs available. *Faculty:* 5 full-time (0 women). *Students:* 10 full-time (5 women), 2 part-time (both women), 8 international. Average age 24. 13 applicants, 62% accepted, 6 enrolled. In 2009, 1 master's awarded. *Degree requirements:* For master's, thesis; for doctorate, thesis/dissertation. *Entrance requirements:* Additional exam requirements/recommendations for international students: Required—TOEFL (minimum score 550 paper-based). *Application deadline:* For fall admission, 4/15 priority date for domestic students. Applications are processed on a rolling basis. Application fee: $45 ($60 for international students). *Financial support:* In 2009–10, 4 research assistantships with full tuition reimbursements (averaging $19,000 per year), 5 teaching assistantships with full tuition reimbursements (averaging $19,000 per year) were awarded; career-related internships or fieldwork, Federal Work-Study, and institutionally sponsored loans also available. Financial award application deadline: 4/15. *Unit head:* Dr. John Hershberger, Chair, 701-231-7678, Fax: 701-231-8831, E-mail: john.hershberger@ndsu.edu. *Application contact:* Dr. Seth Rasmussen, Chair, Graduate Admissions, 701-231-8747, Fax: 701-231-8831, E-mail: seth.rasmussen@ndsu.edu.

Northeastern University, College of Science, Department of Chemistry and Chemical Biology, Boston, MA 02115-5096. Offers analytical chemistry (PhD); chemistry (MS, PhD); inorganic chemistry (PhD); organic chemistry (PhD); physical chemistry (PhD). Part-time and evening/weekend programs available. *Faculty:* 24 full-time (5 women), 7 part-time/adjunct (0 women). *Students:* 86 full-time (48 women), 31 part-time (14 women); includes 9 minority (1 African American, 1 American Indian/Alaska Native, 7 Asian Americans or Pacific Islanders), 36 international. 190 applicants, 22% accepted, 15 enrolled. In 2009, 17 master's, 9 doctorates awarded. Terminal master's awarded for partial completion of doctoral program. *Degree requirements:* For master's, thesis (for some programs); for doctorate, thesis/dissertation, qualifying exam in specialty area. *Entrance requirements:* Additional exam requirements/recommendations for international students: Required—TOEFL. *Application deadline:* For fall admission, 2/1 priority date for domestic and international students. Applications are processed on a rolling basis. Application fee: $50. Electronic applications accepted. *Financial support:* In 2009–10, 41 research assistantships with tuition reimbursements (averaging $18,285 per year), 38 teaching assistantships with tuition reimbursements (averaging $18,285 per year) were awarded; fellowships with tuition reimbursements, career-related internships or fieldwork, Federal Work-Study, scholarships/grants, tuition waivers (partial), and unspecified assistantships also available. Financial award application deadline: 3/1; financial award applicants required to submit FAFSA. *Faculty research:* Bioanalysis, biorganic and medicinal chemistry, biophysical chemistry, nanomaterials, proteonics. *Unit head:* Dr. Robert Hanson, Graduate Coordinator, 617-373-3313, Fax: 617-373-8795, E-mail: chemistry-grad-info@neu.edu. *Application contact:* Jo-Anne Dickinson, Admissions Contact, 617-373-5990, Fax: 617-373-7281, E-mail: gsas@neu.edu.

Northwestern University, The Graduate School and Judd A. and Marjorie Weinberg College of Arts and Sciences, Interdepartmental Biological Sciences Program (IBiS), Evanston, IL

60208. Offers biochemistry, molecular biology, and cell biology (PhD), including biochemistry, cell and molecular biology, molecular biophysics, structural biology; biotechnology (PhD); cell and molecular biology (PhD); developmental biology and genetics (PhD); hormone action and signal transduction (PhD); neuroscience (PhD); structural biology, biochemistry, and biophysics (PhD). Program participants include the Departments of Biochemistry, Molecular Biology, and Cell Biology; Chemistry; Neurobiology and Physiology; Chemical Engineering; Civil Engineering; and Evanston Hospital. *Degree requirements:* For doctorate, thesis/dissertation, qualifying exam. *Entrance requirements:* For doctorate, GRE General Test. Additional exam requirements/recommendations for international students: Required—TOEFL (minimum score 600 paper-based). Electronic applications accepted. *Faculty research:* Developmental genetics, gene regulation, DNA-protein interactions, biological clocks, bioremediation.

Northwestern University, Northwestern University Feinberg School of Medicine and Interdepartmental Programs, Integrated Graduate Programs in the Life Sciences, Chicago, IL 60611. Offers cancer biology (PhD); cell biology (PhD); developmental biology (PhD); evolutionary biology (PhD); immunology and microbial pathogenesis (PhD); molecular biology and genetics (PhD); neurobiology (PhD); pharmacology and toxicology (PhD); structural biology and biochemistry (PhD). *Degree requirements:* For doctorate, comprehensive exam, thesis/dissertation, written and oral qualifying exams. *Entrance requirements:* For doctorate, GRE General Test. Additional exam requirements/recommendations for international students: Required—TOEFL (minimum score 600 paper-based; 250 computer-based). Electronic applications accepted.

OGI School of Science & Engineering at Oregon Health & Science University, Graduate Studies, Department of Environmental and Biomolecular Systems, Beaverton, OR 97006-8921. Offers biochemistry and molecular biology (MS, PhD); environmental health systems (MS); environmental information technology (MS, PhD); environmental science and engineering (MS, PhD). Part-time programs available. Terminal master's awarded for partial completion of doctoral program. *Degree requirements:* For master's, thesis optional; for doctorate, comprehensive exam, oral defense of dissertation. *Entrance requirements:* For master's and doctorate, GRE General Test. Additional exam requirements/recommendations for international students: Required—TOEFL. Electronic applications accepted. *Faculty research:* Air and water science, hydrogeology, estuarine and coastal modeling, environmental microbiology, contaminant transport, biochemistry, biomolecular systems.

The Ohio State University, Graduate School, Ohio State Biochemistry Program, Columbus, OH 43210. Offers MS, PhD. *Faculty:* 100. *Students:* 40 full-time (18 women), 43 part-time (19 women); includes 3 minority (all African Americans), 51 international. Average age 27. In 2009, 4 master's, 6 doctorates awarded. *Degree requirements:* For master's, thesis optional. *Entrance requirements:* For master's, GRE General Test. Additional exam requirements/recommendations for international students: Required—TOEFL (minimum score 620 paper-based; 250 computer-based). *Application deadline:* Applications are processed on a rolling basis. Application fee: $40 ($50 for international students). Electronic applications accepted. *Expenses:* Tuition, state resident: full-time $10,683. Tuition, nonresident: full-time $25,923. Tuition and fees vary according to course load and program. *Financial support:* Fellowships, research assistantships, teaching assistantships available. *Unit head:* Jill Rafael-Fortney, Program Director, 614-292-1463, Fax: 614-292-6511, E-mail: rafael-fortney.1@osu.edu. *Application contact:* 614-292-9444, Fax: 614-292-3895, E-mail: domestic.grad@osu.edu.

Ohio University, Graduate College, College of Arts and Sciences, Department of Chemistry and Biochemistry, Athens, OH 45701-2979. Offers MS, PhD. *Faculty:* 18 full-time (4 women), 2 part-time/adjunct (0 women). *Students:* 59 full-time (27 women), 7 part-time (2 women); includes 3 minority (1 African American, 1 American Indian/Alaska Native, 1 Asian American or Pacific Islander), 46 international. 138 applicants, 17% accepted, 19 enrolled. In 2009, 1 master's, 5 doctorates awarded. *Degree requirements:* For master's, comprehensive exam, thesis, exam; for doctorate, comprehensive exam, thesis/dissertation, exam. *Entrance requirements:* For master's and doctorate, GRE. Additional exam requirements/recommendations for international students: Required—TOEFL (minimum score 550 paper-based; 80 iBT) or IELTS (minimum score 6.5). *Application deadline:* For fall admission, 2/1 priority date for domestic and international students. Application fee: $50 ($55 for international students). Electronic applications accepted. *Expenses:* Tuition, state resident: full-time $7839; part-time $323 per quarter hour. Tuition, nonresident: full-time $15,831; part-time $654 per quarter hour. Required fees: $2931. *Financial support:* Fellowships, research assistantships with full tuition reimbursements, teaching assistantships with full tuition reimbursements, Federal Work-Study and institutionally sponsored loans available. Financial award application deadline: 2/1. *Faculty research:* Materials, RNA, synthesis, carbohydrate, mass spectrometry. Total annual research expenditures: $3.5 million. *Unit head:* Dr. Tadeusz Malinski, Chair, 740-593-1737, Fax: 740-593-0148, E-mail: malinski@ohio.edu. *Application contact:* Dr. Stephen C. Bergmeier, Graduate Chair, 740-597-6949, Fax: 740-593-0148, E-mail: bergmeis@ohio.edu.

Oklahoma State University, College of Agricultural Science and Natural Resources, Department of Biochemistry and Molecular Biology, Stillwater, OK 74078. Offers MS, PhD. *Faculty:* 37 full-time (16 women), 1 part-time/adjunct (0 women). *Students:* 9 full-time (5 women), 27 part-time (17 women); includes 4 minority (1 African American, 2 American Indian/Alaska Native, 1 Hispanic American), 24 international. Average age 27. 86 applicants, 16% accepted, 5 enrolled. In 2009, 3 master's, 1 doctorate awarded. *Degree requirements:* For master's, thesis, oral exam; for doctorate, comprehensive exam, thesis/dissertation. *Entrance requirements:* For master's and doctorate, GRE or GMAT. Additional exam requirements/recommendations for international students: Required—TOEFL (minimum score 550 paper-based; 79 iBT). *Application deadline:* For fall admission, 3/1 priority date for international students; for spring admission, 8/1 priority date for international students. Applications are processed on a rolling basis. Application fee: $40 ($75 for international students). Electronic applications accepted. *Expenses:* Tuition, state resident: full-time $3716; part-time $154.85 per credit hour. Tuition, nonresident: full-time $14,448; part-time $602 per credit hour. Required fees: $1772; $73.85 per credit hour. One-time fee: $50. Tuition and fees vary according to course load and campus/location. *Financial support:* In 2009–10, 36 research assistantships (averaging $17,710 per year), 2 teaching assistantships (averaging $13,614 per year) were awarded; career-related internships or fieldwork, Federal Work-Study, scholarships/grants, health care benefits, tuition waivers (partial), and unspecified assistantships also available. Support available to part-time students. Financial award application deadline: 3/1; financial award applicants required to submit FAFSA. *Unit head:* Dr. Gary Thompson, Head, 405-744-9320, Fax: 405-744-7799. *Application contact:* Dr. Gordon Emslie, Dean, 405-744-6368, Fax: 405-744-0355, E-mail: grad-i@okstate.edu.

Old Dominion University, College of Sciences, Program in Chemistry, Norfolk, VA 23529. Offers analytical chemistry (MS); biochemistry (MS); chemistry (PhD); environmental chemistry (MS); organic chemistry (MS); physical chemistry (MS). Part-time and evening/weekend programs available. *Faculty:* 14 full-time (5 women), 2 part-time/adjunct (0 women). *Students:* 30 full-time (19 women), 10 part-time (5 women); includes 3 minority (1 African American, 1 Asian American or Pacific Islander, 1 Hispanic American), 17 international. Average age 29. 35 applicants, 60% accepted, 8 enrolled. In 2009, 1 degree awarded. *Degree requirements:* For master's, comprehensive exam, thesis. *Entrance requirements:* For master's, GRE General Test, minimum GPA of 3.0 in major, 2.5 overall; for doctorate, GRE General Test. Additional exam requirements/recommendations for international students: Required—TOEFL. *Application deadline:* For fall admission, 7/1 for domestic students, 1/15 for international students; for spring admission, 11/1 for domestic students, 8/15 for international students. Applications are processed on a rolling basis. Application fee: $30. Electronic applications accepted. *Expenses:* Tuition, state resident: full-time $8112; part-time $338 per credit. Tuition, nonresident: full-time $20,256; part-time $844 per credit. Required fees: $119 per semester. One-time fee: $50. *Financial support:* In 2009–10, 6 students received support, including fellowships (averaging $18,000 per year), research assistantships with tuition reimbursements available (averaging $21,000 per year), teaching assistantships with tuition reimbursements available (averaging $18,000 per year); career-related internships or fieldwork, scholarships/grants, and unspecified assistantships also available. Financial award application deadline: 2/15; financial award applicants required to submit FAFSA. *Faculty research:* Biogeochemistry, materials chemistry, bioanalytical chemistry, computational chemistry, organic chemistry. Total annual research expenditures: $2.6 million. *Unit head:* Dr. Craig A. Bayse, Graduate Program Director, 757-683-4097, Fax: 757-683-4628, E-mail: chemgpd@odu.edu. *Application contact:* Valerie DeCosta, Grants and Graduate Program Assistant, 757-683-6979, Fax: 757-683-4628, E-mail: chemgpd@odu.edu.

Oregon Health & Science University, School of Medicine, Graduate Programs in Medicine, Department of Biochemistry and Molecular Biology, Portland, OR 97239-3098. Offers PhD. *Degree requirements:* For doctorate, comprehensive exam, thesis/dissertation, qualifying exam. *Entrance requirements:* For doctorate, GRE General Test (minimum scores: 500 Verbal/600 Quantitative/4.5 Analytical). Additional exam requirements/recommendations for international students: Required—TOEFL. Application fee: $65. Electronic applications accepted. Tuition and fees vary according to course level, course load, degree level, program and reciprocity agreements. *Financial support:* Stipend and paid tuition available. *Faculty research:* Protein structure and function, enzymology, metabolism, membranes transport. *Unit head:* David Farrens, PhD, Program Director, 503-494-7781, E-mail: farrensd@ohsu.edu. *Application contact:* Jeni Wroblewski, Administrative Coordinator, 503-494-2541, E-mail: wroblews@ohsu.edu.

Oregon Health & Science University, School of Medicine, Graduate Programs in Medicine, Department of Environmental and Biomolecular Systems, Portland, OR 97239-3098. Offers biochemistry and molecular biology (MS, PhD); environmental science and engineering (MS, PhD). Part-time programs available. *Degree requirements:* For master's, thesis (for some programs); for doctorate, comprehensive exam, thesis/dissertation. *Entrance requirements:* For master's and doctorate, GRE General Test (minimum scores: 500 Verbal/600 Quantitative/4.5 Analytical) or MCAT (for some programs). Additional exam requirements/recommendations for international students: Required—TOEFL. *Application deadline:* For fall admission, 7/15 for domestic students, 5/15 for international students; for winter admission, 10/15 for domestic students, 9/15 for international students; for spring admission, 1/15 for domestic students, 12/15 for international students. Applications are processed on a rolling basis. Application fee: $65. Electronic applications accepted. Tuition and fees vary according to course level, course load, degree level, program and reciprocity agreements. *Financial support:* PhD students have paid tuition and receive stipends available. *Unit head:* Paul Tratnyek, PhD, Program Director, 503-748-1070, E-mail: info@ebs.ogi.edu. *Application contact:* Nancy Christie, Program Coordinator, 503-748-1070, E-mail: info@ebs.ogi.edu.

Oregon State University, Graduate School, College of Science, Department of Biochemistry and Biophysics, Corvallis, OR 97331. Offers MA, MAIS, MS, PhD. *Faculty:* 9 full-time (1 woman), 1 part-time/adjunct (0 women). *Students:* 19 full-time (7 women); includes 2 minority (1 American Indian/Alaska Native, 1 Asian American or Pacific Islander), 7 international. Average age 27. In 2009, 1 master's, 2 doctorates awarded. *Degree requirements:* For master's, thesis optional; for doctorate, thesis/dissertation, exams. *Entrance requirements:* For master's, GRE General Test, minimum GPA of 3.0; for doctorate, GRE Subject Test, minimum GPA of 3.0. Additional exam requirements/recommendations for international students: Required—TOEFL. *Application deadline:* For fall admission, 4/15 priority date for domestic students. Applications are processed on a rolling basis. Application fee: $50. *Expenses:* Tuition, state resident: full-time $9774; part-time $362 per credit. Tuition, nonresident: full-time $15,849; part-time $587 per credit. Required fees: $1639. Full-time tuition and fees vary according to course load and program. *Financial support:* Research assistantships, teaching assistantships, institutionally sponsored loans available. Support available to part-time students. Financial award application deadline: 2/1. *Faculty research:* DNA and deoxyribonucleotide metabolism, cell growth control, receptors and membranes, protein structure and function. *Unit head:* Dr. Pui Shing Ho, Chair, 541-737-2769, Fax: 541-737-0481. *Application contact:* Dr. W. Curtis Johnson, Chairman, Graduate Committee, 541-737-4511, Fax: 541-737-0481, E-mail: johnsowc@ucs.orst.edu.

Penn State Hershey Medical Center, College of Medicine, Graduate School Programs in the Biomedical Sciences, Graduate Program in Biochemistry and Molecular Biology, Hershey, PA 17033. Offers MS, PhD, MD/PhD. *Students:* 131 applicants, 5% accepted, 3 enrolled. Terminal master's awarded for partial completion of doctoral program. *Degree requirements:* For master's, thesis or alternative; for doctorate, comprehensive exam, thesis/dissertation. *Entrance requirements:* For master's, GRE General Test; for doctorate, GRE General Test, minimum GPA of 3.0. Additional exam requirements/recommendations for international students: Required—TOEFL (minimum score 550 paper-based; 213 computer-based). *Application deadline:* For fall admission, 1/31 priority date for domestic students, 2/1 priority date for international students. Applications are processed on a rolling basis. Application fee: $65. Electronic applications accepted. *Expenses:* Tuition, state resident: part-time $644 per credit. Tuition, nonresident: part-time $1142 per credit. Required fees: $22 per semester. *Financial support:* In 2009–10, research assistantships with full tuition reimbursements (averaging $22,260 per year); fellowships with full tuition reimbursements, scholarships/grants, health care benefits, tuition waivers, and unspecified assistantships also available. Financial award applicants required to submit FAFSA. *Faculty research:* X-ray crystallography of proteins, glycosphingolipid interactions with viruses and toxins, DNA replication and repair, tobacco and environmental carcinogenesis, gene regulation. *Unit head:* Dr. Judith S. Bond, Chair, 717-531-8585, Fax: 717-531-7072, E-mail: bchem-grad-hmc@psu.edu. *Application contact:* Ruth Dean, Administrative Assistant, 717-531-8586, Fax: 717-531-7072, E-mail: bchem-grad-hmc@psu.edu.

Penn State University Park, Graduate School, Eberly College of Science, Department of Biochemistry and Molecular Biology, Program in Biochemistry, Microbiology, and Molecular Biology, State College, University Park, PA 16802-1503. Offers MS, PhD. *Unit head:* Dr. Ronald Porter, Director of Graduate Studies, 814-863-4903, E-mail: rdp1@psu.edu. *Application contact:* Dr. Ronald Porter, Director of Graduate Studies, 814-863-4903, E-mail: rdp1@psu.edu.

Penn State University Park, Graduate School, Intercollege Graduate Programs, State College, University Park, PA 16802-1503. Offers acoustics (M Eng, MS, PhD); bioengineering (MS, PhD); biogeochemistry (dual) (PhD); business administration (MBA); cell and developmental biology (PhD); demography (dual) (MA); ecology (MS, PhD); environmental pollution control (MEPC, MS); genetics (MS, PhD); human dimensions of natural resources and the environment (dual) (MA, MS, PhD); immunology and infectious diseases (MS); integrative biosciences (MS, PhD), including integrative biosciences; materials science and engineering (PhD); operations research (dual) (M Eng, MA, MS, PhD); physiology (MS, PhD); plant physiology (MS, PhD); quality and manufacturing management (MMM). *Students:* 371 full-time (157 women), 22 part-time (7 women). Average age 27. 1,074 applicants, 18% accepted, 130 enrolled. *Entrance requirements:* Additional exam requirements/recommendations for international students: Required—TOEFL (minimum score 550 paper-based; 213 computer-based; 80 iBT). *Application deadline:* Applications are processed on a rolling basis. Application fee: $45. Electronic applications accepted. *Financial support:* Fellowships, research assistantships, teaching assistantships available. Financial award applicants required to submit FAFSA. *Unit head:* Dr. Regina Vasilatos-Younken, Senior Associate Dean, 814-865-2516, Fax: 814-863-4627, E-mail: rxv@psu.edu. *Application contact:* Cynthia E. Nicosia, Director, Graduate Enrollment Services, 814-865-1795, Fax: 814-865-4627, E-mail: cey1@psu.edu.

Purdue University, College of Pharmacy and Pharmacal Sciences and Graduate School, Graduate Programs in Pharmacy and Pharmacal Sciences, Department of Medicinal Chemistry and Molecular Pharmacology, West Lafayette, IN 47907. Offers analytical medicinal chemistry (PhD); computational and biophysical medicinal chemistry (PhD); medicinal and bioorganic chemistry (PhD); medicinal biochemistry and molecular biology (PhD); molecular pharmacology and toxicology (PhD); natural products and pharmacognosy (PhD); nuclear pharmacy (MS); radiopharmaceutical chemistry and nuclear pharmacy (PhD); MS/PhD. Terminal master's awarded for partial completion of doctoral program. *Degree requirements:* For master's,

Biochemistry

Purdue University (continued)
thesis; for doctorate, thesis/dissertation. *Entrance requirements:* For master's, GRE General Test, minimum B average; BS in biology, chemistry, or pharmacy; for doctorate, GRE General Test, minimum B average; BS in biology, chemistry, or pharmacology. Additional exam requirements/recommendations for international students: Required—TOEFL. Electronic applications accepted. *Faculty research:* Drug design and development, cancer research, drug synthesis and analysis, chemical pharmacology, environmental toxicology.

Purdue University, Graduate School, College of Agriculture, Department of Biochemistry, West Lafayette, IN 47907. Offers MS, PhD. Terminal master's awarded for partial completion of doctoral program. *Degree requirements:* For master's, thesis; for doctorate, thesis/dissertation, preliminary and qualifying exams. *Entrance requirements:* For master's and doctorate, GRE General Test. Additional exam requirements/recommendations for international students: Required—TOEFL. Electronic applications accepted. *Faculty research:* Molecular biology and post-translational modifications of neuropeptides, membrane transport proteins.

Queens College of the City University of New York, Division of Graduate Studies, Mathematics and Natural Sciences Division, Department of Chemistry and Biochemistry, Flushing, NY 11367-1597. Offers biochemistry (MA); chemistry (MA). Part-time and evening/weekend programs available. *Faculty:* 14 full-time (4 women). *Students:* 8 part-time (6 women). 13 applicants, 38% accepted, 2 enrolled. In 2009, 4 master's awarded. *Degree requirements:* For master's, comprehensive exam. *Entrance requirements:* For master's, GRE, previous course work in calculus and physics, minimum GPA of 3.0. Additional exam requirements/recommendations for international students: Required—TOEFL. *Application deadline:* For fall admission, 4/1 for domestic students; for spring admission, 11/1 for domestic students. Applications are processed on a rolling basis. Application fee: $125. *Expenses:* Tuition, state resident: full-time $7360; part-time $310 per credit. Tuition, nonresident: part-time $575 per credit. One-time fee: $195 full-time; $145.25 part-time. *Financial support:* Career-related internships or fieldwork, Federal Work-Study, institutionally sponsored loans, and tuition waivers (partial) available. Support available to part-time students. Financial award application deadline: 4/1; financial award applicants required to submit FAFSA. *Unit head:* Dr. William Hersh, Chairperson, 718-997-4144. *Application contact:* Graduate Adviser, 718-997-4100.

Queen's University at Kingston, School of Graduate Studies and Research, Faculty of Health Sciences, Department of Biochemistry, Kingston, ON K7L 3N6, Canada. Offers M Sc, PhD. Part-time programs available. *Degree requirements:* For master's, thesis, research proposal; for doctorate, comprehensive exam, thesis/dissertation, research proposal. *Entrance requirements:* For master's, GRE (if undergraduate degree is not from a Canadian University); for doctorate, GRE required if undergraduate degree is not from a Canadian University. Additional exam requirements/recommendations for international students: Required—TOEFL (minimum score 580 paper-based; 237 computer-based). Electronic applications accepted. *Faculty research:* Gene expression, protein structure, enzyme activity, signal transduction.

Rensselaer Polytechnic Institute, Graduate School, School of Science, Program in Biochemistry and Biophysics, Troy, NY 12180-3590. Offers biochemistry (MS, PhD); biophysics (MS, PhD). Part-time programs available. *Faculty:* 19 full-time (7 women). *Students:* 6 full-time (2 women). 19 applicants, 21% accepted, 3 enrolled. Terminal master's awarded for partial completion of doctoral program. *Degree requirements:* For master's, thesis (for some programs); for doctorate, comprehensive exam, thesis/dissertation. *Entrance requirements:* For master's, GRE General Test, GRE Subject Test (biology, chemistry or biochemistry). Additional exam requirements/recommendations for international students: Required—TOEFL. *Application deadline:* For fall admission, 1/15 priority date for domestic students. Applications are processed on a rolling basis. Application fee: $45. Electronic applications accepted. *Expenses:* Tuition: Full-time $38,100. *Financial support:* In 2009–10, 6 students received support, including 3 research assistantships with full tuition reimbursements available (averaging $16,500 per year), 3 teaching assistantships with full tuition reimbursements available (averaging $16,500 per year); traineeships and unspecified assistantships also available. Financial award application deadline: 2/1. *Faculty research:* Biopolymers, photosynthesis, cellular bioengineering. Total annual research expenditures: $450,000. *Application contact:* Jody Malm, Administrative Coordinator, 518-276-2808, Fax: 518-276-2344, E-mail: malmj@rpi.edu.

Rensselaer Polytechnic Institute, Graduate School, School of Science, Program in Chemistry, Troy, NY 12180-3590. Offers analytical chemistry (MS, PhD); biochemistry (MS, PhD); inorganic chemistry (MS, PhD); organic chemistry (MS, PhD); physical chemistry (MS, PhD); polymer chemistry (MS, PhD). Part-time and evening/weekend programs available. *Faculty:* 16 full-time (2 women). *Students:* 68 full-time (31 women); includes 1 African American, 6 Asian Americans or Pacific Islanders, 1 Hispanic American, 31 international. Average age 24. 85 applicants, 19% accepted, 5 enrolled. In 2009, 5 master's, 6 doctorates awarded. Terminal master's awarded for partial completion of doctoral program. *Degree requirements:* For master's, thesis (for some programs); for doctorate, comprehensive exam, thesis/dissertation. *Entrance requirements:* For master's, GRE General Test, GRE Subject Test (strongly recommended); for doctorate, GRE General Test, GRE Subject Test (chemistry or biochemistry strongly recommended). Additional exam requirements/recommendations for international students: Required—TOEFL (minimum score 600 paper-based). *Application deadline:* For fall admission, 2/1 priority date for domestic students; for spring admission, 11/15 for domestic students. Applications are processed on a rolling basis. Application fee: $75. Electronic applications accepted. *Expenses:* Tuition: Full-time $38,100. *Financial support:* In 2009–10, 1 fellowship with full tuition reimbursement (averaging $22,500 per year), 18 research assistantships with full tuition reimbursements (averaging $22,500 per year), 24 teaching assistantships with full tuition reimbursements (averaging $22,500 per year) were awarded; institutionally sponsored loans and tuition waivers (full and partial) also available. Financial award application deadline: 2/1. *Faculty research:* Synthetic polymer and biopolymer chemistry, physical chemistry of polymeric systems, bioanalytical chemistry, synthetic and computational drug design, protein folding and protein design. Total annual research expenditures: $1.1 million. *Unit head:* Dr. Curtis M. Breneman, Chair, 518-276-3264, Fax: 518-276-4887, E-mail: brenec@rpi.edu. *Application contact:* Sharon E. Gardner, Graduate Program Administrator, 518-276-2140, Fax: 518-276-4887, E-mail: derris@rpi.edu.

Rice University, Graduate Programs, Wiess School of Natural Sciences, Department of Biochemistry and Cell Biology, Houston, TX 77251-1892. Offers MA, PhD. *Faculty:* 26 full-time (8 women). *Students:* 52 full-time (18 women); includes 24 minority (1 African American, 16 Asian Americans or Pacific Islanders, 7 Hispanic Americans), 15 international. Average age 23. 177 applicants, 18% accepted, 12 enrolled. In 2009, 5 master's, 12 doctorates awarded. Terminal master's awarded for partial completion of doctoral program. *Degree requirements:* For master's, thesis; for doctorate, thesis/dissertation. *Entrance requirements:* For master's and doctorate, GRE. Additional exam requirements/recommendations for international students: Required—TOEFL (minimum score 600 paper-based; 250 computer-based; 90 iBT). *Application deadline:* For fall admission, 2/1 priority date for domestic students, 2/1 for international students. Applications are processed on a rolling basis. Application fee: $0 ($70 for international students). Electronic applications accepted. *Expenses:* Contact institution. *Financial support:* In 2009–10, 12 students received support, including 12 fellowships with full tuition reimbursements available (averaging $26,000 per year); tuition waivers (full) also available. Financial award application deadline: 2/1. *Faculty research:* Steroid metabolism, protein structure NMR, biophysics, cell growth and movement. Total annual research expenditures: $5 million. *Unit head:* Dr. Janet Braam, Chair, 713-348-4015, Fax: 713-348-5154, E-mail: bioc@rice.edu. *Application contact:* Dr. Susan Cates, Recruiting Administrator, 713-348-5777, Fax: 713-348-5154, E-mail: bioc@rice.edu.

Rosalind Franklin University of Medicine and Science, School of Graduate and Post-doctoral Studies—Interdisciplinary Graduate Program in Biomedical Sciences, Department of Biochemistry and Molecular Biology, North Chicago, IL 60064-3095. Offers MS, PhD, MD/PhD. Terminal master's awarded for partial completion of doctoral program. *Degree requirements:*

For master's, comprehensive exam, thesis; for doctorate, comprehensive exam, thesis/dissertation. *Entrance requirements:* For master's and doctorate, GRE General Test, minimum GPA of 3.0. Additional exam requirements/recommendations for international students: Required—TOEFL, TWE. Electronic applications accepted. *Faculty research:* Structure of control enzymes, extracellular matrix, glucose metabolism, gene expression, ATP synthesis.

Rush University, Graduate College, Division of Biochemistry, Chicago, IL 60612-3832. Offers PhD, MD/PhD. *Degree requirements:* For doctorate, thesis/dissertation, preliminary exam. *Entrance requirements:* For doctorate, GRE General Test. Additional exam requirements/recommendations for international students: Required—TOEFL. Electronic applications accepted. *Faculty research:* Biochemistry of extracellular matrix, connective tissue biosynthesis and degradation, molecular biology of connective tissue components, cartilage, arthritis.

Rutgers, The State University of New Jersey, Newark, Graduate School, Program in Chemistry, Newark, NJ 07102. Offers analytical chemistry (MS, PhD); biochemistry (MS, PhD); inorganic chemistry (MS, PhD); organic chemistry (MS, PhD); physical chemistry (MS, PhD). Part-time and evening/weekend programs available. Terminal master's awarded for partial completion of doctoral program. *Degree requirements:* For master's, thesis optional, cumulative exams; for doctorate, thesis/dissertation, exams, research proposal. *Entrance requirements:* For master's and doctorate, GRE General Test, minimum undergraduate B average. Additional exam requirements/recommendations for international students: Required—TOEFL. Electronic applications accepted. *Faculty research:* Medicinal chemistry, natural products, isotope effects, biophysics and biorganic approaches to enzyme mechanisms, organic and organometallic synthesis.

Rutgers, The State University of New Jersey, New Brunswick, Graduate School-New Brunswick, Department of Chemistry and Chemical Biology, Piscataway, NJ 08854-8097. Offers biological chemistry (MS, PhD); inorganic chemistry (MS, PhD); organic chemistry (MS, PhD); physical chemistry (MS, PhD). Part-time and evening/weekend programs available. Terminal master's awarded for partial completion of doctoral program. *Degree requirements:* For master's, thesis or alternative, exam; for doctorate, thesis/dissertation, 1 year residency. *Entrance requirements:* For master's and doctorate, GRE General Test, GRE Subject Test. Additional exam requirements/recommendations for international students: Required—TOEFL. Electronic applications accepted. *Faculty research:* Biophysical organic/bioorganic, inorganic/bioinorganic, theoretical, and solid-state/surface chemistry.

Rutgers, The State University of New Jersey, New Brunswick, Graduate School-New Brunswick, Programs in the Molecular Biosciences, Program in Biochemistry, Piscataway, NJ 08854-8097. Offers PhD. *Degree requirements:* For doctorate, thesis/dissertation, written qualifying exam. *Entrance requirements:* For doctorate, GRE General Test, GRE Subject Test (recommended), minimum GPA of 3.0. Additional exam requirements/recommendations for international students: Required—TOEFL. Electronic applications accepted. *Faculty research:* DNA replication and transcription, virus gene expression, tumor biology, structural biochemistry, signal transduction and molecular targeting.

Saint Joseph College, Department of Chemistry, West Hartford, CT 06117-2700. Offers biochemistry (MS); chemistry (MS). Part-time and evening/weekend programs available. Post-baccalaureate distance learning degree programs offered. *Students:* 1 (woman) full-time, 30 part-time (21 women); includes 11 minority (4 African Americans, 4 Asian Americans or Pacific Islanders, 3 Hispanic Americans). *Degree requirements:* For master's, comprehensive exam, thesis optional. *Entrance requirements:* For master's, 2 letters of recommendation. *Application deadline:* Applications are processed on a rolling basis. Application fee: $50. Electronic applications accepted. *Expenses:* Tuition: Part-time $595 per credit. Required fees: $30 per credit. Tuition and fees vary according to program. *Financial support:* Career-related internships or fieldwork and unspecified assistantships available. Support available to part-time students. Financial award applicants required to submit FAFSA. *Application contact:* Graduate Admissions Office, 860-231-5261, E-mail: graduate@sjc.edu.

Saint Louis University, Graduate School and School of Medicine, Graduate Program in Biomedical Sciences and Graduate School, Department of Biochemistry and Molecular Biology, St. Louis, MO 63103-2097. Offers PhD. *Degree requirements:* For doctorate, comprehensive exam, thesis/dissertation, departmental qualifying exams. *Entrance requirements:* For doctorate, GRE General Test, GRE Subject Test (optional), letters of recommendation, resume, interview. Additional exam requirements/recommendations for international students: Required—TOEFL (minimum score 525 paper-based; 194 computer-based). Electronic applications accepted. *Faculty research:* Transcription, chromatin modification and regulation of gene expression; structure/function of proteins and enzymes, including x-ray crystallography; inflammatory mediators in pathenogenesis of diabetes and arteriosclerosis; cellular signaling in response to growth factors, opiates and angiogenic mediators; genomics and proteomics of Cryptococcus neoformans.

San Francisco State University, Division of Graduate Studies, College of Science and Engineering, Department of Chemistry and Biochemistry, San Francisco, CA 94132-1722. Offers chemistry (MS), including biochemistry. Part-time programs available. Electronic applications accepted.

Seton Hall University, College of Arts and Sciences, Department of Chemistry and Biochemistry, South Orange, NJ 07079-2697. Offers analytical chemistry (MS, PhD); biochemistry (MS, PhD); chemistry (MS); inorganic chemistry (MS, PhD); organic chemistry (MS, PhD); physical chemistry (MS, PhD). Part-time and evening/weekend programs available. *Faculty:* 10 full-time (1 woman). *Students:* 24 full-time (14 women), 47 part-time (15 women); includes 22 minority (10 African Americans, 8 Asian Americans or Pacific Islanders, 4 Hispanic Americans), 11 international. Average age 33. 31 applicants, 68% accepted, 10 enrolled. In 2009, 7 master's, 4 doctorates awarded. Terminal master's awarded for partial completion of doctoral program. *Degree requirements:* For master's, thesis optional; for doctorate, comprehensive exam, thesis/dissertation. *Entrance requirements:* Additional exam requirements/recommendations for international students: Required—TOEFL. *Application deadline:* For fall admission, 7/1 priority date for domestic and international students; for spring admission, 11/1 priority date for domestic and international students. Applications are processed on a rolling basis. Application fee: $50. Electronic applications accepted. *Financial support:* Research assistantships, teaching assistantships with full tuition reimbursements, Federal Work-Study and unspecified assistantships available. Financial award applicants required to submit FAFSA. *Faculty research:* DNA metal reactions; chromatography; bioinorganic, biophysical, organometallic, polymer chemistry; heterogeneous catalyst; synthetic organic and carbohydrate chemistry. *Unit head:* Dr. Nicholas Snow, Chair, 973-761-9414, Fax: 973-761-9772, E-mail: snownich@shu.edu. *Application contact:* Dr. Stephen Kelty, Director of Graduate Studies, 973-761-9129, Fax: 973-761-9772, E-mail: keltyste@shu.edu.

Simon Fraser University, Graduate Studies, Faculty of Science, Department of Molecular Biology and Biochemistry, Burnaby, BC V5A 1S6, Canada. Offers M Sc, PhD. *Degree requirements:* For master's, thesis; for doctorate, thesis/dissertation. *Entrance requirements:* For master's, minimum GPA of 3.0; for doctorate, minimum GPA of 3.5. Additional exam requirements/recommendations for international students: Required—TWE or IELTS. *Faculty research:* Molecular genetics and development, biochemistry, molecular physiology, genomics, molecular phylogenetics and population genetics, bioinformation.

Southern Illinois University Carbondale, Graduate School, College of Science, Department of Chemistry and Biochemistry, Carbondale, IL 62901-4701. Offers MS, PhD. Part-time programs available. Terminal master's awarded for partial completion of doctoral program. *Degree requirements:* For master's, one foreign language, thesis; for doctorate, variable foreign language requirement, thesis/dissertation. *Entrance requirements:* For master's, minimum GPA of 2.7; for doctorate, GRE General Test, minimum GPA of 3.25. Additional exam requirements/recommendations for international students: Required—TOEFL. *Faculty research:* Materials, separations, computational chemistry, synthetics.

Southern Illinois University Carbondale, Graduate School, College of Science, Program in Molecular Biology, Microbiology, and Biochemistry, Carbondale, IL 62901-4701. Offers MS, PhD. *Degree requirements:* For master's, thesis; for doctorate, thesis/dissertation. *Entrance requirements:* For master's, GRE, minimum GPA of 2.7; for doctorate, GRE, minimum GPA of 3.25. Additional exam requirements/recommendations for international students: Required—TOEFL. *Faculty research:* Prokaryotic gene regulation and expression; eukaryotic gene regulation; microbial, phylogenetic, and metabolic diversity; immune responses to tumors, pathogens, and autoantigens; protein folding and structure.

Southern University and Agricultural and Mechanical College, Graduate School, College of Sciences, Department of Chemistry, Baton Rouge, LA 70813. Offers analytical chemistry (MS); biochemistry (MS); environmental sciences (MS); inorganic chemistry (MS); organic chemistry (MS); physical chemistry (MS). *Degree requirements:* For master's, thesis. *Entrance requirements:* For master's, GMAT or GRE General Test. Additional exam requirements/ recommendations for international students: Required—TOEFL (minimum score 525 paper-based; 193 computer-based). *Faculty research:* Synthesis of macrocyclic ligands, latex accelerators, anticancer drugs, biosensors, absorption isotheums, isolation of specific enzymes from plants.

Stanford University, School of Medicine, Graduate Programs in Medicine, Department of Biochemistry, Stanford, CA 94305-9991. Offers PhD. *Degree requirements:* For doctorate, thesis/dissertation. *Entrance requirements:* For doctorate, GRE General Test, GRE Subject Test (biology or chemistry). Additional exam requirements/recommendations for international students: Required—TOEFL. Electronic applications accepted. *Expenses:* Tuition: Full-time $37,380; part-time $2760 per quarter. Required fees: $501. *Faculty research:* DNA replication, recombination, and gene regulation; methods of isolating, analyzing, and altering genes and genomes; protein structure, protein folding, and protein processing; protein targeting and transport in the cell; intercellular signaling.

State University of New York College of Environmental Science and Forestry, Department of Chemistry, Syracuse, NY 13210-2779. Offers biochemistry (MPS, MS, PhD); environmental and forest chemistry (MPS, MS, PhD); organic chemistry (MPS); organic chemistry of natural products (MS, PhD); polymer chemistry (MPS, MS, PhD). *Faculty:* 15 full-time (1 woman). *Students:* 40 full-time (23 women), 12 international. Average age 28. 35 applicants, 46% accepted, 5 enrolled. In 2009, 1 master's, 8 doctorates awarded. *Degree requirements:* For master's, thesis; for doctorate, comprehensive exam, thesis/dissertation. *Entrance requirements:* For master's and doctorate, GRE General Test, GRE Subject Test, minimum GPA of 3.0. Additional exam requirements/recommendations for international students: Required—TOEFL (minimum score 550 paper-based; 213 computer-based; 80 iBT), IELTS (minimum score 6). *Application deadline:* For fall admission, 2/1 priority date for domestic and international students; for spring admission, 11/1 priority date for domestic and international students. Applications are processed on a rolling basis. Application fee: $60. Electronic applications accepted. *Financial support:* In 2009–10, 32 students received support, including 2 fellowships with full tuition reimbursements available (averaging $17,500 per year), 7 research assistantships with full tuition reimbursements available (averaging $17,500 per year), 23 teaching assistantships with full tuition reimbursements available (averaging $17,500 per year); Federal Work-Study, institutionally sponsored loans, scholarships/grants, health care benefits, and unspecified assistantships also available. Financial award application deadline: 6/30; financial award applicants required to submit FAFSA. *Faculty research:* Polymer chemistry, biochemistry. Total annual research expenditures: $1.8 million. *Unit head:* Dr. Arthur J. Stipanovic, Chair, 315-470-6855, Fax: 315-470-6856, E-mail: astipano@esf.edu. *Application contact:* Scott S. Shannon, Dean, Instruction and Graduate Studies, 315-470-6599, Fax: 315-470-6978, E-mail: esfgrad@esf.edu.

State University of New York Upstate Medical University, College of Graduate Studies, Program in Biochemistry and Molecular Biology, Syracuse, NY 13210-2334. Offers biochemistry (MS); biochemistry and molecular biology (PhD); MD/PhD. *Faculty:* 16 full-time (3 women). *Students:* 30 full-time (19 women), 1 (woman) part-time; includes 5 minority (1 African American, 3 Asian Americans or Pacific Islanders, 1 Hispanic American), 15 international. In 2009, 1 master's, 4 doctorates awarded. Terminal master's awarded for partial completion of doctoral program. *Degree requirements:* For master's, thesis; for doctorate, comprehensive exam, thesis/dissertation. *Entrance requirements:* For master's, GRE General Test, interview; for doctorate, GRE General Test, telephone interview. Additional exam requirements/ recommendations for international students: Required—TOEFL. *Application deadline:* Applications are processed on a rolling basis. Application fee: $40. Electronic applications accepted. *Financial support:* In 2009–10, fellowships with tuition reimbursements (averaging $21,514 per year), research assistantships with tuition reimbursements (averaging $21,514 per year) were awarded; Federal Work-Study, scholarships/grants, health care benefits, tuition waivers, and unspecified assistantships also available. Financial award application deadline: 4/15; financial award applicants required to submit FAFSA. *Faculty research:* Enzymology, membrane structure and functions, developmental biochemistry. *Unit head:* Dr. Patricia Kane, Chair, 315-464-5127. *Application contact:* Sandra Tillotson, Coordinator of Graduate Recruitment, 315-464-7655.

See Close-Up on page 157.

Stevens Institute of Technology, Graduate School, Charles V. Schaefer Jr. School of Engineering, Department of Chemistry, Chemical Biology and Biomedical Engineering, Hoboken, NJ 07030. Offers analytical chemistry (PhD, Certificate); bioinformatics (PhD, Certificate); biomedical chemistry (Certificate); biomedical engineering (M Eng, Certificate); chemical biology (MS, PhD, Certificate); chemical physiology (Certificate); chemistry (MS, PhD); organic chemistry (PhD); physical chemistry (PhD); polymer chemistry (PhD, Certificate). Part-time and evening/ weekend programs available. Postbaccalaureate distance learning degree programs offered (no on-campus study). Terminal master's awarded for partial completion of doctoral program. *Degree requirements:* For master's, thesis or alternative; for doctorate, one foreign language, thesis/dissertation; for Certificate, project or thesis. *Entrance requirements:* Additional exam requirements/recommendations for international students: Required—TOEFL. Electronic applications accepted. *Expenses:* Tuition: Full-time $9900; part-time $1100 per credit. Required fees: $286 per semester. *Faculty research:* Biochemical reaction engineering, polymerization engineering, reactor design, biochemical process control and synthesis.

Stony Brook University, State University of New York, Graduate School, College of Arts and Sciences, Department of Biochemistry and Cell Biology, Molecular and Cellular Biology Program, Specialization in Biochemistry and Molecular Biology, Stony Brook, NY 11794. Offers PhD. *Degree requirements:* For doctorate, comprehensive exam, thesis/dissertation, teaching experience. *Entrance requirements:* For doctorate, GRE General Test, GRE Subject Test. Additional exam requirements/recommendations for international students: Required—TOEFL. *Application deadline:* For fall admission, 1/15 for domestic students. Application fee: $60. *Expenses:* Tuition, state resident: full-time $8370; part-time $349 per credit. Tuition, nonresident: full-time $13,250; part-time $552 per credit. Required fees: $933. *Financial support:* Fellowships, research assistantships, teaching assistantships, Federal Work-Study available. *Unit head:* Prof. Robert Haltiwanger, Chair, 631-632-8560. *Application contact:* Director, Graduate Program, 631-632-1210, E-mail: mcbprog@life.bio.sunysb.edu.

Stony Brook University, State University of New York, Graduate School, College of Arts and Sciences, Department of Biochemistry and Cell Biology, Program in Biochemistry and Structural Biology, Stony Brook, NY 11794. Offers PhD. *Students:* 26 full-time (14 women); includes 1 African American, 1 Asian American or Pacific Islander, 19 international. Average age 27. 94 applicants, 22% accepted. In 2009, 8 doctorates awarded. *Expenses:* Tuition, state resident: full-time $8370; part-time $349 per credit. Tuition, nonresident: full-time $13,250; part-time $552 per credit. Required fees: $933. *Financial support:* In 2009–10, 19 research assistantships, 5 teaching assistantships were awarded. *Unit head:* Prof. Robert Haltiwanger, Chair, 631-632-8560. *Application contact:* Director, Graduate Program, 631-632-8533, Fax: 631-632-9730, E-mail: mcbprog@life.bio.sunysb.edu.

Syracuse University, College of Arts and Sciences, Program in Structural Biology, Biochemistry and Biophysics, Syracuse, NY 13244. Offers PhD. *Students:* 5 full-time (3 women), 3 part-time (0 women); includes 1 minority (African American), 4 international. Average age 31. 18 applicants, 0% accepted, 0 enrolled. *Degree requirements:* For doctorate, thesis/dissertation, exam. *Entrance requirements:* For doctorate, GRE General Test, GRE Subject Test. Additional exam requirements/recommendations for international students: Required—TOEFL (minimum score 100 iBT). *Application deadline:* For fall admission, 1/10 priority date for domestic and international students. Application fee: $75. Electronic applications accepted. *Expenses:* Tuition: Full-time $26,808; part-time $1117 per credit. Required fees: $1024. *Financial support:* Fellowships with tuition reimbursements, research assistantships, teaching assistantships with tuition reimbursements, tuition waivers available. Financial award application deadline: 1/1; financial award applicants required to submit FAFSA. *Unit head:* Scott Pitnick, Director, 315-443-5128, Fax: 315-443-2012, E-mail: sspitnic@syr.edu. *Application contact:* Evelyn Lott, Information Contact, 315-443-9154, Fax: 315-443-2012, E-mail: ealott@syr.edu.

Temple University, Health Sciences Center, School of Medicine and Graduate School, Graduate Programs in Medicine, Department of Biochemistry, Philadelphia, PA 19122-6096. Offers MS, PhD. *Degree requirements:* For master's, thesis, research seminar; for doctorate, thesis/ dissertation, research seminars. *Entrance requirements:* For master's and doctorate, GRE General Test, GRE Subject Test, minimum GPA of 3.0. Additional exam requirements/ recommendations for international students: Required—TOEFL (minimum score 650 paper-based; 280 computer-based). Electronic applications accepted. *Faculty research:* Metabolism, enzymology, molecular biology, membranology, biophysics.

Texas A&M University, College of Agriculture and Life Sciences, Department of Biochemistry and Biophysics, College Station, TX 77843. Offers biochemistry (MS, PhD); biophysics (MS). *Faculty:* 32. *Students:* 135 full-time (59 women), 6 part-time (0 women); includes 17 minority (3 African Americans, 1 American Indian/Alaska Native, 2 Asian Americans or Pacific Islanders, 11 Hispanic Americans), 55 international. Average age 27. In 2009, 7 master's, 11 doctorates awarded. *Entrance requirements:* For master's and doctorate, GRE General Test. Additional exam requirements/recommendations for international students: Required—TOEFL. *Application deadline:* For fall admission, 2/1 priority date for domestic students, 12/1 priority date for international students. Applications are processed on a rolling basis. Application fee: $50 ($75 for international students). Electronic applications accepted. *Expenses:* Tuition, state resident: full-time $3991; part-time $221.74 per credit hour. Tuition, nonresident: full-time $9049; part-time $502.74 per credit hour. *Financial support:* In 2009–10, 6 fellowships with tuition reimbursements (averaging $20,000 per year), 70 research assistantships with partial tuition reimbursements (averaging $20,000 per year) were awarded; teaching assistantships with partial tuition reimbursements, institutionally sponsored loans, scholarships/grants, traineeships, and unspecified assistantships also available. Financial award application deadline: 2/1; financial award applicants required to submit FAFSA. *Faculty research:* Enzymology, gene expression, protein structure, plant biochemistry. *Unit head:* Department Head, 979-862-2263, Fax: 979-845-9274, E-mail: biobiograd@tamu.edu. *Application contact:* Academic Advisor, 979-845-1779, Fax: 979-845-9274, E-mail: biobiograd@tamu.edu.

Texas State University–San Marcos, Graduate School, College of Science, Department of Chemistry and Biochemistry, Program in Biochemistry, San Marcos, TX 78666. Offers MS. *Faculty:* 6 full-time (3 women). *Students:* 9 full-time (4 women), 5 part-time (2 women); includes 4 minority (1 African American, 3 Hispanic Americans), 2 international. Average age 27. 14 applicants, 86% accepted, 6 enrolled. In 2009, 3 master's awarded. *Degree requirements:* For master's, thesis. *Entrance requirements:* For master's, minimum GPA of 2.75 in last 60 hours of course work. Additional exam requirements/recommendations for international students: Required—TOEFL (minimum score 550 paper-based; 213 computer-based). *Application deadline:* For fall admission, 6/15 priority date for domestic students, 6/1 priority date for international students; for spring admission, 10/15 priority date for domestic students, 10/1 priority date for international students. Applications are processed on a rolling basis. Application fee: $40 ($90 for international students). Electronic applications accepted. *Expenses:* Tuition, state resident: full-time $5784; part-time $241 per credit hour. Tuition, nonresident: full-time $13,224; part-time $551 per credit hour. Required fees: $1728; $48 per credit hour. $306. Tuition and fees vary according to course load. *Financial support:* In 2009–10, 8 students received support, including 7 teaching assistantships (averaging $5,906 per year); research assistantships. Financial award application deadline: 4/1; financial award applicants required to submit FAFSA. *Unit head:* Dr. Chad Booth, Chair, 512-245-2156, Fax: 512-245-2374, E-mail: chadbooth@txstate.edu. *Application contact:* Dr. Chad Booth, Chair, 512-245-2156, Fax: 512-245-2374, E-mail: chadbooth@txstate.edu.

Texas Tech University Health Sciences Center, Graduate School of Biomedical Sciences, Department of Cell Biology and Biochemistry, Program in Biochemistry and Molecular Genetics, Lubbock, TX 79430. Offers MS, PhD, MD/PhD, MS/PhD. Terminal master's awarded for partial completion of doctoral program. *Degree requirements:* For master's, comprehensive exam, thesis, preliminary, comprehensive, and final exams; for doctorate, comprehensive exam, thesis/dissertation, preliminary, comprehensive, and final exams. *Entrance requirements:* For master's and doctorate, GRE General Test, minimum GPA of 3.0. Additional exam requirements/ recommendations for international students: Required—TOEFL. Electronic applications accepted. *Faculty research:* Reproductive endocrinology, immunology, developmental biochemistry, biochemistry and genetics of cancer, molecular genetics and cell cycle.

Thomas Jefferson University, Jefferson College of Graduate Studies, PhD Program in Biochemistry and Molecular Biology, Philadelphia, PA 19107. Offers PhD. *Faculty:* 42 full-time (13 women). *Students:* 18 full-time (10 women), 1 (woman) part-time; includes 3 minority (1 Asian American or Pacific Islander, 2 Hispanic Americans), 2 international. Average age 24. 40 applicants, 18% accepted, 3 enrolled. In 2009, 2 doctorates awarded. *Degree requirements:* For doctorate, comprehensive exam, thesis/dissertation. *Entrance requirements:* For doctorate, GRE General Test or MCAT, minimum GPA of 3.2. Additional exam requirements/ recommendations for international students: Required—TOEFL (minimum score 250 computer-based; 100 iBT) or IELTS. *Application deadline:* For fall admission, 1/15 priority date for domestic students, 1/1 priority date for international students. Applications are processed on a rolling basis. Application fee: $50. Electronic applications accepted. *Expenses:* Tuition: Full-time $26,858; part-time $879 per credit. Required fees: $525. *Financial support:* In 2009–10, 18 students received support, including 18 fellowships with full tuition reimbursements available (averaging $52,883 per year); Federal Work-Study, institutionally sponsored loans, scholarships/ grants, traineeships, and stipends also available. Financial award application deadline: 5/1; financial award applicants required to submit FAFSA. *Faculty research:* Signal transduction and molecular genetics, translational biochemistry, human mitochondrial genetics, molecular biology of protein-RNA interaction, mammalian mitochondrial biogenesis and function. Total annual research expenditures: $17.4 million. *Unit head:* Dr. Diane E. Merry, Program Director, 215-503-4907, Fax: 215-923-9162, E-mail: diane.merry@jefferson.edu. *Application contact:* Marc E. Stearns, Director of Admissions, 215-503-0155, Fax: 215-503-9920, E-mail: jcgs-info@jefferson.edu.

See Close-Up on page 159.

Tufts University, Sackler School of Graduate Biomedical Sciences, Department of Biochemistry, Medford, MA 02155. Offers PhD. *Faculty:* 28 full-time (8 women). *Students:* 16 full-time (6 women); includes 2 minority (both Asian Americans or Pacific Islanders), 5 international. Average age 29. In 2009, 5 doctorates awarded. Terminal master's awarded for partial completion of doctoral program. *Degree requirements:* For doctorate, thesis/dissertation. *Entrance requirements:* For doctorate, GRE, 3 letters of recommendation. Additional exam requirements/ recommendations for international students: Required—TOEFL. *Application deadline:* For fall admission, 12/15 for domestic and international students. Applications are processed on a rolling basis. Application fee: $70. Electronic applications accepted. *Expenses:* Tuition: Full-time $38,096; part-time $3962 per credit. Required fees: $686; $40 per year. Tuition and fees vary according to course level, course load, degree level, program and student level. *Financial*

Biochemistry

Tufts University (continued)
support: In 2009–10, 16 students received support, including 16 research assistantships with full tuition reimbursements available (averaging $28,500 per year); scholarships/grants and health care benefits also available. *Faculty research:* Enzymes and mechanisms, signal transduction, NMR spectroscopy, DNA biosynthesis, membrane function. *Unit head:* Dr. Larry Feig, Program Director, 617-636-6956, Fax: 617-636-2409, E-mail: larry.feig@tufts.edu. *Application contact:* 617-636-6767, Fax: 617-636-0375, E-mail: sackler-school@tufts.edu.

Tufts University, Sackler School of Graduate Biomedical Sciences, Integrated Studies Program, Medford, MA 02155. Offers PhD. *Students:* 10 full-time (7 women); includes 1 minority (Asian American or Pacific Islander), 2 international. Average age 25. 333 applicants, 6% accepted. *Entrance requirements:* For doctorate, GRE General Test, 3 letters of reference. Additional exam requirements/recommendations for international students: Required—TOEFL. *Application deadline:* For fall admission, 12/15 for domestic and international students. Applications are processed on a rolling basis. Application fee: $70. Electronic applications accepted. *Expenses:* Tuition: Full-time $38,096; part-time $3962 per credit. Required fees: $686; $40 per year. Tuition and fees vary according to course level, course load, degree level, program and student level. *Financial support:* In 2009–10, 10 students received support, including 10 research assistantships with tuition reimbursements available (averaging $28,250 per year); scholarships/grants and health care benefits also available. *Unit head:* Dr. Karina Meiri, Program Director, 617-636-6707, E-mail: james.dice@tufts.edu. *Application contact:* Kellie Johnston, Associate Director of Admissions, 617-636-6767, Fax: 617-636-0375, E-mail: sackler-school@tufts.edu.

Tulane University, School of Medicine and School of Liberal Arts, Graduate Programs in Biomedical Sciences, Department of Biochemistry, New Orleans, LA 70118-5669. Offers MS, PhD, MD/PhD. MS and PhD offered through the Graduate School. *Degree requirements:* For master's, thesis; for doctorate, 2 foreign languages, thesis/dissertation. *Entrance requirements:* For master's, GRE General Test, GRE Subject Test, minimum B average in undergraduate course work; for doctorate, GRE General Test, GRE Subject Test. Additional exam requirements/recommendations for international students: Required—TOEFL. Electronic applications accepted. *Faculty research:* Nucleic acid chemistry, complex carbohydrates biochemistry.

Universidad Central del Caribe, School of Medicine, Program in Biomedical Sciences, Bayamón, PR 00960-6032. Offers anatomy and cell biology (MA, MS); biochemistry (MS); biomedical sciences (MA); microbiology and immunology (MA, MS); pharmacology (MS); physiology (MA, MS).

Université de Moncton, Faculty of Science, Department of Chemistry and Biochemistry, Moncton, NB E1A 3E9, Canada. Offers biochemistry (M Sc); chemistry (M Sc). Part-time programs available. *Degree requirements:* For master's, one foreign language, thesis. *Entrance requirements:* For master's, minimum GPA of 3.0. Electronic applications accepted. *Faculty research:* Environmental contaminants, natural products synthesis, nutraceutical, organic catalysis, molecular biology of cancer.

Université de Montréal, Faculty of Medicine, Department of Biochemistry, Montréal, QC H3C 3J7, Canada. Offers biochemistry (M Sc, PhD); clinical biochemistry (DEPD). *Faculty:* 38 full-time (8 women). *Students:* 78 full-time (36 women), 138 part-time (68 women). 130 applicants, 32% accepted, 35 enrolled. In 2009, 25 master's, 12 doctorates, 3 other advanced degrees awarded. Terminal master's awarded for partial completion of doctoral program. *Degree requirements:* For master's, thesis; for doctorate, thesis/dissertation, general exam. *Entrance requirements:* For master's and doctorate, proficiency in French, knowledge of English; for DEPD, proficiency in French. *Application deadline:* For fall admission, 2/1 priority date for domestic students; for winter admission, 11/1 priority date for domestic students; for spring admission, 2/1 priority date for domestic students. Application fee: $100. Electronic applications accepted. *Unit head:* Christian Baron, Director, 514-343-6372, Fax: 514-373-2210, E-mail: christian.baron@umontreal.ca. *Application contact:* Luc DesGroseillers, Graduate Chair, 514-343-5802, Fax: 514-343-2210, E-mail: desgros@bcm.umontreal.ca or luc.desgroseillers@umontreal.ca.

Université de Montréal, Faculty of Medicine, Program in Specialized Studies, Montréal, QC H3C 3J7, Canada. Offers anesthesia (DES); diagnostic radiology (DES); family medicine (DES); gastroenterology (DES); geriatry (DES); intensive care (DES); medical biochemistry (DES); medical genetics (DES); medicine (DES); microbiology and infectious diseases (DES); nuclear medicine (DES); obstetrics and gynecology (DES); ophthalmology (DES); pediatrics (DES); pneumology (DES); psychiatry (DES); radiology-oncology (DES); rheumatology (DES); surgery (DES). *Faculty:* 154 full-time (40 women), 333 part-time/adjunct (100 women). *Students:* 930 full-time (580 women), 7 part-time (all women). 74 applicants, 77% accepted, 29 enrolled. *Application deadline:* For fall admission, 2/1 priority date for domestic students; for winter admission, 11/1 priority date for domestic students; for spring admission, 2/1 priority date for domestic students. Application fee: $100. Electronic applications accepted. *Unit head:* Lorraine Locas, Assistant to the Vice Dean of Graduate Studies, 514-343-6269, Fax: 514-343-5751, E-mail: lorraine.locas@umontreal.ca. *Application contact:* Dr. Andre Ferron, Vice Dean of Graduate Studies, 514-343-6111 Ext. 0933, Fax: 514-343-5751, E-mail: andre.ferron@umontreal.ca.

Université de Sherbrooke, Faculty of Medicine and Health Sciences, Graduate Programs in Medicine, Department of Biochemistry, Sherbrooke, QC J1H 5N4, Canada. Offers M Sc, PhD. Terminal master's awarded for partial completion of doctoral program. *Degree requirements:* For master's, thesis; for doctorate, thesis/dissertation. Electronic applications accepted. *Faculty research:* RNA structure-function, chromatin and gene expression, genetic diseases.

Université Laval, Faculty of Medicine, Post-Professional Programs in Medical Studies, Québec, QC G1K 7P4, Canada. Offers anatomy–pathology (DESS); anesthesiology (DESS); cardiology (DESS); care of older people (Diploma); clinical research (DESS); community health (DESS); dermatology (DESS); diagnostic radiology (DESS); emergency medicine (Diploma); family medicine (DESS); general surgery (DESS); geriatrics (DESS); hematology (DESS); internal medicine (DESS); maternal and fetal medicine (Diploma); medical biochemistry (DESS); medical microbiology and infectious diseases (DESS); medical oncology (DESS); nephrology (DESS); neurology (DESS); neurosurgery (DESS); obstetrics and gynecology (DESS); ophthalmology (DESS); orthopedic surgery (DESS); oto-rhino-laryngology (DESS); palliative medicine (Diploma); pediatrics (DESS); plastic surgery (DESS); psychiatry (DESS); pulmonary medicine (DESS); radiology–oncology (DESS); thoracic surgery (DESS); urology (DESS). *Degree requirements:* For other advanced degree, comprehensive exam. *Entrance requirements:* For degree, knowledge of French. Electronic applications accepted.

Université Laval, Faculty of Sciences and Engineering, Department of Biochemistry and Microbiology, Programs in Biochemistry, Québec, QC G1K 7P4, Canada. Offers M Sc, PhD. Terminal master's awarded for partial completion of doctoral program. *Degree requirements:* For master's, thesis; for doctorate, comprehensive exam, thesis/dissertation. *Entrance requirements:* For master's and doctorate, knowledge of French, comprehension of written English. Electronic applications accepted.

University at Albany, State University of New York, School of Public Health, Department of Biomedical Sciences, Program in Biochemistry, Molecular Biology, and Genetics, Albany, NY 12222-0001. Offers MS, PhD. *Degree requirements:* For master's, thesis; for doctorate, thesis/dissertation. *Entrance requirements:* For master's and doctorate, GRE General Test, GRE Subject Test.

University at Buffalo, the State University of New York, Graduate School, School of Medicine and Biomedical Sciences, Graduate Programs in Medicine and Biomedical Sciences, Department of Biochemistry, Buffalo, NY 14260. Offers MA, PhD. *Faculty:* 17 full-time (5 women), 3 part-time/adjunct (all women). *Students:* 24 full-time (13 women), 5 part-time (all women); includes 2 minority (1 American Indian/Alaska Native, 1 Asian American or Pacific Islander), 7 international. Average age 26. 24 applicants, 50% accepted, 0 enrolled. In 2009, 2 master's, 10 doctorates awarded. Terminal master's awarded for partial completion of doctoral program. *Degree requirements:* For doctorate, thesis/dissertation. *Entrance requirements:* For master's, GRE General Test; for doctorate, GRE General Test, 3 letters of recommendation. Additional exam requirements/recommendations for international students: Required—TOEFL (minimum score 600 paper-based; 250 computer-based; 100 iBT). *Application deadline:* For fall admission, 2/1 priority date for domestic and international students. Applications are processed on a rolling basis. Application fee: $50. Electronic applications accepted. *Financial support:* In 2009–10, 2 fellowships with full tuition reimbursements (averaging $4,000 per year), 20 research assistantships with full tuition reimbursements (averaging $21,000 per year), 4 teaching assistantships with full tuition reimbursements (averaging $21,000 per year) were awarded; Federal Work-Study, institutionally sponsored loans, scholarships/grants, health care benefits, and unspecified assistantships also available. Financial award application deadline: 2/1; financial award applicants required to submit FAFSA. *Faculty research:* Gene expression, proteins and metalloenzymes, biochemical endocrinology. Total annual research expenditures: $3.3 million. *Unit head:* Dr. Kenneth M. Blumenthal, Chair, 716-829-2727, Fax: 716-829-2725, E-mail: kblumen@buffalo.edu. *Application contact:* Dr. Daniel Kosman, Director of Graduate Studies, 716-829-2842, Fax: 716-829-2725, E-mail: camkos@acsu.buffalo.edu.

The University of Alabama at Birmingham, Graduate Programs in Joint Health Sciences, Program in Biochemistry and Molecular Genetics, Birmingham, AL 35294. Offers PhD. *Degree requirements:* For doctorate, thesis/dissertation. *Entrance requirements:* For doctorate, GRE General Test, interview. Electronic applications accepted.

University of Alaska Fairbanks, College of Natural Sciences and Mathematics, Department of Chemistry and Biochemistry, Fairbanks, AK 99775-6160. Offers biochemistry and molecular biology (MS, PhD); chemistry (MA, MS); environmental chemistry (MS, PhD). Part-time programs available. *Faculty:* 12 full-time (4 women), 2 part-time/adjunct (1 woman). *Students:* 32 full-time (21 women), 9 part-time (5 women); includes 9 minority (2 African Americans, 2 American Indian/Alaska Native, 2 Asian Americans or Pacific Islanders, 3 Hispanic Americans), 5 international. Average age 35. 26 applicants, 38% accepted, 8 enrolled. In 2009, 3 master's, 3 doctorates awarded. *Degree requirements:* For master's, comprehensive exam, thesis or alternative; for doctorate, comprehensive exam, thesis/dissertation, oral defense. *Entrance requirements:* Additional exam requirements/recommendations for international students: Required—TOEFL (minimum score 550 paper-based; 213 computer-based). *Application deadline:* For fall admission, 6/1 for domestic students, 3/1 for international students; for spring admission, 10/15 for domestic students, 9/1 for international students. Applications are processed on a rolling basis. Application fee: $60. Electronic applications accepted. *Expenses:* Tuition, state resident: full-time $7584; part-time $316 per credit. Tuition, nonresident: full-time $15,504; part-time $646 per credit. Required fees: $23 per credit. $135 per semester. Tuition and fees vary according to course level, course load and reciprocity agreements. *Financial support:* In 2009–10, 1 fellowship (averaging $13,500 per year), 15 research assistantships (averaging $14,179 per year), 11 teaching assistantships (averaging $13,937 per year) were awarded; Federal Work-Study, scholarships/grants, health care benefits, and unspecified assistantships also available. Support available to part-time students. Financial award application deadline: 7/1; financial award applicants required to submit FAFSA. *Faculty research:* Atmospheric aerosols, cold adaptation, hibernation and neuroprotection, liganogated ion channels, arctic contaminants. *Unit head:* Dr. John Keller, Department Chair, 907-474-5510, Fax: 907-474-5640, E-mail: fychem@uaf.edu. *Application contact:* Dr. John Keller, Department Chair, 907-474-5510, Fax: 907-474-5640, E-mail: fychem@uaf.edu.

University of Alberta, Faculty of Medicine and Dentistry and Faculty of Graduate Studies and Research, Graduate Programs in Medicine, Department of Biochemistry, Edmonton, AB T6G 2E1, Canada. Offers M Sc, PhD. *Faculty:* 24 full-time, 6 part-time/adjunct. *Students:* 68 full-time (20 women), 1 (woman) part-time. Average age 27. 100 applicants, 21% accepted. In 2009, 1 master's, 7 doctorates awarded. Terminal master's awarded for partial completion of doctoral program. *Degree requirements:* For master's, thesis; for doctorate, thesis/dissertation. *Entrance requirements:* For master's and doctorate, minimum GPA of 3.3. Additional exam requirements/recommendations for international students: Required—TOEFL (minimum score 550 paper-based). *Application deadline:* Applications are processed on a rolling basis. Application fee: $0. Tuition and fees charges are reported in Canadian dollars. *Expenses:* Tuition, area resident: Full-time $4626 Canadian dollars; part-time $99.72 Canadian dollars per unit. International tuition: $8216 Canadian dollars full-time. Required fees: $3590 Canadian dollars; $99.72 Canadian dollars per unit. $215 Canadian dollars per term. *Financial support:* In 2009–10, 25 fellowships with full tuition reimbursements, 15 research assistantships with full tuition reimbursements were awarded; teaching assistantships, institutionally sponsored loans, tuition waivers (full and partial), and tuition bursaries also available. *Faculty research:* Proteins, nucleic acids, membranes, regulation of gene expression, receptors. Total annual research expenditures: $10 million. *Unit head:* Dr. Marek Michalak, Chair, 780-492-2256, Fax: 780-492-0886, E-mail: marek.michalak@ualberta.ca. *Application contact:* Marion Benedict, Graduate Secretary, 780-492-7834, Fax: 780-492-0095, E-mail: gradinfo@biochem.ualberta.ca.

The University of Arizona, College of Medicine, Graduate Programs in Medicine and Graduate College, Department of Biochemistry and Molecular Biophysics, Tucson, AZ 85721. Offers MS, PhD. Terminal master's awarded for partial completion of doctoral program. *Degree requirements:* For master's, thesis optional; for doctorate, thesis/dissertation. *Entrance requirements:* For master's and doctorate, GRE General Test. *Expenses:* Tuition, state resident: full-time $9028. Tuition, nonresident: full-time $24,890. *Faculty research:* Membrane biochemistry, lipid biochemistry, neurobiochemistry, protein synthesis and degradation, bioenergetics.

University of Arkansas for Medical Sciences, Graduate School, Graduate Programs in Biomedical Sciences, Program in Biochemistry and Molecular Biology, Little Rock, AR 72205-7199. Offers MS, PhD, MD/PhD. *Faculty:* 18 full-time (4 women), 10 part-time/adjunct (2 women). *Students:* 19 full-time, 3 part-time. In 2009, 3 doctorates awarded. *Degree requirements:* For master's, comprehensive exam, thesis; for doctorate, thesis/dissertation, qualifying exam. *Entrance requirements:* For master's, GRE General Test, bachelor's degree in biology, chemistry, or related field; for doctorate, GRE General Test. Additional exam requirements/recommendations for international students: Required—TOEFL. *Application deadline:* Applications are processed on a rolling basis. Application fee: $0. *Financial support:* In 2009–10, research assistantships with full tuition reimbursements (averaging $24,000 per year); unspecified assistantships and stipend and tuition for doctoral students also available. Support available to part-time students. *Faculty research:* Gene regulation, growth factors, oncogenes, metabolic diseases, hormone regulation. *Application contact:* Dr. Wayne Wahls, Program Director, 501-686-5787, E-mail: wahlswaynep@uams.edu.

The University of British Columbia, Faculty of Medicine, Department of Biochemistry and Molecular Biology, Vancouver, BC V6T 1Z1, Canada. Offers M Sc, PhD. *Degree requirements:* For master's, thesis; for doctorate, comprehensive exam, thesis/dissertation. *Entrance requirements:* For master's, first class B Sc; for doctorate, master's or first class honors bachelor's degree in biochemistry. Additional exam requirements/recommendations for international students: Required—TOEFL (minimum score 625 paper-based; 263 computer-based), GRE. Electronic applications accepted. *Faculty research:* Membrane biochemistry, protein structure/function, signal transduction, biochemistry.

University of Calgary, Faculty of Medicine and Faculty of Graduate Studies, Department of Biochemistry and Molecular Biology, Calgary, AB T2N 1N4, Canada. Offers M Sc, PhD. *Degree requirements:* For master's, thesis; for doctorate, thesis/dissertation, candidacy exam. *Entrance requirements:* For master's and doctorate, GRE General Test, minimum GPA of 3.2. Additional exam requirements/recommendations for international students: Required—TOEFL. Electronic applications accepted. *Faculty research:* Molecular and developmental genetics; molecular biology of disease; genomics, proteomics and bioinformatics; ceu signaling and structure.

University of California, Berkeley, Graduate Division, Group in Comparative Biochemistry, Berkeley, CA 94720-1500. Offers PhD. *Students:* 16 full-time (5 women). Average age 28. 9 applicants, 3 enrolled. In 2009, 6 doctorates awarded. *Degree requirements:* For doctorate, thesis/dissertation, qualifying exam. *Entrance requirements:* For doctorate, GRE General Test, GRE Subject Test, minimum GPA of 3.0, 3 letters of recommendation. Additional exam requirements/recommendations for international students: Required—TOEFL. *Application deadline:* For fall admission, 1/5 for domestic students. Application fee: $70 ($90 for international students). *Financial support:* Unspecified assistantships available. *Unit head:* Prof. Fenyong Liu, Chair, 510-643-1711, E-mail: compbio@nature.berkeley.edu. *Application contact:* Information Contact, 510-643-1711, E-mail: comparbiochem@berkeley.edu.

University of California, Davis, Graduate Studies, Graduate Group in Biochemistry and Molecular Biology, Davis, CA 95616. Offers MS, PhD. Terminal master's awarded for partial completion of doctoral program. *Degree requirements:* For master's, comprehensive exam (for some programs), thesis (for some programs); for doctorate, thesis/dissertation. *Entrance requirements:* For master's and doctorate, GRE General Test, GRE Subject Test. Additional exam requirements/recommendations for international students: Required—TOEFL (minimum score 550 paper-based; 213 computer-based). Electronic applications accepted. *Faculty research:* Gene expression, protein structure, molecular virology, protein synthesis, enzymology, membrane transport and structural biology.

University of California, Irvine, Office of Graduate Studies, School of Biological Sciences, Department of Molecular Biology and Biochemistry, Irvine, CA 92697. Offers biological science (MS); biological sciences (PhD); biotechnology (MS); MD/PhD. *Students:* 86 full-time (43 women); includes 31 minority (2 African Americans, 20 Asian Americans or Pacific Islanders, 9 Hispanic Americans), 10 international. Average age 27. In 2009, 13 master's, 12 doctorates awarded. *Degree requirements:* For doctorate, thesis/dissertation. *Entrance requirements:* For master's, GRE, minimum GPA of 3.0; for doctorate, GRE General Test, GRE Subject Test, minimum GPA of 3.0. Additional exam requirements/recommendations for international students: Required—TOEFL (minimum score 550 paper-based; 213 computer-based). *Application deadline:* For fall admission, 12/15 priority date for domestic students, 12/15 for international students. Applications are processed on a rolling basis. Application fee: $70 ($90 for international students). Electronic applications accepted. *Financial support:* Fellowships, research assistantships with full tuition reimbursements, teaching assistantships, institutionally sponsored loans, traineeships, health care benefits, and unspecified assistantships available. Financial award application deadline: 3/1; financial award applicants required to submit FAFSA. *Faculty research:* Structure and synthesis of nucleic acids and proteins, regulation, virology, biochemical genetics, gene organization. *Unit head:* Jerry Manning, Chair, 949-824-5578, Fax: 949-824-8551, E-mail: jemannin@uci.edu. *Application contact:* Kimberly McKinney, Administrator, 949-824-8145, Fax: 949-824-1965, E-mail: kamckinn@uci.edu.

University of California, Irvine, Office of Graduate Studies, School of Biological Sciences and School of Medicine, Graduate Program in Molecular Biology, Genetics, and Biochemistry, Irvine, CA 92697. Offers biological sciences (PhD). *Degree requirements:* For doctorate, thesis/dissertation, teaching assignment, preliminary exam. *Entrance requirements:* For doctorate, GRE General Test, minimum GPA of 3.0, research experience. Additional exam requirements/recommendations for international students: Required—TOEFL, IELTS, SPEAK test. Electronic applications accepted. *Expenses:* Contact institution. *Faculty research:* Cellular biochemistry; gene structure and expression; protein structure, function, and design; molecular genetics; pathogenesis and inherited disease.

University of California, Irvine, School of Medicine and School of Biological Sciences, Department of Biological Chemistry, Irvine, CA 92697. Offers biological sciences (MS, PhD). Students apply through the Graduate Program in Molecular Biology, Genetics, and Biochemistry. *Students:* 40 full-time (24 women); includes 13 minority (11 Asian Americans or Pacific Islanders, 2 Hispanic Americans), 6 international. Average age 28. In 2009, 6 doctorates awarded. *Degree requirements:* For doctorate, thesis/dissertation. *Entrance requirements:* For master's, minimum GPA of 3.0; for doctorate, GRE General Test, GRE Subject Test, minimum GPA of 3.0. Additional exam requirements/recommendations for international students: Required—TOEFL (minimum score 550 paper-based; 213 computer-based). *Application deadline:* For fall admission, 1/15 priority date for domestic students, 1/15 for international students. Application fee: $70 ($90 for international students). Electronic applications accepted. *Financial support:* Fellowships, research assistantships with full tuition reimbursements, teaching assistantships, institutionally sponsored loans, traineeships, health care benefits, and unspecified assistantships available. Financial award application deadline: 3/1; financial award applicants required to submit FAFSA. *Faculty research:* RNA splicing, mammalian chromosomal organization, membrane-hormone interactions, regulation of protein synthesis, molecular genetics of metabolic processes. *Unit head:* Suzanne Sandmeyer, Chair, 949-824-7571, Fax: 949-824-7407, E-mail: sbsandme@uci.edu. *Application contact:* Kimberly McKinney, Administrator, 949-824-8145, Fax: 949-824-1965, E-mail: kamckinn@uci.edu.

University of California, Los Angeles, David Geffen School of Medicine and Graduate Division, Graduate Programs in Medicine, Department of Biological Chemistry, Los Angeles, CA 90095. Offers MS, PhD. *Degree requirements:* For master's, comprehensive exam or thesis; for doctorate, thesis/dissertation, oral and written qualifying exams. *Entrance requirements:* For master's and doctorate, GRE General Test.

University of California, Los Angeles, Graduate Division, College of Letters and Science, Department of Chemistry and Biochemistry, Program in Biochemistry and Molecular Biology, Los Angeles, CA 90034. Offers MS, PhD. MS admission to program only under exceptional circumstances. *Students:* 99 full-time (46 women); includes 31 minority (1 African American, 20 Asian Americans or Pacific Islanders, 10 Hispanic Americans), 10 international. Average age 28. 89 applicants, 30% accepted, 14 enrolled. In 2009, 6 master's, 20 doctorates awarded. Terminal master's awarded for partial completion of doctoral program. *Degree requirements:* For master's, comprehensive exam or thesis; for doctorate, thesis/dissertation, oral and written exams, 1 year teaching experience. *Entrance requirements:* For master's, GRE General Test, GRE Subject Test, minimum GPA of 3.0; for doctorate, GRE General Test, GRE Subject Test, minimum undergraduate GPA of 3.0. *Application deadline:* For fall admission, 1/15 for domestic and international students. Application fee: $70 ($90 for international students). Electronic applications accepted. *Financial support:* In 2009–10, 89 fellowships with full and partial tuition reimbursements, 71 research assistantships with full and partial tuition reimbursements, 43 teaching assistantships with full and partial tuition reimbursements were awarded; Federal Work-Study, scholarships/grants, health care benefits, tuition waivers (full and partial), and unspecified assistantships also available. Financial award applicants required to submit FAFSA. *Unit head:* Dr. Albert Courey, 310- 825-3958. *Application contact:* Department Office, 310-825-3150, E-mail: grad@chem.ucla.edu.

University of California, Los Angeles, Graduate Division, College of Letters and Science and David Geffen School of Medicine, UCLA ACCESS to Programs in the Molecular, Cellular and Integrative Life Sciences, Los Angeles, CA 90095. Offers biochemistry and molecular biology (PhD); biological chemistry (PhD); cellular and molecular pathology (PhD); human genetics (PhD); microbiology, immunology, and molecular genetics (PhD); molecular biology (PhD); molecular toxicology (PhD); molecular, cellular and integrative physiology (PhD); neurobiology (PhD); oral biology (PhD); physiology (PhD). ACCESS is an umbrella program for first-year coursework in 12 PhD programs. *Students:* 39 full-time (25 women); includes 14 minority (1 African American, 1 American Indian/Alaska Native, 8 Asian Americans or Pacific Islanders, 4 Hispanic Americans), 10 international. Average age 25. 437 applicants, 22% accepted, 30 enrolled. *Degree requirements:* For doctorate, thesis/dissertation, oral and written qualifying exams. *Entrance requirements:* For doctorate, GRE General Test, minimum undergraduate GPA of 3.0. Additional exam requirements/recommendations for international students: Required—TOEFL. *Application deadline:* For fall admission, 12/15 for domestic and international students. Application fee: $70 ($90 for international students). Electronic applications accepted. *Financial support:* In 2009–10, 56 fellowships with full and partial tuition

reimbursements, 16 research assistantships with full and partial tuition reimbursements were awarded; teaching assistantships with full and partial tuition reimbursements, Federal Work-Study, institutionally sponsored loans, scholarships/grants, health care benefits, tuition waivers (full and partial), and unspecified assistantships also available. Financial award application deadline: 3/1; financial award applicants required to submit FAFSA. *Faculty research:* Molecular, cellular, and developmental biology; immunology; microbiology; integrative biology. *Unit head:* Dr. Greg I. Payne, Chair, 310-206-3121. *Application contact:* Coordinator, 310-206-3121, Fax: 310-206-5280, E-mail: uclaaccess@mednet.ucla.edu.

See Close-Up on page 239.

University of California, Riverside, Graduate Division, Department of Biochemistry, Riverside, CA 92521-0102. Offers biochemistry and molecular biology (MS, PhD). Part-time programs available. *Faculty:* 39 full-time (11 women). *Students:* 59 full-time (25 women); includes 23 minority (2 African Americans, 18 Asian Americans or Pacific Islanders, 3 Hispanic Americans), 7 international. Average age 26. 147 applicants, 21% accepted, 21 enrolled. In 2009, 32 master's, 2 doctorates awarded. Terminal master's awarded for partial completion of doctoral program. *Degree requirements:* For master's, comprehensive exams or thesis; for doctorate, comprehensive exam, thesis/dissertation, 2 quarters of teaching experience, qualifying exams. *Entrance requirements:* For master's and doctorate, GRE General Test, minimum GPA of 3.25. Additional exam requirements/recommendations for international students: Required—TOEFL (minimum score 550 paper-based; 213 computer-based; 80 iBT). *Application deadline:* For fall admission, 1/5 priority date for domestic and international students; for winter admission, 12/1 for domestic students, 7/1 for international students; for spring admission, 3/1 for domestic students, 10/1 for international students. Applications are processed on a rolling basis. Application fee: $80 ($100 for international students). Electronic applications accepted. *Financial support:* In 2009–10, fellowships with full tuition reimbursements (averaging $16,000 per year), research assistantships with full tuition reimbursements (averaging $18,000 per year), teaching assistantships with full tuition reimbursements (averaging $16,500 per year) were awarded; career-related internships or fieldwork, Federal Work-Study, institutionally sponsored loans, scholarships/grants, and tuition waivers (full and partial) also available. Financial award application deadline: 1/5; financial award applicants required to submit FAFSA. *Faculty research:* Structural biology and molecular biophysics, signal transduction, plant biochemistry and molecular biology, gene expression and metabolic regulation, molecular toxicology and pathogenesis. *Unit head:* Dr. Russ Hille, Chair, 951-827-6354, Fax: 951-827-4294, E-mail: russ.hille.@ucr.edu. *Application contact:* Dawn Huffman Loyola, Graduate Student Affairs Officer, 951-827-4116, Fax: 951-827-5517, E-mail: biochem@ucr.edu.

University of California, San Diego, Office of Graduate Studies, Department of Chemistry and Biochemistry, La Jolla, CA 92093. Offers chemistry (MS, PhD). *Degree requirements:* For doctorate, thesis/dissertation. *Entrance requirements:* For doctorate, GRE General Test, GRE Subject Test. Electronic applications accepted.

University of California, San Diego, Office of Graduate Studies, Division of Biological Sciences, Program in Biochemistry, La Jolla, CA 92093-0348. Offers PhD. Offered in association with the Salk Institute. *Degree requirements:* For doctorate, thesis/dissertation, qualifying exam. Electronic applications accepted.

University of California, San Francisco, Graduate Division and School of Medicine, Department of Biochemistry and Biophysics, Program in Biochemistry and Molecular Biology, San Francisco, CA 94143. Offers PhD, MD/PhD. *Degree requirements:* For doctorate, thesis/dissertation. *Entrance requirements:* For doctorate, GRE General Test, GRE Subject Test. Additional exam requirements/recommendations for international students: Required—TOEFL. *Expenses:* Contact institution. *Faculty research:* Structural biology, genetics, cell biology, cell physiology, metabolism.

University of California, San Francisco, School of Pharmacy and Graduate Division, Chemistry and Chemical Biology Graduate Program, San Francisco, CA 94143. Offers PhD. *Faculty:* 45 full-time (9 women). *Students:* 48 full-time (23 women); includes 18 minority (2 African Americans, 9 Asian Americans or Pacific Islanders, 7 Hispanic Americans), 4 international. Average age 27. 111 applicants, 19% accepted, 9 enrolled. In 2009, 8 doctorates awarded. *Degree requirements:* For doctorate, thesis/dissertation. *Entrance requirements:* For doctorate, GRE General Test, GRE Subject Test, minimum GPA of 3.0. Additional exam requirements/recommendations for international students: Required—TOEFL (minimum score 550 paper-based; 213 computer-based; 80 iBT). *Application deadline:* For fall admission, 12/1 for domestic and international students. Applications are processed on a rolling basis. Application fee: $70 ($90 for international students). Electronic applications accepted. *Financial support:* In 2009–10, 48 students received support, including 41 fellowships with partial tuition reimbursements available (averaging $19,365 per year), 16 research assistantships with full tuition reimbursements available (averaging $27,000 per year), 2 teaching assistantships with partial tuition reimbursements available (averaging $16,000 per year); institutionally sponsored loans, scholarships/grants, traineeships, and tuition waivers (full) also available. Financial award application deadline: 5/15. *Faculty research:* Biochemistry, macromolecular structure, cellular and molecular pharmacology, physical chemistry and computational biology, synthetic chemistry. *Unit head:* Dr. Charles S. Craik, Director, 415-476-8146, E-mail: craik@cgl.ucsf.edu. *Application contact:* Christine Olson, Senior Administrative Analyst, 415-476-1914, Fax: 415-514-1546, E-mail: olson@cmp.ucsf.edu.

University of California, Santa Barbara, Graduate Division, College of Letters and Sciences, Division of Mathematics, Life, and Physical Sciences, Interdepartmental Graduate Program in Biomolecular Science and Engineering, Santa Barbara, CA 93106-9611. Offers biochemistry and molecular biology (MS, PhD), including biochemistry and molecular biology, biomolecular science and engineering (MS). *Faculty:* 40 full-time (5 women), 2 part-time/adjunct (1 woman). *Students:* 33 full-time (12 women). Average age 28. 62 applicants, 29% accepted, 5 enrolled. In 2009, 3 master's, 2 doctorates awarded. Terminal master's awarded for partial completion of doctoral program. *Degree requirements:* For master's, comprehensive exam (for some programs), thesis (for some programs); for doctorate, comprehensive exam, thesis/dissertation. *Entrance requirements:* For master's, GRE General Test, GRE Subject Test, bachelor's degree in a related science, 3 letters of recommendation, statement of purpose, personal achievements/contributions statement, resume/curriculum vitae, transcripts for post-secondary institutions attended; for doctorate, GRE General Test, GRE Subject Test, bachelor's degree in a related science, 3 letters of recommendation, resume/curriculum vitae. Additional exam requirements/recommendations for international students: Required—TOEFL (minimum score 630 paper-based; 267 computer-based; 109 iBT) or IELTS (minimum score 7). *Application deadline:* For fall admission, 12/15 for domestic and international students. Application fee: $70 ($90 for international students). Electronic applications accepted. *Financial support:* In 2009–10, 33 students received support, including 12 fellowships with full and partial tuition reimbursements available (averaging $15,300 per year), 100 research assistantships with full and partial tuition reimbursements available (averaging $9,500 per year), 92 teaching assistantships with partial tuition reimbursements available (averaging $8,700 per year); career-related internships or fieldwork, Federal Work-Study, institutionally sponsored loans, scholarships/grants, traineeships, health care benefits, tuition waivers (full and partial), and unspecified assistantships also available. Financial award applicants required to submit FAFSA. *Faculty research:* Biochemistry and molecular biology, biophysics, biomaterials, bioengineering, systems biology. *Unit head:* Prof. Philip A. Pincus, Chair, 805-893-4685, E-mail: fyl@mrl.ucsb.edu. *Application contact:* Azure Stewart, Graduate Program Advisor, 805-893-6083, Fax: 805-893-4724, E-mail: azstewart@lifesci.ucsb.edu.

University of California, Santa Cruz, Division of Graduate Studies, Division of Physical and Biological Sciences, Department of Chemistry and Biochemistry, Santa Cruz, CA 95064. Offers MS, PhD. *Degree requirements:* For master's, thesis optional; for doctorate, one foreign language, thesis/dissertation, qualifying exam. *Entrance requirements:* For master's and doctorate, GRE General Test, GRE Subject Test. *Faculty research:* Marine chemistry; biochemistry; inorganic, organic, and physical chemistry.

Biochemistry

University of Chicago, Division of the Biological Sciences, Department of Molecular Biosciences, Department of Biochemistry and Molecular Biology, Chicago, IL 60637-1513. Offers PhD, MD/PhD. *Faculty:* 31 full-time (8 women). *Students:* 35 full-time (14 women); includes 5 minority (2 American Indian/Alaska Native, 3 Asian Americans or Pacific Islanders), 6 international. Average age 28. 44 applicants, 7% accepted, 3 enrolled. In 2009, 8 doctorates awarded. *Degree requirements:* For doctorate, thesis/dissertation, ethics class, 2 teaching assistantships. *Entrance requirements:* For doctorate, GRE General Test, GRE Subject Test. Additional exam requirements/recommendations for international students: Required—TOEFL (minimum score 600 paper-based; 250 computer-based; 104 iBT), IELTS (minimum score 7). *Application deadline:* For fall admission, 12/1 priority date for domestic and international students. Application fee: $55. Electronic applications accepted. *Financial support:* In 2009–10, 35 students received support, including fellowships with tuition reimbursements available (averaging $29,781 per year), research assistantships with tuition reimbursements available (averaging $29,781 per year); institutionally sponsored loans, scholarships/grants, traineeships, and health care benefits also available. Financial award applicants required to submit FAFSA. *Faculty research:* Molecular biology, gene expression, and DNA-protein interactions; membrane biochemistry, molecular endocrinology, and transmembrane signaling; enzyme mechanisms, physical biochemistry, and structural biology. Total annual research expenditures: $5 million. *Unit head:* Dr. Anthony A. Kossiakoff, Chairman, 773-702-9297, Fax: 773-702-0439, E-mail: koss@cummings.uchicago.edu. *Application contact:* Lisa Anderson, Graduate Student Administrator, 773-834-3586, Fax: 773-702-0439, E-mail: landerso@bsd.uchicago.edu.

University of Cincinnati, Graduate School, College of Medicine, Graduate Programs in Biomedical Sciences, Department of Molecular Genetics, Biochemistry and Microbiology, Cincinnati, OH 45221. Offers MS, PhD. Terminal master's awarded for partial completion of doctoral program. *Degree requirements:* For master's, thesis or alternative; for doctorate, thesis/dissertation, qualifying exam. *Entrance requirements:* For master's and doctorate, GRE General Test. Additional exam requirements/recommendations for international students: Required—TOEFL (minimum score 600 paper-based; 250 computer-based; 100 iBT), TWE. Electronic applications accepted. *Faculty research:* Cancer biology and developmental genetics, gene regulation and chromosome structure, microbiology and pathogenic mechanisms, structural biology, membrane biochemistry and signal transduction.

University of Cincinnati, Graduate School, McMicken College of Arts and Sciences, Department of Chemistry, Cincinnati, OH 45221. Offers analytical chemistry (MS, PhD); biochemistry (MS, PhD); inorganic chemistry (MS, PhD); organic chemistry (MS, PhD); physical chemistry (MS, PhD); polymer chemistry (MS, PhD); sensors (PhD). Part-time and evening/weekend programs available. Terminal master's awarded for partial completion of doctoral program. *Degree requirements:* For master's, thesis optional; for doctorate, comprehensive exam, thesis/dissertation. *Entrance requirements:* For master's and doctorate, GRE General Test. Additional exam requirements/recommendations for international students: Required—TOEFL (minimum score 580 paper-based; 237 computer-based). Electronic applications accepted. *Faculty research:* Biomedical chemistry, laser chemistry, surface science, chemical sensors, synthesis.

University of Colorado at Boulder, Graduate School, College of Arts and Sciences, Department of Chemistry and Biochemistry, Boulder, CO 80309. Offers biochemistry (PhD); chemistry (MS). *Faculty:* 44 full-time (7 women). *Students:* 127 full-time (49 women), 71 part-time (36 women); includes 20 minority (4 African Americans, 3 American Indian/Alaska Native, 7 Asian Americans or Pacific Islanders, 6 Hispanic Americans), 30 international. Average age 27. 464 applicants, 10% accepted, 47 enrolled. In 2009, 3 master's, 17 doctorates awarded. *Degree requirements:* For master's, comprehensive exam or thesis; for doctorate, comprehensive exam, thesis/dissertation, cumulative exam. *Entrance requirements:* For master's, GRE General Test, GRE Subject Test, minimum undergraduate GPA of 2.75; for doctorate, GRE General Test, GRE Subject Test, minimum GPA of 3.0. *Application deadline:* For fall admission, 1/15 priority date for domestic students, 1/15 for international students. Applications are processed on a rolling basis. Application fee: $50 ($60 for international students). *Financial support:* In 2009–10, 48 fellowships with full tuition reimbursements (averaging $12,195 per year), 110 research assistantships with full tuition reimbursements (averaging $16,014 per year) were awarded; institutionally sponsored loans, traineeships, and tuition waivers (full) also available. Support available to part-time students. *Faculty research:* Analytical, atmospheric, biochemistry, biophysical, chemical physics, environmental, inorganic, organic and physical chemistry. Total annual research expenditures: $18.1 million.

University of Colorado Denver, School of Medicine, Biochemistry Program, Denver, CO 80217-3364. Offers PhD. *Students:* 27 full-time (12 women); includes 1 minority (Asian American or Pacific Islander), 6 international. In 2009, 3 doctorates awarded. *Degree requirements:* For doctorate, thesis/dissertation. *Entrance requirements:* For doctorate, GRE General Test. Additional exam requirements/recommendations for international students: Required—TOEFL (minimum score 550 paper-based; 213 computer-based). *Application deadline:* For fall admission, 1/15 for domestic students. Application fee: $50. Electronic applications accepted. *Financial support:* Fellowships available. Financial award application deadline: 3/15; financial award applicants required to submit FAFSA. *Faculty research:* DNA damage, cancer and neurodegeneration, molecular mechanisms of pro-MRNA splicing, yeast RNA polymerases, DNA replication. *Unit head:* Dr. Mark Johnston, Chair, 303-724-3201, Fax: 303-724-3215, E-mail: mark.johnston@ucdenver.edu. *Application contact:* Deanne Sylvester, Administrative Assistant, 303-724-3201, E-mail: deanne.sylvester@ucdenver.edu.

University of Connecticut, Graduate School, College of Liberal Arts and Sciences, Department of Molecular and Cell Biology, Field of Biochemistry, Storrs, CT 06269. Offers MS, PhD. *Faculty:* 21 full-time (7 women). *Students:* 26 full-time (14 women); includes 2 minority (both Asian Americans or Pacific Islanders), 11 international. Average age 27. 70 applicants, 11% accepted, 2 enrolled. In 2009, 4 master's, 1 doctorate awarded. Terminal master's awarded for partial completion of doctoral program. *Degree requirements:* For master's, comprehensive exam; for doctorate, thesis/dissertation. *Entrance requirements:* For master's and doctorate, GRE General Test, GRE Subject Test. Additional exam requirements/recommendations for international students: Required—TOEFL (minimum score 550 paper-based; 213 computer-based). *Application deadline:* For fall admission, 2/1 priority date for domestic and international students; for spring admission, 11/1 for domestic students, 10/1 for international students. Applications are processed on a rolling basis. Application fee: $55. Electronic applications accepted. *Expenses:* Tuition, state resident: full-time $4725; part-time $525 per credit. Tuition, nonresident: full-time $12,267; part-time $1363 per credit. Required fees: $346 per semester. Tuition and fees vary according to course load. *Financial support:* In 2009–10, 11 research assistantships with full tuition reimbursements, 13 teaching assistantships with full tuition reimbursements were awarded; fellowships, Federal Work-Study, scholarships/grants, health care benefits, and unspecified assistantships also available. Financial award application deadline: 2/1; financial award applicants required to submit FAFSA. *Unit head:* David Benson, Head, 860-486-4258, Fax: 860-486-4331, E-mail: david.benson@uconn.edu. *Application contact:* Anne St. Onje, Graduate Coordinator, 860-486-4314, Fax: 860-486-3943, E-mail: anne.st_onje@uconn.edu.

See Close-Up on page 187.

University of Connecticut Health Center, Graduate School, Programs in Biomedical Sciences, Program in Molecular Biology and Biochemistry, Farmington, CT 06030. Offers PhD, DMD/PhD, MD/PhD. *Faculty:* 30. *Students:* 22 full-time (13 women); includes 3 minority (1 African American, 2 Asian Americans or Pacific Islanders), 8 international. Average age 29. 165 applicants, 35% accepted. In 2009, 5 doctorates awarded. *Degree requirements:* For doctorate, comprehensive exam, thesis/dissertation. *Entrance requirements:* For doctorate, GRE General Test. Additional exam requirements/recommendations for international students: Required—TOEFL (minimum score 600 paper-based; 250 computer-based). *Application deadline:* For fall admission, 12/15 for domestic students. Application fee: $55. Electronic applications accepted. *Financial support:* In 2009–10, 22 students received support, including 22 research assistantships with full tuition reimbursements available (averaging $27,000 per year); fellowships, health care benefits also available. *Faculty research:* Molecular biology, structural biology, protein biochemistry, microbial physiology and pathogenesis. *Unit head:* Dr. Stephen King, Director, 860-679-3347, Fax: 860-679-1239, E-mail: sking@nso2.uchc.edu. *Application contact:* Tricia Avolt, Graduate Admissions Coordinator, 860-679-2175, Fax: 860-679-1899, E-mail: robertson@nso2.uchc.edu.

See Close-Up on page 243.

University of Delaware, College of Arts and Sciences, Department of Chemistry and Biochemistry, Newark, DE 19716. Offers biochemistry (MA, MS, PhD); chemistry (MA, MS, PhD). Part-time programs available. Terminal master's awarded for partial completion of doctoral program. *Degree requirements:* For master's, one foreign language, thesis (for some programs); for doctorate, one foreign language, thesis/dissertation, cumulative exam. *Entrance requirements:* For master's and doctorate, GRE General Test. Additional exam requirements/recommendations for international students: Required—TOEFL (minimum score 600 paper-based; 260 computer-based). Electronic applications accepted. *Faculty research:* Micro-organisms, bone, cancer metastosis, developmental biology, cell biology, molecular biology.

University of Detroit Mercy, College of Engineering and Science, Department of Chemistry and Biochemistry, Detroit, MI 48221. Offers chemistry (MS). Evening/weekend programs available. *Degree requirements:* For master's, thesis. *Entrance requirements:* For master's, GRE General Test, minimum GPA of 3.0. *Faculty research:* Polymer and physical chemistry, industrial aspects of chemistry.

University of Florida, College of Medicine, Department of Biochemistry and Molecular Biology, Gainesville, FL 32611. Offers biochemistry and molecular biology (MS, PhD); imaging science and technology (MS, PhD). *Degree requirements:* For doctorate, thesis/dissertation. *Entrance requirements:* For doctorate, GRE General Test, minimum GPA of 3.0. Additional exam requirements/recommendations for international students: Required—TOEFL. Electronic applications accepted. *Faculty research:* Gene expression, metabolic regulation, structural biology, enzyme mechanism, membrane transporters.

University of Florida, College of Medicine and Graduate School, Interdisciplinary Program in Biomedical Sciences, Concentration in Biochemistry and Molecular Biology, Gainesville, FL 32611. Offers PhD. *Degree requirements:* For doctorate, thesis/dissertation. *Entrance requirements:* For doctorate, GRE General Test, minimum GPA of 3.0. Additional exam requirements/recommendations for international students: Required—TOEFL. Electronic applications accepted. *Faculty research:* Gene expression, metabolic regulation, structural biology, enzyme mechanism, membrane transporters.

See Close-Up on page 161.

University of Georgia, Graduate School, College of Arts and Sciences, Department of Biochemistry and Molecular Biology, Athens, GA 30602. Offers MS, PhD. *Faculty:* 34 full-time (3 women). *Students:* 63 full-time (25 women), 4 part-time (3 women); includes 7 minority (4 African Americans, 2 Asian Americans or Pacific Islanders, 1 Hispanic American), 21 international. 96 applicants, 16% accepted, 14 enrolled. In 2009, 3 master's, 2 doctorates awarded. *Degree requirements:* For master's, one foreign language, thesis; for doctorate, one foreign language, thesis/dissertation. *Entrance requirements:* For master's and doctorate, GRE General Test. Additional exam requirements/recommendations for international students: Required—TOEFL. *Application deadline:* For fall admission, 1/1 priority date for domestic and international students. Application fee: $50. Electronic applications accepted. *Expenses:* Tuition, state resident: full-time $6000; part-time $250 per credit hour. Tuition, nonresident: full-time $20,904; part-time $871 per credit hour. Required fees: $730 per semester. *Financial support:* Fellowships, research assistantships, teaching assistantships, scholarships/grants and unspecified assistantships available. Financial award application deadline: 1/1. *Unit head:* Dr. Stephen L. Hajduk, Head, 706-542-1676, Fax: 706-542-0182, E-mail: shajduk@bmb.uga.edu. *Application contact:* Dr. Walter K. Schmidt, Graduate Coordinator, 706-583-8241, Fax: 706-542-1738, E-mail: gradcoordinator@bmb.uga.edu.

University of Guelph, Graduate Program Services, College of Biological Science, Department of Molecular and Cellular Biology, Guelph, ON N1G 2W1, Canada. Offers biochemistry (M Sc, PhD); biophysics (M Sc, PhD); botany (M Sc, PhD); microbiology (M Sc, PhD); molecular biology and genetics (M Sc, PhD). *Degree requirements:* For master's, thesis, research proposal; for doctorate, comprehensive exam, thesis/dissertation, research proposal. *Entrance requirements:* For master's, minimum B-average during previous 2 years of coursework; for doctorate, minimum A-average. Additional exam requirements/recommendations for international students: Required—TOEFL (minimum score 550 paper-based; 213 computer-based), IELTS (minimum score 6.5). Electronic applications accepted. *Faculty research:* Physiology, structure, genetics, and ecology of microbes; virology and microbial technology.

University of Guelph, Graduate Program Services, College of Physical and Engineering Science, Guelph-Waterloo Centre for Graduate Work in Chemistry and Biochemistry, Guelph, ON N1G 2W1, Canada. Offers M Sc, PhD. Part-time programs available. *Degree requirements:* For master's, thesis; for doctorate, thesis/dissertation. *Faculty research:* Inorganic, analytical, biological, physical/theoretical, polymer, and organic chemistry.

University of Houston, College of Natural Sciences and Mathematics, Department of Biology and Biochemistry, Houston, TX 77204. Offers biology (MS). *Faculty:* 28 full-time (9 women), 1 part-time/adjunct (0 women). *Students:* 82 full-time (48 women), 8 part-time (2 women); includes 10 minority (3 African Americans, 3 Asian Americans or Pacific Islanders, 4 Hispanic Americans), 59 international. Average age 28. 16 applicants, 100% accepted, 13 enrolled. In 2009, 4 master's, 11 doctorates awarded. Terminal master's awarded for partial completion of doctoral program. *Degree requirements:* For master's, comprehensive exam (for some programs), thesis optional; for doctorate, comprehensive exam (for some programs), thesis/dissertation. *Entrance requirements:* For master's and doctorate, GRE. Additional exam requirements/recommendations for international students: Required—TOEFL (minimum score 550 paper-based; 213 computer-based; 79 iBT), IELTS (minimum score 6.5). *Application deadline:* For fall admission, 4/1 for domestic and international students; for spring admission, 10/1 for domestic and international students. Application fee: $75 for international students. Electronic applications accepted. *Expenses:* Tuition, state resident: full-time $7676; part-time $320 per credit hour. Tuition, nonresident: full-time $14,324; part-time $597 per credit hour. Required fees: $3034. *Financial support:* In 2009–10, 45 fellowships with full tuition reimbursements (averaging $14,300 per year), 39 research assistantships with full tuition reimbursements (averaging $14,300 per year) were awarded; career-related internships or fieldwork, Federal Work-Study, institutionally sponsored loans, scholarships/grants, health care benefits, and unspecified assistantships also available. Support available to part-time students. Financial award application deadline: 2/1. *Faculty research:* Cell and molecular biology, ecology and evolution, biochemical and biophysical sciences, chemical biology. *Unit head:* Dr. Stuart Dryer, Chairman, 713-743-2697, E-mail: sdryer@uh.edu. *Application contact:* Amanda Paul, Academic Advisor, 713-743-2633, Fax: 713-743-2636, E-mail: biogradaffair@nsm.uh.edu.

University of Idaho, College of Graduate Studies, College of Agricultural and Life Sciences, Department of Microbiology, Molecular Biology and Biochemistry, Moscow, ID 83844-2282. Offers microbiology, molecular biology and biochemistry (PhD). *Faculty:* 15 full-time, 1 part-time/adjunct. *Students:* 21 full-time, 4 part-time. In 2009, 6 master's, 4 doctorates awarded. *Degree requirements:* For master's, thesis; for doctorate, one foreign language, thesis/dissertation. *Entrance requirements:* For master's, minimum GPA of 2.8; for doctorate, minimum undergraduate GPA of 2.8, 3.0 graduate. *Application deadline:* For fall admission, 8/1 for domestic students; for spring admission, 12/15 for domestic students. Application fee: $55 ($60 for international students). *Expenses:* Tuition, state resident: full-time $6120. Tuition, nonresident: full-time $17,712. *Financial support:* Research assistantships, teaching assistantships available. Financial award application deadline: 2/15. *Faculty research:* Bioremediation, biodegradation and molecular ecology, developmental and cellular biology, cell cycle regulation, molecular machines, pathogenic mechanisms in infectious disease. *Unit head:* Dr. Bruce

Miller, Interim Chair, 208-885-7966, E-mail: mmbb@uidaho.edu. *Application contact:* Dr. Bruce Miller, Interim Chair, 208-885-7966, E-mail: mmbb@uidaho.edu.

University of Illinois at Chicago, College of Medicine and Graduate College, Graduate Programs in Medicine, Department of Biochemistry and Molecular Genetics, Chicago, IL 60607-7128. Offers PhD, MD/PhD. Terminal master's awarded for partial completion of doctoral program. *Degree requirements:* For doctorate, thesis/dissertation. *Entrance requirements:* For doctorate, GRE General Test. Additional exam requirements/recommendations for international students: Required—TOEFL. Electronic applications accepted. *Faculty research:* Nature of cellular components, control of metabolic processes, regulation of gene expression.

University of Illinois at Urbana–Champaign, Graduate College, College of Liberal Arts and Sciences, School of Chemical Sciences, Champaign, IL 61820. Offers MA, MS, PhD, MS/JD, MS/MBA. *Faculty:* 50 full-time (8 women). *Students:* 423 full-time (138 women), 8 part-time (1 woman); includes 49 minority (9 African Americans, 3 American Indian/Alaska Native, 27 Asian Americans or Pacific Islanders, 10 Hispanic Americans), 132 international. 883 applicants, 16% accepted, 91 enrolled. In 2009, 20 master's, 71 doctorates awarded. *Entrance requirements:* For master's, minimum GPA of 3.0. *Application deadline:* Applications are processed on a rolling basis. Application fee: $60 ($75 for international students). Electronic applications accepted. *Expenses:* Contact institution. *Financial support:* In 2009–10, 131 fellowships, 292 research assistantships, 204 teaching assistantships were awarded; tuition waivers (full and partial) also available. *Unit head:* Andrew A. Gewirth, Director, 217-333-8329, Fax: 217-333-2685, E-mail: agewirth@illinois.edu. *Application contact:* Cheryl Kappes, Office Manager, 217-333-5070, Fax: 217-333-3120, E-mail: dambache@illinois.edu.

University of Illinois at Urbana–Champaign, Graduate College, College of Liberal Arts and Sciences, School of Molecular and Cellular Biology, Department of Biochemistry, Champaign, IL 61820. Offers MS, PhD. *Faculty:* 10 full-time (1 woman). *Students:* 65 full-time (32 women); includes 17 minority (1 African American, 12 Asian Americans or Pacific Islanders, 4 Hispanic Americans), 26 international. In 2009, 6 master's, 15 doctorates awarded. *Entrance requirements:* For master's, GRE General Test, minimum GPA of 3.0; for doctorate, GRE General Test, minimum GPA of 3.0. Additional exam requirements/recommendations for international students: Required—TOEFL (minimum score 590 paper-based; 243 computer-based; 96 iBT). *Application deadline:* Applications are processed on a rolling basis. Application fee: $60 ($75 for international students). Electronic applications accepted. *Financial support:* In 2009–10, 17 fellowships, 59 research assistantships, 30 teaching assistantships were awarded; tuition waivers (full and partial) also available. *Unit head:* Colin A. Wraight, Head, 217-333-3945, Fax: 217-333-8920, E-mail: cwraight@illinois.edu. *Application contact:* Louise R. Cox, Assistant to the Head, 217-333-7149, Fax: 217-244-5858, E-mail: l-cox1@illinois.edu.

The University of Iowa, Roy J. and Lucille A. Carver College of Medicine and Graduate College, Graduate Programs in Medicine, Department of Biochemistry, Iowa City, IA 52242-1316. Offers MS, PhD, MD/PhD. *Faculty:* 19 full-time (4 women), 5 part-time/adjunct (4 women). *Students:* 18 full-time (7 women), 5 international. Average age 27. 128 applicants, 16% accepted, 4 enrolled. In 2009, 3 doctorates awarded. Terminal master's awarded for partial completion of doctoral program. *Degree requirements:* For master's, thesis; for doctorate, comprehensive exam, thesis/dissertation, research project, one semester of teaching. *Entrance requirements:* For master's and doctorate, GRE General Test. Additional exam requirements/recommendations for international students: Required—TOEFL (minimum score 600 paper-based; 250 computer-based; 100 iBT). *Application deadline:* For fall admission, 1/15 priority date for domestic and international students. Applications are processed on a rolling basis. Application fee: $60 ($85 for international students). Electronic applications accepted. *Financial support:* In 2009–10, fellowships with full tuition reimbursements (averaging $24,250 per year), research assistantships with full tuition reimbursements (averaging $24,250 per year), teaching assistantships with full tuition reimbursements (averaging $24,250 per year) were awarded; institutionally sponsored loans, scholarships/grants, traineeships, tuition waivers, and unspecified assistantships also available. *Faculty research:* Regulation of gene expression, protein structure, membrane structure/function, DNA structure and replication. Total annual research expenditures: $4.8 million. *Unit head:* Dr. Charles M. Brenner, Head, 319-335-7934, Fax: 319-335-9570, E-mail: charles-brenner@uiowa.edu. *Application contact:* Admissions Committee, 319-335-7932, Fax: 319-335-9570, E-mail: biochem@uiowa.edu.

The University of Kansas, Graduate Studies, College of Liberal Arts and Sciences, Department of Molecular Biosciences, Lawrence, KS 66044. Offers biochemistry and biophysics (MA, PhD); microbiology (MA, PhD); molecular, cellular, and developmental biology (MA, PhD). *Students:* 58 full-time (30 women), 2 part-time (1 woman); includes 4 minority (1 American Indian/Alaska Native, 1 Asian American or Pacific Islander, 2 Hispanic Americans), 24 international. Average age 27. 49 applicants, 29% accepted, 4 enrolled. In 2009, 2 master's, 7 doctorates awarded. Terminal master's awarded for partial completion of doctoral program. *Degree requirements:* For master's, comprehensive exam, thesis; for doctorate, comprehensive exam, thesis/dissertation. *Entrance requirements:* For master's and doctorate, GRE General Test. Additional exam requirements/recommendations for international students: Required—TOEFL (minimum score 24 iBT). *Application deadline:* For fall admission, 12/15 for domestic and international students. Application fee: $45 ($55 for international students). Electronic applications accepted. *Expenses:* Tuition, state resident: full-time $6492; part-time $270.50 per credit hour. Tuition, nonresident: full-time $15,510; part-time $646.25 per credit hour. Required fees: $847; $70.56 per credit hour. Tuition and fees vary according to course load and program. *Financial support:* Fellowships with tuition reimbursements, research assistantships with tuition reimbursements, teaching assistantships with tuition reimbursements, health care benefits and unspecified assistantships available. Financial award application deadline: 3/1. *Faculty research:* Structure and function of proteins, genetics of organism development, molecular genetics, neurophysiology, molecular virology and pathogenics, developmental biology, cell biology. *Unit head:* Dr. Mark Richter, Chair, 785-864-4311, Fax: 785-864-5294, E-mail: richter@ku.edu. *Application contact:* John P. Connolly, Graduate Program Assistant, 785-864-4311, Fax: 785-864-5294, E-mail: jconnolly@ku.edu.

The University of Kansas, University of Kansas Medical Center, School of Medicine, Department of Biochemistry and Molecular Biology, Kansas City, KS 66160. Offers MS, PhD, MD/PhD. *Faculty:* 14 full-time, 5 part-time/adjunct. *Students:* 8 part-time (1 woman), 4 international. Average age 28. In 2009, 2 doctorates awarded. Terminal master's awarded for partial completion of doctoral program. *Degree requirements:* For master's, oral defense of thesis; for doctorate, comprehensive oral and written exam. *Entrance requirements:* Additional exam requirements/recommendations for international students: Required—TOEFL. Application fee: $0. Electronic applications accepted. *Expenses:* Tuition, state resident: full-time $6492; part-time $270.50 per credit hour. Tuition, nonresident: full-time $15,510; part-time $646.25 per credit hour. Required fees: $847; $70.56 per credit hour. Tuition and fees vary according to course load and program. *Financial support:* In 2009–10, research assistantships with partial tuition reimbursements (averaging $24,000 per year), teaching assistantships with full and partial tuition reimbursements (averaging $24,000 per year) were awarded; fellowships, traineeships, health care benefits, and unspecified assistantships also available. *Faculty research:* Determination of portion structure, underlying bases for interaction of proteins with their target, mapping allosteric circuiting within proteins, mechanism of action of transcription factors, renal signal transduction. Total annual research expenditures: $4.2 million. *Unit head:* Dr. Gerald M. Carlson, Chairman, 913-588-6574, Fax: 913-588-7007, E-mail: gcarlson@kumc.edu. *Application contact:* Dr. Liskin Swint-Kruse, Associate Professor, 913-588-0399, Fax: 913-588-9896, E-mail: lswint-kruse@kumc.edu.

University of Kentucky, Graduate School, Graduate School Programs from the College of Medicine, Program in Molecular and Cellular Biochemistry, Lexington, KY 40506-0032. Offers biochemistry (PhD); MD/PhD. *Degree requirements:* For doctorate, comprehensive exam, thesis/dissertation. *Entrance requirements:* For doctorate, GRE General Test, minimum undergraduate GPA of 2.75. Additional exam requirements/recommendations for international students: Required—TOEFL (minimum score 550 paper-based; 213 computer-based). Electronic applications accepted.

University of Lethbridge, School of Graduate Studies, Lethbridge, AB T1K 3M4, Canada. Offers accounting (MScM); addictions counseling (M Sc); agricultural biotechnology (M Sc); agricultural studies (M Sc, MA); anthropology (MA); archaeology (MA); art (MA, MFA); biochemistry (M Sc); biological sciences (M Sc); biomolecular science (PhD); biosystems and biodiversity (PhD); Canadian studies (MA); chemistry (M Sc); computer science (M Sc); computer science and geographical information science (M Sc); counseling psychology (M Ed); dramatic arts (MA); earth, space, and physical science (PhD); economics (MA); educational leadership (M Ed); English (MA); environmental science (M Sc); evolution and behavior (PhD); exercise science (M Sc); finance (MScM); French (MA); French/German (MA); French/Spanish (MA); general education (M Ed); general management (MScM); geography (M Sc, MA); German (MA); health science (M Sc); history (MA); human resource management and labour relations (MScM); individualized multidisciplinary (M Sc, MA); information systems (MScM); international management (MScM); kinesiology (M Sc, MA); management (M Sc, MA); marketing (MScM); mathematics (M Sc); music (M Mus, MA); Native American studies (MA); neuroscience (M Sc, PhD); new media (MA); nursing (M Sc); philosophy (MA); physics (M Sc); policy and strategy (MScM); political science (MA); psychology (M Sc, MA); religious studies (MA); social sciences (MA); sociology (MA); theatre and dramatic arts (MFA); theoretical and computational science (PhD); urban and regional studies (MA); women's studies (MA). Part-time and evening/weekend programs available. *Degree requirements:* For doctorate, comprehensive exam, thesis/dissertation. *Entrance requirements:* For master's, GMAT (M Sc in management), bachelor's degree in related field, minimum GPA of 3.0 during previous 20 graded semester courses, 2 years teaching or related experience (M Ed); for doctorate, master's degree, minimum graduate GPA of 3.5. Additional exam requirements/recommendations for international students: Required—TOEFL. *Faculty research:* Movement and brain plasticity, gibberellin physiology, photosynthesis, carbon cycling, molecular properties of main-group ring components.

University of Louisville, Graduate School, College of Arts and Sciences, Department of Chemistry, Louisville, KY 40292-0001. Offers analytical chemistry (MS, PhD); biochemistry (MS, PhD); chemical physics (PhD); inorganic chemistry (MS, PhD); organic chemistry (MS, PhD); physical chemistry (MS, PhD). *Students:* 57 full-time (27 women), 4 part-time (1 woman); includes 2 minority (1 African American, 1 Asian American or Pacific Islander), 43 international. Average age 29. 62 applicants, 31% accepted, 13 enrolled. In 2009, 6 master's, 7 doctorates awarded. *Median time to degree:* Of those who began their doctoral program in fall 2001, 0% received their degree in 8 years or less. *Degree requirements:* For master's, thesis; for doctorate, comprehensive exam, thesis/dissertation. *Entrance requirements:* For master's and doctorate, GRE General Test. Additional exam requirements/recommendations for international students: Required—TOEFL. *Application deadline:* Applications are processed on a rolling basis. Application fee: $50. *Financial support:* Fellowships, research assistantships, teaching assistantships available. *Unit head:* Dr. George R. Pack, Chair, 502-852-6798, Fax: 502-852-8149, E-mail: george.pack@louisville.edu. *Application contact:* Libby Leggett, Director, Graduate Admissions, 502-852-3101, Fax: 502-852-6536, E-mail: gradadm@louisville.edu.

University of Louisville, School of Medicine, Department of Biochemistry and Molecular Biology, Louisville, KY 40292-0001. Offers MS, PhD, MD/PhD. *Faculty:* 33 full-time (7 women), 2 part-time/adjunct (1 woman). *Students:* 35 full-time (16 women), 5 part-time (4 women); includes 3 minority (2 African Americans, 1 Hispanic American), 10 international. Average age 29. 44 applicants, 23% accepted, 10 enrolled. In 2009, 12 master's, 5 doctorates awarded. Terminal master's awarded for partial completion of doctoral program. *Degree requirements:* For master's, thesis; for doctorate, comprehensive exam, thesis/dissertation, one first author publication. *Entrance requirements:* For master's, GRE General Test (minimum score 1000 verbal and quantitiative), minimum GPA of 3.0; for doctorate, GRE General Test (minimum Verbal and Quantitative score of 1000), minimum GPA of 3.0. Additional exam requirements/recommendations for international students: Required—TOEFL. *Application deadline:* For fall admission, 4/15 for domestic and international students. Applications are processed on a rolling basis. Application fee: $50. Electronic applications accepted. *Financial support:* In 2009–10, 35 students received support, including 12 fellowships with full tuition reimbursements available (averaging $22,000 per year), 23 research assistantships with full tuition reimbursements available (averaging $22,000 per year); teaching assistantships with tuition reimbursements available, scholarships/grants, traineeships, tuition waivers (full and partial), and unspecified assistantships also available. Financial award application deadline: 4/15. *Faculty research:* Genetic regulatory mechanisms, microRNAs, vesicular trafficking in cancer metastasis and angiogenesis, ribosome biogenesis and disease, regulation of foreign compound metabolism/lipid and steroid metabolism. *Unit head:* Dr. Ronald G. Gregg, Chair, 502-852-5217, Fax: 502-852-6222, E-mail: rggreg02@gwise.louisville.edu. *Application contact:* Dr. William L. Dean, Information Contact, 502-852-5227, Fax: 502-852-6222, E-mail: wldean01@gwise.louisville.edu.

University of Maine, Graduate School, College of Natural Sciences, Forestry, and Agriculture, Department of Biochemistry, Molecular Biology, and Microbiology, Orono, ME 04469. Offers biochemistry (MPS, MS); biochemistry and molecular biology (PhD); microbiology (MPS, MS, PhD). *Faculty:* 9 full-time (4 women), 5 part-time/adjunct (3 women). *Students:* 19 full-time (11 women), 22 part-time (16 women); includes 3 minority (1 American Indian/Alaska Native, 1 Asian American or Pacific Islander, 1 Hispanic American), 6 international. Average age 30. 42 applicants, 33% accepted, 10 enrolled. In 2009, 5 master's, 2 doctorates awarded. *Degree requirements:* For doctorate, thesis/dissertation. *Entrance requirements:* For master's and doctorate, GRE General Test. Additional exam requirements/recommendations for international students: Required—TOEFL. *Application deadline:* For fall admission, 2/1 priority date for domestic students. Applications are processed on a rolling basis. Application fee: $65. Electronic applications accepted. *Financial support:* In 2009–10, 5 research assistantships with tuition reimbursements (averaging $20,893 per year), 12 teaching assistantships with tuition reimbursements (averaging $19,296 per year) were awarded; tuition waivers (full and partial) also available. Financial award application deadline: 3/1. *Unit head:* Dr. Robert Gundersen, Chair, 207-581-2802, Fax: 207-581-2801. *Application contact:* Scott G. Delcourt, Associate Dean of the Graduate School, 207-581-3291, Fax: 207-581-3232, E-mail: graduate@maine.edu.

University of Manitoba, Faculty of Medicine and Faculty of Graduate Studies, Graduate Programs in Medicine, Department of Biochemistry and Medical Genetics, Winnipeg, MB R3T 2N2, Canada. Offers M Sc, PhD. Terminal master's awarded for partial completion of doctoral program. *Degree requirements:* For master's, thesis; for doctorate, thesis/dissertation. *Faculty research:* Cancer, gene expression, membrane lipids, metabolic control, genetic diseases.

University of Maryland, Baltimore, Graduate School, Graduate Program in Life Sciences, Program in Biochemistry and Molecular Biology, Baltimore, MD 21201. Offers biochemistry (MS, PhD); MD/PhD. *Students:* 13 full-time (9 women), 18 part-time (9 women); includes 9 minority (2 African Americans, 1 American Indian/Alaska Native, 3 Asian Americans or Pacific Islanders, 3 Hispanic Americans), 3 international. Average age 27. 64 applicants, 16% accepted, 2 enrolled. In 2009, 1 doctorate awarded. *Entrance requirements:* For doctorate, GRE General Test. Additional exam requirements/recommendations for international students: Required—TOEFL (minimum score 550 paper-based; 80 iBT); Recommended—IELTS (minimum score 7). *Application deadline:* For fall admission, 1/15 for domestic and international students. Application fee: $50. Electronic applications accepted. *Expenses:* Tuition, state resident: full-time $7290; part-time $405 per credit hour. Tuition, nonresident: full-time $12,780; part-time $710 per credit hour. Required fees: $774; $10 per credit hour. $297 per semester. Tuition and fees vary according to course load, degree level and program. *Financial support:* In 2009–10, research assistantships with full tuition reimbursements (averaging $25,000 per year); fellowships, health care benefits and unspecified assistantships also available. Financial award application deadline: 3/1. *Faculty research:* Membrane transport, hormonal regulation, protein structure, molecular virology. *Unit head:* Dr. David Weber, Professor/Director, 410-706-4354,

Biochemistry

University of Maryland, Baltimore (continued)
E-mail: dweber@umaryland.edu. *Application contact:* Foyeke Daramola, Program Coordinator, 410-706-8417, Fax: 410-706-8297, E-mail: fdaramola@som.umaryland.edu.

University of Maryland, Baltimore County, Graduate School, College of Natural and Mathematical Sciences, Department of Chemistry and Biochemistry, Program in Biochemistry, Baltimore, MD 21201. Offers MS, PhD. *Faculty:* 43 full-time (4 women). *Students:* 47 full-time (30 women); includes 21 minority (8 African Americans, 1 American Indian/Alaska Native, 9 Asian Americans or Pacific Islanders, 3 Hispanic Americans), 4 international. Average age 25. 62 applicants, 27% accepted, 10 enrolled. In 2009, 90 doctorates awarded. Terminal master's awarded for partial completion of doctoral program. *Degree requirements:* For master's, comprehensive exam (for some programs), thesis (for some programs); for doctorate, comprehensive exam, thesis/dissertation. *Entrance requirements:* For doctorate, GRE General Test, minimum GPA of 3.0. Additional exam requirements/recommendations for international students: Required—TOEFL (minimum score 550 paper-based; 213 computer-based). *Application deadline:* For fall admission, 2/1 priority date for domestic and international students. Applications are processed on a rolling basis. Application fee: $50. Electronic applications accepted. *Financial support:* In 2009–10, 10 fellowships with full tuition reimbursements (averaging $25,000 per year), 35 research assistantships with full tuition reimbursements (averaging $25,000 per year) were awarded; health care benefits and tuition waivers (full) also available. *Faculty research:* Protein structure, metabolism, molecular biology, physical biochemistry, enzymology. *Unit head:* Dr. Michael F. Summers, Professor, 410-455-2880, Fax: 410-455-1174, E-mail: summers@hhmi.umbc.edu. *Application contact:* Foyeke A. Daramola, Coordinator, 410-706-8417, Fax: 410-706-8297, E-mail: fdaramola@som.umaryland.edu.

University of Maryland, College Park, Academic Affairs, College of Chemical and Life Sciences, Department of Chemistry and Biochemistry, Biochemistry Program, College Park, MD 20742. Offers MS, PhD. Part-time and evening/weekend programs available. *Students:* 44 full-time (23 women), 1 (woman) part-time; includes 9 minority (4 African Americans, 3 Asian Americans or Pacific Islanders, 2 Hispanic Americans), 18 international. 110 applicants, 23% accepted, 9 enrolled. In 2009, 1 master's, 5 doctorates awarded. Terminal master's awarded for partial completion of doctoral program. *Degree requirements:* For master's, thesis or alternative; for doctorate, thesis/dissertation, 2 seminar presentations, oral exam. *Entrance requirements:* For master's and doctorate, GRE General Test, GRE Subject Test (recommended), minimum GPA of 3.0, 3 letters of recommendation. Additional exam requirements/recommendations for international students: Required—TOEFL. *Application deadline:* For fall admission, 2/1 for domestic and international students. Applications are processed on a rolling basis. Application fee: $60. Electronic applications accepted. *Expenses:* Tuition, area resident: Part-time $471 per credit hour. Tuition, state resident: part-time $471 per credit hour. Tuition, nonresident: part-time $1016 per credit hour. Required fees: $337.04 per term. *Financial support:* In 2009–10, 2 fellowships (averaging $10,800 per year), 14 research assistantships (averaging $20,569 per year), 24 teaching assistantships with partial tuition reimbursements (averaging $19,079 per year) were awarded; Federal Work-Study also available. Support available to part-time students. Financial award applicants required to submit FAFSA. *Faculty research:* Analytical biochemistry, immunochemistry, drug metabolism, biosynthesis of proteins, mass spectrometry. *Unit head:* Dr. Michael Doyle, Chairperson, 301-405-1795, Fax: 301-314-2779, E-mail: mdoyle3@umd.edu. *Application contact:* Dean of Graduate School, 301-405-0358, Fax: 301-314-9305.

University of Massachusetts Amherst, Graduate School, College of Natural Sciences, Department of Biochemistry and Molecular Biology, Amherst, MA 01003. Offers biochemistry (MS). Only current UMass students are eligible for terminal MS. PhD offered through the Program in Molecular and Cellular Biology. Part-time programs available. *Faculty:* 17 full-time (6 women). *Students:* 2 full-time (0 women); includes 1 minority (Asian American or Pacific Islander). Average age 23. 3 applicants, 67% accepted, 2 enrolled. In 2009, 1 master's awarded. Terminal master's awarded for partial completion of doctoral program. *Degree requirements:* For master's, thesis or alternative. *Entrance requirements:* Additional exam requirements/recommendations for international students: Required—TOEFL (minimum score 550 paper-based; 213 computer-based; 80 iBT), IELTS (minimum score 6.5). *Application deadline:* For fall admission, 2/1 for domestic and international students. Applications are processed on a rolling basis. Application fee: $50 ($65 for international students). Electronic applications accepted. *Expenses:* Tuition, state resident: full-time $2640; part-time $110 per credit. Tuition, nonresident: full-time $9936; part-time $414 per credit. Tuition and fees vary according to course load. *Financial support:* In 2009–10, 26 research assistantships with full tuition reimbursements (averaging $14,338 per year), 7 teaching assistantships with full tuition reimbursements (averaging $13,422 per year) were awarded; fellowships, career-related internships or fieldwork, Federal Work-Study, scholarships/grants, traineeships, health care benefits, tuition waivers (full), and unspecified assistantships also available. Support available to part-time students. Financial award application deadline: 2/1. *Unit head:* Dr. Lila M. Gierasch, Graduate Program Director, 413-545-0353, Fax: 413-545-3291. *Application contact:* Jean M. Ames, Supervisor of Admissions, 413-545-0722, Fax: 413-577-0010, E-mail: gradadm@grad.umass.edu.

University of Massachusetts Amherst, Graduate School, Interdisciplinary Programs, Program in Molecular and Cellular Biology, Amherst, MA 01003. Offers biological chemistry and molecular biophysics (PhD); biomedicine (PhD); cellular and developmental biology (PhD). Part-time programs available. *Faculty:* 2 full-time (0 women). *Students:* 30 full-time (16 women), 48 part-time (26 women); includes 15 minority (4 African Americans, 1 American Indian/Alaska Native, 3 Asian Americans or Pacific Islanders, 7 Hispanic Americans), 23 international. Average age 27. 140 applicants, 23% accepted, 19 enrolled. In 2009, 12 doctorates awarded. Terminal master's awarded for partial completion of doctoral program. *Degree requirements:* For doctorate, comprehensive exam, thesis/dissertation. *Entrance requirements:* For doctorate, GRE General Test. Additional exam requirements/recommendations for international students: Required—TOEFL (minimum score 550 paper-based; 213 computer-based; 80 iBT), IELTS (minimum score 6.5). *Application deadline:* For fall admission, 12/1 for domestic and international students. Applications are processed on a rolling basis. Application fee: $50 ($65 for international students). Electronic applications accepted. *Expenses:* Tuition, state resident: full-time $2640; part-time $110 per credit. Tuition, nonresident: full-time $9936; part-time $414 per credit. Tuition and fees vary according to course load. *Financial support:* In 2009–10, 11 research assistantships with full tuition reimbursements (averaging $2,590 per year), 3 teaching assistantships with full tuition reimbursements (averaging $3,303 per year) were awarded; fellowships, career-related internships or fieldwork, Federal Work-Study, scholarships/grants, traineeships, health care benefits, tuition waivers (full), and unspecified assistantships also available. Support available to part-time students. Financial award application deadline: 12/1. *Unit head:* Dr. David J. Gross, Graduate Program Director, 413-545-3246, Fax: 413-545-1812. *Application contact:* Jean M. Ames, Supervisor of Admissions, 413-545-0722, Fax: 413-577-0010, E-mail: gradadm@grad.umass.edu.

University of Massachusetts Amherst, Graduate School, Interdisciplinary Programs, Program in Plant Biology, Amherst, MA 01003. Offers biochemistry and metabolism (MS, PhD); cell biology and physiology (MS, PhD); environmental, ecological and integrative (MS, PhD); genetics and evolution (MS, PhD). *Students:* 3 full-time (2 women), 12 part-time (5 women); includes 2 minority (both Asian Americans or Pacific Islanders), 8 international. Average age 27. 32 applicants, 41% accepted, 3 enrolled. In 2009, 3 master's, 1 doctorate awarded. *Degree requirements:* For master's, thesis; for doctorate, 2 foreign languages, comprehensive exam, thesis/dissertation. *Entrance requirements:* For master's and doctorate, GRE General Test. Additional exam requirements/recommendations for international students: Required—TOEFL (minimum score 550 paper-based; 213 computer-based; 80 iBT), IELTS (minimum score 6.5). *Application deadline:* For fall admission, 12/15 for domestic and international students; for spring admission, 10/1 for domestic and international students. Applications are processed on a rolling basis. Application fee: $50 ($65 for international students). Electronic applications accepted. *Expenses:* Tuition, state resident: full-time $2640; part-time $110 per credit. Tuition, nonresident: full-time $9936; part-time $414 per credit. Tuition and fees vary according to course load. *Financial support:* In 2009–10, 11 research assistantships with full tuition reimbursements (averaging $8,884 per year) were awarded; fellowships, teaching assistantships, career-related internships or fieldwork, Federal Work-Study, scholarships/grants, traineeships, health care benefits, tuition waivers (full), and unspecified assistantships also available. Support available to part-time students. Financial award application deadline: 12/15. *Unit head:* Dr. Elsbeth L. Walker, Graduate Program Director, 413-577-3217, Fax: 413-545-3243. *Application contact:* Jean M. Ames, Supervisor of Admissions, 413-545—0722, Fax: 413-577-0010, E-mail: gradadm@grad.umass.edu.

University of Massachusetts Lowell, College of Arts and Sciences, Department of Biological Sciences, Lowell, MA 01854-2881. Offers biochemistry (PhD); biological sciences (MS); biotechnology (MS). Part-time programs available. *Degree requirements:* For master's, thesis; for doctorate, thesis/dissertation. *Entrance requirements:* For master's and doctorate, GRE General Test. Electronic applications accepted.

University of Massachusetts Lowell, College of Arts and Sciences, Department of Chemistry, Lowell, MA 01854-2881. Offers analytical chemistry (PhD); biochemistry (PhD); chemistry (MS, PhD); environmental studies (PhD); green chemistry (PhD); inorganic chemistry (PhD); organic chemistry (PhD); polymer science (MS). Terminal master's awarded for partial completion of doctoral program. *Degree requirements:* For master's, thesis; for doctorate, 2 foreign languages, thesis/dissertation. *Entrance requirements:* For master's and doctorate, GRE General Test. Electronic applications accepted.

University of Massachusetts Worcester, Graduate School of Biomedical Sciences, Program in Biochemistry and Molecular Pharmacology, Worcester, MA 01655-0115. Offers PhD. *Degree requirements:* For doctorate, comprehensive exam, thesis/dissertation. *Entrance requirements:* For doctorate, GRE General Test. Additional exam requirements/recommendations for international students: Required—TOEFL (minimum score 600 paper-based; 250 computer-based). Electronic applications accepted. *Faculty research:* RNA; molecular, cellular, and regulatory biochemistry; molecular biophysics; chemical biology; structural biology.

University of Medicine and Dentistry of New Jersey, Graduate School of Biomedical Sciences, Graduate Programs in Biomedical Sciences–Newark, Department of Biochemistry and Molecular Biology, Newark, NJ 07107. Offers MS, PhD. *Students:* 17 full-time (11 women); includes 1 Hispanic American, 10 international. *Degree requirements:* For master's, thesis; for doctorate, thesis/dissertation, qualifying exam. *Entrance requirements:* For master's and doctorate, GRE General Test. Additional exam requirements/recommendations for international students: Required—TOEFL. *Application deadline:* For fall admission, 2/1 for domestic students. Applications are processed on a rolling basis. Application fee: $40. Electronic applications accepted. *Financial support:* Fellowships, research assistantships, Federal Work-Study, institutionally sponsored loans, and tuition waivers (full and partial) available. Financial award application deadline: 5/1. *Unit head:* Dr. Carol Lutz, Program Director, 973-972-0899, Fax: 973-972-5594, E-mail: lutzls@umdnj.edu. *Application contact:* Dr. Carol Lutz, Program Director, 973-972-0899, Fax: 973-972-5594, E-mail: lutzls@umdnj.edu.

University of Medicine and Dentistry of New Jersey, Graduate School of Biomedical Sciences, Graduate Programs in Biomedical Sciences–Piscataway, Program in Biochemistry and Molecular Biology, Piscataway, NJ 08854-5635. Offers MS, PhD, MD/PhD. Terminal master's awarded for partial completion of doctoral program. *Degree requirements:* For master's, thesis, qualifying exam; for doctorate, thesis/dissertation, qualifying exam. *Entrance requirements:* For master's and doctorate, GRE General Test. Additional exam requirements/recommendations for international students: Required—TOEFL. *Application deadline:* For fall admission, 1/5 for domestic students. Applications are processed on a rolling basis. Application fee: $40. Electronic applications accepted. *Financial support:* Fellowships, research assistantships, teaching assistantships available. Financial award application deadline: 5/1. *Faculty research:* Signal transduction, regulation of RNA, polymerase II transcribed genes, developmental gene expression. *Unit head:* Dr. Kiran Madura, Director, 732-235-5602, Fax: 732-235-5417, E-mail: maduraki@umdnj.edu. *Application contact:* University Registrar, 973-972-5338.

University of Miami, Graduate School, Miller School of Medicine, Graduate Programs in Medicine, Department of Biochemistry and Molecular Biology, Coral Gables, FL 33124. Offers PhD, MD/PhD. *Faculty:* 27 full-time (5 women). *Students:* 34 full-time (16 women); includes 1 Asian American or Pacific Islander, 5 Hispanic Americans, 19 international. Average age 26. *Degree requirements:* For doctorate, comprehensive exam, thesis/dissertation, proposition exams. *Financial support:* In 2009–10, 34 fellowships with full tuition reimbursements (averaging $25,500 per year) were awarded; research assistantships, scholarships/grants and tuition waivers (full) also available. *Faculty research:* Macromolecule metabolism, molecular genetics, protein folding and 3-D structure, regulation of gene expression and enzyme function, signal transduction and developmental biology. Total annual research expenditures: $3 million. *Unit head:* Dr. Louis J. Elsas, Department Chair, 305-243-1456, Fax: 305-243-3955, E-mail: lelsas@med.miami.edu. *Application contact:* Dr. Zafar Nawaz, Director, 305-243-1456, Fax: 305-243-3955, E-mail: znawaz@med.miami.edu.

University of Michigan, Horace H. Rackham School of Graduate Studies, Chemical Biology Program, Ann Arbor, MI 48109. Offers PhD. *Faculty:* 43 full-time (9 women). *Students:* 56 full-time (28 women). 70 applicants, 39% accepted, 13 enrolled. *Degree requirements:* For doctorate, thesis/dissertation. *Entrance requirements:* Additional exam requirements/recommendations for international students: Required—TOEFL (minimum score 600 paper-based; 250 computer-based; 102 iBT). *Application deadline:* For fall admission, 1/15 priority date for domestic and international students. Application fee: $0 ($75 for international students). Electronic applications accepted. *Expenses:* Tuition, state resident: full-time $17,286; part-time $1099 per credit hour. Tuition, nonresident: full-time $34,944; part-time $2080 per credit hour. Required fees: $95 per semester. Tuition and fees vary according to course load, degree level and program. *Financial support:* In 2009–10, 56 students received support, including fellowships with full tuition reimbursements available (averaging $26,500 per year), research assistantships with full tuition reimbursements available (averaging $26,500 per year); health care benefits also available. *Faculty research:* Chemical genetics, structural enzymology, signal transduction, biological catalysis, biomolecular structure, function and recognition. *Unit head:* Prof. Anna Mapp, Program Director, 734-763-7175, Fax: 734-615-1252, E-mail: chemicalbiology@umich.edu. *Application contact:* Prof. Anna Mapp, Program Director, 734-763-7175, Fax: 734-615-1252, E-mail: chemicalbiology@umich.edu.

University of Michigan, Horace H. Rackham School of Graduate Studies, College of Literature, Science, and the Arts, Department of Chemistry, Ann Arbor, MI 48109-1055. Offers analytical chemistry (PhD); chemical biology (PhD); inorganic chemistry (PhD); material chemistry (PhD); organic chemistry (PhD); physical chemistry (PhD). *Faculty:* 42 full-time (10 women). *Students:* 192 full-time (105 women); includes 74 minority (4 African Americans, 64 Asian Americans or Pacific Islanders, 6 Hispanic Americans). Average age 26. 558 applicants, 36% accepted, 56 enrolled. In 2009, 28 doctorates awarded. *Degree requirements:* For doctorate, thesis/dissertation, oral defense of dissertation, organic cumulative proficiency exams. *Entrance requirements:* For doctorate, GRE General Test, GRE Subject Test (recommended), 3 letters of recommendation. Additional exam requirements/recommendations for international students: Required—TOEFL (minimum score 560 paper-based; 220 computer-based; 84 iBT). *Application deadline:* For fall admission, 1/15 for domestic students, 12/15 for international students. Applications are processed on a rolling basis. Application fee: $0 ($75 for international students). Electronic applications accepted. *Expenses:* Tuition, state resident: full-time $17,286; part-time $1099 per credit hour. Tuition, nonresident: full-time $34,944; part-time $2080 per credit hour. Required fees: $95 per semester. Tuition and fees vary according to course load, degree level and program. *Financial support:* In 2009–10, 192 students received support, including 20 fellowships with full tuition reimbursements available (averaging $25,000 per year), 75 research assistantships with full tuition reimbursements available (averaging $25,000 per year), 97 teaching assistantships with full tuition reimbursements available (averaging $25,000 per year); career-related internships or fieldwork, scholarships/grants, traineeships, health care benefits, and unspecified assistantships also available. Financial award applicants required to submit FAFSA. *Faculty research:* Biological catalysis, protein engineering, chemical sensors, de novo metalloprotein design, supramolecular architecture. Total annual research expenditures: $15.3 million. *Unit head:* Dr. Carol A. Fierke, Chair, 734-763-9681, Fax: 734-647-4847. *Application contact:* Anna Stryker, Graduate Program Coordinator, 734-764-7278, Fax: 734-647-4865, E-mail: chemadmissions@umich.edu.

University of Michigan, Horace H. Rackham School of Graduate Studies, Program in Biomedical Sciences (PIBS), Department of Biological Chemistry, Ann Arbor, MI 48109. Offers PhD. *Degree requirements:* For doctorate, thesis/dissertation, oral defense of dissertation, preliminary exam. *Entrance requirements:* For doctorate, GRE General Test, GRE Subject Test, minimum GPA of 3.0. Additional exam requirements/recommendations for international students: Required—TOEFL. Electronic applications accepted. *Expenses:* Tuition, state resident: full-time $17,286; part-time $1099 per credit hour. Tuition, nonresident: full-time $34,944; part-time $2080 per credit hour. Required fees: $95 per semester. Tuition and fees vary according to course load, degree level and program. *Faculty research:* Nucleic acids, gene regulation, mechanistic enzymology, protein biochemistry, signal transduction.

University of Minnesota, Duluth, Graduate School, Swenson College of Science and Engineering, Department of Chemistry and Biochemistry, Duluth, MN 55812-2496. Offers MS. Part-time programs available. *Degree requirements:* For master's, thesis. *Entrance requirements:* For master's, bachelor's degree in chemistry, minimum GPA of 3.0. Additional exam requirements/recommendations for international students: Required—TOEFL (minimum score 550 paper-based; 213 computer-based; 79 iBT), IELTS (minimum score 6.5). *Faculty research:* Physical, inorganic, organic, and analytical chemistry; biochemistry and molecular biology.

University of Minnesota, Duluth, Medical School, Department of Biochemistry, Molecular Biology and Biophysics, Duluth, MN 55812-2496. Offers biochemistry, molecular biology and biophysics (MS); biology and biophysics (PhD); social, administrative, and clinical pharmacy (MS, PhD); toxicology (MS, PhD). *Faculty:* 10 full-time (3 women). *Students:* 16 full-time (5 women); includes 3 minority (all Asian Americans or Pacific Islanders). Average age 29. 7 applicants, 29% accepted, 2 enrolled. In 2009, 1 master's, 1 doctorate awarded. Terminal master's awarded for partial completion of doctoral program. *Degree requirements:* For master's, comprehensive exam, thesis; for doctorate, comprehensive exam, thesis/dissertation. *Entrance requirements:* For master's and doctorate, GRE General Test. Additional exam requirements/recommendations for international students: Required—TOEFL. *Application deadline:* For winter admission, 1/3 for domestic students, 1/2 for international students; for spring admission, 3/15 priority date for domestic and international students. Application fee: $75 ($95 for international students). Electronic applications accepted. *Financial support:* In 2009–10, 8 students received support, including research assistantships with full tuition reimbursements available (averaging $27,300 per year), teaching assistantships with full tuition reimbursements available (averaging $27,300 per year); career-related internships or fieldwork, scholarships/grants, health care benefits, and unspecified assistantships also available. Financial award application deadline: 9/1. *Faculty research:* Intestinal cancer biology; hepatotoxins and mitochondriopathies; toxicology; cell cycle regulation in stem cells; neurobiology of brain development, trace metal function and blood-brain barrier; hibernation biology. Total annual research expenditures: $1.5 million. *Unit head:* Dr. Lester R. Drewes, Professor/Head, 218-726-7925, Fax: 218-726-8014, E-mail: ldrewes@d.umn.edu. *Application contact:* Cheryl Beeman, Administrative Assistant, 218-726-6354, Fax: 218-726-8014, E-mail: ahcd@d.umn.edu.

University of Minnesota, Twin Cities Campus, Graduate School, College of Biological Sciences, Biochemistry, Molecular Biology and Biophysics Graduate Program, Minneapolis, MN 55455-0213. Offers PhD. *Faculty:* 69 full-time (14 women), 1 part-time/adjunct (0 women). *Students:* 60 full-time (26 women); includes 20 minority (2 African Americans, 1 American Indian/Alaska Native, 15 Asian Americans or Pacific Islanders, 2 Hispanic Americans). Average age 26. 199 applicants, 20% accepted, 11 enrolled. In 2009, 16 doctorates awarded. *Degree requirements:* For doctorate, thesis/dissertation. *Entrance requirements:* For doctorate, GRE, 3 letters of recommendation, more than 1 semester of laboratory experience. Additional exam requirements/recommendations for international students: Required—TOEFL (minimum score 625 paper-based; 263 computer-based; 108 iBT with writing subsection 25 and reading subsection 25) or IELTS (minimum score 7). *Application deadline:* For fall admission, 12/15 for domestic and international students. Application fee: $75 ($95 for international students). Electronic applications accepted. *Financial support:* Institutionally sponsored loans, scholarships/grants, traineeships, health care benefits, tuition waivers, unspecified assistantships, and stipends available. *Faculty research:* Microbial biochemistry, biotechnology, molecular biology, regulatory biochemistry, structural biology and biophysics, physical biochemistry, enzymology, physiological chemistry. Total annual research expenditures: $10.3 million. *Unit head:* Prof. David A. Bernlohr, Head, 612-624-2712. *Application contact:* Dr. Anja Katrin Bielinsky, Director of Graduate Studies, 612-624-2469, Fax: 612-625-2163, E-mail: bieli003@umn.edu.

University of Mississippi Medical Center, School of Graduate Studies in the Health Sciences, Department of Biochemistry, Jackson, MS 39216-4505. Offers MS, PhD, MD/PhD. Terminal master's awarded for partial completion of doctoral program. *Degree requirements:* For master's, thesis; for doctorate, thesis/dissertation, first authored publication. *Entrance requirements:* For doctorate, GRE General Test, minimum GPA of 3.0. Additional exam requirements/recommendations for international students: Required—TOEFL. *Faculty research:* Structural biology, regulation of gene expression, enzymology of redox reactions, mechanism of anti cancer drugs, function of nuclear substructure.

University of Missouri, Graduate School, College of Agriculture, Food and Natural Resources, Department of Biochemistry, Columbia, MO 65211. Offers MS, PhD. *Faculty:* 40 full-time (20 women), 3 part-time/adjunct (1 woman). *Students:* 27 full-time (10 women), 9 part-time (4 women); includes 4 minority (1 African American, 2 Asian Americans or Pacific Islanders, 1 Hispanic American), 13 international. Average age 25. 32 applicants, 31% accepted, 10 enrolled. In 2009, 3 doctorates awarded. Terminal master's awarded for partial completion of doctoral program. *Degree requirements:* For master's, thesis; for doctorate, comprehensive exam, thesis/dissertation. *Entrance requirements:* For master's and doctorate, minimum GPA of 3.0; undergraduate research. Additional exam requirements/recommendations for international students: Required—TOEFL (minimum score 620 paper-based; 95 iBT). *Application deadline:* For fall admission, 1/15 priority date for domestic students. Application fee: $45 ($60 for international students). Electronic applications accepted. *Financial support:* Fellowships with tuition reimbursements, research assistantships with tuition reimbursements, teaching assistantships with tuition reimbursements, institutionally sponsored loans available. *Faculty research:* Enzymology, plant biochemistry, molecular biochemistry. *Unit head:* Dr. Gerald Hazelbauer, Department Chair, E-mail: hazelbauerg@missouri.edu. *Application contact:* Stacy Colley, Administrative Assistant, 573-882-4846, E-mail: colleys@missouri.edu.

University of Missouri–Kansas City, School of Biological Sciences, Program in Molecular Biology and Biochemistry, Kansas City, MO 64110-2499. Offers PhD. Offered through the School of Graduate Studies. *Degree requirements:* For doctorate, comprehensive exam, thesis/dissertation. *Entrance requirements:* For doctorate, GRE General Test, bachelor's degree in chemistry, biology, or a related discipline; minimum GPA of 3.0. Additional exam requirements/recommendations for international students: Required—TOEFL (minimum score 550 paper-based; 213 computer-based; 80 iBT). *Application deadline:* For fall admission, 2/15 priority date for domestic and international students. Application fee: $45 ($50 for international students). *Expenses:* Tuition, state resident: full-time $5378; part-time $299 per credit hour. Tuition, nonresident: full-time $13,881; part-time $771 per credit hour. Required fees: $641; $71 per credit hour. Tuition and fees vary according to course load and program. *Financial support:* Research assistantships with full tuition reimbursements, teaching assistantships with full and partial tuition reimbursements, scholarships/grants, tuition waivers (full and partial), and unspecified assistantships available. Financial award application deadline: 3/1; financial award applicants required to submit FAFSA. *Unit head:* Dr. Henry Miziorko, Head, 816-235-2235, E-mail: miziorkoh@umkc.edu. *Application contact:* Laura Batenic, Information Contact, 816-235-2352, Fax: 816-235-5158, E-mail: batenicl@umkc.edu.

See Close-Up on page 249.

University of Missouri–St. Louis, College of Arts and Sciences, Department of Biology, St. Louis, MO 63121. Offers biology (MS, PhD), including animal behavior (MS), biochemistry, biochemistry and biotechnology (MS), biotechnology (MS), conservation biology (MS), development (MS), ecology (MS), environmental studies (PhD), evolution (MS), genetics (MS), molecular biology and biochemistry (PhD), molecular/cellular biology (MS), physiology (MS), plant systematics, population biology (MS), tropical biology (MS); biotechnology (Certificate); tropical biology and conservation (Certificate). Part-time programs available. *Faculty:* 43 full-time (13 women), 2 part-time/adjunct (1 woman). *Students:* 54 full-time (27 women), 79 part-time (43 women); includes 15 minority (6 African Americans, 7 Asian Americans or Pacific Islanders, 2 Hispanic Americans), 47 international. Average age 29. 193 applicants, 44% accepted, 44 enrolled. In 2009, 30 master's, 7 doctorates, 9 other advanced degrees awarded. *Degree requirements:* For master's, thesis or alternative; for doctorate, thesis/dissertation, 1 semester of teaching experience. *Entrance requirements:* For master's, 3 letters of recommendation; for doctorate, GRE General Test, 3 letters of recommendation. Additional exam requirements/recommendations for international students: Required—TOEFL. *Application deadline:* For fall admission, 12/1 priority date for domestic and international students; for spring admission, 10/15 priority date for domestic and international students. Applications are processed on a rolling basis. Application fee: $35 ($40 for international students). Electronic applications accepted. *Expenses:* Tuition, state resident: full-time $5377; part-time $297.70 per credit hour. Tuition, nonresident: full-time $13,882; part-time $771.20 per credit hour. Required fees: $220; $12.20 per credit hour. One-time fee: $12. Tuition and fees vary according to course level, campus/location and program. *Financial support:* In 2009–10, 22 research assistantships with full and partial tuition reimbursements (averaging $16,300 per year), 14 teaching assistantships with full and partial tuition reimbursements (averaging $16,727 per year) were awarded; fellowships with full tuition reimbursements, career-related internships or fieldwork and Federal Work-Study also available. Support available to part-time students. Financial award application deadline: 2/1. *Faculty research:* Molecular biology, microbial genetics, animal behavior, tropical ecology, plant systematics. *Unit head:* Dr. Elizabeth Kellogg, Director of Graduate Studies, 314-516-6200, Fax: 314-516-6233, E-mail: tkellogg@umsl.edu. *Application contact:* 314-516-5458, Fax: 314-516-6996, E-mail: gradadm@umsl.edu.

University of Missouri–St. Louis, College of Arts and Sciences, Department of Chemistry and Biochemistry, St. Louis, MO 63121. Offers chemistry (MS, PhD), including biochemistry, inorganic chemistry, organic chemistry, physical chemistry. Part-time and evening/weekend programs available. *Faculty:* 19 full-time (3 women), 6 part-time/adjunct (1 woman). *Students:* 43 full-time (21 women), 19 part-time (8 women); includes 6 minority (4 African Americans, 1 Asian American or Pacific Islander, 1 Hispanic American), 27 international. Average age 29. 81 applicants, 37% accepted, 19 enrolled. In 2009, 9 master's, 6 doctorates awarded. Terminal master's awarded for partial completion of doctoral program. *Degree requirements:* For master's, thesis optional; for doctorate, thesis/dissertation. *Entrance requirements:* For master's, 2 letters of recommendation; for doctorate, GRE General Test, 3 letters of recommendation. Additional exam requirements/recommendations for international students: Required—TOEFL (minimum score 550 paper-based; 213 computer-based). *Application deadline:* For fall admission, 7/1 priority date for domestic and international students; for spring admission, 12/1 priority date for domestic and international students. Applications are processed on a rolling basis. Application fee: $35 ($40 for international students). Electronic applications accepted. *Expenses:* Tuition, state resident: full-time $5377; part-time $297.70 per credit hour. Tuition, nonresident: full-time $13,882; part-time $771.20 per credit hour. Required fees: $220; $12.20 per credit hour. One-time fee: $12. Tuition and fees vary according to course level, campus/location and program. *Financial support:* In 2009–10, 25 research assistantships with full and partial tuition reimbursements (averaging $17,840 per year), 13 teaching assistantships with full and partial tuition reimbursements (averaging $13,300 per year) were awarded; fellowships with full and partial tuition reimbursements also available. *Faculty research:* Metallaborane chemistry, serum transferrin chemistry, natural products chemistry, organic synthesis. *Unit head:* Dr. Cynthia Dupureur, Director of Graduate Studies, 314-516-5311, Fax: 314-516-5342, E-mail: gradchem@umsl.edu. *Application contact:* 314-516-5458, Fax: 314-516-6996, E-mail: gradadm@umsl.edu.

The University of Montana, Graduate School, College of Arts and Sciences, Division of Biological Sciences, Program in Biochemistry and Microbiology, Missoula, MT 59812-0002. Offers biochemistry (MS); integrative microbiology and biochemistry (PhD); microbial ecology (MS, PhD); microbiology (MS). Terminal master's awarded for partial completion of doctoral program. *Degree requirements:* For master's, thesis; for doctorate, variable foreign language requirement, thesis/dissertation. *Entrance requirements:* For master's and doctorate, GRE General Test. *Faculty research:* Ribosome structure, medical microbiology/pathogenesis, microbial ecology/environmental microbiology.

University of Nebraska–Lincoln, Graduate College, College of Agricultural Sciences and Natural Resources and College of Arts and Sciences, Department of Biochemistry, Lincoln, NE 68588. Offers MS, PhD. Terminal master's awarded for partial completion of doctoral program. *Degree requirements:* For master's, thesis optional; for doctorate, comprehensive exam, thesis/dissertation. *Entrance requirements:* For master's and doctorate, GRE General Test, GRE Subject Test. Additional exam requirements/recommendations for international students: Required—TOEFL (minimum score 550 paper-based; 213 computer-based). Electronic applications accepted. *Faculty research:* Molecular genetics, enzymology, photosynthesis, molecular virology, structural biology.

University of Nebraska–Lincoln, Graduate College, College of Arts and Sciences, Department of Chemistry, Lincoln, NE 68588. Offers analytical chemistry (PhD); biochemistry (PhD); chemistry (MS); inorganic chemistry (PhD); materials chemistry (PhD); organic chemistry (PhD); physical chemistry (PhD). *Degree requirements:* For master's, one foreign language, thesis optional, departmental qualifying exam; for doctorate, one foreign language, comprehensive exam, thesis/dissertation, departmental qualifying exams. *Entrance requirements:* For master's and doctorate, GRE. Additional exam requirements/recommendations for international students: Required—TOEFL (minimum score 550 paper-based; 213 computer-based). Electronic applications accepted. *Faculty research:* Bioorganic and bioinorganic chemistry, biophysical and bioanalytical chemistry, structure-function of DNA and proteins, organometallics, mass spectrometry.

University of Nebraska Medical Center, Graduate Studies, Department of Biochemistry and Molecular Biology, Omaha, NE 68198. Offers MS, PhD. Terminal master's awarded for partial completion of doctoral program. *Degree requirements:* For master's, comprehensive exam, thesis; for doctorate, comprehensive exam, thesis/dissertation. *Entrance requirements:* For master's and doctorate, GRE General Test. Additional exam requirements/recommendations for international students: Required—TOEFL (minimum score 550 paper-based; 213 computer-based). Electronic applications accepted. *Faculty research:* Recombinant DNA, cancer biology, diabetes and drug metabolism, biochemical endocrinology.

University of Nevada, Las Vegas, Graduate College, College of Science, Department of Chemistry, Las Vegas, NV 89154-4003. Offers biochemistry (MS); chemistry (MS, PhD); radiochemistry (PhD). Part-time programs available. *Faculty:* 18 full-time (3 women), 1 part-time/adjunct (0 women). *Students:* 40 full-time (16 women), 18 part-time (9 women); includes 11 minority (2 African Americans, 7 Asian Americans or Pacific Islanders, 2 Hispanic Americans), 17 international. Average age 32. 29 applicants, 55% accepted, 10 enrolled. In 2009, 7 master's, 6 doctorates awarded. *Degree requirements:* For master's, thesis. *Entrance requirements:* For master's and doctorate, GRE General Test. Additional exam requirements/recommendations for international students: Required—TOEFL (minimum score 550 paper-based; 213 computer-based; 80 iBT), IELTS (minimum score 7). *Application deadline:* For fall admission, 2/1 priority date for domestic and international students; for spring admission, 10/1 priority date for domestic and international students. Applications are processed on a rolling

Biochemistry

University of Nevada, Las Vegas (continued)
basis. Application fee: $60 ($95 for international students). Electronic applications accepted. *Financial support:* In 2009–10, 23 students received support, including 7 research assistantships with partial tuition reimbursements available (averaging $17,957 per year), 16 teaching assistantships with partial tuition reimbursements available (averaging $11,250 per year); institutionally sponsored loans, scholarships/grants, health care benefits, and unspecified assistantships also available. Financial award application deadline: 3/1. *Faculty research:* Inorganic and organic chemistry, physical chemistry, radio-chemistry, materials science, biochemistry. *Unit head:* Dr. Dennis Lindle, Chair/Professor, 702-895-4426, Fax: 702-895-4072, E-mail: lindle@unlv.nevada.edu. *Application contact:* Graduate Coordinator, 702-895-3320, Fax: 702-895-4180, E-mail: gradcollege@unlv.edu.

University of Nevada, Reno, Graduate School, College of Agriculture, Biotechnology and Natural Resources, Program in Biochemistry, Reno, NV 89557. Offers MS, PhD. Terminal master's awarded for partial completion of doctoral program. *Degree requirements:* For master's, thesis; for doctorate, thesis/dissertation. *Entrance requirements:* For master's, GRE General Test, minimum GPA of 2.75; for doctorate, GRE General Test, minimum GPA of 3.0. Additional exam requirements/recommendations for international students: Required—TOEFL (minimum score 500 paper-based; 173 computer-based; 61 iBT), IELTS (minimum score 6). Electronic applications accepted. *Faculty research:* Cancer research, insect biochemistry, plant biochemistry, enzymology.

University of New Hampshire, Graduate School, College of Life Sciences and Agriculture, Department of Molecular, Cellular and Biomedical Sciences, Program in Biochemistry, Durham, NH 03824. Offers MS, PhD. Part-time programs available. *Faculty:* 12 full-time. *Students:* 9 full-time (3 women), 13 part-time (6 women); includes 4 minority (3 Asian Americans or Pacific Islanders, 1 Hispanic American), 7 international. Average age 29. 27 applicants, 30% accepted, 6 enrolled. In 2009, 2 master's, 3 doctorates awarded. Terminal master's awarded for partial completion of doctoral program. *Degree requirements:* For master's, thesis; for doctorate, one foreign language, thesis/dissertation. *Entrance requirements:* For master's and doctorate, GRE General Test. Additional exam requirements/recommendations for international students: Required—TOEFL (minimum score 550 paper-based; 213 computer-based; 80 iBT). *Application deadline:* For fall admission, 6/1 priority date for domestic students, 4/1 for international students; for spring admission, 12/1 for domestic students. Applications are processed on a rolling basis. Application fee: $65. Electronic applications accepted. *Expenses:* Tuition, state resident: full-time $10,380; part-time $577 per credit hour. Tuition, nonresident: full-time $24,350; part-time $1002 per credit hour. Required fees: $1550; $387.50 per semester. Tuition and fees vary according to course load and program. *Financial support:* In 2009–10, 18 students received support, including 8 research assistantships, 10 teaching assistantships; fellowships, career-related internships or fieldwork, Federal Work-Study, scholarships/grants, and tuition waivers (full and partial) also available. Support available to part-time students. Financial award application deadline: 2/15. *Faculty research:* Developmental biochemistry, biochemistry of natural products, physical biochemistry, biochemical genetics, structure and metabolism of macromolecules. *Unit head:* Rick Cote, Chairperson, 603-862-2470. *Application contact:* Flora Joyal, Administrative Assistant, 603-862-2103, E-mail: biochemistry.dept@unh.edu.

University of New Mexico, School of Medicine, Biomedical Sciences Graduate Program, Albuquerque, NM 87131-5196. Offers biochemistry and molecular biology (MS, PhD); cell biology and physiology (MS, PhD); molecular genetics and microbiology (MS, PhD); neuroscience (MS, PhD); pathology (MS, PhD); toxicology (MS, PhD). Part-time programs available. Terminal master's awarded for partial completion of doctoral program. *Degree requirements:* For master's, thesis; for doctorate, comprehensive exam, thesis/dissertation. *Entrance requirements:* For master's and doctorate, GRE General Test, minimum undergraduate GPA of 3.0. Additional exam requirements/recommendations for international students: Required—TOEFL. Electronic applications accepted. *Expenses:* Tuition, state resident: full-time $2099; part-time $233.20 per credit hour. Tuition, nonresident: full-time $6650. Required fees: $25 per semester. Tuition and fees vary according to course load, program and reciprocity agreements. *Faculty research:* Signal transduction, infectious disease, biology of cancer, structural biology, neuroscience.

The University of North Carolina at Chapel Hill, School of Medicine and Graduate School, Graduate Programs in Medicine, Department of Biochemistry and Biophysics, Chapel Hill, NC 27599. Offers MS, PhD. Terminal master's awarded for partial completion of doctoral program. *Degree requirements:* For master's, comprehensive exam, thesis; for doctorate, comprehensive exam, thesis/dissertation. *Entrance requirements:* For master's and doctorate, GRE General Test, GRE Subject Test (recommended), minimum GPA of 3.0. Additional exam requirements/recommendations for international students: Required—TOEFL. Electronic applications accepted.

The University of North Carolina at Greensboro, Graduate School, College of Arts and Sciences, Department of Chemistry and Biochemistry, Greensboro, NC 27412-5001. Offers biochemistry (MS); chemistry (MS). *Degree requirements:* For master's, one foreign language, thesis. *Entrance requirements:* For master's, GRE General Test. Additional exam requirements/recommendations for international students: Required—TOEFL. Electronic applications accepted. *Faculty research:* Synthesis of novel cyclopentadienes, molybdenum hydroxylase-cata ladder polymers, vinyl silicones.

University of North Dakota, School of Medicine and Health Sciences and Graduate School, Graduate Programs in Medicine, Department of Biochemistry, Grand Forks, ND 58202. Offers MS, PhD. *Degree requirements:* For master's, thesis, final exam; for doctorate, comprehensive exam, thesis/dissertation, final exam. *Entrance requirements:* For master's and doctorate, GRE General Test, minimum GPA of 3.0. Additional exam requirements/recommendations for international students: Required—TOEFL (minimum score 550 paper-based; 213 computer-based; 79 iBT), IELTS (minimum score 6.5). Electronic applications accepted. *Faculty research:* Glucose-6-phosphatase, guanine nucleotides, carbohydrate and lipid metabolism, cytoskeletal proteins, chromatin structure.

University of North Texas, Robert B. Toulouse School of Graduate Studies, College of Arts and Sciences, Department of Biological Sciences, Program in Biochemistry, Denton, TX 76203. Offers MS, PhD. *Students:* 27 applicants, 33% accepted, 6 enrolled.Terminal master's awarded for partial completion of doctoral program. *Degree requirements:* For master's, comprehensive exam, thesis (for some programs), oral defense of thesis; for doctorate, one foreign language, comprehensive exam, thesis/dissertation, oral defense of dissertation. *Entrance requirements:* For master's, GRE General Test, placement exams in 3 areas, admission to Toulouse School of Graduate Studies, letters of recommendation; for doctorate, GRE General Test, placement exams in 4 areas. Additional exam requirements/recommendations for international students: Recommended—TOEFL (minimum score 550 paper-based; 213 computer-based; 79 iBT). *Application deadline:* For fall admission, 7/15 for domestic students; for spring admission, 11/15 for domestic students. Application fee: $50 ($75 for international students). *Expenses:* Tuition, state resident: full-time $4298; part-time $239 per contact hour. Tuition, nonresident: full-time $9878; part-time $549 per contact hour. Required fees: $265 per contact hour. *Financial support:* Career-related internships or fieldwork, Federal Work-Study, institutionally sponsored loans, scholarships/grants, health care benefits, and unspecified assistantships available. Support available to part-time students. Financial award application deadline: 4/1; financial award applicants required to submit FAFSA. *Faculty research:* Microbial and plant metabolism, regulation of prokaryotic and eukaryotic gene expression, protein interaction. *Application contact:* Dr. Dan Kunz, Graduate Advisor, 940-565-2011, Fax: 940-565-3821, E-mail: kunz@unt.edu.

University of North Texas Health Science Center at Fort Worth, Graduate School of Biomedical Sciences, Fort Worth, TX 76107-2699. Offers anatomy and cell biology (MS, PhD); biochemistry and molecular biology (MS, PhD); biomedical sciences (MS, PhD); biotechnology (MS); forensic genetics (MS); integrative physiology (MS, PhD); medical science (MS); microbiology and immunology (MS, PhD); pharmacology (MS, PhD); science education (MS); DO/MS; DO/PhD. Terminal master's awarded for partial completion of doctoral program. *Degree requirements:* For master's, thesis; for doctorate, thesis/dissertation. *Entrance requirements:* For master's and doctorate, GRE General Test. Additional exam requirements/recommendations for international students: Required—TOEFL. *Expenses:* Contact institution. *Faculty research:* Alzheimer's disease, aging, eye diseases, cancer, cardiovascular disease.

University of Notre Dame, Graduate School, College of Science, Department of Chemistry and Biochemistry, Notre Dame, IN 46556. Offers biochemistry (MS, PhD); inorganic chemistry (MS, PhD); organic chemistry (MS, PhD); physical chemistry (MS, PhD). Terminal master's awarded for partial completion of doctoral program. *Degree requirements:* For master's, comprehensive exam, thesis; for doctorate, thesis/dissertation, qualifying exam. *Entrance requirements:* For master's and doctorate, GRE General Test, GRE Subject Test (strongly recommended). Additional exam requirements/recommendations for international students: Required—TOEFL (minimum score 600 paper-based; 250 computer-based; 80 iBT). Electronic applications accepted. *Faculty research:* Reaction design and mechanistic studies; reactive intermediates; synthesis, structure and reactivity of organometallic cluster complexes and biologically active natural products; bioorganic chemistry; enzymology.

University of Oklahoma, Graduate College, College of Arts and Sciences, Department of Chemistry and Biochemistry, Norman, OK 73019. Offers MS, PhD. *Faculty:* 29 full-time (6 women). *Students:* 85 full-time (37 women), 11 part-time (6 women); includes 12 minority (5 African Americans, 2 American Indian/Alaska Native, 4 Asian Americans or Pacific Islanders, 1 Hispanic American), 48 international. 32 applicants, 56% accepted, 18 enrolled. In 2009, 12 master's, 18 doctorates awarded. Terminal master's awarded for partial completion of doctoral program. *Degree requirements:* For master's, thesis optional; for doctorate, thesis/dissertation. *Entrance requirements:* For master's, GRE, BS in chemistry; for doctorate, GRE. Additional exam requirements/recommendations for international students: Required—TOEFL (minimum score 550 paper-based; 213 computer-based). *Application deadline:* For fall admission, 4/1 priority date for domestic students, 4/1 for international students; for spring admission, 9/1 priority date for domestic students, 9/1 for international students. Applications are processed on a rolling basis. Application fee: $40 ($90 for international students). Electronic applications accepted. *Expenses:* Tuition, state resident: full-time $3744; part-time $156 per credit hour. Tuition, nonresident: full-time $13,577; part-time $565.70 per credit hour. Required fees: $2415; $90.10 per credit hour. *Financial support:* In 2009–10, 73 students received support, including 3 fellowships with full tuition reimbursements available (averaging $5,000 per year), 21 research assistantships with partial tuition reimbursements available (averaging $15,232 per year), 71 teaching assistantships with partial tuition reimbursements available (averaging $15,776 per year); scholarships/grants, health care benefits, and unspecified assistantships also available. Financial award application deadline: 4/1; financial award applicants required to submit FAFSA. *Faculty research:* Catalysis, metals in biology, materials science, nucleic acid structure and function, natural products drug discovery. Total annual research expenditures: $4.4 million. *Unit head:* Dr. George Richter-Addo, Chair, 405-325-4811, Fax: 405-325-6111, E-mail: grichteraddo@ou.edu. *Application contact:* Carol Jones, Graduate Program Assistant, 405-325-2946, Fax: 405-325-6111, E-mail: chemadmit@ou.edu.

University of Oklahoma Health Sciences Center, College of Medicine and Graduate College, Graduate Programs in Medicine, Department of Biochemistry and Molecular Biology, Oklahoma City, OK 73190. Offers biochemistry (MS, PhD); molecular biology (MS, PhD). Part-time programs available. *Faculty:* 10 full-time (4 women). *Students:* 4 full-time (3 women), 23 part-time (10 women); includes 1 minority (African American), 15 international. Average age 28. 26 applicants, 8% accepted, 2 enrolled. In 2009, 5 doctorates awarded. Terminal master's awarded for partial completion of doctoral program. *Degree requirements:* For master's, thesis; for doctorate, thesis/dissertation. *Entrance requirements:* For master's, GRE General Test, 2 letters of recommendation; for doctorate, GRE General Test, 3 letters of recommendation. Additional exam requirements/recommendations for international students: Required—TOEFL. *Application deadline:* For fall admission, 1/31 for domestic students. Application fee: $50. *Expenses:* Tuition, state resident: full-time $3120; part-time $156 per credit hour. Tuition, nonresident: full-time $11,314; part-time $409.70 per credit hour. Required fees: $1471; $51.20 per credit hour. $223.25 per term. *Financial support:* In 2009–10, 20 research assistantships (averaging $18,000 per year) were awarded; institutionally sponsored loans also available. Support available to part-time students. Financial award application deadline: 3/31; financial award applicants required to submit FAFSA. *Faculty research:* Gene expression, regulation of transcription, enzyme evolution, melanogenesis, signal transduction. *Unit head:* Dr. Paul H. Weigel, Chair, 405-271-2227, E-mail: paul-weigel@ouhsc.edu. *Application contact:* Dr. Gillian Air, Graduate Liaison, 405-271-2227, Fax: 405-271-3092, E-mail: gillian-air@ouhsc.edu.

University of Oregon, Graduate School, College of Arts and Sciences, Department of Chemistry, Eugene, OR 97403. Offers biochemistry (MA, MS, PhD); chemistry (MA, MS, PhD). Terminal master's awarded for partial completion of doctoral program. *Degree requirements:* For doctorate, thesis/dissertation. *Entrance requirements:* For master's and doctorate, GRE General Test, minimum GPA of 3.0. Additional exam requirements/recommendations for international students: Required—TOEFL. *Faculty research:* Organic chemistry, organometallic chemistry, inorganic chemistry, physical chemistry, materials science, biochemistry, chemical physics, molecular or cell biology.

University of Ottawa, Faculty of Graduate and Postdoctoral Studies, Faculty of Medicine, Department of Biochemistry, Microbiology and Immunology, Ottawa, ON K1N 6N5, Canada. Offers biochemistry (M Sc, PhD); microbiology and immunology (M Sc, PhD). *Degree requirements:* For master's, thesis; for doctorate, comprehensive exam, thesis/dissertation, seminar. *Entrance requirements:* For master's, honors degree or equivalent, minimum B average; for doctorate, master's degree, minimum B+ average. Electronic applications accepted. *Faculty research:* General biochemistry, molecular biology, microbiology, host biology, nutrition and metabolism.

University of Pennsylvania, School of Medicine, Biomedical Graduate Studies, Graduate Group in Biochemistry and Molecular Biophysics, Philadelphia, PA 19104. Offers PhD, MD/PhD, VMD/PhD. *Faculty:* 74. *Students:* 77 full-time (32 women); includes 21 minority (4 African Americans, 10 Asian Americans or Pacific Islanders, 7 Hispanic Americans), 9 international. 108 applicants, 33% accepted, 14 enrolled. In 2009, 11 doctorates awarded. *Degree requirements:* For doctorate, thesis/dissertation. *Entrance requirements:* For doctorate, GRE General Test. Additional exam requirements/recommendations for international students: Required—TOEFL. *Application deadline:* For fall admission, 12/8 priority date for domestic and international students. Applications are processed on a rolling basis. Application fee: $70. Electronic applications accepted. *Expenses:* Tuition: Full-time $25,660; part-time $4758 per course. Required fees: $2152; $270 per course. Tuition and fees vary according to course load, degree level and program. *Financial support:* In 2009–10, 77 students received support; fellowships, research assistantships, scholarships/grants, traineeships, and unspecified assistantships available. *Faculty research:* Biochemistry of cell differentiation, tissue culture, intermediary metabolism, structure of proteins and nucleic acids, biochemical genetics. *Unit head:* Dr. Kathryn Ferguson, Chairperson, 215-573-7288. *Application contact:* Ruth Keris, Graduate Group Administrator, 215-898-4639, Fax: 215-573-2085, E-mail: keris@mail.med.upenn.edu.

University of Pittsburgh, School of Medicine, Graduate Programs in Medicine, Program in Biochemistry and Molecular Genetics, Pittsburgh, PA 15260. Offers MS, PhD. *Faculty:* 50 full-time (8 women). *Students:* 17 full-time (8 women); includes 3 minority (all Asian Americans or Pacific Islanders), 5 international. Average age 27. 655 applicants, 10% accepted. In 2009, 7 doctorates awarded. *Degree requirements:* For doctorate, comprehensive exam, thesis/dissertation. *Entrance requirements:* For doctorate, GRE General Test, GRE Subject Test, minimum QPA of 3.0. Additional exam requirements/recommendations for international students: Required—TOEFL (minimum score 600 paper-based; 250 computer-based; 100 iBT), IELTS (minimum score 7). *Application deadline:* For fall admission, 12/15 priority date for domestic and international students. Application fee: $40. Electronic applications accepted. *Expenses:* Tuition, state resident: full-time $16,402; part-time $665 per credit. Tuition, nonresident: full-time

$28,694; part-time $1175 per credit. Required fees: $690; $175 per term. Tuition and fees vary according to program. *Financial support:* In 2009–10, 17 research assistantships with full tuition reimbursements (averaging $24,650 per year) were awarded; institutionally sponsored loans, scholarships/grants, traineeships, health care benefits, and unspecified assistantships also available. *Faculty research:* Molecular genetics of cancer, gene expression and signal transduction, genomics and proteomics, human gene therapy, structural dynamics and bioinformatics. *Unit head:* Dr. Martin C. Schmidt, Graduate Program Director, 412-648-9243, Fax: 412-624-1401, E-mail: mcs2@pitt.edu. *Application contact:* Graduate Studies Administrator, 412-648-8957, Fax: 412-648-1077, E-mail: gradstudies@medschool.pitt.edu.

University of Puerto Rico, Medical Sciences Campus, School of Medicine, Division of Graduate Studies, Department of Biochemistry, San Juan, PR 00936-5067. Offers MS, PhD. *Degree requirements:* For master's, thesis; for doctorate, comprehensive exam, thesis/dissertation. *Entrance requirements:* For master's and doctorate, GRE General Test, GRE Subject Test, interview, minimum GPA of 3.0. Electronic applications accepted. *Faculty research:* Genetics, cell and molecular biology, cancer biology, protein structure/function, glycosilation of proteins.

University of Regina, Faculty of Graduate Studies and Research, Faculty of Science, Department of Chemistry and Biochemistry, Regina, SK S4S 0A2, Canada. Offers analytical chemistry (M Sc, PhD); biochemistry (M Sc, PhD); inorganic chemistry (M Sc, PhD); organic chemistry (M Sc, PhD); physical chemistry (M Sc, PhD). Part-time programs available. *Faculty:* 11 full-time (2 women), 3 part-time/adjunct (0 women). *Students:* 20 full-time (8 women). 25 applicants, 28% accepted. In 2009, 2 master's awarded. *Degree requirements:* For master's, thesis, departmental qualifying exam; for doctorate, thesis/dissertation, departmental qualifying exam. *Entrance requirements:* For master's and doctorate, GRE. Additional exam requirements/recommendations for international students: Required—TOEFL (minimum score 580 paper-based; 237 computer-based; 80 iBT). *Application deadline:* For fall admission, 1/1 for domestic students; for winter admission, 7/1 for domestic students. Applications are processed on a rolling basis. Application fee: $90 ($100 for international students). *Financial support:* In 2009–10, 5 fellowships (averaging $19,000 per year), 2 research assistantships (averaging $16,910 per year), 4 teaching assistantships (averaging $6,650 per year) were awarded; scholarships/grants also available. Financial award application deadline: 6/15. *Faculty research:* Organic synthesis, organic oxidations, ionic liquids theoretical/computational chemistry, protein biochemistry/biophysics, environmental analytical, photophysical/photochemistry. *Unit head:* Dr. Tanya Dahms, Head, 306-585-4247, E-mail: tanya.dohms@uregina.ca. *Application contact:* Dr. Scott Murphy, Program Coordinator, 306-585-4247, Fax: 306-585-4894, E-mail: scott.murphy@uregina.ca.

University of Rhode Island, Graduate School, College of the Environment and Life Sciences, Department of Cell and Molecular Biology, Kingston, RI 02881. Offers biochemistry (MS, PhD); clinical laboratory sciences (MS), including biotechnology, clinical laboratory science, cytopathology; microbiology (MS, PhD); molecular genetics (MS, PhD). Part-time programs available. *Faculty:* 12 full-time (4 women). *Students:* 29 full-time (17 women), 43 part-time (31 women); includes 13 minority (5 African Americans, 4 Asian Americans or Pacific Islanders, 4 Hispanic Americans), 3 international. In 2009, 5 master's, 2 doctorates awarded. *Degree requirements:* For master's, comprehensive exam (for some programs); for doctorate, comprehensive exam. *Entrance requirements:* For master's and doctorate, GRE, 2 letters of recommendation. Additional exam requirements/recommendations for international students: Required—TOEFL (minimum score 550 paper-based; 213 computer-based). *Application deadline:* For fall admission, 7/15 for domestic students, 2/1 for international students; for spring admission, 11/15 for domestic students, 7/15 for international students. Application fee: $65. Electronic applications accepted. *Expenses:* Tuition, state resident: full-time $8828; part-time $490 per credit hour. Tuition, nonresident: full-time $22,100; part-time $1228 per credit hour. Required fees: $1118; $57 per semester. Tuition and fees vary according to program. *Financial support:* In 2009–10, 2 research assistantships with full and partial tuition reimbursements (averaging $10,535 per year), 10 teaching assistantships with full and partial tuition reimbursements (averaging $13,449 per year) were awarded. Financial award application deadline: 7/15; financial award applicants required to submit FAFSA. *Faculty research:* Genomics and Sequencing Center: an interdisciplinary genomics research and undergraduate and graduate student training program which provides researchers access to cutting-edge technologies in the field of genomics. Total annual research expenditures: $1.2 million. *Unit head:* Dr. Jay Sperry, Chairperson, 401-874-2201, Fax: 401-874-2202, E-mail: jsperry@mail.uri.edu. *Application contact:* Dr. Jay Sperry, Chairperson, 401-874-2201, Fax: 401-874-2202, E-mail: jsperry@mail.uri.edu.

University of Rochester, School of Medicine and Dentistry, Graduate Programs in Medicine and Dentistry, Department of Biochemistry and Biophysics, Program in Biochemistry, Rochester, NY 14627. Offers MS, PhD. Terminal master's awarded for partial completion of doctoral program. *Degree requirements:* For doctorate, thesis/dissertation, qualifying exam. *Entrance requirements:* For master's and doctorate, GRE General Test.

University of Saskatchewan, College of Medicine, Department of Biochemistry, Saskatoon, SK S7N 5A2, Canada. Offers M Sc, PhD. *Degree requirements:* For master's, thesis; for doctorate, thesis/dissertation. *Entrance requirements:* Additional exam requirements/recommendations for international students: Required—TOEFL. Tuition and fees charges are reported in Canadian dollars. *Expenses:* Tuition, area resident: Full-time $3000 Canadian dollars; part-time $500 Canadian dollars per term. Required fees: $700 Canadian dollars; $100 Canadian dollars per term.

The University of Scranton, College of Graduate and Continuing Education, Department of Chemistry, Program in Biochemistry, Scranton, PA 18510. Offers MA, MS. Part-time and evening/weekend programs available. *Faculty:* 10 full-time (3 women), 1 part-time/adjunct (0 women). *Students:* 29 full-time (16 women), 4 part-time (2 women); includes 2 minority (both Hispanic Americans), 8 international. Average age 24. 26 applicants, 96% accepted. In 2009, 8 master's awarded. *Degree requirements:* For master's, comprehensive exam (for some programs), thesis (for some programs), capstone experience. *Entrance requirements:* For master's, minimum GPA of 2.75. Additional exam requirements/recommendations for international students: Required—TOEFL (minimum score 500 paper-based; 173 computer-based), IELTS (minimum score 5.5). *Application deadline:* Applications are processed on a rolling basis. Application fee: $0. *Financial support:* Fellowships, teaching assistantships with full and partial tuition reimbursements, career-related internships or fieldwork, Federal Work-Study, and unspecified assistantships available. Support available to part-time students. Financial award application deadline: 3/1. *Unit head:* Dr. Christopher A. Baumann, Director, 570-941-6389, Fax: 570-941-7510, E-mail: cab@scranton.edu. *Application contact:* Dr. Christopher A. Baumann, Director, 570-941-6389, Fax: 570-941-7510, E-mail: cab@scranton.edu.

University of South Alabama, College of Medicine and Graduate School, Program in Basic Medical Sciences, Specialization in Biochemistry and Molecular Biology, Mobile, AL 36688-0002. Offers PhD. *Degree requirements:* For doctorate, thesis/dissertation. *Entrance requirements:* For doctorate, GRE General Test or MCAT. *Expenses:* Tuition, state resident: part-time $218 per contact hour. Required fees: $1102 per year. *Faculty research:* Biochemistry of aging, mechanisms of metabolic regulation and oxygen metabolism.

University of South Carolina, The Graduate School, College of Arts and Sciences, Department of Chemistry and Biochemistry, Columbia, SC 29208. Offers IMA, MAT, MS, PhD. IMA and MAT offered in cooperation with the College of Education. Part-time programs available. Terminal master's awarded for partial completion of doctoral program. *Degree requirements:* For master's, comprehensive exam, thesis; for doctorate, comprehensive exam, thesis/dissertation. *Entrance requirements:* For master's and doctorate, GRE General Test. Additional exam requirements/recommendations for international students: Required—TOEFL. Electronic applications accepted. *Faculty research:* Spectroscopy, crystallography, organic and organometallic synthesis, analytical chemistry, materials.

University of Southern California, Keck School of Medicine and Graduate School, Graduate Programs in Medicine, Department of Biochemistry and Molecular Biology, Los Angeles, CA 90089. Offers MS, PhD. *Faculty:* 24 full-time (6 women). *Students:* 36 full-time (20 women); includes 9 minority (1 African American, 8 Asian Americans or Pacific Islanders), 24 international. Average age 24. 29 applicants, 24% accepted, 4 enrolled. In 2009, 11 master's, 14 doctorates awarded. Terminal master's awarded for partial completion of doctoral program. *Degree requirements:* For master's, thesis; for doctorate, comprehensive exam, thesis/dissertation. *Entrance requirements:* For master's and doctorate, GRE General Test, minimum GPA of 3.0. Additional exam requirements/recommendations for international students: Required—TOEFL (minimum score 600 paper-based; 250 computer-based; 100 iBT). *Application deadline:* For fall admission, 4/15 priority date for domestic and international students. Application fee: $85. Electronic applications accepted. *Expenses:* Tuition: Full-time $25,980; part-time $1315 per unit. Required fees: $554. One-time fee: $35 full-time. Full-time tuition and fees vary according to degree level and program. *Financial support:* In 2009–10, 16 students received support, including 1 fellowship with tuition reimbursement available (averaging $27,060 per year), 12 research assistantships with tuition reimbursements available (averaging $27,060 per year), 3 teaching assistantships with tuition reimbursements available (averaging $27,060 per year); Federal Work-Study, institutionally sponsored loans, scholarships/grants, health care benefits, and unspecified assistantships also available. Financial award application deadline: 5/5. *Faculty research:* Molecular genetics, gene expression, membrane biochemistry, metabolic regulation, cancer biology. *Unit head:* Dr. Michael R. Stallcup, Chair, 323-442-1145, Fax: 323-442-1224, E-mail: stallcup@usc.edu. *Application contact:* Anne L. Rice, Student Services Coordinator, 323-442-1145, Fax: 323-442-1224, E-mail: annvazqu@usc.edu.

University of Southern Mississippi, Graduate School, College of Science and Technology, Department of Chemistry and Biochemistry, Hattiesburg, MS 39406-0001. Offers analytical chemistry (MS, PhD); biochemistry (MS, PhD); inorganic chemistry (MS, PhD); organic chemistry (MS, PhD); physical chemistry (MS, PhD). *Faculty:* 16 full-time (4 women). *Students:* 14 full-time (0 women), 5 part-time (4 women). Average age 29. 41 applicants, 17% accepted, 6 enrolled. In 2009, 2 master's, 6 doctorates awarded. *Degree requirements:* For master's, comprehensive exam, thesis; for doctorate, comprehensive exam, thesis/dissertation. *Entrance requirements:* For master's, GRE General Test, minimum GPA of 2.75 in last 60 hours; for doctorate, GRE General Test, minimum GPA of 3.5. Additional exam requirements/recommendations for international students: Required—TOEFL. *Application deadline:* For fall admission, 3/1 priority date for domestic students, 3/1 for international students. Applications are processed on a rolling basis. Application fee: $35. *Expenses:* Tuition, state resident: full-time $5096; part-time $284 per hour. Tuition, nonresident: full-time $13,052; part-time $726 per hour. Required fees: $402. Tuition and fees vary according to course level and course load. *Financial support:* In 2009–10, 3 research assistantships with full tuition reimbursements (averaging $17,000 per year), 19 teaching assistantships with full tuition reimbursements (averaging $20,716 per year) were awarded; fellowships, Federal Work-Study and institutionally sponsored loans also available. Support available to part-time students. Financial award application deadline: 3/15; financial award applicants required to submit FAFSA. *Faculty research:* Plant biochemistry, photo chemistry, polymer chemistry, x-ray analysis, enzyme chemistry. *Unit head:* Dr. Robert Bateman, Chair, 601-266-4701, Fax: 601-266-6075. *Application contact:* Dr. Sabine Heinherst, Graduate Coordinator, 601-266-4702, Fax: 601-266-6075.

University of South Florida, Graduate School, College of Arts and Sciences, Department of Chemistry, Tampa, FL 33620-9951. Offers computational chemistry (PhD); analytical chemistry (MS, PhD); biochemistry (MS, PhD); computational chemistry (MS); environmental chemistry (MS, PhD); inorganic chemistry (MS, PhD); organic chemistry (MS); physical chemistry (MS, PhD); polymer chemistry (PhD). Part-time programs available. *Faculty:* 25 full-time (4 women). *Students:* 113 full-time (36 women), 15 part-time (11 women); includes 19 minority (5 African Americans, 6 Asian Americans or Pacific Islanders, 8 Hispanic Americans), 58 international. Average age 32. 112 applicants, 30% accepted, 21 enrolled. In 2009, 8 master's, 11 doctorates awarded. Terminal master's awarded for partial completion of doctoral program. *Degree requirements:* For master's, comprehensive exam, thesis (for some programs); for doctorate, 2 foreign languages, comprehensive exam, thesis/dissertation. *Entrance requirements:* For master's, GRE General Test or GMAT, minimum GPA of 3.0. Additional exam requirements/recommendations for international students: Required—TOEFL (minimum score 550 paper-based; 213 computer-based). *Application deadline:* For fall admission, 2/15 priority date for domestic students, 1/2 priority date for international students; for spring admission, 10/1 priority date for domestic students, 6/1 priority date for international students. Applications are processed on a rolling basis. Application fee: $30. Electronic applications accepted. *Financial support:* In 2009–10, teaching assistantships with tuition reimbursements (averaging $27,522 per year); unspecified assistantships also available. Financial award application deadline: 6/30. *Faculty research:* Synthesis, bio-organic chemistry, bioinorganic chemistry, environmental chemistry, NMR. Total annual research expenditures: $3.2 million. *Unit head:* Dr. Randy Larsen, Chairperson, 813-974-4129, Fax: 813-974-3203, E-mail: rlarsen@cas.usf.edu. *Application contact:* Patricia Muisener, Director, 813-974-1730, Fax: 813-974-3203, E-mail: muisener@cas.usf.edu.

The University of Tennessee, Graduate School, College of Arts and Sciences, Department of Biochemistry, Cellular and Molecular Biology, Knoxville, TN 37996. Offers MS, PhD. Terminal master's awarded for partial completion of doctoral program. *Degree requirements:* For master's, thesis; for doctorate, thesis/dissertation. *Entrance requirements:* For master's and doctorate, GRE General Test, minimum GPA of 2.7. Additional exam requirements/recommendations for international students: Required—TOEFL. Electronic applications accepted. *Expenses:* Tuition, state resident: full-time $6826; part-time $380 per semester hour. Tuition, nonresident: full-time $21,844; part-time $1147 per semester hour. Tuition and fees vary according to program.

The University of Texas at Austin, Graduate School, College of Natural Sciences, Department of Chemistry and Biochemistry, Program in Biochemistry, Austin, TX 78712-1111. Offers MA, PhD. *Entrance requirements:* For master's and doctorate, GRE General Test.

The University of Texas Health Science Center at Houston, Graduate School of Biomedical Sciences, Program in Biochemistry and Molecular Biology, Houston, TX 77225-0036. Offers MS, PhD, MD/PhD. Terminal master's awarded for partial completion of doctoral program. *Degree requirements:* For master's, thesis; for doctorate, thesis/dissertation. *Entrance requirements:* For master's and doctorate, GRE General Test. Additional exam requirements/recommendations for international students: Required—TOEFL. Electronic applications accepted. *Faculty research:* Biochemistry, membrane biology, macromolecular structure, structural biophysics, molecular models of human disease; molecular biology of the cell.

The University of Texas Health Science Center at San Antonio, Graduate School of Biomedical Sciences, Department of Biochemistry, San Antonio, TX 78229. Offers MS, PhD. *Faculty:* 23 full-time (5 women). *Students:* 25 full-time (10 women). Average age 25. In 2009, 8 doctorates awarded. Terminal master's awarded for partial completion of doctoral program. *Degree requirements:* For master's, thesis; for doctorate, comprehensive exam, thesis/dissertation. *Entrance requirements:* For master's and doctorate, GRE General Test. Additional exam requirements/recommendations for international students: Required—TOEFL (minimum score 560 paper-based; 220 computer-based; 68 iBT). *Application deadline:* For fall admission, 4/1 for domestic students; for spring admission, 9/1 for domestic students. Applications are processed on a rolling basis. Application fee: $0. *Expenses:* Tuition, state resident: full-time $2832; part-time $118 per credit hour. Tuition, nonresident: full-time $10,896; part-time $454 per credit hour. Required fees: $884 per semester. One-time fee: $70. *Financial support:* In 2009–10, 25 teaching assistantships (averaging $26,000 per year) were awarded; fellowships, research assistantships also available. Financial award applicants required to submit FAFSA. *Faculty research:* Protein structure and function, lipid biochemistry, metabolic regulation, immunology, membrane assembly. Total annual research expenditures: $11.3 million. *Unit head:* Bruce J. Nicholson, Professor and Chair, 210-567-3770, Fax: 210-567-6595, E-mail: nicholsonb@uthscsa.edu. *Application contact:* Neal C. Robinson, Chairman, Committee on Graduate Studies, 210-567-3754, E-mail: robinson@uthscsa.edu.

Biochemistry

The University of Texas Medical Branch, Graduate School of Biomedical Sciences, Program in Biochemistry and Molecular Biology, Galveston, TX 77555. Offers biochemistry (PhD); bioinformatics (PhD); biophysics (PhD); cell biology (PhD); computational biology (PhD); structural biology (PhD). *Students:* 41 full-time (17 women); includes 6 minority (1 African American, 1 Asian American or Pacific Islander, 4 Hispanic Americans), 22 international. Average age 28. In 2009, 9 doctorates awarded. *Degree requirements:* For doctorate, thesis/dissertation. *Entrance requirements:* Additional exam requirements/recommendations for international students: Required—TOEFL (minimum score 550 paper-based; 213 computer-based). *Application deadline:* Applications are processed on a rolling basis. Application fee: $30 ($75 for international students). Electronic applications accepted. *Financial support:* In 2009–10, fellowships (averaging $25,000 per year), research assistantships (averaging $25,000 per year) were awarded. Financial award applicants required to submit FAFSA. *Unit head:* Dr. Sarita Sastry, Director, 409-747-1915, Fax: 409-747-1938, E-mail: sasastry@utmb.edu. *Application contact:* Debora Botting, Coordinator for Special Programs, 409-772-2769, Fax: 409-772-5102, E-mail: dmbottin@utmb.edu.

The University of Texas Southwestern Medical Center at Dallas, Southwestern Graduate School of Biomedical Sciences, Division of Basic Science, Program in Biological Chemistry, Dallas, TX 75390. Offers PhD. *Faculty:* 44 full-time (9 women), 1 part-time/adjunct (0 women). *Students:* 37 full-time (14 women); includes 8 minority (1 American Indian/Alaska Native, 4 Asian Americans or Pacific Islanders, 3 Hispanic Americans), 12 international. Average age 27. 946 applicants, 22% accepted. In 2009, 4 doctorates awarded. *Degree requirements:* For doctorate, thesis/dissertation, qualifying exam. *Entrance requirements:* For doctorate, GRE General Test, minimum GPA of 3.0. Additional exam requirements/recommendations for international students: Required—TOEFL. *Application deadline:* For fall admission, 12/15 priority date for domestic students. Application fee: $0. Electronic applications accepted. *Financial support:* Fellowships, research assistantships, institutionally sponsored loans available. *Faculty research:* Regulation of gene expression, protein trafficking, molecular neurobiology, protein structure and function, metabolic regulation. *Unit head:* Adam de Pencier. *Application contact:* Dr. Nancy E. Street, Associate Dean, 214-648-6708, Fax: 214-648-2102, E-mail: nancy.street@utsouthwestern.edu.

University of the Sciences in Philadelphia, College of Graduate Studies, Program in Chemistry, Biochemistry and Pharmacognosy, Philadelphia, PA 19104-4495. Offers biochemistry (MS, PhD); chemistry (MS, PhD); pharmacognosy (MS, PhD). Part-time programs available. *Degree requirements:* For master's, thesis, qualifying exams; for doctorate, comprehensive exam, thesis/dissertation, qualifying exams. *Entrance requirements:* For master's and doctorate, GRE General Test, GRE Subject Test. Additional exam requirements/recommendations for international students: Required—TOEFL, TWE. *Expenses:* Contact institution. *Faculty research:* Organic and medicinal synthesis, mass spectroscopy use in protein analysis, study of analogues of taxol, cholesteryl esters.

The University of Toledo, College of Graduate Studies, College of Arts and Sciences, Department of Chemistry, Toledo, OH 43606-3390. Offers analytical chemistry (MS, PhD); biological chemistry (MS, PhD); inorganic chemistry (MS, PhD); organic chemistry (MS, PhD); physical chemistry (MS, PhD). Part-time programs available. *Degree requirements:* For master's, thesis; for doctorate, thesis/dissertation. *Entrance requirements:* For master's and doctorate, GRE General Test, GRE Subject Test. Additional exam requirements/recommendations for international students: Required—TOEFL. Electronic applications accepted. *Faculty research:* Enzymology, materials chemistry, crystallography, theoretical chemistry.

The University of Toledo, College of Graduate Studies, College of Medicine, Biomedical Science Programs, Department of Biochemistry and Molecular Biology, Toledo, OH 43606-3390. Offers medical sciences (MSBS). Part-time programs available. *Degree requirements:* For master's, thesis, qualifying exam. *Entrance requirements:* For master's, GRE General Test, minimum undergraduate GPA of 3.0. Additional exam requirements/recommendations for international students: Required—TOEFL. *Faculty research:* Gene regulation, protein structure, receptors, protein phosphorylation, peptides.

The University of Toledo, College of Graduate Studies, College of Pharmacy, Program in Medicinal and Biological Chemistry, Toledo, OH 43606-3390. Offers MS, PhD. Terminal master's awarded for partial completion of doctoral program. *Degree requirements:* For master's, thesis; for doctorate, thesis/dissertation. *Entrance requirements:* For master's and doctorate, GRE General Test. Additional exam requirements/recommendations for international students: Required—TOEFL (minimum score 550 paper-based; 213 computer-based; 80 iBT). Electronic applications accepted. *Faculty research:* Neuroscience, molecular modeling, immunotoxicology, organic synthesis, peptide biochemistry.

University of Toronto, School of Graduate Studies, Life Sciences Division, Department of Biochemistry, Toronto, ON M5S 1A1, Canada. Offers M Sc, PhD. *Degree requirements:* For master's, thesis, oral examination of thesis; for doctorate, thesis/dissertation, oral defense of thesis. *Entrance requirements:* For master's, GRE General Test and GRE Subject Test in biochemistry/molecular biology (international applicants only), B Sc in biochemistry or molecular biology, minimum B+ average, letters of reference. Additional exam requirements/recommendations for international students: Required—TOEFL (minimum score 580 paper-based; 237 computer-based), TWE (minimum score 5).

University of Tulsa, Graduate School, College of Engineering and Natural Sciences, Department of Chemistry and Biochemistry, Program in Biochemistry, Tulsa, OK 74104-3189. Offers MS. Part-time programs available. *Faculty:* 2 full-time (0 women). *Students:* 4 full-time (3 women), 2 international. Average age 29. 7 applicants, 71% accepted, 3 enrolled. In 2009, 1 master's awarded. *Degree requirements:* For master's, thesis (for some programs). *Entrance requirements:* For master's, GRE General Test. Additional exam requirements/recommendations for international students: Required—TOEFL (minimum score 550 paper-based; 213 computer-based; 80 iBT), IELTS (minimum score 6). *Application deadline:* Applications are processed on a rolling basis. Application fee: $40. Electronic applications accepted. *Expenses:* Tuition: Full-time $16,182; part-time $899 per credit hour. Required fees: $4 per credit hour. Tuition and fees vary according to course load. *Financial support:* In 2009–10, 2 students received support, including 1 research assistantship (averaging $12,020 per year), 1 teaching assistantship (averaging $11,594 per year); career-related internships or fieldwork, Federal Work-Study, scholarships/grants, health care benefits, and unspecified assistantships also available. Support available to part-time students. Financial award application deadline: 2/1; financial award applicants required to submit FAFSA. *Faculty research:* Analytical, organic, inorganic, and physical chemistry; pecialty courses in materials chemistry, polymer chemistry, nanotechnology, medicinal chemistry, environmental chemistry, biochemistry of disease, chemical kinetics, surface chemistry, and spectroscopy. *Unit head:* Dr. Dale C. Teeters, Chairperson and Advisor, 918-631-2515, Fax: 918-631-3404, E-mail: dale-teeters@utulsa.edu. *Application contact:* Dr. Robert Sheaff, Advisor, 918-631-2319, Fax: 918-631-3404, E-mail: robert-sheaff@utulsa.edu.

University of Utah, Graduate School and Graduate Programs in Medicine, Program in Biological Chemistry, Salt Lake City, UT 84112-1107. Offers PhD. *Faculty:* 48 full-time (9 women). *Students:* 13 full-time (4 women), 6 international. Average age 24. 210 applicants, 13% accepted, 13 enrolled. *Degree requirements:* For doctorate, thesis/dissertation. *Entrance requirements:* For doctorate, GRE General Test. Additional exam requirements/recommendations for international students: Required—TOEFL (minimum score 500 paper-based; 173 computer-based; 60 iBT). *Application deadline:* For fall admission, 12/15 for domestic and international students. Application fee: $0. *Expenses:* Tuition, state resident: full-time $4004; part-time $1674 per semester. Tuition, nonresident: full-time $14,134; part-time $5915 per semester. Required fees: $324 per semester. Tuition and fees vary according to course load, degree level and program. *Financial support:* In 2009–10, 12 research assistantships with full tuition reimbursements (averaging $25,000 per year) were awarded; health care benefits also available. *Faculty research:* Protein structure, nucleic acid, enzymes, proteolysis, HIV. *Unit head:* Dr. Dennis Winge, Director, 801-581-5207, Fax: 801-585-2465. *Application contact:* Barb Saffel, Administrative Program Coordinator, 801-581-5207, E-mail: bsaffel@genetics.utah.edu.

University of Utah, School of Medicine and Graduate School, Graduate Programs in Medicine, Department of Biochemistry, Salt Lake City, UT 84112-1107. Offers MS, PhD. Terminal master's awarded for partial completion of doctoral program. *Degree requirements:* For master's, thesis; for doctorate, thesis/dissertation. *Entrance requirements:* For doctorate, GRE Subject Test, minimum GPA of 3.0. Additional exam requirements/recommendations for international students: Required—TOEFL. Electronic applications accepted. *Expenses:* Tuition, state resident: full-time $4004; part-time $1674 per semester. Tuition, nonresident: full-time $14,134; part-time $5915 per semester. Required fees: $324 per semester. Tuition and fees vary according to course load, degree level and program. *Faculty research:* Protein structure and function, nucleic acid structure and function, nucleic acid enzymology, RNA modification, protein turnover.

University of Vermont, College of Medicine and Graduate College, Graduate Programs in Medicine, Department of Biochemistry, Burlington, VT 05405. Offers MS, PhD, MD/MS, MD/PhD. *Students:* 16 (7 women). 35 applicants, 17% accepted, 1 enrolled. In 2009, 1 master's, 3 doctorates awarded. *Degree requirements:* For master's, thesis; for doctorate, thesis/dissertation. *Entrance requirements:* For master's and doctorate, GRE General Test. Additional exam requirements/recommendations for international students: Required—TOEFL (minimum score 550 paper-based; 213 computer-based; 80 iBT). *Application deadline:* For fall admission, 3/1 priority date for domestic students, 3/1 for international students. Applications are processed on a rolling basis. Application fee: $40. Electronic applications accepted. *Expenses:* Tuition, state resident: part-time $508 per credit hour. Tuition, nonresident: part-time $1281 per credit hour. *Financial support:* Fellowships, research assistantships, teaching assistantships, analytical assistantships available. Financial award application deadline: 3/1. *Faculty research:* Endocrinology, protein chemistry, cell-surface signaling. *Unit head:* Dr. Paula Tracy, Interim Chairperson, 802-656-2220. *Application contact:* Dr. Christopher Francklyn, Coordinator, 802-656-2220.

University of Victoria, Faculty of Graduate Studies, Faculty of Science, Department of Biochemistry and Microbiology, Victoria, BC V8W 2Y2, Canada. Offers biochemistry (M Sc, PhD); microbiology (M Sc, PhD). *Degree requirements:* For master's, thesis, seminar; for doctorate, thesis/dissertation, seminar, candidacy exam. *Entrance requirements:* For master's, GRE General Test, minimum B+ average; for doctorate, GRE General Test, minimum B+ average, M Sc. Additional exam requirements/recommendations for international students: Required—TOEFL (minimum score 600 paper-based; 250 computer-based). Electronic applications accepted. *Faculty research:* Molecular pathogenesis, prokaryotic, eukaryotic, macromolecular interactions, microbial surfaces, virology, molecular genetics.

University of Virginia, School of Medicine, Department of Biochemistry and Molecular Genetics, Charlottesville, VA 22903. Offers biochemistry (PhD); MD/PhD. *Faculty:* 26 full-time (6 women), 1 (woman) part-time/adjunct. *Students:* 33 full-time (15 women); includes 3 minority (1 African American, 2 Asian Americans or Pacific Islanders), 9 international. Average age 26. In 2009, 6 doctorates awarded. *Degree requirements:* For doctorate, thesis/dissertation, written research proposal and defense. *Entrance requirements:* For doctorate, GRE General Test, 3 letters of recommendation. Additional exam requirements/recommendations for international students: Recommended—TOEFL (minimum score 630 paper-based; 250 computer-based; 90 iBT). Application fee: $60. Electronic applications accepted. *Financial support:* Fellowships, health care benefits and tuition waivers (full) available. Financial award applicants required to submit FAFSA. *Unit head:* Joyce L. Hamlin, Chair, 434-924-1940, Fax: 434-924-5069. *Application contact:* Associate Dean for Graduate Programs and Research.

University of Washington, Graduate School, School of Medicine and Graduate School, Graduate Programs in Medicine, Department of Biochemistry, Seattle, WA 98195. Offers PhD. *Degree requirements:* For doctorate, thesis/dissertation. *Entrance requirements:* For doctorate, GRE General Test, GRE Subject Test (biology, chemistry, biochemistry, or cell and molecular biology), minimum GPA of 3.0. Additional exam requirements/recommendations for international students: Required—TOEFL. Electronic applications accepted. *Faculty research:* Blood coagulation, structure and function of enzymes, fertilization events, interaction of plants with bacteria, protein structure.

University of Waterloo, Graduate Studies, Faculty of Science, Guelph-Waterloo Centre for Graduate Work in Chemistry and Biochemistry, Waterloo, ON N2L 3G1, Canada. Offers M Sc, PhD. Part-time programs available. *Degree requirements:* For master's and doctorate, project or thesis. *Entrance requirements:* For master's, GRE, honors degree, minimum B average; for doctorate, GRE, master's degree, minimum B average. Additional exam requirements/recommendations for international students: Required—TOEFL, TWE. Electronic applications accepted. *Faculty research:* Polymer, physical, inorganic, organic, and theoretical chemistry.

The University of Western Ontario, Faculty of Graduate Studies, Biosciences Division, Department of Biochemistry, London, ON N6A 5B8, Canada. Offers M Sc, PhD. *Degree requirements:* For master's, thesis; for doctorate, thesis/dissertation. *Entrance requirements:* For master's, minimum B+ average in last 2 years of undergraduate study; for doctorate, M Sc or an external scholarship winner.

University of West Florida, College of Arts and Sciences: Sciences, School of Allied Health and Life Sciences, Department of Biology, Pensacola, FL 32514-5750. Offers biological chemistry (MS); biology (MS); biology education (MST); biotechnology (MS); coastal zone studies (MS); environmental biology (MS). *Faculty:* 7 full-time (2 women), 1 (woman) part-time/adjunct. *Students:* 5 full-time (1 woman), 21 part-time (14 women); includes 2 minority (1 Asian American or Pacific Islander, 1 Hispanic American), 1 international. Average age 28. 19 applicants, 58% accepted, 7 enrolled. In 2009, 12 master's awarded. *Degree requirements:* For master's, thesis. *Entrance requirements:* For master's, GRE General Test. Additional exam requirements/recommendations for international students: Required—TOEFL (minimum score 550 paper-based; 213 computer-based). *Application deadline:* For fall admission, 6/1 for domestic students, 5/15 for international students; for spring admission, 11/1 for domestic students, 10/1 for international students. Applications are processed on a rolling basis. Application fee: $30. *Expenses:* Tuition, state resident: full-time $4982; part-time $260 per credit hour. Tuition, nonresident: full-time $20,059; part-time $919 per credit hour. Required fees: $1247; $52 per credit hour. *Financial support:* In 2009–10, 2 research assistantships with partial tuition reimbursements (averaging $8,500 per year), 10 teaching assistantships with partial tuition reimbursements (averaging $8,176 per year) were awarded; unspecified assistantships also available. Financial award application deadline: 4/15; financial award applicants required to submit FAFSA. *Unit head:* Dr. George L. Stewart, Chairperson, 850-474-2748. *Application contact:* Terry McCray, Assistant Director of Graduate Admissions, 850-473-7718, Fax: 850-473-7714, E-mail: gradadmissions@uwf.edu.

University of Windsor, Faculty of Graduate Studies, Faculty of Science, Department of Chemistry and Biochemistry, Windsor, ON N9B 3P4, Canada. Offers M Sc, PhD. Part-time programs available. *Degree requirements:* For master's, thesis; for doctorate, comprehensive exam, thesis/dissertation. *Entrance requirements:* For master's and doctorate, minimum B average. Additional exam requirements/recommendations for international students: Required—TOEFL (minimum score 560 paper-based; 220 computer-based), GRE. Electronic applications accepted. *Faculty research:* Molecular biology/recombinant DNA techniques (PCR, cloning mutagenesis), No/02 detectors, western immunoblotting and detection, CD/NMR protein/peptide structure determination, confocal/electron microscopes.

University of Wisconsin–Madison, Graduate School, College of Agricultural and Life Sciences, Department of Biochemistry, Madison, WI 53706-1380. Offers PhD. Terminal master's awarded for partial completion of doctoral program. *Degree requirements:* For doctorate, thesis/dissertation. *Entrance requirements:* For doctorate, GRE General Test, GRE Subject Test (recommended). Additional exam requirements/recommendations for international students: Required—TOEFL. Electronic applications accepted. *Expenses:* Tuition, state resident: part-time $594 per credit. Tuition, nonresident: part-time $1504 per credit. Required fees: $65 per credit. Tuition and fees vary according to course load, program and reciprocity agreements. *Faculty* *research:* Molecular structure of vitamins and hormones, enzymology, NMR spectroscopy, protein structure, molecular genetics.

University of Wisconsin–Madison, School of Medicine and Public Health and Graduate School, Graduate Programs in Medicine, Department of Biomolecular Chemistry, Madison, WI 53706-1380. Offers MS, PhD. *Faculty:* 13 full-time (3 women). *Students:* 41 full-time (21 women); includes 1 minority (Asian American or Pacific Islander), 6 international. Average age 25. 307 applicants, 21% accepted, 25 enrolled. In 2009, 7 doctorates awarded. Terminal master's awarded for partial completion of doctoral program. *Degree requirements:* For master's, thesis; for doctorate, thesis/dissertation. *Entrance requirements:* For doctorate, GRE. *Application deadline:* For fall admission, 12/15 priority date for domestic students. Application fee: $56. Electronic applications accepted. *Expenses:* Tuition, state resident: part-time $594 per credit. Tuition, nonresident: part-time $1504 per credit. Required fees: $65 per credit. Tuition and fees vary according to course load, program and reciprocity agreements. *Financial support:* In 2009–10, fellowships with full tuition reimbursements (averaging $20,000 per year), research assistantships with full tuition reimbursements (averaging $24,000 per year), teaching assistantships with full tuition reimbursements (averaging $27,640 per year) were awarded; traineeships, health care benefits, and tuition waivers (full) also available. *Faculty research:* Membrane biochemistry, protein folding and translocation, gene expression, signal transduction, cell growth and differentiation. Total annual research expenditures: $3.4 million. *Unit head:* Dr. Robert H. Fillingame, Chair, 608-262-1347, Fax: 608-262-5253, E-mail: rhfillin@wisc.edu. *Application contact:* Elyse Meuer, Student Services Coordinator, 608-262-1347, Fax: 608-262-5253, E-mail: eemeuer@wisc.edu.

University of Wisconsin–Milwaukee, Graduate School, College of Letters and Sciences, Department of Chemistry, Milwaukee, WI 53201-0413. Offers biogeochemistry (PhD); chemistry (MS, PhD). *Faculty:* 22 full-time (3 women). *Students:* 68 full-time (22 women), 8 part-time (5 women); includes 9 minority (3 African Americans, 6 Asian Americans or Pacific Islanders), 27 international. Average age 30. 55 applicants, 45% accepted, 17 enrolled. In 2009, 4 master's, 16 doctorates awarded. *Degree requirements:* For master's, thesis or alternative; for doctorate, thesis/dissertation. *Entrance requirements:* For doctorate, GRE General Test. Additional exam requirements/recommendations for international students: Required—TOEFL (minimum score 600 paper-based; 79 iBT), IELTS (minimum score 6.5). *Application deadline:* For fall admission, 1/1 priority date for domestic students; for spring admission, 9/1 for domestic students. Applications are processed on a rolling basis. Application fee: $45 ($75 for international students). *Expenses:* Tuition, state resident: full-time $8800. Tuition, nonresident: full-time $20,760. Tuition and fees vary according to program and reciprocity agreements. *Financial support:* In 2009–10, 22 research assistantships, 48 teaching assistantships were awarded; career-related internships or fieldwork and unspecified assistantships also available. Support available to part-time students. Financial award application deadline: 4/15. *Faculty research:* Analytical chemistry, biochemistry, inorganic chemistry, organic chemistry, physical chemistry. Total annual research expenditures: $2.4 million. *Unit head:* Peter Geissinger, Representative, 414-229-5230, Fax: 414-229-5530, E-mail: geissing@uwm.edu. *Application contact:* Joseph Aldstadt, General Information Contact, 414-229-5605, Fax: 414-229-6967, E-mail: aldstadt@uwm.edu.

Utah State University, School of Graduate Studies, College of Science, Department of Chemistry and Biochemistry, Logan, UT 84322. Offers biochemistry (MS, PhD); chemistry (MS, PhD). Part-time programs available. Terminal master's awarded for partial completion of doctoral program. *Degree requirements:* For master's, thesis, oral and written exams; for doctorate, thesis/dissertation, oral and written exams. *Entrance requirements:* For master's and doctorate, GRE General Test, minimum GPA of 3.0. Additional exam requirements/recommendations for international students: Required—TOEFL. *Faculty research:* Analytical, inorganic, organic, and physical chemistry; iron in asbestos chemistry and carcinogenicity; dicopper complexes; photothermal spectrometry; metal molecule clusters.

Vanderbilt University, Graduate School and School of Medicine, Department of Biochemistry, Nashville, TN 37240-1001. Offers MS, PhD, MD/PhD. *Faculty:* 38 full-time (4 women), 1 part-time/adjunct (0 women). *Students:* 30 full-time (20 women); includes 2 minority (1 African American, 1 Asian American or Pacific Islander), 2 international. Average age 28. In 2009, 1 master's, 9 doctorates awarded. Terminal master's awarded for partial completion of doctoral program. *Degree requirements:* For master's, thesis; for doctorate, thesis/dissertation, preliminary, qualifying, and final exams. *Entrance requirements:* For master's, GRE General Test; for doctorate, GRE General Test, GRE Subject Test (recommended). Additional exam requirements/recommendations for international students: Required—TOEFL (minimum score 570 paper-based; 230 computer-based; 88 iBT). *Application deadline:* For fall admission, 1/15 for domestic and international students. Application fee: $0. Electronic applications accepted. *Financial support:* Fellowships with full tuition reimbursements, research assistantships with full tuition reimbursements, Federal Work-Study, institutionally sponsored loans, scholarships/grants, traineeships, and tuition waivers (partial) available. Financial award application deadline: 1/15; financial award applicants required to submit CSS PROFILE or FAFSA. *Faculty research:* Protein chemistry, carcinogenesis, metabolism, toxicology, receptors and signaling, DNA recognition and transcription. *Unit head:* Dr. Michael R. Waterman, Chair, 615-322-3318, E-mail: michael.waterman@vanderbilt.edu. *Application contact:* Dr. David Cortez, Director of Graduate Studies, 615-322-3318, E-mail: david.cortez@vanderbilt.edu.

Vanderbilt University, School of Medicine, Program in Chemical and Physical Biology, Nashville, TN 37240-1001. Offers PhD. *Degree requirements:* For doctorate, comprehensive exam, thesis/dissertation, dissertation defense. *Entrance requirements:* For doctorate, GRE, 3 letters of recommendation, interview by invitation. Additional exam requirements/recommendations for international students: Required—TOEFL. Electronic applications accepted. *Faculty research:* Mathematical modeling, enzyme kinetics, structural biology, genomics, proteomics and mass spectrometry.

Virginia Commonwealth University, Medical College of Virginia-Professional Programs, School of Medicine, School of Medicine Graduate Programs, Department of Biochemistry, Richmond, VA 23284-9005. Offers biochemistry (MS, PhD); molecular biology and genetics (MS, PhD); neuroscience (PhD); MD/PhD. *Degree requirements:* For master's, thesis; for doctorate, thesis/dissertation, comprehensive oral and written exams. *Entrance requirements:* For master's and doctorate, DAT, GRE General Test, MCAT. *Faculty research:* Molecular biology, peptide/protein chemistry, neurochemistry, enzyme mechanisms, macromolecular structure determination.

Virginia Commonwealth University, Program in Pre-Medical Basic Health Sciences, Richmond, VA 23284-9005. Offers anatomy (CBHS); biochemistry (CBHS); human genetics (CBHS); microbiology (CBHS); pharmacology (CBHS); physiology (CBHS). *Entrance requirements:* For degree, GRE or MCAT, course work in organic chemistry, minimum undergraduate GPA of 2.8. Additional exam requirements/recommendations for international students: Required—TOEFL (minimum score 600 paper-based).

Virginia Polytechnic Institute and State University, Graduate School, College of Agriculture and Life Sciences, Department of Biochemistry, Blacksburg, VA 24061. Offers life sciences (MS, PhD). *Faculty:* 18 full-time (3 women). *Students:* 25 full-time (14 women), 2 part-time (0 women); includes 14 minority (1 African American, 9 American Indian/Alaska Native, 2 Asian Americans or Pacific Islanders, 2 Hispanic Americans), 1 international. Average age 28. 60 applicants, 12% accepted, 2 enrolled. In 2009, 3 master's, 6 doctorates awarded. *Entrance requirements:* For master's and doctorate, GRE, GMAT. Additional exam requirements/recommendations for international students: Required—TOEFL (minimum score 550 paper-based; 213 computer-based). *Application deadline:* For fall admission, 5/15 for international students; for spring admission, 10/15 for international students. Applications are processed on a rolling basis. Application fee: $65. Electronic applications accepted. *Expenses:* Contact institution. *Financial support:* In 2009–10, 5 research assistantships with full tuition reimbursements (averaging $20,029 per year), 10 teaching assistantships with full tuition reimbursements (averaging $18,024 per year) were awarded; career-related internships or fieldwork, Federal Work-Study, scholarships/grants, and unspecified assistantships also available. Financial award application deadline: 1/15. *Faculty research:* Molecular biology, molecular entomology, enzymology, signal transduction, protein structure-function. Total annual research expenditures: $3.1 million. *Unit head:* Dr. Peter J. Kennelly, Dean, 540-231-6315, E-mail: pjkennel@vt.edu. *Application contact:* Erin Dolan, Information Contact, 540-231-2692, Fax: 540-231-6315, E-mail: edolan@vt.edu.

Wake Forest University, School of Medicine and Graduate School of Arts and Sciences, Graduate Programs in Medicine, Department of Biochemistry, Winston-Salem, NC 27109. Offers PhD, MD/PhD. *Degree requirements:* For doctorate, thesis/dissertation. *Entrance requirements:* For doctorate, GRE General Test. Additional exam requirements/recommendations for international students: Required—TOEFL. Electronic applications accepted. *Faculty research:* Biomembranes, cancer, biophysics.

Washington State University, Graduate School, College of Sciences, School of Molecular Biosciences, Program in Biochemistry and Biophysics, Pullman, WA 99164. Offers MS, PhD. Terminal master's awarded for partial completion of doctoral program. *Degree requirements:* For master's, thesis or alternative, oral exam; for doctorate, comprehensive exam, thesis/dissertation, oral exam, written exam. *Entrance requirements:* For master's and doctorate, GRE General Test, minimum GPA of 3.0. Additional exam requirements/recommendations for international students: Required—TOEFL (minimum score 550 paper-based; 213 computer-based). Electronic applications accepted. *Faculty research:* Gene regulation, signal transduction, protein export, reproductive biology, DNA repair.

Washington University in St. Louis, Graduate School of Arts and Sciences, Division of Biology and Biomedical Sciences, Program in Biochemistry, St. Louis, MO 63130-4899. Offers PhD. *Degree requirements:* For doctorate, thesis/dissertation. *Entrance requirements:* For doctorate, GRE General Test, GRE Subject Test. Electronic applications accepted.

Washington University in St. Louis, Graduate School of Arts and Sciences, Division of Biology and Biomedical Sciences, Program in Chemical Biology, St. Louis, MO 63130-4899. Offers PhD. *Degree requirements:* For doctorate, thesis/dissertation. *Entrance requirements:* For doctorate, GRE General Test, GRE Subject Test. Electronic applications accepted.

Wayne State University, School of Medicine, Graduate Programs in Medicine, Department of Biochemistry and Molecular Biology, Detroit, MI 48202. Offers MS, PhD. Terminal master's awarded for partial completion of doctoral program. *Degree requirements:* For master's, thesis; for doctorate, one foreign language, thesis/dissertation. *Entrance requirements:* For master's and doctorate, GRE General Test, GRE Subject Test. Additional exam requirements/recommendations for international students: Required—TOEFL (minimum score 550 paper-based; 213 computer-based); Recommended—TWE (minimum score 6). Electronic applications accepted. *Faculty research:* Protein structure, molecular biology, molecular genetics, enzymology, x-ray crystallography.

Wesleyan University, Graduate Programs, Department of Chemistry, Middletown, CT 06459. Offers biochemistry (MA, PhD); chemical physics (MA, PhD); inorganic chemistry (MA, PhD); organic chemistry (MA, PhD); physical chemistry (MA, PhD); theoretical chemistry (MA, PhD). *Faculty:* 14 full-time (2 women), 2 part-time/adjunct (1 woman). *Students:* 19 full-time (8 women), 2 part-time (0 women), 9 international. Average age 26. 40 applicants, 63% accepted, 4 enrolled. In 2009, 3 master's, 5 doctorates awarded. Terminal master's awarded for partial completion of doctoral program. *Degree requirements:* For master's, thesis, proposal; for doctorate, thesis/dissertation, proposal. *Entrance requirements:* For doctorate, GRE General Test, 3 recommendations. Additional exam requirements/recommendations for international students: Required—TOEFL. *Application deadline:* Applications are processed on a rolling basis. Application fee: $0. Electronic applications accepted. *Financial support:* In 2009–10, 4 research assistantships with full tuition reimbursements, 12 teaching assistantships with full tuition reimbursements were awarded; institutionally sponsored loans also available. Financial award application deadline: 4/15; financial award applicants required to submit FAFSA. *Unit head:* Dr. Joseph Knee, Chair, 860-685-2210. *Application contact:* Cait Zinser, Information Contact, 860-685-2573, Fax: 860-685-2211, E-mail: czinser@wesleyan.edu.

Wesleyan University, Graduate Programs, Department of Molecular Biology and Biochemistry, Middletown, CT 06459. Offers biochemistry (PhD); molecular biology (PhD). *Faculty:* 8 full-time (3 women), 1 (woman) part-time/adjunct. *Students:* 20 full-time (14 women); includes 1 minority (Hispanic American), 13 international. Average age 28. 40 applicants, 18% accepted, 4 enrolled. In 2009, 1 doctorate awarded. *Degree requirements:* For doctorate, comprehensive exam, thesis/dissertation. *Entrance requirements:* For doctorate, GRE General Test, GRE Subject Test. Additional exam requirements/recommendations for international students: Required—TOEFL. *Application deadline:* For fall admission, 2/15 for domestic and international students. Applications are processed on a rolling basis. Application fee: $0. Electronic applications accepted. *Financial support:* In 2009–10, 12 research assistantships with full tuition reimbursements, 8 teaching assistantships with full tuition reimbursements were awarded; institutionally sponsored loans also available. Financial award application deadline: 4/15; financial award applicants required to submit FAFSA. *Faculty research:* Genome organization, regulation of gene expression, molecular biology of development, physical biochemistry. *Unit head:* Dr. Michael McAlear, Chair, 860-685-2443, E-mail: mmcalear@wesleyan.edu. *Application contact:* Information Contact, 860-685-2640, E-mail: mbbgrad@wesleyan.edu.

West Virginia University, School of Medicine, Graduate Programs at the Health Sciences Center, Interdisciplinary Graduate Programs in Biomedical Sciences, Program in Biochemistry and Molecular Biology, Morgantown, WV 26506. Offers MS, PhD, MD/PhD. *Degree requirements:* For doctorate, comprehensive exam, thesis/dissertation. *Entrance requirements:* For doctorate, GRE General Test, minimum GPA of 3.0. Additional exam requirements/recommendations for international students: Required—TOEFL. Electronic applications accepted. *Faculty research:* Regulation of gene expression, cell survival mechanisms, signal transduction, regulation of metabolism, sensory neuroscience.

Worcester Polytechnic Institute, Graduate Studies and Research, Department of Chemistry and Biochemistry, Worcester, MA 01609-2280. Offers biochemistry (MS, PhD); chemistry (MS, PhD). Evening/weekend programs available. *Faculty:* 5 full-time (0 women), 4 part-time/adjunct (1 woman). *Students:* 11 full-time (7 women), 9 part-time (1 woman). 55 applicants, 33% accepted, 10 enrolled. In 2009, 6 master's, 2 doctorates awarded. *Degree requirements:* For master's, thesis; for doctorate, comprehensive exam, thesis/dissertation. *Entrance requirements:* For master's, GRE General Test, 3 letters of recommendation; for doctorate, GRE General Test, 3 letters of recommendation, statement of purpose. Additional exam requirements/recommendations for international students: Required—TOEFL (minimum score 550 paper-based; 213 computer-based; 79 iBT), IELTS (minimum score 6.5). *Application deadline:* For fall admission, 1/15 priority date for domestic and international students; for spring admission, 10/15 priority date for domestic and international students. Applications are processed on a rolling basis. Application fee: $70. Electronic applications accepted. *Financial support:* Career-related internships or fieldwork, institutionally sponsored loans, scholarships/grants, and unspecified assistantships available. Financial award application deadline: 1/15. *Faculty research:* Photochemistry, organic and materials synthesis, surface chemistry, ion transport. *Unit head:* Dr. Kristin K. Wobbe, Interim Head, 508-831-5371, Fax: 508-831-5933, E-mail: kwobbe@wpi.edu. *Application contact:* Dr. James Dittami, Graduate Coordinator, 508-831-5371, Fax: 508-831-5933, E-mail: jdittami@wpi.edu.

Wright State University, School of Graduate Studies, College of Science and Mathematics, Department of Biochemistry and Molecular Biology, Dayton, OH 45435. Offers MS. *Degree requirements:* For master's, thesis. *Entrance requirements:* Additional exam requirements/recommendations for international students: Required—TOEFL. *Faculty research:* Regulation of gene expression, macromolecular structural function, NMR imaging, visual biochemistry.

Yale University, Graduate School of Arts and Sciences, Department of Geology and Geophysics, New Haven, CT 06520. Offers biogeochemistry (PhD); climate dynamics (PhD);

Biochemistry

Yale University *(continued)*
geochemistry (PhD); geophysics (PhD); meteorology (PhD); oceanography (PhD); paleontology (PhD); paleooceanography (PhD); petrology (PhD); tectonics (PhD). *Degree requirements:* For doctorate, thesis/dissertation. *Entrance requirements:* For doctorate, GRE General Test. Additional exam requirements/recommendations for international students: Required—TOEFL.

Yale University, Graduate School of Arts and Sciences, Department of Molecular Biophysics and Biochemistry, New Haven, CT 06520. Offers PhD. *Degree requirements:* For doctorate, thesis/dissertation. *Entrance requirements:* For doctorate, GRE General Test, GRE Subject Test.

Yale University, Graduate School of Arts and Sciences, Department of Molecular, Cellular, and Developmental Biology, Program in Biochemistry, Molecular Biology and Chemical Biology, New Haven, CT 06520. Offers PhD. *Degree requirements:* For doctorate, thesis/dissertation. *Entrance requirements:* For doctorate, GRE General Test, GRE Subject Test.

Yale University, School of Medicine and Graduate School of Arts and Sciences, Combined Program in Biological and Biomedical Sciences (BBS), Molecular Biophysics and Biochemistry Track, New Haven, CT 06520. Offers PhD, MD/PhD. *Degree requirements:* For doctorate, thesis/dissertation. *Entrance requirements:* For doctorate, GRE General Test. Additional exam requirements/recommendations for international students: Required—TOEFL. *Application deadline:* For fall admission, 12/6 for domestic and international students. Electronic applications accepted. *Financial support:* Fellowships, research assistantships available. *Unit head:* Dr. Mark Solomon, Director of Graduate Studies, 203-432-5562, Fax: 203-432-5832. *Application contact:* Nessie Stewart, Graduate Registrar, 203-432-5662, Fax: 203-432-6178, E-mail: nessie. stewart@yale.edu.

Youngstown State University, Graduate School, College of Science, Technology, Engineering and Mathematics, Department of Chemistry, Youngstown, OH 44555-0001. Offers analytical chemistry (MS); biochemistry (MS); chemistry education (MS); inorganic chemistry (MS); organic chemistry (MS); physical chemistry (MS). Part-time programs available. *Degree requirements:* For master's, thesis. *Entrance requirements:* For master's, bachelor's degree in chemistry, minimum GPA of 2.7. Additional exam requirements/recommendations for international students: Required—TOEFL. *Faculty research:* Analysis of antioxidants, chromatography, defects and disorder in crystalline oxides, hydrogen bonding, novel organic and organometallic materials.

IOWA STATE UNIVERSITY OF SCIENCE AND TECHNOLOGY

Department of Biochemistry, Biophysics, and Molecular Biology

Programs of Study

The Department of Biochemistry, Biophysics, and Molecular Biology (BBMB) offers programs leading to M.S. and Ph.D. degrees with majors in the fields of biochemistry; bioinformatics and computational biology; biophysics; genetics; immunobiology; molecular, cellular, and developmental biology; plant physiology; and toxicology. Students enter a rotation program that lasts through the end of the first semester. By the second semester, students have identified their area of research and begun work on their research project with their chosen mentor. A minimum of 30 credits is required for the M.S. degree. For the Ph.D. degree, a minimum of three years of full-time study, at least half of which must be spent in residence, is required. Preliminary examinations in the field of specialization are required for admission to candidacy for the Ph.D. degree. The final examination for M.S. and Ph.D. candidates is an oral defense of the thesis. At some time during graduate work, each student is expected to serve as a teaching assistant. More information about individual faculty members' research activities is available on request or from the Departmental Web site.

Research Facilities

The Department is housed in the Molecular Biology Building, a unique structure that integrates 204,000 square feet of research laboratories and classrooms with artwork inspired by genetic engineering and crafted by award-winning national artists. The modular design of the laboratories allows scientists to quickly reconfigure their space as research needs change. State-of-the-art instrumentation facilities for protein chemistry, nucleic acids, flow cytometry, antibody and hybridoma production, and macromolecular structure determination support life sciences research on campus and throughout the state. The W. M. Keck Metabolomics Research Facility is the most recent addition. Supporting instrument services, a fabrication shop, and chemical stores are conveniently located in a nearby building. Molecular Biology Building classrooms are fitted with the latest instructional technology equipment. Students are linked to the University's high-speed computing network through approximately thirty workstations strategically placed throughout the building. For students and faculty members who prefer it, wireless networking is available in all classrooms and other public areas.

Financial Aid

Financial aid is available to graduate students in the form of research assistantships, teaching assistantships, and fellowships. Most Ph.D. students are supported by research assistantships that currently provide $22,500 per year along with a 100 percent tuition credit. Students are eligible for additional fellowships on a competitive basis.

Cost of Study

In 2010–11, tuition for graduate students is $3560 per semester for fall and spring. Ph.D. students on assistantships receive a 100 percent tuition credit; M.S. students on assistantships receive up to a 50 percent tuition credit. Computer fees ($135 for twelve months), Health Center fees ($257.50 for twelve months), and Activities and Service fees ($505.25 for twelve months) are paid by the student. Health insurance for graduate students on assistantships is paid by the Graduate College.

Living and Housing Costs

University student apartments are available at rates of $482 for single occupancy to $584 per month for two-person occupancy. Rooms in the graduate dormitory rent at an annual cost of $5520 for a single suite. Private, off-campus rooms and apartments are available in the vicinity of the campus.

Student Group

The current enrollment of the University is around 27,000 students, including about 4,700 graduate students. More than 3,000 of those graduate students come from all areas of the United States; the remainder are international students representing nearly 100 countries. There are approximately 90 graduate students enrolled in the Department; most are preparing for research careers in industry or universities.

Student Outcomes

Ph.D. graduates typically pursue careers in research as directors of academic, industry, or government laboratories. In this course, Ph.D. graduates normally go on to postdoctoral research appointments prior to seeking assistant professor/laboratory director positions. Other career courses include college/university teaching or research-related administration. M.S. graduates normally go on to Ph.D. programs or research associate positions in industry or academic laboratories.

Location

Ames is a city of about 50,000 residents, including the student body of Iowa State University. The city is located in a rural area 30 miles north of Des Moines, the capital of Iowa. An active cultural life is provided in Ames by local musical and theatrical groups and by the many internationally acclaimed artists who perform on campus. Athletic events at the University provide a year-round focus of interest. The University has a scenic golf course adjacent to the campus and offers facilities for numerous indoor and outdoor sports. The climate is typical of the Midwest: warm to hot in the summer, generally quite cold in the winter, and mild in spring and fall.

The University

Iowa State University of Science and Technology was founded in 1858 as Iowa State College, one of the first land-grant institutions in the nation. Besides the Graduate College, the University has eight undergraduate colleges—Agriculture, Business, Design, Education, Engineering, Family and Consumer Sciences, Liberal Arts and Sciences, and Veterinary Medicine. The scenic campus is a point of pride for students and faculty members and offers a fitting environment for the varied activities of those who work and study at the University.

Applying

Applicants must be graduates of an accredited institution and must normally rank in the upper half of his or her class. GRE General Test scores are required; the Subject Test in biochemistry, cell and molecular biology; chemistry; biology; or physics is recommended. Undergraduate preparation should include emphasis in chemistry, physics, mathematics, and biology. Visits to the Department are encouraged. Preapplications are required and can be requested by sending e-mail to biochem@iastate.edu.

Correspondence and Information

Department of Biochemistry, Biophysics, and Molecular Biology
1210 Molecular Biology Building
Iowa State University of Science and Technology
Ames, Iowa 50011
Phone: 515-294-2231
      800-433-3464 (toll-free from within the United States)
Fax: 515-294-0453
E-mail: biochem@iastate.edu
Web site: http://www.bbmb.iastate.edu/

Iowa State University of Science and Technology

THE FACULTY AND THEIR RESEARCH

Senior Staff of the Department

Gaya Amarasinghe, Assistant Professor; Ph.D., Maryland, Baltimore County, 2001. Biophysical and biochemical studies of protein-RNA interactions.

Linda Ambrosio, Associate Professor; Ph.D., Princeton, 1985. Mechanisms of signal transduction; molecular and genetic characterization of *D-raf;* pattern formation and cellular differentiation in development.

Amy H. Andreotti, Associate Professor of Biochemistry; Ph.D., Princeton, 1994. Nuclear magnetic resonance; macromolecular structure and recognition.

Donald C. Beitz, Distinguished Professor of Biochemistry and Animal Science; Ph.D., Michigan State, 1967. Lipid metabolism; cholesterol homeostasis in animals and humans; nutritional and genetic control of animal-derived food quality; etiology and prevention of fatty liver disease.

Thomas Bobik, Professor of Biochemistry; Ph.D., Illinois at Urbana-Champaign, 1990. Conversion of inactive cobalamins to coenzyme B12.

Alan DiSpirito, Professor; Ph.D., Ohio State, 1983. Bioenergetics of chemoautotrophic and methanotrophic bacteria.

Jack Girton, Professor; Ph.D., Alberta, 1979. Chromatin structure and function; regulation of cell determination.

Mark S. Hargrove, Professor of Biochemistry and Biophysics; Ph.D., Rice, 1995. Heme protein structure and function; regulation of cell determination.

Richard B. Honzatko, Professor of Biochemistry and Biophysics; Ph.D., Harvard, 1982. X-ray crystallography of proteins; enzyme structure-function.

Ted W. Huiatt, Associate Professor of Biochemistry and Animal Science; Ph.D., Iowa State, 1979. Growth and determination of striated muscle during embryonic development.

Robert L. Jernigan, Professor of Biochemistry and Director, Laurence H. Baker Center for Bioinformatics and Biological Statistics; Ph.D., Stanford, 1968. Bioinformatics; genomics; computational biology; interfaces between structure, function, and sequence; motions of proteins and large assemblages; protein and drug design.

Jorgen Johansen, Professor; Ph.D., Copenhagen, 1984. Regulation of nuclear organization and function.

Kristen M. Johansen, Professor; Ph.D., Yale, 1989. Regulation of nuclear organization and function.

Gustavo MacIntosh, Assistant Professor; Ph.D., Buenos Aires, 1997. Gene expression and metabolic changes during plant defense responses to pests; functional genomics of plant nucleases.

Alan M. Myers, Professor of Biochemistry; Ph.D., Duke, 1983. Molecular mechanisms of starch assembly and disassembly.

Scott Nelson, Professor of Biochemistry; Ph.D., Iowa State, 2002. Molecular mechanisms of DNA replication and repair.

Basil J. Nikolau, Professor of Biochemistry; Ph.D., Massey (New Zealand), 1981. Biochemistry and functional genomics of plant metabolism.

Marit Nilsen-Hamilton, Professor of Biochemistry; Ph.D., Cornell, 1973. Nucleic acid, aptamer-based analytical technology; Growth factor function.

Reuben J. Peters, Associate Professor; Ph.D., California, San Francisco, 1998. Enzymatic/metabolic engineering of terpenoid biosynthesis.

Guru Rao, Professor/Chair of Biochemistry; Ph.D., Mysore (India), 1980. Structure-function relationships of plant proteins; protein-protein interactions in plant signal transduction; protein engineering.

Richard M. Robson, Professor of Biochemistry, Molecular Biology, and Animal Science; Ph.D., Iowa State, 1969. Structure and function of muscle contractile and cytosketal proteins.

John F. Robyt, Professor of Biochemistry; Ph.D., Iowa State, 1962. Carbohydrate chemistry and enzymology.

Yeon-Kyun Shin, Professor of Biophysics; Ph.D., Cornell, 1990. SNARE complex assembly and mechanisms of membrane fusion; EPR methods.

Michael Shogren-Knaak, Assistant Professor of Biochemistry; Ph.D., Stanford, 1994. Role and establishment of histone modifications; chromatin structure.

Robert Thornburg, Professor of Biochemistry; Ph.D., South Carolina, 1981. Eukaryotic gene regulations and expression; plant response to insect attack.

Edward Yu, Associate Professor of Biophysics; Ph.D., Michigan, 1997. Structural and mechanistic aspects of membrane transport; X-ray crystallography of membrane proteins; biophysics.

Olga Zabotina, Assistant Professor; Ph.D., Russian Academy of Sciences, 1987. Plant cell wall structure; polysaccharide biosynthesis, modification, and degredation; bioactive carbohydrates.

Affiliates and Collaborators Primarily Associated with This Department

Martha G. James, Adjunct Associate Professor of Biochemistry; Ph.D., Iowa State, 1989. Plant starch metabolism; functional interactions and genetic engineering.

Louisa B. Tabatabai, USDA-ARS Collaborator, Professor of Biochemistry and Research Chemist, National Animal Disease Center; Ph.D., Iowa State, 1976. Protein chemistry and proteomics; vaccines and diagnostics for animal diseases.

Senior Staff Associated Primarily with Other Departments

Andrzej Kloczkowski, Adjunct Professor; Ph.D., Polish Academy of Sciences, 1980. Computational molecular biology; structural bioinformatics; prediction of protein structure, function, and dynamics; biomolecular simulations.

W. Allen Miller, Professor of Plant Pathology and Biochemistry; Ph.D., Wisconsin–Madison, 1984. RNA virus replication and gene expression; translation mechanisms; barley yellow dwarf virus genomics.

The skylit atrium of the Molecular Biology Building provides natural light for its forty-eight research laboratories and eight instrumentation centers.

The 204,000-square-foot Molecular Biology Building is home to the Department of Biochemistry, Biophysics, and Molecular Biology.

STATE UNIVERSITY OF NEW YORK UPSTATE MEDICAL UNIVERSITY

Program in Biochemistry and Molecular Biology

Programs of Study

At SUNY Upstate's College of Graduate Studies, Ph.D. students thrive as they participate in medically relevant research on a campus that is proud of its mentoring and multidisciplinary approach. Students enjoy a student-faculty ratio of nearly 1:1 and publish articles in professional journals during their program.

Students select a department, thesis mentor, and ultimate area of research after their first year, which includes three in-depth laboratory rotations of their choice. All departments support Upstate's four main Research Pillars: cancer; infectious diseases; diabetes, metabolic disorders, and cardiovascular disease; and disorders of the nervous system.

Research in biochemistry and molecular biology covers topics ranging from structural biology and biophysics to development and cell biology. The department has particular interests in membrane proteins and transport, nucleic acid binding proteins, and oxidative stress, often using model systems in investigations.

These studies impact a number of human diseases, ranging from cancer to neurodegenerative disorders, incorporating all of Upstate's research pillars. Recent papers by faculty members and students have appeared in *Science, Nature Cell Biology, Journal of Biological Chemistry, Journal of Cell Biology, Molecular Biology of the Cell,* and *Journal of Molecular Biology.* The department continues to have a strong record of extramural research funding, primarily from the NIH.

Department faculty members have expertise in nuclear magnetic resonance (NMR), electron microscopy, and computational/ molecular modeling approaches for determining protein structure.

Several faculty members also share interests in modern genetics and genomic technologies. Robotics are available to screen large collections of mutants, generated as a result of genome sequencing, for novel phenotypes. Transgenic frogs used to study the visual system were first developed in this department. This system has provided valuable information about mechanisms underlying light transduction and the cellular defects that underlie certain inherited degenerative diseases of the eye.

Research Facilities

SUNY Upstate has world-class facilities for faculty members and students. A major effort to strengthen the program in structural biology was initiated in the last few years with a $1 million federal equipment grant that purchased mass spectrometers for proteomics and equipment for in-house X-ray crystallography. A powerful 200 kV cryo-electron microscope was subsequently added.

In addition to departmental resources, the main core facilities on campus include the Center for Research and Evaluation, Confocal/Two Photon Imaging, Department of Laboratory Animal Resources, DNA Sequencing, Flow Cytometry, Humanized SCID Mouse and Stem Cell Processing, Imaging Research, In Vivo Computed Tomography, Microarray (SUNYMAC), MRI Research, and Proteomics.

SUNY Upstate also maintains a coalition with nearby Cornell University, the University of Rochester Medical Center, and Buffalo's Roswell Park Cancer Institute, which is dedicated to sharing cutting-edge research facilities. There are also full research support services on campus, including laboratory-animal facilities, network access to the SeqWeb suite of software, a computer-age medical library containing more than 183,000 volumes, electronics and machine shops, and photographic and computer services.

SUNY Upstate's growth on the research side is highlighted by a $72 million expansion of its Institute for Human Performance, a high-tech facility housing shared laboratories and core facilities used in basic and clinical research. It also broke ground in 2009 for a dedicated research park facility.

Financial Aid

All accepted Ph.D. students are fully supported throughout their education by full tuition waivers and a stipend ($21,514 per year). Support comes from graduate assistantships, departmental assistantships, and NIH and NSF grants.

Cost of Study

Stipends and full tuition waivers are granted to all students accepted into the Ph.D. program. There is no teaching requirement. Student fees, which include health service, were $552 for the 2009–10 academic year. Tuition and fees for master's students for the 2009–10 academic year were $8370 for in-state students and $13,250 for out-of-state students.

Living and Housing Costs

On-campus housing is available in Clark Tower, a ten-story apartment building with attractive, fully furnished standard rooms, studio apartments, and two-bedroom suites. Costs ranged from $4127 (double occupancy) to $8618 (married/family accommodations) for 2009–10. Clark Tower also has study rooms, computer rooms, private and shared kitchens, lounges, a recreation room, laundry, and storage. Clark Tower is next door to the Campus Activities Building, which houses athletic facilities, a bookstore, and snack bar.

Many students rent nearby houses or apartments and bicycle or walk to campus. Syracuse has a low cost of living and abundant affordable housing.

Student Group

There are 124 graduate students in the biomedical sciences (58 percent women; 100 percent full-time) and approximately 600 medical students, 200 nursing students, and 200 students in the health professions enrolled at Upstate Medical University. Twenty-five percent of the graduate students come from Canada, Europe, and Asia. Syracuse University and the SUNY College of Environmental Science are located within a quarter mile of SUNY Upstate, resulting in a population of approximately 23,000 students in the immediate area.

Location

Syracuse is New York's fourth-largest city and is located in the scenic center of the state. A naturally beautiful setting, the area offers excellent hiking, biking, boating, and skiing. Nearby are the Finger Lakes region, the Adirondack and the Catskill Mountains, and Lake Ontario. Syracuse's cultural activities include a professional theater, symphony orchestra and opera company, noted author lecture series, chamber music groups, and several top-notch music festivals (classical, blues, and jazz) as well as art and history museums. The area also offers high-quality family life with many excellent school districts and Upstate's own day care center. Syracuse University's top-level collegiate sporting events are a major recreational activity. Syracuse is easily reached by air, rail, and car.

The University

SUNY Upstate is the only academic medical center in the central New York region and is part of the dynamic University Hill community. In addition to the College of Graduate Studies, SUNY Upstate Medical University includes three other colleges—Medicine, Nursing, and Health Professions—its own University Hospital, and a regional campus in Binghamton, New York. The University is growing with new leadership, degree programs, and further plans for expansion. SUNY Upstate Medical University is close to downtown Syracuse and is adjacent to (but not affiliated with) the campus of Syracuse University. SUNY Upstate's Campus Activities Building houses a swimming pool, sauna, gymnasium, squash courts, handball/paddleball court, weight-lifting area with a Universal Gym and a full Nautilus room, billiards, table tennis, television room, bookstore, snack bar, and lounge. Conference rooms are also available for student use.

Applying

The Admissions Committee for the College of Graduate Studies at SUNY Upstate begins reviewing applications in December prior to entry and continues until all positions are filled, which can be as early as early April. The State University of New York requires a $40 application fee. Competitive applicants must have a bachelor's degree or its equivalent, a minimum 3.0 GPA, and course work that includes biology, calculus, chemistry, and physics. GRE General Test scores are required (combined score 1000 minimum), and scores from the Subject Test in chemistry or biology are recommended. International applicants must provide clear evidence of English proficiency (including speaking) by taking the Test of English as a Foreign Language (TOEFL). Candidates for admission are selected on the basis of their record and qualifications for independent scholarship in a specialized field of study. Selected applicants will be invited to campus to meet with faculty, students and tour lab facilities.

Correspondence and Information

Office of Graduate Studies
State University of New York Upstate Medical University
750 East Adams Street
Syracuse, New York 13210
Phone: 315-464-7655
Fax: 315-464-4544
E-mail: biosci@upstate.edu
Web site: http://www.upstate.edu/grad/

State University of New York Upstate Medical University

THE FACULTY AND THEIR RESEARCH

David C. Amberg, Ph.D., Associate Professor. Regulation of actin dynamics and analysis of genomic influences on actin function.

Edward A. Berry, Ph.D., Assistant Professor. Structure and function of membrane protein complexes from energy-transducing biological electron transfer chains.

Peter Calvert, Ph.D., Assistant Professor. Molecular mechanisms of protein transport and localization in retinal neurons; mechanisms of retinal degenerative diseases.

Xin Jie Chen, Ph.D., Associate Professor. Mitochondrial biogenesis and inheritance; aging and aging-related degenerative diseases.

Richard L. Cross, Ph.D., Professor. The mechanism of mitochondrial oxidation phosphorylation; biological rotary motors.

Thomas Duncan, Ph.D., Associate Professor. Bioenergetics; enzymology; structural biology; membrane protein function.

Steven Goodman, Ph.D., Professor and Dean. Proteomic assessment of sickle cell severity.

Patricia M. Kane, Ph.D., Professor and Chair. Mechanisms and regulation of cellular pH control; V-type ATPases.

Barry Knox, Ph.D., Professor. Visual transduction; gene expression; membrane proteins.

Stewart N. Loh, Ph.D., Professor. Mechanism and kinetics of protein folding; structure and function of the p53 tumor suppressor; design of proteins with new or enhanced functions; protein-based molecular switches.

Francesa Pignoni, Ph.D., Associate Professor. Neurogenesis; retinal progenitor cells specification and proliferation; genetic control of stem cell identity and maintenance; genetic pathways in RPE formation; disease genes analysis in *Drosophila.*

Mark E. Schmitt, Ph.D., Associate Professor. Ribonucleoprotein assembly and biogenesis; mitochondrial RNA import; mRNA degradation; cell-cycle control.

Andrea Viczian, Ph.D., Assistant Professor. Mammalian retinal stem cells formation; molecular mechanism of retinal cell fate decisions; using cell replacement therapy to heal the blinded eye.

Stephan Wilkens, Ph.D., Associate Professor. Structure and mechanism of membrane-bound transport proteins.

Michael Zuber, Ph.D., Assistant Professor. Molecular basis of retinal stem cell formation; regulating retinal stem/progenitor cell proliferation; using retinal stem/progenitor cells to heal the injured or degenerating retina.

THOMAS JEFFERSON UNIVERSITY

Jefferson College of Graduate Studies
Kimmel Cancer Center
Department of Biochemistry and Molecular Biology
Graduate Program in Biochemistry and Molecular Biology

Programs of Study

The Ph.D. Program in Biochemistry and Molecular Biology is offered through the Department of Biochemistry and Molecular Biology at Thomas Jefferson University. The Ph.D. Program in Biochemistry and Molecular Biology is designed to provide students with the basis for successful careers as independent scientists and scholars in either the academic or industrial sector. Students entering with a baccalaureate degree take core curriculum courses in biochemistry, molecular biology, cell biology, and genetics. Advanced courses in structural biology, molecular pharmacology, molecular biology, and genetics can be taken in both the first and second years, and the curriculum is flexible to accommodate the individual student's background and interests. All course work is generally completed by the end of the second year. Research rotations are included in the first-year curriculum. Current research interests of the faculty members include molecular biology of cancer, structure-function relationships for tRNA, mitochondrial genetics and related diseases, the role of post-translational modifications in protein function, MAP kinase pathways in meiotic regulatory pathways, protein misfolding in neurodegenerative disease, nucleotide chemistry in therapeutics and gene therapy, combinatorial drug discovery, molecular regulation of G-protein–coupled receptors, biochemical aspects of viral entry and transport, and many more. In addition, several weekly seminar series, frequent laboratory seminars, and invited lectureships form an integral part of the student's education. Students take a comprehensive examination at the end of the second year. Success in this examination allows the student to continue with the thesis program and research. The thesis research is performed under the supervision of a faculty adviser chosen by the student and the written thesis describing the experimental work and its significance is defended before the degree is attained.

The Graduate Program in Biochemistry and Molecular Biology, along with the Programs in Genetics, Molecular Pharmacology and Structural Biology, and Immunology and Microbial Pathogenesis, make up the four Graduate Programs of the Kimmel Cancer Center. There is also an M.S. Program in Biomedical Sciences–Molecular Biology and Biochemistry. This 40-credit program may be completed on a part-time or full-time basis over a two- to four-year period.

Research Facilities

Research laboratories are primarily located in the Department of Biochemistry and Molecular Biology, which is housed in the Bluemle Life Sciences Building. In addition to extensive basic equipment and facilities, the program provides access to numerous specialized resources. These include facilities for peptide and oligonucleotide synthesis and sequencing; cell sorting by flow cytometry; a CD spectrometer; state-of-the-art X-ray detectors for macromolecular crystallography, protein purification and characterization; proteomics and microarray analysis; and biomolecular imaging. Interaction with the faculties of other departments of the University is encouraged as part of the students' education.

Financial Aid

Financial support is available to full-time Ph.D. students in the form of University fellowships. Most types of aid include a stipend ($26,300 in 2010–11) and remission of tuition plus health insurance benefits for a single person. Also available to students demonstrating financial need are Title IV funds and University loan programs.

Cost of Study

Tuition and fees are $28,423 per year in 2010–11.

Living and Housing Costs

Apartments are available in University residences for graduate students enrolled in the program; early rental application is advised. Reasonable alternative housing near the University in the Philadelphia area can also be found.

Student Group

The incoming class size in the Graduate Program in Biochemistry and Molecular Biology is expected to be 3 to 4. At present, the University enrolls more than 2,500 students. The College of Graduate Studies enrolls about 630 students, about half of whom are women. A low ratio of students to faculty members is maintained in order to encourage close interaction.

Location

Thomas Jefferson University is centrally located in Philadelphia within walking distance of many places of cultural interest, including concert halls, theaters, museums, art galleries, and historic sites. There are numerous intercollegiate and professional sports events. Convenient bus and subway lines connect the University with other local universities and colleges and with several outstanding libraries. The proximity of the New Jersey shore and the Pennsylvania mountains offers year-round recreational opportunities, and New York City and Washington, D.C., are each just 2 hours away.

The University

Thomas Jefferson University is an academic health center emphasizing the biological sciences. It evolved from the Jefferson Medical College, which was founded in 1824, and includes the College of Graduate Studies, the College of Health Professions, the University hospital, and various affiliated hospitals and institutions. Jefferson Alumni Hall houses the TJU Fitness and Recreation Facility, study lounges, a swimming pool, a gymnasium, and a handball/squash court.

Applying

Applicants must have at least a bachelor's degree, with a strong educational record in biochemistry, chemistry, and molecular biology. The deadline to submit Ph.D. applications and all supporting materials is January 5. Applications received after this date are considered at the discretion of the admissions committee. Admission is based on GRE scores, undergraduate performance, letters of recommendation, research accomplishments, and interview evaluations. Applications from minority group candidates are encouraged. Application forms can be obtained from the Web site and submitted online.

Correspondence and Information

For applications:

Marc Stearns
Director of Admissions and Recruitment
Jefferson College of Graduate Studies
Thomas Jefferson University
1020 Locust Street, M-60
Philadelphia, Pennsylvania 19107-6799

Phone: 215-503-4400
Fax: 215-503-3433
E-mail: cgs-info@jefferson.edu
Web site: http://www.jefferson.edu/jcgs

For program information:

Joanne Balitzky
Training Programs Coordinator
Kimmel Cancer Center
Thomas Jefferson University
233 South 10th Street, 910 BLSB
Philadelphia, Pennsylvania 19107-5541

Phone: 215-503-6687
Fax: 215-503-0622
E-mail: joanne.balitzky@jefferson.edu
Web site: http://www.jefferson.edu/jcgs/phd/bmb/

Thomas Jefferson University

THE FACULTY AND THEIR RESEARCH

Emad S. Alnemri, Professor; Ph.D., Temple, 1991. Molecular mechanisms of programmed cell death (apoptosis); pattern recognition receptors and inflammasome activation in innate immune responses to molecular danger signals; role of mitochondria in survival, cell death, and aging.

Andrew E. Aplin, Associate Professor; Ph.D., King's College, London, 1996. Mutant BRAF and integrin signaling transduction in melanoma initiation and progression.

Jeffrey L. Benovic, Professor and Chairperson; Ph.D., Duke, 1986. Molecular and regulatory properties of G-protein–coupled receptors; role of receptor dysregulation in cancer and neurological disorders.

Mon-Li Chu, Professor; Ph.D., Florida, 1975. Role of extracellular matrix genes in development and disease, with emphasis on cardiovascular, skin, and musculoskeletal systems; molecular basis and therapies of congenital muscular dystrophy.

Gino Cingolani, Associate Professor; Ph.D., European Molecular Biology Laboratory, 1999. Molecular cell biology of nucleocytoplasmic transport; X-ray crystallography and biophysical analysis of viral DNA-pumping machinery; structure of multi-subunit ATP synthases.

Mark E. Fortini, Associate Professor; Ph.D., Berkeley, 1990. Developmental signaling pathways involved in normal cellular patterning and cancer; proteolytic mechanisms in neurogenesis and neurodegeneration; trafficking and post-translational regulation of cell-surface receptors and ligands.

Philippe G Frank, Assistant Professor; Ph.D., 1998, Ottawa. Plasma lipoproteins and cholesterol transport in human diseases.

Linda E. Greenbaum, Associate Professor; M.D., 1987, Columbia. Mechanisms of liver regeneration and repair by hepatocytes and liver progenitor/stem cells; contribution of these processes to the development of liver fibrosis and hepatocellular carcinoma.

Gerald B. Grunwald, Professor; Ph.D., Wisconsin–Madison, 1981. Developmental biology and neuroscience; eye development and disease; analysis of the role of cadherin cell adhesion molecules in normal and abnormal embryonic development and in proliferative diseases of the nervous system and the eye; investigation of cellular and molecular regulatory mechanisms of cadherin expression and function.

Noreen J. Hickok, Associate Professor; Ph.D., Brandeis, 1981. Development of surfaces for combating peri-prosthetic infection; bacterial-osteoblastic cell interactions; role of extracellular bone matrix in bone formation, bacterial adhesion, and latent infections.

Shiu-Ying Ho, Research Assistant Professor; Ph.D., Rutgers, 2000. Genetic and molecular mechanisms regulating lipid and glucose metabolisms using zebrafish as a model system.

Jan B. Hoek, Professor; Ph.D., Amsterdam, 1972. Systems biology of intracellular signal transduction networks; deregulation of cytokine and growth-factor signaling in the liver associated with chronic alcohol consumption; early signaling responses during liver regeneration; bioenergetics and mitochondrial metabolism and its role in intracellular signaling and apoptosis.

Michael Holinstat; Ph.D., Illinois at Chicago, 2004. Regulation of protease-activated receptor (PAR) function in the platelet; signal transduction and regulation of hemostasis and thrombosis in the platelet; regulation of the small GTPase Rap1 in vascular function; regulation of platelet-mediated hemostasis and thrombosis and signal transduction by 12-lipoxygenase; how platelet function regulates the progression of a number of cardiovascular risks such as diabetes and acute coronary syndrome.

Ya-Ming Hou, Professor; Ph.D., Berkeley, 1986. Genetic and biochemical studies of tRNA, including structure and function mechanism of tRNA aminoacylation; maintenance of the tRNA 3' end, maturation and processing, editing and repair, decoding on the ribosome, and development of bacterial pathogenesis in infectious diseases; targeting tRNAs as strategies against metabolic and neurodegenerative disorders.

Koichi Iijima, Assistant Professor; Ph.D., Tokyo, 2001. Alzheimer's disease; tauopathies; human neurodegenerative diseases; circadian rhythm in *Drosophila;* neurobiology; genetics.

Kanae Iijima-Ando, Assistant Professor; Ph.D., Tokyo, 2001. Pathobiology of tauopathies and Alzheimer's disease; *Drosophila* model of degenerative diseases; circadian rhythm-regulated behavior.

James B. Jaynes, Associate Professor; Ph.D., Washington (Seattle), 1980. Developmental genetics and molecular biology of gene regulation by epigenetic transcriptional memory and chromosomal architecture.

Erica S. Johnson, Associate Professor; Ph.D., MIT, 1992. The ubiquitin-related protein Smt3/SUMO and its conjugation pathway and function in yeast.

Hideko Kaji, Professor; Ph.D., Purdue, 1958. Molecular mechanisms and functions of ribosome recycling in prokaryotes (RRF) and eukaryotes; arginylation of proteins by arginyl tRNA protein transferase (ATE1).

James H. Keen, Professor; Ph.D., Cornell, 1976. Molecular mechanisms coupling signal transduction with receptor-mediated endocytosis and exocytosis; membrane transport studied by biochemical, molecular biological, and morphological approaches.

Michael P. King, Associate Professor; Ph.D., Caltech, 1987. Mammalian mitochondrial biogenesis; molecular genetics of mtDNA mutations resulting in human disease; mtDNA recombination; posttranscriptional modification of mitochondrial RNAs; mitochondrial translation.

Erik S. Knudsen, Professor, Ph.D., California, San Diego, 1991. Functional role of the retinoblastoma tumor suppressor pathway in tumorigenesis, tumor progression and the response to cancer therapies.

Karen E. Knudsen, Professor; Ph.D., California, San Diego, 1996. Translational prostate cancer research, cell cycle control, hormonal control of gene transcription, chromatin remodeling.

Michael Lisanti, Professor; M.D., 1991, Ph.D., 1992, Cornell. Functional role of caveolae and the caveolin genes in normal signal transduction and in a variety of pathogenic disease states, most notably the development of breast and prostate cancers.

My G. Mahoney, Associate Professor; Ph.D., Massachusetts Amherst, 1993. Roles of desmosomal proteins in regulating epithelial cell adhesion, growth, and survival; deregulation of desmosomal proteins in autoimmune, infectious, and inherited diseases associated with fragility and abnormality in diverse tissues such as the skin, hair, and heart; mechanisms by which desmosomal cadherins can modulate mitogenic signaling pathways; genetically manipulated animal models to study human diseases.

Alexander Mazo, Professor; Ph.D., Russian Academy of Sciences, 1976. Chromatin modifications by epigenetic factors and nuclear hormone receptors.

Steven McMahon, Associate Professor; Ph.D., Pennsylvania, 1994. Biochemical and genetic pathways regulated by the MYC oncoprotein and the p53 tumor suppressor.

Diane E. Merry, Associate Professor and Program Director; Ph.D., Pennsylvania, 1991. Molecular pathogenesis of Kennedy's disease and other polyglutamine expansion diseases; protein misfolding and aggregation in neurodegenerative disease; mouse models of neurologic disease; domain function in trafficking and degradation of the androgen receptor; gene and pharmacological therapies for neurodegenerative diseases.

Andrea Morrione, Research Associate Professor; Ph.D., Milan, 1992. Characterization of insulin-like growth factor receptor I (IGF-IR) function in bladder cancer initiation and progression; role of the growth factor progranulin (proepithelin) and its receptor in bladder and prostate cancer; characterization of the role of adaptor protein Grb10 in the regulation of IGF-IR ubiquitination, trafficking, and signaling.

John M. Pascal, Assistant Professor; Ph.D., Texas at Austin, 2000. Structural biology of DNA replication, repair, and signaling mechanisms; mechanisms of genome maintenance and chromosomal metabolism; biochemical and biophysical studies of nucleic acid enzymes; macromolecular X-ray crystallography.

Piera Pasinelli, Assistant Professor; Ph.D., Utrecht (Netherlands), 1996. Molecular mechanisms of motor neuron degeneration and death in amyotrophic lateral sclerosis (ALS); role of superoxide dismutase in cell survival and death; mitochondrial dysfunction in neurodegeneration and neurodegenerative diseases; animal models of ALS; development of cell-based assays for drug screening.

Richard G. Pestell, Professor, Ph.D., 1991, M.D., 1997, Melbourne (Australia), FRACP, 1991, FACP, 2009. Molecular mechanisms and gene therapy of breast and prostate cancer; cancer stem cells.

Natalia A. Riobo, Assistant Professor; Ph.D., Buenos Aires, 2001. Signal transduction mechanisms employed by mammalian Hedgehog proteins in cardiomyocytes, endothelium, cancer cells and stromal fibroblasts in the context of cardiovascular regenerative medicine and cancer.

Ulrich Rodeck, Professor; M.D., Ph.D., Germany, 1981. Regulation of epithelial cell survival by the epidermal growth-factor receptor; coordinate regulation of cell-cycle progression and cell survival by growth factor– and adhesion-dependent signal transduction; targeted therapies in cancer treatment; mitigation of normal tissue toxicity of cancer therapeutics; genotoxic stress responses of vertebrate organisms using zebrafish embryos.

Peter Ronner, Associate Professor; Ph.D., Swiss Federal Institute of Technology, 1978. Control of insulin and glucagon secretion; regulation of ATP-sensitive K channels and voltage-dependent Ca channels; role of cellular metabolism in signal transduction.

Michael Root, Assistant Professor; M.D./Ph.D., Harvard, 1997. Structure and function of glycoproteins involved in viral and cell-cell membrane fusion; design of viral entry inhibitors and immunogens for vaccine development; antibody-antigen interactions.

Charles P. Scott, Assistant Professor; Ph.D., Pennsylvania, 1997. Combinatorial drug discovery; rational drug design; chemical genomics of host-pathogen interactions and cancer.

Davide Trotti, Associate Professor; Ph.D., Milan (Italy), 1997. Molecular pathogenesis of amyotrophic lateral sclerosis (ALS); glutamate transporter regulation and excitotoxic mechanisms in neurodegenerative diseases; biophysics of mitochondria conductances in ALS.

Jouni Uitto, Professor; Ph.D./M.D., Helsinki, 1970. Molecular genetics of the cutaneous basement membrane zone; regulation of collagen and elastin gene expression and the molecular basis of heritable and acquired connective tissue diseases.

Scott A. Waldman, Professor; Ph.D., Thomas Jefferson, 1980; M.D., Stanford, 1987. Molecular mechanisms of signal transduction, with emphasis on receptor-effector coupling and postreceptor signaling mechanisms; molecular mechanisms underlying tissue-specific transcriptional regulation; translation of molecular signaling mechanisms to novel diagnostic and therapeutic approaches to patients with cancer.

Philip B. Wedegaertner, Associate Professor; Ph.D., California, San Diego, 1991. Heterotrimeric G-protein, Rho GTPase, and Rho guanine-nucleotide exchange factor (RhoGEF) signaling and cell biology; mechanisms and functions of regulated subcellular localization and trafficking.

Eric Wickstrom, Professor; Ph.D., Berkeley, 1972. Sensing, imaging, regulation, and control of oncogene expression in cells and animal models with nucleic acid derivatives; permanent bonding of drugs to implants.

Edward Winter, Associate Professor; Ph.D., SUNY at Stony Brook, 1984. Analysis of meiotic development using molecular genetics in yeast; signal transduction and protein kinases; transcriptional regulation.

UNIVERSITY OF FLORIDA

College of Medicine
Advanced Concentration in Biochemistry and Molecular Biology

Program of Study	The College of Medicine at the University of Florida (UF) offers graduate training in biomedical research leading to a Ph.D. degree through the Interdisciplinary Program (IDP) in Biomedical Sciences. The goal of the Interdisciplinary Program is to prepare students for a diversity of careers in research and teaching in academic and commercial settings. The program provides a modern, comprehensive graduate education in biomedical science while providing both maximum program flexibility as well as appropriate specialization for graduate students. During the first year of study, incoming graduate students undertake a common, comprehensive interdisciplinary core curriculum of classroom study developed in a cooperative effort by all of the graduate programs in the College of Medicine. In addition, students select from any of the College of Medicine faculty members for participation in several laboratory rotations conducted throughout the first year, concurrent with the core curriculum. By the end of their first year, students select a laboratory in which to conduct their dissertation research and, once again, they may choose from any of the graduate faculty members in the College of Medicine. Formal selection of a graduate program and mentor is made after completion of the core curriculum to maximize flexibility and facilitate an informed decision; however, students may make an informal commitment to a program or lab at any time.

The Advanced Concentration in Biochemistry and Molecular Biology provides students with an intellectually challenging and rewarding environment for research training in the molecular life sciences. Students can pursue a broad range of investigative opportunities, including gene regulation, enzymology, metabolic regulation, intracellular trafficking, membrane biology, and macromolecular structure. Research groups are most frequently composed of several faculty members and coworkers collaboratively engaged in multidisciplinary research on the molecular basis of disease. Students take additional course work to prepare for qualifying examinations prior to advancement to candidacy for the Doctor of Philosophy degree.

Research Facilities	The College of Medicine houses state-of-the-art research facilities maintained by the Interdisciplinary Center for Biomedical Research (ICBR), the McKnight Brain Institute, the Clinical Research Center, several other University of Florida Research Centers, and individual research laboratories. Together these facilities provide services for DNA and protein synthesis and sequencing, hybridoma production, confocal and electron microscopy, NMR spectroscopy, computing and molecular modeling, flow cytometry, transgenic mouse production, and gene therapy vector construction. The University of Florida libraries, including the Health Center library, form the largest information resource system in the state of Florida and support up-to-date computer-based bibliographic retrieval services.

UF's nine libraries offer more than 4 million catalogued volumes and links to full-text articles in more than 34,000 journals. Of national significance are the Baldwin Library of Historical Children's Literature, the Latin American Collection, the Map and Imagery Library, the P. K. Yonge Library of Florida History (preeminent Floridiana collection), the Price Library of Judaica, and holdings on architectural preservation and eighteenth-century American architecture, late nineteenth- and early twentieth-century German state documents, rural sociology of Florida, and tropical and subtropical agriculture.

Financial Aid	Students accepted into the Interdisciplinary Program receive a stipend of $25,750 per annum. Students also receive a waiver that covers tuition.
Cost of Study	Graduate research assistants pay fees of approximately $1400 per year. Books and supplies cost about $1600.
Living and Housing Costs	Married student housing is available in six apartment villages operated by the University; dormitories for single students are available in limited quantities. The cost of housing for a single graduate student is approximately $5000 per year. Most graduate students live in abundant and comfortable off-campus housing that is near the University; rents vary but are low on a national scale.
Student Group	Enrollment at the University of Florida is both culturally and geographically diverse and numbers about 50,000, including about 10,000 graduate students. There are about 300 graduate students in the College of Medicine.
Location	Situated in north-central Florida, midway between the Atlantic Ocean and the Gulf of Mexico, Gainesville is a nationally recognized academic and research center and was rated the number one place to live in the U.S. in a 1995 *Money* magazine survey. There are about 200,000 residents in the Gainesville metropolitan area, excluding University of Florida students. The climate is moderate, permitting outdoor activities the year around. The University and the Gainesville community also host numerous cultural events, including music, dance, theater, lectures, and art exhibits. Many of the men's and women's athletic programs are considered to be in the top ten programs in the country.
The University and The College	The University of Florida, located on 2,000 acres, is among the nation's leading research universities as categorized by the Carnegie Commission on Higher Education. UF is a member of the Association of American Universities, the nation's most prestigious higher education organization. UF is also one of the nation's top three universities in the breadth of academic programs offered on a single campus. It has twenty colleges and schools and 100 interdisciplinary research and education centers, bureaus, and institutes. The College of Medicine, opened in 1956, has become a nationally recognized leader in medical education and research.
Applying	The Interdisciplinary Program in Biomedical Sciences seeks promising students with undergraduate training in chemistry, biology, psychology, or related disciplines in the life sciences. Applicants are selected on the basis of previous academic work, research experience, GRE General Test scores, letters of recommendation, the personal statement, and a personal interview. Students are admitted for the fall semester, which begins in late August. The application deadline is December 15.
Correspondence and Information	Robert McKenna, Ph.D., Co-Director Department of Biochemistry and Molecular Biology University of Florida College of Medicine P.O. Box 100245 Gainesville, Florida 32610-0245 Phone: 352-392-5696 E-mail: rmckenna@ufl.edu Web site: http://idp.med.ufl.edu/BMB/index.html	Linda Bloom, Ph.D., Co-Director Department of Biochemistry and Molecular Biology University of Florida College of Medicine P.O. Box 100245 Gainesville, Florida 32610-0245 Phone: 352-392-8708 E-mail: lbloom@ufl.edu Web site: http://idp.med.ufl.edu/BMB/index.html

University of Florida

THE FACULTY AND THEIR RESEARCH

Mavis Agbandje-McKenna, Associate Professor; Ph.D., London, 1989. Structural studies of ssDNA viruses, Parvoviridae, Geminiviridae, Microviridae, and Circoviridae. Adeno-associated virus type 2 contains an integrin $\alpha5\beta1$ binding domain essential for viral cell entry. *J. Virol.* 80:8961–9, 2006 (with Asokan, Hamra, Govindasamy, and Samulski).

Charles M. Allen, Professor Emeritus; Ph.D., Brandeis, 1964. Protein prenyl transferase.

R. Donald Allison, Associate Scientist; Ph.D., California, Santa Barbara, 1979. Enzyme mechanisms.

Linda B. Bloom, Associate Professor; Ph.D., Florida, 1990. DNA replication and repair. Contribution of a conserved phenylalanine residue to the activity of *Escherichia coli* uracil DNA glycosylase. *DNA Repair* 3:1273–83, 2004 (with Shaw and Feller).

Kevin D. Brown, Associate Professor; Ph.D., Alabama, 1991. DNA damage response. Inactivation of Wnt inhibitory factor–1 (WIF1) expression by epigenetic silencing is a common event in breast cancer. *Carcinogenesis* 27:1341–48, 2006 (with Ai et al.).

Jorg Bungert, Associate Professor; Ph.D., Philipps, 1992. Molecular genetics. Locus control region elements HS2 and HS3 in combination with chromatin boundaries confer high-level expression of a human beta-globin transgene in a centromeric region. *Genes Cells* 9(11):1043–53, 2004 (with Kang et al.).

Brian D. Cain, Professor; Ph.D., Illinois, 1983. Biochemistry.

Paul W. Chun, Professor Emeritus; Ph.D., Missouri, 1965. Biochemical thermodynamics: elucidation of the Planck-Benzinger thermal work function in biological systems. Why does the human body maintain a constant 37-degree temperature? Thermodynamic switch controls chemical equilibrium in biological systems. *Phys. Scr.* 71:1–4, 2005.

Robert J. Cohen, Associate Professor; Ph.D., Yale, 1969. Theoretical and mathematical biology.

Ben M. Dunn, Distinguished Professor; Ph.D., California, Santa Barbara, 1971. Protein structure-function. Initial cleavage of the human immunodeficiency virus type 1 GagPol precursor by its activated protease occurs by an intramolecular mechanism. *J. Virol.* 78(16):8477–85, 2004 (with Pettit, Everitt, Choudhury, and Kaplan).

Arthur S. Edison, Associate Professor; Ph.D., Wisconsin–Madison, 1993. NMR; structural biology; neurochemistry.

J. Bert Flanegan, Professor and Chair; Ph.D., Michigan, 1975. Replication of RNA viruses. Relationship between poliovirus negative-strand RNA synthesis and the length of the 3' poly(A) tail. *Virology* 345:509–19, 2006 (with Silvestri, Parilla, Morasco, and Ogram).

Susan C. Frost, Professor; Ph.D., Arizona, 1979. Glucose transport and insulin receptor processing.

Suming Huang, Assistant Professor; Ph.D., Mississippi State, 1996. Epigenetic regulation of chromatin structure and gene expression.

Michael S. Kilberg, Professor; Ph.D., South Dakota, 1977. Nutrient control of transcription; drug resistance in leukemia. Characterization of the amino acid response element within the human SNAT2 system A transporter gene. *Biochem. J.* 395:517–27, 2006 (with Palii, Thiaville, Pan, and Zhong).

Michael P. Kladde, Associate Professor; Ph.D., Wisconsin, 1991. Biochemistry.

Mary Jo Koroly, Associate Scientist; Ph.D., Bryn Mawr, 1969. Membrane biology.

Philip J. Laipis, Professor and Associate Chair; Ph.D., Stanford, 1972. Eukaryotic gene regulation, organization, and evolution. A murine model for human sepiapterin-reductase deficiency. *Am. J. Hum. Genet.* 78(4):575–87, 2006 (with Yang et al.).

Joanna R. Long, Assistant Professor; Ph.D., MIT, 1997. NMR; structural biology.

Jianrong Lu, Assistant Professor; Ph.D., Texas, 2000. Chromatin regulators in control of E2F activity and cell proliferation; chromatin association and remodeling.

Thomas H. Mareci, Professor; D.Phil., Oxford, 1982. Structure and function in the nervous system.

Peter M. McGuire, Associate Professor; Ph.D., North Carolina, 1970. Molecular genetics.

Robert McKenna, Associate Professor; Ph.D., London, 1989. Structural studies of carbonic anhydrase, carnitine acetyltransferase, prenylating enzymes, actin complexes, and the replication proteins of adeno-associated virus. Identification of the sialic acid structures recognized by minute virus of mice and the role of binding affinity in virulence adaptation. *J. Biol. Chem.* 281:25670–7, 2006 (with Nam et al.).

Thomas W. O'Brien, Professor Emeritus; Ph.D., Marquette, 1964. Structure, function, and evolution of mammalian mitochondrial ribosomes.

Daniel L. Purich, Professor; Ph.D., Iowa State, 1973. Mechanism of actin-based motility.

Keith D. Robertson, Assistant Professor; Ph.D., Johns Hopkins, 1996. Cancer epigenetics and DNA methylation. An EBF3-mediated transcriptional program that induces cell cycle arrest and apoptosis. *Cancer Res.* 66(19):9445–52, 2006 (with Zhao et al.).

Thomas P. Yang, Professor; Ph.D., California, Irvine, 1982. Epigenetic regulation of transcription. Characterization of cis- and trans-acting elements in the imprinted human SNURF-SNRPN locus. *Nucleic Acids Res.* 33(15):4740–53, 2005 (with Rodriguez-Jato, Nicholls, and Driscoll).

Section 4
Biophysics

This section contains a directory of institutions offering graduate work in biophysics, followed by in-depth entries submitted by institutions that chose to prepare detailed program descriptions. Additional information about programs listed in the directory but not augmented by an in-depth entry may be obtained by writing directly to the dean of a graduate school or chair of a department at the address given in the directory.

For programs offering related work, see also in this book *Biochemistry; Biological and Biomedical Sciences; Cell, Molecular, and Structural Biology; Neuroscience and Neurobiology;* and *Physiology.* In the other guides in this series:

Graduate Programs in the Physical Sciences, Mathematics, Agricultural Sciences, the Environment & Natural Resources
See *Chemistry* and *Physics*

Graduate Programs in Engineering & Applied Sciences
See *Agricultural Engineering and Bioengineering* and *Biomedical Engineering and Biotechnology*

Graduate Programs in Business, Education, Health, Information Studies, Law & Social Work
See *Allied Health, Optometry and Vision Sciences,* and *Public Health*

CONTENTS

Biophysics

Albert Einstein College of Medicine, Sue Golding Graduate Division of Medical Sciences, Department of Physiology and Biophysics, Bronx, NY 10461. Offers PhD, MD/PhD. *Degree requirements:* For doctorate, thesis/dissertation. *Entrance requirements:* For doctorate, GRE General Test. Additional exam requirements/recommendations for international students: Required—TOEFL. *Faculty research:* Biophysical and biochemical basis of body function at the subcellular, cellular, organ, and whole-body level.

Baylor College of Medicine, Graduate School of Biomedical Sciences, Department of Molecular Physiology and Biophysics, Houston, TX 77030-3498. Offers PhD, MD/PhD. *Faculty:* 31 full-time (10 women). *Students:* 21 full-time (14 women); includes 2 minority (1 African American, 1 Hispanic American), 12 international. Average age 26. In 2009, 2 doctorates awarded. *Degree requirements:* For doctorate, thesis/dissertation, public defense. *Entrance requirements:* For doctorate, GRE General Test, GRE Subject Test (strongly recommended), minimum GPA of 3.0. Additional exam requirements/recommendations for international students: Required—TOEFL. *Application deadline:* For fall admission, 1/1 priority date for domestic students. Electronic applications accepted. *Financial support:* Fellowships, research assistantships, career-related internships or fieldwork, Federal Work-Study, institutionally sponsored loans, health care benefits, and students receive a scholarship unless there are grant funds available to pay tuition available. Financial award applicants required to submit FAFSA. *Faculty research:* Multi-photon imaging, magnetic resonance imaging (MRI), structure and function of ion channels and transport proteins, signal transduction, synaptic plasticity, cell-cycle control, reactive oxygen species, neurodegenerative diseases and cardiac development. *Unit head:* Dr. Robia Pautler, Director, 713-798-5630, Fax: 713-798-3475. *Application contact:* Cherrie McGlory, Graduate Program Administrator, 713-798-5109, Fax: 713-798-3475, E-mail: molphysgrad@bcm.edu.

Boston University, Graduate School of Arts and Sciences, Program in Cellular Biophysics, Boston, MA 02215. Offers PhD. *Students:* 5 full-time (1 woman), 3 international. Average age 27. 4 applicants, 0% accepted. *Degree requirements:* For doctorate, one foreign language, comprehensive exam, thesis/dissertation. *Entrance requirements:* For doctorate, GRE General Test, GRE Subject Test, 3 letters of recommendation. Additional exam requirements/recommendations for international students: Required—TOEFL (minimum score 550 paper-based; 213 computer-based; 84 iBT). *Application deadline:* For fall admission, 7/1 for domestic and international students; for spring admission, 10/15 for domestic and international students. Application fee: $70. Electronic applications accepted. *Expenses:* Tuition: Full-time $37,910; part-time $1184 per credit hour. Required fees: $386; $40 per semester. Part-time tuition and fees vary according to class time, course level, degree level and program. *Financial support:* Career-related internships or fieldwork available. Support available to part-time students. Financial award application deadline: 1/15; financial award applicants required to submit FAFSA. *Unit head:* Dr. M. Carter Cornwall, Director, 617-638-4256, Fax: 617-638-4273, E-mail: cornwall@bu.edu. *Application contact:* Rebekah Alexander, Assistant Director of Admissions and Financial Aid, 617-353-2696, Fax: 617-358-5492, E-mail: grs@bu.edu.

Brandeis University, Graduate School of Arts and Sciences, Program in Biophysics and Structural Biology, Waltham, MA 02454-9110. Offers MS, PhD. *Faculty:* 24 full-time (8 women). *Students:* 16 full-time (4 women); includes 1 minority (Hispanic American), 5 international. Average age 26. 32 applicants, 25% accepted, 5 enrolled. *Degree requirements:* For master's, thesis; for doctorate, one foreign language, thesis/dissertation. *Entrance requirements:* For doctorate, GRE General Test, resume, 3 letters of recommendation. Additional exam requirements/recommendations for international students: Required—TOEFL (minimum score 600 paper-based; 250 computer-based; 100 iBT); Recommended—IELTS (minimum score 7). *Application deadline:* For fall admission, 1/15 priority date for domestic students. Applications are processed on a rolling basis. Application fee: $75. Electronic applications accepted. *Financial support:* In 2009–10, 12 students received support, including 5 fellowships with full tuition reimbursements available (averaging $27,500 per year), 11 research assistantships with full tuition reimbursements available (averaging $27,500 per year), teaching assistantships with partial tuition reimbursements available (averaging $3,200 per year); scholarships/grants, traineeships, health care benefits, and tuition waivers (full and partial) also available. Support available to part-time students. Financial award application deadline: 4/15; financial award applicants required to submit FAFSA. *Faculty research:* Biophysical chemistry, macromolecular structure and function, single molecule biophysics, macromolecules. *Unit head:* Dr. Dorothee Kern, Chair, 781-736-2354, Fax: 781-736-2349, E-mail: dkern@brandeis.edu. *Application contact:* Marcia Cabral, Department Administrator, 781-736-3100, Fax: 781-736-3107, E-mail: cabral@brandeis.edu.

California Institute of Technology, Division of Biology, Program in Cell Biology and Biophysics, Pasadena, CA 91125-0001. Offers PhD. *Degree requirements:* For doctorate, thesis/dissertation, qualifying exam. *Entrance requirements:* For doctorate, GRE General Test.

Carnegie Mellon University, Mellon College of Science, Department of Biological Sciences, Pittsburgh, PA 15213-3891. Offers biochemistry (PhD); biophysics (PhD); cell biology (PhD); computational biology (MS, PhD); developmental biology (PhD); genetics (PhD); molecular biology (PhD); neuroscience (PhD). *Degree requirements:* For doctorate, comprehensive exam, thesis/dissertation. *Entrance requirements:* For doctorate, GRE General Test, GRE Subject Test, interview. Electronic applications accepted. *Faculty research:* Genetic structure, function, and regulation; protein structure and function; biological membranes; biological spectroscopy.

Carnegie Mellon University, Mellon College of Science, Department of Chemistry, Pittsburgh, PA 15213-3891. Offers biotechnology and management (MS); chemistry (PhD), including bioinorganic, bioorganic, organic and materials, biophysics and spectroscopy, computational and theoretical, polymer; colloids, polymers and surfaces (MS). Part-time programs available. Terminal master's awarded for partial completion of doctoral program. *Degree requirements:* For doctorate, thesis/dissertation, departmental qualifying and oral exams, teaching experience. *Entrance requirements:* For master's, GRE General Test; for doctorate, GRE General Test, GRE Subject Test. Additional exam requirements/recommendations for international students: Required—TOEFL. Electronic applications accepted. *Faculty research:* Physical and theoretical chemistry, chemical synthesis, biophysical/bioinorganic chemistry.

Case Western Reserve University, School of Medicine and School of Graduate Studies, Graduate Programs in Medicine, Department of Physiology and Biophysics, Cleveland, OH 44106. Offers cell and molecular physiology (MS); cell physiology (PhD); molecular/cellular biophysics (PhD); physiology and biophysics (PhD); systems physiology (PhD); MD/PhD. Terminal master's awarded for partial completion of doctoral program. *Degree requirements:* For master's, thesis; for doctorate, thesis/dissertation. *Entrance requirements:* For master's, GRE General Test, minimum GPA of 3.28; for doctorate, GRE General Test, minimum GPA of 3.6. Additional exam requirements/recommendations for international students: Required—TOEFL. Electronic applications accepted. *Faculty research:* Cardiovascular physiology, calcium metabolism, epithelial cell biology.

See Close-Up on page 487.

Clemson University, Graduate School, College of Engineering and Science, Department of Physics and Astronomy, Clemson, SC 29634. Offers physics (MS, PhD), including astronomy and astrophysics, atmospheric physics, biophysics. Part-time programs available. *Faculty:* 25 full-time (4 women), 1 part-time/adjunct (0 women). *Students:* 46 full-time (11 women), 3 part-time (0 women); includes 1 minority (African American), 22 international. Average age 27. 71 applicants, 62% accepted, 17 enrolled. In 2009, 8 master's, 5 doctorates awarded. Terminal master's awarded for partial completion of doctoral program. *Degree requirements:* For master's, thesis or alternative; for doctorate, thesis/dissertation. *Entrance requirements:* For master's and doctorate, GRE General Test. Additional exam requirements/recommendations for international students: Required—TOEFL. *Application deadline:* For fall admission, 1/15 priority date for domestic students; for spring admission, 9/15 priority date for domestic students. Applications are processed on a rolling basis. Application fee: $70 ($80 for international students). Electronic applications accepted. *Expenses:* Tuition, state resident: full-time $8684; part-time $528 per credit hour. Tuition, nonresident: full-time $15,330; part-time $1078 per credit hour. Required fees: $736; $37 per semester. Part-time tuition and fees vary according to course load and program. *Financial support:* In 2009–10, 45 students received support, including 1 fellowship with full and partial tuition reimbursement available (averaging $10,000 per year), 13 research assistantships with partial tuition reimbursements available (averaging $21,423 per year), 32 teaching assistantships with partial tuition reimbursements available (averaging $16,490 per year); career-related internships or fieldwork, institutionally sponsored loans, scholarships/grants, health care benefits, and unspecified assistantships also available. Support available to part-time students. Financial award application deadline: 6/1; financial award applicants required to submit FAFSA. *Faculty research:* Radiation physics, solid-state physics, nuclear physics, radar and lidar studies of atmosphere. Total annual research expenditures: $3.1 million. *Unit head:* Dr. Peter Barnes, Chair, 864-656-3419, Fax: 864-656-0805, E-mail: peterb@clemson.edu. *Application contact:* Dr. Murray Daw, Graduate Coordinator, 864-656-6702, Fax: 864-656-0805, E-mail: physgradinfo-l@clemson.edu.

Columbia University, College of Physicians and Surgeons, Department of Biochemistry and Molecular Biophysics, New York, NY 10032. Offers biochemistry and molecular biophysics (M Phil, PhD); biophysics (PhD); MD/PhD. Only candidates for the PhD are admitted. *Degree requirements:* For doctorate, one foreign language, thesis/dissertation. *Entrance requirements:* For master's and doctorate, GRE General Test. Additional exam requirements/recommendations for international students: Required—TOEFL.

Columbia University, College of Physicians and Surgeons, Department of Physiology and Cellular Biophysics, New York, NY 10032. Offers M Phil, MA, PhD, MD/PhD. Only candidates for the PhD are admitted. Terminal master's awarded for partial completion of doctoral program. *Degree requirements:* For doctorate, thesis/dissertation. *Entrance requirements:* For master's and doctorate, GRE General Test. Additional exam requirements/recommendations for international students: Required—TOEFL. *Faculty research:* Membrane physiology, cellular biology, cardiovascular physiology, neurophysiology.

Columbia University, College of Physicians and Surgeons, Integrated Program in Cellular, Molecular and Biophysical Studies, New York, NY 10032. Offers M Phil, MA, PhD, MD/PhD. Only candidates for the PhD are admitted. Terminal master's awarded for partial completion of doctoral program. *Degree requirements:* For doctorate, thesis/dissertation. *Entrance requirements:* For master's, GRE General Test; for doctorate, GRE General Test, GRE Subject Test. Additional exam requirements/recommendations for international students: Required—TOEFL. *Expenses:* Contact institution. *Faculty research:* Transcription, macromolecular sorting, gene expression during development, cellular interaction.

Cornell University, Graduate School, Graduate Fields of Agriculture and Life Sciences, Field of Biochemistry, Molecular and Cell Biology, Ithaca, NY 14853-0001. Offers biochemistry (PhD); biophysics (PhD); cell biology (PhD); molecular and cell biology (PhD); molecular biology (PhD). *Faculty:* 64 full-time (14 women). *Students:* 91 full-time (43 women); includes 11 minority (2 African Americans, 6 Asian Americans or Pacific Islanders, 3 Hispanic Americans), 28 international. Average age 27. 150 applicants, 11% accepted, 15 enrolled. In 2009, 17 doctorates awarded. *Degree requirements:* For doctorate, comprehensive exam, thesis/dissertation, 2 semesters of teaching experience. *Entrance requirements:* For doctorate, GRE General Test, GRE Subject Test (biology, chemistry, physics, biochemistry, cell and molecular biology), 3 letters of recommendation. Additional exam requirements/recommendations for international students: Required—TOEFL (minimum score 600 paper-based; 250 computer-based; 77 iBT). *Application deadline:* For fall admission, 1/5 for domestic students. Application fee: $70. Electronic applications accepted. *Expenses:* Tuition: Full-time $29,500. Required fees: $70. Full-time tuition and fees vary according to degree level, program and student level. *Financial support:* In 2009–10, 88 students received support, including 13 fellowships with full tuition reimbursements available, 1 research assistantship with full tuition reimbursement available; teaching assistantships with full tuition reimbursements available, institutionally sponsored loans, scholarships/grants, health care benefits, tuition waivers (full and partial), and unspecified assistantships also available. Financial award applicants required to submit FAFSA. *Faculty research:* Biophysics, structural biology. *Unit head:* Director of Graduate Studies, 607-255-2100, Fax: 607-255-2100. *Application contact:* Graduate Field Assistant, 607-255-2100, Fax: 607-255-2100, E-mail: bmcb@cornell.edu.

Cornell University, Graduate School, Graduate Fields of Agriculture and Life Sciences, Graduate Field of Biophysics, Ithaca, NY 14853-0001. Offers PhD. *Faculty:* 31 full-time (5 women). *Students:* 18 full-time (7 women); includes 2 minority (1 African American, 1 Asian American or Pacific Islander), 9 international. Average age 26. 16 applicants, 56% accepted, 3 enrolled. In 2009, 1 doctorate awarded. *Degree requirements:* For doctorate, comprehensive exam, thesis/dissertation. *Entrance requirements:* For doctorate, GRE General Test, GRE Subject Test (physics or chemistry preferred), 3 letters of recommendation. Additional exam requirements/recommendations for international students: Required—TOEFL (minimum score 550 paper-based; 213 computer-based; 77 iBT). *Application deadline:* For fall admission, 1/15 for domestic students. Application fee: $70. Electronic applications accepted. *Expenses:* Tuition: Full-time $29,500. Required fees: $70. Full-time tuition and fees vary according to degree level, program and student level. *Financial support:* In 2009–10, 17 students received support, including 2 fellowships with full tuition reimbursements available; research assistantships with full tuition reimbursements available, teaching assistantships with full tuition reimbursements available, institutionally sponsored loans, scholarships/grants, health care benefits, tuition waivers (full and partial), and unspecified assistantships also available. Financial award applicants required to submit FAFSA. *Faculty research:* Protein structure and function, biomolecular and cellular function, membrane biophysics, signal transduction, computational biology. *Unit head:* Director of Graduate Studies, 607-255-2100, E-mail: biophysics@cornell.edu. *Application contact:* Graduate Field Assistant, 610-255-2100, E-mail: biophysics@cornell.edu.

Cornell University, Joan and Sanford I. Weill Medical College and Graduate School of Medical Sciences, Weill Cornell Graduate School of Medical Sciences, Physiology, Biophysics and Systems Biology Program, New York, NY 10065. Offers MS, PhD. *Faculty:* 33 full-time (9 women). *Students:* 43 full-time (18 women); includes 8 minority (2 African Americans, 5 Asian Americans or Pacific Islanders, 1 Hispanic American), 21 international. Average age 23. 54 applicants, 28% accepted, 5 enrolled. In 2009, 5 doctorates awarded. Terminal master's awarded for partial completion of doctoral program. *Degree requirements:* For master's, comprehensive exam; for doctorate, thesis/dissertation, final exam. *Entrance requirements:* For doctorate, GRE General Test, introductory courses in biology, inorganic and organic chemistry, physics, and mathematics. Additional exam requirements/recommendations for international students: Required—TOEFL. *Application deadline:* For fall admission, 12/1 for domestic students. Application fee: $60. *Expenses:* Tuition: Full-time $44,650. Required fees: $2805. *Financial support:* In 2009–10, 3 fellowships (averaging $27,992 per year) were awarded; scholarships/grants, health care benefits, and stipends (given to all students) also available. *Faculty research:* Receptor mediated regulation of cell function, molecular properties of channels or receptors, bioinformatics, mathematical modeling. *Unit head:* Dr. Emre Aksay, Co-Director, 212-746-6207, E-mail: ema2004@med.cornell.edu. *Application contact:* Audrey Rivera, Program Coordinator, 212-746-6361, E-mail: ajr2004@med.cornell.edu.

Dalhousie University, Faculty of Medicine, Department of Physiology and Biophysics, Halifax, NS B3H 1X5, Canada. Offers M Sc, PhD, M Sc/PhD. *Degree requirements:* For master's, thesis; for doctorate, thesis/dissertation. *Entrance requirements:* For master's and doctorate, GRE Subject Test (for international students). Additional exam requirements/recommendations for international students: Required—TOEFL, IELTS, 1 of the following 5 approved tests:

TOEFL, IELTS, CANTEST, CAEL, Michigan English Language Assessment Battery. Electronic applications accepted. *Faculty research:* Computer modeling, reproductive and endocrine physiology, cardiovascular physiology, neurophysiology, membrane biophysics.

East Carolina University, Graduate School, Thomas Harriot College of Arts and Sciences, Department of Physics, Greenville, NC 27858-4353. Offers applied and biomedical physics (MS); medical physics (MS); physics (PhD). Part-time programs available. *Degree requirements:* For master's, one foreign language, comprehensive exam. *Entrance requirements:* For master's, GRE General Test. Additional exam requirements/recommendations for international students: Required—TOEFL.

East Tennessee State University, James H. Quillen College of Medicine, Biomedical Science Graduate Program, Johnson City, TN 37614. Offers anatomy (MS, PhD); biochemistry (MS, PhD); biophysics (MS, PhD); microbiology (MS, PhD); pharmacology (MS, PhD); physiology (MS, PhD). Part-time programs available. Terminal master's awarded for partial completion of doctoral program. *Degree requirements:* For master's, one foreign language, thesis, comprehensive qualifying exam; for doctorate, 2 foreign languages, thesis/dissertation. *Entrance requirements:* For master's, GRE General Test, minimum GPA of 3.0, bachelor's degree in biological or related science; for doctorate, GRE General Test, GRE Subject Test. Additional exam requirements/recommendations for international students: Required—TOEFL (minimum score 550 paper-based; 213 computer-based). *Expenses:* Contact institution.

Emory University, Graduate School of Arts and Sciences, Department of Physics, Atlanta, GA 30322-1100. Offers biophysics (PhD); condensed matter physics (PhD); non-linear physics (PhD); radiological physics (PhD); soft condensed matter physics (PhD); solid-state physics (PhD); statistical physics (PhD); MS/PhD. *Degree requirements:* For doctorate, thesis/dissertation, qualifier proposal (PhD). *Entrance requirements:* For doctorate, GRE General Test, minimum GPA of 3.0. Additional exam requirements/recommendations for international students: Required—TOEFL (minimum score 600 paper-based). Electronic applications accepted. *Faculty research:* Experimental studies of the structure and function of metalloproteins, soft condensed matter, granular materials, biophotonics and fluorescence correlation spectroscopy, single molecule studies of DNA-protein systems.

Georgetown University, Graduate School of Arts and Sciences, Programs in Biomedical Sciences, Department of Physiology and Biophysics, Washington, DC 20057. Offers MS, PhD, MD/PhD. *Degree requirements:* For doctorate, thesis/dissertation. *Entrance requirements:* For master's, GRE General Test, MCAT; for doctorate, GRE General Test. Additional exam requirements/recommendations for international students: Required—TOEFL.

Harvard University, Graduate School of Arts and Sciences, Committee on Biophysics, Cambridge, MA 02138. Offers PhD. *Degree requirements:* For doctorate, thesis/dissertation, exam, qualifying paper. *Entrance requirements:* For doctorate, GRE General Test, GRE Subject Test (recommended). Additional exam requirements/recommendations for international students: Required—TOEFL. *Expenses:* Tuition: Full-time $33,696. Required fees: $1126. Full-time tuition and fees vary according to program. *Faculty research:* Structural molecular biology, cell and membrane biophysics, molecular genetics, physical biochemistry, mathematical biophysics.

See Close-Up on page 173.

Howard University, Graduate School, Department of Physiology and Biophysics, Washington, DC 20059-0002. Offers biophysics (PhD); physiology (PhD). *Degree requirements:* For doctorate, comprehensive exam, thesis/dissertation. *Entrance requirements:* For doctorate, GRE General Test, minimum B average in field. *Faculty research:* Cardiovascular physiology, pulmonary physiology, renal physiology, neurophysiology, endocrinology.

Illinois State University, Graduate School, College of Arts and Sciences, Department of Biological Sciences, Normal, IL 61790-2200. Offers animal behavior (MS); bacteriology (MS); biochemistry (MS); biological sciences (MS); biology (PhD); biophysics (MS); biotechnology (MS); botany (MS, PhD); cell biology (MS); conservation biology (MS); developmental biology (MS); ecology (MS, PhD); entomology (MS); evolutionary biology (MS); genetics (MS, PhD); immunology (MS); microbiology (MS, PhD); molecular biology (MS); molecular genetics (MS); neurobiology (MS); neuroscience (MS); parasitology (MS); physiology (MS, PhD); plant biology (MS); plant molecular biology (MS); plant sciences (MS); structural biology (MS); zoology (MS, PhD). Part-time programs available. *Degree requirements:* For master's, thesis or alternative; for doctorate, variable foreign language requirement, thesis/dissertation, 2 terms of residency. *Entrance requirements:* For master's, GRE General Test, minimum GPA of 2.6 in last 60 hours of course work; for doctorate, GRE General Test. *Faculty research:* Redoc balance and drug development in schistosoma mansoni, control of the growth of listeria monocytogenes at low temperature, regulation of cell expansion and microtubule function by SPRI, CRUI: physiology and fitness consequences of different life history phenotypes.

Iowa State University of Science and Technology, Graduate College, College of Agriculture and College of Liberal Arts and Sciences, Department of Biochemistry, Biophysics, and Molecular Biology, Ames, IA 50011. Offers biochemistry (MS, PhD); biophysics (MS, PhD); genetics (MS, PhD); molecular, cellular, and developmental biology (MS, PhD); toxicology (MS, PhD). *Faculty:* 24 full-time (6 women), 1 (woman) part-time/adjunct. *Students:* 77 full-time (30 women), 3 part-time (2 women); includes 3 minority (1 African American, 1 Asian American or Pacific Islander, 1 Hispanic American), 56 international. 41 applicants, 32% accepted, 13 enrolled. In 2009, 2 master's, 7 doctorates awarded. *Degree requirements:* For master's, thesis; for doctorate, thesis/dissertation. *Entrance requirements:* For master's and doctorate, GRE General Test. Additional exam requirements/recommendations for international students: Required—TOEFL (minimum score 550 paper-based; 79 iBT) or IELTS (minimum score 6.5). *Application deadline:* For fall admission, 1/15 priority date for domestic and international students; for spring admission, 10/15 for domestic and international students. Application fee: $40 ($90 for international students). Electronic applications accepted. *Expenses:* Tuition, state resident: full-time $6716. Tuition, nonresident: full-time $8908. Tuition and fees vary according to course level, course load, program and student level. *Financial support:* In 2009–10, 52 research assistantships with full and partial tuition reimbursements (averaging $18,750 per year) were awarded; teaching assistantships with full and partial tuition reimbursements, scholarships/grants, health care benefits, and unspecified assistantships also available. *Unit head:* Dr. Guru Rao, Interim Chair, 515-294-6116, E-mail: biochem@iastate.edu. *Application contact:* Dr. Reuben Peters, Director of Graduate Education, 515-294-6116, E-mail: biochem@iastate.edu.

See Close-Up on page 155.

The Johns Hopkins University, National Institutes of Health Sponsored Programs, Baltimore, MD 21218-2699. Offers biology (PhD), including biochemistry, biophysics, cell biology, developmental biology, genetic biology, molecular biology; cell, molecular, and developmental biology and biophysics (PhD). *Faculty:* 25 full-time (4 women). *Students:* 126 full-time (72 women); includes 36 minority (3 African Americans, 1 American Indian/Alaska Native, 21 Asian Americans or Pacific Islanders, 11 Hispanic Americans), 19 international. 282 applicants, 26% accepted, 36 enrolled. In 2009, 15 doctorates awarded. *Degree requirements:* For doctorate, comprehensive exam, thesis/dissertation. *Entrance requirements:* For doctorate, GRE General Test. Additional exam requirements/recommendations for international students: Required—TOEFL (minimum score 600 paper-based; 250 computer-based), TWE. *Application deadline:* For fall admission, 12/15 priority date for domestic students. Application fee: $60. Electronic applications accepted. *Financial support:* In 2009–10, 24 fellowships (averaging $23,000 per year), 93 research assistantships (averaging $23,000 per year), 22 teaching assistantships (averaging $23,000 per year) were awarded; Federal Work-Study, institutionally sponsored loans, scholarships/grants, traineeships, health care benefits, tuition waivers (partial), and unspecified assistantships also available. Financial award application deadline: 4/15; financial award applicants required to submit FAFSA. *Faculty research:* Protein and nucleic acid biochemistry and biophysical chemistry, molecular biology and development. Total annual research expenditures: $11.2 million. *Unit head:* Dr. Allen Shearn, Chair, 410-516-4693, Fax:

410-516-5213, E-mail: bio_cals@jhu.edu. *Application contact:* Joan Miller, Academic Affairs Manager, 410-516-5502, Fax: 410-516-5213, E-mail: joan@jhu.edu.

The Johns Hopkins University, Zanvyl Krieger School of Arts and Sciences, Program in Molecular Biophysics, Baltimore, MD 21218-2699. Offers PhD. *Faculty:* 9 full-time (3 women). *Students:* 43 full-time (17 women); includes 2 minority (both Asian Americans or Pacific Islanders), 9 international. Average age 26. 73 applicants, 15% accepted, 11 enrolled. In 2009, 7 doctorates awarded. *Degree requirements:* For doctorate, comprehensive exam, thesis/dissertation. *Entrance requirements:* For doctorate, GRE General Test. Additional exam requirements/recommendations for international students: Required—TOEFL (minimum score 600 paper-based; 250 computer-based), IELTS; Recommended—TWE.. *Application deadline:* For fall admission, 1/4 priority date for domestic and international students. Applications are processed on a rolling basis. Application fee: $75. Electronic applications accepted. *Financial support:* In 2009–10, 2 students received support, including fellowships with full tuition reimbursements available (averaging $27,532 per year), research assistantships with full tuition reimbursements available (averaging $27,532 per year); teaching assistantships, institutionally sponsored loans, scholarships/grants, traineeships, health care benefits, tuition waivers (full), and unspecified assistantships also available. Financial award application deadline: 4/15; financial award applicants required to submit FAFSA. *Faculty research:* Protein folding and dynamics; membranes and membrane proteins; structural biology and prediction; RNA biophysics; enzymes and metabolic pathways; single molecule studies; DNA-protein interactions. Total annual research expenditures: $3.7 million. *Unit head:* Dr. Juliette Lecomte, Director, 410-516-5197, Fax: 410-516-4118, E-mail: juliette@jhu.edu. *Application contact:* Ranice Crosby, Coordinator, Graduate Admissions, 410-516-5197, Fax: 410-516-4118, E-mail: crosbyr@jhu.edu.

Medical College of Wisconsin, Graduate School of Biomedical Sciences, Department of Biophysics, Milwaukee, WI 53226-0509. Offers PhD, MD/PhD. *Degree requirements:* For doctorate, comprehensive exam, thesis/dissertation. *Entrance requirements:* For doctorate, GRE. Additional exam requirements/recommendations for international students: Required—TOEFL. Electronic applications accepted.

Medical College of Wisconsin, Graduate School of Biomedical Sciences, Program in Biophysics, Milwaukee, WI 53226-0509. Offers PhD, MD/PhD. Part-time programs available. *Faculty:* 22 full-time (4 women). *Students:* 27 full-time (9 women), 2 part-time (1 woman); includes 2 minority (1 African American, 1 Asian American or Pacific Islander), 10 international. Average age 28. 19 applicants, 26% accepted, 3 enrolled. In 2009, 3 doctorates awarded. *Degree requirements:* For doctorate, thesis/dissertation, oral exam. *Entrance requirements:* For doctorate, GRE General Test. Additional exam requirements/recommendations for international students: Required—TOEFL. *Application deadline:* For fall admission, 2/15 priority date for domestic and international students. Applications are processed on a rolling basis. Application fee: $40. Electronic applications accepted. *Financial support:* In 2009–10, 2 fellowships with full tuition reimbursements (averaging $26,265 per year), 28 research assistantships with full tuition reimbursements (averaging $26,265 per year) were awarded. *Faculty research:* X-ray crystallography, electron spin resonance and membrane structure, protein and membrane dynamics, magnetic resonance imaging, free radical biology. *Unit head:* Dr. Balaraman Kalyanaraman. *Application contact:* Dr. Neil Hogg, Director of Recruitment, 414-456-4012, Fax: 414-456-6512, E-mail: nhogg@mcw.edu.

Northwestern University, The Graduate School and Judd A. and Marjorie Weinberg College of Arts and Sciences, Interdepartmental Biological Sciences Program (IBiS), Evanston, IL 60208. Offers biochemistry, molecular biology, and cell biology (PhD), including biochemistry, cell and molecular biology, molecular biophysics, structural biology; biotechnology (PhD); cell and molecular biology (PhD); developmental biology and genetics (PhD); hormone action and signal transduction (PhD); neuroscience (PhD); structural biology, biochemistry, and biophysics (PhD). Program participants include the Departments of Biochemistry, Molecular Biology, and Cell Biology; Chemistry; Neurobiology and Physiology; Chemical Engineering; Civil Engineering; and Evanston Hospital. *Degree requirements:* For doctorate, thesis/dissertation, qualifying exam. *Entrance requirements:* For doctorate, GRE General Test. Additional exam requirements/recommendations for international students: Required—TOEFL (minimum score 600 paper-based). Electronic applications accepted. *Faculty research:* Developmental genetics, gene regulation, DNA-protein interactions, biological clocks, bioremediation.

The Ohio State University, Graduate School, College of Biological Sciences, Program in Biophysics, Columbus, OH 43210. Offers MS, PhD. *Faculty:* 57. *Students:* 25 full-time (10 women), 26 part-time (8 women); includes 4 minority (all Asian Americans or Pacific Islanders), 24 international. Average age 28. In 2009, 7 master's, 10 doctorates awarded. *Degree requirements:* For master's, thesis optional; for doctorate, thesis/dissertation. *Entrance requirements:* For master's and doctorate, GRE General Test. Additional exam requirements/recommendations for international students: Required—TOEFL (minimum score 600 paper-based; 250 computer-based). *Application deadline:* For fall admission, 8/15 priority date for domestic students, 7/1 priority date for international students; for winter admission, 12/1 priority date for domestic students, 11/1 priority date for international students; for spring admission, 3/1 priority date for domestic students, 2/1 priority date for international students. Applications are processed on a rolling basis. Application fee: $40 ($50 for international students). Electronic applications accepted. *Expenses:* Tuition, state resident: full-time $10,683. Tuition, nonresident: full-time $25,923. Tuition and fees vary according to course load and program. *Financial support:* Fellowships, research assistantships, teaching assistantships, Federal Work-Study and institutionally sponsored loans available. Support available to part-time students. *Unit head:* Ralf Bundschuh, Graduate Studies Committee Chair, 614-292-9480, Fax: 614-292-8772, E-mail: bundschuh.2@osu.edu. *Application contact:* 614-292-9444, Fax: 614-292-3895, E-mail: domestic.grad@osu.edu.

Oregon State University, Graduate School, College of Science, Department of Biochemistry and Biophysics, Corvallis, OR 97331. Offers MA, MAIS, MS, PhD. *Faculty:* 9 full-time (1 woman), 1 part-time/adjunct (0 women). *Students:* 19 full-time (7 women); includes 2 minority (1 American Indian/Alaska Native, 1 Asian American or Pacific Islander), 7 international. Average age 27. In 2009, 1 master's, 2 doctorates awarded. *Degree requirements:* For master's, thesis optional; for doctorate, thesis/dissertation, exams. *Entrance requirements:* For master's, GRE General Test, minimum GPA of 3.0; for doctorate, GRE Subject Test, minimum GPA of 3.0. Additional exam requirements/recommendations for international students: Required—TOEFL. *Application deadline:* For fall admission, 4/15 priority date for domestic students. Applications are processed on a rolling basis. Application fee: $50. *Expenses:* Tuition, state resident: full-time $9774; part-time $362 per credit. Tuition, nonresident: full-time $15,849; part-time $587 per credit. Required fees: $1639. Full-time tuition and fees vary according to course load and program. *Financial support:* Research assistantships, teaching assistantships, institutionally sponsored loans available. Support available to part-time students. Financial award application deadline: 2/1. *Faculty research:* DNA and deoxyribonucleotide metabolism, cell growth control, receptors and membranes, protein structure and function. *Unit head:* Dr. Pui Shing Ho, Chair, 541-737-2769, Fax: 541-737-0481. *Application contact:* Dr. W. Curtis Johnson, Chairman, Graduate Committee, 541-737-4511, Fax: 541-737-0481, E-mail: johnsowc@ucs.orst.edu.

Purdue University, Graduate School, College of Science, Department of Biological Sciences, West Lafayette, IN 47907. Offers biochemistry (PhD); biophysics (PhD); cell and developmental biology (PhD); ecology, evolutionary and population biology (MS, PhD), including ecology, evolutionary biology, population biology; genetics (MS, PhD); microbiology (MS, PhD); molecular biology (PhD); neurobiology (MS, PhD); plant physiology (PhD). Terminal master's awarded for partial completion of doctoral program. *Degree requirements:* For master's, thesis (for some programs); for doctorate, thesis/dissertation, seminars, teaching experience. *Entrance requirements:* For master's and doctorate, GRE General Test. Additional exam requirements/recommendations for international students: Required—TOEFL. Electronic applications accepted.

Biophysics

Rensselaer Polytechnic Institute, Graduate School, School of Science, Program in Biochemistry and Biophysics, Troy, NY 12180-3590. Offers biochemistry (MS, PhD); biophysics (MS, PhD). Part-time programs available. *Faculty:* 19 full-time (7 women). *Students:* 6 full-time (2 women). 19 applicants, 21% accepted, 3 enrolled. Terminal master's awarded for partial completion of doctoral program. *Degree requirements:* For master's, thesis (for some programs); for doctorate, comprehensive exam, thesis/dissertation. *Entrance requirements:* For master's, GRE General Test, GRE Subject Test (biology, chemistry or biochemistry). Additional exam requirements/recommendations for international students: Required—TOEFL. *Application deadline:* For fall admission, 1/15 priority date for domestic students. Applications are processed on a rolling basis. Application fee: $45. Electronic applications accepted. *Expenses:* Tuition: Full-time $38,100. *Financial support:* In 2009–10, 6 students received support, including 3 research assistantships with full tuition reimbursements available (averaging $16,500 per year), 3 teaching assistantships with full tuition reimbursements available (averaging $16,500 per year); traineeships and unspecified assistantships also available. Financial award application deadline: 2/1. *Faculty research:* Biopolymers, photosynthesis, cellular bioengineering. Total annual research expenditures: $450,000. *Application contact:* Jody Malm, Administrative Coordinator, 518-276-2808, Fax: 518-276-2344, E-mail: malmj@rpi.edu.

Rosalind Franklin University of Medicine and Science, School of Graduate and Postdoctoral Studies—Interdisciplinary Graduate Program in Biomedical Sciences, Department of Physiology and Biophysics, North Chicago, IL 60064-3095. Offers MS, PhD, MD/PhD. Terminal master's awarded for partial completion of doctoral program. *Degree requirements:* For master's, comprehensive exam, thesis; for doctorate, comprehensive exam, thesis/dissertation. *Entrance requirements:* For master's and doctorate, GRE General Test. Additional exam requirements/recommendations for international students: Required—TOEFL, TWE. *Faculty research:* Membrane transport, mechanisms of cellular regulation, brain metabolism, peptide metabolism.

Simon Fraser University, Graduate Studies, Faculty of Science, Department of Physics, Burnaby, BC V5A 1S6, Canada. Offers biophysics (M Sc, PhD); chemical physics (M Sc, PhD); physics (M Sc, PhD). *Degree requirements:* For master's, thesis; for doctorate, thesis/dissertation. *Entrance requirements:* For master's, minimum GPA of 3.0; for doctorate, minimum GPA of 3.5. Additional exam requirements/recommendations for international students: Required—TOEFL or IELTS. *Faculty research:* Solid-state physics, magnetism, energy research, superconductivity, nuclear physics.

Stanford University, School of Humanities and Sciences, Program in Biophysics, Stanford, CA 94305-9991. Offers PhD. *Degree requirements:* For doctorate, thesis/dissertation, oral exam. *Entrance requirements:* For doctorate, GRE General Test, GRE Subject Test. Additional exam requirements/recommendations for international students: Required—TOEFL. Electronic applications accepted. *Expenses:* Tuition: Full-time $37,380; part-time $2760 per quarter. Required fees: $501.

Stony Brook University, State University of New York, Stony Brook University Medical Center, School of Medicine and Graduate School, Graduate Programs in Medicine, Department of Physiology and Biophysics, Stony Brook, NY 11794. Offers PhD. *Students:* 14 full-time (9 women); includes 3 minority (all Asian Americans or Pacific Islanders), 5 international. Average age 29. 39 applicants, 41% accepted. In 2009, 6 doctorates awarded. *Degree requirements:* For doctorate, comprehensive exam, thesis/dissertation. *Entrance requirements:* For doctorate, GRE General Test, GRE Subject Test, BS in related field, minimum GPA of 3.0. Additional exam requirements/recommendations for international students: Required—TOEFL. *Application deadline:* For fall admission, 1/15 for domestic students. Application fee: $60. *Expenses:* Tuition, state resident: full-time $8370; part-time $349 per credit. Tuition, nonresident: full-time $13,250; part-time $552 per credit. Required fees: $933. *Financial support:* Fellowships, research assistantships, teaching assistantships, Federal Work-Study available. Financial award application deadline: 3/15. *Faculty research:* Cellular electrophysiology, membrane permeation and transport, metabolic endocrinology. Total annual research expenditures: $6 million. *Unit head:* Dr. Peter Brink, Chair, 631-444-2299, Fax: 631-444-3432. *Application contact:* Melanie Bonnette, Graduate Program Administrator, 631-444-2299, Fax: 631-444-3432.

Syracuse University, College of Arts and Sciences, Program in Structural Biology, Biochemistry and Biophysics, Syracuse, NY 13244. Offers PhD. *Students:* 5 full-time (3 women), 3 part-time (0 women); includes 1 minority (African American), 4 international. Average age 31. 18 applicants, 0% accepted, 0 enrolled. *Degree requirements:* For doctorate, thesis/dissertation, exam. *Entrance requirements:* For doctorate, GRE General Test, GRE Subject Test. Additional exam requirements/recommendations for international students: Required—TOEFL (minimum score 100 iBT). *Application deadline:* For fall admission, 1/10 priority date for domestic and international students. Application fee: $75. Electronic applications accepted. *Expenses:* Tuition: Full-time $26,808; part-time $1117 per credit. Required fees: $1024. *Financial support:* Fellowships with tuition reimbursements, research assistantships, teaching assistantships with tuition reimbursements, tuition waivers available. Financial award application deadline: 1/1; financial award applicants required to submit FAFSA. *Unit head:* Scott Pitnick, Director, 315-443-5128, Fax: 315-443-2012, E-mail: sspitnic@syr.edu. *Application contact:* Evelyn Lott, Information Contact, 315-443-9154, Fax: 315-443-2012, E-mail: ealott@syr.edu.

Texas A&M University, College of Agriculture and Life Sciences, Department of Biochemistry and Biophysics, College Station, TX 77843. Offers biochemistry (MS, PhD); biophysics (MS). *Faculty:* 32. *Students:* 135 full-time (59 women), 6 part-time (0 women); includes 17 minority (3 African Americans, 1 American Indian/Alaska Native, 2 Asian Americans or Pacific Islanders, 11 Hispanic Americans), 55 international. Average age 27. In 2009, 7 master's, 11 doctorates awarded. *Entrance requirements:* For master's and doctorate, GRE General Test. Additional exam requirements/recommendations for international students: Required—TOEFL. *Application deadline:* For fall admission, 2/1 priority date for domestic students, 12/1 priority date for international students. Applications are processed on a rolling basis. Application fee: $50 ($75 for international students). Electronic applications accepted. *Expenses:* Tuition, state resident: full-time $3991; part-time $221.74 per credit hour. Tuition, nonresident: full-time $9049; part-time $502.74 per credit hour. *Financial support:* In 2009–10, 6 fellowships with partial tuition reimbursements (averaging $20,000 per year), 70 research assistantships with partial tuition reimbursements (averaging $20,000 per year) were awarded; teaching assistantships with partial tuition reimbursements, institutionally sponsored loans, scholarships/grants, traineeships, and unspecified assistantships also available. Financial award application deadline: 2/1; financial award applicants required to submit FAFSA. *Faculty research:* Enzymology, gene expression, protein structure, plant biochemistry. *Unit head:* Department Head, 979-862-2263, Fax: 979-845-9274, E-mail: biobiograd@tamu.edu. *Application contact:* Academic Advisor, 979-845-1779, Fax: 979-845-9274, E-mail: biobiograd@tamu.edu.

Thomas Jefferson University, Jefferson College of Graduate Studies, Program in Molecular Physiology and Biophysics, Philadelphia, PA 19107. Offers PhD. *Faculty:* 13 full-time (5 women). *Students:* 2 full-time (1 woman). 4 applicants, 0% accepted, 0 enrolled. *Degree requirements:* For doctorate, comprehensive exam, thesis/dissertation. *Entrance requirements:* For doctorate, GRE General Test, minimum GPA of 3.2. Additional exam requirements/recommendations for international students: Required—TOEFL (minimum score 250 computer-based; 100 iBT). *Application deadline:* For fall admission, 1/15 priority date for domestic and international students. Applications are processed on a rolling basis. Application fee: $50. Electronic applications accepted. *Expenses:* Tuition: Full-time $26,858; part-time $879 per credit. Required fees: $525. *Financial support:* In 2009–10, 2 students received support, including 2 fellowships with full tuition reimbursements available (averaging $52,883 per year); Federal Work-Study, institutionally sponsored loans, scholarships/grants, traineeships, and stipend also available. Support available to part-time students. Financial award application deadline: 5/1; financial award applicants required to submit FAFSA. *Faculty research:* Cardiovascular physiology, smooth muscle physiology, pathophysiology of myocardial ischemia, endothelial cell physiology, molecular biology of ion channel physiology. Total annual research expenditures: $3.2 million. *Unit head:* Dr. Thomas M. Butler, Program Director, 215-503-6583, E-mail: thomas.butler@jefferson.edu. *Application contact:* Marc E. Stearns, Director of Admissions, 215-503-0155, Fax: 215-503-9920, E-mail: jcgs-info@jefferson.edu.

Université de Sherbrooke, Faculty of Medicine and Health Sciences, Graduate Programs in Medicine, Department of Physiology and Biophysics, Sherbrooke, QC J1H 5N4, Canada. Offers M Sc, PhD. Terminal master's awarded for partial completion of doctoral program. *Degree requirements:* For master's, thesis; for doctorate, thesis/dissertation. Electronic applications accepted. *Faculty research:* Ion channels, neurological basis of pain, insulin resistance, obesity.

Université du Québec à Trois-Rivières, Graduate Programs, Program in Biophysics and Cellular Biology, Trois-Rivières, QC G9A 5H7, Canada. Offers M Sc, PhD. Part-time programs available. *Degree requirements:* For master's, thesis; for doctorate, thesis/dissertation. *Entrance requirements:* For master's, appropriate bachelor's degree, proficiency in French; for doctorate, appropriate master's degree, proficiency in French.

University at Buffalo, the State University of New York, Graduate School, Graduate Programs in Cancer Research and Biomedical Sciences at Roswell Park Cancer Institute, Department of Molecular and Cellular Biophysics and Biochemistry at Roswell Park Cancer Institute, Buffalo, NY 14260. Offers PhD. *Faculty:* 25 full-time (3 women). *Students:* 16 full-time (9 women), 1 part-time (0 women); includes 2 minority (1 African American, 1 Asian American or Pacific Islander), 8 international. Average age 25. 20 applicants, 40% accepted, 4 enrolled. In 2009, 3 doctorates awarded. *Degree requirements:* For doctorate, comprehensive exam, thesis/dissertation. *Entrance requirements:* For doctorate, GRE General Test. Additional exam requirements/recommendations for international students: Required—TOEFL (minimum score 600 paper-based; 250 computer-based; 100 iBT). *Application deadline:* For fall admission, 2/1 priority date for domestic students. Applications are processed on a rolling basis. Application fee: $50. Electronic applications accepted. *Financial support:* In 2009–10, 4 fellowships with full tuition reimbursements (averaging $24,000 per year), 21 research assistantships with full tuition reimbursements (averaging $24,000 per year) were awarded; Federal Work-Study, institutionally sponsored loans, and health care benefits also available. Financial award application deadline: 2/1; financial award applicants required to submit FAFSA. *Faculty research:* MRI research, structural and function of biomolecules, photodynamic therapy, DNA damage and repair, heat-shock proteins and vaccine research. Total annual research expenditures: $5.5 million. *Unit head:* Dr. Arindam Sen, Director of Graduate Studies, 716-845-8911, E-mail: arindam.sen@roswellpark.org. *Application contact:* Craig R. Johnson, Director of Admissions, 716-845-2339, Fax: 716-845-8178, E-mail: craig.johnson@roswellpark.org.

University at Buffalo, the State University of New York, Graduate School, School of Medicine and Biomedical Sciences, Graduate Programs in Medicine and Biomedical Sciences, Department of Physiology and Biophysics, Buffalo, NY 14260. Offers biophysics (MS, PhD); physiology (MA, PhD). *Faculty:* 24 full-time (4 women), 1 part-time/adjunct (0 women). *Students:* 16 full-time (7 women), 1 (woman) part-time, 7 international. Average age 28. 8 applicants, 75% accepted. In 2009, 2 master's, 2 doctorates awarded. Terminal master's awarded for partial completion of doctoral program. *Degree requirements:* For master's, thesis, oral exam, project; for doctorate, thesis/dissertation, oral and written qualifying exam or 2 research proposals. *Entrance requirements:* For master's and doctorate, GRE General Test. Additional exam requirements/recommendations for international students: Required—TOEFL (minimum score 600 paper-based; 250 computer-based; 100 iBT). *Application deadline:* For fall admission, 2/1 priority date for domestic and international students. Applications are processed on a rolling basis. Application fee: $50. Electronic applications accepted. *Financial support:* In 2009–10, fellowships with tuition reimbursements (averaging $21,000 per year), 17 research assistantships with tuition reimbursements (averaging $21,000 per year) were awarded; Federal Work-Study, institutionally sponsored loans, health care benefits, and unspecified assistantships also available. Financial award application deadline: 2/1; financial award applicants required to submit FAFSA. *Faculty research:* Neurosciences, ion channels, cardiac physiology, renal/epithelial transport, cardiopulmonary exercise. Total annual research expenditures: $5.4 million. *Unit head:* Dr. Harold C. Strauss, Chair, 716-829-2738, Fax: 716-829-2344, E-mail: hstrauss@buffalo.edu. *Application contact:* Dora Horbachevsky, Program Administrator, 716-829-2189, Fax: 716-829-2364, E-mail: dh26@buffalo.edu.

University of Arkansas for Medical Sciences, Graduate School, Graduate Programs in Biomedical Sciences, Department of Physiology and Biophysics, Little Rock, AR 72205-7199. Offers MS, PhD, MD/PhD. *Faculty:* 20 full-time (4 women), 21 part-time/adjunct (4 women). *Students:* 10 full-time, 3 part-time. In 2009, 1 master's, 4 doctorates awarded. *Degree requirements:* For master's, thesis; for doctorate, thesis/dissertation. *Entrance requirements:* For master's and doctorate, GRE General Test. Additional exam requirements/recommendations for international students: Required—TOEFL. *Application deadline:* For fall admission, 3/15 for domestic and international students. Application fee: $0. *Financial support:* In 2009–10, research assistantships with full tuition reimbursements (averaging $24,000 per year); stipend and tuition for doctoral students also available. Support available to part-time students. *Faculty research:* Gene transcription, protein targeting, membrane biology, cell-cell communication. *Unit head:* Dr. Michael L. Jennings, Chairman, 501-686-5123. *Application contact:* Dr. Richard Kurten, Program Director, 501-686-8269, E-mail: kurtenrichardc@uams.edu.

University of California, Berkeley, Graduate Division, College of Letters and Science, Group in Biophysics, Berkeley, CA 94720-1500. Offers PhD. *Students:* 53 full-time (21 women). Average age 27. 87 applicants, 8 enrolled. In 2009, 12 doctorates awarded. *Degree requirements:* For doctorate, thesis/dissertation, qualifying exam. *Entrance requirements:* For doctorate, GRE General Test, minimum GPA of 3.0, 3 letters of recommendation. *Application deadline:* For fall admission, 12/15 for domestic students. Application fee: $70 ($90 for international students). *Financial support:* Fellowships, research assistantships, teaching assistantships, scholarships/grants, unspecified assistantships, and research service awards available. *Unit head:* Prof. Ehud Isacoff, Chair, 510-642-0379. *Application contact:* Kate Chase, Student Affairs Officer, 510-642-0379, E-mail: biophysicsgrad@berkeley.edu.

University of California, Davis, Graduate Studies, Graduate Group in Biophysics, Davis, CA 95616. Offers MS, PhD. *Degree requirements:* For doctorate, thesis/dissertation. *Entrance requirements:* For master's and doctorate, GRE General Test, GRE Subject Test. Additional exam requirements/recommendations for international students: Required—TOEFL (minimum score 550 paper-based; 213 computer-based). Electronic applications accepted. *Faculty research:* Molecular structure, protein structure/function relationships, spectroscopy.

University of California, Irvine, School of Medicine and School of Biological Sciences, Department of Physiology and Biophysics, Irvine, CA 92697. Offers biological sciences (PhD); MD/PhD. Students apply through the Graduate Program in Molecular Biology, Genetics, and Biochemistry. *Students:* 9 full-time (3 women); includes 3 minority (2 Asian Americans or Pacific Islanders, 1 Hispanic American), 2 international. Average age 27. *Degree requirements:* For doctorate, thesis/dissertation. *Entrance requirements:* For doctorate, GRE General Test, GRE Subject Test, minimum GPA of 3.0. Additional exam requirements/recommendations for international students: Required—TOEFL (minimum score 550 paper-based; 213 computer-based). *Application deadline:* For fall admission, 1/15 priority date for domestic students, 1/15 for international students. Application fee: $70 ($90 for international students). Electronic applications accepted. *Financial support:* Fellowships, research assistantships with full tuition reimbursements, teaching assistantships, institutionally sponsored loans, traineeships, health care benefits, and unspecified assistantships available. Financial award application deadline: 3/1; financial award applicants required to submit FAFSA. *Faculty research:* Membrane physiology, exercise physiology, regulation of hormone biosynthesis and action, endocrinology, ion channels and signal transduction. *Unit head:* Dr. Janos K. Lanyi, Chair, 949-824-7150, Fax: 949-824-8540, E-mail: jklanyi@uci.edu. *Application contact:* Kimberly McKinney, Administrator, 949-824-8145, Fax: 949-824-1965, E-mail: kamckinn@uci.edu.

University of California, San Diego, Office of Graduate Studies, Department of Physics, La Jolla, CA 92093. Offers biophysics (MS, PhD); physics (MS, PhD); physics/materials physics

(MS). *Degree requirements:* For doctorate, thesis/dissertation. *Entrance requirements:* For master's and doctorate, GRE General Test, GRE Subject Test. Additional exam requirements/recommendations for international students: Required—TOEFL. Electronic applications accepted.

University of California, San Francisco, School of Pharmacy and School of Medicine, Graduate Group in Biophysics, San Francisco, CA 94143. Offers PhD. *Faculty:* 42 full-time (9 women). *Students:* 48 full-time (17 women); includes 8 minority (4 Asian Americans or Pacific Islanders, 4 Hispanic Americans), 5 international. Average age 25. 37 applicants, 65% accepted, 8 enrolled. In 2009, 8 doctorates awarded. *Degree requirements:* For doctorate, thesis/dissertation. *Entrance requirements:* For doctorate, GRE General Test; GRE Subject Test (recommended). Additional exam requirements/recommendations for international students: Required—TOEFL. *Application deadline:* For fall admission, 12/1 for domestic students. Application fee: $60 ($80 for international students). Electronic applications accepted. *Financial support:* In 2009–10, fellowships with full tuition reimbursements (averaging $28,000 per year), research assistantships with full tuition reimbursements (averaging $28,000 per year) were awarded; traineeships, health care benefits, tuition waivers (full), unspecified assistantships, and stipends also available. *Faculty research:* Structural and computational biology; proteomic, genomic, and cell biology; chemistry; systems biology. *Unit head:* Dr. Matthew Jacobson, Program Director, 415-514-9881, E-mail: matt.jacobson@ucsf.edu. *Application contact:* Rebecca Brown, Program Administrator, 415-514-0249, Fax: 415-514-0502, E-mail: rbrown@cgl.ucsf.edu.

University of Chicago, Division of the Physical Sciences, Graduate Program in Biophysical Science, Chicago, IL 60637-1513. Offers PhD. *Degree requirements:* For doctorate, comprehensive exam, thesis/dissertation, ethics class, 2 teaching assistantships. *Entrance requirements:* Additional exam requirements/recommendations for international students: Required—IELTS (minimum score 7); Recommended—TOEFL (minimum score 600 paper-based; 250 computer-based; 104 iBT). Electronic applications accepted.

University of Cincinnati, Graduate School, College of Medicine, Graduate Programs in Biomedical Sciences, Department of Pharmacology and Cell Biophysics, Cincinnati, OH 45221. Offers cell biophysics (PhD); pharmacology (PhD). *Degree requirements:* For doctorate, thesis/dissertation, qualifying exam. *Entrance requirements:* For doctorate, GRE General Test. Additional exam requirements/recommendations for international students: Required—TOEFL. Electronic applications accepted. *Faculty research:* Lipoprotein research, enzyme regulation, electrophysiology, gene actuation.

University of Connecticut, Graduate School, College of Liberal Arts and Sciences, Department of Molecular and Cell Biology, Field of Biophysics and Structural Biology, Storrs, CT 06269. Offers MS, PhD. *Faculty:* 23 full-time (9 women). *Students:* 11 full-time (5 women); includes 1 minority (African American), 4 international. Average age 29. 18 applicants, 17% accepted, 2 enrolled.Terminal master's awarded for partial completion of doctoral program. *Degree requirements:* For master's, comprehensive exam; for doctorate, thesis/dissertation. *Entrance requirements:* For master's and doctorate, GRE General Test, GRE Subject Test. Additional exam requirements/recommendations for international students: Required—TOEFL (minimum score 550 paper-based; 213 computer-based). *Application deadline:* For fall admission, 2/1 priority date for domestic and international students; for spring admission, 11/1 for domestic students, 10/1 for international students. Applications are processed on a rolling basis. Application fee: $55. Electronic applications accepted. *Expenses:* Tuition, state resident: full-time $4725; part-time $525 per credit. Tuition, nonresident: full-time $12,267; part-time $1363 per credit. Required fees: $346 per semester. Tuition and fees vary according to course load. *Financial support:* In 2009–10, 4 research assistantships with full tuition reimbursements, 6 teaching assistantships with full tuition reimbursements were awarded; fellowships, Federal Work-Study, scholarships/grants, health care benefits, and unspecified assistantships also available. Financial award application deadline: 2/1; financial award applicants required to submit FAFSA. *Unit head:* David Benson, Head, 860-486-4258, Fax: 860-486-4331, E-mail: david.benson@uconn.edu. *Application contact:* Anne St. Onje, Graduate Coordinator, 860-486-4314, Fax: 860-486-3943, E-mail: anne.st_onje@uconn.edu.

See Close-Up on page 187.

University of Guelph, Graduate Program Services, Biophysics Interdepartmental Group, Guelph, ON N1G 2W1, Canada. Offers M Sc, PhD. *Degree requirements:* For master's, thesis; for doctorate, comprehensive exam, thesis/dissertation. *Entrance requirements:* For master's, minimum B average during previous 2 years of course work; for doctorate, minimum B+ average. Additional exam requirements/recommendations for international students: Required—TOEFL (minimum score 550 paper-based; 213 computer-based). Electronic applications accepted. *Faculty research:* Molecular, cellular, structural, and computational biophysics.

University of Guelph, Graduate Program Services, College of Biological Science, Department of Molecular and Cellular Biology, Guelph, ON N1G 2W1, Canada. Offers biochemistry (M Sc, PhD); biophysics (M Sc, PhD); botany (M Sc, PhD); microbiology (M Sc, PhD); molecular biology and genetics (M Sc, PhD). *Degree requirements:* For master's, thesis, research proposal; for doctorate, comprehensive exam, thesis/dissertation, research proposal. *Entrance requirements:* For master's, minimum B-average during previous 2 years of coursework; for doctorate, minimum A-average. Additional exam requirements/recommendations for international students: Required—TOEFL (minimum score 550 paper-based; 213 computer-based), IELTS (minimum score 6.5). Electronic applications accepted. *Faculty research:* Physiology, structure, genetics, and ecology of microbes; virology and microbial technology.

University of Illinois at Chicago, College of Medicine and Graduate College, Graduate Programs in Medicine, Department of Physiology and Biophysics, Chicago, IL 60607-7128. Offers MS, PhD. Terminal master's awarded for partial completion of doctoral program. *Degree requirements:* For master's, thesis; for doctorate, thesis/dissertation. *Entrance requirements:* For master's and doctorate, GRE General Test. Additional exam requirements/recommendations for international students: Required—TOEFL. Electronic applications accepted. *Faculty research:* Neuroscience, endocrinology and reproduction, cell physiology, exercise physiology, NMR.

University of Illinois at Urbana–Champaign, Graduate College, College of Liberal Arts and Sciences, School of Molecular and Cellular Biology, Center for Biophysics and Computational Biology, Champaign, IL 61820. Offers MS, PhD. *Students:* 71 full-time (16 women); includes 9 minority (7 Asian Americans or Pacific Islanders, 2 Hispanic Americans), 45 international. 88 applicants, 14% accepted, 12 enrolled. In 2009, 11 doctorates awarded. *Entrance requirements:* For doctorate, GRE, minimum GPA of 3.0. Additional exam requirements/recommendations for international students: Required—TOEFL. *Application deadline:* Applications are processed on a rolling basis. Application fee: $60 ($75 for international students). Electronic applications accepted. *Financial support:* In 2009–10, 17 fellowships, 63 research assistantships, 19 teaching assistantships were awarded; tuition waivers (full and partial) also available. *Unit head:* Martin Gruebele, Director, 217-333-1624, Fax: 217-244-3186, E-mail: mgruebel@illinois.edu. *Application contact:* Cynthia Dodds, Office Administrator, 217-333-1630, Fax: 217-244-6615, E-mail: dodds@illinois.edu.

The University of Iowa, Roy J. and Lucille A. Carver College of Medicine and Graduate College, Graduate Programs in Medicine, Department of Molecular Physiology and Biophysics, Iowa City, IA 52242-1316. Offers MS, PhD. *Faculty:* 17 full-time (3 women), 16 part-time/adjunct (2 women). *Students:* 20 full-time (6 women); includes 3 minority (all Asian Americans or Pacific Islanders), 3 international. Average age 25. 8 applicants, 100% accepted, 8 enrolled. In 2009, 1 master's, 8 doctorates awarded. Terminal master's awarded for partial completion of doctoral program. *Degree requirements:* For master's, comprehensive exam; for doctorate, comprehensive exam, thesis/dissertation, teaching experience. *Entrance requirements:* For master's, GRE; for doctorate, GRE General Test, minimum GPA of 3.0. Additional exam requirements/recommendations for international students: Required—TOEFL. *Application deadline:* For fall admission, 4/1 for domestic students, 3/1 for international students; for spring admission, 10/1 for domestic students, 9/1 for international students. Applications are processed on a rolling basis. Application fee: $60 ($80 for international students). Electronic applications accepted. *Financial support:* In 2009–10, 4 fellowships with full tuition reimbursements (averaging $24,250 per year), 13 research assistantships with full tuition reimbursements (averaging $24,250 per year) were awarded; traineeships also available. Financial award application deadline: 4/1. *Faculty research:* Cellular and molecular endocrinology, membrane structure and function, cardiac cell electrophysiology, regulation of gene expression, neurophysiology. *Unit head:* Dr. Kevin P. Campbell, Head, 319-335-7800, Fax: 319-335-7330, E-mail: kevin-campbell@uiowa.edu. *Application contact:* Dr. Michael Anderson, Director of Graduate Studies, 319-335-7839, Fax: 319-335-7330, E-mail: michael-g-anderson@uiowa.edu.

The University of Kansas, Graduate Studies, College of Liberal Arts and Sciences, Department of Molecular Biosciences, Lawrence, KS 66044. Offers biochemistry and biophysics (MA, PhD); microbiology (MA, PhD); molecular, cellular, and developmental biology (MA, PhD). *Students:* 58 full-time (30 women), 2 part-time (1 woman); includes 4 minority (1 American Indian/Alaska Native, 1 Asian American or Pacific Islander, 2 Hispanic Americans), 24 international. Average age 27. 49 applicants, 29% accepted, 4 enrolled. In 2009, 2 master's, 7 doctorates awarded. Terminal master's awarded for partial completion of doctoral program. *Degree requirements:* For master's, comprehensive exam, thesis; for doctorate, comprehensive exam, thesis/dissertation. *Entrance requirements:* For master's and doctorate, GRE General Test. Additional exam requirements/recommendations for international students: Required—TOEFL (minimum score 24 iBT). *Application deadline:* For fall admission, 12/15 for domestic and international students. Application fee: $45 ($55 for international students). Electronic applications accepted. *Expenses:* Tuition, state resident: full-time $6492; part-time $270.50 per credit hour. Tuition, nonresident: full-time $15,510; part-time $646.25 per credit hour. Required fees: $847; $70.56 per credit hour. Tuition and fees vary according to course load and program. *Financial support:* Fellowships with tuition reimbursements, research assistantships with tuition reimbursements, teaching assistantships with tuition reimbursements, health care benefits and unspecified assistantships available. Financial award application deadline: 3/1. *Faculty research:* Structure and function of proteins, genetics of organism development, molecular genetics, neurophysiology, molecular virology and pathogenics, developmental biology, cell biology. *Unit head:* Dr. Mark Richter, Chair, 785-864-4311, Fax: 785-864-5294, E-mail: richter@ku.edu. *Application contact:* John P. Connolly, Graduate Program Assistant, 785-864-4311, Fax: 785-864-5294, E-mail: jconnolly@ku.edu.

University of Louisville, School of Medicine, Department of Physiology and Biophysics, Louisville, KY 40292-0001. Offers MS, PhD, MD/PhD. *Faculty:* 23 full-time (0 women). *Students:* 37 full-time (19 women), 4 part-time (1 woman); includes 8 minority (3 African Americans, 5 Asian Americans or Pacific Islanders), 9 international. Average age 28. 33 applicants, 67% accepted, 19 enrolled. In 2009, 15 master's, 5 doctorates awarded. Terminal master's awarded for partial completion of doctoral program. *Degree requirements:* For master's, thesis; for doctorate, comprehensive exam, thesis/dissertation. *Entrance requirements:* For master's, GRE General Test (minimum score 1000 verbal and quantitative), minimum GPA of 3.0; for doctorate, GRE General Test (Verbal and Quantitative minimum score of 1000), minimum GPA of 3.0. Additional exam requirements/recommendations for international students: Required—TOEFL. *Application deadline:* For fall admission, 1/15 priority date for domestic students. Applications are processed on a rolling basis. Application fee: $50. Electronic applications accepted. *Financial support:* In 2009–10, 24 students received support, including 7 fellowships with full tuition reimbursements available (averaging $22,000 per year), 17 research assistantships with full tuition reimbursements available (averaging $22,000 per year). Financial award application deadline: 4/15. *Faculty research:* Control of microvascular function during normal and disease states; mechanisms of cellular adhesive interactions on endothelial cells lining blood vessels; changes in blood rheological properties and mechanisms associated with increased blood fibrinogen content; role of nutrition in microvascular control mechanisms; mechanism of cardiovascular-renal remodeling in hypertension, diabetes, and heart failure. *Unit head:* Dr. Irving G. Joshua, Chair, 502-852-5371, Fax: 502-852-6239, E-mail: igjosh01@gwise.louisville.edu. *Application contact:* Dr. William Wead, Director of Admissions, 502-852-7571, Fax: 502-852-6849, E-mail: wbwead01@gwise.louisville.edu.

University of Maryland, College Park, Academic Affairs, College of Computer, Mathematical and Physical Sciences, Institute for Physical Science and Technology, Program in Biophysics, College Park, MD 20742. Offers PhD. *Students:* 6 full-time (4 women), 4 international. 17 applicants, 47% accepted, 5 enrolled. *Application deadline:* For fall admission, 1/15 for domestic and international students. Application fee: $60. *Expenses:* Tuition, area resident: Part-time $471 per credit hour. Tuition, state resident: part-time $471 per credit hour. Tuition, nonresident: part-time $1016 per credit hour. Required fees: $337.04 per term. *Financial support:* In 2009–10, 1 research assistantship (averaging $19,280 per year), 5 teaching assistantships (averaging $17,133 per year) were awarded. *Unit head:* Dr. Devarajan Thirumalai, Professor, 301-405-4803. *Application contact:* Dean of the Graduate School, 301-405-0376.

University of Miami, Graduate School, Miller School of Medicine, Graduate Programs in Medicine, Department of Physiology and Biophysics, Coral Gables, FL 33124. Offers PhD, MD/PhD. *Faculty:* 16 full-time (4 women). *Students:* 8 full-time (7 women); includes 5 Asian Americans or Pacific Islanders. Average age 26. In 2009, 2 doctorates awarded. *Degree requirements:* For doctorate, thesis/dissertation, qualifying exam. *Entrance requirements:* For doctorate, GRE General Test, minimum GPA of 3.0 in sciences. Additional exam requirements/recommendations for international students: Required—TOEFL. *Financial support:* In 2009–10, 8 students received support, including fellowships with full tuition reimbursements available (averaging $25,500 per year); research assistantships, tuition waivers (full) also available. *Faculty research:* Cell and membrane physiology, cell-to-cell communication, molecular neurobiology, neuroimmunology, neural development. *Unit head:* Dr. Karl Magleby, Chairman, 305-243-6821, Fax: 305-243-6898, E-mail: kmagleby@miami.edu. *Application contact:* Dr. David Landowne, Director of Graduate Studies, 305-243-6821, Fax: 305-243-5931, E-mail: dl@miami.edu.

University of Michigan, Horace H. Rackham School of Graduate Studies, Interdepartmental Program in Biophysics, Ann Arbor, MI 48109. Offers PhD. *Faculty:* 43 full-time (7 women). *Students:* 34 full-time (11 women); includes 8 minority (2 African Americans, 4 Asian Americans or Pacific Islanders, 2 Hispanic Americans), 9 international. Average age 22. 41 applicants, 20% accepted, 4 enrolled. In 2009, 2 doctorates awarded. *Degree requirements:* For doctorate, thesis/dissertation, oral defense of dissertation, preliminary exam. *Entrance requirements:* For doctorate, GRE General Test, GRE Subject Test. Additional exam requirements/recommendations for international students: Required—TOEFL. *Application deadline:* For fall admission, 1/10 for domestic and international students. Application fee: $60 ($75 for international students). Electronic applications accepted. *Expenses:* Tuition, state resident: full-time $17,286; part-time $1099 per credit hour. Tuition, nonresident: full-time $34,944; part-time $2080 per credit hour. Required fees: $95 per semester. Tuition and fees vary according to course load, degree level and program. *Financial support:* In 2009–10, 14 fellowships with full tuition reimbursements (averaging $20,000 per year), 6 research assistantships with full tuition reimbursements (averaging $20,000 per year), teaching assistantships with full tuition reimbursements (averaging $20,000 per year) were awarded; scholarships/grants, traineeships, health care benefits, and unspecified assistantships also available. Financial award application deadline: 3/15. *Faculty research:* Structural biology, computational biophysics, physical chemistry, cellular biophysics. *Unit head:* Dr. Jens-Christian Meiners, Program Director, 734-764-1146, E-mail: meiners@umich.edu. *Application contact:* Sara Grosky, Student Services Administrator, 734-763-6722, E-mail: saramin@umich.edu.

University of Minnesota, Duluth, Medical School, Department of Biochemistry, Molecular Biology and Biophysics, Duluth, MN 55812-2496. Offers biochemistry, molecular biology and biophysics (MS); biology and biophysics (PhD); social, administrative, and clinical pharmacy (MS, PhD); toxicology (MS, PhD). *Faculty:* 10 full-time (3 women). *Students:* 16 full-time (5 women); includes 3 minority (all Asian Americans or Pacific Islanders). Average age 29. 7 applicants, 29% accepted, 2 enrolled. In 2009, 1 master's, 1 doctorate awarded. Terminal master's awarded for partial completion of doctoral program. *Degree requirements:* For master's,

Biophysics

University of Minnesota, Duluth (continued)
comprehensive exam, thesis; for doctorate, comprehensive exam, thesis/dissertation. *Entrance requirements:* For master's and doctorate, GRE General Test. Additional exam requirements/recommendations for international students: Required—TOEFL. *Application deadline:* For winter admission, 1/3 for domestic students, 1/2 for international students; for spring admission, 3/15 priority date for domestic and international students. Application fee: $75 ($95 for international students). Electronic applications accepted. *Financial support:* In 2009–10, 8 students received support, including research assistantships with full tuition reimbursements available (averaging $27,300 per year), teaching assistantships with full tuition reimbursements available (averaging $27,300 per year); career-related internships or fieldwork, scholarships/grants, health care benefits, and unspecified assistantships also available. Financial award application deadline: 9/1. *Faculty research:* Intestinal cancer biology; hepatotoxins and mitochondriopathies; toxicology; cell cycle regulation in stem cells; neurobiology of brain development, trace metal function and blood-brain barrier; hibernation biology. Total annual research expenditures: $1.5 million. *Unit head:* Dr. Lester R. Drewes, Professor/Head, 218-726-7925, Fax: 218-726-8014, E-mail: ldrewes@d.umn.edu. *Application contact:* Cheryl Beeman, Administrative Assistant, 218-726-6354, Fax: 218-726-8014, E-mail: ahcd@d.umn.edu.

University of Minnesota, Twin Cities Campus, Graduate School, College of Biological Sciences, Biochemistry, Molecular Biology and Biophysics Graduate Program, Minneapolis, MN 55455-0213. Offers PhD. *Faculty:* 69 full-time (14 women), 1 part-time/adjunct (0 women). *Students:* 60 full-time (26 women); includes 20 minority (2 African Americans, 1 American Indian/Alaska Native, 15 Asian Americans or Pacific Islanders, 2 Hispanic Americans). Average age 26. 199 applicants, 20% accepted, 11 enrolled. In 2009, 16 doctorates awarded. *Degree requirements:* For doctorate, thesis/dissertation. *Entrance requirements:* For doctorate, GRE, 3 letters of recommendation, more than 1 semester of laboratory experience. Additional exam requirements/recommendations for international students: Required—TOEFL (minimum score 625 paper-based; 263 computer-based; 108 iBT with writing subsection 25 and reading subsection 25) or IELTS (minimum score 7). *Application deadline:* For fall admission, 12/15 for domestic and international students. Application fee: $75 ($95 for international students). Electronic applications accepted. *Financial support:* Institutionally sponsored loans, scholarships/grants, traineeships, health care benefits, tuition waivers, unspecified assistantships, and stipends available. *Faculty research:* Microbial biochemistry, biotechnology, molecular biology, regulatory biochemistry, structural biology and biophysics, physical biochemistry, enzymology, physiological chemistry. Total annual research expenditures: $10.3 million. *Unit head:* Prof. David A. Bernlohr, Head, 612-624-2712. *Application contact:* Dr. Anja Katrin Bielinsky, Director of Graduate Studies, 612-624-2469, Fax: 612-625-2163, E-mail: bieli003@umn.edu.

University of Minnesota, Twin Cities Campus, Graduate School, Program in Biophysical Sciences and Medical Physics, Minneapolis, MN 55455-0213. Offers MS, PhD. Part-time programs available. *Degree requirements:* For master's, thesis optional, research paper, oral exam; for doctorate, thesis/dissertation, oral/written preliminary exam, oral final exam. *Faculty research:* Theoretical biophysics, radiological physics, cellular and molecular biophysics.

See Display below.

University of Mississippi Medical Center, School of Graduate Studies in the Health Sciences, Department of Physiology and Biophysics, Jackson, MS 39216-4505. Offers MS, PhD, MD/PhD. *Degree requirements:* For master's, thesis; for doctorate, thesis/dissertation, first authored publication. *Entrance requirements:* For master's and doctorate, GRE General Test, minimum GPA of 3.0. *Faculty research:* Cardiovascular, renal, endocrine, and cellular neurophysiology; molecular physiology.

University of Missouri–Kansas City, School of Biological Sciences, Program in Cell Biology and Biophysics, Kansas City, MO 64110-2499. Offers PhD. PhD offered through the School of Graduate Studies. *Degree requirements:* For doctorate, comprehensive exam, thesis/dissertation. *Entrance requirements:* For doctorate, GRE General Test, bachelor's degree in chemistry, biology or related field; minimum GPA of 3.0. Additional exam requirements/recommendations for international students: Required—TOEFL (minimum score 550 paper-based; 213 computer-based; 80 iBT). *Application deadline:* For fall admission, 2/15 priority date for domestic and international students. Applications are processed on a rolling basis. Application fee: $45 ($50 for international students). Electronic applications accepted. *Expenses:* Tuition, state resident: full-time $5378; part-time $299 per credit hour. Tuition, nonresident: full-time $13,881; part-time $771 per credit hour. Required fees: $641; $71 per credit hour. Tuition and fees vary according to course load and program. *Financial support:* Fellowships with full tuition reimbursements, research assistantships with full tuition reimbursements, teaching assistantships with full and partial tuition reimbursements, scholarships/grants, tuition waivers (full and partial), and unspecified assistantships available. Financial award application deadline: 3/1; financial award applicants required to submit FAFSA. *Unit head:* Dr. George J. Thomas, Head, 816-235-2352, E-mail: sbsgradrecruit@umkc.edu. *Application contact:* Laura Batenic, Information Contact, 816-235-2352, Fax: 816-235-5158, E-mail: batenicl@umkc.edu.

See Close-Up on page 247.

University of New Mexico, Graduate School, College of Arts and Sciences, Department of Physics and Astronomy, Albuquerque, NM 87131-2039. Offers biomedical physics (MS, PhD); physics (MS, PhD). Part-time programs available. *Faculty:* 39 full-time (4 women), 2 part-time/adjunct (0 women). *Students:* 71 full-time (19 women), 10 part-time (0 women); includes 7 minority (4 Asian Americans or Pacific Islanders, 3 Hispanic Americans), 30 international. Average age 28. 110 applicants, 35% accepted, 16 enrolled. In 2009, 7 master's, 11 doctorates awarded. Terminal master's awarded for partial completion of doctoral program. *Degree requirements:* For master's, comprehensive exam (for some programs), thesis optional; for doctorate, comprehensive exam, thesis/dissertation. *Entrance requirements:* For master's, GRE; for doctorate, GRE General Test; GRE Subject Test in physics (recommended). Additional exam requirements/recommendations for international students: Required—TOEFL (minimum score 550 paper-based; 213 computer-based; 80 iBT). *Application deadline:* For fall admission, 1/15 for domestic and international students; for spring admission, 8/1 for domestic and international students. Application fee: $50. Electronic applications accepted. *Expenses:* Tuition, state resident: full-time $2099; part-time $233.20 per credit hour. Tuition, nonresident: full-time $6650. Required fees: $25 per semester. Tuition and fees vary according to course load, program and reciprocity agreements. *Financial support:* In 2009–10, 15 students received support, including 3 fellowships with full tuition reimbursements available (averaging $30,000 per year), 54 research assistantships with full tuition reimbursements available (averaging $15,550 per year), 37 teaching assistantships with full tuition reimbursements available (averaging $13,814 per year); career-related internships or fieldwork, scholarships/grants, traineeships, health care benefits, and unspecified assistantships also available. Support available to part-time students. Financial award application deadline: 2/1; financial award applicants required to submit FAFSA. *Faculty research:* Astronomy and astrophysics, biological physics, condensed-matter physics, nonlinear science and complexity, optics and photonics, quantum information, subatomic physics. Total annual research expenditures: $6 million. *Unit head:* Dr. Bernd Bassalleck, Chair, 505-277-1517, Fax: 505-277-1520, E-mail: bossek@unm.edu. *Application contact:* Alisia Gibson, Program Advisement Coordinator, 505-277-1514, Fax: 505-277-1514, E-mail: agibson@unm.edu.

The University of North Carolina at Chapel Hill, School of Medicine and Graduate School, Graduate Programs in Medicine, Department of Biochemistry and Biophysics, Chapel Hill, NC

27599. Offers MS, PhD. Terminal master's awarded for partial completion of doctoral program. *Degree requirements:* For master's, comprehensive exam, thesis; for doctorate, comprehensive exam, thesis/dissertation. *Entrance requirements:* For master's and doctorate, GRE General Test, GRE Subject Test (recommended), minimum GPA of 3.0. Additional exam requirements/recommendations for international students: Required—TOEFL. Electronic applications accepted.

University of Rochester, School of Medicine and Dentistry, Graduate Programs in Medicine and Dentistry, Department of Biochemistry and Biophysics, Program in Biophysics, Rochester, NY 14627. Offers MS, PhD. Terminal master's awarded for partial completion of doctoral program. *Degree requirements:* For doctorate, thesis/dissertation, qualifying exam. *Entrance requirements:* For master's and doctorate, GRE General Test.

University of Southern California, Keck School of Medicine and Graduate School, Graduate Programs in Medicine, Department of Physiology and Biophysics, Los Angeles, CA 90089. Offers MS, PhD, MD/PhD. *Faculty:* 13 full-time (3 women). *Students:* 8 full-time (3 women); includes 1 minority (Asian American or Pacific Islander), 6 international. Average age 28. 11 applicants, 27% accepted, 3 enrolled. In 2009, 2 master's, 2 doctorates awarded. Terminal master's awarded for partial completion of doctoral program. *Degree requirements:* For master's, thesis optional; for doctorate, comprehensive exam, thesis/dissertation. *Entrance requirements:* For master's and doctorate, GRE General Test, minimum GPA of 3.0. Additional exam requirements/recommendations for international students: Required—TOEFL (minimum score 600 paper-based; 250 computer-based; 100 iBT). *Application deadline:* For fall admission, 2/1 priority date for domestic and international students. Application fee: $85. Electronic applications accepted. *Expenses:* Tuition: Full-time $25,980; part-time $1315 per unit. Required fees: $554. One-time fee: $35 full-time. Full-time tuition and fees vary according to degree level and program. *Financial support:* In 2009–10, 1 student received support, including 7 research assistantships with full tuition reimbursements available (averaging $27,060 per year); Federal Work-Study, institutionally sponsored loans, scholarships/grants, traineeships, health care benefits, and unspecified assistantships also available. Financial award application deadline: 5/5. *Faculty research:* Endocrinology and metabolism, neurophysiology, mathematical modeling, cell transport, autoimmunity and cancer immunotherapy. Total annual research expenditures: $4.2 million. *Unit head:* Dr. Richard N. Bergman, Chair, 323-442-1920, Fax: 323-442-1918, E-mail: rbergman@usc.edu. *Application contact:* Elena Camarena, Graduate Coordinator, 323-442-1039, Fax: 323-442-2283, E-mail: physiol@hsc.usc.edu.

The University of Texas Medical Branch, Graduate School of Biomedical Sciences, Program in Biochemistry and Molecular Biology, Galveston, TX 77555. Offers biochemistry (PhD); bioinformatics (PhD); biophysics (PhD); cell biology (PhD); computational biology (PhD); structural biology (PhD). *Students:* 41 full-time (17 women); includes 6 minority (1 African American, 1 Asian American or Pacific Islander, 4 Hispanic Americans), 22 international. Average age 28. In 2009, 9 doctorates awarded. *Degree requirements:* For doctorate, thesis/dissertation. *Entrance requirements:* Additional exam requirements/recommendations for international students: Required—TOEFL (minimum score 550 paper-based; 213 computer-based). *Application deadline:* Applications are processed on a rolling basis. Application fee: $30 ($75 for international students). Electronic applications accepted. *Financial support:* In 2009–10, fellowships (averaging $25,000 per year), research assistantships (averaging $25,000 per year) were awarded. Financial award applicants required to submit FAFSA. *Unit head:* Dr. Sarita Sastry, Director, 409-747-1915, Fax: 409-747-1938, E-mail: sasastry@utmb.edu. *Application contact:* Debora Botting, Coordinator for Special Programs, 409-772-2769, Fax: 409-772-5102, E-mail: dmbottin@utmb.edu.

University of Toronto, School of Graduate Studies, Life Sciences Division, Department of Medical Biophysics, Toronto, ON M5S 1A1, Canada. Offers M Sc, PhD. *Degree requirements:* For master's, thesis; for doctorate, thesis/dissertation. *Entrance requirements:* For master's, resume, 2 letters of reference; for doctorate, resumé, 2 letters of reference. Additional exam requirements/recommendations for international students: Required—TOEFL (minimum score 620 paper-based; 260 computer-based), TWE (minimum score 5), GRE General Test, GRE Subject Test.

University of Vermont, College of Medicine and Graduate College, Graduate Programs in Medicine, Department of Molecular Physiology and Biophysics, Burlington, VT 05405. Offers MS, PhD, MD/MS, MD/PhD. *Students:* 2 (both women), 1 international. 4 applicants, 25% accepted, 0 enrolled. In 2009, 1 master's awarded. *Degree requirements:* For master's, thesis; for doctorate, thesis/dissertation. *Entrance requirements:* For master's and doctorate, GRE General Test. Additional exam requirements/recommendations for international students: Required—TOEFL (minimum score 550 paper-based; 213 computer-based; 80 iBT). *Application deadline:* For fall admission, 4/1 priority date for domestic students, 4/1 for international students. Applications are processed on a rolling basis. Application fee: $40. Electronic applications accepted. *Expenses:* Tuition, state resident: part-time $508 per credit hour. Tuition, nonresident: part-time $1281 per credit hour. *Financial support:* Fellowships, research assistantships, teaching assistantships available. Financial award application deadline: 3/1. *Unit head:* Dr. D. Warshaw, Chairperson, 802-656-2540. *Application contact:* Dr. Terese Ruiz, Coordinator, 802-656-2540.

University of Virginia, School of Medicine, Department of Molecular Physiology and Biological Physics, Charlottesville, VA 22903. Offers biological and physical sciences (MS); physiology (PhD); MD/PhD. *Faculty:* 30 full-time (6 women), 1 part-time/adjunct (0 women). *Students:* 16 full-time (7 women); includes 2 minority (both African Americans). Average age 28. 1 applicant, 100% accepted, 1 enrolled. In 2009, 22 master's, 5 doctorates awarded. *Entrance requirements:* For doctorate, GRE General Test, GRE Subject Test. Additional exam requirements/recommendations for international students: Required—TOEFL. *Application deadline:* For fall admission, 2/15 for domestic and international students. Applications are processed on a rolling basis. Application fee: $60. Electronic applications accepted. *Financial support:* Fellowships, research assistantships, teaching assistantships available. Financial award applicants required to submit FAFSA. *Unit head:* Dr. Mark Yeager, Chair, 434-924-5108, Fax: 434-982-1616, E-mail: my3r@virginia.edu. *Application contact:* Dr. Mark Yeager, Chair, 434-924-5108, Fax: 434-982-1616, E-mail: my3r@virginia.edu.

University of Virginia, School of Medicine, Interdisciplinary Program in Biophysics, Charlottesville, VA 22908. Offers PhD. *Students:* 18 full-time (3 women); includes 3 minority (2 Asian Americans or Pacific Islanders, 1 Hispanic American), 11 international. Average age 28. In 2009, 5 doctorates awarded. *Degree requirements:* For doctorate, thesis/dissertation, research proposal and oral defense. *Entrance requirements:* For doctorate, GRE General Test, GRE Subject Test (recommended), 2 or more letters of recommendation. Additional exam requirements/recommendations for international students: Required—TOEFL. *Application deadline:* For fall admission, 4/15 for domestic and international students. Applications are processed on a rolling basis. Application fee: $60. Electronic applications accepted. *Financial support:* Fellowships with full tuition reimbursements, research assistantships with full tuition reimbursements, teaching assistantships with full tuition reimbursements, tuition waivers (full) available. Financial award application deadline: 1/15; financial award applicants required to submit FAFSA. *Faculty research:* Structural biology and structural genomics, structural biology of membrane proteins and membrane biophysics, spectroscopy and thermodynamics of macromolecular interactions, high Resolution imaging and cell biophysics. *Unit head:* Robert K. Nakamoto, Director, 434-982-6390. *Application contact:* Pam Mullinex, Program Coordinator, 434-243-7248, Fax: 434-982-1616, E-mail: prm8b@virginia.edu.

University of Washington, Graduate School, School of Medicine and Graduate School, Graduate Programs in Medicine, Department of Physiology and Biophysics, Seattle, WA 98195. Offers PhD. *Degree requirements:* For doctorate, thesis/dissertation. *Entrance requirements:* For doctorate, GRE General Test. Additional exam requirements/recommendations for international students: Required—TOEFL (minimum score 580 paper-based; 237 computer-based; 70 iBT). *Faculty research:* Membrane and cell biophysics, neuroendocrinology, cardiovascular and respiratory physiology, systems neurophysiology and behavior, molecular physiology.

The University of Western Ontario, Faculty of Graduate Studies, Biosciences Division, Department of Medical Biophysics, London, ON N6A 5B8, Canada. Offers M Sc, PhD. *Degree requirements:* For master's, thesis; for doctorate, thesis/dissertation. *Entrance requirements:* Additional exam requirements/recommendations for international students: Required—TOEFL. *Faculty research:* Haemodynamics and cardiovascular biomechanics, microcirculation, orthopedic biomechanics, radiobiology, medical imaging.

University of Wisconsin–Madison, Graduate School, Program in Biophysics, Madison, WI 53706-1380. Offers PhD. *Degree requirements:* For doctorate, comprehensive exam, thesis/dissertation. *Entrance requirements:* For doctorate, GRE General Test, minimum GPA of 3.0. Additional exam requirements/recommendations for international students: Required—TOEFL (minimum score 600 paper-based). Electronic applications accepted. *Expenses:* Tuition, state resident: part-time $594 per credit. Tuition, nonresident: part-time $1504 per credit. Required fees: $65 per credit. Tuition and fees vary according to course load, program and reciprocity agreements. *Faculty research:* NMR spectroscopy, high-speed automated DNA sequencing, x-ray crystallography, neuronal signaling and exocytosis, protein structure.

Vanderbilt University, Graduate School and School of Medicine, Department of Molecular Physiology and Biophysics, Nashville, TN 37240-1001. Offers MS, PhD, MD/PhD. *Faculty:* 80 full-time (22 women). *Students:* 29 full-time (21 women), 1 part-time (0 women); includes 6 minority (3 African Americans, 1 American Indian/Alaska Native, 2 Hispanic Americans), 8 international. Average age 30. In 2009, 1 master's, 6 doctorates awarded. *Degree requirements:* For doctorate, comprehensive exam, thesis/dissertation, preliminary, qualifying, and final exams. *Entrance requirements:* For doctorate, GRE General Test, GRE Subject Test (recommended). Additional exam requirements/recommendations for international students: Required—TOEFL (minimum score 570 paper-based; 230 computer-based; 88 iBT). *Application deadline:* For fall admission, 1/15 for domestic and international students. Application fee: $0. Electronic applications accepted. *Financial support:* Fellowships with full tuition reimbursements, research assistantships with full tuition reimbursements, Federal Work-Study, institutionally sponsored loans, scholarships/grants, traineeships, health care benefits, and tuition waivers (partial) available. Financial award application deadline: 1/15; financial award applicants required to submit CSS PROFILE or FAFSA. *Faculty research:* Biophysics, cell signaling and gene regulation, human genetics, diabetes and obesity, neuroscience. *Unit head:* Roger Cone, Chair, 615-322-7000, Fax: 615-343-0490. *Application contact:* Michelle Grundy, Assistant Director, 800-373-0675, E-mail: michelle.grundy@vanderbilt.edu.

Vanderbilt University, School of Medicine, Program in Chemical and Physical Biology, Nashville, TN 37240-1001. Offers PhD. *Degree requirements:* For doctorate, comprehensive exam, thesis/dissertation, dissertation defense. *Entrance requirements:* For doctorate, GRE, 3 letters of recommendation, interview by invitation. Additional exam requirements/recommendations for international students: Required—TOEFL. Electronic applications accepted. *Faculty research:* Mathematical modeling, enzyme kinetics, structural biology, genomics, proteomics and mass spectrometry.

Washington State University, Graduate School, College of Sciences, School of Molecular Biosciences, Program in Biochemistry and Biophysics, Pullman, WA 99164. Offers MS, PhD. Terminal master's awarded for partial completion of doctoral program. *Degree requirements:* For master's, thesis or alternative, oral exam; for doctorate, comprehensive exam, thesis/dissertation, oral exam, written exam. *Entrance requirements:* For master's and doctorate, GRE General Test, minimum GPA of 3.0. Additional exam requirements/recommendations for international students: Required—TOEFL (minimum score 550 paper-based; 213 computer-based). Electronic applications accepted. *Faculty research:* Gene regulation, signal transduction, protein export, reproductive biology, DNA repair.

Wright State University, School of Graduate Studies, College of Science and Mathematics, Department of Neuroscience, Cell Biology, and Physiology, Dayton, OH 45435. Offers anatomy (MS); physiology and biophysics (MS). *Degree requirements:* For master's, thesis optional. *Entrance requirements:* Additional exam requirements/recommendations for international students: Required—TOEFL. *Faculty research:* Reproductive cell biology, neurobiology of pain, neurohistochemistry.

Yale University, Graduate School of Arts and Sciences, Department of Molecular Biophysics and Biochemistry, New Haven, CT 06520. Offers PhD. *Degree requirements:* For doctorate, thesis/dissertation. *Entrance requirements:* For doctorate, GRE General Test, GRE Subject Test.

Molecular Biophysics

Baylor College of Medicine, Graduate School of Biomedical Sciences, Program in Structural and Computational Biology and Molecular Biophysics, Houston, TX 77030-3498. Offers PhD, MD/PhD. *Faculty:* 71 full-time (11 women). *Students:* 48 full-time (19 women); includes 5 minority (3 Asian Americans or Pacific Islanders, 2 Hispanic Americans), 18 international. Average age 25. In 2009, 6 doctorates awarded. *Degree requirements:* For doctorate, thesis/dissertation, public defense. *Entrance requirements:* For doctorate, GRE General Test, GRE Subject Test (strongly recommended), minimum GPA of 3.0. Additional exam requirements/recommendations for international students: Required—TOEFL. *Application deadline:* For fall admission, 1/1 for domestic students. Application fee: $0. Electronic applications accepted. *Financial support:* In 2009–10, 48 students received support; fellowships, research assistantships, career-related internships or fieldwork, Federal Work-Study, institutionally sponsored loans, health care benefits, and students receive a scholarship unless there are grant funds available to pay tuition available. Financial award applicants required to submit FAFSA. *Faculty research:* X-ray and electron crystallography, light and electron microscopy, computer image reconstruction, molecular spectroscopy. *Unit head:* Dr. Wah Chiu, Director, 713-798-6985. *Application contact:* Lourdes Fernandez, Graduate Program Administrator, 713-798-6557, Fax: 713-798-6325.

See Close-Up on page 259.

California Institute of Technology, Division of Biology and Division of Chemistry and Chemical Engineering, Biochemistry and Molecular Biophysics Graduate Option, Pasadena, CA 91125-0001. Offers PhD. *Degree requirements:* For doctorate, thesis/dissertation, qualifying exam. *Entrance requirements:* For doctorate, GRE General Test. Additional exam requirements/recommendations for international students: Required—TOEFL. Electronic applications accepted.

California Institute of Technology, Division of Chemistry and Chemical Engineering, Program in Biochemistry and Molecular Biophysics, Pasadena, CA 91125-0001. Offers MS, PhD.

Molecular Biophysics

California Institute of Technology (continued)

Part-time and evening/weekend programs available. Postbaccalaureate distance learning degree programs offered (minimal on-campus study). *Faculty:* 16 full-time (5 women). *Students:* 51 full-time (20 women). Average age 27. 114 applicants, 23% accepted, 11 enrolled. In 2009, 1 master's, 5 doctorates awarded. Terminal master's awarded for partial completion of doctoral program. *Degree requirements:* For master's, thesis; for doctorate, thesis/dissertation. *Entrance requirements:* Additional exam requirements/recommendations for international students: Required—TOEFL; Recommended—IELTS, TWE. *Application deadline:* For fall admission, 1/1 for domestic and international students. Application fee: $80. Electronic applications accepted. *Financial support:* Fellowships, research assistantships, teaching assistantships, Federal Work-Study, institutionally sponsored loans, scholarships/grants, traineeships, health care benefits, and unspecified assistantships available. Financial award application deadline: 1/1. *Unit head:* Prof. Jacqueline K. Barton, Chair, Chemistry and Chemical Engineering, 626-395-3646, Fax: 626-568-8824, E-mail: jkbarton@caltech.edu. *Application contact:* Alison Ross, Option Secretary, 626-395-6446, E-mail: aross@caltech.edu.

Carnegie Mellon University, Mellon College of Science, Joint Pitt + CMU Molecular Biophysics and Structural Biology Graduate Program, Pittsburgh, PA 15213-3891. Offers PhD. *Degree requirements:* For doctorate, comprehensive exam, thesis/dissertation. *Entrance requirements:* For doctorate, GRE General Test. Additional exam requirements/recommendations for international students: Required—TOEFL (minimum score 600 paper-based; 250 computer-based; 100 iBT), IELTS (minimum score 7). Electronic applications accepted. *Faculty research:* Structural biology, protein dynamics and folding, computational biophysics, molecular informatics, membrane biophysics and ion channels, NMR, x-ray crystallography cryaelectron microscopy.

Duke University, Graduate School, Program in Structural Biology and Biophysics, Durham, NC 27710. Offers Certificate. Students must be enrolled in a participating PhD program. *Faculty:* 25 full-time. *Students:* 1 (woman) full-time. 26 applicants, 23% accepted, 0 enrolled. *Entrance requirements:* For degree, GRE General Test, GRE Subject Test. Additional exam requirements/recommendations for international students: Required—TOEFL (minimum score 550 paper-based; 213 computer-based; 83 iBT), IELTS (minimum score 7). *Application deadline:* For fall admission, 12/8 priority date for domestic and international students. Application fee: $75. *Financial support:* Application deadline: 12/31. *Unit head:* David Richardson, Director of Graduate Studies, 919-684-6559, Fax: 919-684-8346, E-mail: cmbtgp@biochem.duke.edu. *Application contact:* Cynthia Robertson, Associate Dean for Enrollment Services, 919-684-3913, E-mail: grad-admissions@duke.edu.

Florida State University, The Graduate School, College of Arts and Sciences, Program in Molecular Biophysics, Tallahassee, FL 32306. Offers biochemistry, molecular and cell biology (PhD); computational structural biology (PhD); molecular biophysics (PhD). *Faculty:* 49 full-time (6 women). *Students:* 22 full-time (8 women); includes 6 minority (5 Asian Americans or Pacific Islanders, 1 Hispanic American). Average age 28. 30 applicants, 33% accepted, 7 enrolled. In 2009, 5 doctorates awarded. *Degree requirements:* For doctorate, comprehensive exam, thesis/dissertation, teaching 1 term in professor's major department. *Entrance requirements:* For doctorate, GRE General Test. Additional exam requirements/recommendations for international students: Required—TOEFL (minimum score 600 paper-based; 250 computer-based; 100 iBT). *Application deadline:* For fall admission, 2/15 for domestic students, 3/15 for international students; for spring admission, 11/2 for international students. Applications are processed on a rolling basis. Application fee: $30. Electronic applications accepted. *Expenses:* Tuition, state resident: full-time $7413. Tuition, nonresident: full-time $22,567. *Financial support:* In 2009–10, 21 students received support, including fellowships with partial tuition reimbursements available (averaging $21,000 per year), 18 research assistantships with partial tuition reimbursements available (averaging $21,000 per year), 4 teaching assistantships with partial tuition reimbursements available (averaging $21,000 per year); scholarships/grants, health care benefits, and unspecified assistantships also available. Financial award applicants required to submit FAFSA. *Faculty research:* Protein and nucleic acid structure and function, membrane protein structure, computational biophysics, 3-D image reconstruction. Total annual research expenditures: $1.4 million. *Unit head:* Dr. Geoffrey Strouse, Director, 850-644-0056, Fax: 850-644-7244, E-mail: strouse@chem.fsu.edu. *Application contact:* Dr. Kerry Maddox, Academic Coordinator, Graduate Programs, 850-644-1012, Fax: 850-644-7244, E-mail: bkmaddox@sb.fsu.edu.

Illinois Institute of Technology, Graduate College, College of Science and Letters, Department of Biological, Chemical and Physical Sciences, Biology Division, Chicago, IL 60616-3793. Offers biology (MBS, MS, PhD); molecular biochemistry and biophysics (MS, PhD). Part-time and evening/weekend programs available. Postbaccalaureate distance learning degree programs offered (no on-campus study). *Faculty:* 12 full-time (4 women), 2 part-time/adjunct (0 women). *Students:* 98 full-time (50 women), 80 part-time (45 women); includes 15 minority (6 African Americans, 6 Asian Americans or Pacific Islanders, 3 Hispanic Americans), 119 international. Average age 27. 330 applicants, 43% accepted, 57 enrolled. In 2009, 30 master's, 5 doctorates awarded. Terminal master's awarded for partial completion of doctoral program. *Degree requirements:* For master's, comprehensive exam, thesis (for some programs); for doctorate, comprehensive exam, thesis/dissertation. *Entrance requirements:* For master's and doctorate, GRE General Test, minimum undergraduate GPA of 3.0. Additional exam requirements/recommendations for international students: Required—TOEFL (minimum score 550 paper-based; 213 computer-based; 80 iBT). *Application deadline:* For fall admission, 5/1 for domestic and international students; for spring admission, 1/5 for domestic and international students. Applications are processed on a rolling basis. Application fee: $40. Electronic applications accepted. *Expenses:* Tuition: Full-time $17,550; part-time $888 per credit hour. Required fees: $850; $7.50 per credit hour. One-time fee: $50 full-time. Full-time tuition and fees vary according to program. *Financial support:* In 2009–10, 1 fellowship with full tuition reimbursement (averaging $18,000 per year), 6 research assistantships with full tuition reimbursements (averaging $15,500 per year), 11 teaching assistantships with full tuition reimbursements (averaging $15,500 per year) were awarded; career-related internships or fieldwork, Federal Work-Study, institutionally sponsored loans, scholarships/grants, traineeships, health care benefits, tuition waivers (partial), and unspecified assistantships also available. Support available to part-time students. Financial award applicants required to submit FAFSA. *Faculty research:* Structure of muscle and collagen using x-ray scattering, prostate cancer, identification and analysis of anti-cancer drugs, x-ray crystallography of proteins, developmental biology of olfaction, molecular analysis of foodbourne pathogens. Total annual research expenditures: $10.5 million. *Unit head:* Dr. Benjamin C. Stark, Professor and Associate Chair, 312-567-3488, Fax: 312-567-3494, E-mail: starkb@iit.edu. *Application contact:* Morgan Frederick, Assistant Director of Graduate Communications, 866-472-3448, Fax: 312-567-3138, E-mail: inquiry.grad@iit.edu.

The Johns Hopkins University, School of Medicine, Graduate Programs in Medicine, Program in Molecular Biophysics, Baltimore, MD 21218-2699. Offers molecular biophysics (MS, PhD). *Faculty:* 45 full-time (10 women). *Students:* 24 full-time (9 women); includes 6 minority (4 Asian Americans or Pacific Islanders, 2 Hispanic Americans), 1 international. Average age 25. 82 applicants, 38% accepted, 11 enrolled. In 2009, 7 doctorates awarded. *Degree requirements:* For doctorate, comprehensive exam, thesis/dissertation, oral exam, thesis defense. *Entrance requirements:* For doctorate, GRE. Additional exam requirements/recommendations for international students: Required—TOEFL (minimum score 600 paper-based; 250 computer-based), IELTS; Recommended—TWE. *Application deadline:* For winter admission, 1/15 for domestic students. Applications are processed on a rolling basis. Application fee: $65. Electronic applications accepted. *Financial support:* In 2009–10, 2 fellowships with full tuition reimbursements (averaging $27,125 per year), 22 research assistantships (averaging $25,200 per year) were awarded; scholarships/grants, traineeships, health care benefits, and tuition waivers (full) also available. *Faculty research:* Protein folding and dynamics; membranes and membrane proteins; structural biology and prediction; RNA biophysics; enzymes and metabolic pathways; computation and theory; DNA protein interactions; single molecule studies; protein design and evolution. *Unit head:* Dr. L. Mario Amzel, Professor and Director, 410-955-8712, Fax: 410-502-6910, E-mail: mario@neruda.med.jhmi.edu. *Application contact:* Kathleen M. Kolish, Administrative Manager, 410-955-8712, Fax: 410-502-6910, E-mail: kkolish@jhmi.edu.

Rutgers, The State University of New Jersey, New Brunswick, Graduate School-New Brunswick, BioMaPS Institute for Quantitative Biology, Piscataway, NJ 08854-8097. Offers computational biology and molecular biophysics (PhD). *Degree requirements:* For doctorate, comprehensive exam, thesis/dissertation. *Entrance requirements:* For doctorate, GRE. Additional exam requirements/recommendations for international students: Required—TOEFL. Electronic applications accepted. *Faculty research:* Structural biology, systems biology, bioinformatics, translational medicine, genomics.

Texas Tech University Health Sciences Center, Graduate School of Biomedical Sciences, Department of Cell Physiology and Molecular Biophysics, Lubbock, TX 79430. Offers MS, PhD, MD/PhD. Terminal master's awarded for partial completion of doctoral program. *Degree requirements:* For master's, thesis; for doctorate, thesis/dissertation. *Entrance requirements:* For master's and doctorate, GRE General Test, minimum GPA of 3.4. Additional exam requirements/recommendations for international students: Required—TOEFL. Electronic applications accepted. *Faculty research:* Cardiovascular physiology, neurophysiology, renal physiology, respiratory physiology.

University of Massachusetts Amherst, Graduate School, Interdisciplinary Programs, Program in Molecular and Cellular Biology, Amherst, MA 01003. Offers biological chemistry and molecular biophysics (PhD); biomedicine (PhD); cellular and developmental biology (PhD). Part-time programs available. *Faculty:* 2 full-time (0 women). *Students:* 30 full-time (16 women), 48 part-time (26 women); includes 15 minority (4 African Americans, 1 American Indian/Alaska Native, 3 Asian Americans or Pacific Islanders, 7 Hispanic Americans), 23 international. Average age 27. 140 applicants, 23% accepted, 19 enrolled. In 2009, 12 doctorates awarded. Terminal master's awarded for partial completion of doctoral program. *Degree requirements:* For doctorate, comprehensive exam, thesis/dissertation. *Entrance requirements:* For doctorate, GRE General Test. Additional exam requirements/recommendations for international students: Required—TOEFL (minimum score 550 paper-based; 213 computer-based; 80 iBT), IELTS (minimum score 6.5). *Application deadline:* For fall admission, 12/1 for domestic and international students. Applications are processed on a rolling basis. Application fee: $50 ($65 for international students). Electronic applications accepted. *Expenses:* Tuition, state resident: full-time $2640; part-time $110 per credit. Tuition, nonresident: full-time $9936; part-time $414 per credit. Tuition and fees vary according to course load. *Financial support:* In 2009–10, 11 research assistantships with full tuition reimbursements (averaging $2,590 per year), 3 teaching assistantships with full tuition reimbursements (averaging $3,303 per year) were awarded; fellowships, career-related internships or fieldwork, Federal Work-Study, scholarships/grants, traineeships, health care benefits, tuition waivers (full), and unspecified assistantships also available. Support available to part-time students. Financial award application deadline: 12/1. *Unit head:* Dr. David J. Gross, Graduate Program Director, 413-545-3246, Fax: 413-545-1812. *Application contact:* Jean M. Ames, Supervisor of Admissions, 413-545-0722, Fax: 413-577-0010, E-mail: gradadm@grad.umass.edu.

University of Pennsylvania, School of Medicine, Biomedical Graduate Studies, Graduate Group in Biochemistry and Molecular Biophysics, Philadelphia, PA 19104. Offers PhD, MD/PhD, VMD/PhD. *Faculty:* 74. *Students:* 77 full-time (32 women); includes 21 minority (4 African Americans, 10 Asian Americans or Pacific Islanders, 7 Hispanic Americans), 9 international. 108 applicants, 33% accepted, 14 enrolled. In 2009, 11 doctorates awarded. *Degree requirements:* For doctorate, thesis/dissertation. *Entrance requirements:* For doctorate, GRE General Test. Additional exam requirements/recommendations for international students: Required—TOEFL. *Application deadline:* For fall admission, 12/8 priority date for domestic and international students. Applications are processed on a rolling basis. Application fee: $70. Electronic applications accepted. *Expenses:* Tuition: Full-time $25,660; part-time $4758 per course. Required fees: $2152; $270 per course. Tuition and fees vary according to course load, degree level and program. *Financial support:* In 2009–10, 77 students received support; fellowships, research assistantships, scholarships/grants, traineeships, and unspecified assistantships available. *Faculty research:* Biochemistry of cell differentiation, tissue culture, intermediary metabolism, structure of proteins and nucleic acids, biochemical genetics. *Unit head:* Dr. Kathryn Ferguson, Chairperson, 215-573-7288. *Application contact:* Ruth Keris, Graduate Group Administrator, 215-898-4639, Fax: 215-573-2085, E-mail: keris@mail.med.upenn.edu.

University of Pittsburgh, School of Medicine and School of Arts and Sciences, Joint Pitt + CMU Molecular Biophysics and Structural Biology Graduate Program, Pittsburgh, PA 15260. Offers PhD. *Faculty:* 51 full-time (16 women). *Students:* 19 full-time (6 women); includes 3 minority (2 Asian Americans or Pacific Islanders, 1 Hispanic American), 6 international. Average age 26. 70 applicants, 11% accepted, 6 enrolled. *Degree requirements:* For doctorate, comprehensive exam, thesis/dissertation. *Entrance requirements:* For doctorate, GRE General Test. Additional exam requirements/recommendations for international students: Required—TOEFL (minimum score 600 paper-based; 250 computer-based; 100 iBT), IELTS (minimum score 7). *Application deadline:* For fall admission, 12/15 priority date for domestic and international students. Application fee: $0. Electronic applications accepted. *Expenses:* Tuition, state resident: full-time $16,402; part-time $665 per credit. Tuition, nonresident: full-time $28,694; part-time $1175 per credit. Required fees: $690; $175 per term. Tuition and fees vary according to program. *Financial support:* In 2009–10, 3 fellowships with full tuition reimbursements (averaging $27,326 per year), 13 research assistantships with full tuition reimbursements (averaging $24,650 per year) were awarded; institutionally sponsored loans, scholarships/grants, traineeships, and unspecified assistantships also available. *Faculty research:* Structural biology, protein dynamics and folding, computational biophysics, molecular informatics, membrane biophysics and ion channels, x-ray crystallography cryaelectron microscopy. *Unit head:* Dr. Angela M. Gronenborn, Director, 412-648-8957, Fax: 412-648-1077, E-mail: mbsbinfo@medschool.pitt.edu. *Application contact:* Jennifer L. Walker, Program Coordinator, 412-648-8957, Fax: 412-648-1077, E-mail: mbsbinfo@medschool.pitt.edu.

The University of Texas Medical Branch, Graduate School of Biomedical Sciences, Program in Cellular Physiology and Molecular Biophysics, Galveston, TX 77555. Offers MS, PhD. *Students:* 3 full-time (0 women), 2 international. Average age 30. In 2009, 3 doctorates awarded. *Degree requirements:* For master's, thesis or alternative; for doctorate, thesis/dissertation. *Entrance requirements:* For master's and doctorate, GRE General Test. Additional exam requirements/recommendations for international students: Required—TOEFL (minimum score 550 paper-based; 213 computer-based). *Application deadline:* Applications are processed on a rolling basis. Application fee: $30 ($75 for international students). Electronic applications accepted. *Financial support:* In 2009–10, fellowships (averaging $25,000 per year), research assistantships with full tuition reimbursements (averaging $25,000 per year) were awarded. Financial award applicants required to submit FAFSA. *Unit head:* Dr. Mark R. Hellmich, Director, 409-772-2124, Fax: 409-762-1826, E-mail: mhellmic@utmb.edu. *Application contact:* Lisa Davis, Coordinator for Special Programs, 409-772-2124, Fax: 409-762-1826, E-mail: limdavis@utmb.edu.

The University of Texas Southwestern Medical Center at Dallas, Southwestern Graduate School of Biomedical Sciences, Division of Basic Science, Program in Molecular Biophysics, Dallas, TX 75390. Offers PhD. *Faculty:* 34 full-time (6 women). *Students:* 31 full-time (12 women), 1 part-time (0 women); includes 8 minority (2 African Americans, 3 Asian Americans or Pacific Islanders, 3 Hispanic Americans), 13 international. Average age 26. 946 applicants, 22% accepted. In 2009, 8 doctorates awarded. *Degree requirements:* For doctorate, thesis/dissertation, qualifying exam. *Entrance requirements:* For doctorate, GRE General Test, minimum GPA of 3.0. Additional exam requirements/recommendations for international students: Required—TOEFL. *Application deadline:* For fall admission, 12/15 priority date for domestic students. Applications are processed on a rolling basis. Application fee: $0. Electronic applications accepted. *Financial support:* Fellowships, research assistantships, institutionally sponsored loans and traineeships available. *Faculty research:* Optical spectroscopy, x-ray crystallography, protein chemistry, ion channels, contractile and cytoskeletal proteins. *Unit head:* Dr.

Kevin Gardner, Chair, 214-645-6365, Fax: 214-645-6353, E-mail: kevin.gardner@utsouthwestern.edu. *Application contact:* Dr. Nancy E. Street, Associate Dean, 214-648-6708, Fax: 214-648-2102, E-mail: nancy.street@utsouthwestern.edu.

Washington University in St. Louis, Graduate School of Arts and Sciences, Division of Biology and Biomedical Sciences, Program in Molecular Biophysics, St. Louis, MO 63130-4899. Offers PhD. *Degree requirements:* For doctorate, thesis/dissertation. *Entrance requirements:* For doctorate, GRE General Test, GRE Subject Test. Electronic applications accepted.

Yale University, School of Medicine and Graduate School of Arts and Sciences, Combined Program in Biological and Biomedical Sciences (BBS), Molecular Biophysics and Biochemistry Track, New Haven, CT 06520. Offers PhD, MD/PhD. *Degree requirements:* For doctorate, thesis/dissertation. *Entrance requirements:* For doctorate, GRE General Test. Additional exam requirements/recommendations for international students: Required—TOEFL. *Application deadline:* For fall admission, 12/6 for domestic and international students. Electronic applications accepted. *Financial support:* Fellowships, research assistantships available. *Unit head:* Dr. Mark Solomon, Director of Graduate Studies, 203-432-5562, Fax: 203-432-5832. *Application contact:* Nessie Stewart, Graduate Registrar, 203-432-5662, Fax: 203-432-6178, E-mail: nessie.stewart@yale.edu.

Radiation Biology

Auburn University, College of Veterinary Medicine and Graduate School, Graduate Programs in Veterinary Medicine, Auburn University, AL 36849. Offers biomedical sciences (MS, PhD), including anatomy, physiology and pharmacology (MS), biomedical sciences (PhD), clinical sciences (MS), large animal surgery and medicine (MS), pathobiology (MS), radiology (MS), small animal surgery and medicine (MS); DVM/MS. Part-time programs available. *Faculty:* 100 full-time (40 women), 5 part-time/adjunct (1 woman). *Students:* 17 full-time (6 women), 51 part-time (35 women); includes 8 minority (2 African Americans, 1 American Indian/Alaska Native, 3 Asian Americans or Pacific Islanders, 2 Hispanic Americans), 22 international. Average age 31. 70 applicants, 34% accepted, 10 enrolled. In 2009, 12 master's, 7 doctorates awarded. *Degree requirements:* For doctorate, thesis/dissertation. *Entrance requirements:* For master's, GRE General Test; for doctorate, GRE General Test, GRE Subject Test. *Application deadline:* For fall admission, 7/7 for domestic students; for spring admission, 11/24 for domestic students. Applications are processed on a rolling basis. Application fee: $50 ($60 for international students). Electronic applications accepted. *Expenses:* Tuition, state resident: full-time $6240. Tuition, nonresident: full-time $18,720. International tuition: $18,938 full-time. Required fees: $492. Tuition and fees vary according to course load, program and reciprocity agreements. *Financial support:* Research assistantships, teaching assistantships, Federal Work-Study available. Support available to part-time students. Financial award application deadline: 3/15; financial award applicants required to submit FAFSA. *Unit head:* Dr. Timothy R. Boosinger, Dean, 334-844-4546. *Application contact:* Dr. George Flowers, Dean of the Graduate School, 334-844-2125.

Austin Peay State University, College of Graduate Studies, College of Science and Mathematics, Department of Biology, Clarksville, TN 37044. Offers clinical laboratory science (MS); radiologic science (MS). Part-time programs available. *Faculty:* 6 full-time (1 woman). *Students:* 5 full-time (all women), 18 part-time (11 women); includes 6 minority (1 African American, 5 Hispanic Americans), 1 international. Average age 29. 19 applicants, 100% accepted, 9 enrolled. In 2009, 4 master's awarded. *Degree requirements:* For master's, comprehensive exam, thesis optional. *Entrance requirements:* For master's, GRE General Test, 3 letters of recommendation, minimum undergraduate GPA of 2.5. Additional exam requirements/recommendations for international students: Required—TOEFL (minimum score 500 paper-based; 173 computer-based). *Application deadline:* For fall admission, 7/27 priority date for domestic students; for spring admission, 12/17 priority date for domestic students. Applications are processed on a rolling basis. Application fee: $25. Electronic applications accepted. *Expenses:* Tuition, state resident: full-time $6160; part-time $608 per credit hour. Tuition, nonresident: full-time $17,080; part-time $854 per credit hour. Required fees: $1224; $61.20 per credit hour. *Financial support:* In 2009–10, 10 students received support, including 10 research assistantships with full tuition reimbursements available (averaging $5,184 per year); career-related internships or fieldwork, Federal Work-Study, institutionally sponsored loans, scholarships/grants, and unspecified assistantships also available. Support available to part-time students. Financial award application deadline: 3/1. *Faculty research:* Non-paint source pollution, amphibian biomonitoring, aquatic toxicology, biological indicators of water quality, taxonomy. *Unit head:* Dr. Don Dailey, Chair, 931-221-7781, Fax: 931-221-6323, E-mail: daileyd@apsu.edu. *Application contact:* Dr. Dixie Dennis Pinder, Dean, College of Graduate Studies, 931-221-7662, Fax: 931-221-7641, E-mail: dennisdi@apsu.edu.

Colorado State University, College of Veterinary Medicine and Biomedical Sciences, Department of Environmental and Radiological Health Sciences, Fort Collins, CO 80523-1681. Offers environmental health (MS, PhD); radiological health sciences (MS, PhD). *Faculty:* 22 full-time (8 women), 3 part-time/adjunct (0 women). *Students:* 66 full-time (39 women), 37 part-time (22 women); includes 12 minority (4 African Americans, 2 American Indian/Alaska Native, 4 Asian Americans or Pacific Islanders, 2 Hispanic Americans), 8 international. Average age 29. 88 applicants, 76% accepted, 49 enrolled. In 2009, 25 master's, 4 doctorates awarded. Terminal master's awarded for partial completion of doctoral program. *Degree requirements:* For master's, thesis (for some programs), publishable paper; for doctorate, comprehensive exam, thesis/dissertation, publishable paper. *Entrance requirements:* For master's, GRE General Test, 1 year of course work in biology lab and chemistry lab, 1 semester of course work in organic chemistry, course work in calculus, resume, letters of recommendation; for doctorate, GRE General Test, 1 year of course work in biology lab and chemistry lab, 1 semester of course work in organic chemistry, course work in calculus, resume, letters of recommendation, evidence of research capability. Additional exam requirements/recommendations for international students: Required—TOEFL (minimum score 550 paper-based; 213 computer-based). *Application deadline:* For fall admission, 3/1 for domestic students, 2/1 priority date for international students; for spring admission, 10/1 for domestic students. Application fee: $50. Electronic applications accepted. *Expenses:* Tuition, state resident: full-time $6434; part-time $359.10 per credit. Tuition, nonresident: full-time $18,116; part-time $1006.45 per credit. Required fees: $1496; $83 per credit. *Financial support:* In 2009–10, 23 students received support, including 5 fellowships with partial tuition reimbursements available (averaging $38,888 per year), 14 research assistantships (averaging $16,063 per year), 4 teaching assistantships with full tuition reimbursements available (averaging $10,688 per year); career-related internships or fieldwork, Federal Work-Study, institutionally sponsored loans, traineeships, and unspecified assistantships also available. Support available to part-time students. Financial award application deadline: 2/1. *Faculty research:* Epidemiology, toxicology, industrial hygiene,

occupational health, radiation therapy. Total annual research expenditures: $9 million. *Unit head:* Dr. Jac A. Nickoloff, Head, 970-491-6674, Fax: 970-491-0623, E-mail: j.nickoloff@colostate.edu. *Application contact:* Jeanne A. Brockway, Graduate Program Coordinator, 970-491-5003, Fax: 970-491-0623, E-mail: jeanne.brockway@colostate.edu.

Georgetown University, Graduate School of Arts and Sciences, Programs in Biomedical Sciences, Department of Health Physics, Washington, DC 20057. Offers health physics (MS); radiobiology (MS). *Degree requirements:* For master's, thesis. *Entrance requirements:* Additional exam requirements/recommendations for international students: Required—TOEFL.

Université de Sherbrooke, Faculty of Medicine and Health Sciences, Graduate Programs in Medicine, Program in Radiobiology, Sherbrooke, QC J1H 5N4, Canada. Offers M Sc, PhD. Terminal master's awarded for partial completion of doctoral program. *Degree requirements:* For master's, thesis; for doctorate, thesis/dissertation. Electronic applications accepted. *Faculty research:* DNA repair, physiochemical actions of radiation, radiopharmacy, phototherapy, imaging.

The University of Iowa, Roy J. and Lucille A. Carver College of Medicine and Graduate College, Graduate Programs in Medicine, Program in Free Radical and Radiation Biology, Iowa City, IA 52242-1316. Offers MS, PhD. Part-time programs available. *Faculty:* 6 full-time (2 women). *Students:* 15 full-time (5 women). Average age 26. 6 applicants, 67% accepted, 4 enrolled. In 2009, 1 master's, 1 doctorate awarded. *Degree requirements:* For doctorate, thesis/dissertation. *Entrance requirements:* For master's and doctorate, GRE. *Application deadline:* For fall admission, 5/31 priority date for domestic and international students; for spring admission, 10/31 for domestic and international students. Applications are processed on a rolling basis. Application fee: $60 ($85 for international students). *Financial support:* In 2009–10, fellowships with partial tuition reimbursements (averaging $23,500 per year), research assistantships with tuition reimbursements (averaging $23,500 per year) were awarded; traineeships, health care benefits, tuition waivers (partial), and unspecified assistantships also available. *Faculty research:* Radiation injury and cellular repair, cell proliferation kinetics, free radical biology, tumor control, PET imaging, EPR. Total annual research expenditures: $1 million. *Unit head:* Dr. Douglas R. Spitz, Head, 319-335-8019, Fax: 319-335-8039. *Application contact:* Jennifer K. DeWitte, Grant/Program Administrator, 319-335-8164, Fax: 319-335-8039, E-mail: jennifer-dewitte@uiowa.edu.

University of Oklahoma Health Sciences Center, College of Medicine and Graduate College, Graduate Programs in Medicine, Department of Radiological Sciences, Oklahoma City, OK 73190. Offers medical radiation physics (MS, PhD), including diagnostic radiology, nuclear medicine, radiation therapy, ultrasound. Part-time programs available. *Faculty:* 10 full-time (4 women). *Students:* 11 part-time (2 women), 2 international. Average age 28. 53 applicants, 19% accepted, 3 enrolled. In 2009, 4 master's awarded. Terminal master's awarded for partial completion of doctoral program. *Degree requirements:* For master's, thesis; for doctorate, thesis/dissertation. *Entrance requirements:* For master's, GRE General Test; for doctorate, GRE General Test, 3 letters of recommendation. Additional exam requirements/recommendations for international students: Required—TOEFL. *Application deadline:* For fall admission, 4/1 priority date for domestic students; for spring admission, 10/1 for domestic students. Applications are processed on a rolling basis. Application fee: $50. *Expenses:* Tuition, state resident: full-time $3120; part-time $156 per credit hour. Tuition, nonresident: full-time $11,314; part-time $409.70 per credit hour. Required fees: $1471; $51.20 per credit hour. $223.25 per term. *Financial support:* In 2009–10, 2 research assistantships (averaging $17,000 per year) were awarded; fellowships, career-related internships or fieldwork and institutionally sponsored loans also available. Support available to part-time students. Financial award application deadline: 7/1. *Faculty research:* Monte Carlo applications in radiation therapy, observer-performed studies in diagnostic radiology, error analysis in gated cardiac nuclear medicine studies, nuclear medicine absorbed fraction determinations. *Unit head:* Dr. Susan Edwards, Chair, 405-271-5132, E-mail: susan-edwards@ouhsc.edu. *Application contact:* Dr. Dee Wu, Graduate Liaison, 405-270-8001, E-mail: dee-wu@ouhsc.edu.

The University of Texas Southwestern Medical Center at Dallas, Southwestern Graduate School of Biomedical Sciences, Division of Clinical Science, Radiological Sciences Program, Dallas, TX 75390. Offers MS, PhD. *Faculty:* 23 full-time (0 women), 2 part-time/adjunct (0 women). *Students:* 14 full-time (4 women), 1 part-time (0 women); includes 1 minority (Asian American or Pacific Islander), 3 international. Average age 26. 42 applicants, 7% accepted, 0 enrolled. In 2009, 1 doctorate awarded. Terminal master's awarded for partial completion of doctoral program. *Degree requirements:* For master's, thesis; for doctorate, comprehensive exam, thesis/dissertation. *Entrance requirements:* For master's and doctorate, GRE General Test. Additional exam requirements/recommendations for international students: Required—TOEFL. *Application deadline:* For fall admission, 5/15 for domestic students. Application fee: $0. *Financial support:* In 2009–10, 2 research assistantships were awarded; institutionally sponsored loans and scholarships/grants also available. Financial award application deadline: 3/1; financial award applicants required to submit FAFSA. *Faculty research:* Medical physics, nuclear medicine, noninvasive NMR methods, ultrasound, pathophysiological ITin vivo RO investigation. *Unit head:* Dr. Peter P. Antich, Chair, 214-648-2856, Fax: 214-648-2991, E-mail: peter.antich@utsouthwestern.edu. *Application contact:* Kay Emerson, Program Assistant, 214-648-2503, Fax: 214-648-2991, E-mail: kay.emerson@utsouthwestern.edu.

HARVARD UNIVERSITY

Biophysics Program

Program of Study	The Committee on Higher Degrees in Biophysics offers a program of study leading to the Ph.D. degree. The committee comprises senior representatives of the Departments of Chemistry and Chemical Biology, Physics, and Molecular and Cellular Biology; the Division of Engineering and Applied Physics; and the Division of Medical Sciences. Students receive sufficient training in physics, biology, and chemistry to enable them to apply the concepts and methods of the physical sciences to the solution of biological problems.

An initial goal of the Biophysics Program is to provide an introduction through courses and seminars to several of the diverse areas of biophysics, such as structural molecular biology, cell and membrane biophysics, neurobiology, molecular genetics, physical biochemistry, and theoretical biophysics. The program is flexible, and special effort has been devoted to minimizing course work and other formal requirements. Students engage in several research rotations during their first two years. The qualifying examination is taken at the end of the second year to determine admission to candidacy. Students undertake dissertation research as early as possible in the field and subject of their choice. Opportunities for dissertation research are available in a number of special fields. The Ph.D. requires not less than three years devoted to advanced studies, including dissertation research and the dissertation. The Committee on Higher Degrees in Biophysics anticipates that it takes an average of five years, with the maximum being six years, to complete this program.

Research Facilities
Many more of the University's modern research facilities are available to the biophysics student because of the interdepartmental nature of the program. Research programs may be pursued in the Departments of Chemistry and Chemical Biology, Molecular and Cellular Biology, Applied Physics, and Engineering Sciences in Cambridge as well as in the Departments of Biological Chemistry and Molecular Pharmacology, Genetics, Microbiology and Molecular Genetics, Neurobiology, Virology, and Cell Biology in the Harvard Medical School Division of Medical Sciences. Research may also be pursued in the Harvard School of Public Health, the Dana Farber Cancer Institute, Children's Hospital, Massachusetts General Hospital, Beth Israel Hospital, and more than ten other Harvard-affiliated institutions located throughout the cities.

Financial Aid
In 2010–11, all graduate students receive a stipend ($30,600 for twelve months) and full tuition and health fees ($37,930). A semester of teaching is required in the second year. Students are strongly encouraged to apply for fellowships from such sources as the National Science Foundation, the NDSEG, the Hertz Foundation, and the Ford Foundation. Full-time Ph.D. candidates in good academic standing are guaranteed full financial support through their sixth year of study or throughout their academic program if less than six years.

Cost of Study
Tuition and health fees for the 2010–11 academic year are $37,930. After two years in residence, students are eligible for a reduced rate (currently $12,048).

Living and Housing Costs
Accommodations in graduate residence halls are available at rents ranging from $5674 to $8910 per academic year. In addition, there are approximately 1,500 apartments available for graduate students in Harvard-owned buildings. Applications may be obtained from the Harvard University Housing Office, which also maintains a list of available private rooms, houses, and apartments in the vicinity.

Student Group
On average, the program enrolls 50 students annually. Currently, 16 women and 8 international students are enrolled in the program. Biophysics students intermingle in both their research and their social life with graduate students from the many other departments where research in the biophysical sciences is carried out.

Location
The Biophysics Program maintains a dual-campus orientation in the neighboring cities of Cambridge and Boston. Their proximity provides for a wide range of academic, cultural, extracurricular, and recreational opportunities, and the large numbers of theaters, museums, libraries, and universities contribute to enrich the scientific and cultural life of students. Because New England is compact in area, it is easy to reach countryside, mountains, and seacoast for winter and summer sports or just for a change of scenery.

The University
Established in 1636 in the Massachusetts Bay Colony, Harvard has grown to become a complex of many facilities whose educational vitality, social commitment, and level of cultural achievement contribute to make the University a leader in the academic world. Comprising more than 15,000 students and 3,000 faculty members, Harvard appeals to self-directed, resourceful students of diverse beliefs and backgrounds.

Applying
Students must apply by December 8, 2010, to be considered for admission in September 2011. Scores on the General Test of the Graduate Record Examinations are required except in rare circumstances. GRE Subject Tests are recommended. Due to the early application deadline, applicants should plan to take the GRE test no later than October to ensure that original scores are received by December 8. Information about Graduate School fellowships and scholarships, admission procedures, and graduate study at Harvard may be obtained by writing to the Admissions Office.

Correspondence and Information

For information on the program:
Harvard Biophysics Program
Building C2, Room 122
Harvard Medical School Campus
240 Longwood Avenue
Boston, Massachusetts 02115
E-mail: biophys@fas.harvard.edu
Web site: http://fas.harvard.edu/~biophys

For application forms for admission and financial aid:
Admissions Office
Graduate School of Arts and Sciences
Holyoke Center
Harvard University
1350 Massachusetts Avenue
Cambridge, Massachusetts 02138
E-mail: admiss@fas.harvard.edu
Web site: http://www.gsas.harvard.edu

Harvard University

THE FACULTY AND THEIR RESEARCH

The following faculty members accept students for degree work in biophysics. Thesis research with other faculty members is possible by arrangement.

John Assad, Ph.D., Professor of Neurobiology. Mechanisms of visual processing in the visual cortex of awake behaving monkeys.

Frederick M. Ausubel, Ph.D., Professor of Genetics. Molecular biology of microbial pathogenesis in plants and animals.

Howard Berg, Ph.D., Herchel Smith Professor of Physics and Professor of Molecular and Cellular Biology. Motile behavior of bacteria.

Stephen C. Blacklow, M.D., Ph.D., Professor of Pathology. Molecular basis for specificity in protein folding and protein-protein interactions.

Martha L. Bulyk, Ph.D., Associate Professor of Medicine and Health Sciences and Technology and of Pathology. Computational methods; genomic and proteomic technologies in the study of DNA-protein interactions.

Lewis Cantley, Ph.D., Professor of Cell Biology and Systems Biology. Structural basis for specificity in eukaryotic signal transduction pathways.

James J. Chou, Ph.D., Associate Professor of Biological Chemistry and Molecular Pharmacology. NMR spectroscopy on membrane-associated proteins and peptides.

George McDonald Church, Ph.D., Professor of Genetics. Human and microbial functional genomics; genotyping; gene expression regulatory network models.

David E. Clapham, M.D., Ph.D., Professor of Pediatrics and of Neurobiology. Intracellular signal transduction.

Jon Clardy, Ph.D., Professor of Biological Chemistry and Molecular Pharmacology. Chemical ecology; biosynthesis; structure-based design.

Adam E. Cohen, Ph.D., Assistant Professor of Chemistry and Chemical Biology and of Physics. Analysis of structure and function of nicotinic acetylcholine receptors.

Jonathan B. Cohen, Ph.D., Professor of Neurobiology. Structure and function of ligand-gated ion channels.

David P. Corey, Ph.D., Professor of Neurobiology. Ion channels in neural cell membranes.

Vladimir Denic, Ph.D., Assistant Professor of Molecular and Cellular Biology. Structural diversification of very long-chain fatty acids.

Michael J. Eck, M.D., Ph.D., Professor of Biological Chemistry and Molecular Pharmacology. Structural studies of proteins involved in signal transduction pathways.

Florian Engert, Ph.D., Associate Professor of Molecular and Cellular Biology. Synaptic plasticity and neuronal networks.

Rachelle Gaudet, Ph.D., Associate Professor of Molecular and Cellular Biology. Structural studies of the stereochemistry of signaling and transport through biological membranes.

David E. Golan, M.D., Ph.D., Professor of Biological Chemistry and Molecular Pharmacology and of Medicine. Membrane dynamics; membrane structure; cellular adhesion.

Stephen C. Harrison, Ph.D., Professor of Biological Chemistry and Molecular Pharmacology. Structure of viruses and viral membranes; protein-DNA interactions; structural aspects of signal transduction and membrane traffic; X-ray diffraction.

James M. Hogle, Ph.D., Professor of Biological Chemistry and Molecular Pharmacology. Structure and function of viruses and virus-related proteins; X-ray crystallography.

Donald E. Ingber, M.D., Ph.D., Professor of Bioengineering and Judah Folkman Professor of Vascular Biology. Research in integrin signaling, cytoskeleton, and control of angiogenesis.

David Jeruzalmi, Ph.D., Associate Professor of Molecular and Cellular Biology. Structural studies of nucleoprotein assemblies.

Tomas Kirchhausen, Ph.D., Professor of Cell Biology. Molecular mechanisms of membrane traffic; X-ray crystallography; chemical genetics.

Nancy Kleckner, Ph.D., Herchel Smith Professor of Molecular Biology. Chromosome metabolism in bacteria and yeast.

Roberto G. Kolter, Ph.D., Professor of Microbiology and Molecular Genetics. DNA protection from oxidative damage; cell-cell communication in biofilms; microbial evolution.

Andres Leschziner, Ph.D., Assistant Professor of Molecular and Cellular Biology. Structural biology of ATP-dependent chromatin remodeling.

David R. Liu, Ph.D., Professor of Chemistry and Chemical Biology. Organic chemistry and chemical biology.

Jun S. Liu, Ph.D., Professor of Statistics. Stochastic processes, probability theory, and statistical inference.

Gavin MacBeath, Ph.D., Associate Professor of Chemistry and Chemical Biology. Molecular recognition in complex processes: protein trafficking, intercellular communication, and apoptosis.

Markus Meister, Ph.D., Jeff C. Tarr Professor of Molecular and Cellular Biology. Function of neuronal circuits.

Keith W. Miller, Ph.D., Mallinckrodt Professor of Pharmacology, Department of Anesthesia. Molecular mechanisms of regulatory conformation changes and drug action on membrane receptors and channels, using rapid kinetics, time-resolved photolabeling, and spectroscopy (EPR, fluorescence, NMR); characterization of lipid-protein interactions in membrane proteins.

Timothy Mitchison, Ph.D., Hasib Sabbagh Professor of Systems Biology. Cytoskeleton dynamics; mechanism of mitosis and cell locomotion; small-molecule inhibitors.

Venkatesh N. Murthy, Ph.D., Morris Khan Associate Professor of Molecular and Cellular Biology. Mechanisms of synaptic transmission and plasticity.

Erin K. O'Shea, Ph.D., Professor of Molecular and Cellular Biology and of Chemistry and Chemical Biology. Quantitative analysis of regulatory networks.

David Pellman, M.D., Professor of Cell Biology. The mechanics and regulation of mitosis.

Mara Prentiss, Ph.D., Professor of Physics. Exploitation of optical manipulation to measure adhesion properties, including virus cell binding.

Tom A. Rapoport, Ph.D., Professor of Cell Biology. Mechanism of how proteins are transported across the endoplasmic reticulum membrane.

Samara L. Reck-Peterson, Ph.D., Assistant Professor of Cell Biology. Single molecule studies of cellular motors.

Frederick P. Roth, Ph.D., Associate Professor of Biological Chemistry and Molecular Pharmacology. Computational molecular biology.

Gary Ruvkun, Ph.D., Professor of Genetics. Genetic control of developmental timing, neurogenesis, and neural function.

Bernardo L. Sabatini, Ph.D., Associate Professor of Neurobiology. Regulation of synaptic transmission and dendritic function in the mammalian brain.

Aravinthan D. T. Samuel, Ph.D., Associate Professor of Physics. Topics in biophysics, neurobiology, and animal behavior.

Stuart L. Schreiber, Ph.D., Morris Loeb Professor of Chemistry and Chemical Biology. Forward and reverse chemical genetics: using small molecules to explore biology.

Brian Seed, Ph.D., Professor of Genetics. Genetic analysis of signal transduction in the immune system.

Eugene Shakhnovich, Ph.D., Professor of Chemistry and Chemical Biology. Theory and experiments in protein folding and design; theory of molecular evolution; rational drug design and physical chemistry of protein-ligand interactions; theory of complex systems.

William Shih, Ph.D., Assistant Professor of Biological Chemistry and Molecular Pharmacology. Biomolecular nanotechnology.

Steven E. Shoelson, M.D., Ph.D., Professor of Medicine. Structural and cellular biology of insulin signal transduction, insulin, resistance, diabetes, and obesity.

Pamela Silver, Ph.D., Professor of Systems Biology. Nucleocytoplasmic transport; RNA-protein interactions; protein methylation; cell-based small-molecule screens.

Timothy A. Springer, Ph.D., Latham Family Professor of Pathology. Molecular biology of immune cell interactions.

Shamil R. Sunyaev, Ph.D., Assistant Professor of Genetics. Population genetic variation and genomic divergence, with a focus on protein coding regions.

Jack W. Szostak, Ph.D., Professor of Genetics. Directed evolution; information content and molecular function; self-replicating systems.

Gregory L. Verdine, Ph.D., Erving Professor of Chemistry. Protein–nucleic acid interactions; transcriptional regulation; X-ray crystallography.

Gerhard Wagner, Ph.D., Elkan Blout Professor of Biological Chemistry and Molecular Pharmacology. Protein and nucleic acid structure, interaction, and mobility; NMR spectroscopy.

John R. Wakeley, Ph.D., Professor of Organismic and Evolutionary Biology. Theoretical population genetics.

Thomas Walz, Ph.D., Professor of Cell Biology. High-resolution electron microscopy.

George M. Whitesides, Ph.D., Mallinckrodt Professor of Chemistry. Molecular pharmacology; biosurface chemistry; virology.

Xiaoliang Sunney Xie, Ph.D., Mallinckrodt Professor of Chemistry and Chemical Biology. Single-molecule spectroscopy and dynamics; molecular interaction and chemical dynamics in biological systems.

Gary Yellen, Ph.D., Professor of Neurobiology. Molecular physiology of ion channels: functional motions, drug interactions, and electrophysiological mechanisms.

Xaiowei Zhuang, Ph.D., Professor of Chemistry and Chemical Biology and of Physics. Single-molecule biophysics.

Section 5
Botany and Plant Biology

This section contains a directory of institutions offering graduate work in botany and plant biology, followed by an in-depth entry submitted by an institution that chose to prepare a detailed program description. Additional information about programs listed in the directory but not augmented by an in-depth entry may be obtained by writing directly to the dean of a graduate school or chair of a department at the address given in the directory. For programs offering related work, see also in this book *Biochemistry; Biological and Biomedical Sciences; Cell, Molecular, and Structural Biology; Ecology, Environmental Biology, and Evolutionary Biology; Entomology; Genetics, Developmental Biology, and Reproductive Biology;* and *Microbiological Sciences.* In the other guides in this series:

Graduate Programs in the Humanities, Arts & Social Sciences
See *Architecture (Landscape Architecture)* and *Economics (Agricultural Economics and Agribusiness)*
Graduate Programs in the Physical Sciences, Mathematics, Agricultural Sciences, the Environment & Natural Resources
See *Agricultural and Food Sciences*
Graduate Programs in Engineering & Applied Sciences
See *Agricultural Engineering* and *Bioengineering*

CONTENTS

Program Directories

Close-Up

Botany

Auburn University, Graduate School, College of Sciences and Mathematics, Department of Biological Sciences, Auburn University, AL 36849. Offers botany (MS, PhD); microbiology (MS, PhD); zoology (MS, PhD). *Faculty:* 33 full-time (8 women), 1 (woman) part-time/adjunct. *Students:* 42 full-time (17 women), 60 part-time (36 women); includes 9 minority (4 African Americans, 1 American Indian/Alaska Native, 3 Asian Americans or Pacific Islanders, 1 Hispanic American), 21 international. Average age 28. 134 applicants, 20% accepted, 18 enrolled. In 2009, 22 master's, 11 doctorates awarded. *Entrance requirements:* For master's and doctorate, GRE General Test. Additional exam requirements/recommendations for international students: Required—TOEFL. *Application deadline:* For fall admission, 7/7 for domestic students; for spring admission, 11/24 for domestic students. Application fee: $50 ($60 for international students). Electronic applications accepted. *Expenses:* Tuition, state resident: full-time $6240. Tuition, nonresident: full-time $18,720. International tuition: $18,938 full-time. Required fees: $492. Tuition and fees vary according to course load, program and reciprocity agreements. *Financial support:* Research assistantships, teaching assistantships available. Financial award applicants required to submit FAFSA. *Unit head:* Dr. James M. Barbaree, Chair, 334-844-1647, Fax: 334-844-1645. *Application contact:* Dr. George Flowers, Dean of the Graduate School, 334-844-2125.

California State University, Chico, Graduate School, College of Natural Sciences, Department of Biological Sciences, Program in Botany, Chico, CA 95929-0722. Offers MS. *Students:* 1 (woman) full-time. Average age 32. 1 applicant, 100% accepted, 1 enrolled. In 2009, 2 master's awarded. *Degree requirements:* For master's, thesis, seminar presentation. *Entrance requirements:* For master's, GRE General Test, GRE Subject Test (biology), 2 letters of recommendation. Additional exam requirements/recommendations for international students: Required—TOEFL (minimum score 550 paper-based; 213 computer-based; 80 iBT), IELTS (minimum score 6.5). *Application deadline:* For fall admission, 3/1 priority date for domestic students, 3/1 for international students; for spring admission, 9/15 priority date for domestic students, 9/15 for international students. Applications are processed on a rolling basis. Application fee: $55. Electronic applications accepted. *Financial support:* Fellowships, career-related internships or fieldwork available. *Unit head:* Dr. Jonathan Day, Graduate Coordinator, 530-898-6303. *Application contact:* Larry Hanne, Graduate Coordinator, 530-898-5356.

Claremont Graduate University, Graduate Programs, Program in Botany, Claremont, CA 91711-6160. Offers MS, PhD. Part-time programs available. *Faculty:* 7 full-time (4 women). *Students:* 15 full-time (11 women); includes 2 minority (1 Asian American or Pacific Islander, 1 Hispanic American), 6 international. Average age 32.Terminal master's awarded for partial completion of doctoral program. *Entrance requirements:* For master's and doctorate, GRE General Test. Additional exam requirements/recommendations for international students: Required—TOEFL (minimum score 550 paper-based; 213 computer-based; 80 iBT). *Application deadline:* For fall admission, 2/1 priority date for domestic students. Applications are processed on a rolling basis. Application fee: $60. Electronic applications accepted. *Expenses:* Tuition: Full-time $35,046; part-time $1524 per credit. Required fees: $161 per semester. *Financial support:* Fellowships, research assistantships, Federal Work-Study, institutionally sponsored loans, scholarships/grants, and tuition waivers (full) available. Support available to part-time students. Financial award application deadline: 2/15; financial award applicants required to submit FAFSA. *Unit head:* Lucinda McDade, Director of Research/Chair, 909-625-8767 Ext. 234, Fax: 909-626-3489, E-mail: lucinda.mcdade@cgu.edu. *Application contact:* Linda Worlow, Program Coordinator, 909-625-8767 Ext. 241, Fax: 909-626-3489, E-mail: botany@cgu.edu.

Colorado State University, Graduate School, College of Natural Sciences, Department of Biology, Fort Collins, CO 80523-1878. Offers botany (MS, PhD); zoology (MS, PhD). Post-baccalaureate distance learning degree programs offered (no on-campus study). *Faculty:* 25 full-time (10 women), 1 part-time/adjunct (0 women). *Students:* 31 full-time (15 women), 20 part-time (11 women); includes 4 minority (1 American Indian/Alaska Native, 1 Asian American or Pacific Islander, 2 Hispanic Americans), 7 international. Average age 29. 38 applicants, 26% accepted, 9 enrolled. In 2009, 8 master's, 2 doctorates awarded. Terminal master's awarded for partial completion of doctoral program. *Degree requirements:* For master's, comprehensive exam (for some programs), thesis (for some programs); for doctorate, comprehensive exam, thesis/dissertation. *Entrance requirements:* For master's, GRE General Test, minimum GPA of 3.0; 3 letters of recommendation; for doctorate, GRE General Test, minimum GPA of 3.0; statement of purpose; 2 transcripts; 3 letters of recommendation. Additional exam requirements/recommendations for international students: Required—TOEFL (minimum score 550 paper-based; 213 computer-based; 80 iBT). *Application deadline:* For fall admission, 9/15 priority date for domestic students, 8/15 priority date for international students; for spring admission, 1/15 priority date for domestic and international students. Applications are processed on a rolling basis. Application fee: $50. Electronic applications accepted. *Expenses:* Tuition, state resident: full-time $6434; part-time $359.10 per credit. Tuition, nonresident: full-time $18,116; part-time $1006.45 per credit. Required fees: $1496; $83 per credit. *Financial support:* In 2009–10, 15 fellowships (averaging $26,286 per year), 26 research assistantships with full tuition reimbursements (averaging $11,410 per year), 48 teaching assistantships with full tuition reimbursements (averaging $12,007 per year) were awarded; health care benefits also available. Financial award application deadline: 1/15; financial award applicants required to submit FAFSA. *Faculty research:* Aquatic and terrestrial ecology, cell biology and genetics, plant/animal physiology, developmental biology, evolutionary biology. Total annual research expenditures: $5 million. *Unit head:* Dr. Daniel R. Bush, Chair, 970-491-7013, Fax: 970-491-0649, E-mail: dbush@colostate.edu. *Application contact:* Dorothy Ramirez, Graduate Coordinator, 970-491-1923, Fax: 970-491-0649, E-mail: dorothy.ramirez@colostate.edu.

Connecticut College, Graduate School, Department of Botany, New London, CT 06320-4196. Offers MA. Part-time programs available. *Degree requirements:* For master's, thesis. *Entrance requirements:* For master's, GRE General Test and GRE Subject Test. Additional exam requirements/recommendations for international students: Required—TOEFL (minimum score 600 paper-based). *Expenses:* Tuition: Full-time $11,480; part-time $1640 per course. *Faculty research:* Tidal marsh ecology, upland vegetation dynamics, plant development, phycology, paleo limnology and ethno botany.

Emporia State University, School of Graduate Studies, College of Liberal Arts and Sciences, Department of Biological Sciences, Emporia, KS 66801-5087. Offers botany (MS); environmental biology (MS); general biology (MS); microbial and cellular biology (MS); zoology (MS). Part-time programs available. *Faculty:* 13 full-time (3 women). *Students:* 9 full-time (7 women), 17 part-time (11 women); includes 1 minority (African American), 8 international. 22 applicants, 95% accepted, 18 enrolled. In 2009, 24 master's awarded. *Degree requirements:* For master's, comprehensive exam or thesis. *Entrance requirements:* For master's, GRE, appropriate undergraduate degree, interview, letters of reference. Additional exam requirements/recommendations for international students: Required—TOEFL (minimum score 520 paper-based; 133 computer-based; 68 iBT). *Application deadline:* For fall admission, 8/15 priority date for domestic students. Applications are processed on a rolling basis. Application fee: $30 ($75 for international students). Electronic applications accepted. *Expenses:* Tuition, state resident: full-time $4154; part-time $173 per credit hour. Tuition, nonresident: full-time $12,864; part-time $536 per credit hour. Required fees: $948; $58 per credit hour. Tuition and fees vary according to campus/location. *Financial support:* In 2009–10, 7 research assistantships with full tuition reimbursements (averaging $6,876 per year), 10 teaching assistantships with full tuition reimbursements (averaging $7,419 per year) were awarded; career-related internships or fieldwork, Federal Work-Study, institutionally sponsored loans, health care benefits, and unspecified assistantships also available. Financial award application deadline: 3/15; financial award applicants required to submit FAFSA. *Faculty research:* Fisheries, range, and wildlife management; aquatic, plant, grassland, vertebrate, and invertebrate ecology; mammalian and plant systematics, taxonomy, and evolution; immunology, virology, and molecular biology. *Unit head:* Dr. R. Brent Thomas, Interim Chair, 620-341-5311, Fax: 620-341-5608, E-mail: rthomas2@emporia.edu. *Application contact:* Dr. Scott Crupper, Graduate Coordinator, 620-341-5621, Fax: 620-341-5607, E-mail: scrupper@emporia.edu.

Illinois State University, Graduate School, College of Arts and Sciences, Department of Biological Sciences, Normal, IL 61790-2200. Offers animal behavior (MS); bacteriology (MS); biochemistry (MS); biological sciences (MS); biology (PhD); biophysics (MS); biotechnology (MS); botany (MS, PhD); cell biology (MS); conservation biology (MS); developmental biology (MS); ecology (MS, PhD); entomology (MS); evolutionary biology (MS); genetics (MS, PhD); immunology (MS); microbiology (MS, PhD); molecular biology (MS); molecular genetics (MS); neurobiology (MS); neuroscience (MS); parasitology (MS); physiology (MS, PhD); plant biology (MS); plant molecular biology (MS); plant sciences (MS); structural biology (MS); zoology (MS, PhD). Part-time programs available. *Degree requirements:* For master's, thesis or alternative; for doctorate, variable foreign language requirement, thesis/dissertation, 2 terms of residency. *Entrance requirements:* For master's, GRE General Test, minimum GPA of 2.6 in last 60 hours of course work; for doctorate, GRE General Test. *Faculty research:* Redoc balance and drug development in schistosoma mansoni, control of the growth of listeria monocytogenes at low temperature, regulation of cell expansion and microtubule function by SPRI, CRUI: physiology and fitness consequences of different life history phenotypes.

Miami University, Graduate School, College of Arts and Science, Department of Botany, Oxford, OH 45056. Offers MA, MAT, MS, PhD. *Students:* 29 full-time (17 women), 14 international. *Entrance requirements:* For master's, GRE General Test, GRE Subject Test (recommended), minimum undergraduate GPA of 3.0 during previous 2 years or 2.75 overall; for doctorate, GRE General Test, GRE Subject Test (recommended), minimum undergraduate GPA of 2.75, 3.0 graduate. Additional exam requirements/recommendations for international students: Required—TOEFL (minimum score 550 paper-based). *Application deadline:* Applications are processed on a rolling basis. Application fee: $50. Electronic applications accepted. *Expenses:* Tuition, state resident: full-time $11,280. Tuition, nonresident: full-time $24,912. Required fees: $516. *Financial support:* Research assistantships, teaching assistantships with full tuition reimbursements, Federal Work-Study, institutionally sponsored loans, health care benefits, and unspecified assistantships available. Financial award application deadline: 3/1; financial award applicants required to submit FAFSA. *Faculty research:* Evolution of plants, fungi and algae; bioinformatics; molecular biology of plants and cyanobacteria; food web dynamics; plant science education. *Unit head:* Dr. John Kiss, Chair, 513-529-4200, E-mail: kissjz@muohio.edu. *Application contact:* Dr. R. James Hickey, Graduate Coordinator, 513-529-6000, E-mail: hickeyrj@muohio.edu.

North Carolina State University, Graduate School, College of Agriculture and Life Sciences, Department of Plant Biology, Raleigh, NC 27695. Offers MS, PhD. Part-time programs available. Terminal master's awarded for partial completion of doctoral program. *Degree requirements:* For master's, thesis (for some programs); for doctorate, thesis/dissertation. *Entrance requirements:* For master's and doctorate, GRE. Additional exam requirements/recommendations for international students: Required—TOEFL. Electronic applications accepted. *Faculty research:* Plant molecular and cell biology, aquatic ecology, community ecology, restoration, systematics plant pathogen and environmental interactions.

North Dakota State University, College of Graduate and Interdisciplinary Studies, College of Science and Mathematics, Department of Biological Sciences, Fargo, ND 58108. Offers biology (MS); botany (MS, PhD); cellular and molecular biology (PhD); environmental and conservation sciences (MS, PhD); genomics (PhD); natural resources management (MS, PhD); zoology (MS, PhD). *Students:* 32 full-time (21 women), 14 part-time (10 women); includes 1 Asian American or Pacific Islander, 14 international. In 2009, 12 master's, 9 doctorates awarded. *Degree requirements:* For master's, thesis; for doctorate, thesis/dissertation. *Entrance requirements:* For master's and doctorate, GRE General Test. Additional exam requirements/recommendations for international students: Required—TOEFL. *Application deadline:* For fall admission, 3/15 priority date for domestic students; for spring admission, 10/30 priority date for domestic students. Applications are processed on a rolling basis. Application fee: $45 ($60 for international students). Electronic applications accepted. *Financial support:* Fellowships with full tuition reimbursements, research assistantships with full tuition reimbursements, teaching assistantships with full tuition reimbursements, career-related internships or fieldwork, Federal Work-Study, institutionally sponsored loans, scholarships/grants, tuition waivers (full), and unspecified assistantships available. Support available to part-time students. Financial award application deadline: 4/15; financial award applicants required to submit FAFSA. *Faculty research:* Comparative endocrinology, physiology, behavioral ecology, plant cell biology, aquatic biology. Total annual research expenditures: $675,000. *Unit head:* Dr. Marinus L. Otte, Head, 701-231-7087, E-mail: marinus.otte@ndsu.edu. *Application contact:* Dr. Marinus L. Otte, Head, 701-231-7087, E-mail: marinus.otte@ndsu.edu.

Nova Scotia Agricultural College, Research and Graduate Studies, Truro, NS B2N 5E3, Canada. Offers agriculture (M Sc), including air quality, animal behavior, animal molecular genetics, animal nutrition, animal technology, aquaculture, botany, crop management, crop physiology, ecology, environmental microbiology, food science, horticulture, nutrient management, pest management, physiology, plant biotechnology, plant pathology, soil chemistry, soil fertility, waste management and composting, water quality. Part-time programs available. *Degree requirements:* For master's, thesis, ATC Exam Teaching Assistantship. *Entrance requirements:* For master's, honors B Sc, minimum GPA of 3.0. Additional exam requirements/recommendations for international students: Required—TOEFL (minimum score 580 paper-based; 237 computer-based; 92 iBT), IELTS, Michigan English Language Assessment Battery, CanTEST, CAEL. *Faculty research:* Bio-product development, organic agriculture, nutrient management, air and water quality, agricultural biotechnology.

Oklahoma State University, College of Arts and Sciences, Department of Botany, Stillwater, OK 74078. Offers botany (MS); environmental science (MS, PhD); plant science (PhD). *Faculty:* 17 full-time (5 women). *Students:* 12 part-time (4 women); includes 1 minority (American Indian/Alaska Native), 2 international. Average age 31. 10 applicants, 40% accepted, 4 enrolled. In 2009, 1 master's awarded. *Degree requirements:* For master's, thesis; for doctorate, comprehensive exam, thesis/dissertation. *Entrance requirements:* For master's and doctorate, GRE or GMAT. Additional exam requirements/recommendations for international students: Required—TOEFL (minimum score 550 paper-based; 79 iBT). *Application deadline:* For fall admission, 3/1 priority date for international students; for spring admission, 8/1 priority date for international students. Applications are processed on a rolling basis. Application fee: $40 ($75 for international students). Electronic applications accepted. *Expenses:* Tuition, state resident: full-time $3716; part-time $154.85 per credit hour. Tuition, nonresident: full-time $14,448; part-time $602 per credit hour. Required fees: $1772; $73.85 per credit hour. One-time fee: $50. Tuition and fees vary according to course load and campus/location. *Financial support:* In 2009–10, 3 research assistantships (averaging $15,770 per year), 10 teaching assistantships (averaging $15,469 per year) were awarded; career-related internships or fieldwork, Federal Work-Study, scholarships/grants, health care benefits, tuition waivers (partial), and unspecified assistantships also available. Support available to part-time students. Financial award application deadline: 3/1; financial award applicants required to submit FAFSA. *Faculty research:* Ethnobotany, developmental genetics of Arabidopsis, biological roles of Plasmodesmata, community ecology and biodiversity, nutrient cycling in grassland ecosystems. *Unit head:* Dr. Linda Watson, Head, 405-744-5559, Fax: 405-744-7074. *Application contact:* Dr. Gordon Emslie, Dean, 405-744-6368, Fax: 405-744-0355, E-mail: grad-i@okstate.edu.

Oregon State University, Graduate School, College of Science, Department of Botany and Plant Pathology, Corvallis, OR 97331. Offers ecology (MA, MAIS, MS, PhD); genetics (MA, MAIS, MS, PhD); molecular and cellular biology (MA, MAIS, MS, PhD); mycology (MA, MAIS, MS, PhD); plant pathology (MA, MAIS, MS, PhD); plant physiology (MA, MAIS, MS, PhD); structural botany (MA, MAIS, MS, PhD); systematics (MA, MAIS, MS, PhD). Part-time programs available. *Faculty:* 11 full-time (1 woman), 2 part-time/adjunct (1 woman). *Students:* 32 full-time (19 women), 2 part-time (1 woman); includes 2 minority (both Asian Americans or Pacific Islanders), 3 international. Average age 30. In 2009, 4 master's, 3 doctorates awarded. *Degree requirements:* For master's, variable foreign language requirement, thesis optional; for doctorate, thesis/dissertation. *Entrance requirements:* For master's and doctorate, GRE General Test, minimum GPA of 3.0 in last 90 hours. Additional exam requirements/recommendations for international students: Required—TOEFL. *Application deadline:* For fall admission, 2/1 priority date for domestic students. Applications are processed on a rolling basis. Application fee: $50. *Expenses:* Tuition, state resident: full-time $9774; part-time $362 per credit. Tuition, nonresident: full-time $15,849; part-time $587 per credit. Required fees: $1639. Full-time tuition and fees vary according to course load and program. *Financial support:* Fellowships, research assistantships, teaching assistantships, career-related internships or fieldwork, Federal Work-Study, institutionally sponsored loans, and scholarships/grants available. Support available to part-time students. Financial award application deadline: 2/1. *Faculty research:* Plant ecology, plant molecular biology, systematic botany, epidemiology, host-pathogen interaction. *Unit head:* Dr. Daniel J. Arp, Chair, 541-737-1297, Fax: 541-737-3573, E-mail: arpd@science.oregonstate.edu. *Application contact:* Dr. John E. Fowler, Associate Professor, 541-737-5307, Fax: 541-737-3573, E-mail: fowlerj@science.oregonstate.edu.

Purdue University, Graduate School, College of Agriculture, Department of Botany and Plant Pathology, West Lafayette, IN 47907. Offers MS, PhD. Part-time programs available. Terminal master's awarded for partial completion of doctoral program. *Degree requirements:* For master's, thesis; for doctorate, thesis/dissertation. *Entrance requirements:* For master's and doctorate, GRE. Additional exam requirements/recommendations for international students: Required—TOEFL. Electronic applications accepted. *Faculty research:* Biotechnology, plant growth, weed control, crop improvement, plant physiology.

Texas A&M University, College of Science, Department of Biology, College Station, TX 77843. Offers biology (MS, PhD); botany (MS, PhD); microbiology (MS, PhD); molecular and cell biology (PhD); neuroscience (MS, PhD); zoology (MS, PhD). *Faculty:* 37. *Students:* 101 full-time (59 women), 5 part-time (3 women); includes 8 minority (1 African American, 3 Asian Americans or Pacific Islanders, 4 Hispanic Americans), 40 international. Average age 28. In 2009, 9 master's, 5 doctorates awarded. *Degree requirements:* For master's, thesis or alternative; for doctorate, comprehensive exam, thesis/dissertation. *Entrance requirements:* For master's and doctorate, GRE General Test. Additional exam requirements/recommendations for international students: Required—TOEFL. *Application deadline:* For fall admission, 1/15 for domestic students. Applications are processed on a rolling basis. Application fee: $50 ($75 for international students). Electronic applications accepted. *Expenses:* Tuition, state resident: full-time $3991; part-time $221.74 per credit hour. Tuition, nonresident: full-time $9049; part-time $502.74 per credit hour. *Financial support:* Fellowships, research assistantships, teaching assistantships available. Financial award application deadline: 4/1; financial award applicants required to submit FAFSA. *Unit head:* Dr. Jack McMahan, Department Head, 979-845-2301, E-mail: granster@mail.bio.tamu.edu. *Application contact:* Graduate Advisor, 979-845-7755.

University of Alaska Fairbanks, College of Natural Sciences and Mathematics, Department of Biology and Wildlife, Fairbanks, AK 99775-6100. Offers biological sciences (MS, PhD), including biology, botany, wildlife biology (PhD), zoology; biology (MAT, MS); wildlife biology (MS). Part-time programs available. *Faculty:* 27 full-time (9 women), 2 part-time/adjunct (0 women). *Students:* 95 full-time (61 women), 32 part-time (18 women); includes 13 minority (1 African American, 3 American Indian/Alaska Native, 4 Asian Americans or Pacific Islanders, 5 Hispanic Americans), 9 international. Average age 35. 76 applicants, 32% accepted, 24 enrolled. In 2009, 10 master's, 13 doctorates awarded. *Degree requirements:* For master's, comprehensive exam, thesis, oral exam, oral defense; for doctorate, comprehensive exam, thesis/dissertation, oral exam, oral defense. *Entrance requirements:* For master's and doctorate, GRE General Test, GRE Subject Test (biology). Additional exam requirements/recommendations for international students: Required—TOEFL (minimum score 550 paper-based; 213 computer-based; 80 iBT), TWE. *Application deadline:* For fall admission, 6/1 for domestic students, 3/1 for international students; for spring admission, 10/15 for domestic students, 9/1 for international students. Applications are processed on a rolling basis. Application fee: $60. Electronic applications accepted. *Expenses:* Tuition, state resident: full-time $7584; part-time $316 per credit. Tuition, nonresident: full-time $15,504; part-time $646 per credit. Required fees: $23 per credit. $135 per semester. Tuition and fees vary according to course level, course load and reciprocity agreements. *Financial support:* In 2009–10, 46 research assistantships (averaging $13,543 per year), 24 teaching assistantships (averaging $7,495 per year) were awarded; fellowships, career-related internships or fieldwork, Federal Work-Study, scholarships/grants, health care benefits, and unspecified assistantships also available. Support available to part-time students. Financial award application deadline: 7/1; financial award applicants required to submit FAFSA. *Faculty research:* Plant-herbivore interactions, plant metabolic defenses, insect manufacture of glycerol, ice nucleators, structure and functions of arctic and subarctic freshwater ecosystems. *Unit head:* Dr. Richard E. Boone, Chair, 907-474-7671, Fax: 907-474-6716, E-mail: fybio@uaf.edu. *Application contact:* Dr. Richard E. Boone, Chair, 907-474-7671, Fax: 907-474-6716, E-mail: fybio@uaf.edu.

The University of British Columbia, Faculty of Science, Department of Botany, Vancouver, BC V6T 1Z1, Canada. Offers M Sc, PhD. *Degree requirements:* For master's, thesis; for doctorate, comprehensive exam, thesis/dissertation. *Entrance requirements:* Additional exam requirements/recommendations for international students: Required—TOEFL. Electronic applications accepted. *Faculty research:* Plant ecology, evolution and systematics, cell and developmental biology, plant physiology/biochemistry, genetics.

University of California, Riverside, Graduate Division, Department of Botany and Plant Sciences, Riverside, CA 92521-0102. Offers plant biology (MS, PhD), including plant genetics (PhD). Part-time programs available. *Faculty:* 40 full-time (13 women). *Students:* 52 full-time (34 women); includes 7 minority (1 African American, 4 Asian Americans or Pacific Islanders, 2 Hispanic Americans), 22 international. Average age 29. In 2009, 3 master's, 3 doctorates awarded. Terminal master's awarded for partial completion of doctoral program. *Degree requirements:* For master's, comprehensive exams or thesis; for doctorate, thesis/dissertation, qualifying exams. *Entrance requirements:* For master's and doctorate, GRE General Test, minimum GPA of 3.2. Additional exam requirements/recommendations for international students: Required—TOEFL (minimum score 550 paper-based; 213 computer-based; 80 iBT). *Application deadline:* For fall admission, 5/1 for domestic students, 2/1 for international students; for winter admission, 2/1 for domestic students, 7/1 for international students; for spring admission, 12/1 for domestic students, 10/1 for international students. Applications are processed on a rolling basis. Application fee: $80 ($100 for international students). Electronic applications accepted. *Financial support:* In 2009–10, fellowships with tuition reimbursements (averaging $12,000 per year), research assistantships with tuition reimbursements (averaging $23,000 per year), teaching assistantships with tuition reimbursements (averaging $16,500 per year) were awarded; career-related internships or fieldwork, Federal Work-Study, institutionally sponsored loans, scholarships/grants, and tuition waivers (full and partial) also available. Financial award application deadline: 2/1; financial award applicants required to submit FAFSA. *Faculty research:* Agricultural plant biology; biochemistry and physiology; cellular, molecular and developmental biology; ecology, evolution, systematics and ethnobotany; genetics, genomics and bioinformatics. *Unit head:* Dr. Jodie S. Holt, Chair, 951-827-3801. *Application contact:* Deidra Kornfeld, Graduate Program Assistant, 800-735-0717, Fax: 951-827-5517, E-mail: deidra.kornfeld@ucr.edu.

University of Connecticut, Graduate School, College of Liberal Arts and Sciences, Department of Ecology and Evolutionary Biology, Field of Botany, Storrs, CT 06269. Offers MS, PhD. *Faculty:* 12 full-time (3 women). *Students:* 3 full-time (2 women), 1 international. Average age 29. 4 applicants, 0% accepted, 0 enrolled.Terminal master's awarded for partial completion of doctoral program. *Degree requirements:* For master's, comprehensive exam; for doctorate, thesis/dissertation. *Entrance requirements:* For master's and doctorate, GRE General Test, GRE Subject Test. Additional exam requirements/recommendations for international students: Required—TOEFL (minimum score 550 paper-based; 213 computer-based). *Application deadline:* For fall admission, 2/1 priority date for domestic and international students; for spring admission, 11/1 for domestic students, 10/1 for international students. Applications are processed on a rolling basis. Application fee: $55. Electronic applications accepted. *Expenses:* Tuition, state resident: full-time $4725; part-time $525 per credit. Tuition, nonresident: full-time $12,267; part-time $1363 per credit. Required fees: $346 per semester. Tuition and fees vary according to course load. *Financial support:* In 2009–10, 1 research assistantship, 2 teaching assistantships were awarded; fellowships, Federal Work-Study, scholarships/grants, health care benefits, and unspecified assistantships also available. Financial award application deadline: 2/1; financial award applicants required to submit FAFSA. *Unit head:* Kentwood Wells, Head, 860-486-4319, Fax: 860-486-6364, E-mail: kentwood.wells@uconn.edu. *Application contact:* Anne St. Onje, Graduate Coordinator, 860-486-4314, Fax: 860-486-3943, E-mail: anne.st_onje@uconn.edu.

University of Florida, Graduate School, College of Liberal Arts and Sciences and College of Agricultural and Life Sciences, Department of Botany, Gainesville, FL 32611. Offers M Ag, MS, MST, PhD. Part-time programs available. *Degree requirements:* For doctorate, thesis/dissertation. *Entrance requirements:* For master's and doctorate, GRE General Test, minimum GPA of 3.0. Additional exam requirements/recommendations for international students: Required—TOEFL (minimum score 550 paper-based; 213 computer-based). Electronic applications accepted. *Faculty research:* Ecology, physiology, systematics, biochemistry, ecological genetics.

University of Guelph, Graduate Program Services, College of Biological Science, Department of Integrative Biology, Botany and Zoology, Guelph, ON N1G 2W1, Canada. Offers botany (M Sc, PhD); zoology (M Sc, PhD). Part-time programs available. *Degree requirements:* For master's, thesis, research proposal; for doctorate, thesis/dissertation, research proposal, qualifying exam. *Entrance requirements:* For master's, minimum B average during previous 2 years of course work. Additional exam requirements/recommendations for international students: Required—TOEFL (minimum score 550 paper-based; 213 computer-based), IELTS (minimum score 6.5). Electronic applications accepted. *Faculty research:* Aquatic science, environmental physiology, parasitology, wildlife biology, management.

University of Guelph, Graduate Program Services, College of Biological Science, Department of Molecular and Cellular Biology, Guelph, ON N1G 2W1, Canada. Offers biochemistry (M Sc, PhD); biophysics (M Sc, PhD); botany (M Sc, PhD); microbiology (M Sc, PhD); molecular biology and genetics (M Sc, PhD). *Degree requirements:* For master's, thesis, research proposal; for doctorate, comprehensive exam, thesis/dissertation, research proposal. *Entrance requirements:* For master's, minimum B-average during previous 2 years of coursework; for doctorate, minimum A-average. Additional exam requirements/recommendations for international students: Required—TOEFL (minimum score 550 paper-based; 213 computer-based), IELTS (minimum score 6.5). Electronic applications accepted. *Faculty research:* Physiology, structure, genetics, and ecology of microbes; virology and microbial technology.

University of Hawaii at Manoa, Graduate Division, College of Natural Sciences, Department of Botany, Honolulu, HI 96822. Offers MS, PhD. Part-time programs available. *Faculty:* 24 full-time (7 women), 4 part-time/adjunct (0 women). *Students:* 55 full-time (30 women), 12 part-time (5 women); includes 16 minority (14 Asian Americans or Pacific Islanders, 2 Hispanic Americans), 12 international. Average age 30. 39 applicants, 18% accepted, 4 enrolled. In 2009, 14 master's, 6 doctorates awarded. Terminal master's awarded for partial completion of doctoral program. *Degree requirements:* For master's, one foreign language, thesis optional, presentation; for doctorate, one foreign language, comprehensive exam, thesis/dissertation, presentation. *Entrance requirements:* For master's and doctorate, GRE General Test, GRE Subject Test (biology). Additional exam requirements/recommendations for international students: Required—TOEFL (minimum score 540 paper-based; 207 computer-based; 76 iBT), IELTS (minimum score 5). *Application deadline:* For fall admission, 2/1 for domestic students, 1/15 for international students. Application fee: $60. *Expenses:* Tuition, state resident: full-time $8900; part-time $372 per credit. Tuition, nonresident: full-time $21,400; part-time $898 per credit. Required fees: $207 per semester. *Financial support:* In 2009–10, 2 students received support, including 7 fellowships (averaging $14,023 per year), 26 research assistantships (averaging $19,721 per year), 14 teaching assistantships (averaging $16,108 per year); tuition waivers (full and partial) also available. *Faculty research:* Plant ecology, evolution, systematics, conservation biology, ethnobotany. Total annual research expenditures: $14.3 million. *Application contact:* Tom Ranker, Graduate Field Chair, 808-956-8369, Fax: 808-956-3923, E-mail: ranker@hawaii.edu.

The University of Kansas, Graduate Studies, College of Liberal Arts and Sciences, Department of Ecology and Evolutionary Biology, Lawrence, KS 66045. Offers botany (MA, PhD); ecology and evolutionary biology (MA, PhD); entomology (MA, PhD). *Faculty:* 17 full-time (7 women), 29 part-time/adjunct (6 women). *Students:* 57 full-time (24 women), 4 part-time (1 woman); includes 1 minority (Hispanic American), 16 international. Average age 29. 49 applicants, 33% accepted, 8 enrolled. In 2009, 5 master's, 8 doctorates awarded. Terminal master's awarded for partial completion of doctoral program. *Degree requirements:* For master's, comprehensive exam, thesis (for some programs), 30-36 credits, thesis presentation; for doctorate, comprehensive exam, thesis/dissertation, residency, foreign language or other research skills, final exam and dissertation defense. *Entrance requirements:* For master's, GRE General Test, bachelor's degree with minimum undergraduate GPA of 3.0; for doctorate, GRE General Test, bachelor's degree; minimum undergraduate/graduate GPA of 3.0. Additional exam requirements/recommendations for international students: Required—TOEFL, IELTS. *Application deadline:* For fall admission, 12/15 priority date for domestic and international students. Applications are processed on a rolling basis. Application fee: $45 ($55 for international students). Electronic applications accepted. *Expenses:* Tuition, state resident: full-time $6492; part-time $270.50 per credit hour. Tuition, nonresident: full-time $15,510; part-time $646.25 per credit hour. Required fees: $847; $70.56 per credit hour. Tuition and fees vary according to course load and program. *Financial support:* Fellowships with tuition reimbursements, research assistantships with full and partial tuition reimbursements, teaching assistantships with full and partial tuition reimbursements, scholarships/grants, traineeships, health care benefits, and unspecified assistantships available. *Faculty research:* Biodiversity and macroevolution, ecology and global change, evolutionary mechanisms. *Unit head:* Dr. Christopher H. Haufler, Chair, 785-864-3255, Fax: 785-864-5860, E-mail: vulgare@ku.edu. *Application contact:* Jaime Rochelle Keeler, Graduate Coordinator, 785-864-2362, Fax: 785-864-5860, E-mail: jrkeeler@ku.edu.

University of Maine, Graduate School, College of Natural Sciences, Forestry, and Agriculture, Department of Biological Sciences, Program in Botany and Plant Pathology, Orono, ME 04469. Offers MS. Part-time programs available. *Students:* 3 full-time (all women). Average age 25. In 2009, 1 master's awarded. *Degree requirements:* For master's, thesis. *Entrance requirements:* For master's, GRE General Test. Additional exam requirements/recommendations for international students: Required—TOEFL. *Application deadline:* For fall admission, 2/1 priority date for domestic students. Applications are processed on a rolling basis. Application fee: $60. Electronic applications accepted. *Financial support:* Career-related internships or fieldwork, Federal Work-Study, institutionally sponsored loans, and tuition waivers (full) available. Financial award application deadline: 3/1. *Faculty research:* Molecular biology of viral and fungal pathogens, marine ecology, paleoecology and acid systematics and evolution. *Unit head:* Dr. Stellos Tavantiz, Coordinator, 207-581-2986. *Application contact:* Scott G. Delcourt, Associate Dean of the Graduate School, 207-581-3291, Fax: 207-581-3232, E-mail: graduate@maine.edu.

University of Manitoba, Faculty of Graduate Studies, Faculty of Science, Department of Biological Sciences, Winnipeg, MB R3T 2N2, Canada. Offers botany (M Sc, PhD); ecology (M Sc, PhD); zoology (M Sc, PhD).

University of Missouri–St. Louis, College of Arts and Sciences, Department of Biology, St. Louis, MO 63121. Offers biology (MS, PhD), including animal behavior (MS), biochemistry, biochemistry and biotechnology (MS), biotechnology (MS), conservation biology (MS), development (MS), ecology (MS), environmental studies (PhD), evolution (MS), genetics (MS),

Botany

University of Missouri–St. Louis (continued)

molecular biology and biochemistry (PhD), molecular/cellular biology (MS), physiology (MS), plant systematics, population biology (MS), tropical biology (MS); biotechnology (Certificate); tropical biology and conservation (Certificate). Part-time programs available. *Faculty:* 43 full-time (13 women), 2 part-time/adjunct (1 woman). *Students:* 54 full-time (27 women), 79 part-time (43 women); includes 15 minority (6 African Americans, 7 Asian Americans or Pacific Islanders, 2 Hispanic Americans), 47 international. Average age 29. 193 applicants, 44% accepted, 44 enrolled. In 2009, 30 master's, 7 doctorates, 9 other advanced degrees awarded. *Degree requirements:* For master's, thesis or alternative; for doctorate, thesis/dissertation, 1 semester of teaching experience. *Entrance requirements:* For master's, 3 letters of recommendation; for doctorate, GRE General Test, 3 letters of recommendation. Additional exam requirements/recommendations for international students: Required—TOEFL. *Application deadline:* For fall admission, 12/1 priority date for domestic and international students; for spring admission, 10/15 priority date for domestic and international students. Applications are processed on a rolling basis. Application fee: $35 ($40 for international students). Electronic applications accepted. *Expenses:* Tuition, state resident: full-time $5377; part-time $297.70 per credit hour. Tuition, nonresident: full-time $13,882; part-time $771.20 per credit hour. Required fees: $220; $12.20 per credit hour. One-time fee: $12. Tuition and fees vary according to course level, campus/location and program. *Financial support:* In 2009–10, 22 research assistantships with full and partial tuition reimbursements (averaging $16,300 per year), 14 teaching assistantships with full and partial tuition reimbursements (averaging $16,727 per year) were awarded; fellowships with full tuition reimbursements, career-related internships or fieldwork and Federal Work-Study also available. Support available to part-time students. Financial award application deadline: 2/1. *Faculty research:* Molecular biology, microbial genetics, animal behavior, tropical ecology, plant systematics. *Unit head:* Dr. Elizabeth Kellogg, Director of Graduate Studies, 314-516-6200, Fax: 314-516-6233, E-mail: tkellogg@umsl.edu. *Application contact:* 314-516-5458, Fax: 314-516-6996, E-mail: gradadm@umsl.edu.

The University of North Carolina at Chapel Hill, Graduate School, College of Arts and Sciences, Department of Biology, Program in Botany, Chapel Hill, NC 27599. Offers MA, MS, PhD. Terminal master's awarded for partial completion of doctoral program. *Degree requirements:* For master's, comprehensive exam, thesis (for some programs); for doctorate, comprehensive exam, thesis/dissertation. *Entrance requirements:* For master's and doctorate, GRE General Test, GRE Subject Test. Additional exam requirements/recommendations for international students: Required—TOEFL (minimum score 550 paper-based; 213 computer-based).

University of North Dakota, Graduate School, College of Arts and Sciences, Department of Biology, Grand Forks, ND 58202. Offers botany (MS, PhD); ecology (MS, PhD); entomology (MS, PhD); environmental biology (MS, PhD); fisheries/wildlife (MS, PhD); genetics (MS, PhD); zoology (MS, PhD). Terminal master's awarded for partial completion of doctoral program. *Degree requirements:* For master's, thesis, final exam; for doctorate, comprehensive exam, thesis/dissertation, final exam. *Entrance requirements:* For master's, GRE General Test, GRE Subject Test, minimum GPA of 3.0; for doctorate, GRE General Test, GRE Subject Test, minimum GPA of 3.5. Additional exam requirements/recommendations for international students: Required—TOEFL (minimum score 550 paper-based; 213 computer-based; 79 iBT), IELTS (minimum score 6.5). Electronic applications accepted. *Faculty research:* Population biology, wildlife ecology, RNA processing, hormonal control of behavior.

University of Oklahoma, Graduate College, College of Arts and Sciences, Department of Botany and Microbiology, Program in Botany, Norman, OK 73019. Offers MS, PhD. *Students:* 16 full-time (5 women), 2 part-time (both women); includes 1 minority (Asian American or Pacific Islander), 10 international. 7 applicants, 43% accepted, 2 enrolled. In 2009, 2 doctorates awarded. Terminal master's awarded for partial completion of doctoral program. *Degree requirements:* For master's, thesis, oral exam; for doctorate, one foreign language, thesis/dissertation, general exam. *Entrance requirements:* Additional exam requirements/recommendations for international students: Required—TOEFL (minimum score 550 paper-based; 213 computer-based). *Application deadline:* For fall admission, 4/1 for domestic and international students; for spring admission, 12/1 for domestic students, 9/1 for international students. Applications are processed on a rolling basis. Application fee: $40 ($90 for international students). Electronic applications accepted. *Expenses:* Tuition, state resident: full-time $3744; part-time $156 per credit hour. Tuition, nonresident: full-time $13,577; part-time $565.70 per credit hour. Required fees: $2415; $90.10 per credit hour. *Financial support:* In 2009–10, 16 students received support. Federal Work-Study, institutionally sponsored loans, scholarships/grants, health care benefits, and unspecified assistantships available. Support available to part-time students. Financial award applicants required to submit FAFSA. *Faculty research:* Plant molecular biology, global change biology, systematics and evolution of plant species, plant reproductive biology, science education. *Unit head:* Dr. Gordon Uno, Chair, 405-325-4321, Fax: 405-325-7619, E-mail: guno@ou.edu. *Application contact:* Adell Hopper, Staff Assistant, 405-325-4322, Fax: 405-325-7619, E-mail: ahopper@ou.edu.

University of Wisconsin–Madison, Graduate School, College of Letters and Science, Department of Botany, Madison, WI 53706-1380. Offers MS, PhD. Part-time programs available. Terminal master's awarded for partial completion of doctoral program. *Degree requirements:* For master's, thesis; for doctorate, one foreign language, thesis/dissertation. *Entrance requirements:* For master's and doctorate, GRE General Test. Electronic applications accepted. *Expenses:* Tuition, state resident: part-time $594 per credit. Tuition, nonresident: part-time $1504 per credit. Required fees: $65 per credit. Tuition and fees vary according to course load, program and reciprocity agreements. *Faculty research:* Taxonomy and systematics; ecology; structural botany; physiological, cellular, and molecular biology.

University of Wisconsin–Oshkosh, The Office of Graduate Studies, College of Letters and Science, Department of Biology and Microbiology, Oshkosh, WI 54901. Offers biology (MS), including botany, microbiology, zoology. *Degree requirements:* For master's, comprehensive exam, thesis. *Entrance requirements:* For master's, GRE General Test, minimum GPA of 3.0, BS in biology. Additional exam requirements/recommendations for international students: Required—TOEFL (minimum score 550 paper-based; 213 computer-based; 79 iBT). Electronic applications accepted.

University of Wyoming, College of Arts and Sciences, Department of Botany, Laramie, WY 82070. Offers botany (MS, PhD); botany/water resources (MS). Part-time programs available. Terminal master's awarded for partial completion of doctoral program. *Degree requirements:* For master's, thesis; for doctorate, thesis/dissertation. *Entrance requirements:* For master's and doctorate, GRE General Test, minimum GPA of 3.0. Additional exam requirements/recommendations for international students: Required—TOEFL. Electronic applications accepted. *Faculty research:* Ecology, systematics, physiology, mycology, genetics.

Virginia Polytechnic Institute and State University, Graduate School, College of Science, Department of Biological Sciences, Blacksburg, VA 24061. Offers botany (MS, PhD); ecology and evolutionary biology (MS, PhD); genetics and developmental biology (MS, PhD); microbiology (MS, PhD); zoology (MS, PhD). *Faculty:* 42 full-time (11 women). *Students:* 76 full-time (45 women), 5 part-time (1 woman); includes 28 minority (23 American Indian/Alaska Native, 2 Asian Americans or Pacific Islanders, 3 Hispanic Americans). Average age 28. 117 applicants, 15% accepted, 15 enrolled. In 2009, 11 master's, 11 doctorates awarded. *Entrance requirements:* For master's and doctorate, GRE, GMAT. Additional exam requirements/recommendations for international students: Required—TOEFL (minimum score 550 paper-based; 213 computer-based). *Application deadline:* For fall admission, 5/15 for international students; for spring admission, 10/15 for international students. Applications are processed on a rolling basis. Application fee: $65. Electronic applications accepted. *Expenses:* Tuition, area resident: full-time $10,228; part-time $459 per credit hour. Tuition, nonresident: full-time $17,892; part-time $865 per credit hour. Required fees: $1966; $451 per semester. *Financial support:* In 2009–10, 37 research assistantships with full tuition reimbursements (averaging $17,929 per year), 41 teaching assistantships with full tuition reimbursements (averaging $17,344 per year) were awarded; career-related internships or fieldwork, Federal Work-Study, scholarships/grants, and unspecified assistantships also available. Financial award application deadline: 1/15. *Faculty research:* Freshwater ecology, cell cycle regulation, behavioral ecology, motor proteins. Total annual research expenditures: $4.8 million. *Unit head:* Dr. Bob H. Jones, Dean, 540-231-9514, Fax: 540-231-9307, E-mail: rhjones@vt.edu. *Application contact:* Erik Nilsen, Information Contact, 540-231-5671, Fax: 540-231-9307, E-mail: enilsen@vt.edu.

Washington State University, Graduate School, College of Sciences, School of Biological Sciences, Department of Botany, Pullman, WA 99164. Offers MS, PhD. *Faculty:* 33. *Students:* 22 full-time (11 women). Average age 30. 27 applicants, 26% accepted, 7 enrolled. In 2009, 1 master's, 6 doctorates awarded. *Degree requirements:* For master's, comprehensive exam (for some programs), thesis (for some programs), oral exam; for doctorate, comprehensive exam, thesis/dissertation, oral exam. *Entrance requirements:* For master's and doctorate, GRE General Test, GRE Subject Test (recommended), three letters of recommendation, official transcripts from each university-level school attended, minimum GPA of 3.0. Additional exam requirements/recommendations for international students: Required—TOEFL, IELTS. *Application deadline:* For fall admission, 1/10 priority date for domestic students, 1/15 for international students; for spring admission, 9/15 for domestic students, 7/1 for international students. Applications are processed on a rolling basis. Application fee: $50. *Financial support:* In 2009–10, 3 fellowships (averaging $4,000 per year), 4 research assistantships with full and partial tuition reimbursements (averaging $13,917 per year), 21 teaching assistantships with full and partial tuition reimbursements (averaging $13,056 per year) were awarded; career-related internships or fieldwork, Federal Work-Study, institutionally sponsored loans, health care benefits, and tuition waivers (partial) also available. Financial award application deadline: 2/15; financial award applicants required to submit FAFSA. *Unit head:* Dr. Gary Thorgaard, Director, 509-335-3553, Fax: 509-335-3184, E-mail: sbs@wsu.edu. *Application contact:* Graduate School Admissions, 800-GRADWSU, Fax: 509-335-1949, E-mail: gradsch@wsu.edu.

Plant Biology

Arizona State University, Graduate College, College of Liberal Arts and Sciences, Division of Natural Sciences, School of Life Sciences, Tempe, AZ 85287. Offers biological design (PhD); biology (MNS, MS, PhD); biology and society (PhD); human and social dimensions of science and technology (PhD); microbiology (MNS, MS, PhD); molecular and cellular biology (MS, PhD); neuroscience (PhD); plant biology (MNS, MS, PhD). Accreditation: NAACLS. *Degree requirements:* For master's, thesis (MS); for doctorate, one foreign language, thesis/dissertation. *Entrance requirements:* For master's and doctorate, GRE.

Clemson University, Graduate School, College of Agriculture, Forestry and Life Sciences, Department of Entomology, Soils, and Plant Sciences, Program in Plant and Environmental Sciences, Clemson, SC 29634. Offers MS, PhD. *Students:* 34 full-time (14 women), 10 part-time (1 woman); includes 2 minority (both Hispanic Americans), 11 international. Average age 29. 35 applicants, 49% accepted, 14 enrolled. In 2009, 9 master's, 6 doctorates awarded. *Degree requirements:* For master's, thesis; for doctorate, thesis/dissertation. *Entrance requirements:* For master's, GRE General Test, bachelor's degree in biological science or chemistry; for doctorate, GRE General Test. Additional exam requirements/recommendations for international students: Required—TOEFL, IELTS. *Application deadline:* Applications are processed on a rolling basis. Application fee: $70 ($80 for international students). Electronic applications accepted. *Expenses:* Contact institution. *Financial support:* In 2009–10, 28 students received support, including 3 fellowships with full and partial tuition reimbursements available (averaging $11,033 per year), 21 research assistantships with partial tuition reimbursements available (averaging $16,366 per year), 7 teaching assistantships with partial tuition reimbursements available (averaging $14,566 per year); career-related internships or fieldwork, institutionally sponsored loans, scholarships/grants, health care benefits, and unspecified assistantships also available. Support available to part-time students. Financial award application deadline: 3/15; financial award applicants required to submit FAFSA. *Faculty research:* Systematics, aquatic botany, plant ecology, plant-fungus interactions, plant developmental genetics. *Unit head:* Dr. Patricia A. Zungoli, Chair, 864-656-3137, Fax: 864-656-5065, E-mail: pzngl@clemson.edu. *Application contact:* Dr. Halina Knap, Plant and Environmental Sciences Graduate Coordinator, 864-656-3102, Fax: 864-656-5065, E-mail: hskrpsk@clemson.edu.

Cornell University, Graduate School, Graduate Fields of Agriculture and Life Sciences, Field of Plant Biology, Ithaca, NY 14853-0001. Offers cytology (MS, PhD); paleobotany (MS, PhD); plant cell biology (MS, PhD); plant ecology (MS, PhD); plant molecular biology (MS, PhD); plant morphology, anatomy and biomechanics (MS, PhD); plant physiology (MS, PhD); systematic botany (MS, PhD). *Faculty:* 55 full-time (13 women). *Students:* 40 full-time (19 women); includes 3 minority (2 African Americans, 1 Hispanic American), 10 international. Average age 28. 54 applicants, 22% accepted, 6 enrolled. In 2009, 4 doctorates awarded. *Degree requirements:* For doctorate, comprehensive exam, thesis/dissertation. *Entrance requirements:* For doctorate, GRE General Test, GRE Subject Test in biology (recommended), 3 letters of recommendation. Additional exam requirements/recommendations for international students: Required—TOEFL (minimum score 610 paper-based; 253 computer-based; 77 iBT). *Application deadline:* For fall admission, 1/15 priority date for domestic students. Application fee: $70. Electronic applications accepted. *Expenses:* Tuition: Full-time $29,500. Required fees: $70. Full-time tuition and fees vary according to degree level, program and student level. *Financial support:* In 2009–10, 38 students received support, including 6 fellowships with full tuition reimbursements available; research assistantships with full tuition reimbursements available, teaching assistantships with full tuition reimbursements available, institutionally sponsored loans, scholarships/grants, health care benefits, tuition waivers (full and partial), and unspecified assistantships also available. Financial award applicants required to submit FAFSA. *Faculty research:* Plant cell biology/cytology; plant molecular biology; plant morphology/anatomy/biomechanics; plant physiology, systematic botany, paleobotany; plant ecology, ethnobotany, plant biochemistry, photosynthesis. *Unit head:* Director of Graduate Studies, 607-255-2131. *Application contact:* Graduate Field Assistant, 607-255-2131, E-mail: plbio@cornell.edu.

Illinois State University, Graduate School, College of Arts and Sciences, Department of Biological Sciences, Normal, IL 61790-2200. Offers animal behavior (MS); bacteriology (MS); biochemistry (MS); biological sciences (MS); biology (PhD); biophysics (MS); biotechnology (MS); botany (MS, PhD); cell biology (MS); conservation biology (MS); developmental biology (MS); ecology (MS, PhD); entomology (MS); evolutionary biology (MS); genetics (MS, PhD); immunology (MS); microbiology (MS, PhD); molecular biology (MS); molecular genetics (MS); neurobiology (MS); neuroscience (MS); parasitology (MS); physiology (MS, PhD); plant biology (MS); plant molecular biology (MS); plant sciences (MS); structural biology (MS); zoology (MS, PhD). Part-time programs available. *Degree requirements:* For master's, thesis or alternative;

for doctorate, variable foreign language requirement, thesis/dissertation, 2 terms of residency. *Entrance requirements:* For master's, GRE General Test, minimum GPA of 2.6 in last 60 hours of course work; for doctorate, GRE General Test. *Faculty research:* Redoc balance and drug development in schistosoma mansoni, control of the growth of listeria monocytogenes at low temperature, regulation of cell expansion and microtubule function by SPRI, CRUI: physiology and fitness consequences of different life history phenotypes.

Indiana University Bloomington, University Graduate School, College of Arts and Sciences, Department of Biology, Bloomington, IN 47405. Offers biology teaching (MAT); biotechnology (MA); evolution, ecology, and behavior (MA, PhD); genetics (PhD); microbiology (MA, PhD); molecular, cellular, and developmental biology (PhD); plant sciences (MA, PhD); zoology (MA, PhD). *Faculty:* 58 full-time (15 women), 21 part-time/adjunct (6 women). *Students:* 165 full-time (95 women); includes 14 minority (6 African Americans, 1 American Indian/Alaska Native, 7 Asian Americans or Pacific Islanders), 56 international. Average age 27. 312 applicants, 19% accepted, 24 enrolled. In 2009, 4 master's, 22 doctorates awarded. Terminal master's awarded for partial completion of doctoral program. *Degree requirements:* For master's, thesis, oral defense; for doctorate, thesis/dissertation, oral defense. *Entrance requirements:* For master's and doctorate, GRE General Test. Additional exam requirements/recommendations for international students: Required—TOEFL (minimum score 100 iBT). *Application deadline:* For fall admission, 1/5 priority date for domestic students, 12/1 priority date for international students. Application fee: $55 ($65 for international students). Electronic applications accepted. *Financial support:* In 2009–10, 165 students received support, including 62 fellowships with tuition reimbursements available (averaging $19,484 per year), 27 research assistantships with tuition reimbursements available (averaging $22,605 per year), 76 teaching assistantships with tuition reimbursements available (averaging $20,528 per year); scholarships/grants, traineeships, health care benefits, and unspecified assistantships also available. Financial award application deadline: 1/5. *Faculty research:* Evolution, ecology and behavior; microbiology; molecular biology and genetics; plant biology. *Unit head:* Dr. Roger Innes, Chair, 812-855-2219, Fax: 812-855-6082, E-mail: rinnes@indiana.edu. *Application contact:* Tracey D. Stohr, Graduate Student Recruitment Coordinator, 812-856-6303, Fax: 812-855-6082, E-mail: gradbio@indiana.edu.

Iowa State University of Science and Technology, Graduate College, Interdisciplinary Programs, Program in Plant Biology, Ames, IA 50011. Offers MS, PhD. *Students:* 23 full-time (6 women), 1 part-time (0 women); includes 2 minority (1 African American, 1 Asian American or Pacific Islander), 15 international. In 2009, 3 master's, 4 doctorates awarded. *Degree requirements:* For master's, thesis; for doctorate, thesis/dissertation. *Entrance requirements:* For master's and doctorate, GRE General Test. Additional exam requirements/recommendations for international students: Required—TOEFL (minimum score 550 paper-based; 79 iBT) or IELTS (minimum score 6.5). *Application deadline:* For fall admission, 1/15 priority date for domestic and international students. Applications are processed on a rolling basis. Application fee: $40 ($90 for international students). Electronic applications accepted. *Expenses:* Tuition, state resident: full-time $6716. Tuition, nonresident: full-time $8908. Tuition and fees vary according to course level, course load, program and student level. *Financial support:* In 2009–10, 21 research assistantships with full and partial tuition reimbursements (averaging $18,330 per year), 1 teaching assistantship with full and partial tuition reimbursement (averaging $16,750 per year) were awarded; scholarships/grants, health care benefits, and unspecified assistantships also available. *Unit head:* Dr. Steven Whitman, Supervisory Committee Chair, 515-294-9052, E-mail: ippm@iastate.edu. *Application contact:* Information Contact, 515-294-5836, Fax: 515-294-2592, E-mail: grad_admissions@iastate.edu.

Miami University, Graduate School, College of Arts and Science, Department of Botany, Oxford, OH 45056. Offers MA, MAT, MS, PhD. *Students:* 29 full-time (17 women), 14 international. *Entrance requirements:* For master's, GRE General Test, GRE Subject Test (recommended), minimum undergraduate GPA of 3.0 during previous 2 years or 2.75 overall; for doctorate, GRE General Test, GRE Subject Test (recommended), minimum undergraduate GPA of 2.75, 3.0 graduate. Additional exam requirements/recommendations for international students: Required—TOEFL (minimum score 550 paper-based). *Application deadline:* Applications are processed on a rolling basis. Application fee: $50. Electronic applications accepted. *Expenses:* Tuition, state resident: full-time $11,280. Tuition, nonresident: full-time $24,912. Required fees: $516. *Financial support:* Research assistantships, teaching assistantships with full tuition reimbursements, Federal Work-Study, institutionally sponsored loans, health care benefits, and unspecified assistantships available. Financial award application deadline: 3/1; financial award applicants required to submit FAFSA. *Faculty research:* Evolution of plants, fungi and algae; bioinformatics; molecular biology of plants and cyanobacteria; food web dynamics; plant science education. *Unit head:* Dr. John Kiss, Chair, 513-529-4200, E-mail: kissjz@muohio.edu. *Application contact:* Dr. R. James Hickey, Graduate Coordinator, 513-529-6000, E-mail: hickeyrj@muohio.edu.

Michigan State University, The Graduate School, College of Natural Science and College of Agriculture and Natural Resources, Department of Plant Biology, East Lansing, MI 48824. Offers plant biology (MS, PhD); plant breeding, genetics and biotechnology—plant biology (MS, PhD). *Faculty:* 17 full-time (6 women), 1 part-time/adjunct (0 women). *Students:* 51 full-time (29 women), 3 part-time (0 women); includes 4 minority (3 Asian Americans or Pacific Islanders, 1 Hispanic American), 17 international. Average age 28. 62 applicants, 23% accepted. In 2009, 4 master's, 2 doctorates awarded. *Entrance requirements:* Additional exam requirements/recommendations for international students: Required—TOEFL. Electronic applications accepted. *Expenses:* Tuition, state resident: part-time $478.25 per credit hour. Tuition, nonresident: part-time $966.50 per credit hour. Part-time tuition and fees vary according to program. *Financial support:* In 2009–10, 21 research assistantships with tuition reimbursements (averaging $8,107 per year), 17 teaching assistantships with tuition reimbursements (averaging $7,703 per year) were awarded. *Faculty research:* Physiological, molecular, and biochemical mechanisms; systematics; inheritance; ecology and geohistory. Total annual research expenditures: $5.4 million. *Unit head:* Dr. Richard E. Triemer, Chairperson, 517-353-4683, Fax: 517-353-1926, E-mail: triemer@msu.edu. *Application contact:* Kasey Baldwin, Graduate Secretary, 517-432-4429, Fax: 517-353-1926, E-mail: plntbiol@msu.edu.

New York University, Graduate School of Arts and Science, Department of Biology, New York, NY 10012-1019. Offers biology (PhD); biomedical journalism (MS); cancer and molecular biology (PhD); computational biology (PhD); computers in biological research (MS); developmental genetics (PhD); general biology (MS); immunology and microbiology (PhD); molecular genetics (PhD); neurobiology (PhD); oral biology (MS); plant biology (PhD); recombinant DNA technology (MS); MS/MBA. Part-time programs available. *Faculty:* 24 full-time (5 women). *Students:* 142 full-time (79 women), 44 part-time (28 women); includes 34 minority (1 African American, 25 Asian Americans or Pacific Islanders, 8 Hispanic Americans), 82 international. Average age 27. 362 applicants, 71% accepted, 72 enrolled. In 2009, 43 master's, 9 doctorates awarded. Terminal master's awarded for partial completion of doctoral program. *Degree requirements:* For master's, thesis or alternative, qualifying paper; for doctorate, comprehensive exam, thesis/dissertation. *Entrance requirements:* For master's, GRE General Test; for doctorate, GRE General Test, GRE Subject Test. Additional exam requirements/recommendations for international students: Required—TOEFL. *Application deadline:* For fall admission, 12/12 priority date for domestic students. Application fee: $90. *Expenses:* Tuition: Full-time $30,528; part-time $1272 per credit. Required fees: $2177. *Financial support:* Fellowships with tuition reimbursements, research assistantships with tuition reimbursements, teaching assistantships with tuition reimbursements, career-related internships or fieldwork, Federal Work-Study, institutionally sponsored loans, scholarships/grants, health care benefits, and unspecified assistantships available. Financial award application deadline: 12/12; financial award applicants required to submit FAFSA. *Faculty research:* Genomics, molecular and cell biology, development and molecular genetics, molecular evolution of plants and animals. *Unit head:* Gloria Coruzzi, Chair, 212-998-8200, Fax: 212-995-4015, E-mail: biology@nyu.edu. *Application contact:* Stephen Small, Director of Graduate Studies, 212-998-8200, Fax: 212-995-4015, E-mail: biology@nyu.edu.

North Carolina State University, Graduate School, College of Agriculture and Life Sciences, Department of Plant Biology, Raleigh, NC 27695. Offers MS, PhD. Part-time programs available. Terminal master's awarded for partial completion of doctoral program. *Degree requirements:* For master's, thesis (for some programs); for doctorate, thesis/dissertation. *Entrance requirements:* For master's and doctorate, GRE. Additional exam requirements/recommendations for international students: Required—TOEFL. Electronic applications accepted. *Faculty research:* Plant molecular and cell biology, aquatic ecology, community ecology, restoration, systematics plant pathogen and environmental interactions.

The Ohio State University, Graduate School, College of Biological Sciences, Department of Plant Cellular and Molecular Biology, Columbus, OH 43210. Offers plant biology (MS, PhD). *Faculty:* 18. *Students:* 7 full-time (4 women), 17 part-time (11 women), 22 international. Average age 28. In 2009, 1 doctorate awarded. *Degree requirements:* For master's, thesis optional; for doctorate, one foreign language, thesis/dissertation. *Entrance requirements:* For master's and doctorate, GRE General Test. Additional exam requirements/recommendations for international students: Required—TOEFL (minimum score 600 paper-based; 250 computer-based). *Application deadline:* For fall admission, 8/15 priority date for domestic students, 7/1 priority date for international students; for winter admission, 12/1 priority date for domestic students, 11/1 priority date for international students; for spring admission, 3/1 priority date for domestic students, 2/1 priority date for international students. Applications are processed on a rolling basis. Application fee: $40 ($50 for international students). Electronic applications accepted. *Expenses:* Tuition, state resident: full-time $10,683. Tuition, nonresident: full-time $25,923. Tuition and fees vary according to course load and program. *Financial support:* Fellowships, research assistantships, teaching assistantships, Federal Work-Study and institutionally sponsored loans available. Support available to part-time students. *Faculty research:* Regulatory, environmental, structural, systematic, and evolutionary botany. *Unit head:* David E. Somers, Graduate Studies Committee Chair, 614-292-8952, Fax: 614-292-6345, E-mail: somers.24@osu.edu. *Application contact:* 614-292-9444, Fax: 614-292-3895, E-mail: domestic.grad@osu.edu.

Ohio University, Graduate College, College of Arts and Sciences, Department of Environmental and Plant Biology, Athens, OH 45701-2979. Offers MS, PhD. Part-time programs available. *Faculty:* 12 full-time (2 women). *Students:* 25 full-time (11 women); includes 1 minority (African American), 10 international. Average age 25. 19 applicants, 32% accepted, 4 enrolled. In 2009, 1 master's, 2 doctorates awarded. *Degree requirements:* For master's, thesis, 2 quarters of teaching experience; for doctorate, comprehensive exam, thesis/dissertation, 2 quarters of teaching experience. *Entrance requirements:* For master's, GRE General Test, minimum GPA of 3.0; for doctorate, GRE General Test, minimum GPA of 3.2. Additional exam requirements/recommendations for international students: Required—TOEFL (minimum score 620 paper-based; 260 computer-based; 105 iBT) or IELTS (minimum score 7.5). *Application deadline:* For fall admission, 1/15 priority date for domestic and international students. Applications are processed on a rolling basis. Application fee: $50 ($55 for international students). Electronic applications accepted. *Expenses:* Tuition, state resident: full-time $7839; part-time $323 per quarter hour. Tuition, nonresident: full-time $15,831; part-time $654 per quarter hour. Required fees: $2931. *Financial support:* Fellowships with full tuition reimbursements, research assistantships with full tuition reimbursements, teaching assistantships with full tuition reimbursements, Federal Work-Study, institutionally sponsored loans, and scholarships/grants available. Financial award application deadline: 1/15. *Faculty research:* Eastern deciduous forest ecology, evolutionary developmental plant biology, phylogenetic systematics, plant cell wall biotechnology. Total annual research expenditures: $859,166. *Unit head:* Dr. Gar W. Rothwell, Chair, 740-593-1126, Fax: 740-593-1130, E-mail: rothwell@ohio.edu. *Application contact:* Dr. Allan Showalter, Graduate Chair, 740-593-1135, Fax: 740-593-1130, E-mail: showalte@ohio.edu.

Rutgers, The State University of New Jersey, New Brunswick, Graduate School-New Brunswick, Program in Plant Biology, Piscataway, NJ 08854-8097. Offers horticulture and plant technology (MS, PhD); molecular and cellular biology (MS, PhD); organismal and population biology (MS, PhD); plant pathology (MS, PhD). Part-time programs available. Terminal master's awarded for partial completion of doctoral program. *Degree requirements:* For master's, comprehensive exam, thesis or alternative; for doctorate, comprehensive exam, thesis/dissertation. *Entrance requirements:* For master's and doctorate, GRE General Test, GRE Subject Test (recommended). Additional exam requirements/recommendations for international students: Required—TOEFL (minimum score 600 paper-based; 250 computer-based). Electronic applications accepted. *Faculty research:* Molecular biology and biochemistry of plants, plant development and genomics, plant protection, plant improvement, plant management of horticultural and field crops.

Southern Illinois University Carbondale, Graduate School, College of Science, Department of Plant Biology, Carbondale, IL 62901-4701. Offers MS, PhD. *Degree requirements:* For master's, thesis; for doctorate, one foreign language, thesis/dissertation. *Entrance requirements:* For master's, GRE General Test, minimum GPA of 2.7; for doctorate, GRE General Test, minimum GPA of 3.25. Additional exam requirements/recommendations for international students: Required—TOEFL. *Faculty research:* Algal toxins, ethnobotany, community and wetland ecology, morphogenesis, systematics and evolution.

Texas A&M University, College of Agriculture and Life Sciences, Department of Soil and Crop Sciences, College Station, TX 77843. Offers agronomy (M Agr, MS, PhD); genetics (PhD); molecular and environmental plant sciences (MS, PhD); soil science (MS, PhD). *Faculty:* 36. *Students:* 82 full-time (28 women), 25 part-time (6 women); includes 16 minority (4 African Americans, 1 American Indian/Alaska Native, 1 Asian American or Pacific Islander, 10 Hispanic Americans), 33 international. Average age 26. In 2009, 6 master's, 2 doctorates awarded. *Degree requirements:* For master's, thesis; for doctorate, thesis/dissertation. *Entrance requirements:* For master's and doctorate, GRE General Test. Additional exam requirements/recommendations for international students: Required—TOEFL. *Application deadline:* For fall admission, 3/1 priority date for domestic students; for spring admission, 8/1 for domestic students. Applications are processed on a rolling basis. Application fee: $50 ($75 for international students). *Expenses:* Tuition, state resident: full-time $3991; part-time $221.74 per credit hour. Tuition, nonresident: full-time $9049; part-time $502.74 per credit hour. *Financial support:* In 2009–10, fellowships (averaging $16,000 per year), research assistantships with partial tuition reimbursements (averaging $15,000 per year) were awarded; career-related internships or fieldwork, Federal Work-Study, and institutionally sponsored loans also available. *Faculty research:* Soil and crop management, turfgrass science, weed science, cereal chemistry, food protein chemistry. *Unit head:* Department Head, 979-845-3041, E-mail: soilcrop@tamu.edu. *Application contact:* Department Head, 979-845-3041, E-mail: soilcrop@tamu.edu.

Université Laval, Faculty of Agricultural and Food Sciences, Program in Plant Biology, Québec, QC G1K 7P4, Canada. Offers M Sc, PhD. Terminal master's awarded for partial completion of doctoral program. *Degree requirements:* For master's, thesis (for some programs); for doctorate, comprehensive exam, thesis/dissertation. *Entrance requirements:* For master's and doctorate, knowledge of French and English. Electronic applications accepted.

University of Alberta, Faculty of Graduate Studies and Research, Department of Biological Sciences, Edmonton, AB T6G 2E1, Canada. Offers environmental biology and ecology (M Sc, PhD); microbiology and biotechnology (M Sc, PhD); molecular biology and genetics (M Sc, PhD); physiology and cell biology (M Sc, PhD); plant biology (M Sc, PhD); systematics and evolution (M Sc, PhD). *Faculty:* 72 full-time (15 women), 15 part-time/adjunct (4 women). *Students:* 238 full-time (117 women), 32 part-time (15 women), 31 international. 206 applicants, 42% accepted. In 2009, 29 master's, 31 doctorates awarded. Terminal master's awarded for partial completion of doctoral program. *Degree requirements:* For master's, thesis; for doctorate, thesis/dissertation. *Entrance requirements:* Additional exam requirements/recommendations for international students: Required—TOEFL. *Application deadline:* For fall admission, 3/1 priority date for domestic students. Applications are processed on a rolling basis. Application fee: $0. Tuition and fees charges are reported in Canadian dollars. *Expenses:* Tuition, area

Plant Biology

University of Alberta (continued)

resident: Full-time $4626 Canadian dollars; part-time $99.72 Canadian dollars per unit. International tuition: $8216 Canadian dollars full-time. Required fees: $3590 Canadian dollars; $99.72 Canadian dollars per unit. $215 Canadian dollars per term. *Financial support:* In 2009–10, 4 research assistantships with partial tuition reimbursements (averaging $12,000 per year), 103 teaching assistantships with partial tuition reimbursements (averaging $12,300 per year) were awarded; career-related internships or fieldwork and scholarships/grants also available. *Unit head:* Laura Frost, Chair, 780-492-1904. *Application contact:* Dr. John P. Chang, Associate Chair for Graduate Studies, 780-492-1257, Fax: 780-492-9457, E-mail: bio.grad.coordinator@ualberta.ca.

University of California, Berkeley, Graduate Division, College of Natural Resources, Department of Plant and Microbial Biology, Berkeley, CA 94720-1500. Offers plant biology (PhD). *Students:* 41 full-time (22 women). Average age 29. 61 applicants, 6 enrolled. In 2009, 4 doctorates awarded. *Degree requirements:* For doctorate, thesis/dissertation, qualifying exam, seminar presentation. *Entrance requirements:* For doctorate, GRE General Test, minimum GPA of 3.0, 3 letters of recommendation. *Application deadline:* For fall admission, 12/1 for domestic students. Application fee: $60 ($80 for international students). *Financial support:* Fellowships, research assistantships, teaching assistantships, unspecified assistantships available. *Faculty research:* Development, molecular biology, genetics, microbial biology, mycology. *Unit head:* Prof. Brian Staskawicz, Head, 510-642-9999, E-mail: pmbadvisor@nature.berkeley.edu. *Application contact:* Dana Jantz, Director of Student Services, 510-642-5167, Fax: 510-642-4995, E-mail: pmbadvisor@nature.berkeley.edu.

University of California, Davis, Graduate Studies, Graduate Group in Plant Biology, Davis, CA 95616. Offers MS, PhD. *Degree requirements:* For master's, comprehensive exam (for some programs), thesis (for some programs); for doctorate, thesis/dissertation. *Entrance requirements:* For master's, GRE General Test, GRE Subject Test (biology), minimum GPA of 3.0; for doctorate, GRE General Test, GRE Subject Test (biology). Additional exam requirements/recommendations for international students: Required—TOEFL (minimum score 550 paper-based; 213 computer-based). Electronic applications accepted. *Faculty research:* Cell and molecular biology, ecology, systematics and evolution, integrative plant and crop physiology, plant development and structure.

University of California, Riverside, Graduate Division, Department of Botany and Plant Sciences, Riverside, CA 92521-0102. Offers plant biology (MS, PhD), including plant genetics (PhD). Part-time programs available. *Faculty:* 40 full-time (13 women). *Students:* 52 full-time (34 women); includes 7 minority (1 African American, 4 Asian Americans or Pacific Islanders, 2 Hispanic Americans), 22 international. Average age 29. In 2009, 3 master's, 3 doctorates awarded. Terminal master's awarded for partial completion of doctoral program. *Degree requirements:* For master's, comprehensive exams or thesis; for doctorate, thesis/dissertation, qualifying exams. *Entrance requirements:* For master's and doctorate, GRE General Test, minimum GPA of 3.2. Additional exam requirements/recommendations for international students: Required—TOEFL (minimum score 550 paper-based; 213 computer-based; 80 iBT). *Application deadline:* For fall admission, 5/1 for domestic students, 2/1 for international students; for winter admission, 2/1 for domestic students, 7/1 for international students; for spring admission, 12/1 for domestic students, 10/1 for international students. Applications are processed on a rolling basis. Application fee: $80 ($100 for international students). Electronic applications accepted. *Financial support:* In 2009–10, fellowships with tuition reimbursements (averaging $12,000 per year), research assistantships with tuition reimbursements (averaging $23,000 per year), teaching assistantships with tuition reimbursements (averaging $16,500 per year) were awarded; career-related internships or fieldwork, Federal Work-Study, institutionally sponsored loans, scholarships/grants, and tuition waivers (full and partial) also available. Financial award application deadline: 2/1; financial award applicants required to submit FAFSA. *Faculty research:* Agricultural plant biology; biochemistry and physiology; cellular, molecular and developmental biology; ecology, evolution, systematics and ethnobotany; genetics, genomics and bioinformatics. *Unit head:* Dr. Jodie S. Holt, Chair, 951-827-3801. *Application contact:* Deidra Kornfeld, Graduate Program Assistant, 800-735-0717, Fax: 951-827-5517, E-mail: deidra.kornfeld@ucr.edu.

University of California, San Diego, Office of Graduate Studies, Division of Biological Sciences, Program in Plant Systems Biology, La Jolla, CA 92093. Offers PhD.

University of Connecticut, Graduate School, College of Liberal Arts and Sciences, Department of Molecular and Cell Biology, Field of Plant Cell and Molecular Biology, Storrs, CT 06269. Offers MS, PhD. *Faculty:* 1 full-time (0 women). *Students:* 3 full-time (0 women), all international. Average age 23. 14 applicants, 14% accepted, 1 enrolled. In 2009, 1 master's awarded. *Degree requirements:* For doctorate, thesis/dissertation. *Entrance requirements:* For master's and doctorate, GRE General Test, GRE Subject Test. Additional exam requirements/recommendations for international students: Required—TOEFL. *Application deadline:* For fall admission, 3/1 priority date for domestic students; for spring admission, 11/1 for domestic students. Applications are processed on a rolling basis. Application fee: $40 ($45 for international students). *Expenses:* Tuition, state resident: full-time $4725; part-time $525 per credit. Tuition, nonresident: full-time $12,267; part-time $1363 per credit. Required fees: $346 per semester. Tuition and fees vary according to course load. *Financial support:* In 2009–10, 1 research assistantship with full tuition reimbursement, 1 teaching assistantship with full tuition reimbursement were awarded; fellowships, Federal Work-Study, scholarships/grants, and unspecified assistantships also available. Financial award application deadline: 2/15. *Unit head:* David Benson, Head, 860-486-4258, Fax: 860-486-4331, E-mail: david.benson@uconn.edu. *Application contact:* Anne St. Onje, Graduate Coordinator, 860-486-4314, Fax: 860-486-3943, E-mail: anne.st_onje@uconn.edu.

See Close-Up on page 187.

University of Florida, Graduate School, College of Agricultural and Life Sciences and College of Liberal Arts and Sciences, Program in Plant Molecular and Cellular Biology, Gainesville, FL 32611. Offers MS, PhD. *Degree requirements:* For master's, thesis; for doctorate, thesis/dissertation. *Entrance requirements:* For master's and doctorate, GRE General Test, minimum GPA of 3.0. Electronic applications accepted. *Faculty research:* Plant pathology, genetics, biochemistry, microbiology.

University of Georgia, Graduate School, College of Arts and Sciences, Department of Plant Biology, Athens, GA 30602. Offers MS, PhD. *Faculty:* 21 full-time (8 women), 1 part-time/adjunct (0 women). *Students:* 41 full-time (21 women); includes 3 minority (1 Asian American or Pacific Islander, 2 Hispanic Americans), 16 international. 50 applicants, 24% accepted, 7 enrolled. In 2009, 1 master's, 9 doctorates awarded. *Degree requirements:* For master's, thesis; for doctorate, one foreign language, thesis/dissertation. *Entrance requirements:* For master's and doctorate, GRE General Test. *Application deadline:* For fall admission, 1/1 priority date for domestic students. Application fee: $50. Electronic applications accepted. *Expenses:* Tuition, state resident: full-time $6000; part-time $250 per credit hour. Tuition, nonresident: full-time $20,904; part-time $871 per credit hour. Required fees: $730 per semester. *Financial support:* Fellowships, research assistantships, teaching assistantships, unspecified assistantships available. *Unit head:* Dr. Michelle Momany, Head, 706-542-2014, Fax: 706-542-1805, E-mail: momany@plantbio.uga.edu. *Application contact:* Dr. Gregory W. Schmidt, Graduate Coordinator, 706-542-0280, Fax: 706-542-1805, E-mail: schmidt@plantbio.uga.edu.

University of Illinois at Urbana–Champaign, Graduate College, College of Liberal Arts and Sciences, School of Integrative Biology, Department of Plant Biology, Champaign, IL 61820. Offers MS, PhD. *Faculty:* 15 full-time (2 women). *Students:* 27 full-time (16 women), 13 part-time (7 women); includes 4 minority (1 African American, 1 American Indian/Alaska Native, 2 Asian Americans or Pacific Islanders), 3 international. 57 applicants, 23% accepted, 11 enrolled. In 2009, 6 master's, 2 doctorates awarded. *Entrance requirements:* For master's, GRE General Test, minimum GPA of 3.0; for doctorate, GRE, minimum GPA of 3.0. Additional exam requirements/recommendations for international students: Required—TOEFL (minimum score 600 paper-based; 250 computer-based; 102 iBT). *Application deadline:* Applications are processed on a rolling basis. Application fee: $60 ($75 for international students). Electronic applications accepted. *Financial support:* In 2009–10, 3 fellowships, 32 research assistantships, 18 teaching assistantships were awarded; tuition waivers (full and partial) also available. *Unit head:* Feng Sheng Hu, Head, 217-244-2982, Fax: 217-244-7246, E-mail: fhu@illinois.edu. *Application contact:* Lisa Boise, Office Administrator, 217-333-3261, Fax: 217-244-7246, E-mail: boise@illinois.edu.

University of Illinois at Urbana–Champaign, Graduate College, College of Liberal Arts and Sciences, School of Integrative Biology, Program in Physiological and Molecular Plant Biology, Champaign, IL 61820. Offers PhD. *Students:* 10 full-time (4 women); includes 1 minority (Hispanic American), 6 international. 2 applicants, 0% accepted. In 2009, 3 doctorates awarded. *Entrance requirements:* For doctorate, GRE, minimum GPA of 3.0. Additional exam requirements/recommendations for international students: Required—TOEFL (minimum score 570 paper-based; 230 computer-based; 89 iBT). *Application deadline:* Applications are processed on a rolling basis. Application fee: $60 ($75 for international students). Electronic applications accepted. *Financial support:* In 2009–10, 1 fellowship, 6 research assistantships, 4 teaching assistantships were awarded; tuition waivers (full and partial) also available. *Unit head:* Stephen Moose, Director, 217-244-6308, Fax: 217-244-1224, E-mail: smoose@illinois.edu. *Application contact:* Carol Hall, Office Manager, 217-333-8208, Fax: 217-244-1224, E-mail: cahall@illinois.edu.

The University of Iowa, Graduate College, College of Liberal Arts and Sciences, Department of Biology, Iowa City, IA 52242-1316. Offers biology (MS, PhD); cell and developmental biology (MS, PhD); evolution (MS, PhD); genetics (MS, PhD); neurobiology (MS, PhD); plant biology (MS, PhD). Terminal master's awarded for partial completion of doctoral program. *Degree requirements:* For master's, thesis optional, exam; for doctorate, comprehensive exam, thesis/dissertation. *Entrance requirements:* For master's and doctorate, GRE General Test, minimum GPA of 3.0. Additional exam requirements/recommendations for international students: Required—TOEFL (minimum score 600 paper-based; 250 computer-based; 100 iBT). Electronic applications accepted. *Faculty research:* Developmental neurobiology, evolutionary biology, signal transduction, cell motility, molecular genetics (plant and animal).

University of Maine, Graduate School, College of Natural Sciences, Forestry, and Agriculture, Department of Biological Sciences, Program in Plant Science, Orono, ME 04469. Offers PhD. Part-time programs available. *Students:* 1 full-time (0 women), 2 part-time (1 woman), 2 international. Average age 28. 1 applicant, 100% accepted, 1 enrolled. *Degree requirements:* For doctorate, thesis/dissertation. *Entrance requirements:* For doctorate, GRE General Test. Additional exam requirements/recommendations for international students: Required—TOEFL. *Application deadline:* For fall admission, 2/1 priority date for domestic students. Applications are processed on a rolling basis. Application fee: $65. Electronic applications accepted. *Financial support:* Career-related internships or fieldwork, Federal Work-Study, institutionally sponsored loans, and tuition waivers (full) available. Financial award application deadline: 3/1. *Unit head:* Dr. Stellos Tavantiz, Coordinator, 207-581-2986. *Application contact:* Scott G. Delcourt, Associate Dean of the Graduate School, 207-581-3291, Fax: 207-581-3232, E-mail: graduate@maine.edu.

University of Maine, Graduate School, College of Natural Sciences, Forestry, and Agriculture, Department of Plant, Soil, and Environmental Sciences, Orono, ME 04469. Offers biological sciences (PhD); ecology and environmental sciences (MS, PhD); forest resources (PhD); horticulture (MS); plant science (PhD); plant, soil, and environmental sciences (MS); resource utilization (MS). *Faculty:* 8 full-time (2 women), 9 part-time/adjunct (3 women). *Students:* 6 full-time (3 women), 3 part-time (2 women), 1 international. Average age 31. 6 applicants, 17% accepted, 0 enrolled. In 2009, 2 master's awarded. *Entrance requirements:* For master's and doctorate, GRE General Test. Additional exam requirements/recommendations for international students: Required—TOEFL. *Application deadline:* Applications are processed on a rolling basis. Application fee: $65. Electronic applications accepted. *Financial support:* In 2009–10, 16 research assistantships with tuition reimbursements (averaging $16,260 per year), 3 teaching assistantships with tuition reimbursements (averaging $12,790 per year) were awarded; scholarships/grants, tuition waivers (full and partial), and unspecified assistantships also available. *Unit head:* Dr. Gregory Porter, Chair, 207-581-2943, Fax: 207-581-3207. *Application contact:* Scott G. Delcourt, Associate Dean of the Graduate School, 207-581-3291, Fax: 207-581-3232, E-mail: graduate@maine.edu.

University of Maryland, College Park, Academic Affairs, College of Chemical and Life Sciences, Department of Cell Biology and Molecular Genetics, Program in Plant Biology, College Park, MD 20742. Offers MS, PhD. Part-time and evening/weekend programs available. *Application deadline:* For fall admission, 1/11 for domestic and international students. Applications are processed on a rolling basis. Application fee: $60. Electronic applications accepted. *Expenses:* Tuition, area resident: Part-time $471 per credit hour. Tuition, state resident: part-time $471 per credit hour. Tuition, nonresident: part-time $1016 per credit hour. Required fees: $337.04 per term. *Financial support:* Fellowships, research assistantships, teaching assistantships available. Financial award applicants required to submit FAFSA. *Faculty research:* Genetics and molecular biology, virology, plant pathology, mycology, nematology. *Unit head:* Dr. Stephen M. Wolniak, Acting Chair, 301-405-5435, Fax: 301-314-9489, E-mail: swolniak@umd.edu. *Application contact:* Dean of Graduate School, 301-405-0376, Fax: 301-314-9305.

University of Massachusetts Amherst, Graduate School, Interdisciplinary Programs, Program in Plant Biology, Amherst, MA 01003. Offers biochemistry and metabolism (MS, PhD); cell biology and physiology (MS, PhD); environmental, ecological and integrative (MS, PhD); genetics and evolution (MS, PhD). *Students:* 3 full-time (2 women), 12 part-time (5 women); includes 2 minority (both Asian Americans or Pacific Islanders), 8 international. Average age 27. 32 applicants, 41% accepted, 3 enrolled. In 2009, 3 master's, 1 doctorate awarded. *Degree requirements:* For master's, thesis; for doctorate, 2 foreign languages, comprehensive exam, thesis/dissertation. *Entrance requirements:* For master's and doctorate, GRE General Test. Additional exam requirements/recommendations for international students: Required—TOEFL (minimum score 550 paper-based; 213 computer-based; 80 iBT), IELTS (minimum score 6.5). *Application deadline:* For fall admission, 12/15 for domestic and international students; for spring admission, 10/1 for domestic and international students. Applications are processed on a rolling basis. Application fee: $50 ($65 for international students). Electronic applications accepted. *Expenses:* Tuition, state resident: full-time $2640; part-time $110 per credit. Tuition, nonresident: full-time $9936; part-time $414 per credit. Tuition and fees vary according to course load. *Financial support:* In 2009–10, 11 research assistantships with full tuition reimbursements (averaging $8,884 per year) were awarded; fellowships, teaching assistantships, career-related internships or fieldwork, Federal Work-Study, scholarships/grants, traineeships, health care benefits, tuition waivers (full), and unspecified assistantships also available. Support available to part-time students. Financial award application deadline: 12/15. *Unit head:* Dr. Elsbeth L. Walker, Graduate Program Director, 413-577-3217, Fax: 413-545-3243. *Application contact:* Jean M. Ames, Supervisor of Admissions, 413-545—0722, Fax: 413-577-0010, E-mail: gradadm@grad.umass.edu.

University of Minnesota, Twin Cities Campus, Graduate School, College of Biological Sciences, Program in Plant Biological Sciences, Minneapolis, MN 55455-0213. Offers MS, PhD. Part-time programs available. *Faculty:* 58 full-time (17 women). *Students:* 37 full-time (23 women); includes 12 minority (1 African American, 11 Asian Americans or Pacific Islanders). Average age 24. 51 applicants, 39% accepted, 7 enrolled. In 2009, 2 master's, 4 doctorates awarded. Terminal master's awarded for partial completion of doctoral program. *Degree requirements:* For master's, thesis or alternative; for doctorate, thesis/dissertation, written and oral preliminary exams. *Entrance requirements:* For master's and doctorate, GRE General Test. Additional exam requirements/recommendations for international students: Required—TOEFL. *Application deadline:* For fall admission, 12/15 priority date for domestic and international students. Applications are processed on a rolling basis. Application fee: $75 ($95 for international students). Electronic applications accepted. *Financial support:* In 2009–10, 35 students received support, including 2 fellowships with full tuition reimbursements available (averaging $22,765 per year), 23 research assistantships with full tuition reimbursements available (averaging $22,765 per year), 10 teaching assistantships with full tuition reimbursements available (averaging $22,765 per year); career-related internships or fieldwork, Federal Work-Study, scholarships/grants, traineeships, tuition waivers (full and partial), and unspecified assistantships also available. Financial award application deadline: 1/1; financial award applicants required to submit FAFSA. *Faculty research:* Cell and molecular biology; plant physiology; plant structure, diversity, and development; ecology, systematics, evolution and genomics. Total annual research expenditures: $14.9 million. *Unit head:* Prof. Kathryn VandenBosch, Head, 612-625-1234, Fax: 612-625-1738, E-mail: kvandenb@cbs.umn.edu. *Application contact:* Prof. Jane Glazebrook, Director of Graduate Studies, 612-624-5194, Fax: 612-625-1738, E-mail: jglazebr@umn.edu.

University of Missouri, Graduate School, College of Agriculture, Food and Natural Resources, Division of Plant Sciences, Program in Plant Biology and Genetics, Columbia, MO 65211. Offers MS, PhD. Terminal master's awarded for partial completion of doctoral program. *Degree requirements:* For master's, thesis; for doctorate, thesis/dissertation. *Entrance requirements:* For master's and doctorate, GRE General Test, minimum GPA of 3.0. *Application deadline:* For fall admission, 3/1 priority date for domestic students. Applications are processed on a rolling basis. Application fee: $45 ($60 for international students). *Financial support:* Research assistantships, teaching assistantships, institutionally sponsored loans available. *Unit head:* Dr. Jeanne Mihail, Director of Graduate Studies, 573-882-0574, E-mail: mihailj@missouri.edu. *Application contact:* Dr. Jeanne Mihail, Director of Graduate Studies, 573-882-0574, E-mail: mihailj@missouri.edu.

University of New Hampshire, Graduate School, College of Life Sciences and Agriculture, Department of Biological Sciences, Program in Plant Biology, Durham, NH 03824. Offers MS, PhD. Part-time programs available. *Faculty:* 22 full-time. *Students:* 8 full-time (4 women), 9 part-time (6 women), 4 international. Average age 31. 20 applicants, 15% accepted, 3 enrolled. In 2009, 3 master's, 1 doctorate awarded. Terminal master's awarded for partial completion of doctoral program. *Degree requirements:* For master's, thesis; for doctorate, thesis/dissertation. *Entrance requirements:* For master's and doctorate, GRE General Test, GRE Subject Test. Additional exam requirements/recommendations for international students: Required—TOEFL (minimum score 550 paper-based; 213 computer-based; 80 iBT). *Application deadline:* For fall admission, 6/1 priority date for domestic students, 4/1 for international students; for spring admission, 12/1 for domestic students. Applications are processed on a rolling basis. Application fee: $65. Electronic applications accepted. *Expenses:* Tuition, state resident: full-time $10,380; part-time $577 per credit hour. Tuition, nonresident: full-time $24,350; part-time $1002 per credit hour. Required fees: $1550; $387.50 per semester. Tuition and fees vary according to course load and program. *Financial support:* In 2009–10, 13 students received support, including 4 research assistantships, 9 teaching assistantships; fellowships, career-related internships or fieldwork, Federal Work-Study, scholarships/grants, and tuition waivers (full and partial) also available. Support available to part-time students. Financial award application deadline: 2/15. *Unit head:* Christopher Neefus, Chairperson, 603-862-3205. *Application contact:* Diane Lavalliere, Administrative Assistant, 603-862-4095, E-mail: diane.lavallier@unh.edu.

The University of Texas at Austin, Graduate School, College of Natural Sciences, School of Biological Sciences, Program in Plant Biology, Austin, TX 78712-1111. Offers MA, PhD. *Entrance requirements:* For master's and doctorate, GRE General Test, minimum GPA of 3.0. Additional exam requirements/recommendations for international students: Required—TOEFL. Electronic applications accepted. *Faculty research:* Systematics, plant molecular biology, psychology, ecology, evolution.

University of Vermont, Graduate College, College of Agriculture and Life Sciences, Department of Plant Biology, Plant Biology Program, Burlington, VT 05405. Offers MS, PhD. *Faculty:* 11 full-time (4 women). *Students:* 12 (6 women), 1 international. 39 applicants, 21% accepted, 0 enrolled. In 2009, 3 master's awarded. *Degree requirements:* For master's, comprehensive exam, thesis; for doctorate, comprehensive exam, thesis/dissertation. *Entrance requirements:* For master's and doctorate, GRE General Test. Additional exam requirements/recommendations for international students: Required—TOEFL (minimum score 550 paper-based; 213 computer-based; 80 iBT). *Application deadline:* For fall admission, 1/1 priority date for domestic and international students. Applications are processed on a rolling basis. Application fee: $40. Electronic applications accepted. *Expenses:* Tuition, state resident: part-time $508 per credit hour. Tuition, nonresident: part-time $1281 per credit hour. *Financial support:* In 2009–10, research assistantships with full tuition reimbursements (averaging $21,800 per year), teaching assistantships with full tuition reimbursements (averaging $21,800 per year) were awarded; fellowships, health care benefits, tuition waivers (full and partial), and stipends also available. Financial award application deadline: 1/1. *Faculty research:* Systematics, biochemistry, ecology and evolution, physiology, development and molecular genetics. Total annual research expenditures: $739,761. *Unit head:* Dr. Thomas Vogelmann, Chairperson, 802-656-2930, Fax: 802-656-0440. *Application contact:* Dr. C. Paris, Coordinator, 802-656-2930, Fax: 802-656-0440.

The University of Western Ontario, Faculty of Graduate Studies, Biosciences Division, Department of Plant Sciences, London, ON N6A 5B8, Canada. Offers plant and environmental sciences (M Sc); plant sciences (M Sc, PhD); plant sciences and environmental sciences (PhD); plant sciences and molecular biology (M Sc, PhD). *Degree requirements:* For master's, thesis; for doctorate, thesis/dissertation. *Entrance requirements:* For doctorate, M Sc or equivalent. Additional exam requirements/recommendations for international students: Required—TOEFL. *Faculty research:* Ecology systematics, plant biochemistry and physiology, yeast genetics, molecular biology.

Washington University in St. Louis, Graduate School of Arts and Sciences, Division of Biology and Biomedical Sciences, Program in Plant Biology, St. Louis, MO 63130-4899. Offers PhD. *Degree requirements:* For doctorate, thesis/dissertation. *Entrance requirements:* For doctorate, GRE General Test, GRE Subject Test. Electronic applications accepted.

Yale University, Graduate School of Arts and Sciences, Department of Molecular, Cellular, and Developmental Biology, Program in Plant Sciences, New Haven, CT 06520. Offers PhD. *Degree requirements:* For doctorate, thesis/dissertation. *Entrance requirements:* For doctorate, GRE General Test, GRE Subject Test.

Plant Molecular Biology

Cornell University, Graduate School, Graduate Fields of Agriculture and Life Sciences, Field of Plant Biology, Ithaca, NY 14853-0001. Offers cytology (MS, PhD); paleobotany (MS, PhD); plant cell biology (MS, PhD); plant ecology (MS, PhD); plant molecular biology (MS, PhD); plant morphology, anatomy and biomechanics (MS, PhD); plant physiology (MS, PhD); systematic botany (MS, PhD). *Faculty:* 55 full-time (13 women). *Students:* 40 full-time (19 women); includes 3 minority (2 African Americans, 1 Hispanic American), 10 international. Average age 28. 54 applicants, 22% accepted, 6 enrolled. In 2009, 4 doctorates awarded. *Degree requirements:* For doctorate, comprehensive exam, thesis/dissertation. *Entrance requirements:* For doctorate, GRE General Test, GRE Subject Test in biology (recommended), 3 letters of recommendation. Additional exam requirements/recommendations for international students: Required—TOEFL (minimum score 610 paper-based; 253 computer-based; 77 iBT). *Application deadline:* For fall admission, 1/15 priority date for domestic students. Application fee: $70. Electronic applications accepted. *Expenses:* Tuition: Full-time $29,500. Required fees: $70. Full-time tuition and fees vary according to degree level, program and student level. *Financial support:* In 2009–10, 38 students received support, including 6 fellowships with full tuition reimbursements available; research assistantships with full tuition reimbursements available, teaching assistantships with full tuition reimbursements available, institutionally sponsored loans, scholarships/grants, health care benefits, tuition waivers (full and partial), and unspecified assistantships also available. Financial award applicants required to submit FAFSA. *Faculty research:* Plant cell biology/cytology; plant molecular biology; plant morphology/anatomy/biomechanics; plant physiology, systematic botany, paleobotany; plant ecology, ethnobotany, plant biochemistry, photosynthesis. *Unit head:* Director of Graduate Studies, 607-255-2131. *Application contact:* Graduate Field Assistant, 607-255-2131, E-mail: plbio@cornell.edu.

Illinois State University, Graduate School, College of Arts and Sciences, Department of Biological Sciences, Normal, IL 61790-2200. Offers animal behavior (MS); bacteriology (MS); biochemistry (MS); biological sciences (MS); biology (PhD); biophysics (MS); biotechnology (MS); botany (MS, PhD); cell biology (MS); conservation biology (MS); developmental biology (MS); ecology (MS, PhD); entomology (MS); evolutionary biology (MS); genetics (MS, PhD); immunology (MS); microbiology (MS, PhD); molecular biology (MS); molecular genetics (MS); neurobiology (MS); neuroscience (MS); parasitology (MS); physiology (MS, PhD); plant biology (MS); plant molecular biology (MS); plant sciences (MS); structural biology (MS); zoology (MS, PhD). Part-time programs available. *Degree requirements:* For master's, thesis or alternative; for doctorate, variable foreign language requirement, thesis/dissertation, 2 terms of residency. *Entrance requirements:* For master's, GRE General Test, minimum GPA of 2.6 in last 60 hours of course work; for doctorate, GRE General Test. *Faculty research:* Redoc balance and drug development in schistosoma mansoni, control of the growth of listeria monocytogenes at low temperature, regulation of cell expansion and microtubule function by SPRI, CRUI: physiology and fitness consequences of different life history phenotypes.

Michigan Technological University, Graduate School, School of Forest Resources and Environmental Science, Program in Forest Molecular Genetics and Biotechnology, Houghton, MI 49931. Offers MS, PhD. Part-time programs available. Terminal master's awarded for partial completion of doctoral program. *Degree requirements:* For master's, thesis (for some programs); for doctorate, comprehensive exam, thesis/dissertation. *Entrance requirements:* For master's, GRE. Additional exam requirements/recommendations for international students: Required—TOEFL (minimum score 550 paper-based; 213 computer-based). Electronic applications accepted.

Rutgers, The State University of New Jersey, New Brunswick, Graduate School-New Brunswick, Program in Plant Biology, Piscataway, NJ 08854-8097. Offers horticulture and plant technology (MS, PhD); molecular and cellular biology (MS, PhD); organismal and population biology (MS, PhD); plant pathology (MS, PhD). Part-time programs available. Terminal master's awarded for partial completion of doctoral program. *Degree requirements:* For master's, comprehensive exam, thesis or alternative; for doctorate, comprehensive exam, thesis/dissertation. *Entrance requirements:* For master's and doctorate, GRE General Test, GRE Subject Test (recommended). Additional exam requirements/recommendations for international students: Required—TOEFL (minimum score 600 paper-based; 250 computer-based). Electronic applications accepted. *Faculty research:* Molecular biology and biochemistry of plants, plant development and genomics, plant protection, plant improvement, plant management of horticultural and field crops.

University of California, San Diego, Office of Graduate Studies, Division of Biological Sciences, Program in Plant Molecular Biology, La Jolla, CA 92093. Offers PhD. Offered in association with the Salk Institute. *Degree requirements:* For doctorate, thesis/dissertation, qualifying exam. Electronic applications accepted.

University of Connecticut, Graduate School, College of Liberal Arts and Sciences, Department of Molecular and Cell Biology, Field of Plant Cell and Molecular Biology, Storrs, CT 06269. Offers MS, PhD. *Faculty:* 1 full-time (0 women). *Students:* 3 full-time (0 women), all international. Average age 23. 14 applicants, 14% accepted, 1 enrolled. In 2009, 1 master's awarded. *Degree requirements:* For doctorate, thesis/dissertation. *Entrance requirements:* For master's and doctorate, GRE General Test, GRE Subject Test. Additional exam requirements/recommendations for international students: Required—TOEFL. *Application deadline:* For fall admission, 3/1 priority date for domestic students; for spring admission, 11/1 for domestic students. Applications are processed on a rolling basis. Application fee: $40 ($45 for international students). *Expenses:* Tuition, state resident: full-time $4725; part-time $525 per credit. Tuition, nonresident: full-time $12,267; part-time $1363 per credit. Required fees: $346 per semester. Tuition and fees vary according to course load. *Financial support:* In 2009–10, 1 research assistantship with full tuition reimbursement, 1 teaching assistantship with full tuition reimbursement were awarded; fellowships, Federal Work-Study, scholarships/grants, and unspecified assistantships also available. Financial award application deadline: 2/15. *Unit head:* David Benson, Head, 860-486-4258, Fax: 860-486-4331, E-mail: david.benson@uconn.edu. *Application contact:* Anne St. Onje, Graduate Coordinator, 860-486-4314, Fax: 860-486-3943, E-mail: anne.st_onje@uconn.edu.

See Close-Up on page 187.

University of Florida, Graduate School, College of Agricultural and Life Sciences and College of Liberal Arts and Sciences, Program in Plant Molecular and Cellular Biology, Gainesville, FL 32611. Offers MS, PhD. *Degree requirements:* For master's, thesis; for doctorate, thesis/dissertation. *Entrance requirements:* For master's and doctorate, GRE General Test, minimum GPA of 3.0. Electronic applications accepted. *Faculty research:* Plant pathology, genetics, biochemistry, microbiology.

University of Massachusetts Amherst, Graduate School, Interdisciplinary Programs, Program in Plant Biology, Amherst, MA 01003. Offers biochemistry and metabolism (MS, PhD); cell biology and physiology (MS, PhD); environmental, ecological and integrative (MS, PhD); genetics and evolution (MS, PhD). *Students:* 3 full-time (2 women), 12 part-time (5 women); includes 2 minority (both Asian Americans or Pacific Islanders), 8 international. Average age 27. 32 applicants, 41% accepted, 3 enrolled. In 2009, 3 master's, 1 doctorate awarded. *Degree requirements:* For master's, thesis; for doctorate, 2 foreign languages, comprehensive exam, thesis/dissertation. *Entrance requirements:* For master's and doctorate, GRE General Test. Additional exam requirements/recommendations for international students: Required—TOEFL (minimum score 550 paper-based; 213 computer-based; 80 iBT), IELTS (minimum score 6.5). *Application deadline:* For fall admission, 12/15 for domestic and international students; for spring admission, 10/1 for domestic and international students. Applications are processed on a rolling basis. Application fee: $50 ($65 for international students). Electronic applications accepted. *Expenses:* Tuition, state resident: full-time $2640; part-time $110 per credit. Tuition, nonresident: full-time $9936; part-time $414 per credit. Tuition and fees vary according to course load. *Financial support:* In 2009–10, 11 research assistantships with full tuition reimbursements (averaging $8,884 per year) were awarded; fellowships, teaching assistantships, career-related internships or fieldwork, Federal Work-Study, scholarships/

Plant Molecular Biology

University of Massachusetts Amherst (continued)
grants, traineeships, health care benefits, tuition waivers (full), and unspecified assistantships also available. Support available to part-time students. Financial award application deadline: 12/15. *Unit head:* Dr. Elsbeth L. Walker, Graduate Program Director, 413-577-3217, Fax: 413-545-3243. *Application contact:* Jean M. Ames, Supervisor of Admissions, 413-545—0722, Fax: 413-577-0010, E-mail: gradadm@grad.umass.edu.

Washington State University, Graduate School, College of Agricultural, Human, and Natural Resource Sciences, Program in Molecular Plant Sciences, Pullman, WA 99164. Offers MS, PhD. *Faculty:* 23. *Students:* 42 full-time (16 women), 2 part-time (both women); includes 1 minority (African American), 18 international. Average age 27. 70 applicants, 24% accepted, 10 enrolled. In 2009, 1 master's, 4 doctorates awarded. Terminal master's awarded for partial completion of doctoral program. *Degree requirements:* For master's, comprehensive exam (for some programs), thesis (for some programs), oral exam, written exam; for doctorate, comprehensive exam, thesis/dissertation, oral exam, written exam. *Entrance requirements:* For master's and doctorate, GRE General Test. Additional exam requirements/recommendations for international students: Required—TOEFL, IELTS. *Application deadline:* For fall admission, 1/1 priority date for domestic students, 1/1 for international students. Applications are processed on a rolling basis. Application fee: $50. *Financial support:* In 2009–10, 4 fellowships (averaging $4,500 per year), 18 research assistantships with full and partial tuition reimbursements (averaging $13,917 per year), 4 teaching assistantships with full and partial tuition reimbursements (averaging $13,056 per year) were awarded; career-related internships or fieldwork, Federal Work-Study, institutionally sponsored loans, and tuition waivers (partial) also available. Financial award application deadline: 4/1; financial award applicants required to submit FAFSA. *Faculty research:* Cell response to environmental signals, transport of amino acids, regulation of synthesis of defense proteins. *Unit head:* Dr. Michael Neff, Chair, 509-335-7705, Fax: 509-335-1949, E-mail: mmneff@wsu.edu. *Application contact:* Graduate School Admissions, 800-GRADWSU, Fax: 509-335-1949, E-mail: gradsch@wsu.edu.

Plant Pathology

Auburn University, Graduate School, College of Agriculture, Department of Entomology and Plant Pathology, Auburn University, AL 36849. Offers entomology (M Ag, MS, PhD); plant pathology (M Ag, MS, PhD). Part-time programs available. *Faculty:* 17 full-time (6 women). *Students:* 24 full-time (10 women), 11 part-time (4 women); includes 3 minority (1 African American, 2 Asian Americans or Pacific Islanders), 17 international. Average age 30. 21 applicants, 57% accepted, 7 enrolled. In 2009, 3 master's, 2 doctorates awarded. *Degree requirements:* For master's, thesis (for some programs); for doctorate, one foreign language, thesis/dissertation. *Entrance requirements:* For master's, GRE General Test; for doctorate, GRE General Test, GRE Subject Test, master's degree with thesis. *Application deadline:* For fall admission, 7/7 for domestic students; for spring admission, 11/24 for domestic students. Applications are processed on a rolling basis. Application fee: $50 ($60 for international students). Electronic applications accepted. *Expenses:* Tuition, state resident: full-time $6240. Tuition, nonresident: full-time $18,720. International tuition: $18,938 full-time. Required fees: $492. Tuition and fees vary according to course load, program and reciprocity agreements. *Financial support:* Research assistantships, teaching assistantships, Federal Work-Study available. Support available to part-time students. Financial award application deadline: 3/15; financial award applicants required to submit FAFSA. *Faculty research:* Pest management, biological control, systematics, medical entomology. *Unit head:* Dr. Arthur Appel, Chair, 334-844-5006. *Application contact:* Dr. George Flowers, Dean of the Graduate School, 334-844-2125.

Colorado State University, Graduate School, College of Agricultural Sciences, Department of Bioagricultural Sciences and Pest Management, Fort Collins, CO 80523-1177. Offers entomology (MS, PhD); plant pathology and weed science (MS, PhD). Part-time programs available. *Faculty:* 19 full-time (3 women). *Students:* 19 full-time (8 women), 13 part-time (5 women); includes 3 minority (2 American Indian/Alaska Native, 1 Hispanic American), 2 international. Average age 31. 26 applicants, 31% accepted, 4 enrolled. In 2009, 5 master's, 1 doctorate awarded. *Degree requirements:* For master's, comprehensive exam, thesis; for doctorate, comprehensive exam, thesis/dissertation, 72 credits. *Entrance requirements:* For master's, GRE General Test, minimum GPA of 3.0, letters of recommendation; for doctorate, GRE General Test, minimum GPA of 3.0, letters of recommendation, essay. Additional exam requirements/recommendations for international students: Required—TOEFL (minimum score 550 paper-based; 213 computer-based). *Application deadline:* For fall admission, 1/15 priority date for domestic and international students; for spring admission, 9/1 priority date for domestic and international students. Applications are processed on a rolling basis. Application fee: $50. Electronic applications accepted. *Expenses:* Tuition, state resident: full-time $6434; part-time $359.10 per credit. Tuition, nonresident: full-time $18,116; part-time $1006.45 per credit. Required fees: $1496; $83 per credit. *Financial support:* In 2009–10, 7 fellowships with partial tuition reimbursements (averaging $32,685 per year), 22 research assistantships with full tuition reimbursements (averaging $14,370 per year), 8 teaching assistantships with full tuition reimbursements (averaging $11,230 per year) were awarded; career-related internships or fieldwork, scholarships/grants, unspecified assistantships, and fellowships also available. Financial award application deadline: 1/15; financial award applicants required to submit FAFSA. *Faculty research:* Biological control of post-insect plant pathogens and weeds, integrated pest management, weed ecology and biology, pest genomes of plants. Total annual research expenditures: $2.6 million. *Unit head:* Thomas O. Holtzer, Head, 970-491-5261, Fax: 970-491-3862, E-mail: tholtzer@lamar.colostate.edu. *Application contact:* Janet Dill, Education Coordinator, 970-491-0402, Fax: 970-491-3862, E-mail: janet.dill@colostate.edu.

Cornell University, Graduate School, Graduate Fields of Agriculture and Life Sciences, Field of Plant Pathology and Plant-Microbe Biology, Ithaca, NY 14853-0001. Offers ecological and environmental plant pathology (MPS, MS, PhD); epidemiological plant pathology (MPS, MS, PhD); molecular plant pathology (MPS, MS, PhD); mycology (MPS, MS, PhD); plant disease epidemiology (MPS, MS, PhD); plant pathology (MPS, MS, PhD). *Faculty:* 44 full-time (12 women). *Students:* 30 full-time (17 women); includes 2 minority (both Hispanic Americans), 8 international. Average age 31. 32 applicants, 28% accepted, 6 enrolled. In 2009, 1 master's, 4 doctorates awarded. *Degree requirements:* For master's, thesis (MS), project paper (MPS); for doctorate, comprehensive exam, thesis/dissertation. *Entrance requirements:* For master's and doctorate, GRE General Test, GRE Subject Test (biology recommended), 3 letters of recommendation. Additional exam requirements/recommendations for international students: Required—TOEFL (minimum score 550 paper-based; 213 computer-based; 77 iBT). *Application deadline:* For fall admission, 1/15 priority date for domestic students. Applications are processed on a rolling basis. Application fee: $70. Electronic applications accepted. *Expenses:* Tuition: Full-time $29,500. Required fees: $70. Full-time tuition and fees vary according to degree level, program and student level. *Financial support:* In 2009–10, 26 students received support, including 2 fellowships with full tuition reimbursements available, 4 research assistantships with full tuition reimbursements available; teaching assistantships with full tuition reimbursements available, institutionally sponsored loans, scholarships/grants, health care benefits, tuition waivers (full and partial), and unspecified assistantships also available. Financial award applicants required to submit FAFSA. *Faculty research:* Plant pathology; mycology; molecular plant pathology; plant disease epidemiology, ecological and environmental plant pathology; plant disease epidemiology and simulation modeling. *Unit head:* Director of Graduate Studies, 607-255-3259, Fax: 607-255-4471. *Application contact:* Graduate Field Assistant, 607-255-3259, Fax: 607-255-4471, E-mail: plpathology@cornell.edu.

Iowa State University of Science and Technology, Graduate College, College of Agriculture, Department of Plant Pathology, Ames, IA 50011. Offers MS, PhD. *Faculty:* 18 full-time (4 women). *Students:* 35 full-time (19 women), 2 part-time (1 woman); includes 3 minority (2 African Americans, 1 Asian American or Pacific Islander), 17 international. 28 applicants, 18% accepted, 5 enrolled. In 2009, 2 master's, 4 doctorates awarded. *Degree requirements:* For master's, thesis or alternative; for doctorate, thesis/dissertation. *Entrance requirements:* For master's and doctorate, GRE General Test, resume. Additional exam requirements/recommendations for international students: Required—TOEFL (minimum score 550 paper-based; 79 iBT) or IELTS (minimum score 6.5). *Application deadline:* For fall admission, 3/15 priority date for domestic and international students; for spring admission, 9/1 for domestic and international students. Applications are processed on a rolling basis. Application fee: $40 ($90 for international students). Electronic applications accepted. *Expenses:* Tuition, state resident: full-time $6716. Tuition, nonresident: full-time $8908. Tuition and fees vary according to course level, course load, program and student level. *Financial support:* In 2009–10, 12 research assistantships with full and partial tuition reimbursements (averaging $15,630 per year) were awarded; fellowships, teaching assistantships with full and partial tuition reimbursements, scholarships/grants, health care benefits, and unspecified assistantships also available. *Unit head:* Dr. Thomas Baum, Chair, 515-294-1741, Fax: 515-294-9420, E-mail: plantpath@iastate.edu. *Application contact:* Information Contact, 515-294-5836, Fax: 515-294-2592, E-mail: grad_admissions@iastate.edu.

Kansas State University, Graduate School, College of Agriculture, Department of Plant Pathology, Manhattan, KS 66506. Offers genetics (MS, PhD); plant pathology (MS, PhD). *Faculty:* 21 full-time (6 women), 2 part-time/adjunct (0 women). *Students:* 2 full-time (0 women), 26 part-time (12 women); includes 3 minority (1 African American, 2 Hispanic Americans), 21 international. Average age 28. 28 applicants, 25% accepted, 6 enrolled. In 2009, 2 master's, 2 doctorates awarded. Terminal master's awarded for partial completion of doctoral program. *Degree requirements:* For master's, thesis, oral exam; for doctorate, thesis/dissertation, preliminary exams. *Entrance requirements:* For master's and doctorate, minimum undergraduate GPA of 3.0. Additional exam requirements/recommendations for international students: Required—TOEFL (minimum score 550 paper-based; 213 computer-based). *Application deadline:* For fall admission, 2/1 priority date for domestic and international students; for spring admission, 8/1 priority date for domestic and international students. Applications are processed on a rolling basis. Application fee: $40 ($55 for international students). Electronic applications accepted. *Financial support:* In 2009–10, 28 research assistantships (averaging $16,407 per year) were awarded; teaching assistantships, Federal Work-Study, institutionally sponsored loans, and scholarships/grants also available. Support available to part-time students. Financial award application deadline: 3/1; financial award applicants required to submit FAFSA. *Faculty research:* Applied microbiology, microbial genetics, microbial ecology/epidemiology, integrated pest management, plant genetics/genomics/molecular biology. Total annual research expenditures: $4 million. *Unit head:* Dr. John Leslie, Head, 785-532-6176, Fax: 785-532-5692, E-mail: jfl@ksu.edu. *Application contact:* Dr. Bill Bockus, Director, 785-532-1378, Fax: 785-532-5692, E-mail: bockus@ksu.edu.

Louisiana State University and Agricultural and Mechanical College, Graduate School, College of Agriculture, Department of Plant Pathology and Crop Physiology, Baton Rouge, LA 70803. Offers plant health (MS, PhD). *Faculty:* 20 full-time (1 woman). *Students:* 21 full-time (11 women), 2 part-time (0 women); includes 2 minority (1 American Indian/Alaska Native, 1 Hispanic American), 15 international. Average age 31. 22 applicants, 27% accepted, 5 enrolled. Terminal master's awarded for partial completion of doctoral program. *Degree requirements:* For master's, thesis; for doctorate, thesis/dissertation. *Entrance requirements:* For master's and doctorate, GRE General Test, minimum GPA of 3.0. Additional exam requirements/recommendations for international students: Required—TOEFL (minimum score 550 paper-based; 213 computer-based; 79 iBT) or IELTS (minimum score 6.5). *Application deadline:* For fall admission, 1/25 priority date for domestic students, 5/15 for international students; for spring admission, 10/15 for international students. Applications are processed on a rolling basis. Application fee: $50 ($70 for international students). Electronic applications accepted. *Financial support:* In 2009–10, 23 students received support, including 21 research assistantships with partial tuition reimbursements available (averaging $16,935 per year); fellowships, teaching assistantships with partial tuition reimbursements available, career-related internships or fieldwork, Federal Work-Study, health care benefits, and tuition waivers (full) also available. Support available to part-time students. Financial award applicants required to submit FAFSA. *Faculty research:* Plant health and protection, weed biology and management, crop physiology and biotechnology. Total annual research expenditures: $66,995. *Unit head:* Dr. Lawrence Datnoff, Head, 225-765-2876, Fax: 225-578-1415, E-mail: ldatno1@lsu.edu. *Application contact:* Dr. Raymond Schneider, Graduate Adviser, 225-578-4880, Fax: 225-578-1415, E-mail: rschneider@agcenter.lsu.edu.

Michigan State University, The Graduate School, College of Agriculture and Natural Resources and College of Natural Science, Department of Plant Pathology, East Lansing, MI 48824. Offers MS, PhD. *Faculty:* 11 full-time (2 women). *Students:* 21 full-time (13 women), 2 part-time (1 woman); includes 1 minority (African American), 10 international. Average age 28. 10 applicants, 30% accepted. In 2009, 5 master's, 2 doctorates awarded. *Entrance requirements:* Additional exam requirements/recommendations for international students: Required—TOEFL. Application fee: $0. *Expenses:* Tuition, state resident: part-time $478.25 per credit hour. Tuition, nonresident: part-time $966.50 per credit hour. Part-time tuition and fees vary according to program. *Financial support:* In 2009–10, 21 research assistantships with tuition reimbursements (averaging $6,857 per year), 1 teaching assistantship with tuition reimbursement (averaging $6,061 per year) were awarded. Total annual research expenditures: $4.1 million. *Unit head:* Dr. R. Hammerschmidt, Chairperson, 517-355-8624, Fax: 517-353-1781, E-mail: hammers1@msu.edu. *Application contact:* Linda Colon, Graduate Admissions Secretary, 517-432-4592, Fax: 517-353-1781, E-mail: colon@msu.edu.

Mississippi State University, College of Agriculture and Life Sciences, Department of Entomology and Plant Pathology, Mississippi State, MS 39762. Offers agricultural life sciences (MS), including entomology and plant pathology (MS, PhD); life sciences (PhD), including entomology and plant pathology (MS, PhD). *Faculty:* 18 full-time (1 woman). *Students:* 16 full-time (5 women), 5 part-time (3 women); includes 2 minority (1 Asian American or Pacific Islander, 1 Hispanic American), 4 international. Average age 35. 12 applicants, 33% accepted, 2 enrolled. In 2009, 3 master's, 3 doctorates awarded. *Degree requirements:* For master's, thesis; for doctorate, thesis/dissertation. *Entrance requirements:* For master's, GRE General Test, minimum GPA of 2.75; for doctorate, GRE General Test. Additional exam requirements/recommendations for international students: Required—TOEFL (minimum score 475 paper-based; 153 computer-based; 53 iBT); Recommended—IELTS (minimum score 4.5). *Application deadline:* For fall admission, 7/1 for domestic students, 5/1 for international students; for spring admission, 11/1 for domestic students, 9/1 for international students. Applications are processed on a rolling basis. Application fee: $40. Electronic applications accepted. *Expenses:* Tuition, state resident: full-time $2575.50; part-time $286.25 per credit hour. Tuition, nonresident: full-time $6510; part-time $723.50 per credit hour. Tuition and fees vary according to course load. *Financial support:* In 2009–10, 15 research assistantships (averaging $13,924 per year) were awarded; Federal Work-Study, institutionally sponsored loans, and unspecified assistantships also available. Financial award applicants required to submit FAFSA. *Unit head:* Dr. Clarence H. Collison, Professor and Department Head, 662-325-2085, Fax: 662-325-8837, E-mail: ccollison@entomology.msstate.edu. *Application contact:* Dr. Clarence H. Collison, Professor and Department Head, 662-325-2085, Fax: 662-325-8837, E-mail: ccollison@entomology.msstate.edu.

Montana State University, College of Graduate Studies, College of Agriculture, Department of Plant Sciences and Plant Pathology, Bozeman, MT 59717. Offers plant pathology (MS); plant sciences (MS, PhD), including plant genetics (PhD), plant pathology (PhD). Part-time programs available. *Faculty:* 23 full-time (4 women), 3 part-time/adjunct (1 woman). *Students:* 7 full-time (3 women), 11 part-time (5 women), 6 international. Average age 30. 19 applicants, 16% accepted, 3 enrolled. In 2009, 5 master's, 2 doctorates awarded. *Degree requirements:* For master's, comprehensive exam; for doctorate, comprehensive exam, thesis/dissertation. *Entrance requirements:* For master's, GRE General Test, minimum GPA of 3.0; for doctorate, GRE General Test. Additional exam requirements/recommendations for international students: Required—TOEFL (minimum score 550 paper-based; 213 computer-based). *Application deadline:* For fall admission, 7/15 priority date for domestic students, 5/15 priority date for international students; for spring admission, 12/1 priority date for domestic students, 10/1 priority date for international students. Applications are processed on a rolling basis. Application fee: $30. Electronic applications accepted. *Expenses:* Tuition, state resident: full-time $5635; part-time $3492 per year. Tuition, nonresident: full-time $17,212; part-time $7865.10 per year. Required fees: $1441; $153.15 per credit. Tuition and fees vary according to course load and program. *Financial support:* In 2009–10, 9 students received support, including 5 research assistantships with tuition reimbursements available (averaging $36,000 per year), 4 teaching assistantships with tuition reimbursements available (averaging $17,000 per year); health care benefits and unspecified assistantships also available. Financial award application deadline: 3/1; financial award applicants required to submit FAFSA. *Faculty research:* Plant genetics, plant metabolism, plant microbe interactions, plant pathology, entomology. Total annual research expenditures: $2.9 million. *Unit head:* Dr. John Sherwood, Head, 406-994-5153, Fax: 406-994-7600, E-mail: sherwood@montana.edu. *Application contact:* Dr. Carl A. Fox, Vice Provost for Graduate Education, 406-994-4145, Fax: 406-994-7433, E-mail: gradstudy@montana.edu.

New Mexico State University, Graduate School, College of Agricultural, Consumer and Environmental Sciences, Department of Entomology, Plant Pathology and Weed Science, Las Cruces, NM 88003-8001. Offers agricultural biology (MS). Part-time programs available. *Faculty:* 8 full-time (2 women). *Students:* 8 full-time (2 women), 2 part-time (1 woman); includes 2 minority (both Hispanic Americans), 2 international. Average age 26. 8 applicants, 88% accepted, 3 enrolled. In 2009, 4 master's awarded. *Degree requirements:* For master's, comprehensive exam, thesis. *Entrance requirements:* For master's, GRE General Test. *Application deadline:* For fall admission, 7/1 priority date for domestic students; for spring admission, 11/1 priority date for domestic students. Applications are processed on a rolling basis. Application fee: $30 ($50 for international students). Electronic applications accepted. *Expenses:* Tuition, state resident: full-time $4080; part-time $223 per credit. Tuition, nonresident: full-time $14,256; part-time $647 per credit. Required fees: $1278; $639 per semester. *Financial support:* In 2009–10, 5 research assistantships with partial tuition reimbursements (averaging $18,450 per year), 1 teaching assistantship with partial tuition reimbursement (averaging $20,500 per year) were awarded; career-related internships or fieldwork and health care benefits also available. Financial award application deadline: 3/1. *Faculty research:* Integrated pest management, pesticide application and safety, livestock ectoparasite research, biotechnology, nematology. *Unit head:* Dr. David Thompson, Head, 575-646-3225, Fax: 575-646-8087, E-mail: dathomps@nmsu.edu. *Application contact:* Dr. David Thompson, Head, 575-646-3225, Fax: 575-646-8087, E-mail: dathomps@nmsu.edu.

North Carolina State University, Graduate School, College of Agriculture and Life Sciences, Department of Plant Pathology, Raleigh, NC 27695. Offers MS, PhD. Terminal master's awarded for partial completion of doctoral program. *Degree requirements:* For master's, thesis (for some programs); for doctorate, thesis/dissertation. *Entrance requirements:* For master's and doctorate, GRE. Additional exam requirements/recommendations for international students: Required—TOEFL. Electronic applications accepted. *Faculty research:* Microbe-plant interactions, biology of plant pathogens, pathogen evaluation, host-plant resistance, genomics.

North Dakota State University, College of Graduate and Interdisciplinary Studies, College of Agriculture, Food Systems, and Natural Resources, Department of Plant Pathology, Fargo, ND 58108. Offers MS, PhD. Part-time programs available. *Faculty:* 14 full-time (1 woman), 4 part-time/adjunct (0 women). *Students:* 16 full-time (5 women), 8 part-time (3 women); includes 15 minority (1 African American, 10 Asian Americans or Pacific Islanders, 4 Hispanic Americans). Average age 23. 4 applicants, 50% accepted, 2 enrolled. In 2009, 1 master's, 1 doctorate awarded. *Degree requirements:* For master's, thesis; for doctorate, thesis/dissertation. *Entrance requirements:* Additional exam requirements/recommendations for international students: Required—TOEFL (minimum score 550 paper-based; 213 computer-based; 79 iBT). *Application deadline:* Applications are processed on a rolling basis. Application fee: $45 ($60 for international students). Electronic applications accepted. *Financial support:* In 2009–10, 19 research assistantships with full tuition reimbursements were awarded; Federal Work-Study and institutionally sponsored loans also available. Financial award application deadline: 4/15. *Faculty research:* Electron microscopy, disease physiology, molecular biology, genetic resistance, tissue culture. *Unit head:* Dr. Jack Rasmussen, Chair, 701-231-8362, Fax: 701-231-7851, E-mail: jack.rasmussen@ndsu.edu. *Application contact:* Dr. Jack Rasmussen, Chair, 701-231-8362, Fax: 701-231-7851, E-mail: jack.rasmussen@ndsu.edu.

Nova Scotia Agricultural College, Research and Graduate Studies, Truro, NS B2N 5E3, Canada. Offers agriculture (M Sc), including air quality, animal behavior, animal molecular genetics, animal nutrition, animal technology, aquaculture, botany, crop management, crop physiology, ecology, environmental microbiology, food science, horticulture, nutrient management, pest management, physiology, plant biotechnology, plant pathology, soil chemistry, soil fertility, waste management and composting, water quality. Part-time programs available. *Degree requirements:* For master's, thesis, ATC Exam Teaching Assistantship. *Entrance requirements:* For master's, honors B Sc, minimum GPA of 3.0. Additional exam requirements/recommendations for international students: Required—TOEFL (minimum score 580 paper-based; 237 computer-based; 92 iBT), IELTS, Michigan English Language Assessment Battery, CanTEST, CAEL. *Faculty research:* Bio-product development, organic agriculture, nutrient management, air and water quality, agricultural biotechnology.

The Ohio State University, Graduate School, College of Food, Agricultural, and Environmental Sciences, Department of Plant Pathology, Columbus, OH 43210. Offers MS, PhD. *Faculty:* 26. *Students:* 27 full-time (16 women), 6 part-time (4 women), 19 international. Average age 29. In 2009, 3 master's, 4 doctorates awarded. *Degree requirements:* For master's, thesis optional; for doctorate, thesis/dissertation. *Entrance requirements:* For master's and doctorate, GRE General Test. Additional exam requirements/recommendations for international students: Required—TOEFL (minimum score 550 paper-based; 213 computer-based), IELTS (minimum score 7), or Michigan English Language Assessment Battery (minimum score 88). *Application deadline:* For fall admission, 8/15 priority date for domestic students, 7/1 priority date for international students; for winter admission, 12/1 priority date for domestic students, 11/1 priority date for international students; for spring admission, 3/1 priority date for domestic students, 2/1 priority date for international students. Applications are processed on a rolling basis. Application fee: $40 ($50 for international students). Electronic applications accepted. *Expenses:* Tuition, state resident: full-time $10,683. Tuition, nonresident: full-time $25,923. Tuition and fees vary according to course load and program. *Financial support:* Fellowships, research assistantships, teaching assistantships, Federal Work-Study and institutionally sponsored loans available. Support available to part-time students. *Unit head:* Terrence Graham, Graduate Studies Committee Chair, E-mail: graham.1@osu.edu. *Application contact:* Graduate Admissions, 614-292-9444, Fax: 614-292-3895, E-mail: domestic.grad@osu.edu.

Oklahoma State University, College of Agricultural Science and Natural Resources, Department of Entomology and Plant Pathology, Stillwater, OK 74078. Offers entomology (PhD); entomology and plant pathology (MS); plant pathology (PhD). *Faculty:* 34 full-time (10 women). *Students:* 5 full-time (1 woman), 32 part-time (19 women); includes 2 minority (both Asian Americans or Pacific Islanders), 17 international. Average age 29. 36 applicants, 33% accepted, 9 enrolled. In 2009, 2 master's, 1 doctorate awarded. *Degree requirements:* For master's, thesis or alternative; for doctorate, comprehensive exam, thesis/dissertation. *Entrance requirements:* For master's and doctorate, GRE or GMAT. Additional exam requirements/recommendations for international students: Required—TOEFL (minimum score 550 paper-based; 79 iBT). *Application deadline:* For fall admission, 3/1 priority date for international students; for spring admission, 8/1 priority date for international students. Applications are processed on a rolling basis. Application fee: $40 ($75 for international students). Electronic applications accepted. *Expenses:* Tuition, state resident: full-time $3716; part-time $154.85 per credit hour. Tuition, nonresident: full-time $14,448; part-time $602 per credit hour. Required fees: $1772; $73.85 per credit hour. One-time fee: $50. Tuition and fees vary according to course load and campus/location. *Financial support:* In 2009–10, 30 research assistantships (averaging $17,365 per year), 1 teaching assistantship (averaging $16,584 per year) were awarded; career-related internships or fieldwork, Federal Work-Study, scholarships/grants, health care benefits, tuition waivers (partial), and unspecified assistantships also available. Support available to part-time students. Financial award application deadline: 3/1; financial award applicants required to submit FAFSA. *Unit head:* Dr. Phil Mulder, Head, 405-744-5527, Fax: 405-744-6039. *Application contact:* Dr. Brad Kard, Graduate Coordinator, 405-744-2142, Fax: 405-744-6039, E-mail: brad.kard@okstate.edu.

Oregon State University, Graduate School, College of Science, Department of Botany and Plant Pathology, Corvallis, OR 97331. Offers ecology (MA, MAIS, MS, PhD); genetics (MA, MAIS, MS, PhD); molecular and cellular biology (MA, MAIS, MS, PhD); mycology (MA, MAIS, MS, PhD); plant pathology (MA, MAIS, MS, PhD); plant physiology (MA, MAIS, MS, PhD); structural botany (MA, MAIS, MS, PhD); systematics (MA, MAIS, MS, PhD). Part-time programs available. *Faculty:* 11 full-time (1 woman), 2 part-time/adjunct (1 woman). *Students:* 32 full-time (19 women), 2 part-time (1 woman); includes 2 minority (both Asian Americans or Pacific Islanders), 3 international. Average age 30. In 2009, 4 master's, 3 doctorates awarded. *Degree requirements:* For master's, variable foreign language requirement, thesis optional; for doctorate, thesis/dissertation. *Entrance requirements:* For master's and doctorate, GRE General Test, minimum GPA of 3.0 in last 90 hours. Additional exam requirements/recommendations for international students: Required—TOEFL. *Application deadline:* For fall admission, 2/1 priority date for domestic students. Applications are processed on a rolling basis. Application fee: $50. *Expenses:* Tuition, state resident: full-time $9774; part-time $362 per credit. Tuition, nonresident: full-time $15,849; part-time $587 per credit. Required fees: $1639. Full-time tuition and fees vary according to course load and program. *Financial support:* Fellowships, research assistantships, teaching assistantships, career-related internships or fieldwork, Federal Work-Study, institutionally sponsored loans, and scholarships/grants available. Support available to part-time students. Financial award application deadline: 2/1. *Faculty research:* Plant ecology, plant molecular biology, systematic botany, epidemiology, host-pathogen interaction. *Unit head:* Dr. Daniel J. Arp, Chair, 541-737-1297, Fax: 541-737-3573, E-mail: arpd@science.oregonstate.edu. *Application contact:* Dr. John E. Fowler, Associate Professor, 541-737-5307, Fax: 541-737-3573, E-mail: fowlerj@science.oregonstate.edu.

Penn State University Park, Graduate School, College of Agricultural Sciences, Department of Plant Pathology, State College, University Park, PA 16802-1503. Offers MS, PhD.

Purdue University, Graduate School, College of Agriculture, Department of Botany and Plant Pathology, West Lafayette, IN 47907. Offers MS, PhD. Part-time programs available. Terminal master's awarded for partial completion of doctoral program. *Degree requirements:* For master's, thesis; for doctorate, thesis/dissertation. *Entrance requirements:* For master's and doctorate, GRE. Additional exam requirements/recommendations for international students: Required—TOEFL. Electronic applications accepted. *Faculty research:* Biotechnology, plant growth, weed control, crop improvement, plant physiology.

Rutgers, The State University of New Jersey, New Brunswick, Graduate School-New Brunswick, Program in Plant Biology, Piscataway, NJ 08854-8097. Offers horticulture and plant technology (MS, PhD); molecular and cellular biology (MS, PhD); organismal and population biology (MS, PhD); plant pathology (MS, PhD). Part-time programs available. Terminal master's awarded for partial completion of doctoral program. *Degree requirements:* For master's, comprehensive exam, thesis or alternative; for doctorate, comprehensive exam, thesis/dissertation. *Entrance requirements:* For master's and doctorate, GRE General Test, GRE Subject Test (recommended). Additional exam requirements/recommendations for international students: Required—TOEFL (minimum score 600 paper-based; 250 computer-based). Electronic applications accepted. *Faculty research:* Molecular biology and biochemistry of plants, plant development and genomics, plant protection, plant improvement, plant management of horticultural and field crops.

State University of New York College of Environmental Science and Forestry, Department of Environmental and Forest Biology, Syracuse, NY 13210-2779. Offers applied ecology (MPS); chemical ecology (MPS, MS, PhD); conservation biology (MPS, MS, PhD); ecology (MPS, MS, PhD); entomology (MPS, MS, PhD); environmental interpretation (MPS, MS, PhD); environmental physiology (MPS, MS, PhD); fish and wildlife biology (MPS, MS, PhD); forest pathology and mycology (MPS, MS, PhD); plant biotechnology (MPS); plant science and biotechnology (MPS, MS, PhD). *Degree requirements:* For master's, thesis (for some programs); for doctorate, comprehensive exam, thesis/dissertation. *Entrance requirements:* For master's and doctorate, GRE General Test, GRE Subject Test, minimum GPA of 3.0. Additional exam requirements/recommendations for international students: Required—TOEFL (minimum score 550 paper-based; 213 computer-based; 80 iBT), IELTS (minimum score 6). *Faculty research:* Ecology, fish and wildlife biology and management, plant science, entomology.

Texas A&M University, College of Agriculture and Life Sciences, Department of Plant Pathology and Microbiology, College Station, TX 77843. Offers plant pathology (MS, PhD); plant protection (M Agr). Part-time programs available. Postbaccalaureate distance learning degree programs offered. *Faculty:* 18. *Students:* 32 full-time (17 women), 3 part-time (1 woman); includes 7 minority (1 African American, 6 Hispanic Americans), 14 international. Average age 31. In 2009, 1 master's, 1 doctorate awarded. *Degree requirements:* For master's, comprehensive exam (for some programs), thesis; for doctorate, comprehensive exam, thesis/dissertation. *Entrance requirements:* For master's and doctorate, GRE General Test, letters of recommendation, BS/BA in biological sciences. *Application deadline:* Applications are processed on a rolling basis. Application fee: $50 ($75 for international students). *Expenses:* Tuition, state resident: full-time $3991; part-time $221.74 per credit hour. Tuition, nonresident: full-time $9049; part-time $502.74 per credit hour. *Financial support:* In 2009–10, research assistantships with partial tuition reimbursements (averaging $16,800 per year), teaching assistantships with partial tuition reimbursements (averaging $16,800 per year) were awarded; fellowships, career-related internships or fieldwork, Federal Work-Study, institutionally sponsored loans, and unspecified assistantships also available. Support available to part-time students. Financial award application deadline: 4/1; financial award applicants required to submit FAFSA. *Faculty research:* Plant disease control, population biology of plant pathogens, disease epidemiology, molecular genetics of host/parasite interactions. *Unit head:* Professor and Head, 979-845-7311, Fax: 979-845-6483, E-mail: plpm-head@ag.tamu.edu. *Application contact:* Dr., Chair, Graduate Program Committee, 979-845-7311, E-mail: plpm-head@ag.tamu.edu.

Plant Pathology

The University of Arizona, Graduate College, College of Agriculture and Life Sciences, Department of Plant Sciences, Program in Plant Pathology, Tucson, AZ 85721. Offers MS, PhD. Part-time programs available. *Students:* 14 full-time (8 women), 8 international. Average age 32. 6 applicants. In 2009, 1 master's, 4 doctorates awarded. *Degree requirements:* For master's, thesis optional; for doctorate, thesis/dissertation. *Entrance requirements:* For master's, GRE (recommended), minimum GPA of 3.0, academic resume, 3 letters of recommendation; for doctorate, GRE (recommended), minimum GPA of 3.0, academic resume, statement of purpose, 3 letters of recommendation. Additional exam requirements/recommendations for international students: Required—TOEFL. *Application deadline:* For fall admission, 12/1 for domestic and international students; for spring admission, 6/1 for domestic and international students. Applications are processed on a rolling basis. Application fee: $75. *Expenses:* Tuition, state resident: full-time $9028. Tuition, nonresident: full-time $24,890. *Financial support:* Fellowships, research assistantships, teaching assistantships, Federal Work-Study and institutionally sponsored loans available. *Faculty research:* Fungal molecular biology, ecology of soil-borne plant pathogens, plant virology, plant bacteriology, plant/pathogen interactions. *Unit head:* Dr. Leland S. Pierson, Chair, 520-621-1828, E-mail: lsp@u.arizona.edu. *Application contact:* Dr. Rachel W. Pfister, Graduate Coordinator/Advisor, 520-621-8423, Fax: 520-621-7186, E-mail: pfister@ag.arizona.edu.

University of Arkansas, Graduate School, Dale Bumpers College of Agricultural, Food and Life Sciences, Department of Plant Pathology, Fayetteville, AR 72701-1201. Offers MS. *Students:* 5 full-time (4 women), 7 part-time (5 women), 6 international. In 2009, 2 master's awarded. *Degree requirements:* For master's, thesis. Application fee: $40 ($50 for international students). *Expenses:* Tuition, state resident: full-time $7355; part-time $356.58 per hour. Tuition, nonresident: full-time $17,401; part-time $775.17 per hour. Required fees: $1203. *Financial support:* In 2009–10, 10 research assistantships were awarded; fellowships, teaching assistantships, career-related internships or fieldwork and Federal Work-Study also available. Support available to part-time students. Financial award application deadline: 4/1; financial award applicants required to submit FAFSA. *Unit head:* Dr. A. Rick Bennett, Department Head, 479-575-2445, E-mail: rbennett@uark.edu. *Application contact:* Dr. Craig S. Rothrock, Graduate Coordinator, 479-575-6687, E-mail: rothrock@uark.edu.

University of California, Davis, Graduate Studies, Program in Plant Pathology, Davis, CA 95616. Offers MS, PhD. Terminal master's awarded for partial completion of doctoral program. *Degree requirements:* For master's, comprehensive exam (for some programs), thesis (for some programs); for doctorate, thesis/dissertation. *Entrance requirements:* For master's and doctorate, GRE General Test. Additional exam requirements/recommendations for international students: Required—TOEFL (minimum score 550 paper-based; 213 computer-based). Electronic applications accepted. *Faculty research:* Soil microbiology; diagnosis etiology and control of plant diseases; genomics and molecular biology of plant microbe interactions; biotechnology, ecology of plant pathogens and epidemiology of diseases in agricultural and native ecosystems.

University of California, Riverside, Graduate Division, Department of Plant Pathology, Riverside, CA 92521-0102. Offers MS, PhD. *Faculty:* 15 full-time (3 women). *Students:* 12 full-time (8 women); includes 2 minority (1 Asian American or Pacific Islander, 1 Hispanic American), 9 international. Average age 30. 29 applicants, 24% accepted, 3 enrolled. In 2009, 1 master's, 3 doctorates awarded. Terminal master's awarded for partial completion of doctoral program. *Degree requirements:* For master's, comprehensive exams or thesis; for doctorate, thesis/dissertation, qualifying exams. *Entrance requirements:* For master's and doctorate, GRE General Test (minimum score 1100), minimum GPA of 3.2. Additional exam requirements/recommendations for international students: Required—TOEFL (minimum score 550 paper-based; 213 computer-based; 80 iBT). *Application deadline:* For fall admission, 5/1 for domestic students, 2/1 for international students; for winter admission, 9/1 for domestic students, 7/1 for international students; for spring admission, 12/1 for domestic students, 10/1 for international students. Applications are processed on a rolling basis. Application fee: $85 ($100 for international students). Electronic applications accepted. *Financial support:* In 2009–10, 7 students received support, including fellowships with full and partial tuition reimbursements available (averaging $12,000 per year), research assistantships with full and partial tuition reimbursements available (averaging $18,081 per year), teaching assistantships with full and partial tuition reimbursements available (averaging $16,500 per year); career-related internships or fieldwork, institutionally sponsored loans, scholarships/grants, health care benefits, tuition waivers (full and partial), and unspecified assistantships also available. Financial award application deadline: 3/1; financial award applicants required to submit FAFSA. *Faculty research:* Host-pathogen interactions, biological control and integrated approaches to disease management, fungicide behavior, molecular genetics. *Unit head:* Dr. James Baldwin, Chair, 951-827-4432. *Application contact:* Estella Davalos, Student Affairs Officer, 800-735-0717, Fax: 951-827-5913, E-mail: plantpa@urc.edu.

University of Florida, Graduate School, College of Agricultural and Life Sciences, Department of Plant Pathology, Gainesville, FL 32611. Offers MS, PhD. *Degree requirements:* For master's, thesis optional; for doctorate, thesis/dissertation. *Entrance requirements:* For master's and doctorate, GRE General Test, minimum GPA of 3.0. Electronic applications accepted. *Faculty research:* Causes of development of disease in plants, molecular and biochemical aspects of disease, biological control of pathogens and weeds, genetic engineering of resistant plants.

University of Georgia, Graduate School, College of Agricultural and Environmental Sciences, Department of Plant Pathology, Athens, GA 30602. Offers MS, PhD. *Faculty:* 18 full-time (3 women), 3 part-time/adjunct (1 woman). *Students:* 29 full-time (16 women), 5 part-time (2 women); includes 1 minority (Hispanic American), 16 international. 20 applicants, 35% accepted, 6 enrolled. In 2009, 4 master's, 3 doctorates awarded. *Degree requirements:* For master's, thesis (MS); for doctorate, one foreign language; thesis/dissertation. *Entrance requirements:* For master's and doctorate, GRE General Test. *Application deadline:* For fall admission, 7/1 priority date for domestic students; for spring admission, 11/15 for domestic students. Application fee: $50. Electronic applications accepted. *Expenses:* Tuition, state resident: full-time $6000; part-time $250 per credit hour. Tuition, nonresident: full-time $20,904; part-time $871 per credit hour. Required fees: $730 per semester. *Financial support:* Fellowships, research assistantships, teaching assistantships, unspecified assistantships available. *Unit head:* Dr. John L. Sherwood, Head, 706-542-1246, E-mail: sherwood@uga.edu. *Application contact:* Dr. Scott E. Gold, Graduate Coordinator, 706-542-1259, Fax: 706-542-1262, E-mail: sgold@uga.edu.

University of Guelph, Graduate Program Services, Ontario Agricultural College, Department of Environmental Biology, Guelph, ON N1G 2W1, Canada. Offers entomology (M Sc, PhD); environmental microbiology and biotechnology (M Sc, PhD); environmental toxicology (M Sc, PhD); plant and forest systems (M Sc, PhD); plant pathology (M Sc, PhD). Part-time programs available. *Degree requirements:* For master's, thesis; for doctorate, comprehensive exam, thesis/dissertation. *Entrance requirements:* For master's, minimum 75% average during previous 2 years of course work; for doctorate, minimum 75% average. Additional exam requirements/recommendations for international students: Required—TOEFL or IELTS. Electronic applications accepted. *Faculty research:* Entomology, environmental microbiology and biotechnology, environmental toxicology, forest ecology, plant pathology.

University of Hawaii at Manoa, Graduate Division, College of Tropical Agriculture and Human Resources, Department of Plant and Environmental Protection Sciences, Program in Tropical Plant Pathology, Honolulu, HI 96822. Offers MS, PhD. Part-time programs available. *Faculty:* 13 full-time (2 women), 3 part-time/adjunct (1 woman). *Students:* 7 full-time (3 women), 2 part-time (1 woman); includes 1 minority (Asian American or Pacific Islander), 7 international. Average age 32. 9 applicants, 78% accepted, 1 enrolled. In 2009, 2 master's, 3 doctorates awarded. *Degree requirements:* For master's, thesis optional; for doctorate, comprehensive exam, thesis/dissertation. *Entrance requirements:* For master's and doctorate, GRE General Test. Additional exam requirements/recommendations for international students:

Required—TOEFL (minimum score 540 paper-based; 207 computer-based; 76 iBT), IELTS (minimum score 5). *Application deadline:* For fall admission, 3/1 for domestic and international students; for spring admission, 9/1 for domestic and international students. Application fee: $60. *Expenses:* Tuition, state resident: full-time $8900; part-time $372 per credit. Tuition, nonresident: full-time $21,400; part-time $898 per credit. Required fees: $207 per semester. *Financial support:* In 2009–10, 2 fellowships (averaging $1,575 per year), 6 research assistantships (averaging $18,081 per year) were awarded. Total annual research expenditures: $1.8 million. *Application contact:* Dr. Brent Sipes, Graduate Chairperson, 808-956-7076, Fax: 808-956-2832, E-mail: sipes@hawaii.edu.

University of Kentucky, Graduate School, College of Agriculture, Program in Plant Pathology, Lexington, KY 40506-0032. Offers MS, PhD. *Degree requirements:* For master's, comprehensive exam, thesis; for doctorate, comprehensive exam, thesis/dissertation. *Entrance requirements:* For master's, GRE General Test, minimum undergraduate GPA of 2.75; for doctorate, GRE General Test, minimum graduate GPA of 3.0. Additional exam requirements/recommendations for international students: Required—TOEFL (minimum score 550 paper-based; 213 computer-based). Electronic applications accepted. *Faculty research:* Molecular biology of viruses and fungi, biochemistry and physiology of disease resistance, plant transformation, disease ecology, forest pathology.

University of Maine, Graduate School, College of Natural Sciences, Forestry, and Agriculture, Department of Biological Sciences, Program in Botany and Plant Pathology, Orono, ME 04469. Offers MS. Part-time programs available. *Students:* 3 full-time (all women). Average age 25. In 2009, 1 master's awarded. *Degree requirements:* For master's, thesis. *Entrance requirements:* For master's, GRE General Test. Additional exam requirements/recommendations for international students: Required—TOEFL. *Application deadline:* For fall admission, 2/1 priority date for domestic students. Applications are processed on a rolling basis. Application fee: $60. Electronic applications accepted. *Financial support:* Career-related internships or fieldwork, Federal Work-Study, institutionally sponsored loans, and tuition waivers (full) available. Financial award application deadline: 3/1. *Faculty research:* Molecular biology of viral and fungal pathogens, marine ecology, paleoecology and acid systematics and evolution. *Unit head:* Dr. Stellos Tavantiz, Coordinator, 207-581-2986. *Application contact:* Scott G. Delcourt, Associate Dean of the Graduate School, 207-581-3291, Fax: 207-581-3232, E-mail: graduate@maine.edu.

University of Minnesota, Twin Cities Campus, Graduate School, College of Food, Agricultural and Natural Resource Sciences, Department of Plant Pathology, Minneapolis, MN 55455-0213. Offers MS, PhD. Part-time programs available. Terminal master's awarded for partial completion of doctoral program. *Degree requirements:* For master's, comprehensive exam, thesis (for some programs); for doctorate, comprehensive exam, thesis/dissertation. *Entrance requirements:* For master's and doctorate, GRE General Test. Additional exam requirements/recommendations for international students: Required—TOEFL (minimum score 575 paper-based; 232 computer-based; 79 iBT). Electronic applications accepted. *Faculty research:* Plant disease management, disease resistance, product deterioration, international agriculture, molecular biology.

The University of Tennessee, Graduate School, College of Agricultural Sciences and Natural Resources, Department of Entomology and Plant Pathology, Knoxville, TN 37996. Offers entomology (MS, PhD); integrated pest management and bioactive natural products (PhD); plant pathology (MS, PhD). Part-time programs available. *Degree requirements:* For master's, thesis, seminar. *Entrance requirements:* For master's, GRE General Test, minimum GPA of 2.7, 3 reference letters, letter of intent; for doctorate, GRE General Test, minimum GPA of 2.7, 3 reference letters, letter of intent, proposed dissertation research. Additional exam requirements/recommendations for international students: Required—TOEFL. Electronic applications accepted. *Expenses:* Tuition, state resident: full-time $6826; part-time $380 per semester hour. Tuition, nonresident: full-time $21,844; part-time $1147 per semester hour. Tuition and fees vary according to program.

University of Wisconsin–Madison, Graduate School, College of Agricultural and Life Sciences, Department of Plant Pathology, Madison, WI 53706-1380. Offers MS, PhD. Part-time programs available. Terminal master's awarded for partial completion of doctoral program. *Degree requirements:* For master's, thesis; for doctorate, thesis/dissertation. *Entrance requirements:* For master's and doctorate, GRE. Additional exam requirements/recommendations for international students: Required—TOEFL. Electronic applications accepted. *Expenses:* Tuition, state resident: part-time $594 per credit. Tuition, nonresident: part-time $1504 per credit. Required fees: $65 per credit. Tuition and fees vary according to course load, program and reciprocity agreements. *Faculty research:* Plant disease, plant health, plant-microbe interactions, plant disease management, biological control.

Virginia Polytechnic Institute and State University, Graduate School, College of Agriculture and Life Sciences, Department of Plant Pathology, Physiology and Weed Science, Blacksburg, VA 24061. Offers plant pathology (MS, PhD); plant physiology and weed science (MS, PhD); plant protection (MS). *Faculty:* 17 full-time (6 women), 1 (woman) part-time/adjunct. *Students:* 25 full-time (12 women); includes 9 minority (8 American Indian/Alaska Native, 1 Hispanic American). Average age 28. 16 applicants, 25% accepted, 3 enrolled. In 2009, 5 master's, 3 doctorates awarded. *Entrance requirements:* For master's and doctorate, GRE, GMAT. Additional exam requirements/recommendations for international students: Required—TOEFL (minimum score 550 paper-based; 213 computer-based). *Application deadline:* For fall admission, 5/15 for international students; for spring admission, 10/15 for international students. Applications are processed on a rolling basis. Application fee: $65. Electronic applications accepted. *Expenses:* Tuition, area resident: Full-time $10,228; part-time $459 per credit hour. Tuition, nonresident: full-time $17,892; part-time $865 per credit hour. Required fees: $1966; $451 per semester. *Financial support:* In 2009–10, 16 research assistantships with full tuition reimbursements (averaging $18,290 per year) were awarded; career-related internships or fieldwork, Federal Work-Study, scholarships/grants, and unspecified assistantships also available. Financial award application deadline: 1/15. *Faculty research:* Biotechnology, Dutch elm disease, weed control, plant pathogenic microorganisms, agronomic crop resistance to fungal and viral pathogens. Total annual research expenditures: $1.8 million. *Unit head:* Dr. Elizabeth A. Grabau, Dean, 540-231-6361, Fax: 540-231-7477, E-mail: egrabau@vt.edu. *Application contact:* Jim Westwood, Information Contact, 540-231-7519, Fax: 540-231-7477, E-mail: westwood@vt.edu.

Washington State University, Graduate School, College of Agricultural, Human, and Natural Resource Sciences, Department of Plant Pathology, Pullman, WA 99164. Offers MS, PhD. *Faculty:* 33. *Students:* 36 full-time (22 women); includes 5 minority (4 Asian Americans or Pacific Islanders, 1 Hispanic American), 21 international. Average age 31. 57 applicants, 19% accepted, 10 enrolled. In 2009, 4 master's, 1 doctorate awarded. Terminal master's awarded for partial completion of doctoral program. *Degree requirements:* For master's, comprehensive exam (for some programs), thesis (for some programs), oral exam; for doctorate, comprehensive exam, thesis/dissertation, oral exam. *Entrance requirements:* For master's and doctorate, GRE, statement of purpose. Additional exam requirements/recommendations for international students: Required—TOEFL (minimum score 550 paper-based; 213 computer-based), IELTS. *Application deadline:* For fall admission, 1/10 priority date for domestic students, 1/10 for international students; for spring admission, 7/1 for domestic and international students. Applications are processed on a rolling basis. Application fee: $50. Electronic applications accepted. *Financial support:* In 2009–10, 25 students received support, including 1 fellowship (averaging $14,057 per year), 24 research assistantships with full and partial tuition reimbursements available (averaging $13,917 per year), teaching assistantships with full and partial tuition reimbursements available (averaging $13,056 per year); career-related internships or fieldwork, Federal Work-Study, institutionally sponsored loans, scholarships/grants, and teaching associateships also available. Financial award application deadline: 4/1; financial award applicants required to submit FAFSA. *Faculty research:* Biology of fungi, bacteria, and viruses; diseases of plants; genetics of fungi, bacteria, and viruses. Total annual research expenditures: $3.4 million. *Unit head:* Dr. Hanu R. Pappu, Chair, 509-335-9541, Fax: 509-335-9581, E-mail: hrp@wsu.edu. *Application contact:* Graduate School Admissions, 800-GRADWSU, Fax: 509-335-1949, E-mail: gradsch@wsu.edu.

West Virginia University, Davis College of Agriculture, Forestry and Consumer Sciences, Division of Plant and Soil Sciences, Morgantown, WV 26506. Offers agricultural sciences (PhD), including animal and food sciences, plant and soil sciences; agronomy (MS); entomology (MS); environmental microbiology (MS); horticulture (MS); plant pathology (MS). *Degree requirements:* For master's, thesis. *Entrance requirements:* For master's, GRE, minimum GPA of 2.5. Additional exam requirements/recommendations for international students: Required—TOEFL. *Faculty research:* Water quality, reclamation of disturbed land, crop production, pest control, environmental protection.

Plant Physiology

Cornell University, Graduate School, Graduate Fields of Agriculture and Life Sciences, Field of Plant Biology, Ithaca, NY 14853-0001. Offers cytology (MS, PhD); paleobotany (MS, PhD); plant cell biology (MS, PhD); plant ecology (MS, PhD); plant molecular biology (MS, PhD); plant morphology, anatomy and biomechanics (MS, PhD); plant physiology (MS, PhD); systematic botany (MS, PhD). *Faculty:* 55 full-time (13 women). *Students:* 40 full-time (19 women); includes 3 minority (2 African Americans, 1 Hispanic American), 10 international. Average age 28. 54 applicants, 22% accepted, 6 enrolled. In 2009, 4 doctorates awarded. *Degree requirements:* For doctorate, comprehensive exam, thesis/dissertation. *Entrance requirements:* For doctorate, GRE General Test, GRE Subject Test in biology (recommended), 3 letters of recommendation. Additional exam requirements/recommendations for international students: Required—TOEFL (minimum score 610 paper-based; 253 computer-based; 77 iBT). *Application deadline:* For fall admission, 1/15 priority date for domestic students. Application fee: $70. Electronic applications accepted. *Expenses:* Tuition: Full-time $29,500. Required fees: $70. Full-time tuition and fees vary according to degree level, program and student level. *Financial support:* In 2009–10, 38 students received support, including 6 fellowships with full tuition reimbursements available; research assistantships with full tuition reimbursements available, teaching assistantships with full tuition reimbursements available, institutionally sponsored loans, scholarships/grants, health care benefits, tuition waivers (full and partial), and unspecified assistantships also available. Financial award applicants required to submit FAFSA. *Faculty research:* Plant cell biology/cytology; plant molecular biology; plant morphology/anatomy/biomechanics; plant physiology, systematic botany, paleobotany; plant ecology, ethnobotany, plant biochemistry, photosynthesis. *Unit head:* Director of Graduate Studies, 607-255-2131. *Application contact:* Graduate Field Assistant, 607-255-2131, E-mail: plbio@cornell.edu.

Nova Scotia Agricultural College, Research and Graduate Studies, Truro, NS B2N 5E3, Canada. Offers agriculture (M Sc), including air quality, animal behavior, animal molecular genetics, animal nutrition, animal technology, aquaculture, botany, crop management, crop physiology, ecology, environmental microbiology, food science, horticulture, nutrient management, pest management, physiology, plant biotechnology, plant pathology, soil chemistry, soil fertility, waste management and composting, water quality. Part-time programs available. *Degree requirements:* For master's, thesis, ATC Exam Teaching Assistantship. *Entrance requirements:* For master's, honors B Sc, minimum GPA of 3.0. Additional exam requirements/recommendations for international students: Required—TOEFL (minimum score 580 paper-based; 237 computer-based; 92 iBT), IELTS, Michigan English Language Assessment Battery, CanTEST, CAEL. *Faculty research:* Bio-product development, organic agriculture, nutrient management, air and water quality, agricultural biotechnology.

Oregon State University, Graduate School, College of Science, Department of Botany and Plant Pathology, Corvallis, OR 97331. Offers ecology (MA, MAIS, MS, PhD); genetics (MA, MAIS, MS, PhD); molecular and cellular biology (MA, MAIS, MS, PhD); mycology (MA, MAIS, MS, PhD); plant pathology (MA, MAIS, MS, PhD); plant physiology (MA, MAIS, MS, PhD); structural botany (MA, MAIS, MS, PhD); systematics (MA, MAIS, MS, PhD). Part-time programs available. *Faculty:* 11 full-time (1 woman), 2 part-time/adjunct (1 woman). *Students:* 32 full-time (19 women), 2 part-time (1 woman); includes 2 minority (both Asian Americans or Pacific Islanders), 3 international. Average age 30. In 2009, 4 master's, 3 doctorates awarded. *Degree requirements:* For master's, variable foreign language requirement, thesis optional; for doctorate, thesis/dissertation. *Entrance requirements:* For master's and doctorate, GRE General Test, minimum GPA of 3.0 in last 90 hours. Additional exam requirements/recommendations for international students: Required—TOEFL. *Application deadline:* For fall admission, 2/1 priority date for domestic students. Applications are processed on a rolling basis. Application fee: $50. *Expenses:* Tuition, state resident: full-time $9774; part-time $362 per credit. Tuition, nonresident: full-time $15,849; part-time $587 per credit. Required fees: $1639. Full-time tuition and fees vary according to course load and program. *Financial support:* Fellowships, research assistantships, teaching assistantships, career-related internships or fieldwork, Federal Work-Study, institutionally sponsored loans, and scholarships/grants available. Support available to part-time students. Financial award application deadline: 2/1. *Faculty research:* Plant ecology, plant molecular biology, systematic botany, epidemiology, host-pathogen interaction. *Unit head:* Dr. Daniel J. Arp, Chair, 541-737-1297, Fax: 541-737-3573, E-mail: arpd@science.oregonstate.edu. *Application contact:* Dr. John E. Fowler, Associate Professor, 541-737-5307, Fax: 541-737-3573, E-mail: fowlerj@science.oregonstate.edu.

Oregon State University, Graduate School, Program in Plant Physiology, Corvallis, OR 97331. Offers MS, PhD. *Students:* 1 (woman) full-time, all international. Average age 39. In 2009, 1 doctorate awarded. *Degree requirements:* For master's, thesis; for doctorate, thesis/dissertation. *Entrance requirements:* For master's, BS in related area; for doctorate, BS or MS in related area, minimum GPA of 3.0 in last 90 hours of course work. Additional exam requirements/recommendations for international students: Required—TOEFL. *Application deadline:* For fall admission, 3/1 for domestic students. Applications are processed on a rolling basis. Application fee: $50. *Expenses:* Tuition, state resident: full-time $9774; part-time $362 per credit. Tuition, nonresident: full-time $15,849; part-time $587 per credit. Required fees: $1639. Full-time tuition and fees vary according to course load and program. *Financial support:* Fellowships, research assistantships, teaching assistantships, career-related internships or fieldwork, Federal Work-Study, and institutionally sponsored loans available. Support available to part-time students. Financial award application deadline: 2/1. *Faculty research:* Nitrogen metabolism, physiological ecology, phloem transport, mineral nutrition, plant hormones. *Unit head:* Dr. Daniel J. Arp, Chair, 541-737-1297, Fax: 541-737-3573, E-mail: arpd@science.oregonstate.edu. *Application contact:* Dr. Daniel J. Arp, Chair, 541-737-1297, Fax: 541-737-3573, E-mail: arpd@science.oregonstate.edu.

Penn State University Park, Graduate School, Intercollege Graduate Programs, Intercollege Graduate Program in Plant Physiology, State College, University Park, PA 16802-1503. Offers MS, PhD. *Unit head:* Dr. Teh-hui Kao, Head, 814-823-1042, Fax: 814-863-9416, E-mail: txk3@psu.edu. *Application contact:* Dr. Teh-hui Kao, Head, 814-823-1042, Fax: 814-863-9416, E-mail: txk3@psu.edu.

Purdue University, Graduate School, College of Science, Department of Biological Sciences, West Lafayette, IN 47907. Offers biochemistry (PhD); biophysics (PhD); cell and developmental biology (PhD); ecology, evolutionary and population biology (MS, PhD), including ecology, evolutionary biology, population biology; genetics (MS, PhD); microbiology (MS, PhD); molecular biology (PhD); neurobiology (MS, PhD); plant physiology (PhD). Terminal master's awarded for partial completion of doctoral program. *Degree requirements:* For master's, thesis (for some programs); for doctorate, thesis/dissertation, seminars, teaching experience. *Entrance requirements:* For master's and doctorate, GRE General Test. Additional exam requirements/recommendations for international students: Required—TOEFL. Electronic applications accepted.

University of Kentucky, Graduate School, College of Agriculture, Program in Plant Physiology, Lexington, KY 40506-0032. Offers PhD. *Degree requirements:* For doctorate, comprehensive exam, thesis/dissertation. *Entrance requirements:* For doctorate, GRE General Test, minimum graduate GPA of 3.0, undergraduate 2.75. Additional exam requirements/recommendations for international students: Required—TOEFL (minimum score 550 paper-based; 213 computer-based). Electronic applications accepted. *Faculty research:* Biochemistry and biophysics of photosynthesis, biochemical and molecular basis for resistance of plants to pathogens, plant gene expression, physiological aspects of crop production.

University of Manitoba, Faculty of Graduate Studies, Faculty of Agricultural and Food Sciences, Department of Plant Science, Winnipeg, MB R3T 2N2, Canada. Offers agronomy and plant protection (M Sc, PhD); horticulture (M Sc, PhD); plant breeding and genetics (M Sc, PhD); plant physiology-biochemistry (M Sc, PhD). *Degree requirements:* For master's, thesis; for doctorate, one foreign language, thesis/dissertation.

University of Massachusetts Amherst, Graduate School, Interdisciplinary Programs, Program in Plant Biology, Amherst, MA 01003. Offers biochemistry and metabolism (MS, PhD); cell biology and physiology (MS, PhD); environmental, ecological and integrative (MS, PhD); genetics and evolution (MS, PhD). *Students:* 3 full-time (2 women), 12 part-time (5 women); includes 2 minority (both Asian Americans or Pacific Islanders), 8 international. Average age 27. 32 applicants, 41% accepted, 3 enrolled. In 2009, 3 master's, 1 doctorate awarded. *Degree requirements:* For master's, thesis; for doctorate, 2 foreign languages, comprehensive exam, thesis/dissertation. *Entrance requirements:* For master's and doctorate, GRE General Test. Additional exam requirements/recommendations for international students: Required—TOEFL (minimum score 550 paper-based; 213 computer-based; 80 iBT), IELTS (minimum score 6.5). *Application deadline:* For fall admission, 12/15 for domestic and international students; for spring admission, 10/1 for domestic and international students. Applications are processed on a rolling basis. Application fee: $50 ($65 for international students). Electronic applications accepted. *Expenses:* Tuition, state resident: full-time $2640; part-time $110 per credit. Tuition, nonresident: full-time $9936; part-time $414 per credit. Tuition and fees vary according to course load. *Financial support:* In 2009–10, 11 research assistantships with full tuition reimbursements (averaging $8,884 per year) were awarded; fellowships, teaching assistantships, career-related internships or fieldwork, Federal Work-Study, scholarships/grants, traineeships, health care benefits, tuition waivers (full), and unspecified assistantships also available. Support available to part-time students. Financial award application deadline: 12/15. *Unit head:* Dr. Elsbeth L. Walker, Graduate Program Director, 413-577-3217, Fax: 413-545-3243. *Application contact:* Jean M. Ames, Supervisor of Admissions, 413-545—0722, Fax: 413-577-0010, E-mail: gradadm@grad.umass.edu.

The University of Tennessee, Graduate School, College of Arts and Sciences, Program in Life Sciences, Knoxville, TN 37996. Offers genome science and technology (MS, PhD); plant physiology and genetics (MS, PhD). *Degree requirements:* For doctorate, one foreign language, thesis/dissertation. *Entrance requirements:* For master's and doctorate, GRE General Test, minimum GPA of 2.7. Additional exam requirements/recommendations for international students: Required—TOEFL. Electronic applications accepted. *Expenses:* Tuition, state resident: full-time $6826; part-time $380 per semester hour. Tuition, nonresident: full-time $21,844; part-time $1147 per semester hour. Tuition and fees vary according to program.

Virginia Polytechnic Institute and State University, Graduate School, College of Agriculture and Life Sciences, Department of Plant Pathology, Physiology and Weed Science, Blacksburg, VA 24061. Offers plant pathology (MS, PhD); plant physiology and weed science (MS, PhD); plant protection (MS). *Faculty:* 17 full-time (6 women), 1 (woman) part-time/adjunct. *Students:* 25 full-time (12 women); includes 9 minority (8 American Indian/Alaska Native, 1 Hispanic American). Average age 28. 16 applicants, 25% accepted, 3 enrolled. In 2009, 5 master's, 3 doctorates awarded. *Entrance requirements:* For master's and doctorate, GRE, GMAT. Additional exam requirements/recommendations for international students: Required—TOEFL (minimum score 550 paper-based; 213 computer-based). *Application deadline:* For fall admission, 5/15 for international students; for spring admission, 10/15 for international students. Applications are processed on a rolling basis. Application fee: $65. Electronic applications accepted. *Expenses:* Tuition, area resident: Full-time $10,228; part-time $459 per credit hour. Tuition, nonresident: full-time $17,892; part-time $865 per credit hour. Required fees: $1966; $451 per semester. *Financial support:* In 2009–10, 16 research assistantships with full tuition reimbursements (averaging $18,290 per year) were awarded; career-related internships or fieldwork, Federal Work-Study, scholarships/grants, and unspecified assistantships also available. Financial award application deadline: 1/15. *Faculty research:* Biotechnology, Dutch elm disease, weed control, plant pathogenic microorganisms, agronomic crop resistance to fungal and viral pathogens. Total annual research expenditures: $1.8 million. *Unit head:* Dr. Elizabeth A. Grabau, Dean, 540-231-6361, Fax: 540-231-7477, E-mail: egrabau@vt.edu. *Application contact:* Jim Westwood, Information Contact, 540-231-7519, Fax: 540-231-7477, E-mail: westwood@vt.edu.

UNIVERSITY OF CONNECTICUT

Department of Molecular and Cell Biology

Programs of Study

The faculty members in the Department of Molecular and Cell Biology at the University of Connecticut participate in five interrelated fields of study—biochemistry, biophysics/structural biology, cell biology, genetics, and microbiology—which each lead to the M.S. and Ph.D. degrees. The faculty members maintain federally and privately funded research programs, generally with research groups of moderate size, assuring direct faculty guidance for graduate students. Individual faculty members also participate in the interdisciplinary area of applied genetics. Within each field of study, a variety of specific research themes exists.

The field of biochemistry furnishes students with an extensive education in the structure and function of biological macromolecules, particularly in the areas of protein/peptide structure and macromolecular interactions. Biophysics/structural biology provides an exciting program that focuses on the structure and interactions of proteins, both soluble and membrane-bound, and uses state-of-the-art instrumentation. Cell biology emphasizes the interaction of cells with the extracellular environment and the homeostatic mechanisms that maintain fundamental cell functions, such as motility, signal transduction, and membrane integrity. Genetics offers research training with an emphasis on the structure and regulation of heritable macromolecules, and on the practical application of genetic investigations. Microbiology trains students in many areas of modern microbial biology, including the physiology, genetics, molecular biology, and ecology of prokaryotes; biotechnology; bioremediation; and pathogenesis. Offering these diverse fields of study within the Department results in excellent opportunities for interdisciplinary research experience. Two professional science master's (PSM) programs have recently been added to the academic opportunities within the Department—applied genomics and microbial systems analysis.

Research Facilities

The principal research facilities are housed in the recently constructed Biological Sciences/Physics Building, the Torrey Life Sciences Building, and Beach Hall. Exceptional facilities within the Department include a center for analytical ultracentrifugation, a cell-culture facility, a laboratory for flow cytometry and confocal microscopy, facilities for macromolecular characterization (including peptide and DNA sequencing and synthesis), and a protein crystallographic laboratory. An extensive collection of journals is available in the University of Connecticut Library and via electronic journal subscription. The University has an excellent computer center, and Internet access is available in all buildings used by the Department. The University has been nationally recognized for its campuswide network.

Financial Aid

Financial support is available to graduate students in several forms. For 2010–11, nine-month teaching assistantships pay $19,384 for beginning graduate students, $20,396 for those with an M.S. or the equivalent, and $22,676 for Ph.D. candidates who have passed the General Examination. All students with an assistantship also receive the option to purchase highly subsidized health benefits and a tuition waiver. University fellowships and research assistantships are also offered, and a summer stipend is available for most doctoral students.

Cost of Study

Graduate tuition for 2010–11 is $9972 for legal residents of Connecticut and $25,884 for out-of-state students. Fees of about $1850 are also assessed. Tuition is prorated for students registering for fewer than 9 credits per semester. Tuition, but not the general University fee, is waived for graduate assistants.

Living and Housing Costs

University-operated and privately owned apartments are available on and near the campus at moderate rents. Houses and apartments for rent can also be found in surrounding communities.

Student Group

Approximately 16,000 undergraduates and 8,000 graduate students are enrolled on the main campus at Storrs. About 80 percent of the undergraduate students and 33 percent of the graduate students are from Connecticut. The rest of the student body represents numerous other states and more than 100 different countries. The Department of Molecular and Cell Biology has a total of approximately 175 graduate students in five fields of study and two professional science master's programs.

Location

The University is located in a scenic countryside setting of small villages, streams, and rolling hills. There is easy access by automobile and bus to major urban and cultural centers, such as Hartford, New Haven, Boston, and New York, and to other educational institutions, such as Yale, Harvard, and MIT. Bradley International Airport is 40 minutes from campus by car.

Recreational opportunities in the area include fishing, skiing, sailing, hiking, ice-skating, and kayaking. The community's cultural life includes film series, plays, concerts, public lectures, and art exhibits. A small shopping center is within walking distance of the campus, and several large centers are nearby.

The University

The University of Connecticut is a land-grant institution, so designated in 1893. The lineage of the University reaches back to 1881, when the Storrs Agricultural School was founded. The transition to university status, achieved in 1939, has been followed by substantial growth of the University, including an ongoing $2.3-billion building and renovation effort.

Applying

A completed application form, official transcripts of all previous college or university work, scores on the Graduate Record Examinations, a personal statement of research interests, and three letters of reference are required before consideration of the application can begin. For the academic year 2011–12 the deadline for applicants to the doctoral programs is December 15, 2010, and for applicants to the master's programs the deadline is March 1, 2011. The University does not discriminate in admissions on the basis of race, sex, age, or national origin.

Correspondence and Information

Anne St. Onge
Department of Molecular and Cell Biology, U-3042
University of Connecticut
Storrs, Connecticut 06269-3042
Phone: 860-486-4314
E-mail: Anne.St_Onge@uconn.edu
Web site: http://www.mcb.uconn.edu

University of Connecticut

THE FACULTY AND THEIR RESEARCH

Lee Aggison, Associate Professor-in-Residence; Ph.D. Role streptococcal species play in establishing biofilms and damaging endothelial cells; protein-protein interactions; molecular chaperones involved in the cellular trafficking of renin.

Arlene D. Albert, Professor; Ph.D. Biochemistry of vision; signal transduction in rod outer segments; lipid organization in photoreceptors; rhodopsin structure; protein-lipid interactions.

Nathan N. Alder, Assistant Professor; Ph.D. Biochemical and biophysical approaches to studying the structure, function, and biogenesis of membrane proteins; fluorescence-based investigation of membrane protein complexes and protein trafficking in mitochondria; membrane bioenergetics; organelle biogenesis.

Andrei T. Alexandrescu, Assistant Professor; Ph.D. High-resolution solution NMR investigations of protein structure, folding, dynamics, and association; conserved physical properties of OB-fold proteins; HIV regulatory/accessory proteins.

David R. Benson, Professor and Department Head; Ph.D. Microbial physiology, biochemistry, and molecular genetics of symbiotic nitrogen fixation; steroidal transformations in foods.

Robert Birge, Professor (Chemistry, joint MCB appointment); Ph.D. Molecular mechanisms of light absorption.

Peter Burkhard, Associate Professor; Ph.D. Structure-based rational design of self-assembling small proteins; biophysical properties and medical applications of these nanoparticles.

Thomas T. Chen, Professor and Director, Biotechnology Center; Ph.D. Structure, evolution, regulation, and molecular actions of growth hormone and insulin-like growth factor genes; regulation of foreign genes in transgenic fish; development of model transgenic fish.

James Cole, Associate Professor and Head, National Ultracentrifugation Facility; Ph.D. Biophysical and biochemical analysis of protein kinase PKR; mechanism of HIV entry; structure and function of retroviral integrases; analytical ultracentrifugation.

Daniel J. Gage, Associate Professor; Ph.D. Molecular genetics of plant-microbe interactions; bacterial physiology; regulation of bacterial gene expression in response to extracellular signals.

Steven J. Geary, Professor (Pathobiology, joint appointment in MCB); Ph.D. Molecular biology of mycoplasmas.

Charles Giardina, Associate Professor; Ph.D. Studies of eukaryotic RNA polymerase II transcription regulation; mechanisms governing transcription of stress-response genes; the nature of RNA polymerase II interactions at the promoter.

J. Peter Gogarten, Professor; Ph.D. Membrane transport; function and evolution of vacuolar type H+-ATPases; the role of cell-wall-bound enzymes in the long-distance transport in plants.

David J. Goldhamer, Associate Professor; Ph.D. Regulation of cell fates in mammalian development; transcriptional control and function of skeletal muscle regulatory genes; muscle stem cell function and plasticity; mechanism of heterotopic bone formation in human disease.

Jörg Graf, Assistant Professor; Ph.D. Molecular genetics of bacteria-animal interactions; identification of bacterial genes required for host symbiosis; pathogenesis, evolution of virulence factors.

David A. Knecht, Professor; Ph.D. Actin cytoskeleton dynamics; small G proteins and signal transduction; phagocytosis; endocytosis; cell motility and chemotaxis.

Juliet Lee, Associate Professor; Ph.D. The regulation of cell movement; mechanochemical signal transduction; the role of intracellular calcium; cellular force production and its relationship to adhesion formation and cytoskeletal dynamics.

Michael A. Lynes, Professor and Associate Department Head for Research and Graduate Education; Ph.D. Genetic and biochemical control of the immune response; membrane structure and function during development; mechanisms of autoimmune dysfunction; multiplexed surface plasmon resonance imaging microarray assessments of biological signatures.

Philip I. Marcus, Board of Trustees Distinguished Professor and Interim Director, Biotechnology, Bioservices Center; Ph.D. Animal virus-cell interactions; viral interference; the interferon system; regulation of interferon induction-suppression by viruses; cell killing by viruses; development of the avian interferon system; inducible ds RNase.

Barbara Mellone, Assistant Professor; Ph.D. Molecular and cell biology of chromosome segregation; molecular dissection of centromere formation and transmission; cell-cycle regulation of centromere-associated proteins; high-resolution and time-lapse microscopy of chromosome dynamics.

Craig E. Nelson, Assistant Professor; Ph.D. Molecular biological, genetic, genomic, and computational analysis of the evolution of developmental processes and organismal complexity.

Kenneth M. Noll, Professor and Associate Department Head for Undergraduate Research and Education; Ph.D. Biochemistry and molecular biology of thermophilic bacteria and archaebacteria; physiology of extremely thermophilic anaerobes; evolution of genome organization in prokaryotes.

Spencer V. Nyholm, Assistant Professor; Ph.D. Host-microbe interactions; symbiosis; relationship between beneficial bacteria and the innate immune system; comparative immunology.

Michael J. O'Neill, Associate Professor; Ph.D. Molecular genetics of vertebrate development; molecular mechanisms of genomic imprinting; evolution of genomic imprinting; genetics of imprinting and behavior.

Rachel J. Waugh O'Neill, Associate Professor; Ph.D. Genetics of speciation; mammalian chromosome evolution; genome evolution and remodeling; transposable elements and retroelements; hybridogenesis and clonal inheritance in vertebrates; epigenetics.

R. Thane Papke, Assistant Professor; Ph.D. Ecology and evolution of bacteria that live in extreme environments; community structure and function; bacterial species and speciation; comparative genomics; bacterial population genetics.

Andrew J. Pask, Associate Professor; Ph.D. Comparative genetics; molecular mechanisms of sex determination and sexual differentiation; mammalian development; reproductive physiology.

Wolf-Dieter D. Reiter, Associate Professor; Ph.D. Molecular genetics of cell-wall synthesis in *Arabidopsis;* structure and function of plant cell walls; developmental regulation of cell-wall deposition; biochemistry of plant carbohydrates.

Victoria Robinson, Assistant Professor; Ph.D. Genetic, biochemical, and structural methodologies to study novel families of bacterial GTPases as targets for antimicrobial development.

Margaret J. Sekellick, Professor-in-Residence; Ph.D. Animal virology and the interferon system; cloning and genomic organization of avian interferons; role of interferon system and growth-factor expression in embryonic development.

Linda D. Strausbaugh, Professor and Director, Center for Applied Genetics and Technology; Ph.D. Structure, function, and evolution of multigene families; molecular genetics of insects.

Carolyn M. Teschke; Associate Professor; Ph.D. Biochemical, biophysical, and genetic analyses of protein folding; interaction of folding intermediates with molecular chaperones; assembly of viral capsids.

Ruth Washington Associate Professor-in-Residence;, Ph.D. Mitochondrial population genetics and diseases; pericytes and their role in vascular injuries; adherence of *Streptococcus sanguis;* health disparities.

Ping Zhang, Associate Professor; Ph.D. *Drosophila* chromosome structure and function; P element insertional mutagenesis; unusual transcriptional regulation of heterochromatin; Y chromosome genes required for spermatogenesis.

Adam Zweifach, Associate Professor, Ph.D. Lymphocyte physiology and cell biology; role of intracellular calcium dynamics in lymphocyte function; molecular mechanisms of exocytosis; signaling in the immune system.

Emeritus Faculty

Emory H. Braswell, Professor and Head, National Analytical Ultracentrifugation Facility; Ph.D. Biophysical chemistry; interactions of macromolecules.

Lawrence E. Hightower, Professor; Ph.D. Molecular and cellular responses of animal cells to environmental stress; heat shock proteins, growth factors, and cellular stress responses; analysis of regulatory signals and functions of induced proteins.

Judith A. Kelly, Professor; Ph.D. Enzyme structure and function, using X-ray crystallography, kinetic studies, and interactive computer graphics.

James R. Knox, Professor; Ph.D. Protein structure determination by X-ray crystallography; drug target enzymes of bacterial cell-wall synthesis.

Hans Laufer, Professor; Ph.D. Developmental and cell biology; hormonal control and signal transduction during development.

Edward R. Leadbetter, Professor; Ph.D. Microbial ecology, physiology, and biochemistry; gliding motility in prokaryotes; sulfonate biotransformations.

Philip L. Yeagle, Professor; Ph.D. Structure and function of biological membranes; high-resolution structure determination of a G-protein receptor, rhodopsin; cholesterol in mammalian cell biology.

Teaching Faculty

Thomas D. Abbott, Assistant Professor in Residence; Ph.D.

Mary K. Bruno, Assistant Professor in Residence; Ph.D.

Kathleen A. Feldman, Assistant Professor in Residence; Ph.D.

Colleen Spurling, Assistant Professor in Residence; Ph.D.

Associated and Adjunct Faculty

Hedley C. Freake, Professor (Nutritional Sciences); Ph.D. Regulation of fatty-acid synthesis; zinc metabolism.

Carll Ladd, Adjunct Assistant Professor; Ph.D. Connecticut State Police Forensic Science Laboratory.

Thomas Laue, Adjunct Professor; Ph.D. University of New Hampshire.

Alexandros Makriyannis, Professor Emeritus (Pharmaceutical Sciences); Ph.D. Drug design; membrane biophysics; NMR spectroscopy.

Theodore Rasmussen, Associate Professor (Animal Sciences, Center for Regenerative Biology); Ph.D.

Daniel Rosenberg, Professor (Medicine/UCONN Health Center); Ph.D. Chemically induced cancer and the genetics of susceptibility.

Lawrence Silbart, Professor and Department Head (Allied Health Sciences); Ph.D. Mucosal immunity and vaccine development.

Xiuchun (Cindy) Tian, Associate Professor (Animal Sciences, Center for Regenerative Biology); Ph.D.

Pieter Visscher, Professor and Director (Marine Sciences); Ph.D. Applied environmental microbiology.

Susanne Beck von Bodman, Associate Professor (Plant Science); Ph.D. Host-pathogen interactions; bacterial virulence factors.

Steven A. Zinn, Professor (Animal Science); Ph.D. Genetics and physiology of growth factor expression.

Section 6
Cell, Molecular, and Structural Biology

This section contains a directory of institutions offering graduate work in cell, molecular, and structural biology, followed by in-depth entries submitted by institutions that chose to prepare detailed program descriptions. Additional information about programs listed in the directory but not augmented by an in-depth entry may be obtained by writing directly to the dean of a graduate school or chair of a department at the address given in the directory.

For programs offering related work, see also in this book *Anatomy; Biochemistry; Biological and Biomedical Sciences; Biophysics; Botany and Plant Biology; Genetics, Developmental Biology, and Reproductive Biology; Microbiological Sciences; Pathology and Pathobiology; Pharmacology and Toxicology;* and *Physiology.* In the other guides in this series:

Graduate Programs in the Physical Sciences, Mathematics, Agricultural Sciences, the Environment & Natural Resources
See *Chemistry*

Graduate Programs in Engineering & Applied Sciences
See *Agricultural Engineering and Bioengineering* and *Biomedical Engineering and Biotechnology*

Graduate Programs in Business, Education, Health, Information Studies, Law & Social Work
See *Pharmacy and Pharmaceutical Sciences* and *Veterinary Medicine and Sciences*

CONTENTS

Cancer Biology/Oncology

Baylor College of Medicine, Graduate School of Biomedical Sciences, Program in Translational Biology and Molecular Medicine, Houston, TX 77030-3498. Offers PhD. *Faculty:* 151 full-time (48 women). *Students:* 48 full-time (23 women); includes 13 minority (4 African Americans, 4 Asian Americans or Pacific Islanders, 5 Hispanic Americans), 14 international. Average age 24. *Degree requirements:* For doctorate, thesis/dissertation, public defense. *Entrance requirements:* For doctorate, GRE, minimum GPA of 3.0. Additional exam requirements/recommendations for international students: Required—TOEFL. *Application deadline:* For fall admission, 1/1 for domestic students. Application fee: $0. Electronic applications accepted. *Financial support:* In 2009–10, 48 students received support; fellowships, research assistantships, career-related internships or fieldwork, Federal Work-Study, health care benefits, and students receive a scholarship unless there are grant funds available to pay tuition available. Financial award applicants required to submit FAFSA. *Unit head:* Dr. Mary Estes, Director, 713-798-3585, Fax: 713-798-3586, E-mail: tbmm@bcm.edu. *Application contact:* Wanda Waguespack, Graduate Program Administrator, 713-798-1077, Fax: 713-798-3586, E-mail: wandaw@bcm.edu.

See Close-Up on page 261.

Brown University, Graduate School, Division of Biology and Medicine, Program in Pathology and Laboratory Medicine, Providence, RI 02912. Offers biology (PhD); cancer biology (PhD); immunology and infection (PhD); medical science (PhD); pathobiology (Sc M); toxicology and environmental pathology (PhD). Terminal master's awarded for partial completion of doctoral program. *Degree requirements:* For doctorate, thesis/dissertation, preliminary exam. *Entrance requirements:* For master's and doctorate, GRE General Test, GRE Subject Test. Additional exam requirements/recommendations for international students: Required—TOEFL. Electronic applications accepted. *Faculty research:* Environmental pathology, carcinogenesis, immunopathology, signal transduction, innate immunity.

Case Western Reserve University, School of Medicine and School of Graduate Studies, Graduate Programs in Medicine, Programs in Molecular and Cellular Basis of Disease/Pathology, Cancer Biology Training Program, Cleveland, OH 44106. Offers PhD, MD/PhD. *Degree requirements:* For doctorate, comprehensive exam, thesis/dissertation. *Entrance requirements:* For doctorate, GRE. Additional exam requirements/recommendations for international students: Required—TOEFL (minimum score 550 paper-based; 213 computer-based).

Dartmouth College, Program in Experimental and Molecular Medicine, Cancer Biology and Molecular Therapeutics Track, Hanover, NH 03755. Offers PhD.

Duke University, Graduate School, Department of Molecular Cancer Biology, Durham, NC 27710. Offers PhD. *Faculty:* 20 full-time. *Students:* 49 full-time (30 women); includes 4 minority (3 Asian Americans or Pacific Islanders, 1 Hispanic American), 14 international. 83 applicants, 17% accepted, 3 enrolled. In 2009, 10 doctorates awarded. *Degree requirements:* For doctorate, thesis/dissertation. *Entrance requirements:* For doctorate, GRE General Test, GRE Subject Test (recommended). Additional exam requirements/recommendations for international students: Required—TOEFL (minimum score 550 paper-based; 213 computer-based; 83 iBT), IELTS (minimum score 7). *Application deadline:* For fall admission, 12/8 priority date for domestic and international students. Application fee: $75. Electronic applications accepted. *Financial support:* Fellowships, research assistantships available. Financial award application deadline: 12/31. *Unit head:* Ann Marie Pendergast, Director of Graduate Studies, 919-681-8601, Fax: 919-681-7767, E-mail: means003@mc.duke.edu. *Application contact:* Cynthia Robertson, Associate Dean for Enrollment Services, 919-684-3913, E-mail: grad-admissions@duke.edu.

Emory University, Graduate School of Arts and Sciences, Division of Biological and Biomedical Sciences, Program in Cancer Biology, Atlanta, GA 30322-1100. Offers PhD.

Gerstner Sloan-Kettering Graduate School of Biomedical Sciences, Program in Cancer Biology, New York, NY 10021. Offers PhD. *Faculty research:* Biochemistry and molecular biology, biophysics/structural biology, computational biology, genetics, immunology.

See Close-Up on page 235.

Mayo Graduate School, Graduate Programs in Biomedical Sciences, Program in Tumor Biology, Rochester, MN 55905. Offers PhD. *Degree requirements:* For doctorate, oral defense of dissertation, qualifying oral and written exam. *Entrance requirements:* For doctorate, GRE, 1 year of chemistry, biology, calculus, and physics. Additional exam requirements/recommendations for international students: Required—TOEFL. Electronic applications accepted.

McMaster University, Faculty of Health Sciences and School of Graduate Studies, Program in Medical Sciences, Genetics and Cancer Area, Hamilton, ON L8S 4M2, Canada. Offers M Sc, PhD, MD/PhD. *Degree requirements:* For master's, thesis; for doctorate, comprehensive exam, thesis/dissertation. *Entrance requirements:* For master's, honors B Sc, B+ average in related field; for doctorate, M Sc, minimum B+ average, students with proven research experience and an A average may be admitted with a B Sc degree. Additional exam requirements/recommendations for international students: Required—TOEFL (minimum score 580 paper-based; 237 computer-based; 92 iBT).

Medical University of South Carolina, College of Graduate Studies, Program in Molecular and Cellular Biology and Pathobiology, Charleston, SC 29425. Offers cancer biology (PhD); cardiovascular biology (PhD); cardiovascular imaging (PhD); cell regulation (PhD); craniofacial biology (PhD); genetics and development (PhD); marine biomedicine (PhD); DMD/PhD; MD/PhD. *Faculty:* 137 full-time (33 women). *Students:* 39 full-time (25 women); includes 6 minority (4 African Americans, 1 Asian American or Pacific Islander, 1 Hispanic American), 9 international. Average age 28. In 2009, 16 doctorates awarded. *Degree requirements:* For doctorate, thesis/dissertation, oral and written exams. *Entrance requirements:* For doctorate, GRE General Test, interview, minimum GPA of 3.0. Additional exam requirements/recommendations for international students: Required—TOEFL (minimum score 600 paper-based; 250 computer-based; 100 iBT). *Application deadline:* For fall admission, 1/15 priority date for domestic and international students. Applications are processed on a rolling basis. Application fee: $0 ($85 for international students). Electronic applications accepted. *Financial support:* In 2009–10, 39 students received support, including 39 research assistantships with partial tuition reimbursements available (averaging $23,000 per year); Federal Work-Study and scholarships/grants also available. Support available to part-time students. Financial award application deadline: 3/10; financial award applicants required to submit FAFSA. *Unit head:* Dr. Donald R. Menick, Director, 843-876-5045, Fax: 843-792-6590, E-mail: menickd@musc.edu. *Application contact:* Dr. Cynthia F. Wright, Associate Dean for Admissions and Career Development, 843-792-2564, Fax: 843-792-6590, E-mail: wrightcf@musc.edu.

Meharry Medical College, School of Graduate Studies, Program in Biomedical Sciences, Cancer Biology Emphasis, Nashville, TN 37208-9989. Offers PhD, MD/PhD. *Degree requirements:* For doctorate, comprehensive exam, thesis/dissertation. *Entrance requirements:* For doctorate, GRE. *Faculty research:* Regulation of metabolism, enzymology, signal transduction, physical biochemistry.

Memorial University of Newfoundland, Faculty of Medicine and School of Graduate Studies, Graduate Programs in Medicine, Division of Biomedical Sciences, St. John's, NL A1C 5S7, Canada. Offers cancer (M Sc, PhD); cardiovascular (M Sc, PhD); immunology (M Sc, PhD); neuroscience (M Sc, PhD). Part-time programs available. *Degree requirements:* For master's, thesis; for doctorate, comprehensive exam, thesis/dissertation, oral defense of thesis. *Entrance requirements:* For master's, MD or B Sc; for doctorate, MD or M Sc. Additional exam requirements/recommendations for international students: Required—TOEFL. *Faculty research:* Neuroscience, immunology, cardiovascular, and cancer.

New York University, Graduate School of Arts and Science, Department of Biology, New York, NY 10012-1019. Offers biology (PhD); biomedical journalism (MS); cancer and molecular biology (PhD); computational biology (PhD); computers in biological research (MS); developmental genetics (PhD); general biology (MS); immunology and microbiology (PhD); molecular genetics (PhD); neurobiology (PhD); oral biology (MS); plant biology (PhD); recombinant DNA technology (MS); MS/MBA. Part-time programs available. *Faculty:* 24 full-time (5 women). *Students:* 142 full-time (79 women), 44 part-time (28 women); includes 34 minority (1 African American, 25 Asian Americans or Pacific Islanders, 8 Hispanic Americans), 82 international. Average age 27. 362 applicants, 71% accepted, 72 enrolled. In 2009, 43 master's, 9 doctorates awarded. Terminal master's awarded for partial completion of doctoral program. *Degree requirements:* For master's, thesis or alternative, qualifying paper; for doctorate, comprehensive exam, thesis/dissertation. *Entrance requirements:* For master's, GRE General Test; for doctorate, GRE General Test, GRE Subject Test. Additional exam requirements/recommendations for international students: Required—TOEFL. *Application deadline:* For fall admission, 12/12 priority date for domestic students. Application fee: $90. *Expenses:* Tuition: Full-time $30,528; part-time $1272 per credit. Required fees: $2177. *Financial support:* Fellowships with tuition reimbursements, research assistantships with tuition reimbursements, teaching assistantships with tuition reimbursements, career-related internships or fieldwork, Federal Work-Study, institutionally sponsored loans, scholarships/grants, health care benefits, and unspecified assistantships available. Financial award application deadline: 12/12; financial award applicants required to submit FAFSA. *Faculty research:* Genomics, molecular and cell biology, development and molecular genetics, molecular evolution of plants and animals. *Unit head:* Gloria Coruzzi, Chair, 212-998-8200, Fax: 212-995-4015, E-mail: biology@nyu.edu. *Application contact:* Stephen Small, Director of Graduate Studies, 212-998-8200, Fax: 212-995-4015, E-mail: biology@nyu.edu.

New York University, School of Medicine, New York, NY 10012-1019. Offers biomedical sciences (PhD), including biomedical imaging, cellular and molecular biology, computational biology, developmental genetics, medical and molecular parasitology, microbiology, molecular oncobiology and immunology, neuroscience and physiology, pathobiology, pharmacology, structural biology; clinical investigation (MS); medicine (MD); MD/MA; MD/MPA; MD/MS; MD/PhD. *Accreditation:* LCME/AMA (one or more programs are accredited). *Faculty:* 1,493 full-time (558 women), 327 part-time/adjunct (122 women). *Students:* 747 full-time (360 women); includes 275 minority (23 African Americans, 5 American Indian/Alaska Native, 199 Asian Americans or Pacific Islanders, 48 Hispanic Americans), 2 international. Average age 24. 7,568 applicants, 7% accepted, 213 enrolled. In 2009, 164 first professional degrees, 13 master's, 50 doctorates awarded. *Degree requirements:* For master's, comprehensive exam, thesis; for doctorate, comprehensive exam, thesis/dissertation. *Entrance requirements:* MCAT. Additional exam requirements/recommendations for international students: Required—TOEFL. *Application deadline:* For fall admission, 10/15 for domestic students; for winter admission, 12/18 for domestic students, 12/15 for international students. Application fee: $100. *Expenses:* Contact institution. *Financial support:* In 2009–10, 524 students received support, including 29 fellowships with full tuition reimbursements available (averaging $31,000 per year), 47 research assistantships with full tuition reimbursements available (averaging $31,000 per year); teaching assistantships, Federal Work-Study, institutionally sponsored loans, and health care benefits also available. Financial award application deadline: 3/1; financial award applicants required to submit FAFSA. *Faculty research:* AIDS, cancer, neuroscience, molecular biology, neuroscience, cell biology and molecular genetics, structural biology, microbial pathogenesis and host defense, pharmacology, molecular oncology and immunology. Total annual research expenditures: $201.1 million. *Unit head:* Dr. Robert Grossman, Dean, 212-263-3269, Fax: 212-263- 1828. *Application contact:* Dr. Nancy Genieser, Associate Dean, Admissions, 212-263-5290, Fax: 212-263-0720, E-mail: nancy.genieser@nyumc.org.

New York University, School of Medicine and Graduate School of Arts and Science, Sackler Institute of Graduate Biomedical Sciences, Programs in Molecular Oncology and Immunology, New York, NY 10012-1019. Offers immunology (PhD); molecular oncology (PhD); MD/PhD. *Degree requirements:* For doctorate, one foreign language, thesis/dissertation, qualifying exam. *Entrance requirements:* For doctorate, GRE General Test, GRE Subject Test. Additional exam requirements/recommendations for international students: Required—TOEFL. Electronic applications accepted. *Expenses:* Tuition: Full-time $30,528; part-time $1272 per credit. Required fees: $2177. *Faculty research:* Stem cells, immunology, genome instability, DNA damage checkpoints.

Northwestern University, Northwestern University Feinberg School of Medicine and Interdepartmental Programs, Integrated Graduate Programs in the Life Sciences, Chicago, IL 60611. Offers cancer biology (PhD); cell biology (PhD); developmental biology (PhD); evolutionary biology (PhD); immunology and microbial pathogenesis (PhD); molecular biology and genetics (PhD); neurobiology (PhD); pharmacology and toxicology (PhD); structural biology and biochemistry (PhD). *Degree requirements:* For doctorate, comprehensive exam, thesis/dissertation, written and oral qualifying exams. *Entrance requirements:* For doctorate, GRE General Test. Additional exam requirements/recommendations for international students: Required—TOEFL (minimum score 600 paper-based; 250 computer-based). Electronic applications accepted.

Queen's University at Kingston, School of Graduate Studies and Research, Faculty of Health Sciences, Department of Anatomy and Cell Biology, Kingston, ON K7L 3N6, Canada. Offers biology of reproduction (M Sc, PhD); cancer (M Sc, PhD); cardiovascular pathophysiology (M Sc, PhD); cell and molecular biology (M Sc, PhD); drug metabolism (M Sc, PhD); endocrinology (M Sc, PhD); motor control (M Sc, PhD); neural regeneration (M Sc, PhD); neurophysiology (M Sc, PhD). Part-time programs available. *Degree requirements:* For master's, thesis; for doctorate, one foreign language, comprehensive exam, thesis/dissertation. *Entrance requirements:* Additional exam requirements/recommendations for international students: Required—TOEFL. Electronic applications accepted. *Faculty research:* Human kinetics, neuroscience, reproductive biology, cardiovascular.

Rutgers, The State University of New Jersey, New Brunswick, Graduate School-New Brunswick, Program in Endocrinology and Animal Biosciences, Piscataway, NJ 08854-8097. Offers MS, PhD. Terminal master's awarded for partial completion of doctoral program. *Degree requirements:* For master's, thesis; for doctorate, comprehensive exam, thesis/dissertation. *Entrance requirements:* For master's and doctorate, GRE General Test. Additional exam requirements/recommendations for international students: Required—TOEFL. Electronic applications accepted. *Faculty research:* Comparative and behavioral endocrinology, epigenetic regulation of the endocrine system, exercise physiology and immunology, fetal and neonatal developmental programming, mammary gland biology and breast cancer, neuroendocrinology and alcohol studies, reproductive and developmental toxicology.

Stanford University, School of Medicine, Graduate Programs in Medicine, Program in Cancer Biology, Stanford, CA 94305-9991. Offers PhD. *Degree requirements:* For doctorate, thesis/dissertation, qualifying examination. *Entrance requirements:* For doctorate, GRE General Test, GRE Subject Test. Additional exam requirements/recommendations for international students: Required—TOEFL. Electronic applications accepted. *Expenses:* Tuition: Full-time $37,380; part-time $2760 per quarter. Required fees: $501.

State University of New York Upstate Medical University, College of Graduate Studies, Major Research Areas of the College of Graduate Studies, Syracuse, NY 13210-2334. *Unit head:* Dr. Steven R. Goodman, Dean, College of Graduate Studies, 315-464-4538. *Application contact:* Sandra Tillotson, Coordinator of Graduate Recruitment, 315-464-7655, Fax: 315-464-4544, E-mail: tillotss@upstate.edu.

Université de Montréal, Faculty of Medicine, Program in Specialized Studies, Montréal, QC H3C 3J7, Canada. Offers anesthesia (DES); diagnostic radiology (DES); family medicine

(DES); gastroenterology (DES); geriatry (DES); intensive care (DES); medical biochemistry (DES); medical genetics (DES); medicine (DES); microbiology and infectious diseases (DES); nuclear medicine (DES); obstetrics and gynecology (DES); ophthalmology (DES); pediatrics (DES); pneumology (DES); psychiatry (DES); radiology-oncology (DES); rheumatology (DES); surgery (DES). *Faculty:* 154 full-time (40 women), 333 part-time/adjunct (100 women). *Students:* 930 full-time (580 women), 7 part-time (all women). 74 applicants, 77% accepted, 29 enrolled. *Application deadline:* For fall admission, 2/1 priority date for domestic students; for winter admission, 11/1 priority date for domestic students; for spring admission, 2/1 priority date for domestic students. Application fee: $100. Electronic applications accepted. *Unit head:* Lorraine Locas, Assistant to the Vice Dean of Graduate Studies, 514-343-6269, Fax: 514-343-5751, E-mail: lorraine.locas@umontreal.ca. *Application contact:* Dr. Andre Ferron, Vice Dean of Graduate Studies, 514-343-6111 Ext. 0933, Fax: 514-343-5751, E-mail: andre.ferron@umontreal.ca.

Université Laval, Faculty of Medicine, Post-Professional Programs in Medical Studies, Québec, QC G1K 7P4, Canada. Offers anatomy-pathology (DESS); anesthesiology (DESS); cardiology (DESS); care of older people (Diploma); clinical research (DESS); community health (DESS); dermatology (DESS); diagnostic radiology (DESS); emergency medicine (Diploma); family medicine (DESS); general surgery (DESS); geriatrics (DESS); hematology (DESS); internal medicine (DESS); maternal and fetal medicine (Diploma); medical biochemistry (DESS); medical microbiology and infectious diseases (DESS); medical oncology (DESS); nephrology (DESS); neurology (DESS); neurosurgery (DESS); obstetrics and gynecology (DESS); ophthalmology (DESS); orthopedic surgery (DESS); oto-rhino-laryngology (DESS); palliative medicine (Diploma); pediatrics (DESS); plastic surgery (DESS); psychiatry (DESS); pulmonary medicine (DESS); radiology-oncology (DESS); thoracic surgery (DESS); urology (DESS). *Degree requirements:* For other advanced degree, comprehensive exam. *Entrance requirements:* For degree, knowledge of French. Electronic applications accepted.

University at Buffalo, the State University of New York, Graduate School, Graduate Programs in Cancer Research and Biomedical Sciences at Roswell Park Cancer Institute, Department of Molecular Pharmacology and Cancer Therapeutics at Roswell Park Cancer Institute, Program in Molecular Pharmacology and Cancer Therapeutics, Buffalo, NY 14260. Offers PhD. *Faculty:* 30 full-time (8 women). *Students:* 21 full-time (11 women); includes 11 minority (1 African American, 9 Asian Americans or Pacific Islanders, 1 Hispanic American), 1 international. Average age 26. 26 applicants, 35% accepted, 4 enrolled. In 2009, 1 doctorate awarded. *Degree requirements:* For doctorate, thesis/dissertation, departmental qualifying exam, grant proposal. *Entrance requirements:* For doctorate, GRE General Test (recommended). Additional exam requirements/recommendations for international students: Required—TOEFL; Recommended—TWE. *Application deadline:* For fall admission, 2/1 priority date for domestic students. Applications are processed on a rolling basis. Application fee: $35. Electronic applications accepted. *Financial support:* In 2009–10, 21 students received support, including 6 fellowships with full tuition reimbursements available (averaging $20,772 per year), 15 research assistantships with full tuition reimbursements available (averaging $20,772 per year). *Faculty research:* Molecular pharmacology, cancer cell biology, molecular biology, biochemistry, chemotherapy. Total annual research expenditures: $6.5 million. *Application contact:* Dr. Adam Karpf, Director of Graduate Studies, 716-845-8225, Fax: 716-845-3879, E-mail: adam.karpf@roswellpark.org.

University of Alberta, Faculty of Medicine and Dentistry and Faculty of Graduate Studies and Research, Graduate Programs in Medicine, Department of Oncology, Edmonton, AB T6G 2E1, Canada. Offers M Sc, PhD. *Faculty:* 27 full-time (7 women). *Students:* 23 full-time. Average age 29. 28 applicants, 21% accepted. In 2009, 1 doctorate awarded. Terminal master's awarded for partial completion of doctoral program. *Degree requirements:* For master's, thesis; for doctorate, thesis/dissertation. *Entrance requirements:* For master's and doctorate, minimum GPA of 7.0 on a 9.0 scale, B SC. Additional exam requirements/recommendations for international students: Required—TOEFL (minimum score 600 paper-based). *Application deadline:* For fall admission, 7/1 priority date for domestic students. Applications are processed on a rolling basis. Application fee: $0. Electronic applications accepted. Tuition and fees charges are reported in Canadian dollars. *Expenses:* Tuition, area resident: Full-time $4626 Canadian dollars; part-time $99.72 Canadian dollars per unit. International tuition: $8216 Canadian dollars full-time. Required fees: $3590 Canadian dollars; $99.72 Canadian dollars per unit. $215 Canadian dollars per term. *Financial support:* In 2009–10, 16 students received support, including 5 fellowships (averaging $17,200 per year), 1 research assistantship (averaging $7,014 per year); scholarships/grants also available. Financial award application deadline: 9/1. *Faculty research:* Experimental oncology, radiation oncology, medical physics, medical oncology. Total annual research expenditures: $3.5 million. *Unit head:* Dr. Carol E. Cass, Chair, 780-432-8320, Fax: 780-432-8425, E-mail: carol.cass@cancerboard.ab.ca. *Application contact:* Dr. Roseline Godbout, Graduate Coordinator, 780-432-8901, Fax: 780-432-8425, E-mail: roseline@cancerboard.ab.ca.

The University of Arizona, Graduate College, Graduate Interdisciplinary Programs, Graduate Interdisciplinary Program in Cancer Biology, Tucson, AZ 85721. Offers PhD. *Students:* 18 full-time (9 women), 2 part-time (both women); includes 5 minority (all Hispanic Americans), 4 international. Average age 28. 49 applicants, 6% accepted, 3 enrolled. In 2009, 6 doctorates awarded. *Degree requirements:* For doctorate, comprehensive exam, thesis/dissertation. *Entrance requirements:* For doctorate, GRE General Test, 3 letters of recommendation. Additional exam requirements/recommendations for international students: Required—TOEFL (minimum score 550 paper-based; 213 computer-based; 79 iBT). *Application deadline:* For fall admission, 12/1 for domestic and international students. Applications are processed on a rolling basis. Application fee: $65. Electronic applications accepted. *Expenses:* Tuition, state resident: full-time $9028. Tuition, nonresident: full-time $24,890. *Financial support:* Institutionally sponsored loans, scholarships/grants, traineeships, health care benefits, tuition waivers (full), and unspecified assistantships available. *Faculty research:* Differential gene expression, DNA-protein cross linking, cell growth regulation steroid, receptor proteins. *Unit head:* Dr. G. Tim Bowden, Chairman, 520-626-7479, E-mail: bowden@azcc.arizona.edu. *Application contact:* Anne Cione, Senior Program Coordinator, 520-626-7479, Fax: 520-626-4979, E-mail: acione@azcc.arizona.edu.

University of Calgary, Faculty of Medicine and Faculty of Graduate Studies, Department of Medical Science, Calgary, AB T2N 1N4, Canada. Offers cancer biology (M Sc, PhD); immunology (M Sc, PhD); joint injury and arthritis research (M Sc, PhD); medical education (M Sc, PhD); medical science (M Sc, PhD); mountain medicine and high altitude physiology (M Sc). *Degree requirements:* For master's, thesis; for doctorate, thesis/dissertation, candidacy exam. *Entrance requirements:* For master's, minimum undergraduate GPA of 3.2; for doctorate, minimum graduate GPA of 3.2. Additional exam requirements/recommendations for international students: Required—TOEFL (minimum score 600 paper-based; 250 computer-based). Electronic applications accepted. *Faculty research:* Cancer biology, immunology, joint injury and arthritis, medical education, population genomics.

University of California, San Diego, Office of Graduate Studies, Division of Biological Sciences, Program in Immunology, Virology, and Cancer Biology, La Jolla, CA 92093. Offers PhD. Offered in association with the Salk Institute. *Degree requirements:* For doctorate, thesis/dissertation, qualifying exam. Electronic applications accepted.

University of California, San Diego, School of Medicine and Office of Graduate Studies, Molecular Pathology Program, La Jolla, CA 92093. Offers bioinformatics (PhD); cancer biology/oncology (PhD); cardiovascular sciences and disease (PhD); microbiology (PhD); molecular pathology (PhD); neurological disease (PhD); stem cell and developmental biology (PhD); structural biology/drug design (PhD). *Entrance requirements:* For doctorate, GRE General Test, GRE Subject Test. Additional exam requirements/recommendations for international students: Required—TOEFL. Electronic applications accepted.

University of Chicago, Division of the Biological Sciences, Biomedical Sciences Cluster: Cancer Biology, Immunology, Molecular Metabolism and Nutrition, Pathology, and Micro-

biology, Committee on Cancer Biology, Chicago, IL 60637-1513. Offers PhD. *Faculty:* 52 full-time (14 women). *Students:* 35 full-time (19 women); includes 10 minority (9 Asian Americans or Pacific Islanders, 1 Hispanic American), 4 international. Average age 28. 74 applicants, 22% accepted, 5 enrolled. In 2009, 7 doctorates awarded. *Degree requirements:* For doctorate, thesis/dissertation, ethics class, 2 teaching assistantships. *Entrance requirements:* For doctorate, GRE General Test. Additional exam requirements/recommendations for international students: Required—TOEFL (minimum score 600 paper-based; 250 computer-based; 104 iBT), IELTS (minimum score 7). *Application deadline:* For fall admission, 12/1 priority date for domestic and international students. Application fee: $55. Electronic applications accepted. *Financial support:* In 2009–10, 35 students received support, including fellowships with full tuition reimbursements available (averaging $29,781 per year), research assistantships with full tuition reimbursements available (averaging $29,781 per year); institutionally sponsored loans and traineeships also available. Financial award applicants required to submit FAFSA. *Faculty research:* Cancer genetics, apoptosis, signal transduction, tumor biology, cell cycle regulation. Total annual research expenditures: $58 million. *Unit head:* Dr. Geoffrey Greene, Chair, 773-702-6964, E-mail: ggreene@uchicago.edu. *Application contact:* Kristin Reepmeyer, Administrative Assistant, 773-702-3940, Fax: 773-702-4634, E-mail: reepmeyer@bsd.uchicago.edu.

University of Cincinnati, Graduate School, College of Medicine, Graduate Programs in Biomedical Sciences, Graduate Program in Cell and Cancer Biology, Cincinnati, OH 45221. Offers PhD. *Degree requirements:* For doctorate, thesis/dissertation, qualifying exam. *Entrance requirements:* For doctorate, GRE General Test. Additional exam requirements/recommendations for international students: Required—TOEFL. Electronic applications accepted. *Faculty research:* Cancer biology, cell and molecular biology, breast cancer, pancreatic cancer, drug discovery.

University of Colorado Denver, School of Medicine, Program in Pathology Cancer Biology, Denver, CO 80217-3364. Offers cancer biology (PhD); pathology (PhD). *Students:* 16 full-time (12 women); includes 1 minority (Hispanic American), 1 international. *Degree requirements:* For doctorate, comprehensive exam, thesis/dissertation, 3 laboratory rotations. *Entrance requirements:* For doctorate, GRE General Test, interview, minimum undergraduate GPA of 3.0. Additional exam requirements/recommendations for international students: Required—TOEFL (minimum score 550 paper-based; 213 computer-based). *Application deadline:* For fall admission, 2/1 for domestic students. Application fee: $50. Electronic applications accepted. *Financial support:* Fellowships, research assistantships, teaching assistantships, Federal Work-Study and institutionally sponsored loans available. Support available to part-time students. Financial award application deadline: 3/1; financial award applicants required to submit FAFSA. *Faculty research:* Signal transduction by tyrosine kinases, estrogen and progesterone receptors in breast cancer, mechanism of mitochondrial DNA replication in the mammalian cell. *Unit head:* Dr. Steven Nordeen, Director, 303-724-4301, E-mail: steven.nordeen@ucdenver.edu. *Application contact:* Gary Brown, Program Administrator, 303-724-3700, E-mail: gary.brown@ucdenver.edu.

University of Delaware, College of Arts and Sciences, Department of Biological Sciences, Newark, DE 19716. Offers biotechnology (MS); cancer biology (MS, PhD); cell and extracellular matrix biology (MS, PhD); cell and systems physiology (MS, PhD); developmental biology (MS, PhD); ecology and evolution (MS, PhD); microbiology (MS, PhD); molecular biology and genetics (MS, PhD). Terminal master's awarded for partial completion of doctoral program. *Degree requirements:* For master's, thesis, preliminary exam; for doctorate, comprehensive exam, thesis/dissertation, preliminary exam. *Entrance requirements:* For master's and doctorate, GRE General Test. Additional exam requirements/recommendations for international students: Required—TOEFL (minimum score 600 paper-based; 250 computer-based); Recommended—TWE. Electronic applications accepted. *Faculty research:* Microorganisms, bone, cancer metastasis, developmental biology, cell biology, DNA.

University of Manitoba, Faculty of Graduate Studies, Faculty of Nursing, Winnipeg, MB R3T 2N2, Canada. Offers cancer nursing (MN); nursing (MN). *Degree requirements:* For master's, thesis.

University of Maryland, Baltimore, Graduate School, Graduate Program in Life Sciences, Program in Molecular Medicine, Baltimore, MD 21201. Offers cancer biology (PhD); cell and molecular physiology (PhD); human genetics and genomic medicine (PhD); molecular medicine (MS); molecular toxicology and pharmacology (PhD); MD/PhD. *Students:* 61 full-time (37 women), 9 part-time (5 women); includes 19 minority (7 African Americans, 9 Asian Americans or Pacific Islanders, 3 Hispanic Americans), 8 international. Average age 26. 324 applicants, 15% accepted, 20 enrolled. In 2009, 4 master's, 1 doctorate awarded. *Entrance requirements:* Additional exam requirements/recommendations for international students: Required—TOEFL (minimum score 600 paper-based; 100 iBT); Recommended—IELTS (minimum score 7). *Application deadline:* For fall admission, 1/15 for domestic and international students. Application fee: $50. Electronic applications accepted. *Expenses:* Tuition, state resident: full-time $7290; part-time $405 per credit hour. Tuition, nonresident: full-time $12,780; part-time $710 per credit hour. Required fees: $774; $10 per credit hour. $297 per semester. Tuition and fees vary according to course load, degree level and program. *Financial support:* In 2009–10, research assistantships with partial tuition reimbursements (averaging $25,000 per year); fellowships also available. Financial award application deadline: 3/1. *Unit head:* Dr. Dudley Strickland, Director, 410-706-8010, E-mail: dstrickland@som.umaryland.edu. *Application contact:* Sharron Graves, Program Coordinator, 410-706-6044, Fax: 410-706-6040, E-mail: sgraves@som.umaryland.edu.

University of Massachusetts Worcester, Graduate School of Biomedical Sciences, Program in Cancer Biology, Worcester, MA 01655-0115. Offers PhD. *Degree requirements:* For doctorate, comprehensive exam, thesis/dissertation. *Entrance requirements:* For doctorate, GRE General Test. Additional exam requirements/recommendations for international students: Required—TOEFL (minimum score 600 paper-based; 250 computer-based). Electronic applications accepted. *Faculty research:* Breast cancer research, cancer epidemiology, cell death and cell survival in cancer, leukemia/lymphoma research, molecular pathogenesis of tumors from stem cells, prostate cancer research.

University of Miami, Graduate School, Miller School of Medicine, Program in Cancer Biology, Coral Gables, FL 33124. Offers PhD, MD/PhD.

University of Minnesota, Twin Cities Campus, Graduate School, PhD Program in Microbiology, Immunology and Cancer Biology, Minneapolis, MN 55455-0213. Offers PhD. *Degree requirements:* For doctorate, thesis/dissertation. *Entrance requirements:* For doctorate, GRE General Test. Additional exam requirements/recommendations for international students: Required—TOEFL (minimum score 600 paper-based; 250 computer-based). Electronic applications accepted. *Faculty research:* Virology, microbiology, cancer biology, immunology.

University of Nebraska Medical Center, Graduate Studies, Program in Cancer Research, Omaha, NE 68198. Offers PhD. Terminal master's awarded for partial completion of doctoral program. *Degree requirements:* For doctorate, comprehensive exam, thesis/dissertation. *Entrance requirements:* For doctorate, GRE, 3 letters of reference; course work in chemistry, biology, physics and mathematics. Additional exam requirements/recommendations for international students: Required—TOEFL (minimum score 550 paper-based; 213 computer-based). Electronic applications accepted. *Faculty research:* DNA repair, tumor immunology, signal transduction, structural biology, gene expression.

University of Pennsylvania, School of Medicine, Biomedical Graduate Studies, Graduate Group in Cell and Molecular Biology, Philadelphia, PA 19104. Offers cancer biology (PhD); cell biology and physiology (PhD); developmental stem cell regenerative biology (PhD); gene therapy and vaccines (PhD); genetics and gene regulation (PhD); microbiology, virology, and parasitology (PhD); MD/PhD; VMD/PhD. *Faculty:* 296. *Students:* 307 full-time (167 women); includes 78 minority (13 African Americans, 1 American Indian/Alaska Native, 45 Asian Americans or Pacific Islanders, 19 Hispanic Americans), 33 international. 576 applicants, 19% accepted, 40 enrolled. In 2009, 32 doctorates awarded. *Degree requirements:* For doctorate, thesis/

Cancer Biology/Oncology

University of Pennsylvania (continued)

dissertation. *Entrance requirements:* For doctorate, GRE General Test. Additional exam requirements/recommendations for international students: Required—TOEFL. *Application deadline:* For fall admission, 12/8 priority date for domestic and international students. Applications are processed on a rolling basis. Application fee: $70. Electronic applications accepted. *Expenses:* Tuition: Full-time $25,660; part-time $4758 per course. Required fees: $2152; $270 per course. Tuition and fees vary according to course load, degree level and program. *Financial support:* In 2009–10, 307 students received support; fellowships, research assistantships, scholarships/grants, traineeships, and unspecified assistantships available. Financial award application deadline: 1/2. *Unit head:* Dr. Daniel Kessler, Graduate Group Chair, E-mail: raperj@mail.med.upenn.edu. *Application contact:* Meagan Schofer, Coordinator, 215-895-9536, Fax: 215-573-2104, E-mail: camb@mailmed.upenn.edu.

University of South Florida, Graduate School, College of Arts and Sciences, Program in Cancer Biology, Tampa, FL 33620-9951. Offers PhD. *Students:* 29 full-time (21 women), 1 (woman) part-time; includes 3 minority (1 Asian American or Pacific Islander, 2 Hispanic Americans), 5 international. Average age 34. 62 applicants, 10% accepted, 6 enrolled. In 2009, 4 doctorates awarded. *Entrance requirements:* For doctorate, GRE General Test. Additional exam requirements/recommendations for international students: Required—TOEFL (minimum score 550 paper-based; 213 computer-based). *Application deadline:* For fall admission, 2/1 for domestic students, 1/1 for international students. Application fee: $30. *Financial support:* Research assistantships with full tuition reimbursements, career-related internships or fieldwork, health care benefits, and unspecified assistantships available. Financial award application deadline: 4/3. *Faculty research:* Immunology, cancer control, signal transduction, drug discovery, genomics. *Unit head:* Kenneth Wright, Director, 813-745-6876, Fax: 813-745-7264, E-mail: ken.wright@moffitt.org. *Application contact:* Kenneth Wright, Director, 813-745-6876, Fax: 813-745-7264, E-mail: ken.wright@moffitt.org.

The University of Texas Health Science Center at Houston, Graduate School of Biomedical Sciences, Program in Cancer Biology, Houston, TX 77225-0036. Offers MS, PhD, MD/PhD. Terminal master's awarded for partial completion of doctoral program. *Degree requirements:* For master's, thesis; for doctorate, thesis/dissertation. *Entrance requirements:* For master's and doctorate, GRE General Test. Additional exam requirements/recommendations for international students: Required—TOEFL. Electronic applications accepted. *Faculty research:* Cancer metastasis, signal transduction, therapeutic resistance, cell cycle deregulation, cancer markers and target.

The University of Texas Health Science Center at Houston, Graduate School of Biomedical Sciences, Program in Molecular Carcinogenesis, Houston, TX 77225-0036. Offers MS, PhD, MD/PhD. Terminal master's awarded for partial completion of doctoral program. *Degree requirements:* For master's, thesis; for doctorate, thesis/dissertation. *Entrance requirements:* For master's and doctorate, GRE General Test. Additional exam requirements/recommendations for international students: Required—TOEFL. Electronic applications accepted. *Faculty research:* Carcinogenesis, mutagenesis, epigenetics, mouse models, cancer prevention.

The University of Texas Southwestern Medical Center at Dallas, Southwestern Graduate School of Biomedical Sciences, Division of Basic Science, Program in Cancer Biology, Dallas, TX 75390. Offers PhD. *Degree requirements:* For doctorate, thesis/dissertation, qualifying examination. *Unit head:* Jerry Shay, Program Chair, 214-648-3282, E-mail: jerry.shay@utsouthwestern.edu. *Application contact:* Jerry Shay, Program Chair, 214-648-3282, E-mail: jerry.shay@utsouthwestern.edu.

University of the District of Columbia, College of Arts and Sciences, Department of Biological and Environmental Sciences, Program in Cancer Biology, Prevention and Control, Washington, DC 20008-1175. Offers MS. Program offered in partnership with Lombardi Comprehensive Cancer Center at Georgetown University. *Students:* 9 full-time (5 women), 1 (woman) part-time; includes 2 African Americans, 1 Asian American or Pacific Islander, 2 Hispanic Americans. Average age 31. *Expenses:* Tuition, state resident: full-time $7580. Tuition, nonresident: full-time $14,580. Required fees: $620. *Unit head:* Dr. Freddie Dixon, Head, 202-274-7401. *Application contact:* Ann Marie Waterman, Associate Vice President of Admission, Recruitment and Financial Aid, 202-274-6069.

The University of Toledo, College of Graduate Studies, College of Medicine, Biomedical Science Programs, Program in Cancer Biology, Toledo, OH 43606-3390. Offers MSBS, PhD.

University of Utah, School of Medicine and Graduate School, Graduate Programs in Medicine, Department of Oncological Sciences, Salt Lake City, UT 84112-1107. Offers M Phil, MS, PhD. Terminal master's awarded for partial completion of doctoral program. *Degree requirements:* For master's, thesis (for some programs); for doctorate, thesis/dissertation. *Entrance requirements:* For master's and doctorate, GRE General Test, GRE Subject Test, minimum GPA of 3.0. Additional exam requirements/recommendations for international students: Required—TOEFL. *Expenses:* Tuition, state resident: full-time $4004; part-time $1674 per semester. Tuition, nonresident: full-time $14,134; part-time $5915 per semester. Required fees: $324 per semester. Tuition and fees vary according to course load, degree level and program. *Faculty research:* Molecular basis of cell growth and differences, regulation of gene expression, biochemical mechanics of DNA replication, molecular biology and biochemistry of signal transduction, somatic cell genetics.

University of Wisconsin–Madison, School of Medicine and Public Health and Graduate School, Graduate Programs in Medicine, Program in Cancer Biology, Madison, WI 53706-1380. Offers PhD. *Faculty:* 43 full-time (14 women). *Students:* 37 full-time (19 women); includes 2 minority (both Asian Americans or Pacific Islanders), 9 international. 259 applicants, 8% accepted, 9 enrolled. In 2009, 5 doctorates awarded. *Degree requirements:* For doctorate, comprehensive exam, thesis/dissertation. *Entrance requirements:* For doctorate, GRE General Test. Additional exam requirements/recommendations for international students: Required—TOEFL (minimum score 580 paper-based; 237 computer-based; 92 iBT). *Application deadline:* For fall admission, 12/1 priority date for domestic and international students. Applications are processed on a rolling basis. Application fee: $56. Electronic applications accepted. *Expenses:* Tuition, state resident: part-time $594 per credit. Tuition, nonresident: part-time $1504 per credit. Required fees: $65 per credit. Tuition and fees vary according to course load, program and reciprocity agreements. *Financial support:* In 2009–10, 34 students received support,

including 16 fellowships with full tuition reimbursements available (averaging $23,500 per year), 19 research assistantships with full tuition reimbursements available (averaging $23,500 per year); traineeships, health care benefits, and unspecified assistantships also available. Financial award application deadline: 12/1. *Faculty research:* Cancer genetics, tumor virology, chemical carcinogenesis, signal transduction, cell cycle. Total annual research expenditures: $15 million. *Unit head:* Dr. James Shull, Director, 608-262-2177, Fax: 608-262-2824, E-mail: shull@oncology.wisc.edu. *Application contact:* Bette Sheehan, Administrative Program Manager, 608-262-8651, Fax: 608-262-2824, E-mail: bsheehan@oncology.wisc.edu.

Vanderbilt University, Graduate School, Department of Cancer Biology, Nashville, TN 37240-1001. Offers MS, PhD, MD/PhD. *Faculty:* 33 full-time (12 women), 1 part-time/adjunct (0 women). *Students:* 49 full-time (33 women); includes 9 minority (5 African Americans, 3 Asian Americans or Pacific Islanders, 1 Hispanic American), 18 international. Average age 28. In 2009, 2 master's, 5 doctorates awarded. *Degree requirements:* For doctorate, thesis/dissertation, final and qualifying exams. *Entrance requirements:* For master's and doctorate, GRE General Test. Additional exam requirements/recommendations for international students: Required—TOEFL (minimum score 570 paper-based; 230 computer-based; 88 iBT). *Application deadline:* For fall admission, 1/15 for domestic and international students. Application fee: $0. Electronic applications accepted. *Financial support:* Fellowships with full and partial tuition reimbursements, research assistantships with full and partial tuition reimbursements, Federal Work-Study, institutionally sponsored loans, scholarships/grants, traineeships, and health care benefits available. Financial award application deadline: 1/15; financial award applicants required to submit CSS PROFILE or FAFSA. *Faculty research:* Microenvironmental influences on cellular phenotype, in particular as it relates to host/tumor interactions, tumor-stroma interactions, angiogenesis, growth factor and cytokine signaling, oncogenes, tumor suppressors, matrix and matrix degradation, cell adhesion, metastasis. *Unit head:* Dr. Lynn M. Matrisian, Chair, 615-322-0375, Fax: 615-936-2911, E-mail: lynn.matrisian@vanderbilt.edu. *Application contact:* Jin Chen, Director of Graduate Studies, 615-322-0375, Fax: 615-936-2911, E-mail: jin.chen@vanderbilt.edu.

Wake Forest University, School of Medicine and Graduate School of Arts and Sciences, Graduate Programs in Medicine, Department of Cancer Biology, Winston-Salem, NC 27109. Offers PhD, MD/PhD. *Degree requirements:* For doctorate, thesis/dissertation. *Entrance requirements:* For doctorate, GRE General Test. Additional exam requirements/recommendations for international students: Required—TOEFL. Electronic applications accepted. *Faculty research:* Cancer research, mechanisms of carcinogenesis, signal transduction and regulation of cell growth.

Wayne State University, School of Medicine, Graduate Programs in Medicine, Department of Radiation Oncology, Detroit, MI 48202. Offers medical physics (PhD); radiological physics (MS). Part-time and evening/weekend programs available. Terminal master's awarded for partial completion of doctoral program. *Degree requirements:* For master's, thesis, essay, exit exam; for doctorate, thesis/dissertation, qualifying exam. *Entrance requirements:* For master's, GRE General Test, BS in physics or related area; for doctorate, GRE General Test, GRE Subject Test, BS in physics or related area. Additional exam requirements/recommendations for international students: Required—TOEFL (minimum score 550 paper-based; 213 computer-based); Recommended—TWE (minimum score 6). Electronic applications accepted. *Faculty research:* Radiotherapy physics, hyperthermia, magnetic resonance imaging and spectroscopy, clinical ultrasound, x-ray physics.

Wayne State University, School of Medicine, Graduate Programs in Medicine, Program in Cancer Biology, Detroit, MI 48202. Offers MS, PhD. *Degree requirements:* For doctorate, thesis/dissertation. *Entrance requirements:* For doctorate, GRE General Test. Additional exam requirements/recommendations for international students: Required—TOEFL (minimum score 550 paper-based; 213 computer-based); Recommended—TWE (minimum score 6). Electronic applications accepted. *Faculty research:* Molecular oncology and carcinogenesis; cellular interactions and signaling; proteases in neoplasia; therapeutics and prevention; translational research.

See Close-Up on page 253.

West Virginia University, Davis College of Agriculture, Forestry and Consumer Sciences, Interdisciplinary Program in Genetics and Developmental Biology, Morgantown, WV 26506. Offers animal breeding (MS, PhD); biochemical and molecular genetics (MS, PhD); cytogenetics (MS, PhD); descriptive embryology (MS, PhD); developmental genetics (MS); experimental morphogenesis/teratology (MS); human genetics (MS, PhD); immunogenetics (MS, PhD); life cycles of animals and plants (MS, PhD); molecular aspects of development (MS, PhD); mutagenesis (MS, PhD); oncology (MS, PhD); plant genetics (MS, PhD); population and quantitative genetics (MS, PhD); regeneration (MS, PhD); teratology (PhD); toxicology (MS, PhD). *Degree requirements:* For master's, thesis; for doctorate, comprehensive exam, thesis/dissertation. *Entrance requirements:* For master's, GRE or MCAT, minimum GPA of 2.75. Additional exam requirements/recommendations for international students: Required—TOEFL.

West Virginia University, School of Medicine, Graduate Programs at the Health Sciences Center, Interdisciplinary Graduate Programs in Biomedical Sciences, Program in Cancer Cell Biology, Morgantown, WV 26506. Offers PhD, MD/PhD. *Degree requirements:* For doctorate, comprehensive exam, thesis/dissertation. *Entrance requirements:* For doctorate, GRE General Test, minimum GPA of 3.0. Additional exam requirements/recommendations for international students: Required—TOEFL. Electronic applications accepted. *Faculty research:* Cellular signaling, tumor microenvironment, cancer therapeutics.

Yale University, School of Medicine and Graduate School of Arts and Sciences, Combined Program in Biological and Biomedical Sciences (BBS), Pharmacological Sciences and Molecular Medicine Track, New Haven, CT 06520. Offers PhD, MD/PhD. *Degree requirements:* For doctorate, thesis/dissertation. *Entrance requirements:* For doctorate, GRE General Test. Additional exam requirements/recommendations for international students: Required—TOEFL. *Application deadline:* For fall admission, 12/6 for domestic and international students. Electronic applications accepted. *Financial support:* Fellowships, research assistantships available. *Unit head:* Dr. Gerry Shadel, Co-Director, 203-785-2475, E-mail: bbs.pharm@yale.edu. *Application contact:* Dr. Gerry Shadel, Co-Director, 203-785-2475, E-mail: bbs.pharm@yale.edu.

Cell Biology

Albany Medical College, Center for Cell Biology and Cancer Research, Albany, NY 12208-3479. Offers MS, PhD. Part-time programs available. *Faculty:* 16 full-time (4 women). *Students:* 19 full-time (14 women); includes 6 minority (1 African American, 4 Asian Americans or Pacific Islanders, 1 Hispanic American). Average age 26. 25 applicants, 28% accepted, 6 enrolled. In 2009, 2 master's, 2 doctorates awarded. Terminal master's awarded for partial completion of doctoral program. *Degree requirements:* For master's, thesis; for doctorate, comprehensive exam, thesis/dissertation. *Entrance requirements:* For master's, GRE General Test, all transcripts, letters of recommendation; for doctorate, GRE General Test, letters of recommendation. Additional exam requirements/recommendations for international students: Required—TOEFL. *Application deadline:* For fall admission, 3/15 priority date for domestic and international students. Applications are processed on a rolling basis. *Expenses:* Tuition: Full-time $18,820.

Financial support: In 2009–10, 10 research assistantships (averaging $24,000 per year) were awarded; Federal Work-Study, scholarships/grants, and tuition waivers (full) also available. Financial award applicants required to submit FAFSA. *Faculty research:* Cancer cell biology, angiogenesis, tissue remodeling, signal transduction, cell adhesion. *Unit head:* Dr. C. Michael DiPersio, Graduate Director, 518-262-5916, Fax: 518-262-5669, E-mail: dipersm@mail.amc.edu. *Application contact:* Dr. C. Michael DiPersio, Graduate Director, 518-262-5916, Fax: 518-262-5669, E-mail: dipersm@mail.amc.edu.

Albert Einstein College of Medicine, Sue Golding Graduate Division of Medical Sciences, Department of Anatomy and Structural Biology, Bronx, NY 10461. Offers anatomy (PhD); cell and developmental biology (PhD); MD/PhD. *Degree requirements:* For doctorate, thesis/dissertation. *Entrance requirements:* For doctorate, GRE General Test. Additional exam requirements/recommendations for international students: Required—TOEFL. Electronic applications accepted. *Faculty research:* Cell motility, cell membranes and membrane-cytoskeletal interactions as applied to processing of pancreatic hormones, mechanisms of secretion.

Albert Einstein College of Medicine, Sue Golding Graduate Division of Medical Sciences, Division of Biological Sciences, Department of Cell Biology, Bronx, NY 10461. Offers PhD, MD/PhD. *Degree requirements:* For doctorate, thesis/dissertation. *Entrance requirements:* For doctorate, GRE General Test. Additional exam requirements/recommendations for international students: Required—TOEFL. *Faculty research:* Molecular and genetic basis of gene expression in animal cells; expression of differentiated traits of albumin, hemoglobin, myosin, and immunoglobin.

Appalachian State University, Cratis D. Williams Graduate School, Department of Biology, Boone, NC 28608. Offers cell and molecular (MS); general (MS). Part-time programs available. *Faculty:* 27 full-time (11 women). *Students:* 28 full-time (14 women), 7 part-time (3 women); includes 2 minority (both Asian Americans or Pacific Islanders), 24 applicants, 29% accepted, 7 enrolled. In 2009, 10 master's awarded. *Degree requirements:* For master's, comprehensive exam, thesis. *Entrance requirements:* For master's, GRE General Test, 3 letters of recommendation. Additional exam requirements/recommendations for international students: Required—TOEFL (minimum score 570 paper-based; 230 computer-based; 79 iBT), IELTS (minimum score 6.5). *Application deadline:* For fall admission, 7/1 for domestic students, 2/1 for international students; for spring admission, 11/1 for domestic students, 7/1 for international students. Applications are processed on a rolling basis. Application fee: $50. Electronic applications accepted. *Expenses:* Tuition, state resident: full-time $2960. Tuition, nonresident: full-time $14,051. Required fees: $2320. *Financial support:* In 2009–10, 25 teaching assistantships (averaging $9,500 per year) were awarded; fellowships, research assistantships, career-related internships or fieldwork, Federal Work-Study, scholarships/grants, and unspecified assistantships also available. Financial award application deadline: 4/1; financial award applicants required to submit FAFSA. *Faculty research:* Aquatic and terrestrial ecology, animal and plant physiology, behavior and systematics, immunology and cell biology, molecular biology and microbiology. Total annual research expenditures: $451,508. *Unit head:* Dr. Steven Seagle, Chairman, 828-262-3025, E-mail: seaglesw@appstate.edu. *Application contact:* Dr. Gary Walker, Graduate Coordinator, 828-262-3025, E-mail: walkergl@appstate.edu.

Arizona State University, Graduate College, College of Liberal Arts and Sciences, Division of Natural Sciences, School of Life Sciences, Tempe, AZ 85287. Offers biological design (PhD); biology (MNS, MS, PhD); biology and society (PhD); human and social dimensions of science and technology (PhD); microbiology (MNS, MS, PhD); molecular and cellular biology (MS, PhD); neuroscience (PhD); plant biology (MNS, MS, PhD). *Accreditation:* NAACLS. *Degree requirements:* For master's, thesis (MS); for doctorate, one foreign language, thesis/dissertation. *Entrance requirements:* For master's and doctorate, GRE.

Auburn University, Graduate School, Interdepartmental Programs, Auburn University, AL 36849. Offers cell and molecular biology (PhD); integrated textile and apparel sciences (PhD); sociology and rural sociology (MA, MS), including rural sociology (MS), sociology. Part-time programs available. *Students:* 25 full-time (12 women), 19 part-time (13 women); includes 4 minority (1 African American, 1 American Indian/Alaska Native, 2 Asian Americans or Pacific Islanders), 26 international. Average age 28. 88 applicants, 35% accepted, 12 enrolled. In 2009, 4 master's, 3 doctorates awarded. *Entrance requirements:* For master's, GRE General Test. *Application deadline:* For fall admission, 7/7 for domestic students; for spring admission, 11/24 for domestic students. Applications are processed on a rolling basis. Application fee: $50 ($60 for international students). Electronic applications accepted. *Expenses:* Tuition, state resident: full-time $6240. Tuition, nonresident: full-time $18,720. International tuition: $18,938 full-time. Required fees: $492. Tuition and fees vary according to course load, program and reciprocity agreements. *Financial support:* Fellowships, research assistantships, teaching assistantships, Federal Work-Study available. Support available to part-time students. Financial award application deadline: 3/15; financial award applicants required to submit FAFSA. *Unit head:* Interim Dean of the Graduate School. *Application contact:* Dr. George Flowers, Dean of the Graduate School, 334-844-2125.

Baylor College of Medicine, Graduate School of Biomedical Sciences, Department of Molecular and Cellular Biology, Houston, TX 77030-3498. Offers PhD, MD/PhD. *Faculty:* 74 full-time (19 women). *Students:* 66 full-time (36 women); includes 8 minority (2 African Americans, 1 Asian American or Pacific Islander, 5 Hispanic Americans), 19 international. Average age 25. In 2009, 14 doctorates awarded. *Degree requirements:* For doctorate, thesis/dissertation, public defense, qualifying exam. *Entrance requirements:* For doctorate, GRE General Test, GRE Subject Test (strongly recommended), minimum GPA of 3.0. Additional exam requirements/recommendations for international students: Required—TOEFL. *Application deadline:* For fall admission, 1/1 priority date for domestic students. Application fee: $0. Electronic applications accepted. *Financial support:* Fellowships, research assistantships, career-related internships or fieldwork, Federal Work-Study, institutionally sponsored loans, health care benefits, and tuition waivers (full) available. Financial award applicants required to submit FAFSA. *Faculty research:* Gene regulation, cell structure/function, developmental biology, neurobiology, reproductive endocrinology. *Unit head:* Dr. JoAnne Richards, Director, 713-798-4598. *Application contact:* Caroline Kosnik, Graduate Program Administrator, 713-798-4598, Fax: 713-790-0545, E-mail: ckosnik@bcm.edu.

Baylor College of Medicine, Graduate School of Biomedical Sciences, Interdepartmental Program in Cell and Molecular Biology, Houston, TX 77030-3498. Offers biochemistry (PhD); cell and molecular biology (PhD); genetics (PhD); human genetics (PhD); immunology (PhD); microbiology (PhD); virology (PhD); MD/PhD. *Faculty:* 100 full-time (31 women). *Students:* 59 full-time (37 women); includes 24 minority (5 African Americans, 1 American Indian/Alaska Native, 7 Asian Americans or Pacific Islanders, 11 Hispanic Americans), 6 international. Average age 25. In 2009, 9 doctorates awarded. *Degree requirements:* For doctorate, thesis/dissertation, public defense. *Entrance requirements:* For doctorate, GRE General Test, GRE Subject Test (strongly recommended), minimum GPA of 3.0. Additional exam requirements/recommendations for international students: Required—TOEFL. *Application deadline:* For fall admission, 1/1 priority date for domestic students. Applications are processed on a rolling basis. Application fee: $0. Electronic applications accepted. *Financial support:* In 2009–10, 59 students received support; fellowships, research assistantships, teaching assistantships, Federal Work-Study, institutionally sponsored loans, health care benefits, and tuition waivers (full) available. Financial award applicants required to submit FAFSA. *Faculty research:* Gene expression and regulation, developmental biology and genetics, signal transduction and membrane biology, aging process, molecular virology. *Unit head:* Dr. Susan Marriott, Director, 713-798-6557. *Application contact:* Lourdes Fernandez, Graduate Program Administrator, 713-798-6557, Fax: 713-798-6325, E-mail: cmbprog@bcm.edu.

See Close-Up on page 231.

Baylor College of Medicine, Graduate School of Biomedical Sciences, Program in Developmental Biology, Houston, TX 77030-3498. Offers PhD, MD/PhD. *Faculty:* 52 full-time (16 women). *Students:* 51 full-time (26 women); includes 9 minority (1 American Indian/Alaska Native, 6 Asian Americans or Pacific Islanders, 2 Hispanic Americans), 29 international. Average age 25. In 2009, 4 doctorates awarded. *Degree requirements:* For doctorate, thesis/dissertation, public defense. *Entrance requirements:* For doctorate, GRE General Test, GRE Subject Test (strongly recommended), minimum GPA of 3.0. Additional exam requirements/recommendations for international students: Required—TOEFL. *Application deadline:* For fall admission, 1/1 priority date for domestic students. Application fee: $0. Electronic applications accepted. *Financial support:* Fellowships, research assistantships, career-related internships or fieldwork, Federal Work-Study, institutionally sponsored loans, health care benefits, tuition waivers (full), and stipends available. *Faculty research:* Molecular and genetic approaches to study pattern formation in Dictyostelium, Drosophila, C.elegans, mouse, Xenopus, and zebrafish; cross-species approach. *Unit head:* Dr. Hugo Bellen, Director, 713-798-6410. *Application*

contact: Catherine Tasnier, Graduate Program Administrator, 713-798-6410, Fax: 713-798-5386, E-mail: cat@bcm.edu.

See Close-Up on page 315.

Baylor College of Medicine, Program in Cell and Molecular Biology of Aging, Houston, TX 77030-3498. Offers PhD, MD/PhD. *Application contact:* Dr. Lloyd H. Michael, Senior Associate Dean of the Medical School, 713-798-4842, Fax: 713-798-5563, E-mail: lmichael@bcm.edu.

Boston University, Graduate School of Arts and Sciences, Molecular Biology, Cell Biology, and Biochemistry Program (MCBB), Boston, MA 02215. Offers MA, PhD. *Students:* 34 full-time (20 women), 1 (woman) part-time; includes 6 minority (2 African Americans, 2 Asian Americans or Pacific Islanders, 2 Hispanic Americans), 4 international. Average age 29. 77 applicants, 18% accepted, 5 enrolled. In 2009, 2 doctorates awarded. Terminal master's awarded for partial completion of doctoral program. *Degree requirements:* For master's, one foreign language, thesis (for some programs); for doctorate, one foreign language, comprehensive exam, thesis/dissertation. *Entrance requirements:* For master's and doctorate, GRE General Test, GRE Subject Test. Additional exam requirements/recommendations for international students: Required—TOEFL (minimum score 600 paper-based; 250 computer-based). *Application deadline:* For fall admission, 12/7 for domestic and international students. Application fee: $70. Electronic applications accepted. *Expenses:* Tuition: Full-time $37,910; part-time $1184 per credit hour. Required fees: $386; $40 per semester. Part-time tuition and fees vary according to class time, course level, degree level and program. *Financial support:* In 2009–10, 9 students received support, including 1 fellowship with full tuition reimbursement available (averaging $18,900 per year), 7 research assistantships with full tuition reimbursements available (averaging $14,800 per year), 1 teaching assistantship with full tuition reimbursement available (averaging $18,400 per year); Federal Work-Study, scholarships/grants, and traineeships also available. Financial award application deadline: 12/7; financial award applicants required to submit FAFSA. *Unit head:* Dr. Ulla Hansen, Director, 617-353-2432, Fax: 617-353-6340, E-mail: mccall@bu.edu. *Application contact:* Meredith Canode, Academic Administrator, 617-353-2432, Fax: 617-353-6340, E-mail: mcanode@bu.edu.

Boston University, School of Medicine, Division of Graduate Medical Sciences, Department of Biochemistry, Boston, MA 02118. Offers MA, PhD, MD/PhD. Part-time programs available. Terminal master's awarded for partial completion of doctoral program. *Degree requirements:* For master's, thesis or alternative, qualifying exam; for doctorate, thesis/dissertation, qualifying exam. *Entrance requirements:* For master's and doctorate, GRE General Test, GRE Subject Test. Additional exam requirements/recommendations for international students: Required—TOEFL. *Application deadline:* For fall admission, 1/15 priority date for domestic students; for spring admission, 10/15 priority date for domestic students. Electronic applications accepted. *Expenses:* Tuition: Full-time $37,910; part-time $1184 per credit hour. Required fees: $386; $40 per semester. Part-time tuition and fees vary according to class time, course level, degree level and program. *Financial support:* Fellowships, research assistantships, Federal Work-Study, scholarships/grants, and traineeships available. *Faculty research:* Extracellular matrix, gene expression, receptors, growth control. *Unit head:* Dr. Carl Franzblau, Associate Dean, 617-638-5120, Fax: 617-638-4842, E-mail: medsci@bu.edu. *Application contact:* Dr. Barbara Schreiber, Information Contact, 617-638-5094, Fax: 617-638-5339, E-mail: schreibe@biochem. bumc.bu.edu.

Boston University, School of Medicine, Division of Graduate Medical Sciences, Program in Cell and Molecular Biology, Boston, MA 02118. Offers PhD, MD/PhD. *Degree requirements:* For doctorate, thesis/dissertation. *Entrance requirements:* For doctorate, GRE General Test, GRE Subject Test. Additional exam requirements/recommendations for international students: Required—TOEFL. *Application deadline:* For fall admission, 1/15 priority date for domestic students; for spring admission, 10/15 priority date for domestic students. Electronic applications accepted. *Expenses:* Tuition: Full-time $37,910; part-time $1184 per credit hour. Required fees: $386; $40 per semester. Part-time tuition and fees vary according to class time, course level, degree level and program. *Financial support:* Fellowships, research assistantships, Federal Work-Study, scholarships/grants, and traineeships available. *Unit head:* Dr. Vickery Trinkaus Randall, Director, 617-638-6099, Fax: 617-638-5337, E-mail: vickery@bu.edu. *Application contact:* Dr. Mary Jo Murnane, Admissions Director, 617-638-4926, Fax: 617-638-4085, E-mail: mmurnane@bu.edu.

Brandeis University, Graduate School of Arts and Sciences, Program in Molecular and Cell Biology, Waltham, MA 02454-9110. Offers genetics (PhD); microbiology (PhD); molecular and cell biology (MS, PhD); molecular biology (PhD); neurobiology (PhD). *Faculty:* 28 full-time (12 women), 1 (woman) part-time/adjunct. *Students:* 46 full-time (26 women), 1 part-time (0 women); includes 3 minority (2 African Americans, 1 Hispanic American), 7 international. Average age 27. 146 applicants, 21% accepted, 12 enrolled. In 2009, 4 master's, 6 doctorates awarded. Terminal master's awarded for partial completion of doctoral program. *Degree requirements:* For master's, thesis optional, research project; for doctorate, comprehensive exam, thesis/dissertation, teaching assistant experience. *Entrance requirements:* For master's and doctorate, GRE General Test, resume, 3 letters of recommendation. Additional exam requirements/recommendations for international students: Required—TOEFL (minimum score 600 paper-based; 250 computer-based; 100 iBT); Recommended—IELTS (minimum score 7). *Application deadline:* For fall admission, 1/15 priority date for domestic students. Applications are processed on a rolling basis. Application fee: $75. Electronic applications accepted. *Financial support:* In 2009–10, 41 students received support, including 13 fellowships with full tuition reimbursements available (averaging $27,500 per year), 27 research assistantships with full tuition reimbursements available (averaging $27,500 per year), 1 teaching assistantship with partial tuition reimbursement available (averaging $3,200 per year); scholarships/grants, traineeships, health care benefits, and tuition waivers (full and partial) also available. Financial award application deadline: 4/15; financial award applicants required to submit FAFSA. *Faculty research:* Regulation of gene expression by transcription factors, molecular neurobiology, immunology, molecular mechanisms of genetic recombination, cell differentiation. *Unit head:* Dr. Piali Sengupta, Chair, 781-736-2686, Fax: 781-736-3107, E-mail: piali@brandeis.edu. *Application contact:* Marcia Cabral, Department Administrator, 781-736-3100, Fax: 781-736-3107, E-mail: cabral@brandeis.edu.

Brown University, Graduate School, Division of Biology and Medicine, Program in Molecular Biology, Cell Biology, and Biochemistry, Providence, RI 02912. Offers biochemistry (M Med Sc, Sc M, PhD), including biochemistry (Sc M, PhD), biology (Sc M, PhD), medical science (M Med Sc, PhD); biology (MA); cell biology (M Med Sc, Sc M, PhD), including biochemistry (Sc M, PhD), biology (Sc M, PhD), medical science (M Med Sc, PhD); developmental biology (M Med Sc, Sc M, PhD), including biochemistry (Sc M, PhD), biology (Sc M, PhD), medical science (M Med Sc, PhD); immunology (M Med Sc, Sc M, PhD), including biochemistry (Sc M, PhD), biology (Sc M, PhD), medical science (M Med Sc, PhD); molecular microbiology (M Med Sc, Sc M, PhD), including biochemistry (Sc M, PhD), biology (Sc M, PhD), medical science (M Med Sc, PhD); MD/PhD. Part-time programs available. Terminal master's awarded for partial completion of doctoral program. *Degree requirements:* For master's, thesis (for some programs); for doctorate, one foreign language, thesis/dissertation, preliminary exam. *Entrance requirements:* For master's and doctorate, GRE General Test, GRE Subject Test. Additional exam requirements/recommendations for international students: Required—TOEFL. Electronic applications accepted. *Faculty research:* Molecular genetics, gene regulation.

California Institute of Technology, Division of Biology, Program in Cell Biology and Biophysics, Pasadena, CA 91125-0001. Offers PhD. *Degree requirements:* For doctorate, thesis/dissertation, qualifying exam. *Entrance requirements:* For doctorate, GRE General Test.

Carnegie Mellon University, Mellon College of Science, Department of Biological Sciences, Pittsburgh, PA 15213-3891. Offers biochemistry (PhD); biophysics (PhD); cell biology (PhD); computational biology (MS, PhD); developmental biology (PhD); genetics (PhD); molecular biology (PhD); neuroscience (PhD). *Degree requirements:* For doctorate, comprehensive exam, thesis/dissertation. *Entrance requirements:* For doctorate, GRE General Test, GRE

Cell Biology

Carnegie Mellon University (continued)
Subject Test, interview. Electronic applications accepted. *Faculty research:* Genetic structure, function, and regulation; protein structure and function; biological membranes; biological spectroscopy.

Case Western Reserve University, School of Medicine and School of Graduate Studies, Graduate Programs in Medicine, Department of Anatomy, Cleveland, OH 44106. Offers applied anatomy (MS); biological anthropology (MS); cellular biology (MS); MD/MS. Part-time programs available. *Degree requirements:* For master's, comprehensive exam, thesis (for some programs). *Entrance requirements:* For master's, GRE General Test. Additional exam requirements/recommendations for international students: Required—TOEFL. *Faculty research:* Hypoxia, cell injury, biochemical aberration occurrences in ischemic tissue, human functional morphology, evolutionary morphology.

Case Western Reserve University, School of Medicine and School of Graduate Studies, Graduate Programs in Medicine, Department of Molecular Biology and Microbiology, Cleveland, OH 44106-4960. Offers cellular biology (PhD); microbiology (PhD); molecular biology (PhD); molecular virology (PhD); MD/PhD. Students are admitted to an integrated Biomedical Sciences Training Program involving 11 basic science programs at Case Western Reserve University. *Degree requirements:* For doctorate, thesis/dissertation. *Entrance requirements:* For doctorate, GRE General Test, GRE Subject Test. Additional exam requirements/recommendations for international students: Required—TOEFL. Electronic applications accepted. *Faculty research:* Gene expression in eukaryotic and prokaryotic systems; microbial physiology; intracellular transport and signaling; mechanisms of oncogenesis; molecular mechanisms of RNA processing, editing, and catalysis.

Case Western Reserve University, School of Medicine and School of Graduate Studies, Graduate Programs in Medicine, Program in Cell Biology, Cleveland, OH 44106. Offers PhD. *Degree requirements:* For doctorate, thesis/dissertation. *Entrance requirements:* For doctorate, GRE General Test, GRE Subject Test, previous course work in biochemistry. Additional exam requirements/recommendations for international students: Required—TOEFL. Electronic applications accepted. *Faculty research:* Macromolecular transport, membrane traffic, signal transduction, nuclear organization, lipid metabolism.

Case Western Reserve University, School of Medicine and School of Graduate Studies, Graduate Programs in Medicine, Programs in Molecular and Cellular Basis of Disease/Pathology, Cleveland, OH 44106. Offers cancer biology (PhD); cell biology (MS, PhD); immunology (MS, PhD); pathology (MS, PhD); MD/PhD. Terminal master's awarded for partial completion of doctoral program. *Degree requirements:* For master's, thesis; for doctorate, thesis/dissertation. *Entrance requirements:* For master's and doctorate, GRE General Test, GRE Subject Test. Additional exam requirements/recommendations for international students: Required—TOEFL (minimum score 550 paper-based; 213 computer-based). Electronic applications accepted. *Faculty research:* Neurobiology, molecular biology, cancer biology, biomaterials, biocompatibility.

The Catholic University of America, School of Arts and Sciences, Department of Biology, Washington, DC 20064. Offers cell and microbial biology (MS, PhD), including cell biology, microbiology; clinical laboratory science (MS, PhD); MSLS/MS. Part-time programs available. *Faculty:* 7 full-time (4 women), 2 part-time/adjunct (both women). *Students:* 3 full-time (2 women), 23 part-time (15 women); includes 8 minority (2 African Americans, 3 Asian Americans or Pacific Islanders, 3 Hispanic Americans), 8 international. Average age 29. 30 applicants, 47% accepted, 3 enrolled. In 2009, 3 doctorates awarded. *Degree requirements:* For master's, comprehensive exam, thesis or alternative; for doctorate, comprehensive exam, thesis/dissertation. *Entrance requirements:* For master's and doctorate, GRE General Test, GRE Subject Test, statement of purpose, official copies of academic transcripts, three letters of recommendation. Additional exam requirements/recommendations for international students: Required—TOEFL (minimum score 580 paper-based; 237 computer-based). *Application deadline:* For fall admission, 8/1 priority date for domestic students, 7/15 for international students; for spring admission, 12/1 priority date for domestic students, 10/15 for international students. Applications are processed on a rolling basis. Application fee: $55. Electronic applications accepted. *Expenses:* Tuition: Full-time $31,740; part-time $1245 per credit hour. One-time fee: $425 full-time. *Financial support:* Fellowships, research assistantships, teaching assistantships, Federal Work-Study, scholarships/grants, tuition waivers (full and partial), and unspecified assistantships available. Financial award application deadline: 2/1; financial award applicants required to submit FAFSA. *Faculty research:* Cell and microbiology, microbial pathogenesis, molecular biology of cell proliferation, cellular effects of electromagnetic radiation, biotechnology. Total annual research expenditures: $853,913. *Unit head:* Dr. Venigalla Rao, Chair, 202-319-5271, Fax: 202-319-5721, E-mail: rao@cua.edu. *Application contact:* Julie Schwing, Director of Graduate Admissions, 202-319-5057, Fax: 202-319-6533, E-mail: cua-admissions@cua.edu.

Colorado State University, Graduate School, Program in Cell and Molecular Biology, Fort Collins, CO 80523-1618. Offers MS, PhD. *Students:* 27 full-time (13 women), 29 part-time (15 women); includes 11 minority (1 African American, 2 American Indian/Alaska Native, 5 Asian Americans or Pacific Islanders, 3 Hispanic Americans), 15 international. Average age 30. 78 applicants, 12% accepted, 9 enrolled. In 2009, 6 master's, 10 doctorates awarded. *Degree requirements:* For master's, comprehensive exam, thesis; for doctorate, comprehensive exam, thesis/dissertation. *Entrance requirements:* For master's and doctorate, GRE General Test, GRE Subject Test in biology (strongly recommended), minimum GPA of 3.0; BA/BS in biology, biochemistry, physics; calculus sequence, letters of recommendation. Additional exam requirements/recommendations for international students: Required—TOEFL (minimum score 625 paper-based; 263 computer-based; 107 iBT). *Application deadline:* For fall admission, 1/1 priority date for domestic and international students. Applications are processed on a rolling basis. Application fee: $50. Electronic applications accepted. *Expenses:* Tuition, state resident: full-time $6434; part-time $359.10 per credit. Tuition, nonresident: full-time $18,116; part-time $1006.45 per credit. Required fees: $1496; $83 per credit. *Financial support:* In 2009–10, 7 students received support, including 1 research assistantship with full tuition reimbursement available (averaging $20,770 per year), 6 teaching assistantships with full tuition reimbursements available (averaging $16,313 per year); fellowships with partial tuition reimbursements available, traineeships and unspecified assistantships also available. Financial award application deadline: 1/1; financial award applicants required to submit FAFSA. *Faculty research:* Regulation of gene expression, cancer biology, plant molecular genetics, reproductive physiology, infectious diseases. Total annual research expenditures: $1,650. *Unit head:* Dr. Paul J. Laybourn, Director, 970-491-5100, Fax: 970-491-0623, E-mail: paul.laybourn@colostate.edu. *Application contact:* Lori Williams, Administrative Assistant, 970-491-0241, Fax: 970-491-0623, E-mail: cmb@colostate.edu.

Columbia University, College of Physicians and Surgeons, Department of Anatomy and Cell Biology, New York, NY 10032. Offers anatomy (M Phil, MA, PhD); anatomy and cell biology (PhD); MD/PhD. Only candidates for the PhD are admitted. Terminal master's awarded for partial completion of doctoral program. *Degree requirements:* For doctorate, thesis/dissertation, oral exam. *Entrance requirements:* For master's and doctorate, GRE General Test. Additional exam requirements/recommendations for international students: Required—TOEFL. *Faculty research:* Protein sorting, membrane biophysics, muscle energetics, neuroendocrinology, developmental biology, cytoskeleton, transcription factors.

Columbia University, College of Physicians and Surgeons, Integrated Program in Cellular, Molecular and Biophysical Studies, New York, NY 10032. Offers M Phil, MA, PhD, MD/PhD. Only candidates for the PhD are admitted. Terminal master's awarded for partial completion of doctoral program. *Degree requirements:* For doctorate, thesis/dissertation. *Entrance requirements:* For master's, GRE General Test; for doctorate, GRE General Test, GRE Subject Test. Additional exam requirements/recommendations for international students: Required—TOEFL. *Expenses:* Contact institution. *Faculty research:* Transcription, macromolecular sorting, gene expression during development, cellular interaction.

Cornell University, Graduate School, Graduate Fields of Agriculture and Life Sciences, Field of Biochemistry, Molecular and Cell Biology, Ithaca, NY 14853-0001. Offers biochemistry (PhD); biophysics (PhD); cell biology (PhD); molecular and cell biology (PhD); molecular biology (PhD). *Faculty:* 64 full-time (14 women). *Students:* 91 full-time (43 women); includes 11 minority (2 African Americans, 6 Asian Americans or Pacific Islanders, 3 Hispanic Americans), 28 international. Average age 27. 150 applicants, 11% accepted, 15 enrolled. In 2009, 17 doctorates awarded. *Degree requirements:* For doctorate, comprehensive exam, thesis/dissertation, 2 semesters of teaching experience. *Entrance requirements:* For doctorate, GRE General Test, GRE Subject Test (biology, chemistry, physics, biochemistry, cell and molecular biology), 3 letters of recommendation. Additional exam requirements/recommendations for international students: Required—TOEFL (minimum score 600 paper-based; 250 computer-based; 77 iBT). *Application deadline:* For fall admission, 1/5 for domestic students. Application fee: $70. Electronic applications accepted. *Expenses:* Tuition: Full-time $29,500. Required fees: $70. Full-time tuition and fees vary according to degree level, program and student level. *Financial support:* In 2009–10, 88 students received support, including 13 fellowships with full tuition reimbursements available, 1 research assistantship with full tuition reimbursement available; teaching assistantships with full tuition reimbursements available, institutionally sponsored loans, scholarships/grants, health care benefits, tuition waivers (full and partial), and unspecified assistantships also available. Financial award applicants required to submit FAFSA. *Faculty research:* Biophysics, structural biology. *Unit head:* Director of Graduate Studies, 607-255-2100, Fax: 607-255-2100. *Application contact:* Graduate Field Assistant, 607-255-2100, Fax: 607-255-2100, E-mail: bmcb@cornell.edu.

Cornell University, Graduate School, Graduate Fields of Agriculture and Life Sciences, Field of Computational Biology, Ithaca, NY 14853-0001. Offers computational behavioral biology (PhD); computational biology (PhD); computational cell biology (PhD); computational ecology (PhD); computational macromolecular biology (PhD); computational organismal biology (PhD). *Faculty:* 40 full-time (5 women). *Students:* 17 full-time (4 women); includes 4 minority (3 Asian Americans or Pacific Islanders, 1 Hispanic American), 4 international. Average age 28. 142 applicants, 11% accepted, 6 enrolled. *Degree requirements:* For doctorate, comprehensive exam, thesis/dissertation, 2 semesters of teaching experience. *Entrance requirements:* For doctorate, GRE General Test, GRE Subject Test (biology), 2 letters of recommendation. Additional exam requirements/recommendations for international students: Required—TOEFL (minimum score 550 paper-based; 213 computer-based; 77 iBT). *Application deadline:* For fall admission, 2/1 priority date for domestic students. Application fee: $70. Electronic applications accepted. *Expenses:* Tuition: Full-time $29,500. Required fees: $70. Full-time tuition and fees vary according to degree level, program and student level. *Financial support:* In 2009–10, 6 fellowships with full tuition reimbursements were awarded; research assistantships with full tuition reimbursements, teaching assistantships with full tuition reimbursements, institutionally sponsored loans, scholarships/grants, health care benefits, tuition waivers (full and partial), and unspecified assistantships also available. Financial award applicants required to submit FAFSA. *Faculty research:* Computational behavioral biology, computational biology, computational cell biology, computational ecology, computational genetics, computational macromolecular biology, computational organismal biology. *Unit head:* Dr. Andrew Clark, Director of Graduate Studies, 607-255-5488, E-mail: ac347@cornell.edu. *Application contact:* Graduate School Application Requests, 607-255-5816, E-mail: gradadmissions@cornell.edu.

Cornell University, Graduate School, Graduate Fields of Agriculture and Life Sciences, Field of Zoology, Ithaca, NY 14853-0001. Offers animal cytology (MS, PhD); comparative and functional anatomy (MS, PhD); developmental biology (MS, PhD); ecology (MS, PhD); histology (MS, PhD). *Faculty:* 24 full-time (5 women). *Students:* 4 full-time (all women); includes 1 minority (Hispanic American), 1 international. Average age 34. 7 applicants, 0% accepted, 0 enrolled. *Degree requirements:* For doctorate, comprehensive exam, thesis/dissertation, 2 semesters of teaching experience. *Entrance requirements:* For doctorate, GRE General Test, GRE Subject Test (biology), 2 letters of recommendation. Additional exam requirements/recommendations for international students: Required—TOEFL (minimum score 550 paper-based; 213 computer-based; 77 iBT). *Application deadline:* For fall admission, 2/1 priority date for domestic students. Application fee: $70. Electronic applications accepted. *Expenses:* Tuition: Full-time $29,500. Required fees: $70. Full-time tuition and fees vary according to degree level, program and student level. *Financial support:* In 2009–10, 3 students received support; fellowships with full tuition reimbursements available, research assistantships with full tuition reimbursements available, teaching assistantships with full tuition reimbursements available, institutionally sponsored loans, scholarships/grants, health care benefits, tuition waivers (full and partial), and unspecified assistantships available. Financial award applicants required to submit FAFSA. *Faculty research:* Organismal biology, functional morphology, biomechanics, comparative vertebrate anatomy, comparative invertebrate anatomy, paleontology. *Unit head:* Director of Graduate Studies, 607-253-3276, Fax: 607-253-3756. *Application contact:* Graduate Field Assistant, 607-253-3276, Fax: 607-253-3756, E-mail: graduate_edcvm@cornell.edu.

Cornell University, Joan and Sanford I. Weill Medical College and Graduate School of Medical Sciences, Weill Cornell Graduate School of Medical Sciences, Biochemistry, Cell and Molecular Biology Allied Program, New York, NY 10065. Offers MS, PhD. *Faculty:* 100 full-time (26 women). *Students:* 148 full-time (96 women); includes 16 minority (2 African Americans, 8 Asian Americans or Pacific Islanders, 6 Hispanic Americans), 71 international. Average age 22. 295 applicants, 16% accepted, 17 enrolled. In 2009, 19 doctorates awarded. Terminal master's awarded for partial completion of doctoral program. *Degree requirements:* For master's, comprehensive exam; for doctorate, thesis/dissertation, final exam. *Entrance requirements:* For doctorate, GRE General Test, background in genetics, molecular biology, chemistry, or biochemistry. Additional exam requirements/recommendations for international students: Required—TOEFL. *Application deadline:* For fall admission, 12/1 for domestic students. Application fee: $60. Electronic applications accepted. *Expenses:* Tuition: Full-time $44,650. Required fees: $2805. *Financial support:* In 2009–10, 12 fellowships (averaging $21,900 per year) were awarded; scholarships/grants, health care benefits, and stipends (given to all students) also available. *Faculty research:* Molecular structure determination, protein structure, gene structure, stem cell biology, control of gene expression, DNA replication, chromosome maintenance, RNA biosynthesis. *Unit head:* Dr. David Eliezer, Co-Director, 212-746-6557, Fax: 212-717-3047. *Application contact:* Linda Smith, Assistant Dean of Admissions, 212-746-6565, Fax: 212-746-8906, E-mail: lis2025@med.cornell.edu.

Dartmouth College, Graduate Program in Molecular and Cellular Biology, Hanover, NH 03755. Offers PhD, MD/PhD. *Faculty:* 69 full-time (15 women). *Students:* 148 full-time (74 women); includes 7 African Americans, 1 Asian American or Pacific Islander, 3 Hispanic Americans, 55 international. Average age 27. 280 applicants, 22% accepted, 25 enrolled. In 2009, 25 doctorates awarded. *Entrance requirements:* For doctorate, GRE General Test, letters of recommendation. Additional exam requirements/recommendations for international students: Required—TOEFL (minimum score 450 paper-based; 90 iBT) or IELTS (minimum score 7). *Application deadline:* For fall admission, 1/4 for domestic and international students. Applications are processed on a rolling basis. Application fee: $75. Electronic applications accepted. *Financial support:* Scholarships/grants, health care benefits, and stipends ($25,500) available. *Unit head:* Barbara Conradt, Chair, 603-650-1612, Fax: 603-650-1006, E-mail: mcb@dartmouth.edu. *Application contact:* Janet Cheney, Program Coordinator, 603-650-1612, Fax: 603-650-1006, E-mail: molecular.and.cellular.biology@dartmouth.edu.

Drexel University, College of Medicine, Biomedical Graduate Programs, Interdisciplinary Program in Molecular and Cell Biology and Genetics, Philadelphia, PA 19104-2875. Offers MS, PhD, MD/PhD. Terminal master's awarded for partial completion of doctoral program. *Degree requirements:* For master's, comprehensive exam, thesis; for doctorate, thesis/dissertation, qualifying exam. *Entrance requirements:* For master's, GRE General Test, minimum GPA of 2.75; for doctorate, GRE General Test, minimum GPA of 3.0. Additional exam requirements/recommendations for international students: Required—TOEFL. Electronic applications accepted. *Faculty research:* Molecular anatomy, biochemistry, medical biotechnology, molecular pathology, microbiology and immunology.

Duke University, Graduate School, Department of Biological Anthropology and Anatomy, Durham, NC 27710. Offers cellular and molecular biology (PhD); gross anatomy and physical anthropology (PhD), including comparative morphology of human and non-human primates, primate social behavior, vertebrate paleontology; neuroanatomy (PhD). *Faculty:* 8 full-time. *Students:* 14 full-time (9 women); includes 2 minority (1 African American, 1 Hispanic American), 1 international. 39 applicants, 15% accepted, 4 enrolled. In 2009, 4 doctorates awarded. *Degree requirements:* For doctorate, one foreign language, thesis/dissertation. *Entrance requirements:* For doctorate, GRE General Test. Additional exam requirements/recommendations for international students: Required—TOEFL (minimum score 550 paper-based; 213 computer-based; 83 iBT), IELTS (minimum score 7). *Application deadline:* For fall admission, 12/8 priority date for domestic and international students. Application fee: $75. Electronic applications accepted. *Financial support:* Fellowships, teaching assistantships, Federal Work-Study available. Financial award application deadline: 12/31. *Unit head:* Daniel Schmitt, Director of Graduate Studies, 919-684-5664, Fax: 919-684-4124, E-mail: mlsquire@duke.edu. *Application contact:* Cynthia Robertson, Associate Dean for Enrollment Services, 919-684-3913, E-mail: grad-admissions@duke.edu.

Duke University, Graduate School, Department of Cell Biology, Durham, NC 27710. Offers PhD. *Faculty:* 21 full-time. *Students:* 35 full-time (22 women); includes 4 minority (1 African American, 2 Asian Americans or Pacific Islanders, 1 Hispanic American), 6 international. In 2009, 3 doctorates awarded. *Degree requirements:* For doctorate, thesis/dissertation. *Entrance requirements:* For doctorate, GRE General Test, GRE Subject Test (recommended). Additional exam requirements/recommendations for international students: Required—TOEFL or IELTS (preferred). Application fee: $75. *Financial support:* Fellowships, research assistantships, teaching assistantships, Federal Work-Study available. Financial award application deadline: 12/31. *Unit head:* Chris Nicchitta, Director of Graduate Studies, 919-684-8085, Fax: 919-684-8090, E-mail: teresa.jenkins@duke.edu. *Application contact:* Cynthia Robertson, Associate Dean for Enrollment Services, 919-684-3913, E-mail: grad-admissions@duke.edu.

Duke University, Graduate School, Program in Cellular and Molecular Biology, Durham, NC 27710. Offers PhD, Certificate. Certificate students must be enrolled in a participating PhD program. *Faculty:* 144 full-time. *Students:* 21 full-time (16 women); includes 2 minority (1 Asian American or Pacific Islander, 1 Hispanic American), 4 international. 222 applicants, 20% accepted, 18 enrolled. *Entrance requirements:* For degree, GRE General Test, GRE Subject Test (recommended). Additional exam requirements/recommendations for international students: Required—TOEFL (minimum score 550 paper-based; 213 computer-based; 83 iBT), IELTS (minimum score 7). *Application deadline:* For fall admission, 12/8 priority date for domestic and international students. Application fee: $75. Electronic applications accepted. *Financial support:* Fellowships available. Financial award application deadline: 12/31. *Unit head:* Dr. Margarethe Kuehn, Director of Graduate Studies, 919-684-6554, Fax: 919-684-8346, E-mail: carol.richardson@duke.edu. *Application contact:* Cynthia Robertson, Associate Dean for Enrollment Services, 919-684-3913, E-mail: grad-admissions@duke.edu.

East Carolina University, Brody School of Medicine, Department of Anatomy and Cell Biology, Greenville, NC 27858-4353. Offers PhD. *Degree requirements:* For doctorate, comprehensive exam, thesis/dissertation. *Entrance requirements:* For doctorate, GRE General Test. Additional exam requirements/recommendations for international students: Required—TOEFL. *Faculty research:* Kinesin motors during slow matogensis, mitochondria and peroxisomes in obesity, ovarian innervation, tight junction function and regulation.

Eastern Michigan University, Graduate School, College of Arts and Sciences, Department of Biology, Ypsilanti, MI 48197. Offers cell and molecular biology (MS); community college biology teaching (MS); ecology and organismal biology (MS); general biology (MS); water resources (MS). Part-time and evening/weekend programs available. Postbaccalaureate distance learning degree programs offered (minimal on-campus study). *Faculty:* 20 full-time (5 women). *Students:* 10 full-time (8 women), 35 part-time (21 women); includes 3 minority (2 African Americans, 1 Asian American or Pacific Islander), 7 international. Average age 28. 57 applicants, 63% accepted, 20 enrolled. In 2009, 17 master's awarded. *Entrance requirements:* For master's, GRE General Test, GRE Subject Test. Additional exam requirements/recommendations for international students: Required—TOEFL. *Application deadline:* Applications are processed on a rolling basis. Application fee: $35. Tuition and fees vary according to course level. *Financial support:* In 2009–10, 22 teaching assistantships with full tuition reimbursements (averaging $8,660 per year) were awarded; fellowships, research assistantships with full tuition reimbursements, career-related internships or fieldwork, Federal Work-Study, institutionally sponsored loans, scholarships/grants, tuition waivers (partial), and unspecified assistantships also available. Support available to part-time students. Financial award applicants required to submit FAFSA. *Unit head:* Dr. Marianne Laporte, Department Head, 734-487-4242, Fax: 734-487-9235, E-mail: mlaporte@emich.edu. *Application contact:* Dr. Marianne Laporte, Department Head, 734-487-4242, Fax: 734-487-9235, E-mail: mlaporte@emich.edu.

Emory University, Graduate School of Arts and Sciences, Division of Biological and Biomedical Sciences, Program in Biochemistry, Cell and Developmental Biology, Atlanta, GA 30322-1100. Offers PhD. *Faculty:* 51 full-time (10 women). *Students:* 62 full-time (42 women); includes 9 minority (3 African Americans, 5 Asian Americans or Pacific Islanders, 1 Hispanic American), 17 international. Average age 27. 107 applicants, 12% accepted, 6 enrolled. In 2009, 10 doctorates awarded. *Degree requirements:* For doctorate, comprehensive exam, thesis/dissertation. *Entrance requirements:* For doctorate, GRE General Test, minimum GPA of 3.0 in science course work (recommended). Additional exam requirements/recommendations for international students: Required—TOEFL. *Application deadline:* For fall admission, 1/3 for domestic and international students. Application fee: $50. Electronic applications accepted. *Financial support:* In 2009–10, 24 students received support, including 24 fellowships with full tuition reimbursements available (averaging $24,500 per year); institutionally sponsored loans, scholarships/grants, and health care benefits also available. *Faculty research:* Signal transduction, molecular biology, enzymes and cofactors, receptor and ion channel function, membrane biology. *Unit head:* Richard Kahn, Director, 404-727-3561, Fax: 404-727-3746, E-mail: rkahn@emory.edu. *Application contact:* 404-727-2545, Fax: 404-727-3322, E-mail: gdbbs@emory.edu.

Emporia State University, School of Graduate Studies, College of Liberal Arts and Sciences, Department of Biological Sciences, Emporia, KS 66801-5087. Offers botany (MS); environmental biology (MS); general biology (MS); microbial and cellular biology (MS); zoology (MS). Part-time programs available. *Faculty:* 13 full-time (3 women). *Students:* 9 full-time (7 women), 17 part-time (11 women); includes 1 minority (African American), 8 international. 22 applicants, 95% accepted, 18 enrolled. In 2009, 24 master's awarded. *Degree requirements:* For master's, comprehensive exam or thesis. *Entrance requirements:* For master's, GRE, appropriate undergraduate degree, interview, letters of reference. Additional exam requirements/recommendations for international students: Required—TOEFL (minimum score 520 paper-based; 133 computer-based; 68 iBT). *Application deadline:* For fall admission, 8/15 priority date for domestic students. Applications are processed on a rolling basis. Application fee: $30 ($75 for international students). Electronic applications accepted. *Expenses:* Tuition, state resident: full-time $4154; part-time $173 per credit hour. Tuition, nonresident: full-time $12,864; part-time $536 per credit hour. Required fees: $948; $58 per credit hour. Tuition and fees vary according to campus/location. *Financial support:* In 2009–10, 7 research assistantships with full tuition reimbursements (averaging $6,876 per year), 10 teaching assistantships with full tuition reimbursements (averaging $7,419 per year) were awarded; career-related internships or fieldwork, Federal Work-Study, institutionally sponsored loans, health care benefits, and unspecified assistantships also available. Financial award application deadline: 3/15; financial award applicants required to submit FAFSA. *Faculty research:* Fisheries, range, and wildlife management; aquatic, plant, grassland, vertebrate, and invertebrate ecology; mammalian and plant systematics, taxonomy, and evolution; immunology, virology, and molecular biology. *Unit head:* Dr. R. Brent Thomas, Interim Chair, 620-341-5311, Fax: 620-341-5608, E-mail: rthomas2@emporia.edu. *Application contact:* Dr. Scott Crupper, Graduate Coordinator, 620-341-5621, Fax: 620-341-5607, E-mail: scrupper@emporia.edu.

Florida Institute of Technology, Graduate Programs, College of Science, Department of Biological Sciences, Program in Cell and Molecular Biology, Melbourne, FL 32901-6975. Offers MS, PhD. Part-time programs available. *Application deadline:* Applications are processed on a rolling basis. Electronic applications accepted. *Expenses:* Tuition: Part-time $1015 per credit. Tuition and fees vary according to campus/location and program. *Financial support:* Research assistantships with full and partial tuition reimbursements, teaching assistantships with full and partial tuition reimbursements, career-related internships or fieldwork and tuition remissions available. Financial award application deadline: 3/1; financial award applicants required to submit FAFSA. *Faculty research:* Changes in DNA molecule and differential expression of genetic information during aging. *Application contact:* Carolyn P. Shea.

See Close-Up on page 233.

Florida State University, The Graduate School, College of Arts and Sciences, Department of Biological Science, Specialization in Cell and Molecular Biology and Genetics, Tallahassee, FL 32306-4295. Offers MS, PhD. *Faculty:* 28 full-time (6 women). *Students:* 44 full-time (23 women); includes 6 minority (2 African Americans, 1 Asian American or Pacific Islander, 3 Hispanic Americans), 10 international. 118 applicants, 17% accepted, 11 enrolled. In 2009, 6 master's, 4 doctorates awarded. Terminal master's awarded for partial completion of doctoral program. *Degree requirements:* For master's, comprehensive exam, thesis, teaching experience, seminar presentation; for doctorate, comprehensive exam, thesis/dissertation, teaching experience; seminar presentation. *Entrance requirements:* For master's, GRE General Test (minimum combined score 1100, 500 verbal, 500 quantitative), minimum upper-division GPA of 3.0; for doctorate, GRE General Test (minimum combined score 1100, Verbal 500, Quantitative 500), minimum upper-division GPA of 3.0. Additional exam requirements/recommendations for international students: Required—TOEFL (minimum score 600 paper-based; 250 computer-based; 92 iBT). *Application deadline:* For fall admission, 12/15 for domestic and international students. Application fee: $30. Electronic applications accepted. *Expenses:* Tuition, state resident: full-time $7413. Tuition, nonresident: full-time $22,567. *Financial support:* In 2009–10, 14 research assistantships with full tuition reimbursements (averaging $20,000 per year), 30 teaching assistantships with full tuition reimbursements (averaging $18,540 per year) were awarded. Financial award application deadline: 12/15; financial award applicants required to submit FAFSA. *Faculty research:* Molecular biology; genetics and genomics; developmental biology and gene expression; cell structure, function, and motility; cellular and organismal physiology; biophysical and structural biology. *Application contact:* Judy Bowers, Coordinator, Graduate Affairs, 850-644-3023, Fax: 850-644-9829, E-mail: gradinfo@bio.fsu.edu.

George Mason University, College of Science, Fairfax, VA 22030. Offers biodefense (MS, PhD); bioinformatics and computational biology (MS, PhD, Certificate); biology (MS, PhD), including bioinformatics (MS), ecology, systematics and evolution (MS), interpretive biology (MS), molecular and cellular biology (MS), molecular and microbiology (PhD), organismal biology (MS); chemistry and biochemistry (MS), including chemistry; climate dynamics (PhD); computational and data sciences (MS, PhD, Certificate); computational social science (PhD); computational techniques and applications (Certificate); earth systems and geoinformation sciences (MS, PhD, Certificate); environmental science and policy (MS, PhD); geography (MS), including geographic and cartographic sciences; mathematical sciences (MS, PhD), including mathematics; nanotechnology and nanoscience (Certificate); neuroscience (PhD); physical sciences (PhD); physics and astronomy (MS), including applied and engineering physics; remote sensing and earth image processing (Certificate). Part-time and evening/weekend programs available. *Degree requirements:* For doctorate, comprehensive exam, thesis/dissertation. *Entrance requirements:* For master's and doctorate, GRE General Test, minimum GPA of 3.0 in last 60 hours. Additional exam requirements/recommendations for international students: Required—TOEFL. Electronic applications accepted. *Expenses:* Tuition, state resident: full-time $7568; part-time $315.33 per credit hour. Tuition, nonresident: full-time $21,704; part-time $904.33 per credit hour. Required fees: $2184; $91 per credit hour. *Faculty research:* Space sciences and astrophysics, fluid dynamics, materials modeling and simulation, bioinformatics, global changes and statistics.

Georgetown University, Graduate School of Arts and Sciences, Programs in Biomedical Sciences, Department of Cell Biology, Washington, DC 20057. Offers PhD, MD/PhD. *Degree requirements:* For doctorate, comprehensive exam, thesis/dissertation. *Entrance requirements:* For doctorate, GRE General Test. Additional exam requirements/recommendations for international students: Required—TOEFL.

Georgia State University, College of Arts and Sciences, Department of Biology, Program in Cellular and Molecular Biology and Physiology, Atlanta, GA 30302-3083. Offers MS, PhD. Part-time programs available. Terminal master's awarded for partial completion of doctoral program. *Degree requirements:* For master's, thesis or alternative; for doctorate, thesis/dissertation, exam. *Entrance requirements:* For master's and doctorate, GRE General Test. Additional exam requirements/recommendations for international students: Required—TOEFL.

Grand Valley State University, College of Liberal Arts and Sciences, Program in Cell and Molecular Biology, Allendale, MI 49401-9403. Offers MS. *Faculty:* 5 full-time (3 women), 5 part-time/adjunct (3 women). *Students:* 15 full-time (7 women), 14 part-time (9 women); includes 1 minority (American Indian/Alaska Native), 16 international. Average age 25. 40 applicants, 73% accepted, 10 enrolled. In 2009, 5 master's awarded. *Entrance requirements:* For master's, minimum GPA of 3.0. Application fee: $30. *Expenses:* Tuition, state resident: part-time $471 per credit hour. Tuition, nonresident: part-time $646 per credit hour. Tuition and fees vary according to course level. *Financial support:* In 2009–10, 17 students received support, including 2 fellowships (averaging $4,706 per year), 7 research assistantships with tuition reimbursements available (averaging $5,343 per year); unspecified assistantships also available. *Faculty research:* Plant cell biology, plant development, cell/signal integration. *Unit head:* Dr. Mark Staves, Associate Professor/Coordinator, 616-331-2473, E-mail: stavesm@gvsu.edu. *Application contact:* Dr. David Elrod, PSM Coordinator, 616-331-8643, E-mail: elrodd@gvsu.edu.

Harvard University, Graduate School of Arts and Sciences, Department of Molecular and Cellular Biology, Cambridge, MA 02138. Offers PhD. *Degree requirements:* For doctorate, thesis/dissertation, oral exam. *Entrance requirements:* For doctorate, GRE General Test, GRE Subject Test (recommended). Additional exam requirements/recommendations for international students: Required—TOEFL. *Expenses:* Tuition: Full-time $33,696. Required fees: $1126. Full-time tuition and fees vary according to program.

Harvard University, Graduate School of Arts and Sciences, Division of Medical Sciences, Boston, MA 02115. Offers biological chemistry and molecular pharmacology (PhD); cell biology (PhD); genetics (PhD); microbiology and molecular genetics (PhD); pathology (PhD), including experimental pathology. *Degree requirements:* For doctorate, thesis/dissertation. *Entrance requirements:* For doctorate, GRE General Test, GRE Subject Test. Additional exam requirements/recommendations for international students: Required—TOEFL. *Expenses:* Tuition: Full-time $33,696. Required fees: $1126. Full-time tuition and fees vary according to program.

Illinois State University, Graduate School, College of Arts and Sciences, Department of Biological Sciences, Normal, IL 61790-2200. Offers animal behavior (MS); bacteriology (MS); biochemistry (MS); biological sciences (MS); biology (PhD); biophysics (MS); biotechnology (MS); botany (MS, PhD); cell biology (MS); conservation biology (MS); developmental biology (MS); ecology (MS, PhD); entomology (MS); evolutionary biology (MS); genetics (MS, PhD); immunology (MS); microbiology (MS, PhD); molecular biology (MS); molecular genetics (MS); neurobiology (MS); neuroscience (MS); parasitology (MS); physiology (MS, PhD); plant biology (MS); plant molecular biology (MS); plant sciences (MS); structural biology (MS); zoology (MS, PhD). Part-time programs available. *Degree requirements:* For master's, thesis or alternative; for doctorate, variable foreign language requirement, thesis/dissertation, 2 terms of residency.

Cell Biology

Illinois State University (continued)

Entrance requirements: For master's, GRE General Test, minimum GPA of 2.6 in last 60 hours of course work; for doctorate, GRE General Test. *Faculty research:* Redoc balance and drug development in schistosoma mansoni, control of the growth of listeria monocytogenes at low temperature, regulation of cell expansion and microtubule function by SPRI, CRUI: physiology and fitness consequences of different life history phenotypes.

Indiana University Bloomington, University Graduate School, College of Arts and Sciences, Department of Biology, Bloomington, IN 47405. Offers biology teaching (MAT); biotechnology (MA); evolution, ecology, and behavior (MA, PhD); genetics (PhD); microbiology (MA, PhD); molecular, cellular, and developmental biology (PhD); plant sciences (MA, PhD); zoology (MA, PhD). *Faculty:* 58 full-time (15 women), 21 part-time/adjunct (6 women). *Students:* 165 full-time (95 women); includes 14 minority (6 African Americans, 1 American Indian/Alaska Native, 7 Asian Americans or Pacific Islanders), 56 international. Average age 27. 312 applicants, 19% accepted, 24 enrolled. In 2009, 4 master's, 22 doctorates awarded. Terminal master's awarded for partial completion of doctoral program. *Degree requirements:* For master's, thesis, oral defense; for doctorate, thesis/dissertation, oral defense. *Entrance requirements:* For master's and doctorate, GRE General Test. Additional exam requirements/recommendations for international students: Required—TOEFL (minimum score 100 iBT). *Application deadline:* For fall admission, 1/5 priority date for domestic students, 12/1 priority date for international students. Application fee: $55 ($65 for international students). Electronic applications accepted. *Financial support:* In 2009–10, 165 students received support, including 62 fellowships with tuition reimbursements available (averaging $19,484 per year), 27 research assistantships with tuition reimbursements available (averaging $22,605 per year), 76 teaching assistantships with tuition reimbursements available (averaging $20,528 per year); scholarships/grants, traineeships, health care benefits, and unspecified assistantships also available. Financial award application deadline: 1/5. *Faculty research:* Evolution, ecology and behavior; microbiology; molecular biology and genetics; plant biology. *Unit head:* Dr. Roger Innes, Chair, 812-855-2219, Fax: 812-855-6082, E-mail: rinnes@indiana.edu. *Application contact:* Tracey D. Stohr, Graduate Student Recruitment Coordinator, 812-856-6303, Fax: 812-855-6082, E-mail: gradbio@indiana.edu.

Indiana University–Purdue University Indianapolis, Indiana University School of Medicine, Department of Anatomy and Cell Biology, Indianapolis, IN 46202-2896. Offers MS, PhD, MD/PhD. *Faculty:* 14 full-time (1 woman). *Students:* 10 full-time (5 women), 1 international. Average age 31. 21 applicants, 62% accepted, 7 enrolled. In 2009, 1 master's, 3 doctorates awarded. *Degree requirements:* For master's, thesis or alternative; for doctorate, thesis/dissertation. *Entrance requirements:* For master's and doctorate, GRE General Test. *Application deadline:* For fall admission, 1/15 priority date for domestic students. Application fee: $55 ($65 for international students). *Financial support:* In 2009–10, 1 fellowship was awarded; research assistantships, Federal Work-Study, institutionally sponsored loans, tuition waivers (partial), and stipends also available. Financial award application deadline: 2/15. *Faculty research:* Acoustic reflex control, osteoarthritis and bone disease, diabetes, kidney diseases, cellular and molecular neurobiology. *Unit head:* Dr. David B. Burr, Chairman, 317-274-7494, Fax: 317-278-2040, E-mail: dburr@indyvax.iupui.edu. *Application contact:* Dr. James Williams, Graduate Adviser, 317-274-3423, Fax: 317-278-2040, E-mail: williams@anatomy.iupui.edu.

Iowa State University of Science and Technology, Graduate College, College of Agriculture and College of Liberal Arts and Sciences, Department of Biochemistry, Biophysics, and Molecular Biology, Ames, IA 50011. Offers biochemistry (MS, PhD); biophysics (MS, PhD); genetics (MS, PhD); molecular, cellular, and developmental biology (MS, PhD); toxicology (MS, PhD). *Faculty:* 24 full-time (6 women), 1 (woman) part-time/adjunct. *Students:* 77 full-time (30 women), 3 part-time (2 women); includes 3 minority (1 African American, 1 Asian American or Pacific Islander, 1 Hispanic American), 56 international. 41 applicants, 32% accepted, 13 enrolled. In 2009, 2 master's, 7 doctorates awarded. *Degree requirements:* For master's, thesis; for doctorate, thesis/dissertation. *Entrance requirements:* For master's and doctorate, GRE General Test. Additional exam requirements/recommendations for international students: Required—TOEFL (minimum score 550 paper-based; 79 iBT) or IELTS (minimum score 6.5). *Application deadline:* For fall admission, 1/15 priority date for domestic and international students; for spring admission, 10/15 for domestic and international students. Application fee: $40 ($90 for international students). Electronic applications accepted. *Expenses:* Tuition, state resident: full-time $6716. Tuition, nonresident: full-time $8908. Tuition and fees vary according to course level, course load, program and student level. *Financial support:* In 2009–10, 52 research assistantships with full and partial tuition reimbursements (averaging $18,750 per year) were awarded; teaching assistantships with full and partial tuition reimbursements, scholarships/grants, health care benefits, and unspecified assistantships also available. *Unit head:* Dr. Guru Rao, Interim Chair, 515-294-6116, E-mail: biochem@iastate.edu. *Application contact:* Dr. Reuben Peters, Director of Graduate Education, 515-294-6116, E-mail: biochem@iastate.edu.

See Close-Up on page 155.

Iowa State University of Science and Technology, Graduate College, College of Liberal Arts and Sciences and College of Agriculture, Department of Genetics, Developmental and Cell Biology, Ames, IA 50011. Offers MS, PhD. *Faculty:* 30 full-time (5 women), 5 part-time/adjunct (3 women). *Degree requirements:* For master's, thesis; for doctorate, thesis/dissertation. *Entrance requirements:* Additional exam requirements/recommendations for international students: Required—TOEFL (minimum score 570 paper-based; 230 computer-based) or IELTS (minimum score 6.5). Application fee: $40 ($90 for international students). *Expenses:* Tuition, state resident: full-time $6716. Tuition, nonresident: full-time $8908. Tuition and fees vary according to course level, course load, program and student level. *Financial support:* Fellowships with full tuition reimbursements, research assistantships with full and partial tuition reimbursements, teaching assistantships with full and partial tuition reimbursements, scholarships/grants, health care benefits, and unspecified assistantships available. Financial award application deadline: 2/1. *Faculty research:* Animal behavior, animal models of gene therapy, cell biology, comparative physiology, developmental biology. *Unit head:* Dr. Martin Spalding, Chair, 515-294-1749. *Application contact:* Information Contact, 515-294-5836, Fax: 515-294-2592, E-mail: grad_admissions@iastate.edu.

Iowa State University of Science and Technology, Graduate College, Interdisciplinary Programs, Program in Molecular, Cellular, and Developmental Biology, Ames, IA 50011. Offers MS, PhD. *Students:* 34 full-time (16 women), 1 part-time (0 women), 26 international. In 2009, 2 master's, 8 doctorates awarded. *Degree requirements:* For master's, thesis or alternative; for doctorate, thesis/dissertation. *Entrance requirements:* For master's and doctorate, GRE General Test. Additional exam requirements/recommendations for international students: Required—TOEFL (minimum score 580 paper-based; 85 iBT) or IELTS (minimum score 7). *Application deadline:* For fall admission, 1/15 priority date for domestic and international students. Application fee: $40 ($90 for international students). Electronic applications accepted. *Expenses:* Tuition, state resident: full-time $6716. Tuition, nonresident: full-time $8908. Tuition and fees vary according to course level, course load, program and student level. *Financial support:* In 2009–10, 33 research assistantships with full and partial tuition reimbursements (averaging $18,750 per year), 1 teaching assistantship with full and partial tuition reimbursement (averaging $18,750 per year) were awarded; scholarships/grants, health care benefits, and unspecified assistantships also available. *Unit head:* Dr. Jeff Beetham, Supervisory Committee Chair, 515-294-7252, E-mail: idgp@iastate.edu. *Application contact:* Katie Blair, Information Contact, 515-294-7252, Fax: 515-924-6790, E-mail: idgp@iastate.edu.

The Johns Hopkins University, National Institutes of Health Sponsored Programs, Baltimore, MD 21218-2699. Offers biology (PhD), including biochemistry, biophysics, cell biology, developmental biology, genetic biology, molecular biology; cell, molecular, and developmental biology and biophysics (PhD). *Faculty:* 25 full-time (4 women). *Students:* 126 full-time (72 women); includes 36 minority (3 African Americans, 1 American Indian/Alaska Native, 21 Asian Americans or Pacific Islanders, 11 Hispanic Americans), 19 international. 282 applicants, 26% accepted, 36 enrolled. In 2009, 15 doctorates awarded. *Degree requirements:* For doctorate, comprehensive exam, thesis/dissertation. *Entrance requirements:* For doctorate, GRE General Test. Additional exam requirements/recommendations for international students: Required—TOEFL (minimum score 600 paper-based; 250 computer-based), TWE. *Application deadline:* For fall admission, 12/15 priority date for domestic students. Application fee: $60. Electronic applications accepted. *Financial support:* In 2009–10, 24 fellowships (averaging $23,000 per year), 93 research assistantships (averaging $23,000 per year), 22 teaching assistantships (averaging $23,000 per year) were awarded; Federal Work-Study, institutionally sponsored loans, scholarships/grants, traineeships, health care benefits, tuition waivers (partial), and unspecified assistantships also available. Financial award application deadline: 4/15; financial award applicants required to submit FAFSA. *Faculty research:* Protein and nucleic acid biochemistry and biophysical chemistry, molecular biology and development. Total annual research expenditures: $11.2 million. *Unit head:* Dr. Allen Shearn, Chair, 410-516-4693, Fax: 410-516-5213, E-mail: bio_cals@jhu.edu. *Application contact:* Joan Miller, Academic Affairs Manager, 410-516-5502, Fax: 410-516-5213, E-mail: joan@jhu.edu.

The Johns Hopkins University, School of Medicine, Graduate Programs in Medicine, Graduate Program in Cellular and Molecular Medicine, Baltimore, MD 21218-2699. Offers PhD. *Faculty:* 125 full-time (29 women). *Students:* 129 full-time (77 women); includes 50 minority (17 African Americans, 3 American Indian/Alaska Native, 21 Asian Americans or Pacific Islanders, 9 Hispanic Americans), 16 international. Average age 24. 243 applicants, 16% accepted, 21 enrolled. In 2009, 16 doctorates awarded. *Degree requirements:* For doctorate, comprehensive exam, thesis/dissertation, oral exam. *Entrance requirements:* For doctorate, GRE. Additional exam requirements/recommendations for international students: Required—TOEFL. *Application deadline:* For winter admission, 1/1 for domestic students. Application fee: $85. Electronic applications accepted. *Financial support:* In 2009–10, 17 fellowships with tuition reimbursements (averaging $27,125 per year) were awarded; scholarships/grants, health care benefits, and tuition waivers (full) also available. *Faculty research:* Cellular and molecular basis of disease. Total annual research expenditures: $100 million. *Unit head:* Dr. Rajini Rao, Director, 410-955-4732, Fax: 410-614-7294, E-mail: rrao@jhmi.edu. *Application contact:* Leslie Lichter-Mason, Admissions Administrator, 410-614-0391, Fax: 410-614-7294, E-mail: llichte2@jhmi.edu.

The Johns Hopkins University, School of Medicine, Graduate Programs in Medicine, Program in Biochemistry, Cellular and Molecular Biology, Baltimore, MD 21205. Offers PhD. *Faculty:* 101 full-time (35 women). *Students:* 149 full-time (87 women); includes 33 minority (13 African Americans, 1 American Indian/Alaska Native, 17 Asian Americans or Pacific Islanders, 2 Hispanic Americans), 48 international. Average age 25. 299 applicants, 19% accepted, 18 enrolled. In 2009, 19 doctorates awarded. *Degree requirements:* For doctorate, comprehensive exam, thesis/dissertation. *Entrance requirements:* For doctorate, GRE General Test. Additional exam requirements/recommendations for international students: Required—TOEFL. *Application deadline:* For winter admission, 1/10 for domestic and international students. Applications are processed on a rolling basis. Application fee: $80. Electronic applications accepted. *Financial support:* In 2009–10, 5 fellowships with partial tuition reimbursements (averaging $32,000 per year), 144 research assistantships with full and partial tuition reimbursements (averaging $27,125 per year) were awarded; traineeships and tuition waivers (full) also available. Financial award application deadline: 12/31. *Faculty research:* Developmental biology, genomics/proteomics, protein targeting, signal transduction, structural biology. *Unit head:* Dr. Carolyn Machamer, Director, 410-955-3466, Fax: 410-614-8842, E-mail: machamer@jhmi.edu. *Application contact:* Dr. Jeff Corden, Admissions Director, 410-955-3506, Fax: 410-614-8842, E-mail: jcorden@jhmi.edu.

Kent State University, School of Biomedical Sciences, Program in Cellular and Molecular Biology, Kent, OH 44242-0001. Offers MS, PhD. Offered in cooperation with Northeastern Ohio Universities College of Medicine. Terminal master's awarded for partial completion of doctoral program. *Degree requirements:* For master's, thesis; for doctorate, thesis/dissertation. *Entrance requirements:* For master's, GRE General Test, letter of recommendation, minimum GPA of 3.0; for doctorate, GRE General Test, letter of recommendation, minimum GPA of 3.0, MS. Additional exam requirements/recommendations for international students: Required—TOEFL. Electronic applications accepted. *Faculty research:* Molecular genetics, molecular endocrinology, virology and tumor biology, P450 enzymology and catalysis, membrane structure and function.

Louisiana State University Health Sciences Center, School of Graduate Studies in New Orleans, Department of Cell Biology and Anatomy, New Orleans, LA 70112-2223. Offers cell biology and anatomy (MS, PhD), including cell biology, developmental biology, neurobiology and anatomy; MD/PhD. *Degree requirements:* For master's, comprehensive exam, thesis; for doctorate, comprehensive exam, thesis/dissertation. *Entrance requirements:* For master's and doctorate, GRE General Test, GRE Subject Test, minimum undergraduate GPA of 3.0. Additional exam requirements/recommendations for international students: Required—TOEFL. *Faculty research:* Visual system organization, neural development, plasticity of sensory systems, information processing through the nervous system, visuomotor integration.

Louisiana State University Health Sciences Center at Shreveport, Department of Cellular Biology and Anatomy, Shreveport, LA 71130-3932. Offers MS, PhD, MD/PhD. Terminal master's awarded for partial completion of doctoral program. *Degree requirements:* For master's, thesis; for doctorate, thesis/dissertation. *Entrance requirements:* For master's and doctorate, GRE General Test. Additional exam requirements/recommendations for international students: Required—TOEFL. *Faculty research:* Alcohol and immunity, neuroscience, olfactory physiology, extracellular matrix, cancer cell biology and gene therapy.

Loyola University Chicago, Graduate School, Department of Cell Biology, Neurobiology and Anatomy, Chicago, IL 60660. Offers MS, PhD. Part-time programs available. *Faculty:* 16 full-time (6 women), 9 part-time/adjunct (4 women). *Students:* 20 full-time (12 women), 1 (woman) part-time; includes 1 minority (Hispanic American), 1 international. Average age 25. 25 applicants, 40% accepted, 8 enrolled. In 2009, 1 master's, 1 doctorate awarded. Terminal master's awarded for partial completion of doctoral program. *Degree requirements:* For master's, thesis; for doctorate, comprehensive exam, thesis/dissertation. *Entrance requirements:* For master's, GRE General Test, minimum GPA of 3.0; for doctorate, GRE General Test, GRE Subject Test (biology), minimum GPA of 3.0. Additional exam requirements/recommendations for international students: Required—TOEFL (minimum score 600 paper-based; 250 computer-based). *Application deadline:* For fall admission, 5/1 priority date for domestic and international students. Applications are processed on a rolling basis. Application fee: $50. Electronic applications accepted. *Expenses:* Tuition: Full-time $14,220; part-time $790 per credit hour. Required fees: $60 per semester hour. Tuition and fees vary according to program. *Financial support:* In 2009–10, 5 fellowships with full tuition reimbursements (averaging $23,000 per year), 5 research assistantships with full tuition reimbursements (averaging $23,000 per year) were awarded; Federal Work-Study and unspecified assistantships also available. Financial award application deadline: 5/1; financial award applicants required to submit FAFSA. *Faculty research:* Brain steroids, immunology, neuroregeneration, cytokines. Total annual research expenditures: $1 million. *Unit head:* Dr. Phong Le, Head, 708-216-3603, Fax: 708-216-3913, E-mail: ple@lumc.edu. *Application contact:* Ginny Hayes, Graduate Program Secretary, 708-216-3353, Fax: 708-216-3913, E-mail: vhayes@lumc.edu.

Marquette University, Graduate School, College of Arts and Sciences, Department of Biology, Milwaukee, WI 53201-1881. Offers cell biology (MS, PhD); developmental biology (MS, PhD); ecology (MS, PhD); endocrinology (MS, PhD); evolutionary biology (MS, PhD); genetics (MS, PhD); microbiology (MS, PhD); molecular biology (MS, PhD); muscle and exercise physiology (MS, PhD); neurobiology (MS, PhD); reproductive physiology (MS, PhD). *Faculty:* 23 full-time (10 women), 1 part-time/adjunct (0 women). *Students:* 23 full-time (13 women), 16 part-time (9 women); includes 1 minority (Asian American or Pacific Islander), 20 international. Average age 25. 95 applicants, 16% accepted, 10 enrolled. In 2009, 3 master's, 5 doctorates awarded. Terminal master's awarded for partial completion of doctoral program. *Degree requirements:*

For master's, comprehensive exam, thesis, 1 year of teaching experience or equivalent; for doctorate, thesis/dissertation, 1 year of teaching experience or equivalent, qualifying exam. *Entrance requirements:* For master's and doctorate, GRE General Test, GRE Subject Test. Additional exam requirements/recommendations for international students: Required—TOEFL. Application fee: $40. *Financial support:* In 2009–10, 4 fellowships, 22 teaching assistantships were awarded; research assistantships, Federal Work-Study, institutionally sponsored loans, scholarships/grants, and tuition waivers (full and partial) also available. Support available to part-time students. Financial award application deadline: 2/15. *Faculty research:* Microbial and invertebrate ecology, evolution of gene function, DNA methylation, DNA arrangement. *Unit head:* Dr. Robert Fitts, Chair, 414-288-1748, Fax: 414-288-7357. *Application contact:* Debbie Weaver, Administrative Assistant, 414-288-7355, Fax: 414-288-7357.

Massachusetts Institute of Technology, School of Science, Department of Biology, Cambridge, MA 02139-4307. Offers biochemistry (PhD); biological oceanography (PhD); biology (PhD); biophysical chemistry and molecular structure (PhD); cell biology (PhD); computational and systems biology (PhD); developmental biology (PhD); genetics (PhD); immunology (PhD); microbiology (PhD); molecular biology (PhD); neurobiology (PhD). *Faculty:* 54 full-time (14 women). *Students:* 237 full-time (128 women); includes 65 minority (4 African Americans, 2 American Indian/Alaska Native, 33 Asian Americans or Pacific Islanders, 26 Hispanic Americans), 25 international. Average age 26. 645 applicants, 18% accepted, 49 enrolled. In 2009, 41 doctorates awarded. *Degree requirements:* For doctorate, comprehensive exam, thesis/dissertation. *Entrance requirements:* For doctorate, GRE General Test. Additional exam requirements/recommendations for international students: Required—TOEFL (minimum score 577 paper-based; 233 computer-based), IELTS (minimum score 6.5). *Application deadline:* For fall admission, 12/1 for domestic and international students. Application fee: $75. Electronic applications accepted. *Expenses:* Tuition: Full-time $37,510; part-time $585 per unit. Required fees: $272. *Financial support:* In 2009–10, 218 students received support, including 113 fellowships with tuition reimbursements available (averaging $31,816 per year), 109 research assistantships with tuition reimbursements available (averaging $29,254 per year); teaching assistantships with tuition reimbursements available, Federal Work-Study, institutionally sponsored loans, scholarships/grants, traineeships, health care benefits, and unspecified assistantships also available. *Faculty research:* DNA recombination, transcription and gene regulation, signal transduction, cell cycle, neuronal cell fate, replication and repair. Total annual research expenditures: $114 million. *Unit head:* Prof. Chris Kaiser, Head, 617-253-4701, E-mail: mitbio@mit.edu. *Application contact:* Biology Education Office, 617-253-3717, Fax: 617-258-9329, E-mail: gradbio@mit.edu.

Mayo Graduate School, Graduate Programs in Biomedical Sciences, Programs in Biochemistry, Structural Biology, Cell Biology, and Genetics, Rochester, MN 55905. Offers biochemistry and structural biology (PhD); cell biology and genetics (PhD); molecular biology (PhD). *Degree requirements:* For doctorate, oral defense of dissertation, qualifying oral and written exam. *Entrance requirements:* For doctorate, GRE, 1 year of chemistry, biology, calculus, and physics. Additional exam requirements/recommendations for international students: Required—TOEFL. Electronic applications accepted. *Faculty research:* Gene structure and function, membranes and receptors/cytoskeleton, oncogenes and growth factors, protein structure and function, steroid hormonal action.

McGill University, Faculty of Graduate and Postdoctoral Studies, Faculty of Medicine, Department of Anatomy and Cell Biology, Montréal, QC H3A 2T5, Canada. Offers M Sc, PhD.

McMaster University, Faculty of Health Sciences and School of Graduate Studies, Program in Medical Sciences, Metabolism and Nutrition Area, Hamilton, ON L8S 4M2, Canada. Offers M Sc, PhD, MD/PhD. *Degree requirements:* For master's, thesis; for doctorate, comprehensive exam, thesis/dissertation. *Entrance requirements:* For master's, honors B Sc, B+ average in related field; for doctorate, M Sc, minimum B+ average, students with proven research experience and an A average may be admitted with a B Sc degree. Additional exam requirements/recommendations for international students: Required—TOEFL (minimum score 580 paper-based; 237 computer-based; 92 iBT).

Medical College of Georgia, School of Graduate Studies, Program in Cellular Biology and Anatomy, Augusta, GA 30912. Offers PhD. *Degree requirements:* For doctorate, comprehensive exam, thesis/dissertation. *Entrance requirements:* For doctorate, GRE General Test. Additional exam requirements/recommendations for international students: Required—TOEFL (minimum score 550 paper-based; 213 computer-based; 79 iBT). Full-time tuition and fees vary according to campus/location, program and student level. *Faculty research:* Eye disease, developmental biology, cell injury and death, stroke and neurotoxicity, diabetic complications.

Medical College of Wisconsin, Graduate School of Biomedical Sciences, Program in Cell Biology, Neurobiology and Anatomy, Milwaukee, WI 53226-0509. Offers neuroscience (PhD); MD/PhD. Terminal master's awarded for partial completion of doctoral program. *Degree requirements:* For doctorate, comprehensive exam, thesis/dissertation. *Entrance requirements:* For doctorate, GRE General Test. Additional exam requirements/recommendations for international students: Required—TOEFL. *Faculty research:* Neurobiology, development, neuroscience, teratology.

Medical University of South Carolina, College of Graduate Studies, Program in Molecular and Cellular Biology and Pathobiology, Charleston, SC 29425. Offers cancer biology (PhD); cardiovascular biology (PhD); cardiovascular imaging (PhD); cell regulation (PhD); craniofacial biology (PhD); genetics and development (PhD); marine biomedicine (PhD); DMD/PhD; MD/PhD. *Faculty:* 137 full-time (33 women). *Students:* 39 full-time (25 women); includes 6 minority (4 African Americans, 1 Asian American or Pacific Islander, 1 Hispanic American), 9 international. Average age 28. In 2009, 16 doctorates awarded. *Degree requirements:* For doctorate, thesis/dissertation, oral and written exams. *Entrance requirements:* For doctorate, GRE General Test, interview, minimum GPA of 3.0. Additional exam requirements/recommendations for international students: Required—TOEFL (minimum score 600 paper-based; 250 computer-based; 100 iBT). *Application deadline:* For fall admission, 1/15 priority date for domestic and international students. Applications are processed on a rolling basis. Application fee: $0 ($85 for international students). Electronic applications accepted. *Financial support:* In 2009–10, 39 students received support, including 39 research assistantships with partial tuition reimbursements available (averaging $23,000 per year); Federal Work-Study and scholarships/grants also available. Support available to part-time students. Financial award application deadline: 3/10; financial award applicants required to submit FAFSA. *Unit head:* Dr. Donald R. Menick, Director, 843-876-5045, Fax: 843-792-6590, E-mail: menickd@musc.edu. *Application contact:* Dr. Cynthia F. Wright, Associate Dean for Admissions and Career Development, 843-792-2564, Fax: 843-792-6590, E-mail: wrightcf@musc.edu.

Michigan State University, The Graduate School, College of Natural Science, Program in Cell and Molecular Biology, East Lansing, MI 48824. Offers cell and molecular biology (MS, PhD); cell and molecular biology/environmental toxicology (PhD). *Faculty:* 87 full-time (28 women). *Students:* 38 full-time (20 women), 1 (woman) part-time; includes 5 minority (1 African American, 2 Asian Americans or Pacific Islanders, 2 Hispanic Americans), 14 international. Average age 27. 143 applicants, 3% accepted. In 2009, 2 master's, 6 doctorates awarded. *Entrance requirements:* Additional exam requirements/recommendations for international students: Required—TOEFL. Electronic applications accepted. *Expenses:* Tuition, state resident: part-time $478.25 per credit hour. Tuition, nonresident: part-time $966.50 per credit hour. Part-time tuition and fees vary according to program. *Financial support:* In 2009–10, 25 research assistantships with tuition reimbursements (averaging $7,826 per year), 4 teaching assistantships with tuition reimbursements (averaging $7,865 per year) were awarded; scholarships/grants and unspecified assistantships also available. Financial award application deadline: 1/1. *Unit head:* Dr. Susan E. Conrad, Director, 517-353-5161, Fax: 517-432-8813, E-mail: conrad@msu.edu. *Application contact:* Rebecca Mansel, Graduate Secretary, 517-353-8916, Fax: 517-432-8813, E-mail: cmb@msu.edu.

Missouri State University, Graduate College, College of Health and Human Services, Department of Biomedical Sciences, Program in Cell and Molecular Biology, Springfield, MO 65897. Offers MS. Part-time programs available. *Students:* 5 full-time (4 women), 4 part-time (2 women), 2 international. Average age 25. 11 applicants, 55% accepted, 5 enrolled. In 2009, 5 master's awarded. *Degree requirements:* For master's, thesis or alternative, oral and written exams. *Entrance requirements:* For master's, GRE General Test, 2 semesters of course work in organic chemistry and physics, 1 semester of course work in calculus, minimum GPA of 3.0 in last 60 hours of course work. Additional exam requirements/recommendations for international students: Required—TOEFL (minimum score 550 paper-based; 213 computer-based; 79 iBT). *Application deadline:* For fall admission, 7/20 priority date for domestic students, 5/1 for international students; for spring admission, 12/20 priority date for domestic students, 9/1 for international students. Applications are processed on a rolling basis. Application fee: $35 ($50 for international students). Electronic applications accepted. *Expenses:* Tuition, state resident: full-time $3852; part-time $214 per credit hour. Tuition, nonresident: full-time $7524; part-time $418 per credit hour. Required fees: $696; $172 per semester. Tuition and fees vary according to course level, course load, degree level and program. *Financial support:* In 2009–10, 4 teaching assistantships with full tuition reimbursements (averaging $7,340 per year) were awarded; career-related internships or fieldwork, Federal Work-Study, institutionally sponsored loans, scholarships/grants, and unspecified assistantships also available. Support available to part-time students. Financial award application deadline: 3/31; financial award applicants required to submit FAFSA. *Faculty research:* Extracellular matrix membrane protein, P2 nucleotide receptors, double stranded RNA viruses. *Unit head:* Dr. Chris Field, Graduate Program Director, 417-836-5478, E-mail: biomedicalsciences@missouristate.edu. *Application contact:* Eric Eckert, Coordinator of Graduate Admissions and Recruitment, 417-836-6331, Fax: 417-836-6200, E-mail: ericeckert@missouristate.edu.

New York Medical College, Graduate School of Basic Medical Sciences, Department of Cell Biology, Valhalla, NY 10595-1691. Offers cell biology and neuroscience (MS, PhD); MD/PhD. Part-time and evening/weekend programs available. Terminal master's awarded for partial completion of doctoral program. *Degree requirements:* For master's, thesis; for doctorate, comprehensive exam, thesis/dissertation. *Entrance requirements:* For master's and doctorate, GRE General Test. Additional exam requirements/recommendations for international students: Required—TOEFL. *Expenses:* Tuition: Full-time $18,170; part-time $790 per credit. Required fees: $790 per credit. $20 per semester. One-time fee: $100. Tuition and fees vary according to class time, course level, course load, degree level, program, student level and student's religious affiliation. *Faculty research:* Mechanisms of growth control in skeletal muscle, cartilage differentiation, cytoskeletal functions, signal transduction pathways, neuronal development and plasticity.

New York University, School of Medicine, New York, NY 10012-1019. Offers biomedical sciences (PhD), including biomedical imaging, cellular and molecular biology, computational biology, developmental genetics, medical and molecular parasitology, microbiology, molecular oncobiology and immunology, neuroscience and physiology, pathobiology, pharmacology, structural biology; clinical investigation (MS); medicine (MD); MD/MA; MD/MPA; MD/MS; MD/PhD. *Accreditation:* LCME/AMA (one or more programs are accredited). *Faculty:* 1,493 full-time (558 women), 327 part-time/adjunct (122 women). *Students:* 747 full-time (360 women); includes 275 minority (23 African Americans, 5 American Indian/Alaska Native, 199 Asian Americans or Pacific Islanders, 48 Hispanic Americans), 2 international. Average age 24. 7,568 applicants, 7% accepted, 213 enrolled. In 2009, 164 first professional degrees, 13 master's, 50 doctorates awarded. *Degree requirements:* For master's, comprehensive exam, thesis; for doctorate, comprehensive exam, thesis/dissertation. *Entrance requirements:* MCAT. Additional exam requirements/recommendations for international students: Required—TOEFL. *Application deadline:* For fall admission, 10/15 for domestic students; for winter admission, 12/18 for domestic students, 12/15 for international students. Application fee: $100. *Expenses:* Contact institution. *Financial support:* In 2009–10, 524 students received support, including 29 fellowships with full tuition reimbursements available (averaging $31,000 per year), 47 research assistantships with full tuition reimbursements available (averaging $31,000 per year); teaching assistantships, Federal Work-Study, institutionally sponsored loans, and health care benefits also available. Financial award application deadline: 3/1; financial award applicants required to submit FAFSA. *Faculty research:* AIDS, cancer, neuroscience, molecular biology, neuroscience, cell biology and molecular genetics, structural biology, microbial pathogenesis and host defense, pharmacology, molecular oncology and immunology. Total annual research expenditures: $201.1 million. *Unit head:* Dr. Robert Grossman, Dean, 212-263-3269, Fax: 212-263- 1828. *Application contact:* Dr. Nancy Genieser, Associate Dean, Admissions, 212-263-5290, Fax: 212-263-0720, E-mail: nancy.genieser@nyumc.org.

New York University, School of Medicine and Graduate School of Arts and Science, Sackler Institute of Graduate Biomedical Sciences, Program in Cellular and Molecular Biology, New York, NY 10012-1019. Offers PhD, MD/PhD. *Degree requirements:* For doctorate, comprehensive exam, thesis/dissertation, qualifying exams. *Entrance requirements:* For doctorate, GRE General Test. Additional exam requirements/recommendations for international students: Required—TOEFL. *Expenses:* Tuition: Full-time $30,528; part-time $1272 per credit. Required fees: $2177. *Faculty research:* Membrane and organelle structure and biogenesis, intracellular transport and processing of proteins, cellular recognition and cell adhesion, oncogene structure and function, action of growth factors.

North Carolina State University, College of Veterinary Medicine, Program in Comparative Biomedical Sciences, Raleigh, NC 27695. Offers cell biology (MS, PhD); infectious disease (MS, PhD); pathology (MS, PhD); pharmacology (MS, PhD); population medicine (MS, PhD). Part-time programs available. *Degree requirements:* For master's, thesis; for doctorate, thesis/dissertation. *Entrance requirements:* For master's and doctorate, GRE General Test. Additional exam requirements/recommendations for international students: Required—TOEFL (minimum score 550 paper-based; 213 computer-based). Electronic applications accepted. *Expenses:* Contact institution. *Faculty research:* Infectious diseases, cell biology, pharmacology and toxicology, genomics, pathology and population medicine.

North Dakota State University, College of Graduate and Interdisciplinary Studies, College of Science and Mathematics, Department of Biological Sciences, Fargo, ND 58108. Offers biology (MS); botany (MS, PhD); cellular and molecular biology (PhD); environmental and conservation sciences (MS, PhD); genomics (PhD); natural resources management (MS, PhD); zoology (MS, PhD). *Students:* 32 full-time (21 women), 14 part-time (10 women); includes 1 Asian American or Pacific Islander, 14 international. In 2009, 12 master's, 9 doctorates awarded. *Degree requirements:* For master's, thesis; for doctorate, thesis/dissertation. *Entrance requirements:* For master's and doctorate, GRE General Test. Additional exam requirements/recommendations for international students: Required—TOEFL. *Application deadline:* For fall admission, 3/15 priority date for domestic students; for spring admission, 10/30 priority date for domestic students. Applications are processed on a rolling basis. Application fee: $45 ($60 for international students). Electronic applications accepted. *Financial support:* Fellowships with full tuition reimbursements, research assistantships with full tuition reimbursements, teaching assistantships with full tuition reimbursements, career-related internships or fieldwork, Federal Work-Study, institutionally sponsored loans, scholarships/grants, tuition waivers (full), and unspecified assistantships available. Support available to part-time students. Financial award application deadline: 4/15; financial award applicants required to submit FAFSA. *Faculty research:* Comparative endocrinology, physiology, behavioral ecology, plant cell biology, aquatic biology. Total annual research expenditures: $675,000. *Unit head:* Dr. Marinus L. Otte, Head, 701-231-7087, E-mail: marinus.otte@ndsu.edu. *Application contact:* Dr. Marinus L. Otte, Head, 701-231-7087, E-mail: marinus.otte@ndsu.edu.

North Dakota State University, College of Graduate and Interdisciplinary Studies, Interdisciplinary Program in Cellular and Molecular Biology, Fargo, ND 58108. Offers PhD. Offered in cooperation with 11 departments in the university. *Students:* 8 full-time (3 women), 6 international. In 2009, 2 doctorates awarded. *Degree requirements:* For doctorate, thesis/dissertation. *Entrance requirements:* For doctorate, GRE. Additional exam requirements/recommendations for inter-

Cell Biology

North Dakota State University (continued)
national students: Required—TOEFL (minimum score 525 paper-based; 197 computer-based; 71 iBT). *Application deadline:* Applications are processed on a rolling basis. Application fee: $45 ($60 for international students). Electronic applications accepted. *Financial support:* Fellowships with full tuition reimbursements, research assistantships with full tuition reimbursements, teaching assistantships with full tuition reimbursements, unspecified assistantships available. Financial award application deadline: 3/15. *Faculty research:* Plant and animal cell biology, gene regulation, molecular genetics, plant and animal virology. *Unit head:* Dr. Mark Sheridan, Director, 701-231-8110. *Application contact:* Dr. Mark Sheridan, Director, 701-231-8110.

Northwestern University, The Graduate School and Judd A. and Marjorie Weinberg College of Arts and Sciences, Interdepartmental Biological Sciences Program (IBiS), Evanston, IL 60208. Offers biochemistry, molecular biology, and cell biology (PhD), including biochemistry, cell and molecular biology, molecular biophysics, structural biology; biotechnology (PhD); cell and molecular biology (PhD); developmental biology and genetics (PhD); hormone action and signal transduction (PhD); neuroscience (PhD); structural biology, biochemistry, and biophysics (PhD). Program participants include the Departments of Biochemistry, Molecular Biology, and Cell Biology; Chemistry; Neurobiology and Physiology; Chemical Engineering; Civil Engineering; and Evanston Hospital. *Degree requirements:* For doctorate, thesis/dissertation, qualifying exam. *Entrance requirements:* For doctorate, GRE General Test. Additional exam requirements/recommendations for international students: Required—TOEFL (minimum score 600 paper-based). Electronic applications accepted. *Faculty research:* Developmental genetics, gene regulation, DNA-protein interactions, biological clocks, bioremediation.

Northwestern University, Northwestern University Feinberg School of Medicine and Interdepartmental Programs, Integrated Graduate Programs in the Life Sciences, Chicago, IL 60611. Offers cancer biology (PhD); cell biology (PhD); developmental biology (PhD); evolutionary biology (PhD); immunology and microbial pathogenesis (PhD); molecular biology and genetics (PhD); neurobiology (PhD); pharmacology and toxicology (PhD); structural biology and biochemistry (PhD). *Degree requirements:* For doctorate, comprehensive exam, thesis/dissertation, written and oral qualifying exams. *Entrance requirements:* For doctorate, GRE General Test. Additional exam requirements/recommendations for international students: Required—TOEFL (minimum score 600 paper-based; 250 computer-based). Electronic applications accepted.

The Ohio State University, College of Veterinary Medicine, Department of Veterinary Biosciences, Columbus, OH 43210. Offers anatomy and cellular biology (MS, PhD); pathobiology (MS, PhD); pharmacology (MS, PhD); toxicology (MS, PhD); veterinary physiology (MS, PhD). *Faculty:* 45. *Students:* 18 full-time (14 women), 20 part-time (16 women); includes 3 minority (1 African American, 1 Asian American or Pacific Islander, 1 Hispanic American), 16 international. Average age 30. In 2009, 1 master's, 9 doctorates awarded. *Entrance requirements:* For master's and doctorate, GRE General Test. Additional exam requirements/recommendations for international students: Required—TOEFL. *Application deadline:* Applications are processed on a rolling basis. Application fee: $40 ($50 for international students). Electronic applications accepted. *Expenses:* Tuition, state resident: full-time $10,683. Tuition, nonresident: full-time $25,923. Tuition and fees vary according to course load and program. *Faculty research:* Microvasculature, muscle biology, neonatal lung and bone development. *Unit head:* Dr. Michael J. Oglesbee, Graduate Studies Committee Chair, 614-292-5661, Fax: 614-292-6473, E-mail: oglesbee.1@osu.edu. *Application contact:* Graduate Admissions, 614-292-9444, Fax: 614-292-3895, E-mail: domestic.grad@osu.edu.

The Ohio State University, Graduate School, College of Biological Sciences, Department of Molecular Genetics, Columbus, OH 43210. Offers cell and developmental biology (MS, PhD); genetics (MS, PhD); molecular biology (MS, PhD). *Faculty:* 26. *Students:* 8 full-time (5 women), 23 part-time (11 women), 17 international. Average age 27. In 2009, 11 doctorates awarded. *Degree requirements:* For master's, thesis; for doctorate, thesis/dissertation. *Entrance requirements:* For master's and doctorate, GRE General Test, GRE Subject Test in biology or biochemistry (recommended). Additional exam requirements/recommendations for international students: Required—TOEFL (minimum score 600 paper-based; 250 computer-based). *Application deadline:* For fall admission, 8/15 priority date for domestic students, 7/1 priority date for international students; for winter admission, 12/1 priority date for domestic students, 11/1 priority date for international students; for spring admission, 3/1 priority date for domestic students, 2/1 priority date for international students. Applications are processed on a rolling basis. Application fee: $40 ($50 for international students). Electronic applications accepted. *Expenses:* Tuition, state resident: full-time $10,683. Tuition, nonresident: full-time $25,923. Tuition and fees vary according to course load and program. *Financial support:* Fellowships, research assistantships, teaching assistantships, Federal Work-Study and institutionally sponsored loans available. Support available to part-time students. *Unit head:* Dr. Anna Hopper, Chair, 614-292-8084, Fax: 614-292-4466, E-mail: hopper.64@osu.edu. *Application contact:* 614-292-9444, Fax: 614-292-3895, E-mail: domestic.grad@osu.edu.

The Ohio State University, Graduate School, College of Biological Sciences, Program in Molecular, Cellular and Developmental Biology, Columbus, OH 43210. Offers MS, PhD. *Students:* 67 full-time (38 women), 60 part-time (31 women); includes 12 minority (2 African Americans, 5 Asian Americans or Pacific Islanders, 5 Hispanic Americans), 77 international. Average age 28. In 2009, 3 master's, 13 doctorates awarded. *Entrance requirements:* For master's and doctorate, GRE General Test, GRE Subject Test in biology or biochemistry, cell and molecular biology. Additional exam requirements/recommendations for international students: Required—TOEFL (minimum score 573 paper-based; 230 computer-based). *Application deadline:* Applications are processed on a rolling basis. Application fee: $40 ($50 for international students). Electronic applications accepted. *Expenses:* Tuition, state resident: full-time $10,683. Tuition, nonresident: full-time $25,923. Tuition and fees vary according to course load and program. *Unit head:* David M. Bisaro, Graduate Studies Committee Chair, 614-292-2804, Fax: 614-292-8772, E-mail: bisaro.1@osu.edu. *Application contact:* Graduate Admissions, 614-292-9444, Fax: 614-292-3895, E-mail: domestic.grad@osu.edu.

Ohio University, Graduate College, College of Arts and Sciences, Department of Biological Sciences, Athens, OH 45701-2979. Offers biological sciences (MS, PhD); cell biology and physiology (MS, PhD); ecology and evolutionary biology (MS, PhD); exercise physiology and muscle biology (MS, PhD); microbiology (MS, PhD); neuroscience (MS, PhD). *Faculty:* 50 full-time (14 women), 6 part-time/adjunct (1 woman). *Students:* 44 full-time (19 women), 8 part-time (3 women); includes 2 minority (1 African American, 1 Hispanic American), 21 international. 95 applicants, 24% accepted, 10 enrolled. In 2009, 4 master's, 9 doctorates awarded. Terminal master's awarded for partial completion of doctoral program. *Degree requirements:* For master's, comprehensive exam, thesis, 1 quarter of teaching experience; for doctorate, comprehensive exam, thesis/dissertation, 2 quarters of teaching experience. *Entrance requirements:* For master's, GRE General Test, names of three faculty members whose research interests most closely match the applicant's interest; for doctorate, GRE General Test, essay concerning prior training, research interest and career goals, plus names of three faculty members whose research interests most closely match the applicant's interest. Additional exam requirements/recommendations for international students: Required—TOEFL (minimum score 620 paper-based; 105 iBT) or IELTS (minimum score 7.5). *Application deadline:* For fall admission, 1/15 for domestic and international students. Application fee: $50 ($55 for international students). Electronic applications accepted. *Expenses:* Tuition, state resident: full-time $7839; part-time $323 per quarter hour. Tuition, nonresident: full-time $15,831; part-time $654 per quarter hour. Required fees: $2931. *Financial support:* In 2009–10, 1 fellowship with full tuition reimbursement (averaging $18,957 per year), 10 research assistantships with full tuition reimbursements (averaging $18,957 per year), 42 teaching assistantships with full tuition reimbursements (averaging $18,957 per year) were awarded; Federal Work-Study and institutionally sponsored loans also available. Financial award application deadline: 1/15. *Faculty research:* Ecology and evolutionary biology, exercise physiology and muscle biology, neurobiology, cell biology, physiology. Total annual research expenditures: $2.8 million. *Unit head:* Dr. Ralph DiCaprio, Chair, 740-593-2290, Fax: 740-593-0300, E-mail: dicapri@ohio.edu. *Application contact:* Dr. Donald Holzschu, Graduate Chair, 740-593-0425, Fax: 740-593-0300, E-mail: holzschu@ohio.edu.

Ohio University, Graduate College, College of Arts and Sciences, Interdisciplinary Graduate Program in Molecular and Cellular Biology, Athens, OH 45701-2979. Offers MS, PhD. *Faculty:* 47 full-time (12 women). *Students:* 27 full-time (18 women), 2 part-time (1 woman), 25 international. Average age 28. 49 applicants, 24% accepted, 5 enrolled. In 2009, 4 doctorates awarded. *Degree requirements:* For master's, comprehensive exam, thesis, research proposal, teaching experience; for doctorate, comprehensive exam, thesis/dissertation, research proposal, teaching experience. *Entrance requirements:* For master's and doctorate, GRE General Test. Additional exam requirements/recommendations for international students: Required—TOEFL (minimum score 620 paper-based; 260 computer-based; 105 iBT); Recommended—TWE. *Application deadline:* For fall admission, 12/30 priority date for domestic students, 12/30 for international students. Application fee: $50 ($55 for international students). Electronic applications accepted. *Expenses:* Tuition, state resident: full-time $7839; part-time $323 per quarter hour. Tuition, nonresident: full-time $15,831; part-time $654 per quarter hour. Required fees: $2931. *Financial support:* In 2009–10, 25 students received support, including research assistantships with full tuition reimbursements available (averaging $19,500 per year), teaching assistantships with full tuition reimbursements available (averaging $19,500 per year); Federal Work-Study, institutionally sponsored loans, traineeships, and unspecified assistantships also available. Financial award application deadline: 12/30. *Faculty research:* Animal biotechnology, plant molecular biology RNA, immunology, cellular genetics, biochemistry of signal transduction, cancer research, membrane transport, bioinformatics, bioengineering, chemical biology and drug discovery, diabetes, microbiology, neuroscience. Total annual research expenditures: $4.4 million. *Unit head:* Dr. Robert A. Colvin, Chair, 740-593-0198, Fax: 740-593-1569, E-mail: colvin@ohio.edu. *Application contact:* Dr. Xiaozhuo Chen, Graduate Chair, 740-593-9699, Fax: 740-593-1569, E-mail: chenx@ohio.edu.

Oregon Health & Science University, School of Medicine, Graduate Programs in Medicine, Department of Cell and Developmental Biology, Portland, OR 97239-3098. Offers PhD. *Degree requirements:* For doctorate, thesis/dissertation. *Entrance requirements:* For doctorate, GRE General Test, GRE Subject Test, MCAT. Tuition and fees vary according to course level, course load, degree level, program and reciprocity agreements. *Financial support:* Stipend and paid tuition available. *Faculty research:* Developmental mechanisms, molecular biology of cancer, molecular neurobiology, intracellular signaling, growth factors and development. *Unit head:* Richard Maurer, PhD, Interim Chair/Program Director, 503-494-7811, E-mail: maurerr@ohsu.edu. *Application contact:* Elaine Offield, Program Coordinator, 503-494-5824, E-mail: offielde@ohsu.edu.

Oregon State University, Graduate School, Program in Molecular and Cellular Biology, Corvallis, OR 97331. Offers MS, PhD. *Students:* 41 full-time (12 women), 2 part-time (0 women); includes 5 minority (1 American Indian/Alaska Native, 4 Asian Americans or Pacific Islanders), 11 international. Average age 30. In 2009, 1 master's, 4 doctorates awarded. *Degree requirements:* For doctorate, thesis/dissertation, oral and written qualifying exams. *Entrance requirements:* For doctorate, minimum GPA of 3.0 in last 90 hours. Additional exam requirements/recommendations for international students: Required—TOEFL. *Application deadline:* For fall admission, 2/15 for domestic students. Applications are processed on a rolling basis. Application fee: $50. *Expenses:* Tuition, state resident: full-time $9774; part-time $362 per credit. Tuition, nonresident: full-time $15,849; part-time $587 per credit. Required fees: $1639. Full-time tuition and fees vary according to course load and program. *Financial support:* Fellowships, career-related internships or fieldwork, Federal Work-Study, and institutionally sponsored loans available. Support available to part-time students. *Unit head:* Dr. James C. Carrington, Director, 541-737-3347, Fax: 541-737-3045, E-mail: carrington@cgrb.oregonstate.edu. *Application contact:* Dr. James C. Carrington, Director, 541-737-3347, Fax: 541-737-3045, E-mail: carrington@cgrb.oregonstate.edu.

Penn State Hershey Medical Center, College of Medicine, Graduate School Programs in the Biomedical Sciences, Interdepartmental Graduate Program in Cell and Molecular Biology, Hershey, PA 17033. Offers MS, PhD, MD/PhD. *Students:* 37 applicants, 38% accepted, 4 enrolled. In 2009, 4 doctorates awarded. Terminal master's awarded for partial completion of doctoral program. *Degree requirements:* For master's, thesis or alternative; for doctorate, comprehensive exam, thesis/dissertation, oral exam. *Entrance requirements:* For master's, GRE General Test or MCAT; for doctorate, GRE General Test or MCAT, minimum GPA of 3.0. Additional exam requirements/recommendations for international students: Required—TOEFL (minimum score 500 paper-based; 213 computer-based). *Application deadline:* For fall admission, 1/31 priority date for domestic students, 2/1 priority date for international students. Applications are processed on a rolling basis. Application fee: $65. Electronic applications accepted. *Expenses:* Tuition, state resident: part-time $644 per credit. Tuition, nonresident: part-time $1142 per credit. Required fees: $22 per semester. *Financial support:* In 2009–10, research assistantships with full tuition reimbursements (averaging $22,260 per year); fellowships with full tuition reimbursements, career-related internships or fieldwork, scholarships/grants, health care benefits, and unspecified assistantships also available. Financial award applicants required to submit FAFSA. *Faculty research:* Membrane structure, function and modulators; cell division, differentiation and gene expression; Metastasis; intracellular events in the immune system. *Unit head:* Dr. Henry Donahue, Program Director, 717-531-1045, Fax: 717-531-4139, E-mail: cmb-grad-hmc@psu.edu. *Application contact:* Lori Coover, Program Assistant, 717-531-1045, Fax: 717-531-0786, E-mail: cmb-grad-hmc@psu.edu.

Penn State University Park, Graduate School, Intercollege Graduate Programs, State College, University Park, PA 16802-1503. Offers acoustics (M Eng, MS, PhD); bioengineering (MS, PhD); biogeochemistry (dual) (PhD); business administration (MBA); cell and developmental biology (PhD); demography (dual) (MA); ecology (MS, PhD); environmental pollution control (MEPC, MS); genetics (MS, PhD); human dimensions of natural resources and the environment (dual) (MA, MS, PhD); immunology and infectious diseases (MS); integrative biosciences (MS, PhD), including integrative biosciences; materials science and engineering (PhD); operations research (dual) (M Eng, MA, MS, PhD); physiology (MS, PhD); plant physiology (MS, PhD); quality and manufacturing management (MMM). *Students:* 371 full-time (157 women), 22 part-time (7 women). Average age 27. 1,074 applicants, 18% accepted, 130 enrolled. *Entrance requirements:* Additional exam requirements/recommendations for international students: Required—TOEFL (minimum score 550 paper-based; 213 computer-based; 80 iBT). *Application deadline:* Applications are processed on a rolling basis. Application fee: $45. Electronic applications accepted. *Financial support:* Fellowships, research assistantships, teaching assistantships available. Financial award applicants required to submit FAFSA. *Unit head:* Dr. Regina Vasilatos-Younken, Senior Associate Dean, 814-865-2516, Fax: 814-863-4627, E-mail: rxv@psu.edu. *Application contact:* Cynthia E. Nicosia, Director, Graduate Enrollment Services, 814-865-1795, Fax: 814-865-4627, E-mail: cey1@psu.edu.

Purdue University, Graduate School, College of Science, Department of Biological Sciences, West Lafayette, IN 47907. Offers biochemistry (PhD); biophysics (PhD); cell and developmental biology (PhD); ecology, evolutionary and population biology (MS, PhD), including ecology, evolutionary biology, population biology; genetics (MS, PhD); microbiology (MS, PhD); molecular biology (PhD); neurobiology (MS, PhD); plant physiology (PhD). Terminal master's awarded for partial completion of doctoral program. *Degree requirements:* For master's, thesis (for some programs); for doctorate, thesis/dissertation, seminars, teaching experience. *Entrance requirements:* For master's and doctorate, GRE General Test. Additional exam requirements/recommendations for international students: Required—TOEFL. Electronic applications accepted.

Queen's University at Kingston, School of Graduate Studies and Research, Faculty of Health Sciences, Department of Anatomy and Cell Biology, Kingston, ON K7L 3N6, Canada. Offers biology of reproduction (M Sc, PhD); cancer (M Sc, PhD); cardiovascular pathophysiology (M Sc, PhD); cell and molecular biology (M Sc, PhD); drug metabolism (M Sc, PhD); endocrinology (M Sc, PhD); motor control (M Sc, PhD); neural regeneration (M Sc, PhD); neurophysiology (M Sc, PhD). Part-time programs available. *Degree requirements:* For master's, thesis; for doctorate, one foreign language, comprehensive exam, thesis/dissertation. *Entrance requirements:* Additional exam requirements/recommendations for international students: Required—TOEFL. Electronic applications accepted. *Faculty research:* Human kinetics, neuroscience, reproductive biology, cardiovascular.

Quinnipiac University, School of Health Sciences, Program in Molecular and Cell Biology, Hamden, CT 06518-1940. Offers MS. Part-time programs available. *Faculty:* 8 full-time (4 women), 9 part-time/adjunct (2 women). *Students:* 11 full-time (7 women), 15 part-time (9 women); includes 4 minority (1 African American, 1 American Indian/Alaska Native, 2 Asian Americans or Pacific Islanders), 5 international. Average age 26. 21 applicants, 95% accepted, 11 enrolled. In 2009, 8 master's awarded. *Degree requirements:* For master's, thesis optional. *Entrance requirements:* For master's, bachelor's degree in biological, medical, or health sciences; minimum GPA of 2.75. Additional exam requirements/recommendations for international students: Required—TOEFL (minimum score 600 paper-based; 233 computer-based; 90 iBT), IELTS (minimum score 6.5). *Application deadline:* For fall admission, 7/30 priority date for domestic students, 4/30 priority date for international students; for spring admission, 12/15 priority date for domestic students, 9/15 priority date for international students. Applications are processed on a rolling basis. Application fee: $45. Electronic applications accepted. *Expenses:* Tuition: Full-time $16,030; part-time $770 per credit. Required fees: $630; $35 per credit. *Financial support:* Federal Work-Study, tuition waivers, and unspecified assistantships available. Support available to part-time students. Financial award application deadline: 4/15; financial award applicants required to submit FAFSA. *Unit head:* Dr. Gene Wong, Director, 203-582-8467, E-mail: gene.wong@quinnipiac.edu. *Application contact:* Kristin Parent, Assistant Director of Graduate Health Sciences Admissions, 800-462-1944, Fax: 203-582-3443, E-mail: kristin.parent@quinnipiac.edu.

Rice University, Graduate Programs, Wiess School of Natural Sciences, Department of Biochemistry and Cell Biology, Houston, TX 77251-1892. Offers MA, PhD. *Faculty:* 26 full-time (8 women). *Students:* 52 full-time (18 women); includes 24 minority (1 African American, 16 Asian Americans or Pacific Islanders, 7 Hispanic Americans), 15 international. Average age 23. 177 applicants, 18% accepted, 12 enrolled. In 2009, 5 master's, 12 doctorates awarded. Terminal master's awarded for partial completion of doctoral program. *Degree requirements:* For master's, thesis; for doctorate, thesis/dissertation. *Entrance requirements:* For master's and doctorate, GRE. Additional exam requirements/recommendations for international students: Required—TOEFL (minimum score 575 paper-based; 250 computer-based; 90 iBT). *Application deadline:* For fall admission, 2/1 priority date for domestic students, 2/1 for international students. Applications are processed on a rolling basis. Application fee: $0 ($70 for international students). Electronic applications accepted. *Expenses:* Contact institution. *Financial support:* In 2009–10, 12 students received support, including 12 fellowships with full tuition reimbursements available (averaging $26,000 per year); tuition waivers (full) also available. Financial award application deadline: 2/1. *Faculty research:* Steroid metabolism, protein structure NMR, biophysics, cell growth and movement. Total annual research expenditures: $5 million. *Unit head:* Dr. Janet Braam, Chair, 713-348-4015, Fax: 713-348-5154, E-mail: bioc@rice.edu. *Application contact:* Dr. Susan Cates, Recruiting Administrator, 713-348-5777, Fax: 713-348-5154, E-mail: bioc@rice.edu.

Rosalind Franklin University of Medicine and Science, School of Graduate and Postdoctoral Studies—Interdisciplinary Graduate Program in Biomedical Sciences, Department of Cell Biology and Anatomy, North Chicago, IL 60064-3095. Offers MS, PhD, MD/PhD. Terminal master's awarded for partial completion of doctoral program. *Degree requirements:* For master's, comprehensive exam, thesis, qualifying exam; for doctorate, comprehensive exam, thesis/dissertation, original research project. *Entrance requirements:* For master's and doctorate, GRE General Test, minimum GPA of 3.0. Additional exam requirements/recommendations for international students: Required—TOEFL, TWE. *Faculty research:* Neuroscience, molecular biology.

Rush University, Graduate College, Division of Anatomy and Cell Biology, Chicago, IL 60612-3832. Offers MS, PhD, MD/MS, MD/PhD. Terminal master's awarded for partial completion of doctoral program. *Degree requirements:* For master's, thesis; for doctorate, comprehensive exam, thesis/dissertation, preliminary exam, dissertation proposal. *Entrance requirements:* For master's, GRE General Test, minimum GPA of 3.0, bachelor's degree in biology or chemistry (preferred), interview; for doctorate, GRE General Test, minimum GPA of 3.0, interview. Additional exam requirements/recommendations for international students: Required—TOEFL. Electronic applications accepted. *Faculty research:* Incontinence following vaginal distension, knee replacement, biomimetric materials, injured spinal motoneurons, implant fixation.

Rutgers, The State University of New Jersey, New Brunswick, Graduate School-New Brunswick, Programs in the Molecular Biosciences, Program in Cell and Developmental Biology, Piscataway, NJ 08854-8097. Offers MS, PhD. Part-time programs available. Terminal master's awarded for partial completion of doctoral program. *Degree requirements:* For master's, thesis; for doctorate, thesis/dissertation, written qualifying exam. *Entrance requirements:* For master's, GRE General Test; for doctorate, GRE General Test, GRE Subject Test (recommended), minimum GPA of 3.0. Additional exam requirements/recommendations for international students: Required—TOEFL. Electronic applications accepted. *Faculty research:* Signal transduction and regulation of gene expression, developmental biology, cellular biology, developmental genetics, neurobiology.

San Diego State University, Graduate and Research Affairs, College of Sciences, Department of Biology, San Diego, CA 92182. Offers biology (MA, MS), including ecology (MS), molecular biology (MS), physiology (MS), systematics/evolution (MS); cell and molecular biology (PhD); ecology (MS, PhD); microbiology (MS). Terminal master's awarded for partial completion of doctoral program. *Degree requirements:* For master's, thesis; for doctorate, thesis/dissertation. *Entrance requirements:* For master's, GRE General Test, GRE Subject Test, resume or curriculum vitae, 2 letters of recommendation. Additional exam requirements/recommendations for international students: Required—TOEFL. Electronic applications accepted.

San Diego State University, Graduate and Research Affairs, College of Sciences, Molecular Biology Institute, Program in Cell and Molecular Biology, San Diego, CA 92182. Offers PhD. *Degree requirements:* For doctorate, thesis/dissertation, oral comprehensive qualifying exam. *Entrance requirements:* For doctorate, GRE General Test, GRE Subject Test, resumé or curriculum vitae, 3 letters of recommendation. Electronic applications accepted. *Faculty research:* Structure/dynamics of protein kinesis, chromatin structure and DNA methylation membrane biochemistry, secretory protein targeting, molecular biology of cardiac myocytes.

San Francisco State University, Division of Graduate Studies, College of Science and Engineering, Department of Biology, Program in Cell and Molecular Biology, San Francisco, CA 94132-1722. Offers MS.

State University of New York Downstate Medical Center, School of Graduate Studies, Program in Molecular and Cellular Biology, Brooklyn, NY 11203-2098. Offers PhD, MD/PhD. Affiliation with a particular PhD degree-granting program is deferred to the second year. *Degree requirements:* For doctorate, comprehensive exam, thesis/dissertation. *Entrance requirements:* For doctorate, GRE General Test. *Faculty research:* Mechanism of gene regulation, molecular virology.

State University of New York Upstate Medical University, College of Graduate Studies, Program in Anatomy and Cell Biology, Syracuse, NY 13210-2334. Offers anatomy (MS); anatomy and cell biology (PhD); MD/PhD. *Faculty:* 18 full-time (4 women), 1 part-time/adjunct (0 women). *Students:* 17 full-time (7 women), 1 (woman) part-time; includes 1 minority (Asian American or Pacific Islander), 6 international. In 2009, 1 master's awarded. Terminal master's awarded for partial completion of doctoral program. *Degree requirements:* For master's, thesis; for doctorate, comprehensive exam, thesis/dissertation. *Entrance requirements:* For master's, GRE General Test, interview; for doctorate, GRE General Test, telephone interview. Additional exam requirements/recommendations for international students: Required—TOEFL. *Application deadline:* Applications are processed on a rolling basis. Application fee: $40. Electronic applications accepted. *Financial support:* In 2009–10, fellowships with tuition reimbursements (averaging $21,514 per year), research assistantships with tuition reimbursements (averaging $21,514 per year) were awarded; Federal Work-Study, scholarships/grants, health care benefits, and unspecified assistantships also available. Financial award application deadline: 4/15; financial award applicants required to submit FAFSA. *Faculty research:* Cancer, disorders of the nervous system, infectious diseases, diabetes/metabolic disorders/cardiovascular diseases. *Unit head:* Dr. Joseph Sanger, Chair, 315-464-5120. *Application contact:* Sandra Tillotsson, Coordinator of Graduate Recruitment, 315-464-7655, Fax: 315-464-4544.

See Close-Up on page 237.

Stony Brook University, State University of New York, Graduate School, College of Arts and Sciences, Department of Biochemistry and Cell Biology, Molecular and Cellular Biology Program, Stony Brook, NY 11794. Offers biochemistry and molecular biology (PhD); biological sciences (MA); cellular and developmental biology (PhD); immunology and pathology (PhD); molecular and cellular biology (PhD). *Students:* 100 full-time (62 women); includes 8 minority (2 African Americans, 5 Asian Americans or Pacific Islanders, 1 Hispanic American), 60 international. Average age 30. 277 applicants, 15% accepted. In 2009, 15 doctorates awarded. *Degree requirements:* For doctorate, comprehensive exam, thesis/dissertation, teaching experience. *Entrance requirements:* For doctorate, GRE General Test, GRE Subject Test. Additional exam requirements/recommendations for international students: Required—TOEFL. *Application deadline:* For fall admission, 1/15 for domestic students. Application fee: $60. *Expenses:* Tuition, state resident: full-time $8370; part-time $349 per credit. Tuition, nonresident: full-time $13,250; part-time $552 per credit. Required fees: $933. *Financial support:* In 2009–10, 49 research assistantships, 15 teaching assistantships were awarded; fellowships, Federal Work-Study also available. *Unit head:* Prof. Robert Haltiwanger, Chair, 631-632-8560. *Application contact:* Prof. Robert Haltiwanger, Chair, 631-632-8560.

Temple University, Health Sciences Center, School of Medicine and Graduate School, Graduate Programs in Medicine, Department of Anatomy and Cell Biology, Philadelphia, PA 19122-6096. Offers MS, PhD. *Degree requirements:* For doctorate, thesis/dissertation, research seminars. *Entrance requirements:* For master's and doctorate, GRE General Test, GRE Subject Test, minimum GPA of 3.0. Additional exam requirements/recommendations for international students: Required—TOEFL. Electronic applications accepted. *Faculty research:* Neurobiology, reproductive biology, cardiovascular system, musculoskeletal biology, developmental biology.

Texas A&M Health Science Center, Graduate School of Biomedical Sciences, Department of Molecular and Cellular Medicine, College Station, TX 77840. Offers PhD. *Degree requirements:* For doctorate, thesis/dissertation. *Entrance requirements:* For doctorate, GRE General Test. *Faculty research:* Immunology, cell and membrane biology, protein biochemistry, molecular genetics, parasitology, vertebrate embryogenesis and microbiology.

Texas A&M Health Science Center, Graduate School of Biomedical Sciences, Program in Cell and Molecular Biology, College Station, TX 77840. Offers PhD.

Texas A&M University, College of Science, Department of Biology, College Station, TX 77843. Offers biology (MS, PhD); botany (MS, PhD); microbiology (MS, PhD); molecular and cell biology (PhD); neuroscience (MS, PhD); zoology (MS, PhD). *Faculty:* 37. *Students:* 101 full-time (59 women), 5 part-time (3 women); includes 8 minority (1 African American, 3 Asian Americans or Pacific Islanders, 4 Hispanic Americans), 40 international. Average age 28. In 2009, 9 master's, 5 doctorates awarded. *Degree requirements:* For master's, thesis or alternative; for doctorate, comprehensive exam, thesis/dissertation. *Entrance requirements:* For master's and doctorate, GRE General Test. Additional exam requirements/recommendations for international students: Required—TOEFL. *Application deadline:* For fall admission, 1/15 for domestic students. Applications are processed on a rolling basis. Application fee: $50 ($75 for international students). Electronic applications accepted. *Expenses:* Tuition, state resident: full-time $3991; part-time $221.74 per credit hour. Tuition, nonresident: full-time $9049; part-time $502.74 per credit hour. *Financial support:* Fellowships, research assistantships, teaching assistantships available. Financial award application deadline: 4/1; financial award applicants required to submit FAFSA. *Unit head:* Dr. Jack McMahan, Department Head, 979-845-2301, E-mail: granster@mail.bio.tamu.edu. *Application contact:* Graduate Advisor, 979-845-7755.

Texas Tech University Health Sciences Center, Graduate School of Biomedical Sciences, Department of Cell Biology and Biochemistry, Program in Cell and Molecular Biology, Lubbock, TX 79430. Offers MS, PhD, MD/PhD, MS/PhD. Terminal master's awarded for partial completion of doctoral program. *Degree requirements:* For master's, comprehensive exam, thesis; for doctorate, comprehensive exam, thesis/dissertation. *Entrance requirements:* For master's and doctorate, GRE General Test, minimum GPA of 3.0. Additional exam requirements/recommendations for international students: Required—TOEFL. *Faculty research:* Biochemical endocrinology, neurobiology, molecular biology, reproductive biology, biology of developing systems.

Thomas Jefferson University, Jefferson College of Graduate Studies, MS Program in Cell and Developmental Biology, Philadelphia, PA 19107. Offers MS. Part-time and evening/weekend programs available. *Faculty:* 19 full-time (6 women). *Students:* 7 part-time (6 women); includes 1 minority (Asian American or Pacific Islander), 2 international. 12 applicants, 42% accepted, 3 enrolled. In 2009, 1 master's awarded. *Degree requirements:* For master's, thesis, clerkship. *Entrance requirements:* For master's, GRE General Test or MCAT, minimum GPA of 3.0. Additional exam requirements/recommendations for international students: Required—TOEFL (minimum score 250 computer-based; 100 iBT) or IELTS. *Application deadline:* For fall admission, 8/1 priority date for domestic students, 3/1 priority date for international students; for winter admission, 12/1 priority date for domestic students, 6/1 priority date for international students; for spring admission, 4/1 priority date for domestic students. Applications are processed on a rolling basis. Application fee: $50. Electronic applications accepted. *Expenses:* Tuition: Full-time $26,858; part-time $879 per credit. Required fees: $525. *Financial support:* In 2009–10, 3 students received support. Federal Work-Study and institutionally sponsored loans available. Support available to part-time students. Financial award application deadline: 5/1; financial award applicants required to submit FAFSA. *Unit head:* Dr. Gerald Grunwald, Senior Associate Dean and Program Director, 215-503-4191, Fax: 215-503-6690, E-mail: gerald.grunwald@jefferson.edu. *Application contact:* Eleanor M. Gorman, Assistant Coordinator, Graduate Center Programs, 215-503-5799, Fax: 215-503-3433, E-mail: eleanor.gorman@jefferson.edu.

Thomas Jefferson University, Jefferson College of Graduate Studies, PhD Program in Cell and Developmental Biology, Philadelphia, PA 19107. Offers PhD. *Faculty:* 42 full-time (8 women). *Students:* 18 full-time (13 women), 2 international. 21 applicants, 19% accepted, 3 enrolled. In 2009, 4 doctorates awarded. *Degree requirements:* For doctorate, comprehensive exam, thesis/dissertation. *Entrance requirements:* For doctorate, GRE General Test, minimum GPA of 3.2. Additional exam requirements/recommendations for international students: Required—TOEFL (minimum score 250 computer-based; 100 iBT). *Application deadline:* For fall admission, 1/15 priority date for domestic and international students. Applications are processed on a rolling basis. Application fee: $50. Electronic applications accepted. *Expenses:* Tuition: Full-time $26,858; part-time $879 per credit. Required fees: $525. *Financial support:* In 2009–10, 18 students received support, including 18 fellowships with full tuition reimbursements available (averaging $52,883 per year); Federal Work-Study, institutionally sponsored loans, scholarships/grants, traineeships, and stipend also available. Support available to part-time students. Financial award application deadline: 5/1; financial award applicants required to submit FAFSA. Total annual research expenditures: $20 million. *Unit head:* Dr. Theodore F. Taraschi, Program Director, 215-503-5020, Fax: 215-503-0206, E-mail: theodore.taraschi@jefferson.edu. *Application contact:* Marc E. Stearns, Director of Admissions, 215-503-0155, Fax: 215-503-9920, E-mail: jcgs-info@jefferson.edu.

Cell Biology

Tufts University, Sackler School of Graduate Biomedical Sciences, Integrated Studies Program, Medford, MA 02155. Offers PhD. *Students:* 10 full-time (7 women); includes 1 minority (Asian American or Pacific Islander), 2 international. Average age 25. 333 applicants, 6% accepted. *Entrance requirements:* For doctorate, GRE General Test, 3 letters of reference. Additional exam requirements/recommendations for international students: Required—TOEFL. *Application deadline:* For fall admission, 12/15 for domestic and international students. Applications are processed on a rolling basis. Application fee: $70. Electronic applications accepted. *Expenses:* Tuition: Full-time $38,096; part-time $3962 per credit. Required fees: $686; $40 per year. Tuition and fees vary according to course level, course load, degree level, program and student level. *Financial support:* In 2009–10, 10 students received support, including 10 research assistantships with tuition reimbursements available (averaging $28,250 per year); scholarships/grants and health care benefits also available. *Unit head:* Dr. Karina Meiri, Program Director, 617-636-6707, E-mail: james.dice@tufts.edu. *Application contact:* Kellie Johnston, Associate Director of Admissions, 617-636-6767, Fax: 617-636-0375, E-mail: sackler-school@tufts.edu.

Tufts University, Sackler School of Graduate Biomedical Sciences, Program in Cell, Molecular and Developmental Biology, Medford, MA 02155. Offers PhD. *Faculty:* 35 full-time (11 women). *Students:* 25 full-time (13 women); includes 2 minority (both Asian Americans or Pacific Islanders), 2 international. Average age 29. In 2009, 8 doctorates awarded. Terminal master's awarded for partial completion of doctoral program. *Degree requirements:* For doctorate, thesis/dissertation. *Entrance requirements:* For doctorate, GRE General Test, 3 letters of reference. Additional exam requirements/recommendations for international students: Required—TOEFL. *Application deadline:* For fall admission, 12/15 for domestic and international students. Applications are processed on a rolling basis. Application fee: $70. Electronic applications accepted. *Expenses:* Tuition: Full-time $38,096; part-time $3962 per credit. Required fees: $686; $40 per year. Tuition and fees vary according to course level, course load, degree level, program and student level. *Financial support:* In 2009–10, 25 students received support, including 25 research assistantships with full tuition reimbursements available (averaging $28,500 per year); fellowships, scholarships/grants, health care benefits, and tuition waivers (full) also available. *Faculty research:* Reproduction and hormone action, control of gene expression, cell-matrix and cell-cell interactions, growth control and tumorigenesis, cytoskeleton and contractile proteins. *Unit head:* Dr. John Castellot, Program Director, 617-636-0303, Fax: 617-636-0375, E-mail: john.castellot@tufts.edu. *Application contact:* Kellie Johnston, Associate Director of Admissions, 617-636-6767, Fax: 617-636-0375, E-mail: sackler-school@tufts.edu.

Tulane University, School of Medicine and School of Liberal Arts, Graduate Programs in Biomedical Sciences, Department of Structural and Cellular Biology, New Orleans, LA 70118-5669. Offers MS, PhD, MD/PhD. MS and PhD offered through the Graduate School. *Degree requirements:* For master's, one foreign language, thesis; for doctorate, 2 foreign languages, thesis/dissertation. *Entrance requirements:* For master's, GRE General Test, minimum B average in undergraduate course work; for doctorate, GRE General Test. Additional exam requirements/recommendations for international students: Required—TOEFL. Electronic applications accepted. *Faculty research:* Reproductive endocrinology, visual neuroscience, neural response to altered hormones.

Tulane University, School of Medicine and School of Liberal Arts, Graduate Programs in Biomedical Sciences, Interdisciplinary Graduate Program in Molecular and Cellular Biology, New Orleans, LA 70118-5669. Offers PhD, MD/PhD. PhD offered through the Graduate School. *Degree requirements:* For doctorate, thesis/dissertation. *Entrance requirements:* For doctorate, GRE General Test, GRE Subject Test. Additional exam requirements/recommendations for international students: Required—TOEFL. Electronic applications accepted. *Faculty research:* Developmental biology, neuroscience, virology.

Tulane University, School of Science and Engineering, Department of Cell and Molecular Biology, New Orleans, LA 70118-5669. Offers MS, PhD. Terminal master's awarded for partial completion of doctoral program. *Degree requirements:* For doctorate, thesis/dissertation. *Entrance requirements:* For master's, GRE General Test, minimum B average in undergraduate course work; for doctorate, GRE General Test. Additional exam requirements/recommendations for international students: Required—TOEFL. Electronic applications accepted.

Uniformed Services University of the Health Sciences, School of Medicine, Graduate Programs in the Biomedical Sciences and Public Health, Graduate Program in Molecular and Cell Biology, Bethesda, MD 20814-4799. Offers PhD. *Faculty:* 43 full-time (11 women), 3 part-time/adjunct (0 women). *Students:* 20 full-time (9 women); includes 7 minority (4 Asian Americans or Pacific Islanders, 3 Hispanic Americans), 6 international. Average age 26. 30 applicants, 43% accepted, 8 enrolled. In 2009, 2 doctorates awarded. *Degree requirements:* For doctorate, comprehensive exam, thesis/dissertation, qualifying exam. *Entrance requirements:* For doctorate, GRE General Test, minimum GPA of 3.0. Additional exam requirements/recommendations for international students: Required—TOEFL. *Application deadline:* For fall admission, 1/15 priority date for domestic and international students. Applications are processed on a rolling basis. Application fee: $0. Electronic applications accepted. *Financial support:* In 2009–10, fellowships with full tuition reimbursements (averaging $26,000 per year); scholarships/grants, health care benefits, and tuition waivers (full) also available. *Faculty research:* Immunology, biochemistry, cancer biology, stem cell biology. *Unit head:* Dr. Mary Lou Cutler, Graduate Program Director, 301-295-3453, Fax: 301-295-1996. *Application contact:* Elena Marina Sherman, Graduate Program Coordinator, 301-295-3913, Fax: 301-295-6772, E-mail: elena.sherman@usuhs.mil.

Universidad Central del Caribe, School of Medicine, Program in Biomedical Sciences, Bayamón, PR 00960-6032. Offers anatomy and cell biology (MA, MS); biochemistry (MS); biomedical sciences (MA); microbiology and immunology (MA, MS); pharmacology (MS); physiology (MA, MS).

Université de Montréal, Faculty of Medicine, Department of Pathology and Cellular Biology, Montréal, QC H3C 3J7, Canada. Offers M Sc, PhD. *Faculty:* 40 full-time (9 women), 2 part-time/adjunct (1 woman). *Students:* 10 full-time (6 women), 24 part-time (15 women). 38 applicants, 16% accepted, 6 enrolled. In 2009, 3 master's, 2 doctorates awarded. Terminal master's awarded for partial completion of doctoral program. *Degree requirements:* For master's, thesis; for doctorate, thesis/dissertation, general exam. *Entrance requirements:* For master's and doctorate, proficiency in French, knowledge of English. *Application deadline:* For fall admission, 2/1 priority date for domestic students; for winter admission, 11/1 priority date for domestic students; for spring admission, 2/1 priority date for domestic students. Application fee: $100. Electronic applications accepted. *Financial support:* Tuition waivers (full) available. *Faculty research:* Immunopathology, cardiovascular pathology, oncogenetics, cellular neurocytology, muscular dystrophy. *Unit head:* Dr. Pierre Drapeau, Director, 514-343-6294, Fax: 514-343-5755, E-mail: p.drapeau@umontreal.ca. *Application contact:* Dr. Nicole Leclerc, Responsible for Graduate Studies, 514-343-5657, Fax: 514-343-5775, E-mail: nicole.leclerc@umontreal.ca.

Université de Sherbrooke, Faculty of Medicine and Health Sciences, Graduate Programs in Medicine, Department of Anatomy and Cell Biology, Sherbrooke, QC J1H 5N4, Canada. Offers cell biology (M Sc, PhD). Terminal master's awarded for partial completion of doctoral program. *Degree requirements:* For master's, thesis; for doctorate, thesis/dissertation. Electronic applications accepted. *Faculty research:* Biology of the gut epithelium, signal transduction, gene expression and differentiation, intestinal inflammation, vascular and skeletal muscle cell biology.

Université Laval, Faculty of Medicine, Graduate Programs in Medicine, Programs in Cellular and Molecular Biology, Québec, QC G1K 7P4, Canada. Offers M Sc, PhD. Terminal master's awarded for partial completion of doctoral program. *Degree requirements:* For master's, thesis; for doctorate, comprehensive exam, thesis/dissertation. *Entrance requirements:* For master's and doctorate, knowledge of French, comprehension of written English. Electronic applications accepted. *Faculty research:* Oral bacterial metabolism, sugar transport.

University at Albany, State University of New York, College of Arts and Sciences, Department of Biological Sciences, Specialization in Molecular, Cellular, Developmental, and Neural Biology, Albany, NY 12222-0001. Offers MS, PhD. *Degree requirements:* For master's, one foreign language; for doctorate, one foreign language, thesis/dissertation. *Entrance requirements:* For master's and doctorate, GRE General Test.

University at Albany, State University of New York, School of Public Health, Department of Biomedical Sciences, Program in Cell and Molecular Structure, Albany, NY 12222-0001. Offers MS, PhD. *Degree requirements:* For master's, thesis; for doctorate, thesis/dissertation. *Entrance requirements:* For master's and doctorate, GRE General Test, GRE Subject Test.

University at Buffalo, the State University of New York, Graduate School, Graduate Programs in Cancer Research and Biomedical Sciences at Roswell Park Cancer Institute, Department of Cellular and Molecular Biology at Roswell Park Cancer Institute, Buffalo, NY 14260. Offers cellular molecular biology/genetics (PhD). *Faculty:* 23 full-time (3 women). *Students:* 19 full-time (7 women), 5 part-time (4 women); includes 1 minority (Asian American or Pacific Islander), 7 international. Average age 25. 40 applicants, 25% accepted, 4 enrolled. In 2009, 4 doctorates awarded. *Degree requirements:* For doctorate, thesis/dissertation, exam project. *Entrance requirements:* For doctorate, GRE General Test, minimum B average in undergraduate coursework. Additional exam requirements/recommendations for international students: Required—TOEFL (minimum score 600 paper-based; 250 computer-based; 100 iBT) or IELTS. *Application deadline:* For fall admission, 2/1 priority date for domestic and international students. Applications are processed on a rolling basis. Application fee: $50. Electronic applications accepted. *Financial support:* In 2009–10, 24 students received support, including 4 fellowships with full tuition reimbursements available (averaging $24,000 per year), 17 research assistantships with full tuition reimbursements available (averaging $24,000 per year); health care benefits also available. Financial award application deadline: 2/1; financial award applicants required to submit FAFSA. *Faculty research:* Cancer genetics, chromatin structure and replication, regulation of transcription, human gene mapping, genetic and structural approaches to regulation of gene expression. Total annual research expenditures: $5.5 million. *Unit head:* Dr. Rosemary Elliott, Director of Graduate Studies, 716-845-3277, Fax: 716-845-1698, E-mail: rosemary.elliott@roswellpark.org. *Application contact:* Craig R. Johnson, Director of Admissions, 716-845-2339, Fax: 716-845-8178, E-mail: craig.johnson@roswellpark.org.

The University of Alabama at Birmingham, Graduate Programs in Joint Health Sciences, Program in Cell Biology, Birmingham, AL 35294. Offers PhD. *Degree requirements:* For doctorate, variable foreign language requirement, thesis/dissertation, qualifying exam. *Entrance requirements:* For doctorate, GRE General Test, interview. Electronic applications accepted.

The University of Alabama at Birmingham, Graduate Programs in Joint Health Sciences, Program in Cellular and Molecular Physiology, Birmingham, AL 35294. Offers PhD.

University of Alberta, Faculty of Graduate Studies and Research, Department of Biological Sciences, Edmonton, AB T6G 2E1, Canada. Offers environmental biology and ecology (M Sc, PhD); microbiology and biotechnology (M Sc, PhD); molecular biology and genetics (M Sc, PhD); physiology and cell biology (M Sc, PhD); plant biology (M Sc, PhD); systematics and evolution (M Sc, PhD). *Faculty:* 72 full-time (15 women), 15 part-time/adjunct (4 women). *Students:* 238 full-time (117 women), 32 part-time (15 women), 31 international. 206 applicants, 42% accepted. In 2009, 29 master's, 31 doctorates awarded. Terminal master's awarded for partial completion of doctoral program. *Degree requirements:* For master's, thesis; for doctorate, thesis/dissertation. *Entrance requirements:* Additional exam requirements/recommendations for international students: Required—TOEFL. *Application deadline:* For fall admission, 3/1 priority date for domestic students. Applications are processed on a rolling basis. Application fee: $0. Tuition and fees charges are reported in Canadian dollars. *Expenses:* Tuition, area resident: Full-time $4626 Canadian dollars; part-time $99.72 Canadian dollars per unit. International tuition: $8216 Canadian dollars full-time. Required fees: $3590 Canadian dollars; $99.72 Canadian dollars per unit. $215 Canadian dollars per term. *Financial support:* In 2009–10, 4 research assistantships with partial tuition reimbursements (averaging $12,000 per year), 103 teaching assistantships with partial tuition reimbursements (averaging $12,300 per year) were awarded; career-related internships or fieldwork and scholarships/grants also available. *Unit head:* Laura Frost, Chair, 780-492-1904. *Application contact:* Dr. John P. Chang, Associate Chair for Graduate Studies, 780-492-1257, Fax: 780-492-9457, E-mail: bio.grad.coordinator@ualberta.ca.

University of Alberta, Faculty of Medicine and Dentistry and Faculty of Graduate Studies and Research, Graduate Programs in Medicine, Department of Cell Biology, Edmonton, AB T6G 2E1, Canada. Offers cell and molecular biology (M Sc, PhD). *Faculty:* 13 full-time (3 women), 4 part-time/adjunct (0 women). *Students:* 38 full-time (15 women). Average age 29. 33 applicants. In 2009, 1 master's awarded. Terminal master's awarded for partial completion of doctoral program. *Degree requirements:* For master's, thesis; for doctorate, thesis/dissertation. *Entrance requirements:* For master's and doctorate, 3 letters of reference, curriculum vitae. Additional exam requirements/recommendations for international students: Required—TOEFL (minimum score 600 paper-based; 250 computer-based). *Application deadline:* For fall admission, 4/1 for international students; for winter admission, 8/1 for international students. Applications are processed on a rolling basis. Application fee: $100. Tuition and fees charges are reported in Canadian dollars. *Expenses:* Tuition, area resident: Full-time $4626 Canadian dollars; part-time $99.72 Canadian dollars per unit. International tuition: $8216 Canadian dollars full-time. Required fees: $3590 Canadian dollars; $99.72 Canadian dollars per unit. $215 Canadian dollars per term. *Financial support:* In 2009–10, 16 fellowships with full tuition reimbursements (averaging $20,000 per year), 22 research assistantships with full tuition reimbursements (averaging $17,000 per year) were awarded. *Faculty research:* Protein targeting, membrane trafficking, signal transduction, cell growth and division, cell-cell interaction and development. Total annual research expenditures: $3.5 million. *Unit head:* Dr. Richard A. Rachubinski, Chair, 780-492-9868, Fax: 780-492-9278, E-mail: rick.rachubinski@ualberta.ca. *Application contact:* Dr. Paul Melancon, Graduate Coordinator, 780-492-6183, Fax: 780-492-0450, E-mail: paul.melancon@ualberta.ca.

The University of Arizona, College of Medicine, Graduate Programs in Medicine, Department of Cell Biology and Anatomy, Tucson, AZ 85721. Offers PhD. *Degree requirements:* For doctorate, thesis/dissertation. *Entrance requirements:* For doctorate, GRE General Test. *Expenses:* Tuition, state resident: full-time $9028. Tuition, nonresident: full-time $24,890. *Faculty research:* Heart development, neural development, cellular toxicology and microcirculation; membrane traffic and cytoskeleton; cell-surface receptors.

The University of Arizona, Graduate College, College of Science, Department of Molecular and Cellular Biology, Tucson, AZ 85721. Offers applied biosciences (PSM); molecular and cellular biology (MS, PhD). Evening/weekend programs available. *Faculty:* 10. *Students:* 39 full-time (19 women), 13 part-time (6 women); includes 9 minority (2 American Indian/Alaska Native, 5 Asian Americans or Pacific Islanders, 2 Hispanic Americans), 13 international. Average age 29. 160 applicants, 11% accepted, 9 enrolled. In 2009, 10 master's, 10 doctorates awarded. Terminal master's awarded for partial completion of doctoral program. *Degree requirements:* For master's, thesis; for doctorate, thesis/dissertation. *Entrance requirements:* For master's, 3 letters of recommendation; for doctorate, 3 letters of recommendation, statement of purpose. Additional exam requirements/recommendations for international students: Required—TOEFL (minimum score 600 paper-based; 250 computer-based; 90 iBT), IELTS (minimum score 7). *Application deadline:* For fall admission, 1/1 for domestic and international students. Applications are processed on a rolling basis. Application fee: $75. Electronic applications accepted. *Expenses:* Tuition, state resident: full-time $9028. Tuition, nonresident: full-time $24,890. *Financial support:* In 2009–10, 11 research assistantships with full tuition reimbursements (averaging $20,931 per year), 27 teaching assistantships with full tuition reimbursements (averaging $17,501 per year) were awarded; career-related internships or fieldwork, scholarships/grants, health care benefits, and unspecified assistantships also available. *Faculty research:* Plant molecular biology, cellular and molecular aspects of development, genetics of bacteria and lower eukaryotes. Total annual research expenditures: $7 million. *Unit head:*

Kathleen Dixon, Department Head, 520-621-7563, Fax: 520-621-3709, E-mail: dixonk@email.arizona.edu. *Application contact:* Kathleen Dixon, Department Head, 520-621-7563, Fax: 520-621-3709, E-mail: dixonk@email.arizona.edu.

University of Arkansas, Graduate School, Interdisciplinary Program in Cell and Molecular Biology, Fayetteville, AR 72701-1201. Offers MS, PhD. *Students:* 14 full-time (8 women), 51 part-time (29 women); includes 3 minority (1 African American, 2 Asian Americans or Pacific Islanders), 46 international. In 2009, 1 master's, 5 doctorates awarded. *Degree requirements:* For doctorate, thesis/dissertation. Application fee: $40 ($50 for international students). *Expenses:* Tuition, state resident: full-time $7355; part-time $356.58 per hour. Tuition, nonresident: full-time $17,401; part-time $775.17 per hour. Required fees: $1203. *Financial support:* In 2009–10, 4 fellowships with tuition reimbursements, 10 research assistantships were awarded; teaching assistantships. Financial award application deadline: 4/1; financial award applicants required to submit FAFSA. *Unit head:* Dr. Douglas Rhoads, Head, 479-575-7396, Fax: 479-575-5908, E-mail: drhoads@uark.edu. *Application contact:* Graduate Admissions, 479-575-6246, Fax: 479-575-5908, E-mail: gradinfo@uark.edu.

The University of British Columbia, Faculty of Medicine, Department of Cellular and Physiological Sciences, Division of Anatomy and Cell Biology, Vancouver, BC V6T 1Z1, Canada. Offers M Sc, PhD. *Degree requirements:* For master's, thesis, oral defense; for doctorate, comprehensive exam, thesis/dissertation, oral defense. *Entrance requirements:* Additional exam requirements/recommendations for international students: Required—TOEFL (minimum score 550 paper-based; 213 computer-based), IELTS (minimum score 6.2). Electronic applications accepted. *Faculty research:* Cell and developmental biology, membrane biophysics, cellular immunology, cancer, fetal alcohol syndrome.

University of California, Berkeley, Graduate Division, College of Letters and Science, Department of Molecular and Cell Biology, Berkeley, CA 94720-1500. Offers PhD. *Faculty:* 90 full-time (24 women), 1 part-time/adjunct (0 women). *Students:* 261 full-time (144 women); includes 72 minority (5 African Americans, 43 Asian Americans or Pacific Islanders, 24 Hispanic Americans), 17 international. Average age 26. 562 applicants, 24% accepted, 56 enrolled. In 2009, 38 doctorates awarded. *Degree requirements:* For doctorate, comprehensive exam, thesis/dissertation, qualifying exam, 2 semesters of teaching, 3 seminars. *Entrance requirements:* For doctorate, GRE General Test, GRE Subject Test (recommended), minimum GPA of 3.0. Additional exam requirements/recommendations for international students: Required—TOEFL (minimum score 570 paper-based; 230 computer-based; 68 iBT), IELTS (minimum score 7). *Application deadline:* For fall admission, 12/1 for domestic and international students. Applications are processed on a rolling basis. Application fee: $70 ($90 for international students). Electronic applications accepted. *Financial support:* In 2009–10, 129 students received support, including 7 fellowships with full tuition reimbursements available (averaging $24,100 per year), 159 research assistantships with full tuition reimbursements available (averaging $28,000 per year), 88 teaching assistantships with full tuition reimbursements available (averaging $8,315 per year); scholarships/grants, traineeships, health care benefits, tuition waivers (full), and unspecified assistantships also available. Financial award application deadline: 12/1; financial award applicants required to submit FAFSA. *Faculty research:* Biochemistry and molecular biology, cell and developmental biology, genetics, immunology, neurobiology, genomics. *Unit head:* Dr. James M. Berger, Professor, 510-643-9483. *Application contact:* Berta Parra, Student Affairs Officer, 510-642-5252, Fax: 510-642-7000, E-mail: bparra@berkeley.edu.

University of California, Davis, Graduate Studies, Graduate Group in Cell and Developmental Biology, Davis, CA 95616. Offers MS, PhD. *Degree requirements:* For master's, comprehensive exam (for some programs), thesis (for some programs); for doctorate, thesis/dissertation. *Entrance requirements:* For doctorate, GRE General Test, GRE Subject Test. Additional exam requirements/recommendations for international students: Required—TOEFL (minimum score 550 paper-based; 213 computer-based). Electronic applications accepted. *Faculty research:* Molecular basis of cell function and development.

University of California, Irvine, Office of Graduate Studies, School of Biological Sciences, Department of Developmental and Cell Biology, Irvine, CA 92697. Offers biological sciences (MS, PhD). Students apply through the Graduate Program in Molecular Biology, Genetics, and Biochemistry. *Students:* 46 full-time (22 women), 1 part-time (0 women); includes 24 minority (1 African American, 2 American Indian/Alaska Native, 13 Asian Americans or Pacific Islanders, 8 Hispanic Americans), 5 international. Average age 29. In 2009, 3 master's, 7 doctorates awarded. *Degree requirements:* For doctorate, thesis/dissertation. *Entrance requirements:* For master's and doctorate, GRE General Test, GRE Subject Test, minimum GPA of 3.0. Additional exam requirements/recommendations for international students: Required—TOEFL (minimum score 550 paper-based; 213 computer-based). *Application deadline:* For fall admission, 12/15 priority date for domestic and international students. Application fee: $70 ($90 for international students). Electronic applications accepted. *Financial support:* Fellowships, research assistantships with full tuition reimbursements, teaching assistantships, institutionally sponsored loans, traineeships, health care benefits, and unspecified assistantships available. Financial award application deadline: 3/1; financial award applicants required to submit FAFSA. *Faculty research:* Genetics and development, oncogene signaling pathways, gene regulation, tissue regeneration and molecular genetics. *Unit head:* Dr. Arthur D. Lander, Chair, 949-824-1008, Fax: 949-824-4709, E-mail: adlander@uci.edu. *Application contact:* Kimberly McKinney, Administrator, 949-824-8145, Fax: 949-824-1965, E-mail: kamckinn@uci.edu.

University of California, Los Angeles, David Geffen School of Medicine and Graduate Division, Graduate Programs in Medicine, Department of Molecular, Cell and Developmental Biology, Los Angeles, CA 90095. Offers PhD. *Degree requirements:* For doctorate, thesis/dissertation, qualifying exams. *Entrance requirements:* For doctorate, GRE General Test, GRE Subject Test. Additional exam requirements/recommendations for international students: Required—TOEFL.

University of California, Los Angeles, David Geffen School of Medicine and Graduate Division, Graduate Programs in Medicine, Department of Neurobiology, Los Angeles, CA 90095. Offers anatomy and cell biology (PhD). *Degree requirements:* For doctorate, thesis/dissertation, oral and written qualifying exams. *Entrance requirements:* For doctorate, GRE General Test, GRE Subject Test, bachelor's degree in physical or biological science. *Faculty research:* Neuroendocrinology, neurophysiology.

University of California, Los Angeles, Graduate Division, College of Letters and Science and David Geffen School of Medicine, UCLA ACCESS to Programs in the Molecular, Cellular and Integrative Life Sciences, Los Angeles, CA 90095. Offers biochemistry and molecular biology (PhD); biological chemistry (PhD); cellular and molecular pathology (PhD); human genetics (PhD); microbiology, immunology, and molecular genetics (PhD); molecular biology (PhD); molecular toxicology (PhD); molecular, cellular and integrative physiology (PhD); neurobiology (PhD); oral biology (PhD); physiology (PhD). ACCESS is an umbrella program for first-year coursework in 12 PhD programs. *Students:* 39 full-time (25 women); includes 14 minority (1 African American, 1 American Indian/Alaska Native, 8 Asian Americans or Pacific Islanders, 4 Hispanic Americans), 10 international. Average age 25. 437 applicants, 22% accepted, 30 enrolled. *Degree requirements:* For doctorate, thesis/dissertation, oral and written qualifying exams. *Entrance requirements:* For doctorate, GRE General Test, minimum undergraduate GPA of 3.0. Additional exam requirements/recommendations for international students: Required—TOEFL. *Application deadline:* For fall admission, 12/15 for domestic and international students. Application fee: $70 ($90 for international students). Electronic applications accepted. *Financial support:* In 2009–10, 56 fellowships with full and partial tuition reimbursements, 16 research assistantships with full and partial tuition reimbursements were awarded; teaching assistantships with full and partial tuition reimbursements, Federal Work-Study, institutionally sponsored loans, scholarships/grants, health care benefits, tuition waivers (full and partial), and unspecified assistantships also available. Financial award application deadline: 3/1; financial award applicants required to submit FAFSA. *Faculty research:* Molecular, cellular, and developmental biology; immunology; microbiology; integrative biology. *Unit head:* Dr. Greg I. Payne, Chair, 310-206-3121. *Application contact:* Coordinator, 310-206-3121, Fax: 310-206-5280, E-mail: uclaaccess@mednet.ucla.edu.

See Close-Up on page 239.

University of California, Riverside, Graduate Division, Program in Cell, Molecular, and Developmental Biology, Riverside, CA 92521-0102. Offers MS, PhD. *Faculty:* 55 full-time (18 women). *Students:* 47 full-time (28 women); includes 15 minority (2 African Americans, 11 Asian Americans or Pacific Islanders, 2 Hispanic Americans), 15 international. Average age 29. In 2009, 7 doctorates awarded. Terminal master's awarded for partial completion of doctoral program. *Degree requirements:* For master's, thesis, oral defense of thesis; for doctorate, thesis/dissertation, oral defense of thesis, qualifying exams, 2 quarters of teaching experience. *Entrance requirements:* For master's and doctorate, GRE General Test, minimum GPA of 3.2. Additional exam requirements/recommendations for international students: Required—TOEFL (minimum score 550 paper-based; 213 computer-based; 80 iBT). *Application deadline:* For fall admission, 1/5 priority date for domestic and international students. Applications are processed on a rolling basis. Application fee: $60 ($75 for international students). Electronic applications accepted. *Financial support:* In 2009–10, fellowships with full and partial tuition reimbursements (averaging $24,000 per year), research assistantships with full and partial tuition reimbursements (averaging $21,847 per year), teaching assistantships with full and partial tuition reimbursements (averaging $18,485 per year) were awarded; scholarships/grants, traineeships, health care benefits, tuition waivers (partial), and unspecified assistantships also available. Support available to part-time students. Financial award application deadline: 1/5. *Unit head:* Dr. Peter Atkinson, Director, 951-827-4782, E-mail: norman@ucr.edu. *Application contact:* Kathy Redd, Graduate Program Assistant, 800-735-0717, Fax: 951-827-5517, E-mail: cmdb@ucr.edu.

University of California, San Diego, Office of Graduate Studies, Division of Biological Sciences, Program in Cell and Developmental Biology, La Jolla, CA 92093-0348. Offers PhD. Offered in association with the Salk Institute. *Degree requirements:* For doctorate, thesis/dissertation, qualifying exam. Electronic applications accepted.

University of California, San Diego, Office of Graduate Studies, Division of Biological Sciences, Program in Molecular and Cellular Biology, La Jolla, CA 92093. Offers PhD. Offered in association with the Salk Institute. *Degree requirements:* For doctorate, thesis/dissertation, qualifying exam. Electronic applications accepted.

University of California, San Diego, School of Medicine and Office of Graduate Studies, Graduate Studies in Biomedical Sciences, Program in Molecular Cell Biology, La Jolla, CA 92093. Offers PhD. *Degree requirements:* For doctorate, thesis/dissertation, qualifying exam. *Entrance requirements:* For doctorate, GRE General Test. Additional exam requirements/recommendations for international students: Required—TOEFL. Electronic applications accepted. *Faculty research:* Molecular and cellular pharmacology, cell and organ physiology.

University of California, San Diego, School of Medicine and Office of Graduate Studies, Graduate Studies in Biomedical Sciences, Regulatory Biology Program, La Jolla, CA 92093. Offers PhD. *Degree requirements:* For doctorate, thesis/dissertation, 2 qualifying exams. *Entrance requirements:* For doctorate, GRE General Test, GRE Subject Test. Additional exam requirements/recommendations for international students: Required—TOEFL. Electronic applications accepted. *Faculty research:* Eukaryotic regulatory and molecular biology, molecular and cellular pharmacology, cell and organ physiology.

University of California, San Francisco, Graduate Division and School of Medicine, Department of Biochemistry and Biophysics, Program in Cell Biology, San Francisco, CA 94143. Offers PhD, MD/PhD. *Degree requirements:* For doctorate, thesis/dissertation. *Entrance requirements:* For doctorate, GRE General Test, GRE Subject Test. Additional exam requirements/recommendations for international students: Required—TOEFL. *Expenses:* Contact institution.

University of California, Santa Barbara, Graduate Division, College of Letters and Sciences, Division of Mathematics, Life, and Physical Sciences, Department of Molecular, Cellular, and Developmental Biology, Santa Barbara, CA 93106-9625. Offers MA, PhD, MA/PhD. *Faculty:* 21 full-time (3 women), 7 part-time/adjunct (2 women). *Students:* 60 full-time (31 women). Average age 27. 44 applicants, 23% accepted, 6 enrolled. In 2009, 8 master's, 7 doctorates awarded. *Degree requirements:* For master's, comprehensive exam (for some programs), thesis (for some programs); for doctorate, comprehensive exam, thesis/dissertation. *Entrance requirements:* For master's, GRE General Test, GRE Subject Test, 3 letters of recommendation, resume/curriculum vitae; for doctorate, GRE General Test, GRE Subject Test, 3 letters of recommendation, statement of purpose, personal achievements/contributions statement, resume/curriculum vitae, transcripts for post-secondary institutions attended. Additional exam requirements/recommendations for international students: Required—TOEFL (minimum score 610 paper-based; 253 computer-based; 102 iBT) or IELTS (minimum score 7). *Application deadline:* For fall admission, 12/15 for domestic and international students. Application fee: $70 ($90 for international students). Electronic applications accepted. *Financial support:* In 2009–10, 60 students received support, including 19 fellowships with full and partial tuition reimbursements available (averaging $9,800 per year), 39 research assistantships with full and partial tuition reimbursements available (averaging $9,700 per year), 48 teaching assistantships with partial tuition reimbursements available (averaging $7,500 per year); career-related internships or fieldwork, Federal Work-Study, institutionally sponsored loans, scholarships/grants, traineeships, health care benefits, and unspecified assistantships also available. Financial award application deadline: 12/15; financial award applicants required to submit FAFSA. *Faculty research:* Microbiology, neurobiology (including stem cell research), developmental, virology, cell biology. *Unit head:* Dr. Dennis O. Clegg, Chair, 805-893-8490, Fax: 805-893-4724, E-mail: clegg@lifesci.ucsb.edu. *Application contact:* Tony L. Tieu, Staff Graduate Program Advisor, 805-893-8499, Fax: 805-893-4724, E-mail: tieu@lifesci.ucsb.edu.

University of California, Santa Cruz, Division of Graduate Studies, Division of Physical and Biological Sciences, Program in Molecular, Cellular, and Developmental Biology, Santa Cruz, CA 95064. Offers MA, PhD. *Degree requirements:* For master's, thesis; for doctorate, thesis/dissertation, qualifying exam. *Entrance requirements:* For master's and doctorate, GRE General Test, 3 letters of recommendation, interview. Additional exam requirements/recommendations for international students: Required—TOEFL (minimum score 550 paper-based; 220 computer-based; 83 iBT). Electronic applications accepted.

University of Chicago, Division of the Biological Sciences, Department of Molecular Biosciences, Graduate Program in Cell and Molecular Biology, Chicago, IL 60637-1513. Offers PhD. *Faculty:* 31 full-time (8 women). *Students:* 28 full-time (13 women); includes 6 minority (4 Asian Americans or Pacific Islanders, 2 Hispanic Americans). Average age 29. 39 applicants, 10% accepted, 4 enrolled. In 2009, 4 doctorates awarded. *Degree requirements:* For doctorate, thesis/dissertation, ethics class, 2 teaching assistantships. *Entrance requirements:* For doctorate, GRE General Test. Additional exam requirements/recommendations for international students: Required—TOEFL (minimum score 600 paper-based; 250 computer-based; 104 iBT), IELTS (minimum score 7). *Application deadline:* For fall admission, 12/1 priority date for domestic and international students. Application fee: $55. Electronic applications accepted. *Financial support:* In 2009–10, 28 students received support, including fellowships (averaging $29,781 per year), research assistantships (averaging $29,781 per year); institutionally sponsored loans, scholarships/grants, traineeships, and health care benefits also available. Financial award applicants required to submit FAFSA. *Faculty research:* Gene expression, chromosome structure, animal viruses, plant molecular genetics. Total annual research expenditures: $8 million. *Unit head:* Dr. Richard Fehon, Chair, 773-702-5694, E-mail: rfehon@uchicago.edu. *Application contact:* Kristine Gaston, Graduate Administrative Director, 773-702-8037, Fax: 773-702-3172, E-mail: kristine@bsd.uchicago.edu.

University of Cincinnati, Graduate School, College of Medicine, Graduate Programs in Biomedical Sciences, Graduate Program in Cell and Cancer Biology, Cincinnati, OH 45221.

Cell Biology

University of Cincinnati *(continued)*

Offers PhD. *Degree requirements:* For doctorate, thesis/dissertation, qualifying exam. *Entrance requirements:* For doctorate, GRE General Test. Additional exam requirements/recommendations for international students: Required—TOEFL. Electronic applications accepted. *Faculty research:* Cancer biology, cell and molecular biology, breast cancer, pancreatic cancer, drug discovery.

University of Colorado at Boulder, Graduate School, College of Arts and Sciences, Department of Molecular, Cellular, and Developmental Biology, Boulder, CO 80309. Offers cellular structure and function (MA, PhD); developmental biology (MA, PhD); molecular biology (MA, PhD). *Faculty:* 27 full-time (7 women). *Students:* 29 full-time (15 women), 45 part-time (18 women); includes 7 minority (2 American Indian/Alaska Native, 1 Asian American or Pacific Islander, 4 Hispanic Americans), 15 international. Average age 28. 210 applicants, 5% accepted, 11 enrolled. In 2009, 3 master's, 7 doctorates awarded. Terminal master's awarded for partial completion of doctoral program. *Degree requirements:* For master's, comprehensive exam, thesis or alternative; for doctorate, comprehensive exam, thesis/dissertation. *Entrance requirements:* For master's, GRE General Test, GRE Subject Test, minimum undergraduate GPA of 3.0; for doctorate, GRE General Test, GRE Subject Test. *Application deadline:* For fall admission, 1/1 for domestic students, 12/1 for international students. Application fee: $50 ($60 for international students). *Financial support:* In 2009–10, 40 fellowships (averaging $11,628 per year), 53 research assistantships (averaging $14,700 per year) were awarded; tuition waivers (full) also available. Financial award application deadline: 2/1. *Faculty research:* Molecular biology of RNA and DNA, molecular genetics, cell motility and cytoskeleton, cell membranes, developmental genetics, human genetics. Total annual research expenditures: $15.5 million.

University of Colorado Denver, School of Medicine, Program in Cell Biology, Stem Cells, and Developmental Biology, Denver, CO 80217-3364. Offers cell and developmental biology (PhD); cell biology, stem cells and development (PhD); reproductive sciences (PhD). *Students:* 28 full-time (18 women); includes 2 minority (1 Asian American or Pacific Islander, 1 Hispanic American), 8 international. In 2009, 3 doctorates awarded. *Degree requirements:* For doctorate, thesis/dissertation. *Entrance requirements:* For doctorate, GRE, minimum GPA of 3.0, 3 letters of reference. Additional exam requirements/recommendations for international students: Required—TOEFL (minimum score 550 paper-based; 213 computer-based). *Application deadline:* For fall admission, 1/15 for domestic students. Application fee: $50. Electronic applications accepted. *Financial support:* Fellowships, research assistantships, teaching assistantships, Federal Work-Study and institutionally sponsored loans available. Support available to part-time students. Financial award application deadline: 3/15; financial award applicants required to submit FAFSA. *Faculty research:* Human disease, stem cell biology, neuroscience, molecular biology. Total annual research expenditures: $5.7 million. *Unit head:* Dr. Karl Pfenninger, Chair, 303-724-3466, E-mail: karl.pfenninger@ucdenver.edu. *Application contact:* Carmel Hardberg, Program Administrator, 303-724-3426, Fax: 303-724-3420, E-mail: carmel.harberg@ucdenver.edu.

University of Connecticut, Graduate School, College of Liberal Arts and Sciences, Department of Molecular and Cell Biology, Field of Cell and Developmental Biology, Storrs, CT 06269. Offers MS, PhD. *Faculty:* 31 full-time (9 women). *Students:* 42 full-time (16 women), 2 part-time (1 woman); includes 4 minority (1 African American, 2 Asian Americans or Pacific Islanders, 1 Hispanic American), 16 international. Average age 28. 72 applicants, 14% accepted, 5 enrolled. In 2009, 5 master's, 1 doctorate awarded. *Degree requirements:* For doctorate, thesis/dissertation. *Entrance requirements:* For master's and doctorate, GRE General Test, GRE Subject Test. Additional exam requirements/recommendations for international students: Required—TOEFL (minimum score 550 paper-based; 213 computer-based). *Application deadline:* For fall admission, 2/1 priority date for domestic and international students; for spring admission, 11/1 for domestic students, 10/1 for international students. Applications are processed on a rolling basis. Application fee: $55. Electronic applications accepted. *Expenses:* Tuition, state resident: full-time $4725; part-time $525 per credit. Tuition, nonresident: full-time $12,267; part-time $1363 per credit. Required fees: $346 per semester. Tuition and fees vary according to course load. *Financial support:* In 2009–10, 16 research assistantships with full tuition reimbursements, 21 teaching assistantships with full tuition reimbursements were awarded; fellowships, Federal Work-Study, scholarships/grants, health care benefits, and unspecified assistantships also available. Financial award application deadline: 2/1; financial award applicants required to submit FAFSA. *Unit head:* David Benson, Head, 860-486-4258, Fax: 860-486-4331, E-mail: david.benson@uconn.edu. *Application contact:* Anne St. Onje, Graduate Coordinator, 860-486-4314, Fax: 860-486-3943, E-mail: anne.st_onje@uconn.edu.

University of Connecticut Health Center, Graduate School, Graduate Program in Cell Analysis and Modeling, Farmington, CT 06030. Offers PhD.

University of Connecticut Health Center, Graduate School, Programs in Biomedical Sciences, Program in Cell Biology, Farmington, CT 06030. Offers PhD, DMD/PhD, MD/PhD. *Faculty:* 57. *Students:* 26 full-time (17 women); includes 2 minority (1 American Indian/Alaska Native, 1 Asian American or Pacific Islander), 7 international. Average age 28. 165 applicants, 35% accepted. In 2009, 5 doctorates awarded. *Degree requirements:* For doctorate, comprehensive exam, thesis/dissertation. *Entrance requirements:* For doctorate, GRE General Test. Additional exam requirements/recommendations for international students: Required—TOEFL (minimum score 600 paper-based; 250 computer-based). *Application deadline:* For fall admission, 12/15 for domestic students. Application fee: $55. Electronic applications accepted. *Financial support:* In 2009–10, 26 students received support, including 26 research assistantships with tuition reimbursements available (averaging $27,000 per year); fellowships, health care benefits also available. *Faculty research:* Vascular biology, computational biology, cytoskeleton and molecular motors, reproductive biology, signal transduction. *Unit head:* Dr. Kevin Claffey, Director, 860-679-8713, Fax: 860-679-1201, E-mail: claffey@nso2.uchc.edu. *Application contact:* Tricia Avolt, Graduate Admissions Coordinator, 860-679-2175, Fax: 860-679-1899, E-mail: robertson@nso2.uchc.edu.

See Close-Up on page 241.

University of Delaware, College of Arts and Sciences, Department of Biological Sciences, Newark, DE 19716. Offers biotechnology (MS); cancer biology (MS, PhD); cell and extracellular matrix biology (MS, PhD); cell and systems physiology (MS, PhD); developmental biology (MS, PhD); ecology and evolution (MS, PhD); microbiology (MS, PhD); molecular biology and genetics (MS, PhD). Terminal master's awarded for partial completion of doctoral program. *Degree requirements:* For master's, thesis, preliminary exam; for doctorate, comprehensive exam, thesis/dissertation, preliminary exam. *Entrance requirements:* For master's and doctorate, GRE General Test. Additional exam requirements/recommendations for international students: Required—TOEFL (minimum score 600 paper-based; 250 computer-based); Recommended—TWE. Electronic applications accepted. *Faculty research:* Microorganisms, bone, cancer metastasis, developmental biology, cell biology, DNA.

University of Florida, College of Medicine and Graduate School, Interdisciplinary Program in Biomedical Sciences, Concentration in Molecular Cell Biology, Gainesville, FL 32611. Offers PhD. *Degree requirements:* For doctorate, thesis/dissertation. *Entrance requirements:* For doctorate, GRE General Test, minimum GPA of 3.0. Additional exam requirements/recommendations for international students: Required—TOEFL. Electronic applications accepted.

See Close-Up on page 245.

University of Florida, Graduate School, College of Agricultural and Life Sciences, Department of Microbiology and Cell Science, Gainesville, FL 32611. Offers biochemistry and molecular biology (MS, PhD); microbiology and cell science (MS, PhD). *Degree requirements:* For doctorate, thesis/dissertation. *Entrance requirements:* For master's and doctorate, GRE General Test, minimum GPA of 3.0. Electronic applications accepted. *Faculty research:* Biomass conversion, membrane and cell wall chemistry, plant biochemistry and genetics.

University of Florida, Interdisciplinary Concentration in Animal Molecular and Cellular Biology, Gainesville, FL 32611. Offers MS, PhD. Program offered by College of Agricultural and Life Sciences, College of Liberal Arts and Sciences, College of Medicine, and College of Veterinary Medicine.

University of Georgia, Graduate School, College of Arts and Sciences, Department of Cellular Biology, Athens, GA 30602. Offers MS, PhD. *Faculty:* 16 full-time (5 women), 2 part-time/adjunct (1 woman). *Students:* 35 full-time (21 women), 5 part-time (4 women); includes 6 minority (5 African Americans, 1 American Indian/Alaska Native), 19 international. 44 applicants, 27% accepted, 5 enrolled. In 2009, 4 master's, 6 doctorates awarded. *Degree requirements:* For master's, thesis; for doctorate, one foreign language, thesis/dissertation. *Entrance requirements:* For master's and doctorate, GRE General Test. *Application deadline:* For fall admission, 7/1 priority date for domestic students; for spring admission, 11/15 for domestic students. Application fee: $50. Electronic applications accepted. *Expenses:* Tuition, state resident: full-time $6000; part-time $250 per credit hour. Tuition, nonresident: full-time $20,904; part-time $871 per credit hour. Required fees: $730 per semester. *Financial support:* Fellowships, research assistantships, teaching assistantships, unspecified assistantships available. *Unit head:* Dr. Mark A. Farmer, Head, 706-542-3383, E-mail: farmer@cb.uga.edu. *Application contact:* Dr. Marcus Fechheimer, Graduate Coordinator, 706-542-3338, Fax: 706-542-4271, E-mail: fechheim@cb.uga.edu.

University of Guelph, Graduate Program Services, College of Biological Science, Department of Molecular and Cellular Biology, Guelph, ON N1G 2W1, Canada. Offers biochemistry (M Sc, PhD); biophysics (M Sc, PhD); botany (M Sc, PhD); microbiology (M Sc, PhD); molecular biology and genetics (M Sc, PhD). *Degree requirements:* For master's, thesis, research proposal; for doctorate, comprehensive exam, thesis/dissertation, research proposal. *Entrance requirements:* For master's, minimum B-average during previous 2 years of coursework; for doctorate, minimum A-average. Additional exam requirements/recommendations for international students: Required—TOEFL (minimum score 550 paper-based; 213 computer-based), IELTS (minimum score 6.5). Electronic applications accepted. *Faculty research:* Physiology, structure, genetics, and ecology of microbes; virology and microbial technology.

University of Illinois at Chicago, College of Medicine and Graduate College, Graduate Programs in Medicine, Department of Anatomy and Cell Biology, Chicago, IL 60607-7128. Offers neuroscience (PhD), including cellular and systems neuroscience and cell biology; MD/PhD. *Degree requirements:* For doctorate, preliminary oral examination, dissertation and oral defense. *Entrance requirements:* For doctorate, GRE General Test, minimum GPA of 2.75, 3 letters of recommendation, personal statement. Additional exam requirements/recommendations for international students: Required—TOEFL (minimum score 550 paper-based; 213 computer-based). Electronic applications accepted. *Faculty research:* Synapses, axonal transport, neurodegenerative diseases.

See Close-Up on page 401.

University of Illinois at Urbana–Champaign, Graduate College, College of Liberal Arts and Sciences, School of Molecular and Cellular Biology, Department of Cell and Developmental Biology, Champaign, IL 61820. Offers PhD. *Faculty:* 15 full-time (4 women), 1 (woman) part-time/adjunct. *Students:* 49 full-time (25 women); includes 6 minority (4 Asian Americans or Pacific Islanders, 2 Hispanic Americans), 27 international. In 2009, 16 doctorates awarded. *Entrance requirements:* For doctorate, GRE, minimum GPA of 3.0. Additional exam requirements/recommendations for international students: Required—TOEFL (minimum score 590 paper-based; 243 computer-based). *Application deadline:* Applications are processed on a rolling basis. Application fee: $60 ($75 for international students). Electronic applications accepted. *Financial support:* In 2009–10, 7 fellowships, 46 research assistantships, 25 teaching assistantships were awarded; tuition waivers (full and partial) also available. *Unit head:* Andrew Belmont, Head, 217-244-2311, Fax: 217-244-1648, E-mail: asbel@illinois.edu. *Application contact:* Delynn Carter, Assistant to the Head, 217-244-8116, Fax: 217-244-1648, E-mail: dmcarter@illinois.edu.

The University of Iowa, Graduate College, College of Liberal Arts and Sciences, Department of Biology, Iowa City, IA 52242-1316. Offers biology (MS, PhD); cell and developmental biology (MS, PhD); evolution (MS, PhD); genetics (MS, PhD); neurobiology (MS, PhD); plant biology (MS, PhD). Terminal master's awarded for partial completion of doctoral program. *Degree requirements:* For master's, thesis optional, exam; for doctorate, comprehensive exam, thesis/dissertation. *Entrance requirements:* For master's and doctorate, GRE General Test, minimum GPA of 3.0. Additional exam requirements/recommendations for international students: Required—TOEFL (minimum score 600 paper-based; 250 computer-based; 100 iBT). Electronic applications accepted. *Faculty research:* Developmental neurobiology, evolutionary biology, signal transduction, cell motility, molecular genetics (plant and animal).

The University of Iowa, Graduate College, Program in Molecular and Cellular Biology, Iowa City, IA 52242-1316. Offers PhD, MD/PhD. *Degree requirements:* For doctorate, comprehensive exam, thesis/dissertation. *Entrance requirements:* For doctorate, GRE General Test, minimum GPA of 3.0. Additional exam requirements/recommendations for international students: Required—TOEFL (minimum score 600 paper-based; 250 computer-based; 100 iBT). Electronic applications accepted. *Faculty research:* Regulation of gene expression, inherited human genetic diseases, signal transduction mechanisms, structural biology and function.

The University of Iowa, Roy J. and Lucille A. Carver College of Medicine and Graduate College, Graduate Programs in Medicine, Department of Anatomy and Cell Biology, Iowa City, IA 52242-1316. Offers PhD. *Faculty:* 19 full-time (4 women). *Students:* 12 full-time (5 women); includes 1 minority (Asian American or Pacific Islander), 1 international. Average age 28. 154 applicants, 0% accepted. In 2009, 2 doctorates awarded. *Degree requirements:* For doctorate, comprehensive exam, thesis/dissertation. *Entrance requirements:* For doctorate, GRE General Test, minimum GPA of 3.0. Additional exam requirements/recommendations for international students: Required—TOEFL (minimum score 600 paper-based; 250 computer-based; 100 iBT). *Application deadline:* For fall admission, 1/15 priority date for domestic and international students. Applications are processed on a rolling basis. Application fee: $60 ($85 for international students). Electronic applications accepted. *Financial support:* In 2009–10, 12 students received support, including 2 fellowships with full tuition reimbursements available (averaging $23,500 per year), 7 research assistantships with full tuition reimbursements available (averaging $23,500 per year), teaching assistantships with full tuition reimbursements available (averaging $23,500 per year); institutionally sponsored loans, scholarships/grants, and health care benefits also available. Financial award application deadline: 3/1. *Faculty research:* Biology of differentiation and transformation, developmental and vascular cell biology, neurobiology. Total annual research expenditures: $5.8 million. *Unit head:* Dr. John F. Engelhardt, Professor and Head, 319-335-7744, Fax: 319-335-7198, E-mail: john-engelhardt@uiowa.edu. *Application contact:* Julie A. Stark, Program Assistant, 319-335-7744, Fax: 319-335-7198, E-mail: julie-stark@uiowa.edu.

The University of Kansas, Graduate Studies, College of Liberal Arts and Sciences, Department of Molecular Biosciences, Lawrence, KS 66044. Offers biochemistry and biophysics (MA, PhD); microbiology (MA, PhD); molecular, cellular, and developmental biology (MA, PhD). *Students:* 58 full-time (30 women), 2 part-time (1 woman); includes 4 minority (1 American Indian/Alaska Native, 1 Asian American or Pacific Islander, 2 Hispanic Americans), 24 international. Average age 27. 49 applicants, 29% accepted, 4 enrolled. In 2009, 2 master's, 7 doctorates awarded. Terminal master's awarded for partial completion of doctoral program. *Degree requirements:* For master's, comprehensive exam, thesis; for doctorate, comprehensive exam, thesis/dissertation. *Entrance requirements:* For master's and doctorate, GRE General Test. Additional exam requirements/recommendations for international students: Required—TOEFL (minimum score 24 iBT). *Application deadline:* For fall admission, 12/15 for domestic and international students. Application fee: $45 ($55 for international students). Electronic applications accepted. *Expenses:* Tuition, state resident: full-time $6492; part-time $270.50 per credit hour. Tuition, nonresident: full-time $15,510; part-time $646.25 per credit hour.

Required fees: $847; $70.56 per credit hour. Tuition and fees vary according to course load and program. *Financial support:* Fellowships with tuition reimbursements, research assistantships with tuition reimbursements, teaching assistantships with tuition reimbursements, health care benefits and unspecified assistantships available. Financial award application deadline: 3/1. *Faculty research:* Structure and function of proteins, genetics of organism development, molecular genetics, neurophysiology, molecular virology and pathogenics, developmental biology, cell biology. *Unit head:* Dr. Mark Richter, Chair, 785-864-4311, Fax: 785-864-5294, E-mail: richter@ku.edu. *Application contact:* John P. Connolly, Graduate Program Assistant, 785-864-4311, Fax: 785-864-5294, E-mail: jconnolly@ku.edu.

The University of Kansas, University of Kansas Medical Center, School of Medicine, Department of Anatomy and Cell Biology, Kansas City, KS 66160. Offers MA, PhD, MD/PhD. *Faculty:* 23 full-time, 9 part-time/adjunct. *Students:* 2 full-time (1 woman), 12 part-time (10 women); includes 2 minority (both Hispanic Americans), 5 international. Average age 26. In 2009, 4 doctorates awarded. Terminal master's awarded for partial completion of doctoral program. *Degree requirements:* For master's, comprehensive oral exam, oral defense of thesis; for doctorate, comprehensive exam, thesis/dissertation. *Entrance requirements:* For master's and doctorate, GRE. Additional exam requirements/recommendations for international students: Required—TOEFL. *Application deadline:* For fall admission, 1/15 priority date for domestic students. Applications are processed on a rolling basis. Application fee: $0. Electronic applications accepted. *Expenses:* Tuition, state resident: full-time $6492; part-time $270.50 per credit hour. Tuition, nonresident: full-time $15,510; part-time $646.25 per credit hour. Required fees: $847; $70.56 per credit hour. Tuition and fees vary according to course load and program. *Financial support:* In 2009–10, 13 students received support, including 9 research assistantships with full tuition reimbursements available (averaging $21,700 per year), 4 teaching assistantships with full tuition reimbursements available (averaging $21,700 per year); fellowships, institutionally sponsored loans, health care benefits, and unspecified assistantships also available. *Faculty research:* Development of the synapse and neuromuscular junction, pain perception and diabetic neuropathies, cardiovascular and kidney development, reproductive immunology, post-fertilization signaling events. Total annual research expenditures: $9.2 million. *Unit head:* Dr. Dale R. Abrahamson, Chairman, 913-588-7000, Fax: 913-588-2710, E-mail: dabrahamson@kumc.edu. *Application contact:* Dr. Douglas Wright, Professor, 913-588-2713, Fax: 913-588-2710, E-mail: dwright@kumc.edu.

University of Maryland, Baltimore, Graduate School, Graduate Program in Life Sciences, Program in Molecular Medicine, Baltimore, MD 21201. Offers cancer biology (PhD); cell and molecular physiology (PhD); human genetics and genomic medicine (PhD); molecular medicine (MS); molecular toxicology and pharmacology (PhD); MD/PhD. *Students:* 61 full-time (37 women), 9 part-time (5 women); includes 19 minority (7 African Americans, 9 Asian Americans or Pacific Islanders, 3 Hispanic Americans), 8 international. Average age 26. 324 applicants, 15% accepted, 20 enrolled. In 2009, 4 master's, 1 doctorate awarded. *Entrance requirements:* Additional exam requirements/recommendations for international students: Required—TOEFL (minimum score 600 paper-based; 100 iBT); Recommended—IELTS (minimum score 7). *Application deadline:* For fall admission, 1/15 for domestic and international students. Application fee: $50. Electronic applications accepted. *Expenses:* Tuition, state resident: full-time $7290; part-time $405 per credit hour. Tuition, nonresident: full-time $12,780; part-time $710 per credit hour. Required fees: $774; $10 per credit hour. $297 per semester. Tuition and fees vary according to course load, degree level and program. *Financial support:* In 2009–10, research assistantships with partial tuition reimbursements (averaging $25,000 per year); fellowships also available. Financial award application deadline: 3/1. *Unit head:* Dr. Dudley Strickland, Director, 410-706-8010, E-mail: dstrickland@som.umaryland.edu. *Application contact:* Sharron Graves, Program Coordinator, 410-706-6044, Fax: 410-706-6040, E-mail: sgraves@som.umaryland.edu.

University of Maryland, Baltimore County, Graduate School, College of Natural and Mathematical Sciences, Department of Biological Sciences, Program in Molecular and Cell Biology, Baltimore, MD 21250. Offers PhD. *Faculty:* 24 full-time (10 women), 1 part-time/adjunct (0 women). *Students:* 16 full-time (11 women); includes 9 minority (2 African Americans, 7 Asian Americans or Pacific Islanders). Average age 27. 31 applicants, 35% accepted, 0 enrolled. In 2009, 1 doctorate awarded. *Degree requirements:* For doctorate, thesis/dissertation. *Entrance requirements:* For doctorate, GRE General Test, GRE Subject Test, minimum GPA of 3.0. Additional exam requirements/recommendations for international students: Required—TOEFL. *Application deadline:* For fall admission, 1/15 for domestic students, 12/15 for international students. Applications are processed on a rolling basis. Application fee: $50. Electronic applications accepted. *Financial support:* In 2009–10, fellowships with full tuition reimbursements (averaging $23,000 per year), research assistantships with full tuition reimbursements (averaging $22,300 per year), teaching assistantships with full tuition reimbursements (averaging $21,300 per year) were awarded. *Unit head:* Dr. Jeff Leips, Director, 410-455-3669, Fax: 410-455-3875, E-mail: biograd@umbc.edu. *Application contact:* Dr. Phyllis Robinson, Director, 410-455-3669, Fax: 410-455-3875, E-mail: biograd@umbc.edu.

University of Maryland, College Park, Academic Affairs, College of Chemical and Life Sciences, Department of Cell Biology and Molecular Genetics, Program in Cell Biology and Molecular Genetics, College Park, MD 20742. Offers MS, PhD. *Faculty:* 72 full-time (26 women), 5 part-time/adjunct (2 women). *Students:* 77 full-time (44 women), 4 part-time (2 women); includes 9 minority (3 African Americans, 3 Asian Americans or Pacific Islanders, 3 Hispanic Americans), 25 international. 226 applicants, 13% accepted, 15 enrolled. In 2009, 4 master's, 9 doctorates awarded. *Degree requirements:* For master's, thesis; for doctorate, thesis/dissertation, exams. *Entrance requirements:* For master's and doctorate, GRE General Test, 3 letters of recommendation, minimum GPA of 3.0. Additional exam requirements/recommendations for international students: Required—TOEFL. *Application deadline:* For fall admission, 1/6 for domestic and international students. Application fee: $60. *Expenses:* Tuition, area resident: Part-time $471 per credit hour. Tuition, state resident: part-time $471 per credit hour. Tuition, nonresident: part-time $1016 per credit hour. Required fees: $337.04 per term. *Financial support:* In 2009–10, 9 fellowships with full and partial tuition reimbursements (averaging $24,847 per year), 12 research assistantships (averaging $21,075 per year), 52 teaching assistantships (averaging $19,143 per year) were awarded. Financial award applicants required to submit FAFSA. *Faculty research:* Cytoskeletal activity, membrane biology, cell division, genetics and genomics, virology. *Unit head:* Norma Andrews, Chair, 301-405-1605, Fax: 301-314-9489, E-mail: andrewsn@umd.edu. *Application contact:* Dean of Graduate School, 301-405-0358, Fax: 301-314-9305.

University of Maryland, College Park, Academic Affairs, College of Chemical and Life Sciences, Department of Cell Biology and Molecular Genetics, Program in Molecular and Cellular Biology, College Park, MD 20742. Offers PhD. Part-time and evening/weekend programs available. *Students:* 56 full-time (37 women), 2 part-time (1 woman); includes 8 minority (2 African Americans, 4 Asian Americans or Pacific Islanders, 2 Hispanic Americans), 31 international. 97 applicants, 15% accepted, 6 enrolled. In 2009, 7 doctorates awarded. *Degree requirements:* For doctorate, thesis/dissertation, exam, public service. *Entrance requirements:* For doctorate, GRE General Test, 3 letters of reference. Additional exam requirements/recommendations for international students: Required—TOEFL. *Application deadline:* For fall admission, 1/6 for domestic and international students. Applications are processed on a rolling basis. Application fee: $60. Electronic applications accepted. *Expenses:* Tuition, area resident: Part-time $471 per credit hour. Tuition, state resident: part-time $471 per credit hour. Tuition, nonresident: part-time $1016 per credit hour. Required fees: $337.04 per term. *Financial support:* In 2009–10, 2 fellowships with partial tuition reimbursements (averaging $10,800 per year), 8 research assistantships (averaging $18,916 per year), 23 teaching assistantships (averaging $19,246 per year) were awarded. Financial award applicants required to submit FAFSA. *Faculty research:* Monoclonal antibody production, oligonucleotide synthesis, macromolecular processing, signal transduction, developmental biology. *Unit head:* Norma Andrews, 301-405-1605, E-mail: andrewsn@umd.edu. *Application contact:* Dean of Graduate School, 301-405-0358, Fax: 301-314-9305.

University of Massachusetts Amherst, Graduate School, Interdisciplinary Programs, Program in Molecular and Cellular Biology, Amherst, MA 01003. Offers biological chemistry and molecular biophysics (PhD); biomedicine (PhD); cellular and developmental biology (PhD). Part-time programs available. *Faculty:* 2 full-time (0 women). *Students:* 30 full-time (16 women), 48 part-time (26 women); includes 15 minority (4 African Americans, 1 American Indian/Alaska Native, 3 Asian Americans or Pacific Islanders, 7 Hispanic Americans), 23 international. Average age 27. 140 applicants, 23% accepted, 19 enrolled. In 2009, 12 doctorates awarded. Terminal master's awarded for partial completion of doctoral program. *Degree requirements:* For doctorate, comprehensive exam, thesis/dissertation. *Entrance requirements:* For doctorate, GRE General Test. Additional exam requirements/recommendations for international students: Required—TOEFL (minimum score 550 paper-based; 213 computer-based; 80 iBT), IELTS (minimum score 6.5). *Application deadline:* For fall admission, 12/1 for domestic and international students. Applications are processed on a rolling basis. Application fee: $50 ($65 for international students). Electronic applications accepted. *Expenses:* Tuition, state resident: full-time $2640; part-time $110 per credit. Tuition, nonresident: full-time $9936; part-time $414 per credit. Tuition and fees vary according to course load. *Financial support:* In 2009–10, 11 research assistantships with full tuition reimbursements (averaging $2,590 per year), 3 teaching assistantships with full tuition reimbursements (averaging $3,303 per year) were awarded; fellowships, career-related internships or fieldwork, Federal Work-Study, scholarships/grants, traineeships, health care benefits, tuition waivers (full), and unspecified assistantships also available. Support available to part-time students. Financial award application deadline: 12/1. *Unit head:* Dr. David J. Gross, Graduate Program Director, 413-545-3246, Fax: 413-545-1812. *Application contact:* Jean M. Ames, Supervisor of Admissions, 413-545-0722, Fax: 413-577-0010, E-mail: gradadm@grad.umass.edu.

University of Massachusetts Amherst, Graduate School, Interdisciplinary Programs, Program in Plant Biology, Amherst, MA 01003. Offers biochemistry and metabolism (MS, PhD); cell biology and physiology (MS, PhD); environmental, ecological and integrative (MS, PhD); genetics and evolution (MS, PhD). *Students:* 3 full-time (2 women), 12 part-time (5 women); includes 2 minority (both Asian Americans or Pacific Islanders), 8 international. Average age 27. 32 applicants, 41% accepted, 3 enrolled. In 2009, 3 master's, 1 doctorate awarded. *Degree requirements:* For master's, thesis; for doctorate, 2 foreign languages, comprehensive exam, thesis/dissertation. *Entrance requirements:* For master's and doctorate, GRE General Test. Additional exam requirements/recommendations for international students: Required—TOEFL (minimum score 550 paper-based; 213 computer-based; 80 iBT), IELTS (minimum score 6.5). *Application deadline:* For fall admission, 12/15 for domestic and international students; for spring admission, 10/1 for domestic and international students. Applications are processed on a rolling basis. Application fee: $50 ($65 for international students). Electronic applications accepted. *Expenses:* Tuition, state resident: full-time $2640; part-time $110 per credit. Tuition, nonresident: full-time $9936; part-time $414 per credit. Tuition and fees vary according to course load. *Financial support:* In 2009–10, 11 research assistantships with full tuition reimbursements (averaging $8,884 per year) were awarded; fellowships, teaching assistantships, career-related internships or fieldwork, Federal Work-Study, scholarships/grants, traineeships, health care benefits, tuition waivers (full), and unspecified assistantships also available. Support available to part-time students. Financial award application deadline: 12/15. *Unit head:* Dr. Elsbeth L. Walker, Graduate Program Director, 413-577-3217, Fax: 413-545-3243. *Application contact:* Jean M. Ames, Supervisor of Admissions, 413-545—0722, Fax: 413-577-0010, E-mail: gradadm@grad.umass.edu.

University of Massachusetts Boston, Office of Graduate Studies, College of Science and Mathematics, Track in Molecular, Cellular and Organismal Biology, Boston, MA 02125-3393. Offers PhD.

University of Massachusetts Worcester, Graduate School of Biomedical Sciences, Program in Cell Biology, Worcester, MA 01655-0115. Offers PhD. *Degree requirements:* For doctorate, comprehensive exam, thesis/dissertation. *Entrance requirements:* For doctorate, GRE General Test. Additional exam requirements/recommendations for international students: Required—TOEFL (minimum score 600 paper-based; 250 computer-based). Electronic applications accepted. *Faculty research:* Cell growth and differentiation, cell signaling, chromatin structure, transcriptional control of gene expression, cell motility.

University of Medicine and Dentistry of New Jersey, Graduate School of Biomedical Sciences, Graduate Programs in Biomedical Sciences–Newark, Department of Cell Biology and Molecular Medicine, Newark, NJ 07107. Offers PhD. *Students:* 14 full-time (10 women), 10 international. *Degree requirements:* For doctorate, thesis/dissertation, qualifying exam. *Entrance requirements:* For doctorate, GRE General Test. Additional exam requirements/recommendations for international students: Required—TOEFL. *Application deadline:* For fall admission, 2/1 for domestic students. Applications are processed on a rolling basis. Application fee: $40. Electronic applications accepted. *Financial support:* Fellowships, research assistantships, Federal Work-Study, institutionally sponsored loans, and tuition waivers (full and partial) available. Financial award application deadline: 5/1. *Unit head:* Dr. Dorothy Vatner, Program Director, 973-972-1993, Fax: 973-972-7489, E-mail: vatnerdo@umdnj.edu. *Application contact:* Dr. Dorothy Vatner, Program Director, 973-972-1993, Fax: 973-972-7489, E-mail: vatnerdo@umdnj.edu.

University of Medicine and Dentistry of New Jersey, Graduate School of Biomedical Sciences, Graduate Programs in Biomedical Sciences–Stratford, Program in Cell and Molecular Biology, Stratford, NJ 08084-5634. Offers MS, PhD, DO/PhD. *Degree requirements:* For master's, thesis; for doctorate, thesis/dissertation, qualifying exam. *Entrance requirements:* For master's and doctorate, GRE General Test. Additional exam requirements/recommendations for international students: Required—TOEFL. *Application deadline:* For fall admission, 2/1 for domestic students; for spring admission, 10/1 for domestic students. Applications are processed on a rolling basis. Application fee: $40. Electronic applications accepted. *Financial support:* Application deadline: 5/1. *Unit head:* Dr. Sal Caradonna, Program Director, 856-566-6056, Fax: 856-566-6232, E-mail: worraddi@umdnj.edu. *Application contact:* University Registrar, 973-972-5338.

University of Miami, Graduate School, Miller School of Medicine, Graduate Programs in Medicine, Department of Cell Biology and Anatomy, Coral Gables, FL 33124. Offers molecular cell and developmental biology (PhD); MD/PhD. *Degree requirements:* For doctorate, thesis/dissertation. *Entrance requirements:* For doctorate, GRE General Test, GRE Subject Test. Additional exam requirements/recommendations for international students: Required—TOEFL. Electronic applications accepted.

University of Michigan, Horace H. Rackham School of Graduate Studies, College of Literature, Science, and the Arts, Department of Molecular, Cellular, and Developmental Biology, Ann Arbor, MI 48109. Offers MS, PhD. Part-time programs available. *Faculty:* 32 full-time (8 women). *Students:* 74 full-time (39 women), 3 part-time (1 woman); includes 4 minority (2 African Americans, 2 Hispanic Americans), 41 international. Average age 29. 113 applicants, 21% accepted, 14 enrolled. In 2009, 6 master's, 7 doctorates awarded. Terminal master's awarded for partial completion of doctoral program. *Degree requirements:* For doctorate, thesis/dissertation, preliminary exam, oral defense. *Entrance requirements:* For master's and doctorate, GRE General Test. Additional exam requirements/recommendations for international students: Required—TOEFL (minimum score 560 paper-based; 220 computer-based; 83 iBT). *Application deadline:* For fall admission, 1/5 for domestic and international students; for winter admission, 11/1 for domestic and international students. Applications are processed on a rolling basis. Application fee: $60 ($75 for international students). Electronic applications accepted. *Expenses:* Tuition, state resident: full-time $17,286; part-time $1099 per credit hour. Tuition, nonresident: full-time $34,944; part-time $2080 per credit hour. Required fees: $95 per semester. Tuition and fees vary according to course load, degree level and program. *Financial support:* In 2009–10, 64 students received support, including 16 fellowships with full tuition reimbursements available (averaging $26,500 per year), 28 research assistantships with full tuition reimbursements available (averaging $26,500 per year), 20 teaching assistantships

Cell Biology

University of Michigan (continued)
with full tuition reimbursements available (averaging $26,500 per year); health care benefits also available. *Faculty research:* Cell biology, microbiology, neurobiology and physiology, developmental biology and plant molecular biology. Total annual research expenditures: $5.7 million. *Unit head:* Patrick J. Flannery, Administrative Manager, 734-936-2991, Fax: 734-615-6337, E-mail: pjflan@umich.edu. *Application contact:* Mary Carr, Graduate Coordinator, 734-615-1635, Fax: 734-764-0884, E-mail: carrmm@umich.edu.

University of Michigan, Horace H. Rackham School of Graduate Studies, Program in Biomedical Sciences (PIBS), Department of Cell and Developmental Biology, Ann Arbor, MI 48109. Offers PhD. *Degree requirements:* For doctorate, thesis/dissertation, oral defense of dissertation, preliminary exam. *Entrance requirements:* For doctorate, GRE General Test, 3 letters of recommendation, research experience. Additional exam requirements/recommendations for international students: Required—TOEFL (minimum score 84 iBT). Electronic applications accepted. *Expenses:* Tuition, state resident: full-time $17,286; part-time $1099 per credit hour. Tuition, nonresident: full-time $34,944; part-time $2080 per credit hour. Required fees: $95 per semester. Tuition and fees vary according to course load, degree level and program. *Faculty research:* Small stress proteins, cellular stress response, muscle, male reproductive, toxicology, cell cytoskeleton.

University of Michigan, Horace H. Rackham School of Graduate Studies, Program in Biomedical Sciences (PIBS), Interdisciplinary Program in Cellular and Molecular Biology, Ann Arbor, MI 48109. Offers PhD. *Degree requirements:* For doctorate, comprehensive exam, thesis/dissertation, oral defense of dissertation, preliminary exam. *Entrance requirements:* For doctorate, GRE General Test, GRE Subject Test. *Expenses:* Tuition, state resident: full-time $17,286; part-time $1099 per credit hour. Tuition, nonresident: full-time $34,944; part-time $2080 per credit hour. Required fees: $95 per semester. Tuition and fees vary according to course load, degree level and program. *Faculty research:* Genetics, genomics, gene regulation, models of disease, microbes.

University of Minnesota, Twin Cities Campus, Graduate School, Program in Molecular, Cellular, Developmental Biology and Genetics, Minneapolis, MN 55455-0213. Offers genetic counseling (MS); molecular, cellular, developmental biology and genetics (PhD). *Faculty:* 89 full-time (31 women), 19 part-time/adjunct (17 women). *Students:* 86 full-time (49 women); includes 6 minority (1 American Indian/Alaska Native, 4 Asian Americans or Pacific Islanders, 1 Hispanic American), 23 international. Average age 24. 179 applicants, 11% accepted, 19 enrolled. In 2009, 12 master's, 6 doctorates awarded. Terminal master's awarded for partial completion of doctoral program. *Degree requirements:* For master's, thesis optional; for doctorate, thesis/dissertation. *Entrance requirements:* For master's and doctorate, GRE General Test. Additional exam requirements/recommendations for international students: Required—TOEFL (minimum score 625 paper-based; 263 computer-based; 80 iBT). *Application deadline:* For fall admission, 12/15 priority date for domestic and international students. Applications are processed on a rolling basis. Application fee: $55 ($75 for international students). Electronic applications accepted. *Financial support:* In 2009–10, 10 fellowships with full tuition reimbursements (averaging $23,000 per year), 79 research assistantships with full tuition reimbursements (averaging $24,500 per year), 11 teaching assistantships with partial tuition reimbursements (averaging $9,236 per year) were awarded; scholarships/grants, traineeships, and health care benefits also available. Financial award application deadline: 12/15. *Faculty research:* Membrane receptors and membrane transport, cell interactions, cytoskeleton and cell mobility, regulation of gene expression, plant cell and molecular biology. Total annual research expenditures: $9.1 million. *Unit head:* Kathleen Conklin, Director of Graduate Studies, 612-626-0445, Fax: 612-626-6140, E-mail: conkl001@umn.edu. *Application contact:* Sue Knoblauch, Student Support Coordinator, 612-624-7470, Fax: 612-626-6140, E-mail: mcdbg@umn.edu.

University of Minnesota, Twin Cities Campus, Graduate School, Stem Cell Biology Graduate Program, Minneapolis, MN 55455-0213. Offers MS, PhD. *Degree requirements:* For master's, thesis; for doctorate, thesis/dissertation. *Entrance requirements:* For master's and doctorate, BS, BA, or foreign equivalent in biological sciences or related field; minimum undergraduate GPA of 3.2. Additional exam requirements/recommendations for international students: Required—TOEFL (minimum score 580 paper-based; 237 computer-based; 92 iBT), IELTS (minimum score 6.5), TWE (minimum score 4). *Faculty research:* Stem cell and developmental biology; embryonic stem cells; iPS cells; muscle satellite cells; hematopoietic stem cells; neuronal stem cells; cardiovascular, kidney and limb development; regenerating systems.

University of Missouri, Graduate School, College of Arts and Sciences, Division of Biological Sciences, Program in Genetic, Cellular and Developmental Biology, Columbia, MO 65211. Offers MA, PhD.

University of Missouri–Kansas City, School of Biological Sciences, Program in Cell Biology and Biophysics, Kansas City, MO 64110-2499. Offers PhD. PhD offered through the School of Graduate Studies. *Degree requirements:* For doctorate, comprehensive exam, thesis/dissertation. *Entrance requirements:* For doctorate, GRE General Test, bachelor's degree in chemistry, biology or related field; minimum GPA of 3.0. Additional exam requirements/recommendations for international students: Required—TOEFL (minimum score 550 paper-based; 213 computer-based; 80 iBT). *Application deadline:* For fall admission, 2/15 priority date for domestic and international students. Applications are processed on a rolling basis. Application fee: $45 ($50 for international students). Electronic applications accepted. *Expenses:* Tuition, state resident: full-time $5378; part-time $299 per credit hour. Tuition, nonresident: full-time $13,881; part-time $771 per credit hour. Required fees: $641; $71 per credit hour. Tuition and fees vary according to course load and program. *Financial support:* Fellowships with full tuition reimbursements, research assistantships with full tuition reimbursements, teaching assistantships with full and partial tuition reimbursements, scholarships/grants, tuition waivers (full and partial), and unspecified assistantships available. Financial award application deadline: 3/1; financial award applicants required to submit FAFSA. *Unit head:* Dr. George J. Thomas, Head, 816-235-2352, E-mail: sbsgradrecruit@umkc.edu. *Application contact:* Laura Batenic, Information Contact, 816-235-2352, Fax: 816-235-5158, E-mail: batenicl@umkc.edu.

See Close-Up on page 247.

University of Missouri–St. Louis, College of Arts and Sciences, Department of Biology, St. Louis, MO 63121. Offers biology (MS, PhD), including animal behavior (MS), biochemistry, biochemistry and biotechnology (MS), biotechnology (MS), conservation biology (MS), development (MS), ecology (MS), environmental studies (PhD), evolution (MS), genetics (MS), molecular biology and biochemistry (PhD), molecular/cellular biology (MS), physiology (MS), plant systematics, population biology (MS), tropical biology (MS); biotechnology (Certificate); tropical biology and conservation (Certificate). Part-time programs available. *Faculty:* 43 full-time (13 women), 2 part-time/adjunct (1 woman). *Students:* 54 full-time (27 women), 79 part-time (43 women); includes 15 minority (6 African Americans, 7 Asian Americans or Pacific Islanders, 2 Hispanic Americans), 47 international. Average age 29. 193 applicants, 44% accepted, 44 enrolled. In 2009, 30 master's, 7 doctorates, 9 other advanced degrees awarded. *Degree requirements:* For master's, thesis or alternative; for doctorate, thesis/dissertation, 1 semester of teaching experience. *Entrance requirements:* For master's, 3 letters of recommendation; for doctorate, GRE General Test, 3 letters of recommendation. Additional exam requirements/recommendations for international students: Required—TOEFL. *Application deadline:* For fall admission, 12/1 priority date for domestic and international students; for spring admission, 10/15 priority date for domestic and international students. Applications are processed on a rolling basis. Application fee: $35 ($40 for international students). Electronic applications accepted. *Expenses:* Tuition, state resident: full-time $5377; part-time $297.70 per credit hour. Tuition, nonresident: full-time $13,882; part-time $771.20 per credit hour. Required fees: $220; $12.20 per credit hour. One-time fee: $12. Tuition and fees vary according to course level, campus/location and program. *Financial support:* In 2009–10, 22 research assistantships with full and partial tuition reimbursements (averaging $16,300 per year), 14 teaching assistantships with full and partial tuition reimbursements (averaging $16,727 per year) were awarded; fellowships with full tuition reimbursements, career-related internships or fieldwork and Federal Work-Study also available. Support available to part-time students. Financial award application deadline: 2/1. *Faculty research:* Molecular biology, microbial genetics, animal behavior, tropical ecology, plant systematics. *Unit head:* Dr. Elizabeth Kellogg, Director of Graduate Studies, 314-516-6200, Fax: 314-516-6233, E-mail: tkellogg@umsl.edu. *Application contact:* 314-516-5458, Fax: 314-516-6996, E-mail: gradadm@umsl.edu.

University of Nebraska Medical Center, Graduate Studies, Department of Genetics, Cell Biology and Anatomy, Omaha, NE 68198. Offers MS, PhD. Part-time programs available. Terminal master's awarded for partial completion of doctoral program. *Degree requirements:* For master's, comprehensive exam, thesis; for doctorate, comprehensive exam, thesis/dissertation. *Entrance requirements:* For master's and doctorate, GRE General Test. Additional exam requirements/recommendations for international students: Required—TOEFL (minimum score 550 paper-based; 213 computer-based). Electronic applications accepted. *Faculty research:* Hematology, immunology, developmental biology, genetics cancer biology, neuroscience.

University of Nevada, Reno, Graduate School, Interdisciplinary Program in Cell and Molecular Biology, Reno, NV 89557. Offers MS, PhD. Terminal master's awarded for partial completion of doctoral program. *Degree requirements:* For master's, thesis; for doctorate, thesis/dissertation. *Entrance requirements:* For master's, GRE Subject Test (recommended), minimum GPA of 2.75; for doctorate, GRE Subject Test (recommended), minimum GPA of 3.0. Additional exam requirements/recommendations for international students: Required—TOEFL (minimum score 500 paper-based; 173 computer-based; 61 iBT), IELTS (minimum score 6). Electronic applications accepted. *Faculty research:* Cellular biology, biophysics, cancer, microbiology, insect biochemistry.

University of New Haven, Graduate School, College of Arts and Sciences, Program in Cellular and Molecular Biology, West Haven, CT 06516-1916. Offers cellular and molecular biology (MS). *Faculty:* 6 full-time (3 women), 8 part-time/adjunct (2 women). *Students:* 42 full-time (24 women), 16 part-time (7 women); includes 6 minority (3 African Americans, 1 Asian American or Pacific Islander, 2 Hispanic Americans), 35 international. Average age 25. 109 applicants, 68% accepted, 19 enrolled. In 2009, 16 master's awarded. *Degree requirements:* For master's, thesis optional. *Entrance requirements:* Additional exam requirements/recommendations for international students: Required—TOEFL (minimum score 520 paper-based; 190 computer-based; 70 iBT), IELTS (minimum score 5.5). *Application deadline:* For fall admission, 5/31 for international students; for winter admission, 10/15 for international students; for spring admission, 1/15 for international students. Applications are processed on a rolling basis. Application fee: $50. Electronic applications accepted. *Expenses:* Tuition: Part-time $700 per credit. Required fees: $45 per term. One-time fee: $390 part-time. *Financial support:* Career-related internships or fieldwork and Federal Work-Study available. Financial award application deadline: 5/1; financial award applicants required to submit FAFSA. *Unit head:* Dr. Eva Sapi, Coordinator, 203-479-4552. *Application contact:* Eloise Gormley, Director of Graduate Admissions, 203-932-7449, Fax: 203-932-7137, E-mail: gradinfo@newhaven.edu.

University of New Mexico, School of Medicine, Biomedical Sciences Graduate Program, Albuquerque, NM 87131-5196. Offers biochemistry and molecular biology (MS, PhD); cell biology and physiology (MS, PhD); molecular genetics and microbiology (MS, PhD); neuroscience (MS, PhD); pathology (MS, PhD); toxicology (MS, PhD). Part-time programs available. Terminal master's awarded for partial completion of doctoral program. *Degree requirements:* For master's, thesis; for doctorate, comprehensive exam, thesis/dissertation. *Entrance requirements:* For master's and doctorate, GRE General Test, minimum undergraduate GPA of 3.0. Additional exam requirements/recommendations for international students: Required—TOEFL. Electronic applications accepted. *Expenses:* Tuition, state resident: full-time $2099; part-time $233.20 per credit hour. Tuition, nonresident: full-time $6650. Required fees: $25 per semester. Tuition and fees vary according to course load, program and reciprocity agreements. *Faculty research:* Signal transduction, infectious disease, biology of cancer, structural biology, neuroscience.

The University of North Carolina at Chapel Hill, Graduate School, College of Arts and Sciences, Department of Biology, Program in Cell Motility and Cytoskeleton, Chapel Hill, NC 27599. Offers PhD. *Entrance requirements:* For doctorate, GRE General Test.

The University of North Carolina at Chapel Hill, National Institutes of Health Sponsored Programs, NIH-UNC Graduate Partnership Program in Cell Motility and Cytoskeleton, Chapel Hill, NC 27599. Offers PhD.

The University of North Carolina at Chapel Hill, School of Medicine and Graduate School, Graduate Programs in Medicine, Department of Cell and Developmental Biology, Chapel Hill, NC 27599. Offers PhD. *Degree requirements:* For doctorate, comprehensive exam, thesis/dissertation. *Entrance requirements:* For doctorate, GRE General Test, GRE Subject Test. Electronic applications accepted. *Faculty research:* Cell adhesion, motility and cytoskeleton; molecular analysis of signal transduction; development biology and toxicology; reproductive biology; cell and molecular imaging.

University of Notre Dame, Graduate School, College of Science, Department of Biological Sciences, Notre Dame, IN 46556. Offers aquatic ecology, evolution and environmental biology (MS, PhD); cellular and molecular biology (MS, PhD); genetics (MS, PhD); physiology (MS, PhD); vector biology and parasitology (MS, PhD). Terminal master's awarded for partial completion of doctoral program. *Degree requirements:* For master's, comprehensive exam, thesis; for doctorate, comprehensive exam, thesis/dissertation, candidacy exam. *Entrance requirements:* For master's and doctorate, GRE General Test. Additional exam requirements/recommendations for international students: Required—TOEFL (minimum score 600 paper-based; 250 computer-based; 80 iBT). Electronic applications accepted. *Faculty research:* Tropical disease, molecular genetics, neurobiology, evolutionary biology, aquatic biology.

University of Oklahoma Health Sciences Center, College of Medicine and Graduate College, Graduate Programs in Medicine, Department of Cell Biology, Oklahoma City, OK 73190. Offers MS, PhD. *Faculty:* 11 full-time (1 woman). *Students:* 3 full-time (1 woman), 30 part-time (17 women); includes 6 minority (2 African Americans, 4 Asian Americans or Pacific Islanders), 16 international. Average age 29. 17 applicants, 12% accepted, 2 enrolled. In 2009, 1 master's, 12 doctorates awarded. *Degree requirements:* For master's, thesis; for doctorate, thesis/dissertation. *Entrance requirements:* For doctorate, GRE General Test, GRE Subject Test, 3 letters of recommendation. Additional exam requirements/recommendations for international students: Required—TOEFL. *Application deadline:* For fall admission, 1/31 for domestic students. Application fee: $50. *Expenses:* Tuition, state resident: full-time $3120; part-time $156 per credit hour. Tuition, nonresident: full-time $11,314; part-time $409.70 per credit hour. Required fees: $1471; $51.20 per credit hour. $223.25 per term. *Financial support:* In 2009–10, 5 research assistantships (averaging $18,000 per year) were awarded; teaching assistantships, career-related internships or fieldwork and institutionally sponsored loans also available. Support available to part-time students. Financial award application deadline: 7/1. *Faculty research:* Neurobiology, reproductive, neuronal plasticity, extracellular matrix, neuroendocrinology. *Unit head:* Dr. Robert Eugene Anderson, Chair, 405-271-2377, E-mail: robert-anderson@ouhsc.edu. *Application contact:* Dr. Muna Naash, Graduate Liaison, 405-271-2382.

University of Ottawa, Faculty of Graduate and Postdoctoral Studies, Faculty of Medicine, Department of Cellular and Molecular Medicine, Ottawa, ON K1H 8M5, Canada. Offers M Sc, PhD. *Degree requirements:* For master's, thesis, seminar; for doctorate, comprehensive exam, thesis/dissertation, seminar. *Entrance requirements:* For master's, honors degree or equivalent, minimum B average; for doctorate, master's degree, minimum B+ average. Electronic applications accepted. *Faculty research:* Physiology, pharmacology, growth and development.

University of Pennsylvania, School of Medicine, Biomedical Graduate Studies, Graduate Group in Cell and Molecular Biology, Program in Cell Biology and Physiology, Philadelphia, PA 19104. Offers PhD, MD/PhD, VMD/PhD. *Degree requirements:* For doctorate, thesis/dissertation. *Entrance requirements:* For doctorate, GRE General Test. Additional exam requirements/

recommendations for international students: Required—TOEFL. *Application deadline:* For fall admission, 12/8 priority date for domestic students, 12/8 for international students. Applications are processed on a rolling basis. Application fee: $70. Electronic applications accepted. *Expenses:* Tuition: Full-time $25,660; part-time $4758 per course. Required fees: $2152; $270 per course. Tuition and fees vary according to course load, degree level and program. *Financial support:* Fellowships, research assistantships, scholarships/grants, traineeships, and unspecified assistantships available. *Unit head:* Dr. Kevin Koskett, Head. *Application contact:* Kathy O'Connor-Cooley, Coordinator, 215-895-8935, Fax: 215-573-2104, E-mail: camb@mail.med.upenn.edu.

University of Pittsburgh, School of Arts and Sciences, Department of Biological Sciences, Program in Molecular, Cellular, and Developmental Biology, Pittsburgh, PA 15260. Offers PhD. *Faculty:* 23 full-time (6 women). *Students:* 52 full-time (33 women); includes 2 minority (1 African American, 1 Asian American or Pacific Islander), 14 international. Average age 23. 194 applicants, 10% accepted, 9 enrolled. In 2009, 3 doctorates awarded. *Degree requirements:* For doctorate, comprehensive exam, thesis/dissertation. *Entrance requirements:* For doctorate, GRE General Test, GRE Subject Test. Additional exam requirements/recommendations for international students: Required—TOEFL (minimum score 550 paper-based; 213 computer-based). *Application deadline:* For fall admission, 1/15 priority date for domestic students, 12/15 priority date for international students. Applications are processed on a rolling basis. Application fee: $0 ($50 for international students). Electronic applications accepted. *Expenses:* Tuition, state resident: full-time $16,402; part-time $665 per credit. Tuition, nonresident: full-time $28,694; part-time $1175 per credit. Required fees: $690; $175 per term. Tuition and fees vary according to program. *Financial support:* In 2009–10, 31 fellowships with full tuition reimbursements (averaging $27,379 per year), 104 research assistantships with full tuition reimbursements (averaging $24,608 per year), 36 teaching assistantships with full tuition reimbursements (averaging $23,385 per year) were awarded; Federal Work-Study, scholarships/grants, traineeships, health care benefits, and tuition waivers (full) also available. *Faculty research:* Structure and function of genes and proteins, macromolecular interactions, cell-specific gene regulation, regulation of cell proliferation, embryogenesis. *Unit head:* Dr. Gerard L. Campbell, Associate Professor, 412-624-6812, Fax: 412-624-4759, E-mail: camp@pitt.edu. *Application contact:* Cathleen M. Barr, Graduate Administrator, 412-624-4268, Fax: 412-624-4759, E-mail: cbarr@pitt.edu.

University of Pittsburgh, School of Medicine, Graduate Programs in Medicine, Program in Cell Biology and Molecular Physiology, Pittsburgh, PA 15260. Offers MS, PhD. *Faculty:* 42 full-time (12 women). *Students:* 16 full-time (9 women); includes 3 minority (1 African American, 2 Asian Americans or Pacific Islanders), 5 international. Average age 27. 655 applicants, 10% accepted. In 2009, 4 doctorates awarded. *Degree requirements:* For doctorate, comprehensive exam, thesis/dissertation. *Entrance requirements:* For doctorate, GRE General Test, GRE Subject Test, minimum QPA of 3.0. Additional exam requirements/recommendations for international students: Required—TOEFL (minimum score 600 paper-based; 250 computer-based; 100 iBT), IELTS (minimum score 7). *Application deadline:* For fall admission, 12/15 priority date for domestic and international students. Application fee: $40. Electronic applications accepted. *Expenses:* Tuition, state resident: full-time $16,402; part-time $665 per credit. Tuition, nonresident: full-time $28,694; part-time $1175 per credit. Required fees: $690; $175 per term. Tuition and fees vary according to program. *Financial support:* In 2009–10, 10 research assistantships with full tuition reimbursements (averaging $24,650 per year), 6 teaching assistantships with full tuition reimbursements (averaging $24,650 per year) were awarded; institutionally sponsored loans, scholarships/grants, traineeships, health care benefits, and unspecified assistantships also available. *Faculty research:* Genetic disorders of ion channels, regulation of gene expression/development, membrane traffic of proteins and lipids, reproductive biology, signal transduction in diabetes and metabolism. *Unit head:* Dr. William H. Walker, Graduate Program Director, 412-641-7672, Fax: 412-641-7676, E-mail: walkerw@pitt.edu. *Application contact:* Graduate Studies Administrator, 412-648-8957, Fax: 412-648-1077, E-mail: gradstudies@medschool.pitt.edu.

University of Puerto Rico, Río Piedras, College of Natural Sciences, Department of Biology, San Juan, PR 00931-3300. Offers ecology/systematics (MS, PhD); evolution/genetics (MS, PhD); molecular/cellular biology (MS, PhD); neuroscience (MS, PhD). Part-time programs available. *Degree requirements:* For master's, one foreign language, comprehensive exam, thesis; for doctorate, one foreign language, comprehensive exam, thesis/dissertation. *Entrance requirements:* For master's, GRE Subject Test, interview, minimum GPA of 3.0, letter of recommendation; for doctorate, GRE Subject Test, interview, master's degree, minimum GPA of 3.0, letter of recommendation. *Faculty research:* Environmental, poblational and systematic biology.

University of Rhode Island, Graduate School, College of the Environment and Life Sciences, Department of Cell and Molecular Biology, Kingston, RI 02881. Offers biochemistry (MS, PhD); clinical laboratory sciences (MS), including biotechnology, clinical laboratory science, cytopathology; microbiology (MS, PhD); molecular genetics (MS, PhD). Part-time programs available. *Faculty:* 12 full-time (4 women). *Students:* 29 full-time (17 women), 43 part-time (31 women); includes 13 minority (5 African Americans, 4 Asian Americans or Pacific Islanders, 4 Hispanic Americans), 3 international. In 2009, 5 master's, 2 doctorates awarded. *Degree requirements:* For master's, comprehensive exam (for some programs); for doctorate, comprehensive exam. *Entrance requirements:* For master's and doctorate, GRE, 2 letters of recommendation. Additional exam requirements/recommendations for international students: Required—TOEFL (minimum score 550 paper-based; 213 computer-based). *Application deadline:* For fall admission, 7/15 for domestic students, 2/1 for international students; for spring admission, 11/15 for domestic students, 7/15 for international students. Application fee: $65. Electronic applications accepted. *Expenses:* Tuition, state resident: full-time $8828; part-time $490 per credit hour. Tuition, nonresident: full-time $22,100; part-time $1228 per credit hour. Required fees: $1118; $57 per semester. Tuition and fees vary according to program. *Financial support:* In 2009–10, 2 research assistantships with full and partial tuition reimbursements (averaging $10,535 per year), 10 teaching assistantships with full and partial tuition reimbursements (averaging $13,449 per year) were awarded. Financial award application deadline: 7/15; financial award applicants required to submit FAFSA. *Faculty research:* Genomics and Sequencing Center: an interdisciplinary genomics research and undergraduate and graduate student training program which provides researchers access to cutting-edge technologies in the field of genomics. Total annual research expenditures: $1.2 million. *Unit head:* Dr. Jay Sperry, Chairperson, 401-874-2201, Fax: 401-874-2202, E-mail: jsperry@mail.uri.edu. *Application contact:* Dr. Jay Sperry, Chairperson, 401-874-2201, Fax: 401-874-2202, E-mail: jsperry@mail.uri.edu.

University of Saskatchewan, College of Medicine, Department of Anatomy and Cell Biology, Saskatoon, SK S7N 5A2, Canada. Offers M Sc, PhD. *Degree requirements:* For master's, thesis; for doctorate, thesis/dissertation. *Entrance requirements:* Additional exam requirements/recommendations for international students: Required—TOEFL. Tuition and fees charges are reported in Canadian dollars. *Expenses:* Tuition, area resident: Full-time $3000 Canadian dollars; part-time $500 Canadian dollars per term. Required fees: $700 Canadian dollars; $100 Canadian dollars per term.

University of South Alabama, College of Medicine and Graduate School, Program in Basic Medical Sciences, Specialization in Cell Biology and Neuroscience, Mobile, AL 36688-0002. Offers PhD. *Degree requirements:* For doctorate, thesis/dissertation, oral and written preliminary exams, research proposal, qualifying exam. *Entrance requirements:* For doctorate, GRE General Test, minimum GPA of 3.0. Additional exam requirements/recommendations for international students: Required—TOEFL. *Expenses:* Tuition, state resident: part-time $218 per contact hour. Required fees: $1102 per year. *Faculty research:* Cytoskeleton-membrane interactions, neural basis of oral motor behavior, microtubule organizing centers, molecular biology of human chromosomes, mechanisms of synaptic transmissions.

University of South Carolina, The Graduate School, College of Arts and Sciences, Department of Biological Sciences, Graduate Training Program in Molecular, Cellular, and Developmental Biology, Columbia, SC 29208. Offers MS, PhD. *Degree requirements:* For master's, one foreign language, thesis; for doctorate, one foreign language, thesis/dissertation. *Entrance requirements:* For master's and doctorate, GRE General Test, minimum GPA of 3.0 in science. Electronic applications accepted. *Faculty research:* Marine ecology, population and evolutionary biology, molecular biology and genetics, development.

The University of South Dakota, School of Medicine and Health Sciences and Graduate School, Biomedical Sciences Graduate Program, Cellular and Molecular Biology Group, Vermillion, SD 57069-2390. Offers MS, PhD. Terminal master's awarded for partial completion of doctoral program. *Degree requirements:* For master's, thesis; for doctorate, comprehensive exam, thesis/dissertation. *Entrance requirements:* For master's and doctorate, GRE General Test, GRE Subject Test, minimum GPA of 3.0. Additional exam requirements/recommendations for international students: Required—TOEFL (minimum score 550 paper-based; 213 computer-based; 80 iBT), IELTS (minimum score 6). Electronic applications accepted. *Expenses:* Contact institution. *Faculty research:* Molecular aspects of protein and DNA, neurochemistry and energy transduction, gene regulation, cellular development.

University of Southern California, Keck School of Medicine and Graduate School, Graduate Programs in Medicine, Department of Cell and Neurobiology, Los Angeles, CA 90089. Offers MS, PhD. *Faculty:* 28 full-time (5 women), 1 (woman) part-time/adjunct. *Students:* 3 full-time (2 women); includes 1 minority (Asian American or Pacific Islander). Average age 24. 5 applicants, 20% accepted, 1 enrolled.Terminal master's awarded for partial completion of doctoral program. *Degree requirements:* For master's, thesis or alternative; for doctorate, thesis/dissertation. *Entrance requirements:* For master's, GRE General Test, minimum GPA of 3.0; for doctorate, GRE General Test. *Application deadline:* For fall admission, 3/1 priority date for domestic and international students. Application fee: $85. Electronic applications accepted. *Expenses:* Tuition: Full-time $25,980; part-time $1315 per unit. Required fees: $554. One-time fee: $35 full-time. Full-time tuition and fees vary according to degree level and program. *Financial support:* In 2009–10, 1 student received support, including 1 fellowship (averaging $27,060 per year), 4 research assistantships (averaging $27,060 per year); teaching assistantships, Federal Work-Study and institutionally sponsored loans also available. Support available to part-time students. *Faculty research:* Neurobiology and development, gene therapy in vision, lachrymal glands, neuroendocrinology, signal transduction mechanisms. *Unit head:* Dr. Mikel Henry Snow, Vice-Chair, 323-442-1881, Fax: 323-442-3466. *Application contact:* Darlene Marie Campbell, Project Specialist, 323-442-2843, Fax: 323-442-0466, E-mail: dmc@usc.edu.

University of South Florida, Graduate School, College of Arts and Sciences, Department of Biology, Tampa, FL 33620-9951. Offers cell biology and molecular biology (MS); coastal marine biology (MS); coastal marine biology and ecology (PhD); conservation biology (MS, PhD); molecular and cell biology (PhD). Part-time programs available. *Faculty:* 34 full-time (7 women). *Students:* 72 full-time (43 women), 18 part-time (8 women); includes 9 minority (1 African American, 2 American Indian/Alaska Native, 4 Asian Americans or Pacific Islanders, 2 Hispanic Americans), 7 international. Average age 32. 99 applicants, 20% accepted, 14 enrolled. In 2009, 8 master's, 4 doctorates awarded. *Degree requirements:* For master's, comprehensive exam, thesis (for some programs); for doctorate, comprehensive exam, thesis/dissertation. *Entrance requirements:* For master's and doctorate, GRE General Test, minimum GPA of 3.0. Additional exam requirements/recommendations for international students: Required—TOEFL (minimum score 570 paper-based; 213 computer-based). *Application deadline:* For fall admission, 2/15 priority date for domestic students, 1/2 for international students; for spring admission, 8/1 for domestic students, 6/1 for international students. Application fee: $30. Electronic applications accepted. *Financial support:* In 2009–10, teaching assistantships with tuition reimbursements (averaging $58,627 per year); unspecified assistantships also available. Financial award application deadline: 6/30; financial award applicants required to submit FAFSA. Total annual research expenditures: $1.2 million. *Unit head:* Susan Bell, Co-Chairperson, 813-974-6210, Fax: 813-974-2876, E-mail: sbell@cas.usf.edu. *Application contact:* James Garey, Graduate Advisor, 813-974-8434, Fax: 813-974-3263, E-mail: grarey@cas.usf.edu.

The University of Texas at Austin, Graduate School, Institute for Cellular and Molecular Biology, Austin, TX 78712-1111. Offers PhD.

The University of Texas at Dallas, School of Natural Sciences and Mathematics, Program in Biology, Richardson, TX 75080. Offers bioinformatics and computational biology (MS); biotechnology (MS); molecular and cell biology (MS, PhD). Part-time and evening/weekend programs available. *Faculty:* 16 full-time (3 women). *Students:* 89 full-time (50 women), 16 part-time (11 women); includes 19 minority (16 Asian Americans or Pacific Islanders, 3 Hispanic Americans), 62 international. Average age 26. 313 applicants, 31% accepted, 42 enrolled. In 2009, 36 master's, 4 doctorates awarded. *Degree requirements:* For master's, thesis optional; for doctorate, thesis/dissertation, publishable paper. *Entrance requirements:* For master's and doctorate, GRE General Test. Additional exam requirements/recommendations for international students: Required—TOEFL (minimum score 550 paper-based; 213 computer-based). *Application deadline:* For fall admission, 7/15 for domestic students, 5/1 priority date for international students; for spring admission, 11/15 for domestic students, 9/1 priority date for international students. Applications are processed on a rolling basis. Application fee: $50 ($100 for international students). Electronic applications accepted. *Expenses:* Tuition, state resident: full-time $11,068; part-time $461 per credit hour. Tuition, nonresident: full-time $21,178; part-time $882 per credit hour. Tuition and fees vary according to course load. *Financial support:* In 2009–10, 15 research assistantships with full tuition reimbursements (averaging $14,347 per year), 27 teaching assistantships with full tuition reimbursements (averaging $13,511 per year) were awarded; fellowships, career-related internships or fieldwork, Federal Work-Study, institutionally sponsored loans, scholarships/grants, and unspecified assistantships also available. Support available to part-time students. Financial award application deadline: 4/30; financial award applicants required to submit FAFSA. *Faculty research:* DNA replication, regulation of gene expression, subcellular organelles, physical chemistry of macromolecules, damage and repair of cellular DNA. *Unit head:* Dr. Li Zhang, Department Head, 972-883-6032, Fax: 972-883-2502, E-mail: li.zhang@utdallas.edu. *Application contact:* Dr. Lawrence Reitzer, Graduate Advisor, 972-883-2502, Fax: 972-883-2402, E-mail: reitzer@utdallas.edu.

The University of Texas at San Antonio, College of Sciences, Department of Biology, San Antonio, TX 78249-0617. Offers biology (MS, PhD), including cellular and molecular biology (PhD), neurobiology (PhD); biotechnology (MS). Part-time programs available. *Faculty:* 37 full-time (6 women), 7 part-time/adjunct (1 woman). *Students:* 144 full-time (82 women), 45 part-time (28 women); includes 57 minority (6 African Americans, 13 Asian Americans or Pacific Islanders, 38 Hispanic Americans), 69 international. Average age 28. 263 applicants, 58% accepted, 72 enrolled. In 2009, 40 master's, 6 doctorates awarded. *Degree requirements:* For master's, comprehensive exam, thesis; for doctorate, comprehensive exam, thesis/dissertation. *Entrance requirements:* For master's, GRE General Test, minimum GPA of 3.0; for doctorate, GRE General Test, minimum GPA of 3.3. Additional exam requirements/recommendations for international students: Required—TOEFL (minimum score 500 paper-based; 173 computer-based; 61 iBT), IELTS (minimum score 5). *Application deadline:* For fall admission, 7/1 for domestic students, 4/1 for international students; for spring admission, 11/1 for domestic students, 9/1 for international students. Applications are processed on a rolling basis. Application fee: $45 ($80 for international students). Electronic applications accepted. *Expenses:* Tuition, state resident: full-time $3975; part-time $221 per contact hour. Tuition, nonresident: full-time $13,947; part-time $775 per contact hour. Required fees: $1853. *Financial support:* In 2009–10, 66 students received support, including 13 fellowships (averaging $31,063 per year), 87 research assistantships (averaging $15,279 per year), 66 teaching assistantships (averaging $10,368 per year); career-related internships or fieldwork, scholarships/grants, and unspecified assistantships also available. Support available to part-time students. *Faculty research:* Cell and molecular biology, neurobiology, microbiology, integrative biology, environmental science. Total annual research expenditures: $1.7 million. *Unit head:* Dr. Edwin J. Barea-Rodriguez, Interim Chair, 210-458-5481, Fax: 210-458-7498, E-mail: edwin.barea@

Cell Biology

The University of Texas at San Antonio (continued)
utsa.edu. *Application contact:* Dr. Dorothy A. Flannagan, Dean of the Graduate School, 210-458-4330, Fax: 210-458-4332, E-mail: dorothy.flannagan@utsa.edu.

See Close-Up on page 121.

The University of Texas Health Science Center at Houston, Graduate School of Biomedical Sciences, Program in Cell and Regulatory Biology, Houston, TX 77225-0036. Offers MS, PhD, MD/PhD. Terminal master's awarded for partial completion of doctoral program. *Degree requirements:* For master's, thesis; for doctorate, thesis/dissertation. *Entrance requirements:* For master's and doctorate, GRE General Test. Additional exam requirements/recommendations for international students: Required—TOEFL. Electronic applications accepted. *Faculty research:* Pharmacology, cell biology, physiology, signal transduction, systems biology.

The University of Texas Health Science Center at San Antonio, Graduate School of Biomedical Sciences, Department of Cellular and Structural Biology, San Antonio, TX 78229-3900. Offers MS, PhD. *Faculty:* 55 full-time (20 women). *Students:* 52 full-time (38 women), 4 part-time (3 women); includes 25 minority (21 Asian Americans or Pacific Islanders, 4 Hispanic Americans), 10 international. Average age 27. In 2009, 5 master's, 7 doctorates awarded. *Degree requirements:* For master's, thesis, oral qualifying exam; for doctorate, comprehensive exam, thesis/dissertation, oral qualifying exam. *Entrance requirements:* For doctorate, GRE General Test, previous course work in biology, chemistry, physics, and calculus. Additional exam requirements/recommendations for international students: Required—TOEFL (minimum score 550 paper-based; 213 computer-based). *Application deadline:* For fall admission, 4/1 for domestic and international students; for spring admission, 10/1 for domestic and international students. Applications are processed on a rolling basis. Application fee: $0. Electronic applications accepted. *Expenses:* Tuition, state resident: full-time $2832; part-time $118 per credit hour. Tuition, nonresident: full-time $10,896; part-time $454 per credit hour. Required fees: $884 per semester. One-time fee: $70. *Financial support:* In 2009–10, 28 students received support, including 28 teaching assistantships (averaging $26,000 per year). Financial award application deadline: 2/1; financial award applicants required to submit FAFSA. *Faculty research:* Human/molecular genetics, endocrinology and neurobiology, cell biology, cancer biology, biology of aging. Total annual research expenditures: $10.3 million. *Unit head:* Christi A. Walter, Professor and Chair, 210-567-3800, Fax: 210-567-0073, E-mail: walter@uthscsa.edu. *Application contact:* Susan Naylor, Chair, Committee on Graduate Studies, 210-567-3842, Fax: 210-567-3803, E-mail: naylor@uthscsa.edu.

The University of Texas Medical Branch, Graduate School of Biomedical Sciences, Program in Biochemistry and Molecular Biology, Galveston, TX 77555. Offers biochemistry (PhD); bioinformatics (PhD); biophysics (PhD); cell biology (PhD); computational biology (PhD); structural biology (PhD). *Students:* 41 full-time (17 women); includes 6 minority (1 African American, 1 Asian American or Pacific Islander, 4 Hispanic Americans), 22 international. Average age 28. In 2009, 9 doctorates awarded. *Degree requirements:* For doctorate, thesis/dissertation. *Entrance requirements:* Additional exam requirements/recommendations for international students: Required—TOEFL (minimum score 550 paper-based; 213 computer-based). *Application deadline:* Applications are processed on a rolling basis. Application fee: $30 ($75 for international students). Electronic applications accepted. *Financial support:* In 2009–10, fellowships (averaging $25,000 per year), research assistantships (averaging $25,000 per year) were awarded. Financial award applicants required to submit FAFSA. *Unit head:* Dr. Sarita Sastry, Director, 409-747-1915, Fax: 409-747-1938, E-mail: sasastry@utmb.edu. *Application contact:* Debora Botting, Coordinator for Special Programs, 409-772-2769, Fax: 409-772-5102, E-mail: dmbottin@utmb.edu.

The University of Texas Southwestern Medical Center at Dallas, Southwestern Graduate School of Biomedical Sciences, Division of Basic Science, Program in Cell Regulation, Dallas, TX 75390. Offers PhD. *Faculty:* 53 full-time (8 women). *Students:* 52 full-time (25 women), 2 part-time (0 women); includes 10 minority (3 African Americans, 2 American Indian/Alaska Native, 1 Asian American or Pacific Islander, 4 Hispanic Americans), 19 international. 946 applicants, 22% accepted. In 2009, 14 doctorates awarded. *Degree requirements:* For doctorate, thesis/dissertation, qualifying exam. *Entrance requirements:* For doctorate, GRE General Test, minimum GPA of 3.0. Additional exam requirements/recommendations for international students: Required—TOEFL. *Application deadline:* For fall admission, 12/15 priority date for domestic students. Applications are processed on a rolling basis. Application fee: $0. Electronic applications accepted. *Financial support:* Fellowships, research assistantships, institutionally sponsored loans and traineeships available. *Faculty research:* Molecular and cellular approaches to regulatory biology, receptor-effector coupling, membrane structure, function, and assembly. *Unit head:* Dr. Paul Sternweis, Chair, 214-645-6149, Fax: 214-645-6131, E-mail: paul.sternweis@utsouthwestern.edu. *Application contact:* Dr. Nancy E. Street, Associate Dean, 214-648-6708, Fax: 214-648-2102, E-mail: nancy.street@utsouthwestern.edu.

University of the Sciences in Philadelphia, College of Graduate Studies, Misher College of Arts and Sciences, Program in Cell and Molecular Biology, Philadelphia, PA 19104-4495. Offers PhD. *Expenses:* Tuition: Full-time $22,230; part-time $1235 per credit. Tuition and fees vary according to program.

University of the Sciences in Philadelphia, College of Graduate Studies, Program in Cell Biology and Biotechnology, Philadelphia, PA 19104-4495. Offers cell and molecular biology (PhD); cell biology (MS). Part-time and evening/weekend programs available. *Degree requirements:* For master's, thesis (for some programs). *Entrance requirements:* For master's, GRE General Test. Additional exam requirements/recommendations for international students: Required—TOEFL, TWE. *Expenses:* Contact institution. *Faculty research:* Invertebrate cell adhesion, plant-microbe interactions, natural product mechanisms, cell signal transduction, gene regulation and organization.

University of Toronto, School of Graduate Studies, Life Sciences Division, Department of Cell and Systems Biology, Toronto, ON M5S 1A1, Canada. Offers M Sc, PhD. *Degree requirements:* For master's, thesis, thesis defense; for doctorate, thesis/dissertation, thesis defense, oral thesis examination. *Entrance requirements:* For master's, minimum B+ average in final year, B overall, 3 letters of reference. Additional exam requirements/recommendations for international students: Required—TOEFL (minimum score 580 paper-based; 237 computer-based), TWE (minimum score 5).

University of Vermont, Graduate College, Cell and Molecular Biology Program, Burlington, VT 05405. Offers MS, PhD. *Students:* 39 (16 women); includes 6 minority (2 Asian Americans or Pacific Islanders, 4 Hispanic Americans), 7 international. 81 applicants, 23% accepted, 9 enrolled. In 2009, 4 master's, 8 doctorates awarded. *Degree requirements:* For master's, thesis; for doctorate, thesis/dissertation. *Entrance requirements:* For master's and doctorate, GRE General Test. Additional exam requirements/recommendations for international students: Required—TOEFL (minimum score 550 paper-based; 213 computer-based; 80 iBT). *Application deadline:* For fall admission, 1/15 priority date for domestic students. Applications are processed on a rolling basis. Application fee: $40. Electronic applications accepted. *Expenses:* Tuition, state resident: part-time $508 per credit hour. Tuition, nonresident: part-time $1281 per credit hour. *Financial support:* Fellowships, research assistantships, teaching assistantships, career-related internships or fieldwork available. Financial award application deadline: 3/1. *Unit head:* Dr. Karen Lounsbury, Coordinator, 802-656-9673. *Application contact:* Dr. Karen Lounsbury, Coordinator, 802-656-9673.

University of Virginia, School of Medicine, Department of Cell Biology, Charlottesville, VA 22903. Offers PhD, MD/PhD. *Faculty:* 22 full-time (8 women), 3 part-time/adjunct (1 woman). *Students:* 23 full-time (12 women); includes 3 minority (2 Asian Americans or Pacific Islanders, 1 Hispanic American), 5 international. Average age 28. In 2009, 1 doctorate awarded. *Degree requirements:* For doctorate, one foreign language, thesis/dissertation. *Entrance requirements:* For doctorate, GRE General Test, GRE Subject Test (recommended), 2 letters of recommendation. Additional exam requirements/recommendations for international students: Required—TOEFL. *Application deadline:* For fall admission, 4/15 for domestic and international students. Applications are processed on a rolling basis. Application fee: $60. Electronic applications accepted. *Financial support:* Application deadline: 1/15. *Unit head:* Dr. Barry M. Gumbiner, Chairman, 434-924-2731, Fax: 434-982-3912. *Application contact:* Dr. Barry M. Gumbiner, Chairman, 434-924-2731, Fax: 434-982-3912.

University of Washington, Graduate School, School of Medicine and Graduate School, Graduate Programs in Medicine, Program in Molecular and Cellular Biology, Seattle, WA 98195. Offers PhD. Offered jointly with Fred Hutchinson Cancer Research Center. *Degree requirements:* For doctorate, thesis/dissertation. *Entrance requirements:* For doctorate, GRE General Test, GRE Subject Test. Additional exam requirements/recommendations for international students: Required—TOEFL. Electronic applications accepted.

See Close-Up on page 251.

The University of Western Ontario, Faculty of Graduate Studies, Biosciences Division, Department of Biology, London, ON N6A 5B8, Canada. Offers M Sc, PhD. *Degree requirements:* For master's, thesis; for doctorate, comprehensive exam, thesis/dissertation. *Entrance requirements:* For master's, honors degree or equivalent in biological sciences; for doctorate, master's degree. Additional exam requirements/recommendations for international students: Required—TOEFL. *Faculty research:* Cell and molecular biology, developmental biology, neuroscience, immunobiology and cancer.

University of Wisconsin–La Crosse, Office of University Graduate Studies, College of Science and Health, Department of Biology, La Crosse, WI 54601-3742. Offers aquatic sciences (MS); biology (MS); cellular and molecular biology (MS); clinical microbiology (MS); microbiology (MS); nurse anesthesia (MS); physiology (MS). Part-time programs available. *Faculty:* 27 full-time (7 women). *Students:* 19 full-time (8 women), 35 part-time (20 women); includes 1 minority (Asian American or Pacific Islander), 2 international. Average age 28. 87 applicants, 32% accepted, 21 enrolled. In 2009, 18 master's awarded. *Degree requirements:* For master's, comprehensive exam, thesis. *Entrance requirements:* For master's, GRE General Test, minimum GPA of 2.85. Additional exam requirements/recommendations for international students: Required—TOEFL (minimum score 550 paper-based; 213 computer-based; 79 iBT). Application fee: $56. Electronic applications accepted. *Financial support:* In 2009–10, 19 research assistantships with partial tuition reimbursements (averaging $10,021 per year) were awarded; career-related internships or fieldwork, Federal Work-Study, health care benefits, unspecified assistantships, and grant-funded positions also available. Support available to part-time students. Financial award application deadline: 3/15; financial award applicants required to submit FAFSA. *Unit head:* Dr. David Howard, Chair, 608-785-6455, E-mail: howard.davi@uwlax.edu. *Application contact:* Kathryn Kiefer, Director of Admissions, 608-785-8939, E-mail: admissions@uwlax.edu.

University of Wisconsin–Madison, Graduate School, Program in Cellular and Molecular Biology, Madison, WI 53706-1596. Offers PhD. *Degree requirements:* For doctorate, comprehensive exam, thesis/dissertation. *Entrance requirements:* For doctorate, GRE General Test, GRE Subject Test (recommended), minimum GPA of 3.0, lab experience. Additional exam requirements/recommendations for international students: Required—TOEFL (minimum score 580 paper-based; 237 computer-based; 92 iBT). Electronic applications accepted. *Expenses:* Tuition, state resident: part-time $594 per credit. Tuition, nonresident: part-time $1504 per credit. Required fees: $65 per credit. Tuition and fees vary according to course load, program and reciprocity agreements. *Faculty research:* Virology, cancer biology, transcriptional mechanisms, plant biology, immunology.

University of Wyoming, Graduate Program in Molecular and Cellular Life Sciences, Laramie, WY 82070. Offers PhD. *Degree requirements:* For doctorate, thesis/dissertation, four eight-week laboratory rotations, comprehensive basic practical exam, two-part qualifying exam, seminars, symposium.

Vanderbilt University, Graduate School and School of Medicine, Department of Cell and Developmental Biology, Nashville, TN 37240-1001. Offers MS, PhD, MD/PhD. *Faculty:* 42 full-time (14 women), 3 part-time/adjunct (0 women). *Students:* 72 full-time (39 women); includes 4 minority (all Asian Americans or Pacific Islanders), 6 international. Average age 28. In 2009, 3 master's, 4 doctorates awarded. Terminal master's awarded for partial completion of doctoral program. *Degree requirements:* For master's, thesis or alternative; for doctorate, thesis/dissertation, preliminary, qualifying, and final exams. *Entrance requirements:* For master's, GRE General Test; for doctorate, GRE General Test, GRE Subject Test (recommended). Additional exam requirements/recommendations for international students: Required—TOEFL (minimum score 570 paper-based; 230 computer-based; 88 iBT). *Application deadline:* For fall admission, 1/15 for domestic and international students. Application fee: $0. Electronic applications accepted. *Financial support:* Fellowships with full and partial tuition reimbursements, research assistantships with full and partial tuition reimbursements, career-related internships or fieldwork, Federal Work-Study, institutionally sponsored loans, scholarships/grants, traineeships, health care benefits, and tuition waivers (partial) available. Financial award application deadline: 1/15; financial award applicants required to submit CSS PROFILE or FAFSA. *Faculty research:* Cancer biology, cell cycle regulation, cell signaling, cytoskeletal biology, developmental biology, neurobiology, proteomics, stem cell biology, structural biology, reproductive biology, trafficking and transport, medical education and gross anatomy. *Unit head:* Dr. Susan R. Wente, Chair, 615-322-2134, Fax: 615-343-4539. *Application contact:* Dr. Kathy Gould, Director of Graduate Studies, 615-322-2134, Fax: 615-343-4539, E-mail: kathy.gould@vanderbilt.edu.

Washington State University, Graduate School, College of Sciences, School of Molecular Biosciences, Program in Genetics and Cell Biology, Pullman, WA 99164. Offers MS, PhD. Terminal master's awarded for partial completion of doctoral program. *Degree requirements:* For master's, thesis or alternative, oral exam; for doctorate, comprehensive exam, thesis/dissertation, oral exam. *Entrance requirements:* For master's and doctorate, GRE General Test, minimum GPA of 3.0. Additional exam requirements/recommendations for international students: Required—TOEFL (minimum score 550 paper-based; 213 computer-based). Electronic applications accepted. *Faculty research:* Plant molecular biology, growth factors, cancer induction and DNA repair, gene regulation and genetic engineering.

Washington University in St. Louis, Graduate School of Arts and Sciences, Division of Biology and Biomedical Sciences, Program in Molecular Cell Biology, St. Louis, MO 63130-4899. Offers PhD. *Degree requirements:* For doctorate, thesis/dissertation. *Entrance requirements:* For doctorate, GRE General Test, GRE Subject Test. Electronic applications accepted.

Wesleyan University, Graduate Programs, Department of Biology, Middletown, CT 06459. Offers animal behavior (PhD); bioformatics/genomics (PhD); cell biology (PhD); developmental biology (PhD); evolution/ecology (PhD); genetics (PhD); neurobiology (PhD); population biology (PhD). *Faculty:* 13 full-time (4 women). *Students:* 23 full-time (11 women); includes 1 minority (African American), 3 international. Average age 26. 29 applicants, 10% accepted, 2 enrolled. In 2009, 3 doctorates awarded. *Degree requirements:* For doctorate, variable foreign language requirement, thesis/dissertation. *Entrance requirements:* For doctorate, GRE. Additional exam requirements/recommendations for international students: Required—TOEFL. *Application deadline:* For fall admission, 1/15 for domestic and international students. Applications are processed on a rolling basis. Application fee: $0. *Financial support:* In 2009–10, 3 research assistantships with full tuition reimbursements, 19 teaching assistantships with full tuition reimbursements were awarded; stipends also available. Financial award application deadline: 4/15; financial award applicants required to submit FAFSA. *Faculty research:* Microbial population genetics, genetic basis of evolutionary adaptation, genetic regulation of differentiation and pattern formation in *drosophila*. *Unit head:* Dr. Sonia E. Sultan, Chair/Professor, 860-685-3493, E-mail: jnaegele@wesleyan.edu. *Application contact:* Marjorie Fitzgibbons, Information Contact, 860-685-2140, E-mail: mfitzgibbons@wesleyan.edu.

West Virginia University, Eberly College of Arts and Sciences, Department of Biology, Morgantown, WV 26506. Offers cell and molecular biology (MS, PhD); environmental and evolutionary biology (MS, PhD); forensic biology (MS, PhD); genomic biology (MS, PhD); neurobiology (MS, PhD). Terminal master's awarded for partial completion of doctoral program. *Degree requirements:* For master's, thesis, final exam; for doctorate, thesis/dissertation, preliminary and final exams. *Entrance requirements:* For master's, GRE General Test, GRE Subject Test, minimum GPA of 3.0; for doctorate, GRE General Test, minimum GPA of 3.0. Additional exam requirements/recommendations for international students: Required—TOEFL. *Faculty research:* Environmental biology, genetic engineering, developmental biology, global change, biodiversity.

Yale University, Graduate School of Arts and Sciences, Department of Cell Biology, New Haven, CT 06520. Offers PhD. *Degree requirements:* For doctorate, thesis/dissertation. *Entrance requirements:* For doctorate, GRE General Test. *Expenses:* Contact institution.

Yale University, Graduate School of Arts and Sciences, Department of Molecular, Cellular, and Developmental Biology, Program in Cellular and Developmental Biology, New Haven, CT 06520. Offers PhD. *Degree requirements:* For doctorate, thesis/dissertation. *Entrance requirements:* For doctorate, GRE General Test, GRE Subject Test.

Yale University, School of Medicine and Graduate School of Arts and Sciences, Combined Program in Biological and Biomedical Sciences (BBS), Molecular Cell Biology, Genetics, and Development Track, New Haven, CT 06520. Offers PhD, MD/PhD. *Entrance requirements:* Additional exam requirements/recommendations for international students: Required—TOEFL. *Application deadline:* For fall admission, 12/6 for domestic and international students. *Unit head:* Dr. Shirleen Roeder, Co-Director, 203-432-3501. *Application contact:* Shirlene Scott, Graduate Registrar, 203-785-2404, E-mail: shirlene.scott@yale.edu.

Molecular Biology

Albany Medical College, Center for Cell Biology and Cancer Research, Albany, NY 12208-3479. Offers MS, PhD. Part-time programs available. *Faculty:* 16 full-time (4 women). *Students:* 19 full-time (14 women); includes 6 minority (1 African American, 4 Asian Americans or Pacific Islanders, 1 Hispanic American). Average age 26. 25 applicants, 28% accepted, 6 enrolled. In 2009, 2 master's, 2 doctorates awarded. Terminal master's awarded for partial completion of doctoral program. *Degree requirements:* For master's, thesis; for doctorate, comprehensive exam, thesis/dissertation. *Entrance requirements:* For master's, GRE General Test, all transcripts, letters of recommendation; for doctorate, GRE General Test, letters of recommendation. Additional exam requirements/recommendations for international students: Required—TOEFL. *Application deadline:* For fall admission, 3/15 priority date for domestic and international students. Applications are processed on a rolling basis. *Expenses:* Tuition: Full-time $18,820. *Financial support:* In 2009–10, 10 research assistantships (averaging $24,000 per year) were awarded; Federal Work-Study, scholarships/grants, and tuition waivers (full) also available. Financial award applicants required to submit FAFSA. *Faculty research:* Cancer cell biology, angiogenesis, tissue remodeling, signal transduction, cell adhesion. *Unit head:* Dr. C. Michael DiPersio, Graduate Director, 518-262-5916, Fax: 518-262-5669, E-mail: dipersm@mail.amc.edu. *Application contact:* Dr. C. Michael DiPersio, Graduate Director, 518-262-5916, Fax: 518-262-5669, E-mail: dipersm@mail.amc.edu.

Albert Einstein College of Medicine, Sue Golding Graduate Division of Medical Sciences, Division of Biological Sciences, Department of Developmental and Molecular Biology, Bronx, NY 10461. Offers PhD, MD/PhD. *Degree requirements:* For doctorate, thesis/dissertation. *Entrance requirements:* For doctorate, GRE General Test. Additional exam requirements/recommendations for international students: Required—TOEFL. *Faculty research:* DNA, RNA, and protein synthesis in prokaryotes and eukaryotes; chemical and enzymatic alteration of RNA; glycoproteins.

Appalachian State University, Cratis D. Williams Graduate School, Department of Biology, Boone, NC 28608. Offers cell and molecular (MS); general (MS). Part-time programs available. *Faculty:* 27 full-time (11 women). *Students:* 28 full-time (14 women), 7 part-time (3 women); includes 2 minority (both Asian Americans or Pacific Islanders). 24 applicants, 29% accepted, 7 enrolled. In 2009, 10 master's awarded. *Degree requirements:* For master's, comprehensive exam, thesis. *Entrance requirements:* For master's, GRE General Test, 3 letters of recommendation. Additional exam requirements/recommendations for international students: Required—TOEFL (minimum score 570 paper-based; 230 computer-based; 79 iBT), IELTS (minimum score 6.5). *Application deadline:* For fall admission, 7/1 for domestic students, 2/1 for international students; for spring admission, 11/1 for domestic students, 7/1 for international students. Applications are processed on a rolling basis. Application fee: $50. Electronic applications accepted. *Expenses:* Tuition, state resident: full-time $2960. Tuition, nonresident: full-time $14,051. Required fees: $2320. *Financial support:* In 2009–10, 25 teaching assistantships (averaging $9,500 per year) were awarded; fellowships, research assistantships, career-related internships or fieldwork, Federal Work-Study, scholarships/grants, and unspecified assistantships also available. Financial award application deadline: 4/1; financial award applicants required to submit FAFSA. *Faculty research:* Aquatic and terrestrial ecology, animal and plant physiology, behavior and systematics, immunology and cell biology, molecular biology and microbiology. Total annual research expenditures: $451,508. *Unit head:* Dr. Steven Seagle, Chairman, 828-262-3025, E-mail: seaglesw@appstate.edu. *Application contact:* Dr. Gary Walker, Graduate Coordinator, 828-262-3025, E-mail: walkergl@appstate.edu.

Arizona State University, Graduate College, College of Liberal Arts and Sciences, Division of Natural Sciences, School of Life Sciences, Tempe, AZ 85287. Offers biological design (PhD); biology (MNS, MS, PhD); biology and society (PhD); human and social dimensions of science and technology (PhD); microbiology (MNS, MS, PhD); molecular and cellular biology (MS, PhD); neuroscience (PhD); plant biology (MNS, MS, PhD). *Accreditation:* NAACLS. *Degree requirements:* For master's, thesis (MS); for doctorate, one foreign language, thesis/dissertation. *Entrance requirements:* For master's and doctorate, GRE.

Arkansas State University—Jonesboro, Graduate School, College of Sciences and Mathematics, Program in Molecular Biosciences, Jonesboro, State University, AR 72467. Offers PhD. Part-time programs available. *Faculty:* 2 full-time (1 woman), 3 part-time/adjunct (1 woman). *Students:* 15 full-time (3 women), 2 part-time (1 woman); includes 2 minority (both American Indian/Alaska Native), 11 international. Average age 28. 1 applicant, 100% accepted, 1 enrolled. *Degree requirements:* For doctorate, comprehensive exam, thesis/dissertation. *Entrance requirements:* For doctorate, GRE, appropriate bachelor's or master's degree, interview, letters of reference. Additional exam requirements/recommendations for international students: Required—TOEFL (minimum score 550 paper-based; 213 computer-based; 79 iBT), IELTS (minimum score 6). *Application deadline:* For fall admission, 2/15 for domestic and international students. Applications are processed on a rolling basis. Application fee: $50. Electronic applications accepted. *Expenses:* Tuition, state resident: full-time $3744; part-time $208 per credit hour. Tuition, nonresident: full-time $9540; part-time $530 per credit hour. Required fees: $896; $47 per credit hour. $25 per term. One-time fee: $50. Tuition and fees vary according to course load and program. *Financial support:* In 2009–10, 11 students received support; fellowships, research assistantships, teaching assistantships, career-related internships or fieldwork, scholarships/grants, and unspecified assistantships available. Financial award application deadline: 7/1; financial award applicants required to submit FAFSA. *Unit head:* Dr. Roger Buchanan, Director, 870-972-2007, Fax: 870-972-2008, E-mail: rbuck@astate.edu. *Application contact:* Dr. Andrew Sustich, Dean of the Graduate School, 870-972-3029, Fax: 870-972-3857, E-mail: sustich@astate.edu.

Auburn University, Graduate School, Interdepartmental Programs, Auburn University, AL 36849. Offers cell and molecular biology (PhD); integrated textile and apparel sciences (PhD); sociology and rural sociology (MA, MS), including rural sociology (MS), sociology. Part-time programs available. *Students:* 25 full-time (12 women), 19 part-time (13 women); includes 4 minority (1 African American, 1 American Indian/Alaska Native, 2 Asian Americans or Pacific Islanders), 26 international. Average age 28. 88 applicants, 35% accepted, 12 enrolled. In 2009, 4 master's, 3 doctorates awarded. *Entrance requirements:* For master's, GRE General Test. *Application deadline:* For fall admission, 7/7 for domestic students; for spring admission, 11/24 for domestic students. Applications are processed on a rolling basis. Application fee: $50 ($60 for international students). Electronic applications accepted. *Expenses:* Tuition, state resident: full-time $6240. Tuition, nonresident: full-time $18,720. International tuition: $18,938 full-time. Required fees: $492. Tuition and fees vary according to course load, program and reciprocity agreements. *Financial support:* Fellowships, research assistantships, teaching assistantships, Federal Work-Study available. Support available to part-time students. Financial award application deadline: 3/15; financial award applicants required to submit FAFSA. *Unit head:* Interim Dean of the Graduate School. *Application contact:* Dr. George Flowers, Dean of the Graduate School, 334-844-2125.

Baylor College of Medicine, Graduate School of Biomedical Sciences, Department of Biochemistry and Molecular Biology, Houston, TX 77030-3498. Offers PhD, MD/PhD. *Faculty:* 34 full-time (7 women). *Students:* 53 full-time (26 women); includes 7 minority (1 African American, 1 American Indian/Alaska Native, 1 Asian American or Pacific Islander, 4 Hispanic Americans), 30 international. Average age 25. In 2009, 8 doctorates awarded. *Degree requirements:* For doctorate, thesis/dissertation, public defense. *Entrance requirements:* For doctorate, GRE General Test, GRE Subject Test (strongly recommended), minimum GPA of 3.0. Additional exam requirements/recommendations for international students: Required—TOEFL. *Application deadline:* For fall admission, 1/1 priority date for domestic students. Application fee: $30. Electronic applications accepted. *Financial support:* Fellowships, research assistantships, career-related internships or fieldwork, Federal Work-Study, institutionally sponsored loans, health care benefits, and students receive a scholarship unless there are grant funds available to pay tuition available. Financial award applicants required to submit FAFSA. *Faculty research:* Mechanisms of enzyme action, nucleic acid enzymology, and mutagenesis; biochemistry of connective tissue, proteins, and polysaccharides; chemical metabolism of lipids and lipoproteins. *Unit head:* Dr. John Wilson, Director, 713-798-5760. *Application contact:* Monica Bagos, Graduate Program Administrator, 713-798-0124, Fax: 713-796-9438, E-mail: bagos@bcm.edu.

Baylor College of Medicine, Graduate School of Biomedical Sciences, Department of Molecular and Cellular Biology, Houston, TX 77030-3498. Offers PhD, MD/PhD. *Faculty:* 74 full-time (19 women). *Students:* 66 full-time (36 women); includes 8 minority (2 African Americans, 1 Asian American or Pacific Islander, 5 Hispanic Americans), 19 international. Average age 25. In 2009, 14 doctorates awarded. *Degree requirements:* For doctorate, thesis/dissertation, public defense, qualifying exam. *Entrance requirements:* For doctorate, GRE General Test, GRE Subject Test (strongly recommended), minimum GPA of 3.0. Additional exam requirements/recommendations for international students: Required—TOEFL. *Application deadline:* For fall admission, 1/1 priority date for domestic students. Application fee: $0. Electronic applications accepted. *Financial support:* Fellowships, research assistantships, career-related internships or fieldwork, Federal Work-Study, institutionally sponsored loans, health care benefits, and tuition waivers (full) available. Financial award applicants required to submit FAFSA. *Faculty research:* Gene regulation, cell structure/function, developmental biology, neurobiology, reproductive endocrinology. *Unit head:* Dr. JoAnne Richards, Director, 713-798-4598. *Application contact:* Caroline Kosnik, Graduate Program Administrator, 713-798-4598, Fax: 713-790-0545, E-mail: ckosnik@bcm.edu.

Baylor College of Medicine, Graduate School of Biomedical Sciences, Interdepartmental Program in Cell and Molecular Biology, Houston, TX 77030-3498. Offers biochemistry (PhD); cell and molecular biology (PhD); genetics (PhD); human genetics (PhD); immunology (PhD); microbiology (PhD); virology (PhD); MD/PhD. *Faculty:* 100 full-time (31 women). *Students:* 59 full-time (37 women); includes 24 minority (5 African Americans, 1 American Indian/Alaska Native, 7 Asian Americans or Pacific Islanders, 11 Hispanic Americans), 6 international. Average age 25. In 2009, 9 doctorates awarded. *Degree requirements:* For doctorate, thesis/dissertation, public defense. *Entrance requirements:* For doctorate, GRE General Test, GRE Subject Test (strongly recommended), minimum GPA of 3.0. Additional exam requirements/recommendations for international students: Required—TOEFL. *Application deadline:* For fall admission, 1/1 priority date for domestic students. Applications are processed on a rolling basis. Application fee: $0. Electronic applications accepted. *Financial support:* In 2009–10, 59 students received support; fellowships, research assistantships, teaching assistantships, Federal Work-Study, institutionally sponsored loans, health care benefits, and tuition waivers (full) available. Financial award applicants required to submit FAFSA. *Faculty research:* Gene expression and regulation, developmental biology and genetics, signal transduction and membrane biology, aging process, molecular virology. *Unit head:* Dr. Susan Marriott, Director, 713-798-6557. *Application contact:* Lourdes Fernandez, Graduate Program Administrator, 713-798-6557, Fax: 713-798-6325, E-mail: cmbprog@bcm.edu.

See Close-Up on page 231.

Baylor College of Medicine, Graduate School of Biomedical Sciences, Program in Developmental Biology, Houston, TX 77030-3498. Offers PhD, MD/PhD. *Faculty:* 52 full-time (16 women). *Students:* 51 full-time (26 women); includes 9 minority (1 American Indian/Alaska Native, 6 Asian Americans or Pacific Islanders, 2 Hispanic Americans), 29 international. Average age 25. In 2009, 4 doctorates awarded. *Degree requirements:* For doctorate, thesis/dissertation, public defense. *Entrance requirements:* For doctorate, GRE General Test, GRE Subject Test (strongly recommended), minimum GPA of 3.0. Additional exam requirements/recommendations for international students: Required—TOEFL. *Application deadline:* For fall admission, 1/1 priority date for domestic students. Application fee: $0. Electronic applications accepted. *Financial support:* Fellowships, research assistantships, career-related internships or fieldwork, Federal Work-Study, institutionally sponsored loans, health care benefits, tuition waivers (full), and stipends available. *Faculty research:* Molecular and genetic approaches to study pattern formation in Dictyostelium, Drosophila, C.elegans, mouse, Xenopus, and zebrafish; cross-species approach. *Unit head:* Dr. Hugo Bellen, Director, 713-798-6410. *Application contact:* Catherine Tasnier, Graduate Program Administrator, 713-798-6410, Fax: 713-798-5386, E-mail: cat@bcm.edu.

See Close-Up on page 315.

Boston University, Graduate School of Arts and Sciences, Molecular Biology, Cell Biology, and Biochemistry Program (MCBB), Boston, MA 02215. Offers MA, PhD. *Students:* 34 full-time (20 women), 1 (woman) part-time; includes 6 minority (2 African Americans, 2 Asian Americans

Molecular Biology

Boston University (continued)

or Pacific Islanders, 2 Hispanic Americans), 4 international. Average age 29. 77 applicants, 18% accepted, 5 enrolled. In 2009, 2 doctorates awarded. Terminal master's awarded for partial completion of doctoral program. *Degree requirements:* For master's, one foreign language, thesis (for some programs); for doctorate, one foreign language, comprehensive exam, thesis/dissertation. *Entrance requirements:* For master's and doctorate, GRE General Test, GRE Subject Test. Additional exam requirements/recommendations for international students: Required—TOEFL (minimum score 600 paper-based; 250 computer-based). *Application deadline:* For fall admission, 12/7 for domestic and international students. Application fee: $70. Electronic applications accepted. *Expenses:* Tuition: Full-time $37,910; part-time $1184 per credit hour. Required fees: $386; $40 per semester. Part-time tuition and fees vary according to class time, course level, degree level and program. *Financial support:* In 2009–10, 9 students received support, including 1 fellowship with full tuition reimbursement available (averaging $18,900 per year), 7 research assistantships with full tuition reimbursements available (averaging $14,800 per year), 1 teaching assistantship with full tuition reimbursement available (averaging $18,400 per year); Federal Work-Study, scholarships/grants, and traineeships also available. Financial award application deadline: 12/7; financial award applicants required to submit FAFSA. *Unit head:* Dr. Ulla Hansen, Director, 617-353-2432, Fax: 617-353-6340, E-mail: mccall@bu.edu. *Application contact:* Meredith Canode, Academic Administrator, 617-353-2432, Fax: 617-353-6340, E-mail: mcanode@bu.edu.

Boston University, School of Medicine, Division of Graduate Medical Sciences, Department of Biochemistry, Boston, MA 02118. Offers MA, PhD, MD/PhD. Part-time programs available. Terminal master's awarded for partial completion of doctoral program. *Degree requirements:* For master's, thesis or alternative, qualifying exam; for doctorate, thesis/dissertation, qualifying exam. *Entrance requirements:* For master's and doctorate, GRE General Test, GRE Subject Test. Additional exam requirements/recommendations for international students: Required—TOEFL. *Application deadline:* For fall admission, 1/15 priority date for domestic students; for spring admission, 10/15 priority date for domestic students. Electronic applications accepted. *Expenses:* Tuition: Full-time $37,910; part-time $1184 per credit hour. Required fees: $386; $40 per semester. Part-time tuition and fees vary according to class time, course level, degree level and program. *Financial support:* Fellowships, research assistantships, Federal Work-Study, scholarships/grants, and traineeships available. *Faculty research:* Extracellular matrix, gene expression, receptors, growth control. *Unit head:* Dr. Carl Franzblau, Associate Dean, 617-638-5120, Fax: 617-638-4842, E-mail: medsci@bu.edu. *Application contact:* Dr. Barbara Schreiber, Information Contact, 617-638-5094, Fax: 617-638-5339, E-mail: schreibe@biochem.bumc.bu.edu.

Boston University, School of Medicine, Division of Graduate Medical Sciences, Program in Cell and Molecular Biology, Boston, MA 02118. Offers PhD, MD/PhD. *Degree requirements:* For doctorate, thesis/dissertation. *Entrance requirements:* For doctorate, GRE General Test, GRE Subject Test. Additional exam requirements/recommendations for international students: Required—TOEFL. *Application deadline:* For fall admission, 1/15 priority date for domestic students; for spring admission, 10/15 priority date for domestic students. Electronic applications accepted. *Expenses:* Tuition: Full-time $37,910; part-time $1184 per credit hour. Required fees: $386; $40 per semester. Part-time tuition and fees vary according to class time, course level, degree level and program. *Financial support:* Fellowships, research assistantships, Federal Work-Study, scholarships/grants, and traineeships available. *Unit head:* Dr. Vickery Trinkaus Randall, Director, 617-638-6099, Fax: 617-638-5337, E-mail: vickery@bu.edu. *Application contact:* Dr. Mary Jo Murnane, Admissions Director, 617-638-4926, Fax: 617-638-4085, E-mail: mmurnane@bu.edu.

Brandeis University, Graduate School of Arts and Sciences, Program in Molecular and Cell Biology, Waltham, MA 02454-9110. Offers genetics (PhD); microbiology (PhD); molecular and cell biology (MS, PhD); molecular biology (PhD); neurobiology (PhD). *Faculty:* 28 full-time (12 women), 1 (woman) part-time/adjunct. *Students:* 46 full-time (26 women), 1 part-time (0 women); includes 3 minority (2 African Americans, 1 Hispanic American), 7 international. Average age 27. 146 applicants, 21% accepted, 12 enrolled. In 2009, 4 master's, 6 doctorates awarded. Terminal master's awarded for partial completion of doctoral program. *Degree requirements:* For master's, thesis optional, research project; for doctorate, comprehensive exam, thesis/dissertation, teaching assistant experience. *Entrance requirements:* For master's and doctorate, GRE General Test, resume, 3 letters of recommendation. Additional exam requirements/recommendations for international students: Required—TOEFL (minimum score 600 paper-based; 250 computer-based; 100 iBT); Recommended—IELTS (minimum score 7). *Application deadline:* For fall admission, 1/15 priority date for domestic students. Applications are processed on a rolling basis. Application fee: $75. Electronic applications accepted. *Financial support:* In 2009–10, 41 students received support, including 13 fellowships with full tuition reimbursements available (averaging $27,500 per year), 27 research assistantships with full tuition reimbursements available (averaging $27,500 per year), 1 teaching assistantship with partial tuition reimbursement available (averaging $3,200 per year); scholarships/grants, traineeships, health care benefits, and tuition waivers (full and partial) also available. Financial award application deadline: 4/15; financial award applicants required to submit FAFSA. *Faculty research:* Regulation of gene expression by transcription factors, molecular neurobiology, immunology, molecular mechanisms of genetic recombination, cell differentiation. *Unit head:* Dr. Piali Sengupta, Chair, 781-736-2686, Fax: 781-736-3107, E-mail: piali@brandeis.edu. *Application contact:* Marcia Cabral, Department Administrator, 781-736-3100, Fax: 781-736-3107, E-mail: cabral@brandeis.edu.

Brigham Young University, Graduate Studies, College of Life Sciences, Department of Microbiology and Molecular Biology, Provo, UT 84602-1001. Offers microbiology (MS, PhD); molecular biology (MS, PhD). *Faculty:* 18 full-time (3 women). *Students:* 20 full-time (7 women); includes 1 minority (Asian American or Pacific Islander), 4 international. Average age 30. 13 applicants, 62% accepted, 7 enrolled. In 2009, 2 master's, 2 doctorates awarded. *Degree requirements:* For master's, comprehensive exam, thesis; for doctorate, comprehensive exam, thesis/dissertation. *Entrance requirements:* For master's, GRE General Test, minimum GPA of 3.0 during previous 2 years; for doctorate, GRE General Test, minimum GPA of 3.0. Additional exam requirements/recommendations for international students: Required—TOEFL (minimum score 580 paper-based; 85 iBT), IELTS (minimum score 7). *Application deadline:* For fall admission, 12/15 priority date for domestic and international students. Application fee: $50. Electronic applications accepted. *Expenses:* Tuition: Full-time $5580; part-time $301 per credit hour. Tuition and fees vary according to student's religious affiliation. *Financial support:* In 2009–10, 17 students received support, including 8 research assistantships with full and partial tuition reimbursements available (averaging $18,000 per year), 7 teaching assistantships with full and partial tuition reimbursements available (averaging $18,000 per year); institutionally sponsored loans, scholarships/grants, health care benefits, and unspecified assistantships also available. Financial award application deadline: 2/1. *Faculty research:* Immunobiology, molecular genetics, molecular virology, cancer biology, pathogenic and environmental microbiology. Total annual research expenditures: $501,070. *Unit head:* Dr. Brent L. Nielsen, Chair, 801-422-1102, Fax: 801-422-0519, E-mail: brent_nielsen@byu.edu. *Application contact:* Dr. Richard A. Robison, Graduate Coordinator, 801-422-2416, Fax: 801-422-0519, E-mail: richard_robison@byu.edu.

Brown University, Graduate School, Division of Biology and Medicine, Program in Molecular Biology, Cell Biology, and Biochemistry, Providence, RI 02912. Offers biochemistry (M Med Sc, Sc M, PhD), including biochemistry (Sc M, PhD), biology (Sc M, PhD), medical science (M Med Sc, PhD); biology (MA); cell biology (M Med Sc, Sc M, PhD), including biochemistry (Sc M, PhD), biology (Sc M, PhD), medical science (M Med Sc, PhD); developmental biology (M Med Sc, Sc M, PhD), including biochemistry (Sc M, PhD), biology (Sc M, PhD), medical science (M Med Sc, PhD); immunology (M Med Sc, Sc M, PhD), including biochemistry (Sc M, PhD), biology (Sc M, PhD), medical science (M Med Sc, PhD); molecular microbiology (M Med Sc, Sc M, PhD), including biochemistry (Sc M, PhD), biology (Sc M, PhD), medical science (M Med Sc, PhD); MD/PhD. Part-time programs available. Terminal master's awarded for partial completion of doctoral program. *Degree requirements:* For master's, thesis (for some programs); for doctorate, one foreign language, thesis/dissertation, preliminary exam. *Entrance requirements:* For master's and doctorate, GRE General Test, GRE Subject Test. Additional exam requirements/recommendations for international students: Required—TOEFL. Electronic applications accepted. *Faculty research:* Molecular genetics, gene regulation.

California Institute of Technology, Division of Biology, Program in Molecular Biology, Pasadena, CA 91125-0001. Offers PhD. *Degree requirements:* For doctorate, thesis/dissertation, qualifying exam. *Entrance requirements:* For doctorate, GRE General Test.

Carnegie Mellon University, Mellon College of Science, Department of Biological Sciences, Pittsburgh, PA 15213-3891. Offers biochemistry (PhD); biophysics (PhD); cell biology (PhD); computational biology (MS, PhD); developmental biology (PhD); genetics (PhD); molecular biology (PhD); neuroscience (PhD). *Degree requirements:* For doctorate, comprehensive exam, thesis/dissertation. *Entrance requirements:* For doctorate, GRE General Test, GRE Subject Test, interview. Electronic applications accepted. *Faculty research:* Genetic structure, function, and regulation; protein structure and function; biological membranes; biological spectroscopy.

Case Western Reserve University, School of Medicine and School of Graduate Studies, Graduate Programs in Medicine, Department of Molecular Biology and Microbiology, Cleveland, OH 44106-4960. Offers cellular biology (PhD); microbiology (PhD); molecular biology (PhD); molecular virology (PhD); MD/PhD. Students are admitted to an integrated Biomedical Sciences Training Program involving 11 basic science programs at Case Western Reserve University. *Degree requirements:* For doctorate, thesis/dissertation. *Entrance requirements:* For doctorate, GRE General Test, GRE Subject Test. Additional exam requirements/recommendations for international students: Required—TOEFL. Electronic applications accepted. *Faculty research:* Gene expression in eukaryotic and prokaryotic systems; microbial physiology; intracellular transport and signaling; mechanisms of oncogenesis; molecular mechanisms of RNA processing, editing, and catalysis.

Central Connecticut State University, School of Graduate Studies, School of Technology, Department of Biomolecular Sciences, New Britain, CT 06050-4010. Offers MS. Part-time and evening/weekend programs available. *Faculty:* 9 full-time (4 women), 3 part-time/adjunct (2 women). *Students:* 8 full-time (3 women), 19 part-time (11 women); includes 6 minority (3 African Americans, 3 Hispanic Americans). Average age 26. 19 applicants, 58% accepted, 9 enrolled. In 2009, 9 master's awarded. *Degree requirements:* For master's, comprehensive exam, thesis or alternative. *Entrance requirements:* For master's, minimum undergraduate GPA of 2.7. Additional exam requirements/recommendations for international students: Required—TOEFL. *Application deadline:* For fall admission, 7/1 for domestic students; for spring admission, 12/1 for domestic students. Applications are processed on a rolling basis. Application fee: $50. Electronic applications accepted. *Expenses:* Tuition, area resident: Full-time $4662; part-time $440 per credit. Tuition, state resident: full-time $6994; part-time $440 per credit. Tuition, nonresident: full-time $12,988; part-time $440 per credit. Required fees: $3606. One-time fee: $62 part-time. *Financial support:* In 2009–10, 7 students received support, including 2 research assistantships; career-related internships or fieldwork, Federal Work-Study, scholarships/grants, and unspecified assistantships also available. Support available to part-time students. Financial award application deadline: 3/1; financial award applicants required to submit FAFSA. *Unit head:* Dr. James Mulrooney, Chair, 860-832-3560. *Application contact:* Dr. James Mulrooney, Chair, 860-832-3560.

Clemson University, Graduate School, College of Agriculture, Forestry and Life Sciences, Department of Genetics and Biochemistry, Program in Biochemistry and Molecular Biology, Clemson, SC 29634. Offers PhD. *Students:* 15 full-time (11 women), 8 international. Average age 27. 23 applicants, 0% accepted, 0 enrolled. *Degree requirements:* For doctorate, comprehensive exam, thesis/dissertation. *Entrance requirements:* For doctorate, GRE General Test. Additional exam requirements/recommendations for international students: Required—TOEFL. *Application deadline:* For fall admission, 1/1 for domestic students; for spring admission, 9/1 for domestic students. Applications are processed on a rolling basis. Application fee: $70 ($80 for international students). Electronic applications accepted. *Expenses:* Contact institution. *Financial support:* In 2009–10, 15 students received support, including 6 fellowships with full and partial tuition reimbursements available (averaging $6,999 per year), 5 research assistantships with partial tuition reimbursements available (averaging $16,400 per year), 10 teaching assistantships with partial tuition reimbursements available (averaging $19,600 per year); career-related internships or fieldwork, institutionally sponsored loans, scholarships/grants, health care benefits, and unspecified assistantships also available. Support available to part-time students. Financial award application deadline: 3/15; financial award applicants required to submit FAFSA. *Faculty research:* Biomembranes, protein structure, molecular biology of plants, APYA and stress response. Total annual research expenditures: $670,000. *Unit head:* Dr. Keith Murphy, Chair, 864-656-6237, Fax: 864-656-0435, E-mail: kmurph2@clemson.edu. *Application contact:* Sheryl Banks, Administrative Coordinator, 866-656-6878, E-mail: sherylb@clemson.edu.

Colorado State University, Graduate School, Program in Cell and Molecular Biology, Fort Collins, CO 80523-1618. Offers MS, PhD. *Students:* 27 full-time (13 women), 29 part-time (15 women); includes 11 minority (1 African American, 2 American Indian/Alaska Native, 5 Asian Americans or Pacific Islanders, 3 Hispanic Americans), 15 international. Average age 30. 78 applicants, 12% accepted, 9 enrolled. In 2009, 6 master's, 10 doctorates awarded. *Degree requirements:* For master's, comprehensive exam, thesis; for doctorate, comprehensive exam, thesis/dissertation. *Entrance requirements:* For master's and doctorate, GRE General Test, GRE Subject Test in biology (strongly recommended), minimum GPA of 3.0; BA/BS in biology, biochemistry, physics; calculus sequence, letters of recommendation. Additional exam requirements/recommendations for international students: Required—TOEFL (minimum score 625 paper-based; 263 computer-based; 107 iBT). *Application deadline:* For fall admission, 1/1 priority date for domestic and international students. Applications are processed on a rolling basis. Application fee: $50. Electronic applications accepted. *Expenses:* Tuition, state resident: full-time $6434; part-time $359.10 per credit. Tuition, nonresident: full-time $18,116; part-time $1006.45 per credit. Required fees: $1496; $83 per credit. *Financial support:* In 2009–10, 7 students received support, including 1 research assistantship with full tuition reimbursement available (averaging $20,770 per year), 6 teaching assistantships with full tuition reimbursements available (averaging $16,313 per year); fellowships with partial tuition reimbursements available, traineeships and unspecified assistantships also available. Financial award application deadline: 1/1; financial award applicants required to submit FAFSA. *Faculty research:* Regulation of gene expression, cancer biology, plant molecular genetics, reproductive physiology, infectious diseases. Total annual research expenditures: $1,650. *Unit head:* Dr. Paul J. Laybourn, Director, 970-491-5100, Fax: 970-491-0623, E-mail: paul.laybourn@colostate.edu. *Application contact:* Lori Williams, Administrative Assistant, 970-491-0241, Fax: 970-491-0623, E-mail: cmb@colostate.edu.

Columbia University, College of Physicians and Surgeons, Integrated Program in Cellular, Molecular and Biophysical Studies, New York, NY 10032. Offers M Phil, MA, PhD, MD/PhD. Only candidates for the PhD are admitted. Terminal master's awarded for partial completion of doctoral program. *Degree requirements:* For doctorate, thesis/dissertation. *Entrance requirements:* For master's, GRE General Test; for doctorate, GRE General Test, GRE Subject Test. Additional exam requirements/recommendations for international students: Required—TOEFL. *Expenses:* Contact institution. *Faculty research:* Transcription, macromolecular sorting, gene expression during development, cellular interaction.

Cornell University, Graduate School, Graduate Fields of Agriculture and Life Sciences, Field of Biochemistry, Molecular and Cell Biology, Ithaca, NY 14853-0001. Offers biochemistry (PhD); biophysics (PhD); cell biology (PhD); molecular and cell biology (PhD); molecular biology (PhD). *Faculty:* 64 full-time (14 women). *Students:* 91 full-time (43 women); includes 11 minority (2 African Americans, 6 Asian Americans or Pacific Islanders, 3 Hispanic Americans), 28 international. Average age 27. 150 applicants, 11% accepted, 15 enrolled. In 2009, 17 doctorates awarded. *Degree requirements:* For doctorate, comprehensive exam, thesis/dissertation, 2 semesters of teaching experience. *Entrance requirements:* For doctorate, GRE General Test, GRE Subject Test (biology, chemistry, physics, biochemistry, cell and molecular biology), 3 letters of recommendation. Additional exam requirements/recommendations for international students: Required—TOEFL (minimum score 600 paper-based; 250 computer-based; 77 iBT). *Application deadline:* For fall admission, 1/5 for domestic students. Application fee: $70. Electronic applications accepted. *Expenses:* Tuition: Full-time $29,500. Required fees: $70. Full-time tuition and fees vary according to degree level, program and student level. *Financial support:* In 2009–10, 88 students received support, including 13 fellowships with full tuition reimbursements available, 1 research assistantship with full tuition reimbursement available; teaching assistantships with full tuition reimbursements available, institutionally sponsored loans, scholarships/grants, health care benefits, tuition waivers (full and partial), and unspecified assistantships also available. Financial award applicants required to submit FAFSA. *Faculty research:* Biophysics, structural biology. *Unit head:* Director of Graduate Studies, 607-255-2100, Fax: 607-255-2100. *Application contact:* Graduate Field Assistant, 607-255-2100, Fax: 607-255-2100, E-mail: bmcb@cornell.edu.

Cornell University, Joan and Sanford I. Weill Medical College and Graduate School of Medical Sciences, Weill Cornell Graduate School of Medical Sciences, Cell and Molecular Biology Allied Program, New York, NY 10065. Offers MS, PhD. *Faculty:* 100 full-time (26 women). *Students:* 148 full-time (96 women); includes 16 minority (2 African Americans, 8 Asian Americans or Pacific Islanders, 6 Hispanic Americans), 71 international. Average age 22. 295 applicants, 16% accepted, 17 enrolled. In 2009, 19 doctorates awarded. Terminal master's awarded for partial completion of doctoral program. *Degree requirements:* For master's, comprehensive exam; for doctorate, thesis/dissertation, final exam. *Entrance requirements:* For doctorate, GRE General Test, background in genetics, molecular biology, chemistry, or biochemistry. Additional exam requirements/recommendations for international students: Required—TOEFL. *Application deadline:* For fall admission, 12/1 for domestic students. Application fee: $60. Electronic applications accepted. *Expenses:* Tuition: Full-time $44,650. Required fees: $2805. *Financial support:* In 2009–10, 12 fellowships (averaging $21,900 per year) were awarded; scholarships/grants, health care benefits, and stipends (given to all students) also available. *Faculty research:* Molecular structure determination, protein structure, gene structure, stem cell biology, control of gene expression, DNA replication, chromosome maintenance, RNA biosynthesis. *Unit head:* Dr. David Eliezer, Co-Director, 212-746-6557, Fax: 212-717-3047. *Application contact:* Linda Smith, Assistant Dean of Admissions, 212-746-6565, Fax: 212-746-8906, E-mail: lis2025@med.cornell.edu.

Dartmouth College, Graduate Program in Molecular and Cellular Biology, Hanover, NH 03755. Offers PhD, MD/PhD. *Faculty:* 69 full-time (15 women). *Students:* 148 full-time (74 women); includes 7 African Americans, 1 Asian American or Pacific Islander, 3 Hispanic Americans, 55 international. Average age 27. 280 applicants, 22% accepted, 25 enrolled. In 2009, 25 doctorates awarded. *Entrance requirements:* For doctorate, GRE General Test, letters of recommendation. Additional exam requirements/recommendations for international students: Required—TOEFL (minimum score 450 paper-based; 90 iBT) or IELTS (minimum score 7). *Application deadline:* For fall admission, 1/4 for domestic and international students. Applications are processed on a rolling basis. Application fee: $75. Electronic applications accepted. *Financial support:* Scholarships/grants, health care benefits, and stipends ($25,500) available. *Unit head:* Barbara Conradt, Chair, 603-650-1612, Fax: 603-650-1006, E-mail: mcb@dartmouth.edu. *Application contact:* Janet Cheney, Program Coordinator, 603-650-1612, Fax: 603-650-1006, E-mail: molecular.and.cellular.biology@dartmouth.edu.

Drexel University, College of Medicine, Biomedical Graduate Programs, Interdisciplinary Program in Molecular and Cell Biology and Genetics, Philadelphia, PA 19104-2875. Offers MS, PhD, MD/PhD. Terminal master's awarded for partial completion of doctoral program. *Degree requirements:* For master's, comprehensive exam, thesis; for doctorate, thesis/dissertation, qualifying exam. *Entrance requirements:* For master's, GRE General Test, minimum GPA of 2.75; for doctorate, GRE General Test, minimum GPA of 3.0. Additional exam requirements/recommendations for international students: Required—TOEFL. Electronic applications accepted. *Faculty research:* Molecular anatomy, biochemistry, medical biotechnology, molecular pathology, microbiology and immunology.

Duke University, Graduate School, Department of Biological Anthropology and Anatomy, Durham, NC 27710. Offers cellular and molecular biology (PhD); gross anatomy and physical anthropology (PhD), including comparative morphology of human and non-human primates, primate social behavior, vertebrate paleontology; neuroanatomy (PhD). *Faculty:* 8 full-time. *Students:* 14 full-time (9 women); includes 2 minority (1 African American, 1 Hispanic American), 1 international. 39 applicants, 15% accepted, 4 enrolled. In 2009, 4 doctorates awarded. *Degree requirements:* For doctorate, one foreign language, thesis/dissertation. *Entrance requirements:* For doctorate, GRE General Test. Additional exam requirements/recommendations for international students: Required—TOEFL (minimum score 550 paper-based; 213 computer-based; 83 iBT), IELTS (minimum score 7). *Application deadline:* For fall admission, 12/8 priority date for domestic and international students. Application fee: $75. Electronic applications accepted. *Financial support:* Fellowships, teaching assistantships, Federal Work-Study available. Financial award application deadline: 12/31. *Unit head:* Daniel Schmitt, Director of Graduate Studies, 919-684-5664, Fax: 919-684-4124, E-mail: mlsquire@duke.edu. *Application contact:* Cynthia Robertson, Associate Dean for Enrollment Services, 919-684-3913, E-mail: grad-admissions@duke.edu.

Duke University, Graduate School, Program in Cellular and Molecular Biology, Durham, NC 27710. Offers PhD, Certificate. Certificate students must be enrolled in a participating PhD program. *Faculty:* 144 full-time. *Students:* 21 full-time (16 women); includes 2 minority (1 Asian American or Pacific Islander, 1 Hispanic American), 4 international. 222 applicants, 20% accepted, 18 enrolled. *Entrance requirements:* For degree, GRE General Test, GRE Subject Test (recommended). Additional exam requirements/recommendations for international students: Required—TOEFL (minimum score 550 paper-based; 213 computer-based; 83 iBT), IELTS (minimum score 7). *Application deadline:* For fall admission, 12/8 priority date for domestic and international students. Application fee: $75. Electronic applications accepted. *Financial support:* Fellowships available. Financial award application deadline: 12/31. *Unit head:* Dr. Margarethe Kuehn, Director of Graduate Studies, 919-684-6554, Fax: 919-684-8346, E-mail: carol.richardson@duke.edu. *Application contact:* Cynthia Robertson, Associate Dean for Enrollment Services, 919-684-3913, E-mail: grad-admissions@duke.edu.

East Carolina University, Brody School of Medicine, Department of Biochemistry and Molecular Biology, Greenville, NC 27858-4353. Offers PhD. *Degree requirements:* For doctorate, comprehensive exam, thesis/dissertation. *Entrance requirements:* For doctorate, GRE General Test. Additional exam requirements/recommendations for international students: Required—TOEFL. *Faculty research:* Gene regulation, development and differentiation, contractility and motility, macromolecular interactions, cancer.

East Carolina University, Graduate School, Thomas Harriot College of Arts and Sciences, Department of Biology, Greenville, NC 27858-4353. Offers biology (MS); molecular biology/biotechnology (MS). Part-time programs available. *Degree requirements:* For master's, one foreign language, comprehensive exam, thesis. *Entrance requirements:* For master's, GRE General Test, GRE Subject Test. Additional exam requirements/recommendations for international students: Required—TOEFL. *Faculty research:* Biochemistry, microbiology, cell biology.

Eastern Michigan University, Graduate School, College of Arts and Sciences, Department of Biology, Ypsilanti, MI 48197. Offers cell and molecular biology (MS); community college biology teaching (MS); ecology and organismal biology (MS); general biology (MS); water resources (MS). Part-time and evening/weekend programs available. Postbaccalaureate distance learning degree programs offered (minimal on-campus study). *Faculty:* 20 full-time (5 women). *Students:* 10 full-time (8 women), 35 part-time (21 women); includes 3 minority (2 African Americans, 1 Asian American or Pacific Islander), 7 international. Average age 28. 57 applicants, 63% accepted, 20 enrolled. In 2009, 17 master's awarded. *Entrance requirements:* For master's, GRE General Test, GRE Subject Test. Additional exam requirements/recommendations for international students: Required—TOEFL. *Application deadline:* Applications are processed on a rolling basis. Application fee: $35. Tuition and fees vary according to course level. *Financial support:* In 2009–10, 22 teaching assistantships with full tuition reimbursements (averaging $8,660 per year) were awarded; fellowships, research assistantships with full tuition reimbursements, career-related internships or fieldwork, Federal Work-Study, institutionally sponsored loans, scholarships/grants, tuition waivers (partial), and unspecified assistantships also available. Support available to part-time students. Financial award applicants required to submit FAFSA. *Unit head:* Dr. Marianne Laporte, Department Head, 734-487-4242, Fax: 734-487-9235, E-mail: mlaporte@emich.edu. *Application contact:* Dr. Marianne Laporte, Department Head, 734-487-4242, Fax: 734-487-9235, E-mail: mlaporte@emich.edu.

Emory University, Graduate School of Arts and Sciences, Division of Biological and Biomedical Sciences, Program in Genetics and Molecular Biology, Atlanta, GA 30322-1100. Offers PhD. *Faculty:* 46 full-time (7 women). *Students:* 59 full-time (39 women); includes 9 minority (8 African Americans, 1 Hispanic American), 14 international. Average age 27. 94 applicants, 22% accepted, 7 enrolled. In 2009, 9 doctorates awarded. *Degree requirements:* For doctorate, comprehensive exam, thesis/dissertation. *Entrance requirements:* For doctorate, GRE General Test, minimum GPA of 3.0 in science course work (recommended). Additional exam requirements/recommendations for international students: Required—TOEFL. *Application deadline:* For fall admission, 1/3 for domestic and international students. Application fee: $50. Electronic applications accepted. *Financial support:* In 2009–10, 15 students received support, including 15 fellowships with full tuition reimbursements available (averaging $24,500 per year); institutionally sponsored loans, scholarships/grants, and health care benefits also available. *Faculty research:* Gene regulation, genetic combination, developmental regulation. *Unit head:* Dr. Andreas Fritz, Director, 404-727-9012, Fax: 404-727-2880, E-mail: afritz@biology.emory.edu. *Application contact:* Dr. Iain Shepherd, Recruiter, 404-727-2632, Fax: 404-727-2880, E-mail: ishephe@emory.edu.

Florida Institute of Technology, Graduate Programs, College of Science, Department of Biological Sciences, Program in Cell and Molecular Biology, Melbourne, FL 32901-6975. Offers MS, PhD. Part-time programs available. *Application deadline:* Applications are processed on a rolling basis. Electronic applications accepted. *Expenses:* Tuition: Part-time $1015 per credit. Tuition and fees vary according to campus/location and program. *Financial support:* Research assistantships with full and partial tuition reimbursements, teaching assistantships with full and partial tuition reimbursements, career-related internships or fieldwork and tuition remissions available. Financial award application deadline: 3/1; financial award applicants required to submit FAFSA. *Faculty research:* Changes in DNA molecule and differential expression of genetic information during aging. *Application contact:* Carolyn P. Shea.

See Close-Up on page 233.

Florida State University, The Graduate School, College of Arts and Sciences, Department of Biological Science, Specialization in Cell and Molecular Biology and Genetics, Tallahassee, FL 32306-4295. Offers MS, PhD. *Faculty:* 28 full-time (6 women). *Students:* 44 full-time (23 women); includes 6 minority (2 African Americans, 1 Asian American or Pacific Islander, 3 Hispanic Americans), 10 international. 118 applicants, 17% accepted, 11 enrolled. In 2009, 6 master's, 4 doctorates awarded. Terminal master's awarded for partial completion of doctoral program. *Degree requirements:* For master's, comprehensive exam, thesis, teaching experience, seminar presentation; for doctorate, comprehensive exam, thesis/dissertation, teaching experience; seminar presentation. *Entrance requirements:* For master's, GRE General Test (minimum combined score 1100, 500 verbal, 500 quantitative), minimum upper-division GPA of 3.0; for doctorate, GRE General Test (minimum combined score 1100, Verbal 500, Quantitative 500), minimum upper-division GPA of 3.0. Additional exam requirements/recommendations for international students: Required—TOEFL (minimum score 600 paper-based; 250 computer-based; 92 iBT). *Application deadline:* For fall admission, 12/15 for domestic and international students. Application fee: $30. Electronic applications accepted. *Expenses:* Tuition, state resident: full-time $7413. Tuition, nonresident: full-time $22,567. *Financial support:* In 2009–10, 14 research assistantships with full tuition reimbursements (averaging $20,000 per year), 30 teaching assistantships with full tuition reimbursements (averaging $18,540 per year) were awarded. Financial award application deadline: 12/15; financial award applicants required to submit FAFSA. *Faculty research:* Molecular biology; genetics and genomics; developmental biology and gene expression; cell structure, function, and motility; cellular and organismal physiology; biophysical and structural biology. *Application contact:* Judy Bowers, Coordinator, Graduate Affairs, 850-644-3023, Fax: 850-644-9829, E-mail: gradinfo@bio.fsu.edu.

Florida State University, The Graduate School, College of Arts and Sciences, Program in Molecular Biophysics, Tallahassee, FL 32306. Offers biochemistry, molecular and cell biology (PhD); computational structural biology (PhD); molecular biophysics (PhD). *Faculty:* 49 full-time (6 women). *Students:* 22 full-time (8 women); includes 6 minority (5 Asian Americans or Pacific Islanders, 1 Hispanic American). Average age 28. 30 applicants, 33% accepted, 7 enrolled. In 2009, 5 doctorates awarded. *Degree requirements:* For doctorate, comprehensive exam, thesis/dissertation, teaching 1 term in professor's major department. *Entrance requirements:* For doctorate, GRE General Test. Additional exam requirements/recommendations for international students: Required—TOEFL (minimum score 600 paper-based; 250 computer-based; 100 iBT). *Application deadline:* For fall admission, 2/15 for domestic students, 3/15 for international students; for spring admission, 11/2 for international students. Applications are processed on a rolling basis. Application fee: $30. Electronic applications accepted. *Expenses:* Tuition, state resident: full-time $7413. Tuition, nonresident: full-time $22,567. *Financial support:* In 2009–10, 21 students received support, including fellowships with partial tuition reimbursements available (averaging $21,000 per year), 18 research assistantships with partial tuition reimbursements available (averaging $21,000 per year), 4 teaching assistantships with partial tuition reimbursements available (averaging $21,000 per year); scholarships/grants, health care benefits, and unspecified assistantships also available. Financial award applicants required to submit FAFSA. *Faculty research:* Protein and nucleic acid structure and function, membrane protein structure, computational biophysics, 3-D image reconstruction. Total annual research expenditures: $1.4 million. *Unit head:* Dr. Geoffrey Strouse, Director, 850-644-0056, Fax: 850-644-7244, E-mail: strouse@chem.fsu.edu. *Application contact:* Dr. Kerry Maddox, Academic Coordinator, Graduate Programs, 850-644-1012, Fax: 850-644-7244, E-mail: bkmaddox@sb.fsu.edu.

George Mason University, College of Science, Fairfax, VA 22030. Offers biodefense (MS, PhD); bioinformatics and computational biology (MS, PhD, Certificate); biology (MS, PhD), including bioinformatics (MS), ecology, systematics and evolution (MS), interpretive biology (MS), molecular and cellular biology (MS), molecular and microbiology (PhD), organismal biology (MS); chemistry and biochemistry (MS), including chemistry; climate dynamics (PhD); computational and data sciences (MS, PhD, Certificate); computational social science (PhD); computational techniques and applications (Certificate); earth systems and geoinformation sciences (MS, PhD, Certificate); environmental science and policy (MS, PhD); geography (MS), including geographic and cartographic sciences; mathematical sciences (MS, PhD), including mathematics; nanotechnology and nanoscience (Certificate); neuroscience (PhD); physical sciences (PhD); physics and astronomy (MS), including applied and engineering physics; remote sensing and earth image processing (Certificate). Part-time and evening/weekend programs available. *Degree requirements:* For doctorate, comprehensive exam, thesis/dissertation. *Entrance requirements:* For master's and doctorate, GRE General Test, minimum GPA of 3.0 in last 60 hours. Additional exam requirements/recommendations for international students: Required—TOEFL. Electronic applications accepted. *Expenses:* Tuition, state resident: full-time $7568; part-time $315.33 per credit hour. Tuition, nonresident: full-time $21,704; part-time $904.33 per credit hour. Required fees: $2184; $91 per credit hour. *Faculty research:* Space sciences and astrophysics, fluid dynamics, materials modeling and simulation, bioinformatics, global changes and statistics.

Georgetown University, Graduate School of Arts and Sciences, Programs in Biomedical Sciences, Department of Biochemistry and Molecular Biology, Washington, DC 20057. Offers

Molecular Biology

Georgetown University (continued)
MS, PhD. *Degree requirements:* For doctorate, comprehensive exam, thesis/dissertation. *Entrance requirements:* For doctorate, GRE General Test. Additional exam requirements/recommendations for international students: Required—TOEFL.

The George Washington University, School of Medicine and Health Sciences, Department of Biochemistry and Molecular Biology, Washington, DC 20037. Offers biochemistry and molecular biology (MS); biochemistry and molecular genetics (PhD); genomics and bioinformatics (MS). *Faculty:* 20 full-time (3 women), 30 part-time/adjunct (9 women). *Students:* 20 full-time (9 women), 16 part-time (6 women); includes 2 minority (both Asian Americans or Pacific Islanders), 20 international. Average age 27. 57 applicants, 88% accepted, 15 enrolled. In 2009, 17 master's awarded. *Degree requirements:* For master's, comprehensive exam; for doctorate, thesis/dissertation, general exam. *Entrance requirements:* For master's, GRE General Test, interview, minimum GPA of 3.0; for doctorate, GRE General Test, minimum GPA of 3.0. Additional exam requirements/recommendations for international students: Required—TOEFL (minimum score 550 paper-based; 213 computer-based). *Application deadline:* For fall admission, 4/1 priority date for domestic and international students; for spring admission, 10/1 priority date for domestic and international students. Application fee: $60. *Financial support:* Fellowships available. Financial award application deadline: 2/1. *Unit head:* Dr. Allan L. Goldstein, Chair, 202-994-3171, E-mail: bcmalg@gwumc.edu. *Application contact:* Information Contact, 202-994-2179, Fax: 202-994-0967, E-mail: gwibs@gwu.edu.

Georgia State University, College of Arts and Sciences, Department of Biology, Program in Cellular and Molecular Biology and Physiology, Atlanta, GA 30302-3083. Offers MS, PhD. Part-time programs available. Terminal master's awarded for partial completion of doctoral program. *Degree requirements:* For master's, thesis or alternative; for doctorate, thesis/dissertation, exam. *Entrance requirements:* For master's and doctorate, GRE General Test. Additional exam requirements/recommendations for international students: Required—TOEFL.

Grand Valley State University, College of Liberal Arts and Sciences, Program in Cell and Molecular Biology, Allendale, MI 49401-9403. Offers MS. *Faculty:* 5 full-time (3 women), 5 part-time/adjunct (3 women). *Students:* 15 full-time (7 women), 14 part-time (9 women); includes 1 minority (American Indian/Alaska Native), 16 international. Average age 25. 40 applicants, 73% accepted, 10 enrolled. In 2009, 5 master's awarded. *Entrance requirements:* For master's, minimum GPA of 3.0. Application fee: $30. *Expenses:* Tuition, state resident: part-time $471 per credit hour. Tuition, nonresident: part-time $646 per credit hour. Tuition and fees vary according to course level. *Financial support:* In 2009–10, 17 students received support, including 2 fellowships (averaging $4,706 per year), 7 research assistantships with tuition reimbursements available (averaging $5,343 per year); unspecified assistantships also available. *Faculty research:* Plant cell biology, plant development, cell/signal integration. *Unit head:* Dr. Mark Staves, Associate Professor/Coordinator, 616-331-2473, E-mail: stavesm@gvsu.edu. *Application contact:* Dr. David Elrod, PSM Coordinator, 616-331-8643, E-mail: elrodd@gvsu.edu.

Harvard University, Graduate School of Arts and Sciences, Department of Molecular and Cellular Biology, Cambridge, MA 02138. Offers PhD. *Degree requirements:* For doctorate, thesis/dissertation, oral exam. *Entrance requirements:* For doctorate, GRE General Test, GRE Subject Test (recommended). Additional exam requirements/recommendations for international students: Required—TOEFL. *Expenses:* Tuition: Full-time $33,696. Required fees: $1126. Full-time tuition and fees vary according to program.

Harvard University, Graduate School of Arts and Sciences, Program in Chemical Biology, Cambridge, MA 02138. Offers PhD. *Expenses:* Tuition: Full-time $33,696. Required fees: $1126. Full-time tuition and fees vary according to program.

Hood College, Graduate School, Program in Biomedical Science, Frederick, MD 21701-8575. Offers biomedical science (MS), including biotechnology/molecular biology, microbiology/immunology/virology, regulatory compliance; regulatory compliance (Certificate). Part-time and evening/weekend programs available. *Faculty:* 3 full-time (1 woman), 4 part-time/adjunct (2 women). *Students:* 9 full-time (2 women), 82 part-time (54 women); includes 23 minority (17 African Americans, 2 Asian Americans or Pacific Islanders, 4 Hispanic Americans), 7 international. Average age 29. 51 applicants, 67% accepted, 28 enrolled. In 2009, 11 master's, 10 other advanced degrees awarded. *Degree requirements:* For master's, comprehensive exam, thesis or alternative. *Entrance requirements:* For master's, bachelor's degree in biology; minimum GPA of 2.75; undergraduate course work in cell biology, chemistry, organic chemistry, and genetics. Additional exam requirements/recommendations for international students: Required—TOEFL (minimum score 575 paper-based; 231 computer-based; 89 iBT). *Application deadline:* For fall admission, 7/15 for domestic and international students; for spring admission, 12/15 for domestic and international students. Applications are processed on a rolling basis. Application fee: $35. Electronic applications accepted. *Expenses:* Tuition: Full-time $6480; part-time $360 per credit. Required fees: $100; $50 per term. *Financial support:* In 2009–10, 3 research assistantships with full tuition reimbursements (averaging $10,609 per year) were awarded. Financial award applicants required to submit FAFSA. *Unit head:* Dr. Oney Smith, Director, 301-696-3653, Fax: 301-696-3597, E-mail: osmith@hood.edu. *Application contact:* Dr. Allen P. Flora, Dean of Graduate School, 301-696-3811, Fax: 301-696-3597, E-mail: gofurther@hood.edu.

Howard University, College of Medicine, Department of Biochemistry and Molecular Biology, Washington, DC 20059-0002. Offers biochemistry and molecular biology (PhD); biotechnology (MS); MD/PhD. Part-time programs available. *Degree requirements:* For master's, externship; for doctorate, comprehensive exam, thesis/dissertation. *Entrance requirements:* For master's and doctorate, GRE General Test, minimum GPA of 3.0. *Faculty research:* Cellular and molecular biology of olfaction, gene regulation and expression, enzymology, NMR spectroscopy of molecular structure, hormone regulation/metabolism.

Illinois Institute of Technology, Graduate College, College of Science and Letters, Department of Biological, Chemical and Physical Sciences, Biology Division, Chicago, IL 60616-3793. Offers biology (MBS, MS, PhD); molecular biochemistry and biophysics (MS, PhD). Part-time and evening/weekend programs available. Postbaccalaureate distance learning degree programs offered (no on-campus study). *Faculty:* 12 full-time (4 women), 2 part-time/adjunct (0 women). *Students:* 98 full-time (50 women), 80 part-time (45 women); includes 15 minority (6 African Americans, 6 Asian Americans or Pacific Islanders, 3 Hispanic Americans), 119 international. Average age 27. 330 applicants, 43% accepted, 57 enrolled. In 2009, 30 master's, 5 doctorates awarded. Terminal master's awarded for partial completion of doctoral program. *Degree requirements:* For master's, comprehensive exam, thesis (for some programs); for doctorate, comprehensive exam, thesis/dissertation. *Entrance requirements:* For master's and doctorate, GRE General Test, minimum undergraduate GPA of 3.0. Additional exam requirements/recommendations for international students: Required—TOEFL (minimum score 550 paper-based; 213 computer-based; 80 iBT). *Application deadline:* For fall admission, 5/1 for domestic and international students; for spring admission, 1/5 for domestic and international students. Applications are processed on a rolling basis. Application fee: $40. Electronic applications accepted. *Expenses:* Tuition: Full-time $17,550; part-time $888 per credit hour. Required fees: $850; $7.50 per credit hour. One-time fee: $50 full-time. Full-time tuition and fees vary according to program. *Financial support:* In 2009–10, 1 fellowship with full tuition reimbursement (averaging $18,000 per year), 6 research assistantships with full tuition reimbursements (averaging $15,500 per year), 11 teaching assistantships with full tuition reimbursements (averaging $15,500 per year) were awarded; career-related internships or fieldwork, Federal Work-Study, institutionally sponsored loans, scholarships/grants, traineeships, health care benefits, tuition waivers (partial), and unspecified assistantships also available. Support available to part-time students. Financial award applicants required to submit FAFSA. *Faculty research:* Structure of muscle and collagen using x-ray scattering, prostate cancer, identification and analysis of anti-cancer drugs, x-ray crystallography of proteins, developmental biology of olfaction, molecular analysis of foodbourne pathogens. Total annual research expenditures: $10.5 million. *Unit head:* Dr. Benjamin C. Stark, Professor and Associate Chair, 312-567-3488, Fax: 312-567-3494, E-mail: starkb@iit.edu. *Application contact:* Morgan Frederick, Assistant Director of Graduate Communications, 866-472-3448, Fax: 312-567-3138, E-mail: inquiry.grad@iit.edu.

Illinois State University, Graduate School, College of Arts and Sciences, Department of Biological Sciences, Normal, IL 61790-2200. Offers animal behavior (MS); bacteriology (MS); biochemistry (MS); biological sciences (MS); biology (PhD); biophysics (MS); biotechnology (MS); botany (MS, PhD); cell biology (MS); conservation biology (MS); developmental biology (MS); ecology (MS, PhD); entomology (MS); evolutionary biology (MS); genetics (MS, PhD); immunology (MS); microbiology (MS, PhD); molecular biology (MS); molecular genetics (MS); neurobiology (MS); neuroscience (MS); parasitology (MS); physiology (MS, PhD); plant biology (MS); plant molecular biology (MS); plant sciences (MS); structural biology (MS); zoology (MS, PhD). Part-time programs available. *Degree requirements:* For master's, thesis or alternative; for doctorate, variable foreign language requirement, thesis/dissertation, 2 terms of residency. *Entrance requirements:* For master's, GRE General Test, minimum GPA of 2.6 in last 60 hours of course work; for doctorate, GRE General Test. *Faculty research:* Redoc balance and drug development in schistosoma mansoni, control of the growth of listeria monocytogenes at low temperature, regulation of cell expansion and microtubule function by SPRI, CRUI: physiology and fitness consequences of different life history phenotypes.

Indiana University Bloomington, University Graduate School, College of Arts and Sciences, Department of Biology, Bloomington, IN 47405. Offers biology teaching (MAT); biotechnology (MA); evolution, ecology, and behavior (MA, PhD); genetics (PhD); microbiology (MA, PhD); molecular, cellular, and developmental biology (PhD); plant sciences (MA, PhD); zoology (MA, PhD). *Faculty:* 58 full-time (15 women), 21 part-time/adjunct (6 women). *Students:* 165 full-time (95 women); includes 14 minority (6 African Americans, 1 American Indian/Alaska Native, 7 Asian Americans or Pacific Islanders), 56 international. Average age 27. 312 applicants, 19% accepted, 24 enrolled. In 2009, 4 master's, 22 doctorates awarded. Terminal master's awarded for partial completion of doctoral program. *Degree requirements:* For master's, thesis, oral defense; for doctorate, thesis/dissertation, oral defense. *Entrance requirements:* For master's and doctorate, GRE General Test. Additional exam requirements/recommendations for international students: Required—TOEFL (minimum score 100 iBT). *Application deadline:* For fall admission, 1/5 priority date for domestic students, 12/1 priority date for international students. Application fee: $55 ($65 for international students). Electronic applications accepted. *Financial support:* In 2009–10, 165 students received support, including 62 fellowships with tuition reimbursements available (averaging $19,484 per year), 27 research assistantships with tuition reimbursements available (averaging $22,605 per year), 76 teaching assistantships with tuition reimbursements available (averaging $20,528 per year); scholarships/grants, traineeships, health care benefits, and unspecified assistantships also available. Financial award application deadline: 1/5. *Faculty research:* Evolution, ecology and behavior; microbiology; molecular biology and genetics; plant biology. *Unit head:* Dr. Roger Innes, Chair, 812-855-2219, Fax: 812-855-6082, E-mail: rinnes@indiana.edu. *Application contact:* Tracey D. Stohr, Graduate Student Recruitment Coordinator, 812-856-6303, Fax: 812-855-6082, E-mail: gradbio@indiana.edu.

Indiana University–Purdue University Indianapolis, Indiana University School of Medicine, Department of Biochemistry and Molecular Biology, Indianapolis, IN 46202-2896. Offers PhD, MD/MS, MD/PhD. *Faculty:* 17 full-time (4 women). *Students:* 48 full-time (26 women), 16 part-time (10 women); includes 4 minority (1 African American, 3 Asian Americans or Pacific Islanders), 26 international. Average age 31. 21 applicants, 71% accepted, 15 enrolled. In 2009, 7 doctorates awarded. Terminal master's awarded for partial completion of doctoral program. *Degree requirements:* For doctorate, thesis/dissertation. *Entrance requirements:* For doctorate, GRE General Test, GRE Subject Test (recommended), previous course work in organic chemistry. *Application deadline:* For fall admission, 1/15 priority date for domestic students. Applications are processed on a rolling basis. Application fee: $55 ($65 for international students). *Financial support:* In 2009–10, 8 teaching assistantships (averaging $14,949 per year) were awarded; fellowships with tuition reimbursements, research assistantships with tuition reimbursements, Federal Work-Study, institutionally sponsored loans, scholarships/grants, and tuition waivers (partial) also available. Support available to part-time students. Financial award application deadline: 2/1. *Faculty research:* Metabolic regulation, enzymology, peptide and protein chemistry, cell biology, signal transduction. *Unit head:* Dr. Zhong-Yin Zhang, Chairman, 317-274-7151. *Application contact:* Dr. Zhong-Yin Zhang, Chairman, 317-274-7151.

Inter American University of Puerto Rico, Metropolitan Campus, Graduate Programs, Program in Medical Technology, San Juan, PR 00919-1293. Offers administration of clinical laboratories (MS); molecular microbiology (MS). *Accreditation:* NAACLS. Part-time programs available. *Degree requirements:* For master's, comprehensive exam. *Entrance requirements:* For master's, BS in medical technology, minimum GPA of 2.5. Electronic applications accepted.

Iowa State University of Science and Technology, Graduate College, College of Agriculture and College of Liberal Arts and Sciences, Department of Biochemistry, Biophysics, and Molecular Biology, Ames, IA 50011. Offers biochemistry (MS, PhD); biophysics (MS, PhD); genetics (MS, PhD); molecular, cellular, and developmental biology (MS, PhD); toxicology (MS, PhD). *Faculty:* 24 full-time (6 women), 1 (woman) part-time/adjunct. *Students:* 77 full-time (30 women), 3 part-time (2 women); includes 3 minority (1 African American, 1 Asian American or Pacific Islander, 1 Hispanic American), 56 international. 41 applicants, 32% accepted, 13 enrolled. In 2009, 2 master's, 7 doctorates awarded. *Degree requirements:* For master's, thesis; for doctorate, thesis/dissertation. *Entrance requirements:* For master's and doctorate, GRE General Test. Additional exam requirements/recommendations for international students: Required—TOEFL (minimum score 550 paper-based; 79 iBT) or IELTS (minimum score 6.5). *Application deadline:* For fall admission, 1/15 priority date for domestic and international students; for spring admission, 10/15 for domestic and international students. Application fee: $40 ($90 for international students). Electronic applications accepted. *Expenses:* Tuition, state resident: full-time $6716. Tuition, nonresident: full-time $8908. Tuition and fees vary according to course level, course load, program and student level. *Financial support:* In 2009–10, 52 research assistantships with full and partial tuition reimbursements (averaging $18,750 per year) were awarded; teaching assistantships with full and partial tuition reimbursements, scholarships/grants, health care benefits, and unspecified assistantships also available. *Unit head:* Dr. Guru Rao, Interim Chair, 515-294-6116, E-mail: biochem@iastate.edu. *Application contact:* Dr. Reuben Peters, Director of Graduate Education, 515-294-6116, E-mail: biochem@iastate.edu.

See Close-Up on page 155.

Iowa State University of Science and Technology, Graduate College, Interdisciplinary Programs, Bioinformatics and Computational Biology Program, Ames, IA 50011. Offers MS, PhD. *Students:* 52 full-time (19 women), 2 part-time (1 woman); includes 3 minority (all Asian Americans or Pacific Islanders), 34 international. In 2009, 2 master's, 11 doctorates awarded. *Degree requirements:* For doctorate, thesis/dissertation. *Entrance requirements:* For doctorate, GRE General Test. Additional exam requirements/recommendations for international students: Required—TOEFL (minimum score 550 paper-based; 213 computer-based; 79 iBT) or IELTS (minimum score 6.5). *Application deadline:* For fall admission, 1/15 priority date for domestic students, 1/15 for international students; for spring admission, 10/15 for domestic and international students. Application fee: $40 ($90 for international students). Electronic applications accepted. *Expenses:* Tuition, state resident: full-time $6716. Tuition, nonresident: full-time $8908. Tuition and fees vary according to course level, course load, program and student level. *Financial support:* In 2009–10, 48 research assistantships with full and partial tuition reimbursements (averaging $18,330 per year), 3 teaching assistantships (averaging $17,000 per year) were awarded; fellowships with full tuition reimbursements, scholarships/grants, traineeships, health care benefits, and unspecified assistantships also available. *Faculty research:* Functional and structural genomics, genome evolution, macromolecular structure and function, mathematical biology and biological statistics, metabolic and developmental networks. *Unit head:* Dr. Volker Brendel, Chair, Supervising Committee, 515-294-5122, Fax: 515-294-6790, E-mail: bcb@iastate.edu. *Application contact:* Dr. Volker Brendel, Chair, Supervising Committee, 515-294-5122, Fax: 515-294-6790, E-mail: bcb@iastate.edu.

Iowa State University of Science and Technology, Graduate College, Interdisciplinary Programs, Program in Molecular, Cellular, and Developmental Biology, Ames, IA 50011. Offers MS, PhD. *Students:* 34 full-time (16 women), 1 part-time (0 women), 26 international. In 2009, 2 master's, 8 doctorates awarded. *Degree requirements:* For master's, thesis or alternative; for doctorate, thesis/dissertation. *Entrance requirements:* For master's and doctorate, GRE General Test. Additional exam requirements/recommendations for international students: Required—TOEFL (minimum score 580 paper-based; 85 iBT) or IELTS (minimum score 7). *Application deadline:* For fall admission, 1/15 priority date for domestic and international students. Application fee: $40 ($90 for international students). Electronic applications accepted. *Expenses:* Tuition, state resident: full-time $6716. Tuition, nonresident: full-time $8908. Tuition and fees vary according to course level, course load, program and student level. *Financial support:* In 2009–10, 33 research assistantships with full and partial tuition reimbursements (averaging $18,750 per year), 1 teaching assistantship with full and partial tuition reimbursement (averaging $18,750 per year) were awarded; scholarships/grants, health care benefits, and unspecified assistantships also available. *Unit head:* Dr. Jeff Beetham, Supervisory Committee Chair, 515-294-7252, E-mail: idgp@iastate.edu. *Application contact:* Katie Blair, Information Contact, 515-294-7252, Fax: 515-924-6790, E-mail: idgp@iastate.edu.

The Johns Hopkins University, Bloomberg School of Public Health, Department of Biochemistry and Molecular Biology, Baltimore, MD 21205. Offers MHS, Sc M, PhD. Part-time programs available. *Faculty:* 19 full-time (3 women), 6 part-time/adjunct (4 women). *Students:* 64 full-time (41 women), 3 part-time (1 woman); includes 13 minority (1 African American, 9 Asian Americans or Pacific Islanders, 3 Hispanic Americans), 8 international. Average age 25. 108 applicants, 47% accepted, 26 enrolled. In 2009, 27 master's, 6 doctorates awarded. *Degree requirements:* For master's, thesis; for doctorate, comprehensive exam, thesis/ dissertation, oral and written exams. *Entrance requirements:* For master's, MCAT or GRE, 3 letters of recommendation, curriculum vitae; for doctorate, GRE General Test, 3 letters of recommendation, curriculum vitae. Additional exam requirements/recommendations for international students: Required—TOEFL (minimum score 600 paper-based; 250 computer-based). *Application deadline:* For fall admission, 12/22 priority date for domestic students; for winter admission, 6/1 for domestic students. Applications are processed on a rolling basis. Application fee: $45. Electronic applications accepted. *Financial support:* In 2009–10, 63 students received support, including 17 fellowships with tuition reimbursements available (averaging $26,800 per year), 19 research assistantships with tuition reimbursements available (averaging $26,800 per year), 7 teaching assistantships (averaging $1,000 per year); Federal Work-Study, institutionally sponsored loans, scholarships/grants, health care benefits, and stipends also available. Financial award application deadline: 3/15; financial award applicants required to submit FAFSA. *Faculty research:* DNA replication, repair, structure, carcinogenesis, protein structure, enzyme catalysts, reproductive biology. Total annual research expenditures: $6 million. *Unit head:* Dr. Pierre Coulombe, Chairman, 410-955-3671, Fax: 410-955-2926, E-mail: pcoulomb@jhsph.edu. *Application contact:* Sharon Warner, Senior Academic Program Coordinator, 410-955-3672, Fax: 410-955-2926, E-mail: swarner@jhsph.edu.

The Johns Hopkins University, National Institutes of Health Sponsored Programs, Baltimore, MD 21218-2699. Offers biology (PhD), including biochemistry, biophysics, cell biology, developmental biology, genetic biology, molecular biology; cell, molecular, and developmental biology and biophysics (PhD). *Faculty:* 25 full-time (4 women). *Students:* 126 full-time (72 women); includes 36 minority (3 African Americans, 1 American Indian/Alaska Native, 21 Asian Americans or Pacific Islanders, 11 Hispanic Americans), 19 international. 282 applicants, 26% accepted, 36 enrolled. In 2009, 15 doctorates awarded. *Degree requirements:* For doctorate, comprehensive exam, thesis/dissertation. *Entrance requirements:* For doctorate, GRE General Test. Additional exam requirements/recommendations for international students: Required— TOEFL (minimum score 600 paper-based; 250 computer-based), TWE. *Application deadline:* For fall admission, 12/15 priority date for domestic students. Application fee: $60. Electronic applications accepted. *Financial support:* In 2009–10, 24 fellowships (averaging $23,000 per year), 93 research assistantships (averaging $23,000 per year), 22 teaching assistantships (averaging $23,000 per year) were awarded; Federal Work-Study, institutionally sponsored loans, scholarships/grants, traineeships, health care benefits, tuition waivers (partial), and unspecified assistantships also available. Financial award application deadline: 4/15; financial award applicants required to submit FAFSA. *Faculty research:* Protein and nucleic acid biochemistry and biophysical chemistry, molecular biology and development. Total annual research expenditures: $11.2 million. *Unit head:* Dr. Allen Shearn, Chair, 410-516-4693, Fax: 410-516-5213, E-mail: bio_cals@jhu.edu. *Application contact:* Joan Miller, Academic Affairs Manager, 410-516-5502, Fax: 410-516-5213, E-mail: joan@jhu.edu.

The Johns Hopkins University, School of Medicine, Graduate Programs in Medicine, Department of Pharmacology and Molecular Sciences, Baltimore, MD 21205. Offers PhD. *Faculty:* 42 full-time (8 women). *Students:* 60 full-time (27 women); includes 16 minority (7 African Americans, 8 Asian Americans or Pacific Islanders, 1 Hispanic American), 16 international. 180 applicants, 10% accepted, 9 enrolled. In 2009, 4 doctorates awarded. *Degree requirements:* For doctorate, comprehensive exam, thesis/dissertation, departmental seminar. *Entrance requirements:* For doctorate, GRE General Test. Additional exam requirements/recommendations for international students: Required—TOEFL. *Application deadline:* For fall admission, 1/10 for domestic and international students. Application fee: $85. Electronic applications accepted. *Unit head:* Dr. Philip A. Cole, Chairman, 410-614-0540, Fax: 410-614-7717, E-mail: pcole@jhmi.edu. *Application contact:* Dr. James T. Stivers, Director of Admissions, 410-955-7117, Fax: 410-955-3023, E-mail: jstivers@jhmi.edu.

See Close-Up on page 463.

The Johns Hopkins University, School of Medicine, Graduate Programs in Medicine, Predoctoral Training Program in Human Genetics, Baltimore, MD 21218-2699. Offers PhD, MD/PhD. *Faculty:* 59 full-time (14 women). *Students:* 77 full-time (55 women); includes 28 minority (7 African Americans, 15 Asian Americans or Pacific Islanders, 6 Hispanic Americans), 17 international. Average age 24. 172 applicants, 11% accepted, 10 enrolled. In 2009, 9 doctorates awarded. Terminal master's awarded for partial completion of doctoral program. *Degree requirements:* For doctorate, comprehensive exam, thesis/dissertation. *Entrance requirements:* For doctorate, GRE General Test, GRE Subject Test. *Application deadline:* For fall admission, 12/31 priority date for domestic and international students. Application fee: $85. Electronic applications accepted. *Financial support:* In 2009–10, 1 fellowship with full tuition reimbursement (averaging $26,855 per year) was awarded; teaching assistantships with full tuition reimbursements, health care benefits also available. *Faculty research:* Human, mammalian, and molecular genetics, bioinformatics, genomics. *Unit head:* Dr. David Valle, Director, 410-955-4260, Fax: 410-955-7397, E-mail: muscelli@jhmi.edu. *Application contact:* Sandy Muscelli, Program Administrator, 410-955-4260, Fax: 410-955-7397, E-mail: muscelli@jhmi.edu.

The Johns Hopkins University, School of Medicine, Graduate Programs in Medicine, Program in Biochemistry, Cellular and Molecular Biology, Baltimore, MD 21205. Offers PhD. *Faculty:* 101 full-time (35 women). *Students:* 149 full-time (87 women); includes 33 minority (13 African Americans, 1 American Indian/Alaska Native, 17 Asian Americans or Pacific Islanders, 2 Hispanic Americans), 48 international. Average age 25. 299 applicants, 19% accepted, 18 enrolled. In 2009, 19 doctorates awarded. *Degree requirements:* For doctorate, comprehensive exam, thesis/dissertation. *Entrance requirements:* For doctorate, GRE General Test. Additional exam requirements/recommendations for international students: Required—TOEFL. *Application deadline:* For winter admission, 1/10 for domestic and international students. Applications are processed on a rolling basis. Application fee: $80. Electronic applications accepted. *Financial support:* In 2009–10, 5 fellowships with partial tuition reimbursements (averaging $32,000 per

year), 144 research assistantships with full and partial tuition reimbursements (averaging $27,125 per year) were awarded; traineeships and tuition waivers (full) also available. Financial award application deadline: 12/31. *Faculty research:* Developmental biology, genomics/ proteomics, protein targeting, signal transduction, structural biology. *Unit head:* Dr. Carolyn Machamer, Director, 410-955-3466, Fax: 410-614-8842, E-mail: machamer@jhmi.edu. *Application contact:* Dr. Jeff Corden, Admissions Director, 410-955-3506, Fax: 410-614-8842, E-mail: jcorden@jhmi.edu.

Kent State University, School of Biomedical Sciences, Program in Cellular and Molecular Biology, Kent, OH 44242-0001. Offers MS, PhD. Offered in cooperation with Northeastern Ohio Universities College of Medicine. Terminal master's awarded for partial completion of doctoral program. *Degree requirements:* For master's, thesis; for doctorate, thesis/dissertation. *Entrance requirements:* For master's, GRE General Test, letter of recommendation, minimum GPA of 3.0; for doctorate, GRE General Test, letter of recommendation, minimum GPA of 3.0, MS. Additional exam requirements/recommendations for international students: Required— TOEFL. Electronic applications accepted. *Faculty research:* Molecular genetics, molecular endocrinology, virology and tumor biology, P450 enzymology and catalysis, membrane structure and function.

Lehigh University, College of Arts and Sciences, Department of Biological Sciences, Bethlehem, PA 18015. Offers biochemistry (PhD); integrative biology and neuroscience (PhD); molecular biology (MS, PhD). Part-time programs available. Postbaccalaureate distance learning degree programs offered (no on-campus study). *Faculty:* 17 full-time (6 women), 1 (woman) part-time/ adjunct. *Students:* 33 full-time (15 women), 37 part-time (25 women); includes 7 minority (1 African American, 3 Asian Americans or Pacific Islanders, 3 Hispanic Americans), 6 international. Average age 29. 45 applicants, 24% accepted, 11 enrolled. In 2009, 20 master's, 4 doctorates awarded. Terminal master's awarded for partial completion of doctoral program. *Degree requirements:* For master's, research report; for doctorate, comprehensive exam, thesis/ dissertation. *Entrance requirements:* For doctorate, GRE General Test. Additional exam requirements/recommendations for international students: Required—TOEFL. *Application deadline:* For fall admission, 12/15 for domestic and international students. Applications are processed on a rolling basis. Application fee: $65. Electronic applications accepted. *Financial support:* In 2009–10, 34 students received support, including 4 fellowships with full tuition reimbursements available (averaging $23,000 per year), 6 research assistantships with full tuition reimbursements available (averaging $23,000 per year), 16 teaching assistantships with full tuition reimbursements available (averaging $23,000 per year); scholarships/grants, tuition waivers (full and partial), and unspecified assistantships also available. Financial award application deadline: 1/15. *Faculty research:* Gene expression, cytoskeleton and cell structure, cell cycle and growth regulation, neuroscience, animal behavior. Total annual research expenditures: $2 million. *Unit head:* Dr. Murray Itzkowitz, Chairperson, 610-758-3680, Fax: 610-758-4004, E-mail: mi00@lehigh.edu. *Application contact:* Dr. Jennifer M. Swann, Graduate Coordinator, 610-758-5484, Fax: 610-758-4004, E-mail: jms5@lehigh.edu.

Louisiana State University Health Sciences Center at Shreveport, Department of Biochemistry and Molecular Biology, Shreveport, LA 71130-3932. Offers MS, PhD, MD/PhD. *Degree requirements:* For master's, thesis; for doctorate, thesis/dissertation. *Entrance requirements:* For master's and doctorate, GRE General Test. Additional exam requirements/ recommendations for international students: Required—TOEFL. *Faculty research:* Metabolite transport, regulation of translation and transcription, prokaryotic molecular genetics, cell matrix biochemistry, yeast molecular genetics, oncogenes.

Loyola University Chicago, Graduate School, Program in Molecular Biology, Maywood, IL 60153. Offers MS, PhD, MD/PhD. *Faculty:* 28 full-time (5 women). *Students:* 15 full-time (11 women); includes 3 minority (1 American Indian/Alaska Native, 1 Asian American or Pacific Islander, 1 Hispanic American), 9 international. Average age 27. 42 applicants, 14% accepted, 5 enrolled. In 2009, 2 doctorates awarded. Terminal master's awarded for partial completion of doctoral program. *Degree requirements:* For master's, comprehensive exam (for some programs), thesis; for doctorate, comprehensive exam, thesis/dissertation, 48 credit hours. *Entrance requirements:* For master's, GRE General Test, statement of purpose, transcripts, 3 letters of recommendation; for doctorate, GRE General Test, 3 letters of recommendation. Additional exam requirements/recommendations for international students: Required—TOEFL (minimum score 600 paper-based; 250 computer-based). *Application deadline:* For fall admission, 3/1 for domestic and international students. Applications are processed on a rolling basis. Application fee: $40. Electronic applications accepted. *Expenses:* Tuition: Full-time $14,220; part-time $790 per credit hour. Required fees: $60 per semester hour. Tuition and fees vary according to program. *Financial support:* In 2009–10, 7 students received support, including fellowships (averaging $23,000 per year); research assistantships, Federal Work-Study, institutionally sponsored loans, scholarships/grants, and health care benefits also available. Financial award application deadline: 2/15; financial award applicants required to submit FAFSA. *Faculty research:* Cell cycle regulation, molecular immunology, molecular genetics, molecular oncology, molecular virology. Total annual research expenditures: $3,500. *Unit head:* Dr. Manuel O. Diaz, Director, 708-327-3172, Fax: 708-216-6505, E-mail: mdiaz@luc.edu. *Application contact:* Dr. Mitchell Denning, Graduate Program Director, 708-327-3358, E-mail: mdennin@lumc.edu.

Marquette University, Graduate School, College of Arts and Sciences, Department of Biology, Milwaukee, WI 53201-1881. Offers cell biology (MS, PhD); developmental biology (MS, PhD); ecology (MS, PhD); endocrinology (MS, PhD); evolutionary biology (MS, PhD); genetics (MS, PhD); microbiology (MS, PhD); molecular biology (MS, PhD); muscle and exercise physiology (MS, PhD); neurobiology (MS, PhD); reproductive physiology (MS, PhD). *Faculty:* 23 full-time (10 women), 1 part-time/adjunct (0 women). *Students:* 23 full-time (13 women), 16 part-time (9 women); includes 1 minority (Asian American or Pacific Islander), 20 international. Average age 25. 95 applicants, 16% accepted, 10 enrolled. In 2009, 3 master's, 5 doctorates awarded. Terminal master's awarded for partial completion of doctoral program. *Degree requirements:* For master's, comprehensive exam, thesis, 1 year of teaching experience or equivalent; for doctorate, thesis/dissertation, 1 year of teaching experience or equivalent, qualifying exam. *Entrance requirements:* For master's and doctorate, GRE General Test, GRE Subject Test. Additional exam requirements/recommendations for international students: Required—TOEFL. Application fee: $40. *Financial support:* In 2009–10, 4 fellowships, 22 teaching assistantships were awarded; research assistantships, Federal Work-Study, institutionally sponsored loans, scholarships/grants, and tuition waivers (full and partial) also available. Support available to part-time students. Financial award application deadline: 2/15. *Faculty research:* Microbial and invertebrate ecology, evolution of gene function, DNA methylation, DNA arrangement. *Unit head:* Dr. Robert Fitts, Chair, 414-288-1748, Fax: 414-288-7357. *Application contact:* Debbie Weaver, Administrative Assistant, 414-288-7355, Fax: 414-288-7357.

Massachusetts Institute of Technology, School of Science, Department of Biology, Cambridge, MA 02139-4307. Offers biochemistry (PhD); biological oceanography (PhD); biology (PhD); biophysical chemistry and molecular structure (PhD); cell biology (PhD); computational and systems biology (PhD); developmental biology (PhD); genetics (PhD); immunology (PhD); microbiology (PhD); molecular biology (PhD); neurobiology (PhD). *Faculty:* 54 full-time (14 women). *Students:* 237 full-time (128 women); includes 65 minority (4 African Americans, 2 American Indian/Alaska Native, 33 Asian Americans or Pacific Islanders, 26 Hispanic Americans), 25 international. Average age 26. 645 applicants, 18% accepted, 49 enrolled. In 2009, 41 doctorates awarded. *Degree requirements:* For doctorate, comprehensive exam, thesis/ dissertation. *Entrance requirements:* For doctorate, GRE General Test. Additional exam requirements/recommendations for international students: Required—TOEFL (minimum score 577 paper-based; 233 computer-based), IELTS (minimum score 6.5). *Application deadline:* For fall admission, 12/1 for domestic and international students. Application fee: $75. Electronic applications accepted. *Expenses:* Tuition: Full-time $37,510; part-time $585 per unit. Required fees: $272. *Financial support:* In 2009–10, 218 students received support, including 113 fellowships with tuition reimbursements available (averaging $31,816 per year), 109 research assistantships with tuition reimbursements available (averaging $29,254 per year); teaching

Molecular Biology

Massachusetts Institute of Technology (continued)
assistantships with tuition reimbursements available, Federal Work-Study, institutionally sponsored loans, scholarships/grants, traineeships, health care benefits, and unspecified assistantships also available. *Faculty research:* DNA recombination, transcription and gene regulation, signal transduction, cell cycle, neuronal cell fate, replication and repair. Total annual research expenditures: $114 million. *Unit head:* Prof. Chris Kaiser, Head, 617-253-4701, E-mail: mitbio@mit.edu. *Application contact:* Biology Education Office, 617-253-3717, Fax: 617-258-9329, E-mail: gradbio@mit.edu.

Mayo Graduate School, Graduate Programs in Biomedical Sciences, Programs in Biochemistry, Structural Biology, Cell Biology, and Genetics, Rochester, MN 55905. Offers biochemistry and structural biology (PhD); cell biology and genetics (PhD); molecular biology (PhD). *Degree requirements:* For doctorate, oral defense of dissertation, qualifying oral and written exam. *Entrance requirements:* For doctorate, GRE, 1 year of chemistry, biology, calculus, and physics. Additional exam requirements/recommendations for international students: Required—TOEFL. Electronic applications accepted. *Faculty research:* Gene structure and function, membranes and receptors/cytoskeleton, oncogenes and growth factors, protein structure and function, steroid hormonal action.

McMaster University, Faculty of Health Sciences and School of Graduate Studies, Program in Medical Sciences, Hamilton, ON L8S 4M2, Canada. Offers blood and vascular (M Sc, PhD); genetics and cancer (M Sc, PhD); immunity and infection (M Sc, PhD); metabolism and nutrition (M Sc, PhD); neurosciences and behavioral sciences (M Sc, PhD); physiology/pharmacology (M Sc, PhD); MD/PhD. *Degree requirements:* For master's, thesis; for doctorate, comprehensive exam, thesis/dissertation. *Entrance requirements:* For master's, honors B Sc, B+ average in related field; for doctorate, M Sc, minimum B+ average. Additional exam requirements/recommendations for international students: Required—TOEFL (minimum score 580 paper-based; 237 computer-based; 92 iBT).

Medical College of Georgia, School of Graduate Studies, Program in Biochemistry and Molecular Biology, Augusta, GA 30912. Offers PhD. *Degree requirements:* For doctorate, comprehensive exam, thesis/dissertation. *Entrance requirements:* For doctorate, GRE General Test. Additional exam requirements/recommendations for international students: Required—TOEFL (minimum score 550 paper-based; 213 computer-based; 79 iBT). Electronic applications accepted. Full-time tuition and fees vary according to campus/location, program and student level. *Faculty research:* Bacterial pathogenesis, eye diseases, vitamins and amino acid transporters, transcriptional control and molecular oncology, tumor biology.

Medical University of South Carolina, College of Graduate Studies, Department of Biochemistry and Molecular Biology, Charleston, SC 29425. Offers MS, PhD, MD/PhD. *Faculty:* 21 full-time (3 women), 3 part-time/adjunct (1 woman). *Students:* 19 full-time (9 women), 2 part-time (0 women); includes 1 Asian American or Pacific Islander, 1 Hispanic American, 4 international. Average age 29. 9 applicants, 22% accepted, 2 enrolled. In 2009, 2 master's, 4 doctorates awarded. Terminal master's awarded for partial completion of doctoral program. *Degree requirements:* For master's, thesis; for doctorate, thesis/dissertation, oral and written exams. *Entrance requirements:* For master's, GRE General Test; for doctorate, GRE General Test, interview, minimum GPA of 3.0. Additional exam requirements/recommendations for international students: Required—TOEFL (minimum score 600 paper-based; 250 computer-based; 100 iBT). *Application deadline:* For fall admission, 1/15 priority date for domestic and international students. Applications are processed on a rolling basis. Application fee: $0 ($85 for international students). Electronic applications accepted. *Financial support:* In 2009–10, 17 research assistantships with partial tuition reimbursements (averaging $23,000 per year) were awarded; Federal Work-Study and scholarships/grants also available. Support available to part-time students. Financial award application deadline: 3/10; financial award applicants required to submit FAFSA. *Faculty research:* Lipid biochemistry, DNA replication, nucleic acids, protein structure. *Unit head:* Dr. Yusuf A. Hannun, Chairman, 843-792-9318, Fax: 843-792-6590, E-mail: hannun@musc.edu. *Application contact:* Dr. Maurizio Del Poeta, Associate Professor, 843-792-8381, Fax: 843-792-6590, E-mail: delpoeta@musc.edu.

Medical University of South Carolina, College of Graduate Studies, Program in Molecular and Cellular Biology and Pathobiology, Charleston, SC 29425. Offers cancer biology (PhD); cardiovascular biology (PhD); cardiovascular imaging (PhD); cell regulation (PhD); craniofacial biology (PhD); genetics and development (PhD); marine biomedicine (PhD); DMD/PhD; MD/PhD. *Faculty:* 137 full-time (33 women). *Students:* 39 full-time (25 women); includes 6 minority (4 African Americans, 1 Asian American or Pacific Islander, 1 Hispanic American), 9 international. Average age 28. In 2009, 16 doctorates awarded. *Degree requirements:* For doctorate, thesis/dissertation, oral and written exams. *Entrance requirements:* For doctorate, GRE General Test, interview, minimum GPA of 3.0. Additional exam requirements/recommendations for international students: Required—TOEFL (minimum score 600 paper-based; 250 computer-based; 100 iBT). *Application deadline:* For fall admission, 1/15 priority date for domestic and international students. Applications are processed on a rolling basis. Application fee: $0 ($85 for international students). Electronic applications accepted. *Financial support:* In 2009–10, 39 students received support, including 39 research assistantships with partial tuition reimbursements available (averaging $23,000 per year); Federal Work-Study and scholarships/grants also available. Support available to part-time students. Financial award application deadline: 3/10; financial award applicants required to submit FAFSA. *Unit head:* Dr. Donald R. Menick, Director, 843-876-5045, Fax: 843-792-6590, E-mail: menickd@musc.edu. *Application contact:* Dr. Cynthia F. Wright, Associate Dean for Admissions and Career Development, 843-792-2564, Fax: 843-792-6590, E-mail: wrightcf@musc.edu.

Michigan State University, The Graduate School, College of Natural Science and Graduate Programs in Human Medicine and Graduate Studies in Osteopathic Medicine, Department of Biochemistry and Molecular Biology, East Lansing, MI 48824. Offers biochemistry and molecular biology (MS, PhD); biochemistry and molecular biology/environmental toxicology (PhD). *Faculty:* 26 full-time (5 women). *Students:* 64 full-time (26 women); includes 2 minority (1 African American, 1 Asian American or Pacific Islander), 38 international. Average age 27. 111 applicants, 9% accepted. In 2009, 10 doctorates awarded. *Entrance requirements:* Additional exam requirements/recommendations for international students: Required—TOEFL. Electronic applications accepted. *Expenses:* Tuition, state resident: part-time $478.25 per credit hour. Tuition, nonresident: part-time $966.50 per credit hour. Part-time tuition and fees vary according to program. *Financial support:* In 2009–10, 48 research assistantships with tuition reimbursements (averaging $8,017 per year), 3 teaching assistantships with tuition reimbursements (averaging $8,033 per year) were awarded; scholarships/grants and unspecified assistantships also available. Total annual research expenditures: $6.4 million. *Unit head:* Dr. Thomas Sharkey, Chairperson, 517-353-0804, Fax: 517-353-9334, E-mail: tsharkey@msu.edu. *Application contact:* Jessica Lawrence, Graduate Program Secretary, 517-353-0807, Fax: 517-353-9334, E-mail: bmbgrad@cns.msu.edu.

Michigan State University, The Graduate School, College of Natural Science, Program in Cell and Molecular Biology, East Lansing, MI 48824. Offers cell and molecular biology (MS, PhD); cell and molecular biology/environmental toxicology (PhD). *Faculty:* 87 full-time (28 women). *Students:* 38 full-time (20 women), 1 (woman) part-time; includes 5 minority (1 African American, 2 Asian Americans or Pacific Islanders, 2 Hispanic Americans), 14 international. Average age 27. 143 applicants, 3% accepted. In 2009, 2 master's, 6 doctorates awarded. *Entrance requirements:* Additional exam requirements/recommendations for international students: Required—TOEFL. Electronic applications accepted. *Expenses:* Tuition, state resident: part-time $478.25 per credit hour. Tuition, nonresident: part-time $966.50 per credit hour. Part-time tuition and fees vary according to program. *Financial support:* In 2009–10, 25 research assistantships with tuition reimbursements (averaging $7,826 per year), 4 teaching assistantships with tuition reimbursements (averaging $7,865 per year) were awarded; scholarships/grants and unspecified assistantships also available. Financial award application deadline: 1/1. *Unit head:* Dr. Susan E. Conrad, Director, 517-353-5161, Fax: 517-432-8813, E-mail: conrad@msu.edu. *Application contact:* Rebecca Mansel, Graduate Secretary, 517-353-8916, Fax: 517-432-8813, E-mail: cmb@msu.edu.

Mississippi State University, College of Agriculture and Life Sciences, Department of Biochemistry and Molecular Biology, Mississippi State, MS 39762. Offers agriculture life sciences (MS), including biochemistry; molecular biology (PhD). *Faculty:* 7 full-time (0 women). *Students:* 23 full-time (7 women), 4 part-time (3 women); includes 3 minority (1 African American, 1 American Indian/Alaska Native, 1 Asian American or Pacific Islander), 14 international. Average age 27. 20 applicants, 40% accepted, 2 enrolled. In 2009, 2 master's, 3 doctorates awarded. Terminal master's awarded for partial completion of doctoral program. *Degree requirements:* For master's, thesis (for some programs), comprehensive oral or written exam; for doctorate, thesis/dissertation, comprehensive oral and written exam. *Entrance requirements:* For master's, GRE General Test, minimum GPA of 2.75; for doctorate, GRE. Additional exam requirements/recommendations for international students: Required—TOEFL (minimum score 550 paper-based; 213 computer-based; 79 iBT); Recommended—IELTS (minimum score 6.5). *Application deadline:* For fall admission, 7/1 for domestic students, 5/1 for international students; for spring admission, 11/1 for domestic students, 9/1 for international students. Applications are processed on a rolling basis. Application fee: $40. Electronic applications accepted. *Expenses:* Tuition, state resident: full-time $2575.50; part-time $286.25 per credit hour. Tuition, nonresident: full-time $6510; part-time $723.50 per credit hour. Tuition and fees vary according to course load. *Financial support:* In 2009–10, 16 research assistantships with full tuition reimbursements (averaging $11,115 per year) were awarded; Federal Work-Study, institutionally sponsored loans, and unspecified assistantships also available. Financial award applicants required to submit FAFSA. *Faculty research:* Fish nutrition, plant and animal molecular biology, plant biochemistry, enzymology, lipid metabolism. *Unit head:* Dr. Scott T. Willard, Professor and Department Head, 662-325-2640, Fax: 662-325-8664, E-mail: swilliard@ads.msstate.edu. *Application contact:* Dr. Din-Pow Ma, Professor/Graduate Coordinator, 662-325-7739, Fax: 662-325-8664, E-mail: dm1@ra.msstate.edu.

Missouri State University, Graduate College, College of Health and Human Services, Department of Biomedical Sciences, Program in Cell and Molecular Biology, Springfield, MO 65897. Offers MS. Part-time programs available. *Students:* 5 full-time (4 women), 4 part-time (2 women), 2 international. Average age 25. 11 applicants, 55% accepted, 5 enrolled. In 2009, 5 master's awarded. *Degree requirements:* For master's, thesis or alternative, oral and written exams. *Entrance requirements:* For master's, GRE General Test, 2 semesters of course work in organic chemistry and physics, 1 semester of course work in calculus, minimum GPA of 3.0 in last 60 hours of course work. Additional exam requirements/recommendations for international students: Required—TOEFL (minimum score 550 paper-based; 213 computer-based; 79 iBT). *Application deadline:* For fall admission, 7/20 priority date for domestic students, 5/1 for international students; for spring admission, 12/20 priority date for domestic students, 9/1 for international students. Applications are processed on a rolling basis. Application fee: $35 ($50 for international students). Electronic applications accepted. *Expenses:* Tuition, state resident: full-time $3852; part-time $214 per credit hour. Tuition, nonresident: full-time $7524; part-time $418 per credit hour. Required fees: $696; $172 per semester. Tuition and fees vary according to course level, course load, degree level and program. *Financial support:* In 2009–10, 4 teaching assistantships with full tuition reimbursements (averaging $7,340 per year) were awarded; career-related internships or fieldwork, Federal Work-Study, institutionally sponsored loans, scholarships/grants, and unspecified assistantships also available. Support available to part-time students. Financial award application deadline: 3/31; financial award applicants required to submit FAFSA. *Faculty research:* Extracellular matrix membrane protein, P2 nucleotide receptors, double stranded RNA viruses. *Unit head:* Dr. Chris Field, Graduate Program Director, 417-836-5478, E-mail: biomedicalsciences@missouristate.edu. *Application contact:* Eric Eckert, Coordinator of Graduate Admissions and Recruitment, 417-836-6331, Fax: 417-836-6200, E-mail: ericeckert@missouristate.edu.

Montana State University, College of Graduate Studies, College of Agriculture, Department of Veterinary Molecular Biology, Bozeman, MT 59717. Offers MS, PhD. Part-time programs available. *Faculty:* 7 full-time (2 women), 1 (woman) part-time/adjunct. *Students:* 2 full-time (both women), 9 part-time (4 women), 2 international. Average age 29. 5 applicants. In 2009, 5 doctorates awarded. *Degree requirements:* For master's, comprehensive exam; for doctorate, comprehensive exam, thesis/dissertation. *Entrance requirements:* For master's, GRE General Test; for doctorate, GRE General Test, BS or BA. Additional exam requirements/recommendations for international students: Required—TOEFL (minimum score 550 paper-based; 213 computer-based). *Application deadline:* For fall admission, 7/15 priority date for domestic students, 5/15 for international students; for spring admission, 12/1 priority date for domestic students, 10/1 priority date for international students. Applications are processed on a rolling basis. Application fee: $30. Electronic applications accepted. *Expenses:* Tuition, state resident: full-time $5635; part-time $3492 per year. Tuition, nonresident: full-time $17,212; part-time $7865.10 per year. Required fees: $1441; $153.15 per credit. Tuition and fees vary according to course load and program. *Financial support:* In 2009–10, 11 students received support, including 2 fellowships with full tuition reimbursements available (averaging $21,000 per year), 4 teaching assistantships with full tuition reimbursements available (averaging $5,700 per year); health care benefits and unspecified assistantships also available. Financial award application deadline: 3/1; financial award applicants required to submit FAFSA. *Faculty research:* Infectious disease pathogenesis, immunology, developmental biology, vaccine development, complementary and alternative medicine. Total annual research expenditures: $7.8 million. *Unit head:* Dr. Mark G. Quinn, Head, 406-994-5721, Fax: 406-994-4303, E-mail: mquinn@montana.edu. *Application contact:* Dr. Carl A. Fox, Vice Provost for Graduate Education, 406-994-4145, Fax: 406-994-7433, E-mail: gradstudy@montana.edu.

Montclair State University, The Graduate School, College of Science and Mathematics, Department of Biology and Molecular Biology, Montclair, NJ 07043-1624. Offers biology (MS), including biology science education, molecular biology; molecular biology (Certificate). Part-time and evening/weekend programs available. *Faculty:* 21 full-time (8 women), 27 part-time/adjunct (13 women). *Students:* 35 full-time (23 women), 57 part-time (44 women). Average age 28. 53 applicants, 64% accepted, 23 enrolled. In 2009, 26 master's, 2 other advanced degrees awarded. *Degree requirements:* For master's, comprehensive exam, thesis or alternative. *Entrance requirements:* For master's, GRE General Test, 24 credits of course work in undergraduate biology, 2 letters of recommendation, teaching certificate (biology sciences education concentration). Additional exam requirements/recommendations for international students: Required—TOEFL (minimum iBT score of 83) or IELTS. *Application deadline:* For fall admission, 6/1 for international students; for spring admission, 10/1 for international students. Applications are processed on a rolling basis. Application fee: $60. Electronic applications accepted. *Expenses:* Tuition, area resident: Part-time $486.74 per credit. Tuition, state resident: part-time $486.74 per credit. Tuition, nonresident: part-time $751.34 per credit. Tuition and fees vary according to degree level and program. *Financial support:* In 2009–10, 13 research assistantships with full tuition reimbursements (averaging $7,000 per year) were awarded; Federal Work-Study, scholarships/grants, and unspecified assistantships also available. Support available to part-time students. Financial award application deadline: 3/1; financial award applicants required to submit FAFSA. *Faculty research:* Cells, algae blooms, scallops, New Jersey bays, Barnegat Bay. *Unit head:* Dr. Quinn Vega, Chairperson, 973-655-7178. *Application contact:* Amy Aiello, Director of Graduate Admissions and Operations, 973-655-5147, Fax: 973-655-7869, E-mail: graduate.school@montclair.edu.

New Mexico State University, Graduate School, Program in Molecular Biology, Las Cruces, NM 88003-8001. Offers MS, PhD. *Students:* 25 full-time (10 women), 5 part-time (4 women); includes 7 minority (2 African Americans, 5 Hispanic Americans), 16 international. Average age 32. 23 applicants, 87% accepted, 8 enrolled. In 2009, 4 master's, 6 doctorates awarded. *Degree requirements:* For master's, thesis, oral seminars; for doctorate, comprehensive exam, thesis/dissertation, oral seminars. *Entrance requirements:* For master's and doctorate, GRE General Test, minimum GPA of 3.3. Additional exam requirements/recommendations for international students: Required—TOEFL. *Application deadline:* For fall admission, 12/15 for domestic and international students; for spring admission, 1/15 for domestic and international students.

Applications are processed on a rolling basis. Application fee: $30 ($50 for international students). Electronic applications accepted. *Expenses:* Tuition, state resident: full-time $4080; part-time $223 per credit. Tuition, nonresident: full-time $14,256; part-time $647 per credit. Required fees: $1278; $639 per semester. *Financial support:* In 2009–10, 13 research assistantships (averaging $16,413 per year), 10 teaching assistantships (averaging $1,104 per year) were awarded; fellowships, career-related internships or fieldwork, health care benefits, and unspecified assistantships also available. Financial award application deadline: 3/1. *Faculty research:* Emerging pathogens, plant-molecular biology and virology, molecular symbiotic interactions, cell and organismal biology, applied and environmental microbiology. *Unit head:* Dr. Rebecca Creamer, Director, 575-646-3068, Fax: 575-646-8087, E-mail: creamer@nmsu.edu. *Application contact:* Nancy McDow, Program Secretary, 575-646-3437, Fax: 575-646-5170, E-mail: nancyt@nmsu.edu.

New York Medical College, Graduate School of Basic Medical Sciences, Program in Biochemistry and Molecular Biology, Valhalla, NY 10595-1691. Offers MS, PhD, MD/PhD. Part-time and evening/weekend programs available. Terminal master's awarded for partial completion of doctoral program. *Degree requirements:* For master's, thesis; for doctorate, comprehensive exam, thesis/dissertation. *Entrance requirements:* For master's and doctorate, GRE General Test. Additional exam requirements/recommendations for international students: Required—TOEFL. *Expenses:* Tuition: Full-time $18,170; part-time $790 per credit. Required fees: $790 per credit. $20 per semester. One-time fee: $100. Tuition and fees vary according to class time, course level, course load, degree level, program, student level and student's religious affiliation. *Faculty research:* Mechanisms of control of blood coagulation, molecular neurobiology, molecular probes for infectious disease, protein-DNA interactions, molecular biology and biochemistry of double-stranded RNA-dependent enzymes.

New York University, Graduate School of Arts and Science, Department of Biology, New York, NY 10012-1019. Offers biology (PhD); biomedical journalism (MS); cancer and molecular biology (PhD); computational biology (PhD); computers in biological research (MS); developmental genetics (PhD); general biology (MS); immunology and microbiology (PhD); molecular genetics (PhD); neurobiology (PhD); oral biology (MS); plant biology (PhD); recombinant DNA technology (MS); MS/MBA. Part-time programs available. *Faculty:* 24 full-time (5 women). *Students:* 142 full-time (79 women), 44 part-time (28 women); includes 34 minority (1 African American, 25 Asian Americans or Pacific Islanders, 8 Hispanic Americans), 82 international. Average age 27. 362 applicants, 71% accepted, 72 enrolled. In 2009, 43 master's, 9 doctorates awarded. Terminal master's awarded for partial completion of doctoral program. *Degree requirements:* For master's, thesis or alternative, qualifying paper; for doctorate, comprehensive exam, thesis/dissertation. *Entrance requirements:* For master's, GRE General Test; for doctorate, GRE General Test, GRE Subject Test. Additional exam requirements/recommendations for international students: Required—TOEFL. *Application deadline:* For fall admission, 12/12 priority date for domestic students. Application fee: $90. *Expenses:* Tuition: Full-time $30,528; part-time $1272 per credit. Required fees: $2177. *Financial support:* Fellowships with tuition reimbursements, research assistantships with tuition reimbursements, teaching assistantships with tuition reimbursements, career-related internships or fieldwork, Federal Work-Study, institutionally sponsored loans, scholarships/grants, health care benefits, and unspecified assistantships available. Financial award application deadline: 12/12; financial award applicants required to submit FAFSA. *Faculty research:* Genomics, molecular and cell biology, development and molecular genetics, molecular evolution of plants and animals. *Unit head:* Gloria Coruzzi, Chair, 212-998-8200, Fax: 212-995-4015, E-mail: biology@nyu.edu. *Application contact:* Stephen Small, Director of Graduate Studies, 212-998-8200, Fax: 212-995-4015, E-mail: biology@nyu.edu.

New York University, School of Medicine, New York, NY 10012-1019. Offers biomedical sciences (PhD), including biomedical imaging, cellular and molecular biology, computational biology, developmental genetics, medical and molecular parasitology, microbiology, molecular oncobiology and immunology, neuroscience and physiology, pathobiology, pharmacology, structural biology; clinical investigation (MS); medicine (MD); MD/MA; MD/MPA; MD/MS; MD/PhD. *Accreditation:* LCME/AMA (one or more programs are accredited). *Faculty:* 1,493 full-time (558 women), 327 part-time/adjunct (122 women). *Students:* 747 full-time (360 women); includes 275 minority (23 African Americans, 5 American Indian/Alaska Native, 199 Asian Americans or Pacific Islanders, 48 Hispanic Americans), 2 international. Average age 24. 7,568 applicants, 7% accepted, 213 enrolled. In 2009, 164 first professional degrees, 13 master's, 50 doctorates awarded. *Degree requirements:* For master's, comprehensive exam, thesis; for doctorate, comprehensive exam, thesis/dissertation. *Entrance requirements:* MCAT. Additional exam requirements/recommendations for international students: Required—TOEFL. *Application deadline:* For fall admission, 10/15 for domestic students; for winter admission, 12/18 for domestic students, 12/15 for international students. Application fee: $100. *Expenses:* Contact institution. *Financial support:* In 2009–10, 524 students received support, including 29 fellowships with full tuition reimbursements available (averaging $31,000 per year), 47 research assistantships with full tuition reimbursements available (averaging $31,000 per year); teaching assistantships, Federal Work-Study, institutionally sponsored loans, and health care benefits also available. Financial award application deadline: 3/1; financial award applicants required to submit FAFSA. *Faculty research:* AIDS, cancer, neuroscience, molecular biology, neuroscience, cell biology and molecular genetics, structural biology, microbial pathogenesis and host defense, pharmacology, molecular oncology and immunology. Total annual research expenditures: $201.1 million. *Unit head:* Dr. Robert Grossman, Dean, 212-263-3269, Fax: 212-263- 1828. *Application contact:* Dr. Nancy Genieser, Associate Dean, Admissions, 212-263-5290, Fax: 212-263-0720, E-mail: nancy.genieser@nyumc.org.

New York University, School of Medicine and Graduate School of Arts and Science, Sackler Institute of Graduate Biomedical Sciences, Program in Cellular and Molecular Biology, New York, NY 10012-1019. Offers PhD, MD/PhD. *Degree requirements:* For doctorate, comprehensive exam, thesis/dissertation, qualifying exams. *Entrance requirements:* For doctorate, GRE General Test. Additional exam requirements/recommendations for international students: Required—TOEFL. *Expenses:* Tuition: Full-time $30,528; part-time $1272 per credit. Required fees: $2177. *Faculty research:* Membrane and organelle structure and biogenesis, intracellular transport and processing of proteins, cellular recognition and cell adhesion, oncogene structure and function, action of growth factors.

North Dakota State University, College of Graduate and Interdisciplinary Studies, College of Science and Mathematics, Department of Biological Sciences, Fargo, ND 58108. Offers biology (MS); botany (MS, PhD); cellular and molecular biology (PhD); environmental and conservation sciences (MS, PhD); genomics (PhD); natural resources management (MS, PhD); zoology (MS, PhD). *Students:* 32 full-time (21 women), 14 part-time (10 women); includes 1 Asian American or Pacific Islander, 14 international. In 2009, 12 master's, 9 doctorates awarded. *Degree requirements:* For master's, thesis; for doctorate, thesis/dissertation. *Entrance requirements:* For master's and doctorate, GRE General Test. Additional exam requirements/recommendations for international students: Required—TOEFL. *Application deadline:* For fall admission, 3/15 priority date for domestic students; for spring admission, 10/30 priority date for domestic students. Applications are processed on a rolling basis. Application fee: $45 ($60 for international students). Electronic applications accepted. *Financial support:* Fellowships with full tuition reimbursements, research assistantships with full tuition reimbursements, teaching assistantships with full tuition reimbursements, career-related internships or fieldwork, Federal Work-Study, institutionally sponsored loans, scholarships/grants, tuition waivers (full), and unspecified assistantships available. Support available to part-time students. Financial award application deadline: 4/15; financial award applicants required to submit FAFSA. *Faculty research:* Comparative endocrinology, physiology, behavioral ecology, plant cell biology, aquatic biology. Total annual research expenditures: $675,000. *Unit head:* Dr. Marinus L. Otte, Head, 701-231-7087, E-mail: marinus.otte@ndsu.edu. *Application contact:* Dr. Marinus L. Otte, Head, 701-231-7087, E-mail: marinus.otte@ndsu.edu.

North Dakota State University, College of Graduate and Interdisciplinary Studies, Interdisciplinary Program in Cellular and Molecular Biology, Fargo, ND 58108. Offers PhD. Offered in cooperation with 11 departments in the university. *Students:* 8 full-time (3 women), 6 international. In 2009, 2 doctorates awarded. *Degree requirements:* For doctorate, thesis/dissertation. *Entrance requirements:* For doctorate, GRE. Additional exam requirements/recommendations for international students: Required—TOEFL (minimum score 525 paper-based; 197 computer-based; 71 iBT). *Application deadline:* Applications are processed on a rolling basis. Application fee: $45 ($60 for international students). Electronic applications accepted. *Financial support:* Fellowships with full tuition reimbursements, research assistantships with full tuition reimbursements, teaching assistantships with full tuition reimbursements, unspecified assistantships available. Financial award application deadline: 3/15. *Faculty research:* Plant and animal cell biology, gene regulation, molecular genetics, plant and animal virology. *Unit head:* Dr. Mark Sheridan, Director, 701-231-8110. *Application contact:* Dr. Mark Sheridan, Director, 701-231-8110.

Northwestern University, The Graduate School and Judd A. and Marjorie Weinberg College of Arts and Sciences, Interdepartmental Biological Sciences Program (IBiS), Evanston, IL 60208. Offers biochemistry, molecular biology, and cell biology (PhD), including biochemistry, cell and molecular biology, molecular biophysics, structural biology; biotechnology (PhD); cell and molecular biology (PhD); developmental biology and genetics (PhD); hormone action and signal transduction (PhD); neuroscience (PhD); structural biology, biochemistry, and biophysics (PhD). Program participants include the Departments of Biochemistry, Molecular Biology, and Cell Biology; Chemistry; Neurobiology and Physiology; Chemical Engineering; Civil Engineering; and Evanston Hospital. *Degree requirements:* For doctorate, thesis/dissertation, qualifying exam. *Entrance requirements:* For doctorate, GRE General Test. Additional exam requirements/recommendations for international students: Required—TOEFL (minimum score 600 paper-based). Electronic applications accepted. *Faculty research:* Developmental genetics, gene regulation, DNA-protein interactions, biological clocks, bioremediation.

Northwestern University, Northwestern University Feinberg School of Medicine and Interdepartmental Programs, Integrated Graduate Programs in the Life Sciences, Chicago, IL 60611. Offers cancer biology (PhD); cell biology (PhD); developmental biology (PhD); evolutionary biology (PhD); immunology and microbial pathogenesis (PhD); molecular biology and genetics (PhD); neurobiology (PhD); pharmacology and toxicology (PhD); structural biology and biochemistry (PhD). *Degree requirements:* For doctorate, comprehensive exam, thesis/dissertation, written and oral qualifying exams. *Entrance requirements:* For doctorate, GRE General Test. Additional exam requirements/recommendations for international students: Required—TOEFL (minimum score 600 paper-based; 250 computer-based). Electronic applications accepted.

OGI School of Science & Engineering at Oregon Health & Science University, Graduate Studies, Department of Environmental and Biomolecular Systems, Beaverton, OR 97006-8921. Offers biochemistry and molecular biology (MS, PhD); environmental health systems (MS); environmental information technology (MS, PhD); environmental science and engineering (MS, PhD). Part-time programs available. Terminal master's awarded for partial completion of doctoral program. *Degree requirements:* For master's, thesis optional; for doctorate, comprehensive exam, oral defense of dissertation. *Entrance requirements:* For master's and doctorate, GRE General Test. Additional exam requirements/recommendations for international students: Required—TOEFL. Electronic applications accepted. *Faculty research:* Air and water science, hydrogeology, estuarine and coastal modeling, environmental microbiology, contaminant transport, biochemistry, biomolecular systems.

The Ohio State University, Graduate School, College of Biological Sciences, Department of Molecular Genetics, Columbus, OH 43210. Offers cell and developmental biology (MS, PhD); genetics (MS, PhD); molecular biology (MS, PhD). *Faculty:* 26. *Students:* 8 full-time (5 women), 23 part-time (11 women), 17 international. Average age 27. In 2009, 11 doctorates awarded. *Degree requirements:* For master's, thesis; for doctorate, thesis/dissertation. *Entrance requirements:* For master's and doctorate, GRE General Test, GRE Subject Test in biology or biochemistry (recommended). Additional exam requirements/recommendations for international students: Required—TOEFL (minimum score 600 paper-based; 250 computer-based). *Application deadline:* For fall admission, 8/15 priority date for domestic students, 7/1 priority date for international students; for winter admission, 12/1 priority date for domestic students, 11/1 priority date for international students; for spring admission, 3/1 priority date for domestic students, 2/1 priority date for international students. Applications are processed on a rolling basis. Application fee: $40 ($50 for international students). Electronic applications accepted. *Expenses:* Tuition, state resident: full-time $10,683. Tuition, nonresident: full-time $25,923. Tuition and fees vary according to course load and program. *Financial support:* Fellowships, research assistantships, teaching assistantships, Federal Work-Study and institutionally sponsored loans available. Support available to part-time students. *Unit head:* Dr. Anna Hopper, Chair, 614-292-8084, Fax: 614-292-4466, E-mail: hopper.64@osu.edu. *Application contact:* 614-292-9444, Fax: 614-292-3895, E-mail: domestic.grad@osu.edu.

The Ohio State University, Graduate School, College of Biological Sciences, Program in Molecular, Cellular and Developmental Biology, Columbus, OH 43210. Offers MS, PhD. *Students:* 67 full-time (38 women), 60 part-time (31 women); includes 12 minority (2 African Americans, 5 Asian Americans or Pacific Islanders, 5 Hispanic Americans), 77 international. Average age 28. In 2009, 3 master's, 13 doctorates awarded. *Entrance requirements:* For master's and doctorate, GRE General Test, GRE Subject Test in biology or biochemistry, cell and molecular biology. Additional exam requirements/recommendations for international students: Required—TOEFL (minimum score 573 paper-based; 230 computer-based). *Application deadline:* Applications are processed on a rolling basis. Application fee: $40 ($50 for international students). Electronic applications accepted. *Expenses:* Tuition, state resident: full-time $10,683. Tuition, nonresident: full-time $25,923. Tuition and fees vary according to course load and program. *Unit head:* David M. Bisaro, Graduate Studies Committee Chair, 614-292-2804, Fax: 614-292-8772, E-mail: bisaro.1@osu.edu. *Application contact:* Graduate Admissions, 614-292-9444, Fax: 614-292-3895, E-mail: domestic.grad@osu.edu.

Ohio University, Graduate College, College of Arts and Sciences, Interdisciplinary Graduate Program in Molecular and Cellular Biology, Athens, OH 45701-2979. Offers MS, PhD. *Faculty:* 47 full-time (12 women). *Students:* 27 full-time (18 women), 2 part-time (1 woman), 25 international. Average age 28. 49 applicants, 24% accepted, 5 enrolled. In 2009, 4 doctorates awarded. *Degree requirements:* For master's, comprehensive exam, thesis, research proposal, teaching experience; for doctorate, comprehensive exam, thesis/dissertation, research proposal, teaching experience. *Entrance requirements:* For master's and doctorate, GRE General Test. Additional exam requirements/recommendations for international students: Required—TOEFL (minimum score 620 paper-based; 260 computer-based; 105 iBT); Recommended—TWE. *Application deadline:* For fall admission, 12/30 priority date for domestic students, 12/30 for international students. Application fee: $50 ($55 for international students). Electronic applications accepted. *Expenses:* Tuition, state resident: full-time $7839; part-time $323 per quarter hour. Tuition, nonresident: full-time $15,831; part-time $654 per quarter hour. Required fees: $2931. *Financial support:* In 2009–10, 25 students received support, including research assistantships with full tuition reimbursements available (averaging $19,500 per year), teaching assistantships with full tuition reimbursements available (averaging $19,500 per year); Federal Work-Study, institutionally sponsored loans, traineeships, and unspecified assistantships also available. Financial award application deadline: 12/30. *Faculty research:* Animal biotechnology, plant molecular biology RNA, immunology, cellular genetics, biochemistry of signal transduction, cancer research, membrane transport, bioinformatics, bioengineering, chemical biology and drug discovery, diabetes, microbiology, neuroscience. Total annual research expenditures: $4.4 million. *Unit head:* Dr. Robert A. Colvin, Chair, 740-593-0198, Fax: 740-593-1569, E-mail: colvin@ohio.edu. *Application contact:* Dr. Xiaozhuo Chen, Graduate Chair, 740-593-9699, Fax: 740-593-1569, E-mail: chenx@ohio.edu.

Oklahoma State University, College of Agricultural Science and Natural Resources, Department of Biochemistry and Molecular Biology, Stillwater, OK 74078. Offers MS, PhD. *Faculty:* 37

Molecular Biology

Oklahoma State University (continued)
full-time (16 women), 1 part-time/adjunct (0 women). *Students:* 9 full-time (5 women), 27 part-time (17 women); includes 4 minority (1 African American, 2 American Indian/Alaska Native, 1 Hispanic American), 24 international. Average age 27. 86 applicants, 16% accepted, 5 enrolled. In 2009, 3 master's, 1 doctorate awarded. *Degree requirements:* For master's, thesis, oral exam; for doctorate, comprehensive exam, thesis/dissertation. *Entrance requirements:* For master's and doctorate, GRE or GMAT. Additional exam requirements/recommendations for international students: Required—TOEFL (minimum score 550 paper-based; 79 iBT). *Application deadline:* For fall admission, 3/1 priority date for international students; for spring admission, 8/1 priority date for international students. Applications are processed on a rolling basis. Application fee: $40 ($75 for international students). Electronic applications accepted. *Expenses:* Tuition, state resident: full-time $3716; part-time $154.85 per credit hour. Tuition, nonresident: full-time $14,448; part-time $602 per credit hour. Required fees: $1772; $73.85 per credit hour. One-time fee: $50. Tuition and fees vary according to course load and campus/location. *Financial support:* In 2009–10, 36 research assistantships (averaging $17,710 per year), 2 teaching assistantships (averaging $13,614 per year) were awarded; career-related internships or fieldwork, Federal Work-Study, scholarships/grants, health care benefits, tuition waivers (partial), and unspecified assistantships also available. Support available to part-time students. Financial award application deadline: 3/1; financial award applicants required to submit FAFSA. *Unit head:* Dr. Gary Thompson, Head, 405-744-9320, Fax: 405-744-7799. *Application contact:* Dr. Gordon Emslie, Dean, 405-744-6368, Fax: 405-744-0355, E-mail: grad-i@okstate.edu.

Oklahoma State University Center for Health Sciences, Graduate Program in Forensic Sciences, Tulsa, OK 74107-1898. Offers forensic DNA/molecular biology (MS); forensic examination of questioned documents (MFSA, Certificate); forensic pathology (MS); forensic psychology (MS); forensic sciences (MFSA); forensic toxicology (MS). Part-time and evening/weekend programs available. Postbaccalaureate distance learning degree programs offered (no on-campus study). *Degree requirements:* For master's, comprehensive exam (for some programs), thesis (for some programs). *Entrance requirements:* For master's, MAT (MFSA) or GRE General Test, professional experience (MFSA). Additional exam requirements/recommendations for international students: Required—TOEFL (minimum score 600 paper-based; 250 computer-based), TWE (minimum score 5). *Faculty research:* DNA typing, DNA polymorphism, identification through DNA, disease transmission, forensic dentistry, neurotoxicity of HIV, forensic toxicology method development, toxin detection and characterization.

Oregon Health & Science University, School of Medicine, Graduate Programs in Medicine, Department of Biochemistry and Molecular Biology, Portland, OR 97239-3098. Offers PhD. *Degree requirements:* For doctorate, comprehensive exam, thesis/dissertation, qualifying exam. *Entrance requirements:* For doctorate, GRE General Test (minimum scores: 500 Verbal/600 Quantitative/4.5 Analytical). Additional exam requirements/recommendations for international students: Required—TOEFL. Application fee: $65. Electronic applications accepted. Tuition and fees vary according to course level, course load, degree level, program and reciprocity agreements. *Financial support:* Stipend and paid tuition available. *Faculty research:* Protein structure and function, enzymology, metabolism, membranes transport. *Unit head:* David Farrens, PhD, Program Director, 503-494-7781, E-mail: farrensd@ohsu.edu. *Application contact:* Jeni Wroblewski, Administrative Coordinator, 503-494-2541, E-mail: wroblews@ohsu.edu.

Oregon Health & Science University, School of Medicine, Graduate Programs in Medicine, Department of Environmental and Biomolecular Systems, Portland, OR 97239-3098. Offers biochemistry and molecular biology (MS, PhD); environmental science and engineering (MS, PhD). Part-time programs available. *Degree requirements:* For master's, thesis (for some programs); for doctorate, comprehensive exam, thesis/dissertation. *Entrance requirements:* For master's and doctorate, GRE General Test (minimum scores: 500 Verbal/600 Quantitative/4.5 Analytical) or MCAT (for some programs). Additional exam requirements/recommendations for international students: Required—TOEFL. *Application deadline:* For fall admission, 7/15 for domestic students, 5/15 for international students; for winter admission, 10/15 for domestic students, 9/15 for international students; for spring admission, 1/15 for domestic students, 12/15 for international students. Applications are processed on a rolling basis. Application fee: $65. Electronic applications accepted. Tuition and fees vary according to course level, course load, degree level, program and reciprocity agreements. *Financial support:* PhD students have paid tuition and receive stipends available. *Unit head:* Paul Tratnyek, PhD, Program Director, 503-748-1070, E-mail: info@ebs.ogi.edu. *Application contact:* Nancy Christie, Program Coordinator, 503-748-1070, E-mail: info@ebs.ogi.edu.

Oregon State University, Graduate School, Program in Molecular and Cellular Biology, Corvallis, OR 97331. Offers MS, PhD. *Students:* 41 full-time (12 women), 2 part-time (0 women); includes 5 minority (1 American Indian/Alaska Native, 4 Asian Americans or Pacific Islanders), 11 international. Average age 30. In 2009, 1 master's, 4 doctorates awarded. *Degree requirements:* For doctorate, thesis/dissertation, oral and written qualifying exams. *Entrance requirements:* For doctorate, minimum GPA of 3.0 in last 90 hours. Additional exam requirements/recommendations for international students: Required—TOEFL. *Application deadline:* For fall admission, 2/15 for domestic students. Applications are processed on a rolling basis. Application fee: $50. *Expenses:* Tuition, state resident: full-time $9774; part-time $362 per credit. Tuition, nonresident: full-time $15,849; part-time $587 per credit. Required fees: $1639. Full-time tuition and fees vary according to course load and program. *Financial support:* Fellowships, career-related internships or fieldwork, Federal Work-Study, and institutionally sponsored loans available. Support available to part-time students. *Unit head:* Dr. James C. Carrington, Director, 541-737-3347, Fax: 541-737-3045, E-mail: carrington@cgrb.oregonstate.edu. *Application contact:* Dr. James C. Carrington, Director, 541-737-3347, Fax: 541-737-3045, E-mail: carrington@cgrb.oregonstate.edu.

Penn State Hershey Medical Center, College of Medicine, Graduate School Programs in the Biomedical Sciences, Graduate Program in Biochemistry and Molecular Biology, Hershey, PA 17033. Offers MS, PhD, MD/PhD. *Students:* 131 applicants, 5% accepted, 3 enrolled. Terminal master's awarded for partial completion of doctoral program. *Degree requirements:* For master's, thesis or alternative; for doctorate, comprehensive exam, thesis/dissertation. *Entrance requirements:* For master's, GRE General Test; for doctorate, GRE General Test, minimum GPA of 3.0. Additional exam requirements/recommendations for international students: Required—TOEFL (minimum score 550 paper-based; 213 computer-based). *Application deadline:* For fall admission, 1/31 priority date for domestic students, 2/1 priority date for international students. Applications are processed on a rolling basis. Application fee: $65. Electronic applications accepted. *Expenses:* Tuition, state resident: part-time $644 per credit. Tuition, nonresident: part-time $1142 per credit. Required fees: $22 per semester. *Financial support:* In 2009–10, research assistantships with full tuition reimbursements (averaging $22,260 per year); fellowships with full tuition reimbursements, scholarships/grants, health care benefits, tuition waivers, and unspecified assistantships also available. Financial award applicants required to submit FAFSA. *Faculty research:* X-ray crystallography of proteins, glycosphingolipid interactions with viruses and toxins, DNA replication and repair, tobacco and environmental carcinogenesis, gene regulation. *Unit head:* Dr. Judith S. Bond, Chair, 717-531-8585, Fax: 717-531-7072, E-mail: bchem-grad-hmc@psu.edu. *Application contact:* Ruth Dean, Administrative Assistant, 717-531-8586, Fax: 717-531-7072, E-mail: bchem-grad-hmc@psu.edu.

Penn State Hershey Medical Center, College of Medicine, Graduate School Programs in the Biomedical Sciences, Graduate Program in Microbiology and Immunology, Hershey, PA 17033. Offers genetics (PhD); immunology (MS, PhD); microbiology (MS); microbiology/virology (PhD); molecular biology (PhD); MD/PhD. *Students:* 12 applicants, 75% accepted, 3 enrolled. In 2009, 1 doctorate awarded. Terminal master's awarded for partial completion of doctoral program. *Degree requirements:* For master's, thesis or alternative; for doctorate, comprehensive exam, thesis/dissertation, oral exam. *Entrance requirements:* For doctorate, GRE General Test, minimum GPA of 3.0. Additional exam requirements/recommendations for international students: Required—TOEFL. *Application deadline:* For fall admission, 1/31 priority date for domestic students, 2/1 priority date for international students. Applications are processed on a rolling basis. Application fee: $45. Electronic applications accepted. *Expenses:* Tuition, state resident: part-time $644 per credit. Tuition, nonresident: part-time $1142 per credit. Required fees: $22 per semester. *Financial support:* In 2009–10, research assistantships with full tuition reimbursements (averaging $22,260 per year); fellowships with full tuition reimbursements, scholarships/grants, health care benefits, and unspecified assistantships also available. Financial award applicants required to submit FAFSA. *Faculty research:* Virus replication and assembly, oncogenesis, interactions of viruses with host cells and animal model systems. *Unit head:* Dr. Richard J. Courtney, Chair, 717-531-7659, Fax: 717-531-6522, E-mail: micro-grad-hmc@psu.edu. *Application contact:* Billie Burns, Secretary, 717-531-7659, Fax: 717-531-6522, E-mail: micro-grad-hmc@psu.edu.

Penn State Hershey Medical Center, College of Medicine, Graduate School Programs in the Biomedical Sciences, Interdepartmental Graduate Program in Cell and Molecular Biology, Hershey, PA 17033. Offers MS, PhD, MD/PhD. *Students:* 37 applicants, 38% accepted, 4 enrolled. In 2009, 4 doctorates awarded. Terminal master's awarded for partial completion of doctoral program. *Degree requirements:* For master's, thesis or alternative; for doctorate, comprehensive exam, thesis/dissertation, oral exam. *Entrance requirements:* For master's, GRE General Test or MCAT; for doctorate, GRE General Test or MCAT, minimum GPA of 3.0. Additional exam requirements/recommendations for international students: Required—TOEFL (minimum score 500 paper-based; 213 computer-based). *Application deadline:* For fall admission, 1/31 priority date for domestic students, 2/1 priority date for international students. Applications are processed on a rolling basis. Application fee: $65. Electronic applications accepted. *Expenses:* Tuition, state resident: part-time $644 per credit. Tuition, nonresident: part-time $1142 per credit. Required fees: $22 per semester. *Financial support:* In 2009–10, research assistantships with full tuition reimbursements (averaging $22,260 per year); fellowships with full tuition reimbursements, career-related internships or fieldwork, scholarships/grants, health care benefits, and unspecified assistantships also available. Financial award applicants required to submit FAFSA. *Faculty research:* Membrane structure, function and modulators; cell division, differentiation and gene expression; Metastasis; intracellular events in the immune system. *Unit head:* Dr. Henry Donahue, Program Director, 717-531-1045, Fax: 717-531-4139, E-mail: cmb-grad-hmc@psu.edu. *Application contact:* Lori Coover, Program Assistant, 717-531-1045, Fax: 717-531-0786, E-mail: cmb-grad-hmc@psu.edu.

Penn State University Park, Graduate School, Eberly College of Science, Department of Biochemistry and Molecular Biology, Program in Biochemistry, Microbiology, and Molecular Biology, State College, University Park, PA 16802-1503. Offers MS, PhD. *Unit head:* Dr. Ronald Porter, Director of Graduate Studies, 814-863-4903, E-mail: rdp1@psu.edu. *Application contact:* Dr. Ronald Porter, Director of Graduate Studies, 814-863-4903, E-mail: rdp1@psu.edu.

Princeton University, Graduate School, Department of Molecular Biology, Princeton, NJ 08544-1019. Offers PhD. *Degree requirements:* For doctorate, thesis/dissertation. *Entrance requirements:* For doctorate, GRE General Test. Additional exam requirements/recommendations for international students: Required—TOEFL (minimum score 600 paper-based; 250 computer-based). Electronic applications accepted. *Faculty research:* Genetics, virology, biochemistry.

Purdue University, College of Pharmacy and Pharmacal Sciences and Graduate School, Graduate Programs in Pharmacy and Pharmacal Sciences, Department of Medicinal Chemistry and Molecular Pharmacology, West Lafayette, IN 47907. Offers analytical medicinal chemistry (PhD); computational and biophysical medicinal chemistry (PhD); medicinal and bioorganic chemistry (PhD); medicinal biochemistry and molecular biology (PhD); molecular pharmacology and toxicology (PhD); natural products and pharmacognosy (PhD); nuclear pharmacy (MS); radiopharmaceutical chemistry and nuclear pharmacy (PhD); MS/PhD. Terminal master's awarded for partial completion of doctoral program. *Degree requirements:* For master's, thesis; for doctorate, thesis/dissertation. *Entrance requirements:* For master's, GRE General Test, minimum B average; BS in biology, chemistry, or pharmacy; for doctorate, GRE General Test, minimum B average; BS in biology, chemistry, or pharmacology. Additional exam requirements/recommendations for international students: Required—TOEFL. Electronic applications accepted. *Faculty research:* Drug design and development, cancer research, drug synthesis and analysis, chemical pharmacology, environmental toxicology.

Purdue University, Graduate School, College of Science, Department of Biological Sciences, West Lafayette, IN 47907. Offers biochemistry (PhD); biophysics (PhD); cell and developmental biology (PhD); ecology, evolutionary and population biology (MS, PhD), including ecology, evolutionary biology, population biology; genetics (MS, PhD); microbiology (MS, PhD); molecular biology (PhD); neurobiology (MS, PhD); plant physiology (PhD). Terminal master's awarded for partial completion of doctoral program. *Degree requirements:* For master's, thesis (for some programs); for doctorate, thesis/dissertation, seminars, teaching experience. *Entrance requirements:* For master's and doctorate, GRE General Test. Additional exam requirements/recommendations for international students: Required—TOEFL. Electronic applications accepted.

Queen's University at Kingston, School of Graduate Studies and Research, Faculty of Health Sciences, Department of Anatomy and Cell Biology, Kingston, ON K7L 3N6, Canada. Offers biology of reproduction (M Sc, PhD); cancer (M Sc, PhD); cardiovascular pathophysiology (M Sc, PhD); cell and molecular biology (M Sc, PhD); drug metabolism (M Sc, PhD); endocrinology (M Sc, PhD); motor control (M Sc, PhD); neural regeneration (M Sc, PhD); neurophysiology (M Sc, PhD). Part-time programs available. *Degree requirements:* For master's, thesis; for doctorate, one foreign language, comprehensive exam, thesis/dissertation. *Entrance requirements:* Additional exam requirements/recommendations for international students: Required—TOEFL. Electronic applications accepted. *Faculty research:* Human kinetics, neuroscience, reproductive biology, cardiovascular.

Quinnipiac University, School of Health Sciences, Program in Molecular and Cell Biology, Hamden, CT 06518-1940. Offers MS. Part-time programs available. *Faculty:* 8 full-time (4 women), 9 part-time/adjunct (2 women). *Students:* 11 full-time (7 women), 15 part-time (9 women); includes 4 minority (1 African American, 1 American Indian/Alaska Native, 2 Asian Americans or Pacific Islanders), 5 international. Average age 26. 21 applicants, 95% accepted, 11 enrolled. In 2009, 8 master's awarded. *Degree requirements:* For master's, thesis optional. *Entrance requirements:* For master's, bachelor's degree in biological, medical, or health sciences; minimum GPA of 2.75. Additional exam requirements/recommendations for international students: Required—TOEFL (minimum score 575 paper-based; 233 computer-based; 90 iBT), IELTS (minimum score 6.5). *Application deadline:* For fall admission, 7/30 priority date for domestic students, 4/30 priority date for international students; for spring admission, 12/15 priority date for domestic students, 9/15 priority date for international students. Applications are processed on a rolling basis. Application fee: $45. Electronic applications accepted. *Expenses:* Tuition: Full-time $16,030; part-time $770 per credit. Required fees: $630; $35 per credit. *Financial support:* Federal Work-Study, tuition waivers, and unspecified assistantships available. Support available to part-time students. Financial award application deadline: 4/15; financial award applicants required to submit FAFSA. *Unit head:* Dr. Gene Wong, Director, 203-582-8467, E-mail: gene.wong@quinnipiac.edu. *Application contact:* Kristin Parent, Assistant Director of Graduate Health Sciences Admissions, 800-462-1944, Fax: 203-582-3443, E-mail: kristin.parent@quinnipiac.edu.

Rosalind Franklin University of Medicine and Science, School of Graduate and Postdoctoral Studies—Interdisciplinary Graduate Program in Biomedical Sciences, Department of Biochemistry and Molecular Biology, North Chicago, IL 60064-3095. Offers MS, PhD, MD/PhD. Terminal master's awarded for partial completion of doctoral program. *Degree requirements:* For master's, comprehensive exam, thesis; for doctorate, comprehensive exam, thesis/dissertation. *Entrance requirements:* For master's and doctorate, GRE General Test, minimum GPA of 3.0. Additional exam requirements/recommendations for international students: Required—TOEFL, TWE. Electronic applications accepted. *Faculty research:* Structure of control enzymes, extracellular matrix, glucose metabolism, gene expression, ATP synthesis.

Rutgers, The State University of New Jersey, New Brunswick, Graduate School-New Brunswick, Programs in the Molecular Biosciences, Piscataway, NJ 08854-8097. Offers biochemistry (PhD); cell and developmental biology (MS, PhD); microbiology and molecular genetics (MS, PhD), including applied microbiology, clinical microbiology (MS), clinical mircobiology (PhD), computational molecular biology (PhD), immunology, microbial biochemistry, molecular genetics, virology.

Saint Louis University, Graduate School and School of Medicine, Graduate Program in Biomedical Sciences and Graduate School, Department of Biochemistry and Molecular Biology, St. Louis, MO 63103-2097. Offers PhD. *Degree requirements:* For doctorate, comprehensive exam, thesis/dissertation, departmental qualifying exams. *Entrance requirements:* For doctorate, GRE General Test, GRE Subject Test (optional), letters of recommendation, resume, interview. Additional exam requirements/recommendations for international students: Required—TOEFL (minimum score 525 paper-based; 194 computer-based). Electronic applications accepted. *Faculty research:* Transcription, chromatin modification and regulation of gene expression; structure/function of proteins and enzymes, including x-ray crystallography; inflammatory mediators in pathenogenesis of diabetes and arteriosclerosis; cellular signaling in response to growth factors, opiates and angiogenic mediators; genomics and proteomics of Cryptococcus neoformans.

San Diego State University, Graduate and Research Affairs, College of Sciences, Department of Biology, San Diego, CA 92182. Offers biology (MA, MS), including ecology (MS), molecular biology (MS), physiology (MS), systematics/evolution (MS); cell and molecular biology (PhD); ecology (MS, PhD); microbiology (MS). Terminal master's awarded for partial completion of doctoral program. *Degree requirements:* For master's, thesis; for doctorate, thesis/dissertation. *Entrance requirements:* For master's, GRE General Test, GRE Subject Test, resume or curriculum vitae, 2 letters of recommendation. Additional exam requirements/recommendations for international students: Required—TOEFL. Electronic applications accepted.

San Diego State University, Graduate and Research Affairs, College of Sciences, Molecular Biology Institute, Program in Cell and Molecular Biology, San Diego, CA 92182. Offers PhD. *Degree requirements:* For doctorate, thesis/dissertation, oral comprehensive qualifying exam. *Entrance requirements:* For doctorate, GRE General Test, GRE Subject Test, resumé or curriculum vitae, 3 letters of recommendation. Electronic applications accepted. *Faculty research:* Structure/dynamics of protein kinesis, chromatin structure and DNA methylation membrane biochemistry, secretory protein targeting, molecular biology of cardiac myocytes.

San Francisco State University, Division of Graduate Studies, College of Science and Engineering, Department of Biology, Program in Cell and Molecular Biology, San Francisco, CA 94132-1722. Offers MS.

San Jose State University, Graduate Studies and Research, College of Science, Department of Biological Sciences, San Jose, CA 95192-0001. Offers biological sciences (MA, MS); molecular biology and microbiology (MS); organismal biology, conservation and ecology (MS); physiology (MS). Part-time programs available. *Students:* 53 full-time (41 women), 48 part-time (30 women); includes 48 minority (2 African Americans, 1 American Indian/Alaska Native, 36 Asian Americans or Pacific Islanders, 9 Hispanic Americans), 10 international. Average age 30. 158 applicants, 28% accepted, 43 enrolled. In 2009, 36 master's awarded. *Entrance requirements:* For master's, GRE. *Application deadline:* For fall admission, 6/29 for domestic students; for spring admission, 11/30 for domestic students. Applications are processed on a rolling basis. Application fee: $59. Electronic applications accepted. *Financial support:* Teaching assistantships, Federal Work-Study available. Financial award applicants required to submit FAFSA. *Faculty research:* Systemic physiology, molecular genetics, SEM studies, toxicology, large mammal ecology. *Unit head:* Dr. John Boothby, Chair, 408-924-4850, Fax: 408-924-4840, E-mail: jboothby@email.sjsu.edu. *Application contact:* Daniel Holley, Graduate Coordinator, 408-924-4844, E-mail: dholley@email.sjsu.edu.

Seton Hall University, College of Arts and Sciences, Department of Biological Sciences, South Orange, NJ 07079-2697. Offers biology (MS); biology/business administration (MS); microbiology (MS); molecular bioscience (PhD); molecular bioscience/neuroscience (PhD). Part-time and evening/weekend programs available. *Faculty:* 17 full-time (9 women), 1 part-time/adjunct (0 women). *Students:* 19 full-time (8 women), 47 part-time (33 women); includes 13 minority (5 African Americans, 5 Asian Americans or Pacific Islanders, 3 Hispanic Americans), 5 international. Average age 29. 51 applicants, 76% accepted, 12 enrolled. In 2009, 11 master's awarded. *Degree requirements:* For master's, thesis optional; for doctorate, comprehensive exam, thesis/dissertation. *Entrance requirements:* For master's and doctorate, GRE or MS from accredited university in the U.S. Additional exam requirements/recommendations for international students: Required—TOEFL. *Application deadline:* For fall admission, 7/1 priority date for domestic and international students; for spring admission, 11/1 priority date for domestic and international students. Applications are processed on a rolling basis. Application fee: $50. Electronic applications accepted. *Financial support:* Research assistantships, teaching assistantships with full tuition reimbursements, career-related internships or fieldwork, Federal Work-Study, and unspecified assistantships available. Financial award applicants required to submit FAFSA. *Faculty research:* Neurobiology, genetics, immunology, molecular biology, cellular physiology, toxicology, microbiology, bioinformatics. *Unit head:* Dr. Carolyn Bentivegna, Chair, 973-761-9044, Fax: 973-275-2905, E-mail: bentivca@shu.edu. *Application contact:* Dr. Carroll D. Rawn, Director of Graduate Studies, 973-761-9054, Fax: 973-275-2905, E-mail: rawncarr@shu.edu.

Simon Fraser University, Graduate Studies, Faculty of Science, Department of Molecular Biology and Biochemistry, Burnaby, BC V5A 1S6, Canada. Offers M Sc, PhD. *Degree requirements:* For master's, thesis; for doctorate, thesis/dissertation. *Entrance requirements:* For master's, minimum GPA of 3.0; for doctorate, minimum GPA of 3.5. Additional exam requirements/recommendations for international students: Required—TWE or IELTS. *Faculty research:* Molecular genetics and development, biochemistry, molecular physiology, genomics, molecular phylogenetics and population genetics, bioinformation.

Southern Illinois University Carbondale, Graduate School, College of Science, Program in Molecular Biology, Microbiology, and Biochemistry, Carbondale, IL 62901-4701. Offers MS, PhD. *Degree requirements:* For master's, thesis; for doctorate, thesis/dissertation. *Entrance requirements:* For master's, GRE, minimum GPA of 2.7; for doctorate, GRE, minimum GPA of 3.25. Additional exam requirements/recommendations for international students: Required—TOEFL. *Faculty research:* Prokaryotic gene regulation and expression; eukaryotic gene regulation; microbial, phylogenetic, and metabolic diversity; immune responses to tumors, pathogens, and autoantigens; protein folding and structure.

State University of New York Downstate Medical Center, School of Graduate Studies, Program in Molecular and Cellular Biology, Brooklyn, NY 11203-2098. Offers PhD, MD/PhD. Affiliation with a particular PhD degree-granting program is deferred to the second year. *Degree requirements:* For doctorate, comprehensive exam, thesis/dissertation. *Entrance requirements:* For doctorate, GRE General Test. *Faculty research:* Mechanism of gene regulation, molecular virology.

State University of New York Upstate Medical University, College of Graduate Studies, Program in Biochemistry and Molecular Biology, Syracuse, NY 13210-2334. Offers biochemistry (MS); biochemistry and molecular biology (PhD); MD/PhD. *Faculty:* 16 full-time (3 women). *Students:* 30 full-time (19 women), 1 (woman) part-time; includes 5 minority (1 African American, 3 Asian Americans or Pacific Islanders, 1 Hispanic American), 15 international. In 2009, 1 master's, 4 doctorates awarded. Terminal master's awarded for partial completion of doctoral program. *Degree requirements:* For master's, thesis; for doctorate, comprehensive exam, thesis/dissertation. *Entrance requirements:* For master's, GRE General Test, interview; for doctorate, GRE General Test, telephone interview. Additional exam requirements/recommendations for international students: Required—TOEFL. *Application deadline:* Applications are processed on a rolling basis. Application fee: $40. Electronic applications accepted. *Financial support:* In 2009–10, fellowships with tuition reimbursements (averaging $21,514 per year), research assistantships with tuition reimbursements (averaging $21,514 per year) were awarded; Federal Work-Study, scholarships/grants, health care benefits, tuition waivers, and unspecified assistantships also available. Financial award application deadline: 4/15; financial award applicants required to submit FAFSA. *Faculty research:* Enzymology, membrane structure and functions, developmental biochemistry. *Unit head:* Dr. Patricia Kane, Chair, 315-464-5127. *Application contact:* Sandra Tillotson, Coordinator of Graduate Recruitment, 315-464-7655.

See Close-Up on page 157.

Stony Brook University, State University of New York, Graduate School, College of Arts and Sciences, Department of Biochemistry and Cell Biology, Molecular and Cellular Biology Program, Stony Brook, NY 11794. Offers biochemistry and molecular biology (PhD); biological sciences (MA); cellular and developmental biology (PhD); immunology and pathology (PhD); molecular and cellular biology (PhD). *Students:* 100 full-time (62 women); includes 8 minority (2 African Americans, 5 Asian Americans or Pacific Islanders, 1 Hispanic American), 60 international. Average age 30. 277 applicants, 15% accepted. In 2009, 15 doctorates awarded. *Degree requirements:* For doctorate, comprehensive exam, thesis/dissertation, teaching experience. *Entrance requirements:* For doctorate, GRE General Test, GRE Subject Test. Additional exam requirements/recommendations for international students: Required—TOEFL. *Application deadline:* For fall admission, 1/15 for domestic students. Application fee: $60. *Expenses:* Tuition, state resident: full-time $8370; part-time $349 per credit. Tuition, nonresident: full-time $13,250; part-time $552 per credit. Required fees: $933. *Financial support:* In 2009–10, 49 research assistantships, 15 teaching assistantships were awarded; fellowships, Federal Work-Study also available. *Unit head:* Prof. Robert Haltiwanger, Chair, 631-632-8560. *Application contact:* Prof. Robert Haltiwanger, Chair, 631-632-8560.

Temple University, Health Sciences Center, School of Medicine and Graduate School, Graduate Programs in Medicine, Program in Molecular Biology and Genetics, Philadelphia, PA 19122-6096. Offers PhD, MD/PhD. *Degree requirements:* For doctorate, thesis/dissertation, presentation research/literature seminars distinct from area of concentration. *Entrance requirements:* For doctorate, GRE General Test, GRE Subject Test, minimum GPA of 3.0. Additional exam requirements/recommendations for international students: Required—TOEFL (minimum score 620 paper-based; 260 computer-based). Electronic applications accepted. *Faculty research:* Molecular genetics of normal and malignant cell growth, regulation of gene expression, DNA repair systems and carcinogenesis, hormone-receptor interactions and signal transduction systems, structural biology.

Texas A&M Health Science Center, Graduate School of Biomedical Sciences, Department of Microbial and Molecular Pathogenesis, College Station, TX 77840. Offers immunology (PhD); microbiology (PhD); molecular biology (PhD); virology (PhD). *Degree requirements:* For doctorate, thesis/dissertation. *Entrance requirements:* For doctorate, GRE General Test, minimum GPA of 3.0. *Faculty research:* Molecular pathogenesis, microbial therapeutics.

Texas A&M Health Science Center, Graduate School of Biomedical Sciences, Program in Cell and Molecular Biology, College Station, TX 77840. Offers PhD.

Texas Woman's University, Graduate School, College of Arts and Sciences, Department of Biology, Denton, TX 76201. Offers biology (MS); biology teaching (MS); molecular biology (PhD). Part-time programs available. *Faculty:* 12 full-time (8 women), 1 (woman) part-time/adjunct. *Students:* 25 full-time (17 women), 16 part-time (9 women); includes 6 minority (4 African Americans, 2 Hispanic Americans), 29 international. Average age 28. 29 applicants, 79% accepted, 12 enrolled. In 2009, 2 master's, 4 doctorates awarded. Terminal master's awarded for partial completion of doctoral program. *Degree requirements:* For master's, comprehensive exam, thesis (for some programs); for doctorate, comprehensive exam, thesis/dissertation, residency. *Entrance requirements:* For master's, GRE General Test (minimum score 425 verbal, 425 quantitative), 3 letters of reference; for doctorate, GRE General Test (minimum score: Verbal 425, Quantitative 425), 3 letters of reference, letter of interest. Additional exam requirements/recommendations for international students: Required—TOEFL (minimum score 550 paper-based; 213 computer-based; 79 iBT). *Application deadline:* For fall admission, 7/1 priority date for domestic students, 3/1 for international students; for spring admission, 12/1 priority date for domestic students, 7/1 for international students. Applications are processed on a rolling basis. Application fee: $50. Electronic applications accepted. *Expenses:* Tuition, state resident: full-time $3564; part-time $198 per credit hour. Tuition, nonresident: full-time $8550; part-time $475 per credit hour. Required fees: $69.26 per credit hour. Tuition and fees vary according to course load. *Financial support:* In 2009–10, 5 students received support, including 47 research assistantships (averaging $11,862 per year); career-related internships or fieldwork, Federal Work-Study, institutionally sponsored loans, scholarships/grants, traineeships, health care benefits, and unspecified assistantships also available. Support available to part-time students. Financial award application deadline: 3/1; financial award applicants required to submit FAFSA. *Faculty research:* Interacerebral effects of 8-OH-DPAT, rna purification, mechanisms in pathogenesis of gatroduodenal disorders, HHS MBRS program. *Unit head:* Dr. Sarah McIntire, Chair, 940-898-2351, Fax: 940-898-2382, E-mail: biology@twu.edu. *Application contact:* Samuel Wheeler, Assistant Director of Admissions, 940-898-3188, Fax: 940-898-3081, E-mail: wheelersr@twu.edu.

Thomas Jefferson University, Jefferson College of Graduate Studies, PhD Program in Biochemistry and Molecular Biology, Philadelphia, PA 19107. Offers PhD. *Faculty:* 42 full-time (13 women). *Students:* 18 full-time (10 women), 1 (woman) part-time; includes 3 minority (1 Asian American or Pacific Islander, 2 Hispanic Americans), 2 international. Average age 24. 40 applicants, 18% accepted, 3 enrolled. In 2009, 2 doctorates awarded. *Degree requirements:* For doctorate, comprehensive exam, thesis/dissertation. *Entrance requirements:* For doctorate, GRE General Test or MCAT, minimum GPA of 3.2. Additional exam requirements/recommendations for international students: Required—TOEFL (minimum score 250 computer-based; 100 iBT) or IELTS. *Application deadline:* For fall admission, 1/15 priority date for domestic students, 1/1 priority date for international students. Applications are processed on a rolling basis. Application fee: $50. Electronic applications accepted. *Expenses:* Tuition: Full-time $26,858; part-time $879 per credit. Required fees: $525. *Financial support:* In 2009–10, 18 students received support, including 18 fellowships with full tuition reimbursements available (averaging $52,883 per year); Federal Work-Study, institutionally sponsored loans, scholarships/grants, traineeships, and stipends also available. Financial award application deadline: 5/1; financial award applicants required to submit FAFSA. *Faculty research:* Signal transduction and molecular genetics, translational biochemistry, human mitochondrial genetics, molecular biology of protein-RNA interaction, mammalian mitochondrial biogenesis and function. Total annual research expenditures: $17.4 million. *Unit head:* Dr. Diane E. Merry, Program Director, 215-503-4907, Fax: 215-923-9162, E-mail: diane.merry@jefferson.edu. *Application contact:* Marc E. Stearns, Director of Admissions, 215-503-0155, Fax: 215-503-9920, E-mail: jcgs-info@jefferson.edu.

See Close-Up on page 159.

Tufts University, Sackler School of Graduate Biomedical Sciences, Department of Molecular Biology and Microbiology, Medford, MA 02155. Offers molecular microbiology (PhD), including microbiology, molecular biology, molecular microbiology. *Faculty:* 18 full-time (7 women). *Students:* 29 full-time (21 women); includes 8 minority (2 African Americans, 4 Asian Americans or Pacific Islanders, 2 Hispanic Americans), 1 international. Average age 27. 80 applicants, 18% accepted, 5 enrolled. In 2009, 4 doctorates awarded. Terminal master's awarded for partial completion of doctoral program. *Degree requirements:* For doctorate, comprehensive exam, thesis/dissertation. *Entrance requirements:* For doctorate, GRE General Test, 3 letters of reference. Additional exam requirements/recommendations for international students: Required—TOEFL. *Application deadline:* For fall admission, 12/15 priority date for domestic and international students. Applications are processed on a rolling basis. Application fee: $70. Electronic applications accepted. *Expenses:* Tuition: Full-time $38,096; part-time $3962 per credit. Required fees: $686; $40 per year. Tuition and fees vary according to course level,

Molecular Biology

Tufts University (continued)
course load, degree level, program and student level. *Financial support:* In 2009–10, 29 students received support, including 29 research assistantships with full tuition reimbursements available (averaging $28,500 per year); scholarships/grants, health care benefits, and tuition waivers (full) also available. Financial award application deadline: 12/15. *Faculty research:* Fundamental problems of molecular biology of prokaryotes, eukaryotes and their viruses. *Unit head:* Dr. Michael Malamy, Director, 617-636-6750, Fax: 617-636-0337, E-mail: michael.malamy@tufts.edu. *Application contact:* Kellie Johnston, Associate Director of Admissions, 617-636-6767, Fax: 617-633-0375, E-mail: sackler-school@tufts.edu.

Tufts University, Sackler School of Graduate Biomedical Sciences, Program in Cell, Molecular and Developmental Biology, Medford, MA 02155. Offers PhD. *Faculty:* 35 full-time (11 women). *Students:* 25 full-time (13 women); includes 2 minority (both Asian Americans or Pacific Islanders), 2 international. Average age 29. In 2009, 8 doctorates awarded. Terminal master's awarded for partial completion of doctoral program. *Degree requirements:* For doctorate, thesis/dissertation. *Entrance requirements:* For doctorate, GRE General Test, 3 letters of reference. Additional exam requirements/recommendations for international students: Required—TOEFL. *Application deadline:* For fall admission, 12/15 for domestic and international students. Applications are processed on a rolling basis. Application fee: $70. Electronic applications accepted. *Expenses:* Tuition: Full-time $38,096; part-time $3962 per credit. Required fees: $686; $40 per year. Tuition and fees vary according to course level, course load, degree level, program and student level. *Financial support:* In 2009–10, 25 students received support, including 25 research assistantships with full tuition reimbursements available (averaging $28,500 per year); fellowships, scholarships/grants, health care benefits, and tuition waivers (full) also available. *Faculty research:* Reproduction and hormone action, control of gene expression, cell-matrix and cell-cell interactions, growth control and tumorigenesis, cytoskeleton and contractile proteins. *Unit head:* Dr. John Castellot, Program Director, 617-636-0303, Fax: 617-636-0375, E-mail: john.castellot@tufts.edu. *Application contact:* Kellie Johnston, Associate Director of Admissions, 617-636-6767, Fax: 617-636-0375, E-mail: sackler-school@tufts.edu.

Tulane University, School of Medicine and School of Liberal Arts, Graduate Programs in Biomedical Sciences, Interdisciplinary Graduate Program in Molecular and Cellular Biology, New Orleans, LA 70118-5669. Offers PhD, MD/PhD. PhD offered through the Graduate School. *Degree requirements:* For doctorate, thesis/dissertation. *Entrance requirements:* For doctorate, GRE General Test, GRE Subject Test. Additional exam requirements/recommendations for international students: Required—TOEFL. Electronic applications accepted. *Faculty research:* Developmental biology, neuroscience, virology.

Tulane University, School of Science and Engineering, Department of Cell and Molecular Biology, New Orleans, LA 70118-5669. Offers MS, PhD. Terminal master's awarded for partial completion of doctoral program. *Degree requirements:* For doctorate, thesis/dissertation. *Entrance requirements:* For master's, GRE General Test, minimum B average in undergraduate course work; for doctorate, GRE General Test. Additional exam requirements/recommendations for international students: Required—TOEFL. Electronic applications accepted.

Uniformed Services University of the Health Sciences, School of Medicine, Graduate Programs in the Biomedical Sciences and Public Health, Graduate Program in Molecular and Cell Biology, Bethesda, MD 20814-4799. Offers PhD. *Faculty:* 43 full-time (11 women), 3 part-time/adjunct (0 women). *Students:* 20 full-time (9 women); includes 7 minority (4 Asian Americans or Pacific Islanders, 3 Hispanic Americans), 6 international. Average age 26. 30 applicants, 43% accepted, 8 enrolled. In 2009, 2 doctorates awarded. *Degree requirements:* For doctorate, comprehensive exam, thesis/dissertation, qualifying exam. *Entrance requirements:* For doctorate, GRE General Test, minimum GPA of 3.0. Additional exam requirements/recommendations for international students: Required—TOEFL. *Application deadline:* For fall admission, 1/15 priority date for domestic and international students. Applications are processed on a rolling basis. Application fee: $0. Electronic applications accepted. *Financial support:* In 2009–10, fellowships with full tuition reimbursements (averaging $26,000 per year); scholarships/grants, health care benefits, and tuition waivers (full) also available. *Faculty research:* Immunology, biochemistry, cancer biology, stem cell biology. *Unit head:* Dr. Mary Lou Cutler, Graduate Program Director, 301-295-3453, Fax: 301-295-1996. *Application contact:* Elena Marina Sherman, Graduate Program Coordinator, 301-295-3913, Fax: 301-295-6772, E-mail: elena.sherman@usuhs.mil.

Université de Montréal, Faculty of Medicine, Program in Molecular Biology, Montréal, QC H3C 3J7, Canada. Offers M Sc, PhD. *Students:* 44 full-time (30 women), 80 part-time (45 women). 63 applicants, 21% accepted, 10 enrolled. In 2009, 20 master's, 9 doctorates awarded. Terminal master's awarded for partial completion of doctoral program. *Degree requirements:* For master's, thesis; for doctorate, thesis/dissertation, general exam. *Entrance requirements:* For master's and doctorate, proficiency in French, knowledge of English. *Application deadline:* For fall admission, 2/1 priority date for domestic students; for winter admission, 11/1 priority date for domestic students; for spring admission, 2/1 priority date for domestic students. Application fee: $100. Electronic applications accepted. *Faculty research:* Protein interactions, intracellular signaling, development and differentiation, hematopoiesis, stem cells. *Unit head:* Trang Hoang, Director, 514-343-6970, Fax: 514-343-6945, E-mail: trang.hoang@umontreal.ca. *Application contact:* Viviane Jodoin, Information Contact, 514-343-6111 Ext. 0916, Fax: 514-343-7383, E-mail: vivianne.jodoin@umontreal.ca.

Université Laval, Faculty of Medicine, Graduate Programs in Medicine, Programs in Cellular and Molecular Biology, Québec, QC G1K 7P4, Canada. Offers M Sc, PhD. Terminal master's awarded for partial completion of doctoral program. *Degree requirements:* For master's, thesis; for doctorate, comprehensive exam, thesis/dissertation. *Entrance requirements:* For master's and doctorate, knowledge of French, comprehension of written English. Electronic applications accepted. *Faculty research:* Oral bacterial metabolism, sugar transport.

University at Albany, State University of New York, College of Arts and Sciences, Department of Biological Sciences, Specialization in Molecular, Cellular, Developmental, and Neural Biology, Albany, NY 12222-0001. Offers MS, PhD. *Degree requirements:* For master's, one foreign language; for doctorate, one foreign language, thesis/dissertation. *Entrance requirements:* For master's and doctorate, GRE General Test.

University at Albany, State University of New York, School of Public Health, Department of Biomedical Sciences, Program in Biochemistry, Molecular Biology, and Genetics, Albany, NY 12222-0001. Offers MS, PhD. *Degree requirements:* For master's, thesis; for doctorate, thesis/dissertation. *Entrance requirements:* For master's and doctorate, GRE General Test, GRE Subject Test.

University at Buffalo, the State University of New York, Graduate School, Graduate Programs in Cancer Research and Biomedical Sciences at Roswell Park Cancer Institute, Department of Cellular and Molecular Biology at Roswell Park Cancer Institute, Buffalo, NY 14260. Offers cellular molecular biology/genetics (PhD). *Faculty:* 23 full-time (3 women). *Students:* 19 full-time (7 women), 5 part-time (4 women); includes 1 minority (Asian American or Pacific Islander), 7 international. Average age 25. 40 applicants, 25% accepted, 4 enrolled. In 2009, 4 doctorates awarded. *Degree requirements:* For doctorate, thesis/dissertation, exam project. *Entrance requirements:* For doctorate, GRE General Test, minimum B average in undergraduate coursework. Additional exam requirements/recommendations for international students: Required—TOEFL (minimum score 600 paper-based; 250 computer-based; 100 iBT) or IELTS. *Application deadline:* For fall admission, 2/1 priority date for domestic and international students. Applications are processed on a rolling basis. Application fee: $50. Electronic applications accepted. *Financial support:* In 2009–10, 24 students received support, including 4 fellowships with full tuition reimbursements available (averaging $24,000 per year), 17 research assistantships with full tuition reimbursements available (averaging $24,000 per year); health care benefits also available. Financial award application deadline: 2/1; financial award applicants required to submit FAFSA. *Faculty research:* Cancer genetics, chromatin structure and replication, regulation of transcription, human gene mapping, genetic and structural approaches to regulation of gene expression. Total annual research expenditures: $5.5 million. *Unit head:* Dr. Rosemary Elliott, Director of Graduate Studies, 716-845-3277, Fax: 716-845-1698, E-mail: rosemary.elliott@roswellpark.org. *Application contact:* Craig R. Johnson, Director of Admissions, 716-845-2339, Fax: 716-845-8178, E-mail: craig.johnson@roswellpark.org.

The University of Alabama at Birmingham, Graduate Programs in Joint Health Sciences, Program in Cellular and Molecular Physiology, Birmingham, AL 35294. Offers PhD.

University of Alberta, Faculty of Graduate Studies and Research, Department of Biological Sciences, Edmonton, AB T6G 2E1, Canada. Offers environmental biology and ecology (M Sc, PhD); microbiology and biotechnology (M Sc, PhD); molecular biology and genetics (M Sc, PhD); physiology and cell biology (M Sc, PhD); plant biology (M Sc, PhD); systematics and evolution (M Sc, PhD). *Faculty:* 72 full-time (15 women), 15 part-time/adjunct (4 women). *Students:* 238 full-time (117 women), 32 part-time (15 women), 31 international. 206 applicants, 42% accepted. In 2009, 29 master's, 31 doctorates awarded. Terminal master's awarded for partial completion of doctoral program. *Degree requirements:* For master's, thesis; for doctorate, thesis/dissertation. *Entrance requirements:* Additional exam requirements/recommendations for international students: Required—TOEFL. *Application deadline:* For fall admission, 3/1 priority date for domestic students. Applications are processed on a rolling basis. Application fee: $0. Tuition and fee charges are reported in Canadian dollars. *Expenses:* Tuition, area resident: Full-time $4626 Canadian dollars; part-time $99.72 Canadian dollars per unit. International tuition: $8216 Canadian dollars full-time. Required fees: $3590 Canadian dollars; $99.72 Canadian dollars per unit. $215 Canadian dollars per term. *Financial support:* In 2009–10, 4 research assistantships with partial tuition reimbursements (averaging $12,000 per year), 103 teaching assistantships with partial tuition reimbursements (averaging $12,300 per year) were awarded; career-related internships or fieldwork and scholarships/grants also available. *Unit head:* Laura Frost, Chair, 780-492-1904. *Application contact:* Dr. John P. Chang, Associate Chair for Graduate Studies, 780-492-1257, Fax: 780-492-9457, E-mail: bio.grad.coordinator@ualberta.ca.

University of Alberta, Faculty of Medicine and Dentistry and Faculty of Graduate Studies and Research, Graduate Programs in Medicine, Department of Cell Biology, Edmonton, AB T6G 2E1, Canada. Offers cell and molecular biology (M Sc, PhD). *Faculty:* 13 full-time (3 women), 4 part-time/adjunct (0 women). *Students:* 38 full-time (15 women). Average age 29. 33 applicants. In 2009, 1 master's awarded. Terminal master's awarded for partial completion of doctoral program. *Degree requirements:* For master's, thesis; for doctorate, thesis/dissertation. *Entrance requirements:* For master's and doctorate, 3 letters of reference, curriculum vitae. Additional exam requirements/recommendations for international students: Required—TOEFL (minimum score 600 paper-based; 250 computer-based). *Application deadline:* For fall admission, 4/1 for international students; for winter admission, 8/1 for international students. Applications are processed on a rolling basis. Application fee: $100. Tuition and fee charges are reported in Canadian dollars. *Expenses:* Tuition, area resident: Full-time $4626 Canadian dollars; part-time $99.72 Canadian dollars per unit. International tuition: $8216 Canadian dollars full-time. Required fees: $3590 Canadian dollars; $99.72 Canadian dollars per unit. $215 Canadian dollars per term. *Financial support:* In 2009–10, 16 fellowships with full tuition reimbursements (averaging $20,000 per year), 22 research assistantships with full tuition reimbursements (averaging $17,000 per year) were awarded. *Faculty research:* Protein targeting, membrane trafficking, signal transduction, cell growth and division, cell-cell interaction and development. Total annual research expenditures: $3.5 million. *Unit head:* Dr. Richard A. Rachubinski, Chair, 780-492-9868, Fax: 780-492-9278, E-mail: rick.rachubinski@ualberta.ca. *Application contact:* Dr. Paul Melancon, Graduate Coordinator, 780-492-6183, Fax: 780-492-0450, E-mail: paul.melancon@ualberta.ca.

The University of Arizona, Graduate College, College of Science, Department of Molecular and Cellular Biology, Tucson, AZ 85721. Offers applied biosciences (PSM); molecular and cellular biology (MS, PhD). Evening/weekend programs available. *Faculty:* 10. *Students:* 39 full-time (19 women), 13 part-time (6 women); includes 9 minority (2 American Indian/Alaska Native, 5 Asian Americans or Pacific Islanders, 2 Hispanic Americans), 13 international. Average age 29. 160 applicants, 11% accepted, 9 enrolled. In 2009, 10 master's, 10 doctorates awarded. Terminal master's awarded for partial completion of doctoral program. *Degree requirements:* For master's, thesis; for doctorate, thesis/dissertation. *Entrance requirements:* For master's, 3 letters of recommendation; for doctorate, 3 letters of recommendation, statement of purpose. Additional exam requirements/recommendations for international students: Required—TOEFL (minimum score 600 paper-based; 250 computer-based; 90 iBT), IELTS (minimum score 7). *Application deadline:* For fall admission, 1/1 for domestic and international students. Applications are processed on a rolling basis. Application fee: $75. Electronic applications accepted. *Expenses:* Tuition, state resident: full-time $9028. Tuition, nonresident: full-time $24,890. *Financial support:* In 2009–10, 11 research assistantships with full tuition reimbursements (averaging $20,931 per year), 27 teaching assistantships with full tuition reimbursements (averaging $17,501 per year) were awarded; career-related internships or fieldwork, scholarships/grants, health care benefits, and unspecified assistantships also available. *Faculty research:* Plant molecular biology, cellular and molecular aspects of development, genetics of bacteria and lower eukaryotes. Total annual research expenditures: $7 million. *Unit head:* Kathleen Dixon, Department Head, 520-621-7563, Fax: 520-621-3709, E-mail: dixonk@email.arizona.edu. *Application contact:* Kathleen Dixon, Department Head, 520-621-7563, Fax: 520-621-3709, E-mail: dixonk@email.arizona.edu.

University of Arkansas, Graduate School, Interdisciplinary Program in Cell and Molecular Biology, Fayetteville, AR 72701-1201. Offers MS, PhD. *Students:* 14 full-time (8 women), 51 part-time (29 women); includes 3 minority (1 African American, 2 Asian Americans or Pacific Islanders), 46 international. In 2009, 1 master's, 5 doctorates awarded. *Degree requirements:* For doctorate, thesis/dissertation. Application fee: $40 ($50 for international students). *Expenses:* Tuition, state resident: full-time $7355; part-time $356.58 per hour. Tuition, nonresident: full-time $17,401; part-time $775.17 per hour. Required fees: $1203. *Financial support:* In 2009–10, 4 fellowships with tuition reimbursements, 10 research assistantships were awarded; teaching assistantships. Financial award application deadline: 4/1; financial award applicants required to submit FAFSA. *Unit head:* Dr. Douglas Rhoads, Head, 479-575-7396, Fax: 479-575-5908, E-mail: drhoads@uark.edu. *Application contact:* Graduate Admissions, 479-575-6246, Fax: 479-575-5908, E-mail: gradinfo@uark.edu.

University of Arkansas for Medical Sciences, Graduate School, Graduate Programs in Biomedical Sciences, Program in Biochemistry and Molecular Biology, Little Rock, AR 72205-7199. Offers MS, PhD, MD/PhD. *Faculty:* 18 full-time (4 women), 10 part-time/adjunct (2 women). *Students:* 19 full-time, 3 part-time. In 2009, 3 doctorates awarded. *Degree requirements:* For master's, comprehensive exam, thesis; for doctorate, thesis/dissertation, qualifying exam. *Entrance requirements:* For master's, GRE General Test, bachelor's degree in biology, chemistry, or related field; for doctorate, GRE General Test. Additional exam requirements/recommendations for international students: Required—TOEFL. *Application deadline:* Applications are processed on a rolling basis. Application fee: $0. *Financial support:* In 2009–10, research assistantships with full tuition reimbursements (averaging $24,000 per year); unspecified assistantships and stipend and tuition for doctoral students also available. Support available to part-time students. *Faculty research:* Gene regulation, growth factors, oncogenes, metabolic diseases, hormone regulation. *Application contact:* Dr. Wayne Wahls, Program Director, 501-686-5787, E-mail: wahlswaynep@uams.edu.

The University of British Columbia, Faculty of Medicine, Department of Biochemistry and Molecular Biology, Vancouver, BC V6T 1Z1, Canada. Offers M Sc, PhD. *Degree requirements:* For master's, thesis; for doctorate, comprehensive exam, thesis/dissertation. *Entrance requirements:* For master's, first class B Sc; for doctorate, master's or first class honors bachelor's degree in biochemistry. Additional exam requirements/recommendations for international students: Required—TOEFL (minimum score 625 paper-based; 263 computer-based), GRE. Electronic applications accepted. *Faculty research:* Membrane biochemistry, protein structure/function, signal transduction, biochemistry.

University of Calgary, Faculty of Medicine and Faculty of Graduate Studies, Department of Biochemistry and Molecular Biology, Calgary, AB T2N 1N4, Canada. Offers M Sc, PhD. *Degree requirements:* For master's, thesis; for doctorate, thesis/dissertation, candidacy exam. *Entrance requirements:* For master's and doctorate, GRE General Test, minimum GPA of 3.2. Additional exam requirements/recommendations for international students: Required—TOEFL. Electronic applications accepted. *Faculty research:* Molecular and developmental genetics; molecular biology of disease; genomics, proteomics and bioinformatics; ceu signaling and structure.

University of California, Berkeley, Graduate Division, College of Letters and Science, Department of Molecular and Cell Biology, Berkeley, CA 94720-1500. Offers PhD. *Faculty:* 90 full-time (24 women), 1 part-time/adjunct (0 women). *Students:* 261 full-time (144 women); includes 72 minority (5 African Americans, 43 Asian Americans or Pacific Islanders, 24 Hispanic Americans), 17 international. Average age 26. 562 applicants, 24% accepted, 56 enrolled. In 2009, 38 doctorates awarded. *Degree requirements:* For doctorate, comprehensive exam, thesis/dissertation, qualifying exam, 2 semesters of teaching, 3 seminars. *Entrance requirements:* For doctorate, GRE General Test, GRE Subject Test (recommended), minimum GPA of 3.0. Additional exam requirements/recommendations for international students: Required—TOEFL (minimum score 570 paper-based; 230 computer-based; 68 iBT), IELTS (minimum score 7). *Application deadline:* For fall admission, 12/1 for domestic and international students. Applications are processed on a rolling basis. Application fee: $70 ($90 for international students). Electronic applications accepted. *Financial support:* In 2009–10, 129 students received support, including 7 fellowships with full tuition reimbursements available (averaging $24,100 per year), 159 research assistantships with full tuition reimbursements available (averaging $28,000 per year), 88 teaching assistantships with full tuition reimbursements available (averaging $8,315 per year); scholarships/grants, traineeships, health care benefits, tuition waivers (full), and unspecified assistantships also available. Financial award application deadline: 12/1; financial award applicants required to submit FAFSA. *Faculty research:* Biochemistry and molecular biology, cell and developmental biology, genetics, immunology, neurobiology, genomics. *Unit head:* Dr. James M. Berger, Professor, 510-643-9483. *Application contact:* Berta Parra, Student Affairs Officer, 510-642-5252, Fax: 510-642-7000, E-mail: bparra@berkeley.edu.

University of California, Davis, Graduate Studies, Graduate Group in Biochemistry and Molecular Biology, Davis, CA 95616. Offers MS, PhD. Terminal master's awarded for partial completion of doctoral program. *Degree requirements:* For master's, comprehensive exam (for some programs), thesis (for some programs); for doctorate, thesis/dissertation. *Entrance requirements:* For master's and doctorate, GRE General Test, GRE Subject Test. Additional exam requirements/recommendations for international students: Required—TOEFL (minimum score 550 paper-based; 213 computer-based). Electronic applications accepted. *Faculty research:* Gene expression, protein structure, molecular virology, protein synthesis, enzymology, membrane transport and structural biology.

University of California, Irvine, Office of Graduate Studies, School of Biological Sciences, Department of Molecular Biology and Biochemistry, Irvine, CA 92697. Offers biological science (MS); biological sciences (PhD); biotechnology (MS); MD/PhD. *Students:* 86 full-time (43 women); includes 31 minority (2 African Americans, 20 Asian Americans or Pacific Islanders, 9 Hispanic Americans), 10 international. Average age 27. In 2009, 13 master's, 12 doctorates awarded. *Degree requirements:* For doctorate, thesis/dissertation. *Entrance requirements:* For master's, GRE, minimum GPA of 3.0; for doctorate, GRE General Test, GRE Subject Test, minimum GPA of 3.0. Additional exam requirements/recommendations for international students: Required—TOEFL (minimum score 550 paper-based; 213 computer-based). *Application deadline:* For fall admission, 12/15 priority date for domestic students, 12/15 for international students. Applications are processed on a rolling basis. Application fee: $70 ($90 for international students). Electronic applications accepted. *Financial support:* Fellowships, research assistantships with full tuition reimbursements, teaching assistantships, institutionally sponsored loans, traineeships, health care benefits, and unspecified assistantships available. Financial award application deadline: 3/1; financial award applicants required to submit FAFSA. *Faculty research:* Structure and synthesis of nucleic acids and proteins, regulation, virology, biochemical genetics, gene organization. *Unit head:* Jerry Manning, Chair, 949-824-5578, Fax: 949-824-8551, E-mail: jemannin@uci.edu. *Application contact:* Kimberly McKinney, Administrator, 949-824-8145, Fax: 949-824-1965, E-mail: kamckinn@uci.edu.

University of California, Irvine, Office of Graduate Studies, School of Biological Sciences and School of Medicine, Graduate Program in Molecular Biology, Genetics, and Biochemistry, Irvine, CA 92697. Offers biological sciences (PhD). *Degree requirements:* For doctorate, thesis/dissertation, teaching assignment, preliminary exam. *Entrance requirements:* For doctorate, GRE General Test, minimum GPA of 3.0, research experience. Additional exam requirements/recommendations for international students: Required—TOEFL, IELTS, SPEAK test. Electronic applications accepted. *Expenses:* Contact institution. *Faculty research:* Cellular biochemistry; gene structure and expression; protein structure, function, and design; molecular genetics; pathogenesis and inherited disease.

University of California, Los Angeles, David Geffen School of Medicine and Graduate Division, Graduate Programs in Medicine, Department of Molecular, Cell and Developmental Biology, Los Angeles, CA 90095. Offers PhD. *Degree requirements:* For doctorate, thesis/dissertation, qualifying exams. *Entrance requirements:* For doctorate, GRE General Test, GRE Subject Test. Additional exam requirements/recommendations for international students: Required—TOEFL.

University of California, Los Angeles, Graduate Division, College of Letters and Science, Department of Chemistry and Biochemistry, Program in Biochemistry and Molecular Biology, Los Angeles, CA 90034. Offers MS, PhD. MS admission to program only under exceptional circumstances. *Students:* 99 full-time (46 women); includes 31 minority (1 African American, 20 Asian Americans or Pacific Islanders, 10 Hispanic Americans), 10 international. Average age 28. 89 applicants, 30% accepted, 14 enrolled. In 2009, 6 master's, 20 doctorates awarded. Terminal master's awarded for partial completion of doctoral program. *Degree requirements:* For master's, comprehensive exam or thesis; for doctorate, thesis/dissertation, oral and written exams, 1 year teaching experience. *Entrance requirements:* For master's, GRE General Test, GRE Subject Test, minimum GPA of 3.0; for doctorate, GRE General Test, GRE Subject Test, minimum undergraduate GPA of 3.0. *Application deadline:* For fall admission, 1/15 for domestic and international students. Application fee: $70 ($90 for international students). Electronic applications accepted. *Financial support:* In 2009–10, 89 fellowships with full and partial tuition reimbursements, 71 research assistantships with full and partial tuition reimbursements, 43 teaching assistantships with full and partial tuition reimbursements were awarded; Federal Work-Study, scholarships/grants, health care benefits, tuition waivers (full and partial), and unspecified assistantships also available. Financial award applicants required to submit FAFSA. *Unit head:* Dr. Albert Courey, 310- 825-3958. *Application contact:* Department Office, 310-825-3150, E-mail: grad@chem.ucla.edu.

University of California, Los Angeles, Graduate Division, College of Letters and Science, Program in Molecular Biology, Los Angeles, CA 90095. Offers PhD, MD/PhD. *Students:* 73 full-time (33 women); includes 22 minority (2 African Americans, 1 American Indian/Alaska Native, 13 Asian Americans or Pacific Islanders, 6 Hispanic Americans), 6 international. Average age 27. 13 applicants, 31% accepted, 3 enrolled. In 2009, 12 doctorates awarded. *Degree requirements:* For doctorate, thesis/dissertation, oral and written qualifying exams, teaching experience. *Entrance requirements:* For doctorate, GRE General Test, GRE Subject Test (biochemistry, chemistry, biology, or physics). *Application deadline:* For fall admission, 1/10 for domestic and international students. Application fee: $70 ($90 for international students). Electronic applications accepted. *Financial support:* In 2009–10, 54 fellowships with full and partial tuition reimbursements, 54 research assistantships with full and partial tuition reimbursements, 27 teaching assistantships with full and partial tuition reimbursements were awarded; Federal Work-Study, institutionally sponsored loans, scholarships/grants, health care benefits, tuition waivers (full and partial), and unspecified assistantships also available. Financial award application deadline: 3/1; financial award applicants required to submit FAFSA. *Unit head:* Dr. James Tidball, Director, 310-206-3395. *Application contact:* Department Office, 800-206-3395, E-mail: mbigrad@mednet.ucla.edu.

University of California, Los Angeles, Graduate Division, College of Letters and Science, Program in Molecular, Cellular and Integrative Physiology, Los Angeles, CA 90095. Offers PhD. *Students:* 34 full-time (20 women); includes 7 minority (5 Asian Americans or Pacific Islanders, 2 Hispanic Americans), 10 international. Average age 29. 14 applicants, 50% accepted, 4 enrolled. In 2009, 5 doctorates awarded. *Degree requirements:* For doctorate, thesis/dissertation, oral and written exams, student teaching. *Entrance requirements:* For doctorate, GRE General Test, GRE Subject Test (biology or applicant's undergraduate major), minimum GPA of 3.0, bachelor's degree in biological or physical sciences. Application fee: $70 ($90 for international students). Electronic applications accepted. *Financial support:* In 2009–10, 18 fellowships with full and partial tuition reimbursements, 25 research assistantships with full and partial tuition reimbursements, 8 teaching assistantships with full and partial tuition reimbursements were awarded; Federal Work-Study, institutionally sponsored loans, scholarships/grants, health care benefits, tuition waivers (full and partial), and unspecified assistantships also available. Financial award applicants required to submit FAFSA. *Unit head:* James Tidbell, Chair, 310-825-3891. *Application contact:* Department Office, 310-825-3891, E-mail: mcarr@physci.ucla.edu.

University of California, Los Angeles, Graduate Division, College of Letters and Science and David Geffen School of Medicine, UCLA ACCESS to Programs in the Molecular, Cellular and Integrative Life Sciences, Los Angeles, CA 90095. Offers biochemistry and molecular biology (PhD); biological chemistry (PhD); cellular and molecular pathology (PhD); human genetics (PhD); microbiology, immunology, and molecular genetics (PhD); molecular biology (PhD); molecular toxicology (PhD); molecular, cellular and integrative physiology (PhD); neurobiology (PhD); oral biology (PhD); physiology (PhD). ACCESS is an umbrella program for first-year coursework in 12 PhD programs. *Students:* 39 full-time (25 women); includes 14 minority (1 African American, 1 American Indian/Alaska Native, 8 Asian Americans or Pacific Islanders, 4 Hispanic Americans), 10 international. Average age 25. 437 applicants, 22% accepted, 30 enrolled. *Degree requirements:* For doctorate, thesis/dissertation, oral and written qualifying exams. *Entrance requirements:* For doctorate, GRE General Test, minimum undergraduate GPA of 3.0. Additional exam requirements/recommendations for international students: Required—TOEFL. *Application deadline:* For fall admission, 12/15 for domestic and international students. Application fee: $70 ($90 for international students). Electronic applications accepted. *Financial support:* In 2009–10, 56 fellowships with full and partial tuition reimbursements, 16 research assistantships with full and partial tuition reimbursements were awarded; teaching assistantships with full and partial tuition reimbursements, Federal Work-Study, institutionally sponsored loans, scholarships/grants, health care benefits, tuition waivers (full and partial), and unspecified assistantships also available. Financial award application deadline: 3/1; financial award applicants required to submit FAFSA. *Faculty research:* Molecular, cellular, and developmental biology; immunology; microbiology; integrative biology. *Unit head:* Dr. Greg I. Payne, Chair, 310-206-3121. *Application contact:* Coordinator, 310-206-3121, Fax: 310-206-5280, E-mail: uclaaccess@mednet.ucla.edu.

See Close-Up on page 239.

University of California, Riverside, Graduate Division, Program in Cell, Molecular, and Developmental Biology, Riverside, CA 92521-0102. Offers MS, PhD. *Faculty:* 55 full-time (18 women). *Students:* 47 full-time (28 women); includes 15 minority (2 African Americans, 11 Asian Americans or Pacific Islanders, 2 Hispanic Americans), 15 international. Average age 29. In 2009, 7 doctorates awarded. Terminal master's awarded for partial completion of doctoral program. *Degree requirements:* For master's, thesis, oral defense of thesis; for doctorate, thesis/dissertation, oral defense of thesis, qualifying exams, 2 quarters of teaching experience. *Entrance requirements:* For master's and doctorate, GRE General Test, minimum GPA of 3.2. Additional exam requirements/recommendations for international students: Required—TOEFL (minimum score 550 paper-based; 213 computer-based; 80 iBT). *Application deadline:* For fall admission, 1/5 priority date for domestic and international students. Applications are processed on a rolling basis. Application fee: $60 ($75 for international students). Electronic applications accepted. *Financial support:* In 2009–10, fellowships with full and partial tuition reimbursements (averaging $24,000 per year), research assistantships with full and partial tuition reimbursements (averaging $21,847 per year), teaching assistantships with full and partial tuition reimbursements (averaging $18,485 per year) were awarded; scholarships/grants, traineeships, health care benefits, tuition waivers (partial), and unspecified assistantships also available. Support available to part-time students. Financial award application deadline: 1/5. *Unit head:* Dr. Peter Atkinson, Director, 951-827-4782, E-mail: norman@ucr.edu. *Application contact:* Kathy Redd, Graduate Program Assistant, 800-735-0717, Fax: 951-827-5517, E-mail: cmdb@ucr.edu.

University of California, San Diego, Office of Graduate Studies, Division of Biological Sciences, Program in Genetics and Molecular Biology, La Jolla, CA 92093-0348. Offers PhD. Offered in association with the Salk Institute. *Degree requirements:* For doctorate, thesis/dissertation, qualifying exam. Electronic applications accepted.

University of California, San Diego, Office of Graduate Studies, Division of Biological Sciences, Program in Molecular and Cellular Biology, La Jolla, CA 92093. Offers PhD. Offered in association with the Salk Institute. *Degree requirements:* For doctorate, thesis/dissertation, qualifying exam. Electronic applications accepted.

University of California, San Diego, School of Medicine and Office of Graduate Studies, Graduate Studies in Biomedical Sciences, Program in Molecular Cell Biology, La Jolla, CA 92093. Offers PhD. *Degree requirements:* For doctorate, thesis/dissertation, qualifying exam. *Entrance requirements:* For doctorate, GRE General Test. Additional exam requirements/recommendations for international students: Required—TOEFL. Electronic applications accepted. *Faculty research:* Molecular and cellular pharmacology, cell and organ physiology.

University of California, San Diego, School of Medicine and Office of Graduate Studies, Graduate Studies in Biomedical Sciences, Regulatory Biology Program, La Jolla, CA 92093. Offers PhD. *Degree requirements:* For doctorate, thesis/dissertation, 2 qualifying exams. *Entrance requirements:* For doctorate, GRE General Test, GRE Subject Test. Additional exam requirements/recommendations for international students: Required—TOEFL. Electronic applications accepted. *Faculty research:* Eukaryotic regulatory and molecular biology, molecular and cellular pharmacology, cell and organ physiology.

University of California, San Francisco, Graduate Division and School of Medicine, Department of Biochemistry and Biophysics, Program in Biochemistry and Molecular Biology, San Francisco, CA 94143. Offers PhD, MD/PhD. *Degree requirements:* For doctorate, thesis/dissertation. *Entrance requirements:* For doctorate, GRE General Test, GRE Subject Test. Additional exam requirements/recommendations for international students: Required—TOEFL. *Expenses:* Contact institution. *Faculty research:* Structural biology, genetics, cell biology, cell physiology, metabolism.

University of California, Santa Barbara, Graduate Division, College of Letters and Sciences, Division of Mathematics, Life, and Physical Sciences, Department of Molecular, Cellular, and Developmental Biology, Santa Barbara, CA 93106-9625. Offers MA, PhD, MA/PhD. *Faculty:* 21 full-time (3 women), 7 part-time/adjunct (2 women). *Students:* 60 full-time (31 women). Average age 27. 44 applicants, 23% accepted, 6 enrolled. In 2009, 8 master's, 7 doctorates awarded. *Degree requirements:* For master's, comprehensive exam (for some programs), thesis (for some programs); for doctorate, comprehensive exam, thesis/dissertation. *Entrance requirements:* For master's, GRE General Test, GRE Subject Test, 3 letters of recommendation, resume/curriculum vitae; for doctorate, GRE General Test, GRE Subject Test, 3

Molecular Biology

University of California, Santa Barbara (continued)
letters of recommendation, statement of purpose, personal achievements/contributions statement, resume/curriculum vitae, transcripts for post-secondary institutions attended. Additional exam requirements/recommendations for international students: Required—TOEFL (minimum score 610 paper-based; 253 computer-based; 102 iBT) or IELTS (minimum score 7). *Application deadline:* For fall admission, 12/15 for domestic and international students. Application fee: $70 ($90 for international students). Electronic applications accepted. *Financial support:* In 2009–10, 60 students received support, including 19 fellowships with full and partial tuition reimbursements available (averaging $9,800 per year), 39 research assistantships with full and partial tuition reimbursements available (averaging $9,700 per year), 48 teaching assistantships with partial tuition reimbursements available (averaging $7,500 per year); career-related internships or fieldwork, Federal Work-Study, institutionally sponsored loans, scholarships/grants, traineeships, health care benefits, and unspecified assistantships also available. Financial award application deadline: 12/15; financial award applicants required to submit FAFSA. *Faculty research:* Microbiology, neurobiology (including stem cell research), developmental, virology, cell biology. *Unit head:* Dr. Dennis O. Clegg, Chair, 805-893-8490, Fax: 805-893-4724, E-mail: clegg@lifesci.ucsb.edu. *Application contact:* Tony L. Tieu, Staff Graduate Program Advisor, 805-893-8499, Fax: 805-893-4724, E-mail: tieu@lifesci.ucsb.edu.

University of California, Santa Barbara, Graduate Division, College of Letters and Sciences, Division of Mathematics, Life, and Physical Sciences, Interdepartmental Graduate Program in Biomolecular Science and Engineering, Santa Barbara, CA 93106-9611. Offers biochemistry and molecular biology (MS, PhD), including biochemistry and molecular biology, biomolecular science and engineering (MS). *Faculty:* 40 full-time (5 women), 2 part-time/adjunct (1 woman). *Students:* 33 full-time (12 women). Average age 28. 62 applicants, 29% accepted, 5 enrolled. In 2009, 3 master's, 2 doctorates awarded. Terminal master's awarded for partial completion of doctoral program. *Degree requirements:* For master's, comprehensive exam (for some programs), thesis (for some programs); for doctorate, comprehensive exam, thesis/dissertation. *Entrance requirements:* For master's, GRE General Test, GRE Subject Test, bachelor's degree in a related science, 3 letters of recommendation, statement of purpose, personal achievements/contributions statement, resume/curriculum vitae, transcripts for post-secondary institutions attended; for doctorate, GRE General Test, GRE Subject Test, bachelor's degree in a related science, 3 letters of recommendation, resume/curriculum vitae. Additional exam requirements/recommendations for international students: Required—TOEFL (minimum score 630 paper-based; 267 computer-based; 109 iBT) or IELTS (minimum score 7). *Application deadline:* For fall admission, 12/15 for domestic and international students. Application fee: $70 ($90 for international students). Electronic applications accepted. *Financial support:* In 2009–10, 33 students received support, including 12 fellowships with full and partial tuition reimbursements available (averaging $15,300 per year), 100 research assistantships with full and partial tuition reimbursements available (averaging $9,500 per year), 92 teaching assistantships with partial tuition reimbursements available (averaging $8,700 per year); career-related internships or fieldwork, Federal Work-Study, institutionally sponsored loans, scholarships/grants, traineeships, health care benefits, tuition waivers (full and partial), and unspecified assistantships also available. Financial award applicants required to submit FAFSA. *Faculty research:* Biochemistry and molecular biology, biophysics, biomaterials, bioengineering, systems biology. *Unit head:* Prof. Philip A. Pincus, Chair, 805-893-4685, E-mail: fyl@mrl.ucsb.edu. *Application contact:* Azure Stewart, Graduate Program Advisor, 805-893-6083, Fax: 805-893-4724, E-mail: azstewart@lifesci.ucsb.edu.

University of California, Santa Cruz, Division of Graduate Studies, Division of Physical and Biological Sciences, Program in Molecular, Cellular, and Developmental Biology, Santa Cruz, CA 95064. Offers MA, PhD. *Degree requirements:* For master's, thesis; for doctorate, thesis/dissertation, qualifying exam. *Entrance requirements:* For master's and doctorate, GRE General Test, 3 letters of recommendation, interview. Additional exam requirements/recommendations for international students: Required—TOEFL (minimum score 550 paper-based; 220 computer-based; 83 iBT). Electronic applications accepted.

University of Central Florida, College of Medicine, Burnett School of Biomedical Sciences, Program in Molecular Biology and Microbiology, Orlando, FL 32816. Offers MS. Part-time and evening/weekend programs available. *Students:* 26 full-time (16 women); includes 7 minority (3 Asian Americans or Pacific Islanders, 4 Hispanic Americans), 10 international. Average age 27. 49 applicants, 43% accepted, 13 enrolled. In 2009, 14 master's awarded. *Degree requirements:* For master's, comprehensive exam, thesis. *Entrance requirements:* For master's, GRE General Test, minimum GPA of 3.0 in last 60 hours. Additional exam requirements/recommendations for international students: Required—TOEFL. *Application deadline:* For fall admission, 3/15 priority date for domestic students; for spring admission, 12/1 for domestic students. Electronic applications accepted. *Expenses:* Tuition, state resident: part-time $306.31 per credit hour. Tuition, nonresident: part-time $1099.01 per credit hour. Part-time tuition and fees vary according to degree level and program. *Financial support:* In 2009–10, 13 students received support, including 1 fellowship with partial tuition reimbursement available (averaging $10,000 per year), 5 research assistantships with partial tuition reimbursements available (averaging $7,200 per year), 9 teaching assistantships with partial tuition reimbursements available (averaging $9,100 per year); career-related internships or fieldwork, Federal Work-Study, institutionally sponsored loans, tuition waivers (partial), and unspecified assistantships also available. Financial award application deadline: 3/1; financial award applicants required to submit FAFSA. *Application contact:* Dr. Saleh A. Naser, Graduate Coordinator, 407-823-0955, E-mail: nasersi@mail.ucf.edu.

University of Chicago, Division of the Biological Sciences, Department of Molecular Biosciences, Department of Biochemistry and Molecular Biology, Chicago, IL 60637-1513. Offers PhD, MD/PhD. *Faculty:* 31 full-time (8 women). *Students:* 35 full-time (14 women); includes 5 minority (2 American Indian/Alaska Native, 3 Asian Americans or Pacific Islanders), 6 international. Average age 28. 44 applicants, 7% accepted, 3 enrolled. In 2009, 8 doctorates awarded. *Degree requirements:* For doctorate, thesis/dissertation, ethics class, 2 teaching assistantships. *Entrance requirements:* For doctorate, GRE General Test, GRE Subject Test. Additional exam requirements/recommendations for international students: Required—TOEFL (minimum score 600 paper-based; 250 computer-based; 104 iBT), IELTS (minimum score 7). *Application deadline:* For fall admission, 12/1 priority date for domestic and international students. Application fee: $55. Electronic applications accepted. *Financial support:* In 2009–10, 35 students received support, including fellowships with tuition reimbursements available (averaging $29,781 per year), research assistantships with tuition reimbursements available (averaging $29,781 per year); institutionally sponsored loans, scholarships/grants, traineeships, and health care benefits also available. Financial award applicants required to submit FAFSA. *Faculty research:* Molecular biology, gene expression, and DNA-protein interactions; membrane biochemistry, molecular endocrinology, and transmembrane signaling; enzyme mechanisms, physical biochemistry, and structural biology. Total annual research expenditures: $5 million. *Unit head:* Dr. Anthony A. Kossiakoff, Chairman, 773-702-9297, Fax: 773-702-0439, E-mail: koss@cummings.uchicago.edu. *Application contact:* Lisa Anderson, Graduate Student Administrator, 773-834-3586, Fax: 773-702-0439, E-mail: landerso@bsd.uchicago.edu.

University of Chicago, Division of the Biological Sciences, Department of Molecular Biosciences, Graduate Program in Cell and Molecular Biology, Chicago, IL 60637-1513. Offers PhD. *Faculty:* 31 full-time (8 women). *Students:* 28 full-time (13 women); includes 6 minority (4 Asian Americans or Pacific Islanders, 2 Hispanic Americans). Average age 29. 39 applicants, 10% accepted, 4 enrolled. In 2009, 4 doctorates awarded. *Degree requirements:* For doctorate, thesis/dissertation, ethics class, 2 teaching assistantships. *Entrance requirements:* For doctorate, GRE General Test. Additional exam requirements/recommendations for international students: Required—TOEFL (minimum score 600 paper-based; 250 computer-based; 104 iBT), IELTS (minimum score 7). *Application deadline:* For fall admission, 12/1 priority date for domestic and international students. Application fee: $55. Electronic applications accepted. *Financial support:* In 2009–10, 28 students received support, including fellowships (averaging $29,781 per year), research assistantships (averaging $29,781 per year); institutionally sponsored loans, scholarships/grants, traineeships, and health care benefits also available. Financial award applicants required to submit FAFSA. *Faculty research:* Gene expression, chromosome structure, animal viruses, plant molecular genetics. Total annual research expenditures: $8 million. *Unit head:* Dr. Richard Fehon, Chair, 773-702-5694, E-mail: rfehon@uchicago.edu. *Application contact:* Kristine Gaston, Graduate Administrative Director, 773-702-8037, Fax: 773-702-3172, E-mail: kristine@bsd.uchicago.edu.

University of Cincinnati, Graduate School, College of Medicine, Graduate Programs in Biomedical Sciences, Department of Environmental Health, Programs in Environmental Genetics and Molecular Toxicology, Cincinnati, OH 45221. Offers MS, PhD. *Degree requirements:* For doctorate, thesis/dissertation. *Entrance requirements:* For master's, GRE, minimum GPA of 3.0, 3 letters of recommendation. Additional exam requirements/recommendations for international students: Required—TOEFL (minimum score 520 paper-based; 190 computer-based).

University of Cincinnati, Graduate School, College of Medicine, Graduate Programs in Biomedical Sciences, Department of Molecular Genetics, Biochemistry and Microbiology, Cincinnati, OH 45221. Offers MS, PhD. Terminal master's awarded for partial completion of doctoral program. *Degree requirements:* For master's, thesis or alternative; for doctorate, thesis/dissertation, qualifying exam. *Entrance requirements:* For master's and doctorate, GRE General Test. Additional exam requirements/recommendations for international students: Required—TOEFL (minimum score 600 paper-based; 250 computer-based; 100 iBT), TWE. Electronic applications accepted. *Faculty research:* Cancer biology and developmental genetics, gene regulation and chromosome structure, microbiology and pathogenic mechanisms, structural biology, membrane biochemistry and signal transduction.

University of Cincinnati, Graduate School, College of Medicine, Graduate Programs in Biomedical Sciences, Department of Pediatrics, Program in Molecular and Developmental Biology, Cincinnati, OH 45221. Offers PhD. *Degree requirements:* For doctorate, thesis/dissertation, qualifying exam. *Entrance requirements:* For doctorate, GRE General Test, minimum GPA of 3.2. Additional exam requirements/recommendations for international students: Required—TOEFL (minimum score 520 paper-based; 190 computer-based). Electronic applications accepted. *Faculty research:* Cancer biology, cardiovascular biology, developmental biology, human genetics, gene therapy, genomics and bioinformatics, immunobiology, molecular medicine, neuroscience, pulmonary biology, reproductive biology, stem cell biology.

University of Colorado at Boulder, Graduate School, College of Arts and Sciences, Department of Molecular, Cellular, and Developmental Biology, Boulder, CO 80309. Offers cellular structure and function (MA, PhD); developmental biology (MA, PhD); molecular biology (MA, PhD). *Faculty:* 27 full-time (7 women). *Students:* 29 full-time (15 women), 45 part-time (18 women); includes 7 minority (2 American Indian/Alaska Native, 1 Asian American or Pacific Islander, 4 Hispanic Americans), 15 international. Average age 28. 210 applicants, 5% accepted, 11 enrolled. In 2009, 3 master's, 7 doctorates awarded. Terminal master's awarded for partial completion of doctoral program. *Degree requirements:* For master's, comprehensive exam, thesis or alternative; for doctorate, comprehensive exam, thesis/dissertation. *Entrance requirements:* For master's, GRE General Test, GRE Subject Test, minimum undergraduate GPA of 3.0; for doctorate, GRE General Test, GRE Subject Test. *Application deadline:* For fall admission, 1/1 for domestic students, 12/1 for international students. Application fee: $50 ($60 for international students). *Financial support:* In 2009–10, 40 fellowships (averaging $11,628 per year), 53 research assistantships (averaging $14,700 per year) were awarded; tuition waivers (full) also available. Financial award application deadline: 2/1. *Faculty research:* Molecular biology of RNA and DNA, molecular genetics, cell motility and cytoskeleton, cell membranes, developmental genetics, human genetics. Total annual research expenditures: $15.5 million.

University of Colorado Denver, School of Medicine, Program in Molecular Biology, Denver, CO 80217-3364. Offers PhD. *Students:* 36 full-time (19 women); includes 2 minority (both Hispanic Americans), 4 international. *Degree requirements:* For doctorate, thesis/dissertation. *Entrance requirements:* For doctorate, GRE, minimum GPA of 3.0, 4 letters of recommendation. Additional exam requirements/recommendations for international students: Required—TOEFL (minimum score 550 paper-based; 213 computer-based). *Application deadline:* For fall admission, 1/15 for domestic students. Application fee: $50. Electronic applications accepted. *Financial support:* Fellowships, research assistantships, teaching assistantships, Federal Work-Study and institutionally sponsored loans available. Support available to part-time students. Financial award application deadline: 3/15; financial award applicants required to submit FAFSA. *Faculty research:* Gene transcription, RNA processing, chromosome dynamics, DNA damage and repair, chromatin assembly. *Unit head:* Dr. James DeGregori, Director, 303-724-3245, E-mail: james.degregori@uchsc.edu. *Application contact:* Jean Sibley, Administrator, 303-724-3245, Fax: 303-724-3247, E-mail: jean.sibley@uchsc.edu.

University of Connecticut, Graduate School, College of Liberal Arts and Sciences, Department of Molecular and Cell Biology, Field of Microbial Systems Analysis, Storrs, CT 06269. Offers MS, PSM. *Students:* 5 full-time (3 women), 2 part-time (1 woman); includes 2 minority (1 African American, 1 Asian American or Pacific Islander), 3 international. Average age 25. 7 applicants, 71% accepted, 2 enrolled. *Degree requirements:* For master's, comprehensive exam. *Entrance requirements:* For master's, GRE General Test, GRE Subject Test. Additional exam requirements/recommendations for international students: Required—TOEFL (minimum score 550 paper-based; 213 computer-based). *Application deadline:* For fall admission, 2/1 priority date for domestic and international students; for spring admission, 11/1 for domestic students, 10/1 for international students. Applications are processed on a rolling basis. Electronic applications accepted. *Expenses:* Tuition, state resident: full-time $4725; part-time $525 per credit. Tuition, nonresident: full-time $12,267; part-time $1363 per credit. Required fees: $346 per semester. Tuition and fees vary according to course load. *Financial support:* In 2009–10, 1 teaching assistantship with full tuition reimbursement was awarded; research assistantships with full tuition reimbursements, Federal Work-Study, scholarships/grants, health care benefits, and unspecified assistantships also available. Financial award application deadline: 2/1. *Unit head:* David Benson, Head, 860-486-4258, Fax: 860-486-4331, E-mail: david.benson@uconn.edu. *Application contact:* Anne St. Onje, Graduate Coordinator, 860-486-4314, Fax: 860-486-3943, E-mail: anne.st_onje@uconn.edu.

University of Connecticut Health Center, Graduate School, Programs in Biomedical Sciences, Program in Molecular Biology and Biochemistry, Farmington, CT 06030. Offers PhD, DMD/PhD, MD/PhD. *Faculty:* 30. *Students:* 22 full-time (13 women); includes 3 minority (1 African American, 2 Asian Americans or Pacific Islanders), 8 international. Average age 29. 165 applicants, 35% accepted. In 2009, 5 doctorates awarded. *Degree requirements:* For doctorate, comprehensive exam, thesis/dissertation. *Entrance requirements:* For doctorate, GRE General Test. Additional exam requirements/recommendations for international students: Required—TOEFL (minimum score 600 paper-based; 250 computer-based). *Application deadline:* For fall admission, 12/15 for domestic students. Application fee: $55. Electronic applications accepted. *Financial support:* In 2009–10, 22 students received support, including 22 research assistantships with full tuition reimbursements available (averaging $27,000 per year); fellowships, health care benefits also available. *Faculty research:* Molecular biology, structural biology, protein biochemistry, microbial physiology and pathogenesis. *Unit head:* Dr. Stephen King, Director, 860-679-3347, Fax: 860-679-1239, E-mail: sking@nso2.uchc.edu. *Application contact:* Tricia Avolt, Graduate Admissions Coordinator, 860-679-2175, Fax: 860-679-1899, E-mail: robertson@nso2.uchc.edu.

See Close-Up on page 243.

University of Delaware, College of Arts and Sciences, Department of Biological Sciences, Newark, DE 19716. Offers biotechnology (MS); cancer biology (MS, PhD); cell and extracellular matrix biology (MS, PhD); cell and systems physiology (MS, PhD); developmental biology (MS, PhD); ecology and evolution (MS, PhD); microbiology (MS, PhD); molecular biology and genetics (MS, PhD). Terminal master's awarded for partial completion of doctoral program. *Degree requirements:* For master's, thesis, preliminary exam; for doctorate, comprehensive exam, thesis/dissertation, preliminary exam. *Entrance requirements:* For master's and doctorate, GRE General Test. Additional exam requirements/recommendations for international students: Required—TOEFL (minimum score 600 paper-based; 250 computer-based); Recommended—TWE. Electronic applications accepted. *Faculty research:* Microorganisms, bone, cancer metastasis, developmental biology, cell biology, DNA.

University of Florida, College of Medicine, Department of Biochemistry and Molecular Biology, Gainesville, FL 32611. Offers biochemistry and molecular biology (MS, PhD); imaging science and technology (MS, PhD). *Degree requirements:* For doctorate, thesis/dissertation. *Entrance requirements:* For doctorate, GRE General Test, minimum GPA of 3.0. Additional exam requirements/recommendations for international students: Required—TOEFL. Electronic applications accepted. *Faculty research:* Gene expression, metabolic regulation, structural biology, enzyme mechanism, membrane transporters.

University of Florida, College of Medicine and Graduate School, Interdisciplinary Program in Biomedical Sciences, Concentration in Biochemistry and Molecular Biology, Gainesville, FL 32611. Offers PhD. *Degree requirements:* For doctorate, thesis/dissertation. *Entrance requirements:* For doctorate, GRE General Test, minimum GPA of 3.0. Additional exam requirements/recommendations for international students: Required—TOEFL. Electronic applications accepted. *Faculty research:* Gene expression, metabolic regulation, structural biology, enzyme mechanism, membrane transporters.

See Close-Up on page 161.

University of Florida, Interdisciplinary Concentration in Animal Molecular and Cellular Biology, Gainesville, FL 32611. Offers MS, PhD. Program offered by College of Agricultural and Life Sciences, College of Liberal Arts and Sciences, College of Medicine, and College of Veterinary Medicine.

University of Georgia, Graduate School, College of Arts and Sciences, Department of Biochemistry and Molecular Biology, Athens, GA 30602. Offers MS, PhD. *Faculty:* 34 full-time (3 women). *Students:* 63 full-time (25 women), 4 part-time (3 women); includes 7 minority (4 African Americans, 2 Asian Americans or Pacific Islanders, 1 Hispanic American), 21 international. 96 applicants, 16% accepted, 14 enrolled. In 2009, 3 master's, 2 doctorates awarded. *Degree requirements:* For master's, one foreign language, thesis; for doctorate, one foreign language, thesis/dissertation. *Entrance requirements:* For master's and doctorate, GRE General Test. Additional exam requirements/recommendations for international students: Required—TOEFL. *Application deadline:* For fall admission, 1/1 priority date for domestic and international students. Application fee: $50. Electronic applications accepted. *Expenses:* Tuition, state resident: full-time $6000; part-time $250 per credit hour. Tuition, nonresident: full-time $20,904; part-time $871 per credit hour. Required fees: $730 per semester. *Financial support:* Fellowships, research assistantships, teaching assistantships, scholarships/grants and unspecified assistantships available. Financial award application deadline: 1/1. *Unit head:* Dr. Stephen L. Hajduk, Head, 706-542-1676, Fax: 706-542-0182, E-mail: shajduk@bmb.uga.edu. *Application contact:* Dr. Walter K. Schmidt, Graduate Coordinator, 706-583-8241, Fax: 706-542-1738, E-mail: gradcoordinator@bmb.uga.edu.

University of Guelph, Graduate Program Services, College of Biological Science, Department of Molecular and Cellular Biology, Guelph, ON N1G 2W1, Canada. Offers biochemistry (M Sc, PhD); biophysics (M Sc, PhD); botany (M Sc, PhD); microbiology (M Sc, PhD); molecular biology and genetics (M Sc, PhD). *Degree requirements:* For master's, thesis, research proposal; for doctorate, comprehensive exam, thesis/dissertation, research proposal. *Entrance requirements:* For master's, minimum B-average during previous 2 years of coursework; for doctorate, minimum A-average. Additional exam requirements/recommendations for international students: Required—TOEFL (minimum score 550 paper-based; 213 computer-based), IELTS (minimum score 6.5). Electronic applications accepted. *Faculty research:* Physiology, structure, genetics, and ecology of microbes; virology and microbial technology.

University of Hawaii at Manoa, Graduate Division, College of Tropical Agriculture and Human Resources, Department of Molecular Biosciences and Bioengineering, Honolulu, HI 96822. Offers bioengineering (MS); molecular bioscience and bioengineering (MS); molecular biosciences and bioengineering (PhD). Part-time programs available. *Faculty:* 58 full-time (10 women), 15 part-time/adjunct (6 women). *Students:* 72 full-time (38 women), 8 part-time (3 women); includes 26 minority (1 African American, 1 American Indian/Alaska Native, 22 Asian Americans or Pacific Islanders, 2 Hispanic Americans), 34 international. Average age 28. 38 applicants, 68% accepted, 17 enrolled. In 2009, 3 master's, 2 doctorates awarded. *Degree requirements:* For master's, thesis optional; for doctorate, comprehensive exam, thesis/dissertation. *Entrance requirements:* For master's and doctorate, GRE General Test. Additional exam requirements/recommendations for international students: Required—TOEFL (minimum score 550 paper-based; 213 computer-based; 79 iBT), IELTS (minimum score 5). *Application deadline:* For fall admission, 5/30 for domestic students, 4/30 for international students; for spring admission, 10/30 for domestic students, 9/30 for international students. Application fee: $60. *Expenses:* Tuition, state resident: full-time $8900; part-time $372 per credit. Tuition, nonresident: full-time $21,400; part-time $898 per credit. Required fees: $207 per semester. *Financial support:* In 2009–10, 7 fellowships (averaging $2,622 per year), 49 research assistantships (averaging $18,205 per year), 9 teaching assistantships (averaging $15,699 per year) were awarded; Federal Work-Study, institutionally sponsored loans, and tuition waivers (full) also available. *Faculty research:* Mechanization, agricultural systems, waste management, water management, cell culture. Total annual research expenditures: $1.4 million. *Application contact:* Dulal Borthakur, Graduate Chair, 808-956-8384, Fax: 808-956-3542, E-mail: dulal@hawaii.edu.

University of Hawaii at Manoa, John A. Burns School of Medicine, Department of Cell and Molecular Biology, Honolulu, HI 96813. Offers MS, PhD. Part-time programs available. *Faculty:* 48 full-time (13 women), 14 part-time/adjunct (6 women). *Students:* 36 full-time (20 women), 2 part-time (both women); includes 14 minority (13 Asian Americans or Pacific Islanders, 1 Hispanic American), 6 international. Average age 28. 62 applicants, 34% accepted, 11 enrolled. In 2009, 1 master's, 4 doctorates awarded. Terminal master's awarded for partial completion of doctoral program. *Degree requirements:* For master's, thesis optional; for doctorate, comprehensive exam, thesis/dissertation. *Entrance requirements:* For master's and doctorate, GRE General Test, minimum GPA of 3.0. Additional exam requirements/recommendations for international students: Required—TOEFL (minimum score 500 paper-based; 173 computer-based; 61 iBT), IELTS (minimum score 5). *Application deadline:* For fall admission, 1/15 for domestic and international students. Applications are processed on a rolling basis. Application fee: $60. *Expenses:* Tuition, state resident: full-time $8900; part-time $372 per credit. Tuition, nonresident: full-time $21,400; part-time $898 per credit. Required fees: $207 per semester. *Financial support:* In 2009–10, 1 student received support, including 6 fellowships (averaging $1,280 per year), 29 research assistantships (averaging $20,526 per year); Federal Work-Study and institutionally sponsored loans also available. Financial award application deadline: 2/1. Total annual research expenditures: $2.7 million. *Application contact:* Marla Berry, Graduate Co-Chair, 808-692-1506, Fax: 808-692-1968, E-mail: mberry@hawaii.edu.

University of Idaho, College of Graduate Studies, College of Agricultural and Life Sciences, Department of Microbiology, Molecular Biology and Biochemistry, Moscow, ID 83844-2282. Offers microbiology, molecular biology and biochemistry (PhD). *Faculty:* 15 full-time, 1 part-time/adjunct. *Students:* 21 full-time, 4 part-time. In 2009, 6 master's, 4 doctorates awarded. *Degree requirements:* For master's, thesis; for doctorate, one foreign language, thesis/dissertation. *Entrance requirements:* For master's, minimum GPA of 2.8; for doctorate, minimum undergraduate GPA of 2.8, 3.0 graduate. *Application deadline:* For fall admission, 8/1 for domestic students; for spring admission, 12/15 for domestic students. Application fee: $55 ($60 for international students). *Expenses:* Tuition, state resident: full-time $6120. Tuition, nonresident: full-time $17,712. *Financial support:* Research assistantships, teaching assistantships available. Financial award application deadline: 2/15. *Faculty research:* Bioremediation, biodegradation and molecular ecology, developmental and cellular biology, cell cycle regulation, molecular machines, pathogenic mechanisms in infectious disease. *Unit head:* Dr. Bruce Miller, Interim Chair, 208-885-7966, E-mail: mmbb@uidaho.edu. *Application contact:* Dr. Bruce Miller, Interim Chair, 208-885-7966, E-mail: mmbb@uidaho.edu.

University of Illinois at Chicago, College of Medicine and Graduate College, Graduate Programs in Medicine, Department of Biochemistry and Molecular Genetics, Chicago, IL 60607-7128. Offers PhD, MD/PhD. Terminal master's awarded for partial completion of doctoral program. *Degree requirements:* For doctorate, thesis/dissertation. *Entrance requirements:* For doctorate, GRE General Test. Additional exam requirements/recommendations for international students: Required—TOEFL. Electronic applications accepted. *Faculty research:* Nature of cellular components, control of metabolic processes, regulation of gene expression.

The University of Iowa, Graduate College, Program in Molecular and Cellular Biology, Iowa City, IA 52242-1316. Offers PhD, MD/PhD. *Degree requirements:* For doctorate, comprehensive exam, thesis/dissertation. *Entrance requirements:* For doctorate, GRE General Test, minimum GPA of 3.0. Additional exam requirements/recommendations for international students: Required—TOEFL (minimum score 600 paper-based; 250 computer-based; 100 iBT). Electronic applications accepted. *Faculty research:* Regulation of gene expression, inherited human genetic diseases, signal transduction mechanisms, structural biology and function.

The University of Kansas, Graduate Studies, College of Liberal Arts and Sciences, Department of Molecular Biosciences, Lawrence, KS 66044. Offers biochemistry and biophysics (MA, PhD); microbiology (MA, PhD); molecular, cellular, and developmental biology (MA, PhD). *Students:* 58 full-time (30 women), 2 part-time (1 woman); includes 4 minority (1 American Indian/Alaska Native, 1 Asian American or Pacific Islander, 2 Hispanic Americans), 24 international. Average age 27. 49 applicants, 29% accepted, 4 enrolled. In 2009, 2 master's, 7 doctorates awarded. Terminal master's awarded for partial completion of doctoral program. *Degree requirements:* For master's, comprehensive exam, thesis; for doctorate, comprehensive exam, thesis/dissertation. *Entrance requirements:* For master's and doctorate, GRE General Test. Additional exam requirements/recommendations for international students: Required—TOEFL (minimum score 24 iBT). *Application deadline:* For fall admission, 12/15 for domestic and international students. Application fee: $45 ($55 for international students). Electronic applications accepted. *Expenses:* Tuition, state resident: full-time $6492; part-time $270.50 per credit hour. Tuition, nonresident: full-time $15,510; part-time $646.25 per credit hour. Required fees: $847; $70.56 per credit hour. Tuition and fees vary according to course load and program. *Financial support:* Fellowships with tuition reimbursements, research assistantships with tuition reimbursements, teaching assistantships with tuition reimbursements, health care benefits and unspecified assistantships available. Financial award application deadline: 3/1. *Faculty research:* Structure and function of proteins, genetics of organism development, molecular genetics, neurophysiology, molecular virology and pathogenics, developmental biology, cell biology. *Unit head:* Dr. Mark Richter, Chair, 785-864-4311, Fax: 785-864-5294, E-mail: richter@ku.edu. *Application contact:* John P. Connolly, Graduate Program Assistant, 785-864-4311, Fax: 785-864-5294, E-mail: jconnolly@ku.edu.

The University of Kansas, University of Kansas Medical Center, School of Medicine, Department of Biochemistry and Molecular Biology, Kansas City, KS 66160. Offers MS, PhD, MD/PhD. *Faculty:* 14 full-time, 5 part-time/adjunct. *Students:* 8 part-time (1 woman), 4 international. Average age 28. In 2009, 2 doctorates awarded. Terminal master's awarded for partial completion of doctoral program. *Degree requirements:* For master's, oral defense of thesis; for doctorate, comprehensive oral and written exam. *Entrance requirements:* Additional exam requirements/recommendations for international students: Required—TOEFL. Application fee: $0. Electronic applications accepted. *Expenses:* Tuition, state resident: full-time $6492; part-time $270.50 per credit hour. Tuition, nonresident: full-time $15,510; part-time $646.25 per credit hour. Required fees: $847; $70.56 per credit hour. Tuition and fees vary according to course load and program. *Financial support:* In 2009–10, research assistantships with partial tuition reimbursements (averaging $24,000 per year), teaching assistantships with full and partial tuition reimbursements (averaging $24,000 per year) were awarded; fellowships, traineeships, health care benefits, and unspecified assistantships also available. *Faculty research:* Determination of portion structure, underlying bases for interaction of proteins with their target, mapping allosteric circuiting within proteins, mechanism of action of transcription factors, renal signal transduction. Total annual research expenditures: $4.2 million. *Unit head:* Dr. Gerald M. Carlson, Chairman, 913-588-6574, Fax: 913-588-7007, E-mail: gcarlson@kumc.edu. *Application contact:* Dr. Liskin Swint-Kruse, Associate Professor, 913-588-0399, Fax: 913-588-9896, E-mail: lswint-kruse@kumc.edu.

University of Lethbridge, School of Graduate Studies, Lethbridge, AB T1K 3M4, Canada. Offers accounting (MScM); addictions counseling (M Sc); agricultural biotechnology (M Sc); agricultural studies (M Sc, MA); anthropology (MA); archaeology (MA); art (MA, MFA); biochemistry (M Sc); biological sciences (M Sc); biomolecular science (PhD); biosystems and biodiversity (PhD); Canadian studies (MA); chemistry (M Sc); computer science (M Sc); computer science and geographical information science (M Sc); counseling psychology (M Ed); dramatic arts (MA); earth, space, and physical science (PhD); economics (MA); educational leadership (M Ed); English (MA); environmental science (M Sc); evolution and behavior (PhD); exercise science (M Sc); finance (MScM); French (MA); French/German (MA); French/Spanish (MA); general education (M Ed); general management (MScM); geography (M Sc, MA); German (MA); health science (M Sc); history (MA); human resource management and labour relations (MScM); individualized multidisciplinary (M Sc, MA); information systems (MScM); international management (MScM); kinesiology (M Sc, MA); management (M Sc, MA); marketing (MScM); mathematics (M Sc); music (M Mus, MA); Native American studies (MA); neuroscience (M Sc, PhD); new media (MA); nursing (M Sc); philosophy (MA); physics (M Sc); policy and strategy (MScM); political science (MA); psychology (M Sc, MA); religious studies (MA); social sciences (MA); sociology (MA); theatre and dramatic arts (MFA); theoretical and computational science (PhD); urban and regional studies (MA); women's studies (MA). Part-time and evening/weekend programs available. *Degree requirements:* For doctorate, comprehensive exam, thesis/dissertation. *Entrance requirements:* For master's, GMAT (M Sc in management), bachelor's degree in related field, minimum GPA of 3.0 during previous 20 graded semester courses, 2 years teaching or related experience (M Ed); for doctorate, master's degree, minimum graduate GPA of 3.5. Additional exam requirements/recommendations for international students: Required—TOEFL. *Faculty research:* Movement and brain plasticity, gibberellin physiology, photosynthesis, carbon cycling, molecular properties of main-group ring components.

University of Louisville, School of Medicine, Department of Biochemistry and Molecular Biology, Louisville, KY 40292-0001. Offers MS, PhD, MD/PhD. *Faculty:* 33 full-time (7 women), 2 part-time/adjunct (1 woman). *Students:* 35 full-time (16 women), 5 part-time (4 women); includes 3 minority (2 African Americans, 1 Hispanic American), 10 international. Average age 29. 44 applicants, 23% accepted, 10 enrolled. In 2009, 12 master's, 5 doctorates awarded. Terminal master's awarded for partial completion of doctoral program. *Degree requirements:* For master's, thesis; for doctorate, comprehensive exam, thesis/dissertation, one first author publication. *Entrance requirements:* For master's, GRE General Test (minimum score 1000 verbal and quantitative), minimum GPA of 3.0; for doctorate, GRE General Test (minimum Verbal and Quantitative score of 1000), minimum GPA of 3.0. Additional exam requirements/recommendations for international students: Required—TOEFL. *Application deadline:* For fall admission, 4/15 for domestic and international students. Applications are processed on a rolling basis. Application fee: $50. Electronic applications accepted. *Financial support:* In 2009–10, 35 students received support, including 12 fellowships with full tuition reimbursements available (averaging $22,000 per year), 23 research assistantships with full tuition reimbursements available (averaging $22,000 per year); teaching assistantships with tuition reimbursements available, scholarships/grants, traineeships, tuition waivers (full and partial), and unspecified assistantships also available. Financial award application deadline: 4/15. *Faculty research:* Genetic regulatory mechanisms, microRNAs, vesicular trafficking in cancer metastasis and angiogenesis, ribosome biogenesis and disease, regulation of foreign compound metabolism/lipid and steroid metabolism. *Unit head:* Dr. Ronald G. Gregg, Chair, 502-852-

Molecular Biology

University of Louisville (continued)
5217, Fax: 502-852-6222, E-mail: rggreg02@gwise.louisville.edu. *Application contact:* Dr. William L. Dean, Information Contact, 502-852-5227, Fax: 502-852-6222, E-mail: wldean01@gwise.louisville.edu.

University of Maine, Graduate School, College of Natural Sciences, Forestry, and Agriculture, Department of Biochemistry, Molecular Biology, and Microbiology, Orono, ME 04469. Offers biochemistry (MPS, MS); biochemistry and molecular biology (PhD); microbiology (MPS, MS, PhD). *Faculty:* 9 full-time (4 women), 5 part-time/adjunct (3 women). *Students:* 19 full-time (11 women), 22 part-time (16 women); includes 3 minority (1 American Indian/Alaska Native, 1 Asian American or Pacific Islander, 1 Hispanic American), 6 international. Average age 30. 42 applicants, 33% accepted, 10 enrolled. In 2009, 5 master's, 2 doctorates awarded. *Degree requirements:* For doctorate, thesis/dissertation. *Entrance requirements:* For master's and doctorate, GRE General Test. Additional exam requirements/recommendations for international students: Required—TOEFL. *Application deadline:* For fall admission, 2/1 priority date for domestic students. Applications are processed on a rolling basis. Application fee: $65. Electronic applications accepted. *Financial support:* In 2009–10, 5 research assistantships with tuition reimbursements (averaging $20,893 per year), 12 teaching assistantships with tuition reimbursements (averaging $19,296 per year) were awarded; tuition waivers (full and partial) also available. Financial award application deadline: 3/1. *Unit head:* Dr. Robert Gundersen, Chair, 207-581-2802, Fax: 207-581-2801. *Application contact:* Scott G. Delcourt, Associate Dean of the Graduate School, 207-581-3291, Fax: 207-581-3232, E-mail: graduate@maine.edu.

University of Maryland, Baltimore, Graduate School, Graduate Program in Life Sciences, Program in Biochemistry and Molecular Biology, Baltimore, MD 21201. Offers biochemistry (MS, PhD); MD/PhD. *Students:* 13 full-time (9 women), 18 part-time (9 women); includes 9 minority (2 African Americans, 1 American Indian/Alaska Native, 3 Asian Americans or Pacific Islanders, 3 Hispanic Americans), 3 international. Average age 27. 64 applicants, 16% accepted, 2 enrolled. In 2009, 1 doctorate awarded. *Entrance requirements:* For doctorate, GRE General Test. Additional exam requirements/recommendations for international students: Required—TOEFL (minimum score 550 paper-based; 80 iBT); Recommended—IELTS (minimum score 7). *Application deadline:* For fall admission, 1/15 for domestic and international students. Application fee: $50. Electronic applications accepted. *Expenses:* Tuition, state resident: full-time $7290; part-time $405 per credit hour. Tuition, nonresident: full-time $12,780; part-time $710 per credit hour. Required fees: $774; $10 per credit hour. $297 per semester. Tuition and fees vary according to course load, degree level and program. *Financial support:* In 2009–10, research assistantships with full tuition reimbursements (averaging $25,000 per year); fellowships, health care benefits and unspecified assistantships also available. Financial award application deadline: 3/1. *Faculty research:* Membrane transport, hormonal regulation, protein structure, molecular virology. *Unit head:* Dr. David Weber, Professor/Director, 410-706-4354, E-mail: dweber@umaryland.edu. *Application contact:* Foyeke Daramola, Program Coordinator, 410-706-8417, Fax: 410-706-8297, E-mail: fdaramola@som.umaryland.edu.

University of Maryland, Baltimore, Graduate School, Graduate Program in Life Sciences, Program in Molecular Medicine, Baltimore, MD 21201. Offers cancer biology (PhD); cell and molecular physiology (PhD); human genetics and genomic medicine (PhD); molecular medicine (MS); molecular toxicology and pharmacology (PhD); MD/PhD. *Students:* 61 full-time (37 women), 9 part-time (5 women); includes 19 minority (7 African Americans, 9 Asian Americans or Pacific Islanders, 3 Hispanic Americans), 8 international. Average age 26. 324 applicants, 15% accepted, 20 enrolled. In 2009, 4 master's, 1 doctorate awarded. *Entrance requirements:* Additional exam requirements/recommendations for international students: Required—TOEFL (minimum score 600 paper-based; 100 iBT); Recommended—IELTS (minimum score 7). *Application deadline:* For fall admission, 1/15 for domestic and international students. Application fee: $50. Electronic applications accepted. *Expenses:* Tuition, state resident: full-time $7290; part-time $405 per credit hour. Tuition, nonresident: full-time $12,780; part-time $710 per credit hour. Required fees: $774; $10 per credit hour. $297 per semester. Tuition and fees vary according to course load, degree level and program. *Financial support:* In 2009–10, research assistantships with partial tuition reimbursements (averaging $25,000 per year); fellowships also available. Financial award application deadline: 3/1. *Unit head:* Dr. Dudley Strickland, Director, 410-706-8010, E-mail: dstrickland@som.umaryland.edu. *Application contact:* Sharron Graves, Program Coordinator, 410-706-6044, Fax: 410-706-6040, E-mail: sgraves@som.umaryland.edu.

University of Maryland, Baltimore County, Graduate School, College of Natural and Mathematical Sciences, Department of Biological Sciences, Program in Applied Molecular Biology, Baltimore, MD 21250. Offers MS. *Faculty:* 24 full-time (10 women), 1 part-time/adjunct (0 women). *Students:* 9 full-time (5 women), 2 part-time (both women); includes 4 minority (3 Asian Americans or Pacific Islanders, 1 Hispanic American). Average age 24. 238 applicants, 6% accepted, 11 enrolled. In 2009, 11 master's awarded. *Entrance requirements:* For master's, GRE General Test, GRE Subject Test (recommended), minimum GPA of 3.0. Additional exam requirements/recommendations for international students: Required—TOEFL. *Application deadline:* For fall admission, 4/1 priority date for domestic and international students. Applications are processed on a rolling basis. Application fee: $50. Electronic applications accepted. *Financial support:* In 2009–10, 4 students received support, including 4 teaching assistantships with full and partial tuition reimbursements available (averaging $12,000 per year); tuition waivers (partial) also available. *Faculty research:* Structure-function of RNA, genetics and molecular biology, biological chemistry. *Unit head:* Dr. Richard E. Wolf, Director, Graduate Program, 410-455-3669, Fax: 410-455-3875, E-mail: biograd@umbc.edu. *Application contact:* Dr. Richard E. Wolf, Director, Graduate Program, 410-455-3669, Fax: 410-455-3875, E-mail: biograd@umbc.edu.

University of Maryland, Baltimore County, Graduate School, College of Natural and Mathematical Sciences, Department of Biological Sciences, Program in Molecular and Cell Biology, Baltimore, MD 21250. Offers PhD. *Faculty:* 24 full-time (10 women), 1 part-time/adjunct (0 women). *Students:* 16 full-time (11 women); includes 9 minority (2 African Americans, 7 Asian Americans or Pacific Islanders). Average age 27. 31 applicants, 35% accepted, 0 enrolled. In 2009, 1 doctorate awarded. *Degree requirements:* For doctorate, thesis/dissertation. *Entrance requirements:* For doctorate, GRE General Test, GRE Subject Test, minimum GPA of 3.0. Additional exam requirements/recommendations for international students: Required—TOEFL. *Application deadline:* For fall admission, 1/15 for domestic students, 12/15 for international students. Applications are processed on a rolling basis. Application fee: $50. Electronic applications accepted. *Financial support:* In 2009–10, fellowships with full tuition reimbursements (averaging $23,000 per year), research assistantships with full tuition reimbursements (averaging $22,300 per year), teaching assistantships with full tuition reimbursements (averaging $21,300 per year) were awarded. *Unit head:* Dr. Jeff Leips, Director, 410-455-3669, Fax: 410-455-3875, E-mail: biograd@umbc.edu. *Application contact:* Dr. Phyllis Robinson, Director, 410-455-3669, Fax: 410-455-3875, E-mail: biograd@umbc.edu.

University of Maryland, College Park, Academic Affairs, College of Chemical and Life Sciences, Department of Cell Biology and Molecular Genetics, Program in Molecular and Cellular Biology, College Park, MD 20742. Offers PhD. Part-time and evening/weekend programs available. *Students:* 56 full-time (37 women), 2 part-time (1 woman); includes 8 minority (2 African Americans, 4 Asian Americans or Pacific Islanders, 2 Hispanic Americans), 31 international. 97 applicants, 15% accepted, 6 enrolled. In 2009, 7 doctorates awarded. *Degree requirements:* For doctorate, thesis/dissertation, exam, public service. *Entrance requirements:* For doctorate, GRE General Test, 3 letters of reference. Additional exam requirements/recommendations for international students: Required—TOEFL. *Application deadline:* For fall admission, 1/6 for domestic and international students. Applications are processed on a rolling basis. Application fee: $60. Electronic applications accepted. *Expenses:* Tuition, area resident: Part-time $471 per credit hour. Tuition, state resident: part-time $471 per credit hour. Tuition, nonresident: part-time $1016 per credit hour. Required fees: $337.04 per term. *Financial*

support: In 2009–10, 2 fellowships with partial tuition reimbursements (averaging $10,800 per year), 8 research assistantships (averaging $18,916 per year), 23 teaching assistantships (averaging $19,246 per year) were awarded. Financial award applicants required to submit FAFSA. *Faculty research:* Monoclonal antibody production, oligonucleotide synthesis, macronolular processing, signal transduction, developmental biology. *Unit head:* Norma Andrews, 301-405-1605, E-mail: andrewsn@umd.edu. *Application contact:* Dean of Graduate School, 301-405-0358, Fax: 301-314-9305.

University of Massachusetts Boston, Office of Graduate Studies, College of Science and Mathematics, Track in Molecular, Cellular and Organismal Biology, Boston, MA 02125-3393. Offers PhD.

University of Medicine and Dentistry of New Jersey, Graduate School of Biomedical Sciences, Graduate Programs in Biomedical Sciences–Newark, Department of Biochemistry and Molecular Biology, Newark, NJ 07107. Offers MS, PhD. *Students:* 17 full-time (11 women); includes 1 Hispanic American, 10 international. *Degree requirements:* For master's, thesis; for doctorate, thesis/dissertation, qualifying exam. *Entrance requirements:* For master's and doctorate, GRE General Test. Additional exam requirements/recommendations for international students: Required—TOEFL. *Application deadline:* For fall admission, 2/1 for domestic students. Applications are processed on a rolling basis. Application fee: $40. Electronic applications accepted. *Financial support:* Fellowships, research assistantships, Federal Work-Study, institutionally sponsored loans, and tuition waivers (full and partial) available. Financial award application deadline: 5/1. *Unit head:* Dr. Carol Lutz, Program Director, 973-972-0899, Fax: 973-972-5594, E-mail: lutzls@umdnj.edu. *Application contact:* Dr. Carol Lutz, Program Director, 973-972-0899, Fax: 973-972-5594, E-mail: lutzls@umdnj.edu.

University of Medicine and Dentistry of New Jersey, Graduate School of Biomedical Sciences, Graduate Programs in Biomedical Sciences–Piscataway, Program in Biochemistry and Molecular Biology, Piscataway, NJ 08854-5635. Offers MS, PhD, MD/PhD. Terminal master's awarded for partial completion of doctoral program. *Degree requirements:* For master's, thesis, qualifying exam; for doctorate, thesis/dissertation, qualifying exam. *Entrance requirements:* For master's and doctorate, GRE General Test. Additional exam requirements/recommendations for international students: Required—TOEFL. *Application deadline:* For fall admission, 1/5 for domestic students. Applications are processed on a rolling basis. Application fee: $40. Electronic applications accepted. *Financial support:* Fellowships, research assistantships, teaching assistantships available. Financial award application deadline: 5/1. *Faculty research:* Signal transduction, regulation of RNA, polymerase II transcribed genes, developmental gene expression. *Unit head:* Dr. Kiran Madura, Director, 732-235-5602, Fax: 732-235-5417, E-mail: maduraki@umdnj.edu. *Application contact:* University Registrar, 973-972-5338.

University of Medicine and Dentistry of New Jersey, Graduate School of Biomedical Sciences, Graduate Programs in Biomedical Sciences–Stratford, Program in Cell and Molecular Biology, Stratford, NJ 08084-5634. Offers MS, PhD, DO/PhD. *Degree requirements:* For master's, thesis; for doctorate, thesis/dissertation, qualifying exam. *Entrance requirements:* For master's and doctorate, GRE General Test. Additional exam requirements/recommendations for international students: Required—TOEFL. *Application deadline:* For fall admission, 2/1 for domestic students; for spring admission, 10/1 for domestic students. Applications are processed on a rolling basis. Application fee: $40. Electronic applications accepted. *Financial support:* Application deadline: 5/1. *Unit head:* Dr. Sal Caradonna, Program Director, 856-566-6056, Fax: 856-566-6232, E-mail: worraddi@umdnj.edu. *Application contact:* University Registrar, 973-972-5338.

University of Medicine and Dentistry of New Jersey, Graduate School of Biomedical Sciences, Programs in the Molecular Biosciences, Piscataway, NJ 08854-5696. Offers PhD. *Entrance requirements:* Additional exam requirements/recommendations for international students: Required—TOEFL. Electronic applications accepted.

University of Miami, Graduate School, Miller School of Medicine, Graduate Programs in Medicine, Department of Biochemistry and Molecular Biology, Coral Gables, FL 33124. Offers PhD, MD/PhD. *Faculty:* 27 full-time (5 women). *Students:* 34 full-time (16 women); includes 1 Asian American or Pacific Islander, 5 Hispanic Americans, 19 international. Average age 26. *Degree requirements:* For doctorate, comprehensive exam, thesis/dissertation, proposition exams. *Financial support:* In 2009–10, 34 fellowships with full tuition reimbursements (averaging $25,500 per year) were awarded; research assistantships, scholarships/grants and tuition waivers (full) also available. *Faculty research:* Macromolecule metabolism, molecular genetics, protein folding and 3-D structure, regulation of gene expression and enzyme function, signal transduction and developmental biology. Total annual research expenditures: $3 million. *Unit head:* Dr. Louis J. Elsas, Department Chair, 305-243-1456, Fax: 305-243-3955, E-mail: lelsas@med.miami.edu. *Application contact:* Dr. Zafar Nawaz, Director, 305-243-1456, Fax: 305-243-3955, E-mail: znawaz@med.miami.edu.

University of Miami, Graduate School, Miller School of Medicine, Graduate Programs in Medicine, Department of Cell Biology and Anatomy, Coral Gables, FL 33124. Offers molecular cell and developmental biology (PhD); MD/PhD. *Degree requirements:* For doctorate, thesis/dissertation. *Entrance requirements:* For doctorate, GRE General Test, GRE Subject Test. Additional exam requirements/recommendations for international students: Required—TOEFL. Electronic applications accepted.

University of Michigan, Horace H. Rackham School of Graduate Studies, College of Literature, Science, and the Arts, Department of Molecular, Cellular, and Developmental Biology, Ann Arbor, MI 48109. Offers MS, PhD. Part-time programs available. *Faculty:* 32 full-time (8 women). *Students:* 74 full-time (39 women), 3 part-time (1 woman); includes 4 minority (2 African Americans, 2 Hispanic Americans), 41 international. Average age 29. 113 applicants, 21% accepted, 14 enrolled. In 2009, 6 master's, 7 doctorates awarded. Terminal master's awarded for partial completion of doctoral program. *Degree requirements:* For doctorate, thesis/dissertation, preliminary exam, oral defense. *Entrance requirements:* For master's and doctorate, GRE General Test. Additional exam requirements/recommendations for international students: Required—TOEFL (minimum score 560 paper-based; 220 computer-based; 83 iBT). *Application deadline:* For fall admission, 1/5 for domestic and international students; for winter admission, 11/1 for domestic and international students. Applications are processed on a rolling basis. Application fee: $60 ($75 for international students). Electronic applications accepted. *Expenses:* Tuition, state resident: full-time $17,286; part-time $1099 per credit hour. Tuition, nonresident: full-time $34,944; part-time $2080 per credit hour. Required fees: $95 per semester. Tuition and fees vary according to course load, degree level and program. *Financial support:* In 2009–10, 64 students received support, including 16 fellowships with full tuition reimbursements available (averaging $26,500 per year), 28 research assistantships with full tuition reimbursements available (averaging $26,500 per year), 20 teaching assistantships with full tuition reimbursements available (averaging $26,500 per year); health care benefits also available. *Faculty research:* Cell biology, microbiology, neurobiology and physiology, developmental biology and plant molecular biology. Total annual research expenditures: $5.7 million. *Unit head:* Patrick J. Flannery, Administrative Manager, 734-936-2991, Fax: 734-615-6337, E-mail: pjflan@umich.edu. *Application contact:* Mary Carr, Graduate Coordinator, 734-615-1635, Fax: 734-764-0884, E-mail: carrmm@umich.edu.

University of Michigan, Horace H. Rackham School of Graduate Studies, Program in Biomedical Sciences (PIBS), Interdisciplinary Program in Cellular and Molecular Biology, Ann Arbor, MI 48109. Offers PhD. *Degree requirements:* For doctorate, comprehensive exam, thesis/dissertation, oral defense of dissertation, preliminary exam. *Entrance requirements:* For doctorate, GRE General Test, GRE Subject Test. *Expenses:* Tuition, state resident: full-time $17,286; part-time $1099 per credit hour. Tuition, nonresident: full-time $34,944; part-time $2080 per credit hour. Required fees: $95 per semester. Tuition and fees vary according to course load, degree level and program. *Faculty research:* Genetics, genomics, gene regulation, models of disease, microbes.

University of Minnesota, Duluth, Medical School, Department of Biochemistry, Molecular Biology and Biophysics, Duluth, MN 55812-2496. Offers biochemistry, molecular biology and biophysics (MS); biology and biophysics (PhD); social, administrative, and clinical pharmacy (MS, PhD); toxicology (MS, PhD). *Faculty:* 10 full-time (3 women). *Students:* 16 full-time (5 women); includes 3 minority (all Asian Americans or Pacific Islanders). Average age 29. 7 applicants, 29% accepted, 2 enrolled. In 2009, 1 master's, 1 doctorate awarded. Terminal master's awarded for partial completion of doctoral program. *Degree requirements:* For master's, comprehensive exam, thesis; for doctorate, comprehensive exam, thesis/dissertation. *Entrance requirements:* For master's and doctorate, GRE General Test. Additional exam requirements/recommendations for international students: Required—TOEFL. *Application deadline:* For winter admission, 1/3 for domestic students, 1/2 for international students; for spring admission, 3/15 priority date for domestic and international students. Application fee: $75 ($95 for international students). Electronic applications accepted. *Financial support:* In 2009–10, 8 students received support, including research assistantships with full tuition reimbursements available (averaging $27,300 per year), teaching assistantships with full tuition reimbursements available (averaging $27,300 per year); career-related internships or fieldwork, scholarships/grants, health care benefits, and unspecified assistantships also available. Financial award application deadline: 9/1. *Faculty research:* Intestinal cancer biology; hepatotoxins and mitochondriopathies; toxicology; cell cycle regulation in stem cells; neurobiology of brain development, trace metal function and blood-brain barrier; hibernation biology. Total annual research expenditures: $1.5 million. *Unit head:* Dr. Lester R. Drewes, Professor/Head, 218-726-7925, Fax: 218-726-8014, E-mail: ldrewes@d.umn.edu. *Application contact:* Cheryl Beeman, Administrative Assistant, 218-726-6354, Fax: 218-726-8014, E-mail: ahcd@d.umn.edu.

University of Minnesota, Twin Cities Campus, Graduate School, College of Biological Sciences, Biochemistry, Molecular Biology and Biophysics Graduate Program, Minneapolis, MN 55455-0213. Offers PhD. *Faculty:* 69 full-time (14 women), 1 part-time/adjunct (0 women). *Students:* 60 full-time (26 women); includes 20 minority (2 African Americans, 1 American Indian/Alaska Native, 15 Asian Americans or Pacific Islanders, 2 Hispanic Americans). Average age 26. 199 applicants, 20% accepted, 11 enrolled. In 2009, 16 doctorates awarded. *Degree requirements:* For doctorate, thesis/dissertation. *Entrance requirements:* For doctorate, GRE, 3 letters of recommendation, more than 1 semester of laboratory experience. Additional exam requirements/recommendations for international students: Required—TOEFL (minimum score 625 paper-based; 263 computer-based; 108 iBT with writing subsection 25 and reading subsection 25) or IELTS (minimum score 7). *Application deadline:* For fall admission, 12/15 for domestic and international students. Application fee: $75 ($95 for international students). Electronic applications accepted. *Financial support:* Institutionally sponsored loans, scholarships/grants, traineeships, health care benefits, tuition waivers, unspecified assistantships, and stipends available. *Faculty research:* Microbial biochemistry, biotechnology, molecular biology, regulatory biochemistry, structural biology and biophysics, physical biochemistry, enzymology, physiological chemistry. Total annual research expenditures: $10.3 million. *Unit head:* Prof. David A. Bernlohr, Head, 612-624-2712. *Application contact:* Dr. Anja Katrin Bielinsky, Director of Graduate Studies, 612-624-2469, Fax: 612-625-2163, E-mail: bieli003@umn.edu.

University of Minnesota, Twin Cities Campus, Graduate School, Program in Molecular, Cellular, Developmental Biology and Genetics, Minneapolis, MN 55455-0213. Offers genetic counseling (MS); molecular, cellular, developmental biology and genetics (PhD). *Faculty:* 89 full-time (31 women), 19 part-time/adjunct (17 women). *Students:* 86 full-time (49 women); includes 6 minority (1 American Indian/Alaska Native, 4 Asian Americans or Pacific Islanders, 1 Hispanic American), 23 international. Average age 24. 179 applicants, 11% accepted, 19 enrolled. In 2009, 12 master's, 6 doctorates awarded. Terminal master's awarded for partial completion of doctoral program. *Degree requirements:* For master's, thesis optional; for doctorate, thesis/dissertation. *Entrance requirements:* For master's and doctorate, GRE General Test. Additional exam requirements/recommendations for international students: Required—TOEFL (minimum score 625 paper-based; 263 computer-based; 80 iBT). *Application deadline:* For fall admission, 12/15 priority date for domestic and international students. Applications are processed on a rolling basis. Application fee: $55 ($75 for international students). Electronic applications accepted. *Financial support:* In 2009–10, 10 fellowships with full tuition reimbursements (averaging $23,000 per year), 79 research assistantships with full tuition reimbursements (averaging $24,500 per year), 11 teaching assistantships with partial tuition reimbursements (averaging $9,236 per year) were awarded; scholarships/grants, traineeships, and health care benefits also available. Financial award application deadline: 12/15. *Faculty research:* Membrane receptors and membrane transport, cell interactions, cytoskeleton and cell mobility, regulation of gene expression, plant cell and molecular biology. Total annual research expenditures: $9.1 million. *Unit head:* Kathleen Conklin, Director of Graduate Studies, 612-626-0445, Fax: 612-626-6140, E-mail: conkl001@umn.edu. *Application contact:* Sue Knoblauch, Student Support Coordinator, 612-624-7470, Fax: 612-626-6140, E-mail: mcdbg@umn.edu.

University of Missouri–Kansas City, School of Biological Sciences, Program in Molecular Biology and Biochemistry, Kansas City, MO 64110-2499. Offers PhD. Offered through the School of Graduate Studies. *Degree requirements:* For doctorate, comprehensive exam, thesis/dissertation. *Entrance requirements:* For doctorate, GRE General Test, bachelor's degree in chemistry, biology, or a related discipline; minimum GPA of 3.0. Additional exam requirements/recommendations for international students: Required—TOEFL (minimum score 550 paper-based; 213 computer-based; 80 iBT). *Application deadline:* For fall admission, 2/15 priority date for domestic and international students. Application fee: $45 ($50 for international students). *Expenses:* Tuition, state resident: full-time $5378; part-time $299 per credit hour. Tuition, nonresident: full-time $13,881; part-time $771 per credit hour. Required fees: $641; $71 per credit hour. Tuition and fees vary according to course load and program. *Financial support:* Research assistantships with full tuition reimbursements, teaching assistantships with full and partial tuition reimbursements, scholarships/grants, tuition waivers (full and partial), and unspecified assistantships available. Financial award application deadline: 3/1; financial award applicants required to submit FAFSA. *Unit head:* Dr. Henry Miziorko, Head, 816-235-2235, E-mail: miziorkoh@umkc.edu. *Application contact:* Laura Batenic, Information Contact, 816-235-2352, Fax: 816-235-5158, E-mail: bateniel@umkc.edu.

See Close-Up on page 249.

University of Missouri–St. Louis, College of Arts and Sciences, Department of Biology, St. Louis, MO 63121. Offers biology (MS, PhD), including animal behavior (MS), biochemistry, biochemistry and biotechnology (MS), biotechnology (MS), conservation biology (MS), development (MS), ecology (MS), environmental studies (PhD), evolution (MS), genetics (MS), molecular biology and biochemistry (PhD), molecular/cellular biology (MS), physiology (MS), plant systematics, population biology (MS), tropical biology (MS); biotechnology (Certificate); tropical biology and conservation (Certificate). Part-time programs available. *Faculty:* 43 full-time (13 women), 2 part-time/adjunct (1 woman). *Students:* 54 full-time (27 women), 79 part-time (43 women); includes 15 minority (6 African Americans, 7 Asian Americans or Pacific Islanders, 2 Hispanic Americans), 47 international. Average age 29. 193 applicants, 44% accepted, 44 enrolled. In 2009, 30 master's, 7 doctorates, 9 other advanced degrees awarded. *Degree requirements:* For master's, thesis or alternative; for doctorate, thesis/dissertation, 1 semester of teaching experience. *Entrance requirements:* For master's, 3 letters of recommendation; for doctorate, GRE General Test, 3 letters of recommendation. Additional exam requirements/recommendations for international students: Required—TOEFL. *Application deadline:* For fall admission, 12/1 priority date for domestic and international students; for spring admission, 10/15 priority date for domestic and international students. Applications are processed on a rolling basis. Application fee: $35 ($40 for international students). Electronic applications accepted. *Expenses:* Tuition, state resident: full-time $5377; part-time $297.70 per credit hour. Tuition, nonresident: full-time $13,882; part-time $771.20 per credit hour. Required fees: $220; $12.20 per credit hour. One-time fee: $12. Tuition and fees vary according to course level, campus/location and program. *Financial support:* In 2009–10, 22 research assistantships with full and partial tuition reimbursements (averaging $16,300 per year), 14 teaching assistantships with full and partial tuition reimbursements (averaging $16,727 per year) were awarded; fellowships with full tuition reimbursements, career-related internships or fieldwork and Federal Work-Study also available. Support available to part-time students. Financial award application deadline: 2/1. *Faculty research:* Molecular biology, microbial genetics, animal behavior, tropical ecology, plant systematics. *Unit head:* Dr. Elizabeth Kellogg, Director of Graduate Studies, 314-516-6200, Fax: 314-516-6233, E-mail: tkellogg@umsl.edu. *Application contact:* 314-516-5458, Fax: 314-516-6996, E-mail: gradadm@umsl.edu.

University of Nebraska Medical Center, Graduate Studies, Department of Biochemistry and Molecular Biology, Omaha, NE 68198. Offers MS, PhD. Terminal master's awarded for partial completion of doctoral program. *Degree requirements:* For master's, comprehensive exam, thesis; for doctorate, comprehensive exam, thesis/dissertation. *Entrance requirements:* For master's and doctorate, GRE General Test. Additional exam requirements/recommendations for international students: Required—TOEFL (minimum score 550 paper-based; 213 computer-based). Electronic applications accepted. *Faculty research:* Recombinant DNA, cancer biology, diabetes and drug metabolism, biochemical endocrinology.

University of Nevada, Reno, Graduate School, Interdisciplinary Program in Cell and Molecular Biology, Reno, NV 89557. Offers MS, PhD. Terminal master's awarded for partial completion of doctoral program. *Degree requirements:* For master's, thesis; for doctorate, thesis/dissertation. *Entrance requirements:* For master's, GRE Subject Test (recommended), minimum GPA of 2.75; for doctorate, GRE Subject Test (recommended), minimum GPA of 3.0. Additional exam requirements/recommendations for international students: Required—TOEFL (minimum score 500 paper-based; 173 computer-based; 61 iBT), IELTS (minimum score 6). Electronic applications accepted. *Faculty research:* Cellular biology, biophysics, cancer, microbiology, insect biochemistry.

University of New Haven, Graduate School, College of Arts and Sciences, Program in Cellular and Molecular Biology, West Haven, CT 06516-1916. Offers cellular and molecular biology (MS). *Faculty:* 6 full-time (3 women), 8 part-time/adjunct (2 women). *Students:* 42 full-time (24 women), 16 part-time (7 women); includes 6 minority (3 African Americans, 1 Asian American or Pacific Islander, 2 Hispanic Americans), 35 international. Average age 25. 109 applicants, 68% accepted, 19 enrolled. In 2009, 16 master's awarded. *Degree requirements:* For master's, thesis optional. *Entrance requirements:* Additional exam requirements/recommendations for international students: Required—TOEFL (minimum score 520 paper-based; 190 computer-based; 70 iBT), IELTS (minimum score 5.5). *Application deadline:* For fall admission, 5/31 for international students; for winter admission, 10/15 for international students; for spring admission, 1/15 for international students. Applications are processed on a rolling basis. Application fee: $50. Electronic applications accepted. *Expenses:* Tuition: Part-time $700 per credit. Required fees: $45 per term. One-time fee: $390 part-time. *Financial support:* Career-related internships or fieldwork and Federal Work-Study available. Financial award application deadline: 5/1; financial award applicants required to submit FAFSA. *Unit head:* Dr. Eva Sapi, Coordinator, 203-479-4552. *Application contact:* Eloise Gormley, Director of Graduate Admissions, 203-932-7449, Fax: 203-932-7137, E-mail: gradinfo@newhaven.edu.

University of New Mexico, School of Medicine, Biomedical Sciences Graduate Program, Albuquerque, NM 87131-5196. Offers biochemistry and molecular biology (MS, PhD); cell biology and physiology (MS, PhD); molecular genetics and microbiology (MS, PhD); neuroscience (MS, PhD); pathology (MS, PhD); toxicology (MS, PhD). Part-time programs available. Terminal master's awarded for partial completion of doctoral program. *Degree requirements:* For master's, thesis; for doctorate, comprehensive exam, thesis/dissertation. *Entrance requirements:* For master's and doctorate, GRE General Test, minimum undergraduate GPA of 3.0. Additional exam requirements/recommendations for international students: Required—TOEFL. Electronic applications accepted. *Expenses:* Tuition, state resident: full-time $2099; part-time $233.20 per credit hour. Tuition, nonresident: full-time $6650. Required fees: $25 per semester. Tuition and fees vary according to course load, program and reciprocity agreements. *Faculty research:* Signal transduction, infectious disease, biology of cancer, structural biology, neuroscience.

The University of North Carolina at Chapel Hill, Graduate School, College of Arts and Sciences, Department of Biology, Chapel Hill, NC 27599. Offers botany (MA, MS, PhD); cell biology, development, and physiology (MA, MS, PhD); cell motility and cytoskeleton (PhD); ecology and behavior (MA, MS, PhD); genetics and molecular biology (MA, MS, PhD); morphology, systematics, and evolution (MA, MS, PhD). Terminal master's awarded for partial completion of doctoral program. *Degree requirements:* For master's, comprehensive exam, thesis (for some programs); for doctorate, comprehensive exam, thesis/dissertation. *Entrance requirements:* For master's, GRE General Test, GRE Subject Test, 2 semesters of calculus or statistics; 2 semesters of physics, organic chemistry; 3 semesters of biology; for doctorate, GRE General Test, GRE Subject Test, 2 semesters calculus or statistics, 2 semesters physics, organic chemistry, 3 semesters of biology. Additional exam requirements/recommendations for international students: Required—TOEFL (minimum score 550 paper-based; 213 computer-based). Electronic applications accepted. *Faculty research:* Gene expression, biomechanics, yeast genetics, plant ecology, plant molecular biology.

The University of North Carolina at Chapel Hill, School of Medicine and Graduate School, Graduate Programs in Medicine, Curriculum in Genetics and Molecular Biology, Chapel Hill, NC 27599. Offers MS, PhD. *Degree requirements:* For doctorate, comprehensive exam, thesis/dissertation. *Entrance requirements:* For doctorate, minimum GPA of 3.0. Additional exam requirements/recommendations for international students: Required—TOEFL. Electronic applications accepted.

University of North Texas, Robert B. Toulouse School of Graduate Studies, College of Arts and Sciences, Department of Biological Sciences, Program in Molecular Biology, Denton, TX 76203. Offers MA, MS, PhD. *Students:* Average age 31. *Degree requirements:* For master's, variable foreign language requirement, comprehensive exam, thesis (for some programs), oral defense of thesis; for doctorate, one foreign language, comprehensive exam, thesis/dissertation, oral defense of dissertation. *Entrance requirements:* For master's and doctorate, GRE General Test, admission to Toulouse School of Graduate Studies, letters of recommendation. Additional exam requirements/recommendations for international students: Recommended—TOEFL (minimum score 550 paper-based; 213 computer-based). *Application deadline:* Applications are processed on a rolling basis. Application fee: $50 ($75 for international students). *Expenses:* Tuition, state resident: full-time $4298; part-time $239 per contact hour. Tuition, nonresident: full-time $9878; part-time $549 per contact hour. Required fees: $265 per contact hour. *Financial support:* Applicants required to submit FAFSA. *Faculty research:* Pyrimidine metabolism, enzymology mammalian/plant gene structure, organization and expression. Total annual research expenditures: $2.7 million. *Application contact:* Graduate Advisor, 940-565-2011, Fax: 940-565-3821.

University of North Texas Health Science Center at Fort Worth, Graduate School of Biomedical Sciences, Fort Worth, TX 76107-2699. Offers anatomy and cell biology (MS, PhD); biochemistry and molecular biology (MS, PhD); biomedical sciences (MS, PhD); biotechnology (MS); forensic genetics (MS); integrative physiology (MS, PhD); medical science (MS); microbiology and immunology (MS, PhD); pharmacology (MS, PhD); science education (MS); DO/MS; DO/PhD. Terminal master's awarded for partial completion of doctoral program. *Degree requirements:* For master's, thesis; for doctorate, thesis/dissertation. *Entrance requirements:* For master's and doctorate, GRE General Test. Additional exam requirements/recommendations for international students: Required—TOEFL. *Expenses:* Contact institution. *Faculty research:* Alzheimer's disease, aging, eye diseases, cancer, cardiovascular disease.

University of Notre Dame, Graduate School, College of Science, Department of Biological Sciences, Notre Dame, IN 46556. Offers aquatic ecology, evolution and environmental biology (MS, PhD); cellular and molecular biology (MS, PhD); genetics (MS, PhD); physiology (MS, PhD); vector biology and parasitology (MS, PhD). Terminal master's awarded for partial completion of doctoral program. *Degree requirements:* For master's, comprehensive exam, thesis; for doctorate, comprehensive exam, thesis/dissertation, candidacy exam. *Entrance requirements:* For master's and doctorate, GRE General Test. Additional exam requirements/

Molecular Biology

University of Notre Dame (continued)
recommendations for international students: Required—TOEFL (minimum score 600 paper-based; 250 computer-based; 80 iBT). Electronic applications accepted. *Faculty research:* Tropical disease, molecular genetics, neurobiology, evolutionary biology, aquatic biology.

University of Oklahoma Health Sciences Center, College of Medicine and Graduate College, Graduate Programs in Medicine, Department of Biochemistry and Molecular Biology, Oklahoma City, OK 73190. Offers biochemistry (MS, PhD); molecular biology (MS, PhD). Part-time programs available. *Faculty:* 10 full-time (4 women). *Students:* 4 full-time (3 women), 23 part-time (10 women); includes 1 minority (African American), 15 international. Average age 28. 26 applicants, 8% accepted, 2 enrolled. In 2009, 5 doctorates awarded. Terminal master's awarded for partial completion of doctoral program. *Degree requirements:* For master's, thesis; for doctorate, thesis/dissertation. *Entrance requirements:* For master's, GRE General Test, 2 letters of recommendation; for doctorate, GRE General Test, 3 letters of recommendation. Additional exam requirements/recommendations for international students: Required—TOEFL. *Application deadline:* For fall admission, 1/31 for domestic students. Application fee: $50. *Expenses:* Tuition, state resident: full-time $3120; part-time $156 per credit hour. Tuition, nonresident: full-time $11,314; part-time $409.70 per credit hour. Required fees: $1471; $51.20 per credit hour. $223.25 per term. *Financial support:* In 2009–10, 20 research assistantships (averaging $18,000 per year) were awarded; institutionally sponsored loans also available. Support available to part-time students. Financial award application deadline: 3/31; financial award applicants required to submit FAFSA. *Faculty research:* Gene expression, regulation of transcription, enzyme evolution, melanogenesis, signal transduction. *Unit head:* Dr. Paul H. Weigel, Chair, 405-271-2227, E-mail: paul-weigel@ouhsc.edu. *Application contact:* Dr. Gillian Air, Graduate Liaison, 405-271-2227, Fax: 405-271-3092, E-mail: gillian-air@ouhsc.edu.

University of Oregon, Graduate School, College of Arts and Sciences, Department of Biology, Eugene, OR 97403. Offers ecology and evolution (MA, MS, PhD); marine biology (MA, MS, PhD); molecular, cellular and genetic biology (PhD); neuroscience and development (PhD). Terminal master's awarded for partial completion of doctoral program. *Degree requirements:* For master's, thesis (for some programs); for doctorate, thesis/dissertation. *Entrance requirements:* For master's and doctorate, GRE General Test, minimum GPA of 3.2. Additional exam requirements/recommendations for international students: Required—TOEFL. *Faculty research:* Developmental neurobiology; evolution, population biology, and quantitative genetics; regulation of gene expression; biochemistry of marine organisms.

University of Ottawa, Faculty of Graduate and Postdoctoral Studies, Faculty of Medicine, Department of Cellular and Molecular Medicine, Ottawa, ON K1H 8M5, Canada. Offers M Sc, PhD. *Degree requirements:* For master's, thesis, seminar; for doctorate, comprehensive exam, thesis/dissertation, seminar. *Entrance requirements:* For master's, honors degree or equivalent, minimum B average; for doctorate, master's degree, minimum B+ average. Electronic applications accepted. *Faculty research:* Physiology, pharmacology, growth and development.

University of Pennsylvania, School of Medicine, Biomedical Graduate Studies, Graduate Group in Cell and Molecular Biology, Philadelphia, PA 19104. Offers cancer biology (PhD); cell biology and physiology (PhD); developmental stem cell regenerative biology (PhD); gene therapy and vaccines (PhD); genetics and gene regulation (PhD); microbiology, virology, and parasitology (PhD); MD/PhD; VMD/PhD. *Faculty:* 296. *Students:* 307 full-time (167 women); includes 78 minority (13 African Americans, 1 American Indian/Alaska Native, 45 Asian Americans or Pacific Islanders, 19 Hispanic Americans), 33 international. 576 applicants, 19% accepted, 40 enrolled. In 2009, 32 doctorates awarded. *Degree requirements:* For doctorate, thesis/dissertation. *Entrance requirements:* For doctorate, GRE General Test. Additional exam requirements/recommendations for international students: Required—TOEFL. *Application deadline:* For fall admission, 12/8 priority date for domestic and international students. Applications are processed on a rolling basis. Application fee: $70. Electronic applications accepted. *Expenses:* Tuition: Full-time $25,660; part-time $4758 per course. Required fees: $2152; $270 per course. Tuition and fees vary according to course load, degree level and program. *Financial support:* In 2009–10, 307 students received support; fellowships, research assistantships, scholarships/grants, traineeships, and unspecified assistantships available. Financial award application deadline: 1/2. *Unit head:* Dr. Daniel Kessler, Graduate Group Chair, E-mail: raperj@mail.med.upenn.edu. *Application contact:* Meagan Schofer, Coordinator, 215-895-9536, Fax: 215-573-2104, E-mail: camb@mailmed.upenn.edu.

University of Pittsburgh, School of Arts and Sciences, Department of Biological Sciences, Program in Molecular, Cellular, and Developmental Biology, Pittsburgh, PA 15260. Offers PhD. *Faculty:* 23 full-time (6 women). *Students:* 52 full-time (33 women); includes 2 minority (1 African American, 1 Asian American or Pacific Islander), 14 international. Average age 23. 194 applicants, 10% accepted, 9 enrolled. In 2009, 3 doctorates awarded. *Degree requirements:* For doctorate, comprehensive exam, thesis/dissertation. *Entrance requirements:* For doctorate, GRE General Test, GRE Subject Test. Additional exam requirements/recommendations for international students: Required—TOEFL (minimum score 550 paper-based; 213 computer-based). *Application deadline:* For fall admission, 1/15 priority date for domestic students, 12/15 priority date for international students. Applications are processed on a rolling basis. Application fee: $0 ($50 for international students). Electronic applications accepted. *Expenses:* Tuition, state resident: full-time $16,402; part-time $665 per credit. Tuition, nonresident: full-time $28,694; part-time $1175 per credit. Required fees: $690; $175 per term. Tuition and fees vary according to program. *Financial support:* In 2009–10, 31 fellowships with full tuition reimbursements (averaging $27,379 per year), 104 research assistantships with full tuition reimbursements (averaging $24,608 per year), 36 teaching assistantships with full tuition reimbursements (averaging $23,385 per year) were awarded; Federal Work-Study, scholarships/grants, traineeships, health care benefits, and tuition waivers (full) also available. *Faculty research:* Structure and function of genes and proteins, macromolecular interactions, cell-specific gene regulation, regulation of cell proliferation, embryogenesis. *Unit head:* Dr. Gerard L. Campbell, Associate Professor, 412-624-6812, Fax: 412-624-4759, E-mail: camp@pitt.edu. *Application contact:* Cathleen M. Barr, Graduate Administrator, 412-624-4268, Fax: 412-624-4759, E-mail: cbarr@pitt.edu.

University of Pittsburgh, School of Medicine and School of Arts and Sciences, Program in Integrative Molecular Biology, Pittsburgh, PA 15260. Offers PhD. *Faculty:* 29 full-time (11 women). *Students:* 17 full-time (11 women); includes 1 minority (Asian American or Pacific Islander), 11 international. Average age 25. 42 applicants, 29% accepted, 5 enrolled. In 2009, 1 doctorate awarded. *Degree requirements:* For doctorate, comprehensive exam, thesis/dissertation. *Entrance requirements:* For doctorate, GRE, minimum GPA of 3.7, 3 letters of reference. Additional exam requirements/recommendations for international students: Required—TOEFL (minimum score 650 paper-based; 280 computer-based; 114 iBT), IELTS (minimum score 7.5). *Application deadline:* For fall admission, 1/7 for domestic and international students. Application fee: $0. Electronic applications accepted. *Expenses:* Tuition, state resident: full-time $16,402; part-time $665 per credit. Tuition, nonresident: full-time $28,694; part-time $1175 per credit. Required fees: $690; $175 per term. Tuition and fees vary according to program. *Financial support:* In 2009–10, 5 fellowships with full tuition reimbursements (averaging $27,326 per year), 12 research assistantships with full tuition reimbursements (averaging $24,650 per year) were awarded; institutionally sponsored loans, scholarships/grants, traineeships, and unspecified assistantships also available. *Faculty research:* Cellular, molecular, developmental biology; genomics; proteomics and gene function. *Unit head:* Dr. Karen Arndt, Program Director, 412-648-8975, Fax: 412-648-1077, E-mail: arndt@pitt.edu. *Application contact:* Jennifer L. Walker, Program Coordinator, 412-648-8957, Fax: 412-648-1077, E-mail: pimbinfo@medschool.pitt.edu.

University of Puerto Rico, Río Piedras, College of Natural Sciences, Department of Biology, San Juan, PR 00931-3300. Offers ecology/systematics (MS, PhD); evolution/genetics (MS, PhD); molecular/cellular biology (MS, PhD); neuroscience (MS, PhD). Part-time programs available. *Degree requirements:* For master's, one foreign language, comprehensive exam, thesis; for doctorate, one foreign language, comprehensive exam, thesis/dissertation. *Entrance requirements:* For master's, GRE Subject Test, interview, minimum GPA of 3.0, letter of recommendation; for doctorate, GRE Subject Test, interview, master's degree, minimum GPA of 3.0, letter of recommendation. *Faculty research:* Environmental, poblational and systematic biology.

University of Rhode Island, Graduate School, College of the Environment and Life Sciences, Department of Cell and Molecular Biology, Kingston, RI 02881. Offers biochemistry (MS, PhD); clinical laboratory sciences (MS), including biotechnology, clinical laboratory science, cytopathology; microbiology (MS, PhD); molecular genetics (MS, PhD). Part-time programs available. *Faculty:* 12 full-time (4 women). *Students:* 29 full-time (17 women), 43 part-time (31 women); includes 13 minority (5 African Americans, 4 Asian Americans or Pacific Islanders, 4 Hispanic Americans), 3 international. In 2009, 5 master's, 2 doctorates awarded. *Degree requirements:* For master's, comprehensive exam (for some programs); for doctorate, comprehensive exam. *Entrance requirements:* For master's and doctorate, GRE, 2 letters of recommendation. Additional exam requirements/recommendations for international students: Required—TOEFL (minimum score 550 paper-based; 213 computer-based). *Application deadline:* For fall admission, 7/15 for domestic students, 2/1 for international students; for spring admission, 11/15 for domestic students, 7/15 for international students. Application fee: $65. Electronic applications accepted. *Expenses:* Tuition, state resident: full-time $8828; part-time $490 per credit hour. Tuition, nonresident: full-time $22,100; part-time $1228 per credit hour. Required fees: $1118; $57 per semester. Tuition and fees vary according to program. *Financial support:* In 2009–10, 2 research assistantships with full and partial tuition reimbursements (averaging $10,535 per year), 10 teaching assistantships with full and partial tuition reimbursements (averaging $13,449 per year) were awarded. Financial award application deadline: 7/15; financial award applicants required to submit FAFSA. *Faculty research:* Genomics and Sequencing Center: an interdisciplinary genomics research and undergraduate and graduate student training program which provides researchers access to cutting-edge technologies in the field of genomics. Total annual research expenditures: $1.2 million. *Unit head:* Dr. Jay Sperry, Chairperson, 401-874-2201, Fax: 401-874-2202, E-mail: jsperry@mail.uri.edu. *Application contact:* Dr. Jay Sperry, Chairperson, 401-874-2201, Fax: 401-874-2202, E-mail: jsperry@mail.uri.edu.

University of South Alabama, College of Medicine and Graduate School, Program in Basic Medical Sciences, Specialization in Biochemistry and Molecular Biology, Mobile, AL 36688-0002. Offers PhD. *Degree requirements:* For doctorate, thesis/dissertation. *Entrance requirements:* For doctorate, GRE General Test or MCAT. *Expenses:* Tuition, state resident: part-time $218 per contact hour. Required fees: $1102 per year. *Faculty research:* Biochemistry of aging, mechanisms of metabolic regulation and oxygen metabolism.

University of South Carolina, The Graduate School, College of Arts and Sciences, Department of Biological Sciences, Graduate Training Program in Molecular, Cellular, and Developmental Biology, Columbia, SC 29208. Offers MS, PhD. *Degree requirements:* For master's, one foreign language, thesis; for doctorate, one foreign language, thesis/dissertation. *Entrance requirements:* For master's and doctorate, GRE General Test, minimum GPA of 3.0 in science. Electronic applications accepted. *Faculty research:* Marine ecology, population and evolutionary biology, molecular biology and genetics, development.

The University of South Dakota, School of Medicine and Health Sciences and Graduate School, Biomedical Sciences Graduate Program, Cellular and Molecular Biology Group, Vermillion, SD 57069-2390. Offers MS, PhD. Terminal master's awarded for partial completion of doctoral program. *Degree requirements:* For master's, thesis; for doctorate, comprehensive exam, thesis/dissertation. *Entrance requirements:* For master's and doctorate, GRE General Test, GRE Subject Test, minimum GPA of 3.0. Additional exam requirements/recommendations for international students: Required—TOEFL (minimum score 550 paper-based; 213 computer-based; 80 iBT), IELTS (minimum score 6). Electronic applications accepted. *Expenses:* Contact institution. *Faculty research:* Molecular aspects of protein and DNA, neurochemistry and energy transduction, gene regulation, cellular development.

University of Southern California, Graduate School, College of Letters, Arts and Sciences, Department of Biological Sciences, Program in Molecular and Computational Biology, Los Angeles, CA 90089. Offers computational biology and bioinformatics (PhD); molecular biology (PhD). *Faculty:* 43 full-time (8 women). *Students:* 131 full-time (67 women), 3 part-time (1 woman); includes 23 minority (2 African Americans, 1 American Indian/Alaska Native, 13 Asian Americans or Pacific Islanders, 7 Hispanic Americans), 53 international. 158 applicants, 29% accepted, 18 enrolled. In 2009, 15 doctorates awarded. Terminal master's awarded for partial completion of doctoral program. *Degree requirements:* For doctorate, thesis/dissertation, qualifying examination, dissertation defense. *Entrance requirements:* For doctorate, GRE, 3 letters of recommendation, personal statement, resume, minimum GPA of 3.0. Additional exam requirements/recommendations for international students: Required—TOEFL (minimum score 600 paper-based; 250 computer-based; 100 iBT). *Application deadline:* For fall admission, 12/1 priority date for domestic students, 11/1 priority date for international students. Application fee: $85. Electronic applications accepted. *Expenses:* Tuition: Full-time $25,980; part-time $1315 per unit. Required fees: $554. One-time fee: $35 full-time. Full-time tuition and fees vary according to degree level and program. *Financial support:* In 2009–10, 57 students received support, including 8 fellowships with full tuition reimbursements available (averaging $27,000 per year), 44 research assistantships with full tuition reimbursements available (averaging $25,333 per year), 5 teaching assistantships with full tuition reimbursements available (averaging $25,333 per year); scholarships/grants, traineeships, health care benefits, and tuition waivers also available. *Faculty research:* Cell and developmental biology, cancer biology, computational biology and bioinformatics, genetics, computational neurobiology. *Unit head:* Dr. Myron Goodman, Professor of Biological Sciences and Chemistry/Director of the MCB Research Section, 213-740-5190, E-mail: mgoodman@usc.edu. *Application contact:* Catherine Atienza, Student Services Advisor I, 213-740-5188, E-mail: catherine.atienza@usc.edu.

University of Southern California, Keck School of Medicine and Graduate School, Graduate Programs in Medicine, Department of Biochemistry and Molecular Biology, Los Angeles, CA 90089. Offers MS, PhD. *Faculty:* 24 full-time (6 women). *Students:* 36 full-time (20 women); includes 9 minority (1 African American, 8 Asian Americans or Pacific Islanders), 24 international. Average age 24. 29 applicants, 24% accepted, 4 enrolled. In 2009, 11 master's, 14 doctorates awarded. Terminal master's awarded for partial completion of doctoral program. *Degree requirements:* For master's, thesis; for doctorate, comprehensive exam, thesis/dissertation. *Entrance requirements:* For master's and doctorate, GRE General Test, minimum GPA of 3.0. Additional exam requirements/recommendations for international students: Required—TOEFL (minimum score 600 paper-based; 250 computer-based; 100 iBT). *Application deadline:* For fall admission, 4/15 priority date for domestic and international students. Application fee: $85. Electronic applications accepted. *Expenses:* Tuition: Full-time $25,980; part-time $1315 per unit. Required fees: $554. One-time fee: $35 full-time. Full-time tuition and fees vary according to degree level and program. *Financial support:* In 2009–10, 16 students received support, including 1 fellowship with tuition reimbursement available (averaging $27,060 per year), 12 research assistantships with tuition reimbursements available (averaging $27,060 per year), 3 teaching assistantships with tuition reimbursements available (averaging $27,060 per year); Federal Work-Study, institutionally sponsored loans, scholarships/grants, health care benefits, and unspecified assistantships also available. Financial award application deadline: 5/5. *Faculty research:* Molecular genetics, gene expression, membrane biochemistry, metabolic regulation, cancer biology. *Unit head:* Dr. Michael R. Stallcup, Chair, 323-442-1145, Fax: 323-442-1224, E-mail: stallcup@usc.edu. *Application contact:* Anne L. Rice, Student Services Coordinator, 323-442-1145, Fax: 323-442-1224, E-mail: annvazqu@usc.edu.

University of Southern California, Keck School of Medicine and Graduate School, Graduate Programs in Medicine, Department of Preventive Medicine, Division of Biostatistics, Los Angeles, CA 90089. Offers applied biostatistics/epidemiology (MS); biostatistics (MS, PhD); epidemiology (PhD); genetic epidemiology and statistical genetics (PhD); molecular epidemiology (MS, PhD). *Faculty:* 71 full-time (30 women). *Students:* 108 full-time (63 women); includes 24 minority (18 Asian Americans or Pacific Islanders, 6 Hispanic Americans), 58 international. Average age 29. 79 applicants, 52% accepted, 18 enrolled. In 2009, 12 master's, 4 doctorates awarded. Terminal master's awarded for partial completion of doctoral program. *Degree requirements:* For master's, thesis; for doctorate, thesis/dissertation. *Entrance requirements:* For master's and doctorate, GRE General Test, GRE Subject Test, minimum GPA of 3.0. Additional exam requirements/recommendations for international students: Required—TOEFL (minimum score 600 paper-based; 250 computer-based; 100 iBT). *Application deadline:* For fall admission, 12/1 priority date for domestic students, 12/1 for international students. Application fee: $85. Electronic applications accepted. *Expenses:* Tuition: Full-time $25,980; part-time $1315 per unit. Required fees: $554. One-time fee: $35 full-time. Full-time tuition and fees vary according to degree level and program. *Financial support:* In 2009–10, 3 fellowships with full tuition reimbursements (averaging $27,060 per year), 55 research assistantships with full tuition reimbursements (averaging $27,060 per year), 19 teaching assistantships with full and partial tuition reimbursements (averaging $13,530 per year) were awarded; career-related internships or fieldwork, Federal Work-Study, institutionally sponsored loans, scholarships/grants, health care benefits, and unspecified assistantships also available. Financial award application deadline: 5/5. *Faculty research:* Clinical trials in ophthalmology and cancer research, methods of analysis for epidemiological studies, genetic epidemiology. Total annual research expenditures: $1.3 million. *Unit head:* Dr. Stanley P. Azen, Co-Director, 323-442-1810, Fax: 323-442-2993, E-mail: mtrujill@usc.edu. *Application contact:* Mary L. Trujillo, Student Adviser, 323-442-1810, Fax: 323-442-2993; E-mail: mtrujill@usc.edu.

University of Southern California, Keck School of Medicine and Graduate School, Program in Genetic, Molecular and Cellular Biology, Los Angeles, CA 90089. Offers PhD. *Faculty:* 213 full-time (54 women). *Students:* 123 full-time (67 women); includes 24 minority (2 African Americans, 15 Asian Americans or Pacific Islanders, 7 Hispanic Americans), 70 international. 328 applicants, 32% accepted, 47 enrolled. *Degree requirements:* For doctorate, comprehensive exam, thesis/dissertation. *Entrance requirements:* For doctorate, GRE, minimum GPA of 3.0. Additional exam requirements/recommendations for international students: Required—TOEFL (minimum score 600 paper-based; 250 computer-based; 100 iBT). *Application deadline:* For fall admission, 12/1 priority date for domestic and international students. Application fee: $85. Electronic applications accepted. *Expenses:* Tuition: Full-time $25,980; part-time $1315 per unit. Required fees: $554. One-time fee: $35 full-time. Full-time tuition and fees vary according to degree level and program. *Financial support:* In 2009–10, 122 students received support, including 10 fellowships (averaging $27,060 per year), 110 research assistantships with full tuition reimbursements available (averaging $27,060 per year), 2 teaching assistantships with full tuition reimbursements available (averaging $27,060 per year); institutionally sponsored loans, scholarships/grants, traineeships, health care benefits, and unspecified assistantships also available. Financial award application deadline: 5/5; financial award applicants required to submit FAFSA. *Unit head:* Dr. Henry Sucov, Director, 323-442-1475, Fax: 323-442-1199, E-mail: sucov@usc.edu. *Application contact:* Dawn Burke, Student Program Coordinator, 323-442-1475, Fax: 323-442-1199, E-mail: pibbs@usc.edu.

University of Southern Maine, School of Applied Science, Engineering, and Technology, Program in Applied Medical Sciences, Portland, ME 04104-9300. Offers MS. Part-time programs available. *Degree requirements:* For master's, thesis. *Entrance requirements:* For master's, GRE General Test, minimum GPA of 3.0. Additional exam requirements/recommendations for international students: Required—TOEFL. Electronic applications accepted. *Faculty research:* Flow cytometry, cancer, epidemiology, monoclonal antibodies, DNA diagnostics.

University of Southern Mississippi, Graduate School, College of Science and Technology, Department of Biological Sciences, Hattiesburg, MS 39406-0001. Offers environmental biology (MS, PhD); marine biology (MS, PhD); microbiology (MS, PhD); molecular biology (MS, PhD). *Faculty:* 27 full-time (6 women). *Students:* 55 full-time (27 women), 5 part-time (3 women); includes 7 minority (2 African Americans, 1 American Indian/Alaska Native, 2 Asian Americans or Pacific Islanders, 2 Hispanic Americans), 15 international. Average age 32. 53 applicants, 28% accepted, 10 enrolled. In 2009, 8 master's, 4 doctorates awarded. *Degree requirements:* For master's, comprehensive exam, thesis; for doctorate, comprehensive exam, thesis/dissertation. *Entrance requirements:* For master's, GRE General Test, minimum GPA of 3.0; for doctorate, GRE General Test, minimum GPA of 3.5. Additional exam requirements/recommendations for international students: Required—TOEFL. *Application deadline:* For fall admission, 3/1 priority date for domestic students, 3/1 for international students. Applications are processed on a rolling basis. Application fee: $35. *Expenses:* Tuition, state resident: full-time $5096; part-time $284 per hour. Tuition, nonresident: full-time $13,052; part-time $726 per hour. Required fees: $402. Tuition and fees vary according to course level and course load. *Financial support:* In 2009–10, 25 research assistantships with full tuition reimbursements (averaging $9,625 per year), 33 teaching assistantships with full tuition reimbursements (averaging $10,599 per year) were awarded; Federal Work-Study also available. Financial award application deadline: 3/15; financial award applicants required to submit FAFSA. *Unit head:* Dr. Frank Moore, Chair, 601-266-4748, Fax: 601-266-5797. *Application contact:* Dr. Chia Wang, Graduate Coordinator, 601-266-4748, Fax: 601-266-5797.

University of South Florida, Graduate School, College of Arts and Sciences, Department of Biology, Tampa, FL 33620-9951. Offers cell biology and molecular biology (MS); coastal marine biology (MS); coastal marine biology and ecology (PhD); conservation biology (MS, PhD); molecular and cell biology (PhD). Part-time programs available. *Faculty:* 34 full-time (7 women). *Students:* 72 full-time (43 women), 18 part-time (8 women); includes 9 minority (1 African American, 2 American Indian/Alaska Native, 4 Asian Americans or Pacific Islanders, 2 Hispanic Americans), 7 international. Average age 32. 99 applicants, 20% accepted, 14 enrolled. In 2009, 8 master's, 4 doctorates awarded. *Degree requirements:* For master's, comprehensive exam, thesis (for some programs); for doctorate, comprehensive exam, thesis/dissertation. *Entrance requirements:* For master's and doctorate, GRE General Test, minimum GPA of 3.0. Additional exam requirements/recommendations for international students: Required—TOEFL (minimum score 570 paper-based; 213 computer-based). *Application deadline:* For fall admission, 2/15 priority date for domestic students, 1/2 for international students; for spring admission, 8/1 for domestic students, 6/1 for international students. Application fee: $30. Electronic applications accepted. *Financial support:* In 2009–10, teaching assistantships with tuition reimbursements (averaging $58,627 per year); unspecified assistantships also available. Financial award application deadline: 6/30; financial award applicants required to submit FAFSA. Total annual research expenditures: $1.2 million. *Unit head:* Susan Bell, Co-Chairperson, 813-974-6210, Fax: 813-974-2876, E-mail: sbell@cas.usf.edu. *Application contact:* James Garey, Graduate Advisor, 813-974-8434, Fax: 813-974-3263, E-mail: grarey@cas.usf.edu.

The University of Texas at Austin, Graduate School, Institute for Cellular and Molecular Biology, Austin, TX 78712-1111. Offers PhD.

The University of Texas at Dallas, School of Natural Sciences and Mathematics, Program in Biology, Richardson, TX 75080. Offers bioinformatics and computational biology (MS); biotechnology (MS); molecular and cell biology (MS, PhD). Part-time and evening/weekend programs available. *Faculty:* 16 full-time (3 women). *Students:* 89 full-time (50 women), 16 part-time (11 women); includes 19 minority (16 Asian Americans or Pacific Islanders, 3 Hispanic Americans), 62 international. Average age 26. 313 applicants, 31% accepted, 42 enrolled. In 2009, 36 master's, 4 doctorates awarded. *Degree requirements:* For master's, thesis optional; for doctorate, thesis/dissertation, publishable paper. *Entrance requirements:* For master's and doctorate, GRE General Test. Additional exam requirements/recommendations for international students: Required—TOEFL (minimum score 550 paper-based; 213 computer-based). *Application deadline:* For fall admission, 7/15 for domestic students, 5/1 priority date for international students; for spring admission, 11/15 for domestic students, 9/1 priority date for international students. Applications are processed on a rolling basis. Application fee: $50 ($100 for international students). Electronic applications accepted. *Expenses:* Tuition, state resident: full-time $11,068; part-time $461 per credit hour. Tuition, nonresident: full-time $21,178; part-time $882 per credit hour. Tuition and fees vary according to course load. *Financial*

support: In 2009–10, 15 research assistantships with full tuition reimbursements (averaging $14,347 per year), 27 teaching assistantships with full tuition reimbursements (averaging $13,511 per year) were awarded; fellowships, career-related internships or fieldwork, Federal Work-Study, institutionally sponsored loans, scholarships/grants, and unspecified assistantships also available. Support available to part-time students. Financial award application deadline: 4/30; financial award applicants required to submit FAFSA. *Faculty research:* DNA replication, regulation of gene expression, subcellular organelles, physical chemistry of macromolecules, damage and repair of cellular DNA. *Unit head:* Dr. Li Zhang, Department Head, 972-883-6032, Fax: 972-883-2502, E-mail: li.zhang@utdallas.edu. *Application contact:* Dr. Lawrence Reitzer, Graduate Advisor, 972-883-2502, Fax: 972-883-2402, E-mail: reitzer@utdallas.edu.

The University of Texas at San Antonio, College of Sciences, Department of Biology, San Antonio, TX 78249-0617. Offers biology (MS, PhD), including cellular and molecular biology (PhD), neurobiology (PhD); biotechnology (MS). Part-time programs available. *Faculty:* 37 full-time (6 women), 7 part-time/adjunct (1 woman). *Students:* 144 full-time (82 women), 45 part-time (28 women); includes 57 minority (6 African Americans, 13 Asian Americans or Pacific Islanders, 38 Hispanic Americans), 69 international. Average age 28. 263 applicants, 58% accepted, 72 enrolled. In 2009, 40 master's, 6 doctorates awarded. *Degree requirements:* For master's, comprehensive exam, thesis; for doctorate, comprehensive exam, thesis/dissertation. *Entrance requirements:* For master's, GRE General Test, minimum GPA of 3.0; for doctorate, GRE General Test, minimum GPA of 3.3. Additional exam requirements/recommendations for international students: Required—TOEFL (minimum score 500 paper-based; 173 computer-based; 61 iBT), IELTS (minimum score 5). *Application deadline:* For fall admission, 7/1 for domestic students, 4/1 for international students; for spring admission, 11/1 for domestic students, 9/1 for international students. Applications are processed on a rolling basis. Application fee: $45 ($80 for international students). Electronic applications accepted. *Expenses:* Tuition, state resident: full-time $3975; part-time $221 per contact hour. Tuition, nonresident: full-time $13,947; part-time $775 per contact hour. Required fees: $1853. *Financial support:* In 2009–10, 66 students received support, including 13 fellowships (averaging $31,063 per year), 87 research assistantships (averaging $15,279 per year), 66 teaching assistantships (averaging $10,368 per year); career-related internships or fieldwork, scholarships/grants, and unspecified assistantships also available. Support available to part-time students. *Faculty research:* Cell and molecular biology, neurobiology, microbiology, integrative biology, environmental science. Total annual research expenditures: $1.7 million. *Unit head:* Dr. Edwin J. Barea-Rodriguez, Interim Chair, 210-458-5481, Fax: 210-458-7498, E-mail: edwin.barea@utsa.edu. *Application contact:* Dr. Dorothy A. Flannagan, Dean of the Graduate School, 210-458-4330, Fax: 210-458-4332, E-mail: dorothy.flannagan@utsa.edu.

See Close-Up on page 121.

The University of Texas Health Science Center at Houston, Graduate School of Biomedical Sciences, Program in Biochemistry and Molecular Biology, Houston, TX 77225-0036. Offers MS, PhD, MD/PhD. Terminal master's awarded for partial completion of doctoral program. *Degree requirements:* For master's, thesis; for doctorate, thesis/dissertation. *Entrance requirements:* For master's and doctorate, GRE General Test. Additional exam requirements/recommendations for international students: Required—TOEFL. Electronic applications accepted. *Faculty research:* Biochemistry, membrane biology, macromolecular structure, structural biophysics, molecular models of human disease, molecular biology of the cell.

The University of Texas Health Science Center at Houston, Graduate School of Biomedical Sciences, Program in Cell and Regulatory Biology, Houston, TX 77225-0036. Offers MS, PhD, MD/PhD. Terminal master's awarded for partial completion of doctoral program. *Degree requirements:* For master's, thesis; for doctorate, thesis/dissertation. *Entrance requirements:* For master's and doctorate, GRE General Test. Additional exam requirements/recommendations for international students: Required—TOEFL. Electronic applications accepted. *Faculty research:* Pharmacology, cell biology, physiology, signal transduction, systems biology.

University of the Sciences in Philadelphia, College of Graduate Studies, Misher College of Arts and Sciences, Program in Cell and Molecular Biology, Philadelphia, PA 19104-4495. Offers PhD. *Expenses:* Tuition: Full-time $22,230; part-time $1235 per credit. Tuition and fees vary according to program.

The University of Toledo, College of Graduate Studies, College of Medicine, Biomedical Science Programs, Department of Biochemistry and Molecular Biology, Toledo, OH 43606-3390. Offers medical sciences (MSBS). Part-time programs available. *Degree requirements:* For master's, thesis, qualifying exam. *Entrance requirements:* For master's, GRE General Test, minimum undergraduate GPA of 3.0. Additional exam requirements/recommendations for international students: Required—TOEFL. *Faculty research:* Gene regulation, protein structure, receptors, protein phosphorylation, peptides.

University of Utah, School of Medicine, Program in Molecular Biology, Salt Lake City, UT 84132. Offers PhD. *Faculty:* 120 full-time (31 women), 1 part-time/adjunct (0 women). *Students:* 21 full-time (13 women), 1 (woman) part-time; includes 2 minority (both Hispanic Americans), 6 international. Average age 28. 490 applicants, 15% accepted. *Degree requirements:* For doctorate, thesis/dissertation, preliminary exams. *Entrance requirements:* For doctorate, GRE General Test, minimum GPA of 3.0. Additional exam requirements/recommendations for international students: Required—TOEFL (minimum score 500 paper-based; 173 computer-based; 60 iBT). *Application deadline:* For fall admission, 12/15 for domestic and international students. Application fee: $0. Electronic applications accepted. *Expenses:* Tuition, state resident: full-time $4004; part-time $1674 per semester. Tuition, nonresident: full-time $14,134; part-time $5915 per semester. Required fees: $324 per semester. Tuition and fees vary according to course load, degree level and program. *Financial support:* In 2009–10, 30 research assistantships with full tuition reimbursements (averaging $25,000 per year) were awarded. *Faculty research:* Biochemistry; cellular, viral, and molecular biology; human genetics; pathology; procaryotic development. *Unit head:* Dr. Brad Cairns, Director, 801-581-5207, Fax: 801-585-2465. *Application contact:* Tami Brunson, Administrative Program Coordinator, 801-581-5207, Fax: 801-585-2465, E-mail: tami.brunson@genetics.utah.edu.

University of Vermont, Graduate College, Cell and Molecular Biology Program, Burlington, VT 05405. Offers MS, PhD. *Students:* 39 (16 women); includes 6 minority (2 Asian Americans or Pacific Islanders, 4 Hispanic Americans), 7 international. 81 applicants, 23% accepted, 9 enrolled. In 2009, 4 master's, 8 doctorates awarded. *Degree requirements:* For master's, thesis; for doctorate, thesis/dissertation. *Entrance requirements:* For master's and doctorate, GRE General Test. Additional exam requirements/recommendations for international students: Required—TOEFL (minimum score 550 paper-based; 213 computer-based; 80 iBT). *Application deadline:* For fall admission, 1/15 priority date for domestic students. Applications are processed on a rolling basis. Application fee: $40. Electronic applications accepted. *Expenses:* Tuition, state resident: part-time $508 per credit hour. Tuition, nonresident: part-time $1281 per credit hour. *Financial support:* Fellowships, research assistantships, teaching assistantships, career-related internships or fieldwork available. Financial award application deadline: 3/1. *Unit head:* Dr. Karen Lounsbury, Coordinator, 802-656-9673. *Application contact:* Dr. Karen Lounsbury, Coordinator, 802-656-9673.

University of Washington, Graduate School, School of Medicine and Graduate School, Graduate Programs in Medicine, Program in Molecular and Cellular Biology, Seattle, WA 98195. Offers PhD. Offered jointly with Fred Hutchinson Cancer Research Center. *Degree requirements:* For doctorate, thesis/dissertation. *Entrance requirements:* For doctorate, GRE General Test, GRE Subject Test. Additional exam requirements/recommendations for international students: Required—TOEFL. Electronic applications accepted.

See Close-Up on page 251.

The University of Western Ontario, Faculty of Graduate Studies, Biosciences Division, Department of Plant Sciences, London, ON N6A 5B8, Canada. Offers plant and environmental

Molecular Biology

The University of Western Ontario (continued)
sciences (M Sc); plant sciences (M Sc, PhD); plant sciences and environmental sciences (PhD); plant sciences and molecular biology (M Sc, PhD). *Degree requirements:* For master's, thesis; for doctorate, thesis/dissertation. *Entrance requirements:* For doctorate, M Sc or equivalent. Additional exam requirements/recommendations for international students: Required—TOEFL. *Faculty research:* Ecology systematics, plant biochemistry and physiology, yeast genetics, molecular biology.

University of Wisconsin–La Crosse, Office of University Graduate Studies, College of Science and Health, Department of Biology, La Crosse, WI 54601-3742. Offers aquatic sciences (MS); biology (MS); cellular and molecular biology (MS); clinical microbiology (MS); microbiology (MS); nurse anesthesia (MS); physiology (MS). Part-time programs available. *Faculty:* 27 full-time (7 women). *Students:* 19 full-time (8 women), 35 part-time (20 women); includes 1 minority (Asian American or Pacific Islander), 2 international. Average age 28. 87 applicants, 32% accepted, 21 enrolled. In 2009, 18 master's awarded. *Degree requirements:* For master's, comprehensive exam, thesis. *Entrance requirements:* For master's, GRE General Test, minimum GPA of 2.85. Additional exam requirements/recommendations for international students: Required—TOEFL (minimum score 550 paper-based; 213 computer-based; 79 iBT). Application fee: $56. Electronic applications accepted. *Financial support:* In 2009–10, 19 research assistantships with partial tuition reimbursements (averaging $10,021 per year) were awarded; career-related internships or fieldwork, Federal Work-Study, health care benefits, unspecified assistantships, and grant-funded positions also available. Support available to part-time students. Financial award application deadline: 3/15; financial award applicants required to submit FAFSA. *Unit head:* Dr. David Howard, Chair, 608-785-6455, E-mail: howard.davi@uwlax.edu. *Application contact:* Kathryn Kiefer, Director of Admissions, 608-785-8939, E-mail: admissions@uwlax.edu.

University of Wisconsin–Madison, Graduate School, Program in Cellular and Molecular Biology, Madison, WI 53706-1596. Offers PhD. *Degree requirements:* For doctorate, comprehensive exam, thesis/dissertation. *Entrance requirements:* For doctorate, GRE General Test, GRE Subject Test (recommended), minimum GPA of 3.0, lab experience. Additional exam requirements/recommendations for international students: Required—TOEFL (minimum score 580 paper-based; 237 computer-based; 92 iBT). Electronic applications accepted. *Expenses:* Tuition, state resident: part-time $594 per credit. Tuition, nonresident: part-time $1504 per credit. Required fees: $65 per credit. Tuition and fees vary according to course load, program and reciprocity agreements. *Faculty research:* Virology, cancer biology, transcriptional mechanisms, plant biology, immunology.

University of Wisconsin–Parkside, College of Arts and Sciences, Program in Applied Molecular Biology, Kenosha, WI 53141-2000. Offers MAMB. Part-time programs available. *Degree requirements:* For master's, thesis, oral exam. *Entrance requirements:* For master's, GRE General Test, minimum GPA of 3.0; course work in biology, chemistry, math, physics. Additional exam requirements/recommendations for international students: Required—TOEFL (minimum score 550 paper-based; 213 computer-based). Electronic applications accepted. *Faculty research:* Gene cloning, genome structure, cell cycle effects on gene expression, molecular biology of plant hormones, laboratory toxin production and resistance. RNA stability, pathogencity.

University of Wyoming, College of Agriculture, Department of Molecular Biology, Laramie, WY 82070. Offers MS, PhD. Terminal master's awarded for partial completion of doctoral program. *Degree requirements:* For master's, comprehensive exam (for some programs), thesis; for doctorate, comprehensive exam, thesis/dissertation. *Entrance requirements:* For master's and doctorate, GRE General Test, GRE Subject Test (recommended), minimum GPA of 3.0. Additional exam requirements/recommendations for international students: Required—TOEFL. Electronic applications accepted. *Faculty research:* Protein structure/function, developmental regulation, yeast genetics, bacterial pathogenesis.

University of Wyoming, Graduate Program in Molecular and Cellular Life Sciences, Laramie, WY 82070. Offers PhD. *Degree requirements:* For doctorate, thesis/dissertation, four eight-week laboratory rotations, comprehensive basic practical exam, two-part qualifying exam, seminars, symposium.

Utah State University, School of Graduate Studies, College of Agriculture, Department of Nutrition and Food Sciences, Logan, UT 84322. Offers dietetic administration (MDA); food microbiology and safety (MFMS); nutrition and food sciences (MS, PhD); nutrition science (MS, PhD), including molecular biology. Postbaccalaureate distance learning degree programs offered. *Degree requirements:* For master's, thesis; for doctorate, comprehensive exam, thesis/dissertation, teaching experience. *Entrance requirements:* For master's, GRE General Test, minimum GPA of 3.0, course work in chemistry, biochemistry, physics, math, bacteriology, physiology; for doctorate, GRE General Test, minimum GPA of 3.2, course work in chemistry, MS or manuscript in referred journal. Additional exam requirements/recommendations for international students: Required—TOEFL (minimum score 550 paper-based). Electronic applications accepted. *Faculty research:* Mineral balance, meat microbiology and nitrate interactions, milk ultrafiltration, lactic culture, milk coagulation.

Vanderbilt University, Graduate School and School of Medicine, Department of Molecular Physiology and Biophysics, Nashville, TN 37240-1001. Offers MS, PhD, MD/PhD. *Faculty:* 80 full-time (22 women). *Students:* 29 full-time (21 women), 1 part-time (0 women); includes 6 minority (3 African Americans, 1 American Indian/Alaska Native, 2 Hispanic Americans), 8 international. Average age 30. In 2009, 1 master's, 6 doctorates awarded. *Degree requirements:* For doctorate, comprehensive exam, thesis/dissertation, preliminary, qualifying, and final exams. *Entrance requirements:* For doctorate, GRE General Test, GRE Subject Test (recommended). Additional exam requirements/recommendations for international students: Required—TOEFL (minimum score 570 paper-based; 230 computer-based; 88 iBT). *Application deadline:* For fall admission, 1/15 for domestic and international students. Application fee: $0. Electronic applications accepted. *Financial support:* Fellowships with full tuition reimbursements, research assistantships with full tuition reimbursements, Federal Work-Study, institutionally sponsored loans, scholarships/grants, traineeships, health care benefits, and tuition waivers (partial) available. Financial award application deadline: 1/15; financial award applicants required to submit CSS PROFILE or FAFSA. *Faculty research:* Biophysics, cell signaling and gene regulation, human genetics, diabetes and obesity, neuroscience. *Unit head:* Roger Cone, Chair, 615-322-7000, Fax: 615-343-0490. *Application contact:* Michelle Grundy, Assistant Director, 800-373-0675, E-mail: michelle.grundy@vanderbilt.edu.

Virginia Commonwealth University, Medical College of Virginia-Professional Programs, School of Medicine, School of Medicine Graduate Programs, Department of Biochemistry, Richmond, VA 23284-9005. Offers biochemistry (MS, PhD); molecular biology and genetics (MS, PhD); neuroscience (PhD); MD/PhD. *Degree requirements:* For master's, thesis; for doctorate, thesis/dissertation, comprehensive oral and written exams. *Entrance requirements:* For master's and doctorate, DAT, GRE General Test, MCAT. *Faculty research:* Molecular biology, peptide/protein chemistry, neurochemistry, enzyme mechanisms, macromolecular structure determination.

Virginia Commonwealth University, Medical College of Virginia-Professional Programs, School of Medicine, School of Medicine Graduate Programs, Department of Human and Molecular Genetics, Richmond, VA 23284-9005. Offers genetic counseling (MS); human genetics (PhD); molecular biology and genetics (MS, PhD); MD/PhD. *Degree requirements:* For master's, thesis; for doctorate, thesis/dissertation, comprehensive oral and written exams. *Entrance requirements:* For master's, DAT, GRE General Test, or MCAT; for doctorate, GRE General Test, DAT, MCAT. *Faculty research:* Genetic epidemiology, biochemical genetics, quantitative genetics, human cytogenetics, molecular genetics.

Virginia Commonwealth University, Medical College of Virginia-Professional Programs, School of Medicine, School of Medicine Graduate Programs, Department of Microbiology and Immunology, Richmond, VA 23284-9005. Offers microbiology and immunology (MS, PhD); molecular biology and genetics (MS, PhD); MD/PhD. *Degree requirements:* For master's, thesis; for doctorate, thesis/dissertation, comprehensive oral and written exams. *Entrance requirements:* For master's, GRE General Test or MCAT; for doctorate, GRE General Test, MCAT. *Faculty research:* Microbial physiology and genetics, molecular biology, crystallography of biological molecules, antibiotics and chemotherapy, membrane transport.

Virginia Commonwealth University, Medical College of Virginia-Professional Programs, School of Medicine, School of Medicine Graduate Programs, Department of Pharmacology and Toxicology, Richmond, VA 23284-9005. Offers molecular biology and genetics (PhD); neuroscience (PhD); pharmacology (PhD); pharmacology and toxicology (MS); MD/PhD. Terminal master's awarded for partial completion of doctoral program. *Degree requirements:* For master's, thesis; for doctorate, thesis/dissertation, comprehensive oral and written exams. *Entrance requirements:* For master's, DAT, GRE General Test, or MCAT; for doctorate, GRE General Test, MCAT, DAT. *Faculty research:* Drug abuse, drug metabolism, pharmacodynamics, peptide synthesis, receptor mechanisms.

Virginia Polytechnic Institute and State University, Graduate School, Intercollege, Program in Molecular Plant Sciences, Blacksburg, VA 24061. Offers PhD. *Expenses:* Tuition, area resident: Full-time $10,228; part-time $459 per credit hour. Tuition, nonresident: full-time $17,892; part-time $865 per credit hour. Required fees: $1966; $451 per semester.

Wake Forest University, School of Medicine and Graduate School of Arts and Sciences, Graduate Programs in Medicine, Molecular Genetics and Genomics Program, Winston-Salem, NC 27109. Offers PhD, MD/PhD. *Degree requirements:* For doctorate, thesis/dissertation. *Entrance requirements:* For doctorate, GRE General Test. Additional exam requirements/recommendations for international students: Required—TOEFL. Electronic applications accepted. *Faculty research:* Control of gene expression, molecular pathogenesis, protein biosynthesis, cell development, clinical cytogenetics.

Washington State University, Graduate School, College of Sciences, School of Molecular Biosciences, Pullman, WA 99164. Offers MS, PhD. *Faculty:* 30. *Students:* 24 full-time (14 women); includes 1 American Indian/Alaska Native, 1 Asian American or Pacific Islander, 1 Hispanic American, 3 international. 194 applicants, 15% accepted, 16 enrolled. In 2009, 8 master's, 10 doctorates awarded. *Entrance requirements:* For master's and doctorate, GRE, personal statement describing qualifications, goals, and objectives in pursuing graduate research in molecular biosciences; official transcripts from all colleges attended; three letters of recommendation. Additional exam requirements/recommendations for international students: Required—TOEFL, IELTS. *Application deadline:* For fall admission, 12/15 for domestic students. Application fee: $50. *Financial support:* In 2009–10, research assistantships (averaging $13,917 per year), teaching assistantships (averaging $13,056 per year) were awarded. Financial award application deadline: 2/15; financial award applicants required to submit FAFSA. Total annual research expenditures: $8 million. *Unit head:* Dr. John H. Nilson, Director, 509-335-8724, Fax: 509-335-9688, E-mail: jhn@wsu.edu. *Application contact:* Graduate School Admissions, 800-GRADWSU, Fax: 509-335-1949, E-mail: gradsch@wsu.edu.

Washington University in St. Louis, Graduate School of Arts and Sciences, Division of Biology and Biomedical Sciences, Program in Molecular Cell Biology, St. Louis, MO 63130-4899. Offers PhD. *Degree requirements:* For doctorate, thesis/dissertation. *Entrance requirements:* For doctorate, GRE General Test, GRE Subject Test. Electronic applications accepted.

Wayne State University, Graduate School, Program in Molecular Biology and Genetics, Detroit, MI 48202. Offers MS, PhD. Terminal master's awarded for partial completion of doctoral program. *Degree requirements:* For master's, thesis; for doctorate, thesis/dissertation. *Entrance requirements:* For master's and doctorate, GRE General Test, contingent upon admission to the graduate programs of the school of medicine; references. Additional exam requirements/recommendations for international students: Required—TOEFL (minimum score 550 paper-based; 213 computer-based); Recommended—TWE (minimum score 6). Electronic applications accepted. *Faculty research:* Human gene mapping, genome organization and sequencing, gene regulation, molecular evolution.

Wayne State University, School of Medicine, Graduate Programs in Medicine, Department of Biochemistry and Molecular Biology, Detroit, MI 48202. Offers MS, PhD. Terminal master's awarded for partial completion of doctoral program. *Degree requirements:* For master's, thesis; for doctorate, one foreign language, thesis/dissertation. *Entrance requirements:* For master's and doctorate, GRE General Test, GRE Subject Test. Additional exam requirements/recommendations for international students: Required—TOEFL (minimum score 550 paper-based; 213 computer-based); Recommended—TWE (minimum score 6). Electronic applications accepted. *Faculty research:* Protein structure, molecular biology, molecular genetics, enzymology, x-ray crystallography.

Wesleyan University, Graduate Programs, Department of Molecular Biology and Biochemistry, Middletown, CT 06459. Offers biochemistry (PhD); molecular biology (PhD). *Faculty:* 8 full-time (3 women), 1 (woman) part-time/adjunct. *Students:* 20 full-time (14 women); includes 1 minority (Hispanic American), 13 international. Average age 28. 40 applicants, 18% accepted, 4 enrolled. In 2009, 1 doctorate awarded. *Degree requirements:* For doctorate, comprehensive exam, thesis/dissertation. *Entrance requirements:* For doctorate, GRE General Test, GRE Subject Test. Additional exam requirements/recommendations for international students: Required—TOEFL. *Application deadline:* For fall admission, 2/15 for domestic and international students. Applications are processed on a rolling basis. Application fee: $0. Electronic applications accepted. *Financial support:* In 2009–10, 12 research assistantships with full tuition reimbursements, 8 teaching assistantships with full tuition reimbursements were awarded; institutionally sponsored loans also available. Financial award application deadline: 4/15; financial award applicants required to submit FAFSA. *Faculty research:* Genome organization, regulation of gene expression, molecular biology of development, physical biochemistry. *Unit head:* Dr. Michael McAlear, Chair, 860-685-2443, E-mail: mmcalear@wesleyan.edu. *Application contact:* Information Contact, 860-685-2640, E-mail: mbbgrad@wesleyan.edu.

West Virginia University, Eberly College of Arts and Sciences, Department of Biology, Morgantown, WV 26506. Offers cell and molecular biology (MS, PhD); environmental and evolutionary biology (MS, PhD); forensic biology (MS, PhD); genomic biology (MS, PhD); neurobiology (MS, PhD). Terminal master's awarded for partial completion of doctoral program. *Degree requirements:* For master's, thesis, final exam; for doctorate, thesis/dissertation, preliminary and final exams. *Entrance requirements:* For master's, GRE General Test, GRE Subject Test, minimum GPA of 3.0; for doctorate, GRE General Test, minimum GPA of 3.0. Additional exam requirements/recommendations for international students: Required—TOEFL. *Faculty research:* Environmental biology, genetic engineering, developmental biology, global change, biodiversity.

West Virginia University, School of Medicine, Graduate Programs at the Health Sciences Center, Interdisciplinary Graduate Programs in Biomedical Sciences, Program in Biochemistry and Molecular Biology, Morgantown, WV 26506. Offers MS, PhD, MD/PhD. *Degree requirements:* For doctorate, comprehensive exam, thesis/dissertation. *Entrance requirements:* For doctorate, GRE General Test, minimum GPA of 3.0. Additional exam requirements/recommendations for international students: Required—TOEFL. Electronic applications accepted. *Faculty research:* Regulation of gene expression, cell survival mechanisms, signal transduction, regulation of metabolism, sensory neuroscience.

Wright State University, School of Graduate Studies, College of Science and Mathematics, Department of Biochemistry and Molecular Biology, Dayton, OH 45435. Offers MS. *Degree requirements:* For master's, thesis. *Entrance requirements:* Additional exam requirements/recommendations for international students: Required—TOEFL. *Faculty research:* Regulation of gene expression, macromolecular structural function, NMR imaging, visual biochemistry.

Yale University, Graduate School of Arts and Sciences, Department of Molecular, Cellular, and Developmental Biology, Program in Biochemistry, Molecular Biology and Chemical Biology, New Haven, CT 06520. Offers PhD. *Degree requirements:* For doctorate, thesis/dissertation. *Entrance requirements:* For doctorate, GRE General Test, GRE Subject Test.

Yale University, School of Medicine and Graduate School of Arts and Sciences, Combined Program in Biological and Biomedical Sciences (BBS), Molecular Cell Biology, Genetics, and Development Track, New Haven, CT 06520. Offers PhD, MD/PhD. *Entrance requirements:* Additional exam requirements/recommendations for international students: Required—TOEFL. *Application deadline:* For fall admission, 12/6 for domestic and international students. *Unit head:* Dr. Shirleen Roeder, Co-Director, 203-432-3501. *Application contact:* Shirlene Scott, Graduate Registrar, 203-785-2404, E-mail: shirlene.scott@yale.edu.

Youngstown State University, Graduate School, College of Science, Technology, Engineering and Mathematics, Department of Biological Sciences, Youngstown, OH 44555-0001. Offers environmental biology (MS); molecular biology, microbiology, and genetic (MS); physiology and anatomy (MS). Part-time programs available. *Degree requirements:* For master's, comprehensive exam, thesis, oral review. *Entrance requirements:* For master's, GRE General Test, minimum GPA of 2.7. Additional exam requirements/recommendations for international students: Required—TOEFL. *Faculty research:* Cell biology, neurophysiology, molecular biology, neurobiology, gene regulation.

Molecular Medicine

Baylor College of Medicine, Graduate School of Biomedical Sciences, Program in Translational Biology and Molecular Medicine, Houston, TX 77030-3498. Offers PhD. *Faculty:* 151 full-time (48 women). *Students:* 48 full-time (23 women); includes 13 minority (4 African Americans, 4 Asian Americans or Pacific Islanders, 5 Hispanic Americans), 14 international. Average age 24. *Degree requirements:* For doctorate, thesis/dissertation, public defense. *Entrance requirements:* For doctorate, GRE, minimum GPA of 3.0. Additional exam requirements/recommendations for international students: Required—TOEFL. *Application deadline:* For fall admission, 1/1 for domestic students. Application fee: $0. Electronic applications accepted. *Financial support:* In 2009–10, 48 students received support; fellowships, research assistantships, career-related internships or fieldwork, Federal Work-Study, health care benefits, and students receive a scholarship unless there are grant funds available to pay tuition available. Financial award applicants required to submit FAFSA. *Unit head:* Dr. Mary Estes, Director, 713-798-3585, Fax: 713-798-3586, E-mail: tbmm@bcm.edu. *Application contact:* Wanda Waguespack, Graduate Program Administrator, 713-798-1077, Fax: 713-798-3586, E-mail: wandaw@bcm.edu.

See Close-Up on page 261.

Boston University, School of Medicine, Division of Graduate Medical Sciences, Program in Molecular Medicine, Boston, MA 02215. Offers PhD, MD/PhD. *Degree requirements:* For doctorate, thesis/dissertation, qualifying exam. *Application deadline:* For fall admission, 1/15 priority date for domestic students; for spring admission, 10/15 priority date for domestic students. Electronic applications accepted. *Expenses:* Tuition: Full-time $37,910; part-time $1184 per credit hour. Required fees: $386; $40 per semester. Part-time tuition and fees vary according to class time, course level, degree level and program. *Financial support:* Fellowships, research assistantships, Federal Work-Study, scholarships/grants, and traineeships available. *Unit head:* Dr. Joseph Loscalzo, Director, 617-414-1519, Fax: 617-414-1515, E-mail: gpmm@med-med1.bu.edu. *Application contact:* Michelle Hall, Assistant Director of Admissions, 617-638-5121, Fax: 617-638-5740, E-mail: natashah@bu.edu.

Case Western Reserve University, School of Graduate Studies, Cleveland Clinic Lerner Research Institute–Molecular Medicine PhD Program, Cleveland, OH 44106. Offers PhD. *Faculty:* 125 full-time (35 women). *Students:* 18 full-time (8 women), 8 part-time (6 women); includes 9 minority (3 African Americans, 5 Asian Americans or Pacific Islanders, 1 Hispanic American), 6 international. Average age 25. 53 applicants, 28% accepted, 10 enrolled. *Degree requirements:* For doctorate, comprehensive exam, thesis/dissertation, seminar. *Entrance requirements:* For doctorate, GRE, 3 letters of reference, prior research experience. Additional exam requirements/recommendations for international students: Required—TOEFL (minimum score 550 paper-based; 213 computer-based; 79 iBT). *Application deadline:* For fall admission, 1/15 for domestic and international students. Application fee: $50. Electronic applications accepted. *Financial support:* Fellowships with full tuition reimbursements, health care benefits and stipends available. *Faculty research:* Cancer, cardiovascular disease, neuroscience, molecular biology, genetics. *Unit head:* Dr. Martha Cathcart, Director, 216-444-5222, E-mail: molmedphd@ccf.org. *Application contact:* Dr. Marcia Takacs Jarrett, Director of Research Education, 216-445-6690, E-mail: molmedphd@ccf.org.

Case Western Reserve University, School of Medicine and School of Graduate Studies, Graduate Programs in Medicine, Department of Molecular Medicine at the Lerner Research Institute, Cleveland, OH 44106. Offers PhD. *Degree requirements:* For doctorate, comprehensive exam, thesis/dissertation. *Entrance requirements:* For doctorate, GRE. Additional exam requirements/recommendations for international students: Required—TOEFL. Electronic applications accepted.

Cleveland State University, College of Graduate Studies, College of Science, Department of Chemistry, Cleveland, OH 44115. Offers analytical chemistry (MS); clinical chemistry (MS); clinical/bioanalytical chemistry (PhD), including clinical chemistry, molecular medicine; environmental chemistry (MS); inorganic chemistry (MS); organic chemistry (MS); physical chemistry (MS). Part-time and evening/weekend programs available. *Degree requirements:* For master's, thesis (for some programs); for doctorate, thesis/dissertation. *Entrance requirements:* For master's and doctorate, GRE General Test. Additional exam requirements/recommendations for international students: Required—TOEFL (minimum score 525 paper-based; 197 computer-based; 65 iBT). Electronic applications accepted. *Faculty research:* MALDI-TOF based DNA sequencing, development of ionic focusing HPLC, synthetic and structural studies of vanadium.

Cornell University, Graduate School, Graduate Fields of Comparative Biomedical Sciences, Field of Comparative Biomedical Sciences, Ithaca, NY 14853-0001. Offers cellular and molecular medicine (MS, PhD); developmental and reproductive biology (MS, PhD); infectious diseases (MS, PhD); population medicine and epidemiology (MS, PhD); structural and functional biology (MS, PhD). *Faculty:* 106 full-time (29 women). *Students:* 41 full-time (28 women); includes 1 minority (African American), 17 international. Average age 32. 32 applicants, 31% accepted, 9 enrolled. In 2009, 1 master's, 10 doctorates awarded. *Degree requirements:* For master's, thesis; for doctorate, comprehensive exam, thesis/dissertation. *Entrance requirements:* For master's and doctorate, GRE General Test, 2 letters of recommendation. Additional exam requirements/recommendations for international students: Required—TOEFL (minimum score 550 paper-based; 213 computer-based; 77 iBT). *Application deadline:* For fall admission, 12/15 for domestic students. Application fee: $70. Electronic applications accepted. *Expenses:* Tuition: Full-time $29,500. Required fees: $70. Full-time tuition and fees vary according to degree level, program and student level. *Financial support:* In 2009–10, 4 fellowships with full tuition reimbursements, 2 research assistantships with full tuition reimbursements were awarded; teaching assistantships with full tuition reimbursements, institutionally sponsored loans, scholarships/grants, health care benefits, tuition waivers (full and partial), and unspecified assistantships also available. Financial award applicants required to submit FAFSA. *Faculty research:* Receptors and signal transduction, viral and bacterial infectious diseases, tumor metastasis, clinical sciences/nutritional disease, developmental/neurological disorders. *Unit head:* Director of Graduate Studies, 607-253-3276, Fax: 607-253-3756. *Application contact:* Graduate Field Assistant, 607-253-3276, Fax: 607-253-3756, E-mail: graduate_edcvm@cornell.edu.

Dartmouth College, Arts and Sciences Graduate Programs, Program in Experimental and Molecular Medicine, Hanover, NH 03755. Offers biomedical physiology (PhD); cancer biology and molecular therapeutics (PhD); cardiovascular diseases (PhD); molecular pharmacology, toxicology and experimental therapeutics (PhD); neuroscience (PhD); MD/PhD. *Faculty:* 63 full-time (11 women). *Students:* 37 full-time (23 women); includes 3 minority (1 African American, 1 Asian American or Pacific Islander, 1 Hispanic American), 16 international. Average age 26. 128 applicants, 19% accepted, 15 enrolled. *Degree requirements:* For doctorate, comprehensive exam, thesis/dissertation. *Entrance requirements:* For doctorate, GRE, 3 letters of recommendation, interview, minimum GPA of 3.0. Additional exam requirements/recommendations for international students: Required—TOEFL (minimum score 620 paper-based; 260 computer-based; 105 iBT). *Application deadline:* For fall admission, 1/15 for domestic and international students. Application fee: $75. Electronic applications accepted. *Financial support:* In 2009–10, 31 students received support, including fellowships (averaging $25,500 per year), research assistantships (averaging $25,500 per year), teaching assistantships (averaging $25,500 per year); Dartmouth Fellowship (full tuition scholarship and prepaid health insurance plan with student stipends of $25,500) also available. *Unit head:* Dr. Allan Eastman, Director, 603-650-4933, Fax: 603-650-4932. *Application contact:* Gail L. Paige, Program Coordinator, 603-650-4933, Fax: 603-650-4932, E-mail: molecular.medicine@dartmouth.edu.

Dartmouth College, Program in Experimental and Molecular Medicine, Hanover, NH 03755. Offers biomedical physiology (PhD); cancer biology and molecular therapeutics (PhD); cardiovascular diseases (PhD); molecular pharmacology, toxicology and experimental therapeutics (PhD); neuroscience (PhD); MD/PhD. *Faculty:* 63 full-time (11 women). *Students:* 37 full-time (23 women); includes 3 minority (1 African American, 1 Asian American or Pacific Islander, 1 Hispanic American), 16 international. Average age 26. 128 applicants, 19% accepted, 15 enrolled. *Degree requirements:* For doctorate, comprehensive exam, thesis/dissertation. *Entrance requirements:* For doctorate, GRE General Test, 3 letters of recommendation. Additional exam requirements/recommendations for international students: Required—TOEFL (minimum score 620 paper-based; 260 computer-based; 105 iBT). *Application deadline:* For fall admission, 1/15 for domestic students, 10/1 for international students. Application fee: $75. Electronic applications accepted. *Financial support:* In 2009–10, 31 students received support, including fellowships with full tuition reimbursements available (averaging $25,500 per year), research assistantships with full tuition reimbursements available (averaging $25,500 per year), teaching assistantships with full tuition reimbursements available (averaging $25,500 per year); institutionally sponsored loans, traineeships, and unspecified assistantships also available. *Unit head:* Dr. Allan Eastman, Director, 603-650-4933, Fax: 603-650-6122. *Application contact:* Gail L. Paige, Program Coordinator, 603-650-4933, Fax: 603-650-6122, E-mail: molecular.medicine@dartmouth.edu.

Drexel University, College of Medicine, Biomedical Graduate Programs, Molecular Medicine Program, Philadelphia, PA 19129. Offers MS.

The George Washington University, Columbian College of Arts and Sciences, Institute for Biomedical Sciences, Program in Molecular Medicine, Washington, DC 20052. Offers molecular and cellular oncology (PhD); neurosciences (PhD); pharmacology and physiology (PhD). *Students:* 10 full-time (4 women), 15 part-time (11 women); includes 4 minority (2 African Americans, 2 Asian Americans or Pacific Islanders), 2 international. Average age 29. In 2009, 1 doctorate awarded. *Degree requirements:* For doctorate, comprehensive exam, thesis/dissertation, general exams. *Entrance requirements:* For doctorate, GRE General Test, interview, minimum GPA of 3.0. Additional exam requirements/recommendations for international students: Required—TOEFL (minimum score 600 paper-based; 250 computer-based). *Application deadline:* For fall admission, 1/2 priority date for domestic and international students. Applications are processed on a rolling basis. Application fee: $60. Electronic applications accepted. *Financial support:* In 2009–10, 10 students received support; fellowships with tuition reimbursements available, Federal Work-Study, institutionally sponsored loans, and tuition waivers available. Financial award application deadline: 2/1. *Unit head:* Bernard Bouscarel, Director, 202-994-2114, E-mail: beb@gwu.edu. *Application contact:* 202-994-2179, Fax: 202-994-0967, E-mail: gwibs@gwu.edu.

The Johns Hopkins University, School of Medicine, Graduate Programs in Medicine, Graduate Program in Cellular and Molecular Medicine, Baltimore, MD 21218-2699. Offers PhD. *Faculty:* 125 full-time (29 women). *Students:* 129 full-time (77 women); includes 50 minority (17 African Americans, 3 American Indian/Alaska Native, 21 Asian Americans or Pacific Islanders, 9 Hispanic Americans), 16 international. Average age 24. 243 applicants, 16% accepted, 21 enrolled. In 2009, 16 doctorates awarded. *Degree requirements:* For doctorate, comprehensive exam, thesis/dissertation, oral exam. *Entrance requirements:* For doctorate, GRE. Additional exam requirements/recommendations for international students: Required—TOEFL. *Application deadline:* For winter admission, 1/1 for domestic students. Application fee: $85. Electronic applications accepted. *Financial support:* In 2009–10, 17 fellowships with tuition reimbursements (averaging $27,125 per year) were awarded; scholarships/grants, health care benefits, and tuition waivers (full) also available. *Faculty research:* Cellular and molecular basis of disease. Total annual research expenditures: $100 million. *Unit head:* Dr. Rajini Rao, Director, 410-955-4732, Fax: 410-614-7294, E-mail: rrao@jhmi.edu. *Application contact:* Leslie Lichter-Mason, Admissions Administrator, 410-614-0391, Fax: 410-614-7294, E-mail: llichte2@jhmi.edu.

Medical College of Georgia, School of Graduate Studies, Program in Molecular Medicine, Augusta, GA 30912. Offers PhD. *Degree requirements:* For doctorate, comprehensive exam, thesis/dissertation. *Entrance requirements:* For doctorate, GRE General Test. Additional exam requirements/recommendations for international students: Required—TOEFL (minimum score 550 paper-based; 213 computer-based; 79 iBT). Electronic applications accepted. Full-time tuition and fees vary according to campus/location, program and student level. *Faculty research:* Developmental neurobiology, cancer, regenerative medicine, molecular chaperones molecular immunology.

North Shore–LIJ Graduate School of Molecular Medicine, Graduate Program, Manhasset, NY 11030. Offers PhD. *Faculty:* 40 full-time (14 women). *Students:* 12 full-time (3 women). Average age 30. 8 applicants, 13% accepted, 1 enrolled. *Degree requirements:* For doctorate, comprehensive exam, thesis/dissertation. *Entrance requirements:* For doctorate, MD. *Application deadline:* Applications are processed on a rolling basis. Application fee: $25. *Financial support:* In 2009–10, 9 students received support, including 9 fellowships with tuition reimbursements available (averaging $50,000 per year); health care benefits and tuition waivers (full) also available. *Faculty research:* Cardiopulmonary disease, cancer, inflammation, genetics of complex disorders, cytokine biology. Total annual research expenditures: $20 million. *Unit head:* Dr. Bettie M. Steinberg, Dean, 516-562-1159, Fax: 516-562-1022, E-mail: bsteinbe@lij.edu.

Molecular Medicine

North Shore–LIJ Graduate School of Molecular Medicine (continued)
Application contact: Emilia C. Hristis, Associate Dean, 516-562-3405, Fax: 516-562-1022, E-mail: ehristis@nshs.edu.

Penn State Hershey Medical Center, College of Medicine, Graduate School Programs in the Biomedical Sciences, The Huck Institutes of the Life Sciences, Intercollege Graduate Program in Molecular Medicine, Hershey, PA 17033. Offers MS, PhD, MD/PhD. *Students:* 57 applicants, 5% accepted, 3 enrolled. In 2009, 9 master's awarded. Terminal master's awarded for partial completion of doctoral program. *Degree requirements:* For master's, thesis or alternative; for doctorate, comprehensive exam, thesis/dissertation. *Application deadline:* For fall admission, 1/31 for domestic students, 2/1 priority date for international students. Applications are processed on a rolling basis. Application fee: $65. Electronic applications accepted. *Expenses:* Tuition, state resident: part-time $644 per credit. Tuition, nonresident: part-time $1142 per credit. Required fees: $22 per semester. *Financial support:* In 2009–10, research assistantships with full tuition reimbursements (averaging $22,260 per year); fellowships with full tuition reimbursements, career-related internships or fieldwork, scholarships/grants, health care benefits, and unspecified assistantships also available. *Faculty research:* Transitional research, diabetes and retinal vessels, stem cell differentiation/ osteogenesis, cancer, malaria. *Unit head:* Dr. Charles Lang, Head, 717-531-8982, E-mail: grad-hmc@psu.edu. *Application contact:* Kathy Shuey, Administrative Assistant, 717-531-8982, Fax: 717-531-0786, E-mail: grad-hmc@psu.edu.

Queen's University at Kingston, School of Graduate Studies and Research, Faculty of Health Sciences, Department of Pathology and Molecular Medicine, Kingston, ON K7L 3N6, Canada. Offers M Sc, PhD. Part-time programs available. *Degree requirements:* For master's, thesis; for doctorate, comprehensive exam, thesis/dissertation. *Entrance requirements:* Additional exam requirements/recommendations for international students: Required—TOEFL. *Faculty research:* Immunopathology, cancer biology, immunology and metastases, cell differentiation, blood coagulation.

Texas A&M Health Science Center, Graduate School of Biomedical Sciences, Department of Molecular and Cellular Medicine, College Station, TX 77840. Offers PhD. *Degree requirements:* For doctorate, thesis/dissertation. *Entrance requirements:* For doctorate, GRE General Test. *Faculty research:* Immunology, cell and membrane biology, protein biochemistry, molecular genetics, parasitology, vertebrate embryogenesis and microbiology.

University of Chicago, Division of the Biological Sciences, Biomedical Sciences Cluster: Cancer Biology, Immunology, Molecular Metabolism and Nutrition, Pathology, and Microbiology, Department of Pathology, Chicago, IL 60637-1513. Offers molecular pathogenesis and molecular medicine (PhD). *Faculty:* 47 full-time (10 women). *Students:* 30 full-time (13 women); includes 7 minority (1 African American, 5 Asian Americans or Pacific Islanders, 1 Hispanic American). Average age 28. 37 applicants, 22% accepted, 4 enrolled. In 2009, 6 doctorates awarded. *Degree requirements:* For doctorate, thesis/dissertation, ethics class, 2 teaching assistantships. *Entrance requirements:* For doctorate, GRE General Test. Additional exam requirements/recommendations for international students: Required—IELTS (minimum score 7); Recommended—TOEFL (minimum score 600 paper-based; 250 computer-based; 104 iBT). *Application deadline:* For fall admission, 12/1 priority date for domestic and international students. Application fee: $55. Electronic applications accepted. *Financial support:* In 2009–10, 30 students received support, including fellowships with full tuition reimbursements available (averaging $29,781 per year), research assistantships with full tuition reimbursements available (averaging $29,781 per year); institutionally sponsored loans, scholarships/grants, traineeships, and health care benefits also available. Financial award applicants required to submit FAFSA. *Faculty research:* Vascular biology, apolipoproteins, cardiovascular disease, immunopathology. Total annual research expenditures: $18 million. *Unit head:* Dr. Stephen Meredith, Program Director, 773-702-1267, Fax: 773-834-5251. *Application contact:* Kristin Reepmeyer, Administrative Assistant, 773-702-3940, Fax: 773-702-4634, E-mail: reepmeyer@bsd.uchicago.edu.

University of Cincinnati, Graduate School, College of Medicine, Graduate Programs in Biomedical Sciences, Program in Pathobiology and Molecular Medicine, Cincinnati, OH 45221. Offers pathology (PhD), including anatomic pathology, laboratory medicine, pathobiology and molecular medicine. *Degree requirements:* For doctorate, thesis/dissertation, qualifying exam. *Entrance requirements:* For doctorate, GRE General Test. Additional exam requirements/recommendations for international students: Required—TOEFL (minimum score 620 paper-based; 260 computer-based). Electronic applications accepted. *Faculty research:* Cardiovascular and lipid disorders, digestive and kidney disease, endocrine and metabolic disorders, hematologic and oncogenic, immunology and infectious disease.

University of Maryland, Baltimore, Graduate School, Graduate Program in Life Sciences, Program in Molecular Medicine, Baltimore, MD 21201. Offers cancer biology (PhD); cell and molecular physiology (PhD); human genetics and genomic medicine (PhD); molecular medicine (MS); molecular toxicology and pharmacology (PhD); MD/PhD. *Students:* 61 full-time (37 women), 9 part-time (5 women); includes 19 minority (7 African Americans, 9 Asian Americans or Pacific Islanders, 3 Hispanic Americans), 8 international. Average age 26. 324 applicants, 15% accepted, 20 enrolled. In 2009, 4 master's, 1 doctorate awarded. *Entrance requirements:* Additional exam requirements/recommendations for international students: Required—TOEFL (minimum score 600 paper-based; 100 iBT); Recommended—IELTS (minimum score 7). *Application deadline:* For fall admission, 1/15 for domestic and international students. Application fee: $50. Electronic applications accepted. *Expenses:* Tuition, state resident: full-time $7290; part-time $405 per credit hour. Tuition, nonresident: full-time $12,780; part-time $710 per credit hour. Required fees: $774; $10 per credit hour. $297 per semester. Tuition and fees vary according to course load, degree level and program. *Financial support:* In 2009–10, research assistantships with partial tuition reimbursements (averaging $25,000 per year); fellowships also available. Financial award application deadline: 3/1. *Unit head:* Dr. Dudley Strickland, Director, 410-706-8010, E-mail: dstrickland@som.umaryland.edu. *Application contact:* Sharron Graves, Program Coordinator, 410-706-6044, Fax: 410-706-6040, E-mail: sgraves@som.umaryland.edu.

University of Medicine and Dentistry of New Jersey, Graduate School of Biomedical Sciences, Graduate Programs in Biomedical Sciences–Newark, Department of Cell Biology and Molecular Medicine, Newark, NJ 07107. Offers PhD. *Students:* 14 full-time (10 women), 10 international. *Degree requirements:* For doctorate, thesis/dissertation, qualifying exam. *Entrance requirements:* For doctorate, GRE General Test. Additional exam requirements/recommendations for international students: Required—TOEFL. *Application deadline:* For fall admission, 2/1 for domestic students. Applications are processed on a rolling basis. Application fee: $40. Electronic applications accepted. *Financial support:* Fellowships, research assistantships, Federal Work-Study, institutionally sponsored loans, and tuition waivers (full and partial) available. Financial award application deadline: 5/1. *Unit head:* Dr. Dorothy Vatner, Program Director, 973-972-1993, Fax: 973-972-7489, E-mail: vatnerdo@umdnj.edu. *Application contact:* Dr. Dorothy Vatner, Program Director, 973-972-1993, Fax: 973-972-7489, E-mail: vatnerdo@umdnj.edu.

The University of Texas Health Science Center at San Antonio, Graduate School of Biomedical Sciences, Program in Molecular Medicine, San Antonio, TX 78245-3207. Offers MS, PhD. *Faculty:* 11 full-time (5 women). *Students:* 36 full-time (15 women); includes 4 minority (2 African Americans, 1 Asian American or Pacific Islander, 1 Hispanic American), 26 international. Average age 24. 37 applicants, 32% accepted, 6 enrolled. In 2009, 1 master's, 7 doctorates awarded. Terminal master's awarded for partial completion of doctoral program. *Degree requirements:* For master's, comprehensive exam, thesis, written and oral qualifying exam; for doctorate, comprehensive exam, thesis/dissertation, written and oral qualifying exam. *Entrance requirements:* For master's and doctorate, GRE General Test. Additional exam requirements/recommendations for international students: Required—TOEFL (minimum score 560 paper-based; 220 computer-based; 68 iBT). *Application deadline:* For fall admission, 2/1 priority date for domestic and international students. Applications are processed on a rolling basis. Application fee: $0. Electronic applications accepted. *Expenses:* Tuition, state resident: full-time $2832; part-time $118 per credit hour. Tuition, nonresident: full-time $10,896; part-time $454 per credit hour. Required fees: $884 per semester. One-time fee: $70. *Financial support:* In 2009–10, 3 fellowships with full and partial tuition reimbursements (averaging $30,000 per year), 33 teaching assistantships (averaging $26,000 per year) were awarded; career-related internships or fieldwork, health care benefits, and unspecified assistantships also available. Financial award application deadline: 3/9; financial award applicants required to submit FAFSA. *Faculty research:* DNA repair, tumor suppressor genes, vision in drosophila, gene expression (nervous system), cell-type specific gene regulation and development. Total annual research expenditures: $3.3 million. *Unit head:* Zelton Dave Sharp, Chair, 210-567-7200, Fax: 210-567-7277, E-mail: sharp@uthscsa.edu. *Application contact:* Barbara A. Christy, Chair, Committee on Graduate Studies, 210-567-7227, Fax: 210-567-7277, E-mail: christy@uthscsa.edu.

University of Washington, Graduate School, School of Public Health, Department of Global Health, Graduate Program in Pathobiology, Seattle, WA 98195. Offers PhD. *Students:* 35 full-time (27 women), 3 part-time (all women); includes 5 minority (2 African Americans, 1 Asian American or Pacific Islander, 2 Hispanic Americans), 7 international. Average age 29. 50 applicants, 18% accepted, 5 enrolled. In 2009, 7 doctorates awarded. Terminal master's awarded for partial completion of doctoral program. *Degree requirements:* For doctorate, comprehensive exam, thesis/dissertation. *Entrance requirements:* For doctorate, GRE General Test, minimum GPA of 3.0. Additional exam requirements/recommendations for international students: Required—TOEFL. *Application deadline:* For fall admission, 10/1 for domestic students, 11/1 for international students. Application fee: $50. Electronic applications accepted. *Financial support:* In 2009–10, 34 students received support, including 3 fellowships with full tuition reimbursements available (averaging $27,348 per year), 26 research assistantships with full tuition reimbursements available (averaging $27,348 per year); career-related internships or fieldwork, institutionally sponsored loans, scholarships/grants, traineeships, and unspecified assistantships also available. Financial award application deadline: 12/1; financial award applicants required to submit FAFSA. *Faculty research:* Pathogenesis of chlamydiae, molecular biology of parasites, signal transduction, antigenic analysis, molecular biology of tumor viruses, malaria. *Unit head:* Dr. Andreas Stergachis, Acting Chair, 206-543-8350, Fax: 206-543-3873, E-mail: stergach@u.washington.edu. *Application contact:* Mary Conrad, Manager of Student Services, 206-543-4338, Fax: 206-543-3873, E-mail: pathobio@u.washington.edu.

Wake Forest University, School of Medicine and Graduate School of Arts and Sciences, Graduate Programs in Medicine, Molecular Genetics and Genomics Program, Winston-Salem, NC 27109. Offers PhD, MD/PhD. *Degree requirements:* For doctorate, thesis/dissertation. *Entrance requirements:* For doctorate, GRE General Test. Additional exam requirements/recommendations for international students: Required—TOEFL. Electronic applications accepted. *Faculty research:* Control of gene expression, molecular pathogenesis, protein biosynthesis, cell development, clinical cytogenetics.

Wake Forest University, School of Medicine and Graduate School of Arts and Sciences, Graduate Programs in Medicine, Program in Molecular Medicine, Winston-Salem, NC 27109. Offers MS, PhD, MD/PhD. *Degree requirements:* For master's, thesis; for doctorate, thesis/dissertation. *Entrance requirements:* For master's and doctorate, GRE General Test. Additional exam requirements/recommendations for international students: Required—TOEFL. Electronic applications accepted. *Faculty research:* Human biology and disease, scientific basis of medicine, cellular and molecular mechanisms of health and disease.

Yale University, School of Medicine and Graduate School of Arts and Sciences, Combined Program in Biological and Biomedical Sciences (BBS), Pharmacological Sciences and Molecular Medicine Track, New Haven, CT 06520. Offers PhD, MD/PhD. *Degree requirements:* For doctorate, thesis/dissertation. *Entrance requirements:* For doctorate, GRE General Test. Additional exam requirements/recommendations for international students: Required—TOEFL. *Application deadline:* For fall admission, 12/6 for domestic and international students. Electronic applications accepted. *Financial support:* Fellowships, research assistantships available. *Unit head:* Dr. Gerry Shadel, Co-Director, 203-785-2475, E-mail: bbs.pharm@yale.edu. *Application contact:* Dr. Gerry Shadel, Co-Director, 203-785-2475, E-mail: bbs.pharm@yale.edu.

Structural Biology

Baylor College of Medicine, Graduate School of Biomedical Sciences, Program in Structural and Computational Biology and Molecular Biophysics, Houston, TX 77030-3498. Offers PhD, MD/PhD. *Faculty:* 71 full-time (11 women). *Students:* 48 full-time (19 women); includes 5 minority (3 Asian Americans or Pacific Islanders, 2 Hispanic Americans), 18 international. Average age 25. In 2009, 6 doctorates awarded. *Degree requirements:* For doctorate, thesis/dissertation, public defense. *Entrance requirements:* For doctorate, GRE General Test, GRE Subject Test (strongly recommended), minimum GPA of 3.0. Additional exam requirements/recommendations for international students: Required—TOEFL. *Application deadline:* For fall admission, 1/1 for domestic students. Application fee: $0. Electronic applications accepted. *Financial support:* In 2009–10, 48 students received support; fellowships, research assistantships, career-related internships or fieldwork, Federal Work-Study, institutionally sponsored loans, health care benefits, and students receive a scholarship unless there are grant funds available to pay tuition available. Financial award applicants required to submit FAFSA. *Faculty research:* X-ray and electron crystallography, light and electron microscopy, computer image reconstruction, molecular spectroscopy. *Unit head:* Dr. Wah Chiu, Director, 713-798-6985. *Application contact:* Lourdes Fernandez, Graduate Program Administrator, 713-798-6557, Fax: 713-798-6325.

See Close-Up on page 259.

Brandeis University, Graduate School of Arts and Sciences, Program in Biophysics and Structural Biology, Waltham, MA 02454-9110. Offers MS, PhD. *Faculty:* 24 full-time (8 women). *Students:* 16 full-time (4 women); includes 1 minority (Hispanic American), 5 international. Average age 26. 32 applicants, 25% accepted, 5 enrolled. *Degree requirements:* For master's, thesis; for doctorate, one foreign language, thesis/dissertation. *Entrance requirements:* For doctorate, GRE General Test, resume, 3 letters of recommendation. Additional exam requirements/recommendations for international students: Required—TOEFL (minimum score 600 paper-based; 250 computer-based; 100 iBT); Recommended—IELTS (minimum score 7). *Application deadline:* For fall admission, 1/15 priority date for domestic students. Applications are processed on a rolling basis. Application fee: $75. Electronic applications accepted. *Financial support:* In 2009–10, 12 students received support, including 5 fellowships with full tuition reimbursements available (averaging $27,500 per year), 11 research assistantships with full tuition reimbursements available (averaging $27,500 per year), teaching assistantships with partial tuition reimbursements available (averaging $3,200 per year); scholarships/grants, traineeships, health care benefits, and tuition waivers (full and partial) also available. Support available to part-time students. Financial award application deadline: 4/15; financial award applicants required to submit FAFSA. *Faculty research:* Biophysical chemistry, macromolecular structure and function, single molecule biophysics, macromolecules. *Unit head:* Dr. Dorothee Kern, Chair, 781-736-2354, Fax: 781-736-2349, E-mail: dkern@brandeis.edu. *Application contact:* Marcia Cabral, Department Administrator, 781-736-3100, Fax: 781-736-3107, E-mail: cabral@brandeis.edu.

Carnegie Mellon University, Mellon College of Science, Joint Pitt + CMU Molecular Biophysics and Structural Biology Graduate Program, Pittsburgh, PA 15213-3891. Offers PhD. *Degree requirements:* For doctorate, comprehensive exam, thesis/dissertation. *Entrance requirements:* For doctorate, GRE General Test. Additional exam requirements/recommendations for international students: Required—TOEFL (minimum score 600 paper-based; 250 computer-based; 100 iBT), IELTS (minimum score 7). Electronic applications accepted. *Faculty research:* Structural biology, protein dynamics and folding, computational biophysics, molecular informatics, membrane biophysics and ion channels, NMR, x-ray crystallography cryaelectron microscopy.

Cornell University, Graduate School, Graduate Fields of Comparative Biomedical Sciences, Field of Comparative Biomedical Sciences, Ithaca, NY 14853-0001. Offers cellular and molecular medicine (MS, PhD); developmental and reproductive biology (MS, PhD); infectious diseases (MS, PhD); population medicine and epidemiology (MS, PhD); structural and functional biology (MS, PhD). *Faculty:* 106 full-time (29 women). *Students:* 41 full-time (28 women); includes 1 minority (African American), 17 international. Average age 32. 32 applicants, 31% accepted, 9 enrolled. In 2009, 1 master's, 10 doctorates awarded. *Degree requirements:* For master's, thesis; for doctorate, comprehensive exam, thesis/dissertation. *Entrance requirements:* For master's and doctorate, GRE General Test, 2 letters of recommendation. Additional exam requirements/recommendations for international students: Required—TOEFL (minimum score 550 paper-based; 213 computer-based; 77 iBT). *Application deadline:* For fall admission, 12/15 for domestic students. Application fee: $70. Electronic applications accepted. *Expenses:* Tuition: Full-time $29,500. Required fees: $70. Full-time tuition and fees vary according to degree level, program and student level. *Financial support:* In 2009–10, 4 fellowships with full tuition reimbursements, 2 research assistantships with full tuition reimbursements were awarded; teaching assistantships with full tuition reimbursements, institutionally sponsored loans, scholarships/grants, health care benefits, tuition waivers (full and partial), and unspecified assistantships also available. Financial award applicants required to submit FAFSA. *Faculty research:* Receptors and signal transduction, viral and bacterial infectious diseases, tumor metastasis, clinical sciences/nutritional disease, developmental/neurological disorders. *Unit head:* Director of Graduate Studies, 607-253-3276, Fax: 607-253-3756. *Application contact:* Graduate Field Assistant, 607-253-3276, Fax: 607-253-3756, E-mail: graduate_edcvm@cornell.edu.

Cornell University, Joan and Sanford I. Weill Medical College and Graduate School of Medical Sciences, Weill Cornell Graduate School of Medical Sciences, Biochemistry, Cell and Molecular Biology Allied Program, New York, NY 10065. Offers MS, PhD. *Faculty:* 100 full-time (26 women). *Students:* 148 full-time (96 women); includes 16 minority (2 African Americans, 8 Asian Americans or Pacific Islanders, 6 Hispanic Americans), 71 international. Average age 22. 295 applicants, 16% accepted, 17 enrolled. In 2009, 19 doctorates awarded. Terminal master's awarded for partial completion of doctoral program. *Degree requirements:* For master's, comprehensive exam; for doctorate, thesis/dissertation; final exam. *Entrance requirements:* For doctorate, GRE General Test, background in genetics, molecular biology, chemistry, or biochemistry. Additional exam requirements/recommendations for international students: Required—TOEFL. *Application deadline:* For fall admission, 12/1 for domestic students. Application fee: $60. Electronic applications accepted. *Expenses:* Tuition: Full-time $44,650. Required fees: $2805. *Financial support:* In 2009–10, 12 fellowships (averaging $21,900 per year) were awarded; scholarships/grants, health care benefits, and stipends (given to all students) also available. *Faculty research:* Molecular structure determination, protein structure, gene structure, stem cell biology, control of gene expression, DNA replication, chromosome maintenance, RNA biosynthesis. *Unit head:* Dr. David Eliezer, Co-Director, 212-746-6557, Fax: 212-717-3047. *Application contact:* Linda Smith, Assistant Dean of Admissions, 212-746-6565, Fax: 212-746-8906, E-mail: lis2025@med.cornell.edu.

Duke University, Graduate School, Program in Structural Biology and Biophysics, Durham, NC 27710. Offers Certificate. Students must be enrolled in a participating PhD program. *Faculty:* 25 full-time. *Students:* 1 (woman) full-time. 26 applicants, 23% accepted, 0 enrolled. *Entrance requirements:* For degree, GRE General Test, GRE Subject Test. Additional exam requirements/recommendations for international students: Required—TOEFL (minimum score 550 paper-based; 213 computer-based; 83 iBT), IELTS (minimum score 7). *Application deadline:* For fall admission, 12/8 priority date for domestic and international students. Application fee: $75. *Financial support:* Application deadline: 12/31. *Unit head:* David Richardson, Director of Graduate Studies, 919-684-6559, Fax: 919-684-8346, E-mail: cmbtgp@biochem.duke.edu. *Application contact:* Cynthia Robertson, Associate Dean for Enrollment Services, 919-684-3913, E-mail: grad-admissions@duke.edu.

Florida State University, The Graduate School, College of Arts and Sciences, Program in Molecular Biophysics, Tallahassee, FL 32306. Offers biochemistry, molecular and cell biology (PhD); computational structural biology (PhD); molecular biophysics (PhD). *Faculty:* 49 full-time (6 women). *Students:* 22 full-time (8 women); includes 6 minority (5 Asian Americans or Pacific Islanders, 1 Hispanic American). Average age 28. 30 applicants, 33% accepted, 7 enrolled. In 2009, 5 doctorates awarded. *Degree requirements:* For doctorate, comprehensive exam, thesis/dissertation, teaching 1 term in professor's major department. *Entrance requirements:* For doctorate, GRE General Test. Additional exam requirements/recommendations for international students: Required—TOEFL (minimum score 600 paper-based; 250 computer-based; 100 iBT). *Application deadline:* For fall admission, 2/15 for domestic students, 3/15 for international students; for spring admission, 11/2 for international students. Applications are processed on a rolling basis. Application fee: $30. Electronic applications accepted. *Expenses:* Tuition, state resident: full-time $7413. Tuition, nonresident: full-time $22,567. *Financial support:* In 2009–10, 21 students received support, including fellowships with partial tuition reimbursements available (averaging $21,000 per year), 18 research assistantships with partial tuition reimbursements available (averaging $21,000 per year), 4 teaching assistantships with partial tuition reimbursements available (averaging $21,000 per year); scholarships/grants, health care benefits, and unspecified assistantships also available. Financial award applicants required to submit FAFSA. *Faculty research:* Protein and nucleic acid structure and function, membrane protein structure, computational biophysics, 3-D image reconstruction. Total annual research expenditures: $1.4 million. *Unit head:* Dr. Geoffrey Strouse, Director, 850-644-0056, Fax: 850-644-7244, E-mail: strouse@chem.fsu.edu. *Application contact:* Dr. Kerry Maddox, Academic Coordinator, Graduate Programs, 850-644-1012, Fax: 850-644-7244, E-mail: bkmaddox@sb.fsu.edu.

Harvard University, Graduate School of Arts and Sciences, Department of Systems Biology, Cambridge, MA 02138. Offers PhD. *Degree requirements:* For doctorate, thesis/dissertation, lab rotation, qualifying examination. *Entrance requirements:* For doctorate, GRE. Additional exam requirements/recommendations for international students: Required—TOEFL. Electronic applications accepted. *Expenses:* Tuition: Full-time $33,696. Required fees: $1126. Full-time tuition and fees vary according to program.

Illinois State University, Graduate School, College of Arts and Sciences, Department of Biological Sciences, Normal, IL 61790-2200. Offers animal behavior (MS); bacteriology (MS); biochemistry (MS); biological sciences (MS); biology (PhD); biophysics (MS); biotechnology (MS); botany (MS, PhD); cell biology (MS); conservation biology (MS); developmental biology (MS); ecology (MS, PhD); entomology (MS); evolutionary biology (MS); genetics (MS, PhD); immunology (MS); microbiology (MS, PhD); molecular biology (MS); molecular genetics (MS); neurobiology (MS); neuroscience (MS); parasitology (MS); physiology (MS, PhD); plant biology (MS); plant molecular biology (MS); plant sciences (MS); structural biology (MS); zoology (MS, PhD). Part-time programs available. *Degree requirements:* For master's, thesis or alternative; for doctorate, variable foreign language requirement, thesis/dissertation, 2 terms of residency. *Entrance requirements:* For master's, GRE General Test, minimum GPA of 2.6 in last 60 hours of course work; for doctorate, GRE General Test. *Faculty research:* Redoc balance and drug development in schistosoma mansoni, control of the growth of listeria monocytogenes at low temperature, regulation of cell expansion and microtubule function by SPRI, CRUI: physiology and fitness consequences of different life history phenotypes.

Iowa State University of Science and Technology, Graduate College, Interdisciplinary Programs, Bioinformatics and Computational Biology Program, Ames, IA 50011. Offers MS, PhD. *Students:* 52 full-time (19 women), 2 part-time (1 woman); includes 3 minority (all Asian Americans or Pacific Islanders), 34 international. In 2009, 2 master's, 11 doctorates awarded. *Degree requirements:* For doctorate, thesis/dissertation. *Entrance requirements:* For doctorate, GRE General Test. Additional exam requirements/recommendations for international students: Required—TOEFL (minimum score 550 paper-based; 213 computer-based; 79 iBT) or IELTS (minimum score 6.5). *Application deadline:* For fall admission, 1/15 priority date for domestic students, 1/15 for international students; for spring admission, 10/15 for domestic and international students. Application fee: $40 ($90 for international students). Electronic applications accepted. *Expenses:* Tuition, state resident: full-time $6716. Tuition, nonresident: full-time $8908. Tuition and fees vary according to course level, course load, program and student level. *Financial support:* In 2009–10, 48 research assistantships with full and partial tuition reimbursements (averaging $18,330 per year), 3 teaching assistantships (averaging $17,000 per year) were awarded; fellowships with full tuition reimbursements, scholarships/grants, traineeships, health care benefits, and unspecified assistantships also available. *Faculty research:* Functional and structural genomics, genome evolution, macromolecular structure and function, mathematical biology and biological statistics, metabolic and developmental networks. *Unit head:* Dr. Volker Brendel, Chair, Supervising Committee, 515-294-5122, Fax: 515-294-6790, E-mail: bcb@iastate.edu. *Application contact:* Dr. Volker Brendel, Chair, Supervising Committee, 515-294-5122, Fax: 515-294-6790, E-mail: bcb@iastate.edu.

Massachusetts Institute of Technology, School of Science, Department of Biology, Cambridge, MA 02139-4307. Offers biochemistry (PhD); biological oceanography (PhD); biology (PhD); biophysical chemistry and molecular structure (PhD); cell biology (PhD); computational and systems biology (PhD); developmental biology (PhD); genetics (PhD); immunology (PhD); microbiology (PhD); molecular biology (PhD); neurobiology (PhD). *Faculty:* 54 full-time (14 women). *Students:* 237 full-time (128 women); includes 65 minority (4 African Americans, 2 American Indian/Alaska Native, 33 Asian Americans or Pacific Islanders, 26 Hispanic Americans), 25 international. Average age 26. 645 applicants, 18% accepted, 49 enrolled. In 2009, 41 doctorates awarded. *Degree requirements:* For doctorate, comprehensive exam, thesis/dissertation. *Entrance requirements:* For doctorate, GRE General Test. Additional exam requirements/recommendations for international students: Required—TOEFL (minimum score 577 paper-based; 233 computer-based), IELTS (minimum score 6.5). *Application deadline:* For fall admission, 12/1 for domestic and international students. Application fee: $75. Electronic applications accepted. *Expenses:* Tuition: Full-time $37,510; part-time $585 per unit. Required fees: $272. *Financial support:* In 2009–10, 218 students received support, including 113 fellowships with tuition reimbursements available (averaging $31,816 per year), 109 research assistantships with tuition reimbursements available (averaging $29,254 per year); teaching assistantships with tuition reimbursements available, Federal Work-Study, institutionally sponsored loans, scholarships/grants, traineeships, health care benefits, and unspecified assistantships also available. *Faculty research:* DNA recombination, transcription and gene regulation, signal transduction, cell cycle, neuronal cell fate, replication and repair. Total annual research expenditures: $114 million. *Unit head:* Prof. Chris Kaiser, Head, 617-253-4701, E-mail: mitbio@mit.edu. *Application contact:* Biology Education Office, 617-253-3717, Fax: 617-258-9329, E-mail: gradbio@mit.edu.

Mayo Graduate School, Graduate Programs in Biomedical Sciences, Programs in Biochemistry, Structural Biology, Cell Biology, and Genetics, Rochester, MN 55905. Offers biochemistry and structural biology (PhD); cell biology and genetics (PhD); molecular biology (PhD). *Degree requirements:* For doctorate, oral defense of dissertation, qualifying oral and written exam. *Entrance requirements:* For doctorate, GRE, 1 year of chemistry, biology, calculus, and physics. Additional exam requirements/recommendations for international students: Required—TOEFL. Electronic applications accepted. *Faculty research:* Gene structure and function, membranes and receptors/cytoskeleton, oncogenes and growth factors, protein structure and function, steroid hormonal action.

Michigan State University, The Graduate School, College of Natural Science, Quantitative Biology Program, East Lansing, MI 48824. Offers PhD. *Faculty:* 4 full-time (0 women). *Students:* 10 full-time (5 women), 8 international. Average age 27. *Expenses:* Tuition, state resident: part-time $478.25 per credit hour. Tuition, nonresident: part-time $966.50 per credit hour. Part-time tuition and fees vary according to program. Total annual research expenditures: $21.6 million. *Unit head:* Dr. Robert Hausinger, Co-Director, 517-884-5404, E-mail: hausinge@msu.edu. *Application contact:* Helen Geiger, Administrative Assistant, 517-432-9895, Fax: 517-353-9334, E-mail: qbmi@msu.edu.

New York University, School of Medicine, New York, NY 10012-1019. Offers biomedical sciences (PhD), including biomedical imaging, cellular and molecular biology, computational biology, developmental genetics, medical and molecular parasitology, microbiology, molecular oncobiology and immunology, neuroscience and physiology, pathobiology, pharmacology, structural biology; clinical investigation (MS); medicine (MD); MD/MA; MD/MPA; MD/MS; MD/PhD. *Accreditation:* LCME/AMA (one or more programs are accredited). *Faculty:* 1,493 full-time (558 women), 327 part-time/adjunct (122 women). *Students:* 747 full-time (360 women); includes 275 minority (23 African Americans, 5 American Indian/Alaska Native, 199 Asian Americans or Pacific Islanders, 48 Hispanic Americans), 2 international. Average age 24. 7,568 applicants, 7% accepted, 213 enrolled. In 2009, 164 first professional degrees, 13 master's, 50 doctorates awarded. *Degree requirements:* For master's, comprehensive exam, thesis; for doctorate, comprehensive exam, thesis/dissertation. *Entrance requirements:* MCAT. Additional exam requirements/recommendations for international students: Required—TOEFL. *Application deadline:* For fall admission, 10/15 for domestic students; for winter admission, 12/18 for domestic students, 12/15 for international students. Application fee: $100. *Expenses:* Contact institution. *Financial support:* In 2009–10, 524 students received support, including 29 fellowships with full tuition reimbursements available (averaging $31,000 per year), 47 research assistantships with full tuition reimbursements available (averaging $31,000 per year); teaching assistantships, Federal Work-Study, institutionally sponsored loans, and health care benefits also available. Financial award application deadline: 3/1; financial award applicants required to submit FAFSA. *Faculty research:* AIDS, cancer, neuroscience, molecular biology, neuroscience, cell biology and molecular genetics, structural biology, microbial pathogenesis and host defense, pharmacology, molecular oncology and immunology. Total annual research expenditures: $201.1 million. *Unit head:* Dr. Robert Grossman, Dean, 212-263-3269, Fax: 212-263- 1828. *Application contact:* Dr. Nancy Genieser, Associate Dean, Admissions, 212-263-5290, Fax: 212-263-0720, E-mail: nancy.genieser@nyumc.org.

New York University, School of Medicine and Graduate School of Arts and Science, Sackler Institute of Graduate Biomedical Sciences, Program in Structural Biology, New York, NY 10012-1019. Offers PhD. *Degree requirements:* For doctorate, thesis/dissertation, qualifying examination. *Entrance requirements:* For doctorate, GRE General Test, GRE Subject Test in biology or chemistry (recommended). Additional exam requirements/recommendations for international students: Required—TOEFL. *Expenses:* Tuition: Full-time $30,528; part-time $1272 per credit. Required fees: $2177.

Northwestern University, The Graduate School and Judd A. and Marjorie Weinberg College of Arts and Sciences, Interdepartmental Biological Sciences Program (IBiS), Evanston, IL

Structural Biology

Northwestern University (continued)

60208. Offers biochemistry, molecular biology, and cell biology (PhD), including biochemistry, cell and molecular biology, molecular biophysics, structural biology; biotechnology (PhD); cell and molecular biology (PhD); developmental biology and genetics (PhD); hormone action and signal transduction (PhD); neuroscience (PhD); structural biology, biochemistry, and biophysics (PhD). Program participants include the Departments of Biochemistry, Molecular Biology, and Cell Biology; Chemistry; Neurobiology and Physiology; Chemical Engineering; Civil Engineering; and Evanston Hospital. *Degree requirements:* For doctorate, thesis/dissertation, qualifying exam. *Entrance requirements:* For doctorate, GRE General Test. Additional exam requirements/recommendations for international students: Required—TOEFL (minimum score 600 paper-based). Electronic applications accepted. *Faculty research:* Developmental genetics, gene regulation, DNA-protein interactions, biological clocks, bioremediation.

Northwestern University, Northwestern University Feinberg School of Medicine and Interdepartmental Programs, Integrated Graduate Programs in the Life Sciences, Chicago, IL 60611. Offers cancer biology (PhD); cell biology (PhD); developmental biology (PhD); evolutionary biology (PhD); immunology and microbial pathogenesis (PhD); molecular biology and genetics (PhD); neurobiology (PhD); pharmacology and toxicology (PhD); structural biology and biochemistry (PhD). *Degree requirements:* For doctorate, comprehensive exam, thesis/dissertation, written and oral qualifying exams. *Entrance requirements:* For doctorate, GRE General Test. Additional exam requirements/recommendations for international students: Required—TOEFL (minimum score 600 paper-based; 250 computer-based). Electronic applications accepted.

Stanford University, School of Medicine, Graduate Programs in Medicine, Department of Structural Biology, Stanford, CA 94305-9991. Offers PhD. *Degree requirements:* For doctorate, thesis/dissertation. *Entrance requirements:* For doctorate, GRE General Test, GRE Subject Test. Additional exam requirements/recommendations for international students: Required—TOEFL. Electronic applications accepted. *Expenses:* Tuition: Full-time $37,380; part-time $2760 per quarter. Required fees: $501.

Stony Brook University, State University of New York, Graduate School, College of Arts and Sciences, Department of Biochemistry and Cell Biology, Program in Biochemistry and Structural Biology, Stony Brook, NY 11794. Offers PhD. *Students:* 26 full-time (14 women); includes 1 African American, 1 Asian American or Pacific Islander, 19 international. Average age 27. 94 applicants, 22% accepted. In 2009, 8 doctorates awarded. *Expenses:* Tuition, state resident: full-time $8370; part-time $349 per credit. Tuition, nonresident: full-time $13,250; part-time $552 per credit. Required fees: $933. *Financial support:* In 2009–10, 19 research assistantships, 5 teaching assistantships were awarded. *Unit head:* Prof. Robert Haltiwanger, Chair, 631-632-8560. *Application contact:* Director, Graduate Program, 631-632-8533, Fax: 631-632-9730, E-mail: mcbprog@life.bio.sunysb.edu.

Syracuse University, College of Arts and Sciences, Program in Structural Biology, Biochemistry and Biophysics, Syracuse, NY 13244. Offers PhD. *Students:* 5 full-time (3 women), 3 part-time (0 women); includes 1 minority (African American), 4 international. Average age 31. 18 applicants, 0% accepted, 0 enrolled. *Degree requirements:* For doctorate, thesis/dissertation, exam. *Entrance requirements:* For doctorate, GRE General Test, GRE Subject Test. Additional exam requirements/recommendations for international students: Required—TOEFL (minimum score 100 iBT). *Application deadline:* For fall admission, 1/10 priority date for domestic and international students. Application fee: $75. Electronic applications accepted. *Expenses:* Tuition: Full-time $26,808; part-time $1117 per credit. Required fees: $1024. *Financial support:* Fellowships with tuition reimbursements, research assistantships, teaching assistantships with tuition reimbursements, tuition waivers available. Financial award application deadline: 1/1; financial award applicants required to submit FAFSA. *Unit head:* Scott Pitnick, Director, 315-443-5128, Fax: 315-443-2012, E-mail: sspitnic@syr.edu. *Application contact:* Evelyn Lott, Information Contact, 315-443-9154, Fax: 315-443-2012, E-mail: ealott@syr.edu.

Thomas Jefferson University, Jefferson College of Graduate Studies, PhD Program in Molecular Pharmacology and Structural Biology, Philadelphia, PA 19107. Offers PhD. *Faculty:* 34 full-time (5 women). *Students:* 14 full-time (7 women); includes 2 minority (both Asian Americans or Pacific Islanders), 3 international. 24 applicants, 25% accepted, 3 enrolled. In 2009, 5 doctorates awarded. *Degree requirements:* For doctorate, comprehensive exam, thesis/dissertation. *Entrance requirements:* For doctorate, GRE General Test, minimum GPA of 3.2. Additional exam requirements/recommendations for international students: Required—TOEFL (minimum score 250 computer-based; 100 iBT) or IELTS. *Application deadline:* For fall admission, 1/15 priority date for domestic and international students. Applications are processed on a rolling basis. Application fee: $50. Electronic applications accepted. *Expenses:* Tuition: Full-time $26,858; part-time $879 per credit. Required fees: $525. *Financial support:* In 2009–10, 14 students received support, including 14 fellowships with full tuition reimbursements available (averaging $52,883 per year); Federal Work-Study, institutionally sponsored loans, scholarships/grants, traineeships, and stipend also available. Support available to part-time students. Financial award application deadline: 5/1; financial award applicants required to submit FAFSA. *Faculty research:* Biochemistry and cell, molecular and structural biology of cell-surface and intracellular receptors, molecular modeling, signal transduction. Total annual research expenditures: $19.2 million. *Unit head:* Dr. Philip Wedegaertner, Program Director, 215-503-3137, Fax: 215-923-2117, E-mail: philip.wedegaertner@mail.tju.edu. *Application contact:* Marc E. Stearns, Director of Admissions, 215-503-0155, Fax: 215-503-9920, E-mail: jcgs-info@jefferson.edu.

See Close-Up on page 467.

Tulane University, School of Medicine and School of Liberal Arts, Graduate Programs in Biomedical Sciences, Department of Structural and Cellular Biology, New Orleans, LA 70118-5669. Offers MS, PhD, MD/PhD. MS and PhD offered through the Graduate School. *Degree requirements:* For master's, one foreign language, thesis; for doctorate, 2 foreign languages, thesis/dissertation. *Entrance requirements:* For master's, GRE General Test, minimum B average in undergraduate course work; for doctorate, GRE General Test. Additional exam requirements/recommendations for international students: Required—TOEFL. Electronic applications accepted. *Faculty research:* Reproductive endocrinology, visual neuroscience, neural response to altered hormones.

University at Albany, State University of New York, School of Public Health, Department of Biomedical Sciences, Program in Cell and Molecular Structure, Albany, NY 12222-0001. Offers MS, PhD. *Degree requirements:* For master's, thesis; for doctorate, thesis/dissertation. *Entrance requirements:* For master's and doctorate, GRE General Test, GRE Subject Test.

University at Buffalo, the State University of New York, Graduate School, School of Medicine and Biomedical Sciences, Graduate Programs in Medicine and Biomedical Sciences, Department of Structural Biology, Buffalo, NY 14260. Offers MS, PhD. *Faculty:* 6 part-time/adjunct (1 woman). *Students:* 7 full-time (0 women), 1 (woman) part-time; includes 1 minority (Hispanic American). Average age 27. 4 applicants, 75% accepted. In 2009, 2 doctorates awarded. *Degree requirements:* For master's, comprehensive exam, thesis; for doctorate, comprehensive exam, thesis/dissertation. *Entrance requirements:* For master's, BS or BA in science, engineering, or math; for doctorate, GRE General Test, BS or BA in science, engineering, or math. Additional exam requirements/recommendations for international students: Required—TOEFL (minimum score 600 paper-based; 250 computer-based; 100 iBT). *Application deadline:* For fall admission, 2/1 priority date for domestic and international students. Applications are processed on a rolling basis. Application fee: $50. Electronic applications accepted. *Financial support:* Federal Work-Study, scholarships/grants, traineeships, and unspecified assistantships available. Financial award application deadline: 2/1; financial award applicants required to submit FAFSA. *Faculty research:* Biomacromolecular structure and function at the level of three-dimensional atomic architecture. Total annual research expenditures: $3.5 million. *Unit head:* Dr. Robert H. Blessing, Interim Department Chair and Professor, 716-898-8613, Fax: 716-898-8660, E-mail: blessing@hwi.buffalo.edu. *Application contact:* Dr. Robert H. Blessing, Director of Graduate Studies, 716-898-8613, Fax: 716-898-8660, E-mail: blessing@hwi.buffalo.edu.

University of California, San Diego, School of Medicine and Office of Graduate Studies, Molecular Pathology Program, La Jolla, CA 92093. Offers bioinformatics (PhD); cancer biology/oncology (PhD); cardiovascular sciences and disease (PhD); microbiology (PhD); molecular pathology (PhD); neurological disease (PhD); stem cell and developmental biology (PhD); structural biology/drug design (PhD). *Entrance requirements:* For doctorate, GRE General Test, GRE Subject Test. Additional exam requirements/recommendations for international students: Required—TOEFL. Electronic applications accepted.

University of Connecticut, Graduate School, College of Liberal Arts and Sciences, Department of Molecular and Cell Biology, Field of Biophysics and Structural Biology, Storrs, CT 06269. Offers MS, PhD. *Faculty:* 23 full-time (9 women). *Students:* 11 full-time (5 women); includes 1 minority (African American), 4 international. Average age 29. 18 applicants, 17% accepted, 2 enrolled.Terminal master's awarded for partial completion of doctoral program. *Degree requirements:* For master's, comprehensive exam; for doctorate, thesis/dissertation. *Entrance requirements:* For master's and doctorate, GRE General Test, GRE Subject Test. Additional exam requirements/recommendations for international students: Required—TOEFL (minimum score 550 paper-based; 213 computer-based). *Application deadline:* For fall admission, 2/1 priority date for domestic and international students; for spring admission, 11/1 for domestic students, 10/1 for international students. Applications are processed on a rolling basis. Application fee: $55. Electronic applications accepted. *Expenses:* Tuition, state resident: full-time $4725; part-time $525 per credit. Tuition, nonresident: full-time $12,267; part-time $1363 per credit. Required fees: $346 per semester. Tuition and fees vary according to course load. *Financial support:* In 2009–10, 4 research assistantships with full tuition reimbursements, 6 teaching assistantships with full tuition reimbursements were awarded; fellowships, Federal Work-Study, scholarships/grants, health care benefits, and unspecified assistantships also available. Financial award application deadline: 2/1; financial award applicants required to submit FAFSA. *Unit head:* David Benson, Head, 860-486-4258, Fax: 860-486-4331, E-mail: david.benson@uconn.edu. *Application contact:* Anne St. Onje, Graduate Coordinator, 860-486-4314, Fax: 860-486-3943, E-mail: anne.st_onje@uconn.edu.

See Close-Up on page 187.

University of Minnesota, Twin Cities Campus, Graduate School, College of Biological Sciences, Biochemistry, Molecular Biology and Biophysics Graduate Program, Minneapolis, MN 55455-0213. Offers PhD. *Faculty:* 69 full-time (14 women), 1 part-time/adjunct (0 women). *Students:* 60 full-time (26 women); includes 20 minority (2 African Americans, 1 American Indian/Alaska Native, 15 Asian Americans or Pacific Islanders, 2 Hispanic Americans). Average age 26. 199 applicants, 20% accepted, 11 enrolled. In 2009, 16 doctorates awarded. *Degree requirements:* For doctorate, thesis/dissertation. *Entrance requirements:* For doctorate, GRE, 3 letters of recommendation, more than 1 semester of laboratory experience. Additional exam requirements/recommendations for international students: Required—TOEFL (minimum score 625 paper-based; 263 computer-based; 108 iBT with writing subsection 25 and reading subsection 25) or IELTS (minimum score 7). *Application deadline:* For fall admission, 12/15 for domestic and international students. Application fee: $75 ($95 for international students). Electronic applications accepted. *Financial support:* Institutionally sponsored loans, scholarships/grants, traineeships, health care benefits, tuition waivers, unspecified assistantships, and stipends available. *Faculty research:* Microbial biochemistry, biotechnology, molecular biology, regulatory biochemistry, structural biology and biophysics, physical biochemistry, enzymology, physiological chemistry. Total annual research expenditures: $10.3 million. *Unit head:* Prof. David A. Bernlohr, Head, 612-624-2712. *Application contact:* Dr. Anja Katrin Bielinsky, Director of Graduate Studies, 612-624-2469, Fax: 612-625-2163, E-mail: bieli003@umn.edu.

University of Pittsburgh, School of Medicine and School of Arts and Sciences, Joint Pitt + CMU Molecular Biophysics and Structural Biology Graduate Program, Pittsburgh, PA 15260. Offers PhD. *Faculty:* 51 full-time (16 women). *Students:* 19 full-time (6 women); includes 3 minority (2 Asian Americans or Pacific Islanders, 1 Hispanic American), 6 international. Average age 26. 70 applicants, 11% accepted, 6 enrolled. *Degree requirements:* For doctorate, comprehensive exam, thesis/dissertation. *Entrance requirements:* For doctorate, GRE General Test. Additional exam requirements/recommendations for international students: Required—TOEFL (minimum score 600 paper-based; 250 computer-based; 100 iBT), IELTS (minimum score 7). *Application deadline:* For fall admission, 12/15 priority date for domestic and international students. Application fee: $0. Electronic applications accepted. *Expenses:* Tuition, state resident: full-time $16,402; part-time $665 per credit. Tuition, nonresident: full-time $28,694; part-time $1175 per credit. Required fees: $690; $175 per term. Tuition and fees vary according to program. *Financial support:* In 2009–10, 3 fellowships with full tuition reimbursements (averaging $27,326 per year), 13 research assistantships with full tuition reimbursements (averaging $24,650 per year) were awarded; institutionally sponsored loans, scholarships/grants, traineeships, and unspecified assistantships also available. *Faculty research:* Structural biology, protein dynamics and folding, computational biophysics, molecular informatics, membrane biophysics and ion channels, x-ray crystallography cryaelectron microscopy. *Unit head:* Dr. Angela M. Gronenborn, Director, 412-648-8957, Fax: 412-648-1077, E-mail: mbsbinfo@medschool.pitt.edu. *Application contact:* Jennifer L. Walker, Program Coordinator, 412-648-8957, Fax: 412-648-1077, E-mail: mbsbinfo@medschool.pitt.edu.

The University of Texas Health Science Center at San Antonio, Graduate School of Biomedical Sciences, Department of Cellular and Structural Biology, San Antonio, TX 78229-3900. Offers MS, PhD. *Faculty:* 55 full-time (20 women). *Students:* 52 full-time (38 women), 4 part-time (3 women); includes 25 minority (21 Asian Americans or Pacific Islanders, 4 Hispanic Americans), 10 international. Average age 27. In 2009, 5 master's, 7 doctorates awarded. *Degree requirements:* For master's, thesis, oral qualifying exam; for doctorate, comprehensive exam, thesis/dissertation, oral qualifying exam. *Entrance requirements:* For doctorate, GRE General Test, previous course work in biology, chemistry, physics, and calculus. Additional exam requirements/recommendations for international students: Required—TOEFL (minimum score 550 paper-based; 213 computer-based). *Application deadline:* For fall admission, 4/1 for domestic and international students; for spring admission, 10/1 for domestic and international students. Applications are processed on a rolling basis. Application fee: $0. Electronic applications accepted. *Expenses:* Tuition, state resident: full-time $2832; part-time $118 per credit hour. Tuition, nonresident: full-time $10,896; part-time $454 per credit hour. Required fees: $884 per semester. One-time fee: $70. *Financial support:* In 2009–10, 28 students received support, including 28 teaching assistantships (averaging $26,000 per year). Financial award application deadline: 2/1; financial award applicants required to submit FAFSA. *Faculty research:* Human/molecular genetics, endocrinology and neurobiology, cell biology, cancer biology, biology of aging. Total annual research expenditures: $10.3 million. *Unit head:* Christi A. Walter, Professor and Chair, 210-567-3800, Fax: 210-567-0073, E-mail: walter@uthscsa.edu. *Application contact:* Susan Naylor, Chair, Committee on Graduate Studies, 210-567-3842, Fax: 210-567-3803, E-mail: naylor@uthscsa.edu.

The University of Texas Medical Branch, Graduate School of Biomedical Sciences, Program in Biochemistry and Molecular Biology, Galveston, TX 77555. Offers biochemistry (PhD); bioinformatics (PhD); biophysics (PhD); cell biology (PhD); computational biology (PhD); structural biology (PhD). *Students:* 41 full-time (17 women); includes 6 minority (1 African American, 1 Asian American or Pacific Islander, 4 Hispanic Americans), 22 international. Average age 28. In 2009, 9 doctorates awarded. *Degree requirements:* For doctorate, thesis/dissertation. *Entrance requirements:* Additional exam requirements/recommendations for international students: Required—TOEFL (minimum score 550 paper-based; 213 computer-based). *Application deadline:* Applications are processed on a rolling basis. Application fee: $30 ($75 for international students). Electronic applications accepted. *Financial support:* In 2009–10, fellowships (averaging $25,000 per year), research assistantships (averaging $25,000 per year) were awarded. Financial award applicants required to submit FAFSA. *Unit head:* Dr.

Sarita Sastry, Director, 409-747-1915, Fax: 409-747-1938, E-mail: sasastry@utmb.edu. *Application contact:* Debora Botting, Coordinator for Special Programs, 409-772-2769, Fax: 409-772-5102, E-mail: dmbottin@utmb.edu.

University of Washington, Graduate School, School of Medicine and Graduate School, Graduate Programs in Medicine, Department of Biological Structure, Seattle, WA 98195. Offers PhD. *Degree requirements:* For doctorate, thesis/dissertation. *Faculty research:* Cellular and developmental biology, experimental immunology and hematology, molecular structure and molecular biology, neurobiology, x-rays.

Yale University, School of Medicine and Graduate School of Arts and Sciences, Combined Program in Biological and Biomedical Sciences (BBS), Molecular Biophysics and Biochemistry Track, New Haven, CT 06520. Offers PhD, MD/PhD. *Degree requirements:* For doctorate, thesis/dissertation. *Entrance requirements:* For doctorate, GRE General Test. Additional exam requirements/recommendations for international students: Required—TOEFL. *Application deadline:* For fall admission, 12/6 for domestic and international students. Electronic applications accepted. *Financial support:* Fellowships, research assistantships available. *Unit head:* Dr. Mark Solomon, Director of Graduate Studies, 203-432-5562, Fax: 203-432-5832. *Application contact:* Nessie Stewart, Graduate Registrar, 203-432-5662, Fax: 203-432-6178, E-mail: nessie.stewart@yale.edu.

BAYLOR COLLEGE OF MEDICINE

Interdepartmental Program in Cell and Molecular Biology

Program of Study

In 1988, a group of faculty members at Baylor College of Medicine set out to design the ideal biomedical graduate program from a student's perspective. This effort has produced a multidisciplinary environment that provides the brightest and most ambitious students with the skills needed to navigate overlapping scientific disciplines. More than 95 participating faculty members from eleven different departments provide students in the Interdepartmental Program in Cell and Molecular Biology (CMB) with a diverse set of choices for thesis research, leading to the Ph.D. degree. The range of research interests includes molecular mechanisms of inherited diseases, cancer and cell-cycle regulation, biology of aging, human gene therapy, signal transduction and membrane biology, large-scale genome sequencing and bioinformatics, functional genomics, structural and computational biology, gene expression and regulation, developmental biology, molecular virology, and immunology.

A wide range of courses are available during the first year. Core courses (taught by the Graduate School) and specialty courses (offered by individual departments) allow students to acquire depth and breadth in a number of different areas. These courses are combined with advanced courses that allow intensive investigation into topics of particular interest to each student. Course selection is flexible, with multiple choices for each requirement. Course requirements can be easily fulfilled by the end of the first year. This means that, during the second year, no required courses stand in the way of conducting research.

An additional unique feature of the CMB program is the first-year Director's Course. In this small seminar course, consisting of 10 to 12 students and taught by 4 faculty members (one for each term), students develop both practical and intellectual skills as they learn to critically evaluate the primary scientific literature, design and interpret experiments, and give lucid presentations. The intimate format also enables students to get to know the CMB Co-Directors at the beginning of their graduate career, and encourages close working relationships with fellow first-year CMB classmates. The program is supported by a competitive training grant from the National Institute of General Medical Sciences (GM 008231), which is in its eighteenth consecutive year.

Research Facilities

The participating faculty members in the program occupy extensive research space with state-of-the-art equipment and core facilities. In addition to a large number of common laboratory instruments such as ultracentrifuges, scintillation counters, spectrophotometers, and cell-culture facilities, the faculty members are also in charge of sophisticated equipment for transmission and scanning electron microscopy, protein sequencing, mass spectrometry, microarray construction and data analysis, peptide and nucleic acid synthesis, genome sequencing and analysis, knockout and transgenic mouse facilities, flow cytometry, and X-ray diffraction. There are also extensive computing and imaging facilities.

Financial Aid

All students in the CMB program receive competitive stipends of $26,000 per year. This stipend is provided during each year of study, and there are no linked teaching requirements. In addition, full health insurance and tuition are completely covered. Top-performing students each receive a $500 Claude W. Smith Fellowship Award. Although the stipend is always guaranteed, students are also encouraged to apply for outside funding. The Dean recognizes every student who receives outside funding with an additional $2000-per-year supplement to the $26,000 yearly stipend.

Cost of Study

Tuition is supported by Baylor College of Medicine and the training grant. Students pay a one-time matriculation fee of $25, a one-time graduation fee of $190, and an annual Education Resource Center fee of $150 for the first year and $20 for each subsequent year.

Living and Housing Costs

Most students and faculty members live within a few miles of the Medical Center. Housing is not provided for graduate students because a variety of affordable outstanding housing options are readily available. Some CMB students pool their resources to rent a nearby private house, while others choose to rent their own one-bedroom apartments. Numerous apartment complexes are located very close to the Texas Medical Center. Because the cost of living in Houston is well below that of every major city in the U.S., graduate students can afford to enjoy the many recreational and cultural opportunities available in Houston and even buy their own condo or town house.

Student Group

Unlike other interdisciplinary programs, the CMB program accepts only 10 to 12 carefully selected students each year. This means that training, particularly during the first year, involves one-on-one interactions with some of the best scientists in the world in an intimate environment that teaches students how to think like a scientist. Starting in the second year, CMB students present their research once a year in a formal seminar setting. This seminar course, which is attended by CMB students at all stages of training, helps students develop intellectual vigor as well as learn how to present research in a lucid way. CMB students leave Baylor with seminar skills that rival those of any Ph.D. student in the country.

Student Outcomes

Following graduation from this program, students have pursued postdoctoral training in excellent laboratories and high-quality institutions throughout the U.S. and abroad.

Location

Houston is a dynamic city that is both affordable and fun for graduate student life. Symphony concerts, opera, ballet, live theater, year-round major-league sports, and great restaurants are all a part of living in Houston, the fourth-largest city in the United States. From fall through spring, the average temperature ranges between 50°F and 75°F, with the temperatures rarely dropping below freezing, and it does not snow. Average highs during the summer are in the 90s, although it cools down into the 70s each evening, and air conditioning is present in virtually all homes, the Medical Center, indoor sporting events, etc.

The College

Baylor College of Medicine was established as an independent, private university committed to excellence in the training and education of scholars and physicians. The major area of growth for the College continues to be research. The College is located in the Texas Medical Center, which comprises more than 675 acres and includes forty-two independent institutions. The University of Texas Health Science Center, the School of Public Health, and the M. D. Anderson Cancer Center are also on campus. The Texas Medical Center is one of the most actively growing science centers in the country. The influx of new colleagues and the opportunities created by an atmosphere of expansion provide a stimulating academic environment. More information on Baylor College of Medicine can be found on the College's Web site at http://www.bcm.edu/.

Applying

Applicants are required to have a bachelor's degree or the equivalent in a relevant area of science. Most students who join the CMB program have an undergraduate degree in some aspect of the biological sciences or in chemistry, although students with degrees in other areas, such as engineering, have also joined the program. Applications are due on January 1 and should be accompanied by three letters of recommendation from people who are familiar with the applicant's scholastic qualifications and/or research abilities, as well as a personal statement that describes research experience and career goals. Official GRE scores (not more than three years old) and transcripts from all colleges and universities attended must also be provided. Applications can be made online through the Graduate School Web site at http://www.bcm.edu/gradschool/ or the CMB Web site at http://www.bcm.edu/cmb/. There is no fee for online applications. Applicants are invited to visit Baylor to meet with the participating faculty members and students, in order to have a firsthand look at the research and educational opportunities available to students in the CMB program. Expenses for travel and accommodations during the visit are provided by Baylor College of Medicine. Questions regarding the application process can be directed through e-mail to cmbprog@bcm.edu.

Correspondence and Information

Interdepartmental Program in Cell and Molecular Biology
Graduate School of Biomedical Sciences
Baylor College of Medicine
One Baylor Plaza, MS: BCM215
Houston, Texas 77030
Phone: 713-798-6557
E-mail: cmbprog@bcm.edu
Web site: http://www.bcm.edu/cmb/

Baylor College of Medicine

THE FACULTY AND THEIR RESEARCH

Department of Biochemistry and Molecular Biology
Wah Chiu, Ph.D. Structural and computational biology of macromolecular machines and cells.
Ido Golding, Ph.D. Decision-making in living cells: Lessons from simple systems.
Adam Kuspa, Ph.D. Molecular genetics of development in *Dictyostelium*.
B. V. Venkataram Prasad, Ph.D. Structural biology of viruses and viral proteins.
Jun Qin, Ph.D. Network analysis proteomics.
Florante A. Quiocho, Ph.D. Protein structure, molecular recognition, and function; structural biophysics and biology: X-ray crystallography of proteins.
Shelley Sazer, Ph.D. Eukaryotic cell-cycle control; spindle assembly checkpoint; Ran GTPase; nuclear division.
Anna Sokac, Ph.D. Shaping cells, shaping embryos: Coordinated actin and membrane dynamics in flies and frogs.
Zhou Songyang, Ph.D. Molecular mechanisms of signal transduction.
Francis T. F. Tsai, D.Phil. Structural and functional studies of protein complexes and macromolecular assemblies.
Salih Wakil, Ph.D. Mechanism and regulation of fatty acid metabolism.
Theodore G. Wensel, Ph.D. G-protein signaling in neurons.
Thomas Westbrook, Ph.D. RNAi-based strategies to cancer gene discovery; REST tumor suppressor pathway.
John H. Wilson, Ph.D. Instability of trinucleotide repeats; knock-in mouse models for retinitis pigmentosa; gene therapy of dominant rhodopsin mutations.
Zheng Zhou, Ph.D. Molecular genetic studies of clearance of apoptotic cells in *C. elegans*.

Department of Medicine
Lawrence Chan, D.Sc. Molecular biology, genetics, and gene therapy of atherosclerosis; lipid disorders and diabetes mellitus.
N. Tony Eissa, M.D. Innate immunity and inflammation.
Henry Pownall, Ph.D. Identification of the molecular basis of disorders associated with atherosclerosis, obesity, alcoholic hepatitis, and hypertriglyceridemia; dietary studies in human subjects and in animal models; cell culture and gene regulation.
Matthew H. Wilson, M.D., Ph.D. Transposons and kidney gene therapy.
Li-Yuan Yu-Lee, Ph.D. Signaling pathways in immune and inflammatory responses and cancer.

Department of Molecular and Cellular Biology
William (B. R.) Brinkley, Ph.D. Factors in the nucleus and mitotic apparatus affecting genomic instability in cancer.
Keith Syson Chan, Ph.D., Department of Urology. Bladder cancer stem cells in invasion and metastasis.
Eric Chang, Ph.D. Growth and signaling regulation by Ras G-proteins.
Orla Conneely, Ph.D. Developmental control mechanisms.
Francesco J. DeMayo, Ph.D. Molecular and developmental biology of the lung and uterus.
Xin-Hua Feng, Ph.D. Protein modifications and cell signaling in cell fate determination, development, and cancer.
Loning Fu, Ph.D. Role of the circadian clock in cancer development and therapy.
Suzanne A.W. Fuqua, Ph.D., Department of Medicine. The role of estrogen receptors and estrogen-regulated proteins in breast tumor progression.
Milan A. Jamrich, Ph.D. Role of homeobox and forkhead genes in vertebrate eye development.
Weei-Chin Lin, M.D., Ph.D., Department of Medicine. Cell-cycle regulators and novel cancer therapeutic targets.
David D. Moore, Ph.D. Function of nuclear hormone receptors.
Hoang Nguyen, Ph.D. Skin epithelial stem cell fate maintenance and lineage determination.
Bert W. O'Malley, M.D. Steroid receptors and coactivators regulate gene expression in normal and disease states.
Paul Overbeek, Ph.D. Cell fate determination.
Fred A. Pereira, Ph.D. Signaling pathways in auditory development, aging, and cancer.
JoAnne S. Richards, Ph.D. Hormonal control of ovarian gene expression.
Jeffrey M. Rosen, Ph.D. Mammary gland development and breast cancer.
David R. Rowley, Ph.D. The tumor microenvironment in cancer progression.
Ming-Jer Tsai, Ph.D. Transcription factors in development and diseases.
Li Xin, Ph.D. Prostate stem cells and cells of origin for prostate cancer.
Thomas P. Zwaka, M.D., Ph.D. The nature of embryonic stem cell pluripotency.

Department of Molecular and Human Genetics
David B. Bates, Ph.D. Chromosome dynamics and DNA replication control in *E. coli*.
Arthur L. Beaudet, M.D. Role of genomic imprinting and epigenetics in disease, including Prader-Willi and Angelman syndromes and autism; hepatocyte gene therapy.
Richard A. Gibbs, Ph.D. Genomics; genome sequencing; molecular basis of human genetic diseases.
Xiangwei He, Ph.D. Chromosome segregation: Interaction between spindle and kinetochores.
Christophe Herman, Ph.D. Regulation of cellular processes and quality control by an ATP dependent membrane protease.
Grzegors Ira, Ph.D. DNA recombination is ubiquitous and essential for DNA-based life.
Monica Justice, Ph.D. Genetic analysis of mouse development and disease.
Brendan Lee, M.D., Ph.D. Translational studies in skeletal development; gene and cell therapies for inborn errors of metabolism.
Olivier Lichtarge, M.D., Ph.D. Computational and systems biology; rational protein engineering; inhibition of protein interactions and drug design.
James R. Lupski, M.D., Ph.D. Molecular mechanisms for copy number variation (CNV) and genomic disorders.
Michael L. Metzker, Ph.D. Next-generation technology for genome sequencing; novel fluorescence imaging; molecular genetics of diabetics; phylogenetic analysis of HIV-1 transmission between individuals.

David L. Nelson, Ph.D. Human genetic disorders; fragile X syndrome; unstable DNA and neurodegeneration.
Susan Rosenberg, Ph.D. Genome instability in evolution; cancer and antibiotic resistance.
Kenneth Scott, Ph.D. Cancer gene discovery; pathways governing tumor metastasis; animal models for cancer.
Gad Shaulsky, Ph.D. Developmental genetics in *Dictyostelium*; intercellular communication during development; functional genomics; microarray analysis of gene expression; evolution of sociality.
Jue D. Wang, Ph.D. Elongation of DNA replication and implications for genomic stability.
Hui Zheng, Ph.D. Molecular genetics of Alzheimer's disease and age-related disorders.

Department of Molecular Physiology and Biophysics
Mary Dickinson, Ph.D. Imaging the role of fluid mechanics in early cardiovascular development.
Jeannette Kunz, Ph.D. Phosphoinositide phosphate kinases in cell polarization and cell motility.
Steen E. Pedersen, Ph.D. Ion channel function and structure.
Xander H. T. Wehrens, M.D., Ph.D. Regulation of cardiac ion channels in normal and diseased hearts.
Pumin Zhang, Ph.D. Cell-cycle regulation in development and disease.

Department of Molecular Virology and Microbiology
Janet S. Butel, Ph.D. Polyomaviruses and pathogenesis of infection and disease.
Lawrence A. Donehower, Ph.D. Tumor suppressors and mouse cancer and aging models.
Mary K. Estes, Ph.D. Molecular mechanisms regulating virus–intestinal cell interactions and pathogenesis.
Ronald Javier, Ph.D. Adenoviruses and viral oncology.
Jason T. Kimata, Ph.D. Retroviral replication and pathogenesis.
Richard E. Lloyd, Ph.D. Translation regulation in cancer, apoptosis, and viral infection.
Anthony W. Maresso, Ph.D. Pathogenesis of bacterial infections.
Susan J. Marriott, Ph.D. Cellular transformation mediated by human retroviruses.
Robert F. (Frank) Ramig, Ph.D. Genetics, replication, and pathogenesis of *Reoviridae*.
Betty L. Slagle, Ph.D. Hepatitis B virus pathogenesis.
Lynn Zechiedrich, Ph.D. Protein-DNA interactions, genomic instability, and antibiotic resistance.

Department of Neurology
Jeffrey L. Noebels, M.D., Ph.D. Gene control of neuronal excitability.

Department of Neuroscience
Andrew K. Groves, Ph.D. Development and regeneration of the inner ear.
P. Read Montague, Ph.D. Computational neuroscience; neuroimaging; neural economics.
Kimberley R. Tolias, Ph.D. Molecular signaling pathways in structural development and plasticity of dendrites and synapses.

Department of Pathology and Immunology
Thomas A. Cooper, M.D. Alternative splicing regulation in development and disease.
Gretchen J. Darlington, Ph.D. Mouse models of aging.
Shuhua Han, M.D. B-cell activation and differentiation; inflammation; autoimmunity.
H. Daniel Lacorazza, Ph.D. Genetic control of hematopoiesis and developmental immunology.
Dario Marchetti, Ph.D. Invasive, angiogenic, and metastatic mechanisms of brain cancers; brain invasion/metastasis in breast, melanoma, and medulloblastoma; the biology of circulating tumor cells.
Graeme Mardon, Ph.D. Molecular mechanisms controlling retinal development.
Richard N. Sifers, Ph.D. Glycobiology; posttranslational disease modifiers; conformational disease.
David M. Spencer, Ph.D. Prostate cancer progression and immunotherapy; gene therapy.
Tse-Hua Tan, Ph.D. Signal transduction by MAP kinases and phosphatases in cancer and immunity.
Nikolai A. Timchenko, Ph.D. Role of C/EBP proteins and RNA binding proteins in liver biology.
James Versalovic, M.D., Ph.D. The human microbiome; beneficial microbes and host interactions; probiotics, innate immunity, and intestinal inflammation.
Jin Wang, Ph.D. Molecular regulation of immune responses by apoptosis and autophagy.
Laising Yen, Ph.D. RNA-based molecular switches and biosensors; cancer biomarker discovery.
Biao Zheng, M.D., Ph.D. Somatic genetics and development of immune responses; immunosenescence; autoimmunity.

Department of Pediatrics
Alison Bertuch, M.D., Ph.D. Telomere structure, maintenance and function, and DNA double-strand break repair.
Margaret A. Goodell, Ph.D. Hematopoietic stem cells: basic biology and gene therapy.
Karen Hirschi, Ph.D. Molecular regulation of vascular development; vascular regeneration and engineering.
Kendal Hirschi, Ph.D. Plant biology related to human nutrition and environmental issues.
Sharon E. Plon, M.D., Ph.D. Genetic susceptibility to cancer; molecular mechanisms that control genomic stability.
Jason T. Yustein, M.D., Ph.D. Insights into molecular pathogenesis of pediatric sarcomas.
Huda Y. Zoghbi, M.D. Molecular pathogenesis of neurodegenerative and neurodevelopmental disorders.

Department of Pharmacology
Pui-Kwong Chan, Ph.D. Antitumor agents and mechanism
Timothy G. Palzkill, Ph.D. Protein structure-function; protein-protein interactions.

FLORIDA INSTITUTE OF TECHNOLOGY

College of Science
Department of Biological Sciences
Graduate Program in Cell and Molecular Biology

Program of Study

The Department of Biological Sciences offers a program of graduate study leading to the Master of Science and Doctor of Philosophy degrees in cell and molecular biology. The broad areas of study include molecular and cellular biology, molecular genetics, biochemistry, population genetics, developmental biology, sensory biology, and microbiology. These programs emphasize the preparation of scientists for research careers in academic or industrial settings.

Each student's program is designed independently and is based on his or her background and needs. The diverse interests of the participating faculty members and the excellent student–faculty member ratio ensure a broad spectrum of research opportunities and a great deal of personal attention.

Research Facilities

The Department of Biology occupies approximately 45,000 square feet of laboratory and office space. Available facilities support most modern research areas of cell and molecular biology, including DNA purification and analysis, gene cloning, cell culture, and protein isolation and characterization. The department also features a High Resolution Microscopy and Advanced Imaging Center containing confocal and electron microscopes.

Financial Aid

Graduate teaching and research assistantships are available to qualified students. For 2010–11, stipends are approximately $15,000 for nine months. Computer-based information on scholarships, loan funds, and other student assistance may be obtained from the Financial Aid Office. A limited number of assistantships providing tuition remission only or stipend only are also available.

Cost of Study

The 2010–11 tuition is $1040 per semester credit hour for all graduate students. Tuition is remitted for some graduate assistants.

Living and Housing Costs

Room and board on campus costs approximately $4500 per semester in 2010–11. On-campus housing (dormitories and apartments) is available for full-time single and married graduate students, but priority for dormitory rooms is given to undergraduate students. Many apartment complexes and rental houses are available near the campus.

Student Group

The Department currently has an enrollment of 65 graduate students from colleges throughout the United States and around the world. Approximately one half of the graduate students are women, and approximately one fourth are married. Most graduate students receive financial support.

Student Outcomes

Graduates of the Department of Biological Sciences are employed by organizations such as Dynamac, Bionetics, Brigham and Women's Hospital, Dartmouth Medical School, University of Miami Medical School, Pfizer Foundation, SRI International, Autec, Kistler-Morse, DuPont Pharmaceuticals, Midwest Research Institute, Goodwin Bioscience, Invitrogen, and Johns Hopkins University.

Location

Florida Tech's main campus is located in Melbourne, a residential community on Florida's Space Coast. Melbourne is the key city in south Brevard County, which also encompasses nine other smaller communities on the mainland and beachside. The Kennedy Space Center and Disney World are within a 90-minute drive of the Institute. The area's economy is a well-balanced mix of electronics, aviation, light manufacturing, opticals, communications, agriculture, and tourism.

The Institute

Florida Tech was founded in 1958 and has developed rapidly into a university that provides both undergraduate and graduate education in the sciences and engineering for selected students from throughout the United States and many other countries. In addition to cell and molecular biology, Florida Tech offers graduate programs in marine biology, conservation biology, applied mathematics, chemical engineering, chemistry, civil engineering, computer science, electrical engineering, environmental engineering, mechanical engineering, ocean engineering, oceanography, operations research, physics, science education, space sciences, and systems engineering.

Applying

Further information and application forms for admission to the Graduate School may be obtained from the Office of Graduate Admissions. Applicants must take the Graduate Record Examinations and arrange to have the scores sent to the Office of Graduate Admissions. Separate application for financial aid must be made on forms available from the Department or the Graduate School and must be submitted to the Department by March 1.

Correspondence and Information

Office of Graduate Admissions
Florida Institute of Technology
150 West University Boulevard
Melbourne, Florida 32901
Phone: 321-674-8027
      800-944-4348 (toll-free in the U.S.)
Fax: 321-723-9468
E-mail: grad-admissions@fit.edu
Web site: http://www.fit.edu

Dr. Richard Aronson, Head
Department of Biological Sciences
Florida Institute of Technology
150 West University Boulevard
Melbourne, Florida 32901
Phone: 321-674-8034
E-mail: raronson@fit.edu
Web site: http://www.bio.fit.edu

Florida Institute of Technology

THE FACULTY AND THEIR RESEARCH

David J. Carroll, Associate Professor; Ph.D., Connecticut, 1996. Molecular control of signal transduction at fertilization, with focus on egg activation during fertilization and how this activation relieves the cell-cycle block to initiate development.

Combining microinjection and immunoblotting to analyze MAP kinase phosphorylation in single starfish oocytes and eggs. *Meth. Mol. Biol.* 518:57–66, 2009. With Wei.

Tristan J. Fiedler, Research Assistant Professor; Ph.D., Miami, 2001. Genome biology; bioinformatics; marine biochemistry.

The transcriptome of the early life history stages of the California sea hare *Aplysia californica. Comp Biochem Physiol Genom Proteomics* 5(2):165–70, 2010. With Hudder et al.

Michael S. Grace, Associate Professor; Ph.D., Emory, 1991. Behavioral neuroscience; cellular and molecular mechanisms of vision, non-visual photoreception, and infrared imaging in vertebrate animals; laser-based systems for cancer detection and treatment.

Neural correlates of complex behavior: Vision and infrared imaging in boas and pythons. In *Biology of the Boas, Pythons and Related Taxa*, eds. R. L. Henderson and G. Schuett. Eagle Mountain, Utah: Eagle Mountain Publishers, 2007. With Matsushita.

Julia E. Grimwade, Professor; Ph.D., SUNY at Buffalo, 1987. Control of DNA replication; cell-cycle control; DNA-protein interactions.

Bacterial origin recognition complexes direct assembly of higher-order DnaA oligomeric structures. *Proc. Natl. Acad. Sci. Unit. States Am.* 106:18479–84, 2009. With Miller et al.

Alan C. Leonard, Professor; Ph.D., SUNY at Buffalo, 1979. Use of molecular genetic techniques to study the biology of microbial growth control; DNA-protein interaction and temporal gene expression during the bacterial cell division cycle; molecular regulation of plasmid and minichromosome replication in *E. coli.*

Initiating chromosome replication in *E. coli.* it makes sense to recycle. *Gene. Dev.* 23:1145–50, 2009. With Grimwade.

Lisa K. Moore, Research Assistant Professor; Ph.D., Arizona, 1993. Effects of epinephrine and its metabolites on the regulation of connexins in the vasculature.

Modulation of vascular connexins by stress catecholamines and their metabolites. *Faseb J.* 21(6), A912, 2007. With Novak et al.

Charles D. Polson, Associate Professor; Ph.D., Florida Tech, 1979. Development and application of biotechnology techniques in undergraduate education, especially in the areas of cloning, synthesis, and sequencing; electrophoretic separation of large DNA molecules by pulse-field electrophoresis.

Richard R. Sinden, Professor; Ph.D., Georgia, 1978. Alternative DNA structures; mechanisms of spontaneous mutagenesis; mechanisms of DNA repeat expansion associated with human neurodegenerative diseases.

A Z-DNA sequence at the myotonic dystrophy type 2 gene locus prevents slipped strand structure formation in the (CCTG)-(CAGG) repeat. *Proc. Natl. Acad. Sci., U.S.A.* 106:3270–5, 2009. With Edwards et al.

Shaohua Xu, Associate Professor; Ph.D., Purdue, 1989. AFM, TEM, and confocal microscopy of molecular events, biochemical analysis of protein self assembly and formation of amyloid fibers in Alzheimer's disease.

Aggregation drives "misfolding" in protein amyloid fiber formation. *Amyloid* 14(2):119–31, 2007.

GERSTNER SLOAN-KETTERING
GRADUATE SCHOOL OF BIOMEDICAL SCIENCES

Ph.D. in Cancer Biology Program

Program of Study

The mission of the Gerstner Sloan-Kettering Graduate School is to advance the frontiers of knowledge by providing an interactive, innovative, and collegial environment that educates and trains students to make new discoveries in the biological sciences. The recent explosion in new knowledge about the biological functions of disease, including cancer, is rooted in fundamental laboratory discoveries. Research has been performed in genetics, cell biology, immunology, and other disciplines to contribute to the understanding of how disease affects the human body.

The curriculum places special emphasis on the development of a self-reliant research approach, critical analysis, and the integration of basic science knowledge with human disease physiology. During the first year, students complete a thirty-two-week core course (sixteen weeks per semester), which introduces recent findings in relevant topics through didactic lecture and discussion; three laboratory rotations, with each one culminating in a written summary and oral presentation of their findings; four visits with clinicians in the clinic; course work in logic and critical analysis and responsible conduct of research; and two semesters of the President's Research Seminar Series Journal Club, which introduces students to the published works of world-renowned speakers. Following the end of the spring semester, students are expected to choose a research mentor.

During the second year, students begin their full-time dissertation research and present a written and oral thesis proposal. They are also expected to take part in the Current Topics Journal Club as well as the Graduate Student Seminar, in which students present their own research. At the beginning of the third year, students can select a clinical mentor who serves as a conduit for hospital-based academic activities. Sometime during their fifth or sixth year of study, students must complete their research and present and defend their findings in a dissertation.

Research Facilities

The library subscribes to a full range of databases that encompass key science, medical, and health-care information. Students have access to more than 1,100 journal titles, with over 80 percent of these titles accessible and available electronically. The library's Web site provides access to an extensive collection of resources, including an online catalog, databases, electronic books, and electronic journals.

Sloan-Kettering Institute's thirty-nine cutting-edge research core facilities serve both basic and clinical research needs, offering state-of-the-art instruments and technical staff support to students as they train and conduct research. These facilities include the High-Throughput Screening Facility, which screens potential anticancer compounds against targets; the Genomics Core Laboratory, which extracts and analyzes microarrays; the Stem Cell Research Facility, which characterizes and distributes human embryonic stem cells; the Gene Transfer and Somatic Cell Engineering Facility, which develops, validates, and implements procedures critical to gene transfer–related clinical research; the Antitumor Assessment Facility, which provides advisory services related to the evaluation of agents with potential antitumor activity; and the Pathology Core Facility, which performs research involving human tissue.

Financial Aid

All students receive a fellowship package that includes an annual stipend ($32,637 for 2010–11); a first-year allowance to be used for books, journals, and other school expenses; a scholarship that covers tuition and fees; comprehensive medical and dental insurance; a laptop computer; relocation costs of up to $500; and membership in the New York Academy of Sciences. Students may also apply for independent funding from agencies such as the National Institutes of Health and the National Science Foundation. Recipients of one of these fellowships receive an additional award of $5000 from the school; this is in addition to any supplement necessary to bring the stipend to the common level. Travel awards are given to students who present a poster or a short talk at a scientific meeting.

Cost of Study

As highlighted in the Financial Aid section, all tuition expenses are covered by a full fellowship, which is awarded to all students who matriculate in the school. Students are also provided with health insurance at no cost to them.

Living and Housing Costs

Affordable housing in proximity to the research buildings is provided to all students by Memorial Sloan-Kettering. There is a wide range of costs, which vary depending on the size of the housing unit.

Student Group

The graduate students enrolled at Gerstner Sloan-Kettering are drawn from a pool of applicants who comprise a variety of backgrounds and nationalities. Applicants are expected to hold an undergraduate degree from an accredited institution and must have completed sufficient course work in biology, chemistry, genetics, molecular biology, etc.

Student Outcomes

Graduates of the program are expected to enter into careers as researchers, scientists, and educators in excellent laboratories, hospitals, medical schools, and research institutions throughout the country and around the world.

Location

The campus is located in Manhattan's Upper East Side, home to some of New York City's best shopping and dining. Several world-famous museums are within walking distance, and Central Park is a few blocks away. New York also offers theater, live music, outdoor recreation, and cultural attractions such as the Empire State building, all accessible by public transportation.

The Graduate School

The Gerstner Sloan-Kettering Graduate School of Biomedical Sciences offers the next generation of basic scientists an intensive Ph.D. program to study the biological sciences through the lens of cancer—while giving students the tools they need to put them in the vanguard of research that can be applied in any area of human disease. The faculty members of the School have the exceptional ability to present novel perspectives on the molecular pathophysiology of disease to gifted young men and women eager to be part of shaping the future of research and treatment.

Applying

Prospective students must complete and submit the online application form and submit the following: official transcripts from all colleges previously attended; three letters of recommendation from advisers and/or research mentors; and official GRE scores. An in-person interview is requested from those applicants being seriously considered for admission, but the requirement may be waived if geographical constraints are overwhelming and may be substituted with video interviews. The deadline to apply is December 10, and interviews take place the following January.

Correspondence and Information

Gerstner Sloan-Kettering Graduate School of Biomedical Sciences
1275 York Avenue, Box 441
New York, New York 10065

Phone: 646-888-6639
Fax: 646-422-2351
E-mail: gradstudies@sloankettering.edu
Web site: http://www.sloankettering.edu

Gerstner Sloan-Kettering Graduate School of Biomedical Sciences

THE FACULTY AND THEIR RESEARCH

C. David Allis, Molecular Biology. The histone code and its impact on gene regulation and chromosome dynamics.

James P. Allison, Immunology. The T-cell antigen receptor complex and its effect on T-cell proliferation, survival, and cytokine production.

Grégoire Altan-Bonnet, Computational Biology. Robustness and adaptability in T-cell ligand discrimination.

Kathryn V. Anderson, Developmental Biology. Genetic pathways that direct embryonic patterning and morphogenesis in the mouse embryo.

Zhirong Bao, Developmental Biology. How the genome dictates development, with *C. elegans* as model.

Boris C. Bastian, Human Oncology and Pathogenesis. Genetic and biologic characterization of cutaneous neoplasia.

Mary K. Baylies, Developmental Biology. Mechanisms underlying the specification and morphogenesis of organ systems, using *Drosophila* muscle development as a model system.

Robert Benezra, Cancer Biology and Genetics. Molecular mechanisms of tumor growth and progression, using mouse Id1 and Id3 knockout models and analysis of the spindle assembly checkpoint.

Peter Besmer, Developmental Biology. Normal and oncogenic receptor tyrosine kinase signaling in vitro and in vivo in mice.

Ronald G. Blasberg, Molecular Pharmacology and Chemistry. Development of noninvasive imaging paradigms in living organisms, using radionuclide and optical reporter systems.

Jacqueline Bromberg, Medicine. Aberrantly activated Stat3 and the mechanisms of Stat3-mediated transformation.

Luca Cartegni, Molecular Pharmacology and Chemistry. Role of alternative splicing events in the development and/or maintenance of cancer.

Raju S. K. Chaganti, Cell Biology. Genomic instability in cancer cells and its implications for clinical behavior of tumors and normal cellular developmental pathways.

Timothy A. Chan, Human Oncology and Pathogenesis. Identification and characterization of tumor suppressors in GBM and breast cancer.

Jayanta Chaudhuri, Immunology. Mechanistic elucidation of immunoglobulin gene diversification.

Nai-Kong V. Cheung, Pediatrics. Development of curative therapies for the treatment of metastatic childhood solid tumors, with special emphasis on antibody-based strategies.

Gabriela Chiosis, Molecular Pharmacology and Chemistry. Pharmacological modulation of molecular chaperones in transformed systems.

Samuel J. Danishefsky, Molecular Pharmacology and Chemistry. Synthesis of antitumor natural products and of fully synthetic carbohydrate-based vaccines.

Bo Dupont, Immunology. Receptor-ligand interactions regulating NK cell activation/inhibition; signal transduction pathways in NK cells; NK cells in tumor immunosurveillance and hematopoietic stem cell transplantation.

James Fagin, Human Oncology and Pathogenesis. Pathogenesis of thyroid cancer; role of oncogenic kinases.

Yuman Fong, Surgery. Herpes-based oncolytic viral therapies in the treatment of malignancy.

Zvi Fuks, Molecular Pharmacology and Chemistry. Mechanisms of radiation-induced damage; clinical basis of radiation resistance.

Hironori Funabiki, Cell Biology. Regulation of structure and configuration of chromosomes during the cell division cycle.

Filippo Giancotti, Cell Biology. Signaling by adhesion receptors during tumor progression and angiogenesis.

David Y. Gin, Molecular Pharmacology and Chemistry. Synthesis of complex glycoconjugate immunostimulants and anticancer, antiviral natural products.

Michael Glickman, Immunology. Molecular mechanisms underlying the pathogenesis of *Mycobacterium tuberculosis* and mechanisms of nonhomologous end-joining in mycobacteria.

Jonathan Goldberg, Structural Biology. Structural and biochemical characterization of intracellular vesicle transport.

Jan Grimm, Molecular Pharmacology and Chemistry. Developing novel imaging approaches for improved detection and monitoring of disease.

Anna-Katerina Hadjantonakis, Developmental Biology. Using mouse genetics and high-resolution imaging of living samples to study developmental pathways that direct and orchestrate establishment of the mammalian body plan.

Alan Hall, Cell Biology. Rho and Ras GTPases and the control of cell migration, morphogenesis, and polarity.

Ulrich G. Hammerling, Immunology. Mechanisms underlying immunodeficiency caused by vitamin A deprivation.

Cole Haynes, Cell Biology. Molecular mechanisms that protect mitochondrial function, molecular chaperones, and proteases.

Eric C. Holland, Cancer Biology and Genetics. Molecular mechanisms underlying pathogenesis of CNS tumors and modeling of these cancers in mice.

Alan N. Houghton, Immunology. Immune response to cancer; immune recognition of self and mutated molecules; development of new immunotherapies.

Hedvig Hricak, Radiology. Methodologies of molecular imaging of prostate and gynecologic tumors.

Jerard Hurwitz, Molecular Biology. Mechanisms of eukaryotic DNA replication and the isolation and characterization of proteins involved.

Morgan Huse, Immunology. Study of intracellular signaling dynamics in lymphocytes.

Prasad V. Jallepalli, Molecular Biology. Mechanisms of high-fidelity chromosome segregation in human cells.

Maria Jasin, Developmental Biology. Double-strand break repair and genomic integrity in mammalian cells and the relationship to tumor suppression.

Xuejun Jiang, Cell Biology. Programmed cell death, molecular mechanisms, and its roles in tumorigenesis.

Johanna Joyce, Cancer Biology and Genetics. Understanding how a tumor cell co-opts its environment to promote its growth and progression.

Alexandra L. Joyner, Developmental Biology. Genetic and cellular regulation of neural development and adult stem cell biology.

Julia A. Kaltschmidt, Developmental Biology. Understanding the mechanisms of synaptic specificity underlying neuronal circuit formation.

Scott N. Keeney, Molecular Biology. Molecular mechanisms of the initiation of meiotic recombination.

Thomas J. Kelly, Molecular Biology. Regulatory mechanisms that control DNA replication during the cell cycle of eukaryotic cells.

Anna Marie Kenney, Cancer Biology and Genetics. Signaling pathways regulating proliferation in brain development and cancer.

Robert J. Klein, Cancer Biology and Genetics. Identification of genes responsible for inherited predisposition to cancer.

Andrew Koff, Molecular Biology. Role of cell-cycle inhibitors in differentiation and how their loss affects tumorigenesis.

Richard N. Kolesnick, Molecular Pharmacology and Chemistry. Role of ceramide signaling in radiation-induced vascular dysfunction and tumor regression.

Jason A. Koutcher, Medicine. Application of magnetic resonance spectroscopy and imaging to enhance therapeutic gain of different antineoplastic modalities.

Elizabeth H. Lacy, Developmental Biology. Mechanisms of gastrulation and organogenesis during mouse development.

Marc Ladanyi, Human Oncology and Pathogenesis. Molecular pathogenesis of human translocation-associated sarcomas.

Eric Lai, Developmental Biology. Control of developmental patterning by notch signaling and microRNAs.

Steven M. Larson, Molecular Pharmacology and Chemistry. Molecular imaging in animals and humans, using high-resolution diagnostic instruments.

Christina Leslie, Computational Biology. Machine learning algorithms for computational and systems biology.

Ross L. Levine, Human Oncology and Pathogenesis. Investigation of genetic basis of hematopoietic malignancies.

Jason S. Lewis, Molecular Pharmacology and Chemistry. Development of radiopharmaceuticals for the imaging and therapy of cancer.

Ming Li, Immunology. Mechanisms of T-cell homeostasis, tolerance, and immunity and their relevance to autoimmune diseases and cancer.

Yueming Li, Molecular Pharmacology and Chemistry. Function and regulation of transmembrane proteases; development of novel protease-based cancer therapies.

Christopher D. Lima, Structural Biology. Structural biology of posttranslational protein modification and RNA processing.

Jidong Liu, Cell Biology. Molecular mechanism of RNA interference, function, and regulation of mammalian cytoplasmic processing bodies.

Philip O. Livingston, Medicine. Tumor vaccinology; approaches to augmenting antibody and T-cell responses to defined cancer antigens.

Stephen B. Long, Structural Biology. Structural biology of ion channels and enzymatic membrane proteins.

Minkui Luo, Molecular Pharmacology and Chemistry. Developing chemical tools to elucidate protein posttranslational modification and designing inhibitors for cancer therapies.

Kenneth J. Marians, Molecular Biology. Mechanisms of replication restart and chromosome segregation.

Joan Massagué, Cancer Biology and Genetics. Control of cell growth and phenotype; delineating mechanisms of relevance to tumor progression, metastasis, and response to therapy.

Christine Mayr, Cancer Biology and Genetics. Role of the 3' UTR for gene regulation.

Ingo K. Mellinghoff, Human Oncology and Pathogenesis. Molecular determinants in drug response and growth factor signaling.

Malcolm A. S. Moore, Cell Biology. Biology of hematopoietic stem cells in normal and malignant lymphohematopoiesis.

Dimitar B. Nikolov, Structural Biology. Structural, biophysical, and biochemical characterization of molecular mechanisms of cell-cell interactions and signal transduction in the nervous system.

Stephen D. Nimer, Molecular Pharmacology and Chemistry. Defining molecular and biological abnormalities and underlying transcriptional regulation mechanisms involved in development and growth of hematologic cancers.

Kenneth Offit, Medicine. Cancer genetics; gene characterization; genetic/epidemiologic studies of cancer-predisposing alleles; therapeutic, prognostic, and psychosocial translation of these findings.

Richard J. O'Reilly, Immunology. Genetic disparities and cellular interactions between donor and host that affect allogeneic hematopoietic cell transplantation.

Michael Overholtzer, Cell Biology. Mechanisms of tumor initiation/progression; cell adhesion; cell death.

Eric G. Pamer, Immunology. T-cell and innate inflammatory responses to bacterial and fungal infections.

Gavril W. Pasternak, Molecular Pharmacology and Chemistry. Molecular mechanisms of opioid receptor actions, analgesics, and G-protein–coupled receptors.

Dinshaw Patel, Structural Biology. Structural biology of macromolecular recognition: RNA catalysis, RNA interference, and bypass of DNA damage.

Nikola P. Pavletich, Structural Biology. Structural biology of oncogenes and tumor suppressors.

John H. J. Petrini, Molecular Biology. Repair of chromosomal breaks and activation of DNA damage-induced cell-cycle checkpoints.

Simon N. Powell, Molecular Biology, Radiation Oncology. DNA replication and recombination; chromosome dynamics; human genetics.

Mark S. Ptashne, Molecular Biology. Mechanisms of gene regulation.

Marilyn Resh, Cell Biology. Regulation of protein function by fatty acylation; mechanism of retroviral particle assembly; mechanisms of normal and malignant glial cell growth.

Neal Rosen, Molecular Pharmacology and Chemistry. Understanding biochemical mechanisms underlying phenotypes caused by tyrosine kinase activation in epithelial tumors and development of new therapeutic strategies.

Alexander Y. Rudensky, Immunology. Immunological tolerance; T cell differentiation and function.

Michael Sadelain, Immunology. Mechanisms governing transgene expression, stem cell engineering, and genetic strategies to enhance immunity against cancer.

Chris Sander, Computational Biology. Using computational biology to analyze and simulate biological processes at different levels of organization.

Charles L. Sawyers, Human Oncology and Pathogenesis. Molecularly targeted cancer therapy.

David A. Scheinberg, Molecular Pharmacology and Chemistry. Discovery and development of novel, specific immunotherapeutic agents and targeted nanodevices for cancer therapy.

Gary K. Schwartz, Medicine. Identification of cell-cycle inhibitors that promote chemotherapy-induced apoptosis and their use in cancer therapy.

Songhai Shi, Developmental Biology. Molecular and cellular mechanisms underlying mammalian neuronal development and circuit formation.

Stewart Shuman, Molecular Biology. Mechanisms and structures of mRNA cap-forming enzymes and means by which capping is coupled to transcription.

Samuel Singer, Surgery. Development of a novel clinically relevant biochemical and molecular system of prognostic determinants for soft-tissue sarcoma.

David Solit, Human Oncology and Pathogenesis. Human oncology and pathogenesis; genomics; oncogenes and tumor suppressors; cancer therapeutics; clinical trials.

David R. Spriggs, Medicine. Molecular mechanisms of drug resistance in ovarian cancer.

Lorenz P. Studer, Developmental Biology. Stem cells as a tool to understand normal and pathological development in CNS and to develop cell-based strategies for neural repair.

Joseph Sun, Immunology. Natural killer cell development and responses against infection.

Viviane Tabar, Neurosurgery. In vivo applications of neural derivatives of pluripotent stem cells (iPS, ES); cancer stem cells in human brain tumors.

Derek S. Tan, Molecular Pharmacology and Chemistry. Diversity-oriented synthesis and rational design for cancer chemical biology and drug discovery.

Paul J. Tempst, Molecular Biology. Development of proteomic technologies and approaches for studying eukaryotic transcriptional machineries and for cancer biomarker discovery.

Meng-Fu Bryan Tsou, Cell Biology. Cell cycle control of centrosome duplication and degeneration.

Marcel van den Brink, Immunology. Immunology of bone marrow transplantation.

Andrea Ventura, Cancer Biology and Genetics. Biological functions of cancer-relevant microRNAs.

Harel Weinstein, Computational Biology. Structural, dynamic, and integrative determinants of molecular and cellular mechanisms underlying physiological function and pharmacological activity.

Hans-Guido Wendel, Cancer Biology and Genetics. Modeling genetics of tumor initiation, progression, and treatment response in vivo.

Iestyn Whitehouse, Molecular Biology. Chromatin structure and the function of ATP-dependent chromatin remodeling enzymes.

Joao Xavier, Computational Biology. Computational models and quantitative experiments of biofilm and cancer growth.

James W. Young, Medicine. Innate and adaptive immunity against tumors and viruses stimulated by human dendritic cells.

Jennifer A. Zallen, Developmental Biology. Generation of tissue structure through the collective action of cell populations.

Xiaolan Zhao, Molecular Biology. Chromosomal organization and function; role of sumoylation in chromosomal metabolism.

STATE UNIVERSITY OF NEW YORK
UPSTATE MEDICAL UNIVERSITY
Program in Cell and Developmental Biology

Programs of Study	At SUNY Upstate's College of Graduate Studies, Ph.D. students thrive as they participate in medically relevant research on a campus that is proud of its mentoring and multidisciplinary approach. Students enjoy a student-faculty ratio of nearly 1:1 and publish articles in professional journals during their program.
	Students select a department, thesis mentor, and ultimate area of research after their first year, which includes three in-depth laboratory rotations of their choice. All departments support Upstate's four main Research Pillars: cancer; infectious diseases; diabetes, metabolic disorders, and cardiovascular disease; and disorders of the nervous system.
	The Department of Cell and Developmental Biology explores the molecular and biochemical mechanisms of cellular function and development. Research is focused in two main areas. One centers on the function of the actin and microtubule-based cytoskeleton and the role of cell adhesion in regulating the cytoskeleton and cell motility. This includes work on the formation and dynamics of myofibrils in living cells, regulation of the leukocyte actin cytoskeleton by integrin activation, regulation of fibroblast adhesion to the extracellular matrix through the formation of focal adhesion complexes, and regulation of flagellar motility in response to changes in intracellular calcium ion signaling. Other projects include studies of cellular polarity, cytokinesis, and signaling cascades that control cellular proliferation and differentiation.
	The other main research area—mammalian neural development and regeneration—includes the ability of stem cells to repair injuries in the central nervous system, the role of specific genes in development of somatosensory connections in the neonate, and development of the embryonic blood vessels and organ asymmetry.
Research Facilities	SUNY Upstate has world-class facilities for faculty members and students. Students and faculty use a variety of research methods including sophisticated light microscopy (automated motility tracking, laser confocal microscopy, high-resolution dark-field imaging, real-time fluorescence microscopy, high-sensitivity digital cameras and image processing), electron microscopy, tissue culture, stereotactic surgery, flow cytometry, and a complete range of molecular and biochemical techniques.
	In addition to departmental resources, the main core facilities on campus include the Center for Research and Evaluation, Confocal/Two Photon Imaging, Department of Laboratory Animal Resources, DNA Sequencing, Flow Cytometry, Humanized SCID Mouse and Stem Cell Processing, Imaging Research, In Vivo Computed Tomography, Microarray (SUNYMAC), MRI Research, and Proteomics.
	SUNY Upstate also maintains a coalition with nearby Cornell University, the University of Rochester Medical Center, and Buffalo's Roswell Park Cancer Institute, which is dedicated to sharing cutting-edge research facilities. There are also full research support services on campus, including laboratory-animal facilities, network access to the SeqWeb suite of software, a computer-age medical library containing more than 183,000 volumes, electronics and machine shops, and photographic and computer services.
	SUNY Upstate's growth on the research side is highlighted by a $72 million expansion of its Institute for Human Performance, a high-tech facility housing shared laboratories and core facilities used in basic and clinical research. It also broke ground in 2009 for a dedicated research park facility.
Financial Aid	All accepted Ph.D. students are fully supported throughout their education by full tuition waivers and a stipend ($21,514 per year). Support comes from graduate assistantships, departmental assistantships, and NIH and NSF grants.
Cost of Study	Stipends and full tuition waivers are granted to all students accepted into the Ph.D. program. There is no teaching requirement. Student fees, which include health service, were $552 for the 2009–10 academic year. Tuition and fees for master's students for the 2009–10 academic year were $8370 for in-state students and $13,250 for out-of-state students.
Living and Housing Costs	On-campus housing is available in Clark Tower, a ten-story apartment building with attractive, fully furnished standard rooms, studio apartments, and two-bedroom suites. Costs ranged from $4127 (double occupancy) to $8618 (married/family accommodations) for 2009–10. Clark Tower also has study rooms, computer rooms, private and shared kitchens, lounges, a recreation room, laundry, and storage. Clark Tower is next door to the Campus Activities Building, which houses athletic facilities, a bookstore, and snack bar.
	Many students rent nearby houses or apartments and bicycle or walk to campus. Syracuse has a low cost of living and abundant affordable housing.
Student Group	There are 124 graduate students in the biomedical sciences (58 percent women; 100 percent full-time) and approximately 600 medical students, 200 nursing students, and 200 students in the health professions enrolled at Upstate Medical University. Twenty-five percent of the graduate students come from Canada, Europe, and Asia. Syracuse University and the SUNY College of Environmental Science are located within a quarter mile of SUNY Upstate, resulting in a population of approximately 23,000 students in the immediate area.
Location	Syracuse is New York's fourth-largest city and is located in the scenic center of the state. A naturally beautiful setting, the area offers excellent hiking, biking, boating, and skiing. Nearby are the Finger Lakes region, the Adirondack and the Catskill Mountains, and Lake Ontario. Syracuse's cultural activities include a professional theater, symphony orchestra and opera company, noted author lecture series, chamber music groups, and several top-notch music festivals (classical, blues, and jazz) as well as art and history museums. The area also offers high-quality family life with many excellent school districts and Upstate's own day care center. Syracuse University's top-level collegiate sporting events are a major recreational activity. Syracuse is easily reached by air, rail, and car.
The University	SUNY Upstate is the only academic medical center in the central New York region and is part of the dynamic University Hill community. In addition to the College of Graduate Studies, SUNY Upstate Medical University includes three other colleges—Medicine, Nursing, and Health Professions—its own University Hospital, and a regional campus in Binghamton, New York. The University is growing with new leadership, degree programs, and further plans for expansion. SUNY Upstate Medical University is close to downtown Syracuse and is adjacent to (but not affiliated with) the campus of Syracuse University. SUNY Upstate's Campus Activities Building houses a swimming pool, sauna, gymnasium, squash courts, handball/paddleball court, weight-lifting area with a Universal Gym and a full Nautilus room, billiards, table tennis, television room, bookstore, snack bar, and lounge. Conference rooms are also available for student use.
Applying	The Admissions Committee for the College of Graduate Studies at SUNY Upstate begins reviewing applications in December prior to entry and continues until all positions are filled, which can be as early as early April. The State University of New York requires a $40 application fee. Competitive applicants must have a bachelor's degree or its equivalent, a minimum 3.0 GPA, and course work that includes biology, calculus, chemistry, and physics. GRE General Test scores are required (combined score 1000 minimum), and scores from the Subject Test in chemistry or biology are recommended. International applicants must provide clear evidence of English proficiency (including speaking) by taking the Test of English as a Foreign Language (TOEFL). Candidates for admission are selected on the basis of their record and qualifications for independent scholarship in a specialized field of study. Selected applicants will be invited to campus to meet with faculty, students and tour lab facilities.
Correspondence and Information	Office of Graduate Studies State University of New York Upstate Medical University 750 East Adams Street Syracuse, New York 13210 Phone: 315-464-7655 Fax: 315-464-4544 E-mail: biosci@upstate.edu Web site: http://www.upstate.edu/grad/

State University of New York Upstate Medical University

THE FACULTY AND THEIR RESEARCH

Jeffrey Amack, Ph.D., Assistant Professor. Genetics and cell biology of organ morphogenesis during embryonic development.

Scott D. Blystone, Ph.D., Associate Professor. Actin cytoskeletal dynamics in the leukocyte inflammatory phenotype.

Blair Calancie, Ph.D., Professor. CNS plasticity after trauma; intraoperative electrophysiology.

Timothy A. Damron, M.D., Professor. Radioprotectant strategies for protecting the pediatric growth plate.

Dipak Dube, Ph.D., Professor. Molecular mechanism of cardiac myofibrillogenesis in vertebrates.

Russell G. Durkovic, Ph.D., Professor. Examination of processes underlying recovery from spinal cord injury in the salamander.

Eileen A. Friedman, Ph.D., Adjunct Professor. Role of the serine/theonine kinase Mirk/dyrk1B in cancers of the pancreas, ovary, and colon.

Mira Krendel, Ph.D., Assistant Professor. Physiological functions of myosin motors and their roles in diabetic kidney disease and cancer.

Michael J. Lyon, Ph.D., Associate Professor. Age-related changes in the laryngeal muscles and vocal folds.

James S. McCasland, Ph.D., Professor. Cortical plasticity; development of somatotopic representations in cortex.

David R. Mitchell, Ph.D., Professor. Regulation of ciliary dynein activity and assembly; role of the central pair complex in ciliary motility regulation.

Thomas J. Poole, Ph.D., Associate Professor. Vascular development and the alignment of growing nerves and blood vessels in quail and zebrafish embryos.

David Pruyne, Ph.D., Assistant Professor. Biochemistry and cell biology of formins as actin cytoskeleton organizers, using *Caenorhabditis elegans* as a model system.

Jean M. Sanger, Ph.D., Professor. Analysis of the assembly of the actin/myosin cytoskeleton in muscle and nonmuscle cells.

Joseph W. Sanger, Ph.D., Professor and Chair. Cellular analysis of the formation of myofibrils, stress fibers, and cleavage furrows in living cells.

Vladimir Sirotkin, Ph.D., Assistant Professor. Mechanisms of the actin cytoskeleton assembly and role of myosin-1 during endocytosis in fission yeast.

Dennis J. Stelzner, Ph.D., Professor. CNS regeneration; spinal cord injury research; neural plasticity.

Christopher E. Turner, Ph.D., Professor. Regulation of cell migration by focal adhesion adapter proteins and their role in cancer cell metastasis.

UNIVERSITY OF CALIFORNIA, LOS ANGELES

UCLA ACCESS
Programs in Molecular, Cellular, and Integrative Life Sciences

Programs of Study

UCLA ACCESS represents a program of maximal choice in research opportunities in the molecular and cellular life sciences on the UCLA campus. It provides incoming graduate students with the opportunity to choose from 290 faculty members, comprising twenty affinity groups, for studies leading to the Ph.D. degree. The first-year program for ACCESS students consists of three 1-quarter laboratory rotations together with a highly flexible interdisciplinary curriculum. At the end of this period, students choose their thesis adviser, thereby becoming a member of the corresponding department or interdepartmental program (IDP).

In addition to the first-year curriculum, requirements include training in teaching for two quarters (in years two and three, respectively), as well as fulfilling the examination requirements of the thesis adviser's department or IDP. These generally include an oral qualifying examination, a midstream seminar, and submission of a dissertation based on the results of original research. Most students complete their research and receive their Ph.D. degree near the end of the fifth year.

Admission to UCLA ACCESS is the mechanism whereby students can ultimately become affiliated with the following departments: Biochemistry and Molecular Biology; Microbiology, Immunology, and Molecular Genetics; Molecular Biology IDP; Molecular, Cell, and Developmental Biology; and Molecular, Cellular, and Integrative Physiology within the College of Letters and Science as well as Biological Chemistry, Cellular and Molecular Pathology, Human Genetics, Molecular and Medical Pharmacology, Molecular Toxicology, Neurobiology, and Oral Biology within the School of Medicine.

Research Facilities

Laboratories of UCLA ACCESS faculty members are conveniently clustered within a Life Science/Health Science complex on the southern end of the UCLA campus. Facilities within the College of Letters and Science as well as the School of Medicine provide students with state-of-the-art laboratories, equipment, core services, and computer and library resources.

Financial Aid

Student support is guaranteed for five years and is derived from a variety of University sources, including individual fellowships, training grants, teaching assistantships, and research assistantships. The 2010–11 annual stipend (four quarters, or twelve months) was $28,000. Student registration fees and nonresident tuition (where applicable) were also paid in full. Students who receive funding from outside agencies (minimum amount to be determined) are awarded an annual bonus for the duration of the fellowship. In addition to the stipend and fee awards, funds to support research supplies and scholarly travel are also available to graduate students.

Cost of Study

As outlined in the Financial Aid section, costs are covered for graduate students in the programs.

Living and Housing Costs

University-owned town homes, in the heart of Westwood Village, are available for rental. In addition, convenient University-owned apartments are available for both single and married students. Numerous non-University-owned rentals are available adjacent to the campus in Westwood as well as in local outside communities, such as Santa Monica, West Los Angeles, Mar Vista, and Beverly Hills. For additional information, students should contact the Housing Assignment Office at 310-825-4271.

Student Group

The diverse student population of UCLA is made up of 24,000 undergraduates and 12,000 graduate and professional students. UCLA ACCESS admits approximately 60 students per year. During the first year, students associate with small faculty and student affinity groups until a thesis adviser and department are chosen.

Location

UCLA is located at the foot of the Santa Monica Mountains, 5 miles from the Pacific Ocean, in one of the most attractive and affluent suburban neighborhoods in Los Angeles. Within a short driving distance are local ski resorts, the high desert, and numerous bike trails, beaches, and other recreational amenities. Lively interactions exist between UCLA and other outstanding universities and research institutes in southern California, including Caltech; Salk and Scripps institutes; the UC campuses at San Diego, Irvine, Riverside, and Santa Barbara; and the University of Southern California.

The University

Known for its academic excellence, UCLA ranks among the top ten research universities, and many of UCLA's programs are rated among the best in the nation. UCLA is ranked in the top six nationwide for extramural research funding. The UCLA library is ranked third among all research libraries in the nation and contains more than 5 million volumes.

Applying

Applications are accepted for the fall quarter only. The deadline is December 5, and applicants are encouraged to apply early. Students are also urged to apply for the National Science Foundation and Ford Foundation fellowships, if eligible, by the deadline in November. The application comprises official transcripts, scores on the GRE General Test (the Subject Test is optional), three letters of recommendation, and a statement of purpose. International students whose native language is not English must submit results of the TOEFL. Applications are available online and can be completed at the UCLA ACCESS Web site.

Correspondence and Information

UCLA ACCESS
Programs in Molecular, Cellular, and Integrative Life Sciences
172 Boyer Hall
University of California, Los Angeles
P.O. Box 951570
Los Angeles, California 90095-1570
Web site: http://www.uclaaccess.ucla.edu

University of California, Los Angeles

FACULTY RESEARCH

ACCESS offers research leading to the Ph.D. through the following affinity-group areas. For further information, students should consult the Web site at http://www.uclaaccess.ucla.edu.

Biochemistry and Molecular Biology
Bioinformatics
Cancer Biology
Cardiovascular and Metabolic Program
Cell Biology
Developmental Biology
Gene-Environment Interaction
Gene Regulation
Genetics and Genomics
Hematopoiesis
Immunology
Microbial Physiology and Pathogenesis
Molecular and Medical Pharmacology
Molecular Basis of Disease
Molecular, Cellular, and Integrative Physiology
Molecular Evolution and Phylogenomics
Molecular Parasitology
Nanobiology
Neurobiology
Plant Molecular Biology
Stem Cell Biology
Structural Biology and Proteomics
Virology and Gene Therapy
Vision Science

UNIVERSITY OF CONNECTICUT HEALTH CENTER
Graduate Program in Cell Biology

Program of Study

The program offers training leading to a Ph.D. in biomedical sciences and includes faculty members from the Department of Cell Biology as well as eight other Health Center departments. Faculty members' research spans a broad range of interests in the areas of eukaryotic cell biology and related clinical aspects. The program is particularly strong in the following areas of research: angiogenesis, cancer biology, gene expression, molecular medicine, reproductive biology, signal transduction, vascular biology, optical methods, proteomics, and computer modeling of complex biological systems. The curriculum for the first year is tailored to the individual student and can include core courses in the basic biomedical sciences that have been specially formulated to acquaint the student with the principles and practice of modern biomedical research as well as more specialized, analytical courses. In consultation with their advisory committee, students work out a supplementary program of advanced courses, laboratory experiences, and independent study designed to prepare them for general examinations near the end of their second year. Thesis research begins in the second or third year, and research and thesis writing normally occupy the third and fourth years.

Research Facilities

The program is situated in the modern Health Center in Farmington. This complex provides excellent physical facilities for research in both basic and clinical sciences, a computer center, and the Lyman Maynard Stowe Library. The program provides research facilities and guidance for graduate and postdoctoral work in cell biology—particularly membrane and surface function, membrane protein synthesis and turnover, cytoskeleton structure and function, stimulus-response coupling, gene expression and regulation, vascular biology, fertilization, bone biology, molecular medicine, early development, signal transduction, angiogenesis, computer modeling, and tumor biology. Facilities for training in cell culture, electron microscopy, electrophysiology, fluorescence spectroscopy, molecular biology, molecular modeling, fluorescence imaging, and intravital microscopy are available.

Financial Aid

Support for doctoral students engaged in full-time degree programs at the Health Center is provided on a competitive basis. Graduate research assistantships for 2010–11 provide a stipend of $28,000 per year, which includes a waiver of tuition/University fees for the fall and spring semesters and a student health insurance plan. While financial aid is offered competitively, the Health Center makes every possible effort to address the financial needs of all students during their period of training.

Cost of Study

For 2010–11, tuition is $4455 per semester ($8910 per year) for full-time students who are Connecticut residents and $11,565 per semester ($23,130 per year) for full-time out-of-state residents. General University fees are added to the cost of tuition for students who do not receive a tuition waiver. These costs are usually met by traineeships or research assistantships for doctoral students.

Living and Housing Costs

There is a wide range of affordable housing options in the greater Hartford area within easy commuting distance of the campus, including an extensive complex that is adjacent to the Health Center. Costs range from $600 to $900 per month for a one-bedroom unit; 2 or more students sharing an apartment usually pay less. University housing is not available at the Health Center.

Student Group

Currently, 20 students are pursuing doctoral studies in the program. The total number of Ph.D. students at the Health Center is approximately 150, while the medical and dental schools combined currently enroll 130 students per class.

Location

The Health Center is located in the historic town of Farmington, Connecticut. Set in the beautiful New England countryside on a hill overlooking the Farmington Valley, it is close to ski areas, hiking trails, and facilities for boating, fishing, and swimming. Connecticut's capital city of Hartford, 7 miles east of Farmington, is the center of an urban region of approximately 800,000 people. The beaches of the Long Island Sound are about 50 minutes away to the south, and the beautiful Berkshires are a short drive to the northwest. New York City and Boston can be reached within 2½ hours by car. Hartford is the home of the acclaimed Hartford Stage Company, TheatreWorks, the Hartford Symphony and Chamber orchestras, two ballet companies, an opera company, the Wadsworth Atheneum (the oldest public art museum in the nation), the Mark Twain house, the Hartford Civic Center, and many other interesting cultural and recreational facilities. The area is also home to several branches of the University of Connecticut, Trinity College, and the University of Hartford, which includes the Hartt School of Music. Bradley International Airport (about 30 minutes from campus) serves the Hartford/Springfield area with frequent airline connections to major cities in this country and abroad. Frequent bus and rail service is also available from Hartford.

The Health Center

The 200-acre Health Center campus at Farmington houses a division of the University of Connecticut Graduate School, as well as the School of Medicine and Dental Medicine. The campus also includes the John Dempsey Hospital, associated clinics, and extensive medical research facilities, all in a centralized facility with more than 1 million square feet of floor space. The Health Center's newest research addition, the Academic Research Building, was opened in 1999. This impressive eleven-story structure provides 170,000 square feet of state-of-the-art laboratory space. The faculty at the center includes more than 260 full-time members. The institution has a strong commitment to graduate study within an environment that promotes social and intellectual interaction among the various educational programs. Graduate students are represented on various administrative committees concerned with curricular affairs, and the Graduate Student Organization (GSO) represents graduate students' needs and concerns to the faculty and administration, in addition to fostering social contact among graduate students in the Health Center.

Applying

Applications for admission should be submitted on standard forms obtained from the Graduate Admissions Office at the UConn Health Center or on the Web site. The application should be filed together with transcripts, three letters of recommendation, a personal statement, and recent results from the General Test of the Graduate Record Examinations. International students must take the Test of English as a Foreign Language (TOEFL) to satisfy Graduate School requirements. The deadline for completed applications and receipt of all supplemental materials is December 15. In accordance with the laws of the state of Connecticut and of the United States, the University of Connecticut Health Center does not discriminate against any person in its educational and employment activities on the grounds of race, color, creed, national origin, sex, age, or physical disability.

Correspondence and Information

Dr. Kevin Claffey
Director, Cell Biology Graduate Program
MC 3501
University of Connecticut Health Center
Farmington, Connecticut 06030-3501
Phone: 860-679-8713
E-mail: claffey@nso2.uchc.edu
Web site: http://grad.uchc.edu

University of Connecticut Health Center

THE FACULTY AND THEIR RESEARCH

Andrew Arnold, Professor and Director, Center for Molecular Medicine; M.D., Harvard, 1978. Structure and function of the cyclin D1 oncogene and cell-cycle regulator; molecular genetics and biology of endocrine tumors; inherited endocrine neoplastic diseases.

Rashmi Bansal, Associate Professor of Neuroscience; Ph.D., Central Drug Research Institute, 1976. Developmental, cellular, and molecular biology of oligodendrocytes (OLs), the cells that synthesize myelin membrane in the central nervous system.

Gordon G. Carmichael, Professor of Microbiology; Ph.D., Harvard, 1975. Regulation of gene expression in eukaryotes.

Joan M. Caron, Assistant Professor of Cell Biology; Ph.D., Connecticut, 1982. Biochemistry and cell biology of microtubules; palmitoylation of tubulin and cell function; functional role of palmitoylation of signaling proteins.

Kevin P. Claffey, Associate Professor of Cell Biology and Center for Vascular Biology; Ph.D., Boston University, 1989. Angiogenesis in human cancer progression and metastasis; vascular endothelial growth factor (VEGF) expression; hypoxia-mediated gene regulation.

Robert B. Clark, Associate Professor of Medicine, Division of Rheumatic Diseases; M.D., Stanford, 1975. Basic T-lymphocyte biology, especially as it relates to autoimmune diseases, such as multiple sclerosis and rheumatoid arthritis; molecular biology and structure of the T-cell antigen receptor; T-cell function; T-cell activation.

Ann Cowan, Assistant Professor of Biochemistry and Deputy Director of the Center for Biomedical Imaging Technology; Ph.D., Colorado, 1984. Mammalian sperm development.

Kimberly Dodge-Kafka, Assistant Professor of Cell Biology, Center for Cardiology and Cardiovascular Research; Ph.D., Texas–Houston Health Science Center, 1999. Molecular mechanism of signaling pathways in the heart.

David I. Dorsky, Assistant Professor of Medicine; M.D./Ph.D., Harvard, 1982. The structure and function of herpesvirus DNA polymerases and their roles in viral DNA replication.

Paul Epstein, Associate Professor of Cell Biology; Ph.D., Yeshiva (Einstein), 1975. Signal transduction in relation to leukemia and breast cancer; purification and cloning of cyclic nucleotide phosphodiesterases.

Alan Fein, Professor of Cell Biology; Ph.D., Johns Hopkins, 1973. Molecular basis of visual excitation and adaptation; signal transduction and calcium homeostasis in platelets.

Guo-Hua Fong, Associate Professor of Cell Biology and Center for Vascular Biology; Ph.D., Illinois, 1988. Cardiovascular biology.

Brenton R. Graveley, Assistant Professor, Department of Genetics and Developmental Biology; Ph.D., Vermont, 1996. Regulation of alternative splicing in the mammalian nervous system and mechanisms of alternative splicing.

David Han, Associate Professor of Cell Biology and Center for Vascular Biology; Ph.D., George Washington, 1994. Proteomic analysis of complex protein mixtures.

Marc Hansen, Professor of Medicine; Ph.D., Cincinnati, 1986. Analysis of genes involved in the development of the bone tumor osteosarcoma.

Marja Hurley, Professor of Medicine; M.D., Connecticut Health Center, 1972. Molecular mechanisms by which members of the fibroblast growth factor (FGFs) and fibroblast growth factor receptor (FGFR) families (produced by osteoblasts, osteoclasts, and stromal cells) regulate bone development, remodeling, and disorders of bone: Fgf2 knockout and Fgf2 transgenic mice are utilized in loss and gain of function experiments to elucidate the role of FGF-2 in disorders of bone, including osteoporosis.

Laurinda A. Jaffe, Professor of Cell Biology; Ph.D., UCLA, 1977. Physiology of fertilization, in particular the mechanisms by which membrane potential regulates sperm-egg fusion; transduction mechanisms coupling sperm-egg interaction to egg exocytosis; opening of ion channels in the egg membrane.

Stephen M. King, Associate Professor of Biochemistry; Ph.D., London, 1982. Cell biology; biochemistry and function of molecular motors; dynein structure and function.

Dennis E. Koppel, Professor of Biochemistry; Ph.D., Columbia, 1973. Application of biophysical techniques to membrane dynamics; mechanisms by which specialized cell-surface domains are produced and maintained.

Bruce Liang, Professor of Cardiopulmonary Medicine; M.D., Harvard, 1982. Signal transduction; cardiac and vascular cell biology; receptors; G proteins; transgenic mice.

Leslie M. Loew, Professor of Cell Biology and Director, Center for Cell Analysis and Modeling; Ph.D., Cornell, 1974. Spectroscopic methods for measuring spatial and temporal variations in membrane potential; electric field effects on cell membranes; membrane pores induced by toxins and antibiotics.

Nilanjana Maulik, Associate Professor of Surgery; Ph.D., Calcutta, 1990. Molecular and cellular signaling during myocardial ischemia and reperfusion.

Lisa Mehlman, Assistant Professor of Cell Biology; Ph.D., Kent State, 1996. Cell signaling events that regulate oocyte maturation and fertilization; maintenance of oocyte meiotic arrest by G-protein receptors; hormonal regulation of oocyte maturation.

Flavia O'Rourke, Assistant Professor of Cell Biology; Ph.D., Connecticut, 1976. Signal transduction in human platelets, with specific interest in the inositol phosphate signaling pathway and its regulation.

Joel Pachter, Professor of Cell Biology; Ph.D., NYU, 1983. Elucidating the mechanisms by which leukocytes and pathogens invade the central nervous system.

Achilles Pappano, Professor of Cell Biology; Ph.D., Pennsylvania. Cardiac membrane receptors and regulation of ion channels.

John J. Peluso, Professor of Cell Biology and Obstetrics and Gynecology; Ph.D., West Virginia, 1974. Cell and molecular mechanisms involving the regulating ovarian cell mitosis and apoptosis; cell-cell interaction as a regulator of ovarian cell function; identification and characterization of a putative membrane receptor for progesterone.

Carol C. Pilbeam, Associate Professor of Medicine; M.D./Ph.D., Yale, 1982. Regulation and function of prostaglandins in bone; transcriptional regulation of cyclooxygenase-2; role of cytokines and estrogen in bone physiology and osteoporosis.

Vladimir Rodionov, Assistant Professor of Cell Biology; Ph.D., Moscow, 1980. Dynamics of cytoskeleton; self-organization of microtubule arrays; regulation of the activity of microtubule motors.

Daniel Rosenberg, Professor of Medicine; Ph.D., Michigan. Molecular genetics of colorectal cancer; signaling pathways in the development of tumors; toxicogenomics.

David W. Rowe, Professor of Pediatrics; M.D., Vermont, 1969. Hormonal and genetic regulation of Type I collagen synthesis in bone, using molecular biological techniques.

John B. Schenkman, Professor of Pharmacology; Ph.D., SUNY Upstate Medical Center, 1964. The cytochrome P450 monooxygenase system; homeostatic control of the hepatic microsomal enzymes.

Linda H. Shapiro, Associate Professor of Cell Biology and Center for Vascular Biology; Ph.D., Michigan, 1984. Regulation and function of CD 13/aminopeptidase N in angiogenic vasculature and early myeloid cells; control of tumor and myocardial angiogenesis by peptidases; inflammatory regulation of angiogenesis.

Mark R. Terasaki, Assistant Professor of Cell Biology; Ph.D., Berkeley, 1983. Structure and function of the endoplasmic reticulum; confocal microscopy.

Jennifer Tirnauer, Assistant Professor of Medicine, Center for Molecular Medicine; M.D., Maryland, 1989. Role of the microtubule cytoskeleton in cancer biology; molecular mechanisms of microtubule regulation.

James Watras, Associate Professor of Medicine; Ph.D., Washington State, 1979. The mechanisms by which the sarcoplasmic reticulum regulates intracellular calcium concentration in vascular smooth muscle.

Bruce A. White, Professor of Cell Biology; Ph.D., Berkeley, 1980. Regulation of prolactin gene expression by Ca and calmodulin in rat pituitary tumor cells; examination of nuclear DNA-binding proteins, nuclear calmodulin-binding proteins, and nuclear Ca-calmodulin-dependent protein kinase activity.

Charles Wolgemuth, Assistant Professor of Cell Biology; Ph.D., Arizona. Using physics to understand biological systems; morphology; propulsion; growth and fluid dynamics.

Catherine H.-y. Wu, Associate Professor of Medicine; Ph.D., CUNY, Brooklyn, 1976. Mechanisms of procollagen propeptide feedback inhibition of collagen synthesis; pretranslational control.

George Y. Wu, Professor of Medicine; M.D./Ph.D., Yeshiva (Einstein), 1976. Receptor-mediated endocytosis of glycoproteins; drug delivery by endocytic targeting; targeted gene delivery and expression.

Lixia Yue, Assistant Professor of Cell Biology and Center for Cardiovascular Research; Ph.D., McGill, 1999. TRP channels and Ca^{2+} signaling mechanisms in cardiac remodeling.

UNIVERSITY OF CONNECTICUT HEALTH CENTER

Graduate Program in Molecular Biology and Biochemistry

Program of Study
The Graduate Program in Molecular Biology and Biochemistry uniquely bridges modern molecular biology, microbiology, biochemistry, cell biology, and structural biology, leading to a Ph.D. in the biomedical sciences. The goals of the graduate program are to provide rigorous research training in an environment dedicated to advancing excellence in teaching and research. Whether graduates enter academic research, the biotechnology industry, liberal arts college teaching, patent law, or other disciplines, they bring to that career a solid base of knowledge, an ability to learn independently and think independently, and an enduring desire to use their full range of professional skills and experience in creative ways. Graduates are expected to have demonstrated a high degree of competence in research, as judged by publications in first-rank journals, and to have developed essential skills in identifying important research problems, planning research projects and scientific writing. In addition, students are expected to have incorporated ethical principles of scientific conduct into their professional attitudes and activities and to be sensitive to such issues throughout their careers. The success of this training approach is indicated by the high percentage of students who have developed successful independent careers in biomedical research. The current program offers an unparalleled opportunity to study a wide variety of biological problems at the biochemical, molecular, cellular, and structural levels. The interests of the faculty are summarized below.

Research Facilities
In addition to the general facilities of the Health Center (see page describing programs in the Biological and Biomedical Sciences), the program offers complete physical research facilities. There is research equipment, as well as expertise, for all areas of genetic, biochemical, molecular, cellular, and biophysical investigation. The department houses the UConn Health Center NMR Structural Biology Facility (http://structbio.uchc.edu), which includes a 400-MHz NMR spectrometer and cryoprobe-equipped 500- and 600-MHz NMR spectrometers, as well as a circular dichroism spectropolarimeter, isothermal titration calorimeter, and multi-angle laser light scattering facilities. An 800-MHz NMR spectrometer and X-ray crystallography facilities are planned. The department also houses the UConn Health Center Structural Biology Computational Facility, which includes a bank of Mac and Linux desktop computers connected to ultrafast servers with the latest structural biology software. Facilities are also available for electron and confocal laser scanning microscopy, low-light-level imaging microscopy (in the state-of-the-art Center for Cell Analysis and Modeling), protein purification and sequencing, cell culture, monoclonal antibody production, DNA oligonucleotide and peptide synthesis and sequencing, and gene silencing using RNAI.

Financial Aid
Support for doctoral students engaged in full-time degree programs at the Health Center is provided on a competitive basis. Graduate research assistantships for 2010–11 provide a stipend of $28,000 per year, which includes a waiver of tuition/University fees for the fall and spring semesters and a student health insurance plan. While financial aid is offered competitively, the Health Center makes every possible effort to address the financial needs of all students during their period of training.

Cost of Study
For 2010–11, tuition is $4455 per semester ($8910 per year) for full-time students who are Connecticut residents and $11,565 per semester ($23,130 per year) for full-time out-of-state residents. General University fees are added to the cost of tuition for students who do not receive a tuition waiver. These costs are usually met by traineeships or research assistantships for doctoral students.

Living and Housing Costs
There is a wide range of affordable housing options in the greater Hartford area within easy commuting distance of the campus, including an extensive complex that is adjacent to the Health Center. Costs range from $600 to $900 per month for a one-bedroom unit; 2 or more students sharing an apartment usually pay less. University housing is not available at the Health Center.

Student Group
There are approximately 30 graduate students in the molecular biology and biochemistry program. There are approximately 150 graduate students in Ph.D. programs on the Health Center campus, and the total enrollment is about 1,000.

Location
The Health Center is located in the historic town of Farmington, Connecticut. Set in the beautiful New England countryside on a hill overlooking the Farmington Valley, it is close to ski areas, hiking trails, and facilities for boating, fishing, and swimming. Connecticut's capital city of Hartford, 7 miles east of Farmington, is the center of an urban region of approximately 800,000 people. The beaches of the Long Island Sound are about 50 minutes away to the south, and the beautiful Berkshires are a short drive to the northwest. New York City and Boston can be reached within 2½ hours by car. Hartford is the home of the acclaimed Hartford Stage Company, TheatreWorks, the Hartford Symphony and Chamber orchestras, two ballet companies, an opera company, the Wadsworth Athenaeum (the oldest public art museum in the nation), the Mark Twain house, the Hartford Civic Center, and many other interesting cultural and recreational facilities. The area is also home to several branches of the University of Connecticut, Trinity College, and the University of Hartford, which includes the Hartt School of Music. Bradley International Airport (about 30 minutes from campus) serves the Hartford/Springfield area with frequent airline connections to major cities in this country and abroad. Frequent bus and rail service is also available from Hartford.

The Health Center
The 200-acre Health Center campus at Farmington houses a division of the University of Connecticut Graduate School, as well as the School of Medicine and Dental Medicine. The campus also includes the John Dempsey Hospital, associated clinics, and extensive medical research facilities, all in a centralized facility with more than 1 million square feet of floor space. The Health Center's newest research addition, the Academic Research Building, was opened in 1999. This impressive eleven-story structure provides 170,000 square feet of state-of-the-art laboratory space. The faculty at the center includes more than 260 full-time members. The institution has a strong commitment to graduate study within an environment that promotes social and intellectual interaction among the various educational programs. Graduate students are represented on various administrative committees concerned with curricular affairs, and the Graduate Student Organization (GSO) represents graduate students' needs and concerns to the faculty and administration, in addition to fostering social contact among graduate students in the Health Center.

Applying
Applications should be submitted on standard forms obtained from the Graduate Admissions Office at the UConn Health Center or the Web site. The application should be filed together with transcripts, three letters of recommendation, a personal statement, and recent results from the General Test of the Graduate Record Examinations. International students must take the Test of English as a Foreign Language (TOEFL) to satisfy Graduate School requirements. The deadline for completed applications and receipt of all supplemental materials is December 15. In accordance with the laws of the state of Connecticut and of the United States, the University of Connecticut Health Center does not discriminate against any person in its educational and employment activities on the grounds of race, color, creed, national origin, sex, age, or physical disability.

Correspondence and Information
Dr. Stephen King
Program Director for Molecular Biology and Biochemistry
University of Connecticut Health Center
Farmington, Connecticut 06030-3305

Phone: 860-679-3347
Fax: 860-679-1862
E-mail: sking@nso2.uchc.edu
Web site: http://grad.uchc.edu

University of Connecticut Health Center

THE FACULTY AND THEIR RESEARCH

Gordon G. Carmichael, Professor; Ph.D., Harvard. Regulation of viral gene expression and function.

John H. Carson, Professor; Ph.D., MIT. RNA transport in cells of the nervous system.

Ann Cowan, Associate Professor; Ph.D., Colorado at Boulder. Plasma membrane proteins in sperm.

Asis Das, Professor; Ph.D., Calcutta. Gene control in bacterial adaptive response.

Betty Eipper, Professor; Ph.D., Harvard. Biosynthesis and secretion of peptides by neurons and endocrine cells.

Shlomo Eisenberg, Professor; Ph.D., McGill. Biochemistry of DNA replication in yeast.

Michael Gryk, Assistant Professor; Ph.D., Stanford. Three-dimensional structure and function of proteins involved in DNA repair.

Arthur Günzl, Associate Professor; Ph.D., Tübingen (Germany). Transcription and antigenic variation in the mammalian parasite *Trypanosoma brucei*.

Bing Hao, Assistant Professor of Molecular, Microbial, and Structural Biology; Ph.D., Ohio State. Understanding how the cell cycle is regulated by ubiquitin-mediated proteolysis using X-ray crystallography as a primary tool.

Christopher Heinen, Assistant Professor of Medicine; Ph.D., Cincinnati. Biochemical and cellular defects of the DNA mismatch repair pathway during tumorigenesis.

Jeffrey Hoch, Associate Professor; Ph.D., Harvard. Biophysical chemistry of proteins.

Stephen M. King, Associate Professor; Ph.D., University College, London. Structure and function of microtubule-based molecular motor proteins.

Lawrence A. Klobutcher, Professor and Associate Dean of the Graduate School; Ph.D., Yale. DNA rearrangement, programmed translational frameshifting, and phagocytosis in ciliated protozoa.

Dennis E. Koppel, Professor; Ph.D., Columbia. Biophysical studies of membrane dynamics.

Mark Maciejewski, Assistant Professor; Ph.D., Ohio State. Enzymes of DNA replication, repair, and recombination.

Mary Jane Osborn, Professor, Department of Microbiology; Ph.D., Washington (Seattle). Biogenesis of the outer membrane of *Salmonella*.

Juris Ozols, Professor; Ph.D., Washington (Seattle). Isolation and structure of membranous proteins.

Lawrence I. Rothfield, Professor; Ph.D., NYU. Membrane biology and biochemistry; bacterial cell division.

Peter Setlow, Professor; Ph.D., Brandeis. Biochemistry of bacterial spore germination.

Sandra K. Weller, Professor and Department Head; Ph.D., Wisconsin. Mechanisms of DNA replication and DNA encapsidation in herpes simplex virus; virus-host interactions.

UNIVERSITY OF FLORIDA

College of Medicine
Advanced Concentration in Molecular Cell Biology

Program of Study

The College of Medicine at the University of Florida (UF) offers graduate training in biomedical research leading to a Ph.D. degree through the Interdisciplinary Program (IDP) in Biomedical Sciences. The goal of the Interdisciplinary Program is to prepare students for a diversity of careers in research and teaching in academic and commercial settings. The program provides a modern, comprehensive graduate education in biomedical science while providing both maximum program flexibility as well as appropriate specialization for graduate students. During the first year of study, incoming graduate students undertake a common, comprehensive interdisciplinary core curriculum of classroom study developed in a cooperative effort by all of the graduate programs in the College of Medicine. In addition, students select from any of the College of Medicine faculty members for participation in several laboratory rotations conducted throughout the first year, concurrent with the core curriculum. By the end of their first year, students select a laboratory in which to conduct their dissertation research and, once again, they may choose from any of the graduate faculty members in the College of Medicine. Formal selection of a graduate program and mentor is made after completion of the core curriculum to maximize flexibility and facilitate an informed decision; however, students may make an informal commitment to a program or lab at any time.

The Advanced Concentration in Molecular Cell Biology (MCB) prepares investigators for careers in biomedical research in academic or industrial settings. This multidisciplinary program has nearly 60 participating faculty members and offers an extraordinary range of opportunities for advanced study of life at the molecular and cellular levels. The diverse faculty shares common interests in the molecular interactions that account for the functionally integrated subcellular, cellular, and tissue organization found in living organisms. The model systems in use range from yeast and cellular slime molds through *Drosophila* to birds and mammals. These systems are manipulated and analyzed employing a wide range of powerful molecular, genetic, protein chemical, immunological, pharmacological, nuclear magnetic resonance (NMR), and microscopic imaging strategies. Students who select the MCB program take advanced course work and initiate independent research during the second year. This arrangement ensures maximum flexibility for students to custom-design a training program best suited to their own needs.

Research Facilities

The College of Medicine houses state-of-the-art research facilities maintained by the Interdisciplinary Center for Biomedical Research (ICBR), the McKnight Brain Institute, the Clinical Research Center, several other University of Florida Research Centers, and individual research laboratories. Together these facilities provide services for DNA and protein synthesis and sequencing, hybridoma production, confocal and electron microscopy, NMR spectroscopy, computing and molecular modeling, flow cytometry, transgenic mouse production, and gene therapy vector construction. The University of Florida libraries, including the Health Center library, form the largest information resource system in the state of Florida and support up-to-date computer-based bibliographic retrieval services.

UF's nine libraries offer more than 4 million catalogued volumes and links to full-text articles in more than 34,000 journals. Of national significance are the Baldwin Library of Historical Children's Literature, the Latin American Collection, the Map and Imagery Library, the P. K. Yonge Library of Florida History (preeminent Floridiana collection), the Price Library of Judaica, and holdings on architectural preservation and eighteenth-century American architecture, late nineteenth- and early twentieth-century German state documents, rural sociology of Florida, and tropical and subtropical agriculture.

Financial Aid

Students accepted into the Interdisciplinary Program receive a stipend of $25,750 per annum. Students also receive a waiver that covers tuition.

Cost of Study

Graduate research assistants pay fees of approximately $1400 per year. Books and supplies cost about $1600.

Living and Housing Costs

Married student housing is available in six apartment villages operated by the University; dormitories for single students are available in limited quantities. The cost of housing for a single graduate student is approximately $5000 per year. Most graduate students live in abundant and comfortable off-campus housing that is near the University; rents vary but are low on a national scale.

Student Group

Enrollment at the University of Florida is both culturally and geographically diverse and numbers about 50,000, including about 10,000 graduate students. There are about 300 graduate students in the College of Medicine.

Location

Situated in north-central Florida, midway between the Atlantic Ocean and the Gulf of Mexico, Gainesville is a nationally recognized academic and research center and was rated the number one place to live in the U.S. in a 1995 *Money* magazine survey. There are about 200,000 residents in the Gainesville metropolitan area, excluding University of Florida students. The climate is moderate, permitting outdoor activities the year around. The University and the Gainesville community also host numerous cultural events, including music, dance, theater, lectures, and art exhibits. Many of the men's and women's athletic programs are considered to be in the top ten programs in the country.

The University and The College

The University of Florida, located on 2,000 acres, is among the nation's leading research universities as categorized by the Carnegie Commission on Higher Education. UF is a member of the Association of American Universities, the nation's most prestigious higher education organization. UF is also one of the nation's top three universities in the breadth of academic programs offered on a single campus. It has twenty colleges and schools and 100 interdisciplinary research and education centers, bureaus, and institutes. The College of Medicine, opened in 1956, has become a nationally recognized leader in medical education and research.

Applying

The Interdisciplinary Program in Biomedical Sciences seeks promising students with undergraduate training in chemistry, biology, psychology, or related disciplines in the life sciences. Applicants are selected on the basis of previous academic work, research experience, GRE General Test scores, letters of recommendation, the personal statement, and a personal interview. Students are admitted for the fall semester, which begins in late August. The application deadline is December 15.

Correspondence and Information

Michael Edwin Boulton, Ph.D., Director
Interdisciplinary Program in Biomedical Sciences
University of Florida College of Medicine
P.O. Box 100235
Gainesville, Florida 32610-0235

Phone: 352-273-8546
Fax: 352-392-3305
E-mail: meboulton@ufl.edu
Web site: http://idp.med.ufl.edu/MCB/index.html

Alexander Ishov, Ph.D., Co-Director
Interdisciplinary Program in Biomedical Sciences
University of Florida College of Medicine
P.O. Box 100235
Gainesville, Florida 32610-0235

Phone: 352-273-8202
Fax: 352-392-3305
E-mail: ishov@ufl.edu
Web site: http://idp.med.ufl.edu/MCB/index.html

University of Florida

THE FACULTY AND THEIR RESEARCH

John P. Aris, Associate Professor; Ph.D., Stanford, 1985. Cellular mechanisms of aging; yeast *(Saccharomyces cerevisiae)* model system.
  Autophagy and amino acid homeostasis are required for chronological longevity in *Saccharomyces cerevisiae*. *Aging Cell,* in press. With Alvers et al.

Michael E. Boulton, Professor; Ph.D., Westminster (London), 1982. Physiology and pathology of the retina with emphasis on neovascularization, oxidative damage, diabetic retinopathy and age-related macular degeneration.

Mark Brantly, Professor and Chief; M.D., Florida, 1979. Inflammatory mediators of lung injury in alpha-1 antitrypsin deficiency; unfold protein response.

Brian E. Burke, Professor; Ph.D., London, 1980. Nucleocytoplasmic transport and nuclear pore complex structure; nuclear pore complex dynamics during mitosis; the function of the nuclear lamina and its involvement in human disease.

Jun Cai, Research Assistant Professor, Ph.D., Cardiff (UK), 2000. The regulatory mechanisms of pathological angiogenesis.
  Pigment epithelium-derived factor inhibits angiogenesis via regulated intracellular proteolysis of vascular endothelial growth factor receptor 1. *J. Biol. Chem.* 281:3604–13, 2006. With Jiang, Grant, and Boulton.

Nasser Chegini, Professor, Ph.D., Florida. The expression and regulation of growth factors, cytokines, and receptors in human reproductive tract tissues in health and disease states.

Christopher R. Cogle, Associate Professor, M.D., Florida. Laboratory research in stem cell biology and cancer; translational aspects of stem cell plasticity; cancer development; identifying novel agents for treatment of blood cancers.

William A. Dunn Jr., Professor and Interim Chair; Ph.D., Penn State, 1979. Autophagy.
  Emerging role for autophagy in the removal of aggresomes in Schwann cells. *J. Neurosci.* 23:10672–80, 2003. With Fortun, Joy, Li, and Notterpek.

Alexander M. Ishov, Assistant Professor, Ph.D., Russian Academy of Science, 1994. Nuclear structure and function; epigenetic regulation of gene expression; tumor suppression function of the protein Daxx.
  The cellular protein Daxx interacts with avian sarcoma virus integrase and viral DNA to repress viral transcription. *J. Virol.* 79(8):4610–8, 2005. With Greger, Katz, Maul, and Skalka.

Moira Jackson, Ph.D., Lecturer and Director.

Aruna Jaiswal, Ph.D., Research Assistant Professor.

Eric D. Laywell, Assistant Professor; Ph.D., Tennessee, 1993. Medical neuroscience.
  Neural trans-differentiation potential of hepatic oval cells in the neonatal mouse brain. *Exp. Neurol.* 182:373–82, 2003. With Deng, Steindler, and Petersen.

Daiqing Liao, Associate Professor; Ph.D., British Columbia, 1993. Understanding function and regulation of tumor suppressor p53 and its homologous transcriptional activators by viral oncogenes and cellular proteins.
  Negative regulation of p53 functions by Daxx and the involvement of MDM2. *J. Biol. Chem.* 279(48):50566–79, 2004. With Zhao et al.

Paul J. Linser, Professor; Ph.D., Cincinnati, 1977. The regulation of genes that serve to distinguish and define specific cell types in maturing tissues.
  Carbonic anhydrase in the adult mosquito midgut. *J. Exp. Biol.* 208:3263–73, 2005. With Corena et al.

Olga Malakhova, Assistant Scholar; Ph.D., Russian Academy of Sciences, 1981. Neuromorphology.
  Functional and structural analysis of the visual system in the rhesus monkey model of optic nerve head ischemia. *Invest. Ophthalmol. Vis. Sci.* 45(6):1830–40, 2004. With Brooks et al.

Satya Narayan, Professor; Ph.D., Punjab (India), 1987. Mechanism of colorectal carcinogenesis; mechanism of cigarette smoke carcinogens–induced breast carcinogenesis; chemotherapeutic intervention of colorectal and breast cancers.
  Tumor suppressor APC blocks DNA polymerase beta-dependent strand-displacement synthesis and increases sensitivity to DNA methylation. *J. Biol. Chem.* 280:6942–9, 2005. With Jaiswal and Balusu.

Venkatesh Nonabur, M.D., Assistant Scholar. Anatomy.
  Lymph sampling and lymphangiography via EUS-guided transesophageal thoracic duct puncture in a swine model. *Gastrointest. Endosc.* 59:564–7, 2004. With Parsher et al.

Yi Qiu, Ph.D., Research Assistant Professor.

Kyle E. Rarey, Ph.D., Senior Associate Dean, Education.

Kyle Roux, Research Assistant Professor; Ph.D., Florida, 2004.

Kelly Selman, Associate Professor; Ph.D., Harvard, 1972. Oogenesis and oocyte growth in lower vertebrates (mainly teleost fish).
  Bafilomycin A1 inhibits proteolytic cleavage and hydration but not yolk crystal disassembly or meiosis during maturation of sea bass oocytes. *J. Exp. Zool.* 290:265–78, 2001.

Stephen P. Sugrue, Professor and Senior Associate Dean for Research; Ph.D., Cincinnati, 1979. Molecular determinants of the regulation of cell-cell adhesion in epithelium.
  Reduction of Pnn by RNAi induces loss of cell-cell adhesion between human corneal epithelial cells. *Mol. Vis.* 11:133–42, 2005. With Joo et al.

Silvia Tornaletti, Ph.D., Research Assistant Professor.

Shanna Williams, Ph.D., Lecturer.

UNIVERSITY OF MISSOURI–KANSAS CITY

School of Biological Sciences
Program in Cell Biology and Biophysics

Program of Study

The graduate program in cell biology and biophysics at the University of Missouri–Kansas City (UMKC) leads to the Ph.D. degree. The program functions within the interdisciplinary Ph.D. framework of the University and is associated with the M.S. program in cell and molecular biology. The graduate program is designed to prepare students for research-oriented careers in academia, government, or the private sector. An original independent research project under the supervision of a faculty adviser is the core of these programs.

Programs of study provide a background of course work tailored to the interests of each student. Opportunity for research experience begins immediately as a component of the first-year curriculum, with each student being assigned short research projects. By the end of the first academic year, the student is also expected to have acquired a general understanding of the basis of molecular and cellular biology. At that time, the student selects a faculty research adviser and makes further course selections. To qualify for doctoral degree candidacy, students take a written comprehensive examination and prepare and defend an original research proposal. The culmination of the graduate degree programs is the preparation and oral defense of a research dissertation, typically five years after entry into the program.

The areas of research interest of participating faculty members are included in the Faculty and Their Research section. Extensive possibilities for collaboration exist with the School's program in molecular biology and biochemistry and with regional research associates. Opportunities for postdoctoral research are abundant.

Research Facilities

Research facilities for cell, molecular and structural biology, and biochemistry are primarily located in the Biological Sciences and Chemistry buildings. Modern research is conducted in laboratories assigned to individual faculty members and in specialized central facilities. Sophisticated instrumentation in these facilities includes automated DNA and protein synthesizers and sequencers, mass spectrometers, macromolecular X-ray, low-intensity electron microscope and 600-MHz NMR imaging facilities, molecular graphics equipment, and Fourier-transform infrared and EPR spectrometers. Raman and UV-resonance Raman spectrometers, differential scanning and titration microcalorimeters, analytical ultracentrifuge, HPLCs, amino acid and carbohydrate analyzers, low-intensity fluorescence imaging and confocal microscopes, and a large assortment of scanning spectrophotometers, ELISA readers, gel scanners, centrifuges, and related instrumentation associated with modern biochemical research are available. Students also enjoy the use of Linda Hall Library, one of the country's premier private science libraries; central animal facilities; and a fully integrated computer network with on-site and off-site access to national and international databases and the Internet.

Financial Aid

All fully admitted U.S. citizen and resident doctoral students receive financial support as teaching or research assistants. Support is provided for up to five years for students who are progressing satisfactorily. For the 2010–11 year, stipends were $23,000. Other forms of financial aid may be available through the Student Financial Aid Office. The metropolitan area offers many career and educational opportunities for spouses and other family members.

Cost of Study

In 2010–11, in-state tuition was about $6500 per year, while out-of-state fees were approximately $15,000 per year. Full-time doctoral students, as a general rule, receive basic tuition support.

Living and Housing Costs

A wide variety of off-campus housing is available in every price range. The overall cost of living in Kansas City is low compared with metropolitan areas in other parts of the country.

Student Group

The cell biology and biophysics graduate program has a very active graduate student organization. UMKC has approximately 10,000 students, of whom about half are graduate and professional students. The School of Biological Sciences currently has about 80 graduate students and 15 postdoctoral fellows as well as more than 200 undergraduate majors. Eight to 12 new doctoral students are admitted each year.

Student Outcomes

The majority of doctoral graduates transfer to nationally known research institutions, typically as postdoctoral associates, or undertake advanced professional training. A short transitional postdoctoral research period within the School is not uncommon.

Location

Kansas City, "The Heart of America," is the center of a metropolitan area with a population of more than 1 million. The University is adjacent to the elegant Country Club Plaza, the city's entertainment and shopping center. Major-league sports, historical and art museums, and many musical, theatrical, and cultural events as well as an extensive parks system provide entertainment throughout the year. A relaxed, Midwestern lifestyle is also an advantage of the setting, which, with its many fountains, boulevards, unusually clean air, and more days of sunshine than in most large U.S. cities, provides an enjoyable quality of life.

The University and The School

UMKC is part of the four-campus University of Missouri System, and it is the only comprehensive research university in western Missouri. It has a strong life science mission. The School of Biological Sciences was established in 1985 to develop strong research and graduate programs in the modern life sciences. The School has been cited by the Board of Curators of the University of Missouri System as an area of eminence for its programs in molecular biology and biochemistry and in cell biology and biophysics. Program improvement funds have facilitated the hiring of many research-oriented faculty members and the creation of excellent research facilities. An innovative interdisciplinary doctoral program has also been initiated, creating a stimulating environment that offers outstanding research opportunities to graduate students.

Applying

The deadline for applications from U.S. applicants is July 1, but applications received before March 1 have priority for financial support. The deadline for international applications is February 15. A bachelor's degree in biology, chemistry, physics, or a related discipline with a minimum 3.0 grade point average is required for full admission. The General Test of the Graduate Record Examinations is also required. The TOEFL is required for international applicants whose native language is not English.

Correspondence and Information

Graduate Advisor
School of Biological Sciences
University of Missouri–Kansas City
Kansas City, Missouri 64110-2499
Phone: 816-235-2352
Fax: 816-235-5158
E-mail: sbs-grad@umkc.edu
Web site: http://sbs.umkc.edu/graduate/

University of Missouri–Kansas City

THE FACULTY AND THEIR RESEARCH

Professors
Lawrence A. Dreyfus, Ph.D., Kansas. Molecular biology; bacterial toxin structure-function.
Henry M. Miziorko, Ph.D., Pennsylvania. Study of enzyme catalysis and regulation using chemical, biophysical, and molecular biology approaches; lipid biosynthesis; enzymes in inherited disease.
Anthony J. Persechini, Ph.D., Carnegie Mellon. Calcium-calmodulin signaling pathways; intracellular interactions.
G. Sullivan Read, Ph.D., Penn State. RNA turnover control; gene regulation; herpes virus.
Ann Smith, Ph.D., London. Receptor-mediated endocytosis; protein-receptor interactions; intercellular heme transport.

Associate Professors
Karen J. Bame, Ph.D., UCLA. Metabolism of heparan sulfate proteoglycans.
Leonard L. Dobens Jr., Ph.D., Dartmouth. Pattern formation; cell-cell signaling.
Michael B. Ferrari, Ph.D., Texas at Austin. Regulation of skeletal muscle development.
Brian Geisbrecht, Ph.D., Johns Hopkins. Structure and function studies of bacterial virulence factors; X-ray crystallography.
Edward P. Gogol, Ph.D., Yale. Structure of macromolecular assemblies; cryoelectron microscopy.
Saul M. Honigberg, Ph.D., Yale. Signal transduction; cell-cycle control and cell differentiation.
Chi-ming Huang, Ph.D., UCLA. Evolution neurobiology of the cerebellum.
Stephen J. King, Ph.D., Colorado at Boulder. Protein interactions during intracellular motility.
John H. Laity, Ph.D., Cornell. Molecular recognition; NMR spectroscopy; protein biophysical chemistry.
Thomas M. Menees, Ph.D., Yale. Replication of retroviral elements and transposons; yeast molecular genetics.
Michael O'Connor, Ph.D., Ireland. Structure and function of the bacterial ribosome, ribosomal subunits, and the translational reading frame.
Lynda S. Plamann, Ph.D., Iowa. Cell-cell communication during fruiting body formation and sporulation in the soil bacterium *Myxococcus xanthus*.
Michael D. Plamann, Ph.D., Iowa. Microtubule-associated motors; organelle movement; growth polarity; cytoskeleton.
Jeffrey L. Price, Ph.D., Johns Hopkins. *Drosophila* genes involved in chronobiology and circadian rhythms.
Garth Resch, Ph.D., Missouri–Columbia. Neurophysiology and behavior patterns of alcoholism.
Jakob H. Waterborg, Ph.D., Nijmegen (Netherlands). Plant histones; chromatin conformation and gene expression.
Gerald J. Wyckoff, Ph.D., Chicago. Bioinformatics and study of molecular evolution through large-scale comparative genomics in sexual selection.
Marilyn D. Yoder, Ph.D., California, Riverside. X-ray crystallography; protein structure.
Xiao-Qiang Yu, Ph.D., Kansas State. Insect molecular biology and biochemistry of immune responses, pattern recognition proteins, and protein-protein–protein-ligand interactions.

Assistant Professors
Samuel Bouyain, D.Phil., Oxford. Structure and function of the protein tyrosine phosphatase family of cell surface receptors; X-ray crystallography.
Julia Chekanova, Ph.D. Moscow State. Relationships between mRNA quality control, processing, and export in *Saccharomyces cerevisiae*.
Erika Geisbrecht, Ph.D., Johns Hopkins. Myoblast fusion in *Drosophila* embryogenesis.
Alexander Idnurm, Ph.D., Melbourne. Molecular pathogenesis of fungal parasites.
Xiaolan Yao, Ph.D., Iowa State.

Regional Associates
Mark Fisher, Ph.D., Illinois. Chaperonin-assisted protein folding and oligomer assembly.

UNIVERSITY OF MISSOURI–KANSAS CITY

School of Biological Sciences
Program in Molecular Biology and Biochemistry

Programs of Study

The graduate program in molecular biology and biochemistry at the University of Missouri–Kansas City (UMKC) leads to the Ph.D. degree. The program functions within the interdisciplinary Ph.D. framework of the University and is associated with the M.S. program in cell and molecular biology. The graduate program is designed to prepare students for research-oriented careers in academia, government, or the private sector. An original independent research project under the supervision of a faculty adviser is the core of these programs.

Programs of study provide a background of course work tailored to the interests of each student. Opportunity for research experience begins immediately as a component of the first-year curriculum, with each student being assigned short research projects. By the end of the first academic year, the student is also expected to have acquired a general understanding of the basis of molecular and cellular biology. At that time, the student selects a faculty research adviser and makes further course selections. To qualify for doctoral degree candidacy, students take a written comprehensive examination and prepare and defend an original research proposal. The culmination of the graduate degree programs is the preparation and oral defense of a research dissertation, typically five years after entry into the program.

The areas of research interest of participating faculty members are included in the Faculty and Their Research section. Extensive possibilities for collaboration exist with the School's program in cell biology and biophysics and with regional research associates. Opportunities for postdoctoral research are abundant.

Research Facilities

Research facilities for cell, molecular, and structural biology and biochemistry are located primarily in the Biological Sciences and Chemistry buildings. Modern research is done in laboratories assigned to individual faculty members or in specialized central facilities. Sophisticated instrumentation in these facilities includes automated DNA and protein synthesizers and sequencers, mass spectrometers, macromolecular X-ray, low-intensity electron microscope and 600-MHz NMR imaging facilities, molecular graphics equipment, and Fourier-transform infrared and EPR spectrometers. Raman and UV-resonance Raman spectrometers, differential scanning and titration microcalorimeters, analytical ultracentrifuge, HPLCs, amino-acid and carbohydrate analyzers, low-intensity fluorescence imaging and confocal microscopes, and a large assortment of scanning spectrophotometers, ELISA readers, gel scanners, centrifuges, and related instrumentation associated with modern biochemical research are also available. Students enjoy the use of Linda Hall Library, one of the country's premier private science libraries; central animal facilities; and a fully integrated computer network with on-site and off-site access to national and international databases and the Internet.

Financial Aid

All fully admitted U.S. citizen and resident doctoral students receive financial support as teaching or research assistants. Support is provided up to five years for students who are progressing satisfactorily. For the 2010–11 year, stipends were $23,000. Other forms of financial aid may be available through the Student Financial Aid Office. The metropolitan area offers many career and educational opportunities for spouses and other family members.

Cost of Study

In 2010–11, in-state tuition was about $6500 per year, while out-of-state fees were approximately $15,000 per year. Full-time doctoral students, as a general rule, receive basic tuition support.

Living and Housing Costs

A wide variety of off-campus housing is available in every price range. The overall cost of living in Kansas City is low compared with metropolitan areas in other parts of the country.

Student Group

The molecular biology and biochemistry graduate program has a very active graduate student organization. UMKC has approximately 10,000 students, of whom about half are graduate and professional students. The School of Biological Sciences currently has about 80 graduate students and 15 postdoctoral fellows as well as more than 200 undergraduate majors. Eight to 12 new doctoral students are admitted each year.

Student Outcomes

The majority of doctoral graduates transfer to nationally known research institutions, typically as postdoctoral associates, or undertake advanced professional training. A short transitional postdoctoral research period within the School is not uncommon.

Location

Kansas City, "The Heart of America," is the center of a metropolitan area with a population of more than 1 million. The University is adjacent to the elegant Country Club Plaza, the city's entertainment and shopping center. Major-league sports, historical and art museums, and many musical, theatrical, and cultural events as well as an extensive parks system provide entertainment throughout the year. A relaxed, Midwestern lifestyle is also an advantage of the setting, which, with its many fountains, boulevards, unusually clean air, and more days of sunshine than in most large U.S. cities, provides an enjoyable quality of life.

The University and The School

UMKC is part of the four-campus University of Missouri System, and it is the only comprehensive research university in western Missouri. It has a strong life science mission. The School of Biological Sciences was established in 1985 to develop strong research and graduate programs in the modern life sciences. The School has been cited by the Board of Curators of the University of Missouri System as an area of eminence for its programs in molecular biology and biochemistry and in cell biology and biophysics. Program improvement funds have facilitated the hiring of many research-oriented faculty members and the creation of excellent research facilities. An innovative interdisciplinary doctoral program has also been initiated, creating a stimulating environment that offers outstanding research opportunities to graduate students.

Applying

The deadline for applications from U.S. applicants is July 1, but applications received before March 1 have priority for financial support. The deadline for international applications is February 15. A bachelor's degree in biology, chemistry, physics, or a related discipline with a minimum 3.0 grade point average is required for full admission. The General Test of the Graduate Record Examinations is also required. The TOEFL is required for international applicants whose native language is not English.

Correspondence and Information

Graduate Advisor
School of Biological Sciences
University of Missouri–Kansas City
Kansas City, Missouri 64110-2499

Phone: 816-235-2352
Fax: 816-235-5158
E-mail: sbs-grad@umkc.edu
Web site: http://sbs.umkc.edu/graduate/

University of Missouri–Kansas City

THE FACULTY AND THEIR RESEARCH

Professors

Lawrence A. Dreyfus, Ph.D., Kansas. Molecular biology; bacterial toxin structure-function.

Henry M. Miziorko, Ph.D., Pennsylvania. Study of enzyme catalysis and regulation using chemical, biophysical, and molecular biology approaches; lipid biosynthesis; enzymes in inherited disease.

Anthony J. Persechini, Ph.D., Carnegie Mellon. Calcium-calmodulin signaling pathways; intracellular interactions.

G. Sullivan Read, Ph.D., Penn State. RNA turnover control; gene regulation; herpes virus.

Ann Smith, Ph.D., London. Receptor-mediated endocytosis; protein-receptor interactions; intercellular heme transport.

Associate Professors

Karen J. Bame, Ph.D., UCLA. Metabolism of heparan sulfate proteoglycans.

Leonard L. Dobens Jr., Ph.D., Dartmouth. Pattern formation; cell-cell signaling.

Michael B. Ferrari, Ph.D., Texas at Austin. Regulation of skeletal muscle development.

Brian Geisbrecht, Ph.D., Johns Hopkins. Structure and function studies of bacterial virulence factors; X-ray crystallography.

Edward P. Gogol, Ph.D., Yale. Structure of macromolecular assemblies; cryoelectron microscopy.

Saul M. Honigberg, Ph.D., Yale. Signal transduction; cell-cycle control and cell differentiation.

Chi-ming Huang, Ph.D., UCLA. Evolution neurobiology of the cerebellum.

Stephen J. King, Ph.D., Colorado at Boulder. Protein interactions during intracellular motility.

John H. Laity, Ph.D., Cornell. Molecular recognition; NMR spectroscopy; protein biophysical chemistry.

Thomas M. Menees, Ph.D., Yale. Replication of retroviral elements and transposons; yeast molecular genetics.

Michael O'Connor, Ph.D., Ireland. Structure and function of the bacterial ribosome, ribosomal subunits, and the translational reading frame.

Lynda S. Plamann, Ph.D., Iowa. Cell-cell communication during fruiting body formation and sporulation in the soil bacterium *Myxococcus xanthus*.

Michael D. Plamann, Ph.D., Iowa. Microtubule-associated motors; organelle movement; growth polarity; cytoskeleton.

Jeffrey L. Price, Ph.D., Johns Hopkins. *Drosophila* genes involved in chronobiology and circadian rhythms.

Garth Resch, Ph.D., Missouri–Columbia. Neurophysiology and behavior patterns of alcoholism.

Jakob H. Waterborg, Ph.D., Nijmegen (Netherlands). Plant histones; chromatin conformation and gene expression.

Gerald J. Wyckoff, Ph.D., Chicago. Bioinformatics and study of molecular evolution through large-scale comparative genomics in sexual selection.

Marilyn D. Yoder, Ph.D., California, Riverside. X-ray crystallography; protein structure.

Xiao-Qiang Yu, Ph.D., Kansas State. Insect molecular biology and biochemistry of immune responses, pattern recognition proteins, and protein-protein–protein-ligand interactions.

Assistant Professors

Samuel Bouyain, D.Phil., Oxford. Structure and function of the protein tyrosine phosphatase family of cell surface receptors; X-ray crystallography.

Julia Chekanova, Ph.D. Moscow State. Relationships between mRNA quality control, processing, and export in *Saccharomyces cerevisiae*.

Erika Geisbrecht, Ph.D., Johns Hopkins. Myoblast fusion in *Drosophila* embryogenesis.

Alexander Idnurm, Ph.D., Melbourne. Molecular pathogenesis of fungal parasites.

Xiaolan Yao, Ph.D., Iowa State. Structure and dynamic bases of protein function; NMR spectroscopy.

Regional Associates

Gerald M. Carlson, Ph.D., Iowa State. Biophysical, biochemical, and chemical approaches in the study of macromolecular assemblies.

UNIVERSITY OF WASHINGTON / FRED HUTCHINSON CANCER RESEARCH CENTER
Molecular and Cellular Biology Program

Program of Study

The University of Washington and the Fred Hutchinson Cancer Research Center offer a program of graduate studies in molecular and cellular biology leading to the Ph.D. degree. More than 200 faculty members participate in the program and are located on the University of Washington campus in the Departments of Biochemistry, Bioengineering, Biological Structure, Biology, Genome Sciences, Immunology, Microbiology, Pathobiology, Pathology, Pharmacology, and Physiology and Biophysics, as well as on the Day campus at the Hutchinson Center, primarily in the Division of Basic Sciences and the Division of Human Biology. Recently, the Institute for Systems Biology (ISB), a nonprofit research institute headed by Dr. Leroy Hood, and the Seattle Biomedical Research Institute (SBRI), an infectious disease research center led by Dr. Ken Stuart, have joined the Molecular and Cellular Biology (MCB) program.

The goals of the program are to give the student a sound background in molecular and cellular biology and to provide access to the research expertise of all faculty members and laboratories working in this area. These goals are accomplished through the basic elements of the program, which include three quarters of core conjoint courses, a two-quarter literature review course, one quarter of grant writing, three or more quarter-long lab rotations, advanced elective courses in molecular and cellular biology, and a series of informal workshops and seminars on topics in diverse areas of molecular biology and cellular biology. Emphasis is placed on critical evaluation of the literature, exposure to current research methods, and creative thinking through independent research. Students are expected to begin active research in their first year through their lab rotations and to choose a permanent thesis adviser at the end of their first year.

Research Facilities

The program uses the research facilities of the individual departments, Hutchinson Center, ISB, and SBRI. The School of Medicine is housed in the Health Sciences Center and the South Lake Union research hub (SLU). The University Hospital and the College of Arts and Sciences are located in adjoining or nearby buildings. The Hutchinson Center's Day campus and SLU are a 15-minute shuttle ride from the University. The laboratories of participating faculty members are well equipped with the latest in research equipment and are funded by external support. The ISB and the SBRI are located within easy commuting distance. Some of the other facilities available are two Howard Hughes Medical Institute research units, the Markey Molecular Medicine Center, animal quarters, shared major instrument facilities, oligonucleotide and peptide synthesis facilities, a marine biology station at Friday Harbor in the San Juan Islands, and an extensive Health Sciences Library.

Financial Aid

The program offers a salary of approximately $27,348 for twelve months. Students with satisfactory academic progress can anticipate funding that includes tuition and health insurance for the duration of their studies.

Cost of Study

Tuition, salary, and medical, dental, and vision benefits are funded for the duration of the program for students in good standing.

Living and Housing Costs

The University has a wide variety of housing available for single and married students as well as families. Students should call the University Housing Office at 206-543-4059 for further information. Private accommodations may be found within easy walking or bicycling distance.

Student Group

At the University of Washington, approximately 2,500 full-time faculty members serve a student population of 35,000 that is drawn from all over the United States and many other countries.

More than 20 new students are admitted to the program each year. There are approximately 500 graduate students in the biological sciences at the University of Washington.

Student Outcomes

The Molecular and Cellular Biology Program received degree-granting status in 1994. The majority of students upon earning Ph.D. degrees secure postdoctoral research positions.

Location

All around Seattle, there is an abundance of opportunity for outdoor recreation. Unsurpassed sailing, hiking, mountain climbing, skiing, and camping are all a short distance away. Because of the saltwater expanse of the Puget Sound and the mountains both to the east and to the west, Seattle enjoys a moderate climate, with precipitation averaging 32 inches per year, mostly during the winter and early spring. The city's downtown area offers many cultural and educational advantages, including theater, museums, symphony, films, and opera, while the waterfront is home to a large marketplace, galleries, and fresh seafood restaurants. The University itself sponsors many public lectures, concerts, exhibits, film festivals, and theatrical performances.

The University

The University of Washington is located in a residential section of Seattle near the downtown area. It is bordered by two lakes and is one of the largest and most scenic institutions of higher education in the country. The University is a research-intensive institution, regularly ranking first overall among public universities in externally funded research programs. It is recognized for graduate instruction of high quality, offering more than ninety graduate and professional programs that enroll more than 7,300 graduate students on campus. The Hutchinson Center's research laboratories are located by Lake Union near downtown Seattle.

Applying

Applicants must have completed a baccalaureate or advanced degree by the time of matriculation; degrees emphasizing biology, physical or natural sciences, and mathematics are preferred. It is advisable to take the GRE (the General Test) no later than October so that scores can be recorded before the deadline (code for MCB is 0206, code for UW is 4854, on the GRE registration form). New students enter the graduate program in the autumn quarter. The deadline for completion of applications is currently December 1 of the academic year preceding entrance. Students must apply via the online application available at the MCB Program Web site (http://depts.washington.edu/mcb/applicantsinfo.php).

Correspondence and Information

Graduate Program Specialist
Molecular and Cellular Biology Program, Box 357275
University of Washington
Seattle, Washington 98195-7275

Phone: 206-685-3155
Fax: 206-685-8174
E-mail: mcb@u.washington.edu
Web site: http://www.mcb-seattle.edu

University of Washington/Fred Hutchinson Cancer Research Center

THE FACULTY AND THEIR RESEARCH

UNIVERSITY OF WASHINGTON

Cancer Biology
Charles Asbury, Philip Greenberg, Brian Iritani, Lawrence Loeb, Raymond Monnat, Linda Wordeman.

Cell Biology, Signaling, and Cell/Environment Interactions
John Aitchison, Charles Asbury, Sandra Bajjalieh, Nitin Baliga, Joseph Beavo, Karol Bomsztyk, Karin Bornfeldt, Mark Bothwell, Susan Brockerhoff, Peter Byers, John Clark, Trisha Davis, Michael Gelb, Cecilia Giachelli, Sharona Gordon, E. Peter Greenberg, Ted Gross, Bertil Hille, Matthew Kaeberlein, Brian Kennedy, David Kimelman, Michael Laflamme, John Leigh, Jaisri Lingappa, Stanley McKnight, Alex Merz, Neil Nathanson, Jennifer Nemhauser, William Parks, Marilyn Parsons, Andrew Scharenberg, Lynn Schnapp, John Scott, Rong Tian, Keiko Torii, Zhengui Xia, Ning Zheng.

Developmental Biology and Stem Cells
Chris Amemiya, Mark Bothwell, Jeffrey Chamberlain, Michael Cunningham, Ajay Dhaka, Cecilia Giachelli, Marshall Horwitz, David Kimelman, Michael Laflamme, Alex Merz, Raymond Monnat, Randall Moon, Jennifer Nemhauser, David Parichy, David Raible, Billie Swalla, Keiko Torii, Barbara Wakimoto, Zhengui Xia.

Gene Expression, Cell Cycle, and Chromosome Biology
John Aitchison, Charles Asbury, Karol Bomsztyk, Stanley Fields, Raymond Monnat, David Morris, Jennifer Nemhauser, Keiko Torii, Gabriele Varani, Alan Weiner, Linda Wordeman.

Genetics, Genomics, and Evolution
Chris Amemiya, Nitin Baliga, Peter Byers, Jeffrey Chamberlain, Michael Cunningham, Trisha Davis, Aimee Dudley, Stanley Fields, Marshall Horwitz, Matthew Kaeberlein, John Leigh, Mary Lidstrom, Raymond Monnat, David Parichy, David Raible, Lalita Ramakrishnan, Jay Shendure, David Sherman, Ilya Shmulevich, Kenneth Stuart, Billie Swalla, Bruce Tempel, Rong Tian, Keiko Torii, Jeffrey Vieira, Barbara Wakimoto, Alan Weiner, Theodore White.

Microbiology, Infection, and Immunity
James Champoux, Edward Clark, Brad Cookson, Richard Darveau, Ferric Fang, Pamela Fink, Michael Gale, Michael Gelb, E. Peter Greenberg, Philip Greenberg, Jessica Hamerman, Brian Iritani, Michael Katze, Michael Lagunoff, Mary Lidstrom, Jaisri Lingappa, Joseph Mougous, James Mullins, William Parks, Matthew Parsek, Marilyn Parsons, Lakshmi Rajgopal, Lalita Ramakrishnan, Jay Shendure, David Sherman, Jason Smith, Joseph Smith, Kelly Smith, Leonidas Stamatatos, Daniel Stetson, Kenneth Stuart, Theodore White, Tuofu Zhu.

Molecular Structure and Computational Biology
John Aitchison, Charles Asbury, David Baker, James Champoux, John Clark, Michael Gelb, Bertil Hille, Wim Hol, Rachel Klevit, Raymond Monnat, Ilya Shmulevich, Leonidas Stamatatos, Ronald Stenkamp, Gabriele Varani, Ning Zheng.

Neuroscience
Sandra Bajjalieh, Andres Barria, Joseph Beavo, Olivia Bermingham-McDonogh, Susan Brockerhoff, William Catterall, Jeffrey Chamberlain, Charles Chavkin, Ajay Dhaka, Sharona Gordon, Matthew Kaeberlein, Stanley McKnight, Neil Nathanson, John Neumaier, Richard Palmiter, Paul Phillips, David Raible, Nephi Stella, Bruce Tempel, Rachel Wong, Zhengui Xia.

FRED HUTCHINSON CANCER RESEARCH CENTER

Cancer Biology
Antonio Bedalov, Laura Beretta, Jason Bielas, Bruce Clurman, Steven Collins, Robert Eisenman, Matthew Fero, Denise Galloway, David Hockenbery, Christopher Kemp, Beatrice Knudsen, Paul Lampe, Dusty Miller, Peter Nelson, James Olson, Amanda Paulovich, Peggy Porter, Nina Salama, Akiko Shimamura, Julian Simon, Toshiyasu Taniguchi, Stephen Tapscott, Muneesh Tewari, Valeri Vasioukhin, Edus Warren, Cassian Yee.

Cell Biology, Signaling, and Cell/Environment Interactions
Linda Breeden, Steven Collins, Jonathan Cooper, Robert Eisenman, Daniel Gottschling, David Hockenbery, Paul Lampe, Susan Parkhurst, James Priess, Mark Roth, Wenying Shou, Marc Van Gilst, Valeri Vasioukhin.

Developmental Biology and Stem Cells
Jonathan Cooper, Robert Eisenman, Cecilia Moens, Patrick Paddison, Susan Parkhurst, James Priess.

Gene Expression, Cell Cycle, and Chromosome Biology
Antonio Bedalov, Sue Biggins, Linda Breeden, Robert Eisenman, Matthew Fero, Adam Geballe, Daniel Gottschling, Mark Groudine, Steven Hahn, Steven Henikoff, Amanda Paulovich, Mark Roth, Gerald Smith, Stephen Tapscott, Barbara Trask, Toshio Tsukiyama.

Genetics, Genomics, and Evolution
Antonio Bedalov, Michael Emerman, Adam Geballe, Daniel Gottschling, Steven Hahn, Steven Henikoff, Harmit Malik, Peter Nelson, Amanda Paulovich, Katie Peichel, Wenying Shou, Muneesh Tewari, Barbara Trask.

Microbiology, Infection, and Immunity
Laura Beretta, Michael Emerman, Denise Galloway, Adam Geballe, Keith Jerome, Hans-Peter Kiem, Maxine Linial, Dusty Miller, Julie Overbaugh, Nina Salama, Roland Strong, Edus Warren.

Molecular Structure and Computational Biology
Adrian Ferre-D'Amare, Steven Hahn, Barry Stoddard, Roland Strong.

Neuroscience
Linda Buck, Cecilia Moens, James Olson.

WAYNE STATE UNIVERSITY

School of Medicine
Graduate Program in Cancer Biology

Program of Study

This nationally recognized Ph.D. in Cancer Biology–granting program was established in 1989. The program's multidisciplinary and interdisciplinary faculty is mostly in the School of Medicine and the Barbara Ann Karmanos Cancer Institute (BAKCI). The program's faculty members are from basic and clinical science departments, their research is well supported with national competitive funding, and they are experienced in graduate student/Ph.D. candidate education and research training. The scope of the faculty's cutting-edge cancer biology research is broad, encompassing basic and translational cancer biology research in areas including drug discovery and development, proteases and metastasis, molecular oncology and human genetics, breast cancer, chemical carcinogenesis and toxicology, and prevention. Their research is on specific topics, such as mechanisms of cell proliferation control, apoptosis, DNA repair, cell-cell interactions, invasion, and metastasis. Cancer biology is a new multi- and interdisciplinary field that requires education and research training in many disciplines, including cellular biology, molecular biology, pharmacology, and oncology. Students' first year is devoted primarily to courses, research explorations, and seminars, and by the end, the student chooses a graduate adviser who guides the initial research. During the second year, each student completes most of the course requirements, progresses to dissertation research, and fulfills the dissertation prospectus requirement. Subsequent years as a predoctoral candidate are devoted primarily to dissertation research. Additional details are available at the program's Web site. The average time to degree is less than five years.

Research Facilities

The cancer biology faculty has more than 100,000 square feet of modern laboratory space. Besides typical laboratory instruments, there are many specialized core facilities (e.g., molecular biology and genetics, biostatistics, flow cytometry/cell sorting, and confocal imaging) equipment (e.g., DNA and protein synthesis and sequencing, X-ray crystallography, and spectroscopy), science libraries, and computer facilities.

Financial Aid

Support is awarded on a competitive basis to first-year graduate students, who receive full financial support until completion provided the program's standards of progress are met. A significant addition to the stipend is available to U.S. citizens and permanent residents who can qualify for support from training grants and individual fellowships. Support includes full tuition (see Cost of Study section), insurances (medical, dental, and vision) and annual stipend of more than $20,389, for an approximate total value of at least $37,000 for Michigan residents and $47,500 for nonresidents. Applicants who are U.S. citizens or permanent residents are encouraged to also apply for an Undergraduate Summer Cancer Biology Research Fellowship.

Cost of Study

Supported students have their tuition and fees covered (approximately $11,300 and $23,500 per year for Michigan and nonresident students, respectively).

Living and Housing Costs

WSU has a variety of furnished and unfurnished graduate student apartments. The metropolitan area has high-quality housing within a modest price range. The University Housing Office assists students in locating housing. Living costs, food, and recreation are modest. There are abundant employment opportunities for spouses.

Student Group

The program annually has over 25 enrolled students and Ph.D. candidates. Current students are from several states (Michigan, Minnesota, Mississippi, New York, Washington D.C., Wisconsin, Utah) and other countries (Canada, India, Thailand). They are a significant component of the School of Medicine's approximately 180 Ph.D. students.

Student Outcomes

The vast majority of the program's over 60 Ph.D. in Cancer Biology alumni progressed to postdoctoral training in excellent laboratories at prestigious institutions such as Duke, Harvard, Johns Hopkins, Yale, University of Michigan, National Institutes of Health, and Scripps Research Institute. Many graduates have progressed to faculty appointments (e.g., Grand Valley State, Loma Linda, Michigan State, Northwestern, and Wake Forest Universities) or to investigator positions at research institutes (e.g., Scripps Research Institute) or pharmaceutical enterprises (e.g., Millennium Pharmaceuticals).

Location

WSU is in the University Cultural Center with the Institute of Arts, Orchestra Hall, Public Library, theaters, schools of art and music, and the African-American Museum. Nearby are major sports (baseball, hockey, football) facilities. The riverfront, lakes, and parks are in driving distance.

The University

WSU is a major public urban research university with nine major schools and colleges. BAKCI is a National Cancer Institute–designated Comprehensive Cancer Center, a nationally recognized institution of basic, translational, and clinical cancer research excellence.

Applying

Applications are encouraged from U.S. citizens or permanent residents, particularly diverse individuals, as well as international students. A copy of official transcripts from all previously attended institutions must include one that reports at least a bachelor's degree from an accredited school or evidence that the degree requirements will be completed before matriculation. The cumulative degree posted grade point average should be at least 3.0 (on a 4.0 scale). Transcripts must report one full year each of general/inorganic chemistry, organic chemistry, and biology; one full year of calculus and of physics are recommended but not required. The GRE General Test is required, and a score report is mandatory. International applicants must provide a copy of the TOEFL or an equivalent exam score report. Three letters of evaluation are required; they may be mailed directly or submitted via the online application mechanism. A brief (one-page) Statement of Purpose is required (a description of the applicant's background, goals, and objectives). A brief description of research experiences should be detailed in a one-page addendum. Complete applications should be submitted well in advance of March 1.

Correspondence and Information

Dr. Robert J. Pauley, Director
Graduate Program in Cancer Biology
School of Medicine
Wayne State University
550 East Canfield Avenue, Room 329
Detroit, Michigan 48202
Phone: 313-577-1065
E-mail: rpauley@med.wayne.edu
　　　ad3340@wayne.edu (to send applications)
Web site: http://www.med.wayne.edu/cancer/

Wayne State University

THE FACULTY AND THEIR RESEARCH

Ayad M. Al-Katib, Professor of Medicine; M.D., Mosul Medical College (Iraq), 1974. Biology and experimental therapeutics of human lymphoid tumors.

Julie L. Boerner, Assistant Professor of Pharmacology, Karmanos Cancer Institute; Ph.D., Mayo, 2000. Ligand-independent EGFR signaling.

George S. Brush, Associate Professor of Pathology, Karmanos Cancer Institute; Ph.D., Johns Hopkins, 1991. DNA damage and DNA replication checkpoints.

Angelika M. Burger, Professor of Pharmacology, Karmanos Cancer Institute; Ph.D., Johannes Gutenberg (Germany), 1992; Ph.D., Bradford (UK), 2005. Molecular targets and cancer therapeutics.

Ben D.-M. Chen, Professor of Medicine; Ph.D., Vanderbilt, 1977. Regulation of macrophage production and differentiation by hematopoietic growth factor; growth-factor receptor; signal transduction.

Michael L. Cher, Professor of Urology and Pathology, Karmanos Cancer Institute; M.D., Washington (St. Louis), 1986. Biology of prostate cancer bone metastasis.

Sreenivasa R. Chinni, Assistant Professor, Departments of Urology and Pathology and Karmanos Cancer Institute; Ph.D., Louisville, 1997. Chemokine signaling; prostate cancer bone metastasis.

Q. Ping Dou, Professor of Pathology; Ph.D., Rutgers, 1988. Chemoprevention and molecular targeting.

James F. Eliason, Associate Professor of Medicine and Oncology; Ph.D., Chicago, 1978. Mechanisms of drug resistance and prediction of patient response to therapy.

Stephen P. Ethier, Professor of Pathology; Associate Center Director, Basic Research; and Deputy Director, Karmanos Cancer Institute; Ph.D., Tennessee–Oak Ridge, 1982. Breast cancer genetics, cell biology, and cell signaling.

David R. Evans, Professor of Biochemistry; Ph.D., Wayne State, 1968. Structure and control mechanisms of enzymes that regulate mammalian pyrimidine biosynthesis.

Joseph A. Fontana, Professor of Medicine; Ph.D., Johns Hopkins, 1969; M.D., Pennsylvania, 1975. Retinoids and their signaling pathways.

Rafael Fridman, Professor of Pathology; Ph.D., Jerusalem, 1986. Role of tumor proteases in tumor cell invasion.

Craig N. Giroux, Associate Professor of Institute of Environmental Health; Ph.D., MIT, 1979. Molecular biology of germ line differentiation; genome stability; developmental genetics; mechanisms of mutation and tumor prevention.

David H. Gorski, Associate Professor of Surgery, Karmanos Cancer Institute; M.D., Michigan, 1988; Ph.D., Case Western Reserve, 1994. Breast cancer and regulation of tumor angiogenesis.

Miriam L. Greenberg, Professor of Biological Sciences; Ph.D., Yeshiva (Einstein), 1980. Regulation of membrane biogenesis; genetic control of phospholipid biosynthesis; inositol phosphate metabolism in yeast.

Ahmad R. Heydari, Associate Professor of Nutrition and Food Science; Ph.D., Illinois State, 1990. Nutrient-gene interactions in aging and neoplasia; nutrients and DNA damage and repair.

Kenneth V. Honn, Professor of Radiation Oncology and Pathology; Ph.D., Wayne State, 1977. Cancer biology: role of kinases, eicosanoids, and integrin receptors in tumor invasion/metastasis.

Michael C. Joiner, Professor of Radiation Oncology; Ph.D., London, 1980. Mechanisms underlying variation in response to ionizing radiation.

David H. Kessel, Professor of Pharmacology and of Medicine; Ph.D., Michigan, 1959. Photosensitization of neoplastic cells; photobiology; mechanisms of drug resistance.

Hyeong-Reh C. Kim, Professor of Pathology; Ph.D., Northwestern, 1989. Growth factor signaling and regulation of apoptosis.

Thomas A. Kocarek, Associate Professor, Institute of Chemical Toxicology; Ph.D., Ohio State, 1988. Regulation of cytochrome P-450 gene expression

Adhip N. Majumdar, Professor of Internal Medicine; Ph.D., London, 1968. Aging and carcinogenesis of the gastrointestinal tract, in particular, the role of EGF-receptor family in regulating growth and transformation.

Larry H. Matherly, Professor of Pharmacology and Associate Member, Karmanos Cancer Institute; Ph.D., Penn State, 1981. Cancer chemotherapy: mechanisms of action of antitumor agents; mechanisms of drug resistance.

Raymond R. Mattingly, Associate Professor of Pharmacology; Ph.D., Virginia, 1993. Signal transduction through Ras and heterotrimeric GTP-binding proteins.

Fred R. Miller, Professor, Karmanos Cancer Institute; Ph.D., Wisconsin–Madison, 1976. Progression of preneoplastic breast disease; stromal-epithelial interactions; mechanisms of metastasis.

Ramzi Mohammad, Professor of Hematology and Oncology; Ph.D., Utah State, 1987. Developmental therapeutic program.

Raymond F. Novak, Professor of Pharmacology and Director, Institute of Environmental Health Sciences; Ph.D., Case Western Reserve, 1973. Role of intracellular and extracellular matrix signaling in gene expression; cell function and tumorigenesis; microarray analysis and global gene expression profiling.

Robert J. Pauley, Professor; Ph.D., Marquette, 1975. Molecular oncology: *Mtv* (mammary tumor virus) and oncogenes; human breast neoplasia.

Izabela Podgorski, Assistant Professor, Department of Pharmacology and Karmanos Cancer Institute; Ph.D., Oakland, 2001. Obesity; inflammation; prostate cancer.

Venuprasad K. Poojary, Assistant Professor, Karmanos Cancer Institute and Department of Immunolagy and Microbiology; Ph.D., National Center for Cell Science (India), 2002. Cell signaling in the immune system; regulation of inflammation; anti-tumor immune response.

Avraham Raz, Professor of Radiation Oncology and Pathology and Director, Cancer Metastasis Program, Karmanos Cancer Institute; Ph.D., Weizmann (Israel), 1978. Tumor metastasis: role of adhesion molecule in tumor spread

John J. Reiners Jr., Professor of Pharmacology and Associate Professor, Environmental Health Science; Ph.D., Purdue, 1977. Mechanisms of chemical-induced carcinogenesis, signal transduction, and immunomodulation.

James H. Rigby, Professor of Chemistry; Ph.D., Wisconsin–Madison, 1977. Total synthesis and structure-activity studies on tumor-promoting diterpenes and alkaloids; total synthesis of antitumor natural products.

Arun K. Rishi, Associate Professor of Internal Medicine; Ph.D., London, 1987. Retinoid-dependent and -independent cell-cycle and apoptosis regulatory pathways.

Louis J. Romano, Professor of Chemistry; Ph.D., Rutgers, 1976. Chemical carcinogenesis; mutagenesis; replication of damaged DNA.

Melissa Runge-Morris, Associate Professor, Institute of Chemical Toxicology; M.D., Michigan, 1979. Molecular regulation of the sulfotransferase multigene family.

Fazlul H. Sarkar, Professor of Pathology; Ph.D., Banaras Hindu (India), 1978. Molecular biology of human adenocarcinoma; gene expression and regulation, activation and inactivation, and mutation; tumor angiogenesis; invasion and metastasis.

Ann G. Schwartz, Professor, Internal Medicine and Cancer Institute, and Associate Center Director, Population Sciences, Karmanos Cancer Institute; Ph.D., Michigan, 1986. Genetic epidemiology of lung cancer.

Malathy Shekhar, Associate Professor of Pathology; Ph.D., Indian Institute of Science, 1985. Breast cancer.

Shijie Sheng, Associate Professor of Pathology; Ph.D., Florida, 1993. Tumor invasion and metastasis/proteolysis.

Anthony Shields, Professor of Internal Medicine; M.D., Harvard, 1979; Ph.D., MIT, 1979. Positron emission tomography.

Debra F. Skafar, Associate Professor of Physiology; Ph.D., Vanderbilt, 1983. Estrogen receptor signaling mechanisms.

Bonnie F. Sloane, Professor and Chair of Pharmacology; Ph.D., Rutgers, 1976. Cancer biology: role of cysteine proteinases and their inhibitors in malignant progression.

Michael A. Tainsky, Professor of Pathology and Member, Karmanos Cancer Institute; Ph.D., Cornell, 1977. Molecular oncology and genetics.

Jeffrey W. Taub, M.D., Associate Professor of Pediatrics; M.D., Western Ontario, 1987. Molecular epidemiology and pharmacology of childhood leukemia.

Wei-Zen Wei, Professor of Immunology, Karmanos Cancer Institute; Ph.D., Brown, 1978. Host immunity in mammary tumorigenesis; modulation of mammary-tumor progression.

Gen Sheng Wu, Assistant Professor of Cancer Biology and Immunology; Ph.D., Chinese Academy of Medical Sciences (Beijing), 1992. Tumor suppressor genes and chemosensitivity.

Guojun Wu, Assistant Professor of Pathology, Karmanos Cancer Institute; Ph.D., Fudan (China), 1998. Oncogene, tumor suppressor gene, and breast cancer metastasis.

Hai-Young Wu, Associate Professor of Pharmacology; Ph.D., CUNY Graduate Center, 1985. DNA topology; DNA conformation; gene expression regulation.

Youming Xie, Assistant Professor of Pathology, Karmanos Cancer Institute; Ph.D., Texas, 1996. The ubiquitin-proteasome system.

Fayth Yoshimura, Associate Professor of Immunology and Microbiology; Ph.D., Yale, 1972. Pathogenesis of oncogenic murine retroviruses.

Section 7
Computational, Systems, and Translational Biology

This section contains a directory of institutions offering graduate work in computational, systems, and translational biology, followed by in-depth entries submitted by institutions that chose to prepare detailed program descriptions. Additional information about programs listed in the directory but not augmented by an in-depth entry may be obtained by writing directly to the dean of a graduate school or chair of a department at the address given in the directory.

CONTENTS

Program Directories

Close-Ups

Computational Biology

Arizona State University, Graduate College, College of Liberal Arts and Sciences, Division of Natural Sciences, Department of Mathematics and Statistics, Program in Computational Biosciences, Tempe, AZ 85287. Offers PSM.

Baylor College of Medicine, Graduate School of Biomedical Sciences, Program in Structural and Computational Biology and Molecular Biophysics, Houston, TX 77030-3498. Offers PhD, MD/PhD. *Faculty:* 71 full-time (11 women). *Students:* 48 full-time (19 women); includes 5 minority (3 Asian Americans or Pacific Islanders, 2 Hispanic Americans), 18 international. Average age 25. In 2009, 6 doctorates awarded. *Degree requirements:* For doctorate, thesis/dissertation, public defense. *Entrance requirements:* For doctorate, GRE General Test, GRE Subject Test (strongly recommended), minimum GPA of 3.0. Additional exam requirements/recommendations for international students: Required—TOEFL. *Application deadline:* For fall admission, 1/1 for domestic students. Application fee: $0. Electronic applications accepted. *Financial support:* In 2009–10, 48 students received support; fellowships, research assistantships, career-related internships or fieldwork, Federal Work-Study, institutionally sponsored loans, health care benefits, and students receive a scholarship unless there are grant funds available to pay tuition available. Financial award applicants required to submit FAFSA. *Faculty research:* X-ray and electron crystallography, light and electron microscopy, computer image reconstruction, molecular spectroscopy. *Unit head:* Dr. Wah Chiu, Director, 713-798-6985. *Application contact:* Lourdes Fernandez, Graduate Program Administrator, 713-798-6557, Fax: 713-798-6325.

See Close-Up on page 259.

Carnegie Mellon University, Joint CMU-Pitt PhD Program in Computational Biology, Pittsburgh, PA 15213-3891. Offers PhD.

Carnegie Mellon University, Mellon College of Science, Department of Biological Sciences, Program in Computational Biology, Pittsburgh, PA 15213-3891. Offers MS. *Entrance requirements:* For master's, GRE General Test, GRE Subject Test, interview.

Claremont Graduate University, Graduate Programs, School of Mathematical Sciences, Claremont, CA 91711-6160. Offers computational and systems biology (PhD); computational mathematics and numerical analysis (MA, MS); computational science (PhD); engineering and industrial applied mathematics (PhD); mathematics (PhD); operations research and statistics (MA, MS); physical applied mathematics (MA, MS); pure mathematics (MA, MS); scientific computing (MA, MS); systems and control theory (MA, MS). Part-time programs available. *Faculty:* 5 full-time (0 women), 2 part-time/adjunct (0 women). *Students:* 56 full-time (20 women), 12 part-time (3 women); includes 13 minority (2 African Americans, 6 Asian Americans or Pacific Islanders, 5 Hispanic Americans), 25 international. Average age 33. In 2009, 7 master's, 7 doctorates awarded. Terminal master's awarded for partial completion of doctoral program. *Entrance requirements:* For master's and doctorate, GRE General Test. Additional exam requirements/recommendations for international students: Required—TOEFL (minimum score 550 paper-based; 213 computer-based; 80 iBT). *Application deadline:* For fall admission, 2/1 priority date for domestic students. Applications are processed on a rolling basis. Application fee: $60. Electronic applications accepted. *Expenses:* Tuition: Full-time $35,046; part-time $1524 per credit. Required fees: $161 per semester. *Financial support:* Fellowships, research assistantships, Federal Work-Study, institutionally sponsored loans, scholarships/grants, and tuition waivers (full and partial) available. Support available to part-time students. Financial award application deadline: 2/15; financial award applicants required to submit FAFSA. *Unit head:* John Angus, Dean, 909-621-8080, Fax: 909-607-8261, E-mail: john.angus@cgu.edu. *Application contact:* Susan Townzen, Program Coordinator, 909-621-8080, Fax: 909-607-8261, E-mail: susan.n.townzen@cgu.edu.

Cornell University, Graduate School, Graduate Fields of Agriculture and Life Sciences, Field of Computational Biology, Ithaca, NY 14853-0001. Offers computational behavioral biology (PhD); computational biology (PhD); computational cell biology (PhD); computational ecology (PhD); computational macromolecular biology (PhD); computational organismal biology (PhD). *Faculty:* 40 full-time (5 women). *Students:* 17 full-time (4 women); includes 4 minority (3 Asian Americans or Pacific Islanders, 1 Hispanic American), 4 international. Average age 28. 142 applicants, 11% accepted, 6 enrolled. *Degree requirements:* For doctorate, comprehensive exam, thesis/dissertation, 2 semesters of teaching experience. *Entrance requirements:* For doctorate, GRE General Test, GRE Subject Test (biology), 2 letters of recommendation. Additional exam requirements/recommendations for international students: Required—TOEFL (minimum score 550 paper-based; 213 computer-based; 77 iBT). *Application deadline:* For fall admission, 2/1 priority date for domestic students. Application fee: $70. Electronic applications accepted. *Expenses:* Tuition: Full-time $29,500. Required fees: $70. Full-time tuition and fees vary according to degree level, program and student level. *Financial support:* In 2009–10, 6 fellowships with full tuition reimbursements were awarded; research assistantships with full tuition reimbursements, teaching assistantships with full tuition reimbursements, institutionally sponsored loans, scholarships/grants, health care benefits, tuition waivers (full and partial), and unspecified assistantships also available. Financial award applicants required to submit FAFSA. *Faculty research:* Computational behavioral biology, computational biology, computational cell biology, computational ecology, computational genetics, computational macromolecular biology, computational organismal biology. *Unit head:* Dr. Andrew Clark, Director of Graduate Studies, 607-255-5488, E-mail: ac347@cornell.edu. *Application contact:* Graduate School Application Requests, 607-255-5816, E-mail: gradadmissions@cornell.edu.

Cornell University, Joan and Sanford I. Weill Medical College and Graduate School of Medical Sciences, Weill Cornell Graduate School of Medical Sciences, Tri-Institutional Training Program in Computational Biology and Medicine, New York, NY 10065. Offers PhD. *Faculty:* 45 full-time (7 women). *Students:* 34 full-time (12 women); includes 8 minority (1 African American, 7 Asian Americans or Pacific Islanders), 12 international. 142 applicants, 11% accepted, 6 enrolled.Terminal master's awarded for partial completion of doctoral program. *Degree requirements:* For doctorate, comprehensive exam, thesis/dissertation. *Entrance requirements:* For doctorate, GRE. Additional exam requirements/recommendations for international students: Required—TOEFL. *Application deadline:* For winter admission, 1/1 for domestic and international students. Application fee: $70. Electronic applications accepted. *Expenses:* Tuition: Full-time $44,650. Required fees: $2805. *Financial support:* In 2009–10, 34 students received support, including 34 fellowships with full tuition reimbursements available (averaging $37,000 per year). *Faculty research:* Biophysics/structural biology; genomics/bioinformatics; modeling/systems biology; neuroscience; cancer biology. *Unit head:* Kathleen E. Pickering, Executive Director, 212-746-6049, Fax: 212-746-8992, E-mail: cbm@triiprograms.org. *Application contact:* Margie H. Mendoza, Program Administrator, 212-746-5267, Fax: 212-746-8992, E-mail: cbm@triiprograms.org.

Florida State University, The Graduate School, College of Arts and Sciences, Program in Molecular Biophysics, Tallahassee, FL 32306. Offers biochemistry, molecular and cell biology (PhD); computational structural biology (PhD); molecular biophysics (PhD). *Faculty:* 49 full-time (6 women). *Students:* 22 full-time (8 women); includes 6 minority (5 Asian Americans or Pacific Islanders, 1 Hispanic American). Average age 28. 30 applicants, 33% accepted, 7 enrolled. In 2009, 5 doctorates awarded. *Degree requirements:* For doctorate, comprehensive exam, thesis/dissertation, teaching 1 term in professor's major department. *Entrance requirements:* For doctorate, GRE General Test. Additional exam requirements/recommendations for international students: Required—TOEFL (minimum score 600 paper-based; 250 computer-based; 100 iBT). *Application deadline:* For fall admission, 2/15 for domestic students, 3/15 for international students; for spring admission, 11/2 for international students. Applications are processed on a rolling basis. Application fee: $30. Electronic applications accepted. *Expenses:* Tuition, state resident: full-time $7413. Tuition, nonresident: full-time $22,567. *Financial support:* In 2009–10, 21 students received support, including fellowships with partial tuition reimbursements available (averaging $21,000 per year), 18 research assistantships with partial tuition reimbursements available (averaging $21,000 per year), 4 teaching assistantships with partial tuition reimbursements available (averaging $21,000 per year); scholarships/grants, health care benefits, and unspecified assistantships also available. Financial award applicants required to submit FAFSA. *Faculty research:* Protein and nucleic acid structure and function, membrane protein structure, computational biophysics, 3-D image reconstruction. Total annual research expenditures: $1.4 million. *Unit head:* Dr. Geoffrey Strouse, Director, 850-644-0056, Fax: 850-644-7244, E-mail: strouse@chem.fsu.edu. *Application contact:* Dr. Kerry Maddox, Academic Coordinator, Graduate Programs, 850-644-1012, Fax: 850-644-7244, E-mail: bkmaddox@sb.fsu.edu.

George Mason University, College of Science, Department of Bioinformatics and Computational Biology, Fairfax, VA 22030. Offers MS, PhD, Certificate. *Expenses:* Tuition, state resident: full-time $7568; part-time $315.33 per credit hour. Tuition, nonresident: full-time $21,704; part-time $904.33 per credit hour. Required fees: $2184; $91 per credit hour.

Iowa State University of Science and Technology, Graduate College, Interdisciplinary Programs, Bioinformatics and Computational Biology Program, Ames, IA 50011. Offers MS, PhD. *Students:* 52 full-time (19 women), 2 part-time (1 woman); includes 3 minority (all Asian Americans or Pacific Islanders), 34 international. In 2009, 2 master's, 11 doctorates awarded. *Degree requirements:* For doctorate, thesis/dissertation. *Entrance requirements:* For doctorate, GRE General Test. Additional exam requirements/recommendations for international students: Required—TOEFL (minimum score 550 paper-based; 213 computer-based; 79 iBT) or IELTS (minimum score 6.5). *Application deadline:* For fall admission, 1/15 priority date for domestic students, 1/15 for international students; for spring admission, 10/15 for domestic and international students. Application fee: $40 ($90 for international students). Electronic applications accepted. *Expenses:* Tuition, state resident: full-time $6716. Tuition, nonresident: full-time $8908. Tuition and fees vary according to course level, course load, program and student level. *Financial support:* In 2009–10, 48 research assistantships with full and partial tuition reimbursements (averaging $18,330 per year), 3 teaching assistantships (averaging $17,000 per year) were awarded; fellowships with full tuition reimbursements, scholarships/grants, traineeships, health care benefits, and unspecified assistantships also available. *Faculty research:* Functional and structural genomics, genome evolution, macromolecular structure and function, mathematical biology and biological statistics, metabolic and developmental networks. *Unit head:* Dr. Volker Brendel, Chair, Supervising Committee, 515-294-5122, Fax: 515-294-6790, E-mail: bcb@iastate.edu. *Application contact:* Dr. Volker Brendel, Chair, Supervising Committee, 515-294-5122, Fax: 515-294-6790, E-mail: bcb@iastate.edu.

Keck Graduate Institute of Applied Life Sciences, Bioscience Program, Claremont, CA 91711. Offers applied life science (PhD); bioscience (MBS); bioscience management (Certificate); computational systems biology (PhD). *Degree requirements:* For master's, comprehensive exam, project. *Entrance requirements:* For master's, GRE General Test or MCAT. Additional exam requirements/recommendations for international students: Required—TOEFL. Electronic applications accepted. *Faculty research:* Computational biology, drug discovery and development, molecular and cellular biology, biomedical engineering, biomaterials and tissue engineering.

Massachusetts Institute of Technology, School of Engineering and School of Science, Program in Computational and Systems Biology, Cambridge, MA 02139-4307. Offers PhD. *Students:* 36 full-time (14 women); includes 6 minority (1 African American, 4 Asian Americans or Pacific Islanders, 1 Hispanic American), 19 international. Average age 26. 148 applicants, 4% accepted, 6 enrolled. In 2009, 1 doctorate awarded. *Degree requirements:* For doctorate, comprehensive exam, thesis/dissertation. *Entrance requirements:* For doctorate, GRE General Test. Additional exam requirements/recommendations for international students: Required—IELTS (minimum score 6); Recommended—TOEFL (minimum score 577 paper-based; 233 computer-based). *Application deadline:* For fall admission, 12/15 for domestic and international students. Application fee: $75. Electronic applications accepted. *Expenses:* Tuition: Full-time $37,510; part-time $585 per unit. Required fees: $272. *Financial support:* In 2009–10, 33 students received support, including 16 fellowships (averaging $34,670 per year), 14 research assistantships (averaging $31,337 per year), 1 teaching assistantship; Federal Work-Study, institutionally sponsored loans, scholarships/grants, health care benefits, and unspecified assistantships also available. *Faculty research:* Computational biology and bioinformatics, biological design and synthetic biology, gene and protein networks, systems biology of cancer, nanobiology and microsystems. *Unit head:* Prof. Douglas A. Lauffenberger, Director, 617-324-0074, E-mail: csbi@mit.edu. *Application contact:* Academic Office, 617-324-0055, Fax: 617-253-8699, E-mail: csbphd@mit.edu.

Massachusetts Institute of Technology, School of Science, Department of Biology, Cambridge, MA 02139-4307. Offers biochemistry (PhD); biological oceanography (PhD); biology (PhD); biophysical chemistry and molecular structure (PhD); cell biology (PhD); computational and systems biology (PhD); developmental biology (PhD); genetics (PhD); immunology (PhD); microbiology (PhD); molecular biology (PhD); neurobiology (PhD). *Faculty:* 54 full-time (14 women). *Students:* 237 full-time (128 women); includes 65 minority (4 African Americans, 2 American Indian/Alaska Native, 33 Asian Americans or Pacific Islanders, 26 Hispanic Americans), 25 international. Average age 26. 645 applicants, 18% accepted, 49 enrolled. In 2009, 41 doctorates awarded. *Degree requirements:* For doctorate, comprehensive exam, thesis/dissertation. *Entrance requirements:* For doctorate, GRE General Test. Additional exam requirements/recommendations for international students: Required—TOEFL (minimum score 577 paper-based; 233 computer-based), IELTS (minimum score 6.5). *Application deadline:* For fall admission, 12/1 for domestic and international students. Application fee: $75. Electronic applications accepted. *Expenses:* Tuition: Full-time $37,510; part-time $585 per unit. Required fees: $272. *Financial support:* In 2009–10, 218 students received support, including 113 fellowships with tuition reimbursements available (averaging $31,816 per year), 109 research assistantships with tuition reimbursements available (averaging $29,254 per year); teaching assistantships with tuition reimbursements available, Federal Work-Study, institutionally sponsored loans, scholarships/grants, traineeships, health care benefits, and unspecified assistantships also available. *Faculty research:* DNA recombination, transcription and gene regulation, signal transduction, cell cycle, neuronal cell fate, replication and repair. Total annual research expenditures: $114 million. *Unit head:* Prof. Chris Kaiser, Head, 617-253-4701, E-mail: mitbio@mit.edu. *Application contact:* Biology Education Office, 617-253-3717, Fax: 617-258-9329, E-mail: gradbio@mit.edu.

New Jersey Institute of Technology, Office of Graduate Studies, College of Science and Liberal Arts, Department of Mathematical Science, Program in Computational Biology, Newark, NJ 07102. Offers MS. Part-time and evening/weekend programs available. *Entrance requirements:* For master's, GRE General Test. Additional exam requirements/recommendations for international students: Required—TOEFL (minimum score 550 paper-based; 213 computer-based; 79 iBT). Electronic applications accepted. *Faculty research:* Technological, computational, and mathematical aspects of biology and bioengineering.

New York University, Graduate School of Arts and Science, Department of Biology, Program in Computational Biology, New York, NY 10012-1019. Offers PhD. *Students:* 21 full-time (8 women), 4 part-time (2 women); includes 2 minority (both Asian Americans or Pacific Islanders), 6 international. Average age 31. 72 applicants, 15% accepted, 3 enrolled. In 2009, 2 doctorates awarded. *Entrance requirements:* For doctorate, GRE. Additional exam requirements/recommendations for international students: Required—TOEFL. Application fee: $90. *Expenses:* Tuition: Full-time $30,528; part-time $1272 per credit. Required fees: $2177. *Financial support:* Fellowships, research assistantships, teaching assistantships, Federal Work-Study, institutionally sponsored loans, scholarships/grants, health care benefits, and unspecified assistantships available. *Unit head:* Mike Shelley, Director, 212-998-4856, Fax: 212-995-4121, E-mail: fas.computational.biology@nyu.edu. *Application contact:* Susan Mrsic, Program Administrator, 212-998-4856, Fax: 212-995-4121, E-mail: fas.computational.biology@nyu.edu.

New York University, School of Medicine and Graduate School of Arts and Science, Sackler Institute of Graduate Biomedical Sciences, New York, NY 10012-1019. Offers cellular and molecular biology (PhD); computational biology (PhD); developmental genetics (PhD); medical and molecular parasitology (PhD); microbiology (PhD); molecular oncology and immunology (PhD), including immunology, molecular oncology; neuroscience and physiology (PhD); pathobiology (PhD); pharmacology (PhD), including molecular pharmacology; structural biology (PhD); MD/PhD. *Degree requirements:* For doctorate, comprehensive exam, thesis/dissertation, qualifying exam. *Entrance requirements:* For doctorate, GRE General Test. Additional exam requirements/recommendations for international students: Required—TOEFL. Electronic applications accepted. *Expenses:* Contact institution.

Northwestern University, McCormick School of Engineering and Applied Science, Program in Computational Biology and Bioinformatics, Evanston, IL 60208. Offers MS. Part-time programs available. *Degree requirements:* For master's, thesis. *Entrance requirements:* For master's, GRE General Test, 2 letters of reference. Additional exam requirements/recommendations for international students: Required—TOEFL (minimum score 600 paper-based; 250 computer-based). Electronic applications accepted. *Faculty research:* Mathematical models of protein signaling, high throughput DNA sequencing, macromolecule interactions, chemoinformatics, genome DNA sequence evolution.

Princeton University, Graduate School, Department of Molecular Biology, Princeton, NJ 08544-1019. Offers PhD. *Degree requirements:* For doctorate, thesis/dissertation. *Entrance requirements:* For doctorate, GRE General Test. Additional exam requirements/recommendations for international students: Required—TOEFL (minimum score 600 paper-based; 250 computer-based). Electronic applications accepted. *Faculty research:* Genetics, virology, biochemistry.

Rutgers, The State University of New Jersey, Newark, Graduate School, Program in Computational Biology, Newark, NJ 07102. Offers MS. *Entrance requirements:* For master's, GRE, minimum undergraduate B average. Additional exam requirements/recommendations for international students: Required—TOEFL.

Rutgers, The State University of New Jersey, New Brunswick, Graduate School-New Brunswick, BioMaPS Institute for Quantitative Biology, Piscataway, NJ 08854-8097. Offers computational biology and molecular biophysics (PhD). *Degree requirements:* For doctorate, comprehensive exam, thesis/dissertation. *Entrance requirements:* For doctorate, GRE. Additional exam requirements/recommendations for international students: Required—TOEFL. Electronic applications accepted. *Faculty research:* Structural biology, systems biology, bioinformatics, translational medicine, genomics.

University of Colorado Denver, Colorado School of Public Health, Health Services Research Program, Denver, CO 80217-3364. Offers computational bioscience (PhD); epidemiology (PhD); health services research (PhD). *Students:* 35 full-time (17 women), 3 part-time (all women); includes 3 minority (all Hispanic Americans), 3 international. In 2009, 3 doctorates awarded. *Degree requirements:* For doctorate, comprehensive exam, thesis/dissertation. *Entrance requirements:* For doctorate, GRE, interview, 3 letters of recommendation. Additional exam requirements/recommendations for international students: Required—TOEFL (minimum score 550 paper-based; 213 computer-based). *Application deadline:* For fall admission, 2/1 for domestic students. Application fee: $50. *Financial support:* Application deadline: 3/1. *Faculty research:* Biochemical functions of proteins, description and classification of enzymatic functions, optimization of genome-shuffling in gram negative bacteria. *Application contact:* Information Contact, 303-724-4613, Fax: 303-724-4620, E-mail: colorado.sph@ucdenver.edu.

University of Idaho, College of Graduate Studies, Program in Bioinformatics and Computational Biology, Moscow, ID 83844-2282. Offers MS, PhD. *Students:* 3 full-time, 1 part-time. In 2009, 1 master's awarded. *Entrance requirements:* For master's, GRE, minimum GPA of 2.8. *Application deadline:* For fall admission, 8/1 for domestic students; for spring admission, 12/15 for domestic students. Application fee: $55 ($60 for international students). *Expenses:* Tuition, state resident: full-time $6120. Tuition, nonresident: full-time $17,712. *Financial support:* Application deadline: 2/15. *Unit head:* Dr. Christopher Williams, Director, 208-885-6242, Fax: 208-885-6198, E-mail: bcb@uidaho.edu. *Application contact:* Dr. Christopher Williams, Director, 208-885-6242, Fax: 208-885-6198, E-mail: bcb@uidaho.edu.

University of Illinois at Urbana–Champaign, Graduate College, College of Liberal Arts and Sciences, School of Molecular and Cellular Biology, Center for Biophysics and Computational Biology, Champaign, IL 61820. Offers MS, PhD. *Students:* 71 full-time (16 women); includes 9 minority (7 Asian Americans or Pacific Islanders, 2 Hispanic Americans), 45 international. 88 applicants, 14% accepted, 12 enrolled. In 2009, 11 doctorates awarded. *Entrance requirements:* For doctorate, GRE, minimum GPA of 3.0. Additional exam requirements/recommendations for international students: Required—TOEFL. *Application deadline:* Applications are processed on a rolling basis. Application fee: $60 ($75 for international students). Electronic applications accepted. *Financial support:* In 2009–10, 17 fellowships, 63 research assistantships, 19 teaching assistantships were awarded; tuition waivers (full and partial) also available. *Unit head:* Martin Gruebele, Director, 217-333-1624, Fax: 217-244-3186, E-mail: mgruebel@illinois.edu. *Application contact:* Cynthia Dodds, Office Administrator, 217-333-1630, Fax: 217-244-6615, E-mail: dodds@illinois.edu.

The University of Iowa, Graduate College, Program in Informatics, Iowa City, IA 52242-1316. Offers bioinformatics and computational biology (Certificate); health informatics (MS, PhD, Certificate); information science (MS, PhD, Certificate). *Degree requirements:* For master's, thesis optional; for doctorate, comprehensive exam, thesis/dissertation. *Entrance requirements:* For master's and doctorate, GRE General Test, minimum GPA of 3.0. Additional exam requirements/recommendations for international students: Required—TOEFL (minimum score 550 paper-based; 213 computer-based; 81 iBT). Electronic applications accepted.

University of Pennsylvania, School of Medicine, Biomedical Graduate Studies, Graduate Group in Genomics and Computational Biology, Philadelphia, PA 19104. Offers PhD, MD/PhD, VMD/PhD. *Faculty:* 57. *Students:* 35 full-time (8 women); includes 11 minority (2 African Americans, 7 Asian Americans or Pacific Islanders, 2 Hispanic Americans), 9 international. 54 applicants, 19% accepted, 6 enrolled. In 2009, 5 doctorates awarded. *Degree requirements:* For doctorate, thesis/dissertation optional. *Entrance requirements:* For doctorate, GRE. Additional exam requirements/recommendations for international students: Required—TOEFL. *Application deadline:* For fall admission, 12/8 priority date for domestic and international students. Applications are processed on a rolling basis. Application fee: $70. Electronic applications accepted. *Expenses:* Tuition: Full-time $25,660; part-time $4758 per course. Required fees: $2152; $270 per course. Tuition and fees vary according to course load, degree level and program. *Financial support:* In 2009–10, 19 students received support; fellowships, research assistantships, scholarships/grants, traineeships, and unspecified assistantships available. *Unit head:* Dr. Maja Bucan, Chairperson, 215-898-0020. *Application contact:* Hannah Chervitz, Graduate Coordinator, 215-746-2807, E-mail: gcbcoord@pcbi.upenn.edu.

University of Pittsburgh, Joint CMU-Pitt PhD Program in Computational and Systems Biology, Pittsburgh, PA 15260. Offers PhD. *Faculty:* 76 full-time (10 women). *Students:* 44 full-time (9 women); includes 27 minority (all Asian Americans or Pacific Islanders). Average age 25. 206 applicants, 9% accepted, 7 enrolled. *Degree requirements:* For doctorate, comprehensive exam, thesis/dissertation, ethics training service as course assistant, seminar. *Entrance requirements:* For doctorate, GRE Subject Test (recommended), GRE General Test, 3 letters of recommendation, resume. Additional exam requirements/recommendations for international students: Required—TOEFL (minimum score 600 paper-based; 250 computer-based; 100 iBT). *Application deadline:* For fall admission, 1/15 priority date for domestic and international students. Application fee: $50. Electronic applications accepted. *Expenses:* Tuition, state resident: full-time $16,402; part-time $665 per credit. Tuition, nonresident: full-time $28,694; part-time $1175 per credit. Required fees: $690; $175 per term. Tuition and fees vary according to program. *Financial support:* In 2009–10, 44 students received support, including 7 fellowships with tuition reimbursements available, 37 research assistantships with full tuition reimbursements available (averaging $24,650 per year). *Faculty research:* Computational structural biology, computational genomics, cell and systems modeling, bioimage informatics, computational neurobiology. *Unit head:* Dr. Takis Benos, Director, 412-648-3315, Fax: 412-648-3163, E-mail: benos@pitt.edu. *Application contact:* Kelly Gentille, Assistant Programs Coordinator, 412-648-8107, Fax: 412-648-3163, E-mail: kmg120@pitt.edu.

University of Rochester, School of Medicine and Dentistry, Graduate Programs in Medicine and Dentistry, Department of Biostatistics and Computational Biology, Rochester, NY 14627. Offers medical statistics (MS); statistics (MA, PhD). Terminal master's awarded for partial completion of doctoral program. *Degree requirements:* For doctorate, thesis/dissertation, qualifying exam. *Entrance requirements:* For master's and doctorate, GRE General Test. Additional exam requirements/recommendations for international students: Required—TOEFL.

University of Southern California, Graduate School, College of Letters, Arts and Sciences, Department of Biological Sciences, Program in Molecular and Computational Biology, Los Angeles, CA 90089. Offers computational biology and bioinformatics (PhD); molecular biology (PhD). *Faculty:* 43 full-time (8 women). *Students:* 131 full-time (67 women), 3 part-time (1 woman); includes 23 minority (2 African Americans, 1 American Indian/Alaska Native, 13 Asian Americans or Pacific Islanders, 7 Hispanic Americans), 53 international. 158 applicants, 29% accepted, 18 enrolled. In 2009, 15 doctorates awarded. Terminal master's awarded for partial completion of doctoral program. *Degree requirements:* For doctorate, thesis/dissertation, qualifying examination, dissertation defense. *Entrance requirements:* For doctorate, GRE, 3 letters of recommendation, personal statement, resume, minimum GPA of 3.0. Additional exam requirements/recommendations for international students: Required—TOEFL (minimum score 600 paper-based; 250 computer-based; 100 iBT). *Application deadline:* For fall admission, 12/1 priority date for domestic students, 11/1 priority date for international students. Application fee: $85. Electronic applications accepted. *Expenses:* Tuition: Full-time $25,980; part-time $1315 per unit. Required fees: $554. One-time fee: $35 full-time. Full-time tuition and fees vary according to degree level and program. *Financial support:* In 2009–10, 57 students received support, including 8 fellowships with full tuition reimbursements available (averaging $27,000 per year), 44 research assistantships with full tuition reimbursements available (averaging $25,333 per year), 5 teaching assistantships with full tuition reimbursements available (averaging $25,333 per year); scholarships/grants, traineeships, health care benefits, and tuition waivers also available. *Faculty research:* Cell and developmental biology, cancer biology, computational biology and bioinformatics, genetics, computational neurobiology. *Unit head:* Dr. Myron Goodman, Professor of Biological Sciences and Chemistry/Director of the MCB Research Section, 213-740-5190, E-mail: mgoodman@usc.edu. *Application contact:* Catherine Atienza, Student Services Advisor I, 213-740-5188, E-mail: catherine.atienza@usc.edu.

The University of Texas Medical Branch, Graduate School of Biomedical Sciences, Program in Biochemistry and Molecular Biology, Galveston, TX 77555. Offers biochemistry (PhD); bioinformatics (PhD); biophysics (PhD); cell biology (PhD); computational biology (PhD); structural biology (PhD). *Students:* 41 full-time (17 women); includes 6 minority (1 African American, 1 Asian American or Pacific Islander, 4 Hispanic Americans), 22 international. Average age 28. In 2009, 9 doctorates awarded. *Degree requirements:* For doctorate, thesis/dissertation. *Entrance requirements:* Additional exam requirements/recommendations for international students: Required—TOEFL (minimum score 550 paper-based; 213 computer-based). *Application deadline:* Applications are processed on a rolling basis. Application fee: $30 ($75 for international students). Electronic applications accepted. *Financial support:* In 2009–10, fellowships (averaging $25,000 per year), research assistantships (averaging $25,000 per year) were awarded. Financial award applicants required to submit FAFSA. *Unit head:* Dr. Sarita Sastry, Director, 409-747-1915, Fax: 409-747-1938, E-mail: sasastry@utmb.edu. *Application contact:* Debora Botting, Coordinator for Special Programs, 409-772-2769, Fax: 409-772-5102, E-mail: dmbottin@utmb.edu.

University of Wyoming, Graduate Program in Molecular and Cellular Life Sciences, Laramie, WY 82070. Offers PhD. *Degree requirements:* For doctorate, thesis/dissertation, four eight-week laboratory rotations, comprehensive basic practical exam, two-part qualifying exam, seminars, symposium.

Virginia Polytechnic Institute and State University, Graduate School, Intercollege, Program in Genetics, Bioinformatics and Computational Biology, Blacksburg, VA 24061. Offers PhD. *Students:* 40 full-time (20 women), 3 part-time (2 women); includes 34 minority (26 American Indian/Alaska Native, 6 Asian Americans or Pacific Islanders, 2 Hispanic Americans). Average age 29. 39 applicants, 33% accepted, 8 enrolled. In 2009, 6 doctorates awarded. *Entrance requirements:* For doctorate, GRE, GMAT. Additional exam requirements/recommendations for international students: Required—TOEFL (minimum score 550 paper-based; 213 computer-based). *Application deadline:* For fall admission, 5/15 for international students; for spring admission, 10/15 for international students. Applications are processed on a rolling basis. Application fee: $65. Electronic applications accepted. *Expenses:* Tuition, area resident: Full-time $10,228; part-time $459 per credit hour. Tuition, nonresident: full-time $17,892; part-time $865 per credit hour. Required fees: $1966; $451 per semester. *Financial support:* Career-related internships or fieldwork, Federal Work-Study, scholarships/grants, and unspecified assistantships available. Financial award application deadline: 1/15. *Unit head:* Dr. David R. Bevan, Dean, 540-231-5040, Fax: 540-231-3010, E-mail: drbevan@vt.edu. *Application contact:* Dennie Munson, Information Contact, 540-231-1928, Fax: 540-231-3010, E-mail: dennie@vt.edu.

Washington University in St. Louis, Graduate School of Arts and Sciences, Division of Biology and Biomedical Sciences, Program in Computational Biology, St. Louis, MO 63130-4899. Offers PhD. *Degree requirements:* For doctorate, thesis/dissertation. Electronic applications accepted.

Yale University, School of Medicine and Graduate School of Arts and Sciences, Combined Program in Biological and Biomedical Sciences (BBS), Computational Biology and Bioinformatics Track, New Haven, CT 06520. Offers PhD, MD/PhD. *Students:* 3 full-time. *Entrance requirements:* Additional exam requirements/recommendations for international students: Required—TOEFL. *Application deadline:* For fall admission, 12/6 for domestic and international students. *Unit head:* Dr. Perry Miller, Director of Graduate Studies, 203-737-2903. *Application contact:* Lisa Sobel, Graduate Registrar, 203-737-6029.

Systems Biology

Cornell University, Joan and Sanford I. Weill Medical College and Graduate School of Medical Sciences, Weill Cornell Graduate School of Medical Sciences, Physiology, Biophysics and Systems Biology Program, New York, NY 10065. Offers MS, PhD. *Faculty:* 33 full-time (9 women). *Students:* 43 full-time (18 women); includes 8 minority (2 African Americans, 5 Asian Americans or Pacific Islanders, 1 Hispanic American), 21 international. Average age 23. 54 applicants, 28% accepted, 5 enrolled. In 2009, 5 doctorates awarded. Terminal master's awarded for partial completion of doctoral program. *Degree requirements:* For master's, comprehensive exam; for doctorate, thesis/dissertation, final exam. *Entrance requirements:* For doctorate, GRE General Test, introductory courses in biology, inorganic and organic chemistry, physics, and mathematics. Additional exam requirements/recommendations for international students: Required—TOEFL. *Application deadline:* For fall admission, 12/1 for domestic students. Application fee: $60. *Expenses:* Tuition: Full-time $44,650. Required fees: $2805. *Financial support:* In 2009–10, 3 fellowships (averaging $27,992 per year) were awarded; scholarships/grants, health care benefits, and stipends (given to all students) also available. *Faculty research:* Receptor mediated regulation of cell function, molecular properties of channels or receptors, bioinformatics, mathematical modeling. *Unit head:* Dr. Emre Aksay, Co-Director, 212-746-6207, E-mail: ema2004@med.cornell.edu. *Application contact:* Audrey Rivera, Program Coordinator, 212-746-6361, E-mail: ajr2004@med.cornell.edu.

Dartmouth College, Program in Experimental and Molecular Medicine, Biomedical Physiology Track, Hanover, NH 03755. Offers PhD.

Harvard University, Graduate School of Arts and Sciences, Department of Systems Biology, Cambridge, MA 02138. Offers PhD. *Degree requirements:* For doctorate, thesis/dissertation, lab rotation, qualifying examination. *Entrance requirements:* For doctorate, GRE. Additional exam requirements/recommendations for international students: Required—TOEFL. Electronic applications accepted. *Expenses:* Tuition: Full-time $33,696. Required fees: $1126. Full-time tuition and fees vary according to program.

Massachusetts Institute of Technology, School of Engineering and School of Science, Program in Computational and Systems Biology, Cambridge, MA 02139-4307. Offers PhD. *Students:* 36 full-time (14 women); includes 6 minority (1 African American, 4 Asian Americans or Pacific Islanders, 1 Hispanic American), 19 international. Average age 26. 148 applicants, 4% accepted, 6 enrolled. In 2009, 1 doctorate awarded. *Degree requirements:* For doctorate, comprehensive exam, thesis/dissertation. *Entrance requirements:* For doctorate, GRE General Test. Additional exam requirements/recommendations for international students: Required—IELTS (minimum score 6); Recommended—TOEFL (minimum score 577 paper-based; 233 computer-based). *Application deadline:* For fall admission, 12/15 for domestic and international students. Application fee: $75. Electronic applications accepted. *Expenses:* Tuition: Full-time $37,510; part-time $585 per unit. Required fees: $272. *Financial support:* In 2009–10, 33 students received support, including 16 fellowships (averaging $34,670 per year), 14 research assistantships (averaging $31,337 per year), 1 teaching assistantship; Federal Work-Study, institutionally sponsored loans, scholarships/grants, health care benefits, and unspecified assistantships also available. *Faculty research:* Computational biology and bioinformatics, biological design and synthetic biology, gene and protein networks, systems biology of cancer, nanobiology and microsystems. *Unit head:* Prof. Douglas A. Lauffenberger, Director, 617-324-0074, E-mail: csbi@mit.edu. *Application contact:* Academic Office, 617-324-0055, Fax: 617-253-8699, E-mail: csbphd@mit.edu.

Michigan State University, The Graduate School, College of Natural Science, Quantitative Biology Program, East Lansing, MI 48824. Offers PhD. *Faculty:* 4 full-time (0 women). *Students:* 10 full-time (5 women), 8 international. Average age 27. *Expenses:* Tuition, state resident: part-time $478.25 per credit hour. Tuition, nonresident: part-time $966.50 per credit hour. Part-time tuition and fees vary according to program. Total annual research expenditures: $21.6 million. *Unit head:* Dr. Robert Hausinger, Co-Director, 517-884-5404, E-mail: hausinge@msu.edu. *Application contact:* Helen Geiger, Administrative Assistant, 517-432-9895, Fax: 517-353-9334, E-mail: qbmi@msu.edu.

Rutgers, The State University of New Jersey, New Brunswick, Graduate School-New Brunswick, BioMaPS Institute for Quantitative Biology, Piscataway, NJ 08854-8097. Offers computational biology and molecular biophysics (PhD). *Degree requirements:* For doctorate, comprehensive exam, thesis/dissertation. *Entrance requirements:* For doctorate, GRE. Additional exam requirements/recommendations for international students: Required—TOEFL. Electronic applications accepted. *Faculty research:* Structural biology, systems biology, bioinformatics, translational medicine, genomics.

Texas A&M Health Science Center, Graduate School of Biomedical Sciences, Department of Systems Biology and Translational Medicine, College Station, TX 77840. Offers PhD. *Degree requirements:* For doctorate, thesis/dissertation. *Entrance requirements:* For doctorate, GRE General Test. *Faculty research:* Cardiovascular physiology, vascular cell and molecular biology.

University of California, Merced, Division of Graduate Studies, School of Natural Sciences, Merced, CA 95343. Offers applied mathematics (MS, PhD); biological engineering and small-scale technologies (MS, PhD); environmental systems (MS, PhD); mechanical engineering and applied mechanics (MS, PhD); physics and chemistry (PhD); quantitative and systems biology (MS, PhD). *Expenses:* Tuition, nonresident: full-time $15,102. Required fees: $10,919.

University of California, San Diego, Office of Graduate Studies, Division of Biological Sciences, Program in Plant Systems Biology, La Jolla, CA 92093. Offers PhD.

University of Chicago, Division of the Biological Sciences, Department of Molecular Biosciences, Committee on Genetics, Genomics and Systems Biology, Chicago, IL 60637-1513. Offers PhD. *Faculty:* 65 full-time (24 women). *Students:* 21 full-time (11 women); includes 6 minority (1 African American, 4 Asian Americans or Pacific Islanders, 1 Hispanic American). Average age 28. 35 applicants, 11% accepted, 4 enrolled. In 2009, 3 doctorates awarded. *Degree requirements:* For doctorate, thesis/dissertation, ethics class, 2 teaching assistantships. *Entrance requirements:* For doctorate, GRE General Test, minimum GPA of 3.0. Additional exam requirements/recommendations for international students: Required—TOEFL (minimum score 600 paper-based; 250 computer-based; 104 iBT), IELTS (minimum score 7). *Application deadline:* For fall admission, 12/1 priority date for domestic and international students. Application fee: $55. Electronic applications accepted. *Financial support:* In 2009–10, 21 students received support, including fellowships with tuition reimbursements available (averaging $29,781 per year), research assistantships with tuition reimbursements available (averaging $29,781 per year); institutionally sponsored loans, scholarships/grants, traineeships, and health care benefits also available. Financial award applicants required to submit FAFSA. *Faculty research:* Molecular genetics, developmental genetics, population genetics, human genetics. *Unit head:* Dr. Richard Hudson, Chair, 773-834-2978, Fax: 773-702-8093, E-mail: committee-on-genetics@uchicago.edu. *Application contact:* Sue Levison, Administrator, 773-702-2464, Fax: 773-702-3172, E-mail: committee-on-genetics@uchicago.edu.

University of Pittsburgh, Joint CMU-Pitt PhD Program in Computational and Systems Biology, Pittsburgh, PA 15260. Offers PhD. *Faculty:* 76 full-time (10 women). *Students:* 44 full-time (9 women); includes 27 minority (all Asian Americans or Pacific Islanders). Average age 25. 206 applicants, 9% accepted, 7 enrolled. *Degree requirements:* For doctorate, comprehensive exam, thesis/dissertation, ethics training service as course assistant, seminar. *Entrance requirements:* For doctorate, GRE Subject Test (recommended), GRE General Test, 3 letters of recommendation, resume. Additional exam requirements/recommendations for international students: Required—TOEFL (minimum score 600 paper-based; 250 computer-based; 100 iBT). *Application deadline:* For fall admission, 1/15 priority date for domestic and international students. Application fee: $50. Electronic applications accepted. *Expenses:* Tuition, state resident: full-time $16,402; part-time $665 per credit. Tuition, nonresident: full-time $28,694; part-time $1175 per credit. Required fees: $690; $175 per term. Tuition and fees vary according to program. *Financial support:* In 2009–10, 44 students received support, including 7 fellowships with tuition reimbursements available, 37 research assistantships with full tuition reimbursements available (averaging $24,650 per year). *Faculty research:* Computational structural biology, computational genomics, cell and systems modeling, bioimage informatics, computational neurobiology. *Unit head:* Dr. Takis Benos, Director, 412-648-3315, Fax: 412-648-3163, E-mail: benos@pitt.edu. *Application contact:* Kelly Gentille, Assistant Programs Coordinator, 412-648-8107, Fax: 412-648-3163, E-mail: kmg120@pitt.edu.

University of Southern California, Keck School of Medicine and Graduate School, Program in Systems Biology and Disease, Los Angeles, CA 90089. Offers PhD. *Faculty:* 213 full-time (54 women). *Students:* 29 full-time (16 women); includes 7 minority (1 African American, 3 Asian Americans or Pacific Islanders, 3 Hispanic Americans), 7 international. Average age 32. 3 applicants, 33% accepted, 1 enrolled. In 2009, 3 doctorates awarded. *Degree requirements:* For doctorate; comprehensive exam, thesis/dissertation. *Entrance requirements:* For doctorate, GRE, minimum GPA of 3.0. Additional exam requirements/recommendations for international students: Required—TOEFL (minimum score 600 paper-based; 250 computer-based; 100 iBT). *Application deadline:* For fall admission, 12/1 priority date for domestic and international students. Application fee: $85. Electronic applications accepted. *Expenses:* Tuition: Full-time $25,980; part-time $1315 per unit. Required fees: $554. One-time fee: $35 full-time. Full-time tuition and fees vary according to degree level and program. *Financial support:* In 2009–10, 27 students received support, including 5 fellowships (averaging $27,060 per year), 22 research assistantships with full tuition reimbursements available (averaging $27,060 per year); institutionally sponsored loans, scholarships/grants, traineeships, health care benefits, and unspecified assistantships also available. Financial award application deadline: 5/5; financial award applicants required to submit FAFSA. *Unit head:* Dr. Alicia McDonough, Director, 323-442-1475, Fax: 323-442-1199, E-mail: mcdonoug@usc.edu. *Application contact:* Dawn Burke, Student Program Coordinator, 323-442-1475, Fax: 323-442-1199, E-mail: pibbs@usc.edu.

University of Toronto, School of Graduate Studies, Life Sciences Division, Department of Cell and Systems Biology, Toronto, ON M5S 1A1, Canada. Offers M Sc, PhD. *Degree requirements:* For master's, thesis, thesis defense; for doctorate, thesis/dissertation, thesis defense, oral thesis examination. *Entrance requirements:* For master's, minimum B+ average in final year, B overall, 3 letters of reference. Additional exam requirements/recommendations for international students: Required—TOEFL (minimum score 580 paper-based; 237 computer-based), TWE (minimum score 5).

Virginia Commonwealth University, Graduate School, School of Life Sciences, Doctoral Program in Integrative Life Sciences, Richmond, VA 23284-9005. Offers PhD. *Entrance requirements:* For doctorate, GRE, minimum GPA of 3.0 in last 60 credits of undergraduate work or in graduate degree, 3 letters of recommendation. Additional exam requirements/recommendations for international students: Required—TOEFL.

Translational Biology

Baylor College of Medicine, Graduate School of Biomedical Sciences, Program in Translational Biology and Molecular Medicine, Houston, TX 77030-3498. Offers PhD. *Faculty:* 151 full-time (48 women). *Students:* 48 full-time (23 women); includes 13 minority (4 African Americans, 4 Asian Americans or Pacific Islanders, 5 Hispanic Americans), 14 international. Average age 24. *Degree requirements:* For doctorate, thesis/dissertation, public defense. *Entrance requirements:* For doctorate, GRE, minimum GPA of 3.0. Additional exam requirements/recommendations for international students: Required—TOEFL. *Application deadline:* For fall admission, 1/1 for domestic students. Application fee: $0. Electronic applications accepted. *Financial support:* In 2009–10, 48 students received support; fellowships, research assistantships, career-related internships or fieldwork, Federal Work-Study, health care benefits, and students receive a scholarship unless there are grant funds available to pay tuition available. Financial award applicants required to submit FAFSA. *Unit head:* Dr. Mary Estes, Director, 713-798-3585, Fax: 713-798-3586, E-mail: tbmm@bcm.edu. *Application contact:* Wanda Waguespack, Graduate Program Administrator, 713-798-1077, Fax: 713-798-3586, E-mail: wandaw@bcm.edu.

See Close-Up on page 261.

Cedars-Sinai Medical Center, Graduate Program in Biomedical Sciences and Translational Medicine, Los Angeles, CA 90048. Offers PhD. *Degree requirements:* For doctorate, comprehensive exam, thesis/dissertation. *Entrance requirements:* For doctorate, GRE, 3 letters of recommendation. Additional exam requirements/recommendations for international students: Required—TOEFL (minimum score 560 paper-based; 220 computer-based; 87 iBT). *Faculty research:* Immunology and infection, neuroscience, cardiovascular science, cancer, human genetics.

Texas A&M Health Science Center, Graduate School of Biomedical Sciences, Department of Systems Biology and Translational Medicine, College Station, TX 77840. Offers PhD. *Degree requirements:* For doctorate, thesis/dissertation. *Entrance requirements:* For doctorate, GRE General Test. *Faculty research:* Cardiovascular physiology, vascular cell and molecular biology.

The University of Iowa, Graduate College, Program in Translational Biomedicine, Iowa City, IA 52242-1316. Offers MS, PhD. Terminal master's awarded for partial completion of doctoral program. *Degree requirements:* For master's, comprehensive exam; for doctorate, comprehensive exam, thesis/dissertation. *Entrance requirements:* For master's and doctorate, minimum GPA of 3.0. Additional exam requirements/recommendations for international students: Required—TOEFL (minimum score 550 paper-based; 213 computer-based; 81 iBT). Electronic applications accepted.

BAYLOR COLLEGE OF MEDICINE

Structural and Computational Biology and Molecular Biophysics

Program of Study

The Structural and Computational Biology and Molecular Biophysics (SCBMB) program is an interdisciplinary and interdepartmental program that offers a Ph.D. in structural and computational biology and molecular biophysics. This program is designed to train students by employing a strong research emphasis in these areas while also providing a solid background in biochemistry and cellular and molecular biology.

Faculty research activities cover development of state-of-the-art structural and computational techniques, protein design and engineering, biophysical chemistry of macromolecules, DNA structure and topology, membrane biophysics, and genome informatics. Over 70 faculty members in this program, from different departments at Baylor College of Medicine (BCM), Rice University, the University of Houston (UH), the University of Texas–Houston Health Science Center (UT–HSC), the University of Texas–M. D. Anderson Cancer Center (MDACC), and the University of Texas Medical Branch in Galveston (UTMB) are involved in teaching and supervising students' research.

The program seeks applicants with undergraduate degrees in physical, chemical, mathematical, computational, and engineering sciences as well as students with traditional backgrounds in biochemistry and molecular biology. The first-year curriculum is tailored to each student's background; undergraduate courses in science, mathematics, and engineering are available at Rice University and the University of Houston. Courses not available at Baylor can be taken free of charge at the other institutions. Students participate in three to five laboratory rotations to experience different research areas. Seminars of student research and distinguished scientists enhance the educational experience.

Research Facilities

Through participating faculty members, students have access to a number of research centers, each uniquely equipped and staffed. These include the W. M. Keck Center for Interdisciplinary Bioscience Training of the Gulf Coast Consortia, National Center for Macromolecular Imaging, Institute for Molecular Design, Center for High Performance Software Research, Houston Area Computational Science Consortium, Computer and Information Technology Institute, and Texas Learning and Computation Center. These facilities offer students access to state-of-the-art hardware and software for X-ray and electron crystallography, magnetic resonance spectroscopy, genomics, proteomics, computational biophysics, and advanced optical and MRI imaging techniques.

Financial Aid

All students enrolled in the program receive an annual stipend for $26,000 and paid individual health insurance. Separate offices assist students with additional needs.

Cost of Study

Full-tuition scholarships are supported by Baylor College of Medicine. Students pay a one-time matriculation fee of $25, a graduation fee of $190 (due in the fourth year), and an Educational Resource Center fee of $150 for the first year and $20 for each following year. International students pay additional yearly visa fees: $75 for an F-1 and $100 for a J-1.

Living and Housing Costs

There are numerous apartment complexes located very close to the Texas Medical Center. Students frequently bike or walk to the campus from these apartments. The cost of living in Houston is less than in most major U.S. cities. The cost for food and recreation is modest, and there are many opportunities for employment of spouses in the Texas Medical Center.

Student Group

The SCBMB program currently has 37 graduate students and enrolls 6 to 8 students per year. Approximately 550 students are enrolled in the graduate school. Students interact with predoctoral and postdoctoral fellows and with staff members in a variety of research centers. These centers sponsor annual symposia, workshops, seminars, and informal discussion groups.

Location

Houston is a dynamic city, with a population of approximately 5 million people. With its large seaport and modern airport, it is a center of international travel. Mexico City is 90 minutes away by air, and the Gulf of Mexico is only an hour's ride by car. The climate offers very pleasant cool and dry weather from fall through spring. The temperature during winter rarely drops below freezing, and it does not normally snow. Although summer temperatures are in the 90s with moderately high humidity, comfort is ensured by air-conditioning in all homes and workplaces. Symphony, opera, ballet, live theater, year-round major-league sports, and a large number of diverse ethnic groups and restaurants help to make Houston an entertaining and exciting city in which to live and work.

The College

Baylor College of Medicine was established as an independent, private university committed to excellence in the training and education of scholars and physicians. The College is located in the Texas Medical Center, which is composed of more than 645 acres and includes forty-two independent institutions. The University of Texas Health Science Center, the School of Public Health, and the M. D. Anderson Cancer Center are also on the campus, together with numerous hospitals and research institutes. The Texas Medical Center is one of the most actively growing science centers in the country. The influx of new colleagues and the opportunities created by an atmosphere of expansion provide a stimulating academic environment. More information on Baylor College of Medicine can be found on the College's Web site at http://www.bcm.edu.

Applying

Applicants must be in excellent academic standing and have a bachelor's degree, with extensive course work in biology, chemistry, physics, and mathematics. GRE scores less than three years old at the time of application must be provided. Applications should be accompanied by transcripts from all colleges and universities attended, plus three letters of recommendation and a statement of research interest and career goals.

Applications, catalogs, and instructions can be obtained via the Internet through the graduate school's Web site at http://www.bcm.edu/gradschool/ or the SCBMB Web site. There is no application fee for electronic submission. The application deadline is January 1 for fall admission. Successful candidates are invited for either a phone interview or a visit BCM to meet with the participating faculty members and students in order to have a firsthand look at the SCBMB program. Expenses for travel and accommodations during the visit are provided by Baylor College of Medicine. Questions regarding the application process can be directed to the admissions e-mail address at gradappboss@bcm.edu.

Correspondence and Information

Dr. Wah Chiu, Director
Graduate Program in Structural and Computational Biology and Molecular Biophysics
Graduate School of Biomedical Sciences, Room N204T
Baylor College of Medicine
One Baylor Plaza, MS: BCM 215
Houston, Texas 77030
Phone: 713-798-5197
Fax: 713-798-6325
E-mail: scb@bcm.edu
Web site: http://www.bcm.edu/scbmb

Baylor College of Medicine

THE FACULTY AND THEIR RESEARCH

Jonas Almeida, Ph.D.; Bioinformatics and Computational Biology at UTMDA. Integrative bioinformatics; systems biology; biomarker identification; drug/target discovery; statistical mechanics.

Patrick Barth, Ph.D.; Pharmacology and Biochemistry and Molecular Biology at BCM. Signaling mechanisms across biological membranes by computational modeling, design, and experimental biophysics.

Hugo Bellen, Ph.D.; Molecular and Human Genetics at BCM. Genetic and molecular analysis of neurotransmitter release and nervous system development in *Drosophila*.

John Belmont, M.D., Ph.D.; Molecular and Human Genetics at BCM. Structural congenital heart defects including abnormalities in laterality and hypoplastic left heart syndrome; functional studies of Zic3; genetics of human immune responses; medical population genetics.

Elmer V. Bernstam, M.D., Ph.D.; Internal Medicine at UT–HSC. Biomedical informatics.

Penelope Bonnen, Ph.D., Molecular and Human Genetics at BCM. Genomics and population genetics; genetics of infectious disease; genetics of metabolic disease.

Aladin M. Boriek, Ph.D.; Medicine and Molecular Physiology and Biophysics at BCM. Respiratory muscle mechanics; computational models of tissue mechanics; mechanical role of structural proteins in skeletal and smooth muscles; mechanical signal transduction in skeletal and smooth muscles.

James M. Briggs, Ph.D.; Biology and Biochemistry at UH. Computer-aided drug design; molecular modeling; computational biophysics.

William R. Brinkley, Ph.D.; Molecular and Cellular Biology at BCM. Structure and assembly of the mitotic apparatus; molecular mechanisms for aneuploidy and genomic instability in tumor cells.

William E. Brownell, Ph.D.; Otorhinolaryngology and Communicative Sciences at BCM. Cochlear biophysics and the mechanism of outer hair cell electromotility.

Wah Chiu, Ph.D.; Biochemistry and Molecular Biology at BCM. Structural and computational biology of biological machines.

John W. Clark Jr., Ph.D.; Electrical and Computer Engineering at Rice. Cell modeling; engineering in critical care medicine.

Cecilia Clementi, Ph.D.; Chemistry at Rice. Theory of protein folding; protein modeling and simulations; folding/function relationship.

John A. Dani, Ph.D.; Neuroscience at BCM. In vivo, cellular, and molecular studies of synaptic communication and of circuits underlying reward and behavior.

Anne H. Delcour, Ph.D.; Biology and Biochemistry at UH. Molecular mechanisms of bacterial ion channels.

Mary E. Dickinson, Ph.D.; Molecular Physiology and Molecular Biophysics at BCM. In vivo optical microscopy; analysis of vascular networks; role of mechanical forces in vertebrate development.

Henry F. Epstein, M.D.; Neuroscience and Cell Biology at UTMB. Structural biology of myosin filaments, molecular chaperones, and protein kinase complexes.

Mary K. Estes, Ph.D.; Molecular Virology and Microbiology at BCM. Molecular biology and structure of virus assembly.

Mauro Ferrari, Ph.D.; Biomedical Engineering at UT–HSC. Nanotechnology in Biomedical Applications.

George E. Fox, Ph.D.; Biology and Biochemistry at UH. RNA structure, function, and evolution; bioinformatics.

Fabrizio Gabbiani, Ph.D.; Neuroscience at BCM. Biophysics of information processing in the nervous system.

Xiaolian Gao, Ph.D.; Biology and Biochemistry at UH. Biophysical and bioorganic chemistry of nucleic acids; NMR of nucleic acids, proteins, antitumor antibiotics, and their complexes; development of biochips for genetic screening.

Richard A. Gibbs, Ph.D.; Molecular and Human Genetics at BCM, Human Genome Project; molecular basis of human genetic diseases; molecular evolution.

Hiram F. Gilbert, Ph.D.; Biochemistry and Molecular Biology at BCM. Protein folding and catalysis of disulfide formation during protein secretion in yeast.

Ido Golding, Ph.D. Biochemistry and Molecular Biology at BCM. Spatiotemporal dynamics in living cells.

David Gorenstein, Ph.D.; Biochemistry and Molecular Biology at UTMB. Proteomics and nanomedicine for both diagnostics and therapeutics in cancer and infectious diseases.

Dan Graur, Ph.D.; Biology and Biochemistry at UH. Theoretical, statistical, and analytical topics within the area of molecular evolution.

Rudy Guerra, Ph.D.; Statistics at Rice. Meta-analysis for genetic linkage studies; case-control studies using haplotype blocks; identification of multiple genetic markers influencing a single trait.

Susan L. Hamilton, Ph.D.; Molecular Physiology and Biophysics at BCM. Calcium release channel structure and function.

Frank Horrigan, Ph.D.; Molecular Physiology and Biophysics at BCM. Molecular and biophysical mechanisms of ion channel gating. Allosteric regulation of BK potassium channel function.

S. Lennart Johnsson, Ph.D.; Computer Science at UH. Computational science.

Lydia E. Kavraki, Ph.D.; Computer Science and Bioengineering at Rice. Computation of shape and motion in biology; computer-assisted drug design.

Ching-Hwa Kiang, Ph.D.; Physics and Astronomy at Rice. Single-molecule force spectroscopy of biomolecules.

Choel Kim, Ph.D.; Pharmacology and Biochemistry and Molecular Biology at BCM Signal transduction; protein-protein recognition; assembly of higher order signal transduction complexes; localized cyclic nucleotide signaling.

Marek Kimmel, Ph.D.; Statistics at Rice. Informatics and statistical modeling of genome dynamics.

Stephen LaConte, Ph.D.; Neuroscience at BCM. Utilization of functional magnetic resonance imaging (fMRI) in machine learning for interpretation of mental representations and enhancement of fMRI for biofeedback in neural rehabilitation.

Ching C. Lau, M.D., Ph.D.; Pediatrics and Cancer Genomics Program at BCM. Genomics and proteomics of cancer, bioinformatics, and development of targeted therapy.

Suzanne M. Leal, Ph.D.; Molecular and Human Genetics at BCM. Statistical genetics and genetic epidemiology.

Wei Li, Ph.D.; Molecular and Cellular Biology at BCM. A genomic view of epigenetic and transcriptional regulation.

Olivier Lichtarge, M.D., Ph.D.; Molecular and Human Genetics at BCM. Annotation and designed perturbation of protein function and pathways.

Jun Liu, Ph.D.; Pathology and Laboratory Medicine at UT-HSC. Three-dimensional structure/function of macromolecular assemblies; intact bacteria and enveloped viruses; AIDS virus; viral entry and antibody neutralization.

Steven Ludtke, Ph.D.; Biochemistry and Molecular Biology at BCM. Cryoelectron microscopy and single particle reconstruction.

Jianpeng Ma, Ph.D.; Biochemistry and Molecular Biology at BCM. Computational molecular biophysics and structural biology.

Whee Ky "Wei Ji" Ma, Ph.D., Neuroscience at BCM. Theoretical and behavioral studies of perceptual computation.

Michael A. Mancini, Ph.D.; Molecular and Cellular Biology at BCM. Transcription analyses at the single-cell level.

Aleksandar Milosavljevic, Ph.D.; Molecular and Human Genetics at BCM. Bioinformatics and comparative genomics.

P. Read Montague, Ph.D.; Neuroscience at BCM. Computational neuroscience; neuroimaging; neural economics.

Joel D. Morrisett, Ph.D.; Medicine and Biochemistry and Molecular Biology at BCM. Imaging, genomics, and proteomics of human atherosclerosis.

Luay Nakhleh, Ph.D.; Computer Science at Rice. Computational biology and bioinformatics.

Timothy G. Palzkill, Ph.D.; Molecular Virology and Microbiology at BCM. Molecular basis of antibiotic resistance; functional genomics of bacterial pathogens.

Steen E. Pedersen, Ph.D.; Molecular Physiology and Biophysics at BCM. Allosteric mechanisms of ion channel function.

Pawel A. Penczek, Ph.D.; Biochemistry and Molecular Biology at UT–HSC. Structural determination of proteins and molecular assemblies.

B. Montgomery Pettitt, Ph.D.; Chemistry at UH. Theoretical and computational biology and biochemistry.

Paul J. Pfaffinger, Ph.D.; Neuroscience at BCM. Molecular biology and biophysics of potassium ion channels.

Henry J. Pownall, Ph.D.; Medicine at BCM. Structures of native and model plasma lipoproteins.

B. V. Venkataram Prasad, Ph.D.; Biochemistry and Molecular Biology at BCM. Structural biology of replication mechanisms in pathogens such as rotavirus, norovirus, and influenza virus.

Jun Qin, Ph.D.; Biochemistry and Molecular Biology at BCM. Network analysis proteomics: the human DNA damage-signaling network.

Florante A. Quiocho, Ph.D.; Biochemistry and Molecular Biology at BCM. Protein atomic structure; molecular recognition and function.

Robert Raphael, Ph.D.; Bioengineering at Rice. Cell membrane mechanics; thermodynamics and biophysics.

Peter Saggau, Ph.D.; Neuroscience at BCM. Mechanisms and modulation of synaptic transmission; single neuron computation; advanced optical imaging techniques in neuroscience.

Michael F. Schmid, Ph.D.; Biochemistry and Molecular Biology at BCM. Image processing and electron crystallography of macromolecular machines.

Gad Shaulsky, Ph.D.; Molecular and Human Genetics at BCM. Functional genomics and new data mining tools; the evolution of social behavior and allorecognition in *Dictyostelium*.

Chad Shaw, Ph.D.; Molecular and Human Genetics at BCM. Devising new statistical methods for genome scale data using a systems biology approach.

Richard N. Sifers, Ph.D.; Pathology and Molecular and Cellular Biology at BCM. Glycobiology; regulation of endoplasmic reticulum degradation; conformational disease; alpha1-antitrypsin deficiency.

Stelios Manolis Smirnakis, Ph.D.; Neurology and Neuroscience at BCM. In vivo functional magnetic resonance imaging, electrophysiology, and two-photon techniques in the study of cortical network function in health and disease.

Jack W. Smith, M.D., Ph.D.; Health Informatics at UT–HSC. Decision support systems and intelligent tutoring.

Daniel C. Sorensen, Ph.D.; Computational and Applied Mathematics at Rice. Numerical linear algebra and optimization; parallel computing; large-scale eigenanalysis.

John L. Spudich, Ph.D.; Center for Membrane Biology at UT–MS. Photosensory receptors and signal transduction/microbial rhodopsins.

David States, M.D., Ph.D; School of Health Information Sciences at UT–HSC. Multidisciplinary computational applications for biomedicine.

Andreas Tolias, Ph.D. Neuroscience at BCM. Electrophysiological, computational, and functional imaging approaches to processing of visual information in the cerebral cortex of alert-behaving primates.

Francis T. F. Tsai, D.Phil.; Biochemistry and Molecular Biology at BCM. Structure and function of macromolecular complexes and supramolecular assemblies.

Salih J. Wakil, Ph.D.; Biochemistry and Molecular Biology at BCM. Structure, function, and regulation of the multifunctional enzymes, acetyl-CoA carboxylase, and fatty acid synthase.

Ted Wensel, Ph.D.; Biochemistry and Ophthalmology at BCM. Structure and dynamics of signal transducing membranes.

Richard Willson, Ph.D.; Chemical Engineering and Biochemical and Biophysical Sciences at UH. Biology and biochemistry.

John H. Wilson, Ph.D.; Biochemistry and Molecular Biology at BCM. Instability of trinucleotide repeats in human disease; gene therapy for diseases of the eye.

Steve Wong, Ph.D.; Chief Research Informatics Officer at The Methodist Hospital. Computational biology; high throughput cell imaging and medical imaging.

Samuel M. Wu, Ph.D.; Ophthalmology at BCM. Retinal neurophysiology.

E. Lynn Zechiedrich, Ph.D.; Molecular Virology and Microbiology at BCM. DNA topoisomereases and antimicrobial resistance.

BCM
Baylor College of Medicine

BAYLOR COLLEGE OF MEDICINE
Translational Biology and Molecular Medicine Graduate Program

Program of Study

The interdepartmental Translational Biology and Molecular Medicine (TBMM) graduate program is a new complimentary approach to train individuals in translational biology and to promote collaborations between more than 130 clinical and basic science faculty members. The Ph.D. program aims to develop a new workforce with firsthand experience in translational research and leadership training to serve as a catalyst to move discoveries effectively between bench and bedside. One of the unique aspects of the program is that students have 2 mentors, 1 basic scientist and 1 clinical scientist. The courses have been created to teach molecular mechanisms and clinical aspects of human health problems in an integrated fashion. During their second year, students participate in clinical rotations, which provide them with direct knowledge of human health issues. Journal clubs emphasize in-depth discussions of disease mechanisms. In addition, the program provides training in ethics, the approval process for human health research, grant writing, statistics, and high-throughput technologies.

The Translational Biology and Molecular Medicine graduate program emphasizes research in human health problems and diseases and is closely aligned with centers and other areas of translational research strength at Baylor College of Medicine. The first-year courses are designed to provide the background. In the second year, the clinical rotations and electives are specifically targeted to health and diseases, including cancer, digestive system disorders, diseases of cardiac muscle, diseases of skeletal muscle, endocrine diseases and diabetes, genetic disorders, hemodynamic disorders, thrombosis and shock, infectious diseases, inflammation and immune disorders, neurological disorders, psychiatric disorders, renal system disorders, reproductive disorders, respiratory system disorders, and vascular system diseases. Students participate in at least three laboratory rotations and select their mentor pairs and thesis project by the end of their first year. The program is supported in part by the Howard Hughes Medical Research Institute Med into Grad Initiative.

Research Facilities

Baylor College of Medicine is one of several biomedical institutions within the Texas Medical Center. The participating faculty members in the program utilize state-of-the-art research facilities housed in one of the seventy nationally recognized research centers. More than 1 million square feet of space is devoted to the research and teaching activities of the 1,700 full-time faculty members, who conduct more than $400 million worth of sponsored research annually.

Financial Aid

All students in the TBMM program receive competitive stipends of $26,000 per year. This stipend is provided to students for each year of study, without any teaching assistantship requirements. In addition, full health insurance and tuition are completely covered. Although the stipend is always guaranteed, applying for outside funding is encouraged. Students who receive outside funding are recognized with a Dean's award, which is an additional $2000-per-year supplement to the $26,000 yearly stipend.

Cost of Study

Tuition is supported by the College. Students pay a one-time matriculation fee of $25, a one-time graduation fee of $140 during the fourth year, and an annual student fee of $150 for the first year and $20 for subsequent years. Students on temporary visas also pay an annual international services fee of $75 for an F-1 visa or $100 for a J-1 visa.

Living and Housing Costs

Most students live within a few miles of the Medical Center. Housing is not provided for graduate students because a variety of affordable excellent housing options are readily available. Some students choose to rent a private house nearby, while others choose to rent or buy a one-bedroom apartment or condo of their own. Numerous apartment complexes are located very close to the Medical Center. Houston's cost of living is well below that of every major city in the U.S., so graduate students can afford to enjoy the many recreational and cultural opportunities available.

Student Group

The TBMM program accepts 10 to 12 carefully selected students per year. The smaller class size allows for a more personalized one-on-one approach to learning and training in an environment with some of the best scientists in the country. Several specialized courses in the area of translational biology are part of the curriculum.

Student Outcomes

Graduates typically go on to postdoctoral research appointments, followed by careers in academics, medicine, and industry. Other options include careers in science education and government.

Location

Houston is a young and dynamic city that is both fun and affordable for graduate student life. Extensive and affordable cultural and recreational facilities and opportunities are available, including symphony concerts, operas, ballets, live theaters, museums, professional year-round sports, and numerous restaurants, which are all part of living in Houston, the fourth-largest city in the United States. From fall through spring, temperatures average between 50°F and 75°F, with temperatures rarely dropping below freezing, and it does not snow. Average highs during the summer are in the 90s, although it cools down in the evenings, and air conditioning is present in virtually all homes, the Medical Center, indoor sporting venues, etc.

The College

Baylor College of Medicine was established as an independent, private university committed to excellence in the training and education of scholars and physicians. The College is located in the heart of the Texas Medical Center, one of the largest medical centers in the world. The Medical Center, adjacent to residential areas, covers more than 675 acres and includes forty-two independent institutions. The Graduate School is committed to excellence in graduate training. There is a high degree of interdisciplinary cooperation not only among the faculty members in basic science areas but also with clinical investigators in the College and associated institutions in the Texas Medical Center. Ongoing research programs carried out by productive and widely recognized investigators in both the basic sciences and the clinical faculty, coupled with the favorable faculty-student ratio, permit students to be directly involved in and contribute to significant research projects.

Applying

Applicants must hold a bachelor's degree or the equivalent in a relevant area of science. Most of the students who join the program have a variety of undergraduate degrees in any area of the biological sciences, as well as in chemistry, engineering, and physics. Applications are due by January 1 each year and should be accompanied by three letters of recommendation from people who are familiar with the applicant's scholastic qualifications and/or research abilities, as well as a personal statement that describes research experience and career goals. Official GRE scores (not more than three years old) and transcripts from all colleges and universities attended must also be provided. Applications can be made online through the Graduate School Web site at http://www.bcm.edu/gradschool or the TBMM Web site at http://www.bcm.edu/tbmm/. There is no fee for online applications. Top applicants are invited to visit Baylor to meet with the participating faculty members and students, in order to have a firsthand look at the research and educational opportunities available to students in the TBMM program. Expenses for travel and accommodations during the visit are provided by Baylor College of Medicine. Applications from members of underrepresented populations, including women, are encouraged. Questions regarding the application process can be directed through e-mail to tbmm@bcm.edu.

Correspondence and Information

Translational Biology and Molecular Medicine Graduate Program
Baylor College of Medicine
One Baylor Plaza
Mail Stop: BCM215
Houston, Texas 77030
Phone: 713-798-1077
Fax: 713-798-6325
E-mail: tbmm@bcm.edu
Web site: http://www.bcm.edu/tbmm/

Baylor College of Medicine

THE FACULTY AND THEIR RESEARCH

Department of Biochemistry and Molecular Biology
Francis T. F. Tsai, D.Phil. Structural biochemistry of protein quality control systems.
John H. Wilson, Ph.D. Neurological diseases: genomic instability and gene therapy.

Department of Medicine
Roberto C. Arduino, M.D. HIV treatment strategies and new antiretroviral drugs.
Robert Atmar, M.D. Respiratory and enteric viruses, therapeutics and vaccines.
Mandeep Bajaj, M.D. Obesity and insulin resistance.
Ashok Balasubramanyam, M.D. Diabetes; molecular pathology; mouse models; human metabolic studies.
Christie Ballantyne, M.D. Inflammation; vascular disease; genetics; biomarkers; obesity.
Biykem Bozkurt, M.D., Ph.D. Predictors of outcome and remodeling in heart failure.
Malcolm K. Brenner, M.B., Ch.B., Ph.D. Cell and gene therapy of cancer.
Lawrence C. B. Chan, M.B., D.Sc. Diabetes: molecular cell biology, physiology and therapy.
Jenny C. N. Chang, M.D. Therapeutic resistance; breast cancer stem cells.
David B. Corry, M.D. Asthma; cytokine receptors; T cells; microRNAs; proteases.
Farhad R. Danesh, M.D. RhoA and stem cell regulation in kidney diseases.
Jing-Fei Dong, M.D., Ph.D. Platelets and adhesion ligands in hemostasis and thrombosis.
Gianpietro Dotti, M.D. Immunotherapy and T-cell therapy of human malignancies.
Tony N. Eissa, M.D. Airway inflammation; innate immunity; lung diseases; autophagy; nitric oxide.
Mark L. Entman, M.D. Molecular mechanisms of cardiac injury and repair.
Suzanne A. Fuqua, Ph.D. Estrogen receptors; microarray profiling; metastasis; hormone resistance.
David Y. Graham, M.D. *Helicobacter pylori;* virulence; treatment; epidemiology; vaccines; resistance.
Teresa Hayes, M.D., Ph.D. Cancer prevention; cancer clinical research.
Helen E. Heslop, M.D., M.B., Ch.B. Adoptive immunotherapy; lymphoproliferative disorders.
Susan G. Hilsenbeck, Ph.D. Design/statistical analysis of translational/clinical experiments.
Farrah Kheradmand, M.D. Lung inflammation; asthma; COPD; infection; autoimmunity.
Weei-Chin Lin, M.D., Ph.D. Cell cycle regulators; novel cancer therapeutic targets.
Martha P. Mims, M.D., Ph.D. Genetic markers of prostate cancer risk in African Americans.
William E. Mitch, M.D. Control of protein metabolism in catabolic conditions.
C. Kent Osborne, M.D. Molecular mechanisms of treatment resistance in breast cancer.
Mothaffar F. Rimawi, M.D. Targeted therapy and biomarkers in breast cancer.
Rolando E. Rumbaut, M.D., Ph.D. Microvascular dysfunction in inflammation.
Rachel Schiff, Ph.D. Breast cancer endocrine; targeted therapies.
David Sheikh-Hamad, M.D. Stanniocalcin; inflammation; SMADs; cardiac failure; osmoregulation; dysnatremias.
George E. Taffet, M.D. Aging and cardiovascular function; arterial rigidity; mouse models.
David J. Tweardy, M.D. STAT 3 function, activation, and specific inhibitors; hemorrhagic shock; cancer.
Vinod K. Vijayan, M.D. Serine/threonine phosphatases in platelet and endothelial cell activation.
Matthew H. Wilson, M.D., Ph.D. Transposons and gene therapy for renal diseases.
Li-Yuan Yu-Lee, Ph.D. Immune-inflammatory responses; mitotic regulators; cancer.

Department of Molecular and Cellular Biology
Francisco J. DeMayo, Ph.D. Molecular regulation of cellular differentiation and physiology.
Yi Li, Ph.D. Breast cancer; stem cells; Wnt; differentiation.
Daniel Medina, M.D. Mammary premalignant progression; mechanisms of cancer chemoprevention.
Hoang Nguyen, Ph.D. Skin stem cell maintenance, differentiation, and tumorigenesis.
Bert W. O'Malley, M.D. Steroid hormone action; gene regulation; transcription factors.

Frederick A. Pereira, Ph.D. Signaling pathways in auditory development, aging, and cancer.
Jeffrey M. Rosen, Ph.D. Mammary gland development; stem cells and breast cancer.
David R. Rowley, Ph.D. Tumor microenvironment regulation of cancer progression.
Carolyn L. Smith, Ph.D. Estrogen receptor molecular pharmacology; breast/bladder cancer.
Nancy L. Weigel, Ph.D. Nuclear receptors and coactivators in prostate cancer.

Department of Molecular and Human Genetics
Arthur L. Beaudet, M.D. Epigenetics; autism; clinical array CGH; hepatocyte gene therapy.
William J. Craigen, M.D., Ph.D. Energy metabolism; mitochondrial function; transgenic models.
Richard A. Gibbs, Ph.D. Genomic sequencing; haplotype maps; rare genetic variation.
Brett H. Graham, M.D., Ph.D. Models of mitochondrial disease in fly/mouse.
Monica J. Justice, Ph.D. Mouse molecular genetics; blood diseases; leukemia.
Brendan Lee, M.D., Ph.D. Gene therapy; skeletal dysplasias; biochemical genetics.
James R. Lupski, M.D., Ph.D. Genomic disorders; gene dosage and recombination.
Aleksandar Milosavljevic, Ph.D. Bioinformatics and comparative genomics.
Philip Ng, Ph.D. Gene therapy for genetic diseases.
Richard E. Paylor, Ph.D. Behavioral analysis of mutant mouse models of human disease.
Susan M. Rosenberg, Ph.D. Genomic instability in evolution, cancer, and antibiotic resistance.
Lee-Jun C. Wong, Ph.D. Genetics and pathogenic mechanism of mitochondrial disorders.
Hui Zheng, Ph.D. Genetic studies of Alzheimer's disease using mouse models.
Huda Y. Zoghbi, M.D. Neurodegenerative disease; ataxia; Rett syndrome; autism; mouse models.

Department of Molecular Physiology and Biophysics
Mary Dickinson, Ph.D. Hemodynamic forces in vascular development and remodeling.
Susan L. Hamilton, Ph.D. Mechanisms of malignant hyperthermia and central core diseases.
Jeanette Kunz, Ph.D. Regulation of cell migration, adhesion, and invasion; phosphoinositide signaling.
Robia Pautler, Ph.D. MRI; Nanotechnology; technology development; Alzheimer's disease.
Xander Wehrens, M.D., Ph.D. Molecular mechanisms of cardiac arrhythmias and heart failure.
Gang-Yi Wu, Ph.D. Activity-dependent signal transduction in neurons.
Pumin Zhang, Ph.D. Cell-cycle regulation; myogenesis; lens development; rhabdomyosarcoma.

Department of Molecular Virology and Microbiology
Janet S. Butel, Ph.D. SV40 pathogenesis of infection and cancer; hamster model.
Margaret E. Conner, Ph.D. Mucosal immunity; rotavirus pathogenesis; intestinal intussusception.
Lawrence A. Donehower, Ph.D. The p53 tumor suppressor gene in cancer and aging.
Mary K. Estes, Ph.D. GI virus-host interactions: pathogenesis, immunity, and vaccines.
Wendy A. Keitel, M.D. Immunization; vaccine evaluation; infection and immunity.
Jason T. Kimata, Ph.D. HIV replication and pathogenesis; HIV model development.
Joseph Petrosino, Ph.D. Human microbiome and infectious disease systems biology.
Andrew P. Rice, Ph.D. Viral gene expression and pathogenesis.
Lynn Zechiedrich, Ph.D. DNA structure-function; gene therapy vectors; fluoroquinolone and multidrug resistance.

Department of Neurology
Rachelle Doody, M.D., Ph.D. Progression and treatment of Alzheimer's disease and mild cognitive impairment.
Thomas A. Kent, M.D. Translational stroke models; cerebrovascular regulation; oxygen radicals.
Jeffrey L. Noebels, M.D., Ph.D. Epilepsy; ion channel genes; mutant gene expression.

Department of Neuroscience
John A. Dani, Ph.D. Addiction; learning and memory; degenerative dysfunction.

Mariella De Biasi, Ph.D. Molecular basis of nicotine addiction; mouse models; ubiquitin-like proteins; receptor trafficking.
Benjamin Deneen, Ph.D. Glial cell development and the generation of gliomas.
Joanna L. Jankowsky, Ph.D. Pathogenesis and treatment of Alzheimer's disease.

Department of Neurosurgery
Claudia S. Robertson, M.D. Cerebral vascular flow; brain injury; imaging; biomarkers.
H. David Shine, Ph.D. Gene therapy and nervous system repair.

Department of Obstetrics and Gynecology
Kjersti M. Aagaard-Tillery, M.D., Ph.D. The in-utero environment and epigenetics in fetal programming and development.
Matthew L. Anderson, M.D., Ph.D. Noncoding RNAs in reproductive tract cancers; novel miRNA-based therapeutics.
William E. Gibbons, M.D. Folliculogenesis; endometrial function; ART outcomes; fertility preservation.
Shannon M. Hawkins, M.D., Ph.D. The role of microRNAs and genomic variants in endometriosis.
Ignatia B. Van den Veyver, M.D. Genetic and epigenetic developmental disorders; prenatal genetic diagnosis.

Department of Ophthalmology
Patricia Chevez-Barrios, M.D. Retinoblastoma biology, predictive factors, and targeted therapies.

Department of Orthopedic Surgery
Michael H. Heggeness, M.D., Ph.D. Pathophysiology of the spine during degenerative disease states.

Department of Otolaryngology
William E. Brownell, Ph.D. Electromechanics of hearing: membrane-based motor mechanisms.

Department of Pathology and Immunology
Thomas A. Cooper, M.D. Myotonic dystrophy pathogenesis; pre-mRNA alternative splicing.
Milton Finegold, M.D. Molecular genetics of liver cancer.
Michael M. Ittman, M.D., Ph.D. Molecular genetics of prostate cancer.
H. Daniel Lacorazza, Ph.D. Transcriptional control of hematopoiesis and development of immunity.
Dario Marchetti, Ph.D. Mechanisms and molecular determinants of brain metastasis.
Martin M. Matzuk, M.D., Ph.D. Ovarian and testicular function; dysfunction in mammals.
Richard N. Sifers, Ph.D. Glycoprotein quality control as disease modifier.
David M. Spencer, Ph.D. Immunogenetic therapy; DCs; prostate cancer; signaling; apoptosis.
James Versalovic, M.D., Ph.D. Probiotics; intestinal inflammation; human microbiome and metagenomics.
Jin Wang, Ph.D. Molecular regulation of immune responses by apoptosis and autophagy.
Rongfu Wang, Ph.D. Cancer immunology; inflammation; immune regulation.
Biao Zheng, M.D., Ph.D. Germinal center biology; autoimmunity; immunosenescence.

Department of Pediatrics
Stuart L. Abramson, M.D., Ph.D. Environmental determinants in asthma pathophysiology and epidemiology.
Nabil M. Ahmed, M.D., M.P.H. Immunotherapy for brain tumors.
Anne Anderson, M.D. Signaling mechanisms in epilepsy; potassium channels; transcription.
Susan M. Blaney, M.D. Novel therapies for pediatric cancer.
Catherine Bollard, M.B., Ch.B., M.D. Developing immunotherapies for viral and malignant diseases.
Malcolm K. Brenner, M.B., Ch.B., Ph.D. Cell and gene therapy of cancer.
Douglas Burrin, Ph.D. Translational research in pediatric nutrition and gastroenterology.
Murali M. Chintagumpala, M.D. Clinical research in brain tumors, retinoblastoma, and Wilms' tumor.
Alan R. Davis, Ph.D. Bone stem cell recruitment, function, and differentiation; tissue engineering.
Elizabeth A. Davis, Ph.D. Tissue engineering of endochondral bone.
George D. Ferry, M.D. Inflammatory bowel disease.

Aaron E. Foster, Ph.D. Identification and immunotherapeutic targeting of cancer stem cells.
M. Waleed Gaber, Ph.D. Animal imaging of microvascular changes caused by tumors and radiotherapy.
Margaret A. Goodell, Ph.D. Regulation of hematopoietic stem cells.
Stephen M. G. Gottschalk, M.D. Immunotherapy for malignancies and viral-associated diseases.
Xinfu Guan, Ph.D. Neuropeptide receptor-mediated cell function and signaling network.
Karen Hirschi, Ph.D. Regulation of vascular development; vascular regeneration.
Terzah M. Horton, M.D., Ph.D. Treatment therapies for childhood leukemias and lymphomas.
Richard L. Hurwitz, M.D. Gene therapy; retinoblastoma; retinal degeneration.
Saul Karpen, M.D., Ph.D. Liver; nuclear receptors; cholestasis; inflammation; treatment.
Mark W. Kline, M.D. International pediatric HIV/AIDS care and treatment.
Ann M. Leen, Ph.D. T-cell immunotherapy for viruses and cancer.
Bhagavatula Moorthy, Ph.D. Cytochrome P450 regulation; hyperoxia; lung injury; carcinogenesis.
Jeffrey N. Neul, M.D., Ph.D. Models of neurodevelopmental diseases; Rett syndrome.
Debananda Pati, Ph.D. Molecular basis of aneuploidy and apoptosis; mammary carcinogenesis; pediatric tumors; immunotherapy.
Mary E. Paul, M.D. Pediatric and adolescent HIV/AIDS and clinical trials.
David G. Poplack, M.D. Childhood leukemia; cancer survivorship; clinical pharmacology of anticancer agents in children.
Cliona M. Rooney, Ph.D. T cell therapy for virus infections and cancer; tumor immune evasion strategies.
Jason M. Shohet, M.D., Ph.D. Apoptosis pathways and oncogenes in pediatric cancers.
John W. Swann, Ph.D. Molecular mechanisms of early-onset epilepsy.
Sundararajah Thevananther, Ph.D. Molecular mechanisms of liver regeneration.
Qiang Tong, Ph.D. Molecular mechanisms of metabolic regulation and aging.
Lisa L. Wang, M.D. Molecular basis of osteosarcoma, RECQL4.
Jianhua Yang, Ph.D. Molecular targets in cancer.
Jason T. Yustein, M.D., Ph.D. Investigations into the molecular pathogenesis of pediatric sarcomas.

Department of Psychiatry and Behavioral Sciences
Thomas R. Kosten, M.D. Neurobiology of mental health and addictions.

Department of Radiology
Juliet A. Wendt, M.D. Multimodality molecular imaging.

Department of Surgery
David H. Berger, M.D. Impact of obesity and diabetes on survival in colorectal cancer; epithelial motility; colon cancer.
F. Charles Brunicardi, M.D. Pancreatic and neuroendocrine cancer; personalized genomic medicine.
Changyi (Johnny) Chen, M.D., Ph.D. Vascular tissue engineering; HIV; endothelial dysfunction.
Xin-Hua Feng, Ph.D. Cell signaling; protein modifications; cancer.
John A. Goss, M.D. Genomics or hepatocellular carcinoma.
Mimi Leong, M.D. Role of immune system in abnormal or impaired wound healing.
Peter H. Lin, M.D. Endovascular treatment outcome; vascular disease progression.
Vijay Nambi, M.D. Vascular disease; atherosclerosis; atherosclerosis imaging; preventive cardiology.
Qizhi (Cathy) Yao, M.D., Ph.D. Vaccines for HIV, cardiovascular disease, and cancers.

Department of Urology
Keith S. Chan, Ph.D. Role of cancer stem cells in tumor progression.
Dolores J. Lamb, Ph.D. Male infertility; genitourinary defects; prostate cancer; receptors.
Seth P. Lerner, M.D. Bladder cancer; estrogen receptor–targeted therapy.
Kevin M. Slawin, M.D. Urologic oncology; benign and malignant diseases of the prostate.

Section 8
Ecology, Environmental Biology, and Evolutionary Biology

This section contains a directory of institutions offering graduate work in ecology, environmental biology, and evolutionary biology, followed by in-depth entries submitted by institutions that chose to prepare detailed program descriptions. Additional information about programs listed in the directory but not augmented by an in-depth entry may be obtained by writing directly to the dean of a graduate school or chair of a department at the address given in the directory.

For programs offering related work, see also in this book *Biological and Biomedical Sciences; Botany and Plant Biology; Entomology; Genetics, Developmental Biology, and Reproductive Biology; Microbiological Sciences; Pharmacology and Toxicology;* and *Zoology.* In the other guides in this series:

Graduate Programs in the Humanities, Arts & Social Sciences
See *Sociology, Anthropology, and Archaeology*

Graduate Programs in the Physical Sciences, Mathematics, Agricultural Sciences, the Environment & Natural Resources
See *Agricultural and Food Sciences, Geosciences, Marine Sciences and Oceanography,* and *Mathematical Sciences*

Graduate Programs in Engineering & Applied Sciences
See *Civil and Environmental Engineering, Management of Engineering and Technology,* and *Ocean Engineering*

Graduate Programs in Business, Education, Health, Information Studies, Law & Social Work
See *Public Health*

CONTENTS

Program Directories

Close-Up

See also:

Conservation Biology

Antioch University New England, Graduate School, Department of Environmental Studies, Program in Conservation Biology, Keene, NH 03431-3552. Offers MS. *Degree requirements:* For master's, thesis or project. *Entrance requirements:* For master's, resume, 3 letters of recommendation.

Central Michigan University, College of Graduate Studies, College of Science and Technology, Department of Biology, Mount Pleasant, MI 48859. Offers biology (MS); conservation biology (MS). Part-time programs available. *Degree requirements:* For master's, thesis or alternative. *Entrance requirements:* For master's, GRE, bachelor's degree with a major in biological science, minimum GPA of 3.0. Electronic applications accepted. *Faculty research:* Conservation biology, morphology and taxonomy of aquatic plants, molecular biology and genetics, microbials and invertebrate ecology, vertebrates.

Colorado State University, Graduate School, Warner College of Natural Resources, Department of Fishery and Wildlife Biology, Fort Collins, CO 80523-1474. Offers fish, wildlife and conservation biology (MFWCB); fishery and wildlife biology (MFWB, MS, PhD). *Faculty:* 15 full-time (4 women). *Students:* 11 full-time (3 women), 12 part-time (5 women). Average age 31. 23 applicants, 17% accepted, 4 enrolled. In 2009, 9 master's, 1 doctorate awarded. Terminal master's awarded for partial completion of doctoral program. *Degree requirements:* For master's, comprehensive exam, thesis (for some programs); for doctorate, comprehensive exam, thesis/dissertation. *Entrance requirements:* For master's, GRE General Test (combined minimum score of 1200 on the Verbal and Quantitative sections), minimum GPA of 3.0, BA or BS in related field, letters of recommendation, personal narrative, resume, transcripts; for doctorate, GRE General Test (minimum score 1000 verbal and quantitative), minimum GPA of 3.0, MS in related field. Additional exam requirements/recommendations for international students: Required—TOEFL (minimum score 550 paper-based; 213 computer-based; 80 iBT). *Application deadline:* For fall admission, 2/15 priority date for domestic and international students. Applications are processed on a rolling basis. Application fee: $50. Electronic applications accepted. *Expenses:* Tuition, state resident: full-time $6434; part-time $359.10 per credit. Tuition, nonresident: full-time $18,116; part-time $1006.45 per credit. Required fees: $1496; $83 per credit. *Financial support:* In 2009–10, 21 students received support, including 3 fellowships with full and partial tuition reimbursements available (averaging $32,645 per year), 15 research assistantships with full and partial tuition reimbursements available (averaging $13,957 per year), 3 teaching assistantships with full and partial tuition reimbursements available (averaging $7,524 per year); institutionally sponsored loans, scholarships/grants, tuition waivers (full and partial), and unspecified assistantships also available. Financial award application deadline: 3/1; financial award applicants required to submit FAFSA. *Faculty research:* Conservation biology, aquatic ecology, animal behavior, population modeling, habitat evaluation and management. Total annual research expenditures: $3.5 million. *Unit head:* Dr. Kenneth R. Wilson, Head, 970-491-7755, Fax: 970-491-5091, E-mail: kenneth.wilson@colostate.edu. *Application contact:* Kathy Bowers, Graduate Affairs Coordinator, 970-491-5020, Fax: 970-491-5091, E-mail: fwb@cnr.colostate.edu.

Columbia University, Graduate School of Arts and Sciences, Division of Natural Sciences, Department of Ecology and Evolutionary Biology, New York, NY 10027. Offers conservation biology (Certificate); ecology and evolutionary biology (PhD); environmental policy (Certificate). *Degree requirements:* For doctorate, one foreign language, thesis/dissertation, teaching experience. *Entrance requirements:* For doctorate, GRE General Test, previous course work in biology. Additional exam requirements/recommendations for international students: Required—TOEFL. Electronic applications accepted. *Faculty research:* Tropical ecology, ethnobotany, global change, systematics.

See Close-Up on page 281.

Columbia University, Graduate School of Arts and Sciences, Program in Conservation Biology, New York, NY 10027. Offers MA. *Degree requirements:* For master's, thesis.

See Close-Up on page 281.

Frostburg State University, Graduate School, College of Liberal Arts and Sciences, Department of Biology, Program in Applied Ecology and Conservation Biology, Frostburg, MD 21532-1099. Offers MS. *Faculty:* 10. *Students:* 9 full-time (5 women), 1 (woman) part-time; includes 1 minority (American Indian/Alaska Native). Average age 25. 16 applicants, 6% accepted, 1 enrolled. In 2009, 4 master's awarded. *Degree requirements:* For master's, thesis. *Entrance requirements:* For master's, GRE General Test, resume. Additional exam requirements/recommendations for international students: Required—TOEFL. *Application deadline:* For fall admission, 7/15 priority date for domestic students. Applications are processed on a rolling basis. Application fee: $30. Electronic applications accepted. *Expenses:* Tuition, state resident: full-time $5706; part-time $317 per credit hour. Tuition, nonresident: full-time $6948; part-time $386 per credit hour. Required fees: $1476; $82 per credit hour. $11 per term. One-time fee: $30 full-time. *Financial support:* In 2009–10, 8 research assistantships with full tuition reimbursements (averaging $5,000 per year) were awarded; career-related internships or fieldwork and Federal Work-Study also available. Financial award application deadline: 4/1; financial award applicants required to submit FAFSA. *Faculty research:* Forest ecology, microbiology of man-made wetlands, invertebrate zoology and entomology, wildlife and carnivore ecology, aquatic pollution ecology. *Unit head:* Dr. R. Scott Fritz, Coordinator, 301-687-4166. *Application contact:* Vickie Mazer, Director, Graduate Services, 301-687-7053, Fax: 301-687-4597, E-mail: vmmazer@frostburg.edu.

Illinois State University, Graduate School, College of Arts and Sciences, Department of Biological Sciences, Normal, IL 61790-2200. Offers animal behavior (MS); bacteriology (MS); biochemistry (MS); biological sciences (MS); biology (PhD); biophysics (MS); biotechnology (MS); botany (MS, PhD); cell biology (MS); conservation biology (MS); developmental biology (MS); ecology (MS, PhD); entomology (MS); evolutionary biology (MS); genetics (MS, PhD); immunology (MS); microbiology (MS, PhD); molecular biology (MS); molecular genetics (MS); neurobiology (MS); neuroscience (MS); parasitology (MS); physiology (MS, PhD); plant biology (MS); plant molecular biology (MS); plant sciences (MS); structural biology (MS); zoology (MS, PhD). Part-time programs available. *Degree requirements:* For master's, thesis or alternative; for doctorate, variable foreign language requirement, thesis/dissertation, 2 terms of residency. *Entrance requirements:* For master's, GRE General Test, minimum GPA of 2.6 in last 60 hours of course work; for doctorate, GRE General Test. *Faculty research:* Redoc balance and drug development in schistosoma mansoni, control of the growth of listeria monocytogenes at low temperature, regulation of cell expansion and microtubule function by SPRI, CRUI: physiology and fitness consequences of different life history phenotypes.

North Dakota State University, College of Graduate and Interdisciplinary Studies, College of Agriculture, Food Systems, and Natural Resources, Department of Entomology, Fargo, ND 58108. Offers entomology (MS, PhD); environment and conservation science (MS, PhD); natural resource management (MS, PhD). Part-time programs available. *Faculty:* 7 full-time (3 women), 8 part-time/adjunct (0 women). *Students:* 2 full-time (1 woman), 12 part-time (8 women); includes 2 Asian Americans or Pacific Islanders, 4 international. Average age 34. 5 applicants, 20% accepted, 1 enrolled. In 2009, 5 doctorates awarded. *Degree requirements:* For master's, thesis; for doctorate, comprehensive exam, thesis/dissertation. *Entrance requirements:* For master's and doctorate, minimum GPA of 3.0. Additional exam requirements/recommendations for international students: Required—TOEFL (minimum score 550 paper-based; 213 computer-based; 79 iBT). *Application deadline:* Applications are processed on a rolling basis. Application fee: $45 ($60 for international students). Electronic applications accepted. *Financial support:* In 2009–10, 11 research assistantships with full tuition reimbursements (averaging $13,800 per year) were awarded; Federal Work-Study, institutionally sponsored loans, and unspecified assistantships also available. Financial award application deadline: 4/15. *Faculty research:* Insect systematics, conservation biology, integrated pest management, insect behavior, insect biology. *Unit head:* Dr. David A. Rider, Chair, 701-231-7908, Fax: 701-231-8557, E-mail: david.rider@ndsu.edu. *Application contact:* Dr. David A. Rider, Chair, 701-231-7908, Fax: 701-231-8557, E-mail: david.rider@ndsu.edu.

North Dakota State University, College of Graduate and Interdisciplinary Studies, College of Science and Mathematics, Department of Biological Sciences, Fargo, ND 58108. Offers biology (MS); botany (MS, PhD); cellular and molecular biology (PhD); environmental and conservation sciences (MS, PhD); genomics (PhD); natural resources management (MS, PhD); zoology (MS, PhD). *Students:* 32 full-time (21 women), 14 part-time (10 women); includes 1 Asian American or Pacific Islander, 14 international. In 2009, 12 master's, 9 doctorates awarded. *Degree requirements:* For master's, thesis; for doctorate, thesis/dissertation. *Entrance requirements:* For master's and doctorate, GRE General Test. Additional exam requirements/recommendations for international students: Required—TOEFL. *Application deadline:* For fall admission, 3/15 priority date for domestic students; for spring admission, 10/30 priority date for domestic students. Applications are processed on a rolling basis. Application fee: $45 ($60 for international students). Electronic applications accepted. *Financial support:* Fellowships with full tuition reimbursements, research assistantships with full tuition reimbursements, teaching assistantships with full tuition reimbursements, career-related internships or fieldwork, Federal Work-Study, institutionally sponsored loans, scholarships/grants, tuition waivers (full), and unspecified assistantships available. Support available to part-time students. Financial award application deadline: 4/15; financial award applicants required to submit FAFSA. *Faculty research:* Comparative endocrinology, physiology, behavioral ecology, plant cell biology, aquatic biology. Total annual research expenditures: $675,000. *Unit head:* Dr. Marinus L. Otte, Head, 701-231-7087, E-mail: marinus.otte@ndsu.edu. *Application contact:* Dr. Marinus L. Otte, Head, 701-231-7087, E-mail: marinus.otte@ndsu.edu.

San Francisco State University, Division of Graduate Studies, College of Science and Engineering, Department of Biology, Program in Conservation Biology, San Francisco, CA 94132-1722. Offers MS.

State University of New York College of Environmental Science and Forestry, Department of Environmental and Forest Biology, Syracuse, NY 13210-2779. Offers applied ecology (MPS); chemical ecology (MPS, MS, PhD); conservation biology (MPS, MS, PhD); ecology (MPS, MS, PhD); entomology (MPS, MS, PhD); environmental interpretation (MPS, MS, PhD); environmental physiology (MPS, MS, PhD); fish and wildlife biology (MPS, MS, PhD); forest pathology and mycology (MPS, MS, PhD); plant biotechnology (MPS); plant science and biotechnology (MPS, MS, PhD). *Degree requirements:* For master's, thesis (for some programs); for doctorate, comprehensive exam, thesis/dissertation. *Entrance requirements:* For master's and doctorate, GRE General Test, GRE Subject Test, minimum GPA of 3.0. Additional exam requirements/recommendations for international students: Required—TOEFL (minimum score 550 paper-based; 213 computer-based; 80 iBT), IELTS (minimum score 6). *Faculty research:* Ecology, fish and wildlife biology and management, plant science, entomology.

Texas State University–San Marcos, Graduate School, College of Science, Department of Biology, Program in Population and Conservation Biology, San Marcos, TX 78666. Offers MS. *Faculty:* 4 full-time (1 woman). *Students:* 17 full-time (11 women), 4 part-time (0 women); includes 4 minority (2 Asian Americans or Pacific Islanders, 2 Hispanic Americans). Average age 27. 14 applicants, 93% accepted, 9 enrolled. In 2009, 4 master's awarded. *Degree requirements:* For master's, thesis. *Entrance requirements:* For master's, GRE (preferred minimum combined score of 1000 Verbal and Quantitative), bachelor's degree in biology or related discipline, minimum GPA of 3.0 in last 60 hours of undergraduate course work. Additional exam requirements/recommendations for international students: Required—TOEFL (minimum score 550 paper-based; 213 computer-based). *Application deadline:* For fall admission, 6/15 for domestic students, 6/1 for international students; for spring admission, 10/15 for domestic students, 10/1 for international students. Applications are processed on a rolling basis. Application fee: $40 ($90 for international students). Electronic applications accepted. *Expenses:* Tuition, state resident: full-time $5784; part-time $241 per credit hour. Tuition, nonresident: full-time $13,224; part-time $551 per credit hour. Required fees: $1728; $48 per credit hour. $306. Tuition and fees vary according to course load. *Financial support:* In 2009–10, 8 students received support, including 1 research assistantship (averaging $5,364 per year), 15 teaching assistantships (averaging $5,187 per year). Financial award application deadline: 4/1. *Unit head:* Dr. Chris Nice, Graduate Advisor, 512-245-2321, E-mail: ccnice@txstate.edu. *Application contact:* Dr. J. Michael Willoughby, Dean of the Graduate School, 512-245-2581, Fax: 512-245-8365, E-mail: jw02@swt.edu.

Tropical Agriculture Research and Higher Education Center, Graduate School, Turrialba, Costa Rica. Offers agribusiness management (MS); agroforestry systems (PhD); ecological agriculture (MS); environmental socioeconomics (MS); forestry in tropical and subtropical zones (PhD); integrated watershed management (MS); management and conservation of tropical rainforests and biodiversity (MS); tropical agriculture (PhD); tropical agroforestry (MS). *Entrance requirements:* For master's, GRE, 2 years of related professional experience, letters of recommendation; for doctorate, GRE, 4 letters of recommendation, letter of support from employing organization, master's degree in agronomy, biological sciences, forestry, natural resources or related field. Additional exam requirements/recommendations for international students: Required—TOEFL (minimum score 550 paper-based; 213 computer-based). Electronic applications accepted. *Faculty research:* Biodiversity in fragmented landscapes, ecosystem management, integrated pest management, environmental livestock production, biotechnology carbon balances in diverse land uses.

University at Albany, State University of New York, College of Arts and Sciences, Department of Biological Sciences, Program in Biodiversity, Conservation, and Policy, Albany, NY 12222-0001. Offers MS. *Degree requirements:* For master's, one foreign language. *Entrance requirements:* For master's, GRE General Test. *Faculty research:* Aquatic ecology, plant community ecology, biodiversity and public policy, restoration ecology, coastal and estuarine science.

University of Alberta, Faculty of Graduate Studies and Research, Department of Renewable Resources, Edmonton, AB T6G 2E1, Canada. Offers agroforestry (M Ag, M Sc, MF); conservation biology (M Sc, PhD); forest biology and management (M Sc, PhD); land reclamation and remediation (M Sc, PhD); protected areas and wildlands management (M Sc, PhD); soil science (M Ag, M Sc, PhD); water and land resources (M Ag, M Sc, PhD); wildlife ecology and management (M Sc, PhD); MBA/M Ag; MBA/MF. Part-time programs available. *Faculty:* 26 full-time (4 women), 22 part-time/adjunct (3 women). *Students:* 63 full-time (33 women), 50 part-time (20 women), 14 international. 122 applicants, 24% accepted, 22 enrolled. In 2009, 16 master's, 8 doctorates awarded. *Degree requirements:* For master's, thesis (for some programs); for doctorate, comprehensive exam, thesis/dissertation. *Entrance requirements:* For master's, minimum 2 years of relevant professional experiences, minimum GPA of 3.0; for doctorate, minimum GPA of 3.0. Additional exam requirements/recommendations for international students: Required—TOEFL (minimum score 550 paper-based; 213 computer-based). *Application deadline:* For fall admission, 7/1 priority date for domestic students, 6/1 priority date for international students. Applications are processed on a rolling basis. Application fee: $0. Electronic applications accepted. Tuition and fees charges are reported in Canadian dollars. *Expenses:* Tuition, area resident: Full-time $4626 Canadian dollars; part-time $99.72 Canadian dollars per unit. International tuition: $8216 Canadian dollars full-time. Required fees: $3590 Canadian dollars; $99.72 Canadian dollars per unit. $215 Canadian dollars per term. *Financial support:* In 2009–10, 63 students received support, including 21 research assistantships with partial tuition reimbursements available (averaging $2,800 per year), 28 teaching assistantships with partial tuition reimbursements available (averaging $1,900 per year); scholarships/grants and unspecified assistantships also available. *Faculty research:* Natural and managed landscapes. Total annual research expenditures: $6.1 million. *Unit head:* Dr. John R. Spence,

Chair, 780-492-2820, Fax: 780-492-4323, E-mail: john.spence@ualberta.ca. *Application contact:* Sandy Nakashima, Graduate Program Secretary, 780-492-2820, Fax: 780-492-4323, E-mail: rrgrads.inquiry@ualberta.ca.

University of Central Florida, College of Sciences, Department of Biology, Orlando, FL 32816. Offers biology (MS); conservation biology (PhD, Certificate). Part-time and evening/weekend programs available. *Faculty:* 22 full-time (5 women). *Students:* 55 full-time (36 women), 24 part-time (16 women); includes 6 minority (1 African American, 3 Asian Americans or Pacific Islanders, 2 Hispanic Americans), 6 international. 59 applicants, 47% accepted, 15 enrolled. In 2009, 17 master's, 2 doctorates awarded. *Degree requirements:* For master's, comprehensive exam, thesis or alternative, field exam. *Entrance requirements:* For master's, GRE General Test, minimum GPA of 3.0 in last 60 hours. Additional exam requirements/recommendations for international students: Required—TOEFL. *Application deadline:* For fall admission, 3/1 priority date for domestic students; for spring admission, 10/15 for domestic students. Application fee: $30. Electronic applications accepted. *Expenses:* Tuition, state resident: part-time $306.31 per credit hour. Tuition, nonresident: part-time $1099.01 per credit hour. Part-time tuition and fees vary according to degree level and program. *Financial support:* In 2009–10, 12 students received support, including 12 fellowships with partial tuition reimbursements available (averaging $5,500 per year), 8 research assistantships with partial tuition reimbursements available (averaging $8,400 per year), 37 teaching assistantships with partial tuition reimbursements available (averaging $10,600 per year); career-related internships or fieldwork, Federal Work-Study, institutionally sponsored loans, tuition waivers (partial), and unspecified assistantships also available. Financial award application deadline: 3/1; financial award applicants required to submit FAFSA. *Unit head:* Dr. Ross Hinkle, Chair, 407-823-2976, Fax: 407-823-5769, E-mail: thinkle@mail.ucf.edu. *Application contact:* Dr. Ross Hinkle, Chair, 407-823-2976, Fax: 407-823-5769, E-mail: thinkle@mail.ucf.edu.

University of Hawaii at Hilo, Program in Tropical Conservation Biology and Environmental Science, Hilo, HI 96720-4091. Offers MS.

University of Hawaii at Manoa, Graduate Division, Interdisciplinary Specialization in Ecology, Evolution and Conservation Biology, Honolulu, HI 96822. Offers MS, PhD. *Degree requirements:* For doctorate, thesis/dissertation. *Expenses:* Tuition, state resident: full-time $8900; part-time $372 per credit. Tuition, nonresident: full-time $21,400; part-time $898 per credit. Required fees: $207 per semester. *Faculty research:* Agronomy and soil science, zoology, entomology, genetics and molecular biology, botanical sciences.

University of Illinois at Urbana–Champaign, Graduate College, College of Liberal Arts and Sciences, School of Integrative Biology, Program in Ecology, Evolution and Conservation Biology, Champaign, IL 61820. Offers MS, PhD. *Students:* 25 full-time (14 women), 10 part-time (8 women); includes 4 minority (1 African American, 2 Asian Americans or Pacific Islanders, 1 Hispanic American), 2 international. 40 applicants, 23% accepted, 6 enrolled. In 2009, 1 master's, 4 doctorates awarded. *Entrance requirements:* For master's and doctorate, GRE. Additional exam requirements/recommendations for international students: Required—TOEFL (minimum score 613 paper-based; 257 computer-based; 103 iBT). *Application deadline:* Applications are processed on a rolling basis. Application fee: $60 ($75 for international students). Electronic applications accepted. *Financial support:* In 2009–10, 9 fellowships, 19 research assistantships, 15 teaching assistantships were awarded; tuition waivers (full and partial) also available. *Unit head:* Carla E. Caceres, Director, 217-244-2139, Fax: 217-244-1224, E-mail: cecacere@illinois.edu. *Application contact:* Carol Hall, Secretary, 217-333-8208, Fax: 217-244-1224, E-mail: cahall@illinois.edu.

University of Maryland, College Park, Academic Affairs, College of Chemical and Life Sciences, Department of Biology, Program in Sustainable Development and Conservation Biology, College Park, MD 20742. Offers MS. Part-time and evening/weekend programs available. *Students:* 21 full-time (12 women), 6 part-time (5 women); includes 1 minority (Hispanic American), 5 international. 55 applicants, 33% accepted, 12 enrolled. In 2009, 14 master's awarded. *Degree requirements:* For master's, internship, scholarly paper. *Entrance requirements:* For master's, GRE General Test, minimum GPA of 3.0, 3 letters of recommendation. *Application deadline:* For fall admission, 2/15 priority date for domestic students, 2/1 for international students. Applications are processed on a rolling basis. Application fee: $60. Electronic applications accepted. *Expenses:* Tuition, area resident: Part-time $471 per credit hour. Tuition, state resident: part-time $471 per credit hour. Tuition, nonresident: part-time $1016 per credit hour. Required fees: $337.04 per term. *Financial support:* In 2009–10, 1 research assistantship (averaging $18,519 per year), 16 teaching assistantships (averaging $18,653 per year) were awarded; fellowships also available. Financial award application deadline: 2/1; financial award applicants required to submit FAFSA. *Faculty research:* Biodiversity, global change, conservation. *Unit head:* Dr. David W. Inouye, Director, 301-405-9358, Fax: 301-314-9358, E-mail: inouye@umd.edu. *Application contact:* Dean of Graduate School, 301-405-0358, Fax: 301-314-9305.

University of Michigan, School of Natural Resources and Environment, Program in Natural Resources and Environment, Ann Arbor, MI 48109. Offers aquatic sciences: research and management (MS); behavior, education and communication (MS); conservation biology (MS); environmental informatics (MS); environmental justice (MS); environmental policy and planning (MS); natural resources and environment (PhD); sustainable systems (MS); terrestrial ecosystems (MS); MS/AM; MS/JD; MS/MBA. *Students:* Average age 27. In 2009, 87 master's, 14 doctorates awarded. Terminal master's awarded for partial completion of doctoral program. *Degree requirements:* For master's, practicum or group project; for doctorate, comprehensive exam, thesis/dissertation, oral defense of dissertation, preliminary exam. *Entrance requirements:* For master's, GRE General Test; for doctorate, GRE General Test, master's degree. Additional exam requirements/recommendations for international students: Required—TOEFL (minimum score 560 paper-based; 220 computer-based; 84 iBT). *Application deadline:* For fall admission, 1/5 priority date for domestic and international students. Applications are processed on a rolling basis. Application fee: $60 ($75 for international students). Electronic applications accepted. *Expenses:* Tuition, state resident: full-time $17,286; part-time $1099 per credit hour. Tuition, nonresident: full-time $34,944; part-time $2080 per credit hour. Required fees: $95 per semester. Tuition and fees vary according to course load, degree level and program. *Financial support:* Fellowships with tuition reimbursements, research assistantships with tuition reimbursements, teaching assistantships with tuition reimbursements, career-related internships or fieldwork, Federal Work-Study, institutionally sponsored loans, scholarships/grants, health care benefits, and unspecified assistantships available. Support available to part-time students. Financial award application deadline: 1/5; financial award applicants required to submit FAFSA. *Faculty research:* Stream ecology, plant-insect interactions, fish biology, resource control and reproductive success, remote sensing. *Application contact:* Graduate Admissions Team, 734-764-6453, Fax: 734-936-2195, E-mail: snre.admissions@umich.edu.

University of Minnesota, Twin Cities Campus, Graduate School, College of Food, Agricultural and Natural Resource Sciences, Program in Conservation Biology, Minneapolis, MN 55455-

0213. Offers MS, PhD. Part-time programs available. *Faculty:* 97 full-time (26 women), 8 part-time/adjunct (2 women). *Students:* 67 full-time (41 women), 17 part-time (6 women); includes 6 minority (1 African American, 1 American Indian/Alaska Native, 3 Asian Americans or Pacific Islanders, 1 Hispanic American), 10 international. Average age 28. 75 applicants, 16% accepted, 9 enrolled. In 2009, 12 master's, 9 doctorates awarded. Terminal master's awarded for partial completion of doctoral program. *Degree requirements:* For master's, comprehensive exam, thesis (for some programs); for doctorate, comprehensive exam, thesis/dissertation. *Entrance requirements:* For master's and doctorate, GRE, advanced ecology course. Additional exam requirements/recommendations for international students: Required—TOEFL (minimum score 550 paper-based; 213 computer-based; 79 iBT). *Application deadline:* For fall admission, 12/15 priority date for domestic and international students; for spring admission, 10/15 for domestic and international students. Application fee: $55 ($75 for international students). Electronic applications accepted. *Financial support:* In 2009–10, 3 fellowships with full tuition reimbursements (averaging $22,000 per year), 17 research assistantships with full and partial tuition reimbursements (averaging $18,000 per year), 17 teaching assistantships with full and partial tuition reimbursements (averaging $18,000 per year) were awarded; scholarships/grants, health care benefits, and unspecified assistantships also available. *Faculty research:* Wildlife conservation, fisheries and aquatic biology, invasive species, human dimensions, GIS, restoration ecology. Total annual research expenditures: $3 million. *Unit head:* Dr. Karen Oberhauser, Co-Director of Graduate Studies, 612-642-8706, E-mail: oberh001@umn.edu. *Application contact:* Anup Joshi, Program Coordinator, 612-524-7751, E-mail: consbio@umn.edu.

University of Missouri–St. Louis, College of Arts and Sciences, Department of Biology, St. Louis, MO 63121. Offers biology (MS, PhD), including animal behavior (MS), biochemistry, biochemistry and biotechnology (MS), biotechnology (MS), conservation biology (MS), development (MS), ecology (MS), environmental studies (PhD), evolution (MS), genetics (MS), molecular biology and biochemistry (PhD), molecular/cellular biology (MS), physiology (MS), plant systematics, population biology (MS), tropical biology (MS); biotechnology (Certificate); tropical biology and conservation (Certificate). Part-time programs available. *Faculty:* 43 full-time (13 women), 2 part-time/adjunct (1 woman). *Students:* 54 full-time (27 women), 79 part-time (43 women); includes 15 minority (6 African Americans, 7 Asian Americans or Pacific Islanders, 2 Hispanic Americans), 47 international. Average age 29. 193 applicants, 44% accepted, 44 enrolled. In 2009, 30 master's, 7 doctorates, 9 other advanced degrees awarded. *Degree requirements:* For master's, thesis or alternative; for doctorate, thesis/dissertation, 1 semester of teaching experience. *Entrance requirements:* For master's, 3 letters of recommendation; for doctorate, GRE General Test, 3 letters of recommendation. Additional exam requirements/recommendations for international students: Required—TOEFL. *Application deadline:* For fall admission, 12/1 priority date for domestic and international students; for spring admission, 10/15 priority date for domestic and international students. Applications are processed on a rolling basis. Application fee: $35 ($40 for international students). Electronic applications accepted. *Expenses:* Tuition, state resident: full-time $5377; part-time $297.70 per credit hour. Tuition, nonresident: full-time $13,882; part-time $771.20 per credit hour. Required fees: $220; $12.20 per credit hour. One-time fee: $12. Tuition and fees vary according to course level, campus/location and program. *Financial support:* In 2009–10, 22 research assistantships with full and partial tuition reimbursements (averaging $16,300 per year), 14 teaching assistantships with full and partial tuition reimbursements (averaging $16,727 per year) were awarded; fellowships with full tuition reimbursements, career-related internships or fieldwork and Federal Work-Study also available. Support available to part-time students. Financial award application deadline: 2/1. *Faculty research:* Molecular biology, microbial genetics, animal behavior, tropical ecology, plant systematics. *Unit head:* Dr. Elizabeth Kellogg, Director of Graduate Studies, 314-516-6200, Fax: 314-516-6233, E-mail: tkellogg@umsl.edu. *Application contact:* 314-516-5458, Fax: 314-516-6996, E-mail: gradadm@umsl.edu.

University of Nevada, Reno, Graduate School, Interdisciplinary Program in Ecology, Evolution, and Conservation Biology, Reno, NV 89557. Offers PhD. Offered through the College of Arts and Science, the M. C. Fleischmann College of Agriculture, and the Desert Research Institute. *Degree requirements:* For doctorate, thesis/dissertation. *Entrance requirements:* For doctorate, GRE General Test, GRE Subject Test, minimum GPA of 3.0. Additional exam requirements/recommendations for international students: Required—TOEFL (minimum score 500 paper-based; 173 computer-based; 61 iBT), IELTS (minimum score 6). Electronic applications accepted. *Faculty research:* Population biology, behavioral ecology, plant response to climate change, conservation of endangered species, restoration of natural ecosystems.

University of South Florida, Graduate School, College of Arts and Sciences, Department of Biology, Tampa, FL 33620-9951. Offers cell biology and molecular biology (MS); coastal marine biology (MS); coastal marine biology and ecology (PhD); conservation biology (MS, PhD); molecular and cell biology (PhD). Part-time programs available. *Faculty:* 34 full-time (7 women). *Students:* 72 full-time (43 women), 18 part-time (8 women); includes 9 minority (1 African American, 2 American Indian/Alaska Native, 4 Asian Americans or Pacific Islanders, 2 Hispanic Americans), 7 international. Average age 32. 99 applicants, 20% accepted, 14 enrolled. In 2009, 8 master's, 4 doctorates awarded. *Degree requirements:* For master's, comprehensive exam, thesis (for some programs); for doctorate, comprehensive exam, thesis/dissertation. *Entrance requirements:* For master's and doctorate, GRE General Test, minimum GPA of 3.0. Additional exam requirements/recommendations for international students: Required—TOEFL (minimum score 570 paper-based; 213 computer-based). *Application deadline:* For fall admission, 2/15 priority date for domestic students, 1/2 for international students; for spring admission, 8/1 for domestic students, 6/1 for international students. Application fee: $30. Electronic applications accepted. *Financial support:* In 2009–10, teaching assistantships with tuition reimbursements (averaging $58,627 per year); unspecified assistantships also available. Financial award application deadline: 6/30; financial award applicants required to submit FAFSA. Total annual research expenditures: $1.2 million. *Unit head:* Susan Bell, Co-Chairperson, 813-974-6210, Fax: 813-974-2876, E-mail: sbell@cas.usf.edu. *Application contact:* James Garey, Graduate Advisor, 813-974-8434, Fax: 813-974-3263, E-mail: grarey@cas.usf.edu.

University of Wisconsin–Madison, Graduate School, Gaylord Nelson Institute for Environmental Studies, Conservation Biology and Sustainable Development Program, Madison, WI 53706-1380. Offers MS. Part-time programs available. *Degree requirements:* For master's, thesis or alternative, exit seminar. *Entrance requirements:* For master's, GRE General Test. Additional exam requirements/recommendations for international students: Required—TOEFL (minimum score 550 paper-based; 213 computer-based; 79 iBT). Electronic applications accepted. *Expenses:* Tuition, state resident: part-time $594 per credit. Tuition, nonresident: part-time $1504 per credit. Required fees: $65 per credit. Tuition and fees vary according to course load, program and reciprocity agreements. *Faculty research:* Ornithology, forestry, sociology, rural sociology, plant ecology.

Ecology

Baylor University, Graduate School, College of Arts and Sciences, The Institute of Ecological, Earth and Environmental Sciences, Waco, TX 76798. Offers PhD. *Students:* 5 full-time (2 women), 3 international. *Unit head:* Dr. Joseph D. White, Director, 254-710-2911, E-mail: joseph_d_white@baylor.edu. *Application contact:* Suzanne Keener, Administrative Assistant, 254-710-3588, Fax: 254-710-3870.

Brown University, Graduate School, Division of Biology and Medicine, Program in Ecology and Evolutionary Biology, Providence, RI 02912. Offers PhD. *Degree requirements:* For doctorate, thesis/dissertation, preliminary exam. *Entrance requirements:* For doctorate, GRE General Test, GRE Subject Test. Additional exam requirements/recommendations for international students: Required—TOEFL. Electronic applications accepted. *Faculty research:* Marine ecology, behavioral ecology, population genetics, evolutionary morphology, plant ecology.

California State University, Stanislaus, College of Natural Sciences, Department of Biological Sciences, Turlock, CA 95382. Offers ecology and sustainability (MS); genetic counseling (MS); marine sciences (MS). Part-time programs available. *Degree requirements:* For master's, thesis. *Entrance requirements:* For master's, GRE General Test, GRE Subject Test, minimum GPA of 3.0, 3 letters of reference. Additional exam requirements/recommendations for international students: Required—TOEFL (minimum score 550 paper-based; 213 computer-based). Electronic applications accepted. *Faculty research:* Long-term smoking and pregnancy rate, vertebrate paleobiology, terrestrial animals, benthic invertebrates of central California coastline.

Clemson University, Graduate School, College of Agriculture, Forestry and Life Sciences, Department of Biological Sciences, Program in Biological Sciences, Clemson, SC 29634. Offers MS, PhD. *Students:* 38 full-time (21 women), 2 part-time (1 woman); includes 3 minority (2 Asian Americans or Pacific Islanders, 1 Hispanic American), 11 international. Average age 28. 38 applicants, 21% accepted, 6 enrolled. In 2009, 2 master's, 4 doctorates awarded. *Degree requirements:* For master's, thesis optional; for doctorate, comprehensive exam, thesis/dissertation. *Entrance requirements:* For master's and doctorate, GRE General Test. Additional exam requirements/recommendations for international students: Required—TOEFL, IELTS. *Application deadline:* For fall admission, 1/15 for domestic students, 4/15 for international students. Applications are processed on a rolling basis. Application fee: $70 ($80 for international students). Electronic applications accepted. *Expenses:* Tuition, state resident: full-time $8684; part-time $528 per credit hour. Tuition, nonresident: full-time $15,330; part-time $1078 per credit hour. Required fees: $736; $37 per semester. Part-time tuition and fees vary according to course load and program. *Financial support:* In 2009–10, 39 students received support, including 12 fellowships with full and partial tuition reimbursements available (averaging $9,529 per year), 11 research assistantships with partial tuition reimbursements available (averaging $18,008 per year), 28 teaching assistantships with partial tuition reimbursements available (averaging $17,393 per year); career-related internships or fieldwork, institutionally sponsored loans, scholarships/grants, health care benefits, and unspecified assistantships also available. Support available to part-time students. Financial award application deadline: 3/15; financial award applicants required to submit FAFSA. *Unit head:* Dr. Alfred Wheeler, Department Chair, 864-656-1415, Fax: 864-656-0435, E-mail: wheeler@clemson.edu. *Application contact:* Jay Lyn Martin, Coordinator for Graduate Program, 864-656-3587, Fax: 864-656-0435, E-mail: gradbio@clemson.edu.

Colorado State University, Graduate School, Graduate Degree Program in Ecology, Fort Collins, CO 80523-1401. Offers MS, PhD. Part-time programs available. *Students:* 58 full-time (37 women), 53 part-time (32 women); includes 10 minority (2 African Americans, 1 American Indian/Alaska Native, 5 Asian Americans or Pacific Islanders, 2 Hispanic Americans), 5 international. Average age 32. 118 applicants, 21% accepted, 25 enrolled. In 2009, 7 master's, 7 doctorates awarded. Terminal master's awarded for partial completion of doctoral program. *Degree requirements:* For master's, comprehensive exam, thesis; for doctorate, comprehensive exam, thesis/dissertation. *Entrance requirements:* For master's, GRE General Test, minimum GPA of 3.0, BA/BS in agriculture, anthropology, biology, biochemistry, math or physical sciences (preferred), letters of recommendation; for doctorate, GRE General Test, minimum GPA of 3.0, BA/BS in agriculture, anthropology, biology, biochemistry, math or physical sciences (preferred), letters of recommendation, personal statement. Additional exam requirements/recommendations for international students: Required—TOEFL (minimum score 550 paper-based; 213 computer-based; 80 iBT). *Application deadline:* For fall admission, 1/1 priority date for domestic and international students; for spring admission, 9/1 for domestic students. Applications are processed on a rolling basis. Application fee: $50. Electronic applications accepted. *Expenses:* Tuition, state resident: full-time $6434; part-time $359.10 per credit. Tuition, nonresident: full-time $18,116; part-time $1006.45 per credit. Required fees: $1496; $83 per credit. *Financial support:* Fellowships, research assistantships, teaching assistantships with full tuition reimbursements available. Financial award applicants required to submit FAFSA. *Faculty research:* Plant and animal ecology at organismal, population, community, and ecosystem levels. *Unit head:* Dr. N. Leroy Poff, Interim Director, 970-491-2079, Fax: 970-491-2796, E-mail: poff@lamar.colostate.edu. *Application contact:* Jeri Morgan, Program Assistant, 970-491-4373, Fax: 970-491-2796, E-mail: ecology@colostate.edu.

Columbia University, Graduate School of Arts and Sciences, Division of Natural Sciences, Department of Ecology and Evolutionary Biology, New York, NY 10027. Offers conservation biology (Certificate); ecology and evolutionary biology (PhD); environmental policy (Certificate). *Degree requirements:* For doctorate, one foreign language, thesis/dissertation, teaching experience. *Entrance requirements:* For doctorate, GRE General Test, previous course work in biology. Additional exam requirements/recommendations for international students: Required—TOEFL. Electronic applications accepted. *Faculty research:* Tropical ecology, ethnobotany, global change, systematics.

See Close-Up on page 281.

Cornell University, Graduate School, Graduate Fields of Agriculture and Life Sciences, Field of Computational Biology, Ithaca, NY 14853-0001. Offers computational behavioral biology (PhD); computational biology (PhD); computational cell biology (PhD); computational ecology (PhD); computational macromolecular biology (PhD); computational organismal biology (PhD). *Faculty:* 40 full-time (5 women). *Students:* 17 full-time (4 women); includes 4 minority (3 Asian Americans or Pacific Islanders, 1 Hispanic American), 4 international. Average age 28. 142 applicants, 11% accepted, 6 enrolled. *Degree requirements:* For doctorate, comprehensive exam, thesis/dissertation, 2 semesters of teaching experience. *Entrance requirements:* For doctorate, GRE General Test, GRE Subject Test (biology), 2 letters of recommendation. Additional exam requirements/recommendations for international students: Required—TOEFL (minimum score 550 paper-based; 213 computer-based; 77 iBT). *Application deadline:* For fall admission, 2/1 priority date for domestic students. Application fee: $70. Electronic applications accepted. *Expenses:* Tuition: Full-time $29,500. Required fees: $70. Full-time tuition and fees vary according to degree level, program and student level. *Financial support:* In 2009–10, 6 fellowships with full tuition reimbursements were awarded; research assistantships with full tuition reimbursements, teaching assistantships with full tuition reimbursements, institutionally sponsored loans, scholarships/grants, health care benefits, tuition waivers (full and partial), and unspecified assistantships also available. Financial award applicants required to submit FAFSA. *Faculty research:* Computational behavioral biology, computational biology, computational cell biology, computational ecology, computational genetics, computational macromolecular biology, computational organismal biology. *Unit head:* Dr. Andrew Clark, Director of Graduate Studies, 607-255-5488, E-mail: ac347@cornell.edu. *Application contact:* Graduate School Application Requests, 607-255-5816, E-mail: gradadmissions@cornell.edu.

Cornell University, Graduate School, Graduate Fields of Agriculture and Life Sciences, Field of Ecology and Evolutionary Biology, Ithaca, NY 14853-0001. Offers ecology (PhD), including animal ecology, applied ecology, biogeochemistry, community and ecosystem ecology, limnology,

oceanography, physiological ecology, plant ecology, population ecology, theoretical ecology, vertebrate zoology; evolutionary biology (PhD), including ecological genetics, paleobiology, population biology, systematics. *Faculty:* 53 full-time (14 women). *Students:* 57 full-time (43 women); includes 4 minority (2 Asian Americans or Pacific Islanders, 2 Hispanic Americans), 8 international. Average age 29. 99 applicants, 11% accepted, 8 enrolled. In 2009, 12 doctorates awarded. *Degree requirements:* For doctorate, comprehensive exam, thesis/dissertation, 2 semesters of teaching experience. *Entrance requirements:* For doctorate, GRE General Test, GRE Subject Test (biology), 2 letters of recommendation. Additional exam requirements/ recommendations for international students: Required—TOEFL (minimum score 550 paper-based; 213 computer-based; 77 iBT). *Application deadline:* For fall admission, 12/15 for domestic students. Application fee: $70. Electronic applications accepted. *Expenses:* Tuition: Full-time $29,500. Required fees: $70. Full-time tuition and fees vary according to degree level, program and student level. *Financial support:* In 2009–10, 56 students received support, including 7 fellowships with full tuition reimbursements available, 1 teaching assistantship with full tuition reimbursement available; research assistantships with full tuition reimbursements available, institutionally sponsored loans, scholarships/grants, health care benefits, tuition waivers (full and partial), and unspecified assistantships also available. Financial award applicants required to submit FAFSA. *Faculty research:* Population and organismal biology, population and evolutionary genetics, systematics and macroevolution, biochemistry, conservation biology. *Unit head:* Director of Graduate Studies, 607-254-4230. *Application contact:* Graduate Field Assistant, 607-254-4230, E-mail: eeb_grad_req@cornell.edu.

Cornell University, Graduate School, Graduate Fields of Agriculture and Life Sciences, Field of Zoology, Ithaca, NY 14853-0001. Offers animal cytology (MS, PhD); comparative and functional anatomy (MS, PhD); developmental biology (MS, PhD); ecology (MS, PhD); histology (MS, PhD). *Faculty:* 24 full-time (5 women). *Students:* 4 full-time (all women); includes 1 minority (Hispanic American), 1 international. Average age 34. 7 applicants, 0% accepted, 0 enrolled. *Degree requirements:* For doctorate, comprehensive exam, thesis/dissertation, 2 semesters of teaching experience. *Entrance requirements:* For doctorate, GRE General Test, GRE Subject Test (biology), 2 letters of recommendation. Additional exam requirements/ recommendations for international students: Required—TOEFL (minimum score 550 paper-based; 213 computer-based; 77 iBT). *Application deadline:* For fall admission, 2/1 priority date for domestic students. Application fee: $70. Electronic applications accepted. *Expenses:* Tuition: Full-time $29,500. Required fees: $70. Full-time tuition and fees vary according to degree level, program and student level. *Financial support:* In 2009–10, 3 students received support; fellowships with full tuition reimbursements available, research assistantships with full tuition reimbursements available, teaching assistantships with full tuition reimbursements available, institutionally sponsored loans, scholarships/grants, health care benefits, tuition waivers (full and partial), and unspecified assistantships available. Financial award applicants required to submit FAFSA. *Faculty research:* Organismal biology, functional morphology, biomechanics, comparative vertebrate anatomy, comparative invertebrate anatomy, paleontology. *Unit head:* Director of Graduate Studies, 607-253-3276, Fax: 607-253-3756. *Application contact:* Graduate Field Assistant, 607-253-3276, Fax: 607-253-3756, E-mail: graduate_edcvm@cornell.edu.

Dartmouth College, Arts and Sciences Graduate Programs, Program in Ecology and Evolutionary Biology, Hanover, NH 03755. Offers PhD. *Faculty:* 16 full-time (3 women). *Students:* 16 full-time (9 women); includes 3 minority (1 American Indian/Alaska Native, 1 Asian American or Pacific Islander, 1 Hispanic American), 1 international. Average age 27. 49 applicants, 16% accepted, 5 enrolled. In 2009, 5 doctorates awarded. *Entrance requirements:* For doctorate, GRE General Test, GRE Subject Test in biology (highly recommended). Additional exam requirements/recommendations for international students: Required—TOEFL. *Application deadline:* For fall admission, 12/1 for domestic students. Application fee: $25. *Financial support:* In 2009–10, 12 students received support, including fellowships (averaging $23,832 per year), research assistantships with full tuition reimbursements available (averaging $23,832 per year), teaching assistantships with full tuition reimbursements available (averaging $23,832 per year); institutionally sponsored loans, traineeships, and unspecified assistantships also available. Financial award applicants required to submit FAFSA. *Unit head:* Dr. Matthew Ayres, 603-646-2788, Fax: 603-646-3488. *Application contact:* Amy Layne, 603-646-3847, Fax: 603-646-3488.

See Close-Up on page 91.

Duke University, Graduate School, Department of Ecology, Durham, NC 27708-0342. Offers PhD, Certificate. *Faculty:* 31 full-time. *Students:* 29 full-time (14 women); includes 5 minority (1 African American, 2 Asian Americans or Pacific Islanders, 2 Hispanic Americans), 3 international. 55 applicants, 13% accepted, 4 enrolled. In 2009, 9 doctorates awarded. *Degree requirements:* For doctorate, thesis/dissertation. *Entrance requirements:* For doctorate, GRE General Test. Additional exam requirements/recommendations for international students: Required—TOEFL (minimum score 550 paper-based; 213 computer-based; 83 iBT), IELTS (minimum score 7). *Application deadline:* For fall admission, 12/8 priority date for domestic and international students. Application fee: $75. Electronic applications accepted. *Unit head:* Dan Richter, Director of Graduate Studies, 919-613-8031, Fax: 919-684-8741, E-mail: drichter@duke.edu. *Application contact:* Cynthia Robertson, Associate Dean for Enrollment Services, 919-684-3913, E-mail: grad-admissions@duke.edu.

Duke University, Graduate School, Department of Environment, Durham, NC 27708. Offers natural resource economics/policy (AM, PhD); natural resource science/ecology (AM, PhD); natural resource systems science (AM, PhD); JD/AM. Part-time programs available. *Faculty:* 28 full-time. *Students:* 66 full-time (39 women); includes 3 minority (2 African Americans, 1 Asian American or Pacific Islander), 25 international. 126 applicants, 26% accepted, 19 enrolled. In 2009, 4 master's, 11 doctorates awarded. *Degree requirements:* For doctorate, variable foreign language requirement, thesis/dissertation. *Entrance requirements:* For master's and doctorate, GRE General Test. Additional exam requirements/recommendations for international students: Required—TOEFL (minimum score 550 paper-based; 213 computer-based; 83 iBT), IELTS (minimum score 7). *Application deadline:* For fall admission, 12/8 priority date for domestic and international students. Application fee: $75. Electronic applications accepted. *Financial support:* Fellowships, research assistantships, teaching assistantships, Federal Work-Study available. Financial award application deadline: 12/31. *Unit head:* Kenneth Reckhow, Director of Graduate Studies, Fax: 919-660-1884, E-mail: meg.stephens@duke.edu. *Application contact:* Cynthia Robertson, Associate Dean for Enrollment Services, 919-684-3913, E-mail: grad-admissions@duke.edu.

Duke University, Nicholas School of the Environment, Durham, NC 27708-0328. Offers coastal environmental management (MEM); DEL-environmental leadership (MEM); energy and environment (MEM); environmental economics and policy (MEM); environmental health and security (MEM); forest resource management (MF); global environmental change (MEM); resource ecology (MEM); water and air resources (MEM); JD/AM; JD/MEM; JD/MF; MAT/MEM; MBA/MEM; MBA/MF; MEM/MPP; MF/MPP. *Accreditation:* SAF (one or more programs are accredited). Part-time programs available. *Degree requirements:* For master's, thesis. *Entrance requirements:* For master's, GRE General Test, previous course work in biology or ecology, calculus, statistics, and microeconomics; computer familiarity with word processing and data analysis. Additional exam requirements/recommendations for international students: Required—TOEFL (minimum score 550 paper-based; 213 computer-based). Electronic applications accepted. *Expenses:* Contact institution. *Faculty research:* Ecosystem management, conservation ecology, earth systems, risk assessment.

Eastern Kentucky University, The Graduate School, College of Arts and Sciences, Department of Biological Sciences, Richmond, KY 40475-3102. Offers biological sciences (MS); ecology (MS). Part-time programs available. *Degree requirements:* For master's, thesis. *Entrance requirements:* For master's, GRE General Test, minimum GPA of 2.5. *Faculty research:*

Systematics, ecology, and biodiversity; animal behavior; protein structure and molecular genetics; biomonitoring and aquatic toxicology; pathogenesis of microbes and parasites.

Eastern Michigan University, Graduate School, College of Arts and Sciences, Department of Biology, Ypsilanti, MI 48197. Offers cell and molecular biology (MS); community college biology teaching (MS); ecology and organismal biology (MS); general biology (MS); water resources (MS). Part-time and evening/weekend programs available. Postbaccalaureate distance learning degree programs offered (minimal on-campus study). *Faculty:* 20 full-time (5 women). *Students:* 10 full-time (8 women), 35 part-time (21 women); includes 3 minority (2 African Americans, 1 Asian American or Pacific Islander), 7 international. Average age 28. 57 applicants, 63% accepted, 20 enrolled. In 2009, 17 master's awarded. *Entrance requirements:* For master's, GRE General Test, GRE Subject Test. Additional exam requirements/recommendations for international students: Required—TOEFL. *Application deadline:* Applications are processed on a rolling basis. Application fee: $35. Tuition and fees vary according to course level. *Financial support:* In 2009–10, 22 teaching assistantships with full tuition reimbursements (averaging $8,660 per year) were awarded; fellowships, research assistantships with full tuition reimbursements, career-related internships or fieldwork, Federal Work-Study, institutionally sponsored loans, scholarships/grants, tuition waivers (partial), and unspecified assistantships also available. Support available to part-time students. Financial award applicants required to submit FAFSA. *Unit head:* Dr. Marianne Laporte, Department Head, 734-487-4242, Fax: 734-487-9235, E-mail: mlaporte@emich.edu. *Application contact:* Dr. Marianne Laporte, Department Head, 734-487-4242, Fax: 734-487-9235, E-mail: mlaporte@emich.edu.

Emory University, Graduate School of Arts and Sciences, Division of Biological and Biomedical Sciences, Program in Population Biology, Ecology and Evolution, Atlanta, GA 30322-1100. Offers PhD. *Faculty:* 29 full-time (4 women). *Students:* 27 full-time (18 women); includes 6 minority (2 Asian Americans or Pacific Islanders, 4 Hispanic Americans), 5 international. Average age 27. 37 applicants, 19% accepted, 5 enrolled. In 2009, 4 doctorates awarded. *Degree requirements:* For doctorate, comprehensive exam, thesis/dissertation. *Entrance requirements:* For doctorate, GRE General Test, minimum GPA of 3.0 in science course work (recommended). Additional exam requirements/recommendations for international students: Required—TOEFL. *Application deadline:* For fall admission, 1/3 for domestic and international students. Application fee: $50. Electronic applications accepted. *Financial support:* In 2009–10, 14 students received support, including 14 fellowships with full tuition reimbursements available (averaging $24,500 per year); institutionally sponsored loans, scholarships/grants, and health care benefits also available. *Faculty research:* Evolution of microbes, infectious disease, the immune system, genetic disease in humans, evolution of behavior. *Unit head:* Dr. Michael Zwick, Director, 404-727-9924, Fax: 404-727-3949, E-mail: mzwick@emory.edu. *Application contact:* Dr. Yun Tao, 404-727-0815, Fax: 404-727-2880, E-mail: ytao3@emory.edu.

Florida Institute of Technology, Graduate Programs, College of Science, Department of Biological Sciences, Program in Ecology, Melbourne, FL 32901-6975. Offers MS. Part-time programs available. *Degree requirements:* For master's, thesis. *Entrance requirements:* For master's, GRE General Test, minimum GPA of 3.0. *Application deadline:* Applications are processed on a rolling basis. Electronic applications accepted. *Expenses:* Tuition: Part-time $1015 per credit. Tuition and fees vary according to campus/location and program. *Financial support:* In 2009–10, research assistantships with full and partial tuition reimbursements (averaging $5,844 per year), teaching assistantships (averaging $4,267 per year) were awarded; career-related internships or fieldwork and tuition remissions also available. Financial award application deadline: 3/1; financial award applicants required to submit FAFSA. *Faculty research:* Endangered or threatened avian and mammalian species, hydroacoustics and feeding preference of the West Indian manatee, habitat preference of the Florida scrub jay. *Application contact:* Carolyn P. Shea.

See Close-Up on page 329.

Florida State University, The Graduate School, College of Arts and Sciences, Department of Biological Science, Specialization in Ecology and Evolutionary Biology, Tallahassee, FL 32306-4295. Offers MS, PhD. *Faculty:* 24 full-time (9 women). *Students:* 55 full-time (31 women); includes 8 minority (1 American Indian/Alaska Native, 3 Asian Americans or Pacific Islanders, 4 Hispanic Americans), 2 international. 133 applicants, 15% accepted, 16 enrolled. In 2009, 2 doctorates awarded. Terminal master's awarded for partial completion of doctoral program. *Degree requirements:* For master's, comprehensive exam, thesis, teaching experience, seminar presentation; for doctorate, comprehensive exam, thesis/dissertation, teaching experience; seminar presentation. *Entrance requirements:* For master's, GRE General Test (minimum combined score 1100, 500 verbal, 500 quantitative), minimum upper-division GPA of 3.0; for doctorate, GRE General Test (minimum combined score 1100, Verbal 500, Quantitative 500), minimum upper-division GPA of 3.0. Additional exam requirements/recommendations for international students: Required—TOEFL (minimum score 600 paper-based; 250 computer-based; 92 iBT). *Application deadline:* For fall admission, 12/15 for domestic and international students. Application fee: $30. Electronic applications accepted. *Expenses:* Tuition, state resident: full-time $7413. Tuition, nonresident: full-time $22,567. *Financial support:* In 2009–10, 43 students received support, including 4 fellowships with full tuition reimbursements available (averaging $22,000 per year), 13 research assistantships with full tuition reimbursements available (averaging $20,000 per year), 38 teaching assistantships with full tuition reimbursements available (averaging $18,540 per year). Financial award application deadline: 12/15; financial award applicants required to submit FAFSA. *Faculty research:* Ecology and conservation biology, evolution, marine biology, phylogeny and systematics, theoretical, computational and mathematical biology. *Application contact:* Judy Bowers, Coordinator, Graduate Affairs, 850-644-3023, Fax: 850-644-9829, E-mail: gradinfo@bio.fsu.edu.

Frostburg State University, Graduate School, College of Liberal Arts and Sciences, Department of Biology, Program in Applied Ecology and Conservation Biology, Frostburg, MD 21532-1099. Offers MS. *Faculty:* 10. *Students:* 9 full-time (5 women), 1 (woman) part-time; includes 1 minority (American Indian/Alaska Native). Average age 25. 16 applicants, 6% accepted, 1 enrolled. In 2009, 4 master's awarded. *Degree requirements:* For master's, thesis. *Entrance requirements:* For master's, GRE General Test, resume. Additional exam requirements/recommendations for international students: Required—TOEFL. *Application deadline:* For fall admission, 7/15 priority date for domestic students. Applications are processed on a rolling basis. Application fee: $30. Electronic applications accepted. *Expenses:* Tuition, state resident: full-time $5706; part-time $317 per credit hour. Tuition, nonresident: full-time $6948; part-time $386 per credit hour. Required fees: $1476; $82 per credit hour. $11 per term. One-time fee: $30 full-time. *Financial support:* In 2009–10, 8 research assistantships with full tuition reimbursements (averaging $5,000 per year) were awarded; career-related internships or fieldwork and Federal Work-Study also available. Financial award application deadline: 4/1; financial award applicants required to submit FAFSA. *Faculty research:* Forest ecology, microbiology of man-made wetlands, invertebrate zoology and entomology, wildlife and carnivore ecology, aquatic pollution ecology. *Unit head:* Dr. R. Scott Fritz, Coordinator, 301-687-4166. *Application contact:* Vickie Mazer, Director, Graduate Services, 301-687-7053, Fax: 301-687-4597, E-mail: vmmazer@frostburg.edu.

Illinois State University, Graduate School, College of Arts and Sciences, Department of Biological Sciences, Normal, IL 61790-2200. Offers animal behavior (MS); bacteriology (MS); biochemistry (MS); biological sciences (MS); biology (PhD); biophysics (MS); biotechnology (MS); botany (MS, PhD); cell biology (MS); conservation biology (MS); developmental biology (MS); ecology (MS, PhD); entomology (MS); evolutionary biology (MS); genetics (MS, PhD); immunology (MS); microbiology (MS, PhD); molecular biology (MS); molecular genetics (MS); neurobiology (MS); neuroscience (MS); parasitology (MS); physiology (MS, PhD); plant biology (MS); plant molecular biology (MS); plant sciences (MS); structural biology (MS); zoology (MS, PhD). Part-time programs available. *Degree requirements:* For master's, thesis or alternative; for doctorate, variable foreign language requirement, thesis/dissertation, 2 terms of residency. *Entrance requirements:* For master's, GRE General Test, minimum GPA of 2.6 in last 60 hours of course work; for doctorate, GRE General Test. *Faculty research:* Redoc balance and drug development in schistosoma mansoni, control of the growth of listeria monocytogenes at low temperature, regulation of cell expansion and microtubule function by SPRI, CRUI: physiology and fitness consequences of different life history phenotypes.

Indiana State University, School of Graduate Studies, College of Arts and Sciences, Department of Biology, Terre Haute, IN 47809. Offers ecology (PhD); life sciences (MS); microbiology (PhD); physiology (PhD); science education (MS). *Degree requirements:* For master's, thesis (for some programs); for doctorate, comprehensive exam, thesis/dissertation. *Entrance requirements:* For master's and doctorate, GRE General Test. Electronic applications accepted.

Indiana University Bloomington, University Graduate School, College of Arts and Sciences, Department of Biology, Bloomington, IN 47405. Offers biology teaching (MAT); biotechnology (MA); evolution, ecology, and behavior (MA, PhD); genetics (PhD); microbiology (MA, PhD); molecular, cellular, and developmental biology (PhD); plant sciences (MA, PhD); zoology (MA, PhD). *Faculty:* 58 full-time (15 women), 21 part-time/adjunct (6 women). *Students:* 165 full-time (95 women); includes 14 minority (6 African Americans, 1 American Indian/Alaska Native, 7 Asian Americans or Pacific Islanders), 56 international. Average age 27. 312 applicants, 19% accepted, 24 enrolled. In 2009, 4 master's, 22 doctorates awarded. Terminal master's awarded for partial completion of doctoral program. *Degree requirements:* For master's, thesis, oral defense; for doctorate, thesis/dissertation, oral defense. *Entrance requirements:* For master's and doctorate, GRE General Test. Additional exam requirements/recommendations for international students: Required—TOEFL (minimum score 100 iBT). *Application deadline:* For fall admission, 1/5 priority date for domestic students, 12/1 priority date for international students. Application fee: $55 ($65 for international students). Electronic applications accepted. *Financial support:* In 2009–10, 165 students received support, including 62 fellowships with tuition reimbursements available (averaging $19,484 per year), 27 research assistantships with tuition reimbursements available (averaging $22,605 per year), 76 teaching assistantships with tuition reimbursements available (averaging $20,528 per year); scholarships/grants, traineeships, health care benefits, and unspecified assistantships also available. Financial award application deadline: 1/5. *Faculty research:* Evolution, ecology and behavior; microbiology; molecular biology and genetics; plant biology. *Unit head:* Dr. Roger Innes, Chair, 812-855-2219, Fax: 812-855-6082, E-mail: rinnes@indiana.edu. *Application contact:* Tracey D. Stohr, Graduate Student Recruitment Coordinator, 812-856-6303, Fax: 812-855-6082, E-mail: gradbio@indiana.edu.

Inter American University of Puerto Rico, Bayamón Campus, Graduate School, Bayamón, PR 00957. Offers biology (MS), including environmental sciences and ecology, molecular biotechnology; electronic commerce (MBA); human resources (MBA). Part-time and evening/weekend programs available. *Faculty:* 6 full-time (1 woman), 5 part-time/adjunct (2 women). *Students:* 99 part-time (61 women); includes all Hispanic Americans. Average age 31. *Degree requirements:* For master's, comprehensive exam, research project. *Entrance requirements:* For master's, EXADEP, GRE General Test, letters of recommendation. *Application deadline:* For fall admission, 7/1 for domestic students, 5/1 priority date for international students; for winter admission, 11/15 priority date for domestic and international students; for spring admission, 2/15 priority date for domestic and international students. Application fee: $31. *Expenses:* Tuition: Part-time $195 per credit. Required fees: $148 per trimester. *Unit head:* Prof. Juan F. Martinez, Rector, 787-279-1200 Ext. 2295, Fax: 787-279-2205, E-mail: jmartinez@bc.inter.edu. *Application contact:* Carlos Alicea, Director of Admission, 787-279-1200 Ext. 2017, Fax: 787-279-2205, E-mail: calicea@bc.inter.edu.

Iowa State University of Science and Technology, Graduate College, College of Liberal Arts and Sciences, Department of Ecology, Evolution, and Organismal Biology, Ames, IA 50011. Offers MS, PhD. *Faculty:* 28 full-time (9 women), 2 part-time/adjunct (1 woman). *Degree requirements:* For master's, thesis or alternative; for doctorate, thesis/dissertation. *Entrance requirements:* For master's and doctorate, GRE General Test. Additional exam requirements/recommendations for international students: Required—TOEFL. Application fee: $40 ($90 for international students). Electronic applications accepted. *Expenses:* Tuition, state resident: full-time $6716. Tuition, nonresident: full-time $8908. Tuition and fees vary according to course level, course load, program and student level. *Financial support:* Fellowships, research assistantships with partial tuition reimbursements, teaching assistantships with partial tuition reimbursements, scholarships/grants, health care benefits, and unspecified assistantships available. *Faculty research:* Aquatic and wetland ecology, cytology, ecology, physiology and molecular biology, systematics and evolution. *Unit head:* Dr. Jonathan Wendel, Chair, 515-294-7172. *Application contact:* Information Contact, 515-294-5836, Fax: 515-294-2592, E-mail: grad_admissions@iastate.edu.

Iowa State University of Science and Technology, Graduate College, Interdisciplinary Programs, Program in Ecology and Evolutionary Biology, Ames, IA 50011. Offers MS, PhD. *Students:* 51 full-time (24 women), 3 part-time (1 woman); includes 4 minority (1 American Indian/Alaska Native, 1 Asian American or Pacific Islander, 2 Hispanic Americans), 9 international. In 2009, 5 master's, 5 doctorates awarded. *Degree requirements:* For master's, thesis or alternative; for doctorate, thesis/dissertation. *Entrance requirements:* For master's and doctorate, GRE General Test, application to cooperating department. Additional exam requirements/recommendations for international students: Required—TOEFL (minimum score 550 paper-based; 79 iBT) or IELTS (minimum score 6.5). *Application deadline:* For fall admission, 1/1 priority date for domestic and international students. Application fee: $40 ($90 for international students). Electronic applications accepted. *Expenses:* Tuition, state resident: full-time $6716. Tuition, nonresident: full-time $8908. Tuition and fees vary according to course level, course load, program and student level. *Financial support:* In 2009–10, 33 research assistantships with full and partial tuition reimbursements (averaging $16,750 per year), 16 teaching assistantships with full and partial tuition reimbursements (averaging $16,750 per year) were awarded; scholarships/grants, health care benefits, and unspecified assistantships also available. *Faculty research:* Landscape ecology, aquatic and method ecology, physiological ecology, population genetics and evolution, systematics. *Unit head:* Dr. Kirk Moloney, Supervisory Committee Chair, 515-294-6518, E-mail: eeboffice@iastate.edu. *Application contact:* Charles Sauer, Information Contact, 515-294-6518, E-mail: eeboffice@iastate.edu.

Kent State University, College of Arts and Sciences, Department of Biological Sciences, Program in Ecology, Kent, OH 44242-0001. Offers MS, PhD. *Degree requirements:* For master's, thesis; for doctorate, thesis/dissertation. *Entrance requirements:* For master's, GRE General Test, minimum GPA of 3.0; for doctorate, GRE General Test, minimum GPA of 3.25. Additional exam requirements/recommendations for international students: Required—TOEFL (minimum score 600 paper-based; 287 computer-based). Electronic applications accepted.

Laurentian University, School of Graduate Studies and Research, Programme in Biology, Sudbury, ON P3E 2C6, Canada. Offers biology (M Sc); boreal ecology (PhD). Part-time programs available. *Degree requirements:* For master's, thesis. *Entrance requirements:* For master's, honors degree with second class or better. *Faculty research:* Recovery of acid-stressed lakes, effects of climate change, origin and maintenance of biocomplexity, radionuclide dynamics, cytogenetic studies of plants.

Lesley University, Graduate School of Arts and Social Sciences, Cambridge, MA 02138-2790. Offers clinical mental health counseling (MA), including expressive therapies counseling, holistic counseling, school and community counseling; counseling psychology (MA, CAGS), including professional counseling (MA), school counseling (MA); creative arts in learning (CAGS); creative writing (MFA); ecological teaching and learning (MS); environmental education (MS); expressive therapies (MA, PhD, CAGS), including art (MA), dance (MA), expressive therapies, music (MA); independent studies (CAGS); independent study (MA); intercultural relations (MA, CAGS); interdisciplinary studies (MA), including individualized studies, integrative holistic health, women's studies; urban environmental leadership (MA); visual arts (MFA). Part-time and evening/weekend programs available. Postbaccalaureate distance learning degree programs offered (minimal on-campus study). *Degree requirements:* For master's, internship, practicum, thesis (expressive therapies); for doctorate, thesis/dissertation, arts apprenticeship,

Ecology

Lesley University (continued)

field placement; for CAGS, thesis, internship (counseling psychology, expressive therapies). *Entrance requirements:* For master's, MAT (counseling psychology), interview, writing samples, art portfolio; for doctorate, GRE or MAT; for CAGS, interview, master's degree. Additional exam requirements/recommendations for international students: Required—TOEFL (minimum score 550 paper-based; 213 computer-based; 80 iBT). Electronic applications accepted. *Faculty research:* Psychotherapy and culture; psychotherapy and psychological trauma; women's issues in art, teaching and psychotherapy; community based art, psycho-spiritual inquiry.

Marquette University, Graduate School, College of Arts and Sciences, Department of Biology, Milwaukee, WI 53201-1881. Offers cell biology (MS, PhD); developmental biology (MS, PhD); ecology (MS, PhD); endocrinology (MS, PhD); evolutionary biology (MS, PhD); genetics (MS, PhD); microbiology (MS, PhD); molecular biology (MS, PhD); muscle and exercise physiology (MS, PhD); neurobiology (MS, PhD); reproductive physiology (MS, PhD). *Faculty:* 23 full-time (10 women), 1 part-time/adjunct (0 women). *Students:* 23 full-time (13 women), 16 part-time (9 women); includes 1 minority (Asian American or Pacific Islander), 20 international. Average age 25. 95 applicants, 16% accepted, 10 enrolled. In 2009, 3 master's, 5 doctorates awarded. Terminal master's awarded for partial completion of doctoral program. *Degree requirements:* For master's, comprehensive exam, thesis, 1 year of teaching experience or equivalent; for doctorate, thesis/dissertation, 1 year of teaching experience or equivalent, qualifying exam. *Entrance requirements:* For master's and doctorate, GRE General Test, GRE Subject Test. Additional exam requirements/recommendations for international students: Required—TOEFL. Application fee: $40. *Financial support:* In 2009–10, 4 fellowships, 22 teaching assistantships were awarded; research assistantships, Federal Work-Study, institutionally sponsored loans, scholarships/grants, and tuition waivers (full and partial) also available. Support available to part-time students. Financial award application deadline: 2/15. *Faculty research:* Microbial and invertebrate ecology, evolution of gene function, DNA methylation, DNA arrangement. *Unit head:* Dr. Robert Fitts, Chair, 414-288-1748, Fax: 414-288-7357. *Application contact:* Debbie Weaver, Administrative Assistant, 414-288-7355, Fax: 414-288-7357.

Michigan State University, The Graduate School, College of Natural Science, Interdepartmental Program in Ecology, Evolutionary Biology and Behavior, East Lansing, MI 48824. Offers PhD. *Faculty:* 98 full-time (23 women). *Students:* 81 full-time (43 women), 6 part-time (1 woman); includes 5 minority (3 Asian Americans or Pacific Islanders, 2 Hispanic Americans), 11 international. Average age 29. *Entrance requirements:* Additional exam requirements/recommendations for international students: Required—TOEFL. Electronic applications accepted. *Expenses:* Tuition, state resident: part-time $478.25 per credit hour. Tuition, nonresident: part-time $966.50 per credit hour. Part-time tuition and fees vary according to program. *Financial support:* In 2009–10, 1 research assistantship with tuition reimbursement (averaging $6,379 per year) was awarded. *Unit head:* Dr. Kay E. Holekamp, Director, 517-432-1359, E-mail: holekamp@msu.edu. *Application contact:* Patricia Resler, Program Secretary, 517-432-1359, E-mail: eebb@msu.edu.

Michigan Technological University, Graduate School, School of Forest Resources and Environmental Science, Program in Applied Ecology, Houghton, MI 49931. Offers MS. Part-time programs available. *Degree requirements:* For master's, thesis (for some programs). *Entrance requirements:* For master's, GRE. Additional exam requirements/recommendations for international students: Required—TOEFL (minimum score 550 paper-based; 213 computer-based). Electronic applications accepted.

Montana State University, College of Graduate Studies, College of Letters and Science, Department of Ecology, Bozeman, MT 59717. Offers ecological and environmental statistics (MS); ecology and environmental sciences (PhD); fish and wildlife biology (PhD); fish and wildlife management (MS). Part-time programs available. *Faculty:* 12 full-time (2 women), 2 part-time/adjunct (0 women). *Students:* 8 full-time (2 women), 48 part-time (18 women). Average age 31. 18 applicants, 33% accepted, 6 enrolled. In 2009, 6 master's, 7 doctorates awarded. *Degree requirements:* For master's, comprehensive exam, thesis (for some programs); for doctorate, comprehensive exam, thesis/dissertation. *Entrance requirements:* For master's, GRE General Test, letters of recommendation, essay; for doctorate, GRE General Test, letters of recommendation. Additional exam requirements/recommendations for international students: Required—TOEFL (minimum score 550 paper-based; 213 computer-based). *Application deadline:* For fall admission, 7/15 priority date for domestic students, 5/15 priority date for international students; for spring admission, 12/1 priority date for domestic students, 10/1 priority date for international students. Applications are processed on a rolling basis. Application fee: $30. Electronic applications accepted. *Expenses:* Tuition, state resident: full-time $5635; part-time $3492 per year. Tuition, nonresident: full-time $17,212; part-time $7865.10 per year. Required fees: $1441; $153.15 per credit. Tuition and fees vary according to course load and program. *Financial support:* In 2009–10, 2 fellowships with full tuition reimbursements (averaging $17,725 per year), 29 research assistantships with full and partial tuition reimbursements (averaging $19,500 per year), 20 teaching assistantships with full tuition reimbursements (averaging $12,321 per year) were awarded; career-related internships or fieldwork, scholarships/grants, health care benefits, tuition waivers (partial), and unspecified assistantships also available. Support available to part-time students. Financial award application deadline: 3/1; financial award applicants required to submit FAFSA. *Faculty research:* Evolutionary biology, conservation ecology, human impact on ecosystems, biodiversity, applied wildlife and fisheries research, plant and animal community ecology. Total annual research expenditures: $2.6 million. *Unit head:* Dr. David Roberts, Head, 406-994-4548, Fax: 406-994-3190, E-mail: droberts@montana.edu. *Application contact:* Dr. Carl A. Fox, Vice Provost for Graduate Education, 406-994-4145, Fax: 406-994-7433, E-mail: gradstudy@montana.edu.

North Dakota State University, College of Graduate and Interdisciplinary Studies, Interdisciplinary Program in Environmental and Conservation Sciences, Fargo, ND 58108. Offers MS, PhD. *Faculty:* 59. *Students:* 3 full-time (0 women), 2 part-time (0 women). *Degree requirements:* For master's, comprehensive exam, thesis. *Entrance requirements:* Additional exam requirements/recommendations for international students: Required—TOEFL (minimum score 550 paper-based; 213 computer-based; 79 iBT). *Unit head:* Dr. Wei Lin, Director, 701-231-8785, Fax: 701-231-7149, E-mail: wei.lin@ndsu.edu. *Application contact:* Ruth Ann Faulkner, Administrative Assistant, 701-231-6727, E-mail: ruthann.faulkner@ndsu.edu.

Nova Scotia Agricultural College, Research and Graduate Studies, Truro, NS B2N 5E3, Canada. Offers agriculture (M Sc), including air quality, animal behavior, animal molecular genetics, animal nutrition, animal technology, aquaculture, botany, crop management, crop physiology, ecology, environmental microbiology, food science, horticulture, nutrient management, pest management, physiology, plant biotechnology, plant pathology, soil chemistry, soil fertility, waste management and composting, water quality. Part-time programs available. *Degree requirements:* For master's, thesis, ATC Exam Teaching Assistantship. *Entrance requirements:* For master's, honors B Sc, minimum GPA of 3.0. Additional exam requirements/recommendations for international students: Required—TOEFL (minimum score 580 paper-based; 237 computer-based; 92 iBT), IELTS, Michigan English Language Assessment Battery, CanTEST, CAEL. *Faculty research:* Bio-product development, organic agriculture, nutrient management, air and water quality, agricultural biotechnology.

The Ohio State University, Graduate School, College of Biological Sciences, Department of Evolution, Ecology, and Organismal Biology, Columbus, OH 43210. Offers MS, PhD. *Faculty:* 43. *Students:* 19 full-time (13 women), 38 part-time (20 women); includes 2 minority (1 African American, 1 Hispanic American), 7 international. Average age 27. In 2009, 2 master's, 13 doctorates awarded. *Degree requirements:* For master's, thesis optional; for doctorate, thesis/dissertation. *Entrance requirements:* For master's and doctorate, GRE General Test. Additional exam requirements/recommendations for international students: Required—TOEFL (minimum score 600 paper-based; 250 computer-based). *Application deadline:* For fall admission, 8/15 priority date for domestic students, 7/1 priority date for international students; for winter admission, 12/1 priority date for domestic students, 11/1 priority date for international students; for spring admission, 3/1 priority date for domestic students, 2/1 priority date for international students. Applications are processed on a rolling basis. Application fee: $40 ($50 for international students). Electronic applications accepted. *Expenses:* Tuition, state resident: full-time $10,683. Tuition, nonresident: full-time $25,923. Tuition and fees vary according to course load and program. *Financial support:* Fellowships, research assistantships, teaching assistantships, Federal Work-Study and institutionally sponsored loans available. Support available to part-time students. *Unit head:* H. Lisle Gibbs, Graduate Studies Committee Chair, 614-292-8088, Fax: 614-292-2030, E-mail: gibbs.128@osu.edu. *Application contact:* 614-292-9444, Fax: 614-292-3895, E-mail: domestic.grad@osu.edu.

Ohio University, Graduate College, College of Arts and Sciences, Department of Biological Sciences, Athens, OH 45701-2979. Offers biological sciences (MS, PhD); cell biology and physiology (MS, PhD); ecology and evolutionary biology (MS, PhD); exercise physiology and muscle biology (MS, PhD); microbiology (MS, PhD); neuroscience (MS, PhD). *Faculty:* 50 full-time (14 women), 6 part-time/adjunct (1 woman). *Students:* 44 full-time (19 women), 8 part-time (3 women); includes 2 minority (1 African American, 1 Hispanic American), 21 international. 95 applicants, 24% accepted, 10 enrolled. In 2009, 4 master's, 9 doctorates awarded. Terminal master's awarded for partial completion of doctoral program. *Degree requirements:* For master's, comprehensive exam, thesis, 1 quarter of teaching experience; for doctorate, comprehensive exam, thesis/dissertation, 2 quarters of teaching experience. *Entrance requirements:* For master's, GRE General Test, names of three faculty members whose research interests most closely match the applicant's interest; for doctorate, GRE General Test, essay concerning prior training, research interest and career goals, plus names of three faculty members whose research interests most closely match the applicant's interest. Additional exam requirements/recommendations for international students: Required—TOEFL (minimum score 620 paper-based; 105 iBT) or IELTS (minimum score 7.5). *Application deadline:* For fall admission, 1/15 for domestic and international students. Application fee: $50 ($55 for international students). Electronic applications accepted. *Expenses:* Tuition, state resident: full-time $7839; part-time $323 per quarter hour. Tuition, nonresident: full-time $15,831; part-time $654 per quarter hour. Required fees: $2931. *Financial support:* In 2009–10, 1 fellowship with full tuition reimbursement (averaging $18,957 per year), 10 research assistantships with full tuition reimbursements (averaging $18,957 per year), 42 teaching assistantships with full tuition reimbursements (averaging $18,957 per year) were awarded; Federal Work-Study and institutionally sponsored loans also available. Financial award application deadline: 1/15. *Faculty research:* Ecology and evolutionary biology, exercise physiology and muscle biology, neurobiology, cell biology, physiology. Total annual research expenditures: $2.8 million. *Unit head:* Dr. Ralph DiCaprio, Chair, 740-593-2290, Fax: 740-593-0300, E-mail: dicaprir@ohio.edu. *Application contact:* Dr. Donald Holzschu, Graduate Chair, 740-593-0425, Fax: 740-593-0300, E-mail: holzschu@ohio.edu.

Old Dominion University, College of Sciences, Program in Ecological Sciences, Norfolk, VA 23529. Offers PhD. *Faculty:* 14 full-time (2 women), 41 part-time/adjunct (7 women). *Students:* 12 full-time (5 women), 12 part-time (6 women); includes 1 minority (Asian American or Pacific Islander), 3 international. Average age 32. 10 applicants, 70% accepted, 7 enrolled. In 2009, 4 doctorates awarded. *Degree requirements:* For doctorate, one foreign language, comprehensive exam, thesis/dissertation. *Entrance requirements:* For doctorate, GRE General Test, 3 letters of recommendation. Additional exam requirements/recommendations for international students: Required—TOEFL (minimum score 550 paper-based). *Application deadline:* For fall admission, 2/1 priority date for domestic and international students. Applications are processed on a rolling basis. Application fee: $40. Electronic applications accepted. *Expenses:* Tuition, state resident: full-time $8112; part-time $338 per credit. Tuition, nonresident: full-time $20,256; part-time $844 per credit. Required fees: $119 per semester. One-time fee: $50. *Financial support:* In 2009–10, 2 fellowships with full tuition reimbursements (averaging $15,000 per year), 4 research assistantships with full tuition reimbursements (averaging $15,750 per year), 12 teaching assistantships with full tuition reimbursements (averaging $15,000 per year) were awarded; scholarships/grants also available. Financial award application deadline: 2/15; financial award applicants required to submit FAFSA. *Faculty research:* Marine ecology, physiological ecology, systematics and speciation, ecological and evolutionary processes, molecular genetics. Total annual research expenditures: $2 million. *Unit head:* Dr. Ian Bartol, Graduate Program Director, 757-683-4737, Fax: 757-683-5283, E-mail: ecolgpd@odu.edu. *Application contact:* Dr. Ian Bartol, Graduate Program Director, 757-683-4737, Fax: 757-683-5283, E-mail: ecolgpd@odu.edu.

Penn State University Park, Graduate School, Intercollege Graduate Programs, Intercollege Graduate Program in Ecology, State College, University Park, PA 16802-1503. Offers MS, PhD. *Unit head:* Dr. David Eissenstat, Chair, 814-863-3371, Fax: 814-865-9451. *Application contact:* Dr. David Eissenstat, Chair, 814-863-3371, Fax: 814-865-9451.

Princeton University, Graduate School, Department of Ecology and Evolutionary Biology, Princeton, NJ 08544-1019. Offers PhD. *Degree requirements:* For doctorate, thesis/dissertation. *Entrance requirements:* For doctorate, GRE General Test, GRE Subject Test. Additional exam requirements/recommendations for international students: Required—TOEFL (minimum score 600 paper-based; 250 computer-based). Electronic applications accepted.

Purdue University, Graduate School, College of Science, Department of Biological Sciences, West Lafayette, IN 47907. Offers biochemistry (PhD); biophysics (PhD); cell and developmental biology (PhD); ecology, evolutionary and population biology (MS, PhD), including ecology, evolutionary biology, population biology; genetics (MS, PhD); microbiology (MS, PhD); molecular biology (PhD); neurobiology (MS, PhD); plant physiology (PhD). Terminal master's awarded for partial completion of doctoral program. *Degree requirements:* For master's, thesis (for some programs); for doctorate, thesis/dissertation, seminars, teaching experience. *Entrance requirements:* For master's and doctorate, GRE General Test. Additional exam requirements/recommendations for international students: Required—TOEFL. Electronic applications accepted.

Rice University, Graduate Programs, Wiess School of Natural Sciences, Department of Ecology and Evolutionary Biology, Houston, TX 77251-1892. Offers MA, MS, PhD. Terminal master's awarded for partial completion of doctoral program. *Degree requirements:* For master's, comprehensive exam (for some programs), thesis (for some programs); for doctorate, comprehensive exam, thesis/dissertation. *Entrance requirements:* For master's and doctorate, GRE General Test, GRE Subject Test. Additional exam requirements/recommendations for international students: Required—TOEFL (minimum score 600 paper-based; 250 computer-based; 90 iBT). Electronic applications accepted. *Faculty research:* Trace gas emissions, wetlands, biology, community ecology of forests and grasslands, conservation biology specialization.

Rutgers, The State University of New Jersey, New Brunswick, Graduate School-New Brunswick, Program in Ecology and Evolution, Piscataway, NJ 08854-8097. Offers MS, PhD. Part-time programs available. Terminal master's awarded for partial completion of doctoral program. *Degree requirements:* For master's, comprehensive exam; for doctorate, comprehensive exam, thesis/dissertation. *Entrance requirements:* For master's and doctorate, GRE General Test, minimum GPA of 3.0. Additional exam requirements/recommendations for international students: Required—TOEFL (minimum score 550 paper-based; 213 computer-based). Electronic applications accepted. *Faculty research:* Population and community ecology, population genetics, evolutionary biology, conservation biology, ecosystem ecology.

San Diego State University, Graduate and Research Affairs, College of Sciences, Department of Biology, Program in Ecology, San Diego, CA 92182. Offers MS, PhD. *Degree requirements:* For master's, thesis; for doctorate, thesis/dissertation. *Entrance requirements:* For master's, GRE General Test, resumé or curriculum vitae, 2 letters of recommendation.; for doctorate, GRE General Test, GRE Subject Test, resume or curriculum vitae, 3 letters of recommendation. Electronic applications accepted. *Faculty research:* Conservation and restoration ecology, coastal and marine ecology, global change and ecosystem ecology.

San Francisco State University, Division of Graduate Studies, College of Science and Engineering, Department of Biology, Program in Ecology and Systematic Biology, San Francisco, CA 94132-1722. Offers MS.

San Jose State University, Graduate Studies and Research, College of Science, Department of Biological Sciences, San Jose, CA 95192-0001. Offers biological sciences (MA, MS); molecular biology and microbiology (MS); organismal biology, conservation and ecology (MS); physiology (MS). Part-time programs available. *Students:* 53 full-time (41 women), 48 part-time (30 women); includes 48 minority (2 African Americans, 1 American Indian/Alaska Native, 36 Asian Americans or Pacific Islanders, 9 Hispanic Americans), 10 international. Average age 30. 158 applicants, 28% accepted, 43 enrolled. In 2009, 36 master's awarded. *Entrance requirements:* For master's, GRE. *Application deadline:* For fall admission, 6/29 for domestic students; for spring admission, 11/30 for domestic students. Applications are processed on a rolling basis. Application fee: $59. Electronic applications accepted. *Financial support:* Teaching assistantships, Federal Work-Study available. Financial award applicants required to submit FAFSA. *Faculty research:* Systemic physiology, molecular genetics, SEM studies, toxicology, large mammal ecology. *Unit head:* Dr. John Boothby, Chair, 408-924-4850, Fax: 408-924-4840, E-mail: jboothby@email.sjsu.edu. *Application contact:* Daniel Holley, Graduate Coordinator, 408-924-4844, E-mail: dholley@email.sjsu.edu.

State University of New York College of Environmental Science and Forestry, Department of Environmental and Forest Biology, Syracuse, NY 13210-2779. Offers applied ecology (MPS); chemical ecology (MPS, MS, PhD); conservation biology (MPS, MS, PhD); ecology (MPS, MS, PhD); entomology (MPS, MS, PhD); environmental interpretation (MPS, MS, PhD); environmental physiology (MPS, MS, PhD); fish and wildlife biology (MPS, MS, PhD); forest pathology and mycology (MPS, MS, PhD); plant biotechnology (MPS); plant science and biotechnology (MPS, MS, PhD). *Degree requirements:* For master's, thesis (for some programs); for doctorate, comprehensive exam, thesis/dissertation. *Entrance requirements:* For master's and doctorate, GRE General Test, GRE Subject Test, minimum GPA of 3.0. Additional exam requirements/recommendations for international students: Required—TOEFL (minimum score 550 paper-based; 213 computer-based; 80 iBT), IELTS (minimum score 6). *Faculty research:* Ecology, fish and wildlife biology and management, plant science, entomology.

Stony Brook University, State University of New York, Graduate School, College of Arts and Sciences, Department of Ecology and Evolution, Stony Brook, NY 11794. Offers applied ecology (MA); ecology and evolution (PhD). *Faculty:* 18 full-time (5 women), 1 part-time/adjunct (0 women). *Students:* 50 full-time (27 women); includes 7 minority (3 Asian Americans or Pacific Islanders, 4 Hispanic Americans), 9 international. Average age 28. 91 applicants, 32% accepted. In 2009, 4 doctorates awarded. *Degree requirements:* For doctorate, one foreign language, comprehensive exam, thesis/dissertation, teaching experience. *Entrance requirements:* For doctorate, GRE General Test, GRE Subject Test. Additional exam requirements/recommendations for international students: Required—TOEFL. *Application deadline:* For fall admission, 1/15 for domestic students. Application fee: $60. *Expenses:* Tuition, state resident: full-time $8370; part-time $349 per credit. Tuition, nonresident: full-time $13,250; part-time $552 per credit. Required fees: $933. *Financial support:* In 2009–10, 7 research assistantships, 35 teaching assistantships were awarded; fellowships, Federal Work-Study also available. *Faculty research:* Theoretical and experimental population genetics, numerical taxonomy, biostatistics, population and community ecology, plant ecology. Total annual research expenditures: $985,740. *Unit head:* Dr. Jessica Gurevitch, Chair, 631-632-8600. *Application contact:* Dr. Dan Dykhuizen, Director, 631-246-8604, E-mail: dandyk@life.bio.sunysb.edu.

Tulane University, School of Science and Engineering, Department of Ecology and Evolutionary Biology, New Orleans, LA 70118-5669. Offers MS, PhD. Terminal master's awarded for partial completion of doctoral program. *Degree requirements:* For master's, thesis or alternative; for doctorate, thesis/dissertation. *Entrance requirements:* For master's, GRE General Test, minimum B average in undergraduate course work; for doctorate, GRE General Test. Additional exam requirements/recommendations for international students: Required—TOEFL. Electronic applications accepted. *Faculty research:* Ichthyology, plant systematics, crustacean endocrinology, ecotoxicology, ornithology.

University at Albany, State University of New York, College of Arts and Sciences, Department of Biological Sciences, Specialization in Ecology, Evolution, and Behavior, Albany, NY 12222-0001. Offers MS, PhD. *Degree requirements:* For master's, one foreign language; for doctorate, one foreign language, thesis/dissertation. *Entrance requirements:* For master's and doctorate, GRE General Test.

University at Buffalo, the State University of New York, Graduate School, College of Arts and Sciences, Program in Evolution, Ecology and Behavior, Buffalo, NY 14260. Offers MS, PhD, Certificate. *Faculty:* 12 full-time (2 women). *Students:* 14 full-time (9 women), 1 (woman) part-time; includes 1 minority (Hispanic American), 1 international. Average age 28. 34 applicants, 47% accepted, 6 enrolled. In 2009, 4 master's, 1 doctorate awarded. Terminal master's awarded for partial completion of doctoral program. *Degree requirements:* For master's, project; for doctorate, comprehensive exam, thesis/dissertation. *Entrance requirements:* For master's, GRE, minimum undergraduate GPA of 3.0; for doctorate, GRE, minimum GPA of 3.0. Additional exam requirements/recommendations for international students: Required—TOEFL (minimum score 79 iBT). *Application deadline:* For fall admission, 1/15 priority date for domestic and international students. Applications are processed on a rolling basis. Application fee: $75. Electronic applications accepted. *Financial support:* In 2009–10, 2 fellowships with full tuition reimbursements (averaging $23,000 per year), 3 research assistantships with full tuition reimbursements (averaging $20,000 per year), 4 teaching assistantships with full tuition reimbursements (averaging $17,000 per year) were awarded; Federal Work-Study, scholarships/grants, health care benefits, and unspecified assistantships also available. Financial award application deadline: 1/15; financial award applicants required to submit FAFSA. *Faculty research:* Coral reef ecology, evolution and ecology of aquatic invertebrates, animal communication, paleobiology, primate behavior. *Unit head:* Dr. Howard Lasker, Program Director, 716-645-4870, Fax: 716-645-3999, E-mail: ub-evb@buffalo.edu. *Application contact:* Marty Roth, Secretary 1, 716-645-3489, Fax: 716-345-3999, E-mail: mlroth@buffalo.edu.

University of Alberta, Faculty of Graduate Studies and Research, Department of Biological Sciences, Edmonton, AB T6G 2E1, Canada. Offers environmental biology and ecology (M Sc, PhD); microbiology and biotechnology (M Sc, PhD); molecular biology and genetics (M Sc, PhD); physiology and cell biology (M Sc, PhD); plant biology (M Sc, PhD); systematics and evolution (M Sc, PhD). *Faculty:* 72 full-time (15 women), 15 part-time/adjunct (4 women). *Students:* 238 full-time (117 women), 32 part-time (15 women), 31 international. 206 applicants, 42% accepted. In 2009, 29 master's, 31 doctorates awarded. Terminal master's awarded for partial completion of doctoral program. *Degree requirements:* For master's, thesis; for doctorate, thesis/dissertation. *Entrance requirements:* Additional exam requirements/recommendations for international students: Required—TOEFL. *Application deadline:* For fall admission, 3/1 priority date for domestic students. Applications are processed on a rolling basis. Application fee: $0. Tuition and fees charges are reported in Canadian dollars. *Expenses:* Tuition, area resident: Full-time $4626 Canadian dollars; part-time $99.72 Canadian dollars per unit. International tuition: $8216 Canadian dollars full-time. Required fees: $3590 Canadian dollars; $99.72 Canadian dollars per unit. $215 Canadian dollars per term. *Financial support:* In 2009–10, 4 research assistantships with partial tuition reimbursements (averaging $12,000 per year), 103 teaching assistantships with partial tuition reimbursements (averaging $12,300 per year) were awarded; career-related internships or fieldwork and scholarships/grants also available. *Unit head:* Laura Frost, Chair, 780-492-1904. *Application contact:* Dr. John P. Chang, Associate Chair for Graduate Studies, 780-492-1257, Fax: 780-492-9457, E-mail: bio.grad.coordinator@ualberta.ca.

The University of Arizona, Graduate College, College of Science, Department of Ecology and Evolutionary Biology, Tucson, AZ 85721. Offers MS, PhD. *Faculty:* 21. *Students:* 18 full-time (8 women), 50 part-time (31 women); includes 4 minority (1 African American, 1 American Indian/Alaska Native, 1 Asian American or Pacific Islander, 1 Hispanic American), 10 international. Average age 31. 87 applicants, 15% accepted, 9 enrolled. In 2009, 3 master's, 5 doctorates awarded. Terminal master's awarded for partial completion of doctoral program. *Degree requirements:* For master's, thesis optional; for doctorate, one foreign language, comprehensive exam, thesis/dissertation. *Entrance requirements:* For master's, GRE General Test, GRE Subject Test, statement of purpose, curriculum vitae, 3 letters of recommendation; for doctorate, GRE General Test, GRE Subject Test, curriculum vitae, 3 letters of recommendation. Additional exam requirements/recommendations for international students: Required—TOEFL (minimum score 550 paper-based; 213 computer-based; 79 iBT). *Application deadline:* For fall admission, 12/8 for domestic and international students. Application fee: $75. *Expenses:* Tuition, state resident: full-time $9028. Tuition, nonresident: full-time $24,890. *Financial support:* In 2009–10, 4 research assistantships with full tuition reimbursements (averaging $16,483 per year), 17 teaching assistantships with full tuition reimbursements (averaging $16,557 per year) were awarded; career-related internships or fieldwork, scholarships/grants, health care benefits, and unspecified assistantships also available. *Faculty research:* Biological diversity, evolutionary history, evolutionary mechanisms, community structure. Total annual research expenditures: $4.5 million. *Unit head:* Dr. Richard E. Michod, Head, 520-621-7509, Fax: 520-621-9190, E-mail: michod@email.arizona.edu. *Application contact:* Carol Burleson, Administrative Associate, 520-621-1165, Fax: 520-621-9190, E-mail: burleson@email.arizona.edu.

University of California, Davis, Graduate Studies, Graduate Group in Ecology, Davis, CA 95616. Offers MS, PhD. *Degree requirements:* For master's, comprehensive exam (for some programs), thesis (for some programs); for doctorate, thesis/dissertation. *Entrance requirements:* For master's and doctorate, GRE General Test. Additional exam requirements/recommendations for international students: Required—TOEFL (minimum score 550 paper-based; 213 computer-based). Electronic applications accepted. *Faculty research:* Agricultural conservation, physiological restoration, environmental policy, ecotoxicology.

University of California, Irvine, Office of Graduate Studies, School of Biological Sciences, Department of Ecology and Evolutionary Biology, Irvine, CA 92697. Offers biological sciences (MS, PhD). *Students:* 43 full-time (30 women); includes 3 minority (all Hispanic Americans), 6 international. Average age 27. 38 applicants, 26% accepted, 5 enrolled. In 2009, 4 master's, 7 doctorates awarded. *Degree requirements:* For master's, thesis; for doctorate, thesis/dissertation. *Entrance requirements:* For master's and doctorate, GRE General Test, GRE Subject Test, minimum GPA of 3.0. Additional exam requirements/recommendations for international students: Required—TOEFL (minimum score 550 paper-based; 213 computer-based). *Application deadline:* For fall admission, 1/15 priority date for domestic students, 1/15 for international students. Applications are processed on a rolling basis. Application fee: $70 ($90 for international students). Electronic applications accepted. *Financial support:* Fellowships, research assistantships with full tuition reimbursements, teaching assistantships, career-related internships or fieldwork, institutionally sponsored loans, traineeships, health care benefits, and unspecified assistantships available. Financial award application deadline: 3/1; financial award applicants required to submit FAFSA. *Faculty research:* Ecological energetics, quantitative genetics, life history evolution, plant-herbivore and plant-pollinator interactions, molecular evolution. *Unit head:* Albert F. Bennett, Chair, 949-824-6930, E-mail: abennett@uci.edu. *Application contact:* Pam McDonald, Administrative Assistant, 949-824-4743, E-mail: pmcdonal@uci.edu.

University of California, Los Angeles, Graduate Division, College of Letters and Science, Department of Ecology and Evolutionary Biology, Los Angeles, CA 90095. Offers MA, PhD. *Faculty:* 26 full-time (8 women), 8 part-time/adjunct (1 woman). *Students:* 64 full-time (39 women); includes 8 minority (1 African American, 1 American Indian/Alaska Native, 3 Asian Americans or Pacific Islanders, 3 Hispanic Americans), 9 international. Average age 29. 88 applicants, 19% accepted, 13 enrolled. In 2009, 5 master's, 16 doctorates awarded. Terminal master's awarded for partial completion of doctoral program. *Degree requirements:* For master's, comprehensive exam or thesis; for doctorate, thesis/dissertation, oral and written qualifying exams; teaching experience. *Entrance requirements:* For master's and doctorate, GRE General Test, GRE Subject Test (biology), minimum GPA of 3.0, 3 letters of recommendation. *Application deadline:* For fall admission, 12/1 for domestic and international students. Application fee: $70 ($90 for international students). Electronic applications accepted. *Financial support:* In 2009–10, 61 fellowships with full and partial tuition reimbursements, 18 research assistantships with full and partial tuition reimbursements, 42 teaching assistantships with full and partial tuition reimbursements were awarded; Federal Work-Study, institutionally sponsored loans, scholarships/grants, health care benefits, tuition waivers (full and partial), and unspecified assistantships also available. Financial award application deadline: 3/1; financial award applicants required to submit FAFSA. *Faculty research:* Molecular, cell, and developmental biology; interactive biology; organisms and populations. *Unit head:* Victoria Sork, Chair, 310-825-7755, Fax: 310-206-0484, E-mail: vlsork@ucla.edu. *Application contact:* Department Office, 310-825-1959, Fax: 310-206-5280, E-mail: eebgrad@eeb.ucla.edu.

University of California, San Diego, Office of Graduate Studies, Division of Biological Sciences, Program in Ecology, Behavior, and Evolution, La Jolla, CA 92093. Offers PhD. *Degree requirements:* For doctorate, thesis/dissertation, qualifying exam. Electronic applications accepted.

University of California, Santa Barbara, Graduate Division, College of Letters and Sciences, Division of Mathematics, Life, and Physical Sciences, Department of Ecology, Evolution, and Marine Biology, Santa Barbara, CA 93106-9620. Offers computational science and engineering (PhD); MA/PhD. *Faculty:* 39 full-time (8 women). *Students:* 56 full-time (35 women). Average age 30. 135 applicants, 13% accepted, 7 enrolled. In 2009, 7 master's, 15 doctorates awarded. Terminal master's awarded for partial completion of doctoral program. *Degree requirements:* For master's, comprehensive exam (for some programs), thesis (for some programs); for doctorate, comprehensive exam, thesis/dissertation. *Entrance requirements:* For master's, GRE General Test, 3 letters of recommendation, resume/curriculum vitae; for doctorate, GRE General Test, 3 letters of recommendation, statement of purpose, personal achievements/contributions statement, resume/curriculum vitae, transcripts for post-secondary institutions attended. Additional exam requirements/recommendations for international students: Required—TOEFL (minimum score 550 paper-based; 213 computer-based; 80 iBT) or IELTS. *Application deadline:* For fall admission, 12/15 for domestic and international students. Application fee: $70 ($90 for international students). Electronic applications accepted. *Financial support:* In 2009–10, 54 students received support, including 26 fellowships with full and partial tuition reimbursements available (averaging $17,900 per year), 16 research assistantships with full and partial tuition reimbursements available (averaging $7,300 per year), 35 teaching assistantships with partial tuition reimbursements available (averaging $9,100 per year); Federal Work-Study, institutionally sponsored loans, scholarships/grants, traineeships, health care benefits, tuition waivers (full and partial), and unspecified assistantships also available. Financial award applicants required to submit FAFSA. *Faculty research:* Ecology, population genetics, stream ecology, evolution, marine biology. *Unit head:* Robert Warner, Chair, 805-893-2415, Fax: 805-893-4724, E-mail: eembchair@lifesci.ucsb.edu. *Application contact:* Alina Haas, Staff Graduate Advisor, 805-893-3023, Fax: 805-893-5885, E-mail: haas@lifesci.ucsb.edu.

University of California, Santa Cruz, Division of Graduate Studies, Division of Physical and Biological Sciences, Department of Ecology and Evolutionary Biology, Santa Cruz, CA 95064. Offers MA, PhD. *Degree requirements:* For master's, thesis; for doctorate, thesis/dissertation. *Entrance requirements:* For master's and doctorate, GRE General Test, GRE Subject Test, 3 letters of recommendation. Additional exam requirements/recommendations for international students: Required—TOEFL (minimum score 550 paper-based); Recommended—IELTS. Electronic applications accepted.

University of Chicago, Division of the Biological Sciences, Darwinian Sciences Cluster: Ecological, Integrative and Evolutionary Biology, Department of Ecology and Evolution, Chicago, IL 60637-1513. Offers PhD. *Faculty:* 14 full-time (2 women). *Students:* 22 full-time (9 women); includes 5 minority (4 Asian Americans or Pacific Islanders, 1 Hispanic American). Average age 28. 26 applicants, 35% accepted, 4 enrolled. In 2009, 5 doctorates awarded. *Degree requirements:* For doctorate, thesis/dissertation, ethics class, 2 teaching assistantships. *Entrance requirements:* For doctorate, GRE General Test. Additional exam requirements/recommendations

Ecology

University of Chicago *(continued)*
for international students: Required—TOEFL (minimum score 600 paper-based; 250 computer-based; 104 iBT), IELTS (minimum score 7). *Application deadline:* For fall admission, 12/1 priority date for domestic and international students. Application fee: $55. Electronic applications accepted. *Financial support:* In 2009–10, 22 students received support, including fellowships with tuition reimbursements available (averaging $29,781 per year), research assistantships with tuition reimbursements available (averaging $29,781 per year); institutionally sponsored loans, scholarships/grants, traineeships, and health care benefits also available. Financial award applicants required to submit FAFSA. *Faculty research:* Population genetics, molecular evolution, behavior. *Unit head:* Dr. Joy Bergelson, Chair, 773-702-3855, Fax: 773-702-9740, E-mail: j-bergelson@uchicago.edu. *Application contact:* Jeffrey Heller, Graduate Program Administrator, 773-702-9011, Fax: 773-702-9740, E-mail: j-heller@uchicago.edu.

University of Colorado at Boulder, Graduate School, College of Arts and Sciences, Department of Ecology and Evolutionary Biology, Boulder, CO 80309. Offers animal behavior (MA); biology (MA, PhD); environmental biology (MA, PhD); evolutionary biology (MA, PhD); neurobiology (MA); population biology (MA); population genetics (PhD). *Faculty:* 32 full-time (10 women). *Students:* 64 full-time (36 women), 15 part-time (9 women); includes 12 minority (1 American Indian/Alaska Native, 3 Asian Americans or Pacific Islanders, 8 Hispanic Americans), 4 international. Average age 29. 145 applicants, 14% accepted, 21 enrolled. In 2009, 9 master's, 6 doctorates awarded. Terminal master's awarded for partial completion of doctoral program. *Degree requirements:* For master's, comprehensive exam, thesis or alternative; for doctorate, comprehensive exam, thesis/dissertation. *Entrance requirements:* For master's, GRE General Test, GRE Subject Test, minimum undergraduate GPA of 3.0; for doctorate, GRE General Test, GRE Subject Test. *Application deadline:* For fall admission, 12/30 priority date for domestic students, 12/1 for international students. Application fee: $50 ($60 for international students). *Financial support:* In 2009–10, 25 fellowships (averaging $17,876 per year), 27 research assistantships (averaging $15,070 per year) were awarded; Federal Work-Study, institutionally sponsored loans, and tuition waivers (full) also available. *Faculty research:* Behavior, ecology, genetics, morphology, endocrinology, physiology, systematics. Total annual research expenditures: $3.1 million.

University of Connecticut, Graduate School, College of Liberal Arts and Sciences, Department of Ecology and Evolutionary Biology, Field of Ecology, Storrs, CT 06269. Offers MS, PhD. *Faculty:* 30 full-time (7 women). *Students:* 31 full-time (20 women), 4 part-time (2 women); includes 4 minority (1 African American, 3 Hispanic Americans), 8 international. Average age 31. 42 applicants, 12% accepted, 3 enrolled. Terminal master's awarded for partial completion of doctoral program. *Degree requirements:* For master's, comprehensive exam; for doctorate, thesis/dissertation. *Entrance requirements:* For master's and doctorate, GRE General Test, GRE Subject Test. Additional exam requirements/recommendations for international students: Required—TOEFL (minimum score 550 paper-based; 213 computer-based). *Application deadline:* For fall admission, 2/1 priority date for domestic and international students; for spring admission, 11/1 for domestic students, 10/1 for international students. Applications are processed on a rolling basis. Application fee: $55. Electronic applications accepted. *Expenses:* Tuition, state resident: full-time $4725; part-time $525 per credit. Tuition, nonresident: full-time $12,267; part-time $1363 per credit. Required fees: $346 per semester. Tuition and fees vary according to course load. *Financial support:* In 2009–10, 18 research assistantships with full tuition reimbursements, 13 teaching assistantships with full tuition reimbursements were awarded; fellowships, Federal Work-Study, scholarships/grants, health care benefits, and unspecified assistantships also available. Financial award application deadline: 2/1; financial award applicants required to submit FAFSA. *Unit head:* Kentwood Wells, Head, 860-486-4319, Fax: 860-486-6364, E-mail: kentwood.wells@uconn.edu. *Application contact:* Anne St. Onje, Graduate Coordinator, 860-486-4314, Fax: 860-486-3943, E-mail: anne.st_onje@uconn.edu.

University of Connecticut, Graduate School, College of Liberal Arts and Sciences, Department of Psychology, Storrs, CT 06269. Offers behavioral neuroscience (PhD); biopsychology (PhD); clinical psychology (MA, PhD); cognition and instruction (PhD); developmental psychology (MA, PhD); ecological psychology (PhD); experimental psychology (PhD); general psychology (MA, PhD); health psychology (Graduate Certificate); industrial/organizational psychology (PhD); language and cognition (PhD); neuroscience (PhD); occupational health psychology (Graduate Certificate); social psychology (MA, PhD). *Accreditation:* APA. *Faculty:* 59 full-time (26 women). *Students:* 194 full-time (133 women), 24 part-time (12 women); includes 48 minority (12 African Americans, 21 Asian Americans or Pacific Islanders, 15 Hispanic Americans), 25 international. Average age 28. 585 applicants, 4% accepted, 14 enrolled. In 2009, 22 master's, 24 doctorates awarded. Terminal master's awarded for partial completion of doctoral program. *Degree requirements:* For master's, comprehensive exam; for doctorate, thesis/dissertation. *Entrance requirements:* For master's and doctorate, GRE General Test, GRE Subject Test. Additional exam requirements/recommendations for international students: Required—TOEFL (minimum score 550 paper-based; 213 computer-based). *Application deadline:* For fall admission, 2/1 priority date for domestic and international students; for spring admission, 11/1 for domestic students, 10/1 for international students. Applications are processed on a rolling basis. Application fee: $55. Electronic applications accepted. *Expenses:* Tuition, state resident: full-time $4725; part-time $525 per credit. Tuition, nonresident: full-time $12,267; part-time $1363 per credit. Required fees: $346 per semester. Tuition and fees vary according to course load. *Financial support:* In 2009–10, 109 research assistantships with full tuition reimbursements, 72 teaching assistantships with full tuition reimbursements were awarded; fellowships, career-related internships or fieldwork, Federal Work-Study, scholarships/grants, health care benefits, and unspecified assistantships also available. Financial award application deadline: 2/1; financial award applicants required to submit FAFSA. *Unit head:* Charles A. Lowe, Head, 860-486-3517, Fax: 860-486-2760, E-mail: charles.lowe@uconn.edu. *Application contact:* Charles A. Lowe, Head, 860-486-3517, Fax: 860-486-2760, E-mail: charles.lowe@uconn.edu.

University of Delaware, College of Agriculture and Natural Resources, Department of Entomology and Wildlife Ecology, Newark, DE 19716. Offers entomology and applied ecology (MS, PhD), including avian ecology, evolution and taxonomy, insect biological control, insect ecology and behavior (MS), insect genetics, pest management, plant-insect interactions, wildlife ecology and management. Part-time programs available. *Degree requirements:* For master's, comprehensive exam, thesis, oral exam, seminar; for doctorate, comprehensive exam, thesis/dissertation, qualifying exam, seminar. *Entrance requirements:* For master's, GRE General Test, minimum GPA of 3.0 in field, 2.8 overall; for doctorate, GRE General Test, GRE Subject Test (biology), minimum GPA of 3.0 in field, 2.8 overall. Additional exam requirements/recommendations for international students: Required—TOEFL. Electronic applications accepted. *Faculty research:* Ecology and evolution of plant-insect interactions, ecology of wildlife conservation management, habitat restoration, biological control, applied ecosystem management.

University of Delaware, College of Arts and Sciences, Department of Biological Sciences, Newark, DE 19716. Offers biotechnology (MS); cancer biology (MS, PhD); cell and extracellular matrix biology (MS, PhD); cell and systems physiology (MS, PhD); developmental biology (MS, PhD); ecology and evolution (MS, PhD); microbiology (MS, PhD); molecular biology and genetics (MS, PhD). Terminal master's awarded for partial completion of doctoral program. *Degree requirements:* For master's, thesis, preliminary exam; for doctorate, comprehensive exam, thesis/dissertation, preliminary exam. *Entrance requirements:* For master's and doctorate, GRE General Test. Additional exam requirements/recommendations for international students: Required—TOEFL (minimum score 600 paper-based; 250 computer-based); Recommended—TWE. Electronic applications accepted. *Faculty research:* Microorganisms, bone, cancer metastasis, developmental biology, cell biology, DNA.

University of Florida, Graduate School, College of Agricultural and Life Sciences, Department of Wildlife Ecology and Conservation, Gainesville, FL 32611. Offers MS, PhD. *Degree requirements:* For master's, thesis optional; for doctorate, thesis/dissertation. *Entrance requirements:* For master's and doctorate, GRE General Test, minimum GPA of 3.3. Electronic applications accepted. *Faculty research:* Wildlife biology and management, tropical ecology and conservation, conservation biology, landscape ecology and restoration, conservation education.

University of Florida, Graduate School, School of Natural Resources and Environment, Gainesville, FL 32611. Offers interdisciplinary ecology (MS, PhD). *Degree requirements:* For master's, thesis optional; for doctorate, thesis/dissertation. *Entrance requirements:* For master's and doctorate, GRE General Test, minimum GPA of 3.0. Additional exam requirements/recommendations for international students: Required—TOEFL (minimum score 550 paper-based; 213 computer-based). Electronic applications accepted.

University of Georgia, Graduate School, School of Ecology, Athens, GA 30602. Offers conservation ecology and sustainable development (MS); ecology (MS, PhD). *Faculty:* 21 full-time (6 women), 7 part-time/adjunct (2 women). *Students:* 59 full-time (33 women), 22 part-time (11 women); includes 4 minority (1 African American, 3 Hispanic Americans), 3 international. 138 applicants, 19% accepted, 21 enrolled. In 2009, 13 master's, 10 doctorates awarded. *Degree requirements:* For master's, thesis; for doctorate, one foreign language, thesis/dissertation. *Entrance requirements:* For master's and doctorate, GRE General Test. *Application deadline:* For fall admission, 7/1 priority date for domestic students; for spring admission, 11/15 for domestic students. Application fee: $50. Electronic applications accepted. *Expenses:* Tuition, state resident: full-time $6000; part-time $250 per credit hour. Tuition, nonresident: full-time $20,904; part-time $871 per credit hour. Required fees: $730 per semester. *Financial support:* Fellowships, research assistantships, teaching assistantships, unspecified assistantships available. *Unit head:* Dr. John L. Gittleman, Dean, 706-542-2968, Fax: 706-542-4819, E-mail: ecohead@uga.edu. *Application contact:* Dr. C. Ronald Carroll, Graduate Coordinator, 706-338-1366, Fax: 706-542-4819, E-mail: rcarroll@uga.edu.

University of Guelph, Graduate Program Services, College of Biological Science, Department of Integrative Biology, Botany and Zoology, Guelph, ON N1G 2W1, Canada. Offers botany (M Sc, PhD); zoology (M Sc, PhD). Part-time programs available. *Degree requirements:* For master's, thesis, research proposal; for doctorate, thesis/dissertation, research proposal, qualifying exam. *Entrance requirements:* For master's, minimum B average during previous 2 years of course work. Additional exam requirements/recommendations for international students: Required—TOEFL (minimum score 550 paper-based; 213 computer-based), IELTS (minimum score 6.5). Electronic applications accepted. *Faculty research:* Aquatic science, environmental physiology, parasitology, wildlife biology, management.

University of Hawaii at Manoa, Graduate Division, Interdisciplinary Specialization in Ecology, Evolution and Conservation Biology, Honolulu, HI 96822. Offers MS, PhD. *Degree requirements:* For doctorate, thesis/dissertation. *Expenses:* Tuition, state resident: full-time $8900; part-time $372 per credit. Tuition, nonresident: full-time $21,400; part-time $898 per credit. Required fees: $207 per semester. *Faculty research:* Agronomy and soil science, zoology, entomology, genetics and molecular biology, botanical sciences.

University of Illinois at Urbana–Champaign, Graduate College, College of Liberal Arts and Sciences, School of Integrative Biology, Department of Animal Biology, Champaign, IL 61820. Offers animal biology (ecology, ethology and evolution) (MS, PhD). *Faculty:* 10 full-time (5 women). *Students:* 10 full-time (6 women), 4 part-time (2 women); includes 1 minority (Asian American or Pacific Islander), 3 international. 13 applicants, 15% accepted, 1 enrolled. In 2009, 1 doctorate awarded. *Entrance requirements:* For master's and doctorate, GRE. Additional exam requirements/recommendations for international students: Required—TOEFL (minimum score 570 paper-based; 230 computer-based; 88 iBT). *Application deadline:* Applications are processed on a rolling basis. Application fee: $60 ($75 for international students). Electronic applications accepted. *Financial support:* In 2009–10, 2 fellowships, 3 research assistantships, 11 teaching assistantships were awarded; tuition waivers (full and partial) also available. *Unit head:* Ken Paige, Head, 217-244-6606, Fax: 217-244-4565, E-mail: k-paige@illinois.edu. *Application contact:* Kathy Jennings, Office Support Specialist, 217-333-7801, Fax: 217-244-4565, E-mail: ab@life.uiuc.edu.

University of Illinois at Urbana–Champaign, Graduate College, College of Liberal Arts and Sciences, School of Integrative Biology, Program in Ecology, Evolution and Conservation Biology, Champaign, IL 61820. Offers MS, PhD. *Students:* 25 full-time (14 women), 10 part-time (8 women); includes 4 minority (1 African American, 2 Asian Americans or Pacific Islanders, 1 Hispanic American), 2 international. 40 applicants, 23% accepted, 6 enrolled. In 2009, 1 master's, 4 doctorates awarded. *Entrance requirements:* For master's and doctorate, GRE. Additional exam requirements/recommendations for international students: Required—TOEFL (minimum score 613 paper-based; 257 computer-based; 103 iBT). *Application deadline:* Applications are processed on a rolling basis. Application fee: $60 ($75 for international students). Electronic applications accepted. *Financial support:* In 2009–10, 9 fellowships, 19 research assistantships, 15 teaching assistantships were awarded; tuition waivers (full and partial) also available. *Unit head:* Carla E. Caceres, Director, 217-244-2139, Fax: 217-244-1224, E-mail: cecacere@illinois.edu. *Application contact:* Carol Hall, Secretary, 217-333-8208, Fax: 217-244-1224, E-mail: cahall@illinois.edu.

The University of Kansas, Graduate Studies, College of Liberal Arts and Sciences, Department of Ecology and Evolutionary Biology, Lawrence, KS 66045. Offers botany (MA, PhD); ecology and evolutionary biology (MA, PhD); entomology (MA, PhD). *Faculty:* 17 full-time (7 women), 29 part-time/adjunct (6 women). *Students:* 57 full-time (24 women), 4 part-time (1 woman); includes 1 minority (Hispanic American), 16 international. Average age 29. 49 applicants, 33% accepted, 8 enrolled. In 2009, 5 master's, 8 doctorates awarded. Terminal master's awarded for partial completion of doctoral program. *Degree requirements:* For master's, comprehensive exam, thesis (for some programs), 30-36 credits, thesis presentation; for doctorate, comprehensive exam, thesis/dissertation, residency, foreign language or other research skills, final exam and dissertation defense. *Entrance requirements:* For master's, GRE General Test, bachelor's degree with minimum undergraduate GPA of 3.0; for doctorate, GRE General Test, bachelor's degree; minimum undergraduate/graduate GPA of 3.0. Additional exam requirements/recommendations for international students: Required—TOEFL, IELTS. *Application deadline:* For fall admission, 12/15 priority date for domestic and international students. Applications are processed on a rolling basis. Application fee: $45 ($55 for international students). Electronic applications accepted. *Expenses:* Tuition, state resident: full-time $6492; part-time $270.50 per credit hour. Tuition, nonresident: full-time $15,510; part-time $646.25 per credit hour. Required fees: $847; $70.56 per credit hour. Tuition and fees vary according to course load and program. *Financial support:* Fellowships with tuition reimbursements, research assistantships with full and partial tuition reimbursements, teaching assistantships with full and partial tuition reimbursements, scholarships/grants, traineeships, health care benefits, and unspecified assistantships available. *Faculty research:* Biodiversity and macroevolution, ecology and global change, evolutionary mechanisms. *Unit head:* Dr. Christopher H. Haufler, Chair, 785-864-3255, Fax: 785-864-5860, E-mail: vulgare@ku.edu. *Application contact:* Jaime Rochelle Keeler, Graduate Coordinator, 785-864-2362, Fax: 785-864-5860, E-mail: jrkeeler@ku.edu.

University of Maine, Graduate School, College of Natural Sciences, Forestry, and Agriculture, Department of Biological Sciences, Program in Ecology and Environmental Science, Orono, ME 04469. Offers MS, PhD. Part-time programs available. *Students:* 28 full-time (23 women), 9 part-time (6 women). Average age 29. 67 applicants, 16% accepted, 10 enrolled. In 2009, 5 master's, 1 doctorate awarded. *Degree requirements:* For doctorate, thesis/dissertation. *Entrance requirements:* For master's and doctorate, GRE General Test. Additional exam requirements/recommendations for international students: Required—TOEFL. *Application deadline:* For fall admission, 2/1 priority date for domestic students. Applications are processed on a rolling basis. Application fee: $65. Electronic applications accepted. *Financial support:* Career-related internships or fieldwork, Federal Work-Study, institutionally sponsored loans, and tuition waivers (full) available. Financial award application deadline: 3/1. *Unit head:* Dr. Chris Cronan, Coordinator, 207-581-3235. *Application contact:* Scott G. Delcourt, Associate Dean of the Graduate School, 207-581-3291, Fax: 207-581-3232, E-mail: graduate@maine.edu.

University of Maine, Graduate School, College of Natural Sciences, Forestry, and Agriculture, Department of Plant, Soil, and Environmental Sciences, Orono, ME 04469. Offers biological sciences (PhD); ecology and environmental sciences (MS, PhD); forest resources (PhD); horticulture (MS); plant science (PhD); plant, soil, and environmental sciences (MS); resource utilization (MS). *Faculty:* 8 full-time (2 women), 9 part-time/adjunct (3 women). *Students:* 6 full-time (3 women), 3 part-time (2 women), 1 international. Average age 31. 6 applicants, 17% accepted, 0 enrolled. In 2009, 2 master's awarded. *Entrance requirements:* For master's and doctorate, GRE General Test. Additional exam requirements/recommendations for international students: Required—TOEFL. *Application deadline:* Applications are processed on a rolling basis. Application fee: $65. Electronic applications accepted. *Financial support:* In 2009–10, 16 research assistantships with tuition reimbursements (averaging $16,260 per year), 3 teaching assistantships with tuition reimbursements (averaging $12,790 per year) were awarded; scholarships/grants, tuition waivers (full and partial), and unspecified assistantships also available. *Unit head:* Dr. Gregory Porter, Chair, 207-581-2943, Fax: 207-581-3207. *Application contact:* Scott G. Delcourt, Associate Dean of the Graduate School, 207-581-3291, Fax: 207-581-3232, E-mail: graduate@maine.edu.

University of Manitoba, Faculty of Graduate Studies, Faculty of Science, Department of Biological Sciences, Winnipeg, MB R3T 2N2, Canada. Offers botany (M Sc, PhD); ecology (M Sc, PhD); zoology (M Sc, PhD).

University of Maryland, College Park, Academic Affairs, College of Chemical and Life Sciences, Department of Biology, Behavior, Ecology, Evolution, and Systematics Program, College Park, MD 20742. Offers MS, PhD. *Students:* 34 full-time (20 women), 1 part-time (0 women); includes 2 minority (both Asian Americans or Pacific Islanders), 2 international. 47 applicants, 9% accepted, 4 enrolled. In 2009, 1 master's, 7 doctorates awarded. *Degree requirements:* For master's, thesis, oral defense, seminar; for doctorate, thesis/dissertation, exam, 4 seminars. *Entrance requirements:* For master's and doctorate, GRE General Test, GRE Subject Test (biology), 3 letters of recommendation. Additional exam requirements/recommendations for international students: Required—TOEFL. *Application deadline:* For fall admission, 12/1 for domestic and international students. Applications are processed on a rolling basis. Application fee: $60. Electronic applications accepted. *Expenses:* Tuition, area resident: Part-time $471 per credit hour. Tuition, state resident: part-time $471 per credit hour. Tuition, nonresident: part-time $1016 per credit hour. Required fees: $337.04 per term. *Financial support:* In 2009–10, 6 fellowships with full and partial tuition reimbursements (averaging $13,373 per year), 4 research assistantships with tuition reimbursements (averaging $19,418 per year), 18 teaching assistantships with tuition reimbursements (averaging $19,479 per year) were awarded; Federal Work-Study and scholarships/grants also available. Support available to part-time students. Financial award applicants required to submit FAFSA. *Faculty research:* Animal behavior, biostatistics, ecology, evolution, neurothology. *Unit head:* Dr. Michele Dudash, Director, 301-405-1642, Fax: 301-314-9358, E-mail: mdudash@umd.edu. *Application contact:* Dean of Graduate School, 301-405-0358, Fax: 301-314-9305.

University of Massachusetts Amherst, Graduate School, Interdisciplinary Programs, Program in Organismic and Evolutionary Biology, Amherst, MA 01003. Offers animal behavior (PhD); ecology (PhD); evolutionary biology (PhD); organismal biology (PhD); organismic and evolutionary biology (MS). Part-time programs available. *Faculty:* 2 full-time (1 woman). *Students:* 33 full-time (21 women), 3 part-time (0 women); includes 2 minority (both Hispanic Americans), 6 international. Average age 27. 53 applicants, 15% accepted, 5 enrolled. In 2009, 2 master's, 4 doctorates awarded. Terminal master's awarded for partial completion of doctoral program. *Degree requirements:* For master's, thesis or alternative; for doctorate, comprehensive exam, thesis/dissertation. *Entrance requirements:* For master's and doctorate, GRE General Test, 3 letters of recommendation. Additional exam requirements/recommendations for international students: Required—TOEFL (minimum score 550 paper-based; 213 computer-based; 80 iBT), IELTS (minimum score 6.5). *Application deadline:* For fall admission, 12/1 for domestic and international students. Applications are processed on a rolling basis. Application fee: $50 ($65 for international students). Electronic applications accepted. *Expenses:* Tuition, state resident: full-time $2640; part-time $110 per credit. Tuition, nonresident: full-time $9936; part-time $414 per credit. Tuition and fees vary according to course load. *Financial support:* Fellowships, research assistantships, teaching assistantships, career-related internships or fieldwork, Federal Work-Study, scholarships/grants, traineeships, health care benefits, tuition waivers (full), and unspecified assistantships available. Support available to part-time students. Financial award application deadline: 12/1. *Unit head:* Dr. Elizabeth M. Jakob, Graduate Program Director, 413-545-0928, Fax: 413-545-3243. *Application contact:* Jean M. Ames, Supervisor of Admissions, 413-545-0722, Fax: 413-577-0010, E-mail: gradadm@grad.umass.edu.

University of Michigan, Horace H. Rackham School of Graduate Studies, College of Literature, Science, and the Arts, Department of Ecology and Evolutionary Biology, Ann Arbor, MI 48109. Offers ecology and evolutionary biology (MS, PhD); ecology and evolutionary biology-Frontiers (MS). Part-time programs available. *Faculty:* 47 full-time (13 women). *Students:* 67 full-time (40 women); includes 11 minority (3 African Americans, 1 American Indian/Alaska Native, 5 Asian Americans or Pacific Islanders, 2 Hispanic Americans), 20 international. Average age 28. 107 applicants, 25% accepted, 7 enrolled. In 2009, 6 master's, 5 doctorates awarded. Terminal master's awarded for partial completion of doctoral program. *Degree requirements:* For master's, thesis (for some programs), two seminars; for doctorate, comprehensive exam, thesis/dissertation, 2 semesters of teaching. *Entrance requirements:* For master's and doctorate, GRE. Additional exam requirements/recommendations for international students: Required—TOEFL (minimum score 560 paper-based; 220 computer-based; 84 iBT). *Application deadline:* For fall admission, 12/1 priority date for domestic and international students; for winter admission, 10/15 priority date for domestic and international students. Applications are processed on a rolling basis. Application fee: $65 ($75 for international students). Electronic applications accepted. *Expenses:* Tuition, state resident: full-time $17,286; part-time $1099 per credit hour. Tuition, nonresident: full-time $34,944; part-time $2080 per credit hour. Required fees: $95 per semester. Tuition and fees vary according to course load, degree level and program. *Financial support:* In 2009–10, 60 students received support, including 18 fellowships with full tuition reimbursements available (averaging $21,944 per year), 8 research assistantships with full tuition reimbursements available (averaging $21,944 per year), 34 teaching assistantships with full tuition reimbursements available (averaging $21,944 per year); scholarships/grants, traineeships, health care benefits, and unspecified assistantships also available. Financial award applicants required to submit FAFSA. *Faculty research:* Community ecology, molecular evolution, theoretical ecology, systematics, evolutionary genetics. Total annual research expenditures: $3.1 million. *Unit head:* Deborah Goldberg, Chair, 734-615-4912, Fax: 734-763-0544. *Application contact:* Jane Sullivan, Graduate Coordinator, 734-615-7338, Fax: 734-763-0544, E-mail: eeb.gradcoord@umich.edu.

University of Minnesota, Twin Cities Campus, Graduate School, College of Biological Sciences, Department of Ecology, Evolution, and Behavior, Minneapolis, MN 55455-0213. Offers ecology, evolution, and behavior (MS, PhD). Terminal master's awarded for partial completion of doctoral program. *Degree requirements:* For master's, comprehensive exam, thesis or projects; for doctorate, comprehensive exam, thesis/dissertation. *Entrance requirements:* For master's and doctorate, GRE General Test, minimum GPA of 3.0. Additional exam requirements/recommendations for international students: Required—TOEFL (minimum score 550 paper-based; 213 computer-based), Michigan English Language Assessment Battery. Electronic applications accepted. *Faculty research:* Behavioral ecology, community ecology, community genetics, ecosystem and global change, evolution and systematics.

University of Missouri, Graduate School, College of Arts and Sciences, Division of Biological Sciences, Program in Evolutionary Biology and Ecology, Columbia, MO 65211. Offers MA, PhD.

University of Missouri–St. Louis, College of Arts and Sciences, Department of Biology, St. Louis, MO 63121. Offers biology (MS, PhD), including animal behavior (MS), biochemistry, biochemistry and biotechnology (MS), biotechnology (MS), conservation biology (MS), development (MS), ecology (MS), environmental studies (PhD), evolution (MS), genetics (MS), molecular biology and biochemistry (PhD), molecular/cellular biology (MS), physiology (MS), plant systematics, population biology (MS), tropical biology (MS); biotechnology (Certificate); tropical biology and conservation (Certificate). Part-time programs available. *Faculty:* 43 full-time (13 women), 2 part-time/adjunct (1 woman). *Students:* 54 full-time (27 women), 79 part-time (43 women); includes 15 minority (6 African Americans, 7 Asian Americans or Pacific Islanders, 2 Hispanic Americans), 47 international. Average age 29. 193 applicants, 44% accepted, 44 enrolled. In 2009, 30 master's, 7 doctorates, 9 other advanced degrees awarded. *Degree requirements:* For master's, thesis or alternative; for doctorate, thesis/dissertation, 1 semester of teaching experience. *Entrance requirements:* For master's, 3 letters of recommendation; for doctorate, GRE General Test, 3 letters of recommendation. Additional exam requirements/recommendations for international students: Required—TOEFL. *Application deadline:* For fall admission, 12/1 priority date for domestic and international students; for spring admission, 10/15 priority date for domestic and international students. Applications are processed on a rolling basis. Application fee: $35 ($40 for international students). Electronic applications accepted. *Expenses:* Tuition, state resident: full-time $5377; part-time $297.70 per credit hour. Tuition, nonresident: full-time $13,882; part-time $771.20 per credit hour. Required fees: $220; $12.20 per credit hour. One-time fee: $12. Tuition and fees vary according to course level, campus/location and program. *Financial support:* In 2009–10, 22 research assistantships with full and partial tuition reimbursements (averaging $16,300 per year), 14 teaching assistantships with full and partial tuition reimbursements (averaging $16,727 per year) were awarded; fellowships with full tuition reimbursements, career-related internships or fieldwork and Federal Work-Study also available. Support available to part-time students. Financial award application deadline: 2/1. *Faculty research:* Molecular biology, microbial genetics, animal behavior, tropical ecology, plant systematics. *Unit head:* Dr. Elizabeth Kellogg, Director of Graduate Studies, 314-516-6200, Fax: 314-516-6233, E-mail: tkellogg@umsl.edu. *Application contact:* 314-516-5458, Fax: 314-516-6996, E-mail: gradadm@umsl.edu.

The University of Montana, Graduate School, College of Arts and Sciences, Division of Biological Sciences, Program in Ecology of Infectious Disease, Missoula, MT 59812-0002. Offers PhD.

The University of Montana, Graduate School, College of Arts and Sciences, Division of Biological Sciences, Program in Organismal Biology and Ecology, Missoula, MT 59812-0002. Offers MS, PhD. Terminal master's awarded for partial completion of doctoral program. *Degree requirements:* For master's, one foreign language, thesis; for doctorate, 2 foreign languages, thesis/dissertation. *Entrance requirements:* For master's and doctorate, GRE General Test. *Faculty research:* Conservation biology, ecology and behavior, evolutionary genetics, avian biology.

University of Nevada, Reno, Graduate School, Interdisciplinary Program in Ecology, Evolution, and Conservation Biology, Reno, NV 89557. Offers PhD. Offered through the College of Arts and Science, the M. C. Fleischmann College of Agriculture, and the Desert Research Institute. *Degree requirements:* For doctorate, thesis/dissertation. *Entrance requirements:* For doctorate, GRE General Test, GRE Subject Test, minimum GPA of 3.0. Additional exam requirements/recommendations for international students: Required—TOEFL (minimum score 500 paper-based; 173 computer-based; 61 iBT), IELTS (minimum score 6). Electronic applications accepted. *Faculty research:* Population biology, behavioral ecology, plant response to climate change, conservation of endangered species, restoration of natural ecosystems.

University of New Haven, Graduate School, College of Arts and Sciences, Program in Environmental Sciences, West Haven, CT 06516-1916. Offers environmental ecology (Certificate); environmental geoscience (MS); environmental health and management (MS); environmental science (MS); geographical information systems (Certificate). Part-time and evening/weekend programs available. *Faculty:* 6 full-time (3 women), 8 part-time/adjunct (2 women). *Students:* 8 full-time (5 women), 21 part-time (9 women); includes 2 minority (both African Americans), 4 international. Average age 27. 28 applicants, 79% accepted, 4 enrolled. In 2009, 7 master's, 5 other advanced degrees awarded. *Degree requirements:* For master's, thesis or alternative. *Entrance requirements:* Additional exam requirements/recommendations for international students: Required—TOEFL (minimum score 520 paper-based; 190 computer-based; 70 iBT); Recommended—IELTS (minimum score 5.5). *Application deadline:* For fall admission, 5/31 for international students; for winter admission, 10/15 for international students; for spring admission, 1/15 for international students. Applications are processed on a rolling basis. Application fee: $50. Electronic applications accepted. *Expenses:* Tuition: Part-time $700 per credit. Required fees: $45 per term. One-time fee: $390 part-time. *Financial support:* Research assistantships with partial tuition reimbursements, teaching assistantships with partial tuition reimbursements, career-related internships or fieldwork, Federal Work-Study, scholarships/grants, tuition waivers, and unspecified assistantships available. Support available to part-time students. Financial award applicants required to submit FAFSA. *Faculty research:* Mapping and assessing geological and living resources in Long Island Sound, geology, San Salvador Island, Bahamas. *Unit head:* Dr. Roman Zajac, Coordinator, 203-932-7108. *Application contact:* Eloise Gormley, Director of Graduate Admissions, 203-932-7449, Fax: 203-932-7137, E-mail: gradinfo@newhaven.edu.

The University of North Carolina at Chapel Hill, Graduate School, College of Arts and Sciences, Curriculum in Ecology, Chapel Hill, NC 27599. Offers MA, MS, PhD. *Degree requirements:* For master's, comprehensive exam, thesis (for some programs), oral defense of thesis; for doctorate, comprehensive exam, thesis/dissertation, oral exams, oral defense of dissertation. *Entrance requirements:* For master's and doctorate, GRE General Test. Additional exam requirements/recommendations for international students: Required—TOEFL (minimum score 550 paper-based; 213 computer-based). Electronic applications accepted. *Faculty research:* Community and population ecology and ecosystems, human ecology, landscape ecology, conservation ecology, marine ecology.

The University of North Carolina at Chapel Hill, Graduate School, College of Arts and Sciences, Department of Biology, Chapel Hill, NC 27599. Offers botany (MA, MS, PhD); cell biology, development, and physiology (MA, MS, PhD); cell motility and cytoskeleton (PhD); ecology and behavior (MA, MS, PhD); genetics and molecular biology (MA, MS, PhD); morphology, systematics, and evolution (MA, MS, PhD). Terminal master's awarded for partial completion of doctoral program. *Degree requirements:* For master's, comprehensive exam, thesis (for some programs); for doctorate, comprehensive exam, thesis/dissertation. *Entrance requirements:* For master's, GRE General Test, GRE Subject Test, 2 semesters of calculus or statistics; 2 semesters of physics, organic chemistry; 3 semesters of biology; for doctorate, GRE General Test, GRE Subject Test, 2 semesters calculus or statistics, 2 semesters physics, organic chemistry, 3 semesters of biology. Additional exam requirements/recommendations for international students: Required—TOEFL (minimum score 550 paper-based; 213 computer-based). Electronic applications accepted. *Faculty research:* Gene expression, biomechanics, yeast genetics, plant ecology, plant molecular biology.

University of North Dakota, Graduate School, College of Arts and Sciences, Department of Biology, Grand Forks, ND 58202. Offers botany (MS, PhD); ecology (MS, PhD); entomology (MS, PhD); environmental biology (MS, PhD); fisheries/wildlife (MS, PhD); genetics (MS, PhD); zoology (MS, PhD). Terminal master's awarded for partial completion of doctoral program. *Degree requirements:* For master's, thesis, final exam; for doctorate, comprehensive exam, thesis/dissertation, final exam. *Entrance requirements:* For master's, GRE General Test, GRE Subject Test, minimum GPA of 3.0; for doctorate, GRE General Test, GRE Subject Test, minimum GPA of 3.5. Additional exam requirements/recommendations for international students: Required—TOEFL (minimum score 550 paper-based; 213 computer-based; 79 iBT), IELTS (minimum score 6.5). Electronic applications accepted. *Faculty research:* Population biology, wildlife ecology, RNA processing, hormonal control of behavior.

University of Notre Dame, Graduate School, College of Science, Department of Biological Sciences, Notre Dame, IN 46556. Offers aquatic ecology, evolution and environmental biology (MS, PhD); cellular and molecular biology (MS, PhD); genetics (MS, PhD); physiology (MS,

Ecology

University of Notre Dame (continued)
PhD); vector biology and parasitology (MS, PhD). Terminal master's awarded for partial completion of doctoral program. *Degree requirements:* For master's, comprehensive exam, thesis; for doctorate, comprehensive exam, thesis/dissertation, candidacy exam. *Entrance requirements:* For master's and doctorate, GRE General Test. Additional exam requirements/recommendations for international students: Required—TOEFL (minimum score 600 paper-based; 250 computer-based; 80 iBT). Electronic applications accepted. *Faculty research:* Tropical disease, molecular genetics, neurobiology, evolutionary biology, aquatic biology.

University of Oklahoma, Graduate College, College of Arts and Sciences, Department of Botany and Microbiology, Program in Ecology and Evolutionary Biology, Norman, OK 73019. Offers PhD. *Students:* 5 full-time (3 women), all international. 7 applicants, 71% accepted, 2 enrolled. *Entrance requirements:* Additional exam requirements/recommendations for international students: Required—TOEFL (minimum score 550 paper-based; 213 computer-based). *Application deadline:* For fall admission, 4/1 for domestic and international students; for spring admission, 11/1 for domestic students, 9/1 for international students. Applications are processed on a rolling basis. Application fee: $40 ($90 for international students). Electronic applications accepted. *Expenses:* Tuition, state resident: full-time $3744; part-time $156 per credit hour. Tuition, nonresident: full-time $13,577; part-time $565.70 per credit hour. Required fees: $2415; $90.10 per credit hour. *Financial support:* Federal Work-Study, institutionally sponsored loans, scholarships/grants, health care benefits, and unspecified assistantships available. Support available to part-time students. *Faculty research:* Global change biology, plant physiological ecology, bioremediation, soil ecosystems, community structure. *Unit head:* Dr. Gordon Uno, Chair, 405-325-4321, Fax: 405-325-7619, E-mail: guno@ou.edu. *Application contact:* Adell Hopper, Staff Assistant, 405-325-4322, Fax: 405-325-7619, E-mail: ahopper@ou.edu.

University of Oklahoma, Graduate College, College of Arts and Sciences, Department of Zoology, Program in Ecology and Evolutionary Biology, Norman, OK 73019. Offers PhD. *Students:* 12 full-time (7 women), 1 part-time (0 women), 4 international. 7 applicants, 71% accepted, 1 enrolled. In 2009, 1 doctorate awarded. *Entrance requirements:* Additional exam requirements/recommendations for international students: Required—TOEFL (minimum score 550 paper-based; 213 computer-based). *Application deadline:* For fall admission, 12/15 for domestic students, 4/1 for international students; for spring admission, 10/1 for domestic students, 9/1 for international students. Applications are processed on a rolling basis. Application fee: $40 ($90 for international students). Electronic applications accepted. *Expenses:* Tuition, state resident: full-time $3744; part-time $156 per credit hour. Tuition, nonresident: full-time $13,577; part-time $565.70 per credit hour. Required fees: $2415; $90.10 per credit hour. *Financial support:* Federal Work-Study, institutionally sponsored loans, scholarships/grants, health care benefits, and unspecified assistantships available. Support available to part-time students. *Faculty research:* Behavioral ecology, community ecology, molecular ecology, population ecology, systematics. *Unit head:* Don Wilson, Assistant Chair, 405-325-4821, Fax: 405-325-6202, E-mail: dwilson@ou.edu. *Application contact:* Michael Kaspari, Professor/Director, 405-325-3371, Fax: 405-325-6202, E-mail: zoologygrad@ou.edu.

University of Oregon, Graduate School, College of Arts and Sciences, Department of Biology, Eugene, OR 97403. Offers ecology and evolution (MA, MS, PhD); marine biology (MA, MS, PhD); molecular, cellular and genetic biology (PhD); neuroscience and development (PhD). Terminal master's awarded for partial completion of doctoral program. *Degree requirements:* For master's, thesis (for some programs); for doctorate, thesis/dissertation. *Entrance requirements:* For master's and doctorate, GRE General Test, minimum GPA of 3.2. Additional exam requirements/recommendations for international students: Required—TOEFL. *Faculty research:* Developmental neurobiology; evolution, population biology, and quantitative genetics; regulation of gene expression; biochemistry of marine organisms.

University of Pittsburgh, School of Arts and Sciences, Department of Biological Sciences, Program in Ecology and Evolution, Pittsburgh, PA 15260. Offers PhD. *Faculty:* 7 full-time (2 women). *Students:* 14 full-time (5 women); includes 3 minority (1 Asian American or Pacific Islander, 2 Hispanic Americans), 1 international. Average age 23. 40 applicants, 18% accepted, 4 enrolled. In 2009, 1 doctorate awarded. *Degree requirements:* For doctorate, comprehensive exam, thesis/dissertation, completion of research integrity module. *Entrance requirements:* For doctorate, GRE General Test, GRE Subject Test. Additional exam requirements/recommendations for international students: Required—TOEFL (minimum score 550 paper-based; 213 computer-based). *Application deadline:* For fall admission, 1/15 priority date for domestic students, 12/15 priority date for international students. Applications are processed on a rolling basis. Application fee: $0 ($50 for international students). Electronic applications accepted. *Expenses:* Tuition, state resident: full-time $16,402; part-time $665 per credit. Tuition, nonresident: full-time $28,694; part-time $1175 per credit. Required fees: $690; $175 per term. Tuition and fees vary according to program. *Financial support:* In 2009–10, 12 fellowships with full tuition reimbursements (averaging $27,379 per year), 6 research assistantships with full tuition reimbursements (averaging $24,608 per year), 20 teaching assistantships with full tuition reimbursements (averaging $23,385 per year) were awarded; Federal Work-Study, scholarships/grants, traineeships, health care benefits, and tuition waivers (full) also available. *Faculty research:* Ecological and population genetics, tropical and community ecology, evolutionary ecology, phylogeny of birds, evolution of dispersal and dormancy. *Unit head:* Dr. Gerard L. Campbell, Associate Professor, 412-624-6812, Fax: 412-624-4759, E-mail: camp@pitt.edu. *Application contact:* Cathleen M. Barr, Graduate Administrator, 412-624-4268, Fax: 412-624-4759, E-mail: cbarr@pitt.edu.

University of Puerto Rico, Río Piedras, College of Natural Sciences, Department of Biology, San Juan, PR 00931-3300. Offers ecology/systematics (MS, PhD); evolution/genetics (MS, PhD); molecular/cellular biology (MS, PhD); neuroscience (MS, PhD). Part-time programs available. *Degree requirements:* For master's, one foreign language, comprehensive exam, thesis; for doctorate, one foreign language, comprehensive exam, thesis/dissertation. *Entrance requirements:* For master's, GRE Subject Test, interview, minimum GPA of 3.0, letter of recommendation; for doctorate, GRE Subject Test, interview, master's degree, minimum GPA of 3.0, letter of recommendation. *Faculty research:* Environmental, poblational and systematic biology.

University of South Carolina, The Graduate School, College of Arts and Sciences, Department of Biological Sciences, Graduate Training Program in Ecology, Evolution, and Organismal Biology, Columbia, SC 29208. Offers MS, PhD. *Degree requirements:* For master's, one foreign language, comprehensive exam, thesis; for doctorate, one foreign language, comprehensive exam, thesis/dissertation. *Entrance requirements:* For master's and doctorate, GRE General Test, minimum GPA of 3.0 in science. Additional exam requirements/recommendations for international students: Required—TOEFL (minimum score 570 paper-based; 230 computer-based). Electronic applications accepted.

The University of Tennessee, Graduate School, College of Arts and Sciences, Department of Ecology and Evolutionary Biology, Knoxville, TN 37996. Offers behavior (MS, PhD); ecology (MS, PhD); evolutionary biology (MS, PhD). Part-time programs available. *Degree requirements:* For master's, thesis; for doctorate, thesis/dissertation. *Entrance requirements:* For master's and doctorate, GRE General Test, minimum GPA of 2.7. Additional exam requirements/recommendations for international students: Required—TOEFL. Electronic applications accepted. *Expenses:* Tuition, state resident: full-time $6826; part-time $380 per semester hour. Tuition, nonresident: full-time $21,844; part-time $1147 per semester hour. Tuition and fees vary according to program.

The University of Tennessee, Graduate School, College of Arts and Sciences, Department of Mathematics, Knoxville, TN 37996. Offers applied mathematics (MS); mathematical ecology (PhD); mathematics (M Math, MS, PhD). Part-time programs available. *Degree requirements:* For master's, thesis or alternative; for doctorate, one foreign language, thesis/dissertation. *Entrance requirements:* For master's and doctorate, minimum GPA of 2.7. Additional exam requirements/recommendations for international students: Required—TOEFL. Electronic applications accepted. *Expenses:* Tuition, state resident: full-time $6826; part-time $380 per semester hour. Tuition, nonresident: full-time $21,844; part-time $1147 per semester hour. Tuition and fees vary according to program.

The University of Texas at Austin, Graduate School, College of Natural Sciences, School of Biological Sciences, Program in Ecology, Evolution and Behavior, Austin, TX 78712-1111. Offers MA, PhD. *Entrance requirements:* For doctorate, GRE General Test. Additional exam requirements/recommendations for international students: Required—TOEFL. Electronic applications accepted.

The University of Toledo, College of Graduate Studies, College of Arts and Sciences, Department of Environmental Sciences, Toledo, OH 43606-3390. Offers biology (ecology track) (MS, PhD); geology (MS), including earth surface processes, general geology. Part-time programs available. *Degree requirements:* For master's, thesis. *Entrance requirements:* For master's, GRE General Test. Additional exam requirements/recommendations for international students: Required—TOEFL. Electronic applications accepted. *Faculty research:* Environmental geochemistry, geophysics, petrology and mineralogy, paleontology, geohydrology.

University of Toronto, School of Graduate Studies, Life Sciences Division, Department of Ecology and Evolutionary Biology, Toronto, ON M5S 1A1, Canada. Offers M Sc, PhD. *Degree requirements:* For master's, thesis, thesis defense; for doctorate, thesis/dissertation, thesis defense. *Entrance requirements:* For master's, minimum B average in last 2 years; knowledge of physics, chemistry, and biology.

University of Washington, Graduate School, College of Forest Resources, Seattle, WA 98195. Offers bioresource science and engineering (MS, PhD); environmental horticulture (MEH); environmental horticulture and urban forestry (MS, PhD); forest ecology (MS, PhD); forest management (MFR); forest soils (MS, PhD); forest systems and bioenergy (MS, PhD); restoration ecology (MS, PhD); social sciences (MS, PhD); sustainable resource management (MS, PhD); wildlife science (MS, PhD); MFR/MAIS; MPA/MS. *Accreditation:* SAF. *Degree requirements:* For master's, thesis (for some programs); for doctorate, comprehensive exam (for some programs), thesis/dissertation. *Entrance requirements:* For master's and doctorate, GRE, minimum GPA of 3.0. Additional exam requirements/recommendations for international students: Required—TOEFL. Electronic applications accepted. *Faculty research:* Ecosystem analysis, silviculture and forest protection, paper science and engineering, environmental horticulture and urban forestry, natural resource policy and economics.

University of Wisconsin–Madison, Graduate School, College of Agricultural and Life Sciences, Agroecology Program, Madison, WI 53706-1380. Offers MS. *Degree requirements:* For master's, thesis (for some programs). *Entrance requirements:* For master's, GRE. Additional exam requirements/recommendations for international students: Required—TOEFL (minimum score 580 paper-based; 237 computer-based; 92 iBT), IELTS (minimum score 7). Electronic applications accepted. *Expenses:* Tuition, state resident: part-time $594 per credit. Tuition, nonresident: part-time $1504 per credit. Required fees: $65 per credit. Tuition and fees vary according to course load, program and reciprocity agreements. *Faculty research:* Multifunctional landscape, socio-ecological systems, participatory solutions to environmental problems.

University of Wyoming, Program in Ecology, Laramie, WY 82070. Offers MS, PhD. *Entrance requirements:* For master's and doctorate, GRE.

Utah State University, School of Graduate Studies, College of Natural Resources, Department of Aquatic, Watershed, and Earth Resources, Logan, UT 84322. Offers ecology (MS, PhD); fisheries biology (MS, PhD); watershed science (MS, PhD). *Degree requirements:* For master's, thesis (for some programs); for doctorate, thesis/dissertation. *Entrance requirements:* For master's and doctorate, GRE General Test, minimum GPA of 3.2. Additional exam requirements/recommendations for international students: Required—TOEFL. Electronic applications accepted. *Faculty research:* Behavior, population ecology, habitat, conservation biology, restoration, aquatic ecology, fisheries management, fluvial geomorphology, remote sensing, conservation biology.

Utah State University, School of Graduate Studies, College of Natural Resources, Department of Environment and Society, Logan, UT 84322. Offers bioregional planning (MS); geography (MA, MS); human dimensions of ecosystem science and management (MS, PhD); recreation resource management (MS, PhD). *Degree requirements:* For master's, comprehensive exam, thesis (for some programs). *Entrance requirements:* For master's and doctorate, GRE General Test, minimum GPA of 3.0. Additional exam requirements/recommendations for international students: Required—TOEFL. Electronic applications accepted. *Faculty research:* Geographic information systems/geographic and environmental education, bioregional planning, natural resource and environmental policy, outdoor recreation and tourism, natural resource and environmental management.

Utah State University, School of Graduate Studies, College of Natural Resources, Department of Wildland Resources, Logan, UT 84322. Offers ecology (MS, PhD); forestry (MS, PhD); range science (MS, PhD); wildlife biology (MS, PhD). Part-time programs available. *Degree requirements:* For master's, thesis; for doctorate, comprehensive exam, thesis/dissertation. *Entrance requirements:* For master's and doctorate, GRE General Test, minimum GPA of 3.0. Additional exam requirements/recommendations for international students: Required—TOEFL. *Faculty research:* Range plant ecophysiology, plant community ecology, ruminant nutrition, population ecology.

Utah State University, School of Graduate Studies, College of Science, Department of Biology, Logan, UT 84322. Offers biology (MS, PhD); ecology (MS, PhD). Part-time programs available. *Degree requirements:* For master's, thesis; for doctorate, thesis/dissertation. *Entrance requirements:* For master's and doctorate, GRE General Test, minimum GPA of 3.0. Additional exam requirements/recommendations for international students: Required—TOEFL (minimum score 575 paper-based). *Faculty research:* Plant, insect, microbial, and animal biology.

Virginia Polytechnic Institute and State University, Graduate School, College of Science, Department of Biological Sciences, Blacksburg, VA 24061. Offers botany (MS, PhD); ecology and evolutionary biology (MS, PhD); genetics and developmental biology (MS, PhD); microbiology (MS, PhD); zoology (MS, PhD). *Faculty:* 42 full-time (11 women). *Students:* 76 full-time (45 women), 5 part-time (1 woman); includes 28 minority (23 American Indian/Alaska Native, 2 Asian Americans or Pacific Islanders, 3 Hispanic Americans). Average age 28. 117 applicants, 15% accepted, 15 enrolled. In 2009, 11 master's, 11 doctorates awarded. *Entrance requirements:* For master's and doctorate, GRE, GMAT. Additional exam requirements/recommendations for international students: Required—TOEFL (minimum score 550 paper-based; 213 computer-based). *Application deadline:* For fall admission, 5/15 for international students; for spring admission, 10/15 for international students. Applications are processed on a rolling basis. Application fee: $65. Electronic applications accepted. *Expenses:* Tuition, area resident: Full-time $10,228; part-time $459 per credit hour. Tuition, nonresident: full-time $17,892; part-time $865 per credit hour. Required fees: $1966; $451 per semester. *Financial support:* In 2009–10, 37 research assistantships with full tuition reimbursements (averaging $17,929 per year), 41 teaching assistantships with full tuition reimbursements (averaging $17,344 per year) were awarded; career-related internships or fieldwork, Federal Work-Study, scholarships/grants, and unspecified assistantships also available. Financial award application deadline: 1/15. *Faculty research:* Freshwater ecology, cell cycle regulation, behavioral ecology, motor proteins. Total annual research expenditures: $4.8 million. *Unit head:* Dr. Bob H. Jones, Dean, 540-231-9514, Fax: 540-231-9307, E-mail: rhjones@vt.edu. *Application contact:* Erik Nilsen, Information Contact, 540-231-5671, Fax: 540-231-9307, E-mail: enilsen@vt.edu.

Washington University in St. Louis, Graduate School of Arts and Sciences, Division of Biology and Biomedical Sciences, Program in Evolution, Ecology and Population Biology, St. Louis, MO 63130-4899. Offers ecology (PhD); environmental biology (PhD); evolutionary biology (PhD); genetics (PhD). *Degree requirements:* For doctorate, thesis/dissertation. *Entrance requirements:* For doctorate, GRE General Test, GRE Subject Test. Electronic applications accepted.

Wesleyan University, Graduate Programs, Department of Biology, Middletown, CT 06459. Offers animal behavior (PhD); bioformatics/genomics (PhD); cell biology (PhD); developmental biology (PhD); evolution/ecology (PhD); genetics (PhD); neurobiology (PhD); population biology (PhD). *Faculty:* 13 full-time (4 women). *Students:* 23 full-time (11 women); includes 1 minority (African American), 3 international. Average age 26. 29 applicants, 10% accepted, 2 enrolled. In 2009, 3 doctorates awarded. *Degree requirements:* For doctorate, variable foreign language requirement, thesis/dissertation. *Entrance requirements:* For doctorate, GRE. Additional exam requirements/recommendations for international students: Required—TOEFL. *Application deadline:* For fall admission, 1/15 for domestic and international students. Applications are processed on a rolling basis. Application fee: $0. *Financial support:* In 2009–10, 3 research assistantships with full tuition reimbursements, 19 teaching assistantships with full tuition reimbursements were awarded; stipends also available. Financial award application deadline: 4/15; financial award applicants required to submit FAFSA. *Faculty research:* Microbial population genetics, genetic basis of evolutionary adaptation, genetic regulation of differentiation and pattern formation in *drosophila*. *Unit head:* Dr. Sonia E. Sultan, Chair/Professor, 860-685-3493, E-mail: jnaegele@wesleyan.edu. *Application contact:* Marjorie Fitzgibbons, Information Contact, 860-685-2140, E-mail: mfitzgibbons@wesleyan.edu.

Yale University, Graduate School of Arts and Sciences, Department of Ecology and Evolutionary Biology, New Haven, CT 06520. Offers PhD. *Entrance requirements:* For doctorate, GRE General Test, GRE Subject Test (biology).

Environmental Biology

Baylor University, Graduate School, College of Arts and Sciences, Department of Biology, Waco, TX 76798. Offers biology (MA, MS, PhD); environmental biology (MS); limnology (MS). Part-time programs available. *Faculty:* 13 full-time (3 women). *Students:* 34 full-time (15 women); includes 1 minority (Asian American or Pacific Islander), 10 international. In 2009, 8 master's, 4 doctorates awarded. *Degree requirements:* For master's, thesis (for some programs); for doctorate, thesis/dissertation. *Entrance requirements:* For master's and doctorate, GRE General Test. *Application deadline:* For fall admission, 1/31 priority date for domestic students. Applications are processed on a rolling basis. Application fee: $25. *Financial support:* Teaching assistantships, career-related internships or fieldwork, Federal Work-Study, institutionally sponsored loans, and tuition waivers (full and partial) available. Support available to part-time students. Financial award application deadline: 2/28. *Faculty research:* Terrestrial ecology, aquatic ecology, genetics. *Unit head:* Dr. Myeongwoo Lee, Graduate Program Director, 254-710-2141, Fax: 254-710-2969, E-mail: myeongwoo_lee@baylor.edu. *Application contact:* Tamara Lehmann, Administrative Assistant, 254-710-2911, Fax: 254-710-2969, E-mail: tamara_lehmann@baylor.edu.

Chatham University, Program in Biology, Pittsburgh, PA 15232-2826. Offers environmental biology-non-thesis track (MS); environmental biology-thesis track (MS); human biology-non-thesis track (MS); human biology-thesis track (MS). Part-time programs available. *Students:* 23 full-time (18 women). Average age 25. 30 applicants, 83% accepted, 13 enrolled. In 2009, 8 master's awarded. *Degree requirements:* For master's, thesis optional. *Entrance requirements:* For master's, 3 letters of recommendation. Additional exam requirements/recommendations for international students: Required—TOEFL (minimum score 600 paper-based; 250 computer-based; 100 iBT), IELTS (minimum score 6.5), TWE. *Application deadline:* For fall admission, 5/1 priority date for domestic and international students; for spring admission, 11/1 priority date for domestic and international students. Applications are processed on a rolling basis. Application fee: $45. Electronic applications accepted. *Financial support:* Applicants required to submit FAFSA. *Faculty research:* Molecular evolution of iron homeostasis, characteristics of soil bacterial communities, gene flow through seed movement, role of gonadotropins in spermatogonial proliferation, phosphatid/linositol metabolism in epithelial cells. *Unit head:* Dr. Lisa Lambert, Director, 412-365-1217, E-mail: lambert@chatham.edu. *Application contact:* Maureen Stokan, Assistant Director of Graduate Admissions, 412-365-2988, Fax: 412-365-1609, E-mail: gradadmissions@chatham.edu.

Emporia State University, School of Graduate Studies, College of Liberal Arts and Sciences, Department of Biological Sciences, Emporia, KS 66801-5087. Offers botany (MS); environmental biology (MS); general biology (MS); microbial and cellular biology (MS); zoology (MS). Part-time programs available. *Faculty:* 13 full-time (3 women). *Students:* 9 full-time (7 women), 17 part-time (11 women); includes 1 minority (African American), 8 international. 22 applicants, 95% accepted, 18 enrolled. In 2009, 24 master's awarded. *Degree requirements:* For master's, comprehensive exam or thesis. *Entrance requirements:* For master's, GRE, appropriate undergraduate degree, interview, letters of reference. Additional exam requirements/recommendations for international students: Required—TOEFL (minimum score 520 paper-based; 133 computer-based; 68 iBT). *Application deadline:* For fall admission, 8/15 priority date for domestic students. Applications are processed on a rolling basis. Application fee: $30 ($75 for international students). Electronic applications accepted. *Expenses:* Tuition, state resident: full-time $4154; part-time $173 per credit hour. Tuition, nonresident: full-time $12,864; part-time $536 per credit hour. Required fees: $948; $58 per credit hour. Tuition and fees vary according to campus/location. *Financial support:* In 2009–10, 7 research assistantships with full tuition reimbursements (averaging $6,876 per year), 10 teaching assistantships with full tuition reimbursements (averaging $7,419 per year) were awarded; career-related internships or fieldwork, Federal Work-Study, institutionally sponsored loans, health care benefits, and unspecified assistantships also available. Financial award application deadline: 3/15; financial award applicants required to submit FAFSA. *Faculty research:* Fisheries, range, and wildlife management; aquatic, plant, grassland, vertebrate, and invertebrate ecology; mammalian and plant systematics, taxonomy, and evolution; immunology, virology, and molecular biology. *Unit head:* Dr. R. Brent Thomas, Interim Chair, 620-341-5311, Fax: 620-341-5608, E-mail: rthomas2@emporia.edu. *Application contact:* Dr. Scott Crupper, Graduate Coordinator, 620-341-5621, Fax: 620-341-5607, E-mail: scrupper@emporia.edu.

Georgia State University, College of Arts and Sciences, Department of Biology, Program in Applied and Environmental Microbiology, Atlanta, GA 30302-3083. Offers MS, PhD. Part-time programs available. Terminal master's awarded for partial completion of doctoral program. *Degree requirements:* For master's, thesis or alternative; for doctorate, thesis/dissertation, exam. *Entrance requirements:* For master's and doctorate, GRE General Test. Additional exam requirements/recommendations for international students: Required—TOEFL. Electronic applications accepted.

Governors State University, College of Arts and Sciences, Program in Environmental Biology, University Park, IL 60466-0975. Offers MS. Part-time and evening/weekend programs available. *Degree requirements:* For master's, thesis or alternative. *Faculty research:* Animal physiology, cell biology, animal behavior, plant physiology, plant populations.

Hampton University, Graduate College, Department of Biological Sciences, Hampton, VA 23668. Offers biology (MS); environmental science (MS); medical science (MS). Part-time and evening/weekend programs available. *Degree requirements:* For master's, thesis optional. *Entrance requirements:* For master's, GRE General Test. *Faculty research:* Marine ecology, microbial and chemical pollution, pesticide problems.

Hood College, Graduate School, Program in Environmental Biology, Frederick, MD 21701-8575. Offers MS. Part-time and evening/weekend programs available. *Faculty:* 2 full-time (0 women), 5 part-time/adjunct (2 women). *Students:* 4 full-time (all women), 54 part-time (42 women); includes 4 minority (2 African Americans, 1 Asian American or Pacific Islander, 1 Hispanic American). Average age 31. 18 applicants, 89% accepted, 12 enrolled. In 2009, 9 master's awarded. *Degree requirements:* For master's, thesis or alternative. *Entrance requirements:* For master's, minimum GPA of 2.75, 1 year of undergraduate biology and chemistry, 1 semester of mathematics. Additional exam requirements/recommendations for international students: Required—TOEFL (minimum score 575 paper-based; 231 computer-based; 89 iBT). *Application deadline:* For fall admission, 7/15 for domestic and international students; for spring admission, 12/15 for domestic and international students. Applications are processed on a rolling basis. Application fee: $35. Electronic applications accepted. *Expenses:* Tuition: Full-time $6480; part-time $360 per credit. Required fees: $100; $50 per term. *Financial support:* Applicants required to submit FAFSA. *Unit head:* Dr. Drew Ferrier, Director, 301-696-3649, Fax: 301-694-3597, E-mail: dferrier@hood.edu. *Application contact:* Dr. Allen P. Flora, Dean of Graduate School, 301-696-3811, Fax: 301-696-3597, E-mail: gofurther@hood.edu.

Inter American University of Puerto Rico, San Germán Campus, Graduate Studies Center, Program in Environmental Sciences, San Germán, PR 00683-5008. Offers environmental biology (MS); environmental chemistry (MS); water analysis (MS). Part-time and evening/weekend programs available. *Degree requirements:* For master's, comprehensive exam, thesis. *Entrance requirements:* For master's, GRE General Test or EXADEP, minimum GPA of 3.0. *Faculty research:* Environmental biology, environmental chemistry, water resources and unit operations.

Massachusetts Institute of Technology, School of Engineering, Department of Civil and Environmental Engineering, Cambridge, MA 02139-4307. Offers biological oceanography (PhD, Sc D); chemical oceanography (PhD, Sc D); civil and environmental engineering (M Eng, SM, PhD, Sc D); civil and environmental systems (PhD, Sc D); civil engineering (PhD, Sc D, CE); coastal engineering (PhD, Sc D); construction engineering and management (PhD, Sc D); environmental biology (PhD, Sc D); environmental chemistry (PhD, Sc D); environmental engineering (PhD, Sc D); environmental fluid mechanics (PhD, Sc D); geotechnical and geoenvironmental engineering (PhD, Sc D); hydrology (PhD, Sc D); information technology (PhD, Sc D); oceanographic engineering (PhD, Sc D); structures and materials (PhD, Sc D); transportation (PhD, Sc D); SM/MBA. *Faculty:* 36 full-time (5 women). *Students:* 190 full-time (59 women); includes 22 minority (2 African Americans, 14 Asian Americans or Pacific Islanders, 6 Hispanic Americans), 103 international. Average age 26. 478 applicants, 25% accepted, 76 enrolled. In 2009, 72 master's, 14 doctorates awarded. *Degree requirements:* For master's and CE, thesis; for doctorate, comprehensive exam, thesis/dissertation. *Entrance requirements:* For master's and doctorate, GRE General Test. Additional exam requirements/recommendations for international students: Required—TOEFL (minimum score 577 paper-based; 233 computer-based; 90 iBT), IELTS (minimum score 7). *Application deadline:* For fall admission, 1/2 for domestic and international students. Application fee: $75. Electronic applications accepted. *Expenses:* Tuition: Full-time $37,510; part-time $585 per unit. Required fees: $272. *Financial support:* In 2009–10, 185 students received support, including 40 fellowships with tuition reimbursements available (averaging $27,725 per year), 97 research assistantships with tuition reimbursements available (averaging $28,035 per year), 21 teaching assistantships with tuition reimbursements available (averaging $24,802 per year); career-related internships or fieldwork, Federal Work-Study, institutionally sponsored loans, scholarships/grants, health care benefits, and unspecified assistantships also available. *Faculty research:* Environmental chemistry, environmental microbiology, environmental fluid mechanics and coastal engineering, geotechnical engineering and geomechanics, hydrology and hydroclimatology, mechanics of materials and structures, operations research/supply chain, transportation. Total annual research expenditures: $16.6 million. *Unit head:* Prof. Andrew Whittle, Department Head, 617-253-7101. *Application contact:* Patricia Glidden, Graduate Admissions Coordinator, 617-253-7119, Fax: 617-258-6775, E-mail: cee-admissions@mit.edu.

Missouri University of Science and Technology, Graduate School, Department of Biological Sciences, Rolla, MO 65409. Offers applied and environmental biology (MS). *Entrance requirements:* For master's, GRE (minimum score 600 quantitative, 4 writing). Additional exam requirements/recommendations for international students: Required—TOEFL (minimum score 570 paper-based; 230 computer-based).

Morgan State University, School of Graduate Studies, School of Computer, Mathematical, and Natural Sciences, Department of Biology, Program in Bioenvironmental Science, Baltimore, MD 21251. Offers PhD. *Degree requirements:* For doctorate, comprehensive exam, thesis/dissertation, oral defense of dissertation. *Entrance requirements:* For doctorate, GRE General Test, GRE Subject Test (biology, chemistry, or related science), bachelor's or master's degree in biology, chemistry, physics or related field; minimum GPA of 3.0. Additional exam requirements/recommendations for international students: Required—TOEFL (minimum score 550 paper-based; 213 computer-based).

Nicholls State University, Graduate Studies, College of Arts and Sciences, Department of Biological Sciences, Thibodaux, LA 70310. Offers marine and environmental biology (MS). Part-time programs available. *Degree requirements:* For master's, comprehensive exam, thesis. *Entrance requirements:* For master's, GRE. Additional exam requirements/recommendations for international students: Required—TOEFL (minimum score 600 paper-based). *Faculty research:* Bioremediation, ecology, public health, biotechnology, physiology.

Nova Scotia Agricultural College, Research and Graduate Studies, Truro, NS B2N 5E3, Canada. Offers agriculture (M Sc), including air quality, animal behavior, animal molecular genetics, animal nutrition, animal technology, aquaculture, botany, crop management, crop physiology, ecology, environmental microbiology, food science, horticulture, nutrient management, pest management, physiology, plant biotechnology, plant pathology, soil chemistry, soil fertility, waste management and composting, water quality. Part-time programs available. *Degree requirements:* For master's, thesis, ATC Exam Teaching Assistantship. *Entrance requirements:* For master's, honors B Sc, minimum GPA of 3.0. Additional exam requirements/recommendations for international students: Required—TOEFL (minimum score 580 paper-based; 237 computer-based; 92 iBT), IELTS, Michigan English Language Assessment Battery, CanTEST, CAEL. *Faculty research:* Bio-product development, organic agriculture, nutrient management, air and water quality, agricultural biotechnology.

Ohio University, Graduate College, College of Arts and Sciences, Department of Environmental and Plant Biology, Athens, OH 45701-2979. Offers MS, PhD. Part-time programs available. *Faculty:* 12 full-time (2 women). *Students:* 25 full-time (11 women); includes 1 minority (African American), 10 international. Average age 25. 19 applicants, 32% accepted, 4 enrolled. In 2009, 1 master's, 2 doctorates awarded. *Degree requirements:* For master's, thesis, 2 quarters of teaching experience; for doctorate, comprehensive exam, thesis/dissertation, 2 quarters of teaching experience. *Entrance requirements:* For master's, GRE General Test, minimum GPA of 3.0; for doctorate, GRE General Test, minimum GPA of 3.2. Additional exam requirements/recommendations for international students: Required—TOEFL

Environmental Biology

Ohio University (continued)

(minimum score 620 paper-based; 260 computer-based; 105 iBT) or IELTS (minimum score 7.5). *Application deadline:* For fall admission, 1/15 priority date for domestic and international students. Applications are processed on a rolling basis. Application fee: $50 ($55 for international students). Electronic applications accepted. *Expenses:* Tuition, state resident: full-time $7839; part-time $323 per quarter hour. Tuition, nonresident: full-time $15,831; part-time $654 per quarter hour. Required fees: $2931. *Financial support:* Fellowships with full tuition reimbursements, research assistantships with full tuition reimbursements, teaching assistantships with full tuition reimbursements, Federal Work-Study, institutionally sponsored loans, and scholarships/grants available. Financial award application deadline: 1/15. *Faculty research:* Eastern deciduous forest ecology, evolutionary developmental plant biology, phylogenetic systematics, plant cell wall biotechnology. Total annual research expenditures: $859,166. *Unit head:* Dr. Gar W. Rothwell, Chair, 740-593-1126, Fax: 740-593-1130, E-mail: rothwell@ohio.edu. *Application contact:* Dr. Allan Showalter, Graduate Chair, 740-593-1135, Fax: 740-593-1130, E-mail: showalte@ohio.edu.

Rutgers, The State University of New Jersey, New Brunswick, Graduate School-New Brunswick, Department of Environmental Sciences, Piscataway, NJ 08854-8097. Offers air pollution and resources (MS, PhD); aquatic biology (MS, PhD); aquatic chemistry (MS, PhD); atmospheric science (MS, PhD); chemistry and physics of aerosol and hydrosol systems (MS, PhD); environmental chemistry (MS, PhD); environmental microbiology (MS, PhD); environmental toxicology (PhD); exposure assessment (PhD); fate and effects of pollutants (MS, PhD); pollution prevention and control (MS, PhD); water and wastewater treatment (MS, PhD); water resources (MS, PhD). Terminal master's awarded for partial completion of doctoral program. *Degree requirements:* For master's, comprehensive exam, thesis or alternative, oral final exam; for doctorate, comprehensive exam, thesis/dissertation, thesis defense, qualifying exam. *Entrance requirements:* For master's and doctorate, GRE General Test. Additional exam requirements/recommendations for international students: Required—TOEFL. Electronic applications accepted. *Faculty research:* Biological waste treatment; contaminant fate and transport; air, soil and water quality.

Sonoma State University, School of Science and Technology, Department of Biology, Rohnert Park, CA 94928. Offers environmental biology (MA); general biology (MA). Part-time programs available. *Faculty:* 8 full-time (2 women). *Students:* 19 part-time (12 women); includes 2 minority (1 American Indian/Alaska Native, 1 Hispanic American), 1 international. Average age 27. 23 applicants, 43% accepted, 6 enrolled. In 2009, 7 master's awarded. *Degree requirements:* For master's, thesis or alternative, oral exam. *Entrance requirements:* For master's, GRE General Test, GRE Subject Test, minimum GPA of 3.0. Additional exam requirements/recommendations for international students: Required—TOEFL (minimum score 500 paper-based; 173 computer-based). *Application deadline:* For fall admission, 11/30 for domestic students. Applications are processed on a rolling basis. Application fee: $55. *Expenses:* Tuition, nonresident: full-time $11,160. Required fees: $6226. Full-time tuition and fees vary according to course load. *Financial support:* In 2009–10, 5 fellowships (averaging $6,010 per year), 7 research assistantships (averaging $9,286 per year), 20 teaching assistantships (averaging $5,298 per year) were awarded; career-related internships or fieldwork, Federal Work-Study, and tuition waivers (full) also available. Financial award application deadline: 3/2; financial award applicants required to submit FAFSA. *Faculty research:* Plant physiology, comparative physiology, community ecology, restoration ecology, marine ecology, conservation genetics, primate behavior, behavioral ecology, developmental biology, plant and animal systematics. Total annual research expenditures: $238,000. *Unit head:* Dr. Dan Crocker, Chair, 707-664-2189, E-mail: james.christmann@sonoma.edu. *Application contact:* John Hopkirk, Graduate Adviser, 707-664-2180.

State University of New York College of Environmental Science and Forestry, Department of Environmental and Forest Biology, Syracuse, NY 13210-2779. Offers applied ecology (MPS); chemical ecology (MPS, MS, PhD); conservation biology (MPS, MS, PhD); ecology (MPS, MS, PhD); entomology (MPS, MS, PhD); environmental interpretation (MPS, MS, PhD); environmental physiology (MPS, MS, PhD); fish and wildlife biology (MPS, MS, PhD); forest pathology and mycology (MPS, MS, PhD); plant biotechnology (MPS); plant science and biotechnology (MPS, MS, PhD). *Degree requirements:* For master's, thesis (for some programs); for doctorate, comprehensive exam, thesis/dissertation. *Entrance requirements:* For master's and doctorate, GRE General Test, GRE Subject Test, minimum GPA of 3.0. Additional exam requirements/recommendations for international students: Required—TOEFL (minimum score 550 paper-based; 213 computer-based; 80 iBT), IELTS (minimum score 6). *Faculty research:* Ecology, fish and wildlife biology and management, plant science, entomology.

Universidad del Turabo, Graduate Programs, Programs in Science and Technology, Gurabo, PR 00778-3030. Offers environmental analysis (MSE), including environmental chemistry; environmental management (MSE), including pollution management; environmental science (D Sc), including environmental biology. *Students:* 8 full-time (7 women), 110 part-time (76 women); includes 115 Hispanic Americans. Average age 37. 52 applicants, 65% accepted, 30 enrolled. In 2009, 6 master's awarded. *Entrance requirements:* For master's, GRE, EXADEP, interview. *Application deadline:* For fall admission, 8/5 for domestic students. Application fee: $25. *Application contact:* Virginia Gonzalez, Admissions Officer, 787-746-3009.

University of Alberta, Faculty of Graduate Studies and Research, Department of Biological Sciences, Edmonton, AB T6G 2E1, Canada. Offers environmental biology and ecology (M Sc, PhD); microbiology and biotechnology (M Sc, PhD); molecular biology and genetics (M Sc, PhD); physiology and cell biology (M Sc, PhD); plant biology (M Sc, PhD); systematics and evolution (M Sc, PhD). *Faculty:* 72 full-time (15 women), 15 part-time/adjunct (4 women). *Students:* 238 full-time (117 women), 32 part-time (15 women), 31 international. 206 applicants, 42% accepted. In 2009, 29 master's, 31 doctorates awarded. Terminal master's awarded for partial completion of doctoral program. *Degree requirements:* For master's, thesis; for doctorate, thesis/dissertation. *Entrance requirements:* Additional exam requirements/recommendations for international students: Required—TOEFL. *Application deadline:* For fall admission, 3/1 priority date for domestic students. Applications are processed on a rolling basis. Application fee: $0. Tuition and fees charges are reported in Canadian dollars. *Expenses:* Tuition, area resident: Full-time $4626 Canadian dollars; part-time $99.72 Canadian dollars per unit. International tuition: $8216 Canadian dollars full-time. Required fees: $3590 Canadian dollars; $99.72 Canadian dollars per unit. $215 Canadian dollars per term. *Financial support:* In 2009–10, 4 research assistantships with partial tuition reimbursements (averaging $12,000 per year), 103 teaching assistantships with partial tuition reimbursements (averaging $12,300 per year) were awarded; career-related internships or fieldwork and scholarships/grants also available. *Unit head:* Laura Frost, Chair, 780-492-1904. *Application contact:* Dr. John P. Chang, Associate Chair for Graduate Studies, 780-492-1257, Fax: 780-492-9457, E-mail: bio.grad.coordinator@ualberta.ca.

University of California, Santa Cruz, Division of Graduate Studies, Division of Physical and Biological Sciences, Environmental Toxicology Department, Santa Cruz, CA 95064. Offers MS, PhD. *Degree requirements:* For master's, comprehensive exam, thesis; for doctorate, thesis/dissertation, qualifying exams. *Entrance requirements:* For master's and doctorate, GRE.

University of Guelph, Graduate Program Services, Ontario Agricultural College, Department of Environmental Biology, Guelph, ON N1G 2W1, Canada. Offers entomology (M Sc, PhD); environmental microbiology and biotechnology (M Sc, PhD); environmental toxicology (M Sc, PhD); plant and forest systems (M Sc, PhD); plant pathology (M Sc, PhD). Part-time programs available. *Degree requirements:* For master's, thesis; for doctorate, comprehensive exam, thesis/dissertation. *Entrance requirements:* For master's, minimum 75% average during previous 2 years of course work; for doctorate, minimum 75% average. Additional exam requirements/recommendations for international students: Required—TOEFL or IELTS. Electronic applications accepted. *Faculty research:* Entomology, environmental microbiology and biotechnology, environmental toxicology, forest ecology, plant pathology.

University of Louisiana at Lafayette, College of Sciences, Department of Biology, Lafayette, LA 70504. Offers biology (MS); environmental and evolutionary biology (PhD). Terminal master's awarded for partial completion of doctoral program. *Degree requirements:* For master's, thesis; for doctorate, 2 foreign languages, comprehensive exam, thesis/dissertation. *Entrance requirements:* For master's, GRE General Test, minimum GPA of 2.75; for doctorate, GRE General Test, GRE Subject Test, minimum GPA of 3.0. Additional exam requirements/recommendations for international students: Required—TOEFL (minimum score 550 paper-based; 213 computer-based). Electronic applications accepted. *Faculty research:* Structure and ultrastructure, system biology, ecology, processes, environmental physiology.

University of Louisville, Graduate School, College of Arts and Sciences, Department of Biology, Louisville, KY 40292-0001. Offers biology (MS); environmental biology (PhD). *Students:* 38 full-time (19 women), 10 part-time (8 women); includes 1 minority (Asian American or Pacific Islander), 9 international. Average age 32. 49 applicants, 53% accepted, 9 enrolled. In 2009, 7 master's, 6 doctorates awarded. *Degree requirements:* For master's, thesis (for some programs); for doctorate, thesis/dissertation. *Entrance requirements:* For master's and doctorate, GRE General Test. *Application deadline:* Applications are processed on a rolling basis. Application fee: $50. *Unit head:* Dr. Ronald Fell, Chair, 502-852-6771, Fax: 502-852-0725, E-mail: rdfell@louisville.edu. *Application contact:* Dr. Joseph M. Steffen, Director of Graduate Studies, 502-852-6771, Fax: 502-852-0725, E-mail: joe.steffen@louisville.edu.

University of Massachusetts Amherst, Graduate School, College of Natural Sciences, Department of Natural Resources Conservation, Program in Wildlife and Fisheries Conservation, Amherst, MA 01003. Offers MS, PhD. Part-time programs available. *Students:* 32 full-time (17 women), 32 part-time (11 women); includes 2 minority (1 African American, 1 American Indian/Alaska Native), 10 international. Average age 32. 43 applicants, 26% accepted, 9 enrolled. In 2009, 8 master's, 3 doctorates awarded. Terminal master's awarded for partial completion of doctoral program. *Degree requirements:* For master's, thesis optional; for doctorate, comprehensive exam, thesis/dissertation. *Entrance requirements:* For master's and doctorate, GRE General Test. Additional exam requirements/recommendations for international students: Required—TOEFL (minimum score 550 paper-based; 213 computer-based; 80 iBT), IELTS (minimum score 6.5). *Application deadline:* For fall admission, 2/1 for domestic and international students; for spring admission, 10/1 for domestic and international students. Applications are processed on a rolling basis. Application fee: $50 ($65 for international students). Electronic applications accepted. *Expenses:* Tuition, state resident: full-time $2640; part-time $110 per credit. Tuition, nonresident: full-time $9936; part-time $414 per credit. Tuition and fees vary according to course load. *Financial support:* Fellowships, research assistantships, teaching assistantships, career-related internships or fieldwork, Federal Work-Study, scholarships/grants, traineeships, health care benefits, tuition waivers (full), and unspecified assistantships available. Support available to part-time students. Financial award application deadline: 2/1. *Unit head:* Dr. Kevin McGarigal, Graduate Program Director, 413-545-2666, Fax: 413-545-4358. *Application contact:* Jean M. Ames, Supervisor of Admissions, 413-545-0722, Fax: 413-577-0010, E-mail: gradadm@grad.umass.edu.

University of Massachusetts Boston, Office of Graduate Studies, College of Science and Mathematics, Department of Environmental, Earth and Ocean Sciences, Program in Environmental Biology, Boston, MA 02125-3393. Offers PhD. Part-time and evening/weekend programs available. *Degree requirements:* For doctorate, comprehensive exam, thesis/dissertation, oral exams. *Entrance requirements:* For doctorate, GRE General Test, minimum GPA of 2.75. *Faculty research:* Polychoets biology, predator and prey relationships, population and evolutionary biology, neurobiology, biodiversity.

University of North Dakota, Graduate School, College of Arts and Sciences, Department of Biology, Grand Forks, ND 58202. Offers botany (MS, PhD); ecology (MS, PhD); entomology (MS, PhD); environmental biology (MS, PhD); fisheries/wildlife (MS, PhD); genetics (MS, PhD); zoology (MS, PhD). Terminal master's awarded for partial completion of doctoral program. *Degree requirements:* For master's, thesis, final exam; for doctorate, comprehensive exam, thesis/dissertation, final exam. *Entrance requirements:* For master's, GRE General Test, GRE Subject Test, minimum GPA of 3.0; for doctorate, GRE General Test, GRE Subject Test, minimum GPA of 3.5. Additional exam requirements/recommendations for international students: Required—TOEFL (minimum score 550 paper-based; 213 computer-based; 79 iBT), IELTS (minimum score 6.5). Electronic applications accepted. *Faculty research:* Population biology, wildlife ecology, RNA processing, hormonal control of behavior.

University of Southern California, Graduate School, College of Letters, Arts and Sciences, Department of Biological Sciences, Program in Marine Biology and Biological Oceanography, Los Angeles, CA 90089. Offers marine and environmental biology (MS); marine biology and biological oceanography (PhD). *Faculty:* 27 full-time (8 women), 7 part-time/adjunct (2 women). *Students:* 2 full-time (1 woman), 1 international. 36 applicants, 50% accepted. In 2009, 1 master's awarded. Terminal master's awarded for partial completion of doctoral program. *Degree requirements:* For master's, comprehensive exam (for some programs), research paper; for doctorate, thesis/dissertation, qualifying examination, dissertation defense. *Entrance requirements:* For master's and doctorate, GRE, 3 letters of recommendation, personal statement, resume, minimum GPA of 3.0. Additional exam requirements/recommendations for international students: Required—TOEFL (minimum score 600 paper-based; 250 computer-based; 100 iBT). *Application deadline:* For fall admission, 12/1 priority date for domestic and international students. Application fee: $85. Electronic applications accepted. *Expenses:* Tuition: Full-time $25,980; part-time $1315 per unit. Required fees: $554. One-time fee: $35 full-time. Full-time tuition and fees vary according to degree level and program. *Financial support:* In 2009–10, 10 fellowships with full tuition reimbursements (averaging $25,333 per year), 14 research assistantships with full tuition reimbursements (averaging $25,333 per year), 14 teaching assistantships with full tuition reimbursements (averaging $25,333 per year) were awarded; scholarships/grants, traineeships, health care benefits, and tuition waivers also available. *Faculty research:* Adaptation, evolution, and population dynamics; marine microbiology; global biogeochemical cycles; coastal water quality; marine environmental genomics. *Unit head:* Dr. David A. Caron, Professor of Biological Sciences/Director of the MBBO Graduate Program, 213-740-0203, E-mail: dcaron@usc.edu. *Application contact:* Adolfo dela Rosa, Student Services Advisor I, 213-821-3164, Fax: 213-740-1380, E-mail: adolfode@usc.edu.

University of Southern Mississippi, Graduate School, College of Science and Technology, Department of Biological Sciences, Hattiesburg, MS 39406-0001. Offers environmental biology (MS, PhD); marine biology (MS, PhD); microbiology (MS, PhD); molecular biology (MS, PhD). *Faculty:* 27 full-time (6 women). *Students:* 55 full-time (27 women), 5 part-time (3 women); includes 7 minority (2 African Americans, 1 American Indian/Alaska Native, 2 Asian Americans or Pacific Islanders, 2 Hispanic Americans), 15 international. Average age 32. 53 applicants, 28% accepted, 10 enrolled. In 2009, 8 master's, 4 doctorates awarded. *Degree requirements:* For master's, comprehensive exam, thesis; for doctorate, comprehensive exam, thesis/dissertation. *Entrance requirements:* For master's, GRE General Test, minimum GPA of 3.0; for doctorate, GRE General Test, minimum GPA of 3.5. Additional exam requirements/recommendations for international students: Required—TOEFL. *Application deadline:* For fall admission, 3/1 priority date for domestic students, 3/1 for international students. Applications are processed on a rolling basis. Application fee: $35. *Expenses:* Tuition, state resident: full-time $5096; part-time $284 per hour. Tuition, nonresident: full-time $13,052; part-time $726 per hour. Required fees: $402. Tuition and fees vary according to course level and course load. *Financial support:* In 2009–10, 25 research assistantships with full tuition reimbursements (averaging $9,625 per year), 33 teaching assistantships with full tuition reimbursements (averaging $10,599 per year) were awarded; Federal Work-Study also available. Financial award application deadline: 3/15; financial award applicants required to submit FAFSA. *Unit head:* Dr. Frank Moore, Chair, 601-266-4748, Fax: 601-266-5797. *Application contact:* Dr. Chia Wang, Graduate Coordinator, 601-266-4748, Fax: 601-266-5797.

University of West Florida, College of Arts and Sciences: Sciences, School of Allied Health and Life Sciences, Department of Biology, Pensacola, FL 32514-5750. Offers biological chemistry

(MS); biology (MS); biology education (MST); biotechnology (MS); coastal zone studies (MS); environmental biology (MS). *Faculty:* 7 full-time (2 women), 1 (woman) part-time/adjunct. *Students:* 5 full-time (1 woman), 21 part-time (14 women); includes 2 minority (1 Asian American or Pacific Islander, 1 Hispanic American), 1 international. Average age 28. 19 applicants, 58% accepted, 7 enrolled. In 2009, 12 master's awarded. *Degree requirements:* For master's, thesis. *Entrance requirements:* For master's, GRE General Test. Additional exam requirements/recommendations for international students: Required—TOEFL (minimum score 550 paper-based; 213 computer-based). *Application deadline:* For fall admission, 6/1 for domestic students, 5/15 for international students; for spring admission, 11/1 for domestic students, 10/1 for international students. Applications are processed on a rolling basis. Application fee: $30. *Expenses:* Tuition, state resident: full-time $4982; part-time $260 per credit hour. Tuition, nonresident: full-time $20,059; part-time $919 per credit hour. Required fees: $1247; $52 per credit hour. *Financial support:* In 2009–10, 2 research assistantships with partial tuition reimbursements (averaging $8,500 per year), 10 teaching assistantships with partial tuition reimbursements (averaging $8,176 per year) were awarded; unspecified assistantships also available. Financial award application deadline: 4/15; financial award applicants required to submit FAFSA. *Unit head:* Dr. George L. Stewart, Chairperson, 850-474-2748. *Application contact:* Terry McCray, Assistant Director of Graduate Admissions, 850-473-7718, Fax: 850-473-7714, E-mail: gradadmissions@uwf.edu.

University of Wisconsin–Madison, School of Medicine and Public Health, Molecular and Environmental Toxicology Center, Madison, WI 53706. Offers MS, PhD. *Faculty:* 71 full-time (22 women), 1 part-time/adjunct (0 women). *Students:* 40 full-time (25 women); includes 5 minority (1 American Indian/Alaska Native, 2 Asian Americans or Pacific Islanders, 2 Hispanic Americans), 10 international. Average age 29. 52 applicants, 29% accepted, 6 enrolled. In 2009, 1 master's, 3 doctorates awarded. Terminal master's awarded for partial completion of doctoral program. *Degree requirements:* For master's, thesis; for doctorate, thesis/dissertation. *Entrance requirements:* For master's and doctorate, bachelor's degree in science-related field. Additional exam requirements/recommendations for international students: Required—TOEFL. *Application deadline:* For fall admission, 12/1 priority date for domestic and international students. Application fee: $56. Electronic applications accepted. *Expenses:* Tuition, state resident: part-time $594 per credit. Tuition, nonresident: part-time $1504 per credit. Required fees: $65 per credit. Tuition and fees vary according to course load, program and reciprocity agreements. *Financial support:* In 2009–10, 6 research assistantships with tuition reimbursements (averaging $22,500 per year) were awarded; fellowships with tuition reimbursements, traineeships, health care benefits, and unspecified assistantships also available. *Faculty research:* Toxicology, cancer, genetics, cell cycle, xenobotic metabolism. *Unit head:* Dr. Christopher Bradfield, Director, 608-262-2024, E-mail: bradfield@oncology.wisc.edu. *Application*

contact: Eileen M. Stevens, Program Administrator, 608-263-4580, Fax: 608-262-5245, E-mail: emstevens@wisc.edu.

Washington University in St. Louis, Graduate School of Arts and Sciences, Division of Biology and Biomedical Sciences, Program in Evolution, Ecology and Population Biology, St. Louis, MO 63130-4899. Offers ecology (PhD); environmental biology (PhD); evolutionary biology (PhD); genetics (PhD). *Degree requirements:* For doctorate, thesis/dissertation. *Entrance requirements:* For doctorate, GRE General Test, GRE Subject Test. Electronic applications accepted.

West Virginia University, Davis College of Agriculture, Forestry and Consumer Sciences, Division of Plant and Soil Sciences, Morgantown, WV 26506. Offers agricultural sciences (PhD), including animal and food sciences, plant and soil sciences; agronomy (MS); entomology (MS); environmental microbiology (MS); horticulture (MS); plant pathology (MS). *Degree requirements:* For master's, thesis. *Entrance requirements:* For master's, GRE, minimum GPA of 2.5. Additional exam requirements/recommendations for international students: Required—TOEFL. *Faculty research:* Water quality, reclamation of disturbed land, crop production, pest control, environmental protection.

West Virginia University, Eberly College of Arts and Sciences, Department of Biology, Morgantown, WV 26506. Offers cell and molecular biology (MS, PhD); environmental and evolutionary biology (MS, PhD); forensic biology (MS, PhD); genomic biology (MS, PhD); neurobiology (MS, PhD). Terminal master's awarded for partial completion of doctoral program. *Degree requirements:* For master's, thesis, final exam; for doctorate, thesis/dissertation, preliminary and final exams. *Entrance requirements:* For master's, GRE General Test, GRE Subject Test, minimum GPA of 3.0; for doctorate, GRE General Test, minimum GPA of 3.0. Additional exam requirements/recommendations for international students: Required—TOEFL. *Faculty research:* Environmental biology, genetic engineering, developmental biology, global change, biodiversity.

Youngstown State University, Graduate School, College of Science, Technology, Engineering and Mathematics, Department of Biological Sciences, Youngstown, OH 44555-0001. Offers environmental biology (MS); molecular biology, microbiology, and genetic (MS); physiology and anatomy (MS). Part-time programs available. *Degree requirements:* For master's, comprehensive exam, thesis, oral review. *Entrance requirements:* For master's, GRE General Test, minimum GPA of 2.7. Additional exam requirements/recommendations for international students: Required—TOEFL. *Faculty research:* Cell biology, neurophysiology, molecular biology, neurobiology, gene regulation.

Evolutionary Biology

Brown University, Graduate School, Division of Biology and Medicine, Program in Ecology and Evolutionary Biology, Providence, RI 02912. Offers PhD. *Degree requirements:* For doctorate, thesis/dissertation, preliminary exam. *Entrance requirements:* For doctorate, GRE General Test, GRE Subject Test. Additional exam requirements/recommendations for international students: Required—TOEFL. Electronic applications accepted. *Faculty research:* Marine ecology, behavioral ecology, population genetics, evolutionary morphology, plant ecology.

Clemson University, Graduate School, College of Agriculture, Forestry and Life Sciences, Department of Biological Sciences, Program in Biological Sciences, Clemson, SC 29634. Offers MS, PhD. *Students:* 38 full-time (21 women), 2 part-time (1 woman); includes 3 minority (2 Asian Americans or Pacific Islanders, 1 Hispanic American), 11 international. Average age 28. 38 applicants, 21% accepted, 6 enrolled. In 2009, 2 master's, 4 doctorates awarded. *Degree requirements:* For master's, thesis optional; for doctorate, comprehensive exam, thesis/dissertation. *Entrance requirements:* For master's and doctorate, GRE General Test. Additional exam requirements/recommendations for international students: Required—TOEFL, IELTS. *Application deadline:* For fall admission, 1/15 for domestic students, 4/15 for international students. Applications are processed on a rolling basis. Application fee: $70 ($80 for international students). Electronic applications accepted. *Expenses:* Tuition, state resident: full-time $8684; part-time $528 per credit hour. Tuition, nonresident: full-time $15,330; part-time $1078 per credit hour. Required fees: $736; $37 per semester. Part-time tuition and fees vary according to course load and program. *Financial support:* In 2009–10, 39 students received support, including 12 fellowships with full and partial tuition reimbursements available (averaging $9,529 per year), 11 research assistantships with partial tuition reimbursements available (averaging $18,008 per year), 28 teaching assistantships with partial tuition reimbursements available (averaging $17,393 per year); career-related internships or fieldwork, institutionally sponsored loans, scholarships/grants, health care benefits, and unspecified assistantships also available. Support available to part-time students. Financial award application deadline: 3/15; financial award applicants required to submit FAFSA. *Unit head:* Dr. Alfred Wheeler, Department Chair, 864-656-1415, Fax: 864-656-0435, E-mail: wheeler@clemson.edu. *Application contact:* Jay Lyn Martin, Coordinator for Graduate Program, 864-656-3587, Fax: 864-656-0435, E-mail: gradbio@clemson.edu.

Columbia University, Graduate School of Arts and Sciences, Division of Natural Sciences, Department of Ecology and Evolutionary Biology, New York, NY 10027. Offers conservation biology (Certificate); ecology and evolutionary biology (PhD); environmental policy (Certificate). *Degree requirements:* For doctorate, one foreign language, thesis/dissertation, teaching experience. *Entrance requirements:* For doctorate, GRE General Test, previous course work in biology. Additional exam requirements/recommendations for international students: Required—TOEFL. Electronic applications accepted. *Faculty research:* Tropical ecology, ethnobotany, global change, systematics.

See Close-Up on page 281.

Cornell University, Graduate School, Graduate Fields of Agriculture and Life Sciences, Field of Ecology and Evolutionary Biology, Ithaca, NY 14853-0001. Offers ecology (PhD), including animal ecology, applied ecology, biogeochemistry, community and ecosystem ecology, limnology, oceanography, physiological ecology, plant ecology, population ecology, theoretical ecology, vertebrate zoology; evolutionary biology (PhD), including ecological genetics, paleobiology, population biology, systematics. *Faculty:* 53 full-time (14 women). *Students:* 57 full-time (43 women); includes 4 minority (2 Asian Americans or Pacific Islanders, 2 Hispanic Americans), 8 international. Average age 29. 99 applicants, 11% accepted, 8 enrolled. In 2009, 12 doctorates awarded. *Degree requirements:* For doctorate, comprehensive exam, thesis/dissertation, 2 semesters of teaching experience. *Entrance requirements:* For doctorate, GRE General Test, GRE Subject Test (biology), 2 letters of recommendation. Additional exam requirements/recommendations for international students: Required—TOEFL (minimum score 550 paper-based; 213 computer-based; 77 iBT). *Application deadline:* For fall admission, 12/15 for domestic students. Application fee: $70. Electronic applications accepted. *Expenses:* Tuition: Full-time $29,500. Required fees: $70. Full-time tuition and fees vary according to degree level, program and student level. *Financial support:* In 2009–10, 56 students received support, including 7 fellowships with full tuition reimbursements available, 1 teaching assistantship with full tuition reimbursement available; research assistantships with full tuition reimbursements available, institutionally sponsored loans, scholarships/grants, health care benefits, tuition waivers (full and partial), and unspecified assistantships also available. Financial award applicants required to submit FAFSA. *Faculty research:* Population and organismal biology,

population and evolutionary genetics, systematics and macroevolution, biochemistry, conservation biology. *Unit head:* Director of Graduate Studies, 607-254-4230. *Application contact:* Graduate Field Assistant, 607-254-4230, E-mail: eeb_grad_req@cornell.edu.

Dartmouth College, Arts and Sciences Graduate Programs, Program in Ecology and Evolutionary Biology, Hanover, NH 03755. Offers PhD. *Faculty:* 16 full-time (3 women). *Students:* 16 full-time (9 women); includes 3 minority (1 American Indian/Alaska Native, 1 Asian American or Pacific Islander, 1 Hispanic American), 1 international. Average age 27. 49 applicants, 16% accepted, 5 enrolled. In 2009, 5 doctorates awarded. *Entrance requirements:* For doctorate, GRE General Test, GRE Subject Test in biology (highly recommended). Additional exam requirements/recommendations for international students: Required—TOEFL. *Application deadline:* For fall admission, 12/1 for domestic students. Application fee: $25. *Financial support:* In 2009–10, 12 students received support, including fellowships (averaging $23,832 per year), research assistantships with full tuition reimbursements available (averaging $23,832 per year), teaching assistantships with full tuition reimbursements available (averaging $23,832 per year); institutionally sponsored loans, traineeships, and unspecified assistantships also available. Financial award applicants required to submit FAFSA. *Unit head:* Dr. Matthew Ayres, 603-646-2788, Fax: 603-646-3488. *Application contact:* Amy Layne, 603-646-3847, Fax: 603-646-3488.

See Close-Up on page 91.

Emory University, Graduate School of Arts and Sciences, Division of Biological and Biomedical Sciences, Program in Population Biology, Ecology and Evolution, Atlanta, GA 30322-1100. Offers PhD. *Faculty:* 29 full-time (4 women). *Students:* 27 full-time (18 women); includes 6 minority (2 Asian Americans or Pacific Islanders, 4 Hispanic Americans), 5 international. Average age 27. 37 applicants, 19% accepted, 5 enrolled. In 2009, 4 doctorates awarded. *Degree requirements:* For doctorate, comprehensive exam, thesis/dissertation. *Entrance requirements:* For doctorate, GRE General Test, minimum GPA of 3.0 in science course work (recommended). Additional exam requirements/recommendations for international students: Required—TOEFL. *Application deadline:* For fall admission, 1/3 for domestic and international students. Application fee: $50. Electronic applications accepted. *Financial support:* In 2009–10, 14 students received support, including 14 fellowships with full tuition reimbursements available (averaging $24,500 per year); institutionally sponsored loans, scholarships/grants, and health care benefits also available. *Faculty research:* Evolution of microbes, infectious disease, the immune system, genetic disease in humans, evolution of behavior. *Unit head:* Dr. Michael Zwick, Director, 404-727-9924, Fax: 404-727-3949, E-mail: mzwick@emory.edu. *Application contact:* Dr. Yun Tao, 404-727-0815, Fax: 404-727-2880, E-mail: ytao3@emory.edu.

Florida State University, The Graduate School, College of Arts and Sciences, Department of Biological Science, Specialization in Ecology and Evolutionary Biology, Tallahassee, FL 32306-4295. Offers MS, PhD. *Faculty:* 24 full-time (9 women). *Students:* 55 full-time (31 women); includes 8 minority (1 American Indian/Alaska Native, 3 Asian Americans or Pacific Islanders, 4 Hispanic Americans), 2 international. 133 applicants, 15% accepted, 16 enrolled. In 2009, 2 doctorates awarded. Terminal master's awarded for partial completion of doctoral program. *Degree requirements:* For master's, comprehensive exam, thesis, teaching experience, seminar presentation; for doctorate, comprehensive exam, thesis/dissertation, teaching experience; seminar presentation. *Entrance requirements:* For master's, GRE General Test (minimum combined score 1100, 500 verbal, 500 quantitative), minimum upper-division GPA of 3.0; for doctorate, GRE General Test (minimum combined score 1100, Verbal 500, Quantitative 500), minimum upper-division GPA of 3.0. Additional exam requirements/recommendations for international students: Required—TOEFL (minimum score 600 paper-based; 250 computer-based; 92 iBT). *Application deadline:* For fall admission, 12/15 for domestic and international students. Application fee: $30. Electronic applications accepted. *Expenses:* Tuition, state resident: full-time $7413. Tuition, nonresident: full-time $22,567. *Financial support:* In 2009–10, 43 students received support, including 4 fellowships with full tuition reimbursements available (averaging $22,000 per year), 13 research assistantships with full tuition reimbursements available (averaging $20,000 per year), 38 teaching assistantships with full tuition reimbursements available (averaging $18,540 per year). Financial award application deadline: 12/15; financial award applicants required to submit FAFSA. *Faculty research:* Ecology and conservation biology, evolution, marine biology, phylogeny and systematics, theoretical, computational and mathematical biology. *Application contact:* Judy Bowers, Coordinator, Graduate Affairs, 850-644-3023, Fax: 850-644-9829, E-mail: gradinfo@bio.fsu.edu.

George Mason University, College of Science, Fairfax, VA 22030. Offers biodefense (MS, PhD); bioinformatics and computational biology (MS, PhD, Certificate); biology (MS, PhD);

Evolutionary Biology

George Mason University (continued)
including bioinformatics (MS), ecology, systematics and evolution (MS), interpretive biology (MS), molecular and cellular biology (MS), molecular and microbiology (PhD), organismal biology (MS); chemistry and biochemistry (MS), including chemistry; climate dynamics (PhD); computational and data sciences (MS, PhD, Certificate); computational social science (PhD); computational techniques and applications (Certificate); earth systems and geoinformation sciences (MS, PhD, Certificate); environmental science and policy (MS, PhD); geography (MS), including geographic and cartographic sciences; mathematical sciences (MS, PhD), including mathematics; nanotechnology and nanoscience (Certificate); neuroscience (PhD); physical sciences (PhD); physics and astronomy (MS), including applied and engineering physics; remote sensing and earth image processing (Certificate). Part-time and evening/weekend programs available. *Degree requirements:* For doctorate, comprehensive exam, thesis/dissertation. *Entrance requirements:* For master's and doctorate, GRE General Test, minimum GPA of 3.0 in last 60 hours. Additional exam requirements/recommendations for international students: Required—TOEFL. Electronic applications accepted. *Expenses:* Tuition, state resident: full-time $7568; part-time $315.33 per credit hour. Tuition, nonresident: full-time $21,704; part-time $904.33 per credit hour. Required fees: $2184; $91 per credit hour. *Faculty research:* Space sciences and astrophysics, fluid dynamics, materials modeling and simulation, bioinformatics, global changes and statistics.

Harvard University, Graduate School of Arts and Sciences, Department of Organismic and Evolutionary Biology, Cambridge, MA 02138. Offers biology (PhD). *Degree requirements:* For doctorate, 2 foreign languages, public presentation of thesis research, exam. *Entrance requirements:* For doctorate, GRE General Test, GRE Subject Test (recommended), 7 courses in biology, chemistry, physics, mathematics, computer science, or geology. Additional exam requirements/recommendations for international students: Required—TOEFL. *Expenses:* Tuition: Full-time $33,696. Required fees: $1126. Full-time tuition and fees vary according to program.

Illinois State University, Graduate School, College of Arts and Sciences, Department of Biological Sciences, Normal, IL 61790-2200. Offers animal behavior (MS); bacteriology (MS); biochemistry (MS); biological sciences (MS); biology (PhD); biophysics (MS); biotechnology (MS); botany (MS, PhD); cell biology (MS); conservation biology (MS); developmental biology (MS); ecology (MS, PhD); entomology (MS); evolutionary biology (MS); genetics (MS, PhD); immunology (MS); microbiology (MS, PhD); molecular biology (MS); molecular genetics (MS); neurobiology (MS); neuroscience (MS); parasitology (MS); physiology (MS, PhD); plant biology (MS); plant molecular biology (MS); plant sciences (MS); structural biology (MS); zoology (MS, PhD). Part-time programs available. *Degree requirements:* For master's, thesis or alternative; for doctorate, variable foreign language requirement, thesis/dissertation, 2 terms of residency. *Entrance requirements:* For master's, GRE General Test, minimum GPA of 2.6 in last 60 hours of course work; for doctorate, GRE General Test. *Faculty research:* Redoc balance and drug development in schistosoma mansoni, control of the growth of listeria monocytogenes at low temperature, regulation of cell expansion and microtubule function by SPRI, CRUI: physiology and fitness consequences of different life history phenotypes.

Indiana University Bloomington, University Graduate School, College of Arts and Sciences, Department of Biology, Bloomington, IN 47405. Offers biology teaching (MAT); biotechnology (MA); evolution, ecology, and behavior (MA, PhD); genetics (PhD); microbiology (MA, PhD); molecular, cellular, and developmental biology (PhD); plant sciences (MA, PhD); zoology (MA, PhD). *Faculty:* 58 full-time (15 women), 21 part-time/adjunct (6 women). *Students:* 165 full-time (95 women); includes 14 minority (6 African Americans, 1 American Indian/Alaska Native, 7 Asian Americans or Pacific Islanders), 56 international. Average age 27. 312 applicants, 19% accepted, 24 enrolled. In 2009, 4 master's, 22 doctorates awarded. Terminal master's awarded for partial completion of doctoral program. *Degree requirements:* For master's, thesis, oral defense; for doctorate, thesis/dissertation, oral defense. *Entrance requirements:* For master's and doctorate, GRE General Test. Additional exam requirements/recommendations for international students: Required—TOEFL (minimum score 100 iBT). *Application deadline:* For fall admission, 1/5 priority date for domestic students, 12/1 priority date for international students. Application fee: $55 ($65 for international students). Electronic applications accepted. *Financial support:* In 2009–10, 165 students received support, including 62 fellowships with tuition reimbursements available (averaging $19,484 per year), 27 research assistantships with tuition reimbursements available (averaging $22,605 per year), 76 teaching assistantships with tuition reimbursements available (averaging $20,528 per year); scholarships/grants, traineeships, health care benefits, and unspecified assistantships also available. Financial award application deadline: 1/5. *Faculty research:* Evolution, ecology and behavior; microbiology; molecular biology and genetics; plant biology. *Unit head:* Dr. Roger Innes, Chair, 812-855-2219, Fax: 812-855-6082, E-mail: rinnes@indiana.edu. *Application contact:* Tracey D. Stohr, Graduate Student Recruitment Coordinator, 812-856-6303, Fax: 812-855-6082, E-mail: gradbio@indiana.edu.

Iowa State University of Science and Technology, Graduate College, College of Liberal Arts and Sciences, Department of Ecology, Evolution, and Organismal Biology, Ames, IA 50011. Offers MS, PhD. *Faculty:* 28 full-time (9 women), 2 part-time/adjunct (1 woman). *Degree requirements:* For master's, thesis or alternative; for doctorate, thesis/dissertation. *Entrance requirements:* For master's and doctorate, GRE General Test. Additional exam requirements/recommendations for international students: Required—TOEFL. Application fee: $40 ($90 for international students). Electronic applications accepted. *Expenses:* Tuition, state resident: full-time $6716. Tuition, nonresident: full-time $8908. Tuition and fees vary according to course level, course load, program and student level. *Financial support:* Fellowships, research assistantships with partial tuition reimbursements, teaching assistantships with partial tuition reimbursements, scholarships/grants, health care benefits, and unspecified assistantships available. *Faculty research:* Aquatic and wetland ecology, cytology, ecology, physiology and molecular biology, systematics and evolution. *Unit head:* Dr. Jonathan Wendel, Chair, 515-294-7172. *Application contact:* Information Contact, 515-294-5836, Fax: 515-294-2592, E-mail: grad_admissions@iastate.edu.

Iowa State University of Science and Technology, Graduate College, Interdisciplinary Programs, Program in Ecology and Evolutionary Biology, Ames, IA 50011. Offers MS, PhD. *Students:* 51 full-time (24 women), 3 part-time (1 woman); includes 4 minority (1 American Indian/Alaska Native, 1 Asian American or Pacific Islander, 2 Hispanic Americans), 9 international. In 2009, 5 master's, 5 doctorates awarded. *Degree requirements:* For master's, thesis or alternative; for doctorate, thesis/dissertation. *Entrance requirements:* For master's and doctorate, GRE General Test, application to cooperating department. Additional exam requirements/recommendations for international students: Required—TOEFL (minimum score 550 paper-based; 79 iBT) or IELTS (minimum score 6.5). *Application deadline:* For fall admission, 1/1 priority date for domestic and international students. Application fee: $40 ($90 for international students). Electronic applications accepted. *Expenses:* Tuition, state resident: full-time $6716. Tuition, nonresident: full-time $8908. Tuition and fees vary according to course level, course load, program and student level. *Financial support:* In 2009–10, 33 research assistantships with full and partial tuition reimbursements (averaging $16,750 per year), 16 teaching assistantships with full and partial tuition reimbursements (averaging $16,750 per year) were awarded; scholarships/grants, health care benefits, and unspecified assistantships also available. *Faculty research:* Landscape ecology, aquatic and method ecology, physiological ecology, population genetics and evolution, systematics. *Unit head:* Dr. Kirk Moloney, Supervisory Committee Chair, 515-294-6518, E-mail: eeboffice@iastate.edu. *Application contact:* Charles Sauer, Information Contact, 515-294-6518, E-mail: eeboffice@iastate.edu.

The Johns Hopkins University, School of Medicine, Graduate Programs in Medicine, Center for Functional Anatomy and Evolution, Baltimore, MD 21218-2699. Offers PhD. *Faculty:* 5 full-time (1 woman), 2 part-time/adjunct (1 woman). *Students:* 9 full-time (6 women). Average age 25. 26 applicants, 15% accepted, 2 enrolled. In 2009, 2 doctorates awarded. *Degree requirements:* For doctorate, comprehensive exam, thesis/dissertation, oral exams. *Entrance requirements:* For doctorate, GRE. Additional exam requirements/recommendations for international students: Required—TOEFL. *Application deadline:* For fall admission, 1/10 for domestic and international students. Application fee: $85. *Financial support:* In 2009–10, 1 fellowship with partial tuition reimbursement (averaging $30,000 per year), 8 teaching assistantships with full tuition reimbursements (averaging $26,855 per year) were awarded; career-related internships or fieldwork, institutionally sponsored loans, health care benefits, and tuition waivers (full) also available. *Faculty research:* Vertebrate evolution, functional anatomy, primate evolution, vertebrate paleobiology, vertebrate morphology. *Unit head:* Dr. Kenneth D. Rose, Director, 410-955-7172, Fax: 410-614-9030, E-mail: kdrose@jhmi.edu. *Application contact:* Catherine L. Will, Coordinator, Graduate Student Affairs, 410-614-3385, E-mail: grad_study@som.adm.jhu.edu.

Marquette University, Graduate School, College of Arts and Sciences, Department of Biology, Milwaukee, WI 53201-1881. Offers cell biology (MS, PhD); developmental biology (MS, PhD); ecology (MS, PhD); endocrinology (MS, PhD); evolutionary biology (MS, PhD); genetics (MS, PhD); microbiology (MS, PhD); molecular biology (MS, PhD); muscle and exercise physiology (MS, PhD); neurobiology (MS, PhD); reproductive physiology (MS, PhD). *Faculty:* 23 full-time (10 women), 1 part-time/adjunct (0 women). *Students:* 23 full-time (13 women), 16 part-time (9 women); includes 1 minority (Asian American or Pacific Islander), 20 international. Average age 25. 95 applicants, 16% accepted, 10 enrolled. In 2009, 3 master's, 5 doctorates awarded. Terminal master's awarded for partial completion of doctoral program. *Degree requirements:* For master's, comprehensive exam, thesis, 1 year of teaching experience or equivalent; for doctorate, thesis/dissertation, 1 year of teaching experience or equivalent, qualifying exam. *Entrance requirements:* For master's and doctorate, GRE General Test, GRE Subject Test. Additional exam requirements/recommendations for international students: Required—TOEFL. Application fee: $40. *Financial support:* In 2009–10, 4 fellowships, 22 teaching assistantships were awarded; research assistantships, Federal Work-Study, institutionally sponsored loans, scholarships/grants, and tuition waivers (full and partial) also available. Support available to part-time students. Financial award application deadline: 2/15. *Faculty research:* Microbial and invertebrate ecology, evolution of gene function, DNA methylation, DNA arrangement. *Unit head:* Dr. Robert Fitts, Chair, 414-288-1748, Fax: 414-288-7357. *Application contact:* Debbie Weaver, Administrative Assistant, 414-288-7355, Fax: 414-288-7357.

Michigan State University, The Graduate School, College of Natural Science, Interdepartmental Program in Ecology, Evolutionary Biology and Behavior, East Lansing, MI 48824. Offers PhD. *Faculty:* 98 full-time (23 women). *Students:* 81 full-time (43 women), 6 part-time (1 woman); includes 5 minority (3 Asian Americans or Pacific Islanders, 2 Hispanic Americans), 11 international. Average age 29. *Entrance requirements:* Additional exam requirements/recommendations for international students: Required—TOEFL. Electronic applications accepted. *Expenses:* Tuition, state resident: part-time $478.25 per credit hour. Tuition, nonresident: part-time $966.50 per credit hour. Part-time tuition and fees vary according to program. *Financial support:* In 2009–10, 1 research assistantship with tuition reimbursement (averaging $6,379 per year) was awarded. *Unit head:* Dr. Kay E. Holekamp, Director, 517-432-1359, E-mail: holekamp@msu.edu. *Application contact:* Patricia Resler, Program Secretary, 517-432-1359, E-mail: eebb@msu.edu.

Northwestern University, Northwestern University Feinberg School of Medicine and Interdepartmental Programs, Integrated Graduate Programs in the Life Sciences, Chicago, IL 60611. Offers cancer biology (PhD); cell biology (PhD); developmental biology (PhD); evolutionary biology (PhD); immunology and microbial pathogenesis (PhD); molecular biology and genetics (PhD); neurobiology (PhD); pharmacology and toxicology (PhD); structural biology and biochemistry (PhD). *Degree requirements:* For doctorate, comprehensive exam, thesis/dissertation, written and oral qualifying exams. *Entrance requirements:* For doctorate, GRE General Test. Additional exam requirements/recommendations for international students: Required—TOEFL (minimum score 600 paper-based; 250 computer-based). Electronic applications accepted.

The Ohio State University, Graduate School, College of Biological Sciences, Department of Evolution, Ecology, and Organismal Biology, Columbus, OH 43210. Offers MS, PhD. *Faculty:* 43. *Students:* 19 full-time (13 women), 38 part-time (20 women); includes 2 minority (1 African American, 1 Hispanic American), 7 international. Average age 27. In 2009, 2 master's, 13 doctorates awarded. *Degree requirements:* For master's, thesis optional; for doctorate, thesis/dissertation. *Entrance requirements:* For master's and doctorate, GRE General Test. Additional exam requirements/recommendations for international students: Required—TOEFL (minimum score 600 paper-based; 250 computer-based). *Application deadline:* For fall admission, 8/15 priority date for domestic students, 7/1 priority date for international students; for winter admission, 12/1 priority date for domestic students, 11/1 priority date for international students; for spring admission, 3/1 priority date for domestic students, 2/1 priority date for international students. Applications are processed on a rolling basis. Application fee: $40 ($50 for international students). Electronic applications accepted. *Expenses:* Tuition, state resident: full-time $10,683. Tuition, nonresident: full-time $25,923. Tuition and fees vary according to course load and program. *Financial support:* Fellowships, research assistantships, teaching assistantships, Federal Work-Study and institutionally sponsored loans available. Support available to part-time students. *Unit head:* H. Lisle Gibbs, Graduate Studies Committee Chair, 614-292-8088, Fax: 614-292-2030, E-mail: gibbs.128@osu.edu. *Application contact:* 614-292-9444, Fax: 614-292-3895, E-mail: domestic.grad@osu.edu.

Ohio University, Graduate College, College of Arts and Sciences, Department of Biological Sciences, Athens, OH 45701-2979. Offers biological sciences (MS, PhD); cell biology and physiology (MS, PhD); ecology and evolutionary biology (MS, PhD); exercise physiology and muscle biology (MS, PhD); microbiology (MS, PhD); neuroscience (MS, PhD). *Faculty:* 50 full-time (14 women), 6 part-time/adjunct (1 woman). *Students:* 44 full-time (19 women), 8 part-time (3 women); includes 2 minority (1 African American, 1 Hispanic American), 21 international. 95 applicants, 24% accepted, 10 enrolled. In 2009, 4 master's, 9 doctorates awarded. Terminal master's awarded for partial completion of doctoral program. *Degree requirements:* For master's, comprehensive exam, thesis, 1 quarter of teaching experience; for doctorate, comprehensive exam, thesis/dissertation, 2 quarters of teaching experience. *Entrance requirements:* For master's, GRE General Test, names of three faculty members whose research interests most closely match the applicant's interest; for doctorate, GRE General Test, essay concerning prior training, research interest and career goals, plus names of three faculty members whose research interests most closely match the applicant's interest. Additional exam requirements/recommendations for international students: Required—TOEFL (minimum score 620 paper-based; 105 iBT) or IELTS (minimum score 7.5). *Application deadline:* For fall admission, 1/15 for domestic and international students. Application fee: $50 ($55 for international students). Electronic applications accepted. *Expenses:* Tuition, state resident: full-time $7839; part-time $323 per quarter hour. Tuition, nonresident: full-time $15,831; part-time $654 per quarter hour. Required fees: $2931. *Financial support:* In 2009–10, 1 fellowship with full tuition reimbursement (averaging $18,957 per year), 10 research assistantships with full tuition reimbursements (averaging $18,957 per year), 42 teaching assistantships with full tuition reimbursements (averaging $18,957 per year) were awarded; Federal Work-Study and institutionally sponsored loans also available. Financial award application deadline: 1/15. *Faculty research:* Ecology and evolutionary biology, exercise physiology and muscle biology, neurobiology, cell biology, physiology. Total annual research expenditures: $2.8 million. *Unit head:* Dr. Ralph DiCaprio, Chair, 740-593-2290, Fax: 740-593-0300, E-mail: dicaprir@ohio.edu. *Application contact:* Dr. Donald Holzschu, Graduate Chair, 740-593-0425, Fax: 740-593-0300, E-mail: holzschu@ohio.edu.

Princeton University, Graduate School, Department of Ecology and Evolutionary Biology, Princeton, NJ 08544-1019. Offers PhD. *Degree requirements:* For doctorate, thesis/dissertation. *Entrance requirements:* For doctorate, GRE General Test, GRE Subject Test. Additional exam requirements/recommendations for international students: Required—TOEFL (minimum score 600 paper-based; 250 computer-based). Electronic applications accepted.

Purdue University, Graduate School, College of Science, Department of Biological Sciences, West Lafayette, IN 47907. Offers biochemistry (PhD); biophysics (PhD); cell and developmental biology (PhD); ecology, evolutionary and population biology (MS, PhD), including ecology, evolutionary biology, population biology; genetics (MS, PhD); microbiology (MS, PhD); molecular biology (PhD); neurobiology (MS, PhD); plant physiology (PhD). Terminal master's awarded for partial completion of doctoral program. *Degree requirements:* For master's, thesis (for some programs); for doctorate, thesis/dissertation, seminars, teaching experience. *Entrance requirements:* For master's and doctorate, GRE General Test. Additional exam requirements/recommendations for international students: Required—TOEFL. Electronic applications accepted.

Rice University, Graduate Programs, Wiess School of Natural Sciences, Department of Ecology and Evolutionary Biology, Houston, TX 77251-1892. Offers MA, MS, PhD. Terminal master's awarded for partial completion of doctoral program. *Degree requirements:* For master's, comprehensive exam (for some programs), thesis (for some programs); for doctorate, comprehensive exam, thesis/dissertation. *Entrance requirements:* For master's and doctorate, GRE General Test, GRE Subject Test. Additional exam requirements/recommendations for international students: Required—TOEFL (minimum score 600 paper-based; 250 computer-based; 90 iBT). Electronic applications accepted. *Faculty research:* Trace gas emissions, wetlands, biology, community ecology of forests and grasslands, conservation biology specialization.

Rutgers, The State University of New Jersey, New Brunswick, Graduate School-New Brunswick, Program in Ecology and Evolution, Piscataway, NJ 08854-8097. Offers MS, PhD. Part-time programs available. Terminal master's awarded for partial completion of doctoral program. *Degree requirements:* For master's, comprehensive exam; for doctorate, comprehensive exam, thesis/dissertation. *Entrance requirements:* For master's and doctorate, GRE General Test, minimum GPA of 3.0. Additional exam requirements/recommendations for international students: Required—TOEFL (minimum score 550 paper-based; 213 computer-based). Electronic applications accepted. *Faculty research:* Population and community ecology, population genetics, evolutionary biology, conservation biology, ecosystem ecology.

Rutgers, The State University of New Jersey, New Brunswick, Graduate School-New Brunswick, Program in Plant Biology, Piscataway, NJ 08854-8097. Offers horticulture and plant technology (MS, PhD); molecular and cellular biology (MS, PhD); organismal and population biology (MS, PhD); plant pathology (MS, PhD). Part-time programs available. Terminal master's awarded for partial completion of doctoral program. *Degree requirements:* For master's, comprehensive exam, thesis or alternative; for doctorate, comprehensive exam, thesis/dissertation. *Entrance requirements:* For master's and doctorate, GRE General Test, GRE Subject Test (recommended). Additional exam requirements/recommendations for international students: Required—TOEFL (minimum score 600 paper-based; 250 computer-based). Electronic applications accepted. *Faculty research:* Molecular biology and biochemistry of plants, plant development and genomics, plant protection, plant improvement, plant management of horticultural and field crops.

Stony Brook University, State University of New York, Graduate School, College of Arts and Sciences, Department of Ecology and Evolution, Stony Brook, NY 11794. Offers applied ecology (MA); ecology and evolution (PhD). *Faculty:* 18 full-time (5 women), 1 part-time/adjunct (0 women). *Students:* 50 full-time (27 women); includes 7 minority (3 Asian Americans or Pacific Islanders, 4 Hispanic Americans), 9 international. Average age 28. 91 applicants, 32% accepted. In 2009, 4 doctorates awarded. *Degree requirements:* For doctorate, one foreign language, comprehensive exam, thesis/dissertation, teaching experience. *Entrance requirements:* For doctorate, GRE General Test, GRE Subject Test. Additional exam requirements/recommendations for international students: Required—TOEFL. *Application deadline:* For fall admission, 1/15 for domestic students. Application fee: $60. *Expenses:* Tuition, state resident: full-time $8370; part-time $349 per credit. Tuition, nonresident: full-time $13,250; part-time $552 per credit. Required fees: $933. *Financial support:* In 2009–10, 7 research assistantships, 35 teaching assistantships were awarded; fellowships, Federal Work-Study also available. *Faculty research:* Theoretical and experimental population genetics, numerical taxonomy, biostatistics, population and community ecology, plant ecology. Total annual research expenditures: $985,740. *Unit head:* Dr. Jessica Gurevitch, Chair, 631-632-8600. *Application contact:* Dr. Dan Dykhuizen, Director, 631-246-8604, E-mail: dandyk@life.bio.sunysb.edu.

Tulane University, School of Science and Engineering, Department of Ecology and Evolutionary Biology, New Orleans, LA 70118-5669. Offers MS, PhD. Terminal master's awarded for partial completion of doctoral program. *Degree requirements:* For master's, thesis or alternative; for doctorate, thesis/dissertation. *Entrance requirements:* For master's, GRE General Test, minimum B average in undergraduate course work; for doctorate, GRE General Test. Additional exam requirements/recommendations for international students: Required—TOEFL. Electronic applications accepted. *Faculty research:* Ichthyology, plant systematics, crustacean endocrinology, ecotoxicology, ornithology.

University at Albany, State University of New York, College of Arts and Sciences, Department of Biological Sciences, Specialization in Ecology, Evolution, and Behavior, Albany, NY 12222-0001. Offers MS, PhD. *Degree requirements:* For master's, one foreign language; for doctorate, one foreign language, thesis/dissertation. *Entrance requirements:* For master's and doctorate, GRE General Test.

University at Buffalo, the State University of New York, Graduate School, College of Arts and Sciences, Program in Evolution, Ecology and Behavior, Buffalo, NY 14260. Offers MS, PhD, Certificate. *Faculty:* 12 full-time (2 women). *Students:* 14 full-time (9 women), 1 (woman) part-time; includes 1 minority (Hispanic American), 1 international. Average age 28. 34 applicants, 47% accepted, 6 enrolled. In 2009, 4 master's, 1 doctorate awarded. Terminal master's awarded for partial completion of doctoral program. *Degree requirements:* For master's, project; for doctorate, comprehensive exam, thesis/dissertation. *Entrance requirements:* For master's, GRE, minimum undergraduate GPA of 3.0; for doctorate, GRE, minimum GPA of 3.0. Additional exam requirements/recommendations for international students: Required—TOEFL (minimum score 79 iBT). *Application deadline:* For fall admission, 1/15 priority date for domestic and international students. Applications are processed on a rolling basis. Application fee: $75. Electronic applications accepted. *Financial support:* In 2009–10, 2 fellowships with full tuition reimbursements (averaging $23,000 per year), 3 research assistantships with full tuition reimbursements (averaging $20,000 per year), 4 teaching assistantships with full tuition reimbursements (averaging $17,000 per year) were awarded; Federal Work-Study, scholarships/grants, health care benefits, and unspecified assistantships also available. Financial award application deadline: 1/15; financial award applicants required to submit FAFSA. *Faculty research:* Coral reef ecology, evolution and ecology of aquatic invertebrates, animal communication, paleobiology, primate behavior. *Unit head:* Dr. Howard Lasker, Program Director, 716-645-4870, Fax: 716-645-3999, E-mail: ub-evb@buffalo.edu. *Application contact:* Marty Roth, Secretary 1, 716-645-3489, Fax: 716-345-3999, E-mail: mlroth@buffalo.edu.

University of Alberta, Faculty of Graduate Studies and Research, Department of Biological Sciences, Edmonton, AB T6G 2E1, Canada. Offers environmental biology and ecology (M Sc, PhD); microbiology and biotechnology (M Sc, PhD); molecular biology and genetics (M Sc, PhD); physiology and cell biology (M Sc, PhD); plant biology (M Sc, PhD); systematics and evolution (M Sc, PhD). *Faculty:* 72 full-time (15 women), 15 part-time/adjunct (4 women). *Students:* 238 full-time (117 women), 32 part-time (15 women), 31 international. 206 applicants, 42% accepted. In 2009, 29 master's, 31 doctorates awarded. Terminal master's awarded for partial completion of doctoral program. *Degree requirements:* For master's, thesis; for doctorate, thesis/dissertation. *Entrance requirements:* Additional exam requirements/recommendations for international students: Required—TOEFL. *Application deadline:* For fall admission, 3/1 priority date for domestic students. Applications are processed on a rolling basis. Application fee: $0. Tuition and fees charges are reported in Canadian dollars. *Expenses:* Tuition, area resident: Full-time $4626 Canadian dollars; part-time $99.72 Canadian dollars per unit. International tuition: $8216 Canadian dollars full-time. Required fees: $3590 Canadian dollars; $99.72 Canadian dollars per unit. $215 Canadian dollars per term. *Financial support:* In 2009–10, 4 research assistantships with partial tuition reimbursements (averaging $12,000 per

year), 103 teaching assistantships with partial tuition reimbursements (averaging $12,300 per year) were awarded; career-related internships or fieldwork and scholarships/grants also available. *Unit head:* Laura Frost, Chair, 780-492-1904. *Application contact:* Dr. John P. Chang, Associate Chair for Graduate Studies, 780-492-1257, Fax: 780-492-9457, E-mail: bio.grad.coordinator@ualberta.ca.

The University of Arizona, Graduate College, College of Science, Department of Ecology and Evolutionary Biology, Tucson, AZ 85721. Offers MS, PhD. *Faculty:* 21. *Students:* 18 full-time (8 women), 50 part-time (31 women); includes 4 minority (1 African American, 1 American Indian/Alaska Native, 1 Asian American or Pacific Islander, 1 Hispanic American), 10 international. Average age 31. 87 applicants, 15% accepted, 9 enrolled. In 2009, 3 master's, 5 doctorates awarded. Terminal master's awarded for partial completion of doctoral program. *Degree requirements:* For master's, thesis optional; for doctorate, one foreign language, comprehensive exam, thesis/dissertation. *Entrance requirements:* For master's, GRE General Test, GRE Subject Test, statement of purpose, curriculum vitae, 3 letters of recommendation; for doctorate, GRE General Test, GRE Subject Test, curriculum vitae, 3 letters of recommendation. Additional exam requirements/recommendations for international students: Required—TOEFL (minimum score 550 paper-based; 213 computer-based; 79 iBT). *Application deadline:* For fall admission, 12/8 for domestic and international students. Application fee: $75. *Expenses:* Tuition, state resident: full-time $9028. Tuition, nonresident: full-time $24,890. *Financial support:* In 2009–10, 4 research assistantships with full tuition reimbursements (averaging $16,483 per year), 17 teaching assistantships with full tuition reimbursements (averaging $16,557 per year) were awarded; career-related internships or fieldwork, scholarships/grants, health care benefits, and unspecified assistantships also available. *Faculty research:* Biological diversity, evolutionary history, evolutionary mechanisms, community structure. Total annual research expenditures: $4.5 million. *Unit head:* Dr. Richard E. Michod, Head, 520-621-7509, Fax: 520-621-9190, E-mail: michod@email.arizona.edu. *Application contact:* Carol Burleson, Administrative Associate, 520-621-1165, Fax: 520-621-9190, E-mail: burleson@email.arizona.edu.

University of California, Davis, Graduate Studies, Graduate Group in Population Biology, Davis, CA 95616. Offers PhD. *Degree requirements:* For doctorate, thesis/dissertation. *Entrance requirements:* For doctorate, GRE General Test, GRE Subject Test. Additional exam requirements/recommendations for international students: Required—TOEFL (minimum score 550 paper-based; 213 computer-based). Electronic applications accepted. *Faculty research:* Population ecology, population genetics, systematics, evolution, community ecology.

University of California, Irvine, Office of Graduate Studies, School of Biological Sciences, Department of Ecology and Evolutionary Biology, Irvine, CA 92697. Offers biological sciences (MS, PhD). *Students:* 43 full-time (30 women); includes 3 minority (all Hispanic Americans), 6 international. Average age 27. 38 applicants, 26% accepted, 5 enrolled. In 2009, 4 master's, 7 doctorates awarded. *Degree requirements:* For master's, thesis; for doctorate, thesis/dissertation. *Entrance requirements:* For master's and doctorate, GRE General Test, GRE Subject Test, minimum GPA of 3.0. Additional exam requirements/recommendations for international students: Required—TOEFL (minimum score 550 paper-based; 213 computer-based). *Application deadline:* For fall admission, 1/15 priority date for domestic students, 1/15 for international students. Applications are processed on a rolling basis. Application fee: $70 ($90 for international students). Electronic applications accepted. *Financial support:* Fellowships, research assistantships with full tuition reimbursements, teaching assistantships, career-related internships or fieldwork, institutionally sponsored loans, traineeships, health care benefits, and unspecified assistantships available. Financial award application deadline: 3/1; financial award applicants required to submit FAFSA. *Faculty research:* Ecological energetics, quantitative genetics, life history evolution, plant-herbivore and plant-pollinator interactions, molecular evolution. *Unit head:* Albert F. Bennett, Chair, 949-824-6930, E-mail: abennett@uci.edu. *Application contact:* Pam McDonald, Administrative Assistant, 949-824-4743, E-mail: pmcdonal@uci.edu.

University of California, Los Angeles, Graduate Division, College of Letters and Science, Department of Ecology and Evolutionary Biology, Los Angeles, CA 90095. Offers MA, PhD. *Faculty:* 26 full-time (8 women), 8 part-time/adjunct (1 woman). *Students:* 64 full-time (39 women); includes 8 minority (1 African American, 1 American Indian/Alaska Native, 3 Asian Americans or Pacific Islanders, 3 Hispanic Americans), 9 international. Average age 29. 88 applicants, 19% accepted, 13 enrolled. In 2009, 5 master's, 16 doctorates awarded. Terminal master's awarded for partial completion of doctoral program. *Degree requirements:* For master's, comprehensive exam or thesis; for doctorate, thesis/dissertation, oral and written qualifying exams; teaching experience. *Entrance requirements:* For master's and doctorate, GRE General Test, GRE Subject Test (biology), minimum GPA of 3.0, 3 letters of recommendation. *Application deadline:* For fall admission, 12/1 for domestic and international students. Application fee: $70 ($90 for international students). Electronic applications accepted. *Financial support:* In 2009–10, 61 fellowships with full and partial tuition reimbursements, 18 research assistantships with full and partial tuition reimbursements, 42 teaching assistantships with full and partial tuition reimbursements were awarded; Federal Work-Study, institutionally sponsored loans, scholarships/grants, health care benefits, tuition waivers (full and partial), and unspecified assistantships also available. Financial award application deadline: 3/1; financial award applicants required to submit FAFSA. *Faculty research:* Molecular, cell, and developmental biology; interactive biology; organisms and populations. *Unit head:* Victoria Sork, Chair, 310-825-7755, Fax: 310-206-0484, E-mail: vlsork@ucla.edu. *Application contact:* Department Office, 310-825-1959, Fax: 310-206-5280, E-mail: eebgrad@eeb.ucla.edu.

University of California, Riverside, Graduate Division, Department of Biology, Riverside, CA 92521-0102. Offers biology (MS, PhD); evolution, ecology and organismal biology (MS, PhD). Department also affiliated with following interdepartmental graduate programs: Cell, Molecular, and Developmental Biology; Evolution and Ecology; Genetics. Terminal master's awarded for partial completion of doctoral program. *Degree requirements:* For master's, oral defense of thesis; for doctorate, thesis/dissertation, 3 quarters of teaching experience, qualifying exams. *Entrance requirements:* For master's and doctorate, GRE General Test, minimum GPA of 3.2. Additional exam requirements/recommendations for international students: Required—TOEFL (minimum score 550 paper-based; 213 computer-based; 80 iBT). Electronic applications accepted. *Faculty research:* Molecular genetics, neurophysiology, evolutionary biology, physiology and organismal biology, signal transduction.

University of California, San Diego, Office of Graduate Studies, Division of Biological Sciences, Program in Ecology, Behavior, and Evolution, La Jolla, CA 92093. Offers PhD. *Degree requirements:* For doctorate, thesis/dissertation, qualifying exam. Electronic applications accepted.

University of California, Santa Barbara, Graduate Division, College of Letters and Sciences, Division of Mathematics, Life, and Physical Sciences, Department of Ecology, Evolution, and Marine Biology, Santa Barbara, CA 93106-9620. Offers computational science and engineering (PhD); MA/PhD. *Faculty:* 39 full-time (8 women). *Students:* 56 full-time (35 women). Average age 30. 135 applicants, 13% accepted, 7 enrolled. In 2009, 7 master's, 15 doctorates awarded. Terminal master's awarded for partial completion of doctoral program. *Degree requirements:* For master's, comprehensive exam (for some programs), thesis (for some programs); for doctorate, comprehensive exam, thesis/dissertation. *Entrance requirements:* For master's, GRE General Test, 3 letters of recommendation, resume/curriculum vitae; for doctorate, GRE General Test, 3 letters of recommendation, statement of purpose, personal achievements/contributions statement, resume/curriculum vitae, transcripts for post-secondary institutions attended. Additional exam requirements/recommendations for international students: Required—TOEFL (minimum score 550 paper-based; 213 computer-based; 80 iBT) or IELTS. *Application deadline:* For fall admission, 12/15 for domestic and international students. Application fee: $70 ($90 for international students). Electronic applications accepted. *Financial support:* In 2009–10, 54 students received support, including 26 fellowships with full and partial tuition reimbursements available (averaging $17,900 per year), 16 research assistantships with full and partial tuition reimbursements available (averaging $7,300 per year), 35 teaching assistant-

Evolutionary Biology

University of California, Santa Barbara (continued)
ships with partial tuition reimbursements available (averaging $9,100 per year); Federal Work-Study, institutionally sponsored loans, scholarships/grants, traineeships, health care benefits, tuition waivers (full and partial), and unspecified assistantships also available. Financial award applicants required to submit FAFSA. *Faculty research:* Ecology, population genetics, stream ecology, evolution, marine biology. *Unit head:* Robert Warner, Chair, 805-893-2415, Fax: 805-893-4724, E-mail: eembchair@lifesci.ucsb.edu. *Application contact:* Alina Haas, Staff Graduate Advisor, 805-893-3023, Fax: 805-893-5885, E-mail: haas@lifesci.ucsb.edu.

University of California, Santa Cruz, Division of Graduate Studies, Division of Physical and Biological Sciences, Department of Ecology and Evolutionary Biology, Santa Cruz, CA 95064. Offers MA, PhD. *Degree requirements:* For master's, thesis; for doctorate, thesis/dissertation. *Entrance requirements:* For master's and doctorate, GRE General Test, GRE Subject Test, 3 letters of recommendation. Additional exam requirements/recommendations for international students: Required—TOEFL (minimum score 550 paper-based); Recommended—IELTS. Electronic applications accepted.

University of Chicago, Division of the Biological Sciences, Darwinian Sciences Cluster: Ecological, Integrative and Evolutionary Biology, Committee on Evolutionary Biology, Chicago, IL 60637-1513. Offers functional and evolutionary biology (PhD). *Faculty:* 49 full-time (7 women). *Students:* 29 full-time (12 women); includes 2 minority (both African Americans), 2 international. Average age 29. 16 applicants, 31% accepted, 4 enrolled. In 2009, 8 doctorates awarded. Terminal master's awarded for partial completion of doctoral program. *Degree requirements:* For doctorate, thesis/dissertation, ethics class, 2 teaching assistantships. *Entrance requirements:* For doctorate, GRE General Test. Additional exam requirements/recommendations for international students: Required—TOEFL (minimum score 600 paper-based; 250 computer-based; 104 iBT), IELTS (minimum score 7). *Application deadline:* For fall admission, 12/1 priority date for domestic and international students. Application fee: $55. Electronic applications accepted. *Financial support:* In 2009–10, 29 students received support, including fellowships with tuition reimbursements available (averaging $29,781 per year), research assistantships (averaging $29,781 per year); institutionally sponsored loans, scholarships/grants, traineeships, and health care benefits also available. Financial award applicants required to submit FAFSA. *Faculty research:* Systematics and evolutionary theory, genetics, functional morphology and physiology, behavior, ecology and biogeography. *Unit head:* Dr. Michael Coates, Chairman, 773-834-8417, Fax: 773-702-4699, E-mail: mcoates@uchicago.edu. *Application contact:* Carolyn Johnson, Graduate Administrative Director, 773-702-9474, Fax: 773-702-4699, E-mail: csjohnso@uchicago.edu.

University of Colorado at Boulder, Graduate School, College of Arts and Sciences, Department of Ecology and Evolutionary Biology, Boulder, CO 80309. Offers animal behavior (MA); biology (MA, PhD); environmental biology (MA, PhD); evolutionary biology (MA, PhD); neurobiology (MA); population biology (MA); population genetics (PhD). *Faculty:* 32 full-time (10 women). *Students:* 64 full-time (36 women), 15 part-time (9 women); includes 12 minority (1 American Indian/Alaska Native, 3 Asian Americans or Pacific Islanders, 8 Hispanic Americans), 4 international. Average age 29. 145 applicants, 14% accepted, 21 enrolled. In 2009, 9 master's, 6 doctorates awarded. Terminal master's awarded for partial completion of doctoral program. *Degree requirements:* For master's, comprehensive exam, thesis or alternative; for doctorate, comprehensive exam, thesis/dissertation. *Entrance requirements:* For master's, GRE General Test, GRE Subject Test, minimum undergraduate GPA of 3.0; for doctorate, GRE General Test, GRE Subject Test. *Application deadline:* For fall admission, 12/30 priority date for domestic students, 12/1 for international students. Application fee: $50 ($60 for international students). *Financial support:* In 2009–10, 25 fellowships (averaging $17,876 per year), 27 research assistantships (averaging $15,070 per year) were awarded; Federal Work-Study, institutionally sponsored loans, and tuition waivers (full) also available. *Faculty research:* Behavior, ecology, genetics, morphology, endocrinology, physiology, systematics. Total annual research expenditures: $3.1 million.

University of Delaware, College of Arts and Sciences, Department of Biological Sciences, Newark, DE 19716. Offers biotechnology (MS); cancer biology (MS, PhD); cell and extra-cellular matrix biology (MS, PhD); cell and systems physiology (MS, PhD); developmental biology (MS, PhD); ecology and evolution (MS, PhD); microbiology (MS, PhD); molecular biology and genetics (MS, PhD). Terminal master's awarded for partial completion of doctoral program. *Degree requirements:* For master's, thesis, preliminary exam; for doctorate, comprehensive exam, thesis/dissertation, preliminary exam. *Entrance requirements:* For master's and doctorate, GRE General Test. Additional exam requirements/recommendations for international students: Required—TOEFL (minimum score 600 paper-based; 250 computer-based); Recommended—TWE. Electronic applications accepted. *Faculty research:* Microorganisms, bone, cancer metastasis, developmental biology, cell biology, DNA.

University of Guelph, Graduate Program Services, College of Biological Science, Department of Integrative Biology, Botany and Zoology, Guelph, ON N1G 2W1, Canada. Offers botany (M Sc, PhD); zoology (M Sc, PhD). Part-time programs available. *Degree requirements:* For master's, thesis, research proposal; for doctorate, thesis/dissertation, research proposal, qualifying exam. *Entrance requirements:* For master's, minimum B average during previous 2 years of course work. Additional exam requirements/recommendations for international students: Required—TOEFL (minimum score 550 paper-based; 213 computer-based), IELTS (minimum score 6.5). Electronic applications accepted. *Faculty research:* Aquatic science, environmental physiology, parasitology, wildlife biology, management.

University of Hawaii at Manoa, Graduate Division, Interdisciplinary Specialization in Ecology, Evolution and Conservation Biology, Honolulu, HI 96822. Offers MS, PhD. *Degree requirements:* For doctorate, thesis/dissertation. *Expenses:* Tuition, state resident: full-time $8900; part-time $372 per credit. Tuition, nonresident: full-time $21,400; part-time $898 per credit. Required fees: $207 per semester. *Faculty research:* Agronomy and soil science, zoology, entomology, genetics and molecular biology, botanical sciences.

University of Illinois at Urbana–Champaign, Graduate College, College of Liberal Arts and Sciences, School of Integrative Biology, Department of Animal Biology, Champaign, IL 61820. Offers animal biology (ecology, ethology and evolution) (MS, PhD). *Faculty:* 10 full-time (5 women). *Students:* 10 full-time (6 women), 4 part-time (2 women); includes 1 minority (Asian American or Pacific Islander), 3 international. 13 applicants, 15% accepted, 1 enrolled. In 2009, 1 doctorate awarded. *Entrance requirements:* For master's and doctorate, GRE. Additional exam requirements/recommendations for international students: Required—TOEFL (minimum score 570 paper-based; 230 computer-based; 88 iBT). *Application deadline:* Applications are processed on a rolling basis. Application fee: $60 ($75 for international students). Electronic applications accepted. *Financial support:* In 2009–10, 2 fellowships, 3 research assistantships, 11 teaching assistantships were awarded; tuition waivers (full and partial) also available. *Unit head:* Ken Paige, Head, 217-244-6606, Fax: 217-244-4565, E-mail: k-paige@illinois.edu. *Application contact:* Kathy Jennings, Office Support Specialist, 217-333-7801, Fax: 217-244-4565, E-mail: ab@life.uiuc.edu.

University of Illinois at Urbana–Champaign, Graduate College, College of Liberal Arts and Sciences, School of Integrative Biology, Program in Ecology, Evolution and Conservation Biology, Champaign, IL 61820. Offers MS, PhD. *Students:* 25 full-time (14 women), 10 part-time (8 women); includes 4 minority (1 African American, 2 Asian Americans or Pacific Islanders, 1 Hispanic American), 2 international. 40 applicants, 23% accepted, 6 enrolled. In 2009, 1 master's, 4 doctorates awarded. *Entrance requirements:* For master's and doctorate, GRE. Additional exam requirements/recommendations for international students: Required—TOEFL (minimum score 613 paper-based; 257 computer-based; 103 iBT). *Application deadline:* Applications are processed on a rolling basis. Application fee: $60 ($75 for international students). Electronic applications accepted. *Financial support:* In 2009–10, 9 fellowships, 19 research assistantships, 15 teaching assistantships were awarded; tuition waivers (full and partial) also available. *Unit head:* Carla E. Caceres, Director, 217-244-2139, Fax: 217-244-1224, E-mail: cecacere@illinois.edu. *Application contact:* Carol Hall, Secretary, 217-333-8208, Fax: 217-244-1224, E-mail: cahall@illinois.edu.

The University of Iowa, Graduate College, College of Liberal Arts and Sciences, Department of Biology, Iowa City, IA 52242-1316. Offers biology (MS, PhD); cell and developmental biology (MS, PhD); evolution (MS, PhD); genetics (MS, PhD); neurobiology (MS, PhD); plant biology (MS, PhD). Terminal master's awarded for partial completion of doctoral program. *Degree requirements:* For master's, thesis optional, exam; for doctorate, comprehensive exam, thesis/dissertation. *Entrance requirements:* For master's and doctorate, GRE General Test, minimum GPA of 3.0. Additional exam requirements/recommendations for international students: Required—TOEFL (minimum score 600 paper-based; 250 computer-based; 100 iBT). Electronic applications accepted. *Faculty research:* Developmental neurobiology, evolutionary biology, signal transduction, cell motility, molecular genetics (plant and animal).

The University of Kansas, Graduate Studies, College of Liberal Arts and Sciences, Department of Ecology and Evolutionary Biology, Lawrence, KS 66045. Offers botany (MA, PhD); ecology and evolutionary biology (MA, PhD); entomology (MA, PhD). *Faculty:* 17 full-time (7 women), 29 part-time/adjunct (6 women). *Students:* 57 full-time (24 women), 4 part-time (1 woman); includes 1 minority (Hispanic American), 16 international. Average age 29. 49 applicants, 33% accepted, 8 enrolled. In 2009, 5 master's, 8 doctorates awarded. Terminal master's awarded for partial completion of doctoral program. *Degree requirements:* For master's, comprehensive exam, thesis (for some programs), 30-36 credits, thesis presentation; for doctorate, comprehensive exam, thesis/dissertation, residency, foreign language or other research skills, final exam and dissertation defense. *Entrance requirements:* For master's, GRE General Test, bachelor's degree with minimum undergraduate GPA of 3.0; for doctorate, GRE General Test, bachelor's degree; minimum undergraduate/graduate GPA of 3.0. Additional exam requirements/recommendations for international students: Required—TOEFL, IELTS. *Application deadline:* For fall admission, 12/15 priority date for domestic and international students. Applications are processed on a rolling basis. Application fee: $45 ($55 for international students). Electronic applications accepted. *Expenses:* Tuition, state resident: full-time $6492; part-time $270.50 per credit hour. Tuition, nonresident: full-time $15,510; part-time $646.25 per credit hour. Required fees: $847; $70.56 per credit hour. Tuition and fees vary according to course load and program. *Financial support:* Fellowships with tuition reimbursements, research assistantships with full and partial tuition reimbursements, teaching assistantships with full and partial tuition reimbursements, scholarships/grants, traineeships, health care benefits, and unspecified assistantships available. *Faculty research:* Biodiversity and macroevolution, ecology and global change, evolutionary mechanisms. *Unit head:* Dr. Christopher H. Haufler, Chair, 785-864-3255, Fax: 785-864-5860, E-mail: vulgare@ku.edu. *Application contact:* Jaime Rochelle Keeler, Graduate Coordinator, 785-864-2362, Fax: 785-864-5860, E-mail: jrkeeler@ku.edu.

University of Louisiana at Lafayette, College of Sciences, Department of Biology, Lafayette, LA 70504. Offers biology (MS); environmental and evolutionary biology (PhD). Terminal master's awarded for partial completion of doctoral program. *Degree requirements:* For master's, thesis; for doctorate, 2 foreign languages, comprehensive exam, thesis/dissertation. *Entrance requirements:* For master's, GRE General Test, minimum GPA of 2.75; for doctorate, GRE General Test, GRE Subject Test, minimum GPA of 3.0. Additional exam requirements/recommendations for international students: Required—TOEFL (minimum score 550 paper-based; 213 computer-based). Electronic applications accepted. *Faculty research:* Structure and ultrastructure, system biology, ecology, processes, environmental physiology.

University of Maryland, College Park, Academic Affairs, College of Chemical and Life Sciences, Department of Biology, Behavior, Ecology, Evolution, and Systematics Program, College Park, MD 20742. Offers MS, PhD. *Students:* 34 full-time (20 women), 1 part-time (0 women); includes 2 minority (both Asian Americans or Pacific Islanders), 2 international. 47 applicants, 9% accepted, 4 enrolled. In 2009, 1 master's, 7 doctorates awarded. *Degree requirements:* For master's, thesis, oral defense, seminar; for doctorate, thesis/dissertation, exam, 4 seminars. *Entrance requirements:* For master's and doctorate, GRE General Test, GRE Subject Test (biology), 3 letters of recommendation. Additional exam requirements/recommendations for international students: Required—TOEFL. *Application deadline:* For fall admission, 12/1 for domestic and international students. Applications are processed on a rolling basis. Application fee: $60. Electronic applications accepted. *Expenses:* Tuition, area resident: Part-time $471 per credit hour. Tuition, state resident: part-time $471 per credit hour. Tuition, nonresident: part-time $1016 per credit hour. Required fees: $337.04 per term. *Financial support:* In 2009–10, 6 fellowships with full and partial tuition reimbursements (averaging $13,373 per year), 4 research assistantships with tuition reimbursements (averaging $19,418 per year), 18 teaching assistantships with tuition reimbursements (averaging $19,479 per year) were awarded; Federal Work-Study and scholarships/grants also available. Support available to part-time students. Financial award applicants required to submit FAFSA. *Faculty research:* Animal behavior, biostatistics, ecology, evolution, neurothology. *Unit head:* Dr. Michele Dudash, Director, 301-405-1642, Fax: 301-314-9358, E-mail: mdudash@umd.edu. *Application contact:* Dean of Graduate School, 301-405-0358, Fax: 301-314-9305.

University of Massachusetts Amherst, Graduate School, Interdisciplinary Programs, Program in Organismic and Evolutionary Biology, Amherst, MA 01003. Offers animal behavior (PhD); ecology (PhD); evolutionary biology (PhD); organismal biology (PhD); organismic and evolutionary biology (MS). Part-time programs available. *Faculty:* 2 full-time (1 woman). *Students:* 33 full-time (21 women), 3 part-time (0 women); includes 2 minority (both Hispanic Americans), 6 international. Average age 27. 53 applicants, 15% accepted, 5 enrolled. In 2009, 2 master's, 4 doctorates awarded. Terminal master's awarded for partial completion of doctoral program. *Degree requirements:* For master's, thesis or alternative; for doctorate, comprehensive exam, thesis/dissertation. *Entrance requirements:* For master's and doctorate, GRE General Test, 3 letters of recommendation. Additional exam requirements/recommendations for international students: Required—TOEFL (minimum score 550 paper-based; 213 computer-based; 80 iBT), IELTS (minimum score 6.5). *Application deadline:* For fall admission, 12/1 for domestic and international students. Applications are processed on a rolling basis. Application fee: $50 ($65 for international students). Electronic applications accepted. *Expenses:* Tuition, state resident: full-time $2640; part-time $110 per credit. Tuition, nonresident: full-time $9936; part-time $414 per credit. Tuition and fees vary according to course load. *Financial support:* Fellowships, research assistantships, teaching assistantships, career-related internships or fieldwork, Federal Work-Study, scholarships/grants, traineeships, health care benefits, tuition waivers (full), and unspecified assistantships available. Support available to part-time students. Financial award application deadline: 12/1. *Unit head:* Dr. Elizabeth M. Jakob, Graduate Program Director, 413-545-0928, Fax: 413-545-3243. *Application contact:* Jean M. Ames, Supervisor of Admissions, 413-545-0722, Fax: 413-577-0010, E-mail: gradadm@grad.umass.edu.

University of Massachusetts Amherst, Graduate School, Interdisciplinary Programs, Program in Plant Biology, Amherst, MA 01003. Offers biochemistry and metabolism (MS, PhD); cell biology and physiology (MS, PhD); environmental, ecological and integrative (MS, PhD); genetics and evolution (MS, PhD). *Students:* 3 full-time (2 women), 12 part-time (5 women); includes 2 minority (both Asian Americans or Pacific Islanders), 8 international. Average age 27. 32 applicants, 41% accepted, 3 enrolled. In 2009, 3 master's, 1 doctorate awarded. *Degree requirements:* For master's, thesis; for doctorate, 2 foreign languages, comprehensive exam, thesis/dissertation. *Entrance requirements:* For master's and doctorate, GRE General Test. Additional exam requirements/recommendations for international students: Required—TOEFL (minimum score 550 paper-based; 213 computer-based; 80 iBT), IELTS (minimum score 6.5). *Application deadline:* For fall admission, 12/15 for domestic and international students; for spring admission, 10/1 for domestic and international students. Applications are processed on a rolling basis. Application fee: $50 ($65 for international students). Electronic applications accepted. *Expenses:* Tuition, state resident: full-time $2640; part-time $110 per credit. Tuition, nonresident: full-time $9936; part-time $414 per credit. Tuition and fees vary according to course load. *Financial support:* In 2009–10, 11 research assistantships with full tuition reimbursements (averaging $8,884 per year) were awarded; fellowships, teaching assistantships, career-related internships or fieldwork, Federal Work-Study, scholarships/

grants, traineeships, health care benefits, tuition waivers (full), and unspecified assistantships also available. Support available to part-time students. Financial award application deadline: 12/15. *Unit head:* Dr. Elsbeth L. Walker, Graduate Program Director, 413-577-3217, Fax: 413-545-3243. *Application contact:* Jean M. Ames, Supervisor of Admissions, 413-545—0722, Fax: 413-577-0010, E-mail: gradadm@grad.umass.edu.

University of Miami, Graduate School, College of Arts and Sciences, Department of Biology, Coral Gables, FL 33124. Offers biology (MS, PhD); genetics and evolution (MS, PhD). Terminal master's awarded for partial completion of doctoral program. *Degree requirements:* For master's, comprehensive exam (for some programs), thesis (for some programs); for doctorate, thesis/dissertation, oral and written qualifying exam. *Entrance requirements:* For master's, GRE General Test, 3 letters of recommendation, research papers; for doctorate, GRE General Test, 3 letters of recommendation, research papers, sponsor letter. Additional exam requirements/recommendations for international students: Required—TOEFL (minimum score 550 paper-based; 213 computer-based; 59 iBT). Electronic applications accepted. *Faculty research:* Neuroscience to ethology; plants, vertebrates and mycorrhizae; phylogenies, life histories and species interactions; molecular biology, gene expression and populations; cells, auditory neurons and vertebrate locomotion.

University of Michigan, Horace H. Rackham School of Graduate Studies, College of Literature, Science, and the Arts, Department of Ecology and Evolutionary Biology, Ann Arbor, MI 48109. Offers ecology and evolutionary biology (MS, PhD); ecology and evolutionary biology-Frontiers (MS). Part-time programs available. *Faculty:* 47 full-time (13 women). *Students:* 67 full-time (40 women); includes 11 minority (3 African Americans, 1 American Indian/Alaska Native, 5 Asian Americans or Pacific Islanders, 2 Hispanic Americans), 20 international. Average age 28. 107 applicants, 25% accepted, 7 enrolled. In 2009, 6 master's, 5 doctorates awarded. Terminal master's awarded for partial completion of doctoral program. *Degree requirements:* For master's, thesis (for some programs), two seminars; for doctorate, comprehensive exam, thesis/dissertation, 2 semesters of teaching. *Entrance requirements:* For master's and doctorate, GRE. Additional exam requirements/recommendations for international students: Required—TOEFL (minimum score 560 paper-based; 220 computer-based; 84 iBT). *Application deadline:* For fall admission, 12/1 priority date for domestic and international students; for winter admission, 10/15 priority date for domestic and international students. Applications are processed on a rolling basis. Application fee: $65 ($75 for international students). Electronic applications accepted. *Expenses:* Tuition, state resident: full-time $17,286; part-time $1099 per credit hour. Tuition, nonresident: full-time $34,944; part-time $2080 per credit hour. Required fees: $95 per semester. Tuition and fees vary according to course load, degree level and program. *Financial support:* In 2009–10, 60 students received support, including 18 fellowships with full tuition reimbursements available (averaging $21,944 per year), 8 research assistantships with full tuition reimbursements available (averaging $21,944 per year), 34 teaching assistantships with full tuition reimbursements available (averaging $21,944 per year); scholarships/grants, traineeships, health care benefits, and unspecified assistantships also available. Financial award applicants required to submit FAFSA. *Faculty research:* Community ecology, molecular evolution, theoretical ecology, systematics, evolutionary genetics. Total annual research expenditures: $3.1 million. *Unit head:* Deborah Goldberg, Chair, 734-615-4912, Fax: 734-763-0544. *Application contact:* Jane Sullivan, Graduate Coordinator, 734-615-7338, Fax: 734-763-0544, E-mail: eeb.gradcoord@umich.edu.

University of Minnesota, Twin Cities Campus, Graduate School, College of Biological Sciences, Department of Ecology, Evolution, and Behavior, Minneapolis, MN 55455-0213. Offers ecology, evolution, and behavior (MS, PhD). Terminal master's awarded for partial completion of doctoral program. *Degree requirements:* For master's, comprehensive exam, thesis or projects; for doctorate, comprehensive exam, thesis/dissertation. *Entrance requirements:* For master's and doctorate, GRE General Test, minimum GPA of 3.0. Additional exam requirements/recommendations for international students: Required—TOEFL (minimum score 550 paper-based; 213 computer-based), Michigan English Language Assessment Battery. Electronic applications accepted. *Faculty research:* Behavioral ecology, community ecology, community genetics, ecosystem and global change, evolution and systematics.

University of Missouri, Graduate School, College of Arts and Sciences, Division of Biological Sciences, Program in Evolutionary Biology and Ecology, Columbia, MO 65211. Offers MA, PhD.

University of Missouri–St. Louis, College of Arts and Sciences, Department of Biology, St. Louis, MO 63121. Offers biology (MS, PhD), including animal behavior (MS), biochemistry, biochemistry and biotechnology (MS), biotechnology (MS), conservation biology (MS), development (MS), ecology (MS), environmental studies (PhD), evolution (MS), genetics (MS), molecular biology and biochemistry (PhD), molecular/cellular biology (MS), physiology (MS), plant systematics, population biology (MS), tropical biology (MS); biotechnology (Certificate); tropical biology and conservation (Certificate). Part-time programs available. *Faculty:* 43 full-time (13 women), 2 part-time/adjunct (1 woman). *Students:* 54 full-time (27 women), 79 part-time (43 women); includes 15 minority (6 African Americans, 7 Asian Americans or Pacific Islanders, 2 Hispanic Americans), 47 international. Average age 29. 193 applicants, 44% accepted, 44 enrolled. In 2009, 30 master's, 7 doctorates, 9 other advanced degrees awarded. *Degree requirements:* For master's, thesis or alternative; for doctorate, thesis/dissertation, 1 semester of teaching experience. *Entrance requirements:* For master's, 3 letters of recommendation; for doctorate, GRE General Test, 3 letters of recommendation. Additional exam requirements/recommendations for international students: Required—TOEFL. *Application deadline:* For fall admission, 12/1 priority date for domestic and international students; for spring admission, 10/15 priority date for domestic and international students. Applications are processed on a rolling basis. Application fee: $35 ($40 for international students). Electronic applications accepted. *Expenses:* Tuition, state resident: full-time $5377; part-time $297.70 per credit hour. Tuition, nonresident: full-time $13,882; part-time $771.20 per credit hour. Required fees: $220; $12.20 per credit hour. One-time fee: $12. Tuition and fees vary according to course level, campus/location and program. *Financial support:* In 2009–10, 22 research assistantships with full and partial tuition reimbursements (averaging $16,300 per year), 14 teaching assistantships with full and partial tuition reimbursements (averaging $16,727 per year) were awarded; fellowships with full tuition reimbursements, career-related internships or fieldwork and Federal Work-Study also available. Support available to part-time students. Financial award application deadline: 2/1. *Faculty research:* Molecular biology, microbial genetics, animal behavior, tropical ecology, plant systematics. *Unit head:* Dr. Elizabeth Kellogg, Director of Graduate Studies, 314-516-6200, Fax: 314-516-6233, E-mail: tkellogg@umsl.edu. *Application contact:* 314-516-5458, Fax: 314-516-6996, E-mail: gradadm@umsl.edu.

University of Nevada, Reno, Graduate School, Interdisciplinary Program in Ecology, Evolution, and Conservation Biology, Reno, NV 89557. Offers PhD. Offered through the College of Arts and Science, the M. C. Fleischmann College of Agriculture, and the Desert Research Institute. *Degree requirements:* For doctorate, thesis/dissertation. *Entrance requirements:* For doctorate, GRE General Test, GRE Subject Test, minimum GPA of 3.0. Additional exam requirements/recommendations for international students: Required—TOEFL (minimum score 500 paper-based; 173 computer-based; 61 iBT), IELTS (minimum score 6). Electronic applications accepted. *Faculty research:* Population biology, behavioral ecology, plant response to climate change, conservation of endangered species, restoration of natural ecosystems.

The University of North Carolina at Chapel Hill, Graduate School, College of Arts and Sciences, Department of Biology, Chapel Hill, NC 27599. Offers botany (MA, MS, PhD); cell biology, development, and physiology (MA, MS, PhD); cell motility and cytoskeleton (PhD); ecology and behavior (MA, MS, PhD); genetics and molecular biology (MA, MS, PhD); morphology, systematics, and evolution (MA, MS, PhD). Terminal master's awarded for partial completion of doctoral program. *Degree requirements:* For master's, comprehensive exam, thesis (for some programs); for doctorate, comprehensive exam, thesis/dissertation. *Entrance requirements:* For master's, GRE General Test, GRE Subject Test, 2 semesters of calculus or statistics; 2 semesters of physics, organic chemistry; 3 semesters of biology; for doctorate, GRE General Test, GRE Subject Test, 2 semesters calculus or statistics, 2 semesters physics, organic chemistry, 3 semesters of biology. Additional exam requirements/recommendations for international students: Required—TOEFL (minimum score 550 paper-based; 213 computer-based). Electronic applications accepted. *Faculty research:* Gene expression, biomechanics, yeast genetics, plant ecology, plant molecular biology.

University of Notre Dame, Graduate School, College of Science, Department of Biological Sciences, Notre Dame, IN 46556. Offers aquatic ecology, evolution and environmental biology (MS, PhD); cellular and molecular biology (MS, PhD); genetics (MS, PhD); physiology (MS, PhD); vector biology and parasitology (MS, PhD). Terminal master's awarded for partial completion of doctoral program. *Degree requirements:* For master's, comprehensive exam, thesis; for doctorate, comprehensive exam, thesis/dissertation, candidacy exam. *Entrance requirements:* For master's and doctorate, GRE General Test. Additional exam requirements/recommendations for international students: Required—TOEFL (minimum score 600 paper-based; 250 computer-based; 80 iBT). Electronic applications accepted. *Faculty research:* Tropical disease, molecular genetics, neurobiology, evolutionary biology, aquatic biology.

University of Oklahoma, Graduate College, College of Arts and Sciences, Department of Botany and Microbiology, Program in Ecology and Evolutionary Biology, Norman, OK 73019. Offers PhD. *Students:* 5 full-time (3 women), all international. 7 applicants, 71% accepted, 2 enrolled. *Entrance requirements:* Additional exam requirements/recommendations for international students: Required—TOEFL (minimum score 550 paper-based; 213 computer-based). *Application deadline:* For fall admission, 4/1 for domestic and international students; for spring admission, 11/1 for domestic students, 9/1 for international students. Applications are processed on a rolling basis. Application fee: $40 ($90 for international students). Electronic applications accepted. *Expenses:* Tuition, state resident: full-time $3744; part-time $156 per credit hour. Tuition, nonresident: full-time $13,577; part-time $565.70 per credit hour. Required fees: $2415; $90.10 per credit hour. *Financial support:* Federal Work-Study, institutionally sponsored loans, scholarships/grants, health care benefits, and unspecified assistantships available. Support available to part-time students. *Faculty research:* Global change biology, plant physiological ecology, bioremediation, soil ecosystems, community structure. *Unit head:* Dr. Gordon Uno, Chair, 405-325-4321, Fax: 405-325-7619, E-mail: guno@ou.edu. *Application contact:* Adell Hopper, Staff Assistant, 405-325-4322, Fax: 405-325-7619, E-mail: ahopper@ou.edu.

University of Oklahoma, Graduate College, College of Arts and Sciences, Department of Zoology, Program in Ecology and Evolutionary Biology, Norman, OK 73019. Offers PhD. *Students:* 12 full-time (7 women), 1 part-time (0 women), 4 international. 7 applicants, 71% accepted, 1 enrolled. In 2009, 1 doctorate awarded. *Entrance requirements:* Additional exam requirements/recommendations for international students: Required—TOEFL (minimum score 550 paper-based; 213 computer-based). *Application deadline:* For fall admission, 12/15 for domestic students, 4/1 for international students; for spring admission, 10/1 for domestic students, 9/1 for international students. Applications are processed on a rolling basis. Application fee: $40 ($90 for international students). Electronic applications accepted. *Expenses:* Tuition, state resident: full-time $3744; part-time $156 per credit hour. Tuition, nonresident: full-time $13,577; part-time $565.70 per credit hour. Required fees: $2415; $90.10 per credit hour. *Financial support:* Federal Work-Study, institutionally sponsored loans, scholarships/grants, health care benefits, and unspecified assistantships available. Support available to part-time students. *Faculty research:* Behavioral ecology, community ecology, molecular ecology, population ecology, systematics. *Unit head:* Don Wilson, Assistant Chair, 405-325-4821, Fax: 405-325-6202, E-mail: dwilson@ou.edu. *Application contact:* Michael Kaspari, Professor/Director, 405-325-3371, Fax: 405-325-6202, E-mail: zoologygrad@ou.edu.

University of Oregon, Graduate School, College of Arts and Sciences, Department of Biology, Eugene, OR 97403. Offers ecology and evolution (MA, MS, PhD); marine biology (MA, MS, PhD); molecular, cellular and genetic biology (PhD); neuroscience and development (PhD). Terminal master's awarded for partial completion of doctoral program. *Degree requirements:* For master's, thesis (for some programs); for doctorate, thesis/dissertation. *Entrance requirements:* For master's and doctorate, GRE General Test, minimum GPA of 3.2. Additional exam requirements/recommendations for international students: Required—TOEFL. *Faculty research:* Developmental neurobiology; evolution, population biology, and quantitative genetics; regulation of gene expression; biochemistry of marine organisms.

University of Pittsburgh, School of Arts and Sciences, Department of Biological Sciences, Program in Ecology and Evolution, Pittsburgh, PA 15260. Offers PhD. *Faculty:* 7 full-time (2 women). *Students:* 14 full-time (5 women); includes 3 minority (1 Asian American or Pacific Islander, 2 Hispanic Americans), 1 international. Average age 23. 40 applicants, 18% accepted, 4 enrolled. In 2009, 1 doctorate awarded. *Degree requirements:* For doctorate, comprehensive exam, thesis/dissertation, completion of research integrity module. *Entrance requirements:* For doctorate, GRE General Test, GRE Subject Test. Additional exam requirements/recommendations for international students: Required—TOEFL (minimum score 550 paper-based; 213 computer-based). *Application deadline:* For fall admission, 1/15 priority date for domestic students, 12/15 priority date for international students. Applications are processed on a rolling basis. Application fee: $0 ($50 for international students). Electronic applications accepted. *Expenses:* Tuition, state resident: full-time $16,402; part-time $665 per credit. Tuition, nonresident: full-time $28,694; part-time $1175 per credit. Required fees: $690; $175 per term. Tuition and fees vary according to program. *Financial support:* In 2009–10, 12 fellowships with full tuition reimbursements (averaging $27,379 per year), 6 research assistantships with full tuition reimbursements (averaging $24,608 per year), 20 teaching assistantships with full tuition reimbursements (averaging $23,385 per year) were awarded; Federal Work-Study, scholarships/grants, traineeships, health care benefits, and tuition waivers (full) also available. *Faculty research:* Ecological and population genetics, tropical and community ecology, evolutionary ecology, phylogeny of birds, evolution of dispersal and dormancy. *Unit head:* Dr. Gerard L. Campbell, Associate Professor, 412-624-6812, Fax: 412-624-4759, E-mail: camp@pitt.edu. *Application contact:* Cathleen M. Barr, Graduate Administrator, 412-624-4268, Fax: 412-624-4759, E-mail: cbarr@pitt.edu.

University of Puerto Rico, Río Piedras, College of Natural Sciences, Department of Biology, San Juan, PR 00931-3300. Offers ecology/systematics (MS, PhD); evolution/genetics (MS, PhD); molecular/cellular biology (MS, PhD); neuroscience (MS, PhD). Part-time programs available. *Degree requirements:* For master's, one foreign language, comprehensive exam, thesis; for doctorate, one foreign language, comprehensive exam, thesis/dissertation. *Entrance requirements:* For master's, GRE Subject Test, interview, minimum GPA of 3.0, letter of recommendation; for doctorate, GRE Subject Test, interview, master's degree, minimum GPA of 3.0, letter of recommendation. *Faculty research:* Environmental, poblational and systematic biology.

University of South Carolina, The Graduate School, College of Arts and Sciences, Department of Biological Sciences, Graduate Training Program in Ecology, Evolution, and Organismal Biology, Columbia, SC 29208. Offers MS, PhD. *Degree requirements:* For master's, one foreign language, comprehensive exam, thesis; for doctorate, one foreign language, comprehensive exam, thesis/dissertation. *Entrance requirements:* For master's and doctorate, GRE General Test, minimum GPA of 3.0 in science. Additional exam requirements/recommendations for international students: Required—TOEFL (minimum score 570 paper-based; 230 computer-based). Electronic applications accepted.

University of Southern California, Graduate School, College of Letters, Arts and Sciences, Department of Biological Sciences, Program in Integrative and Evolutionary Biology, Los Angeles, CA 90089. Offers PhD. *Faculty:* 25 full-time (6 women), 3 part-time/adjunct (0 women). *Students:* 17 full-time (9 women), 1 part-time (0 women); includes 3 minority (2 Asian Americans or Pacific Islanders, 1 Hispanic American), 6 international. 23 applicants, 22% accepted, 2 enrolled.Terminal master's awarded for partial completion of doctoral program. *Degree requirements:* For doctorate, thesis/dissertation, qualifying examination, dissertation defense. *Entrance requirements:* For doctorate, GRE, 3 letters of recommendation, personal

Evolutionary Biology

University of Southern California (continued)
statement, resume, minimum GPA of 3.0. Additional exam requirements/recommendations for international students: Required—TOEFL (minimum score 600 paper-based; 250 computer-based; 100 iBT). *Application deadline:* For fall admission, 12/1 priority date for domestic and international students. Application fee: $85. Electronic applications accepted. *Expenses:* Tuition: Full-time $25,980; part-time $1315 per unit. Required fees: $554. One-time fee: $35 full-time. Full-time tuition and fees vary according to degree level and program. *Financial support:* In 2009–10, 12 students received support, including 3 fellowships with full tuition reimbursements available (averaging $25,333 per year), 1 research assistantship with full tuition reimbursement available (averaging $25,333 per year), 8 teaching assistantships with full tuition reimbursements available (averaging $25,333 per year); scholarships/grants, traineeships, health care benefits, and tuition waivers also available. *Unit head:* Dr. Jill L. McNitt-Gray, Professor of Kinesiology, Biological Sciences, and Biomedical Engineering/Director, 213-740-7902, E-mail: mcnitt@usc.edu. *Application contact:* Adolfo dela Rosa, Student Services Advisor I, 213-821-3164, Fax: 213-740-1380, E-mail: adolfode@usc.edu.

The University of Tennessee, Graduate School, College of Arts and Sciences, Department of Ecology and Evolutionary Biology, Knoxville, TN 37996. Offers behavior (MS, PhD); ecology (MS, PhD); evolutionary biology (MS, PhD). Part-time programs available. *Degree requirements:* For master's, thesis; for doctorate, thesis/dissertation. *Entrance requirements:* For master's and doctorate, GRE General Test, minimum GPA of 2.7. Additional exam requirements/recommendations for international students: Required—TOEFL. Electronic applications accepted. *Expenses:* Tuition, state resident: full-time $6826; part-time $380 per semester hour. Tuition, nonresident: full-time $21,844; part-time $1147 per semester hour. Tuition and fees vary according to program.

The University of Texas at Austin, Graduate School, College of Natural Sciences, School of Biological Sciences, Program in Ecology, Evolution and Behavior, Austin, TX 78712-1111. Offers MA, PhD. *Entrance requirements:* For doctorate, GRE General Test. Additional exam requirements/recommendations for international students: Required—TOEFL. Electronic applications accepted.

University of Toronto, School of Graduate Studies, Life Sciences Division, Department of Ecology and Evolutionary Biology, Toronto, ON M5S 1A1, Canada. Offers M Sc, PhD. *Degree requirements:* For master's, thesis, thesis defense; for doctorate, thesis/dissertation, thesis defense. *Entrance requirements:* For master's, minimum B average in last 2 years; knowledge of physics, chemistry, and biology.

Virginia Polytechnic Institute and State University, Graduate School, College of Science, Department of Biological Sciences, Blacksburg, VA 24061. Offers botany (MS, PhD); ecology and evolutionary biology (MS, PhD); genetics and developmental biology (MS, PhD); microbiology (MS, PhD); zoology (MS, PhD). *Faculty:* 42 full-time (11 women). *Students:* 76 full-time (45 women), 5 part-time (1 woman); includes 28 minority (23 American Indian/Alaska Native, 2 Asian Americans or Pacific Islanders, 3 Hispanic Americans). Average age 28. 117 applicants, 15% accepted, 15 enrolled. In 2009, 11 master's, 11 doctorates awarded. *Entrance requirements:* For master's and doctorate, GRE, GMAT. Additional exam requirements/recommendations for international students: Required—TOEFL (minimum score 550 paper-based; 213 computer-based). *Application deadline:* For fall admission, 5/15 for international students; for spring admission, 10/15 for international students. Applications are processed on a rolling basis. Application fee: $65. Electronic applications accepted. *Expenses:* Tuition, area resident: Full-time $10,228; part-time $459 per credit hour. Tuition, nonresident: full-time $17,892; part-time $865 per credit hour. Required fees: $1966; $451 per semester. *Financial support:* In 2009–10, 37 research assistantships with full tuition reimbursements (averaging $17,929 per year), 41 teaching assistantships with full tuition reimbursements (averaging $17,344 per year) were awarded; career-related internships or fieldwork, Federal Work-Study, scholarships/grants, and unspecified assistantships also available. Financial award application deadline: 1/15. *Faculty research:* Freshwater ecology, cell cycle regulation, behavioral ecology, motor proteins. Total annual research expenditures: $4.8 million. *Unit head:* Dr. Bob H. Jones, Dean, 540-231-9514, Fax: 540-231-9307, E-mail: rhjones@vt.edu. *Application contact:* Erik Nilsen, Information Contact, 540-231-5671, Fax: 540-231-9307, E-mail: enilsen@vt.edu.

Washington University in St. Louis, Graduate School of Arts and Sciences, Division of Biology and Biomedical Sciences, Program in Evolution, Ecology and Population Biology, St. Louis, MO 63130-4899. Offers ecology (PhD); environmental biology (PhD); evolutionary biology (PhD); genetics (PhD). *Degree requirements:* For doctorate, thesis/dissertation. *Entrance requirements:* For doctorate, GRE General Test, GRE Subject Test. Electronic applications accepted.

Wesleyan University, Graduate Programs, Department of Biology, Middletown, CT 06459. Offers animal behavior (PhD); bioinformatics/genomics (PhD); cell biology (PhD); developmental biology (PhD); evolution/ecology (PhD); genetics (PhD); neurobiology (PhD); population biology (PhD). *Faculty:* 13 full-time (4 women). *Students:* 23 full-time (11 women); includes 1 minority (African American), 3 international. Average age 26. 29 applicants, 10% accepted, 2 enrolled. In 2009, 3 doctorates awarded. *Degree requirements:* For doctorate, variable foreign language requirement, thesis/dissertation. *Entrance requirements:* For doctorate, GRE. Additional exam requirements/recommendations for international students: Required—TOEFL. *Application deadline:* For fall admission, 1/15 for domestic and international students. Applications are processed on a rolling basis. Application fee: $0. *Financial support:* In 2009–10, 3 research assistantships with full tuition reimbursements, 19 teaching assistantships with full tuition reimbursements were awarded; stipends also available. Financial award application deadline: 4/15; financial award applicants required to submit FAFSA. *Faculty research:* Microbial population genetics, genetic basis of evolutionary adaptation, genetic regulation of differentiation and pattern formation in *drosophila*. *Unit head:* Dr. Sonia E. Sultan, Chair/Professor, 860-685-3493, E-mail: jnaegele@wesleyan.edu. *Application contact:* Marjorie Fitzgibbons, Information Contact, 860-685-2140, E-mail: mfitzgibbons@wesleyan.edu.

West Virginia University, Eberly College of Arts and Sciences, Department of Biology, Morgantown, WV 26506. Offers cell and molecular biology (MS, PhD); environmental and evolutionary biology (MS, PhD); forensic biology (MS, PhD); genomic biology (MS, PhD); neurobiology (MS, PhD). Terminal master's awarded for partial completion of doctoral program. *Degree requirements:* For master's, thesis, final exam; for doctorate, thesis/dissertation, preliminary and final exams. *Entrance requirements:* For master's, GRE General Test, GRE Subject Test, minimum GPA of 3.0; for doctorate, GRE General Test, minimum GPA of 3.0. Additional exam requirements/recommendations for international students: Required—TOEFL. *Faculty research:* Environmental biology, genetic engineering, developmental biology, global change, biodiversity.

Yale University, Graduate School of Arts and Sciences, Department of Ecology and Evolutionary Biology, New Haven, CT 06520. Offers PhD. *Entrance requirements:* For doctorate, GRE General Test, GRE Subject Test (biology).

COLUMBIA UNIVERSITY

Department of Ecology, Evolution, and Environmental Biology

Programs of Study

The Department of Ecology, Evolution, and Environmental Biology (E3B) was established in 2001 in response to the recognition of the importance of these fields in modern society and the realization that they have their own set of intellectual foci, theoretical foundations, scales of analysis, and methodologies. Its mission is to educate a new generation of scientists, professionals, and practitioners in the theory and methods of these disciplines. It emphasizes a multidisciplinary perspective on the study of the Earth's declining biodiversity, integrating insights from relevant fields in biology and the social sciences. Faculty members are based at the University and at partner institutions, including the American Museum of Natural History, the New York Botanical Garden, the Wildlife Conservation Society, and Wildlife Trust.

The M.A. in conservation biology integrates the biological sciences with a foundation in environmental policy and economics. The program offers three tracks: academic, professional, and educational; and two programs: thesis-based and course-based. The tracks and the programs can be matched in any combination to meet students' interests and needs. Students in the course-based program are required to complete 47 credits and those in the thesis-based program 49 credits. Core courses for all tracks and all programs include two semesters in conservation biology and environmental policy, four semesters of the Research (E3B/CERC) Seminar, three electives in conservation science and two electives in environmental policy, and two more electives in either area. Students following the course-based program will register for additional classes and complete their requirements by writing a take-home essay at the end of their second year. Students in the thesis-based program must complete additional credits with a research project that leads to a final thesis. Research projects are generally carried out over the summer.

Doctoral candidates may elect to pursue a degree in ecology and evolutionary biology or evolutionary primatology. Unique to the Ph.D. program in ecology and evolutionary biology is course work leading to proficiency in environmental policy which can be formalized into a separate Environmental Policy Certificate. Candidates in both degrees are required to complete 6 units of full-time residency (six semesters), two core courses, two broader context requirements, and a thesis development seminar which will include performing an in-depth review of the scholarly literature that is most relevant to the proposed dissertation research. Additional requirements include demonstrating proficiency in a foreign language, as needed for their specific fieldwork locations; serving as teaching assistants for two to four semesters; an oral general knowledge exam; a proposal defense; and orally defending their dissertation. Upon advancing to candidacy, students are expected to submit their proposals to granting agencies for outside funding.

Research Facilities

The Department of Ecology, Evolution, and Environmental Biology (E3B) has two large common research labs with wet and dry areas, equipped with state-of-the-art equipment, as well as advanced computer facilities. The Biological Sciences Library houses more than 52,000 volumes, subscribes to about 335 serials, and has digital subscriptions to hundreds of other serials. The print collection is particularly strong in the areas of molecular biology, biochemistry, cell biology, genetics, and neurobiology. Scientific literature in the areas of population and evolutionary biology and plant physiology is also collected at research level. The Center for Environmental Research and Conservation (CERC) conducts research to find long-term solutions to combat the loss of biological diversity and natural resource depletion while meeting the needs of a growing worldwide human population. Black Rock Forest comprises nearly 3,800 acres of land on the west bank of the Hudson River and is dedicated to scientific research and conservation of the ecosystems that once covered the region.

Financial Aid

Ph.D. fellowships for up to five years are available through the Faculty Fellows program. Students are expected to find their own funding for their dissertation research year (for research and stipend expenses). There are no fellowships for the master's program. However, applicants are strongly encouraged to apply for outside sources of funding, such as the EPA Science to Achieve Results Fellowship Program and the NSF Graduate Fellowship Program).

Cost of Study

In the 2010–11 academic year, full-time tuition is $18,230 per semester for the Ph.D. program and $19,312 per semester for the first year of the M.A. program. Health insurance, health services, and student fees were $2654 for the entire academic year. A part-time option is available for students in the M.A. program. Full-time second-year master's students register for Extended Residence, which costs about half as much as regular full-time tuition.

Living and Housing Costs

In 2010–11, students living on campus paid $18,252 during the academic year for room and board, $3626 for personal expenses, and $2000 for books and supplies. Students living off campus paid $850 to $1200 per month for a one-bedroom apartment or $1100 to $1600 per month for a two-bedroom apartment. These are approximate costs and can vary, depending on individual needs.

Student Group

There are currently 34 doctoral candidates and 44 master's students in the program. They come from a variety of backgrounds, but the majority of them hold undergraduate degrees in the biological sciences and related disciplines.

Student Outcomes

Students develop the skills to conduct ecological, behavioral, systematic, molecular, and other evolutionary biological research as well as to formulate and implement environmental policy. Graduates of the programs have pursued academic careers as researchers and teachers or have entered the job market directly as scientific researchers, teachers, or administrators in government agencies or in national or international conservation, environmental, and multilateral aid organizations dedicated to the conservation of biodiversity.

Location

The campus is located in New York City's Morningside Heights neighborhood. Residents are a short walk from Riverside Park, Central Park, St. John the Divine Cathedral, and other landmarks. The subway, just outside the campus main gate on Broadway, connects to world-famous sites like the Empire State Building or Times Square, neighborhoods such as Greenwich Village or Little Italy, or one of New York's many museums, theaters, or restaurants.

The University

Columbia University, the fifth-oldest university in the United States, was founded in 1754 as King's College; the first class, led by Samuel Johnson, had 8 students. Today, the University is one of the most competitive in the nation, enrolling more than 23,000 students in three undergraduate schools, thirteen graduate and professional schools, and a school of continuing education. It is also a premier research institute, where faculty members engage in groundbreaking research in medicine, science, the arts, and the humanities.

Applying

Prospective students must submit an application for admission, a statement of academic purpose, official transcripts, three letters of recommendation, a statistical form, a fellowship statement, a curriculum vitae or resume, and an application fee of $85. Applicants should have an undergraduate degree in one of the natural sciences, with course work in calculus, physics, chemistry, statistics, genetics, ecology, and organismal biology. The GRE General Test is required, and the biology Subject Test is recommended. The application deadline for admission to the M.A. program is January 15. The application deadline for the Ph.D. program is December 1.

Correspondence and Information

Eleanor Sterling, Director of Graduate Studies
Department of Ecology, Evolution, and Environmental Biology
Columbia University
1200 Amsterdam Avenue
New York, New York 10027
Phone: 212-854-9987
Fax: 212-854-8188
E-mail: es443@columbia.edu
    e3b@columbia.edu (Departmental e-mail)
Web site: http://www.columbia.edu/cu/e3b/

Fabio Corsi, M.A. Program Advisor
Department of Ecology, Evolution, and Environmental Biology
Columbia University
1200 Amsterdam Avenue
New York, New York 10027
Phone: 212-854-7807
Fax: 212-854-8188
E-mail: fc2257@columbia.edu
    e3b@columbia.edu (Departmental e-mail)
Web site: http://www.columbia.edu/cu/e3b/

Columbia University

THE FACULTY AND THEIR RESEARCH

For a full listing of all E3B faculty members who are approved advisers and are part of the Department's consortium partnership, students should consult the Departmental Web site.

Walter J. Bock, Professor of Biological Science; Ph.D., Harvard, 1959. Theoretical aspects of evolution and systematics; feeding apparatus of birds; origin of avian flight.

Hilary S. Callahan, Assistant Professor; Ph.D. (botany), Wisconsin–Madison, 1996. Ability of a genotype to express different phenotypes in response to different environments; phenotypic plasticity of flowering time in the model organism *Arabidopsis thaliana*.

Joel Cohen, Professor; Ph.D. (population sciences and tropical public health), Harvard, 1973. Role of the food web, body sizes, and species abundances in describing ecological communities; new inequalities arising in information theory and operations research; frequency-domain analysis of nonlinear stochastic population models.

Steven A. Cohen, Director, Graduate Program in Earth Systems; Ph.D. (political science), Buffalo, SUNY, 1979. Organizational management; workforce planning; quality management and management innovation.

Marina Cords, Professor; Ph.D. (zoology), Berkeley, 1984. Understanding the mating system of blue monkeys in the Kakamega Forest, western Kenya; social behavior and behavioral ecology of primates; proximate and ultimate explanations of social systems.

Fabio Corsi, Lecturer and M.A. Program Adviser; Ph.D. (spatial ecology), Wageningen (The Netherlands), 2004. Patterns to processes, spatial explicit models to explore ecological and biological phenomena, data integration and biodiversity informatics, species distribution modeling.

Ruth DeFries, Professor; Ph.D., Johns Hopkins, 1980. Consequences of anthropogenic land-use change on ecological processes; characterization of land cover and anthropogenic land-use change with remote sensing; interactions between human activities, the land surface, and ecosystem services that regulate the Earth's habitability.

James Gibbs, Adjunct Professor; Ph.D. (forestry and environmental studies), Yale, 1995. Biological monitoring, population biology, conservation genetics, and landscape ecology; improving conservation biology education, particularly in tropical, developing countries.

John Glendinning, Associate Professor; Ph.D., Florida, 1989. Chemosensory mechanisms that control the feeding behavior of insects and mammals; contribution of taste and viscerosensory response mechanisms to this coping process.

Kevin Griffin, Associate Professor; Ph.D. (earth and environmental science), Duke, 1994. Plant respiration; global carbon cycle; forest ecology.

Paul E. Hertz, Professor; Ph.D. (biology), Harvard, 1977. Evolution and interaction of behavioral and physiological traits that compensate for geographic and seasonal shifts in operative temperatures; extent and effectiveness of temperature regulation and its effect on resource partitioning in West Indian anoles; role of light intensity in microhabitat selection.

Ralph L. Holloway, Professor; Ph.D. (anthropology), Berkeley, 1964. Brain endocasts of fossil hominids; ape brain endocast morphology and variation; biostereometric analysis of the brain; cerebral asymmetry, lateralization, and cognition.

Darcy Kelley, Professor; Ph.D. (biological sciences), Rockefeller, 1975. Neural systems and behavior; hormonal effects; sexual differentiation.

Don J. Melnick, Professor; Ph.D. (physical anthropology), Yale, 1981. Genetic consequences of habitat fragmentation in vertebrates; genetic indicators for setting conservation priorities.

Brian Morton, Assistant Professor; Ph.D. (genetics), California, Riverside, 1993. How selective constraints on codon usage interact with other structural features; how rate heterogeneity among sites is affected by variation in context or the composition of nucleotides flanking those sites.

Shahid Naeem, Professor and Chair; Ph.D. (zoology), Berkeley, 1989. How extrinsic factors interact with plant biodiversity to regulate the spread of invasive plant species in old fields; how mathematical models developed for reliability engineering can be used for understanding the reliability of ecosystems.

Paul E. Olsen, Arthur D. Stroke Memorial Professor of Geological Sciences; Ph.D. (biology), Yale, 1984. Evolution of continental ecosystems; pattern, causes, and effects of climate change on geological time scales and mass extinctions; effects of evolutionary innovations on global biogeochemical cycles.

Matthew Palmer, Lecturer and Director of Undergraduate Studies; Ph.D. (plant diversity), Rutgers, 2005. Community ecology; plant conservation biology; local controls on plant diversity.

Miguel Pinedo-Vasquez, Lecturer and Associate Research Scientist; Ph.D. (forestry and environmental studies), Yale, 1995. Patterns and effects of small-holder management of tropical ecosystems and landscapes.

Jeanne Poindexter, Assistant Professor; Ph.D. (bacteriology), Berkeley, 1963. Ecophysiology of oligotrophic bacteria; effects of nutrient fluxes on physiologic, morphologic, and behavioral properties of bacteria.

Robert E. Pollack, Professor; Ph.D. (biology), Brandeis, 1966. The future of medical research in the U.S.; approaches of medicine to aging; social and political consequences of medical genetics and DNA-based medicine.

Dustin Rubenstein, Assistant Professor; Ph.D. (neurobiology and behavior), Cornell, 2006. Behavioral ecology, evolutionary ecology, behavioral neuroendocrinology, evolutionary biology, population biology, integrative biology, animal behavior.

William Schuster, Executive Director, Black Rock Forest Consortium; Ph.D. (biology), Colorado, 1989. Forest structure, composition, ecological processes, and how these factors and overall forest health change over timescales; consequences of various human activities for forest ecosystems.

Jill Shapiro, Lecturer and coordinator of biological anthropology major; Ph.D. (anthropology), Columbia, 1995. Analysis of interpopulational cranial variation in the orangutan, as compared with that present in the African apes.

Eleanor Sterling, Director, Center for Biodiversity Conservation, American Museum of Natural History and Director of Graduate Studies, Ph.D. (physical anthropology and forestry), Yale, 1993. Optimal techniques for mammals surveys to studies of the distribution of patterns of biodiversity in tropical regions of the world.

Maria Uriarte, Assistant Professor; Ph.D. (ecology and evolutionary biology), Cornell, 2002. Role that neighborhood interactions play in the assembly and composition of natural plant communities.

Paige West, Assistant Professor; Ph.D. (cultural anthropology), Rutgers. Hunting practices of rural peoples and the population ecology of prey species in Papua New Guinea; commodity ecumene for coffee as the first step in understanding commodity flows from rural Papua New Guinea to urban areas.

Section 9
Entomology

This section contains a directory of institutions offering graduate work in entomology. Additional information about programs listed in the directory may be obtained by writing directly to the dean of a graduate school or chair of a department at the address given in the directory.

For programs offering related work, see also in this book *Biochemistry; Biological and Biomedical Sciences; Botany and Plant Biology; Ecology, Environmental Biology, and Evolutionary Biology; Genetics, Developmental Biology, and Reproductive Biology; Microbiological Sciences; Physiology;* and *Zoology.* In the other guides in this series:

Graduate Programs in the Humanities, Arts & Social Sciences
See *Economics (Agricultural Economics and Agribusiness)*

Graduate Programs in the Physical Sciences, Mathematics, Agricultural Sciences, the Environment & Natural Resources
See *Agricultural and Food Sciences* and *Environmental Sciences and Management*

Graduate Programs in Engineering & Applied Sciences
See *Agricultural Engineering* and *Bioengineering*

CONTENTS

Program Directory

Entomology

Auburn University, Graduate School, College of Agriculture, Department of Entomology and Plant Pathology, Auburn University, AL 36849. Offers entomology (M Ag, MS, PhD); plant pathology (M Ag, MS, PhD). Part-time programs available. *Faculty:* 17 full-time (6 women). *Students:* 24 full-time (10 women), 11 part-time (4 women); includes 3 minority (1 African American, 2 Asian Americans or Pacific Islanders), 17 international. Average age 30. 21 applicants, 57% accepted, 7 enrolled. In 2009, 3 master's, 2 doctorates awarded. *Degree requirements:* For master's, thesis (for some programs); for doctorate, one foreign language, thesis/dissertation. *Entrance requirements:* For master's, GRE General Test; for doctorate, GRE General Test, GRE Subject Test, master's degree with thesis. *Application deadline:* For fall admission, 7/7 for domestic students; for spring admission, 11/24 for domestic students. Applications are processed on a rolling basis. Application fee: $50 ($60 for international students). Electronic applications accepted. *Expenses:* Tuition, state resident: full-time $6240. Tuition, nonresident: full-time $18,720. International tuition: $18,938 full-time. Required fees: $492. Tuition and fees vary according to course load, program and reciprocity agreements. *Financial support:* Research assistantships, teaching assistantships, Federal Work-Study available. Support available to part-time students. Financial award application deadline: 3/15; financial award applicants required to submit FAFSA. *Faculty research:* Pest management, biological control, systematics, medical entomology. *Unit head:* Dr. Arthur Appel, Chair, 334-844-5006. *Application contact:* Dr. George Flowers, Dean of the Graduate School, 334-844-2125.

Clemson University, Graduate School, College of Agriculture, Forestry and Life Sciences, Department of Entomology, Soils, and Plant Sciences, Program in Entomology, Clemson, SC 29634. Offers MS, PhD. *Students:* 10 full-time (5 women), 3 international. Average age 27. 9 applicants, 33% accepted, 1 enrolled. In 2009, 7 master's, 4 doctorates awarded. *Degree requirements:* For master's, thesis; for doctorate, thesis/dissertation. *Entrance requirements:* For master's, GRE General Test, bachelor's degree in biological science or chemistry; for doctorate, GRE General Test. Additional exam requirements/recommendations for international students: Required—TOEFL. *Application deadline:* Applications are processed on a rolling basis. Application fee: $70 ($80 for international students). Electronic applications accepted. *Expenses:* Contact institution. *Financial support:* In 2009–10, 9 students received support, including 2 fellowships with full and partial tuition reimbursements available (averaging $15,333 per year), 6 research assistantships with partial tuition reimbursements available (averaging $19,161 per year), 2 teaching assistantships with partial tuition reimbursements available (averaging $18,000 per year); career-related internships or fieldwork, institutionally sponsored loans, scholarships/grants, health care benefits, and unspecified assistantships also available. Support available to part-time students. *Unit head:* Dr. Patricia A. Zungoli, Chair, 864-656-3137, Fax: 864-656-5065, E-mail: pzngl@clemson.edu. *Application contact:* Dr. Matthew Turnbull, Coordinator, 864-656-5038, Fax: 864-656-5065, E-mail: turnbul@clemson.edu.

Colorado State University, Graduate School, College of Agricultural Sciences, Department of Bioagricultural Sciences and Pest Management, Fort Collins, CO 80523-1177. Offers entomology (MS, PhD); plant pathology and weed science (MS, PhD). Part-time programs available. *Faculty:* 19 full-time (3 women). *Students:* 19 full-time (8 women), 13 part-time (5 women); includes 3 minority (2 American Indian/Alaska Native, 1 Hispanic American), 2 international. Average age 31. 26 applicants, 31% accepted, 4 enrolled. In 2009, 5 master's, 1 doctorate awarded. *Degree requirements:* For master's, comprehensive exam, thesis; for doctorate, comprehensive exam, thesis/dissertation, 72 credits. *Entrance requirements:* For master's, GRE General Test, minimum GPA of 3.0, letters of recommendation; for doctorate, GRE General Test, minimum GPA of 3.0, letters of recommendation, essay. Additional exam requirements/recommendations for international students: Required—TOEFL (minimum score 550 paper-based; 213 computer-based). *Application deadline:* For fall admission, 1/15 priority date for domestic and international students; for spring admission, 9/1 priority date for domestic and international students. Applications are processed on a rolling basis. Application fee: $50. Electronic applications accepted. *Expenses:* Tuition, state resident: full-time $6434; part-time $359.10 per credit. Tuition, nonresident: full-time $18,116; part-time $1006.45 per credit. Required fees: $1496; $83 per credit. *Financial support:* In 2009–10, 7 fellowships with partial tuition reimbursements (averaging $32,685 per year), 22 research assistantships with full tuition reimbursements (averaging $14,370 per year), 8 teaching assistantships with full tuition reimbursements (averaging $11,230 per year) were awarded; career-related internships or fieldwork, scholarships/grants, unspecified assistantships, and fellowships also available. Financial award application deadline: 1/15; financial award applicants required to submit FAFSA. *Faculty research:* Biological control of post-insect plant pathogens and weeds, integrated pest management, weed ecology and biology, pest genomes of plants. Total annual research expenditures: $2.6 million. *Unit head:* Thomas O. Holtzer, Head, 970-491-5261, Fax: 970-491-3862, E-mail: tholtzer@lamar.colostate.edu. *Application contact:* Janet Dill, Education Coordinator, 970-491-0402, Fax: 970-491-3862, E-mail: janet.dill@colostate.edu.

Cornell University, Graduate School, Graduate Fields of Agriculture and Life Sciences, Field of Entomology, Ithaca, NY 14853-0001. Offers acarology (MS, PhD); apiculture (MS, PhD); applied entomology (MS, PhD); aquatic entomology (MS, PhD); biological control (MS, PhD); insect behavior (MS, PhD); insect biochemistry (MS, PhD); insect ecology (MS, PhD); insect genetics (MS, PhD); insect morphology (MS, PhD); insect pathology (MS, PhD); insect physiology (MS, PhD); insect systematics (MS, PhD); insect toxicology and insecticide chemistry (MS, PhD); integrated pest management (MS, PhD); medical and veterinary entomology (MS, PhD). *Faculty:* 47 full-time (7 women). *Students:* 31 full-time (13 women); includes 3 minority (1 Asian American or Pacific Islander, 2 Hispanic Americans), 12 international. Average age 29. 26 applicants, 23% accepted, 6 enrolled. In 2009, 1 master's, 6 doctorates awarded. *Degree requirements:* For master's, thesis; for doctorate, comprehensive exam, thesis/dissertation. *Entrance requirements:* For master's and doctorate, GRE General Test, GRE Subject Test (biology), 3 letters of recommendation. Additional exam requirements/recommendations for international students: Required—TOEFL (minimum score 550 paper-based; 213 computer-based; 77 iBT). *Application deadline:* For fall admission, 12/1 for domestic students. Application fee: $70. Electronic applications accepted. *Expenses:* Tuition: Full-time $29,500. Required fees: $70. Full-time tuition and fees vary according to degree level, program and student level. *Financial support:* In 2009–10, 28 students received support, including 2 fellowships with full tuition reimbursements available, 2 research assistantships with full tuition reimbursements available; teaching assistantships with full tuition reimbursements available, institutionally sponsored loans, scholarships/grants, health care benefits, tuition waivers (full and partial), and unspecified assistantships also available. Financial award applicants required to submit FAFSA. *Faculty research:* Systematics and biodiversity, integrated pest management, pathology and biological control, toxicology and physiology, ecology and behavior. *Unit head:* Director of Graduate Studies, 607-255-6198, Fax: 607-255-0939. *Application contact:* Graduate Field Assistant, 607-255-6198, Fax: 607-255-0939, E-mail: fieldofent2@cornell.edu.

Florida Agricultural and Mechanical University, Division of Graduate Studies, Research, and Continuing Education, College of Engineering Science, Technology, and Agriculture, Division of Agricultural Sciences, Tallahassee, FL 32307-3200. Offers agribusiness (MS); animal science (MS); engineering technology (MS); entomology (MS); food science (MS); international programs (MS); plant science (MS). *Faculty:* 31 full-time (2 women). *Students:* 14 full-time (8 women), 8 part-time (4 women); includes 17 minority (16 African Americans, 1 Asian American or Pacific Islander), 3 international. In 2009, 7 master's awarded. *Degree requirements:* For master's, thesis. *Entrance requirements:* For master's, GRE General Test, minimum GPA of 3.0. Additional exam requirements/recommendations for international students: Required—TOEFL (minimum score 500 paper-based). *Application deadline:* For fall admission, 5/18 for domestic students, 12/18 for international students; for spring admission, 11/12 for domestic students, 5/12 for international students. Application fee: $20. *Financial support:* Application deadline: 2/15. *Unit head:* Dr. Mitwe N. Musingo, Graduate Coordinator, 850-561-2309, Fax: 850-599-8821. *Application contact:* Dr. Chanta M. Haywood, Dean of Graduate Studies, Research, and Continuing Education, 850-599-3315, Fax: 850-599-3727.

Illinois State University, Graduate School, College of Arts and Sciences, Department of Biological Sciences, Normal, IL 61790-2200. Offers animal behavior (MS); bacteriology (MS); biochemistry (MS); biological sciences (MS); biology (PhD); biophysics (MS); biotechnology (MS); botany (MS, PhD); cell biology (MS); conservation biology (MS); developmental biology (MS); ecology (MS, PhD); entomology (MS); evolutionary biology (MS); genetics (MS, PhD); immunology (MS); microbiology (MS, PhD); molecular biology (MS); molecular genetics (MS); neurobiology (MS); neuroscience (MS); parasitology (MS); physiology (MS, PhD); plant biology (MS); plant molecular biology (MS); plant sciences (MS); structural biology (MS); zoology (MS, PhD). Part-time programs available. *Degree requirements:* For master's, thesis or alternative; for doctorate, variable foreign language requirement, thesis/dissertation, 2 terms of residency. *Entrance requirements:* For master's, GRE General Test, minimum GPA of 2.6 in last 60 hours of course work; for doctorate, GRE General Test. *Faculty research:* Redoc balance and drug development in schistosoma mansoni, control of the growth of listeria monocytogenes at low temperature, regulation of cell expansion and microtubule function by SPRI, CRUI: physiology and fitness consequences of different life history phenotypes.

Iowa State University of Science and Technology, Graduate College, College of Agriculture, Department of Entomology, Ames, IA 50011. Offers MS, PhD. *Faculty:* 16 full-time (5 women), 1 part-time/adjunct (0 women). *Students:* 26 full-time (12 women), 4 part-time (0 women), 5 international. 10 applicants, 50% accepted, 5 enrolled. In 2009, 1 master's, 2 doctorates awarded. *Degree requirements:* For master's, thesis; for doctorate, thesis/dissertation. *Entrance requirements:* For master's and doctorate, GRE General Test, GRE Subject Test (biology). Additional exam requirements/recommendations for international students: Required—TOEFL (minimum score 550 paper-based; 79 iBT) or IELTS (minimum score 6.5). *Application deadline:* Applications are processed on a rolling basis. Application fee: $40 ($90 for international students). Electronic applications accepted. *Expenses:* Tuition, state resident: full-time $6716. Tuition, nonresident: full-time $8908. Tuition and fees vary according to course level, course load, program and student level. *Financial support:* In 2009–10, 13 research assistantships with full and partial tuition reimbursements (averaging $15,710 per year) were awarded; fellowships, teaching assistantships with full and partial tuition reimbursements, scholarships/grants, health care benefits, and unspecified assistantships also available. *Unit head:* Dr. Leslie Lewis, Chair, 515-294-7400, Fax: 515-294-2125, E-mail: entomology@iastate.edu. *Application contact:* Dr. Joel Coats, Director of Graduate Education, 515-294-7400, E-mail: entomology@iastate.edu.

Kansas State University, Graduate School, College of Agriculture, Department of Entomology, Manhattan, KS 66506. Offers MS, PhD. *Faculty:* 19 full-time (0 women), 10 part-time/adjunct (1 woman). *Students:* 28 full-time (14 women); includes 3 minority (1 African American, 1 American Indian/Alaska Native, 1 Hispanic American), 15 international. Average age 33. 9 applicants, 56% accepted, 3 enrolled. In 2009, 1 master's, 3 doctorates awarded. *Degree requirements:* For master's, thesis, oral exam; for doctorate, thesis/dissertation, written and oral exams. *Application deadline:* For fall admission, 2/1 priority date for domestic and international students; for spring admission, 8/1 priority date for domestic and international students. Applications are processed on a rolling basis. Application fee: $40 ($55 for international students). Electronic applications accepted. *Financial support:* In 2009–10, 22 research assistantships (averaging $16,286 per year) were awarded; teaching assistantships with partial tuition reimbursements, career-related internships or fieldwork, Federal Work-Study, institutionally sponsored loans, scholarships/grants, and tuition waivers (partial) also available. Support available to part-time students. Financial award application deadline: 3/1; financial award applicants required to submit FAFSA. *Faculty research:* Molecular genetics, biologically-based pest management, host plant resistance, ecological genomics, stored product entomology. Total annual research expenditures: $1.6 million. *Unit head:* Tom Phillips, Head, 785-532-6154, Fax: 785-532-6232, E-mail: twp1@ksu.edu. *Application contact:* Evelyn Kennedy, Application Contact, 785-532-4702, Fax: 785-532-6232, E-mail: ekennedy@ksu.edu.

Louisiana State University and Agricultural and Mechanical College, Graduate School, College of Agriculture, Department of Entomology, Baton Rouge, LA 70803. Offers MS, PhD. *Faculty:* 24 full-time (5 women). *Students:* 21 full-time (4 women), 9 part-time (1 woman); includes 1 Asian American or Pacific Islander, 1 Hispanic American, 8 international. Average age 30. 7 applicants, 71% accepted, 4 enrolled. In 2009, 2 master's awarded. *Degree requirements:* For master's, thesis; for doctorate, thesis/dissertation. *Entrance requirements:* For master's and doctorate, GRE General Test, minimum GPA of 3.0. Additional exam requirements/recommendations for international students: Required—TOEFL (minimum score 550 paper-based; 213 computer-based; 79 iBT) or IELTS (minimum score 6.5). *Application deadline:* For fall admission, 1/25 priority date for domestic students, 5/15 for international students; for spring admission, 10/15 for international students. Applications are processed on a rolling basis. Application fee: $50 ($70 for international students). Electronic applications accepted. *Financial support:* In 2009–10, 28 students received support, including 20 research assistantships with partial tuition reimbursements available (averaging $18,125 per year); fellowships, teaching assistantships with partial tuition reimbursements available, Federal Work-Study, institutionally sponsored loans, scholarships/grants, health care benefits, and unspecified assistantships also available. Support available to part-time students. Financial award applicants required to submit FAFSA. *Faculty research:* Conservation biology, insect systematics, insect ecology, urban entomology, agricultural pest management, insect genomics. Total annual research expenditures: $15,045. *Unit head:* Dr. Timothy Schowalter, Head, 225-578-1628, Fax: 225-578-2257, E-mail: tschowalter@agcenter.lsu.edu. *Application contact:* Paula Beecher, Recruiting Coordinator, 225-578-2468, E-mail: pbeeche@lsu.edu.

McGill University, Faculty of Graduate and Postdoctoral Studies, Faculty of Agricultural and Environmental Sciences, Department of Natural Resource Sciences, Montréal, QC H3A 2T5, Canada. Offers entomology (M Sc, PhD); environmental assessment (M Sc); forest science (M Sc, PhD); microbiology (M Sc, PhD); micrometeorology (M Sc, PhD); neotropical environment (M Sc, PhD); soil science (M Sc, PhD); wildlife biology (M Sc, PhD).

Michigan State University, The Graduate School, College of Agriculture and Natural Resources and College of Natural Science, Department of Entomology, East Lansing, MI 48824. Offers entomology (MS, PhD); integrated pest management (MS). *Faculty:* 18 full-time (5 women). *Students:* 39 full-time (16 women), 2 part-time (0 women); includes 1 minority (Asian American or Pacific Islander), 8 international. Average age 29. 21 applicants, 24% accepted. In 2009, 8 master's, 6 doctorates awarded. *Entrance requirements:* Additional exam requirements/recommendations for international students: Required—TOEFL (minimum score 550 paper-based; 213 computer-based), Michigan State University ELT (minimum score 85), Michigan English Language Assessment Battery (minimum score 83). Electronic applications accepted. *Expenses:* Tuition, state resident: part-time $478.25 per credit hour. Tuition, nonresident: part-time $966.50 per credit hour. Part-time tuition and fees vary according to program. *Financial support:* In 2009–10, 22 research assistantships with tuition reimbursements (averaging $7,135 per year), 9 teaching assistantships with tuition reimbursements (averaging $7,374 per year) were awarded. Total annual research expenditures: $8.8 million. *Unit head:* Dr. Ernest S. Delfosse, Chairperson, 517-355-4665, Fax: 517-353-4354, E-mail: delfosse@msu.edu. *Application contact:* Heather Lenartson-Kluge, Graduate Secretary, 517-355-4665, Fax: 517-353-4354, E-mail: lenartso@msu.edu.

Mississippi State University, College of Agriculture and Life Sciences, Department of Entomology and Plant Pathology, Mississippi State, MS 39762. Offers agricultural life sciences (MS), including entomology and plant pathology (MS, PhD); life sciences (PhD), including entomology and plant pathology (MS, PhD). *Faculty:* 18 full-time (1 woman). *Students:* 16 full-time (5 women), 5 part-time (3 women); includes 2 minority (1 Asian American or Pacific

Islander, 1 Hispanic American), 4 international. Average age 35. 12 applicants, 33% accepted, 2 enrolled. In 2009, 3 master's, 3 doctorates awarded. *Degree requirements:* For master's, thesis; for doctorate, thesis/dissertation. *Entrance requirements:* For master's, GRE General Test, minimum GPA of 2.75; for doctorate, GRE General Test. Additional exam requirements/recommendations for international students: Required—TOEFL (minimum score 475 paper-based; 153 computer-based; 53 iBT); Recommended—IELTS (minimum score 4.5). *Application deadline:* For fall admission, 7/1 for domestic students, 5/1 for international students; for spring admission, 11/1 for domestic students, 9/1 for international students. Applications are processed on a rolling basis. Application fee: $40. Electronic applications accepted. *Expenses:* Tuition, state resident: full-time $2575.50; part-time $286.25 per credit hour. Tuition, nonresident: full-time $6510; part-time $723.50 per credit hour. Tuition and fees vary according to course load. *Financial support:* In 2009–10, 15 research assistantships (averaging $13,924 per year) were awarded; Federal Work-Study, institutionally sponsored loans, and unspecified assistantships also available. Financial award applicants required to submit FAFSA. *Unit head:* Dr. Clarence H. Collison, Professor and Department Head, 662-325-2085, Fax: 662-325-8837, E-mail: ccollison@entomology.msstate.edu. *Application contact:* Dr. Clarence H. Collison, Professor and Department Head, 662-325-2085, Fax: 662-325-8837, E-mail: ccollison@entomology.msstate.edu.

New Mexico State University, Graduate School, College of Agricultural, Consumer and Environmental Sciences, Department of Entomology, Plant Pathology and Weed Science, Las Cruces, NM 88003-8001. Offers agricultural biology (MS). Part-time programs available. *Faculty:* 8 full-time (2 women). *Students:* 8 full-time (2 women), 2 part-time (1 woman); includes 2 minority (both Hispanic Americans), 2 international. Average age 26. 8 applicants, 88% accepted, 3 enrolled. In 2009, 4 master's awarded. *Degree requirements:* For master's, comprehensive exam, thesis. *Entrance requirements:* For master's, GRE General Test. *Application deadline:* For fall admission, 7/1 priority date for domestic students; for spring admission, 11/1 priority date for domestic students. Applications are processed on a rolling basis. Application fee: $30 ($50 for international students). Electronic applications accepted. *Expenses:* Tuition, state resident: full-time $4080; part-time $223 per credit. Tuition, nonresident: full-time $14,256; part-time $647 per credit. Required fees: $1278; $639 per semester. *Financial support:* In 2009–10, 5 research assistantships with partial tuition reimbursements (averaging $18,450 per year), 1 teaching assistantship with partial tuition reimbursement (averaging $20,500 per year) were awarded; career-related internships or fieldwork and health care benefits also available. Financial award application deadline: 3/1. *Faculty research:* Integrated pest management, pesticide application and safety, livestock ectoparasite research, biotechnology, nematology. *Unit head:* Dr. David Thompson, Head, 575-646-3225, Fax: 575-646-8087, E-mail: dathomps@nmsu.edu. *Application contact:* Dr. David Thompson, Head, 575-646-3225, Fax: 575-646-8087, E-mail: dathomps@nmsu.edu.

North Carolina State University, Graduate School, College of Agriculture and Life Sciences, Department of Entomology, Raleigh, NC 27695. Offers MS, PhD. Terminal master's awarded for partial completion of doctoral program. *Degree requirements:* For master's, thesis (for some programs); for doctorate, thesis/dissertation. *Entrance requirements:* For master's and doctorate, GRE General Test. Electronic applications accepted. *Faculty research:* Physiology, biocontrol, ecology, forest entomology, apiculture.

North Dakota State University, College of Graduate and Interdisciplinary Studies, College of Agriculture, Food Systems, and Natural Resources, Department of Entomology, Fargo, ND 58108. Offers entomology (MS, PhD); environment and conservation science (MS, PhD); natural resource management (MS, PhD). Part-time programs available. *Faculty:* 7 full-time (3 women), 8 part-time/adjunct (0 women). *Students:* 2 full-time (1 woman), 12 part-time (8 women); includes 2 Asian Americans or Pacific Islanders, 4 international. Average age 34. 5 applicants, 20% accepted, 1 enrolled. In 2009, 5 doctorates awarded. *Degree requirements:* For master's, thesis; for doctorate, comprehensive exam, thesis/dissertation. *Entrance requirements:* For master's and doctorate, minimum GPA of 3.0. Additional exam requirements/recommendations for international students: Required—TOEFL (minimum score 550 paper-based; 213 computer-based; 79 iBT). *Application deadline:* Applications are processed on a rolling basis. Application fee: $45 ($60 for international students). Electronic applications accepted. *Financial support:* In 2009–10, 11 research assistantships with full tuition reimbursements (averaging $13,800 per year) were awarded; Federal Work-Study, institutionally sponsored loans, and unspecified assistantships also available. Financial award application deadline: 4/15. *Faculty research:* Insect systematics, conservation biology, integrated pest management, insect behavior, insect biology. *Unit head:* Dr. David A. Rider, Chair, 701-231-7908, Fax: 701-231-8557, E-mail: david.rider@ndsu.edu. *Application contact:* Dr. David A. Rider, Chair, 701-231-7908, Fax: 701-231-8557, E-mail: david.rider@ndsu.edu.

The Ohio State University, Graduate School, College of Biological Sciences, Department of Entomology, Columbus, OH 43210. Offers MS, PhD. *Faculty:* 33. *Students:* 12 full-time (6 women), 15 part-time (6 women), 14 international. Average age 28. In 2009, 5 master's, 4 doctorates awarded. *Degree requirements:* For master's, variable foreign language requirement, thesis optional; for doctorate, variable foreign language requirement, thesis/dissertation. *Entrance requirements:* For master's and doctorate, GRE General Test. Additional exam requirements/recommendations for international students: Required—TOEFL (minimum score 600 paper-based; 250 computer-based). *Application deadline:* For fall admission, 8/15 priority date for domestic students, 7/1 priority date for international students; for winter admission, 12/1 priority date for domestic students, 11/1 priority date for international students; for spring admission, 3/1 priority date for domestic students, 2/1 priority date for international students. Applications are processed on a rolling basis. Application fee: $40 ($50 for international students). Electronic applications accepted. *Expenses:* Tuition, state resident: full-time $10,683. Tuition, nonresident: full-time $25,923. Tuition and fees vary according to course load and program. *Financial support:* Fellowships, research assistantships, teaching assistantships, Federal Work-Study and institutionally sponsored loans available. Support available to part-time students. *Faculty research:* Acarology, insect systematics, soil ecology, integrated pest management, chemical ecology. *Unit head:* Susan Fisher, Chair, 614-292-1617, Fax: 614-292-2180, E-mail: fisher.14@osu.edu. *Application contact:* 614-292-9444, Fax: 614-292-3895, E-mail: domestic.grad@osu.edu.

Oklahoma State University, College of Agricultural Science and Natural Resources, Department of Entomology and Plant Pathology, Stillwater, OK 74078. Offers entomology (PhD); entomology and plant pathology (MS); plant pathology (PhD). *Faculty:* 34 full-time (10 women). *Students:* 5 full-time (1 woman), 32 part-time (19 women); includes 2 minority (both Asian Americans or Pacific Islanders), 17 international. Average age 29. 36 applicants, 33% accepted, 9 enrolled. In 2009, 2 master's, 1 doctorate awarded. *Degree requirements:* For master's, thesis or alternative; for doctorate, comprehensive exam, thesis/dissertation. *Entrance requirements:* For master's and doctorate, GRE or GMAT. Additional exam requirements/recommendations for international students: Required—TOEFL (minimum score 550 paper-based; 79 iBT). *Application deadline:* For fall admission, 3/1 priority date for international students; for spring admission, 8/1 priority date for international students. Applications are processed on a rolling basis. Application fee: $40 ($75 for international students). Electronic applications accepted. *Expenses:* Tuition, state resident: full-time $3716; part-time $154.85 per credit hour. Tuition, nonresident: full-time $14,448; part-time $602 per credit hour. Required fees: $1772; $73.85 per credit hour. One-time fee: $50. Tuition and fees vary according to course load and campus/location. *Financial support:* In 2009–10, 30 research assistantships (averaging $17,365 per year), 1 teaching assistantship (averaging $16,584 per year) were awarded; career-related internships or fieldwork, Federal Work-Study, scholarships/grants, health care benefits, tuition waivers (partial), and unspecified assistantships also available. Support available to part-time students. Financial award application deadline: 3/1; financial award applicants required to submit FAFSA. *Unit head:* Dr. Phil Mulder, Head, 405-744-5527, Fax: 405-744-6039. *Application contact:* Dr. Brad Kard, Graduate Coordinator, 405-744-2142, Fax: 405-744-6039, E-mail: brad.kard@okstate.edu.

Penn State University Park, Graduate School, College of Agricultural Sciences, Department of Entomology, State College, University Park, PA 16802-1503. Offers MS, PhD.

Purdue University, Graduate School, College of Agriculture, Department of Entomology, West Lafayette, IN 47907. Offers MS, PhD. Part-time programs available. *Degree requirements:* For master's, thesis (for some programs), seminar; for doctorate, thesis/dissertation, seminar. *Entrance requirements:* For master's and doctorate, GRE. Additional exam requirements/recommendations for international students: Required—TOEFL. Electronic applications accepted. *Faculty research:* Insect biochemistry, nematology, aquatic diptera, behavioral ecology, insect physiology.

Rutgers, The State University of New Jersey, New Brunswick, Graduate School-New Brunswick, Program in Entomology, Piscataway, NJ 08854-8097. Offers MS, PhD. *Degree requirements:* For master's, thesis or alternative; for doctorate, thesis/dissertation. *Entrance requirements:* For master's and doctorate, GRE General Test, GRE Subject Test (recommended). Additional exam requirements/recommendations for international students: Required—TOEFL. Electronic applications accepted. *Faculty research:* Insect toxicology, biolorial control, pathology, IPM and ecology, insect systematics.

Simon Fraser University, Graduate Studies, Faculty of Science, Department of Biological Sciences, Burnaby, BC V5A 1S6, Canada. Offers biological sciences (M Sc, PhD); environmental toxicology (MET); pest management (MPM). *Degree requirements:* For master's, thesis; for doctorate, thesis/dissertation. *Entrance requirements:* For master's, minimum GPA of 3.0; for doctorate, minimum GPA of 3.5. Additional exam requirements/recommendations for international students: Required—TOEFL or IELTS. Electronic applications accepted. *Faculty research:* Molecular biology, marine biology, ecology, wildlife biology, endocrinology.

State University of New York College of Environmental Science and Forestry, Department of Environmental and Forest Biology, Syracuse, NY 13210-2779. Offers applied ecology (MPS); chemical ecology (MPS, MS, PhD); conservation biology (MPS, MS, PhD); ecology (MPS, MS, PhD); entomology (MPS, MS, PhD); environmental interpretation (MPS, MS, PhD); environmental physiology (MPS, MS, PhD); fish and wildlife biology (MPS, MS, PhD); forest pathology and mycology (MPS, MS, PhD); plant biotechnology (MPS); plant science and biotechnology (MPS, MS, PhD). *Degree requirements:* For master's, thesis (for some programs); for doctorate, comprehensive exam, thesis/dissertation. *Entrance requirements:* For master's and doctorate, GRE General Test, GRE Subject Test, minimum GPA of 3.0. Additional exam requirements/recommendations for international students: Required—TOEFL (minimum score 550 paper-based; 213 computer-based; 80 iBT), IELTS (minimum score 6). *Faculty research:* Ecology, fish and wildlife biology and management, plant science, entomology.

Texas A&M University, College of Agriculture and Life Sciences, Department of Entomology, College Station, TX 77843. Offers M Agr, MS, PhD. *Faculty:* 21. *Students:* 42 full-time (18 women), 8 part-time (2 women); includes 9 minority (2 African Americans, 1 American Indian/Alaska Native, 6 Hispanic Americans), 10 international. Average age 34. In 2009, 8 master's, 2 doctorates awarded. *Degree requirements:* For master's, comprehensive exam, thesis (for some programs); for doctorate, comprehensive exam, thesis/dissertation. *Entrance requirements:* For master's and doctorate, GRE General Test. Additional exam requirements/recommendations for international students: Required—TOEFL. *Application deadline:* For fall admission, 2/1 priority date for domestic students; for spring admission, 10/1 for domestic students. Applications are processed on a rolling basis. Application fee: $50 ($75 for international students). Electronic applications accepted. *Expenses:* Tuition, state resident: full-time $3991; part-time $221.74 per credit hour. Tuition, nonresident: full-time $9049; part-time $502.74 per credit hour. *Financial support:* In 2009–10, research assistantships with partial tuition reimbursements (averaging $16,500 per year), teaching assistantships with partial tuition reimbursements (averaging $16,500 per year) were awarded; fellowships, Federal Work-Study also available. Financial award application deadline: 3/1; financial award applicants required to submit FAFSA. *Faculty research:* Biology, biological control, integrated pest management, systematics, host plant resistance. *Unit head:* Head, 979-845-2516, Fax: 979-845-6305, E-mail: entomain@tamuu.edu. *Application contact:* Advisor, 979-845-9349, Fax: 979-845-9938, E-mail: entomain@tamuu.edu.

Texas Tech University, Graduate School, College of Agricultural Sciences and Natural Resources, Department of Plant and Soil Science, Lubbock, TX 79409. Offers crop science (MS); entomology (MS); horticulture (MS); plant and soil science (PhD); soil science (MS); JD/MS. Part-time programs available. *Faculty:* 15 full-time (3 women), 6 part-time/adjunct (0 women). *Students:* 48 full-time (21 women), 42 part-time (18 women); includes 6 minority (2 African Americans, 4 Hispanic Americans), 26 international. Average age 33. 58 applicants, 72% accepted, 27 enrolled. In 2009, 13 master's, 4 doctorates awarded. *Degree requirements:* For master's, thesis or alternative; for doctorate, thesis/dissertation. *Entrance requirements:* For master's and doctorate, GRE General Test. Additional exam requirements/recommendations for international students: Required—TOEFL (minimum score 550 paper-based; 213 computer-based). *Application deadline:* For fall admission, 3/1 priority date for international students; for spring admission, 11/1 priority date for international students. Applications are processed on a rolling basis. Application fee: $50 ($75 for international students). Electronic applications accepted. *Expenses:* Tuition, state resident: full-time $5100; part-time $213 per credit hour. Tuition, nonresident: full-time $11,748; part-time $490 per credit hour. Required fees: $2298; $50 per credit hour. $555 per semester. *Financial support:* In 2009–10, 23 research assistantships with partial tuition reimbursements (averaging $20,991 per year) were awarded; teaching assistantships with partial tuition reimbursements, Federal Work-Study and institutionally sponsored loans also available. Support available to part-time students. Financial award application deadline: 4/15; financial award applicants required to submit FAFSA. *Faculty research:* Molecular and cellular biology of plant stress, physiology/genetics of crop production in semiarid conditions, agricultural bioterrorism, improvement of native plants, soil science and management. Total annual research expenditures: $3.4 million. *Unit head:* Dr. Thomas Thompson, Chair, 806-742-2837, Fax: 806-742-0775, E-mail: thomas.thompson@ttu.edu. *Application contact:* Dr. Eric Hequet, Graduate Adviser, 806-742-2837, Fax: 806-742-0775, E-mail: eric.hequet@ttu.edu.

The University of Arizona, Graduate College, Graduate Interdisciplinary Programs, Department of Entomology, Tucson, AZ 85721. Offers MS, PhD. Part-time programs available. *Faculty:* 9. *Students:* 12 full-time (7 women), 3 part-time (2 women); includes 1 minority (Asian American or Pacific Islander), 7 international. Average age 29. 21 applicants, 10% accepted, 1 enrolled. In 2009, 3 master's, 2 doctorates awarded. *Degree requirements:* For master's, thesis; for doctorate, comprehensive exam, thesis/dissertation. *Entrance requirements:* For master's, GRE General Test, GRE Subject Test, minimum GPA of 3.0, 3 letters of recommendation; for doctorate, GRE General Test, GRE Subject Test, minimum GPA of 3.0, 3 letters of recommendation, statement of purpose. Additional exam requirements/recommendations for international students: Required—TOEFL (minimum score 550 paper-based; 213 computer-based). *Application deadline:* For fall admission, 1/1 for domestic students, 12/1 for international students. Applications are processed on a rolling basis. Application fee: $75. *Expenses:* Tuition, state resident: full-time $9028. Tuition, nonresident: full-time $24,890. *Financial support:* In 2009–10, 1 student received support, including 5 research assistantships with full and partial tuition reimbursements available (averaging $17,954 per year); fellowships, teaching assistantships, Federal Work-Study, institutionally sponsored loans, scholarships/grants, health care benefits, tuition waivers (full and partial), and unspecified assistantships also available. Financial award application deadline: 3/1. *Faculty research:* Toxicology and physiology, plant/insect relations, vector biology, insect pest management, chemical ecology. Total annual research expenditures: $2.4 million. *Unit head:* Dr. Bruce E. Tabashnik, Professor and Head, 520-621-1141, Fax: 520-621-1150, E-mail: brucet@ag.arizona.edu. *Application contact:* Patricia L. Baldewiez, Graduate Coordinator, 520-621-1151, Fax: 520-621-1150, E-mail: pbaldewi@ag.arizona.edu.

University of Arkansas, Graduate School, Dale Bumpers College of Agricultural, Food and Life Sciences, Department of Entomology, Fayetteville, AR 72701-1201. Offers MS, PhD. *Faculty:* 14 full-time (0 women). *Students:* 5 full-time (3 women), 12 part-time (4 women); includes 3 minority (2 Asian Americans or Pacific Islanders, 1 Hispanic American), 1 international.

Entomology

University of Arkansas (continued)

In 2009, 8 master's, 1 doctorate awarded. *Degree requirements:* For master's, thesis; for doctorate, one foreign language, thesis/dissertation. *Entrance requirements:* For master's, GRE, minimum GPA of 3.0; for doctorate, GRE, minimum GPA of 3.25. Application fee: $40 ($50 for international students). *Expenses:* Tuition, state resident: full-time $7355; part-time $356.58 per hour. Tuition, nonresident: full-time $17,401; part-time $775.17 per hour. Required fees: $1203. *Financial support:* In 2009–10, 4 fellowships with tuition reimbursements, 17 research assistantships were awarded; teaching assistantships, career-related internships or fieldwork and Federal Work-Study also available. Support available to part-time students. Financial award application deadline: 4/1; financial award applicants required to submit FAFSA. *Faculty research:* Integrated pest management, insect virology, insect taxonomy. *Unit head:* Dr. Robert Wiedenmann, Chair, 479-575-6628, E-mail: rwieden@uark.edu. *Application contact:* Janet Funk, Administrative Assistant I, 479-575-6628, E-mail: jfunk@uark.edu.

University of California, Davis, Graduate Studies, Graduate Group in Integrated Pest Management, Davis, CA 95616. Offers MS. *Degree requirements:* For master's, comprehensive exam (for some programs), thesis (for some programs). *Entrance requirements:* For master's, GRE General Test, GRE Subject Test (biology), minimum GPA of 3.0. Additional exam requirements/recommendations for international students: Required—TOEFL (minimum score 550 paper-based; 213 computer-based). Electronic applications accepted.

University of California, Davis, Graduate Studies, Program in Entomology, Davis, CA 95616. Offers MS, PhD. Terminal master's awarded for partial completion of doctoral program. *Degree requirements:* For master's, comprehensive exam (for some programs), thesis (for some programs); for doctorate, thesis/dissertation. *Entrance requirements:* For master's and doctorate, GRE General Test, GRE Subject Test (biology). Additional exam requirements/recommendations for international students: Required—TOEFL (minimum score 550 paper-based; 213 computer-based). Electronic applications accepted. *Faculty research:* Bee biology, biological control, systematics, medical/veterinary entomology, pest management.

University of California, Riverside, Graduate Division, Department of Entomology, Riverside, CA 92521-0102. Offers MS, PhD. Part-time programs available. Terminal master's awarded for partial completion of doctoral program. *Degree requirements:* For master's, thesis; for doctorate, thesis/dissertation, qualifying exams. *Entrance requirements:* For master's and doctorate, GRE General Test, minimum GPA of 3.2. Additional exam requirements/recommendations for international students: Required—TOEFL (minimum score 550 paper-based; 213 computer-based; 80 iBT). Electronic applications accepted. *Faculty research:* Agricultural, urban, medical, and veterinary entomology; biological control; chemical ecology; insect pathogens; novel toxicants.

University of Connecticut, Graduate School, College of Liberal Arts and Sciences, Department of Ecology and Evolutionary Biology, Field of Entomology, Storrs, CT 06269. Offers MS, PhD. *Faculty:* 9 full-time (2 women). *Students:* 2 full-time (0 women), 2 part-time (1 woman); includes 1 minority (Hispanic American), 1 international. Average age 34. 1 applicant, 0% accepted, 0 enrolled.Terminal master's awarded for partial completion of doctoral program. *Degree requirements:* For master's, comprehensive exam; for doctorate, thesis/dissertation. *Entrance requirements:* For master's and doctorate, GRE General Test, GRE Subject Test. Additional exam requirements/recommendations for international students: Required—TOEFL (minimum score 550 paper-based; 213 computer-based). *Application deadline:* For fall admission, 2/1 priority date for domestic and international students; for spring admission, 11/1 for domestic students, 10/1 for international students. Applications are processed on a rolling basis. Application fee: $55. Electronic applications accepted. *Expenses:* Tuition, state resident: full-time $4725; part-time $525 per credit. Tuition, nonresident: full-time $12,267; part-time $1363 per credit. Required fees: $346 per semester. Tuition and fees vary according to course load. *Financial support:* In 2009–10, 1 research assistantship with full tuition reimbursement, 1 teaching assistantship with full tuition reimbursement were awarded; fellowships, Federal Work-Study, scholarships/grants, health care benefits, and unspecified assistantships also available. Financial award application deadline: 2/1; financial award applicants required to submit FAFSA. *Unit head:* Kentwood Wells, Head, 860-486-4319, Fax: 860-486-6364, E-mail: kentwood.wells@uconn.edu. *Application contact:* Anne St. Onje, Graduate Coordinator, 860-486-4314, Fax: 860-486-3943, E-mail: anne.st_onje@uconn.edu.

University of Delaware, College of Agriculture and Natural Resources, Department of Entomology and Wildlife Ecology, Newark, DE 19716. Offers entomology and applied ecology (MS, PhD), including avian ecology, evolution and taxonomy, insect biological control, insect ecology and behavior (MS), insect genetics, pest management, plant-insect interactions, wildlife ecology and management. Part-time programs available. *Degree requirements:* For master's, comprehensive exam, thesis, oral exam, seminar; for doctorate, comprehensive exam, thesis/dissertation, qualifying exam, seminar. *Entrance requirements:* For master's, GRE General Test, minimum GPA of 3.0 in field, 2.8 overall; for doctorate, GRE General Test, GRE Subject Test (biology), minimum GPA of 3.0 in field, 2.8 overall. Additional exam requirements/recommendations for international students: Required—TOEFL. Electronic applications accepted. *Faculty research:* Ecology and evolution of plant-insect interactions, ecology of wildlife conservation management, habitat restoration, biological control, applied ecosystem management.

University of Florida, Graduate School, College of Agricultural and Life Sciences, Department of Entomology and Nematology, Gainesville, FL 32611. Offers MS, PhD. Terminal master's awarded for partial completion of doctoral program. *Degree requirements:* For master's, thesis optional; for doctorate, thesis/dissertation. *Entrance requirements:* For master's and doctorate, GRE General Test, GRE Subject Test (biology), minimum GPA of 3.0. Electronic applications accepted. *Faculty research:* Medical, veterinary, and urban entomology; genetics; biology and management; biocontrol; insect ecology.

University of Georgia, Graduate School, College of Agricultural and Environmental Sciences, Department of Entomology, Athens, GA 30602. Offers entomology (MS, PhD); plant protection and pest management (MPPPM). *Faculty:* 24 full-time (3 women). *Students:* 39 full-time (14 women), 3 part-time (1 woman); includes 2 minority (1 African American, 1 Hispanic American), 17 international. 20 applicants, 50% accepted, 8 enrolled. In 2009, 5 master's, 6 doctorates awarded. *Degree requirements:* For master's, thesis (MS); for doctorate, one foreign language, thesis/dissertation. *Entrance requirements:* For master's and doctorate, GRE General Test. *Application deadline:* For fall admission, 7/1 priority date for domestic students; for spring admission, 11/15 for domestic students. Application fee: $50. Electronic applications accepted. *Expenses:* Tuition, state resident: full-time $6000; part-time $250 per credit hour. Tuition, nonresident: full-time $20,904; part-time $871 per credit hour. Required fees: $730 per semester. *Financial support:* Unspecified assistantships available. *Faculty research:* Apiculture, acarology, aquatic and soil biology, ecology, systematics. *Unit head:* Dr. Raymond Noblet, Head, 706-542-1238, Fax: 706-542-2279, E-mail: rnoblet@uga.edu. *Application contact:* Dr. Mark Brown, Graduate Coordinator, 706-542-2317, E-mail: mbrown@uga.edu.

University of Guelph, Graduate Program Services, Ontario Agricultural College, Department of Environmental Biology, Guelph, ON N1G 2W1, Canada. Offers entomology (M Sc, PhD); environmental microbiology and biotechnology (M Sc, PhD); environmental toxicology (M Sc, PhD); plant and forest systems (M Sc, PhD); plant pathology (M Sc, PhD). Part-time programs available. *Degree requirements:* For master's, thesis; for doctorate, comprehensive exam, thesis/dissertation. *Entrance requirements:* For master's, minimum 75% average during previous 2 years of course work; for doctorate, minimum 75% average. Additional exam requirements/recommendations for international students: Required—TOEFL or IELTS. Electronic applications accepted. *Faculty research:* Entomology, environmental microbiology and biotechnology, environmental toxicology, forest ecology, plant pathology.

University of Hawaii at Manoa, Graduate Division, College of Tropical Agriculture and Human Resources, Department of Plant and Environmental Protection Sciences, Program in Entomology, Honolulu, HI 96822. Offers MS, PhD. Part-time programs available. *Faculty:* 13 full-time (1 woman), 9 part-time/adjunct (2 women). *Students:* 14 full-time (7 women), 1 part-time (0 women); includes 2 minority (both Asian Americans or Pacific Islanders), 6 international. Average age 30. 13 applicants, 46% accepted, 4 enrolled. *Degree requirements:* For master's, thesis optional; for doctorate, comprehensive exam, thesis/dissertation. *Entrance requirements:* For master's and doctorate, GRE General Test, GRE Subject Test (biology). Additional exam requirements/recommendations for international students: Required—TOEFL (minimum score 500 paper-based; 173 computer-based; 61 iBT), IELTS (minimum score 5). *Application deadline:* For fall admission, 3/1 for domestic and international students; for spring admission, 10/1 for domestic and international students. Application fee: $50. *Expenses:* Tuition, state resident: full-time $8900; part-time $372 per credit. Tuition, nonresident: full-time $21,400; part-time $898 per credit. Required fees: $207 per semester. *Financial support:* In 2009–10, 1 fellowship (averaging $3,150 per year), 13 research assistantships (averaging $19,383 per year) were awarded; tuition waivers (full) also available. *Faculty research:* Integrated pest management, biological control, urban entomology, medical/forensic entomology resistance. Total annual research expenditures: $200,000. *Application contact:* Julian Yates, Graduate Chair, 808-956-7076, Fax: 808-956-2428, E-mail: yates@hawaii.edu.

University of Idaho, College of Graduate Studies, College of Agricultural and Life Sciences, Department of Plant, Soil, and Entomological Sciences, Program in Entomology, Moscow, ID 83844-2282. Offers MS, PhD. *Students:* 8 full-time, 1 part-time. In 2009, 2 master's, 3 doctorates awarded. *Degree requirements:* For master's, thesis (for some programs); for doctorate, one foreign language, thesis/dissertation. *Entrance requirements:* For master's and doctorate, GRE General Test, minimum GPA of 3.0. *Application deadline:* For fall admission, 8/1 for domestic students; for spring admission, 12/15 for domestic students. Application fee: $55 ($60 for international students). *Expenses:* Tuition, state resident: full-time $6120. Tuition, nonresident: full-time $17,712. *Financial support:* Application deadline: 2/15. *Faculty research:* Biological control of insect pests/weeds, aquatic entomology-resource management, hop pest management, mosquito reproductive physiology, landscape ecology for sustainability and biological conservation. *Unit head:* Dr. Sanford Eigenbrode, Chair, 208-885-2972. *Application contact:* Dr. Sanford Eigenbrode, Chair, 208-885-2972.

University of Illinois at Urbana–Champaign, Graduate College, College of Liberal Arts and Sciences, School of Integrative Biology, Department of Entomology, Champaign, IL 61820. Offers MS, PhD. *Faculty:* 10 full-time (3 women). *Students:* 28 full-time (14 women), 6 part-time (4 women); includes 4 minority (1 African American, 2 Asian Americans or Pacific Islanders, 1 Hispanic American), 11 international. 27 applicants, 44% accepted, 9 enrolled. In 2009, 5 master's, 7 doctorates awarded. Terminal master's awarded for partial completion of doctoral program. *Entrance requirements:* For master's and doctorate, GRE General Test, GRE Subject Test, minimum GPA of 3.0. Additional exam requirements/recommendations for international students: Required—TOEFL (minimum score 550 paper-based). *Application deadline:* Applications are processed on a rolling basis. Application fee: $60 ($75 for international students). Electronic applications accepted. *Financial support:* In 2009–10, 2 fellowships, 28 research assistantships, 16 teaching assistantships were awarded; tuition waivers (full and partial) also available. *Unit head:* Dr. May R. Berenbaum, Head, 217-333-7784, Fax: 217-244-3499, E-mail: maybe@illinois.edu. *Application contact:* Audra Weinstein, Office Administrator, 217-244-2888, Fax: 217-244-3499, E-mail: audra@illinois.edu.

The University of Kansas, Graduate Studies, College of Liberal Arts and Sciences, Department of Ecology and Evolutionary Biology, Lawrence, KS 66045. Offers botany (MA, PhD); ecology and evolutionary biology (MA, PhD); entomology (MA, PhD). *Faculty:* 17 full-time (7 women), 29 part-time/adjunct (6 women). *Students:* 57 full-time (24 women), 4 part-time (1 woman); includes 1 minority (Hispanic American), 16 international. Average age 29. 49 applicants, 33% accepted, 8 enrolled. In 2009, 5 master's, 8 doctorates awarded. Terminal master's awarded for partial completion of doctoral program. *Degree requirements:* For master's, comprehensive exam, thesis (for some programs), 30-36 credits, thesis presentation; for doctorate, comprehensive exam, thesis/dissertation, residency, foreign language or other research skills, final exam and dissertation defense. *Entrance requirements:* For master's, GRE General Test, bachelor's degree with minimum undergraduate GPA of 3.0; for doctorate, GRE General Test, bachelor's degree; minimum undergraduate/graduate GPA of 3.0. Additional exam requirements/recommendations for international students: Required—TOEFL, IELTS. *Application deadline:* For fall admission, 12/15 priority date for domestic and international students. Applications are processed on a rolling basis. Application fee: $45 ($55 for international students). Electronic applications accepted. *Expenses:* Tuition, state resident: full-time $6492; part-time $270.50 per credit hour. Tuition, nonresident: full-time $15,510; part-time $646.25 per credit hour. Required fees: $847; $70.56 per credit hour. Tuition and fees vary according to course load and program. *Financial support:* Fellowships with tuition reimbursements, research assistantships with full and partial tuition reimbursements, teaching assistantships with full and partial tuition reimbursements, scholarships/grants, traineeships, health care benefits, and unspecified assistantships available. *Faculty research:* Biodiversity and macroevolution, ecology and global change, evolutionary mechanisms. *Unit head:* Dr. Christopher H. Haufler, Chair, 785-864-3255, Fax: 785-864-5860, E-mail: vulgare@ku.edu. *Application contact:* Jaime Rochelle Keeler, Graduate Coordinator, 785-864-2362, Fax: 785-864-5860, E-mail: jrkeeler@ku.edu.

University of Kentucky, Graduate School, College of Agriculture, Program in Entomology, Lexington, KY 40506-0032. Offers MS, PhD. *Degree requirements:* For master's, comprehensive exam, thesis optional; for doctorate, comprehensive exam, thesis/dissertation. *Entrance requirements:* For master's, GRE General Test, minimum undergraduate GPA of 2.75; for doctorate, GRE General Test, minimum graduate GPA of 3.0. Additional exam requirements/recommendations for international students: Required—TOEFL (minimum score 550 paper-based; 213 computer-based). Electronic applications accepted. *Faculty research:* Applied entomology, behavior, insect biology and ecology, biological control, insect physiology and molecular biology.

University of Maine, Graduate School, College of Natural Sciences, Forestry, and Agriculture, Department of Biological Sciences, Program in Entomology, Orono, ME 04469. Offers MS. Part-time programs available. *Students:* 1 applicant, 0% accepted, 0 enrolled. *Entrance requirements:* For master's, GRE General Test. Additional exam requirements/recommendations for international students: Required—TOEFL. *Application deadline:* For fall admission, 2/1 priority date for domestic students. Applications are processed on a rolling basis. Application fee: $65. Electronic applications accepted. *Financial support:* Career-related internships or fieldwork, Federal Work-Study, institutionally sponsored loans, and tuition waivers (full) available. Financial award application deadline: 3/1. *Unit head:* Dr. Stellos Tavantiz, Coordinator, 207-581-2986. *Application contact:* Scott G. Delcourt, Associate Dean of the Graduate School, 207-581-3291, Fax: 207-581-3232, E-mail: graduate@maine.edu.

University of Manitoba, Faculty of Graduate Studies, Faculty of Agricultural and Food Sciences, Department of Entomology, Winnipeg, MB R3T 2N2, Canada. Offers M Sc, PhD. *Degree requirements:* For master's, thesis; for doctorate, one foreign language, thesis/dissertation.

University of Maryland, College Park, Academic Affairs, College of Chemical and Life Sciences, Department of Entomology, College Park, MD 20742. Offers MS, PhD. Part-time and evening/weekend programs available. *Faculty:* 32 full-time (13 women), 1 (woman) part-time/adjunct. *Students:* 12 full-time (3 women), 3 part-time (2 women); includes 2 minority (1 African American, 1 Asian American or Pacific Islander), 5 international. 24 applicants, 21% accepted, 3 enrolled. In 2009, 2 master's, 3 doctorates awarded. Terminal master's awarded for partial completion of doctoral program. *Degree requirements:* For master's, thesis; for doctorate, thesis/dissertation, oral qualifying exam. *Entrance requirements:* For master's and doctorate, GRE General Test, minimum GPA of 3.0, 3 letters of recommendation. *Application deadline:* For fall admission, 2/1 for domestic and international students. Applications are processed on a rolling basis. Application fee: $60. Electronic applications accepted. *Expenses:* Tuition, area resident: Part-time $471 per credit hour. Tuition, state resident: part-time $471 per credit hour. Tuition, nonresident: part-time $1016 per credit hour. Required fees: $337.04 per term. *Financial support:* In 2009–10, 11 teaching assistantships with tuition reimbursements (averaging $20,031 per year) were awarded; fellowships, research assistantships, career-related internships or fieldwork and Federal Work-Study also available. Support available to part-time students. Financial award applicants required to submit FAFSA. *Faculty research:* Pest management, biosystematics, physiology and morphology, toxicology. Total annual research expenditures: $1.5 million. *Unit head:* Dr. Charles Mitter, Chair, 301-405-3912, Fax: 301-314-9290, E-mail: cmitter@umd.edu. *Application contact:* Dean of Graduate School, 301-405-0358, Fax: 301-314-9305.

University of Massachusetts Amherst, Graduate School, College of Natural Sciences, Department of Plant, Soil and Insect Sciences, Program in Entomology, Amherst, MA 01003. Offers MS, PhD. Part-time programs available. *Faculty:* 9 full-time (2 women). *Students:* 5 full-time (2 women), 1 international. Average age 27. 9 applicants, 56% accepted, 2 enrolled. In 2009, 1 doctorate awarded. Terminal master's awarded for partial completion of doctoral program. *Degree requirements:* For master's, thesis or alternative; for doctorate, comprehensive exam, thesis/dissertation. *Entrance requirements:* For master's and doctorate, GRE General Test. Additional exam requirements/recommendations for international students: Required—TOEFL (minimum score 550 paper-based; 213 computer-based; 80 iBT), IELTS (minimum score 6.5). *Application deadline:* For fall admission, 1/2 for domestic and international students; for spring admission, 10/1 for domestic and international students. Applications are processed on a rolling basis. Application fee: $50 ($65 for international students). Electronic applications accepted. *Expenses:* Tuition, state resident: full-time $2640; part-time $110 per credit. Tuition, nonresident: full-time $9936; part-time $414 per credit. Tuition and fees vary according to course load. *Financial support:* Fellowships, research assistantships, teaching assistantships, career-related internships or fieldwork, Federal Work-Study, scholarships/grants, traineeships, health care benefits, tuition waivers (full), and unspecified assistantships available. Support available to part-time students. Financial award application deadline: 1/2. *Unit head:* Dr. Benjamin Normark, Graduate Program Director, 413-545-1059, Fax: 413-545-2115. *Application contact:* Jean M. Ames, Supervisor of Admissions, 413-545-0722, Fax: 413-577-0010, E-mail: gradadm@grad.umass.edu.

University of Minnesota, Twin Cities Campus, Graduate School, College of Food, Agricultural and Natural Resource Sciences, Program in Entomology, Minneapolis, MN 55455-0213. Offers MS, PhD. Part-time programs available. *Degree requirements:* For master's, comprehensive exam, thesis; for doctorate, comprehensive exam, thesis/dissertation. *Entrance requirements:* For master's, GRE, minimum undergraduate GPA of 3.0; for doctorate, GRE, minimum undergraduate GPA of 3.0, graduate 3.5. Additional exam requirements/recommendations for international students: Required—TOEFL. Electronic applications accepted. *Faculty research:* Behavior, ecology, molecular genetics, physiology, systematics and taxonomy.

University of Missouri, Graduate School, College of Agriculture, Food and Natural Resources, Division of Plant Sciences, Program in Entomology, Columbia, MO 65211. Offers MS, PhD. *Degree requirements:* For doctorate, thesis/dissertation. *Application deadline:* Applications are processed on a rolling basis. *Financial support:* Research assistantships, teaching assistantships, institutionally sponsored loans available. *Application contact:* Dr. Jeanne Mihail, Director of Graduate Studies, 573-882-0574, E-mail: mihailj@missouri.edu.

University of Nebraska–Lincoln, Graduate College, College of Agricultural Sciences and Natural Resources, Department of Entomology, Lincoln, NE 68588. Offers MS, PhD. Postbaccalaureate distance learning degree programs offered (no on-campus study). *Degree requirements:* For master's, thesis optional; for doctorate, comprehensive exam, thesis/dissertation. *Entrance requirements:* For master's and doctorate, GRE General Test. Additional exam requirements/recommendations for international students: Required—TOEFL (minimum score 550 paper-based; 213 computer-based). Electronic applications accepted. *Faculty research:* Ecology and behavior, insect-plant interactions, integrated pest management, genetics, urban entomology.

University of North Dakota, Graduate School, College of Arts and Sciences, Department of Biology, Grand Forks, ND 58202. Offers botany (MS, PhD); ecology (MS, PhD); entomology (MS, PhD); environmental biology (MS, PhD); fisheries/wildlife (MS, PhD); genetics (MS, PhD); zoology (MS, PhD). Terminal master's awarded for partial completion of doctoral program. *Degree requirements:* For master's, thesis, final exam; for doctorate, comprehensive exam, thesis/dissertation, final exam. *Entrance requirements:* For master's, GRE General Test, GRE Subject Test, minimum GPA of 3.0; for doctorate, GRE General Test, GRE Subject Test, minimum GPA of 3.5. Additional exam requirements/recommendations for international students: Required—TOEFL (minimum score 550 paper-based; 213 computer-based; 79 iBT), IELTS (minimum score 6.5). Electronic applications accepted. *Faculty research:* Population biology, wildlife ecology, RNA processing, hormonal control of behavior.

University of Rhode Island, Graduate School, College of the Environment and Life Sciences, Department of Plant Sciences, Kingston, RI 02881. Offers entomology (MS, PhD); plant sciences (MS, PhD). Part-time programs available. *Faculty:* 9 full-time (2 women). *Students:* 1 full-time (0 women), all international. *Degree requirements:* For master's, comprehensive exam (for some programs), thesis optional; for doctorate, comprehensive exam, thesis/dissertation. *Entrance requirements:* For master's and doctorate, GRE, 2 letters of recommendation. Additional exam requirements/recommendations for international students: Required—TOEFL (minimum score 550 paper-based; 213 computer-based). *Application deadline:* For fall admission, 7/15 for domestic students, 2/1 for international students; for spring admission, 11/15 for domestic students, 7/15 for international students. Application fee: $65. Electronic applications accepted. *Expenses:* Tuition, state resident: full-time $8828; part-time $490 per credit hour. Tuition, nonresident: full-time $22,100; part-time $1228 per credit hour. Required fees: $1118; $57 per semester. Tuition and fees vary according to program. *Financial support:* In 2009–10, 2 research assistantships with full and partial tuition reimbursements (averaging $9,263 per year), 4 teaching assistantships with full and partial tuition reimbursements (averaging $11,389 per year) were awarded. Financial award application deadline: 7/15; financial award applicants required to submit FAFSA. *Faculty research:* Plant development and management; pest management; tick biology, ecology, and control; identification and replacement of invasive ornamentals. Total annual research expenditures: $1.3 million. *Unit head:* Dr. Brian K. Maynard, Interim Chair, 401-874-2928, Fax: 401-874-2494, E-mail: bmaynard@uri.edu. *Application contact:* Dr. Thomas Mather, Director of Graduate Studies, 401-874-5616, Fax: 401-874-2494, E-mail: tmather@uri.edu.

The University of Tennessee, Graduate School, College of Agricultural Sciences and Natural Resources, Department of Entomology and Plant Pathology, Knoxville, TN 37996. Offers entomology (MS, PhD); integrated pest management and bioactive natural products (PhD); plant pathology (MS, PhD). Part-time programs available. *Degree requirements:* For master's, thesis, seminar. *Entrance requirements:* For master's, GRE General Test, minimum GPA of 2.7, 3 reference letters, letter of intent; for doctorate, GRE General Test, minimum GPA of 2.7, 3 reference letters, letter of intent, proposed dissertation research. Additional exam requirements/recommendations for international students: Required—TOEFL. Electronic applications accepted. *Expenses:* Tuition, state resident: full-time $6826; part-time $380 per semester hour. Tuition, nonresident: full-time $21,844; part-time $1147 per semester hour. Tuition and fees vary according to program.

University of Wisconsin–Madison, Graduate School, College of Agricultural and Life Sciences, Department of Entomology, Madison, WI 53706-1380. Offers MS, PhD. *Degree requirements:* For master's, thesis; for doctorate, thesis/dissertation. *Entrance requirements:* For master's and doctorate, GRE General Test, minimum GPA of 3.0. Additional exam requirements/recommendations for international students: Required—TOEFL (minimum score 237 computer-based). Electronic applications accepted. *Expenses:* Tuition, state resident: part-time $594 per credit. Tuition, nonresident: part-time $1504 per credit. Required fees: $65 per credit. Tuition and fees vary according to course load, program and reciprocity agreements. *Faculty research:* Ecology, biocontrol, molecular.

University of Wyoming, College of Agriculture, Department of Renewable Resources, Program in Entomology, Laramie, WY 82070. Offers MS, PhD. *Degree requirements:* For master's, thesis; for doctorate, thesis/dissertation. *Entrance requirements:* For master's and doctorate, GRE General Test, minimum GPA of 3.0. Additional exam requirements/recommendations for international students: Required—TOEFL. Electronic applications accepted. *Faculty research:* Insect pest management, taxonomy, biocontrol of weeds, forest insects, insects affecting humans and animals.

Virginia Polytechnic Institute and State University, Graduate School, College of Agriculture and Life Sciences, Department of Entomology, Blacksburg, VA 24061. Offers MS, PhD. *Faculty:* 14 full-time (2 women). *Students:* 41 full-time (27 women); includes 13 minority (10 American Indian/Alaska Native, 2 Asian Americans or Pacific Islanders, 1 Hispanic American), 1 international. Average age 29. 11 applicants, 82% accepted, 6 enrolled. In 2009, 4 master's, 4 doctorates awarded. *Entrance requirements:* For master's and doctorate, GRE, GMAT. Additional exam requirements/recommendations for international students: Required—TOEFL (minimum score 550 paper-based; 213 computer-based). *Application deadline:* For fall admission, 5/15 for international students; for spring admission, 10/15 for international students. Applications are processed on a rolling basis. Application fee: $65. Electronic applications accepted. *Expenses:* Tuition, area resident: Full-time $10,228; part-time $459 per credit hour. Tuition, nonresident: full-time $17,892; part-time $865 per credit hour. Required fees: $1966; $451 per semester. *Financial support:* In 2009–10, 22 research assistantships with full tuition reimbursements (averaging $17,013 per year), 9 teaching assistantships with full tuition reimbursements (averaging $14,015 per year) were awarded; career-related internships or fieldwork, Federal Work-Study, scholarships/grants, and unspecified assistantships also available. Financial award application deadline: 1/15. *Faculty research:* Physiology, ecology, biocontrol, genetics, taxonomy. Total annual research expenditures: $2.7 million. *Unit head:* Dr. Loke T. Kok, Dean, 540-231-6341, Fax: 540-231-9131, E-mail: ltkok@vt.edu. *Application contact:* Don Mullins, Information Contact, 540-231-5978, Fax: 540-231-9131, E-mail: mullinsd@vt.edu.

Washington State University, Graduate School, College of Agricultural, Human, and Natural Resource Sciences, Department of Entomology, Pullman, WA 99164. Offers MS, PhD. Part-time programs available. *Faculty:* 22. *Students:* 23 full-time (9 women), 1 (woman) part-time; includes 1 minority (Asian American or Pacific Islander), 7 international. Average age 31. 24 applicants, 63% accepted, 8 enrolled. In 2009, 3 master's, 3 doctorates awarded. Terminal master's awarded for partial completion of doctoral program. *Degree requirements:* For master's, comprehensive exam (for some programs), thesis (for some programs), oral exam; for doctorate, comprehensive exam, thesis/dissertation, oral exam, written exam. *Entrance requirements:* For master's, GRE General Test, GRE Subject Test in advanced biology (recommended), minimum GPA of 3.0, 3 letters of recommendation; for doctorate, GRE General Test, minimum GPA of 3.0, 3 letters of recommendation. Additional exam requirements/recommendations for international students: Required—TOEFL (minimum score 550 paper-based; 213 computer-based), IELTS. *Application deadline:* For fall admission, 1/10 priority date for domestic and international students; for spring admission, 7/1 priority date for domestic and international students. Applications are processed on a rolling basis. Application fee: $50. Electronic applications accepted. *Financial support:* In 2009–10, 2 fellowships (averaging $5,306 per year), 17 research assistantships with full and partial tuition reimbursements (averaging $14,634 per year), 1 teaching assistantship with full and partial tuition reimbursement (averaging $13,383 per year) were awarded; career-related internships or fieldwork, Federal Work-Study, institutionally sponsored loans, tuition waivers (partial), unspecified assistantships, and teaching associateships also available. Financial award application deadline: 2/5; financial award applicants required to submit FAFSA. *Faculty research:* Apiculture, biological control of arthropods, integrated pest management, ecology, physiology and systematics of insects. Total annual research expenditures: $2.8 million. *Unit head:* Dr. W. Steve Sheppard, Chair, 509-335-5180, Fax: 509-335-1009, E-mail: shepp@wsu.edu. *Application contact:* Graduate School Admissions, 800-GRADWSU, Fax: 509-335-1949, E-mail: gradsch@wsu.edu.

West Virginia University, Davis College of Agriculture, Forestry and Consumer Sciences, Division of Plant and Soil Sciences, Morgantown, WV 26506. Offers agricultural sciences (PhD), including animal and food sciences, plant and soil sciences; agronomy (MS); entomology (MS); environmental microbiology (MS); horticulture (MS); plant pathology (MS). *Degree requirements:* For master's, thesis. *Entrance requirements:* For master's, GRE, minimum GPA of 2.5. Additional exam requirements/recommendations for international students: Required—TOEFL. *Faculty research:* Water quality, reclamation of disturbed land, crop production, pest control, environmental protection.

Section 10
Genetics, Developmental Biology, and Reproductive Biology

This section contains a directory of institutions offering graduate work in genetics, developmental biology, and reproductive biology, followed by in-depth entries submitted by institutions that chose to prepare detailed program descriptions. Additional information about programs listed in the directory but not augmented by an in-depth entry may be obtained by writing directly to the dean of a graduate school or chair of a department at the address given in the directory.

For programs offering related work, see also all other sections of this book. In the other guides in this series:

Graduate Programs in the Physical Sciences, Mathematics, Agricultural Sciences, the Environment & Natural Resources

See *Agricultural and Food Sciences, Chemistry,* and *Environmental Sciences and Management*

Graduate Programs in Engineering & Applied Sciences

See *Agricultural Engineering and Bioengineering* and *Biomedical Engineering and Biotechnology*

Graduate Programs in Business, Education, Health, Information Studies, Law & Social Work

See *Veterinary Medicine and Sciences*

CONTENTS

Developmental Biology

Albert Einstein College of Medicine, Sue Golding Graduate Division of Medical Sciences, Department of Anatomy and Structural Biology, Bronx, NY 10461. Offers anatomy (PhD); cell and developmental biology (PhD); MD/PhD. *Degree requirements:* For doctorate, thesis/dissertation. *Entrance requirements:* For doctorate, GRE General Test. Additional exam requirements/recommendations for international students: Required—TOEFL. Electronic applications accepted. *Faculty research:* Cell motility, cell membranes and membrane-cytoskeletal interactions as applied to processing of pancreatic hormones, mechanisms of secretion.

Albert Einstein College of Medicine, Sue Golding Graduate Division of Medical Sciences, Division of Biological Sciences, Department of Developmental and Molecular Biology, Bronx, NY 10461. Offers PhD, MD/PhD. *Degree requirements:* For doctorate, thesis/dissertation. *Entrance requirements:* For doctorate, GRE General Test. Additional exam requirements/recommendations for international students: Required—TOEFL. *Faculty research:* DNA, RNA, and protein synthesis in prokaryotes and eukaryotes; chemical and enzymatic alteration of RNA; glycoproteins.

Baylor College of Medicine, Graduate School of Biomedical Sciences, Program in Developmental Biology, Houston, TX 77030-3498. Offers PhD. *Faculty:* 52 full-time (16 women). *Students:* 51 full-time (26 women); includes 9 minority (1 American Indian/Alaska Native, 6 Asian Americans or Pacific Islanders, 2 Hispanic Americans), 29 international. Average age 25. In 2009, 4 doctorates awarded. *Degree requirements:* For doctorate, thesis/dissertation, public defense. *Entrance requirements:* For doctorate, GRE General Test, GRE Subject Test (strongly recommended), minimum GPA of 3.0. Additional exam requirements/recommendations for international students: Required—TOEFL. *Application deadline:* For fall admission, 1/1 priority date for domestic students. Application fee: $0. Electronic applications accepted. *Financial support:* Fellowships, research assistantships, career-related internships or fieldwork, Federal Work-Study, institutionally sponsored loans, health care benefits, tuition waivers (full), and stipends available. *Faculty research:* Molecular and genetic approaches to study pattern formation in Dictyostelium, Drosophila, C.elegans, mouse, Xenopus, and zebrafish; cross-species approach. *Unit head:* Dr. Hugo Bellen, Director, 713-798-6410. *Application contact:* Catherine Tasnier, Graduate Program Administrator, 713-798-6410, Fax: 713-798-5386, E-mail: cat@bcm.edu.

See Display on this page and Close-Up on page 315.

Brigham Young University, Graduate Studies, College of Life Sciences, Department of Physiology and Developmental Biology, Provo, UT 84602. Offers neuroscience (MS, PhD); physiology and developmental biology (MS, PhD). Part-time programs available. *Faculty:* 19 full-time (0 women). *Students:* 25 full-time (11 women); includes 3 minority (1 American Indian/Alaska Native, 1 Asian American or Pacific Islander, 1 Hispanic American). Average age 30. 14 applicants, 43% accepted, 3 enrolled. In 2009, 3 master's, 3 doctorates awarded. Terminal master's awarded for partial completion of doctoral program. *Degree requirements:* For master's, thesis; for doctorate, thesis/dissertation. *Entrance requirements:* For master's, GRE General Test, minimum GPA of 3.0 during previous 2 years; for doctorate, GRE General Test, minimum GPA of 3.0 overall. Additional exam requirements/recommendations for international students: Required—TOEFL. *Application deadline:* For fall admission, 2/1 priority date for domestic and international students; for winter admission, 9/10 priority date for domestic and international students. Application fee: $50. Electronic applications accepted. *Expenses:* Tuition: Full-time $5580; part-time $301 per credit hour. Tuition and fees vary according to student's religious affiliation. *Financial support:* In 2009–10, 25 students received support, including 1 fellowship with partial tuition reimbursement available (averaging $7,100 per year), 12 research assistantships with full tuition reimbursements available (averaging $15,500 per year), 13 teaching assistantships with partial tuition reimbursements available (averaging $14,900 per year); career-related internships or fieldwork, institutionally sponsored loans, scholarships/grants, tuition waivers (full and partial), unspecified assistantships, and tuition awards also available. Financial award application deadline: 2/1. *Faculty research:* Sex differentiation of the brain, exercise physiology, developmental biology, membrane biophysics, neuroscience. Total annual research expenditures: $848,996. *Unit head:* Dr. William W. Winder, Chair, 801-422-3093, Fax: 801-422-0700, E-mail: william_winder@byu.edu. *Application contact:* Dr. Dixon J. Woodbury, Graduate Coordinator, 801-422-7562, Fax: 801-422-0700, E-mail: dixon_woodbury@byu.edu.

Brown University, Graduate School, Division of Biology and Medicine, Program in Molecular Biology, Cell Biology, and Biochemistry, Providence, RI 02912. Offers biochemistry (M Med Sc, Sc M, PhD), including biochemistry (Sc M, PhD), biology (Sc M, PhD), medical science (M Med Sc, PhD); biology (MA); cell biology (M Med Sc, Sc M, PhD), including biochemistry (Sc M, PhD), biology (Sc M, PhD), medical science (M Med Sc, PhD); developmental biology (M Med Sc, Sc M, PhD), including biochemistry (Sc M, PhD), biology (Sc M, PhD), medical science (M Med Sc, PhD); immunology (M Med Sc, Sc M, PhD), including biochemistry (Sc M, PhD), biology (Sc M, PhD), medical science (M Med Sc, PhD); molecular microbiology (M Med Sc, Sc M, PhD), including biochemistry (Sc M, PhD), biology (Sc M, PhD), medical science (M Med Sc, PhD); MD/PhD. Part-time programs available. Terminal master's awarded for partial completion of doctoral program. *Degree requirements:* For master's, thesis (for some programs); for doctorate, one foreign language, thesis/dissertation, preliminary exam. *Entrance requirements:* For master's and doctorate, GRE General Test, GRE Subject Test. Additional exam requirements/recommendations for international students: Required—TOEFL. Electronic applications accepted. *Faculty research:* Molecular genetics, gene regulation.

California Institute of Technology, Division of Biology, Program in Developmental Biology, Pasadena, CA 91125-0001. Offers PhD. *Degree requirements:* For doctorate, thesis/dissertation, qualifying exam. *Entrance requirements:* For doctorate, GRE General Test.

Carnegie Mellon University, Mellon College of Science, Department of Biological Sciences, Pittsburgh, PA 15213-3891. Offers biochemistry (PhD); biophysics (PhD); cell biology (PhD); computational biology (MS, PhD); developmental biology (PhD); genetics (PhD); molecular biology (PhD); neuroscience (PhD). *Degree requirements:* For doctorate, comprehensive exam, thesis/dissertation. *Entrance requirements:* For doctorate, GRE General Test, GRE Subject Test, interview. Electronic applications accepted. *Faculty research:* Genetic structure, function, and regulation; protein structure and function; biological membranes; biological spectroscopy.

Columbia University, College of Physicians and Surgeons, Department of Genetics and Development, New York, NY 10032. Offers genetics (M Phil, MA, PhD); MD/PhD. Only candidates for the PhD are admitted. Terminal master's awarded for partial completion of doctoral program. *Degree requirements:* For doctorate, thesis/dissertation. *Entrance requirements:* For master's and doctorate, GRE General Test. Additional exam requirements/recommendations for international students: Required—TOEFL. *Faculty research:* Mammalian cell differentiation and meiosis, developmental genetics, yeast and human genetics, chromosome structure, molecular and cellular biology.

Cornell University, Graduate School, Graduate Fields of Agriculture and Life Sciences, Field of Genetics and Development, Ithaca, NY 14853-0001. Offers developmental biology (PhD); genetics (PhD). *Faculty:* 58 full-time (14 women). *Students:* 60 full-time (33 women); includes 5 minority (2 Asian Americans or Pacific Islanders, 3 Hispanic Americans), 22 international. Average age 27. 64 applicants, 33% accepted, 12 enrolled. In 2009, 5 doctorates awarded. *Degree requirements:* For doctorate, comprehensive exam, thesis/dissertation, 2 semesters of teaching experience. *Entrance requirements:* For doctorate, GRE General Test, GRE Subject Test in biology or biochemistry (recommended), 2 letters of recommendation. Additional exam requirements/recommendations for international students: Required—TOEFL (minimum score 550 paper-based; 213 computer-based; 77 iBT). *Application deadline:* For fall admission, 1/5 for domestic students. Application fee: $70. Electronic applications accepted. *Expenses:* Tuition:

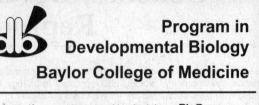
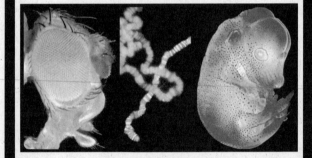

Full-time $29,500. Required fees: $70. Full-time tuition and fees vary according to degree level, program and student level. *Financial support:* In 2009–10, 54 students received support, including 7 fellowships with full tuition reimbursements available, 2 research assistantships with full tuition reimbursements available, 1 teaching assistantship with full tuition reimbursement available; institutionally sponsored loans, scholarships/grants, health care benefits, tuition waivers (full and partial), and unspecified assistantships also available. Financial award applicants required to submit FAFSA. *Faculty research:* Molecular and general genetics, developmental biology and developmental genetics, evolution and population genetics, plant genetics, microbial genetics. *Unit head:* Director of Graduate Studies, 607-254-2100. *Application contact:* Graduate Field Assistant, 607-254-2100, E-mail: gendev@cornell.edu.

Cornell University, Graduate School, Graduate Fields of Agriculture and Life Sciences, Field of Zoology, Ithaca, NY 14853-0001. Offers animal cytology (MS, PhD); comparative and functional anatomy (MS, PhD); developmental biology (MS, PhD); ecology (MS, PhD); histology (MS, PhD). *Faculty:* 24 full-time (5 women). *Students:* 4 full-time (all women); includes 1 minority (Hispanic American), 1 international. Average age 34. 7 applicants, 0% accepted, 0 enrolled. *Degree requirements:* For doctorate, comprehensive exam, thesis/dissertation, 2 semesters of teaching experience. *Entrance requirements:* For doctorate, GRE General Test, GRE Subject Test (biology), 2 letters of recommendation. Additional exam requirements/recommendations for international students: Required—TOEFL (minimum score 550 paper-based; 213 computer-based; 77 iBT). *Application deadline:* For fall admission, 2/1 priority date for domestic students. Application fee: $70. Electronic applications accepted. *Expenses:* Tuition: Full-time $29,500. Required fees: $70. Full-time tuition and fees vary according to degree level, program and student level. *Financial support:* In 2009–10, 3 students received support; fellowships with full tuition reimbursements available, research assistantships with full tuition reimbursements available, teaching assistantships with full tuition reimbursements available, institutionally sponsored loans, scholarships/grants, health care benefits, tuition waivers (full and partial), and unspecified assistantships available. Financial award applicants required to submit FAFSA. *Faculty research:* Organismal biology, functional morphology, biomechanics, comparative vertebrate anatomy, comparative invertebrate anatomy, paleontology. *Unit head:* Director of Graduate Studies, 607-253-3276, Fax: 607-253-3756. *Application contact:* Graduate Field Assistant, 607-253-3276, Fax: 607-253-3756, E-mail: graduate_edcvm@cornell.edu.

Cornell University, Graduate School, Graduate Fields of Comparative Biomedical Sciences, Field of Comparative Biomedical Sciences, Ithaca, NY 14853-0001. Offers cellular and molecular medicine (MS, PhD); developmental and reproductive biology (MS, PhD); infectious diseases (MS, PhD); population medicine and epidemiology (MS, PhD); structural and functional biology (MS, PhD). *Faculty:* 106 full-time (29 women). *Students:* 41 full-time (28 women); includes 1 minority (African American), 17 international. Average age 32. 32 applicants, 31% accepted, 9 enrolled. In 2009, 1 master's, 10 doctorates awarded. *Degree requirements:* For master's, thesis; for doctorate, comprehensive exam, thesis/dissertation. *Entrance requirements:* For master's and doctorate, GRE General Test, 2 letters of recommendation. Additional exam requirements/recommendations for international students: Required—TOEFL (minimum score 550 paper-based; 213 computer-based; 77 iBT). *Application deadline:* For fall admission, 12/15 for domestic students. Application fee: $70. Electronic applications accepted. *Expenses:* Tuition: Full-time $29,500. Required fees: $70. Full-time tuition and fees vary according to degree level, program and student level. *Financial support:* In 2009–10, 4 fellowships with full tuition reimbursements, 2 research assistantships with full tuition reimbursements were awarded; teaching assistantships with full tuition reimbursements, institutionally sponsored loans, scholarships/grants, health care benefits, tuition waivers (full and partial), and unspecified assistantships also available. Financial award applicants required to submit FAFSA. *Faculty research:* Receptors and signal transduction, viral and bacterial infectious diseases, tumor metastasis, clinical sciences/nutritional disease, developmental/neurological disorders. *Unit head:* Director of Graduate Studies, 607-253-3276, Fax: 607-253-3756. *Application contact:* Graduate Field Assistant, 607-253-3276, Fax: 607-253-3756, E-mail: graduate_edcvm@cornell.edu.

Duke University, Graduate School, Program in Developmental Biology, Durham, NC 27710. Offers PhD, Certificate. *Faculty:* 45 full-time. *Students:* 10 full-time (6 women); includes 1 minority (Asian American or Pacific Islander), 3 international. 51 applicants, 31% accepted, 9 enrolled. *Entrance requirements:* For doctorate, GRE General Test, GRE Subject Test (recommended); for Certificate, GRE General Test, GRE Subject Test. Additional exam requirements/recommendations for international students: Required—TOEFL (minimum score 550 paper-based; 213 computer-based; 83 iBT), IELTS (minimum score 7). *Application deadline:* For fall admission, 12/8 priority date for domestic and international students. Application fee: $75. *Unit head:* John Klingensmith, Head, 919-684-6629, Fax: 919-684-8346, E-mail: andrea.lanahan@duke.edu. *Application contact:* Cynthia Robertson, Associate Dean for Enrollment Services, 919-684-3913, E-mail: grad-admissions@duke.edu.

Emory University, Graduate School of Arts and Sciences, Division of Biological and Biomedical Sciences, Program in Biochemistry, Cell and Developmental Biology, Atlanta, GA 30322-1100. Offers PhD. *Faculty:* 51 full-time (10 women). *Students:* 62 full-time (42 women); includes 9 minority (3 African Americans, 5 Asian Americans or Pacific Islanders, 1 Hispanic American), 17 international. Average age 27. 107 applicants, 12% accepted, 6 enrolled. In 2009, 10 doctorates awarded. *Degree requirements:* For doctorate, comprehensive exam, thesis/dissertation. *Entrance requirements:* For doctorate, GRE General Test, minimum GPA of 3.0 in science course work (recommended). Additional exam requirements/recommendations for international students: Required—TOEFL. *Application deadline:* For fall admission, 1/3 for domestic and international students. Application fee: $50. Electronic applications accepted. *Financial support:* In 2009–10, 24 students received support, including 24 fellowships with full tuition reimbursements available (averaging $24,500 per year); institutionally sponsored loans, scholarships/grants, and health care benefits also available. *Faculty research:* Signal transduction, molecular biology, enzymes and cofactors, receptor and ion channel function, membrane biology. *Unit head:* Richard Kahn, Director, 404-727-3561, Fax: 404-727-3746, E-mail: rkahn@emory.edu. *Application contact:* 404-727-2545, Fax: 404-727-3322, E-mail: gdbbs@emory.edu.

Illinois State University, Graduate School, College of Arts and Sciences, Department of Biological Sciences, Normal, IL 61790-2200. Offers animal behavior (MS); bacteriology (MS); biochemistry (MS); biological sciences (MS); biology (PhD); biophysics (MS); biotechnology (MS); botany (MS, PhD); cell biology (MS); conservation biology (MS); developmental biology (MS); ecology (MS, PhD); entomology (MS); evolutionary biology (MS); genetics (MS, PhD); immunology (MS); microbiology (MS, PhD); molecular biology (MS); molecular genetics (MS); neurobiology (MS); neuroscience (MS); parasitology (MS); physiology (MS, PhD); plant biology (MS); plant molecular biology (MS); plant sciences (MS); structural biology (MS); zoology (MS, PhD). Part-time programs available. *Degree requirements:* For master's, thesis or alternative; for doctorate, variable foreign language requirement, thesis/dissertation, 2 terms of residency. *Entrance requirements:* For master's, GRE General Test, minimum GPA of 2.6 in last 60 hours of course work; for doctorate, GRE General Test. *Faculty research:* Redoc balance and drug development in schistosoma mansoni, control of the growth of listeria monocytogenes at low temperature, regulation of cell expansion and microtubule function by SPRI, CRUI: physiology and fitness consequences of different life history phenotypes.

Iowa State University of Science and Technology, Graduate College, College of Liberal Arts and Sciences and College of Agriculture, Department of Genetics, Developmental and Cell Biology, Ames, IA 50011. Offers MS, PhD. *Faculty:* 30 full-time (5 women), 5 part-time/adjunct (3 women). *Degree requirements:* For master's, thesis; for doctorate, thesis/dissertation. *Entrance requirements:* Additional exam requirements/recommendations for international students: Required—TOEFL (minimum score 570 paper-based; 230 computer-based) or IELTS (minimum score 6.5). Application fee: $40 ($90 for international students). *Expenses:* Tuition, state resident: full-time $6716. Tuition, nonresident: full-time $8908. Tuition and fees vary according to course level, course load, program and student level. *Financial support:* Fellowships with full tuition reimbursements, research assistantships with full and partial tuition reimbursements, teaching assistantships with full and partial tuition reimbursements, scholarships/grants, health care benefits, and unspecified assistantships available. Financial award application deadline: 2/1. *Faculty research:* Animal behavior, animal models of gene therapy, cell biology, comparative physiology, developmental biology. *Unit head:* Dr. Martin Spalding, Chair, 515-294-1749. *Application contact:* Information Contact, 515-294-5836, Fax: 515-294-2592, E-mail: grad_admissions@iastate.edu.

Iowa State University of Science and Technology, Graduate College, Interdisciplinary Programs, Program in Molecular, Cellular, and Developmental Biology, Ames, IA 50011. Offers MS, PhD. *Students:* 34 full-time (16 women), 1 part-time (0 women), 26 international. In 2009, 2 master's, 8 doctorates awarded. *Degree requirements:* For master's, thesis or alternative; for doctorate, thesis/dissertation. *Entrance requirements:* For master's and doctorate, GRE General Test. Additional exam requirements/recommendations for international students: Required—TOEFL (minimum score 580 paper-based; 85 iBT) or IELTS (minimum score 7). *Application deadline:* For fall admission, 1/15 priority date for domestic and international students. Application fee: $40 ($90 for international students). Electronic applications accepted. *Expenses:* Tuition, state resident: full-time $6716. Tuition, nonresident: full-time $8908. Tuition and fees vary according to course level, course load, program and student level. *Financial support:* In 2009–10, 33 research assistantships with full and partial tuition reimbursements (averaging $18,750 per year), 1 teaching assistantship with full and partial tuition reimbursement (averaging $18,750 per year) were awarded; scholarships/grants, health care benefits, and unspecified assistantships also available. *Unit head:* Dr. Jeff Beetham, Supervisory Committee Chair, 515-294-7252, E-mail: idgp@iastate.edu. *Application contact:* Katie Blair, Information Contact, 515-294-7252, Fax: 515-924-6790, E-mail: idgp@iastate.edu.

The Johns Hopkins University, National Institutes of Health Sponsored Programs, Baltimore, MD 21218-2699. Offers biology (PhD), including biochemistry, biophysics, cell biology, developmental biology, genetic biology, molecular biology; cell, molecular, and developmental biology and biophysics (PhD). *Faculty:* 25 full-time (4 women). *Students:* 126 full-time (72 women); includes 36 minority (3 African Americans, 1 American Indian/Alaska Native, 21 Asian Americans or Pacific Islanders, 11 Hispanic Americans), 19 international. 282 applicants, 26% accepted, 36 enrolled. In 2009, 15 doctorates awarded. *Degree requirements:* For doctorate, comprehensive exam, thesis/dissertation. *Entrance requirements:* For doctorate, GRE General Test. Additional exam requirements/recommendations for international students: Required—TOEFL (minimum score 600 paper-based; 250 computer-based), TWE. *Application deadline:* For fall admission, 12/15 priority date for domestic students. Application fee: $60. Electronic applications accepted. *Financial support:* In 2009–10, 24 fellowships (averaging $23,000 per year), 93 research assistantships (averaging $23,000 per year), 22 teaching assistantships (averaging $23,000 per year) were awarded; Federal Work-Study, institutionally sponsored loans, scholarships/grants, traineeships, health care benefits, tuition waivers (partial), and unspecified assistantships also available. Financial award application deadline: 4/15; financial award applicants required to submit FAFSA. *Faculty research:* Protein and nucleic acid biochemistry and biophysical chemistry, molecular biology and development. Total annual research expenditures: $11.2 million. *Unit head:* Dr. Allen Shearn, Chair, 410-516-4693, Fax: 410-516-5213, E-mail: bio_cals@jhu.edu. *Application contact:* Joan Miller, Academic Affairs Manager, 410-516-5502, Fax: 410-516-5213, E-mail: joan@jhu.edu.

Louisiana State University Health Sciences Center, School of Graduate Studies in New Orleans, Department of Cell Biology and Anatomy, New Orleans, LA 70112-2223. Offers cell biology and anatomy (MS, PhD), including cell biology, developmental biology, neurobiology and anatomy; MD/PhD. *Degree requirements:* For master's, comprehensive exam, thesis; for doctorate, comprehensive exam, thesis/dissertation. *Entrance requirements:* For master's and doctorate, GRE General Test, GRE Subject Test, minimum undergraduate GPA of 3.0. Additional exam requirements/recommendations for international students: Required—TOEFL. *Faculty research:* Visual system organization, neural development, plasticity of sensory systems, information processing through the nervous system, visuomotor integration.

Marquette University, Graduate School, College of Arts and Sciences, Department of Biology, Milwaukee, WI 53201-1881. Offers cell biology (MS, PhD); developmental biology (MS, PhD); ecology (MS, PhD); endocrinology (MS, PhD); evolutionary biology (MS, PhD); genetics (MS, PhD); microbiology (MS, PhD); molecular biology (MS, PhD); muscle and exercise physiology (MS, PhD); neurobiology (MS, PhD); reproductive physiology (MS, PhD). *Faculty:* 23 full-time (10 women), 1 part-time/adjunct (0 women). *Students:* 23 full-time (13 women), 16 part-time (9 women); includes 1 minority (Asian American or Pacific Islander), 20 international. Average age 25. 95 applicants, 16% accepted, 10 enrolled. In 2009, 3 master's, 5 doctorates awarded. Terminal master's awarded for partial completion of doctoral program. *Degree requirements:* For master's, comprehensive exam, thesis, 1 year of teaching experience or equivalent; for doctorate, thesis/dissertation, 1 year of teaching experience or equivalent, qualifying exam. *Entrance requirements:* For master's and doctorate, GRE General Test, GRE Subject Test. Additional exam requirements/recommendations for international students: Required—TOEFL. Application fee: $40. *Financial support:* In 2009–10, 4 fellowships, 22 teaching assistantships were awarded; research assistantships, Federal Work-Study, institutionally sponsored loans, scholarships/grants, and tuition waivers (full and partial) also available. Support available to part-time students. Financial award application deadline: 2/15. *Faculty research:* Microbial and invertebrate ecology, evolution of gene function, DNA methylation, DNA arrangement. *Unit head:* Dr. Robert Fitts, Chair, 414-288-1748, Fax: 414-288-7357. *Application contact:* Debbie Weaver, Administrative Assistant, 414-288-7355, Fax: 414-288-7357.

Massachusetts Institute of Technology, School of Science, Department of Biology, Cambridge, MA 02139-4307. Offers biochemistry (PhD); biological oceanography (PhD); biology (PhD); biophysical chemistry and molecular structure (PhD); cell biology (PhD); computational and systems biology (PhD); developmental biology (PhD); genetics (PhD); immunology (PhD); microbiology (PhD); molecular biology (PhD); neurobiology (PhD). *Faculty:* 54 full-time (14 women). *Students:* 237 full-time (128 women); includes 65 minority (4 African Americans, 2 American Indian/Alaska Native, 33 Asian Americans or Pacific Islanders, 26 Hispanic Americans), 25 international. Average age 26. 645 applicants, 18% accepted, 49 enrolled. In 2009, 41 doctorates awarded. *Degree requirements:* For doctorate, comprehensive exam, thesis/dissertation. *Entrance requirements:* For doctorate, GRE General Test. Additional exam requirements/recommendations for international students: Required—TOEFL (minimum score 577 paper-based; 233 computer-based), IELTS (minimum score 6.5). *Application deadline:* For fall admission, 12/1 for domestic and international students. Application fee: $75. Electronic applications accepted. *Expenses:* Tuition: Full-time $37,510; part-time $585 per unit. Required fees: $272. *Financial support:* In 2009–10, 218 students received support, including 113 fellowships with tuition reimbursements available (averaging $31,816 per year), 109 research assistantships with tuition reimbursements available (averaging $29,254 per year); teaching assistantships with tuition reimbursements available, Federal Work-Study, institutionally sponsored loans, scholarships/grants, traineeships, health care benefits, and unspecified assistantships also available. *Faculty research:* DNA recombination, transcription and gene regulation, signal transduction, cell cycle, neuronal cell fate, replication and repair. Total annual research expenditures: $114 million. *Unit head:* Prof. Chris Kaiser, Head, 617-253-4701, E-mail: mitbio@mit.edu. *Application contact:* Biology Education Office, 617-253-3717, Fax: 617-258-9329, E-mail: gradbio@mit.edu.

Medical College of Wisconsin, Graduate School of Biomedical Sciences, Program in Cell Biology, Neurobiology and Anatomy, Milwaukee, WI 53226-0509. Offers neuroscience (PhD); MD/PhD. Terminal master's awarded for partial completion of doctoral program. *Degree requirements:* For doctorate, comprehensive exam, thesis/dissertation. *Entrance requirements:* For doctorate, GRE General Test. Additional exam requirements/recommendations for international students: Required—TOEFL. *Faculty research:* Neurobiology, development, neuroscience, teratology.

Medical University of South Carolina, College of Graduate Studies, Program in Molecular and Cellular Biology and Pathobiology, Charleston, SC 29425. Offers cancer biology (PhD); cardiovascular biology (PhD); cardiovascular imaging (PhD); cell regulation (PhD); craniofacial

Developmental Biology

Medical University of South Carolina (continued)

biology (PhD); genetics and development (PhD); marine biomedicine (PhD); DMD/PhD; MD/PhD. *Faculty:* 137 full-time (33 women). *Students:* 39 full-time (25 women); includes 6 minority (4 African Americans, 1 Asian American or Pacific Islander, 1 Hispanic American), 9 international. Average age 28. In 2009, 16 doctorates awarded. *Degree requirements:* For doctorate, thesis/dissertation, oral and written exams. *Entrance requirements:* For doctorate, GRE General Test, interview, minimum GPA of 3.0. Additional exam requirements/recommendations for international students: Required—TOEFL (minimum score 600 paper-based; 250 computer-based; 100 iBT). *Application deadline:* For fall admission, 1/15 priority date for domestic and international students. Applications are processed on a rolling basis. Application fee: $0 ($85 for international students). Electronic applications accepted. *Financial support:* In 2009–10, 39 students received support, including 39 research assistantships with partial tuition reimbursements available (averaging $23,000 per year); Federal Work-Study and scholarships/grants also available. Support available to part-time students. Financial award application deadline: 3/10; financial award applicants required to submit FAFSA. *Unit head:* Dr. Donald R. Menick, Director, 843-876-5045, Fax: 843-792-6590, E-mail: menickd@musc.edu. *Application contact:* Dr. Cynthia F. Wright, Associate Dean for Admissions and Career Development, 843-792-2564, Fax: 843-792-6590, E-mail: wrightcf@musc.edu.

New York University, Graduate School of Arts and Science, Department of Biology, New York, NY 10012-1019. Offers biology (PhD); biomedical journalism (MS); cancer and molecular biology (PhD); computational biology (PhD); computers in biological research (MS); developmental genetics (PhD); general biology (MS); immunology and microbiology (PhD); molecular genetics (PhD); neurobiology (PhD); oral biology (MS); plant biology (PhD); recombinant DNA technology (MS); MS/MBA. Part-time programs available. *Faculty:* 24 full-time (5 women). *Students:* 142 full-time (79 women), 44 part-time (28 women); includes 34 minority (1 African American, 25 Asian Americans or Pacific Islanders, 8 Hispanic Americans), 82 international. Average age 27. 362 applicants, 71% accepted, 72 enrolled. In 2009, 43 master's, 9 doctorates awarded. Terminal master's awarded for partial completion of doctoral program. *Degree requirements:* For master's, thesis or alternative, qualifying paper; for doctorate, comprehensive exam, thesis/dissertation. *Entrance requirements:* For master's, GRE General Test; for doctorate, GRE General Test, GRE Subject Test. Additional exam requirements/recommendations for international students: Required—TOEFL. *Application deadline:* For fall admission, 12/12 priority date for domestic students. Application fee: $90. *Expenses:* Tuition: Full-time $30,528; part-time $1272 per credit. Required fees: $2177. *Financial support:* Fellowships with tuition reimbursements, research assistantships with tuition reimbursements, teaching assistantships with tuition reimbursements, career-related internships or fieldwork, Federal Work-Study, institutionally sponsored loans, scholarships/grants, health care benefits, and unspecified assistantships available. Financial award application deadline: 12/12; financial award applicants required to submit FAFSA. *Faculty research:* Genomics, molecular and cell biology, development and molecular genetics, molecular evolution of plants and animals. *Unit head:* Gloria Coruzzi, Chair, 212-998-8200, Fax: 212-995-4015, E-mail: biology@nyu.edu. *Application contact:* Stephen Small, Director of Graduate Studies, 212-998-8200, Fax: 212-995-4015, E-mail: biology@nyu.edu.

New York University, School of Medicine and Graduate School of Arts and Science, Sackler Institute of Graduate Biomedical Sciences, New York, NY 10012-1019. Offers cellular and molecular biology (PhD); computational biology (PhD); developmental genetics (PhD); medical and molecular parasitology (PhD); microbiology (PhD); molecular oncology and immunology (PhD), including immunology, molecular oncology; neuroscience and physiology (PhD); pathobiology (PhD); pharmacology (PhD), including molecular pharmacology; structural biology (PhD); MD/PhD. *Degree requirements:* For doctorate, comprehensive exam, thesis/dissertation, qualifying exam. *Entrance requirements:* For doctorate, GRE General Test. Additional exam requirements/recommendations for international students: Required—TOEFL. Electronic applications accepted. *Expenses:* Contact institution.

Northwestern University, The Graduate School and Judd A. and Marjorie Weinberg College of Arts and Sciences, Interdepartmental Biological Sciences Program (IBiS), Evanston, IL 60208. Offers biochemistry, molecular biology, and cell biology (PhD), including biochemistry, cell and molecular biology, molecular biophysics, structural biology; biotechnology (PhD); cell and molecular biology (PhD); developmental biology and genetics (PhD); hormone action and signal transduction (PhD); neuroscience (PhD); structural biology, biochemistry, and biophysics (PhD). Program participants include the Departments of Biochemistry, Molecular Biology, and Cell Biology; Chemistry; Neurobiology and Physiology; Chemical Engineering; Civil Engineering; and Evanston Hospital. *Degree requirements:* For doctorate, thesis/dissertation, qualifying exam. *Entrance requirements:* For doctorate, GRE General Test. Additional exam requirements/recommendations for international students: Required—TOEFL (minimum score 600 paper-based). Electronic applications accepted. *Faculty research:* Developmental genetics, gene regulation, DNA-protein interactions, biological clocks, bioremediation.

Northwestern University, Northwestern University Feinberg School of Medicine and Interdepartmental Programs, Integrated Graduate Programs in the Life Sciences, Chicago, IL 60611. Offers cancer biology (PhD); cell biology (PhD); developmental biology (PhD); evolutionary biology (PhD); immunology and microbial pathogenesis (PhD); molecular biology and genetics (PhD); neurobiology (PhD); pharmacology and toxicology (PhD); structural biology and biochemistry (PhD). *Degree requirements:* For doctorate, comprehensive exam, thesis/dissertation, written and oral qualifying exams. *Entrance requirements:* For doctorate, GRE General Test. Additional exam requirements/recommendations for international students: Required—TOEFL (minimum score 600 paper-based; 250 computer-based). Electronic applications accepted.

The Ohio State University, Graduate School, College of Biological Sciences, Department of Molecular Genetics, Columbus, OH 43210. Offers cell and developmental biology (MS, PhD); genetics (MS, PhD); molecular biology (MS, PhD). *Faculty:* 26. *Students:* 8 full-time (5 women), 23 part-time (11 women), 17 international. Average age 27. In 2009, 11 doctorates awarded. *Degree requirements:* For master's, thesis; for doctorate, thesis/dissertation. *Entrance requirements:* For master's and doctorate, GRE General Test, GRE Subject Test in biology or biochemistry (recommended). Additional exam requirements/recommendations for international students: Required—TOEFL (minimum score 600 paper-based; 250 computer-based). *Application deadline:* For fall admission, 8/15 priority date for domestic students, 7/1 priority date for international students; for winter admission, 12/1 priority date for domestic students, 11/1 priority date for international students; for spring admission, 3/1 priority date for domestic students, 2/1 priority date for international students. Applications are processed on a rolling basis. Application fee: $40 ($50 for international students). Electronic applications accepted. *Expenses:* Tuition, state resident: full-time $10,683. Tuition, nonresident: full-time $25,923. Tuition and fees vary according to course load and program. *Financial support:* Fellowships, research assistantships, teaching assistantships, Federal Work-Study and institutionally sponsored loans available. Support available to part-time students. *Unit head:* Dr. Anna Hopper, Chair, 614-292-8084, Fax: 614-292-4466, E-mail: hopper.64@osu.edu. *Application contact:* 614-292-9444, Fax: 614-292-3895, E-mail: domestic.grad@osu.edu.

The Ohio State University, Graduate School, College of Biological Sciences, Program in Molecular, Cellular and Developmental Biology, Columbus, OH 43210. Offers MS, PhD. *Students:* 67 full-time (38 women), 60 part-time (31 women); includes 12 minority (2 African Americans, 5 Asian Americans or Pacific Islanders, 5 Hispanic Americans), 77 international. Average age 28. In 2009, 3 master's, 13 doctorates awarded. *Entrance requirements:* For master's and doctorate, GRE General Test, GRE Subject Test in biology or biochemistry, cell and molecular biology. Additional exam requirements/recommendations for international students: Required—TOEFL (minimum score 573 paper-based; 230 computer-based). *Application deadline:* Applications are processed on a rolling basis. Application fee: $40 ($50 for international students). Electronic applications accepted. *Expenses:* Tuition, state resident: full-time $10,683. Tuition, nonresident: full-time $25,923. Tuition and fees vary according to course load and program. *Unit head:* David M. Bisaro, Graduate Studies Committee Chair, 614-292-2804, Fax: 614-292-8772, E-mail: bisaro.1@osu.edu. *Application contact:* Graduate Admissions, 614-292-9444, Fax: 614-292-3895, E-mail: domestic.grad@osu.edu.

Oregon Health & Science University, School of Medicine, Graduate Programs in Medicine, Department of Cell and Developmental Biology, Portland, OR 97239-3098. Offers PhD. *Degree requirements:* For doctorate, thesis/dissertation. *Entrance requirements:* For doctorate, GRE General Test, GRE Subject Test, MCAT. Tuition and fees vary according to course level, course load, degree level, program and reciprocity agreements. *Financial support:* Stipend and paid tuition available. *Faculty research:* Developmental mechanisms, molecular biology of cancer, molecular neurobiology, intracellular signaling, growth factors and development. *Unit head:* Richard Maurer, PhD, Interim Chair/Program Director, 503-494-7811, E-mail: maurerr@ohsu.edu. *Application contact:* Elaine Offield, Program Coordinator, 503-494-5824, E-mail: offielde@ohsu.edu.

Penn State University Park, Graduate School, Intercollege Graduate Programs, State College, University Park, PA 16802-1503. Offers acoustics (M Eng, MS, PhD); bioengineering (MS, PhD); biogeochemistry (dual) (PhD); business administration (MBA); cell and developmental biology (PhD); demography (dual) (MA); ecology (MS, PhD); environmental pollution control (MEPC, MS); genetics (MS, PhD); human dimensions of natural resources and the environment (dual) (MA, MS, PhD); immunology and infectious diseases (MS); integrative biosciences (MS, PhD), including integrative biosciences; materials science and engineering (PhD); operations research (dual) (M Eng, MA, MS, PhD); physiology (MS, PhD); plant physiology (MS, PhD); quality and manufacturing management (MMM). *Students:* 371 full-time (157 women), 22 part-time (7 women). Average age 27. 1,074 applicants, 18% accepted, 130 enrolled. *Entrance requirements:* Additional exam requirements/recommendations for international students: Required—TOEFL (minimum score 550 paper-based; 213 computer-based; 80 iBT). *Application deadline:* Applications are processed on a rolling basis. Application fee: $45. Electronic applications accepted. *Financial support:* Fellowships, research assistantships, teaching assistantships available. Financial award applicants required to submit FAFSA. *Unit head:* Dr. Regina Vasilatos-Younken, Senior Associate Dean, 814-865-2516, Fax: 814-863-4627, E-mail: rxv@psu.edu. *Application contact:* Cynthia E. Nicosia, Director, Graduate Enrollment Services, 814-865-1795, Fax: 814-865-4627, E-mail: cey1@psu.edu.

Purdue University, Graduate School, College of Science, Department of Biological Sciences, West Lafayette, IN 47907. Offers biochemistry (PhD); biophysics (PhD); cell and developmental biology (PhD); ecology, evolutionary and population biology (MS, PhD), including ecology, evolutionary biology, population biology; genetics (MS, PhD); microbiology (MS, PhD); molecular biology (PhD); neurobiology (MS, PhD); plant physiology (PhD). Terminal master's awarded for partial completion of doctoral program. *Degree requirements:* For master's, thesis (for some programs); for doctorate, thesis/dissertation, seminars, teaching experience. *Entrance requirements:* For master's and doctorate, GRE General Test. Additional exam requirements/recommendations for international students: Required—TOEFL. Electronic applications accepted.

Rutgers, The State University of New Jersey, New Brunswick, Graduate School-New Brunswick, Programs in the Molecular Biosciences, Program in Cell and Developmental Biology, Piscataway, NJ 08854-8097. Offers MS, PhD. Part-time programs available. Terminal master's awarded for partial completion of doctoral program. *Degree requirements:* For master's, thesis; for doctorate, thesis/dissertation, written qualifying exam. *Entrance requirements:* For master's, GRE General Test; for doctorate, GRE General Test, GRE Subject Test (recommended), minimum GPA of 3.0. Additional exam requirements/recommendations for international students: Required—TOEFL. Electronic applications accepted. *Faculty research:* Signal transduction and regulation of gene expression, developmental biology, cellular biology, developmental genetics, neurobiology.

Stanford University, School of Medicine, Graduate Programs in Medicine, Department of Developmental Biology, Stanford, CA 94305-9991. Offers PhD. *Degree requirements:* For doctorate, thesis/dissertation, qualifying examination. *Entrance requirements:* For doctorate, GRE General Test, GRE Subject Test. Additional exam requirements/recommendations for international students: Required—TOEFL. Electronic applications accepted. *Expenses:* Tuition: Full-time $37,380; part-time $2760 per quarter. Required fees: $501. *Faculty research:* Mammalian embryology, developmental genetics with particular emphasis on microbial systems, *Dictyostelium, Drosophila*, the nematode, and the mouse.

Stony Brook University, State University of New York, Graduate School, College of Arts and Sciences, Department of Biochemistry and Cell Biology, Stony Brook, NY 11794. Offers biochemistry and structural biology (PhD); molecular and cellular biology (MA, PhD), including biochemistry and molecular biology (PhD), biological sciences (MA), cellular and developmental biology (PhD), immunology and pathology (PhD), molecular and cellular biology (PhD). *Faculty:* 22 full-time (5 women). *Students:* 126 full-time (76 women); includes 10 minority (2 African Americans, 7 Asian Americans or Pacific Islanders, 1 Hispanic American), 79 international. Average age 28. 371 applicants, 17% accepted. In 2009, 11 master's, 24 doctorates awarded. *Degree requirements:* For doctorate, comprehensive exam, thesis/dissertation, teaching experience. *Entrance requirements:* For doctorate, GRE General Test, GRE Subject Test. Additional exam requirements/recommendations for international students: Required—TOEFL. *Application deadline:* For fall admission, 1/15 for domestic students. Application fee: $60. *Expenses:* Tuition, state resident: full-time $8370; part-time $349 per credit. Tuition, nonresident: full-time $13,250; part-time $552 per credit. Required fees: $933. *Financial support:* In 2009–10, 68 research assistantships, 20 teaching assistantships were awarded; fellowships, Federal Work-Study also available. *Faculty research:* Genome organization and replication, cell surface dynamics, enzyme structure and mechanism, developmental and regulatory biology. Total annual research expenditures: $8.8 million. *Unit head:* Prof. Robert Haltiwanger, Chair, 631-632-8560. *Application contact:* Director, Graduate Program, 631-632-8533, Fax: 631-632-9730, E-mail: mcbprog@life.bio.sunysb.edu.

Stony Brook University, State University of New York, Graduate School, College of Arts and Sciences, Department of Biochemistry and Cell Biology, Molecular and Cellular Biology Program, Specialization in Cellular and Developmental Biology, Stony Brook, NY 11794. Offers PhD. In 2009, 1 doctorate awarded. *Degree requirements:* For doctorate, one foreign language, comprehensive exam, thesis/dissertation, teaching experience. *Entrance requirements:* For doctorate, GRE General Test, GRE Subject Test. Additional exam requirements/recommendations for international students: Required—TOEFL. *Application deadline:* For fall admission, 1/15 for domestic students. Application fee: $60. *Expenses:* Tuition, state resident: full-time $8370; part-time $349 per credit. Tuition, nonresident: full-time $13,250; part-time $552 per credit. Required fees: $933. *Financial support:* Fellowships, research assistantships, teaching assistantships available. *Unit head:* Director, Graduate Program, 631-632-8533, Fax: 631-632-9730, E-mail: mcbprog@life.bio.sunysb.edu. *Application contact:* Director, Graduate Program, 631-632-8533, Fax: 631-632-9730, E-mail: mcbprog@life.bio.sunysb.edu.

Thomas Jefferson University, Jefferson College of Graduate Studies, MS Program in Cell and Developmental Biology, Philadelphia, PA 19107. Offers MS. Part-time and evening/weekend programs available. *Faculty:* 19 full-time (6 women). *Students:* 7 part-time (6 women); includes 1 minority (Asian American or Pacific Islander), 2 international. 12 applicants, 42% accepted, 3 enrolled. In 2009, 1 master's awarded. *Degree requirements:* For master's, thesis, clerkship. *Entrance requirements:* For master's, GRE General Test or MCAT, minimum GPA of 3.0. Additional exam requirements/recommendations for international students: Required—TOEFL (minimum score 250 computer-based; 100 iBT) or IELTS. *Application deadline:* For fall admission, 8/1 priority date for domestic students, 3/1 priority date for international students; for winter admission, 12/1 priority date for domestic students, 6/1 priority date for international students; for spring admission, 4/1 priority date for domestic students. Applications are processed on a rolling basis. Application fee: $50. Electronic applications accepted. *Expenses:* Tuition: Full-time $26,858; part-time $879 per credit. Required fees: $525. *Financial support:* In 2009–10, 3 students received support. Federal Work-Study and institutionally sponsored loans available.

Support available to part-time students. Financial award application deadline: 5/1; financial award applicants required to submit FAFSA. *Unit head:* Dr. Gerald Grunwald, Senior Associate Dean and Program Director, 215-503-4191, Fax: 215-503-6690, E-mail: gerald.grunwald@jefferson.edu. *Application contact:* Eleanor M. Gorman, Assistant Coordinator, Graduate Center Programs, 215-503-5799, Fax: 215-503-3433, E-mail: eleanor.gorman@jefferson.edu.

Thomas Jefferson University, Jefferson College of Graduate Studies, PhD Program in Cell and Developmental Biology, Philadelphia, PA 19107. Offers PhD. *Faculty:* 42 full-time (8 women). *Students:* 18 full-time (13 women), 2 international. 21 applicants, 19% accepted, 3 enrolled. In 2009, 4 doctorates awarded. *Degree requirements:* For doctorate, comprehensive exam, thesis/dissertation. *Entrance requirements:* For doctorate, GRE General Test, minimum GPA of 3.2. Additional exam requirements/recommendations for international students: Required—TOEFL (minimum score 250 computer-based; 100 iBT). *Application deadline:* For fall admission, 1/15 priority date for domestic and international students. Applications are processed on a rolling basis. Application fee: $50. Electronic applications accepted. *Expenses:* Tuition: Full-time $26,858; part-time $879 per credit. Required fees: $525. *Financial support:* In 2009–10, 18 students received support, including 18 fellowships with full tuition reimbursements available (averaging $52,883 per year); Federal Work-Study, institutionally sponsored loans, scholarships/grants, traineeships, and stipend also available. Support available to part-time students. Financial award application deadline: 5/1; financial award applicants required to submit FAFSA. Total annual research expenditures: $20 million. *Unit head:* Dr. Theodore F. Taraschi, Program Director, 215-503-5020, Fax: 215-503-0206, E-mail: theodore.taraschi@jefferson.edu. *Application contact:* Marc E. Stearns, Director of Admissions, 215-503-0155, Fax: 215-503-9920, E-mail: jcgs-info@jefferson.edu.

Tufts University, Sackler School of Graduate Biomedical Sciences, Program in Cell, Molecular, and Developmental Biology, Medford, MA 02155. Offers PhD. *Faculty:* 35 full-time (11 women). *Students:* 25 full-time (13 women); includes 2 minority (both Asian Americans or Pacific Islanders), 2 international. Average age 29. In 2009, 8 doctorates awarded. Terminal master's awarded for partial completion of doctoral program. *Degree requirements:* For doctorate, thesis/dissertation. *Entrance requirements:* For doctorate, GRE General Test, 3 letters of reference. Additional exam requirements/recommendations for international students: Required—TOEFL. *Application deadline:* For fall admission, 12/15 for domestic and international students. Applications are processed on a rolling basis. Application fee: $70. Electronic applications accepted. *Expenses:* Tuition: Full-time $38,096; part-time $3962 per credit. Required fees: $686; $40 per year. Tuition and fees vary according to course level, course load, degree level, program and student level. *Financial support:* In 2009–10, 25 students received support, including 25 research assistantships with full tuition reimbursements available (averaging $28,500 per year); fellowships, scholarships/grants, health care benefits, and tuition waivers (full) also available. *Faculty research:* Reproduction and hormone action, control of gene expression, cell-matrix and cell-cell interactions, growth control and tumorigenesis, cytoskeleton and contractile proteins. *Unit head:* Dr. John Castellot, Program Director, 617-636-0303, Fax: 617-636-0375, E-mail: john.castellot@tufts.edu. *Application contact:* Kellie Johnston, Associate Director of Admissions, 617-636-6767, Fax: 617-636-0375, E-mail: sackler-school@tufts.edu.

University at Albany, State University of New York, College of Arts and Sciences, Department of Biological Sciences, Specialization in Molecular, Cellular, Developmental, and Neural Biology, Albany, NY 12222-0001. Offers MS, PhD. *Degree requirements:* For master's, one foreign language; for doctorate, one foreign language, thesis/dissertation. *Entrance requirements:* For master's and doctorate, GRE General Test.

University of California, Davis, Graduate Studies, Graduate Group in Cell and Developmental Biology, Davis, CA 95616. Offers MS, PhD. *Degree requirements:* For master's, comprehensive exam (for some programs), thesis (for some programs); for doctorate, thesis/dissertation. *Entrance requirements:* For doctorate, GRE General Test, GRE Subject Test. Additional exam requirements/recommendations for international students: Required—TOEFL (minimum score 550 paper-based; 213 computer-based). Electronic applications accepted. *Faculty research:* Molecular basis of cell function and development.

University of California, Irvine, Office of Graduate Studies, School of Biological Sciences, Department of Developmental and Cell Biology, Irvine, CA 92697. Offers biological sciences (MS, PhD). Students apply through the Graduate Program in Molecular Biology, Genetics, and Biochemistry. *Students:* 46 full-time (22 women), 1 part-time (0 women); includes 24 minority (1 African American, 2 American Indian/Alaska Native, 13 Asian Americans or Pacific Islanders, 8 Hispanic Americans), 5 international. Average age 29. In 2009, 3 master's, 7 doctorates awarded. *Degree requirements:* For doctorate, thesis/dissertation. *Entrance requirements:* For master's and doctorate, GRE General Test, GRE Subject Test, minimum GPA of 3.0. Additional exam requirements/recommendations for international students: Required—TOEFL (minimum score 550 paper-based; 213 computer-based). *Application deadline:* For fall admission, 12/15 priority date for domestic and international students. Application fee: $70 ($90 for international students). Electronic applications accepted. *Financial support:* Fellowships, research assistantships with full tuition reimbursements, teaching assistantships, institutionally sponsored loans, traineeships, health care benefits, and unspecified assistantships available. Financial award application deadline: 3/1; financial award applicants required to submit FAFSA. *Faculty research:* Genetics and development, oncogene signaling pathways, gene regulation, tissue regeneration and molecular genetics. *Unit head:* Dr. Arthur D. Lander, Chair, 949-824-1008, Fax: 949-824-4709, E-mail: adlander@uci.edu. *Application contact:* Kimberly McKinney, Administrator, 949-824-8145, Fax: 949-824-1965, E-mail: kamckinn@uci.edu.

University of California, Los Angeles, David Geffen School of Medicine and Graduate Division, Graduate Programs in Medicine, Department of Molecular, Cell and Developmental Biology, Los Angeles, CA 90095. Offers PhD. *Degree requirements:* For doctorate, thesis/dissertation, qualifying exams. *Entrance requirements:* For doctorate, GRE General Test, GRE Subject Test. Additional exam requirements/recommendations for international students: Required—TOEFL.

University of California, Riverside, Graduate Division, Program in Cell, Molecular, and Developmental Biology, Riverside, CA 92521-0102. Offers MS, PhD. *Faculty:* 55 full-time (18 women). *Students:* 47 full-time (28 women); includes 15 minority (2 African Americans, 11 Asian Americans or Pacific Islanders, 2 Hispanic Americans), 15 international. Average age 29. In 2009, 7 doctorates awarded. Terminal master's awarded for partial completion of doctoral program. *Degree requirements:* For master's, thesis, oral defense of thesis; for doctorate, thesis/dissertation, oral defense of thesis, qualifying exams, 2 quarters of teaching experience. *Entrance requirements:* For master's and doctorate, GRE General Test, minimum GPA of 3.2. Additional exam requirements/recommendations for international students: Required—TOEFL (minimum score 550 paper-based; 213 computer-based; 80 iBT). *Application deadline:* For fall admission, 1/5 priority date for domestic and international students. Applications are processed on a rolling basis. Application fee: $60 ($75 for international students). Electronic applications accepted. *Financial support:* In 2009–10, fellowships with full and partial tuition reimbursements (averaging $24,000 per year), research assistantships with full and partial tuition reimbursements (averaging $21,847 per year), teaching assistantships with full and partial tuition reimbursements (averaging $18,485 per year) were awarded; scholarships/grants, traineeships, health care benefits, tuition waivers (partial), and unspecified assistantships also available. Support available to part-time students. Financial award application deadline: 1/5. *Unit head:* Dr. Peter Atkinson, Director, 951-827-4782, E-mail: norman@ucr.edu. *Application contact:* Kathy Redd, Graduate Program Assistant, 800-735-0717, Fax: 951-827-5517, E-mail: cmdb@ucr.edu.

University of California, San Diego, Office of Graduate Studies, Division of Biological Sciences, Program in Cell and Developmental Biology, La Jolla, CA 92093-0348. Offers PhD. Offered in association with the Salk Institute. *Degree requirements:* For doctorate, thesis/dissertation, qualifying exam. Electronic applications accepted.

University of California, San Diego, School of Medicine and Office of Graduate Studies, Molecular Pathology Program, La Jolla, CA 92093. Offers bioinformatics (PhD); cancer biology/oncology (PhD); cardiovascular sciences and disease (PhD); microbiology (PhD); molecular pathology (PhD); neurological disease (PhD); stem cell and developmental biology (PhD); structural biology/drug design (PhD). *Entrance requirements:* For doctorate, GRE General Test, GRE Subject Test. Additional exam requirements/recommendations for international students: Required—TOEFL. Electronic applications accepted.

University of California, San Francisco, Graduate Division and School of Medicine, Department of Biochemistry and Biophysics, San Francisco, CA 94143. Offers biochemistry and molecular biology (PhD); cell biology (PhD); developmental biology (PhD); genetics (PhD); MD/PhD. *Degree requirements:* For doctorate, thesis/dissertation. *Entrance requirements:* For doctorate, GRE General Test, GRE Subject Test. Additional exam requirements/recommendations for international students: Required—TOEFL. *Expenses:* Contact institution.

University of California, Santa Barbara, Graduate Division, College of Letters and Sciences, Division of Mathematics, Life, and Physical Sciences, Department of Molecular, Cellular, and Developmental Biology, Santa Barbara, CA 93106-9625. Offers MA, PhD, MA/PhD. *Faculty:* 21 full-time (3 women), 7 part-time/adjunct (2 women). *Students:* 60 full-time (31 women). Average age 27. 44 applicants, 23% accepted, 6 enrolled. In 2009, 8 master's, 7 doctorates awarded. *Degree requirements:* For master's, comprehensive exam (for some programs), thesis (for some programs); for doctorate, comprehensive exam, thesis/dissertation. *Entrance requirements:* For master's, GRE General Test, GRE Subject Test, 3 letters of recommendation, resume/curriculum vitae; for doctorate, GRE General Test, GRE Subject Test, 3 letters of recommendation, statement of purpose, personal achievements/contributions statement, resume/curriculum vitae, transcripts for post-secondary institutions attended. Additional exam requirements/recommendations for international students: Required—TOEFL (minimum score 610 paper-based; 253 computer-based; 102 iBT) or IELTS (minimum score 7). *Application deadline:* For fall admission, 12/15 for domestic and international students. Application fee: $70 ($90 for international students). Electronic applications accepted. *Financial support:* In 2009–10, 60 students received support, including 19 fellowships with full and partial tuition reimbursements available (averaging $9,800 per year), 39 research assistantships with full and partial tuition reimbursements available (averaging $9,700 per year), 48 teaching assistantships with partial tuition reimbursements available (averaging $7,500 per year); career-related internships or fieldwork, Federal Work-Study, institutionally sponsored loans, scholarships/grants, traineeships, health care benefits, and unspecified assistantships also available. Financial award application deadline: 12/15; financial award applicants required to submit FAFSA. *Faculty research:* Microbiology, neurobiology (including stem cell research), developmental, virology, cell biology. *Unit head:* Dr. Dennis O. Clegg, Chair, 805-893-8490, Fax: 805-893-4724, E-mail: clegg@lifesci.ucsb.edu. *Application contact:* Tony L. Tieu, Staff Graduate Program Advisor, 805-893-8499, Fax: 805-893-4724, E-mail: tieu@lifesci.ucsb.edu.

University of California, Santa Cruz, Division of Graduate Studies, Division of Physical and Biological Sciences, Program in Molecular, Cellular, and Developmental Biology, Santa Cruz, CA 95064. Offers MA, PhD. *Degree requirements:* For master's, thesis; for doctorate, thesis/dissertation, qualifying exam. *Entrance requirements:* For master's and doctorate, GRE General Test, 3 letters of recommendation, interview. Additional exam requirements/recommendations for international students: Required—TOEFL (minimum score 550 paper-based; 220 computer-based; 83 iBT). Electronic applications accepted.

University of Chicago, Division of the Biological Sciences, Department of Molecular Biosciences, Committee on Developmental Biology, Chicago, IL 60637-1513. Offers cellular differentiation (PhD); developmental endocrinology (PhD); developmental genetics (PhD); developmental neurobiology (PhD); gene expression (PhD). *Faculty:* 23 full-time (11 women), 11 part-time/adjunct (0 women). *Students:* 16 full-time (10 women); includes 7 minority (1 African American, 5 Asian Americans or Pacific Islanders, 1 Hispanic American). Average age 28. 54 applicants, 76% accepted, 1 enrolled. In 2009, 1 doctorate awarded. *Degree requirements:* For doctorate, thesis/dissertation, ethics class, 2 teaching assistantships. *Entrance requirements:* For doctorate, GRE General Test. Additional exam requirements/recommendations for international students: Required—TOEFL (minimum score 600 paper-based; 250 computer-based; 104 iBT), IELTS (minimum score 7). *Application deadline:* For fall admission, 12/1 priority date for domestic and international students. Application fee: $55. Electronic applications accepted. *Financial support:* In 2009–10, 16 students received support, including fellowships with full tuition reimbursements available (averaging $29,781 per year), research assistantships with full tuition reimbursements available (averaging $29,781 per year); institutionally sponsored loans, scholarships/grants, traineeships, and health care benefits also available. Financial award applicants required to submit FAFSA. *Faculty research:* Epidermal differentiation, neural lineages, pattern formation. *Unit head:* Dr. Victoria Prince, Chair, 773-834-2100, E-mail: vprince@uchicago.edu. *Application contact:* Kristine Gaston, Graduate Administrative Director, 773-702-8037, Fax: 773-702-3172, E-mail: kristine@bsd.uchicago.edu.

University of Cincinnati, Graduate School, College of Medicine, Graduate Programs in Biomedical Sciences, Department of Pediatrics, Program in Molecular and Developmental Biology, Cincinnati, OH 45221. Offers PhD. *Degree requirements:* For doctorate, thesis/dissertation, qualifying exam. *Entrance requirements:* For doctorate, GRE General Test, minimum GPA of 3.2. Additional exam requirements/recommendations for international students: Required—TOEFL (minimum score 520 paper-based; 190 computer-based). Electronic applications accepted. *Faculty research:* Cancer biology, cardiovascular biology, developmental biology, human genetics, gene therapy, genomics and bioinformatics, immunobiology, molecular medicine, neuroscience, pulmonary biology, reproductive biology, stem cell biology.

University of Colorado at Boulder, Graduate School, College of Arts and Sciences, Department of Molecular, Cellular, and Developmental Biology, Boulder, CO 80309. Offers cellular structure and function (MA, PhD); developmental biology (MA, PhD); molecular biology (MA, PhD). *Faculty:* 27 full-time (7 women). *Students:* 29 full-time (15 women), 45 part-time (18 women); includes 7 minority (2 American Indian/Alaska Native, 1 Asian American or Pacific Islander, 4 Hispanic Americans), 15 international. Average age 28. 210 applicants, 5% accepted, 11 enrolled. In 2009, 3 master's, 7 doctorates awarded. Terminal master's awarded for partial completion of doctoral program. *Degree requirements:* For master's, comprehensive exam, thesis or alternative; for doctorate, comprehensive exam, thesis/dissertation. *Entrance requirements:* For master's, GRE General Test, GRE Subject Test, minimum undergraduate GPA of 3.0; for doctorate, GRE General Test, GRE Subject Test. *Application deadline:* For fall admission, 1/1 for domestic students, 12/1 for international students. Application fee: $50 ($60 for international students). *Financial support:* In 2009–10, 40 fellowships (averaging $11,628 per year), 53 research assistantships (averaging $14,700 per year) were awarded; tuition waivers (full) also available. Financial award application deadline: 2/1. *Faculty research:* Molecular biology of RNA and DNA, molecular genetics, cell motility and cytoskeleton, cell membranes, developmental genetics, human genetics. Total annual research expenditures: $15.5 million.

University of Colorado Denver, School of Medicine, Program in Cell Biology, Stem Cells, and Developmental Biology, Denver, CO 80217-3364. Offers cell and developmental biology (PhD); cell biology, stem cells and development (PhD); reproductive sciences (PhD). *Students:* 28 full-time (18 women); includes 2 minority (1 Asian American or Pacific Islander, 1 Hispanic American), 8 international. In 2009, 3 doctorates awarded. *Degree requirements:* For doctorate, thesis/dissertation. *Entrance requirements:* For doctorate, GRE, minimum GPA of 3.0, 3 letters of reference. Additional exam requirements/recommendations for international students: Required—TOEFL (minimum score 550 paper-based; 213 computer-based). *Application deadline:* For fall admission, 1/15 for domestic students. Application fee: $50. Electronic applications accepted. *Financial support:* Fellowships, research assistantships, teaching assistantships, Federal Work-Study and institutionally sponsored loans available. Support available to part-time students. Financial award application deadline: 3/15; financial award applicants required to submit FAFSA. *Faculty research:* Human disease, stem cell biology,

Developmental Biology

University of Colorado Denver (continued)
neuroscience, molecular biology. Total annual research expenditures: $5.7 million. *Unit head:* Dr. Karl Pfenninger, Chair, 303-724-3466, E-mail: karl.pfenninger@ucdenver.edu. *Application contact:* Carmel Hardberg, Program Administrator, 303-724-3426, Fax: 303-724-3420, E-mail: carmel.harberg@ucdenver.edu.

University of Connecticut, Graduate School, College of Liberal Arts and Sciences, Department of Molecular and Cell Biology, Storrs, CT 06269. Offers applied genomics (MS, PSM); biochemistry (MS, PhD); biophysics and structural biology (MS, PhD); cell and developmental biology (MS, PhD); genetics, genomics, and bioinformatics (MS, PhD); microbial systems analysis (MS, PSM); microbiology (MS, PhD); plant cell and molecular biology (MS, PhD). *Faculty:* 73 full-time (19 women). *Students:* 174 full-time (84 women), 25 part-time (18 women); includes 27 minority (9 African Americans, 1 American Indian/Alaska Native, 13 Asian Americans or Pacific Islanders, 4 Hispanic Americans), 54 international. Average age 28. 383 applicants, 16% accepted, 26 enrolled. In 2009, 34 master's, 9 doctorates awarded. Terminal master's awarded for partial completion of doctoral program. *Degree requirements:* For master's, comprehensive exam; for doctorate, thesis/dissertation. *Entrance requirements:* For master's and doctorate, GRE General Test, GRE Subject Test. Additional exam requirements/recommendations for international students: Required—TOEFL (minimum score 550 paper-based; 213 computer-based). *Application deadline:* For fall admission, 2/1 priority date for domestic and international students; for spring admission, 11/1 for domestic students, 10/1 for international students. Applications are processed on a rolling basis. Application fee: $55. Electronic applications accepted. *Expenses:* Tuition, state resident: full-time $4725; part-time $525 per credit. Tuition, nonresident: full-time $12,267; part-time $1363 per credit. Required fees: $346 per semester. Tuition and fees vary according to course load. *Financial support:* In 2009–10, 61 research assistantships with full tuition reimbursements, 76 teaching assistantships with full tuition reimbursements were awarded; fellowships, Federal Work-Study, scholarships/grants, health care benefits, and unspecified assistantships also available. Financial award application deadline: 2/1; financial award applicants required to submit FAFSA. *Unit head:* David Benson, Head, 860-486-4258, Fax: 860-486-4331, E-mail: david.benson@uconn.edu. *Application contact:* Anne St. Onje, Graduate Coordinator, 860-486-4314, Fax: 860-486-3943, E-mail: anne.st_onje@uconn.edu.

University of Connecticut Health Center, Graduate School, Programs in Biomedical Sciences, Program in Genetics and Developmental Biology, Farmington, CT 06030. Offers PhD, DMD/PhD, MD/PhD. *Faculty:* 46. *Students:* 20 full-time (11 women); includes 1 minority (Asian American or Pacific Islander), 7 international. Average age 30. 165 applicants, 35% accepted. In 2009, 4 doctorates awarded. *Degree requirements:* For doctorate, comprehensive exam, thesis/dissertation. *Entrance requirements:* For doctorate, GRE General Test, GRE Subject Test. Additional exam requirements/recommendations for international students: Required—TOEFL (minimum score 600 paper-based; 250 computer-based). *Application deadline:* For fall admission, 12/15 for domestic students. Application fee: $55. Electronic applications accepted. *Financial support:* In 2009–10, 20 students received support, including 20 research assistantships with tuition reimbursements available (averaging $27,000 per year); fellowships, health care benefits also available. *Faculty research:* Developmental biology, genomic imprinting, RNA biology, RNA alternative splicing, human embryonic stem cells. *Unit head:* Dr. William Mohler, Director, 860-679-7947, E-mail: wmohler@neuron.uchc.edu. *Application contact:* Tricia Avolt, Graduate Admissions Coordinator, 860-679-2175, Fax: 860-679-1899, E-mail: robertson@nso2.uchc.edu.

See Close-Up on page 319.

University of Delaware, College of Arts and Sciences, Department of Biological Sciences, Newark, DE 19716. Offers biotechnology (MS); cancer biology (MS, PhD); cell and extracellular matrix biology (MS, PhD); cell and systems physiology (MS, PhD); developmental biology (MS, PhD); ecology and evolution (MS, PhD); microbiology (MS, PhD); molecular biology and genetics (MS, PhD). Terminal master's awarded for partial completion of doctoral program. *Degree requirements:* For master's, thesis, preliminary exam; for doctorate, comprehensive exam, thesis/dissertation, preliminary exam. *Entrance requirements:* For master's and doctorate, GRE General Test. Additional exam requirements/recommendations for international students: Required—TOEFL (minimum score 600 paper-based; 250 computer-based); Recommended—TWE. Electronic applications accepted. *Faculty research:* Microorganisms, bone, cancer metastasis, developmental biology, cell biology, DNA.

University of Hawaii at Manoa, John A. Burns School of Medicine, Program in Developmental and Reproductive Biology, Honolulu, HI 96813. Offers MS, PhD. Part-time programs available. *Faculty:* 19 full-time (2 women), 7 part-time/adjunct (4 women). *Students:* 18 full-time (9 women), 8 part-time (3 women); includes 17 minority (all Asian Americans or Pacific Islanders), 2 international. Average age 27. 20 applicants, 70% accepted, 10 enrolled. In 2009, 10 master's awarded. *Degree requirements:* For doctorate, thesis/dissertation. *Entrance requirements:* For doctorate, GRE General Test, GRE Subject Test. Application fee: $50. *Expenses:* Tuition, state resident: full-time $8900; part-time $372 per credit. Tuition, nonresident: full-time $21,400; part-time $898 per credit. Required fees: $207 per semester. *Financial support:* In 2009–10, 1 fellowship (averaging $1,000 per year), 9 research assistantships (averaging $17,109 per year), 3 teaching assistantships (averaging $14,382 per year) were awarded. *Faculty research:* Biology of gametes and fertilization, reproductive endocrinology. Total annual research expenditures: $5.4 million. *Application contact:* Steve Ward, Graduate Chair, 808-956-6598, Fax: 808-956-7316.

University of Illinois at Urbana–Champaign, Graduate College, College of Liberal Arts and Sciences, School of Molecular and Cellular Biology, Department of Cell and Developmental Biology, Champaign, IL 61820. Offers PhD. *Faculty:* 15 full-time (4 women), 1 (woman) part-time/adjunct. *Students:* 49 full-time (25 women); includes 6 minority (4 Asian Americans or Pacific Islanders, 2 Hispanic Americans), 27 international. In 2009, 16 doctorates awarded. *Entrance requirements:* For doctorate, GRE, minimum GPA of 3.0. Additional exam requirements/recommendations for international students: Required—TOEFL (minimum score 590 paper-based; 243 computer-based). *Application deadline:* Applications are processed on a rolling basis. Application fee: $60 ($75 for international students). Electronic applications accepted. *Financial support:* In 2009–10, 7 fellowships, 46 research assistantships, 25 teaching assistantships were awarded; tuition waivers (full and partial) also available. *Unit head:* Andrew Belmont, Head, 217-244-2311, Fax: 217-244-1648, E-mail: asbel@illinois.edu. *Application contact:* Delynn Carter, Assistant to the Head, 217-244-8116, Fax: 217-244-1648, E-mail: dmcarter@illinois.edu.

The University of Kansas, Graduate Studies, College of Liberal Arts and Sciences, Department of Molecular Biosciences, Lawrence, KS 66044. Offers biochemistry and biophysics (MA, PhD); microbiology (MA, PhD); molecular, cellular, and developmental biology (MA, PhD). *Students:* 58 full-time (30 women), 2 part-time (1 woman); includes 4 minority (1 American Indian/Alaska Native, 1 Asian American or Pacific Islander, 2 Hispanic Americans), 24 international. Average age 27. 49 applicants, 29% accepted, 4 enrolled. In 2009, 2 master's, 7 doctorates awarded. Terminal master's awarded for partial completion of doctoral program. *Degree requirements:* For master's, comprehensive exam, thesis; for doctorate, comprehensive exam, thesis/dissertation. *Entrance requirements:* For master's and doctorate, GRE General Test. Additional exam requirements/recommendations for international students: Required—TOEFL (minimum score 24 iBT). *Application deadline:* For fall admission, 12/15 for domestic and international students. Application fee: $45 ($55 for international students). Electronic applications accepted. *Expenses:* Tuition, state resident: full-time $6492; part-time $270.50 per credit hour. Tuition, nonresident: full-time $15,510; part-time $646.25 per credit hour. Required fees: $847; $70.56 per credit hour. Tuition and fees vary according to course load and program. *Financial support:* Fellowships with tuition reimbursements, research assistantships with tuition reimbursements, teaching assistantships with tuition reimbursements, health care benefits and unspecified assistantships available. Financial award application deadline: 3/1. *Faculty research:* Structure and function of proteins, genetics of organism development, molecular genetics, neurophysiology, molecular virology and pathogenics, developmental biology, cell biology. *Unit head:* Dr. Mark Richter, Chair, 785-864-4311, Fax: 785-864-5294, E-mail: richter@ku.edu. *Application contact:* John P. Connolly, Graduate Program Assistant, 785-864-4311, Fax: 785-864-5294, E-mail: jconnolly@ku.edu.

University of Massachusetts Amherst, Graduate School, Interdisciplinary Programs, Program in Molecular and Cellular Biology, Amherst, MA 01003. Offers biological chemistry and molecular biophysics (PhD); biomedicine (PhD); cellular and developmental biology (PhD). Part-time programs available. *Faculty:* 2 full-time (0 women). *Students:* 30 full-time (16 women), 48 part-time (26 women); includes 15 minority (4 African Americans, 1 American Indian/Alaska Native, 3 Asian Americans or Pacific Islanders, 7 Hispanic Americans), 23 international. Average age 27. 140 applicants, 23% accepted, 19 enrolled. In 2009, 12 doctorates awarded. Terminal master's awarded for partial completion of doctoral program. *Degree requirements:* For doctorate, comprehensive exam, thesis/dissertation. *Entrance requirements:* For doctorate, GRE General Test. Additional exam requirements/recommendations for international students: Required—TOEFL (minimum score 550 paper-based; 213 computer-based; 80 iBT), IELTS (minimum score 6.5). *Application deadline:* For fall admission, 12/1 for domestic and international students. Applications are processed on a rolling basis. Application fee: $50 ($65 for international students). Electronic applications accepted. *Expenses:* Tuition, state resident: full-time $2640; part-time $110 per credit. Tuition, nonresident: full-time $9936; part-time $414 per credit. Tuition and fees vary according to course load. *Financial support:* In 2009–10, 11 research assistantships with full tuition reimbursements (averaging $2,590 per year), 3 teaching assistantships with full tuition reimbursements (averaging $3,303 per year) were awarded; fellowships, career-related internships or fieldwork, Federal Work-Study, scholarships/grants, traineeships, health care benefits, tuition waivers (full), and unspecified assistantships also available. Support available to part-time students. Financial award application deadline: 12/1. *Unit head:* Dr. David J. Gross, Graduate Program Director, 413-545-3246, Fax: 413-545-1812. *Application contact:* Jean M. Ames, Supervisor of Admissions, 413-545-0722, Fax: 413-577-0010, E-mail: gradadm@grad.umass.edu.

University of Medicine and Dentistry of New Jersey, Graduate School of Biomedical Sciences, Graduate Programs in Biomedical Sciences–Newark, Newark, NJ 07107. Offers biochemistry and molecular biology (MS, PhD); biodefense (Certificate); biomedical engineering (Certificate); biomedical sciences (interdisciplinary) (PhD); cell biology and molecular medicine (PhD); integrative neuroscience (PhD); microbiology and molecular genetics (PhD); molecular pathology and immunology (PhD); neuroscience (Certificate); pharmaceutical sciences (Certificate); pharmacology and physiology (PhD); stem cell (Certificate); DMD/PhD; MD/PhD. *Students:* 337 full-time (191 women), 68 part-time (42 women); includes 133 minority (24 African Americans, 2 American Indian/Alaska Native, 83 Asian Americans or Pacific Islanders, 24 Hispanic Americans), 78 international. Average age 26. 576 applicants, 57% accepted, 177 enrolled. In 2009, 95 master's, 27 doctorates awarded. Terminal master's awarded for partial completion of doctoral program. *Degree requirements:* For master's, thesis (for some programs); for doctorate, thesis/dissertation, qualifying exam. *Entrance requirements:* For master's, GRE General Test, MCAT or DAT; for doctorate, GRE General Test. Additional exam requirements/recommendations for international students: Required—TOEFL. *Application deadline:* For fall admission, 1/15 for domestic students. Applications are processed on a rolling basis. Application fee: $40. Electronic applications accepted. *Financial support:* Fellowships, research assistantships, teaching assistantships, career-related internships or fieldwork, Federal Work-Study, institutionally sponsored loans, and tuition waivers (full and partial) available. Financial award application deadline: 5/1. *Unit head:* Dr. Andrew Thomas, Senior Associate Dean, 973-972-4511, Fax: 973-972-7148, E-mail: thomas@umdnj.edu. *Application contact:* Dr. B. J. Wagner, 973-972-5335, Fax: 973-972-7148, E-mail: wagner@umdnj.edu.

University of Miami, Graduate School, Miller School of Medicine, Graduate Programs in Medicine, Department of Cell Biology and Anatomy, Coral Gables, FL 33124. Offers molecular cell and developmental biology (PhD); MD/PhD. *Degree requirements:* For doctorate, thesis/dissertation. *Entrance requirements:* For doctorate, GRE General Test, GRE Subject Test. Additional exam requirements/recommendations for international students: Required—TOEFL. Electronic applications accepted.

University of Michigan, Horace H. Rackham School of Graduate Studies, College of Literature, Science, and the Arts, Department of Molecular, Cellular, and Developmental Biology, Ann Arbor, MI 48109. Offers MS, PhD. Part-time programs available. *Faculty:* 32 full-time (8 women). *Students:* 74 full-time (39 women), 3 part-time (1 woman); includes 4 minority (2 African Americans, 2 Hispanic Americans), 41 international. Average age 29. 113 applicants, 21% accepted, 14 enrolled. In 2009, 6 master's, 7 doctorates awarded. Terminal master's awarded for partial completion of doctoral program. *Degree requirements:* For doctorate, thesis/dissertation, preliminary exam, oral defense. *Entrance requirements:* For master's and doctorate, GRE General Test. Additional exam requirements/recommendations for international students: Required—TOEFL (minimum score 560 paper-based; 220 computer-based; 83 iBT). *Application deadline:* For fall admission, 1/5 for domestic and international students; for winter admission, 11/1 for domestic and international students. Applications are processed on a rolling basis. Application fee: $60 ($75 for international students). Electronic applications accepted. *Expenses:* Tuition, state resident: full-time $17,286; part-time $1099 per credit hour. Tuition, nonresident: full-time $34,944; part-time $2080 per credit hour. Required fees: $95 per semester. Tuition and fees vary according to course load, degree level and program. *Financial support:* In 2009–10, 64 students received support, including 16 fellowships with full tuition reimbursements available (averaging $26,500 per year), 28 research assistantships with full tuition reimbursements available (averaging $26,500 per year), 20 teaching assistantships with full tuition reimbursements available (averaging $26,500 per year); health care benefits also available. *Faculty research:* Cell biology, microbiology, neurobiology and physiology, developmental biology and plant molecular biology. Total annual research expenditures: $5.7 million. *Unit head:* Patrick J. Flannery, Administrative Manager, 734-936-2991, Fax: 734-615-6337, E-mail: pjflan@umich.edu. *Application contact:* Mary Carr, Graduate Coordinator, 734-615-1635, Fax: 734-764-0884, E-mail: carrmm@umich.edu.

University of Michigan, Horace H. Rackham School of Graduate Studies, Program in Biomedical Sciences (PIBS), Department of Cell and Developmental Biology, Ann Arbor, MI 48109. Offers PhD. *Degree requirements:* For doctorate, thesis/dissertation, oral defense of dissertation, preliminary exam. *Entrance requirements:* For doctorate, GRE General Test, 3 letters of recommendation, research experience. Additional exam requirements/recommendations for international students: Required—TOEFL (minimum score 84 iBT). Electronic applications accepted. *Expenses:* Tuition, state resident: full-time $17,286; part-time $1099 per credit hour. Tuition, nonresident: full-time $34,944; part-time $2080 per credit hour. Required fees: $95 per semester. Tuition and fees vary according to course load, degree level and program. *Faculty research:* Small stress proteins, cellular stress response, muscle, male reproductive, toxicology, cell cytoskeleton.

University of Minnesota, Twin Cities Campus, Graduate School, Program in Molecular, Cellular, Developmental Biology and Genetics, Minneapolis, MN 55455-0213. Offers genetic counseling (MS); molecular, cellular, developmental biology and genetics (PhD). *Faculty:* 89 full-time (31 women), 19 part-time/adjunct (17 women). *Students:* 86 full-time (49 women); includes 6 minority (1 American Indian/Alaska Native, 4 Asian Americans or Pacific Islanders, 1 Hispanic American), 23 international. Average age 24. 179 applicants, 11% accepted, 19 enrolled. In 2009, 12 master's, 6 doctorates awarded. Terminal master's awarded for partial completion of doctoral program. *Degree requirements:* For master's, thesis optional; for doctorate, thesis/dissertation. *Entrance requirements:* For master's and doctorate, GRE General Test. Additional exam requirements/recommendations for international students: Required—TOEFL (minimum score 625 paper-based; 263 computer-based; 80 iBT). *Application deadline:* For fall admission, 12/15 priority date for domestic and international students. Applications are processed on a rolling basis. Application fee: $55 ($75 for international students). Electronic applications accepted. *Financial support:* In 2009–10, 10 fellowships with full tuition reimbursements (averaging $23,000 per year), 79 research assistantships with full tuition reimbursements (averaging $24,500 per year), 11 teaching assistantships with partial tuition reimbursements (averaging $9,236 per year) were awarded; scholarships/grants, traineeships, and health care benefits also available. Financial award application deadline: 12/15. *Faculty research:* Membrane receptors and membrane transport, cell interactions, cytoskeleton and cell mobility, regulation of gene expression, plant cell and molecular biology. Total annual research expenditures: $9.1 million. *Unit head:* Kathleen Conklin, Director of Graduate Studies, 612-626-0445, Fax: 612-626-6140, E-mail: conkl001@umn.edu. *Application contact:* Sue Knoblauch, Student Support Coordinator, 612-624-7470, Fax: 612-626-6140, E-mail: mcdbg@umn.edu.

University of Minnesota, Twin Cities Campus, Graduate School, Stem Cell Biology Graduate Program, Minneapolis, MN 55455-0213. Offers MS, PhD. *Degree requirements:* For master's, thesis; for doctorate, thesis/dissertation. *Entrance requirements:* For master's and doctorate, BS, BA, or foreign equivalent in biological sciences or related field; minimum undergraduate GPA of 3.2. Additional exam requirements/recommendations for international students: Required—TOEFL (minimum score 580 paper-based; 237 computer-based; 92 iBT), IELTS (minimum score 6.5), TWE (minimum score 4). *Faculty research:* Stem cell and developmental biology; embryonic stem cells; iPS cells; muscle satellite cells; hematopoietic stem cells; neuronal stem cells; cardiovascular, kidney and limb development; regenerating systems.

University of Missouri–St. Louis, College of Arts and Sciences, Department of Biology, St. Louis, MO 63121. Offers biology (MS, PhD), including animal behavior (MS), biochemistry, biochemistry and biotechnology (MS), biotechnology (MS), conservation biology (MS), development (MS), ecology (MS), environmental studies (PhD), evolution (MS), genetics (MS), molecular biology and biochemistry (PhD), molecular/cellular biology (MS), physiology (MS), plant systematics, population biology (MS), tropical biology (MS); biotechnology (Certificate); tropical biology and conservation (Certificate). Part-time programs available. *Faculty:* 43 full-time (13 women), 2 part-time/adjunct (1 woman). *Students:* 54 full-time (27 women), 79 part-time (43 women); includes 15 minority (6 African Americans, 7 Asian Americans or Pacific Islanders, 2 Hispanic Americans), 47 international. Average age 29. 193 applicants, 44% accepted, 44 enrolled. In 2009, 30 master's, 7 doctorates, 9 other advanced degrees awarded. *Degree requirements:* For master's, thesis or alternative; for doctorate, thesis/dissertation, 1 semester of teaching experience. *Entrance requirements:* For master's, 3 letters of recommendation; for doctorate, GRE General Test, 3 letters of recommendation. Additional exam requirements/recommendations for international students: Required—TOEFL. *Application deadline:* For fall admission, 12/1 priority date for domestic and international students; for spring admission, 10/15 priority date for domestic and international students. Applications are processed on a rolling basis. Application fee: $35 ($40 for international students). Electronic applications accepted. *Expenses:* Tuition, state resident: full-time $5377; part-time $297.70 per credit hour. Tuition, nonresident: full-time $13,882; part-time $771.20 per credit hour. Required fees: $220; $12.20 per credit hour. One-time fee: $12. Tuition and fees vary according to course level, campus/location and program. *Financial support:* In 2009–10, 22 research assistantships with full and partial tuition reimbursements (averaging $16,300 per year), 14 teaching assistantships with full and partial tuition reimbursements (averaging $16,727 per year) were awarded; fellowships with full tuition reimbursements, career-related internships or fieldwork and Federal Work-Study also available. Support available to part-time students. Financial award application deadline: 2/1. *Faculty research:* Molecular biology, microbial genetics, animal behavior, tropical ecology, plant systematics. *Unit head:* Dr. Elizabeth Kellogg, Director of Graduate Studies, 314-516-6200, Fax: 314-516-6233, E-mail: tkellogg@umsl.edu. *Application contact:* 314-516-5458, Fax: 314-516-6996, E-mail: gradadm@umsl.edu.

The University of North Carolina at Chapel Hill, Graduate School, College of Arts and Sciences, Department of Biology, Chapel Hill, NC 27599. Offers botany (MA, MS, PhD); cell biology, development, and physiology (MA, MS, PhD); cell motility and cytoskeleton (PhD); ecology and behavior (MA, MS, PhD); genetics and molecular biology (MA, MS, PhD); morphology, systematics, and evolution (MA, MS, PhD). Terminal master's awarded for partial completion of doctoral program. *Degree requirements:* For master's, comprehensive exam, thesis (for some programs); for doctorate, comprehensive exam, thesis/dissertation. *Entrance requirements:* For master's, GRE General Test, GRE Subject Test, 2 semesters of calculus or statistics; 2 semesters of physics, organic chemistry; 3 semesters of biology; for doctorate, GRE General Test, GRE Subject Test, 2 semesters calculus or statistics, 2 semesters physics, organic chemistry, 3 semesters of biology. Additional exam requirements/recommendations for international students: Required—TOEFL (minimum score 550 paper-based; 213 computer-based). Electronic applications accepted. *Faculty research:* Gene expression, biomechanics, yeast genetics, plant ecology, plant molecular biology.

The University of North Carolina at Chapel Hill, School of Medicine and Graduate School, Graduate Programs in Medicine, Department of Cell and Developmental Biology, Chapel Hill, NC 27599. Offers PhD. *Degree requirements:* For doctorate, comprehensive exam, thesis/dissertation. *Entrance requirements:* For doctorate, GRE General Test, GRE Subject Test. Electronic applications accepted. *Faculty research:* Cell adhesion, motility and cytoskeleton; molecular analysis of signal transduction; development biology and toxicology; reproductive biology; cell and molecular imaging.

University of Pennsylvania, School of Medicine, Biomedical Graduate Studies, Graduate Group in Cell and Molecular Biology, Program in Developmental Biology, Philadelphia, PA 19104. Offers PhD, MD/PhD, VMD/PhD. *Degree requirements:* For doctorate, thesis/dissertation. *Entrance requirements:* For doctorate, GRE General Test. Additional exam requirements/recommendations for international students: Required—TOEFL. *Application deadline:* For fall admission, 12/8 priority date for domestic and international students. Applications are processed on a rolling basis. Application fee: $70. Electronic applications accepted. *Expenses:* Tuition: Full-time $25,660; part-time $4758 per course. Required fees: $2152; $270 per course. Tuition and fees vary according to course load, degree level and program. *Financial support:* Fellowships, research assistantships, scholarships/grants, traineeships, and unspecified assistantships available. *Unit head:* Dr. Sarah Millar, Chair, 215-898-1478. *Application contact:* Meagan Schofer, Coordinator, 215-895-9536, Fax: 215-573-2104, E-mail: camb@mailmed.upenn.edu.

University of Pittsburgh, School of Arts and Sciences, Department of Biological Sciences, Program in Molecular, Cellular, and Developmental Biology, Pittsburgh, PA 15260. Offers PhD. *Faculty:* 23 full-time (6 women). *Students:* 52 full-time (33 women); includes 2 minority (1 African American, 1 Asian American or Pacific Islander), 14 international. Average age 23. 194 applicants, 10% accepted, 9 enrolled. In 2009, 3 doctorates awarded. *Degree requirements:* For doctorate, comprehensive exam, thesis/dissertation. *Entrance requirements:* For doctorate, GRE General Test, GRE Subject Test. Additional exam requirements/recommendations for international students: Required—TOEFL (minimum score 550 paper-based; 213 computer-based). *Application deadline:* For fall admission, 1/15 priority date for domestic students, 12/15 priority date for international students. Applications are processed on a rolling basis. Application fee: $0 ($50 for international students). Electronic applications accepted. *Expenses:* Tuition, state resident: full-time $16,402; part-time $665 per credit. Tuition, nonresident: full-time $28,694; part-time $1175 per credit. Required fees: $690; $175 per term. Tuition and fees vary according to program. *Financial support:* In 2009–10, 31 fellowships with full tuition reimbursements (averaging $27,379 per year), 104 research assistantships with full tuition reimbursements (averaging $24,608 per year), 36 teaching assistantships with full tuition reimbursements (averaging $23,385 per year) were awarded; Federal Work-Study, scholarships/grants, traineeships, health care benefits, and tuition waivers (full) also available. *Faculty research:* Structure and function of genes and proteins, macromolecular interactions, cell-specific gene regulation, regulation of cell proliferation, embryogenesis. *Unit head:* Dr. Gerard L. Campbell, Associate Professor, 412-624-6812, Fax: 412-624-4759, E-mail: camp@pitt.edu. *Application contact:* Cathleen M. Barr, Graduate Administrator, 412-624-4268, Fax: 412-624-4759, E-mail: cbarr@pitt.edu.

University of South Carolina, The Graduate School, College of Arts and Sciences, Department of Biological Sciences, Graduate Training Program in Molecular, Cellular, and Developmental Biology, Columbia, SC 29208. Offers MS, PhD. *Degree requirements:* For master's, one foreign language, thesis; for doctorate, one foreign language, thesis/dissertation. *Entrance requirements:* For master's and doctorate, GRE General Test, minimum GPA of 3.0 in science. Electronic applications accepted. *Faculty research:* Marine ecology, population and evolutionary biology, molecular biology and genetics, development.

The University of Texas Health Science Center at Houston, Graduate School of Biomedical Sciences, Program in Genes and Development, Houston, TX 77030. Offers MS, PhD, MD/PhD. Terminal master's awarded for partial completion of doctoral program. *Degree requirements:* For master's, thesis; for doctorate, thesis/dissertation. *Entrance requirements:* For master's and doctorate, GRE General Test. Additional exam requirements/recommendations for international students: Required—TOEFL. Electronic applications accepted. *Faculty research:* Developmental biology, genetics, cell biology, structural biology, cancer.

The University of Texas Southwestern Medical Center at Dallas, Southwestern Graduate School of Biomedical Sciences, Division of Basic Science, Program in Genetics and Development, Dallas, TX 75390. Offers PhD. *Faculty:* 85 full-time (16 women), 2 part-time/adjunct (0 women). *Students:* 102 full-time (52 women), 4 part-time (1 woman); includes 25 minority (1 African American, 1 American Indian/Alaska Native, 12 Asian Americans or Pacific Islanders, 11 Hispanic Americans), 38 international. Average age 28. 946 applicants, 22% accepted, 87 enrolled. In 2009, 19 doctorates awarded. *Degree requirements:* For doctorate, thesis/dissertation, qualifying exam. *Entrance requirements:* For doctorate, GRE General Test, minimum GPA of 3.0. Additional exam requirements/recommendations for international students: Required—TOEFL. *Application deadline:* For fall admission, 12/15 priority date for domestic students. Application fee: $0. Electronic applications accepted. *Financial support:* Fellowships, research assistantships, institutionally sponsored loans available. *Faculty research:* Human molecular genetics, chromosome structure, gene regulation, molecular biology, gene expression. *Unit head:* Dr. Nancy E. Street, Associate Dean, 214-648-6708, Fax: 214-648-2102, E-mail: nancy.street@utsouthwestern.edu. *Application contact:* Dr. Nancy E. Street, Associate Dean, 214-648-6708, Fax: 214-648-2102, E-mail: nancy.street@utsouthwestern.edu.

Virginia Polytechnic Institute and State University, Graduate School, College of Science, Department of Biological Sciences, Blacksburg, VA 24061. Offers botany (MS, PhD); ecology and evolutionary biology (MS, PhD); genetics and developmental biology (MS, PhD); microbiology (MS, PhD); zoology (MS, PhD). *Faculty:* 42 full-time (11 women). *Students:* 76 full-time (45 women), 5 part-time (1 woman); includes 28 minority (23 American Indian/Alaska Native, 2 Asian Americans or Pacific Islanders, 3 Hispanic Americans). Average age 28. 117 applicants, 15% accepted, 15 enrolled. In 2009, 11 master's, 11 doctorates awarded. *Entrance requirements:* For master's and doctorate, GRE, GMAT. Additional exam requirements/recommendations for international students: Required—TOEFL (minimum score 550 paper-based; 213 computer-based). *Application deadline:* For fall admission, 5/15 for international students; for spring admission, 10/15 for international students. Applications are processed on a rolling basis. Application fee: $65. Electronic applications accepted. *Expenses:* Tuition, area resident: Full-time $10,228; part-time $459 per credit hour. Tuition, nonresident: full-time $17,892; part-time $865 per credit hour. Required fees: $1966; $451 per semester. *Financial support:* In 2009–10, 37 research assistantships with full tuition reimbursements (averaging $17,929 per year), 41 teaching assistantships with full tuition reimbursements (averaging $17,344 per year) were awarded; career-related internships or fieldwork, Federal Work-Study, scholarships/grants, and unspecified assistantships also available. Financial award application deadline: 1/15. *Faculty research:* Freshwater ecology, cell cycle regulation, behavioral ecology, motor proteins. Total annual research expenditures: $4.8 million. *Unit head:* Dr. Bob H. Jones, Dean, 540-231-9514, Fax: 540-231-9307, E-mail: rhjones@vt.edu. *Application contact:* Erik Nilsen, Information Contact, 540-231-5671, Fax: 540-231-9307, E-mail: enilsen@vt.edu.

Washington University in St. Louis, Graduate School of Arts and Sciences, Division of Biology and Biomedical Sciences, Program in Developmental Biology, St. Louis, MO 63130-4899. Offers PhD. *Degree requirements:* For doctorate, thesis/dissertation. *Entrance requirements:* For doctorate, GRE General Test, GRE Subject Test. Electronic applications accepted.

Wesleyan University, Graduate Programs, Department of Biology, Middletown, CT 06459. Offers animal behavior (PhD); bioformatics/genomics (PhD); cell biology (PhD); developmental biology (PhD); evolution/ecology (PhD); genetics (PhD); neurobiology (PhD); population biology (PhD). *Faculty:* 13 full-time (4 women). *Students:* 23 full-time (11 women); includes 1 minority (African American), 3 international. Average age 26. 29 applicants, 10% accepted, 2 enrolled. In 2009, 3 doctorates awarded. *Degree requirements:* For doctorate, variable foreign language requirement, thesis/dissertation. *Entrance requirements:* For doctorate, GRE. Additional exam requirements/recommendations for international students: Required—TOEFL. *Application deadline:* For fall admission, 1/15 for domestic and international students. Applications are processed on a rolling basis. Application fee: $0. *Financial support:* In 2009–10, 3 research assistantships with full tuition reimbursements, 19 teaching assistantships with full tuition reimbursements were awarded; stipends also available. Financial award application deadline: 4/15; financial award applicants required to submit FAFSA. *Faculty research:* Microbial population genetics, genetic basis of evolutionary adaptation, genetic regulation of differentiation and pattern formation in *drosophila*. *Unit head:* Dr. Sonia E. Sultan, Chair/Professor, 860-685-3493, E-mail: jnaegele@wesleyan.edu. *Application contact:* Marjorie Fitzgibbons, Information Contact, 860-685-2140, E-mail: mfitzgibbons@wesleyan.edu.

West Virginia University, Davis College of Agriculture, Forestry and Consumer Sciences, Interdisciplinary Program in Genetics and Developmental Biology, Morgantown, WV 26506. Offers animal breeding (MS, PhD); biochemical and molecular genetics (MS, PhD); cytogenetics (MS, PhD); descriptive embryology (MS, PhD); developmental genetics (MS); experimental morphogenesis/teratology (MS); human genetics (MS, PhD); immunogenetics (MS, PhD); life cycles of animals and plants (MS, PhD); molecular aspects of development (MS, PhD); mutagenesis (MS, PhD); oncology (MS, PhD); plant genetics (MS, PhD); population and quantitative genetics (MS, PhD); regeneration (MS, PhD); teratology (PhD); toxicology (MS, PhD). *Degree requirements:* For master's, thesis; for doctorate, comprehensive exam, thesis/dissertation. *Entrance requirements:* For master's, GRE or MCAT, minimum GPA of 2.75. Additional exam requirements/recommendations for international students: Required—TOEFL.

Yale University, Graduate School of Arts and Sciences, Department of Molecular, Cellular, and Developmental Biology, New Haven, CT 06520. Offers biochemistry, molecular biology and chemical biology (PhD); cellular and developmental biology (PhD); genetics (PhD); neurobiology (PhD); plant sciences (PhD). *Degree requirements:* For doctorate, thesis/dissertation. *Entrance requirements:* For doctorate, GRE General Test, GRE Subject Test.

Genetics

Albert Einstein College of Medicine, Sue Golding Graduate Division of Medical Sciences, Division of Biological Sciences, Department of Genetics, Bronx, NY 10461. Offers computational genetics (PhD); molecular genetics (PhD); translational genetics (PhD); MD/PhD. *Degree requirements:* For doctorate, thesis/dissertation. *Entrance requirements:* For doctorate, GRE General Test. Additional exam requirements/recommendations for international students: Required—TOEFL. *Faculty research:* Neurologic genetics in *Drosophila*, biochemical genetics of yeast, developmental genetics in the mouse.

Baylor College of Medicine, Graduate School of Biomedical Sciences, Department of Molecular and Human Genetics, Houston, TX 77030-3498. Offers PhD, MD/PhD. *Faculty:* 68 full-time (16 women). *Students:* 78 full-time (46 women); includes 5 minority (2 African Americans, 1 Asian American or Pacific Islander, 2 Hispanic Americans), 39 international. Average age 24. In 2009, 11 doctorates awarded. *Degree requirements:* For doctorate, thesis/dissertation, public defense. *Entrance requirements:* For doctorate, GRE General Test, GRE Subject Test (strongly recommended), minimum GPA of 3.0. Additional exam requirements/recommendations for international students: Required—TOEFL. *Application deadline:* For fall admission, 1/1 priority date for domestic students. Application fee: $0. Electronic applications accepted. *Financial support:* Fellowships, research assistantships, career-related internships or fieldwork, Federal Work-Study, institutionally sponsored loans, health care benefits, and students receive a scholarship unless there are grant funds available to pay tuition available. Financial award applicants required to submit FAFSA. *Faculty research:* Cytogenetics, biochemical genetics, somatic cell genetics, gene therapy. *Unit head:* Dr. Gad Shaulsky, Director, 713-798-5056. *Application contact:* Judi Coleman, Graduate Program Administrator, 713-798-5056, Fax: 713-798-8597, E-mail: genetics-gradprm@bcm.edu.

See Close-Up on page 313.

Baylor College of Medicine, Graduate School of Biomedical Sciences, Interdepartmental Program in Cell and Molecular Biology, Houston, TX 77030-3498. Offers biochemistry (PhD); cell and molecular biology (PhD); genetics (PhD); human genetics (PhD); immunology (PhD); microbiology (PhD); virology (PhD); MD/PhD. *Faculty:* 100 full-time (31 women). *Students:* 59 full-time (37 women); includes 24 minority (5 African Americans, 1 American Indian/Alaska Native, 7 Asian Americans or Pacific Islanders, 11 Hispanic Americans), 6 international. Average age 25. In 2009, 9 doctorates awarded. *Degree requirements:* For doctorate, thesis/dissertation, public defense. *Entrance requirements:* For doctorate, GRE General Test, GRE Subject Test (strongly recommended), minimum GPA of 3.0. Additional exam requirements/recommendations for international students: Required—TOEFL. *Application deadline:* For fall admission, 1/1 priority date for domestic students. Applications are processed on a rolling basis. Application fee: $0. Electronic applications accepted. *Financial support:* In 2009–10, 59 students received support; fellowships, research assistantships, teaching assistantships, Federal Work-Study, institutionally sponsored loans, health care benefits, and tuition waivers (full) available. Financial award applicants required to submit FAFSA. *Faculty research:* Gene expression and regulation, developmental biology and genetics, signal transduction and membrane biology, aging process, molecular virology. *Unit head:* Dr. Susan Marriott, Director, 713-798-6557. *Application contact:* Lourdes Fernandez, Graduate Program Administrator, 713-798-6557, Fax: 713-798-6325, E-mail: cmbprog@bcm.edu.

See Close-Up on page 231.

Baylor College of Medicine, Graduate School of Biomedical Sciences, Program in Developmental Biology, Houston, TX 77030-3498. Offers PhD, MD/PhD. *Faculty:* 52 full-time (16 women). *Students:* 51 full-time (26 women); includes 9 minority (1 American Indian/Alaska Native, 6 Asian Americans or Pacific Islanders, 2 Hispanic Americans), 29 international. Average age 25. In 2009, 4 doctorates awarded. *Degree requirements:* For doctorate, thesis/dissertation, public defense. *Entrance requirements:* For doctorate, GRE General Test, GRE Subject Test (strongly recommended), minimum GPA of 3.0. Additional exam requirements/recommendations for international students: Required—TOEFL. *Application deadline:* For fall admission, 1/1 priority date for domestic students. Application fee: $0. Electronic applications accepted. *Financial support:* Fellowships, research assistantships, career-related internships or fieldwork, Federal Work-Study, institutionally sponsored loans, health care benefits, tuition waivers (full), and stipends available. *Faculty research:* Molecular and genetic approaches to study pattern formation in Dictyostelium, Drosophila, C.elegans, mouse, Xenopus, and zebrafish; cross-species approach. *Unit head:* Dr. Hugo Bellen, Director, 713-798-6410. *Application contact:* Catherine Tasnier, Graduate Program Administrator, 713-798-6410, Fax: 713-798-5386, E-mail: cat@bcm.edu.

See Close-Up on page 315.

Baylor College of Medicine, Graduate School of Biomedical Sciences, Program in Translational Biology and Molecular Medicine, Houston, TX 77030-3498. Offers PhD. *Faculty:* 151 full-time (48 women). *Students:* 48 full-time (23 women); includes 13 minority (4 African Americans, 4 Asian Americans or Pacific Islanders, 5 Hispanic Americans), 14 international. Average age 24. *Degree requirements:* For doctorate, thesis/dissertation, public defense. *Entrance requirements:* For doctorate, GRE, minimum GPA of 3.0. Additional exam requirements/recommendations for international students: Required—TOEFL. *Application deadline:* For fall admission, 1/1 for domestic students. Application fee: $0. Electronic applications accepted. *Financial support:* In 2009–10, 48 students received support; fellowships, research assistantships, career-related internships or fieldwork, Federal Work-Study, health care benefits, and students receive a scholarship unless there are grant funds available to pay tuition available. Financial award applicants required to submit FAFSA. *Unit head:* Dr. Mary Estes, Director, 713-798-3585, Fax: 713-798-3586, E-mail: tbmm@bcm.edu. *Application contact:* Wanda Waguespack, Graduate Program Administrator, 713-798-1077, Fax: 713-798-3586, E-mail: wandaw@bcm.edu.

See Close-Up on page 261.

Brandeis University, Graduate School of Arts and Sciences, Program in Molecular and Cell Biology, Waltham, MA 02454-9110. Offers genetics (PhD); microbiology (PhD); molecular and cell biology (MS, PhD); molecular biology (PhD); neurobiology (PhD). *Faculty:* 28 full-time (12 women), 1 (woman) part-time/adjunct. *Students:* 46 full-time (26 women), 1 part-time (0 women); includes 3 minority (2 African Americans, 1 Hispanic American), 7 international. Average age 27. 146 applicants, 21% accepted, 12 enrolled. In 2009, 4 master's, 6 doctorates awarded. Terminal master's awarded for partial completion of doctoral program. *Degree requirements:* For master's, thesis optional, research project; for doctorate, comprehensive exam, thesis/dissertation, teaching assistant experience. *Entrance requirements:* For master's and doctorate, GRE General Test, resume, 3 letters of recommendation. Additional exam requirements/recommendations for international students: Required—TOEFL (minimum score 600 paper-based; 250 computer-based; 100 iBT); Recommended—IELTS (minimum score 7). *Application deadline:* For fall admission, 1/15 priority date for domestic students. Applications are processed on a rolling basis. Application fee: $75. Electronic applications accepted. *Financial support:* In 2009–10, 41 students received support, including 13 fellowships with full tuition reimbursements available (averaging $27,500 per year), 27 research assistantships with full tuition reimbursements available (averaging $27,500 per year), 1 teaching assistantship with partial tuition reimbursement available (averaging $3,200 per year); scholarships/grants, traineeships, health care benefits, and tuition waivers (full and partial) also available. Financial award application deadline: 4/15; financial award applicants required to submit FAFSA. *Faculty research:* Regulation of gene expression by transcription factors, molecular neurobiology, immunology, molecular mechanisms of genetic recombination, cell differentiation. *Unit head:* Dr. Piali Sengupta, Chair, 781-736-2686, Fax: 781-736-3107, E-mail: piali@brandeis.edu. *Application contact:* Marcia Cabral, Department Administrator, 781-736-3100, Fax: 781-736-3107, E-mail: cabral@brandeis.edu.

California Institute of Technology, Division of Biology, Program in Genetics, Pasadena, CA 91125-0001. Offers PhD. *Degree requirements:* For doctorate, thesis/dissertation, qualifying exam. *Entrance requirements:* For doctorate, GRE General Test.

Carnegie Mellon University, Mellon College of Science, Department of Biological Sciences, Pittsburgh, PA 15213-3891. Offers biochemistry (PhD); biophysics (PhD); cell biology (PhD); computational biology (MS, PhD); developmental biology (PhD); genetics (PhD); molecular biology (PhD); neuroscience (PhD). *Degree requirements:* For doctorate, comprehensive exam, thesis/dissertation. *Entrance requirements:* For doctorate, GRE General Test, GRE Subject Test, interview. Electronic applications accepted. *Faculty research:* Genetic structure, function, and regulation; protein structure and function; biological membranes; biological spectroscopy.

Case Western Reserve University, School of Medicine and School of Graduate Studies, Graduate Programs in Medicine, Department of Genetics, Program in Human, Molecular, and Developmental Genetics and Genomics, Cleveland, OH 44106. Offers PhD, MD/PhD. *Degree requirements:* For doctorate, comprehensive exam, thesis/dissertation. *Entrance requirements:* For doctorate, GRE General Test, GRE Subject Test. Additional exam requirements/recommendations for international students: Required—TOEFL. *Faculty research:* Regulation of gene expression, molecular control of development, genomics.

Clemson University, Graduate School, College of Agriculture, Forestry and Life Sciences, Department of Genetics and Biochemistry, Program in Genetics, Clemson, SC 29634. Offers PhD. *Students:* 20 full-time (12 women), 3 part-time (2 women), 7 international. Average age 30. 22 applicants, 23% accepted, 3 enrolled. In 2009, 3 doctorates awarded. *Degree requirements:* For doctorate, thesis/dissertation. *Entrance requirements:* For doctorate, GRE General Test, minimum GPA of 3.2. Additional exam requirements/recommendations for international students: Required—TOEFL, IELTS. *Application deadline:* For fall admission, 1/1 for domestic students; for spring admission, 9/1 for domestic students. Applications are processed on a rolling basis. Application fee: $70 ($80 for international students). Electronic applications accepted. *Expenses:* Contact institution. *Financial support:* In 2009–10, 20 students received support, including 7 fellowships with full and partial tuition reimbursements available (averaging $11,238 per year), 13 research assistantships with partial tuition reimbursements available (averaging $18,148 per year), 7 teaching assistantships with partial tuition reimbursements available (averaging $21,929 per year). Financial award application deadline: 3/15; financial award applicants required to submit FAFSA. *Faculty research:* Animal, plant, microbial, molecular, and biometrical genetics. *Unit head:* Dr. Keith Murphy, Chair, 864-656-6237, E-mail: kmurph2@clemson.edu. *Application contact:* Sheryl Banks, Administrative Coordinator, 866-656-6878, E-mail: sherylb@clemson.edu.

Clemson University, Graduate School, College of Health, Education, and Human Development, School of Nursing, Clemson, SC 29634. Offers healthcare genetics (PhD); nursing (MS). *Accreditation:* AACN. Part-time programs available. Postbaccalaureate distance learning degree programs offered. *Faculty:* 15 full-time (all women), 1 (woman) part-time/adjunct. *Students:* 44 full-time (42 women), 37 part-time (34 women); includes 7 minority (4 African Americans, 2 Asian Americans or Pacific Islanders, 1 Hispanic American), 3 international. Average age 34. 39 applicants, 38% accepted, 10 enrolled. In 2009, 32 master's awarded. *Degree requirements:* For master's, thesis or alternative; for doctorate, comprehensive exam, thesis/dissertation. *Entrance requirements:* For master's, GRE General Test, RN license; for doctorate, GRE General Test. Additional exam requirements/recommendations for international students: Required—TOEFL. *Application deadline:* For fall admission, 4/1 for domestic students; for spring admission, 10/1 for domestic students. Applications are processed on a rolling basis. Application fee: $70 ($80 for international students). Electronic applications accepted. *Expenses:* Contact institution. *Financial support:* In 2009–10, 24 students received support, including 1 research assistantship with partial tuition reimbursement available (averaging $15,600 per year), 20 teaching assistantships with partial tuition reimbursements available (averaging $10,341 per year); fellowships with full and partial tuition reimbursements available, career-related internships or fieldwork, institutionally sponsored loans, scholarships/grants, health care benefits, and unspecified assistantships also available. Support available to part-time students. Financial award applicants required to submit FAFSA. *Faculty research:* Risk behaviors and chronic risk-taking in early adolescents, stress in older caregivers, home care of elderly, cancer awareness, pain. Total annual research expenditures: $414,950. *Unit head:* Dr. Rosanne Pruitt, Director, 864-656-7622, Fax: 864-656-5488, E-mail: prosan@clemson.edu. *Application contact:* Dr. Margaret Ann Wetsel, Graduate Studies Coordinator, 864-656-5527, Fax: 864-656-5488, E-mail: mwetsel@clemson.edu.

Columbia University, College of Physicians and Surgeons, Department of Genetics and Development, New York, NY 10032. Offers genetics (M Phil, MA, PhD); MD/PhD. Only candidates for the PhD are admitted. Terminal master's awarded for partial completion of doctoral program. *Degree requirements:* For doctorate, thesis/dissertation. *Entrance requirements:* For master's and doctorate, GRE General Test. Additional exam requirements/recommendations for international students: Required—TOEFL. *Faculty research:* Mammalian cell differentiation and meiosis, developmental genetics, yeast and human genetics, chromosome structure, molecular and cellular biology.

Cornell University, Graduate School, Graduate Fields of Agriculture and Life Sciences, Field of Genetics and Development, Ithaca, NY 14853-0001. Offers developmental biology (PhD); genetics (PhD). *Faculty:* 58 full-time (14 women). *Students:* 60 full-time (33 women); includes 5 minority (2 Asian Americans or Pacific Islanders, 3 Hispanic Americans), 22 international. Average age 27. 64 applicants, 33% accepted, 12 enrolled. In 2009, 5 doctorates awarded. *Degree requirements:* For doctorate, comprehensive exam, thesis/dissertation, 2 semesters of teaching experience. *Entrance requirements:* For doctorate, GRE General Test, GRE Subject Test in biology or biochemistry (recommended), 2 letters of recommendation. Additional exam requirements/recommendations for international students: Required—TOEFL (minimum score 550 paper-based; 213 computer-based; 77 iBT). *Application deadline:* For fall admission, 1/5 for domestic students. Application fee: $70. Electronic applications accepted. *Expenses:* Tuition: Full-time $29,500. Required fees: $70. Full-time tuition and fees vary according to degree level, program and student level. *Financial support:* In 2009–10, 54 students received support, including 7 fellowships with full tuition reimbursements available, 2 research assistantships with full tuition reimbursements available, 1 teaching assistantship with full tuition reimbursement available; institutionally sponsored loans, scholarships/grants, health care benefits, tuition waivers (full and partial), and unspecified assistantships also available. Financial award applicants required to submit FAFSA. *Faculty research:* Molecular and general genetics, developmental biology and developmental genetics, evolution and population genetics, plant genetics, microbial genetics. *Unit head:* Director of Graduate Studies, 607-254-2100. *Application contact:* Graduate Field Assistant, 607-254-2100, E-mail: gendev@cornell.edu.

Dartmouth College, Graduate Program in Molecular and Cellular Biology, Department of Genetics, Hanover, NH 03755. Offers PhD, MD/PhD. *Faculty:* 17 full-time (4 women). *Students:* 47 full-time (21 women); includes 1 African American, 1 Hispanic American, 23 international. Average age 27. 275 applicants, 22% accepted, 25 enrolled. In 2009, 5 doctorates awarded. *Entrance requirements:* For doctorate, GRE General Test, letters of recommendation. Additional exam requirements/recommendations for international students: Required—TOEFL (minimum score 450 paper-based; 90 iBT) or IELTS (minimum score 7). *Application deadline:* For fall admission, 1/4 for domestic and international students. Applications are processed on a rolling basis. Application fee: $75. Electronic applications accepted. *Financial support:* Scholarships/grants, health care benefits, and stipends ($25,500) available. *Unit head:* Dr. Jay C. Dunlap, Chair and Professor, 603-650-1108, E-mail: genetics@dartmouth.edu. *Application contact:* Janet Cheney, Program Coordinator, 603-650-1612, Fax: 603-650-1006, E-mail: mcb@dartmouth.edu.

Drexel University, College of Medicine, Biomedical Graduate Programs, Interdisciplinary Program in Molecular and Cell Biology and Genetics, Philadelphia, PA 19104-2875. Offers MS, PhD, MD/PhD. Terminal master's awarded for partial completion of doctoral program. *Degree requirements:* For master's, comprehensive exam, thesis; for doctorate, thesis/dissertation, qualifying exam. *Entrance requirements:* For master's, GRE General Test, minimum GPA of 2.75; for doctorate, GRE General Test, minimum GPA of 3.0. Additional exam requirements/recommendations for international students: Required—TOEFL. Electronic applications accepted. *Faculty research:* Molecular anatomy, biochemistry, medical biotechnology, molecular pathology, microbiology and immunology.

Duke University, Graduate School, Department of Biochemistry, Durham, NC 27710. Offers crystallography of macromolecules (PhD); enzyme mechanisms (PhD); lipid biochemistry (PhD); membrane structure and function (PhD); molecular genetics (PhD); neurochemistry (PhD); nucleic acid structure and function (PhD); protein structure and function (PhD). *Faculty:* 29 full-time. *Students:* 68 full-time (25 women); includes 6 minority (2 African Americans, 4 Asian Americans or Pacific Islanders), 21 international. 101 applicants, 23% accepted, 12 enrolled. In 2009, 8 doctorates awarded. *Degree requirements:* For doctorate, thesis/dissertation. *Entrance requirements:* For doctorate, GRE General Test, GRE Subject Test (recommended). Additional exam requirements/recommendations for international students: Required—TOEFL (minimum score 550 paper-based; 213 computer-based; 83 iBT), IELTS (minimum score 7). *Application deadline:* For fall admission, 12/8 priority date for domestic and international students. Application fee: $75. Electronic applications accepted. *Financial support:* Fellowships, research assistantships, teaching assistantships, Federal Work-Study available. Financial award application deadline: 12/8. *Unit head:* Leonard Spicer, Director of Graduate Studies, 919-681-8770, Fax: 919-684-8885, E-mail: anorfleet@biochem.duke.edu. *Application contact:* Cynthia Robertson, Associate Dean for Enrollment Services, 919-684-3913, E-mail: grad-admissions@duke.edu.

Duke University, Graduate School, Program in Genetics and Genomics, Durham, NC 27710. Offers PhD. *Faculty:* 105 full-time. *Students:* 84 full-time (52 women); includes 9 minority (3 African Americans, 4 Asian Americans or Pacific Islanders, 2 Hispanic Americans), 14 international. 103 applicants, 27% accepted, 8 enrolled. In 2009, 5 doctorates awarded. *Degree requirements:* For doctorate, variable foreign language requirement, thesis/dissertation. *Entrance requirements:* For doctorate, GRE General Test, GRE Subject Test (recommended). Additional exam requirements/recommendations for international students: Required—TOEFL (minimum score 550 paper-based; 213 computer-based; 83 iBT), IELTS (minimum score 7). *Application deadline:* For fall admission, 12/8 priority date for domestic and international students. Application fee: $75. *Financial support:* Fellowships available. Financial award application deadline: 12/31. *Unit head:* Dr. Michael Hauser, Director of Graduate Studies, 919-684-3508, Fax: 919-684-6629, E-mail: genetics@biochem.duke.edu. *Application contact:* Cynthia Robertson, Associate Dean for Enrollment Services, 919-684-3913, E-mail: grad-admissions@duke.edu.

Emory University, Graduate School of Arts and Sciences, Division of Biological and Biomedical Sciences, Program in Genetics and Molecular Biology, Atlanta, GA 30322-1100. Offers PhD. *Faculty:* 46 full-time (7 women). *Students:* 59 full-time (39 women); includes 9 minority (8 African Americans, 1 Hispanic American), 14 international. Average age 27. 94 applicants, 22% accepted, 7 enrolled. In 2009, 9 doctorates awarded. *Degree requirements:* For doctorate, comprehensive exam, thesis/dissertation. *Entrance requirements:* For doctorate, GRE General Test, minimum GPA of 3.0 in science course work (recommended). Additional exam requirements/recommendations for international students: Required—TOEFL. *Application deadline:* For fall admission, 1/3 for domestic and international students. Application fee: $50. Electronic applications accepted. *Financial support:* In 2009–10, 15 students received support, including 15 fellowships with full tuition reimbursements available (averaging $24,500 per year); institutionally sponsored loans, scholarships/grants, and health care benefits also available. *Faculty research:* Gene regulation, genetic combination, developmental regulation. *Unit head:* Dr. Andreas Fritz, Director, 404-727-9012, Fax: 404-727-2880, E-mail: afritz@biology.emory.edu. *Application contact:* Dr. Iain Shepherd, Recruiter, 404-727-2632, Fax: 404-727-2880, E-mail: ishephe@emory.edu.

Florida State University, The Graduate School, College of Arts and Sciences, Department of Biological Science, Specialization in Cell and Molecular Biology and Genetics, Tallahassee, FL 32306-4295. Offers MS, PhD. *Faculty:* 28 full-time (6 women). *Students:* 44 full-time (23 women); includes 6 minority (2 African Americans, 1 Asian American or Pacific Islander, 3 Hispanic Americans), 10 international. 118 applicants, 17% accepted, 11 enrolled. In 2009, 6 master's, 4 doctorates awarded. Terminal master's awarded for partial completion of doctoral program. *Degree requirements:* For master's, comprehensive exam, thesis, teaching experience, seminar presentation; for doctorate, comprehensive exam, thesis/dissertation, teaching experience, seminar presentation. *Entrance requirements:* For master's, GRE General Test (minimum combined score 1100, 500 verbal, 500 quantitative), minimum upper-division GPA of 3.0; for doctorate, GRE General Test (minimum combined score 1100, Verbal 500, Quantitative 500), minimum upper-division GPA of 3.0. Additional exam requirements/recommendations for international students: Required—TOEFL (minimum score 600 paper-based; 250 computer-based; 92 iBT). *Application deadline:* For fall admission, 12/15 for domestic and international students. Application fee: $30. Electronic applications accepted. *Expenses:* Tuition, state resident: full-time $7413. Tuition, nonresident: full-time $22,567. *Financial support:* In 2009–10, 14 research assistantships with full tuition reimbursements (averaging $20,000 per year), 30 teaching assistantships with full tuition reimbursements (averaging $18,540 per year) were awarded. Financial award application deadline: 12/15; financial award applicants required to submit FAFSA. *Faculty research:* Molecular biology; genetics and genomics; developmental biology and gene expression; cell structure, function, and motility; cellular and organismal physiology; biophysical and structural biology. *Application contact:* Judy Bowers, Coordinator, Graduate Affairs, 850-644-3023, Fax: 850-644-9829, E-mail: gradinfo@bio.fsu.edu.

The George Washington University, Columbian College of Arts and Sciences, Institute for Biomedical Sciences, Program in Biochemistry and Molecular Genetics, Washington, DC 20052. Offers PhD. Part-time and evening/weekend programs available. *Students:* 3 full-time (all women), 4 part-time (2 women). Average age 29. 19 applicants, 68% accepted, 6 enrolled. In 2009, 1 doctorate awarded. Terminal master's awarded for partial completion of doctoral program. *Degree requirements:* For doctorate, thesis/dissertation, general exam. *Entrance requirements:* For doctorate, GRE General Test, interview, minimum GPA of 3.0. Additional exam requirements/recommendations for international students: Required—TOEFL (minimum score 600 paper-based; 250 computer-based). *Application deadline:* For fall admission, 1/2 priority date for domestic and international students; for spring admission, 10/1 priority date for domestic and international students. Applications are processed on a rolling basis. Application fee: $60. Electronic applications accepted. *Financial support:* In 2009–10, 4 students received support; fellowships, Federal Work-Study, institutionally sponsored loans, and tuition waivers available. Financial award application deadline: 2/1. *Unit head:* Valerie W. Hu, Director, 202-994-8431, E-mail: valhu@gwu.edu. *Application contact:* Information Contact, 202-994-7120, Fax: 202-994-6100, E-mail: genetics@gwu.edu.

Harvard University, Graduate School of Arts and Sciences, Division of Medical Sciences, Boston, MA 02115. Offers biological chemistry and molecular pharmacology (PhD); cell biology (PhD); genetics (PhD); microbiology and molecular genetics (PhD); pathology (PhD), including experimental pathology. *Degree requirements:* For doctorate, thesis/dissertation. *Entrance requirements:* For doctorate, GRE General Test, GRE Subject Test. Additional exam requirements/recommendations for international students: Required—TOEFL. *Expenses:* Tuition: Full-time $33,696. Required fees: $1126. Full-time tuition and fees vary according to program.

Harvard University, School of Public Health, Department of Genetics and Complex Diseases, Boston, MA 02115-6096. Offers PhD. *Faculty:* 7 full-time (2 women). *Degree requirements:* For doctorate, thesis/dissertation, qualifying exam. *Entrance requirements:* For doctorate, GRE. Additional exam requirements/recommendations for international students: Required—TOEFL

(minimum score 600 paper-based; 240 computer-based; 100 iBT); Recommended—IELTS (minimum score 7). *Application deadline:* For fall admission, 12/8 for domestic and international students. Application fee: $115. Electronic applications accepted. *Expenses:* Tuition: Full-time $33,696. Required fees: $1126. Full-time tuition and fees vary according to program. *Financial support:* Fellowships, research assistantships, Federal Work-Study, scholarships/grants, traineeships, tuition waivers (partial), and unspecified assistantships available. Financial award application deadline: 2/8; financial award applicants required to submit FAFSA. *Faculty research:* Toxicology, radiation biology. *Unit head:* Dr. Gokhan Hotamisligil, Chair, 617-432-0054, Fax: 617-432-5236, E-mail: ghotamis@hsph.harvard.edu. *Application contact:* Vincent W. James, Director of Admissions, 617-432-1031, Fax: 617-432-7080, E-mail: admisofc@hsph.harvard.edu.

Illinois State University, Graduate School, College of Arts and Sciences, Department of Biological Sciences, Normal, IL 61790-2200. Offers animal behavior (MS); bacteriology (MS); biochemistry (MS); biological sciences (MS); biology (PhD); biophysics (MS); biotechnology (MS); botany (MS, PhD); cell biology (MS); conservation biology (MS); developmental biology (MS); ecology (MS, PhD); entomology (MS); evolutionary biology (MS); genetics (MS, PhD); immunology (MS); microbiology (MS, PhD); molecular biology (MS); molecular genetics (MS); neurobiology (MS); neuroscience (MS); parasitology (MS); physiology (MS, PhD); plant biology (MS); plant molecular biology (MS); plant sciences (MS); structural biology (MS); zoology (MS, PhD). Part-time programs available. *Degree requirements:* For master's, thesis or alternative; for doctorate, variable foreign language requirement, thesis/dissertation, 2 terms of residency. *Entrance requirements:* For master's, GRE General Test, minimum GPA of 2.6 in last 60 hours of course work; for doctorate, GRE General Test. *Faculty research:* Redoc balance and drug development in schistosoma mansoni, control of the growth of listeria monocytogenes at low temperature, regulation of cell expansion and microtubule function by SPRI, CRUI: physiology and fitness consequences of different life history phenotypes.

Indiana University Bloomington, University Graduate School, College of Arts and Sciences, Department of Biology, Bloomington, IN 47405. Offers biology teaching (MAT); biotechnology (MA); evolution, ecology, and behavior (MA, PhD); genetics (PhD); microbiology (MA, PhD); molecular, cellular, and developmental biology (PhD); plant sciences (MA, PhD); zoology (MA, PhD). *Faculty:* 58 full-time (15 women), 21 part-time/adjunct (6 women). *Students:* 165 full-time (95 women); includes 14 minority (6 African Americans, 1 American Indian/Alaska Native, 7 Asian Americans or Pacific Islanders), 56 international. Average age 27. 312 applicants, 19% accepted, 24 enrolled. In 2009, 4 master's, 22 doctorates awarded. Terminal master's awarded for partial completion of doctoral program. *Degree requirements:* For master's, thesis, oral defense; for doctorate, thesis/dissertation, oral defense. *Entrance requirements:* For master's and doctorate, GRE General Test. Additional exam requirements/recommendations for international students: Required—TOEFL (minimum score 100 iBT). *Application deadline:* For fall admission, 1/5 priority date for domestic students, 12/1 priority date for international students. Application fee: $55 ($65 for international students). Electronic applications accepted. *Financial support:* In 2009–10, 165 students received support, including 62 fellowships with tuition reimbursements available (averaging $19,484 per year), 27 research assistantships with tuition reimbursements available (averaging $22,605 per year), 76 teaching assistantships with tuition reimbursements available (averaging $20,528 per year); scholarships/grants, traineeships, health care benefits, and unspecified assistantships also available. Financial award application deadline: 1/5. *Faculty research:* Evolution, ecology and behavior; microbiology; molecular biology and genetics; plant biology. *Unit head:* Dr. Roger Innes, Chair, 812-855-2219, Fax: 812-855-6082, E-mail: rinnes@indiana.edu. *Application contact:* Tracey D. Stohr, Graduate Student Recruitment Coordinator, 812-856-6303, Fax: 812-855-6082, E-mail: gradbio@indiana.edu.

Iowa State University of Science and Technology, Graduate College, College of Liberal Arts and Sciences and College of Agriculture, Department of Genetics, Developmental and Cell Biology, Ames, IA 50011. Offers MS, PhD. *Faculty:* 30 full-time (5 women), 5 part-time/adjunct (3 women). *Degree requirements:* For master's, thesis; for doctorate, thesis/dissertation. *Entrance requirements:* Additional exam requirements/recommendations for international students: Required—TOEFL (minimum score 570 paper-based; 230 computer-based) or IELTS (minimum score 6.5). Application fee: $40 ($90 for international students). *Expenses:* Tuition, state resident: full-time $6716. Tuition, nonresident: full-time $8908. Tuition and fees vary according to course level, course load, program and student level. *Financial support:* Fellowships with full tuition reimbursements, research assistantships with full and partial tuition reimbursements, teaching assistantships with full and partial tuition reimbursements, scholarships/grants, health care benefits, and unspecified assistantships available. Financial award application deadline: 2/1. *Faculty research:* Animal behavior, animal models of gene therapy, cell biology, comparative physiology, developmental biology. *Unit head:* Dr. Martin Spalding, Chair, 515-294-1749. *Application contact:* Information Contact, 515-294-5836, Fax: 515-294-2592, E-mail: grad_admissions@iastate.edu.

Iowa State University of Science and Technology, Graduate College, Interdisciplinary Programs, Bioinformatics and Computational Biology Program, Ames, IA 50011. Offers MS, PhD. *Students:* 52 full-time (19 women), 2 part-time (1 woman); includes 3 minority (all Asian Americans or Pacific Islanders), 34 international. In 2009, 2 master's, 11 doctorates awarded. *Degree requirements:* For doctorate, thesis/dissertation. *Entrance requirements:* For doctorate, GRE General Test. Additional exam requirements/recommendations for international students: Required—TOEFL (minimum score 550 paper-based; 213 computer-based; 79 iBT) or IELTS (minimum score 6.5). *Application deadline:* For fall admission, 1/15 priority date for domestic students, 1/15 for international students; for spring admission, 10/15 for domestic and international students. Application fee: $40 ($90 for international students). Electronic applications accepted. *Expenses:* Tuition, state resident: full-time $6716. Tuition, nonresident: full-time $8908. Tuition and fees vary according to course level, course load, program and student level. *Financial support:* In 2009–10, 48 research assistantships with full and partial tuition reimbursements (averaging $18,330 per year), 3 teaching assistantships (averaging $17,000 per year) were awarded; fellowships with full tuition reimbursements, scholarships/grants, traineeships, health care benefits, and unspecified assistantships also available. *Faculty research:* Functional and structural genomics, genome evolution, macromolecular structure and function, mathematical biology and biological statistics, metabolic and developmental networks. *Unit head:* Dr. Volker Brendel, Chair, Supervising Committee, 515-294-5122, Fax: 515-294-6790, E-mail: bcb@iastate.edu. *Application contact:* Dr. Volker Brendel, Chair, Supervising Committee, 515-294-5122, Fax: 515-294-6790, E-mail: bcb@iastate.edu.

Iowa State University of Science and Technology, Graduate College, Interdisciplinary Programs, Program in Genetics, Ames, IA 50011. Offers MS, PhD. *Students:* 97 full-time (55 women), 3 part-time (all women); includes 6 minority (4 African Americans, 2 Hispanic Americans), 60 international. In 2009, 4 master's, 6 doctorates awarded. Terminal master's awarded for partial completion of doctoral program. *Degree requirements:* For master's, thesis; for doctorate, thesis/dissertation. *Entrance requirements:* For master's and doctorate, GRE General Test. Additional exam requirements/recommendations for international students: Required—TOEFL (minimum score 550 paper-based; 79 iBT) or IELTS (minimum score 6.5). *Application deadline:* For fall admission, 2/1 priority date for domestic and international students; for spring admission, 9/1 priority date for domestic and international students. Applications are processed on a rolling basis. Application fee: $40 ($90 for international students). *Expenses:* Tuition, state resident: full-time $6716. Tuition, nonresident: full-time $8908. Tuition and fees vary according to course level, course load, program and student level. *Financial support:* In 2009–10, 81 research assistantships with full and partial tuition reimbursements (averaging $18,340 per year), 11 teaching assistantships with full and partial tuition reimbursements (averaging $16,750 per year) were awarded; fellowships, scholarships/grants, health care benefits, and unspecified assistantships also available. *Unit head:* Dr. Phil Becraft, Supervisory Committee Chair, 515-294-7697, Fax: 515-294-6669, E-mail: genetics@iastate.edu. *Application contact:* Linda Wild, Program Coordinator, 800-499-1972, Fax: 515-294-6669, E-mail: genetics@iastate.edu.

Genetics

The Johns Hopkins University, Bloomberg School of Public Health, Department of Epidemiology, Baltimore, MD 21205. Offers cancer epidemiology (MHS, Sc M, PhD, Sc D); cardiovascular disease epidemiology (MHS, Sc M, PhD, Sc D); clinical epidemiology (MHS, Sc M, PhD, Sc D); clinical trials (PhD, Sc D); epidemiology (Dr PH); epidemiology (general) (MHS, Sc M, PhD, Sc D); epidemiology of aging (MHS, Sc M, PhD, Sc D); human genetics/genetic epidemiology (MHS, Sc M, PhD, Sc D); infectious disease epidemiology (MHS, Sc M, PhD, Sc D); occupational/environmental epidemiology (MHS, Sc M, PhD, Sc D). Part-time programs available. *Faculty:* 80 full-time (44 women), 82 part-time/adjunct (36 women). *Students:* 142 full-time (102 women), 24 part-time (17 women); includes 44 minority (13 African Americans, 28 Asian Americans or Pacific Islanders, 3 Hispanic Americans), 41 international. Average age 30. 263 applicants, 41% accepted, 52 enrolled. In 2009, 61 master's, 25 doctorates awarded. *Degree requirements:* For master's, comprehensive exam, thesis, 1 year full-time residency; for doctorate, comprehensive exam, thesis/dissertation, 2 years full-time residency, oral and written exams, student teaching. *Entrance requirements:* For master's, GRE General Test or MCAT, 3 letters of recommendation, curriculum vitae; for doctorate, GRE General Test, minimum 1 year of work experience, 3 letters of recommendation, curriculum vitae, academic records from all schools. Additional exam requirements/recommendations for international students: Required—TOEFL (minimum score 600 paper-based; 250 computer-based; 100 iBT); Recommended—IELTS (minimum score 7.5), TWE. *Application deadline:* For fall admission, 12/1 priority date for domestic students. Applications are processed on a rolling basis. Application fee: $45. Electronic applications accepted. *Financial support:* In 2009–10, 2 fellowships (averaging $28,859 per year) were awarded; Federal Work-Study, institutionally sponsored loans, scholarships/grants, traineeships, tuition waivers (partial), and stipends also available. Support available to part-time students. Financial award application deadline: 3/15; financial award applicants required to submit FAFSA. *Faculty research:* Cancer and congenital malformations, nutritional epidemiology, AIDS, tuberculosis, cardiovascular disease, risk assessment. Total annual research expenditures: $70.1 million. *Unit head:* Dr. David D. Celentano, Chair, 410-955-3286, Fax: 410-955-0863, E-mail: dcelenta@jhsph.edu. *Application contact:* Frances S. Burman, Academic Program Manager, 410-955-3926, Fax: 410-955-0863, E-mail: fburman@jhsph.edu.

The Johns Hopkins University, National Institutes of Health Sponsored Programs, Baltimore, MD 21218-2699. Offers biology (PhD), including biochemistry, biophysics, cell biology, developmental biology, genetic biology, molecular biology; cell, molecular, and developmental biology and biophysics (PhD). *Faculty:* 25 full-time (4 women). *Students:* 126 full-time (72 women); includes 36 minority (3 African Americans, 1 American Indian/Alaska Native, 21 Asian Americans or Pacific Islanders, 11 Hispanic Americans), 19 international. 282 applicants, 26% accepted, 36 enrolled. In 2009, 15 doctorates awarded. *Degree requirements:* For doctorate, comprehensive exam, thesis/dissertation. *Entrance requirements:* For doctorate, GRE General Test. Additional exam requirements/recommendations for international students: Required—TOEFL (minimum score 600 paper-based; 250 computer-based), TWE. *Application deadline:* For fall admission, 12/15 priority date for domestic students. Application fee: $60. Electronic applications accepted. *Financial support:* In 2009–10, 24 fellowships (averaging $23,000 per year), 93 research assistantships (averaging $23,000 per year), 22 teaching assistantships (averaging $23,000 per year) were awarded; Federal Work-Study, institutionally sponsored loans, scholarships/grants, traineeships, health care benefits, tuition waivers (partial), and unspecified assistantships also available. Financial award application deadline: 4/15; financial award applicants required to submit FAFSA. *Faculty research:* Protein and nucleic acid biochemistry and biophysical chemistry, molecular biology and development. Total annual research expenditures: $11.2 million. *Unit head:* Dr. Allen Shearn, Chair, 410-516-4693, Fax: 410-516-5213, E-mail: bio_cals@jhu.edu. *Application contact:* Joan Miller, Academic Affairs Manager, 410-516-5502, Fax: 410-516-5213, E-mail: joan@jhu.edu.

Kansas State University, Graduate School, College of Agriculture, Department of Plant Pathology, Manhattan, KS 66506. Offers genetics (MS, PhD); plant pathology (MS, PhD). *Faculty:* 21 full-time (6 women), 2 part-time/adjunct (0 women). *Students:* 2 full-time (0 women), 26 part-time (12 women); includes 3 minority (1 African American, 2 Hispanic Americans), 21 international. Average age 28. 28 applicants, 25% accepted, 6 enrolled. In 2009, 2 master's, 2 doctorates awarded. Terminal master's awarded for partial completion of doctoral program. *Degree requirements:* For master's, thesis, oral exam; for doctorate, thesis/dissertation, preliminary exams. *Entrance requirements:* For master's and doctorate, minimum undergraduate GPA of 3.0. Additional exam requirements/recommendations for international students: Required—TOEFL (minimum score 550 paper-based; 213 computer-based). *Application deadline:* For fall admission, 2/1 priority date for domestic and international students; for spring admission, 8/1 priority date for domestic and international students. Applications are processed on a rolling basis. Application fee: $40 ($55 for international students). Electronic applications accepted. *Financial support:* In 2009–10, 28 research assistantships (averaging $16,407 per year) were awarded; teaching assistantships, Federal Work-Study, institutionally sponsored loans, and scholarships/grants also available. Support available to part-time students. Financial award application deadline: 3/1; financial award applicants required to submit FAFSA. *Faculty research:* Applied microbiology, microbial genetics, microbial ecology/epidemiology, integrated pest management, plant genetics/genomics/molecular biology. Total annual research expenditures: $4 million. *Unit head:* Dr. John Leslie, Head, 785-532-6176, Fax: 785-532-5692, E-mail: jfl@ksu.edu. *Application contact:* Dr. Bill Bockus, Director, 785-532-1378, Fax: 785-532-5692, E-mail: bockus@ksu.edu.

Marquette University, Graduate School, College of Arts and Sciences, Department of Biology, Milwaukee, WI 53201-1881. Offers cell biology (MS, PhD); developmental biology (MS, PhD); ecology (MS, PhD); endocrinology (MS, PhD); evolutionary biology (MS, PhD); genetics (MS, PhD); microbiology (MS, PhD); molecular biology (MS, PhD); muscle and exercise physiology (MS, PhD); neurobiology (MS, PhD); reproductive physiology (MS, PhD). *Faculty:* 23 full-time (10 women), 1 part-time/adjunct (0 women). *Students:* 23 full-time (13 women), 16 part-time (9 women); includes 1 minority (Asian American or Pacific Islander), 20 international. Average age 25. 95 applicants, 16% accepted, 10 enrolled. In 2009, 3 master's, 5 doctorates awarded. Terminal master's awarded for partial completion of doctoral program. *Degree requirements:* For master's, comprehensive exam, thesis, 1 year of teaching experience or equivalent; for doctorate, thesis/dissertation, 1 year of teaching experience or equivalent, qualifying exam. *Entrance requirements:* For master's and doctorate, GRE General Test, GRE Subject Test. Additional exam requirements/recommendations for international students: Required—TOEFL. Application fee: $40. *Financial support:* In 2009–10, 4 fellowships, 22 teaching assistantships were awarded; research assistantships, Federal Work-Study, institutionally sponsored loans, scholarships/grants, and tuition waivers (full and partial) also available. Support available to part-time students. Financial award application deadline: 2/15. *Faculty research:* Microbial and invertebrate ecology, evolution of gene function, DNA methylation, DNA arrangement. *Unit head:* Dr. Robert Fitts, Chair, 414-288-1748, Fax: 414-288-7357. *Application contact:* Debbie Weaver, Administrative Assistant, 414-288-7355, Fax: 414-288-7357.

Massachusetts Institute of Technology, School of Science, Department of Biology, Cambridge, MA 02139-4307. Offers biochemistry (PhD); biological oceanography (PhD); biology (PhD); biophysical chemistry and molecular structure (PhD); cell biology (PhD); computational and systems biology (PhD); developmental biology (PhD); genetics (PhD); immunology (PhD); microbiology (PhD); molecular biology (PhD); neurobiology (PhD). *Faculty:* 54 full-time (14 women). *Students:* 237 full-time (128 women); includes 65 minority (4 African Americans, 2 American Indian/Alaska Native, 33 Asian Americans or Pacific Islanders, 26 Hispanic Americans), 25 international. Average age 26. 645 applicants, 18% accepted, 49 enrolled. In 2009, 41 doctorates awarded. *Degree requirements:* For doctorate, comprehensive exam, thesis/dissertation. *Entrance requirements:* For doctorate, GRE General Test. Additional exam requirements/recommendations for international students: Required—TOEFL (minimum score 577 paper-based; 233 computer-based), IELTS (minimum score 6.5). *Application deadline:* For fall admission, 12/1 for domestic and international students. Application fee: $75. Electronic applications accepted. *Expenses:* Tuition: Full-time $37,510; part-time $585 per unit. Required fees: $272. *Financial support:* In 2009–10, 218 students received support, including 113 fellowships with tuition reimbursements available (averaging $31,816 per year), 109 research assistantships with tuition reimbursements available (averaging $29,254 per year); teaching assistantships with tuition reimbursements available, Federal Work-Study, institutionally sponsored loans, scholarships/grants, traineeships, health care benefits, and unspecified assistantships also available. *Faculty research:* DNA recombination, transcription and gene regulation, signal transduction, cell cycle, neuronal cell fate, replication and repair. Total annual research expenditures: $114 million. *Unit head:* Prof. Chris Kaiser, Head, 617-253-4701, E-mail: mitbio@mit.edu. *Application contact:* Biology Education Office, 617-253-3717, Fax: 617-258-9329, E-mail: gradbio@mit.edu.

Mayo Graduate School, Graduate Programs in Biomedical Sciences, Program in Virology and Gene Therapy, Rochester, MN 55905. Offers PhD.

Mayo Graduate School, Graduate Programs in Biomedical Sciences, Programs in Biochemistry, Structural Biology, Cell Biology, and Genetics, Rochester, MN 55905. Offers biochemistry and structural biology (PhD); cell biology and genetics (PhD); molecular biology (PhD). *Degree requirements:* For doctorate, oral defense of dissertation, qualifying oral and written exam. *Entrance requirements:* For doctorate, GRE, 1 year of chemistry, biology, calculus, and physics. Additional exam requirements/recommendations for international students: Required—TOEFL. Electronic applications accepted. *Faculty research:* Gene structure and function, membranes and receptors/cytoskeleton, oncogenes and growth factors, protein structure and function, steroid hormonal action.

McMaster University, Faculty of Health Sciences and School of Graduate Studies, Program in Medical Sciences, Genetics and Cancer Area, Hamilton, ON L8S 4M2, Canada. Offers M Sc, PhD, MD/PhD. *Degree requirements:* For master's, thesis; for doctorate, comprehensive exam, thesis/dissertation. *Entrance requirements:* For master's, honors B Sc, B+ average in related field; for doctorate, M Sc, minimum B+ average, students with proven research experience and an A average may be admitted with a B Sc degree. Additional exam requirements/recommendations for international students: Required—TOEFL (minimum score 580 paper-based; 237 computer-based; 92 iBT).

Medical University of South Carolina, College of Graduate Studies, Program in Molecular and Cellular Biology and Pathobiology, Charleston, SC 29425. Offers cancer biology (PhD); cardiovascular biology (PhD); cardiovascular imaging (PhD); cell regulation (PhD); craniofacial biology (PhD); genetics and development (PhD); marine biomedicine (PhD); DMD/PhD; MD/PhD. *Faculty:* 137 full-time (33 women). *Students:* 39 full-time (25 women); includes 6 minority (4 African Americans, 1 Asian American or Pacific Islander, 1 Hispanic American), 9 international. Average age 28. In 2009, 16 doctorates awarded. *Degree requirements:* For doctorate, thesis/dissertation, oral and written exams. *Entrance requirements:* For doctorate, GRE General Test, interview, minimum GPA of 3.0. Additional exam requirements/recommendations for international students: Required—TOEFL (minimum score 600 paper-based; 250 computer-based; 100 iBT). *Application deadline:* For fall admission, 1/15 priority date for domestic and international students. Applications are processed on a rolling basis. Application fee: $0 ($85 for international students). Electronic applications accepted. *Financial support:* In 2009–10, 39 students received support, including 39 research assistantships with partial tuition reimbursements available (averaging $23,000 per year); Federal Work-Study and scholarships/grants also available. Support available to part-time students. Financial award application deadline: 3/10; financial award applicants required to submit FAFSA. *Unit head:* Dr. Donald R. Menick, Director, 843-876-5045, Fax: 843-792-6590, E-mail: menickd@musc.edu. *Application contact:* Dr. Cynthia F. Wright, Associate Dean for Admissions and Career Development, 843-792-2564, Fax: 843-792-6590, E-mail: wrightcf@musc.edu.

Michigan State University, College of Veterinary Medicine and The Graduate School, Graduate Programs in Veterinary Medicine and College of Natural Science and Graduate Programs in Human Medicine, Department of Microbiology and Molecular Genetics, East Lansing, MI 48824. Offers industrial microbiology (MS, PhD); microbiology (MS, PhD); microbiology and molecular genetics (MS, PhD); microbiology–environmental toxicology (PhD). *Faculty:* 32 full-time (9 women). *Students:* 50 full-time (22 women), 5 part-time (1 woman); includes 7 minority (2 African Americans, 4 Asian Americans or Pacific Islanders, 1 Hispanic American), 21 international. Average age 27. 104 applicants, 14% accepted. In 2009, 6 master's, 5 doctorates awarded. *Entrance requirements:* For master's, GRE General Test. Additional exam requirements/recommendations for international students: Required—TOEFL (minimum score 550 paper-based; 213 computer-based), Michigan State University ELT (minimum score 85), Michigan English Language Assessment Battery (minimum score 83). Electronic applications accepted. *Expenses:* Tuition, state resident: part-time $478.25 per credit hour. Tuition, nonresident: part-time $966.50 per credit hour. Part-time tuition and fees vary according to program. *Financial support:* In 2009–10, 34 research assistantships with tuition reimbursements (averaging $7,765 per year), 6 teaching assistantships with tuition reimbursements (averaging $7,544 per year) were awarded. Total annual research expenditures: $5.5 million. *Unit head:* Dr. Walter Esselman, Chairperson, 517-884-5292, Fax: 517-353-8957, E-mail: mmgchair@msu.edu. *Application contact:* Suzanne Peacock, Graduate Program Coordinator, 517-884-5287, Fax: 517-353-8957, E-mail: micgrad@msu.edu.

Michigan State University, The Graduate School, College of Natural Science, Program in Genetics, East Lansing, MI 48824. Offers genetics (MS, PhD); genetics–environmental toxicology (PhD). *Faculty:* 111 full-time (33 women), 1 part-time/adjunct (0 women). *Students:* 54 full-time (26 women), 1 part-time (0 women); includes 5 minority (2 African Americans, 1 Asian American or Pacific Islander, 2 Hispanic Americans), 32 international. Average age 28. 41 applicants, 17% accepted. In 2009, 3 master's, 10 doctorates awarded. *Entrance requirements:* Additional exam requirements/recommendations for international students: Required—TOEFL. Electronic applications accepted. *Expenses:* Tuition, state resident: part-time $478.25 per credit hour. Tuition, nonresident: part-time $966.50 per credit hour. Part-time tuition and fees vary according to program. *Financial support:* In 2009–10, 36 research assistantships with tuition reimbursements (averaging $7,896 per year), 8 teaching assistantships with tuition reimbursements (averaging $8,115 per year) were awarded. Total annual research expenditures: $59,433. *Unit head:* Dr. Barbara Sears, Director, 517-353-9845, Fax: 517-355-0112, E-mail: sears@msu.edu. *Application contact:* Jeannine Lee, Graduate Secretary, 517-353-9845, Fax: 517-355-0112, E-mail: genetics@msu.edu.

Mississippi State University, College of Agriculture and Life Sciences, Department of Animal Dairy Sciences, Mississippi State, MS 39762. Offers agricultural life sciences (MS), including animal physiology (MS, PhD), genetics (MS, PhD); agricultural science (PhD), including animal dairy sciences, animal nutrition (MS, PhD); agriculture (MS), including animal nutrition (MS, PhD); life sciences (PhD), including animal physiology (MS, PhD), genetics (MS, PhD). *Faculty:* 13 full-time (4 women). *Students:* 28 full-time (10 women), 12 part-time (7 women); includes 4 minority (2 African Americans, 2 Hispanic Americans), 7 international. Average age 29. 25 applicants, 36% accepted, 9 enrolled. In 2009, 8 master's, 1 doctorate awarded. *Degree requirements:* For master's, thesis, comprehensive oral or written exam; for doctorate, thesis/dissertation, comprehensive oral or written exam. *Entrance requirements:* For master's, GRE General Test, minimum GPA of 3.0; for doctorate, GRE General Test. Additional exam requirements/recommendations for international students: Required—TOEFL (minimum score 575 paper-based). *Application deadline:* For fall admission, 7/1 for domestic students, 5/1 for international students; for spring admission, 11/1 for domestic students, 9/1 for international students. Applications are processed on a rolling basis. Application fee: $40. Electronic applications accepted. *Expenses:* Tuition, state resident: full-time $2575.50; part-time $286.25 per credit hour. Tuition, nonresident: full-time $6510; part-time $723.50 per credit hour. Tuition and fees vary according to course load. *Financial support:* In 2009–10, 13 research assistantships (averaging $10,389 per year), 2 teaching assistantships (averaging $8,110 per year) were awarded; Federal Work-Study, institutionally sponsored loans, and unspecified assistantships also available. Financial award applicants required to submit FAFSA. *Faculty research:* Ecology and population dynamics, physiology, biochemistry and behavior, systematics. *Unit head:* Dr. Terry Kiser, Professor and Department Head, 662-325-2802, Fax: 662-325-8873, E-mail:

tkiser@ads.msstate.edu. *Application contact:* Dr. Peter Ryan, Graduate Coordinator, 662-325-2802, Fax: 662-325-8873, E-mail: pryan@ads.msstate.edu.

New York University, Graduate School of Arts and Science, Department of Biology, New York, NY 10012-1019. Offers biology (PhD); biomedical journalism (MS); cancer and molecular biology (PhD); computational biology (PhD); computers in biological research (MS); developmental genetics (PhD); general biology (MS); immunology and microbiology (PhD); molecular genetics (PhD); neurobiology (PhD); oral biology (MS); plant biology (PhD); recombinant DNA technology (MS); MS/MBA. Part-time programs available. *Faculty:* 24 full-time (5 women). *Students:* 142 full-time (79 women), 44 part-time (28 women); includes 34 minority (1 African American, 25 Asian Americans or Pacific Islanders, 8 Hispanic Americans), 82 international. Average age 27. 362 applicants, 71% accepted, 72 enrolled. In 2009, 43 master's, 9 doctorates awarded. Terminal master's awarded for partial completion of doctoral program. *Degree requirements:* For master's, thesis or alternative, qualifying paper; for doctorate, comprehensive exam, thesis/dissertation. *Entrance requirements:* For master's, GRE General Test; for doctorate, GRE General Test, GRE Subject Test. Additional exam requirements/recommendations for international students: Required—TOEFL. *Application deadline:* For fall admission, 12/12 priority date for domestic students. Application fee: $90. *Expenses:* Tuition: Full-time $30,528; part-time $1272 per credit. Required fees: $2177. *Financial support:* Fellowships with tuition reimbursements, research assistantships with tuition reimbursements, teaching assistantships with tuition reimbursements, career-related internships or fieldwork, Federal Work-Study, institutionally sponsored loans, scholarships/grants, health care benefits, and unspecified assistantships available. Financial award application deadline: 12/12; financial award applicants required to submit FAFSA. *Faculty research:* Genomics, molecular and cell biology, development and molecular genetics, molecular evolution of plants and animals. *Unit head:* Gloria Coruzzi, Chair, 212-998-8200, Fax: 212-995-4015, E-mail: biology@nyu.edu. *Application contact:* Stephen Small, Director of Graduate Studies, 212-998-8200, Fax: 212-995-4015, E-mail: biology@nyu.edu.

North Carolina State University, Graduate School, College of Agriculture and Life Sciences, Department of Genetics, Raleigh, NC 27695. Offers MG, MS, PhD. Terminal master's awarded for partial completion of doctoral program. *Degree requirements:* For master's, thesis (for some programs); for doctorate, thesis/dissertation. *Entrance requirements:* For master's and doctorate, GRE General Test, minimum GPA of 3.0. Electronic applications accepted. *Faculty research:* Population and quantitative genetics, plant molecular genetics, developmental genetics.

Northwestern University, The Graduate School and Judd A. and Marjorie Weinberg College of Arts and Sciences, Interdepartmental Biological Sciences Program (IBiS), Evanston, IL 60208. Offers biochemistry, molecular biology, and cell biology (PhD), including biochemistry, cell and molecular biology, molecular biophysics, structural biology; biotechnology (PhD); cell and molecular biology (PhD); developmental biology and genetics (PhD); hormone action and signal transduction (PhD); neuroscience (PhD); structural biology, biochemistry, and biophysics (PhD). Program participants include the Departments of Biochemistry, Molecular Biology, and Cell Biology; Chemistry; Neurobiology and Physiology; Chemical Engineering; Civil Engineering; and Evanston Hospital. *Degree requirements:* For doctorate, thesis/dissertation, qualifying exam. *Entrance requirements:* For doctorate, GRE General Test. Additional exam requirements/recommendations for international students: Required—TOEFL (minimum score 600 paper-based). Electronic applications accepted. *Faculty research:* Developmental genetics, gene regulation, DNA-protein interactions, biological clocks, bioremediation.

Northwestern University, Northwestern University Feinberg School of Medicine and Interdepartmental Programs, Integrated Graduate Programs in the Life Sciences, Chicago, IL 60611. Offers cancer biology (PhD); cell biology (PhD); developmental biology (PhD); evolutionary biology (PhD); immunology and microbial pathogenesis (PhD); molecular biology and genetics (PhD); neurobiology (PhD); pharmacology and toxicology (PhD); structural biology and biochemistry (PhD). *Degree requirements:* For doctorate, comprehensive exam, thesis/dissertation, written and oral qualifying exams. *Entrance requirements:* For doctorate, GRE General Test. Additional exam requirements/recommendations for international students: Required—TOEFL (minimum score 600 paper-based; 250 computer-based). Electronic applications accepted.

The Ohio State University, College of Medicine, School of Biomedical Science, Integrated Biomedical Science Graduate Program, Columbus, OH 43210. Offers immunology (PhD); medical genetics (PhD); molecular virology (PhD); pharmacology (PhD). *Degree requirements:* For doctorate, thesis/dissertation. *Entrance requirements:* For doctorate, GRE, GRE Subject Test in biochemistry, cell and molecular biology (recommended for some). Additional exam requirements/recommendations for international students: Required—TOEFL (minimum score 600 paper-based; 250 computer-based). Electronic applications accepted. *Expenses:* Tuition, state resident: full-time $10,683. Tuition, nonresident: full-time $25,923. Tuition and fees vary according to course load and program.

The Ohio State University, College of Medicine, School of Biomedical Science, Program in Molecular Virology, Immunology and Medical Genetics, Columbus, OH 43210. Offers MS, PhD. *Entrance requirements:* For master's and doctorate, GRE, GRE Subject Test in biology (recommended). Electronic applications accepted. *Expenses:* Tuition, state resident: full-time $10,683. Tuition, nonresident: full-time $25,923. Tuition and fees vary according to course load and program.

The Ohio State University, Graduate School, College of Biological Sciences, Department of Molecular Genetics, Columbus, OH 43210. Offers cell and developmental biology (MS, PhD); genetics (MS, PhD); molecular biology (MS, PhD). *Faculty:* 26. *Students:* 8 full-time (5 women), 23 part-time (11 women), 17 international. Average age 27. In 2009, 11 doctorates awarded. *Degree requirements:* For master's, thesis; for doctorate, thesis/dissertation. *Entrance requirements:* For master's and doctorate, GRE General Test, GRE Subject Test in biology or biochemistry (recommended). Additional exam requirements/recommendations for international students: Required—TOEFL (minimum score 600 paper-based; 250 computer-based). *Application deadline:* For fall admission, 8/15 priority date for domestic students, 7/1 priority date for international students; for winter admission, 12/1 priority date for domestic students, 11/1 priority date for international students; for spring admission, 3/1 priority date for domestic students, 2/1 priority date for international students. Applications are processed on a rolling basis. Application fee: $40 ($50 for international students). Electronic applications accepted. *Expenses:* Tuition, state resident: full-time $10,683. Tuition, nonresident: full-time $25,923. Tuition and fees vary according to course load and program. *Financial support:* Fellowships, research assistantships, teaching assistantships, Federal Work-Study and institutionally sponsored loans available. Support available to part-time students. *Unit head:* Dr. Anna Hopper, Chair, 614-292-8084, Fax: 614-292-4466, E-mail: hopper.64@osu.edu. *Application contact:* 614-292-9444, Fax: 614-292-3895, E-mail: domestic.grad@osu.edu.

Oregon Health & Science University, School of Medicine, Graduate Programs in Medicine, Department of Molecular and Medical Genetics, Portland, OR 97239-3098. Offers PhD. *Degree requirements:* For doctorate, comprehensive exam, thesis/dissertation. *Entrance requirements:* For doctorate, GRE General Test (minimum scores: 500 Verbal/600 Quantitative/4.5 Analytical) or MCAT (for some programs). Additional exam requirements/recommendations for international students: Required—TOEFL. Application fee: $65. Electronic applications accepted. Tuition and fees vary according to course level, course load, degree level, program and reciprocity agreements. *Financial support:* PhD students have paid tuition and receive stipends available. *Faculty research:* Molecular studies of metabolic diseases, gene therapy, control of mycogenesis, regulation of gene expression, DNA replication and repair. *Unit head:* Susan Olson, PhD, Program Director, 503-494-7703, E-mail: olsonsu@ohsu.edu. *Application contact:* Marissa Utter, Program Coordinator, 503-494-7703, E-mail: utter@ohsu.edu.

Oregon State University, Graduate School, College of Agricultural Sciences, Program in Genetics, Corvallis, OR 97331. Offers MA, MAIS, MS, PhD. Part-time programs available. *Students:* 1 full-time (0 women), all international. Average age 37. In 2009, 3 master's, 1 doctorate awarded. Terminal master's awarded for partial completion of doctoral program. *Degree requirements:* For master's, variable foreign language requirement, thesis or alternative; for doctorate, thesis/dissertation. *Entrance requirements:* For master's and doctorate, GRE General Test, minimum GPA of 3.0 in last 90 hours. Additional exam requirements/recommendations for international students: Required—TOEFL. *Application deadline:* For fall admission, 3/1 for domestic students. Applications are processed on a rolling basis. Application fee: $50. *Expenses:* Tuition, state resident: full-time $9774; part-time $362 per credit. Tuition, nonresident: full-time $15,849; part-time $587 per credit. Required fees: $1639. Full-time tuition and fees vary according to course load and program. *Financial support:* Fellowships, research assistantships, teaching assistantships, Federal Work-Study and institutionally sponsored loans available. Financial award application deadline: 2/1. *Faculty research:* Molecular genetics, cytogenetics, population and quantitative genetics, microbial genetics, plant genetics. *Unit head:* Dr. Lloyd W. Ream, Director, 541-737-1791, Fax: 541-737-0496, E-mail: reamw@oregonstate.edu. *Application contact:* Dr. Stella Coakley, Associate Dean, 541-737-5264, Fax: 541-737-3178, E-mail: stella.coakley@oregonstate.edu.

Penn State Hershey Medical Center, College of Medicine, Graduate School Programs in the Biomedical Sciences, Graduate Program in Microbiology and Immunology, Hershey, PA 17033. Offers genetics (PhD); immunology (MS, PhD); microbiology (MS); microbiology/virology (PhD); molecular biology (PhD); MD/PhD. *Students:* 12 applicants, 75% accepted, 3 enrolled. In 2009, 1 doctorate awarded. Terminal master's awarded for partial completion of doctoral program. *Degree requirements:* For master's, thesis or alternative; for doctorate, comprehensive exam, thesis/dissertation, oral exam. *Entrance requirements:* For doctorate, GRE General Test, minimum GPA of 3.0. Additional exam requirements/recommendations for international students: Required—TOEFL. *Application deadline:* For fall admission, 1/31 priority date for domestic students, 2/1 priority date for international students. Applications are processed on a rolling basis. Application fee: $45. Electronic applications accepted. *Expenses:* Tuition, state resident: part-time $644 per credit. Tuition, nonresident: part-time $1142 per credit. Required fees: $22 per semester. *Financial support:* In 2009–10, research assistantships with full tuition reimbursements (averaging $22,260 per year); fellowships with full tuition reimbursements, scholarships/grants, health care benefits, and unspecified assistantships also available. Financial award applicants required to submit FAFSA. *Faculty research:* Virus replication and assembly, oncogenesis, interactions of viruses with host cells and animal model systems. *Unit head:* Dr. Richard J. Courtney, Chair, 717-531-7659, Fax: 717-531-6522, E-mail: micro-grad-hmc@psu.edu. *Application contact:* Billie Burns, Secretary, 717-531-7659, Fax: 717-531-6522, E-mail: micro-grad-hmc@psu.edu.

Penn State Hershey Medical Center, College of Medicine, Graduate School Programs in the Biomedical Sciences, The Huck Institutes of the Life Sciences, Intercollege Graduate Program in Genetics, Hershey, PA 17033. Offers MS, PhD, MD/PhD. *Students:* 173 applicants, 4% accepted, 2 enrolled. In 2009, 4 doctorates awarded. Terminal master's awarded for partial completion of doctoral program. *Degree requirements:* For master's, thesis or alternative; for doctorate, comprehensive exam, thesis/dissertation, oral exam. *Entrance requirements:* For master's, GRE General Test; for doctorate, GRE General Test, minimum GPA of 3.0. Additional exam requirements/recommendations for international students: Required—TOEFL (minimum score 500 paper-based; 213 computer-based). *Application deadline:* For fall admission, 1/31 priority date for domestic students, 2/1 priority date for international students. Applications are processed on a rolling basis. Application fee: $65. Electronic applications accepted. *Expenses:* Tuition, state resident: part-time $644 per credit. Tuition, nonresident: part-time $1142 per credit. Required fees: $22 per semester. *Financial support:* In 2009–10, research assistantships with full tuition reimbursements (averaging $22,260 per year); fellowships with full tuition reimbursements, scholarships/grants, health care benefits, and unspecified assistantships also available. Financial award applicants required to submit FAFSA. *Faculty research:* Genome structure/stability, gene expression, cellular sorting of macromolecules, signal transduction, stem cell differentiation. *Unit head:* Dr. Ralph Keil, Co-Director, 717-531-8982, E-mail: grad-hmc@psu.edu. *Application contact:* Kathy Shuey, Administrative Assistant, 717-531-8982, Fax: 717-531-0786, E-mail: grad-hmc@psu.edu.

Penn State University Park, Graduate School, Intercollege Graduate Programs, Intercollege Graduate Program in Genetics, State College, University Park, PA 16802-1503. Offers MS, PhD. *Unit head:* Dr. Richard Ordway, Chair, 814-863-5693, Fax: 814-865-9131, E-mail: rordway@psu.edu. *Application contact:* Cynthia E. Nicosia, Director, Graduate Enrollment Services, 814-865-1795, Fax: 814-865-4627, E-mail: cey1@psu.edu.

Purdue University, Graduate School, College of Science, Department of Biological Sciences, West Lafayette, IN 47907. Offers biochemistry (PhD); biophysics (PhD); cell and developmental biology (PhD); ecology, evolutionary and population biology (MS, PhD), including ecology, evolutionary biology, population biology; genetics (MS, PhD); microbiology (MS, PhD); molecular biology (PhD); neurobiology (MS, PhD); plant physiology (PhD). Terminal master's awarded for partial completion of doctoral program. *Degree requirements:* For master's, thesis (for some programs); for doctorate, thesis/dissertation, seminars, teaching experience. *Entrance requirements:* For master's and doctorate, GRE General Test. Additional exam requirements/recommendations for international students: Required—TOEFL. Electronic applications accepted.

Rutgers, The State University of New Jersey, New Brunswick, Graduate School-New Brunswick, Programs in the Molecular Biosciences, Program in Microbiology and Molecular Genetics, Piscataway, NJ 08854-8097. Offers applied microbiology (MS, PhD); clinical microbiology (MS, PhD); computational molecular biology (PhD); immunology (MS, PhD); microbial biochemistry (MS, PhD); molecular genetics (MS, PhD); virology (MS, PhD). Part-time programs available. Terminal master's awarded for partial completion of doctoral program. *Degree requirements:* For master's, comprehensive exam, thesis or alternative; for doctorate, comprehensive exam, thesis/dissertation, written qualifying exam. *Entrance requirements:* For master's, GRE General Test, minimum GPA of 3.0; for doctorate, GRE General Test, GRE Subject Test (recommended), minimum GPA of 3.0. Additional exam requirements/recommendations for international students: Required—TOEFL. Electronic applications accepted. *Faculty research:* Molecular genetics and microbial physiology; virology and pathogenic microbiology; applied, environmental and industrial microbiology; computers in molecular biology.

Stanford University, School of Medicine, Graduate Programs in Medicine, Department of Genetics, Stanford, CA 94305-9991. Offers PhD. *Degree requirements:* For doctorate, thesis/dissertation, qualifying examination. *Entrance requirements:* For doctorate, GRE General Test, GRE Subject Test. Additional exam requirements/recommendations for international students: Required—TOEFL. Electronic applications accepted. *Expenses:* Tuition: Full-time $37,380; part-time $2760 per quarter. Required fees: $501. *Faculty research:* Molecular biology of DNA replication in human cells, analysis of existing and search for new DNA polymorphisms in humans, molecular genetics of prokaryotic and eukaryotic genetic elements, proteins in DNA replication.

Stony Brook University, State University of New York, Graduate School, College of Arts and Sciences, Graduate Program in Genetics, Stony Brook, NY 11794. Offers PhD. *Students:* 53 full-time (34 women); includes 9 minority (2 African Americans, 2 Asian Americans or Pacific Islanders, 5 Hispanic Americans), 21 international. Average age 27. 129 applicants, 16% accepted. In 2009, 14 doctorates awarded. *Degree requirements:* For doctorate, comprehensive exam, thesis/dissertation, teaching experience. *Entrance requirements:* For doctorate, GRE General Test, GRE Subject Test. Additional exam requirements/recommendations for international students: Required—TOEFL. *Application deadline:* For fall admission, 1/15 for domestic students. Application fee: $60. *Expenses:* Tuition, state resident: full-time $8370; part-time $349 per credit. Tuition, nonresident: full-time $13,250; part-time $552 per credit. Required fees: $933. *Financial support:* In 2009–10, 7 teaching assistantships were awarded; fellowships, research assistantships, Federal Work-Study also available. *Faculty research:* Gene structure, gene regulation. *Application contact:* Dr. Kent Marks, Assistant Dean, Admissions and Records, 631-632-4723, Fax: 631-632-7243, E-mail: kmarks@notes.cc.sunysb.edu.

Genetics

Temple University, Health Sciences Center, School of Medicine and Graduate School, Graduate Programs in Medicine, Program in Molecular Biology and Genetics, Philadelphia, PA 19122-6096. Offers PhD, MD/PhD. *Degree requirements:* For doctorate, thesis/dissertation, presentation research/literature seminars distinct from area of concentration. *Entrance requirements:* For doctorate, GRE General Test, GRE Subject Test, minimum GPA of 3.0. Additional exam requirements/recommendations for international students: Required—TOEFL (minimum score 620 paper-based; 260 computer-based). Electronic applications accepted. *Faculty research:* Molecular genetics of normal and malignant cell growth, regulation of gene expression, DNA repair systems and carcinogenesis, hormone-receptor interactions and signal transduction systems, structural biology.

Texas A&M University, College of Veterinary Medicine, Department of Veterinary Pathobiology, College Station, TX 77843. Offers genetics (MS, PhD); veterinary microbiology (MS, PhD); veterinary parasitology (MS); veterinary pathology (MS, PhD). Part-time programs available. Postbaccalaureate distance learning degree programs offered. *Faculty:* 27. *Students:* 31 full-time (20 women), 15 part-time (12 women); includes 6 minority (2 African Americans, 1 Asian American or Pacific Islander, 3 Hispanic Americans), 13 international. Average age 33. In 2009, 1 master's, 4 doctorates awarded. Terminal master's awarded for partial completion of doctoral program. *Degree requirements:* For master's, thesis, seminars; for doctorate, thesis/dissertation, seminars. *Entrance requirements:* For master's and doctorate, GRE General Test, minimum GPA of 3.0 in last 60 hours. Additional exam requirements/recommendations for international students: Required—TOEFL. *Application deadline:* For fall admission, 3/1 priority date for domestic students; for spring admission, 8/1 priority date for domestic students. Applications are processed on a rolling basis. Application fee: $50 ($75 for international students). Electronic applications accepted. *Expenses:* Tuition, state resident: full-time $3991; part-time $221.74 per credit hour. Tuition, nonresident: full-time $9049; part-time $502.74 per credit hour. *Financial support:* In 2009–10, fellowships with partial tuition reimbursements (averaging $16,000 per year), research assistantships with partial tuition reimbursements (averaging $15,400 per year), teaching assistantships with partial tuition reimbursements (averaging $16,000 per year) were awarded; Federal Work-Study, institutionally sponsored loans, scholarships/grants, traineeships, health care benefits, and unspecified assistantships also available. Support available to part-time students. Financial award applicants required to submit FAFSA. *Faculty research:* Infectious and noninfectious diseases of animals and birds, animal genetics, molecular biology, immunology, virology. *Unit head:* Dr. Fuller Bazer, Interim Head, 979-845-5941, Fax: 979-845-9231, E-mail: fbazer@tamu.edu. *Application contact:* Dr. G. G. Wagner, Graduate Advisor, 979-845-2851, Fax: 979-862-1147, E-mail: gwagner@cvm.tamu.edu.

Thomas Jefferson University, Jefferson College of Graduate Studies, PhD Program in Genetics, Philadelphia, PA 19107. Offers PhD. *Faculty:* 33 full-time (8 women), 2 part-time/adjunct (both women). *Students:* 25 full-time (14 women); includes 3 minority (all African Americans), 5 international. 32 applicants, 28% accepted, 6 enrolled. In 2009, 5 doctorates awarded. *Degree requirements:* For doctorate, comprehensive exam, thesis/dissertation. *Entrance requirements:* For doctorate, GRE General Test, minimum GPA of 3.2. Additional exam requirements/recommendations for international students: Required—TOEFL (minimum score 250 computer-based; 100 iBT) or IELTS. *Application deadline:* For fall admission, 1/15 priority date for domestic and international students. Applications are processed on a rolling basis. Application fee: $50. Electronic applications accepted. *Expenses:* Tuition: Full-time $26,858; part-time $879 per credit. Required fees: $525. *Financial support:* In 2009–10, 25 students received support, including 25 fellowships with full tuition reimbursements available (averaging $52,883 per year); Federal Work-Study, institutionally sponsored loans, scholarships/grants, traineeships, and stipend also available. Support available to part-time students. Financial award application deadline: 5/1; financial award applicants required to submit FAFSA. *Faculty research:* Functional genomics, cancer susceptibility, cell cycle, regulation oncogenes and tumor suppressor genes, genetics of neoplastic disease. Total annual research expenditures: $20.2 million. *Unit head:* Dr. Linda D. Siracusa, Program Director, 215-503-4536, E-mail: linda.siracusa@jefferson.edu. *Application contact:* Marc E. Stearns, Director of Admissions, 215-503-0155, Fax: 215-503-9920, E-mail: jcgs-info@jefferson.edu.

See Close-Up on page 317.

Tufts University, Sackler School of Graduate Biomedical Sciences, Graduate Program in Genetics, Medford, MA 02155. Offers PhD. *Faculty:* 47 full-time (17 women). *Students:* 29 full-time (20 women); includes 5 minority (1 African American, 3 Asian Americans or Pacific Islanders, 1 Hispanic American), 6 international. Average age 28. 77 applicants, 10% accepted, 3 enrolled. In 2009, 3 doctorates awarded. Terminal master's awarded for partial completion of doctoral program. *Degree requirements:* For doctorate, thesis/dissertation, qualifying exam. *Entrance requirements:* For doctorate, GRE General Test, 3 letters of reference. Additional exam requirements/recommendations for international students: Required—TOEFL. *Application deadline:* For fall admission, 12/15 for domestic and international students. Applications are processed on a rolling basis. Application fee: $70. Electronic applications accepted. *Expenses:* Tuition: Full-time $38,096; part-time $3962 per credit. Required fees: $686; $40 per year. Tuition and fees vary according to course level, course load, degree level, program and student level. *Financial support:* In 2009–10, 29 students received support, including 29 research assistantships with full tuition reimbursements available (averaging $28,250 per year); scholarships/grants and health care benefits also available. *Faculty research:* Cancer, human and developmental genetics. *Unit head:* Dr. Erik Selsing, Program Director, 617-636-0467, E-mail: erik.selsing@tufts.edu. *Application contact:* Kellie Johnston, Associate Director of Admissions, 617-636-6767, Fax: 617-636-0375.

Université de Montréal, Faculty of Medicine, Program in Specialized Studies, Montréal, QC H3C 3J7, Canada. Offers anesthesia (DES); diagnostic radiology (DES); family medicine (DES); gastroenterology (DES); geriatry (DES); intensive care (DES); medical biochemistry (DES); medical genetics (DES); medicine (DES); microbiology and infectious diseases (DES); nuclear medicine (DES); obstetrics and gynecology (DES); ophthalmology (DES); pediatrics (DES); pneumology (DES); psychiatry (DES); radiology-oncology (DES); rheumatology (DES); surgery (DES). *Faculty:* 154 full-time (40 women), 333 part-time/adjunct (100 women). *Students:* 930 full-time (580 women), 7 part-time (all women). 74 applicants, 77% accepted, 29 enrolled. *Application deadline:* For fall admission, 2/1 priority date for domestic students; for winter admission, 11/1 priority date for domestic students; for spring admission, 2/1 priority date for domestic students. Application fee: $100. Electronic applications accepted. *Unit head:* Lorraine Locas, Assistant to the Vice Dean of Graduate Studies, 514-343-6269, Fax: 514-343-5751, E-mail: lorraine.locas@umontreal.ca. *Application contact:* Dr. Andre Ferron, Vice Dean of Graduate Studies, 514-343-6111 Ext. 0933, Fax: 514-343-5751, E-mail: andre.ferron@umontreal.ca.

Université de Montréal, Faculty of Medicine, Programs in Medical Genetics, Montréal, QC H3C 3J7, Canada.

Université du Québec à Chicoutimi, Graduate Programs, Program in Experimental Medicine, Chicoutimi, QC G7H 2B1, Canada. Offers genetics (M Sc). *Degree requirements:* For master's, thesis. *Entrance requirements:* For master's, appropriate bachelor's degree, proficiency in French.

University at Albany, State University of New York, School of Public Health, Department of Biomedical Sciences, Program in Biochemistry, Molecular Biology, and Genetics, Albany, NY 12222-0001. Offers MS, PhD. *Degree requirements:* For master's, thesis; for doctorate, thesis/dissertation. *Entrance requirements:* For master's and doctorate, GRE General Test, GRE Subject Test.

The University of Alabama at Birmingham, Graduate Programs in Joint Health Sciences, Program in Genetics, Birmingham, AL 35294. Offers PhD. *Degree requirements:* For doctorate, thesis/dissertation. *Entrance requirements:* For doctorate, GRE, interview. Electronic applications accepted. *Faculty research:* Clinical cytogenetics, cancer cytogenetics, prenatal diagnosis.

University of Alberta, Faculty of Graduate Studies and Research, Department of Biological Sciences, Edmonton, AB T6G 2E1, Canada. Offers environmental biology and ecology (M Sc, PhD); microbiology and biotechnology (M Sc, PhD); molecular biology and genetics (M Sc, PhD); physiology and cell biology (M Sc, PhD); plant biology (M Sc, PhD); systematics and evolution (M Sc, PhD). *Faculty:* 72 full-time (15 women), 15 part-time/adjunct (4 women). *Students:* 238 full-time (117 women), 32 part-time (15 women), 31 international. 206 applicants, 42% accepted. In 2009, 29 master's, 31 doctorates awarded. Terminal master's awarded for partial completion of doctoral program. *Degree requirements:* For master's, thesis; for doctorate, thesis/dissertation. *Entrance requirements:* Additional exam requirements/recommendations for international students: Required—TOEFL. *Application deadline:* For fall admission, 3/1 priority date for domestic students. Applications are processed on a rolling basis. Application fee: $0. Tuition and fees charges are reported in Canadian dollars. *Expenses:* Tuition, area resident: Full-time $4626 Canadian dollars; part-time $99.72 Canadian dollars per unit. International tuition: $8216 Canadian dollars full-time. Required fees: $3590 Canadian dollars; $99.72 Canadian dollars per unit. $215 Canadian dollars per term. *Financial support:* In 2009–10, 4 research assistantships with partial tuition reimbursements (averaging $12,000 per year), 103 teaching assistantships with partial tuition reimbursements (averaging $12,300 per year) were awarded; career-related internships or fieldwork and scholarships/grants also available. *Unit head:* Laura Frost, Chair, 780-492-1904. *Application contact:* Dr. John P. Chang, Associate Chair for Graduate Studies, 780-492-1257, Fax: 780-492-9457, E-mail: bio.grad.coordinator@ualberta.ca.

University of Alberta, Faculty of Medicine and Dentistry and Faculty of Graduate Studies and Research, Graduate Programs in Medicine, Department of Medical Genetics, Edmonton, AB T6G 2E1, Canada. Offers M Sc, PhD. *Faculty:* 6 full-time (4 women), 3 part-time/adjunct (1 woman). *Students:* 21 full-time (12 women). Average age 24. 17 applicants, 35% accepted, 4 enrolled. In 2009, 1 doctorate awarded. *Degree requirements:* For master's, comprehensive exam, thesis; for doctorate, comprehensive exam, thesis/dissertation. *Entrance requirements:* For master's and doctorate, minimum GPA of 3.2. *Application deadline:* For fall admission, 2/28 priority date for domestic students. Applications are processed on a rolling basis. Application fee: $100. Tuition and fees charges are reported in Canadian dollars. *Expenses:* Tuition, area resident: Full-time $4626 Canadian dollars; part-time $99.72 Canadian dollars per unit. International tuition: $8216 Canadian dollars full-time. Required fees: $3590 Canadian dollars; $99.72 Canadian dollars per unit. $215 Canadian dollars per term. *Financial support:* In 2009–10, 1 fellowship with tuition reimbursement (averaging $19,000 per year), research assistantships with partial tuition reimbursements (averaging $16,592 per year) were awarded; scholarships/grants also available. Financial award application deadline: 10/1. *Faculty research:* Clinical and molecular cytogenetics, ocular genetics, Prader-Willi syndrome, genomic instability, developmental genetics. Total annual research expenditures: $2,500. *Unit head:* Dr. Michael Walter, Chair, 780-492-9044, Fax: 780-492-6934, E-mail: mwalter@ualberta.ca. *Application contact:* Shari Barham, Administrative Coordinator, 780-492-9104, Fax: 780-492-1998, E-mail: shari.barham@ualberta.ca.

The University of Arizona, Graduate College, Graduate Interdisciplinary Programs, Graduate Interdisciplinary Program in Genetics, Tucson, AZ 85719. Offers MS, PhD. *Students:* 8 full-time (3 women), 3 part-time (all women); includes 2 minority (1 American Indian/Alaska Native, 1 Asian American or Pacific Islander). Average age 31. 15 applicants, 13% accepted, 1 enrolled. In 2009, 1 doctorate awarded. Terminal master's awarded for partial completion of doctoral program. *Degree requirements:* For master's, thesis; for doctorate, one foreign language, comprehensive exam, thesis/dissertation. *Entrance requirements:* For master's, GRE General Test, 3 letters of recommendation; for doctorate, GRE General Test, statement of purpose, 3 letters of recommendation. Additional exam requirements/recommendations for international students: Required—TOEFL (minimum score 550 paper-based; 213 computer-based; 79 iBT). *Application deadline:* For fall admission, 6/1 for domestic students, 12/1 for international students. Applications are processed on a rolling basis. Application fee: $65. Electronic applications accepted. *Expenses:* Tuition, state resident: full-time $9028. Tuition, nonresident: full-time $24,890. *Financial support:* Career-related internships or fieldwork, scholarships/grants, health care benefits, and unspecified assistantships available. *Faculty research:* Cancer research; DNA repair; plant and animal cytogenetics; molecular, population, and ecological genetics. *Unit head:* Dr. Murray Brilliant, Chairman, 520-626-3305, Fax: 520-626-5097, E-mail: mhb@peds.arizona.edu. *Application contact:* Lori Taylor, Program Coordinator, 520-626-9821, Fax: 520-626-5097, E-mail: lltaylor@arizona.edu.

The University of British Columbia, Faculty of Medicine, Department of Medical Genetics, Medical Genetics Graduate Program, Vancouver, BC V6T 1Z1, Canada. Offers M Sc, PhD.

The University of British Columbia, Genetics Graduate Program, Vancouver, BC V6T 1Z1, Canada. Offers M Sc, PhD. *Degree requirements:* For master's, comprehensive exam, thesis, thesis defense; for doctorate, comprehensive exam, thesis/dissertation, qualifying exam, oral and written comprehensive exams. *Entrance requirements:* Additional exam requirements/recommendations for international students: Required—TOEFL (minimum score 600 paper-based; 250 computer-based; 100 iBT). *Faculty research:* Prokaryote and eukaryote genetics.

University of California, Davis, Graduate Studies, Graduate Group in Genetics, Davis, CA 95616. Offers MS, PhD. Terminal master's awarded for partial completion of doctoral program. *Degree requirements:* For master's, comprehensive exam (for some programs), thesis (for some programs); for doctorate, thesis/dissertation. *Entrance requirements:* For master's and doctorate, GRE General Test, GRE Subject Test. Additional exam requirements/recommendations for international students: Required—TOEFL (minimum score 550 paper-based; 213 computer-based). Electronic applications accepted. *Faculty research:* Molecular, quantitative, and developmental genetics; cytogenetics; plant breeding.

University of California, Irvine, Office of Graduate Studies, School of Biological Sciences and School of Medicine, Graduate Program in Molecular Biology, Genetics, and Biochemistry, Irvine, CA 92697. Offers biological sciences (PhD). *Degree requirements:* For doctorate, thesis/dissertation, teaching assignment, preliminary exam. *Entrance requirements:* For doctorate, GRE General Test, minimum GPA of 3.0, research experience. Additional exam requirements/recommendations for international students: Required—TOEFL, IELTS, SPEAK test. Electronic applications accepted. *Expenses:* Contact institution. *Faculty research:* Cellular biochemistry; gene structure and expression; protein structure, function, and design; molecular genetics; pathogenesis and inherited disease.

University of California, Riverside, Graduate Division, Graduate Program in Genetics, Genomics, and Bioinformatics, Riverside, CA 92521-0102. Offers genomics and bioinformatics (PhD); molecular genetics (PhD); population and evolutionary genetics (PhD). *Degree requirements:* For doctorate, thesis/dissertation, qualifying exams, teaching experience. *Entrance requirements:* For doctorate, GRE General Test, minimum GPA of 3.2. Additional exam requirements/recommendations for international students: Required—TOEFL (minimum score 550 paper-based; 213 computer-based; 80 iBT). Electronic applications accepted. *Faculty research:* Molecular Genetics, Evolution and Population Genetics, Genomics and Bioinformatics.

University of California, San Diego, Office of Graduate Studies, Division of Biological Sciences, Program in Genetics and Molecular Biology, La Jolla, CA 92093-0348. Offers PhD. Offered in association with the Salk Institute. *Degree requirements:* For doctorate, thesis/dissertation, qualifying exam. Electronic applications accepted.

University of California, San Francisco, Graduate Division and School of Medicine, Department of Biochemistry and Biophysics, Program in Genetics, San Francisco, CA 94143. Offers PhD, MD/PhD. *Degree requirements:* For doctorate, thesis/dissertation. *Entrance requirements:* For doctorate, GRE General Test, GRE Subject Test. Additional exam requirements/recommendations for international students: Required—TOEFL. *Expenses:* Contact institution. *Faculty research:* Gene expression; chromosome structure and mechanics; medical, somatic cell, and radiation genetics.

University of Chicago, Division of the Biological Sciences, Department of Molecular Biosciences, Committee on Genetics, Genomics and Systems Biology, Chicago, IL 60637-1513. Offers PhD. *Faculty:* 65 full-time (24 women). *Students:* 21 full-time (11 women); includes 6 minority (1 African American, 4 Asian Americans or Pacific Islanders, 1 Hispanic American). Average age 28. 35 applicants, 11% accepted, 4 enrolled. In 2009, 3 doctorates awarded. *Degree requirements:* For doctorate, thesis/dissertation, ethics class, 2 teaching assistantships. *Entrance requirements:* For doctorate, GRE General Test, minimum GPA of 3.0. Additional exam requirements/recommendations for international students: Required—TOEFL (minimum score 600 paper-based; 250 computer-based; 104 iBT), IELTS (minimum score 7). *Application deadline:* For fall admission, 12/1 priority date for domestic and international students. Application fee: $55. Electronic applications accepted. *Financial support:* In 2009–10, 21 students received support, including fellowships with tuition reimbursements available (averaging $29,781 per year), research assistantships with tuition reimbursements available (averaging $29,781 per year); institutionally sponsored loans, scholarships/grants, traineeships, and health care benefits also available. Financial award applicants required to submit FAFSA. *Faculty research:* Molecular genetics, developmental genetics, population genetics, human genetics. *Unit head:* Dr. Richard Hudson, Chair, 773-834-2978, Fax: 773-702-8093, E-mail: committee-on-genetics@uchicago.edu. *Application contact:* Sue Levison, Administrator, 773-702-2464, Fax: 773-702-3172, E-mail: committee-on-genetics@uchicago.edu.

University of Colorado at Boulder, Graduate School, College of Arts and Sciences, Department of Ecology and Evolutionary Biology, Boulder, CO 80309. Offers animal behavior (MA); biology (MA, PhD); environmental biology (MA, PhD); evolutionary biology (MA, PhD); neurobiology (MA); population biology (MA); population genetics (PhD). *Faculty:* 32 full-time (10 women). *Students:* 64 full-time (36 women), 15 part-time (9 women); includes 12 minority (1 American Indian/Alaska Native, 3 Asian Americans or Pacific Islanders, 8 Hispanic Americans), 4 international. Average age 29. 145 applicants, 14% accepted, 21 enrolled. In 2009, 9 master's, 6 doctorates awarded. Terminal master's awarded for partial completion of doctoral program. *Degree requirements:* For master's, comprehensive exam, thesis or alternative; for doctorate, comprehensive exam, thesis/dissertation. *Entrance requirements:* For master's, GRE General Test, GRE Subject Test, minimum undergraduate GPA of 3.0; for doctorate, GRE General Test, GRE Subject Test. *Application deadline:* For fall admission, 12/30 priority date for domestic students, 12/1 for international students. Application fee: $50 ($60 for international students). *Financial support:* In 2009–10, 25 fellowships (averaging $17,876 per year), 27 research assistantships (averaging $15,070 per year) were awarded; Federal Work-Study, institutionally sponsored loans, and tuition waivers (full) also available. *Faculty research:* Behavior, ecology, genetics, morphology, endocrinology, physiology, systematics. Total annual research expenditures: $3.1 million.

University of Colorado Denver, School of Medicine, Program in Medical Genetics and Genetic Counseling, Denver, CO 80217-3364. Offers genetic counseling (MS); human medical genetics (PhD). *Students:* 22 full-time (17 women). In 2009, 6 master's, 14 doctorates awarded. *Degree requirements:* For doctorate, thesis/dissertation, 3 laboratory rotations. *Entrance requirements:* For doctorate, GRE General Test, minimum GPA of 3.0, 4 letters of recommendation. Additional exam requirements/recommendations for international students: Required—TOEFL (minimum score 550 paper-based; 213 computer-based). *Application deadline:* For fall admission, 1/1 for domestic students. Application fee: $50. *Financial support:* Fellowships, research assistantships, teaching assistantships, Federal Work-Study and institutionally sponsored loans available. Support available to part-time students. Financial award application deadline: 3/15; financial award applicants required to submit FAFSA. *Faculty research:* Genetics of colon cancer, cancer cytogenetics, tumor suppressor genes and cancer, molecular basis of inherited human disease, neurodevelopmental genetics. *Unit head:* Dr. Richard A. Spritz, Director, 303-724-3107, E-mail: richard.spritz@ucdenver.edu. *Application contact:* M. J. Stewart, Administrator, 303-724-3102, Fax: 303-724-3100, E-mail: mj.stewart@ucdenver.edu.

University of Connecticut, Graduate School, College of Liberal Arts and Sciences, Department of Molecular and Cell Biology, Field of Genetics, Genomics, and Bioinformatics, Storrs, CT 06269. Offers MS, PhD. *Faculty:* 28 full-time (8 women). *Students:* 43 full-time (17 women), 3 part-time (0 women); includes 7 minority (2 African Americans, 5 Asian Americans or Pacific Islanders), 11 international. Average age 28. 106 applicants, 9% accepted, 6 enrolled. In 2009, 4 master's, 5 doctorates awarded. Terminal master's awarded for partial completion of doctoral program. *Degree requirements:* For master's, comprehensive exam; for doctorate, thesis/dissertation. *Entrance requirements:* For master's and doctorate, GRE General Test, GRE Subject Test. Additional exam requirements/recommendations for international students: Required—TOEFL (minimum score 550 paper-based; 213 computer-based). *Application deadline:* For fall admission, 2/1 priority date for domestic and international students; for spring admission, 11/1 for domestic students, 10/1 for international students. Applications are processed on a rolling basis. Application fee: $55. Electronic applications accepted. *Expenses:* Tuition, state resident: full-time $4725; part-time $525 per credit. Tuition, nonresident: full-time $12,267; part-time $1363 per credit. Required fees: $346 per semester. Tuition and fees vary according to course load. *Financial support:* In 2009–10, 18 research assistantships with full tuition reimbursements, 23 teaching assistantships with full tuition reimbursements were awarded; fellowships, Federal Work-Study, scholarships/grants, health care benefits, and unspecified assistantships also available. Financial award application deadline: 2/1; financial award applicants required to submit FAFSA. *Unit head:* David Benson, Head, 860-486-4258, Fax: 860-486-4331, E-mail: david.benson@uconn.edu. *Application contact:* Anne St. Onje, Graduate Coordinator, 860-486-4314, Fax: 860-486-3943, E-mail: anne.st_onje@uconn.edu.

See Close-Up on page 187.

University of Connecticut Health Center, Graduate School, Programs in Biomedical Sciences, Program in Genetics and Developmental Biology, Farmington, CT 06030. Offers PhD, DMD/PhD, MD/PhD. *Faculty:* 46. *Students:* 20 full-time (11 women); includes 1 minority (Asian American or Pacific Islander), 7 international. Average age 30. 165 applicants, 35% accepted. In 2009, 4 doctorates awarded. *Degree requirements:* For doctorate, comprehensive exam, thesis/dissertation. *Entrance requirements:* For doctorate, GRE General Test, GRE Subject Test. Additional exam requirements/recommendations for international students: Required—TOEFL (minimum score 600 paper-based; 250 computer-based). *Application deadline:* For fall admission, 12/15 for domestic students. Application fee: $55. Electronic applications accepted. *Financial support:* In 2009–10, 20 students received support, including 20 research assistantships with tuition reimbursements available (averaging $27,000 per year); fellowships, health care benefits also available. *Faculty research:* Developmental biology, genomic imprinting, RNA biology, RNA alternative splicing, human embryonic stem cells. *Unit head:* Dr. William Mohler, Director, 860-679-7947, E-mail: wmohler@neuron.uchc.edu. *Application contact:* Tricia Avolt, Graduate Admissions Coordinator, 860-679-2175, Fax: 860-679-1899, E-mail: robertson@nso2.uchc.edu.

See Close-Up on page 319.

University of Connecticut Health Center, Graduate School, Programs in Biomedical Sciences, Program in Molecular Biology and Biochemistry, Farmington, CT 06030. Offers PhD, DMD/PhD, MD/PhD. *Faculty:* 30. *Students:* 22 full-time (13 women); includes 3 minority (1 African American, 2 Asian Americans or Pacific Islanders), 8 international. Average age 29. 165 applicants, 35% accepted. In 2009, 5 doctorates awarded. *Degree requirements:* For doctorate, comprehensive exam, thesis/dissertation. *Entrance requirements:* For doctorate, GRE General Test. Additional exam requirements/recommendations for international students: Required—TOEFL (minimum score 600 paper-based; 250 computer-based). *Application deadline:* For fall admission, 12/15 for domestic students. Application fee: $55. Electronic applications accepted. *Financial support:* In 2009–10, 22 students received support, including 22 research assistantships with full tuition reimbursements available (averaging $27,000 per year); fellowships, health care benefits also available. *Faculty research:* Molecular biology, structural biology, protein biochemistry, microbial physiology and pathogenesis. *Unit head:* Dr. Stephen King, Director, 860-679-3347, Fax: 860-679-1239, E-mail: sking@nso2.uchc.edu.

Application contact: Tricia Avolt, Graduate Admissions Coordinator, 860-679-2175, Fax: 860-679-1899, E-mail: robertson@nso2.uchc.edu.

See Close-Up on page 243.

University of Delaware, College of Arts and Sciences, Department of Biological Sciences, Newark, DE 19716. Offers biotechnology (MS); cancer biology (MS, PhD); cell and extracellular matrix biology (MS, PhD); cell and systems physiology (MS, PhD); developmental biology (MS, PhD); ecology and evolution (MS, PhD); microbiology (MS, PhD); molecular biology and genetics (MS, PhD). Terminal master's awarded for partial completion of doctoral program. *Degree requirements:* For master's, thesis, preliminary exam; for doctorate, comprehensive exam, thesis/dissertation, preliminary exam. *Entrance requirements:* For master's and doctorate, GRE General Test. Additional exam requirements/recommendations for international students: Required—TOEFL (minimum score 600 paper-based; 250 computer-based); Recommended—TWE. Electronic applications accepted. *Faculty research:* Microorganisms, bone, cancer metastasis, developmental biology, cell biology, DNA.

University of Florida, College of Medicine and Graduate School, Interdisciplinary Program in Biomedical Sciences, Concentration in Genetics, Gainesville, FL 32611. Offers PhD. *Degree requirements:* For doctorate, thesis/dissertation. *Entrance requirements:* For doctorate, GRE General Test, minimum GPA of 3.0. Additional exam requirements/recommendations for international students: Required—TOEFL. Electronic applications accepted.

See Close-Up on page 321.

University of Georgia, Graduate School, College of Arts and Sciences, Department of Genetics, Athens, GA 30602. Offers MS, PhD. *Faculty:* 20 full-time (5 women). *Students:* 45 full-time (32 women); includes 2 minority (1 African American, 1 Hispanic American), 7 international. 104 applicants, 19% accepted, 9 enrolled. In 2009, 2 master's, 5 doctorates awarded. Terminal master's awarded for partial completion of doctoral program. *Degree requirements:* For master's, thesis; for doctorate, comprehensive exam, thesis/dissertation. *Entrance requirements:* For master's and doctorate, GRE General Test. Additional exam requirements/recommendations for international students: Required—TOEFL. *Application deadline:* For fall admission, 1/1 priority date for domestic and international students; for spring admission, 11/15 for domestic students. Application fee: $50. Electronic applications accepted. *Expenses:* Tuition, state resident: full-time $6000; part-time $250 per credit hour. Tuition, nonresident: full-time $20,904; part-time $871 per credit hour. Required fees: $730 per semester. *Financial support:* In 2009–10, fellowships with full tuition reimbursements (averaging $19,000 per year), research assistantships with full tuition reimbursements (averaging $19,000 per year), teaching assistantships with full tuition reimbursements (averaging $19,000 per year) were awarded; scholarships/grants and unspecified assistantships also available. *Unit head:* Dr. Robert D. Ivarie, Head, 706-542-1692, Fax: 706-542-3910, E-mail: ivarie@uga.edu. *Application contact:* Dr. R. Kelly Dawe, Director of Graduate Studies, 706-542-0288, Fax: 706-542-3910, E-mail: gencoord@uga.edu.

University of Hawaii at Manoa, John A. Burns School of Medicine, Department of Cell and Molecular Biology, Honolulu, HI 96813. Offers MS, PhD. Part-time programs available. *Faculty:* 48 full-time (13 women), 14 part-time/adjunct (6 women). *Students:* 36 full-time (20 women), 2 part-time (both women); includes 14 minority (13 Asian Americans or Pacific Islanders, 1 Hispanic American), 6 international. Average age 28. 62 applicants, 34% accepted, 11 enrolled. In 2009, 1 master's, 4 doctorates awarded. Terminal master's awarded for partial completion of doctoral program. *Degree requirements:* For master's, thesis optional; for doctorate, comprehensive exam, thesis/dissertation. *Entrance requirements:* For master's and doctorate, GRE General Test, minimum GPA of 3.0. Additional exam requirements/recommendations for international students: Required—TOEFL (minimum score 500 paper-based; 173 computer-based; 61 iBT), IELTS (minimum score 5). *Application deadline:* For fall admission, 1/15 for domestic and international students. Applications are processed on a rolling basis. Application fee: $60. *Expenses:* Tuition, state resident: full-time $8900; part-time $372 per credit. Tuition, nonresident: full-time $21,400; part-time $898 per credit. Required fees: $207 per semester. *Financial support:* In 2009–10, 1 student received support, including 6 fellowships (averaging $1,280 per year), 29 research assistantships (averaging $20,526 per year); Federal Work-Study and institutionally sponsored loans also available. Financial award application deadline: 2/1. Total annual research expenditures: $2.7 million. *Application contact:* Marla Berry, Graduate Co-Chair, 808-692-1506, Fax: 808-692-1968, E-mail: mberry@hawaii.edu.

University of Illinois at Chicago, College of Medicine and Graduate College, Graduate Programs in Medicine, Department of Biochemistry and Molecular Genetics, Chicago, IL 60607-7128. Offers PhD, MD/PhD. Terminal master's awarded for partial completion of doctoral program. *Degree requirements:* For doctorate, thesis/dissertation. *Entrance requirements:* For doctorate, GRE General Test. Additional exam requirements/recommendations for international students: Required—TOEFL. Electronic applications accepted. *Faculty research:* Nature of cellular components, control of metabolic processes, regulation of gene expression.

The University of Iowa, Graduate College, College of Liberal Arts and Sciences, Department of Biology, Iowa City, IA 52242-1316. Offers biology (MS, PhD); cell and developmental biology (MS, PhD); evolution (MS, PhD); genetics (MS, PhD); neurobiology (MS, PhD); plant biology (MS, PhD). Terminal master's awarded for partial completion of doctoral program. *Degree requirements:* For master's, thesis optional, exam; for doctorate, comprehensive exam, thesis/dissertation. *Entrance requirements:* For master's and doctorate, GRE General Test, minimum GPA of 3.0. Additional exam requirements/recommendations for international students: Required—TOEFL (minimum score 600 paper-based; 250 computer-based; 100 iBT). Electronic applications accepted. *Faculty research:* Developmental neurobiology, evolutionary biology, signal transduction, cell motility, molecular genetics (plant and animal).

The University of Iowa, Graduate College, Program in Genetics, Iowa City, IA 52242-1316. Offers PhD, MD/PhD. *Degree requirements:* For doctorate, comprehensive exam, thesis/dissertation. *Entrance requirements:* For doctorate, GRE General Test, minimum GPA of 3.0. Additional exam requirements/recommendations for international students: Required—TOEFL (minimum score 600 paper-based; 250 computer-based; 100 iBT). Electronic applications accepted. *Expenses:* Contact institution. *Faculty research:* Developmental genetics, eukaryotic gene expression, human genetics, molecular and biochemical genetics, evolutionary genetics.

The University of Iowa, Roy J. and Lucille A. Carver College of Medicine and Graduate College, Graduate Programs in Medicine, Department of Microbiology, Iowa City, IA 52242-1316. Offers general microbiology and microbial physiology (MS, PhD); immunology (MS, PhD); microbial genetics (MS, PhD); pathogenic bacteriology (MS, PhD); virology (MS, PhD). *Faculty:* 24 full-time (3 women), 8 part-time/adjunct (2 women). *Students:* 36 full-time (20 women); includes 3 minority (2 American Indian/Alaska Native, 1 Hispanic American), 5 international. Average age 25. 87 applicants, 14% accepted, 5 enrolled. In 2009, 3 master's, 7 doctorates awarded. *Degree requirements:* For master's, thesis; for doctorate, comprehensive exam, thesis/dissertation. *Entrance requirements:* For master's and doctorate, GRE General Test. Additional exam requirements/recommendations for international students: Required—TOEFL (minimum score 600 paper-based; 250 computer-based). *Application deadline:* For fall admission, 2/1 for domestic and international students. Application fee: $60 ($85 for international students). Electronic applications accepted. *Financial support:* In 2009–10, 4 fellowships with full tuition reimbursements (averaging $24,250 per year), 32 research assistantships with full tuition reimbursements (averaging $24,250 per year) were awarded; institutionally sponsored loans, scholarships/grants, traineeships, and health care benefits also available. *Faculty research:* Gene regulation, processing and transport of HIV, retroviral pathogenesis, biodegradation, biofilm. Total annual research expenditures: $11.7 million. *Unit head:* Dr. Michael A. Apicella, Head, 319-335-7810, E-mail: grad-micro-info@uiowa.edu. *Application contact:* Dr. Michael A. Apicella, Head, 319-335-7810, E-mail: grad-micro-info@uiowa.edu.

University of Massachusetts Amherst, Graduate School, Interdisciplinary Programs, Program in Plant Biology, Amherst, MA 01003. Offers biochemistry and metabolism (MS, PhD); cell

Genetics

University of Massachusetts Amherst (continued)

biology and physiology (MS, PhD); environmental, ecological and integrative (MS, PhD); genetics and evolution (MS, PhD). *Students:* 3 full-time (2 women), 12 part-time (5 women); includes 2 minority (both Asian Americans or Pacific Islanders), 8 international. Average age 27. 32 applicants, 41% accepted, 3 enrolled. In 2009, 3 master's, 1 doctorate awarded. *Degree requirements:* For master's, thesis; for doctorate, 2 foreign languages, comprehensive exam, thesis/dissertation. *Entrance requirements:* For master's and doctorate, GRE General Test. Additional exam requirements/recommendations for international students: Required—TOEFL (minimum score 550 paper-based; 213 computer-based; 80 iBT), IELTS (minimum score 6.5). *Application deadline:* For fall admission, 12/15 for domestic and international students; for spring admission, 10/1 for domestic and international students. Applications are processed on a rolling basis. Application fee: $50 ($65 for international students). Electronic applications accepted. *Expenses:* Tuition, state resident: full-time $2640; part-time $110 per credit. Tuition, nonresident: full-time $9936; part-time $414 per credit. Tuition and fees vary according to course load. *Financial support:* In 2009–10, 11 research assistantships with full tuition reimbursements (averaging $8,884 per year) were awarded; fellowships, teaching assistantships, career-related internships or fieldwork, Federal Work-Study, scholarships/grants, traineeships, health care benefits, tuition waivers (full), and unspecified assistantships also available. Support available to part-time students. Financial award application deadline: 12/15. *Unit head:* Dr. Elsbeth L. Walker, Graduate Program Director, 413-577-3217, Fax: 413-545-3243. *Application contact:* Jean M. Ames, Supervisor of Admissions, 413-545—0722, Fax: 413-577-0010, E-mail: gradadm@grad.umass.edu.

University of Miami, Graduate School, College of Arts and Sciences, Department of Biology, Coral Gables, FL 33124. Offers biology (MS, PhD); genetics and evolution (MS, PhD). Terminal master's awarded for partial completion of doctoral program. *Degree requirements:* For master's, comprehensive exam (for some programs), thesis (for some programs); for doctorate, thesis/dissertation, oral and written qualifying exam. *Entrance requirements:* For master's, GRE General Test, 3 letters of recommendation, research papers; for doctorate, GRE General Test, 3 letters of recommendation, research papers, sponsor letter. Additional exam requirements/recommendations for international students: Required—TOEFL (minimum score 550 paper-based; 213 computer-based; 59 iBT). Electronic applications accepted. *Faculty research:* Neuroscience to ethology; plants, vertebrates and mycorrhizae; phylogenies, life histories and species interactions; molecular biology, gene expression and populations; cells, auditory neurons and vertebrate locomotion.

University of Minnesota, Twin Cities Campus, Graduate School, Program in Molecular, Cellular, Developmental Biology and Genetics, Minneapolis, MN 55455-0213. Offers genetic counseling (MS); molecular, cellular, developmental biology and genetics (PhD). *Faculty:* 89 full-time (31 women), 19 part-time/adjunct (17 women). *Students:* 86 full-time (49 women); includes 6 minority (1 American Indian/Alaska Native, 4 Asian Americans or Pacific Islanders, 1 Hispanic American), 23 international. Average age 24. 179 applicants, 11% accepted, 19 enrolled. In 2009, 12 master's, 6 doctorates awarded. Terminal master's awarded for partial completion of doctoral program. *Degree requirements:* For master's, thesis optional; for doctorate, thesis/dissertation. *Entrance requirements:* For master's and doctorate, GRE General Test. Additional exam requirements/recommendations for international students: Required—TOEFL (minimum score 625 paper-based; 263 computer-based; 80 iBT). *Application deadline:* For fall admission, 12/15 priority date for domestic and international students. Applications are processed on a rolling basis. Application fee: $55 ($75 for international students). Electronic applications accepted. *Financial support:* In 2009–10, 10 fellowships with full tuition reimbursements (averaging $23,000 per year), 79 research assistantships with full tuition reimbursements (averaging $24,500 per year), 11 teaching assistantships with partial tuition reimbursements (averaging $9,236 per year) were awarded; scholarships/grants, traineeships, and health care benefits also available. Financial award application deadline: 12/15. *Faculty research:* Membrane receptors and membrane transport, cell interactions, cytoskeleton and cell mobility, regulation of gene expression, plant cell and molecular biology. Total annual research expenditures: $9.1 million. *Unit head:* Kathleen Conklin, Director of Graduate Studies, 612-626-0445, Fax: 612-626-6140, E-mail: conkl001@umn.edu. *Application contact:* Sue Knoblauch, Student Support Coordinator, 612-624-7470, Fax: 612-626-6140, E-mail: mcdbg@umn.edu.

University of Missouri, Graduate School, College of Arts and Sciences, Division of Biological Sciences, Program in Genetic, Cellular and Developmental Biology, Columbia, MO 65211. Offers MA, PhD.

University of Missouri, Graduate School, Genetics Area Program, Columbia, MO 65211. Offers PhD. *Degree requirements:* For doctorate, comprehensive exam, thesis/dissertation. *Entrance requirements:* For doctorate, GRE General Test, minimum GPA of 3.0. Additional exam requirements/recommendations for international students: Required—TOEFL (minimum score 580 paper-based; 237 computer-based; 92 iBT).

University of Missouri–St. Louis, College of Arts and Sciences, Department of Biology, St. Louis, MO 63121. Offers biology (MS, PhD), including animal behavior (MS), biochemistry, biochemistry and biotechnology (MS), biotechnology (MS), conservation biology (MS), development (MS), ecology (MS), environmental studies (PhD), evolution (MS), genetics (MS), molecular biology and biochemistry (PhD), molecular/cellular biology (MS), physiology (MS), plant systematics, population biology (MS), tropical biology (MS); biotechnology (Certificate); tropical biology and conservation (Certificate). Part-time programs available. *Faculty:* 43 full-time (13 women), 2 part-time/adjunct (1 woman). *Students:* 54 full-time (27 women), 79 part-time (43 women); includes 15 minority (6 African Americans, 7 Asian Americans or Pacific Islanders, 2 Hispanic Americans), 47 international. Average age 29. 193 applicants, 44% accepted, 44 enrolled. In 2009, 30 master's, 7 doctorates, 9 other advanced degrees awarded. *Degree requirements:* For master's, thesis or alternative; for doctorate, thesis/dissertation, 1 semester of teaching experience. *Entrance requirements:* For master's, 3 letters of recommendation; for doctorate, GRE General Test, 3 letters of recommendation. Additional exam requirements/recommendations for international students: Required—TOEFL. *Application deadline:* For fall admission, 12/1 priority date for domestic and international students; for spring admission, 10/15 priority date for domestic and international students. Applications are processed on a rolling basis. Application fee: $35 ($40 for international students). Electronic applications accepted. *Expenses:* Tuition, state resident: full-time $5377; part-time $297.70 per credit hour. Tuition, nonresident: full-time $13,882; part-time $771.20 per credit hour. Required fees: $220; $12.20 per credit hour. One-time fee: $12. Tuition and fees vary according to course level, campus/location and program. *Financial support:* In 2009–10, 22 research assistantships with full and partial tuition reimbursements (averaging $16,300 per year), 14 teaching assistantships with full and partial tuition reimbursements (averaging $16,727 per year) were awarded; fellowships with full tuition reimbursements, career-related internships or fieldwork and Federal Work-Study also available. Support available to part-time students. Financial award application deadline: 2/1. *Faculty research:* Molecular biology, microbial genetics, animal behavior, tropical ecology, plant systematics. *Unit head:* Dr. Elizabeth Kellogg, Director of Graduate Studies, 314-516-6200, Fax: 314-516-6233, E-mail: tkellogg@umsl.edu. *Application contact:* 314-516-5458, Fax: 314-516-6996, E-mail: gradadm@umsl.edu.

University of Nebraska Medical Center, Graduate Studies, Department of Genetics, Cell Biology and Anatomy, Omaha, NE 68198. Offers MS, PhD. Part-time programs available. Terminal master's awarded for partial completion of doctoral program. *Degree requirements:* For master's, comprehensive exam, thesis; for doctorate, comprehensive exam, thesis/dissertation. *Entrance requirements:* For master's and doctorate, GRE General Test. Additional exam requirements/recommendations for international students: Required—TOEFL (minimum score 550 paper-based; 213 computer-based). Electronic applications accepted. *Faculty research:* Hematology, immunology, developmental biology, genetics cancer biology, neuroscience.

University of New Hampshire, Graduate School, College of Life Sciences and Agriculture, Department of Molecular, Cellular and Biomedical Sciences, Program in Genetics, Durham, NH 03824. Offers MS, PhD. Part-time programs available. *Faculty:* 12 full-time. *Students:* 7 full-time (5 women), 7 part-time (4 women), 6 international. Average age 32. 15 applicants, 27% accepted, 4 enrolled. In 2009, 1 doctorate awarded. *Degree requirements:* For master's, thesis; for doctorate, thesis/dissertation. *Entrance requirements:* For master's and doctorate, GRE General Test, GRE Subject Test. Additional exam requirements/recommendations for international students: Required—TOEFL (minimum score 550 paper-based; 213 computer-based; 80 iBT). *Application deadline:* For fall admission, 6/1 priority date for domestic students, 4/1 for international students; for spring admission, 12/1 for domestic students. Applications are processed on a rolling basis. Application fee: $65. Electronic applications accepted. *Expenses:* Tuition, state resident: full-time $10,380; part-time $577 per credit hour. Tuition, nonresident: full-time $24,350; part-time $1002 per credit hour. Required fees: $1550; $387.50 per semester. Tuition and fees vary according to course load and program. *Financial support:* In 2009–10, 12 students received support, including 4 research assistantships, 7 teaching assistantships; fellowships, career-related internships or fieldwork, Federal Work-Study, and scholarships/grants also available. Support available to part-time students. Financial award application deadline: 2/15. *Unit head:* Dr. Rick Cote, Chair, 603-862-3217. *Application contact:* Flora Joyal, Administrative Assistant, 603-862-2250, E-mail: genetics.dept@unh.edu.

University of New Mexico, School of Medicine, Biomedical Sciences Graduate Program, Albuquerque, NM 87131-5196. Offers biochemistry and molecular biology (MS, PhD); cell biology and physiology (MS, PhD); molecular genetics and microbiology (MS, PhD); neuroscience (MS, PhD); pathology (MS, PhD); toxicology (MS, PhD). Part-time programs available. Terminal master's awarded for partial completion of doctoral program. *Degree requirements:* For master's, thesis; for doctorate, comprehensive exam, thesis/dissertation. *Entrance requirements:* For master's and doctorate, GRE General Test, minimum undergraduate GPA of 3.0. Additional exam requirements/recommendations for international students: Required—TOEFL. Electronic applications accepted. *Expenses:* Tuition, state resident: full-time $2099; part-time $233.20 per credit hour. Tuition, nonresident: full-time $6650. Required fees: $25 per semester. Tuition and fees vary according to course load, program and reciprocity agreements. *Faculty research:* Signal transduction, infectious disease, biology of cancer, structural biology, neuroscience.

The University of North Carolina at Chapel Hill, Graduate School, College of Arts and Sciences, Department of Biology, Chapel Hill, NC 27599. Offers botany (MA, MS, PhD); cell biology, development, and physiology (MA, MS, PhD); cell motility and cytoskeleton (PhD); ecology and behavior (MA, MS, PhD); genetics and molecular biology (MA, MS, PhD); morphology, systematics, and evolution (MA, MS, PhD). Terminal master's awarded for partial completion of doctoral program. *Degree requirements:* For master's, comprehensive exam, thesis (for some programs); for doctorate, comprehensive exam, thesis/dissertation. *Entrance requirements:* For master's, GRE General Test, GRE Subject Test, 2 semesters of calculus or statistics; 2 semesters of physics, organic chemistry; 3 semesters of biology; for doctorate, GRE General Test, GRE Subject Test, 2 semesters calculus or statistics, 2 semesters physics, organic chemistry, 3 semesters of biology. Additional exam requirements/recommendations for international students: Required—TOEFL (minimum score 550 paper-based; 213 computer-based). Electronic applications accepted. *Faculty research:* Gene expression, biomechanics, yeast genetics, plant ecology, plant molecular biology.

The University of North Carolina at Chapel Hill, School of Medicine and Graduate School, Graduate Programs in Medicine, Curriculum in Genetics and Molecular Biology, Chapel Hill, NC 27599. Offers MS, PhD. *Degree requirements:* For doctorate, comprehensive exam, thesis/dissertation. *Entrance requirements:* For doctorate, minimum GPA of 3.0. Additional exam requirements/recommendations for international students: Required—TOEFL. Electronic applications accepted.

University of North Dakota, Graduate School, College of Arts and Sciences, Department of Biology, Grand Forks, ND 58202. Offers botany (MS, PhD); ecology (MS, PhD); entomology (MS, PhD); environmental biology (MS, PhD); fisheries/wildlife (MS, PhD); genetics (MS, PhD); zoology (MS, PhD). Terminal master's awarded for partial completion of doctoral program. *Degree requirements:* For master's, thesis, final exam; for doctorate, comprehensive exam, thesis/dissertation, final exam. *Entrance requirements:* For master's, GRE General Test, GRE Subject Test, minimum GPA of 3.0; for doctorate, GRE General Test, GRE Subject Test, minimum GPA of 3.5. Additional exam requirements/recommendations for international students: Required—TOEFL (minimum score 550 paper-based; 213 computer-based; 79 iBT), IELTS (minimum score 6.5). Electronic applications accepted. *Faculty research:* Population biology, wildlife ecology, RNA processing, hormonal control of behavior.

University of North Texas Health Science Center at Fort Worth, Graduate School of Biomedical Sciences, Fort Worth, TX 76107-2699. Offers anatomy and cell biology (MS, PhD); biochemistry and molecular biology (MS, PhD); biomedical sciences (MS, PhD); biotechnology (MS); forensic genetics (MS); integrative physiology (MS, PhD); medical science (MS); microbiology and immunology (MS, PhD); pharmacology (MS, PhD); science education (MS); DO/MS; DO/PhD. Terminal master's awarded for partial completion of doctoral program. *Degree requirements:* For master's, thesis; for doctorate, thesis/dissertation. *Entrance requirements:* For master's and doctorate, GRE General Test. Additional exam requirements/recommendations for international students: Required—TOEFL. *Expenses:* Contact institution. *Faculty research:* Alzheimer's disease, aging, eye diseases, cancer, cardiovascular disease.

University of Notre Dame, Graduate School, College of Science, Department of Biological Sciences, Notre Dame, IN 46556. Offers aquatic ecology, evolution and environmental biology (MS, PhD); cellular and molecular biology (MS, PhD); genetics (MS, PhD); physiology (MS, PhD); vector biology and parasitology (MS, PhD). Terminal master's awarded for partial completion of doctoral program. *Degree requirements:* For master's, comprehensive exam, thesis; for doctorate, comprehensive exam, thesis/dissertation, candidacy exam. *Entrance requirements:* For master's and doctorate, GRE General Test. Additional exam requirements/recommendations for international students: Required—TOEFL (minimum score 600 paper-based; 250 computer-based; 80 iBT). Electronic applications accepted. *Faculty research:* Tropical disease, molecular genetics, neurobiology, evolutionary biology, aquatic biology.

University of Oregon, Graduate School, College of Arts and Sciences, Department of Biology, Eugene, OR 97403. Offers ecology and evolution (MA, MS, PhD); marine biology (MA, MS, PhD); molecular, cellular and genetic biology (PhD); neuroscience and development (PhD). Terminal master's awarded for partial completion of doctoral program. *Degree requirements:* For master's, thesis (for some programs); for doctorate, thesis/dissertation. *Entrance requirements:* For master's and doctorate, GRE General Test, minimum GPA of 3.2. Additional exam requirements/recommendations for international students: Required—TOEFL. *Faculty research:* Developmental neurobiology; evolution, population biology, and quantitative genetics; regulation of gene expression; biochemistry of marine organisms.

University of Pennsylvania, School of Medicine, Biomedical Graduate Studies, Graduate Group in Cell and Molecular Biology, Program in Gene Therapy and Vaccines, Philadelphia, PA 19104. Offers PhD, MD/PhD, VMD/PhD. *Degree requirements:* For doctorate, thesis/dissertation. *Entrance requirements:* For doctorate, GRE General Test. Additional exam requirements/recommendations for international students: Required—TOEFL. *Application deadline:* For fall admission, 12/8 priority date for domestic and international students. Applications are processed on a rolling basis. Application fee: $70. Electronic applications accepted. *Expenses:* Tuition: Full-time $25,660; part-time $4758 per course. Required fees: $2152; $270 per course. Tuition and fees vary according to course load, degree level and program. *Financial support:* Fellowships, research assistantships, scholarships/grants, traineeships, and unspecified assistantships available. *Unit head:* Dr. David M. Weiner, Chair, 215-349-8365. *Application contact:* Anna Klein, Coordinator, 215-898-3918, Fax: 215-573-2104, E-mail: camb@mail.med.upenn.edu.

University of Pennsylvania, School of Medicine, Biomedical Graduate Studies, Graduate Group in Cell and Molecular Biology, Program in Genetics and Gene Regulation, Philadelphia, PA 19104. Offers PhD, MD/PhD, VMD/PhD. *Degree requirements:* For doctorate, thesis/

dissertation. *Entrance requirements:* For doctorate, GRE General Test. Additional exam requirements/recommendations for international students: Required—TOEFL. *Application deadline:* For fall admission, 12/8 priority date for domestic and international students. Applications are processed on a rolling basis. Application fee: $70. Electronic applications accepted. *Expenses:* Tuition: Full-time $25,660; part-time $4758 per course. Required fees: $2152; $270 per course. Tuition and fees vary according to course load, degree level and program. *Financial support:* Fellowships, research assistantships, scholarships/grants, traineeships, and unspecified assistantships available. *Unit head:* Dr. Doug Epstein, Chair, 215-573-4527. *Application contact:* Meagan Schofer, Coordinator, 215-895-9536, Fax: 215-573-2104, E-mail: camb@mailmed.upenn.edu.

University of Puerto Rico, Río Piedras, College of Natural Sciences, Department of Biology, San Juan, PR 00931-3300. Offers ecology/systematics (MS, PhD); evolution/genetics (MS, PhD); molecular/cellular biology (MS, PhD); neuroscience (MS, PhD). Part-time programs available. *Degree requirements:* For master's, one foreign language, comprehensive exam, thesis; for doctorate, one foreign language, comprehensive exam, thesis/dissertation. *Entrance requirements:* For master's, GRE Subject Test, interview, minimum GPA of 3.0, letter of recommendation; for doctorate, GRE Subject Test, interview, master's degree, minimum GPA of 3.0, letter of recommendation. *Faculty research:* Environmental, poblational and systematic biology.

University of Rochester, School of Medicine and Dentistry, Graduate Programs in Medicine and Dentistry, Department of Biomedical Genetics, Rochester, NY 14627. Offers MS, PhD. *Degree requirements:* For doctorate, thesis/dissertation, qualifying exam. *Entrance requirements:* For doctorate, GRE General Test.

University of Southern California, Keck School of Medicine and Graduate School, Graduate Programs in Medicine, Department of Preventive Medicine, Division of Biostatistics, Los Angeles, CA 90089. Offers applied biostatistics/epidemiology (MS); biostatistics (MS, PhD); epidemiology (PhD); genetic epidemiology and statistical genetics (PhD); molecular epidemiology (MS, PhD). *Faculty:* 71 full-time (30 women). *Students:* 108 full-time (63 women); includes 24 minority (18 Asian Americans or Pacific Islanders, 6 Hispanic Americans), 58 international. Average age 29. 79 applicants, 52% accepted, 18 enrolled. In 2009, 12 master's, 4 doctorates awarded. Terminal master's awarded for partial completion of doctoral program. *Degree requirements:* For master's, thesis; for doctorate, thesis/dissertation. *Entrance requirements:* For master's and doctorate, GRE General Test, GRE Subject Test, minimum GPA of 3.0. Additional exam requirements/recommendations for international students: Required—TOEFL (minimum score 600 paper-based; 250 computer-based; 100 iBT). *Application deadline:* For fall admission, 12/1 priority date for domestic students, 12/1 for international students. Application fee: $85. Electronic applications accepted. *Expenses:* Tuition: Full-time $25,980; part-time $1315 per unit. Required fees: $554. One-time fee: $35 full-time. Full-time tuition and fees vary according to degree level and program. *Financial support:* In 2009–10, 3 fellowships with full tuition reimbursements (averaging $27,060 per year), 55 research assistantships with full tuition reimbursements (averaging $27,060 per year), 19 teaching assistantships with full and partial tuition reimbursements (averaging $13,530 per year) were awarded; career-related internships or fieldwork, Federal Work-Study, institutionally sponsored loans, scholarships/grants, health care benefits, and unspecified assistantships also available. Financial award application deadline: 5/5. *Faculty research:* Clinical trials in ophthalmology and cancer research, methods of analysis for epidemiological studies, genetic epidemiology. Total annual research expenditures: $1.3 million. *Unit head:* Dr. Stanley P. Azen, Co-Director, 323-442-1810, Fax: 323-442-2993, E-mail: mtrujill@usc.edu. *Application contact:* Mary L. Trujillo, Student Adviser, 323-442-1810, Fax: 323-442-2993, E-mail: mtrujill@usc.edu.

University of Southern California, Keck School of Medicine and Graduate School, Program in Genetic, Molecular and Cellular Biology, Los Angeles, CA 90089. Offers PhD. *Faculty:* 213 full-time (54 women). *Students:* 123 full-time (67 women); includes 24 minority (2 African Americans, 15 Asian Americans or Pacific Islanders, 7 Hispanic Americans), 70 international. 328 applicants, 32% accepted, 47 enrolled. *Degree requirements:* For doctorate, comprehensive exam, thesis/dissertation. *Entrance requirements:* For doctorate, GRE, minimum GPA of 3.0. Additional exam requirements/recommendations for international students: Required—TOEFL (minimum score 600 paper-based; 250 computer-based; 100 iBT). *Application deadline:* For fall admission, 12/1 priority date for domestic and international students. Application fee: $85. Electronic applications accepted. *Expenses:* Tuition: Full-time $25,980; part-time $1315 per unit. Required fees: $554. One-time fee: $35 full-time. Full-time tuition and fees vary according to degree level and program. *Financial support:* In 2009–10, 122 students received support, including 10 fellowships (averaging $27,060 per year), 110 research assistantships with full tuition reimbursements available (averaging $27,060 per year), 2 teaching assistantships with full tuition reimbursements available (averaging $27,060 per year); institutionally sponsored loans, scholarships/grants, traineeships, health care benefits, and unspecified assistantships also available. Financial award application deadline: 5/5; financial award applicants required to submit FAFSA. *Unit head:* Dr. Henry Sucov, Director, 323-442-1475, Fax: 323-442-1199, E-mail: sucov@usc.edu. *Application contact:* Dawn Burke, Student Program Coordinator, 323-442-1475, Fax: 323-442-1199, E-mail: pibbs@usc.edu.

The University of Tennessee, Graduate School, College of Arts and Sciences, Program in Life Sciences, Knoxville, TN 37996. Offers genome science and technology (MS, PhD); plant physiology and genetics (MS, PhD). *Degree requirements:* For doctorate, one foreign language, thesis/dissertation. *Entrance requirements:* For master's and doctorate, GRE General Test, minimum GPA of 2.7. Additional exam requirements/recommendations for international students: Required—TOEFL. Electronic applications accepted. *Expenses:* Tuition, state resident: full-time $6826; part-time $380 per semester hour. Tuition, nonresident: full-time $21,844; part-time $1147 per semester hour. Tuition and fees vary according to program.

The University of Texas Health Science Center at Houston, Graduate School of Biomedical Sciences, Program in Genes and Development, Houston, TX 77030. Offers MS, PhD, MD/PhD. Terminal master's awarded for partial completion of doctoral program. *Degree requirements:* For master's, thesis; for doctorate, thesis/dissertation. *Entrance requirements:* For master's and doctorate, GRE General Test. Additional exam requirements/recommendations for international students: Required—TOEFL. Electronic applications accepted. *Faculty research:* Developmental biology, genetics, cell biology, structural biology, cancer.

The University of Texas Medical Branch, Graduate School of Biomedical Sciences, Program in Biochemistry and Molecular Biology, Galveston, TX 77555. Offers biochemistry (PhD); bioinformatics (PhD); biophysics (PhD); cell biology (PhD); computational biology (PhD); structural biology (PhD). *Students:* 41 full-time (17 women); includes 6 minority (1 African American, 1 Asian American or Pacific Islander, 4 Hispanic Americans), 22 international. Average age 28. In 2009, 9 doctorates awarded. *Degree requirements:* For doctorate, thesis/dissertation. *Entrance requirements:* Additional exam requirements/recommendations for international students: Required—TOEFL (minimum score 550 paper-based; 213 computer-based). *Application deadline:* Applications are processed on a rolling basis. Application fee: $30 ($75 for international students). Electronic applications accepted. *Financial support:* In 2009–10, fellowships (averaging $25,000 per year), research assistantships (averaging $25,000 per year) were awarded. Financial award applicants required to submit FAFSA. *Unit head:* Dr. Sarita Sastry, Director, 409-747-1915, Fax: 409-747-1938, E-mail: sasastry@utmb.edu. *Application contact:* Debora Botting, Coordinator for Special Programs, 409-772-2769, Fax: 409-772-5102, E-mail: dmbottin@utmb.edu.

The University of Texas Southwestern Medical Center at Dallas, Southwestern Graduate School of Biomedical Sciences, Division of Basic Science, Program in Genetics and Development, Dallas, TX 75390. Offers PhD. *Faculty:* 85 full-time (16 women), 2 part-time/adjunct (0 women). *Students:* 102 full-time (52 women), 4 part-time (1 woman); includes 25 minority (1 African American, 1 American Indian/Alaska Native, 12 Asian Americans or Pacific Islanders, 11 Hispanic Americans), 38 international. Average age 28. 946 applicants, 22% accepted, 87 enrolled. In 2009, 19 doctorates awarded. *Degree requirements:* For doctorate, thesis/dissertation, qualifying exam. *Entrance requirements:* For doctorate, GRE General Test, minimum GPA of 3.0. Additional exam requirements/recommendations for international students: Required—TOEFL. *Application deadline:* For fall admission, 12/15 priority date for domestic students. Application fee: $0. Electronic applications accepted. *Financial support:* Fellowships, research assistantships, institutionally sponsored loans available. *Faculty research:* Human molecular genetics, chromosome structure, gene regulation, molecular biology, gene expression. *Unit head:* Dr. Nancy E. Street, Associate Dean, 214-648-6708, Fax: 214-648-2102, E-mail: nancy.street@utsouthwestern.edu. *Application contact:* Dr. Nancy E. Street, Associate Dean, 214-648-6708, Fax: 214-648-2102, E-mail: nancy.street@utsouthwestern.edu.

University of Toronto, School of Graduate Studies, Life Sciences Division, Department of Molecular and Medical Genetics, Toronto, ON M5S 1A1, Canada. Offers genetic counseling (M Sc); molecular and medical genetics (M Sc, PhD). *Degree requirements:* For master's, thesis; for doctorate, thesis/dissertation. *Entrance requirements:* For master's, B Sc or equivalent; for doctorate, M Sc or equivalent, minimum B+ average. Additional exam requirements/recommendations for international students: Required—TOEFL, IELTS (minimum score: 7), Michigan English Language Assessment Battery (minimum score: 85) or COPE (minimum score: 4). *Faculty research:* Structural biology, developmental genetics, molecular medicine, genetic counseling.

University of Washington, Graduate School, School of Public Health, Department of Epidemiology, Institute for Public Health Genetics, Seattle, WA 98195. Offers genetic epidemiology (MS); public health genetics (MPH, PhD). Part-time programs available. *Students:* 24 full-time (19 women), 6 part-time (2 women); includes 8 minority (5 Asian Americans or Pacific Islanders, 3 Hispanic Americans), 2 international. Average age 30. 49 applicants, 33% accepted, 8 enrolled. In 2009, 11 master's, 1 doctorate awarded. Terminal master's awarded for partial completion of doctoral program. *Degree requirements:* For master's, thesis, practicum (MPH); for doctorate, comprehensive exam, thesis/dissertation. *Entrance requirements:* For master's and doctorate, GRE General Test, experience in health sciences (preferred), minimum GPA of 3.0. Additional exam requirements/recommendations for international students: Required—TOEFL (minimum score 583 paper-based; 237 computer-based). *Application deadline:* For fall admission, 1/15 for domestic students, 11/1 for international students. Application fee: $50. *Financial support:* In 2009–10, 4 students received support, including 3 research assistantships with full tuition reimbursements available (averaging $13,725 per year), 1 teaching assistantship with full tuition reimbursement available (averaging $1,375 per year). Financial award application deadline: 1/15; financial award applicants required to submit FAFSA. *Faculty research:* Genetic epidemiology; ethical, legal, social issues of genetics; ecogenetics; health policy. Total annual research expenditures: $400,000. *Unit head:* Dr. Melissa A. Austin, Director, 206-543-1065. *Application contact:* Barb Snyder, Student Services Advisor, 206-616-9286, Fax: 206-685-9651, E-mail: phgen@u.washington.edu.

University of Wisconsin–Madison, Graduate School, College of Agricultural and Life Sciences and Graduate Programs in Medicine, Department of Genetics, Program in Genetics, Madison, WI 53706-1380. Offers PhD. *Degree requirements:* For doctorate, thesis/dissertation. *Expenses:* Tuition, state resident: part-time $594 per credit. Tuition, nonresident: part-time $1504 per credit. Required fees: $65 per credit. Tuition and fees vary according to course load, program and reciprocity agreements.

See Display on page 304 and Close-Up on page 323.

University of Wisconsin–Madison, School of Medicine and Public Health and Graduate School, Graduate Programs in Medicine, Madison, WI 53705. Offers biomolecular chemistry (MS, PhD); cancer biology (PhD); genetics and medical genetics (MS, PhD), including genetics (PhD), medical genetics (MS); medical physics (MS, PhD), including health physics (MS), medical physics; microbiology (PhD); molecular and cellular pharmacology (PhD); pathology and laboratory medicine (PhD); physiology (PhD); population health sciences (MPH, MS, PhD), including clinical research (MS, PhD), epidemiology (MS, PhD), health services research (MS, PhD), population health sciences (MPH), social and behavioral health sciences (MS, PhD); DPT/MPH; DVM/MPH; MD/MPH; MD/PhD; MPA/MPH; MS/MPH; Pharm D/MPH. Part-time programs available. Postbaccalaureate distance learning degree programs offered (minimal on-campus study). Terminal master's awarded for partial completion of doctoral program. Application fee: $45. Electronic applications accepted. *Expenses:* Contact institution. *Financial support:* Fellowships with full tuition reimbursements, research assistantships with full tuition reimbursements, teaching assistantships with full tuition reimbursements, scholarships/grants, traineeships, and tuition waivers (full) available. *Unit head:* Dr. Richard L. Moss, Senior Associate Dean for Basic Research, Biotechnology and Graduate Studies, 608-265-0523, Fax: 608-265-0522, E-mail: rlmoss@wisc.edu. *Application contact:* Information Contact, 608-262-2433, Fax: 608-262-5134, E-mail: gradadmiss@mail.bascom.wisc.edu.

University of Wyoming, Graduate Program in Molecular and Cellular Life Sciences, Laramie, WY 82070. Offers PhD. *Degree requirements:* For doctorate, thesis/dissertation, four eight-week laboratory rotations, comprehensive basic practical exam, two-part qualifying exam, seminars, symposium.

Virginia Commonwealth University, Medical College of Virginia-Professional Programs, School of Medicine, School of Medicine Graduate Programs, Department of Biochemistry, Richmond, VA 23284-9005. Offers biochemistry (MS, PhD); molecular biology and genetics (MS, PhD); neuroscience (PhD); MD/PhD. *Degree requirements:* For master's, thesis; for doctorate, thesis/dissertation, comprehensive oral and written exams. *Entrance requirements:* For master's and doctorate, DAT, GRE General Test, MCAT. *Faculty research:* Molecular biology, peptide/protein chemistry, neurochemistry, enzyme mechanisms, macromolecular structure determination.

Virginia Commonwealth University, Medical College of Virginia-Professional Programs, School of Medicine, School of Medicine Graduate Programs, Department of Human and Molecular Genetics, Richmond, VA 23284-9005. Offers genetic counseling (MS); human genetics (PhD); molecular biology and genetics (MS, PhD); MD/PhD. *Degree requirements:* For master's, thesis; for doctorate, thesis/dissertation, comprehensive oral and written exams. *Entrance requirements:* For master's, DAT, GRE General Test, or MCAT; for doctorate, GRE General Test, DAT, MCAT. *Faculty research:* Genetic epidemiology, biochemical genetics, quantitative genetics, human cytogenetics, molecular genetics.

Virginia Commonwealth University, Medical College of Virginia-Professional Programs, School of Medicine, School of Medicine Graduate Programs, Department of Microbiology and Immunology, Richmond, VA 23284-9005. Offers microbiology and immunology (MS, PhD); molecular biology and genetics (MS, PhD); MD/PhD. *Degree requirements:* For master's, thesis; for doctorate, thesis/dissertation, comprehensive oral and written exams. *Entrance requirements:* For master's, GRE General Test or MCAT; for doctorate, GRE General Test, MCAT. *Faculty research:* Microbial physiology and genetics, molecular biology, crystallography of biological molecules, antibiotics and chemotherapy, membrane transport.

Virginia Commonwealth University, Medical College of Virginia-Professional Programs, School of Medicine, School of Medicine Graduate Programs, Department of Pharmacology and Toxicology, Richmond, VA 23284-9005. Offers molecular biology and genetics (PhD); neuroscience (PhD); pharmacology (PhD); pharmacology and toxicology (MS); MD/PhD. Terminal master's awarded for partial completion of doctoral program. *Degree requirements:* For master's, thesis; for doctorate, thesis/dissertation, comprehensive oral and written exams. *Entrance requirements:* For master's, DAT, GRE General Test, or MCAT; for doctorate, GRE General Test, MCAT, DAT. *Faculty research:* Drug abuse, drug metabolism, pharmacodynamics, peptide synthesis, receptor mechanisms.

Virginia Polytechnic Institute and State University, Graduate School, College of Science, Department of Biological Sciences, Blacksburg, VA 24061. Offers botany (MS, PhD); ecology and evolutionary biology (MS, PhD); genetics and developmental biology (MS, PhD); microbiology (MS, PhD); zoology (MS, PhD). *Faculty:* 42 full-time (11 women). *Students:* 76 full-time

Genetics

Virginia Polytechnic Institute and State University *(continued)*
(45 women), 5 part-time (1 woman); includes 28 minority (23 American Indian/Alaska Native, 2 Asian Americans or Pacific Islanders, 3 Hispanic Americans). Average age 28. 117 applicants, 15% accepted, 15 enrolled. In 2009, 11 master's, 11 doctorates awarded. *Entrance requirements:* For master's and doctorate, GRE, GMAT. Additional exam requirements/recommendations for international students: Required—TOEFL (minimum score 550 paper-based; 213 computer-based). *Application deadline:* For fall admission, 5/15 for international students; for spring admission, 10/15 for international students. Applications are processed on a rolling basis. Application fee: $65. Electronic applications accepted. *Expenses:* Tuition, area resident: Full-time $10,228; part-time $459 per credit hour. Tuition, nonresident: full-time $17,892; part-time $865 per credit hour. Required fees: $1966; $451 per semester. *Financial support:* In 2009–10, 37 research assistantships with full tuition reimbursements (averaging $17,929 per year), 41 teaching assistantships with full tuition reimbursements (averaging $17,344 per year) were awarded; career-related internships or fieldwork, Federal Work-Study, scholarships/grants, and unspecified assistantships also available. Financial award application deadline: 1/15. *Faculty research:* Freshwater ecology, cell cycle regulation, behavioral ecology, motor proteins. Total annual research expenditures: $4.8 million. *Unit head:* Dr. Bob H. Jones, Dean, 540-231-9514, Fax: 540-231-9307, E-mail: rhjones@vt.edu. *Application contact:* Erik Nilsen, Information Contact, 540-231-5671, Fax: 540-231-9307, E-mail: enilsen@vt.edu.

Virginia Polytechnic Institute and State University, Graduate School, Intercollege, Program in Genetics, Bioinformatics and Computational Biology, Blacksburg, VA 24061. Offers PhD. *Students:* 40 full-time (20 women), 3 part-time (2 women); includes 34 minority (26 American Indian/Alaska Native, 6 Asian Americans or Pacific Islanders, 2 Hispanic Americans). Average age 29. 39 applicants, 33% accepted, 8 enrolled. In 2009, 6 doctorates awarded. *Entrance requirements:* For doctorate, GRE, GMAT. Additional exam requirements/recommendations for international students: Required—TOEFL (minimum score 550 paper-based; 213 computer-based). *Application deadline:* For fall admission, 5/15 for international students; for spring admission, 10/15 for international students. Applications are processed on a rolling basis. Application fee: $65. Electronic applications accepted. *Expenses:* Tuition, area resident: Full-time $10,228; part-time $459 per credit hour. Tuition, nonresident: full-time $17,892; part-time $865 per credit hour. Required fees: $1966; $451 per semester. *Financial support:* Career-related internships or fieldwork, Federal Work-Study, scholarships/grants, and unspecified assistantships available. Financial award application deadline: 1/15. *Unit head:* Dr. David R. Bevan, Dean, 540-231-5040, Fax: 540-231-3010, E-mail: drbevan@vt.edu. *Application contact:* Dennie Munson, Information Contact, 540-231-1928, Fax: 540-231-3010, E-mail: dennie@vt.edu.

Washington State University, Graduate School, College of Sciences, School of Molecular Biosciences, Program in Genetics and Cell Biology, Pullman, WA 99164. Offers MS, PhD. Terminal master's awarded for partial completion of doctoral program. *Degree requirements:* For master's, thesis or alternative, oral exam; for doctorate, comprehensive exam, thesis/dissertation, oral exam. *Entrance requirements:* For master's and doctorate, GRE General Test, minimum GPA of 3.0. Additional exam requirements/recommendations for international students: Required—TOEFL (minimum score 550 paper-based; 213 computer-based). Electronic applications accepted. *Faculty research:* Plant molecular biology, growth factors, cancer induction and DNA repair, gene regulation and genetic engineering.

Washington University in St. Louis, Graduate School of Arts and Sciences, Division of Biology and Biomedical Sciences, Program in Evolution, Ecology and Population Biology, St. Louis, MO 63130-4899. Offers ecology (PhD); environmental biology (PhD); evolutionary biology (PhD); genetics (PhD). *Degree requirements:* For doctorate, thesis/dissertation. *Entrance requirements:* For doctorate, GRE General Test, GRE Subject Test. Electronic applications accepted.

Washington University in St. Louis, School of Medicine, Program in Genetic Epidemiology, St. Louis, MO 63130-4899. Offers clinical (MS); computational (MS); genetic epidemiology (Certificate). Part-time programs available. *Faculty:* 29 full-time (11 women). *Students:* 8 full-time (3 women), 8 part-time (7 women); includes 8 minority (2 African Americans, 5 Asian Americans or Pacific Islanders, 1 Hispanic American), 1 international. Average age 32. 18 applicants, 61% accepted, 10 enrolled. In 2009, 7 master's awarded. *Degree requirements:* For master's, thesis, research paper. *Entrance requirements:* For master's, proficiency in computer programming, statistics and biology/genetics. Additional exam requirements/recommendations for international students: Required—TOEFL (minimum score 600 paper-based; 250 computer-based; 100 iBT). *Application deadline:* For fall admission, 5/1 priority date for domestic and international students. Applications are processed on a rolling basis. Application fee: $50. *Expenses:* Contact institution. *Financial support:* Research assistantships with partial tuition reimbursements, Federal Work-Study, institutionally sponsored loans, scholarships/grants, health care benefits, tuition waivers (partial), and unspecified assistantships available. Financial award application deadline: 4/1; financial award applicants required to submit FAFSA. *Faculty research:* Biostatistics, clinical trials, cardiovascular diseases, genetics, genetic epidemiology. *Unit head:* Dr. Dabeeru C. Rao, Professor/Director of Biostatistics, 314-362-3608, Fax: 314-362-2693, E-mail: rao@wubios.wustl.edu. *Application contact:* June C. Mueller, Program Manager, 314-362-1052, Fax: 314-362-2693, E-mail: june@wubios.wustl.edu.

Wayne State University, Graduate School, Program in Molecular Biology and Genetics, Detroit, MI 48202. Offers MS, PhD. Terminal master's awarded for partial completion of doctoral program. *Degree requirements:* For master's, thesis; for doctorate, thesis/dissertation. *Entrance requirements:* For master's and doctorate, GRE General Test, contingent upon admission to the graduate programs of the school of medicine; references. Additional exam requirements/recommendations for international students: Required—TOEFL (minimum score 550 paper-based; 213 computer-based); Recommended—TWE (minimum score 6). Electronic applications accepted. *Faculty research:* Human gene mapping, genome organization and sequencing, gene regulation, molecular evolution.

Wesleyan University, Graduate Programs, Department of Biology, Middletown, CT 06459. Offers animal behavior (PhD); bioformatics/genomics (PhD); cell biology (PhD); developmental biology (PhD); evolution/ecology (PhD); genetics (PhD); neurobiology (PhD); population biology (PhD). *Faculty:* 13 full-time (4 women). *Students:* 23 full-time (11 women); includes 1 minority (African American), 3 international. Average age 26. 29 applicants, 10% accepted, 2 enrolled. In 2009, 3 doctorates awarded. *Degree requirements:* For doctorate, variable foreign language requirement, thesis/dissertation. *Entrance requirements:* For doctorate, GRE. Additional exam requirements/recommendations for international students: Required—TOEFL. *Application deadline:* For fall admission, 1/15 for domestic and international students. Applications are processed on a rolling basis. Application fee: $0. *Financial support:* In 2009–10, 3 research assistantships with full tuition reimbursements, 19 teaching assistantships with full tuition reimbursements were awarded; stipends also available. Financial award application deadline: 4/15; financial award applicants required to submit FAFSA. *Faculty research:* Microbial population genetics, genetic basis of evolutionary adaptation, genetic regulation of differentiation and pattern formation in *drosophila*. *Unit head:* Dr. Sonia E. Sultan, Chair/Professor, 860-685-3493, E-mail: jnaegele@wesleyan.edu. *Application contact:* Marjorie Fitzgibbons, Information Contact, 860-685-2140, E-mail: mfitzgibbons@wesleyan.edu.

West Virginia University, Davis College of Agriculture, Forestry and Consumer Sciences, Interdisciplinary Program in Genetics and Developmental Biology, Morgantown, WV 26506. Offers animal breeding (MS, PhD); biochemical and molecular genetics (MS, PhD); cytogenetics (MS, PhD); descriptive embryology (MS, PhD); developmental genetics (MS); experimental morphogenesis/teratology (MS); human genetics (MS, PhD); immunogenetics

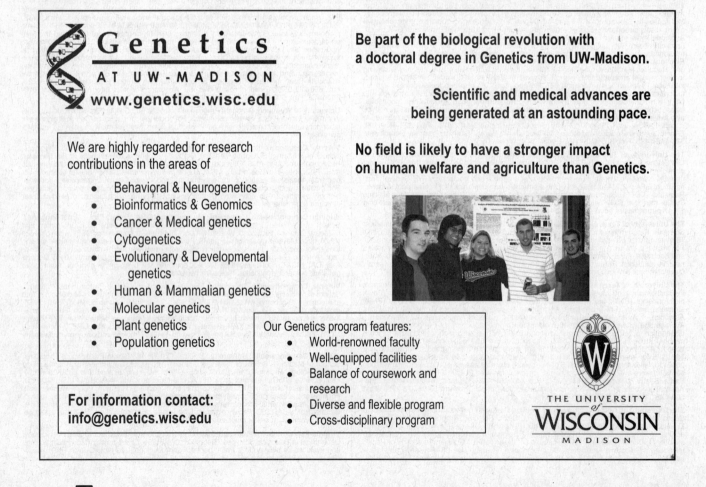

(MS, PhD); life cycles of animals and plants (MS, PhD); molecular aspects of development (MS, PhD); mutagenesis (MS, PhD); oncology (MS, PhD); plant genetics (MS, PhD); population and quantitative genetics (MS, PhD); regeneration (MS, PhD); teratology (PhD); toxicology (MS, PhD). *Degree requirements:* For master's, thesis; for doctorate, comprehensive exam, thesis/dissertation. *Entrance requirements:* For master's, GRE or MCAT, minimum GPA of 2.75. Additional exam requirements/recommendations for international students: Required—TOEFL.

Yale University, Graduate School of Arts and Sciences, Department of Genetics, New Haven, CT 06520. Offers PhD, MD/PhD. *Degree requirements:* For doctorate, thesis/dissertation. *Entrance requirements:* For doctorate, GRE General Test, GRE Subject Test.

Yale University, Graduate School of Arts and Sciences, Department of Molecular, Cellular, and Developmental Biology, Program in Genetics, New Haven, CT 06520. Offers PhD. *Degree requirements:* For doctorate, thesis/dissertation. *Entrance requirements:* For doctorate, GRE General Test, GRE Subject Test.

Yale University, School of Medicine and Graduate School of Arts and Sciences, Combined Program in Biological and Biomedical Sciences (BBS), Molecular Cell Biology, Genetics, and Development Track, New Haven, CT 06520. Offers PhD, MD/PhD. *Entrance requirements:* Additional exam requirements/recommendations for international students: Required—TOEFL. *Application deadline:* For fall admission, 12/6 for domestic and international students. *Unit head:* Dr. Shirleen Roeder, Co-Director, 203-432-3501. *Application contact:* Shirlene Scott, Graduate Registrar, 203-785-2404, E-mail: shirlene.scott@yale.edu.

Genomic Sciences

Albert Einstein College of Medicine, Sue Golding Graduate Division of Medical Sciences, Division of Biological Sciences, Department of Genetics, Bronx, NY 10461. Offers computational genetics (PhD); molecular genetics (PhD); translational genetics (PhD); MD/PhD. *Degree requirements:* For doctorate, thesis/dissertation. *Entrance requirements:* For doctorate, GRE General Test. Additional exam requirements/recommendations for international students: Required—TOEFL. *Faculty research:* Neurologic genetics in *Drosophila*, biochemical genetics of yeast, developmental genetics in the mouse.

Black Hills State University, Graduate Studies, Program in Integrative Genomics, Spearfish, SD 57799. Offers MS. *Faculty:* 4 full-time (0 women), 1 (woman) part-time/adjunct. *Students:* 8 full-time (2 women), 1 international. Average age 27. 13 applicants, 100% accepted, 2 enrolled. In 2009, 3 master's awarded. *Entrance requirements:* Additional exam requirements/recommendations for international students: Required—TOEFL (minimum score 500 paper-based; 171 computer-based; 60 iBT). *Application deadline:* For fall admission, 4/15 for domestic students. Application fee: $35. *Expenses:* Tuition, state resident: full-time $4170; part-time $139 per credit hour. Tuition, nonresident: full-time $8828; part-time $294 per credit. Required fees: $3476; $116 per credit hour. *Application contact:* Dr. George Earley, Director of Graduate Studies, 605-642-6270, Fax: 605-642-6273, E-mail: georgeearley@bhsu.edu.

Case Western Reserve University, School of Medicine and School of Graduate Studies, Graduate Programs in Medicine, Department of Genetics, Program in Human, Molecular, and Developmental Genetics and Genomics, Cleveland, OH 44106. Offers PhD, MD/PhD. *Degree requirements:* For doctorate, comprehensive exam, thesis/dissertation. *Entrance requirements:* For doctorate, GRE General Test, GRE Subject Test. Additional exam requirements/recommendations for international students: Required—TOEFL. *Faculty research:* Regulation of gene expression, molecular control of development, genomics.

Concordia University, School of Graduate Studies, Faculty of Arts and Science, Department of Biology, Montréal, QC H3G 1M8, Canada. Offers biology (M Sc, PhD); biotechnology and genomics (Diploma). *Degree requirements:* For master's, thesis; for doctorate, thesis/dissertation, pedagogical training. *Entrance requirements:* For master's, honors degree in biology; for doctorate, M Sc in life science. *Faculty research:* Cell biology, animal physiology, ecology, microbiology/molecular biology, plant physiology/biochemistry and biotechnology.

The George Washington University, School of Medicine and Health Sciences, Department of Biochemistry and Molecular Biology, Program in Genomics and Bioinformatics, Washington, DC 20052. Offers MS. Part-time programs available. *Students:* 13 full-time (8 women), 5 part-time (1 woman); includes 1 minority (Asian American or Pacific Islander), 11 international. Average age 26. 31 applicants, 84% accepted, 9 enrolled. In 2009, 7 master's awarded. *Entrance requirements:* For master's, GRE General Test, minimum GPA of 3.0. Additional exam requirements/recommendations for international students: Required—TOEFL (minimum score 550 paper-based; 213 computer-based). *Application deadline:* For fall admission, 4/1 priority date for domestic and international students; for spring admission, 10/1 priority date for domestic and international students. Applications are processed on a rolling basis. Application fee: $60. Electronic applications accepted. *Unit head:* Dr. Jack Vanderhoek, Director, 202-994-2929, E-mail: jyvdh@gwu.edu. *Application contact:* Dr. Fatah Kashanchi, Director, 202-994-1781, Fax: 202-994-6213, E-mail: bcmfxk@gwumc.edu.

Harvard University, Graduate School of Arts and Sciences, Department of Systems Biology, Cambridge, MA 02138. Offers PhD. *Degree requirements:* For doctorate, thesis/dissertation, lab rotation, qualifying examination. *Entrance requirements:* For doctorate, GRE. Additional exam requirements/recommendations for international students: Required—TOEFL. Electronic applications accepted. *Expenses:* Tuition: Full-time $33,696. Required fees: $1126. Full-time tuition and fees vary according to program.

Medical College of Georgia, School of Graduate Studies, Program in Genomic Medicine, Augusta, GA 30912. Offers PhD. *Degree requirements:* For doctorate, comprehensive exam, thesis/dissertation. *Entrance requirements:* For doctorate, GRE General Test. Additional exam requirements/recommendations for international students: Required—TOEFL (minimum score 550 paper-based; 213 computer-based; 79 iBT). Electronic applications accepted. Full-time tuition and fees vary according to campus/location, program and student level. *Faculty research:* Genetic and genomic basis of diseases (diabetes, cancer, autoimmunity), development of diagnostic markers, bioinformatics, computational biology.

North Carolina State University, Graduate School, College of Agriculture and Life Sciences, Graduate Program in Genomic Sciences, Raleigh, NC 27695. Offers MS, PhD.

North Carolina State University, Graduate School, College of Agriculture and Life Sciences, Program in Functional Genomics, Raleigh, NC 27695. Offers MFG, MS, PhD. *Degree requirements:* For master's, thesis (for some programs); for doctorate, thesis/dissertation. *Entrance requirements:* For master's and doctorate, GRE, minimum B average. Additional exam requirements/recommendations for international students: Required—TOEFL. Electronic applications accepted. *Faculty research:* Genome structure, genome expression, molecular evolution, nucleic acid structure/function, proteomics.

North Dakota State University, College of Graduate and Interdisciplinary Studies, College of Science and Mathematics, Department of Biological Sciences, Fargo, ND 58108. Offers biology (MS); botany (MS, PhD); cellular and molecular biology (PhD); environmental and conservation sciences (MS, PhD); genomics (PhD); natural resources management (MS, PhD); zoology (MS, PhD). *Students:* 32 full-time (21 women), 14 part-time (10 women); includes 1 Asian American or Pacific Islander, 14 international. In 2009, 12 master's, 9 doctorates awarded. *Degree requirements:* For master's, thesis; for doctorate, thesis/dissertation. *Entrance requirements:* For master's and doctorate, GRE General Test. Additional exam requirements/recommendations for international students: Required—TOEFL. *Application deadline:* For fall admission, 3/15 priority date for domestic students; for spring admission, 10/30 priority date for domestic students. Applications are processed on a rolling basis. Application fee: $45 ($60 for international students). Electronic applications accepted. *Financial support:* Fellowships with full tuition reimbursements, research assistantships with full tuition reimbursements, teaching assistantships with full tuition reimbursements, career-related internships or fieldwork, Federal Work-Study, institutionally sponsored loans, scholarships/grants, tuition waivers (full), and unspecified assistantships available. Support available to part-time

students. Financial award application deadline: 4/15; financial award applicants required to submit FAFSA. *Faculty research:* Comparative endocrinology, physiology, behavioral ecology, plant cell biology, aquatic biology. Total annual research expenditures: $675,000. *Unit head:* Dr. Marinus L. Otte, Head, 701-231-7087, E-mail: marinus.otte@ndsu.edu. *Application contact:* Dr. Marinus L. Otte, Head, 701-231-7087, E-mail: marinus.otte@ndsu.edu.

North Dakota State University, College of Graduate and Interdisciplinary Studies, Interdisciplinary Program in Genomics and Bioinformatics, Fargo, ND 58108. Offers MS, PhD. Part-time programs available. *Faculty:* 21 full-time (3 women). *Students:* 6 full-time (2 women), 7 part-time (5 women), 11 international. 2 applicants, 100% accepted, 2 enrolled. *Degree requirements:* For master's, thesis; for doctorate, comprehensive exam, thesis/dissertation. *Entrance requirements:* For master's and doctorate, minimum GPA of 3.0. Additional exam requirements/recommendations for international students: Required—TOEFL (minimum score 525 paper-based; 197 computer-based; 71 iBT). *Application deadline:* Applications are processed on a rolling basis. Application fee: $45 ($60 for international students). Electronic applications accepted. *Financial support:* In 2009–10, 12 research assistantships with full tuition reimbursements (averaging $15,000 per year) were awarded; unspecified assistantships also available. *Faculty research:* Genome evolution, genome mapping, genome expression, bioinformatics, data mining. Total annual research expenditures: $300,000. *Unit head:* Dr. Phillip E. McClean, Director, 701-231-8443, Fax: 701-231-8474. *Application contact:* Dr. Phillip E. McClean, Director, 701-231-8443, Fax: 701-231-8474.

Texas Tech University, Center for Biotechnology and Genomics, Lubbock, TX 79409. Offers biotechnology (MS); science and agricultural biotechnology (MS); JD/MS. Part-time programs available. *Faculty:* 2 full-time (1 woman). *Students:* 22 full-time (10 women), 2 part-time (1 woman), 23 international. Average age 23. 114 applicants, 61% accepted, 16 enrolled. In 2009, 8 master's awarded. *Degree requirements:* For master's, thesis or alternative. *Entrance requirements:* For master's, GRE General Test. Additional exam requirements/recommendations for international students: Required—TOEFL (minimum score 550 paper-based; 213 computer-based). *Application deadline:* For fall admission, 3/1 priority date for international students; for spring admission, 11/1 priority date for international students. Application fee: $50 ($75 for international students). *Expenses:* Tuition, state resident: full-time $5100; part-time $213 per credit hour. Tuition, nonresident: full-time $11,748; part-time $490 per credit hour. Required fees: $2298; $50 per credit hour. $555 per semester. *Financial support:* In 2009–10, 4 students received support, including 2 research assistantships with partial tuition reimbursements available (averaging $15,037 per year). Financial award application deadline: 4/15. *Faculty research:* Biotechnology and applied science. *Unit head:* Dr. David B. Knaff, Advisor, 806-742-0288, Fax: 806-742-1289, E-mail: david.knaff@ttu.edu. *Application contact:* Jatindra Tripathy, Senior Research Associate, 806-742-3722 Ext. 229, Fax: 806-742-3788, E-mail: jatindra.tripathy@ttu.edu.

University of California, Riverside, Graduate Division, Graduate Program in Genetics, Genomics, and Bioinformatics, Riverside, CA 92521-0102. Offers genomics and bioinformatics (PhD); molecular genetics (PhD); population and evolutionary genetics (PhD). *Degree requirements:* For doctorate, thesis/dissertation, qualifying exams, teaching experience. *Entrance requirements:* For doctorate, GRE General Test, minimum GPA of 3.2. Additional exam requirements/recommendations for international students: Required—TOEFL (minimum score 550 paper-based; 213 computer-based; 80 iBT). Electronic applications accepted. *Faculty research:* Molecular Genetics, Evolution and Population Genetics, Genomics and Bioinformatics.

University of California, San Francisco, School of Pharmacy and Graduate Division, Pharmaceutical Sciences and Pharmacogenomics Graduate Group, San Francisco, CA 94158-0775. Offers PhD. *Faculty:* 51 full-time (14 women). *Students:* 43 full-time (22 women); includes 15 minority (14 Asian Americans or Pacific Islanders, 1 Hispanic American). Average age 24. 69 applicants, 23% accepted, 6 enrolled. In 2009, 5 doctorates awarded. *Degree requirements:* For doctorate, comprehensive exam, thesis/dissertation. *Entrance requirements:* For doctorate, GRE General Test, minimum GPA of 3.0. Additional exam requirements/recommendations for international students: Required—TOEFL. *Application deadline:* For fall admission, 12/31 for domestic students. Application fee: $60 ($80 for international students). Electronic applications accepted. *Financial support:* In 2009–10, 4 fellowships with full tuition reimbursements (averaging $27,000 per year), 23 research assistantships with full tuition reimbursements (averaging $27,000 per year), 6 teaching assistantships with full tuition reimbursements (averaging $27,000 per year) were awarded; career-related internships or fieldwork, institutionally sponsored loans, scholarships/grants, traineeships, tuition waivers (full), and unspecified assistantships also available. Financial award application deadline: 4/6. *Faculty research:* Drug development, drug delivery, molecular pharmacology. *Unit head:* Francis C. Szoka, Program Director, 415-476-3895, Fax: 415-476-0688, E-mail: szoka@cgl.ucsf.edu. *Application contact:* Debbie Acoba-Idlebi, Program Coordinator, 415-476-1947, Fax: 415-476-6022, E-mail: debbie.acoba@ucsf.edu.

University of Chicago, Division of the Biological Sciences, Department of Molecular Biosciences, Committee on Genetics, Genomics and Systems Biology, Chicago, IL 60637-1513. Offers PhD. *Faculty:* 65 full-time (24 women). *Students:* 21 full-time (11 women); includes 6 minority (1 African American, 4 Asian Americans or Pacific Islanders, 1 Hispanic American). Average age 28. 35 applicants, 11% accepted, 4 enrolled. In 2009, 3 doctorates awarded. *Degree requirements:* For doctorate, thesis/dissertation, ethics class, 2 teaching assistantships. *Entrance requirements:* For doctorate, GRE General Test, minimum GPA of 3.0. Additional exam requirements/recommendations for international students: Required—TOEFL (minimum score 600 paper-based; 250 computer-based; 104 iBT), IELTS (minimum score 7). *Application deadline:* For fall admission, 12/1 priority date for domestic and international students. Application fee: $55. Electronic applications accepted. *Financial support:* In 2009–10, 21 students received support, including fellowships with tuition reimbursements available (averaging $29,781 per year), research assistantships with tuition reimbursements available (averaging $29,781 per year); institutionally sponsored loans, scholarships/grants, traineeships, and health care benefits also available. Financial award applicants required to submit FAFSA. *Faculty research:* Molecular genetics, developmental genetics, population genetics, human genetics. *Unit head:* Dr. Richard Hudson, Chair, 773-834-2978, Fax: 773-702-8093, E-mail: committee-on-genetics@uchicago.edu. *Application contact:* Sue Levison, Administrator, 773-702-2464, Fax: 773-702-3172, E-mail: committee-on-genetics@uchicago.edu.

Genomic Sciences

University of Cincinnati, Graduate School, College of Medicine, Graduate Programs in Biomedical Sciences, Department of Environmental Health, Programs in Environmental Genetics and Molecular Toxicology, Cincinnati, OH 45221. Offers MS, PhD. *Degree requirements:* For doctorate, thesis/dissertation. *Entrance requirements:* For master's, GRE, minimum GPA of 3.0, 3 letters of recommendation. Additional exam requirements/recommendations for international students: Required—TOEFL (minimum score 520 paper-based; 190 computer-based).

University of Connecticut, Graduate School, College of Liberal Arts and Sciences, Department of Molecular and Cell Biology, Field of Applied Genomics, Storrs, CT 06269. Offers MS, PSM. *Students:* 18 full-time (14 women), 16 part-time (14 women); includes 5 minority (2 African Americans, 2 Asian Americans or Pacific Islanders, 1 Hispanic American), 1 international. Average age 29. 22 applicants, 41% accepted, 3 enrolled. In 2009, 11 master's awarded. *Degree requirements:* For master's, comprehensive exam. *Entrance requirements:* For master's, GRE General Test, GRE Subject Test. Additional exam requirements/recommendations for international students: Required—TOEFL (minimum score 550 paper-based; 213 computer-based). *Application deadline:* For fall admission, 2/1 priority date for domestic and international students; for spring admission, 11/1 for domestic students, 10/1 for international students. Applications are processed on a rolling basis. Application fee: $55. Electronic applications accepted. *Expenses:* Tuition, state resident: full-time $4725; part-time $525 per credit. Tuition, nonresident: full-time $12,267; part-time $1363 per credit. Required fees: $346 per semester. Tuition and fees vary according to course load. *Financial support:* In 2009–10, 1 research assistantship with full tuition reimbursement, 2 teaching assistantships with full tuition reimbursements were awarded; fellowships, Federal Work-Study, scholarships/grants, health care benefits, and unspecified assistantships also available. Financial award application deadline: 2/1; financial award applicants required to submit FAFSA. *Unit head:* David Benson, Head, 860-486-4258, Fax: 860-486-4331, E-mail: david.benson@uconn.edu. *Application contact:* Anne St. Onje, Graduate Coordinator, 860-486-4314, Fax: 860-486-3943, E-mail: anne.st_onje@uconn.edu.

University of Florida, College of Medicine, Department of Physiology and Functional Genomics, Gainesville, FL 32611. Offers PhD. *Degree requirements:* For doctorate, thesis/dissertation. *Entrance requirements:* For doctorate, GRE General Test, minimum GPA of 3.0. Additional exam requirements/recommendations for international students: Required—TOEFL. Electronic applications accepted. *Faculty research:* Cell and general endocrinology, neuroendocrinology, neurophysiology, respiration, membrane transport and ion channels.

University of Maryland, Baltimore, School of Medicine, Department of Epidemiology and Preventive Medicine, Baltimore, MD 21201. Offers biostatistics (MS); clinical research (MS); epidemiology (PhD); epidemiology and preventive medicine (MPH, MS); gerontology (PhD); human genetics and genomic (MS, PhD); molecular epidemiology (PhD); toxicology (MS, PhD); JD/MS; MD/PhD; MS/PhD. *Accreditation:* CEPH. Part-time programs available. *Students:* 64 full-time (42 women), 60 part-time (40 women); includes 40 minority (17 African Americans, 19 Asian Americans or Pacific Islanders, 4 Hispanic Americans), 16 international. Average age 31. 207 applicants, 48% accepted, 50 enrolled. In 2009, 24 master's, 9 doctorates awarded. *Entrance requirements:* For master's and doctorate, GRE General Test, minimum GPA of 3.0. Additional exam requirements/recommendations for international students: Required—TOEFL; Recommended—IELTS. *Application deadline:* For fall admission, 1/15 for domestic and international students. Application fee: $50. Electronic applications accepted. *Expenses:* Tuition, state resident: full-time $7290; part-time $405 per credit hour. Tuition, nonresident: full-time $12,780; part-time $710 per credit hour. Required fees: $774; $10 per credit hour. $297 per semester. Tuition and fees vary according to course load, degree level and program. *Financial support:* In 2009–10, research assistantships with partial tuition reimbursements (averaging $25,000 per year); fellowships also available. Financial award application deadline: 3/1. *Unit head:* Dr. Patricia Langenberg, Program Director, 410-706-3251, Fax: 410-706-8013. *Application contact:* Rachael Holmes, Academic Coordinator, 410-706-8492, Fax: 410-706-4225, E-mail: rholmes@epi.umaryland.edu.

University of Pennsylvania, School of Medicine, Biomedical Graduate Studies, Graduate Group in Genomics and Computational Biology, Philadelphia, PA 19104. Offers PhD, MD/PhD, VMD/PhD. *Faculty:* 57. *Students:* 35 full-time (8 women); includes 11 minority (2 African Americans, 7 Asian Americans or Pacific Islanders, 2 Hispanic Americans), 9 international. 54 applicants, 19% accepted, 6 enrolled. In 2009, 5 doctorates awarded. *Degree requirements:* For doctorate, thesis/dissertation optional. *Entrance requirements:* For doctorate, GRE. Additional exam requirements/recommendations for international students: Required—TOEFL. *Application deadline:* For fall admission, 12/8 priority date for domestic and international students. Applications are processed on a rolling basis. Application fee: $70. Electronic applications accepted. *Expenses:* Tuition: Full-time $25,660; part-time $4758 per course. Required fees: $2152; $270 per course. Tuition and fees vary according to course load, degree level and program. *Financial support:* In 2009–10, 19 students received support; fellowships, research assistantships, scholarships/grants, traineeships, and unspecified assistantships available. *Unit head:* Dr. Maja Bucan, Chairperson, 215-898-0020. *Application contact:* Hannah Chervitz, Graduate Coordinator, 215-746-2807, E-mail: gcbcoord@pcbi.upenn.edu.

The University of Tennessee, Graduate School, College of Arts and Sciences, Program in Life Sciences, Knoxville, TN 37996. Offers genome science and technology (MS, PhD); plant physiology and genetics (MS, PhD). *Degree requirements:* For doctorate, one foreign language, thesis/dissertation. *Entrance requirements:* For master's and doctorate, GRE General Test, minimum GPA of 2.7. Additional exam requirements/recommendations for international students: Required—TOEFL. Electronic applications accepted. *Expenses:* Tuition, state resident: full-time $6826; part-time $380 per semester hour. Tuition, nonresident: full-time $21,844; part-time $1147 per semester hour. Tuition and fees vary according to program.

The University of Tennessee–Oak Ridge National Laboratory Graduate School of Genome Science and Technology, Graduate Program, Oak Ridge, TN 37830-8026. Offers life sciences (MS, PhD). *Degree requirements:* For master's, thesis; for doctorate, comprehensive exam, thesis/dissertation. *Entrance requirements:* For master's and doctorate, GRE General Test. Additional exam requirements/recommendations for international students: Required—TOEFL (minimum score 550 paper-based; 213 computer-based). Electronic applications accepted. *Faculty research:* Genetics/genomics, structural biology/proteomics, computational biology/bioinformatics, bioanalytical technologies.

The University of Toledo, College of Graduate Studies, College of Medicine, Biomedical Science Programs, Program in Bioinformatics and Proteomics/Genomics, Toledo, OH 43606-3390. Offers MSBS, Certificate, MD/MSBS. Part-time programs available. *Degree requirements:* For master's, thesis, qualifying exam. *Entrance requirements:* For master's, GRE General Test, minimum Undergraduate GPA of 3.0.

University of Washington, Graduate School, School of Medicine and Graduate School, Graduate Programs in Medicine, Department of Genome Sciences, Seattle, WA 98195. Offers PhD. *Degree requirements:* For doctorate, thesis/dissertation, general exam. *Entrance requirements:* For doctorate, GRE General Test, minimum GPA of 3.0. Additional exam requirements/recommendations for international students: Required—TOEFL. Electronic applications accepted. *Faculty research:* Model organism genetics, human and medical genetics, genomics and proteomics, computational biology.

Wake Forest University, School of Medicine and Graduate School of Arts and Sciences, Graduate Programs in Medicine, Molecular Genetics and Genomics Program, Winston-Salem, NC 27109. Offers PhD, MD/PhD. *Degree requirements:* For doctorate, thesis/dissertation. *Entrance requirements:* For doctorate, GRE General Test. Additional exam requirements/recommendations for international students: Required—TOEFL. Electronic applications accepted. *Faculty research:* Control of gene expression, molecular pathogenesis, protein biosynthesis, cell development, clinical cytogenetics.

Wesleyan University, Graduate Programs, Department of Biology, Middletown, CT 06459. Offers animal behavior (PhD); bioformatics/genomics (PhD); cell biology (PhD); developmental biology (PhD); evolution/ecology (PhD); genetics (PhD); neurobiology (PhD); population biology (PhD). *Faculty:* 13 full-time (4 women). *Students:* 23 full-time (11 women); includes 1 minority (African American), 3 international. Average age 26. 29 applicants, 10% accepted, 2 enrolled. In 2009, 3 doctorates awarded. *Degree requirements:* For doctorate, variable foreign language requirement, thesis/dissertation. *Entrance requirements:* For doctorate, GRE. Additional exam requirements/recommendations for international students: Required—TOEFL. *Application deadline:* For fall admission, 1/15 for domestic and international students. Applications are processed on a rolling basis. Application fee: $0. *Financial support:* In 2009–10, 3 research assistantships with full tuition reimbursements, 19 teaching assistantships with full tuition reimbursements were awarded; stipends also available. Financial award application deadline: 4/15; financial award applicants required to submit FAFSA. *Faculty research:* Microbial population genetics, genetic basis of evolutionary adaptation, genetic regulation of differentiation and pattern formation in *drosophila*. *Unit head:* Dr. Sonia E. Sultan, Chair/Professor, 860-685-3493, E-mail: jnaegele@wesleyan.edu. *Application contact:* Marjorie Fitzgibbons, Information Contact, 860-685-2140, E-mail: mfitzgibbons@wesleyan.edu.

West Virginia University, Eberly College of Arts and Sciences, Department of Biology, Morgantown, WV 26506. Offers cell and molecular biology (MS, PhD); environmental and evolutionary biology (MS, PhD); forensic biology (MS, PhD); genomic biology (MS, PhD); neurobiology (MS, PhD). Terminal master's awarded for partial completion of doctoral program. *Degree requirements:* For master's, thesis, final exam; for doctorate, thesis/dissertation, preliminary and final exams. *Entrance requirements:* For master's, GRE General Test, GRE Subject Test, minimum GPA of 3.0; for doctorate, GRE General Test, minimum GPA of 3.0. Additional exam requirements/recommendations for international students: Required—TOEFL. *Faculty research:* Environmental biology, genetic engineering, developmental biology, global change, biodiversity.

Yale University, School of Medicine and Graduate School of Arts and Sciences, Combined Program in Biological and Biomedical Sciences (BBS), Computational Biology and Bioinformatics Track, New Haven, CT 06520. Offers PhD, MD/PhD. *Students:* 3 full-time. *Entrance requirements:* Additional exam requirements/recommendations for international students: Required—TOEFL. *Application deadline:* For fall admission, 12/6 for domestic and international students. *Unit head:* Dr. Perry Miller, Director of Graduate Studies, 203-737-2903. *Application contact:* Lisa Sobel, Graduate Registrar, 203-737-6029.

Human Genetics

Baylor College of Medicine, Graduate School of Biomedical Sciences, Department of Molecular and Human Genetics, Houston, TX 77030-3498. Offers PhD, MD/PhD. *Faculty:* 68 full-time (16 women). *Students:* 78 full-time (46 women); includes 5 minority (2 African Americans, 1 Asian American or Pacific Islander, 2 Hispanic Americans), 39 international. Average age 24. In 2009, 11 doctorates awarded. *Degree requirements:* For doctorate, thesis/dissertation, public defense. *Entrance requirements:* For doctorate, GRE General Test, GRE Subject Test (strongly recommended), minimum GPA of 3.0. Additional exam requirements/recommendations for international students: Required—TOEFL. *Application deadline:* For fall admission, 1/1 priority date for domestic students. Application fee: $0. Electronic applications accepted. *Financial support:* Fellowships, research assistantships, career-related internships or fieldwork, Federal Work-Study, institutionally sponsored loans, health care benefits, and students receive a scholarship unless there are grant funds available to pay tuition available. Financial award applicants required to submit FAFSA. *Faculty research:* Cytogenetics, biochemical genetics, somatic cell genetics, gene therapy. *Unit head:* Dr. Gad Shaulsky, Director, 713-798-5056. *Application contact:* Judi Coleman, Graduate Program Administrator, 713-798-5056, Fax: 713-798-8597, E-mail: genetics-gradprm@bcm.edu.

See Close-Up on page 313.

Baylor College of Medicine, Graduate School of Biomedical Sciences, Interdepartmental Program in Cell and Molecular Biology, Houston, TX 77030-3498. Offers biochemistry (PhD); cell and molecular biology (PhD); genetics (PhD); human genetics (PhD); immunology (PhD); microbiology (PhD); virology (PhD); MD/PhD. *Faculty:* 100 full-time (31 women). *Students:* 59 full-time (37 women); includes 24 minority (5 African Americans, 1 American Indian/Alaska Native, 7 Asian Americans or Pacific Islanders, 11 Hispanic Americans), 6 international. Average age 25. In 2009, 9 doctorates awarded. *Degree requirements:* For doctorate, thesis/dissertation, public defense. *Entrance requirements:* For doctorate, GRE General Test, GRE Subject Test (strongly recommended), minimum GPA of 3.0. Additional exam requirements/recommendations for international students: Required—TOEFL. *Application deadline:* For fall admission, 1/1 priority date for domestic students. Applications are processed on a rolling basis. Application fee: $0. Electronic applications accepted. *Financial support:* In 2009–10, 59 students received support; fellowships, research assistantships, teaching assistantships, Federal Work-Study, institutionally sponsored loans, health care benefits, and tuition waivers (full) available. Financial award applicants required to submit FAFSA. *Faculty research:* Gene expression and regulation, developmental biology and genetics, signal transduction and membrane biology, aging process, molecular virology. *Unit head:* Dr. Susan Marriott, Director, 713-798-6557. *Application contact:* Lourdes Fernandez, Graduate Program Administrator, 713-798-6557, Fax: 713-798-6325, E-mail: cmbprog@bcm.edu.

See Close-Up on page 231.

Case Western Reserve University, School of Medicine and School of Graduate Studies, Graduate Programs in Medicine, Department of Genetics, Program in Human, Molecular, and Developmental Genetics and Genomics, Cleveland, OH 44106. Offers PhD, MD/PhD. *Degree requirements:* For doctorate, comprehensive exam, thesis/dissertation. *Entrance requirements:* For doctorate, GRE General Test, GRE Subject Test. Additional exam requirements/recommendations for international students: Required—TOEFL. *Faculty research:* Regulation of gene expression, molecular control of development, genomics.

The Johns Hopkins University, School of Medicine, Graduate Programs in Medicine, Predoctoral Training Program in Human Genetics, Baltimore, MD 21218-2699. Offers PhD, MD/PhD. *Faculty:* 59 full-time (14 women). *Students:* 77 full-time (55 women); includes 28 minority (7 African Americans, 15 Asian Americans or Pacific Islanders, 6 Hispanic Americans), 17 international. Average age 24. 172 applicants, 11% accepted, 10 enrolled. In 2009, 9 doctorates awarded. Terminal master's awarded for partial completion of doctoral program. *Degree requirements:* For doctorate, comprehensive exam, thesis/dissertation. *Entrance requirements:* For doctorate, GRE General Test, GRE Subject Test. *Application deadline:* For fall admission, 12/31 priority date for domestic and international students. Application fee: $85.

Electronic applications accepted. *Financial support:* In 2009–10, 1 fellowship with full tuition reimbursement (averaging $26,855 per year) was awarded; teaching assistantships with full tuition reimbursements, health care benefits also available. *Faculty research:* Human, mammalian, and molecular genetics, bioinformatics, genomics. *Unit head:* Dr. David Valle, Director, 410-955-4260, Fax: 410-955-7397, E-mail: muscelli@jhmi.edu. *Application contact:* Sandy Muscelli, Program Administrator, 410-955-4260, Fax: 410-955-7397, E-mail: muscelli@jhmi.edu.

Louisiana State University Health Sciences Center, School of Graduate Studies in New Orleans, Department of Human Genetics, New Orleans, LA 70112-2223. Offers MS, PhD, MD/PhD. Part-time programs available. Terminal master's awarded for partial completion of doctoral program. *Degree requirements:* For master's, comprehensive exam, thesis; for doctorate, comprehensive exam, thesis/dissertation. *Entrance requirements:* For master's and doctorate, GRE General Test. Additional exam requirements/recommendations for international students: Required—TOEFL. *Faculty research:* Genetic epidemiology, segregation and linkage analysis, gene mapping.

McGill University, Faculty of Graduate and Postdoctoral Studies, Faculty of Medicine, Department of Human Genetics, Montréal, QC H3A 2T5, Canada. Offers genetic counseling (M Sc); human genetics (M Sc, PhD).

Memorial University of Newfoundland, Faculty of Medicine and School of Graduate Studies, Graduate Programs in Medicine, Division of Human Genetics, St. John's, NL A1C 5S7, Canada. Offers M Sc, PhD, MD/PhD. Part-time programs available. *Degree requirements:* For master's, thesis; for doctorate, comprehensive exam, thesis/dissertation, oral defense of thesis. *Entrance requirements:* For master's, MD or B Sc; for doctorate, MD or M Sc. Additional exam requirements/recommendations for international students: Required—TOEFL. *Faculty research:* Cancer genetics, gene mapping, medical genetics, birth defects, population genetics.

Sarah Lawrence College, Graduate Studies, Joan H. Marks Graduate Program in Human Genetics, Bronxville, NY 10708-5999. Offers MS. Part-time programs available. *Faculty:* 21 part-time/adjunct (16 women). *Students:* 41 full-time (40 women), 5 part-time (all women); includes 5 minority (3 Asian Americans or Pacific Islanders, 2 Hispanic Americans), 13 international. 137 applicants, 30% accepted, 24 enrolled. In 2009, 16 master's awarded. *Degree requirements:* For master's, thesis, fieldwork. *Entrance requirements:* For master's, previous course work in biology, chemistry, developmental biology, genetics, probability and statistics. *Application deadline:* For fall admission, 1/15 for domestic students. Application fee: $60. *Expenses:* Contact institution. *Financial support:* In 2009–10, 26 students received support, including 38 fellowships; career-related internships or fieldwork, Federal Work-Study, scholarships/grants, and unspecified assistantships also available. Support available to part-time students. Financial award application deadline: 3/1; financial award applicants required to submit CSS PROFILE or FAFSA. *Unit head:* Caroline Lieber, Director, 914-395-2371. *Application contact:* Susan Guma, Dean of Graduate Studies, 914-395-2373, E-mail: sguma@mail.slc.edu.

Tulane University, School of Medicine and School of Liberal Arts, Graduate Programs in Biomedical Sciences, Program in Human Genetics, New Orleans, LA 70118-5669. Offers MBS, PhD, MD/PhD. MS and PhD offered through the Graduate School. *Degree requirements:* For master's, thesis; for doctorate, thesis/dissertation. *Entrance requirements:* For master's, GRE, MCAT; for doctorate, GRE General Test. Additional exam requirements/recommendations for international students: Required—TOEFL. Electronic applications accepted. *Faculty research:* Inborn errors of metabolism, DNA methylation, gene therapy.

University of California, Los Angeles, David Geffen School of Medicine and Graduate Division, Graduate Programs in Medicine, Department of Human Genetics, Los Angeles, CA 90095. Offers MS, PhD. *Entrance requirements:* For master's and doctorate, GRE General Test.

University of California, Los Angeles, Graduate Division, College of Letters and Science and David Geffen School of Medicine, UCLA ACCESS to Programs in the Molecular, Cellular and Integrative Life Sciences, Los Angeles, CA 90095. Offers biochemistry and molecular biology (PhD); biological chemistry (PhD); cellular and molecular pathology (PhD); human genetics (PhD); microbiology, immunology, and molecular genetics (PhD); molecular biology (PhD); molecular toxicology (PhD); molecular, cellular and integrative physiology (PhD); neurobiology (PhD); oral biology (PhD); physiology (PhD). ACCESS is an umbrella program for first-year coursework in 12 PhD programs. *Students:* 39 full-time (25 women); includes 14 minority (1 African American, 1 American Indian/Alaska Native, 8 Asian Americans or Pacific Islanders, 4 Hispanic Americans), 10 international. Average age 25. 437 applicants, 22% accepted, 30 enrolled. *Degree requirements:* For doctorate, thesis/dissertation, oral and written qualifying exams. *Entrance requirements:* For doctorate, GRE General Test, minimum undergraduate GPA of 3.0. Additional exam requirements/recommendations for international students: Required—TOEFL. *Application deadline:* For fall admission, 12/15 for domestic and international students. Application fee: $70 ($90 for international students). Electronic applications accepted. *Financial support:* In 2009–10, 56 fellowships with full and partial tuition reimbursements, 16 research assistantships with full and partial tuition reimbursements were awarded; teaching assistantships with full and partial tuition reimbursements, Federal Work-Study, institutionally sponsored loans, scholarships/grants, health care benefits, tuition waivers (full and partial), and unspecified assistantships also available. Financial award application deadline: 3/1; financial award applicants required to submit FAFSA. *Faculty research:* Molecular, cellular, and developmental biology; immunology; microbiology; integrative biology. *Unit head:* Dr. Greg I. Payne, Chair, 310-206-3121. *Application contact:* Coordinator, 310-206-3121, Fax: 310-206-5280, E-mail: uclaaccess@mednet.ucla.edu.

See Close-Up on page 239.

University of Chicago, Division of the Biological Sciences, Department of Human Genetics, Chicago, IL 60637-1513. Offers PhD. *Faculty:* 19 full-time (11 women). *Students:* 27 full-time (16 women); includes 5 minority (1 African American, 4 Asian Americans or Pacific Islanders). Average age 28. 42 applicants, 10% accepted, 4 enrolled. In 2009, 5 doctorates awarded. *Degree requirements:* For doctorate, thesis/dissertation, ethics class, 2 teaching assistantships. *Entrance requirements:* For doctorate, GRE General Test. Additional exam requirements/recommendations for international students: Required—TOEFL (minimum score 600 paper-based; 250 computer-based; 104 iBT), IELTS (minimum score 7). *Application deadline:* For fall admission, 12/1 priority date for domestic and international students. Application fee: $55. Electronic applications accepted. *Financial support:* In 2009–10, 27 students received support, including fellowships with tuition reimbursements available (averaging $29,781 per year), research assistantships with tuition reimbursements available (averaging $29,781 per year); institutionally sponsored loans, scholarships/grants, traineeships, and health care benefits also available. Financial award applicants required to submit FAFSA. *Unit head:* Dr. Carole Ober, Chair, 773-834-0735, Fax: 773-834-0505. *Application contact:* Justin Shelton, Graduate Administrative Director, 773-834-8073, Fax: 773-702-3172, E-mail: jshelton@bsd.uchicago.edu.

University of Chicago, Division of the Biological Sciences, Department of Molecular Biosciences, Chicago, IL 60637-1513. Offers biochemistry and molecular biology (PhD); cell and molecular biology (PhD); developmental biology (PhD), including cellular differentiation, developmental endocrinology, developmental genetics, developmental neurobiology, gene expression; genetics, genomics and systems biology (PhD); human genetics (PhD); MD/PhD. *Faculty:* 92 full-time (23 women). *Students:* 127 full-time (64 women); includes 30 minority (3 African Americans, 2 American Indian/Alaska Native, 20 Asian Americans or Pacific Islanders, 5 Hispanic Americans). Average age 28. 234 applicants, 24% accepted, 16 enrolled. In 2009, 21 doctorates awarded. *Degree requirements:* For doctorate, thesis/dissertation, ethics class, 2 teaching assistantships. *Entrance requirements:* For doctorate, GRE General Test. Additional exam requirements/recommendations for international students: Required—TOEFL (minimum score 600 paper-based; 250 computer-based; 104 iBT), IELTS (minimum score 7). *Application*

deadline: For fall admission, 12/1 priority date for domestic and international students. Application fee: $55. Electronic applications accepted. *Financial support:* In 2009–10, 127 students received support, including fellowships with tuition reimbursements available (averaging $29,781 per year), research assistantships with tuition reimbursements available (averaging $29,781 per year); institutionally sponsored loans, scholarships/grants, traineeships, and health care benefits also available. Financial award applicants required to submit FAFSA. *Unit head:* Graduate Administrative Director. *Application contact:* Kristine Gaston, 773-702-8037, Fax: 773-702-3172, E-mail: kristine@bsd.uchicago.edu.

University of Manitoba, Faculty of Medicine and Faculty of Graduate Studies, Graduate Programs in Medicine, Department of Biochemistry and Medical Genetics, Winnipeg, MB R3T 2N2, Canada. Offers M Sc, PhD. Terminal master's awarded for partial completion of doctoral program. *Degree requirements:* For master's, thesis; for doctorate, thesis/dissertation. *Faculty research:* Cancer, gene expression, membrane lipids, metabolic control, genetic diseases.

University of Maryland, Baltimore, School of Medicine, Department of Epidemiology and Preventive Medicine, Baltimore, MD 21201. Offers biostatistics (MS); clinical research (MS); epidemiology (PhD); epidemiology and preventive medicine (MPH, MS); gerontology (PhD); human genetics and genomic (MS, PhD); molecular epidemiology (PhD); toxicology (MS, PhD); JD/MS; MD/PhD; MS/PhD. *Accreditation:* CEPH. Part-time programs available. *Students:* 64 full-time (42 women), 60 part-time (40 women); includes 40 minority (17 African Americans, 19 Asian Americans or Pacific Islanders, 4 Hispanic Americans), 16 international. Average age 31. 207 applicants, 48% accepted, 50 enrolled. In 2009, 24 master's, 9 doctorates awarded. *Entrance requirements:* For master's and doctorate, GRE General Test, minimum GPA of 3.0. Additional exam requirements/recommendations for international students: Required—TOEFL; Recommended—IELTS. *Application deadline:* For fall admission, 1/15 for domestic and international students. Application fee: $50. Electronic applications accepted. *Expenses:* Tuition, state resident: full-time $7290; part-time $405 per credit hour. Tuition, nonresident: full-time $12,780; part-time $710 per credit hour. Required fees: $774; $10 per credit hour. $297 per semester. Tuition and fees vary according to course load, degree level and program. *Financial support:* In 2009–10, research assistantships with partial tuition reimbursements (averaging $25,000 per year); fellowships also available. Financial award application deadline: 3/1. *Unit head:* Dr. Patricia Langenberg, Program Director, 410-706-3251, Fax: 410-706-8013. *Application contact:* Rachael Holmes, Academic Coordinator, 410-706-8492, Fax: 410-706-4225, E-mail: rholmes@epi.umaryland.edu.

University of Michigan, Horace H. Rackham School of Graduate Studies, Program in Biomedical Sciences (PIBS), Department of Human Genetics, Ann Arbor, MI 48109. Offers human genetics (MS, PhD), including genetic counseling (PhD). Part-time programs available. Terminal master's awarded for partial completion of doctoral program. *Degree requirements:* For master's, research project; for doctorate, thesis/dissertation, oral defense of dissertation, oral preliminary exam. *Entrance requirements:* For master's, GRE General Test, 3 letters of recommendation; for doctorate, GRE General Test, GRE Subject Test (biology, biochemistry recommended), 3 letters of recommendation. Additional exam requirements/recommendations for international students: Required—TOEFL (minimum score 84 iBT). Electronic applications accepted. *Expenses:* Tuition, state resident: full-time $17,286; part-time $1099 per credit hour. Tuition, nonresident: full-time $34,944; part-time $2080 per credit hour. Required fees: $95 per semester. Tuition and fees vary according to course load, degree level and program. *Faculty research:* Molecular, developmental, statistical, and population genetics.

University of Pittsburgh, Graduate School of Public Health, Department of Human Genetics, Pittsburgh, PA 15260. Offers genetic counseling (MS); human genetics (MS, PhD); public health genetics (MPH, Certificate). *Faculty:* 9 full-time (5 women), 5 part-time/adjunct (2 women). *Students:* 37 full-time (26 women), 15 part-time (12 women); includes 9 minority (3 African Americans, 5 Asian Americans or Pacific Islanders, 1 Hispanic American), 23 international. Average age 30. 69 applicants, 65% accepted, 18 enrolled. In 2009, 5 master's, 7 doctorates awarded. Terminal master's awarded for partial completion of doctoral program. *Degree requirements:* For master's, thesis (for some programs); for doctorate, thesis/dissertation. *Entrance requirements:* For master's, GRE General Test, previous course work in biochemistry, calculus, and genetics; for doctorate, GRE General Test. Additional exam requirements/recommendations for international students: Required—TOEFL (minimum score 550 paper-based; 213 computer-based; 80 iBT). *Application deadline:* For fall admission, 4/1 for international students; for winter admission, 9/1 for international students; for spring admission, 2/1 for international students. Applications are processed on a rolling basis. Application fee: $95. Electronic applications accepted. *Expenses:* Tuition, state resident: full-time $16,402; part-time $665 per credit. Tuition, nonresident: full-time $28,694; part-time $1175 per credit. Required fees: $690; $175 per term. Tuition and fees vary according to program. *Financial support:* In 2009–10, 18 students received support, including 18 research assistantships with full tuition reimbursements available (averaging $31,140 per year). *Faculty research:* Genetic mechanisms related to the transition from normal to disease states, how genes and the environment interact to affect the distribution of health and disease in human populations. Total annual research expenditures: $4 million. *Unit head:* Dr. Mohammad Kamboh, Chairman, 412-624-3066, Fax: 412-624-3020, E-mail: kamboh@pitt.edu. *Application contact:* Jeanette Norbut, Administrative Secretary, 412-624-3018, Fax: 412-624-3020, E-mail: jeanette.norbut@hgen.pitt.edu.

The University of Texas Health Science Center at Houston, Graduate School of Biomedical Sciences, Program in Human and Molecular Genetics, Houston, TX 77225-0036. Offers MS, PhD, MD/PhD. Terminal master's awarded for partial completion of doctoral program. *Degree requirements:* For master's, thesis; for doctorate, thesis/dissertation. *Entrance requirements:* For master's and doctorate, GRE General Test. Additional exam requirements/recommendations for international students: Required—TOEFL. Electronic applications accepted. *Faculty research:* Computational genomics, cancer genetics, complex disease genetics, medical genetics.

University of Utah, School of Medicine and Graduate School, Graduate Programs in Medicine, Department of Human Genetics, Salt Lake City, UT 84112-1107. Offers MS, PhD. Terminal master's awarded for partial completion of doctoral program. *Degree requirements:* For master's, comprehensive exam, thesis optional; for doctorate, comprehensive exam, thesis/dissertation. Electronic applications accepted. *Expenses:* Tuition, state resident: full-time $4004; part-time $1674 per semester. Tuition, nonresident: full-time $14,134; part-time $5915 per semester. Required fees: $324 per semester. Tuition and fees vary according to course load, degree level and program. *Faculty research:* RNA metabolism, drosophilia genetics, mouse genetics, protein synthesis.

Vanderbilt University, Graduate School, Program in Human Genetics, Nashville, TN 37240-1001. Offers PhD, MD/PhD. *Faculty:* 43 full-time (15 women). *Students:* 17 full-time (9 women), 1 (woman) part-time; includes 2 minority (1 African American, 1 American Indian/Alaska Native), 4 international. Average age 28. In 2009, 3 doctorates awarded. *Degree requirements:* For doctorate, comprehensive exam, thesis/dissertation. *Entrance requirements:* For doctorate, GRE General Test. Additional exam requirements/recommendations for international students: Required—TOEFL (minimum score 570 paper-based; 230 computer-based; 88 iBT). *Application deadline:* For fall admission, 1/15 for domestic and international students. Application fee: $0. Electronic applications accepted. *Financial support:* Fellowships with full and partial tuition reimbursements, research assistantships with full and partial tuition reimbursements, Federal Work-Study, institutionally sponsored loans, traineeships, and health care benefits available. Financial award application deadline: 1/15; financial award applicants required to submit CSS PROFILE or FAFSA. *Faculty research:* Disease gene discovery, computational genomics, translational genetics. *Unit head:* Roger G. Chalkley, Senior Associate Dean, Vanderbilt School of Medicine, 615-343-7290, Fax: 615-343-0749, E-mail: roger.g.chalkley@vanderbilt.edu. *Application contact:* Scott Williams, Director of Graduate Studies, 615-343-8555, Fax: 615-343-8619, E-mail: scott.m.williams@vanderbilt.edu.

Virginia Commonwealth University, Medical College of Virginia-Professional Programs, School of Medicine, School of Medicine Graduate Programs, Department of Human and Molecular Genetics, Richmond, VA 23284-9005. Offers genetic counseling (MS); human genetics

Human Genetics

Virginia Commonwealth University (continued)
(PhD); molecular biology and genetics (MS, PhD); MD/PhD. *Degree requirements:* For master's, thesis; for doctorate, thesis/dissertation, comprehensive oral and written exams. *Entrance requirements:* For master's, DAT, GRE General Test, or MCAT; for doctorate, GRE General Test, DAT, MCAT. *Faculty research:* Genetic epidemiology, biochemical genetics, quantitative genetics, human cytogenetics, molecular genetics.

Virginia Commonwealth University, Program in Pre-Medical Basic Health Sciences, Richmond, VA 23284-9005. Offers anatomy (CBHS); biochemistry (CBHS); human genetics (CBHS); microbiology (CBHS); pharmacology (CBHS); physiology (CBHS). *Entrance requirements:* For degree, GRE or MCAT, course work in organic chemistry, minimum undergraduate GPA of 2.8. Additional exam requirements/recommendations for international students: Required—TOEFL (minimum score 600 paper-based).

Wake Forest University, School of Medicine and Graduate School of Arts and Sciences, Graduate Programs in Medicine, Molecular Genetics and Genomics Program, Winston-Salem, NC 27109. Offers PhD, MD/PhD. *Degree requirements:* For doctorate, thesis/dissertation. *Entrance requirements:* For doctorate, GRE General Test. Additional exam requirements/recommendations for international students: Required—TOEFL. Electronic applications accepted. *Faculty research:* Control of gene expression, molecular pathogenesis, protein biosynthesis, cell development, clinical cytogenetics.

West Virginia University, Davis College of Agriculture, Forestry and Consumer Sciences, Interdisciplinary Program in Genetics and Developmental Biology, Morgantown, WV 26506. Offers animal breeding (MS, PhD); biochemical and molecular genetics (MS, PhD); cytogenetics (MS, PhD); descriptive embryology (MS, PhD); developmental genetics (MS); experimental morphogenesis/teratology (MS); human genetics (MS, PhD); immunogenetics (MS, PhD); life cycles of animals and plants (MS, PhD); molecular aspects of development (MS, PhD); mutagenesis (MS, PhD); oncology (MS, PhD); plant genetics (MS, PhD); population and quantitative genetics (MS, PhD); regeneration (MS, PhD); teratology (PhD); toxicology (MS, PhD). *Degree requirements:* For master's, thesis; for doctorate, comprehensive exam, thesis/dissertation. *Entrance requirements:* For master's, GRE or MCAT, minimum GPA of 2.75. Additional exam requirements/recommendations for international students: Required—TOEFL.

Molecular Genetics

Albert Einstein College of Medicine, Sue Golding Graduate Division of Medical Sciences, Division of Biological Sciences, Department of Genetics, Bronx, NY 10461. Offers computational genetics (PhD); molecular genetics (PhD); translational genetics (PhD); MD/PhD. *Degree requirements:* For doctorate, thesis/dissertation. *Entrance requirements:* For doctorate, GRE General Test. Additional exam requirements/recommendations for international students: Required—TOEFL. *Faculty research:* Neurologic genetics in *Drosophila*, biochemical genetics of yeast, developmental genetics in the mouse.

Duke University, Graduate School, Department of Molecular Genetics and Microbiology, Durham, NC 27710. Offers PhD. *Faculty:* 25 full-time. *Students:* 39 full-time (24 women); includes 6 minority (4 African Americans, 2 Asian Americans or Pacific Islanders), 11 international. Average age 22. 69 applicants, 26% accepted, 9 enrolled. In 2009, 4 doctorates awarded. *Degree requirements:* For doctorate, thesis/dissertation. *Entrance requirements:* For doctorate, GRE General Test, GRE Subject Test (recommended). Additional exam requirements/recommendations for international students: Required—TOEFL (minimum score 550 paper-based; 213 computer-based; 83 iBT), IELTS (minimum score 7). *Application deadline:* For fall admission, 12/8 priority date for domestic and international students. Application fee: $75. Electronic applications accepted. *Financial support:* In 2009–10, fellowships with full tuition reimbursements (averaging $19,350 per year), research assistantships with full tuition reimbursements (averaging $19,350 per year) were awarded; Federal Work-Study also available. Financial award application deadline: 12/31. *Unit head:* Dr. Raphael Valdivia, Director of Graduate Studies, 919-684-3290, Fax: 919-684-6629, E-mail: andrea.lanahan@duke.edu. *Application contact:* Cynthia Robertson, Associate Dean for Enrollment Services, 919-684-3913, E-mail: grad-admissions@duke.edu.

Emory University, Graduate School of Arts and Sciences, Division of Biological and Biomedical Sciences, Program in Microbiology and Molecular Genetics, Atlanta, GA 30322-1100. Offers PhD. *Faculty:* 33 full-time (7 women). *Students:* 43 full-time (28 women); includes 7 minority (3 African Americans, 1 Asian American or Pacific Islander, 3 Hispanic Americans), 6 international. Average age 27. 78 applicants, 18% accepted, 5 enrolled. In 2009, 4 doctorates awarded. *Degree requirements:* For doctorate, comprehensive exam, thesis/dissertation. *Entrance requirements:* For doctorate, GRE General Test, minimum GPA of 3.0 in science course work (recommended). Additional exam requirements/recommendations for international students: Required—TOEFL. *Application deadline:* For fall admission, 1/3 for domestic and international students. Application fee: $50. Electronic applications accepted. *Financial support:* In 2009–10, 17 students received support, including 17 fellowships with full tuition reimbursements available (averaging $24,500 per year); institutionally sponsored loans, scholarships/grants, and health care benefits also available. *Faculty research:* Bacterial genetics and physiology, microbial development, molecular biology of viruses and bacterial pathogens, DNA recombination. *Unit head:* Dr. Phil Rather, Director, 404-728-5079, Fax: 404-728-7780, E-mail: prather@emory.edu. *Application contact:* Dr. Martin Moore, Recruiter, 404-727-8943, Fax: 404-727-3322, E-mail: martin.moore@emory.edu.

The George Washington University, Columbian College of Arts and Sciences, Institute for Biomedical Sciences, Program in Biochemistry and Molecular Genetics, Washington, DC 20052. Offers PhD. Part-time and evening/weekend programs available. *Students:* 3 full-time (all women), 4 part-time (2 women). Average age 29. 19 applicants, 68% accepted, 6 enrolled. In 2009, 1 doctorate awarded. Terminal master's awarded for partial completion of doctoral program. *Degree requirements:* For doctorate, thesis/dissertation, general exam. *Entrance requirements:* For doctorate, GRE General Test, interview, minimum GPA of 3.0. Additional exam requirements/recommendations for international students: Required—TOEFL (minimum score 600 paper-based; 250 computer-based). *Application deadline:* For fall admission, 1/2 priority date for domestic and international students; for spring admission, 10/1 priority date for domestic and international students. Applications are processed on a rolling basis. Application fee: $60. Electronic applications accepted. *Financial support:* In 2009–10, 4 students received support; fellowships, Federal Work-Study, institutionally sponsored loans, and tuition waivers available. Financial award application deadline: 2/1. *Unit head:* Valerie W. Hu, Director, 202-994-8431, E-mail: valhu@gwu.edu. *Application contact:* Information Contact, 202-994-7120, Fax: 202-994-6100, E-mail: genetics@gwu.edu.

Georgia State University, College of Arts and Sciences, Department of Biology, Program in Molecular Genetics and Biochemistry, Atlanta, GA 30302-3083. Offers MS, PhD. Part-time programs available. Terminal master's awarded for partial completion of doctoral program. *Degree requirements:* For master's, thesis or alternative; for doctorate, thesis/dissertation, exam. *Entrance requirements:* For master's and doctorate, GRE General Test. Additional exam requirements/recommendations for international students: Required—TOEFL. Electronic applications accepted.

Harvard University, Graduate School of Arts and Sciences, Division of Medical Sciences, Boston, MA 02115. Offers biological chemistry and molecular pharmacology (PhD); cell biology (PhD); genetics (PhD); microbiology and molecular genetics (PhD); pathology (PhD), including experimental pathology. *Degree requirements:* For doctorate, thesis/dissertation. *Entrance requirements:* For doctorate, GRE General Test, GRE Subject Test. Additional exam requirements/recommendations for international students: Required—TOEFL. *Expenses:* Tuition: Full-time $33,696. Required fees: $1126. Full-time tuition and fees vary according to program.

Illinois State University, Graduate School, College of Arts and Sciences, Department of Biological Sciences, Normal, IL 61790-2200. Offers animal behavior (MS); bacteriology (MS); biochemistry (MS); biological sciences (MS); biology (PhD); biophysics (MS); biotechnology (MS); botany (MS, PhD); cell biology (MS); conservation biology (MS); developmental biology (MS); ecology (MS, PhD); entomology (MS); evolutionary biology (MS); genetics (MS, PhD); immunology (MS); microbiology (MS, PhD); molecular biology (MS); molecular genetics (MS); neurobiology (MS); neuroscience (MS); parasitology (MS); physiology (MS, PhD); plant biology (MS); plant molecular biology (MS); plant sciences (MS); structural biology (MS); zoology (MS, PhD). Part-time programs available. *Degree requirements:* For master's, thesis or alternative; for doctorate, variable foreign language requirement, thesis/dissertation, 2 terms of residency. *Entrance requirements:* For master's, GRE General Test, minimum GPA of 2.6 in last 60 hours of course work; for doctorate, GRE General Test. *Faculty research:* Redoc balance and drug development in schistosoma mansoni, control of the growth of listeria monocytogenes at low temperature, regulation of cell expansion and microtubule function by SPRI, CRUI: physiology and fitness consequences of different life history phenotypes.

Indiana University–Purdue University Indianapolis, Indiana University School of Medicine, Department of Medical and Molecular Genetics, Indianapolis, IN 46202-2896. Offers genetic counseling (MS); medical and molecular genetics (MS, PhD); MD/MS; MD/PhD. Part-time programs available. *Faculty:* 8 full-time (2 women). *Students:* 25 full-time (17 women), 4 part-time (3 women); includes 2 minority (both Asian Americans or Pacific Islanders), 5 international. Average age 27. 78 applicants, 22% accepted, 13 enrolled. In 2009, 6 master's, 1 doctorate awarded. Terminal master's awarded for partial completion of doctoral program. *Degree requirements:* For master's, thesis optional; for doctorate, thesis/dissertation, research ethics. *Entrance requirements:* For master's and doctorate, GRE General Test, minimum GPA of 3.2. *Application deadline:* For fall admission, 1/15 priority date for domestic students. Application fee: $55 ($65 for international students). *Financial support:* In 2009–10, 11 students received support, including 2 fellowships with tuition reimbursements available (averaging $12,750 per year), 2 teaching assistantships (averaging $22,000 per year); research assistantships with tuition reimbursements available, Federal Work-Study and institutionally sponsored loans also available. Support available to part-time students. Financial award application deadline: 1/15. *Faculty research:* Twins, human gene mapping, chromosomes and malignancy, clinical genetics. Total annual research expenditures: $2.1 million. *Unit head:* Dr. Joe Christlan, Chairman, 317-274-2241. *Application contact:* Kathleen Wilhelm, Admissions Secretary, 317-274-2241, Fax: 317-274-2387, E-mail: medgen@iupui.edu.

Medical College of Wisconsin, Graduate School of Biomedical Sciences, Department of Microbiology and Molecular Genetics, Milwaukee, WI 53226-0509. Offers MS, PhD, MD/PhD. *Degree requirements:* For doctorate, comprehensive exam, thesis/dissertation. *Entrance requirements:* For doctorate, GRE General Test. Additional exam requirements/recommendations for international students: Required—TOEFL. *Faculty research:* Virology, immunology, bacterial toxins, regulation of gene expression.

Michigan State University, College of Human Medicine and The Graduate School, Graduate Programs in Human Medicine, East Lansing, MI 48824. Offers biochemistry and molecular biology (MS, PhD); epidemiology (MS, PhD); microbiology (MS); microbiology and molecular genetics (PhD); pharmacology and toxicology (MS, PhD); physiology (MS, PhD); public health (MPH). *Students:* 58 full-time (31 women), 31 part-time (25 women); includes 17 minority (7 African Americans, 1 American Indian/Alaska Native, 6 Asian Americans or Pacific Islanders, 3 Hispanic Americans), 22 international. Average age 30. In 2009, 8 master's, 9 doctorates awarded. *Entrance requirements:* Additional exam requirements/recommendations for international students: Required—TOEFL. *Expenses:* Tuition, state resident: part-time $478.25 per credit hour. Tuition, nonresident: part-time $966.50 per credit hour. Part-time tuition and fees vary according to program. *Financial support:* In 2009–10, 17 research assistantships with tuition reimbursements (averaging $7,053 per year), 3 teaching assistantships with tuition reimbursements (averaging $6,607 per year) were awarded. *Unit head:* Margo K. Smith, Director of Graduate Studies, 517-432-5112, E-mail: smithmk@msu.edu. *Application contact:* Margo K. Smith, Director of Graduate Studies, 517-432-5112, E-mail: smithmk@msu.edu.

Michigan State University, College of Osteopathic Medicine and The Graduate School, Graduate Studies in Osteopathic Medicine, East Lansing, MI 48824. Offers biochemistry and molecular biology (MS, PhD); microbiology (MS); microbiology and molecular genetics (PhD); pharmacology and toxicology (MS, PhD), including integrative pharmacology (MS), pharmacology and toxicology, pharmacology and toxicology-environmental toxicology (PhD); physiology (MS, PhD). *Students:* 6 full-time (1 woman), 39 part-time (22 women); includes 8 minority (2 African Americans, 2 Asian Americans or Pacific Islanders, 4 Hispanic Americans), 3 international. Average age 30. *Expenses:* Tuition, state resident: part-time $478.25 per credit hour. Tuition, nonresident: part-time $966.50 per credit hour. Part-time tuition and fees vary according to program. *Financial support:* In 2009–10, 1 research assistantship with tuition reimbursement (averaging $7,894 per year) was awarded. *Application contact:* Bethany Heinlen, Information Contact, 517-353-7785, Fax: 517-353-9004, E-mail: heinlen@msu.edu.

New York University, Graduate School of Arts and Science, Department of Biology, New York, NY 10012-1019. Offers biology (PhD); biomedical journalism (MS); cancer and molecular biology (PhD); computational biology (PhD); computers in biological research (MS); developmental genetics (PhD); general biology (MS); immunology and microbiology (PhD); molecular genetics (PhD); neurobiology (PhD); oral biology (MS); plant biology (PhD); recombinant DNA technology (MS); MS/MBA. Part-time programs available. *Faculty:* 24 full-time (5 women). *Students:* 142 full-time (79 women), 44 part-time (28 women); includes 34 minority (1 African American, 25 Asian Americans or Pacific Islanders, 8 Hispanic Americans), 82 international. Average age 27. 362 applicants, 71% accepted, 72 enrolled. In 2009, 43 master's, 9 doctorates awarded. Terminal master's awarded for partial completion of doctoral program. *Degree requirements:* For master's, thesis or alternative, qualifying paper; for doctorate, comprehensive exam, thesis/dissertation. *Entrance requirements:* For master's, GRE General Test; for doctorate, GRE General Test, GRE Subject Test. Additional exam requirements/recommendations for international students: Required—TOEFL. *Application deadline:* For fall admission, 12/12 priority date for domestic students. Application fee: $90. *Expenses:* Tuition: Full-time $30,528; part-time $1272 per credit. Required fees: $2177. *Financial support:* Fellowships with tuition reimbursements, research assistantships with tuition reimbursements, teaching assistantships with tuition reimbursements, career-related internships or fieldwork, Federal Work-Study, institutionally sponsored loans, scholarships/grants, health care benefits, and unspecified assistantships available. Financial award application deadline: 12/12; financial award applicants required to submit FAFSA. *Faculty research:* Genomics, molecular and cell biology, development and molecular genetics, molecular evolution of plants and animals. *Unit head:* Gloria Coruzzi,

Chair, 212-998-8200, Fax: 212-995-4015, E-mail: biology@nyu.edu. *Application contact:* Stephen Small, Director of Graduate Studies, 212-998-8200, Fax: 212-995-4015, E-mail: biology@nyu.edu.

The Ohio State University, Graduate School, College of Biological Sciences, Department of Molecular Genetics, Columbus, OH 43210. Offers cell and developmental biology (MS, PhD); genetics (MS, PhD); molecular biology (MS, PhD). *Faculty:* 26. *Students:* 8 full-time (5 women), 23 part-time (11 women), 17 international. Average age 27. In 2009, 11 doctorates awarded. *Degree requirements:* For master's, thesis; for doctorate, thesis/dissertation. *Entrance requirements:* For master's and doctorate, GRE General Test, GRE Subject Test in biology or biochemistry (recommended). Additional exam requirements/recommendations for international students: Required—TOEFL (minimum score 600 paper-based; 250 computer-based). *Application deadline:* For fall admission, 8/15 priority date for domestic students, 7/1 priority date for international students; for winter admission, 12/1 priority date for domestic students, 11/1 priority date for international students; for spring admission, 3/1 priority date for domestic students, 2/1 priority date for international students. Applications are processed on a rolling basis. Application fee: $40 ($50 for international students). Electronic applications accepted. *Expenses:* Tuition, state resident: full-time $10,683. Tuition, nonresident: full-time $25,923. Tuition and fees vary according to course load and program. *Financial support:* Fellowships, research assistantships, teaching assistantships, Federal Work-Study and institutionally sponsored loans available. Support available to part-time students. *Unit head:* Dr. Anna Hopper, Chair, 614-292-8084, Fax: 614-292-4466, E-mail: hopper.64@osu.edu. *Application contact:* 614-292-9444, Fax: 614-292-3895, E-mail: domestic.grad@osu.edu.

Oklahoma State University, College of Arts and Sciences, Department of Microbiology and Molecular Genetics, Stillwater, OK 74078. Offers MS, PhD. *Faculty:* 20 full-time (4 women), 1 (woman) part-time/adjunct. *Students:* 10 full-time (5 women), 18 part-time (10 women); includes 2 minority (1 American Indian/Alaska Native, 1 Asian American or Pacific Islander), 12 international. Average age 28. 88 applicants, 11% accepted, 7 enrolled. In 2009, 2 master's, 2 doctorates awarded. *Degree requirements:* For master's, thesis; for doctorate, comprehensive exam, thesis/dissertation. *Entrance requirements:* For master's, GRE General Test; for doctorate, GRE General Test. Additional exam requirements/recommendations for international students: Required—TOEFL (minimum score 550 paper-based; 79 iBT). *Application deadline:* For fall admission, 3/1 priority date for international students; for spring admission, 8/1 priority date for international students. Applications are processed on a rolling basis. Application fee: $40 ($75 for international students). Electronic applications accepted. *Expenses:* Tuition, state resident: full-time $3716; part-time $154.85 per credit hour. Tuition, nonresident: full-time $14,448; part-time $602 per credit hour. Required fees: $1772; $73.85 per credit hour. One-time fee: $50. Tuition and fees vary according to course load and campus/location. *Financial support:* In 2009–10, 13 research assistantships (averaging $18,761 per year), 12 teaching assistantships (averaging $16,275 per year) were awarded; career-related internships or fieldwork, Federal Work-Study, scholarships/grants, health care benefits, tuition waivers (partial), and unspecified assistantships also available. Support available to part-time students. Financial award application deadline: 3/1; financial award applicants required to submit FAFSA. *Faculty research:* Bioinformatics, genomics-genetics, virology, environmental microbiology, development-molecular mechanisms. *Unit head:* Dr. Bill Picking, Head, 405-744-7180, Fax: 405-744-6790. *Application contact:* Dr. Gordon Emslie, Dean, 405-744-6368, Fax: 405-744-0355, E-mail: grad-i@okstate.edu.

Rutgers, The State University of New Jersey, New Brunswick, Graduate School-New Brunswick, Programs in the Molecular Biosciences, Program in Microbiology and Molecular Genetics, Piscataway, NJ 08854-8097. Offers applied microbiology (MS, PhD); clinical microbiology (MS, PhD); computational molecular biology (PhD); immunology (MS, PhD); microbial biochemistry (MS, PhD); molecular genetics (MS, PhD); virology (MS, PhD). Part-time programs available. Terminal master's awarded for partial completion of doctoral program. *Degree requirements:* For master's, comprehensive exam, thesis or alternative; for doctorate, comprehensive exam, thesis/dissertation, written qualifying exam. *Entrance requirements:* For master's, GRE General Test, minimum GPA of 3.0; for doctorate, GRE General Test, GRE Subject Test (recommended), minimum GPA of 3.0. Additional exam requirements/recommendations for international students: Required—TOEFL. Electronic applications accepted. *Faculty research:* Molecular genetics and microbial physiology; virology and pathogenic microbiology; applied, environmental and industrial microbiology; computers in molecular biology.

Stony Brook University, State University of New York, Stony Brook University Medical Center, School of Medicine and Graduate School, Graduate Programs in Medicine, Department of Molecular Genetics and Microbiology, Stony Brook, NY 11794. Offers molecular microbiology (PhD). *Students:* 26 full-time (16 women); includes 3 minority (1 African American, 1 Asian American or Pacific Islander, 1 Hispanic American), 5 international. Average age 27. 110 applicants, 13% accepted. In 2009, 6 doctorates awarded. *Degree requirements:* For doctorate, comprehensive exam, thesis/dissertation. *Entrance requirements:* For doctorate, GRE General Test, GRE Subject Test. Additional exam requirements/recommendations for international students: Required—TOEFL. *Application deadline:* For fall admission, 1/15 for domestic students. Application fee: $60. *Expenses:* Tuition, state resident: full-time $8370; part-time $349 per credit. Tuition, nonresident: full-time $13,250; part-time $552 per credit. Required fees: $933. *Financial support:* Fellowships, research assistantships, teaching assistantships, Federal Work-Study available. Financial award application deadline: 3/15. *Faculty research:* Adenovirus molecular genetics, molecular biology of tumors, virus SV40, mechanism of tumor infection by SAV virus. Total annual research expenditures: $8 million. *Unit head:* Dr. Jorge Benach, Interim Chair, 631-632-8812, Fax: 631-632-9797. *Application contact:* Dr. Patrick Hearing, Director, 631-632-8813, Fax: 631-632-9797, E-mail: hearing@asterix.bio.sunysb.edu.

Texas Tech University Health Sciences Center, Graduate School of Biomedical Sciences, Department of Cell Biology and Biochemistry, Program in Biochemistry and Molecular Genetics, Lubbock, TX 79430. Offers MS, PhD, MD/PhD, MS/PhD. Terminal master's awarded for partial completion of doctoral program. *Degree requirements:* For master's, comprehensive exam, thesis, preliminary, comprehensive, and final exams; for doctorate, comprehensive exam, thesis/dissertation, preliminary, comprehensive, and final exams. *Entrance requirements:* For master's and doctorate, GRE General Test, minimum GPA of 3.0. Additional exam requirements/recommendations for international students: Required—TOEFL. Electronic applications accepted. *Faculty research:* Reproductive endocrinology, immunology, developmental biochemistry, biochemistry and genetics of cancer, molecular genetics and cell cycle.

The University of Alabama at Birmingham, Graduate Programs in Joint Health Sciences, Program in Biochemistry and Molecular Genetics, Birmingham, AL 35294. Offers PhD. *Degree requirements:* For doctorate, thesis/dissertation. *Entrance requirements:* For doctorate, GRE General Test, interview. Electronic applications accepted.

University of California, Irvine, School of Medicine and School of Biological Sciences, Department of Microbiology and Molecular Genetics, Irvine, CA 92697. Offers biological sciences (MS, PhD); MD/PhD. Students apply through the Graduate Program in Molecular Biology, Genetics, and Biochemistry. *Students:* 77 full-time (49 women); includes 36 minority (1 African American, 22 Asian Americans or Pacific Islanders, 13 Hispanic Americans), 2 international. Average age 26. 401 applicants, 24% accepted, 38 enrolled. In 2009, 4 master's, 8 doctorates awarded. *Degree requirements:* For doctorate, thesis/dissertation. *Entrance requirements:* For doctorate, GRE General Test, GRE Subject Test, minimum GPA of 3.0. Additional exam requirements/recommendations for international students: Required—TOEFL (minimum score 550 paper-based; 213 computer-based). *Application deadline:* For fall admission, 12/15 priority date for domestic students, 12/15 for international students. Application fee: $70 ($90 for international students). Electronic applications accepted. *Financial support:* Fellowships, research assistantships with full tuition reimbursements, teaching assistantships, institutionally sponsored loans, traineeships, health care benefits, and unspecified assistantships available. Financial award applicants required to submit FAFSA. *Faculty research:* Molecular biology and genetics of viruses, bacteria, and yeast; immune response; molecular biology of cultured animal cells; genetic basis of cancer; genetics and physiology of infectious agents. *Unit head:* Bert L. Semler, Chair, 949-824-7573 Ext. 6058, Fax: 949-824-8598, E-mail: blsemler@uci.edu. *Application contact:* Kimberly McKinney, Administrator, 949-824-8145, Fax: 949-824-1965, E-mail: kamckinn@uci.edu.

University of California, Los Angeles, David Geffen School of Medicine and Graduate Division, Graduate Programs in Medicine, Department of Microbiology, Immunology and Molecular Genetics, Los Angeles, CA 90095. Offers MS, PhD. *Degree requirements:* For doctorate, thesis/dissertation, oral and written qualifying exams. *Entrance requirements:* For doctorate, GRE General Test, GRE Subject Test. Additional exam requirements/recommendations for international students: Required—TOEFL.

University of California, Riverside, Graduate Division, Graduate Program in Genetics, Genomics, and Bioinformatics, Riverside, CA 92521-0102. Offers genomics and bioinformatics (PhD); molecular genetics (PhD); population and evolutionary genetics (PhD). *Degree requirements:* For doctorate, thesis/dissertation, qualifying exams, teaching experience. *Entrance requirements:* For doctorate, GRE General Test, minimum GPA of 3.2. Additional exam requirements/recommendations for international students: Required—TOEFL (minimum score 550 paper-based; 213 computer-based; 80 iBT). Electronic applications accepted. *Faculty research:* Molecular Genetics, Evolution and Population Genetics, Genomics and Bioinformatics.

University of Cincinnati, Graduate School, College of Medicine, Graduate Programs in Biomedical Sciences, Department of Molecular Genetics, Biochemistry and Microbiology, Cincinnati, OH 45221. Offers MS, PhD. Terminal master's awarded for partial completion of doctoral program. *Degree requirements:* For master's, thesis or alternative; for doctorate, thesis/dissertation, qualifying exam. *Entrance requirements:* For master's and doctorate, GRE General Test. Additional exam requirements/recommendations for international students: Required—TOEFL (minimum score 600 paper-based; 250 computer-based; 100 iBT), TWE. Electronic applications accepted. *Faculty research:* Cancer biology and developmental genetics, gene regulation and chromosome structure, microbiology and pathogenic mechanisms, structural biology, membrane biochemistry and signal transduction.

University of Florida, College of Medicine, Department of Molecular Genetics and Microbiology, Gainesville, FL 32611. Offers MS, PhD. Terminal master's awarded for partial completion of doctoral program. *Degree requirements:* For master's, thesis; for doctorate, thesis/dissertation. *Entrance requirements:* For master's and doctorate, GRE General Test, minimum GPA of 3.0. Additional exam requirements/recommendations for international students: Required—TOEFL. Electronic applications accepted.

University of Guelph, Graduate Program Services, College of Biological Science, Department of Molecular and Cellular Biology, Guelph, ON N1G 2W1, Canada. Offers biochemistry (M Sc, PhD); biophysics (M Sc, PhD); botany (M Sc, PhD); microbiology (M Sc, PhD); molecular biology and genetics (M Sc, PhD). *Degree requirements:* For master's, thesis, research proposal; for doctorate, comprehensive exam, thesis/dissertation, research proposal. *Entrance requirements:* For master's, minimum B-average during previous 2 years of coursework; for doctorate, minimum A-average. Additional exam requirements/recommendations for international students: Required—TOEFL (minimum score 550 paper-based; 213 computer-based), IELTS (minimum score 6.5). Electronic applications accepted. *Faculty research:* Physiology, structure, genetics, and ecology of microbes; virology and microbial technology.

University of Illinois at Chicago, College of Medicine and Graduate College, Graduate Programs in Medicine, Department of Biochemistry and Molecular Genetics, Chicago, IL 60607-7128. Offers PhD, MD/PhD. Terminal master's awarded for partial completion of doctoral program. *Degree requirements:* For doctorate, thesis/dissertation. *Entrance requirements:* For doctorate, GRE General Test. Additional exam requirements/recommendations for international students: Required—TOEFL. Electronic applications accepted. *Faculty research:* Nature of cellular components, control of metabolic processes, regulation of gene expression.

The University of Kansas, University of Kansas Medical Center, School of Medicine, Department of Microbiology, Molecular Genetics and Immunology, Kansas City, KS 66160. Offers microbiology (PhD); MD/PhD. *Faculty:* 12 full-time, 1 part-time/adjunct. *Students:* 1 (woman) full-time, 13 part-time (5 women), 9 international. Average age 29. In 2009, 2 degrees awarded. *Median time to degree:* Of those who began their doctoral program in fall 2001, 100% received their degree in 8 years or less. *Degree requirements:* For doctorate, comprehensive exam, thesis/dissertation, research skills. *Entrance requirements:* For doctorate, GRE General Test, B Sc. Additional exam requirements/recommendations for international students: Required—TOEFL. *Application deadline:* For fall admission, 1/15 priority date for international students. *Expenses:* Tuition, state resident: full-time $6492; part-time $270.50 per credit hour. Tuition, nonresident: full-time $15,510; part-time $646.25 per credit hour. Required fees: $847; $70.56 per credit hour. Tuition and fees vary according to course load and program. *Financial support:* In 2009–10, 1 fellowship with tuition reimbursement (averaging $24,000 per year), 9 research assistantships with partial tuition reimbursements (averaging $24,000 per year), 3 teaching assistantships with full and partial tuition reimbursements (averaging $24,000 per year) were awarded; scholarships/grants and unspecified assistantships also available. *Faculty research:* Immunology, infectious disease, virology, molecular genetics, bacteriology. Total annual research expenditures: $4 million. *Unit head:* Dr. Michael Parmely, Interim Chair, 913-588-7010, Fax: 913-588-7295, E-mail: mparmely@kumc.edu. *Application contact:* Dr. Joe Lutkenhaus, Microbiology Graduate Studies Director, 913-588-7054, Fax: 913-588-7295, E-mail: jlutkenh@kumc.edu.

University of Maryland, College Park, Academic Affairs, College of Chemical and Life Sciences, Department of Cell Biology and Molecular Genetics, Program in Cell Biology and Molecular Genetics, College Park, MD 20742. Offers MS, PhD. *Faculty:* 72 full-time (26 women), 5 part-time/adjunct (2 women). *Students:* 77 full-time (44 women), 4 part-time (2 women); includes 9 minority (3 African Americans, 3 Asian Americans or Pacific Islanders, 3 Hispanic Americans), 25 international. 226 applicants, 13% accepted, 15 enrolled. In 2009, 4 master's, 9 doctorates awarded. *Degree requirements:* For master's, thesis; for doctorate, thesis/dissertation, exams. *Entrance requirements:* For master's and doctorate, GRE General Test, 3 letters of recommendation, minimum GPA of 3.0. Additional exam requirements/recommendations for international students: Required—TOEFL. *Application deadline:* For fall admission, 1/6 for domestic and international students. Application fee: $60. *Expenses:* Tuition, area resident: Part-time $471 per credit hour. Tuition, state resident: part-time $471 per credit hour. Tuition, nonresident: part-time $1016 per credit hour. Required fees: $337.04 per term. *Financial support:* In 2009–10, 9 fellowships with full and partial tuition reimbursements (averaging $24,847 per year), 12 research assistantships (averaging $21,075 per year), 52 teaching assistantships (averaging $19,143 per year) were awarded. Financial award applicants required to submit FAFSA. *Faculty research:* Cytoskeletal activity, membrane biology, cell division, genetics and genomics, virology. *Unit head:* Norma Andrews, Chair, 301-405-1605, Fax: 301-314-9489, E-mail: andrewsn@umd.edu. *Application contact:* Dean of Graduate School, 301-405-0358, Fax: 301-314-9305.

University of Massachusetts Worcester, Graduate School of Biomedical Sciences, Program in Molecular Genetics and Microbiology, Worcester, MA 01655-0115. Offers PhD. *Degree requirements:* For doctorate, comprehensive exam, thesis/dissertation. *Entrance requirements:* For doctorate, GRE General Test. Additional exam requirements/recommendations for international students: Required—TOEFL (minimum score 600 paper-based; 250 computer-based). Electronic applications accepted. *Faculty research:* Contemporary molecular biology, bacterial and yeast genetics, eukaryotic and cellular immunology, virology and bacterial pathogenesis.

University of Medicine and Dentistry of New Jersey, Graduate School of Biomedical Sciences, Graduate Programs in Biomedical Sciences–Newark, Department of Microbiology and Molecular Genetics, Newark, NJ 07107. Offers PhD. *Students:* 21 full-time (14 women); includes 3 Asian Americans or Pacific Islanders, 4 international. *Degree requirements:* For

Molecular Genetics

University of Medicine and Dentistry of New Jersey (continued)
doctorate, thesis/dissertation, qualifying exam. *Entrance requirements:* For doctorate, GRE General Test. Additional exam requirements/recommendations for international students: Required—TOEFL. *Application deadline:* For fall admission, 2/1 for domestic students. Applications are processed on a rolling basis. Application fee: $40. Electronic applications accepted. *Financial support:* Fellowships, research assistantships, Federal Work-Study, institutionally sponsored loans, and tuition waivers (full and partial) available. Financial award application deadline: 5/1. *Faculty research:* Molecular genetics of yeast, mutagenesis and carcinogenesis of DNA, bacterial protein synthesis, mammalian cell genetics, adenovirus gene expression. *Unit head:* Dr. Stephen Garrett, Program Director, 973-972-4391, Fax: 973-972-8981. *Application contact:* Dr. Stephen Garrett, Program Director, 973-972-4391, Fax: 973-972-8981.

University of Medicine and Dentistry of New Jersey, Graduate School of Biomedical Sciences, Graduate Programs in Biomedical Sciences–Piscataway, Program in Molecular Genetics, Microbiology and Immunology, Piscataway, NJ 08854-5635. Offers MS, PhD, MD/PhD. Terminal master's awarded for partial completion of doctoral program. *Degree requirements:* For master's, thesis, qualifying exam; for doctorate, thesis/dissertation, qualifying exam. *Entrance requirements:* For master's and doctorate, GRE General Test. Additional exam requirements/recommendations for international students: Required—TOEFL. Electronic applications accepted. *Faculty research:* Interferon, receptors, retrovirus evolution, Arbo virus/host cell interactions.

University of Pittsburgh, School of Medicine, Graduate Programs in Medicine, Program in Biochemistry and Molecular Genetics, Pittsburgh, PA 15260. Offers MS, PhD. *Faculty:* 50 full-time (8 women). *Students:* 17 full-time (8 women); includes 3 minority (all Asian Americans or Pacific Islanders), 5 international. Average age 27. 655 applicants, 10% accepted. In 2009, 7 doctorates awarded. *Degree requirements:* For doctorate, comprehensive exam, thesis/dissertation. *Entrance requirements:* For doctorate, GRE General Test, GRE Subject Test, minimum QPA of 3.0. Additional exam requirements/recommendations for international students: Required—TOEFL (minimum score 600 paper-based; 250 computer-based; 100 iBT), IELTS (minimum score 7). *Application deadline:* For fall admission, 12/15 priority date for domestic and international students. Application fee: $40. Electronic applications accepted. *Expenses:* Tuition, state resident: full-time $16,402; part-time $665 per credit. Tuition, nonresident: full-time $28,694; part-time $1175 per credit. Required fees: $690; $175 per term. Tuition and fees vary according to program. *Financial support:* In 2009–10, 17 research assistantships with full tuition reimbursements (averaging $24,650 per year) were awarded; institutionally sponsored loans, scholarships/grants, traineeships, health care benefits, and unspecified assistantships also available. *Faculty research:* Molecular genetics of cancer, gene expression and signal transduction, genomics and proteomics, human gene therapy, structural dynamics and bioinformatics. *Unit head:* Dr. Martin C. Schmidt, Graduate Program Director, 412-648-9243, Fax: 412-624-1401, E-mail: mcs2@pitt.edu. *Application contact:* Graduate Studies Administrator, 412-648-8957, Fax: 412-648-1077, E-mail: gradstudies@medschool.pitt.edu.

University of Rhode Island, Graduate School, College of the Environment and Life Sciences, Department of Cell and Molecular Biology, Kingston, RI 02881. Offers biochemistry (MS, PhD); clinical laboratory sciences (MS), including biotechnology, clinical laboratory science, cytopathology; microbiology (MS, PhD); molecular genetics (MS, PhD). Part-time programs available. *Faculty:* 12 full-time (4 women). *Students:* 29 full-time (17 women), 43 part-time (31 women); includes 13 minority (5 African Americans, 4 Asian Americans or Pacific Islanders, 4 Hispanic Americans), 3 international. In 2009, 5 master's, 2 doctorates awarded. *Degree requirements:* For master's, comprehensive exam (for some programs); for doctorate, comprehensive exam. *Entrance requirements:* For master's and doctorate, GRE, 2 letters of recommendation. Additional exam requirements/recommendations for international students: Required—TOEFL (minimum score 550 paper-based; 213 computer-based). *Application deadline:* For fall admission, 7/15 for domestic students, 2/1 for international students; for spring admission, 11/15 for domestic students, 7/15 for international students. Application fee: $65. Electronic applications accepted. *Expenses:* Tuition, state resident: full-time $8828; part-time $490 per credit hour. Tuition, nonresident: full-time $22,100; part-time $1228 per credit hour. Required fees: $1118; $57 per semester. Tuition and fees vary according to program. *Financial support:* In 2009–10, 2 research assistantships with full and partial tuition reimbursements (averaging $10,535 per year), 10 teaching assistantships with full and partial tuition reimbursements (averaging $13,449 per year) were awarded. Financial award application deadline: 7/15; financial award applicants required to submit FAFSA. *Faculty research:* Genomics and Sequencing Center: an interdisciplinary genomics research and undergraduate and graduate student training program which provides researchers access to cutting-edge technologies in the field of genomics. Total annual research expenditures: $1.2 million. *Unit head:* Dr. Jay Sperry, Chairperson, 401-874-2201, Fax: 401-874-2202, E-mail: jsperry@mail.uri.edu. *Application contact:* Dr. Jay Sperry, Chairperson, 401-874-2201, Fax: 401-874-2202, E-mail: jsperry@mail.uri.edu.

The University of Texas Health Science Center at Houston, Graduate School of Biomedical Sciences, Program in Human and Molecular Genetics, Houston, TX 77225-0036. Offers MS, PhD, MD/PhD. Terminal master's awarded for partial completion of doctoral program. *Degree requirements:* For master's, thesis; for doctorate, thesis/dissertation. *Entrance requirements:* For master's and doctorate, GRE General Test. Additional exam requirements/recommendations for international students: Required—TOEFL. Electronic applications accepted. *Faculty research:* Computational genomics, cancer genetics, complex disease genetics, medical genetics.

The University of Texas Health Science Center at Houston, Graduate School of Biomedical Sciences, Program in Microbiology and Molecular Genetics, Houston, TX 77225-0036. Offers MS, PhD, MD/PhD. Terminal master's awarded for partial completion of doctoral program. *Degree requirements:* For master's, thesis; for doctorate, thesis/dissertation. *Entrance requirements:* For master's and doctorate, GRE General Test. Additional exam requirements/recommendations for international students: Required—TOEFL. Electronic applications accepted. *Faculty research:* Disease causation, environmental signaling, gene regulation, cell growth and division, cell structure and architecture.

University of Vermont, College of Medicine and Graduate College, Graduate Programs in Medicine, Department of Microbiology and Molecular Genetics, Burlington, VT 05405. Offers MS, PhD, MD/MS, MD/PhD. *Faculty:* 18 full-time (5 women). *Students:* 23 (13 women), 12 international. 49 applicants, 33% accepted, 3 enrolled. In 2009, 4 doctorates awarded. *Degree requirements:* For master's, thesis; for doctorate, thesis/dissertation. *Entrance requirements:* For master's and doctorate, GRE General Test. Additional exam requirements/recommendations for international students: Required—TOEFL (minimum score 550 paper-based; 213 computer-based; 80 iBT). *Application deadline:* For fall admission, 1/16 priority date for domestic students, 1/16 for international students. Applications are processed on a rolling basis. Application fee: $40. Electronic applications accepted. *Expenses:* Tuition, state resident: part-time $508 per credit hour. Tuition, nonresident: part-time $1281 per credit hour. *Financial support:* Fellowships, research assistantships, teaching assistantships available. Financial award application deadline: 3/1. *Unit head:* Dr. Susan S. Wallace, Chairperson, 802-656-2164. *Application contact:* Dr. David Pederson, Coordinator, 802-656-2164.

University of Vermont, Graduate College, College of Agriculture and Life Sciences and College of Medicine, Department of Microbiology and Molecular Genetics, Burlington, VT 05405. Offers MS, PhD, MD/MS, MD/PhD. *Faculty:* 18 full-time (5 women). *Degree requirements:* For master's, thesis; for doctorate, thesis/dissertation. *Entrance requirements:* For master's and doctorate, GRE General Test. Additional exam requirements/recommendations for international students: Required—TOEFL (minimum score 550 paper-based; 213 computer-based; 80 iBT). *Application deadline:* For fall admission, 2/1 priority date for domestic students. Applications are processed on a rolling basis. Application fee: $40. Electronic applications accepted. *Expenses:* Tuition, state resident: part-time $508 per credit hour. Tuition, nonresident: part-time $1281 per credit hour. *Financial support:* Fellowships, research assistantships, teaching assistantships available. Financial award application deadline: 3/1. *Unit head:* Dr. Susan S. Wallace, Chairperson, 802-656-2164. *Application contact:* Dr. S. Doublie, Coordinator, 802-656-2164.

University of Virginia, School of Medicine, Department of Biochemistry and Molecular Genetics, Charlottesville, VA 22903. Offers biochemistry (PhD); MD/PhD. *Faculty:* 26 full-time (6 women), 1 (woman) part-time/adjunct. *Students:* 33 full-time (15 women); includes 3 minority (1 African American, 2 Asian Americans or Pacific Islanders), 9 international. Average age 26. In 2009, 6 doctorates awarded. *Degree requirements:* For doctorate, thesis/dissertation, written research proposal and defense. *Entrance requirements:* For doctorate, GRE General Test, 3 letters of recommendation. Additional exam requirements/recommendations for international students: Recommended—TOEFL (minimum score 630 paper-based; 250 computer-based; 90 iBT). Application fee: $60. Electronic applications accepted. *Financial support:* Fellowships, health care benefits and tuition waivers (full) available. Financial award applicants required to submit FAFSA. *Unit head:* Joyce L. Hamlin, Chair, 434-924-1940, Fax: 434-924-5069. *Application contact:* Associate Dean for Graduate Programs and Research.

Wake Forest University, School of Medicine and Graduate School of Arts and Sciences, Graduate Programs in Medicine, Molecular Genetics and Genomics Program, Winston-Salem, NC 27109. Offers PhD, MD/PhD. *Degree requirements:* For doctorate, thesis/dissertation. *Entrance requirements:* For doctorate, GRE General Test. Additional exam requirements/recommendations for international students: Required—TOEFL. Electronic applications accepted. *Faculty research:* Control of gene expression, molecular pathogenesis, protein biosynthesis, cell development, clinical cytogenetics.

Washington University in St. Louis, Graduate School of Arts and Sciences, Division of Biology and Biomedical Sciences, Program in Molecular Genetics, St. Louis, MO 63130-4899. Offers PhD. *Degree requirements:* For doctorate, thesis/dissertation. *Entrance requirements:* For doctorate, GRE General Test, GRE Subject Test. Electronic applications accepted.

Reproductive Biology

Cornell University, Graduate School, Graduate Fields of Comparative Biomedical Sciences, Field of Comparative Biomedical Sciences, Ithaca, NY 14853-0001. Offers cellular and molecular medicine (MS, PhD); developmental and reproductive biology (MS, PhD); infectious diseases (MS, PhD); population medicine and epidemiology (MS, PhD); structural and functional biology (MS, PhD). *Faculty:* 106 full-time (29 women). *Students:* 41 full-time (28 women); includes 1 minority (African American), 17 international. Average age 32. 32 applicants, 31% accepted, 9 enrolled. In 2009, 1 master's, 10 doctorates awarded. *Degree requirements:* For master's, thesis; for doctorate, comprehensive exam, thesis/dissertation. *Entrance requirements:* For master's and doctorate, GRE General Test, 2 letters of recommendation. Additional exam requirements/recommendations for international students: Required—TOEFL (minimum score 550 paper-based; 213 computer-based; 77 iBT). *Application deadline:* For fall admission, 12/15 for domestic students. Application fee: $70. Electronic applications accepted. *Expenses:* Tuition: Full-time $29,500. Required fees: $70. Full-time tuition and fees vary according to degree level, program and student level. *Financial support:* In 2009–10, 4 fellowships with full tuition reimbursements, 2 research assistantships with full tuition reimbursements were awarded; teaching assistantships with full tuition reimbursements, institutionally sponsored loans, scholarships/grants, health care benefits, tuition waivers (full and partial), and unspecified assistantships also available. Financial award applicants required to submit FAFSA. *Faculty research:* Receptors and signal transduction, viral and bacterial infectious diseases, tumor metastasis, clinical sciences/nutritional disease, developmental/neurological disorders. *Unit head:* Director of Graduate Studies, 607-253-3276, Fax: 607-253-3756. *Application contact:* Graduate Field Assistant, 607-253-3276, Fax: 607-253-3756, E-mail: graduate_edcvm@cornell.edu.

Eastern Virginia Medical School, Master's Program in Biomedical Sciences (Clinical Embryology and Andrology), Norfolk, VA 23501-1980. Offers MS. Postbaccalaureate distance learning degree programs offered (minimal on-campus study). *Faculty:* 12 full-time, 8 part-time/adjunct. *Students:* 55 full-time (41 women); includes 6 African Americans, 8 Asian Americans or Pacific Islanders, 9 Hispanic Americans. 32 applicants, 75% accepted, 21 enrolled. In 2009, 11 master's awarded. *Entrance requirements:* Additional exam requirements/recommendations for international students: Required—TOEFL (minimum score 550 paper-based; 213 computer-based; 80 iBT). *Application deadline:* For fall admission, 1/1 for domestic and international students. Applications are processed on a rolling basis. Application fee: $60. Electronic applications accepted. *Expenses:* Contact institution. *Unit head:* Dr. Jacob Mayer, Director, 757-446-5049, Fax: 757-446-5905. *Application contact:* Nancy Garcia, Administrator, 757-446-8935, Fax: 757-446-5905, E-mail: garcianw@evms.edu.

Northwestern University, The Graduate School and Judd A. and Marjorie Weinberg College of Arts and Sciences, Interdepartmental Biological Sciences Program (IBiS), Evanston, IL 60208. Offers biochemistry, molecular biology, and cell biology (PhD), including biochemistry, cell and molecular biology, molecular biophysics, structural biology; biotechnology (PhD); cell and molecular biology (PhD); developmental biology and genetics (PhD); hormone action and signal transduction (PhD); neuroscience (PhD); structural biology, biochemistry, and biophysics (PhD). Program participants include the Departments of Biochemistry, Molecular Biology, and Cell Biology; Chemistry; Neurobiology and Physiology; Chemical Engineering; Civil Engineering; and Evanston Hospital. *Degree requirements:* For doctorate, thesis/dissertation, qualifying exam. *Entrance requirements:* For doctorate, GRE General Test. Additional exam requirements/recommendations for international students: Required—TOEFL (minimum score 600 paper-based). Electronic applications accepted. *Faculty research:* Developmental genetics, gene regulation, DNA-protein interactions, biological clocks, bioremediation.

Queen's University at Kingston, School of Graduate Studies and Research, Faculty of Health Sciences, Department of Anatomy and Cell Biology, Kingston, ON K7L 3N6, Canada. Offers biology of reproduction (M Sc, PhD); cancer (M Sc, PhD); cardiovascular pathophysiology (M Sc, PhD); cell and molecular biology (M Sc, PhD); drug metabolism (M Sc, PhD); endocrinology (M Sc, PhD); motor control (M Sc, PhD); neural regeneration (M Sc, PhD); neurophysiology (M Sc, PhD). Part-time programs available. *Degree requirements:* For master's, thesis; for doctorate, one foreign language, comprehensive exam, thesis/dissertation. *Entrance requirements:* Additional exam requirements/recommendations for international students: Required—TOEFL. Electronic applications accepted. *Faculty research:* Human kinetics, neuroscience, reproductive biology, cardiovascular.

Rutgers, The State University of New Jersey, New Brunswick, Graduate School-New Brunswick, Program in Endocrinology and Animal Biosciences, Piscataway, NJ 08854-8097.

Offers MS, PhD. Terminal master's awarded for partial completion of doctoral program. *Degree requirements:* For master's, thesis; for doctorate, comprehensive exam, thesis/dissertation. *Entrance requirements:* For master's and doctorate, GRE General Test. Additional exam requirements/recommendations for international students: Required—TOEFL. Electronic applications accepted. *Faculty research:* Comparative and behavioral endocrinology, epigenetic regulation of the endocrine system, exercise physiology and immunology, fetal and neonatal developmental programming, mammary gland biology and breast cancer, neuroendocrinology and alcohol studies, reproductive and developmental toxicology.

The University of British Columbia, Faculty of Medicine, Department of Obstetrics and Gynecology, Program in Reproductive and Developmental Sciences, Vancouver, BC V6H 3N1, Canada. Offers M Sc, PhD. Terminal master's awarded for partial completion of doctoral program. *Degree requirements:* For master's, thesis; for doctorate, thesis/dissertation. *Entrance requirements:* For master's, BSc or equivalent, MD, DVM, DDS; for doctorate, B Sc with first class honors, M Sc, MD, DVM, DDS. Additional exam requirements/recommendations for international students: Required—TOEFL (paper-based 550) or IELTS (paper-based 7). Electronic applications accepted. *Faculty research:* Reproductive and placental endocrinology; immunology of reproductive, fertilization, and embryonic development; perinatal metabolism; neonatal development.

University of Colorado Denver, School of Medicine, Program in Cell Biology, Stem Cells, and Developmental Biology, Denver, CO 80217-3364. Offers cell and developmental biology (PhD); cell biology, stem cells and development (PhD); reproductive sciences (PhD). *Students:* 28 full-time (18 women); includes 2 minority (1 Asian American or Pacific Islander, 1 Hispanic American), 8 international. In 2009, 3 doctorates awarded. *Degree requirements:* For doctorate, thesis/dissertation. *Entrance requirements:* For doctorate, GRE, minimum GPA of 3.0, 3 letters of reference. Additional exam requirements/recommendations for international students: Required—TOEFL (minimum score 550 paper-based; 213 computer-based). *Application deadline:* For fall admission, 1/15 for domestic students. Application fee: $50. Electronic applications accepted. *Financial support:* Fellowships, research assistantships, teaching assistantships, Federal Work-Study and institutionally sponsored loans available. Support available to part-time students. Financial award application deadline: 3/15; financial award applicants required to submit FAFSA. *Faculty research:* Human disease, stem cell biology, neuroscience, molecular biology. Total annual research expenditures: $5.7 million. *Unit head:* Dr. Karl Pfenninger, Chair, 303-724-3466, E-mail: karl.pfenninger@ucdenver.edu. *Application contact:* Carmel Hardberg, Program Administrator, 303-724-3426, Fax: 303-724-3420, E-mail: carmel.harberg@ucdenver.edu.

University of Hawaii at Manoa, John A. Burns School of Medicine, Program in Developmental and Reproductive Biology, Honolulu, HI 96813. Offers MS, PhD. Part-time programs available.

Faculty: 19 full-time (2 women), 7 part-time/adjunct (4 women). *Students:* 18 full-time (9 women), 8 part-time (3 women); includes 17 minority (all Asian Americans or Pacific Islanders), 2 international. Average age 27. 20 applicants, 70% accepted, 10 enrolled. In 2009, 10 master's awarded. *Degree requirements:* For doctorate, thesis/dissertation. *Entrance requirements:* For doctorate, GRE General Test, GRE Subject Test. Application fee: $50. *Expenses:* Tuition, state resident: full-time $8900; part-time $372 per credit. Tuition, nonresident: full-time $21,400; part-time $898 per credit. Required fees: $207 per semester. *Financial support:* In 2009–10, 1 fellowship (averaging $1,000 per year), 9 research assistantships (averaging $17,109 per year), 3 teaching assistantships (averaging $14,382 per year) were awarded. *Faculty research:* Biology of gametes and fertilization, reproductive endocrinology. Total annual research expenditures: $5.4 million. *Application contact:* Steve Ward, Graduate Chair, 808-956-6598, Fax: 808-956-7316.

University of Saskatchewan, College of Medicine, Department of Obstetrics, Gynecology and Reproductive Services, Saskatoon, SK S7N 5A2, Canada. Offers M Sc, PhD. *Degree requirements:* For master's, thesis; for doctorate, thesis/dissertation. Additional exam requirements/recommendations for international students: Required—TOEFL. Tuition and fees charges are reported in Canadian dollars. *Expenses:* Tuition, area resident: Full-time $3000 Canadian dollars; part-time $500 Canadian dollars per term. Required fees: $700 Canadian dollars; $100 Canadian dollars per term.

University of Wyoming, College of Agriculture, Department of Animal Sciences, Program in Reproductive Biology, Laramie, WY 82070. Offers MS, PhD. *Degree requirements:* For master's, thesis; for doctorate, thesis/dissertation. *Entrance requirements:* For master's, GRE General Test, minimum GPA of 3.0; for doctorate, GRE General Test, minimum GPA of 3.0 or MS degree. Additional exam requirements/recommendations for international students: Required—TOEFL. *Faculty research:* Fetal programming, chemical suppression, ovaria function, genetics.

West Virginia University, Davis College of Agriculture, Forestry and Consumer Sciences, Interdisciplinary Program in Genetics and Developmental Biology, Morgantown, WV 26506. Offers animal breeding (MS, PhD); biochemical and molecular genetics (MS, PhD); cytogenetics (MS, PhD); descriptive embryology (MS, PhD); developmental genetics (MS); experimental morphogenesis/teratology (MS); human genetics (MS, PhD); immunogenetics (MS, PhD); life cycles of animals and plants (MS, PhD); molecular aspects of development (MS, PhD); mutagenesis (MS, PhD); oncology (MS, PhD); plant genetics (MS, PhD); population and quantitative genetics (MS, PhD); regeneration (MS, PhD); teratology (PhD); toxicology (MS, PhD). *Degree requirements:* For master's, thesis; for doctorate, comprehensive exam, thesis/dissertation. *Entrance requirements:* For master's, GRE or MCAT, minimum GPA of 2.75. Additional exam requirements/recommendations for international students: Required—TOEFL.

Teratology

West Virginia University, Davis College of Agriculture, Forestry and Consumer Sciences, Interdisciplinary Program in Genetics and Developmental Biology, Morgantown, WV 26506. Offers animal breeding (MS, PhD); biochemical and molecular genetics (MS, PhD); cytogenetics (MS, PhD); descriptive embryology (MS, PhD); developmental genetics (MS); experimental morphogenesis/teratology (MS); human genetics (MS, PhD); immunogenetics (MS, PhD); life cycles of animals and plants (MS, PhD); molecular aspects of development (MS, PhD); mutagenesis (MS, PhD); oncology (MS, PhD); plant genetics (MS, PhD); population and quantitative genetics (MS, PhD); regeneration (MS, PhD); teratology (MS, PhD); toxicology (MS, PhD). *Degree requirements:* For master's, thesis; for doctorate, comprehensive exam, thesis/dissertation. *Entrance requirements:* For master's, GRE or MCAT, minimum GPA of 2.75. Additional exam requirements/recommendations for international students: Required—TOEFL.

BAYLOR COLLEGE OF MEDICINE

Department of Molecular and Human Genetics

Programs of Study	The Department of Molecular and Human Genetics offers an NIGMS-supported training program leading to the Ph.D. degree. The Department also cooperates in the Medical Scientist Training Program that leads to a combined M.D./Ph.D. degree.

The research interests of the Department span a broad range, including the principles of DNA replication and repair, DNA recombination, cell division, aging, cancer, development, learning, memory, and social behavior. A variety of model organisms are used, from *E. coli* to yeast and *Dictyostelium* to flies and mice, and there is a strong research program in bioinformatics and genomics as well. Studies in model organisms are tightly integrated with studies on the genetic basis of the human condition. The research program addresses a variety of genetic diseases, and the unique environment of a large medical center allows students to obtain experience in aspects of both basic and clinical research.

The Graduate Program in Molecular and Human Genetics provides outstanding educational opportunities for students who wish to pursue a career in the broad field of genetics. Students in the program obtain rigorous training in modern biology, with an emphasis on genetics. They participate in cutting-edge research on a variety of topics and publish their work in the some of the best peer-reviewed journals in the world. Students are expected to devote full-time to this course of study. In the first year, they concentrate on course work and laboratory rotations designed to provide a firm basis in fundamental genetic concepts and cover recent developments in molecular biology. The program design permits students to move quickly into their thesis research project. The second year and subsequent years are devoted to independent thesis research and elective course work. Seminar programs, literature review meetings, and research presentations enable students to learn about faculty research programs and the current status of various fields of study in the larger scientific community. An annual two-day Departmental research retreat provides an excellent opportunity for students and faculty members to share information in an informal setting.

Students first enrolled in the program in 1987. To date, 146 degrees have been awarded, and the 2010–11 academic year is scheduled to begin with 78 students in training. The Department continues to rank first in the number of NIH grants and first in total NIH funding among genetics departments at U.S. medical schools.

The Department of Molecular and Human Genetics interacts closely with other departments at Baylor and with other institutions in the Texas Medical Center. Course credit reciprocity among Baylor, Rice University, Texas A&M University, the University of Houston, and the University of Texas Health Science Center expands the scholastic horizon of Baylor students. |
Research Facilities	Faculty members in the Department occupy research laboratories furnished with state-of-the-art equipment. The arrangement of laboratories consists of centralized core facilities in which instrumentation serves several investigators. Cooperative and collaborative interactions among Department faculty members and between the Department of Molecular and Human Genetics and other departments and organizations enable students to take full advantage of the facilities at the Texas Medical Center.
Financial Aid	A stipend and fringe-benefits package is awarded to all graduate students enrolled at Baylor College of Medicine. The current stipend is $26,000 per year and health insurance is provided at no cost. Tuition scholarships are awarded to students who are admitted to the program. Following admission to candidacy, students receive a $1000 travel grant from the Department to initiate participation in national meetings.
Cost of Study	Tuition costs are covered in full by tuition scholarships or training grants.
Living and Housing Costs	Most students and faculty members live within a few miles of the Texas Medical Center. Numerous housing options are available. The cost of living in Houston is lower than most major cities. Excellent job opportunities for spouses are available in the many institutions of the Texas Medical Center and throughout the city of Houston.
Student Group	Students in the Department of Molecular and Human Genetics may seek either the Ph.D. degree or the combined M.D./Ph.D. degree. In the past three years, about 15 students per year on average have joined the program. There are approximately 580 students enrolled in the Graduate School; the Medical School has about 680 students. Admission policies at Baylor offer equal opportunity to all, without regard to race, sex, age, religion, country of origin, or handicap.
Location	Baylor College of Medicine is located within the Texas Medical Center, a large and vigorous professional community that also includes the University of Texas Health Science Center, eight teaching hospitals, and the M. D. Anderson Cancer Center. Rice University is nearby. Houston is also the home of Houston Baptist University and the University of Houston. The fourth-largest city in the nation, Houston is an exciting cultural and metropolitan center. Ballet, opera, symphony, and theater are excellent and accessible to the general population. Many fine museums and parks enhance city life. Professional and amateur sports are very popular. The climate permits participation in a wide variety of outdoor activities, and Gulf Coast beaches are a short drive from the city.
The College	Baylor College of Medicine is an independent, private institution dedicated to training in basic and medical sciences. It has promoted the development of interdisciplinary research programs and has consistently identified and encouraged outstanding investigators and medical practitioners. The climate of interaction benefits the graduate student body by expanding its learning opportunities.
Applying	Applicants must have earned a bachelor's degree and have a strong background in biology and biochemistry. Candidates for admission must complete the application form of the Graduate School. The application should contain Graduate Record Examinations scores (less than three years old), three letters of recommendation, and official undergraduate transcripts. Applications receive two reviews, one by a faculty committee of the Department and a second by the Admissions Committee of the Graduate School. The application deadline for admission is January 1. Applications can be obtained through the Graduate School Web site listed in the Costs/Admission Information section.
Correspondence and Information	For an application:

Admissions Office
Graduate School
Baylor College of Medicine
Houston, Texas 77030

Phone: 713-798-4060
Web site: http://www.bcm.edu/gradschool/ |

For information:

Director of Graduate Studies
Department of Molecular and Human Genetics
Baylor College of Medicine
One Baylor Plaza
Houston, Texas 77030

Phone: 713-798-5056
E-mail: genetics-gradprgm@bcm.tmc.edu
Web site: http://www.bcm.tmc.edu/molgen/

Baylor College of Medicine

THE FACULTY AND THEIR RESEARCH

David Bates, Assistant Professor; Ph.D., New Mexico, 1998. Chromosome dynamics, molecular mechanisms of DNA replication, and cell-cycle control in *E. coli*.

Arthur L. Beaudet, Professor and Chair; M.D., Yale, 1967. Role of genomic imprinting in evolution and disease, including Prader-Willi and Angelman syndromes and autism; hepatocyte gene therapy.

Hugo J. Bellen, Professor; D.V.M./Ph.D., California, Davis, 1986. Genetic and molecular analysis of neurotransmitter release and neural development in *Drosophila*.

John W. Belmont, Professor; M.D./Ph.D., Baylor College of Medicine, 1981. Immunogenetics; congenital heart defects.

Alison A. Bertuch, Assistant Professor; M.D./Ph.D., Rochester, 1993. Telomere biology and DNA repair in yeast and vertebrates.

Penelope M. Bonnen, Assistant Professor; Ph.D., Baylor College of Medicine, 2002. Population genetics and genomics of disease-causing alleles.

Juan Botas, Professor; Ph.D., Madrid, 1986. Molecular mechanisms of pathogenesis in neurological disorders: a system biology approach.

Malcolm K. Brenner, Professor; M.D./Ph.D., Cambridge, 1981. Use of gene therapy to improve responses to cancer.

Chester W. Brown, Assistant Professor; M.D./Ph.D., Cincinnati, 1993. Molecular mechanisms that control adiposity, growth, and development.

Rui Chen, Assistant Professor; Ph.D., Baylor, 1999. Genetic network of human retinal diseases and development.

William J. Craigen, Professor; M.D./Ph.D., Baylor College of Medicine, 1988. Regulation of cellular energy metabolism; mouse models of metabolic diseases.

Gretchen J. Darlington, Professor; Ph.D., Michigan, 1970. Molecular mechanisms determining tissue-specific gene expression; gene transcription; molecular basis of cellular and organismal aging.

Herman A. Dierick, Assistant Professor; M.D., Catholic University of Louvain (Belgium), 1991. Genetic and neurobiological mechanisms of *Drosophila* aggression.

Richard A. Gibbs, Professor; Ph.D., Melbourne (Australia), 1985. Human genome analysis; molecular analysis of genetic and infectious disease.

Scott Goode, Assistant Professor; Ph.D., Chicago, 1991. Epithelial morphogenesis, cell migrations, and tumor cell invasion of *Drosophila* and humans.

Margaret A. Goodell, Professor; Ph.D., Cambridge, 1991. Murine and human hematopoietic stem cells: regulation, development, and gene therapy.

Brett H. Graham, Assistant Professor; M.D./Ph.D., Emory, 1998. Genetics of inborn errors of metabolism; genetic models of mitochondrial disease in *Drosophila* and vertebrates.

Andrew Groves, Associate Professor; Ph.D., Ludwig Institute for Cancer Research (London), 1992. Development and regeneration of the inner ear.

Philip Hastings, Professor; Ph.D., Cambridge, 1965. Molecular mechanisms of gene amplification, genome instability, and recombination in *E. coli*.

Xiangwei He, Assistant Professor; Ph.D., Baylor College of Medicine, 1997. Molecular mechanisms of mitotic chromosome segregation.

Christophe Herman, Assistant Professor; Ph.D., Bruxelles (Belgium), 1996. Epigenetics; stress response; membrane quality control mechanism.

Kendal D. Hirschi, Professor; Ph.D., Arizona, 1993. Nutrient bioavailability in plants.

Grzegorz Ira, Assistant Professor, Ph.D., Copernicus, 1999. Mechanisms of DNA recombination.

Milan Jamrich, Professor; Ph.D., Heidelberg, 1978. Pattern formation in vertebrate embryos; ocular development; gene therapy.

Monica J. Justice, Professor; Ph.D., Kansas State, 1987. Using mouse mutagenesis to analyze gene function and establish models of human disease.

Richard L. Kelley, Associate Professor; Ph.D., Stanford, 1984. Noncoding RNAs and chromatin structure.

Adam Kuspa, Professor and Chair of Biochemistry and Molecular Biology; Ph.D., Stanford, 1989. Genomic studies of cell signaling and development in *Dictyostelium*.

Suzanne M. Leal, Professor; Ph.D., Columbia, 1994. Statistical genetics and genetic epidemiology; methods development; complex trait association studies of rare variants; the genetics of nonsyndromic hearing loss.

Brendan Lee, Professor; M.D./Ph.D., SUNY Downstate Medical Center, 1993. Molecular determinants of cartilage and skeletal development and their associated human genetic conditions; adenoviral hepatocyte gene therapy for treatment of inborn errors of metabolism; urea cycle disorders as a model of nitric oxide dysregulation.

Olivier Lichtarge, Professor; M.D./Ph.D., Stanford, 1990. Computational studies of protein sequence, structure, and function; G protein signaling; protein design; functional genomics.

James R. Lupski, Professor and Vice Chair; M.D./Ph.D., NYU, 1985. DNA fingerprinting of bacteria; molecular genetics of Charcot-Marie-Tooth disease and related inherited neuropathies; inherited eye diseases; molecular mechanisms for human DNA rearrangements; genomic disorders.

Graeme Mardon, Professor; Ph.D., MIT, 1990. Retinal cell fate determination, development, and disease in *Drosophila*, mice, and humans.

Martin M. Matzuk, Professor; M.D./Ph.D., Washington (St. Louis), 1989. Mammalian reproduction and cancer.

Michael L. Metzker, Associate Professor; Ph.D., Baylor College of Medicine, 1996. Next-generation technology for genome sequencing; novel fluorescence imaging; molecular genetics of diabetes; phylogenetic analysis of HIV-1 transmission between individuals.

Aleksandar Milosavljevic, Associate Professor; Ph.D., California, Santa Cruz, 1990. Bioinformatics; genomics; cancer genomics; epigenomics.

David D. Moore, Professor; Ph.D., Wisconsin–Madison. Functions of the nuclear hormone receptor superfamily.

Paolo M. Moretti, Assistant Professor; M.D., Padua, 1990. Neurodegeneration; Parkinson's disease; epigenetics; DNA methylation; Rett syndrome.

David L. Nelson, Professor; Ph.D., MIT, 1984. Fragile-X syndrome; FXTAS neurodegeneration; incontinentia pigmenti; mouse and fly models.

Jeffrey L. Neul, Assistant Professor; M.D./Ph.D., Chicago, 2000. Rett syndrome pathophysiology and treatment.

Philip Ng, Associate Professor; Ph.D., Guelph, 1999. Gene therapy for genetic and acquired disorders.

Jeffrey L. Noebels, Professor; Ph.D., Stanford, 1977; M.D., Yale, 1981. Gene control of neuronal excitability within the developing mammalian CNS.

William E. O'Brien, Professor; Ph.D., Georgia, 1971. Inborn errors of metabolism.

Paul A. Overbeek, Professor; Ph.D., Michigan, 1980. Gene regulation in transgenic mice; ocular development; growth factors; insertional mutagenesis.

Xuewen Pan, Assistant Professor; Ph.D., Duke, 2001. Genetic networking; chemical genomics; technology development.

Donald W. Parsons, Assistant Professor; M.D./Ph.D., Ohio State, 2001. Development of large-scale (genomic) methods to identify and evaluate cancer-causing mutations in human tumors.

Richard E. Paylor, Professor; Ph.D., Colorado, 1991. Genetic basis of complex behavioral traits in mice.

Sharon E. Plon, Professor; M.D./Ph.D., Harvard, 1987. Genetic basis of cancer susceptibility; control of genomic stability.

Frank Probst, Assistant Professor, M.D./Ph.D., Michigan, 2001. The use of the house mouse (*Mus musculus*) as a model system for human genetic disorders.

Antony Rodriguez, Assistant Professor; Ph.D., Texas Southwestern Medical Center at Dallas, 2002. Roles of miRNAs in stem cells and cancer; microRNA regulatory networks (targetomics); identification of disease genes regulated by microRNAs.

Susan M. Rosenberg, Professor; Ph.D., Oregon, 1986. Molecular mechanisms of genome instability, mutation, DNA repair, and recombination in *E. coli*; cancer; antibiotic resistance.

Christian Rosenmund, Associate Professor; Ph.D., Oregon Health Sciences, 1993. Molecular mechanisms of synaptic transmission and plasticity at central mammalian synapses.

Marco Sardiello, Assistant Professor; Ph.D., Bari (Italy), 2003. Development of innovative therapies for lysosomal storage disorders (LSDs).

Daryl Scott, Assistant Professor; M.D./Ph.D., Iowa, 2000. Molecular genetics of common birth defects.

Kenneth L. Scott, Assistant Professor; Ph.D. Baylor College of Medicine, 2005. Cancer gene discovery; mechanisms for cancer metastasis.

Gad Shaulsky, Professor; Ph.D., Weizmann (Israel), 1991. Developmental genetics in *Dictyostelium*; functional genomics; the molecular basis of social behavior.

Pawel Stankiewicz, Assistant Professor; M.D., Warsaw, 1991; Ph.D., 1999, Dr.Habil. (D.Sc.), 2006, Institute of Mother and Child (Poland). Better understanding molecular mechanisms and phenotypic effects of genomic rearrangements; unraveling pathogenetics of FOX transcription factor gene cluster on 16q24.1 in alveolar capillary dysplasia/misalignment of pulmonary veins and a broad spectrum of congenital malformations.

Ignatia B. Van den Veyver, Associate Professor; M.D., Antwerp (Belgium), 1986. Role of epigenetics and genomic imprinting in development and disease; X-linked developmental disorders.

James Versalovic, Professor; M.D./Ph.D., Baylor College of Medicine, 1995. The human microbiome; functional genomics of probiotics.

Jue D. (Jade) Wang, Assistant Professor; Ph.D., California, San Francisco, 2002. Control of elongation of DNA replication in bacteria and its implications for genomic integrity.

Robert A. Waterland, Assistant Professor; Ph.D., Cornell, 2000. Early nutritional influences on mammalian epigenetic gene regulation.

Thomas Westbrook, Assistant Professor; Ph.D., Rochester, 2003. Functional genetic screens for cancer gene networks and therapeutic targets; the REST tumor suppressor network.

John H. Wilson, Professor; Ph.D., Caltech, 1971. Instability of trinucleotide repeats; knock-in mouse models for retinitis pigmentosa; gene therapy of dominant rhodopsin mutations.

Lee-Jun C. Wong, Professor; Ph.D., Ohio State, 1975. Understanding the role of mitochondrial genetics and function in diseases, cancer, and aging.

Hui Zheng, Professor; Ph.D., Baylor, 1990. Molecular genetics of Alzheimer's disease.

Huda Zoghbi, Professor; M.D., Meharry Medical College, 1979. Molecular basis of degenerative and developmental neurologic disorders; nervous system development.

Thomas P. Zwaka, Associate Professor; M.D./Ph.D., Ulm (Germany), 2000. Embryonic stem cells; pluripotency; differentiation of embryonic stem cells into ectoderm and mesoderm.

BAYLOR COLLEGE OF MEDICINE

Graduate Program in Developmental Biology

Program of Study	The Graduate Program in Developmental Biology (DB Program) awards a Ph.D. degree and is designed to prepare students both intellectually and technologically to pursue a successful career in biological and/or biomedical research. The program also participates in the Medical Scientist Training Program, which leads to a combined M.D./Ph.D. degree.
	The DB Program provides a wide spectrum of exciting research possibilities and a broad cross-disciplinary training. In order to understand how a single cell develops into a complex organism, the program laboratories use molecular biology, cell biology, biochemistry, imaging, physiology, genetics, and genomics. Studies of organisms as diverse as social molds, worms, flies, frogs, chickens, fish, mice, and humans are conducted using a wide variety of approaches, instruments, and techniques of modern biological research. Members of the DB Program study basic biological mechanisms of direct and fundamental relevance to human development, disease, and stem cell therapy. This allows students to unravel the principles and mechanisms that guide embryonic development, the maintenance and differentiation of stem cells, the differentiation of adult cell types, regeneration of organs and tissues, and the mechanisms underlying aging and neurodegeneration. The major research interests are neurobiology; cancer biology; cell death; aging; neurodegenerative and other human diseases; stem cell biology; gene therapy; reproductive development; oogenesis; skin, muscle, heart, blood, kidney, bone, limb, and eye development; cell lineage specification; X chromosome dosage compensation; and plant differentiation.
	During their first year, students take core courses in classical and molecular genetics, cell biology, molecular biology, and biochemistry, as well as several courses and seminars in developmental biology. They also sample several areas of research by doing rotations in the program's laboratories. Before the end of the first year, students take a qualifying exam and select a laboratory in which they carry out their dissertation research. Subsequently, students meet every six months with their thesis committee to evaluate the research accomplished and redefine goals necessary to complete the thesis project. In the final year, students defend their theses in a public seminar. Study for the Ph.D. degree generally requires five years of graduate work, most of which is spent on the dissertation research. The program is supported by a competitive NIH training grant, the local chapter of the March of Dimes, Texas Children's Hospital, and the College.
Research Facilities	DB Program faculty members are well-funded and drawn from eleven departments and four institutions, including Baylor College of Medicine (BCM), the University of Texas M. D. Anderson Cancer Center, the University of Texas Health Science Center, and Rice University, all within easy walking distance of the Texas Medical Center. They occupy extensive research space with state-of-the-art instrumentation and computing equipment. Cooperative and collaborative interactions among program laboratories and institutions enable students to take full advantage of the facilities of the Texas Medical Center.
Financial Aid	Students enrolled in the program receive a competitive stipend of $29,000 per year plus health insurance at no extra cost. Tuition scholarships are awarded to all students admitted to the program. Separate offices provide assistance to international students and students with financial hardships.
Cost of Study	Tuition is fully covered by the program, the College, or training grants.
Living and Housing Costs	Numerous affordable housing options are available within a few miles of the medical center. Some students rent a nearby house while others rent or buy their own apartment, condo, or townhome. The cost of living in Houston is below that of most large U.S. cities, and there are ample opportunities for employment of spouses in the Texas Medical Center.
Student Group	The DB Program currently has 53 full-time graduate students, including 25 women and 31 international students. Each year, 7–10 students join the program. Because of the program's commitment to excellence, it favors a low student-faculty ratio. In addition to the laboratories in the program, students have contact with students, postdoctoral fellows, and faculty members in other programs and departments throughout the school and the medical center. The BCM graduate school has approximately 550 students, the medical school about 700 students.
Student Outcomes	The Career Resource Center of the graduate school provides career information and counseling for all BCM graduate and postdoctoral students in biomedical sciences. DB students typically graduate with an excellent-to-outstanding publication record and go on to successful careers. The average number of publications per graduate student is above 4.5, with an average of more than 2.5 first-author papers. The average impact factor per graduate student publication is more than 10. The DB graduates have subsequently pursued postdoctoral training in excellent laboratories and high-quality institutions. A substantial number of former graduate students are now faculty members at universities and teaching colleges around the world.
Location	Houston is a dynamic city with an exciting cultural and metropolitan center. Ballet, opera, symphony, theater, and art museums are excellent and accessible to the general population. In addition, there are more than a thousand bars and restaurants, which are moderately priced. Recreation opportunities abound, with facilities for a wide range of professional and amateur sports. The climate offers very pleasant weather from fall through spring and permits participation in a wide variety of outdoor activities. Gulf Coast beaches are a short drive from the city.
The College	Baylor College of Medicine is an independent, private institution dedicated to training in basic and medical sciences. It is located in the heart of the Texas Medical Center, one of the largest medical centers in the world. It has promoted the development of interdisciplinary, interdepartmental, and interinstitutional programs and has consistently identified and encouraged outstanding investigators. Considered one of the top research institutions in the nation, the College continues to develop programs and services that meet new needs and trends, making higher education one of the most exciting and rewarding of human experiences.
Applying	Applicants must have a bachelor's degree, preferably with course work in biology and genetics. GRE General Test scores less than three years old at the time of application must be provided. Applications should be accompanied by transcripts, three letters of recommendation, and a statement of research interest and career goals; they must be complete by January 1, with a preferred deadline of December 15. Successful candidates are invited to meet with the participating faculty members and students to have a firsthand look at the DB Program. Expenses for travel and accommodations during the visit are provided for domestic and international students. Admission policies at BCM offer equal opportunity to all, without regard to race, sex, age, religion, country of origin, or handicap. Questions regarding the application process can be directed to cat@bcm.edu.
Correspondence and Information	Graduate Program in Developmental Biology Baylor College of Medicine, BCM 225 One Baylor Plaza Houston, Texas 77030 Phone: 713-798-7696 E-mail: cat@bcm.edu Web site: http://www.bcm.edu/db/

Baylor College of Medicine

THE FACULTY AND THEIR RESEARCH

Benjamin R. Arenkiel, Assistant Professor of Molecular and Human Genetics, Neurological Research Institute; Ph.D., Utah, 2004. Mechanisms of neuronal connectivity and maintenance of synapses during development and adulthood.

Richard R. Behringer, Professor of Genetics, University of Texas M. D. Anderson Cancer Center; Ph.D., South Carolina, 1986. Molecular genetics of female reproductive tract development.

Hugo J. Bellen, Professor of Molecular and Human Genetics and Neuroscience; Director, Program in Developmental Biology; and Investigator, Howard Hughes Medical Institute; D.V.M./Ph.D., California, Davis, 1986. Nervous system development and neurotransmitter release in *Drosophila*.

John W. Belmont, Professor of Molecular and Human Genetics and Immunology; M.D./Ph.D., Baylor College of Medicine, 1981. Hematopoietic and immune development and cardiovascular genetics.

Andreas Bergmann, Associate Professor of Biochemistry and Molecular Biology, University of Texas M. D. Anderson Cancer Center; Ph.D., Max Planck Institute for Developmental Biology (Germany), 1996. Genetic control of programmed cell death (apoptosis) in *Drosophila*.

Janet Braam, Professor and Chair of Biochemistry and Cell Biology, Rice University; Ph.D., Cornell, 1985. Molecular and developmental responses of plants to environmental stresses: roles of calmodulin-related proteins and cell wall modifying enzymes.

Rui Chen, Assistant Professor of Molecular and Human Genetics, Human Genome Sequencing Center; Ph.D., Baylor College of Medicine, 1999. System biology; genetics network controlling retinal development in *Drosophila*.

Thomas A. Cooper, Professor of Pathology and Molecular and Cellular Biology; M.D., Temple, 1982. Alternative splicing regulation in development and disease.

Francesco J. DeMayo, Professor of Molecular and Cellular Biology; Ph.D., Michigan, 1983. Molecular and developmental biology of the lung and uterus; cancer; reproductive biology.

Benjamin Deneen, Assistant Professor of Neuroscience, Center for Cell and Gene Therapy and Stem Cells and Regenerative Medicine Center; Ph.D., UCLA, 2002. Glial cell development and disease.

Mary E. Dickinson, Associate Professor of Molecular Physiology and Biophysics; Ph.D., Columbia, 1996. Vascular remodeling and heart morphogenesis in early vertebrate embryos.

Margaret A. Goodell, Professor of Pediatrics, Molecular and Human Genetics, and Immunology; Director, Center for Cell and Gene Therapy and Stem Cells and Regenerative Medicine Center; Ph.D., Cambridge, 1991. Adult and embryonic stem cell biology.

Andy K. Groves, Associate Professor of Neuroscience and Molecular and Human Genetics; Ph.D., Ludwig Institute for Cancer Research (United Kingdom), 1992. Development and regeneration of the inner ear.

Georg Halder, Associate Professor of Biochemistry and Molecular Biology, University of Texas M. D. Anderson Cancer Center; Ph.D., Basel (Switzerland), 1996. Tumor suppressor genes and organ size control; *Drosophila* genetics.

Karen K. Hirschi, Professor of Pediatrics and Molecular and Cellular Biology, Center for Cell and Gene Therapy and Stem Cells and Regenerative Medicine Center; Ph.D., Arizona, 1990. Vascular development and vascular progenitors in adult tissues.

Hamed Jafar-Nejad, Assistant Professor of Molecular Medicine, University of Texas Health Science Center; M.D., Tehran (Iran), 1994. Cell biological regulation of developmental signaling pathways.

Milan Jamrich, Professor of Molecular and Human Genetics and Molecular and Cellular Biology; Ph.D., Heidelberg (Germany), 1978. Molecular basis of embryonic pattern formation.

Randy L. Johnson, Associate Professor of Biochemistry and Molecular Biology, University of Texas M. D. Anderson Cancer Center; Ph.D., Columbia, 1991. Mouse developmental genetics.

Monica J. Justice, Professor of Molecular and Human Genetics; Ph.D., Kansas, 1987. Genetic analysis of mouse development and disease.

Richard L. Kelley, Associate Professor of Molecular and Human Genetics; Ph.D., Stanford, 1984. Noncoding RNAs and chromatin structure.

Adam Kuspa, Professor and Chair of Biochemistry and Molecular Biology and Molecular and Human Genetics; Ph.D., Stanford, 1989. Genomic studies of cell signaling and development in *Dictyostelium*.

Brendan Lee, Professor of Molecular and Human Genetics and Investigator, Howard Hughes Medical Institute; M.D./Ph.D., SUNY Health Science Center at Brooklyn, 1993. Human and mouse developmental genetics; cartilage and skeletal development.

Michael T. Lewis, Associate Professor of Molecular and Cellular Biology, Lester and Sue Smith Breast Center; Ph.D., California, Santa Cruz, 1995. Genetic regulation of mammary gland development and early-stage breast cancer.

Olivier Lichtarge, Professor of Molecular and Human Genetics and Biochemistry and Molecular Biology; M.D./Ph.D., Stanford, 1990. Evolutionary studies of sequence, structure, and function in biological macromolecules; bioinformatics.

Hui-Chen Lu, Assistant Professor of Pediatrics–Neurology and Neuroscience; Ph.D., Baylor College of Medicine, 1997. Molecular mechanisms of cortical development.

Peter Y. Lwigale, Assistant Professor of Biochemistry and Cell Biology, Rice University; Ph.D., Kansas, 2001. Eye development; cellular interactions and molecular regulation of neural crest cells as they form the cornea.

Mirjana Maletic-Savatic, Assistant Professor of Pediatrics; M.D./Ph.D., Belgrade (Serbia), 1996. Imaging and metabolomics and neurogenesis.

Graeme Mardon, Professor of Pathology, Molecular and Human Genetics, and Neuroscience; Ph.D., MIT, 1990. Neural cell-fate determination, development, and degeneration in *Drosophila* and vertebrates.

Martin M. Matzuk, Professor of Pathology, Molecular and Human Genetics, and Molecular and Cellular Biology; M.D./Ph.D., Washington (St. Louis), 1989. Mammalian reproduction, oncogenesis, and development.

David D. Moore, Professor of Molecular and Cellular Biology and Molecular and Human Genetics; Ph.D., Wisconsin–Madison, 1979. Functions of the nuclear hormone receptor superfamily.

Jeffrey L. Neul, Assistant Professor of Pediatrics; M.D./Ph.D., Chicago, 1998. Rett Syndrome; the role of MECP2 in the medulla and the regulation of autonomic function.

Hoang Nguyen, Assistant Professor of Molecular and Cellular Biology, Center for Cell and Gene Therapy and Stem Cells and Regenerative Medicine Center; Ph.D., Cornell/Sloan-Kettering, 2002. Skin epithelial stem cell fate maintenance and lineage determination.

Paul A. Overbeek, Professor of Molecular and Cellular Biology, Molecular and Human Genetics, and Neuroscience; Ph.D., Michigan, 1980. Transgenic mice; ocular development; transposon-mediated insertional mutagenesis in mice.

Matthew N. Rasband, Associate Professor of Neuroscience; Ph.D., Rochester, 1999. Role of neuronal-glial signaling in brain development, function, injury, and disease.

Antony Rodriguez, Assistant Professor of Molecular and Human Genetics; Ph.D., Texas Southwestern Medical Center at Dallas, 2002. Molecular genetics of mammalian microRNAs.

Jeffrey M. Rosen, Professor of Molecular and Cellular Biology; Ph.D., SUNY at Buffalo, 1971. Mammary gland development, stem cells, and breast cancer.

Gad Shaulsky, Professor of Molecular and Human Genetics; Ph.D., Weizmann (Israel), 1991. Developmental genetics in *Dictyostelium*; functional genomics; molecular basis of social behavior.

Anna Marie Sokac, Assistant Professor of Biochemistry and Molecular Biology; Ph.D., Wisconsin–Madison, 2001. Coordinated actin and membrane dynamics in flies and frogs.

Kimberly R. Tolias, Assistant Professor of Neuroscience; Ph.D., Harvard, 1998. Molecular signaling pathways in structural development and plasticity of dendrites and synapses.

Ming-Jer Tsai, Professor of Molecular and Cellular Biology; Ph.D., California, Davis, 1971. Pancreas and neural development; organogenesis steroid hormone action; prostate cancer.

Sophia Y. Tsai, Professor of Molecular and Cellular Biology; Ph.D., California, Davis, 1969. Nuclear orphan receptor in mouse development and organogenesis.

Meng Wang, Assistant Professor of Molecular and Human Genetics, and Huffington Center on Aging; Ph.D., Rochester, 2005. Systemic studies of endocrine and metabolic signaling in promoting healthy aging.

Thomas F. Westbrook, Assistant Professor of Biochemistry and Molecular Biology and Molecular and Human Genetics; Ph.D., Rochester, 2003. Genetic regulation of human tumorigenesis and hematopoiesis.

Hui Zheng, Professor of Molecular and Human Genetics, Molecular and Cellular Biology, and Neuroscience, Huffington Center on Aging; Ph.D., Baylor College of Medicine, 1990. Molecular genetics of Alzheimer's disease.

Zheng Zhou, Associate Professor of Biochemistry and Molecular Biology; Ph.D., Baylor College of Medicine, 1994. Clearance of apoptotic cells in *C. elegans*.

Huda Y. Zoghbi, Professor of Pediatrics, Molecular and Human Genetics, and Neuroscience; Director, Neurological Research Institute; and Investigator, Howard Hughes Medical Institute; M.D., Meharry Medical College, 1979. Pathogenesis of polyglutamine neurodegenerative diseases and Rett syndrome; genes essential for neurodevelopment.

Thomas P. Zwaka, Associate Professor of Molecular and Cellular Biology and Molecular and Human Genetics, Center for Cell and Gene Therapy and Stem Cells and Regenerative Medicine Center; M.D./Ph.D., Ulm (Germany), 2000. The nature of embryonic stem cell pluripotency.

THOMAS JEFFERSON UNIVERSITY

Jefferson College of Graduate Studies
Kimmel Cancer Center
Department of Microbiology and Immunology
Graduate Program in Genetics

Program of Study

The Graduate Program in Genetics is an interdepartmental program that focuses on training in the rapidly expanding field of molecular genetics and functional genomics. The program of study leading to a Ph.D. degree is designed to provide graduate students with comprehensive training and research experience to pursue careers as independent scientific investigators in academic, government, or industrial settings. Students entering with a baccalaureate degree take core courses in genetics, biochemistry, bioinformatics, molecular biology, and cell biology. Advanced courses and special-topics courses in the genetic basis of human disease; the genetics of yeast, fruit flies, zebrafish, and mice; and the genetic basis of cancer are offered as well. A weekly journal club is led by a student presenter, facilitating open discussion between faculty members and peers about current topics. Course work during the first year is supplemented by three rotations in the laboratories of faculty mentors who conduct active research programs on diverse problems in the genetics of cancer, development, and disease. During this time, students learn state-of-the-art research techniques and the principles of sound methods of scientific investigation. Besides frequent laboratory seminars where faculty mentors, postdoctoral fellows, and graduate students present their current research, a wide variety of joint-program and Departmental seminars and lectureships by eminent scientists from outside the Jefferson academic community form an integral part of this program. A thesis laboratory is chosen after the first year of study, and formal course work is completed by the end of the second year of study. The curriculum is flexible enough to accommodate the diverse backgrounds and the special interests of individual students. The Graduate Program in Genetics, with the Graduate Programs in Immunology and Microbial Pathogenesis, Molecular Pharmacology and Structural Biology, and Biochemistry and Molecular Biology, constitute the four graduate programs of the Kimmel Cancer Center.

Current research interests of the genetics program faculty include cancer biology, chromatin organization, functional genomics, genetics of cancer susceptibility, genetics of human disease, genetics of the immune system, developmental genetics and epigenetics, mitochondrial genetics, model systems of human disease, molecular determinants of therapeutic response, molecular genomics of hematopoietic neoplasias and solid tumors, molecular mechanisms regulated by oncogenes and tumor suppressor genes, nuclear hormone receptors, regulation of transcription, and translational research.

Research Facilities

Research laboratories are primarily located in the Kimmel Cancer Center, which occupies 70,000 square feet in the Bluemle Life Sciences Building and 25,000 square feet in the adjacent Jefferson Alumni Hall. In addition to having extensive basic equipment and facilities, the program has access to numerous specialized resources. These include peptide synthesis and sequencing facilities, microarray and proteomics facilities, a flow cytometry facility, a pathogen-free animal facility, a facility for generating transgenic and gene-targeted mice, a bioimaging facility, a pathology facility and tumor bank, extensive computer facilities, and an X-ray crystallography facility.

Financial Aid

Financial support is available to full-time Ph.D. students in the form of University fellowships and training grants. In 2010–11, students granted full fellowship support receive funds for payment of tuition and fees, along with a stipend of $26,300. Also available to students demonstrating financial need are Title IV funds. University loan programs are also available to qualifying students.

Cost of Study

Tuition and fees for full-time Ph.D. students are $28,423 per year in 2010–11.

Living and Housing Costs

Campus housing is available to graduate students in the program. In addition, there is reasonable alternative housing located near Thomas Jefferson University.

Student Group

The incoming class size in the Graduate Program in Genetics is expected to be 3; the program currently has 26 Ph.D. students. The College of Graduate Studies enrolls approximately 630 students, about half of whom are women. The University enrolls about 2,500 students.

Student Outcomes

Recent Ph.D. graduates have accepted postdoctoral positions in prestigious academic institutions, such as Harvard, Johns Hopkins, Tufts, Baylor, UC Davis, the University of Texas M. D. Anderson Cancer Center, and the National Institutes of Health, and in industry, including Bristol-Meyers Squibb, Merck, and Pfizer.

Location

The 13-acre campus of Thomas Jefferson University is located in the historic downtown area of Philadelphia within walking distance of many places of cultural interest, including concert halls, theaters, museums, art galleries, and historic sites. There are numerous intercollegiate and professional sports teams and events. Convenient bus and subway lines connect the University with other local universities and colleges and with several outstanding libraries. The New Jersey shore and the Pennsylvania mountains offer year-round recreational opportunities, and New York City and Washington, D.C., are just a few hours away.

The University

Thomas Jefferson University is an academic health center. It evolved from the Jefferson Medical College, which was founded in 1824, and besides the Medical College, includes the College of Graduate Studies, the College of Health Professions, the University Hospital, and various affiliated hospitals and institutions. Jefferson Alumni Hall houses the TJU Fitness and Recreation Facility, the graduate student lounge, an indoor swimming pool, a sauna, a gymnasium, a handball/squash court, and volleyball courts. The Graduate Student Association (GSA) is a voice for graduate students within the University as well as organizers of intellectual, professional, social, and community service programs.

Applying

The deadline to submit Ph.D. applications and all supporting materials is January 5. Applications received after this date are considered at the discretion of the admissions committee. Scores on the General Test of the Graduate Record Examinations (GRE), three letters of recommendation, and academic transcripts are required of all applicants. For those students whose native language is not English, scores on the Test of English as a Foreign Language (TOEFL) are required. Scores on an appropriate Subject Test of the GRE are strongly recommended. Prospective students are encouraged to visit the Department and to discuss the graduate program with members of the faculty.

Correspondence and Information

For applications:
Marc Stearns
Director of Admissions and Recruitment
College of Graduate Studies
Thomas Jefferson University
1020 Locust Street, M-46
Philadelphia, Pennsylvania 19107-6799
Phone: 215-503-4400
Fax: 215-503-3433
E-mail: cgs-info@jefferson.edu
Web site: http://www.jefferson.edu/cgs

For program information:
Joanne Balitzky
Training Programs Coordinator
Kimmel Cancer Center
Thomas Jefferson University
233 South 10th Street, 910 BLSB
Philadelphia, Pennsylvania 19107-5541
Phone: 215-503-6687
Fax: 215-503-0622
E-mail: joanne.balitzky@jefferson.edu
Web site: http://www.jefferson.edu/jcgs/phd/genetics/

Thomas Jefferson University

THE FACULTY AND THEIR RESEARCH

David Abraham, Professor; Ph.D., Pennsylvania, 1983. Parasite immunology; role of eosinophils, neutrophils, and macrophages in innate and adaptive immunity to helminth parasite infections; development of vaccines against nematode infections; genetic control of protective immunity to parasites; chemotherapy of leishmaniasis; diagnosis of strongyloidiasis.

Emad S. Alnemri, Professor; Ph.D., Temple, 1991. Molecular mechanisms of programmed cell death (apoptosis); pattern recognition receptors and inflammasome activation in innate immune responses to molecular danger signals; role of mitochondria in survival, cell death, and aging.

Andrew E. Aplin, Associate Professor; Ph.D., King's College, London, 1996. Genetic alterations underlying melanoma initiation and progression.

Renato Baserga, Professor; M.D., Milan, 1949. Genetic analysis of G1-phase and control of cell proliferation; growth factors and their receptors; apoptosis; anticancer therapy.

Jeffrey L. Benovic, Professor and Chairperson; Ph.D., Duke, 1986. Molecular and regulatory properties of G-protein–coupled receptors; role of receptor dysregulation in cancer and neurological disorders.

Arthur M. Buchberg, Associate Professor; Ph.D., SUNY at Buffalo, 1983. Genetics of cancer susceptibility; mouse models of cancer; identification and characterization of genes involved in cancer initiation and progression.

Bruno Calabretta, Professor; M.D., Modena (Italy), 1977; Ph.D., Rome, 1987. Molecular mechanisms of normal hematopoiesis and BCR/ABL-dependent leukemogenesis.

Franco Capozza, Assistant Professor; Ph.D., Rome, 1999. Mechanisms of skin cancer initiation and progression; mouse models of human disease.

Gregory E. Gonye, Research Assistant Professor; Ph.D., Connecticut Health Center, 1993. Transcriptional network analysis downstream of angiotensin II receptor activation and hypertension; computational and high dimensional analysis of gene regulation networks.

Linda E. Greenbaum, Associate Professor; M.D., Columbia, 1987. Mechanisms of liver regeneration and repair by hepatocytes and liver progenitor/stem cells; contribution of these processes to the development of liver fibrosis and hepatocellular carcinoma.

Ya Ming Hou, Professor; Ph.D., Berkeley, 1986. Genetic and biochemical studies of tRNA, including structure and function mechanisms of tRNA aminoacylation, maintenance of the tRNA 3' end, maturation and processing, editing and repair, decoding on the ribosome, and development of bacterial pathogenesis in infectious diseases; targeting tRNAs as strategies against metabolic and neurodegenerative disorders.

James B. Jaynes, Associate Professor; Ph.D., Washington (Seattle), 1980. Developmental genetics and molecular biology of gene regulation by epigenetic transcriptional memory and chromosomal architecture.

Erica S. Johnson, Associate Professor; Ph.D., MIT, 1992. The ubiquitin-related protein Smt3/SUMO and its conjugation pathway and function in yeast.

James H. Keen, Professor; Ph.D., Cornell, 1976. Molecular mechanisms coupling signal transduction with receptor-mediated endocytosis and exocytosis; membrane transport studied by biochemical, molecular biological, and morphological approaches.

Michael P. King, Associate Professor; Ph.D., Caltech, 1987. Mammalian mitochondrial biogenesis; molecular genetics of mtDNA mutations resulting in human disease; mtDNA recombination; mitochondrial translation.

Erik S. Knudsen, Professor; Ph.D., California, San Diego, 1991. Functional role of the retinoblastoma tumor suppressor pathway in tumorigenesis; tumor progression and the response to cancer therapies.

Karen E. Knudsen, Professor; Ph.D., California, San Diego, 1996. Translational prostate cancer research; cell cycle control; hormonal control of gene transcription; chromatin remodeling.

Carlisle P. Landel, Research Assistant Professor; Ph.D., Colorado at Boulder, 1982. Mouse genetics and rodent transgenesis; using the laboratory mouse as a model system to examine the genetics of sperm cryopreservation.

Michael Lisanti, Professor; M.D., 1991, Ph.D., 1992, Cornell. Functional role of caveolae and the caveolin genes in normal signal transduction and in a variety of pathogenic disease states, most notably the development of breast and prostate cancers.

Alexander Mazo, Professor; Ph.D., Russian Academy of Sciences, 1976. Chromatin modifications by epigenetic factors and nuclear hormone receptors.

Steven McKenzie, Professor; M.D./Ph.D., Pennsylvania, 1985. Murine models of immune-mediated thrombocytopenia and thrombosis syndromes; molecular genetics of Fc receptor evolution and function; genetically modified mouse models of autoimmune disease and host defense.

Steven McMahon, Associate Professor; Ph.D., Pennsylvania, 1994. Biochemical and genetic pathways regulated by the MYC oncoprotein and the p53 tumor suppressor.

Diane S. Merry, Associate Professor; Ph.D., Pennsylvania, 1991. Molecular pathogenesis of Kennedy's disease and other polyglutamine expansion diseases; protein misfolding and aggregation in neurodegenerative disease; mouse models of neurologic disease; domain function in trafficking and degradation of the androgen receptor; gene and pharmacological therapies for neurodegenerative diseases.

Andrea Morrione, Research Associate Professor; Ph.D., Milan, 1992. Characterization of insulin-like growth factor receptor I (IGF-IR) function in bladder cancer initiation and progression; role of the growth factor progranulin (proepithelin) and its receptor in bladder and prostate cancer; characterization of the role of adaptor protein Grb10 in the regulation of IGF-IR ubiquitination, trafficking, and signaling.

Marja T. Nevalainen, Associate Professor; M.D., 1992, Ph.D., 1997, Turku (Finland). Stat transcription factors in prostate cancer.

Richard G. Pestell, Professor, Ph.D., 1991, M.D., 1997, Melbourne (Australia), FRACP, 1991, FACP, 2009. Molecular mechanisms and gene therapy of breast and prostate cancer; cancer stem cells.

Isidore Rigoutsos, Professor; Ph.D., NYU, 1992. Non-coding RNAs and their roles in the regulation of cellular processes and the onset and progression of disease; organism-specific regulatory motifs; computational methods for solving problems from genomics, genetics, molecular biology, and medicine.

Linda D. Siracusa, Professor and Program Director; Ph.D., Buffalo, SUNY, 1985. Genetics of cancer susceptibility; identification and characterization of genes affecting cancer risk; molecular genomics and biology of the gastrointestinal tract, with special emphasis on pathways leading to intestinal and colorectal cancers.

Jouni Uitto, Professor; Ph.D./M.D., Helsinki, 1970. Molecular genetics of the cutaneous basement membrane zone; regulation of collagen and elastin gene expression and the molecular basis of heritable and acquired connective tissue diseases.

Scott A. Waldman, Professor; Ph.D., Thomas Jefferson, 1980; M.D., Stanford, 1987. Molecular mechanisms of signal transduction, with emphasis on receptor-effector coupling and postreceptor signaling mechanisms; molecular mechanisms underlying tissue-specific transcriptional regulation; translation of molecular signaling mechanisms to novel diagnostic and therapeutic approaches to patients with cancer.

Chenguang Wang, Assistant Professor; Ph.D., Chinese Academy of Sciences, 1998. Mechanisms of steroid nuclear receptors in regulation of cellular proliferation and progression; role of steroid nuclear receptor signaling in tumorigenesis and differentiation.

Edward P. Winter, Associate Professor; Ph.D., SUNY at Stony Brook, 1984. Analysis of meiotic development using molecular/genetics in yeast; signal transduction and protein kinases; transcriptional regulation.

UNIVERSITY OF CONNECTICUT HEALTH CENTER

Graduate Program in Genetics and Developmental Biology

Program of Study

The genetics and developmental biology graduate program provides students with fundamental interdisciplinary training in modern molecular genetics and developmental biology, emphasizing cellular and molecular aspects as well as tissue interactions. The program is intended for students pursuing a Ph.D. degree and prepares students to compete for job opportunities in traditional medical and dental school departments as well as a productive research career in either academia or industry. Combined M.D./Ph.D. and D.M.D/Ph.D. programs are also available. Students are encouraged to obtain in-depth training through research and courses in biochemistry, molecular biology, cell biology, developmental biology, and genetics. Faculty members are from several basic science and clinical departments and study a wide range of organisms including yeast, worms, fruit flies, mice, and humans. Areas of research include the biology of human embryonic stem cells, mapping and cloning of genes responsible for human disease, RNA processing (including RNA editing, alternative splicing, antisense regulation, and RNA interference), the molecular mechanisms of aging, signal transduction pathways, microbial pathogenesis, developmental neurobiology, cell differentiation, musculoskeletal development, morphogenesis and pattern formation, reproductive biology, and endocrinology.

Research Facilities

The Department of Genetics and Developmental Biology is the academic home of the genetics and developmental biology graduate program. The Department of Genetics and Developmental Biology occupies three floors of the state-of-the-art Academic Research Building, which opened in 1999, as well as laboratory space in adjacent buildings. The department houses equipment and facilities for mouse transgenics, ES cell manipulation, DNA microarrays, nucleic acid sequencing, fluorescence microscopy, and digital imaging. Students also have ready access to first-rate flow cytometry and confocal microscopy facilities. Other institutional resources include a computer center and a library containing approximately 200,000 volumes and subscribing to more than 1,400 current periodicals. Students of the program therefore have an excellent opportunity for research and training in cutting-edge areas of genetics and developmental biology.

Financial Aid

Support for doctoral students engaged in full-time degree programs at the Health Center is provided on a competitive basis. Graduate research assistantships for 2010–11 provide a stipend of $28,000 per year, which includes a waiver of tuition/University fees for the fall and spring semesters and a student health insurance plan. While financial aid is offered competitively, the Health Center makes every possible effort to address the financial needs of all students during their period of training.

Cost of Study

For 2010–11, tuition is $4455 per semester ($8910 per year) for full-time students who are Connecticut residents and $11,565 per semester ($23,130 per year) for full-time out-of-state residents. General University fees are added to the cost of tuition for students who do not receive a tuition waiver. These costs are usually met by traineeships or research assistantships for doctoral students.

Living and Housing Costs

There is a wide range of affordable housing options in the greater Hartford area within easy commuting distance of the campus, including an extensive complex that is adjacent to the Health Center. Costs range from $600 to $900 per month for a one-bedroom unit; 2 or more students sharing an apartment usually pay less. University housing is not available at the Health Center.

Student Group

At UCHC, there are about 500 students in the Schools of Medicine and Dental Medicine, 150 Ph.D. students, and 50 postdoctoral fellows. There are no restrictions on the admission of out-of-state graduate students.

Location

The Health Center is located in the historic town of Farmington, Connecticut. Set in the beautiful New England countryside on a hill overlooking the Farmington Valley, it is close to ski areas, hiking trails, and facilities for boating, fishing, and swimming. Connecticut's capital city of Hartford, 7 miles east of Farmington, is the center of an urban region of approximately 800,000 people. The beaches of the Long Island Sound are about 50 minutes away to the south, and the beautiful Berkshires are a short drive to the northwest. New York City and Boston can be reached within 2½ hours by car. Hartford is the home of the acclaimed Hartford Stage Company, TheatreWorks, the Hartford Symphony and Chamber orchestras, two ballet companies, an opera company, the Wadsworth Athenaeum (the oldest public art museum in the nation), the Mark Twain house, the Hartford Civic Center, and many other interesting cultural and recreational facilities. The area is also home to several branches of the University of Connecticut, Trinity College, and the University of Hartford, which includes the Hartt School of Music. Bradley International Airport (about 30 minutes from campus) serves the Hartford/Springfield area with frequent airline connections to major cities in this country and abroad. Frequent bus and rail service is also available from Hartford.

The Health Center

The 200-acre Health Center campus at Farmington houses a division of the University of Connecticut Graduate School, as well as the School of Medicine and Dental Medicine. The campus also includes the John Dempsey Hospital, associated clinics, and extensive medical research facilities, all in a centralized facility with more than 1 million square feet of floor space. The Health Center's newest research addition, the Academic Research Building, was opened in 1999. This impressive eleven-story structure provides 170,000 square feet of state-of-the-art laboratory space. The faculty at the center includes more than 260 full-time members. The institution has a strong commitment to graduate study within an environment that promotes social and intellectual interaction among the various educational programs. Graduate students are represented on various administrative committees concerned with curricular affairs, and the Graduate Student Organization (GSO) represents graduate students' needs and concerns to the faculty and administration, in addition to fostering social contact among graduate students in the Health Center.

Applying

Applications for admission should be submitted on standard forms obtained from the Graduate Admissions Office at the UConn Health Center or the Web site. The application should be filed together with transcripts, three letters of recommendation, a personal statement, and recent results from the General Test of the Graduate Record Examinations. International students must take the Test of English as a Foreign Language (TOEFL) to satisfy Graduate School requirements. The deadline for completed applications and receipt of all supplemental materials is December 15. In accordance with the laws of the state of Connecticut and of the United States, the University of Connecticut Health Center does not discriminate against any person in its educational and employment activities on the grounds of race, color, creed, national origin, sex, age, or physical disability.

Correspondence and Information

Dr. James Li
Program Director
Department of Genetics and Developmental Biology
University of Connecticut Health Center
Farmington, Connecticut 06030-3301
Phone: 860-679-3836
E-mail: jali@uchc.edu
Web site: http://grad.uchc.edu

University of Connecticut Health Center

THE FACULTY AND THEIR RESEARCH

Alexander Amerik, Ph.D., Assistant Professor of Genetics and Developmental Biology. Deubiquitinating enzymes and ubiquitin homeostasis in the yeast *Saccharomyces cerevisiae*.

Andrew Arnold, M.D., Professor of Medicine and Murray-Heilig Chair in Molecular Medicine. Molecular genetic underpinnings of tumors of the endocrine glands; role of the cyclin D1 oncogene.

Gordon Carmichael, Ph.D., Professor of Genetics and Developmental Biology. Regulation of gene expression in eukaryotes.

Kevin Claffey, Ph.D., Assistant Professor of Cell Biology. Angiogenesis in cancer progression and metastasis; vascular endothelial growth factor (VEGF) expression; hypoxia-mediated gene regulation.

Stephen Clark, Ph.D., Associate Professor of Medicine. Characterization of mutations affecting connective tissues; molecular genetic mapping; generation and analysis of transgenic mice.

Asis Das, Ph.D., Professor of Microbiology. Basic genetic and biomechanical mechanisms that govern the elongation-termination and decision in transcription.

Caroline N. Dealy, Ph.D., Assistant Professor of Anatomy. Roles of various growth factors and signaling molecules, particularly IGF-I and insulin, in the regulation of chick limb development.

Paul Epstein, Ph.D., Associate Professor of Pharmacology. Receptor signal transduction, second messengers, and protein phosphorylation in control of cell growth and regulation; purification and regulation of cyclic nucleotide phosphodiesterases; role of calmodulin in mediating Ca^{2+}-dependent cell processes.

Guo-Hua Fong, Ph.D., Assistant Professor of Cell Biology. Developmental biology of the vascular system, VEGF-A receptor signal transduction, embryonic stem cells, and gene knock-out in mice.

Brenton R. Graveley, Ph.D., Associate Professor of Genetics and Developmental Biology. Regulation of alternative splicing in the mammalian nervous system and mechanisms of alternative splicing.

Arthur Günzl, Ph.D., Associate Professor, Center for Microbial Pathogenesis. Transcription and antigenic variation in the mammalian parasite *Trypanosoma brucei*.

Marc Hansen, Ph.D., Professor of Medicine. Molecular genetics of osteosarcoma and related bone diseases.

Laurinda Jaffe, Ph.D., Professor of Cell Biology. Physiology of fertilization.

Robert A. Kosher, Ph.D., Professor of Anatomy. Limb development; role of extracellular matrix, cytoskeleton, and cyclic nucleotides in chondrogenesis; molecular regulation of gene activity during cartilage differentiation.

Barbara Kream, Ph.D., Professor of Medicine. Hormonal regulation of collagen gene expression in bone.

Marc Lalande, Ph.D., Professor of Genetics and Developmental Biology. Genomic imprinting; Angelman syndrome; mechanism of tissue-specific silencing of the Angelman ubiquitin ligase in mouse and human.

James Li, Ph.D., Assistant Professor of Genetics and Developmental Biology. Identifying the molecular mechanisms underlying formation of the mammalian cerebellum.

Alexander Lichtler, Ph.D., Associate Professor of Pediatrics. Regulation of collagen gene transcription; retrovirus vectors; role of homeobox genes in limb development.

Bruce Mayer, Ph.D., Associate Professor of Genetics and Developmental Biology. Biologically relevant Nck-interacting proteins.

Mina Mina, D.M.D., Ph.D., Associate Professor of Pediatric Dentistry. Characterization of genetic and epigenetic influences involved in pattern formation and skeletogenesis of the chick mandible and mouse tooth germ.

William Mohler, Ph.D., Assistant Professor of Genetics and Developmental Biology. Molecular and cellular mechanisms of cell fusion.

D. Kent Morest, M.D., Professor of Neuroscience. Role of cell and tissue interactions in the migration and differentiation of neurons; structure and function of neurons during development and synapse formation.

Achilles Pappano, Ph.D., Professor of Pharmacology. Development of electrical properties of the heart; maturation of cardiac autonomic receptors; neurogenesis in the embryonic heart.

John Peluso, Ph.D., Professor of Cell Biology. Control of ovarian follicle growth steroidogenesis in vitro; proto-oncogene expression and ovarian follicular growth.

Justin D. Radolf, M.D., Professor of Medicine and Genetics and Developmental Biology. Molecular pathogenesis and immunobiology of spirochetal infections.

Blanka Rogina, Ph.D., Assistant Professor of Genetics and Developmental Biology. Molecular mechanism underlying aging process in *Drosophila melanogaster*.

Edward F. Rossomando, D.D.S., Ph.D., Professor of BioStructure and Function. Control of gene expression in tumor and nontumor cell lines in response to stimulation by monokines; coding, transmission, and processing of environmental signals in normal and abnormal development.

David Rowe, M.D., Professor of Pediatrics. Hormonal regulation of Type I collagen in mature and developing bone; heritable disorders of bone formation.

Mansoor Sarfarazi, Ph.D., Associate Professor of Surgery. Positional mapping and mutation analysis of human genetic disorders; primary open angle glaucoma; primary congenital glaucoma; synpolydactyly; dyslexia; mitral valve prolapse and ascending aortic aneurysm.

Marvin Tanzer, M.D., Professor of BioStructure and Function. Role of the extracellular matrix in developing systems; regulation of the expression of collagens, proteoglycans, laminin, and fibronectin.

Petros Tsipouras, M.D., Professor of Pediatrics. Heritable disorders of connective tissue, nosology, and genetics; genetic linkage studies; molecular mechanisms of mutations in human collagen genes.

William B. Upholt, Ph.D., Professor of BioStructure and Function. Regulation of gene expression during embryonic development; procollagen gene expression and regulation in limb chondrogenesis and skeletogenesis; pattern formation; homeobox genes.

Bruce White, Ph.D., Professor of Physiology. Control of prolactin gene expression at pretranslational level in GH3 cells; control of aromatase gene expression in ovarian and testicular tissues.

Ren-He Xu, Ph.D., Associate Professor of Genetics and Developmental Biology. Biology of human embryonic stem cells.

UNIVERSITY OF FLORIDA

College of Medicine
Advanced Concentration in Genetics

Program of Study	The College of Medicine at the University of Florida (UF) offers graduate training in biomedical research leading to a Ph.D. degree through the Interdisciplinary Program (IDP) in Biomedical Sciences. The goal of the Interdisciplinary Program is to prepare students for a diversity of careers in research and teaching in academic and commercial settings. The program provides a modern, comprehensive graduate education in biomedical science while providing both maximum program flexibility as well as appropriate specialization for graduate students. During the first year of study, incoming graduate students undertake a common, comprehensive interdisciplinary core curriculum of classroom study developed in a cooperative effort by all of the graduate programs in the College of Medicine. In addition, students select from any of the College of Medicine faculty members for participation in several laboratory rotations conducted throughout the first year, concurrent with the core curriculum. By the end of their first year, students select a laboratory in which to conduct their dissertation research and, once again, they may choose from any of the graduate faculty members in the College of Medicine. Formal selection of a graduate program and mentor is made after completion of the core curriculum to maximize flexibility and facilitate an informed decision; however, students may make an informal commitment to a program or lab at any time.

The Advanced Concentration in Genetics prepares students to conduct research and assume supervisory and teaching responsibilities in all facets of modern molecular genetics, including human genetics, mammalian genetics, lower eukaryotic genetics, bacterial genetics, viral genetics, and immunogenetics. All Ph.D. candidates must pass a qualifying examination that tests proficiency in genetics and related areas as well as the ability to formulate and defend a research proposal. Dissertation research is conducted with the advice of the student's supervisory committee. The program of study leading to the Ph.D. degree can be completed in four to five years.

Research Facilities	The College of Medicine houses state-of-the-art research facilities maintained by the Interdisciplinary Center for Biomedical Research (ICBR), the McKnight Brain Institute, the Clinical Research Center, the Cancer/Genetics Research Center, several other University of Florida research centers, and individual research laboratories. Together these facilities provide services for DNA and protein synthesis and sequencing, hybridoma production, confocal and electron microscopy, NMR spectroscopy, computing and molecular modeling, flow cytometry, transgenic mouse production, and gene therapy vector construction. The University of Florida libraries, including the Health Center library, form the largest information resource system in the state of Florida and support up-to-date computer-based bibliographic retrieval services.

UF's nine libraries offer more than 4 million catalogued volumes and links to full-text articles in more than 34,000 journals. Of national significance are the Baldwin Library of Historical Children's Literature, the Latin American Collection, the Map and Imagery Library, the P. K. Yonge Library of Florida History (preeminent Floridiana collection), the Price Library of Judaica, and holdings on architectural preservation and eighteenth-century American architecture, late nineteenth- and early twentieth-century German state documents, rural sociology of Florida, and tropical and subtropical agriculture.

Financial Aid	Students accepted into the Interdisciplinary Program receive a stipend of $25,750 per annum. Students also receive a waiver that covers tuition and GatorGradCare health insurance.
Cost of Study	Graduate research assistants pay fees of approximately $1400 per year. Books and supplies cost about $1600.
Living and Housing Costs	Married student housing is available in six apartment villages operated by the University; dormitories for single students are available in limited quantities. The cost of housing for a single graduate student is approximately $6500 per year. Most graduate students live in abundant and comfortable off-campus housing that is near the University; rents vary but are low on a national scale.
Student Group	Enrollment at the University of Florida is both culturally and geographically diverse and numbers about 50,000, including about 10,000 graduate students. There are about 300 graduate students in the College of Medicine.
Location	Situated in north-central Florida, midway between the Atlantic Ocean and the Gulf of Mexico, Gainesville is a nationally recognized academic and research center and was rated the number one place to live in the U.S. in a 1995 *Money* magazine survey. There are about 200,000 residents in the Gainesville metropolitan area, excluding University of Florida students. The climate is moderate, permitting outdoor activities the year around. The University and the Gainesville community also host numerous cultural events, including music, dance, theater, lectures, and art exhibits. Many of the men's and women's athletic programs are considered to be in the top ten programs in the country.
The University and The College	The University of Florida, located on 2,000 acres, is among the nation's leading research universities as categorized by the Carnegie Commission on Higher Education. UF is a member of the Association of American Universities, the nation's most prestigious higher education organization. UF is also one of the nation's top three universities in the breadth of academic programs offered on a single campus. It has twenty colleges and schools and 100 interdisciplinary research and education centers, bureaus, and institutes. The College of Medicine, opened in 1956, has become a nationally recognized leader in medical education and research.
Applying	The Interdisciplinary Program in Biomedical Sciences seeks promising students with undergraduate training in chemistry, biology, psychology, or related disciplines in the life sciences. Applicants are selected on the basis of previous academic work, research experience, GRE General Test scores, letters of recommendation, the personal statement, and a personal interview. Students are admitted for the fall semester, which begins in late August. The application deadline is December 15.
Correspondence and Information	Peggy Wallace, Director Department of Molecular Genetics and Microbiology University of Florida College of Medicine P.O. Box 100266 Gainesville, Florida 32610-0266 Phone: 352-392-3055 Fax: 352-392-3133 E-mail: peggyw@ufl.edu Web site: http://idp.med.ufl.edu/GEN/index.html

University of Florida

THE FACULTY AND THEIR RESEARCH

David Allred, Ph.D., Associate Professor. Cellular and molecular bases of host-parasite interactions; immunology of hemoparasitic diseases.

John Aris, Ph.D., Associate Professor. Mechanisms of cellular aging, yeast model system.

Mark Atkinson, Ph.D., Eminent Scholar, Program Director, and Unit Co-Director, Experimental Pathology. Natural history of insulin-dependent diabetes; cellular immunology; immunoprevention trials; gene therapy; cellular regeneration; transplantation.

Henry V. Baker, Ph.D., Professor and Chair. Functional genomics; gene expression profiling using DNA microarrays to understand phenotype.

Kenneth Berns, M.D., Ph.D., Professor. AAV as a vector for human gene therapy; molecular genetics of AAV.

David Bloom, Ph.D., Associate Professor. Herpesvirus latency and pathogenesis; HSV vectors.

Linda Bloom, Ph.D., Professor. Biochemistry of DNA replication and repair; dynamic protein-DNA interactions and enzyme mechanisms required for these processes.

David Borchelt, Ph.D., Professor and Interim Chair. Transgenic and knockout mouse models and cell models for molecular mechanisms of familial neurodegenerative diseases, including Alzheimer's disease, amyotrophic lateral sclerosis, and Huntington's disease.

Luciano Brocchieri, Ph.D., Assistant Professor. Bioinformatics; molecular evolution; phylogenetic trees; determinants of gene and protein composition; genomics of herpesviruses; chaperonomics.

Kevin Brown, Ph.D., Associate Professor. Cellular mechanisms that maintain stability of the human genome; signal transduction pathways that trigger cell-cycle checkpoints and apoptosis in response to DNA damage.

Jörg Bungert, Ph.D., Associate Professor. The powerful DNA regulatory element composed of five DNase I hypersensitive sites (HS1 to HS5) on the human beta-globin locus control region (LCR), located from 8 to 22 Kbp upstream of the human epsilon-globin gene.

Martha Burt, M.D., Assistant Professor. Forensic toxicology; impact of trauma services on the medical examiner forensic taphonomy; autopsy pathology.

Barry Byrne, M.D., Ph.D., Professor. Cardiovascular gene therapy; adeno-associated viral vectors.

Lung-Ji Chang, Ph.D., Professor. HIV, retroviral, and lentiviral vectors and cancer.

Martin Cohn, Ph.D., Associate Professor. Development of vertebrate external genitalia; evolution of vertebrate limb development; genetic mechanisms of vertebrate skeletal evolution; genetic basis of birth defects.

Richard C. Condit, Ph.D., Professor and Co-Director. Vaccinia virus molecular genetics; transcription elongation.

Daniel Driscoll, M.D., Ph.D., Professor. Neurobehavioral syndromes; genomic imprinting and obesity.

Kenneth Drury, Ph.D., Professor. Preimplantation genetic diagnosis; metabolic requirements and oxidative damage to in vitro cultured human gametes; micromanipulation and chromosomal analysis of preimplantation embryos using FISH.

Pedro Fernandez-Funez, Ph.D., Assistant Professor. Molecular mechanisms of neurodegeneration in Alzheimer's disease; prion disorders in transfenic *Drosophilia* models.

Melissa Elder, M.D., Ph.D., Associate Professor. AAV- or parvovirus B19-mediated correction of human severe combined immunodeficiency syndrome.

Giti Ghaffari, Ph.D., Research Assistant Professor. Molecular pathology of HIV-1.

Steve Ghivizzani, Ph.D., Associate Professor. Gene delivery approaches to the treatment and repair of musculoskeletal disorders.

Jorge A. Giron, Ph.D., Associate Professor. Understanding the molecular basis of the relationship between pathogenic *Escherichia coli* and host cells.

Maureen Goodenow, Ph.D., Professor and Unit Co-Director, Experimental Pathology. Pathogenesis of retroviruses and HIV; signal transduction in lymphocytes and macrophages; genetics of viral drug resistance; evolution of HIV-1.

Paul A. Gulig, Ph.D., Professor. Pathogenesis of *Vibrio vulnificus;* bacteriophage therapy; detection of agents of bioterrorism.

Brian Harfe, Ph.D., Assistant Professor. Molecular pathways of embryonic development; vertebrate model systems of limb development; invertebral disk formation and disease using mouse models.

William Hauswirth, Ph.D., Eminent Scholar. Gene expression; gene delivery; gene therapy and functional genomics in the retina.

Jeffrey Hillman, D.M.D., Ph.D., Professor. Identification, characterization, and modification of bacterial virulence factors for the control or prevention of infections.

Jacqueline Hobbs, M.D., Ph.D., Assistant Professor. Neurovirology and the potential role viruses may play in the pathogenesis of mental illness, focusing on the neurobiology of parvoviruses.

Steven Hochwald, M.D., Assistant Professor. Signal transduction; novel tyrosine kinase inhibitors in pancreatic cancer.

Stephen Hsu, M.D., Ph.D., Associate Professor. Cell-cycle regulation; nephrogenomics/nephroproteomics; clinical trials of novel investigational agents; metabolic syndrome; autoimmune disease.

Suming Huang, Ph.D., Assistant Professor. Epigenetic regulation of chromatin structure and gene expression; structure and function of the globin gene chromatin insulator 5'HS4; regulation of TAL1 oncoprotein activity.

Shouguang Jin, Ph.D., Professor. Type III secretion system of *Pseudomonas* and host-cell apoptosis.

Michael Kilberg, Ph.D., Professor. Nutrient control of gene transcription for human asparagine synthetase; charaterization of chromatin changes and transcription factor complexes during stress.

Michael Kladde, Ph.D., Associate Professor. Regulation of transcription by chromatin; role of DNA methylation in epigenetic silencing in breast cancer; DNA methyltransferases as probes of chromatin structure; yeast and mammalian cell-culture systems.

Phil Laipis, Ph.D., Professor. Structure/function and genetics of carbonic anhydrase; inheritance of mammalian mitochondrial DNA.

Alfred S. Lewin, Ph.D., Professor. RNA-mediated gene therapy; retinal disease; RNA catalysis.

Chen Liu, Ph.D., Associate Professor. Viral hepatitis pathogenesis and hepatocarcinogenesis; oncogenes, signal transduction, and cell transformation; viral immunology and vaccine; alpha-1 antitrypsin deficiency and liver disease.

Jianrong Lu, Ph.D., Assistant Professor. Chromatin regulation in development and cancer, using cell culture and mouse models.

Alexandra Lucas, M.D., Professor. Analysis of serpins in vascular innate immune responses; role of GAGs in viral chemokine modulating protein anti-inflammatory functions; optical analysis of vascular inflammation and atherogenesis.

Clayton Mathews, Ph.D., Professor. Genetics of resistance to autoimmune diabetes; oxidative burden of the beta cell.

Wayne T. McCormack, Ph.D., Associate Professor and Director, Graduate Program. Genetics of susceptibility to autoimmune disease; vitiligo.

Peter McGuire, Ph.D., Professor. Molecular biology; gene regulation.

Lauren McIntyre, Ph.D., Associate Professor. Statistical theory to elucidate the relationship between genotype and phenotype; simple models for gene networks.

Laurence Morel, Ph.D., Associate Professor and Co-Director. Genetic analysis of systemic lupus erythematosus (SLE) susceptibility using mouse models; genetic basis for susceptibility to autoimmunity.

J. Glen Morris Jr., M.D., Professor. Molecular epidemiology and pathogenesis of bacterial enteric pathogens.

Phillippe Moullier, M.D., Adjunct Professor. Basic virology of adeno-associated virus and murine leukemia virus with translational developments in recombinant virus assembly, the preclinical evaluation of recombinant viral vectors in primates and large animals.

Richard W. Moyer, Ph.D., Professor and Senior Associate Dean for Research Development. Poxvirus biology and pathogenesis.

Nicholas Muzyczka, Ph.D., Eminent Scholar. Adeno-associated virus and virus vectors.

Peter Nelson, M.D., Assistant Professor. Human system-wide genomic and proteomic studies investigating the link between systemic inflammation and outcomes following vascular surgical intervention.

Thomas O'Brien, Ph.D., Professor. Mitochondrial ribosome structure/function and gene expression.

Rolf F. Renne, Ph.D., Associate Professor. Kaposi's sarcoma–associated herpesvirus (KSHV/HHV-8) latency and pathogenesis.

James Resnick, Ph.D., Associate Professor. Development and genetic reprogramming of the germline in mammalian embryos; mechanisms regulating genomic imprinting and mouse models of imprinting diseases.

Alberto Riva, Ph.D., Assistant Professor. Development of computational tools and techniques for the representation, storage, and dissemination of biomedical knowledge.

Marco Salemi, Ph.D., Assistant Professor. Molecular evolution of viruses, with special emphasis on HIV and SIV; development and application of new bioinformatics and phylogenetic analysis tools to investigate the molecular epidemiology of pathogenic viruses and to study viral quasispecies.

Desmond Schatz, M.D., Professor. Prediction, immunopathogenesis, genetics, and prevention and care of type I diabetes.

Edward Scott, Ph.D., Professor. Gene regulation; biology of hematopoietic progenitor cells.

Greg Schultz, Ph.D., Professor. Role of growth factors and proteases in ocular and skin wound healing; gene therapy using ribozymes to receptors.

Paul Shirk, Ph.D., Associate Professor. Growth and development of germ cells and gonadal differentiation in insects; development of germline and somatic transformation vectors.

William Slayton, M.D., Assistant Professor. Normal and malignant hematopoiesis.

Richard Snyder, Ph.D., Assistant Professor. Molecular aspects of adeno-associated virus genome packaging; viral gene transfer vectors.

Eric Sobel, M.D., Ph.D., Associate Professor. Mechanisms of autoantibody production.

Arun Srivastava, Ph.D., Professor. Molecular correlates of human parvovirus (AAV and B19) host-cell interactions; development of recombinant human parvovirus vectors for gene therapy.

Sankar Swaminathan, M.D., Associate Professor. Molecular mechanisms of gene regulation in the oncogenic viruses Epstein-Barr virus (EBV) and Kaposi's sarcoma herpesvirus (KSHV).

Maurice S. Swanson, Ph.D., Professor. Mouse models for neuromuscular and neurological diseases; regulation of RNA alternative splicing, transport, and turnover.

Peggy Wallace, Ph.D., Professor and Director. Mapping, cloning, mutation, and functional analysis of human disease genes.

Michael Waters, Ph.D., Assistant Professor. The brain: projects encompass the fields of neurodegeneration, neurodevelopment, and neural repair in the context of neurogenetic discorders such as spinocerebellar atax as well as stroke pathophysiology and recovery.

Lizi Wu, Ph.D., Assistant Professor. Transcriptional regulation of Notch/MAML signaling in development and cancers.

Anthony Yachnis, Ph.D., Associate Professor. Cell survival in the nervous system and CNS development; developmental neuropathology; nervous system tumors; epilepsy neuropathology.

Thomas Yang, Ph.D., Professor. Molecular biology and genetics of the mammalian X-chromosome; molecular biology and genetics of genomic imprinting; regulation of transcription and chromatin structure; DNA methylation and epigenetics.

Lei Zhou, Ph.D., Assistant Professor. Genetic and genomic analysis of irradiation-induced cell death.

Roberto Zori, M.D., Associate Professor. Clinical genetics and cytogenetics; neurodevelopmental diseases.

UNIVERSITY OF WISCONSIN–MADISON

Genetics Training Program

Program of Study	The program in genetics is offered by the Departments of Genetics and Medical Genetics. It offers a broad spectrum of graduate work in genetics, including many aspects of molecular and developmental genetics, immunogenetics, cytogenetics, and viral, bacterial, mammalian, plant, human, behavioral, population, and clinical genetics.

The faculty for the program comes primarily from the Laboratory of Genetics but includes members of other departments with allied interests. Students have access to more than 70 trainers in many different biological departments at the University of Wisconsin–Madison (UW-Madison).

Applicants are selected for their strong interest in and aptitude for genetic research. Students should plan to earn the Ph.D. degree, which normally takes five to six years. The first year is devoted to both research and course work. Formal Ph.D. degree requirements are minimal and can be chosen from a wide range of specialized courses as well as from the fundamental background curriculum. Students are expected to initiate research on their thesis projects during the second semester of their first year and to devote more time to independent research as their careers progress. To fulfill minor requirements, the student may take courses in a single department, or from several departments chosen to meet individual interests. Seminars, journal clubs, and experience in teaching are also an integral part of the formal training. Each student's course program is devised by a certifying committee consisting of the student, the major professor, and 3 other professors from the program.

Research time in the first semester is devoted to a series of research experiences in various laboratories that last approximately three to four weeks each. This rotation through laboratories of the student's choice helps the student decide on a major professor.

In addition to the Ph.D. program, a specialized master's degree is offered in medical genetics that provides training in genetics counseling. Admission is independent of the Ph.D. program. |
Research Facilities	The laboratory location for thesis research depends upon the choice of thesis adviser. Since the program is administratively centered in the Genetics/Biotechnology Building, many students conduct their thesis research in this facility. The Genetics/Biotechnology Building houses laboratories with all the equipment necessary for state-of-the-art genetic research. Students who choose professors with laboratories outside the Genetics/Biotechnology Building use comparable facilities. Ancillary facilities such as greenhouses, constant-environment laboratories, a high-voltage electron microscope, and animal quarters are also available.
Financial Aid	All students accepted into the Ph.D. degree program receive financial aid from either an NIH training grant or graduate school fellowships. In later years, support may be derived from a research assistantship. The net stipend for 2010–11 is $23,000 per year after payment of tuition and fees. Support is awarded on a continuing basis, provided that satisfactory progress is maintained toward completion of Ph.D. requirements, and is contingent upon availability of federal government grants. Limited financial aid is available to international students. Currently, there is no support for the M.S. students in genetics counseling.
Cost of Study	Graduate students appointed as research assistants are considered residents for purposes of tuition, and the cost of resident tuition is paid for students accepted into the Ph.D. program.
Living and Housing Costs	A wide variety of rooms and apartments can be found in the areas surrounding the campus and elsewhere in Madison. Most students live off campus, where rates vary considerably. Furnished rooms for graduate students on campus are available from $605 per month for the 2010–11 academic year, not including board; unfurnished apartments for married students (Eagle Heights) are $670–$745 per month, including heat and hot water.
Student Group	The present enrollment at UW-Madison is approximately 41,000, of whom about 8,700 are graduate students. The standard enrollment in the genetics program is 60–70 students. About 10 new students are usually admitted to the program each year. Students are drawn from all regions of the United States and a number of other countries. Students interact with numerous postdoctoral fellows, who have received their training from a large cross section of outstanding educational institutions.
Location	The city of Madison has a population of about 200,000. It is the capital city of the state and is surrounded by four attractive lakes. Recreational opportunities are excellent all year. Camping, canoeing, backpacking, fishing, hunting, skiing, and bicycling are popular activities in the area. The cosmopolitan population enjoys both city- and University-promoted concerts, recitals, plays and theater productions and excellent dining. There are numerous opportunities for both appreciation of and participation in the arts. In the campus mall area, impromptu art exhibits, musical performances, and local vendors of crafts can be found.
The University	Founded in 1848, the University of Wisconsin has consistently been ranked among the top universities in the country. The community of biologists is one of the largest, most diverse, and best of any educational institution in the country. It is characterized by a dynamic spirit of inquiry and an atmosphere of academic freedom. The University has unusual breadth in its offerings and has pioneered in placing its facilities and staff at the disposal of the state and the nation.
Applying	Most students admitted are selected during January and February. Completed applications must be received by December 1. Midyear admissions are not considered. Admission is based mainly on demonstrated ability, experience, and interest in biology, mathematics, and the physical sciences. Minimum course prerequisites are mathematics through calculus, 1 year of physics, chemistry through organic chemistry, and three of the following four biology courses—cell biology, physiology, development, and population biology—as well as introductory courses in genetics and biochemistry. Scores on the GRE General Test are required and a Subject Test is recommended.
Correspondence and Information	Genetics Ph.D. Admissions Secretary
1432 Genetics/Biotechnology Building
University of Wisconsin–Madison
425-G Henry Mall
Madison, Wisconsin 53706-1580
Phone: 608-262-1069
Web site: http://www.genetics.wisc.edu

University of Wisconsin–Madison

THE FACULTY AND THEIR RESEARCH

Philip Anderson, Professor. Molecular genetics of the nematode, *Caenorhabditis elegans.*

David Baum, Professor (also with Botany). Molecular basis of plant morphological evolution; phylogenetics; evolutionary developmental genetics.

Frederick Blattner, Professor. Mechanisms of DNA replication, transcription, and recombination; cloning of eukaryotic DNA segments in prokaryotic carriers; immunoglobulins; DNA sequencing; phage lambda.

Sean B. Carroll, Professor (also with Molecular Biology). Developmental genetics of pattern formation; molecular evolution.

Qiang Chang, Assistant Professor. Epigenetic regulation of brain functions.

Nansi Jo Colley, Associate Professor (also with Ophthalmology). Molecular and genetic basis of photoreceptor cell function in *Drosophila melanogaster,* with particular emphasis on intracellular targeting and trafficking.

James F. Crow, Professor Emeritus. Population/evolution; *Drosophila;* human and mammalian research.

Michael R. Culbertson, Professor and Chair (also with Molecular Biology). Molecular genetics of yeast.

John Doebley, Professor. Evolutionary genetics; development and evolution.

William F. Dove, Professor (also with Oncology). Cellular and developmental genetics of *Physarum polycephalum* and of the mouse.

Albert H. Ellingboe, Professor Emeritus (also with Plant Pathology). Mendelian and molecular genetics of host-parasite interactions.

William E. Engels, Professor. Genetic and molecular behavior of transposable elements in *Drosophila* chromosomes.

Barry S. Ganetzky, Professor. Neurogenetics; genetic, electrophysiological, and molecular analysis of mutants affecting the *Drosophila* nervous system.

Audrey Gasch, Assistant Professor. The role, regulation, and evolution of fungal genomic expression responses to stress.

F. Michael Hoffmann, Professor (also with Oncology). Roles of proto-oncogenes and growth factors in *Drosophila* development.

Akihiro Ikeda, Associate Professor. Mouse genetics; development and function of the synapse; sensory neuronal disease.

Scott Kennedy, Assistant Professor (also with Pharmacology). Molecular understanding of small RNAs.

Judith E. Kimble, Professor (also with Biochemistry and Molecular Biology). Genetics and molecular biology of development in *C. elegans.*

Ching Kung, Professor (also with Molecular Biology). Ion channels and sensory transduction in *Paramecium,* yeast, and *Escherichia coli.*

Allen Laughon, Professor. Molecular genetics; homeotic and segmentation gene interactions in *Drosophila.*

Kate O'Connor-Giles, Assistant Professor. Regulation of synaptic growth and plasticity.

Patrick Masson, Professor. Maize transposable elements; mutational analysis of gravitropism and phototropism in *Arabidopsis.*

Bret Payseur, Assistant Professor. Population genetics; genetics of speciation; genetics of morphological evolution.

Francisco Pelegri, Associate Professor. Genetic analysis of vertebrate development.

Nicole Perna, Associate Professor. Evolution of bacterial genomes.

Tómas Prolla, Professor. Molecular basis of cancer and DNA repair; generation of mouse models of human disease through gene targeting.

David Schwartz, Professor. Single molecule approaches to whole genome analysis.

Ahna Skop, Assistant Professor. Cytokinesis and cell-cycle proteomics.

Paul Sondel, Professor (also with Human Oncology). Immunogenetics; transplantation immunology; cancer immunology.

Xin Sun, Associate Professor. Molecular genetics of vertebrate organogenesis.

Richard Vierstra, Professor. Molecular, genetic, and biochemical analysis of ubiquitin-dependent protein degradation and photomorphogenesis in plants, especially *Arabidopsis.*

Jerry C. P. Yin, Professor. Molecular genetics of learning and memory formation in *Drosophila* and mice.

Jaehyuk Yu, Associate Professor (also with Bacteriology). Molecular genetics of fungal development and secondary metabolism; signal transduction in fungi.

Members of Other Departments Who Serve As Trainers in the Genetics Training Program

Caroline Alexander, Oncology.
Richard Amasino, Biochemistry.
Jean-Michel Ané, Agronomy.
Aseem Ansari, Biochemistry.
Alan Attie, Veterinary Medicine and Biochemistry.
Arash Bashirullah, Pharmacy.
Andrew Bent, Plant Pathology.
Seth Blair, Zoology.
Grace Boekhoff-Falk, Anatomy.
Christopher Bradfield, Oncology.
David Brow, Biomolecular Chemistry.
Lara Collier, Pharmacy.
Cameron Currie, Bacteriology.
Elizabeth C. Craig, Physiological Chemistry.
Timothy Donohue, Bacteriology.
Diana Downs, Bacteriology.
David Eide, Nutritional Sciences and Biochemistry.
Marcin Filutowicz, Bacteriology.
Catherine Fox, Biomolecular Chemistry.
Michael Gould, Oncology.
Richard L. Gourse, Bacteriology.

Daniel Greenspan, Pathology.
Anne Griep, Anatomy.
Yevgenya Grinblat, Zoology and Anatomy.
Mary Halloran, Zoology and Anatomy.
Jeffrey Hardin, Zoology.
Colleen Hayes, Biochemistry.
Jiming Jiang, Horticulture.
Nancy Keller, Plant Pathology.
Patrick Krysan, Horticulture.
Robert Landick, Biochemistry.
Carol E. Lee, Zoology.
Paul Marker, Pharmacy.
Janet E. Mertz, Oncology.
Amy Moser, Human Oncology.
Marisa Otegui, Botany.
Gary Roberts, Bacteriology.
Michael R. Sussman, Biochemistry.
Donald Waller, Botany.
Karen Wassarman, Bacteriology.
Marvin Wickens, Biochemistry.
Jing Zhang, Oncology.

Section 11
Marine Biology

This section contains a directory of institutions offering graduate work in marine biology, followed by an in-depth entry submitted by an institution that chose to prepare a detailed program description. Additional information about programs listed in the directory but not augmented by an in-depth entry may be obtained by writing directly to the dean of a graduate school or chair of a department at the address given in the directory.

For programs offering related work, see also in this book *Biological and Biomedical Sciences* and *Zoology*. In another guide in this series: ***Graduate Programs in the Physical Sciences, Mathematics, Agricultural Sciences, the Environment & Natural Resources***
See *Marine Sciences and Oceanography*

CONTENTS

Marine Biology

College of Charleston, Graduate School, School of Sciences and Mathematics, Program in Marine Biology, Charleston, SC 29412. Offers MS. *Faculty:* 100. *Students:* 52 full-time (31 women); includes 1 minority (Hispanic American). Average age 26. 88 applicants, 25% accepted, 16 enrolled. In 2009, 14 master's awarded. *Degree requirements:* For master's, comprehensive exam, thesis. *Entrance requirements:* For master's, GRE General Test, 3 letters of recommendation. Additional exam requirements/recommendations for international students: Required—TOEFL. *Application deadline:* For fall admission, 2/1 for domestic and international students; for spring admission, 11/1 for domestic and international students. Application fee: $45. Electronic applications accepted. *Financial support:* In 2009–10, 4 fellowships (averaging $22,000 per year), 22 research assistantships, 19 teaching assistantships were awarded; career-related internships or fieldwork, Federal Work-Study, institutionally sponsored loans, scholarships/grants, and unspecified assistantships also available. Support available to part-time students. Financial award application deadline: 4/1; financial award applicants required to submit FAFSA. *Faculty research:* Ecology, environmental physiology, marine genomics, bioinformatics, toxicology, cell biology, population biology, fisheries science, animal physiology, biodiversity, estuarine ecology, evolution and systematics, microbial processes, plant physiology, immunology. *Unit head:* Dr. Craig J. Plante, Director, 843-953-9187, Fax: 843-953-9199, E-mail: plantec@cofc.edu. *Application contact:* Susan Hallatt, Director of Graduate Admissions, 843-953-5614, Fax: 843-953-1434, E-mail: hallatts@cofc.edu.

Florida Institute of Technology, Graduate Programs, College of Science, Department of Biological Sciences, Program in Marine Biology, Melbourne, FL 32901-6975. Offers MS. Part-time programs available. *Degree requirements:* For master's, thesis. *Entrance requirements:* For master's, GRE General Test, minimum GPA of 3.0. *Application deadline:* Applications are processed on a rolling basis. Electronic applications accepted. *Expenses:* Tuition: Part-time $1015 per credit. Tuition and fees vary according to campus/location and program. *Financial support:* In 2009–10, 8 students received support; research assistantships with full and partial tuition reimbursements available, teaching assistantships with full and partial tuition reimbursements available, career-related internships or fieldwork and tuition remissions available. Financial award application deadline: 3/1; financial award applicants required to submit FAFSA. *Faculty research:* Ecology of coral reef fish communities and biology of Foraminiferida; ecology, physiology, reproduction, and morphology of sea stars, sea urchins, and other echinoderms. *Application contact:* Carolyn P. Shea.

See Close-Up on page 329.

Memorial University of Newfoundland, School of Graduate Studies, Department of Biology, St. John's, NL A1C 5S7, Canada. Offers biology (M Sc, PhD); marine biology (M Sc, PhD). Part-time programs available. *Degree requirements:* For master's, thesis; for doctorate, comprehensive exam, thesis/dissertation, oral defense of thesis. *Entrance requirements:* For master's, honors degree (minimum 2nd class standing) in related field. Electronic applications accepted. *Faculty research:* Northern flora and fauna, especially cold ocean and boreal environments.

Nicholls State University, Graduate Studies, College of Arts and Sciences, Department of Biological Sciences, Thibodaux, LA 70310. Offers marine and environmental biology (MS). Part-time programs available. *Degree requirements:* For master's, comprehensive exam, thesis. *Entrance requirements:* For master's, GRE. Additional exam requirements/recommendations for international students: Required—TOEFL (minimum score 600 paper-based). *Faculty research:* Bioremediation, ecology, public health, biotechnology, physiology.

Northeastern University, College of Science, Department of Biology, Boston, MA 02115-5096. Offers bioinformatics (PMS); biology (MS, PhD); biotechnology (MS); marine biology (MS). Part-time programs available. *Faculty:* 27 full-time (10 women), 5 part-time/adjunct (all women). *Students:* 111 full-time (67 women); includes 2 African Americans, 3 Asian Americans or Pacific Islanders, 3 Hispanic Americans, 39 international. 178 applicants, 28% accepted, 35 enrolled. In 2009, 31 master's, 5 doctorates awarded. Terminal master's awarded for partial completion of doctoral program. *Degree requirements:* For master's, thesis (for some programs); for doctorate, thesis/dissertation, qualifying exam. *Entrance requirements:* For master's and doctorate, GRE General Test. Additional exam requirements/recommendations for international students: Required—TOEFL (minimum score 250 computer-based). *Application deadline:* For fall admission, 1/1 priority date for domestic and international students. Applications are processed on a rolling basis. Application fee: $50. Electronic applications accepted. *Financial support:* In 2009–10, 19 research assistantships with tuition reimbursements (averaging $18,285 per year), 41 teaching assistantships with tuition reimbursements (averaging $18,285 per year) were awarded; fellowships with tuition reimbursements, career-related internships or fieldwork, Federal Work-Study, tuition waivers (full and partial), and unspecified assistantships also available. Financial award application deadline: 3/1; financial award applicants required to submit FAFSA. *Faculty research:* Biochemistry, marine sciences, molecular biology, microbiology and immunology neurobiology, cellular and molecular biology, biochemistry, marine biochemistry and ecology, microbiology, neurobiology, biotechnology. *Unit head:* Dr. Wendy Smith, Graduate Coordinator, 617-373-2260, Fax: 617-373-3724, E-mail: gradbio@neu.edu. *Application contact:* Jo-Anne Dickinson, Admissions Assistant, 617-373-5990, Fax: 617-373-7281, E-mail: gsas@neu.edu.

Nova Southeastern University, Oceanographic Center, Program in Marine Biology, Fort Lauderdale, FL 33314-7796. Offers MS. *Faculty:* 15 full-time (1 woman), 5 part-time/adjunct (0 women). *Students:* 89 full-time (70 women), 33 part-time (20 women); includes 8 minority (1 African American, 7 Hispanic Americans), 3 international. 60 applicants, 97% accepted, 35 enrolled. In 2009, 26 master's awarded. *Degree requirements:* For master's, thesis. *Entrance requirements:* For master's, GRE. Additional exam requirements/recommendations for international students: Required—TOEFL (minimum score 550 paper-based). *Application deadline:* Applications are processed on a rolling basis. Application fee: $50. *Expenses:* Contact institution. *Financial support:* In 2009–10, 6 research assistantships (averaging $4,000 per year), 3 teaching assistantships (averaging $3,500 per year) were awarded; career-related internships or fieldwork, Federal Work-Study, scholarships/grants, and unspecified assistantships also available. Support available to part-time students. Financial award applicants required to submit FAFSA. *Unit head:* Dr. Richard Spieler, Director of Academic Programs, 954-262-3600, Fax: 954-262-4020, E-mail: spieler@nova.edu. *Application contact:* Dr. Richard Spieler, Director of Academic Programs, 954-262-3600, Fax: 954-262-4020, E-mail: spieler@nova.edu.

Nova Southeastern University, Oceanographic Center, Program in Marine Biology and Oceanography, Fort Lauderdale, FL 33314-7796. Offers marine biology (PhD); oceanography (PhD). *Faculty:* 15 full-time (1 woman), 5 part-time/adjunct (0 women). *Students:* 10 full-time (4 women), 5 part-time (4 women); includes 1 minority (African American), 1 international. 5 applicants, 80% accepted, 3 enrolled. In 2009, 1 doctorate awarded. *Degree requirements:* For doctorate, comprehensive exam, thesis/dissertation. *Entrance requirements:* For doctorate, GRE, master's degree. Application fee: $50. *Financial support:* In 2009–10, research assistantships (averaging $18,000 per year); Federal Work-Study, scholarships/grants, and unspecified assistantships also available. Support available to part-time students. *Unit head:* Dr. Richard Dodge, Dean, 954-262-3600, Fax: 954-262-4020, E-mail: dodge@nsu.nova.edu. *Application contact:* Dr. Richard Spieler, Director of Academic Programs, 954-262-3600, Fax: 954-262-4020, E-mail: spieler@nova.edu.

Princeton University, Graduate School, Department of Geosciences, Princeton, NJ 08544-1019. Offers atmospheric and oceanic sciences (PhD); geosciences (PhD); ocean sciences and marine biology (PhD). *Degree requirements:* For doctorate, one foreign language, thesis/dissertation. *Entrance requirements:* For doctorate, GRE General Test. Additional exam requirements/recommendations for international students: Required—TOEFL (minimum score 600 paper-based; 250 computer-based). Electronic applications accepted. *Faculty research:* Biogeochemistry, climate science, earth history, regional geology and tectonics, solid–earth geophysics.

Rutgers, The State University of New Jersey, New Brunswick, Graduate School-New Brunswick, Department of Environmental Sciences, Piscataway, NJ 08854-8097. Offers air pollution and resources (MS, PhD); aquatic biology (MS, PhD); aquatic chemistry (MS, PhD); atmospheric science (MS, PhD); chemistry and physics of aerosol and hydrosol systems (MS, PhD); environmental chemistry (MS, PhD); environmental microbiology (MS, PhD); environmental toxicology (PhD); exposure assessment (PhD); fate and effects of pollutants (MS, PhD); pollution prevention and control (MS, PhD); water and wastewater treatment (MS, PhD); water resources (MS, PhD). Terminal master's awarded for partial completion of doctoral program. *Degree requirements:* For master's, comprehensive exam, thesis or alternative, oral final exam; for doctorate, comprehensive exam, thesis/dissertation, thesis defense, qualifying exam. *Entrance requirements:* For master's and doctorate, GRE General Test. Additional exam requirements/recommendations for international students: Required—TOEFL. Electronic applications accepted. *Faculty research:* Biological waste treatment; contaminant fate and transport; air, soil and water quality.

San Francisco State University, Division of Graduate Studies, College of Science and Engineering, Department of Biology, Program in Marine Science, San Francisco, CA 94132-1722. Offers MS.

Texas A&M University at Galveston, Department of Marine Biology, Galveston, TX 77553-1675. Offers MS, PhD. *Faculty:* 33 full-time (7 women). *Students:* 7 full-time (5 women); includes 2 minority (both Hispanic Americans). Average age 23. 15 applicants, 40% accepted, 2 enrolled. *Entrance requirements:* For master's and doctorate, GRE. Additional exam requirements/recommendations for international students: Required—TOEFL (minimum score 550 paper-based; 213 computer-based). *Application deadline:* For fall admission, 12/15 priority date for domestic students; for spring admission, 5/15 priority date for domestic students. Applications are processed on a rolling basis. Application fee: $50 ($75 for international students). Electronic applications accepted. *Financial support:* In 2009–10, 1 student received support, including 8 teaching assistantships; research assistantships, scholarships/grants, health care benefits, and unspecified assistantships also available. Financial award applicants required to submit FAFSA. *Faculty research:* Fisheries, coastal and wetland ecologies, phytoplankton, marine mammals, seafood safety, marine invertebrates and marine biospeleology. Total annual research expenditures: $3.8 million. *Unit head:* Dr. Bernd Wursig, Professor/Chair of Marine Biology Interdisciplinary Program, 409-740-4413, E-mail: wursigb@tamug.edu. *Application contact:* Nicole Wilkins, Administrative Coordinator for Graduate Studies, 409-740-4937, Fax: 409-740-4754, E-mail: wilkinsn@tamug.edu.

Texas State University–San Marcos, Graduate School, College of Science, Department of Biology, Program in Aquatic Resources, San Marcos, TX 78666. Offers MS, PhD. *Faculty:* 7 full-time (1 woman). *Students:* 39 full-time (22 women), 19 part-time (11 women); includes 10 minority (1 American Indian/Alaska Native, 3 Asian Americans or Pacific Islanders, 6 Hispanic Americans), 4 international. Average age 33. 13 applicants, 69% accepted, 7 enrolled. In 2009, 9 master's, 3 doctorates awarded. *Degree requirements:* For master's, comprehensive exam, thesis, 3 seminars. *Entrance requirements:* For master's, GRE General Test, previous course work in biology, minimum GPA of 2.75 in last 60 hours of course work. Additional exam requirements/recommendations for international students: Required—TOEFL (minimum score 550 paper-based; 213 computer-based). *Application deadline:* For fall admission, 6/15 priority date for domestic students, 6/1 priority date for international students; for spring admission, 10/15 priority date for domestic students, 10/1 priority date for international students. Applications are processed on a rolling basis. Application fee: $40 ($90 for international students). Electronic applications accepted. *Expenses:* Tuition, state resident: full-time $5784; part-time $241 per credit hour. Tuition, nonresident: full-time $13,224; part-time $551 per credit hour. Required fees: $1728; $48 per credit hour. $306. Tuition and fees vary according to course load. *Financial support:* In 2009–10, 31 students received support, including 17 research assistantships (averaging $8,841 per year), 23 teaching assistantships (averaging $10,196 per year). Financial award application deadline: 4/1; financial award applicants required to submit FAFSA. *Unit head:* Dr. Tim Bonner, Advisor, 512-245-1616, Fax: 512-245-8713, E-mail: tb14@txstate.edu. *Application contact:* Dr. J. Michael Willoughby, Dean of the Graduate School, 512-245-2581, Fax: 512-245-8365, E-mail: jw02@swt.edu.

University of Alaska Fairbanks, School of Fisheries and Ocean Sciences, Program in Marine Sciences and Limnology, Fairbanks, AK 99775-7220. Offers marine biology (MS, PhD); oceanography (PhD), including biological oceanography, chemical oceanography, fisheries, geological oceanography, physical oceanography. Part-time programs available. *Faculty:* 12 full-time (5 women), 2 part-time/adjunct (0 women). *Students:* 29 full-time (17 women), 14 part-time (9 women); includes 4 minority (2 Asian Americans or Pacific Islanders, 2 Hispanic Americans), 2 international. Average age 33. 45 applicants, 18% accepted, 8 enrolled. In 2009, 8 master's, 2 doctorates awarded. *Degree requirements:* For master's, comprehensive exam, thesis, oral defense; for doctorate, comprehensive exam, thesis/dissertation, oral defense. *Entrance requirements:* For master's and doctorate, GRE General Test. Additional exam requirements/recommendations for international students: Required—TOEFL (minimum score 550 paper-based; 213 computer-based; 80 iBT). *Application deadline:* For fall admission, 6/1 for domestic students, 3/1 for international students; for spring admission, 10/15 for domestic students, 8/1 for international students. Applications are processed on a rolling basis. Application fee: $60. Electronic applications accepted. *Expenses:* Tuition, state resident: full-time $7584; part-time $316 per credit. Tuition, nonresident: full-time $15,504; part-time $646 per credit. Required fees: $23 per credit. $135 per semester. Tuition and fees vary according to course level, course load and reciprocity agreements. *Financial support:* In 2009–10, 3 fellowships (averaging $10,865 per year), 18 research assistantships (averaging $10,454 per year), 6 teaching assistantships (averaging $10,748 per year) were awarded; career-related internships or fieldwork, Federal Work-Study, scholarships/grants, health care benefits, and unspecified assistantships also available. Support available to part-time students. Financial award application deadline: 7/1; financial award applicants required to submit FAFSA. *Unit head:* Dr. Denis Wiesenberg, Dean, 907-474-7824, Fax: 907-474-7204, E-mail: info@sfos.uaf.edu. *Application contact:* Katie Straub, Recruitment and Retention Coordinator, 907-474-6786, Fax: 907-474-5863, E-mail: kmstraub@alaska.edu.

University of California, San Diego, Office of Graduate Studies, Scripps Institution of Oceanography, La Jolla, CA 92093. Offers earth sciences (PhD); marine biodiversity and conservation (MAS); marine biology (PhD); oceanography (PhD). *Entrance requirements:* For doctorate, GRE General Test, GRE Subject Test. Additional exam requirements/recommendations for international students: Required—TOEFL (minimum score 550 paper-based; 213 computer-based). Electronic applications accepted.

University of California, Santa Barbara, Graduate Division, College of Letters and Sciences, Division of Mathematics, Life, and Physical Sciences, Department of Ecology, Evolution, and Marine Biology, Santa Barbara, CA 93106-9620. Offers computational science and engineering (PhD); MA/PhD. *Faculty:* 39 full-time (8 women). *Students:* 56 full-time (35 women). Average age 30. 135 applicants, 13% accepted, 7 enrolled. In 2009, 7 master's, 15 doctorates awarded. Terminal master's awarded for partial completion of doctoral program. *Degree requirements:* For master's, comprehensive exam (for some programs), thesis (for some programs); for doctorate, comprehensive exam, thesis/dissertation. *Entrance requirements:* For master's, GRE General Test, 3 letters of recommendation, resume/curriculum vitae; for doctorate, GRE

General Test, 3 letters of recommendation, statement of purpose, personal achievements/contributions statement, resume/curriculum vitae, transcripts for post-secondary institutions attended. Additional exam requirements/recommendations for international students: Required—TOEFL (minimum score 550 paper-based; 213 computer-based; 80 iBT) or IELTS. *Application deadline:* For fall admission, 12/15 for domestic and international students. Application fee: $70 ($90 for international students). Electronic applications accepted. *Financial support:* In 2009–10, 54 students received support, including 26 fellowships with full and partial tuition reimbursements available (averaging $17,900 per year), 16 research assistantships with full and partial tuition reimbursements available (averaging $7,300 per year), 35 teaching assistantships with partial tuition reimbursements available (averaging $9,100 per year); Federal Work-Study, institutionally sponsored loans, scholarships/grants, traineeships, health care benefits, tuition waivers (full and partial), and unspecified assistantships also available. Financial award applicants required to submit FAFSA. *Faculty research:* Ecology, population genetics, stream ecology, evolution, marine biology. *Unit head:* Robert Warner, Chair, 805-893-2415, Fax: 805-893-4724, E-mail: eembchair@lifesci.ucsb.edu. *Application contact:* Alina Haas, Staff Graduate Advisor, 805-893-3023, Fax: 805-893-5885, E-mail: haas@lifesci.ucsb.edu.

University of Colorado at Boulder, Graduate School, College of Arts and Sciences, Department of Ecology and Evolutionary Biology, Boulder, CO 80309. Offers animal behavior (MA); biology (MA, PhD); environmental biology (MA, PhD); evolutionary biology (MA, PhD); neurobiology (MA); population biology (MA); population genetics (PhD). *Faculty:* 32 full-time (10 women). *Students:* 64 full-time (36 women), 15 part-time (9 women); includes 12 minority (1 American Indian/Alaska Native, 3 Asian Americans or Pacific Islanders, 8 Hispanic Americans), 4 international. Average age 29. 145 applicants, 14% accepted, 21 enrolled. In 2009, 9 master's, 6 doctorates awarded. Terminal master's awarded for partial completion of doctoral program. *Degree requirements:* For master's, comprehensive exam, thesis or alternative; for doctorate, comprehensive exam, thesis/dissertation. *Entrance requirements:* For master's, GRE General Test, GRE Subject Test, minimum undergraduate GPA of 3.0; for doctorate, GRE General Test, GRE Subject Test. *Application deadline:* For fall admission, 12/30 priority date for domestic students, 12/1 for international students. Application fee: $50 ($60 for international students). *Financial support:* In 2009–10, 25 fellowships (averaging $17,876 per year), 27 research assistantships (averaging $15,070 per year) were awarded; Federal Work-Study, institutionally sponsored loans, and tuition waivers (full) also available. *Faculty research:* Behavior, ecology, genetics, morphology, endocrinology, physiology, systematics. Total annual research expenditures: $3.1 million.

University of Guam, Office of Graduate Studies, College of Natural and Applied Sciences, Program in Biology, Mangilao, GU 96923. Offers tropical marine biology (MS). *Degree requirements:* For master's, comprehensive exam, thesis. *Entrance requirements:* For master's, GRE General Test, GRE Subject Test. Additional exam requirements/recommendations for international students: Required—TOEFL. *Faculty research:* Maintenance and ecology of coral reefs.

University of Hawaii at Hilo, Program in Tropical Conservation Biology and Environmental Science, Hilo, HI 96720-4091. Offers MS.

University of Hawaii at Manoa, Graduate Division, Interdisciplinary Program in Marine Biology, Honolulu, HI 96822. Offers MS, PhD. *Degree requirements:* For master's, thesis, research project; for doctorate, thesis/dissertation, research project. *Entrance requirements:* For master's and doctorate, GRE. Additional exam requirements/recommendations for international students: Required—TOEFL. *Expenses:* Contact institution. *Faculty research:* Ecology, ichthyology, behavior of marine animals, developmental biology.

University of Maine, Graduate School, College of Natural Sciences, Forestry, and Agriculture, School of Marine Sciences, Program in Marine Biology, Orono, ME 04469. Offers MS, PhD. *Students:* 21 full-time (13 women), 9 part-time (5 women); includes 1 minority (Hispanic American), 2 international. Average age 29. 49 applicants, 12% accepted, 3 enrolled. In 2009, 7 master's awarded. *Degree requirements:* For master's, thesis; for doctorate, thesis/dissertation. *Entrance requirements:* For master's and doctorate, GRE General Test. Additional exam requirements/recommendations for international students: Required—TOEFL. *Application deadline:* For fall admission, 2/1 priority date for domestic students. Applications are processed on a rolling basis. Application fee: $65. Electronic applications accepted. *Financial support:* Career-related internships or fieldwork, Federal Work-Study, and tuition waivers (full and partial) available. Support available to part-time students. Financial award application deadline: 3/1. *Unit head:* Dr. Susan Brawley, Coordinator, 207-581-2973. *Application contact:* Scott G. Delcourt, Associate Dean of the Graduate School, 207-581-3291, Fax: 207-581-3232, E-mail: graduate@maine.edu.

University of Massachusetts Dartmouth, Graduate School, College of Arts and Sciences, Department of Biology, North Dartmouth, MA 02747-2300. Offers biology (MS); marine biology (MS). Part-time programs available. *Faculty:* 17 full-time (6 women), 2 part-time/adjunct (1 woman). *Students:* 10 full-time (8 women), 7 part-time (4 women); includes 2 minority (1 Asian American or Pacific Islander, 1 Hispanic American). Average age 28. 17 applicants, 41% accepted, 6 enrolled. In 2009, 3 master's awarded. *Degree requirements:* For master's, thesis. *Entrance requirements:* For master's, GRE General Test, GRE Subject Test, 3 letters of recommendation. Additional exam requirements/recommendations for international students: Required—TOEFL (minimum score 500 paper-based). *Application deadline:* For fall admission, 3/15 for domestic students, 1/15 for international students; for spring admission, 11/15 priority date for domestic students, 9/15 priority date for international students. Application fee: $40 ($60 for international students). Electronic applications accepted. *Expenses:* Tuition, state resident: full-time $2071; part-time $86.29 per credit. Tuition, nonresident: full-time $8099; part-time $337.46 per credit. Required fees: $9446. Tuition and fees vary according to class time, course load and reciprocity agreements. *Financial support:* In 2009–10, 6 research assistantships with full tuition reimbursements (averaging $12,577 per year), 7 teaching assistantships with full tuition reimbursements (averaging $10,340 per year) were awarded; Federal Work-Study and unspecified assistantships also available. Support available to part-time students. Financial award application deadline: 3/1; financial award applicants required to submit FAFSA. *Faculty research:* Fish biology, antibody mediated protection, bottlenose dolphins, adaptations in fish via genetics evolutionary biology. Total annual research expenditures: $774,000. *Unit head:* Dr. Diego Bernal, Director, 508-999-8307, Fax: 508-999-8196, E-mail: dbernal@umassd.edu. *Application contact:* Elan Turcotte-Shamski, Graduate Admissions Officer, 508-999-8604, Fax: 508-999-8183, E-mail: graduate@umassd.edu.

University of Miami, Graduate School, Rosenstiel School of Marine and Atmospheric Science, Division of Marine Biology and Fisheries, Coral Gables, FL 33124. Offers MA, MS, PhD. Terminal master's awarded for partial completion of doctoral program. *Degree requirements:* For master's, comprehensive exam, thesis; for doctorate, comprehensive exam, thesis/dissertation. *Entrance requirements:* For master's and doctorate, GRE General Test. Additional exam requirements/recommendations for international students: Required—TOEFL (minimum score 550 paper-based; 213 computer-based). Electronic applications accepted. *Faculty research:* Biochemistry, physiology, plankton, coral, biology.

The University of North Carolina Wilmington, Center for Marine Science, Wilmington, NC 28403-3297. Offers MS. Part-time programs available. *Degree requirements:* For master's, comprehensive exam, thesis. *Entrance requirements:* For master's, GRE, minimum undergraduate B average. Additional exam requirements/recommendations for international students: Required—TOEFL (minimum score 550 paper-based; 217 computer-based; 79 iBT), IELTS (minimum score 6.5).

The University of North Carolina Wilmington, College of Arts and Sciences, Department of Biology and Marine Biology, Wilmington, NC 28403-3297. Offers biology (MS); marine biology (MS, PhD). Part-time programs available. *Degree requirements:* For master's, comprehensive exam, thesis; for doctorate, comprehensive exam, thesis/dissertation. *Entrance requirements:* For master's, GRE General Test, GRE Subject Test, minimum B average in undergraduate major; for doctorate, GRE General Test, minimum B average in undergraduate major and graduate courses. Additional exam requirements/recommendations for international students: Required—TOEFL (minimum score 550 paper-based; 217 computer-based; 79 iBT), IELTS (minimum score 6.5). Electronic applications accepted. *Faculty research:* Ecology, physiology, cell and molecular biology, systematics, biomechanics.

University of Oregon, Graduate School, College of Arts and Sciences, Department of Biology, Eugene, OR 97403. Offers ecology and evolution (MA, MS, PhD); marine biology (MA, MS, PhD); molecular, cellular and genetic biology (PhD); neuroscience and development (PhD). Terminal master's awarded for partial completion of doctoral program. *Degree requirements:* For master's, thesis (for some programs); for doctorate, thesis/dissertation. *Entrance requirements:* For master's and doctorate, GRE General Test, minimum GPA of 3.2. Additional exam requirements/recommendations for international students: Required—TOEFL. *Faculty research:* Developmental neurobiology; evolution, population biology, and quantitative genetics; regulation of gene expression; biochemistry of marine organisms.

University of Southern California, Graduate School, College of Letters, Arts and Sciences, Department of Biological Sciences, Program in Marine Biology and Biological Oceanography, Los Angeles, CA 90089. Offers marine and environmental biology (MS); marine biology and biological oceanography (PhD). *Faculty:* 27 full-time (8 women), 7 part-time/adjunct (2 women). *Students:* 2 full-time (1 woman), 1 international. 36 applicants, 50% accepted. In 2009, 1 master's awarded. Terminal master's awarded for partial completion of doctoral program. *Degree requirements:* For master's, comprehensive exam (for some programs), research paper; for doctorate, thesis/dissertation, qualifying examination, dissertation defense. *Entrance requirements:* For master's and doctorate, GRE, 3 letters of recommendation, personal statement, resume, minimum GPA of 3.0. Additional exam requirements/recommendations for international students: Required—TOEFL (minimum score 600 paper-based; 250 computer-based; 100 iBT). *Application deadline:* For fall admission, 12/1 priority date for domestic and international students. Application fee: $85. Electronic applications accepted. *Expenses:* Tuition: Full-time $25,980; part-time $1315 per unit. Required fees: $554. One-time fee: $35 full-time. Full-time tuition and fees vary according to degree level and program. *Financial support:* In 2009–10, 10 fellowships with full tuition reimbursements (averaging $25,333 per year), 14 research assistantships with full tuition reimbursements (averaging $25,333 per year), 14 teaching assistantships with full tuition reimbursements (averaging $25,333 per year) were awarded; scholarships/grants, traineeships, health care benefits, and tuition waivers also available. *Faculty research:* Adaptation, evolution, and population dynamics; marine microbiology; global biogeochemical cycles; coastal water quality; marine environmental genomics. *Unit head:* Dr. David A. Caron, Professor of Biological Sciences/Director of the MBBO Graduate Program, 213-740-0203, E-mail: dcaron@usc.edu. *Application contact:* Adolfo dela Rosa, Student Services Advisor I, 213-821-3164, Fax: 213-740-1380, E-mail: adolfode@usc.edu.

University of Southern Mississippi, Graduate School, College of Science and Technology, Department of Biological Sciences, Hattiesburg, MS 39406-0001. Offers environmental biology (MS, PhD); marine biology (MS, PhD); microbiology (MS, PhD); molecular biology (MS, PhD). *Faculty:* 27 full-time (6 women). *Students:* 55 full-time (27 women), 5 part-time (3 women); includes 7 minority (2 African Americans, 1 American Indian/Alaska Native, 2 Asian Americans or Pacific Islanders, 2 Hispanic Americans), 15 international. Average age 32. 53 applicants, 28% accepted, 10 enrolled. In 2009, 8 master's, 4 doctorates awarded. *Degree requirements:* For master's, comprehensive exam, thesis; for doctorate, comprehensive exam, thesis/dissertation. *Entrance requirements:* For master's, GRE General Test, minimum GPA of 3.0; for doctorate, GRE General Test, minimum GPA of 3.5. Additional exam requirements/recommendations for international students: Required—TOEFL. *Application deadline:* For fall admission, 3/1 priority date for domestic students, 3/1 for international students. Applications are processed on a rolling basis. Application fee: $35. *Expenses:* Tuition, state resident: full-time $5096; part-time $284 per hour. Tuition, nonresident: full-time $13,052; part-time $726 per hour. Required fees: $402. Tuition and fees vary according to course level and course load. *Financial support:* In 2009–10, 25 research assistantships with full tuition reimbursements (averaging $9,625 per year), 33 teaching assistantships with full tuition reimbursements (averaging $10,599 per year) were awarded; Federal Work-Study also available. Financial award application deadline: 3/15; financial award applicants required to submit FAFSA. *Unit head:* Dr. Frank Moore, Chair, 601-266-4748, Fax: 601-266-5797. *Application contact:* Dr. Chia Wang, Graduate Coordinator, 601-266-4748, Fax: 601-266-5797.

University of South Florida, Graduate School, College of Arts and Sciences, Department of Biology, Tampa, FL 33620-9951. Offers cell biology and molecular biology (MS); coastal marine biology (MS); coastal marine biology and ecology (PhD); conservation biology (MS, PhD); molecular and cell biology (PhD). Part-time programs available. *Faculty:* 34 full-time (7 women). *Students:* 72 full-time (43 women), 18 part-time (8 women); includes 9 minority (1 African American, 2 American Indian/Alaska Native, 4 Asian Americans or Pacific Islanders, 2 Hispanic Americans), 7 international. Average age 32. 99 applicants, 20% accepted, 14 enrolled. In 2009, 8 master's, 4 doctorates awarded. *Degree requirements:* For master's, comprehensive exam, thesis (for some programs); for doctorate, comprehensive exam, thesis/dissertation. *Entrance requirements:* For master's and doctorate, GRE General Test, minimum GPA of 3.0. Additional exam requirements/recommendations for international students: Required—TOEFL (minimum score 570 paper-based; 213 computer-based). *Application deadline:* For fall admission, 2/15 priority date for domestic students, 1/2 for international students; for spring admission, 8/1 for domestic students, 6/1 for international students. Application fee: $30. Electronic applications accepted. *Financial support:* In 2009–10, teaching assistantships with tuition reimbursements (averaging $58,627 per year); unspecified assistantships also available. Financial award application deadline: 6/30; financial award applicants required to submit FAFSA. Total annual research expenditures: $1.2 million. *Unit head:* Susan Bell, Co-Chairperson, 813-974-6210, Fax: 813-974-2876, E-mail: sbell@cas.usf.edu. *Application contact:* James Garey, Graduate Advisor, 813-974-8434, Fax: 813-974-3263, E-mail: grarey@cas.usf.edu.

Western Illinois University, School of Graduate Studies, College of Arts and Sciences, Department of Biological Sciences, Macomb, IL 61455-1390. Offers biological sciences (MS); environmental geographic information systems (Certificate); zoo and aquarium studies (Certificate). Part-time programs available. *Students:* 62 full-time (43 women), 28 part-time (17 women); includes 6 minority (2 African Americans, 2 Asian Americans or Pacific Islanders, 2 Hispanic Americans), 10 international. Average age 26. 53 applicants, 72% accepted. In 2009, 25 master's, 15 other advanced degrees awarded. *Degree requirements:* For master's, thesis or alternative. *Entrance requirements:* Additional exam requirements/recommendations for international students: Required—TOEFL (minimum score 550 paper-based; 213 computer-based; 80 iBT). *Application deadline:* Applications are processed on a rolling basis. Application fee: $30. Electronic applications accepted. *Expenses:* Tuition, state resident: full-time $4486; part-time $249.21 per credit hour. Tuition, nonresident: full-time $8972; part-time $498.42 per credit hour. Required fees: $72.62 per credit hour. *Financial support:* In 2009–10, 34 students received support, including 16 research assistantships with full tuition reimbursements available (averaging $7,280 per year), 18 teaching assistantships with full tuition reimbursements available (averaging $8,400 per year). Financial award applicants required to submit FAFSA. *Unit head:* Dr. Michael Romano, Chairperson, 309-298-1546. *Application contact:* Evelyn Hoing, Assistant Director of Graduate Studies, 309-298-1806, Fax: 309-298-2345, E-mail: grad-office@wiu.edu.

Woods Hole Oceanographic Institution, MIT/WHOI Joint Program in Oceanography/Applied Ocean Science and Engineering, Woods Hole, MA 02543-1541. Offers applied ocean sciences (PhD); biological oceanography (PhD, Sc D); chemical oceanography (PhD, Sc D); civil

Marine Biology

Woods Hole Oceanographic Institution (continued)
and environmental and oceanographic engineering (PhD); electrical and oceanographic engineering (PhD); geochemistry (PhD); geophysics (PhD); marine biology (PhD); marine geochemistry (PhD, Sc D); marine geology (PhD, Sc D); marine geophysics (PhD); mechanical and oceanographic engineering (PhD); ocean engineering (PhD); oceanographic engineering (M Eng, MS, PhD, Sc D, Eng); paleoceanography (PhD); physical oceanography (PhD, Sc D).

Terminal master's awarded for partial completion of doctoral program. *Degree requirements:* For master's and Eng, thesis (for some programs); for doctorate, thesis/dissertation. *Entrance requirements:* For master's, GRE General Test; for doctorate, GRE General Test, GRE Subject Test. Additional exam requirements/recommendations for international students: Required—TOEFL. Electronic applications accepted.

FLORIDA INSTITUTE OF TECHNOLOGY

College of Science
Department of Biological Sciences
Graduate Program in Ecology and Marine Biology

Programs of Study

The ecology and marine biology section of the Department of Biological Sciences offers programs leading to the degrees of Master of Science and Doctor of Philosophy. Programs focus on the applied and theoretical biology of the organism and its relationship to its environment. Areas of study and research include marine biology, aquaculture and fisheries, animal behavior, conservation, climate change, community ecology and paleobiology, physiological ecology, life history analysis, taxonomy, habitat management, and population biology.

The programs consist of fundamental studies in the biological sciences, with emphasis on individual research under the supervision of graduate faculty members. Individual programs of study are designed by the student in consultation with a committee of faculty members. Courses include those that contribute to the professional and scientific development of the student, those that correct deficiencies in the student's undergraduate preparation, and those required by the Department. Seminars by visiting scientists and close contact with faculty members prepare the student for an active program of independent research. Students are encouraged to pursue interdisciplinary studies, providing them with a competitive edge in career development. Advisory committees are tailored to individual needs.

Research Facilities

Florida Tech is located in east-central Florida, an area with many opportunities for field research. There is a wide array of ecosystems available, ranging from subtropical upland forests, to salt marshes and mangroves, to estuarine and fully marine subtidal systems. Opportunities exist for fieldwork throughout the Americas and in Antarctica, the Caribbean, and the Indo-Pacific.

Facilities include two new buildings on the Melbourne campus and the Vero Beach Marine Laboratory, located on a barrier island within an hour's drive. Common labs include aquaculture facilities; a museum; an imaging center with electron and confocal microscopes; and an instrumentation lab for spectroscopy and chromatography, biochemistry, and molecular genetics. The Department is home to the Institute for Marine Research, the Sportfish Research Institute, and the Institute for Research on Global Climate Change. The Ralph S. Evinrude Marine Operations Center is located on the Indian River Lagoon near the main campus, where small craft and workboats are maintained for teaching and research.

Financial Aid

Graduate teaching and research assistantships are available to qualified students. For 2010–11, stipends are approximately $15,000 for nine months, plus tuition remission (see below). Computer-based information on scholarships, loan funds, and other student assistance may be obtained from the Financial Aid Office. A limited number of assistantships providing tuition remission only are also available.

Cost of Study

Tuition for 2010–11 is $1040 per semester credit hour. Tuition is remitted for graduate assistants.

Living and Housing Costs

Room and board on campus cost approximately $4500 per semester in 2010–11. On-campus housing (dormitories and apartments) is available for full-time single and married graduate students, but priority for dormitory rooms is given to undergraduate students. Many apartment complexes and rental houses are available near the campus.

Student Group

The Department currently has 65 graduate students enrolled from colleges throughout the United States and around the world. Approximately half of the graduate students are women, and approximately one fourth are married. Most graduate students receive financial support.

Student Outcomes

Many graduates of the Department of Biological Sciences hold academic positions at institutions including Cornell University, Florida Atlantic University, the University of Alaska, and the University of Arkansas. Others are employed by government agencies, industry, and consulting firms, such as NOAA, The Nature Conservancy, and Continental Shelf Associates.

Location

Florida Tech's main campus is located in Melbourne on Florida's east coast. The area's economy is supported by a well-balanced mix of industries in electronics, aviation, light manufacturing, opticals, communications, agriculture, and tourism. The John F. Kennedy Space Center and Disney World are within a 90-minute drive of the campus.

The Institute

Florida Tech was founded in 1958 and has developed rapidly into a university providing both undergraduate and graduate education in the sciences and engineering for students from throughout the U.S. and internationally. Current enrollment on the Melbourne campus is 4,000. Florida Tech also offers graduate programs in applied mathematics, cell and molecular biology, chemical engineering, chemistry, civil engineering, computer science, electrical engineering, environmental engineering, mechanical engineering, ocean engineering, oceanography, operations research, physics, science education, space sciences, and systems engineering.

Applying

Information and application forms are available from the Graduate Admissions Office. Applicants must take the Graduate Record Examinations (General Test) and have the scores sent to the Graduate Admissions Office. Separate application for financial aid must be made on forms available from the Department or the Graduate School and must be submitted to the Department by March 1.

Correspondence and Information

Office of Graduate Admissions
Florida Institute of Technology
150 West University Boulevard
Melbourne, Florida 32901
Phone: 321-674-8027
      800-944-4348 (toll-free in the U.S.)
Fax: 321-723-9468
E-mail: grad-admissions@fit.edu
Web site: http://www.fit.edu

Dr. Richard B. Aronson, Head
Department of Biological Sciences
Florida Institute of Technology
150 West University Boulevard
Melbourne, Florida 32901
Phone: 321-674-8034
E-mail: raronson@fit.edu
Web site: http://www.bio.fit.edu

Florida Institute of Technology

THE FACULTY AND THEIR RESEARCH

Richard B. Aronson, Professor and Head of Department; Ph.D., Harvard, 1985. Coral reef ecology and paleoecology; paleobiology of marine communities in Antarctica; climate change and biological invasions; marine protected areas; salt marsh restoration.

Mark B. Bush, Professor; Ph.D., Hull (England), 1986. Paleoecology and climate change; biogeography; human impacts on neotropical systems.

Michael S. Grace, Associate Professor; Ph.D., Emory, 1992. Animal behavior; development of vision in marine turtles and fish.

Junda Lin, Professor; Ph.D., North Carolina at Chapel Hill, 1989. Molluscan and crustacean aquaculture; marine population and community ecology.

Christin L. Pruett, Assistant Professor; Ph.D., Alaska Fairbanks, 2002. Evolutionary ecology of terrestrial vertebrates; population genetics, speciation, and biodiversity of birds; effects of climate change and habitat fragmentation.

Jonathan M. Shenker, Associate Professor; Ph.D., Oregon State, 1986. Finfish aquaculture; larval and juvenile fish biology; ecology and management of recreational fishery species; coastal ecosystems.

Richard A. Tankersley, Professor; Ph.D., Wake Forest, 1992. Behavioral and physiological ecology of invertebrates; reproductive biology and larval ecology of crustaceans; transport and recruitment of marine organisms.

Ralph G. Turingan, Professor; Ph.D., Puerto Rico, 1993. Environmental biology of fishes; evolution of vertebrate functional morphology; ontogeny of functional morphology in fishes.

Richard L. Turner, Associate Professor; Ph.D., South Florida, 1977. Echinoderm biology; reproduction and ecology of the Florida applesnail; physiological ecology of crustaceans.

Robert van Woesik, Professor; Ph.D., James Cook (Australia), 1993. Population and community ecology of corals; quantitative ecology; management of coral reefs.

Associated Graduate Faculty

M. Dennis Hanisak, Director, Division of Marine Science, Harbor Branch Oceanographic Institution; Ph.D., Rhode Island, 1977. Marine botany; physiological ecology of marine plants; biology of deep-water macroalgae; nutrient dynamics; coral reef ecology; aquaculture, particularly marine plant cultivation.

Jose V. Lopez, Assistant Scientist, Division of Biomedical Research, Harbor Branch Oceanographic Institution; Ph.D., George Mason, 1995. Molecular evolution; conservation and biodiversity of marine invertebrates and their microbial associates.

Richard Paperno, Research Administrator I, Florida Fish and Wildlife Conservation Commission, Florida Marine Research Institute; Ph.D., Delaware, 1991.

Dolores R. Piperno, Research Scientist and Curator, Department of Anthropology, National Museum of Natural History, Washington D.C.; Ph.D., Temple, 1983.

Marty A. Riche, Research Fishery Biologist, USDA; Ph.D., Michigan State, 2000. Sustainable marine aquaculture technologies; spawning, nutrition, and physiology of southern flounder and black sea bass.

Hilary M. Swain, Executive Director, Archbold Biological Station, Lake Placid, Florida; Ph.D., Newcastle, 1981. Conservation biology; Florida ecosystems; geographic information systems (GIS); biodiversity; agroecology; restoration ecology.

Section 12
Microbiological Sciences

This section contains a directory of institutions offering graduate work in microbiological sciences, followed by in-depth entries submitted by institutions that chose to prepare detailed program descriptions. Additional information about programs listed in the directory but not augmented by an in-depth entry may be obtained by writing directly to the dean of a graduate school or chair of a department at the address given in the directory.

For programs offering related work, see also in this book *Biochemistry; Biological and Biomedical Sciences; Botany and Plant Biology; Cell, Molecular, and Structural Biology; Ecology, Environmental Biology, and Evolutionary Biology; Entomology; Genetics, Developmental Biology, and Reproductive Biology; Parasitology; Pathology and Pathobiology; Physiology;* and *Zoology.* In the other guides in this series:

Graduate Programs in the Physical Sciences, Mathematics, Agricultural Sciences, the Environment & Natural Resources

See *Agricultural and Food Sciences* and *Chemistry*

Graduate Programs in Engineering & Applied Sciences

See *Agricultural Engineering and Bioengineering* and *Biomedical Engineering and Biotechnology*

Graduate Programs in Business, Education, Health, Information Studies, Law & Social Work

See *Allied Health, Dentistry and Dental Sciences, Pharmacy and Pharmaceutical Sciences, Public Health,* and *Veterinary Medicine and Sciences*

CONTENTS

Program Directories

Close-Ups

Bacteriology

Illinois State University, Graduate School, College of Arts and Sciences, Department of Biological Sciences, Normal, IL 61790-2200. Offers animal behavior (MS); bacteriology (MS); biochemistry (MS); biological sciences (MS); biology (PhD); biophysics (MS); biotechnology (MS); botany (MS, PhD); cell biology (MS); conservation biology (MS); developmental biology (MS); ecology (MS, PhD); entomology (MS); evolutionary biology (MS); genetics (MS, PhD); immunology (MS); microbiology (MS, PhD); molecular biology (MS); molecular genetics (MS); neurobiology (MS); neuroscience (MS); parasitology (MS); physiology (MS, PhD); plant biology (MS); plant molecular biology (MS); plant sciences (MS); structural biology (MS); zoology (MS, PhD). Part-time programs available. *Degree requirements:* For master's, thesis or alternative; for doctorate, variable foreign language requirement, thesis/dissertation, 2 terms of residency. *Entrance requirements:* For master's, GRE General Test, minimum GPA of 2.6 in last 60 hours of course work; for doctorate, GRE General Test. *Faculty research:* Redoc balance and drug development in schistosoma mansoni, control of the growth of listeria monocytogenes at low temperature, regulation of cell expansion and microtubule function by SPRI, CRUI: physiology and fitness consequences of different life history phenotypes.

The University of Iowa, Roy J. and Lucille A. Carver College of Medicine and Graduate College, Graduate Programs in Medicine, Department of Microbiology, Iowa City, IA 52242-1316. Offers general microbiology and microbial physiology (MS, PhD); immunology (MS, PhD); microbial genetics (MS, PhD); pathogenic bacteriology (MS, PhD); virology (MS, PhD). *Faculty:* 24 full-time (3 women), 8 part-time/adjunct (2 women). *Students:* 36 full-time (20 women); includes 3 minority (2 American Indian/Alaska Native, 1 Hispanic American), 5 international. Average age 25. 87 applicants, 14% accepted, 5 enrolled. In 2009, 3 master's, 7 doctorates awarded. *Degree requirements:* For master's, thesis; for doctorate, comprehensive exam, thesis/dissertation. *Entrance requirements:* For master's and doctorate, GRE General Test. Additional exam requirements/recommendations for international students: Required—TOEFL (minimum score 600 paper-based; 250 computer-based). *Application deadline:* For fall admission, 2/1 for domestic and international students. Application fee: $60 ($85 for international students). Electronic applications accepted. *Financial support:* In 2009–10, 4 fellowships with full tuition reimbursements (averaging $24,250 per year), 32 research assistantships with full tuition reimbursements (averaging $24,250 per year) were awarded; institutionally sponsored loans, scholarships/grants, traineeships, and health care benefits also available. *Faculty research:* Gene regulation, processing and transport of HIV, retroviral pathogenesis, biodegradation, biofilm. Total annual research expenditures: $11.7 million. *Unit head:* Dr. Michael A. Apicella, Head, 319-335-7810, E-mail: grad-micro-info@uiowa.edu. *Application contact:* Dr. Michael A. Apicella, Head, 319-335-7810, E-mail: grad-micro-info@uiowa.edu.

University of Prince Edward Island, Atlantic Veterinary College, Graduate Program in Veterinary Medicine, Charlottetown, PE C1A 4P3, Canada. Offers anatomy (M Sc, PhD); bacteriology (M Sc, PhD); clinical pharmacology (M Sc, PhD); clinical sciences (M Sc, PhD); epidemiology (M Sc, PhD), including reproduction; fish health (M Sc, PhD); food animal nutrition (M Sc, PhD); immunology (M Sc, PhD); microanatomy (M Sc, PhD); parasitology (M Sc, PhD); pathology (M Sc, PhD); pharmacology (M Sc, PhD); physiology (M Sc, PhD); toxicology (M Sc, PhD); veterinary science (M Vet Sc); virology (M Sc, PhD). Part-time programs available. *Degree requirements:* For master's, thesis; for doctorate, thesis/dissertation. *Entrance requirements:* For master's, DVM, B Sc honors degree, or equivalent; for doctorate, M Sc. Additional exam requirements/recommendations for international students: Required—TOEFL (minimum score 550 paper-based; 213 computer-based; 80 iBT). *Expenses:* Contact institution. *Faculty research:* Animal health management, infectious diseases, fin fish and shellfish health, basic biomedical sciences, ecosystem health.

The University of Texas Medical Branch, Graduate School of Biomedical Sciences, Center for Biodefense and Emerging Infectious Diseases, Galveston, TX 77555. Offers biodefense training (PhD). *Entrance requirements:* For doctorate, GRE, minimum overall GPA of 3.0. *Financial support:* Tuition waivers and unspecified assistantships available. *Unit head:* Dr. Clarence J. Peters, Executive Director, 409-772-0090, Fax: 409-747-0762, E-mail: cjpeters@utmb.edu. *Application contact:* Dr. Dorian H. Coppenhaver, Associate Dean for Student Affairs, 409-772-2665, Fax: 409-747-0772, E-mail: dcoppenh@utmb.edu.

The University of Texas Medical Branch, Graduate School of Biomedical Sciences, Program in Emerging and Tropical Infectious Diseases, Galveston, TX 77555. Offers PhD, MD/PhD. *Degree requirements:* For doctorate, thesis/dissertation. *Entrance requirements:* For doctorate, GRE General Test. *Application deadline:* Applications are processed on a rolling basis. Application fee: $25 ($50 for international students). *Financial support:* In 2009–10, fellowships (averaging $25,000 per year), research assistantships with full tuition reimbursements (averaging $25,000 per year) were awarded; traineeships and unspecified assistantships also available. *Faculty research:* Emerging diseases, tropical diseases, parasitology, vitology and bacteriology. *Application contact:* Dr. Dorian H. Coppenhaver, Associate Dean for Student Affairs, 409-772-2665, Fax: 409-747-0772, E-mail: dcoppenh@utmb.edu.

University of Washington, Graduate School, School of Public Health, Department of Global Health, Graduate Program in Pathobiology, Seattle, WA 98195. Offers PhD. *Students:* 35 full-time (27 women), 3 part-time (all women); includes 5 minority (2 African Americans, 1 Asian American or Pacific Islander, 2 Hispanic Americans), 7 international. Average age 29. 50 applicants, 18% accepted, 5 enrolled. In 2009, 7 doctorates awarded. Terminal master's awarded for partial completion of doctoral program. *Degree requirements:* For doctorate, comprehensive exam, thesis/dissertation. *Entrance requirements:* For doctorate, GRE General Test, minimum GPA of 3.0. Additional exam requirements/recommendations for international students: Required—TOEFL. *Application deadline:* For fall admission, 10/1 for domestic students, 11/1 for international students. Application fee: $50. Electronic applications accepted. *Financial support:* In 2009–10, 34 students received support, including 3 fellowships with full tuition reimbursements available (averaging $27,348 per year), 26 research assistantships with full tuition reimbursements available (averaging $27,348 per year); career-related internships or fieldwork, institutionally sponsored loans, scholarships/grants, traineeships, and unspecified assistantships also available. Financial award application deadline: 12/1; financial award applicants required to submit FAFSA. *Faculty research:* Pathogenesis of chlamydiae, molecular biology of parasites, signal transduction, antigenic analysis, molecular biology of tumor viruses, malaria. *Unit head:* Dr. Andreas Stergachis, Acting Chair, 206-543-8350, Fax: 206-543-3873, E-mail: stergach@u.washington.edu. *Application contact:* Mary Conrad, Manager of Student Services, 206-543-4338, Fax: 206-543-3873, E-mail: pathobio@u.washington.edu.

University of Wisconsin–Madison, Graduate School, College of Agricultural and Life Sciences, Department of Bacteriology, Madison, WI 53706-1380. Offers MS. Part-time programs available. *Entrance requirements:* Additional exam requirements/recommendations for international students: Required—TOEFL. Electronic applications accepted. *Expenses:* Tuition, state resident: part-time $594 per credit. Tuition, nonresident: part-time $1504 per credit. Required fees: $65 per credit. Tuition and fees vary according to course load, program and reciprocity agreements. *Faculty research:* Microbial physiology, gene regulation, microbial ecology, plant-microbe interactions, symbiosis.

Immunology

Albany Medical College, Center for Immunology and Microbial Disease, Albany, NY 12208-3479. Offers MS, PhD. Part-time programs available. *Faculty:* 22 full-time (3 women), 11 part-time/adjunct (6 women). *Students:* 19 full-time (11 women). Average age 25. 20 applicants, 45% accepted, 6 enrolled. In 2009, 1 doctorate awarded. Terminal master's awarded for partial completion of doctoral program. *Degree requirements:* For master's, thesis; for doctorate, comprehensive exam, thesis/dissertation, oral qualifying exam, written preliminary exam, 1 published paper-peer review. *Entrance requirements:* For master's, GRE General Test, all transcripts, letters of recommendation; for doctorate, GRE General Test, letters of recommendation. Additional exam requirements/recommendations for international students: Required—TOEFL. *Application deadline:* For fall admission, 3/15 priority date for domestic and international students. Applications are processed on a rolling basis. Application fee: $0 ($60 for international students). *Expenses:* Tuition: Full-time $18,820. *Financial support:* In 2009–10, 10 research assistantships (averaging $24,000 per year) were awarded; Federal Work-Study, scholarships/grants, and tuition waivers (full) also available. Financial award applicants required to submit FAFSA. *Faculty research:* Microbial and viral pathogenesis, cancer development and cell transformation, biochemical and genetic mechanisms responsible for human disease. *Unit head:* Dr. Thomas D. Friedrich, Graduate Director, 518-262-6750, Fax: 518-262-6161, E-mail: dgs_cimd@mail.amc.edu. *Application contact:* Dr. Thomas D. Friedrich, Graduate Director, 518-262-6750, Fax: 518-262-6161, E-mail: dgs_cimd@mail.amc.edu.

Albert Einstein College of Medicine, Sue Golding Graduate Division of Medical Sciences, Department of Microbiology and Immunology, Bronx, NY 10461. Offers PhD, MD/PhD. *Degree requirements:* For doctorate, thesis/dissertation. *Entrance requirements:* For doctorate, GRE General Test. Additional exam requirements/recommendations for international students: Required—TOEFL. *Faculty research:* Nature of histocompatibility antigens, lymphoid cell receptors, regulation of immune responses and mechanisms of resistance to infection.

Baylor College of Medicine, Graduate School of Biomedical Sciences, Department of Immunology, Houston, TX 77030-3498. Offers PhD, MD/PhD. *Faculty:* 36 full-time (12 women). *Students:* 29 full-time (18 women); includes 11 minority (3 African Americans, 5 Asian Americans or Pacific Islanders, 3 Hispanic Americans), 15 international. Average age 26. In 2009, 4 doctorates awarded. *Degree requirements:* For doctorate, thesis/dissertation, public defense. *Entrance requirements:* For doctorate, GRE General Test, GRE Subject Test (strongly recommended), minimum GPA of 3.0. Additional exam requirements/recommendations for international students: Required—TOEFL. *Application deadline:* For fall admission, 1/1 priority date for domestic students. Application fee: $0. Electronic applications accepted. *Financial support:* Fellowships, research assistantships, teaching assistantships, career-related internships or fieldwork, Federal Work-Study, institutionally sponsored loans, health care benefits, and students receive a scholarship unless there are grant funds available to pay tuition available. Financial award applicants required to submit FAFSA. *Faculty research:* Structure and function of major histocompatibility antigens, induction and regulation of T-cell immune responses, microbial genetics, pathophysiology of bacterial and viral infections, control and epidemiology of respiratory viruses. *Unit head:* Dr. Biao Zheng, Director, 713-798-8796, Fax: 713-798-7949. *Application contact:* Kelly Levitt, Graduate Program Administrator, 713-798-3921, Fax: 713-798-3900, E-mail: klevitt@bcm.edu.

Baylor College of Medicine, Graduate School of Biomedical Sciences, Interdepartmental Program in Cell and Molecular Biology, Houston, TX 77030-3498. Offers biochemistry (PhD); cell and molecular biology (PhD); genetics (PhD); human genetics (PhD); immunology (PhD); microbiology (PhD); virology (PhD); MD/PhD. *Faculty:* 100 full-time (31 women). *Students:* 59 full-time (37 women); includes 24 minority (5 African Americans, 1 American Indian/Alaska Native, 7 Asian Americans or Pacific Islanders, 11 Hispanic Americans), 6 international. Average age 25. In 2009, 9 doctorates awarded. *Degree requirements:* For doctorate, thesis/dissertation, public defense. *Entrance requirements:* For doctorate, GRE General Test, GRE Subject Test (strongly recommended), minimum GPA of 3.0. Additional exam requirements/recommendations for international students: Required—TOEFL. *Application deadline:* For fall admission, 1/1 priority date for domestic students. Applications are processed on a rolling basis. Application fee: $0. Electronic applications accepted. *Financial support:* In 2009–10, 59 students received support; fellowships, research assistantships, teaching assistantships, Federal Work-Study, institutionally sponsored loans, health care benefits, and tuition waivers (full) available. Financial award applicants required to submit FAFSA. *Faculty research:* Gene expression and regulation, developmental biology and genetics, signal transduction and membrane biology, aging process, molecular virology. *Unit head:* Dr. Susan Marriott, Director, 713-798-6557. *Application contact:* Lourdes Fernandez, Graduate Program Administrator, 713-798-6557, Fax: 713-798-6325, E-mail: cmbprog@bcm.edu.

See Close-Up on page 231.

Boston University, School of Medicine, Division of Graduate Medical Sciences, Department of Microbiology, Boston, MA 02118. Offers immunology (PhD); microbiology (MA); MD/PhD. Terminal master's awarded for partial completion of doctoral program. *Degree requirements:* For master's, thesis; for doctorate, comprehensive exam, thesis/dissertation. *Entrance requirements:* For master's and doctorate, GRE General Test, GRE Subject Test. Additional exam requirements/recommendations for international students: Required—TOEFL. *Application deadline:* For fall admission, 1/15 for domestic students; for spring admission, 10/15 for domestic students. Electronic applications accepted. *Expenses:* Tuition: Full-time $37,910; part-time $1184 per credit hour. Required fees: $386; $40 per semester. Part-time tuition and fees vary according to class time, course level, degree level and program. *Financial support:* Fellowships, research assistantships, Federal Work-Study, scholarships/grants, and traineeships available. *Faculty research:* Eukaryotic cell biology, tumor cell biology, nutrition and cancer, experimental tumor therapy, photobiology. *Unit head:* Dr. Ronald B. Corley, Chairman, 617-638-4284, Fax: 617-638-4286, E-mail: rbcorley@bu.edu. *Application contact:* Dr. Gregory Viglianti, Graduate Director, 617-638-7790, Fax: 617-638-4286, E-mail: gviglian@bu.edu.

Boston University, School of Medicine, Immunology Training Program, Boston, MA 02215. Offers PhD, MD/PhD. *Degree requirements:* For doctorate, thesis/dissertation, qualifying exam. *Entrance requirements:* For doctorate, GRE General Test, GRE Subject Test. Additional exam requirements/recommendations for international students: Required—TOEFL. *Application deadline:* For fall admission, 1/15 priority date for domestic students; for spring admission, 10/15 priority date for domestic students. Electronic applications accepted. *Expenses:* Tuition: Full-time $37,910; part-time $1184 per credit hour. Required fees: $386; $40 per semester. Part-time tuition and fees vary according to class time, course level, degree level and program. *Financial support:* Fellowships with tuition reimbursements, research assistantships with tuition reimbursements, Federal Work-Study, scholarships/grants, and traineeships available. *Unit head:* Dr. Ann Marshak-Rothstein, Director, 617-638-4284, Fax: 617-638-4286, E-mail: itp@bu.edu. *Application contact:* Michelle Hall, Assistant Director of Admissions, 617-638-5121, Fax: 617-638-5740, E-mail: natashah@bu.edu.

Brown University, Graduate School, Division of Biology and Medicine, Program in Molecular Biology, Cell Biology, and Biochemistry, Providence, RI 02912. Offers biochemistry (M Med Sc,

Sc M, PhD), including biochemistry (Sc M, PhD), biology (Sc M, PhD), medical science (M Med Sc, PhD); biology (MA); cell biology (M Med Sc, Sc M, PhD), including biochemistry (Sc M, PhD), biology (Sc M, PhD), medical science (M Med Sc, PhD); developmental biology (M Med Sc, Sc M, PhD), including biochemistry (Sc M, PhD), biology (Sc M, PhD), medical science (M Med Sc, PhD); immunology (M Med Sc, Sc M, PhD), including biochemistry (Sc M, PhD), biology (Sc M, PhD), medical science (M Med Sc, PhD); molecular microbiology (M Med Sc, Sc M, PhD), including biochemistry (Sc M, PhD), biology (Sc M, PhD), medical science (M Med Sc, PhD); MD/PhD. Part-time programs available. Terminal master's awarded for partial completion of doctoral program. *Degree requirements:* For master's, thesis (for some programs); for doctorate, one foreign language, thesis/dissertation, preliminary exam. *Entrance requirements:* For master's and doctorate, GRE General Test, GRE Subject Test. Additional exam requirements/recommendations for international students: Required—TOEFL. Electronic applications accepted. *Faculty research:* Molecular genetics, gene regulation.

Brown University, Graduate School, Division of Biology and Medicine, Program in Pathology and Laboratory Medicine, Providence, RI 02912. Offers biology (PhD); cancer biology (PhD); immunology and infection (PhD); medical science (PhD); pathobiology (Sc M); toxicology and environmental pathology (PhD). Terminal master's awarded for partial completion of doctoral program. *Degree requirements:* For doctorate, thesis/dissertation, preliminary exam. *Entrance requirements:* For master's and doctorate, GRE General Test, GRE Subject Test. Additional exam requirements/recommendations for international students: Required—TOEFL. Electronic applications accepted. *Faculty research:* Environmental pathology, carcinogenesis, immunopathology, signal transduction, innate immunity.

California Institute of Technology, Division of Biology, Program in Immunology, Pasadena, CA 91125-0001. Offers PhD. *Degree requirements:* For doctorate, thesis/dissertation, qualifying exam. *Entrance requirements:* For doctorate, GRE General Test.

Case Western Reserve University, School of Medicine and School of Graduate Studies, Graduate Programs in Medicine, Programs in Molecular and Cellular Basis of Disease/Pathology, Immunology Training Program, Cleveland, OH 44106. Offers MS, PhD, MD/PhD. *Degree requirements:* For doctorate, comprehensive exam, thesis/dissertation. *Entrance requirements:* For doctorate, GRE General Test, GRE Subject Test. Additional exam requirements/recommendations for international students: Required—TOEFL (minimum score 550 paper-based; 213 computer-based). Electronic applications accepted. *Faculty research:* Immunology, immunopathology, immunochemistry, infectious diseases.

Colorado State University, College of Veterinary Medicine and Biomedical Sciences, Department of Microbiology, Immunology and Pathology, Fort Collins, CO 80523-1619. Offers microbiology (MS, PhD); pathology (PhD). *Faculty:* 43 full-time (18 women), 2 part-time/adjunct (1 woman). *Students:* 51 full-time (43 women), 40 part-time (22 women); includes 8 minority (4 Asian Americans or Pacific Islanders, 4 Hispanic Americans), 9 international. Average age 31. 87 applicants, 14% accepted, 12 enrolled. In 2009, 8 master's, 15 doctorates awarded. *Degree requirements:* For master's, thesis; for doctorate, comprehensive exam, thesis/dissertation. *Entrance requirements:* For master's, GRE General Test, minimum GPA of 3.0, BA/BS in biomedical field, reviewer evaluation forms, resume; for doctorate, GRE General Test, minimum GPA of 3.0, BA/BS in biomedical field, reviewer evaluation forms, resume, statement of interest. Additional exam requirements/recommendations for international students: Required—TOEFL (minimum score 550 paper-based). *Application deadline:* For fall admission, 1/1 priority date for domestic students; for spring admission, 10/1 priority date for domestic students. Applications are processed on a rolling basis. Application fee: $50. Electronic applications accepted. *Expenses:* Tuition, state resident: full-time $6434; part-time $359.10 per credit. Tuition, nonresident: full-time $18,116; part-time $1006.45 per credit. Required fees: $1496; $83 per credit. *Financial support:* In 2009–10, 85 students received support, including 34 fellowships with tuition reimbursements available (averaging $29,724 per year), 45 research assistantships with tuition reimbursements available (averaging $21,337 per year), 6 teaching assistantships with tuition reimbursements available (averaging $12,607 per year); Federal Work-Study, scholarships/grants, traineeships, and unspecified assistantships also available. Financial award applicants required to submit FAFSA. *Faculty research:* Medical and veterinary microbiology, pathology of disease, microbial pathogenesis, industrial and environmental microbiology, vector-borne disease. Total annual research expenditures: $32.6 million. *Unit head:* Dr. Edward A. Hoover, Head, 970-491-7587, Fax: 970-491-0603, E-mail: edward.hoover@colostate.edu. *Application contact:* Marcia Boggs, Graduate Program Coordinator, 970-491-3228, Fax: 970-491-1815, E-mail: marcia.boggs@colostate.edu.

Cornell University, Graduate School, Graduate Fields of Comparative Biomedical Sciences, Field of Immunology, Ithaca, NY 14853-0001. Offers cellular immunology (MS, PhD); immunochemistry (MS, PhD); immunogenetics (MS, PhD); immunopathology (MS, PhD); infection and immunity (MS, PhD). *Faculty:* 20 full-time (7 women). *Students:* 13 full-time (10 women); includes 1 minority (African American), 4 international. Average age 28. 43 applicants, 9% accepted, 2 enrolled. In 2009, 2 doctorates awarded. Terminal master's awarded for partial completion of doctoral program. *Degree requirements:* For master's, thesis; for doctorate, comprehensive exam, thesis/dissertation. *Entrance requirements:* For master's and doctorate, GRE General Test, 2 letters of recommendation. Additional exam requirements/recommendations for international students: Required—TOEFL (minimum score 550 paper-based; 213 computer-based; 77 iBT). *Application deadline:* For fall admission, 12/15 for domestic students. Application fee: $70. Electronic applications accepted. *Expenses:* Tuition: Full-time $29,500. Required fees: $70. Full-time tuition and fees vary according to degree level, program and student level. *Financial support:* In 2009–10, 2 research assistantships with full tuition reimbursements were awarded; fellowships with full tuition reimbursements, teaching assistantships with full tuition reimbursements, institutionally sponsored loans, scholarships/grants, health care benefits, tuition waivers (full and partial), and unspecified assistantships also available. Financial award applicants required to submit FAFSA. *Faculty research:* Avian immunology, mucosal immunity, anti-parasite and anti-viral immunity, neutrophil function, reproductive immunology. *Unit head:* Director of Graduate Studies, 607-253-3276, Fax: 607-253-3756. *Application contact:* Graduate Field Assistant, 607-253-3276, Fax: 607-253-3756, E-mail: graduate_edcvm@cornell.edu.

Cornell University, Joan and Sanford I. Weill Medical College and Graduate School of Medical Sciences, Weill Cornell Graduate School of Medical Sciences, Immunology and Microbial Pathogenesis Program, New York, NY 10065. Offers immunology (MS, PhD), including immunology, microbiology, pathology. *Faculty:* 34 full-time (12 women). *Students:* 48 full-time (37 women); includes 8 minority (6 Asian Americans or Pacific Islanders, 2 Hispanic Americans), 27 international. Average age 23. 115 applicants, 16% accepted, 4 enrolled. In 2009, 1 master's, 8 doctorates awarded. Terminal master's awarded for partial completion of doctoral program. *Degree requirements:* For master's, comprehensive exam; for doctorate, thesis/dissertation, final exam. *Entrance requirements:* For doctorate, GRE General Test, laboratory research experience, course work in biological sciences. Additional exam requirements/recommendations for international students: Required—TOEFL. *Application deadline:* For fall admission, 12/1 for domestic students. Application fee: $60. Electronic applications accepted. *Expenses:* Tuition: Full-time $44,650. Required fees: $2805. *Financial support:* In 2009–10, 7 fellowships (averaging $23,571 per year) were awarded; scholarships/grants, health care benefits, and stipends (given to all students) also available. *Faculty research:* Microbial immunity, tumor immunology, lympholyte and leukocyte biology, auto immunity, stem cell/bone marrow transplantation. *Unit head:* Dr. Ulrich Hammerling, Director, 646-888-2303, E-mail: u-hammerling@ski.mskcc.org. *Application contact:* Stephen Nesbit, Assistant Dean of Admissions, 212-746-6565, Fax: 212-746-8906, E-mail: sjn2001@med.cornell.edu.

Creighton University, School of Medicine and Graduate School, Graduate Programs in Medicine, Department of Medical Microbiology and Immunology, Omaha, NE 68178-0001. Offers MS, PhD. Terminal master's awarded for partial completion of doctoral program. *Degree requirements:* For master's, comprehensive exam, thesis; for doctorate, thesis/dissertation, preliminary exams. *Entrance requirements:* For master's and doctorate, GRE General Test. Additional exam requirements/recommendations for international students: Required—TOEFL. *Expenses:* Tuition: Full-time $11,700; part-time $650 per credit hour. Required fees: $126 per semester. *Faculty research:* Infectious diseases, molecular biology, genetics, antimicrobial agents and chemotherapy, virology.

Dalhousie University, Faculty of Medicine, Department of Microbiology and Immunology, Halifax, NS B3H 1X5, Canada. Offers M Sc, PhD. *Degree requirements:* For master's, thesis; for doctorate, comprehensive exam, thesis/dissertation. *Entrance requirements:* For master's, GRE General Test, honors B Sc; for doctorate, GRE General Test, honors B Sc in microbiology, M Sc in discipline or transfer after 1 year in master's program. Additional exam requirements/recommendations for international students: Required—TOEFL, IELTS, 1 of the following 5 approved tests: TOEFL, IELTS, CAEL, CANTEST, Michigan English Language Assessment Battery. Electronic applications accepted. *Faculty research:* Virology, molecular genetics, pathogenesis, bacteriology, immunology.

Dartmouth College, Graduate Program in Molecular and Cellular Biology, Department of Microbiology and Immunology, Program in Immunology, Hanover, NH 03755. Offers MD/PhD. *Faculty research:* Tumor immunotherapy, cell and molecular biology of connective tissue degradation in rheumatoid arthritis and cancer, immunology and immunotherapy of tumors of the central nervous system, transcriptional regulation of hematopoiesis and leukemia, bacterial pathogenesis.

Drexel University, College of Medicine, Biomedical Graduate Programs, Program in Microbiology and Immunology, Philadelphia, PA 19104-2875. Offers MS, PhD, MD/PhD. Terminal master's awarded for partial completion of doctoral program. *Degree requirements:* For master's, comprehensive exam, thesis; for doctorate, thesis/dissertation, qualifying exam. *Entrance requirements:* For master's, GRE General Test, minimum GPA of 2.75; for doctorate, GRE General Test, minimum GPA of 3.0. Additional exam requirements/recommendations for international students: Required—TOEFL. Electronic applications accepted. *Faculty research:* Immunology of malarial parasites, virology, bacteriology, molecular biology, parasitology.

Duke University, Graduate School, Department of Immunology, Durham, NC 27710. Offers PhD. *Faculty:* 48 full-time. *Students:* 39 full-time (25 women); includes 4 minority (2 African Americans, 1 Asian American or Pacific Islander, 1 Hispanic American), 12 international. 69 applicants, 23% accepted, 10 enrolled. In 2009, 5 doctorates awarded. *Degree requirements:* For doctorate, thesis/dissertation. *Entrance requirements:* For doctorate, GRE General Test, GRE Subject Test (recommended). Additional exam requirements/recommendations for international students: Required—TOEFL (minimum score 550 paper-based; 213 computer-based; 83 iBT), IELTS (minimum score 7). *Application deadline:* For fall admission, 12/8 priority date for domestic and international students. Application fee: $75. Electronic applications accepted. *Financial support:* Fellowships, research assistantships available. Financial award application deadline: 12/31. *Unit head:* Yuan Zhuang, Director of Graduate Studies, Fax: 919-613-3578, E-mail: immunologydept@mc.duke.edu. *Application contact:* Tom Steffen, Director of Admissions.

East Carolina University, Brody School of Medicine, Department of Microbiology and Immunology, Greenville, NC 27858-4353. Offers PhD. *Degree requirements:* For doctorate, comprehensive exam, thesis/dissertation. *Entrance requirements:* For doctorate, GRE General Test. Additional exam requirements/recommendations for international students: Required—TOEFL. *Faculty research:* Molecular virology, genetics of bacteria, yeast and somatic cells, bacterial physiology and metabolism, bioterrorism.

Emory University, Graduate School of Arts and Sciences, Division of Biological and Biomedical Sciences, Program in Immunology and Molecular Pathogenesis, Atlanta, GA 30322-1100. Offers PhD. *Faculty:* 50 full-time (8 women). *Students:* 73 full-time (42 women); includes 19 minority (3 African Americans, 1 American Indian/Alaska Native, 12 Asian Americans or Pacific Islanders, 3 Hispanic Americans), 13 international. Average age 27. 120 applicants, 18% accepted, 9 enrolled. In 2009, 12 doctorates awarded. *Degree requirements:* For doctorate, comprehensive exam, thesis/dissertation. *Entrance requirements:* For doctorate, GRE General Test, minimum GPA of 3.0 in science course work (recommended). Additional exam requirements/recommendations for international students: Required—TOEFL. *Application deadline:* For fall admission, 1/3 for domestic and international students. Application fee: $50. Electronic applications accepted. *Financial support:* In 2009–10, 24 students received support, including 24 fellowships with full tuition reimbursements available (averaging $24,500 per year); institutionally sponsored loans, scholarships/grants, and health care benefits also available. *Faculty research:* Transplantation immunology, autoimmunity, microbial pathogenesis. *Unit head:* Dr. Brian Evavold, Director, 404-727-3393, Fax: 404-727-3659, E-mail: evavold@microbio.emory.edu. *Application contact:* Dr. Joshy Jacob, Recruiter, 404-727-7919, Fax: 404-727-8199, E-mail: jjacob3@emory.edu.

Georgetown University, Graduate School of Arts and Sciences, Programs in Biomedical Sciences, Department of Microbiology and Immunology, Washington, DC 20057. Offers biohazardous threat agents and emerging infectious diseases (MS); general microbiology and immunology (MS); global infectious diseases (PhD); microbiology and immunology research (PhD); science policy and advocacy (MS). Part-time programs available. *Degree requirements:* For master's, 30 credit hours of coursework; for doctorate, comprehensive exam, thesis/dissertation. *Entrance requirements:* For master's, GRE General Test, 3 letters of reference, bachelor's degree in related field; for doctorate, GRE General Test, 3 letters of reference, MS/BS in related field. Additional exam requirements/recommendations for international students: Required—TOEFL (minimum score 505 paper-based; 213 computer-based). Electronic applications accepted. *Faculty research:* Pathogenesis and basic biology of the fungus Candida albicans, molecular biology of viral immunopathological mechanisms in Multiple Sclerosis.

The George Washington University, Columbian College of Arts and Sciences, Institute for Biomedical Sciences, Program in Microbiology and Immunology, Washington, DC 20052. Offers PhD. *Students:* 3 full-time (1 woman), 13 part-time (9 women); includes 3 minority (1 American Indian/Alaska Native, 1 Asian American or Pacific Islander, 1 Hispanic American), 4 international. Average age 31. *Degree requirements:* For doctorate, thesis/dissertation. *Entrance requirements:* For doctorate, GRE General Test, minimum GPA of 3.0. Additional exam requirements/recommendations for international students: Required—TOEFL (minimum score 600 paper-based; 250 computer-based). *Application deadline:* For fall admission, 1/2 priority date for domestic and international students. Applications are processed on a rolling basis. Application fee: $60. Electronic applications accepted. *Financial support:* In 2009–10, 10 students received support; fellowships with tuition reimbursements, tuition waivers available. *Unit head:* Dr. David Leitenberg, Director, 202-994-9475, Fax: 202-994-2913, E-mail: dleit@gwu.edu. *Application contact:* Information Contact, 202-994-3532, Fax: 202-994-2913, E-mail: mtmjxl@gwumc.edu.

Harvard University, School of Public Health, Department of Immunology and Infectious Diseases, Boston, MA 02115-6096. Offers PhD, SD. Part-time programs available. *Faculty:* 27 full-time (9 women), 5 part-time/adjunct (0 women). *Students:* 6 applicants, 17% accepted, 0 enrolled. *Degree requirements:* For doctorate, thesis/dissertation, qualifying exam. *Entrance requirements:* For doctorate, GRE. Additional exam requirements/recommendations for international students: Required—TOEFL (minimum score 600 paper-based; 240 computer-based; 100 iBT); Recommended—IELTS (minimum score 7). *Application deadline:* For fall admission, 12/15 for domestic and international students. Application fee: $115. Electronic applications accepted. *Expenses:* Tuition: Full-time $33,696. Required fees: $1126. Full-time tuition and fees vary according to program. *Financial support:* Fellowships, research assistantships, Federal Work-Study, scholarships/grants, traineeships, tuition waivers (partial), and unspecified assistantships available. Financial award application deadline: 2/8; financial award applicants required to submit FAFSA. *Faculty research:* Infectious disease epidemiology and tropical public health, vector biology, ecology and control, virology. *Unit head:* Dr. Dyann F. Wirth, Chair, 617-432-2234, Fax: 617-739-8348, E-mail: rkenwort@hsph.harvard.edu. *Application contact:* Vincent W. James, Director of Admissions, 617-432-1031, Fax: 617-432-7080, E-mail: admisofc@hsph.harvard.edu.

Immunology

Hood College, Graduate School, Program in Biomedical Science, Frederick, MD 21701-8575. Offers biomedical science (MS), including biotechnology/molecular biology, microbiology/immunology/virology, regulatory compliance; regulatory compliance (Certificate). Part-time and evening/weekend programs available. *Faculty:* 3 full-time (1 woman), 4 part-time/adjunct (2 women). *Students:* 9 full-time (2 women), 82 part-time (54 women); includes 23 minority (17 African Americans, 2 Asian Americans or Pacific Islanders, 4 Hispanic Americans), 7 international. Average age 29. 51 applicants, 67% accepted, 28 enrolled. In 2009, 11 master's, 10 other advanced degrees awarded. *Degree requirements:* For master's, comprehensive exam, thesis or alternative. *Entrance requirements:* For master's, bachelor's degree in biology; minimum GPA of 2.75; undergraduate course work in cell biology, chemistry, organic chemistry, and genetics. Additional exam requirements/recommendations for international students: Required—TOEFL (minimum score 575 paper-based; 231 computer-based; 89 iBT). *Application deadline:* For fall admission, 7/15 for domestic and international students; for spring admission, 12/15 for domestic and international students. Applications are processed on a rolling basis. Application fee: $35. Electronic applications accepted. *Expenses:* Tuition: Full-time $6480; part-time $360 per credit. Required fees: $100; $50 per term. *Financial support:* In 2009–10, 3 research assistantships with full tuition reimbursements (averaging $10,609 per year) were awarded. Financial award applicants required to submit FAFSA. *Unit head:* Dr. Oney Smith, Director, 301-696-3653, Fax: 301-696-3597, E-mail: osmith@hood.edu. *Application contact:* Dr. Allen P. Flora, Dean of Graduate School, 301-696-3811, Fax: 301-696-3597, E-mail: gofurther@hood.edu.

Illinois State University, Graduate School, College of Arts and Sciences, Department of Biological Sciences, Normal, IL 61790-2200. Offers animal behavior (MS); bacteriology (MS); biochemistry (MS); biological sciences (MS); biology (PhD); biophysics (MS); biotechnology (MS); botany (MS, PhD); cell biology (MS); conservation biology (MS); developmental biology (MS); ecology (MS, PhD); entomology (MS); evolutionary biology (MS); genetics (MS, PhD); immunology (MS); microbiology (MS, PhD); molecular biology (MS); molecular genetics (MS); neurobiology (MS); neuroscience (MS); parasitology (MS); physiology (MS, PhD); plant biology (MS); plant molecular biology (MS); plant sciences (MS); structural biology (MS); zoology (MS, PhD). Part-time programs available. *Degree requirements:* For master's, thesis or alternative; for doctorate, variable foreign language requirement, thesis/dissertation, 2 terms of residency. *Entrance requirements:* For master's, GRE General Test, minimum GPA of 2.6 in last 60 hours of course work; for doctorate, GRE General Test. *Faculty research:* Redoc balance and drug development in schistosoma mansoni, control of the growth of listeria monocytogenes at low temperature, regulation of cell expansion and microtubule function by SPRI, CRUI: physiology and fitness consequences of different life history phenotypes.

Indiana University–Purdue University Indianapolis, Indiana University School of Medicine, Department of Microbiology and Immunology, Indianapolis, IN 46202-2896. Offers MS, PhD, MD/MS, MD/PhD. *Faculty:* 20 full-time (2 women). *Students:* 31 full-time (24 women); includes 8 minority (6 African Americans, 2 Asian Americans or Pacific Islanders), 9 international. Average age 27. 8 applicants, 100% accepted, 8 enrolled. In 2009, 5 doctorates awarded. Terminal master's awarded for partial completion of doctoral program. *Degree requirements:* For master's, thesis; for doctorate, thesis/dissertation. *Entrance requirements:* For master's and doctorate, GRE General Test, previous course work in calculus, cell biology, chemistry, genetics, physics, and biochemistry. *Application deadline:* For fall admission, 3/1 for domestic students. Applications are processed on a rolling basis. Application fee: $55 ($65 for international students). *Financial support:* In 2009–10, 2 fellowships with full tuition reimbursements (averaging $8,313 per year), 6 teaching assistantships with full tuition reimbursements (averaging $18,391 per year) were awarded; research assistantships with full tuition reimbursements, Federal Work-Study, institutionally sponsored loans, scholarships/grants, traineeships, and tuition waivers (partial) also available. Financial award application deadline: 2/1. *Faculty research:* Host-parasite interactions, molecular biology, cellular and molecular immunology and hematology, viral and bacterial pathogenesis, cancer research. Total annual research expenditures: $4.2 million. *Unit head:* Dr. Hal E. Broxmeyer, Chairman, 317-274-7672, Fax: 317-274-4090, E-mail: hbroxmey@iupui.edu. *Application contact:* 317-274-7671, Fax: 317-274-4090.

Iowa State University of Science and Technology, Graduate College, Interdisciplinary Programs, Program in Immunobiology, Ames, IA 50011. Offers MS, PhD. *Students:* 14 full-time (7 women), 3 part-time (0 women); includes 1 minority (Hispanic American), 5 international. In 2009, 2 master's, 1 doctorate awarded. *Degree requirements:* For master's, one foreign language, thesis; for doctorate, one foreign language, thesis/dissertation. *Entrance requirements:* For master's and doctorate, GRE General Test, resume. Additional exam requirements/recommendations for international students: Required—TOEFL (minimum score 600 paper-based; 85 iBT) or IELTS (minimum score 7). *Application deadline:* For fall admission, 1/15 priority date for domestic and international students. Applications are processed on a rolling basis. Application fee: $40 ($90 for international students). Electronic applications accepted. *Expenses:* Tuition, state resident: full-time $6716. Tuition, nonresident: full-time $8908. Tuition and fees vary according to course level, course load, program and student level. *Financial support:* In 2009–10, 13 research assistantships with full and partial tuition reimbursements (averaging $18,880 per year) were awarded; fellowships, teaching assistantships, scholarships/grants, health care benefits, and unspecified assistantships also available. *Faculty research:* Immunogenetics, cellular and molecular immunology, infectious disease, neuroimmunology. *Unit head:* Dr. Marian Kohut, Supervisory Committee Chair, 515-294-7252, E-mail: idgp@iastate.edu. *Application contact:* Katie Blair, Information Contact, 515-294-7252, Fax: 515-924-6790, E-mail: idgp@iastate.edu.

The Johns Hopkins University, Bloomberg School of Public Health, The W. Harry Feinstone, Department of Molecular Microbiology and Immunology, Baltimore, MD 21218-2699. Offers MHS, Sc M, PhD. *Faculty:* 41 full-time (10 women), 10 part-time/adjunct (1 woman). *Students:* 86 full-time (56 women), 1 part-time (0 women); includes 24 minority (5 African Americans, 1 American Indian/Alaska Native, 14 Asian Americans or Pacific Islanders, 4 Hispanic Americans), 27 international. Average age 26. 184 applicants, 53% accepted, 38 enrolled. In 2009, 19 master's, 11 doctorates awarded. Terminal master's awarded for partial completion of doctoral program. *Degree requirements:* For master's, comprehensive exam, thesis (for some programs), essay, written exams; for doctorate, comprehensive exam, thesis/dissertation, 1 year full-time residency, oral and written exams. *Entrance requirements:* For master's, GRE General Test or MCAT, 3 letters of recommendation, curriculum vitae; for doctorate, GRE General Test, 3 letters of recommendation, transcripts, curriculum vitae. Additional exam requirements/recommendations for international students: Required—TOEFL (minimum score 600 paper-based; 250 computer-based). *Application deadline:* For fall admission, 1/2 priority date for domestic and international students. Applications are processed on a rolling basis. Application fee: $45. Electronic applications accepted. *Financial support:* In 2009–10, 37 fellowships with full and partial tuition reimbursements, 28 research assistantships with tuition reimbursements were awarded; Federal Work-Study, institutionally sponsored loans, scholarships/grants, and stipends also available. Financial award application deadline: 3/15; financial award applicants required to submit FAFSA. *Faculty research:* Immunology, virology, bacteriology, parasitology, vector biology, disease ecology, pathogenesis of infectious disease, immune responses to infectious agents, vector-borne and tropical diseases, biochemistry and molecular biology of infectious agents, population genetics of insect vectors, genetic regulation and immune responses in insect vectors, vaccine development, hormonal effects on pathogenesis and immune responses. Total annual research expenditures: $14.5 million. *Unit head:* Dr. Diane E. Griffin, Chair, 410-955-3459, Fax: 410-955-0105, E-mail: dgriffin@jhsph.edu. *Application contact:* Gail O'Connor, Senior Academic Program Coordinator, 410-614-4232, Fax: 410-955-0105, E-mail: goconnor@jhsph.edu.

The Johns Hopkins University, School of Medicine, Graduate Programs in Medicine, Immunology Training Program, Baltimore, MD 21205. Offers PhD. *Faculty:* 34 full-time (8 women). *Students:* 41 full-time (21 women); includes 13 minority (3 African Americans, 10 Asian Americans or Pacific Islanders), 5 international. Average age 23. 126 applicants, 11% accepted, 5 enrolled. In 2009, 6 doctorates awarded. *Degree requirements:* For doctorate, comprehensive exam, thesis/dissertation, oral exam, final thesis seminar. *Entrance requirements:* For doctorate, GRE General Test, 2 letters of recommendation. Additional exam requirements/recommendations for international students: Required—TOEFL (minimum score 550 paper-based). *Application deadline:* For fall admission, 1/10 for domestic students. Application fee: $85. Electronic applications accepted. *Financial support:* In 2009–10, 9 fellowships with full tuition reimbursements (averaging $20,976 per year), 31 research assistantships with full tuition reimbursements (averaging $27,125 per year) were awarded; scholarships/grants, traineeships, health care benefits, tuition waivers (full), unspecified assistantships, and institutional funds also available. Financial award application deadline: 1/10. *Faculty research:* HIV immunity, tumor immunity, major histocompatibility complex, transplantation, genetics of antibodies and T-cell receptors; immune response to infectious agents; antigen recognition; immune regulation; autoimmune diseases; immune cell signaling. Total annual research expenditures: $22.9 million. *Unit head:* Dr. Mark J. Soloski, Director, 410-550-8493, Fax: 410-550-2072, E-mail: mski@jhmi.edu. *Application contact:* Angela James, Academic Program Coordinator II, 410-955-2709, Fax: 410-955-0964, E-mail: ajames@jhmi.edu.

Long Island University, C.W. Post Campus, School of Health Professions and Nursing, Department of Biomedical Sciences, Brookville, NY 11548-1300. Offers cardiovascular perfusion (MS); clinical laboratory management (MS); medical biology (MS), including hematology, immunology, medical biology, medical chemistry, medical microbiology. Part-time and evening/weekend programs available. Postbaccalaureate distance learning degree programs offered. *Degree requirements:* For master's, thesis. *Entrance requirements:* For master's, minimum GPA of 2.75 in major. Electronic applications accepted.

Louisiana State University Health Sciences Center, School of Graduate Studies in New Orleans, Department of Microbiology, Immunology, and Parasitology, New Orleans, LA 70112-1393. Offers microbiology and immunology (MS, PhD); MD/PhD. Terminal master's awarded for partial completion of doctoral program. *Degree requirements:* For master's, comprehensive exam, thesis; for doctorate, comprehensive exam, thesis/dissertation, preliminary exam, qualifying exam. *Entrance requirements:* For master's and doctorate, GRE General Test. Additional exam requirements/recommendations for international students: Required—TOEFL. *Faculty research:* Microbial physiology, animal virology, vaccine development, AIDS drug studies, pathogenic mechanisms, molecular immunology.

Louisiana State University Health Sciences Center at Shreveport, Department of Microbiology and Immunology, Shreveport, LA 71130-3932. Offers MS, PhD, MD/PhD. Terminal master's awarded for partial completion of doctoral program. *Degree requirements:* For master's, thesis; for doctorate, thesis/dissertation. *Entrance requirements:* For master's and doctorate, GRE General Test. Additional exam requirements/recommendations for international students: Required—TOEFL. *Faculty research:* Infectious disease, pathogenesis, molecular virology and biology.

Loyola University Chicago, Graduate School, Department of Microbiology and Immunology, Maywood, IL 60153. Offers immunology (PhD); microbiology (MS); MD/PhD. *Faculty:* 11 full-time (3 women). *Students:* 36 full-time (24 women); includes 2 minority (both Asian Americans or Pacific Islanders), 7 international. Average age 27. 81 applicants, 21% accepted, 7 enrolled. In 2009, 1 master's, 5 doctorates awarded. Terminal master's awarded for partial completion of doctoral program. *Degree requirements:* For master's, thesis; for doctorate, comprehensive exam, thesis/dissertation. *Entrance requirements:* For master's and doctorate, GRE General Test. Additional exam requirements/recommendations for international students: Required—TOEFL. *Application deadline:* Applications are processed on a rolling basis. Application fee: $50. Electronic applications accepted. *Expenses:* Tuition: Full-time $14,220; part-time $790 per credit hour. Required fees: $60 per semester hour. Tuition and fees vary according to program. *Financial support:* In 2009–10, 5 fellowships with tuition reimbursements (averaging $23,000 per year), 24 research assistantships with tuition reimbursements (averaging $23,000 per year) were awarded; institutionally sponsored loans and scholarships/grants also available. Financial award application deadline: 2/15. *Faculty research:* Viral pathogenesis, microbial physiology and genetics, immunoglobulin genetics and differentiation of the immune response, signal transduction and host-parasite interactions. Total annual research expenditures: $4.2 million. *Unit head:* Dr. Katherine L. Knight, Chair, 708-216-3385, Fax: 708-216-9574, E-mail: kknight@lumc.edu. *Application contact:* Dr. Karen Visick, Graduate Program Director, 708-216-0869, Fax: 708-216-9574, E-mail: kvisick@lumc.edu.

Loyola University Chicago, Graduate School, Program in Infectious Disease and Immunology, Chicago, IL 60660. *Expenses:* Tuition: Full-time $14,220; part-time $790 per credit hour. Required fees: $60 per semester hour. Tuition and fees vary according to program.

Massachusetts Institute of Technology, School of Science, Department of Biology, Cambridge, MA 02139-4307. Offers biochemistry (PhD); biological oceanography (PhD); biology (PhD); biophysical chemistry and molecular structure (PhD); cell biology (PhD); computational and systems biology (PhD); developmental biology (PhD); genetics (PhD); immunology (PhD); microbiology (PhD); molecular biology (PhD); neurobiology (PhD). *Faculty:* 54 full-time (14 women). *Students:* 237 full-time (128 women); includes 65 minority (4 African Americans, 2 American Indian/Alaska Native, 33 Asian Americans or Pacific Islanders, 26 Hispanic Americans), 25 international. Average age 26. 645 applicants, 18% accepted, 49 enrolled. In 2009, 41 doctorates awarded. *Degree requirements:* For doctorate, comprehensive exam, thesis/dissertation. *Entrance requirements:* For doctorate, GRE General Test. Additional exam requirements/recommendations for international students: Required—TOEFL (minimum score 577 paper-based; 233 computer-based), IELTS (minimum score 6.5). *Application deadline:* For fall admission, 12/1 for domestic and international students. Application fee: $75. Electronic applications accepted. *Expenses:* Tuition: Full-time $37,510; part-time $585 per unit. Required fees: $272. *Financial support:* In 2009–10, 218 students received support, including 113 fellowships with tuition reimbursements available (averaging $31,816 per year), 109 research assistantships with tuition reimbursements available (averaging $29,254 per year); teaching assistantships with tuition reimbursements available, Federal Work-Study, institutionally sponsored loans, scholarships/grants, traineeships, health care benefits, and unspecified assistantships also available. *Faculty research:* DNA recombination, transcription and gene regulation, signal transduction, cell cycle, neuronal cell fate, replication and repair. Total annual research expenditures: $114 million. *Unit head:* Prof. Chris Kaiser, Head, 617-253-4701, E-mail: mitbio@mit.edu. *Application contact:* Biology Education Office, 617-253-3717, Fax: 617-258-9329, E-mail: gradbio@mit.edu.

Mayo Graduate School, Graduate Programs in Biomedical Sciences, Program in Immunology, Rochester, MN 55905. Offers PhD. *Degree requirements:* For doctorate, oral defense of dissertation, qualifying oral and written exam. *Entrance requirements:* For doctorate, GRE, 1 year of chemistry, biology, calculus, and physics. Additional exam requirements/recommendations for international students: Required—TOEFL. Electronic applications accepted. *Faculty research:* Immunogenetics, autoimmunity, receptor signal transduction, T lymphocyte activation, transplantation.

McGill University, Faculty of Graduate and Postdoctoral Studies, Faculty of Medicine, Department of Microbiology and Immunology, Montréal, QC H3A 2T5, Canada. Offers M Sc, M Sc A, PhD.

McMaster University, Faculty of Health Sciences and School of Graduate Studies, Program in Medical Sciences, Immunity and Infection Area, Hamilton, ON L8S 4M2, Canada. Offers M Sc, PhD, MD/PhD. *Degree requirements:* For master's, thesis; for doctorate, comprehensive exam, thesis/dissertation. *Entrance requirements:* For master's, honors B Sc, B+ average in related field; for doctorate, M Sc, minimum B+ average, students with proven research experience and an A average may be admitted with a B Sc degree. Additional exam requirements/recommendations for international students: Required—TOEFL (minimum score 580 paper-based; 237 computer-based; 92 iBT).

Medical University of South Carolina, College of Graduate Studies, Department of Microbiology and Immunology, Charleston, SC 29425. Offers MS, PhD, DMD/PhD, MD/PhD. *Faculty:* 14 full-time (4 women). *Students:* 17 full-time (10 women), 1 part-time (0 women); includes 2 African Americans, 2 Hispanic Americans, 1 international. Average age 26. 13 applicants, 31% accepted, 4 enrolled. In 2009, 1 master's, 8 doctorates awarded. Terminal master's awarded for partial completion of doctoral program. *Degree requirements:* For master's, thesis; for doctorate, thesis/dissertation, oral and written exams. *Entrance requirements:* For master's, GRE General Test, MCAT, or DAT, interview; for doctorate, GRE General Test, interview, minimum GPA of 3.0. Additional exam requirements/recommendations for international students: Required—TOEFL (minimum score 600 paper-based; 250 computer-based; 100 iBT). *Application deadline:* For fall admission, 1/15 priority date for domestic and international students. Applications are processed on a rolling basis. Application fee: $0 ($85 for international students). Electronic applications accepted. *Financial support:* In 2009–10, 10 research assistantships with partial tuition reimbursements (averaging $23,000 per year) were awarded; Federal Work-Study and scholarships/grants also available. Support available to part-time students. Financial award application deadline: 3/10; financial award applicants required to submit FAFSA. *Faculty research:* Innate and adaptive immunology, gene therapy/vector development, vaccinology, proteomics of biowarfare agents, bacterial and fungal pathogenesis. *Unit head:* Dr. James S. Norris, Chair, 843-792-7915, Fax: 843-792-6590, E-mail: norrisjs@musc.edu. *Application contact:* Dr. Laura Kasman, Assistant Professor, 843-792-8117, Fax: 843-792-6590, E-mail: kasmanl@musc.edu.

Meharry Medical College, School of Graduate Studies, Program in Biomedical Sciences, Microbiology and Immunology Emphasis, Nashville, TN 37208-9989. Offers PhD, MD/PhD. *Degree requirements:* For doctorate, comprehensive exam, thesis/dissertation. *Entrance requirements:* For doctorate, GRE General Test, GRE Subject Test, undergraduate degree in related science. *Faculty research:* Microbial and bacterial pathogenesis, viral transcription, immune response to viruses and parasites.

Memorial University of Newfoundland, Faculty of Medicine and School of Graduate Studies, Graduate Programs in Medicine, Division of Biomedical Sciences, St. John's, NL A1C 5S7, Canada. Offers cancer (M Sc, PhD); cardiovascular (M Sc, PhD); immunology (M Sc, PhD); neuroscience (M Sc, PhD). Part-time programs available. *Degree requirements:* For master's, thesis; for doctorate, comprehensive exam, thesis/dissertation, oral defense of thesis. *Entrance requirements:* For master's, MD or B Sc; for doctorate, MD or M Sc. Additional exam requirements/recommendations for international students: Required—TOEFL. *Faculty research:* Neuroscience, immunology, cardiovascular, and cancer.

New York Medical College, Graduate School of Basic Medical Sciences, Microbiology and Immunology Department, Valhalla, NY 10595-1691. Offers MS, PhD, MD/PhD. Part-time and evening/weekend programs available. Terminal master's awarded for partial completion of doctoral program. *Degree requirements:* For master's, thesis; for doctorate, comprehensive exam, thesis/dissertation. *Entrance requirements:* For master's and doctorate, GRE General Test. Additional exam requirements/recommendations for international students: Required—TOEFL. *Expenses:* Tuition: Full-time $18,170; part-time $790 per credit. Required fees: $790 per credit. $20 per semester. One-time fee: $100. Tuition and fees vary according to class time, course level, course load, degree level, program, student level and student's religious affiliation. *Faculty research:* Tumor and transplantation immunology, molecular mechanisms of DNA repair, virus-host interactions.

New York University, Graduate School of Arts and Science, Department of Biology, New York, NY 10012-1019. Offers biology (PhD); biomedical journalism (MS); cancer and molecular biology (PhD); computational biology (PhD); computers in biological research (MS); developmental genetics (PhD); general biology (MS); immunology and microbiology (PhD); molecular genetics (PhD); neurobiology (PhD); oral biology (MS); plant biology (PhD); recombinant DNA technology (MS); MS/MBA. Part-time programs available. *Faculty:* 24 full-time (5 women). *Students:* 142 full-time (79 women), 44 part-time (28 women); includes 34 minority (1 African American, 25 Asian Americans or Pacific Islanders, 8 Hispanic Americans), 82 international. Average age 27. 362 applicants, 71% accepted, 72 enrolled. In 2009, 43 master's, 9 doctorates awarded. Terminal master's awarded for partial completion of doctoral program. *Degree requirements:* For master's, thesis or alternative, qualifying paper; for doctorate, comprehensive exam, thesis/dissertation. *Entrance requirements:* For master's, GRE General Test; for doctorate, GRE General Test, GRE Subject Test. Additional exam requirements/recommendations for international students: Required—TOEFL. *Application deadline:* For fall admission, 12/12 priority date for domestic students. Application fee: $90. *Expenses:* Tuition: Full-time $30,528; part-time $1272 per credit. Required fees: $2177. *Financial support:* Fellowships with tuition reimbursements, research assistantships with tuition reimbursements, teaching assistantships with tuition reimbursements, career-related internships or fieldwork, Federal Work-Study, institutionally sponsored loans, scholarships/grants, health care benefits, and unspecified assistantships available. Financial award application deadline: 12/12; financial award applicants required to submit FAFSA. *Faculty research:* Genomics, molecular and cell biology, development and molecular genetics, molecular evolution of plants and animals. *Unit head:* Gloria Coruzzi, Chair, 212-998-8200, Fax: 212-995-4015, E-mail: biology@nyu.edu. *Application contact:* Stephen Small, Director of Graduate Studies, 212-998-8200, Fax: 212-995-4015, E-mail: biology@nyu.edu.

New York University, School of Medicine, New York, NY 10012-1019. Offers biomedical sciences (PhD), including biomedical imaging, cellular and molecular biology, computational biology, developmental genetics, medical and molecular parasitology, microbiology, molecular oncobiology and immunology, neuroscience and physiology, pathobiology, pharmacology, structural biology; clinical investigation (MS); medicine (MD); MD/MA; MD/MPA; MD/MS; MD/PhD. *Accreditation:* LCME/AMA (one or more programs are accredited). *Faculty:* 1,493 full-time (558 women), 327 part-time/adjunct (122 women). *Students:* 747 full-time (360 women); includes 275 minority (23 African Americans, 5 American Indian/Alaska Native, 199 Asian Americans or Pacific Islanders, 48 Hispanic Americans), 2 international. Average age 24. 7,568 applicants, 7% accepted, 213 enrolled. In 2009, 164 first professional degrees, 13 master's, 50 doctorates awarded. *Degree requirements:* For master's, comprehensive exam, thesis; for doctorate, comprehensive exam, thesis/dissertation. *Entrance requirements:* MCAT. Additional exam requirements/recommendations for international students: Required—TOEFL. *Application deadline:* For fall admission, 10/15 for domestic students; for winter admission, 12/18 for domestic students, 12/15 for international students. Application fee: $100. *Expenses:* Contact institution. *Financial support:* In 2009–10, 524 students received support, including 29 fellowships with full tuition reimbursements available (averaging $31,000 per year), 47 research assistantships with full tuition reimbursements available (averaging $31,000 per year); teaching assistantships, Federal Work-Study, institutionally sponsored loans, and health care benefits also available. Financial award application deadline: 3/1; financial award applicants required to submit FAFSA. *Faculty research:* AIDS, cancer, neuroscience, molecular biology, neuroscience, cell biology and molecular genetics, structural biology, microbial pathogenesis and host defense, pharmacology, molecular oncology and immunology. Total annual research expenditures: $201.1 million. *Unit head:* Dr. Robert Grossman, Dean, 212-263-3269, Fax: 212-263- 1828. *Application contact:* Dr. Nancy Genieser, Associate Dean, Admissions, 212-263-5290, Fax: 212-263-0720, E-mail: nancy.genieser@nyumc.org.

New York University, School of Medicine and Graduate School of Arts and Science, Sackler Institute of Graduate Biomedical Sciences, Programs in Molecular Oncology and Immunology, New York, NY 10012-1019. Offers immunology (PhD); molecular oncology (PhD); MD/PhD. *Degree requirements:* For doctorate, one foreign language, thesis/dissertation, qualifying exam. *Entrance requirements:* For doctorate, GRE General Test, GRE Subject Test. Additional exam requirements/recommendations for international students: Required—TOEFL. Electronic applications accepted. *Expenses:* Tuition: Full-time $30,528; part-time $1272 per credit. Required fees: $2177. *Faculty research:* Stem cells, immunology, genome instability, DNA damage checkpoints.

North Carolina State University, Graduate School, College of Agriculture and Life Sciences and College of Veterinary Medicine, Program in Immunology, Raleigh, NC 27695. Offers MS, PhD. *Degree requirements:* For master's, thesis; for doctorate, thesis/dissertation. *Entrance requirements:* For master's and doctorate, GRE General Test. Additional exam requirements/recommendations for international students: Required—TOEFL (minimum score 550 paper-based; 213 computer-based). Electronic applications accepted. *Faculty research:* Immunogenetics, immunopathology, immunotoxicology, immunoparasitology, molecular and infectious disease immunology.

Northwestern University, Northwestern University Feinberg School of Medicine and Interdepartmental Programs, Integrated Graduate Programs in the Life Sciences, Chicago, IL 60611. Offers cancer biology (PhD); cell biology (PhD); developmental biology (PhD); evolutionary biology (PhD); immunology and microbial pathogenesis (PhD); molecular biology and genetics (PhD); neurobiology (PhD); pharmacology and toxicology (PhD); structural biology and biochemistry (PhD). *Degree requirements:* For doctorate, comprehensive exam, thesis/dissertation, written and oral qualifying exams. *Entrance requirements:* For doctorate, GRE General Test. Additional exam requirements/recommendations for international students: Required—TOEFL (minimum score 600 paper-based; 250 computer-based). Electronic applications accepted.

The Ohio State University, College of Medicine, School of Biomedical Science, Integrated Biomedical Science Graduate Program, Columbus, OH 43210. Offers immunology (PhD); medical genetics (PhD); molecular virology (PhD); pharmacology (PhD). *Degree requirements:* For doctorate, thesis/dissertation. *Entrance requirements:* For doctorate, GRE, GRE Subject Test in biochemistry, cell and molecular biology (recommended for some). Additional exam requirements/recommendations for international students: Required—TOEFL (minimum score 600 paper-based; 250 computer-based). Electronic applications accepted. *Expenses:* Tuition, state resident: full-time $10,683. Tuition, nonresident: full-time $25,923. Tuition and fees vary according to course load and program.

The Ohio State University, College of Medicine, School of Biomedical Science, Program in Molecular Virology, Immunology and Medical Genetics, Columbus, OH 43210. Offers MS, PhD. *Entrance requirements:* For master's and doctorate, GRE, GRE Subject Test in biology (recommended). Electronic applications accepted. *Expenses:* Tuition, state resident: full-time $10,683. Tuition, nonresident: full-time $25,923. Tuition and fees vary according to course load and program.

Oregon Health & Science University, School of Medicine, Graduate Programs in Medicine, Department of Molecular Microbiology and Immunology, Portland, OR 97239-3098. Offers PhD. *Degree requirements:* For doctorate, comprehensive exam, thesis/dissertation. *Entrance requirements:* For doctorate, GRE General Test (minimum scores: 500 Verbal/600 Quantitative/4.5 Analytical) or MCAT (for some programs). Additional exam requirements/recommendations for international students: Required—TOEFL. *Application deadline:* For fall admission, 12/1 for domestic students. Electronic applications accepted. Tuition and fees vary according to course level, course load, degree level, program and reciprocity agreements. *Financial support:* PhD students have paid tuition and receive stipends available. *Faculty research:* Molecular biology of bacterial and viral pathogens, cellular and humoral immunology, molecular biology of microbes. *Unit head:* Eric Barklis, PhD, Program Director, 503-494-7768, E-mail: mmi@ohsu.edu. *Application contact:* Kathy Shinall, Program Coordinator, 503-494-7768, E-mail: mmi@ohsu.edu.

Penn State Hershey Medical Center, College of Medicine, Graduate School Programs in the Biomedical Sciences, Graduate Program in Microbiology and Immunology, Hershey, PA 17033. Offers genetics (PhD); immunology (MS, PhD); microbiology (MS); microbiology/virology (PhD); molecular biology (PhD); MD/PhD. *Students:* 12 applicants, 75% accepted, 3 enrolled. In 2009, 1 doctorate awarded. Terminal master's awarded for partial completion of doctoral program. *Degree requirements:* For master's, thesis or alternative; for doctorate, comprehensive exam, thesis/dissertation, oral exam. *Entrance requirements:* For doctorate, GRE General Test, minimum GPA of 3.0. Additional exam requirements/recommendations for international students: Required—TOEFL. *Application deadline:* For fall admission, 1/31 priority date for domestic students, 2/1 priority date for international students. Applications are processed on a rolling basis. Application fee: $45. Electronic applications accepted. *Expenses:* Tuition, state resident: part-time $644 per credit. Tuition, nonresident: part-time $1142 per credit. Required fees: $22 per semester. *Financial support:* In 2009–10, research assistantships with full tuition reimbursements (averaging $22,260 per year); fellowships with full tuition reimbursements, scholarships/grants, health care benefits, and unspecified assistantships also available. Financial award applicants required to submit FAFSA. *Faculty research:* Virus replication and assembly, oncogenesis, interactions of viruses with host cells and animal model systems. *Unit head:* Dr. Richard J. Courtney, Chair, 717-531-7659, Fax: 717-531-6522, E-mail: micro-grad-hmc@psu.edu. *Application contact:* Billie Burns, Secretary, 717-531-7659, Fax: 717-531-6522, E-mail: micro-grad-hmc@psu.edu.

Penn State University Park, Graduate School, Intercollege Graduate Programs, State College, University Park, PA 16802-1503. Offers acoustics (M Eng, MS, PhD); bioengineering (MS, PhD); biogeochemistry (dual) (PhD); business administration (MBA); cell and developmental biology (PhD); demography (dual) (MA); ecology (MS, PhD); environmental pollution control (MEPC, MS); genetics (MS, PhD); human dimensions of natural resources and the environment (dual) (MA, MS, PhD); immunology and infectious diseases (MS); integrative biosciences (MS, PhD), including integrative biosciences; materials science and engineering (PhD); operations research (dual) (M Eng, MA, MS, PhD); physiology (MS, PhD); plant physiology (MS, PhD); quality and manufacturing management (MMM). *Students:* 371 full-time (157 women), 22 part-time (7 women). Average age 27. 1,074 applicants, 18% accepted, 130 enrolled. *Entrance requirements:* Additional exam requirements/recommendations for international students: Required—TOEFL (minimum score 550 paper-based; 213 computer-based; 80 iBT). *Application deadline:* Applications are processed on a rolling basis. Application fee: $45. Electronic applications accepted. *Financial support:* Fellowships, research assistantships, teaching assistantships available. Financial award applicants required to submit FAFSA. *Unit head:* Dr. Regina Vasilatos-Younken, Senior Associate Dean, 814-865-2516, Fax: 814-863-4627, E-mail: rxv@psu.edu. *Application contact:* Cynthia E. Nicosia, Director, Graduate Enrollment Services, 814-865-1795, Fax: 814-865-4627, E-mail: cey1@psu.edu.

Purdue University, School of Veterinary Medicine and Graduate School, Graduate Programs in Veterinary Medicine, Department of Comparative Pathobiology, West Lafayette, IN 47907-2027. Offers comparative epidemiology and public health (MS); comparative epidemiology and public heath (PhD); comparative microbiology and immunology (MS, PhD); comparative pathobiology (MS, PhD); interdisciplinary studies (PhD), including microbial pathogenesis, molecular signaling and cancer biology, molecular virology; lab animal medicine (MS); veterinary anatomic pathology (MS); veterinary clinical pathology (MS). *Faculty:* 37 full-time (10 women), 4 part-time/adjunct (2 women). *Students:* 53 full-time (31 women), 2 part-time (1 woman); includes 3 minority (2 African Americans, 1 Hispanic American), 32 international. Average age 35. In 2009, 6 master's, 2 doctorates awarded. Terminal master's awarded for partial completion of doctoral program. *Degree requirements:* For master's, thesis (for some programs); for doctorate, thesis/dissertation. *Entrance requirements:* For master's and doctorate, GRE General Test. Additional exam requirements/recommendations for international students: Required—TOEFL (minimum score 575 paper-based; 232 computer-based), IELTS (minimum score 6.5), TWE (minimum score 4). *Application deadline:* For fall admission, 8/12 for domestic students, 6/15 for international students; for spring admission, 1/12 for domestic students, 10/15 for international students. Application fee: $55. Electronic applications accepted. *Financial support:* Fellowships, research assistantships, teaching assistantships available. Financial award application deadline: 3/1; financial award applicants required to submit FAFSA. *Unit head:* Dr. Suresh Mittal, Interim Head, 765-494-7543. *Application contact:* Denise A. Ottinger, Director, Student Services and Admissions, 765-494-7893, Fax: 765-496-2891, E-mail: vetadmissions@purdue.edu.

Immunology

Queen's University at Kingston, School of Graduate Studies and Research, Faculty of Health Sciences, Department of Microbiology and Immunology, Kingston, ON K7L 3N6, Canada. Offers M Sc, PhD. Part-time programs available. *Degree requirements:* For master's, thesis; for doctorate, comprehensive exam, thesis/dissertation. *Entrance requirements:* For master's and doctorate, minimum B+ average. Additional exam requirements/recommendations for international students: Required—TOEFL (minimum score 600 paper-based; 250 computer-based). Electronic applications accepted. *Faculty research:* Bacteriology, virology, immunology, education in microbiology and immunology, microbial pathogenesis.

Rosalind Franklin University of Medicine and Science, School of Graduate and Post-doctoral Studies—Interdisciplinary Graduate Program in Biomedical Sciences, Department of Microbiology and Immunology, North Chicago, IL 60064-3095. Offers MS, PhD, MD/PhD. Terminal master's awarded for partial completion of doctoral program. *Degree requirements:* For master's, comprehensive exam, thesis; for doctorate, comprehensive exam, thesis/dissertation. *Entrance requirements:* For master's and doctorate, GRE General Test. Additional exam requirements/recommendations for international students: Required—TOEFL, TWE. *Faculty research:* Molecular biology, parasitology, virology.

Rush University, Graduate College, Division of Immunology and Microbiology, Program in Immunology/Microbiology, Chicago, IL 60612-3832. Offers immunology (MS, PhD); virology (MS, PhD); MD/PhD. Part-time programs available. Terminal master's awarded for partial completion of doctoral program. *Degree requirements:* For master's, thesis; for doctorate, thesis/dissertation, comprehensive preliminary exam. *Entrance requirements:* For master's, GRE General Test; for doctorate, GRE General Test, interview, minimum GPA of 3.0. Additional exam requirements/recommendations for international students: Required—TOEFL. Electronic applications accepted. *Faculty research:* Human genetics, autoimmunity, tumor biology, complement, HIV immunopathology genesis.

Rutgers, The State University of New Jersey, New Brunswick, Graduate School-New Brunswick, Programs in the Molecular Biosciences, Program in Microbiology and Molecular Genetics, Piscataway, NJ 08854-8097. Offers applied microbiology (MS, PhD); clinical microbiology (MS, PhD); computational molecular biology (PhD); immunology (MS, PhD); microbial biochemistry (MS, PhD); molecular genetics (MS, PhD); virology (MS, PhD). Part-time programs available. Terminal master's awarded for partial completion of doctoral program. *Degree requirements:* For master's, comprehensive exam, thesis or alternative; for doctorate, comprehensive exam, thesis/dissertation, written qualifying exam. *Entrance requirements:* For master's, GRE General Test, minimum GPA of 3.0; for doctorate, GRE General Test, GRE Subject Test (recommended), minimum GPA of 3.0. Additional exam requirements/recommendations for international students: Required—TOEFL. Electronic applications accepted. *Faculty research:* Molecular genetics and microbial physiology; virology and pathogenic microbiology; applied, environmental and industrial microbiology; computers in molecular biology.

Saint Louis University, Graduate School and School of Medicine, Graduate Program in Biomedical Sciences, Department of Molecular Microbiology and Immunology, St. Louis, MO 63103-2097. Offers PhD. *Degree requirements:* For doctorate, comprehensive exam, thesis/dissertation, qualifying exams. *Entrance requirements:* For doctorate, GRE General Test (GRE Subject Test optional), letters of recommendation, resume, interview. Additional exam requirements/recommendations for international students: Required—TOEFL (minimum score 525 paper-based; 194 computer-based). Electronic applications accepted. *Faculty research:* Pathogenesis of hepatitis C virus, herperviruses, pox viruses, rheumatoid arthritis, antiviral drugs and vaccines in biodefense, cancer gene therapy, virology and immunology.

Stanford University, School of Medicine, Graduate Programs in Medicine, Department of Microbiology and Immunology, Stanford, CA 94305-9991. Offers PhD. *Degree requirements:* For doctorate, comprehensive exam, thesis/dissertation, 2 quarters teaching assistantship. *Entrance requirements:* For doctorate, GRE General Test, GRE Subject Test (biology or biochemistry). Additional exam requirements/recommendations for international students: Required—TOEFL. Electronic applications accepted. *Expenses:* Tuition: Full-time $37,380; part-time $2760 per quarter. Required fees: $501. *Faculty research:* Molecular pathogenesis of bacteria viruses and parasites, immune system function, autoimmunity, molecular biology.

Stanford University, School of Medicine, Graduate Programs in Medicine, Program in Immunology, Stanford, CA 94305-9991. Offers PhD. *Degree requirements:* For doctorate, thesis/dissertation, qualifying examination. *Entrance requirements:* For doctorate, GRE General Test, GRE Subject Test. Additional exam requirements/recommendations for international students: Required—TOEFL. Electronic applications accepted. *Expenses:* Tuition: Full-time $37,380; part-time $2760 per quarter. Required fees: $501.

State University of New York Upstate Medical University, College of Graduate Studies, Program in Microbiology and Immunology, Syracuse, NY 13210-2334. Offers microbiology (MS); microbiology and immunology (PhD); MD/PhD. *Faculty:* 18 full-time (4 women), 2 part-time/adjunct (1 woman). *Students:* 19 full-time (14 women), 1 (woman) part-time; includes 5 minority (3 Asian Americans or Pacific Islanders, 2 Hispanic Americans), 1 international. In 2009, 1 master's, 1 doctorate awarded. Terminal master's awarded for partial completion of doctoral program. *Degree requirements:* For master's, thesis; for doctorate, comprehensive exam, thesis/dissertation. *Entrance requirements:* For master's, GRE General Test, interview; for doctorate, GRE General Test, telephone interview. Additional exam requirements/recommendations for international students: Required—TOEFL. *Application deadline:* Applications are processed on a rolling basis. Application fee: $40. Electronic applications accepted. *Financial support:* In 2009–10, fellowships with tuition reimbursements (averaging $21,514 per year), research assistantships with tuition reimbursements (averaging $21,514 per year) were awarded; Federal Work-Study, scholarships/grants, health care benefits, tuition waivers, and unspecified assistantships also available. Financial award application deadline: 4/15; financial award applicants required to submit FAFSA. *Faculty research:* Cancer, disorders of the nervous system, infectious diseases, diabetes/metabolic disorders/cardiovascular diseases. *Unit head:* Dr. Rosemary Rochford, Chair, 315-464-5127. *Application contact:* Sandra Tillotson, Coordinator of Graduate Recruitment, 315-464-7655.

See Close-Up on page 359.

Stony Brook University, State University of New York, Graduate School, College of Arts and Sciences, Department of Biochemistry and Cell Biology, Molecular and Cellular Biology Program, Stony Brook, NY 11794. Offers biochemistry and molecular biology (PhD); biological sciences (MA); cellular and developmental biology (PhD); immunology and pathology (PhD); molecular and cellular biology (PhD). *Students:* 100 full-time (62 women); includes 8 minority (2 African Americans, 5 Asian Americans or Pacific Islanders, 1 Hispanic American), 60 international. Average age 30. 277 applicants, 15% accepted. In 2009, 15 doctorates awarded. *Degree requirements:* For doctorate, comprehensive exam, thesis/dissertation, teaching experience. *Entrance requirements:* For doctorate, GRE General Test, GRE Subject Test. Additional exam requirements/recommendations for international students: Required—TOEFL. *Application deadline:* For fall admission, 1/15 for domestic students. Application fee: $60. *Expenses:* Tuition, state resident: full-time $8370; part-time $349 per credit. Tuition, nonresident: full-time $13,250; part-time $552 per credit. Required fees: $933. *Financial support:* In 2009–10, 49 research assistantships, 15 teaching assistantships were awarded; fellowships, Federal Work-Study also available. *Unit head:* Prof. Robert Haltiwanger, Chair, 631-632-8560. *Application contact:* Prof. Robert Haltiwanger, Chair, 631-632-8560.

Temple University, Health Sciences Center, School of Medicine and Graduate School, Graduate Programs in Medicine, Department of Microbiology and Immunology, Philadelphia, PA 19140-5104. Offers MS, PhD, MD/PhD. *Degree requirements:* For master's, thesis; for doctorate, thesis/dissertation, research seminars. *Entrance requirements:* For master's and doctorate, GRE General Test, GRE Subject Test, minimum GPA of 3.0. Additional exam requirements/recommendations for international students: Required—TOEFL (minimum score 600 paper-based; 250 computer-based). Electronic applications accepted. *Faculty research:* Molecular and cellular immunology, molecular and biochemical microbiology, molecular genetics.

Texas A&M Health Science Center, Graduate School of Biomedical Sciences, Department of Microbial and Molecular Pathogenesis, College Station, TX 77840. Offers immunology (PhD); microbiology (PhD); molecular biology (PhD); virology (PhD). *Degree requirements:* For doctorate, thesis/dissertation. *Entrance requirements:* For doctorate, GRE General Test, minimum GPA of 3.0. *Faculty research:* Molecular pathogenesis, microbial therapeutics.

Thomas Jefferson University, Jefferson College of Graduate Studies, PhD Program in Immunology and Microbial Pathogenesis, Philadelphia, PA 19107. Offers PhD. *Faculty:* 34 full-time (5 women), 2 part-time/adjunct (0 women). *Students:* 27 full-time (14 women); includes 4 minority (1 African American, 2 Asian Americans or Pacific Islanders, 1 Hispanic American), 2 international. 58 applicants, 16% accepted, 4 enrolled. In 2009, 3 doctorates awarded. *Degree requirements:* For doctorate, comprehensive exam, thesis/dissertation. *Entrance requirements:* For doctorate, GRE General Test, minimum GPA of 3.2. Additional exam requirements/recommendations for international students: Required—TOEFL (minimum score 250 computer-based; 100 iBT) or IELTS. *Application deadline:* For fall admission, 1/15 priority date for domestic and international students. Applications are processed on a rolling basis. Application fee: $50. Electronic applications accepted. *Expenses:* Tuition: Full-time $26,858; part-time $879 per credit. Required fees: $525. *Financial support:* In 2009–10, 27 students received support, including 27 fellowships with full tuition reimbursements available (averaging $52,883 per year); Federal Work-Study, institutionally sponsored loans, scholarships/grants, traineeships, and stipend also available. Support available to part-time students. Financial award application deadline: 5/1; financial award applicants required to submit FAFSA. Total annual research expenditures: $15.7 million. *Unit head:* Dr. Kishore Alugupalli, Program Director, 215-503-4550, Fax: 215-923-4153, E-mail: kishore.alugupalli@jefferson.edu. *Application contact:* Marc E. Stearns, Director of Admissions, 215-503-0155, Fax: 215-503-9920, E-mail: jcgs-info@jefferson.edu.

See Close-Up on page 361.

Tufts University, Sackler School of Graduate Biomedical Sciences, Program in Immunology, Medford, MA 02155. Offers PhD. *Faculty:* 24 full-time (8 women). *Students:* 29 full-time (15 women); includes 5 minority (1 African American, 3 Asian Americans or Pacific Islanders, 1 Hispanic American), 3 international. Average age 27. 105 applicants, 7% accepted, 4 enrolled. In 2009, 10 doctorates awarded. Terminal master's awarded for partial completion of doctoral program. *Degree requirements:* For doctorate, thesis/dissertation. *Entrance requirements:* For doctorate, GRE General Test, 3 letters of reference. Additional exam requirements/recommendations for international students: Required—TOEFL. *Application deadline:* For fall admission, 12/15 for domestic and international students. Applications are processed on a rolling basis. Application fee: $70. Electronic applications accepted. *Expenses:* Tuition: Full-time $38,096; part-time $3962 per credit. Required fees: $686; $40 per year. Tuition and fees vary according to course level, course load, degree level, program and student level. *Financial support:* In 2009–10, 29 students received support, including 29 research assistantships with full tuition reimbursements available (averaging $28,250 per year); scholarships/grants and tuition waivers (full) also available. *Faculty research:* Genetic analysis of lymphocyte function, ontogeny and activation, transformation of hematopoietic cells, autoimmunity, the immune response to infection. *Unit head:* Dr. Henry H. Wortis, Director, 617-636-6836, Fax: 617-636-2990, E-mail: henry.wortis@tufts.edu. *Application contact:* Kellie Johnston, Associate Director of Admissions, 617-636-6767, Fax: 617-636-0375, E-mail: sackler-school@tufts.edu.

Tulane University, School of Medicine and School of Liberal Arts, Graduate Programs in Biomedical Sciences, Department of Microbiology and Immunology, New Orleans, LA 70118-5669. Offers MS, PhD, MD/PhD. MS and PhD offered through the Graduate School. *Degree requirements:* For master's, thesis; for doctorate, 2 foreign languages, thesis/dissertation. *Entrance requirements:* For master's, GRE General Test, minimum B average in undergraduate course work; for doctorate, GRE General Test, GRE Subject Test. Additional exam requirements/recommendations for international students: Required—TOEFL. Electronic applications accepted. *Faculty research:* Vaccine development, viral pathogenesis, molecular virology, bacterial pathogenesis, fungal pathogenesis.

Uniformed Services University of the Health Sciences, School of Medicine, Graduate Programs in the Biomedical Sciences and Public Health, Graduate Program in Emerging Infectious Diseases, Bethesda, MD 20814-4799. Offers PhD. *Faculty:* 35 full-time (5 women), 17 part-time/adjunct (6 women). *Students:* 37 full-time (24 women); includes 5 minority (1 African American, 3 Asian Americans or Pacific Islanders, 1 Hispanic American), 3 international. Average age 26. 43 applicants, 44% accepted, 11 enrolled. In 2009, 7 doctorates awarded. *Degree requirements:* For doctorate, comprehensive exam, thesis/dissertation, qualifying exam. *Entrance requirements:* For doctorate, GRE General Test. Additional exam requirements/recommendations for international students: Required—TOEFL. *Application deadline:* For fall admission, 1/15 priority date for domestic and international students. Applications are processed on a rolling basis. Application fee: $0. Electronic applications accepted. *Financial support:* In 2009–10, fellowships with full tuition reimbursements (averaging $26,000 per year); scholarships/grants, health care benefits, and tuition waivers (full) also available. *Unit head:* Dr. Christopher Broder, Graduate Program Director, 301-295-3401, E-mail: cbroder@usuhs.mil. *Application contact:* Elena Marina Sherman, Graduate Program Coordinator, 301-295-3913, Fax: 301-295-6772, E-mail: elena.sherman@usuhs.mil.

Universidad Central del Caribe, School of Medicine, Program in Biomedical Sciences, Bayamón, PR 00960-6032. Offers anatomy and cell biology (MA, MS); biochemistry (MS); biomedical sciences (MA); microbiology and immunology (MA, MS); pharmacology (MS); physiology (MA, MS).

Université de Montréal, Faculty of Medicine, Department of Microbiology and Immunology, Montréal, QC H3C 3J7, Canada. Offers M Sc, PhD. *Faculty:* 44 full-time (14 women), 29 part-time/adjunct (8 women). *Students:* 13 full-time (7 women), 120 part-time (69 women). 82 applicants, 21% accepted, 15 enrolled. In 2009, 10 master's, 8 doctorates awarded. Terminal master's awarded for partial completion of doctoral program. *Degree requirements:* For master's, thesis; for doctorate, thesis/dissertation, general exam. *Entrance requirements:* For master's and doctorate, proficiency in French, knowledge of English. *Application deadline:* For fall admission, 2/1 priority date for domestic students; for winter admission, 11/1 priority date for domestic students; for spring admission, 2/1 priority date for domestic students. Application fee: $100. Electronic applications accepted. *Unit head:* Dr. Pierre Belhumeur, Director, 514-343-6273, Fax: 514-343-5701, E-mail: pierre.belhumeur@umontreal.ca. *Application contact:* Dr. George Szatmari, Chairperson, 514-343-5767, Fax: 514-343-5701, E-mail: george.szatmari@umontreal.ca.

Université de Montréal, Faculty of Veterinary Medicine, Program in Virology and Immunology, Montréal, QC H3C 3J7, Canada. Offers PhD. *Students:* 8 full-time (5 women). *Degree requirements:* For doctorate, thesis/dissertation, general exam. *Entrance requirements:* For doctorate, proficiency in French, knowledge of English. *Application deadline:* For fall admission, 2/1 priority date for domestic students; for winter admission, 11/1 priority date for domestic students; for spring admission, 2/1 priority date for domestic students. Application fee: $100. Electronic applications accepted. *Unit head:* Dr. George Szatmari, Chairperson, 514-343-5767, Fax: 514-343-5701, E-mail: george.szatmari@umontreal.ca. *Application contact:* Lamercie Youance, Information Contact, 514-343-6111 Ext. 3129, Fax: 514-343-5701, E-mail: lamercie.youance@umontreal.ca.

Université de Sherbrooke, Faculty of Medicine and Health Sciences, Graduate Programs in Medicine, Program in Immunology, Sherbrooke, QC J1H 5N4, Canada. Offers M Sc, PhD. Electronic applications accepted. *Faculty research:* Cytokine receptor signal transduction, lipid mediators and inflammation, TGFbeta convertases.

Université du Québec, Institut National de la Recherche Scientifique, Graduate Programs, Research Center—INRS—Institut Armand-Frappier—Human Health, Québec, QC G1K 9A9, Canada. Offers applied microbiology (M Sc); biology (PhD); experimental health sciences (M Sc); virology and immunology (M Sc, PhD). Programs given in French. Part-time programs available. *Faculty:* 37. *Students:* 157 full-time (97 women), 4 part-time (all women), 41 international. Average age 30. In 2009, 14 master's, 5 doctorates awarded. *Median time to degree:* Of those who began their doctoral program in fall 2001, 67% received their degree in 8 years or less. *Degree requirements:* For doctorate, thesis/dissertation. *Entrance requirements:* For master's and doctorate, appropriate bachelor's degree, proficiency in French. *Application deadline:* For fall admission, 3/30 for domestic and international students; for winter admission, 11/1 for domestic and international students. Application fee: $30 Canadian dollars. *Financial support:* Fellowships, research assistantships, teaching assistantships available. *Faculty research:* Immunity, infection and cancer; toxicology and environmental biotechnology; molecular pharmacochemistry. *Unit head:* Alain Fournier, Director, 450-687-5010, Fax: 450-686-5501, E-mail: alain.fournier@iaf.inrs.ca. *Application contact:* Yvonne Boisvert, Registrar, 418-654-3861, Fax: 418-654-3858, E-mail: registrariat@adm.inrs.ca.

Université Laval, Faculty of Medicine, Graduate Programs in Medicine, Programs in Microbiology-Immunology, Québec, QC G1K 7P4, Canada. Offers M Sc, PhD. Terminal master's awarded for partial completion of doctoral program. *Degree requirements:* For master's, thesis; for doctorate, comprehensive exam, thesis/dissertation. *Entrance requirements:* For master's and doctorate, knowledge of French, comprehension of written English. Electronic applications accepted.

University at Albany, State University of New York, School of Public Health, Department of Biomedical Sciences, Program in Immunobiology and Immunochemistry, Albany, NY 12222-0001. Offers MS, PhD. *Degree requirements:* For master's, thesis; for doctorate, thesis/dissertation. *Entrance requirements:* For master's and doctorate, GRE General Test, GRE Subject Test.

University at Buffalo, the State University of New York, Graduate School, Graduate Programs in Cancer Research and Biomedical Sciences at Roswell Park Cancer Institute, Department of Immunology at Roswell Park Cancer Institute, Buffalo, NY 14260. Offers cancer immunology (PhD). *Faculty:* 20 full-time (7 women). *Students:* 20 full-time (12 women), 7 part-time (1 woman); includes 1 minority (Asian American or Pacific Islander), 13 international. Average age 27. 32 applicants, 25% accepted, 5 enrolled. In 2009, 5 doctorates awarded. *Degree requirements:* For doctorate, comprehensive exam, thesis/dissertation. *Entrance requirements:* For doctorate, GRE. Additional exam requirements/recommendations for international students: Required—TOEFL (minimum score 600 paper-based; 250 computer-based; 100 iBT) or IELTS. *Application deadline:* For fall admission, 2/1 priority date for domestic students, 2/1 for international students. Applications are processed on a rolling basis. Application fee: $50. Electronic applications accepted. *Financial support:* In 2009–10, 10 students received support, including 4 fellowships with full tuition reimbursements available (averaging $24,000 per year), 6 research assistantships with full tuition reimbursements available (averaging $24,000 per year); Federal Work-Study also available. Financial award application deadline: 2/1; financial award applicants required to submit FAFSA. *Faculty research:* Immunochemistry, immunobiology, molecular immunology, hybridoma studies, recombinant DNA studies. Total annual research expenditures: $4 million. *Unit head:* Dr. Kelvin Lee, Chair, 716-845-4106, E-mail: kelvin.lee@roswellpark.org. *Application contact:* Craig R. Johnson, Director of Admissions, 716-845-2339, Fax: 716-845-8178, E-mail: craig.johnson@roswellpark.org.

University at Buffalo, the State University of New York, Graduate School, School of Medicine and Biomedical Sciences, Graduate Programs in Medicine and Biomedical Sciences, Department of Microbiology and Immunology, Buffalo, NY 14260. Offers MA, PhD. *Faculty:* 16 full-time (4 women), 2 part-time/adjunct (0 women). *Students:* 24 full-time (12 women); includes 2 minority (1 Asian American or Pacific Islander, 1 Hispanic American), 6 international. Average age 28. 10 applicants, 10% accepted. In 2009, 2 master's, 8 doctorates awarded. *Degree requirements:* For master's, comprehensive exam; for doctorate, thesis/dissertation, departmental qualifying exam. *Entrance requirements:* For master's and doctorate, GRE General Test, 3 letters of recommendation. Additional exam requirements/recommendations for international students: Required—TOEFL (minimum score 100 iBT). *Application deadline:* For fall admission, 2/1 priority date for domestic and international students. Applications are processed on a rolling basis. Application fee: $50. Electronic applications accepted. *Financial support:* In 2009–10, 9 fellowships with tuition reimbursements (averaging $24,000 per year), 18 research assistantships with tuition reimbursements (averaging $21,000 per year), 2 teaching assistantships with tuition reimbursements (averaging $21,000 per year) were awarded; Federal Work-Study, institutionally sponsored loans, traineeships, health care benefits, and unspecified assistantships also available. Financial award application deadline: 2/1; financial award applicants required to submit FAFSA. *Faculty research:* Bacteriology, immunology, parasitology, virology, microbial pathogenesis. Total annual research expenditures: $7.9 million. *Unit head:* Dr. John Hay, Interim Chairman, 716-829-2312, Fax: 716-829-2376. *Application contact:* Dr. Anthony Campagnari, Director of Graduate Studies, 716-829-2176, Fax: 716-829-2158.

University of Alberta, Faculty of Medicine and Dentistry and Faculty of Graduate Studies and Research, Graduate Programs in Medicine, Department of Medical Microbiology and Immunology, Edmonton, AB T6G 2E1, Canada. Offers M Sc, PhD. *Faculty:* 16 full-time (5 women), 4 part-time/adjunct (1 woman). *Students:* 40 full-time (23 women); includes 7 minority (1 African American, 5 Asian Americans or Pacific Islanders, 1 Hispanic American), 1 international. Average age 25. 39 applicants, 33% accepted, 9 enrolled. In 2009, 1 master's, 3 doctorates awarded. Terminal master's awarded for partial completion of doctoral program. *Degree requirements:* For master's, thesis; for doctorate, thesis/dissertation. *Entrance requirements:* For master's and doctorate, minimum GPA of 3.3. Additional exam requirements/recommendations for international students: Required—TOEFL (minimum score 600 paper-based; 232 computer-based; 96 iBT). *Application deadline:* For fall admission, 7/1 for domestic students, 2/28 priority date for international students. Tuition and fee charges are reported in Canadian dollars. *Expenses:* Tuition, area resident: Full-time $4626 Canadian dollars; part-time $99.72 Canadian dollars per unit. International tuition: $8216 Canadian dollars full-time. Required fees: $3590 Canadian dollars; $99.72 Canadian dollars per unit. $215 Canadian dollars per term. *Financial support:* In 2009–10, 39 students received support, including 11 fellowships with full tuition reimbursements available (averaging $20,000 per year), 25 research assistantships with full tuition reimbursements available (averaging $17,000 per year), 3 teaching assistantships with full tuition reimbursements available (averaging $17,000 per year); scholarships/grants, traineeships, and unspecified assistantships also available. Financial award application deadline: 1/1. *Faculty research:* Cellular and reproductive immunology, microbial pathogenesis, mechanisms of antibiotic resistance, molecular biology of mammalian viruses, antiviral chemotherapy. Total annual research expenditures: $4.9 million. *Unit head:* Dr. David H. Evans, Chair, 780-492-2308, Fax: 780-492-7521. *Application contact:* Dr. Larry Guilbert, Graduate Director, 780-492-4910, Fax: 780-492-9828, E-mail: larry.guilbert@ualberta.ca.

The University of Arizona, College of Medicine, Graduate Programs in Medicine, Department of Immunobiology, Tucson, AZ 85721. Offers MS, PhD. *Degree requirements:* For master's, thesis; for doctorate, thesis/dissertation. *Entrance requirements:* For master's and doctorate, GRE General Test, minimum GPA of 3.0. *Expenses:* Tuition, state resident: full-time $9028. Tuition, nonresident: full-time $24,890. *Faculty research:* Environmental and pathogenic microbiology, molecular biology.

University of Arkansas for Medical Sciences, Graduate School, Graduate Programs in Biomedical Sciences, Department of Microbiology and Immunology, Little Rock, AR 72205-7199. Offers MS, PhD, MD/PhD. *Faculty:* 19 full-time (4 women), 6 part-time/adjunct (3 women). *Students:* 14 full-time, 2 part-time. In 2009, 3 doctorates awarded. *Degree requirements:* For master's, thesis; for doctorate, thesis/dissertation. *Entrance requirements:* For master's and doctorate, GRE General Test. Additional exam requirements/recommendations for international students: Required—TOEFL. *Application deadline:* For fall admission, 2/15 for domestic and international students. Application fee: $0. *Financial support:* Research assistantships available. Support available to part-time students. *Faculty research:* Tumor immunology and immunotherapy, microbial pathogenesis and genetics, allergy, immune response in infectious diseases. *Unit head:* Dr. Richard Morrison, Chairman, 501-686-8599, E-mail: rpmorrison@uams.edu. *Application contact:* Dr. Marie Chow, Professor, 501-686-5155, E-mail: chowmarie@uams.edu.

The University of British Columbia, Faculty of Science, Department of Microbiology and Immunology, Vancouver, BC V6T 1Z1, Canada. Offers M Sc, PhD. *Degree requirements:* For master's, thesis; for doctorate, comprehensive exam, thesis/dissertation. *Entrance requirements:* For master's and doctorate, GRE General Test. Additional exam requirements/recommendations for international students: Required—TOEFL (minimum score 590 paper-based; 243 computer-based). Electronic applications accepted. *Faculty research:* Bacterial genetics, metabolism, pathogenic bacteriology, virology.

University of Calgary, Faculty of Medicine and Faculty of Graduate Studies, Department of Medical Science, Calgary, AB T2N 1N4, Canada. Offers cancer biology (M Sc, PhD); immunology (M Sc, PhD); joint injury and arthritis research (M Sc, PhD); medical education (M Sc, PhD); medical science (M Sc, PhD); mountain medicine and high altitude physiology (M Sc). *Degree requirements:* For master's, thesis; for doctorate, thesis/dissertation, candidacy exam. *Entrance requirements:* For master's, minimum undergraduate GPA of 3.2; for doctorate, minimum graduate GPA of 3.2. Additional exam requirements/recommendations for international students: Required—TOEFL (minimum score 600 paper-based; 250 computer-based). Electronic applications accepted. *Faculty research:* Cancer biology, immunology, joint injury and arthritis, medical education, population genomics.

University of California, Berkeley, Graduate Division, School of Public Health, Group in Infectious Diseases and Immunity, Berkeley, CA 94720-1500. Offers PhD. *Students:* 14 full-time (8 women). Average age 29. 54 applicants, 2 enrolled. In 2009, 3 doctorates awarded. *Entrance requirements:* For doctorate, GRE General Test, minimum GPA of 3.0, 3 letters of recommendation. *Application deadline:* For fall admission, 12/1 for domestic students. Applications are processed on a rolling basis. Application fee: $70 ($90 for international students). *Financial support:* Fellowships, research assistantships, teaching assistantships, unspecified assistantships available. *Unit head:* Prof. Lee Riley, Head, 510-642-9189, E-mail: idadmin@berkeley.edu. *Application contact:* Teresa Liu, Student Affairs Specialist, 510-642-9189, E-mail: idadmin@berkeley.edu.

University of California, Davis, Graduate Studies, Graduate Group in Immunology, Davis, CA 95616. Offers MS, PhD. Terminal master's awarded for partial completion of doctoral program. *Degree requirements:* For master's, comprehensive exam (for some programs), thesis (for some programs); for doctorate, thesis/dissertation. *Entrance requirements:* For master's and doctorate, GRE General Test. Additional exam requirements/recommendations for international students: Required—TOEFL (minimum score 550 paper-based; 213 computer-based). Electronic applications accepted. *Faculty research:* Immune regulation in autoimmunity, immunopathology, immunotoxicology, tumor immunology, avian immunology.

University of California, Los Angeles, David Geffen School of Medicine and Graduate Division, Graduate Programs in Medicine, Department of Microbiology, Immunology and Molecular Genetics, Los Angeles, CA 90095. Offers MS, PhD. *Degree requirements:* For doctorate, thesis/dissertation, oral and written qualifying exams. *Entrance requirements:* For doctorate, GRE General Test, GRE Subject Test. Additional exam requirements/recommendations for international students: Required—TOEFL.

University of California, Los Angeles, Graduate Division, College of Letters and Science and David Geffen School of Medicine, UCLA ACCESS to Programs in the Molecular, Cellular and Integrative Life Sciences, Los Angeles, CA 90095. Offers biochemistry and molecular biology (PhD); biological chemistry (PhD); cellular and molecular pathology (PhD); human genetics (PhD); microbiology, immunology, and molecular genetics (PhD); molecular biology (PhD); molecular toxicology (PhD); molecular, cellular and integrative physiology (PhD); neurobiology (PhD); oral biology (PhD); physiology (PhD). ACCESS is an umbrella program for first-year coursework in 12 PhD programs. *Students:* 39 full-time (25 women); includes 14 minority (1 African American, 1 American Indian/Alaska Native, 8 Asian Americans or Pacific Islanders, 4 Hispanic Americans), 10 international. Average age 25. 437 applicants, 22% accepted, 30 enrolled. *Degree requirements:* For doctorate, thesis/dissertation, oral and written qualifying exams. *Entrance requirements:* For doctorate, GRE General Test, minimum undergraduate GPA of 3.0. Additional exam requirements/recommendations for international students: Required—TOEFL. *Application deadline:* For fall admission, 12/15 for domestic and international students. Application fee: $70 ($90 for international students). Electronic applications accepted. *Financial support:* In 2009–10, 56 fellowships with full and partial tuition reimbursements, 16 research assistantships with full and partial tuition reimbursements were awarded; teaching assistantships with full and partial tuition reimbursements, Federal Work-Study, institutionally sponsored loans, scholarships/grants, health care benefits, tuition waivers (full and partial), and unspecified assistantships also available. Financial award application deadline: 3/1; financial award applicants required to submit FAFSA. *Faculty research:* Molecular, cellular, and developmental biology; immunology; microbiology; integrative biology. *Unit head:* Dr. Greg I. Payne, Chair, 310-206-3121. *Application contact:* Coordinator, 310-206-3121, Fax: 310-206-5280, E-mail: uclaaccess@mednet.ucla.edu.

See Close-Up on page 239.

University of California, San Diego, Office of Graduate Studies, Division of Biological Sciences, Program in Immunology, Virology, and Cancer Biology, La Jolla, CA 92093. Offers PhD. Offered in association with the Salk Institute. *Degree requirements:* For doctorate, thesis/dissertation, qualifying exam. Electronic applications accepted.

University of California, San Francisco, Graduate Division, Department of Microbiology and Immunology, San Francisco, CA 94143. Offers PhD. *Degree requirements:* For doctorate, thesis/dissertation. *Entrance requirements:* For doctorate, GRE General Test.

University of Chicago, Division of the Biological Sciences, Biomedical Sciences Cluster: Cancer Biology, Immunology, Molecular Metabolism and Nutrition, Pathology, and Microbiology, Committee on Immunology, Chicago, IL 60637-1513. Offers PhD. *Faculty:* 37 full-time (11 women). *Students:* 27 full-time (12 women); includes 7 minority (6 Asian Americans or Pacific Islanders, 1 Hispanic American). Average age 28. 51 applicants, 25% accepted, 8 enrolled. In 2009, 8 doctorates awarded. *Degree requirements:* For doctorate, thesis/dissertation, ethics class, 2 teaching assistantships. *Entrance requirements:* For doctorate, GRE General Test. Additional exam requirements/recommendations for international students: Required—TOEFL (minimum score 600 paper-based; 250 computer-based; 104 iBT), IELTS (minimum score 7). *Application deadline:* For fall admission, 12/1 priority date for domestic and international students. Application fee: $55. Electronic applications accepted. *Financial support:* In 2009–10, 27 students received support, including 10 fellowships with full tuition reimbursements available (averaging $29,781 per year), 16 research assistantships with full tuition reimbursements available (averaging $29,781 per year); institutionally sponsored loans and traineeships also available. Financial award applicants required to submit FAFSA. *Faculty research:* Molecular immunology, transplantation, autoimmunology, neuroimmunology, tumor immunology. Total annual research expenditures: $15 million. *Unit head:* Dr. Alexander Chervonsky, Interim Chairman, 773-702-1371, Fax: 773-834-5251. *Application contact:* Kristin Reepmeyer, Administrative Assistant, 773-702-3940, Fax: 773-702-4634, E-mail: reepmeyer@bsd.uchicago.edu.

University of Cincinnati, Graduate School, College of Medicine, Graduate Programs in Biomedical Sciences, Department of Pediatrics, Cincinnati, OH 45221. Offers immunobiology (PhD); molecular and developmental biology (PhD). *Degree requirements:* For doctorate, thesis/dissertation, qualifying exam. *Entrance requirements:* For doctorate, GRE General Test,

Immunology

University of Cincinnati *(continued)*

minimum GPA of 3.0. Additional exam requirements/recommendations for international students: Required—TOEFL (minimum score 600 paper-based; 250 computer-based; 100 iBT). Electronic applications accepted. *Faculty research:* Pulmonary biology, molecular cardiovascular, developmental biology, cancer biology, genetics.

University of Cincinnati, Graduate School, College of Medicine, Graduate Programs in Biomedical Sciences, Immunobiology Training Program, Cincinnati, OH 45221. Offers MS, PhD. *Degree requirements:* For master's, seminar, thesis with oral defense; for doctorate, seminar, dissertation with oral defense, written and oral candidacy exams.

University of Colorado Denver, School of Medicine, Program in Immunology, Denver, CO 80217-3364. Offers PhD. *Students:* 46 full-time (31 women); includes 7 minority (3 Asian Americans or Pacific Islanders, 4 Hispanic Americans), 3 international. In 2009, 4 doctorates awarded. *Degree requirements:* For doctorate, comprehensive exam, thesis/dissertation, 4 laboratory rotations. *Entrance requirements:* For doctorate, 4 letters of recommendation. Additional exam requirements/recommendations for international students: Required—TOEFL (minimum score 550 paper-based; 213 computer-based). *Application deadline:* For fall admission, 1/15 for domestic students. Application fee: $50. *Financial support:* Applicants required to submit FAFSA. *Unit head:* Dr. John C. Cambier, Chair, 303-398-1325, E-mail: cambierj@njc.org. *Application contact:* Jane Lanners, Administrative Assistant, 303-398-1305, E-mail: lannersj@njc.org.

University of Connecticut Health Center, Graduate School, Programs in Biomedical Sciences, Program in Immunology, Farmington, CT 06030. Offers PhD, DMD/PhD, MD/PhD. *Faculty:* 21. *Students:* 23 full-time (10 women); includes 3 minority (2 Asian Americans or Pacific Islanders, 1 Hispanic American), 10 international. Average age 29. 165 applicants, 35% accepted. In 2009, 4 doctorates awarded. *Degree requirements:* For doctorate, comprehensive exam, thesis/dissertation. *Entrance requirements:* For doctorate, GRE General Test. Additional exam requirements/recommendations for international students: Required—TOEFL (minimum score 600 paper-based; 250 computer-based). *Application deadline:* For fall admission, 12/15 for domestic students. Application fee: $55. Electronic applications accepted. *Financial support:* In 2009–10, 23 students received support, including 23 research assistantships with tuition reimbursements available (averaging $27,000 per year); fellowships also available. *Faculty research:* Developmental immunology, T-cell immunity, lymphoid cell development, tolerance and tumor immunity, leukocyte chemotaxis. *Unit head:* Dr. Anthony Vella, Co-Director, 860-679-4364, Fax: 860-679-1868, E-mail: vella@uchc.edu. *Application contact:* Tricia Avolt, Graduate Admissions Coordinator, 860-679-2175, Fax: 860-679-1899, E-mail: robertson@nso2.uchc.edu.

See Close-Up on page 363.

University of Florida, College of Medicine, Department of Pathology, Immunology and Laboratory Medicine, Gainesville, FL 32611. Offers immunology and molecular pathology (PhD). *Degree requirements:* For doctorate, thesis/dissertation. *Entrance requirements:* For doctorate, GRE General Test, minimum GPA of 3.0. Additional exam requirements/recommendations for international students: Required—TOEFL. Electronic applications accepted. *Faculty research:* Molecular immunology, autoimmunity and transplantation, tumor biology, oncogenic viruses, human immunodeficiency viruses.

University of Florida, College of Medicine and Graduate School, Interdisciplinary Program in Biomedical Sciences, Concentration in Immunology and Microbiology, Gainesville, FL 32611. Offers PhD. *Degree requirements:* For doctorate, thesis/dissertation. *Entrance requirements:* For doctorate, GRE General Test, minimum GPA of 3.0. Additional exam requirements/recommendations for international students: Required—TOEFL. Electronic applications accepted.

See Close-Up on page 365.

University of Guelph, Ontario Veterinary College and Graduate Program Services, Graduate Programs in Veterinary Sciences, Department of Pathobiology, Guelph, ON N1G 2W1, Canada. Offers anatomic pathology (DV Sc, Diploma); clinical pathology (Diploma); comparative pathology (M Sc, PhD); immunology (M Sc, PhD); laboratory animal science (DV Sc); pathology (M Sc, PhD, Diploma); veterinary infectious diseases (M Sc, PhD); zoo animal/wildlife medicine (DV Sc). *Degree requirements:* For master's, thesis; for doctorate, thesis/dissertation. *Entrance requirements:* For master's, DVM with B average or an honours degree in biological sciences; for doctorate, DVM or MSC degree, minimum B+ average. Additional exam requirements/recommendations for international students: Required—TOEFL (minimum score 550 paper-based; 213 computer-based). *Faculty research:* Pathogenesis; diseases of animals, wildlife, fish, and laboratory animals; parasitology; immunology; veterinary infectious diseases; laboratory animal science.

University of Illinois at Chicago, College of Medicine and Graduate College, Graduate Programs in Medicine, Department of Microbiology and Immunology, Chicago, IL 60607-7128. Offers PhD, MD/PhD. *Degree requirements:* For doctorate, thesis/dissertation. *Entrance requirements:* For doctorate, GRE General Test, minimum GPA of 2.75. Additional exam requirements/recommendations for international students: Required—TOEFL.

The University of Iowa, Graduate College, Program in Immunology, Iowa City, IA 52242-1316. Offers PhD, MD/PhD. *Degree requirements:* For doctorate, comprehensive exam, thesis/dissertation. *Entrance requirements:* For doctorate, GRE General Test, minimum GPA of 3.0. Additional exam requirements/recommendations for international students: Required—TOEFL (minimum score 600 paper-based; 250 computer-based; 100 iBT). Electronic applications accepted.

The University of Iowa, Roy J. and Lucille A. Carver College of Medicine and Graduate College, Graduate Programs in Medicine, Department of Microbiology, Iowa City, IA 52242-1316. Offers general microbiology and microbial physiology (MS, PhD); immunology (MS, PhD); microbial genetics (MS, PhD); pathogenic bacteriology (MS, PhD); virology (MS, PhD). *Faculty:* 24 full-time (3 women), 8 part-time/adjunct (2 women). *Students:* 36 full-time (20 women); includes 3 minority (2 American Indian/Alaska Native, 1 Hispanic American), 5 international. Average age 25. 87 applicants, 14% accepted, 5 enrolled. In 2009, 3 master's, 7 doctorates awarded. *Degree requirements:* For master's, thesis; for doctorate, comprehensive exam, thesis/dissertation. *Entrance requirements:* For master's and doctorate, GRE General Test. Additional exam requirements/recommendations for international students: Required—TOEFL (minimum score 600 paper-based; 250 computer-based). *Application deadline:* For fall admission, 2/1 for domestic and international students. Application fee: $60 ($85 for international students). Electronic applications accepted. *Financial support:* In 2009–10, 4 fellowships with full tuition reimbursements (averaging $24,250 per year), 32 research assistantships with full tuition reimbursements (averaging $24,250 per year) were awarded; institutionally sponsored loans, scholarships/grants, traineeships and health care benefits also available. *Faculty research:* Gene regulation, processing and transport of HIV, retroviral pathogenesis, biodegradation, biofilm. Total annual research expenditures: $11.7 million. *Unit head:* Dr. Michael A. Apicella, Head, 319-335-7810, E-mail: grad-micro-info@uiowa.edu. *Application contact:* Dr. Michael A. Apicella, Head, 319-335-7810, E-mail: grad-micro-info@uiowa.edu.

The University of Kansas, University of Kansas Medical Center, School of Medicine, Department of Microbiology, Molecular Genetics and Immunology, Kansas City, KS 66160. Offers microbiology (PhD); MD/PhD. *Faculty:* 12 full-time, 1 part-time/adjunct. *Students:* 1 (woman) full-time, 13 part-time (5 women), 9 international. Average age 29. In 2009, 2 degrees awarded. *Median time to degree:* Of those who began their doctoral program in fall 2001, 100% received their degree in 8 years or less. *Degree requirements:* For doctorate, comprehensive exam, thesis/dissertation, research skills. *Entrance requirements:* For doctorate, GRE General Test, B Sc. Additional exam requirements/recommendations for international students: Required—TOEFL. *Application deadline:* For fall admission, 1/15 priority date for international students. *Expenses:* Tuition, state resident: full-time $6492; part-time $270.50 per

credit hour. Tuition, nonresident: full-time $15,510; part-time $646.25 per credit hour. Required fees: $847; $70.56 per credit hour. Tuition and fees vary according to course load and program. *Financial support:* In 2009–10, 1 fellowship with tuition reimbursement (averaging $24,000 per year), 9 research assistantships with partial tuition reimbursements (averaging $24,000 per year), 3 teaching assistantships with full and partial tuition reimbursements (averaging $24,000 per year) were awarded; scholarships/grants and unspecified assistantships also available. *Faculty research:* Immunology, infectious disease, virology, molecular genetics, bacteriology. Total annual research expenditures: $4 million. *Unit head:* Dr. Michael Parmely, Interim Chair, 913-588-7010, Fax: 913-588-7295, E-mail: mparmely@kumc.edu. *Application contact:* Dr. Joe Lutkenhaus, Microbiology Graduate Studies Director, 913-588-7054, Fax: 913-588-7295, E-mail: jlutkenh@kumc.edu.

University of Louisville, School of Medicine, Department of Microbiology and Immunology, Louisville, KY 40292-0001. Offers MS, PhD, MD/PhD. *Faculty:* 22 full-time (6 women). *Students:* 34 full-time (22 women); includes 6 minority (4 African Americans, 2 Asian Americans or Pacific Islanders), 13 international. Average age 30. 51 applicants, 31% accepted, 10 enrolled. In 2009, 2 master's, 8 doctorates awarded. Terminal master's awarded for partial completion of doctoral program. *Degree requirements:* For master's, thesis; for doctorate, comprehensive exam, thesis/dissertation. *Entrance requirements:* For master's, GRE General Test (minimum score 1000 verbal and quantitative), minimum GPA of 3.0; 1 year of course work in biology, organic chemistry, physics; 1 semester of course work in calculus and quantitative analysis, biochemistry, or molecular biology; for doctorate, GRE General Test (Verbal and Quantitative minimum score of 1000), minimum GPA of 3.0; 1 year of course work in biology, organic chemistry, physics; 1 semester of course work in calculus and quantitative analysis, biochemistry, or molecular biology. Additional exam requirements/recommendations for international students: Required—TOEFL. *Application deadline:* For fall admission, 2/1 priority date for domestic and international students. Applications are processed on a rolling basis. Application fee: $50. Electronic applications accepted. *Financial support:* In 2009–10, 17 fellowships with full tuition reimbursements (averaging $22,000 per year), 18 research assistantships with full tuition reimbursements (averaging $22,000 per year) were awarded. Financial award application deadline: 4/15. *Faculty research:* Opportunistic and emerging infections; biology and regulation of the immune system; cellular and molecular bases of chronic inflammatory response; role of cytokines and chemokines in cancer, autoimmune and infectious disease; host defense and pathogenesis of viral infections. *Unit head:* Dr. Robert D. Stout, Chair, 502-852-5351, Fax: 502-852-7531, E-mail: bobstout@louisville.edu. *Application contact:* Carolyn M Burton, Academic Coordinator, 502-852-6208, Fax: 502-852-7531, E-mail: cmburt01@gwise.louisville.edu.

University of Manitoba, Faculty of Medicine and Faculty of Graduate Studies, Graduate Programs in Medicine, Department of Immunology, Winnipeg, MB R3T 2N2, Canada. Offers M Sc, PhD. Terminal master's awarded for partial completion of doctoral program. *Degree requirements:* For master's, thesis; for doctorate, one foreign language, thesis/dissertation. *Faculty research:* Immediate hypersensitivity, regulation of the immune response, natural immunity, cytokines, inflammation.

University of Maryland, Baltimore, Graduate School, Graduate Program in Life Sciences, Program in Molecular Microbiology and Immunology, Baltimore, MD 21201. Offers PhD, MD/PhD. *Students:* 61 full-time (37 women), 9 part-time (5 women); includes 19 minority (7 African Americans, 9 Asian Americans or Pacific Islanders, 3 Hispanic Americans), 8 international. Average age 27. 167 applicants, 11% accepted, 10 enrolled. In 2009, 5 doctorates awarded. *Entrance requirements:* For doctorate, GRE. Additional exam requirements/recommendations for international students: Required—TOEFL (minimum score 550 paper-based; 80 iBT); Recommended—IELTS (minimum score 7). *Application deadline:* For fall admission, 1/15 for domestic and international students. Application fee: $50. Electronic applications accepted. *Expenses:* Tuition, state resident: full-time $7290; part-time $405 per credit hour. Tuition, nonresident: full-time $12,780; part-time $710 per credit hour. Required fees: $774; $10 per credit hour. $297 per semester. Tuition and fees vary according to course load, degree level and program. *Financial support:* In 2009–10, research assistantships with partial tuition reimbursements (averaging $25,000 per year); fellowships also available. Financial award application deadline: 3/1. *Unit head:* Dr. Nicholas Carbonetti, Director, 410-706-7677, E-mail: ncarbone@umaryland.edu. *Application contact:* June Green, Program Coordinator, 410-706-7126, Fax: 410-706-2129, E-mail: jgreen@umaryland.edu.

University of Massachusetts Worcester, Graduate School of Biomedical Sciences, Program in Immunology and Virology, Worcester, MA 01655-0115. Offers medical sciences (PhD). *Degree requirements:* For doctorate, comprehensive exam, thesis/dissertation. *Entrance requirements:* For doctorate, GRE General Test. Additional exam requirements/recommendations for international students: Required—TOEFL (minimum score 600 paper-based; 250 computer-based). Electronic applications accepted. *Faculty research:* Molecular and immunological studies on viral pathogenesis and oncology, AIDS viruses and other retroviruses, herpes viruses, influenza, Dengue and Newcastle disease viruses.

University of Medicine and Dentistry of New Jersey, Graduate School of Biomedical Sciences, Graduate Programs in Biomedical Sciences–Newark, Program in Molecular Pathology and Immunology, Newark, NJ 07107. Offers PhD. *Students:* 16 full-time (10 women), 3 part-time (1 woman); includes 2 African Americans, 1 Asian American or Pacific Islander, 1 Hispanic American, 10 international. *Entrance requirements:* Additional exam requirements/recommendations for international students: Required—TOEFL. *Application deadline:* For fall admission, 2/1 for domestic students. Applications are processed on a rolling basis. Electronic applications accepted. *Financial support:* Fellowships, research assistantships, Federal Work-Study, institutionally sponsored loans, and tuition waivers (full and partial) available. *Unit head:* Dr. Muriel Lambert, Program Director, 973-972-4405, Fax: 973-972-7293, E-mail: mlambert@umdnj.edu. *Application contact:* Dr. Muriel Lambert, Program Director, 973-972-4405, Fax: 973-972-7293, E-mail: mlambert@umdnj.edu.

University of Medicine and Dentistry of New Jersey, Graduate School of Biomedical Sciences, Graduate Programs in Biomedical Sciences–Piscataway, Program in Molecular Genetics, Microbiology and Immunology, Piscataway, NJ 08854-5635. Offers MS, PhD, MD/PhD. Terminal master's awarded for partial completion of doctoral program. *Degree requirements:* For master's, thesis, qualifying exam; for doctorate, thesis/dissertation, qualifying exam. *Entrance requirements:* For master's and doctorate, GRE General Test. Additional exam requirements/recommendations for international students: Required—TOEFL. Electronic applications accepted. *Faculty research:* Interferon, receptors, retrovirus evolution, Arbo virus/host cell interactions.

University of Medicine and Dentistry of New Jersey, Graduate School of Biomedical Sciences, Graduate Programs in Biomedical Sciences–Stratford, Stratford, NJ 08084-5634. Offers biomedical sciences (MBS, MS); cell and molecular biology (MS, PhD); molecular pathology and immunology (MS); DO/MS; DO/PhD; MS/MPH. *Students:* 79 full-time (43 women), 19 part-time (14 women); includes 44 minority (21 African Americans, 16 Asian Americans or Pacific Islanders, 7 Hispanic Americans), 11 international. Average age 25. 128 applicants, 74% accepted, 64 enrolled. In 2009, 36 master's, 1 doctorate awarded. Terminal master's awarded for partial completion of doctoral program. *Degree requirements:* For master's, thesis (for some programs); for doctorate, thesis/dissertation, qualifying exam. *Entrance requirements:* For master's, GRE General Test, MCAT or DAT; for doctorate, GRE General Test. Additional exam requirements/recommendations for international students: Required—TOEFL. *Application deadline:* For fall admission, 2/1 for domestic students; for spring admission, 11/1 for domestic students. Applications are processed on a rolling basis. Application fee: $40. Electronic applications accepted. *Financial support:* Fellowships, Federal Work-Study available. Financial award application deadline: 5/1. *Unit head:* Dr. Carl E. Hock, Senior Associate Dean, Graduate School, 856-566-6282, Fax: 856-566-6232, E-mail: hock@umdnj.edu. *Application contact:* University Registrar, 973-972-5338.

University of Miami, Graduate School, Miller School of Medicine, Graduate Programs in Medicine, Department of Microbiology and Immunology, Coral Gables, FL 33124. Offers PhD, MD/PhD. *Degree requirements:* For doctorate, thesis/dissertation, oral and written qualifying exams. *Entrance requirements:* For doctorate, GRE General Test. Additional exam requirements/recommendations for international students: Required—TOEFL. Electronic applications accepted. *Faculty research:* Cellular and molecular immunology, molecular and pathogenic virology, pathogenic bacteriology and gene therapy of cancer.

University of Michigan, Horace H. Rackham School of Graduate Studies, Program in Biomedical Sciences (PIBS), Department of Microbiology and Immunology, Ann Arbor, MI 48109. Offers PhD. *Degree requirements:* For doctorate, thesis/dissertation, oral defense of dissertation, preliminary exam. *Entrance requirements:* For doctorate, GRE General Test. Additional exam requirements/recommendations for international students: Required—TOEFL (minimum score 600 paper-based; 220 computer-based; 84 iBT), TWE. Electronic applications accepted. *Expenses:* Tuition, state resident: full-time $17,286; part-time $1099 per credit hour. Tuition, nonresident: full-time $34,944; part-time $2080 per credit hour. Required fees: $95 per semester. Tuition and fees vary according to course load, degree level and program. *Faculty research:* Gene regulation, molecular biology of animal and bacterial viruses, molecular and cellular networks, pathogenesis and microbial genetics.

University of Michigan, Horace H. Rackham School of Graduate Studies, Program in Biomedical Sciences (PIBS), Program in Immunology, Ann Arbor, MI 48109-0619. Offers PhD. *Degree requirements:* For doctorate, thesis/dissertation, oral defense of dissertation, preliminary exam. *Entrance requirements:* For doctorate, GRE General Test, 3 letters of recommendation, research experience. Additional exam requirements/recommendations for international students: Required—TOEFL (minimum score 84 iBT). Electronic applications accepted. *Expenses:* Tuition, state resident: full-time $17,286; part-time $1099 per credit hour. Tuition, nonresident: full-time $34,944; part-time $2080 per credit hour. Required fees: $95 per semester. Tuition and fees vary according to course load, degree level and program. *Faculty research:* Cytokine networks, T and B cell activation, autoimmunity, antigen processing/ presentation, cell signaling.

University of Minnesota, Duluth, Medical School, Microbiology, Immunology and Molecular Pathobiology Section, Duluth, MN 55812-2496. Offers MS, PhD. Terminal master's awarded for partial completion of doctoral program. *Degree requirements:* For master's, thesis, final oral exam; for doctorate, thesis/dissertation, final exam, oral and written preliminary exams. *Entrance requirements:* For master's and doctorate, GRE General Test. Additional exam requirements/recommendations for international students: Required—TOEFL. *Faculty research:* Immunomodulation, molecular diagnosis of rabies, cytokines, cancer immunology, cytomegalovirus infection.

University of Minnesota, Twin Cities Campus, Graduate School, PhD Program in Microbiology, Immunology and Cancer Biology, Minneapolis, MN 55455-0213. Offers PhD. *Degree requirements:* For doctorate, thesis/dissertation. *Entrance requirements:* For doctorate, GRE General Test. Additional exam requirements/recommendations for international students: Required—TOEFL (minimum score 600 paper-based; 250 computer-based). Electronic applications accepted. *Faculty research:* Virology, microbiology, cancer biology, immunology.

University of Missouri, School of Medicine and Graduate School, Graduate Programs in Medicine, Department of Molecular Microbiology and Immunology, Columbia, MO 65211. Offers MS, PhD. Terminal master's awarded for partial completion of doctoral program. *Degree requirements:* For master's, thesis; for doctorate, thesis/dissertation. *Entrance requirements:* For master's and doctorate, GRE General Test, minimum GPA of 3.0. Additional exam requirements/recommendations for international students: Required—TOEFL (minimum score 580 paper-based; 237 computer-based; 92 iBT). *Faculty research:* Molecular biology, host-parasite interactions.

The University of North Carolina at Chapel Hill, School of Medicine and Graduate School, Graduate Programs in Medicine, Department of Microbiology and Immunology, Chapel Hill, NC 27599-7290. Offers immunology (MS, PhD); microbiology (MS, PhD). *Faculty:* 62 full-time (22 women). *Students:* 73 full-time (51 women); includes 12 minority (3 African Americans, 7 Asian Americans or Pacific Islanders, 2 Hispanic Americans), 6 international. Average age 29. 8 applicants, 88% accepted, 7 enrolled. In 2009, 1 master's, 13 doctorates awarded. Terminal master's awarded for partial completion of doctoral program. *Degree requirements:* For master's, comprehensive exam, thesis; for doctorate, comprehensive exam, thesis/dissertation. *Entrance requirements:* For master's and doctorate, GRE General Test, minimum GPA of 3.0. *Application deadline:* For fall admission, 12/1 priority date for domestic and international students. Applications are processed on a rolling basis. Application fee: $100. Electronic applications accepted. *Financial support:* In 2009–10, 3 students received support, including 2 fellowships with full tuition reimbursements available (averaging $26,000 per year), 71 research assistantships with full tuition reimbursements available (averaging $26,000 per year); scholarships/grants, traineeships, health care benefits, and unspecified assistantships also available. Financial award application deadline: 3/1; financial award applicants required to submit FAFSA. *Faculty research:* HIV pathogenesis, immune response, t-cell mediated autoimmunity, alpha-viruses, bacterial chemotaxis. Total annual research expenditures: $9.4 million. *Unit head:* Dr. William Goldman, Chairman, 919-966-1191, Fax: 919-962-8103, E-mail: goldman@med.unc.edu. *Application contact:* Dixie Flannery, Student Services Specialist, 919-966-9005, Fax: 919-962-8103, E-mail: microimm@med.unc.edu.

University of North Dakota, School of Medicine and Health Sciences and Graduate School, Graduate Programs in Medicine, Department of Microbiology and Immunology, Grand Forks, ND 58202. Offers MS, PhD. *Degree requirements:* For master's, comprehensive exam, thesis or alternative; for doctorate, comprehensive exam, thesis/dissertation, final examination. *Entrance requirements:* For master's and doctorate, GRE General Test, minimum GPA of 3.0. Additional exam requirements/recommendations for international students: Required—TOEFL (minimum score 550 paper-based; 213 computer-based; 79 iBT), IELTS (minimum score 6.5). Electronic applications accepted. *Faculty research:* Genetic and immunological aspects of a murine model of human multiple sclerosis, termination of DNA replication, cell division in bacteria, yersinia pestis.

University of North Texas Health Science Center at Fort Worth, Graduate School of Biomedical Sciences, Fort Worth, TX 76107-2699. Offers anatomy and cell biology (MS, PhD); biochemistry and molecular biology (MS, PhD); biomedical sciences (MS, PhD); biotechnology (MS); forensic genetics (MS); integrative physiology (MS, PhD); medical science (MS); microbiology and immunology (MS, PhD); pharmacology (MS, PhD); science education (MS); DO/MS; DO/PhD. Terminal master's awarded for partial completion of doctoral program. *Degree requirements:* For master's, thesis; for doctorate, thesis/dissertation. *Entrance requirements:* For master's and doctorate, GRE General Test. Additional exam requirements/recommendations for international students: Required—TOEFL. *Expenses:* Contact institution. *Faculty research:* Alzheimer's disease, aging, eye diseases, cancer, cardiovascular disease.

University of Oklahoma Health Sciences Center, College of Medicine and Graduate College, Graduate Programs in Medicine, Department of Microbiology and Immunology, Oklahoma City, OK 73190. Offers immunology (MS, PhD); microbiology (MS, PhD). Part-time programs available. *Faculty:* 13 full-time (5 women). *Students:* 7 full-time (4 women), 25 part-time (14 women); includes 4 minority (1 American Indian/Alaska Native, 3 Asian Americans or Pacific Islanders), 2 international. Average age 27. 20 applicants, 5% accepted, 1 enrolled. In 2009, 1 master's, 5 doctorates awarded. Terminal master's awarded for partial completion of doctoral program. *Degree requirements:* For master's, thesis or alternative; for doctorate, one foreign language, thesis/dissertation. *Entrance requirements:* For doctorate, GRE General Test, 3 letters of recommendation. Additional exam requirements/recommendations for international students: Required—TOEFL. *Application deadline:* For fall admission, 12/15 for domestic students. Application fee: $50. *Expenses:* Tuition, state resident: full-time $3120; part-time $156 per credit hour. Tuition, nonresident: full-time $11,314; part-time $409.70 per credit hour. Required fees: $1471; $51.20 per credit hour. $223.25 per term. *Financial support:* In 2009–10, 20 research assistantships (averaging $17,000 per year) were awarded; fellowships, teaching assistantships also available. Financial award applicants required to submit FAFSA. *Faculty research:* Molecular genetics, pathogenesis, streptococcal infections, gram-positive virulence,

monoclonal antibodies. *Unit head:* Dr. John Iandolo, Chairman, 405-271-2133, E-mail: john-iandolo@ouhsc.edu. *Application contact:* Dr. Rebecca Blackstock, Graduate Liaison, 405-271-2133, E-mail: rebecca-blackstock@ouhsc.edu.

University of Ottawa, Faculty of Graduate and Postdoctoral Studies, Faculty of Medicine, Department of Biochemistry, Microbiology and Immunology, Ottawa, ON K1N 6N5, Canada. Offers biochemistry (M Sc, PhD); microbiology and immunology (M Sc, PhD). *Degree requirements:* For master's, thesis; for doctorate, comprehensive exam, thesis/dissertation, seminar. *Entrance requirements:* For master's, honors degree or equivalent, minimum B average; for doctorate, master's degree, minimum B+ average. Electronic applications accepted. *Faculty research:* General biochemistry, molecular biology, microbiology, host biology, nutrition and metabolism.

University of Pennsylvania, School of Medicine, Biomedical Graduate Studies, Graduate Group in Immunology, Philadelphia, PA 19104. Offers PhD, MD/PhD, VMD/PhD. *Faculty:* 106. *Students:* 75 full-time (46 women); includes 19 minority (2 African Americans, 1 American Indian/Alaska Native, 13 Asian Americans or Pacific Islanders, 3 Hispanic Americans), 3 international. 124 applicants, 19% accepted, 13 enrolled. In 2009, 10 doctorates awarded. *Degree requirements:* For doctorate, thesis/dissertation, 2 preliminary exams. *Entrance requirements:* For doctorate, GRE General Test, undergraduate major in natural or physical science. Additional exam requirements/recommendations for international students: Required—TOEFL. *Application deadline:* For fall admission, 12/8 priority date for domestic students, 12/8 for international students. Applications are processed on a rolling basis. Application fee: $70. Electronic applications accepted. *Expenses:* Tuition: Full-time $25,660; part-time $4758 per course. Required fees: $2152; $270 per course. Tuition and fees vary according to course load, degree level and program. *Financial support:* In 2009–10, 75 students received support; fellowships, research assistantships, scholarships/grants, traineeships, and unspecified assistantships available. *Faculty research:* Immunoglobulin structure and function, cell surface receptors, lymphocyte functional transplantation immunology, cellular immunology, molecular biology of immunoglobulins. *Unit head:* Dr. Steven L. Reiner, Chairman. *Application contact:* Kaitlyn Baraldi, Graduate Coordinator, 215-746-5536, E-mail: kbaraldi@mail.med.upenn.edu.

University of Pittsburgh, School of Medicine, Graduate Programs in Medicine, Program in Immunology, Pittsburgh, PA 15260. Offers MS, PhD. *Faculty:* 57 full-time (17 women). *Students:* 45 full-time (28 women); includes 7 minority (1 African American, 5 Asian Americans or Pacific Islanders, 1 Hispanic American), 15 international. Average age 27. 655 applicants, 10% accepted, 20 enrolled. In 2009, 7 doctorates awarded. *Degree requirements:* For doctorate, comprehensive exam, thesis/dissertation. *Entrance requirements:* For doctorate, GRE General Test, GRE Subject Test, minimum QPA of 3.0. Additional exam requirements/recommendations for international students: Required—TOEFL (minimum score 600 paper-based; 250 computer-based; 100 iBT), IELTS (minimum score 7). *Application deadline:* For fall admission, 12/15 priority date for domestic and international students. Application fee: $40. Electronic applications accepted. *Expenses:* Tuition, state resident: full-time $16,402; part-time $665 per credit. Tuition, nonresident: full-time $28,694; part-time $1175 per credit. Required fees: $690; $175 per term. Tuition and fees vary according to program. *Financial support:* In 2009–10, 45 research assistantships with full tuition reimbursements (averaging $24,650 per year) were awarded; institutionally sponsored loans, scholarships/grants, traineeships, health care benefits, and unspecified assistantships also available. *Faculty research:* Human T-cell biology, opportunistic infections associated with AIDS, autoimmunity, immunoglobin gene expression, tumor immunology. *Unit head:* Dr. Russell D. Salter, Graduate Program Director, 412-648-9471, Fax: 412-624-7736, E-mail: rds@pitt.edu. *Application contact:* Graduate Studies Administrator, 412-648-8957, Fax: 412-648-1007, E-mail: gradstudies@medschool.pitt.edu.

University of Prince Edward Island, Atlantic Veterinary College, Graduate Program in Veterinary Medicine, Charlottetown, PE C1A 4P3, Canada. Offers anatomy (M Sc, PhD); bacteriology (M Sc, PhD); clinical pharmacology (M Sc, PhD); clinical sciences (M Sc, PhD); epidemiology (M Sc, PhD), including reproduction; fish health (M Sc, PhD); food animal nutrition (M Sc, PhD); immunology (M Sc, PhD); microanatomy (M Sc, PhD); parasitology (M Sc, PhD); pathology (M Sc, PhD); pharmacology (M Sc, PhD); physiology (M Sc, PhD); toxicology (M Sc, PhD); veterinary science (M Vet Sc); virology (M Sc, PhD). Part-time programs available. *Degree requirements:* For master's, thesis; for doctorate, thesis/dissertation. *Entrance requirements:* For master's, DVM, B Sc honors degree, or equivalent; for doctorate, M Sc. Additional exam requirements/recommendations for international students: Required—TOEFL (minimum score 550 paper-based; 213 computer-based; 80 iBT). *Expenses:* Contact institution. *Faculty research:* Animal health management, infectious diseases, fin fish and shellfish health, basic biomedical sciences, ecosystem health.

University of Rochester, School of Medicine and Dentistry, Graduate Programs in Medicine and Dentistry, Department of Microbiology and Immunology, Rochester, NY 14627. Offers microbiology (MS, PhD); MBA/MS. *Degree requirements:* For doctorate, thesis/dissertation, qualifying exam. *Entrance requirements:* For master's and doctorate, GRE General Test.

University of Saskatchewan, College of Medicine, Department of Microbiology and Immunology, Saskatoon, SK S7N 5A2, Canada. Offers M Sc, PhD. *Degree requirements:* For master's, thesis; for doctorate, thesis/dissertation. *Entrance requirements:* Additional exam requirements/recommendations for international students: Required—TOEFL. Tuition and fees charges are reported in Canadian dollars. *Expenses:* Tuition, area resident: Full-time $3000 Canadian dollars; part-time $500 Canadian dollars per term. Required fees: $700 Canadian dollars; $100 Canadian dollars per term.

University of South Alabama, College of Medicine and Graduate School, Program in Basic Medical Sciences, Specialization in Microbiology and Immunology, Mobile, AL 36688-0002. Offers PhD. *Degree requirements:* For doctorate, thesis/dissertation. *Entrance requirements:* For doctorate, GRE General Test or MCAT. *Expenses:* Tuition, state resident: part-time $218 per contact hour. Required fees: $1102 per year. *Faculty research:* Mechanisms of tumor immunity, host response to infectious agents, virus replication, immune regulation, mechanisms of resistance to viruses and bacteria.

The University of South Dakota, School of Medicine and Health Sciences and Graduate School, Biomedical Sciences Graduate Program, Molecular Microbiology and Immunology Group, Vermillion, SD 57069-2390. Offers MS, PhD. Terminal master's awarded for partial completion of doctoral program. *Degree requirements:* For master's, thesis; for doctorate, comprehensive exam, thesis/dissertation. *Entrance requirements:* For master's and doctorate, GRE General Test, minimum GPA of 3.0. Additional exam requirements/recommendations for international students: Required—TOEFL (minimum score 550 paper-based; 213 computer-based; 80 iBT), IELTS (minimum score 6). Electronic applications accepted. *Expenses:* Contact institution. *Faculty research:* Structure-function membranes, plasmids, immunology, virology, pathogenesis.

University of Southern California, Keck School of Medicine and Graduate School, Graduate Programs in Medicine, Department of Molecular Microbiology and Immunology, Los Angeles, CA 90089. Offers MS, PhD. Part-time programs available. *Faculty:* 15 full-time (3 women), 1 (woman) part-time/adjunct. *Students:* 20 full-time (10 women); includes 17 minority (15 Asian Americans or Pacific Islanders, 2 Hispanic Americans). Average age 27. 19 applicants, 47% accepted, 6 enrolled. In 2009, 5 master's, 4 doctorates awarded. Terminal master's awarded for partial completion of doctoral program. *Degree requirements:* For master's, comprehensive exam (for some programs), thesis optional; for doctorate, comprehensive exam, thesis/dissertation. *Entrance requirements:* For master's, GRE General Test, minimum GPA of 3.0; for doctorate, GRE General Test, GRE Subject Test, minimum GPA of 3.0. Additional exam requirements/recommendations for international students: Required—TOEFL (minimum score 100 iBT). *Application deadline:* Applications are processed on a rolling basis. Application fee: $85. Electronic applications accepted. *Expenses:* Tuition: Full-time $25,980; part-time $1315 per unit. Required fees: $554. One-time fee: $35 full-time. Full-time tuition and fees vary according to degree level and program. *Financial support:* In 2009–10, 4 students received

Immunology

University of Southern California (continued)
support, including 1 fellowship with full tuition reimbursement available (averaging $27,060 per year), 6 research assistantships with full tuition reimbursements available (averaging $27,060 per year), 1 teaching assistantship with full tuition reimbursement available (averaging $27,060 per year); Federal Work-Study, institutionally sponsored loans, scholarships/grants, health care benefits, and unspecified assistantships also available. Financial award application deadline: 5/5; financial award applicants required to submit FAFSA. *Faculty research:* Animal virology, microbial genetics, molecular and cellular immunology, cellular differentiation control of protein synthesis. *Unit head:* Dr. Jae U. Jung, Professor and Chair, 323-442-1713, Fax: 323-442-1721, E-mail: jaeujung@usc.edu. *Application contact:* Silvina V. Campos, Administrative Assistant II, 323-442-1713, Fax: 323-442-1721, E-mail: scampos@usc.edu.

University of Southern Maine, School of Applied Science, Engineering, and Technology, Program in Applied Medical Sciences, Portland, ME 04104-9300. Offers MS. Part-time programs available. *Degree requirements:* For master's, thesis. *Entrance requirements:* For master's, GRE General Test, minimum GPA of 3.0. Additional exam requirements/recommendations for international students: Required—TOEFL. Electronic applications accepted. *Faculty research:* Flow cytometry, cancer, epidemiology, monoclonal antibodies, DNA diagnostics.

The University of Texas Health Science Center at Houston, Graduate School of Biomedical Sciences, Program in Immunology, Houston, TX 77225-0036. Offers MS, PhD, MD/PhD. Terminal master's awarded for partial completion of doctoral program. *Degree requirements:* For master's, thesis; for doctorate, thesis/dissertation. *Entrance requirements:* For master's and doctorate, GRE General Test. Additional exam requirements/recommendations for international students: Required—TOEFL. Electronic applications accepted. *Faculty research:* Cancer immunology, molecular immunology, immune cell signaling, immune disease, immune system development.

The University of Texas Health Science Center at San Antonio, Graduate School of Biomedical Sciences, Department of Microbiology and Immunology, San Antonio, TX 78229-3900. Offers PhD. *Faculty:* 17 full-time (2 women), 9 part-time/adjunct (2 women). *Students:* 39 full-time (21 women); includes 12 minority (2 African Americans, 10 Hispanic Americans), 12 international. Average age 30. In 2009, 1 doctorate awarded. Terminal master's awarded for partial completion of doctoral program. *Degree requirements:* For doctorate, comprehensive exam, thesis/dissertation. *Entrance requirements:* For doctorate, GRE General Test, minimum GPA of 3.0. Additional exam requirements/recommendations for international students: Required—TOEFL (minimum score 560 paper-based; 220 computer-based; 68 iBT). *Application deadline:* For fall admission, 1/15 priority date for domestic and international students. Applications are processed on a rolling basis. Electronic applications accepted. *Expenses:* Tuition, state resident: full-time $2832; part-time $118 per credit hour. Tuition, nonresident: full-time $10,896; part-time $454 per credit hour. Required fees: $884 per semester. One-time fee: $70. *Financial support:* In 2009–10, 38 teaching assistantships (averaging $26,000 per year) were awarded; fellowships, research assistantships, dental scientist awards also available. Financial award applicants required to submit FAFSA. *Faculty research:* Molecular immunology, mechanisms of microbial pathogenesis, molecular genetics, vaccine and immunodiagnostic development. Total annual research expenditures: $6.8 million. *Unit head:* Joel B. Baseman, Chairman, 210-567-3939, Fax: 210-567-6491, E-mail: baseman@uthscsa.edu. *Application contact:* Sophia Pina, Assistant Dean, 210-567-3984, Fax: 210-567-3719, E-mail: pina@uthscsa.edu.

The University of Texas Medical Branch, Graduate School of Biomedical Sciences, Program in Microbiology and Immunology, Galveston, TX 77555. Offers MS, PhD. *Students:* 35 full-time (20 women), 1 part-time (0 women); includes 7 minority (5 African Americans, 2 Hispanic Americans), 11 international. Average age 30. In 2009, 8 doctorates awarded. Terminal master's awarded for partial completion of doctoral program. *Degree requirements:* For master's, thesis or alternative; for doctorate, thesis/dissertation. *Entrance requirements:* For doctorate, GRE General Test, minimum GPA of 3.0. Additional exam requirements/recommendations for international students: Required—TOEFL (minimum score 550 paper-based; 213 computer-based). *Application deadline:* Applications are processed on a rolling basis. Application fee: $30 ($75 for international students). Electronic applications accepted. *Financial support:* In 2009–10, research assistantships with full tuition reimbursements (averaging $25,000 per year). Financial award applicants required to submit FAFSA. *Unit head:* Dr. Rolf Konig, Director, 409-747-0395, Fax: 409-772-5065, E-mail: rokonig@utmb.edu. *Application contact:* Aneth Zertuche, Coordinator for Special Programs, 409-772-2322, Fax: 409-747-6869, E-mail: azertuch@utmb.edu.

The University of Texas Southwestern Medical Center at Dallas, Southwestern Graduate School of Biomedical Sciences, Division of Basic Science, Program in Immunology, Dallas, TX 75390. Offers PhD. *Faculty:* 47 full-time (12 women), 2 part-time/adjunct (0 women). *Students:* 32 full-time (18 women), 2 part-time (0 women); includes 9 minority (1 American Indian/Alaska Native, 3 Asian Americans or Pacific Islanders, 5 Hispanic Americans), 4 international. Average age 27. 946 applicants, 22% accepted. In 2009, 8 doctorates awarded. *Degree requirements:* For doctorate, thesis/dissertation, qualifying exam. *Entrance requirements:* For doctorate, GRE General Test, minimum GPA of 3.0. Additional exam requirements/recommendations for international students: Required—TOEFL. *Application deadline:* For fall admission, 12/15 priority date for domestic students. Applications are processed on a rolling basis. Application fee: $0. Electronic applications accepted. *Financial support:* Fellowships, research assistantships available. *Faculty research:* Antibody diversity and idiotype, cytotoxic effector mechanisms, natural killer cells, biology of immunoglobulins, oncogenes. *Unit head:* Dr. Nicolai Van Oers, Chair, 214-648-1236, Fax: 214-648-1902, E-mail: nicolai.vanoers@utsouthwestern.edu. *Application contact:* Dr. Nancy E. Street, Associate Dean, 214-648-6708, Fax: 214-648-2102, E-mail: nancy.street@utsouthwestern.edu.

The University of Toledo, College of Graduate Studies, College of Medicine, Biomedical Science Programs, Program in Infection, Immunity and Transplantation, Toledo, OH 43606-3390. Offers MSBS, PhD.

University of Toronto, School of Graduate Studies, Life Sciences Division, Department of Immunology, Toronto, ON M5S 1A1, Canada. Offers M Sc, PhD. *Degree requirements:* For master's, thesis, thesis defense; for doctorate, thesis/dissertation, thesis defense. *Entrance requirements:* For master's, resume, 3 letters of reference. Additional exam requirements/recommendations for international students: Required—TOEFL, TWE, GRE.

University of Washington, Graduate School, School of Medicine and Graduate School, Graduate Programs in Medicine, Department of Immunology, Seattle, WA 98195. Offers MS, PhD. Master's offered as terminal degree only. *Faculty:* 24 full-time (6 women). *Students:* 40 full-time (21 women); includes 9 minority (2 African Americans, 6 Asian Americans or Pacific Islanders, 1 Hispanic American), 3 international. Average age 28. 87 applicants, 21% accepted, 8 enrolled. In 2009, 5 doctorates awarded. *Degree requirements:* For doctorate, thesis/dissertation. *Entrance requirements:* For doctorate, GRE General Test, BA or BS in related field. Additional exam requirements/recommendations for international students: Required—TOEFL (minimum score 600 paper-based; 250 computer-based; 100 iBT). *Application deadline:* For fall admission, 12/7 for domestic students, 11/1 for international students. Application fee: $50. Electronic applications accepted. *Financial support:* In 2009–10, 16 fellowships with full tuition reimbursements (averaging $27,348 per year), 24 research assistantships with full tuition reimbursements (averaging $27,348 per year) were awarded; scholarships/grants, traineeships, health care benefits, tuition waivers (full), and stipends also available. *Faculty*

research: Molecular and cellular immunology, regulation of lymphocyte differentiation and responses, genetics of immune recognition genetics and pathogenesis of autoimmune diseases, signal transduction. Total annual research expenditures: $15 million. *Unit head:* Dr. Joan M. Goverman, Professor and Interim Chair, 206-543-1010, Fax: 206-543-1013. *Application contact:* Peggy A. McCune, Training Program Manager, 206-685-3955, Fax: 206-543-1013, E-mail: immgrad@u.washington.edu.

The University of Western Ontario, Faculty of Graduate Studies, Biosciences Division, Department of Microbiology and Immunology, London, ON N6A 5B8, Canada. Offers M Sc, PhD. *Degree requirements:* For master's, thesis, oral and written exam; for doctorate, thesis/dissertation, oral and written exam. *Entrance requirements:* For master's, honors degree or equivalent in microbiology, immunology, or other biological science; minimum B average; for doctorate, M Sc in microbiology and immunology. Additional exam requirements/recommendations for international students: Required—TOEFL. *Faculty research:* Virology, molecular pathogenesis, cellular immunology, molecular biology.

Vanderbilt University, Graduate School and School of Medicine, Department of Microbiology and Immunology, Nashville, TN 37240-1001. Offers MS, PhD, MD/PhD. *Faculty:* 38 full-time (8 women). *Students:* 33 full-time (15 women); includes 5 minority (2 African Americans, 1 Asian American or Pacific Islander, 2 Hispanic Americans), 5 international. Average age 27. In 2009, 2 master's, 9 doctorates awarded. Terminal master's awarded for partial completion of doctoral program. *Degree requirements:* For master's, thesis; for doctorate, thesis/dissertation, final and qualifying exams. *Entrance requirements:* For master's and doctorate, GRE General Test, GRE Subject Test (recommended). Additional exam requirements/recommendations for international students: Required—TOEFL (minimum score 570 paper-based; 230 computer-based; 88 iBT). *Application deadline:* For fall admission, 1/15 for domestic and international students. Application fee: $0. Electronic applications accepted. *Financial support:* Fellowships with full tuition reimbursements, research assistantships with full tuition reimbursements, Federal Work-Study, institutionally sponsored loans, scholarships/grants, traineeships, health care benefits, and tuition waivers (partial) available. Financial award application deadline: 1/15; financial award applicants required to submit CSS PROFILE or FAFSA. *Faculty research:* Cellular and molecular microbiology, viruses, genes, cancer, molecular pathogenesis of microbial diseases, immunobiology. *Unit head:* Jacek Hawiger, Chair, 615-322-2087, E-mail: jacek.hawiger@vanderbilt.edu. *Application contact:* Christopher R. Aiken, Director of Graduate Studies, 615-322-2087, E-mail: chris.aiken@vanderbilt.edu.

Virginia Commonwealth University, Medical College of Virginia-Professional Programs, School of Medicine, School of Medicine Graduate Programs, Department of Microbiology and Immunology, Richmond, VA 23284-9005. Offers microbiology and immunology (MS, PhD); molecular biology and genetics (MS, PhD); MD/PhD. *Degree requirements:* For master's, thesis; for doctorate, thesis/dissertation, comprehensive oral and written exams. *Entrance requirements:* For master's, GRE General Test or MCAT; for doctorate, GRE General Test, MCAT. *Faculty research:* Microbial physiology and genetics, molecular biology, crystallography of biological molecules, antibiotics and chemotherapy, membrane transport.

Wake Forest University, School of Medicine and Graduate School of Arts and Sciences, Graduate Programs in Medicine, Department of Microbiology and Immunology, Winston-Salem, NC 27109. Offers PhD, MD/PhD. *Degree requirements:* For doctorate, thesis/dissertation. *Entrance requirements:* For doctorate, GRE General Test. Additional exam requirements/recommendations for international students: Required—TOEFL. Electronic applications accepted. *Faculty research:* Molecular immunology, bacterial pathogenesis and molecular genetics, viral pathogenesis, regulation of mRNA metabolism, leukocyte biology.

Washington University in St. Louis, Graduate School of Arts and Sciences, Division of Biology and Biomedical Sciences, Program in Immunology, St. Louis, MO 63130-4899. Offers PhD. *Degree requirements:* For doctorate, thesis/dissertation. *Entrance requirements:* For doctorate, GRE General Test, GRE Subject Test. Electronic applications accepted.

Wayne State University, School of Medicine, Graduate Programs in Medicine, Department of Immunology and Microbiology, Detroit, MI 48202. Offers MS, PhD, MD/PhD. Terminal master's awarded for partial completion of doctoral program. *Degree requirements:* For master's, thesis; for doctorate, thesis/dissertation. *Entrance requirements:* For master's, GRE, minimum GPA of 2.5; for doctorate, GRE, minimum GPA of 3.0. Additional exam requirements/recommendations for international students: Required—TOEFL (minimum score 550 paper-based; 213 computer-based); Recommended—TWE (minimum score 6). Electronic applications accepted. *Faculty research:* Immune regulation, bacterial pathophysiology, molecular biology/viruses/bacteria, cellular and molecular immunology, microbial pathogenesis.

West Virginia University, Davis College of Agriculture, Forestry and Consumer Sciences, Interdisciplinary Program in Genetics and Developmental Biology, Morgantown, WV 26506. Offers animal breeding (MS, PhD); biochemical and molecular genetics (MS, PhD); cyto-genetics (MS, PhD); descriptive embryology (MS, PhD); developmental genetics (MS); experimental morphogenesis/teratology (MS); human genetics (MS, PhD); immunogenetics (MS, PhD); life cycles of animals and plants (MS, PhD); molecular aspects of development (MS, PhD); mutagenesis (MS, PhD); oncology (MS, PhD); plant genetics (MS, PhD); population and quantitative genetics (MS, PhD); regeneration (MS, PhD); teratology (PhD); toxicology (MS, PhD). *Degree requirements:* For master's, thesis; for doctorate, comprehensive exam, thesis/dissertation. *Entrance requirements:* For master's, GRE or MCAT, minimum GPA of 2.75. Additional exam requirements/recommendations for international students: Required—TOEFL.

West Virginia University, School of Medicine, Graduate Programs at the Health Sciences Center, Interdisciplinary Graduate Programs in Biomedical Sciences, Program in Immunology and Microbial Pathogenesis, Morgantown, WV 26506. Offers MS, PhD, MD/PhD. *Degree requirements:* For doctorate, comprehensive exam, thesis/dissertation. *Entrance requirements:* For doctorate, GRE General Test, minimum GPA of 3.0. Additional exam requirements/recommendations for international students: Required—TOEFL. Electronic applications accepted. *Faculty research:* Regulation of signal transduction in immune responses, immune responses in bacterial and viral diseases, peptide and DNA vaccines for contraception, inflammatory bowel disease, physiology of pathogenic microbes.

Wright State University, School of Graduate Studies, College of Science and Mathematics, Program in Microbiology and Immunology, Dayton, OH 45435. Offers MS. Part-time programs available. *Degree requirements:* For master's, thesis. *Entrance requirements:* Additional exam requirements/recommendations for international students: Required—TOEFL. *Faculty research:* Reproductive immunology, viral pathogenesis, virus-host cell interactions.

Yale University, Graduate School of Arts and Sciences, Department of Immunobiology, New Haven, CT 06520. Offers PhD. *Degree requirements:* For doctorate, thesis/dissertation. *Entrance requirements:* For doctorate, GRE General Test.

Yale University, School of Medicine and Graduate School of Arts and Sciences, Combined Program in Biological and Biomedical Sciences (BBS), Immunology Track, New Haven, CT 06520. Offers PhD, MD/PhD. *Degree requirements:* For doctorate, thesis/dissertation. *Entrance requirements:* For doctorate, GRE General Test. Additional exam requirements/recommendations for international students: Required—TOEFL. *Application deadline:* For fall admission, 12/6 for domestic and international students. Electronic applications accepted. *Financial support:* Fellowships, research assistantships available. *Unit head:* Dr. Susan Kaech, Director of Graduate Admissions, 203-785-3857. *Application contact:* Barbara Giamattei, Student Services Officer, 203-785-3857, Fax: 203-785-2939, E-mail: barbara.giamattei@yale.edu.

Infectious Diseases

Cornell University, Graduate School, Graduate Fields of Comparative Biomedical Sciences, Field of Comparative Biomedical Sciences, Ithaca, NY 14853-0001. Offers cellular and molecular medicine (MS, PhD); developmental and reproductive biology (MS, PhD); infectious diseases (MS, PhD); population medicine and epidemiology (MS, PhD); structural and functional biology (MS, PhD). *Faculty:* 106 full-time (29 women). *Students:* 41 full-time (28 women); includes 1 minority (African American), 17 international. Average age 32. 32 applicants, 31% accepted, 9 enrolled. In 2009, 1 master's, 10 doctorates awarded. *Degree requirements:* For master's, thesis; for doctorate, comprehensive exam, thesis/dissertation. *Entrance requirements:* For master's and doctorate, GRE General Test, 2 letters of recommendation. Additional exam requirements/recommendations for international students: Required—TOEFL (minimum score 550 paper-based; 213 computer-based; 77 iBT). *Application deadline:* For fall admission, 12/15 for domestic students. Application fee: $70. Electronic applications accepted. *Expenses:* Tuition: Full-time $29,500. Required fees: $70. Full-time tuition and fees vary according to degree level, program and student level. *Financial support:* In 2009–10, 4 fellowships with full tuition reimbursements, 2 research assistantships with full tuition reimbursements were awarded; teaching assistantships with full tuition reimbursements, institutionally sponsored loans, scholarships/grants, health care benefits, tuition waivers (full and partial), and unspecified assistantships also available. Financial award applicants required to submit FAFSA. *Faculty research:* Receptors and signal transduction, viral and bacterial infectious diseases, tumor metastasis, clinical sciences/nutritional disease, developmental/neurological disorders. *Unit head:* Director of Graduate Studies, 607-253-3276, Fax: 607-253-3756. *Application contact:* Graduate Field Assistant, 607-253-3276, Fax: 607-253-3756, E-mail: graduate_edcvm@cornell.edu.

Georgetown University, Graduate School of Arts and Sciences, Programs in Biomedical Sciences, Department of Microbiology and Immunology, Washington, DC 20057. Offers biohazardous threat agents and emerging infectious diseases (MS); general microbiology and immunology (MS); global infectious diseases (PhD); microbiology and immunology research (PhD); science policy and advocacy (MS). Part-time programs available. *Degree requirements:* For master's, 30 credit hours of coursework; for doctorate, comprehensive exam, thesis/dissertation. *Entrance requirements:* For master's, GRE General Test, 3 letters of reference, bachelor's degree in related field; for doctorate, GRE General Test, 3 letters of reference, MS/BS in related field. Additional exam requirements/recommendations for international students: Required—TOEFL (minimum score 505 paper-based; 213 computer-based). Electronic applications accepted. *Faculty research:* Pathogenesis and basic biology of the fungus Candida albicans, molecular biology of viral immunopathological mechanisms in Multiple Sclerosis.

The George Washington University, School of Public Health and Health Services, Department of Epidemiology and Biostatistics, Washington, DC 20052. Offers biostatistics (MPH); epidemiology (MPH); microbiology and emerging infectious diseases (MSPH). *Faculty:* 16 full-time (7 women), 14 part-time/adjunct (8 women). *Students:* 52 full-time (40 women), 53 part-time (37 women); includes 44 minority (14 African Americans, 25 Asian Americans or Pacific Islanders, 5 Hispanic Americans), 5 international. Average age 28. 165 applicants, 85% accepted, 37 enrolled. In 2009, 28 master's awarded. *Degree requirements:* For master's, case study or special project. *Entrance requirements:* For master's, GMAT, GRE General Test, or MCAT. Additional exam requirements/recommendations for international students: Required—TOEFL. *Application deadline:* For fall admission, 4/15 priority date for domestic students, 4/15 for international students; for spring admission, 11/1 for domestic and international students. Applications are processed on a rolling basis. Application fee: $60. *Financial support:* In 2009–10, 6 students received support. Tuition waivers available. Financial award application deadline: 2/15. *Unit head:* Dr. Alan E. Greenberg, Chair, 202-994-0612, E-mail: aeg1@gwu.edu. *Application contact:* Jane Smith, Director of Admissions, 202-994-0248, Fax: 202-994-1860, E-mail: sphhsinfo@gwumc.edu.

Harvard University, School of Public Health, Department of Immunology and Infectious Diseases, Boston, MA 02115-6096. Offers PhD, SD. Part-time programs available. *Faculty:* 27 full-time (9 women), 5 part-time/adjunct (0 women). *Students:* 6 applicants, 17% accepted, 0 enrolled. *Degree requirements:* For doctorate, thesis/dissertation, qualifying exam. *Entrance requirements:* For doctorate, GRE. Additional exam requirements/recommendations for international students: Required—TOEFL (minimum score 600 paper-based; 240 computer-based; 100 iBT); Recommended—IELTS (minimum score 7). *Application deadline:* For fall admission, 12/15 for domestic and international students. Application fee: $115. Electronic applications accepted. *Expenses:* Tuition: Full-time $33,696. Required fees: $1126. Full-time tuition and fees vary according to program. *Financial support:* Fellowships, research assistantships, Federal Work-Study, scholarships/grants, traineeships, tuition waivers (partial), and unspecified assistantships available. Financial award application deadline: 2/8; financial award applicants required to submit FAFSA. *Faculty research:* Infectious disease epidemiology and tropical public health, vector biology, ecology and control, virology. *Unit head:* Dr. Dyann F. Wirth, Chair, 617-432-2234, Fax: 617-739-8348, E-mail: rkenwort@hsph.harvard.edu. *Application contact:* Vincent W. James, Director of Admissions, 617-432-1031, Fax: 617-432-7080, E-mail: admisofc@hsph.harvard.edu.

The Johns Hopkins University, Bloomberg School of Public Health, Department of Epidemiology, Baltimore, MD 21205. Offers cancer epidemiology (MHS, Sc M, PhD, Sc D); cardiovascular disease epidemiology (MHS, Sc M, PhD, Sc D); clinical epidemiology (MHS, Sc M, PhD, Sc D); clinical trials (PhD, Sc D); epidemiology (Dr PH); epidemiology (general) (MHS, Sc M, PhD, Sc D); epidemiology of aging (MHS, Sc M, PhD, Sc D); human genetics/genetic epidemiology (MHS, Sc M, PhD, Sc D); infectious disease epidemiology (MHS, Sc M, PhD, Sc D); occupational/environmental epidemiology (MHS, Sc M, PhD, Sc D). Part-time programs available. *Faculty:* 80 full-time (44 women), 82 part-time/adjunct (36 women). *Students:* 142 full-time (102 women), 24 part-time (17 women); includes 44 minority (13 African Americans, 28 Asian Americans or Pacific Islanders, 3 Hispanic Americans), 41 international. Average age 30. 263 applicants, 41% accepted, 52 enrolled. In 2009, 61 master's, 25 doctorates awarded. *Degree requirements:* For master's, comprehensive exam, thesis, 1 year full-time residency; for doctorate, comprehensive exam, thesis/dissertation, 2 years full-time residency, oral and written exams, student teaching. *Entrance requirements:* For master's, GRE General Test or MCAT, 3 letters of recommendation, curriculum vitae; for doctorate, GRE General Test, minimum 1 year of work experience, 3 letters of recommendation, curriculum vitae, academic records from all schools. Additional exam requirements/recommendations for international students: Required—TOEFL (minimum score 600 paper-based; 250 computer-based; 100 iBT); Recommended—IELTS (minimum score 7.5), TWE. *Application deadline:* For fall admission, 12/1 priority date for domestic students. Applications are processed on a rolling basis. Application fee: $45. Electronic applications accepted. *Financial support:* In 2009–10, 2 fellowships (averaging $28,859 per year) were awarded; Federal Work-Study, institutionally sponsored loans, scholarships/grants, traineeships, tuition waivers (partial), and stipends also available. Support available to part-time students. Financial award application deadline: 3/15; financial award applicants required to submit FAFSA. *Faculty research:* Cancer and congenital malformations, nutritional epidemiology, AIDS, tuberculosis, cardiovascular disease, risk assessment. Total annual research expenditures: $70.1 million. *Unit head:* Dr. David D. Celentano, Chair, 410-955-3286, Fax: 410-955-0863, E-mail: dcelenta@jhsph.edu. *Application contact:* Frances S. Burman, Academic Program Manager, 410-955-3926, Fax: 410-955-0863, E-mail: fburman@jhsph.edu.

Loyola University Chicago, Graduate School, Marcella Niehoff School of Nursing, Population-Based Infection Control and Environmental Safety Program, Chicago, IL 60660. Offers population based infection control (MSN, Certificate). Part-time and evening/weekend programs available. *Students:* 17 part-time (all women); includes 2 minority (1 African American, 1 Asian American or Pacific Islander). Average age 42. 6 applicants, 67% accepted, 2 enrolled. In 2009, 1 master's awarded. *Entrance requirements:* For master's, Illinois nursing license, 3 letters of recommendation, minimum nursing GPA of 3.0, 1000 hours experience before starting clinical. Application fee: $50. *Expenses:* Tuition: Full-time $14,220; part-time $790 per credit hour. Required fees: $60 per semester hour. Tuition and fees vary according to program. *Financial support:* Traineeships available. *Unit head:* Dr. Ida Androwich, Professor, 708-216-9276, Fax: 708-216-9555, E-mail: iandrow@luc.edu. *Application contact:* Dr. Vicki A. Keough, Associate Dean, 773-508-3263, Fax: 773-508-3241, E-mail: vkeough@luc.edu.

North Carolina State University, College of Veterinary Medicine, Program in Comparative Biomedical Sciences, Raleigh, NC 27695. Offers cell biology (MS, PhD); infectious disease (MS, PhD); pathology (MS, PhD); pharmacology (MS, PhD); population medicine (MS, PhD). Part-time programs available. *Degree requirements:* For master's, thesis; for doctorate, thesis/dissertation. *Entrance requirements:* For master's and doctorate, GRE General Test. Additional exam requirements/recommendations for international students: Required—TOEFL (minimum score 550 paper-based; 213 computer-based). Electronic applications accepted. *Expenses:* Contact institution. *Faculty research:* Infectious diseases, cell biology, pharmacology and toxicology, genomics, pathology and population medicine.

State University of New York Upstate Medical University, College of Graduate Studies, Major Research Areas of the College of Graduate Studies, Syracuse, NY 13210-2334. *Unit head:* Dr. Steven R. Goodman, Dean, College of Graduate Studies, 315-464-4538. *Application contact:* Sandra Tillotson, Coordinator of Graduate Recruitment, 315-464-7655, Fax: 315-464-4544, E-mail: tillotss@upstate.edu.

Tulane University, School of Public Health and Tropical Medicine, Department of Tropical Medicine, New Orleans, LA 70118-5669. Offers clinical tropical medicine and travelers health (Diploma); parasitology (MSPH, PhD); public health and tropical medicine (MPHTM); vector borne infectious diseases (MS, PhD); MD/PhD. MS and PhD offered through the Graduate School. *Degree requirements:* For master's, thesis; for doctorate, comprehensive exam, thesis/dissertation. *Entrance requirements:* For master's, GRE General Test, minimum B average in undergraduate course work; for doctorate, GRE General Test. Additional exam requirements/recommendations for international students: Required—TOEFL.

Uniformed Services University of the Health Sciences, School of Medicine, Graduate Programs in the Biomedical Sciences and Public Health, Graduate Program in Emerging Infectious Diseases, Bethesda, MD 20814-4799. Offers PhD. *Faculty:* 35 full-time (5 women), 17 part-time/adjunct (6 women). *Students:* 37 full-time (24 women); includes 5 minority (1 African American, 3 Asian Americans or Pacific Islanders, 1 Hispanic American), 3 international. Average age 26. 43 applicants, 44% accepted, 11 enrolled. In 2009, 7 doctorates awarded. *Degree requirements:* For doctorate, comprehensive exam, thesis/dissertation, qualifying exam. *Entrance requirements:* For doctorate, GRE General Test. Additional exam requirements/recommendations for international students: Required—TOEFL. *Application deadline:* For fall admission, 1/15 priority date for domestic and international students. Applications are processed on a rolling basis. Application fee: $0. Electronic applications accepted. *Financial support:* In 2009–10, fellowships with full tuition reimbursements (averaging $26,000 per year); scholarships/grants, health care benefits, and tuition waivers (full) also available. *Unit head:* Dr. Christopher Broder, Graduate Program Director, 301-295-3401, E-mail: cbroder@usuhs.mil. *Application contact:* Elena Marina Sherman, Graduate Program Coordinator, 301-295-3913, Fax: 301-295-6772, E-mail: elena.sherman@usuhs.mil.

Université de Montréal, Faculty of Medicine, Program in Specialized Studies, Montréal, QC H3C 3J7, Canada. Offers anesthesia (DES); diagnostic radiology (DES); family medicine (DES); gastroenterology (DES); geriatry (DES); intensive care (DES); medical biochemistry (DES); medical genetics (DES); medicine (DES); microbiology and infectious diseases (DES); nuclear medicine (DES); obstetrics and gynecology (DES); ophthalmology (DES); pediatrics (DES); pneumology (DES); psychiatry (DES); radiology-oncology (DES); rheumatology (DES); surgery (DES). *Faculty:* 154 full-time (40 women), 333 part-time/adjunct (100 women). *Students:* 930 full-time (580 women), 7 part-time (all women). 74 applicants, 77% accepted, 29 enrolled. *Application deadline:* For fall admission, 2/1 priority date for domestic students; for winter admission, 11/1 priority date for domestic students; for spring admission, 2/1 priority date for domestic students. Application fee: $100. Electronic applications accepted. *Unit head:* Lorraine Locas, Assistant to the Vice Dean of Graduate Studies, 514-343-6269, Fax: 514-343-5751, E-mail: lorraine.locas@umontreal.ca. *Application contact:* Dr. Andre Ferron, Vice Dean of Graduate Studies, 514-343-6111 Ext. 0933, Fax: 514-343-5751, E-mail: andre.ferron@umontreal.ca.

Université Laval, Faculty of Medicine, Post-Professional Programs in Medical Studies, Québec, QC G1K 7P4, Canada. Offers anatomy–pathology (DESS); anesthesiology (DESS); cardiology (DESS); care of older people (Diploma); clinical research (DESS); community health (DESS); dermatology (DESS); diagnostic radiology (DESS); emergency medicine (Diploma); family medicine (DESS); general surgery (DESS); geriatrics (DESS); hematology (DESS); internal medicine (DESS); maternal and fetal medicine (Diploma); medical biochemistry (DESS); medical microbiology and infectious diseases (DESS); medical oncology (DESS); nephrology (DESS); neurology (DESS); neurosurgery (DESS); obstetrics and gynecology (DESS); ophthalmology (DESS); orthopedic surgery (DESS); oto-rhino-laryngology (DESS); palliative medicine (Diploma); pediatrics (DESS); plastic surgery (DESS); psychiatry (DESS); pulmonary medicine (DESS); radiology–oncology (DESS); thoracic surgery (DESS); urology (DESS). *Degree requirements:* For other advanced degree, comprehensive exam. *Entrance requirements:* For degree, knowledge of French. Electronic applications accepted.

University of Calgary, Faculty of Medicine and Faculty of Graduate Studies, Department of Microbiology and Infectious Diseases, Calgary, AB T2N 1N4, Canada. Offers M Sc, PhD. *Degree requirements:* For master's, thesis, oral thesis exam; for doctorate, thesis/dissertation, candidacy exam, oral thesis exam. *Entrance requirements:* For master's and doctorate, minimum GPA of 3.2. Additional exam requirements/recommendations for international students: Required—TOEFL (minimum score 580 paper-based; 237 computer-based). Electronic applications accepted. *Faculty research:* Bacteriology, virology, parasitology, immunology.

University of California, Berkeley, Graduate Division, School of Public Health, Group in Epidemiology, Berkeley, CA 94720-1500. Offers epidemiology (MS, PhD); infectious diseases (MPH, PhD). *Accreditation:* CEPH (one or more programs are accredited). *Students:* 48 full-time (34 women). Average age 33. 85 applicants, 8 enrolled. In 2009, 2 master's, 17 doctorates awarded. *Degree requirements:* For master's, comprehensive exam; for doctorate, thesis/dissertation, oral and written exam. *Entrance requirements:* For master's, GRE General Test, minimum GPA of 3.0; MD, DDS, DVM, or PhD in biomedical science (MPH); for doctorate, GRE General Test, minimum GPA of 3.0. *Application deadline:* For fall admission, 12/1 for domestic students. Applications are processed on a rolling basis. Application fee: $70 ($90 for international students). *Financial support:* Fellowships, research assistantships, teaching assistantships, Federal Work-Study and unspecified assistantships available. *Unit head:* Prof. Arthur L. Reingold, Head, 510-642-3997, E-mail: robertamyers@berkeley.edu. *Application contact:* Roberta Meyers, Graduate Assistant, 510-643-2731, E-mail: robertamyers@berkeley.edu.

University of California, Berkeley, Graduate Division, School of Public Health, Group in Infectious Diseases and Immunity, Berkeley, CA 94720-1500. Offers PhD. *Students:* 14 full-time (8 women). Average age 29. 54 applicants, 2 enrolled. In 2009, 3 doctorates awarded. *Entrance requirements:* For doctorate, GRE General Test, minimum GPA of 3.0, 3 letters of recommendation. *Application deadline:* For fall admission, 12/1 for domestic students. Applications are processed on a rolling basis. Application fee: $70 ($90 for international students). *Financial support:* Fellowships, research assistantships, teaching assistantships, unspecified assistantships available. *Unit head:* Prof. Lee Riley, Head, 510-642-9189, E-mail: idadmin@berkeley.edu. *Application contact:* Teresa Liu, Student Affairs Specialist, 510-642-9189, E-mail: idadmin@berkeley.edu.

Infectious Diseases

University of Georgia, College of Veterinary Medicine and Graduate School, Graduate Programs in Veterinary Medicine, Department of Infectious Diseases, Athens, GA 30602. Offers MS, PhD. *Faculty:* 19 full-time (6 women), 2 part-time/adjunct (0 women). *Students:* 32 full-time (19 women), 4 part-time (2 women); includes 3 minority (2 African Americans, 1 Asian American or Pacific Islander), 8 international. 38 applicants, 39% accepted, 11 enrolled. In 2009, 5 master's, 5 doctorates awarded. *Degree requirements:* For master's, thesis; for doctorate, one foreign language, thesis/dissertation. *Entrance requirements:* For master's and doctorate, GRE General Test. *Application deadline:* For fall admission, 7/1 priority date for domestic students; for spring admission, 11/15 for domestic students. Application fee: $50. Electronic applications accepted. *Expenses:* Tuition, state resident: full-time $6000; part-time $250 per credit hour. Tuition, nonresident: full-time $20,904; part-time $871 per credit hour. Required fees: $730 per semester. *Financial support:* Fellowships, research assistantships, teaching assistantships, unspecified assistantships available. *Unit head:* Dr. Frederick Quinn, Head, 706-542-5790, Fax: 706-542-5771, E-mail: fquinn@uga.edu. *Application contact:* Dr. Liliana Jaso-Friedman, Graduate Coordinator, 706-542-2875, Fax: 706-542-5771, E-mail: ljaso@uga.edu.

University of Guelph, Ontario Veterinary College and Graduate Program Services, Graduate Programs in Veterinary Sciences, Department of Pathobiology, Guelph, ON N1G 2W1, Canada. Offers anatomic pathology (DV Sc, Diploma); clinical pathology (Diploma); comparative pathology (M Sc, PhD); immunology (M Sc, PhD); laboratory animal science (DV Sc); pathology (M Sc, PhD, Diploma); veterinary infectious diseases (M Sc, PhD); zoo animal/wildlife medicine (DV Sc). *Degree requirements:* For master's, thesis; for doctorate, thesis/dissertation. *Entrance requirements:* For master's, DVM with B average or an honours degree in biological sciences; for doctorate, DVM or MSC degree, minimum B+ average. Additional exam requirements/recommendations for international students: Required—TOEFL (minimum score 550 paper-based; 213 computer-based). *Faculty research:* Pathogenesis; diseases of animals, wildlife, fish, and laboratory animals; parasitology; immunology; veterinary infectious diseases; laboratory animal science.

University of Minnesota, Twin Cities Campus, School of Public Health, Division of Environmental Health Sciences, Area in Environmental Infectious Diseases, Minneapolis, MN 55455-0213. Offers MPH, MS, PhD. *Degree requirements:* For doctorate, thesis/dissertation. *Entrance requirements:* For master's and doctorate, GRE General Test. Electronic applications accepted.

The University of Montana, Graduate School, College of Arts and Sciences, Division of Biological Sciences, Program in Ecology of Infectious Disease, Missoula, MT 59812-0002. Offers PhD.

University of Pittsburgh, Graduate School of Public Health, Department of Infectious Diseases and Microbiology, Pittsburgh, PA 15260. Offers bioscience of infectious diseases (MPH); community and behavioral intervention of infectious diseases (MPH); infectious diseases and microbiology (MS, Dr PH, PhD); LGBT health and wellness (Certificate). Part-time programs available. *Faculty:* 20 full-time (7 women), 2 part-time/adjunct (1 woman). *Students:* 46 full-time (33 women), 8 part-time (6 women); includes 7 minority (2 African Americans, 4 Asian Americans or Pacific Islanders, 1 Hispanic American), 6 international. Average age 28. 176 applicants, 43% accepted, 18 enrolled. In 2009, 11 master's, 9 doctorates awarded. Terminal master's awarded for partial completion of doctoral program. *Degree requirements:* For master's, one foreign language, comprehensive exam (for some programs), thesis; for doctorate, one foreign language, comprehensive exam, thesis/dissertation. *Entrance requirements:* For master's and doctorate, GRE General Test, MCAT, or DAT. Additional exam requirements/recommendations for international students: Required—TOEFL (minimum score 550 paper-based; 213 computer-based; 80 iBT). *Application deadline:* For fall admission, 1/4 for domestic students. Applications are processed on a rolling basis. Application fee: $95. Electronic applications accepted. *Expenses:* Tuition, state resident: full-time $16,402; part-time $665 per credit. Tuition, nonresident: full-time $28,694; part-time $1175 per credit. Required fees: $690; $175 per term. Tuition and fees vary according to program. *Financial support:* In 2009–10, 16 students received support, including 16 research assistantships with full tuition reimbursements available (averaging $23,500 per year). Financial award applicants required to submit FAFSA. *Faculty research:* HIV, Epstein-Barr virus, virology, immunology, malaria. Total annual research expenditures: $13.6 million. *Unit head:* Dr. Charles R. Rinaldo, Chairman, 412-624-3928, Fax: 412-624-4953, E-mail: rinaldo@pitt.edu. *Application contact:* Dr. Jeremy Martinson, Assistant Professor, 412-624-5646, Fax: 412-383-8926, E-mail: jmartins@pitt.edu.

The University of Texas Medical Branch, Graduate School of Biomedical Sciences, Center for Biodefense and Emerging Infectious Diseases, Galveston, TX 77555. Offers biodefense training (PhD). *Entrance requirements:* For doctorate, GRE, minimum overall GPA of 3.0. *Financial support:* Tuition waivers and unspecified assistantships available. *Unit head:* Dr. Clarence J. Peters, Executive Director, 409-772-0090, Fax: 409-747-0762, E-mail: cjpeters@utmb.edu. *Application contact:* Dr. Dorian H. Coppenhaver, Associate Dean for Student Affairs, 409-772-2665, Fax: 409-747-0772, E-mail: dcoppenh@utmb.edu.

The University of Texas Medical Branch, Graduate School of Biomedical Sciences, Program in Emerging and Tropical Infectious Diseases, Galveston, TX 77555. Offers PhD, MD/PhD. *Degree requirements:* For doctorate, thesis/dissertation. *Entrance requirements:* For doctorate, GRE General Test. *Application deadline:* Applications are processed on a rolling basis. Application fee: $25 ($50 for international students). *Financial support:* In 2009–10, fellowships (averaging $25,000 per year), research assistantships with full tuition reimbursements (averaging $25,000 per year) were awarded; traineeships and unspecified assistantships also available. *Faculty research:* Emerging diseases, tropical diseases, parasitology, vitology and bacteriology. *Application contact:* Dr. Dorian H. Coppenhaver, Associate Dean for Student Affairs, 409-772-2665, Fax: 409-747-0772, E-mail: dcoppenh@utmb.edu.

Yale University, School of Medicine and Graduate School of Arts and Sciences, Combined Program in Biological and Biomedical Sciences (BBS), Microbiology Track, New Haven, CT 06520. Offers PhD, MD/PhD. *Degree requirements:* For doctorate, thesis/dissertation. *Entrance requirements:* For doctorate, GRE General Test, GRE Subject Test. Additional exam requirements/recommendations for international students: Required—TOEFL. *Application deadline:* For fall admission, 12/6 for domestic and international students. Electronic applications accepted. *Financial support:* Fellowships, research assistantships available. *Unit head:* Dr. Robert Means, Director of Graduate Admissions, 203-737-2404. *Application contact:* Karen Kavanaugh, Graduate Registrar, 203-737-2404, E-mail: karen.kavanaugh@yale.edu.

Medical Microbiology

Creighton University, School of Medicine and Graduate School, Graduate Programs in Medicine, Department of Medical Microbiology and Immunology, Omaha, NE 68178-0001. Offers MS, PhD. Terminal master's awarded for partial completion of doctoral program. *Degree requirements:* For master's, comprehensive exam, thesis; for doctorate, thesis/dissertation, preliminary exams. *Entrance requirements:* For master's and doctorate, GRE General Test. Additional exam requirements/recommendations for international students: Required—TOEFL. *Expenses:* Tuition: Full-time $11,700; part-time $650 per credit hour. Required fees: $126 per semester. *Faculty research:* Infectious diseases, molecular biology, genetics, antimicrobial agents and chemotherapy, virology.

Idaho State University, Office of Graduate Studies, College of Arts and Sciences, Department of Biological Sciences, Pocatello, ID 83209-8007. Offers biology (MNS, MS, DA, PhD); clinical laboratory science (MS); microbiology (MS). *Accreditation:* NAACLS. Part-time programs available. *Faculty:* 25 full-time (4 women). *Students:* 65 full-time (28 women), 24 part-time (8 women); includes 3 minority (1 American Indian/Alaska Native, 2 Hispanic Americans), 12 international. Average age 31. In 2009, 17 master's, 6 doctorates awarded. *Degree requirements:* For master's, comprehensive exam, thesis; for doctorate, comprehensive exam, thesis/dissertation, 9 credits of internship (for DA). *Entrance requirements:* For master's, GRE General Test, minimum GPA of 3.0 in all upper division classes; for doctorate, GRE General Test, GRE Subject Test (biology), diagnostic exam (DA), minimum GPA of 3.0 in all upper division classes. Additional exam requirements/recommendations for international students: Required—TOEFL (minimum score 550 paper-based; 213 computer-based; 80 iBT). *Application deadline:* For fall admission, 7/1 for domestic students, 6/1 for international students; for spring admission, 12/1 for domestic students, 11/1 for international students. Applications are processed on a rolling basis. Application fee: $55. Electronic applications accepted. *Expenses:* Tuition, state resident: full-time $3318; part-time $297 per credit hour. Tuition, nonresident: full-time $13,120; part-time $437 per credit hour. Required fees: $2530. Tuition and fees vary according to program. *Financial support:* In 2009–10, fellowships with full and partial tuition reimbursements (averaging $12,282 per year), 23 research assistantships with full and partial tuition reimbursements (averaging $12,503 per year), 27 teaching assistantships with full and partial tuition reimbursements (averaging $10,841 per year) were awarded; Federal Work-Study, institutionally sponsored loans, scholarships/grants, health care benefits, tuition waivers (full and partial), and unspecified assistantships also available. Support available to part-time students. Financial award application deadline: 1/1; financial award applicants required to submit FAFSA. *Faculty research:* Ecology, plant and animal physiology, plant and animal developmental biology, immunology, molecular biology, bioinfomatics. *Unit head:* Dr. Terry Bowyer, Chair, 208-282-3765, Fax: 208-282-4570, E-mail: bowyterr@isu.edu. *Application contact:* Tami Carson, Graduate School Technical Records Specialist, 208-282-2150, Fax: 208-282-4847, E-mail: carstami@isu.edu.

Rutgers, The State University of New Jersey, New Brunswick, Graduate School-New Brunswick, Programs in the Molecular Biosciences, Program in Microbiology and Molecular Genetics, Piscataway, NJ 08854-8097. Offers applied microbiology (MS, PhD); clinical microbiology (MS, PhD); computational molecular biology (PhD); immunology (MS, PhD); microbial biochemistry (MS, PhD); molecular genetics (MS, PhD); virology (MS, PhD). Part-time programs available. Terminal master's awarded for partial completion of doctoral program. *Degree requirements:* For master's, comprehensive exam, thesis or alternative; for doctorate, comprehensive exam, thesis/dissertation, written qualifying exam. *Entrance requirements:* For master's, GRE General Test, minimum GPA of 3.0; for doctorate, GRE General Test, GRE Subject Test (recommended), minimum GPA of 3.0. Additional exam requirements/recommendations for international students: Required—TOEFL. Electronic applications accepted. *Faculty research:* Molecular genetics and microbial physiology; virology and pathogenic microbiology; applied, environmental and industrial microbiology; computers in molecular biology.

Texas Tech University Health Sciences Center, Graduate School of Biomedical Sciences, Department of Microbiology and Immunology, Lubbock, TX 79430. Offers medical microbiology (MS, PhD); MD/PhD; MS/PhD. Terminal master's awarded for partial completion of doctoral program. *Degree requirements:* For master's, thesis; for doctorate, thesis/dissertation. *Entrance requirements:* For master's and doctorate, GRE General Test, minimum GPA of 3.0. Additional exam requirements/recommendations for international students: Required—TOEFL (minimum score 550 paper-based; 213 computer-based). Electronic applications accepted. *Faculty research:* Genetics, pathogenic bacteriology, molecular biology, virology, medical mycology.

Université du Québec, Institut National de la Recherche Scientifique, Graduate Programs, Research Center—INRS—Institut Armand-Frappier—Human Health, Québec, QC G1K 9A9, Canada. Offers applied microbiology (M Sc); biology (PhD); experimental health sciences (M Sc); virology and immunology (M Sc, PhD). Programs given in French. Part-time programs available. *Faculty:* 37. *Students:* 157 full-time (97 women), 4 part-time (all women), 41 international. Average age 30. In 2009, 14 master's, 5 doctorates awarded. *Median time to degree:* Of those who began their doctoral program in fall 2001, 67% received their degree in 8 years or less. *Degree requirements:* For doctorate, thesis/dissertation. *Entrance requirements:* For master's and doctorate, appropriate bachelor's degree, proficiency in French. *Application deadline:* For fall admission, 3/30 for domestic and international students; for winter admission, 11/1 for domestic and international students. Application fee: $30 Canadian dollars. *Financial support:* Fellowships, research assistantships, teaching assistantships available. *Faculty research:* Immunity, infection and cancer; toxicology and environmental biotechnology; molecular pharmacochemistry. *Unit head:* Alain Fournier, Director, 450-687-5010, Fax: 450-686-5501, E-mail: alain.fournier@iaf.inrs.ca. *Application contact:* Yvonne Boisvert, Registrar, 418-654-3861, Fax: 418-654-3858, E-mail: registrariat@adm.inrs.ca.

University of Alberta, Faculty of Medicine and Dentistry and Faculty of Graduate Studies and Research, Graduate Programs in Medicine, Department of Medical Microbiology and Immunology, Edmonton, AB T6G 2E1, Canada. Offers M Sc, PhD. *Faculty:* 16 full-time (5 women), 4 part-time/adjunct (1 woman). *Students:* 40 full-time (23 women); includes 7 minority (1 African American, 5 Asian Americans or Pacific Islanders, 1 Hispanic American), 1 international. Average age 25. 39 applicants, 33% accepted, 9 enrolled. In 2009, 1 master's, 3 doctorates awarded. Terminal master's awarded for partial completion of doctoral program. *Degree requirements:* For master's, thesis; for doctorate, thesis/dissertation. *Entrance requirements:* For master's and doctorate, minimum GPA of 3.3. Additional exam requirements/recommendations for international students: Required—TOEFL (minimum score 600 paper-based; 232 computer-based; 96 iBT). *Application deadline:* For fall admission, 7/1 for domestic students, 2/28 priority date for international students. Tuition and fees charges are reported in Canadian dollars. *Expenses:* Tuition, area resident: Full-time $4626 Canadian dollars; part-time $99.72 Canadian dollars per unit. International tuition: $8216 Canadian dollars full-time. Required fees: $3590 Canadian dollars; $99.72 Canadian dollars per unit. $215 Canadian dollars per term. *Financial support:* In 2009–10, 39 students received support, including 11 fellowships with full tuition reimbursements available (averaging $20,000 per year), 25 research assistantships with full tuition reimbursements available (averaging $17,000 per year), 3 teaching assistantships with full tuition reimbursements available (averaging $17,000 per year); scholarships/grants, traineeships, and unspecified assistantships also available. Financial award application deadline: 1/1. *Faculty research:* Cellular and reproductive immunology, microbial pathogenesis, mechanisms of antibiotic resistance, molecular biology of mammalian viruses, antiviral chemotherapy. Total annual research expenditures: $4.9 million. *Unit head:* Dr. David H. Evans, Chair, 780-492-2308, Fax: 780-492-7521. *Application contact:* Dr. Larry Guilbert, Graduate Director, 780-492-4910, Fax: 780-492-9828, E-mail: larry.guilbert@ualberta.ca.

University of Hawaii at Manoa, John A. Burns School of Medicine and Graduate Division, Graduate Programs in Biomedical Sciences, Department of Tropical Medicine, Medical Microbiology and Pharmacology, Honolulu, HI 96822. Offers tropical medicine (MS, PhD). Part-time programs available. *Faculty:* 19 full-time (7 women), 9 part-time/adjunct (5 women). *Students:*

18 full-time (10 women), 4 part-time (2 women); includes 7 minority (all Asian Americans or Pacific Islanders), 7 international. Average age 30. 25 applicants, 32% accepted, 7 enrolled. In 2009, 1 master's, 1 doctorate awarded. Terminal master's awarded for partial completion of doctoral program. *Degree requirements:* For master's, thesis optional; for doctorate, comprehensive exam, thesis/dissertation. *Entrance requirements:* For master's and doctorate, GRE General Test. Additional exam requirements/recommendations for international students: Required—TOEFL (minimum score 580 paper-based; 237 computer-based; 92 iBT), IELTS (minimum score 5). *Application deadline:* For fall admission, 1/15 for domestic and international students; for spring admission, 9/1 for domestic and international students. Application fee: $60. *Expenses:* Tuition, state resident: full-time $8900; part-time $372 per credit. Tuition, nonresident: full-time $21,400; part-time $898 per credit. Required fees: $207 per semester. *Financial support:* In 2009–10, 6 fellowships (averaging $792 per year), 13 research assistantships (averaging $20,160 per year), 2 teaching assistantships (averaging $16,191 per year) were awarded; tuition waivers (full) also available. *Faculty research:* Immunological studies of dengue, malaria, Kawasaki's disease, lupus erythematosus, rheumatoid disease. Total annual research expenditures: $2.4 million. *Application contact:* Sandra Chang, Graduate Chair, 808-692-1617, Fax: 808-692-1979, E-mail: sandrac@hawaii.edu.

University of Manitoba, Faculty of Medicine and Faculty of Graduate Studies, Graduate Programs in Medicine, Department of Medical Microbiology, Winnipeg, MB R3T 2N2, Canada. Offers M Sc, PhD. Part-time programs available. Terminal master's awarded for partial completion of doctoral program. *Degree requirements:* For master's, thesis; for doctorate, one foreign language, thesis/dissertation. *Entrance requirements:* For master's and doctorate, minimum GPA of 3.0. Electronic applications accepted. *Faculty research:* HIV, bacterial adhesion, sexually transmitted diseases, virus structure/function and assembly.

University of Minnesota, Duluth, Medical School, Microbiology, Immunology and Molecular Pathobiology Section, Duluth, MN 55812-2496. Offers MS, PhD. Terminal master's awarded for partial completion of doctoral program. *Degree requirements:* For master's, thesis, final oral exam; for doctorate, thesis/dissertation, final exam, oral and written preliminary exams. *Entrance requirements:* For master's and doctorate, GRE General Test. Additional exam requirements/recommendations for international students: Required—TOEFL. *Faculty research:* Immunomodulation, molecular diagnosis of rabies, cytokines, cancer immunology, cytomegalovirus infection.

University of Wisconsin–La Crosse, Office of University Graduate Studies, College of Science and Health, Department of Biology, Program in Clinical Microbiology, La Crosse, WI 54601-3742. Offers MS. *Students:* 7 full-time (5 women), 7 part-time (6 women); includes 1 minority (Asian American or Pacific Islander), 2 international. Average age 28. 15 applicants, 60% accepted, 3 enrolled. In 2009, 1 master's awarded. *Degree requirements:* For master's, thesis. *Entrance requirements:* For master's, GRE General Test, minimum GPA of 2.85. Additional exam requirements/recommendations for international students: Required—TOEFL (minimum score 550 paper-based; 213 computer-based; 79 iBT). *Application deadline:* For fall admission, 1/20 for domestic students. Applications are processed on a rolling basis. Application fee: $56. Electronic applications accepted. *Financial support:* Research assistantships with partial tuition reimbursements available. *Unit head:* Dr. Mike Hoffman, Head, 608-785-6984, E-mail: hoffman.mic2@uwlax.edu. *Application contact:* Kathryn Kiefer, Director of Admissions, 608-785-8939, E-mail: admissions@uwlax.edu.

University of Wisconsin–Madison, School of Medicine and Public Health and Graduate School, Graduate Programs in Medicine and College of Agricultural and Life Sciences, Microbiology Doctoral Training Program, Madison, WI 53706-1380. Offers PhD. *Faculty:* 92 full-time (27 women). *Students:* 88 full-time (50 women); includes 11 minority (2 African Americans, 2 Asian Americans or Pacific Islanders, 7 Hispanic Americans), 4 international. Average age 24. 212 applicants, 19% accepted, 20 enrolled. In 2009, 18 doctorates awarded. *Degree requirements:* For doctorate, thesis/dissertation, preliminary exam, 2 semesters of teaching. *Entrance requirements:* For doctorate, GRE. Additional exam requirements/recommendations for international students: Required—TOEFL (minimum score 580 paper-based; 237 computer-based). *Application deadline:* For fall admission, 12/1 for domestic and international students. Application fee: $56. Electronic applications accepted. *Expenses:* Tuition, state resident: part-time $594 per credit. Tuition, nonresident: part-time $1504 per credit. Required fees: $65 per credit. Tuition and fees vary according to course load, program and reciprocity agreements. *Financial support:* In 2009–10, 88 students received support, including 12 fellowships with tuition reimbursements available (averaging $23,500 per year), 76 research assistantships with tuition reimbursements available (averaging $23,500 per year); career-related internships or fieldwork, scholarships/grants, traineeships, health care benefits, and tuition waivers (full) also available. Financial award application deadline: 12/1. *Faculty research:* Microbial pathogenesis, gene regulation, immunology, virology, cell biology. Total annual research expenditures: $15.1 million. *Unit head:* Dr. Joseph Dillard, Director, 608-265-2837, Fax: 608-262-8418, E-mail: jpdillard@wisc.edu. *Application contact:* Cathy Davis Gray, Coordinator, 608-265-0689, Fax: 608-262-8418, E-mail: cdg@bact.wisc.edu.

Microbiology

Albany Medical College, Center for Immunology and Microbial Disease, Albany, NY 12208-3479. Offers MS, PhD. Part-time programs available. *Faculty:* 22 full-time (3 women), 11 part-time/adjunct (6 women). *Students:* 19 full-time (11 women). Average age 25. 20 applicants, 45% accepted, 6 enrolled. In 2009, 1 doctorate awarded. Terminal master's awarded for partial completion of doctoral program. *Degree requirements:* For master's, thesis; for doctorate, comprehensive exam, thesis/dissertation, oral qualifying exam, written preliminary exam, 1 published paper-peer review. *Entrance requirements:* For master's, GRE General Test, all transcripts, letters of recommendation; for doctorate, GRE General Test, letters of recommendation. Additional exam requirements/recommendations for international students: Required—TOEFL. *Application deadline:* For fall admission, 3/15 priority date for domestic and international students. Applications are processed on a rolling basis. Application fee: $0 ($60 for international students). *Expenses:* Tuition: Full-time $18,820. *Financial support:* In 2009–10, 10 research assistantships (averaging $24,000 per year) were awarded; Federal Work-Study, scholarships/grants, and tuition waivers (full) also available. Financial award applicants required to submit FAFSA. *Faculty research:* Microbial and viral pathogenesis, cancer development and cell transformation, biochemical and genetic mechanisms responsible for human disease. *Unit head:* Dr. Thomas D. Friedrich, Graduate Director, 518-262-6750, Fax: 518-262-6161, E-mail: dgs_cimd@mail.amc.edu. *Application contact:* Dr. Thomas D. Friedrich, Graduate Director, 518-262-6750, Fax: 518-262-6161, E-mail: dgs_cimd@mail.amc.edu.

Albert Einstein College of Medicine, Sue Golding Graduate Division of Medical Sciences, Department of Microbiology and Immunology, Bronx, NY 10461. Offers PhD, MD/PhD. *Degree requirements:* For doctorate, thesis/dissertation. *Entrance requirements:* For doctorate, GRE General Test. Additional exam requirements/recommendations for international students: Required—TOEFL. *Faculty research:* Nature of histocompatibility antigens, lymphoid cell receptors, regulation of immune responses and mechanisms of resistance to infection.

American University of Beirut, Graduate Programs, Faculty of Medicine, Beirut, Lebanon. Offers biochemistry (MS); human morphology (MS); medicine (MD); microbiology and immunology (MS); neuroscience (MS); pharmacology and therapeutics (MS); physiology (MS). Part-time programs available. *Degree requirements:* For master's, one foreign language, comprehensive exam, thesis (for some programs). *Entrance requirements:* For MD, MCAT, bachelor's degree; for master's, letter of recommendation. Additional exam requirements/recommendations for international students: Required—TOEFL (minimum score 600 paper-based; 250 computer-based; 100 iBT), IELTS (minimum score 7.5). *Faculty research:* Cancer research, stem cell research, genetic research, neuroscience research, bone research.

Arizona State University, Graduate College, College of Liberal Arts and Sciences, Division of Natural Sciences, School of Life Sciences, Tempe, AZ 85287. Offers biological design (PhD); biology (MNS, MS, PhD); biology and society (PhD); human and social dimensions of science and technology (PhD); microbiology (MNS, MS, PhD); molecular and cellular biology (MS, PhD); neuroscience (PhD); plant biology (MNS, MS, PhD). *Accreditation:* NAACLS. *Degree requirements:* For master's, thesis (MS); for doctorate, one foreign language, thesis/dissertation. *Entrance requirements:* For master's and doctorate, GRE.

Auburn University, Graduate School, College of Sciences and Mathematics, Department of Biological Sciences, Auburn University, AL 36849. Offers botany (MS, PhD); microbiology (MS, PhD); zoology (MS, PhD). *Faculty:* 33 full-time (8 women), 1 (woman) part-time/adjunct. *Students:* 42 full-time (17 women), 60 part-time (36 women); includes 9 minority (4 African Americans, 1 American Indian/Alaska Native, 3 Asian Americans or Pacific Islanders, 1 Hispanic American), 21 international. Average age 28. 134 applicants, 20% accepted, 18 enrolled. In 2009, 22 master's, 11 doctorates awarded. *Entrance requirements:* For master's and doctorate, GRE General Test. Additional exam requirements/recommendations for international students: Required—TOEFL. *Application deadline:* For fall admission, 7/7 for domestic students; for spring admission, 11/24 for domestic students. Application fee: $50 ($60 for international students). Electronic applications accepted. *Expenses:* Tuition, state resident: full-time $6240. Tuition, nonresident: full-time $18,720. International tuition: $18,938 full-time. Required fees: $492. Tuition and fees vary according to course load, program and reciprocity agreements. *Financial support:* Research assistantships, teaching assistantships available. Financial award applicants required to submit FAFSA. *Unit head:* Dr. James M. Barbaree, Chair, 334-844-1647, Fax: 334-844-1645. *Application contact:* Dr. George Flowers, Dean of the Graduate School, 334-844-2125.

Baylor College of Medicine, Graduate School of Biomedical Sciences, Department of Molecular Virology and Microbiology, Houston, TX 77030-3498. Offers PhD, MD/PhD. *Faculty:* 42 full-time (13 women). *Students:* 36 full-time (19 women); includes 12 minority (2 African Americans, 5 Asian Americans or Pacific Islanders, 5 Hispanic Americans), 9 international. Average age 26. In 2009, 3 doctorates awarded. *Degree requirements:* For doctorate, thesis/dissertation, public defense. *Entrance requirements:* For doctorate, GRE General Test, GRE Subject Test (strongly recommended), minimum GPA of 3.0. Additional exam requirements/recommendations for international students: Required—TOEFL. *Application deadline:* For fall admission, 1/1 priority date for domestic students. Applications are processed on a rolling basis. Application fee: $0. Electronic applications accepted. *Financial support:* Fellowships, research assistantships, teaching assistantships, career-related internships or fieldwork, Federal Work-Study, institutionally sponsored loans, health care benefits, and tuition waivers (full) available. Financial award applicants required to submit FAFSA. *Faculty research:* Molecular biology of virus replication, viruses and cancer, viral genetics, viral infectious diseases, environmental virology. *Unit head:* Dr. Frank Ramig, Director, 713-798-4830, Fax: 713-798-5075, E-mail: rramig@bcm.edu. *Application contact:* Rosa Banegas, Graduate Program Administrator, 713-798-4472, Fax: 713-798-5075, E-mail: rbanegas@bcm.edu.

Baylor College of Medicine, Graduate School of Biomedical Sciences, Interdepartmental Program in Cell and Molecular Biology, Houston, TX 77030-3498. Offers biochemistry (PhD); cell and molecular biology (PhD); genetics (PhD); human genetics (PhD); immunology (PhD); microbiology (PhD); virology (PhD); MD/PhD. *Faculty:* 100 full-time (31 women). *Students:* 59 full-time (37 women); includes 24 minority (5 African Americans, 1 American Indian/Alaska Native, 7 Asian Americans or Pacific Islanders, 11 Hispanic Americans), 6 international. Average age 25. In 2009, 9 doctorates awarded. *Degree requirements:* For doctorate, thesis/dissertation, public defense. *Entrance requirements:* For doctorate, GRE General Test, GRE Subject Test (strongly recommended), minimum GPA of 3.0. Additional exam requirements/recommendations for international students: Required—TOEFL. *Application deadline:* For fall admission, 1/1 priority date for domestic students. Applications are processed on a rolling basis. Application fee: $0. Electronic applications accepted. *Financial support:* In 2009–10, 59 students received support; fellowships, research assistantships, teaching assistantships, Federal Work-Study, institutionally sponsored loans, health care benefits, and tuition waivers (full) available. Financial award applicants required to submit FAFSA. *Faculty research:* Gene expression and regulation, developmental biology and genetics, signal transduction and membrane biology, aging process, molecular virology. *Unit head:* Dr. Susan Marriott, Director, 713-798-6557. *Application contact:* Lourdes Fernandez, Graduate Program Administrator, 713-798-6557, Fax: 713-798-6325, E-mail: cmbprog@bcm.edu.

See Close-Up on page 231.

Boston University, School of Medicine, Division of Graduate Medical Sciences, Department of Microbiology, Boston, MA 02118. Offers immunology (PhD); microbiology (MA); MD/PhD. Terminal master's awarded for partial completion of doctoral program. *Degree requirements:* For master's, thesis; for doctorate, comprehensive exam, thesis/dissertation. *Entrance requirements:* For master's and doctorate, GRE General Test, GRE Subject Test. Additional exam requirements/recommendations for international students: Required—TOEFL. *Application deadline:* For fall admission, 1/15 for domestic students; for spring admission, 10/15 for domestic students. Electronic applications accepted. *Expenses:* Tuition: Full-time $37,910; part-time $1184 per credit hour. Required fees: $386; $40 per semester. Part-time tuition and fees vary according to class time, course level, degree level and program. *Financial support:* Fellowships, research assistantships, Federal Work-Study, scholarships/grants, and traineeships available. *Faculty research:* Eukaryotic cell biology, tumor cell biology, nutrition and cancer, experimental tumor therapy, photobiology. *Unit head:* Dr. Ronald B. Corley, Chairman, 617-638-4284, Fax: 617-638-4286, E-mail: rbcorley@bu.edu. *Application contact:* Dr. Gregory Viglianti, Graduate Director, 617-638-7790, Fax: 617-638-4286, E-mail: gviglian@bu.edu.

Brandeis University, Graduate School of Arts and Sciences, Program in Molecular and Cell Biology, Waltham, MA 02454-9110. Offers genetics (PhD); microbiology (PhD); molecular and cell biology (MS, PhD); molecular biology (PhD); neurobiology (PhD). *Faculty:* 28 full-time (12 women), 1 (woman) part-time/adjunct. *Students:* 46 full-time (26 women), 1 part-time (0 women); includes 3 minority (2 African Americans, 1 Hispanic American), 7 international. Average age 27. 146 applicants, 21% accepted, 12 enrolled. In 2009, 4 master's, 6 doctorates awarded. Terminal master's awarded for partial completion of doctoral program. *Degree requirements:* For master's, thesis optional, research project; for doctorate, comprehensive exam, thesis/dissertation, teaching assistant experience. *Entrance requirements:* For master's and doctorate, GRE General Test, resume, 3 letters of recommendation. Additional exam requirements/recommendations for international students: Required—TOEFL (minimum score 600 paper-based; 250 computer-based; 100 iBT); Recommended—IELTS (minimum score 7). *Application deadline:* For fall admission, 1/15 priority date for domestic students. Applications are processed on a rolling basis. Application fee: $75. Electronic applications accepted.

Microbiology

Brandeis University (continued)

Financial support: In 2009–10, 41 students received support, including 13 fellowships with full tuition reimbursements available (averaging $27,500 per year), 27 research assistantships with full tuition reimbursements available (averaging $27,500 per year), 1 teaching assistantship with partial tuition reimbursement available (averaging $3,200 per year); scholarships/grants, traineeships, health care benefits, and tuition waivers (full and partial) also available. Financial award application deadline: 4/15; financial award applicants required to submit FAFSA. *Faculty research:* Regulation of gene expression by transcription factors, molecular neurobiology, immunology, molecular mechanisms of genetic recombination, cell differentiation. *Unit head:* Dr. Piali Sengupta, Chair, 781-736-2686, Fax: 781-736-3107, E-mail: piali@brandeis.edu. *Application contact:* Marcia Cabral, Department Administrator, 781-736-3100, Fax: 781-736-3107, E-mail: cabral@brandeis.edu.

Brigham Young University, Graduate Studies, College of Life Sciences, Department of Microbiology and Molecular Biology, Provo, UT 84602-1001. Offers microbiology (MS, PhD); molecular biology (MS, PhD). *Faculty:* 18 full-time (3 women). *Students:* 20 full-time (7 women); includes 1 minority (Asian American or Pacific Islander), 4 international. Average age 30. 13 applicants, 62% accepted, 7 enrolled. In 2009, 2 master's, 2 doctorates awarded. *Degree requirements:* For master's, comprehensive exam, thesis; for doctorate, comprehensive exam, thesis/dissertation. *Entrance requirements:* For master's, GRE General Test, minimum GPA of 3.0 during previous 2 years; for doctorate, GRE General Test, minimum GPA of 3.0. Additional exam requirements/recommendations for international students: Required—TOEFL (minimum score 580 paper-based; 85 iBT), IELTS (minimum score 7). *Application deadline:* For fall admission, 12/15 priority date for domestic and international students. Application fee: $50. Electronic applications accepted. *Expenses:* Tuition: Full-time $5580; part-time $301 per credit hour. Tuition and fees vary according to student's religious affiliation. *Financial support:* In 2009–10, 17 students received support, including 8 research assistantships with full and partial tuition reimbursements available (averaging $18,000 per year), 7 teaching assistantships with full and partial tuition reimbursements available (averaging $18,000 per year); institutionally sponsored loans, scholarships/grants, health care benefits, and unspecified assistantships also available. Financial award application deadline: 2/1. *Faculty research:* Immunobiology, molecular genetics, molecular virology, cancer biology, pathogenic and environmental microbiology. Total annual research expenditures: $501,070. *Unit head:* Dr. Brent L. Nielsen, Chair, 801-422-1102, Fax: 801-422-0519, E-mail: brent_nielsen@byu.edu. *Application contact:* Dr. Richard A. Robison, Graduate Coordinator, 801-422-2416, Fax: 801-422-0519, E-mail: richard_robison@byu.edu.

Brown University, Graduate School, Division of Biology and Medicine, Program in Molecular Biology, Cell Biology, and Biochemistry, Providence, RI 02912. Offers biochemistry (M Med Sc, Sc M, PhD), including biochemistry (Sc M, PhD), biology (Sc M, PhD), medical science (M Med Sc, PhD); biology (MA); cell biology (M Med Sc, Sc M, PhD), including biochemistry (Sc M, PhD), biology (Sc M, PhD), medical science (M Med Sc, PhD); developmental biology (M Med Sc, Sc M, PhD), including biochemistry (Sc M, PhD), biology (Sc M, PhD), medical science (M Med Sc, PhD); immunology (M Med Sc, Sc M, PhD), including biochemistry (Sc M, PhD), biology (Sc M, PhD), medical science (M Med Sc, PhD); molecular microbiology (M Med Sc, Sc M, PhD), including biochemistry (Sc M, PhD), biology (Sc M, PhD), medical science (M Med Sc, PhD); MD/PhD. Part-time programs available. Terminal master's awarded for partial completion of doctoral program. *Degree requirements:* For master's, thesis (for some programs); for doctorate, one foreign language, thesis/dissertation, preliminary exam. *Entrance requirements:* For master's and doctorate, GRE General Test, GRE Subject Test. Additional exam requirements/recommendations for international students: Required—TOEFL. Electronic applications accepted. *Faculty research:* Molecular genetics, gene regulation.

California State University, Long Beach, Graduate Studies, College of Natural Sciences and Mathematics, Department of Biological Sciences, Long Beach, CA 90840. Offers biology (MS); microbiology (MS). Part-time programs available. *Faculty:* 38 full-time (14 women), 1 part-time/adjunct (0 women). *Students:* 11 full-time (9 women), 58 part-time (32 women); includes 25 minority (1 African American, 14 Asian Americans or Pacific Islanders, 10 Hispanic Americans), 7 international. Average age 28. 70 applicants, 39% accepted, 16 enrolled. *Entrance requirements:* For master's, GRE Subject Test, minimum GPA of 3.0. *Application deadline:* For fall admission, 3/15 for domestic students. Applications are processed on a rolling basis. Application fee: $55. Electronic applications accepted. *Expenses:* Required fees: $1802 per semester. Part-time tuition and fees vary according to course load. *Financial support:* Teaching assistantships, Federal Work-Study, institutionally sponsored loans, scholarships/grants, traineeships, and unspecified assistantships available. Financial award application deadline: 3/2. *Unit head:* Dr. Brian Livingston, Chair, 562-985-4807, Fax: 562-985-8878, E-mail: blivings@csulb.edu. *Application contact:* Dr. Christopher Lowe, Graduate Advisor, 562-985-4918, Fax: 562-985-8878, E-mail: clowe@csulb.edu.

Case Western Reserve University, School of Medicine and School of Graduate Studies, Graduate Programs in Medicine, Department of Molecular Biology and Microbiology, Cleveland, OH 44106-4960. Offers cellular biology (PhD); microbiology (PhD); molecular biology (PhD); molecular virology (PhD); MD/PhD. Students are admitted to an integrated Biomedical Sciences Training Program involving 11 basic science programs at Case Western Reserve University. *Degree requirements:* For doctorate, thesis/dissertation. *Entrance requirements:* For doctorate, GRE General Test, GRE Subject Test. Additional exam requirements/recommendations for international students: Required—TOEFL. Electronic applications accepted. *Faculty research:* Gene expression in eukaryotic and prokaryotic systems; microbial physiology; intracellular transport and signaling; mechanisms of oncogenesis; molecular mechanisms of RNA processing, editing, and catalysis.

The Catholic University of America, School of Arts and Sciences, Department of Biology, Washington, DC 20064. Offers cell and microbial biology (MS, PhD), including cell biology, microbiology; clinical laboratory science (MS, PhD); MSLS/MS. Part-time programs available. *Faculty:* 7 full-time (4 women), 2 part-time/adjunct (both women). *Students:* 3 full-time (2 women), 23 part-time (15 women); includes 8 minority (2 African Americans, 3 Asian Americans or Pacific Islanders, 3 Hispanic Americans), 8 international. Average age 29. 30 applicants, 47% accepted, 3 enrolled. In 2009, 3 doctorates awarded. *Degree requirements:* For master's, comprehensive exam, thesis or alternative; for doctorate, comprehensive exam, thesis/dissertation. *Entrance requirements:* For master's and doctorate, GRE General Test, GRE Subject Test, statement of purpose, official copies of academic transcripts, three letters of recommendation. Additional exam requirements/recommendations for international students: Required—TOEFL (minimum score 580 paper-based; 237 computer-based). *Application deadline:* For fall admission, 8/1 priority date for domestic students, 7/15 for international students; for spring admission, 12/1 priority date for domestic students, 10/15 for international students. Applications are processed on a rolling basis. Application fee: $55. Electronic applications accepted. *Expenses:* Tuition: Full-time $31,740; part-time $1245 per credit hour. One-time fee: $425 full-time. *Financial support:* Fellowships, research assistantships, teaching assistantships, Federal Work-Study, scholarships/grants, tuition waivers (full and partial), and unspecified assistantships available. Financial award application deadline: 2/1; financial award applicants required to submit FAFSA. *Faculty research:* Cell and microbiology, microbial pathogenesis, molecular biology of cell proliferation, cellular effects of electromagnetic radiation, biotechnology. Total annual research expenditures: $853,913. *Unit head:* Dr. Venigalla Rao, Chair, 202-319-5271, Fax: 202-319-5721, E-mail: rao@cua.edu. *Application contact:* Julie Schwing, Director of Graduate Admissions, 202-319-5057, Fax: 202-319-6533, E-mail: cua-admissions@cua.edu.

Clemson University, Graduate School, College of Agriculture, Forestry and Life Sciences, Department of Biological Sciences, Program in Microbiology, Clemson, SC 29634. Offers MS, PhD. *Students:* 28 full-time (19 women), 4 part-time (3 women); includes 1 minority (African American), 13 international. Average age 28. 32 applicants, 16% accepted, 3 enrolled. In 2009, 2 master's, 2 doctorates awarded. *Degree requirements:* For master's, thesis; for doctorate, thesis/dissertation. *Entrance requirements:* For master's and doctorate, GRE General Test. Additional exam requirements/recommendations for international students: Required—TOEFL, IELTS. *Application deadline:* For fall admission, 1/15 for domestic students, 4/15 for international students. Applications are processed on a rolling basis. Application fee: $70 ($80 for international students). Electronic applications accepted. *Expenses:* Contact institution. *Financial support:* In 2009–10, 27 students received support, including 2 fellowships with full and partial tuition reimbursements available (averaging $12,000 per year), 9 research assistantships with partial tuition reimbursements available (averaging $17,432 per year), 19 teaching assistantships with partial tuition reimbursements available (averaging $17,474 per year); career-related internships or fieldwork, institutionally sponsored loans, scholarships/grants, health care benefits, and unspecified assistantships also available. Support available to part-time students. Financial award application deadline: 3/1; financial award applicants required to submit FAFSA. *Faculty research:* Anaerobic microbiology, microbiology and ecology of soil and aquatic systems, genetic engineering, monoclonal antibodies and immunomodulation. *Unit head:* Dr. Alfred Wheeler, Department Chair, 864-656-1415, Fax: 864-656-0435, E-mail: wheeler@clemson.edu. *Application contact:* Jay Lyn Martin, Coordinator for Graduate Program, 864-656-3587, Fax: 864-656-0435, E-mail: gradbio@clemson.edu.

Colorado State University, College of Veterinary Medicine and Biomedical Sciences, Department of Microbiology, Immunology and Pathology, Fort Collins, CO 80523-1619. Offers microbiology (MS, PhD); pathology (PhD). *Faculty:* 43 full-time (18 women), 2 part-time/adjunct (1 woman). *Students:* 51 full-time (43 women), 40 part-time (22 women); includes 8 minority (4 Asian Americans or Pacific Islanders, 4 Hispanic Americans), 9 international. Average age 31. 87 applicants, 14% accepted, 12 enrolled. In 2009, 8 master's, 15 doctorates awarded. *Degree requirements:* For master's, thesis; for doctorate, comprehensive exam, thesis/dissertation. *Entrance requirements:* For master's, GRE General Test, minimum GPA of 3.0, BA/BS in biomedical field, reviewer evaluation forms, resume; for doctorate, GRE General Test, minimum GPA of 3.0, BA/BS in biomedical field, reviewer evaluation forms, resume, statement of interest. Additional exam requirements/recommendations for international students: Required—TOEFL (minimum score 550 paper-based). *Application deadline:* For fall admission, 1/1 priority date for domestic students; for spring admission, 10/1 priority date for domestic students. Applications are processed on a rolling basis. Application fee: $50. Electronic applications accepted. *Expenses:* Tuition, state resident: full-time $6434; part-time $359.10 per credit. Tuition, nonresident: full-time $18,116; part-time $1006.45 per credit. Required fees: $1496; $83 per credit. *Financial support:* In 2009–10, 85 students received support, including 34 fellowships with tuition reimbursements available (averaging $29,724 per year), 45 research assistantships with tuition reimbursements available (averaging $21,337 per year), 6 teaching assistantships with tuition reimbursements available (averaging $12,607 per year); Federal Work-Study, scholarships/grants, traineeships, and unspecified assistantships also available. Financial award applicants required to submit FAFSA. *Faculty research:* Medical and veterinary microbiology, pathology of disease, microbial pathogenesis, industrial and environmental microbiology, vector-borne disease. Total annual research expenditures: $32.6 million. *Unit head:* Dr. Edward A. Hoover, Head, 970-491-7587, Fax: 970-491-0603, E-mail: edward.hoover@colostate.edu. *Application contact:* Marcia Boggs, Graduate Program Coordinator, 970-491-3228, Fax: 970-491-1815, E-mail: marcia.boggs@colostate.edu.

Columbia University, College of Physicians and Surgeons, Department of Microbiology, New York, NY 10032. Offers biomedical sciences (M Phil, MA, PhD); MD/PhD. Only candidates for the PhD are admitted. Terminal master's awarded for partial completion of doctoral program. *Degree requirements:* For doctorate, thesis/dissertation. *Entrance requirements:* For master's, GRE General Test; for doctorate, GRE. Additional exam requirements/recommendations for international students: Required—TOEFL. *Faculty research:* Prokaryotic molecular biology, immunology, virology, yeast molecular genetics, regulation of gene expression.

Cornell University, Graduate School, Graduate Fields of Agriculture and Life Sciences, Field of Microbiology, Ithaca, NY 14853-0001. Offers PhD. *Faculty:* 43 full-time (12 women). *Students:* 38 full-time (20 women); includes 2 minority (1 Asian American or Pacific Islander, 1 Hispanic American), 13 international. Average age 27. 60 applicants, 20% accepted, 6 enrolled. In 2009, 11 doctorates awarded. *Degree requirements:* For doctorate, comprehensive exam, thesis/dissertation, 2 semesters of teaching experience. *Entrance requirements:* For doctorate, GRE General Test, 3 letters of recommendation. Additional exam requirements/recommendations for international students: Required—TOEFL (minimum score 550 paper-based; 213 computer-based; 77 iBT). *Application deadline:* For fall admission, 1/15 for domestic students. Application fee: $70. Electronic applications accepted. *Expenses:* Tuition: Full-time $29,500. Required fees: $70. Full-time tuition and fees vary according to degree level, program and student level. *Financial support:* In 2009–10, 1 fellowship with full tuition reimbursement, 1 research assistantship with full tuition reimbursement, 3 teaching assistantships with full tuition reimbursements were awarded; institutionally sponsored loans, scholarships/grants, health care benefits, tuition waivers (full and partial), and unspecified assistantships also available. Financial award applicants required to submit FAFSA. *Faculty research:* Microbial diversity, molecular biology, biotechnology, microbial ecology, phytobacteriology. *Unit head:* Director of Graduate Studies, 607-255-3088. *Application contact:* Graduate Field Assistant, 607-255-3088, E-mail: microfield@cornell.edu.

Dalhousie University, Faculty of Medicine, Department of Microbiology and Immunology, Halifax, NS B3H 1X5, Canada. Offers M Sc, PhD. *Degree requirements:* For master's, thesis; for doctorate, comprehensive exam, thesis/dissertation. *Entrance requirements:* For master's, GRE General Test, honors B Sc; for doctorate, GRE General Test, honors B Sc in microbiology, M Sc in discipline or transfer after 1 year in master's program. Additional exam requirements/recommendations for international students: Required—TOEFL, IELTS, 1 of the following 5 approved tests: TOEFL, IELTS, CAEL, CANTEST, Michigan English Language Assessment Battery. Electronic applications accepted. *Faculty research:* Virology, molecular genetics, pathogenesis, bacteriology, immunology.

Dartmouth College, Graduate Program in Molecular and Cellular Biology, Department of Microbiology and Immunology, Program in Immunology, Hanover, NH 03755. Offers MD/PhD. *Faculty research:* Tumor immunotherapy, cell and molecular biology of connective tissue degradation in rheumatoid arthritis and cancer, immunology and immunotherapy of tumors of the central nervous system, transcriptional regulation of hematopoiesis and leukemia, bacterial pathogenesis.

Dartmouth College, Graduate Program in Molecular and Cellular Biology, Department of Microbiology and Immunology, Program in Molecular Pathogenesis, Hanover, NH 03755. Offers microbiology and immunology (PhD).

Drexel University, College of Medicine, Biomedical Graduate Programs, Program in Microbiology and Immunology, Philadelphia, PA 19104-2875. Offers MS, PhD, MD/PhD. Terminal master's awarded for partial completion of doctoral program. *Degree requirements:* For master's, comprehensive exam, thesis; for doctorate, thesis/dissertation, qualifying exam. *Entrance requirements:* For master's, GRE General Test, minimum GPA of 2.75; for doctorate, GRE General Test, minimum GPA of 3.0. Additional exam requirements/recommendations for international students: Required—TOEFL. Electronic applications accepted. *Faculty research:* Immunology of malarial parasites, virology, bacteriology, molecular biology, parasitology.

Duke University, Graduate School, Department of Molecular Genetics and Microbiology, Durham, NC 27710. Offers PhD. *Faculty:* 25 full-time. *Students:* 39 full-time (24 women); includes 6 minority (4 African Americans, 2 Asian Americans or Pacific Islanders), 11 international. Average age 22. 69 applicants, 26% accepted, 9 enrolled. In 2009, 4 doctorates awarded. *Degree requirements:* For doctorate, thesis/dissertation. *Entrance requirements:* For doctorate, GRE General Test, GRE Subject Test (recommended). Additional exam requirements/recommendations for international students: Required—TOEFL (minimum score 550 paper-based; 213 computer-based; 83 iBT), IELTS (minimum score 7). *Application deadline:* For fall admission, 12/8 priority date for domestic and international students. Application fee: $75. Electronic applications accepted. *Financial support:* In 2009–10, fellowships with full tuition reimbursements (averaging $19,350 per year), research assistantships with full tuition reimbursements (averaging $19,350 per year) were awarded; Federal Work-Study also available. Financial award application deadline: 12/31. *Unit head:* Dr. Raphael Valdivia, Director of Graduate Studies, 919-684-3290, Fax: 919-684-6629, E-mail: andrea.lanahan@duke.edu. *Application contact:* Cynthia Robertson, Associate Dean for Enrollment Services, 919-684-3913, E-mail: grad-admissions@duke.edu.

East Carolina University, Brody School of Medicine, Department of Microbiology and Immunology, Greenville, NC 27858-4353. Offers PhD. *Degree requirements:* For doctorate, comprehensive exam, thesis/dissertation. *Entrance requirements:* For doctorate, GRE General Test. Additional exam requirements/recommendations for international students: Required—TOEFL. *Faculty research:* Molecular virology, genetics of bacteria, yeast and somatic cells, bacterial physiology and metabolism, bioterrorism.

East Tennessee State University, James H. Quillen College of Medicine, Biomedical Science Graduate Program, Johnson City, TN 37614. Offers anatomy (MS, PhD); biochemistry (MS, PhD); biophysics (MS, PhD); microbiology (MS, PhD); pharmacology (MS, PhD); physiology (MS, PhD). Part-time programs available. Terminal master's awarded for partial completion of doctoral program. *Degree requirements:* For master's, one foreign language, thesis, comprehensive qualifying exam; for doctorate, 2 foreign languages, thesis/dissertation. *Entrance requirements:* For master's, GRE General Test, minimum GPA of 3.0, bachelor's degree in biological or related science; for doctorate, GRE General Test, GRE Subject Test. Additional exam requirements/recommendations for international students: Required—TOEFL (minimum score 550 paper-based; 213 computer-based). *Expenses:* Contact institution.

East Tennessee State University, School of Graduate Studies, College of Arts and Sciences, Department of Biological Sciences, Johnson City, TN 37614. Offers biology (MS); microbiology (MS). *Degree requirements:* For master's, comprehensive exam, thesis or alternative. *Entrance requirements:* For master's, GRE General Test or GRE Subject Test, minimum GPA of 3.0. Additional exam requirements/recommendations for international students: Required—TOEFL (minimum score 550 paper-based; 213 computer-based). *Faculty research:* Vertebrate natural history, mutation rates in fruit flies, regulation of plant secondary metabolism, plant biochemistry, timekeeping in honeybees, gene expression in diapausing flies.

Emory University, Graduate School of Arts and Sciences, Division of Biological and Biomedical Sciences, Program in Microbiology and Molecular Genetics, Atlanta, GA 30322-1100. Offers PhD. *Faculty:* 33 full-time (7 women). *Students:* 43 full-time (28 women); includes 7 minority (3 African Americans, 1 Asian American or Pacific Islander, 3 Hispanic Americans), 6 international. Average age 27. 78 applicants, 18% accepted, 5 enrolled. In 2009, 4 doctorates awarded. *Degree requirements:* For doctorate, comprehensive exam, thesis/dissertation. *Entrance requirements:* For doctorate, GRE General Test, minimum GPA of 3.0 in science course work (recommended). Additional exam requirements/recommendations for international students: Required—TOEFL. *Application deadline:* For fall admission, 1/3 for domestic and international students. Application fee: $50. Electronic applications accepted. *Financial support:* In 2009–10, 17 students received support, including 17 fellowships with full tuition reimbursements available (averaging $24,500 per year); institutionally sponsored loans, scholarships/grants, and health care benefits also available. *Faculty research:* Bacterial genetics and physiology, microbial development, molecular biology of viruses and bacterial pathogens, DNA recombination. *Unit head:* Dr. Phil Rather, Director, 404-728-5079, Fax: 404-728-7780, E-mail: prather@emory.edu. *Application contact:* Dr. Martin Moore, Recruiter, 404-727-8943, Fax: 404-727-3322, E-mail: martin.moore@emory.edu.

Emporia State University, School of Graduate Studies, College of Liberal Arts and Sciences, Department of Biological Sciences, Emporia, KS 66801-5087. Offers botany (MS); environmental biology (MS); general biology (MS); microbial and cellular biology (MS); zoology (MS). Part-time programs available. *Faculty:* 13 full-time (3 women). *Students:* 9 full-time (7 women), 17 part-time (11 women); includes 1 minority (African American), 8 international. 22 applicants, 95% accepted, 18 enrolled. In 2009, 24 master's awarded. *Degree requirements:* For master's, comprehensive exam or thesis. *Entrance requirements:* For master's, GRE, appropriate undergraduate degree, interview, letters of reference. Additional exam requirements/recommendations for international students: Required—TOEFL (minimum score 520 paper-based; 133 computer-based; 68 iBT). *Application deadline:* For fall admission, 8/15 priority date for domestic students. Applications are processed on a rolling basis. Application fee: $30 ($75 for international students). Electronic applications accepted. *Expenses:* Tuition, state resident: full-time $4154; part-time $173 per credit hour. Tuition, nonresident: full-time $12,864; part-time $536 per credit hour. Required fees: $948; $58 per credit hour. Tuition and fees vary according to campus/location. *Financial support:* In 2009–10, 7 research assistantships with full tuition reimbursements (averaging $6,876 per year), 10 teaching assistantships with full tuition reimbursements (averaging $7,419 per year) were awarded; career-related internships or fieldwork, Federal Work-Study, institutionally sponsored loans, health care benefits, and unspecified assistantships also available. Financial award application deadline: 3/15; financial award applicants required to submit FAFSA. *Faculty research:* Fisheries, range, and wildlife management; aquatic, plant, grassland, vertebrate, and invertebrate ecology; mammalian and plant systematics, taxonomy, and evolution; immunology, virology, and molecular biology. *Unit head:* Dr. R. Brent Thomas, Interim Chair, 620-341-5311, Fax: 620-341-5608, E-mail: rthomas2@emporia.edu. *Application contact:* Dr. Scott Crupper, Graduate Coordinator, 620-341-5621, Fax: 620-341-5607, E-mail: scrupper@emporia.edu.

George Mason University, College of Science, Fairfax, VA 22030. Offers biodefense (MS, PhD); bioinformatics and computational biology (MS, PhD, Certificate); biology (MS, PhD), including bioinformatics (MS), ecology, systematics and evolution (MS), interpretive biology (MS), molecular and cellular biology (MS), molecular and microbiology (PhD), organismal biology (MS); chemistry and biochemistry (MS), including chemistry; climate dynamics (PhD); computational and data sciences (MS, PhD, Certificate); computational social science (PhD); computational techniques and applications (Certificate); earth systems and geoinformation sciences (MS, PhD, Certificate); environmental science and policy (MS, PhD); geography (MS), including geographic and cartographic sciences; mathematical sciences (MS, PhD), including mathematics; nanotechnology and nanoscience (Certificate); neuroscience (PhD); physical sciences (PhD); physics and astronomy (MS), including applied and engineering physics; remote sensing and earth image processing (Certificate). Part-time and evening/weekend programs available. *Degree requirements:* For doctorate, comprehensive exam, thesis/dissertation. *Entrance requirements:* For master's and doctorate, GRE General Test, minimum GPA of 3.0 in last 60 hours. Additional exam requirements/recommendations for international students: Required—TOEFL. Electronic applications accepted. *Expenses:* Tuition, state resident: full-time $7568; part-time $315.33 per credit hour. Tuition, nonresident: full-time $21,704; part-time $904.33 per credit hour. Required fees: $2184; $91 per credit hour. *Faculty research:* Space sciences and astrophysics, fluid dynamics, materials modeling and simulation, bioinformatics, global changes and statistics.

Georgetown University, Graduate School of Arts and Sciences, Programs in Biomedical Sciences, Department of Microbiology and Immunology, Washington, DC 20057. Offers biohazardous threat agents and emerging infectious diseases (MS); general microbiology and immunology (MS); global infectious diseases (PhD); microbiology and immunology research (PhD); science policy and advocacy (MS). Part-time programs available. *Degree requirements:* For master's, 30 credit hours of coursework; for doctorate, comprehensive exam, thesis/dissertation. *Entrance requirements:* For master's, GRE General Test, 3 letters of reference, bachelor's degree in related field; for doctorate, GRE General Test, 3 letters of reference, MS/BS in related field. Additional exam requirements/recommendations for international students: Required—TOEFL (minimum score 505 paper-based; 213 computer-based). Electronic applications accepted. *Faculty research:* Pathogenesis and basic biology of the fungus Candida albicans, molecular biology of viral immunopathological mechanisms in Multiple Sclerosis.

The George Washington University, Columbian College of Arts and Sciences, Institute for Biomedical Sciences, Program in Microbiology and Immunology, Washington, DC 20052. Offers PhD. *Students:* 3 full-time (1 woman), 13 part-time (9 women); includes 3 minority (1 American Indian/Alaska Native, 1 Asian American or Pacific Islander, 1 Hispanic American), 4 international. Average age 31. *Degree requirements:* For doctorate, thesis/dissertation. *Entrance requirements:* For doctorate, GRE General Test, minimum GPA of 3.0. Additional exam requirements/recommendations for international students: Required—TOEFL (minimum score 600 paper-based; 250 computer-based). *Application deadline:* For fall admission, 1/2 priority date for domestic and international students. Applications are processed on a rolling basis. Application fee: $60. Electronic applications accepted. *Financial support:* In 2009–10, 10 students received support; fellowships with tuition reimbursements available, tuition waivers available. *Unit head:* Dr. David Leitenberg, Director, 202-994-9475, Fax: 202-994-2913, E-mail: dleit@gwu.edu. *Application contact:* Information Contact, 202-994-3532, Fax: 202-994-2913, E-mail: mtmjxl@gwumc.edu.

The George Washington University, School of Medicine and Health Sciences, Health Sciences Programs, Washington, DC 20052. Offers adult nurse practitioner (MSN, Post Master's Certificate); clinical practice management (MSHS); clinical research administration (MSHS); clinical research administration for nurses (MSN); emergency services management (MSHS); end-of-life care (MSHS, MSN); family nurse practitioner (MSN, Post Master's Certificate); immunohematology (MSHS); nursing (DNP); nursing leadership and management (MSN); physical therapy (DPT); physician assistant (MSHS); MSHS/MPH. Postbaccalaureate distance learning degree programs offered (no on-campus study). *Students:* 270 full-time (220 women), 491 part-time (406 women); includes 176 minority (83 African Americans, 5 American Indian/Alaska Native, 62 Asian Americans or Pacific Islanders, 26 Hispanic Americans), 26 international. Average age 35. 1,059 applicants, 47% accepted, 292 enrolled. In 2009, 155 master's, 22 doctorates, 75 other advanced degrees awarded. *Entrance requirements:* Additional exam requirements/recommendations for international students: Required—TOEFL (minimum score 550 paper-based; 213 computer-based). *Application deadline:* Applications are processed on a rolling basis. Application fee: $60. *Expenses:* Contact institution. *Unit head:* Jean E. Johnson, Senior Associate Dean, 202-994-3725, E-mail: jejohns@gwu.edu. *Application contact:* Joke Ogundiran, Director of Admission, 202-994-1668, Fax: 202-994-0870, E-mail: jokeogun@gwu.edu.

The George Washington University, School of Public Health and Health Services, Department of Epidemiology and Biostatistics, Washington, DC 20052. Offers biostatistics (MPH); epidemiology (MPH); microbiology and emerging infectious diseases (MSPH). *Faculty:* 16 full-time (7 women), 14 part-time/adjunct (8 women). *Students:* 52 full-time (40 women), 53 part-time (37 women); includes 44 minority (14 African Americans, 25 Asian Americans or Pacific Islanders, 5 Hispanic Americans), 5 international. Average age 28. 165 applicants, 85% accepted, 37 enrolled. In 2009, 28 master's awarded. *Degree requirements:* For master's, case study or special project. *Entrance requirements:* For master's, GMAT, GRE General Test, or MCAT. Additional exam requirements/recommendations for international students: Required—TOEFL. *Application deadline:* For fall admission, 4/15 priority date for domestic students, 4/15 for international students; for spring admission, 11/1 for domestic and international students. Applications are processed on a rolling basis. Application fee: $60. *Financial support:* In 2009–10, 6 students received support. Tuition waivers available. Financial award application deadline: 2/15. *Unit head:* Dr. Alan E. Greenberg, Chair, 202-994-0612, E-mail: aeg1@gwu.edu. *Application contact:* Jane Smith, Director of Admissions, 202-994-0248, Fax: 202-994-1860, E-mail: sphhsinfo@gwumc.edu.

Georgia State University, College of Arts and Sciences, Department of Biology, Program in Applied and Environmental Microbiology, Atlanta, GA 30302-3083. Offers MS, PhD. Part-time programs available. Terminal master's awarded for partial completion of doctoral program. *Degree requirements:* For master's, thesis or alternative; for doctorate, thesis/dissertation, exam. *Entrance requirements:* For master's and doctorate, GRE General Test. Additional exam requirements/recommendations for international students: Required—TOEFL. Electronic applications accepted.

Harvard University, Graduate School of Arts and Sciences, Division of Medical Sciences, Boston, MA 02115. Offers biological chemistry and molecular pharmacology (PhD); cell biology (PhD); genetics (PhD); microbiology and molecular genetics (PhD); pathology (PhD), including experimental pathology. *Degree requirements:* For doctorate, thesis/dissertation. *Entrance requirements:* For doctorate, GRE General Test, GRE Subject Test. Additional exam requirements/recommendations for international students: Required—TOEFL. *Expenses:* Tuition: Full-time $33,696. Required fees: $1126. Full-time tuition and fees vary according to program.

Hood College, Graduate School, Program in Biomedical Science, Frederick, MD 21701-8575. Offers biomedical science (MS), including biotechnology/molecular biology, microbiology/immunology/virology, regulatory compliance; regulatory compliance (Certificate). Part-time and evening/weekend programs available. *Faculty:* 3 full-time (1 woman), 4 part-time/adjunct (2 women). *Students:* 9 full-time (2 women), 82 part-time (54 women); includes 23 minority (17 African Americans, 2 Asian Americans or Pacific Islanders, 4 Hispanic Americans), 7 international. Average age 29. 51 applicants, 67% accepted, 28 enrolled. In 2009, 11 master's, 10 other advanced degrees awarded. *Degree requirements:* For master's, comprehensive exam, thesis or alternative. *Entrance requirements:* For master's, bachelor's degree in biology; minimum GPA of 2.75; undergraduate course work in cell biology, chemistry, organic chemistry, and genetics. Additional exam requirements/recommendations for international students: Required—TOEFL (minimum score 575 paper-based; 231 computer-based; 89 iBT). *Application deadline:* For fall admission, 7/15 for domestic and international students; for spring admission, 12/15 for domestic and international students. Applications are processed on a rolling basis. Application fee: $35. Electronic applications accepted. *Expenses:* Tuition: Full-time $6480; part-time $360 per credit. Required fees: $100; $50 per term. *Financial support:* In 2009–10, 3 research assistantships with full tuition reimbursements (averaging $10,609 per year) were awarded. Financial award applicants required to submit FAFSA. *Unit head:* Dr. Oney Smith, Director, 301-696-3653, Fax: 301-696-3597, E-mail: osmith@hood.edu. *Application contact:* Dr. Allen P. Flora, Dean of Graduate School, 301-696-3811, Fax: 301-696-3597, E-mail: gofurther@hood.edu.

Howard University, College of Medicine, Department of Microbiology, Washington, DC 20059-0002. Offers PhD. *Degree requirements:* For doctorate, one foreign language, comprehensive exam, thesis/dissertation, qualifying exam, teaching experience. *Entrance requirements:* For doctorate, GRE General Test, minimum GPA of 3.0 in sciences. Additional exam requirements/recommendations for international students: Required—TOEFL. *Faculty research:* Immunology, molecular and cellular microbiology, microbial genetics, microbial physiology, pathogenic bacteriology, medical mycology, medical parasitology, virology.

Idaho State University, Office of Graduate Studies, College of Arts and Sciences, Department of Biological Sciences, Pocatello, ID 83209-8007. Offers biology (MNS, MS, DA, PhD); clinical laboratory science (MS); microbiology (MS). *Accreditation:* NAACLS. Part-time programs available. *Faculty:* 25 full-time (4 women). *Students:* 65 full-time (28 women), 24 part-time (8 women); includes 3 minority (1 American Indian/Alaska Native, 2 Hispanic Americans), 12 international. Average age 31. In 2009, 17 master's, 6 doctorates awarded. *Degree requirements:* For master's, comprehensive exam, thesis; for doctorate, comprehensive exam, thesis/dissertation, 9 credits of internship (for DA). *Entrance requirements:* For master's, GRE General Test, minimum GPA of 3.0 in all upper division classes; for doctorate, GRE General Test, GRE Subject Test (biology), diagnostic exam (DA), minimum GPA of 3.0 in all upper division classes. Additional exam requirements/recommendations for international students: Required—TOEFL (minimum score 550 paper-based; 213 computer-based; 80 iBT). *Application deadline:* For fall admission, 7/1 for domestic students, 6/1 for international students; for spring admission, 12/1 for domestic students, 11/1 for international students. Applications are processed on a rolling basis. Application fee: $55. Electronic applications accepted. *Expenses:* Tuition, state resident: full-time $3318; part-time $297 per credit hour. Tuition, nonresident: full-time $13,120; part-time $437 per credit hour. Required fees: $2530. Tuition and fees vary according to program. *Financial support:* In 2009–10, fellowships with full and partial tuition reimburse-

Microbiology

Idaho State University (continued)
ments (averaging $12,282 per year), 23 research assistantships with full and partial tuition reimbursements (averaging $12,503 per year), 27 teaching assistantships with full and partial tuition reimbursements (averaging $10,841 per year) were awarded; Federal Work-Study, institutionally sponsored loans, scholarships/grants, health care benefits, tuition waivers (full and partial), and unspecified assistantships also available. Support available to part-time students. Financial award application deadline: 1/1; financial award applicants required to submit FAFSA. *Faculty research:* Ecology, plant and animal physiology, plant and animal developmental biology, immunology, molecular biology, bioinfomatics. *Unit head:* Dr. Terry Bowyer, Chair, 208-282-3765, Fax: 208-282-4570, E-mail: bowyterr@isu.edu. *Application contact:* Tami Carson, Graduate School Technical Records Specialist, 208-282-2150, Fax: 208-282-4847, E-mail: carstami@isu.edu.

Illinois State University, Graduate School, College of Arts and Sciences, Department of Biological Sciences, Normal, IL 61790-2200. Offers animal behavior (MS); bacteriology (MS); biochemistry (MS); biological sciences (MS); biology (PhD); biophysics (MS); biotechnology (MS); botany (MS, PhD); cell biology (MS); conservation biology (MS); developmental biology (MS); ecology (MS, PhD); entomology (MS); evolutionary biology (MS); genetics (MS, PhD); immunology (MS); microbiology (MS, PhD); molecular biology (MS); molecular genetics (MS); neurobiology (MS); neuroscience (MS); parasitology (MS); physiology (MS, PhD); plant biology (MS); plant molecular biology (MS); plant sciences (MS); structural biology (MS); zoology (MS, PhD). Part-time programs available. *Degree requirements:* For master's, thesis or alternative; for doctorate, variable foreign language requirement, thesis/dissertation, 2 terms of residency. *Entrance requirements:* For master's, GRE General Test, minimum GPA of 2.6 in last 60 hours of course work; for doctorate, GRE General Test. *Faculty research:* Redoc balance and drug development in schistosoma mansoni, control of the growth of listeria monocytogenes at low temperature, regulation of cell expansion and microtubule function by SPRI, CRUI: physiology and fitness consequences of different life history phenotypes.

Indiana State University, School of Graduate Studies, College of Arts and Sciences, Department of Biology, Terre Haute, IN 47809. Offers ecology (PhD); life sciences (MS); microbiology (PhD); physiology (PhD); science education (MS). *Degree requirements:* For master's, thesis (for some programs); for doctorate, comprehensive exam, thesis/dissertation. *Entrance requirements:* For master's and doctorate, GRE General Test. Electronic applications accepted.

Indiana University Bloomington, University Graduate School, College of Arts and Sciences, Department of Biology, Bloomington, IN 47405. Offers biology teaching (MAT); biotechnology (MA); evolution, ecology, and behavior (MA, PhD); genetics (PhD); microbiology (MA, PhD); molecular, cellular, and developmental biology (PhD); plant sciences (MA, PhD); zoology (MA, PhD). *Faculty:* 58 full-time (15 women), 21 part-time/adjunct (6 women). *Students:* 165 full-time (95 women); includes 14 minority (6 African Americans, 1 American Indian/Alaska Native, 7 Asian Americans or Pacific Islanders), 56 international. Average age 27. 312 applicants, 19% accepted, 24 enrolled. In 2009, 4 master's, 22 doctorates awarded. Terminal master's awarded for partial completion of doctoral program. *Degree requirements:* For master's, thesis, oral defense; for doctorate, thesis/dissertation, oral defense. *Entrance requirements:* For master's and doctorate, GRE General Test. Additional exam requirements/recommendations for international students: Required—TOEFL (minimum score 100 iBT). *Application deadline:* For fall admission, 1/5 priority date for domestic students, 12/1 priority date for international students. Application fee: $55 ($65 for international students). Electronic applications accepted. *Financial support:* In 2009–10, 165 students received support, including 62 fellowships with tuition reimbursements available (averaging $19,484 per year), 27 research assistantships with tuition reimbursements available (averaging $22,605 per year), 76 teaching assistantships with tuition reimbursements available (averaging $20,528 per year); scholarships/grants, traineeships, health care benefits, and unspecified assistantships also available. Financial award application deadline: 1/5. *Faculty research:* Evolution, ecology and behavior; microbiology; molecular biology and genetics; plant biology. *Unit head:* Dr. Roger Innes, Chair, 812-855-2219, Fax: 812-855-6082, E-mail: rinnes@indiana.edu. *Application contact:* Tracey D. Stohr, Graduate Student Recruitment Coordinator, 812-856-6303, Fax: 812-855-6082, E-mail: gradbio@indiana.edu.

Indiana University–Purdue University Indianapolis, Indiana University School of Medicine, Department of Microbiology and Immunology, Indianapolis, IN 46202-2896. Offers MS, PhD, MD/MS, MD/PhD. *Faculty:* 20 full-time (2 women). *Students:* 31 full-time (24 women); includes 8 minority (6 African Americans, 2 Asian Americans or Pacific Islanders), 9 international. Average age 27. 8 applicants, 100% accepted, 8 enrolled. In 2009, 5 doctorates awarded. Terminal master's awarded for partial completion of doctoral program. *Degree requirements:* For master's, thesis; for doctorate, thesis/dissertation. *Entrance requirements:* For master's and doctorate, GRE General Test, previous course work in calculus, cell biology, chemistry, genetics, physics, and biochemistry. *Application deadline:* For fall admission, 3/1 for domestic students. Applications are processed on a rolling basis. Application fee: $55 ($65 for international students). *Financial support:* In 2009–10, 2 fellowships with full tuition reimbursements (averaging $8,313 per year), 6 teaching assistantships with full tuition reimbursements (averaging $18,391 per year) were awarded; research assistantships with full tuition reimbursements, Federal Work-Study, institutionally sponsored loans, scholarships/grants, traineeships, and tuition waivers (partial) also available. Financial award application deadline: 2/1. *Faculty research:* Host-parasite interactions, molecular biology, cellular and molecular immunology and hematology, viral and bacterial pathogenesis, cancer research. Total annual research expenditures: $4.2 million. *Unit head:* Dr. Hal E. Broxmeyer, Chairman, 317-274-7672, Fax: 317-274-4090, E-mail: hbroxmey@iupui.edu. *Application contact:* 317-274-7671, Fax: 317-274-4090.

Inter American University of Puerto Rico, Metropolitan Campus, Graduate Programs, Program in Medical Technology, San Juan, PR 00919-1293. Offers administration of clinical laboratories (MS); molecular microbiology (MS). *Accreditation:* NAACLS. Part-time programs available. *Degree requirements:* For master's, comprehensive exam. *Entrance requirements:* For master's, BS in medical technology, minimum GPA of 2.5. Electronic applications accepted.

Iowa State University of Science and Technology, College of Veterinary Medicine and Graduate College, Graduate Programs in Veterinary Medicine, Department of Veterinary Microbiology and Preventive Medicine, Ames, IA 50011. Offers veterinary microbiology (MS, PhD). *Faculty:* 20 full-time (5 women), 8 part-time/adjunct (4 women). *Students:* 27 full-time (10 women), 14 part-time (6 women); includes 4 minority (1 African American, 3 Asian Americans or Pacific Islanders), 11 international. 14 applicants, 21% accepted, 2 enrolled. In 2009, 2 master's, 4 doctorates awarded. *Degree requirements:* For master's, thesis or alternative; for doctorate, thesis/dissertation. *Entrance requirements:* For master's and doctorate, GRE General Test. Additional exam requirements/recommendations for international students: Required—TOEFL (minimum score 550 paper-based; 79 iBT) or IELTS (minimum score 6.5). *Application deadline:* For fall admission, 2/1 priority date for domestic and international students. Applications are processed on a rolling basis. Application fee: $40 ($90 for international students). Electronic applications accepted. *Expenses:* Tuition, state resident: full-time $6716. Tuition, nonresident: full-time $8908. Tuition and fees vary according to course level, course load, program and student level. *Financial support:* In 2009–10, 8 research assistantships with full and partial tuition reimbursements (averaging $16,480 per year) were awarded; fellowships, teaching assistantships with full and partial tuition reimbursements, scholarships/grants, health care benefits, and unspecified assistantships also available. *Faculty research:* Bacteriology, immunology, virology, public health and food safety. *Unit head:* Dr. Michael Wannemuehler, Chair, 515-294-5776, E-mail: vetmicro@iastate.edu. *Application contact:* Dr. Michael Wannemuehler, Chair, 515-294-5776, E-mail: vetmicro@iastate.edu.

Iowa State University of Science and Technology, Graduate College, Interdisciplinary Programs, Program in Microbiology, Ames, IA 50011. Offers MS, PhD. *Students:* 20 full-time (12 women), 3 part-time (1 woman); includes 6 minority (2 African Americans, 4 Asian Americans or Pacific Islanders), 4 international. In 2009, 2 master's awarded. *Degree requirements:* For master's, thesis or alternative; for doctorate, thesis/dissertation. *Entrance requirements:* For master's and doctorate, GRE General Test. Additional exam requirements/recommendations for international students: Required—TOEFL (minimum score 550 paper-based; 79 iBT) or IELTS (minimum score 6.5). *Application deadline:* For fall admission, 2/1 priority date for domestic and international students. Application fee: $40 ($90 for international students). Electronic applications accepted. *Expenses:* Tuition, state resident: full-time $6716. Tuition, nonresident: full-time $8908. Tuition and fees vary according to course level, course load, program and student level. *Financial support:* In 2009–10, 15 research assistantships with partial tuition reimbursements (averaging $16,660 per year), 2 teaching assistantships with partial tuition reimbursements (averaging $16,660 per year) were awarded; scholarships/grants, health care benefits, and unspecified assistantships also available. *Unit head:* Dr. Adam Bogdanove, Chair, Supervising Committee, 515-294-9052. *Application contact:* Information Contact, 515-294-5836, Fax: 515-294-2592, E-mail: grad_admissions@iastate.edu.

The Johns Hopkins University, Bloomberg School of Public Health, The W. Harry Feinstone, Department of Molecular Microbiology and Immunology, Baltimore, MD 21218-2699. Offers MHS, Sc M, PhD. *Faculty:* 41 full-time (10 women), 10 part-time/adjunct (1 woman). *Students:* 86 full-time (56 women), 1 part-time (0 women); includes 24 minority (5 African Americans, 1 American Indian/Alaska Native, 14 Asian Americans or Pacific Islanders, 4 Hispanic Americans), 27 international. Average age 26. 184 applicants, 53% accepted, 38 enrolled. In 2009, 19 master's, 11 doctorates awarded. Terminal master's awarded for partial completion of doctoral program. *Degree requirements:* For master's, comprehensive exam, thesis (for some programs), essay, written exams; for doctorate, comprehensive exam, thesis/dissertation, 1 year full-time residency, oral and written exams. *Entrance requirements:* For master's, GRE General Test or MCAT, 3 letters of recommendation, curriculum vitae; for doctorate, GRE General Test, 3 letters of recommendation, transcripts, curriculum vitae. Additional exam requirements/recommendations for international students: Required—TOEFL (minimum score 600 paper-based; 250 computer-based). *Application deadline:* For fall admission, 1/2 priority date for domestic and international students. Applications are processed on a rolling basis. Application fee: $45. Electronic applications accepted. *Financial support:* In 2009–10, 37 fellowships with full and partial tuition reimbursements, 28 research assistantships with tuition reimbursements were awarded; Federal Work-Study, institutionally sponsored loans, scholarships/grants, and stipends also available. Financial award application deadline: 3/15; financial award applicants required to submit FAFSA. *Faculty research:* Immunology, virology, bacteriology, parasitology, vector biology, disease ecology, pathogenesis of infectious disease, immune responses to infectious agents, vector-borne and tropical diseases, biochemistry and molecular biology of infectious agents, population genetics of insect vectors, genetic regulation and immune responses in insect vectors, vaccine development, hormonal effects on pathogenesis and immune responses. Total annual research expenditures: $14.5 million. *Unit head:* Dr. Diane E. Griffin, Chair, 410-955-3459, Fax: 410-955-0105, E-mail: dgriffin@jhsph.edu. *Application contact:* Gail O'Connor, Senior Academic Program Coordinator, 410-614-4232, Fax: 410-955-0105, E-mail: goconnor@jhsph.edu.

Kansas State University, Graduate School, College of Arts and Sciences, Division of Biology, Manhattan, KS 66506. Offers biology (MS, PhD); microbiology (PhD). *Faculty:* 40 full-time (12 women), 12 part-time/adjunct (2 women). *Students:* 49 full-time (25 women). Average age 24. 155 applicants, 6% accepted, 9 enrolled. In 2009, 5 master's, 9 doctorates awarded. Terminal master's awarded for partial completion of doctoral program. *Degree requirements:* For master's, thesis; for doctorate, thesis/dissertation. *Entrance requirements:* For master's, GRE General Test, minimum undergraduate GPA of 3.0; for doctorate, GRE General Test, minimum GPA of 3.0. Additional exam requirements/recommendations for international students: Required—TOEFL (minimum score 550 paper-based; 213 computer-based). *Application deadline:* For fall admission, 2/1 priority date for domestic and international students; for spring admission, 8/1 priority date for domestic and international students. Applications are processed on a rolling basis. Application fee: $40 ($55 for international students). Electronic applications accepted. *Financial support:* In 2009–10, 18 research assistantships (averaging $22,305 per year), 30 teaching assistantships with full tuition reimbursements (averaging $14,704 per year) were awarded; institutionally sponsored loans and scholarships/grants also available. Support available to part-time students. Financial award application deadline: 3/1; financial award applicants required to submit FAFSA. *Faculty research:* Ecology, genetics, developmental biology, microbiology, cell biology. Total annual research expenditures: $7.3 million. *Unit head:* David Rintoul, Head, 785-532-6615, Fax: 785-532-6653, E-mail: drintoul@ksu.edu. *Application contact:* S. Keith Chapes, Director, 785-532-6795, Fax: 785-532-6653, E-mail: skcbiol@ksu.edu.

Loma Linda University, School of Medicine, Department of Biochemistry/Microbiology, Loma Linda, CA 92350. Offers MS, PhD. Part-time programs available. *Degree requirements:* For master's, thesis or alternative; for doctorate, thesis/dissertation. *Entrance requirements:* For master's and doctorate, GRE General Test. Additional exam requirements/recommendations for international students: Required—TOEFL (minimum score 550 paper-based; 213 computer-based). *Faculty research:* Physical chemistry of macromolecules, biochemistry of endocrine system, biochemical mechanism of bone volume regulation.

Long Island University, C.W. Post Campus, School of Health Professions and Nursing, Department of Biomedical Sciences, Brookville, NY 11548-1300. Offers cardiovascular perfusion (MS); clinical laboratory management (MS); medical biology (MS), including hematology, immunology, medical biology, medical chemistry, medical microbiology. Part-time and evening/weekend programs available. Postbaccalaureate distance learning degree programs offered. *Degree requirements:* For master's, thesis. *Entrance requirements:* For master's, minimum GPA of 2.75 in major. Electronic applications accepted.

Louisiana State University Health Sciences Center, School of Graduate Studies in New Orleans, Department of Microbiology, Immunology, and Parasitology, New Orleans, LA 70112-1393. Offers microbiology and immunology (MS, PhD); MD/PhD. Terminal master's awarded for partial completion of doctoral program. *Degree requirements:* For master's, comprehensive exam, thesis; for doctorate, comprehensive exam, thesis/dissertation, preliminary exam, qualifying exam. *Entrance requirements:* For master's and doctorate, GRE General Test. Additional exam requirements/recommendations for international students: Required—TOEFL. *Faculty research:* Microbial physiology, animal virology, vaccine development, AIDS drug studies, pathogenic mechanisms, molecular immunology.

Louisiana State University Health Sciences Center at Shreveport, Department of Microbiology and Immunology, Shreveport, LA 71130-3932. Offers MS, PhD, MD/PhD. Terminal master's awarded for partial completion of doctoral program. *Degree requirements:* For master's, thesis; for doctorate, thesis/dissertation. *Entrance requirements:* For master's and doctorate, GRE General Test. Additional exam requirements/recommendations for international students: Required—TOEFL. *Faculty research:* Infectious disease, pathogenesis, molecular virology and biology.

Loyola University Chicago, Graduate School, Department of Microbiology and Immunology, Maywood, IL 60153. Offers immunology (PhD); microbiology (MS); MD/PhD. *Faculty:* 11 full-time (3 women). *Students:* 36 full-time (24 women); includes 2 minority (both Asian Americans or Pacific Islanders), 7 international. Average age 27. 81 applicants, 21% accepted, 7 enrolled. In 2009, 1 master's, 5 doctorates awarded. Terminal master's awarded for partial completion of doctoral program. *Degree requirements:* For master's, thesis; for doctorate, comprehensive exam, thesis/dissertation. *Entrance requirements:* For master's and doctorate, GRE General Test. Additional exam requirements/recommendations for international students: Required—TOEFL. *Application deadline:* Applications are processed on a rolling basis. Application fee: $50. Electronic applications accepted. *Expenses:* Tuition: Full-time $14,220; part-time $790 per credit hour. Required fees: $60 per semester hour. Tuition and fees vary according to program. *Financial support:* In 2009–10, 5 fellowships with tuition reimbursements (averaging $23,000 per year), 24 research assistantships with tuition reimbursements (averaging $23,000 per year) were awarded; institutionally sponsored loans and scholarships/

grants also available. Financial award application deadline: 2/15. *Faculty research:* Viral pathogenesis, microbial physiology and genetics, immunoglobulin genetics and differentiation of the immune response, signal transduction and host-parasite interactions. Total annual research expenditures: $4.2 million. *Unit head:* Dr. Katherine L. Knight, Chair, 708-216-3385, Fax: 708-216-9574, E-mail: kknight@lumc.edu. *Application contact:* Dr. Karen Visick, Graduate Program Director, 708-216-0869, Fax: 708-216-9574, E-mail: kvisick@lumc.edu.

Marquette University, Graduate School, College of Arts and Sciences, Department of Biology, Milwaukee, WI 53201-1881. Offers cell biology (MS, PhD); developmental biology (MS, PhD); ecology (MS, PhD); endocrinology (MS, PhD); evolutionary biology (MS, PhD); genetics (MS, PhD); microbiology (MS, PhD); molecular biology (MS, PhD); muscle and exercise physiology (MS, PhD); neurobiology (MS, PhD); reproductive physiology (MS, PhD). *Faculty:* 23 full-time (10 women), 1 part-time/adjunct (0 women). *Students:* 23 full-time (13 women), 16 part-time (9 women); includes 1 minority (Asian American or Pacific Islander), 20 international. Average age 25. 95 applicants, 16% accepted, 10 enrolled. In 2009, 3 master's, 5 doctorates awarded. Terminal master's awarded for partial completion of doctoral program. *Degree requirements:* For master's, comprehensive exam, thesis, 1 year of teaching experience or equivalent; for doctorate, thesis/dissertation, 1 year of teaching experience or equivalent, qualifying exam. *Entrance requirements:* For master's and doctorate, GRE General Test, GRE Subject Test. Additional exam requirements/recommendations for international students: Required—TOEFL. Application fee: $40. *Financial support:* In 2009–10, 4 fellowships, 22 teaching assistantships were awarded; research assistantships, Federal Work-Study, institutionally sponsored loans, scholarships/grants, and tuition waivers (full and partial) also available. Support available to part-time students. Financial award application deadline: 2/15. *Faculty research:* Microbial and invertebrate ecology, evolution of gene function, DNA methylation, DNA arrangement. *Unit head:* Dr. Robert Fitts, Chair, 414-288-1748, Fax: 414-288-7357. *Application contact:* Debbie Weaver, Administrative Assistant, 414-288-7355, Fax: 414-288-7357.

Massachusetts Institute of Technology, School of Science, Department of Biology, Cambridge, MA 02139-4307. Offers biochemistry (PhD); biological oceanography (PhD); biology (PhD); biophysical chemistry and molecular structure (PhD); cell biology (PhD); computational and systems biology (PhD); developmental biology (PhD); genetics (PhD); immunology (PhD); microbiology (PhD); molecular biology (PhD); neurobiology (PhD). *Faculty:* 54 full-time (14 women). *Students:* 237 full-time (128 women); includes 65 minority (4 African Americans, 2 American Indian/Alaska Native, 33 Asian Americans or Pacific Islanders, 26 Hispanic Americans), 25 international. Average age 26. 645 applicants, 18% accepted, 49 enrolled. In 2009, 41 doctorates awarded. *Degree requirements:* For doctorate, comprehensive exam, thesis/dissertation. *Entrance requirements:* For doctorate, GRE General Test. Additional exam requirements/recommendations for international students: Required—TOEFL (minimum score 577 paper-based; 233 computer-based), IELTS (minimum score 6.5). *Application deadline:* For fall admission, 12/1 for domestic and international students. Application fee: $75. Electronic applications accepted. *Expenses:* Tuition: Full-time $37,510; part-time $585 per unit. Required fees: $272. *Financial support:* In 2009–10, 218 students received support, including 113 fellowships with tuition reimbursements available (averaging $31,816 per year), 109 research assistantships with tuition reimbursements available (averaging $29,254 per year); teaching assistantships with tuition reimbursements available, Federal Work-Study, institutionally sponsored loans, scholarships/grants, traineeships, health care benefits, and unspecified assistantships also available. *Faculty research:* DNA recombination, transcription and gene regulation, signal transduction, cell cycle, neuronal cell fate, replication and repair. Total annual research expenditures: $114 million. *Unit head:* Prof. Chris Kaiser, Head, 617-253-4701, E-mail: mitbio@mit.edu. *Application contact:* Biology Education Office, 617-253-3717, Fax: 617-258-9329, E-mail: gradbio@mit.edu.

McGill University, Faculty of Graduate and Postdoctoral Studies, Faculty of Agricultural and Environmental Sciences, Department of Natural Resource Sciences, Montréal, QC H3A 2T5, Canada. Offers entomology (M Sc, PhD); environmental assessment (M Sc); forest science (M Sc, PhD); microbiology (M Sc, PhD); micrometeorology (M Sc, PhD); neotropical environment (M Sc, PhD); soil science (M Sc, PhD); wildlife biology (M Sc, PhD).

McGill University, Faculty of Graduate and Postdoctoral Studies, Faculty of Medicine, Department of Microbiology and Immunology, Montréal, QC H3A 2T5, Canada. Offers M Sc, M Sc A, PhD.

Medical College of Wisconsin, Graduate School of Biomedical Sciences, Department of Microbiology and Molecular Genetics, Milwaukee, WI 53226-0509. Offers MS, PhD, MD/PhD. *Degree requirements:* For doctorate, comprehensive exam, thesis/dissertation. *Entrance requirements:* For doctorate, GRE General Test. Additional exam requirements/recommendations for international students: Required—TOEFL. *Faculty research:* Virology, immunology, bacterial toxins, regulation of gene expression.

Medical University of South Carolina, College of Graduate Studies, Department of Microbiology and Immunology, Charleston, SC 29425. Offers MS, PhD, DMD/PhD, MD/PhD. *Faculty:* 14 full-time (4 women). *Students:* 17 full-time (10 women), 1 part-time (0 women); includes 2 African Americans, 2 Hispanic Americans, 1 international. Average age 26. 13 applicants, 31% accepted, 4 enrolled. In 2009, 1 master's, 8 doctorates awarded. Terminal master's awarded for partial completion of doctoral program. *Degree requirements:* For master's, thesis; for doctorate, thesis/dissertation, oral and written exams. *Entrance requirements:* For master's, GRE General Test, MCAT, or DAT, interview; for doctorate, GRE General Test, interview, minimum GPA of 3.0. Additional exam requirements/recommendations for international students: Required—TOEFL (minimum score 600 paper-based; 250 computer-based; 100 iBT). *Application deadline:* For fall admission, 1/15 priority date for domestic and international students. Applications are processed on a rolling basis. Application fee: $0 ($85 for international students). Electronic applications accepted. *Financial support:* In 2009–10, 10 research assistantships with partial tuition reimbursements (averaging $23,000 per year) were awarded; Federal Work-Study and scholarships/grants also available. Support available to part-time students. Financial award application deadline: 3/10; financial award applicants required to submit FAFSA. *Faculty research:* Inmate and adaptive immunology, gene therapy/vector development, vaccinology, proteomics of biowarfare agents, bacterial and fungal pathogenesis. *Unit head:* Dr. James S. Norris, Chair, 843-792-7915, Fax: 843-792-6590, E-mail: norrisjs@musc.edu. *Application contact:* Dr. Laura Kasman, Assistant Professor, 843-792-8117, Fax: 843-792-6590, E-mail: kasmanl@musc.edu.

Meharry Medical College, School of Graduate Studies, Program in Biomedical Sciences, Microbiology and Immunology Emphasis, Nashville, TN 37208-9989. Offers PhD, MD/PhD. *Degree requirements:* For doctorate, comprehensive exam, thesis/dissertation. *Entrance requirements:* For doctorate, GRE General Test, GRE Subject Test, undergraduate degree in related science. *Faculty research:* Microbial and bacterial pathogenesis, viral transcription, immune response to viruses and parasites.

Miami University, Graduate School, College of Arts and Science, Department of Microbiology, Oxford, OH 45056. Offers MS, PhD. Part-time programs available. *Students:* 25 full-time (12 women); includes 3 minority (1 African American, 2 Asian Americans or Pacific Islanders), 5 international. *Entrance requirements:* For master's, GRE General Test, minimum undergraduate GPA of 3.0 during previous 2 years or 2.75 overall; for doctorate, GRE General Test, minimum undergraduate GPA of 2.75, 3.0 graduate. Additional exam requirements/recommendations for international students: Required—TOEFL. Application fee: $50. *Expenses:* Tuition, state resident: full-time $11,280. Tuition, nonresident: full-time $24,912. Required fees: $516. *Financial support:* Fellowships with full tuition reimbursements, research assistantships with full tuition reimbursements, teaching assistantships with full tuition reimbursements, Federal Work-Study, institutionally sponsored loans, scholarships/grants, health care benefits, tuition waivers (full), and unspecified assistantships available. Financial award application deadline: 3/1; financial award applicants required to submit FAFSA. *Unit head:* Dr. Louis A. Actis, Chair, 513-529-5421, Fax: 513-529-2431, E-mail: actisla@muohio.edu. *Application contact:* Graduate Admissions Chair, 513-529-5422, E-mail: microbiology@muohio.edu.

Michigan State University, College of Human Medicine and The Graduate School, Graduate Programs in Human Medicine, East Lansing, MI 48824. Offers biochemistry and molecular biology (MS, PhD); epidemiology (MS, PhD); microbiology (MS); microbiology and molecular genetics (PhD); pharmacology and toxicology (MS, PhD); physiology (MS, PhD); public health (MPH). *Students:* 58 full-time (31 women), 31 part-time (25 women); includes 17 minority (7 African Americans, 1 American Indian/Alaska Native, 6 Asian Americans or Pacific Islanders, 3 Hispanic Americans), 22 international. Average age 30. In 2009, 8 master's, 9 doctorates awarded. *Entrance requirements:* Additional exam requirements/recommendations for international students: Required—TOEFL. *Expenses:* Tuition, state resident: part-time $478.25 per credit hour. Tuition, nonresident: part-time $966.50 per credit hour. Part-time tuition and fees vary according to program. *Financial support:* In 2009–10, 17 research assistantships with tuition reimbursements (averaging $7,053 per year), 3 teaching assistantships with tuition reimbursements (averaging $6,607 per year) were awarded. *Unit head:* Margo K. Smith, Director of Graduate Studies, 517-432-5112, E-mail: smithmk@msu.edu. *Application contact:* Margo K. Smith, Director of Graduate Studies, 517-432-5112, E-mail: smithmk@msu.edu.

Michigan State University, College of Osteopathic Medicine and The Graduate School, Graduate Studies in Osteopathic Medicine, East Lansing, MI 48824. Offers biochemistry and molecular biology (MS, PhD); microbiology (MS); microbiology and molecular genetics (PhD); pharmacology and toxicology (MS, PhD), including integrative pharmacology (MS), pharmacology and toxicology, pharmacology and toxicology-environmental toxicology (PhD); physiology (MS, PhD). *Students:* 6 full-time (1 woman), 39 part-time (22 women); includes 8 minority (2 African Americans, 2 Asian Americans or Pacific Islanders, 4 Hispanic Americans), 3 international. Average age 30. *Expenses:* Tuition, state resident: part-time $478.25 per credit hour. Tuition, nonresident: part-time $966.50 per credit hour. Part-time tuition and fees vary according to program. *Financial support:* In 2009–10, 1 research assistantship with tuition reimbursement (averaging $7,894 per year) was awarded. *Application contact:* Bethany Heinlen, Information Contact, 517-353-7785, Fax: 517-353-9004, E-mail: heinlen@msu.edu.

Michigan State University, College of Veterinary Medicine and The Graduate School, Graduate Programs in Veterinary Medicine and College of Natural Science and Graduate Programs in Human Medicine, Department of Microbiology and Molecular Genetics, East Lansing, MI 48824. Offers industrial microbiology (MS, PhD); microbiology (MS, PhD); microbiology and molecular genetics (MS, PhD); microbiology–environmental toxicology (PhD). *Faculty:* 32 full-time (9 women). *Students:* 50 full-time (22 women), 5 part-time (1 woman); includes 7 minority (2 African Americans, 4 Asian Americans or Pacific Islanders, 1 Hispanic American), 21 international. Average age 27. 104 applicants, 14% accepted. In 2009, 6 master's, 5 doctorates awarded. *Entrance requirements:* For master's, GRE General Test. Additional exam requirements/recommendations for international students: Required—TOEFL (minimum score 550 paper-based; 213 computer-based), Michigan State University ELT (minimum score 85), Michigan English Language Assessment Battery (minimum score 83). Electronic applications accepted. *Expenses:* Tuition, state resident: part-time $478.25 per credit hour. Tuition, nonresident: part-time $966.50 per credit hour. Part-time tuition and fees vary according to program. *Financial support:* In 2009–10, 34 research assistantships with tuition reimbursements (averaging $7,765 per year), 6 teaching assistantships with tuition reimbursements (averaging $7,544 per year) were awarded. Total annual research expenditures: $5.5 million. *Unit head:* Dr. Walter Esselman, Chairperson, 517-884-5292, Fax: 517-353-8957, E-mail: mmgchair@msu.edu. *Application contact:* Suzanne Peacock, Graduate Program Coordinator, 517-884-5287, Fax: 517-353-8957, E-mail: micgrad@msu.edu.

Montana State University, College of Graduate Studies, College of Letters and Science, Department of Microbiology, Bozeman, MT 59717. Offers MS, PhD. Part-time programs available. *Faculty:* 6 full-time (1 woman), 5 part-time/adjunct (4 women). *Students:* 1 full-time (0 women), 18 part-time (14 women), 4 international. Average age 32. 25 applicants. In 2009, 4 master's, 2 doctorates awarded. *Degree requirements:* For master's, comprehensive exam; for doctorate, comprehensive exam, thesis/dissertation. *Entrance requirements:* For master's and doctorate, GRE General Test. Additional exam requirements/recommendations for international students: Required—TOEFL (minimum score 550 paper-based; 213 computer-based). *Application deadline:* For fall admission, 2/1 priority date for domestic students, 5/15 priority date for international students; for spring admission, 12/1 priority date for domestic students, 10/1 priority date for international students. Applications are processed on a rolling basis. Application fee: $30. Electronic applications accepted. *Expenses:* Tuition, state resident: full-time $5635; part-time $3492 per year. Tuition, nonresident: full-time $17,212; part-time $7865.10 per year. Required fees: $1441; $153.15 per credit. Tuition and fees vary according to course load and program. *Financial support:* In 2009–10, 4 fellowships with full tuition reimbursements (averaging $25,000 per year), 16 research assistantships with full tuition reimbursements (averaging $15,000 per year), 8 teaching assistantships with full tuition reimbursements (averaging $12,000 per year) were awarded; scholarships/grants, traineeships, health care benefits, and unspecified assistantships also available. Financial award application deadline: 3/1; financial award applicants required to submit FAFSA. *Faculty research:* Environmental microbiology, medical microbiology, biofilms, molecular biology, immunology. Total annual research expenditures: $2.1 million. *Unit head:* Dr. Michael Franklin, Head, 406-994-5658, Fax: 406-994-4926. *Application contact:* Dr. Carl A. Fox, Vice Provost for Graduate Education, 406-994-4145, Fax: 406-994-7433, E-mail: gradstudy@montana.edu.

New York Medical College, Graduate School of Basic Medical Sciences, Microbiology and Immunology Department, Valhalla, NY 10595-1691. Offers MS, PhD, MD/PhD. Part-time and evening/weekend programs available. Terminal master's awarded for partial completion of doctoral program. *Degree requirements:* For master's, thesis; for doctorate, comprehensive exam, thesis/dissertation. *Entrance requirements:* For master's and doctorate, GRE General Test. Additional exam requirements/recommendations for international students: Required—TOEFL. *Expenses:* Tuition: Full-time $18,170; part-time $790 per credit. Required fees: $790 per credit. $20 per semester. One-time fee: $100. Tuition and fees vary according to class time, course level, course load, degree level, program, student level and student's religious affiliation. *Faculty research:* Tumor and transplantation immunology, molecular mechanisms of DNA repair, virus-host interactions.

New York University, Graduate School of Arts and Science, Department of Biology, New York, NY 10012-1019. Offers biology (PhD); biomedical journalism (MS); cancer and molecular biology (PhD); computational biology (PhD); computers in biological research (MS); developmental genetics (PhD); general biology (MS); immunology and microbiology (PhD); molecular genetics (PhD); neurobiology (PhD); oral biology (MS); plant biology (PhD); recombinant DNA technology (MS); MS/MBA. Part-time programs available. *Faculty:* 24 full-time (5 women). *Students:* 142 full-time (79 women), 44 part-time (28 women); includes 34 minority (1 African American, 25 Asian Americans or Pacific Islanders, 8 Hispanic Americans), 82 international. Average age 27. 362 applicants, 71% accepted, 72 enrolled. In 2009, 43 master's, 9 doctorates awarded. Terminal master's awarded for partial completion of doctoral program. *Degree requirements:* For master's, thesis or alternative, qualifying paper; for doctorate, comprehensive exam, thesis/dissertation. *Entrance requirements:* For master's, GRE General Test; for doctorate, GRE General Test, GRE Subject Test. Additional exam requirements/recommendations for international students: Required—TOEFL. *Application deadline:* For fall admission, 12/12 priority date for domestic students. Application fee: $90. *Expenses:* Tuition: Full-time $30,528; part-time $1272 per credit. Required fees: $2177. *Financial support:* Fellowships with tuition reimbursements, research assistantships with tuition reimbursements, teaching assistantships with tuition reimbursements, career-related internships or fieldwork, Federal Work-Study, institutionally sponsored loans, scholarships/grants, health care benefits, and unspecified assistantships available. Financial award application deadline: 12/12; financial award applicants required to submit FAFSA. *Faculty research:* Genomics, molecular and cell biology, development and molecular genetics, molecular evolution of plants and animals. *Unit head:* Gloria Coruzzi, Chair, 212-998-8200, Fax: 212-995-4015, E-mail: biology@nyu.edu. *Application contact:* Stephen Small, Director of Graduate Studies, 212-998-8200, Fax: 212-995-4015, E-mail: biology@nyu.edu.

Microbiology

New York University, School of Medicine, New York, NY 10012-1019. Offers biomedical sciences (PhD), including biomedical imaging, cellular and molecular biology, computational biology, developmental genetics, medical and molecular parasitology, microbiology, molecular oncobiology and immunology, neuroscience and physiology, pathobiology, pharmacology, structural biology; clinical investigation (MS); medicine (MD); MD/MA; MD/MPA; MD/MS; MD/PhD. *Accreditation:* LCME/AMA (one or more programs are accredited). *Faculty:* 1,493 full-time (558 women), 327 part-time/adjunct (122 women). *Students:* 747 full-time (360 women); includes 275 minority (23 African Americans, 5 American Indian/Alaska Native, 199 Asian Americans or Pacific Islanders, 48 Hispanic Americans), 2 international. Average age 24. 7,568 applicants, 7% accepted, 213 enrolled. In 2009, 164 first professional degrees, 13 master's, 50 doctorates awarded. *Degree requirements:* For master's, comprehensive exam, thesis; for doctorate, comprehensive exam, thesis/dissertation. *Entrance requirements:* MCAT. Additional exam requirements/recommendations for international students: Required—TOEFL. *Application deadline:* For fall admission, 10/15 for domestic students; for winter admission, 12/18 for domestic students, 12/15 for international students. Application fee: $100. *Expenses:* Contact institution. *Financial support:* In 2009–10, 524 students received support, including 29 fellowships with full tuition reimbursements available (averaging $31,000 per year), 47 research assistantships with full tuition reimbursements available (averaging $31,000 per year); teaching assistantships, Federal Work-Study, institutionally sponsored loans, and health care benefits also available. Financial award application deadline: 3/1; financial award applicants required to submit FAFSA. *Faculty research:* AIDS, cancer, neuroscience, molecular biology, neuroscience, cell biology and molecular genetics, structural biology, microbial pathogenesis and host defense, pharmacology, molecular oncology and immunology. Total annual research expenditures: $201.1 million. *Unit head:* Dr. Robert Grossman, Dean, 212-263-3269, Fax: 212-263- 1828. *Application contact:* Dr. Nancy Genieser, Associate Dean, Admissions, 212-263-5290, Fax: 212-263-0720, E-mail: nancy.genieser@nyumc.org.

New York University, School of Medicine and Graduate School of Arts and Science, Sackler Institute of Graduate Biomedical Sciences, Department of Microbiology, New York, NY 10012-1019. Offers PhD, MD/PhD. *Degree requirements:* For doctorate, one foreign language, comprehensive exam, thesis/dissertation, qualifying exam. *Entrance requirements:* For doctorate, GRE General Test, GRE Subject Test. Additional exam requirements/recommendations for international students: Required—TOEFL. *Expenses:* Tuition: Full-time $30,528; part-time $1272 per credit. Required fees: $2177. *Faculty research:* Aspects of microbiology, parasitology, and genetics; virology.

North Carolina State University, Graduate School, College of Agriculture and Life Sciences, Department of Microbiology, Program in Microbiology, Raleigh, NC 27695. Offers MS, PhD. *Degree requirements:* For master's, thesis (for some programs); for doctorate, thesis/dissertation. *Entrance requirements:* For master's and doctorate, GRE. Electronic applications accepted.

North Dakota State University, College of Graduate and Interdisciplinary Studies, College of Agriculture, Food Systems, and Natural Resources, Department of Veterinary and Microbiological Sciences, Fargo, ND 58108. Offers food safety (MS); microbiology (MS); molecular pathogenesis (PhD). Part-time programs available. *Students:* 4 full-time (all women), 3 part-time (1 woman). *Degree requirements:* For master's, thesis; for doctorate, thesis/dissertation, oral and written preliminary exams. *Entrance requirements:* For master's and doctorate, GRE. Additional exam requirements/recommendations for international students: Required—TOEFL (minimum score 525 paper-based; 197 computer-based; 71 iBT). *Application deadline:* For fall admission, 3/15 priority date for domestic students. Applications are processed on a rolling basis. Application fee: $25. *Financial support:* Fellowships with full tuition reimbursements, research assistantships with full tuition reimbursements, teaching assistantships with full tuition reimbursements, Federal Work-Study and institutionally sponsored loans available. Financial award application deadline: 4/15. *Faculty research:* Bacterial gene regulation, antibiotic resistance, molecular virology, mechanisms of bacterial pathogenesis, immunology of animals. *Unit head:* Dr. Doug Freeman, Head, 701-231-7511, E-mail: douglas.freeman@ndsu.nodak.edu. *Application contact:* Dr. Eugene S. Berry, Associate Professor, 701-231-7520, Fax: 701-231-7514, E-mail: eugene.berry@ndsu.edu.

Northwestern University, Northwestern University Feinberg School of Medicine and Interdepartmental Programs, Integrated Graduate Programs in the Life Sciences, Chicago, IL 60611. Offers cancer biology (PhD); cell biology (PhD); developmental biology (PhD); evolutionary biology (PhD); immunology and microbial pathogenesis (PhD); molecular biology and genetics (PhD); neurobiology (PhD); pharmacology and toxicology (PhD); structural biology and biochemistry (PhD). *Degree requirements:* For doctorate, comprehensive exam, thesis/dissertation, written and oral qualifying exams. *Entrance requirements:* For doctorate, GRE General Test. Additional exam requirements/recommendations for international students: Required—TOEFL (minimum score 600 paper-based; 250 computer-based). Electronic applications accepted.

The Ohio State University, Graduate School, College of Biological Sciences, Department of Microbiology, Columbus, OH 43210. Offers MS, PhD. *Faculty:* 24. *Students:* 10 full-time (4 women), 37 part-time (20 women); includes 3 minority (1 African American, 1 Asian American or Pacific Islander, 1 Hispanic American), 16 international. Average age 27. In 2009, 4 master's, 6 doctorates awarded. *Degree requirements:* For master's, thesis optional; for doctorate, thesis/dissertation. *Entrance requirements:* For master's, GRE General Test, GRE Subject Test in biology, biochemistry or chemistry (recommended); for doctorate, GRE General Test; GRE Subject Test in biology, biochemistry or chemistry (recommended). Additional exam requirements/recommendations for international students: Required—TOEFL (minimum score 600 paper-based; 250 computer-based). *Application deadline:* For fall admission, 8/15 priority date for domestic students, 7/1 priority date for international students; for winter admission, 12/1 priority date for domestic students, 11/1 priority date for international students; for spring admission, 3/1 priority date for domestic students, 2/1 priority date for international students. Applications are processed on a rolling basis. Application fee: $40 ($50 for international students). Electronic applications accepted. *Expenses:* Tuition, state resident: full-time $10,683. Tuition, nonresident: full-time $25,923. Tuition and fees vary according to course load and program. *Financial support:* Fellowships, research assistantships, teaching assistantships, Federal Work-Study and institutionally sponsored loans available. Support available to part-time students. *Unit head:* Tina M. Henkin, Chair, 614-292-2301, Fax: 614-292-8120, E-mail: henkin.3@osu.edu. *Application contact:* 614-292-9444, Fax: 614-292-3895, E-mail: domestic.grad@osu.edu.

Ohio University, Graduate College, College of Arts and Sciences, Department of Biological Sciences, Athens, OH 45701-2979. Offers biological sciences (MS, PhD); cell biology and physiology (MS, PhD); ecology and evolutionary biology (MS, PhD); exercise physiology and muscle biology (MS, PhD); microbiology (MS, PhD); neuroscience (MS, PhD). *Faculty:* 50 full-time (14 women), 6 part-time/adjunct (1 woman). *Students:* 44 full-time (19 women), 8 part-time (3 women); includes 2 minority (1 African American, 1 Hispanic American), 21 international. 95 applicants, 24% accepted, 10 enrolled. In 2009, 4 master's, 9 doctorates awarded. Terminal master's awarded for partial completion of doctoral program. *Degree requirements:* For master's, comprehensive exam, thesis, 1 quarter of teaching experience; for doctorate, comprehensive exam, thesis/dissertation, 2 quarters of teaching experience. *Entrance requirements:* For master's, GRE General Test, names of three faculty members whose research interests most closely match the applicant's interest; for doctorate, GRE General Test, essay concerning prior training, research interest and career goals, plus names of three faculty members whose research interests most closely match the applicant's interest. Additional exam requirements/recommendations for international students: Required—TOEFL (minimum score 620 paper-based; 105 iBT) or IELTS (minimum score 7.5). *Application deadline:* For fall admission, 1/15 for domestic and international students. Application fee: $50 ($55 for international students). Electronic applications accepted. *Expenses:* Tuition, state resident: full-time $7839; part-time $323 per quarter hour. Tuition, nonresident: full-time $15,831; part-time $654 per quarter hour. Required fees: $2931. *Financial support:* In 2009–10, 1 fellowship with full tuition reimbursement (averaging $18,957 per year), 10 research assistantships with full tuition reimbursements (averaging $18,957 per year), 42 teaching assistantships with full tuition reimbursements (averaging $18,957 per year) were awarded; Federal Work-Study and institutionally sponsored loans also available. Financial award application deadline: 1/15. *Faculty research:* Ecology and evolutionary biology, exercise physiology and muscle biology, neurobiology, cell biology, physiology. Total annual research expenditures: $2.8 million. *Unit head:* Dr. Ralph DiCaprio, Chair, 740-593-2290, Fax: 740-593-0300, E-mail: dicaprir@ohio.edu. *Application contact:* Dr. Donald Holzschu, Graduate Chair, 740-593-0425, Fax: 740-593-0300, E-mail: holzschu@ohio.edu.

Oklahoma State University, College of Arts and Sciences, Department of Microbiology and Molecular Genetics, Stillwater, OK 74078. Offers MS, PhD. *Faculty:* 20 full-time (4 women), 1 (woman) part-time/adjunct. *Students:* 10 full-time (5 women), 18 part-time (10 women); includes 2 minority (1 American Indian/Alaska Native, 1 Asian American or Pacific Islander), 12 international. Average age 28. 88 applicants, 11% accepted, 7 enrolled. In 2009, 2 master's, 2 doctorates awarded. *Degree requirements:* For master's, thesis; for doctorate, comprehensive exam, thesis/dissertation. *Entrance requirements:* For master's, GRE General Test; for doctorate, GRE General Test. Additional exam requirements/recommendations for international students: Required—TOEFL (minimum score 550 paper-based; 79 iBT). *Application deadline:* For fall admission, 3/1 priority date for international students; for spring admission, 8/1 priority date for international students. Applications are processed on a rolling basis. Application fee: $40 ($75 for international students). Electronic applications accepted. *Expenses:* Tuition, state resident: full-time $3716; part-time $154.85 per credit hour. Tuition, nonresident: full-time $14,448; part-time $602 per credit hour. Required fees: $1772; $73.85 per credit hour. One-time fee: $50. Tuition and fees vary according to course load and campus/location. *Financial support:* In 2009–10, 13 research assistantships (averaging $18,761 per year), 12 teaching assistantships (averaging $16,275 per year) were awarded; career-related internships or fieldwork, Federal Work-Study, scholarships/grants, health care benefits, tuition waivers (partial), and unspecified assistantships also available. Support available to part-time students. Financial award application deadline: 3/1; financial award applicants required to submit FAFSA. *Faculty research:* Bioinformatics, genomics-genetics, virology, environmental microbiology, development-molecular mechanisms. *Unit head:* Dr. Bill Picking, Head, 405-744-7180, Fax: 405-744-6790. *Application contact:* Dr. Gordon Emslie, Dean, 405-744-6368, Fax: 405-744-0355, E-mail: grad-i@okstate.edu.

Oregon Health & Science University, School of Medicine, Graduate Programs in Medicine, Department of Molecular Microbiology and Immunology, Portland, OR 97239-3098. Offers PhD. *Degree requirements:* For doctorate, comprehensive exam, thesis/dissertation. *Entrance requirements:* For doctorate, GRE General Test (minimum scores: 500 Verbal/600 Quantitative/4.5 Analytical) or MCAT (for some programs). Additional exam requirements/recommendations for international students: Required—TOEFL. *Application deadline:* For fall admission, 12/1 for domestic students. Electronic applications accepted. Tuition and fees vary according to course level, course load, degree level, program and reciprocity agreements. *Financial support:* PhD students have paid tuition and receive stipends available. *Faculty research:* Molecular biology of bacterial and viral pathogens, cellular and humoral immunology, molecular biology of microbes. *Unit head:* Eric Barklis, PhD, Program Director, 503-494-7768, E-mail: mmi@ohsu.edu. *Application contact:* Kathy Shinall, Program Coordinator, 503-494-7768, E-mail: mmi@ohsu.edu.

Oregon State University, Graduate School, College of Science, Department of Microbiology, Corvallis, OR 97331. Offers MA, MAIS, MS, PhD. Part-time programs available. *Faculty:* 7 full-time (3 women), 2 part-time/adjunct (0 women). *Students:* 32 full-time (15 women), 1 (woman) part-time; includes 4 minority (1 American Indian/Alaska Native, 2 Asian Americans or Pacific Islanders, 1 Hispanic American), 3 international. Average age 28. In 2009, 1 master's awarded. Terminal master's awarded for partial completion of doctoral program. *Degree requirements:* For master's, thesis; for doctorate, one foreign language, thesis/dissertation. *Entrance requirements:* For master's and doctorate, GRE General Test, minimum GPA of 3.0 in last 90 hours. Additional exam requirements/recommendations for international students: Required—TOEFL. *Application deadline:* For fall admission, 3/1 for domestic students. Applications are processed on a rolling basis. Application fee: $50. *Expenses:* Tuition, state resident: full-time $9774; part-time $362 per credit. Tuition, nonresident: full-time $15,849; part-time $587 per credit. Required fees: $1639. Full-time tuition and fees vary according to course load and program. *Financial support:* Fellowships, research assistantships, teaching assistantships, career-related internships or fieldwork, Federal Work-Study, and institutionally sponsored loans available. Support available to part-time students. Financial award application deadline: 2/1. *Faculty research:* Genetics, physiology, biotechnology, pathogenic microbiology, plant virology. *Unit head:* Dr. Theo W. Dreher, Chair, 541-737-1834, Fax: 541-737-0496, E-mail: theo.dreher@oregonstate.edu. *Application contact:* Dina L. Stoneman, Office Specialist 2, 541-737-1830, Fax: 541-737-0496, E-mail: dina.stoneman@oregonstate.edu.

Penn State Hershey Medical Center, College of Medicine, Graduate School Programs in the Biomedical Sciences, Graduate Program in Microbiology and Immunology, Hershey, PA 17033. Offers genetics (PhD); immunology (MS, PhD); microbiology (MS); microbiology/virology (PhD); molecular biology (PhD); MD/PhD. *Students:* 12 applicants, 75% accepted, 3 enrolled. In 2009, 1 doctorate awarded. Terminal master's awarded for partial completion of doctoral program. *Degree requirements:* For master's, thesis or alternative; for doctorate, comprehensive exam, thesis/dissertation, oral exam. *Entrance requirements:* For doctorate, GRE General Test, minimum GPA of 3.0. Additional exam requirements/recommendations for international students: Required—TOEFL. *Application deadline:* For fall admission, 1/31 priority date for domestic students, 2/1 priority date for international students. Applications are processed on a rolling basis. Application fee: $45. Electronic applications accepted. *Expenses:* Tuition, state resident: part-time $644 per credit. Tuition, nonresident: part-time $1142 per credit. Required fees: $22 per semester. *Financial support:* In 2009–10, research assistantships with full tuition reimbursements (averaging $22,260 per year); fellowships with full tuition reimbursements, scholarships/grants, health care benefits, and unspecified assistantships also available. Financial award applicants required to submit FAFSA. *Faculty research:* Virus replication and assembly, oncogenesis, interactions of viruses with host cells and animal model systems. *Unit head:* Dr. Richard J. Courtney, Chair, 717-531-7659, Fax: 717-531-6522, E-mail: micro-grad-hmc@psu.edu. *Application contact:* Billie Burns, Secretary, 717-531-7659, Fax: 717-531-6522, E-mail: micro-grad-hmc@psu.edu.

Penn State University Park, Graduate School, Eberly College of Science, Department of Biochemistry and Molecular Biology, Program in Biochemistry, Microbiology, and Molecular Biology, State College, University Park, PA 16802-1503. Offers MS, PhD. *Unit head:* Dr. Ronald Porter, Director of Graduate Studies, 814-863-4903, E-mail: rdp1@psu.edu. *Application contact:* Dr. Ronald Porter, Director of Graduate Studies, 814-863-4903, E-mail: rdp1@psu.edu.

Purdue University, Graduate School, College of Science, Department of Biological Sciences, West Lafayette, IN 47907. Offers biochemistry (PhD); biophysics (PhD); cell and developmental biology (PhD); ecology, evolutionary and population biology (MS, PhD), including ecology, evolutionary biology, population biology; genetics (MS, PhD); microbiology (MS, PhD); molecular biology (PhD); neurobiology (MS, PhD); plant physiology (PhD). Terminal master's awarded for partial completion of doctoral program. *Degree requirements:* For master's, thesis (for some programs); for doctorate, thesis/dissertation, seminars, teaching experience. *Entrance requirements:* For master's and doctorate, GRE General Test. Additional exam requirements/recommendations for international students: Required—TOEFL. Electronic applications accepted.

Purdue University, School of Veterinary Medicine and Graduate School, Graduate Programs in Veterinary Medicine, Department of Comparative Pathobiology, West Lafayette, IN 47907-2027. Offers comparative epidemiology and public health (MS); comparative epidemiology and public heath (PhD); comparative microbiology and immunology (MS, PhD); comparative pathobiology (MS, PhD); interdisciplinary studies (PhD), including microbial pathogenesis, molecular signaling and cancer biology, molecular virology; lab animal medicine (MS); veterinary anatomic pathology (MS); veterinary clinical pathology (MS). *Faculty:* 37 full-time (10 women), 4 part-time/adjunct (2 women). *Students:* 53 full-time (31 women), 2 part-time (1 woman); includes 3 minority (2 African Americans, 1 Hispanic American), 32 international. Average age 35. In 2009, 6 master's, 2 doctorates awarded. Terminal master's awarded for partial completion of doctoral program. *Degree requirements:* For master's, thesis (for some programs); for doctorate, thesis/dissertation. *Entrance requirements:* For master's and doctorate, GRE General Test. Additional exam requirements/recommendations for international students: Required—TOEFL (minimum score 575 paper-based; 232 computer-based), IELTS (minimum score 6.5), TWE (minimum score 4). *Application deadline:* For fall admission, 8/12 for domestic students, 6/15 for international students; for spring admission, 1/12 for domestic students, 10/15 for international students. Application fee: $55. Electronic applications accepted. *Financial support:* Fellowships, research assistantships, teaching assistantships available. Financial award application deadline: 3/1; financial award applicants required to submit FAFSA. *Unit head:* Dr. Suresh Mittal, Interim Head, 765-494-7543. *Application contact:* Denise A. Ottinger, Director, Student Services and Admissions, 765-494-7893, Fax: 765-496-2891, E-mail: vetadmissions@purdue.edu.

Queen's University at Kingston, School of Graduate Studies and Research, Faculty of Health Sciences, Department of Microbiology and Immunology, Kingston, ON K7L 3N6, Canada. Offers M Sc, PhD. Part-time programs available. *Degree requirements:* For master's, thesis; for doctorate, comprehensive exam, thesis/dissertation. *Entrance requirements:* For master's and doctorate, minimum B+ average. Additional exam requirements/recommendations for international students: Required—TOEFL (minimum score 600 paper-based; 250 computer-based). Electronic applications accepted. *Faculty research:* Bacteriology, virology, immunology, education in microbiology and immunology, microbial pathogenesis.

Quinnipiac University, School of Health Sciences, Program in Medical Laboratory Sciences, Hamden, CT 06518-1940. Offers biomedical sciences (MHS); laboratory management (MHS); microbiology (MHS). *Accreditation:* NAACLS. Part-time programs available. *Faculty:* 9 full-time (5 women), 12 part-time/adjunct (3 women). *Students:* 30 full-time (16 women), 22 part-time (13 women); includes 7 minority (3 African Americans, 1 Asian American or Pacific Islander, 3 Hispanic Americans), 13 international. Average age 28. 44 applicants, 86% accepted, 29 enrolled. In 2009, 15 master's awarded. *Degree requirements:* For master's, comprehensive exam, thesis optional. *Entrance requirements:* For master's, minimum GPA of 2.75; bachelor's degree in biological, medical, or health sciences. Additional exam requirements/recommendations for international students: Required—TOEFL (minimum score 575 paper-based; 233 computer-based; 90 iBT), IELTS (minimum score 6.5). *Application deadline:* For fall admission, 7/30 priority date for domestic students, 4/30 priority date for international students; for spring admission, 12/15 priority date for domestic students, 9/15 priority date for international students. Applications are processed on a rolling basis. Application fee: $45. Electronic applications accepted. *Expenses:* Tuition: Full-time $16,030; part-time $770 per credit. Required fees: $630; $35 per credit. *Financial support:* Federal Work-Study, tuition waivers (partial), and unspecified assistantships available. Support available to part-time students. Financial award application deadline: 4/15; financial award applicants required to submit FAFSA. *Faculty research:* Microbial physiology, fermentation technology. *Unit head:* Dr. Kenneth Kaloustian, Director, 203-582-8676, Fax: 203-582-3443, E-mail: ken.kaloustian@quinnipiac.edu. *Application contact:* Kristin Parent, Assistant Director of Graduate Health Sciences Admissions, 800-462-1944, Fax: 203-582-3443, E-mail: kristin.parent@quinnipiac.edu.

Rosalind Franklin University of Medicine and Science, School of Graduate and Post-doctoral Studies—Interdisciplinary Graduate Program in Biomedical Sciences, Department of Microbiology and Immunology, North Chicago, IL 60064-3095. Offers MS, PhD, MD/PhD. Terminal master's awarded for partial completion of doctoral program. *Degree requirements:* For master's, comprehensive exam, thesis; for doctorate, comprehensive exam, thesis/dissertation. *Entrance requirements:* For master's and doctorate, GRE General Test. Additional exam requirements/recommendations for international students: Required—TOEFL, TWE. *Faculty research:* Molecular biology, parasitology, virology.

Rush University, Graduate College, Division of Immunology and Microbiology, Chicago, IL 60612-3832. Offers microbiology (PhD); virology (MS, PhD), including immunology, virology; MD/PhD. *Degree requirements:* For doctorate, thesis/dissertation, comprehensive preliminary exam. *Entrance requirements:* For doctorate, GRE General Test, interview, minimum GPA of 3.0. Additional exam requirements/recommendations for international students: Required—TOEFL. *Faculty research:* Immune interactions of cells and membranes, HIV immunopathogenesis, autoimmunity, tumor biology.

Rutgers, The State University of New Jersey, New Brunswick, Graduate School-New Brunswick, Programs in the Molecular Biosciences, Program in Microbiology and Molecular Genetics, Piscataway, NJ 08854-8097. Offers applied microbiology (MS, PhD); clinical microbiology (MS, PhD); computational molecular biology (PhD); immunology (MS, PhD); microbial biochemistry (MS, PhD); molecular genetics (MS, PhD); virology (MS, PhD). Part-time programs available. Terminal master's awarded for partial completion of doctoral program. *Degree requirements:* For master's, comprehensive exam, thesis or alternative; for doctorate, comprehensive exam, thesis/dissertation, written qualifying exam. *Entrance requirements:* For master's, GRE General Test, minimum GPA of 3.0; for doctorate, GRE General Test, GRE Subject Test (recommended), minimum GPA of 3.0. Additional exam requirements/recommendations for international students: Required—TOEFL. Electronic applications accepted. *Faculty research:* Molecular genetics and microbial physiology; virology and pathogenic microbiology; applied, environmental and industrial microbiology; computers in molecular biology.

Saint Louis University, Graduate School and School of Medicine, Graduate Program in Biomedical Sciences, Department of Molecular Microbiology and Immunology, St. Louis, MO 63103-2097. Offers PhD. *Degree requirements:* For doctorate, comprehensive exam, thesis/dissertation, qualifying exams. *Entrance requirements:* For doctorate, GRE General Test (GRE Subject Test optional), letters of recommendation, resume, interview. Additional exam requirements/recommendations for international students: Required—TOEFL (minimum score 525 paper-based; 194 computer-based). Electronic applications accepted. *Faculty research:* Pathogenesis of hepatitis C virus, herpervituses, pox viruses, rheumatoid arthritis, antiviral drugs and vaccines in biodefense, cancer gene therapy, virology and immunology.

San Diego State University, Graduate and Research Affairs, College of Sciences, Department of Biology, Program in Microbiology, San Diego, CA 92182. Offers MS. *Degree requirements:* For master's, thesis, oral exam. *Entrance requirements:* For master's, GRE General Test, GRE Subject Test, resume or curriculum vitae, 2 letters of recommendation. Additional exam requirements/recommendations for international students: Required—TOEFL. Electronic applications accepted.

San Francisco State University, Division of Graduate Studies, College of Science and Engineering, Department of Biology, Program in Microbiology, San Francisco, CA 94132-1722. Offers MS.

San Jose State University, Graduate Studies and Research, College of Science, Department of Biological Sciences, San Jose, CA 95192-0001. Offers biological sciences (MA, MS); molecular biology and microbiology (MS); organismal biology, conservation and ecology (MS); physiology (MS). Part-time programs available. *Students:* 53 full-time (41 women), 48 part-time (30 women); includes 48 minority (2 African Americans, 1 American Indian/Alaska Native, 36 Asian Americans or Pacific Islanders, 9 Hispanic Americans), 10 international. Average age 30. 158 applicants, 28% accepted, 43 enrolled. In 2009, 36 master's awarded. *Entrance requirements:* For master's, GRE. *Application deadline:* For fall admission, 6/29 for domestic students; for spring admission, 11/30 for domestic students. Applications are processed on a rolling basis. Application fee: $59. Electronic applications accepted. *Financial support:* Teaching assistantships, Federal Work-Study available. Financial award applicants required to submit FAFSA. *Faculty research:* Systemic physiology, molecular genetics, SEM studies, toxicology, large mammal ecology. *Unit head:* Dr. John Boothby, Chair, 408-924-4850, Fax: 408-924-4840, E-mail: jboothby@email.sjsu.edu. *Application contact:* Daniel Holley, Graduate Coordinator, 408-924-4844, E-mail: dholley@email.sjsu.edu.

Seton Hall University, College of Arts and Sciences, Department of Biological Sciences, South Orange, NJ 07079-2697. Offers biology (MS); biology/business administration (MS); microbiology (MS); molecular bioscience (PhD); molecular bioscience/neuroscience (PhD). Part-time and evening/weekend programs available. *Faculty:* 17 full-time (9 women), 1 part-time/adjunct (0 women). *Students:* 19 full-time (8 women), 47 part-time (33 women); includes 13 minority (5 African Americans, 5 Asian Americans or Pacific Islanders, 3 Hispanic Americans), 5 international. Average age 29. 51 applicants, 76% accepted, 12 enrolled. In 2009, 11 master's awarded. *Degree requirements:* For master's, thesis optional; for doctorate, comprehensive exam, thesis/dissertation. *Entrance requirements:* For master's and doctorate, GRE or MS from accredited university in the U.S. Additional exam requirements/recommendations for international students: Required—TOEFL. *Application deadline:* For fall admission, 7/1 priority date for domestic and international students; for spring admission, 11/1 priority date for domestic and international students. Applications are processed on a rolling basis. Application fee: $50. Electronic applications accepted. *Financial support:* Research assistantships, teaching assistantships with full tuition reimbursements, career-related internships or fieldwork, Federal Work-Study, and unspecified assistantships available. Financial award applicants required to submit FAFSA. *Faculty research:* Neurobiology, genetics, immunology, molecular biology, cellular physiology, toxicology, microbiology, bioinformatics. *Unit head:* Dr. Carolyn Bentivegna, Chair, 973-761-9044, Fax: 973-275-2905, E-mail: bentivca@shu.edu. *Application contact:* Dr. Carroll D. Rawn, Director of Graduate Studies, 973-761-9054, Fax: 973-275-2905, E-mail: rawncarr@shu.edu.

South Dakota State University, Graduate School, College of Agriculture and Biological Sciences, Department of Biology and Microbiology, Brookings, SD 57007. Offers biological sciences (MS, PhD). Part-time programs available. *Degree requirements:* For master's, thesis (for some programs), oral exam; for doctorate, comprehensive exam, thesis/dissertation, oral exam. *Entrance requirements:* For master's and doctorate, GRE General Test. Additional exam requirements/recommendations for international students: Required—TOEFL (minimum score 600 paper-based; 250 computer-based; 100 iBT). *Faculty research:* Ecosystem ecology; plant, animal and microbial genomics; animal infectious disease, microbial bioproducts.

Southern Illinois University Carbondale, Graduate School, College of Science, Program in Molecular Biology, Microbiology, and Biochemistry, Carbondale, IL 62901-4701. Offers MS, PhD. *Degree requirements:* For master's, thesis; for doctorate, thesis/dissertation. *Entrance requirements:* For master's, GRE, minimum GPA of 2.7; for doctorate, GRE, minimum GPA of 3.25. Additional exam requirements/recommendations for international students: Required—TOEFL. *Faculty research:* Prokaryotic gene regulation and expression; eukaryotic gene regulation; microbial, phylogenetic, and metabolic diversity; immune responses to tumors, pathogens, and autoantigens; protein folding and structure.

Southwestern Oklahoma State University, College of Professional and Graduate Studies, School of Behavioral Sciences and Education, Specialization in Health Sciences and Microbiology, Weatherford, OK 73096-3098. Offers M Ed.

Stanford University, School of Medicine, Graduate Programs in Medicine, Department of Microbiology and Immunology, Stanford, CA 94305-9991. Offers PhD. *Degree requirements:* For doctorate, comprehensive exam, thesis/dissertation, 2 quarters teaching assistantship. *Entrance requirements:* For doctorate, GRE General Test, GRE Subject Test (biology or biochemistry). Additional exam requirements/recommendations for international students: Required—TOEFL. Electronic applications accepted. *Expenses:* Tuition: Full-time $37,380; part-time $2760 per quarter. Required fees: $501. *Faculty research:* Molecular pathogenesis of bacteria viruses and parasites, immune system function, autoimmunity, molecular biology.

State University of New York Upstate Medical University, College of Graduate Studies, Program in Microbiology and Immunology, Syracuse, NY 13210-2334. Offers microbiology (MS); microbiology and immunology (PhD); MD/PhD. *Faculty:* 18 full-time (4 women), 2 part-time/adjunct (1 woman). *Students:* 19 full-time (14 women), 1 (woman) part-time; includes 5 minority (3 Asian Americans or Pacific Islanders, 2 Hispanic Americans), 1 international. In 2009, 1 master's, 1 doctorate awarded. Terminal master's awarded for partial completion of doctoral program. *Degree requirements:* For master's, thesis; for doctorate, comprehensive exam, thesis/dissertation. *Entrance requirements:* For master's, GRE General Test, interview; for doctorate, GRE General Test, telephone interview. Additional exam requirements/recommendations for international students: Required—TOEFL. *Application deadline:* Applications are processed on a rolling basis. Application fee: $40. Electronic applications accepted. *Financial support:* In 2009–10, fellowships with tuition reimbursements (averaging $21,514 per year), research assistantships with tuition reimbursements (averaging $21,514 per year) were awarded; Federal Work-Study, scholarships/grants, health care benefits, tuition waivers, and unspecified assistantships also available. Financial award application deadline: 4/15; financial award applicants required to submit FAFSA. *Faculty research:* Cancer, disorders of the nervous system, infectious diseases, diabetes/metabolic disorders/cardiovascular diseases. *Unit head:* Dr. Rosemary Rochford, Chair, 315-464-5127. *Application contact:* Sandra Tillotson, Coordinator of Graduate Recruitment, 315-464-7655.

See Close-Up on page 359.

Stony Brook University, State University of New York, Stony Brook University Medical Center, School of Medicine and Graduate School, Graduate Programs in Medicine, Department of Molecular Genetics and Microbiology, Stony Brook, NY 11794. Offers molecular microbiology (PhD). *Students:* 26 full-time (16 women); includes 3 minority (1 African American, 1 Asian American or Pacific Islander, 1 Hispanic American), 5 international. Average age 27. 110 applicants, 13% accepted. In 2009, 6 doctorates awarded. *Degree requirements:* For doctorate, comprehensive exam, thesis/dissertation. *Entrance requirements:* For doctorate, GRE General Test, GRE Subject Test. Additional exam requirements/recommendations for international students: Required—TOEFL. *Application deadline:* For fall admission, 1/15 for domestic students. Application fee: $60. *Expenses:* Tuition, state resident: full-time $8370; part-time $349 per credit. Tuition, nonresident: full-time $13,250; part-time $552 per credit. Required fees: $933. *Financial support:* Fellowships, research assistantships, teaching assistantships, Federal Work-Study available. Financial award application deadline: 3/15. *Faculty research:* Adenovirus molecular genetics, molecular biology of tumors, virus SV40, mechanism of tumor infection by SAV virus. Total annual research expenditures: $8 million. *Unit head:* Dr. Jorge Benach, Interim Chair, 631-632-8812, Fax: 631-632-9797. *Application contact:* Dr. Patrick Hearing, Director, 631-632-8813, Fax: 631-632-9797, E-mail: hearing@asterix.bio.sunysb.edu.

Temple University, Health Sciences Center, School of Medicine and Graduate School, Graduate Programs in Medicine, Department of Microbiology and Immunology, Philadelphia, PA 19140-5104. Offers MS, PhD, MD/PhD. *Degree requirements:* For master's, thesis; for doctorate, thesis/dissertation, research seminars. *Entrance requirements:* For master's and doctorate, GRE General Test, GRE Subject Test, minimum GPA of 3.0. Additional exam requirements/recommendations for international students: Required—TOEFL (minimum score 600 paper-based; 250 computer-based). Electronic applications accepted. *Faculty research:* Molecular and cellular immunology, molecular and biochemical microbiology, molecular genetics.

Texas A&M Health Science Center, Graduate School of Biomedical Sciences, Department of Microbial and Molecular Pathogenesis, College Station, TX 77840. Offers immunology (PhD); microbiology (PhD); molecular biology (PhD); virology (PhD). *Degree requirements:* For doctorate, thesis/dissertation. *Entrance requirements:* For doctorate, GRE General Test, minimum GPA of 3.0. *Faculty research:* Molecular pathogenesis, microbial therapeutics.

Texas A&M University, College of Science, Department of Biology, College Station, TX 77843. Offers biology (MS, PhD); botany (MS, PhD); microbiology (MS, PhD); molecular and cell biology (PhD); neuroscience (MS, PhD); zoology (MS, PhD). *Faculty:* 37. *Students:* 101

Microbiology

Texas A&M University (continued)
full-time (59 women), 5 part-time (3 women); includes 8 minority (1 African American, 3 Asian Americans or Pacific Islanders, 4 Hispanic Americans), 40 international. Average age 28. In 2009, 9 master's, 5 doctorates awarded. *Degree requirements:* For master's, thesis or alternative; for doctorate, comprehensive exam, thesis/dissertation. *Entrance requirements:* For master's and doctorate, GRE General Test. Additional exam requirements/recommendations for international students: Required—TOEFL. *Application deadline:* For fall admission, 1/15 for domestic students. Applications are processed on a rolling basis. Application fee: $50 ($75 for international students). Electronic applications accepted. *Expenses:* Tuition, state resident: full-time $3991; part-time $221.74 per credit hour. Tuition, nonresident: full-time $9049; part-time $502.74 per credit hour. *Financial support:* Fellowships, research assistantships, teaching assistantships available. Financial award application deadline: 4/1; financial award applicants required to submit FAFSA. *Unit head:* Dr. Jack McMahan, Department Head, 979-845-2301, E-mail: granster@mail.bio.tamu.edu. *Application contact:* Graduate Advisor, 979-845-7755.

Texas A&M University, College of Veterinary Medicine, Department of Veterinary Pathobiology, College Station, TX 77843. Offers genetics (MS, PhD); veterinary microbiology (MS, PhD); veterinary parasitology (MS); veterinary pathology (MS, PhD). Part-time programs available. Postbaccalaureate distance learning degree programs offered. *Faculty:* 27. *Students:* 31 full-time (20 women), 15 part-time (12 women); includes 6 minority (2 African Americans, 1 Asian American or Pacific Islander, 3 Hispanic Americans), 13 international. Average age 33. In 2009, 1 master's, 4 doctorates awarded. Terminal master's awarded for partial completion of doctoral program. *Degree requirements:* For master's, thesis, seminars; for doctorate, thesis/dissertation, seminars. *Entrance requirements:* For master's and doctorate, GRE General Test, minimum GPA of 3.0 in last 60 hours. Additional exam requirements/recommendations for international students: Required—TOEFL. *Application deadline:* For fall admission, 3/1 priority date for domestic students; for spring admission, 8/1 priority date for domestic students. Applications are processed on a rolling basis. Application fee: $50 ($75 for international students). Electronic applications accepted. *Expenses:* Tuition, state resident: full-time $3991; part-time $221.74 per credit hour. Tuition, nonresident: full-time $9049; part-time $502.74 per credit hour. *Financial support:* In 2009–10, fellowships with partial tuition reimbursements (averaging $16,000 per year), research assistantships with partial tuition reimbursements (averaging $15,400 per year), teaching assistantships with partial tuition reimbursements (averaging $16,000 per year) were awarded; Federal Work-Study, institutionally sponsored loans, scholarships/grants, traineeships, health care benefits, and unspecified assistantships also available. Support available to part-time students. Financial award applicants required to submit FAFSA. *Faculty research:* Infectious and noninfectious diseases of animals and birds, animal genetics, molecular biology, immunology, virology. *Unit head:* Dr. Fuller Bazer, Interim Head, 979-845-5941, Fax: 979-845-9231, E-mail: fbazer@tamu.edu. *Application contact:* Dr. G. G. Wagner, Graduate Advisor, 979-845-2851, Fax: 979-862-1147, E-mail: gwagner@cvm.tamu.edu.

Texas Tech University, Graduate School, College of Arts and Sciences, Department of Biological Sciences, Lubbock, TX 79409. Offers biological informatics (MS); biology (MS, PhD); microbiology (MS); zoology (MS, PhD). Part-time programs available. *Faculty:* 31 full-time (6 women). *Students:* 120 full-time (59 women), 5 part-time (3 women); includes 5 minority (1 Asian American or Pacific Islander, 4 Hispanic Americans), 65 international. Average age 29. 121 applicants, 42% accepted, 24 enrolled. In 2009, 17 master's, 6 doctorates awarded. *Degree requirements:* For master's, thesis or alternative; for doctorate, thesis/dissertation. *Entrance requirements:* For master's and doctorate, GRE General Test. Additional exam requirements/recommendations for international students: Required—TOEFL (minimum score 550 paper-based; 213 computer-based). *Application deadline:* For fall admission, 3/1 priority date for international students; for spring admission, 11/1 priority date for international students. Applications are processed on a rolling basis. Application fee: $50 ($75 for international students). Electronic applications accepted. *Expenses:* Tuition, state resident: full-time $5100; part-time $213 per credit hour. Tuition, nonresident: full-time $11,748; part-time $490 per credit hour. Required fees: $2298; $50 per credit hour. $555 per semester. *Financial support:* In 2009–10, 16 research assistantships with partial tuition reimbursements (averaging $21,854 per year), 11 teaching assistantships with partial tuition reimbursements (averaging $19,985 per year) were awarded; career-related internships or fieldwork, Federal Work-Study, and institutionally sponsored loans also available. Support available to part-time students. Financial award application deadline: 4/15; financial award applicants required to submit FAFSA. *Faculty research:* Biodiversity and evolution, climate change in arid ecosystems, plant biology and biotechnology, animal communication and behavior, zoonotic and emerging diseases. Total annual research expenditures: $2.1 million. *Unit head:* Dr. Llewellyn D. Densmore, Chair, 806-742-2715, Fax: 806-742-2963, E-mail: jlou.densmore@ttu.edu. *Application contact:* Dr. Randall M. Jeter, Graduate Adviser, 806-742-2710 Ext. 223, Fax: 806-742-2963, E-mail: randall.jeter@ttu.edu.

Thomas Jefferson University, Jefferson College of Graduate Studies, MS Program in Microbiology, Philadelphia, PA 19107. Offers MS. Part-time and evening/weekend programs available. *Faculty:* 15 full-time (4 women), 9 part-time/adjunct (5 women). *Students:* 25 part-time (15 women); includes 4 minority (2 African Americans, 2 Asian Americans or Pacific Islanders), 2 international. 29 applicants, 62% accepted, 16 enrolled. In 2009, 9 master's awarded. *Degree requirements:* For master's, thesis, clerkship. *Entrance requirements:* For master's, GRE General Test or MCAT, minimum GPA of 3.0. Additional exam requirements/recommendations for international students: Required—TOEFL (minimum score 250 computer-based; 100 iBT). *Application deadline:* For fall admission, 8/1 priority date for domestic students, 3/1 priority date for international students; for winter admission, 12/1 priority date for domestic students, 6/1 priority date for international students; for spring admission, 4/1 priority date for domestic students. Applications are processed on a rolling basis. Application fee: $50. Electronic applications accepted. *Expenses:* Contact institution. *Financial support:* In 2009–10, 12 students received support. Federal Work-Study and institutionally sponsored loans available. Support available to part-time students. Financial award application deadline: 5/1; financial award applicants required to submit FAFSA. *Unit head:* Dr. Jerome G. Buescher, Program Director, 215-503-0159, Fax: 215-503-3433, E-mail: jerome.buescher@jefferson.edu. *Application contact:* Eleanor M. Gorman, Assistant Coordinator, Graduate Center Programs, 215-503-5799, Fax: 215-503-3433, E-mail: eleanor.gorman@jefferson.edu.

Thomas Jefferson University, Jefferson College of Graduate Studies, PhD Program in Immunology and Microbial Pathogenesis, Philadelphia, PA 19107. Offers PhD. *Faculty:* 34 full-time (5 women), 2 part-time/adjunct (0 women). *Students:* 27 full-time (14 women); includes 4 minority (1 African American, 2 Asian Americans or Pacific Islanders, 1 Hispanic American), 2 international. 58 applicants, 16% accepted, 4 enrolled. In 2009, 3 doctorates awarded. *Degree requirements:* For doctorate, comprehensive exam, thesis/dissertation. *Entrance requirements:* For doctorate, GRE General Test, minimum GPA of 3.2. Additional exam requirements/recommendations for international students: Required—TOEFL (minimum score 250 computer-based; 100 iBT) or IELTS. *Application deadline:* For fall admission, 1/15 priority date for domestic and international students. Applications are processed on a rolling basis. Application fee: $50. Electronic applications accepted. *Expenses:* Tuition: Full-time $26,858; part-time $879 per credit. Required fees: $525. *Financial support:* In 2009–10, 27 students received support, including 27 fellowships with full tuition reimbursements available (averaging $52,883 per year); Federal Work-Study, institutionally sponsored loans, scholarships/grants, traineeships, and stipend also available. Support available to part-time students. Financial award application deadline: 5/1; financial award applicants required to submit FAFSA. Total annual research expenditures: $15.7 million. *Unit head:* Dr. Kishore Alugupalli, Program Director, 215-503-4550, Fax: 215-923-4153, E-mail: kishore.alugupalli@jefferson.edu. *Application contact:* Marc E. Stearns, Director of Admissions, 215-503-0155, Fax: 215-503-9920, E-mail: jcgs-info@jefferson.edu.

See Close-Up on page 361.

Tufts University, Sackler School of Graduate Biomedical Sciences, Department of Molecular Biology and Microbiology, Medford, MA 02155. Offers molecular microbiology (PhD), including microbiology, molecular biology, molecular microbiology. *Faculty:* 18 full-time (7 women). *Students:* 29 full-time (21 women); includes 8 minority (2 African Americans, 4 Asian Americans or Pacific Islanders, 2 Hispanic Americans), 1 international. Average age 27. 80 applicants, 18% accepted, 5 enrolled. In 2009, 4 doctorates awarded. Terminal master's awarded for partial completion of doctoral program. *Degree requirements:* For doctorate, comprehensive exam, thesis/dissertation. *Entrance requirements:* For doctorate, GRE General Test, 3 letters of reference. Additional exam requirements/recommendations for international students: Required—TOEFL. *Application deadline:* For fall admission, 12/15 priority date for domestic and international students. Applications are processed on a rolling basis. Application fee: $70. Electronic applications accepted. *Expenses:* Tuition: Full-time $38,096; part-time $3962 per credit. Required fees: $686; $40 per year. Tuition and fees vary according to course level, course load, degree level, program and student level. *Financial support:* In 2009–10, 29 students received support, including 29 research assistantships with full tuition reimbursements available (averaging $28,500 per year); scholarships/grants, health care benefits, and tuition waivers (full) also available. Financial award application deadline: 12/15. *Faculty research:* Fundamental problems of molecular biology of prokaryotes, eukaryotes and their viruses. *Unit head:* Dr. Michael Malamy, Director, 617-636-6750, Fax: 617-636-0337, E-mail: michael.malamy@tufts.edu. *Application contact:* Kellie Johnston, Associate Director of Admissions, 617-636-6767, Fax: 617-633-0375, E-mail: sackler-school@tufts.edu.

Tulane University, School of Medicine and School of Liberal Arts, Graduate Programs in Biomedical Sciences, Department of Microbiology and Immunology, New Orleans, LA 70118-5669. Offers MS, PhD, MD/PhD. MS and PhD offered through the Graduate School. *Degree requirements:* For master's, thesis; for doctorate, 2 foreign languages, thesis/dissertation. *Entrance requirements:* For master's, GRE General Test, minimum B average in undergraduate course work; for doctorate, GRE General Test, GRE Subject Test. Additional exam requirements/recommendations for international students: Required—TOEFL. Electronic applications accepted. *Faculty research:* Vaccine development, viral pathogenesis, molecular virology, bacterial pathogenesis, fungal pathogenesis.

Universidad Central del Caribe, School of Medicine, Program in Biomedical Sciences, Bayamón, PR 00960-6032. Offers anatomy and cell biology (MA, MS); biochemistry (MS); biomedical sciences (MA); microbiology and immunology (MA, MS); pharmacology (MS); physiology (MA, MS).

Université de Montréal, Faculty of Medicine, Department of Microbiology and Immunology, Montréal, QC H3C 3J7, Canada. Offers M Sc, PhD. *Faculty:* 44 full-time (14 women), 29 part-time/adjunct (8 women). *Students:* 13 full-time (7 women), 120 part-time (69 women). 82 applicants, 21% accepted, 15 enrolled. In 2009, 10 master's, 8 doctorates awarded. Terminal master's awarded for partial completion of doctoral program. *Degree requirements:* For master's, thesis; for doctorate, thesis/dissertation, general exam. *Entrance requirements:* For master's and doctorate, proficiency in French, knowledge of English. *Application deadline:* For fall admission, 2/1 priority date for domestic students; for winter admission, 11/1 priority date for domestic students; for spring admission, 2/1 priority date for domestic students. Application fee: $100. Electronic applications accepted. *Unit head:* Dr. Pierre Belhumeur, Director, 514-343-6273, Fax: 514-343-5701, E-mail: pierre.belhumeur@umontreal.ca. *Application contact:* Dr. George Szatmari, Chairperson, 514-343-5767, Fax: 514-343-5701, E-mail: george.szatmari@umontreal.ca.

Université de Montréal, Faculty of Medicine, Program in Specialized Studies, Montréal, QC H3C 3J7, Canada. Offers anesthesia (DES); diagnostic radiology (DES); family medicine (DES); gastroenterology (DES); geriatry (DES); intensive care (DES); medical biochemistry (DES); medical genetics (DES); medicine (DES); microbiology and infectious diseases (DES); nuclear medicine (DES); obstetrics and gynecology (DES); ophthalmology (DES); pediatrics (DES); pneumology (DES); psychiatry (DES); radiology-oncology (DES); rheumatology (DES); surgery (DES). *Faculty:* 154 full-time (40 women), 333 part-time/adjunct (100 women). *Students:* 930 full-time (580 women), 7 part-time (all women). 74 applicants, 77% accepted, 29 enrolled. *Application deadline:* For fall admission, 2/1 priority date for domestic students; for winter admission, 11/1 priority date for domestic students; for spring admission, 2/1 priority date for domestic students. Application fee: $100. Electronic applications accepted. *Unit head:* Lorraine Locas, Assistant to the Vice Dean of Graduate Studies, 514-343-6269, Fax: 514-343-5751, E-mail: lorraine.locas@umontreal.ca. *Application contact:* Dr. Andre Ferron, Vice Dean of Graduate Studies, 514-343-6111 Ext. 0933, Fax: 514-343-5751, E-mail: andre.ferron@umontreal.ca.

Université de Sherbrooke, Faculty of Medicine and Health Sciences, Graduate Programs in Medicine, Program in Microbiology, Sherbrooke, QC J1H 5N4, Canada. Offers M Sc, PhD. Terminal master's awarded for partial completion of doctoral program. *Degree requirements:* For master's, thesis; for doctorate, thesis/dissertation. Electronic applications accepted. *Faculty research:* Oncogenes, alternative splicing mechanisms, genomics, telomerase, DNA repair, Clostridium difficile, Campylobacter jejuni.

Université du Québec, Institut National de la Recherche Scientifique, Graduate Programs, Research Center—INRS—Institut Armand-Frappier—Human Health, Québec, QC G1K 9A9, Canada. Offers applied microbiology (M Sc); biology (PhD); experimental health sciences (M Sc); virology and immunology (M Sc, PhD). Programs given in French. Part-time programs available. *Faculty:* 37. *Students:* 157 full-time (97 women), 4 part-time (all women), 41 international. Average age 30. In 2009, 14 master's, 5 doctorates awarded. *Median time to degree:* Of those who began their doctoral program in fall 2001, 67% received their degree in 8 years or less. *Degree requirements:* For doctorate, thesis/dissertation. *Entrance requirements:* For master's and doctorate, appropriate bachelor's degree, proficiency in French. *Application deadline:* For fall admission, 3/30 for domestic and international students; for winter admission, 11/1 for domestic and international students. Application fee: $30 Canadian dollars. *Financial support:* Fellowships, research assistantships, teaching assistantships available. *Faculty research:* Immunity, infection and cancer; toxicology and environmental biotechnology; molecular pharmacochemistry. *Unit head:* Alain Fournier, Director, 450-687-5010, Fax: 450-686-5501, E-mail: alain.fournier@iaf.inrs.ca. *Application contact:* Yvonne Boisvert, Registrar, 418-654-3861, Fax: 418-654-3858, E-mail: registrariat@adm.inrs.ca.

Université Laval, Faculty of Agricultural and Food Sciences, Program in Agricultural Microbiology, Québec, QC G1K 7P4, Canada. Offers agricultural microbiology (M Sc); agro-food microbiology (PhD). Terminal master's awarded for partial completion of doctoral program. *Degree requirements:* For master's, thesis; for doctorate, comprehensive exam, thesis/dissertation. *Entrance requirements:* For master's and doctorate, knowledge of French and English. Electronic applications accepted.

Université Laval, Faculty of Medicine, Graduate Programs in Medicine, Programs in Microbiology-Immunology, Québec, QC G1K 7P4, Canada. Offers M Sc, PhD. Terminal master's awarded for partial completion of doctoral program. *Degree requirements:* For master's, thesis; for doctorate, comprehensive exam, thesis/dissertation. *Entrance requirements:* For master's and doctorate, knowledge of French, comprehension of written English. Electronic applications accepted.

Université Laval, Faculty of Sciences and Engineering, Department of Biochemistry and Microbiology, Programs in Microbiology, Québec, QC G1K 7P4, Canada. Offers M Sc, PhD. Terminal master's awarded for partial completion of doctoral program. *Degree requirements:* For master's, thesis; for doctorate, comprehensive exam, thesis/dissertation. *Entrance requirements:* For master's and doctorate, knowledge of French, comprehension of written English. Electronic applications accepted.

University at Buffalo, the State University of New York, Graduate School, School of Medicine and Biomedical Sciences, Graduate Programs in Medicine and Biomedical Sciences, Department of Microbiology and Immunology, Buffalo, NY 14260. Offers MA, PhD. *Faculty:* 16 full-time (4 women), 2 part-time/adjunct (0 women). *Students:* 24 full-time (12 women); includes 2 minority (1 Asian American or Pacific Islander, 1 Hispanic American), 6 international. Average age 28. 10 applicants, 10% accepted. In 2009, 2 master's, 8 doctorates awarded. *Degree requirements:* For master's, comprehensive exam; for doctorate, thesis/dissertation, departmental qualifying exam. *Entrance requirements:* For master's and doctorate, GRE General Test, 3 letters of recommendation. Additional exam requirements/recommendations for international students: Required—TOEFL (minimum score 100 iBT). *Application deadline:* For fall admission, 2/1 priority date for domestic and international students. Applications are processed on a rolling basis. Application fee: $50. Electronic applications accepted. *Financial support:* In 2009–10, 9 fellowships with tuition reimbursements (averaging $24,000 per year), 18 research assistantships with tuition reimbursements (averaging $21,000 per year), 2 teaching assistantships with tuition reimbursements (averaging $21,000 per year) were awarded; Federal Work-Study, institutionally sponsored loans, traineeships, health care benefits, and unspecified assistantships also available. Financial award application deadline: 2/1; financial award applicants required to submit FAFSA. *Faculty research:* Bacteriology, immunology, parasitology, virology, microbial pathogenesis. Total annual research expenditures: $7.9 million. *Unit head:* Dr. John Hay, Interim Chairman, 716-829-2312, Fax: 716-829-2376. *Application contact:* Dr. Anthony Campagnari, Director of Graduate Studies, 716-829-2176, Fax: 716-829-2158.

The University of Alabama at Birmingham, Graduate Programs in Joint Health Sciences, Program in Microbiology, Birmingham, AL 35294. Offers PhD. *Degree requirements:* For doctorate, thesis/dissertation. *Entrance requirements:* For doctorate, GRE General Test, interview. Electronic applications accepted.

University of Alberta, Faculty of Graduate Studies and Research, Department of Biological Sciences, Edmonton, AB T6G 2E1, Canada. Offers environmental biology and ecology (M Sc, PhD); microbiology and biotechnology (M Sc, PhD); molecular biology and genetics (M Sc, PhD); physiology and cell biology (M Sc, PhD); plant biology (M Sc, PhD); systematics and evolution (M Sc, PhD). *Faculty:* 72 full-time (15 women), 15 part-time/adjunct (4 women). *Students:* 238 full-time (117 women), 32 part-time (15 women), 31 international. 206 applicants, 42% accepted. In 2009, 29 master's, 31 doctorates awarded. Terminal master's awarded for partial completion of doctoral program. *Degree requirements:* For master's, thesis; for doctorate, thesis/dissertation. *Entrance requirements:* Additional exam requirements/recommendations for international students: Required—TOEFL. *Application deadline:* For fall admission, 3/1 priority date for domestic students. Applications are processed on a rolling basis. Application fee: $0. Tuition and fees charges are reported in Canadian dollars. *Expenses:* Tuition, area resident: Full-time $4626 Canadian dollars; part-time $99.72 Canadian dollars per unit. International tuition: $8216 Canadian dollars full-time. Required fees: $3590 Canadian dollars; $99.72 Canadian dollars per unit. $215 Canadian dollars per term. *Financial support:* In 2009–10, 4 research assistantships with partial tuition reimbursements (averaging $12,000 per year), 103 teaching assistantships with partial tuition reimbursements (averaging $12,300 per year) were awarded; career-related internships or fieldwork and scholarships/grants also available. *Unit head:* Laura Frost, Chair, 780-492-1904. *Application contact:* Dr. John P. Chang, Associate Chair for Graduate Studies, 780-492-1257, Fax: 780-492-9457, E-mail: bio.grad.coordinator@ualberta.ca.

The University of Arizona, College of Medicine, Graduate Programs in Medicine, Department of Immunobiology, Tucson, AZ 85721. Offers MS, PhD. *Degree requirements:* For master's, thesis; for doctorate, thesis/dissertation. *Entrance requirements:* For master's and doctorate, GRE General Test, minimum GPA of 3.0. *Expenses:* Tuition, state resident: full-time $9028. Tuition, nonresident: full-time $24,890. *Faculty research:* Environmental and pathogenic microbiology, molecular biology.

The University of Arizona, Graduate College, College of Agriculture and Life Sciences, Program in Microbiology, Tucson, AZ 85721. Offers MS, PhD. *Faculty:* 7. *Students:* 14 full-time (9 women), 5 part-time (2 women); includes 3 minority (2 African Americans, 1 Hispanic American), 4 international. Average age 32. 31 applicants, 23% accepted, 2 enrolled. In 2009, 1 master's, 3 doctorates awarded. *Degree requirements:* For master's, thesis; for doctorate, comprehensive exam, thesis/dissertation. *Entrance requirements:* For master's and doctorate, GRE, minimum GPA of 3.0, 3 letters of recommendation, letter of intent. Additional exam requirements/recommendations for international students: Required—TOEFL (minimum score 550 paper-based; 213 computer-based). *Application deadline:* For fall admission, 2/28 for domestic students, 12/1 for international students. Application fee: $75. *Expenses:* Tuition, state resident: full-time $9028. Tuition, nonresident: full-time $24,890. *Financial support:* In 2009–10, 5 research assistantships (averaging $17,293 per year), 4 teaching assistantships (averaging $15,210 per year) were awarded. Financial award application deadline: 3/22. Total annual research expenditures: $2.7 million. *Unit head:* Dr. Jack Schmitz, Head, 520-626-5482, E-mail: jschmitz@u.arizona.edu. *Application contact:* Elaine Mattes, 520-621-4466, E-mail: emattes@email.arizona.edu.

The University of Arizona, Graduate College, College of Agriculture and Life Sciences, School of Natural Resources, Program in Microbiology and Pathobiology, Tucson, AZ 85721. Offers MS, PhD. *Students:* 42 full-time (23 women), 43 part-time (22 women); includes 2 American Indian/Alaska Native, 2 Asian Americans or Pacific Islanders, 4 Hispanic Americans, 16 international. Average age 31.Terminal master's awarded for partial completion of doctoral program. *Degree requirements:* For master's, thesis; for doctorate, comprehensive exam, thesis/dissertation. *Entrance requirements:* For master's and doctorate, GRE, minimum GPA of 3.0, 3 letters of recommendation, letter of intent. Additional exam requirements/recommendations for international students: Required—TOEFL (minimum score 550 paper-based; 213 computer-based; 80 iBT); Recommended—IELTS (minimum score 7). *Application deadline:* For fall admission, 2/28 for domestic students, 12/1 for international students. Applications are processed on a rolling basis. Application fee: $75. *Expenses:* Tuition, state resident: full-time $9028. Tuition, nonresident: full-time $24,890. *Financial support:* Research assistantships with tuition reimbursements, teaching assistantships with tuition reimbursements, scholarships/grants available. Financial award application deadline: 3/22. *Faculty research:* Antibiotic resistance, molecular pathogenesis of bacteria, food safety, diagnosis of animal disease, parasitology. *Application contact:* Elaine Mattes, 520-621-4466, E-mail: emattes@email.arizona.edu.

University of Arkansas for Medical Sciences, Graduate School, Graduate Programs in Biomedical Sciences, Department of Microbiology and Immunology, Little Rock, AR 72205-7199. Offers MS, PhD, MD/PhD. *Faculty:* 19 full-time (4 women), 6 part-time/adjunct (3 women). *Students:* 14 full-time, 2 part-time. In 2009, 3 doctorates awarded. *Degree requirements:* For master's, thesis; for doctorate, thesis/dissertation. *Entrance requirements:* For master's and doctorate, GRE General Test. Additional exam requirements/recommendations for international students: Required—TOEFL. *Application deadline:* For fall admission, 2/15 for domestic and international students. Application fee: $0. *Financial support:* Research assistantships available. Support available to part-time students. *Faculty research:* Tumor immunology and immunotherapy, microbial pathogenesis and genetics, allergy, immune response in infectious diseases. *Unit head:* Dr. Richard Morrison, Chairman, 501-686-8599, E-mail: rpmorrison@uams.edu. *Application contact:* Dr. Marie Chow, Professor, 501-686-5155, E-mail: chowmarie@uams.edu.

The University of British Columbia, Faculty of Science, Department of Microbiology and Immunology, Vancouver, BC V6T 1Z1, Canada. Offers M Sc, PhD. *Degree requirements:* For master's, thesis; for doctorate, comprehensive exam, thesis/dissertation. *Entrance requirements:* For master's and doctorate, GRE General Test. Additional exam requirements/recommendations for international students: Required—TOEFL (minimum score 590 paper-based; 243 computer-based). Electronic applications accepted. *Faculty research:* Bacterial genetics, metabolism, pathogenic bacteriology, virology.

University of Calgary, Faculty of Medicine and Faculty of Graduate Studies, Department of Microbiology and Infectious Diseases, Calgary, AB T2N 1N4, Canada. Offers M Sc, PhD. *Degree requirements:* For master's, thesis, oral thesis exam; for doctorate, thesis/dissertation, candidacy exam, oral thesis exam. *Entrance requirements:* For master's and doctorate, minimum GPA of 3.2. Additional exam requirements/recommendations for international students: Required—TOEFL (minimum score 580 paper-based; 237 computer-based). Electronic applications accepted. *Faculty research:* Bacteriology, virology, parasitology, immunology.

University of California, Berkeley, Graduate Division, College of Natural Resources, Group in Microbiology, Berkeley, CA 94720-1500. Offers PhD. *Students:* 44 full-time (28 women). Average age 28. 82 applicants, 4 enrolled. In 2009, 6 doctorates awarded. *Degree requirements:* For doctorate, thesis/dissertation. *Entrance requirements:* For doctorate, GRE General Test, minimum GPA of 3.0, 3 letters of recommendation. *Application deadline:* For fall admission, 12/1 for domestic students. Application fee: $70 ($90 for international students). *Financial support:* Fellowships, research assistantships, teaching assistantships, unspecified assistantships available. *Unit head:* Prof. Steve Lindow, Head, 510-642-5167, E-mail: pmbadvisor@nature.berkeley.edu. *Application contact:* Dana Jantz, Director of Student Services, 510-642-5167, Fax: 510-642-4995, E-mail: pmbadvisor@nature.berkeley.edu.

University of California, Davis, Graduate Studies, Graduate Group in Microbiology, Davis, CA 95616. Offers MS, PhD. Terminal master's awarded for partial completion of doctoral program. *Degree requirements:* For master's, thesis; for doctorate, thesis/dissertation. *Entrance requirements:* For master's and doctorate, GRE General Test, minimum GPA of 3.0. Additional exam requirements/recommendations for international students: Required—TOEFL (minimum score 550 paper-based; 213 computer-based). Electronic applications accepted. *Faculty research:* Microbial physiology and genetics, microbial molecular and cellular biology, microbial ecology, microbial pathogenesis and immunology, urology.

University of California, Irvine, School of Medicine and School of Biological Sciences, Department of Microbiology and Molecular Genetics, Irvine, CA 92697. Offers biological sciences (MS, PhD); MD/PhD. Students apply through the Graduate Program in Molecular Biology, Genetics, and Biochemistry. *Students:* 77 full-time (49 women); includes 36 minority (1 African American, 22 Asian Americans or Pacific Islanders, 13 Hispanic Americans), 2 international. Average age 26. 401 applicants, 24% accepted, 38 enrolled. In 2009, 4 master's, 8 doctorates awarded. *Degree requirements:* For doctorate, thesis/dissertation. *Entrance requirements:* For doctorate, GRE General Test, GRE Subject Test, minimum GPA of 3.0. Additional exam requirements/recommendations for international students: Required—TOEFL (minimum score 550 paper-based; 213 computer-based). *Application deadline:* For fall admission, 12/15 priority date for domestic students, 12/15 for international students. Application fee: $70 ($90 for international students). Electronic applications accepted. *Financial support:* Fellowships, research assistantships with full tuition reimbursements, teaching assistantships, institutionally sponsored loans, traineeships, health care benefits, and unspecified assistantships available. Financial award applicants required to submit FAFSA. *Faculty research:* Molecular biology and genetics of viruses, bacteria, and yeast; immune response; molecular biology of cultured animal cells; genetic basis of cancer; genetics and physiology of infectious agents. *Unit head:* Bert L. Semler, Chair, 949-824-7573 Ext. 6058, Fax: 949-824-8598, E-mail: blsemler@uci.edu. *Application contact:* Kimberly McKinney, Administrator, 949-824-8145, Fax: 949-824-1965, E-mail: kamckinn@uci.edu.

University of California, Los Angeles, David Geffen School of Medicine and Graduate Division, Graduate Programs in Medicine, Department of Microbiology, Immunology and Molecular Genetics, Los Angeles, CA 90095. Offers MS, PhD. *Degree requirements:* For doctorate, thesis/dissertation, oral and written qualifying exams. *Entrance requirements:* For doctorate, GRE General Test, GRE Subject Test. Additional exam requirements/recommendations for international students: Required—TOEFL.

University of California, Riverside, Graduate Division, Program in Microbiology, Riverside, CA 92521-0102. Offers MS, PhD. Part-time programs available. Terminal master's awarded for partial completion of doctoral program. *Degree requirements:* For master's, thesis; for doctorate, thesis/dissertation, qualifying exams. *Entrance requirements:* For master's and doctorate, GRE General Test, minimum GPA of 3.2. Additional exam requirements/recommendations for international students: Required—TOEFL (minimum score 550 paper-based; 213 computer-based; 80 iBT). Electronic applications accepted. *Faculty research:* Host-pathogen interactions; environmental microbiology; bioremediation; molecular microbiology; microbial genetics, physiology, and pathogenesis.

University of California, San Diego, School of Medicine and Office of Graduate Studies, Molecular Pathology Program, La Jolla, CA 92093. Offers bioinformatics (PhD); cancer biology/oncology (PhD); cardiovascular sciences and disease (PhD); microbiology (PhD); molecular pathology (PhD); neurological disease (PhD); stem cell and developmental biology (PhD); structural biology/drug design (PhD). *Entrance requirements:* For doctorate, GRE General Test, GRE Subject Test. Additional exam requirements/recommendations for international students: Required—TOEFL. Electronic applications accepted.

University of California, San Francisco, Graduate Division, Department of Microbiology and Immunology, San Francisco, CA 94143. Offers PhD. *Degree requirements:* For doctorate, thesis/dissertation. *Entrance requirements:* For doctorate, GRE General Test.

University of Central Florida, College of Medicine, Burnett School of Biomedical Sciences, Program in Molecular Biology and Microbiology, Orlando, FL 32816. Offers MS. Part-time and evening/weekend programs available. *Students:* 26 full-time (16 women); includes 7 minority (3 Asian Americans or Pacific Islanders, 4 Hispanic Americans), 10 international. Average age 27. 49 applicants, 43% accepted, 13 enrolled. In 2009, 14 master's awarded. *Degree requirements:* For master's, comprehensive exam, thesis. *Entrance requirements:* For master's, GRE General Test, minimum GPA of 3.0 in last 60 hours. Additional exam requirements/recommendations for international students: Required—TOEFL. *Application deadline:* For fall admission, 3/15 priority date for domestic students; for spring admission, 12/1 for domestic students. Electronic applications accepted. *Expenses:* Tuition, state resident: part-time $306.31 per credit hour. Tuition, nonresident: part-time $1099.01 per credit hour. Part-time tuition and fees vary according to degree level and program. *Financial support:* In 2009–10, 13 students received support, including 1 fellowship with partial tuition reimbursement available (averaging $10,000 per year), 5 research assistantships with partial tuition reimbursements available (averaging $7,200 per year), 9 teaching assistantships with partial tuition reimbursements available (averaging $9,100 per year); career-related internships or fieldwork, Federal Work-Study, institutionally sponsored loans, tuition waivers (partial), and unspecified assistantships also available. Financial award application deadline: 3/1; financial award applicants required to submit FAFSA. *Application contact:* Dr. Saleh A. Naser, Graduate Coordinator, 407-823-0955, E-mail: nasersi@mail.ucf.edu.

University of Chicago, Division of the Biological Sciences, Biomedical Sciences Cluster: Cancer Biology, Immunology, Molecular Metabolism and Nutrition, Pathology, and Microbiology, Committee on Microbiology, Chicago, IL 60637-1513. Offers PhD. *Faculty:* 17 full-time (4 women). *Students:* 26 full-time (12 women); includes 3 minority (1 African American, 2 Asian Americans or Pacific Islanders), 1 international. Average age 27. 48 applicants, 25% accepted, 7 enrolled. In 2009, 5 doctorates awarded. *Degree requirements:* For doctorate, thesis/dissertation, ethics class, 2 teaching assistantships. *Entrance requirements:* For doctorate, GRE General Test. Additional exam requirements/recommendations for international students: Required—TOEFL (minimum score 600 paper-based; 250 computer-based; 104 iBT), IELTS (minimum score 7). *Application deadline:* For fall admission, 12/1 priority date for domestic and international students. Application fee: $55. Electronic applications accepted. *Financial support:* In 2009–10, 26 students received support, including fellowships with full tuition reimbursements available (averaging $29,781 per year), research assistantships with full tuition reimbursements available (averaging $29,781 per year); institutionally sponsored loans and traineeships also available. Financial award application deadline: 1/5; financial award applicants required to submit FAFSA. *Faculty research:* Molecular genetics, herpes virus, adipoviruses, Picarna viruses, ENS viruses. *Unit head:* Dr. Olaf Schneewind, Chairman, 773-834-9060, Fax: 773-834-8150. *Application contact:* Emily Traw, Administrator, 773-834-3550, Fax: 773-834-7473, E-mail: etraw@bsd.uchicago.edu.

Microbiology

University of Cincinnati, Graduate School, College of Medicine, Graduate Programs in Biomedical Sciences, Department of Molecular Genetics, Biochemistry and Microbiology, Cincinnati, OH 45221. Offers MS, PhD. Terminal master's awarded for partial completion of doctoral program. *Degree requirements:* For master's, thesis or alternative; for doctorate, thesis/dissertation, qualifying exam. *Entrance requirements:* For master's and doctorate, GRE General Test. Additional exam requirements/recommendations for international students: Required—TOEFL (minimum score 600 paper-based; 250 computer-based; 100 iBT), TWE. Electronic applications accepted. *Faculty research:* Cancer biology and developmental genetics, gene regulation and chromosome structure, microbiology and pathogenic mechanisms, structural biology, membrane biochemistry and signal transduction.

University of Colorado at Boulder, Graduate School, College of Arts and Sciences, Department of Ecology and Evolutionary Biology, Boulder, CO 80309. Offers animal behavior (MA); biology (MA, PhD); environmental biology (MA, PhD); evolutionary biology (MA, PhD); neurobiology (MA); population biology (MA); population genetics (PhD). *Faculty:* 32 full-time (10 women). *Students:* 64 full-time (36 women), 15 part-time (9 women); includes 12 minority (1 American Indian/Alaska Native, 3 Asian Americans or Pacific Islanders, 8 Hispanic Americans), 4 international. Average age 29. 145 applicants, 14% accepted, 21 enrolled. In 2009, 9 master's, 6 doctorates awarded. Terminal master's awarded for partial completion of doctoral program. *Degree requirements:* For master's, comprehensive exam, thesis or alternative; for doctorate, comprehensive exam, thesis/dissertation. *Entrance requirements:* For master's, GRE General Test, GRE Subject Test, minimum undergraduate GPA of 3.0; for doctorate, GRE General Test, GRE Subject Test. *Application deadline:* For fall admission, 12/30 priority date for domestic students, 12/1 for international students. Application fee: $50 ($60 for international students). *Financial support:* In 2009–10, 25 fellowships (averaging $17,876 per year), 27 research assistantships (averaging $15,070 per year) were awarded; Federal Work-Study, institutionally sponsored loans, and tuition waivers (full) also available. *Faculty research:* Behavior, ecology, genetics, morphology, endocrinology, physiology, systematics. Total annual research expenditures: $3.1 million.

University of Colorado Denver, School of Medicine, Program in Microbiology, Denver, CO 80217-3364. Offers PhD. *Students:* 24 full-time (15 women); includes 4 minority (2 African Americans, 1 Asian American or Pacific Islander, 1 Hispanic American). In 2009, 3 doctorates awarded. *Degree requirements:* For doctorate, comprehensive exam, thesis/dissertation. *Entrance requirements:* For doctorate, GRE, minimum GPA of 3.0, 4 letters of recommendation. Additional exam requirements/recommendations for international students: Required—TOEFL (minimum score 550 paper-based; 213 computer-based). *Application deadline:* For fall admission, 1/1 for domestic students. Application fee: $50. Electronic applications accepted. *Financial support:* Fellowships, research assistantships, teaching assistantships, Federal Work-Study and institutionally sponsored loans available. Support available to part-time students. Financial award application deadline: 3/15; financial award applicants required to submit FAFSA. *Faculty research:* Molecular mechanisms of picornavirus replication, mechanisms of papovavirus assembly, human immune response in multiple sclerosis. *Unit head:* Dr. Randall K. Holmes, Chair, 303-724-4224, E-mail: randall.holmes@ucdenver.edu. *Application contact:* Dr. Ronald E. Gill, Director, 303-724-4227, E-mail: ron.gill@ucdenver.edu.

University of Connecticut, Graduate School, College of Liberal Arts and Sciences, Department of Molecular and Cell Biology, Field of Microbiology, Storrs, CT 06269. Offers MS, PhD. *Faculty:* 19 full-time (5 women). *Students:* 18 full-time (10 women), 2 part-time (both women); includes 4 minority (1 African American, 1 American Indian/Alaska Native, 1 Asian American or Pacific Islander, 1 Hispanic American), 4 international. Average age 28. 65 applicants, 12% accepted, 2 enrolled. In 2009, 2 master's, 2 doctorates awarded. Terminal master's awarded for partial completion of doctoral program. *Degree requirements:* For master's, comprehensive exam; for doctorate, thesis/dissertation. *Entrance requirements:* For master's and doctorate, GRE General Test, GRE Subject Test. Additional exam requirements/recommendations for international students: Required—TOEFL (minimum score 550 paper-based; 213 computer-based). *Application deadline:* For fall admission, 2/1 priority date for domestic and international students; for spring admission, 11/1 for domestic students, 10/1 for international students. Applications are processed on a rolling basis. Application fee: $55. Electronic applications accepted. *Expenses:* Tuition, state resident: full-time $4725; part-time $525 per credit. Tuition, nonresident: full-time $12,267; part-time $1363 per credit. Required fees: $346 per semester. Tuition and fees vary according to course load. *Financial support:* In 2009–10, 9 research assistantships with full tuition reimbursements, 5 teaching assistantships with full tuition reimbursements were awarded; fellowships, Federal Work-Study, scholarships/grants, health care benefits, and unspecified assistantships also available. Financial award application deadline: 2/1; financial award applicants required to submit FAFSA. *Unit head:* David Benson, Head, 860-486-4258, Fax: 860-486-4331, E-mail: david.benson@uconn.edu. *Application contact:* Anne St. Onje, Graduate Coordinator, 860-486-4314, Fax: 860-486-3943, E-mail: anne.st_onje@uconn.edu.

See Close-Up on page 187.

University of Delaware, College of Arts and Sciences, Department of Biological Sciences, Newark, DE 19716. Offers biotechnology (MS); cancer biology (MS, PhD); cell and extracellular matrix biology (MS, PhD); cell and systems physiology (MS, PhD); developmental biology (MS, PhD); ecology and evolution (MS, PhD); microbiology (MS, PhD); molecular biology and genetics (MS, PhD). Terminal master's awarded for partial completion of doctoral program. *Degree requirements:* For master's, thesis, preliminary exam; for doctorate, comprehensive exam, thesis/dissertation, preliminary exam. *Entrance requirements:* For master's and doctorate, GRE General Test. Additional exam requirements/recommendations for international students: Required—TOEFL (minimum score 600 paper-based; 250 computer-based); Recommended—TWE. Electronic applications accepted. *Faculty research:* Microorganisms, bone, cancer metastasis, developmental biology, cell biology, DNA.

University of Florida, College of Medicine, Department of Molecular Genetics and Microbiology, Gainesville, FL 32611. Offers MS, PhD. Terminal master's awarded for partial completion of doctoral program. *Degree requirements:* For master's, thesis; for doctorate, thesis/dissertation. *Entrance requirements:* For master's and doctorate, GRE General Test, minimum GPA of 3.0. Additional exam requirements/recommendations for international students: Required—TOEFL. Electronic applications accepted.

University of Florida, College of Medicine and Graduate School, Interdisciplinary Program in Biomedical Sciences, Concentration in Immunology and Microbiology, Gainesville, FL 32611. Offers PhD. *Degree requirements:* For doctorate, thesis/dissertation. *Entrance requirements:* For doctorate, GRE General Test, minimum GPA of 3.0. Additional exam requirements/recommendations for international students: Required—TOEFL. Electronic applications accepted.

See Close-Up on page 365.

University of Florida, Graduate School, College of Agricultural and Life Sciences, Department of Microbiology and Cell Science, Gainesville, FL 32611. Offers biochemistry and molecular biology (MS, PhD); microbiology and cell science (MS, PhD). *Degree requirements:* For doctorate, thesis/dissertation. *Entrance requirements:* For master's and doctorate, GRE General Test, minimum GPA of 3.0. Electronic applications accepted. *Faculty research:* Biomass conversion, membrane and cell wall chemistry, plant biochemistry and genetics.

University of Georgia, Graduate School, College of Arts and Sciences, Department of Microbiology, Athens, GA 30602. Offers MS, PhD. *Faculty:* 16 full-time (4 women). *Students:* 44 full-time (26 women), 1 (woman) part-time; includes 7 minority (2 African Americans, 2 Asian Americans or Pacific Islanders, 3 Hispanic Americans), 7 international. 66 applicants, 27% accepted, 7 enrolled. In 2009, 1 master's, 9 doctorates awarded. *Degree requirements:* For master's, thesis; for doctorate, one foreign language, thesis/dissertation. *Entrance requirements:* For master's and doctorate, GRE General Test. Additional exam requirements/recommendations for international students: Required—TOEFL (minimum score 550 paper-based; 213 computer-based). *Application deadline:* For fall admission, 7/1 priority date for domestic students; for spring admission, 11/15 for domestic students. Application fee: $50. Electronic applications accepted. *Expenses:* Tuition, state resident: full-time $6000; part-time $250 per credit hour. Tuition, nonresident: full-time $20,904; part-time $871 per credit hour. Required fees: $730 per semester. *Financial support:* In 2009–10, 9 fellowships (averaging $20,000 per year), 20 research assistantships (averaging $18,461 per year), 12 teaching assistantships (averaging $18,461 per year) were awarded; unspecified assistantships also available. Financial award application deadline: 12/15. *Unit head:* Dr. William B. Whitman, Head, 706-542-4219, E-mail: whitman@uga.edu. *Application contact:* Dr. Anna C. Karls, Graduate Coordinator, 706-543-0822, Fax: 706-542-2674, E-mail: akarls@uga.edu.

See Close-Up on page 367.

University of Guelph, Graduate Program Services, College of Biological Science, Department of Molecular and Cellular Biology, Guelph, ON N1G 2W1, Canada. Offers biochemistry (M Sc, PhD); biophysics (M Sc, PhD); botany (M Sc, PhD); microbiology (M Sc, PhD); molecular biology and genetics (M Sc, PhD). *Degree requirements:* For master's, thesis, research proposal; for doctorate, comprehensive exam, thesis/dissertation, research proposal. *Entrance requirements:* For master's, minimum B-average during previous 2 years of coursework; for doctorate, minimum A-average. Additional exam requirements/recommendations for international students: Required—TOEFL (minimum score 550 paper-based; 213 computer-based), IELTS (minimum score 6.5). Electronic applications accepted. *Faculty research:* Physiology, structure, genetics, and ecology of microbes; virology and microbial technology.

University of Hawaii at Manoa, Graduate Division, College of Natural Sciences, Department of Microbiology, Honolulu, HI 96822. Offers MS, PhD. Part-time programs available. *Faculty:* 22 full-time (5 women), 3 part-time/adjunct (2 women). *Students:* 26 full-time (12 women), 4 part-time (2 women); includes 11 minority (all Asian Americans or Pacific Islanders), 8 international. Average age 27. 26 applicants, 27% accepted, 6 enrolled. In 2009, 5 master's, 4 doctorates awarded. *Degree requirements:* For master's, thesis optional; for doctorate, comprehensive exam, thesis/dissertation. *Entrance requirements:* For master's and doctorate, GRE General Test. Additional exam requirements/recommendations for international students: Required—TOEFL (minimum score 580 paper-based; 237 computer-based; 92 iBT), IELTS (minimum score 5). *Application deadline:* For fall admission, 2/1 for domestic and international students; for spring admission, 8/1 for domestic and international students. Application fee: $60. *Expenses:* Tuition, state resident: full-time $8900; part-time $372 per credit. Tuition, nonresident: full-time $21,400; part-time $898 per credit. Required fees: $207 per semester. *Financial support:* In 2009–10, 2 fellowships (averaging $450 per year), 6 research assistantships (averaging $19,132 per year), 17 teaching assistantships (averaging $15,856 per year) were awarded. *Faculty research:* Virology, immunology, microbial physiology, medical microbiology, bacterial genetics. Total annual research expenditures: $852,000. *Application contact:* Dr. Paul Q. Patek, Chairperson, 808-956-8553, Fax: 808-956-5339, E-mail: patek@hawaii.edu.

University of Idaho, College of Graduate Studies, College of Agricultural and Life Sciences, Department of Microbiology, Molecular Biology and Biochemistry, Moscow, ID 83844-2282. Offers microbiology, molecular biology and biochemistry (PhD). *Faculty:* 15 full-time, 1 part-time/adjunct. *Students:* 21 full-time, 4 part-time. In 2009, 6 master's, 4 doctorates awarded. *Degree requirements:* For master's, thesis; for doctorate, one foreign language, thesis/dissertation. *Entrance requirements:* For master's, minimum GPA of 2.8; for doctorate, minimum undergraduate GPA of 2.8, 3.0 graduate. *Application deadline:* For fall admission, 8/1 for domestic students; for spring admission, 12/15 for domestic students. Application fee: $55 ($60 for international students). *Expenses:* Tuition, state resident: full-time $6120. Tuition, nonresident: full-time $17,712. *Financial support:* Research assistantships, teaching assistantships available. Financial award application deadline: 2/15. *Faculty research:* Bioremediation, biodegradation and molecular ecology, developmental and cellular biology, cell cycle regulation, molecular machines, pathogenic mechanisms in infectious disease. *Unit head:* Dr. Bruce Miller, Interim Chair, 208-885-7966, E-mail: mmbb@uidaho.edu. *Application contact:* Dr. Bruce Miller, Interim Chair, 208-885-7966, E-mail: mmbb@uidaho.edu.

University of Illinois at Chicago, College of Medicine and Graduate College, Graduate Programs in Medicine, Department of Microbiology and Immunology, Chicago, IL 60607-7128. Offers PhD, MD/PhD. *Degree requirements:* For doctorate, thesis/dissertation. *Entrance requirements:* For doctorate, GRE General Test, minimum GPA of 2.75. Additional exam requirements/recommendations for international students: Required—TOEFL.

University of Illinois at Urbana–Champaign, Graduate College, College of Liberal Arts and Sciences, School of Molecular and Cellular Biology, Department of Microbiology, Champaign, IL 61820. Offers MS, PhD. *Faculty:* 14 full-time (3 women). *Students:* 67 full-time (40 women); includes 10 minority (2 African Americans, 1 American Indian/Alaska Native, 3 Asian Americans or Pacific Islanders, 4 Hispanic Americans), 23 international. In 2009, 9 master's, 9 doctorates awarded. *Entrance requirements:* For master's and doctorate, GRE, minimum GPA of 3.0. Additional exam requirements/recommendations for international students: Required—TOEFL (minimum score 590 paper-based; 243 computer-based; 96 iBT). *Application deadline:* Applications are processed on a rolling basis. Application fee: $60 ($75 for international students). Electronic applications accepted. *Financial support:* In 2009–10, 18 fellowships, 45 research assistantships, 49 teaching assistantships were awarded; tuition waivers (full and partial) also available. *Faculty research:* Bacterial physiology and genetics, bacterial pathogenesis, host-pathogen interaction, molecular immunology. *Unit head:* John E. Cronan, Head, 217-333-7919, Fax: 217-244-6697, E-mail: jecronan@illinois.edu. *Application contact:* Deb LeBaugh, Office Manager, 217-333-9765, E-mail: lebaugh@illinois.edu.

The University of Iowa, Roy J. and Lucille A. Carver College of Medicine and Graduate College, Graduate Programs in Medicine, Department of Microbiology, Iowa City, IA 52242-1316. Offers general microbiology and microbial physiology (MS, PhD); immunology (MS, PhD); microbial genetics (MS, PhD); pathogenic bacteriology (MS, PhD); virology (MS, PhD). *Faculty:* 24 full-time (3 women), 8 part-time/adjunct (2 women). *Students:* 36 full-time (20 women); includes 3 minority (2 American Indian/Alaska Native, 1 Hispanic American), 5 international. Average age 25. 87 applicants, 14% accepted, 5 enrolled. In 2009, 3 master's, 7 doctorates awarded. *Degree requirements:* For master's, thesis; for doctorate, comprehensive exam, thesis/dissertation. *Entrance requirements:* For master's and doctorate, GRE General Test. Additional exam requirements/recommendations for international students: Required—TOEFL (minimum score 600 paper-based; 250 computer-based). *Application deadline:* For fall admission, 2/1 for domestic and international students. Application fee: $60 ($85 for international students). Electronic applications accepted. *Financial support:* In 2009–10, 4 fellowships with full tuition reimbursements (averaging $24,250 per year), 32 research assistantships with full tuition reimbursements (averaging $24,250 per year) were awarded; institutionally sponsored loans, scholarships/grants, traineeships, and health care benefits also available. *Faculty research:* Gene regulation, processing and transport of HIV, retroviral pathogenesis, biodegradation, biofilm. Total annual research expenditures: $11.7 million. *Unit head:* Dr. Michael A. Apicella, Head, 319-335-7810, E-mail: grad-micro-info@uiowa.edu. *Application contact:* Dr. Michael A. Apicella, Head, 319-335-7810, E-mail: grad-micro-info@uiowa.edu.

The University of Kansas, Graduate Studies, College of Liberal Arts and Sciences, Department of Molecular Biosciences, Lawrence, KS 66044. Offers biochemistry and biophysics (MA, PhD); microbiology (MA, PhD); molecular, cellular, and developmental biology (MA, PhD). *Students:* 58 full-time (30 women), 2 part-time (1 woman); includes 4 minority (1 American Indian/Alaska Native, 1 Asian American or Pacific Islander, 2 Hispanic Americans), 24 international. Average age 27. 49 applicants, 29% accepted, 4 enrolled. In 2009, 2 master's, 7 doctorates awarded. Terminal master's awarded for partial completion of doctoral program. *Degree requirements:* For master's, comprehensive exam, thesis; for doctorate, comprehensive exam, thesis/dissertation. *Entrance requirements:* For master's and doctorate, GRE General Test. Additional exam requirements/recommendations for international students: Required—TOEFL (minimum score 24 iBT). *Application deadline:* For fall admission, 12/15 for domestic and international students. Application fee: $45 ($55 for international students). Electronic applications accepted. *Expenses:* Tuition, state resident: full-time $6492; part-time $270.50

per credit hour. Tuition, nonresident: full-time $15,510; part-time $646.25 per credit hour. Required fees: $847; $70.56 per credit hour. Tuition and fees vary according to course load and program. *Financial support:* Fellowships with tuition reimbursements, research assistantships with tuition reimbursements, teaching assistantships with tuition reimbursements, health care benefits and unspecified assistantships available. Financial award application deadline: 3/1. *Faculty research:* Structure and function of proteins, genetics of organism development, molecular genetics, neurophysiology, molecular virology and pathogenics, developmental biology, cell biology. *Unit head:* Dr. Mark Richter, Chair, 785-864-4311, Fax: 785-864-5294, E-mail: richter@ku.edu. *Application contact:* John P. Connolly, Graduate Program Assistant, 785-864-4311, Fax: 785-864-5294, E-mail: jconnolly@ku.edu.

The University of Kansas, University of Kansas Medical Center, School of Medicine, Department of Microbiology, Molecular Genetics and Immunology, Kansas City, KS 66160. Offers microbiology (PhD); MD/PhD. *Faculty:* 12 full-time, 1 part-time/adjunct. *Students:* 1 (woman) full-time, 13 part-time (5 women), 9 international. Average age 29. In 2009, 2 degrees awarded. *Median time to degree:* Of those who began their doctoral program in fall 2001, 100% received their degree in 8 years or less. *Degree requirements:* For doctorate, comprehensive exam, thesis/dissertation, research skills. *Entrance requirements:* For doctorate, GRE General Test, B Sc. Additional exam requirements/recommendations for international students: Required—TOEFL. *Application deadline:* For fall admission, 1/15 priority date for international students. *Expenses:* Tuition, state resident: full-time $6492; part-time $270.50 per credit hour. Tuition, nonresident: full-time $15,510; part-time $646.25 per credit hour. Required fees: $847; $70.56 per credit hour. Tuition and fees vary according to course load and program. *Financial support:* In 2009–10, 1 fellowship with tuition reimbursement (averaging $24,000 per year), 9 research assistantships with partial tuition reimbursements (averaging $24,000 per year), 3 teaching assistantships with full and partial tuition reimbursements (averaging $24,000 per year) were awarded; scholarships/grants and unspecified assistantships also available. *Faculty research:* Immunology, infectious disease, virology, molecular genetics, bacteriology. Total annual research expenditures: $4 million. *Unit head:* Dr. Michael Parmely, Interim Chair, 913-588-7010, Fax: 913-588-7295, E-mail: mparmely@kumc.edu. *Application contact:* Dr. Joe Lutkenhaus, Microbiology Graduate Studies Director, 913-588-7054, Fax: 913-588-7295, E-mail: jlutkenh@kumc.edu.

University of Kentucky, Graduate School, Graduate School Programs from the College of Medicine, Program in Microbiology and Immunology, Lexington, KY 40506-0032. Offers microbiology (PhD). *Degree requirements:* For doctorate, comprehensive exam, thesis/dissertation. *Entrance requirements:* For doctorate, GRE General Test, minimum undergraduate GPA of 2.75. Additional exam requirements/recommendations for international students: Required—TOEFL (minimum score 550 paper-based; 213 computer-based). Electronic applications accepted.

University of Louisville, School of Medicine, Department of Microbiology and Immunology, Louisville, KY 40292-0001. Offers MS, PhD, MD/PhD. *Faculty:* 22 full-time (6 women). *Students:* 34 full-time (22 women); includes 6 minority (4 African Americans, 2 Asian Americans or Pacific Islanders), 13 international. Average age 30. 51 applicants, 31% accepted, 10 enrolled. In 2009, 2 master's, 8 doctorates awarded. Terminal master's awarded for partial completion of doctoral program. *Degree requirements:* For master's, thesis; for doctorate, comprehensive exam, thesis/dissertation. *Entrance requirements:* For master's, GRE General Test (minimum score 1000 verbal and quantitiative), minimum GPA of 3.0; 1 year of course work in biology, organic chemistry, physics; 1 semester of course work in calculus and quantitative analysis, biochemistry, or molecular biology; for doctorate, GRE General Test (Verbal and Quantitative minimum score of 1000), minimum GPA of 3.0; 1 year of course work in biology, organic chemistry, physics; 1 semester of course work in calculus and quantitative analysis, biochemistry, or molecular biology. Additional exam requirements/recommendations for international students: Required—TOEFL. *Application deadline:* For fall admission, 2/1 priority date for domestic and international students. Applications are processed on a rolling basis. Application fee: $50. Electronic applications accepted. *Financial support:* In 2009–10, 17 fellowships with full tuition reimbursements (averaging $22,000 per year), 18 research assistantships with full tuition reimbursements (averaging $22,000 per year) were awarded. Financial award application deadline: 4/15. *Faculty research:* Opportunistic and emerging infections; biology and regulation of the immune system; cellular and molecular bases of chronic inflammatory response; role of cytokines and chemokines in cancer, autoimmune and infectious disease; host defense and pathogenesis of viral infections. *Unit head:* Dr. Robert D. Stout, Chair, 502-852-5351, Fax: 502-852-7531, E-mail: bobstout@louisville.edu. *Application contact:* Carolyn M Burton, Academic Coordinator, 502-852-6208, Fax: 502-852-7531, E-mail: cmburt01@gwise.louisville.edu.

University of Maine, Graduate School, College of Natural Sciences, Forestry, and Agriculture, Department of Biochemistry, Molecular Biology, and Microbiology, Orono, ME 04469. Offers biochemistry (MPS, MS); biochemistry and molecular biology (PhD); microbiology (MPS, MS, PhD). *Faculty:* 9 full-time (4 women), 5 part-time/adjunct (3 women). *Students:* 19 full-time (11 women), 22 part-time (16 women); includes 3 minority (1 American Indian/Alaska Native, 1 Asian American or Pacific Islander, 1 Hispanic American), 6 international. Average age 30. 42 applicants, 33% accepted, 10 enrolled. In 2009, 5 master's, 2 doctorates awarded. *Degree requirements:* For doctorate, thesis/dissertation. *Entrance requirements:* For master's and doctorate, GRE General Test. Additional exam requirements/recommendations for international students: Required—TOEFL. *Application deadline:* For fall admission, 2/1 priority date for domestic students. Applications are processed on a rolling basis. Application fee: $65. Electronic applications accepted. *Financial support:* In 2009–10, 5 research assistantships with tuition reimbursements (averaging $20,893 per year), 12 teaching assistantships with tuition reimbursements (averaging $19,296 per year) were awarded; tuition waivers (full and partial) also available. Financial award application deadline: 3/1. *Unit head:* Dr. Robert Gundersen, Chair, 207-581-2802, Fax: 207-581-2801. *Application contact:* Scott G. Delcourt, Associate Dean of the Graduate School, 207-581-3291, Fax: 207-581-3232, E-mail: graduate@maine.edu.

University of Manitoba, Faculty of Graduate Studies, Faculty of Science, Department of Microbiology, Winnipeg, MB R3T 2N2, Canada. Offers M Sc, PhD. *Degree requirements:* For master's, thesis; for doctorate, one foreign language, thesis/dissertation.

University of Maryland, Baltimore, Graduate School, Graduate Program in Life Sciences, Program in Molecular Microbiology and Immunology, Baltimore, MD 21201. Offers PhD, MD/PhD. *Students:* 61 full-time (37 women), 9 part-time (5 women); includes 19 minority (7 African Americans, 9 Asian Americans or Pacific Islanders, 3 Hispanic Americans), 8 international. Average age 27. 167 applicants, 11% accepted, 10 enrolled. In 2009, 5 doctorates awarded. *Entrance requirements:* For doctorate, GRE. Additional exam requirements/recommendations for international students: Required—TOEFL (minimum score 550 paper-based; 80 iBT); Recommended—IELTS (minimum score 7). *Application deadline:* For fall admission, 1/15 for domestic and international students. Application fee: $50. Electronic applications accepted. *Expenses:* Tuition, state resident: full-time $7290; part-time $405 per credit hour. Tuition, nonresident: full-time $12,780; part-time $710 per credit hour. Required fees: $774; $10 per credit hour. $297 per semester. Tuition and fees vary according to course load, degree level and program. *Financial support:* In 2009–10, research assistantships with partial tuition reimbursements (averaging $25,000 per year); fellowships also available. Financial award application deadline: 3/1. *Unit head:* Dr. Nicholas Carbonetti, Director, 410-706-7677, E-mail: ncarbone@umaryland.edu. *Application contact:* June Green, Program Coordinator, 410-706-7126, Fax: 410-706-2129, E-mail: jgreen@umaryland.edu.

University of Massachusetts Amherst, Graduate School, College of Natural Sciences, Department of Microbiology, Amherst, MA 01003. Offers MS, PhD. Part-time programs available. *Faculty:* 15 full-time (3 women). *Students:* 30 full-time (21 women), 2 part-time (1 woman); includes 5 minority (1 African American, 3 Asian Americans or Pacific Islanders, 1 Hispanic American), 10 international. Average age 27. 69 applicants, 22% accepted, 9 enrolled. In 2009, 7 master's, 4 doctorates awarded. Terminal master's awarded for partial completion of doctoral program. *Degree requirements:* For master's, thesis or alternative; for doctorate, comprehensive exam, thesis/dissertation. *Entrance requirements:* For master's and doctorate, GRE General Test. Additional exam requirements/recommendations for international students: Required—TOEFL (minimum score 550 paper-based; 213 computer-based; 80 iBT), IELTS (minimum score 6.5). *Application deadline:* For fall admission, 12/1 for domestic and international students; for spring admission, 10/1 for domestic and international students. Applications are processed on a rolling basis. Application fee: $50 ($65 for international students). Electronic applications accepted. *Expenses:* Tuition, state resident: full-time $2640; part-time $110 per credit. Tuition, nonresident: full-time $9936; part-time $414 per credit. Tuition and fees vary according to course load. *Financial support:* In 2009–10, 27 research assistantships with full tuition reimbursements (averaging $12,769 per year), 17 teaching assistantships with full tuition reimbursements (averaging $10,684 per year) were awarded; fellowships, career-related internships or fieldwork, Federal Work-Study, scholarships/grants, traineeships, health care benefits, tuition waivers (full), and unspecified assistantships also available. Support available to part-time students. Financial award application deadline: 12/1. *Unit head:* Dr. Klaus Nusslein, Graduate Program Director, 413-545-6675, Fax: 413-545-1578. *Application contact:* Jean M. Ames, Supervisor of Admissions, 413-545-0722, Fax: 413-577-0010, E-mail: gradadm@grad.umass.edu.

See Close-Up on page 369.

University of Massachusetts Worcester, Graduate School of Biomedical Sciences, Program in Molecular Genetics and Microbiology, Worcester, MA 01655-0115. Offers PhD. *Degree requirements:* For doctorate, comprehensive exam, thesis/dissertation. *Entrance requirements:* For doctorate, GRE General Test. Additional exam requirements/recommendations for international students: Required—TOEFL (minimum score 600 paper-based; 250 computer-based). Electronic applications accepted. *Faculty research:* Contemporary molecular biology, bacterial and yeast genetics, eukaryotic and cellular immunology, virology and bacterial pathogenesis.

University of Medicine and Dentistry of New Jersey, Graduate School of Biomedical Sciences, Graduate Programs in Biomedical Sciences–Newark, Department of Microbiology and Molecular Genetics, Newark, NJ 07107. Offers PhD. *Students:* 21 full-time (14 women); includes 3 Asian Americans or Pacific Islanders, 4 international. *Degree requirements:* For doctorate, thesis/dissertation, qualifying exam. *Entrance requirements:* For doctorate, GRE General Test. Additional exam requirements/recommendations for international students: Required—TOEFL. *Application deadline:* For fall admission, 2/1 for domestic students. Applications are processed on a rolling basis. Application fee: $40. Electronic applications accepted. *Financial support:* Fellowships, research assistantships, Federal Work-Study, institutionally sponsored loans, and tuition waivers (full and partial) available. Financial award application deadline: 5/1. *Faculty research:* Molecular genetics of yeast, mutagenesis and carcinogenesis of DNA, bacterial protein synthesis, mammalian cell genetics, adenovirus gene expression. *Unit head:* Dr. Stephen Garrett, Program Director, 973-972-4391, Fax: 973-972-8981. *Application contact:* Dr. Stephen Garrett, Program Director, 973-972-4391, Fax: 973-972-8981.

University of Medicine and Dentistry of New Jersey, Graduate School of Biomedical Sciences, Graduate Programs in Biomedical Sciences–Piscataway, Program in Molecular Genetics, Microbiology and Immunology, Piscataway, NJ 08854-5635. Offers MS, PhD, MD/PhD. Terminal master's awarded for partial completion of doctoral program. *Degree requirements:* For master's, thesis, qualifying exam; for doctorate, thesis/dissertation, qualifying exam. *Entrance requirements:* For master's and doctorate, GRE General Test. Additional exam requirements/recommendations for international students: Required—TOEFL. Electronic applications accepted. *Faculty research:* Interferon, receptors, retrovirus evolution, Arbo virus/host cell interactions.

University of Miami, Graduate School, Miller School of Medicine, Graduate Programs in Medicine, Department of Microbiology and Immunology, Coral Gables, FL 33124. Offers PhD, MD/PhD. *Degree requirements:* For doctorate, thesis/dissertation, oral and written qualifying exams. *Entrance requirements:* For doctorate, GRE General Test. Additional exam requirements/recommendations for international students: Required—TOEFL. Electronic applications accepted. *Faculty research:* Cellular and molecular immunology, molecular and pathogenic virology, pathogenic bacteriology and gene therapy of cancer.

University of Michigan, Horace H. Rackham School of Graduate Studies, Program in Biomedical Sciences (PIBS), Department of Microbiology and Immunology, Ann Arbor, MI 48109. Offers PhD. *Degree requirements:* For doctorate, thesis/dissertation, oral defense of dissertation, preliminary exam. *Entrance requirements:* For doctorate, GRE General Test. Additional exam requirements/recommendations for international students: Required—TOEFL (minimum score 600 paper-based; 220 computer-based; 84 iBT), TWE. Electronic applications accepted. *Expenses:* Tuition, state resident: full-time $17,286; part-time $1099 per credit hour. Tuition, nonresident: full-time $34,944; part-time $2080 per credit hour. Required fees: $95 per semester. Tuition and fees vary according to course load, degree level and program. *Faculty research:* Gene regulation, molecular biology of animal and bacterial viruses, molecular and cellular networks, pathogenesis and microbial genetics.

University of Minnesota, Twin Cities Campus, Graduate School, PhD Program in Microbiology, Immunology and Cancer Biology, Minneapolis, MN 55455-0213. Offers PhD. *Degree requirements:* For doctorate, thesis/dissertation. *Entrance requirements:* For doctorate, GRE General Test. Additional exam requirements/recommendations for international students: Required—TOEFL (minimum score 600 paper-based; 250 computer-based). Electronic applications accepted. *Faculty research:* Virology, microbiology, cancer biology, immunology.

University of Mississippi Medical Center, School of Graduate Studies in the Health Sciences, Department of Microbiology, Jackson, MS 39216-4505. Offers MS, PhD, MD/PhD. Terminal master's awarded for partial completion of doctoral program. *Degree requirements:* For master's, thesis; for doctorate, thesis/dissertation, first authored publication. *Entrance requirements:* For master's and doctorate, GRE General Test, minimum GPA of 3.0. *Faculty research:* Immunology, virology, microbial physiology/genetics, parasitology.

University of Missouri, School of Medicine and Graduate School, Graduate Programs in Medicine, Department of Molecular Microbiology and Immunology, Columbia, MO 65211. Offers MS, PhD. Terminal master's awarded for partial completion of doctoral program. *Degree requirements:* For master's, thesis; for doctorate, thesis/dissertation. *Entrance requirements:* For master's and doctorate, GRE General Test, minimum GPA of 3.0. Additional exam requirements/recommendations for international students: Required—TOEFL (minimum score 580 paper-based; 237 computer-based; 92 iBT). *Faculty research:* Molecular biology, host-parasite interactions.

The University of Montana, Graduate School, College of Arts and Sciences, Division of Biological Sciences, Program in Biochemistry and Microbiology, Missoula, MT 59812-0002. Offers biochemistry (MS); integrative microbiology and biochemistry (PhD); microbial ecology (MS, PhD); microbiology (MS). Terminal master's awarded for partial completion of doctoral program. *Degree requirements:* For master's, thesis; for doctorate, variable foreign language requirement, thesis/dissertation. *Entrance requirements:* For master's and doctorate, GRE General Test. *Faculty research:* Ribosome structure, medical microbiology/pathogenesis, microbial ecology/environmental microbiology.

University of Nebraska Medical Center, Graduate Studies, Department of Pathology and Microbiology, Omaha, NE 68198. Offers MS, PhD. Part-time programs available. Terminal master's awarded for partial completion of doctoral program. *Degree requirements:* For master's, comprehensive exam, thesis; for doctorate, comprehensive exam, thesis/dissertation. *Entrance requirements:* For master's, previous course work in biology, chemistry, mathematics, and physics; for doctorate, GRE General Test, previous course work in biology, chemistry, mathematics, and physics. Additional exam requirements/recommendations for international students: Required—TOEFL (minimum score 550 paper-based; 213 computer-based). Electronic

Microbiology

University of Nebraska Medical Center (continued)
applications accepted. *Faculty research:* Carcinogenesis, cancer biology, immunobiology, molecular virology, molecular genetics.

University of New Hampshire, Graduate School, College of Life Sciences and Agriculture, Department of Molecular, Cellular and Biomedical Sciences, Program in Microbiology, Durham, NH 03824. Offers MS, PhD. Part-time programs available. *Faculty:* 7 full-time. *Students:* 9 full-time (8 women), 13 part-time (6 women); includes 2 minority (both Asian Americans or Pacific Islanders). Average age 28. 21 applicants, 38% accepted, 4 enrolled. In 2009, 5 master's awarded. Terminal master's awarded for partial completion of doctoral program. *Degree requirements:* For master's, thesis; for doctorate, thesis/dissertation. *Entrance requirements:* For master's and doctorate, GRE General Test. Additional exam requirements/recommendations for international students: Required—TOEFL (minimum score 550 paper-based; 213 computer-based; 80 iBT). *Application deadline:* For fall admission, 1/15 priority date for domestic students, 1/15 for international students; for spring admission, 11/1 for domestic students. Applications are processed on a rolling basis. Application fee: $65. Electronic applications accepted. *Expenses:* Tuition, state resident: full-time $10,380; part-time $577 per credit hour. Tuition, nonresident: full-time $24,350; part-time $1002 per credit hour. Required fees: $1550; $387.50 per semester. Tuition and fees vary according to course load and program. *Financial support:* In 2009–10, 14 students received support, including 1 fellowship, 5 research assistantships, 8 teaching assistantships; career-related internships or fieldwork, Federal Work-Study, scholarships/grants, and tuition waivers (full and partial) also available. Support available to part-time students. Financial award application deadline: 2/15. *Faculty research:* Bacterial host-parasite interactions, immunology, microbial structures, bacterial and bacteriophage genetics, virology. *Unit head:* Dr. Rick Cote, Chairperson, 603-862-0211. *Application contact:* Flora Joyal, Administrative Assistant, 603-862-4095, E-mail: flora.joyal@unh.edu.

University of New Mexico, School of Medicine, Biomedical Sciences Graduate Program, Albuquerque, NM 87131-5196. Offers biochemistry and molecular biology (MS, PhD); cell biology and physiology (MS, PhD); molecular genetics and microbiology (MS, PhD); neuroscience (MS, PhD); pathology (MS, PhD); toxicology (MS, PhD). Part-time programs available. Terminal master's awarded for partial completion of doctoral program. *Degree requirements:* For master's, thesis; for doctorate, comprehensive exam, thesis/dissertation. *Entrance requirements:* For master's and doctorate, GRE General Test, minimum undergraduate GPA of 3.0. Additional exam requirements/recommendations for international students: Required—TOEFL. Electronic applications accepted. *Expenses:* Tuition, state resident: full-time $2099; part-time $233.20 per credit hour. Tuition, nonresident: full-time $6650. Required fees: $25 per semester. Tuition and fees vary according to course load, program and reciprocity agreements. *Faculty research:* Signal transduction, infectious disease, biology of cancer, structural biology, neuroscience.

The University of North Carolina at Chapel Hill, School of Medicine and Graduate School, Graduate Programs in Medicine, Department of Microbiology and Immunology, Chapel Hill, NC 27599-7290. Offers immunology (MS, PhD); microbiology (MS, PhD). *Faculty:* 62 full-time (22 women). *Students:* 73 full-time (51 women); includes 12 minority (3 African Americans, 7 Asian Americans or Pacific Islanders, 2 Hispanic Americans), 6 international. Average age 29. 8 applicants, 88% accepted, 7 enrolled. In 2009, 1 master's, 13 doctorates awarded. Terminal master's awarded for partial completion of doctoral program. *Degree requirements:* For master's, comprehensive exam, thesis; for doctorate, comprehensive exam, thesis/dissertation. *Entrance requirements:* For master's and doctorate, GRE General Test, minimum GPA of 3.0. *Application deadline:* For fall admission, 12/1 priority date for domestic and international students. Applications are processed on a rolling basis. Application fee: $100. Electronic applications accepted. *Financial support:* In 2009–10, 3 students received support, including 2 fellowships with full tuition reimbursements available (averaging $26,000 per year), 71 research assistantships with full tuition reimbursements available (averaging $26,000 per year); scholarships/grants, traineeships, health care benefits, and unspecified assistantships also available. Financial award application deadline: 3/1; financial award applicants required to submit FAFSA. *Faculty research:* HIV pathogenesis, immune response, t-cell mediated autoimmunity, alpha-viruses, bacterial chemotaxis. Total annual research expenditures: $9.4 million. *Unit head:* Dr. William Goldman, Chairman, 919-966-1191, Fax: 919-962-8103, E-mail: goldman@med.unc.edu. *Application contact:* Dixie Flannery, Student Services Specialist, 919-966-9005, Fax: 919-962-8103, E-mail: microimm@med.unc.edu.

University of North Dakota, School of Medicine and Health Sciences and Graduate School, Graduate Programs in Medicine, Department of Microbiology and Immunology, Grand Forks, ND 58202. Offers MS, PhD. *Degree requirements:* For master's, comprehensive exam, thesis or alternative; for doctorate, comprehensive exam, thesis/dissertation, final examination. *Entrance requirements:* For master's and doctorate, GRE General Test, minimum GPA of 3.0. Additional exam requirements/recommendations for international students: Required—TOEFL (minimum score 550 paper-based; 213 computer-based; 79 iBT), IELTS (minimum score 6.5). Electronic applications accepted. *Faculty research:* Genetic and immunological aspects of a murine model of human multiple sclerosis, termination of DNA replication, cell division in bacteria, yersinia pestis.

University of North Texas Health Science Center at Fort Worth, Graduate School of Biomedical Sciences, Fort Worth, TX 76107-2699. Offers anatomy and cell biology (MS, PhD); biochemistry and molecular biology (MS, PhD); biomedical sciences (MS, PhD); biotechnology (MS); forensic genetics (MS); integrative physiology (MS, PhD); medical science (MS); microbiology and immunology (MS, PhD); pharmacology (MS, PhD); science education (MS); DO/MS; DO/PhD. Terminal master's awarded for partial completion of doctoral program. *Degree requirements:* For master's, thesis; for doctorate, thesis/dissertation. *Entrance requirements:* For master's and doctorate, GRE General Test. Additional exam requirements/recommendations for international students: Required—TOEFL. *Expenses:* Contact institution. *Faculty research:* Alzheimer's disease, aging, eye diseases, cancer, cardiovascular disease.

University of Oklahoma, Graduate College, College of Arts and Sciences, Department of Botany and Microbiology, Program in Microbiology, Norman, OK 73019. Offers MS, PhD. *Students:* 36 full-time (17 women), 2 part-time (1 woman); includes 5 minority (2 African Americans, 1 American Indian/Alaska Native, 2 Asian Americans or Pacific Islanders), 10 international. 21 applicants, 57% accepted, 5 enrolled. In 2009, 1 master's, 6 doctorates awarded. *Degree requirements:* For master's, thesis, oral exam; for doctorate, one foreign language, thesis/dissertation, general exam. *Entrance requirements:* For master's and doctorate, GRE. Additional exam requirements/recommendations for international students: Required—TOEFL (minimum score 550 paper-based; 213 computer-based). *Application deadline:* For fall admission, 4/1 for domestic and international students; for spring admission, 11/1 for domestic students, 9/1 for international students. Applications are processed on a rolling basis. Application fee: $40 ($90 for international students). Electronic applications accepted. *Expenses:* Tuition, state resident: full-time $3744; part-time $156 per credit hour. Tuition, nonresident: full-time $13,577; part-time $565.70 per credit hour. Required fees: $2415; $90.10 per credit hour. *Financial support:* Federal Work-Study, institutionally sponsored loans, scholarships/grants, health care benefits, and unspecified assistantships available. Support available to part-time students. Financial award applicants required to submit FAFSA. *Faculty research:* Anaerobic microbiology, bioremediation, microbial ecology, pathogen-host interactions, microbial systematics. *Unit head:* Dr. Gordon Uno, Chair, 405-325-4321, Fax: 405-325-7619, E-mail: guno@ou.edu. *Application contact:* Adell Hopper, Staff Assistant, 405-325-4322, Fax: 405-325-7619, E-mail: ahopper@ou.edu.

University of Oklahoma Health Sciences Center, College of Medicine and Graduate College, Graduate Programs in Medicine, Department of Microbiology and Immunology, Oklahoma City, OK 73190. Offers immunology (MS, PhD); microbiology (MS, PhD). Part-time programs available. *Faculty:* 13 full-time (5 women). *Students:* 7 full-time (4 women), 25 part-time (14 women); includes 4 minority (1 American Indian/Alaska Native, 3 Asian Americans or Pacific Islanders), 2 international. Average age 27. 20 applicants, 5% accepted, 1 enrolled. In 2009, 1 master's, 5 doctorates awarded. Terminal master's awarded for partial completion of doctoral program. *Degree requirements:* For master's, thesis or alternative; for doctorate, one foreign language, thesis/dissertation. *Entrance requirements:* For doctorate, GRE General Test, 3 letters of recommendation. Additional exam requirements/recommendations for international students: Required—TOEFL. *Application deadline:* For fall admission, 12/15 for domestic students. Application fee: $50. *Expenses:* Tuition, state resident: full-time $3120; part-time $156 per credit hour. Tuition, nonresident: full-time $11,314; part-time $409.70 per credit hour. Required fees: $1471; $51.20 per credit hour. $223.25 per term. *Financial support:* In 2009–10, 20 research assistantships (averaging $17,000 per year) were awarded; fellowships, teaching assistantships also available. Financial award applicants required to submit FAFSA. *Faculty research:* Molecular genetics, pathogenesis, streptococcal infections, gram-positive virulence, monoclonal antibodies. *Unit head:* Dr. John Iandolo, Chairman, 405-271-2133, E-mail: john-iandolo@ouhsc.edu. *Application contact:* Dr. Rebecca Blackstock, Graduate Liaison, 405-271-2133, E-mail: rebecca-blackstock@ouhsc.edu.

University of Ottawa, Faculty of Graduate and Postdoctoral Studies, Faculty of Medicine, Department of Biochemistry, Microbiology and Immunology, Ottawa, ON K1N 6N5, Canada. Offers biochemistry (M Sc, PhD); microbiology and immunology (M Sc, PhD). *Degree requirements:* For master's, thesis; for doctorate, comprehensive exam, thesis/dissertation, seminar. *Entrance requirements:* For master's, honors degree or equivalent, minimum B average; for doctorate, master's degree, minimum B+ average. Electronic applications accepted. *Faculty research:* General biochemistry, molecular biology, microbiology, host biology, nutrition and metabolism.

University of Pennsylvania, School of Medicine, Biomedical Graduate Studies, Graduate Group in Cell and Molecular Biology, Program in Microbiology, Virology, and Parasitology, Philadelphia, PA 19104. Offers PhD, MD/PhD, VMD/PhD. *Degree requirements:* For doctorate, thesis/dissertation. *Entrance requirements:* For doctorate, GRE General Test, previous course work in science. Additional exam requirements/recommendations for international students: Required—TOEFL. *Application deadline:* For fall admission, 12/8 priority date for domestic and international students. Applications are processed on a rolling basis. Application fee: $70. Electronic applications accepted. *Expenses:* Tuition: Full-time $25,660; part-time $4758 per course. Required fees: $2152; $270 per course. Tuition and fees vary according to course load, degree level and program. *Financial support:* Fellowships, research assistantships, scholarships/grants, traineeships, and unspecified assistantships available. *Unit head:* Dr. Robert Ricciardi, Chair, 215-898-3965. *Application contact:* Anna Kline, Coordinator, 215-898-3918, Fax: 215-573-2104, E-mail: camb@mail.med.upenn.edu.

University of Pittsburgh, Graduate School of Public Health, Department of Infectious Diseases and Microbiology, Pittsburgh, PA 15260. Offers bioscience of infectious diseases (MPH); community and behavioral intervention of infectious diseases (MPH); infectious diseases and microbiology (MS, Dr PH, PhD); LGBT health and wellness (Certificate). Part-time programs available. *Faculty:* 20 full-time (7 women), 2 part-time/adjunct (1 woman). *Students:* 46 full-time (33 women), 8 part-time (6 women); includes 7 minority (2 African Americans, 4 Asian Americans or Pacific Islanders, 1 Hispanic American), 6 international. Average age 28. 176 applicants, 43% accepted, 18 enrolled. In 2009, 11 master's, 9 doctorates awarded. Terminal master's awarded for partial completion of doctoral program. *Degree requirements:* For master's, one foreign language, comprehensive exam (for some programs), thesis; for doctorate, one foreign language, comprehensive exam, thesis/dissertation. *Entrance requirements:* For master's and doctorate, GRE General Test, MCAT, or DAT. Additional exam requirements/recommendations for international students: Required—TOEFL (minimum score 550 paper-based; 213 computer-based; 80 iBT). *Application deadline:* For fall admission, 1/4 for domestic students. Applications are processed on a rolling basis. Application fee: $95. Electronic applications accepted. *Expenses:* Tuition, state resident: full-time $16,402; part-time $665 per credit. Tuition, nonresident: full-time $28,694; part-time $1175 per credit. Required fees: $690; $175 per term. Tuition and fees vary according to program. *Financial support:* In 2009–10, 16 students received support, including 16 research assistantships with full tuition reimbursements available (averaging $23,500 per year). Financial award applicants required to submit FAFSA. *Faculty research:* HIV, Epstein-Barr virus, virology, immunology, malaria. Total annual research expenditures: $13.6 million. *Unit head:* Dr. Charles R. Rinaldo, Chairman, 412-624-3928, Fax: 412-624-4953, E-mail: rinaldo@pitt.edu. *Application contact:* Dr. Jeremy Martinson, Assistant Professor, 412-624-5646, Fax: 412-383-8926, E-mail: jmartins@pitt.edu.

University of Pittsburgh, School of Medicine, Graduate Programs in Medicine, Program in Molecular Virology and Microbiology, Pittsburgh, PA 15260. Offers MS, PhD. *Faculty:* 39 full-time (7 women). *Students:* 27 full-time (16 women); includes 2 minority (both Hispanic Americans), 5 international. Average age 27. 655 applicants, 10% accepted, 20 enrolled. In 2009, 1 doctorate awarded. *Degree requirements:* For doctorate, comprehensive exam, thesis/dissertation. *Entrance requirements:* For doctorate, GRE General Test, GRE Subject Test, minimum QPA of 3.0. Additional exam requirements/recommendations for international students: Required—TOEFL (minimum score 600 paper-based; 250 computer-based; 100 iBT), IELTS (minimum score 7). *Application deadline:* For fall admission, 12/15 priority date for domestic and international students. Application fee: $40. Electronic applications accepted. *Expenses:* Tuition, state resident: full-time $16,402; part-time $665 per credit. Tuition, nonresident: full-time $28,694; part-time $1175 per credit. Required fees: $690; $175 per term. Tuition and fees vary according to program. *Financial support:* In 2009–10, 27 research assistantships with full tuition reimbursements (averaging $24,650 per year) were awarded; institutionally sponsored loans, scholarships/grants, traineeships, health care benefits, and unspecified assistantships also available. *Faculty research:* Host-pathogen interactions, persistent microbial infections, microbial genetics and gene expression, microbial pathogenesis, anti-bacterial therapeutics. *Unit head:* Dr. Neal A. DeLuca, Graduate Program Director, 412-648-9947, Fax: 412-624-0298, E-mail: ndeluca@pitt.edu. *Application contact:* Graduate Studies Administrator, 412-648-8957, Fax: 412-648-1077, E-mail: gradstudies@medschool.pitt.edu.

University of Puerto Rico, Medical Sciences Campus, School of Medicine, Division of Graduate Studies, Department of Microbiology and Medical Zoology, San Juan, PR 00936-5067. Offers MS, PhD. *Degree requirements:* For master's, one foreign language, thesis; for doctorate, one foreign language, comprehensive exam, thesis/dissertation. *Entrance requirements:* For master's and doctorate, GRE General Test, GRE Subject Test, interview, minimum GPA of 3.0, 3 letters of recommendation. *Faculty research:* Molecular and general parasitology, immunology, development of viral vaccines and antiviral agents, antibiotic resistance, bacteriology.

University of Rhode Island, Graduate School, College of the Environment and Life Sciences, Department of Cell and Molecular Biology, Kingston, RI 02881. Offers biochemistry (MS, PhD); clinical laboratory sciences (MS), including biotechnology, clinical laboratory science, cytopathology; microbiology (MS, PhD); molecular genetics (MS, PhD). Part-time programs available. *Faculty:* 12 full-time (4 women). *Students:* 29 full-time (17 women), 43 part-time (31 women); includes 13 minority (5 African Americans, 4 Asian Americans or Pacific Islanders, 4 Hispanic Americans), 3 international. In 2009, 5 master's, 2 doctorates awarded. *Degree requirements:* For master's, comprehensive exam (for some programs); for doctorate, comprehensive exam. *Entrance requirements:* For master's and doctorate, GRE, 2 letters of recommendation. Additional exam requirements/recommendations for international students: Required—TOEFL (minimum score 550 paper-based; 213 computer-based). *Application deadline:* For fall admission, 7/15 for domestic students, 2/1 for international students; for spring admission, 11/15 for domestic students, 7/15 for international students. Application fee: $65. Electronic applications accepted. *Expenses:* Tuition, state resident: full-time $8828; part-time $490 per credit hour. Tuition, nonresident: full-time $22,100; part-time $1228 per credit hour. Required fees: $1118; $57 per semester. Tuition and fees vary according to program. *Financial support:* In 2009–10, 2 research assistantships with full and partial tuition reimbursements (averaging $10,535 per year), 10 teaching assistantships with full and partial tuition reimbursements (averaging $13,449 per year) were awarded. Financial award application deadline: 7/15; financial award applicants required to submit FAFSA. *Faculty research:* Genomics and Sequencing Center: an interdisciplinary genomics research and undergraduate and graduate student training program which provides researchers access to cutting-edge technologies in the field of genomics. Total annual research expenditures: $1.2 million. *Unit head:* Dr. Jay Sperry, Chairperson, 401-874-2201, Fax: 401-874-2202, E-mail: jsperry@mail.uri.edu. *Application contact:* Dr. Jay Sperry, Chairperson, 401-874-2201, Fax: 401-874-2202, E-mail: jsperry@mail.uri.edu.

University of Rochester, School of Medicine and Dentistry, Graduate Programs in Medicine and Dentistry, Department of Microbiology and Immunology, Rochester, NY 14627. Offers microbiology (MS, PhD); MBA/MS. *Degree requirements:* For doctorate, thesis/dissertation, qualifying exam. *Entrance requirements:* For master's and doctorate, GRE General Test.

University of Saskatchewan, College of Medicine, Department of Microbiology and Immunology, Saskatoon, SK S7N 5A2, Canada. Offers M Sc, PhD. *Degree requirements:* For master's, thesis; for doctorate, thesis/dissertation. *Entrance requirements:* Additional exam requirements/recommendations for international students: Required—TOEFL. Tuition and fees charges are reported in Canadian dollars. *Expenses:* Tuition, area resident: Full-time $3000 Canadian dollars; part-time $500 Canadian dollars per term. Required fees: $700 Canadian dollars; $100 Canadian dollars per term.

University of Saskatchewan, Western College of Veterinary Medicine and College of Graduate Studies and Research, Graduate Programs in Veterinary Medicine, Department of Veterinary Microbiology, Saskatoon, SK S7N 5A2, Canada. Offers M Sc, M Vet Sc, PhD. *Faculty:* 27. *Students:* 32. In 2009, 1 master's, 9 doctorates awarded. *Degree requirements:* For master's, thesis; for doctorate, comprehensive exam (for some programs), thesis/dissertation. *Entrance requirements:* Additional exam requirements/recommendations for international students: Required—TOEFL (minimum score 80 iBT) or IELTS (minimum score 6.5). *Application deadline:* For fall admission, 7/1 priority date for domestic students. Applications are processed on a rolling basis. Application fee: $75. Electronic applications accepted. Tuition and fees charges are reported in Canadian dollars. *Expenses:* Tuition, area resident: Full-time $3000 Canadian dollars; part-time $500 Canadian dollars per term. Required fees: $700 Canadian dollars; $100 Canadian dollars per term. *Financial support:* Fellowships, teaching assistantships available. Financial award application deadline: 1/31. *Faculty research:* Immunology, vaccinology, epidemiology, virology, parasitology. *Unit head:* Dr. Vikram Misra, Head, 306-966-7210, Fax: 306-966-4311, E-mail: vikram.misra@usask.ca. *Application contact:* Dr. Vikram Misra, Graduate Chair, 306-966-7210, E-mail: vikram.misra@usask.ca.

University of South Alabama, College of Medicine and Graduate School, Program in Basic Medical Sciences, Specialization in Microbiology and Immunology, Mobile, AL 36688-0002. Offers PhD. *Degree requirements:* For doctorate, thesis/dissertation. *Entrance requirements:* For doctorate, GRE General Test or MCAT. *Expenses:* Tuition, state resident: part-time $218 per contact hour. Required fees: $1102 per year. *Faculty research:* Mechanisms of tumor immunity, host response to infectious agents, virus replication, immune regulation, mechanisms of resistance to viruses and bacteria.

The University of South Dakota, School of Medicine and Health Sciences and Graduate School, Biomedical Sciences Graduate Program, Molecular Microbiology and Immunology Group, Vermillion, SD 57069-2390. Offers MS, PhD. Terminal master's awarded for partial completion of doctoral program. *Degree requirements:* For master's, thesis; for doctorate, comprehensive exam, thesis/dissertation. *Entrance requirements:* For master's and doctorate, GRE General Test, minimum GPA of 3.0. Additional exam requirements/recommendations for international students: Required—TOEFL (minimum score 550 paper-based; 213 computer-based; 80 iBT), IELTS (minimum score 6). Electronic applications accepted. *Expenses:* Contact institution. *Faculty research:* Structure-function membranes, plasmids, immunology, virology, pathogenesis.

University of Southern California, Keck School of Medicine and Graduate School, Graduate Programs in Medicine, Department of Molecular Microbiology and Immunology, Los Angeles, CA 90089. Offers MS, PhD. Part-time programs available. *Faculty:* 15 full-time (3 women), 1 (woman) part-time/adjunct. *Students:* 20 full-time (10 women); includes 17 minority (15 Asian Americans or Pacific Islanders, 2 Hispanic Americans). Average age 27. 19 applicants, 47% accepted, 6 enrolled. In 2009, 5 master's, 4 doctorates awarded. Terminal master's awarded for partial completion of doctoral program. *Degree requirements:* For master's, comprehensive exam (for some programs), thesis optional; for doctorate, comprehensive exam, thesis/dissertation. *Entrance requirements:* For master's, GRE General Test, minimum GPA of 3.0; for doctorate, GRE General Test, GRE Subject Test, minimum GPA of 3.0. Additional exam requirements/recommendations for international students: Required—TOEFL (minimum score 100 iBT). *Application deadline:* Applications are processed on a rolling basis. Application fee: $85. Electronic applications accepted. *Expenses:* Tuition: Full-time $25,980; part-time $1315 per unit. Required fees: $554. One-time fee: $35 full-time. Full-time tuition and fees vary according to degree level and program. *Financial support:* In 2009–10, 4 students received support, including 1 fellowship with full tuition reimbursement available (averaging $27,060 per year), 6 research assistantships with full tuition reimbursements available (averaging $27,060 per year), 1 teaching assistantship with full tuition reimbursement available (averaging $27,060 per year); Federal Work-Study, institutionally sponsored loans, scholarships/grants, health care benefits, and unspecified assistantships also available. Financial award application deadline: 5/5; financial award applicants required to submit FAFSA. *Faculty research:* Animal virology, microbial genetics, molecular and cellular immunology, cellular differentiation control of protein synthesis. *Unit head:* Dr. Jae U. Jung, Professor and Chair, 323-442-1713, Fax: 323-442-1721, E-mail: jaeujung@usc.edu. *Application contact:* Silvina V. Campos, Administrative Assistant II, 323-442-1713, Fax: 323-442-1721, E-mail: scampos@usc.edu.

University of Southern Mississippi, Graduate School, College of Science and Technology, Department of Biological Sciences, Hattiesburg, MS 39406-0001. Offers environmental biology (MS, PhD); marine biology (MS, PhD); microbiology (MS, PhD); molecular biology (MS, PhD). *Faculty:* 27 full-time (6 women). *Students:* 55 full-time (27 women), 5 part-time (3 women); includes 7 minority (2 African Americans, 1 American Indian/Alaska Native, 2 Asian Americans or Pacific Islanders, 2 Hispanic Americans), 15 international. Average age 32. 53 applicants, 28% accepted, 10 enrolled. In 2009, 8 master's, 4 doctorates awarded. *Degree requirements:* For master's, comprehensive exam, thesis; for doctorate, comprehensive exam, thesis/dissertation. *Entrance requirements:* For master's, GRE General Test, minimum GPA of 3.0; for doctorate, GRE General Test, minimum GPA of 3.5. Additional exam requirements/recommendations for international students: Required—TOEFL. *Application deadline:* For fall admission, 3/1 priority date for domestic students, 3/1 for international students. Applications are processed on a rolling basis. Application fee: $35. *Expenses:* Tuition, state resident: full-time $5096; part-time $284 per hour. Tuition, nonresident: full-time $13,052; part-time $726 per hour. Required fees: $402. Tuition and fees vary according to course level and course load. *Financial support:* In 2009–10, 25 research assistantships with full tuition reimbursements (averaging $9,625 per year), 33 teaching assistantships with full tuition reimbursements (averaging $10,599 per year) were awarded; Federal Work-Study also available. Financial award application deadline: 3/15; financial award applicants required to submit FAFSA. *Unit head:* Dr. Frank Moore, Chair, 601-266-4748, Fax: 601-266-5797. *Application contact:* Dr. Chia Wang, Graduate Coordinator, 601-266-4748, Fax: 601-266-5797.

The University of Tennessee, Graduate School, College of Arts and Sciences, Department of Microbiology, Knoxville, TN 37996. Offers MS, PhD. Part-time programs available. *Degree requirements:* For master's, thesis; for doctorate, thesis/dissertation. *Entrance requirements:* For master's and doctorate, GRE General Test, minimum GPA of 2.7. Additional exam requirements/recommendations for international students: Required—TOEFL. Electronic applications accepted. *Expenses:* Tuition, state resident: full-time $6826; part-time $380 per semester hour. Tuition, nonresident: full-time $21,844; part-time $1147 per semester hour. Tuition and fees vary according to program.

The University of Texas at Austin, Graduate School, College of Natural Sciences, School of Biological Sciences, Program in Microbiology, Austin, TX 78712-1111. Offers PhD. *Entrance requirements:* For doctorate, GRE General Test. Electronic applications accepted.

The University of Texas Health Science Center at Houston, Graduate School of Biomedical Sciences, Program in Microbiology and Molecular Genetics, Houston, TX 77225-0036. Offers MS, PhD, MD/PhD. Terminal master's awarded for partial completion of doctoral program. *Degree requirements:* For master's, thesis; for doctorate, thesis/dissertation. *Entrance requirements:* For master's and doctorate, GRE General Test. Additional exam requirements/recommendations for international students: Required—TOEFL. Electronic applications accepted. *Faculty research:* Disease causation, environmental signaling, gene regulation, cell growth and division, cell structure and architecture.

The University of Texas Health Science Center at San Antonio, Graduate School of Biomedical Sciences, Department of Microbiology and Immunology, San Antonio, TX 78229-3900. Offers PhD. *Faculty:* 17 full-time (2 women), 9 part-time/adjunct (2 women). *Students:* 39 full-time (21 women); includes 12 minority (2 African Americans, 10 Hispanic Americans), 12 international. Average age 30. In 2009, 1 doctorate awarded. Terminal master's awarded for partial completion of doctoral program. *Degree requirements:* For doctorate, comprehensive exam, thesis/dissertation. *Entrance requirements:* For doctorate, GRE General Test, minimum GPA of 3.0. Additional exam requirements/recommendations for international students: Required—TOEFL (minimum score 560 paper-based; 220 computer-based; 68 iBT). *Application deadline:* For fall admission, 1/15 priority date for domestic and international students. Applications are processed on a rolling basis. Electronic applications accepted. *Expenses:* Tuition, state resident: full-time $2832; part-time $118 per credit hour. Tuition, nonresident: full-time $10,896; part-time $454 per credit hour. Required fees: $884 per semester. One-time fee: $70. *Financial support:* In 2009–10, 38 teaching assistantships (averaging $26,000 per year) were awarded; fellowships, research assistantships, dental scientist awards also available. Financial award applicants required to submit FAFSA. *Faculty research:* Molecular immunology, mechanisms of microbial pathogenesis, molecular genetics, vaccine and immunodiagnostic development. Total annual research expenditures: $6.8 million. *Unit head:* Joel B. Baseman, Chairman, 210-567-3939, Fax: 210-567-6491, E-mail: baseman@uthscsa.edu. *Application contact:* Sophia Pina, Assistant Dean, 210-567-3984, Fax: 210-567-3719, E-mail: pina@uthscsa.edu.

The University of Texas Medical Branch, Graduate School of Biomedical Sciences, Program in Microbiology and Immunology, Galveston, TX 77555. Offers MS, PhD. *Students:* 35 full-time (20 women), 1 part-time (0 women); includes 7 minority (5 African Americans, 2 Hispanic Americans), 11 international. Average age 30. In 2009, 8 doctorates awarded. Terminal master's awarded for partial completion of doctoral program. *Degree requirements:* For master's, thesis or alternative; for doctorate, thesis/dissertation. *Entrance requirements:* For doctorate, GRE General Test, minimum GPA of 3.0. Additional exam requirements/recommendations for international students: Required—TOEFL (minimum score 550 paper-based; 213 computer-based). *Application deadline:* Applications are processed on a rolling basis. Application fee: $30 ($75 for international students). Electronic applications accepted. *Financial support:* In 2009–10, research assistantships with full tuition reimbursements (averaging $25,000 per year). Financial award applicants required to submit FAFSA. *Unit head:* Dr. Rolf Konig, Director, 409-747-0395, Fax: 409-772-5065, E-mail: rokonig@utmb.edu. *Application contact:* Aneth Zertuche, Coordinator for Special Programs, 409-772-2322, Fax: 409-747-6869, E-mail: azertuch@utmb.edu.

The University of Texas Southwestern Medical Center at Dallas, Southwestern Graduate School of Biomedical Sciences, Division of Basic Science, Program in Molecular Microbiology, Dallas, TX 75390. Offers PhD. *Faculty:* 34 full-time (10 women), 2 part-time/adjunct (0 women). *Students:* 19 full-time (10 women); includes 2 minority (both Hispanic Americans), 5 international. Average age 28. 946 applicants, 22% accepted. In 2009, 9 degrees awarded. *Degree requirements:* For doctorate, thesis/dissertation, oral and written exams. *Entrance requirements:* For doctorate, GRE General Test, minimum GPA of 3.0. Additional exam requirements/recommendations for international students: Required—TOEFL. *Application deadline:* For fall admission, 12/15 priority date for domestic students. Applications are processed on a rolling basis. Application fee: $0. Electronic applications accepted. *Financial support:* Fellowships, research assistantships, institutionally sponsored loans available. *Faculty research:* Cell and molecular immunology, molecular pathogenesis of infectious disease, virology. *Unit head:* Dr. Vanessa Speraudio, Chair, 214-648-1603, Fax: 214-648-1899, E-mail: vanessa.speraudio@utsouthwestern.edu. *Application contact:* Dr. Nancy E. Street, Associate Dean, 214-648-6708, Fax: 214-648-2102, E-mail: nancy.street@utsouthwestern.edu.

University of Vermont, College of Medicine and Graduate College, Graduate Programs in Medicine, Department of Microbiology and Molecular Genetics, Burlington, VT 05405. Offers MS, PhD, MD/MS, MD/PhD. *Faculty:* 18 full-time (5 women). *Students:* 23 (13 women), 12 international. 49 applicants, 33% accepted, 3 enrolled. In 2009, 4 doctorates awarded. *Degree requirements:* For master's, thesis; for doctorate, thesis/dissertation. *Entrance requirements:* For master's and doctorate, GRE General Test. Additional exam requirements/recommendations for international students: Required—TOEFL (minimum score 550 paper-based; 213 computer-based; 80 iBT). *Application deadline:* For fall admission, 1/16 priority date for domestic students, 1/16 for international students. Applications are processed on a rolling basis. Application fee: $40. Electronic applications accepted. *Expenses:* Tuition, state resident: part-time $508 per credit hour. Tuition, nonresident: part-time $1281 per credit hour. *Financial support:* Fellowships, research assistantships, teaching assistantships available. Financial award application deadline: 3/1. *Unit head:* Dr. Susan S. Wallace, Chairperson, 802-656-2164. *Application contact:* Dr. David Pederson, Coordinator, 802-656-2164.

University of Vermont, Graduate College, College of Agriculture and Life Sciences and College of Medicine, Department of Microbiology and Molecular Genetics, Burlington, VT 05405. Offers MS, PhD, MD/MS, MD/PhD. *Faculty:* 18 full-time (5 women). *Degree requirements:* For master's, thesis; for doctorate, thesis/dissertation. *Entrance requirements:* For master's and doctorate, GRE General Test. Additional exam requirements/recommendations for international students: Required—TOEFL (minimum score 550 paper-based; 213 computer-based; 80 iBT). *Application deadline:* For fall admission, 2/1 priority date for domestic students. Applications are processed on a rolling basis. Application fee: $40. Electronic applications accepted. *Expenses:* Tuition, state resident: part-time $508 per credit hour. Tuition, nonresident: part-time $1281 per credit hour. *Financial support:* Fellowships, research assistantships, teaching assistantships available. Financial award application deadline: 3/1. *Unit head:* Dr. Susan S. Wallace, Chairperson, 802-656-2164. *Application contact:* Dr. S. Doublie, Coordinator, 802-656-2164.

University of Victoria, Faculty of Graduate Studies, Faculty of Science, Department of Biochemistry and Microbiology, Victoria, BC V8W 2Y2, Canada. Offers biochemistry (M Sc, PhD); microbiology (M Sc, PhD). *Degree requirements:* For master's, thesis, seminar; for doctorate, thesis/dissertation, seminar, candidacy exam. *Entrance requirements:* For master's, GRE General Test, minimum B+ average; for doctorate, GRE General Test, minimum B+ average, M Sc. Additional exam requirements/recommendations for international students: Required—TOEFL (minimum score 600 paper-based; 250 computer-based). Electronic applications accepted. *Faculty research:* Molecular pathogenesis, prokaryotic, eukaryotic, macromolecular interactions, microbial surfaces, virology, molecular genetics.

University of Virginia, School of Medicine, Department of Microbiology, Charlottesville, VA 22903. Offers PhD, MD/PhD. *Faculty:* 36 full-time (14 women). *Students:* 70 full-time (44

Microbiology

University of Virginia (continued)
women); includes 12 minority (4 African Americans, 4 Asian Americans or Pacific Islanders, 4 Hispanic Americans), 6 international. Average age 28. In 2009, 16 doctorates awarded. *Degree requirements:* For doctorate, thesis/dissertation. *Entrance requirements:* For doctorate, GRE General Test, 2 or more letters of recommendation. Additional exam requirements/recommendations for international students: Required—TOEFL (minimum score 600 paper-based; 250 computer-based; 90 iBT). *Application deadline:* For fall admission, 2/1 for domestic and international students. Applications are processed on a rolling basis. Application fee: $60. Electronic applications accepted. *Financial support:* Fellowships, traineeships and unspecified assistantships available. Financial award applicants required to submit FAFSA. *Faculty research:* Virology, membrane biology and molecular genetics. *Unit head:* J. Thomas Parsons, Chair, 434-924-1948, Fax: 434-982-1071. *Application contact:* J. Thomas Parsons, Chair, 434-924-1948, Fax: 434-982-1071.

University of Washington, Graduate School, School of Medicine and Graduate School, Graduate Programs in Medicine, Department of Microbiology, Seattle, WA 98195. Offers PhD. *Degree requirements:* For doctorate, thesis/dissertation. *Entrance requirements:* For doctorate, GRE General Test, GRE Subject Test (recommended). Electronic applications accepted. *Faculty research:* Bacterial genetics and physiology, mechanisms of bacterial and viral pathogenesis, bacterial-plant interaction.

The University of Western Ontario, Faculty of Graduate Studies, Biosciences Division, Department of Microbiology and Immunology, London, ON N6A 5B8, Canada. Offers M Sc, PhD. *Degree requirements:* For master's, thesis, oral and written exam; for doctorate, thesis/dissertation, oral and written exam. *Entrance requirements:* For master's, honors degree or equivalent in microbiology, immunology, or other biological science; minimum B average; for doctorate, M Sc in microbiology and immunology. Additional exam requirements/recommendations for international students: Required—TOEFL. *Faculty research:* Virology, molecular pathogenesis, cellular immunology, molecular biology.

University of Wisconsin–La Crosse, Office of University Graduate Studies, College of Science and Health, Department of Biology, La Crosse, WI 54601-3742. Offers aquatic sciences (MS); biology (MS); cellular and molecular biology (MS); clinical microbiology (MS); microbiology (MS); nurse anesthesia (MS); physiology (MS). Part-time programs available. *Faculty:* 27 full-time (7 women). *Students:* 19 full-time (8 women), 35 part-time (20 women); includes 1 minority (Asian American or Pacific Islander), 2 international. Average age 28. 87 applicants, 32% accepted, 21 enrolled. In 2009, 18 master's awarded. *Degree requirements:* For master's, comprehensive exam, thesis. *Entrance requirements:* For master's, GRE General Test, minimum GPA of 2.85. Additional exam requirements/recommendations for international students: Required—TOEFL (minimum score 550 paper-based; 213 computer-based; 79 iBT). Application fee: $56. Electronic applications accepted. *Financial support:* In 2009–10, 19 research assistantships with partial tuition reimbursements (averaging $10,021 per year) were awarded; career-related internships or fieldwork, Federal Work-Study, health care benefits, unspecified assistantships, and grant-funded positions also available. Support available to part-time students. Financial award application deadline: 3/15; financial award applicants required to submit FAFSA. *Unit head:* Dr. David Howard, Chair, 608-785-6455, E-mail: howard.davi@uwlax.edu. *Application contact:* Kathryn Kiefer, Director of Admissions, 608-785-8939, E-mail: admissions@uwlax.edu.

University of Wisconsin–Madison, School of Medicine and Public Health and Graduate School, Graduate Programs in Medicine and College of Agricultural and Life Sciences, Microbiology Doctoral Training Program, Madison, WI 53706-1380. Offers PhD. *Faculty:* 92 full-time (27 women). *Students:* 88 full-time (50 women); includes 11 minority (2 African Americans, 2 Asian Americans or Pacific Islanders, 7 Hispanic Americans), 4 international. Average age 24. 212 applicants, 19% accepted, 20 enrolled. In 2009, 18 doctorates awarded. *Degree requirements:* For doctorate, thesis/dissertation, preliminary exam, 2 semesters of teaching. *Entrance requirements:* For doctorate, GRE. Additional exam requirements/recommendations for international students: Required—TOEFL (minimum score 580 paper-based; 237 computer-based). *Application deadline:* For fall admission, 12/1 for domestic and international students. Application fee: $56. Electronic applications accepted. *Expenses:* Tuition: state resident: part-time $594 per credit. Tuition, nonresident: part-time $1504 per credit. Required fees: $65 per credit. Tuition and fees vary according to course load, program and reciprocity agreements. *Financial support:* In 2009–10, 88 students received support, including 12 fellowships with tuition reimbursements available (averaging $23,500 per year), 76 research assistantships with tuition reimbursements available (averaging $23,500 per year); career-related internships or fieldwork, scholarships/grants, traineeships, health care benefits, and tuition waivers (full) also available. Financial award application deadline: 12/1. *Faculty research:* Microbial pathogenesis, gene regulation, immunology, virology, cell biology. Total annual research expenditures: $15.1 million. *Unit head:* Dr. Joseph Dillard, Director, 608-265-2837, Fax: 608-262-8418, E-mail: jpdillard@wisc.edu. *Application contact:* Cathy Davis Gray, Coordinator, 608-265-0689, Fax: 608-262-8418, E-mail: cdg@bact.wisc.edu.

University of Wisconsin–Oshkosh, The Office of Graduate Studies, College of Letters and Science, Department of Biology and Microbiology, Oshkosh, WI 54901. Offers biology (MS), including botany, microbiology, zoology. *Degree requirements:* For master's, comprehensive exam, thesis. *Entrance requirements:* For master's, GRE General Test, minimum GPA of 3.0, BS in biology. Additional exam requirements/recommendations for international students: Required—TOEFL (minimum score 550 paper-based; 213 computer-based; 79 iBT). Electronic applications accepted.

University of Wyoming, Graduate Program in Molecular and Cellular Life Sciences, Laramie, WY 82070. Offers PhD. *Degree requirements:* For doctorate, thesis/dissertation, four eight-week laboratory rotations, comprehensive basic practical exam, two-part qualifying exam, seminars, symposium.

Utah State University, School of Graduate Studies, College of Agriculture, Department of Nutrition and Food Sciences, Logan, UT 84322. Offers dietetic administration (MDA); food microbiology and safety (MFMS); nutrition and food sciences (MS, PhD); nutrition science (MS, PhD), including molecular biology. Postbaccalaureate distance learning degree programs offered. *Degree requirements:* For master's, thesis; for doctorate, comprehensive exam, thesis/dissertation, teaching experience. *Entrance requirements:* For master's, GRE General Test, minimum GPA of 3.0, course work in chemistry, biochemistry, physics, math, bacteriology, physiology; for doctorate, GRE General Test, minimum GPA of 3.2, course work in chemistry, MS or manuscript in referred journal. Additional exam requirements/recommendations for international students: Required—TOEFL (minimum score 550 paper-based). Electronic applications accepted. *Faculty research:* Mineral balance, meat microbiology and nitrate interactions, milk ultrafiltration, lactic culture, milk coagulation.

Vanderbilt University, Graduate School and School of Medicine, Department of Microbiology and Immunology, Nashville, TN 37240-1001. Offers MS, PhD, MD/PhD. *Faculty:* 38 full-time (8 women). *Students:* 33 full-time (15 women); includes 5 minority (2 African Americans, 1 Asian American or Pacific Islander, 2 Hispanic Americans), 5 international. Average age 27. In 2009, 2 master's, 9 doctorates awarded. Terminal master's awarded for partial completion of doctoral program. *Degree requirements:* For master's, thesis; for doctorate, thesis/dissertation, final and qualifying exams. *Entrance requirements:* For master's and doctorate, GRE General Test, GRE Subject Test (recommended). Additional exam requirements/recommendations for international students: Required—TOEFL (minimum score 570 paper-based; 230 computer-based; 88 iBT). *Application deadline:* For fall admission, 1/15 for domestic and international students. Application fee: $0. Electronic applications accepted. *Financial support:* Fellowships with full tuition reimbursements, research assistantships with full tuition reimbursements, Federal Work-

Study, institutionally sponsored loans, scholarships/grants, traineeships, health care benefits, and tuition waivers (partial) available. Financial award application deadline: 1/15; financial award applicants required to submit CSS PROFILE or FAFSA. *Faculty research:* Cellular and molecular microbiology, viruses, genes, cancer, molecular pathogenesis of microbial diseases, immunobiology. *Unit head:* Jacek Hawiger, Chair, 615-322-2087, E-mail: jacek.hawiger@vanderbilt.edu. *Application contact:* Christopher R. Aiken, Director of Graduate Studies, 615-322-2087, E-mail: chris.aiken@vanderbilt.edu.

Virginia Commonwealth University, Medical College of Virginia-Professional Programs, School of Medicine, School of Medicine Graduate Programs, Department of Microbiology and Immunology, Richmond, VA 23284-9005. Offers microbiology and immunology (MS, PhD); molecular biology and genetics (MS, PhD); MD/PhD. *Degree requirements:* For master's, thesis; for doctorate, thesis/dissertation, comprehensive oral and written exams. *Entrance requirements:* For master's, GRE General Test or MCAT; for doctorate, GRE General Test, MCAT. *Faculty research:* Microbial physiology and genetics, molecular biology, crystallography of biological molecules, antibiotics and chemotherapy, membrane transport.

Virginia Commonwealth University, Program in Pre-Medical Basic Health Sciences, Richmond, VA 23284-9005. Offers anatomy (CBHS); biochemistry (CBHS); human genetics (CBHS); microbiology (CBHS); pharmacology (CBHS); physiology (CBHS). *Entrance requirements:* For degree, GRE or MCAT, course work in organic chemistry, minimum undergraduate GPA of 2.8. Additional exam requirements/recommendations for international students: Required—TOEFL (minimum score 600 paper-based).

Virginia Polytechnic Institute and State University, Graduate School, College of Science, Department of Biological Sciences, Blacksburg, VA 24061. Offers botany (MS, PhD); ecology and evolutionary biology (MS, PhD); genetics and developmental biology (MS, PhD); microbiology (MS, PhD); zoology (MS, PhD). *Faculty:* 42 full-time (11 women). *Students:* 76 full-time (45 women), 5 part-time (1 woman); includes 28 minority (23 American Indian/Alaska Native, 2 Asian Americans or Pacific Islanders, 3 Hispanic Americans). Average age 28. 117 applicants, 15% accepted, 15 enrolled. In 2009, 11 master's, 11 doctorates awarded. *Entrance requirements:* For master's and doctorate, GRE, GMAT. Additional exam requirements/recommendations for international students: Required—TOEFL (minimum score 550 paper-based; 213 computer-based). *Application deadline:* For fall admission, 5/15 for international students; for spring admission, 10/15 for international students. Applications are processed on a rolling basis. Application fee: $65. Electronic applications accepted. *Expenses:* Tuition, area resident: Full-time $10,228; part-time $459 per credit hour. Tuition, nonresident: full-time $17,892; part-time $865 per credit hour. Required fees: $1966; $451 per semester. *Financial support:* In 2009–10, 37 research assistantships with full tuition reimbursements (averaging $17,929 per year), 41 teaching assistantships with full tuition reimbursements (averaging $17,344 per year) were awarded; career-related internships or fieldwork, Federal Work-Study, scholarships/grants, and unspecified assistantships also available. Financial award application deadline: 1/15. *Faculty research:* Freshwater ecology, cell cycle regulation, behavioral ecology, motor proteins. Total annual research expenditures: $4.8 million. *Unit head:* Dr. Bob H. Jones, Dean, 540-231-9514, Fax: 540-231-9307, E-mail: rhjones@vt.edu. *Application contact:* Erik Nilsen, Information Contact, 540-231-5671, Fax: 540-231-9307, E-mail: enilsen@vt.edu.

Virginia Polytechnic Institute and State University, Graduate School, Intercollege, Microbiology Program, Blacksburg, VA 24061. Offers PhD. *Expenses:* Tuition, area resident: Full-time $10,228; part-time $459 per credit hour. Tuition, nonresident: full-time $17,892; part-time $865 per credit hour. Required fees: $1966; $451 per semester.

Wagner College, Division of Graduate Studies, Department of Biological Sciences, Program in Microbiology, Staten Island, NY 10301-4495. Offers MS. Part-time and evening/weekend programs available. *Degree requirements:* For master's, comprehensive exam or thesis. *Entrance requirements:* For master's, minimum GPA of 2.6, proficiency in statistics, undergraduate major in science. Additional exam requirements/recommendations for international students: Required—TOEFL (minimum score 550 paper-based; 217 computer-based). *Expenses:* Tuition: Full-time $15,570; part-time $865 per credit. Required fees: $2.

Wake Forest University, School of Medicine and Graduate School of Arts and Sciences, Graduate Programs in Medicine, Department of Microbiology and Immunology, Winston-Salem, NC 27109. Offers PhD, MD/PhD. *Degree requirements:* For doctorate, thesis/dissertation. *Entrance requirements:* For doctorate, GRE General Test. Additional exam requirements/recommendations for international students: Required—TOEFL. Electronic applications accepted. *Faculty research:* Molecular immunology, bacterial pathogenesis and molecular genetics, viral pathogenesis, regulation of mRNA metabolism, leukocyte biology.

Washington State University, Graduate School, College of Sciences, School of Molecular Biosciences, Program in Microbiology, Pullman, WA 99164. Offers MS, PhD. Terminal master's awarded for partial completion of doctoral program. *Degree requirements:* For master's, thesis, oral exam; for doctorate, comprehensive exam, thesis/dissertation, oral exam. *Entrance requirements:* For master's and doctorate, GRE General Test, minimum GPA of 3.0. Additional exam requirements/recommendations for international students: Required—TOEFL (minimum score 550 paper-based; 213 computer-based). Electronic applications accepted. *Faculty research:* Viral-host interaction, bacterial-host interaction, microbial medicine, microbial pathogenesis, cancer biology.

Washington University in St. Louis, Graduate School of Arts and Sciences, Division of Biology and Biomedical Sciences, Program in Molecular Microbiology and Microbial Pathogenesis, St. Louis, MO 63130-4899. Offers PhD. *Degree requirements:* For doctorate, thesis/dissertation. *Entrance requirements:* For doctorate, GRE General Test, GRE Subject Test. Electronic applications accepted.

Wayne State University, School of Medicine, Graduate Programs in Medicine, Department of Immunology and Microbiology, Detroit, MI 48202. Offers MS, PhD, MD/PhD. Terminal master's awarded for partial completion of doctoral program. *Degree requirements:* For master's, thesis; for doctorate, thesis/dissertation. *Entrance requirements:* For master's, GRE, minimum GPA of 2.5; for doctorate, GRE, minimum GPA of 3.0. Additional exam requirements/recommendations for international students: Required—TOEFL (minimum score 550 paper-based; 213 computer-based); Recommended—TWE (minimum score 6). Electronic applications accepted. *Faculty research:* Immune regulation, bacterial pathophysiology, molecular biology/viruses/bacteria, cellular and molecular immunology, microbial pathogenesis.

West Virginia University, School of Medicine, Graduate Programs at the Health Sciences Center, Interdisciplinary Graduate Programs in Biomedical Sciences, Program in Immunology and Microbial Pathogenesis, Morgantown, WV 26506. Offers MS, PhD, MD/PhD. *Degree requirements:* For doctorate, comprehensive exam, thesis/dissertation. *Entrance requirements:* For doctorate, GRE General Test, minimum GPA of 3.0. Additional exam requirements/recommendations for international students: Required—TOEFL. Electronic applications accepted. *Faculty research:* Regulation of signal transduction in immune responses, immune responses in bacterial and viral diseases, peptide and DNA vaccines for contraception, inflammatory bowel disease, physiology of pathogenic microbes.

Wright State University, School of Graduate Studies, College of Science and Mathematics, Program in Microbiology and Immunology, Dayton, OH 45435. Offers MS. Part-time programs available. *Degree requirements:* For master's, thesis. *Entrance requirements:* Additional exam requirements/recommendations for international students: Required—TOEFL. *Faculty research:* Reproductive immunology, viral pathogenesis, virus-host cell interactions.

Yale University, School of Medicine and Graduate School of Arts and Sciences, Combined Program in Biological and Biomedical Sciences (BBS), Microbiology Track, New Haven, CT 06520. Offers PhD, MD/PhD. *Degree requirements:* For doctorate, thesis/dissertation. *Entrance requirements:* For doctorate, GRE General Test, GRE Subject Test. Additional exam requirements/recommendations for international students: Required—TOEFL. *Application deadline:* For fall admission, 12/6 for domestic and international students. Electronic applications accepted. *Financial support:* Fellowships, research assistantships available. *Unit head:* Dr. Robert Means, Director of Graduate Admissions, 203-737-2404. *Application contact:* Karen Kavanaugh, Graduate Registrar, 203-737-2404, E-mail: karen.kavanaugh@yale.edu.

Youngstown State University, Graduate School, College of Science, Technology, Engineering and Mathematics, Department of Biological Sciences, Youngstown, OH 44555-0001. Offers environmental biology (MS); molecular biology, microbiology, and genetic (MS); physiology and anatomy (MS). Part-time programs available. *Degree requirements:* For master's, comprehensive exam, thesis, oral review. *Entrance requirements:* For master's, GRE General Test, minimum GPA of 2.7. Additional exam requirements/recommendations for international students: Required—TOEFL. *Faculty research:* Cell biology, neurophysiology, molecular biology, neurobiology, gene regulation.

Virology

Baylor College of Medicine, Graduate School of Biomedical Sciences, Department of Molecular Virology and Microbiology, Houston, TX 77030-3498. Offers PhD, MD/PhD. *Faculty:* 42 full-time (13 women). *Students:* 36 full-time (19 women); includes 12 minority (2 African Americans, 5 Asian Americans or Pacific Islanders, 5 Hispanic Americans), 9 international. Average age 26. In 2009, 3 doctorates awarded. *Degree requirements:* For doctorate, thesis/dissertation, public defense. *Entrance requirements:* For doctorate, GRE General Test, GRE Subject Test (strongly recommended), minimum GPA of 3.0. Additional exam requirements/recommendations for international students: Required—TOEFL. *Application deadline:* For fall admission, 1/1 priority date for domestic students. Applications are processed on a rolling basis. Application fee: $0. Electronic applications accepted. *Financial support:* Fellowships, research assistantships, teaching assistantships, career-related internships or fieldwork, Federal Work-Study, institutionally sponsored loans, health care benefits, and tuition waivers (full) available. Financial award applicants required to submit FAFSA. *Faculty research:* Molecular biology of virus replication, viruses and cancer, viral genetics, viral infectious diseases, environmental virology. *Unit head:* Dr. Frank Ramig, Director, 713-798-4830, Fax: 713-798-5075, E-mail: rramig@bcm.edu. *Application contact:* Rosa Banegas, Graduate Program Administrator, 713-798-4472, Fax: 713-798-5075, E-mail: rbanegas@bcm.edu.

Baylor College of Medicine, Graduate School of Biomedical Sciences, Interdepartmental Program in Cell and Molecular Biology, Houston, TX 77030-3498. Offers biochemistry (PhD); cell and molecular biology (PhD); genetics (PhD); human genetics (PhD); immunology (PhD); microbiology (PhD); virology (PhD); MD/PhD. *Faculty:* 100 full-time (31 women). *Students:* 59 full-time (37 women); includes 24 minority (5 African Americans, 1 American Indian/Alaska Native, 7 Asian Americans or Pacific Islanders, 11 Hispanic Americans), 6 international. Average age 25. In 2009, 9 doctorates awarded. *Degree requirements:* For doctorate, thesis/dissertation, public defense. *Entrance requirements:* For doctorate, GRE General Test, GRE Subject Test (strongly recommended), minimum GPA of 3.0. Additional exam requirements/recommendations for international students: Required—TOEFL. *Application deadline:* For fall admission, 1/1 priority date for domestic students. Applications are processed on a rolling basis. Application fee: $0. Electronic applications accepted. *Financial support:* In 2009–10, 59 students received support; fellowships, research assistantships, teaching assistantships, Federal Work-Study, institutionally sponsored loans, health care benefits, and tuition waivers (full) available. Financial award applicants required to submit FAFSA. *Faculty research:* Gene expression and regulation, developmental biology and genetics, signal transduction and membrane biology, aging process, molecular virology. *Unit head:* Dr. Susan Marriott, Director, 713-798-6557. *Application contact:* Lourdes Fernandez, Graduate Program Administrator, 713-798-6557, Fax: 713-798-6325, E-mail: cmbprog@bcm.edu.

See Close-Up on page 231.

Case Western Reserve University, School of Medicine and School of Graduate Studies, Graduate Programs in Medicine, Department of Molecular Biology and Microbiology, Program in Molecular Virology, Cleveland, OH 44106. Offers PhD. *Entrance requirements:* Additional exam requirements/recommendations for international students: Required—TOEFL (minimum score 550 paper-based; 213 computer-based).

Mayo Graduate School, Graduate Programs in Biomedical Sciences, Program in Virology and Gene Therapy, Rochester, MN 55905. Offers PhD.

McMaster University, Faculty of Health Sciences and School of Graduate Studies, Program in Medical Sciences, Hamilton, ON L8S 4M2, Canada. Offers blood and vascular (M Sc, PhD); genetics and cancer (M Sc, PhD); immunity and infection (M Sc, PhD); metabolism and nutrition (M Sc, PhD); neurosciences and behavioral sciences (M Sc, PhD); physiology/ pharmacology (M Sc, PhD); MD/PhD. *Degree requirements:* For master's, thesis; for doctorate, comprehensive exam, thesis/dissertation. *Entrance requirements:* For master's, honors B Sc, B+ average in related field; for doctorate, M Sc, minimum B+ average. Additional exam requirements/recommendations for international students: Required—TOEFL (minimum score 580 paper-based; 237 computer-based; 92 iBT).

The Ohio State University, College of Medicine, School of Biomedical Science, Integrated Biomedical Science Graduate Program, Columbus, OH 43210. Offers immunology (PhD); medical genetics (PhD); molecular virology (PhD); pharmacology (PhD). *Degree requirements:* For doctorate, thesis/dissertation. *Entrance requirements:* For doctorate, GRE, GRE Subject Test in biochemistry, cell and molecular biology (recommended for some). Additional exam requirements/recommendations for international students: Required—TOEFL (minimum score 600 paper-based; 250 computer-based). Electronic applications accepted. *Expenses:* Tuition, state resident: full-time $10,683. Tuition, nonresident: full-time $25,923. Tuition and fees vary according to course load and program.

The Ohio State University, College of Medicine, School of Biomedical Science, Program in Molecular Virology, Immunology and Medical Genetics, Columbus, OH 43210. Offers MS, PhD. *Entrance requirements:* For master's and doctorate, GRE, GRE Subject Test in biology (recommended). Electronic applications accepted. *Expenses:* Tuition, state resident: full-time $10,683. Tuition, nonresident: full-time $25,923. Tuition and fees vary according to course load and program.

Penn State Hershey Medical Center, College of Medicine, Graduate School Programs in the Biomedical Sciences, Graduate Program in Microbiology and Immunology, Hershey, PA 17033. Offers genetics (PhD); immunology (MS, PhD); microbiology (MS); microbiology/virology (PhD); molecular biology (PhD); MD/PhD. *Students:* 12 applicants, 75% accepted, 3 enrolled. In 2009, 1 doctorate awarded. Terminal master's awarded for partial completion of doctoral program. *Degree requirements:* For master's, thesis or alternative; for doctorate, comprehensive exam, thesis/dissertation, oral exam. *Entrance requirements:* For doctorate, GRE General Test, minimum GPA of 3.0. Additional exam requirements/recommendations for international students: Required—TOEFL. *Application deadline:* For fall admission, 1/31 priority date for domestic students, 2/1 priority date for international students. Applications are processed on a rolling basis. Application fee: $45. Electronic applications accepted. *Expenses:* Tuition, state resident: part-time $644 per credit. Tuition, nonresident: part-time $1142 per credit. Required fees: $22 per semester. *Financial support:* In 2009–10, research assistantships with full tuition reimbursements (averaging $22,260 per year); fellowships with full tuition reimbursements, scholarships/grants, health care benefits, and unspecified assistantships also available. Financial

award applicants required to submit FAFSA. *Faculty research:* Virus replication and assembly, oncogenesis, interactions of viruses with host cells and animal model systems. *Unit head:* Dr. Richard J. Courtney, Chair, 717-531-7659, Fax: 717-531-6522, E-mail: micro-grad-hmc@psu.edu. *Application contact:* Billie Burns, Secretary, 717-531-7659, Fax: 717-531-6522, E-mail: micro-grad-hmc@psu.edu.

Purdue University, School of Veterinary Medicine and Graduate School, Graduate Programs in Veterinary Medicine, Department of Comparative Pathobiology, West Lafayette, IN 47907-2027. Offers comparative epidemiology and public health (MS); comparative epidemiology and public heath (PhD); comparative microbiology and immunology (MS, PhD); comparative pathobiology (MS, PhD); interdisciplinary studies (PhD), including microbial pathogenesis, molecular signaling and cancer biology, molecular virology; lab animal medicine (MS); veterinary anatomic pathology (MS); veterinary clinical pathology (MS). *Faculty:* 37 full-time (10 women), 4 part-time/adjunct (2 women). *Students:* 53 full-time (31 women), 2 part-time (1 woman); includes 3 minority (2 African Americans, 1 Hispanic American), 32 international. Average age 35. In 2009, 6 master's, 2 doctorates awarded. Terminal master's awarded for partial completion of doctoral program. *Degree requirements:* For master's, thesis (for some programs); for doctorate, thesis/dissertation. *Entrance requirements:* For master's and doctorate, GRE General Test. Additional exam requirements/recommendations for international students: Required—TOEFL (minimum score 575 paper-based; 232 computer-based), IELTS (minimum score 6.5), TWE (minimum score 4). *Application deadline:* For fall admission, 8/12 for domestic students, 6/15 for international students; for spring admission, 1/12 for domestic students, 10/15 for international students. Application fee: $55. Electronic applications accepted. *Financial support:* Fellowships, research assistantships, teaching assistantships available. Financial award application deadline: 3/1; financial award applicants required to submit FAFSA. *Unit head:* Dr. Suresh Mittal, Interim Head, 765-494-7543. *Application contact:* Denise A. Ottinger, Director, Student Services and Admissions, 765-494-7893, Fax: 765-496-2891, E-mail: vetadmissions@purdue.edu.

Rush University, Graduate College, Division of Immunology and Microbiology, Program in Immunology/Microbiology, Chicago, IL 60612-3832. Offers immunology (MS, PhD); virology (MS, PhD); MD/PhD. Part-time programs available. Terminal master's awarded for partial completion of doctoral program. *Degree requirements:* For master's, thesis; for doctorate, thesis/dissertation, comprehensive preliminary exam. *Entrance requirements:* For master's, GRE General Test; for doctorate, GRE General Test, interview, minimum GPA of 3.0. Additional exam requirements/recommendations for international students: Required—TOEFL. Electronic applications accepted. *Faculty research:* Human genetics, autoimmunity, tumor biology, complement, HIV immunopathology genesis.

Rutgers, The State University of New Jersey, New Brunswick, Graduate School-New Brunswick, Programs in the Molecular Biosciences, Program in Microbiology and Molecular Genetics, Piscataway, NJ 08854-8097. Offers applied microbiology (MS, PhD); clinical microbiology (MS, PhD); computational molecular biology (PhD); immunology (MS, PhD); microbial biochemistry (MS, PhD); molecular genetics (MS, PhD); virology (MS, PhD). Part-time programs available. Terminal master's awarded for partial completion of doctoral program. *Degree requirements:* For master's, comprehensive exam, thesis or alternative; for doctorate, comprehensive exam, thesis/dissertation, written qualifying exam. *Entrance requirements:* For master's, GRE General Test, minimum GPA of 3.0; for doctorate, GRE General Test, GRE Subject Test (recommended), minimum GPA of 3.0. Additional exam requirements/ recommendations for international students: Required—TOEFL. Electronic applications accepted. *Faculty research:* Molecular genetics and microbial physiology; virology and pathogenic microbiology; applied, environmental and industrial microbiology; computers in molecular biology.

Texas A&M Health Science Center, Graduate School of Biomedical Sciences, Department of Microbial and Molecular Pathogenesis, College Station, TX 77840. Offers immunology (PhD); microbiology (PhD); molecular biology (PhD); virology (PhD). *Degree requirements:* For doctorate, thesis/dissertation. *Entrance requirements:* For doctorate, GRE General Test, minimum GPA of 3.0. *Faculty research:* Molecular pathogenesis, microbial therapeutics.

Université de Montréal, Faculty of Veterinary Medicine, Program in Virology and Immunology, Montréal, QC H3C 3J7, Canada. Offers PhD. *Students:* 8 full-time (5 women). *Degree requirements:* For doctorate, thesis/dissertation, general exam. *Entrance requirements:* For doctorate, proficiency in French, knowledge of English. *Application deadline:* For fall admission, 2/1 priority date for domestic students; for winter admission, 11/1 priority date for domestic students; for spring admission, 2/1 priority date for domestic students. Application fee: $100. Electronic applications accepted. *Unit head:* Dr. George Szatmari, Chairperson, 514-343-5767, Fax: 514-343-5701, E-mail: george.szatmari@umontreal.ca. *Application contact:* Lamercie Youance, Information Contact, 514-343-6111 Ext. 3129, Fax: 514-343-5701, E-mail: lamercie.youance@umontreal.ca.

Université du Québec, Institut National de la Recherche Scientifique, Graduate Programs, Research Center—INRS—Institut Armand-Frappier—Human Health, Québec, QC G1K 9A9, Canada. Offers applied microbiology (M Sc); biology (PhD); experimental health sciences (M Sc); virology and immunology (M Sc, PhD). Programs given in French. Part-time programs available. *Faculty:* 37. *Students:* 157 full-time (97 women), 4 part-time (all women), 41 international. Average age 30. In 2009, 14 master's, 5 doctorates awarded. *Median time to degree:* Of those who began their doctoral program in fall 2001, 67% received their degree in 8 years or less. *Degree requirements:* For doctorate, thesis/dissertation. *Entrance requirements:* For master's and doctorate, appropriate bachelor's degree, proficiency in French. *Application deadline:* For fall admission, 3/30 for domestic and international students; for winter admission, 11/1 for domestic and international students. Application fee: $30 Canadian dollars. *Financial support:* Fellowships, research assistantships, teaching assistantships available. *Faculty research:* Immunity, infection and cancer; toxicology and environmental biotechnology; molecular pharmacochemistry. *Unit head:* Alain Fournier, Director, 450-687-5010, Fax: 450-686-5501, E-mail: alain.fournier@iaf.inrs.ca. *Application contact:* Yvonne Boisvert, Registrar, 418-654-3861, Fax: 418-654-3858, E-mail: registrariat@adm.inrs.ca.

University of California, San Diego, Office of Graduate Studies, Division of Biological Sciences, Program in Immunology, Virology, and Cancer Biology, La Jolla, CA 92093. Offers PhD. Offered in association with the Salk Institute. *Degree requirements:* For doctorate, thesis/dissertation, qualifying exam. Electronic applications accepted.

Virology

The University of Iowa, Roy J. and Lucille A. Carver College of Medicine and Graduate College, Graduate Programs in Medicine, Department of Microbiology, Iowa City, IA 52242-1316. Offers general microbiology and microbial physiology (MS, PhD); immunology (MS, PhD); microbial genetics (MS, PhD); pathogenic bacteriology (MS, PhD); virology (MS, PhD). *Faculty:* 24 full-time (3 women), 8 part-time/adjunct (2 women). *Students:* 36 full-time (20 women); includes 3 minority (2 American Indian/Alaska Native, 1 Hispanic American), 5 international. Average age 25. 87 applicants, 14% accepted, 5 enrolled. In 2009, 3 master's, 7 doctorates awarded. *Degree requirements:* For master's, thesis; for doctorate, comprehensive exam, thesis/dissertation. *Entrance requirements:* For master's and doctorate, GRE General Test. Additional exam requirements/recommendations for international students: Required—TOEFL (minimum score 600 paper-based; 250 computer-based). *Application deadline:* For fall admission, 2/1 for domestic and international students. Electronic applications accepted. *Financial support:* In 2009–10, 4 fellowships with full tuition reimbursements (averaging $24,250 per year), 32 research assistantships with full tuition reimbursements (averaging $24,250 per year) were awarded; institutionally sponsored loans, scholarships/grants, traineeships, and health care benefits also available. *Faculty research:* Gene regulation, processing and transport of HIV, retroviral pathogenesis, biodegradation, biofilm. Total annual research expenditures: $11.7 million. *Unit head:* Dr. Michael A. Apicella, Head, 319-335-7810, E-mail: grad-micro-info@uiowa.edu. *Application contact:* Dr. Michael A. Apicella, Head, 319-335-7810, E-mail: grad-micro-info@uiowa.edu.

University of Massachusetts Worcester, Graduate School of Biomedical Sciences, Program in Immunology and Virology, Worcester, MA 01655-0115. Offers medical sciences (PhD). *Degree requirements:* For doctorate, comprehensive exam, thesis/dissertation. *Entrance requirements:* For doctorate, GRE General Test. Additional exam requirements/recommendations for international students: Required—TOEFL (minimum score 600 paper-based; 250 computer-based). Electronic applications accepted. *Faculty research:* Molecular and immunological studies on viral pathogenesis and oncology, AIDS viruses and other retroviruses, herpes viruses, influenza, Dengue and Newcastle disease viruses.

University of Minnesota, Twin Cities Campus, Graduate School, PhD Program in Microbiology, Immunology and Cancer Biology, Minneapolis, MN 55455-0213. Offers PhD. *Degree requirements:* For doctorate, thesis/dissertation. *Entrance requirements:* For doctorate, GRE General Test. Additional exam requirements/recommendations for international students: Required—TOEFL (minimum score 600 paper-based; 250 computer-based). Electronic applications accepted. *Faculty research:* Virology, microbiology, cancer biology, immunology.

University of Pennsylvania, School of Medicine, Biomedical Graduate Studies, Graduate Group in Cell and Molecular Biology, Program in Microbiology, Virology, and Parasitology, Philadelphia, PA 19104. Offers PhD, MD/PhD, VMD/PhD. *Degree requirements:* For doctorate, thesis/dissertation. *Entrance requirements:* For doctorate, GRE General Test, previous course work in science. Additional exam requirements/recommendations for international students: Required—TOEFL. *Application deadline:* For fall admission, 12/8 priority date for domestic and international students. Applications are processed on a rolling basis. Application fee: $70. Electronic applications accepted. *Expenses:* Tuition: Full-time $25,660; part-time $4758 per course. Required fees: $2152; $270 per course. Tuition and fees vary according to course load, degree level and program. *Financial support:* Fellowships, research assistantships, scholarships/grants, traineeships, and unspecified assistantships available. *Unit head:* Dr. Robert Ricciardi, Chair, 215-898-3965. *Application contact:* Anna Kline, Coordinator, 215-898-3918, Fax: 215-573-2104, E-mail: camb@mail.med.upenn.edu.

University of Pittsburgh, School of Medicine, Graduate Programs in Medicine, Program in Molecular Virology and Microbiology, Pittsburgh, PA 15260. Offers MS, PhD. *Faculty:* 39 full-time (7 women). *Students:* 27 full-time (16 women); includes 2 minority (both Hispanic Americans), 5 international. Average age 27. 655 applicants, 10% accepted, 20 enrolled. In 2009, 1 doctorate awarded. *Degree requirements:* For doctorate, comprehensive exam, thesis/dissertation. *Entrance requirements:* For doctorate, GRE General Test, GRE Subject Test, minimum QPA of 3.0. Additional exam requirements/recommendations for international students: Required—TOEFL (minimum score 600 paper-based; 250 computer-based; 100 iBT), IELTS (minimum score 7). *Application deadline:* For fall admission, 12/15 priority date for domestic and international students. Application fee: $40. Electronic applications accepted. *Expenses:*

Tuition, state resident: full-time $16,402; part-time $665 per credit. Tuition, nonresident: full-time $28,694; part-time $1175 per credit. Required fees: $690; $175 per term. Tuition and fees vary according to program. *Financial support:* In 2009–10, 27 research assistantships with full tuition reimbursements (averaging $24,650 per year) were awarded; institutionally sponsored loans, scholarships/grants, traineeships, health care benefits, and unspecified assistantships also available. *Faculty research:* Host-pathogen interactions, persistent microbial infections, microbial genetics and gene expression, microbial pathogenesis, anti-bacterial therapeutics. *Unit head:* Dr. Neal A. DeLuca, Graduate Program Director, 412-648-9947, Fax: 412-624-0298, E-mail: ndeluca@pitt.edu. *Application contact:* Graduate Studies Administrator, 412-648-8957, Fax: 412-648-1077, E-mail: gradstudies@medschool.pitt.edu.

University of Prince Edward Island, Atlantic Veterinary College, Graduate Program in Veterinary Medicine, Charlottetown, PE C1A 4P3, Canada. Offers anatomy (M Sc, PhD); bacteriology (M Sc, PhD); clinical pharmacology (M Sc, PhD); clinical sciences (M Sc, PhD); epidemiology (M Sc, PhD), including reproduction; fish health (M Sc, PhD); food animal nutrition (M Sc, PhD); immunology (M Sc, PhD); microanatomy (M Sc, PhD); parasitology (M Sc, PhD); pathology (M Sc, PhD); pharmacology (M Sc, PhD); physiology (M Sc, PhD); toxicology (M Sc, PhD); veterinary science (M Vet Sc); virology (M Sc, PhD). Part-time programs available. *Degree requirements:* For master's, thesis; for doctorate, thesis/dissertation. *Entrance requirements:* For master's, DVM, B Sc honors degree, or equivalent; for doctorate, M Sc. Additional exam requirements/recommendations for international students: Required—TOEFL (minimum score 550 paper-based; 213 computer-based; 80 iBT). *Expenses:* Contact institution. *Faculty research:* Animal health management, infectious diseases, fin fish and shellfish health, basic biomedical sciences, ecosystem health.

The University of Texas Health Science Center at Houston, Graduate School of Biomedical Sciences, Program in Virology and Gene Therapy, Houston, TX 77225-0036. Offers MS, PhD, MD/PhD. Terminal master's awarded for partial completion of doctoral program. *Degree requirements:* For master's, thesis; for doctorate, thesis/dissertation. *Entrance requirements:* For master's and doctorate, GRE General Test. Additional exam requirements/recommendations for international students: Required—TOEFL. Electronic applications accepted. *Faculty research:* Viruses, infectious diseases, vaccines, gene therapy, cancer.

The University of Texas Medical Branch, Graduate School of Biomedical Sciences, Center for Biodefense and Emerging Infectious Diseases, Galveston, TX 77555. Offers biodefense training (PhD). *Entrance requirements:* For doctorate, GRE, minimum overall GPA of 3.0. *Financial support:* Tuition waivers and unspecified assistantships available. *Unit head:* Dr. Clarence J. Peters, Executive Director, 409-772-0090, Fax: 409-747-0762, E-mail: cjpeters@utmb.edu. *Application contact:* Dr. Dorian H. Coppenhaver, Associate Dean for Student Affairs, 409-772-2665, Fax: 409-747-0772, E-mail: dcoppenh@utmb.edu.

The University of Texas Medical Branch, Graduate School of Biomedical Sciences, Program in Emerging and Tropical Infectious Diseases, Galveston, TX 77555. Offers PhD, MD/PhD. *Degree requirements:* For doctorate, thesis/dissertation. *Entrance requirements:* For doctorate, GRE General Test. *Application deadline:* Applications are processed on a rolling basis. Application fee: $25 ($50 for international students). *Financial support:* In 2009–10, fellowships (averaging $25,000 per year), research assistantships with full tuition reimbursements (averaging $25,000 per year) were awarded; traineeships and unspecified assistantships also available. *Faculty research:* Emerging diseases, tropical diseases, parasitology, vitology and bacteriology. *Application contact:* Dr. Dorian H. Coppenhaver, Associate Dean for Student Affairs, 409-772-2665, Fax: 409-747-0772, E-mail: dcoppenh@utmb.edu.

Yale University, School of Medicine and Graduate School of Arts and Sciences, Combined Program in Biological and Biomedical Sciences (BBS), Microbiology Track, New Haven, CT 06520. Offers PhD, MD/PhD. *Degree requirements:* For doctorate, thesis/dissertation. *Entrance requirements:* For doctorate, GRE General Test, GRE Subject Test. Additional exam requirements/recommendations for international students: Required—TOEFL. *Application deadline:* For fall admission, 12/6 for domestic and international students. Electronic applications accepted. *Financial support:* Fellowships, research assistantships available. *Unit head:* Dr. Robert Means, Director of Graduate Admissions, 203-737-2404. *Application contact:* Karen Kavanaugh, Graduate Registrar, 203-737-2404, E-mail: karen.kavanaugh@yale.edu.

STATE UNIVERSITY OF NEW YORK
UPSTATE MEDICAL UNIVERSITY
Program in Microbiology and Immunology

Programs of Study

At SUNY Upstate's College of Graduate Studies, Ph.D. students thrive as they participate in medically relevant research on a campus that is proud of its mentoring and multidisciplinary approach. Students enjoy a student-faculty ratio of nearly 1:1 and publish articles in professional journals during their program.

Students select a department, thesis mentor, and ultimate area of research after their first year, which includes three in-depth laboratory rotations of their choice. All departments support Upstate's four main Research Pillars: cancer; infectious diseases; diabetes, metabolic disorders, and cardiovascular disease; and disorders of the nervous system.

Major research areas in the Department of Microbiology and Immunology include diseases caused by viruses, the host response to infection, and the development and function of the immune system. A range of viruses is studied: the retrovirus human T-cell leukemia virus (HTLV); dengue virus (DENV); and the herpesviruses, herpes simplex virus-1 (HSV-1), Epstein-Barr virus (EBV), Kaposi's sarcoma-associated herpesvirus (KSHV), and varicella zoster virus (VZV). The focus of the virology research is on pathogenesis, gene regulation, molecular interactions with the host cell, antiviral agents, and DNA replication.

Cancers caused by viruses are also studied, as well as the use of viruses to infect and kill cancer cells. Immunology research focuses on autoimmune diseases such as lupus and multiple sclerosis, macrophage function, T-cell development, antigen processing and presentation, viral immunity, immunotoxicology, and vaccine development. A central theme is understanding how the immune system prevents or causes disease pathogenesis.

Research Facilities

SUNY Upstate has world-class facilities for faculty members and students. Departmental research is conducted at the molecular, biochemical, and genetic levels with goals of developing gene therapies, vaccines, and better treatment of diseases. Research methods include cell culture, animal models, molecular genetics and gene therapy, microarray analysis of gene expression, and protein array analysis of interactions between viral and cellular proteins.

The main core facilities on campus include the Center for Research and Evaluation, Confocal/Two Photon Imaging, Department of Laboratory Animal Resources, DNA Sequencing, Flow Cytometry, Humanized SCID Mouse and Stem Cell Processing, Imaging Research, In Vivo Computed Tomography, Microarray (SUNYMAC), MRI Research, and Proteomics.

SUNY Upstate also maintains a coalition with nearby Cornell University, the University of Rochester Medical Center, and Buffalo's Roswell Park Cancer Institute, which is dedicated to sharing cutting-edge research facilities. There are also full research support services on campus, including laboratory-animal facilities, network access to the SeqWeb suite of software, a computer-age medical library containing more than 183,000 volumes, electronics and machine shops, and photographic and computer services.

SUNY Upstate's growth on the research side is highlighted by a $72 million expansion of its Institute for Human Performance, a high-tech facility housing shared laboratories and core facilities used in basic and clinical research. It also broke ground in 2009 for a dedicated research park facility.

Financial Aid

All accepted Ph.D. students are fully supported throughout their education by full tuition waivers and a stipend ($21,514 per year). Support comes from graduate assistantships, departmental assistantships, and NIH and NSF grants.

Cost of Study

Stipends and full tuition waivers are granted to all students accepted into the Ph.D. program. There is no teaching requirement. Student fees, which include health service, were $552 for the 2009–10 academic year.

Living and Housing Costs

On-campus housing is available in Clark Tower, a ten-story apartment building with attractive, fully furnished standard rooms, studio apartments, and two-bedroom suites. Costs ranged from $4127 (double occupancy) to $8618 (married/family accommodations) for 2009–10. Clark Tower also has study rooms, computer rooms, private and shared kitchens, lounges, a recreation room, laundry, and storage. Clark Tower is next door to the Campus Activities Building, which houses athletic facilities, a bookstore, and snack bar.

Many students rent nearby houses or apartments and bicycle or walk to campus. Syracuse has a low cost of living and abundant affordable housing.

Student Group

There are 124 graduate students in the biomedical sciences (58 percent women; 100 percent full-time) and approximately 600 medical students, 200 nursing students, and 200 students in the health professions enrolled at Upstate Medical University. Twenty-five percent of the graduate students come from Canada, Europe, and Asia. Syracuse University and the SUNY College of Environmental Science are located within a quarter mile of SUNY Upstate, resulting in a population of approximately 23,000 students in the immediate area.

Location

Syracuse is New York's fourth-largest city and is located in the scenic center of the state. A naturally beautiful setting, the area offers excellent hiking, biking, boating, and skiing. Nearby are the Finger Lakes region, the Adirondack and the Catskill Mountains, and Lake Ontario. Syracuse's cultural activities include a professional theater, symphony orchestra and opera company, noted author lecture series, chamber music groups, and several top-notch music festivals (classical, blues, and jazz) as well as art and history museums. The area also offers high-quality family life with many excellent school districts and Upstate's own day care center. Syracuse University's top-level collegiate sporting events are a major recreational activity. Syracuse is easily reached by air, rail, and car.

The University

SUNY Upstate is the only academic medical center in the central New York region and is part of the dynamic University Hill community. In addition to the College of Graduate Studies, SUNY Upstate Medical University includes three other colleges—Medicine, Nursing, and Health Professions—its own University Hospital, and a regional campus in Binghamton, New York. The University is growing with new leadership, degree programs, and further plans for expansion. SUNY Upstate Medical University is close to downtown Syracuse and is adjacent to (but not affiliated with) the campus of Syracuse University. SUNY Upstate's Campus Activities Building houses a swimming pool, sauna, gymnasium, squash courts, handball/paddleball court, weight-lifting area with a Universal Gym and a full Nautilus room, billiards, table tennis, television room, bookstore, snack bar, and lounge. Conference rooms are also available for student use.

Applying

The Admissions Committee for the College of Graduate Studies at SUNY Upstate begins reviewing applications in December prior to entry and continues until all positions are filled, which can be as early as early April. The State University of New York requires a $40 application fee. Competitive applicants must have a bachelor's degree or its equivalent, a minimum 3.0 GPA, and course work that includes biology, calculus, chemistry, and physics. GRE General Test scores are required (combined score 1000 minimum), and scores from the Subject Test in chemistry or biology are recommended. International applicants must provide clear evidence of English proficiency (including speaking) by taking the Test of English as a Foreign Language (TOEFL). Candidates for admission are selected on the basis of their record and qualifications for independent scholarship in a specialized field of study. Selected applicants will be invited to campus to meet with faculty, students and tour lab facilities.

Correspondence and Information

Office of Graduate Studies
State University of New York Upstate Medical University
750 East Adams Street
Syracuse, New York 13210
Phone: 315-464-7655
Fax: 315-464-4544
E-mail: biosci@upstate.edu
Web site: http://www.upstate.edu/grad/

State University of New York Upstate Medical University

THE FACULTY AND THEIR RESEARCH

Joseph Domachowske, M.D., Adjunct Professor. Pneumovirus pathogenesis.

Timothy Endy, M.D., M.P.H., Associate Professor. Understanding the epidemiology and pathogenesis of viral hemorrhagic and encephalitic arboviruses and host-vector interactions.

Gerold Feuer, Ph.D., Associate Professor. HTLV pathogenesis and Tax function; humanized SCID mouse models of hematopoiesis; lentivirus vectors; KSHV/HHV-8 infection and pathogenesis; SCID-hu immune responses against HIV envelope.

Jerrie Gavalchin, Ph.D., Professor. Regulation of pathogenic antibody production in autoimmune glomerulonephritis; cell-surface receptors for retroviruses.

Sandra M. Hayes, Ph.D., Assistant Professor. Determining the roles of gamma/delta TCR structure and signaling potential in gamma/delta T-cell development and function.

Charles B. C. Hwang, Ph.D., Professor. DNA replication of herpes viruses.

Burk Jubelt, M.D., Professor. CNS acute and chronic polio- and entero-virus infections.

William Kerr, Ph.D., Professor. Transplant immunology and stem-cell biology.

Dilip Kittur, M.D., Professor. Xenotransplantation; endothelial cell dysfunction; use of herbal products in transplant biology.

James Listman, M.D., Assistant Professor. Cytomegalovirus and transplantation.

Paul Massa, Ph.D., Professor. Genetic regulation of glial cell differentiation.

Jennifer Moffat, Ph.D., Associate Professor. Varicella zoster pathogenesis.

Andras Perl, M.D., Ph.D., Adjunct Professor. Genes and viruses predisposing to autoimmunity; genetics; apoptosis; endogenous retroviruses; transaldolase.

Dawn Post, Ph.D., Assistant Professor. Cancer treatment, using oncolytic viruses and gene therapy.

Michael F. Princiotta, Ph.D., Assistant Professor. Antigen processing and presentation; cytotoxic T-lymphocyte response to viral and bacterial infections.

Rosemary Rochford, Ph.D., Professor and Chair. Etiology of viral-associated malignancies; gammaherpesvirus pathogenesis.

Edward J. Shillitoe, B.D.S., Ph.D., Professor. Gene therapy for cancer.

Allen E. Silverstone, Ph.D., Professor. How dioxins and estrogens and estrogenic compounds affect the immune system.

Steven M. Taffet, Ph.D., Professor. Regulation of intercellular communication in the heart; gene expression during macrophage activation.

THOMAS JEFFERSON UNIVERSITY

Jefferson College of Graduate Studies
Department of Microbiology and Immunology
Kimmel Cancer Center
Graduate Program in Immunology and Microbial Pathogenesis

Programs of Study

The Graduate Program in Immunology and Microbial Pathogenesis, leading to the Doctor of Philosophy degree, is sponsored by the Department of Microbiology and Immunology in connection with the Kimmel Cancer Center. Students entering with a baccalaureate degree take a core biomedical course in the fall semester, incorporating biochemistry, molecular biology, cell biology, and genetics. With this foundation in place, students continue on with core courses in immunology, virology, and microbiology. Advanced courses are taken in both the first and second years of study. The curriculum is sufficiently flexible to accommodate the individual's background and interests, such as advanced virology, immunopathogenesis, and tumor immunology. Laboratory rotations allow students to experience different areas of research before choosing a preceptor and direction for thesis work by the end of the first year. Concentrated thesis research continues thereafter as the predominant activity of the student's graduate experience. Guidance for students is provided by the research adviser and a thesis faculty committee. Students are given considerable opportunity to continue developing their scientific knowledge base in immunology through weekly journal clubs and research seminars. The Graduate Program in Immunology and Microbial Pathogenesis, with the Graduate Programs in Biochemistry and Molecular Biology, Genetics, and Molecular Pharmacology and Structural Biology, make up the four Graduate Programs of the Kimmel Cancer Center.

Current research interests within the program include antigen presentation, antiviral agents, autoimmunity, B-cell development, cancer immunology, cancer inflammation, cell biology of malaria, cell growth regulation and differentiation, cellular immunology, cell activation and signal transduction, chemical and antigenic structure of virus particles, cytokines, developmental immunology, immunochemistry, immunogenetics, immunoparasitology, immunoregulation, latent virus infections, microbial immunology and pathogenesis, molecular immunology, neuroimmunology, neurovirology, regulation of viral gene expression, reproductive immunology, transplantation immunology, viral oncogenes, viral replication, and virus-cell interactions.

Research Facilities

Research laboratories are primarily located in the Kimmel Cancer Center, occupying 70,000 square feet of the Bluemle Life Sciences Building and 25,000 square feet in the adjacent Jefferson Alumni Hall. The Center is exceptionally well equipped and provides a rich environment for interaction among research disciplines. Facilities are available for cell sorting by flow cytometry, peptide and oligonucleotide synthesis and sequencing, proteomics, microarray, scanning and transmission electron microscopy, transgenic mouse production, and X-ray crystallography. State-of-the-art, high-speed, Internet-ready computer systems are also available.

Financial Aid

Financial support is available to full-time Ph.D. students in the form of University fellowships. In 2010–11, students granted full fellowship support receive funds for payment of tuition, student medical insurance, and a stipend of $26,300. Also available to students demonstrating financial need are Title IV funds. University loan programs are available to qualifying students.

Cost of Study

Tuition and fees for full-time Ph.D. students are $28,423 per year in 2010–11.

Living and Housing Costs

Campus housing is available to graduate students in the program; there is also reasonably priced alternative housing near the University.

Student Group

The incoming class size in the Graduate Program in Immunology and Microbial Pathogenesis is expected to be 3; the program currently has 28 Ph.D. students. The University enrolls about 2,500 students. The College of Graduate Studies enrolls approximately 630 students, about half of whom are women.

Student Outcomes

Recent Ph.D. graduates have accepted postdoctoral positions in prestigious academic institutions, such as Harvard, Baylor, Johns Hopkins, UC Davis, and M. D. Anderson Cancer Center at the University of Texas; at the Trudeau Institute and the NIH; and in industry, including Bristol-Meyers Squibb, Centocor, and Pfizer.

Location

The 13-acre campus of Thomas Jefferson University is located in the vibrant historical downtown area of Philadelphia within walking distance of many places of cultural interest. Numerous intercollegiate and professional athletics events take place nearby, within easy access by bus and subway lines. Philadelphia is located a few hours away from New York City and Washington, D.C., and the nearby Jersey shore and Pennsylvania mountains offer year-round recreational activities.

The University

Thomas Jefferson University is an academic health center. It evolved from the Jefferson Medical College, which was founded in 1824. In addition to the medical college, the University includes the Jefferson College of Graduate Studies, the Jefferson College of Health Professions, the University hospital, and various affiliated hospitals and institutions. Jefferson Alumni Hall houses the TJU Fitness and Recreation Facility, study lounges, a swimming pool, a sauna, a gymnasium, and a handball/squash court.

At present, the University enrolls about 2,500 students. The College of Graduate Studies enrolls approximately 630 students, about half of whom are women.

Applying

The deadline to submit Ph.D. applications and all supporting materials is January 5. Applications received after this date are considered at the discretion of the admissions committee. Scores on the General Test of the Graduate Record Examinations (GRE), three letters of recommendation, and academic transcripts are required of all applicants. For those students whose native language is not English, scores on the Test of English as a Foreign Language (TOEFL) are required. Scores on an appropriate Subject Test of the GRE are strongly recommended. Prospective students are encouraged to visit the Department and discuss the graduate program with members of the faculty.

Correspondence and Information

For applications:

Marc Stearns
Director of Admissions and Recruitment
College of Graduate Studies
Thomas Jefferson University
1020 Locust Street, M-46
Philadelphia, Pennsylvania 19107-6799

Phone: 215-503-4400
Fax: 215-503-3433
E-mail: cgs-info@jefferson.edu
Web site: http://www.jefferson.edu/cgs

For program information:

Joanne Balitzky
Training Programs Coordinator
Kimmel Cancer Center
Thomas Jefferson University
233 South 10th Street, 910 BLSB
Philadelphia, Pennsylvania 19107-5541

Phone: 215-503-6687
Fax: 215-503-0622
E-mail: joanne.balitzky@jefferson.edu
Web site: http://www.jefferson.edu/jcgs/phd/imp/

Thomas Jefferson University

THE FACULTY AND THEIR RESEARCH

David Abraham, Professor; Ph.D., Pennsylvania, 1983. Parasite immunology; role of eosinophils, neutrophils, and macrophages in innate and adaptive immunity to helminth parasite infections; development of vaccines against nematode infections; genetic control of protective immunity to parasites; chemotherapy of leishmaniasis; diagnosis of strongyloidiasis.

Kishore R. Alugupalli, Assistant Professor and Program Director; Ph.D., Lund (Sweden), 1996. Molecular basis of bacterial pathogenesis using murine infection models; B 1 b lymphocytes in T cell–independent IgM memory; role of Toll-like receptors in innate and adaptive immune responses.

Hwyda Arafat, Assistant Professor; M.D., 1982, Ph.D., 1996, Ain Shams (Cairo); Ph.D., University of Medicine and Dentistry of New Jersey, 1996. Molecular interactions of pancreatic beta cells during the inflammatory processes in type 1 diabetes.

Arthur M. Buchberg, Associate Professor; Ph.D., SUNY at Buffalo, 1983. Immunogenetics: dissecting the role the homeoprotein, Meis1, has in contributing to AML development; genetics of the innate immune response to pathogen infection.

Bruno Calabretta, Professor; M.D./Ph.D., Rome, 1987. Regulation of granulocytic differentiation by members of the CCAAT family of transcription factors.

Catherine E. Calkins, Professor; Ph.D., Purdue, 1972. Cellular immunology; immunoregulation of antiself reactivity; autoimmune disease; antiviral immunity; immunopathogenesis of hepatitis B virus.

Kerry Campbell, Associate Professor; Ph.D., Virginia Commonwealth, 1988. Molecular mechanisms by which killer cell immunoglobulin-like receptors (KIR) regulate human natural killer (NK) cell responses; signal transduction in natural killer cells.

Rene Daniel, Associate Professor; M.D., Karlova (Prague), 1991; Ph.D., Temple, 1996. Retrovirus–host cell interactions; gene therapy vectors; HIV-1 replication; stem cells and aging.

Bernhard Dietzschold, Professor; D.V.M., Giessen (Germany), 1967. Study of the pathogenesis of rabies; identification of immune mechanisms involved in rabies virus clearance from the CNS; development of novel recombinant virus vaccines against rabies and other emerging viral diseases such as Nipah virus infection.

Laurence C. Eisenlohr, Professor and Codirector, M.D./Ph.D. Program; V.M.D., 1983, Ph.D., 1988, Pennsylvania. Cell biology of MHC class I– and class II–restricted antigen processing of viral antigens; T-cell responses and memory to viral antigens; antitumor immunity.

Neal Flomenberg, Professor; M.D., Thomas Jefferson, 1976. Marrow transplantation and graft-host interactions; characterization and manipulation of the immune response to malignant disease in an allogeneic setting (such as graft-versus-leukemia responses); approaches to promote graft-host tolerance after marrow or solid organ transplantation and to accelerate immune reconstitution.

Phyllis R. Flomenberg, Associate Professor; M.D., Yeshiva (Einstein), 1980. Adenoviruses; *Vaccinia virus;* viral immunology; tumor immunology; immunotherapy.

Richard R. Hardy, Professor; Ph.D., Caltech, 1980. Developmental immunology of B cells, including their generation from stem cells in fetal liver and bone marrow; regulation of B-cell development by pre-BCR and BCR signaling; development of B-cell subsets, including B-1 B cells, with relevance to autoimmunity and leukemia.

D. Craig Hooper, Associate Professor; Ph.D., McGill, 1983. Neuroimmunology; contribution of free radicals to immunity; central nervous system (CNS) inflammation; immune regulation of blood-brain barrier function; autoimmunity; virus clearance from the CNS; spinal cord injury; CNS tumor immunity; immunopathogenesis; T cell–dependent inflammatory mechanisms; mechanisms of immune cell invasion into the CNS; CD4 T-cell priming; passive immunization; vaccination.

Tim Manser, Plimpton-Pugh Professor and Chair; Ph.D., Utah, 1982. Role of antigen receptor specificity in B-cell selection, tolerance, and memory; germinal center reaction; regulation of B-cell responses by inhibitory Fc receptors.

James P. McGettigan, Research Assistant Professor; Ph.D., Thomas Jefferson, 2002. Vaccine- and naturally-induced B- and T-cell responses against infectious diseases, with an emphasis on rabies virus and HIV; evaluating the role for non-neutralizing antibodies in the design of future vaccines.

Steven McKenzie, Professor; M.D./Ph.D., Pennsylvania, 1985. Murine models of immune-mediated thrombocytopenia and thrombosis syndromes; molecular genetics of Fc receptor evolution and function; genetically modified mouse models of autoimmune disease and host defense.

Fabienne Paumet, Assistant Professor; Ph.D., Pasteur Institute (France), 1999. Understanding the protein machinery regulating membrane fusion during phagocytosis and its corruption during bacterial infection.

Richard G. Pestell, Professor; Ph.D., 1991, M.D., 1997, Melbourne (Australia); FRACP, 1991, FACP, 2009. Molecular mechanisms and gene therapy of breast and prostate cancer; cancer stem cells.

Glenn F. Rall, Associate Professor; Ph.D., Vanderbilt, 1990. Viral spread within neurons; recruitment and function of the immune response to neurotropic viral challenges; transgenic models of viral pathogenesis.

Ulrich Rodeck, Professor; M.D., Ph.D., Germany, 1981. Regulation of epithelial cell survival by the epidermal growth-factor receptor; coordinate regulation of cell-cycle progression and cell survival by growth factor– and adhesion-dependent signal transduction; targeted therapies in cancer treatment; mitigation of normal tissue toxicity of cancer therapeutics; genotoxic stress responses of vertebrate organisms using zebrafish embryos.

Michael J. Root, Assistant Professor; M.D./Ph.D., Harvard, 1997. Structure and function of glycoproteins involved in viral and cell-cell membrane fusion; design of viral entry inhibitors and immunogens for vaccine development; antibody-antigen interactions.

Takami Sato, Professor; M.D., 1980, Ph.D., 1997, Jichi Medical (Japan). Cancer immunotherapies; immunoembolization of hepatic tumors with GM-CSF; antibody-directed natural killer cell therapy.

Matthias J. Schnell, Professor and Director, Jefferson Vaccine Center; Ph.D., Hohenheim (Stuttgart), 1994. Recombinant rhabdoviruses as vaccine vectors for HIV-1 and other IDs; interaction of rhabdoviruses with the immune system; molecular pathogenesis of rabies virus.

Charles P. Scott, Assistant Professor; Ph.D., Pennsylvania, 1997. Combinatorial target and drug discovery; chemical genomics of host-pathogen interactions and cancer.

Luis Sigal, Associate Professor; D.V.M., Buenos Aires, 1984, Ph.D., Nebraska–Lincoln, 1994. Antigen presentation in viral infections and mechanisms of natural and acquired resistance to ectromelia virus.

Linda D. Siracusa, Professor; Ph.D., SUNY at Buffalo, 1985. Immunogenetics: identification and characterization of genes, allelic variants, and mutations involved in mammalian disease processes.

David S. Strayer, Professor; M.D./Ph.D., Chicago, 1976. Gene delivery and gene therapy; use of viral gene transfer to protect bone marrow–derived cells from HIV-1 infection and to protect brain neurons from the effects of HIV-1 infection in the central nervous system; immunizing against botulinum toxin antigens and lentiviral antigens, particularly with application of immunostimulatory cytokines to the process of immunization; developing strategies to protect from and to treat infection by hepatitis B and C viruses, using transgenes designed to improve cellular resistance to these viruses, including single-chain Fv antibodies, interferons alpha and gamma, and inhibitory RNA species (siRNAs, ribozymes, antisense); developing treatment strategies for inherited diseases of the lungs and liver, e.g., hereditary hypercholesterolemia and alpha-1-antitrypsin deficiency.

Yuri Sykulev, Associate Professor; M.D./Ph.D., Pyrogov Moscow State Medical, 1982. Mechanisms of regulation of cytolytic effector activities responding to virus-infected and cancer cells.

Theodore F. Taraschi, Professor; Ph.D., Rutgers, 1980. (1) (Defective) DNA mismatch repair and anti-malarial drug resistance in the human malaria parasite, *Plasmodium falciparum,* and (2) identification and characterization of the pathways that mediate hemoglobin internalization from the host erythrocyte and subsequent transport to the malaria parasite food vacuole, where the obligate degradation of hemoglobin occurs. Understanding the basis of antimalarial drug resistance and the identification of new antimalarial targets and agents are the long-term goals of these projects.

John L. Wagner, Associate Professor; M.D., Temple, 1989. Canine immunogenetics and allogeneic peripheral blood stem cell transplantation; gene expression in graft-versus-host disease post–bone marrow transplantation.

Scott A. Waldman, Professor; Ph.D., Thomas Jefferson, 1980; M.D., Stanford, 1987. Molecular mechanisms of signal transduction, with emphasis on receptor-effector coupling and post-receptor signaling mechanisms; translation of molecular signaling mechanisms to novel diagnostic and therapeutic approaches to patients with cancer; defining cross talk between systemic and mucosal immune systems; exploring the relationship between immune-mediated inflammation and neoplasia; identifying unique antigenic targets to serve as effective antitumor vaccines.

David Wiest, Associate Professor; Ph.D., Duke, 1991. Understanding the molecular basis for control of T lineage development by molecular effectors differentially elicited by distinct TCR isotypes.

Hui Zhang, Professor; M.D., Sun Yatsen Medical Sciences, 1982; Ph.D., SUNY Health Science Center at Syracuse, 1994. Cytidine deaminase APOBEC3G/F and its anti-HIV-1 activity; microRNA and HIV-1 pathogenesis; proteomics; high-throughput assay to screen antiviral drugs; HIV-1 vaccine.

Jianke Zhang, Associate Professor; Ph.D., Purdue, 1993. Immune tolerance and homeostasis; lymphocyte apoptosis; cytokine-receptor signal transduction; lymphocyte development; signal transduction mechanisms by the Fas/TNF receptor family members that mediate apoptosis and growth/proliferation; Toll-like receptor signaling; transgenic and gene targeting (knockout) analyses of protein functions in mice.

UNIVERSITY OF CONNECTICUT HEALTH CENTER

Graduate Program in Immunology

Program of Study

A Ph.D. in immunology is offered through an interdepartmental program consisting of 21 faculty members. The immunology faculty members also participate in training students in the combined M.D./Ph.D. and D.M.D./Ph.D. programs. The central focus of the program is to train students to become independent investigators who will provide meaningful research and educational contributions to the areas of basic, applied, or clinical immunology. This goal is achieved by lectures, seminars, laboratory rotations, research presentations, and a concentration on laboratory research. In addition to basic and advanced immunology courses, students are given a strong foundation in biomedical sciences through the core curriculum in biochemistry, genetics, molecular biology, and cell biology. Research laboratory training aims to provide a foundation in modern laboratory techniques and concentrates on hypothesis-based analysis of problems. Research in the program is focused on the cellular and molecular aspects of immune system structure and function in animal models and in humans. Areas of emphasis include molecular immunology (mechanisms of antigen presentation, major histocompatibility complex genetics and function, cytokines and cytokine receptors, and tumor antigens), cellular immunology (biochemical mechanisms and biological aspects of signal transduction of lymphocytes and granulocytes; cellular and molecular requirements for thymic T-lymphocyte development, selection, and activation; cytokines in B- and T-cell development; regulation of antitumor immunity; immunoparasitology, including parasite genetics and immune recognition of parasite antigens; and mechanisms of inflammation), organ-based immunology (immune effector mechanisms of the intestine, lymphocyte interactions in the lung, and immune regulation of the eye), immunity to infectious agents (viruses, bacteria, parasites, including vector-borne organisms), and autoimmunity (animal models of autoimmune disease and effector mechanisms in human autoimmunity).

Research Facilities

The Graduate Program in Immunology is interdepartmental, and therefore provides a broad base of training possibilities as well as ample shared facilities. State-of-the-art equipment is available in individual laboratories for analysis of molecular and cellular parameters of immune system structure and function. In addition, Health Center–supported facilities provide equipment and expertise in areas of advanced data acquisition and analysis. These facilities include the Center for Cell Analysis and Modeling, the Fluorescence Flow Cytometry Facility, the Gene Targeting and Transgenic Facility, the Molecular Core Facility, the Microarray Facility, the Gregory P. Mullen Structural Biology Facility, and the Electron Microscopy Facility. The Health Center Library is well equipped with extensive journal and book holdings and rapid electronic access to database searching, the World Wide Web, and library holdings. A computer center is also housed in the library for student use and training.

Financial Aid

Support for doctoral students engaged in full-time degree programs at the Health Center is provided on a competitive basis. Graduate research assistantships for 2010–11 provide a stipend of $28,000 per year, which includes a waiver of tuition/University fees for the fall and spring semesters and a student health insurance plan. While financial aid is offered competitively, the Health Center makes every possible effort to address the financial needs of all students.

Cost of Study

For 2010–11, tuition is $4455 per semester ($8910 per year) for full-time students who are Connecticut residents and $11,565 per semester ($23,130 per year) for full-time out-of-state residents. General University fees are added to the cost of tuition for students who do not receive a tuition waiver. These costs are usually met by traineeships or research assistantships for doctoral students.

Living and Housing Costs

There is a wide range of affordable housing options in the greater Hartford area within easy commuting distance of the campus, including an extensive complex that is adjacent to the Health Center. Costs range from $600 to $900 per month for a one-bedroom unit; 2 or more students sharing an apartment usually pay less. University housing is not available.

Student Group

At present, there are 30 students in the Graduate Program in Immunology. There are 150 students in the various Ph.D. programs on the Health Center campus.

Student Outcomes

Graduates have traditionally been accepted into high-quality laboratories for postdoctoral training. Following their training, graduates have accepted a wide range of positions in research in universities, colleges, research institutes, and industry, including the biotechnology sector.

Location

The Health Center is located in the historic town of Farmington, Connecticut. Set in the beautiful New England countryside on a hill overlooking the Farmington Valley, it is close to ski areas, hiking trails, and facilities for boating, fishing, and swimming. Connecticut's capital city of Hartford, 7 miles east of Farmington, is the center of an urban region of approximately 800,000 people. The beaches of the Long Island Sound are about 50 minutes away to the south, and the beautiful Berkshires are a short drive to the northwest. New York City and Boston can be reached within 2½ hours by car. Hartford is the home of the acclaimed Hartford Stage Company, TheatreWorks, the Hartford Symphony and Chamber orchestras, two ballet companies, an opera company, the Wadsworth Athenaeum (the oldest public art museum in the nation), the Mark Twain house, the Hartford Civic Center, and many other interesting cultural and recreational facilities. The area is also home to several branches of the University of Connecticut, Trinity College, and the University of Hartford, which includes the Hartt School of Music. Bradley International Airport (about 30 minutes from campus) serves the Hartford/Springfield area with frequent airline connections to major cities in this country and abroad. Frequent bus and rail service is also available from Hartford.

The Health Center

The 200-acre Health Center campus at Farmington houses a division of the University of Connecticut Graduate School, as well as the School of Medicine and Dental Medicine. The campus also includes the John Dempsey Hospital, associated clinics, and extensive medical research facilities, all in a centralized facility with more than 1 million square feet of floor space. The Health Center's newest research addition, the Academic Research Building, was opened in 1999. This impressive eleven-story structure provides 170,000 square feet of state-of-the-art laboratory space. The faculty at the center includes more than 260 full-time members. The institution has a strong commitment to graduate study within an environment that promotes social and intellectual interaction among the various educational programs. Graduate students are represented on various administrative committees concerned with curricular affairs, and the Graduate Student Organization (GSO) represents graduate students' needs and concerns to the faculty and administration, in addition to fostering social contact among graduate students in the Health Center.

Applying

Applications for admission should be submitted on standard forms obtained from the Graduate Admissions Office at the UConn Health Center or on the Web site. The application should be filed together with transcripts, three letters of recommendation, a personal statement, and recent results from the General Test of the Graduate Record Examinations. International students must take the Test of English as a Foreign Language (TOEFL) to satisfy Graduate School requirements. The deadline for completed applications and receipt of all supplemental materials is December 15. In accordance with the laws of the state of Connecticut and of the United States, the University of Connecticut Health Center does not discriminate against any person in its educational and employment activities on the grounds of race, color, creed, national origin, sex, age, or physical disability.

Correspondence and Information

Dr. Adam Adler, Program Director
Graduate Program in Immunology
Department of Immunology
MC 1601
University of Connecticut Health Center
Farmington, Connecticut 06030-1601
Phone: 860-679-7992
Fax: 860-679-1868
E-mail: aadler@uchc.edu
Web site: http://www.grad.uchc.edu

www.twitter.com/usgradschools

University of Connecticut Health Center

THE FACULTY AND THEIR RESEARCH

Adam J. Adler, Associate Professor of Immunology; Ph.D., Columbia. Mechanisms of T-cell tolerance induction to peripheral self- and tumor-antigens; immunological properties of prostate cancer.

Hector L. Aguila, Assistant Professor of Immunology; Ph.D., Yeshiva (Einstein). Hematopoiesis and bone marrow microenvironment; lymphoid cell development; stem cell biology.

Linda Cauley, Assistant Professor of Immunology; D.Phil., Oxford. T-cell memory and respiratory virus infections.

Robert B. Clark, Associate Professor of Immunology; M.D., Stanford. Autoimmunity; immune regulation; regulatory T cells.

Robert Cone, Professor of Immunology; Ph.D., Michigan. Ocular immunology; regulatory T cells; neuroimmunology.

Irving Goldschneider, Professor of Immunology; M.D., Pennsylvania. T- and B-cell development; acquired thymic tolerance; cytokines.

Chi-Kuang Huang, Associate Professor of Immunology; Ph.D., Connecticut. Signal transduction in stimulated neutrophil and lymphocytes; roles of protein kinase and phosphoproteins in cell activation; chemotaxis.

Donald L. Kreutzer, Professor of Pathology and Surgery; Ph.D., Kansas. Immunopathology and molecular mechanisms of inflammation; mediators and regulators of leukocyte chemotaxis; modulation of inflammatory reactions by the vascular endothelium.

Leo Lefrancois, Professor of Immunology; Ph.D., Wake Forest. T-cell memory; immune response to infection; tolerance; vaccines.

Joseph A. Lorenzo, Professor of Medicine; M.D., SUNY Downstate Medical Center. Relationships between bone-absorbing osteoclasts and immune cells.

Bijay Mukherji, Professor of Medicine; M.D., Calcutta (India). Tumor immunology and cancer vaccines; tumor-specific antigens.

James O'Rourke, Professor of Immunology and Surgery; M.D., Georgetown. Vascular biology; tissue plasminogen activator synthesis, transport, and release.

Lynn Puddington, Associate Professor of Immunology; Ph.D., Wake Forest. Allergic asthma; neonatal immunity and tolerance; developmental immunology.

Justin D. Radolf, Professor of Medicine and Center for Microbial Pathogenesis; M.D., California, San Francisco. Molecular pathogenesis and immunobiology of spirochetal infections.

Pramod K. Srivastava, Professor of Medicine; Ph.D., Hyderabad (India). Heat shock proteins as peptide chaperones; roles in antigen presentation and applications in immunotherapy of cancer, infectious diseases, and autoimmune disorders.

Roger S. Thrall, Professor of Immunology and Surgery; Ph.D., Marquette. Immune cells; pulmonary inflammation.

Anthony T. Vella, Associate Professor of Immunology; Ph.D., Cornell. T-cell immunity; costimulation; adjuvants and cytokines.

Carol A. Wu, Assistant Professor of Immunology; Ph.D., Vanderbilt. Viral respiratory infection and asthma.

Richard A. Zeff, Associate Professor of Immunology; Ph.D., Rush. Major histocompatibility complex; antigen processing and presentation.

UNIVERSITY OF FLORIDA

College of Medicine
Advanced Concentration in Immunology and Microbiology

Program of Study

The College of Medicine at the University of Florida (UF) offers graduate training in biomedical research leading to a Ph.D. degree through the Interdisciplinary Program (IDP) in Biomedical Sciences. The goal of the Interdisciplinary Program is to prepare students for a diversity of careers in research and teaching in academic and commercial settings. The program provides a modern, comprehensive graduate education in biomedical science while providing both maximum program flexibility as well as appropriate specialization for graduate students. During the first year of study, incoming graduate students undertake a common, comprehensive interdisciplinary core curriculum of classroom study developed in a cooperative effort by all of the graduate programs in the College of Medicine. In addition, students select from any of the College of Medicine faculty members for participation in several laboratory rotations conducted throughout the first year, concurrent with the core curriculum. By the end of their first year, students select a laboratory in which to conduct their dissertation research and, once again, they may choose from any of the graduate faculty members in the College of Medicine. Formal selection of a graduate program and mentor is made after completion of the core curriculum to maximize flexibility and facilitate an informed decision; however, students may make an informal commitment to a program or lab at any time.

The Advanced Concentration in Immunology and Microbiology provides graduate training in cellular and molecular immunology, including immunopathology, immunogenetics, and autoimmunity, and in microbiology, including virology, bacteriology, microbial genetics, and microbial pathogenesis. The program is designed for maximum flexibility in the educational experience of the individual student and provides broad opportunities for training in immunology and microbiology, emphasizing both cellular and molecular aspects. Students participate in seminars, journal clubs, and research rotations. Dissertation research is conducted with the advice of a supervisory faculty member and a supervisory committee. The program is expected to require four to five years of graduate study. During this time, students are expected to pass a qualifying examination indicating proficiency in immunology, microbiology, and cellular and molecular biology and to present a dissertation thesis on original research.

Research Facilities

The College of Medicine houses state-of-the-art research facilities maintained by the Interdisciplinary Center for Biomedical Research (ICBR), the McKnight Brain Institute, the Clinical Research Center, the Cancer/Genetics Research Center, several other University of Florida research centers, and individual research laboratories. Together these facilities provide services for DNA and protein synthesis and sequencing, hybridoma production, confocal and electron microscopy, NMR spectroscopy, computing and molecular modeling, flow cytometry, transgenic mouse production, and gene therapy vector construction. The University of Florida libraries, including the Health Center library, form the largest information resource system in the state of Florida and support up-to-date computer-based bibliographic retrieval services.

UF's nine libraries offer more than 4 million catalogued volumes and links to full-text articles in more than 34,000 journals. Of national significance are the Baldwin Library of Historical Children's Literature, the Latin American Collection, the Map and Imagery Library, the P. K. Yonge Library of Florida History (preeminent Floridiana collection), the Price Library of Judaica, and holdings on architectural preservation and eighteenth-century American architecture, late nineteenth- and early twentieth-century German state documents, rural sociology of Florida, and tropical and subtropical agriculture.

Financial Aid

Students accepted into the Interdisciplinary Program receive a stipend of $25,750 per annum. Students also receive a waiver that covers tuition and GatorGradCare health insurance.

Cost of Study

Graduate research assistants pay fees of approximately $1400 per year. Books and supplies cost about $1600.

Living and Housing Costs

Married student housing is available in six apartment villages operated by the University; dormitories for single students are available in limited quantities. The cost of housing for a single graduate student is approximately $6500 per year. Most graduate students live in abundant and comfortable off-campus housing that is near the University; rents vary but are low on a national scale.

Student Group

Enrollment at the University of Florida is both culturally and geographically diverse and numbers about 50,000, including about 10,000 graduate students. There are about 300 graduate students in the College of Medicine.

Location

Situated in north-central Florida, midway between the Atlantic Ocean and the Gulf of Mexico, Gainesville is a nationally recognized academic and research center and was rated the number one place to live in the U.S. in a 1995 *Money* magazine survey. There are about 200,000 residents in the Gainesville metropolitan area, excluding University of Florida students. The climate is moderate, permitting outdoor activities the year around. The University and the Gainesville community also host numerous cultural events, including music, dance, theater, lectures, and art exhibits. Many of the men's and women's athletic programs are considered to be in the top ten programs in the country.

The University and The College

The University of Florida, located on 2,000 acres, is among the nation's leading research universities as categorized by the Carnegie Commission on Higher Education. UF is a member of the Association of American Universities, the nation's most prestigious higher education organization. UF is also one of the nation's top three universities in the breadth of academic programs offered on a single campus. It has twenty colleges and schools and 100 interdisciplinary research and education centers, bureaus, and institutes. The College of Medicine, opened in 1956, has become a nationally recognized leader in medical education and research.

Applying

The Interdisciplinary Program in Biomedical Sciences seeks promising students with undergraduate training in chemistry, biology, psychology, or related disciplines in the life sciences. Applicants are selected on the basis of previous academic work, research experience, GRE General Test scores, letters of recommendation, the personal statement, and a personal interview. Students are admitted for the fall semester, which begins in late August. The application deadline is December 15.

Correspondence and Information

Richard Condit, Co-Director
Department of Molecular Genetics and Microbiology
University of Florida College of Medicine
P.O. Box 100266
Gainesville, Florida 32610-0266
Phone: 352-392-3128
E-mail: condit@mgm.ufl.edu
Web site: http://idp.med.ufl.edu/IMM/index.html

Clayton Mathews, Co-Director
Department of Pathology, Immunology, and Laboratory
  Medicine
University of Florida College of Medicine
P.O. Box 100275
Gainesville, Florida 32610-0275
Phone: 352-392-9803
E-mail: clayton.mathews@pathology.ufl.edu
Web site: http://idp.med.ufl.edu/IMM/index.html

University of Florida

THE FACULTY AND THEIR RESEARCH

David Allred, Ph.D., Associate Professor. Cellular and molecular bases of host-parasite interactions; immunology of hemoparasitic diseases.

Veena Anthony, M.D., Professor and Chief. Molecular recognition of inflammation at epithelial surfaces in the lung.

Mark Atkinson, Ph.D., Eminent Scholar, Program Director, and Unit Co-Director, Experimental Pathology. Natural history of insulin-dependent diabetes; cellular immunology; immunoprevention trials; gene therapy; cellular regeneration; transplantation.

Anthony Barbet, Ph.D., Professor. Molecular biology of parasitic and ehrlichial diseases of cattle; development of recombinant vaccines and diagnostic tests, molecular mechanism of pathogenesis.

Kenneth Berns, M.D., Ph.D., Professor. AAV as a vector for human gene therapy; molecular genetics of AAV.

Arnold Bleiweiss, Ph.D., Graduate Research Professor. Immunochemistry of the cell wall and membrane of oral streptococci, with emphasis on *Streptococcus mutans;* genetics and physiology of gram-positive bacteria.

David Bloom, Ph.D., Associate Professor. Herpesvirus latency and pathogenesis; HSV vectors.

L. Jeannine Brady, Ph.D., Assistant Professor. Host/pathogen interactions; immunomodulation by monoclonal antibodies; structure/function of streptococcal surface antigens; streptococcal protein translocation; stress responses; membrane biogenesis; biofilm formation; bacterial adhesion.

Raul Braylan, M.D., Professor and Chief, Hematopathology. Development and application of immunomicroscopic, flow cytometric, and molecular genetic analyses to diagnosis/detection/biological characterization of human hematological neoplasia.

Luciano Brocchieri, Ph.D., Assistant Professor. Bioinformatics; molecular evolution; phylogenetic trees; determinants of gene and protein composition; genomics of herpesviruses; chaperonomics.

Tom Brown, Ph.D., Professor. Recombinant vaccines; role of IgA in mucosal immunity; microbial IgA1 proteases.

Brian Burke, Ph.D., Professor. Cell biology, nuclear structure, and organization; nucleocytoplasmic transport.

Robert Burne, Ph.D., Professor and Chair. Environmental regulation of bacterial gene expression and virulence.

Barry Byrne, M.D., Ph.D. Professor. Cardiovascular gene therapy; adeno-associated viral vectors.

Martha Campbell-Thompson, D.V.M., Ph.D., Associate Research Professor. Molecular pathology and immunology core; type 1 diabetes; AAV gene therapy.

Edward Chan, Ph.D, Professor. Molecular and cell biology of macromolecules and subcellular organelles that are targets in autoimmunity; RNA interference; GW bodies as related to autoimmunity and cancer.

Lung-Ji Chang, Ph.D., Professor. HIV, retroviral, and lentiviral vectors and cancer.

Michael Clare-Salzler, M.D., Professor. Role of antigen-presenting cells in the pathogenesis of autoimmune diseases, including type 1 diabetes; development of dendritic cell function and interaction with NK T cells.

Richard C. Condit, Ph.D., Professor and Co-Director. Vaccinia virus molecular genetics; transcription elongation.

James M. Crawford, M.D., Ph.D., Professor and Chair. Gene therapy of hepatic disease; stem cell biology of the liver; molecular pathology and tissue bank core laboratory; optical imaging and pathology.

Byron Croker, M.D., Ph.D., Professor and Chief Unit Director, Renal Pathology.

Benn Dunn, Ph.D., Professor. Directed mutagenesis and kinetic/structural analysis of enzymatic specificity, especially for proteolytic enzymes; HIV-AIDS research; proteases in malaria.

Melissa Elder, M.D., Ph.D., Associate Professor. AAV- or parvovirus B19-mediated correction of human severe combined immunodeficiency syndrome.

James Flanegan, Ph.D., Professor. Molecular biology and genetics of RNA virus replication.

Maureen Goodenow, Ph.D., Professor and Unit Co-Director, Experimental Pathology. Pathogenesis of retroviruses and HIV; signal transduction in lymphocytes and macrophages; genetics of viral drug resistance; evolution of HIV-1.

Scott Grieshaber, Ph.D., Assistant Professor. Understanding the unique mechanism by which the obligate intracellular bacteria *Chlamydia trachomatis* hijack the microtubule system during infection; host-pathogen interactions; control of chlamydial infections.

Paul A. Gulig, Ph.D., Professor and Co-Director. Pathogenesis of *Vibrio vulnificus;* bacteriophage therapy; detection of agents of bioterrorism.

Martin Handfield, Ph.D., Associate Professor. Novel molecular biology and genetic tools to study bacterial pathogenesis in vivo; identification, characterization, and modification of bacterial virulence factors for the control or prevention of infections; study of host-pathogen interactions using mic.

Axel Heiser, Ph.D., Assistant Professor. Immunobiology of dendritic cells, T cells, and tumors; applications for tumor therapy.

Roland Herzog, Ph.D., Associate Professor. Gene therapy for the inherited bleeding disorder hemophilia; immunology of in vivo gene transfer; tolerance induction to therapeutic proteins.

Jeffrey Hillman, D.M.D., Ph.D., Professor. Identification, characterization, and modification of bacterial virulence factors for the control or prevention of infections.

Paul Hoffman, M.D., Courtesy Professor. Animal models of neurodegeneration with emphasis on inflammation.

Shouguang Jin, Ph.D., Professor. Type III secretion system of *Pseudomonas* and host-cell apoptosis.

Saeed Khan, Ph.D., Professor; Unit Co-Director, Experimental Pathology; and Director, Center for the Study of Lithiasis. Urolithiasis; biomineralization; role of lipids and proteins in calcification and stone formation; electron microscopy; X-ray microanalysis.

Peter Kima, Ph.D., Associate Professor. Host-parasite interactions; mechanisms by which intracellular pathogens evade activation of the cell-mediated immune response.

Paul A. Klein, Ph.D., Adjunct Professor and Professor Emeritus. Pathogenesis, immunology, and epidemiology of infectious diseases in lower vertebrates; cancer biology; monoclonal antibody applications.

Richard Lamont, Ph.D., Professor. Molecular mechanisms of biofilm formation and communication among biofilm bacteria; invasion of bacteria into oral epithelial cells and host-cell signaling responses to internal bacteria.

Ann Marie LeVine, M.D., Associate Professor. Lung injury and repair with specific emphasis on the immune response; surfactant proteins.

Alfred S. Lewin, Ph.D., Professor. RNA-mediated gene therapy; retinal disease; RNA catalysis.

Chen Liu, Ph.D., Associate Professor. Viral hepatitis pathogenesis and hepatocarcinogenesis; oncogenes, signal transduction, and cell transformation; viral immunology and vaccine; alpha-1 antitrypsin deficiency and liver disease.

Alexandra Lucas, M.D., Professor. Analysis of serpins in vascular innate immune responses; role of GAGs in viral chemokine modulating protein anti-inflammatory functions; optical analysis of vascular inflammation and atherogenesis.

Clayton Mathews, Ph.D., Professor. Genetics of resistance to autoimmune diabetes; oxidative burden of the beta cell.

William McArthur, Ph.D., Professor. Host/parasite interactions in the pathogenesis of inflammatory diseases, specifically periodontal diseases.

Wayne T. McCormack, Ph.D., Associate Professor and Director, Graduate Program. Genetics of susceptibility to autoimmune disease; vitiligo.

Grant McFadden, Ph.D., Professor. Immune evasion by poxviruses; oncolytic virotherapy.

Ayalew Mergia, Ph.D., Professor. Retrovirus vector for gene transfer based on foamy virus; comparative and experimental pathology; veterinary medicine.

Laurence Morel, Ph.D., Associate Professor and Co-Director. Genetic analysis of systemic lupus erythematosus (SLE) susceptibility using mouse models; genetic basis for susceptibility to autoimmunity.

Richard W. Moyer, Ph.D., Professor and Senior Associate Dean for Research Development. Poxvirus biology and pathogenesis.

Nicholas Muzyczka, Ph.D., Eminent Scholar. Adeno-associated virus and virus vectors.

David A. Ostrov, Ph.D., Assistant Professor. Immunological regulation by T cells; structural interactions between ligand pairs linked to T-cell interaction.

Ammon Peck, Ph.D., Professor. Cellular immunology; transplantation immunology; stem cell biology; autoimmune endocrinopathy (diabetes); autoimmune exocrinopathy (Sjogren's syndrome); calcium oxalate urolithiasis.

Ann Progulske-Fox, Ph.D., Professor. Molecular mechanisms of pathogenesis of gram-negative anaerobic bacterial species; bacterial/host-cell interactions.

Reuben Ramphal, M.D., Professor.

Vijay Reddy, M.D., Ph.D., Assistant Professor. Dendritic cells, cytokines, and immune reconstitution after stem cell transplantation.

Westley Reeves, M.D., Eminent Scholar. Pathogenesis of systemic lupus erythematosus in humans and animal models; novel disease markers.

Rolf F. Renne, Ph.D., Associate Professor. Kaposi's sarcoma–associated herpesvirus (KSHV/HHV-8) latency and pathogenesis.

Hanno Richards, M.D., Assistant Professor. Role of cytokines in murine lupus; role of dendritic cells in autoimmunity; urinary markers of lupus nephritis.

Nigel Richards, Ph.D., Professor. Structure/function studies of oxalate-metabolizing enzymes and melanocortin receptor antagonists; asparagine synthetase inhibitors as antileukemia agents; molecular evolution of glutamine-dependent enzymes; antituberculosis agents.

Minoru Satoh, M.D., Ph.D., Research Associate Professor. Mechanisms of autoantibody production in systemic lupus erythematosus; role of genetic and environmental interactions in autoimmunity using chemically (pristane) induced and genetically determined spontaneous models of murine lupus.

Desmond Schatz, M.D., Professor. Prediction, immunopathogenesis, genetics, and prevention and care of type I diabetes.

Edward Scott, Ph.D., Professor. Gene regulation; biology of hematopoietic progenitor cells.

Eric Sobel, M.D., Ph.D., Associate Professor. Mechanisms of autoantibody production.

Fred Southwick, M.D., Professor. Dynamic remodeling of the actin cytoskeleton in motile cells and in *Listeria* and *Shigella* intracellular infections; macrophage and dendritic cell motility; anthrax toxins effects on immune function.

Arun Srivastava, Ph.D., Professor. Molecular correlates of human parvovirus- (AAV and B19) host-cell interactions; development of recombinant human parvovirus vectors for gene therapy.

Danny Strosberg, Ph.D., Courtesy Professor. Study of the role of protein-protein interactions in host-pathogen relationship.

Zhen Su, M.D., Assistant Professor. Development of novel anti-cancer vaccines; cancer vaccines with embryonic stem cells; cancer stem cell markers for immunotherapy; phase I/II clinical trials using tumor mRNA-loaded dendritic cells; immune suppressive cells in late-stage cancer patients.

Sankar Swaminathan, M.D., Associate Professor. Molecular mechanisms of gene regulation in the oncogenic viruses Epstein-Barr virus (EBV) and Kaposi's sarcoma herpesvirus (KSHV).

Clay Walker, Ph.D., Professor. Mechanisms of antibiotic resistance and antibiotic resistance in biofilms.

Shannon Wallet, Ph.D., Assistant Professor. Innate and adaptive immunological concepts of inflammation and autoimmunity, specifically diabetes mellitus.

William Winter, M.D., Professor and Unit Director, Clinical Chemistry. Diabetes research.

LiJun Yang, M.D., Associate Professor. Transdifferentiation of human bone marrow and liver-derived adult stem cells into insulin-producing cells for cell replacement therapy of type 1 diabetes; immune therapy for multiple myeloma; molecular mechanism of acute promyelocytic leukemia.

Ozlem Yilmaz, D.D.S., Ph.D., Assistant Professor. Oral bacterial colonization mechanisms in gingival epithelia and the characterization of the temporal host responses induced by oral bacteria.

Li Yin, M.D., Ph.D., Research Assistant Professor. Alteration of TCRV CDR3 length distribution within CD4 and CD8 subsets in HIV-1 infected children before and after therapy.

James Zucali, Ph.D., Professor.

UNIVERSITY OF GEORGIA

Department of Microbiology

Programs of Study	The Department of Microbiology offers M.S. and Ph.D. degrees. Students with a B.S. may apply directly for either program. Degree requirements include the successful completion of course work and comprehensive exams, fulfillment of the Graduate School residency requirement, and submission of a thesis or dissertation consisting of original, scholarly research in the field of microbiology. Students pursue a variety of disciplines, including microbial physiology and genetics, cell biology, microbial pathogenesis, ecology, evolution, population biology, biotechnology, and bioinformatics. All students take a core curriculum in microbial physiology and metabolism, molecular biology, and microbial diversity. Advanced courses in specialized areas are also available through the Department of Microbiology and the Division of Biological Sciences. The M.S. program is generally completed in two to three years, while the Ph.D. requires approximately five years. The program of study is designed by the student and his or her advisory committee to provide a broad foundation in microbiology, preparing the student for a career in research and/or teaching in academia, industry, or the government.
Research Facilities	The Department of Microbiology occupies more than 34,000 square feet of renovated space in the Biological Sciences Building, as well as research space in the Coverdell Center for Biomedical and Health Sciences and the Riverbend Research Complex. Facilities are also available for environmental studies at the University of Georgia Marine Institute on Sapelo Island and the Savannah River Ecology Laboratory. Departmental laboratories are equipped for state-of-the-art research in microbiology. Students may also use University research facilities for computational analysis, electron and laser-scanning confocal microscopy, flow cytometry, proteomics, mass spectrometry, DNA and protein sequencing and synthesis, large-scale fermentations, monoclonal antibody production, research animal care, and Biosafety level 3 pathogenesis research. Most of these facilities are in the same building, while others are just a few blocks away.
Financial Aid	Graduate students in the Department of Microbiology are supported by assistantships or fellowships, with awards starting at $24,000 per year for Ph.D. candidates and $22,000 per year for M.S. candidates. In addition to these awards, full annual tuition is waived for every graduate student on any kind of fellowship or assistantship; this amounts to an additional value of $30,856. Thus, the total financial package (assistantship/fellowship plus tuition waiver) ranges from $52,856 to $54,856, depending on the type of assistantship/fellowship.
Cost of Study	Student activity fees covering registration, health service, campus transportation, and computer use are $830 for the fall and spring semesters and $584 for the summer.
Living and Housing Costs	The cost of living (including food, clothing, housing, and utilities) is generally quite reasonable in Athens (students can compare the cost of living at various locations at http://homefair.com/homefair/calc/salcalc.html). Dormitory rooms are available. In addition, apartments are available in the University's family housing unit (http://www.uga.edu/housing/gradfam/index.html). A variety of apartments, duplexes, and rental homes can be found off campus.
Student Group	In 2008–09, 39 students were enrolled in graduate studies in the Department of Microbiology, representing Asia, South America, and seventeen U.S. states. The Microbiology Graduate Student Association promotes communication between students and faculty members, sponsors visiting seminar speakers and social events, and participates in the campuswide Graduate Student Association.
Location	The University of Georgia is located in Athens, one of America's great college towns. Athens has a community of 98,000 and is situated in a rolling, wooded area in the Piedmont of northeastern Georgia. The climate is moderate, with mean temperatures ranging from 33°F to 53°F (1°C to 12°C) in January and 68°F to 89°F (20°C to 32°C) in July. The Appalachian Trail begins only 70 miles to the north, and Atlanta lies about the same distance to the southwest. Within a modest drive are the barrier islands of the Georgia coast, the Okefenokee Swamp, and the Chattahoochee National Forest. Numerous recreational and cultural activities are available in the Athens area and nearby.
The University and The Department	Chartered in 1785, the University of Georgia was the nation's first state-supported university. It is composed of thirteen schools and has a total enrollment of 32,500 students. The University campus covers approximately 3,500 acres. Established more than fifty years ago in the Franklin College of Arts and Sciences, the Department of Microbiology, among the top five non–medical school microbiology departments in the nation, is highly regarded for its mastery of a broad range of microbial systems. Among the 15 faculty members, there are 3 recipients of prestigious NSF Presidential Young Investigator Awards, 1 Guggenheim Fellow, and 3 recipients of NIH Research Career Development Awards. Research in the Department of Microbiology usually generates more than $2 million annually from sources such as the NIH, NSF, EPA, USDA, Department of Energy, Office of Naval Research, and several foundations and corporate sponsors. The Department members usually generate more than seventy publications annually in scientific journals.
Applying	Application information is available at the Web site. To ensure consideration for competitive assistantships, the Graduate School application should be submitted online before December 15. A Background and Interest form should be completed for the microbiology program on the Web site by December 15. All recent successful applicants had a baccalaureate in the biological sciences with previous research experience either as an undergraduate or in employment. Generally, undergraduate GPAs are about 3.5, and GRE scores (verbal and quantitative) are greater than 1250. International students whose native language is not English must have a TOEFL Academic Speaking Test (TAST) score of at least 26 for acceptance.
Correspondence and Information	Graduate Coordinator Department of Microbiology 527 Biological Sciences Building University of Georgia Athens, Georgia 30602-2605 Phone: 706-542-2045 E-mail: mibcoord@uga.edu Web site: http://www.uga.edu/mib

University of Georgia

THE FACULTY AND THEIR RESEARCH

Daniel G. Colley, Professor; Ph.D., Tulane, 1968. Immunology of schistosomiasis in people (at the Kenya Medical Research Institute, Kisumu, Kenya); operational research on public health interventions for schistosomiasis.
  Influence of exposure history on the immunology and development of resistance to human schistosomiasis mansoni. *PLoS Neglected Tropical Diseases* 4(3):e637, 2010. doi:10.1371/journal.pntd.0000637.

Harry A. Dailey, Professor; Ph.D., UCLA, 1976. Regulation of heme metabolism; structure-function of heme synthetic enzymes.
  Altered orientation of active site residues in variants of human ferrochelatase. Evidence for a hydrogen bond network involved in catalysis. *Biochemistry* 46:7973–9, 2007. Substrate interactions with human ferrochelatase. *Proc. Natl. Acad. Sci. U.S.A.* 104:1789–93, 2007.

Timothy R. Hoover, Professor; Ph.D., Wisconsin–Madison, 1988. Transcriptional regulation in bacteria.
  Sense and sensibility: Flagellum-mediated gene regulation. Trends Microbiol. 18(1):30–37, 2010. *Helicobacter pylori* FlhB processing-deficient variants affect flagellar assembly but not flagellar gene expression. *Microbiology* 155(4):1170–80, 2009.

Anna C. Glasgow Karls, Associate Professor; Ph.D., Wisconsin–Madison, 1986. Specialized DNA recombination systems and Neisserial pathogenesis.
  Chromosomal context directs high-frequency precise excision of IS*492* in *Pseudoalteromonas atlantica. Proc. Natl. Acad. Sci. U.S.A.* 104:1901, 2007. Piv site-specific invertase requires a DEED motif analogous to the catalytic center of the RuvC Holliday junction resolvases. *J. Bacteriol.* 187:3431–7, 2005.

Duncan C. Krause, Professor; Ph.D., North Carolina at Chapel Hill, 1982. Cell biology and pathogenesis of *Mycoplasma pneumoniae;* nanotechnology-based detection of mycoplasmas.
  Mycoplasma pneumoniae J-domain protein required for terminal organelle function. *Mol. Microbiol.* 71(5):1296–307, 2009. *Mycoplasma pneumoniae* cytoskeletal protein HMW2 and the architecture of the terminal organelle. *J. Bacteriol.* 191(21):6741–8, 2009. Cytoskeletal protein P41 is required to anchor the terminal organelle of the wall-less prokaryote *Mycoplasma pneumoniae. Mol. Microbiol.* 63(1):44–53, 2007.

Robert Maier, Professor and Eminent Scholar; Ph.D., Wisconsin–Madison, 1977. *Helicobacter* and *Salmonella* pathogenesis; oxidative stress resistance; roles and maturation of metalloproteins.
  Oxidative stress-induced peptidoglycan deacetylase in *Helicobacter pylori. J. Biol. Chem.* 284(11):6790–800, 2009. *Salmonella enterica* serovar typhimurium NiFe uptake-type hydrogenases are differentially expressed in vivo. *Infect. Immun.* 76(10):4445–54, 2008.

Jan Mrázek, Assistant Professor; Ph.D., Czechoslovak Academy of Sciences, 1992. DNA sequence analysis; bioinformatics; microbial comparative genomics.
  Phylogenetic signals in DNA composition: Limitations and prospects. *J. Mol. Biol.* 26:1163–9, 2009. AIMIE: A web-based environment for detection and interpretation of significant sequence motifs in prokaryotic genomes. *Bioinformatics* 24:1041–8, 2008. Simple sequence repeats in prokaryotic genomes. *Proc. Natl. Acad. Sci. U.S.A.*104:8472–7, 2007.

Ellen L. Neidle, Professor; Ph.D., Yale, 1987. Biodegradation and transcriptional regulation; gene amplification and genome rearrangement.
  Inducer responses of BenM, a LysR-type transcriptional regulator from *Acinetobacter baylyi* ADP1. *Mol. Microbiol.* 72(4):881–94, 2009. Double trouble: Medical implications of genetic duplication and amplification in bacteria. *Future Microbiol.* 2:309–21, 2007.

Joy Doran-Peterson, Associate Professor; Ph.D., Florida, 1994. Industrial/native fermentations; biomass pretreatments; enzyme digestion; biofuels.
  Mining diversity of the natural biorefinery housed within *Tipula abdominalis* larvae for use in an industrial biorefinery for production of lignocellulosic ethanol. *Insect Sci.* 17(3):303–12, 2010. Microbial conversion of sugars from plant biomass to lactic acid or ethanol. *Plant J.* 54(4):582–92, 2008.

Mark A. Schell, Professor; Ph.D., Cornell, 1979. Host-pathogen interactions; microbial genomics; bioinformatics; gene regulation; protein secretion.
  Type VI secretion is a major virulence determinant in *Burkholderia mallei. Mol. Microbiol.* 64:1466–85, 2007. Ecological genomics of marine *Roseobacters. Appl. Environ. Microbiol.,* 2007.

Lawrence J. Shimkets, Professor; Ph.D., Minnesota, 1980. Cell-cell interactions, biofilm formation, gene regulation, surface motility, and chemotaxis.
  Survival in nuclear waste, extreme resistance, and potential applications gleaned from the genome sequence of *Kineococcus radiotolerans* SRS30216. *PLoS One* 3(12):e3878, 2008. The mosaic genome of *Anaeromyxobacter dehalogenans* strain 2CP-C suggests an aerobic common ancestor to the delta-proteobacteria. *PLoS One* 3(5):e2103, 2008.

Eric V. Stabb, Associate Professor; Ph.D., Wisconsin–Madison, 1997. *Vibrio fischeri–Euprymna scolopes* symbiosis; bioluminescence; MAMPs; genetics.
  Bioluminescence in *Vibrio fischeri* is controlled by the redox-responsive regulator ArcA. *Mol. Microbiol.* 65:538–53, 2007. New rfp- and pES213-derived tools for analyzing symbiotic *Vibrio fischeri* reveal patterns of infection and lux expression in situ. *Appl. Environ. Microbiol.* 72:802–10, 2006.

Vincent J. Starai, Assistant Professor; Ph.D., Wisconsin–Madison, 2004. Bacterial effectors of eukaryotic intracellular membrane fusion; host-pathogen interactions.

Anne O. Summers, Professor; Ph.D., Washington (St. Louis), 1973. Structure-function in metal defense proteins; host cell components of metal resistance; global proteomics of heavy metal shock.
  Structure and conformational dynamics of the metalloregulator MerR upon binding Hg(II). *J. Mol. Biol.* 398(4):555–68, 2010. Damage control: Regulating defenses against toxic metals and metalloids. *Curr. Opin. Microbiol.* 12(2):138–44, 2009. ^{19}F-NMR reveals metal- and operator-induced allostery in MerR. *J. Mol. Biol.* 371(1):79–92, 2007.

William B. Whitman, Professor; Ph.D., Texas at Austin, 1978. Bacterial physiology/evolution; carbon metabolism in methanogens; prokaryotic systematics.
  Development of soil microbial communities during tallgrass prairie restoration. *Soil Biol. Biochem.* 42(2):302–12, 2010. The Sac10b homolog in *Methanococcus maripaludis* binds DNA at specific sites. *J. Bacteriol.* 191(7):2315–29, 2009.

Joint and Adjunct Faculty

Michael W. Adams, Research Professor, Department of Biochemistry and Molecular Biology; Ph.D., London, 1979. Physiology and enzymology of microorganisms growing near 100°C, using structural and functional genomic approaches.

Michael J. Adang, Professor, Department of Entomology; Ph.D., Washington State, 1981. Genetics and toxicology of *Bacillus thuringiensis* insecticidal proteins.

Russell W. Carlson, Professor, Department of Biochemistry and Molecular Biology, and Technical Director, Complex Carbohydrate Research Center; Ph.D., Colorado at Boulder, 1976. Molecular bases for bacterial-plant and bacterial-animal interactions.

Timothy P. Denny, Professor, Department of Plant Pathology; Ph.D., Cornell, 1983. Genetics and biochemistry of *Ralstonia solanacearum*–plant interactions; mechanisms of bacterial type II protein secretion.

Mark A. Eiteman, Professor, Department of Biological and Agricultural Engineering; Ph.D., Virginia, 1991. Fermentation technology and metabolic engineering of the production of biochemicals.

Marcus Fechheimer, Josiah Meigs Professor, Department of Cellular Biology; Ph.D., Johns Hopkins, 1980. Cell biology, molecular biology, and biochemistry of the actin cytoskeleton in nonmuscle cells and in neurodegenerative disease.

Joseph Frank, Professor, Department of Food Science and Technology; Ph.D., Wisconsin–Madison, 1977. Pathogen-food interactions, with an emphasis on direct observation using confocal scanning laser microscopy; food microbiology; food fermentations.

James T. Hollibaugh, Distinguished Research Professor and AAAS Fellow, Department of Marine Sciences; Ph.D., Dalhousie, 1977. Structure and function of microbial communities; role of bacteria in biogeochemical processes; arsenic metabolism; polar oceanography.

Sidney R. Kushner, Distinguished Research Professor, Department of Genetics; Ph.D., Brandeis, 1970. Analysis of the mechanisms of posttranscriptional genetic regulation in *Escherichia coli;* molecular analysis of RNA processing, decay, and polyadenylation; structure-function analysis of DNA helicase II.

Eric R. Lafontaine, Associate Professor, Department of Infectious Diseases; Ph. D., Calgary, 1997. Host pathogen interactions of the respiratory infectious agents *Moraxella catarrhalis, Burkholderia pseudomallei, and Burkholderia mallei.*

John J. Maurer, Professor, Department of Population Health; Ph.D., Texas at San Antonio, 1990. Antibiotic resistance, food safety, and molecular epidemiology of veterinary and food-borne pathogens.

Cory Momany, Associate Professor, Department of Pharmaceutical and Biomedical Sciences; Ph.D., Texas at Austin, 1990. Structural biology of prokaryotic transcriptional regulation, drug discovery, and bioremediation.

Mary Ann Moran, Professor, Department of Marine Sciences; Ph.D., Georgia, 1987. Microbial ecology and biogeochemistry in coastal marine environments; bacterial community structure; ecological genomics.

Boris Striepen, Professor, Department of Cellular Biology; Ph.D., Marburg (Germany), 1995. Cell and molecular biology of intracellular protozoan parasites *(Toxoplasma* and *Cryptosporidium).*

Rick L. Tarleton, Distinguished Research Professor, Department of Cellular Biology; Ph.D., Wake Forest, 1983. Immunology of *Trypanosoma cruzi* infection and Chagas disease; vaccine development; proteomics and bioinformatics for trypanosomes.

UNIVERSITY OF MASSACHUSETTS AMHERST

Department of Microbiology

Programs of Study

The Department of Microbiology at the University of Massachusetts Amherst offers programs of graduate study leading to the M.S. and Ph.D. degrees in microbiology. Postdoctoral training is also available. Courses covering various areas in the field of microbiology are offered by the Departmental faculty members, listed in the Faculty and Their Research section.

In the Ph.D. program, formal course work is generally completed during the first two years. After the first year, an increasing proportion of time is dedicated to research. Students select dissertation problems from a wide spectrum of research areas pursued by the faculty. The following research fields are represented: bioinformatics, physiology, genetics, immunology, parasitology, pathogenic bacteriology, molecular biology, microbial ecology, and environmental microbiology. In addition, close ties are maintained with the Departments of Biochemistry, Biology, and Chemistry through the interdepartmental program for doctoral training in molecular and cellular biology. In the second year, Ph.D. candidates must pass a comprehensive preliminary examination. Degree requirements are completed by submission and defense of a dissertation. There is no foreign language requirement. Completion of the Ph.D. program generally takes four years beyond the bachelor's degree.

Research Facilities

The Department of Microbiology occupies space in the Morrill Science Center. Air-conditioned laboratories are spacious and well equipped for research and teaching. The modern apparatus necessary for investigation into all aspects of microbiology is available within Departmental space. The Department's facilities include tissue- and cell-culture laboratories, animal quarters, and various instrument rooms containing preparative and analytical ultracentrifuges, scintillation counters, fermentors, anaerobic chambers, equipment for DNA sequence analysis and chromatographic and electrophoretic procedures, photography, and other standard laboratory procedures. Centralized facilities provide state-of-the-art equipment and expertise to support research projects, such as the Central Microscopy Facility; Phosphorimager, Genomics and Bioinformatics Facility; High Field NMR Facility; and Mass Spectrometry Facility.

Financial Aid

Financial aid is available in the form of University fellowships and teaching assistantships. Research assistantships are available for advanced graduate students. All assistantships include a waiver of tuition.

Cost of Study

For the academic year 2009–10, annual tuition for in-state residents was $110 per credit; nonresident tuition was $414 per credit. Full-time students register for at least 9 credits per semester. The mandatory fee assessed for full-time graduate students was $4143 per semester for in-state residents and $5745.50 for nonresidents. Fees are subject to change.

Living and Housing Costs

Graduate student housing is available in several twelve-month campus residence halls through University Housing Services. The University owns and manages unfurnished apartments of various sizes for family housing on or near the campus. Off-campus housing is available; rents vary widely and depend on factors such as size and location.

Student Group

The Department has approximately 35 graduate and 140 undergraduate students as well as 35 postdoctoral fellows. Enrollment at the Amherst campus is about 24,000, including 6,000 graduate students.

Location

The 1,450-acre campus of the University provides a rich cultural environment in a rural setting. Amherst is situated in the picturesque Pioneer Valley in historic western Massachusetts. The area is renowned for its natural beauty. Green open land framed by the outline of the Holyoke Range, clear streams, country roads, forests, grazing cattle, and shade trees are characteristic of the region. A broad spectrum of cultural activities and extensive recreational facilities are available within the University and at four neighboring colleges—Smith, Amherst, Mount Holyoke, and Hampshire. Opportunities for outdoor winter sports are exceptional. Amherst is 90 miles west of Boston and 175 miles north of New York City, and Cape Cod is a 3½-hour drive away.

The University

The University of Massachusetts is the state university of the Commonwealth of Massachusetts and is the flagship campus of the five-campus UMass system. Departments affiliated with the ten colleges and schools of the University offer a variety of graduate degrees through the Graduate School. The Amherst campus consists of approximately 150 buildings, including the twenty-eight-story W. E. B. DuBois Library, which is the largest at a state-supported institution in New England. The library features more than 5.8 million items and is home to a state-of-the-art learning commons equipped with PC and Mac workstations and laptop network access.

Applying

Application forms may be obtained from the Graduate Admissions Office, 530 Goodell Building, University of Massachusetts, 140 Hicks Way, Amherst, Massachusetts 01003-9333, or online at http://www.umass.edu/gradschool. Prospective students are required to take the Graduate Record Examinations. Applications for admission should be received by the Graduate Admissions Office by December 1 for September enrollment and by October 1 for January enrollment. Applications received after these dates are considered only if space is available.

Correspondence and Information

Graduate Program Director
Department of Microbiology
Morrill IV, N203
639 North Pleasant Street
University of Massachusetts Amherst
Amherst, Massachusetts 01003-9298

Phone: 413-545-2051
Fax: 413-545-1578
E-mail: microbio-dept@microbio.umass.edu
Web site: http://www.bio.umass.edu/micro/

University of Massachusetts Amherst

THE FACULTY AND THEIR RESEARCH

J. M. Lopes, Professor and Department Head; Ph.D., South Carolina. Regulation of gene expression in eukaryotes. *Mol. Microbiol.* 70:1529, 2008. *Eukaryot. Cell* 6:786, 2007. *Genetics* 173:621, 2006.

C. L. Baldwin, Adjunct Professor; Ph.D., Cornell. Cellular immunity to intracellular microbial parasites, including *Brucella abortus,* with particular interest in the interaction of the microbe with macrophages and the control of infection by T-cell cytokines; stimulation and control of gamma/delta T-cell responses. *Mol. Immunol.* 44:2033–45, 2007. *Eur. J. Immunol.* 37:1204–16, 2007. *Immunogenetics* 58:746–57, 2006. *Crit. Rev. Immunol.* 26:407–42, 2006. *Microbes Infect.* 9:55–62, 2006.

J. Blanchard, Associate Professor; Ph.D., Georgia. Biofuels; modeling cellular processes using genomic data; evolution of cellular networks. *Mol. Biol. Evol.* 26:5–13, 2009. *PLoS ONE* 11:e1186, 2007.

J. P. Burand, Adjunct Associate Professor; Ph.D., Washington State. Biology and molecular biology of insect pathogenic viruses, particularly nonoccluded insect viruses and bee viruses, with emphasis on virus-host interactions that affect the virulence and persistence of these viruses in insects. *Virol. Sin.* 24:428–35, 2009. *Arch. Virol.* 154:909–18, 2009. *Virol. Sin.* 22:128–36, 2007. *Ann. Entomol. Soc. Am.* 99:967, 2006. *J. Insect Sci.* 5:6, 2005.

D. R. Cooley, Adjunct Associate Professor; Ph.D., Massachusetts. Ecology of diseases; plant pathogenic fungi and bacteria; plant disease management; integrated pest management; development of sustainable agricultural systems.

S. Goodwin, Dean, College of Natural Sciences; Ph.D., Wisconsin.

K. L. Griffith, Assistant Professor; Ph.D., Maryland. Cell-cell signaling in bacteria; development of tools for studying regulatory networks. *J. Mol. Bio.* 381:261–75, 2008. *Mol. Microbiol.* 70:1012–25, 2008.

R. Guerrero, Adjunct Professor; Ph.D., Barcelona. Microbial ecology, particularly microbial mats and early ecosystems; polyhydroxyalkanoates; anoxygenic photosynthetic bacteria. *Int. Microbiol.* 11:267, 2008. *Microb. Ecol.* 54:523, 2007. *Arch. Microbiol.* 188:137, 2007. *Proc. Natl. Acad. Sci. U.S.A.* 103:13080, 2006.

J. F. Holden, Associate Professor; Ph.D., Washington (Seattle). Physiology of hyperthermophilic archaea; geomicrobiology of geothermal environments. *Appl. Environ. Microbiol.* 75:242–5, 2009. *Appl. Environ. Microbiol.* 74:396–402, 2008. *Extremophiles* 11:741–6, 2007.

M. M. Klingbeil, Assistant Professor; Ph.D., Toledo. Molecular and biochemical parasitology, replication and repair of mitochondrial DNA (kinetoplast DNA) and nuclear DNA replication initiation in African trypanosomes. *Mol. Cell* 5:398–400, 2009. *Eukaryot. Cell* 7:2141–6, 2008. *Science* 309:409–15, 2005. *Proc. Natl. Acad. Sci. U.S.A.* 101:4333–4, 2004. *J. Biol. Chem.* 278:49095–101, 2003. *Mol. Cell* 10:175–86, 2002. *Protist* 152:255–62, 2001.

S. B. Leschine, Professor; Ph.D., Pittsburgh. Harnessing the diversity of the microbial world and the power of genomics for energy solutions. *Biofuels Technology* 1:37–44, 2008 (with Gorham et al.). *Biofilms,* 2008: doi:10.1017/S1479050508002238 (with Alonso and Pomposiello). In *Handbook on Clostridia,* pp. 101–31, ed. P. Durre, CRC Press, 2005. *Arch. Microbiol.* 180:434–43, 2003 (with Reguera). *Int. J. Syst. Evol. Microbiol.* 52:1155–60, 2002 (with Warnick).

D. R. Lovley, Distinguished University Professor; Ph.D., Michigan State. Genome-enabled study of the physiology, ecology, and evolution of novel anaerobic microorganisms; environmental genomics; bioremediation of metal and organic contamination; microbial fuel cells; in silico cell modeling; life in extreme environments. *Nature Rev. Microbiol.* 4:497–508, 2006. *Nature* 435:1098–101, 2005. *Nature Rev. Microbiol.* 1:35–44, 2003. *Science* 301:934, 2003. *Nature* 416:767–9, 2002. *Science* 295:483–5, 2002. *Nature* 415:312–6, 2002.

W. J. Manning, Adjunct Professor; Ph.D., Delaware. Effects of ozone on plants and associated mycoflora; plants as bioindicators of ozone; effects of ozone and other air pollutants on plants in urban environments; managing invasive plants with fungal pathogens. *Environ. Pollut.* 126:73–81, 2003.

L. Margulis, Adjunct Professor and Distinguished University Professor. Evolution of microbes; symbiogenesis and the origin of the nucleus; evolution of cells. *Handbook of Prototists,* Sudbury, MA: Jones and Bartlett, 2009. *Kingdoms and Domains: An Illustrated Guide to the Phyla of Life on Earth,* Academic Press, 2009. *Proc. Natl. Acad. Sci. U.S.A.* 103:13080–5, 2006. *Proc. Natl. Acad. Sci. U.S.A.* 31:175–91, 2005. *Acquiring Genomes: A Theory of the Origins of Species,* 240 pp., New York: Basic Books, 2002. *Symbiosis in Cell Evolution: Microbial Communities in the Archean and Proterozoic Eons,* 2nd ed., 452 pp., 1993.

K. Nüsslein, Associate Professor; Ph.D., Michigan State. Microbial ecology of terrestrial and aquatic environments; relating the stress of environmental influences to community structure and function, with emphasis on understanding interactions among bacterial communities. *Geomicrobiology* 26:9–20, 2009. *Geology* 36:139–42, 2008. *Chemosphere* 70:329–36. 2007. *Appl. Environ. Microbiol.* 73:4171–9, 2007. *FEMS Microb. Ecol.* 60:60–73, 2006. *Microb. Ecol.* 51:441–52, 2006.

S. T. Petsch, Adjunct Assistant Professor; Ph.D., Yale. Transport, transformation, and biodegradation of natural organic matter in sediments, soils, and sedimentary rocks. *Geology,* in press. *Appl. Environ. Microbiol.* 73:4171–9, 2007. *Geochim. Cosmochim. Acta* 71:4233–50, 2007. *SEPM* 5:5–9, 2007. *Am. J. Sci.* 306:575–615, 2006. *Palaeogeogr. Palaeoclim. Palaeoecol.* 219:157–70, 2005. *Gas Technol. Inst.* GRI-05/0023, 2004. *Am. J. Sci.* 304:234–49, 2004. *Org. Geochem.* 34:731–43, 2003.

M. A. Riley, Adjunct Professor; Ph.D., Harvard. Microbial ecology and evolution and genome evolution. *BMC Microbial.* 2009, in press. *J. Appl. Microbiol.* 2009, in press.

S. J. Sandler, Professor; Ph.D., Berkeley. Molecular genetics of recombination; DNA replication and DNA repair in bacteria. *Mol. Microbiol.* 57:1074, 2005. *Mol. Microbiol.* 53:1343, 2004.

E. Stuart, Associate Professor; Ph.D., Chicago. Infection, immunity, and pathogenesis, with special interest in processes used by chlamydial species for entry into host cells and replication, prevalence of blood cell-borne *Chlamydia,* and susceptibility of blood cells to infection by *Chlamydia;* vaccine components for use with *Chlamydia;* generation, display, and utility of recombinant vaccine components targeting viral or bacterial peptides. *BMC Microbiol.* 8:213, 2008. *Tocotrienols: Vitamin E beyond Tocopherols,* ch. 25 "Tocotrienol in the potential treatment of infectious disease," CRC Press, 2008;. *BMC Biotechnol.* 8:9, 2008. *J. Clin. Apheresis* 21(3):195–201, 2006. *BMC Infect. Dis.* 6:23, 2006. *Am. J. Respir. Crit. Care Med.* 171(10):1083–8, 2005. *BMC Infect. Dis.* 4(1):23, 2004. *Curr. Microbiol.* 49(1):13–21, 2004. *J. Biotechnol.* 114:225–37, 2004. *Exp. Cell Res.* 287(1):67–7, 2003. *J. Biotechnol.* 88(2):119–28, 2001.

W. Webley, Assistant Professor; Ph.D., Massachusetts. Immunology and pathogenic bacteriology; elucidating the role of *Chlamydia* in the initiation and exacerbation of neonatal asthma; evaluation of chlamydial survival and host range; development of novel antigen display and vaccine delivery systems for *Chlamydia* and other pathogenic bacteria of interest to community health; elucidating the role of *Chlamydia* in thromboembolitic diseases. *Eur. Respir. J.,* 33:1–8, 2009. *Biology of AIDS,* 2nd ed., Dubuque, Iowa: Kendall/Hunt Publishing Company, 2008. *CHEST* 132(suppl.), 2008. *CHEST* 134(suppl.):607, 2007. *J. Clin. Apheresis* 3, 2006. *BMC Infect. Dis.* 6:23, 2006. *Am. J. Respir. Crit. Care Med.* 171(10):1083–8, 2005. *BMC Infect. Dis.* 4(1):23, 2004 (with Stuart and Norkin). *Curr. Microbiol.* 49(1):13–21, 2004. *Am. J. Respir. Crit. Care Med.* 169(7):A586, 2004. *J. Clin. Apheresis* 18(2), 2003. *Exp. Cell Res.* 287(1):67–78, 2003.

R. M. Weis, Adjunct Professor; Ph.D., Stanford. Signal transduction in chemotaxis system and chemotaxis-like pathways. *BMC Genom.* 9:471, 2008. *Proc. Natl. Acad. Sci. USA* 105:12289–94, 2008. *Methods Enzymol.* 423:267–98, 2007. *J. Biol. Chem.* 281:30512–23, 2006.

H. Xiao, Adjunct Assistant Professor; Ph.D., Wisconsin–Madison. Cancer preventive dietary components, diet-based strategy for cancer prevention, enhancement of biological activity of dietary components by combination regimen and food processing.

Section 13
Neuroscience and Neurobiology

This section contains a directory of institutions offering graduate work in neuroscience and neurobiology, followed by in-depth entries submitted by institutions that chose to prepare detailed program descriptions. Additional information about programs listed in the directory but not augmented by an in-depth entry may be obtained by writing directly to the dean of a graduate school or chair of a department at the address given in the directory.

For programs offering related work, see also in this book *Anatomy; Biochemistry; Biological and Biomedical Sciences; Biophysics; Cell, Molecular, and Structural Biology; Genetics, Developmental Biology, and Reproductive Biology; Pathology and Pathobiology; Pharmacology and Toxicology; Physiology;* and *Zoology.* In the other guides in this series:

Graduate Programs in the Humanities, Arts & Social Sciences
See *Psychology and Counseling*
Graduate Programs in Business, Education, Health, Information Studies, Law & Social Work
See *Optometry and Vision Sciences*

CONTENTS

Program Directories

Biopsychology

American University, College of Arts and Sciences, Department of Psychology, Program in Psychology, Washington, DC 22016-8062. Offers experimental/biological psychology (MA); general psychology (MA); personality/social psychology (MA). Part-time programs available. *Students:* 30 full-time (27 women), 17 part-time (14 women); includes 9 minority (3 African Americans, 3 Asian Americans or Pacific Islanders, 3 Hispanic Americans), 1 international. Average age 27. 190 applicants, 36% accepted, 17 enrolled. In 2009, 35 master's awarded. *Degree requirements:* For master's, comprehensive exam, thesis or alternative. *Entrance requirements:* For master's, GRE General Test, GRE Subject Test. Additional exam requirements/recommendations for international students: Required—TOEFL. *Application deadline:* For fall admission, 3/1 for domestic students. Applications are processed on a rolling basis. Application fee: $80. *Expenses:* Tuition: Full-time $22,266; part-time $1237 per credit hour. Required fees: $430. Tuition and fees vary according to program. *Financial support:* Research assistantships, teaching assistantships available. Financial award application deadline: 2/1. *Faculty research:* Behavior therapy, cognitive behavior modification, pro-social behavior, conditioning and learning, olfaction. *Application contact:* Sara Holland, Senior Administrative Assistant, 202-885-1717, Fax: 202-885-1023.

Argosy University, Atlanta, College of Psychology and Behavioral Sciences, Atlanta, GA 30328. Offers clinical psychology (MA, Psy D, Postdoctoral Respecialization Certificate), including child and family psychology (Psy D); general adult clinical (Psy D), health psychology (Psy D), neuropsychology/geropsychology (Psy D); community counseling (MA), including marriage and family therapy; counselor education and supervision (Ed D); forensic psychology (MA); industrial organizational psychology (MA); marriage and family therapy (Certificate); sport-exercise psychology (MA). *Accreditation:* APA.

Argosy University, Twin Cities, College of Psychology and Behavioral Sciences, Eagan, MN 55121. Offers clinical psychology (MA, Psy D), including child and family psychology (Psy D), forensic psychology (Psy D), health and neuropsychology (Psy D), trauma (Psy D); forensic counseling (Post-Graduate Certificate); forensic psychology (MA); industrial organizational psychology (MA); marriage and family therapy (MA, DMFT), including forensic counseling (MA). *Accreditation:* APA.

Brown University, Graduate School, Department of Psychology, Providence, RI 02912. Offers behavioral neuroscience (PhD); cognitive processes (PhD); sensation and perception (PhD); social/developmental (PhD); MS/PhD. *Degree requirements:* For doctorate, thesis/dissertation. *Entrance requirements:* For doctorate, GRE General Test, GRE Subject Test.

Carnegie Mellon University, College of Humanities and Social Sciences, Department of Psychology, Area of Cognitive Neuroscience, Pittsburgh, PA 15213-3891. Offers PhD. *Degree requirements:* For doctorate, comprehensive exam, thesis/dissertation. *Entrance requirements:* For doctorate, GRE General Test. Additional exam requirements/recommendations for international students: Required—TOEFL.

Columbia University, Graduate School of Arts and Sciences, Division of Natural Sciences, Department of Psychology, New York, NY 10027. Offers experimental psychology (M Phil, MA, PhD); psychobiology (M Phil, MA, PhD); social psychology (M Phil, MA, PhD); JD/MA; JD/PhD; MD/PhD. *Degree requirements:* For master's, thesis; for doctorate, thesis/dissertation. *Entrance requirements:* For master's and doctorate, GRE General Test. Additional exam requirements/recommendations for international students: Required—TOEFL.

Cornell University, Graduate School, Graduate Fields of Arts and Sciences, Field of Psychology, Ithaca, NY 14853-0001. Offers biopsychology (PhD); human experimental psychology (PhD); personality and social psychology (PhD). *Faculty:* 49 full-time (17 women). *Students:* 37 full-time (24 women); includes 5 minority (1 African American, 2 Asian Americans or Pacific Islanders, 2 Hispanic Americans), 10 international. Average age 29. 221 applicants, 4% accepted, 8 enrolled. In 2009, 3 doctorates awarded. *Degree requirements:* For doctorate, comprehensive exam, thesis/dissertation, 2 semesters of teaching experience. *Entrance requirements:* For doctorate, GRE General Test, 3 letters of recommendation. Additional exam requirements/recommendations for international students: Required—TOEFL (minimum score 550 paper-based; 213 computer-based; 77 iBT). *Application deadline:* For fall admission, 12/15 for domestic students. Application fee: $70. Electronic applications accepted. *Expenses:* Tuition: Full-time $29,500. Required fees: $70. Full-time tuition and fees vary according to degree level, program and student level. *Financial support:* In 2009–10, 36 students received support, including 6 fellowships with full tuition reimbursements available, 2 teaching assistantships with full tuition reimbursements available; research assistantships with full tuition reimbursements available, institutionally sponsored loans, scholarships/grants, health care benefits, tuition waivers (full and partial), and unspecified assistantships also available. Financial award applicants required to submit FAFSA. *Faculty research:* Sensory and perceptual systems, social cognition, cognitive development, quantitative and computational modeling, behavioral neuroscience. *Unit head:* Director of Graduate Studies, 607-255-6364, Fax: 607-255-8433. *Application contact:* Graduate Field Assistant, 607-255-3834, Fax: 607-255-8433, E-mail: psychapp@cornell.edu.

Drexel University, College of Arts and Sciences, Department of Psychology, Philadelphia, PA 19104-2875. Offers clinical psychology (PhD), including clinical psychology, forensic psychology, health psychology, neuropsychology; law-psychology (PhD); psychology (MS); JD/PhD. *Accreditation:* APA (one or more programs are accredited). *Degree requirements:* For doctorate, thesis/dissertation, internship. *Entrance requirements:* For doctorate, GRE General Test. Additional exam requirements/recommendations for international students: Required—TOEFL. Electronic applications accepted. *Expenses:* Contact institution. *Faculty research:* Neurosciences, rehabilitation psychology, cognitive science, neurological assessment.

Duke University, Graduate School, Department of Psychology, Durham, NC 27708-0586. Offers biological psychology (PhD); clinical psychology (PhD); cognitive psychology (PhD); developmental psychology (PhD); experimental psychology (PhD); health psychology (PhD); human social development (PhD); JD/MA. *Accreditation:* APA (one or more programs are accredited). *Faculty:* 40 full-time. *Students:* 92 full-time (70 women); includes 13 minority (5 African Americans, 2 Asian Americans or Pacific Islanders, 6 Hispanic Americans), 14 international. 478 applicants, 8% accepted, 21 enrolled. In 2009, 10 doctorates awarded. *Degree requirements:* For doctorate, thesis/dissertation. *Entrance requirements:* For doctorate, GRE General Test. Additional exam requirements/recommendations for international students: Required—TOEFL (minimum score 550 paper-based; 213 computer-based; 83 iBT), IELTS (minimum score 7). *Application deadline:* For fall admission, 12/8 priority date for domestic and international students. Application fee: $75. Electronic applications accepted. *Financial support:* Fellowships, research assistantships, teaching assistantships, career-related internships or fieldwork and Federal Work-Study available. Financial award application deadline: 12/31. *Unit head:* Melanie Bonner, Director of Graduate Studies, 919-660-5716, Fax: 919-660-5715, E-mail: morrell@duke.edu. *Application contact:* Cynthia Robertson, Associate Dean for Enrollment Services, 919-684-3913, E-mail: grad-admissions@duke.edu.

Graduate School and University Center of the City University of New York, Graduate Studies, Program in Psychology, New York, NY 10016-4039. Offers basic applied neurocognition (PhD); biopsychology (PhD); clinical psychology (PhD); developmental psychology (PhD); environmental psychology (PhD); experimental psychology (PhD); industrial psychology (PhD); learning processes (PhD); neuropsychology (PhD); psychology (PhD); social personality (PhD). *Faculty:* 119 full-time (40 women). *Students:* 559 full-time (414 women), 1 part-time (0 women); includes 101 minority (34 African Americans, 25 Asian Americans or Pacific Islanders, 42 Hispanic Americans), 57 international. Average age 33. 750 applicants, 16% accepted, 84 enrolled. In 2009, 54 doctorates awarded. *Degree requirements:* For doctorate, one foreign language, thesis/dissertation. *Entrance requirements:* For doctorate, GRE General Test. Additional exam requirements/recommendations for international students: Required—TOEFL.

Application deadline: For fall admission, 12/15 priority date for domestic students. Application fee: $125. Electronic applications accepted. *Financial support:* In 2009–10, 371 students received support, including 340 fellowships, 34 research assistantships, 33 teaching assistantships; career-related internships or fieldwork, Federal Work-Study, institutionally sponsored loans, and tuition waivers (full and partial) also available. Financial award application deadline: 2/1; financial award applicants required to submit FAFSA. *Unit head:* Dr. Joseph Glick, Executive Officer, 212-817-8706, Fax: 212-817-1533, E-mail: jglick@gc.cuny.edu. *Application contact:* Les Gribben, Director of Admissions, 212-817-7470, Fax: 212-817-1624, E-mail: lgribben@gc.cuny.edu.

Harvard University, Graduate School of Arts and Sciences, Department of Psychology, Cambridge, MA 02138. Offers psychology (PhD), including behavior and decision analysis, cognition, developmental psychology, experimental psychology, personality, psychobiology, psychopathology; social psychology (PhD). *Accreditation:* APA. *Degree requirements:* For doctorate, thesis/dissertation, general exams. *Entrance requirements:* For doctorate, GRE General Test. Additional exam requirements/recommendations for international students: Required—TOEFL. *Expenses:* Tuition: Full-time $33,696. Required fees: $1126. Full-time tuition and fees vary according to program.

Howard University, Graduate School, Department of Psychology, Washington, DC 20059-0002. Offers clinical psychology (PhD); developmental psychology (PhD); experimental psychology (PhD); neuropsychology (PhD); personality psychology (PhD); psychology (MS); social psychology (PhD). *Accreditation:* APA (one or more programs are accredited). Part-time programs available. *Degree requirements:* For master's, thesis; for doctorate, comprehensive exam, thesis/dissertation, qualifying exam. *Entrance requirements:* For master's, GRE General Test, minimum GPA of 2.5, bachelor's degree in psychology or related field; for doctorate, GRE General Test, minimum GPA of 3.0. *Faculty research:* Personality and psychophysiology, educational and social development of African-American children, child and adult psychopathology.

Hunter College of the City University of New York, Graduate School, School of Arts and Sciences, Department of Psychology, New York, NY 10021-5085. Offers applied and evaluative psychology (MA); biopsychology and comparative psychology (MA); social, cognitive, and developmental psychology (MA). Part-time and evening/weekend programs available. *Faculty:* 18 full-time (9 women), 2 part-time/adjunct (0 women). *Students:* 12 full-time (10 women), 68 part-time (56 women); includes 13 minority (2 African Americans, 3 Asian Americans or Pacific Islanders, 8 Hispanic Americans). Average age 28. 122 applicants, 37% accepted, 24 enrolled. In 2009, 15 master's awarded. *Degree requirements:* For master's, comprehensive exam, thesis. *Entrance requirements:* For master's, GRE General Test, minimum 12 credits of course work in psychology, including statistics and experimental psychology; 2 letters of recommendation. Additional exam requirements/recommendations for international students: Required—TOEFL. *Application deadline:* For fall admission, 4/1 for domestic students, 2/1 for international students; for spring admission, 11/1 for domestic students, 9/1 for international students. Applications are processed on a rolling basis. Application fee: $125. *Expenses:* Tuition, state resident: full-time $7360; part-time $310 per credit. Required fees: $250 per semester. *Financial support:* Federal Work-Study, scholarships/grants, and tuition waivers (partial) available. Support available to part-time students. *Faculty research:* Personality, cognitive and linguistic development, hormonal and neural control of behavior, gender and culture, social cognition of health and attitudes. *Unit head:* Dr. Jeffrey Parsons, Chairperson, 212-772-5550, Fax: 212-772-5620, E-mail: jeffrey.parsons@hunter.cuny.edu. *Application contact:* Martin Braun, Acting Program Director, 212-772-4482, Fax: 212-650-3336, E-mail: cbraun@hunter.cuny.edu.

Indiana University–Purdue University Indianapolis, School of Science, Department of Psychology, Psychobiology of Addictions Program, Indianapolis, IN 46202-2896. Offers MS, PhD. *Faculty:* 7 full-time (3 women). *Students:* 12 full-time (10 women), 5 part-time (3 women); includes 3 minority (all African Americans). Average age 28. *Entrance requirements:* For master's, GRE General Test, minimum undergraduate GPA of 3.2. *Application deadline:* For fall admission, 1/1 for domestic students. Application fee: $50 ($60 for international students). *Financial support:* Fellowships with partial tuition reimbursements, research assistantships with partial tuition reimbursements, teaching assistantships with partial tuition reimbursements, career-related internships or fieldwork and Federal Work-Study available. Financial award application deadline: 3/1; financial award applicants required to submit FAFSA. *Faculty research:* Behavioral genetics, behavior pharmacology, animal models, developmental psychology, neurobehavioral toxicology, neuropsychology of learning and memory, animal models of fetal alcohol syndrome. *Unit head:* Dr. J. Gregor Fetterman, Chairman, 317-274-6945, Fax: 317-274-6756, E-mail: gfetter@iupui.edu. *Application contact:* Dr. J. Gregor Fetterman, Chairman, 317-274-6945, Fax: 317-274-6756, E-mail: gfetter@iupui.edu.

Louisiana State University and Agricultural and Mechanical College, Graduate School, College of Arts and Sciences, Department of Psychology, Baton Rouge, LA 70803. Offers biological psychology (MA, PhD); clinical psychology (MA, PhD); cognitive psychology (MA, PhD); developmental psychology (MA, PhD); industrial/organizational psychology (MA, PhD); school psychology (MA, PhD). *Accreditation:* APA (one or more programs are accredited). *Faculty:* 27 full-time (10 women). *Students:* 94 full-time (68 women), 17 part-time (12 women); includes 14 minority (6 African Americans, 2 American Indian/Alaska Native, 2 Asian Americans or Pacific Islanders, 4 Hispanic Americans), 3 international. Average age 27. 232 applicants, 18% accepted, 29 enrolled. In 2009, 13 master's, 14 doctorates awarded. Terminal master's awarded for partial completion of doctoral program. *Degree requirements:* For master's, thesis; for doctorate, thesis/dissertation, 1 year internship. *Entrance requirements:* For master's and doctorate, GRE General Test, minimum GPA of 3.0. Additional exam requirements/recommendations for international students: Required—TOEFL (minimum score 550 paper-based; 213 computer-based; 79 iBT) or IELTS (minimum score 6.5). *Application deadline:* For fall admission, 1/15 for domestic and international students. Applications are processed on a rolling basis. Application fee: $50 ($70 for international students). Electronic applications accepted. *Financial support:* In 2009–10, 108 students received support, including 5 fellowships (averaging $26,974 per year), 2 research assistantships with partial tuition reimbursements available (averaging $18,000 per year), 74 teaching assistantships with partial tuition reimbursements available (averaging $14,751 per year); career-related internships or fieldwork, Federal Work-Study, institutionally sponsored loans, scholarships/grants, health care benefits, and tuition waivers (full and partial) also available. Financial award applicants required to submit FAFSA. *Faculty research:* Clinical psychology, autism, anxiety, addition, neuropsychology, school psychology, cognitive psychology, experimental psychology. Total annual research expenditures: $1 million. *Unit head:* Dr. Robert Matthews, Chair, 225-578-8745, Fax: 225-578-4125, E-mail: psmath@lsu.edu. *Application contact:* Dr. Jason Hicks, Coordinator of Graduate Studies, 225-578-4109, Fax: 225-578-4125, E-mail: jhicks@lsu.edu.

Memorial University of Newfoundland, School of Graduate Studies, Interdisciplinary Program in Cognitive and Behavioral Ecology, St. John's, NL A1C 5S7, Canada. Offers M Sc, PhD. *Degree requirements:* For master's, thesis, public lecture; for doctorate, comprehensive exam, thesis/dissertation, oral defense of dissertation. *Entrance requirements:* For master's, honors degree (minimum 2nd class standing) in related field; for doctorate, master's degree. Electronic applications accepted. *Faculty research:* Seabird feeding ecology, marine mammal and seabird energetics, systems of fish, seabird/seal/fisheries interaction.

Northwestern University, The Graduate School, Judd A. and Marjorie Weinberg College of Arts and Sciences, Department of Psychology, Evanston, IL 60208. Offers brain, behavior and cognition (PhD); clinical psychology (PhD); cognitive psychology (PhD); personality (PhD); social psychology (PhD); JD/PhD. Admissions and degrees offered through The Graduate School. *Accreditation:* APA (one or more programs are accredited). Part-time programs available. *Degree requirements:* For doctorate, thesis/dissertation. *Entrance requirements:* For doctorate,

GRE General Test, GRE Subject Test. Additional exam requirements/recommendations for international students: Required—TOEFL. Electronic applications accepted. *Faculty research:* Memory and higher order cognition, anxiety and depression, effectiveness of psychotherapy, social cognition, molecular basis of memory.

Northwestern University, The Graduate School and Northwestern University Feinberg School of Medicine, Program in Clinical Psychology, Evanston, IL 60208. Offers clinical psychology (PhD), including clinical neuropsychology, general clinical. PhD admissions and degree offered through The Graduate School. *Accreditation:* APA. *Degree requirements:* For doctorate, thesis/ dissertation, clinical internship. *Entrance requirements:* For doctorate, GRE General Test, GRE Subject Test, minimum GPA of 3.2, course work in psychology. Additional exam requirements/recommendations for international students: Required—TOEFL. *Faculty research:* Cancer and cardiovascular risk reduction, evaluation of mental health services and policy, neuropsychological assessment, outcome of psychotherapy, cognitive therapy, pediatric and clinical child psychology.

Oregon Health & Science University, School of Medicine, Graduate Programs in Medicine, Department of Behavioral Neuroscience, Portland, OR 97239-3098. Offers MS, PhD. *Students:* 58 applicants, 9% accepted, 5 enrolled. In 2009, 1 master's, 2 doctorates awarded. Terminal master's awarded for partial completion of doctoral program. *Degree requirements:* For doctorate, thesis/dissertation, written exam. *Entrance requirements:* For doctorate, GRE General Test (minimum scores: 500 Verbal/600 Quantitative/4.5 Analytical), undergraduate coursework in biopsychology and other basic science areas providing background required for graduate training in behavioral neuroscience. Additional exam requirements/recommendations for international students: Required—TOEFL. Application fee: $65. Electronic applications accepted. Tuition and fees vary according to course level, course load, degree level, program and reciprocity agreements. *Financial support:* Health care benefits, tuition waivers (full), and stipends available. *Faculty research:* Neural basis of behavior, behavioral pharmacology, behavioral genetics, neuropharmacology and neuroendocrinology, biological basis of drug seeking and addiction. *Application contact:* Kris Thomason, Graduate Program Manager, 503-494-8464, E-mail: thomason@ohsu.edu.

Palo Alto University, PGSP-Stanford Psy D Consortium Program, Palo Alto, CA 94303-4232. Offers Psy D. *Degree requirements:* For doctorate, thesis/dissertation. *Entrance requirements:* For doctorate, GRE, BA or MA in psychology or related area, minimum undergraduate GPA of 3.0, minimum graduate GPA of 3.3. Additional exam requirements/recommendations for international students: Required—TOEFL. Electronic applications accepted. *Expenses:* Tuition: Full-time $33,009; part-time $916 per credit hour. Required fees: $1243 per quarter. *Faculty research:* Biopsychosocial research, neurobiology, psychopharmacology.

Penn State University Park, Graduate School, College of Health and Human Development, Department of Biobehavioral Health, State College, University Park, PA 16802-1503. Offers PhD.

Rutgers, The State University of New Jersey, Newark, Graduate School, Program in Integrative Neuroscience, Newark, NJ 07102. Offers PhD. Part-time programs available. *Degree requirements:* For doctorate, thesis/dissertation. *Entrance requirements:* For doctorate, GRE, minimum GPA of 3.0. Electronic applications accepted. *Faculty research:* Systems neuroscience, cognitive neuroscience, molecular neuroscience, behavioral neuroscience.

Rutgers, The State University of New Jersey, Newark, Graduate School, Program in Psychology, Newark, NJ 07102. Offers cognitive neuroscience (PhD); cognitive science (PhD); perception (PhD); psychobiology (PhD); social cognition (PhD). *Degree requirements:* For doctorate, comprehensive exam, thesis/dissertation. *Entrance requirements:* For doctorate, GRE General Test, GRE Subject Test, minimum undergraduate B average. Electronic applications accepted. *Faculty research:* Visual perception (luminance, motion), neuroendocrine mechanisms in behavior (reproduction, pain), attachment theory, connectionist modeling of cognition.

Rutgers, The State University of New Jersey, New Brunswick, Graduate School-New Brunswick, Program in Psychology, Piscataway, NJ 08854-8097. Offers behavioral neuroscience (PhD); clinical psychology (PhD); cognitive psychology (PhD); interdisciplinary health psychology (PhD); social psychology (PhD). *Accreditation:* APA. *Degree requirements:* For doctorate, comprehensive exam, thesis/dissertation. *Entrance requirements:* For doctorate, GRE General Test, 3 letters of recommendation. Additional exam requirements/recommendations for international students: Required—TOEFL (minimum score 577 paper-based; 233 computer-based). Electronic applications accepted. *Faculty research:* Learning and memory, behavioral ecology, hormones and behavior, psychopharmacology, anxiety disorders.

State University of New York at Binghamton, Graduate School, School of Arts and Sciences, Department of Psychology, Specialization in Behavioral Neuroscience, Binghamton, NY 13902-6000. Offers MA, PhD. *Students:* 17 full-time (13 women), 9 part-time (7 women); includes 3 minority (1 African American, 2 Hispanic Americans). Average age 26. 25 applicants, 20% accepted, 4 enrolled. In 2009, 1 master's awarded. *Degree requirements:* For master's, thesis; for doctorate, thesis/dissertation, departmental qualifying exam. *Entrance requirements:* For master's and doctorate, GRE General Test, GRE Subject Test. Additional exam requirements/ recommendations for international students: Required—TOEFL (minimum score 550 paper-based; 213 computer-based; 80 iBT). *Application deadline:* For fall admission, 1/15 priority date for domestic and international students. Applications are processed on a rolling basis. Application fee: $60. Electronic applications accepted. *Financial support:* Fellowships, research assistantships, teaching assistantships, career-related internships or fieldwork, Federal Work-Study, institutionally sponsored loans, health care benefits, and unspecified assistantships available. Financial award application deadline: 2/15; financial award applicants required to submit FAFSA. *Unit head:* Dr. Lisa Savage, Graduate Coordinator, 607-777-4383, E-mail: lsavage@binghamton.edu. *Application contact:* Victoria Williams, Recruiting and Admissions Coordinator, 607-777-2151, Fax: 607-777-2501, E-mail: vwilliam@binghamton.edu.

Stony Brook University, State University of New York, Graduate School, College of Arts and Sciences, Department of Psychology, Program in Biopsychology, Stony Brook, NY 11794. Offers PhD. *Students:* 15 full-time (8 women); includes 4 minority (1 African American, 3 Asian Americans or Pacific Islanders), 5 international. Average age 28. 30 applicants, 17% accepted. In 2009, 3 doctorates awarded. *Degree requirements:* For doctorate, thesis/dissertation. *Entrance requirements:* For doctorate, GRE General Test, GRE Subject Test. Additional exam requirements/recommendations for international students: Required—TOEFL. *Application deadline:* For fall admission, 1/15 for domestic students. Application fee: $60. *Expenses:* Tuition, state resident: full-time $8370; part-time $349 per credit. Tuition, nonresident: full-time $13,250; part-time $552 per credit. Required fees: $933. *Unit head:* Dr. Brenda J. Anderson, Head, 631-632-7821, E-mail: brenda.anderson@stonybrook.edu. *Application contact:* Dr. Arthur Samuel, Graduate Director, 631-632-7792, Fax: 631-632-7876.

Texas A&M University, College of Liberal Arts, Department of Psychology, College Station, TX 77843. Offers behavioral and cellular neuroscience (MS, PhD); clinical psychology (MS, PhD); cognitive psychology (MS, PhD); developmental psychology (MS, PhD); industrial/ organizational psychology (MS, PhD); social psychology (MS, PhD). *Accreditation:* APA (one or more programs are accredited). *Faculty:* 36. *Students:* 84 full-time (58 women), 6 part-time (5 women); includes 26 minority (6 African Americans, 3 Asian Americans or Pacific Islanders, 17 Hispanic Americans), 6 international. In 2009, 12 master's, 8 doctorates awarded. *Degree requirements:* For master's, thesis; for doctorate, comprehensive exam (for some programs), thesis/dissertation. *Entrance requirements:* For master's and doctorate, GRE General Test. Additional exam requirements/recommendations for international students: Required—TOEFL. *Application deadline:* For fall admission, 1/5 for domestic and international students. Application fee: $50 ($75 for international students). Electronic applications accepted. *Expenses:* Tuition, state resident: full-time $3991; part-time $221.74 per credit hour. Tuition, nonresident: full-time $9049; part-time $502.74 per credit hour. *Financial support:* Fellowships with partial tuition reimbursements, research assistantships with partial tuition reimbursements, teaching assistantships with partial tuition reimbursements, career-related internships or fieldwork, institutionally sponsored loans, health care benefits, and unspecified assistantships available. Financial award application deadline: 1/5; financial award applicants required to submit FAFSA. *Unit head:* Dr. Les Morey, Head, 979-845-2581, Fax: 979-845-4727, E-mail: lmorey@psych. tamu.edu. *Application contact:* Sharon Starr, Graduate Admissions Supervisor, 979-458-1710, Fax: 979-845-4727, E-mail: gradadv@psyc.tamu.edu.

University at Albany, State University of New York, College of Arts and Sciences, Department of Psychology, Albany, NY 12222-0001. Offers autism (Certificate); biopsychology (PhD); clinical psychology (PhD); general/experimental psychology (PhD); industrial/organizational psychology (PhD); psychology (MA); social/personality psychology (PhD). *Accreditation:* APA (one or more programs are accredited). *Degree requirements:* For doctorate, thesis/dissertation. *Entrance requirements:* For doctorate, GRE General Test, GRE Subject Test. Additional exam requirements/recommendations for international students: Required—TOEFL (minimum score 550 paper-based; 213 computer-based). Electronic applications accepted.

The University of British Columbia, Faculty of Arts and Faculty of Graduate Studies, Department of Psychology, Vancouver, BC V6T 1Z4, Canada. Offers behavioral neuroscience (MA, PhD); clinical psychology (MA, PhD); cognitive science (MA, PhD); developmental psychology (MA, PhD); health psychology (MA, PhD); quantitative methods (MA, PhD); social/ personality psychology (MA, PhD). *Accreditation:* APA (one or more programs are accredited). Terminal master's awarded for partial completion of doctoral program. *Degree requirements:* For master's, thesis; for doctorate, comprehensive exam, thesis/dissertation. *Entrance requirements:* For master's and doctorate, GRE General Test. Additional exam requirements/ recommendations for international students: Required—TOEFL (minimum score 550 paper-based; 230 computer-based; 80 iBT). Electronic applications accepted. *Faculty research:* Clinical, developmental, social/personality, cognition, behavioral neuroscience.

University of Connecticut, Graduate School, College of Liberal Arts and Sciences, Department of Psychology, Storrs, CT 06269. Offers behavioral neuroscience (PhD); biopsychology (PhD); clinical psychology (MA, PhD); cognition and instruction (PhD); developmental psychology (MA, PhD); ecological psychology (PhD); experimental psychology (PhD); general psychology (MA, PhD); health psychology (Graduate Certificate); industrial/organizational psychology (PhD); language and cognition (PhD); neuroscience (PhD); occupational health psychology (Graduate Certificate); social psychology (MA, PhD). *Accreditation:* APA. *Faculty:* 59 full-time (26 women). *Students:* 194 full-time (133 women), 24 part-time (12 women); includes 48 minority (12 African Americans, 21 Asian Americans or Pacific Islanders, 15 Hispanic Americans), 25 international. Average age 28. 585 applicants, 4% accepted, 14 enrolled. In 2009, 22 master's, 24 doctorates awarded. Terminal master's awarded for partial completion of doctoral program. *Degree requirements:* For master's, comprehensive exam; for doctorate, thesis/dissertation. *Entrance requirements:* For master's and doctorate, GRE General Test, GRE Subject Test. Additional exam requirements/recommendations for international students: Required—TOEFL (minimum score 550 paper-based; 213 computer-based). *Application deadline:* For fall admission, 2/1 priority date for domestic and international students; for spring admission, 11/1 for domestic students, 10/1 for international students. Applications are processed on a rolling basis. Application fee: $55. Electronic applications accepted. *Expenses:* Tuition, state resident: full-time $4725; part-time $525 per credit. Tuition, nonresident: full-time $12,267; part-time $1363 per credit. Required fees: $346 per semester. Tuition and fees vary according to course load. *Financial support:* In 2009–10, 109 research assistantships with full tuition reimbursements, 72 teaching assistantships with full tuition reimbursements were awarded; fellowships, career-related internships or fieldwork, Federal Work-Study, scholarships/grants, health care benefits, and unspecified assistantships also available. Financial award application deadline: 2/1; financial award applicants required to submit FAFSA. *Unit head:* Charles A. Lowe, Head, 860-486-3517, Fax: 860-486-2760, E-mail: charles.lowe@uconn.edu. *Application contact:* Charles A. Lowe, Head, 860-486-3517, Fax: 860-486-2760, E-mail: charles.lowe@uconn.edu.

University of Michigan, Horace H. Rackham School of Graduate Studies, College of Literature, Science, and the Arts, Department of Psychology, Ann Arbor, MI 48451. Offers biopsychology (PhD); clinical psychology (PhD); cognition and perception (PhD); developmental psychology (PhD); personality and social contexts (PhD); social psychology (PhD). *Accreditation:* APA. *Faculty:* 87 full-time (40 women), 28 part-time/adjunct (16 women). *Students:* 147 full-time (101 women); includes 40 minority (15 African Americans, 2 American Indian/Alaska Native, 18 Asian Americans or Pacific Islanders, 5 Hispanic Americans), 25 international. Average age 27. 621 applicants, 10% accepted, 37 enrolled. In 2009, 25 doctorates awarded. *Degree requirements:* For doctorate, comprehensive exam, thesis/dissertation, oral defense of dissertation, preliminary exam. *Entrance requirements:* For doctorate, GRE General Test. Additional exam requirements/recommendations for international students: Required—TOEFL. *Application deadline:* For fall admission, 12/1 for domestic and international students. Application fee: $60 ($75 for international students). Electronic applications accepted. *Expenses:* Tuition, state resident: full-time $17,286; part-time $1099 per credit hour. Tuition, nonresident: full-time $34,944; part-time $2080 per credit hour. Required fees: $95 per semester. Tuition and fees vary according to course load, degree level and program. *Financial support:* In 2009–10, 133 students received support, including 52 fellowships with full tuition reimbursements available (averaging $20,900 per year), 16 research assistantships with full tuition reimbursements available (averaging $20,900 per year), 79 teaching assistantships with full tuition reimbursements available (averaging $16,694 per year); career-related internships or fieldwork also available. Financial award application deadline: 4/15. *Unit head:* Prof. Theresa Lee, Chair, 734-764-7429. *Application contact:* Laurie Brannan, Psychology Student Academic Affairs, 731-764-2580, Fax: 734-615-7584, E-mail: psych.saa@umich.edu.

University of Minnesota, Twin Cities Campus, Graduate School, College of Liberal Arts, Department of Psychology, Program in Cognitive and Biological Psychology, Minneapolis, MN 55455-0213. Offers PhD. *Degree requirements:* For doctorate, comprehensive exam, thesis/ dissertation. *Entrance requirements:* For doctorate, GRE General Test, GRE Subject Test (recommended), 12 credits of upper-level psychology courses, including a course in statistics or psychological measurement. Additional exam requirements/recommendations for international students: Required—TOEFL (minimum score 550 paper-based; 213 computer-based; 79 iBT).

University of Nebraska at Omaha, Graduate Studies, College of Arts and Sciences, Department of Psychology, Omaha, NE 68182. Offers developmental psychology (PhD); industrial/ organizational psychology (MS, PhD); psychobiology (PhD); psychology (MA); school psychology (MS, Ed S). Part-time programs available. *Faculty:* 18 full-time (8 women). *Students:* 44 full-time (36 women), 23 part-time (18 women); includes 3 minority (1 African American, 1 Asian American or Pacific Islander, 1 Hispanic American), 2 international. Average age 26. 116 applicants, 34% accepted, 28 enrolled. In 2009, 30 master's, 5 other advanced degrees awarded. *Degree requirements:* For master's, comprehensive exam, thesis (for some programs). *Entrance requirements:* For master's, GRE General Test, GRE Subject Test, previous course work in psychology, including statistics and a laboratory course; minimum GPA of 3.0, 3 letters of recommendation; for doctorate, GRE General Test. Additional exam requirements/ recommendations for international students: Required—TOEFL (minimum score 500 paper-based; 173 computer-based; 61 iBT). *Application deadline:* For fall admission, 1/5 for domestic students. Application fee: $45. Electronic applications accepted. *Financial support:* In 2009–10, 44 students received support; fellowships, research assistantships with tuition reimbursements available, teaching assistantships with tuition reimbursements available, career-related internships or fieldwork, Federal Work-Study, institutionally sponsored loans, scholarships/grants, tuition waivers (partial), and unspecified assistantships available. Support available to part-time students. Financial award application deadline: 3/1; financial award applicants required to submit FAFSA. *Unit head:* Dr. Kenneth Deffenbacher, Chairperson, 402-554-2592. *Application contact:* Dr. Joseph Brown, Student Contact, 402-554-2592.

University of Nebraska–Lincoln, Graduate College, College of Arts and Sciences, Department of Psychology, Lincoln, NE 68588. Offers biopsychology (PhD); clinical psychology (PhD);

Biopsychology

University of Nebraska–Lincoln (continued)
cognitive psychology (PhD); developmental psychology (PhD); psychology (MA); social/personality psychology (PhD); JD/MA; JD/PhD. *Accreditation:* APA (one or more programs are accredited). *Degree requirements:* For master's, thesis optional; for doctorate, comprehensive exam, thesis/dissertation. *Entrance requirements:* For master's and doctorate, GRE General Test. Additional exam requirements/recommendations for international students: Required—TOEFL (minimum score 550 paper-based; 213 computer-based). Electronic applications accepted. *Faculty research:* Law and psychology, rural mental health, chronic mental illness, neuropsychology, child clinical psychology.

University of Oklahoma Health Sciences Center, College of Medicine and Graduate College, Graduate Programs in Medicine, Department of Psychiatry and Behavioral Sciences, Oklahoma City, OK 73190. Offers biological psychology (MS, PhD). *Faculty:* 3 full-time (all women). *Degree requirements:* For master's, thesis; for doctorate, thesis/dissertation. *Entrance requirements:* For doctorate, GRE General Test, 3 letters of recommendation. Additional exam requirements/recommendations for international students: Required—TOEFL. *Application deadline:* For fall admission, 1/31 for domestic students. Application fee: $50. *Expenses:* Tuition, state resident: full-time $3120; part-time $156 per credit hour. Tuition, nonresident: full-time $11,314; part-time $409.70 per credit hour. Required fees: $1471; $51.20 per credit hour. $223.25 per term. *Financial support:* In 2009–10, research assistantships (averaging $18,000 per year); fellowships, career-related internships or fieldwork, institutionally sponsored loans, and tuition waivers (full and partial) also available. Support available to part-time students. *Faculty research:* Behavioral neuroscience, human neuropsychology, psychophysiology, behavioral medicine, health psychology. *Unit head:* Dr. Frank Holloway, Director, 405-271-2011, E-mail: frank-holloway@ouhsc.edu. *Application contact:* Dr. Larry Gonzalez, Graduate Liaison, 405-271-2011, E-mail: larry-gonzalez@ouhsc.edu.

University of Oregon, Graduate School, College of Arts and Sciences, Department of Psychology, Eugene, OR 97403. Offers clinical psychology (PhD); cognitive psychology (MA, MS, ,PhD); developmental psychology (MA, MS, PhD); physiological psychology (MA, MS, PhD); psychology (MA, MS, PhD); social/personality psychology (MA, MS, PhD). *Accreditation:* APA (one or more programs are accredited). Terminal master's awarded for partial completion of doctoral program. *Degree requirements:* For doctorate, thesis/dissertation. *Entrance requirements:* For master's, GRE General Test, minimum GPA of 3.0; for doctorate, GRE General Test. Additional exam requirements/recommendations for international students: Required—TOEFL.

The University of Texas at Austin, Graduate School, The Institute for Neuroscience, Austin, TX 78712-1111. Offers PhD, MD/PhD. Terminal master's awarded for partial completion of doctoral program. *Degree requirements:* For doctorate, thesis/dissertation. *Entrance requirements:* For doctorate, GRE. Electronic applications accepted. *Faculty research:* Cellular/molecular biology, neurobiology, pharmacology, behavioral neuroscience.

The University of Toledo, College of Graduate Studies, College of Arts and Sciences, Department of Psychology, Toledo, OH 43606-3390. Offers behavioral (PhD), including cognitive, psychobiology and learning, social; clinical psychology (PhD); experimental psychology (MA). *Accreditation:* APA. *Degree requirements:* For master's, thesis; for doctorate, one foreign language, thesis/dissertation. *Entrance requirements:* For master's and doctorate, GRE General Test, GRE Subject Test. *Faculty research:* Neural taste response.

University of Windsor, Faculty of Graduate Studies, Faculty of Arts and Social Sciences, Department of Psychology, Windsor, ON N9B 3P4, Canada. Offers adult clinical (MA, PhD); applied social psychology (MA, PhD); child clinical (MA, PhD); clinical neuropsychology (MA, PhD). *Accreditation:* APA (one or more programs are accredited). *Degree requirements:* For master's, thesis; for doctorate, comprehensive exam, thesis/dissertation. *Entrance requirements:* For master's, GRE General Test, GRE Subject Test in psychology, minimum B average; for doctorate, GRE General Test, GRE Subject Test in psychology, master's degree. Additional exam requirements/recommendations for international students: Required—TOEFL (minimum score 600 paper-based; 250 computer-based). Electronic applications accepted. *Faculty research:* Gambling, suicidology, emotional competence, psychotherapy and trauma.

University of Wisconsin–Madison, Graduate School, College of Letters and Science, Department of Psychology, Program in Biology of Brain and Behavior, Madison, WI 53706-1380. Offers PhD. *Degree requirements:* For doctorate, comprehensive exam, thesis/dissertation. *Entrance requirements:* For doctorate, GRE General Test, minimum undergraduate GPA of 3.0. Additional exam requirements/recommendations for international students: Required—TOEFL. Electronic applications accepted. *Expenses:* Tuition, state resident: part-time $594 per credit. Tuition, nonresident: part-time $1504 per credit. Required fees: $65 per credit. Tuition and fees vary according to course load, program and reciprocity agreements.

Wayne State University, School of Medicine, Graduate Programs in Medicine, Department of Psychiatry and Behavioral Neurosciences, Detroit, MI 48202. Offers psychiatry (MS); translational neuroscience (PhD). *Faculty research:* Substance abuse; brain imaging; schizophrenia; child psychopathy; child development; neurobiology of monoamine systems.

Neurobiology

Albert Einstein College of Medicine, Sue Golding Graduate Division of Medical Sciences, Department of Neuroscience, Bronx, NY 10461. Offers PhD, MD/PhD. *Degree requirements:* For doctorate, thesis/dissertation. *Entrance requirements:* For doctorate, GRE General Test. Additional exam requirements/recommendations for international students: Required—TOEFL. *Faculty research:* Structure-function relations at chemical and electrical synapses, mechanisms of electrogenesis, analysis of neuronal subsystems.

Brandeis University, Graduate School of Arts and Sciences, Program in Molecular and Cell Biology, Waltham, MA 02454-9110. Offers genetics (PhD); microbiology (PhD); molecular and cell biology (MS, PhD); molecular biology (PhD); neurobiology (PhD). *Faculty:* 28 full-time (12 women), 1 (woman) part-time/adjunct. *Students:* 46 full-time (26 women), 1 part-time (0 women); includes 3 minority (2 African Americans, 1 Hispanic American), 7 international. Average age 27. 146 applicants, 21% accepted, 12 enrolled. In 2009, 4 master's, 6 doctorates awarded. Terminal master's awarded for partial completion of doctoral program. *Degree requirements:* For master's, thesis optional, research project; for doctorate, comprehensive exam, thesis/dissertation, teaching assistant experience. *Entrance requirements:* For master's and doctorate, GRE General Test, resume, 3 letters of recommendation. Additional exam requirements/recommendations for international students: Required—TOEFL (minimum score 600 paper-based; 250 computer-based; 100 iBT); Recommended—IELTS (minimum score 7). *Application deadline:* For fall admission, 1/15 priority date for domestic students. Applications are processed on a rolling basis. Application fee: $75. Electronic applications accepted. *Financial support:* In 2009–10, 41 students received support, including 13 fellowships with full tuition reimbursements available (averaging $27,500 per year), 27 research assistantships with full tuition reimbursements available (averaging $27,500 per year), 1 teaching assistantship with partial tuition reimbursement available (averaging $3,200 per year); scholarships/grants, traineeships, health care benefits, and tuition waivers (full and partial) also available. Financial award application deadline: 4/15; financial award applicants required to submit FAFSA. *Faculty research:* Regulation of gene expression by transcription factors, molecular neurobiology, immunology, molecular mechanisms of genetic recombination, cell differentiation. *Unit head:* Dr. Piali Sengupta, Chair, 781-736-2686, Fax: 781-736-3107, E-mail: piali@brandeis.edu. *Application contact:* Marcia Cabral, Department Administrator, 781-736-3100, Fax: 781-736-3107, E-mail: cabral@brandeis.edu.

California Institute of Technology, Division of Biology, Program in Neurobiology, Pasadena, CA 91125-0001. Offers PhD. *Degree requirements:* For doctorate, thesis/dissertation, qualifying exam. *Entrance requirements:* For doctorate, GRE General Test.

Carnegie Mellon University, Mellon College of Science, Department of Biological Sciences, Pittsburgh, PA 15213-3891. Offers biochemistry (PhD); biophysics (PhD); cell biology (PhD); computational biology (MS, PhD); developmental biology (PhD); genetics (PhD); molecular biology (PhD); neuroscience (PhD). *Degree requirements:* For doctorate, comprehensive exam, thesis/dissertation. *Entrance requirements:* For doctorate, GRE General Test, GRE Subject Test, interview. Electronic applications accepted. *Faculty research:* Genetic structure, function, and regulation; protein structure and function; biological membranes; biological spectroscopy.

Case Western Reserve University, School of Medicine and School of Graduate Studies, Graduate Programs in Medicine, Department of Neurosciences, Cleveland, OH 44106. Offers neurobiology (PhD); neuroscience (PhD); MD/PhD. *Degree requirements:* For doctorate, thesis/dissertation. *Entrance requirements:* For doctorate, GRE General Test, 3 letters of recommendation. Additional exam requirements/recommendations for international students: Required—TOEFL. Electronic applications accepted. *Faculty research:* Neurotropic factors, synapse formation, regeneration, determination of cell fate, cellular neuroscience.

Columbia University, College of Physicians and Surgeons, Program in Neurobiology and Behavior, New York, NY 10032. Offers PhD. Only candidates for the PhD are admitted. *Degree requirements:* For doctorate, thesis/dissertation. *Entrance requirements:* For doctorate, GRE General Test. Additional exam requirements/recommendations for international students: Required—TOEFL. *Expenses:* Contact institution. *Faculty research:* Cellular and molecular mechanisms of neural development, neuropathology, neuropharmacology.

Cornell University, Graduate School, Graduate Fields of Agriculture and Life Sciences, Field of Neurobiology and Behavior, Ithaca, NY 14853-0001. Offers behavioral biology (PhD), including behavioral ecology, chemical ecology, ethology, neuroethology, sociobiology; neurobiology (PhD), including cellular and molecular neurobiology, neuroanatomy, neurochemistry, neuropharmacology, neurophysiology, sensory physiology. *Faculty:* 51 full-time (9 women). *Students:* 36 full-time (15 women); includes 4 minority (1 African American, 1 Asian American or Pacific Islander, 2 Hispanic Americans), 3 international. Average age 29. 44 applicants, 30% accepted, 7 enrolled. In 2009, 8 doctorates awarded. *Degree requirements:* For doctorate, comprehensive exam, thesis/dissertation, 1 year of teaching experience, seminar presentation. *Entrance requirements:* For doctorate, GRE General Test, GRE Subject Test (biology), 3 letters of recommendation. Additional exam requirements/recommendations for international students: Required—TOEFL (minimum score 550 paper-based; 213 computer-based; 77 iBT). *Application deadline:* For fall admission, 12/1 for domestic students. Application fee: $70. Electronic applications accepted. *Expenses:* Tuition: Full-time $29,500. Required fees: $70. Full-time tuition and fees vary according to degree level, program and student level. *Financial support:* In 2009–10, 35 students received support, including 7 fellowships with full tuition reimbursements available; research assistantships with full tuition reimbursements available, teaching assistantships with full tuition reimbursements available, institutionally sponsored loans, scholarships/grants, health care benefits, tuition waivers (full and partial), and unspecified assistantships also available. Financial award applicants required to submit FAFSA. *Faculty research:* Cellular neurobiology and neuropharmacology, integrative neurobiology, social behavior, chemical ecology, neuroethology. *Unit head:* Director of Graduate Studies, 607-254-4340, Fax: 607-254-4340. *Application contact:* Graduate Field Assistant, 607-254-4340, Fax: 607-254-4340, E-mail: nbb_field@cornell.edu.

Dalhousie University, Faculty of Graduate Studies and Faculty of Medicine, Graduate Programs in Medicine, Department of Anatomy and Neurobiology, Halifax, NS B3H 4R2, Canada. Offers M Sc, PhD. *Degree requirements:* For master's, thesis; for doctorate, thesis/dissertation. *Entrance requirements:* For master's and doctorate, GRE (recommended), minimum A- average. Additional exam requirements/recommendations for international students: Required—TOEFL, IELTS, 1 of the following 5 approved tests: TOELF, IELTS, CANTEST, CAEL, Michigan English Language Assessment Battery. Electronic applications accepted. *Faculty research:* Neuroscience histology, cell biology, neuroendocrinology, evolutionary biology.

Duke University, Graduate School, Department of Biological Anthropology and Anatomy, Durham, NC 27710. Offers cellular and molecular biology (PhD); gross anatomy and physical anthropology (PhD), including comparative morphology of human and non-human primates, primate social behavior, vertebrate paleontology; neuroanatomy (PhD). *Faculty:* 8 full-time. *Students:* 14 full-time (9 women); includes 2 minority (1 African American, 1 Hispanic American), 1 international. 39 applicants, 15% accepted, 4 enrolled. In 2009, 4 doctorates awarded. *Degree requirements:* For doctorate, one foreign language, thesis/dissertation. *Entrance requirements:* For doctorate, GRE General Test. Additional exam requirements/recommendations for international students: Required—TOEFL (minimum score 550 paper-based; 213 computer-based; 83 iBT), IELTS (minimum score 7). *Application deadline:* For fall admission, 12/8 priority date for domestic and international students. Application fee: $75. Electronic applications accepted. *Financial support:* Fellowships, teaching assistantships, Federal Work-Study available. Financial award application deadline: 12/31. *Unit head:* Daniel Schmitt, Director of Graduate Studies, 919-684-5664, Fax: 919-684-4124, E-mail: mlsquire@duke.edu. *Application contact:* Cynthia Robertson, Associate Dean for Enrollment Services, 919-684-3913, E-mail: grad-admissions@duke.edu.

Duke University, Graduate School, Department of Neurobiology, Durham, NC 27708-0586. Offers PhD. *Faculty:* 62 full-time. *Students:* 47 full-time (18 women); includes 7 minority (2 Asian Americans or Pacific Islanders, 5 Hispanic Americans), 16 international. 112 applicants, 18% accepted, 8 enrolled. In 2009, 10 doctorates awarded. *Degree requirements:* For doctorate, variable foreign language requirement, thesis/dissertation. *Entrance requirements:* For doctorate, GRE General Test. Additional exam requirements/recommendations for international students: Required—TOEFL (minimum score 550 paper-based; 213 computer-based; 83 iBT), IELTS (minimum score 7). *Application deadline:* For fall admission, 12/8 priority date for domestic and international students. Application fee: $75. Electronic applications accepted. *Financial support:* Fellowships, research assistantships, teaching assistantships, Federal Work-Study available. Financial award application deadline: 12/31. *Unit head:* Richard Mooney, Director, Fax: 919-684-4431, E-mail: herbst@neuro.duke.edu. *Application contact:* Cynthia Robertson, Associate Dean for Enrollment Services, 919-684-3913, E-mail: grad-admissions@duke.edu.

Georgia State University, College of Arts and Sciences, Department of Biology, Program in Neurobiology and Behavior, Atlanta, GA 30302-3083. Offers MS, PhD. Part-time programs available. Terminal master's awarded for partial completion of doctoral program. *Degree requirements:* For master's, thesis or alternative; for doctorate, thesis/dissertation, exam. *Entrance requirements:* For master's and doctorate, GRE General Test. Additional exam requirements/recommendations for international students: Required—TOEFL. Electronic applications accepted.

Harvard University, Graduate School of Arts and Sciences, Program in Neuroscience, Boston, MA 02115. Offers neurobiology (PhD). *Degree requirements:* For doctorate, thesis/dissertation, qualifying exam. *Entrance requirements:* For doctorate, GRE General Test, GRE Subject Test. Additional exam requirements/recommendations for international students: Required—TOEFL. *Expenses:* Tuition: Full-time $33,696. Required fees: $1126. Full-time tuition and fees vary according to program. *Faculty research:* Relationship between diseases of the nervous system and basic science.

Illinois State University, Graduate School, College of Arts and Sciences, Department of Biological Sciences, Normal, IL 61790-2200. Offers animal behavior (MS); bacteriology (MS); biochemistry (MS); biological sciences (MS); biology (PhD); biophysics (MS); biotechnology (MS); botany (MS, PhD); cell biology (MS); conservation biology (MS); developmental biology (MS); ecology (MS, PhD); entomology (MS); evolutionary biology (MS); genetics (MS, PhD); immunology (MS); microbiology (MS, PhD); molecular biology (MS); molecular genetics (MS); neurobiology (MS); neuroscience (MS); parasitology (MS); physiology (MS, PhD); plant biology (MS); plant molecular biology (MS); plant sciences (MS); structural biology (MS); zoology (MS, PhD). Part-time programs available. *Degree requirements:* For master's, thesis or alternative; for doctorate, variable foreign language requirement, thesis/dissertation, 2 terms of residency. *Entrance requirements:* For master's, GRE General Test, minimum GPA of 2.6 in last 60 hours of course work; for doctorate, GRE General Test. *Faculty research:* Redoc balance and drug development in schistosoma mansoni, control of the growth of listeria monocytogenes at low temperature, regulation of cell expansion and microtubule function by SPRI, CRUI: physiology and fitness consequences of different life history phenotypes.

Louisiana State University Health Sciences Center, School of Graduate Studies in New Orleans, Department of Cell Biology and Anatomy, New Orleans, LA 70112-2223. Offers cell biology and anatomy (MS, PhD), including cell biology, developmental biology, neurobiology and anatomy; MD/PhD. *Degree requirements:* For master's, comprehensive exam, thesis; for doctorate, comprehensive exam, thesis/dissertation. *Entrance requirements:* For master's and doctorate, GRE General Test, GRE Subject Test, minimum undergraduate GPA of 3.0. Additional exam requirements/recommendations for international students: Required—TOEFL. *Faculty research:* Visual system organization, neural development, plasticity of sensory systems, information processing through the nervous system, visuomotor integration.

Loyola University Chicago, Graduate School, Department of Cell Biology, Neurobiology and Anatomy, Chicago, IL 60660. Offers MS, PhD. Part-time programs available. *Faculty:* 16 full-time (6 women), 9 part-time/adjunct (4 women). *Students:* 20 full-time (12 women), 1 (woman) part-time; includes 1 minority (Hispanic American), 1 international. Average age 25. 25 applicants, 40% accepted, 8 enrolled. In 2009, 1 master's, 1 doctorate awarded. Terminal master's awarded for partial completion of doctoral program. *Degree requirements:* For master's, thesis; for doctorate, comprehensive exam, thesis/dissertation. *Entrance requirements:* For master's, GRE General Test, minimum GPA of 3.0; for doctorate, GRE General Test, GRE Subject Test (biology), minimum GPA of 3.0. Additional exam requirements/recommendations for international students: Required—TOEFL (minimum score 600 paper-based; 250 computer-based). *Application deadline:* For fall admission, 5/1 priority date for domestic and international students. Applications are processed on a rolling basis. Application fee: $50. Electronic applications accepted. *Expenses:* Tuition: Full-time $14,220; part-time $790 per credit hour. Required fees: $60 per semester hour. Tuition and fees vary according to program. *Financial support:* In 2009–10, 5 fellowships with full tuition reimbursements (averaging $23,000 per year), 5 research assistantships with full tuition reimbursements (averaging $23,000 per year) were awarded; Federal Work-Study and unspecified assistantships also available. Financial award application deadline: 5/1; financial award applicants required to submit FAFSA. *Faculty research:* Brain steroids, immunology, neuroregeneration, cytokines. Total annual research expenditures: $1 million. *Unit head:* Dr. Phong Le, Head, 708-216-3603, Fax: 708-216-3913, E-mail: ple@lumc.edu. *Application contact:* Ginny Hayes, Graduate Program Secretary, 708-216-3353, Fax: 708-216-3913, E-mail: vhayes@lumc.edu.

Marquette University, Graduate School, College of Arts and Sciences, Department of Biology, Milwaukee, WI 53201-1881. Offers cell biology (MS, PhD); developmental biology (MS, PhD); ecology (MS, PhD); endocrinology (MS, PhD); evolutionary biology (MS, PhD); genetics (MS, PhD); microbiology (MS, PhD); molecular biology (MS, PhD); muscle and exercise physiology (MS, PhD); neurobiology (MS, PhD); reproductive physiology (MS, PhD). *Faculty:* 23 full-time (10 women), 1 part-time/adjunct (0 women). *Students:* 23 full-time (13 women), 16 part-time (9 women); includes 1 minority (Asian American or Pacific Islander), 20 international. Average age 25. 95 applicants, 16% accepted, 10 enrolled. In 2009, 3 master's, 5 doctorates awarded. Terminal master's awarded for partial completion of doctoral program. *Degree requirements:* For master's, comprehensive exam, thesis, 1 year of teaching experience or equivalent; for doctorate, thesis/dissertation, 1 year of teaching experience or equivalent, qualifying exam. *Entrance requirements:* For master's and doctorate, GRE General Test, GRE Subject Test. Additional exam requirements/recommendations for international students: Required—TOEFL. Application fee: $40. *Financial support:* In 2009–10, 4 fellowships, 22 teaching assistantships were awarded; research assistantships, Federal Work-Study, institutionally sponsored loans, scholarships/grants, and tuition waivers (full and partial) also available. Support available to part-time students. Financial award application deadline: 2/15. *Faculty research:* Microbial and invertebrate ecology, evolution of gene function, DNA methylation, DNA arrangement. *Unit head:* Dr. Robert Fitts, Chair, 414-288-1748, Fax: 414-288-7357. *Application contact:* Debbie Weaver, Administrative Assistant, 414-288-7355, Fax: 414-288-7357.

Massachusetts Institute of Technology, School of Science, Department of Biology, Cambridge, MA 02139-4307. Offers biochemistry (PhD); biological oceanography (PhD); biology (PhD); biophysical chemistry and molecular structure (PhD); cell biology (PhD); computational and systems biology (PhD); developmental biology (PhD); genetics (PhD); immunology (PhD); microbiology (PhD); molecular biology (PhD); neurobiology (PhD). *Faculty:* 54 full-time (14 women). *Students:* 237 full-time (128 women); includes 65 minority (4 African Americans, 2 American Indian/Alaska Native, 33 Asian Americans or Pacific Islanders, 26 Hispanic Americans), 25 international. Average age 26. 645 applicants, 18% accepted, 49 enrolled. In 2009, 41 doctorates awarded. *Degree requirements:* For doctorate, comprehensive exam, thesis/dissertation. *Entrance requirements:* For doctorate, GRE General Test. Additional exam requirements/recommendations for international students: Required—TOEFL (minimum score 577 paper-based; 233 computer-based), IELTS (minimum score 6.5). *Application deadline:* For fall admission, 12/1 for domestic and international students. Application fee: $75. Electronic applications accepted. *Expenses:* Tuition: Full-time $37,510; part-time $585 per unit. Required fees: $272. *Financial support:* In 2009–10, 218 students received support, including 113 fellowships with tuition reimbursements available (averaging $31,816 per year), 109 research assistantships with tuition reimbursements available (averaging $29,254 per year); teaching assistantships with tuition reimbursements available, Federal Work-Study, institutionally sponsored loans, scholarships/grants, traineeships, health care benefits, and unspecified assistantships also available. *Faculty research:* DNA recombination, transcription and gene regulation, signal transduction, cell cycle, neuronal cell fate, replication and repair. Total annual research expenditures: $114 million. *Unit head:* Prof. Chris Kaiser, Head, 617-253-4701, E-mail: mitbio@mit.edu. *Application contact:* Biology Education Office, 617-253-3717, Fax: 617-258-9329, E-mail: gradbio@mit.edu.

New York University, Graduate School of Arts and Science, Department of Biology, New York, NY 10012-1019. Offers biology (PhD); biomedical journalism (MS); cancer and molecular biology (PhD); computational biology (PhD); computers in biological research (MS); developmental genetics (PhD); general biology (MS); immunology and microbiology (PhD); molecular genetics (PhD); neurobiology (PhD); oral biology (MS); plant biology (PhD); recombinant DNA technology (MS); MS/MBA. Part-time programs available. *Faculty:* 24 full-time (5 women). *Students:* 142 full-time (79 women), 44 part-time (28 women); includes 34 minority (1 African American, 25 Asian Americans or Pacific Islanders, 8 Hispanic Americans), 82 international. Average age 27. 362 applicants, 71% accepted, 72 enrolled. In 2009, 43 master's, 9 doctorates awarded. Terminal master's awarded for partial completion of doctoral program. *Degree requirements:* For master's, thesis or alternative, qualifying paper; for doctorate, comprehensive exam, thesis/dissertation. *Entrance requirements:* For master's, GRE General Test; for doctorate, GRE General Test, GRE Subject Test. Additional exam requirements/recommendations for international students: Required—TOEFL. *Application deadline:* For fall admission, 12/12 priority date for domestic students. Application fee: $90. *Expenses:* Tuition: Full-time $30,528; part-time $1272 per credit. Required fees: $2177. *Financial support:* Fellowships with tuition reimbursements, research assistantships with tuition reimbursements, teaching assistantships with tuition reimbursements, career-related internships or fieldwork, Federal Work-Study, institutionally sponsored loans, scholarships/grants, health care benefits, and unspecified assistantships available. Financial award application deadline: 12/12; financial award applicants required to submit FAFSA. *Faculty research:* Genomics, molecular and cell biology, development and molecular genetics, molecular evolution of plants and animals. *Unit head:* Gloria Coruzzi, Chair, 212-998-8200, Fax: 212-995-4015, E-mail: biology@nyu.edu. *Application contact:* Stephen Small, Director of Graduate Studies, 212-998-8200, Fax: 212-995-4015, E-mail: biology@nyu.edu.

Northwestern University, The Graduate School, Judd A. and Marjorie Weinberg College of Arts and Sciences, Department of Neurobiology and Physiology, Evanston, IL 60208. Offers MS. Admissions and degrees offered through The Graduate School. Part-time programs available. *Degree requirements:* For master's, thesis. *Entrance requirements:* For master's, GRE General Test and MCAT (strongly recommended). Additional exam requirements/recommendations for international students: Required—TOEFL. Electronic applications accepted. *Expenses:* Contact institution. *Faculty research:* Sensory neurobiology and neuroendocrinology, reproductive biology, vision physiology and psychophysics, cell and developmental biology.

Northwestern University, Northwestern University Feinberg School of Medicine and Interdepartmental Programs, Integrated Graduate Programs in the Life Sciences, Chicago, IL 60611. Offers cancer biology (PhD); cell biology (PhD); developmental biology (PhD); evolutionary biology (PhD); immunology and microbial pathogenesis (PhD); molecular biology and genetics (PhD); neurobiology (PhD); pharmacology and toxicology (PhD); structural biology and biochemistry (PhD). *Degree requirements:* For doctorate, comprehensive exam, thesis/dissertation, written and oral qualifying exams. *Entrance requirements:* For doctorate, GRE General Test. Additional exam requirements/recommendations for international students: Required—TOEFL (minimum score 600 paper-based; 250 computer-based). Electronic applications accepted.

Purdue University, Graduate School, College of Science, Department of Biological Sciences, West Lafayette, IN 47907. Offers biochemistry (PhD); biophysics (PhD); cell and developmental biology (PhD); ecology, evolutionary and population biology (MS, PhD), including ecology, evolutionary biology, population biology; genetics (MS, PhD); microbiology (MS, PhD); molecular biology (PhD); neurobiology (MS, PhD); plant physiology (PhD). Terminal master's awarded for partial completion of doctoral program. *Degree requirements:* For master's, thesis (for some programs); for doctorate, thesis/dissertation, seminars, teaching experience. *Entrance requirements:* For master's and doctorate, GRE General Test. Additional exam requirements/recommendations for international students: Required—TOEFL. Electronic applications accepted.

Queen's University at Kingston, School of Graduate Studies and Research, Faculty of Health Sciences, Department of Anatomy and Cell Biology, Kingston, ON K7L 3N6, Canada. Offers biology of reproduction (M Sc, PhD); cancer (M Sc, PhD); cardiovascular pathophysiology (M Sc, PhD); cell and molecular biology (M Sc, PhD); drug metabolism (M Sc, PhD); endocrinology (M Sc, PhD); motor control (M Sc, PhD); neural regeneration (M Sc, PhD); neurophysiology (M Sc, PhD). Part-time programs available. *Degree requirements:* For master's, thesis; for doctorate, one foreign language, comprehensive exam, thesis/dissertation. *Entrance requirements:* Additional exam requirements/recommendations for international students: Required—TOEFL. Electronic applications accepted. *Faculty research:* Human kinetics, neuroscience, reproductive biology, cardiovascular.

Université Laval, Faculty of Medicine, Graduate Programs in Medicine, Programs in Neurobiology, Québec, QC G1K 7P4, Canada. Offers M Sc, PhD. Terminal master's awarded for partial completion of doctoral program. *Degree requirements:* For master's, thesis; for doctorate, comprehensive exam, thesis/dissertation. *Entrance requirements:* For master's and doctorate, knowledge of French and English. Electronic applications accepted.

University at Albany, State University of New York, College of Arts and Sciences, Department of Biological Sciences, Specialization in Molecular, Cellular, Developmental, and Neural Biology, Albany, NY 12222-0001. Offers MS, PhD. *Degree requirements:* For master's, one foreign language; for doctorate, one foreign language, thesis/dissertation. *Entrance requirements:* For master's and doctorate, GRE General Test.

The University of Alabama at Birmingham, Graduate Programs in Joint Health Sciences, Program in Neurobiology, Birmingham, AL 35294. Offers PhD. *Degree requirements:* For doctorate, thesis/dissertation. *Entrance requirements:* For doctorate, GRE, interview. Electronic applications accepted.

University of Arkansas for Medical Sciences, Graduate School, Graduate Programs in Biomedical Sciences, Department of Neurobiology and Developmental Sciences, Little Rock, AR 72205-7199. Offers MS, PhD, MD/PhD. *Faculty:* 21 full-time (7 women), 16 part-time/adjunct (9 women). *Students:* 11 full-time, 1 part-time. In 2009, 1 doctorate awarded. *Degree requirements:* For master's, thesis; for doctorate, thesis/dissertation. *Entrance requirements:* For master's, GRE General Test; for doctorate, GRE General Test, GRE Subject Test. Additional exam requirements/recommendations for international students: Required—TOEFL. *Application deadline:* For fall admission, 2/15 for domestic and international students. Application fee: $0. *Financial support:* In 2009–10, research assistantships with full tuition reimbursements (averaging $24,000 per year); stipend and tuition for doctoral students also available. Support available to part-time students. *Faculty research:* Cellular and molecular neuroscience, translation neuroscience. *Unit head:* Dr. Gwen Childs, Chair, 501-686-5180. *Application contact:* Dr. David Davies, Graduate Coordinator, 501-686-5184, E-mail: dldavies@uams.edu.

University of California, Irvine, Office of Graduate Studies, School of Biological Sciences, Department of Neurobiology and Behavior, Irvine, CA 92697. Offers biological sciences (MS, PhD); MD/PhD. *Students:* 61 full-time (36 women); includes 14 minority (7 Asian Americans or Pacific Islanders, 7 Hispanic Americans), 1 international. Average age 26. 185 applicants, 17% accepted, 16 enrolled. In 2009, 6 doctorates awarded. *Degree requirements:* For doctorate, thesis/dissertation. *Entrance requirements:* For master's and doctorate, GRE General Test, GRE Subject Test, minimum GPA of 3.0. Additional exam requirements/recommendations for international students: Required—TOEFL (minimum score 550 paper-based; 213 computer-based). *Application deadline:* For fall admission, 1/15 priority date for domestic students, 1/15 for international students. Applications are processed on a rolling basis. Application fee: $70 ($90 for international students). Electronic applications accepted. *Financial support:* Fellowships, research assistantships with full tuition reimbursements, teaching assistantships, institutionally sponsored loans, traineeships, health care benefits, and unspecified assistantships available. Financial award application deadline: 3/1; financial award applicants required to submit FAFSA. *Faculty research:* Synaptic processes, neurophysiology, neuroendocrinology, neuroanatomy, molecular neurobiology. *Unit head:* Thomas J. Carew, Chair, 949-824-6114, Fax: 949-824-2447, E-mail: tcarew@uci.edu. *Application contact:* Lee Johnson, Graduate Admissions Assistant, 949-824-8519, Fax: 949-824-2447, E-mail: jljohnso@uci.edu.

University of California, Irvine, School of Medicine and School of Biological Sciences, Department of Anatomy and Neurobiology, Irvine, CA 92697. Offers biological sciences (MS, PhD); MD/PhD. *Students:* 28 full-time (18 women); includes 10 minority (4 Asian Americans or Pacific Islanders, 6 Hispanic Americans), 2 international. Average age 28. In 2009, 5 doctorates

Neurobiology

University of California, Irvine (continued)

awarded. *Degree requirements:* For doctorate, thesis/dissertation. *Entrance requirements:* For master's and doctorate, GRE General Test, GRE Subject Test. Additional exam requirements/recommendations for international students: Required—TOEFL (minimum score 550 paper-based; 213 computer-based). *Application deadline:* For fall admission, 1/15 priority date for domestic students, 1/15 for international students. Applications are processed on a rolling basis. Application fee: $70 ($90 for international students). Electronic applications accepted. *Financial support:* Fellowships, research assistantships with full tuition reimbursements, teaching assistantships, institutionally sponsored loans, traineeships, health care benefits, and unspecified assistantships available. Financial award application deadline: 3/1; financial award applicants required to submit FAFSA. *Faculty research:* Neurotransmitter immunocytochemistry, intracellular physiology, molecular neurobiology, forebrain organization and development, structure and function of sensory and motor systems. *Unit head:* Dr. Richard T. Robertson, Professor and Chair, 949-824-6553, Fax: 949-824-1105, E-mail: rtrobert@uci.edu. *Application contact:* Kimberly McKinney, Biological Sciences Contact, 949-824-8145, Fax: 949-824-7407, E-mail: kamckinn@uci.edu.

University of California, Los Angeles, David Geffen School of Medicine and Graduate Division, Graduate Programs in Medicine, Department of Neurobiology, Los Angeles, CA 90095. Offers anatomy and cell biology (PhD). *Degree requirements:* For doctorate, thesis/dissertation, oral and written qualifying exams. *Entrance requirements:* For doctorate, GRE General Test, GRE Subject Test, bachelor's degree in physical or biological science. *Faculty research:* Neuroendocrinology, neurophysiology.

University of California, Los Angeles, Graduate Division, College of Letters and Science and David Geffen School of Medicine, UCLA ACCESS to Programs in the Molecular, Cellular and Integrative Life Sciences, Los Angeles, CA 90095. Offers biochemistry and molecular biology (PhD); biological chemistry (PhD); cellular and molecular pathology (PhD); human genetics (PhD); microbiology, immunology, and molecular genetics (PhD); molecular biology (PhD); molecular toxicology (PhD); molecular, cellular and integrative physiology (PhD); neurobiology (PhD); oral biology (PhD); physiology (PhD). ACCESS is an umbrella program for first-year coursework in 12 PhD programs. *Students:* 39 full-time (25 women); includes 14 minority (1 African American, 1 American Indian/Alaska Native, 8 Asian Americans or Pacific Islanders, 4 Hispanic Americans), 10 international. Average age 25. 437 applicants, 22% accepted, 30 enrolled. *Degree requirements:* For doctorate, thesis/dissertation, oral and written qualifying exams. *Entrance requirements:* For doctorate, GRE General Test, minimum undergraduate GPA of 3.0. Additional exam requirements/recommendations for international students: Required—TOEFL. *Application deadline:* For fall admission, 12/15 for domestic and international students. Application fee: $70 ($90 for international students). Electronic applications accepted. *Financial support:* In 2009–10, 56 fellowships with full and partial tuition reimbursements, 16 research assistantships with full and partial tuition reimbursements were awarded; teaching assistantships with full and partial tuition reimbursements, Federal Work-Study, institutionally sponsored loans, scholarships/grants, health care benefits, tuition waivers (full and partial), and unspecified assistantships also available. Financial award application deadline: 3/1; financial award applicants required to submit FAFSA. *Faculty research:* Molecular, cellular, and developmental biology; immunology; microbiology; integrative biology. *Unit head:* Dr. Greg I. Payne, Chair, 310-206-3121. *Application contact:* Coordinator, 310-206-3121, Fax: 310-206-5280, E-mail: uclaaccess@mednet.ucla.edu.

See Close-Up on page 239.

University of California, San Diego, Office of Graduate Studies, Division of Biological Sciences, Program in Computational Neurobiology, La Jolla, CA 92093-0348. Offers PhD. Offered in association with the Salk Institute. *Degree requirements:* For doctorate, thesis/dissertation, qualifying exam. Electronic applications accepted.

University of California, San Diego, Office of Graduate Studies, Division of Biological Sciences, Program in Neurobiology, La Jolla, CA 92093. Offers PhD. Offered in association with the Salk Institute. *Degree requirements:* For doctorate, thesis/dissertation, qualifying exam. Electronic applications accepted.

University of Chicago, Division of the Biological Sciences, Neuroscience Graduate Programs, Committee on Neurobiology, Chicago, IL 60637-1513. Offers PhD. *Faculty:* 45 full-time (14 women). *Students:* 41 full-time (18 women); includes 11 minority (2 African Americans, 5 Asian Americans or Pacific Islanders, 4 Hispanic Americans), 4 international. Average age 29. 47 applicants, 15% accepted, 7 enrolled. In 2009, 12 doctorates awarded. *Degree requirements:* For doctorate, thesis/dissertation, ethics class, 2 teaching assistantships. *Entrance requirements:* For doctorate, GRE General Test. Additional exam requirements/recommendations for international students: Required—TOEFL (minimum score 600 paper-based; 250 computer-based; 104 iBT), IELTS (minimum score 7). *Application deadline:* For fall admission, 12/1 priority date for domestic and international students. Application fee: $55. Electronic applications accepted. *Financial support:* In 2009–10, 41 students received support, including fellowships with tuition reimbursements available (averaging $29,781 per year), research assistantships with tuition reimbursements available (averaging $29,781 per year); institutionally sponsored loans, scholarships/grants, traineeships, and health care benefits also available. Financial award applicants required to submit FAFSA. *Faculty research:* Immunogenetic aspects of neurologic disease. *Unit head:* Christian Hansel, Chairman, 773-702-1555, E-mail: neurobiology@chicago.edu. *Application contact:* Diane J. Hall, Graduate Administrative Director, 773-702-6371, Fax: 773-702-1216, E-mail: djh8@uchicago.edu.

University of Colorado at Boulder, Graduate School, College of Arts and Sciences, Department of Ecology and Evolutionary Biology, Boulder, CO 80309. Offers animal behavior (MA); biology (MA, PhD); environmental biology (MA, PhD); evolutionary biology (MA, PhD); neurobiology (MA); population biology (MA); population genetics (PhD). *Faculty:* 32 full-time (10 women). *Students:* 64 full-time (36 women), 15 part-time (9 women); includes 12 minority (1 American Indian/Alaska Native, 3 Asian Americans or Pacific Islanders, 8 Hispanic Americans), 4 international. Average age 29. 145 applicants, 14% accepted, 21 enrolled. In 2009, 9 master's, 6 doctorates awarded. Terminal master's awarded for partial completion of doctoral program. *Degree requirements:* For master's, comprehensive exam, thesis or alternative; for doctorate, comprehensive exam, thesis/dissertation. *Entrance requirements:* For master's, GRE General Test, GRE Subject Test, minimum undergraduate GPA of 3.0; for doctorate, GRE General Test, GRE Subject Test. *Application deadline:* For fall admission, 12/30 priority date for domestic students, 12/1 for international students. Application fee: $50 ($60 for international students). *Financial support:* In 2009–10, 25 fellowships (averaging $17,876 per year), 27 research assistantships (averaging $15,070 per year) were awarded; Federal Work-Study, institutionally sponsored loans, and tuition waivers (full) also available. *Faculty research:* Behavior, ecology, genetics, morphology, endocrinology, physiology, systematics. Total annual research expenditures: $3.1 million.

University of Connecticut, Graduate School, College of Liberal Arts and Sciences, Department of Physiology and Neurobiology, Storrs, CT 06269. Offers comparative physiology (MS, PhD); endocrinology (MS, PhD), including comparative physiology (MS), neurobiology (MS); neurobiology (MS, PhD). *Faculty:* 20 full-time (5 women). *Students:* 29 full-time (12 women), 3 part-time (0 women); includes 5 minority (all Asian Americans or Pacific Islanders), 12 international. Average age 28. 46 applicants, 11% accepted, 3 enrolled. In 2009, 5 master's, 2 doctorates awarded. Terminal master's awarded for partial completion of doctoral program. *Degree requirements:* For master's, comprehensive exam; for doctorate, thesis/dissertation. *Entrance requirements:* For master's and doctorate, GRE General Test, GRE Subject Test. Additional exam requirements/recommendations for international students: Required—TOEFL (minimum score 550 paper-based; 213 computer-based). *Application deadline:* For fall admission, 2/1 priority date for domestic and international students; for spring admission, 11/1 for domestic students, 10/1 for international students. Applications are processed on a rolling basis. Application fee: $55. Electronic applications accepted. *Expenses:* Tuition, state resident: full-time $4725; part-time $525 per credit. Tuition, nonresident: full-time $12,267; part-time $1363 per credit. Required fees: $346 per semester. Tuition and fees vary according to course load. *Financial support:* In 2009–10, 12 research assistantships with full tuition reimbursements, 17 teaching assistantships with full tuition reimbursements were awarded; fellowships, Federal Work-Study, scholarships/grants, health care benefits, and unspecified assistantships also available. Financial award application deadline: 2/1. *Unit head:* J. Larry Renfro, Head, 860-486-3285, Fax: 860-486-3303, E-mail: larry.renfro@uconn.edu. *Application contact:* Joseph J. LoTurco, Chairperson, 860-486-3271, Fax: 860-486-3303, E-mail: joseph.loturco@uconn.edu.

See Close-Up on page 491.

University of Illinois at Chicago, Graduate College, Graduate Program in Neuroscience, Chicago, IL 60607-7128. Offers PhD, MD/PhD. Admissions and degrees offered through participating Departments of Anatomy and Cell Biology, Biochemistry, Bioengineering, Biological Sciences, Chemistry, Pathology, Pharmacology, Physiology and Biophysics, and Psychology. *Degree requirements:* For doctorate, thesis/dissertation. *Entrance requirements:* For doctorate, GRE General Test, minimum GPA of 3.75 on a 5.0 scale. Additional exam requirements/recommendations for international students: Required—TOEFL. *Faculty research:* Neurobiology and behavior.

The University of Iowa, Graduate College, College of Liberal Arts and Sciences, Department of Biology, Iowa City, IA 52242-1316. Offers biology (MS, PhD); cell and developmental biology (MS, PhD); evolution (MS, PhD); genetics (MS, PhD); neurobiology (MS, PhD); plant biology (MS, PhD). Terminal master's awarded for partial completion of doctoral program. *Degree requirements:* For master's, thesis optional, exam; for doctorate, comprehensive exam, thesis/dissertation. *Entrance requirements:* For master's and doctorate, GRE General Test, minimum GPA of 3.0. Additional exam requirements/recommendations for international students: Required—TOEFL (minimum score 600 paper-based; 250 computer-based; 100 iBT). Electronic applications accepted. *Faculty research:* Developmental neurobiology, evolutionary biology, signal transduction, cell motility, molecular genetics (plant and animal).

The University of Iowa, Graduate College, College of Liberal Arts and Sciences, Department of Psychology, Iowa City, IA 52242-1316. Offers neural and behavioral sciences (PhD); psychology (MA, PhD). *Degree requirements:* For master's, thesis optional, exam; for doctorate, comprehensive exam, thesis/dissertation. *Entrance requirements:* For master's and doctorate, GRE General Test, minimum GPA of 3.0. Additional exam requirements/recommendations for international students: Required—TOEFL (minimum score 550 paper-based; 213 computer-based; 81 iBT). Electronic applications accepted.

University of Kentucky, Graduate School, Graduate School Programs from the College of Medicine, Program in Anatomy and Neurobiology, Lexington, KY 40506-0032. Offers anatomy (PhD). *Degree requirements:* For doctorate, comprehensive exam, thesis/dissertation. *Entrance requirements:* For doctorate, GRE General Test, minimum undergraduate GPA of 2.75. Additional exam requirements/recommendations for international students: Required—TOEFL (minimum score 550 paper-based; 213 computer-based). Electronic applications accepted. *Faculty research:* Neuroendocrinology, developmental neurobiology, neurotrophic substances, neural plasticity and trauma, neurobiology of aging.

University of Louisville, School of Medicine, Department of Anatomical Sciences and Neurobiology, Louisville, KY 40292-0001. Offers MS, PhD, MD/PhD. *Faculty:* 20 full-time (3 women), 12 part-time/adjunct (1 woman). *Students:* 37 full-time (18 women), 2 part-time (1 woman); includes 1 minority (Hispanic American), 12 international. Average age 28. 32 applicants, 53% accepted, 12 enrolled. In 2009, 6 master's, 3 doctorates awarded. Terminal master's awarded for partial completion of doctoral program. *Degree requirements:* For master's, thesis; for doctorate, comprehensive exam, thesis/dissertation. *Entrance requirements:* For master's, GRE General Test (minimum score 1000 verbal and quantitative), minimum GPA of 3.0; for doctorate, GRE General Test (Verbal and Quantitative minimum score of 1000), minimum GPA of 3.0. Additional exam requirements/recommendations for international students: Required—TOEFL. *Application deadline:* For fall admission, 1/15 priority date for domestic students; for spring admission, 4/15 priority date for domestic and international students. Applications are processed on a rolling basis. Application fee: $50. Electronic applications accepted. *Financial support:* In 2009–10, 32 students received support, including 6 fellowships with full tuition reimbursements available (averaging $22,000 per year), 26 research assistantships with full tuition reimbursements available (averaging $22,000 per year); health care benefits and unspecified assistantships also available. Financial award application deadline: 4/15. *Faculty research:* Human adult neural stem cells, development and plasticity of the nervous system, organization of the dorsal thalamus, electrophysiology/neuroanatomy of central neurons mediating control of reproductive and pelvic organs; normal neural mechanisms and plasticity following injury and/or chronic pain, differentiation and regeneration of motor neurons and oligodendrocytes. Total annual research expenditures: $4 million. *Unit head:* Dr. Fred J. Roisen, Chair, 502-852-5165, Fax: 502-852-6228, E-mail: fjrois01@gwise.louisville.edu. *Application contact:* Dr. Charles Hubscher, Director of Graduate Studies, 502-852-3058, Fax: 502-852-6228, E-mail: chhub01@louisville.edu.

University of Maryland, Baltimore, Graduate School, Graduate Program in Life Sciences, Program in Neuroscience, Baltimore, MD 21201. Offers PhD, MD/PhD. Part-time programs available. *Students:* 52 full-time (32 women); includes 9 minority (3 African Americans, 5 Asian Americans or Pacific Islanders, 1 Hispanic American), 4 international. Average age 27. 89 applicants, 25% accepted, 5 enrolled. In 2009, 5 doctorates awarded. *Entrance requirements:* For doctorate, GRE General Test, minimum GPA of 3.0. Additional exam requirements/recommendations for international students: Required—TOEFL (minimum score 550 paper-based; 80 iBT); Recommended—IELTS (minimum score 7). *Application deadline:* For fall admission, 1/15 for domestic and international students. Application fee: $50. Electronic applications accepted. *Expenses:* Tuition, state resident: full-time $7290; part-time $405 per credit hour. Tuition, nonresident: full-time $12,780; part-time $710 per credit hour. Required fees: $774; $10 per credit hour. $297 per semester. Tuition and fees vary according to course load, degree level and program. *Financial support:* In 2009–10, research assistantships with partial tuition reimbursements (averaging $25,000 per year); fellowships, health care benefits and unspecified assistantships also available. Financial award application deadline: 3/1. *Faculty research:* Molecular, biochemical, and cellular pharmacology; membrane biophysics; synaptology; developmental neurobiology. *Unit head:* Dr. Frank Margolis, Director, 410-706-8913, E-mail: fmargoli@umaryland.edu. *Application contact:* Jennifer Aumiller, Coordinator, 410-706-4701, Fax: 410-706-4724, E-mail: neurosci@umaryland.edu.

University of Minnesota, Twin Cities Campus, Graduate School, Graduate Program in Neuroscience, Minneapolis, MN 55455-0213. Offers MS, PhD. Terminal master's awarded for partial completion of doctoral program. *Degree requirements:* For master's, thesis; for doctorate, thesis/dissertation. *Entrance requirements:* For doctorate, GRE. Additional exam requirements/recommendations for international students: Required—TOEFL. Electronic applications accepted. *Faculty research:* Cellular and molecular neuroscience, behavioral neuroscience, developmental neuroscience, neurodegenerative diseases, pain, addiction, motor control.

University of Missouri, Graduate School, College of Arts and Sciences, Division of Biological Sciences, Program in Neurobiology and Behavior, Columbia, MO 65211. Offers MA, PhD.

The University of North Carolina at Chapel Hill, School of Medicine and Graduate School, Graduate Programs in Medicine, Curriculum in Neurobiology, Chapel Hill, NC 27599. Offers PhD. *Degree requirements:* For doctorate, comprehensive exam, thesis/dissertation. *Entrance requirements:* For doctorate, GRE General Test, minimum GPA of 3.0. Electronic applications accepted.

University of Oklahoma, Graduate College, College of Arts and Sciences, Department of Zoology and School of Aerospace and Mechanical Engineering and Department of Chemistry and Biochemistry, Program in Cellular and Behavioral Neurobiology, Norman, OK 73019. Offers PhD. *Entrance requirements:* Additional exam requirements/recommendations for international students: Required—TOEFL (minimum score 550 paper-based; 213 computer-based). *Application deadline:* For fall admission, 4/1 for domestic and international students; for spring admission, 11/1 for domestic students, 9/1 for international students. Applications are processed on a rolling basis. Application fee: $40 ($90 for international students). Electronic applications accepted. *Expenses:* Tuition, state resident: full-time $3744; part-time $156 per credit hour. Tuition, nonresident: full-time $13,577; part-time $565.70 per credit hour. Required fees: $2415; $90.10 per credit hour. *Financial support:* In 2009–10, 4 students received support. Scholarships/grants, health care benefits, and unspecified assistantships available. *Faculty research:* Neural bases of behavior; signal transduction and plasticity; development and regeneration; behavioral, cellular, systems, molecular and computational neurobiology; sensory and sensorimotor neurophysiology; neural interfaces. *Unit head:* Don Wilson, Assistant Chair, 405-325-4821, Fax: 405-325-6202, E-mail: dwilson@ou.edu. *Application contact:* Dr. Ari Berkowitz, Director, 405-325-3492, Fax: 405-325-6202, E-mail: cbn@ou.edu.

University of Rochester, School of Medicine and Dentistry, Graduate Programs in Medicine and Dentistry, Department of Neurobiology and Anatomy, Program in Neurobiology and Anatomy, Rochester, NY 14627. Offers MS, PhD. *Degree requirements:* For doctorate, thesis/dissertation, qualifying exam. *Entrance requirements:* For master's and doctorate, GRE General Test.

University of Southern California, Graduate School, College of Letters, Arts and Sciences, Department of Biological Sciences, Program in Neurobiology, Los Angeles, CA 90089. Offers PhD. *Faculty:* 17 full-time (5 women). *Students:* 5 full-time (3 women); includes 2 minority (both Asian Americans or Pacific Islanders), 3 international. 27 applicants, 19% accepted, 5 enrolled. *Degree requirements:* For doctorate, thesis/dissertation, qualifying examination. *Entrance requirements:* For doctorate, GRE, 3 letters of recommendation, resume, minimum GPA of 3.0. Additional exam requirements/recommendations for international students: Required—TOEFL (minimum score 600 paper-based; 250 computer-based; 100 iBT). *Application deadline:* For fall admission, 12/1 priority date for domestic and international students. Application fee: $85. Electronic applications accepted. *Expenses:* Tuition: Full-time $25,980; part-time $1315 per unit. Required fees: $554. One-time fee: $35 full-time. Full-time tuition and fees vary according to degree level and program. *Financial support:* In 2009–10, 5 students received support, including fellowships with full tuition reimbursements available (averaging $30,000 per year), 5 research assistantships with full tuition reimbursements available (averaging $27,500 per year), teaching assistantships with full tuition reimbursements available (averaging $27,500 per year); scholarships/grants, traineeships, health care benefits, tuition waivers, and unspecified assistantships also available. *Faculty research:* Behavior, learning and memory; cell biology and physiology of neuronal signaling; sensory processing; development, disease and aging. *Unit head:* Dr. Chien-Ping Ko, Professor of Biological Sciences/Director, 213-740-9182, Fax: 213-740-5687, E-mail: cko@college.usc.edu. *Application contact:* Beatriz Gil, Administrative Assistant II, 213-740-9176, Fax: 213-740-6980, E-mail: bgil@usc.edu.

University of Southern California, Keck School of Medicine and Graduate School, Graduate Programs in Medicine, Department of Cell and Neurobiology, Los Angeles, CA 90089. Offers MS, PhD. *Faculty:* 28 full-time (5 women), 1 (woman) part-time/adjunct. *Students:* 3 full-time (2 women); includes 1 minority (Asian American or Pacific Islander). Average age 24. 5 applicants, 20% accepted, 1 enrolled.Terminal master's awarded for partial completion of doctoral program. *Degree requirements:* For master's, thesis or alternative; for doctorate, thesis/dissertation. *Entrance requirements:* For master's, GRE General Test, minimum GPA of 3.0; for doctorate, GRE General Test. *Application deadline:* For fall admission, 3/1 priority date for domestic and international students. Application fee: $85. Electronic applications accepted. *Expenses:* Tuition: Full-time $25,980; part-time $1315 per unit. Required fees: $554. One-time fee: $35 full-time. Full-time tuition and fees vary according to degree level and program. *Financial support:* In 2009–10, 1 student received support, including 1 fellowship (averaging $27,060 per year), 4 research assistantships (averaging $27,060 per year); teaching assistantships, Federal Work-Study and institutionally sponsored loans also available. Support available to part-time students. *Faculty research:* Neurobiology and development, gene therapy in vision, lachrymal glands, neuroendocrinology, signal transduction mechanisms. *Unit head:* Dr. Mikel Henry Snow, Vice-Chair, 323-442-1881, Fax: 323-442-3466. *Application contact:* Darlene Marie Campbell, Project Specialist, 323-442-2843, Fax: 323-442-0466, E-mail: dmc@usc.edu.

The University of Tennessee Health Science Center, College of Graduate Health Sciences, Department of Anatomy and Neurobiology, Memphis, TN 38163-0002. Offers PhD. *Degree requirements:* For doctorate, thesis/dissertation, oral and written preliminary and comprehensive exams. *Entrance requirements:* For doctorate, GRE General Test, minimum GPA of 3.0. Electronic applications accepted.

The University of Texas at Austin, Graduate School, The Institute for Neuroscience, Austin, TX 78712-1111. Offers PhD, MD/PhD. Terminal master's awarded for partial completion of doctoral program. *Degree requirements:* For doctorate, thesis/dissertation. *Entrance requirements:* For doctorate, GRE. Electronic applications accepted. *Faculty research:* Cellular/molecular biology, neurobiology, pharmacology, behavioral neuroscience.

The University of Texas at San Antonio, College of Sciences, Department of Biology, San Antonio, TX 78249-0617. Offers biology (MS, PhD), including cellular and molecular biology (PhD); neurobiology (PhD); biotechnology (MS). Part-time programs available. *Faculty:* 37 full-time (6 women), 7 part-time/adjunct (1 woman). *Students:* 144 full-time (82 women), 45 part-time (28 women); includes 57 minority (6 African Americans, 13 Asian Americans or Pacific Islanders, 38 Hispanic Americans), 69 international. Average age 28. 263 applicants, 58% accepted, 72 enrolled. In 2009, 40 master's, 6 doctorates awarded. *Degree requirements:* For master's, comprehensive exam, thesis; for doctorate, comprehensive exam, thesis/dissertation. *Entrance requirements:* For master's, GRE General Test, minimum GPA of 3.0; for doctorate, GRE General Test, minimum GPA of 3.3. Additional exam requirements/recommendations for international students: Required—TOEFL (minimum score 500 paper-based; 173 computer-based; 61 iBT), IELTS (minimum score 5). *Application deadline:* For fall admission, 7/1 for domestic students, 4/1 for international students; for spring admission, 11/1 for domestic students, 9/1 for international students. Applications are processed on a rolling basis. Application fee: $45 ($80 for international students). Electronic applications accepted. *Expenses:* Tuition, state resident: full-time $3975; part-time $221 per contact hour. Tuition, nonresident: full-time $13,947; part-time $775 per contact hour. Required fees: $1853. *Financial support:* In 2009–10, 66 students received support, including 13 fellowships (averaging $31,063 per year), 87 research assistantships (averaging $15,279 per year), 66 teaching assistantships (averaging $10,368 per year); career-related internships or fieldwork, scholarships/grants, and unspecified assistantships also available. Support available to part-time students. *Faculty research:* Cell and molecular biology, neurobiology, microbiology, integrative biology, environmental science. Total annual research expenditures: $1.7 million. *Unit head:* Dr. Edwin J. Barea-Rodriguez, Interim Chair, 210-458-5481, Fax: 210-458-7498, E-mail: edwin.barea@utsa.edu. *Application contact:* Dr. Dorothy A. Flannagan, Dean of the Graduate School, 210-458-4330, Fax: 210-458-4332, E-mail: dorothy.flannagan@utsa.edu.

See Close-Up on page 121.

University of Utah, School of Medicine and Graduate School, Graduate Programs in Medicine, Department of Neurobiology and Anatomy, Salt Lake City, UT 84112-1107. Offers PhD. Part-time programs available. Terminal master's awarded for partial completion of doctoral program. *Degree requirements:* For doctorate, comprehensive exam, thesis/dissertation. *Entrance requirements:* For doctorate, GRE General Test. Additional exam requirements/recommendations for international students: Required—TOEFL. *Expenses:* Tuition, state resident: full-time $4004; part-time $1674 per semester. Tuition, nonresident: full-time $14,134; part-time $5915 per semester. Required fees: $324 per semester. Tuition and fees vary according to course load, degree level and program. *Faculty research:* Neuroscience, neuroanatomy, developmental neurobiology, neurogenetics.

University of Washington, Graduate School, School of Medicine and Graduate School, Graduate Programs in Medicine, Graduate Program in Neurobiology and Behavior, Seattle, WA 98195. Offers PhD. *Degree requirements:* For doctorate, thesis/dissertation. *Entrance requirements:* For doctorate, GRE. Additional exam requirements/recommendations for international students: Required—TOEFL. Electronic applications accepted. *Faculty research:* Motor, sensory systems, neuroplasticity, animal behavior, neuroendocrinology, computational neuroscience.

University of Wisconsin–Madison, School of Medicine and Public Health and Graduate School, Graduate Programs in Medicine, Department of Physiology, Madison, WI 53706-1380. Offers PhD. *Faculty:* 16 full-time (5 women). *Students:* 17 full-time (4 women); includes 10 minority (2 African Americans, 6 Asian Americans or Pacific Islanders, 2 Hispanic Americans). Average age 22. 39 applicants, 8% accepted, 2 enrolled. In 2009, 3 doctorates awarded. *Degree requirements:* For doctorate, thesis/dissertation, written exams. *Entrance requirements:* For doctorate, GRE, minimum GPA of 3.0. Additional exam requirements/recommendations for international students: Required—TOEFL (minimum score 580 paper-based; 237 computer-based). *Application deadline:* For fall admission, 1/15 priority date for domestic and international students. Applications are processed on a rolling basis. Application fee: $45. Electronic applications accepted. *Expenses:* Tuition, state resident: part-time $594 per credit. Tuition, nonresident: part-time $1504 per credit. Required fees: $65 per credit. Tuition and fees vary according to course load, program and reciprocity agreements. *Financial support:* In 2009–10, fellowships with tuition reimbursements (averaging $23,500 per year), research assistantships with tuition reimbursements (averaging $23,500 per year), teaching assistantships with tuition reimbursements (averaging $23,500 per year) were awarded. *Faculty research:* Studies in molecular cellular systems, cardiovascular, neuroscience. *Unit head:* Dr. Donata Oertel, Interim Chair, 608-263-6281, Fax: 608-265-5512, E-mail: oertel@physiology.wisc.edu. *Application contact:* Sue S. Krey, Program Assistant, 608-262-9114, Fax: 608-265-5512, E-mail: krey@physiology.wisc.edu.

Virginia Commonwealth University, Medical College of Virginia-Professional Programs, School of Medicine, School of Medicine Graduate Programs, Department of Anatomy and Neurobiology, Program in Anatomy and Neurobiology, Richmond, VA 23284-9005. Offers PhD. *Accreditation:* APTA. *Degree requirements:* For doctorate, thesis/dissertation. *Entrance requirements:* For doctorate, GRE General Test.

Wake Forest University, School of Medicine and Graduate School of Arts and Sciences, Graduate Programs in Medicine, Department of Neurobiology and Anatomy, Winston-Salem, NC 27109. Offers PhD, MD/PhD. *Degree requirements:* For doctorate, thesis/dissertation. *Entrance requirements:* For doctorate, GRE General Test. Additional exam requirements/recommendations for international students: Required—TOEFL. Electronic applications accepted. *Faculty research:* Sensory neurobiology, reproductive endocrinology, regulatory processes in cell biology.

Wesleyan University, Graduate Programs, Department of Biology, Middletown, CT 06459. Offers animal behavior (PhD); bioformatics/genomics (PhD); cell biology (PhD); developmental biology (PhD); evolution/ecology (PhD); genetics (PhD); neurobiology (PhD); population biology (PhD). *Faculty:* 13 full-time (4 women). *Students:* 23 full-time (11 women); includes 1 minority (African American), 3 international. Average age 26. 29 applicants, 10% accepted, 2 enrolled. In 2009, 3 doctorates awarded. *Degree requirements:* For doctorate, variable foreign language requirement, thesis/dissertation. *Entrance requirements:* For doctorate, GRE. Additional exam requirements/recommendations for international students: Required—TOEFL. *Application deadline:* For fall admission, 1/15 for domestic and international students. Applications are processed on a rolling basis. Application fee: $0. *Financial support:* In 2009–10, 3 research assistantships with full tuition reimbursements, 19 teaching assistantships with full tuition reimbursements were awarded; stipends also available. Financial award application deadline: 4/15; financial award applicants required to submit FAFSA. *Faculty research:* Microbial population genetics, genetic basis of evolutionary adaptation, genetic regulation of differentiation and pattern formation in *drosophila*. *Unit head:* Dr. Sonia E. Sultan, Chair/Professor, 860-685-3493, E-mail: jnaegele@wesleyan.edu. *Application contact:* Marjorie Fitzgibbons, Information Contact, 860-685-2140, E-mail: mfitzgibbons@wesleyan.edu.

West Virginia University, Eberly College of Arts and Sciences, Department of Biology, Morgantown, WV 26506. Offers cell and molecular biology (MS, PhD); environmental and evolutionary biology (MS, PhD); forensic biology (MS, PhD); genomic biology (MS, PhD); neurobiology (MS, PhD). Terminal master's awarded for partial completion of doctoral program. *Degree requirements:* For master's, thesis, final exam; for doctorate, thesis/dissertation, preliminary and final exams. *Entrance requirements:* For master's, GRE General Test, GRE Subject Test, minimum GPA of 3.0; for doctorate, GRE General Test, minimum GPA of 3.0. Additional exam requirements/recommendations for international students: Required—TOEFL. *Faculty research:* Environmental biology, genetic engineering, developmental biology, global change, biodiversity.

Yale University, Graduate School of Arts and Sciences, Department of Molecular, Cellular, and Developmental Biology, Program in Neurobiology, New Haven, CT 06520. Offers PhD. *Degree requirements:* For doctorate, thesis/dissertation. *Entrance requirements:* For doctorate, GRE General Test, GRE Subject Test.

Yale University, School of Medicine and Graduate School of Arts and Sciences, Combined Program in Biological and Biomedical Sciences (BBS), Department of Neurobiology, New Haven, CT 06520. Offers PhD. In 2009, 2 doctorates awarded. *Degree requirements:* For doctorate, thesis/dissertation. *Entrance requirements:* For doctorate, GRE General Test, GRE Subject Test. *Application deadline:* For fall admission, 12/6 for domestic and international students. *Financial support:* Fellowships, research assistantships, Federal Work-Study and institutionally sponsored loans available. Support available to part-time students. *Unit head:* Dr. Michael Crair, Director of Graduate Studies, 203-785-5768. *Application contact:* Graduate Admissions Office, 203-432-2771.

Neuroscience

Albany Medical College, Center for Neuropharmacology and Neuroscience, Albany, NY 12208-3479. Offers MS, PhD. *Faculty:* 23 full-time (8 women). *Students:* 18 full-time (7 women); includes 5 minority (2 African Americans, 2 Asian Americans or Pacific Islanders, 1 Hispanic American). Average age 24. 31 applicants, 19% accepted, 6 enrolled. In 2009, 2 master's, 3 doctorates awarded. Terminal master's awarded for partial completion of doctoral program. *Degree requirements:* For master's, thesis; for doctorate, comprehensive exam, thesis/dissertation. *Entrance requirements:* For master's, GRE General Test, all transcripts, letters of recommendation; for doctorate, GRE General Test, letters of recommendation. Additional exam requirements/recommendations for international students: Required—TOEFL. *Application deadline:* For fall admission, 3/15 priority date for domestic and international students. Applications are processed on a rolling basis. Application fee: $0 ($60 for international students). *Expenses:* Tuition: Full-time $18,820. *Financial support:* In 2009–10, 3 fellowships with partial tuition reimbursements (averaging $20,772 per year), 18 research assistantships with full tuition reimbursements (averaging $24,000 per year) were awarded; Federal Work-Study, scholarships/grants, and tuition waivers (full) also available. Financial award applicants required to submit FAFSA. *Faculty research:* Molecular and cellular neuroscience, neuronal development, addiction. *Unit head:* Dr. Stanley D. Glick, Director, 518-262-5303, Fax: 518-262-5799, E-mail: cnninfo@mail.amc.edu. *Application contact:* Dr. Richard Keller, Graduate Director, 518-262-5303, Fax: 518-262-5799, E-mail: cnninfo@mail.amc.edu.

American University, College of Arts and Sciences, Department of Psychology, Program in Behavior, Cognition, and Neuroscience, Washington, DC 22016-8062. Offers psychology (PhD), including behavior, cognition and neuroscience. *Students:* 8 full-time (5 women), 16 part-time (12 women); includes 4 minority (1 African American, 2 Asian Americans or Pacific Islanders, 1 Hispanic American), 3 international. Average age 28. 26 applicants, 23% accepted, 4 enrolled. *Degree requirements:* For doctorate, comprehensive exam, thesis/dissertation, 2 lab rotations, 2 tools of research. *Entrance requirements:* For doctorate, GRE General Test, GRE Subject Test, 3 recommendations. Additional exam requirements/recommendations for international students: Required—TOEFL. *Application deadline:* For fall admission, 1/1 for domestic students. Application fee: $80. *Expenses:* Tuition: Full-time $22,266; part-time $1237 per credit hour. Required fees: $430. Tuition and fees vary according to program. *Financial support:* Fellowships, research assistantships, teaching assistantships, career-related internships or fieldwork, Federal Work-Study, institutionally sponsored loans, and tuition waivers (full and partial) available. Support available to part-time students. Financial award application deadline: 2/1. *Faculty research:* Psychophysics, drug discrimination learning, choice behavior, conditioning and learning, olfaction and taste. *Application contact:* Sara Holland, Senior Administrative Assistant, 202-885-1717, Fax: 202-885-1023.

American University of Beirut, Graduate Programs, Faculty of Medicine, Beirut, Lebanon. Offers biochemistry (MS); human morphology (MS); medicine (MD); microbiology and immunology (MS); neuroscience (MS); pharmacology and therapeutics (MS); physiology (MS). Part-time programs available. *Degree requirements:* For master's, one foreign language, comprehensive exam, thesis (for some programs). *Entrance requirements:* For MD, MCAT, bachelor's degree; for master's, letter of recommendation. Additional exam requirements/recommendations for international students: Required—TOEFL (minimum score 600 paper-based; 250 computer-based; 100 iBT), IELTS (minimum score 7.5). *Faculty research:* Cancer research, stem cell research, genetic research, neuroscience research, bone research.

Argosy University, Chicago, College of Psychology and Behavioral Sciences, Doctoral Program in Clinical Psychology, Chicago, IL 60601. Offers child and adolescent psychology (Psy D); client-centered and experiential psychotherapies (Psy D); diversity and multicultural psychology (Psy D); family psychology (Psy D); forensic psychology (Psy D); health psychology (Psy D); neuropsychology (Psy D); organizational consulting (Psy D); psychoanalytic psychology (Psy D); psychology and spirituality (Psy D). *Accreditation:* APA.

Argosy University, Phoenix, College of Psychology and Behavioral Sciences, Program in Clinical Psychology, Phoenix, AZ 85021. Offers clinical psychology (MA); neuropsychology (Psy D); sports-exercise psychology (Psy D). *Accreditation:* APA (one or more programs are accredited).

Argosy University, Phoenix, College of Psychology and Behavioral Sciences, Program in Neuropsychology, Phoenix, AZ 85021. Offers Psy D.

Argosy University, Schaumburg, College of Psychology and Behavioral Sciences, Schaumburg, IL 60173-5403. Offers clinical health psychology (Post-Graduate Certificate); clinical psychology (MA, Psy D), including child and family psychology (Psy D), clinical health psychology (Psy D), diversity and multicultural psychology (Psy D), forensic psychology (Psy D), neuropsychology (Psy D); community counseling (MA); counseling psychology (Ed D), including counselor education and supervision; counselor education and supervision (Ed D); forensic psychology (Post-Graduate Certificate); industrial organizational psychology (MA). *Accreditation:* ACA; APA.

Argosy University, Tampa, College of Psychology and Behavioral Sciences, Program in Clinical Psychology, Tampa, FL 33607. Offers clinical psychology (MA, Psy D), including child and adolescent psychology (Psy D), geropsychology (Psy D), marriage/couples and family therapy (Psy D), neuropsychology (Psy D). *Accreditation:* APA.

Arizona State University, Graduate College, College of Liberal Arts and Sciences, Division of Natural Sciences, Department of Psychology, Tempe, AZ 85287. Offers behavioral neuroscience (PhD); clinical psychology (PhD); cognition, action and perception (PhD); developmental psychology (PhD); quantitative psychology (PhD); social psychology (PhD). *Accreditation:* APA. *Degree requirements:* For doctorate, thesis/dissertation. *Entrance requirements:* For doctorate, GRE General Test, GRE Subject Test.

Arizona State University, Graduate College, College of Liberal Arts and Sciences, Division of Natural Sciences, School of Life Sciences, Tempe, AZ 85287. Offers biological design (PhD); biology (MNS, MS, PhD); biology and society (PhD); human and social dimensions of science and technology (PhD); microbiology (MNS, MS, PhD); molecular and cellular biology (MS, PhD); neuroscience (PhD); plant biology (MNS, MS, PhD). *Accreditation:* NAACLS. *Degree requirements:* For master's, thesis (MS); for doctorate, one foreign language, thesis/dissertation. *Entrance requirements:* For master's and doctorate, GRE.

Baylor College of Medicine, Graduate School of Biomedical Sciences, Department of Neuroscience, Houston, TX 77030-3498. Offers PhD, MD/PhD. *Faculty:* 47 full-time (11 women). *Students:* 53 full-time (26 women); includes 14 minority (2 African Americans, 5 Asian Americans or Pacific Islanders, 7 Hispanic Americans), 10 international. Average age 25. In 2009, 9 doctorates awarded. *Degree requirements:* For doctorate, thesis/dissertation, public defense. *Entrance requirements:* For doctorate, GRE General Test, GRE Subject Test (strongly recommended), minimum GPA of 3.0. Additional exam requirements/recommendations for international students: Required—TOEFL. *Application deadline:* For fall admission, 1/1 priority date for domestic students. Application fee: $0. Electronic applications accepted. *Financial support:* In 2009–10, 51 students received support; fellowships, research assistantships, Federal Work-Study, institutionally sponsored loans, health care benefits, and students receive a scholarship unless there are grant funds available to pay tuition available. Financial award applicants required to submit FAFSA. *Faculty research:* Molecular and developmental neurobiology, neurobiology of disease, neuroanatomy, neurophysiology, neural systems analysis. *Unit head:* Dr. Mariella DeBiasi, Director, 713-798-7270. *Application contact:* Krista Defalco, Graduate Program Administrator, 713-798-7270, Fax: 713-798-3946, E-mail: kdefalco@bcm.edu.

Baylor College of Medicine, Graduate School of Biomedical Sciences, Program in Developmental Biology, Houston, TX 77030-3498. Offers PhD, MD/PhD. *Faculty:* 52 full-time (16 women). *Students:* 51 full-time (26 women); includes 9 minority (1 American Indian/Alaska Native, 6 Asian Americans or Pacific Islanders, 2 Hispanic Americans), 29 international. Average age 25. In 2009, 4 doctorates awarded. *Degree requirements:* For doctorate, thesis/dissertation, public defense. *Entrance requirements:* For doctorate, GRE General Test, GRE Subject Test (strongly recommended), minimum GPA of 3.0. Additional exam requirements/recommendations for international students: Required—TOEFL. *Application deadline:* For fall admission, 1/1 priority date for domestic students. Application fee: $0. Electronic applications accepted. *Financial support:* Fellowships, research assistantships, career-related internships or fieldwork, Federal Work-Study, institutionally sponsored loans, health care benefits, tuition waivers (full), and stipends available. *Faculty research:* Molecular and genetic approaches to study pattern formation in Dictyostelium, Drosophila, C.elegans, mouse, Xenopus, and zebrafish; cross-species approach. *Unit head:* Dr. Hugo Bellen, Director, 713-798-6410. *Application contact:* Catherine Tasnier, Graduate Program Administrator, 713-798-6410, Fax: 713-798-5386, E-mail: cat@bcm.edu.

See Close-Up on page 315.

Boston University, Graduate School of Arts and Sciences, Department of Cognitive and Neural Systems, Boston, MA 02215. Offers MA, PhD. *Students:* 47 full-time (10 women), 6 part-time (2 women); includes 5 minority (4 Asian Americans or Pacific Islanders, 1 Hispanic American), 18 international. Average age 30. 61 applicants, 31% accepted, 8 enrolled. Terminal master's awarded for partial completion of doctoral program. *Degree requirements:* For master's, one foreign language, comprehensive exam; for doctorate, one foreign language, comprehensive exam, thesis/dissertation. *Entrance requirements:* For master's and doctorate, GRE General Test, GRE Subject Test (recommended), 3 letters of recommendation. Additional exam requirements/recommendations for international students: Required—TOEFL (minimum score 550 paper-based; 213 computer-based). *Application deadline:* For fall admission, 1/15 for domestic and international students; for spring admission, 10/15 for domestic and international students. Application fee: $70. Electronic applications accepted. *Expenses:* Tuition: Full-time $37,910; part-time $1184 per credit hour. Required fees: $386; $40 per semester. Part-time tuition and fees vary according to class time, course level, degree level and program. *Financial support:* In 2009–10, 3 fellowships with full tuition reimbursements (averaging $18,900 per year), 35 research assistantships with full tuition reimbursements (averaging $18,400 per year), 2 teaching assistantships with full tuition reimbursements were awarded; Federal Work-Study and unspecified assistantships also available. Support available to part-time students. Financial award application deadline: 1/15; financial award applicants required to submit FAFSA. *Unit head:* Ennio Mingolla, Chairman, 617-353-9485, Fax: 617-353-7755, E-mail: ennio@bu.edu. *Application contact:* Carol Y. Jefferson, Administrative Assistant, 617-353-7676, Fax: 617-353-7755, E-mail: caroly@bu.edu.

Boston University, Graduate School of Arts and Sciences, Interdepartmental Program in Neuroscience, Boston, MA 02215. Offers MA, PhD. *Students:* 21 full-time (8 women); includes 4 minority (1 African American, 2 Asian Americans or Pacific Islanders, 1 Hispanic American). Average age 27. 110 applicants, 12% accepted, 6 enrolled. In 2009, 3 doctorates awarded. Terminal master's awarded for partial completion of doctoral program. *Degree requirements:* For master's, one foreign language, thesis; for doctorate, one foreign language, comprehensive exam, thesis/dissertation. *Entrance requirements:* For master's and doctorate, GRE General Test, 3 letters of recommendation. Additional exam requirements/recommendations for international students: Required—TOEFL (minimum score 550 paper-based; 213 computer-based). *Application deadline:* For fall admission, 12/15 for domestic and international students. Application fee: $70. Electronic applications accepted. *Expenses:* Tuition: Full-time $37,910; part-time $1184 per credit hour. Required fees: $386; $40 per semester. Part-time tuition and fees vary according to class time, course level, degree level and program. *Financial support:* In 2009–10, 12 students received support, including 1 fellowship with full tuition reimbursement available (averaging $18,900 per year), 7 research assistantships with full tuition reimbursements available (averaging $18,400 per year), 4 teaching assistantships with full tuition reimbursements available (averaging $18,400 per year); Federal Work-Study, scholarships/grants, and traineeships also available. Financial award application deadline: 12/15; financial award applicants required to submit FAFSA. *Unit head:* Dr. William Eldred, Director, 617-353-2439, Fax: 617-358-1857, E-mail: eldred@bu.edu. *Application contact:* Sandi Grasso, Program Administrator, 617-358-1123, Fax: 617-358-1857, E-mail: neurosci@bu.edu.

Brandeis University, Graduate School of Arts and Sciences, Department of Psychology, Waltham, MA 02454-9110. Offers brain, body and behavior (PhD); cognitive neuroscience (PhD); general psychology (MA); social/developmental psychology (PhD). Part-time programs available. *Faculty:* 16 full-time (4 women), 3 part-time/adjunct (2 women). *Students:* 35 full-time (27 women), 1 (woman) part-time; includes 2 minority (both Asian Americans or Pacific Islanders), 7 international. Average age 26. 121 applicants, 31% accepted, 13 enrolled. In 2009, 9 master's, 3 doctorates awarded. *Degree requirements:* For doctorate, comprehensive exam, thesis/dissertation. *Entrance requirements:* For master's, GRE General Test, GRE Subject Test (recommended), 3 letters of recommendation, statement of purpose; for doctorate, GRE General Test, GRE Subject Test (recommended), 3 letters of recommendation. Additional exam requirements/recommendations for international students: Required—TOEFL (minimum score 600 paper-based; 250 computer-based; 100 iBT); Recommended—IELTS (minimum score 7). *Application deadline:* For fall admission, 1/15 for domestic and international students. Applications are processed on a rolling basis. Application fee: $75. Electronic applications accepted. *Financial support:* In 2009–10, 16 fellowships with full tuition reimbursements (averaging $20,000 per year), 3 research assistantships with full tuition reimbursements (averaging $20,000 per year), 9 teaching assistantships with partial tuition reimbursements (averaging $3,200 per year) were awarded; institutionally sponsored loans, scholarships/grants, traineeships, health care benefits, tuition waivers (full), and unspecified assistantships also available. Support available to part-time students. Financial award applicants required to submit FAFSA. *Faculty research:* Development, cognition, social aging, perception, social/developmental psychology, cognitive neuroscience, brain, body and behavior, motor control, visual perception, taste physiology and psychophysics, memory, learning, aggression, emotion, personality and cognition in adulthood and old age, social relations and health, stereotypes and nonverbal communication. *Unit head:* Prof. Paul DiZio, Director of Graduate Studies, 781-736-3300, Fax: 781-736-3291, E-mail: dizio@brandeis.edu. *Application contact:* Donna J. Coletti, Graduate Admissions Coordinator, 781-736-3303, Fax: 781-736-3291, E-mail: coletti@brandeis.edu.

Brandeis University, Graduate School of Arts and Sciences, Program in Neuroscience, Waltham, MA 02454-9110. Offers MS, PhD. *Faculty:* 22 full-time (9 women), 2 part-time/adjunct (1 woman). *Students:* 50 full-time (28 women), 1 part-time (0 women); includes 12 minority (3 African Americans, 5 Asian Americans or Pacific Islanders, 4 Hispanic Americans), 2 international. Average age 24. 97 applicants, 30% accepted, 14 enrolled. In 2009, 6 master's, 8 doctorates awarded. Terminal master's awarded for partial completion of doctoral program. *Degree requirements:* For master's, thesis optional, research project; for doctorate, comprehensive exam, thesis/dissertation, qualifying exams, teaching experience, journal club. *Entrance requirements:* For master's and doctorate, GRE General Test, resume, 3 letters of recommendation. Additional exam requirements/recommendations for international students: Required—TOEFL (minimum score 600 paper-based; 250 computer-based; 100 iBT); Recommended—IELTS (minimum score 7). *Application deadline:* For fall admission, 1/15 priority date for domestic students. Applications are processed on a rolling basis. Application fee: $75. Electronic applications accepted. *Financial support:* In 2009–10, 40 students received support, including 5 fellowships with full tuition reimbursements available (averaging $27,500 per year), 32 research assistantships with full tuition reimbursements available (averaging $27,500 per year), teaching assistantships with partial tuition reimbursements available (averaging $3,200 per year); scholarships/grants, traineeships, health care benefits, and tuition waivers (full and partial) also available. Support available to part-time students. Financial award application deadline: 4/15; financial award applicants required to submit FAFSA. *Faculty* *research:* Behavioral neuroscience, cellular and molecular neuroscience, computational and integrative neuroscience. *Unit head:* Dr. Sacha Nelson, Chair, 781-736-3181, E-mail: nelson@brandeis.edu. *Application contact:* Marcia Cabral, Department Administrator, 781-736-3100, Fax: 781-736-3107, E-mail: cabral@brandeis.edu.

Brigham Young University, Graduate Studies, College of Life Sciences, Department of Physiology and Developmental Biology, Provo, UT 84602. Offers neuroscience (MS, PhD); physiology and developmental biology (MS, PhD). Part-time programs available. *Faculty:* 19 full-time (0 women). *Students:* 25 full-time (11 women); includes 3 minority (1 American Indian/Alaska Native, 1 Asian American or Pacific Islander, 1 Hispanic American). Average age 30. 14 applicants, 43% accepted, 3 enrolled. In 2009, 3 master's, 3 doctorates awarded. Terminal master's awarded for partial completion of doctoral program. *Degree requirements:* For master's, thesis; for doctorate, thesis/dissertation. *Entrance requirements:* For master's, GRE General Test, minimum GPA of 3.0 during previous 2 years; for doctorate, GRE General Test, minimum GPA of 3.0 overall. Additional exam requirements/recommendations for international students: Required—TOEFL. *Application deadline:* For fall admission, 2/1 priority date for domestic and international students; for winter admission, 9/10 priority date for domestic and international students. Application fee: $50. Electronic applications accepted. *Expenses:* Tuition: Full-time $5580; part-time $301 per credit hour. Tuition and fees vary according to student's religious affiliation. *Financial support:* In 2009–10, 25 students received support, including 1 fellowship with partial tuition reimbursement available (averaging $7,100 per year), 12 research assistantships with full tuition reimbursements available (averaging $15,500 per year), 13 teaching assistantships with partial tuition reimbursements available (averaging $14,900 per year); career-related internships or fieldwork, institutionally sponsored loans, scholarships/grants, tuition waivers (full and partial), unspecified assistantships, and tuition awards also available. Financial award application deadline: 2/1. *Faculty research:* Sex differentiation of the brain, exercise physiology, developmental biology, membrane biophysics, neuroscience. Total annual research expenditures: $848,996. *Unit head:* Dr. William W. Winder, Chair, 801-422-3093, Fax: 801-422-0700, E-mail: william_winder@byu.edu. *Application contact:* Dr. Dixon J. Woodbury, Graduate Coordinator, 801-422-7562, Fax: 801-422-0700, E-mail: dixon_woodbury@byu.edu.

Brock University, Faculty of Graduate Studies, Faculty of Social Sciences, Program in Psychology, St. Catharines, ON L2S 3A1, Canada. Offers behavioral neuroscience (MA, PhD); life span development (MA, PhD); social personality (MA, PhD). Part-time programs available. *Degree requirements:* For master's, thesis; for doctorate, thesis/dissertation. *Entrance requirements:* For master's, GRE, honors degree; for doctorate, GRE, master's degree. Additional exam requirements/recommendations for international students: Required—TOEFL (minimum score 550 paper-based; 213 computer-based; 80 iBT), IELTS (minimum score 6.5), TWE (minimum score 4). Electronic applications accepted. *Faculty research:* Social personality, behavioral neuroscience, life-span development.

Brown University, Graduate School, Department of Neuroscience, Providence, RI 02912. Offers PhD. *Degree requirements:* For doctorate, comprehensive exam, thesis/dissertation. *Entrance requirements:* For doctorate, GRE.

Brown University, Graduate School, Department of Psychology, Providence, RI 02912. Offers behavioral neuroscience (PhD); cognitive processes (PhD); sensation and perception (PhD); social/developmental (PhD); MS/PhD. *Degree requirements:* For doctorate, thesis/dissertation. *Entrance requirements:* For doctorate, GRE General Test, GRE Subject Test.

Brown University, Graduate School, Division of Biology and Medicine, Department of Neuroscience, Providence, RI 02912. Offers PhD. *Degree requirements:* For doctorate, thesis/dissertation, preliminary exam. *Entrance requirements:* For doctorate, GRE General Test, GRE Subject Test. Additional exam requirements/recommendations for international students: Required—TOEFL. Electronic applications accepted. *Faculty research:* Neurophysiology, systems neuroscience, membrane biophysics, neuropharmacology, sensory systems.

Brown University, National Institutes of Health Sponsored Programs, Department of Neuroscience, Providence, RI 02912. Offers PhD. *Degree requirements:* For doctorate, comprehensive exam, thesis/dissertation.

California Institute of Technology, Division of Engineering and Applied Science, Option in Computation and Neural Systems, Pasadena, CA 91125-0001. Offers MS, PhD. *Faculty:* 3 full-time (0 women). *Students:* 40 full-time (10 women). 114 applicants, 14% accepted, 7 enrolled. In 2009, 1 master's, 6 doctorates awarded. Terminal master's awarded for partial completion of doctoral program. *Degree requirements:* For doctorate, thesis/dissertation, qualifying exam. *Entrance requirements:* For doctorate, GRE General Test. *Application deadline:* For fall admission, 1/1 for domestic students. Application fee: $0. *Financial support:* In 2009–10, 10 fellowships, 23 research assistantships, 3 teaching assistantships were awarded; Federal Work-Study and institutionally sponsored loans also available. Financial award application deadline: 1/15. *Faculty research:* Biological and artificial computational devices, modeling of sensory processes and learning, theory of collective computation. *Unit head:* Dr. Pietro Perona, Executive Officer, 626-395-4867, E-mail: perona@its.caltech.edu. *Application contact:* Natalie Gilmore, Assistant Dean of Graduate Studies, 626-395-3812, Fax: 626-577-9246, E-mail: ngilmore@caltech.edu.

Carleton University, Faculty of Graduate Studies, Faculty of Arts and Social Sciences, Department of Psychology, Ottawa, ON K1S 5B6, Canada. Offers neuroscience (M Sc); psychology (MA, PhD). Part-time programs available. *Degree requirements:* For master's, thesis; for doctorate, comprehensive exam, thesis/dissertation. *Entrance requirements:* For master's, honors degree; for doctorate, GRE, master's degree. Additional exam requirements/recommendations for international students: Required—TOEFL. *Faculty research:* Behavioral neuroscience, social and personality psychology, cognitive/perception, developmental psychology, computer user research and evaluation, forensic psychology, health psychology.

Carnegie Mellon University, Center for the Neural Basis of Cognition, Pittsburgh, PA 15213-3891. Offers PhD.

Case Western Reserve University, School of Medicine and School of Graduate Studies, Graduate Programs in Medicine, Department of Neurosciences, Cleveland, OH 44106. Offers neurobiology (PhD); neuroscience (PhD); MD/PhD. *Degree requirements:* For doctorate, thesis/dissertation. *Entrance requirements:* For doctorate, GRE General Test, 3 letters of recommendation. Additional exam requirements/recommendations for international students: Required—TOEFL. Electronic applications accepted. *Faculty research:* Neurotropic factors, synapse formation, regeneration, determination of cell fate, cellular neuroscience.

Central Michigan University, College of Graduate Studies, College of Humanities and Social and Behavioral Sciences, Department of Psychology, Program in Neuroscience, Mount Pleasant, MI 48859. Offers MS, PhD. *Degree requirements:* For master's, comprehensive exam, thesis or alternative; for doctorate, thesis/dissertation. *Entrance requirements:* For master's and doctorate, GRE. Electronic applications accepted.

College of Staten Island of the City University of New York, Graduate Programs, Center for Developmental Neuroscience and Developmental Disabilities, Staten Island, NY 10314-6600. Offers neuroscience, mental retardation and developmental disabilities (MS). Part-time and evening/weekend programs available. *Faculty:* 6 full-time (1 woman), 3 part-time/adjunct (1 woman). *Students:* 39 part-time (20 women); includes 6 minority (2 African Americans, 4 Asian Americans or Pacific Islanders), 5 international. Average age 26. 38 applicants, 71% accepted, 20 enrolled. In 2009, 8 master's awarded. *Degree requirements:* For master's, thesis, oral preliminary exam, thesis defense. *Entrance requirements:* For master's, 3 letters of recommendation; minimum GPA of 3.0 in undergraduate biology, mathematics, psychology or other science courses; 2 semesters of course work in biology, chemistry and psychology; 1 semester of course work in calculus and statistics. Additional exam requirements/recommendations for international students: Required—TOEFL (minimum score 550 paper-

based; 213 computer-based; 79 iBT). *Application deadline:* Applications are processed on a rolling basis. Application fee: $125. Electronic applications accepted. *Expenses:* Tuition, state resident: full-time $7360; part-time $310 per credit. Tuition, nonresident: part-time $575 per credit. Required fees: $378; $113 per semester. *Financial support:* Career-related internships or fieldwork, Federal Work-Study, and scholarships/grants available. Support available to part-time students. Financial award applicants required to submit FAFSA. *Unit head:* Dr. Probal Banerjee, Coordinator, 718-982-3950, Fax: 718-982-3953, E-mail: banerjee@mail.csi.cuny.edu. *Application contact:* Sasha Spence, Assistant Director of Graduate Recruitment and Admissions, 718-982-2699, Fax: 718-982-2500, E-mail: sasha.spence@csi.cuny.edu.

Colorado State University, Graduate School, Program in Molecular, Cellular and Integrative Neurosciences, Fort Collins, CO 80523-1617. Offers PhD. *Students:* 6 full-time (4 women). Average age 23. 27 applicants, 19% accepted, 5 enrolled. *Entrance requirements:* For doctorate, GRE, minimum GPA of 3.0, letter of recommendation. Additional exam requirements/recommendations for international students: Required—TOEFL (minimum score 630 paper-based; 267 computer-based; 109 iBT). *Application deadline:* For fall admission, 1/1 priority date for domestic and international students. Application fee: $50. *Expenses:* Tuition, state resident: full-time $6434; part-time $359.10 per credit. Tuition, nonresident: full-time $18,116; part-time $1006.45 per credit. Required fees: $1496; $83 per credit. *Financial support:* In 2009–10, 4 students received support, including 4 research assistantships with partial tuition reimbursements available (averaging $10,598 per year); fellowships, teaching assistantships with partial tuition reimbursements available, scholarships/grants, health care benefits, and unspecified assistantships also available. Financial award application deadline: 1/1; financial award applicants required to submit FAFSA. *Faculty research:* Ion channels, synaptic mechanisms, neuronal circuitry, degeneration and regeneration, artificial neural networks. *Unit head:* Dr. James Bamburg, Professor and Director, 970-491-0425, Fax: 970-491-7907, E-mail: james.bamburg@colostate.edu. *Application contact:* Nancy Graham, Administrative Assistant, 970-491-0425, Fax: 970-491-7907, E-mail: njgraham@colostate.edu.

Cornell University, Joan and Sanford I. Weill Medical College and Graduate School of Medical Sciences, Weill Cornell Graduate School of Medical Sciences, Neuroscience Program, New York, NY 10065. Offers MS, PhD. *Faculty:* 29 full-time (8 women). *Students:* 41 full-time (25 women); includes 8 minority (3 African Americans, 4 Asian Americans or Pacific Islanders, 1 Hispanic American), 8 international. Average age 22. 83 applicants, 19% accepted, 5 enrolled. In 2009, 2 master's, 10 doctorates awarded. Terminal master's awarded for partial completion of doctoral program. *Degree requirements:* For master's, comprehensive exam; for doctorate, thesis/dissertation, final exam. *Entrance requirements:* For doctorate, GRE General Test, undergraduate training in biology, organic chemistry, physics, and mathematics. Additional exam requirements/recommendations for international students: Required—TOEFL. *Application deadline:* For fall admission, 12/1 for domestic students. Application fee: $60. Electronic applications accepted. *Expenses:* Tuition: Full-time $44,650. Required fees: $2805. *Financial support:* In 2009–10, 4 fellowships (averaging $20,976 per year) were awarded; scholarships/grants, health care benefits, and stipends (given to all students) also available. *Faculty research:* Regulation of neuronal development, neuronal stem cells, information processing, behavior, neuronal plasticity. *Unit head:* Dr. Betty Jo Casey, Director, 212-746-5832, E-mail: bjc2002@med.cornell.edu. *Application contact:* Alime Lukaj, Program Coordinator, 212-746-6582, E-mail: alukaj@med.cornell.edu.

Dalhousie University, Faculty of Graduate Studies, Neuroscience Institute, Halifax, NS B3H 4H7, Canada. Offers M Sc, PhD. *Degree requirements:* For doctorate, thesis/dissertation. *Entrance requirements:* For master's and doctorate, 4 year honors degree or equivalent, minimum A- average. Additional exam requirements/recommendations for international students: Required—TOEFL, IELTS, 1 of the following 5 approved tests: TOEFL, IELTS, CANTEST, CAEL, Michigan English Language Assessment Battery. Electronic applications accepted. *Faculty research:* Molecular, cellular, systems, behavioral and clinical neuroscience.

Dalhousie University, Faculty of Science, Department of Psychology, Halifax, NS B3H 4R2, Canada. Offers clinical psychology (PhD); psychology (M Sc, PhD); psychology/neuroscience (M Sc, PhD). *Accreditation:* APA (one or more programs are accredited). *Faculty:* 30 full-time (8 women), 34 part-time/adjunct (14 women). *Students:* 56 full-time (35 women); includes 2 minority (both Asian Americans or Pacific Islanders). 200 applicants, 8% accepted. In 2009, 8 master's, 7 doctorates awarded. *Degree requirements:* For master's, thesis; for doctorate, thesis/dissertation. *Entrance requirements:* For doctorate, GRE General Test. Additional exam requirements/recommendations for international students: Required—TOEFL, IELTS, CANTEST, CAEL, or Michigan English Language Assessment Battery. Application fee: $70. Electronic applications accepted. *Financial support:* In 2009–10, 19 fellowships, 26 teaching assistantships (averaging $1,853 per year) were awarded; career-related internships or fieldwork, scholarships/grants, and health care benefits also available. Financial award application deadline: 2/1. *Faculty research:* Physiological psychology, psychology of learning, learning and behavior, forensic clinical health psychology, development perception and cognition. Total annual research expenditures: $1.9 million. *Unit head:* Dr. Tracy Taylor-Helmick, Graduate Coordinator, 902-494-3001, Fax: 902-494-6585, E-mail: tracy.taylor.helmick@dal.ca. *Application contact:* Mary Macconnachie, Graduate Secretary, 902-494-3839, Fax: 902-494-6585, E-mail: mary.macconnachie@dal.ca.

Dartmouth College, Arts and Sciences Graduate Programs, Department of Psychological and Brain Sciences, Hanover, NH 03755. Offers cognitive neuroscience (PhD); psychology (PhD). *Faculty:* 20 full-time (6 women). *Students:* 32 full-time (16 women); includes 4 minority (1 African American, 2 Asian Americans or Pacific Islanders, 1 Hispanic American), 8 international. Average age 26. 88 applicants, 15% accepted, 8 enrolled. In 2009, 1 doctorate awarded. *Degree requirements:* For doctorate, thesis/dissertation. *Entrance requirements:* For doctorate, GRE General Test, GRE Subject Test. Additional exam requirements/recommendations for international students: Required—TOEFL. *Application deadline:* For fall admission, 1/15 priority date for domestic students. Application fee: $40. *Financial support:* In 2009–10, 24 students received support, including fellowships with full tuition reimbursements available (averaging $23,832 per year), research assistantships with full tuition reimbursements available (averaging $23,832 per year), teaching assistantships (averaging $23,832 per year); institutionally sponsored loans, traineeships, tuition waivers (full), and unspecified assistantships also available. *Faculty research:* Behavioral neuroscience, cognitive neuroscience, cognitive science, social/personality psychology. *Unit head:* Dr. Howard C. Hughes, Chair, 603-646-3181, Fax: 603-646-1419, E-mail: howard.hughes@dartmouth.edu. *Application contact:* Nancy Tenney, Department Administrator, 603-646-3181, E-mail: nancy.tenney@dartmouth.edu.

Dartmouth College, Arts and Sciences Graduate Programs, Program in Experimental and Molecular Medicine, The Neuroscience Center, Hanover, NH 03755. Offers PhD, MD/PhD. Degrees awarded through participating programs. *Students:* 138 applicants, 20% accepted, 13 enrolled. *Entrance requirements:* Additional exam requirements/recommendations for international students: Required—TOEFL (minimum score 620 paper-based; 260 computer-based; 105 iBT). *Application deadline:* For fall admission, 1/15 for domestic students, 10/1 for international students. Application fee: $50. Electronic applications accepted. *Financial support:* In 2009–10, fellowships with full tuition reimbursements (averaging $25,500 per year), research assistantships with full tuition reimbursements (averaging $25,500 per year) were awarded; teaching assistantships with full tuition reimbursements, tuition waivers (full) also available. *Unit head:* Dr. Alan Eastman, Director, 603-650-4933, Fax: 603-650-4932. *Application contact:* Information Contact, 603-650-8561, Fax: 603-650-8449, E-mail: neurosciencecenter@dartmouth.edu.

Dartmouth College, Program in Experimental and Molecular Medicine, Neuroscience Track, Hanover, NH 03755. Offers PhD.

Delaware State University, Graduate Programs, Department of Biology, Dover, DE 19901-2277. Offers biological sciences (MA, MS); biology education (MS); molecular and cellular neuroscience (MS); neuroscience (PhD). Part-time and evening/weekend programs available. *Degree requirements:* For master's, thesis (for some programs). *Entrance requirements:* For

Neuroscience

Delaware State University (continued)
master's, GRE, minimum GPA of 3.0 in major, 2.75 overall. Additional exam requirements/recommendations for international students: Required—TOEFL (minimum score 550 paper-based). Electronic applications accepted. *Faculty research:* Cell biology, immunology, microbiology, genetics, ecology.

Drexel University, College of Arts and Sciences, Department of Psychology, Clinical Psychology Program, Philadelphia, PA 19104-2875. Offers clinical psychology (PhD); forensic psychology (PhD); health psychology (PhD); neuropsychology (PhD). *Accreditation:* APA. Terminal master's awarded for partial completion of doctoral program. *Degree requirements:* For doctorate, thesis/dissertation, qualifying exam. *Entrance requirements:* For doctorate, GRE General Test, GRE Subject Test, minimum GPA of 3.0. Electronic applications accepted. *Expenses:* Contact institution. *Faculty research:* Cognitive behavioral therapy, stress and coping, eating disorders, substance abuse, developmental disabilities.

Drexel University, College of Medicine, Biomedical Graduate Programs, Program in Neuroscience, Philadelphia, PA 19104-2875. Offers MS, PhD, MD/PhD. *Degree requirements:* For doctorate, thesis/dissertation, qualifying exam. *Entrance requirements:* For doctorate, GRE General Test, or MCAT, minimum GPA of 2.75. Additional exam requirements/recommendations for international students: Required—TOEFL. Electronic applications accepted. *Faculty research:* Central monoamine systems, drugs of abuse, anatomy/physiology of sensory systems, neurodegenerative disorders and recovery of function, neuromodulation and synaptic plasticity.

Duke University, Graduate School, Department of Cognitive Neuroscience, Durham, NC 27708-0586. Offers PhD, Certificate. *Faculty:* 39 full-time. *Students:* 6 full-time (3 women); includes 1 minority (African American), 1 international. 59 applicants, 19% accepted, 5 enrolled. *Degree requirements:* For doctorate, thesis/dissertation. *Entrance requirements:* For doctorate, GRE. Additional exam requirements/recommendations for international students: Required—TOEFL (minimum score 550 paper-based; 213 computer-based; 83 iBT), IELTS (minimum score 7). *Application deadline:* For fall admission, 12/8 priority date for domestic and international students. Application fee: $75. Electronic applications accepted. *Financial support:* Fellowships, research assistantships, teaching assistantships available. Financial award application deadline: 12/8. *Unit head:* Elizabeth Brannon, Director of Graduate Studies, 919-668-6201, Fax: 919-684-3422, E-mail: beth.peloquin@duke.edu. *Application contact:* Cynthia Robertson, Associate Dean for Enrollment Services, 919-684-3913, E-mail: grad-admissions@duke.edu.

Emory University, Graduate School of Arts and Sciences, Department of Psychology, Atlanta, GA 30322-1100. Offers clinical psychology (PhD); cognition and development (PhD); neuroscience and animal behavior (PhD). *Accreditation:* APA. *Degree requirements:* For doctorate, comprehensive exam, thesis/dissertation. *Entrance requirements:* For doctorate, GRE General Test, minimum GPA of 3.25. Additional exam requirements/recommendations for international students: Required—TOEFL. Electronic applications accepted. *Faculty research:* Neuroscience and animal behavior; adult and child psychopathology, cognition development assessment.

Emory University, Graduate School of Arts and Sciences, Division of Biological and Biomedical Sciences, Program in Neuroscience, Atlanta, GA 30322-1100. Offers PhD. *Faculty:* 108 full-time (25 women). *Students:* 98 full-time (62 women); includes 16 minority (4 African Americans, 3 Asian Americans or Pacific Islanders, 9 Hispanic Americans), 5 international. Average age 27. 134 applicants, 17% accepted, 13 enrolled. In 2009, 15 doctorates awarded. *Degree requirements:* For doctorate, comprehensive exam, thesis/dissertation. *Entrance requirements:* For doctorate, GRE General Test, minimum GPA of 3.0 in science course work (recommended). Additional exam requirements/recommendations for international students: Required—TOEFL. *Application deadline:* For fall admission, 1/3 for domestic and international students. Application fee: $50. Electronic applications accepted. *Financial support:* In 2009–10, 30 students received support, including 30 fellowships with full tuition reimbursements available (averaging $24,500 per year); institutionally sponsored loans, scholarships/grants, and health care benefits also available. *Faculty research:* Cell and molecular biology, development, behavior, neurodegenerative disease. *Unit head:* Dr. Yoland Smith, Director, 404-727-7519, Fax: 404-727-3278, E-mail: yolands@rmy.emory.edu. *Application contact:* Dr. Gary Bassell, Recruiter, 404-727-3772, Fax: 404-727-6256, E-mail: gary.bassell@emory.edu.

Florida Atlantic University, Charles E. Schmidt College of Science, Center for Complex Systems and Brain Sciences, Boca Raton, FL 33431-0991. Offers PhD. *Faculty:* 3 full-time (1 woman). *Students:* 13 full-time (6 women), 5 part-time (2 women); includes 1 minority (Hispanic American), 5 international. Average age 34. 14 applicants, 21% accepted, 1 enrolled. In 2009, 2 doctorates awarded. *Degree requirements:* For doctorate, thesis/dissertation. *Entrance requirements:* For doctorate, GRE General Test, minimum GPA of 3.0 in last 60 hours of undergraduate course work. Additional exam requirements/recommendations for international students: Required—TOEFL. *Application deadline:* For fall admission, 1/15 priority date for domestic and international students. Application fee: $30. *Expenses:* Tuition, state resident: full-time $7055; part-time $293.94 per credit hour. Tuition, nonresident: full-time $22,096; part-time $920.66 per credit hour. *Financial support:* Fellowships with full tuition reimbursements, research assistantships with partial tuition reimbursements, teaching assistantships with partial tuition reimbursements, Federal Work-Study, traineeships, and unspecified assistantships available. *Faculty research:* Motor behavior, speech perception, nonlinear dynamics and fractals, behavioral neuroscience, cellular and molecular neuroscience. *Unit head:* Dr. Janet Blanks, Director, 561-297-2229, Fax: 561-297-3634, E-mail: blanks@ccs.fau.edu. *Application contact:* Rhona Frankel, Associate Director, 561-297-2230, E-mail: frankel@fau.edu.

Florida State University, College of Medicine, Department of Biomedical Sciences, Tallahassee, FL 32306-4300. Offers biomedical sciences (PhD); neuroscience (PhD). *Faculty:* 31 full-time (10 women). *Students:* 30 full-time (16 women); includes 2 minority (both Hispanic Americans), 12 international. Average age 27. 67 applicants, 13% accepted, 7 enrolled. In 2009, 2 doctorates awarded. *Degree requirements:* For doctorate, thesis/dissertation. *Entrance requirements:* For doctorate, GRE (minimum score: 1000). Additional exam requirements/recommendations for international students: Required—TOEFL (minimum score 550 paper-based; 80 iBT). *Application deadline:* For fall admission, 2/1 for domestic and international students. Application fee: $30. *Expenses:* Tuition, state resident: full-time $7413. Tuition, nonresident: full-time $22,567. *Financial support:* In 2009–10, 30 students received support, including 30 research assistantships with full tuition reimbursements available (averaging $21,500 per year). Financial award applicants required to submit FAFSA. *Unit head:* Dr. Myra M. Hurt, Senior Associate Dean for Research and Graduate Programs, 850-644-2015, Fax: 850-645-7153, E-mail: myra.hurt@med.fsu.edu. *Application contact:* Denise Renee Newsome, Academic Program Specialist, 850-645-6420, Fax: 850-645-7153, E-mail: denise.newsome@med.fsu.edu.

Florida State University, The Graduate School, College of Arts and Sciences, Department of Biological Science, Tallahassee, FL 32306-4295. Offers cell and molecular biology and genetics (MS, PhD); ecology and evolutionary biology (MS, PhD); neuroscience (PhD). *Faculty:* 52 full-time (15 women). *Students:* 106 full-time (58 women); includes 14 minority (2 African Americans, 1 American Indian/Alaska Native, 4 Asian Americans or Pacific Islanders, 7 Hispanic Americans), 12 international. 268 applicants, 16% accepted, 28 enrolled. In 2009, 10 master's, 10 doctorates awarded. Terminal master's awarded for partial completion of doctoral program. *Degree requirements:* For master's, comprehensive exam, thesis, teaching experience, seminar presentations; for doctorate, comprehensive exam, thesis/dissertation, teaching experience; seminar presentations. *Entrance requirements:* For master's, GRE General Test (minimum combined score 1100, 500 verbal, 500 quantitative), minimum upper division GPA of 3.0; for doctorate, GRE General Test (minimum combined score 1100, Verbal 500, Quantitative 500), minimum upper division GPA of 3.0. Additional exam requirements/recommendations for international students: Required—TOEFL (minimum score 600 paper-based; 250 computer-based; 92 iBT). *Application deadline:* For fall admission, 12/15 for domestic and international students. Application fee: $30. Electronic applications accepted. *Expenses:* Tuition, state resident: full-time $7413. Tuition, nonresident: full-time $22,567. *Financial support:* In 2009–10, 104 students received support, including 9 fellowships with full tuition reimbursements available (averaging $22,000 per year), 28 research assistantships with full tuition reimbursements available (averaging $20,000 per year), 67 teaching assistantships with full tuition reimbursements available (averaging $18,540 per year); traineeships and unspecified assistantships also available. Financial award application deadline: 12/15; financial award applicants required to submit FAFSA. *Faculty research:* Cell and molecular biology and genetics, ecology and evolutionary biology. *Unit head:* Dr. George W. Bates, Professor and Associate Chairman, 850-644-5749, Fax: 850-644-9829, E-mail: bates@bio.fsu.edu. *Application contact:* Judy Bowers, Coordinator, Graduate Affairs, 850-644-3023, Fax: 850-644-9829, E-mail: gradinfo@bio.fsu.edu.

Florida State University, The Graduate School, College of Arts and Sciences, Department of Psychology, Interdisciplinary Program in Neuroscience, Tallahassee, FL 32306. Offers PhD. *Faculty:* 11 full-time (4 women). *Students:* 30 full-time (18 women); includes 7 minority (2 African Americans, 2 Asian Americans or Pacific Islanders, 3 Hispanic Americans). Average age 26. 45 applicants, 31% accepted, 9 enrolled. *Degree requirements:* For doctorate, thesis/dissertation, preliminary exam. *Entrance requirements:* For doctorate, GRE General Test, minimum GPA of 3.0, research experience, letters of recommendation. Additional exam requirements/recommendations for international students: Required—TOEFL (minimum score 550 paper-based; 213 computer-based; 80 iBT). *Application deadline:* For fall admission, 12/1 for domestic and international students. Application fee: $30. Electronic applications accepted. *Expenses:* Tuition, state resident: full-time $7413. Tuition, nonresident: full-time $22,567. *Financial support:* In 2009–10, 22 students received support, including 4 fellowships with full tuition reimbursements available (averaging $20,772 per year), 11 research assistantships with full tuition reimbursements available (averaging $20,772 per year), 7 teaching assistantships with full tuition reimbursements available (averaging $17,500 per year); Federal Work-Study, institutionally sponsored loans, scholarships/grants, traineeships, health care benefits, and unspecified assistantships also available. Financial award applicants required to submit FAFSA. *Faculty research:* Sensory processes, neural development and plasticity, circadian rhythms, behavioral and molecular genetics, hormonal control of behavior. Total annual research expenditures: $2.4 million. *Unit head:* Dr. Richard Hyson, Director, 850-644-3076, Fax: 850-645-0349, E-mail: hyson@psy.fsu.edu. *Application contact:* Cherie P. Miller, Graduate Program Assistant, 850-644-2499, Fax: 850-644-7739, E-mail: grad-info@psy.fsu.edu.

George Mason University, College of Science, Fairfax, VA 22030. Offers biodefense (MS, PhD); bioinformatics and computational biology (MS, PhD, Certificate); biology (MS, PhD), including bioinformatics (MS), ecology, systematics and evolution (MS), interpretive biology (MS), molecular and cellular biology (MS), molecular and microbiology (PhD), organismal biology (MS); chemistry and biochemistry (MS), including chemistry; climate dynamics (PhD); computational and data sciences (MS, PhD, Certificate); computational social science (PhD); computational techniques and applications (Certificate); earth systems and geoinformation sciences (MS, PhD, Certificate); environmental science and policy (MS, PhD); geography (MS), including geographic and cartographic sciences; mathematical sciences (MS, PhD), including mathematics; nanotechnology and nanoscience (Certificate); neuroscience (PhD); physical sciences (PhD); physics and astronomy (MS), including applied and engineering physics; remote sensing and earth image processing (Certificate). Part-time and evening/weekend programs available. *Degree requirements:* For doctorate, comprehensive exam, thesis/dissertation. *Entrance requirements:* For master's and doctorate, GRE General Test, minimum GPA of 3.0 in last 60 hours. Additional exam requirements/recommendations for international students: Required—TOEFL. Electronic applications accepted. *Expenses:* Tuition, state resident: full-time $7568; part-time $315.33 per credit hour. Tuition, nonresident: full-time $21,704; part-time $904.33 per credit hour. Required fees: $2184; $91 per credit hour. *Faculty research:* Space sciences and astrophysics, fluid dynamics, materials modeling and simulation, bioinformatics, global changes and statistics.

Georgetown University, Graduate School of Arts and Sciences, Programs in Biomedical Sciences, Program in Neuroscience, Washington, DC 20057. Offers PhD, MD/PhD. *Degree requirements:* For doctorate, thesis/dissertation. *Entrance requirements:* For doctorate, GRE General Test. Additional exam requirements/recommendations for international students: Required—TOEFL.

Graduate School and University Center of the City University of New York, Graduate Studies, Program in Psychology, New York, NY 10016-4039. Offers basic applied neurocognition (PhD); biopsychology (PhD); clinical psychology (PhD); developmental psychology (PhD); environmental psychology (PhD); experimental psychology (PhD); industrial psychology (PhD); learning processes (PhD); neuropsychology (PhD); psychology (PhD); social personality (PhD). *Faculty:* 119 full-time (40 women). *Students:* 559 full-time (414 women), 1 part-time (0 women); includes 101 minority (34 African Americans, 25 Asian Americans or Pacific Islanders, 42 Hispanic Americans), 57 international. Average age 33. 750 applicants, 16% accepted, 84 enrolled. In 2009, 54 doctorates awarded. *Degree requirements:* For doctorate, one foreign language, thesis/dissertation. *Entrance requirements:* For doctorate, GRE General Test. Additional exam requirements/recommendations for international students: Required—TOEFL. *Application deadline:* For fall admission, 12/15 priority date for domestic students. Application fee: $125. Electronic applications accepted. *Financial support:* In 2009–10, 371 students received support, including 340 fellowships, 34 research assistantships, 33 teaching assistantships; career-related internships or fieldwork, Federal Work-Study, institutionally sponsored loans, and tuition waivers (full and partial) also available. Financial award application deadline: 2/1; financial award applicants required to submit FAFSA. *Unit head:* Dr. Joseph Glick, Executive Officer, 212-817-8706, Fax: 212-817-1533, E-mail: jglick@gc.cuny.edu. *Application contact:* Les Gribben, Director of Admissions, 212-817-7470, Fax: 212-817-1624, E-mail: lgribben@gc.cuny.edu.

Harvard University, Graduate School of Arts and Sciences, Program in Neuroscience, Boston, MA 02115. Offers neurobiology (PhD). *Degree requirements:* For doctorate, thesis/dissertation, qualifying exam. *Entrance requirements:* For doctorate, GRE General Test, GRE Subject Test. Additional exam requirements/recommendations for international students: Required—TOEFL. *Expenses:* Tuition: Full-time $33,696. Required fees: $1126. Full-time tuition and fees vary according to program. *Faculty research:* Relationship between diseases of the nervous system and basic science.

Illinois State University, Graduate School, College of Arts and Sciences, Department of Biological Sciences, Normal, IL 61790-2200. Offers animal behavior (MS); bacteriology (MS); biochemistry (MS); biological sciences (MS); biology (PhD); biophysics (MS); biotechnology (MS); botany (MS, PhD); cell biology (MS); conservation biology (MS); developmental biology (MS); ecology (MS, PhD); entomology (MS); evolutionary biology (MS); genetics (MS, PhD); immunology (MS); microbiology (MS, PhD); molecular biology (MS); molecular genetics (MS); neurobiology (MS); neuroscience (MS); parasitology (MS); physiology (MS, PhD); plant biology (MS); plant molecular biology (MS); plant sciences (MS); structural biology (MS); zoology (MS, PhD). Part-time programs available. *Degree requirements:* For master's, thesis or alternative; for doctorate, variable foreign language requirement, thesis/dissertation, 2 terms of residency. *Entrance requirements:* For master's, GRE General Test, minimum GPA of 2.6 in last 60 hours of course work; for doctorate, GRE General Test. *Faculty research:* Redoc balance and drug development in schistosoma mansoni, control of the growth of listeria monocytogenes at low temperature, regulation of cell expansion and microtubule function by SPRI, CRUI: physiology and fitness consequences of different life history phenotypes.

Indiana University Bloomington, University Graduate School, College of Arts and Sciences, Program in Neuroscience, Bloomington, IN 47405-7000. Offers PhD. *Students:* 16 full-time (8 women); includes 1 minority (African American), 4 international. Average age 29. 37 applicants, 11% accepted, 2 enrolled. In 2009, 3 doctorates awarded. Application fee: $55 ($65 for international students). *Financial support:* Fellowships with tuition reimbursements, teaching assistantships with tuition reimbursements available. *Unit head:* George Rebec, Director of Graduate Studies, 812-855-4832, E-mail: rebec@indiana.edu. *Application contact:* Faye Caylor, Administrative Assistant, 812-855-7756, E-mail: fcaylor@indiana.edu.

Iowa State University of Science and Technology, Graduate College, Interdisciplinary Programs, Program in Neuroscience, Ames, IA 50011. Offers MS, PhD. *Students:* 11 full-time (5 women); includes 2 minority (both Asian Americans or Pacific Islanders), 4 international. In 2009, 1 master's, 4 doctorates awarded. Terminal master's awarded for partial completion of doctoral program. *Degree requirements:* For master's, thesis; for doctorate, thesis/dissertation. *Entrance requirements:* For master's and doctorate, GRE General Test, resume. Additional exam requirements/recommendations for international students: Required—TOEFL (minimum score 580 paper-based; 85 iBT) or IELTS (minimum score 7). *Application deadline:* For fall admission, 2/1 priority date for domestic students, 2/1 for international students. Application fee: $40 ($90 for international students). *Expenses:* Tuition, state resident: full-time $6716. Tuition, nonresident: full-time $8908. Tuition and fees vary according to course level, course load, program and student level. *Financial support:* In 2009–10, 9 research assistantships with full and partial tuition reimbursements (averaging $18,340 per year), 2 teaching assistantships with full and partial tuition reimbursements (averaging $16,750 per year) were awarded; scholarships/grants, health care benefits, and unspecified assistantships also available. *Faculty research:* Behavioral pharmacology and immunology, developmental neurobiology, neuroendocrinology, neuroregulatory mechanisms at the cellular level, signal transduction in neurons. *Unit head:* Dr. Donald Sakaguchi, Chair, Supervising Committee, 515-294-7252, E-mail: idgp@iastate.edu. *Application contact:* Katie Blair, Information Contact, 515-294-7252, Fax: 515-924-6790, E-mail: idgp@iastate.edu.

The Johns Hopkins University, School of Medicine, Graduate Programs in Medicine, Neuroscience Training Program, Baltimore, MD 21218-2699. Offers PhD. *Faculty:* 66 full-time (10 women). *Students:* 94 full-time (43 women); includes 18 minority (3 African Americans, 8 Asian Americans or Pacific Islanders, 7 Hispanic Americans), 39 international. Average age 28. 239 applicants, 12% accepted, 13 enrolled. In 2009, 13 doctorates awarded. *Degree requirements:* For doctorate, comprehensive exam, thesis/dissertation, thesis defense. *Entrance requirements:* For doctorate, GRE General Test, bachelor's degree in science or mathematics. Additional exam requirements/recommendations for international students: Required—TOEFL. *Application deadline:* For winter admission, 12/8 for domestic and international students. Application fee: $85. Electronic applications accepted. *Financial support:* In 2009–10, 94 fellowships (averaging $27,125 per year) were awarded; scholarships/grants and tuition waivers (full and partial) also available. Financial award application deadline: 1/1. *Faculty research:* Neurophysiology, neurochemistry, neuroanatomy, pharmacology, development. Total annual research expenditures: $15.5 million. *Unit head:* Dr. David D. Ginty, Professor and Director of Graduate Studies, 410-614-9494, Fax: 410-614-6249, E-mail: dginty@jhmi.edu. *Application contact:* Rita G. Ragan, Graduate Program Manager, 410-955-7947, Fax: 410-614-6249, E-mail: rgragan@jhmi.edu.

Kent State University, School of Biomedical Sciences, Program in Neuroscience, Kent, OH 44242-0001. Offers MS, PhD. Offered in cooperation with Northeastern Ohio Universities College of Medicine. Terminal master's awarded for partial completion of doctoral program. *Degree requirements:* For master's, thesis; for doctorate, thesis/dissertation. *Entrance requirements:* For master's and doctorate, GRE General Test, minimum GPA of 3.0. Additional exam requirements/recommendations for international students: Required—TOEFL. Electronic applications accepted. *Faculty research:* Plasticity of the nervous system, learning and memory processes–neural correlates, neuroendocrinology of cyclic behavior, synaptic neurochemistry.

Lehigh University, College of Arts and Sciences, Department of Biological Sciences, Bethlehem, PA 18015. Offers biochemistry (PhD); integrative biology and neuroscience (PhD); molecular biology (MS, PhD). Part-time programs available. Postbaccalaureate distance learning degree programs offered (no on-campus study). *Faculty:* 17 full-time (6 women), 1 (woman) part-time/adjunct. *Students:* 33 full-time (15 women), 37 part-time (25 women); includes 7 minority (1 African American, 3 Asian Americans or Pacific Islanders, 3 Hispanic Americans), 6 international. Average age 29. 45 applicants, 24% accepted, 11 enrolled. In 2009, 20 master's, 4 doctorates awarded. Terminal master's awarded for partial completion of doctoral program. *Degree requirements:* For master's, research report; for doctorate, comprehensive exam, thesis/dissertation. *Entrance requirements:* For doctorate, GRE General Test. Additional exam requirements/recommendations for international students: Required—TOEFL. *Application deadline:* For fall admission, 12/15 for domestic and international students. Applications are processed on a rolling basis. Application fee: $65. Electronic applications accepted. *Financial support:* In 2009–10, 34 students received support, including 4 fellowships with full tuition reimbursements available (averaging $23,000 per year), 6 research assistantships with full tuition reimbursements available (averaging $23,000 per year), 16 teaching assistantships with full tuition reimbursements available (averaging $23,000 per year); scholarships/grants, tuition waivers (full and partial), and unspecified assistantships also available. Financial award application deadline: 1/15. *Faculty research:* Gene expression, cytoskeleton and cell structure, cell cycle and growth regulation, neuroscience, animal behavior. Total annual research expenditures: $2 million. *Unit head:* Dr. Murray Itzkowitz, Chairperson, 610-758-3680, Fax: 610-758-4004, E-mail: mi00@lehigh.edu. *Application contact:* Dr. Jennifer M. Swann, Graduate Coordinator, 610-758-5484, Fax: 610-758-4004, E-mail: jms5@lehigh.edu.

Louisiana State University Health Sciences Center, School of Graduate Studies in New Orleans, Interdisciplinary Neuroscience Graduate Program, New Orleans, LA 70112-2223. Offers MS, PhD, MD/PhD. *Degree requirements:* For master's, comprehensive exam, thesis; for doctorate, comprehensive exam, thesis/dissertation. *Entrance requirements:* For master's, GRE; for doctorate, GRE General Test, GRE Subject Test, previous course work in chemistry, mathematics, physics, and computer science. Additional exam requirements/recommendations for international students: Required—TOEFL. *Faculty research:* Visual system, second messengers, drugs and behavior, signal transduction, plasticity and development.

Loyola University Chicago, Graduate School, Program in Neuroscience, Maywood, IL 60153. Offers MS, PhD, MD/PhD. *Faculty:* 20 full-time (9 women). *Students:* 19 full-time (14 women), 4 international. Average age 27. 64 applicants, 8% accepted, 4 enrolled. In 2009, 2 doctorates awarded. Terminal master's awarded for partial completion of doctoral program. *Degree requirements:* For master's, comprehensive exam, thesis; for doctorate, comprehensive exam, thesis/dissertation. *Entrance requirements:* For master's, GRE or MCAT; for doctorate, GRE General Test. Additional exam requirements/recommendations for international students: Required—TOEFL (minimum score 600 paper-based; 220 computer-based). *Application deadline:* For fall admission, 3/15 priority date for domestic and international students. Applications are processed on a rolling basis. Application fee: $50. Electronic applications accepted. *Expenses:* Tuition: Full-time $14,220; part-time $790 per credit hour. Required fees: $60 per semester hour. Tuition and fees vary according to program. *Financial support:* In 2009–10, 6 fellowships with full tuition reimbursements (averaging $23,000 per year) were awarded; Federal Work-Study, scholarships/grants, and health care benefits also available. Financial award application deadline: 3/15; financial award applicants required to submit FAFSA. *Faculty research:* Parkinson's disease, drugs of abuse, neuroendocrinology, neuroimmunology, neurotoxicity. Total annual research expenditures: $3.5 million. *Unit head:* Dr. Edward J. Neafsey, Director, 708-216-3355, Fax: 708-216-6823, E-mail: eneafse@lumc.edu. *Application contact:* Peggy Richied, Administrative Secretary, 708-216-4841, Fax: 708-216-6823, E-mail: prichie@lumc.edu.

Massachusetts Institute of Technology, School of Science, Department of Brain and Cognitive Sciences, Cambridge, MA 02139-4307. Offers cognitive science (PhD); neuroscience (PhD). *Faculty:* 38 full-time (14 women). *Students:* 93 full-time (32 women); includes 21 minority (3 African Americans, 1 American Indian/Alaska Native, 9 Asian Americans or Pacific Islanders, 8 Hispanic Americans), 16 international. Average age 27. 371 applicants, 6% accepted, 10 enrolled. In 2009, 13 doctorates awarded. *Degree requirements:* For doctorate, comprehensive exam, thesis/dissertation. *Entrance requirements:* For doctorate, GRE General Test. Additional exam requirements/recommendations for international students: Required—TOEFL (minimum score 577 paper-based; 233 computer-based; 90 iBT), IELTS (minimum score 7). *Application deadline:* For fall admission, 12/10 for domestic and international students. Application fee: $75. Electronic applications accepted. *Expenses:* Tuition: Full-time $37,510; part-time $585 per unit. Required fees: $272. *Financial support:* In 2009–10, 91 students received support, including 61 fellowships with tuition reimbursements available (averaging $27,103 per year), 18 research assistantships with tuition reimbursements available (averaging $29,154 per year), 9 teaching assistantships with tuition reimbursements available (averaging $30,040 per year); Federal Work-Study, institutionally sponsored loans, scholarships/grants, traineeships, health care benefits, and unspecified assistantships also available. *Faculty research:* Vision—perception and physiology, learning, memory, and executive control—molecular and systems approaches, sensorimotor systems—physiology and computation, neural and cognitive development and plasticity, language and high-level cognition—learning, acquisition, and computation. Total annual research expenditures: $19.7 million. *Unit head:* Prof. Mriganka Sur, Head, 617-253-9344, E-mail: bcs-info@mit.edu. *Application contact:* Academic Office, 617-253-7403, Fax: 617-253-9216, E-mail: bcs-admissions@mit.edu.

Mayo Graduate School, Graduate Programs in Biomedical Sciences, Program in Molecular Neuroscience, Rochester, MN 55905. Offers PhD. Program also offered in Jacksonville, FL. *Degree requirements:* For doctorate, oral defense of dissertation, qualifying oral and written exam. *Entrance requirements:* For doctorate, GRE, 1 year of chemistry, biology, calculus, and physics. Additional exam requirements/recommendations for international students: Required—TOEFL. Electronic applications accepted. *Faculty research:* Cholinergic receptor/Alzheimer's; molecular biology, channels, receptors, and mental disease; neuronal cytoskeleton; growth factors; gene regulation.

McGill University, Faculty of Graduate and Postdoctoral Studies, Faculty of Medicine, Department of Neurology and Neurosurgery, Montréal, QC H3A 2T5, Canada. Offers M Sc, PhD.

McMaster University, Faculty of Health Sciences and School of Graduate Studies, Program in Medical Sciences, Neurosciences and Behavioral Sciences Area, Hamilton, ON L8S 4M2, Canada. Offers M Sc, PhD, MD/PhD. *Degree requirements:* For master's, thesis; for doctorate, comprehensive exam, thesis/dissertation. *Entrance requirements:* For master's, honors B Sc, B+ average in related field; for doctorate, M Sc, minimum B+ average, students with proven research experience and an A average may be admitted with a B Sc degree. Additional exam requirements/recommendations for international students: Required—TOEFL (minimum score 580 paper-based; 237 computer-based).

Medical College of Georgia, School of Graduate Studies, Program in Neuroscience, Augusta, GA 30912. Offers PhD. *Degree requirements:* For doctorate, comprehensive exam, thesis/dissertation. *Entrance requirements:* For doctorate, GRE General Test. Additional exam requirements/recommendations for international students: Required—TOEFL (minimum score 550 paper-based; 213 computer-based; 79 iBT). Electronic applications accepted. Full-time tuition and fees vary according to campus/location, program and student level. *Faculty research:* Learning and memory, neuronal migration, synapse formation, regeneration, developmental neurobiology, neurodegeneration and neural repair.

Medical College of Wisconsin, Graduate School of Biomedical Sciences, Program in Cell Biology, Neurobiology and Anatomy, Milwaukee, WI 53226-0509. Offers neuroscience (PhD); MD/PhD. Terminal master's awarded for partial completion of doctoral program. *Degree requirements:* For doctorate, comprehensive exam, thesis/dissertation. *Entrance requirements:* For doctorate, GRE General Test. Additional exam requirements/recommendations for international students: Required—TOEFL. *Faculty research:* Neurobiology, development, neuroscience, teratology.

Medical University of South Carolina, College of Graduate Studies, Department of Neurosciences, Charleston, SC 29425. Offers MS, PhD, DMD/PhD, MD/PhD. *Faculty:* 22 full-time (6 women). *Students:* 14 full-time (3 women), 1 international. Average age 28. 6 applicants, 0% accepted, 0 enrolled.Terminal master's awarded for partial completion of doctoral program. *Degree requirements:* For master's, thesis; for doctorate, thesis/dissertation, oral and written exams. *Entrance requirements:* For master's, GRE General Test; for doctorate, GRE General Test, interview, minimum GPA of 3.0. Additional exam requirements/recommendations for international students: Required—TOEFL (minimum score 600 paper-based; 250 computer-based; 100 iBT). *Application deadline:* For fall admission, 1/15 priority date for domestic and international students. Applications are processed on a rolling basis. Application fee: $0 ($85 for international students). Electronic applications accepted. *Financial support:* In 2009–10, 13 research assistantships with partial tuition reimbursements (averaging $23,000 per year) were awarded; Federal Work-Study and scholarships/grants also available. Support available to part-time students. Financial award application deadline: 3/10; financial award applicants required to submit FAFSA. *Faculty research:* Addiction, aging, movement disorders, membrane physiology, neurotransmission and behavior. *Unit head:* Dr. Peter Kalivas, Chair, 843-792-4400, Fax: 843-792-6590, E-mail: kalivasp@musc.edu. *Application contact:* Dr. L. Judson Chandler, Associate Professor, 843-792-5224, Fax: 843-792-6590, E-mail: chandj@musc.edu.

Meharry Medical College, School of Graduate Studies, Program in Biomedical Sciences, Neuroscience Emphasis, Nashville, TN 37208-9989. Offers PhD, MD/PhD. *Degree requirements:* For doctorate, comprehensive exam, thesis/dissertation. *Entrance requirements:* For doctorate, GRE. *Faculty research:* Neurochemistry, pain, smooth muscle tone, HP axis and peptides neural plasticity.

Memorial University of Newfoundland, Faculty of Medicine and School of Graduate Studies, Graduate Programs in Medicine, Division of Biomedical Sciences, St. John's, NL A1C 5S7, Canada. Offers cancer (M Sc, PhD); cardiovascular (M Sc, PhD); immunology (M Sc, PhD); neuroscience (M Sc, PhD). Part-time programs available. *Degree requirements:* For master's, thesis; for doctorate, comprehensive exam, thesis/dissertation, oral defense of thesis. *Entrance requirements:* For master's, MD or B Sc; for doctorate, MD or M Sc. Additional exam requirements/recommendations for international students: Required—TOEFL. *Faculty research:* Neuroscience, immunology, cardiovascular, and cancer.

Michigan State University, The Graduate School, College of Natural Science, Program in Neuroscience, East Lansing, MI 48824. Offers MS, PhD. *Faculty:* 48 full-time (18 women). *Students:* 25 full-time (15 women), 1 (woman) part-time; includes 4 minority (3 Asian Americans or Pacific Islanders, 1 Hispanic American), 5 international. Average age 26. 57 applicants, 18% accepted. In 2009, 1 master's, 3 doctorates awarded. *Entrance requirements:* Additional exam requirements/recommendations for international students: Required—TOEFL. Electronic applications accepted. *Expenses:* Tuition, state resident: part-time $478.25 per credit hour. Tuition, nonresident: part-time $966.50 per credit hour. Part-time tuition and fees vary according to program. *Financial support:* In 2009–10, 10 research assistantships with tuition reimbursements (averaging $7,514 per year) were awarded; scholarships/grants and unspecified assistantships also available. Total annual research expenditures: $795,917. *Unit head:* Dr. Cheryl L. Sisk, Director, 517-355-5253, Fax: 517-432-2744, E-mail: sisk@msu.edu. *Application contact:* Shari Stockmeyer, Program Support, 517-353-8947, Fax: 517-432-2744, E-mail: neurosci@msu.edu.

Montana State University, College of Graduate Studies, College of Letters and Science, Department of Cell Biology and Neuroscience, Bozeman, MT 59717. Offers biological sciences (PhD); neuroscience (MS, PhD). Part-time programs available. *Faculty:* 6 full-time (1 woman), 2 part-time/adjunct (1 woman). *Students:* 1 full-time (0 women), 4 part-time (1 woman). Average age 28. 31 applicants, 58% accepted. *Degree requirements:* For master's, comprehensive exam; for doctorate, comprehensive exam, thesis/dissertation. *Entrance requirements:* For master's and doctorate, GRE General Test. Additional exam requirements/recommendations for international students: Required—TOEFL (minimum score 550 paper-based; 213 computer-based). *Application deadline:* For fall admission, 7/15 priority date for

Neuroscience

Montana State University (continued)

domestic students, 5/15 priority date for international students; for spring admission, 12/1 priority date for domestic students, 10/1 priority date for international students. Applications are processed on a rolling basis. Application fee: $30. Electronic applications accepted. *Expenses:* Tuition, state resident: full-time $5635; part-time $3492 per year. Tuition, nonresident: full-time $17,212; part-time $7865.10 per year. Required fees: $1441; $153.15 per credit. Tuition and fees vary according to course load and program. *Financial support:* In 2009–10, research assistantships with full and partial tuition reimbursements (averaging $22,000 per year), 8 teaching assistantships (averaging $10,500 per year) were awarded; health care benefits and unspecified assistantships also available. Financial award application deadline: 3/1; financial award applicants required to submit FAFSA. *Faculty research:* Development of the nervous system, neuronal mechanisms of visual perception, ion channel biophysics, mechanisms of sensory coding, neuroinformatics. Total annual research expenditures: $2.7 million. *Unit head:* Dr. Thomas Hughes, Head, 406-994-5395, Fax: 406-994-7077, E-mail: thughes@montana.edu. *Application contact:* Dr. Carl A. Fox, Vice Provost for Graduate Education, 406-994-4145, Fax: 406-994-7433, E-mail: gradstudy@montana.edu.

Mount Sinai School of Medicine of New York University, Graduate School of Biological Sciences, New York, NY 10029-6504. Offers bioethics (MS); biological sciences (PhD); clinical research (MS); community medicine (MPH); genetic counseling (MS); neurosciences (PhD); MD/PhD. Terminal master's awarded for partial completion of doctoral program. *Degree requirements:* For master's, thesis; for doctorate, comprehensive exam, thesis/dissertation. *Entrance requirements:* For master's, GRE General Test; for doctorate, GRE General Test, GRE Subject Test, 3 years of college pre-med course work. Additional exam requirements/recommendations for international students: Required—TOEFL. Electronic applications accepted. *Faculty research:* Cancer, genetics and genomics, immunology, neuroscience, developmental and stem cell biology, translational research.

New York Medical College, Graduate School of Basic Medical Sciences, Department of Cell Biology, Valhalla, NY 10595-1691. Offers cell biology and neuroscience (MS, PhD); MD/PhD. Part-time and evening/weekend programs available. Terminal master's awarded for partial completion of doctoral program. *Degree requirements:* For master's, thesis; for doctorate, comprehensive exam, thesis/dissertation. *Entrance requirements:* For master's and doctorate, GRE General Test. Additional exam requirements/recommendations for international students: Required—TOEFL. *Expenses:* Tuition: Full-time $18,170; part-time $790 per credit. Required fees: $790 per credit. $20 per semester. One-time fee: $100. Tuition and fees vary according to class time, course level, course load, degree level, program, student level and student's religious affiliation. *Faculty research:* Mechanisms of growth control in skeletal muscle, cartilage differentiation, cytoskeletal functions, signal transduction pathways, neuronal development and plasticity.

New York University, Graduate School of Arts and Science, Center for Neural Science, New York, NY 10012-1019. Offers PhD. *Faculty:* 15 full-time (3 women). *Students:* 28 full-time (14 women), 6 part-time (4 women); includes 9 minority (2 African Americans, 6 Asian Americans or Pacific Islanders, 1 Hispanic American), 3 international. Average age 28. 156 applicants, 13% accepted, 7 enrolled. In 2009, 7 doctorates awarded. *Degree requirements:* For doctorate, one foreign language, thesis/dissertation. *Entrance requirements:* For doctorate, GRE, interview. Additional exam requirements/recommendations for international students: Required—TOEFL. *Application deadline:* For fall admission, 12/18 for domestic students. Application fee: $90. *Expenses:* Tuition: Full-time $30,528; part-time $1272 per credit. Required fees: $2177. *Financial support:* Fellowships with tuition reimbursements, research assistantships with tuition reimbursements, career-related internships or fieldwork, Federal Work-Study, institutionally sponsored loans, scholarships/grants, health care benefits, and unspecified assistantships available. Financial award application deadline: 12/18; financial award applicants required to submit FAFSA. *Faculty research:* Systems and integrative neuroscience; combining biology, cognition, computation, and theory. *Unit head:* J. Anthony Movshon, Chair, 212-998-7780, Fax: 212-995-4011, E-mail: cns@nyu.edu. *Application contact:* Nava Rubin, Director of Graduate Studies, 212-998-7780, Fax: 212-995-4011, E-mail: cns@nyu.edu.

New York University, School of Medicine, New York, NY 10012-1019. Offers biomedical sciences (PhD), including biomedical imaging, cellular and molecular biology, computational biology, developmental genetics, medical and molecular parasitology, microbiology, molecular oncobiology and immunology, neuroscience and physiology, pathobiology, pharmacology, structural biology; clinical investigation (MS); medicine (MD); MD/MA; MD/MPA; MD/MS; MD/PhD. *Accreditation:* LCME/AMA (one or more programs are accredited). *Faculty:* 1,493 full-time (558 women), 327 part-time/adjunct (122 women). *Students:* 747 full-time (360 women); includes 275 minority (23 African Americans, 5 American Indian/Alaska Native, 199 Asian Americans or Pacific Islanders, 48 Hispanic Americans), 2 international. Average age 24. 7,568 applicants, 7% accepted, 213 enrolled. In 2009, 164 first professional degrees, 13 master's, 50 doctorates awarded. *Degree requirements:* For master's, comprehensive exam, thesis; for doctorate, comprehensive exam, thesis/dissertation. *Entrance requirements:* MCAT. Additional exam requirements/recommendations for international students: Required—TOEFL. *Application deadline:* For fall admission, 10/15 for domestic students; for winter admission, 12/18 for domestic students, 12/15 for international students. Application fee: $100. *Expenses:* Contact institution. *Financial support:* In 2009–10, 524 students received support, including 29 fellowships with full tuition reimbursements available (averaging $31,000 per year), 47 research assistantships with full tuition reimbursements available (averaging $31,000 per year); teaching assistantships, Federal Work-Study, institutionally sponsored loans, and health care benefits also available. Financial award application deadline: 3/1; financial award applicants required to submit FAFSA. *Faculty research:* AIDS, cancer, neuroscience, molecular biology, neuroscience, cell biology and molecular genetics, structural biology, microbial pathogenesis and host defense, pharmacology, molecular oncology and immunology. Total annual research expenditures: $201.1 million. *Unit head:* Dr. Robert Grossman, Dean, 212-263-3269, Fax: 212-263- 1828. *Application contact:* Dr. Nancy Genieser, Associate Dean, Admissions, 212-263-5290, Fax: 212-263-0720, E-mail: nancy.genieser@nyumc.org.

New York University, School of Medicine and Graduate School of Arts and Science, Sackler Institute of Graduate Biomedical Sciences, Department of Neuroscience and Physiology, New York, NY 10012-1019. Offers PhD, MD/PhD. *Degree requirements:* For doctorate, one foreign language, comprehensive exam, thesis/dissertation, qualifying exam. *Entrance requirements:* For doctorate, GRE General Test. Additional exam requirements/recommendations for international students: Required—TOEFL. *Expenses:* Tuition: Full-time $30,528; part-time $1272 per credit. Required fees: $2177. *Faculty research:* Synaptic transmission, retinal physiology, signal transduction, CNS intrinsic properties, cerebellar function.

Northwestern University, The Graduate School, Institute for Neuroscience, Evanston, IL 60208. Offers PhD. Admissions and degree offered through The Graduate School. *Degree requirements:* For doctorate, thesis/dissertation. *Entrance requirements:* For doctorate, GRE General Test. Additional exam requirements/recommendations for international students: Required—TOEFL. *Faculty research:* Circadian rhythms, synaptic neurotransmissions, cognitive neuroscience, sensory/motor systems, cell biology and structure/function, neurobiology of disease.

Northwestern University, The Graduate School and Judd A. and Marjorie Weinberg College of Arts and Sciences, Interdepartmental Biological Sciences Program (IBiS), Evanston, IL 60208. Offers biochemistry, molecular biology, and cell biology (PhD), including biochemistry, cell and molecular biology, molecular biophysics, structural biology; biotechnology (PhD); cell and molecular biology (PhD); developmental biology and genetics (PhD); hormone action and signal transduction (PhD); neuroscience (PhD); structural biology, biochemistry, and biophysics (PhD). Program participants include the Departments of Biochemistry, Molecular Biology, and Cell Biology; Chemistry; Neurobiology and Physiology; Chemical Engineering; Civil Engineering; and Evanston Hospital. *Degree requirements:* For doctorate, thesis/dissertation, qualifying exam. *Entrance requirements:* For doctorate, GRE General Test. Additional exam requirements/recommendations for international students: Required—TOEFL (minimum score 600 paper-based). Electronic applications accepted. *Faculty research:* Developmental genetics, gene regulation, DNA-protein interactions, biological clocks, bioremediation.

The Ohio State University, College of Medicine, School of Biomedical Science, Neuroscience Graduate Studies Program, Columbus, OH 43210. Offers PhD. *Degree requirements:* For doctorate, comprehensive exam, thesis/dissertation. *Entrance requirements:* For doctorate, GRE General Test, GRE Subject Test. Additional exam requirements/recommendations for international students: Required—TOEFL (minimum score 600 paper-based; 250 computer-based). Electronic applications accepted. *Expenses:* Tuition, state resident: full-time $10,683. Tuition, nonresident: full-time $25,923. Tuition and fees vary according to course load and program. *Faculty research:* Neurotrauma and disease, behavioral neuroscience, systems neuroscience, stress and neuroimmunology, molecular and cellular neuroscience.

The Ohio State University, Graduate School, College of Social and Behavioral Sciences, School of Social and Behavioral Science, Department of Psychology, Columbus, OH 43210. Offers behavioral neuroscience (PhD); clinical psychology (PhD); cognitive psychology (PhD); developmental psychology (PhD); mental retardation and developmental disabilities (PhD); psychology (MA); quantitative psychology (PhD); social psychology (PhD). *Accreditation:* APA (one or more programs are accredited). *Faculty:* 60. *Students:* 88 full-time (59 women), 47 part-time (31 women); includes 20 minority (7 African Americans, 1 American Indian/Alaska Native, 5 Asian Americans or Pacific Islanders, 7 Hispanic Americans), 20 international. Average age 27. In 2009, 15 master's, 20 doctorates awarded. *Degree requirements:* For doctorate, thesis/dissertation. *Entrance requirements:* For master's and doctorate, GRE General Test. Additional exam requirements/recommendations for international students: Required—TOEFL (minimum score 600 paper-based; 250 computer-based). *Application deadline:* For fall admission, 12/31 for domestic students, 11/30 for international students. Applications are processed on a rolling basis. Application fee: $40 ($50 for international students). Electronic applications accepted. *Expenses:* Tuition, state resident: full-time $10,683. Tuition, nonresident: full-time $25,923. Tuition and fees vary according to course load and program. *Financial support:* Fellowships, research assistantships, teaching assistantships available. *Unit head:* Michael Vasey, Graduate Studies Committee Chair, E-mail: vasey.1@osu.edu. *Application contact:* 614-292-9444, Fax: 614-292-3895, E-mail: domestic.grad@osu.edu.

Ohio University, Graduate College, College of Arts and Sciences, Department of Biological Sciences, Athens, OH 45701-2979. Offers biological sciences (MS, PhD); cell biology and physiology (MS, PhD); ecology and evolutionary biology (MS, PhD); exercise physiology and muscle biology (MS, PhD); microbiology (MS, PhD); neuroscience (MS, PhD). *Faculty:* 50 full-time (14 women), 6 part-time/adjunct (1 woman). *Students:* 44 full-time (19 women), 8 part-time (3 women); includes 2 minority (1 African American, 1 Hispanic American), 21 international. 95 applicants, 24% accepted, 10 enrolled. In 2009, 4 master's, 9 doctorates awarded. Terminal master's awarded for partial completion of doctoral program. *Degree requirements:* For master's, comprehensive exam, thesis, 1 quarter of teaching experience; for doctorate, comprehensive exam, thesis/dissertation, 2 quarters of teaching experience. *Entrance requirements:* For master's, GRE General Test, names of three faculty members whose research interests most closely match the applicant's interest; for doctorate, GRE General Test, essay concerning prior training, research interest and career goals, plus names of three faculty members whose research interests most closely match the applicant's interest. Additional exam requirements/recommendations for international students: Required—TOEFL (minimum score 620 paper-based; 105 iBT) or IELTS (minimum score 7.5). *Application deadline:* For fall admission, 1/15 for domestic and international students. Application fee: $50 ($55 for international students). Electronic applications accepted. *Expenses:* Tuition, state resident: full-time $7839; part-time $323 per quarter hour. Tuition, nonresident: full-time $15,831; part-time $654 per quarter hour. Required fees: $2931. *Financial support:* In 2009–10, 1 fellowship with full tuition reimbursement (averaging $18,957 per year), 10 research assistantships with full tuition reimbursements (averaging $18,957 per year), 42 teaching assistantships with full tuition reimbursements (averaging $18,957 per year) were awarded; Federal Work-Study and institutionally sponsored loans also available. Financial award application deadline: 1/15. *Faculty research:* Ecology and evolutionary biology, exercise physiology and muscle biology, neurobiology, cell biology, physiology. Total annual research expenditures: $2.8 million. *Unit head:* Dr. Ralph DiCaprio, Chair, 740-593-2290, Fax: 740-593-0300, E-mail: dicapri@ohio.edu. *Application contact:* Dr. Donald Holzschu, Graduate Chair, 740-593-0425, Fax: 740-593-0300, E-mail: holzschu@ohio.edu.

Oregon Health & Science University, School of Medicine, Graduate Programs in Medicine, Department of Behavioral Neuroscience, Portland, OR 97239-3098. Offers MS, PhD. *Students:* 58 applicants, 9% accepted, 5 enrolled. In 2009, 1 master's, 2 doctorates awarded. Terminal master's awarded for partial completion of doctoral program. *Degree requirements:* For doctorate, thesis/dissertation, written exam. *Entrance requirements:* For doctorate, GRE General Test (minimum scores: 500 Verbal/600 Quantitative/4.5 Analytical), undergraduate coursework in biopsychology and other basic science areas providing background required for graduate training in behavioral neuroscience. Additional exam requirements/recommendations for international students: Required—TOEFL. Application fee: $65. Electronic applications accepted. Tuition and fees vary according to course level, course load, degree level, program and reciprocity agreements. *Financial support:* Health care benefits, tuition waivers (full), and stipends available. *Faculty research:* Neural basis of behavior, behavioral pharmacology, behavioral genetics, neuropharmacology and neuroendocrinology, biological basis of drug seeking and addiction. *Application contact:* Kris Thomason, Graduate Program Manager, 503-494-8464, E-mail: thomason@ohsu.edu.

Oregon Health & Science University, School of Medicine, Graduate Programs in Medicine, Neuroscience Graduate Program, Portland, OR 97239-3098. Offers PhD. *Degree requirements:* For doctorate, comprehensive exam, thesis/dissertation. *Entrance requirements:* For doctorate, GRE General Test (minimum scores: 500 Verbal/600 Quantitative/4.5 Analytical) or MCAT (for some programs). Additional exam requirements/recommendations for international students: Required—TOEFL. *Application deadline:* For fall admission, 12/15 for domestic students. Application fee: $65. Electronic applications accepted. Tuition and fees vary according to course level, course load, degree level, program and reciprocity agreements. *Financial support:* PhD students have paid tuition and receive stipends available. *Faculty research:* Signal transduction, receptors and ion channels, transcriptional regulation, drug abuse, systems, behavioral neuroscience. *Unit head:* Gary Westbrook, PhD, Program Director, 503-494-6932, E-mail: ngp@ohsu.edu. *Application contact:* Liz Lawson-Weber, Program Coordinator, 503-494-6932, E-mail: ngp@ohsu.edu.

See Close-Up on page 391.

Penn State Hershey Medical Center, College of Medicine, Graduate School Programs in the Biomedical Sciences, The Huck Institutes of the Life Sciences, Intercollege Graduate Program in Neuroscience, Hershey, PA 17033. Offers MS, PhD, MD/PhD. *Students:* 96 applicants, 4% accepted, 2 enrolled. In 2009, 2 master's, 4 doctorates awarded. Terminal master's awarded for partial completion of doctoral program. *Degree requirements:* For master's, thesis or alternative; for doctorate, comprehensive exam, thesis/dissertation, oral exam. *Entrance requirements:* For master's, GRE General Test; for doctorate, GRE General Test, minimum GPA of 3.0. Additional exam requirements/recommendations for international students: Required—TOEFL (minimum score 500 paper-based; 213 computer-based). *Application deadline:* For fall admission, 1/31 priority date for domestic students, 2/1 priority date for international students. Applications are processed on a rolling basis. Application fee: $65. Electronic applications accepted. *Expenses:* Tuition, state resident: part-time $644 per credit. Tuition, nonresident: part-time $1142 per credit. Required fees: $22 per semester. *Financial support:* In 2009–10, research assistantships with full tuition reimbursements (averaging $22,260 per year); fellowships with full tuition reimbursements, career-related internships or fieldwork, institutionally sponsored loans, scholarships/grants, health care benefits, and unspecified assistantships also available. Financial award applicants required to submit FAFSA. *Faculty research:* Behavioral neuroscience, growth factors and neuropeptides, molecular neurobiology and neurogenetics, neuronal aging and brain metabolism, neuronal and glial development. *Unit head:* Dr. Patricia Grigson, Program Director, 717-531-1045, Fax: 717-531-0786, E-mail: neuro-grad-hmc@psu.edu. *Application contact:* Lori Coover, Program Assistant, 717-531-1045, Fax: 717-531-0786, E-mail: neuro-grad-hmc@psu.edu.

Princeton University, Graduate School, Department of Psychology, Princeton, NJ 08544-1019. Offers neuroscience (PhD); psychology (PhD). *Degree requirements:* For doctorate, thesis/dissertation. *Entrance requirements:* For doctorate, GRE General Test, GRE Subject Test. Additional exam requirements/recommendations for international students: Required—TOEFL (minimum score 550 paper-based). Electronic applications accepted.

Princeton University, Princeton Neuroscience Institute, Princeton, NJ 08544-1019. Offers PhD. Electronic applications accepted.

Queen's University at Kingston, School of Graduate Studies and Research, Faculty of Health Sciences, Department of Anatomy and Cell Biology, Kingston, ON K7L 3N6, Canada. Offers biology of reproduction (M Sc, PhD); cancer (M Sc, PhD); cardiovascular pathophysiology (M Sc, PhD); cell and molecular biology (M Sc, PhD); drug metabolism (M Sc, PhD); endocrinology (M Sc, PhD); motor control (M Sc, PhD); neural regeneration (M Sc, PhD); neurophysiology (M Sc, PhD). Part-time programs available. *Degree requirements:* For master's, thesis; for doctorate, one foreign language, comprehensive exam, thesis/dissertation. *Entrance requirements:* Additional exam requirements/recommendations for international students: Required—TOEFL. Electronic applications accepted. *Faculty research:* Human kinetics, neuroscience, reproductive biology, cardiovascular.

Rosalind Franklin University of Medicine and Science, School of Graduate and Post-doctoral Studies—Interdisciplinary Graduate Program in Biomedical Sciences, Department of Neuroscience, North Chicago, IL 60064-3095. Offers PhD, MD/PhD. *Degree requirements:* For doctorate, comprehensive exam, thesis/dissertation, original research project. *Entrance requirements:* For doctorate, GRE General Test. Additional exam requirements/recommendations for international students: Required—TOEFL, TWE.

Rush University, Graduate College, Division of Neuroscience, Chicago, IL 60612-3832. Offers MS, PhD. Terminal master's awarded for partial completion of doctoral program. *Degree requirements:* For master's, thesis; for doctorate, thesis/dissertation. *Entrance requirements:* For master's and doctorate, GRE General Test. Additional exam requirements/recommendations for international students: Required—TOEFL. Electronic applications accepted. *Faculty research:* Neurodegenerative disorders, neurobiology of memory, aging, pathology and genetics of Alzheimer's disease.

Rutgers, The State University of New Jersey, Newark, Graduate School, Program in Integrative Neuroscience, Newark, NJ 07102. Offers PhD. Part-time programs available. *Degree requirements:* For doctorate, thesis/dissertation. *Entrance requirements:* For doctorate, GRE, minimum GPA of 3.0. Electronic applications accepted. *Faculty research:* Systems neuroscience, cognitive neuroscience, molecular neuroscience, behavioral neuroscience.

Rutgers, The State University of New Jersey, Newark, Graduate School, Program in Psychology, Newark, NJ 07102. Offers cognitive neuroscience (PhD); cognitive science (PhD); perception (PhD); psychobiology (PhD); social cognition (PhD). *Degree requirements:* For doctorate, comprehensive exam, thesis/dissertation. *Entrance requirements:* For doctorate, GRE General Test, GRE Subject Test, minimum undergraduate B average. Electronic applications accepted. *Faculty research:* Visual perception (luminance, motion), neuroendocrine mechanisms in behavior (reproduction, pain), attachment theory, connectionist modeling of cognition.

Rutgers, The State University of New Jersey, New Brunswick, Graduate School-New Brunswick, Program in Endocrinology and Animal Biosciences, Piscataway, NJ 08854-8097. Offers MS, PhD. Terminal master's awarded for partial completion of doctoral program. *Degree requirements:* For master's, thesis; for doctorate, comprehensive exam, thesis/dissertation. *Entrance requirements:* For master's and doctorate, GRE General Test. Additional exam requirements/recommendations for international students: Required—TOEFL. Electronic applications accepted. *Faculty research:* Comparative and behavioral endocrinology, epigenetic regulation of the endocrine system, exercise physiology and immunology, fetal and neonatal developmental programming, mammary gland biology and breast cancer, neuroendocrinology and alcohol studies, reproductive and developmental toxicology.

Rutgers, The State University of New Jersey, New Brunswick, Graduate School-New Brunswick, Program in Neuroscience, Piscataway, NJ 08854-8097. Offers PhD. *Degree requirements:* For doctorate, thesis/dissertation, qualifying exam, research project. *Entrance requirements:* For doctorate, GRE General Test, 3 letters of recommendation. Additional exam requirements/recommendations for international students: Required—TOEFL. Electronic applications accepted. *Faculty research:* Neural patterning, neurogenesis, neurogenetics, cell population behavior, regeneration.

Seton Hall University, College of Arts and Sciences, Department of Biological Sciences, South Orange, NJ 07079-2697. Offers biology (MS); biology/business administration (MS); microbiology (MS); molecular bioscience (PhD); molecular bioscience/neuroscience (PhD). Part-time and evening/weekend programs available. *Faculty:* 17 full-time (9 women), 1 part-time/adjunct (0 women). *Students:* 19 full-time (8 women), 47 part-time (33 women); includes 13 minority (5 African Americans, 5 Asian Americans or Pacific Islanders, 3 Hispanic Americans), 5 international. Average age 29. 51 applicants, 76% accepted, 12 enrolled. In 2009, 11 master's awarded. *Degree requirements:* For master's, thesis optional; for doctorate, comprehensive exam, thesis/dissertation. *Entrance requirements:* For master's and doctorate, GRE or MS from accredited university in the U.S. Additional exam requirements/recommendations for international students: Required—TOEFL. *Application deadline:* For fall admission, 7/1 priority date for domestic and international students; for spring admission, 11/1 priority date for domestic and international students. Applications are processed on a rolling basis. Application fee: $50. Electronic applications accepted. *Financial support:* Research assistantships, teaching assistantships with full tuition reimbursements, career-related internships or fieldwork, Federal Work-Study, and unspecified assistantships available. Financial award applicants required to submit FAFSA. *Faculty research:* Neurobiology, genetics, immunology, molecular biology, cellular physiology, toxicology, microbiology, bioinformatics. *Unit head:* Dr. Carolyn Bentivegna, Chair, 973-761-9044, Fax: 973-275-2905, E-mail: bentivca@shu.edu. *Application contact:* Dr. Carroll D. Rawn, Director of Graduate Studies, 973-761-9054, Fax: 973-275-2905, E-mail: rawncarr@shu.edu.

Seton Hall University, College of Arts and Sciences, Department of Psychology, South Orange, NJ 07079-2697. Offers experimental psychology (MS), including behavioral neuroscience. Part-time and evening/weekend programs available. *Faculty:* 12 full-time (7 women). *Students:* 14 full-time (7 women); includes 3 minority (2 Asian Americans or Pacific Islanders, 1 Hispanic American). Average age 25. 28 applicants, 71% accepted, 10 enrolled. In 2009, 5 master's awarded. *Entrance requirements:* For master's, GRE. Additional exam requirements/recommendations for international students: Required—TOEFL. *Application deadline:* For fall admission, 7/1 priority date for domestic and international students. Applications are processed on a rolling basis. Application fee: $50. Electronic applications accepted. *Financial support:* Research assistantships, teaching assistantships with full tuition reimbursements, career-related internships or fieldwork, Federal Work-Study, scholarships/grants, and unspecified assistantships available. Financial award applicants required to submit FAFSA. *Faculty research:* Behavioral neuroscience, cognitive psychology, social psychology, perception/motor skills, memory, depression, anxiety. *Unit head:* Dr. Susan A. Nolan, Chair, 973-761-9484, Fax: 973-275-5829, E-mail: nolansus@shu.edu. *Application contact:* Dr. Janine P. Buckner, Director of Graduate Studies, 973-761-9484, Fax: 973-275-5829, E-mail: buckneja@shu.edu.

Stanford University, School of Medicine, Graduate Programs in Medicine, Neurosciences Program, Stanford, CA 94305-9991. Offers PhD. *Degree requirements:* For doctorate, thesis/dissertation. *Entrance requirements:* For doctorate, GRE General Test, GRE Subject Test. Additional exam requirements/recommendations for international students: Required—TOEFL. Electronic applications accepted. *Expenses:* Tuition: Full-time $37,380; part-time $2760 per quarter. Required fees: $501.

State University of New York Downstate Medical Center, School of Graduate Studies, Program in Neural and Behavioral Science, Brooklyn, NY 11203-2098. Offers PhD, MD/PhD. *Degree requirements:* For doctorate, comprehensive exam, thesis/dissertation. *Entrance requirements:* For doctorate, GRE. *Faculty research:* Molecular neuroscience, cellular neuroscience, systems neuroscience, behavioral neuroscience, behavior.

State University of New York Upstate Medical University, College of Graduate Studies, Program in Neuroscience, Syracuse, NY 13210-2334. Offers PhD. *Faculty:* 31 full-time (4 women), 2 part-time/adjunct (0 women). *Students:* 18 full-time (9 women), 1 (woman) part-time; includes 1 minority (Asian American or Pacific Islander), 4 international. In 2009, 1 doctorate awarded. *Degree requirements:* For doctorate, comprehensive exam, thesis/dissertation. *Entrance requirements:* For doctorate, GRE General Test, telephone interview. Additional exam requirements/recommendations for international students: Required—TOEFL. *Application deadline:* Applications are processed on a rolling basis. Application fee: $40. Electronic applications accepted. *Financial support:* In 2009–10, fellowships with tuition reimbursements (averaging $21,514 per year), research assistantships with tuition reimbursements (averaging $21,514 per year) were awarded; Federal Work-Study, institutionally sponsored loans, scholarships/grants, health care benefits, and unspecified assistantships also available. Financial award application deadline: 4/15; financial award applicants required to submit FAFSA. *Faculty research:* Cancer, disorders of the nervous system, infectious diseases, diabetes/metabolic disorders/cardiovascular diseases. *Unit head:* Dr. Michael W. Miller, Chair, 315-464-4413. *Application contact:* Sandra Tillotson, Coordinator of Graduate Recruitment, 315-464-7655.

See Close-Up on page 393.

Stony Brook University, State University of New York, Graduate School, College of Arts and Sciences, Department of Neurobiology and Behavior, Stony Brook, NY 11794. Offers neuroscience (PhD). *Faculty:* 17 full-time (3 women), 1 part-time/adjunct (0 women). *Students:* 36 full-time (18 women); includes 5 minority (3 Asian Americans or Pacific Islanders, 2 Hispanic Americans), 16 international. Average age 27. 92 applicants, 17% accepted. In 2009, 3 doctorates awarded. *Degree requirements:* For doctorate, comprehensive exam, thesis/dissertation, teaching experience. *Entrance requirements:* For doctorate, GRE General Test, GRE Subject Test, minimum GPA of 3.0. Additional exam requirements/recommendations for international students: Required—TOEFL. *Application deadline:* For fall admission, 1/15 for domestic students. Application fee: $60. *Expenses:* Tuition, state resident: full-time $8370; part-time $349 per credit. Tuition, nonresident: full-time $13,250; part-time $552 per credit. Required fees: $933. *Financial support:* In 2009–10, 21 research assistantships, 6 teaching assistantships were awarded; fellowships, Federal Work-Study also available. *Faculty research:* Biophysics; neurochemistry; cellular, developmental, and integrative neurobiology. Total annual research expenditures: $4.1 million. *Unit head:* Dr. Lorna Role, Interim Chair, 631-632-8616, Fax: 631-632-6661. *Application contact:* Dr. Gary G. Matthews, Director, 631-632-8616, Fax: 631-632-6661, E-mail: ggmatthews@notes.cc.sunysb.edu.

Teachers College, Columbia University, Graduate Faculty of Education, Department of Biobehavioral Studies, Program in Neuroscience and Education, New York, NY 10027-6696. Offers Ed M, Ed D. *Students:* 9 full-time (8 women), 18 part-time (16 women); includes 7 minority (3 African Americans, 3 Asian Americans or Pacific Islanders, 1 Hispanic American), 4 international. Average age 27. 33 applicants, 85% accepted, 13 enrolled. In 2009, 17 master's awarded. *Application deadline:* For fall admission, 5/15 for domestic students. Application fee: $65. *Financial support:* Career-related internships or fieldwork, Federal Work-Study, institutionally sponsored loans, and tuition waivers (full and partial) available. Support available to part-time students. Financial award application deadline: 2/1. *Faculty research:* Neuropsychological diagnosis and intervention. *Unit head:* John H. Saxman, Chair, 212-678-3895, E-mail: jhs37@columbia.edu. *Application contact:* Debbie Lesperance, Assistant Director of Admission, 212-678-3710, Fax: 212-678-4171.

Temple University, Health Sciences Center, School of Medicine and Graduate School, Graduate Programs in Medicine, Department of Neuroscience, Philadelphia, PA 19122-6096. Offers MS, PhD. *Entrance requirements:* For master's and doctorate, GRE or MCAT, minimum GPA of 3.0. Additional exam requirements/recommendations for international students: Required—TOEFL. Electronic applications accepted.

Texas A&M Health Science Center, Graduate School of Biomedical Sciences, Department of Neuroscience and Experimental Therapeutics, College Station, TX 77840. Offers PhD.

Texas A&M University, College of Liberal Arts, Department of Psychology, College Station, TX 77843. Offers behavioral and cellular neuroscience (MS, PhD); clinical psychology (MS, PhD); cognitive psychology (MS, PhD); developmental psychology (MS, PhD); industrial/organizational psychology (MS, PhD); social psychology (MS, PhD). *Accreditation:* APA (one or more programs are accredited). *Faculty:* 36. *Students:* 84 full-time (58 women), 6 part-time (5 women); includes 26 minority (6 African Americans, 3 Asian Americans or Pacific Islanders, 17 Hispanic Americans), 6 international. In 2009, 12 master's, 8 doctorates awarded. *Degree requirements:* For master's, thesis; for doctorate, comprehensive exam (for some programs), thesis/dissertation. *Entrance requirements:* For master's and doctorate, GRE General Test. Additional exam requirements/recommendations for international students: Required—TOEFL. *Application deadline:* For fall admission, 1/5 for domestic and international students. Application fee: $50 ($75 for international students). Electronic applications accepted. *Expenses:* Tuition, state resident: full-time $3991; part-time $221.74 per credit hour. Tuition, nonresident: full-time $9049; part-time $502.74 per credit hour. *Financial support:* Fellowships with partial tuition reimbursements, research assistantships with partial tuition reimbursements, teaching assistantships with partial tuition reimbursements, career-related internships or fieldwork, institutionally sponsored loans, health care benefits, and unspecified assistantships available. Financial award application deadline: 1/5; financial award applicants required to submit FAFSA. *Unit head:* Dr. Les Morey, Head, 979-845-2581, Fax: 979-845-4727, E-mail: lmorey@psych.tamu.edu. *Application contact:* Sharon Starr, Graduate Admissions Supervisor, 979-458-1710, Fax: 979-845-4727, E-mail: gradadv@psyc.tamu.edu.

Texas A&M University, College of Science, Department of Biology, College Station, TX 77843. Offers biology (MS, PhD); botany (MS, PhD); microbiology (MS, PhD); molecular and cell biology (PhD); neuroscience (MS, PhD); zoology (MS, PhD). *Faculty:* 37. *Students:* 101 full-time (59 women), 5 part-time (3 women); includes 8 minority (1 African American, 3 Asian Americans or Pacific Islanders, 4 Hispanic Americans), 40 international. Average age 28. In 2009, 9 master's, 5 doctorates awarded. *Degree requirements:* For master's, thesis or alternative; for doctorate, comprehensive exam, thesis/dissertation. *Entrance requirements:* For master's and doctorate, GRE General Test. Additional exam requirements/recommendations for international students: Required—TOEFL. *Application deadline:* For fall admission, 1/15 for domestic students. Applications are processed on a rolling basis. Application fee: $50 ($75 for international students). Electronic applications accepted. *Expenses:* Tuition, state resident: full-time $3991; part-time $221.74 per credit hour. Tuition, nonresident: full-time $9049; part-time $502.74 per credit hour. *Financial support:* Fellowships, research assistantships, teaching assistantships available. Financial award application deadline: 4/1; financial award applicants required to submit FAFSA. *Unit head:* Dr. Jack McMahan, Department Head, 979-845-2301, E-mail: granster@mail.bio.tamu.edu. *Application contact:* Graduate Advisor, 979-845-7755.

Texas Christian University, College of Science and Engineering, Department of Psychology, Fort Worth, TX 76129-0002. Offers experimental psychology (PhD), including cognitive

Neuroscience

Texas Christian University (continued)

psychology, learning, neuropsychology, social psychology; psychology (MA, MS). *Degree requirements:* For master's, thesis; for doctorate, thesis/dissertation. *Entrance requirements:* For master's and doctorate, GRE General Test. Additional exam requirements/recommendations for international students: Required—TOEFL. *Application deadline:* For fall admission, 3/1 for domestic and international students; for spring admission, 12/1 for domestic students. Applications are processed on a rolling basis. Application fee: $50. *Expenses:* Tuition: Full-time $17,640; part-time $980 per credit hour. Tuition and fees vary according to program. *Financial support:* In 2009–10, 20 students received support; teaching assistantships with full tuition reimbursements available, unspecified assistantships available. Financial award application deadline: 3/1. *Unit head:* Dr. Charles Lord, Graduate Director, 817-257-7410, E-mail: c.lord@tcu.edu. *Application contact:* Marilyn Eudaly, Department Manager, 817-257-6437.

Texas Tech University Health Sciences Center, Graduate School of Biomedical Sciences, Department of Pharmacology and Neuroscience, Lubbock, TX 79430. Offers MS, PhD, MD/PhD, MS/PhD. Terminal master's awarded for partial completion of doctoral program. *Degree requirements:* For master's, thesis; for doctorate, thesis/dissertation. *Entrance requirements:* For master's and doctorate, GRE General Test, minimum GPA of 3.0. Additional exam requirements/recommendations for international students: Required—TOEFL. Electronic applications accepted. *Faculty research:* Neuroscience, neuropsychopharmacology, autonomic pharmacology, cardiovascular pharmacology, molecular pharmacology.

Thomas Jefferson University, Jefferson College of Graduate Studies, PhD Program in Neuroscience, Philadelphia, PA 19107. Offers PhD. Offered in conjunction with the Farber Institute for Neuroscience. *Faculty:* 30 full-time (9 women). *Students:* 14 full-time (9 women); includes 2 minority (both Asian Americans or Pacific Islanders), 1 international. 40 applicants, 20% accepted, 3 enrolled. *Degree requirements:* For doctorate, comprehensive exam, thesis/dissertation. *Entrance requirements:* For doctorate, GRE General Test, strong background in the sciences, interview, previous research experience. Additional exam requirements/recommendations for international students: Required—TOEFL (minimum score 250 computer-based; 100 iBT) or IELTS. *Application deadline:* For fall admission, 1/15 priority date for domestic and international students. Application fee: $50. *Expenses:* Tuition: Full-time $26,858; part-time $879 per credit. Required fees: $525. *Financial support:* In 2009–10, 14 students received support, including 14 fellowships with full tuition reimbursements available (averaging $52,883 per year); institutionally sponsored loans, scholarships/grants, and stipend also available. Financial award application deadline: 5/1. Total annual research expenditures: $12.7 million. *Unit head:* Dr. Elisabeth J. Van Bockstaele, Program Director, 215-503-1245, Fax: 215-503-9238, E-mail: elisabeth.vanbockstaele@jefferson.edu. *Application contact:* Marc E. Stearns, Director of Admissions and Recruitment, 215-503-4400, Fax: 215-503-9920, E-mail: jcgs-info@jefferson.edu.

Tufts University, Sackler School of Graduate Biomedical Sciences, Program in Neuroscience, Medford, MA 02155. Offers PhD. *Faculty:* 29 full-time (8 women). *Students:* 12 full-time (10 women); includes 1 minority (Hispanic American), 1 international. Average age 26. In 2009, 3 doctorates awarded. *Degree requirements:* For doctorate, thesis/dissertation. *Entrance requirements:* For doctorate, GRE General Test, 3 letters of reference. Additional exam requirements/recommendations for international students: Required—TOEFL. *Application deadline:* For fall admission, 12/15 for domestic students, 12/15 priority date for international students. Applications are processed on a rolling basis. Application fee: $70. Electronic applications accepted. *Expenses:* Tuition: Full-time $38,096; part-time $3962 per credit. Required fees: $686; $40 per year. Tuition and fees vary according to course level, course load, degree level, program and student level. *Financial support:* In 2009–10, 12 students received support, including 12 research assistantships with full tuition reimbursements available (averaging $28,250 per year); fellowships, scholarships/grants, health care benefits, and tuition waivers (full) also available. *Faculty research:* Electrophysiology, molecular neurobiology, structure and function of sensory systems, neural regulation of development. *Unit head:* Dr. Kathleen Dunlap, Director, 617-636-4942. *Application contact:* Kellie Johnston, Associate Director of Admissions, 617-636-6767, Fax: 617-636-0375, E-mail: sackler-school@tufts.edu.

Tulane University, School of Medicine and School of Liberal Arts, Graduate Programs in Biomedical Sciences, Program in Neuroscience, New Orleans, LA 70118-5669. Offers MS, PhD, MD/PhD. MS and PhD offered through the Graduate School. *Degree requirements:* For doctorate, thesis/dissertation, qualifying exam. *Entrance requirements:* For doctorate, GRE General Test. Additional exam requirements/recommendations for international students: Required—TOEFL. Electronic applications accepted. *Faculty research:* Neuroendocrinology, ion channels, neuropeptides.

Tulane University, School of Science and Engineering, Neuroscience Program, New Orleans, LA 70118-5669. Offers MS, PhD.

Uniformed Services University of the Health Sciences, School of Medicine, Graduate Programs in the Biomedical Sciences and Public Health, Graduate Program in Neuroscience, Bethesda, MD 20814-4799. Offers PhD. *Faculty:* 35 full-time (13 women), 6 part-time/adjunct (2 women). *Students:* 21 full-time (6 women); includes 1 minority (African American), 3 international. Average age 26. 22 applicants, 32% accepted, 5 enrolled. In 2009, 5 doctorates awarded. *Degree requirements:* For doctorate, comprehensive exam, thesis/dissertation, qualifying exams. *Entrance requirements:* For doctorate, GRE General Test, minimum GPA of 3.0; course work in biology, general chemistry, organic chemistry. Additional exam requirements/recommendations for international students: Required—TOEFL. *Application deadline:* For fall admission, 1/15 priority date for domestic students, 1/15 for international students. Applications are processed on a rolling basis. Application fee: $0. Electronic applications accepted. *Financial support:* In 2009–10, fellowships with full tuition reimbursements (averaging $26,000 per year); scholarships/grants, health care benefits, and tuition waivers (full) also available. *Faculty research:* Neuronal development and plasticity, molecular neurobiology, environmental adaptations, stress and injury. *Unit head:* Dr. Sharon Juliano, Graduate Program Director, 301-295-3673, Fax: 301-295-1996, E-mail: sjuliano@usuhs.mil. *Application contact:* Elena Marina Sherman, Graduate Program Coordinator, 301-295-3913, Fax: 301-295-6772, E-mail: elena.sherman@usuhs.mil.

Universidad de Iberoamerica, Graduate School, San Jose, Costa Rica. Offers clinical neuropsychology (PhD); clinical psychology (M Psych); educational psychology (M Psych); forensic psychology (M Psych); hospital management (MHA); intensive care nursing (MN); medicine (MD). *Entrance requirements:* For master's, 2 letters of recommendation, interview.

Université de Montréal, Faculty of Medicine, Department of Physiology, Program in Neurological Sciences, Montréal, QC H3C 3J7, Canada. Offers M Sc, PhD. *Students:* 30 full-time (12 women), 46 part-time (29 women). 21 applicants, 48% accepted, 7 enrolled. In 2009, 10 master's, 5 doctorates awarded. Terminal master's awarded for partial completion of doctoral program. *Degree requirements:* For master's, thesis; for doctorate, thesis/dissertation, general exam. *Entrance requirements:* For master's and doctorate, proficiency in French, knowledge of English. *Application deadline:* For fall admission, 2/1 priority date for domestic students; for winter admission, 11/1 priority date for domestic students; for spring admission, 2/1 priority date for domestic students. Application fee: $100. Electronic applications accepted. *Financial support:* Fellowships, research assistantships available. *Unit head:* John Kalaska, Head, 514-343-6349, Fax: 514-343-7072, E-mail: john.francis.kalaska@umontreal.ca. *Application contact:* Joanne Payette, Student Files Management Technician, 514-343-2481, Fax: 514-343-7072, E-mail: joanne.payette@umontreal.ca.

University at Albany, State University of New York, School of Public Health, Department of Biomedical Sciences, Program in Neuroscience, Albany, NY 12222-0001. Offers MS, PhD. *Degree requirements:* For master's, thesis; for doctorate, thesis/dissertation. *Entrance requirements:* For master's and doctorate, GRE General Test, GRE Subject Test.

University at Buffalo, the State University of New York, Graduate School, College of Arts and Sciences, Department of Psychology, Buffalo, NY 14260. Offers behavioral neuroscience (PhD); clinical psychology (PhD); cognitive psychology (PhD); general psychology (MA); social-personality psychology (PhD). *Accreditation:* APA (one or more programs are accredited). *Faculty:* 32 full-time (12 women), 8 part-time/adjunct (6 women). *Students:* 94 full-time (64 women), 7 part-time (2 women); includes 5 minority (2 African Americans, 3 Hispanic Americans), 12 international. Average age 27. 353 applicants, 11% accepted. In 2009, 18 master's, 7 doctorates awarded. Terminal master's awarded for partial completion of doctoral program. *Degree requirements:* For master's, project; for doctorate, thesis/dissertation. *Entrance requirements:* For master's and doctorate, GRE General Test. Additional exam requirements/recommendations for international students: Required—TOEFL (minimum score 550 paper-based; 213 computer-based; 79 iBT). *Application deadline:* For fall admission, 1/5 for domestic and international students. Application fee: $50. Electronic applications accepted. *Financial support:* In 2009–10, 81 students received support, including 20 fellowships with full tuition reimbursements available (averaging $14,400 per year), 1 research assistantship with full tuition reimbursement available (averaging $10,400 per year), 38 teaching assistantships with full tuition reimbursements available (averaging $10,400 per year); career-related internships or fieldwork, Federal Work-Study, institutionally sponsored loans, scholarships/grants, and tuition waivers (partial) also available. Financial award application deadline: 1/5; financial award applicants required to submit FAFSA. *Faculty research:* Neural, endocrine, and molecular bases of behavior; adult mood and anxiety disorders; relationship dysfunction; attention deficit/hyperactivity disorder; psycho-linguistics. Total annual research expenditures: $7.9 million. *Unit head:* Dr. Paul A. Luce, Chair, 716-645-3650 Ext. 203, Fax: 716-645-3801, E-mail: psychair@acsu.buffalo.edu. *Application contact:* Michele Nowacki, Coordinator of Admissions, 716-645-3650 Ext. 209, Fax: 716-645-3801, E-mail: psych@acsu.buffalo.edu.

University at Buffalo, the State University of New York, Graduate School, School of Medicine and Biomedical Sciences, Graduate Programs in Medicine and Biomedical Sciences, Program in Neuroscience, Buffalo, NY 14260. Offers MS, PhD. Part-time programs available. *Students:* 17 full-time (8 women), 9 international. Average age 25. 13 applicants, 46% accepted. In 2009, 3 master's, 2 doctorates awarded. Terminal master's awarded for partial completion of doctoral program. *Degree requirements:* For master's, thesis or alternative; for doctorate, comprehensive exam, thesis/dissertation. *Entrance requirements:* For master's, GRE General Test; for doctorate, GRE General Test, 3 letters of recommendation. Additional exam requirements/recommendations for international students: Required—TOEFL (minimum score 79 iBT). *Application deadline:* For fall admission, 2/1 priority date for domestic and international students. Application fee: $50. *Financial support:* In 2009–10, 17 students received support, including 17 research assistantships with full tuition reimbursements available (averaging $21,000 per year). *Faculty research:* Neural plasticity, development, synapse, neurodisease, genetics of neuropathology. Total annual research expenditures: $6 million. *Unit head:* Dr. Malcolm Slaughter, Professor, 716-829-3240, Fax: 716-829-2364, E-mail: mslaught@buffalo.edu. *Application contact:* Kristen Kahi, Program Administrator, 716-829-2419, Fax: 716-829-3849, E-mail: kkms@buffalo.edu.

The University of Alabama at Birmingham, Graduate Programs in Joint Health Sciences, Program in Neurobiology, Birmingham, AL 35294. Offers PhD. *Degree requirements:* For doctorate, thesis/dissertation. *Entrance requirements:* For doctorate, GRE, interview. Electronic applications accepted.

University of Alberta, Faculty of Medicine and Dentistry and Faculty of Graduate Studies and Research, Graduate Programs in Medicine, Centre for Neuroscience, Edmonton, AB T6G 2E1, Canada. Offers M Sc, PhD. *Faculty:* 54 part-time/adjunct (10 women). *Students:* 32 full-time (16 women). Average age 27. 28 applicants, 32% accepted, 9 enrolled. In 2009, 3 master's, 3 doctorates awarded. Terminal master's awarded for partial completion of doctoral program. *Degree requirements:* For master's, thesis; for doctorate, thesis/dissertation. *Entrance requirements:* For master's and doctorate, minimum GPA of 3.3. Additional exam requirements/recommendations for international students: Required—TOEFL (minimum score 600 paper-based; 250 computer-based). *Application deadline:* For fall admission, 7/1 priority date for domestic students, 5/1 priority date for international students; for winter admission, 11/30 priority date for domestic students, 10/31 priority date for international students. Applications are processed on a rolling basis. Application fee: $0. Electronic applications accepted. Tuition and fees charges are reported in Canadian dollars. *Expenses:* Tuition, area resident: Full-time $4626 Canadian dollars; part-time $99.72 Canadian dollars per unit. International tuition: $8216 Canadian dollars full-time. Required fees: $3590 Canadian dollars; $99.72 Canadian dollars per unit. $215 Canadian dollars per term. *Financial support:* In 2009–10, 5 students received support, including 1 research assistantship with tuition reimbursement available (averaging $12,000 per year); fellowships with tuition reimbursements available also available. *Faculty research:* Sensory and motor mechanisms, neural growth and regeneration, molecular neurobiology, synaptic mechanisms, behavioral and psychiatric neuroscience. *Unit head:* Dr. Keir G. Pearson, Director, 780-492-5628, Fax: 780-492-1617, E-mail: keir.pearson@ualberta.ca. *Application contact:* Dr. Teresa Krukoff, Professor, 780-492-4996, Fax: 780-492-1617, E-mail: neurosci@ualberta.ca.

The University of Arizona, Graduate College, Graduate Interdisciplinary Programs, Graduate Interdisciplinary Program in Neuroscience, Tucson, AZ 85719. Offers PhD. *Faculty:* 6 full-time (1 woman). *Students:* 22 full-time (14 women), 2 part-time (1 woman); includes 4 minority (2 Asian Americans or Pacific Islanders, 2 Hispanic Americans), 8 international. Average age 28. 49 applicants, 12% accepted, 4 enrolled. In 2009, 6 doctorates awarded. *Degree requirements:* For doctorate, thesis/dissertation. *Entrance requirements:* For doctorate, GRE (minimum score 1100), minimum GPA of 3.5, 3 letters of recommendation. Additional exam requirements/recommendations for international students: Required—TOEFL (minimum score 550 paper-based; 213 computer-based; 79 iBT). *Application deadline:* For fall admission, 12/1 for domestic and international students. Application fee: $65. Electronic applications accepted. *Expenses:* Tuition, state resident: full-time $9028. Tuition, nonresident: full-time $24,890. *Financial support:* In 2009–10, 10 research assistantships with full tuition reimbursements (averaging $44,615 per year) were awarded; health care benefits, tuition waivers (full), and unspecified assistantships also available. Financial award application deadline: 12/1. *Faculty research:* Cognitive neuroscience, developmental neurobiology, speech and hearing, motor control, insect neurobiology. Total annual research expenditures: $1.8 million. *Unit head:* Dr. Konrad E. Zinsmaier, Chairman, 520-621-1343, Fax: 520-621-8282, E-mail: kez@neurobio.arizona.edu. *Application contact:* Erin Wolfe, Graduate Coordinator, 520-621-8380, Fax: 520-626-2618, E-mail: nrsc@u.arizona.edu.

The University of British Columbia, Faculty of Arts and Faculty of Graduate Studies, Department of Psychology, Vancouver, BC V6T 1Z4, Canada. Offers behavioral neuroscience (MA, PhD); clinical psychology (MA, PhD); cognitive science (MA, PhD); developmental psychology (MA, PhD); health psychology (MA, PhD); quantitative methods (MA, PhD); social/personality psychology (MA, PhD). *Accreditation:* APA (one or more programs are accredited). Terminal master's awarded for partial completion of doctoral program. *Degree requirements:* For master's, thesis; for doctorate, comprehensive exam, thesis/dissertation. *Entrance requirements:* For master's and doctorate, GRE General Test. Additional exam requirements/recommendations for international students: Required—TOEFL (minimum score 550 paper-based; 230 computer-based; 80 iBT). Electronic applications accepted. *Faculty research:* Clinical, developmental, social/personality, cognition, behavioral neuroscience.

University of Calgary, Faculty of Medicine and Faculty of Graduate Studies, Department of Neuroscience, Calgary, AB T2N 1N4, Canada. Offers M Sc, PhD. *Degree requirements:* For master's, thesis, oral thesis exam; for doctorate, thesis/dissertation, candidacy exam, oral thesis exam. *Entrance requirements:* For master's and doctorate, minimum GPA of 3.2 during previous 2 years. Additional exam requirements/recommendations for international students: Required—TOEFL (minimum score 580 paper-based; 237 computer-based). Electronic applications accepted. *Faculty research:* Cellular pharmacology and neurotoxicology, developmental neurobiology, molecular basis of neurodegenerative diseases, neural systems, ion channels.

University of California, Berkeley, Graduate Division, Group in Neuroscience, Berkeley, CA 94720-3200. Offers PhD. *Faculty:* 43 full-time, 3 part-time/adjunct. *Students:* 50 full-time (29 women). Average age 26. 234 applicants, 11 enrolled. In 2009, 8 doctorates awarded. *Degree requirements:* For doctorate, qualifying exam, teaching, research thesis/dissertation. *Entrance requirements:* For doctorate, GRE General Test, minimum GPA of 3.0, 3 letters of recommendation, at least one year of laboratory experience. Additional exam requirements/recommendations for international students: Required—TOEFL or IELTS. *Application deadline:* For fall admission, 12/1 for domestic and international students. Application fee: $70 ($90 for international students). Electronic applications accepted. *Financial support:* Fellowships, research assistantships, teaching assistantships, scholarships/grants, traineeships, and health care benefits available. *Faculty research:* Analysis of ion channels, signal transduction mechanisms, and gene regulation; development of neurons, synapses, and circuits; synapse function and plasticity; mechanisms of sensory processing; principles of function of cerebral cortex; neural basis for learning, attention, and sleep; neural basis for human emotion, language, motor control, and other high-level cognitive processes. *Unit head:* Prof. John J. Ngai, Chair, 510-642-9885, E-mail: neurosci@berkeley.edu. *Application contact:* Kati S. Markowitz, Information Contact, 510-642-8915, Fax: 510-643-4966, E-mail: neurosci@berkeley.edu.

See Close-Up on page 395.

University of California, Davis, Graduate Studies, Graduate Group in Neuroscience, Davis, CA 95616. Offers PhD. *Degree requirements:* For doctorate, thesis/dissertation. *Entrance requirements:* For doctorate, GRE General Test, GRE Subject Test. Additional exam requirements/recommendations for international students: Required—TOEFL (minimum score 550 paper-based; 213 computer-based). Electronic applications accepted. *Faculty research:* Neuroethology, cognitive neurosciences, cortical neurophysics, cellular and molecular neurobiology.

University of California, Los Angeles, David Geffen School of Medicine and Graduate Division, Graduate Programs in Medicine, Neuroscience Program, Los Angeles, CA 90095. Offers PhD. *Degree requirements:* For doctorate, thesis/dissertation, oral and written qualifying exams. *Entrance requirements:* For doctorate, GRE General Test.

University of California, Riverside, Graduate Division, Program in Neuroscience, Riverside, CA 92521-0102. Offers PhD. *Faculty:* 25 full-time (10 women). *Students:* 24 full-time (11 women), 1 part-time (0 women); includes 5 minority (1 African American, 2 Asian Americans or Pacific Islanders, 2 Hispanic Americans), 1 international. Average age 29. 47 applicants, 21% accepted, 5 enrolled. *Degree requirements:* For doctorate, comprehensive exam, thesis/dissertation, 2 quarters of teaching experience, qualifying exams. *Entrance requirements:* For doctorate, GRE General Test, minimum GPA of 3.2. Additional exam requirements/recommendations for international students: Required—TOEFL (minimum score 550 paper-based; 213 computer-based; 80 iBT). *Application deadline:* For fall admission, 1/5 priority date for domestic and international students. Applications are processed on a rolling basis. Application fee: $80 ($100 for international students). Electronic applications accepted. *Financial support:* In 2009–10, 5 students received support, including 5 fellowships with full tuition reimbursements available (averaging $22,000 per year), 3 research assistantships with partial tuition reimbursements available (averaging $14,240 per year), 17 teaching assistantships with partial tuition reimbursements available (averaging $16,637 per year); tuition waivers (full and partial) also available. Financial award application deadline: 1/5; financial award applicants required to submit FAFSA. *Faculty research:* Cellular and molecular neuroscience, development and plasticity, systems neuroscience and behavior, computational neuroscience, cognitive neuroscience, medical neuroscience. *Unit head:* Dr. Michael Adams, Director, 951-827-4746, Fax: 951-827-3087, E-mail: michael.adams@ucr.edu. *Application contact:* Perla Fabelo, Graduate Student Affairs Assistant, 951-827-4716, Fax: 951-827-5517, E-mail: neuro@ucr.edu.

University of California, San Diego, Office of Graduate Studies, Interdisciplinary Program in Cognitive Science, La Jolla, CA 92093. Offers cognitive science/anthropology (PhD); cognitive science/communication (PhD); cognitive science/computer science and engineering (PhD); cognitive science/linguistics (PhD); cognitive science/neuroscience (PhD); cognitive science/philosophy (PhD); cognitive science/psychology (PhD); cognitive science/sociology (PhD). Admissions offered through affiliated departments. *Degree requirements:* For doctorate, thesis/dissertation. *Entrance requirements:* For doctorate, GRE General Test, acceptance into one of the eight participating departments. *Faculty research:* Language and cognition, philosophy of mind, visual perception, biological anthropology, sociolinguistics.

University of California, San Diego, School of Medicine and Office of Graduate Studies, Molecular Pathology Program, La Jolla, CA 92093. Offers bioinformatics (PhD); cancer biology/oncology (PhD); cardiovascular sciences and disease (PhD); microbiology (PhD); molecular pathology (PhD); neurological disease (PhD); stem cell and developmental biology (PhD); structural biology/drug design (PhD). *Entrance requirements:* For doctorate, GRE General Test, GRE Subject Test. Additional exam requirements/recommendations for international students: Required—TOEFL. Electronic applications accepted.

University of California, San Diego, School of Medicine and Office of Graduate Studies, Neurosciences Program, La Jolla, CA 92093. Offers PhD. *Degree requirements:* For doctorate, thesis/dissertation, qualifying exam. *Entrance requirements:* For doctorate, GRE General Test, GRE Subject Test. Additional exam requirements/recommendations for international students: Required—TOEFL. Electronic applications accepted. *Faculty research:* Neurophysiology, neuropharmacology, neurochemistry.

University of California, San Francisco, Graduate Division, Program in Neuroscience, San Francisco, CA 94143. Offers PhD. *Degree requirements:* For doctorate, thesis/dissertation. *Entrance requirements:* For doctorate, GRE General Test, GRE Subject Test. *Faculty research:* Molecular neurobiology, synaptic plasticity, mechanisms of motor learning.

University of Chicago, Division of the Biological Sciences, Neuroscience Graduate Programs, Committee on Computational Neuroscience, Chicago, IL 60637-1513. Offers PhD. *Faculty:* 27 full-time (5 women), 2 part-time/adjunct (1 woman). *Students:* 21 full-time (7 women); includes 2 minority (1 African American, 1 Asian American or Pacific Islander). Average age 28. 24 applicants, 13% accepted, 3 enrolled. In 2009, 7 doctorates awarded. *Degree requirements:* For doctorate, thesis/dissertation, ethics class, 2 teaching assistantships. *Entrance requirements:* For doctorate, GRE General Test. Additional exam requirements/recommendations for international students: Required—TOEFL (minimum score 600 paper-based; 250 computer-based; 104 iBT), IELTS (minimum score 7). *Application deadline:* For fall admission, 12/1 for domestic students, 12/1 priority date for international students. Application fee: $55. Electronic applications accepted. *Financial support:* In 2009–10, 21 students received support, including fellowships with tuition reimbursements available (averaging $29,781 per year), research assistantships with tuition reimbursements available (averaging $29,781 per year); institutionally sponsored loans, scholarships/grants, traineeships, and health care benefits also available. Financial award applicants required to submit FAFSA. *Unit head:* Dr. Nicholas Hatsopoulos, Chair, 773-702-5594. *Application contact:* Diane J. Hall, Graduate Administrative Director, 773-702-6371, Fax: 773-702-1216, E-mail: djh8@uchicago.edu.

University of Chicago, Division of the Biological Sciences, Neuroscience Graduate Programs, Department of Integrative Neuroscience, Chicago, IL 60637-1513. Offers cell physiology (PhD); pharmacological and physiological sciences (PhD). *Faculty:* 8 full-time (all women). *Students:* Average age 30. *Degree requirements:* For doctorate, thesis/dissertation, preliminary exam. *Entrance requirements:* For doctorate, GRE General Test. Additional exam requirements/recommendations for international students: Required—TOEFL. *Application deadline:* For fall admission, 12/28 priority date for domestic and international students. Application fee: $55. Electronic applications accepted. *Financial support:* In 2009–10, fellowships with tuition reimbursements (averaging $26,301 per year), research assistantships with tuition reimbursements (averaging $26,301 per year) were awarded; institutionally sponsored loans, scholarships/grants, traineeships, and health care benefits also available. Financial award applicants required to submit FAFSA. *Faculty research:* Psychopharmacology, neuropharmacology. *Unit head:* Dr. Steven Shevell, Chairman, 773-834-2900, Fax: 773-702-8842, E-mail: shevell@uchicago.edu. *Application contact:* Diane J. Hall, Graduate Administrative Director, 773-702-6371, Fax: 773-702-1216, E-mail: d-hall@uchicago.edu.

University of Cincinnati, Graduate School, Interdisciplinary PhD Study Program in Neuroscience, Cincinnati, OH 45221. Offers PhD. *Degree requirements:* For doctorate, thesis/dissertation, qualifying exam. *Entrance requirements:* For doctorate, GRE General Test. Additional exam requirements/recommendations for international students: Required—TOEFL. Electronic applications accepted. *Faculty research:* Developmental neurobiology, membrane and channel biophysics, molecular neurobiology, neuroendocrinology, neuronal cell biology.

University of Colorado Denver, School of Medicine, Program in Neuroscience, Denver, CO 80217-3364. Offers PhD. *Students:* 35 full-time (23 women); includes 3 minority (2 Asian Americans or Pacific Islanders, 1 Hispanic American), 1 international. In 2009, 4 doctorates awarded. *Degree requirements:* For doctorate, comprehensive exam, thesis/dissertation, lab rotations. *Entrance requirements:* For doctorate, GRE, minimum GPA of 3.0. Additional exam requirements/recommendations for international students: Required—TOEFL (minimum score 570 paper-based; 230 computer-based). *Application deadline:* For fall admission, 12/15 priority date for domestic students, 1/1 priority date for international students. Applications are processed on a rolling basis. Application fee: $65. Electronic applications accepted. *Financial support:* In 2009–10, 1 fellowship with full tuition reimbursement (averaging $4,000 per year) was awarded; institutionally sponsored loans, scholarships/grants, traineeships, health care benefits, and tuition waivers (full) also available. Financial award application deadline: 3/15; financial award applicants required to submit FAFSA. *Faculty research:* Neurobiology of olfaction, ion channels, schizophrenia, spinal cord regeneration, neurotransplantation. *Unit head:* Dr. Diego Restrepo, Director, 303-724-3405, Fax: 303-724-3420, E-mail: diego.restrepo@ucdenver.edu. *Application contact:* Mellodee Phillips, Program Administrator, 303-724-3120, Fax: 303-724-3121, E-mail: mellodee.phillips@ucdenver.edu.

University of Connecticut, Graduate School, College of Liberal Arts and Sciences, Department of Psychology, Storrs, CT 06269. Offers behavioral neuroscience (PhD); biopsychology (PhD); clinical psychology (MA, PhD); cognition and instruction (PhD); developmental psychology (MA, PhD); ecological psychology (PhD); experimental psychology (PhD); general psychology (MA, PhD); health psychology (Graduate Certificate); industrial/organizational psychology (PhD); language and cognition (PhD); neuroscience (PhD); occupational health psychology (Graduate Certificate); social psychology (MA, PhD). *Accreditation:* APA. *Faculty:* 59 full-time (26 women). *Students:* 194 full-time (133 women), 24 part-time (12 women); includes 48 minority (12 African Americans, 21 Asian Americans or Pacific Islanders, 15 Hispanic Americans), 25 international. Average age 28. 585 applicants, 4% accepted, 14 enrolled. In 2009, 22 master's, 24 doctorates awarded. Terminal master's awarded for partial completion of doctoral program. *Degree requirements:* For master's, comprehensive exam; for doctorate, thesis/dissertation. *Entrance requirements:* For master's and doctorate, GRE General Test, GRE Subject Test. Additional exam requirements/recommendations for international students: Required—TOEFL (minimum score 550 paper-based; 213 computer-based). *Application deadline:* For fall admission, 2/1 priority date for domestic and international students; for spring admission, 11/1 for domestic students, 10/1 for international students. Applications are processed on a rolling basis. Application fee: $55. Electronic applications accepted. *Expenses:* Tuition, state resident: full-time $4725; part-time $525 per credit. Tuition, nonresident: full-time $12,267; part-time $1363 per credit. Required fees: $346 per semester. Tuition and fees vary according to course load. *Financial support:* In 2009–10, 109 research assistantships with full tuition reimbursements, 72 teaching assistantships with full tuition reimbursements were awarded; fellowships, career-related internships or fieldwork, Federal Work-Study, scholarships/grants, health care benefits, and unspecified assistantships also available. Financial award application deadline: 2/1; financial award applicants required to submit FAFSA. *Unit head:* Charles A. Lowe, Head, 860-486-3517, Fax: 860-486-2760, E-mail: charles.lowe@uconn.edu. *Application contact:* Charles A. Lowe, Head, 860-486-3517, Fax: 860-486-2760, E-mail: charles.lowe@uconn.edu.

University of Connecticut Health Center, Graduate School, Programs in Biomedical Sciences, Program in Neuroscience, Farmington, CT 06030. Offers PhD, DMD/PhD, MD/PhD. *Faculty:* 24. *Students:* 21 full-time (12 women); includes 3 minority (2 African Americans, 1 Asian American or Pacific Islander), 5 international. Average age 28. 165 applicants, 35% accepted. In 2009, 2 doctorates awarded. *Degree requirements:* For doctorate, comprehensive exam, thesis/dissertation. *Entrance requirements:* For doctorate, GRE General Test, interview (recommended). Additional exam requirements/recommendations for international students: Required—TOEFL (minimum score 600 paper-based; 250 computer-based). *Application deadline:* For fall admission, 12/15 for domestic students. Application fee: $55. Electronic applications accepted. *Financial support:* In 2009–10, 21 students received support, including 21 research assistantships with full tuition reimbursements available (averaging $27,000 per year); fellowships, health care benefits also available. *Faculty research:* Molecular and systems neuroscience, neuroanatomy, neurophysiology, neurochemistry, neuropathology. *Unit head:* Dr. James Hewett, Director, 860-679-4131, Fax: 860-679-1885, E-mail: jhewett@nso1.uchc.edu. *Application contact:* Tricia Avolt, Graduate Admissions Coordinator, 860-679-2175, Fax: 860-679-1899, E-mail: robertson@nso2.uchc.edu.

See Close-Up on page 397.

University of Delaware, College of Arts and Sciences, Department of Psychology, Newark, DE 19716. Offers behavioral neuroscience (PhD); clinical psychology (PhD); cognitive psychology (PhD); social psychology (PhD). *Accreditation:* APA. *Degree requirements:* For doctorate, thesis/dissertation. *Entrance requirements:* For doctorate, GRE General Test. Additional exam requirements/recommendations for international students: Required—TOEFL (minimum score 600 paper-based; 250 computer-based). Electronic applications accepted. *Faculty research:* Emotion development, neural and cognitive aspects of memory, neural control of feeding, intergroup relations, social cognition and communication.

University of Florida, College of Medicine, Department of Neuroscience, Gainesville, FL 32611. Offers MS, PhD. Terminal master's awarded for partial completion of doctoral program. *Degree requirements:* For master's, thesis; for doctorate, thesis/dissertation. *Entrance requirements:* For master's and doctorate, GRE General Test, minimum GPA of 3.0. Additional exam requirements/recommendations for international students: Required—TOEFL. Electronic applications accepted. *Faculty research:* Neural injury and repair, neuroimmunology and endocrinology, neurophysiology, neurotoxicology, cellular and molecular neurobiology.

University of Florida, College of Medicine and Graduate School, Interdisciplinary Program in Biomedical Sciences, Concentration in Neuroscience, Gainesville, FL 32611. Offers PhD. *Degree requirements:* For doctorate, thesis/dissertation. *Entrance requirements:* For doctorate, GRE General Test, minimum GPA of 3.0. Additional exam requirements/recommendations for international students: Required—TOEFL. Electronic applications accepted. *Faculty research:* Neural injury and repair, neurophysiology, neurotoxicology, cellular and molecular neurobiology, neuroimmunology and endocrinology.

See Close-Up on page 399.

University of Florida, Graduate School, College of Liberal Arts and Sciences, Department of Psychology, Gainesville, FL 32611. Offers behavior analysis (PhD); behavioral neuroscience (MS, PhD); cognitive and sensory processes (PhD); counseling psychology (PhD); developmental psychology (PhD); social psychology (MS, PhD); JD/PhD. *Degree requirements:* For master's, thesis or alternative; for doctorate, thesis/dissertation. *Entrance requirements:* For master's and doctorate, GRE General Test, minimum GPA of 3.0. Additional exam requirements/recommendations for international students: Required—TOEFL (minimum score 550 paper-based; 213 computer-based). Electronic applications accepted. *Faculty research:* Experimental analysis of behavior, psychobiology, cognition and sensory processes, counseling psychology, social psychology, developmental psychology.

Neuroscience

University of Georgia, Graduate School, Biomedical and Health Sciences Institute, Athens, GA 30602. Offers neuroscience (PhD). *Entrance requirements:* For doctorate, GRE, official transcripts, 3 letters of recommendation, statement of interest. Additional exam requirements/recommendations for international students: Required—TOEFL. *Expenses:* Tuition, state resident: full-time $6000; part-time $250 per credit hour. Tuition, nonresident: full-time $20,904; part-time $871 per credit hour. Required fees: $730 per semester. *Financial support:* Unspecified assistantships available. Financial award application deadline: 12/31. *Unit head:* Dr. Gaylen Edwards, Chair, 706-542-5922, Fax: 706-542-5285, E-mail: gedwards@uga.edu. *Application contact:* Philip V. Holmes, Graduate Coordinator, 706-542-5922.

University of Guelph, Ontario Veterinary College and Graduate Program Services, Graduate Programs in Veterinary Sciences, Department of Biomedical Sciences, Guelph, ON N1G 2W1, Canada. Offers morphology (M Sc, DV Sc, PhD); neuroscience (M Sc, DV Sc, PhD); pharmacology (M Sc, DV Sc, PhD); physiology (M Sc, DV Sc, PhD); toxicology (M Sc, DV Sc, PhD). Part-time programs available. *Degree requirements:* For master's, thesis; for doctorate, comprehensive exam, thesis/dissertation. *Entrance requirements:* For master's, honors B Sc, minimum 75% average in last 20 courses; for doctorate, M Sc with thesis from accredited institution. Additional exam requirements/recommendations for international students: Required—TOEFL (minimum score 550 paper-based; 213 computer-based; 89 iBT). Electronic applications accepted. *Faculty research:* Cellular morphology; endocrine, vascular and reproductive physiology; clinical pharmacology; veterinary toxicology; developmental biology, neuroscience.

University of Guelph, Ontario Veterinary College and Graduate Program Services, Graduate Programs in Veterinary Sciences, Department of Clinical Studies, Guelph, ON N1G 2W1, Canada. Offers anesthesiology (M Sc, DV Sc); cardiology (DV Sc, Diploma); clinical studies (Diploma); dermatology (M Sc); diagnostic imaging (M Sc, DV Sc); emergency/critical care (M Sc, DV Sc, Diploma); medicine (M Sc, DV Sc); neurology (M Sc, DV Sc); ophthalmology (M Sc, DV Sc); surgery (M Sc, DV Sc). *Degree requirements:* For master's, thesis; for doctorate, comprehensive exam, thesis/dissertation. *Entrance requirements:* Additional exam requirements/recommendations for international students: Required—TOEFL (minimum score 550 paper-based; 213 computer-based), IELTS (minimum score 6.5). Electronic applications accepted. *Faculty research:* Orthopedics, respirology, oncology, exercise physiology, cardiology.

University of Hartford, College of Arts and Sciences, Department of Biology, Program in Neuroscience, West Hartford, CT 06117-1599. Offers MS. Part-time and evening/weekend programs available. *Degree requirements:* For master's, comprehensive exam, thesis optional, oral exams. *Entrance requirements:* For master's, GRE General Test, GRE Subject Test, MCAT. Additional exam requirements/recommendations for international students: Required—TOEFL (minimum score 550 paper-based; 213 computer-based). Electronic applications accepted. *Faculty research:* Neurobiology of aging, central actions of neural steroids, neuroendocrine control of reproduction, retinopathies in sharks, plasticity in the central nervous system.

University of Idaho, College of Graduate Studies, Program in Neuroscience, Moscow, ID 83844-2282. Offers MS, PhD. *Faculty:* 6 full-time, 1 part-time/adjunct. *Students:* 9 full-time, 2 part-time. In 2009, 1 doctorate awarded. *Expenses:* Tuition, state resident: full-time $6120. Tuition, nonresident: full-time $17,712. *Unit head:* Dr. Margrit von Braun, Dean of the College of Graduate Studies, 208-885-6243, Fax: 208-885-6198, E-mail: uigrad@uidaho.edu. *Application contact:* Dr. Margrit von Braun, Dean of the College of Graduate Studies, 208-885-6243, Fax: 208-885-6198, E-mail: uigrad@uidaho.edu.

University of Illinois at Chicago, College of Medicine and Graduate College, Graduate Programs in Medicine, Department of Anatomy and Cell Biology, Program in Neuroscience, Chicago, IL 60607-7128. Offers cellular and systems neuroscience and cell biology (PhD).

See Close-Up on page 401.

University of Illinois at Urbana–Champaign, Graduate College, College of Liberal Arts and Sciences, School of Molecular and Cellular Biology, Neuroscience Program, Champaign, IL 61820. Offers PhD. *Students:* 50 full-time (29 women), 5 part-time (3 women); includes 20 minority (1 African American, 15 Asian Americans or Pacific Islanders, 4 Hispanic Americans), 9 international. 93 applicants, 15% accepted, 8 enrolled. In 2009, 10 doctorates awarded. *Entrance requirements:* For doctorate, GRE, minimum GPA of 3.0. Additional exam requirements/recommendations for international students: Required—TOEFL (minimum score 570 paper-based; 230 computer-based). *Application deadline:* Applications are processed on a rolling basis. Application fee: $60 ($75 for international students). Electronic applications accepted. *Financial support:* In 2009–10, 20 fellowships, 27 research assistantships, 18 teaching assistantships were awarded; tuition waivers (full and partial) also available. *Unit head:* Gene Robinson, Director, 217-333-4971, Fax: 217-244-3499, E-mail: generobi@illinois.edu. *Application contact:* Sam Beshers, Program Coordinator, 217-333-4971, Fax: 217-244-3499, E-mail: beshers@illinois.edu.

The University of Iowa, Graduate College, Program in Neuroscience, Iowa City, IA 52242-1316. Offers PhD, MD/PhD. *Degree requirements:* For doctorate, comprehensive exam, thesis/dissertation. *Entrance requirements:* For doctorate, GRE General Test, minimum GPA of 3.0. Additional exam requirements/recommendations for international students: Required—TOEFL (minimum score 600 paper-based; 250 computer-based; 100 iBT). Electronic applications accepted. *Faculty research:* Molecular, cellular, and developmental systems; behavioral neurosciences.

The University of Kansas, Graduate Studies, School of Pharmacy, Program in Neurosciences, Lawrence, KS 66045. Offers MS, PhD. *Students:* 9 full-time (6 women); includes 1 minority (Asian American or Pacific Islander), 2 international. Average age 27. 26 applicants, 4% accepted, 1 enrolled. In 2009, 1 master's, 1 doctorate awarded. *Degree requirements:* For doctorate, comprehensive exam, thesis/dissertation. *Entrance requirements:* For master's and doctorate, GRE. Additional exam requirements/recommendations for international students: Required—TOEFL. *Application deadline:* For fall admission, 1/5 priority date for domestic and international students. Applications are processed on a rolling basis. Application fee: $45 ($55 for international students). Electronic applications accepted. *Expenses:* Tuition, state resident: full-time $6492; part-time $270.50 per credit hour. Tuition, nonresident: full-time $15,510; part-time $646.25 per credit hour. Required fees: $847; $70.56 per credit hour. Tuition and fees vary according to course load and program. *Financial support:* Fellowships, research assistantships with full tuition reimbursements available. Financial award application deadline: 1/15. *Unit head:* Prof. Elias Michaelis, 785-864-4001, Fax: 785-864-5219, E-mail: emichaelis@ku.edu. *Application contact:* Prof. Elias K. Michaelis, 785-864-4001, E-mail: emichaelis@ku.edu.

The University of Kansas, University of Kansas Medical Center, School of Medicine, Department of Molecular and Integrative Physiology, Neuroscience Graduate Program, Lawrence, KS 66045-7582. Offers MS, PhD. *Students:* 1 (woman) part-time. Average age 32. *Entrance requirements:* Additional exam requirements/recommendations for international students: Required—TOEFL. *Expenses:* Tuition, state resident: full-time $6492; part-time $270.50 per credit hour. Tuition, nonresident: full-time $15,510; part-time $646.25 per credit hour. Required fees: $847; $70.56 per credit hour. Tuition and fees vary according to course load and program. *Unit head:* Dr. Paul D. Cheney, Chairman, 913-588-7400, Fax: 913-588-7430, E-mail: pcheney@kumc.edu. *Application contact:* Marcia Jones, Director of Graduate Studies, 913-588-1238, Fax: 913-588-5242, E-mail: mjones@kumc.edu.

University of Lethbridge, School of Graduate Studies, Lethbridge, AB T1K 3M4, Canada. Offers accounting (MScM); addictions counseling (M Sc); agricultural biotechnology (M Sc); agricultural studies (M Sc, MA); anthropology (MA); archaeology (MA); art (MA, MFA); biochemistry (M Sc); biological sciences (M Sc); biomolecular science (PhD); biosystems and biodiversity (PhD); Canadian studies (MA); chemistry (M Sc); computer science (M Sc); computer science and geographical information science (M Sc); counseling psychology (M Ed); dramatic arts (MA); earth, space, and physical science (PhD); economics (MA); educational leadership (M Ed); English (MA); environmental science (M Sc); evolution and behavior (PhD); exercise science (M Sc); finance (MScM); French (MA); French/German (MA); French/Spanish (MA); general education (M Ed); general management (MScM); geography (M Sc, MA); German (MA); health science (M Sc); history (MA); human resource management and labour relations (MScM); individualized multidisciplinary (M Sc, MA); information systems (MScM); international management (MScM); kinesiology (M Sc, MA); management (M Sc, MA); marketing (MScM); mathematics (M Sc); music (M Mus, MA); Native American studies (MA); neuroscience (M Sc, PhD); new media (MA); nursing (M Sc); philosophy (MA); physics (M Sc); policy and strategy (MScM); political science (MA); psychology (M Sc, MA); religious studies (MA); social sciences (MA); sociology (MA); theatre and dramatic arts (MFA); theoretical and computational science (PhD); urban and regional studies (MA); women's studies (MA). Part-time and evening/weekend programs available. *Degree requirements:* For doctorate, comprehensive exam, thesis/dissertation. *Entrance requirements:* For master's, GMAT (M Sc in management), bachelor's degree in related field, minimum GPA of 3.0 during previous 20 graded semester courses, 2 years teaching or related experience (M Ed); for doctorate, master's degree, minimum graduate GPA of 3.5. Additional exam requirements/recommendations for international students: Required—TOEFL. *Faculty research:* Movement and brain plasticity, gibberellin physiology, photosynthesis, carbon cycling, molecular properties of main-group ring components.

University of Maryland, Baltimore, Graduate School, Graduate Program in Life Sciences, Program in Neuroscience, Baltimore, MD 21201. Offers PhD, MD/PhD. Part-time programs available. *Students:* 52 full-time (32 women); includes 9 minority (3 African Americans, 5 Asian Americans or Pacific Islanders, 1 Hispanic American), 4 international. Average age 27. 89 applicants, 25% accepted, 5 enrolled. In 2009, 5 doctorates awarded. *Entrance requirements:* For doctorate, GRE General Test, minimum GPA of 3.0. Additional exam requirements/recommendations for international students: Required—TOEFL (minimum score 550 paper-based; 80 iBT); Recommended—IELTS (minimum score 7). *Application deadline:* For fall admission, 1/15 for domestic and international students. Application fee: $50. Electronic applications accepted. *Expenses:* Tuition, state resident: full-time $7290; part-time $405 per credit hour. Tuition, nonresident: full-time $12,780; part-time $710 per credit hour. Required fees: $774; $10 per credit hour. $297 per semester. Tuition and fees vary according to course load, degree level and program. *Financial support:* In 2009–10, research assistantships with partial tuition reimbursements (averaging $25,000 per year); fellowships, health care benefits and unspecified assistantships also available. Financial award application deadline: 3/1. *Faculty research:* Molecular, biochemical, and cellular pharmacology; membrane biophysics; synaptology; developmental neurobiology. *Unit head:* Dr. Frank Margolis, Director, 410-706-8913, E-mail: fmargoli@umaryland.edu. *Application contact:* Jennifer Aumiller, Coordinator, 410-706-4701, Fax: 410-706-4724, E-mail: neurosci@umaryland.edu.

University of Maryland, Baltimore County, Graduate School, College of Natural and Mathematical Sciences, Department of Biological Sciences and Department of Psychology, Program in Neurosciences and Cognitive Sciences, Baltimore, MD 21250. Offers PhD. *Faculty:* 18 full-time (8 women). *Students:* 5 full-time (4 women); includes 3 minority (2 Asian Americans or Pacific Islanders, 1 Hispanic American). 13 applicants, 23% accepted, 0 enrolled. In 2009, 1 doctorate awarded. *Degree requirements:* For doctorate, comprehensive exam (for some programs), thesis/dissertation. *Entrance requirements:* For doctorate, GRE General Test, minimum GPA of 3.0. Additional exam requirements/recommendations for international students: Required—TOEFL. *Application deadline:* For fall admission, 1/15 for domestic students, 12/15 for international students. Applications are processed on a rolling basis. Application fee: $50. Electronic applications accepted. *Financial support:* In 2009–10, 5 students received support, including 3 research assistantships with full tuition reimbursements available (averaging $22,300 per year), 2 teaching assistantships with full tuition reimbursements available (averaging $21,300 per year). *Unit head:* Dr. Phyllis Robinson, Director, 410-455-3669, Fax: 410-455-3875, E-mail: biograd@umbc.edu. *Application contact:* Dr. Phyllis Robinson, Director, 410-455-3669, Fax: 410-455-3875, E-mail: biograd@umbc.edu.

University of Maryland, College Park, Academic Affairs, College of Behavioral and Social Sciences, Department of Hearing and Speech Sciences, College Park, MD 20742. Offers audiology (MA, PhD); hearing and speech sciences (Au D); language pathology (MA, PhD); neuroscience (PhD); speech (MA, PhD). *Accreditation:* ASHA (one or more programs are accredited). *Faculty:* 19 full-time (18 women), 13 part-time/adjunct (11 women). *Students:* 82 full-time (76 women), 18 part-time (all women); includes 20 minority (9 African Americans, 8 Asian Americans or Pacific Islanders, 3 Hispanic Americans), 2 international. 260 applicants, 46% accepted, 36 enrolled. In 2009, 23 master's, 11 doctorates awarded. *Degree requirements:* For master's, thesis optional; for doctorate, thesis/dissertation, written and oral exams. *Entrance requirements:* For master's, GRE General Test, minimum GPA of 3.5, 3 letters of recommendation; for doctorate, GRE General Test, minimum GPA of 3.5. Additional exam requirements/recommendations for international students: Required—TOEFL. *Application deadline:* For fall admission, 1/15 for domestic and international students. Applications are processed on a rolling basis. Application fee: $60. Electronic applications accepted. *Expenses:* Tuition, area resident: Part-time $471 per credit hour. Tuition, state resident: part-time $471 per credit hour. Tuition, nonresident: part-time $1016 per credit hour. Required fees: $337.04 per term. *Financial support:* In 2009–10, 3 fellowships with partial tuition reimbursements (averaging $10,848 per year), 2 research assistantships (averaging $15,614 per year), 34 teaching assistantships with tuition reimbursements (averaging $15,709 per year) were awarded; career-related internships or fieldwork, Federal Work-Study, scholarships/grants, and health care benefits also available. Support available to part-time students. Financial award applicants required to submit FAFSA. *Faculty research:* Speech perception, language acquisition, bilingualism, hearing loss. Total annual research expenditures: $491,296. *Unit head:* Dr. Nan B. Bernstein-Ratner, Chair, 301-405-4217, Fax: 301-314-2023, E-mail: nratner@umd.edu. *Application contact:* Dean of Graduate School, 301-405-0358, Fax: 301-314-9305.

University of Maryland, College Park, Academic Affairs, College of Behavioral and Social Sciences, Program in Neurosciences and Cognitive Sciences, College Park, MD 20742. Offers PhD. *Faculty:* 1 (woman) full-time. *Students:* 52 full-time (32 women); includes 5 minority (3 African Americans, 2 Asian Americans or Pacific Islanders), 14 international. 68 applicants, 25% accepted, 11 enrolled. In 2009, 4 doctorates awarded. *Degree requirements:* For doctorate, comprehensive exam, thesis/dissertation. *Entrance requirements:* For doctorate, GRE General Test, 3 letters of recommendation. Additional exam requirements/recommendations for international students: Required—TOEFL. *Application deadline:* For fall admission, 12/15 for domestic and international students. Applications are processed on a rolling basis. Application fee: $60. Electronic applications accepted. *Expenses:* Tuition, area resident: Part-time $471 per credit hour. Tuition, state resident: part-time $471 per credit hour. Tuition, nonresident: part-time $1016 per credit hour. Required fees: $337.04 per term. *Financial support:* In 2009–10, 7 fellowships with full and partial tuition reimbursements (averaging $17,343 per year), 15 research assistantships with tuition reimbursements (averaging $19,143 per year), 26 teaching assistantships (averaging $17,254 per year) were awarded; Federal Work-Study and scholarships/grants also available. Support available to part-time students. Financial award applicants required to submit FAFSA. *Faculty research:* Molecular neurobiology, cognition, neural and behavioral systems language, memory, human development. *Unit head:* Dr. Cynthia F. Moss, Director, 301-405-0353, Fax: 301-405-7104, E-mail: moss@umd.edu. *Application contact:* Dean of Graduate School, 301-405-0358, Fax: 301-314-9305.

University of Massachusetts Amherst, Graduate School, Interdisciplinary Programs, Program in Neuroscience and Behavior, Amherst, MA 01003. Offers animal behavior and learning (PhD); molecular and cellular neuroscience (PhD); neural and behavioral development (PhD); neuroendocrinology (PhD); neuroscience and behavior (MS); sensorimotor, cognitive, and computational neuroscience (PhD). *Students:* 28 full-time (19 women); includes 4 minority (1 African American, 2 Asian Americans or Pacific Islanders, 1 Hispanic American), 3 international. Average age 26. 70 applicants, 26% accepted, 5 enrolled. In 2009, 4 master's, 5 doctorates awarded. Terminal master's awarded for partial completion of doctoral program. *Degree requirements:* For master's, thesis or alternative; for doctorate, comprehensive exam, thesis/dissertation. *Entrance requirements:* For master's and doctorate, GRE General Test. Additional exam requirements/recommendations for international students: Required—TOEFL (minimum score 550 paper-based; 213 computer-based; 80 iBT), IELTS (minimum score 6.5). *Application deadline:* For fall admission, 1/2 for domestic and international students. Applications are processed on a rolling basis. Application fee: $50 ($65 for international students). Electronic applications accepted. *Expenses:* Tuition, state resident: full-time $2640; part-time $110 per credit. Tuition, nonresident: full-time $9936; part-time $414 per credit. Tuition and fees vary according to course load. *Financial support:* In 2009–10, 1 fellowship with full tuition reimbursement (averaging $11,144 per year), 3 research assistantships with full tuition reimbursements (averaging $1,477 per year) were awarded; teaching assistantships, career-related internships or fieldwork, Federal Work-Study, scholarships/grants, traineeships, health care benefits, tuition waivers (full), and unspecified assistantships also available. Support available to part-time students. Financial award application deadline: 1/2. *Unit head:* Dr. Elizabeth A. Connor, Graduate Program Director, 413-545-2046, Fax: 413-545-3243. *Application contact:* Jean M. Ames, Supervisor of Admissions, 413-545-0722, Fax: 413-577-0010, E-mail: gradadm@grad.umass.edu.

University of Massachusetts Worcester, Graduate School of Biomedical Sciences, Program in Neuroscience, Worcester, MA 01655-0115. Offers PhD. *Degree requirements:* For doctorate, comprehensive exam, thesis/dissertation. *Entrance requirements:* For doctorate, GRE General Test. Additional exam requirements/recommendations for international students: Required—TOEFL (minimum score 600 paper-based; 250 computer-based). Electronic applications accepted. *Faculty research:* Molecular, biophysical, and cellular techniques to investigate cell function with emphasis on signal transduction processes, cell growth, and proliferation.

University of Medicine and Dentistry of New Jersey, Graduate School of Biomedical Sciences, Graduate Programs in Biomedical Sciences–Newark, Program in Integrative Neuroscience, Newark, NJ 07107. Offers PhD. *Students:* 12 full-time (8 women); includes 1 African American, 1 Asian American or Pacific Islander, 1 international. *Degree requirements:* For doctorate, thesis/dissertation, qualifying exam. *Entrance requirements:* For doctorate, GRE General Test, minimum GPA of 3.5. Additional exam requirements/recommendations for international students: Required—TOEFL. *Application deadline:* For fall admission, 2/1 for domestic students. Applications are processed on a rolling basis. Application fee: $40. Electronic applications accepted. *Financial support:* Fellowships, research assistantships available. Financial award application deadline: 5/1. *Unit head:* Dr. Richard Servatius, Program Director, 973-676-1000 Ext. 3678, E-mail: richard.servatius@va.gov. *Application contact:* Dr. Richard Servatius, Program Director, 973-676-1000 Ext. 3678, E-mail: richard.servatius@va.gov.

University of Medicine and Dentistry of New Jersey, Graduate School of Biomedical Sciences, Graduate Programs in Biomedical Sciences–Piscataway, Program in Neuroscience, Piscataway, NJ 08854-5635. Offers MS, PhD, MD/PhD. *Degree requirements:* For master's, thesis, qualifying exam; for doctorate, thesis/dissertation, qualifying exam. *Entrance requirements:* Additional exam requirements/recommendations for international students: Required—TOEFL. *Application deadline:* For fall admission, 1/5 for domestic students. Applications are processed on a rolling basis. Application fee: $40. Electronic applications accepted. *Unit head:* Dr. John Pintar, Director, 732-235-4250, Fax: 732-235-4990, E-mail: pintar@umdnj.edu. *Application contact:* University Registrar, 973-972-5338.

University of Miami, Graduate School, College of Arts and Sciences, Department of Psychology, Coral Gables, FL 33124. Offers adult clinical (PhD); behavioral neuroscience (PhD); child clinical (PhD); developmental psychology (PhD); health clinical (PhD); psychology (MS). *Accreditation:* APA (one or more programs are accredited). *Degree requirements:* For doctorate, comprehensive exam, thesis/dissertation. *Entrance requirements:* For doctorate, GRE General Test, minimum GPA of 3.5. Additional exam requirements/recommendations for international students: Required—TOEFL. Electronic applications accepted. *Faculty research:* Behavioral factors in cardiovascular disease and cancer adult psychopathology, developmental disabilities, social and emotional development, mechanisms of coping.

University of Miami, Graduate School, Miller School of Medicine, Graduate Programs in Medicine, Neuroscience Program, Coral Gables, FL 33124. Offers PhD, MD/PhD. *Faculty:* 42 full-time (9 women). *Students:* 27 full-time (12 women). Average age 28. 66 applicants, 17% accepted, 5 enrolled. In 2009, 1 doctorate awarded. *Degree requirements:* For doctorate, thesis/dissertation, qualifying exam. *Entrance requirements:* For doctorate, GRE General Test. Additional exam requirements/recommendations for international students: Required—TOEFL (minimum score 550 paper-based; 213 computer-based). *Application deadline:* For fall admission, 1/15 priority date for domestic and international students. Applications are processed on a rolling basis. Application fee: $50. Electronic applications accepted. *Financial support:* In 2009–10, 17 fellowships with tuition reimbursements (averaging $22,000 per year), 4 research assistantships with tuition reimbursements (averaging $22,000 per year) were awarded; institutionally sponsored loans also available. *Faculty research:* Cellular and molecular biology, transduction, nerve regeneration and embryonic development, membrane biophysics. Total annual research expenditures: $6 million. *Unit head:* Dr. John L. Bixby, Chairman, Neuroscience Program Steering Committee, 305-243-4874, Fax: 305-243-2970, E-mail: jbixby@miami.edu. *Application contact:* Samone Welch, Graduate Coordinator, 305-243-3368, Fax: 305-243-2970, E-mail: neurosci@med.miami.edu.

University of Michigan, Horace H. Rackham School of Graduate Studies, Program in Biomedical Sciences (PIBS), Neuroscience Program, Ann Arbor, MI 48072-2215. Offers PhD. *Degree requirements:* For doctorate, thesis/dissertation, oral defense of dissertation, preliminary exam. *Entrance requirements:* For doctorate, GRE General Test, 3 letters of recommendation, research experience. Additional exam requirements/recommendations for international students: Required—TOEFL (minimum score 84 iBT). Electronic applications accepted. *Expenses:* Tuition, state resident: full-time $17,286; part-time $1099 per credit hour. Tuition, nonresident: full-time $34,944; part-time $2080 per credit hour. Required fees: $95 per semester. Tuition and fees vary according to course load, degree level and program. *Faculty research:* Developmental neurobiology, cellular and molecular neurobiology, cognitive neuroscience, sensory neuroscience, behavioral neuroscience.

University of Minnesota, Twin Cities Campus, Graduate School, Graduate Program in Neuroscience, Minneapolis, MN 55455-0213. Offers MS, PhD. Terminal master's awarded for partial completion of doctoral program. *Degree requirements:* For master's, thesis; for doctorate, thesis/dissertation. *Entrance requirements:* For doctorate, GRE. Additional exam requirements/recommendations for international students: Required—TOEFL. Electronic applications accepted. *Faculty research:* Cellular and molecular neuroscience, behavioral neuroscience, developmental neuroscience, neurodegenerative diseases, pain, addiction, motor control.

University of Missouri, Graduate School, Neuroscience Interdisciplinary Program, Columbia, MO 65211. Offers MS, PhD. *Entrance requirements:* Additional exam requirements/recommendations for international students: Required—TOEFL (minimum score 600 paper-based; 250 computer-based; 100 iBT).

University of Missouri–St. Louis, College of Arts and Sciences, Department of Psychology, St. Louis, MO 63121. Offers behavioral neuroscience (PhD); clinical psychology respecialization (Certificate); community psychology (PhD); general psychology (MA); industrial/organizational psychology (PhD). *Accreditation:* APA (one or more programs are accredited). Evening/weekend programs available. *Faculty:* 21 full-time (10 women), 5 part-time/adjunct (3 women). *Students:* 35 full-time (29 women), 39 part-time (30 women); includes 4 minority (1 American Indian/Alaska Native, 1 Asian American or Pacific Islander, 2 Hispanic Americans). Average age 28. 208 applicants, 9% accepted, 13 enrolled. In 2009, 16 master's, 6 doctorates awarded. Terminal master's awarded for partial completion of doctoral program. *Degree requirements:* For master's, thesis; for doctorate, thesis/dissertation. *Entrance requirements:* For master's and doctorate, GRE General Test, GRE Subject Test, 3 letters of recommendation. Additional exam requirements/recommendations for international students: Required—TOEFL (minimum score 550 paper-based; 213 computer-based). *Application deadline:* For fall admission, 1/15 for domestic and international students. Application fee: $35 ($40 for international students). Electronic applications accepted. *Expenses:* Tuition, state resident: full-time $5377; part-time $297.70 per credit hour. Tuition, nonresident: full-time $13,882; part-time $771.20 per credit hour. Required fees: $220; $12.20 per credit hour. One-time fee: $12. Tuition and fees vary according to course level, campus/location and program. *Financial support:* In 2009–10, 7 research assistantships with full and partial tuition reimbursements (averaging $10,600 per year), 20 teaching assistantships with full and partial tuition reimbursements (averaging $9,788 per year) were awarded; fellowships with full tuition reimbursements also available. Financial award applicants required to submit FAFSA. *Faculty research:* Bereavement and loss, neuroscience, post-traumatic stress disorder, conflict and negotiation, social psychology. *Unit head:* Dr. George Taylor, Chair, 314-516-5391, Fax: 314-516-5392, E-mail: umslpsychology@msx.umsl.edu. *Application contact:* 314-516-5458, Fax: 314-516-6996, E-mail: gradadm@umsl.edu.

The University of Montana, Graduate School, College of Health Professions and Biomedical Sciences, Skaggs School of Pharmacy, Department of Biomedical and Pharmaceutical Sciences, Missoula, MT 59812-0002. Offers biomedical sciences (PhD); neuroscience (MS, PhD); pharmaceutical sciences (MS); toxicology (MS, PhD). *Accreditation:* ACPE. *Degree requirements:* For master's, oral defense of thesis; for doctorate, research dissertation defense. *Entrance requirements:* For master's and doctorate, GRE General Test. Additional exam requirements/recommendations for international students: Required—TOEFL (minimum score 540 paper-based; 210 computer-based). Electronic applications accepted. *Faculty research:* Cardiovascular pharmacology, medicinal chemistry, neurosciences, environmental toxicology, pharmacogenetics, cancer.

University of Nebraska Medical Center, Graduate Studies, Department of Pharmacology and Experimental Neuroscience, Omaha, NE 68198. Offers neuroscience (MS, PhD); pharmacology (MS, PhD). Terminal master's awarded for partial completion of doctoral program. *Degree requirements:* For master's, comprehensive exam, thesis; for doctorate, comprehensive exam, thesis/dissertation. *Entrance requirements:* For master's and doctorate, GRE General Test. Additional exam requirements/recommendations for international students: Required—TOEFL (minimum score 600 paper-based; 250 computer-based). Electronic applications accepted. *Faculty research:* Neuropharmacology, molecular pharmacology, toxicology, molecular biology, neuroscience.

University of New Mexico, School of Medicine, Biomedical Sciences Graduate Program, Albuquerque, NM 87131-5196. Offers biochemistry and molecular biology (MS, PhD); cell biology and physiology (MS, PhD); molecular genetics and microbiology (MS, PhD); neuroscience (MS, PhD); pathology (MS, PhD); toxicology (MS, PhD). Part-time programs available. Terminal master's awarded for partial completion of doctoral program. *Degree requirements:* For master's, thesis; for doctorate, comprehensive exam, thesis/dissertation. *Entrance requirements:* For master's and doctorate, GRE General Test, minimum undergraduate GPA of 3.0. Additional exam requirements/recommendations for international students: Required—TOEFL. Electronic applications accepted. *Expenses:* Tuition, state resident: full-time $2099; part-time $233.20 per credit hour. Tuition, nonresident: full-time $6650. Required fees: $25 per semester. Tuition and fees vary according to course load, program and reciprocity agreements. *Faculty research:* Signal transduction, infectious disease, biology of cancer, structural biology, neuroscience.

University of Oklahoma Health Sciences Center, College of Medicine and Graduate College, Graduate Programs in Medicine, Department of Neuroscience, Oklahoma City, OK 73190. Offers MS, PhD. *Faculty:* 5 full-time (2 women). *Students:* 5 full-time (0 women), 7 part-time (6 women); includes 1 minority (African American), 5 international. Average age 27. 12 applicants, 42% accepted, 3 enrolled. In 2009, 1 master's, 1 doctorate awarded. *Degree requirements:* For doctorate, thesis/dissertation. *Entrance requirements:* For master's and doctorate, GRE General Test, 3 letters of recommendation. Additional exam requirements/recommendations for international students: Required—TOEFL. *Application deadline:* For fall admission, 12/1 for domestic students. Application fee: $50. *Expenses:* Tuition, state resident: full-time $3120; part-time $156 per credit hour. Tuition, nonresident: full-time $11,314; part-time $409.70 per credit hour. Required fees: $1471; $51.20 per credit hour. $223.25 per term. *Financial support:* In 2009–10, 3 research assistantships (averaging $18,000 per year) were awarded. *Unit head:* Dr. Beverley Greenwood, Director, 405-271-6267, E-mail: beverley.greenwood@ouhsc.edu. *Application contact:* Dr. Anthony Johnson, Graduate Liaison, 405-271-8244, Fax: 405-271-3552, E-mail: anthony.johnson@ouhsc.edu.

University of Oregon, Graduate School, College of Arts and Sciences, Department of Biology, Eugene, OR 97403. Offers ecology and evolution (MA, MS, PhD); marine biology (MA, MS, PhD); molecular, cellular and genetic biology (PhD); neuroscience and development (PhD). Terminal master's awarded for partial completion of doctoral program. *Degree requirements:* For master's, thesis (for some programs); for doctorate, thesis/dissertation. *Entrance requirements:* For master's and doctorate, GRE General Test, minimum GPA of 3.2. Additional exam requirements/recommendations for international students: Required—TOEFL. *Faculty research:* Developmental neurobiology; evolution, population biology, and quantitative genetics; regulation of gene expression; biochemistry of marine organisms.

University of Pennsylvania, School of Medicine, Biomedical Graduate Studies, Graduate Group in Neuroscience, Philadelphia, PA 19104. Offers PhD, MD/PhD. *Faculty:* 124. *Students:* 122 full-time (60 women); includes 31 minority (5 African Americans, 3 American Indian/Alaska Native, 17 Asian Americans or Pacific Islanders, 6 Hispanic Americans), 9 international. 174 applicants, 21% accepted, 16 enrolled. In 2009, 22 doctorates awarded. *Degree requirements:* For doctorate, thesis/dissertation, research project. *Entrance requirements:* For doctorate, GRE General Test. Additional exam requirements/recommendations for international students: Required—TOEFL. *Application deadline:* For fall admission, 12/8 priority date for domestic and international students. Applications are processed on a rolling basis. Application fee: $70. Electronic applications accepted. *Expenses:* Tuition: Full-time $25,660; part-time $4758 per course. Required fees: $2152; $270 per course. Tuition and fees vary according to course load, degree level and program. *Financial support:* In 2009–10, 122 students received support; fellowships, research assistantships, teaching assistantships, scholarships/grants, traineeships, and unspecified assistantships available. *Faculty research:* Molecular and cellular neuroscience, behavioral neuroscience, developmental neurobiology, systems neuroscience and neurophysiology, neurochemistry. *Unit head:* Dr. Rita Balice-Gordon, Chairperson. *Application contact:* Jane Hoshi, Coordinator, 215-898-8048, Fax: 215-573-2248.

University of Pittsburgh, School of Arts and Sciences and School of Medicine, Center for Neuroscience, Pittsburgh, PA 15260. Offers neurobiology (PhD); neuroscience (PhD). *Faculty:* 91 full-time (23 women). *Students:* 73 full-time (39 women); includes 10 minority (3 African Americans, 6 Asian Americans or Pacific Islanders, 1 Hispanic American), 12 international. Average age 25. 134 applicants, 24% accepted, 16 enrolled. In 2009, 10 doctorates awarded. *Degree requirements:* For doctorate, comprehensive exam, thesis/dissertation. *Entrance requirements:* For doctorate, GRE, interview. Additional exam requirements/recommendations for international students: Required—TOEFL (minimum score 600 paper-based; 250 computer-based; 100 iBT). *Application deadline:* For fall admission, 12/1 priority date for domestic and international students. Application fee: $50. Electronic applications accepted. *Expenses:* Contact institution. *Financial support:* In 2009–10, 31 fellowships with full tuition reimbursements (averaging $24,650 per year), 32 research assistantships with full tuition reimbursements (averaging $24,650 per year), 2 teaching assistantships with full tuition reimbursements (averaging $24,650 per year) were awarded. Financial award application deadline: 12/1. *Faculty research:* Behavioral/systems/cognitive, cell and molecular, development/plasticity/repair, neurobiology of disease. *Unit head:* Dr. Alan Sved, Co-Director, Graduate Program, 412-624-6996, Fax: 412-624-9188. *Application contact:* Joan M. Blaney, Administrator, 412-624-5043, Fax: 412-624-9198, E-mail: jblaney@pitt.edu.

University of Puerto Rico, Río Piedras, College of Natural Sciences, Department of Biology, San Juan, PR 00931-3300. Offers ecology/systematics (MS, PhD); evolution/genetics (MS, PhD); molecular/cellular biology (MS, PhD); neuroscience (MS, PhD). Part-time programs available. *Degree requirements:* For master's, one foreign language, comprehensive exam,

Neuroscience

University of Puerto Rico, Río Piedras (continued)
thesis; for doctorate, one foreign language, comprehensive exam, thesis/dissertation. *Entrance requirements:* For master's, GRE Subject Test, interview, minimum GPA of 3.0, letter of recommendation; for doctorate, GRE Subject Test, interview, master's degree, minimum GPA of 3.0, letter of recommendation. *Faculty research:* Environmental, poblational and systematic biology.

University of Rochester, School of Medicine and Dentistry, Graduate Programs in Medicine and Dentistry, Department of Neurobiology and Anatomy, Interdepartmental Program in Neuroscience, Rochester, NY 14627. Offers MS, PhD. Terminal master's awarded for partial completion of doctoral program. *Degree requirements:* For doctorate, one foreign language, thesis/dissertation, qualifying exam. *Entrance requirements:* For master's and doctorate, GRE General Test.

University of South Alabama, College of Medicine and Graduate School, Program in Basic Medical Sciences, Specialization in Cell Biology and Neuroscience, Mobile, AL 36688-0002. Offers PhD. *Degree requirements:* For doctorate, thesis/dissertation, oral and written preliminary exams, research proposal, qualifying exam. *Entrance requirements:* For doctorate, GRE General Test, minimum GPA of 3.0. Additional exam requirements/recommendations for international students: Required—TOEFL. *Expenses:* Tuition, state resident: part-time $218 per contact hour. Required fees: $1102 per year. *Faculty research:* Cytoskeleton-membrane interactions, neural basis of oral motor behavior, microtubule organizing centers, molecular biology of human chromosomes, mechanisms of synaptic transmissions.

The University of South Dakota, School of Medicine and Health Sciences and Graduate School, Biomedical Sciences Graduate Program, Program in Neuroscience, Vermillion, SD 57069-2390. Offers MS, PhD. Terminal master's awarded for partial completion of doctoral program. *Degree requirements:* For master's, thesis; for doctorate, comprehensive exam, thesis/dissertation. *Entrance requirements:* For master's and doctorate, GRE General Test, minimum GPA of 3.0. Additional exam requirements/recommendations for international students: Required—TOEFL (minimum score 550 paper-based; 213 computer-based; 80 iBT), IELTS (minimum score 6). Electronic applications accepted. *Expenses:* Contact institution. *Faculty research:* Central nervous system learning, neural plasticity, respiratory control.

University of Southern California, Graduate School, College of Letters, Arts and Sciences, Neuroscience Graduate Program, Los Angeles, CA 90089. Offers PhD. *Faculty:* 78 full-time (25 women), 3 part-time/adjunct (2 women). *Students:* 92 full-time (48 women); includes 11 minority (8 Asian Americans or Pacific Islanders, 3 Hispanic Americans), 48 international. 186 applicants, 16% accepted, 14 enrolled. In 2009, 16 doctorates awarded. *Median time to degree:* Of those who began their doctoral program in fall 2001, 100% received their degree in 8 years or less. *Degree requirements:* For doctorate, thesis/dissertation, qualifying exam, ethics course. *Entrance requirements:* For doctorate, GRE, 3 letters of recommendation, resume. Additional exam requirements/recommendations for international students: Required—TOEFL (minimum score 600 paper-based; 250 computer-based; 100 iBT). *Application deadline:* For fall admission, 12/1 priority date for domestic and international students. Application fee: $85. Electronic applications accepted. *Expenses:* Tuition: Full-time $25,980; part-time $1315 per unit. Required fees: $554. One-time fee: $35 full-time. Full-time tuition and fees vary according to degree level and program. *Financial support:* In 2009–10, 85 students received support, including 4 fellowships with full tuition reimbursements available (averaging $30,000 per year), 67 research assistantships with full tuition reimbursements available (averaging $27,500 per year), 14 teaching assistantships with full tuition reimbursements available (averaging $27,500 per year); traineeships, health care benefits, and tuition waivers also available. *Faculty research:* Cellular and molecular neurobiology; behavioral, systems and cognitive neuroscience; computational neuroscience and neural engineering; aging, neurobiology of disease, and translational research; development, plasticity and repair. *Unit head:* Dr. Pat Levitt, Professor of Cell and Neurobiology, Psychiatry and Pharmacy/Director, 323-442-2144, Fax: 323-442-2145, E-mail: plevitt@usc.edu. *Application contact:* Vanessa Clark, Student Services Advisor I, 213-740-2245, Fax: 213-740-6980, E-mail: saydacla@college.usc.edu.

University of South Florida, Graduate School, College of Arts and Sciences, Department of Psychology, Tampa, FL 33620-9951. Offers clinical psychology (PhD); cognitive and neural sciences (PhD); industrial-organizational psychology (PhD). *Accreditation:* APA. *Faculty:* 32 full-time (9 women). *Students:* 98 full-time (55 women), 21 part-time (13 women); includes 16 minority (3 African Americans, 7 Asian Americans or Pacific Islanders, 6 Hispanic Americans), 11 international. Average age 32. 437 applicants, 8% accepted, 24 enrolled. In 2009, 24 doctorates awarded. *Degree requirements:* For doctorate, comprehensive exam, thesis/dissertation, internship. *Entrance requirements:* For doctorate, GRE General Test, minimum GPA of 3.0 in last 60 hours of course work. Additional exam requirements/recommendations for international students: Required—TOEFL (minimum score 550 paper-based; 213 computer-based). *Application deadline:* For fall admission, 12/1 for domestic and international students. Application fee: $30. Electronic applications accepted. *Expenses:* Contact institution. *Financial support:* In 2009–10, teaching assistantships with tuition reimbursements (averaging $27,086 per year); tuition waivers (partial) and unspecified assistantships also available. Financial award applicants required to submit FAFSA. *Faculty research:* Clinical, cognitive, neuroscience, social, industrial/organizational. Total annual research expenditures: $4.7 million. *Unit head:* Michael Brannick, Chairperson, 813-974-0478, Fax: 813-974-4617, E-mail: mbrannick@usf.edu. *Application contact:* William Sacco, Program Director, 813-974-0375, Fax: 813-974-4617, E-mail: sacco@cas.usf.edu.

The University of Texas at Austin, Graduate School, The Institute for Neuroscience, Austin, TX 78712-1111. Offers PhD, MD/PhD. Terminal master's awarded for partial completion of doctoral program. *Degree requirements:* For doctorate, thesis/dissertation. *Entrance requirements:* For doctorate, GRE. Electronic applications accepted. *Faculty research:* Cellular/molecular biology, neurobiology, pharmacology, behavioral neuroscience.

The University of Texas at Dallas, School of Behavioral and Brain Sciences, Program in Cognition and Neuroscience, Richardson, TX 75080. Offers applied cognition and neuroscience (MS); cognition and neuroscience (PhD). Part-time and evening/weekend programs available. *Faculty:* 21 full-time (6 women). *Students:* 79 full-time (35 women), 27 part-time (12 women); includes 25 minority (3 African Americans, 17 Asian Americans or Pacific Islanders, 5 Hispanic Americans), 20 international. Average age 30. 71 applicants, 54% accepted, 31 enrolled. In 2009, 28 master's, 4 doctorates awarded. *Degree requirements:* For master's, internship; for doctorate, thesis/dissertation. *Entrance requirements:* For master's and doctorate, GRE General Test, minimum GPA of 3.0 in upper-level coursework in field. Additional exam requirements/recommendations for international students: Required—TOEFL (minimum score 550 paper-based; 213 computer-based). *Application deadline:* For fall admission, 7/15 for domestic students, 5/1 priority date for international students; for spring admission, 11/15 for domestic students, 9/1 priority date for international students. Applications are processed on a rolling basis. Application fee: $50 ($100 for international students). Electronic applications accepted. *Expenses:* Tuition, state resident: full-time $11,068; part-time $461 per credit hour. Tuition, nonresident: full-time $21,178; part-time $882 per credit hour. Tuition and fees vary according to course load. *Financial support:* In 2009–10, 10 research assistantships with full tuition reimbursements (averaging $13,526 per year), 28 teaching assistantships with full tuition reimbursements (averaging $10,792 per year) were awarded; fellowships, career-related internships or fieldwork, Federal Work-Study, institutionally sponsored loans, scholarships/grants, and unspecified assistantships also available. Support available to part-time students. Financial award application deadline: 4/30; financial award applicants required to submit FAFSA. *Faculty research:* Combination of biological, behavioral, and computational approaches for evaluating biological and artificial information processing systems. *Unit head:* Dr. James C. Bartlett, Head, PhD Program, 972-883-2079, Fax: 972-883-2491, E-mail: jbartlet@utdallas.edu. *Application contact:* Dr. Robert D. Stillman, Head, 972-883-3106, Fax: 972-883-3022, E-mail: stillman@utdallas.edu.

The University of Texas Health Science Center at Houston, Graduate School of Biomedical Sciences, Program in Neuroscience, Houston, TX 77225-0036. Offers MS, PhD, MD/PhD. Terminal master's awarded for partial completion of doctoral program. *Degree requirements:* For master's, thesis; for doctorate, thesis/dissertation. *Entrance requirements:* For master's and doctorate, GRE General Test. Additional exam requirements/recommendations for international students: Required—TOEFL. Electronic applications accepted. *Faculty research:* Behavior, cognitive, computational, neuroimaging, substance abuse.

The University of Texas Medical Branch, Graduate School of Biomedical Sciences, Program in Neuroscience, Galveston, TX 77555. Offers PhD. *Students:* 9 full-time (3 women), 2 international. Average age 27. In 2009, 2 doctorates awarded. *Degree requirements:* For doctorate, thesis/dissertation. *Entrance requirements:* For doctorate, GRE General Test. Additional exam requirements/recommendations for international students: Required—TOEFL (minimum score 550 paper-based; 213 computer-based). *Application deadline:* Applications are processed on a rolling basis. Application fee: $30 ($75 for international students). Electronic applications accepted. *Financial support:* In 2009–10, fellowships (averaging $25,000 per year), research assistantships with full tuition reimbursements (averaging $25,000 per year) were awarded. Financial award applicants required to submit FAFSA. *Unit head:* Dr. Volker E. Neugebauer, Director, 409-772-5259, E-mail: voneugeb@utmb.edu. *Application contact:* Lisa Davis, Program Coordinator, 409-772-2124, E-mail: limdavis@utmb.edu.

The University of Texas Southwestern Medical Center at Dallas, Southwestern Graduate School of Biomedical Sciences, Division of Basic Science, Program in Neuroscience, Dallas, TX 75390. Offers PhD. *Faculty:* 35 full-time (5 women). *Students:* 41 full-time (22 women), 3 part-time (1 woman); includes 13 minority (4 African Americans, 6 Asian Americans or Pacific Islanders, 3 Hispanic Americans), 12 international. Average age 28. 946 applicants, 22% accepted. In 2009, 21 doctorates awarded. *Degree requirements:* For doctorate, thesis/dissertation, qualifying exam. *Entrance requirements:* For doctorate, GRE General Test, minimum GPA of 3.0. Additional exam requirements/recommendations for international students: Required—TOEFL. *Application deadline:* For fall admission, 12/15 priority date for domestic students. Applications are processed on a rolling basis. Application fee: $0. Electronic applications accepted. *Financial support:* Fellowships, research assistantships available. *Faculty research:* Ion channels, sensory transduction, membrane excitability and biophysics, synaptic transmission, developmental neurogenetics. *Unit head:* Dr. Nancy E. Street, Associate Dean, 214-648-6708, Fax: 214-648-2102, E-mail: nancy.street@utsouthwestern.edu. *Application contact:* Dr. Nancy E. Street, Associate Dean, 214-648-6708, Fax: 214-648-2102, E-mail: nancy.street@utsouthwestern.edu.

The University of Toledo, College of Graduate Studies, College of Medicine, Biomedical Science Programs, Program in Neurosciences and Neurological Disorders, Toledo, OH 43606-3390. Offers MS, PhD.

University of Utah, School of Medicine and Graduate School, Graduate Programs in Medicine, Program in Neuroscience, Salt Lake City, UT 84112-1107. Offers PhD. *Degree requirements:* For doctorate, thesis/dissertation. *Entrance requirements:* For doctorate, GRE General Test, minimum GPA of 3.0. Additional exam requirements/recommendations for international students: Required—TOEFL (minimum score 500 paper-based; 173 computer-based); Recommended—TWE (minimum score 6). Electronic applications accepted. *Expenses:* Tuition, state resident: full-time $4004; part-time $1674 per semester. Tuition, nonresident: full-time $14,134; part-time $5915 per semester. Required fees: $324 per semester. Tuition and fees vary according to course load, degree level and program. *Faculty research:* Brain and behavioral neuroscience, cellular neuroscience, molecular neuroscience, neurobiology of disease, developmental neuroscience.

University of Vermont, College of Medicine and Graduate College, Graduate Programs in Medicine, Graduate Program in Neuroscience, Burlington, VT 05405. Offers PhD. *Students:* 19 (12 women); includes 2 Hispanic Americans. 20 applicants, 60% accepted, 5 enrolled. *Degree requirements:* For doctorate, thesis/dissertation. *Entrance requirements:* For doctorate, GRE General Test. Additional exam requirements/recommendations for international students: Required—TOEFL (minimum score 550 paper-based; 213 computer-based; 80 iBT). *Application deadline:* For fall admission, 12/15 priority date for domestic students, 12/15 for international students. Application fee: $40. Electronic applications accepted. *Expenses:* Tuition, state resident: part-time $508 per credit hour. Tuition, nonresident: part-time $1281 per credit hour. *Financial support:* Research assistantships, teaching assistantships available. Financial award application deadline: 3/1. *Unit head:* Dr. Rae Nishi, Director, 802-656-1178, E-mail: rae.nishi@uvm.edu. *Application contact:* Dr. Rae Nishi, Director, 802-656-1178, E-mail: rae.nishi@uvm.edu.

University of Virginia, School of Medicine, Department of Neuroscience, Charlottesville, VA 22903. Offers PhD, MD/PhD. *Faculty:* 11 full-time (5 women). *Students:* 29 full-time (18 women); includes 5 minority (1 African American, 4 Hispanic Americans), 3 international. Average age 28. In 2009, 2 doctorates awarded. *Degree requirements:* For doctorate, thesis/dissertation. *Entrance requirements:* For doctorate, GRE General Test, 2 letters of recommendation. Additional exam requirements/recommendations for international students: Required—TOEFL. *Application deadline:* For fall admission, 4/15 for domestic and international students. Applications are processed on a rolling basis. Application fee: $60. Electronic applications accepted. *Financial support:* Application deadline: 1/15. *Unit head:* Dr. Kevin Lee, Chair, 434-982-2927, Fax: 434-982-4380, E-mail: neurograd@virginia.edu. *Application contact:* Tracy Mourton, Program Coordinator, 434-982-4285, Fax: 434-982-4380, E-mail: neurograd@virginia.edu.

The University of Western Ontario, Faculty of Graduate Studies, Biosciences Division, Department of Clinical Neurological Sciences, London, ON N6A 5B8, Canada. Offers M Sc, PhD. Terminal master's awarded for partial completion of doctoral program. *Degree requirements:* For master's, thesis; for doctorate, thesis/dissertation. *Entrance requirements:* For master's, honors degree or equivalent, minimum B+ average; for doctorate, master's degree, minimum B+ average. *Faculty research:* Behavioral neuroscience, neural regeneration and degeneration, visual development, human motor function.

University of Wisconsin–Madison, Graduate School, College of Letters and Science, Department of Psychology, Program in Cognitive Neurosciences, Madison, WI 53706-1380. Offers PhD. *Degree requirements:* For doctorate, comprehensive exam, thesis/dissertation. *Entrance requirements:* For doctorate, GRE General Test, minimum undergraduate GPA of 3.0. Additional exam requirements/recommendations for international students: Required—TOEFL. Electronic applications accepted. *Expenses:* Tuition, state resident: part-time $594 per credit. Tuition, nonresident: part-time $1504 per credit. Required fees: $65 per credit. Tuition and fees vary according to course load, program and reciprocity agreements.

University of Wisconsin–Madison, Graduate School, Neuroscience Training Program, Madison, WI 53706-1380. Offers PhD. *Degree requirements:* For doctorate, thesis/dissertation. *Entrance requirements:* For doctorate, GRE General Test. Electronic applications accepted. *Expenses:* Tuition, state resident: part-time $594 per credit. Tuition, nonresident: part-time $1504 per credit. Required fees: $65 per credit. Tuition and fees vary according to course load, program and reciprocity agreements.

Virginia Commonwealth University, Medical College of Virginia-Professional Programs, School of Medicine, Graduate Program in Neuroscience, Richmond, VA 23284-9005. Offers PhD. Program offered with Departments of Anatomy, Biochemistry and Molecular Biophysics, Pharmacology and Toxicology, and Physiology.

Virginia Commonwealth University, Medical College of Virginia-Professional Programs, School of Medicine, School of Medicine Graduate Programs, Department of Anatomy and Neurobiology, Richmond, VA 23284-9005. Offers anatomy (MS, PhD); anatomy and neurobiology (PhD); anatomy and physical therapy (PhD); neuroscience (MS, PhD). *Degree requirements:* For master's, thesis; for doctorate, thesis/dissertation, comprehensive oral and written exams. *Entrance requirements:* For master's, DAT, GRE General Test, or MCAT; for doctorate, DAT, GRE General Test, MCAT.

Virginia Commonwealth University, Medical College of Virginia-Professional Programs, School of Medicine, School of Medicine Graduate Programs, Department of Biochemistry, Richmond, VA 23284-9005. Offers biochemistry (MS, PhD); molecular biology and genetics (MS, PhD); neuroscience (PhD); MD/PhD. *Degree requirements:* For master's, thesis; for doctorate, thesis/dissertation, comprehensive oral and written exams. *Entrance requirements:* For master's and doctorate, DAT, GRE General Test, MCAT. *Faculty research:* Molecular biology, peptide/protein chemistry, neurochemistry, enzyme mechanisms, macromolecular structure determination.

Virginia Commonwealth University, Medical College of Virginia-Professional Programs, School of Medicine, School of Medicine Graduate Programs, Department of Pharmacology and Toxicology, Richmond, VA 23284-9005. Offers molecular biology and genetics (PhD); neuroscience (PhD); pharmacology (PhD); pharmacology and toxicology (MS); MD/PhD. Terminal master's awarded for partial completion of doctoral program. *Degree requirements:* For master's, thesis; for doctorate, thesis/dissertation, comprehensive oral and written exams. *Entrance requirements:* For master's, DAT, GRE General Test, or MCAT; for doctorate, GRE General Test, MCAT, DAT. *Faculty research:* Drug abuse, drug metabolism, pharmacodynamics, peptide synthesis, receptor mechanisms.

Virginia Commonwealth University, Medical College of Virginia-Professional Programs, School of Medicine, School of Medicine Graduate Programs, Department of Physiology, Richmond, VA 23284-9005. Offers neuroscience (PhD); physiology (MS, PhD); MD/PhD. Terminal master's awarded for partial completion of doctoral program. *Degree requirements:* For master's, thesis; for doctorate, thesis/dissertation, comprehensive oral and written exams. *Entrance requirements:* For master's, DAT, GRE General Test, or MCAT; for doctorate, GRE General Test, MCAT, DAT.

Wake Forest University, School of Medicine and Graduate School of Arts and Sciences, Graduate Programs in Medicine, Interdisciplinary Program in Neuroscience, Winston-Salem, NC 27109. Offers PhD, MD/PhD. *Degree requirements:* For doctorate, thesis/dissertation. *Entrance requirements:* For doctorate, GRE General Test. Additional exam requirements/recommendations for international students: Required—TOEFL. Electronic applications accepted. *Faculty research:* Neurobiology of substance abuse, learning and memory, aging, sensory neurobiology, nervous system development.

Washington State University, College of Veterinary Medicine and Graduate School, Graduate Programs in Veterinary Science, Pullman, WA 99164. Offers veterinary and comparative anatomy, pharmacology, and physiology (MS, PhD), including neuroscience, veterinary science; veterinary clinical sciences (MS); veterinary microbiology and pathology (MS, PhD), including veterinary science; DVM/MS. Part-time programs available. *Faculty:* 45 full-time (8 women), 15 part-time/adjunct (4 women). *Students:* 108 full-time (59 women), 3 part-time (1 woman); includes 5 minority (4 Asian Americans or Pacific Islanders, 1 Hispanic American), 44 international. Average age 33. 109 applicants, 28% accepted, 22 enrolled. In 2009, 7 master's, 5 doctorates awarded. Terminal master's awarded for partial completion of doctoral program. *Degree requirements:* For master's, thesis, oral exam; for doctorate, thesis/dissertation, oral exam, written exam. *Entrance requirements:* For master's and doctorate, GRE General Test, minimum GPA of 3.0. Additional exam requirements/recommendations for international students: Required—TOEFL (minimum score 550 paper-based; 213 computer-based; 80 iBT). *Application deadline:* For fall admission, 12/31 priority date for domestic and international students; for spring admission, 8/1 for domestic and international students. Applications are processed on a rolling basis. Application fee: $60. Electronic applications accepted. *Expenses:* Contact institution. *Financial support:* In 2009–10, 29 students received support, including 4 fellowships with partial tuition reimbursements available (averaging $28,000 per year), 48 research assistantships with partial tuition reimbursements available (averaging $21,558 per year), 8 teaching assistantships with partial tuition reimbursements available (averaging $21,558 per year); Federal Work-Study, scholarships/grants, health care benefits, and unspecified assistantships also available. Financial award application deadline: 3/1; financial award applicants required to submit FAFSA. *Unit head:* Dr. Bryan K. Slinker, Dean, 509-335-9515, Fax: 509-335-0160, E-mail: vetmed-dean@vetmed.wsu.edu. *Application contact:* Julie K. Smith, Principal Assistant, 509-335-3164, E-mail: jksmith@vetmed.wsu.edu.

Washington State University, College of Veterinary Medicine and Graduate School, Graduate Programs in Veterinary Science, Department of Veterinary and Comparative Anatomy, Pharmacology, and Physiology, Program in Neuroscience, Pullman, WA 99164-6520. Offers MS, PhD. Part-time programs available. *Faculty:* 24 full-time (8 women), 19 part-time/adjunct (7 women). *Students:* 26 full-time (12 women), 1 part-time (0 women); includes 2 minority (1 Asian American or Pacific Islander, 1 Hispanic American), 8 international. Average age 28. 55 applicants, 18% accepted, 5 enrolled. In 2009, 1 doctorate awarded. Terminal master's awarded

for partial completion of doctoral program. *Degree requirements:* For master's, thesis, written exam; for doctorate, thesis/dissertation, written exam, oral exam. *Entrance requirements:* For master's and doctorate, GRE General Test, MCAT, minimum GPA of 3.0. Additional exam requirements/recommendations for international students: Required—TOEFL (minimum score 550 paper-based; 213 computer-based; 80 iBT). *Application deadline:* For fall admission, 12/31 for domestic and international students; for spring admission, 8/1 for domestic and international students. Applications are processed on a rolling basis. Application fee: $50. Electronic applications accepted. *Financial support:* In 2009–10, 22 students received support, including 3 fellowships with full tuition reimbursements available (averaging $28,000 per year), 16 research assistantships with full tuition reimbursements available (averaging $21,558 per year), 8 teaching assistantships with full tuition reimbursements available (averaging $21,558 per year); scholarships/grants, health care benefits, and unspecified assistantships also available. Financial award application deadline: 4/15. *Faculty research:* Addiction, sleep and performance, body weight and energy balance, emotion and well being, learning and memory, reproduction, vision, movement. Total annual research expenditures: $5 million. *Unit head:* Dr. Steve Simasko, Chairman, 509-335-6624, Fax: 509-335-4650, E-mail: simasko@vetmed.wsu.edu. *Application contact:* Heather Cochran, Assistant Director, 509-335-7675, Fax: 509-335-4650, E-mail: hcochran@vetmed.wsu.edu.

Washington University in St. Louis, Graduate School of Arts and Sciences, Department of Philosophy, Program in Philosophy/Neuroscience/Psychology, St. Louis, MO 63130-4899. Offers PhD. *Degree requirements:* For doctorate, thesis/dissertation. *Entrance requirements:* For doctorate, GRE General Test, sample of written work. Electronic applications accepted.

Washington University in St. Louis, Graduate School of Arts and Sciences, Division of Biology and Biomedical Sciences, Program in Neurosciences, St. Louis, MO 63130-4899. Offers PhD. *Degree requirements:* For doctorate, thesis/dissertation. *Entrance requirements:* For doctorate, GRE General Test, GRE Subject Test. Electronic applications accepted.

Wayne State University, School of Medicine, Graduate Programs in Medicine, Department of Psychiatry and Behavioral Neurosciences, Program in Translational Neuroscience, Detroit, MI 48201. Offers PhD. *Degree requirements:* For doctorate, thesis/dissertation, qualifying examination, oral defense of dissertation. *Entrance requirements:* For doctorate, GRE General Test, baccalaureate degree with minimum GPA of 3.0, personal statement, 3 letters of recommendation. Additional exam requirements/recommendations for international students: Required—TOEFL. *Faculty research:* Developmental neurobiology, cellular and molecular neurobiology, neuroimaging, pediatric and adult psychiatry, pre-clinical neuroscience and neuropharmacology.

West Virginia University, School of Medicine, Graduate Programs at the Health Sciences Center, Interdisciplinary Graduate Programs in Biomedical Sciences, Program in Neuroscience, Morgantown, WV 26506. Offers PhD, MD/PhD. *Degree requirements:* For doctorate, comprehensive exam, thesis/dissertation. *Entrance requirements:* For doctorate, GRE General Test, minimum GPA of 3.0. Additional exam requirements/recommendations for international students: Required—TOEFL. Electronic applications accepted. *Faculty research:* Sensory neuroscience, cognitive neuroscience, neural injury, homeostasis, behavioral neuroscience.

Yale University, Graduate School of Arts and Sciences, Department of Psychology, New Haven, CT 06520. Offers behavioral neuroscience (PhD); clinical psychology (PhD); cognitive psychology (PhD); developmental psychology (PhD); social/personality psychology (PhD). *Accreditation:* APA. *Degree requirements:* For doctorate, thesis/dissertation. *Entrance requirements:* For doctorate, GRE General Test.

Yale University, Graduate School of Arts and Sciences, Interdepartmental Neuroscience Program, New Haven, CT 06520. Offers PhD. *Degree requirements:* For doctorate, thesis/dissertation. *Entrance requirements:* For doctorate, GRE General Test. *Expenses:* Contact institution.

Yale University, School of Medicine and Graduate School of Arts and Sciences, Combined Program in Biological and Biomedical Sciences (BBS), Neuroscience Track, New Haven, CT 06520. Offers PhD, MD/PhD. *Degree requirements:* For doctorate, thesis/dissertation. *Entrance requirements:* For doctorate, GRE General Test. Additional exam requirements/recommendations for international students: Required—TOEFL. *Application deadline:* For fall admission, 12/6 for domestic and international students. Electronic applications accepted. *Financial support:* Fellowships, research assistantships available. *Unit head:* Dr. Charles Greer, Co-Director, 203-785-5932, Fax: 203-785-5971. *Application contact:* Carol Russo, Student Services Officer, 203-785-5932, Fax: 203-785-5971, E-mail: bbs.neuro@yale.edu.

OREGON HEALTH & SCIENCE UNIVERSITY

Neuroscience Graduate Program

Program of Study	The Neuroscience Graduate Program (NGP) at Oregon Health & Science University (OHSU) offers training leading to the Doctor of Philosophy (Ph.D.) degree. The program is most appropriate for students intending to pursue a professional career in research and teaching, but the University encourages students to pursue the career path that best matches their interests and skills. Students admitted to the M.D./Ph.D. program at OHSU also can pursue their Ph.D. in the program. Highly qualified students admitted to the M.D. program may apply for concurrent admission to the NGP to pursue a Ph.D. in neuroscience. For further information visit http://www.ohsu.edu/ngp.
	The interdepartmental program is broad and diverse, comprised of 140 faculty members and including members of the National Academy of Sciences, the Institute of Medicine, and investigators of the Howard Hughes Medical Institute. The program offers opportunities for advanced study and research in all areas of modern neuroscience including molecular, cellular, developmental, endocrine, behavioral, and systems neuroscience. As a medical campus, there are numerous opportunities for translational projects as well. The faculty represents basic and clinical departments as well as the Vollum Institute, the Center for Research on Occupational and Environmental Toxicology, the Jungers Center, the Oregon National Primate Research Center, the School of Dentistry, and, the Veterans Administration Medical Center.
	The first year includes required course work as well as laboratory rotations. Course work includes a four-course series that provides a broad foundation for a career in neuroscience (cellular neuroscience; neuronal cell biology, signaling and development; systems neuroscience; and neurobiology of disease). Students also rotate in at least three laboratories and participate in special topics and seminar courses. Four elective courses selected from biochemistry, molecular biology, genetics, cell biology, statistics, or advanced neuroscience topics make up the remainder of the course work, typically completed in the first two years. Students identify their dissertation mentor at the end of the first year and spend most of their time in the laboratory during the second year defining their dissertation project. An oral qualifying exam, which incorporates a written thesis proposal, is taken after the second year. Students require an average of five years to complete the Ph.D.
Research Facilities	The faculty is well funded by extramural research grants and maintain modern laboratories for state-of-the-art biomedical research. Students of the program also have access to specialized resources within OHSU through their individual mentors.
Financial Aid	In 2010–11, incoming full-time Ph.D. students receive stipends of $26,500 per year with several fellowships available to supplement stipends. After passing the oral exam at the end of the second year, the stipend increases. Fees such as health care and hospitalization insurance are paid for students on stipends. After the first year of study, students are supported by funds provided by their thesis adviser or training grants. Many students in the NGP apply for and receive extramural fellowships from NIH or private foundations. Several fellowship programs at OHSU offer stipends for projects in translational neuroscience.
Cost of Study	Graduate students are enrolled as graduate research assistants and thus receive a full tuition waiver.
Living and Housing Costs	Many apartments are within walking distance of the campus or on a campus bus route and rent for $600 to $800 per month.
Student Group	The Oregon Health & Science University has approximately 1,000 students in professional schools and 300 students in graduate programs. The Neuroscience Graduate Program admits about 10 students per year with approximately 60 currently in the program. NGP students also benefit from interactions with students in the molecular and cellular biology program, the M.D./Ph.D. program and the behavioral neuroscience program.
Student Outcomes	Since its inception in 1992, more than 75 students have graduated from the program. Nearly all have pursued biomedical research and a number hold tenure-track faculty positions in the U.S. and Europe. Others hold positions in industry, government, or non-profit agencies.
Location	OHSU is located on Marquam Hill near the center of Portland. The site allows sweeping views of the downtown, the Willamette River and the Cascades, including Mount Hood and Mount St. Helens. An overhead tram connects the main campus to a new clinical/translational campus at the South Waterfront and provides easy public transportation access to OHSU from across Portland. The greater Portland area is a major cultural center with a population of two million, and a reputation for great neighborhoods, sustainable living, bicycle commuting, and all forms of outdoor activities within easy driving. The Willamette River and Columbia river gorge are popular areas for water sports including windsurfing. The high desert of Central Oregon offers rock climbing, whitewater rafting, and great sunny weather. The driving time from Portland to the mountains or high desert (to the east) and ocean beaches (to the west) is just over an hour. Portland's climate is mild, with summer high temperatures in the 70s and 80s and winter temperatures between 40 and 50 degrees. Other colleges and universities located in Portland include Reed College, Lewis and Clark College, Portland State University, and the University of Portland.
The University	The Oregon Health & Science University is the only academic health center in the state of Oregon. It houses the Schools of Medicine, Dentistry, Nursing, and Engineering; the Vollum Institute; the Oregon National Primate Research Center; the University Hospital and Clinics; and Doernbecher Children's Hospital. Affiliations exist with many other institutions, including Portland State University, the Veterans Administration Medical Center, and the Shriners Hospital for Crippled Children.
Applying	Students with a bachelor's degree in the biological or physical sciences and with a strong commitment to research are encouraged to apply. The deadline is December 15. Applicants must submit scores on the Graduate Record Examinations, and international applicants whose native language is not English must submit scores from the Test of English as a Foreign Language (TOEFL). Successful applicants generally have significant research experience. Applicants are notified of acceptance no later than April 1, and accepted students are strongly encouraged to begin research rotations on July 1.
Correspondence and Information	Neuroscience Graduate Program Oregon Health & Science University Vollum Institute, L-474 3181 Southwest Sam Jackson Park Road Portland, Oregon 97239 Phone: 503-494-6932 Fax: 503-494-5518 E-mail: ngp@ohsu.edu Web site: http://www.ohsu.edu/ngp

Oregon Health & Science University

THE FACULTY

Neuroscience is multidisciplinary and becoming even more so, despite increasing technology. Thus most faculty members and most projects in neuroscience no longer fit a single subdiscipline within neuroscience. That is certainly true of the 140 NGP faculty members at OHSU. On the University's Web site at http://www.ohsu.edu/academic/som/ngp/faculty.cfm, faculty members have been listed by traditional subdisciplines in neuroscience as well as areas of particular strength.

STATE UNIVERSITY OF NEW YORK
UPSTATE MEDICAL UNIVERSITY

Programs in Neuroscience

Programs of Study	At SUNY Upstate's College of Graduate Studies, Ph.D. students thrive as they participate in medically relevant research on a campus that is proud of its mentoring and multidisciplinary approach. Students enjoy a student-faculty ratio of nearly 1:1 and publish articles in professional journals during their program.
	Students select a department, thesis mentor, and ultimate area of research after their first year, which includes three in-depth laboratory rotations of their choice. All departments support Upstate's four main Research Pillars: cancer; infectious diseases; diabetes, metabolic disorders, and cardiovascular disease; and disorders of the nervous system.
	The graduate program in neuroscience is a multidisciplinary, interdepartmental program divided into three main areas: cell and molecular neuroscience, development and regeneration, and systems neuroscience.
	The program's research relates to many human diseases and disorders including fetal alcohol syndrome, spinal cord injury, degenerative retinal disease, Alzheimer's disease, multiple sclerosis, cerebral palsy, and amyotrophic lateral sclerosis (ALS), also known as Lou Gehrig's disease.
	The Cell and Molecular Neuroscience group studies the regulation of gene expression in the nervous system, mechanisms of cell signaling, mechanisms of excitability within cells, and the molecular bases of neurological disease and disorders.
	The Development and Regeneration group studies the development of the mammalian cortex, the regulation of gene expression during development, development and regeneration of the vertebrate retina, and the mechanisms of spinal cord regeneration.
	The Systems Neuroscience group studies the neural mechanisms underlying the functions of the olfactory system, visual system, and motor systems in health and disease.
Research Facilities	SUNY Upstate has world-class facilities for faculty members and students. Faculty and students have access to a variety of state-of-the-art research methods, including computational and behavioral techniques, gene array, real-time PCR, transgenesis, optical imaging, single-cell electrophysiology, and cell culture.
	The main core facilities on campus include the Center for Research and Evaluation, Confocal/Two Photon Imaging, Department of Laboratory Animal Resources, DNA Sequencing, Flow Cytometry, Humanized SCID Mouse and Stem Cell Processing, Imaging Research, In Vivo Computed Tomography, Microarray (SUNYMAC), MRI Research, and Proteomics.
	SUNY Upstate also maintains a coalition with nearby Cornell University, the University of Rochester Medical Center, and Buffalo's Roswell Park Cancer Institute, which is dedicated to sharing cutting-edge research facilities. There are also full research support services on campus, including laboratory-animal facilities, network access to the SeqWeb suite of software, a computer-age medical library containing more than 183,000 volumes, electronics and machine shops, and photographic and computer services.
	SUNY Upstate's growth on the research side is highlighted by a $72 million expansion of its Institute for Human Performance, a high-tech facility housing shared laboratories and core facilities used in basic and clinical research. It also broke ground in 2009 for a dedicated research park facility.
Financial Aid	All accepted Ph.D. students are fully supported throughout their education by full tuition waivers and a stipend ($21,514 per year). Support comes from graduate assistantships, departmental assistantships, and NIH and NSF grants.
Cost of Study	Stipends and full tuition waivers are granted to all students accepted into the Ph.D. program. There is no teaching requirement. Student fees, which include health service, were $552 for the 2009–10 academic year.
Living and Housing Costs	On-campus housing is available in Clark Tower, a ten-story apartment building with attractive, fully furnished standard rooms, studio apartments, and two-bedroom suites. Costs ranged from $4127 (double occupancy) to $8618 (married/family accommodations) for 2009–10. Clark Tower also has study rooms, computer rooms, private and shared kitchens, lounges, a recreation room, laundry, and storage. Clark Tower is next door to the Campus Activities Building, which houses athletic facilities, a bookstore, and snack bar.
	Many students rent nearby houses or apartments and bicycle or walk to campus. Syracuse has a low cost of living and abundant affordable housing.
Student Group	There are 124 graduate students in the biomedical sciences (58 percent women; 100 percent full-time) and approximately 600 medical students, 200 nursing students, and 200 students in the health professions enrolled at Upstate Medical University. Twenty-five percent of the graduate students come from Canada, Europe, and Asia. Syracuse University and the SUNY College of Environmental Science are located within a quarter mile of SUNY Upstate, resulting in a population of approximately 23,000 students in the immediate area.
Location	Syracuse is New York's fourth-largest city and is located in the scenic center of the state. A naturally beautiful setting, the area offers excellent hiking, biking, boating, and skiing. Nearby are the Finger Lakes region, the Adirondack and the Catskill Mountains, and Lake Ontario. Syracuse's cultural activities include a professional theater, symphony orchestra and opera company, noted author lecture series, chamber music groups, and several top-notch music festivals (classical, blues, and jazz) as well as art and history museums. The area also offers high-quality family life with many excellent school districts and Upstate's own day care center. Syracuse University's top-level collegiate sporting events are a major recreational activity. Syracuse is easily reached by air, rail, and car.
The University	SUNY Upstate is the only academic medical center in the central New York region and is part of the dynamic University Hill community. In addition to the College of Graduate Studies, SUNY Upstate Medical University includes three other colleges—Medicine, Nursing, and Health Professions—its own University Hospital, and a regional campus in Binghamton, New York. The University is growing with new leadership, degree programs, and further plans for expansion. SUNY Upstate Medical University is close to downtown Syracuse and is adjacent to (but not affiliated with) the campus of Syracuse University. SUNY Upstate's Campus Activities Building houses a swimming pool, sauna, gymnasium, squash courts, handball/paddleball court, weight-lifting area with a Universal Gym and a full Nautilus room, billiards, table tennis, television room, bookstore, snack bar, and lounge. Conference rooms are also available for student use.
Applying	The Admissions Committee for the College of Graduate Studies at SUNY Upstate begins reviewing applications in December prior to entry and continues until all positions are filled, which can be as early as early April. The State University of New York requires a $40 application fee. Competitive applicants must have a bachelor's degree or its equivalent, a minimum 3.0 GPA, and course work that includes biology, calculus, chemistry, and physics. GRE General Test scores are required (combined score 1000 minimum), and scores from the Subject Test in chemistry or biology are recommended. International applicants must provide clear evidence of English proficiency (including speaking) by taking the Test of English as a Foreign Language (TOEFL). Candidates for admission are selected on the basis of their record and qualifications for independent scholarship in a specialized field of study. Selected applicants will be invited to campus to meet with faculty, students and tour lab facilities.
Correspondence and Information	Office of Graduate Studies State University of New York Upstate Medical University 750 East Adams Street Syracuse, New York 13210 Phone: 315-464-7655 Fax: 315-464-4544 E-mail: biosci@upstate.edu Web site: http://www.upstate.edu/grad/

State University of New York Upstate Medical University

THE FACULTY AND THEIR RESEARCH

Robert B. Barlow, Ph.D., Professor. Neural basis of visual behavior; computational models of neural coding; circadian and metabolic modulation of human visual sensitivity.

Blair Calancie, Ph.D., Professor. CNS plasticity after trauma; intraoperative electrophysiology.

Gregory Canute, M.D., Associate Professor. Genetics and gene therapy of brain tumors.

Timothy A. Damron, M.D., Professor. Radioprotectant strategies for protecting the pediatric growth plate.

Russell G. Durkovic, Ph.D., Professor. Examination of processes underlying recovery from spinal cord injury in the salamander.

Jeffrey C. Freedman, Ph.D., Associate Professor. Membrane physiology in normal and sickle human red blood cells; optical indicators of membrane potential and intracellular calcium; membrane biophysics.

Stephen J. Glatt, Ph.D., Assistant Professor. Psychiatric epidemiology and genetics.

Charles J. Hodge, M.D., Professor. Mechanisms of cortical plasticity and cortical reorganization after injury.

Huaiyu Hu, Ph.D., Professor. Molecular studies of brain malformations.

Burk Jubelt, M.D., Professor. CNS acute and chronic polio- and entero-virus infections.

Wendy Kates, Ph.D., Associate Professor. Anatomic and functional imaging investigations of neurodevelopment in individuals with genetic or psychiatric disorders.

Barry Knox, Ph.D., Professor. Visual transduction; gene expression; membrane proteins.

Michael J. Lyon, Ph.D., Associate Professor. Age-related changes in the laryngeal muscles and vocal folds.

Kenneth Mann, Ph.D., Professor. Mechanical and biological factors in total joint replacement.

Paul Massa, Ph.D., Professor. Genetic regulation of glial cell differentiation.

Russell Matthews, Ph.D., Assistant Professor. Role of glycoproteins in oncogenesis and brain development.

James S. McCasland, Ph.D., Professor. Cortical plasticity; development of somatotopic representations in cortex.

Michael M. Meguid, M.D., Adjunct Professor. Neurophysiological regulation of food intake.

Frank Middleton, Ph.D., Associate Professor. Molecular basis of cortical-basal ganglia and cortical-cerebellar circuit and dysfunction in neurological and psychiatric disease.

Michael Miller, Ph.D., Professor and Chair. Factors that regulate the proliferation, migration, and survival/death of neurons in the developing brain; models of fetal alcohol syndrome, autism, and attention-deficit hyperactivity disorder.

Sandra Mooney, Ph.D., Assistant Professor. Cell death and survival in the developing brain; mechanisms of ethanol toxicity; models of fetal alcohol syndrome and autism.

Brad Motter, Ph.D., Research Associate Professor. Visual neurophysiology; visual attention; visual search behavior.

Nancy Nussmeier, M.D., Professor. Stroke after cardiac surgery; cerebral protection during cardiac surgery; gender-related surgical outcomes.

Eric Olson, Ph.D., Assistant Professor. Cellular and molecular mechanisms of cerebral cortex development.

Joseph A. Spadaro, Ph.D., Professor. Electromagnetic and mechanical regulation of bone physiology; skeletal growth and bone density.

Dennis J. Stelzner, Ph.D., Professor. CNS regeneration; spinal cord injury research; neural plasticity.

Daniel Ts'o, Ph.D., Associate Professor. Neuronal mechanisms of visual perception, studied through physiological, anatomical, and functional imaging techniques.

Mary Lou Vallano, Ph.D., Professor. Neuronal survival and development.

Richard D. Veenstra, Ph.D., Professor. Regulation of connexin-specific gap junctions; gap-junction channel biophysics.

Brent Vogt, Ph.D., Professor. Structure, functions, and pathologies of cingulate cortex.

Richard J. H. Wojcikiewicz, Ph.D., Professor. Intracellular signaling via $InsP_3$ receptors and the ubiquitin/proteasome pathway.

Steven Youngentob, Ph.D., Professor. Olfactory neural plasticity in adults; olfactory signal transduction; in utero ethanol experience and olfactory system plasticity; peripheral and central mechanisms of odorant quality coding.

UNIVERSITY OF CALIFORNIA, BERKELEY

Neuroscience Graduate Program

Program of Study
The Neuroscience Graduate Program is a campuswide interdisciplinary organization that includes more than 40 faculty members with state-of-the-art laboratories from the Departments of Molecular and Cell Biology, Psychology, Physics, and Integrative Biology in the College of Letters and Sciences; the Department of Chemical Engineering in the College of Chemistry; the Department of Environmental Science Policy and Management in the College of Natural Resources; the Helen Wills Neuroscience Institute; the School of Public Health; the Department of Electrical Engineering in the College of Engineering; and the School of Optometry's Program in Vision Sciences. Faculty members participate in neuroscience graduate training and research from the molecular and genetic levels to the cognitive and computational levels. Areas of training and research include analysis of ion channels, receptors, and signal transduction mechanisms; formation, function, and plasticity of synapses; control of neural cell fate and pattern formation; neuronal growth cone guidance and target recognition; mechanisms of sensory processing in the visual, auditory, and olfactory systems; development and function of neural networks; motor control; and the neural basis of cognition. The preparations in use range from reductionist models to complex neural systems and include cells in culture, simple invertebrate and vertebrate organisms, model genetic systems, the mammalian cerebral cortex, and human brain imaging.

The graduate training includes a series of graduate-level courses, three laboratory rotations during the first year, placement in a thesis laboratory starting with the second year, a qualifying examination that includes a thesis proposal at the end of the second year, two semesters of teaching assistantship, and approximately three years of in-candidacy, full-time research ending with the thesis presentation and filing.

Research Facilities
In addition to the neuroscience faculty members' research laboratories, the Neuroscience Institute has four technology centers: the Brain Imaging Center, with a 4-Tesla fMRI and a 3-Tesla fMRI, as well as a networked computer system; the Redwood Center for Theoretical Neuroscience; the Functional Genomics Laboratory; and the Molecular Imaging Center. All facilities are used for research and training purposes. Faculty laboratories and the technology centers are housed in various buildings on the UC Berkeley main campus.

Financial Aid
All graduate students are fully supported by the program during their training. Financial aid packages include scholarships, teaching assistantships, and research assistantships. Applicants are strongly encouraged to apply for National Science Foundation fellowships in November during their senior year. University fellowships are also available. The 2010–11 minimum stipend level is set at $28,000 for twelve months.

Cost of Study
In 2010–11, University registration fees for legal California residents amount to approximately $12,950 for the academic year, or two semesters. For nonresidents, tuition and fees for the same period of study amount to approximately $28,050. All admitted students have fees and tuition, as well as health and dental insurance, paid in full by the program.

Living and Housing Costs
Most graduate students live in apartments or houses in the vicinity of the campus. Rents for shared housing range from $800 to $1200 per month. The University maintains a family student housing complex for married couples and single-parent families. The Student Housing Office has its own Web site (http://www.housing.berkeley.edu/) and assists students in locating housing both on and off campus.

Student Group
The Berkeley campus has approximately 35,000 students, including more than 10,000 graduate students. Around 3,000 international students from more than 100 countries add to the cosmopolitan flavor of the campus. The Neuroscience Graduate Program, with more than 100 graduate student affiliates from widely varied backgrounds and with wide-ranging interests and pursuits, is a vigorous, stimulating group within Berkeley's outstanding scientific community. Cohesion within this group is enhanced by weekly seminars, Journal Club activities, and annual off-site neuroscience retreats.

Student Outcomes
Neuroscience graduates find employment as postdoctoral fellows at peer institutions such as Caltech, Columbia, Harvard, MIT, Stanford, the University of California at San Francisco, the University of California at San Diego, and the NIH; as faculty members in academia; and as researchers in both private and public institutions. Some graduates work in biotechnology firms or choose to continue their studies at medical, veterinary, or law schools.

Location
The campus, at the foot of the Berkeley Hills and in the center of the city of Berkeley, is surrounded by business and residential districts. The setting retains a park atmosphere, with wooded glens, spacious plazas, and the picturesque Strawberry Creek running the length of the campus. Many areas and buildings on campus provide panoramic views of San Francisco and the entire nine-county Bay Area, a region renowned for its cultural and recreational activities, including public lectures, concerts, theater and other dramatic presentations, museums, galleries, exhibits, and a wide variety of restaurants, eateries, and cafés. Hiking and biking trails are in abundance, and sailing on the bay is nearby.

The University
The Berkeley campus, which was founded in 1868, is the oldest of the ten University of California campuses. Just to name a few of its outstanding and diverse faculty members, there are 8 out of a total of 20 Nobel laureates who are still active faculty members. The University is home to 213 American Association for the Advancement of Science Fellows, 225 American Academy of Arts and Sciences Fellows, 30 MacArthur Fellows (one of the most recent is Lu Chen, an active faculty member of the Neuroscience Graduate Program), 136 National Academy of Sciences members (including Mu-ming Poo of the Neuroscience Graduate Program), 12 recipients of the National Medal of Science, 1 poet laureate, 14 Howard Hughes Medical Institute Investigators (including Yang Dan from the Neuroscience Graduate Program (Kristin Scott is the recipient of the HHMI Early Career Scientist Award), and 4 Pulitzer Prize winners. Generally considered the leading public university in the nation, with its graduate programs ranked first in the nation in both number (97 percent are in the top ten list) and scholarship (thirty-two "distinguished" programs) according to the National Research Council, Berkeley is continually developing new programs and redefining existing ones, such as the integrated Neuroscience Graduate Program, in an attempt to meet each new challenge and forge new paths.

Applying
The Neuroscience Graduate Program admits students starting in the fall semester only for a Ph.D. course of study exclusively. Inquiries regarding application procedures should be directed to the Graduate Affairs Office. Applicants must use the online application method at https://gradadm.berkeley.edu/grdappl/welcome. The application deadline is December 1 each year, but students can apply as early as September. Graduate Record Examinations scores (Institute Code 4833; Department Code 0213) for the General Test, mandatory, and one Subject Test, highly recommended (same codes; tests in biochemistry and cell biology, chemistry, biology, psychology, computer science, mathematics, or physics), a TOEFL (Institute Code 4833) for international applicants whose first language is not English (with a minimum score of 230 on the CBT or 68 on the iBT), and a minimum GPA of 3.0 are required. At least one year of proven laboratory experience is likewise required. Admitted students have historically scored above the high 80th percentile on the tests and have higher average GPAs. The Neuroscience Graduate Program actively solicits applications from underrepresented groups.

Correspondence and Information
Graduate Affairs Office
Neuroscience Graduate Program
3210F Tolman Hall, MC#3192
University of California, Berkeley
Berkeley, California 94720
Phone: 510-642-8915
Fax: 510-643-4966
E-mail: neurosci@berkeley.edu
Web site: http://neuroscience.berkeley.edu/grad/home/

University of California, Berkeley

THE FACULTY AND THEIR RESEARCH

Faculty members in the Neuroscience Graduate Program are divided into four broad research areas: cellular, molecular, and developmental neuroscience; systems and animal behavior; computational and theoretical neuroscience; and human cognitive neuroscience. Individual faculty members may be involved in more than one research area.

Martin S. Banks, Professor. Visual space perception; psychophysics; modeling of vision; virtual reality.

Shaowen Bao, Assistant Adjunct Professor. Sensory processing.

Diana Bautista, Assistant Professor (McKnight and Pew Scholar). Molecular mechanisms of transduction in touch and pain receptors.

George Bentley, Associate Professor. Neural integration and transduction of environmental cues into endocrine signals.

Sonia Bishop, Assistant Professor. Affective cognitive neuroscience; individual (including genetic) differences in cognitive control.

Silvia Bunge, Associate Professor. Cognitive neuroscience and developmental cognitive neuroscience; cognitive control and prefrontal function.

Jose Carmena, Assistant Professor (Sloan Research Fellow); NSF Faculty Early Career Development Award). Brain-machine interfaces; neural mechanisms of sensorimotor control and learning; neural ensemble computation; neuroprosthetics.

Lu Chen, Associate Professor (MacArthur Fellow). Mechanisms of synapse formation during development and synapse modification in plasticity.

Yang Dan, Professor (HHMI Investigator). Processing and computation of visual information in the thalamus and cortex.

Mark D'Esposito, Professor. Neural basis of working memory in humans; functions of human prefrontal cortex; fMRI.

Michael DeWeese, Assistant Professor. Auditory sensory processing in cortex; cortical mechanisms of selective attention.

Dan Feldman, Associate Professor. Synaptic mechanisms for cortical map plasticity; mechanisms and function of spike timing-dependant synaptic plasticity; sensory coding in the whisker system.

Marla Feller, Associate Professor. Neural activity in assembly of neural circuits; cellular mechanisms that underlie the spontaneous generation of retinal waves; role of retinal waves in the maturation of retinal projection to its primary targets in the CNS; role of retinal waves in the development of receptive fields of retinal ganglion cells.

John Flannery, Professor. Molecular genetics of transduction and retinal degeneration; gene therapy for retinal diseases.

Darlene Francis, Assistant Professor. Behavioral neuroscience; developmental psychobiology; animal models; stress; maternal care; gene-environment interaction.

Jack Gallant, Professor. Neural mechanisms of visual form perception and attention.

Gian Garriga, Professor. Neuronal migration and axonal pathfinding in *C. elegans*.

Donald Glaser, Professor and Nobel Laureate. Computational modeling of human vision.

Xiaohua Gong, Associate Professor. Eye development and disease; cell-to-cell communication; intracellular signaling pathways in the lens.

Thomas Griffiths, Associate Professor. Computational models of cognition, including causality, categorization, inductive inference, probabilistic reasoning, language learning, and language evolution; machine learning; Bayesian statistics.

Ehud Isacoff, Professor. Biophysical properties of ion channels; advanced optical methods.

Richard Ivry, Professor. Neural basis of motor control and motor learning in humans.

Lucia Jacobs, Associate Professor. Neural mechanisms of complex behaviors.

William Jagust, Professor. Structural and functional imaging of aging and dementia.

Daniela Kaufer, Assistant Professor (National Institute of Mental Health BRAINS Award). Molecular mechanisms underlying stress responses in the brain.

Stanley Klein, Professor. Modeling of spatial vision and its application in image compression.

Robert Knight, Professor. Role of human prefrontal cortex in attention and memory control.

Richard Kramer, Professor. Mechanisms of cell signaling mediated by cyclic nucleotides.

Lance Kriegsfeld, Associate Professor. Genetic, cellular, and hormonal mechanisms responsible for the temporal control of motivated behaviors.

Dennis Levi, Professor. Peripheral and central mechanisms of amblyopia.

John Ngai, Professor. Cellular and molecular mechanisms of olfaction; functional genomics.

Bruno Olshausen, Professor. Computational models of perception.

Mu-ming Poo, Professor (Academy of Science member). Mechanisms of axon guidance; synaptic plasticity.

Lynn Robertson, Adjunct Professor. Neural basis of human perception and attention.

David Schaffer, Professor. Mechanisms of stem cell differentiation.

Kristin Scott, Associate Professor (HHMI Early Career Scientist, Merck Fellow). Taste recognition in *Drosophila*.

Arthur Shimamura, Professor (Guggenheim Fellow). Biological basis of memory and cognitive functions in humans.

Michael Silver, Assistant Professor. Neural correlates of human visual perception and attention.

Friedrich Sommer, Associate Adjunct Professor. Models of associative memory; sensory processing.

Mark Tanouye, Professor. Molecular genetics and physiology of behavior in *Drosophila*.

Frédéric Theunissen, Professor. Neural mechanisms underlying complex sound recognition.

Matthew Walker, Associate Professor. Cognitive neuroscience of the sleeping brain.

Jonathan Wallis, Associate Professor. Neuronal mechanisms of goal-directed behavior.

David Whitney, Associate Professor. Visual and visuomotor localization.

Andrew Wurmser, Assistant Professor. Differentiation of neural stem cells.

Robert Zucker, Professor. Role of calcium in transmitter release, synaptic transmission, and plasticity.

UNIVERSITY OF CONNECTICUT HEALTH CENTER

Graduate Program in Neuroscience

Program of Study

The neuroscience graduate program at the University of Connecticut Health Center offers an interdisciplinary training environment that is committed to preparing students for research and teaching careers in both academic and industrial settings. The curriculum and research are dedicated to understanding the normal function and disorders of the nervous system.

All course requirements are fulfilled within the first two years of the program. Introductory core courses establish a strong foundation in molecular, cellular, and systems-level neurobiology.

A wide selection of advanced elective courses on such topics as physiology of excitable tissue, computational neuroscience, neuropharmacology, neuroimmunology, neurobiology of disease, microscopy, biochemistry, immunology, genetics, and cell biology allows tailoring of the curriculum to accommodate the specific needs and diverse interests of students. Participation in weekly journal clubs provides a broad perspective of cutting-edge research in the field.

During the first year of the program, three research rotation projects are performed in laboratories of the student's choice and a laboratory is identified for the dissertation research project by the beginning of the second year. Experimental training opportunities ranging from recombinant DNA to human studies are available. The breadth of these opportunities is shown in a survey of the areas of faculty research, which include regulation of gene expression, signal transduction, and intracellular trafficking in neurons and glia; function of voltage-sensitive ion channels and neurotransmitter receptors; biology of neuropeptides; synaptic transmission and neuroplasticity; development of neurons and glia; synaptic organization and stimulus coding; and sensory perception, behavior, and human psychophysics. Research pertaining to specific maladies of the nervous system includes neuroinflammation, autoimmunity, and neurodegeneration; substance abuse; stroke; epilepsy; multiple sclerosis; and deafness. Approaches employed include genetic engineering; cell and brain slice cultures; stem cells; electrophysiology; confocal microscopy and other imaging; neuroanatomical, virtual cell and mathematical modeling; and behavioral and transgenic animal models.

Research Facilities

Because of the interdepartmental format, the students have access to all of the facilities of modern biomedical research at the University of Connecticut Health Center, including those in clinical and basic science departments. Most of the neuroscience faculty members are housed in the same building on adjoining floors, providing for a congenial atmosphere of informal scientific exchange and collaborations between laboratories. The Center for Cell Analysis and Modeling (CCAM) has state-of-the-art facilities for confocal and two-photon microscopy and image analysis and is available to members of the Program in Neuroscience. The Lyman Maynard Stowe Library has an extensive collection of periodicals and monographs as well as subscriptions to journals of current interest in the field of neuroscience.

Financial Aid

Support for doctoral students engaged in full-time degree programs at the Health Center is provided on a competitive basis. Graduate research assistantships for 2010–11 provide a stipend of $28,000 per year, which includes a waiver of tuition/University fees for the fall and spring semesters and a student health insurance plan. While financial aid is offered competitively, the Health Center makes every possible effort to address the financial needs of all students.

Cost of Study

For 2010–11, tuition is $4455 per semester ($8910 per year) for full-time students who are Connecticut residents and $11,565 per semester ($23,130 per year) for full-time out-of-state residents. General University fees are added to the cost of tuition for students who do not receive a tuition waiver. These costs are usually met by traineeships or research assistantships for doctoral students.

Living and Housing Costs

There is a wide range of affordable housing options in the greater Hartford area within easy commuting distance of the campus, including an extensive complex that is adjacent to the Health Center. Costs range from $600 to $900 per month for a one-bedroom unit; 2 or more students sharing an apartment usually pay less. University housing is not available.

Student Group

Twenty-two students are registered in the Ph.D. program (including combined-degree students). The total number of master's and Ph.D. students at the Health Center is approximately 400, and there are about 125 medical and dental students per class.

Location

The Health Center is located in the historic town of Farmington, Connecticut. Set in the beautiful New England countryside on a hill overlooking the Farmington Valley, it is close to ski areas, hiking trails, and facilities for boating, fishing, and swimming. Connecticut's capital city of Hartford, 7 miles east of Farmington, is the center of an urban region of approximately 800,000 people. The beaches of the Long Island Sound are about 50 minutes away to the south, and the beautiful Berkshires are a short drive to the northwest. New York City and Boston can be reached within 2½ hours by car. Hartford is the home of the acclaimed Hartford Stage Company, TheatreWorks, the Hartford Symphony and Chamber orchestras, two ballet companies, an opera company, the Wadsworth Atheneum (the oldest public art museum in the nation), the Mark Twain house, the Hartford Civic Center, and many other interesting cultural and recreational facilities. The area is also home to several branches of the University of Connecticut, Trinity College, and the University of Hartford, which includes the Hartt School of Music. Bradley International Airport (about 30 minutes from campus) serves the Hartford/Springfield area with frequent airline connections to major cities in this country and abroad. Frequent bus and rail service is also available from Hartford.

The Health Center

The 200-acre Health Center campus at Farmington houses a division of the University of Connecticut Graduate School, as well as the School of Medicine and Dental Medicine. The campus also includes the John Dempsey Hospital, associated clinics, and extensive medical research facilities, all in a centralized facility with more than 1 million square feet of floor space. The Health Center's newest research addition, the Academic Research Building, was opened in 1999. This impressive eleven-story structure provides 170,000 square feet of state-of-the-art laboratory space. The faculty at the center includes more than 260 full-time members. The institution has a strong commitment to graduate study within an environment that promotes social and intellectual interaction among the various educational programs. Graduate students are represented on various administrative committees concerned with curricular affairs, and the Graduate Student Organization (GSO) represents graduate students' needs and concerns to the faculty and administration, in addition to fostering social contact among graduate students in the Health Center.

Applying

Applications for admission should be submitted on standard forms obtained from the Graduate Admissions Office at the UConn Health Center or on the Web site. The application should be filed together with transcripts, three letters of recommendation, a personal statement, and recent results from the General Test of the Graduate Record Examinations. International students must take the Test of English as a Foreign Language (TOEFL) to satisfy Graduate School requirements. The deadline for completed applications and receipt of all supplemental materials is December 15. Earlier submission of applications is recommended, and interviews are considered highly desirable. Applicants should have had undergraduate instruction in chemistry and biology. In accordance with the laws of the state of Connecticut and of the United States, the University of Connecticut Health Center does not discriminate against any person in its educational and employment activities on the grounds of race, color, creed, national origin, sex, age, or physical disability.

Correspondence and Information

Dr. Richard Mains, Neuroscience Program Director
Lori Capozzi, Neuroscience Graduate Program Coordinator
University of Connecticut Health Center, E-4056
Farmington, Connecticut 06030-3401

Phone: 860-679-2658
Fax: 860-679-8766
E-mail: capozzi@uchc.edu
Web site: http://grad.uchc.edu
http://grad.uchc.edu/neuroscience/neuroscience_intro.html

University of Connecticut Health Center

THE FACULTY AND THEIR RESEARCH

Srdjan Antic, Assistant Professor of Neuroscience; M.D., Belgrade. Dendritic integration of synaptic inputs; dopaminergic modulation of dendritic excitability.

Rashmi Bansal, Associate Professor of Neuroscience; Ph.D., Central Drug Research Institute, 1976. Developmental, cellular, and molecular biology of oligodendrocytes; growth-factor regulation of development and function and its relationship to neurodegenerative disease, including multiple sclerosis.

Elisa Barbarese, Professor of Neuroscience and Neurology; Ph.D. McGill, 1978. Molecular and cellular biology of neural cells, with emphasis on RNA trafficking.

Leslie R. Bernstein, Associate Professor of Neuroscience; Ph.D., Illinois, 1984. Behavioral neuroscience: psychoacoustics, binaural hearing.

John H. Carson, Professor of Molecular, Microbial, and Structural Biology; Ph.D., MIT, 1972. Molecular and developmental neurobiology; myelination; intracellular RNA trafficking.

Lisa Conti, Assistant Professor of Psychiatry; Ph.D., Vermont, 1986. Behavioral neuroscience: roles of stress and neuropeptides in animal models of psychiatric disorders.

Jonathan Covault, Associate Professor of Psychiatry; M.D., Ph.D., Iowa, 1982. Genetic correlates of alcohol use disorders; role of neuroactive steroids in the effects of alcohol.

Stephen Crocker, Assistant Professor of Neuroscience; Ph.D., Ottawa. Brain injury and repair in neurodegenerative diseases, with a focus on neuroinflammation; myelin injury; neural stem cell differentiation; signal transduction; glia; matrix metalloproteinases and their tissue inhibitors.

Betty Eipper, Professor of Neuroscience; Ph.D., Harvard, 1973. Cell biology, biochemistry, and physiology of peptide synthesis, storage, and secretion in neurons and endocrine cells.

Marion E. Frank, Professor of BioStructure and Function and Director, Connecticut Chemosensory Clinical Research Center; Ph.D., Brown, 1968. Gustatory neurophysiology, neuroanatomy, behavior, and disorders; chemosensory information processing; clinical testing of oral chemosensory function in humans.

James Hewett, Assistant Professor of Neuroscience; Ph.D., Michigan State, 1991. Mechanisms of cell injury and inflammation in the central nervous system.

Sandra Hewett, Associate Professor of Neuroscience; Ph.D., Michigan State, 1992. Mechanisms underlying acute and chronic cell death in the central nervous system.

Duck O. Kim, Professor of Neuroscience and Biological Engineering Program; D.Sc., Washington (St. Louis), 1972. Neurobiology and biophysics of the auditory system; computational neuroscience of single neurons and neural systems; experimental otolaryngology; biomedical engineering.

Shigeyuki Kuwada, Professor of Neuroscience; Ph.D., Cincinnati, 1973. Neurophysiology and anatomy of mammalian auditory system; principles of binaural signal processing, electrical audiometry in infants.

Eric S. Levine, Associate Professor of Neuroscience; Ph.D., Princeton, 1992. Synapse plasticity and role of neuromodulators in brain development and learning, focusing on neurotrophins and endocannabinoids.

James Li, Professor of Genetics and Developmental Biology; Ph.D., Texas. Development of the central nervous system, with an emphasis on the cellular and molecular mechanisms underlying formation of the mammalian cerebellum.

Xue-Jun Li, Assistant Professor of Neuroscience; Ph.D., Fudan (China). Stem cell biology: mechanisms and pathways underlying the development and degeneration of human motor neurons, using human stem cells as an experimental system.

Leslie Loew, Professor of Cell Biology; Ph.D., Cornell, 1974. Morphological determinants of cell physiology; image-based computational models of cellular biology; spatial variations of cell membrane electrophysiology; new optical methods for probing living cells.

Xin-Ming Ma, Assistant Professor of Neuroscience; Ph.D., Beijing. Synaptogenesis and spine plasticity in hippocampal neurons; estrogen hormones and synaptic plasticity; stress and neuronal plasticity.

Richard Mains, Professor and Chair of Neuroscience; Ph.D., Harvard, 1973. Pituitary; neuronal tissue culture; peptides, vesicles; enzymes; drug abuse; development.

Louise McCullough, Associate Professor of Neurology and Neuroscience; M.D., Ph.D., Connecticut. Effects of estrogens on stroke.

D. Kent Morest, Professor of Neuroscience and Communication Sciences and Director of the Center for Neurological Sciences; M.D., Yale, 1960. Synaptic organization and fine structure of nervous system: plastic changes following activity changes; noise-induced hearing loss; development of synapses; tissue culture; neuronal transplantation.

Douglas L. Oliver, Professor of Neuroscience and Biomedical Engineering; Ph.D., Duke, 1977. Synaptic organization; parallel information processing in CNS; role of ionic currents, channel expression in information processing; neurocytology, morphology, cellular physiology of CNS sensory systems; biology of hearing and deafness.

Joel S. Pachter, Professor of Cell Biology; Ph.D., NYU, 1983. Mechanisms regulating pathogenesis of CNS infectious/inflammatory disease.

David M. Waitzman, Associate Professor of Neurology; M.D./Ph.D., CUNY, Mount Sinai, 1982. Neurophysiology; oculomotor system; gaze control system; modeling of CNS.

Zhaowen Wang, Assistant Professor of Neuroscience; Ph.D., Michigan State, 1993. Molecular mechanisms of synaptic transmission, focusing on neurotransmitter release and mechanisms of potassium channel localization, using *C. elegans* as a model organism.

Ji Yu, Assistant Professor of Genetics and Developmental Biology; Ph.D., Texas, 2002. Optical imaging technology; regulatory mechanisms in dendritic RNA translation; cytoskeletal dynamics.

Nada Zecevic, Assistant Professor of Neuroscience; M.D., 1970, Ph.D., 1978, Belgrade. Cellular and molecular aspects of CNS development; primate cerebral cortex; oligodendrocyte progenitors, stem cells, microglia; multiple sclerosis.

UNIVERSITY OF FLORIDA

College of Medicine
Advanced Concentration in Neuroscience

Program of Study

The College of Medicine at the University of Florida (UF) offers graduate training in biomedical research leading to a Ph.D. degree through the Interdisciplinary Program (IDP) in Biomedical Sciences. The goal of the Interdisciplinary Program is to prepare students for a diversity of careers in research and teaching in academic and commercial settings. The program provides a modern, comprehensive graduate education in biomedical science while providing both maximum program flexibility as well as appropriate specialization for graduate students. During the first year of study, incoming graduate students undertake a common, comprehensive interdisciplinary core curriculum of classroom study developed in a cooperative effort by all of the graduate programs in the College of Medicine. In addition, students select from any of the College of Medicine faculty members for participation in several laboratory rotations conducted throughout the first year, concurrent with the core curriculum. By the end of their first year, students select a laboratory in which to conduct their dissertation research and, once again, they may choose from any of the graduate faculty members in the College of Medicine. Formal selection of a graduate program and mentor is made after completion of the core curriculum to maximize flexibility and facilitate an informed decision; however, students may make an informal commitment to a program or lab at any time.

The Advanced Concentration in Neuroscience strives to provide students with a solid foundation in neuroscience principles and access to a wide array of research techniques that permit rigorous investigations of the normal and diseased nervous system. Neuroscience is a rapidly evolving and dynamic research field that touches all of the medical sciences. To address the diverse needs of the students, two areas of programmatic emphasis have been created: cellular/molecular and behavioral/cognitive neuroscience.

Students whose research includes a large cellular/molecular component investigate fundamental questions in the neurosciences. Areas of study include molecular and cellular studies of the normal and diseased nervous system, the developing and aging nervous system, neurochemistry and pharmacology, neuroimmunology, cellular and membrane neurophysiology, and injury and repair of the nervous system. Faculty members associated with this program represent numerous basic and clinical departments within the College of Medicine, many of whom are involved in multidisciplinary, collaborative research efforts aimed at understanding the basic mechanisms underlying neurobiological disease and developing treatments for these diseases. Students in this program have access to state-of-the-art research facilities to study a wide range of model systems, including cell culture, vertebrate and invertebrate animal models, and human tissues.

Students whose research program includes a large behavioral/cognitive component investigate questions in the neurosciences that bridge basic and clinical neuroscience. Areas of study include the neurobiology of mental illnesses, eating/obesity, sex, addiction, and autism; behavioral neuroscience; neurotoxicity; human perception; and brain functional circuitry and imaging. Faculty members associated with this program come from diverse departmental backgrounds, including the Departments of Neuroscience, Psychiatry, Psychology, Pediatrics, and Aging/Geriatrics. Students in this program have access to state-of-the-art research and clinical facilities that permit studies of research questions directly related to human neuroscience.

All students enrolled in the Neuroscience IDP program, regardless of research focus, must successfully complete the required core IDP courses and those specifically required by the Neuroscience IDP program. Students interested in pursuing neuroscience as an advanced-concentration area of study are encouraged to obtain a broad perspective of basic biomedical sciences during the first year.

Research Facilities

The College of Medicine houses state-of-the-art research facilities maintained by the Interdisciplinary Center for Biomedical Research (ICBR), the McKnight Brain Institute, the Clinical Research Center, several other University of Florida Research Centers, and individual research laboratories. Together these facilities provide services for DNA and protein synthesis and sequencing, hybridoma production, confocal and electron microscopy, NMR spectroscopy, computing and molecular modeling, flow cytometry, transgenic mouse production, and gene therapy vector construction. The University of Florida libraries, including the Health Center library, form the largest information resource system in the state of Florida and support up-to-date computer-based bibliographic retrieval services.

UF's nine libraries offer more than 4 million catalogued volumes and links to full-text articles in more than 34,000 journals. Of national significance are the Baldwin Library of Historical Children's Literature, the Latin American Collection, the Map and Imagery Library, the P. K. Yonge Library of Florida History (preeminent Floridiana collection), the Price Library of Judaica, and holdings on architectural preservation and eighteenth-century American architecture, late nineteenth- and early twentieth-century German state documents, rural sociology of Florida, and tropical and subtropical agriculture.

Financial Aid

Students accepted into the Interdisciplinary Program receive a stipend of $25,750 per annum. Students also receive a waiver that covers tuition.

Cost of Study

Graduate research assistants pay fees of approximately $1400 per year. Books and supplies cost about $1600.

Living and Housing Costs

Married student housing is available in six apartment villages operated by the University; dormitories for single students are available in limited quantities. The cost of housing for a single graduate student is approximately $5000 per year. Most graduate students live in abundant and comfortable off-campus housing that is near the University; rents vary but are low on a national scale.

Student Group

Enrollment at the University of Florida is both culturally and geographically diverse and numbers about 50,000, including about 10,000 graduate students. There are about 300 graduate students in the College of Medicine.

Location

Situated in north-central Florida, midway between the Atlantic Ocean and the Gulf of Mexico, Gainesville is a nationally recognized academic and research center and was rated the number one place to live in the U.S. in a 1995 *Money* magazine survey. There are about 200,000 residents in the Gainesville metropolitan area, excluding University of Florida students. The climate is moderate, permitting outdoor activities the year around. The University and the Gainesville community also host numerous cultural events, including music, dance, theater, lectures, and art exhibits. Many of the men's and women's athletic programs are considered to be in the top ten programs in the country.

The University and The College

The University of Florida, located on 2,000 acres, is among the nation's leading research universities as categorized by the Carnegie Commission on Higher Education. UF is a member of the Association of American Universities, the nation's most prestigious higher education organization. UF is also one of the nation's top three universities in the breadth of academic programs offered on a single campus. It has twenty colleges and schools and 100 interdisciplinary research and education centers, bureaus, and institutes. The College of Medicine, opened in 1956, has become a nationally recognized leader in medical education and research.

Applying

The Interdisciplinary Program in Biomedical Sciences seeks promising students with undergraduate training in chemistry, biology, psychology, or related disciplines in the life sciences. Applicants are selected on the basis of previous academic work, research experience, GRE General Test scores, letters of recommendation, the personal statement, and a personal interview. Students are admitted for the fall semester, which begins in late August. The application deadline is December 15.

Correspondence and Information

Wolfgang J. Streit, Ph.D., Director
Department of Neuroscience
University of Florida College of Medicine
P.O. Box 100244
Gainesville, Florida 32610-0244

Phone: 352-392-3910
E-mail: streit@mbi.ufl.edu
Web site: http://www.neuroscience.ufl.edu/neurogradweb/index.html

University of Florida

THE FACULTY AND THEIR RESEARCH

Barbara Battelle, Professor and Investigator, Whitney Laboratories; Ph.D., Syracuse. Circadian regulation of retinal functions; biochemistry of vision; modulation of the photoresponse.

Steve Blackband, Professor and Investigator, McKnight Brain Institute; Ph.D., Nottingham. Development and application of magnetic resonance imaging (MRI) and spectroscopy (MRS), primarily applied to neuroscience.

David Borchelt, Professor; Investigator, McKnight Brain Institute; and Director, Santa Fe Health Alzheimer's Disease Research Center; Ph.D., Kentucky. Transgenic and knockout mouse models and cell models for molecular mechanisms of familial neurodegenerative diseases, including Alzheimer's disease, amyotrophic lateral sclerosis, and Huntington's disease.

Dirk Bucher, Professor and Investigator, Whitney Laboratories; Ph.D., Berlin. Plasticity and homeostasis of network function; motor pattern generation; dopamine modulation of motor axons.

Thomas Foster, Professor; Investigator, McKnight Brain Institute; and McKnight Chair for Research on Aging and Memory; Ph.D., Wake Forest. Combining behavioral characterization with biochemical, molecular, and electrophysiological techniques to obtain an integrated perspective of brain aging, from molecular to cognitive levels.

Marieta Heaton, Professor and Investigator, McKnight Brain Institute; Ph.D., North Carolina State. Interactions of neurotrophic factors, apoptosis-related genes, and antioxidants in fetal alcohol syndrome.

Dena Howland, Assistant Professor and Investigator, McKnight Brain Institute; Ph.D., Medical College of Pennsylvania. Studies on the cellular, molecular, and behavioral bases of neural plasticity, with emphasis on spinal cord injury and repair; testing of potential therapeutic interventions, including gene transfer, cellular replacement, and enzyme application.

Jeffrey Kleim, Associate Professor and Research Health Scientist, VA Brain Rehabilitation Research Center; Ph.D., Illinois. Examining the neural mechanisms underlying rehabilitation-dependent recovery of motor function after stroke.

Ronald Mandel, Professor and Investigator, McKnight Brain Institute; Ph.D., USC. Application of gene transfer to study animal models of neurodegenerative disorders, including Parkinson's disease, Alzheimer's disease, Huntington's disease, brain tumors, and ischemia.

Leonid Moroz, Professor; Investigator, Whitney Laboratories; and Director, Center of Excellence in Genomic Sciences; Ph.D., Russian Academy of Sciences. Genomic bases of neuronal identity and plasticity; genomics of learning and memory; neuronal evolution; development of innovative bionanotechnologies for direct single-cell genomic and microchemical analysis.

Harry Nick, Professor and Investigator, McKnight Brain Institute; Ph.D., Pennsylvania. Cytokine action in the inflammatory response: tissue-specific gene regulation, gene therapy, diabetes, and spinal cord injury.

Lucia Notterpek, Associate Professor and Investigator, McKnight Brain Institute; Ph.D., UCLA. Studies on the cellular and molecular bases for inherited peripheral neuropathies; Schwann cell biology and myelin formation.

Paul Reier, Associate Professor and Investigator, McKnight Brain Institute; Ph.D., Case Western Reserve. Cell biology of neurons and glia in the developing and injured peripheral and central nervous systems.

Louis Ritz, Associate Professor and Investigator, McKnight Brain Institute; Ph.D., Florida. Structural and functional organization of the normal and injured spinal cord.

Susan L. Semple-Rowland, Professor; Investigator, McKnight Brain Institute; and Director, Interdisciplinary Program in Neuroscience; Ph.D., Florida. Biochemical and molecular mechanisms underlying inherited retinal disease; mechanisms of light entrainment of retinal photoreceptor and pinealocyte circadian oscillators; viral gene replacement strategies for treatment of retinal disease.

Gerry Shaw, Professor and Investigator, McKnight Brain Institute; Ph.D., London. Neuronal cytoskeleton intermediate filaments and their associated proteins in the nervous system; protein signaling modules; computer analysis of protein and nucleic acid sequence.

Dennis Steindler, Professor and Executive Director, McKnight Brain Institute; Ph.D., California, San Francisco. Study of stem cells from the adult brain, including their cell biology and molecular genetics and determining their potential for replacement therapies in neurological disease.

Wolfgang Streit, Professor and Investigator, McKnight Brain Institute; Ph.D., Medical University of South Carolina. Neuroimmunology and experimental neuropathology; neurobiology of microglial cells.

Floyd Thompson, Professor and Investigator, McKnight Brain Institute; Ph.D., Indiana. Fundamental mechanisms that regulate spinal motor systems, how these are altered by brain or spinal cord injury, and how these relate to therapeutic strategies to enhance locomotor recovery.

David Zacharias, Assistant Professor and Investigator, Whitney Laboratories; Ph.D., Mayo. Lipid-related signal transduction, using novel and enlightening methodologies.

UIC

UNIVERSITY OF ILLINOIS AT CHICAGO

College of Medicine
Department of Anatomy and Cell Biology
Program in Neuroscience

Program of Study

The graduate program at the University of Illinois at Chicago (UIC) emphasizes training leading to the Ph.D. degree, emphasizing cellular and systems neurobiology as well as cell biology. Specific areas of research include axonal transport, Alzheimer's and other neurodegenerative diseases, neuroplasticity and neuronal stem cell function, vestibulocochlear physiology and functional anatomy, ion channel regulation, myelination and demyelinating diseases, neuroendocrine control of behavior, neural development, and functional interactions of the plasma membrane with cytoskeletal elements. Students are expected to have a clear desire to enter a research career. The training program provides an intensive experience in fundamental research and frequent opportunities to demonstrate appropriate forward progress. Basic courses in cell and molecular biology and biochemistry are taken in the first year, when students also do rotations through different research laboratories. The first-year curriculum is coordinated through an interdepartmental program in the College of Medicine and the Graduate College called Graduate Education in Medical Sciences (GEMS), thus allowing students from different programs to interact and explore different biomedical disciplines. A wide range of advanced courses in neuroscience, cell biology, and anatomy are available during the second year, which prepare the student to take advantage of the rapidly changing face of science. The course work, along with progress on a thesis research project, prepares the student for preliminary examinations. The average time needed to complete the degree in recent years has been about five years. The training prepares students for a research or teaching career in academia or industry.

Research Facilities

Cellular structure and function, biochemistry, and molecular biology are investigated with electron microscopes, confocal and video microscopy, and quantitative computer-assisted image analysis techniques. A new biochemical and molecular biology core provides a range of equipment for contemporary biology, including phosphorimaging, FPLC, real-time PCR, and cell culture. Electrophysiology is probed with patch clamp and microelectrode techniques, by using cells modified through molecular biology techniques or by using selected sensory systems to reveal the functions of receptors, mechanisms of intracellular trafficking and signal transduction, and characteristics of ion channels. The Library of the Health Sciences' collection of nearly 500,000 volumes and more than 5,100 journals supports education and research. A science library provides additional resources in terms of both books and journals. The libraries provide extensive free access to databases, and professional staff members provide training and computer-assisted searches.

Financial Aid

The successful applicant is anticipated to receive a research or teaching assistantship with a current stipend of $27,000 per year and a tuition waiver. The student is responsible for about $1,300 in fees each semester.

Cost of Study

For the 2009–10 year, in-state tuition and other required fees were nearly $14,000 per year. Out-of-state tuition and fees were approximately $30,000 per year. Living expenses are estimated at $1300 per month. Costs are subject to change.

Living and Housing Costs

Nestled among the health sciences colleges, on-campus housing is available, including an apartment-style residence hall for graduate, professional, and older undergraduate students who are looking for convenience and an intensive study environment. The residence facilities connect directly to the Chicago Illini Union, the recently remodeled swimming pool, and the fitness center. Numerous privately owned rooms and apartments are available in the University area at a wide range of prices.

Student Group

The number of graduate students in the Department of Anatomy and Cell Biology is relatively small, allowing each student a great deal of individual attention and guidance in research training. However, the GEMS program includes 30 to 40 new students each year, which provides a critical mass of students for educational, scientific, and social activities. Thus, the Department combines the best of both large and small programs.

Location

The University of Illinois at Chicago is located in the heart of the cosmopolitan city of Chicago. The city combines the best of the arts, cuisine, entertainment, history, and sports. The campus is centrally located near The Loop and is surrounded by vibrant neighborhoods like Greek Town, Little Italy, Pilsen, and Chinatown. UIC is served by the Blue Line and Pink Line trains and CTA #7 and #157 buses, with ready access to both airports, and is only minutes away from the famed Michigan Avenue and downtown. There is an abundance of cultural activities and institutions in the area, including the Art Institute of Chicago, art galleries, the Chicago Symphony Orchestra, the blues and jazz clubs of a lively music scene, and outstanding theaters that include the Chicago Shakespeare Theater, Steppenwolf Theatre Company, and The Second City.

The University

UIC is the largest institution of higher learning in the Chicago area and is one of only eighty-eight Research I institutions nationally. Its history began in the 1890s, when the Chicago College of Pharmacy and the College of Physicians and Surgeons of Chicago became part of the University of Illinois. Today, UIC is located on approximately 185 acres in an area that includes two historic landmark residential neighborhoods and the West Side Medical Center District, the largest concentration of advanced public and private health-care facilities in the world.

Applying

A general background in biology, chemistry, and physics is expected. Acceptance is based on the student's potential for scholarly research and teaching as shown by his or her undergraduate record, letters of recommendation, and Graduate Record Examinations General Test scores. The Graduate College application deadline for fall admission for degree candidates is May 15, but prospective students are strongly encouraged to apply by January 15 for the Anatomy and Cell Biology (GEMS) program. Applications from international students must be received by February 15 to allow processing. Applications received bearing a postmark later than the application deadline are returned to the applicant.

Correspondence and Information

Director, Graduate Studies Committee
Department of Anatomy and Cell Biology, M/C 512
University of Illinois at Chicago
808 South Wood Street, Room 578
Chicago, Illinois 60612-7308
Phone: 312-996-6791
Fax: 312-413-0354
E-mail: conwell@uic.edu
Web site: http://www.anatomy.uic.edu/index.html (Department)
http://gems.comd.uic.edu/ (GEMS)

University of Illinois at Chicago

THE FACULTY AND THEIR RESEARCH

Conwell H. Anderson, Associate Professor; Ph.D., Kansas, 1969. Neuroendocrinology; morphological aspects of the hypothalamus and its influence on reproduction.

Jonathan J. Art, Associate Professor; Ph.D., Chicago, 1979. Cochlear hair cell physiology to characterize the cellular mechanisms that contribute to sensory transduction and signal processing in the nervous system; confocal laser microscopy.

Ernesto R. Bongarzone, Assistant Professor; Ph.D., Buenos Aires, 1989. Cellular biology of myelination, oligodendrogenesis and neurogenesis in the mammalian central nervous system; molecular mechanisms of dying back axonopathies associated to myelin disorders, neurodegeneration and aging; biodynamics of neural cell responses through membrane microdomains.

Scott T. Brady, Professor and Head; Ph.D., USC, 1978. Molecular mechanisms of axonal transport; specializations of the neuronal cytoskeleton; glial modulation of neuronal function; effects of physiological stress on neuron structure and function.

Maria Irene Givogri, Research Assistant Professor; Ph.D., Cordoba (Argentina), 1994. Molecular and cellular regulation of neurogenic niches and neural progenitors responses in health and in genetic (leukodystrophies) and acquired (multiple sclerosis) demyelinating diseases; role of myelin sulfatides as modulators of neural regenerative responses in the brain.

Naohiko Ikegaki, Associate Professor; Ph.D., Pennsylvania, 1988. Biology and therapeutic approaches of neuroblastoma; functions of MYCN, EPH receptors, and ephrins in neuroblastoma.

Mary Jo LaDu, Associate Professor, Ph.D., Illinois at Chicago, 1991. Alzheimer's disease (AD): structural and functional interactions between the amyloid-beta peptide (AB) and apolipoprotein E (apoE); in vitro and in vivo models to test the various hypotheses that arise from the study of AB and apoE4.

Orly Lazarov, Assistant Professor, Ph.D., Weizmann (Israel), 2000. Physiological roles of proteins associated with Alzheimer's disease and the mechanisms by which mutant forms of these proteins induce AD in vivo.

Anna Lysakowski, Professor; Ph.D., Illinois at Chicago, 1984. Organization, physiology, and function of the vestibular sensory apparatus extending from the cellular to system level.

Gerardo Morfini, Assistant Professor; Ph.D., Cordoba (Argentina), 1997. Axonal transport in neurodegenerative diseases; regulatory mechanisms for microtubule-based motility, identification, and characterization of signal transduction pathways; microtubule-based molecular motors providing novel insights on pathogenic mechanisms for late-onset neurodegenerative conditions such as ALS, Parkinson's, and polyglutamine-expansion diseases.

Yasuko Nakajima, Professor; M.D./Ph.D., Tokyo, 1962. Signal transduction mechanisms of neurotransmitter effects on brain neurons, using a unique method of culturing neurons from specific brain nuclei, such as cholinergic neurons from the basal forebrain and dopaminergic neurons from the substantia nigra (these nuclei are related to Alzheimer's and Parkinson's diseases).

Usha Raj, Professor and Head, Department of Pediatrics; M.D., Bombay (Mumbai), 1977. Developmental mechanisms controlling pulmonary circulation in fetuses and newborns, why some babies develop problems related to lung blood vessels while others do not.

Adrienne A. Rogalski-Wilk, Associate Professor; Ph.D., Illinois, 1981. Cell and molecular biology of novel plasma membrane–actin cytoskeletal linkage.

Xao Tang, Assistant Professor; Ph.D., Pennsylvania, 1993. Favorable neuroblastoma genes and molecular therapeutics of neuroblastoma.

James R. Unnerstall, Associate Professor; Ph.D., Johns Hopkins, 1984. Plasticity and regeneration in central catecholamine systems during the aging process, emphasizing the compensatory responses of specific neural systems following physiological stress, insult, or injury; neurotrophic factors.

Adjunct Research Faculty

C. Sue Carter, Professor and Co-Director, Brain Body Center, Department of Psychiatry; Ph.D., Arkansas, 1969. Rodent models, including the socially monogamous prairie vole, used to examine the behavioral, physiological, and autonomic actions of oxytocin and vasopressin.

Thomas Diekwisch, Professor and Head, Oral Biology; D.D.S., Ph.D., Marburg (Germany), 1990. Craniofacial biology, development, and genetics.

Douglas Feinstein, Research Professor; Ph.D., Johns Hopkins, 1984. Novel therapeutic means to reduce inflammatory damage and neuronal death in multiple sclerosis and Alzheimer's disease.

Anne George, Professor; Ph.D., Madras (India), 1983. Identification and characterization of acidic proteins involved in biomineralization.

Nalin Kumar, Professor; D.Phil., Oxford, 1979. Molecular structure and function of gap junctions; intercellular channels between adjacent cells.

Deborah Little, Adjunct Assistant Professor; Ph.D., Brandeis, 2002. Biological basis of compensatory processes in normal aging and in disease in language comprehension, attention, learning, and memory.

Subhash Pandey, Professor and Director Neuroscience Alcoholism Research; Ph.D., Kanpur (India), 1987. Molecular and cellular neurobiology of alcoholism and drugs of abuse.

Tingyu Qu, Assistant Professor; Ph.D., Kobe (Japan), 1997. Therapeutic potential of stem cells in neurological degenerative diseases.

Neil R. Smalheiser, Associate Professor; M.D./Ph.D., Yeshiva (Einstein), 1982. Biochemical, molecular, developmental, and cellular studies of nerve cells; data-mining techniques in medical informatics and bioinformatics.

William Wolf, Associate Professor; Ph.D., George Washington, 1985. Monoaminergic modulation of neuronal plasticity in neurological disorders such as Parkinson's disease and stroke and psychiatric disorders that include drug abuse, schizophrenia, and affective disorders.

Section 14
Nutrition

This section contains a directory of institutions offering graduate work in nutrition, followed by in-depth entries submitted by institutions that chose to prepare detailed program descriptions. Additional information about programs listed in the directory but not augmented by an in-depth entry may be obtained by writing directly to the dean of a graduate school or chair of a department at the address given in the directory.

For programs offering related work, see also in this book *Biochemistry, Biological and Biomedical Sciences, Botany and Plant Biology, Microbiological Sciences, Pathology and Pathobiology, Pharmacology and Toxicology,* and *Physiology.* In the other guides in this series:

Graduate Programs in the Humanities, Arts & Social Sciences

See *Economics (Agricultural Economics and Agribusiness)* and *Family and Consumer Sciences*

Graduate Programs in the Physical Sciences, Mathematics, Agricultural Sciences, the Environment & Natural Resources

See *Agricultural and Food Sciences* and *Chemistry*

Graduate Programs in Engineering & Applied Sciences

See *Agricultural Engineering and Bioengineering* and *Biomedical Engineering and Biotechnology*

Graduate Programs in Business, Education, Health, Information Studies, Law & Social Work

See *Allied Health, Public Health,* and *Veterinary Medicine and Sciences*

CONTENTS

Program Directory

Close-Ups

Nutrition

American University of Beirut, Graduate Programs, Faculty of Agricultural and Food Sciences, Beirut, Lebanon. Offers agricultural economics (MS); animal sciences (MS); ecosystem management (MSES); food technology (MS); irrigation (MS); mechanization (MS); nutrition (MS); plant protection (MS); plant science (MS); poultry science (MS); soils (MS). Part-time programs available. *Degree requirements:* For master's, one foreign language, comprehensive exam, thesis (for some programs). *Entrance requirements:* For master's, letter of recommendation. Additional exam requirements/recommendations for international students: Required—TOEFL (minimum score 600 paper-based; 250 computer-based; 100 iBT), IELTS (minimum score 7.5). *Faculty research:* Sustainable animal systems/agriculture; natural resource management; community nutrition, obesity and food safety; integrated pest management; ecosystem management.

Andrews University, School of Graduate Studies, College of Arts and Sciences, Department of Nutrition, Berrien Springs, MI 49104. Offers MS. Part-time programs available. *Faculty:* 2 full-time (0 women), 2 part-time/adjunct (both women). *Students:* 6 full-time (4 women), 12 part-time (all women); includes 4 minority (3 African Americans, 1 Hispanic American), 2 international. Average age 31. 19 applicants, 53% accepted, 6 enrolled. In 2009, 2 master's awarded. *Entrance requirements:* For master's, GRE. Additional exam requirements/recommendations for international students: Required—TOEFL (minimum score 550 paper-based). *Application deadline:* Applications are processed on a rolling basis. Application fee: $40. *Unit head:* Dr. Winston Craig, Chairperson, 269-471-3370. *Application contact:* Carolyn Hurst, Supervisor of Graduate Admission, 800-253-2874, Fax: 269-471-6321, E-mail: graduate@andrews.edu.

Appalachian State University, Cratis D. Williams Graduate School, Department of Family and Consumer Sciences, Boone, NC 28608. Offers child development (MA); family and consumer science (MA), including food and nutrition; family and consumer science education (MA). Part-time programs available. Postbaccalaureate distance learning degree programs offered (no on-campus study). *Faculty:* 12 full-time (10 women), 2 part-time/adjunct (1 woman). *Students:* 17 full-time (16 women), 15 part-time (all women); includes 2 minority (both African Americans), 1 international. 29 applicants, 83% accepted, 20 enrolled. In 2009, 6 master's awarded. *Degree requirements:* For master's, comprehensive exam, thesis optional. *Entrance requirements:* For master's, GRE General Test, 3 letters of recommendation. Additional exam requirements/recommendations for international students: Required—TOEFL (minimum score 550 paper-based; 230 computer-based; 79 iBT), IELTS (minimum score 6.5). *Application deadline:* For fall admission, 7/1 for domestic students, 2/1 for international students; for spring admission, 11/1 for domestic students, 7/1 for international students. Applications are processed on a rolling basis. Application fee: $50. Electronic applications accepted. *Expenses:* Tuition, state resident: full-time $2960. Tuition, nonresident: full-time $14,051. Required fees: $2320. *Financial support:* In 2009–10, 5 research assistantships (averaging $8,000 per year) were awarded; career-related internships or fieldwork, scholarships/grants, and unspecified assistantships also available. Financial award application deadline: 7/1; financial award applicants required to submit FAFSA. *Faculty research:* Food antioxidants, preschool curriculum, children with special needs, family child care, FCS curriculum content. *Unit head:* Dr. Sarah Jordan, Chairperson, 828-262-2661, E-mail: jordansr@appstate.edu. *Application contact:* Dr. Sandy Krause, Director of Graduate Admissions and Recruiting, 828-262-2130, E-mail: krausesl@appstate.edu.

Arizona State University, Graduate College, College of Nursing and Healthcare Innovation, Department of Nutrition, Tempe, AZ 85287. Offers MS. Part-time and evening/weekend programs available. *Degree requirements:* For master's, thesis. *Entrance requirements:* For master's, 3 letters of recommendation including 1 from instructor, resume, supplementary information form. Additional exam requirements/recommendations for international students: Required—TOEFL (minimum score 550 paper-based; 213 computer-based; 83 iBT); Recommended—TWE. Electronic applications accepted. *Faculty research:* Vitamin C metabolism, nutrition and exercise, nutrient intakes, nutritional status, metabolic feeding studies.

Auburn University, Graduate School, College of Human Sciences, Department of Nutrition and Food Science, Auburn University, AL 36849. Offers MS, PhD. Part-time programs available. *Faculty:* 16 full-time (7 women). *Students:* 16 full-time (11 women), 13 part-time (6 women); includes 4 minority (all African Americans), 7 international. Average age 31. 79 applicants, 37% accepted, 9 enrolled. In 2009, 10 master's, 5 doctorates awarded. *Degree requirements:* For master's, thesis (for some programs); for doctorate, thesis/dissertation. *Entrance requirements:* For master's and doctorate, GRE General Test. *Application deadline:* For fall admission, 7/7 for domestic students; for spring admission, 11/24 for domestic students. Applications are processed on a rolling basis. Application fee: $50 ($60 for international students). Electronic applications accepted. *Expenses:* Tuition, state resident: full-time $6240. Tuition, nonresident: full-time $18,720. International tuition: $18,938 full-time. Required fees: $492. Tuition and fees vary according to course load, program and reciprocity agreements. *Financial support:* Research assistantships, teaching assistantships, career-related internships or fieldwork and Federal Work-Study available. Support available to part-time students. Financial award application deadline: 3/15; financial award applicants required to submit FAFSA. *Faculty research:* Food quality and safety, diet, food supply, physical activity in maintenance of health, prevention of selected chronic disease states. *Unit head:* Dr. Douglas B. White, Head, 334-844-4261. *Application contact:* Dr. George Flowers, Dean of the Graduate School, 334-844-2125.

Bastyr University, School of Nutrition and Exercise Science, Kenmore, WA 98028-4966. Offers nutrition (MS); nutrition and clinical health psychology (MS). *Accreditation:* ADtA. Part-time programs available. *Students:* 86 full-time (84 women), 20 part-time (18 women). Average age 32. In 2009, 43 master's awarded. *Degree requirements:* For master's, thesis optional. *Entrance requirements:* For master's, 1 year of course work in chemistry, biochemistry, physiology and nutrition. Additional exam requirements/recommendations for international students: Required—TOEFL (minimum score 550 paper-based; 213 computer-based; 79 iBT). *Application deadline:* For fall admission, 3/15 priority date for domestic and international students. Applications are processed on a rolling basis. Application fee: $75. *Expenses:* Tuition: Full-time $23,478. Tuition and fees vary according to course level, course load and program. *Financial support:* Career-related internships or fieldwork, Federal Work-Study, and scholarships/grants available. Support available to part-time students. Financial award application deadline: 4/15; financial award applicants required to submit FAFSA. *Unit head:* Debra Boutin, Chair, 425-823-1300, Fax: 425-823-6222. *Application contact:* Admissions Office, 425-602-3330, Fax: 425-602-3090, E-mail: admissions@bastyr.edu.

See Close-Up on page 419.

Baylor University, Graduate School, Military Programs, Program in Nutrition, Waco, TX 76798. Offers MS. *Students:* 19 full-time (11 women); includes 1 Asian American or Pacific Islander, 2 Hispanic Americans. In 2009, 9 master's awarded. *Unit head:* Lt. Col. Lori Sigrist, Graduate Program Director, 210-221-6274, Fax: 210-221-7306, E-mail: lori.sigrist@us.army.mil. *Application contact:* S. Sgt. Janean Ortega, Administrative Assistant, 210-221-6274, E-mail: janean.ortega@us.army.mil.

Baylor University, Graduate School, School of Education, Department of Health, Human Performance and Recreation, Waco, TX 76798. Offers exercise, nutrition and preventive health (PhD); health, human performance and recreation (MS Ed). *Accreditation:* NCATE. Part-time programs available. *Faculty:* 13 full-time (5 women), 3 part-time/adjunct (1 woman). *Students:* 66 full-time (35 women), 42 part-time (21 women); includes 14 minority (7 African Americans, 3 Asian Americans or Pacific Islanders, 4 Hispanic Americans), 5 international. 30 applicants, 87% accepted. In 2009, 48 master's, 6 doctorates awarded. *Degree requirements:* For master's, thesis optional. *Entrance requirements:* For master's, GRE General Test. *Application deadline:* For fall admission, 4/1 priority date for domestic students; for spring

admission, 10/1 for domestic students. Applications are processed on a rolling basis. Application fee: $25. Electronic applications accepted. *Financial support:* In 2009–10, 35 students received support, including 22 teaching assistantships; career-related internships or fieldwork, Federal Work-Study, institutionally sponsored loans, tuition waivers (partial), and recreation supplements also available. *Faculty research:* Behavior change theory, pedagogy, nutrition and enzyme therapy, exercise testing, health planning. *Unit head:* Dr. Glenn Miller, Graduate Program Director, 254-710-4001, Fax: 254-710-3527, E-mail: glenn_miller@baylor.edu. *Application contact:* Eva Berger-Rhodes, Administrative Assistant, 254-710-4945, Fax: 254-710-3870, E-mail: eva_rhodes@baylor.edu.

Benedictine University, Graduate Programs, Program in Nutrition and Wellness, Lisle, IL 60532-0900. Offers MS. *Students:* 21 full-time (20 women), 20 part-time (all women); includes 4 minority (1 African American, 2 Asian Americans or Pacific Islanders, 1 Hispanic American). 44 applicants, 82% accepted, 15 enrolled. In 2009, 7 master's awarded. *Entrance requirements:* Additional exam requirements/recommendations for international students: Required—TOEFL (minimum score 550 paper-based; 213 computer-based). *Application deadline:* For fall admission, 9/1 for domestic students; for winter admission, 12/1 for domestic students; for spring admission, 2/15 for domestic students. Applications are processed on a rolling basis. Application fee: $40. Electronic applications accepted. *Expenses:* Tuition: Part-time $750 per credit hour. Tuition and fees vary according to campus/location and program. *Financial support:* Career-related internships or fieldwork and health care benefits available. Support available to part-time students. *Faculty research:* Community and corporate wellness risk assessment, health behavior change, self-efficacy, evaluation of health program impact and effectiveness. Total annual research expenditures: $8,335. *Unit head:* Catherine Arnold, Director, 630-829-6534, E-mail: carnold@ben.edu. *Application contact:* Kari Gibbons, Director, Admissions, 630-829-6200, Fax: 630-829-6584, E-mail: kgibbons@ben.edu.

Benedictine University, Graduate Programs, Program in Public Health, Lisle, IL 60532-0900. Offers administration of health care institutions (MPH); dietetics (MPH); disaster management (MPH); health education (MPH); health information systems (MPH); MBA/MPH; MPH/MS. Part-time and evening/weekend programs available. Postbaccalaureate distance learning degree programs offered. *Faculty:* 2 full-time (0 women), 8 part-time/adjunct (3 women). *Students:* 132 full-time (92 women), 354 part-time (286 women); includes 171 minority (112 African Americans, 1 American Indian/Alaska Native, 35 Asian Americans or Pacific Islanders, 23 Hispanic Americans), 14 international. Average age 33. 247 applicants, 94% accepted, 180 enrolled. In 2009, 77 master's awarded. *Entrance requirements:* For master's, MAT, GRE, or GMAT. Additional exam requirements/recommendations for international students: Required—TOEFL (minimum score 550 paper-based; 213 computer-based). *Application deadline:* For fall admission, 9/1 for domestic students; for winter admission, 12/1 for domestic students; for spring admission, 2/15 for domestic students. Application fee: $40. *Expenses:* Tuition: Part-time $750 per credit hour. Tuition and fees vary according to campus/location and program. *Financial support:* Career-related internships or fieldwork and health care benefits available. Support available to part-time students. *Unit head:* Dr. Alan Gorr, Director, 630-829-6566, Fax: 630-960-1126, E-mail: agorr@ben.edu. *Application contact:* Kari Gibbons, Director, Admissions, 630-829-6200, Fax: 630-829-6584, E-mail: kgibbons@ben.edu.

Boston University, College of Health and Rehabilitation Sciences—Sargent College, Department of Health Sciences, Program in Nutrition, Boston, MA 02215. Offers MS. *Faculty:* 10 full-time (9 women), 5 part-time/adjunct (3 women). *Students:* 50 full-time (49 women), 5 part-time (all women); includes 4 minority (1 Asian American or Pacific Islander, 3 Hispanic Americans), 3 international. Average age 25. 116 applicants, 42% accepted, 27 enrolled. In 2009, 23 master's awarded. *Entrance requirements:* For master's, GRE General Test, minimum GPA of 3.0. Additional exam requirements/recommendations for international students: Required—TOEFL (minimum score 550 paper-based; 84 iBT). *Application deadline:* For fall admission, 2/15 priority date for domestic students; for spring admission, 10/1 for domestic students. Applications are processed on a rolling basis. Application fee: $70. Electronic applications accepted. *Expenses:* Tuition: Full-time $37,910; part-time $1184 per credit hour. Required fees: $386; $40 per semester. Part-time tuition and fees vary according to class time, course level, degree level and program. *Financial support:* In 2009–10, 39 students received support, including 21 fellowships with partial tuition reimbursements available (averaging $12,000 per year); career-related internships or fieldwork, Federal Work-Study, institutionally sponsored loans, scholarships/grants, and tuition waivers (partial) also available. Support available to part-time students. Financial award application deadline: 4/15; financial award applicants required to submit FAFSA. *Unit head:* Dr. Kathleen Morgan, Chair, 617-353-2717, E-mail: kmorgan@bu.edu. *Application contact:* Sharon Sankey, Director, Student Services, 617-353-2713, Fax: 617-353-7500, E-mail: ssankey@bu.edu.

Bowling Green State University, Graduate College, College of Education and Human Development, School of Family and Consumer Sciences, Bowling Green, OH 43403. Offers food and nutrition (MFCS); human development and family studies (MFCS). Part-time programs available. *Degree requirements:* For master's, thesis. *Entrance requirements:* For master's, GRE General Test, minimum GPA of 3.0. Additional exam requirements/recommendations for international students: Required—TOEFL. Electronic applications accepted. *Faculty research:* Public health, wellness, social issues and policies, ethnic foods, nutrition and aging.

Brigham Young University, Graduate Studies, College of Life Sciences, Department of Nutrition, Dietetics and Food Science, Provo, UT 84602-1001. Offers food science (MS); nutrition (MS). *Faculty:* 13 full-time (5 women). *Students:* 14 full-time (10 women), 2 part-time (both women); includes 2 minority (1 African American, 1 Asian American or Pacific Islander). Average age 24. 5 applicants, 60% accepted, 1 enrolled. In 2009, 6 master's awarded. *Degree requirements:* For master's, comprehensive exam, thesis. *Entrance requirements:* For master's, GRE General Test. Additional exam requirements/recommendations for international students: Required—TOEFL (minimum score 550 paper-based; 213 computer-based). *Application deadline:* For fall admission, 2/1 for domestic students, 2/1 priority date for international students; for winter admission, 6/30 for domestic students, 6/30 priority date for international students. Application fee: $50. Electronic applications accepted. *Expenses:* Tuition: Full-time $5580; part-time $301 per credit hour. Tuition and fees vary according to student's religious affiliation. *Financial support:* In 2009–10, 9 students received support, including 4 research assistantships (averaging $20,325 per year), 3 teaching assistantships (averaging $20,325 per year); career-related internships or fieldwork, institutionally sponsored loans, and scholarships/grants also available. Financial award application deadline: 4/1. *Faculty research:* Dairy foods, lipid oxidation, food processes, magnesium and selenium nutrition, nutrient effect on gene expression. Total annual research expenditures: $398,048. *Unit head:* Dr. Miochael L. Dunn, Chair, 801-422-6670, Fax: 801-422-0258, E-mail: michael_dunn@byu.edu. *Application contact:* Dr. Susan Fullmer, Graduate Coordinator, 801-422-3349, Fax: 801-422-0258, E-mail: susan_fullmer@byu.edu.

Brooklyn College of the City University of New York, Division of Graduate Studies, Department of Health and Nutrition Science, Program in Nutrition, Brooklyn, NY 11210-2889. Offers MS. Part-time programs available. *Students:* 11 full-time (9 women), 69 part-time (59 women); includes 28 minority (13 African Americans, 11 Asian Americans or Pacific Islanders, 4 Hispanic Americans), 10 international. Average age 33. 42 applicants, 60% accepted, 18 enrolled. In 2009, 16 master's awarded. *Degree requirements:* For master's, thesis or alternative. *Entrance requirements:* For master's, 18 credits in health-related areas, 2 letters of recommendation, essay. Additional exam requirements/recommendations for international students: Required—TOEFL. *Application deadline:* For fall admission, 3/1 priority date for domestic students, 2/1 priority date for international students; for spring admission, 11/1 priority date for domestic students, 10/1 priority date for international students. Applications are processed on a rolling basis. Application fee: $125. Electronic applications accepted. *Expenses:* Tuition, state resident: full-time $7360; part-time $310 per credit hour. Tuition, nonresident: full-time

$13,800; part-time $575 per credit hour. Required fees: $140.10 per semester. *Financial support:* Federal Work-Study, institutionally sponsored loans, and scholarships/grants available. Support available to part-time students. Financial award application deadline: 5/1; financial award applicants required to submit FAFSA. *Faculty research:* Medical ethics, AIDS, history of public health, diet restriction, palliative care, risk reduction/disease prevention, metabolism, diabetes. *Unit head:* Dr. Kathleen Axen, Graduate Deputy Chairperson, 718-951-5909, Fax: 718-951-4670, E-mail: kaxen@brooklyn.cuny.edu. *Application contact:* Hernan Sierra, Graduate Admissions Coordinator, 718-951-4536, Fax: 718-951-4506, E-mail: grads@brooklyn.cuny.edu.

California State University, Chico, Graduate School, College of Natural Sciences, Department of Biological Sciences, Program in Nutritional Sciences, Chico, CA 95929-0722. Offers nutrition education (MS). Part-time programs available. *Students:* 11 full-time (all women), 9 part-time (8 women); includes 3 minority (all Hispanic Americans), 1 international. Average age 26. 20 applicants, 40% accepted, 5 enrolled. In 2009, 9 master's awarded. *Degree requirements:* For master's, thesis, seminar presentation. *Entrance requirements:* For master's, GRE General Test, 2 letters of recommendation. Additional exam requirements/recommendations for international students: Required—TOEFL (minimum score 550 paper-based; 213 computer-based; 80 iBT), IELTS (minimum score 6.5). *Application deadline:* For fall admission, 3/1 priority date for domestic students, 3/1 for international students; for spring admission, 9/15 priority date for domestic students, 9/15 for international students. Applications are processed on a rolling basis. Application fee: $55. Electronic applications accepted. *Financial support:* Teaching assistantships available. *Unit head:* Dr. Kathryn Silliman, Graduate Coordinator, 530-898-6805. *Application contact:* Larry Hanne, Graduate Coordinator, 530-898-5356.

California State University, Long Beach, Graduate Studies, College of Health and Human Services, Department of Family and Consumer Sciences, Master of Science in Nutritional Science Program, Long Beach, CA 90840. Offers food science (MS); hospitality foodservice and hotel management (MS); nutritional science (MS). Part-time programs available. *Students:* 25 full-time (24 women), 22 part-time (all women); includes 14 minority (1 African American, 10 Asian Americans or Pacific Islanders, 3 Hispanic Americans), 1 international. Average age 26. 50 applicants, 62% accepted, 17 enrolled. *Degree requirements:* For master's, thesis, oral presentation of thesis or directed project. *Entrance requirements:* For master's, GRE, minimum GPA of 2.5 in last 60 units. *Application deadline:* For fall admission, 5/1 for domestic students. Applications are processed on a rolling basis. Application fee: $55. Electronic applications accepted. *Expenses:* Required fees: $1802 per semester. Part-time tuition and fees vary according to course load. *Financial support:* Federal Work-Study, institutionally sponsored loans, and scholarships/grants available. Financial award application deadline: 3/2. *Faculty research:* Protein and water-soluble vitamins, sensory evaluation of foods, mineral deficiencies in humans, child nutrition, minerals and blood pressure. *Unit head:* Dr. M. Sue Stanley, Chair, 562-985-4484, Fax: 562-985-4414, E-mail: stanleym@csulb.edu. *Application contact:* Dr. Mary Jacob, Graduate Coordinator, 562-985-4484, Fax: 562-985-4414, E-mail: marjacob@csulb.edu.

California State University, Long Beach, Graduate Studies, College of Health and Human Services, Department of Kinesiology, Long Beach, CA 90840. Offers adapted physical education (MA); coaching and student athlete development (MA); exercise physiology and nutrition (MS); exercise science (MS); individualized studies (MA); kinesiology (MA); pedagogical studies (MA); sport and exercise psychology (MS); sport management (MA); sports medicine and injury studies (MS). Part-time programs available. *Faculty:* 9 full-time (6 women), 1 part-time/adjunct (0 women). *Students:* 34 full-time (22 women), 23 part-time (14 women); includes 22 minority (4 African Americans, 2 American Indian/Alaska Native, 8 Asian Americans or Pacific Islanders, 8 Hispanic Americans), 9 international. Average age 27. 143 applicants, 59% accepted, 20 enrolled. *Degree requirements:* For master's, oral and written comprehensive exams or thesis. *Entrance requirements:* For master's, GRE General Test, minimum GPA of 2.75 during previous 2 years of course work. *Application deadline:* For fall admission, 6/1 for domestic students. Applications are processed on a rolling basis. Application fee: $55. Electronic applications accepted. *Expenses:* Required fees: $1802 per semester. Part-time tuition and fees vary according to course load. *Financial support:* Federal Work-Study, institutionally sponsored loans, and scholarships/grants available. Financial award application deadline: 3/2. *Faculty research:* Pulmonary functioning, feedback and practice structure, strength training, history and politics of sports, special population research issues. *Unit head:* Dr. Sharon R. Guthrie, Chair, 562-985-7487, Fax: 562-985-8067, E-mail: guthrie@csulb.edu. *Application contact:* Dr. Grant Hill, Graduate Advisor, 562-985-8856, Fax: 562-985-8067, E-mail: ghill@csulb.edu.

California State University, Los Angeles, Graduate Studies, College of Health and Human Services, Department of Kinesiology and Nutritional Sciences, Los Angeles, CA 90032-8530. Offers nutritional science (MS); physical education and kinesiology (MA, MS). *Accreditation:* ADtA. Part-time and evening/weekend programs available. *Faculty:* 6 full-time (3 women), 1 part-time/adjunct (0 women). *Students:* 64 full-time (57 women), 49 part-time (38 women); includes 58 minority (10 African Americans, 29 Asian Americans or Pacific Islanders, 19 Hispanic Americans), 11 international. Average age 31. 55 applicants, 100% accepted, 17 enrolled. In 2009, 17 master's awarded. *Degree requirements:* For master's, comprehensive exam, project or thesis. *Entrance requirements:* For master's, minimum GPA of 2.75. Additional exam requirements/recommendations for international students: Required—TOEFL (minimum score 500 paper-based; 173 computer-based). *Application deadline:* For fall admission, 5/1 for domestic and international students. Applications are processed on a rolling basis. Application fee: $55. *Financial support:* Federal Work-Study available. Support available to part-time students. Financial award application deadline: 3/1. *Unit head:* Dr. Nazareth Khodiguian, Chair, 323-343-4650, Fax: 323-343-6482, E-mail: nkhodig@calstatela.edu. *Application contact:* Dr. Cheryl L. Ney, Associate Vice President for Academic Affairs and Dean of Graduate Studies, 323-343-3820, Fax: 323-343-5653, E-mail: cney@cslanet.calstatela.edu.

Case Western Reserve University, School of Medicine and School of Graduate Studies, Graduate Programs in Medicine, Department of Nutrition, Cleveland, OH 44106. Offers dietetics (MS); nutrition (MS, PhD), including molecular nutrition (PhD), nutrition and biochemistry (PhD); public health nutrition (MS). Part-time programs available. Terminal master's awarded for partial completion of doctoral program. *Degree requirements:* For master's, thesis (for some programs); for doctorate, thesis/dissertation. *Entrance requirements:* For master's, GRE General Test; for doctorate, GRE General Test, GRE Subject Test. Additional exam requirements/recommendations for international students: Required—TOEFL. *Faculty research:* Fatty acid metabolism, application of gene therapy to nutritional problems, dietary intake methodology, nutrition and physical fitness, metabolism during infancy and pregnancy.

See Close-Up on page 421.

Central Michigan University, College of Graduate Studies, College of Education and Human Services, Department of Human Environmental Studies, Mount Pleasant, MI 48859. Offers apparel product development and merchandising technology (MS); human development and family studies (MA); nutrition and dietetics (MS). Part-time and evening/weekend programs available. *Degree requirements:* For master's, thesis or alternative. Electronic applications accepted. *Faculty research:* Human growth and development, family studies and human sexuality, human nutrition and dietetics, apparel and textile retailing, computer-aided design for apparel.

Central Washington University, Graduate Studies and Research, College of Education and Professional Studies, Department of Nutrition, Exercise and Health Services, Ellensburg, WA 98926. Offers exercise science (MS); nutrition (MS). *Accreditation:* NCATE. Part-time programs available. *Faculty:* 21 full-time (5 women). *Students:* 26 full-time (13 women), 6 part-time (1 woman), 1 international. 30 applicants, 63% accepted, 19 enrolled. In 2009, 9 master's awarded. *Degree requirements:* For master's, thesis or alternative. *Entrance requirements:* For master's, GRE (nutrition), minimum GPA of 3.0. Additional exam requirements/recommendations for international students: Required—TOEFL (minimum score 550 paper-based; 213 computer-based; 79 iBT). *Application deadline:* For fall admission, 2/1 priority date for domestic students; for winter admission, 10/1 for domestic students; for spring admission, 1/1 for domestic students. Applications are processed on a rolling basis. Application fee: $50. Electronic applications accepted. *Expenses:* Tuition, state resident: full-time $7353; part-time $245 per credit. Tuition, nonresident: full-time $16,383; part-time $546 per credit. Required fees: $882. Tuition and fees vary according to degree level. *Financial support:* In 2009–10, 17 teaching assistantships with full and partial tuition reimbursements (averaging $9,145 per year) were awarded; research assistantships, Federal Work-Study and health care benefits also available. Financial award application deadline: 3/1; financial award applicants required to submit FAFSA. *Unit head:* Dr. Vince Nethery, Chair, 509-963-1911. *Application contact:* Justine Eason, Admissions Program Coordinator, 509-963-3103, Fax: 509-963-1799, E-mail: masters@cwu.edu.

Chapman University, Graduate Studies, Schmid College of Science, Food Science Program, Orange, CA 92866. Offers MS, MBA/MS. Part-time and evening/weekend programs available. *Faculty:* 3 full-time (2 women). *Students:* 12 full-time (8 women), 20 part-time (14 women); includes 7 minority (1 African American, 5 Asian Americans or Pacific Islanders, 1 Hispanic American), 14 international. Average age 25. 35 applicants, 63% accepted, 11 enrolled. In 2009, 12 master's awarded. *Degree requirements:* For master's, comprehensive exam, thesis optional. *Entrance requirements:* For master's, GRE, minimum undergraduate GPA of 2.5. Additional exam requirements/recommendations for international students: Required—TOEFL (minimum score 550 paper-based; 213 computer-based; 80 iBT). *Application deadline:* Applications are processed on a rolling basis. Application fee: $50. Electronic applications accepted. Tuition and fees vary according to course load, degree level and program. *Financial support:* Fellowships, Federal Work-Study and scholarships/grants available. Financial award application deadline: 6/30; financial award applicants required to submit FAFSA. *Unit head:* Dr. Anuradha Prakash, Director, 714-744-7895, E-mail: prakash@chapman.edu. *Application contact:* Priscilla Garcia Powers, Graduate Admission Counselor, 714-997-6711, E-mail: pgarcia@chapman.edu.

Clemson University, Graduate School, College of Agriculture, Forestry and Life Sciences, Department of Food Science and Human Nutrition, Program in Food, Nutrition, and Culinary Science, Clemson, SC 29634. Offers MS. *Students:* 12 full-time (6 women), 10 part-time (3 women); includes 1 minority (African American), 5 international. Average age 28. 53 applicants, 15% accepted, 5 enrolled. In 2009, 5 degrees awarded. *Degree requirements:* For master's, thesis. *Entrance requirements:* For master's, GRE General Test. Additional exam requirements/recommendations for international students: Required—TOEFL, IELTS. *Application deadline:* For fall admission, 6/1 for domestic students, 4/15 for international students; for spring admission, 9/15 for international students. Applications are processed on a rolling basis. Application fee: $70 ($80 for international students). Electronic applications accepted. *Expenses:* Contact institution. *Financial support:* In 2009–10, 8 students received support, including 2 research assistantships with partial tuition reimbursements available (averaging $12,000 per year), 6 teaching assistantships with partial tuition reimbursements available (averaging $15,444 per year); fellowships with full and partial tuition reimbursements available, career-related internships or fieldwork, institutionally sponsored loans, scholarships/grants, health care benefits, and unspecified assistantships also available. Support available to part-time students. Financial award applicants required to submit FAFSA. *Unit head:* Dr. Anthony L. Pometto, Chair, 864-656-4382, Fax: 864-656-3131, E-mail: pometto@clemson.edu. *Application contact:* Dr. Paul Dawson, Coordinator, 864-656-1138, Fax: 864-656-3131, E-mail: pdawson@clemson.edu.

College of Saint Elizabeth, Department of Foods and Nutrition, Morristown, NJ 07960-6989. Offers dietetic internship (Certificate); nutrition (MS). Part-time and evening/weekend programs available. *Faculty:* 1 (woman) full-time, 3 part-time/adjunct (all women). *Students:* 19 full-time (all women), 25 part-time (23 women); includes 1 minority (Asian American or Pacific Islander), 1 international. Average age 34. 27 applicants, 96% accepted, 21 enrolled. In 2009, 3 master's, 20 other advanced degrees awarded. *Application deadline:* Applications are processed on a rolling basis. Application fee: $35. Electronic applications accepted. *Expenses:* Tuition: Part-time $797 per credit hour. Required fees: $65 per credit hour. *Financial support:* Tuition waivers (partial) and unspecified assistantships available. Support available to part-time students. Financial award application deadline: 3/15; financial award applicants required to submit FAFSA. *Faculty research:* Medical nutrition intervention, public policy, obesity, hunger and food security, osteoporosis, nutrition and exercise. *Unit head:* Dr. Jean C. Burge, Director of the Graduate Program in Nutrition, 973-290-4127, Fax: 973-290-4167, E-mail: nutrition@cse.edu. *Application contact:* Donna Tatarka, Dean of Admission, 973-290-4705, Fax: 973-290-4710, E-mail: dtatarka@cse.edu.

Colorado State University, Graduate School, College of Applied Human Sciences, Department of Food Science and Human Nutrition, Fort Collins, CO 80523-1571. Offers MS, PhD. *Accreditation:* ADtA. Part-time programs available. *Faculty:* 15 full-time (6 women), 3 part-time/adjunct (2 women). *Students:* 47 full-time (35 women), 36 part-time (26 women); includes 9 minority (1 African American, 3 Asian Americans or Pacific Islanders, 5 Hispanic Americans), 6 international. Average age 30. 85 applicants, 52% accepted, 23 enrolled. In 2009, 23 master's, 4 doctorates awarded. *Degree requirements:* For master's, thesis; for doctorate, thesis/dissertation. *Entrance requirements:* For master's and doctorate, GRE General Test, minimum GPA of 3.0, resume, 3 letters of recommendation. Additional exam requirements/recommendations for international students: Required—TOEFL (minimum score 550 paper-based; 213 computer-based; 80 iBT). *Application deadline:* For fall admission, 2/1 priority date for domestic and international students; for spring admission, 8/1 priority date for domestic and international students. Application fee: $50. Electronic applications accepted. *Expenses:* Tuition, state resident: full-time $6434; part-time $359.10 per credit. Tuition, nonresident: full-time $18,116; part-time $1006.45 per credit. Required fees: $1496; $83 per credit. *Financial support:* In 2009–10, 19 students received support, including 1 fellowship (averaging $41,500 per year), 9 research assistantships with full and partial tuition reimbursements available (averaging $9,342 per year), 9 teaching assistantships with full and partial tuition reimbursements available (averaging $8,215 per year); Federal Work-Study and scholarships/grants also available. Financial award application deadline: 3/1; financial award applicants required to submit FAFSA. *Faculty research:* Metabolic regulation, nutrition education, food safety, obesity and diabetes, metabolism. Total annual research expenditures: $6 million. *Unit head:* Dr. Christopher Melby, Head, 970-491-6736, Fax: 970-491-7252, E-mail: christopher.melby@colostate.edu. *Application contact:* Paula Coleman, Graduate Coordinator, 970-491-3819, Fax: 970-491-3875, E-mail: pcoleman@cahs.colostate.edu.

Columbia University, College of Physicians and Surgeons, Institute of Human Nutrition, MS Program in Nutrition, New York, NY 10032. Offers MS, MPH/MS. Part-time and evening/weekend programs available. *Degree requirements:* For master's, thesis. *Entrance requirements:* For master's, GRE General Test, TOEFL, MCAT. Additional exam requirements/recommendations for international students: Required—TOEFL.

See Close-Up on page 423.

Columbia University, College of Physicians and Surgeons, Institute of Human Nutrition and Graduate School of Arts and Sciences at the College of Physicians and Surgeons, PhD Program in Nutrition, New York, NY 10032. Offers PhD. *Degree requirements:* For doctorate, thesis/dissertation. *Entrance requirements:* For doctorate, GRE General Test. Additional exam requirements/recommendations for international students: Required—TOEFL. *Faculty research:* Growth and development, nutrition and metabolism.

See Close-Up on page 423.

Cornell University, Graduate School, Graduate Fields of Agriculture and Life Sciences and Graduate Fields of Human Ecology, Field of Nutrition, Ithaca, NY 14853-0001. Offers animal nutrition (MPS, MS, PhD); community nutrition (MPS, MS, PhD); human nutrition (MPS, MS, PhD); international nutrition (MPS, MS, PhD); nutritional biochemistry (MPS, MS, PhD). *Faculty:* 56 full-time (23 women). *Students:* 53 full-time (44 women); includes 7 minority (2 African Americans, 3 Asian Americans or Pacific Islanders, 2 Hispanic Americans), 13 international. Average age 30. 80 applicants. In 2009, 2 master's, 6 doctorates awarded. *Degree requirements:* For master's, thesis (MS), project papers (MPS); for doctorate, comprehensive exam, thesis/

Nutrition

Cornell University (continued)

dissertation. *Entrance requirements:* For master's and doctorate, GRE General Test, previous course work in organic chemistry (with laboratory) and biochemistry; 2 letters of recommendation. Additional exam requirements/recommendations for international students: Required—TOEFL (minimum score 550 paper-based; 213 computer-based; 77 iBT). *Application deadline:* For fall admission, 1/10 priority date for domestic students; for spring admission, 10/1 for domestic students. Application fee: $70. Electronic applications accepted. *Expenses:* Tuition: Full-time $29,500. Required fees: $70. Full-time tuition and fees vary according to degree level, program and student level. *Financial support:* In 2009–10, 46 students received support, including 4 fellowships with full tuition reimbursements available, 1 research assistantship with full tuition reimbursement available; teaching assistantships with full tuition reimbursements available, institutionally sponsored loans, scholarships/grants, health care benefits, tuition waivers (full and partial), and unspecified assistantships also available. Financial award applicants required to submit FAFSA. *Faculty research:* Nutritional biochemistry, experimental human and animal nutrition, international nutrition, community nutrition. *Unit head:* Director of Graduate Studies, 607-255-2528, Fax: 607-255-0178. *Application contact:* Graduate Field Assistant, 607-255-2628, Fax: 607-225-0178, E-mail: nutrition_gfr@cornell.edu.

Cornell University, Graduate School, Graduate Fields of Arts and Sciences, Field of International Development, Ithaca, NY 14853-0001. Offers development policy (MPS); international nutrition (MPS); international planning (MPS); international population (MPS); science and technology policy (MPS). *Faculty:* 54 full-time (18 women). *Students:* 1 (woman) full-time, all international. Average age 33. 31 applicants, 42% accepted, 1 enrolled. In 2009, 15 master's awarded. *Degree requirements:* For master's, project paper. *Entrance requirements:* For master's, GRE General Test (recommended), 2 academic recommendations, 2 years of development experience. Additional exam requirements/recommendations for international students: Required—TOEFL (minimum score 77 iBT). *Application deadline:* Applications are processed on a rolling basis. Application fee: $70. Electronic applications accepted. *Expenses:* Tuition: Full-time $29,500. Required fees: $70. Full-time tuition and fees vary according to degree level, program and student level. *Financial support:* In 2009–10, 1 student received support; fellowships with full tuition reimbursements available, research assistantships with full tuition reimbursements available, teaching assistantships with full tuition reimbursements available, institutionally sponsored loans, scholarships/grants, health care benefits, tuition waivers (full and partial), and unspecified assistantships available. Financial award applicants required to submit FAFSA. *Faculty research:* Development policy, international nutrition, international planning, science and technology policy, international population. *Unit head:* Director of Graduate Studies, 607-255-3037, Fax: 607-255-1005. *Application contact:* Graduate Field Assistant, 607-255-0831, Fax: 607-255-1005, E-mail: mpsid@cornell.edu.

Drexel University, College of Arts and Sciences, Department of Biology, Program in Human Nutrition, Philadelphia, PA 19104-2875. Offers MS. *Accreditation:* ADtA. Part-time programs available. Terminal master's awarded for partial completion of doctoral program. *Degree requirements:* For master's, thesis. *Entrance requirements:* For master's, GRE General Test. Additional exam requirements/recommendations for international students: Required—TOEFL. Electronic applications accepted. *Faculty research:* Metabolism of lipids, W-3 fatty acids, obesity, diabetes and heart disease, mineral metabolism.

D'Youville College, Department of Dietetics, Buffalo, NY 14201-1084. Offers MS. Five-year program that begins at freshman entry. *Accreditation:* ADtA. *Degree requirements:* For master's, thesis. *Entrance requirements:* Additional exam requirements/recommendations for international students: Required—TOEFL (minimum score 500 paper-based; 173 computer-based). Electronic applications accepted. *Faculty research:* Nutrition education, clinical nutrition, herbal supplements, obesity.

East Carolina University, Graduate School, College of Human Ecology, Department of Nutrition and Hospitality Management, Greenville, NC 27858-4353. Offers nutrition (MS). Part-time programs available. *Degree requirements:* For master's, comprehensive exam, thesis optional. *Entrance requirements:* For master's, GRE. Additional exam requirements/recommendations for international students: Required—TOEFL. *Faculty research:* Lifecycle nutrition, nutrition and disease, nutrition for fish species, food service management.

Eastern Illinois University, Graduate School, Lumpkin College of Business and Applied Sciences, School of Family and Consumer Sciences, Charleston, IL 61920-3099. Offers dietetics (MS); family and consumer sciences (MS). Part-time programs available. *Faculty:* 12 full-time (10 women). *Students:* 34 full-time (33 women), 29 part-time (all women). In 2009, 40 master's awarded. *Degree requirements:* For master's, comprehensive exam. *Application deadline:* For fall admission, 3/31 priority date for domestic students. Applications are processed on a rolling basis. Application fee: $30. *Expenses:* Tuition, state resident: full-time $9434; part-time $239 per credit hour. Tuition, nonresident: full-time $23,774; part-time $717 per credit hour. Required fees: $802.63. *Financial support:* In 2009–10, 2 research assistantships with tuition reimbursements (averaging $8,100 per year), 6 teaching assistantships with tuition reimbursements (averaging $8,100 per year) were awarded; career-related internships or fieldwork also available. *Unit head:* Dr. James Painter, Chairperson, 217-581-6076, Fax: 217-581-6090, E-mail: jepainter@eiu.edu. *Application contact:* Dr. Lisa Taylor, Coordinator, 217-581-8584, Fax: 217-581-6090, E-mail: lmtaylor@eiu.edu.

Eastern Kentucky University, The Graduate School, College of Health Sciences, Department of Family and Consumer Sciences, Richmond, KY 40475-3102. Offers community nutrition (MS). Part-time programs available. *Entrance requirements:* For master's, GRE General Test, minimum GPA of 2.5.

Eastern Michigan University, Graduate School, College of Health and Human Services, School of Health Sciences, Programs in Dietetics and Nutrition, Ypsilanti, MI 48197. Offers human nutrition (MS); human nutrition-coordinated program in dietetics (MS). *Accreditation:* ADtA. Part-time and evening/weekend programs available. Postbaccalaureate distance learning degree programs offered (minimal on-campus study). *Students:* 22 full-time (21 women), 62 part-time (59 women); includes 13 minority (6 African Americans, 3 Asian Americans or Pacific Islanders, 4 Hispanic Americans), 1 international. Average age 33. In 2009, 11 master's awarded. *Entrance requirements:* Additional exam requirements/recommendations for international students: Required—TOEFL. *Application deadline:* Applications are processed on a rolling basis. Application fee: $35. Tuition and fees vary according to course level. *Financial support:* Fellowships, research assistantships with full tuition reimbursements, teaching assistantships with full tuition reimbursements, career-related internships or fieldwork, Federal Work-Study, institutionally sponsored loans, scholarships/grants, tuition waivers (partial), and unspecified assistantships available. Support available to part-time students. Financial award applicants required to submit FAFSA. *Unit head:* Lydia Kret, Interim Program Director, 734-487-4096, Fax: 734-487-4095, E-mail: lkret@emich.edu. *Application contact:* Lydia Kret, Interim Program Director, 734-487-4096, Fax: 734-487-4095, E-mail: lkret@emich.edu.

East Tennessee State University, School of Graduate Studies, College of Business and Technology, Department of Family and Consumer Sciences, Johnson City, TN 37614. Offers clinical nutrition (MS). *Degree requirements:* For master's, thesis, oral exam. *Entrance requirements:* For master's, GRE, ADA-approved undergraduate didactic program in dietetics. Additional exam requirements/recommendations for international students: Required—TOEFL (minimum score 550 paper-based; 213 computer-based). *Faculty research:* Kindergarten students, measures of percent body fat during pregnancy, writing to read in preschool children, computer research in food systems management, students' knowledge of aging.

Emory University, Graduate School of Arts and Sciences, Division of Biological and Biomedical Sciences, Program in Nutrition and Health Sciences, Atlanta, GA 30322-1100. Offers PhD. *Faculty:* 43 full-time (23 women). *Students:* 30 full-time (26 women); includes 4 minority (1 African American, 2 Asian Americans or Pacific Islanders, 1 Hispanic American), 6 international. Average age 27. 32 applicants, 28% accepted, 8 enrolled. In 2009, 4 doctorates awarded. *Degree requirements:* For doctorate, comprehensive exam, thesis/dissertation. *Entrance requirements:* For doctorate, GRE General Test, minimum GPA of 3.0 in science course work (recommended). Additional exam requirements/recommendations for international students: Required—TOEFL. *Application deadline:* For fall admission, 1/3 for domestic and international students. Application fee: $50. Electronic applications accepted. *Financial support:* In 2009–10, 15 students received support, including 15 fellowships with full tuition reimbursements available (averaging $24,500 per year); institutionally sponsored loans, scholarships/grants, and health care benefits also available. *Faculty research:* Biochemistry, molecular and cell biology, clinical nutrition, community and preventive health, nutritional epidemiology. *Unit head:* Dr. Usha Ramakrishnan, Director, 404-727-1092, Fax: 404-727-1278, E-mail: uramakr@sph.emory.edu. *Application contact:* Dr. Vin Tangpricha, Recruiter, 404-727-7254, Fax: 404-727-3322, E-mail: vtangpr@emory.edu.

Emory University, Rollins School of Public Health, Hubert Department of Global Health, Atlanta, GA 30322-1100. Offers global demography (MSPH); global environmental health (MPH); public nutrition (MSPH). *Accreditation:* CEPH. Part-time programs available. *Degree requirements:* For master's, thesis, practicum. *Entrance requirements:* For master's, GRE General Test. Additional exam requirements/recommendations for international students: Required—TOEFL (minimum score 550 paper-based; 213 computer-based; 80 iBT). Electronic applications accepted.

Florida International University, Stempel College of Public Health and Social Work, Department of Dietetics and Nutrition, Miami, FL 33199. Offers MS, PhD. Part-time programs available. *Faculty:* 11 full-time (10 women). *Students:* 78 full-time (67 women), 51 part-time (46 women); includes 65 minority (10 African Americans, 9 Asian Americans or Pacific Islanders, 46 Hispanic Americans), 25 international. Average age 31. 68 applicants, 32% accepted, 19 enrolled. In 2009, 10 master's, 3 doctorates awarded. *Degree requirements:* For master's, thesis; for doctorate, comprehensive exam, thesis/dissertation. *Entrance requirements:* For master's, minimum GPA of 3.0; for doctorate, GRE General Test, minimum GPA of 3.0, resume, letters of recommendation, faculty sponsor. Additional exam requirements/recommendations for international students: Required—TOEFL (minimum score 550 paper-based; 80 iBT). *Application deadline:* For fall admission, 6/1 for domestic students, 4/1 for international students; for spring admission, 10/1 for domestic students, 9/1 for international students. Applications are processed on a rolling basis. Application fee: $30. Electronic applications accepted. *Expenses:* Tuition, state resident: full-time $8008; part-time $4004 per year. Tuition, nonresident: full-time $20,104; part-time $10,052 per year. Required fees: $298; $149 per term. *Financial support:* Career-related internships or fieldwork, Federal Work-Study, institutionally sponsored loans, and scholarships/grants available. Financial award application deadline: 3/1; financial award applicants required to submit FAFSA. *Faculty research:* Clinical nutrition, cultural food habits, pediatric nutrition, diabetes, dietetic education. *Unit head:* Dr. Fatma Huffman, Chair, 305-348-3788, Fax: 305-348-1996, E-mail: fatma.ercanli-huffman@fiu.edu. *Application contact:* Nanett Rojas, Assistant Director of Graduate Admissions, 305-348-7442, Fax: 305-348-7441, E-mail: gradadm@fiu.edu.

Florida State University, The Graduate School, College of Human Sciences, Department of Nutrition, Food, and Exercise Sciences, Tallahassee, FL 32306-1493. Offers exercise science (MS, PhD), including exercise physiology; nutrition and food sciences (MS, PhD), including clinical nutrition (MS), food science, human nutrition (PhD), nutrition and sport (MS), nutrition science (MS), nutrition, education and health promotion (MS). Part-time programs available. *Faculty:* 13 full-time (8 women). *Students:* 88 full-time (58 women), 21 part-time (14 women); includes 28 minority (10 African Americans, 5 Asian Americans or Pacific Islanders, 13 Hispanic Americans), 23 international. 128 applicants, 52% accepted, 35 enrolled. In 2009, 30 master's, 8 doctorates awarded. *Degree requirements:* For master's, comprehensive exam (for some programs), thesis optional; for doctorate, thesis/dissertation. *Entrance requirements:* For master's, GRE General Test, minimum upper-division GPA of 3.0; for doctorate, GRE General Test, minimum upper-division GPA of 3.0, MS. Additional exam requirements/recommendations for international students: Required—TOEFL (minimum score 570 paper-based; 80 iBT). *Application deadline:* For fall admission, 7/1 for domestic students, 3/1 for international students; for spring admission, 11/1 for domestic students, 5/1 for international students. Application fee: $30. Electronic applications accepted. *Expenses:* Tuition, state resident: full-time $7413. Tuition, nonresident: full-time $22,567. *Financial support:* In 2009–10, 42 students received support, including 5 fellowships with partial tuition reimbursements available (averaging $10,000 per year), 8 research assistantships with partial tuition reimbursements available (averaging $8,000 per year), 31 teaching assistantships with partial tuition reimbursements available (averaging $8,000 per year); career-related internships or fieldwork, Federal Work-Study, institutionally sponsored loans, scholarships/grants, and unspecified assistantships also available. Financial award application deadline: 1/15; financial award applicants required to submit FAFSA. *Faculty research:* Body composition, functional food, chronic disease and aging response; food safety, food allergy, and safety/quality detection methods; sports nutrition, energy and human performance. *Unit head:* Dr. Bahram H. Arjmandi, Margaret A. Sitton Professor and Chair, 850-645-1517, Fax: 850-645-5000, E-mail: barjmandi@fsu.edu. *Application contact:* Ursula M. Tate, Administrative Support Assistant, 850-644-4800, Fax: 850-645-5000, E-mail: utate@fsu.edu.

Framingham State University, Division of Graduate and Continuing Education, Programs in Food and Nutrition, Coordinated Program in Dietetics, Framingham, MA 01701-9101. Offers MS. *Accreditation:* ADtA.

Framingham State University, Division of Graduate and Continuing Education, Programs in Food and Nutrition, Food Science and Nutrition Science Program, Framingham, MA 01701-9101. Offers MS. Part-time and evening/weekend programs available. *Entrance requirements:* For master's, GRE General Test.

Framingham State University, Division of Graduate and Continuing Education, Programs in Food and Nutrition, Program in Human Nutrition: Education and Media Technologies, Framingham, MA 01701-9101. Offers MS.

George Mason University, College of Health and Human Services, Department of Global and Community Health, Fairfax, VA 22030. Offers biostatistics (Certificate); epidemiology (Certificate); epidemiology and biostatistics (MS); gerontology (Certificate); global health (MS, Certificate); nutrition (Certificate); public health (MPH, Certificate); rehabilitation science (Certificate). *Faculty:* 14 full-time (8 women), 12 part-time/adjunct (8 women). *Students:* 93 full-time (75 women), 106 part-time (92 women); includes 87 minority (46 African Americans, 1 American Indian/Alaska Native, 31 Asian Americans or Pacific Islanders, 9 Hispanic Americans), 22 international. Average age 31. 269 applicants, 69% accepted, 146 enrolled. In 2009, 17 master's, 2 other advanced degrees awarded. *Degree requirements:* For master's, comprehensive exam (for some programs), thesis or practicum. *Entrance requirements:* For master's, GRE, BA with minimum GPA of 3.0, 2 letters of recommendation. Additional exam requirements/recommendations for international students: Required—TOEFL. *Application deadline:* For fall admission, 4/1 priority date for domestic students, 4/1 for international students; for spring admission, 11/1 for domestic and international students. Applications are processed on a rolling basis. Application fee: $75. Electronic applications accepted. *Expenses:* Tuition, state resident: full-time $7568; part-time $315.33 per credit hour. Tuition, nonresident: full-time $21,704; part-time $904.33 per credit hour. Required fees: $2184; $91 per credit hour. *Financial support:* In 2009–10, 4 students received support, including 2 research assistantships with full and partial tuition reimbursements available (averaging $3,500 per year), 2 teaching assistantships with full and partial tuition reimbursements available (averaging $2,790 per year); Federal Work-Study, scholarships/grants, unspecified assistantships, and research awards, health care benefits health care benefits (full-time research or teaching assistantship recipients) also available. Support available to part-time students. Financial award application deadline: 3/1. *Faculty research:* Providing introductory and advanced degrees in health-related disciplines centered in global and community issues, health issues and the needs of affected populations at the regional and global level. *Unit head:* Dr. Shirley S. Travis, Dean, 703-993-1918. *Application contact:* Allan Weiss, Office Manager, 703-993-3126, E-mail: aweiss2@gmu.edu.

Georgia State University, College of Health and Human Sciences, School of Health Professions, Division of Nutrition, Atlanta, GA 30302-3083. Offers MS. *Accreditation:* ADtA. Part-time and evening/weekend programs available. *Degree requirements:* For master's, thesis optional. *Entrance requirements:* For master's, GRE or MAT. Additional exam requirements/recommendations for international students: Required—TOEFL (minimum score 550 paper-based; 213 computer-based). Electronic applications accepted. *Faculty research:* Food safety, sports nutrition, obesity, food fortification, nutrition interventions.

Harvard University, School of Public Health, Department of Nutrition, Boston, MA 02115-6096. Offers nutrition (DPH, PhD, SD); nutritional epidemiology (DPH, SD); public health nutrition (DPH, SD). *Faculty:* 14 full-time (3 women), 7 part-time/adjunct (2 women). *Students:* 30 full-time, 1 part-time; includes 1 minority (Hispanic American), 22 international. Average age 33. 30 applicants, 30% accepted, 6 enrolled. In 2009, 11 doctorates awarded. *Degree requirements:* For doctorate, thesis/dissertation, qualifying exam. *Entrance requirements:* For doctorate, GRE. Additional exam requirements/recommendations for international students: Required—TOEFL (minimum score 595 paper-based; 240 computer-based; 95 iBT); Recommended—IELTS (minimum score 7). *Application deadline:* For fall admission, 12/15 for domestic and international students. Application fee: $115. Electronic applications accepted. *Expenses:* Tuition: Full-time $33,696. Required fees: $1126. Full-time tuition and fees vary according to program. *Financial support:* Fellowships, research assistantships, teaching assistantships, Federal Work-Study, scholarships/grants, traineeships, tuition waivers (partial), and unspecified assistantships available. Support available to part-time students. Financial award application deadline: 2/8; financial award applicants required to submit FAFSA. *Faculty research:* Dietary and genetic factors affecting heart diseases in humans; interactions among nutrition, immunity, and infection; role of diet and lifestyle in preventing macrovascular complications in diabetics. *Unit head:* Dr. Walter Willett, Chair, 617-432-1333, Fax: 617-432-2435, E-mail: walter.willett@channing.harvard.edu. *Application contact:* Vincent W. James, Director of Admissions, 617-432-1031, Fax: 617-432-7080, E-mail: admisofc@hsph.harvard.edu.

Howard University, Graduate School, Department of Nutritional Sciences, Washington, DC 20059-0002. Offers nutrition (MS, PhD). Part-time and evening/weekend programs available. *Degree requirements:* For master's, comprehensive exam, thesis; for doctorate, comprehensive exam, thesis/dissertation. *Entrance requirements:* For master's and doctorate, minimum GPA of 3.0, general chemistry, organic chemistry, biochemistry, nutrition. Additional exam requirements/recommendations for international students: Required—TOEFL (minimum score 213 computer-based). Electronic applications accepted. *Faculty research:* Dietary fiber, phytate, trace minerals, cardio-vascular diseases, overweight/obesity.

Hunter College of the City University of New York, Graduate School, Schools of the Health Professions, School of Health Sciences, Programs in Urban Public Health, Program in Nutrition and Public Health, New York, NY 10021-5085. Offers MPH. *Accreditation:* ADtA. Part-time and evening/weekend programs available. *Faculty:* 27 full-time (17 women), 3 part-time/adjunct (2 women). *Students:* 11 full-time (9 women), 21 part-time (19 women); includes 9 minority (3 African Americans, 6 Asian Americans or Pacific Islanders). Average age 32. 26 applicants, 65% accepted, 8 enrolled. *Degree requirements:* For master's, comprehensive exam, thesis optional, internship. *Entrance requirements:* For master's, GRE General Test, previous course work in calculus and statistics. Additional exam requirements/recommendations for international students: Required—TOEFL. *Application deadline:* For fall admission, 4/1 for domestic students; for spring admission, 11/1 for domestic students. Application fee: $125. *Expenses:* Tuition, state resident: full-time $7360; part-time $310 per credit. Required fees: $250 per semester. *Financial support:* In 2009–10, 6 fellowships were awarded; career-related internships or fieldwork, Federal Work-Study, institutionally sponsored loans, and tuition waivers (partial) also available. Support available to part-time students. *Unit head:* Arlene Spark, Coordinator, 212-481-7950, Fax: 212-481-5260, E-mail: aspark@hunter.cuny.edu. *Application contact:* Milena Solo, Assistant Director for Graduate Admissions, 212-772-4288, Fax: 212-650-3336, E-mail: milena.solo@hunter.cuny.edu.

Huntington College of Health Sciences, Program in Nutrition, Knoxville, TN 37919-7736. Offers MS. Part-time and evening/weekend programs available. Postbaccalaureate distance learning degree programs offered (no on-campus study). *Entrance requirements:* For master's, high school diploma/bachelor's degree.

Idaho State University, Office of Graduate Studies, Kasiska College of Health Professions, Department of Health and Nutrition Sciences, Pocatello, ID 83209-8109. Offers dietetics (Certificate); health education (MHE); public health (MPH). Part-time programs available. *Faculty:* 4 full-time (2 women). *Students:* 29 full-time (18 women), 33 part-time (23 women); includes 8 minority (1 African American, 1 American Indian/Alaska Native, 2 Asian Americans or Pacific Islanders, 4 Hispanic Americans), 8 international. Average age 31. In 2009, 12 master's awarded. *Degree requirements:* For master's, comprehensive exam, internship, thesis or project. *Entrance requirements:* For master's, GRE General Test or GPA greater than 3.5, minimum GPA of 3.0 for upper division classes, 2 letters of recommendation. Additional exam requirements/recommendations for international students: Required—TOEFL (minimum score 600 paper-based; 213 computer-based). *Application deadline:* For fall admission, 7/1 for domestic students, 6/1 for international students; for spring admission, 12/1 for domestic students, 11/1 for international students. Applications are processed on a rolling basis. Application fee: $55. Electronic applications accepted. *Expenses:* Tuition, state resident: full-time $3318; part-time $297 per credit hour. Tuition, nonresident: full-time $13,120; part-time $437 per credit hour. Required fees: $2530. Tuition and fees vary according to program. *Financial support:* In 2009–10, 2 research assistantships with full and partial tuition reimbursements (averaging $10,841 per year) were awarded; teaching assistantships with full and partial tuition reimbursements, career-related internships or fieldwork, Federal Work-Study, institutionally sponsored loans, scholarships/grants, traineeships, health care benefits, tuition waivers (full and partial), and unspecified assistantships also available. Support available to part-time students. Financial award application deadline: 1/1; financial award applicants required to submit FAFSA. *Faculty research:* Epidemiology, environmental health, nutrition and aging, dietetics. *Unit head:* Dr. Willis McAleese, Chairman, 208-282-2729, Fax: 208-282-4000, E-mail: mcalwill@isu.edu. *Application contact:* Tami Carson, Graduate School Technical Records Specialist, 208-282-2150, Fax: 208-282-4847, E-mail: carstami@isu.edu.

Immaculata University, College of Graduate Studies, Program in Nutrition Education, Immaculata, PA 19345. Offers nutrition education (MA); nutrition education/approved pre-professional practice program (MA). Part-time and evening/weekend programs available. *Degree requirements:* For master's, comprehensive exam, thesis optional. *Entrance requirements:* For master's, GRE or MAT, minimum GPA of 3.0. Electronic applications accepted. *Faculty research:* Sports nutrition, pediatric nutrition, changes in food consumption patterns in weight loss, nutritional counseling.

Indiana State University, School of Graduate Studies, College of Arts and Sciences, Department of Family and Consumer Sciences, Terre Haute, IN 47809. Offers dietetics (MS); family and consumer sciences education (MS); inter-area option (MS). *Accreditation:* ADtA. Part-time programs available. *Degree requirements:* For master's, thesis optional. Electronic applications accepted.

Indiana University Bloomington, School of Health, Physical Education and Recreation, Department of Applied Health Science, Bloomington, IN 47405-7000. Offers health behavior (PhD); health promotion (MS); human development/family studies (MS); nutrition science (MS); public health (MPH); safety management (MS); school and college health programs (MS). *Accreditation:* CEPH (one or more programs are accredited). *Faculty:* 24 full-time (12 women). *Students:* 131 full-time (92 women), 22 part-time (20 women); includes 35 minority (22 African Americans, 1 American Indian/Alaska Native, 5 Asian Americans or Pacific Islanders, 7 Hispanic Americans), 29 international. Average age 31. 118 applicants, 71% accepted, 52 enrolled. In 2009, 43 master's, 6 doctorates awarded. *Degree requirements:* For master's, thesis optional; for doctorate, thesis/dissertation. *Entrance requirements:* For master's, GRE (MS in nutrition science), 3 recommendations; for doctorate, GRE, 3 recommendations. Additional exam requirements/recommendations for international students: Required—TOEFL (minimum score 550 paper-based; 213 computer-based; 79 iBT). *Application deadline:* For fall admission, 4/30 priority date for domestic students, 12/1 priority date for international students; for spring admission, 11/15 priority date for domestic students, 9/1 priority date for international students. Application fee: $55 ($65 for international students). *Financial support:* In 2009–10, 80 students received support, including 12 fellowships (averaging $2,316 per year), 50 research assistantships with full and partial tuition reimbursements available (averaging $6,973 per year), 27 teaching assistantships with full and partial tuition reimbursements available (averaging $11,067 per year); career-related internships or fieldwork, Federal Work-Study, institutionally sponsored loans, scholarships/grants, tuition waivers (partial), and fee remissions also available. Financial award application deadline: 3/1. *Faculty research:* Cancer education, HIV/AIDS and drug education, public health, parent-child interactions, safety education. Total annual research expenditures: $2.8 million. *Unit head:* Dr. Mohammad R. Torabi, Chair, 812-855-4808, Fax: 812-855-3936, E-mail: torabi@indiana.edu. *Application contact:* Dr. Mohammad R. Torabi, Chair, 812-855-4808, Fax: 812-855-3936, E-mail: torabi@indiana.edu.

Indiana University of Pennsylvania, School of Graduate Studies and Research, College of Health and Human Services, Department of Food and Nutrition, Program in Food and Nutrition, Indiana, PA 15705-1087. Offers MS. Part-time programs available. *Faculty:* 5 full-time (all women). *Students:* 8 full-time (7 women), 16 part-time (14 women); includes 2 minority (1 American Indian/Alaska Native, 1 Asian American or Pacific Islander), 1 international. Average age 25. 33 applicants, 48% accepted, 13 enrolled. In 2009, 12 master's awarded. *Degree requirements:* For master's, thesis optional. *Entrance requirements:* For master's, GRE General Test, 2 letters of recommendation. Additional exam requirements/recommendations for international students: Required—TOEFL. *Application deadline:* For fall admission, 7/1 priority date for domestic students; for spring admission, 11/1 for domestic students. Applications are processed on a rolling basis. Application fee: $40. *Expenses:* Tuition, state resident: full-time $6666; part-time $370 per credit hour. Tuition, nonresident: full-time $10,666; part-time $593 per credit hour. Required fees: $813 per semester. *Financial support:* In 2009–10, 5 research assistantships with full and partial tuition reimbursements (averaging $4,018 per year) were awarded. Financial award applicants required to submit FAFSA. *Unit head:* Dr. Stephanie Taylor-Davis, Graduate Coordinator, 724-357-7733, E-mail: stdavis@iup.edu. *Application contact:* Dr. Stephanie Taylor-Davis, Graduate Coordinator, 724-357-7733, E-mail: stdavis@iup.edu.

Indiana University–Purdue University Indianapolis, Indiana University School of Medicine, School of Health and Rehabilitation Sciences, Indianapolis, IN 46202-2896. Offers health sciences education (MS); nutrition and dietetics (MS); occupational therapy (MS); physical therapy (DPT). Part-time and evening/weekend programs available. *Faculty:* 8 full-time (5 women). *Students:* 206 full-time (161 women), 11 part-time (8 women); includes 16 minority (5 African Americans, 1 American Indian/Alaska Native, 8 Asian Americans or Pacific Islanders, 2 Hispanic Americans), 1 international. Average age 26. 23 applicants, 83% accepted, 18 enrolled. In 2009, 9 master's, 32 doctorates awarded. *Degree requirements:* For master's, thesis (for some programs). *Entrance requirements:* For master's, GRE General Test, minimum GPA of 3.0. Additional exam requirements/recommendations for international students: Required—TOEFL. *Application deadline:* For fall admission, 1/15 priority date for domestic students; for spring admission, 10/15 for domestic students. Application fee: $55 ($65 for international students). *Financial support:* In 2009–10, 10 fellowships (averaging $2,485 per year), 1 teaching assistantship (averaging $3,600 per year) were awarded; research assistantships, Federal Work-Study, institutionally sponsored loans, and scholarships/grants also available. Support available to part-time students. Financial award applicants required to submit FAFSA. *Unit head:* Dr. Mark S. Sothmann, Dean, 317-274-4702, E-mail: msothman@iupui.edu. *Application contact:* Dr. Mark S. Sothmann, Dean, 317-274-4702, E-mail: msothman@iupui.edu.

Iowa State University of Science and Technology, Graduate College, College of Human Sciences and College of Agriculture, Department of Food Science and Human Nutrition, Ames, IA 50011. Offers food science and technology (MS, PhD); nutrition (MS, PhD). *Faculty:* 31 full-time (19 women), 1 (woman) part-time/adjunct. *Students:* 54 full-time (37 women), 4 part-time (2 women); includes 5 minority (2 African Americans, 2 Asian Americans or Pacific Islanders, 1 Hispanic American), 24 international. 74 applicants, 22% accepted, 15 enrolled. In 2009, 3 master's, 5 doctorates awarded. *Degree requirements:* For master's, thesis; for doctorate, thesis/dissertation. *Entrance requirements:* For master's and doctorate, GRE General Test. Additional exam requirements/recommendations for international students: Required—TOEFL (minimum score 550 paper-based; 79 iBT) or IELTS (minimum score 6.5). *Application deadline:* For fall admission, 1/15 priority date for domestic and international students. Applications are processed on a rolling basis. Application fee: $40 ($90 for international students). Electronic applications accepted. *Expenses:* Tuition, state resident: full-time $6716. Tuition, nonresident: full-time $8908. Tuition and fees vary according to course level, course load, program and student level. *Financial support:* In 2009–10, 21 research assistantships with full and partial tuition reimbursements (averaging $16,240 per year) were awarded; fellowships, teaching assistantships with full and partial tuition reimbursements, scholarships/grants also available. *Unit head:* Dr. Ruth S. MacDonald, Chair, 515-294-5991, Fax: 515-294-8181, E-mail: ruthmacd@iastate.edu. *Application contact:* Dr. Patricia Murphy, Director of Graduate Education, 515-294-6442, E-mail: gradsecretary@iastate.edu.

Iowa State University of Science and Technology, Graduate College, Interdisciplinary Programs, Program in Nutritional Sciences, Ames, IA 50011. Offers MS, PhD. *Students:* 32 full-time (20 women), 2 part-time (both women); includes 1 minority (Asian American or Pacific Islander), 9 international. In 2009, 2 master's, 3 doctorates awarded. *Degree requirements:* For master's, thesis; for doctorate, thesis/dissertation. *Entrance requirements:* For master's and doctorate, GRE General Test. Additional exam requirements/recommendations for international students: Required—TOEFL (minimum score 550 paper-based; 79 iBT) or IELTS (minimum score 6.5). *Application deadline:* For fall admission, 1/15 priority date for domestic and international students. Applications are processed on a rolling basis. Application fee: $40 ($90 for international students). Electronic applications accepted. *Expenses:* Tuition, state resident: full-time $6716. Tuition, nonresident: full-time $8908. Tuition and fees vary according to course level, course load, program and student level. *Financial support:* In 2009–10, 27 research assistantships with full and partial tuition reimbursements (averaging $16,240 per year), 1 teaching assistantship with full and partial tuition reimbursement (averaging $16,240 per year) were awarded. *Unit head:* Dr. Kevin Schalinske, Chair, Supervising Committee, 515-294-8442, E-mail: gradsecretary@iastate.edu. *Application contact:* Dr. Wendy White, Professor, 515-294-6442, E-mail: gradsecretary@iastate.edu.

The Johns Hopkins University, Bloomberg School of Public Health, Department of International Health, Baltimore, MD 21205. Offers global disease epidemiology and control (MHS, PhD); health systems (MHS, PhD); human nutrition (MHS, PhD); international health (Dr PH); social and behavioral interventions (MHS, PhD). *Faculty:* 137 full-time (82 women), 185 part-time/adjunct (63 women). *Students:* 242 full-time (189 women), 1 (woman) part-time; includes 61 minority (9 African Americans, 41 Asian Americans or Pacific Islanders, 11 Hispanic Americans), 71 international. Average age 28. 494 applicants, 48% accepted, 100 enrolled. In 2009, 66 master's, 15 doctorates awarded. *Degree requirements:* For master's, comprehensive exam, thesis (for some programs), 1 year full-time residency, 4-9 month internship; for doctorate, comprehensive exam, thesis/dissertation or alternative, 1.5 years full-time residency, oral and written exams. *Entrance requirements:* For master's, GRE General Test or MCAT, 3 letters of recommendation, resume; for doctorate, GRE General Test or MCAT, 3 letters of recommendation, resume, transcripts. Additional exam requirements/recommendations for international students: Required—TOEFL (minimum score 600 paper-based; 250 computer-based; 100 iBT); Recommended—IELTS (minimum score 7). *Application deadline:* For fall admission, 1/2 priority date for domestic and international students. Applications are processed on a rolling basis. Application fee: $45. Electronic applications accepted. *Financial support:* In

Nutrition

The Johns Hopkins University (continued)
2009–10, 188 students received support, including 15 fellowships (averaging $50,000 per year); Federal Work-Study, institutionally sponsored loans, scholarships/grants, traineeships, and stipends also available. Financial award application deadline: 1/2. *Faculty research:* Nutrition, infectious diseases, health systems, health economics, humanitarian emergencies. Total annual research expenditures: $72 million. *Unit head:* Dr. Robert E. Black, Chairman, 410-955-3934, Fax: 410-955-7159, E-mail: rblack@jhsph.edu. *Application contact:* Cristina G. Salazar, Academic Program Manager, 410-955-3734, Fax: 410-955-7159, E-mail: csalazar@jhsph.edu.

Kansas State University, Graduate School, College of Human Ecology, Department of Human Nutrition, Manhattan, KS 66506. Offers MS, PhD. Part-time programs available. *Faculty:* 17 full-time (8 women), 3 part-time/adjunct (1 woman). *Students:* 20 full-time (15 women), 1 part-time (0 women); includes 2 minority (both African Americans), 14 international. Average age 29. 19 applicants, 42% accepted, 4 enrolled. In 2009, 4 doctorates awarded. *Degree requirements:* For master's, thesis or alternative, residency; for doctorate, thesis/dissertation, residency. *Entrance requirements:* For master's, GRE General Test, minimum undergraduate GPA of 3.0; for doctorate, GRE General Test, minimum graduate GPA of 3.5, course work in biochemistry and statistics. Additional exam requirements/recommendations for international students: Required—TOEFL (minimum score 600 paper-based; 250 computer-based). *Application deadline:* For fall admission, 2/1 priority date for domestic and international students; for spring admission, 8/1 priority date for domestic and international students. Applications are processed on a rolling basis. Application fee: $40 ($55 for international students). Electronic applications accepted. *Financial support:* In 2009–10, 23 research assistantships (averaging $11,737 per year) were awarded; career-related internships or fieldwork, Federal Work-Study, institutionally sponsored loans, scholarships/grants, and tuition waivers (full) also available. Support available to part-time students. Financial award application deadline: 3/1; financial award applicants required to submit FAFSA. *Faculty research:* Sensory analysis and consumer behavior, nutrition education and communication, human metabolism and performance, molecular and biochemical nutrition, public health nutrition. Total annual research expenditures: $936,226. *Unit head:* Denis Medeiros, Head, 785-532-0150, Fax: 785-532-3132, E-mail: medeiros@ksu.edu. *Application contact:* Mark Haub, Director, 785-532-0170, Fax: 785-532-3132, E-mail: haub@ksu.edu.

Kent State University, Graduate School of Education, Health, and Human Services, School of Health Sciences, Program in Nutrition, Kent, OH 44242-0001. Offers dietetic (MS). *Faculty:* 5 full-time (all women). *Students:* 30 full-time (28 women), 13 part-time (12 women); includes 1 minority (African American), 1 international. 44 applicants, 77% accepted. In 2009, 15 master's awarded. *Entrance requirements:* For master's, GRE. Application fee: $30. *Financial support:* In 2009–10, 1 research assistantship (averaging $8,313 per year) was awarded. *Unit head:* Karen Gordon, Coordinator, 330-672-2248, E-mail: klowry@kent.edu. *Application contact:* Nancy Miller, Academic Program Coordinator, Office of Graduate Student Services, 330-672-2576, Fax: 330-672-9162.

Lehman College of the City University of New York, Division of Natural and Social Sciences, Department of Health Sciences, Program in Nutrition, Bronx, NY 10468-1589. Offers clinical nutrition (MS); community nutrition (MS); dietetic internship (MS). *Degree requirements:* For master's, thesis or alternative.

Loma Linda University, School of Public Health, Department of Nutrition, Loma Linda, CA 92350. Offers public health nutrition (MPH, Dr PH). *Accreditation:* ADtA. *Degree requirements:* For doctorate, thesis/dissertation. *Entrance requirements:* For doctorate, GRE General Test. Additional exam requirements/recommendations for international students: Required—Michigan English Language Assessment Battery or TOEFL. *Faculty research:* Sports nutrition in minorities, dietary determinance of chronic disease, protein adequacy in vegetarian diets, relationship of dietary intake to hormone level.

Long Island University, C.W. Post Campus, School of Health Professions and Nursing, Department of Nutrition, Brookville, NY 11548-1300. Offers dietetic internship (Certificate); nutrition (MS). Part-time and evening/weekend programs available. *Degree requirements:* For master's, thesis. *Entrance requirements:* For master's, minimum GPA of 2.75 in major. Electronic applications accepted. *Faculty research:* Hematopoiesis, interleukins in allergy, growth factors effect in metastasis affecting behavioral change for nutrition.

Louisiana Tech University, Graduate School, College of Applied and Natural Sciences, School for Human Ecology, Ruston, LA 71272. Offers dietetics (MS); human ecology (MS). Part-time programs available. *Degree requirements:* For master's, thesis or alternative, Registered Dietician Exam eligibility. *Entrance requirements:* For master's, GRE General Test.

Loyola University Chicago, Graduate School, Marcella Niehoff School of Nursing, Dietetics Program, Chicago, IL 60660. Offers MS, Certificate. *Students:* 12 full-time (all women), 14 part-time (12 women). Average age 26. 4 applicants, 25% accepted, 0 enrolled. In 2009, 2 master's, 1 other advanced degree awarded. *Expenses:* Tuition: Full-time $14,220; part-time $790 per credit hour. Required fees: $60 per semester hour. Tuition and fees vary according to program. *Unit head:* Dr. Joanna Kouba, Director, 708-216-4132, E-mail: jkouba@luc.edu. *Application contact:* Dr. Vicki A. Keough, Associate Professor/Master's Program Director, 708-216-3582, Fax: 708-216-9555, E-mail: vkeough@luc.edu.

Marshall University, Academic Affairs Division, College of Health Professions, Department of Dietetics, Huntington, WV 25755. Offers MS. *Faculty:* 3 full-time (all women), 1 (woman) part-time/adjunct. *Students:* 13 full-time (11 women), 5 part-time (4 women). Average age 26. In 2009, 8 master's awarded. *Unit head:* Dr. Kelli Williams, Chairperson, 304-696-4336, E-mail: williamsk@marshall.edu. *Application contact:* Information Contact, 304-746-1900, Fax: 304-746-1902, E-mail: services@marshall.edu.

Marywood University, Academic Affairs, College of Health and Human Services, Department of Nutrition and Dietetics, Program in Dietetic Internship, Scranton, PA 18509-1598. Offers Certificate. *Students:* 11 part-time (10 women); includes 1 minority (Asian American or Pacific Islander). Average age 25. *Entrance requirements:* Additional exam requirements/recommendations for international students: Required—TOEFL (minimum score 550 paper-based; 213 computer-based; 79 iBT). Application fee: $35. Electronic applications accepted. *Expenses:* Tuition: Part-time $715 per credit. Required fees: $270 per semester. Tuition and fees vary according to degree level, campus/location and program. *Financial support:* Research assistantships, career-related internships or fieldwork, scholarships/grants, and unspecified assistantships available. Support available to part-time students. Financial award application deadline: 6/30; financial award applicants required to submit FAFSA. *Unit head:* Dr. Kathleen Mckee, Co-Chair, 570-348-6211 Ext. 2632, E-mail: khmckee@es.marywood.edu. *Application contact:* Tammy Manka, Assistant Director of Graduate Admissions, 866-279-9663, E-mail: tmanka@marywood.edu.

Marywood University, Academic Affairs, College of Health and Human Services, Department of Nutrition and Dietetics, Program in Nutrition, Scranton, PA 18509-1598. Offers MS. *Students:* 15 full-time (13 women), 7 part-time (6 women); includes 1 minority (African American), 1 international. Average age 29. In 2009, 9 master's awarded. *Entrance requirements:* Additional exam requirements/recommendations for international students: Required—TOEFL (minimum score 550 paper-based; 213 computer-based; 79 iBT). *Application deadline:* For fall admission, 4/1 priority date for domestic students, 3/31 priority date for international students; for spring admission, 11/1 priority date for domestic students, 8/31 priority date for international students. Applications are processed on a rolling basis. Application fee: $35. Electronic applications accepted. *Expenses:* Tuition: Part-time $715 per credit. Required fees: $270 per semester. Tuition and fees vary according to degree level, campus/location and program. *Financial support:* Career-related internships or fieldwork, scholarships/grants, and unspecified assistantships available. Support available to part-time students. Financial award application deadline: 6/30; financial award applicants required to submit FAFSA. *Faculty research:* Obesity and childhood nutrition, dietary supplements (Resveratrol). *Unit head:* Dr. Kathleen Mckee, Co-Chair, 570-348-6211 Ext. 2632, E-mail: khmckee@es.marywood.edu. *Application contact:* Tammy Manka, Assistant Director of Graduate Admissions, 866-279-9663, E-mail: tmanka@marywood.edu.

Marywood University, Academic Affairs, College of Health and Human Services, Department of Nutrition and Dietetics, Program in Sports Nutrition and Exercise Science, Scranton, PA 18509-1598. Offers MS. *Students:* 11 full-time (8 women), 5 part-time (3 women). Average age 26. In 2009, 4 master's awarded. *Entrance requirements:* Additional exam requirements/recommendations for international students: Required—TOEFL (minimum score 550 paper-based; 213 computer-based; 79 iBT). *Application deadline:* For fall admission, 4/1 priority date for domestic students, 3/31 priority date for international students; for spring admission, 11/1 priority date for domestic students, 8/31 priority date for international students. Applications are processed on a rolling basis. Application fee: $35. Electronic applications accepted. *Expenses:* Tuition: Part-time $715 per credit. Required fees: $270 per semester. Tuition and fees vary according to degree level, campus/location and program. *Financial support:* Career-related internships or fieldwork, scholarships/grants, and unspecified assistantships available. Support available to part-time students. Financial award application deadline: 6/30; financial award applicants required to submit FAFSA. *Faculty research:* Lung function studies (pulmonary diffusing capacity of nitric oxide). *Unit head:* Dr. Kathleen Mckee, Co-Chair, 570-348-6211 Ext. 2632, E-mail: khmckee@es.marywood.edu. *Application contact:* Tammy Manka, Assistant Director of Graduate Admissions, 866-279-9663, E-mail: tmanka@marywood.edu.

McGill University, Faculty of Graduate and Postdoctoral Studies, Faculty of Agricultural and Environmental Sciences, School of Dietetics and Human Nutrition, Montréal, QC H3A 2T5, Canada. Offers dietetics (M Sc A, Graduate Diploma); human nutrition (M Sc, M Sc A, PhD).

McMaster University, Faculty of Health Sciences and School of Graduate Studies, Program in Medical Sciences, Metabolism and Nutrition Area, Hamilton, ON L8S 4M2, Canada. Offers M Sc, PhD, MD/PhD. *Degree requirements:* For master's, thesis; for doctorate, comprehensive exam, thesis/dissertation. *Entrance requirements:* For master's, honors B Sc, B+ average in related field; for doctorate, M Sc, minimum B+ average, students with proven research experience and an A average may be admitted with a B Sc degree. Additional exam requirements/recommendations for international students: Required—TOEFL (minimum score 580 paper-based; 237 computer-based; 92 iBT).

McNeese State University, Doré School of Graduate Studies, Burton College of Education, Department of Health and Human Performance, Lake Charles, LA 70609. Offers exercise physiology (MS); health promotion (MS); nutrition and wellness (MS). *Accreditation:* NCATE. Evening/weekend programs available. *Faculty:* 5 full-time (2 women). *Students:* 40 full-time (32 women), 6 part-time (4 women); includes 6 minority (all African Americans), 4 international. In 2009, 22 master's awarded. *Entrance requirements:* For master's, GRE, undergraduate major or minor in health and human performance or related field of study. *Application deadline:* For fall admission, 5/15 priority date for domestic and international students; for spring admission, 10/15 priority date for domestic and international students. Applications are processed on a rolling basis. Application fee: $20 ($30 for international students). *Expenses:* Tuition, area resident: Full-time $2556. Tuition, state resident: full-time $2556. Required fees: $1031. Tuition and fees vary according to course load. *Financial support:* Application deadline: 5/1. *Unit head:* Dr. Michael Soileau, Head, 337-475-5374, Fax: 337-475-5947, E-mail: msoileau@mcneese.edu. *Application contact:* Dr. George F. Mead, Interim Dean of Doré School of Graduate Studies, 337-475-5396, Fax: 337-475-5397, E-mail: admissions@mcneese.edu.

Meredith College, John E. Weems Graduate School, Department of Human Environmental Sciences, Raleigh, NC 27607-5298. Offers dietetic internship (Postbaccalaureate Certificate); nutrition (MS). *Faculty:* 3 full-time (2 women), 1 (woman) part-time/adjunct. *Students:* 37 full-time (all women), 38 part-time (37 women); includes 9 minority (6 African Americans, 2 Asian Americans or Pacific Islanders, 1 Hispanic American). Average age 34. 170 applicants, 25% accepted, 34 enrolled. In 2009, 10 master's, 12 other advanced degrees awarded. *Degree requirements:* For master's, thesis optional. *Entrance requirements:* For master's, GRE, recommendations, interview. Additional exam requirements/recommendations for international students: Required—TOEFL. *Application deadline:* For fall admission, 7/1 priority date for domestic and international students; for spring admission, 11/1 priority date for domestic and international students. Applications are processed on a rolling basis. Application fee: $50. Electronic applications accepted. *Expenses:* Contact institution. *Financial support:* Application deadline: 2/15. *Unit head:* Dr. Deborah Tippett, Head, 919-760-2355, Fax: 919-760-2819, E-mail: tipettd@meredith.edu. *Application contact:* Dr. William H. Landis, Director, 919-760-2355, Fax: 919-760-2819, E-mail: landisb@meredith.edu.

Michigan State University, The Graduate School, College of Agriculture and Natural Resources and College of Natural Science, Department of Food Science and Human Nutrition, East Lansing, MI 48824. Offers food science (MS, PhD); food science—environmental toxicology (PhD); human nutrition (MS, PhD); human nutrition-environmental toxicology (PhD). *Faculty:* 23 full-time (10 women). *Students:* 40 full-time (31 women), 2 part-time (1 woman); includes 4 minority (2 African Americans, 1 Asian American or Pacific Islander, 1 Hispanic American), 15 international. Average age 28. 94 applicants, 9% accepted. In 2009, 9 master's, 6 doctorates awarded. *Entrance requirements:* Additional exam requirements/recommendations for international students: Required—TOEFL (minimum score 550 paper-based; 213 computer-based), Michigan State University ELT (minimum score 85), Michigan English Language Assessment Battery (minimum score 83). Electronic applications accepted. *Expenses:* Tuition, state resident: part-time $478.25 per credit hour. Tuition, nonresident: part-time $966.50 per credit hour. Part-time tuition and fees vary according to program. *Financial support:* In 2009–10, 29 research assistantships with tuition reimbursements (averaging $6,399 per year), 2 teaching assistantships with tuition reimbursements (averaging $5,985 per year) were awarded. Total annual research expenditures: $3 million. *Unit head:* Dr. Frederik Derksen, Acting Chairperson, 517-355-8474 Ext. 100, Fax: 517-353-8963, E-mail: derksen@anr.msu.edu. *Application contact:* Deborah Klein, Graduate Secretary, 517-355-8474 Ext. 182, Fax: 517-353-8963, E-mail: kleinde@msu.edu.

Middle Tennessee State University, College of Graduate Studies, College of Education and Behavioral Science, Department of Human Sciences, Murfreesboro, TN 37132. Offers child development and family studies (MS); nutrition and food science (MS). Part-time and evening/weekend programs available. Postbaccalaureate distance learning degree programs offered. *Faculty:* 7 full-time (all women). *Students:* 24 part-time (all women); includes 5 minority (4 African Americans, 1 Asian American or Pacific Islander). Average age 27. 22 applicants, 82% accepted, 18 enrolled. In 2009, 3 master's awarded. *Degree requirements:* For master's, comprehensive exam, thesis. *Entrance requirements:* For master's, GRE or MAT. Additional exam requirements/recommendations for international students: Required—TOEFL (minimum score 525 paper-based; 195 computer-based; 71 iBT) or IELTS (minimum score 6). *Application deadline:* For fall admission, 6/1 for domestic and international students. Applications are processed on a rolling basis. Application fee: $25 ($30 for international students). Electronic applications accepted. *Expenses:* Tuition, state resident: full-time $4404. Tuition, nonresident: full-time $10,956. *Financial support:* In 2009–10, 5 students received support. Application deadline: 5/1. *Faculty research:* Courtship relationships, feminist methodology and epistemology in family studies, school uniforms, body fat in elderly, asynchronous distance education. *Unit head:* Dr. Dellmar Walker, Chair, 615-898-2884. *Application contact:* Dr. Michael Allen, Dean and Vice Provost for Research, 615-898-2840, Fax: 615-904-8020, E-mail: mallen@mtsu.edu.

Mississippi State University, College of Agriculture and Life Sciences, Department of Food Science, Nutrition and Health Promotion, MS State, MS 39762. Offers food science and technology (PhD); nutrition (MS). Postbaccalaureate distance learning degree programs offered (no on-campus study). *Faculty:* 12 full-time (5 women), 2 part-time/adjunct (0 women). *Students:* 50 full-time (35 women), 28 part-time (20 women); includes 14 minority (10 African Americans, 2 Asian Americans or Pacific Islanders, 2 Hispanic Americans), 18 international. Average age 29. 88 applicants, 48% accepted, 28 enrolled. In 2009, 16 master's, 1 doctorate awarded.

Degree requirements: For master's, comprehensive exam, thesis; for doctorate, comprehensive exam, thesis/dissertation. *Entrance requirements:* For master's, GRE General Test, minimum GPA of 2.8; for doctorate, GRE General Test, minimum GPA of 3.0. Additional exam requirements/recommendations for international students: Required—TOEFL (minimum score 475 paper-based; 153 computer-based; 53 iBT); Recommended—IELTS (minimum score 4.5). *Application deadline:* For fall admission, 7/1 for domestic students, 5/1 for international students; for spring admission, 11/1 for domestic students, 9/1 for international students. Applications are processed on a rolling basis. Application fee: $40. Electronic applications accepted. *Expenses:* Tuition, state resident: full-time $2575.50; part-time $286.25 per credit hour. Tuition, nonresident: full-time $6510; part-time $723.50 per credit hour. Tuition and fees vary according to course load. *Financial support:* In 2009–10, 13 research assistantships with full tuition reimbursements (averaging $9,766 per year), 4 teaching assistantships with full tuition reimbursements (averaging $9,943 per year) were awarded; Federal Work-Study, institutionally sponsored loans, scholarships/grants, and unspecified assistantships also available. Financial award application deadline: 4/1; financial award applicants required to submit FAFSA. *Faculty research:* Food preservation, food chemistry, food safety, food processing, product development. *Unit head:* Dr. Benjy Mikel, Professor and Head, 662-325-3200, Fax: 662-325-8728, E-mail: wmikel@fsnhp.msstate.edu. *Application contact:* Dr. Juan Silva, Professor and Graduate Coordinator, 662-325-3200, Fax: 662-325-8728, E-mail: jls@ra.msstate.edu.

Montana State University, College of Graduate Studies, College of Education, Health, and Human Development, Department of Health and Human Development, Bozeman, MT 59717. Offers health and human development (MS), including counseling, exercise and nutrition sciences, family and consumer sciences, family financial planning, health promotion and education. *Accreditation:* ACA. Part-time programs available. Postbaccalaureate distance learning degree programs offered (no on-campus study). *Faculty:* 27 full-time (18 women), 7 part-time/adjunct (6 women). *Students:* 54 full-time (47 women), 18 part-time (15 women); includes 1 minority (Hispanic American). Average age 30. 32 applicants, 34% accepted, 10 enrolled. In 2009, 26 master's awarded. *Degree requirements:* For master's, comprehensive exam. *Entrance requirements:* For master's, GRE General Test. Additional exam requirements/recommendations for international students: Required—TOEFL (minimum score 550 paper-based; 213 computer-based). *Application deadline:* For fall admission, 7/15 priority date for domestic students, 5/15 priority date for international students; for spring admission, 12/1 priority date for domestic students, 10/1 priority date for international students. Applications are processed on a rolling basis. Application fee: $30. Electronic applications accepted. *Expenses:* Tuition, state resident: full-time $5635; part-time $3492 per year. Tuition, nonresident: full-time $17,212; part-time $7865.10 per year. Required fees: $1441; $153.15 per credit. Tuition and fees vary according to course load and program. *Financial support:* In 2009–10, 24 students received support, including 7 research assistantships (averaging $1,000 per year), 17 teaching assistantships with full tuition reimbursements available (averaging $8,000 per year). Financial award application deadline: 3/1; financial award applicants required to submit FAFSA. *Faculty research:* Gait analysis, cancer prevention, obesity prevention, energy expenditure, decision making. Total annual research expenditures: $2.8 million. *Unit head:* Dr. Tim Dunnagan, Head, 404-994-3242, Fax: 404-994-2013, E-mail: dunnagan@montana.edu. *Application contact:* Dr. Carl Fox.

Montclair State University, The Graduate School, College of Education and Human Services, Department of Exercise Science and Physical Education, Montclair, NJ 07043-1624. Offers health and physical education (Certificate); nutrition and exercise science (Certificate); physical education (MA, Certificate), including coaching and sports administration (MA), exercise science (MA), physical education (MA), teaching and supervision of physical education (MA). Part-time and evening/weekend programs available. *Faculty:* 15 full-time (9 women), 17 part-time/adjunct (10 women). *Students:* 8 full-time (3 women), 38 part-time (19 women). Average age 30. 34 applicants, 56% accepted, 13 enrolled. In 2009, 9 master's awarded. *Degree requirements:* For master's, comprehensive exam. *Entrance requirements:* For master's, GRE General Test, 2 letters of recommendation; for Certificate, 2 letters of recommendation (nutrition and exercise science concentration). Additional exam requirements/recommendations for international students: Required—TOEFL (minimum iBT score of 83) or IELTS. *Application deadline:* For fall admission, 6/1 for international students; for spring admission, 10/1 for international students. Applications are processed on a rolling basis. Application fee: $60. Electronic applications accepted. *Expenses:* Tuition, area resident: Part-time $486.74 per credit. Tuition, state resident: part-time $486.74 per credit. Tuition, nonresident: part-time $751.34 per credit. Tuition and fees vary according to degree level and program. *Financial support:* In 2009–10, 5 research assistantships with full tuition reimbursements (averaging $7,000 per year) were awarded; Federal Work-Study, scholarships/grants, and unspecified assistantships also available. Support available to part-time students. Financial award application deadline: 3/1; financial award applicants required to submit FAFSA. *Unit head:* Dr. Susana Juniu, Chairperson, 973-655-7093. *Application contact:* Amy Aiello, Director of Graduate Admissions and Operations, 973-655-5147, Fax: 973-655-7869, E-mail: graduate.school@montclair.edu.

Montclair State University, The Graduate School, College of Education and Human Services, Department of Health and Nutrition Sciences, Montclair, NJ 07043-1624. Offers American Dietetic Association (Certificate); community health education (MPH); food safety instructor (Certificate); health education (MA); nutrition and exercise science (MS); nutrition and food science (MS). Part-time and evening/weekend programs available. *Faculty:* 15 full-time (10 women), 55 part-time/adjunct (40 women). *Students:* 38 full-time (32 women), 78 part-time (68 women). Average age 32. 53 applicants, 64% accepted, 23 enrolled. In 2009, 19 master's, 2 other advanced degrees awarded. *Degree requirements:* For master's, comprehensive exam, thesis optional. *Entrance requirements:* For master's, GRE, 2 letters of recommendation. Additional exam requirements/recommendations for international students: Required—TOEFL (minimum iBT score of 83) or IELTS. *Application deadline:* For fall admission, 6/1 for international students; for spring admission, 10/1 for international students. Application fee: $60. *Expenses:* Tuition, area resident: Part-time $486.74 per credit. Tuition, state resident: part-time $486.74 per credit. Tuition, nonresident: part-time $751.34 per credit. Tuition and fees vary according to degree level and program. *Financial support:* In 2009–10, 8 research assistantships with full tuition reimbursements (averaging $7,000 per year) were awarded; Federal Work-Study, scholarships/grants, and unspecified assistantships also available. Support available to part-time students. Financial award application deadline: 3/1; financial award applicants required to submit FAFSA. *Faculty research:* Adolescent physical activity. *Unit head:* Dr. Eva Goldfarb, Chairperson, 973-655-4154. *Application contact:* Amy Aiello, Director of Graduate Admissions and Operations, 973-655-5147, Fax: 973-655-7869, E-mail: graduate.school@montclair.edu.

Mount Mary College, Graduate Programs, Program in Dietetics, Milwaukee, WI 53222-4597. Offers administrative dietetics (MS); clinical dietetics (MS); nutrition education (MS). Part-time and evening/weekend programs available. *Faculty:* 1 (woman) full-time, 5 part-time/adjunct (4 women). *Students:* 13 full-time (all women), 20 part-time (all women), 1 international. Average age 28. 60 applicants, 22% accepted, 12 enrolled. In 2009, 1 master's awarded. *Degree requirements:* For master's, thesis. *Entrance requirements:* For master's, minimum GPA of 2.75, completion of ADA and DPD requirements. Additional exam requirements/recommendations for international students: Required—TOEFL (minimum score 500 paper-based; 173 computer-based). *Application deadline:* For fall admission, 2/15 priority date for domestic students. Application fee: $35 ($100 for international students). *Expenses:* Tuition: Part-time $595 per credit. Tuition and fees vary according to program. *Financial support:* In 2009–10, 1 student received support. Career-related internships or fieldwork and Federal Work-Study available. Support available to part-time students. Financial award application deadline: 5/1; financial award applicants required to submit FAFSA. *Unit head:* Lisa Stark, Director, 414-258-4810 Ext. 398, E-mail: starkl@mtmary.edu. *Application contact:* Lisa Stark, Director, 414-258-4810 Ext. 398, E-mail: starkl@mtmary.edu.

Mount Saint Vincent University, Graduate Programs, Department of Applied Human Nutrition, Halifax, NS B3M 2J6, Canada. Offers M Sc AHN, MAHN. Part-time and evening/weekend programs available. *Degree requirements:* For master's, thesis (for some programs). *Entrance requirements:* For master's, bachelor's degree in related field, minimum GPA of 3.0, professional experience. Electronic applications accepted.

New York Chiropractic College, Program in Applied Clinical Nutrition, Seneca Falls, NY 13148-0800. Offers MS. Part-time and evening/weekend programs available. *Faculty:* 4 part-time/adjunct (2 women). *Students:* 78 part-time (45 women); includes 7 minority (3 African Americans, 1 American Indian/Alaska Native, 2 Asian Americans or Pacific Islanders, 1 Hispanic American), 9 international. Average age 32. 59 applicants, 80% accepted, 42 enrolled. In 2009, 34 master's awarded. *Entrance requirements:* For master's, minimum GPA of 2.5, transcripts, writing sample. *Application deadline:* Applications are processed on a rolling basis. Application fee: $60. Electronic applications accepted. *Expenses:* Tuition: Full-time $18,320; part-time $426 per credit hour. Required fees: $680. Tuition and fees vary according to course load and program. *Financial support:* In 2009–10, 56 students received support. Federal Work-Study and scholarships/grants available. Financial award applicants required to submit FAFSA. *Faculty research:* Isagenix research. *Unit head:* Dr. Anna R. Kelles, Director, 315-568-3310. *Application contact:* Michael Lynch, Director of Admissions, 315-568-3040, Fax: 315-568-3087, E-mail: mlynch@nycc.edu.

New York Institute of Technology, Graduate Division, School of Health Professions, Program in Clinical Nutrition, Old Westbury, NY 11568-8000. Offers MS, DO/MS. Part-time and evening/weekend programs available. *Students:* 9 full-time (6 women), 26 part-time (21 women); includes 11 minority (4 African Americans, 1 Asian American or Pacific Islander, 6 Hispanic Americans). Average age 31. In 2009, 12 master's awarded. *Degree requirements:* For master's, comprehensive exam, thesis (for some programs). *Entrance requirements:* For master's, minimum QPA of 2.85. Additional exam requirements/recommendations for international students: Required—TOEFL (minimum score 550 paper-based; 213 computer-based). *Application deadline:* For fall admission, 7/1 priority date for domestic students; for spring admission, 12/1 priority date for domestic students. Applications are processed on a rolling basis. Application fee: $50. Electronic applications accepted. *Expenses:* Tuition: Part-time $825 per credit. *Financial support:* Fellowships, research assistantships with partial tuition reimbursements, career-related internships or fieldwork, institutionally sponsored loans, tuition waivers (full and partial), and unspecified assistantships available. Support available to part-time students. Financial award applicants required to submit FAFSA. *Faculty research:* Medical nutrition training. *Unit head:* Mindy Haar, Chair, 516-686-3818, Fax: 516-686-3795, E-mail: mhaar@nyit.edu. *Application contact:* Dr. Jacquelyn Nealon, Vice President for Enrollment Services, 516-686-7925, Fax: 516-686-7597, E-mail: jnealon@nyit.edu.

New York University, Steinhardt School of Culture, Education, and Human Development, Department of Nutrition, Food Studies, and Public Health, Program in Community Public Health, New York, NY 10012-1019. Offers community public health (MPH), including community health, international community health, public health nutrition; public health (PhD). *Accreditation:* CEPH. Part-time programs available. *Students:* 90 full-time (77 women), 45 part-time (41 women); includes 34 minority (11 African Americans, 17 Asian Americans or Pacific Islanders, 6 Hispanic Americans), 10 international. Average age 28. 257 applicants, 81% accepted, 52 enrolled. In 2009, 36 master's awarded. *Degree requirements:* For master's, thesis (for some programs). *Entrance requirements:* For master's, GRE General Test; for doctorate, GRE General Test, interview. Additional exam requirements/recommendations for international students: Required—TOEFL. *Application deadline:* For fall admission, 12/15 priority date for domestic and international students; for spring admission, 11/1 for domestic and international students. Applications are processed on a rolling basis. Application fee: $75. Electronic applications accepted. *Expenses:* Tuition: Full-time $30,528; part-time $1272 per credit. Required fees: $2177. *Financial support:* Fellowships with full and partial tuition reimbursements, career-related internships or fieldwork, Federal Work-Study, institutionally sponsored loans, scholarships/grants, and tuition waivers (partial) available. Support available to part-time students. Financial award application deadline: 2/1; financial award applicants required to submit FAFSA. *Faculty research:* Social epidemiology, primary health care, global health, immigrants and health, infectious disease prevention, HIV/AIDS. *Unit head:* Director, 212-998-5580, Fax: 212-995-4192. *Application contact:* 212-998-5030, Fax: 212-995-4328, E-mail: steinhardt.gradadmissions@nyu.edu.

New York University, Steinhardt School of Culture, Education, and Human Development, Department of Nutrition, Food Studies, and Public Health, Program in Nutrition and Dietetics, New York, NY 10012-1019. Offers nutrition and dietetics (MS), including clinical nutrition, food and nutrition. Part-time programs available. *Students:* 107 full-time (99 women), 108 part-time (101 women); includes 36 minority (9 African Americans, 15 Asian Americans or Pacific Islanders, 12 Hispanic Americans), 14 international. Average age 28. 209 applicants, 24% accepted, 33 enrolled. In 2009, 49 master's, 2 doctorates awarded. *Degree requirements:* For master's, thesis (for some programs); for doctorate, thesis/dissertation. *Entrance requirements:* For doctorate, GRE General Test, interview. Additional exam requirements/recommendations for international students: Required—TOEFL. *Application deadline:* For fall admission, 12/15 priority date for domestic students, 12/15 for international students; for spring admission, 11/1 for domestic and international students. Applications are processed on a rolling basis. Application fee: $75. Electronic applications accepted. *Expenses:* Tuition: Full-time $30,528; part-time $1272 per credit. Required fees: $2177. *Financial support:* Fellowships with full and partial tuition reimbursements, career-related internships or fieldwork, Federal Work-Study, institutionally sponsored loans, scholarships/grants, tuition waivers (partial), and unspecified assistantships available. Financial award application deadline: 2/1; financial award applicants required to submit FAFSA. *Faculty research:* Nutrition and race, childhood obesity and other eating disorders, nutritional epidemiology, nutrition policy, nutrition and health promotion. *Unit head:* Dr. Lisa Sasson, 212-998-5580, Fax: 212-995-4194. *Application contact:* 212-998-5030, Fax: 212-995-4328, E-mail: steinhardt.gradadmissions@nyu.edu.

North Carolina Agricultural and Technical State University, Graduate School, School of Agriculture and Environmental Sciences, Department of Family and Consumer Sciences, Greensboro, NC 27411. Offers food and nutrition (MS). Part-time and evening/weekend programs available. *Degree requirements:* For master's, comprehensive exam, thesis or alternative, qualifying exam. *Entrance requirements:* For master's, GRE General Test, minimum GPA of 2.6.

North Carolina State University, Graduate School, College of Agriculture and Life Sciences and College of Veterinary Medicine, Program in Nutrition, Raleigh, NC 27695. Offers MN, MS, PhD. Part-time programs available. *Degree requirements:* For master's, thesis (for some programs); for doctorate, thesis/dissertation. *Entrance requirements:* For master's and doctorate, GRE General Test. Additional exam requirements/recommendations for international students: Required—TOEFL (minimum score 550 paper-based; 213 computer-based). Electronic applications accepted. *Faculty research:* Effects of food/feed ingredients and components on health and growth, community nutrition, waste management and reduction, experimental animal nutrition.

North Dakota State University, College of Graduate and Interdisciplinary Studies, College of Human Development and Education, Department of Health, Nutrition, and Exercise Sciences, Fargo, ND 58108. Offers dietetics (MS); entry level athletic training (MS); exercise science (MS); nutrition science (MS); public health (MS); sport pedagogy (MS); sports recreation management (MS). Part-time and evening/weekend programs available. Postbaccalaureate distance learning degree programs offered (no on-campus study). *Faculty:* 12 full-time (6 women). *Students:* 28 full-time (18 women), 23 part-time (16 women); includes 1 African American, 1 Asian American or Pacific Islander, 3 international. 19 applicants, 100% accepted, 15 enrolled. In 2009, 27 master's awarded. *Degree requirements:* For master's, thesis (for some programs). *Entrance requirements:* For master's, minimum GPA of 3.0. Additional exam requirements/recommendations for international students: Required—TOEFL (minimum score 525 paper-based; 197 computer-based; 71 iBT). *Application deadline:* For fall admission, 3/1 priority date for domestic and international students. Application fee: $45 ($60 for international students). Electronic applications accepted. *Financial support:* In 2009–10, 28 students received

Nutrition

North Dakota State University (continued)

support, including 18 teaching assistantships with full tuition reimbursements available (averaging $6,500 per year). Financial award application deadline: 3/31. *Faculty research:* Biomechanics, sport specialization, recreation, nutrition, athletic training. Total annual research expenditures: $10,000. *Unit head:* Brad Strand, Head, 701-231-7474, Fax: 701-231-8872, E-mail: bradford.strand@ndsu.edu. *Application contact:* Brad Strand, Head, 701-231-7474, Fax: 701-231-8872, E-mail: bradford.strand@ndsu.edu.

Northern Illinois University, Graduate School, College of Health and Human Sciences, School of Family, Consumer and Nutrition Sciences, De Kalb, IL 60115-2854. Offers applied family and child studies (MS); nutrition and dietetics (MS). *Accreditation:* AAMFT/COAMFTE. Part-time programs available. *Faculty:* 16 full-time (14 women), 2 part-time/adjunct (1 woman). *Students:* 55 full-time (49 women), 33 part-time (30 women); includes 11 minority (6 African Americans, 3 Asian Americans or Pacific Islanders, 2 Hispanic Americans), 2 international. Average age 26. In 2009, 28 degrees awarded. *Degree requirements:* For master's, comprehensive exam, internship, thesis (nutrition and dietetics). *Entrance requirements:* For master's, GRE General Test, minimum GPA of 2.75. Additional exam requirements/recommendations for international students: Required—TOEFL (minimum score 550 paper-based; 213 computer-based). *Application deadline:* For fall admission, 6/1 for domestic students, 5/1 for international students; for spring admission, 11/1 for domestic students, 10/1 for international students. Applications are processed on a rolling basis. Application fee: $30. Electronic applications accepted. *Expenses:* Tuition, state resident: full-time $6576; part-time $274 per credit hour. Tuition, nonresident: full-time $13,152; part-time $548 per credit hour. Required fees: $1813; $75.53 per credit hour. Part-time tuition and fees vary according to course load. *Financial support:* In 2009–10, 8 teaching assistantships with full tuition reimbursements were awarded; fellowships with full tuition reimbursements, research assistantships with full tuition reimbursements, career-related internships or fieldwork, Federal Work-Study, scholarships/grants, tuition waivers (full), and staff assistantships also available. Support available to part-time students. Financial award applicants required to submit FAFSA. *Faculty research:* Preliminary child development, hospitality administration in Asia, sports nutrition, eating disorders. *Unit head:* Dr. Laura Smart, Acting Chair, 815-753-1960, Fax: 815-753-1321, E-mail: lsmart@niu.edu. *Application contact:* Dr. Laura Smart, Acting Chair, 815-753-1960, Fax: 815-753-1321, E-mail: lsmart@niu.edu.

The Ohio State University, Graduate School, College of Education and Human Ecology, Department of Human Nutrition, Columbus, OH 43210. Offers food service management (MS, PhD); foods (MS, PhD); nutrition (MS, PhD). *Accreditation:* ADtA. *Faculty:* 18. *Students:* 8 full-time (7 women), 4 part-time (3 women); includes 2 minority (both African Americans), 3 international. Average age 30. In 2009, 9 master's awarded. *Degree requirements:* For master's, thesis optional; for doctorate, thesis/dissertation. *Entrance requirements:* For master's and doctorate, GRE General Test. Additional exam requirements/recommendations for international students: Required—TOEFL (minimum score 577 paper-based; 233 computer-based). *Application deadline:* For fall admission, 8/15 priority date for domestic students, 7/1 priority date for international students; for winter admission, 12/1 priority date for domestic students, 11/1 priority date for international students; for spring admission, 3/1 priority date for domestic students, 2/1 priority date for international students. Applications are processed on a rolling basis. Application fee: $40 ($50 for international students). Electronic applications accepted. *Expenses:* Tuition, state resident: full-time $10,683. Tuition, nonresident: full-time $25,923. Tuition and fees vary according to course load and program. *Financial support:* Fellowships, research assistantships, teaching assistantships, Federal Work-Study and institutionally sponsored loans available. Support available to part-time students. *Unit head:* James E. Kinder, Chair, 614-292-4485, Fax: 614-292-8880, E-mail: kinder.15@osu.edu. *Application contact:* 614-292-9444, Fax: 614-292-3895, E-mail: domestic.grad@osu.edu.

The Ohio State University, Graduate School, College of Food, Agricultural, and Environmental Sciences, Department of Food Science and Nutrition, Columbus, OH 43210. Offers MS, PhD. *Accreditation:* ADtA. *Faculty:* 23. *Students:* 40 full-time (28 women), 32 part-time (12 women); includes 9 minority (2 African Americans, 5 Asian Americans or Pacific Islanders, 2 Hispanic Americans), 37 international. Average age 27. In 2009, 21 master's, 5 doctorates awarded. *Degree requirements:* For master's, thesis optional; for doctorate, thesis/dissertation. *Entrance requirements:* For master's and doctorate, GRE General Test. Additional exam requirements/recommendations for international students: Required—TOEFL (minimum score 550 paper-based; 213 computer-based), IELTS (minimum score 7), or Michigan English Language Assessment Battery (minimum score 89). *Application deadline:* For fall admission, 8/15 priority date for domestic students, 7/1 priority date for international students; for winter admission, 12/1 priority date for domestic students, 11/1 priority date for international students; for spring admission, 3/1 priority date for domestic students, 2/1 priority date for international students. Applications are processed on a rolling basis. Application fee: $40 ($50 for international students). Electronic applications accepted. *Expenses:* Tuition, state resident: full-time $10,683. Tuition, nonresident: full-time $25,923. Tuition and fees vary according to course load and program. *Financial support:* Fellowships, research assistantships, Federal Work-Study and institutionally sponsored loans available. Support available to part-time students. *Application contact:* Graduate Admissions, 614-292-9444, Fax: 614-292-3895, E-mail: domestic.grad@osu.edu.

Ohio University, Graduate College, College of Health and Human Services, School of Human and Consumer Sciences, Athens, OH 45701-2979. Offers apparel, textiles, and merchandising (MS); child development and family life (MS); early childhood education (MS); family studies (MS); food and nutrition (MS). Part-time programs available. *Faculty:* 13 full-time (9 women), 5 part-time/adjunct (all women). *Students:* 18 full-time (14 women), 7 part-time (all women); includes 2 minority (1 African American, 1 Asian American or Pacific Islander), 3 international. 21 applicants, 81% accepted, 8 enrolled. In 2009, 6 master's awarded. *Degree requirements:* For master's, comprehensive exam (for some programs), thesis. *Entrance requirements:* For master's, GRE. Additional exam requirements/recommendations for international students: Required—TOEFL (minimum score 550 paper-based; 80 iBT) or IELTS (minimum score 6.5). *Application deadline:* For fall admission, 3/1 priority date for domestic and international students. Applications are processed on a rolling basis. Application fee: $50 ($55 for international students). Electronic applications accepted. *Expenses:* Tuition, state resident: full-time $7839; part-time $323 per quarter hour. Tuition, nonresident: full-time $15,831; part-time $654 per quarter hour. Required fees: $2931. *Financial support:* Research assistantships, teaching assistantships, career-related internships or fieldwork, Federal Work-Study, institutionally sponsored loans, and unspecified assistantships available. Financial award application deadline: 3/15. *Faculty research:* Diversity, developmentally appropriate activities, death and dying, gerontology, sexuality education. *Unit head:* Dr. V. Ann Paulins, Director, 740-593-2880, Fax: 740-593-0289, E-mail: paulins@ohio.edu. *Application contact:* Dr. Annette Graham, Graduate Coordinator, 740-593-0700, E-mail: grahama@ohio.edu.

Oklahoma State University, College of Human Environmental Sciences, Department of Nutritional Sciences, Stillwater, OK 74078. Offers MS, PhD. Postbaccalaureate distance learning degree programs offered. *Faculty:* 19 full-time (16 women). *Students:* 32 full-time (30 women), 22 part-time (18 women); includes 3 minority (2 African Americans, 1 American Indian/Alaska Native), 14 international. Average age 30. 44 applicants, 59% accepted, 21 enrolled. In 2009, 20 master's, 4 doctorates awarded. *Degree requirements:* For master's, thesis (for some programs); for doctorate, comprehensive exam, thesis/dissertation. *Entrance requirements:* For master's and doctorate, GRE or GMAT. Additional exam requirements/recommendations for international students: Required—TOEFL (minimum score 550 paper-based; 79 iBT). *Application deadline:* For fall admission, 3/1 priority date for international students; for spring admission, 8/1 priority date for international students. Applications are processed on a rolling basis. Application fee: $40 ($75 for international students). Electronic applications accepted. *Expenses:* Tuition, state resident: full-time $3716; part-time $154.85 per credit hour. Tuition, nonresident: full-time $14,448; part-time $602 per credit hour. Required fees: $1772; $73.85 per credit hour. One-time fee: $50. Tuition and fees vary according to course load and campus/location. *Financial support:* In 2009–10, 24 research assistantships (averaging $9,151 per year), 13 teaching assistantships (averaging $8,571 per year) were awarded; career-related internships or fieldwork, Federal Work-Study, scholarships/grants, health care benefits, tuition waivers (partial), and unspecified assistantships also available. Support available to part-time students. Financial award application deadline: 3/1; financial award applicants required to submit FAFSA. *Faculty research:* Nutritional sciences, micronutrients and chronic disease, phytochemicals, nutrition education, osteoporosis, food service administration. *Unit head:* Dr. Nancy M. Betts, Head, 405-744-5040, Fax: 405-744-1357. *Application contact:* Dr. Gordon Emslie, Dean, 405-744-6368, Fax: 405-744-0355, E-mail: grad-i@okstate.edu.

Oregon Health & Science University, School of Medicine, Graduate Programs in Medicine, Program in Clinical Nutrition, Portland, OR 97239-3098. Offers MS. Part-time programs available. In 2009, 4 master's awarded. *Entrance requirements:* For master's, GRE. Application fee: $120. Tuition and fees vary according to course level, course load, degree level, program and reciprocity agreements. *Unit head:* Diane Stadler, PhD, Program Director. *Application contact:* Chandra Nautiyal, Administrative Coordinator, 503-494-7596, E-mail: nautiyal@ohsu.edu.

Oregon State University, Graduate School, College of Health and Human Sciences, Department of Nutrition and Exercise Sciences, Corvallis, OR 97331. Offers exercise and sport science (MS, PhD); movement studies in disabilities (MAIS, MS); nutrition and exercise sciences (MAIS); nutrition and food management (MS). *Faculty:* 26 full-time (16 women), 3 part-time/adjunct (all women). *Students:* 47 full-time (26 women), 6 part-time (3 women); includes 2 minority (1 American Indian/Alaska Native, 1 Hispanic American), 7 international. Average age 29. In 2009, 20 master's, 9 doctorates awarded. Terminal master's awarded for partial completion of doctoral program. *Degree requirements:* For master's, thesis; for doctorate, thesis/dissertation. *Entrance requirements:* For master's and doctorate, minimum GPA of 3.0 in last 90 hours. Additional exam requirements/recommendations for international students: Required—TOEFL. Application fee: $50. *Expenses:* Tuition, state resident: full-time $9774; part-time $362 per credit. Tuition, nonresident: full-time $15,849; part-time $587 per credit. Required fees: $1639. Full-time tuition and fees vary according to course load and program. *Financial support:* Research assistantships, teaching assistantships, career-related internships or fieldwork, Federal Work-Study, and institutionally sponsored loans available. Support available to part-time students. Financial award application deadline: 2/1. *Faculty research:* Motor control, sports medicine, exercise physiology, sport psychology, biomechanics. *Unit head:* Dr. Anthony R. Wilcox, Chair, 541-737-2643, Fax: 541-737-6914, E-mail: anthony.wilcox@oregonstate.edu. *Application contact:* Dr. Anthony R. Wilcox, Chair, 541-737-2643, Fax: 541-737-6914, E-mail: anthony.wilcox@oregonstate.edu.

Penn State University Park, Graduate School, College of Health and Human Development, Department of Nutritional Sciences, State College, University Park, PA 16802-1503. Offers MS, PhD.

Purdue University, Graduate School, College of Consumer and Family Sciences, Department of Foods and Nutrition, West Lafayette, IN 47907. Offers nutrition (MS, PhD). *Degree requirements:* For master's, thesis; for doctorate, thesis/dissertation. *Entrance requirements:* For master's and doctorate, GRE General Test. Additional exam requirements/recommendations for international students: Required—TOEFL (minimum score 600 paper-based). Electronic applications accepted. *Faculty research:* Nutrient requirements, nutrient metabolism, nutrition and disease prevention.

Rosalind Franklin University of Medicine and Science, College of Health Professions, Department of Nutrition, North Chicago, IL 60064-3095. Offers clinical nutrition (MS); nutrition education (MS). Part-time and evening/weekend programs available. Postbaccalaureate distance learning degree programs offered (no on-campus study). *Faculty:* 3 full-time (all women), 3 part-time/adjunct (2 women). *Students:* 46; includes 6 minority (2 African Americans, 3 Asian Americans or Pacific Islanders, 1 Hispanic American). Average age 36. 34 applicants, 76% accepted, 23 enrolled. *Degree requirements:* For master's, thesis optional, portfolio. *Entrance requirements:* For master's, minimum GPA of 2.75, registered dietitian (RD), professional certificate or license. Additional exam requirements/recommendations for international students: Required—TOEFL. *Application deadline:* For fall admission, 8/6 priority date for domestic students; for winter admission, 10/29 for domestic students; for spring admission, 2/5 for domestic students. Applications are processed on a rolling basis. Application fee: $50. *Expenses:* Contact institution. *Financial support:* Institutionally sponsored loans available. Support available to part-time students. Financial award application deadline: 6/9; financial award applicants required to submit FAFSA. *Faculty research:* Nutrition education, distance learning, computer-based graduate education, childhood obesity, nutrition medical education. *Unit head:* Dr. Lynn Janas, Chair, 847-578-3324, Fax: 847-578-8623, E-mail: lynn.janas@rosalindfranklin.edu. *Application contact:* Melissa Knox, Admissions Officer, 847-578-8772, Fax: 847-775-6559, E-mail: melissa.knox@rosalindfranklin.edu.

Rush University, College of Health Sciences, Department of Clinical Nutrition, Chicago, IL 60612. Offers MS. Part-time programs available. *Degree requirements:* For master's, thesis. *Entrance requirements:* For master's, GRE General Test, minimum GPA of 3.0, course work in statistics, undergraduate didactic program approved by the American Dietetic Association. Additional exam requirements/recommendations for international students: Required—TOEFL. *Faculty research:* Food service management, chronic disease prevention/treatment, obesity, Alzheimer's.

Rutgers, The State University of New Jersey, New Brunswick, Graduate School-New Brunswick, Program in Nutritional Sciences, Piscataway, NJ 08854-8097. Offers MS, PhD. Part-time programs available. Terminal master's awarded for partial completion of doctoral program. *Degree requirements:* For master's, thesis; for doctorate, thesis/dissertation, written qualifying exam. *Entrance requirements:* For master's and doctorate, GRE General Test, 3 letters of recommendation. Additional exam requirements/recommendations for international students: Required—TOEFL (minimum score 560 paper-based; 220 computer-based; 83 iBT). Electronic applications accepted. *Faculty research:* Nutrition and gene expression, nutrition and disease (obesity, diabetes, cancer, osteoporosis, alcohol), community nutrition and nutrition education, cellular lipid transport and metabolism.

Sacred Heart University, Graduate Programs, College of Education and Health Professions, Department of Physical Therapy and Human Movement and Sports Science, Fairfield, CT 06825-1000. Offers exercise science and nutrition (MS); physical therapy (DPT). *Accreditation:* APTA. *Faculty:* 9 full-time (5 women). *Students:* 146 full-time (95 women); includes 17 minority (4 African Americans, 1 American Indian/Alaska Native, 7 Asian Americans or Pacific Islanders, 5 Hispanic Americans), 2 international. Average age 25. 205 applicants, 58% accepted, 63 enrolled. *Entrance requirements:* Additional exam requirements/recommendations for international students: Required—TOEFL (minimum score 550 paper-based; 213 computer-based). *Application deadline:* For fall admission, 1/15 priority date for domestic students. Applications are processed on a rolling basis. Application fee: $50 ($100 for international students). Electronic applications accepted. *Expenses:* Contact institution. *Financial support:* Career-related internships or fieldwork, institutionally sponsored loans, and unspecified assistantships available. Support available to part-time students. Financial award applicants required to submit FAFSA. *Unit head:* Dr. Michael Emery, Director, 203-365-7656. *Application contact:* Kathy Dilks, Assistant Dean of Graduate Admissions, Health Professions, 203-396-8259, Fax: 203-365-4732, E-mail: gradstudies@sacredheart.edu.

Sage Graduate School, Graduate School, School of Health Sciences, Program in Nutrition, Troy, NY 12180-4115. Offers applied nutrition (MS); dietetic internship (Certificate). Part-time and evening/weekend programs available. *Faculty:* 3 full-time (all women), 2 part-time/adjunct (both women). *Students:* 21 full-time (19 women), 23 part-time (all women), 2 international. Average age 28. 67 applicants, 43% accepted, 13 enrolled. In 2009, 12 master's awarded. *Entrance requirements:* For master's, minimum GPA of 2.75, resume, 2 letters of recommendation, interview with director. Additional exam requirements/recommendations for international students: Required—TOEFL (minimum score 550 paper-based; 213 computer-based). *Application deadline:* Applications are processed on a rolling basis. Application fee: $40. *Expenses:* Tuition: Full-time $10,620; part-time $590 per credit hour. *Financial support:* Fellowships, research assistantships, Federal Work-Study, scholarships/grants, and unspecified assistantships available. Support available to part-time students. *Unit head:* Rayane AbuSabha, Director of Didactic Program Dietetics, 518-244-2396, Fax: 518-244-4586, E-mail: abusar@sage.edu. *Application contact:* Wendy D. Diefendorf, Director of Graduate and Adult Admission, 518-244-2443, Fax: 518-244-6880, E-mail: diefew@sage.edu.

Sage Graduate School, Graduate School, School of Management, Program in Health Services Administration, Troy, NY 12180-4115. Offers dietetic internship (Certificate); gerontology (MS). Part-time and evening/weekend programs available. *Faculty:* 4 full-time (2 women), 6 part-time/adjunct (0 women). *Students:* 7 full-time (6 women), 19 part-time (15 women); includes 4 minority (2 African Americans, 2 Hispanic Americans). Average age 29. 16 applicants. In 2009, 5 master's awarded. *Entrance requirements:* For master's, minimum GPA of 2.75, resume, 2 letters of recommendation. Additional exam requirements/recommendations for international students: Required—TOEFL (minimum score 550 paper-based; 213 computer-based). Application fee: $40. *Expenses:* Tuition: Full-time $10,620; part-time $590 per credit hour. *Financial support:* Fellowships, research assistantships, Federal Work-Study, scholarships/grants, and unspecified assistantships available. Support available to part-time students. Financial award application deadline: 3/1; financial award applicants required to submit FAFSA. *Unit head:* Dr. Kimberly Fredricks, Program Director, 518-292-1700, Fax: 518-292-5414, E-mail: fredek1@sage.edu. *Application contact:* Wendy D. Diefendorf, Director of Graduate and Adult Admission, 518-244-2443, Fax: 518-244-6880, E-mail: diefew@sage.edu.

Saint Joseph College, Department of Nutrition, West Hartford, CT 06117-2700. Offers MS. Part-time and evening/weekend programs available. Postbaccalaureate distance learning degree programs offered. *Students:* 9 full-time (all women), 65 part-time (61 women); includes 8 minority (5 African Americans, 2 Asian Americans or Pacific Islanders, 1 Hispanic American). *Entrance requirements:* For master's, 2 letters of recommendation. *Application deadline:* Applications are processed on a rolling basis. Application fee: $50. Electronic applications accepted. *Expenses:* Tuition: Part-time $595 per credit. Required fees: $30 per credit. Tuition and fees vary according to program. *Financial support:* Career-related internships or fieldwork and unspecified assistantships available. Support available to part-time students. Financial award applicants required to submit FAFSA. *Application contact:* Graduate Admissions Office, 860-231-5261, E-mail: graduate@sjc.edu.

Saint Louis University, Graduate School, Doisy College of Health Sciences and Graduate School, Department of Nutrition and Dietetics, St. Louis, MO 63103-2097. Offers medical dietetics (MS); nutrition and physical performance (MS). Part-time programs available. *Degree requirements:* For master's, comprehensive exam (for some programs). *Entrance requirements:* For master's, GRE General Test, letters of recommendation, resume, interview. Additional exam requirements/recommendations for international students: Required—TOEFL (minimum score 525 paper-based; 194 computer-based). Electronic applications accepted. *Faculty research:* Sustainable food systems, nutrition education, public health nutrition, culinary nutrition and physical performance.

Sam Houston State University, College of Humanities and Social Sciences, Department of Family and Consumer Sciences, Huntsville, TX 77341. Offers dietetics (MS); family and consumer sciences (MS). Part-time and evening/weekend programs available. *Faculty:* 5 full-time (all women). *Students:* 17 full-time (all women), 5 part-time (all women); includes 3 minority (1 American Indian/Alaska Native, 2 Hispanic Americans). Average age 26. 15 applicants, 93% accepted, 12 enrolled. In 2009, 9 master's awarded. *Entrance requirements:* For master's, GRE General Test, minimum GPA of 2.5. Additional exam requirements/recommendations for international students: Required—TOEFL (minimum score 550 paper-based; 213 computer-based; 79 iBT). *Application deadline:* For fall admission, 8/1 for domestic students; for spring admission, 12/1 for domestic students. Application fee: $20. *Expenses:* Tuition, state resident: full-time $3690; part-time $205 per credit hour. Tuition, nonresident: full-time $8676; part-time $482 per credit hour. Required fees: $1474. Tuition and fees vary according to course load and campus/location. *Financial support:* Teaching assistantships available. Financial award application deadline: 5/31; financial award applicants required to submit FAFSA. *Unit head:* Dr. Janis White, Chair, 936-294-1242, Fax: 936-294-4204, E-mail: jwhite@shsu.edu. *Application contact:* Dr. Claudia Sealey-Potts, Advisor, 936-294-1250, E-mail: clapotts@shsu.edu.

San Diego State University, Graduate and Research Affairs, College of Professional Studies and Fine Arts, Department of Exercise and Nutritional Sciences, Program in Nutritional Science, San Diego, CA 92182. Offers nutritional sciences (MS); MS/MS. *Degree requirements:* For master's, thesis. *Entrance requirements:* For master's, GRE General Test, 2 letters of reference. Additional exam requirements/recommendations for international students: Required—TOEFL. Electronic applications accepted.

San Jose State University, Graduate Studies and Research, College of Applied Sciences and Arts, Department of Nutrition, Food Science, and Packaging, San Jose, CA 95192-0001. Offers nutritional science (MS). *Students:* 52 full-time (48 women), 37 part-time (33 women); includes 28 minority (1 African American, 22 Asian Americans or Pacific Islanders, 5 Hispanic Americans), 10 international. Average age 31. 92 applicants, 25% accepted, 19 enrolled. In 2009, 23 master's awarded. *Application deadline:* For fall admission, 6/27 for domestic students; for spring admission, 11/30 for domestic students. Applications are processed on a rolling basis. Application fee: $59. Electronic applications accepted. *Financial support:* Applicants required to submit FAFSA. *Unit head:* Dr. Lucy McProud, Chair, 408-924-3100, Fax: 408-924-3114. *Application contact:* Dr. Panfilo Belo, Graduate Coordinator, 408-924-3108.

Saybrook University, Graduate College of Mind-Body Medicine, San Francisco, CA 94111-1920. Offers MS, PhD, Certificate.

Simmons College, School of Health Sciences, Program in Nutrition and Health Promotion, Boston, MA 02115. Offers didactic program in dietetics (Certificate); nutrition (dietetic internship) (Certificate); nutrition and health promotion (MS); sports nutrition (Certificate). Part-time programs available. Postbaccalaureate distance learning degree programs offered (no on-campus study). *Faculty:* 5 full-time (all women), 4 part-time/adjunct (all women). *Students:* 17 full-time (all women), 40 part-time (37 women); includes 7 minority (1 African American, 1 American Indian/Alaska Native, 3 Asian Americans or Pacific Islanders, 2 Hispanic Americans). Average age 31. 45 applicants, 84% accepted, 35 enrolled. In 2009, 13 master's, 28 other advanced degrees awarded. *Degree requirements:* For master's, research project. *Entrance requirements:* For master's, GRE, courses in community nutrition, nutritional metabolism, introduction to nutrition, organic and inorganic chemistry, statistics, anatomy and physiology; for Certificate, 1 year of anatomy and physiology with lab, half-year of introductory nutrition, bachelor's degree. Additional exam requirements/recommendations for international students: Required—TOEFL (minimum score 570 paper-based; 230 computer-based; 88 iBT). *Application deadline:* For fall admission, 3/1 for domestic and international students; for spring admission, 11/1 for domestic students. Application fee: $50. *Expenses:* Contact institution. *Financial support:* Application deadline: 3/1. *Faculty research:* Good insecurity, chronic disease and nutrition, childhood obesity, dietary assessment, food safety. Total annual research expenditures: $60,000. *Unit head:* Dr. Nancie Herbold, Director, 617-521-2711, Fax: 617-521-3137, E-mail: herbold@simmons.edu. *Application contact:* Carmen Fortin, Assistant Dean/Director of Admission, 617-521-2605, Fax: 617-521-3137, E-mail: shs@simmons.edu.

South Carolina State University, School of Graduate Studies, Department of Family and Consumer Sciences, Orangeburg, SC 29117-0001. Offers individual and family development (MS); nutritional sciences (MS). Part-time and evening/weekend programs available. *Degree requirements:* For master's, comprehensive exam, thesis optional, departmental qualifying exam. *Entrance requirements:* For master's, GRE, MAT, or NTE, minimum GPA of 2.7. Electronic applications accepted. *Expenses:* Tuition, state resident: part-time $470 per credit hour. Tuition, nonresident: part-time $924 per credit hour. *Faculty research:* Societal competence, relationship of parent-child interaction to adult, quality of well-being of rural elders.

South Dakota State University, Graduate School, College of Education and Human Sciences, Department of Nutrition, Food Science and Hospitality, Brookings, SD 57007. Offers dietetics (MS); nutrition, food science and hospitality (MFCS); nutritional sciences (MS, PhD). Part-time programs available. *Degree requirements:* For master's, comprehensive exam (for some programs), thesis (for some programs), oral exam. *Entrance requirements:* Additional exam requirements/recommendations for international students: Required—TOEFL (minimum score 525 paper-based). *Faculty research:* Food chemistry, bone density, functional food, nutrition education, nutrition biochemistry.

Southeast Missouri State University, School of Graduate Studies, Department of Health, Human Performance and Recreation, Cape Girardeau, MO 63701-4799. Offers community wellness and leisure (MPA); nutrition and exercise science (MS). Part-time and evening/weekend programs available. *Degree requirements:* For master's, comprehensive exam (for some programs), thesis or alternative. *Entrance requirements:* For master's, GRE General Test (minimum score 1000 verbal and quantitative) for nutrition and exercise science (MS), minimum undergraduate GPA of 3.0 (MS), 2.7 (MPA). Additional exam requirements/recommendations for international students: Required—TOEFL (minimum score 550 paper-based; 213 computer-based); Recommended—IELTS (minimum score 6). Electronic applications accepted. *Expenses:* Tuition, state resident: full-time $4266; part-time $237 per credit hour. Tuition, nonresident: full-time $7506; part-time $417 per credit hour. Required fees: $427; $427. *Faculty research:* Health issues of athletes, body composition assessment, exercise testing, exercise training, perceptual responses to physical activity.

Southern Illinois University Carbondale, Graduate School, College of Agriculture, Department of Animal Science, Food and Nutrition, Program in Food and Nutrition, Carbondale, IL 62901-4701. Offers MS. *Degree requirements:* For master's, thesis or alternative. *Entrance requirements:* For master's, minimum GPA of 2.7. Additional exam requirements/recommendations for international students: Required—TOEFL. *Faculty research:* Public health nutrition, nutrition physiology, soybean utilization, nutrition education.

State University of New York College at Oneonta, Graduate Education, Department of Human Ecology, Oneonta, NY 13820-4015. Offers nutrition and dietetics (MS). Postbaccalaureate distance learning degree programs offered (no on-campus study). *Students:* 20 full-time (all women). Average age 25. 40 applicants, 38% accepted, 15 enrolled. In 2009, 14 master's awarded. *Application deadline:* For fall admission, 2/15 for domestic students. Application fee: $50. *Expenses:* Tuition, state resident: part-time $349 per credit hour. Tuition, nonresident: full-time $12,870; part-time $552 per credit hour. Required fees: $1280; $15.85 per credit hour. *Unit head:* Dr. Katherine Angell, Chair, 607-436-2068, E-mail: angellkg@oneonta.edu. *Application contact:* Dean, 607-436-2523, Fax: 607-436-3084, E-mail: gradoffice@oneonta.edu.

Syracuse University, College of Human Ecology, Program in Nutrition Science, Syracuse, NY 13244. Offers MA, MS. *Accreditation:* ADtA. Part-time programs available. *Students:* 10 full-time (all women), 4 part-time (all women); includes 2 minority (1 African American, 1 Asian American or Pacific Islander), 3 international. Average age 30. 27 applicants, 59% accepted, 3 enrolled. In 2009, 12 master's awarded. *Degree requirements:* For master's, thesis (for some programs). *Entrance requirements:* For master's, GRE General Test. Additional exam requirements/recommendations for international students: Required—TOEFL (minimum score 100 iBT). *Application deadline:* For fall admission, 3/15 priority date for domestic and international students; for spring admission, 11/1 priority date for domestic and international students. Applications are processed on a rolling basis. Application fee: $75. Electronic applications accepted. *Expenses:* Tuition: Full-time $26,808; part-time $1117 per credit. Required fees: $1024. *Financial support:* Fellowships with tuition reimbursements, research assistantships with full and partial tuition reimbursements, teaching assistantships with tuition reimbursements, tuition waivers (partial) available. Financial award application deadline: 1/1; financial award applicants required to submit FAFSA. *Unit head:* Dr. Kay Bruening, Program Director, 315-443-9326, Fax: 315-443-2562, E-mail: inquire@hshp.syr.edu. *Application contact:* Amy Pangborn, Information Contact, 315-443-5555, E-mail: inquire@hshp.syr.edu.

Teachers College, Columbia University, Graduate Faculty of Education, Department of Health and Behavioral Studies, Program in Applied Physiology Nutrition, New York, NY 10027-6696. Offers Ed M, MA, Ed D.

Teachers College, Columbia University, Graduate Faculty of Education, Department of Health and Behavioral Studies, Program in Behavioral Nutrition, New York, NY 10027-6696. Offers PhD.

Teachers College, Columbia University, Graduate Faculty of Education, Department of Health and Behavioral Studies, Program in Community Nutrition Education, New York, NY 10027-6696. Offers Ed M.

Teachers College, Columbia University, Graduate Faculty of Education, Department of Health and Behavioral Studies, Program in Nutrition and Education, New York, NY 10027-6696. Offers nutrition education (Ed M, MS, Ed D); nutrition education and public health nutrition (Ed M, MS, Ed D), including community nutrition education (Ed M), nutrition and public health (MS, Ed D), nutrition education (MS, Ed D). Part-time and evening/weekend programs available. *Faculty:* 1 (woman) full-time, 3 part-time/adjunct. *Students:* 40 full-time (38 women), 99 part-time (94 women); includes 33 minority (8 African Americans, 18 Asian Americans or Pacific Islanders, 7 Hispanic Americans), 15 international. Average age 30. 87 applicants, 87% accepted, 35 enrolled. In 2009, 27 master's, 5 doctorates awarded. Terminal master's awarded for partial completion of doctoral program. *Degree requirements:* For master's, thesis optional, integrative project; for doctorate, thesis/dissertation. *Entrance requirements:* For master's, GRE General Test or MAT, previous course work in science; for doctorate, GRE General Test, sample of written work, previous course work in science. *Application deadline:* For fall admission, 5/15 for domestic students; for spring admission, 12/1 for domestic students. Application fee: $65. *Financial support:* Fellowships, research assistantships, career-related internships or fieldwork, Federal Work-Study, institutionally sponsored loans, and tuition waivers (full and partial) available. Support available to part-time students. Financial award application deadline: 2/1. *Faculty research:* Psychosocial determinants of eating behavior, food supply and environmental education, development and evaluation of nutrition education. *Unit head:* Dr. Chuck Basch, Chair, 212-678-3964, E-mail: ceb35@columbia.edu. *Application contact:* Peter Shon, Assistant Director of Admission, 212-678-3305, Fax: 212-678-4171, E-mail: shon@exchange.tc.columbia.edu.

Teachers College, Columbia University, Graduate Faculty of Education, Department of Health and Behavioral Studies, Program in Nutrition and Public Health, New York, NY 10027-6696. Offers MS, Ed D.

Texas State University–San Marcos, Graduate School, College of Applied Arts, Department of Family and Consumer Science, San Marcos, TX 78666. Offers family and child studies (MS); human nutrition (MS). Part-time programs available. *Faculty:* 7 full-time (6 women), 3 part-time/adjunct (1 woman). *Students:* 43 full-time (36 women), 27 part-time (26 women); includes 16 minority (2 African Americans, 1 Asian American or Pacific Islander, 13 Hispanic Americans). Average age 26. 49 applicants, 80% accepted, 24 enrolled. In 2009, 7 master's awarded. *Degree requirements:* For master's, comprehensive exam, thesis (for some programs). *Entrance requirements:* For master's, GRE General Test (preferred), minimum GPA of 3.0 in last 60 hours of course work. Additional exam requirements/recommendations for international students: Required—TOEFL (minimum score 550 paper-based; 213 computer-based). *Application deadline:* For fall admission, 6/15 priority date for domestic students; for spring admission, 10/15 priority date for domestic students. Applications are processed on a rolling basis. Application fee: $40 ($90 for international students). Electronic applications accepted. *Expenses:* Tuition, state resident: full-time $5784; part-time $241 per credit hour. Tuition,

Nutrition

Texas State University–San Marcos (continued)
nonresident: full-time $13,224; part-time $551 per credit hour. Required fees: $1728; $48 per credit hour. $306. Tuition and fees vary according to course load. *Financial support:* In 2009–10, 55 students received support, including 6 research assistantships (averaging $5,786 per year), 20 teaching assistantships (averaging $4,572 per year). Financial award application deadline: 4/1. *Faculty research:* Textile CD ROM, hair fiber products, retinol and cancer met, light/color assessment, fair labor monitor. Total annual research expenditures: $656,557. *Unit head:* Dr. Maria E. Canabal, Chair, 512-245-2155, Fax: 512-245-3829, E-mail: me57@txstate.edu. *Application contact:* Dr. Sue Williams, Graduate Adviser, 512-245-2155, Fax: 512-245-3829, E-mail: sw10@txstate.edu.

Texas Tech University, Graduate School, College of Human Sciences, Department of Nutrition, Hospitality, and Retailing, Program in Nutritional Sciences, Lubbock, TX 79409. Offers MS, PhD. Part-time programs available. *Students:* 23 full-time (all women), 16 part-time (15 women); includes 2 minority (both Hispanic Americans), 11 international. Average age 25. 35 applicants, 80% accepted, 13 enrolled. In 2009, 12 master's, 2 doctorates awarded. *Degree requirements:* For master's, thesis or alternative; for doctorate, thesis/dissertation. *Entrance requirements:* For master's and doctorate, GRE General Test. Additional exam requirements/recommendations for international students: Required—TOEFL (minimum score 550 paper-based; 213 computer-based). *Application deadline:* For fall admission, 3/1 priority date for international students; for spring admission, 11/1 priority date for international students. Applications are processed on a rolling basis. Application fee: $50 ($75 for international students). Electronic applications accepted. *Expenses:* Tuition, state resident: full-time $5100; part-time $213 per credit hour. Tuition, nonresident: full-time $11,748; part-time $490 per credit hour. Required fees: $2298; $50 per credit hour. $555 per semester. *Financial support:* Research assistantships with partial tuition reimbursements, teaching assistantships with partial tuition reimbursements, career-related internships or fieldwork, Federal Work-Study, institutionally sponsored loans, and scholarships/grants available. Support available to part-time students. Financial award application deadline: 4/15; financial award applicants required to submit FAFSA. *Faculty research:* Antioxidants and health; health effects of selenium; prevention of obesity; nutrition education for underserved populations; nutritional aspects of inflammation and chronic disease. *Unit head:* Dr. Debra Reed, Graduate Advisor, 806-742-3068, Fax: 806-742-3042, E-mail: debra.reed@ttu.edu. *Application contact:* Dr. Debra Reed, Graduate Advisor, 806-742-3068 Ext. 251, Fax: 806-742-3042, E-mail: debra.reed@ttu.edu.

Texas Woman's University, Graduate School, College of Health Sciences, Department of Nutrition and Food Sciences, Denton, TX 76201. Offers exercise and sports nutrition (MS); food science (MS); food systems administration (MS); nutrition (MS, PhD). Part-time and evening/weekend programs available. *Faculty:* 15 full-time (7 women). *Students:* 88 full-time (78 women), 90 part-time (81 women); includes 44 minority (13 African Americans, 1 American Indian/Alaska Native, 16 Asian Americans or Pacific Islanders, 14 Hispanic Americans), 25 international. Average age 28. 121 applicants, 76% accepted, 57 enrolled. In 2009, 55 master's, 3 doctorates awarded. *Degree requirements:* For master's, comprehensive exam; for doctorate, comprehensive exam, thesis/dissertation, qualifying exam. *Entrance requirements:* For master's, GRE General Test (minimum score 350 verbal, 450 quantitative), minimum GPA of 3.25, resume; for doctorate, GRE General Test (minimum score: 450 Verbal, 550 Quantitative), minimum GPA of 3.5, 2 letters of reference, resume. Additional exam requirements/recommendations for international students: Required—TOEFL (minimum score 550 paper-based; 213 computer-based; 79 iBT). *Application deadline:* For fall admission, 7/1 priority date for domestic students, 3/1 for international students; for spring admission, 12/1 priority date for domestic students, 7/1 for international students. Applications are processed on a rolling basis. Application fee: $50. Electronic applications accepted. *Expenses:* Tuition, state resident: full-time $3564; part-time $198 per credit hour. Tuition, nonresident: full-time $8550; part-time $475 per credit hour. Required fees: $69.26 per credit hour. Tuition and fees vary according to course load. *Financial support:* In 2009–10, 47 students received support, including 18 research assistantships (averaging $10,746 per year), 1 teaching assistantship (averaging $10,746 per year); career-related internships or fieldwork, Federal Work-Study, institutionally sponsored loans, scholarships/grants, traineeships, health care benefits, and unspecified assistantships also available. Support available to part-time students. Financial award application deadline: 3/1; financial award applicants required to submit FAFSA. *Faculty research:* Food science, food safety, clinical nutrition, nutrition and cancer, weight management, chemical and toxicological evaluations, food waste management, nutrition education, processing models and parfrying, elimination of transfats, impact of d-delta-tocotienol on osteoclasts and osteoblasts, osteoarthritis, markers for protective for Diabetes, melanomas. Total annual research expenditures: $1 million. *Unit head:* Dr. Chandan Prasad, Chair, 940-898-2636, Fax: 940-898-2634, E-mail: nutrfdsci@twu.edu. *Application contact:* Samuel Wheeler, Assistant Director of Admissions, 940-898-3188, Fax: 940-898-3081, E-mail: wheelersr@twu.edu.

Tufts University, The Gerald J. and Dorothy R. Friedman School of Nutrition Science and Policy, Medford, MA 02155. Offers humanitarian assistance (MAHA); nutrition (MS, PhD). Part-time programs available. *Degree requirements:* For doctorate, comprehensive exam, thesis/dissertation. *Entrance requirements:* For master's and doctorate, GRE General Test. Additional exam requirements/recommendations for international students: Required—TOEFL. Electronic applications accepted. *Expenses:* Contact institution. *Faculty research:* Nutritional biochemistry and metabolism, cell and molecular biochemistry, epidemiology, policy/planning, applied nutrition.

Tulane University, School of Public Health and Tropical Medicine, Department of Community Health Sciences, Program in Nutrition, New Orleans, LA 70118-5669. Offers MPH. *Degree requirements:* For master's, comprehensive exam. *Entrance requirements:* For master's, GRE General Test. Additional exam requirements/recommendations for international students: Required—TOEFL.

Tuskegee University, Graduate Programs, College of Agricultural, Environmental and Natural Sciences, Department of Food and Nutritional Sciences, Tuskegee, AL 36088. Offers MS. *Faculty:* 4 full-time (3 women). *Students:* 16 full-time (14 women), 1 (woman) part-time; includes 14 minority (all African Americans), 1 international. Average age 28. In 2009, 5 master's awarded. *Degree requirements:* For master's, thesis. *Entrance requirements:* For master's, GRE General Test. Additional exam requirements/recommendations for international students: Required—TOEFL (minimum score 500 paper-based; 69 computer-based). *Application deadline:* For fall admission, 7/15 for domestic students. Applications are processed on a rolling basis. Application fee: $25 ($35 for international students). *Expenses:* Tuition: Full-time $15,630; part-time $940 per credit hour. Required fees: $650. *Financial support:* Application deadline: 4/15. *Unit head:* Dr. Ralphenia Pace, Head, 334-727-8162. *Application contact:* Dr. Robert L. Laney, Vice President/Director of Admissions and Enrollment Management, 334-727-8580, Fax: 334-727-5750, E-mail: planey@tuskegee.edu.

Université de Moncton, School of Food Science, Nutrition and Family Studies, Moncton, NB E1A 3E9, Canada. Offers foods/nutrition (M Sc). Part-time programs available. *Degree requirements:* For master's, one foreign language, thesis. *Entrance requirements:* For master's, previous course work in statistics. Electronic applications accepted. *Faculty research:* Clinic nutrition (anemia, elderly, osteoporosis), applied nutrition, metabolic activities of lactic bacteria, solubility of low density lipoproteins, bile acids.

Université de Montréal, Faculty of Medicine, Department of Nutrition, Montréal, QC H3C 3J7, Canada. Offers M Sc, PhD, DESS. *Faculty:* 23 full-time (13 women), 1 (woman) part-time/adjunct. *Students:* 52 full-time (37 women), 65 part-time (52 women). 89 applicants, 37% accepted, 21 enrolled. In 2009, 16 master's, 2 doctorates, 2 other advanced degrees awarded. Terminal master's awarded for partial completion of doctoral program. *Degree requirements:* For master's, thesis; for doctorate, thesis/dissertation, general exam. *Entrance requirements:* For master's, MD, B Sc in nutrition or equivalent, proficiency in French; for doctorate, M Sc in nutrition or equivalent, proficiency in French. *Application deadline:* For fall admission, 2/1 priority date for domestic students; for winter admission, 11/1 priority date for domestic students; for spring admission, 2/1 priority date for domestic students. Application fee: $100. Electronic applications accepted. *Faculty research:* Nutritional aspects of diabetes, obesity, anorexia nervosa, lipid metabolism, hepatic function. *Unit head:* Marielle Ledoux, Director, 514-343-6401, Fax: 514-343-7395, E-mail: marielle.ledoux@umontreal.ca. *Application contact:* Irene Strychar, Assistant Director of Graduate Studies, 514-343-6111 Ext. 28843, Fax: 514-343-7395, E-mail: irene.strychar@@umontreal.ca.

Université Laval, Faculty of Agricultural and Food Sciences, Department of Food Sciences and Nutrition, Programs in Nutrition, Québec, QC G1K 7P4, Canada. Offers M Sc, PhD. Terminal master's awarded for partial completion of doctoral program. *Degree requirements:* For master's, thesis; for doctorate, comprehensive exam, thesis/dissertation. *Entrance requirements:* For master's and doctorate, knowledge of French and English. Electronic applications accepted.

University at Buffalo, the State University of New York, Graduate School, School of Public Health and Health Professions, Department of Exercise and Nutrition Sciences, Buffalo, NY 14260. Offers exercise science (MS, PhD); nutrition (MS). Part-time programs available. *Faculty:* 16 full-time (4 women), 14 part-time/adjunct (12 women). *Students:* 93 full-time (51 women), 29 part-time (24 women); includes 16 minority (4 African Americans, 9 Asian Americans or Pacific Islanders, 3 Hispanic Americans), 24 international. Average age 24. 72 applicants, 60% accepted. In 2009, 19 master's, 3 doctorates awarded. *Degree requirements:* For master's, comprehensive exam or thesis; for doctorate, comprehensive exam, thesis/dissertation. *Entrance requirements:* For master's, GRE General Test (nutrition), minimum GPA of 3.0; for doctorate, GRE General Test, minimum GPA of 3.0 (PhD). Additional exam requirements/recommendations for international students: Required—TOEFL (minimum score 550 paper-based; 213 computer-based; 79 iBT), IELTS (minimum score 6.5). *Application deadline:* For fall admission, 1/31 for domestic students, 2/1 for international students. Applications are processed on a rolling basis. Application fee: $50. Electronic applications accepted. *Financial support:* In 2009–10, 10 students received support, including 1 research assistantship with tuition reimbursement available (averaging $18,000 per year), 10 teaching assistantships with full and partial tuition reimbursements available (averaging $11,000 per year); career-related internships or fieldwork, Federal Work-Study, institutionally sponsored loans, scholarships/grants, health care benefits, tuition waivers (full and partial), unspecified assistantships, and stipends also available. Financial award application deadline: 3/15; financial award applicants required to submit FAFSA. *Faculty research:* Cardiovascular disease-diet and exercise, respiratory control and muscle function, plasticity of connective and neural tissue, exercise nutrition, diet and cancer. Total annual research expenditures: $409,473. *Unit head:* Dr. Joan Dorn, Chair, 716-829-2975 Ext. 619, Fax: 716-829-2979, E-mail: jdorn@buffalo.edu. *Application contact:* Dr. Gaspar Farkas, Director of Graduate Studies, 76-829-2941 Ext. 311, Fax: 716-829-2428, E-mail: farkas@buffalo.edu.

The University of Akron, Graduate School, College of Health Sciences and Human Services, School of Health and Human Services, Program in Nutrition and Dietetics, Akron, OH 44325. Offers MS. *Students:* 7 full-time (all women), 2 part-time (1 woman); includes 2 minority (1 African American, 1 Asian American or Pacific Islander), 2 international. Average age 25. 8 applicants, 63% accepted, 4 enrolled. In 2009, 4 master's awarded. *Degree requirements:* For master's, comprehensive exam, thesis or project. *Entrance requirements:* For master's, GRE, minimum GPA of 2.75, letters of recommendation, resume. Additional exam requirements/recommendations for international students: Required—TOEFL (minimum score 550 paper-based; 213 computer-based; 79 iBT). *Application deadline:* For fall admission, 3/1 for domestic and international students; for spring admission, 10/1 for domestic and international students. Application fee: $30 ($40 for international students). Electronic applications accepted. *Expenses:* Tuition, state resident: full-time $6570; part-time $365 per credit hour. Tuition, nonresident: full-time $11,250; part-time $625 per credit hour. *Unit head:* Dr. Deborah Marino, Associate Professor, 330-972-6322, E-mail: debora7@uakron.edu. *Application contact:* Dr. Deborah Marino, Associate Professor, 330-972-6322, E-mail: debora7@uakron.edu.

The University of Alabama, Graduate School, College of Human Environmental Sciences, Department of Human Nutrition and Hospitality Management, Tuscaloosa, AL 35487. Offers MSHES. Part-time programs available. Postbaccalaureate distance learning degree programs offered (no on-campus study). *Faculty:* 4 full-time (3 women). *Students:* 18 full-time (17 women), 59 part-time (58 women); includes 6 minority (5 African Americans, 1 Asian American or Pacific Islander), 1 international. Average age 31. 66 applicants, 52% accepted, 28 enrolled. In 2009, 22 degrees awarded. *Degree requirements:* For master's, comprehensive exam, thesis optional. *Entrance requirements:* For master's, minimum GPA of 3.0. Additional exam requirements/recommendations for international students: Required—TOEFL. *Application deadline:* For fall admission, 7/6 for domestic students. Applications are processed on a rolling basis. Application fee: $50 ($60 for international students). Electronic applications accepted. *Expenses:* Tuition, state resident: full-time $7000. Tuition, nonresident: full-time $19,200. *Financial support:* In 2009–10, 4 students received support, including 2 research assistantships (averaging $8,100 per year), 2 teaching assistantships (averaging $8,100 per year); career-related internships or fieldwork also available. Financial award application deadline: 3/15. *Faculty research:* Maternal and child nutrition, childhood obesity, community nutrition interventions, geriatric nutrition, family eating patterns. Total annual research expenditures: $11,473. *Unit head:* Dr. Olivia W. Kendrick, Chair and Associate Professor, 205-348-6150, Fax: 205-348-3789, E-mail: okendric@ches.ua.edu. *Application contact:* Dr. Olivia W. Kendrick, Chair and Associate Professor, 205-348-6150, Fax: 205-348-3789, E-mail: okendric@ches.ua.edu.

The University of Alabama at Birmingham, School of Health Professions, Program in Clinical Nutrition and Dietetics, Birmingham, AL 35294. Offers MS. Part-time programs available. *Degree requirements:* For master's, thesis. *Entrance requirements:* For master's, GRE General Test or MAT, bachelor's degree in dietetics or related field. Electronic applications accepted. *Faculty research:* Clinical assessment, folic acid, energy metabolism, nutrition and cancer, nutrition for children and adolescents with special health care needs.

The University of Alabama at Birmingham, School of Health Professions, Program in Nutrition Sciences, Birmingham, AL 35294. Offers PhD. *Degree requirements:* For doctorate, thesis/dissertation. *Entrance requirements:* For doctorate, GRE General Test. Electronic applications accepted. *Faculty research:* Energy metabolism, obesity, body composition, cancer prevention, bone metabolism.

University of Alaska Fairbanks, School of Fisheries and Ocean Sciences, Fairbanks, AK 99775-7220. Offers fisheries (MS, PhD); marine sciences and limnology (MS, PhD), including marine biology, oceanography (PhD); seafood science and nutrition (MS, PhD). Part-time programs available. *Faculty:* 25 full-time (8 women), 3 part-time/adjunct (1 woman). *Students:* 66 full-time (35 women), 44 part-time (23 women); includes 5 minority (2 American Indian/Alaska Native, 3 Asian Americans or Pacific Islanders), 8 international. Average age 33. 81 applicants. In 2009, 25 master's, 5 doctorates awarded. Terminal master's awarded for partial completion of doctoral program. *Degree requirements:* For master's, comprehensive exam, thesis or alternative; for doctorate, comprehensive exam, thesis/dissertation, oral defense. *Entrance requirements:* For master's and doctorate, GRE General Test. Additional exam requirements/recommendations for international students: Required—TOEFL (minimum score 550 paper-based; 213 computer-based; 80 iBT). *Application deadline:* For fall admission, 6/1 for domestic students, 3/1 for international students; for spring admission, 10/15 for domestic students, 9/1 for international students. Applications are processed on a rolling basis. Application fee: $60. Electronic applications accepted. *Expenses:* Tuition, state resident: full-time $7584; part-time $316 per credit. Tuition, nonresident: full-time $15,504; part-time $646 per credit. Required fees: $23 per credit. $135 per semester. Tuition and fees vary according to course level, course load and reciprocity agreements. *Financial support:* In 2009–10, 37 research assistantships (averaging $11,925 per year), 15 teaching assistantships with tuition reimbursements (averaging $10,395 per year) were awarded; fellowships, career-related internships or fieldwork, Federal Work-Study, scholarships/grants, health care benefits, and unspecified assistantships also available. Support available to part-time students. Financial award application deadline: 2/15; financial award applicants required to submit FAFSA. *Faculty research:* Marine mammals, hydrology, sea ice, harmful algal blooms, polar ecology. Total annual research expenditures: $13.8 million. *Unit head:* Dr. Denis Wiesenberg, Dean, 907-474-7824, Fax: 907-474-7204, E-mail: info@sfos.uaf.edu. *Application contact:* Katie Murra, Recruitment and Retention Coordinator, 907-474-6786, Fax: 907-474-7204, E-mail: murra@sfos.uaf.edu.

The University of Arizona, Graduate College, College of Agriculture and Life Sciences, Department of Nutritional Sciences, Tucson, AZ 85721. Offers MS, PhD. *Faculty:* 9. *Students:* 18 full-time (13 women), 7 part-time (4 women); includes 3 minority (1 African American, 2 Hispanic Americans), 5 international. Average age 30. 26 applicants, 23% accepted, 5 enrolled. In 2009, 2 master's, 3 doctorates awarded. *Entrance requirements:* For master's, GRE, minimum GPA of 3.0, 2 letters of recommendation; for doctorate, GRE, minimum GPA of 3.0, 2 letters of recommendation, statement of purpose. Additional exam requirements/recommendations for international students: Required—TOEFL. *Application deadline:* Applications are processed on a rolling basis. Application fee: $75. Electronic applications accepted. *Expenses:* Tuition, state resident: full-time $9028. Tuition, nonresident: full-time $24,890. *Financial support:* In 2009–10, 5 research assistantships with full and partial tuition reimbursements (averaging $19,428 per year), 9 teaching assistantships with full and partial tuition reimbursements (averaging $18,069 per year) were awarded; fellowships, scholarships/grants, health care benefits, tuition waivers (full and partial), and unspecified assistantships also available. *Faculty research:* Bioactive compounds, nutrients and lifestyle: relationships to cancer; metabolic and behavior factors Influencing body composition; diabetes, obesity, musculoskeletal and cardiovascular diseases. Total annual research expenditures: $3.6 million. *Unit head:* Dr. Cynthia Thomson, Head, E-mail: cthomson@u.arizona.edu. *Application contact:* Nancy Driscoll, Information Contact, 520-626-0970, Fax: 520-621-9446, E-mail: nancya@email.arizona.edu.

University of Arkansas for Medical Sciences, Graduate School, Program in Clinical Nutrition, Little Rock, AR 72205-7199. Offers MS. Part-time programs available. *Faculty:* 13 full-time (8 women). *Students:* 8 full-time, 11 part-time. In 2009, 8 master's awarded. *Degree requirements:* For master's, thesis. *Entrance requirements:* For master's, GRE. Additional exam requirements/recommendations for international students: Required—TOEFL. *Application deadline:* Applications are processed on a rolling basis. Application fee: $0. *Financial support:* Research assistantships available. Support available to part-time students. *Faculty research:* Geriatric nutrition, pediatric nutrition, nutrition and health promotion wellness emphasis, community nutrition. *Unit head:* Dr. Reza Hakkak, Chair and Program Director, 501-686-5715, E-mail: hakkakreza@uams.edu. *Application contact:* Dr. Reza Hakkak, Chair and Program Director, 501-686-5715, E-mail: hakkakreza@uams.edu.

University of Bridgeport, Nutrition Institute, Bridgeport, CT 06604. Offers human nutrition (MS). Part-time and evening/weekend programs available. Postbaccalaureate distance learning degree programs offered (no on-campus study). *Degree requirements:* For master's, thesis, research project. *Entrance requirements:* For master's, previous course work in anatomy, biochemistry, organic chemistry, or physiology. Additional exam requirements/recommendations for international students: Recommended—TOEFL (minimum score 550 paper-based; 213 computer-based; 80 iBT), IELTS (minimum score 6.5). Electronic applications accepted. *Expenses:* Contact institution.

The University of British Columbia, Faculty of Land and Food Systems, Human Nutrition Program, Vancouver, BC V6T 1Z1, Canada. Offers M Sc, PhD. Part-time programs available. Terminal master's awarded for partial completion of doctoral program. *Degree requirements:* For master's, thesis; for doctorate, comprehensive exam, thesis/dissertation. *Entrance requirements:* Additional exam requirements/recommendations for international students: Required—TOEFL (minimum score 577 paper-based; 233 computer-based; 90 iBT), IELTS (minimum score 6.5). Electronic applications accepted. *Faculty research:* Basic nutrition, clinical nutrition, community nutrition, women's health, pediatric nutrition.

University of California, Berkeley, Graduate Division, College of Natural Resources, Group in Molecular and Biochemical Nutrition, Berkeley, CA 94720-1500. Offers PhD. *Students:* 18 full-time (12 women). Average age 28. 49 applicants, 3 enrolled. In 2009, 1 doctorate awarded. *Degree requirements:* For doctorate, thesis/dissertation, qualifying exam. *Entrance requirements:* For doctorate, GRE General Test, minimum GPA of 3.0, 3 letters of recommendation. Additional exam requirements/recommendations for international students: Required—TOEFL. *Application deadline:* For fall admission, 12/1 for domestic students. Application fee: $70 ($90 for international students). Electronic applications accepted. *Financial support:* Fellowships, research assistantships with full tuition reimbursements, teaching assistantships with full tuition reimbursements, unspecified assistantships and stipends available. Financial award applicants required to submit FAFSA. *Faculty research:* Regulation of metabolism; nutritional genomics and nutrient-gene interactions; transport, metabolism and function of minerals; carcinogenesis and dietary anti-carcinogens. *Unit head:* Prof. Joseph Napoli, Chair, 510-642-6490, E-mail: mbn@nature.berkeley.edu. *Application contact:* Graduate Assistant, 510-643-2863, Fax: 510-642-0535, E-mail: mbn@nature.berkeley.edu.

University of California, Davis, Graduate Studies, Graduate Group in Nutritional Biology, Davis, CA 95616. Offers MS, PhD. *Degree requirements:* For master's, thesis; for doctorate, thesis/dissertation. *Entrance requirements:* For master's and doctorate, GRE General Test, minimum GPA of 3.0. Additional exam requirements/recommendations for international students: Required—TOEFL (minimum score 550 paper-based; 213 computer-based). Electronic applications accepted. *Faculty research:* Human/animal nutrition.

University of California, Davis, Graduate Studies, Program in Maternal and Child Nutrition, Davis, CA 95616. Offers MAS. *Degree requirements:* For master's, comprehensive exam. *Entrance requirements:* Additional exam requirements/recommendations for international students: Required—TOEFL (minimum score 550 paper-based; 213 computer-based).

University of Central Oklahoma, College of Graduate Studies and Research, College of Education, Department of Human Environmental Sciences, Edmond, OK 73034-5209. Offers family and child studies (MS); family and consumer science education (MS); interior design (MS); nutrition-food management (MS). Part-time programs available. *Faculty:* 5 full-time (4 women), 7 part-time/adjunct (4 women). *Students:* 51 full-time (49 women), 43 part-time (all women); includes 31 minority (20 African Americans, 7 American Indian/Alaska Native, 1 Asian American or Pacific Islander, 3 Hispanic Americans), 3 international. Average age 30. 21 applicants, 95% accepted. In 2009, 30 master's awarded. *Entrance requirements:* Additional exam requirements/recommendations for international students: Required—TOEFL (minimum score 550 paper-based; 213 computer-based). *Application deadline:* For fall admission, 7/1 for international students; for spring admission, 11/1 for international students. Applications are processed on a rolling basis. Application fee: $25. Electronic applications accepted. *Expenses:* Tuition, state resident: full-time $4128; part-time $172 per credit hour. Tuition, nonresident: full-time $10,373; part-time $432.20 per credit hour. Required fees: $433.20; $18.05 per credit hour. *Financial support:* Career-related internships or fieldwork and unspecified assistantships available. Financial award application deadline: 3/31; financial award applicants required to submit FAFSA. *Faculty research:* Dietetics and food science. *Unit head:* Dr. Kaye Sears, Chairperson, 405-974-5786. *Application contact:* Dr. Richard Bernard, Dean, Graduate College, 405-974-3493, Fax: 405-974-3852, E-mail: gradcoll@uco.edu.

University of Chicago, Division of the Biological Sciences, Biomedical Sciences Cluster: Cancer Biology, Immunology, Molecular Metabolism and Nutrition, Pathology, and Microbiology, Committee on Molecular Metabolism and Nutrition, Chicago, IL 60637-1513. Offers PhD. *Faculty:* 43. *Students:* 21 full-time (13 women); includes 9 minority (6 Asian Americans or Pacific Islanders, 3 Hispanic Americans). Average age 29. 15 applicants, 27% accepted, 3 enrolled. In 2009, 1 doctorate awarded. *Degree requirements:* For doctorate, thesis/dissertation, ethics class, 2 teaching assistantships. *Entrance requirements:* For doctorate, GRE General Test. Additional exam requirements/recommendations for international students: Required—TOEFL (minimum score 600 paper-based; 250 computer-based; 104 iBT), IELTS (minimum

score 7). *Application deadline:* For fall admission, 12/1 priority date for domestic and international students. Application fee: $55. Electronic applications accepted. *Financial support:* In 2009–10, 21 students received support, including fellowships with full tuition reimbursements available (averaging $29,781 per year), research assistantships with full tuition reimbursements available (averaging $29,781 per year); institutionally sponsored loans, scholarships/grants, traineeships, and health care benefits also available. Financial award applicants required to submit FAFSA. *Faculty research:* Regulation of lipoprotein metabolism, cellular vitamin metabolism, obesity and body composition, adipocyte differentiation. *Unit head:* Dr. Christopher J. Rhodes, Chairman, 773-702-8128, Fax: 773-834-0851. *Application contact:* Kristin Reepmeyer, Administrative Assistant, 773-702-3940, Fax: 773-702-4634, E-mail: reepmeyer@bsd.uchicago.edu.

University of Cincinnati, Graduate School, College of Allied Health Sciences, Department of Nutritional Science, Cincinnati, OH 45221. Offers MS. Part-time programs available. *Degree requirements:* For master's, thesis. *Entrance requirements:* For master's, GRE General Test. Additional exam requirements/recommendations for international students: Required—TOEFL (minimum score 550 paper-based; 230 computer-based). Electronic applications accepted. *Faculty research:* Phytochemicals-osteoarthritis, pediatric hypertension and hypercholesterol, cancer prevention/Type II diabetes.

University of Connecticut, Graduate School, College of Agriculture and Natural Resources, Department of Nutritional Sciences, Storrs, CT 06269. Offers MS, PhD. *Faculty:* 15 full-time (8 women). *Students:* 31 full-time (22 women), 6 part-time (all women); includes 4 minority (2 African Americans, 2 Asian Americans or Pacific Islanders), 13 international. Average age 29. 57 applicants, 19% accepted, 7 enrolled. In 2009, 10 master's, 7 doctorates awarded. Terminal master's awarded for partial completion of doctoral program. *Degree requirements:* For master's, comprehensive exam, thesis; for doctorate, thesis/dissertation. *Entrance requirements:* For master's and doctorate, GRE General Test. Additional exam requirements/recommendations for international students: Required—TOEFL (minimum score 550 paper-based; 213 computer-based). *Application deadline:* For fall admission, 2/1 priority date for domestic and international students; for spring admission, 11/1 for domestic students, 10/1 for international students. Applications are processed on a rolling basis. Application fee: $55. Electronic applications accepted. *Expenses:* Tuition, state resident: full-time $4725; part-time $525 per credit. Tuition, nonresident: full-time $12,267; part-time $1363 per credit. Required fees: $346 per semester. Tuition and fees vary according to course load. *Financial support:* In 2009–10, 25 research assistantships with full tuition reimbursements, 2 teaching assistantships with full tuition reimbursements were awarded; fellowships, Federal Work-Study, scholarships/grants, health care benefits, and unspecified assistantships also available. Financial award application deadline: 2/1; financial award applicants required to submit FAFSA. *Unit head:* Sung I. Koo, Head, 860-486-3495, Fax: 860-486-3674, E-mail: skoo@canr.uconn.edu. *Application contact:* Maria-Luz Fernandez, Coordinator, 860-486-5547, Fax: 860-486-3674, E-mail: maria-luz.fernandez@uconn.edu.

University of Delaware, College of Health Sciences, Department of Health, Nutrition, and Exercise Sciences, Newark, DE 19716. Offers exercise science (MS), including biomechanics, exercise physiology, motor control; health promotion (MS); human nutrition (MS). Part-time programs available. *Degree requirements:* For master's, thesis. *Entrance requirements:* For master's, GRE General Test, interview, minimum GPA of 3.0. Additional exam requirements/recommendations for international students: Required—TOEFL (minimum score 550 paper-based; 213 computer-based). Electronic applications accepted. *Faculty research:* Sport biomechanics, rehabilitation biomechanics, vascular dynamics.

University of Florida, Graduate School, College of Agricultural and Life Sciences, Department of Food Science and Human Nutrition, Gainesville, FL 32611. Offers food science (MS, PhD); nutritional sciences (MS, PhD). *Degree requirements:* For master's, thesis optional; for doctorate, thesis/dissertation. *Entrance requirements:* For master's and doctorate, GRE General Test, minimum GPA of 3.0. Additional exam requirements/recommendations for international students: Required—TOEFL. Electronic applications accepted. *Faculty research:* Pesticide research, nutritional biochemistry and microbiology, food safety and toxicology assessment and dietetics, food chemistry.

University of Georgia, Graduate School, College of Family and Consumer Sciences, Department of Foods and Nutrition, Athens, GA 30602. Offers MFCS, MS, PhD. *Faculty:* 13 full-time (9 women). *Students:* 35 full-time (33 women), 3 part-time (all women); includes 3 minority (2 African Americans, 1 Asian American or Pacific Islander), 3 international. 53 applicants, 57% accepted, 23 enrolled. In 2009, 14 master's, 1 doctorate awarded. *Degree requirements:* For master's, thesis (MS); for doctorate, thesis/dissertation. *Entrance requirements:* For master's, GRE General Test, minimum GPA of 3.0, course work in biochemistry and physiology; for doctorate, GRE General Test, master's degree, minimum GPA of 3.0. *Application deadline:* For fall admission, 7/1 priority date for domestic students; for spring admission, 11/15 for domestic students. Application fee: $50. Electronic applications accepted. *Expenses:* Tuition, state resident: full-time $6000; part-time $250 per credit hour. Tuition, nonresident: full-time $20,904; part-time $871 per credit hour. Required fees: $730 per semester. *Financial support:* Fellowships, research assistantships, teaching assistantships, unspecified assistantships available. *Unit head:* Dr. Rebecca M. Mullis, Head, 706-542-4875, Fax: 706-542-5059, E-mail: rmm@fcs.uga.edu. *Application contact:* Dr. Mary Ann Johnson, Graduate Coordinator, 706-542-2292, E-mail: mjohnson@fcs.uga.edu.

University of Guelph, Graduate Program Services, College of Biological Science, Department of Human Health and Nutritional Sciences, Guelph, ON N1G 2W1, Canada. Offers nutritional sciences (M Sc, PhD). Part-time programs available. *Degree requirements:* For master's, thesis (for some programs); for doctorate, comprehensive exam, thesis/dissertation. *Entrance requirements:* For master's, minimum B-average during previous 2 years of coursework; for doctorate, minimum A-average. Additional exam requirements/recommendations for international students: Required—TOEFL (minimum score 550 paper-based; 213 computer-based). Electronic applications accepted. *Faculty research:* Nutrition and biochemistry, exercise metabolism and physiology, toxicology, gene expression, biomechanics and ergonomics.

University of Guelph, Graduate Program Services, College of Social and Applied Human Sciences, Department of Family Relations and Applied Nutrition, Guelph, ON N1G 2W1, Canada. Offers applied nutrition (MAN); family relations and human development (M Sc, PhD), including applied human nutrition, couple and family therapy (M Sc), family relations and human development. *Accreditation:* AAMFT/COAMFTE (one or more programs are accredited). Part-time programs available. *Degree requirements:* For master's, thesis (for some programs); for doctorate, comprehensive exam, thesis/dissertation. *Entrance requirements:* For master's, minimum B+ average; for doctorate, master's degree in family relations and human development or related field with a minimum B+ average or master's degree in applied human nutrition. Additional exam requirements/recommendations for international students: Required—TOEFL (minimum score 600 paper-based; 250 computer-based). Electronic applications accepted. *Faculty research:* Child and adolescent development, social gerontology, family roles and relations, couple and family therapy, applied human nutrition.

University of Hawaii at Manoa, Graduate Division, College of Tropical Agriculture and Human Resources, Department of Human Nutrition, Food and Animal Sciences, Program in Nutrition, Honolulu, HI 96822. Offers PhD. Part-time programs available. *Students:* 1 full-time (0 women), 1 (woman) part-time; includes 1 minority (Asian American or Pacific Islander). Average age 31. 8 applicants, 38% accepted, 1 enrolled. *Degree requirements:* For doctorate, comprehensive exam, thesis/dissertation. *Entrance requirements:* For doctorate, GRE General Test. Additional exam requirements/recommendations for international students: Required—TOEFL (minimum score 580 paper-based; 237 computer-based; 92 iBT), IELTS (minimum score 5). *Application deadline:* For fall admission, 2/1 for domestic and international students; for spring admission, 9/1 for domestic and international students. Application fee: $60. *Expenses:* Tuition, state resident: full-time $8900; part-time $372 per credit. Tuition, nonresident: full-time $21,400; part-time $898 per credit. Required fees: $207 per semester. *Financial support:* In

Nutrition

University of Hawaii at Manoa (continued)
2009–10, 1 fellowship (averaging $3,000 per year), 1 research assistantship (averaging $18,198 per year) were awarded. *Application contact:* Dr. Michael Dunn, Graduate Chair, 808-956-7095, Fax: 808-956-4024, E-mail: mdunn@hawaii.edu.

University of Hawaii at Manoa, Graduate Division, College of Tropical Agriculture and Human Resources, Department of Human Nutrition, Food and Animal Sciences, Program in Nutritional Sciences, Honolulu, HI 96822. Offers MS, PhD. Part-time programs available. *Faculty:* 27 full-time (12 women), 4 part-time/adjunct (2 women). *Students:* 7 full-time (5 women), 2 part-time (both women); includes 6 minority (all Asian Americans or Pacific Islanders), 2 international. Average age 28. 20 applicants, 25% accepted, 3 enrolled. In 2009, 6 master's awarded. *Degree requirements:* For master's, thesis optional; for doctorate, comprehensive exam, thesis/dissertation. *Entrance requirements:* For master's and doctorate, GRE General Test. Additional exam requirements/recommendations for international students: Required—TOEFL (minimum score 580 paper-based; 237 computer-based; 92 iBT), IELTS (minimum score 5). *Application deadline:* For fall admission, 2/1 for domestic and international students; for spring admission, 9/1 for domestic and international students. Application fee: $60. *Expenses:* Tuition, state resident: full-time $8900; part-time $372 per credit. Tuition, nonresident: full-time $21,400; part-time $898 per credit. Required fees: $207 per semester. *Financial support:* In 2009–10, 2 fellowships (averaging $3,125 per year), 3 research assistantships (averaging $16,824 per year), 1 teaching assistantship (averaging $14,382 per year) were awarded; tuition waivers (full) also available. Financial award application deadline: 3/1. *Faculty research:* Nutritional biochemistry, human nutrition, nutrition education, international nutrition, nutritional epidemiology. Total annual research expenditures: $1 million. *Application contact:* Dr. Michael Dunn, Graduate Chairperson, 808-956-7095, Fax: 808-956-4024, E-mail: mdunn@hawaii.edu.

University of Houston, College of Education, Department of Health and Human Performance, Houston, TX 77204. Offers allied health education and administration (M Ed, Ed D); exercise science (MS); health education (M Ed); human nutrition (MS); human space exploration sciences (MS); kinesiology (PhD); physical education (M Ed). *Accreditation:* NCATE (one or more programs are accredited). Part-time and evening/weekend programs available. *Faculty:* 12 full-time (4 women), 4 part-time/adjunct (3 women). *Students:* 53 full-time (26 women), 39 part-time (25 women); includes 21 minority (12 African Americans, 6 Asian Americans or Pacific Islanders, 3 Hispanic Americans), 14 international. Average age 29. 78 applicants, 64% accepted, 26 enrolled. In 2009, 20 master's, 2 doctorates awarded. *Degree requirements:* For master's, comprehensive exam, thesis (for some programs); for doctorate, comprehensive exam, thesis/dissertation, qualifying exam, candidacy paper. *Entrance requirements:* For master's, GRE (minimum 35th percentile on each section), minimum cumulative GPA of 3.0; for doctorate, GRE (minimum 35th percentile on each section), minimum cumulative GPA of 3.3. Additional exam requirements/recommendations for international students: Required—TOEFL (minimum score 550 paper-based; 79 iBT). *Application deadline:* For fall admission, 5/1 for domestic students, 4/1 for international students; for spring admission, 10/1 for domestic and international students. Applications are processed on a rolling basis. Application fee: $45 ($75 for international students). Electronic applications accepted. *Expenses:* Tuition, state resident: full-time $7676; part-time $320 per credit hour. Tuition, nonresident: full-time $14,324; part-time $597 per credit hour. Required fees: $3034. *Financial support:* In 2009–10, 7 fellowships with full tuition reimbursements (averaging $9,500 per year), 8 research assistantships with full tuition reimbursements (averaging $9,850 per year), 12 teaching assistantships with full tuition reimbursements (averaging $9,850 per year) were awarded; career-related internships or fieldwork, Federal Work-Study, institutionally sponsored loans, scholarships/grants, health care benefits, and unspecified assistantships also available. Support available to part-time students. Financial award application deadline: 2/1. *Faculty research:* Biomechanics, exercise physiology, obesity, nutrition, space exploration science. *Unit head:* Dr. Charles Layne, Chairperson, 713-743-9868, Fax: 713-743-9860, E-mail: clayne2@uh.edu. *Application contact:* Todd Boutte, Graduate Admission Counselor, 713-743-0571, Fax: 713-743-0123, E-mail: tboutte@mail.coe.uh.edu.

University of Illinois at Chicago, Graduate College, College of Applied Health Sciences, Program in Nutrition, Chicago, IL 60607-7128. Offers MS, PhD. *Accreditation:* ADtA. *Degree requirements:* For master's, thesis; for doctorate, thesis/dissertation. *Entrance requirements:* For master's and doctorate, GRE General Test, minimum GPA of 2.75. Additional exam requirements/recommendations for international students: Required—TOEFL. Electronic applications accepted. *Faculty research:* Nutrition for the elderly, inborn errors of metabolism, nutrition and cancer, lipid metabolism, dietary fat markers.

University of Illinois at Urbana–Champaign, Graduate College, College of Agricultural, Consumer and Environmental Sciences, Department of Food Science and Human Nutrition, Champaign, IL 61820. Offers food science (MS); food science and human nutrition (MS, PhD), including professional science (MS); human nutrition (MS). Part-time programs available. Postbaccalaureate distance learning degree programs offered (minimal on-campus study). *Faculty:* 28 full-time (12 women), 1 (woman) part-time/adjunct. *Students:* 62 full-time (43 women), 32 part-time (22 women); includes 5 minority (1 African American, 3 Asian Americans or Pacific Islanders, 1 Hispanic American), 44 international. 147 applicants, 28% accepted, 31 enrolled. In 2009, 15 master's, 3 doctorates awarded. *Entrance requirements:* For master's and doctorate, GRE, minimum GPA of 3.0. Additional exam requirements/recommendations for international students: Required—TOEFL (minimum score 550 paper-based; 213 computer-based; 79 iBT) or IELTS (minimum score 6.5). *Application deadline:* Applications are processed on a rolling basis. Application fee: $60 ($75 for international students). Electronic applications accepted. *Financial support:* In 2009–10, 14 fellowships, 38 research assistantships, 18 teaching assistantships were awarded; tuition waivers (full and partial) also available. *Unit head:* Faye L. Dong, Head, 217-244-4498, Fax: 217-265-0925, E-mail: fayedong@illinois.edu. *Application contact:* Barb J. Vandeventer, Office Administrator, 217-333-1324, Fax: 217-265-0925, E-mail: vandvntr@illinois.edu.

University of Illinois at Urbana–Champaign, Graduate College, College of Agricultural, Consumer and Environmental Sciences, Division of Nutritional Sciences, Champaign, IL 61820. Offers MS, PhD. *Students:* 60 full-time (45 women); includes 11 minority (2 African Americans, 5 Asian Americans or Pacific Islanders, 4 Hispanic Americans), 14 international. 69 applicants, 20% accepted, 13 enrolled. In 2009, 11 master's, 11 doctorates awarded. *Entrance requirements:* For master's and doctorate, GRE, minimum GPA of 3.0. Additional exam requirements/recommendations for international students: Required—TOEFL (minimum score 560 paper-based; 220 computer-based; 83 iBT) or IELTS (minimum score 6.5). *Application deadline:* Applications are processed on a rolling basis. Application fee: $60 ($75 for international students). Electronic applications accepted. *Financial support:* In 2009–10, 17 fellowships, 42 research assistantships, 7 teaching assistantships were awarded; tuition waivers (full and partial) also available. *Unit head:* Rodney W. Johnson, Director, 217-333-2118, Fax: 217-333-9368, E-mail: rwjohn@illinois.edu. *Application contact:* Jessica L. Hartke, Visiting Program Coordinator, 217-333-4177, Fax: 217-333-9368, E-mail: jessh@illinois.edu.

The University of Kansas, University of Kansas Medical Center, School of Allied Health, Department of Dietetics and Nutrition, Lawrence, KS 66045. Offers dietetic internship (Certificate); dietetics and nutrition (MS); medical nutrition science (PhD). Part-time programs available. *Faculty:* 12 full-time, 2 part-time/adjunct. *Students:* 37 full-time (34 women), 13 part-time (12 women); includes 4 minority (2 American Indian/Alaska Native, 2 Asian Americans or Pacific Islanders), 7 international. Average age 25. 68 applicants, 50% accepted, 27 enrolled. In 2009, 17 master's awarded. *Degree requirements:* For master's, thesis, oral exam. *Entrance requirements:* For master's, GRE, prerequisite courses in nutrition, biochemistry, and physiology; for Certificate, GRE. Additional exam requirements/recommendations for international students: Required—TOEFL (minimum score 228 computer-based; 92 iBT). *Application deadline:* For fall admission, 8/1 for domestic students, 7/1 for international students; for winter admission, 12/1 for domestic students, 11/1 for international students; for spring admission, 5/1 for domestic students, 4/1 for international students. Applications are processed on a rolling basis. Application fee: $60. Electronic applications accepted. *Expenses:* Tuition, state resident: full-time $6492; part-time $270.50 per credit hour. Tuition, nonresident: full-time $15,510; part-time $646.25 per credit hour. Required fees: $847; $70.56 per credit hour. Tuition and fees vary according to course load and program. *Financial support:* In 2009–10, 23 students received support, including 9 research assistantships with full tuition reimbursements available, 2 teaching assistantships with full tuition reimbursements available; fellowships, career-related internships or fieldwork, Federal Work-Study, institutionally sponsored loans, scholarships/grants, traineeships, tuition waivers, and unspecified assistantships also available. Support available to part-time students. Financial award application deadline: 2/15. *Faculty research:* Obesity prevention and treatment, omega-3 fatty acids impact on infant development and immunity, iron status of infants, appetitive and endocrine responses to food intake, vitamin D and bone metabolism in osteosarcoma cells, food security in individuals with mental illness, cancer prevention and recovery, nutrigenomics. Total annual research expenditures: $1.7 million. *Unit head:* Dr. Debra Kay Sullivan, Chairperson, 913-588-5357, Fax: 913-588-8946, E-mail: dsulliva@kumc.edu. *Application contact:* Dr. Linda Dianne Griffith, Graduate Director, 913-588-7652, Fax: 913-588-8946, E-mail: lgriffith@kumc.edu.

University of Kentucky, Graduate School, College of Agriculture, Program in Hospitality and Dietetic Administration, Lexington, KY 40506-0032. Offers MS. *Degree requirements:* For master's, comprehensive exam, thesis optional. *Entrance requirements:* For master's, GRE General Test, minimum undergraduate GPA of 2.75. Additional exam requirements/recommendations for international students: Required—TOEFL (minimum score 550 paper-based; 213 computer-based). Electronic applications accepted.

University of Kentucky, Graduate School, Program in Nutritional Sciences, Lexington, KY 40506-0032. Offers MSNS, PhD. *Degree requirements:* For doctorate, comprehensive exam, thesis/dissertation. *Entrance requirements:* For master's, GRE General Test, minimum undergraduate GPA of 2.75; for doctorate, GRE General Test, minimum graduate GPA of 3.0. Additional exam requirements/recommendations for international students: Required—TOEFL (minimum score 550 paper-based; 213 computer-based). Electronic applications accepted. *Faculty research:* Nutrition and AIDS, nutrition and alcoholism, nutrition and cardiovascular disease, nutrition and cancer, nutrition and diabetes.

University of Maine, Graduate School, College of Natural Sciences, Forestry, and Agriculture, Department of Food Science and Human Nutrition, Orono, ME 04469. Offers food and nutritional sciences (PhD); food science and human nutrition (MS). Part-time programs available. *Faculty:* 8 full-time (6 women), 2 part-time/adjunct (1 woman). *Students:* 25 full-time (21 women), 6 part-time (all women); includes 1 minority (African American), 4 international. Average age 28. 36 applicants, 44% accepted, 9 enrolled. In 2009, 6 master's, 1 doctorate awarded. *Degree requirements:* For master's, thesis; for doctorate, thesis/dissertation. *Entrance requirements:* For master's, GRE General Test, minimum GPA of 3.0; for doctorate, GRE General Test. Additional exam requirements/recommendations for international students: Required—TOEFL. *Application deadline:* For fall admission, 2/1 priority date for domestic students. Applications are processed on a rolling basis. Application fee: $65. Electronic applications accepted. *Financial support:* In 2009–10, 9 research assistantships with tuition reimbursements (averaging $13,500 per year), 4 teaching assistantships with tuition reimbursements (averaging $12,000 per year) were awarded; scholarships/grants and tuition waivers (full and partial) also available. Financial award application deadline: 3/1. *Faculty research:* Product development of fruit and vegetables, lipid oxidation in fish and meat, analytical methods development, metabolism of potato glycoalkaloids, seafood quality. *Unit head:* Dr. Denise Skonberg, 207-581-1639. *Application contact:* Scott G. Delcourt, Associate Dean of the Graduate School, 207-581-3291, Fax: 207-581-3232, E-mail: graduate@maine.edu.

University of Manitoba, Faculty of Graduate Studies, Faculty of Agricultural and Food Sciences, Department of Food Science, Winnipeg, MB R3T 2N2, Canada. Offers food and nutritional sciences (PhD); food science (M Sc); foods and nutrition (M Sc). *Degree requirements:* For master's, thesis.

University of Manitoba, Faculty of Graduate Studies, Faculty of Human Ecology, Department of Human Nutritional Sciences, Winnipeg, MB R3T 2N2, Canada. Offers M Sc. *Degree requirements:* For master's, thesis.

University of Maryland, College Park, Academic Affairs, College of Agriculture and Natural Resources, Department of Nutrition and Food Science, Program in Nutrition, College Park, MD 20742. Offers MS, PhD. *Students:* 18 full-time (17 women), 3 part-time (2 women); includes 3 minority (2 African Americans, 1 Asian American or Pacific Islander), 8 international. 44 applicants, 20% accepted, 7 enrolled. In 2009, 1 master's, 3 doctorates awarded. *Degree requirements:* For master's, thesis; for doctorate, comprehensive exam, thesis/dissertation, candidacy exam. *Entrance requirements:* For master's, GRE General Test, minimum GPA of 3.0, 3 letters of recommendation; for doctorate, GRE General Test, minimum GPA of 3.0. Additional exam requirements/recommendations for international students: Required—TOEFL. *Application deadline:* For fall admission, 12/15 for domestic and international students; for spring admission, 6/1 for domestic and international students. Applications are processed on a rolling basis. Application fee: $60. Electronic applications accepted. *Expenses:* Tuition, area resident: Part-time $471 per credit hour. Tuition, state resident: part-time $471 per credit hour. Tuition, nonresident: part-time $1016 per credit hour. Required fees: $337.04 per term. *Financial support:* In 2009–10, 2 fellowships with partial tuition reimbursements (averaging $9,844 per year), 1 research assistantship (averaging $15,800 per year), 10 teaching assistantships with tuition reimbursements (averaging $15,750 per year) were awarded. Financial award applicants required to submit FAFSA. *Faculty research:* Nutrition education, carbohydrates and physical activity. *Unit head:* Lucy Yu, Acting Chair, 301-405-0773, E-mail: lyu5@umd.edu. *Application contact:* Dean of Graduate School, 301-405-0376, Fax: 301-314-9305.

University of Massachusetts Amherst, Graduate School, School of Public Health and Health Sciences, Department of Nutrition, Amherst, MA 01003. Offers nutrition (MPH, MS); public health (PhD). Part-time and evening/weekend programs available. Postbaccalaureate distance learning degree programs offered (no on-campus study). *Faculty:* 11 full-time (7 women). *Students:* 7 full-time (all women), 2 part-time (both women); includes 1 minority (Hispanic American), 2 international. Average age 25. 38 applicants, 39% accepted, 5 enrolled. In 2009, 4 master's awarded. Terminal master's awarded for partial completion of doctoral program. *Degree requirements:* For master's, thesis or alternative; for doctorate, comprehensive exam, thesis/dissertation. *Entrance requirements:* For master's, GRE General Test. Additional exam requirements/recommendations for international students: Required—TOEFL (minimum score 550 paper-based; 213 computer-based; 80 iBT), IELTS (minimum score 6.5). *Application deadline:* For fall admission, 2/1 for domestic and international students; for spring admission, 10/1 for domestic and international students. Applications are processed on a rolling basis. Application fee: $50 ($65 for international students). Electronic applications accepted. *Expenses:* Tuition, state resident: full-time $2640; part-time $110 per credit. Tuition, nonresident: full-time $9936; part-time $414 per credit. Tuition and fees vary according to course load. *Financial support:* In 2009–10, 3 research assistantships with full tuition reimbursements (averaging $10,963 per year), 9 teaching assistantships with full tuition reimbursements (averaging $10,887 per year) were awarded; fellowships, career-related internships or fieldwork, Federal Work-Study, scholarships/grants, traineeships, health care benefits, tuition waivers (full), and unspecified assistantships also available. Support available to part-time students. Financial award application deadline: 2/1. *Unit head:* Dr. Elena T. Carbone, Graduate Program Director, 413-545-0740, Fax: 413-545-1074. *Application contact:* Jean M. Ames, Supervisor of Admissions, 413-545-0722, Fax: 413-577-0010, E-mail: gradadm@grad.umass.edu.

University of Massachusetts Amherst, Graduate School, School of Public Health and Health Sciences, Department of Public Health, Amherst, MA 01003. Offers biostatistics (MS, PhD); community health education (MS); environmental health sciences (MPH, MS); epidemiology (MPH, MS); health policy and management (MPH, MS); nutrition (PhD); public health practice (MPH). *Accreditation:* CEPH (one or more programs are accredited). Part-time and evening/weekend programs available. Postbaccalaureate distance learning degree programs offered (no on-campus study). *Faculty:* 38 full-time (23 women). *Students:* 96 full-time (71 women), 232 part-time (153 women); includes 41 minority (14 African Americans, 17 Asian Americans or Pacific Islanders, 10 Hispanic Americans), 65 international. Average age 36. 316 applicants, 61% accepted, 79 enrolled. In 2009, 91 master's, 5 doctorates awarded. Terminal master's awarded for partial completion of doctoral program. *Degree requirements:* For master's, thesis (for some programs); for doctorate, comprehensive exam, thesis/dissertation. *Entrance requirements:* For master's and doctorate, GRE General Test. Additional exam requirements/recommendations for international students: Required—TOEFL (minimum score 550 paper-based; 213 computer-based; 80 iBT), IELTS (minimum score 6.5). *Application deadline:* For fall admission, 2/1 for domestic and international students. Applications are processed on a rolling basis. Application fee: $40 ($65 for international students). Electronic applications accepted. *Expenses:* Tuition, state resident: full-time $2640; part-time $110 per credit. Tuition, nonresident: full-time $9936; part-time $414 per credit. Tuition and fees vary according to course load. *Financial support:* In 2009–10, 3 fellowships with full tuition reimbursements (averaging $2,791 per year), 32 research assistantships with full tuition reimbursements (averaging $9,196 per year), 24 teaching assistantships with full tuition reimbursements (averaging $5,789 per year) were awarded; career-related internships or fieldwork, Federal Work-Study, scholarships/grants, traineeships, health care benefits, tuition waivers (full), and unspecified assistantships also available. Support available to part-time students. Financial award application deadline: 2/1. *Unit head:* Dr. Paula Stamps, Graduate Program Director, 413-545-2861, Fax: 413-545-0964. *Application contact:* Jean M. Ames, Supervisor of Admissions, 413-545-0722, Fax: 413-577-0010, E-mail: gradadm@grad.umass.edu.

University of Massachusetts Lowell, School of Health and Environment, Department of Clinical Laboratory and Nutritional Sciences, Lowell, MA 01854-2881. Offers clinical laboratory sciences (MS); clinical pathology (Graduate Certificate); nutritional sciences (Graduate Certificate); public health laboratory sciences (Graduate Certificate). *Accreditation:* NAACLS. Part-time programs available. Postbaccalaureate distance learning degree programs offered. *Degree requirements:* For master's, thesis optional. *Entrance requirements:* For master's, GRE General Test, minimum GPA of 3.0, letters of recommendation. *Faculty research:* Cardiovascular disease, lipoprotein metabolism, micronutrient evaluation, alcohol metabolism, mycobacterial drug resistance.

University of Medicine and Dentistry of New Jersey, School of Health Related Professions, Department of Interdisciplinary Studies, Program in Health Sciences, Newark, NJ 07107-1709. Offers cardiopulmonary sciences (PhD); clinical laboratory sciences (PhD); health sciences (MS); interdisciplinary studies (PhD); nutrition (PhD); physical therapy/movement science (PhD). *Degree requirements:* For doctorate, thesis/dissertation. *Entrance requirements:* For doctorate, interview, writing sample. Additional exam requirements/recommendations for international students: Required—TOEFL. Electronic applications accepted.

University of Medicine and Dentistry of New Jersey, School of Health Related Professions, Department of Nutritional Sciences, Dietetic Internship Program, Newark, NJ 07107-1709. Offers Certificate. *Entrance requirements:* For degree, bachelor's degree in dietetics, nutrition, or related field; interview; minimum GPA of 2.5. Additional exam requirements/recommendations for international students: Required—TOEFL. Electronic applications accepted.

University of Medicine and Dentistry of New Jersey, School of Health Related Professions, Department of Nutritional Sciences, Program in Clinical Nutrition, Newark, NJ 07107-1709. Offers MS, DCN. *Entrance requirements:* For master's, minimum GPA of 3.0, proof of registered dietician status. Additional exam requirements/recommendations for international students: Required—TOEFL. Electronic applications accepted.

University of Memphis, Graduate School, College of Education, Department of Health and Sport Sciences, Memphis, TN 38152. Offers clinical nutrition (MS); exercise and sport science (MS); health promotion (MS); physical education teacher education (MS), including teacher education; sport and leisure commerce (MS). Part-time and evening/weekend programs available. *Faculty:* 18 full-time (9 women), 3 part-time/adjunct (1 woman). *Students:* 64 full-time (35 women), 36 part-time (23 women); includes 17 African Americans, 1 Asian American or Pacific Islander, 1 Hispanic American, 4 international. Average age 27. 99 applicants, 72% accepted, 50 enrolled. In 2009, 35 master's awarded. *Degree requirements:* For master's, comprehensive exam, thesis. *Entrance requirements:* For master's, GRE General Test or GMAT (sport and leisure commerce). *Application deadline:* For fall admission, 5/1 priority date for domestic students; for spring admission, 11/1 for domestic students. Applications are processed on a rolling basis. Application fee: $35 ($60 for international students). *Expenses:* Tuition, state resident: full-time $6246; part-time $347 per credit hour. Tuition, nonresident: full-time $15,894; part-time $883 per credit hour. Required fees: $1160. Full-time tuition and fees vary according to course load, degree level and program. *Financial support:* In 2009–10, 59 students received support; research assistantships with full tuition reimbursements available, teaching assistantships with full tuition reimbursements available, career-related internships or fieldwork, Federal Work-Study, scholarships/grants, tuition waivers (partial), and unspecified assistantships available. Financial award application deadline: 2/15; financial award applicants required to submit FAFSA. *Faculty research:* Sport marketing and consumer analysis, health psychology, smoking cessation, psychosocial aspects of cardiovascular disease, global health promotion. *Unit head:* Linda H. Clemens, Interim Chair, 901-678-2324, Fax: 901-678-3591, E-mail: lhclemns@memphis.edu. *Application contact:* Dr. Kenneth Ward, Graduate Studies Coordinator, 901-678-1714, E-mail: kdward@memphis.edu.

University of Michigan, School of Public Health, Department of Environmental Health Sciences, Ann Arbor, MI 48109. Offers environmental health sciences (MS, PhD); environmental quality and health (MPH); human nutrition (MPH); industrial hygiene (MPH, MS); nutritional sciences (MS); occupational and environmental epidemiology (MPH); toxicology (MPH, MS, PhD). *Accreditation:* CEPH (one or more programs are accredited). Part-time programs available. Terminal master's awarded for partial completion of doctoral program. *Degree requirements:* For master's, thesis (for some programs); for doctorate, thesis/dissertation, qualifying exam, oral defense of dissertation, preliminary exam. *Entrance requirements:* For master's and doctorate, GRE General Test and/or MCAT. Additional exam requirements/recommendations for international students: Required—TOEFL (minimum score 560 paper-based; 220 computer-based; 100 iBT). Electronic applications accepted. *Expenses:* Tuition, state resident: full-time $17,286; part-time $1099 per credit hour. Tuition, nonresident: full-time $34,944; part-time $2080 per credit hour. Required fees: $95 per semester. Tuition and fees vary according to course load, degree level and program. *Faculty research:* Toxicology; occupational hygiene; nutrition; environmental exposure sciences; environmental epidemiology.

University of Minnesota, Twin Cities Campus, Graduate School, College of Food, Agricultural and Natural Resource Sciences, Program in Nutrition, Minneapolis, MN 55455-0213. Offers MS, PhD. Part-time programs available. *Faculty:* 38 full-time (21 women), 11 part-time/adjunct (6 women). *Students:* 41 full-time (34 women), 18 part-time (15 women); includes 12 minority (9 Asian Americans or Pacific Islanders, 3 Hispanic Americans). Average age 31. 51 applicants, 20% accepted, 8 enrolled. In 2009, 11 master's, 9 doctorates awarded. Terminal master's awarded for partial completion of doctoral program. *Degree requirements:* For master's, comprehensive exam, thesis (for some programs); for doctorate, comprehensive exam, thesis/dissertation. *Entrance requirements:* For master's, GRE General Test, previous course work in general chemistry, organic chemistry, physiology, biology, biochemistry, statistics; minimum GPA of 3.0 (preferred); for doctorate, GRE General Test, previous course work in general chemistry, organic chemistry, calculus, biology, physics, physiology, biochemistry, statistics; minimum GPA of 3.0 (preferred). Additional exam requirements/recommendations for international students: Required—TOEFL (minimum score 550 paper-based; 213 computer-based; 79 iBT). *Application deadline:* For fall admission, 12/15 for domestic and international students; for spring admission, 10/15 for domestic and international students. Applications are processed on a rolling basis. Application fee: $75 ($95 for international students). Electronic applications accepted. *Financial support:* In 2009–10, 36 students received support, including 2 fellowships with full tuition reimbursements available (averaging $20,500 per year), 21 research assistant-

ships with partial tuition reimbursements available (averaging $17,500 per year), 13 teaching assistantships with partial tuition reimbursements available (averaging $17,500 per year); career-related internships or fieldwork, Federal Work-Study, institutionally sponsored loans, scholarships/grants, traineeships, health care benefits, and unspecified assistantships also available. Support available to part-time students. *Faculty research:* Diet and chronic disease: from basic biological and molecular biology approaches to a public health/intervention/ epidemiology perspective. Total annual research expenditures: $1.8 million. *Unit head:* Dr. Mindy S. Kurzer, Director of Graduate Studies, 612-624-9789, Fax: 612-625-5272, E-mail: mkurzer@umn.edu. *Application contact:* Nancy L. Toedt, Program Coordinator, 612-624-6753, Fax: 612-625-5272, E-mail: sviker@umn.edu.

University of Minnesota, Twin Cities Campus, School of Public Health, Major in Public Health Nutrition, Minneapolis, MN 55455-0213. Offers MPH. Part-time programs available. *Degree requirements:* For master's, fieldwork, project. *Entrance requirements:* For master's, GRE General Test. Additional exam requirements/recommendations for international students: Required—TOEFL. Electronic applications accepted. *Expenses:* Contact institution. *Faculty research:* Nutrition and pregnancy outcomes, nutrition and women's health, child growth and nutrition, child and adolescent nutrition and eating behaviors, obesity and eating disorder prevention.

University of Missouri, Graduate School, College of Agriculture, Food and Natural Resources, Department of Food and Hospitality Systems, Columbia, MO 65211. Offers food science (MS, PhD); foods and food systems management (MS); human nutrition (MS). *Faculty:* 17 full-time (4 women), 2 part-time/adjunct (0 women). *Students:* 18 full-time (11 women), 13 part-time (6 women), 15 international. Average age 27. 44 applicants, 36% accepted, 9 enrolled. In 2009, 1 master's awarded. Terminal master's awarded for partial completion of doctoral program. *Degree requirements:* For doctorate, comprehensive exam, thesis/dissertation. *Entrance requirements:* For master's, GRE General Test (minimum score: Verbal and Quantitative 1000 with neither section below 400, Analytical 3.5), minimum GPA of 3.0; BS in food science from accredited university; for doctorate, GRE General Test (minimum score: Verbal and Quantitative 1000 with neither section below 400, Analytical 3.5), minimum GPA of 3.0; BS and MS in food science from accredited university. Additional exam requirements/recommendations for international students: Required—TOEFL (minimum score 550 paper-based; 79 iBT). *Application deadline:* For fall admission, 4/1 priority date for domestic students; for winter admission, 10/1 priority date for domestic students. Applications are processed on a rolling basis. Application fee: $45 ($60 for international students). Electronic applications accepted. *Financial support:* Research assistantships with tuition reimbursements, teaching assistantships with tuition reimbursements, institutionally sponsored loans available. *Unit head:* Dr. Jinglu Tan, Department Chair, E-mail: tanj@missouri.edu. *Application contact:* JoAnn Lewis, 573-882-4113, E-mail: lewisj@missouri.edu.

University of Missouri, Graduate School, College of Human Environmental Science, Department of Nutritional Sciences, Columbia, MO 65211. Offers exercise physiology (MA, PhD); nutritional sciences (MS, PhD). *Degree requirements:* For doctorate, thesis/dissertation. *Entrance requirements:* For master's and doctorate, GRE General Test, minimum GPA of 3.0. Additional exam requirements/recommendations for international students: Required—TOEFL (minimum score 500 paper-based; 173 computer-based; 61 iBT).

University of Nebraska–Lincoln, Graduate College, College of Agricultural Sciences and Natural Resources, Department of Agricultural Leadership, Education and Communication, Lincoln, NE 68588. Offers distance education specialization (MS); leadership development (MS); leadership education (MS); nutrition outreach education specialization (MS); teaching and extension education specialization (MS). *Degree requirements:* For master's, thesis optional. *Entrance requirements:* For master's, resume. Additional exam requirements/recommendations for international students: Required—TOEFL (minimum score 550 paper-based; 213 computer-based). Electronic applications accepted. *Faculty research:* Teaching and instruction, extension education, leadership and human resource development, international agricultural education.

University of Nebraska–Lincoln, Graduate College, College of Agricultural Sciences and Natural Resources, Interdepartmental Area of Nutrition, Lincoln, NE 68588. Offers MS, PhD. *Degree requirements:* For master's, thesis optional; for doctorate, comprehensive exam, thesis/dissertation. *Entrance requirements:* For master's and doctorate, GRE General Test. Additional exam requirements/recommendations for international students: Required—TOEFL (minimum score 550 paper-based; 213 computer-based). Electronic applications accepted. *Faculty research:* Human nutrition and metabolism, animal nutrition and metabolism, biochemistry, community and clinical nutrition.

University of Nebraska–Lincoln, Graduate College, College of Education and Human Sciences, Department of Nutrition and Health Sciences, Lincoln, NE 68588. Offers community nutrition and health promotion (MS); nutrition (MS, PhD); nutrition and exercise (MS); nutrition and health sciences (MS, PhD). *Degree requirements:* For master's, thesis optional. *Entrance requirements:* For master's, GRE General Test. Additional exam requirements/recommendations for international students: Required—TOEFL (minimum score 550 paper-based; 213 computer-based). Electronic applications accepted. *Faculty research:* Foods/food service administration, community nutrition science, diet-health relationships.

University of Nebraska Medical Center, School of Allied Health Professions and College of Medicine, UNMC Dietetic Internship Program (Medical Nutrition Education Division), Omaha, NE 68198. Offers Certificate. *Entrance requirements:* Additional exam requirements/recommendations for international students: Required—TOEFL. *Faculty research:* Nutrition intervention outcomes.

University of Nevada, Reno, Graduate School, College of Agriculture, Biotechnology and Natural Resources, Department of Nutrition, Reno, NV 89557. Offers MS. *Degree requirements:* For master's, thesis optional. *Entrance requirements:* For master's, GRE, minimum GPA of 2.75. Additional exam requirements/recommendations for international students: Required—TOEFL (minimum score 500 paper-based; 173 computer-based; 61 iBT), IELTS (minimum score 6). Electronic applications accepted. *Faculty research:* Nutritional education, food technology, therapeutic human nutrition, human nutritional requirements, diet and disease.

University of New Hampshire, Graduate School, College of Life Sciences and Agriculture, Department of Molecular, Cellular and Biomedical Sciences, Program in Animal and Nutritional Sciences, Durham, NH 03824. Offers PhD. Part-time programs available. *Faculty:* 23 full-time. *Students:* 5 full-time (2 women), 1 (woman) part-time. Average age 37. 4 applicants, 25% accepted, 1 enrolled. *Entrance requirements:* For doctorate, GRE. Additional exam requirements/recommendations for international students: Required—TOEFL (minimum score 550 paper-based; 213 computer-based; 80 iBT). *Application deadline:* For fall admission, 6/1 priority date for domestic students, 4/1 priority date for international students; for spring admission, 12/1 for domestic students. Application fee: $65. Electronic applications accepted. *Expenses:* Tuition, state resident: full-time $10,380; part-time $577 per credit hour. Tuition, nonresident: full-time $24,350; part-time $1002 per credit hour. Required fees: $1550; $387.50 per semester. Tuition and fees vary according to course load and program. *Financial support:* In 2009–10, 4 students received support, including 1 fellowship, 1 research assistantship, 2 teaching assistantships; scholarships/grants, traineeships, and unspecified assistantships also available. Support available to part-time students. *Unit head:* Dr. Rick Cote, Chairperson, 603-862-2458. *Application contact:* Flora Joyal, Administrative Assistant, 603-862-4095, E-mail: ansc.grad.program.info@unh.edu.

University of New Hampshire, Graduate School, College of Life Sciences and Agriculture, Department of Molecular, Cellular and Biomedical Sciences, Program in Nutritional Sciences, Durham, NH 03824. Offers MS. Part-time programs available. *Faculty:* 23 full-time. *Students:* 2 full-time (both women), 5 part-time (4 women). Average age 33. 4 applicants, 50% accepted, 1 enrolled. In 2009, 6 master's awarded. *Degree requirements:* For master's, thesis. *Entrance requirements:* Additional exam requirements/recommendations for international students:

Nutrition

University of New Hampshire (continued)

Required—TOEFL (minimum score 550 paper-based; 213 computer-based; 80 iBT). *Application deadline:* For fall admission, 4/1 priority date for domestic students, 4/1 for international students; for spring admission, 12/1 for domestic students. Applications are processed on a rolling basis. Application fee: $65. Electronic applications accepted. *Expenses:* Tuition, state resident: full-time $10,380; part-time $577 per credit hour. Tuition, nonresident: full-time $24,350; part-time $1002 per credit hour. Required fees: $1550; $387.50 per semester. Tuition and fees vary according to course load and program. *Financial support:* In 2009–10, 5 students received support, including 5 teaching assistantships; fellowships, research assistantships, career-related internships or fieldwork, Federal Work-Study, and scholarships/grants also available. Support available to part-time students. Financial award application deadline: 2/15. *Unit head:* Dr. Rick Cote, Chair, 603-862-2458. *Application contact:* Flora Joyal, Administrative Assistant, 603-862-4095.

University of New Haven, Graduate School, College of Arts and Sciences, Program in Human Nutrition, West Haven, CT 06516-1916. Offers MS. *Faculty:* 1 (woman) full-time, 3 part-time/adjunct (2 women). *Students:* 2 full-time (both women), 18 part-time (16 women); includes 1 minority (Asian American or Pacific Islander), 1 international. Average age 30. 16 applicants, 94% accepted, 9 enrolled. In 2009, 8 master's awarded. *Entrance requirements:* Additional exam requirements/recommendations for international students: Required—TOEFL (minimum score 520 paper-based; 190 computer-based; 70 iBT); Recommended—IELTS (minimum score 5.5). *Application deadline:* For fall admission, 5/31 for international students; for winter admission, 10/15 for international students; for spring admission, 1/15 for international students. Applications are processed on a rolling basis. Application fee: $50. Electronic applications accepted. *Expenses:* Tuition: Part-time $700 per credit. Required fees: $45 per term. One-time fee: $390 part-time. *Financial support:* Research assistantships with partial tuition reimbursements, teaching assistantships with partial tuition reimbursements, career-related internships or fieldwork, Federal Work-Study, scholarships/grants, tuition waivers, and unspecified assistantships available. Support available to part-time students. Financial award applicants required to submit FAFSA. *Unit head:* Dr. Rosa A. Mo, Director, 203-932-7352. *Application contact:* Eloise Gormley, Director of Graduate Admissions, 203-932-7449, Fax: 203-932-7137, E-mail: gradinfo@newhaven.edu.

University of New Mexico, Graduate School, College of Education, Department of Individual, Family and Community Education, Program in Nutrition, Albuquerque, NM 87131-2039. Offers MS. Part-time programs available. *Faculty:* 21 full-time (14 women), 11 part-time/adjunct (9 women). *Students:* 12 full-time (11 women), 9 part-time (8 women); includes 9 minority (2 American Indian/Alaska Native, 1 Asian American or Pacific Islander, 6 Hispanic Americans), 1 international. Average age 31. 13 applicants, 69% accepted, 9 enrolled. In 2009, 9 master's awarded. *Degree requirements:* For master's, comprehensive exam or thesis. *Entrance requirements:* For master's, GRE. *Application deadline:* For fall admission, 2/1 priority date for domestic students; for spring admission, 11/1 priority date for domestic students. Application fee: $50. Electronic applications accepted. *Expenses:* Tuition, state resident: full-time $2099; part-time $233.20 per credit hour. Tuition, nonresident: full-time $6650. Required fees: $25 per semester. Tuition and fees vary according to course load, program and reciprocity agreements. *Financial support:* In 2009–10, 9 students received support, including 4 teaching assistantships with full and partial tuition reimbursements available (averaging $6,111 per year). Financial award application deadline: 3/1; financial award applicants required to submit FAFSA. *Faculty research:* Nutritional needs of children, obesity prevention, phytochemicals, international nutrition. *Unit head:* Dr. Carole Conn, Graduate Coordinator, 505-277-8185, Fax: 505-277-8361, E-mail: cconn@unm.edu. *Application contact:* Cynthia Salas, Program Office, 505-277-4535, Fax: 505-277-8361, E-mail: casalas@unm.edu.

The University of North Carolina at Chapel Hill, Graduate School, School of Public Health, Department of Nutrition, Chapel Hill, NC 27599. Offers nutrition (MPH, Dr PH, PhD); nutritional biochemistry (MS); professional practice program (MPH). *Accreditation:* ADtA. *Degree requirements:* For master's, comprehensive exam, thesis, major paper; for doctorate, comprehensive exam, thesis/dissertation. *Entrance requirements:* For master's and doctorate, GRE General Test, minimum GPA of 3.0. Additional exam requirements/recommendations for international students: Required—TOEFL. Electronic applications accepted. *Faculty research:* Nutrition policy, management and leadership development, lipid and carbohydrate metabolism, dietary trends and determinants, transmembrane signal transduction and carcinogenesis, maternal and child nutrition.

The University of North Carolina at Greensboro, Graduate School, School of Human Environmental Sciences, Department of Nutrition, Greensboro, NC 27412-5001. Offers MS, PhD. *Degree requirements:* For master's, thesis; for doctorate, thesis/dissertation. *Entrance requirements:* For master's and doctorate, GRE General Test. Additional exam requirements/recommendations for international students: Required—TOEFL. Electronic applications accepted.

University of North Florida, Brooks College of Health, Department of Public Health, Jacksonville, FL 32224. Offers community health (MPH); geriatric management (MSH); health administration (MHA); health behavior research and evaluation (Certificate); nutrition (MSH); rehabilitation counseling (MS). *Accreditation:* CEPH. Part-time and evening/weekend programs available. *Faculty:* 23 full-time (17 women). *Students:* 118 full-time (91 women), 82 part-time (61 women); includes 42 minority (23 African Americans, 8 Asian Americans or Pacific Islanders, 11 Hispanic Americans), 9 international. Average age 31. 192 applicants, 26% accepted, 23 enrolled. In 2009, 69 master's awarded. *Degree requirements:* For master's, thesis optional. *Entrance requirements:* For master's, GRE General Test (MSH, MS, MPH); GMAT or GRE General Test (MHA), minimum GPA of 3.0 in last 60 hours. Additional exam requirements/recommendations for international students: Required—TOEFL (minimum score 500 paper-based; 173 computer-based). *Application deadline:* For fall admission, 7/1 priority date for domestic students, 5/1 for international students; for spring admission, 11/1 priority date for domestic students, 10/1 for international students. Applications are processed on a rolling basis. Application fee: $30. Electronic applications accepted. *Expenses:* Tuition, state resident: full-time $6649.20; part-time $277.05 per credit hour. Tuition, nonresident: full-time $22,970; part-time $957.08 per credit hour. Required fees: $985; $41.03 per credit hour. *Financial support:* In 2009–10, 99 students received support, including 1 teaching assistantship (averaging $1,004 per year); research assistantships, career-related internships or fieldwork, Federal Work-Study, scholarships/grants, and tuition waivers (partial) also available. Support available to part-time students. Financial award application deadline: 4/1; financial award applicants required to submit FAFSA. *Faculty research:* Dietary supplements; alcohol, tobacco, and other drug use prevention; turnover among health professionals; aging; psychosocial aspects of disabilities. Total annual research expenditures: $335,106. *Unit head:* Dr. JoAnn Nolin, Chair, 904-620-2840, Fax: 904-620-2848, E-mail: jnolin@unf.edu. *Application contact:* Heather Kenney, Director of Advising, 904-620-2810, Fax: 904-620-1030, E-mail: heather.kenney@unf.edu.

University of Oklahoma Health Sciences Center, Graduate College, College of Allied Health, Department of Nutritional Sciences, Oklahoma City, OK 73190. Offers MS. *Accreditation:* ADtA. *Faculty:* 5 full-time (3 women). *Students:* 35 full-time (31 women), 21 part-time (20 women); includes 15 minority (1 African American, 8 American Indian/Alaska Native, 4 Asian Americans or Pacific Islanders, 2 Hispanic Americans). Average age 26. 46 applicants, 78% accepted, 29 enrolled. In 2009, 18 master's awarded. *Degree requirements:* For master's, comprehensive exam, thesis optional. *Entrance requirements:* For master's, GRE General Test, interview, 3 letters of reference. Additional exam requirements/recommendations for international students: Required—TOEFL (minimum score 550 paper-based). *Application deadline:* For fall admission, 7/1 for domestic students; for winter admission, 5/1 for domestic students; for spring admission, 12/1 for domestic students. Application fee: $50. *Expenses:* Tuition, state resident: full-time $3120; part-time $156 per credit hour. Tuition, nonresident: full-time $11,314; part-time $409.70 per credit hour. Required fees: $1471; $51.20 per credit hour. $223.25 per term. *Unit head:* Dr. Karen Funderburg, Chair, 405-271-2113, E-mail: karen-funderburg@ouhsc.edu. *Application contact:* Dr. Jan Womack, Associate Dean, Academic and Student Affairs, 405-271-6588, Fax: 405-271-3120, E-mail: jan-womack@ouhsc.edu.

University of Pittsburgh, School of Health and Rehabilitation Sciences, Coordinated Master in Dietetics Program, Pittsburgh, PA 15260. Offers MS. *Accreditation:* ADtA. Part-time and evening/weekend programs available. *Students:* 30 full-time (28 women), 1 (woman) part-time; includes 2 minority (1 African American, 1 Asian American or Pacific Islander), 3 international. Average age 27. 37 applicants, 51% accepted, 17 enrolled. In 2009, 11 master's awarded. *Entrance requirements:* Additional exam requirements/recommendations for international students: Required—TOEFL (minimum score 550 paper-based; 213 computer-based; 80 iBT); IELTS (minimum score 6.5). *Application deadline:* For fall admission, 3/15 for domestic students, 1/31 for international students. Application fee: $50. Electronic applications accepted. *Expenses:* Contact institution. *Unit head:* Dr. Scott Lephart, Department Chair and Associate Professor, 412-383-6530, Fax: 412-383-6527, E-mail: lephart@pitt.edu. *Application contact:* Shameem Gangjee, Director of Admissions, 412-383-6558, Fax: 412-383-6535, E-mail: admissions@shrs.pitt.edu.

University of Pittsburgh, School of Health and Rehabilitation Sciences, Master's Programs in Health and Rehabilitation Sciences, Pittsburgh, PA 15260. Offers health and rehabilitation sciences (MS), including clinical dietetics and nutrition, health care supervision and management, health information systems, occupational therapy, physical therapy, rehabilitation counseling, rehabilitation science and technology, sports medicine, wellness and human performance. *Accreditation:* APTA. Part-time and evening/weekend programs available. *Faculty:* 30 full-time (14 women), 4 part-time/adjunct (3 women). *Students:* 81 full-time (47 women), 54 part-time (27 women); includes 10 minority (6 African Americans, 4 Asian Americans or Pacific Islanders), 44 international. Average age 29. 326 applicants, 65% accepted, 130 enrolled. In 2009, 93 master's awarded. *Degree requirements:* For master's, comprehensive exam (for some programs), thesis optional. *Entrance requirements:* For master's, minimum GPA of 3.0. Additional exam requirements/recommendations for international students: Required—TOEFL, IELTS. *Application deadline:* For fall admission, 1/31 for international students; for spring admission, 7/31 for international students. Applications are processed on a rolling basis. Application fee: $50. Electronic applications accepted. *Expenses:* Contact institution. *Financial support:* In 2009–10, 3 research assistantships with full tuition reimbursements (averaging $18,450 per year) were awarded; teaching assistantships, Federal Work-Study, institutionally sponsored loans, traineeships, and unspecified assistantships also available. Financial award applicants required to submit FAFSA. *Faculty research:* Assistive technology, seating and wheeled mobility, cellular neurophysiology, low back syndrome, augmentative communication. Total annual research expenditures: $6.5 million. *Unit head:* Dr. Clifford E. Brubaker, Dean, 412-383-6560, Fax: 412-383-6535, E-mail: cliffb@pitt.edu. *Application contact:* Shameem Gangjee, Director of Admissions, 412-383-6558, Fax: 412-383-6535, E-mail: admissions@shrs.pitt.edu.

University of Puerto Rico, Medical Sciences Campus, Graduate School of Public Health, Program in Nutrition, San Juan, PR 00936-5067. Offers MS. Part-time programs available. *Degree requirements:* For master's, thesis. *Entrance requirements:* For master's, GRE, previous course work in algebra, biochemistry, biology, chemistry, and social sciences.

University of Puerto Rico, Medical Sciences Campus, School of Health Professions, Program in Dietetics Internship, San Juan, PR 00936-5067. Offers Certificate. *Degree requirements:* For Certificate, one foreign language, clinical practice. *Entrance requirements:* For degree, minimum GPA of 2.5, interview, participation in the computer matching process by the American Dietetic Association.

University of Puerto Rico, Medical Sciences Campus, School of Medicine, Division of Graduate Studies, Department of Biochemistry, San Juan, PR 00936-5067. Offers MS, PhD. *Degree requirements:* For master's, thesis; for doctorate, comprehensive exam, thesis/dissertation. *Entrance requirements:* For master's and doctorate, GRE General Test, GRE Subject Test, interview, minimum GPA of 3.0. Electronic applications accepted. *Faculty research:* Genetics, cell and molecular biology, cancer biology, protein structure/function, glycosilation of proteins.

University of Puerto Rico, Río Piedras, College of Education, Program in Family Ecology and Nutrition, San Juan, PR 00931-3300. Offers M Ed. Part-time programs available. *Degree requirements:* For master's, thesis. *Entrance requirements:* For master's, PAEG or GRE, minimum GPA of 3.0, letter of recommendation.

University of Rhode Island, Graduate School, College of the Environment and Life Sciences, Department of Nutrition and Food Sciences, Kingston, RI 02881. Offers food science (MS, PhD); nutrition (MS, PhD). Part-time programs available. *Faculty:* 8 full-time (5 women), 1 (woman) part-time/adjunct. *Students:* 15 full-time (14 women), 13 part-time (12 women); includes 2 minority (1 Asian American or Pacific Islander, 1 Hispanic American), 1 international. In 2009, 5 master's, 2 doctorates awarded. *Degree requirements:* For master's, comprehensive exam (for some programs), thesis optional; for doctorate, thesis/dissertation. *Entrance requirements:* For master's and doctorate, GRE, 2 letters of recommendation. Additional exam requirements/recommendations for international students: Required—TOEFL (minimum score 550 paper-based; 213 computer-based). *Application deadline:* For fall admission, 7/15 for domestic students, 2/1 for international students; for spring admission, 11/15 for domestic students, 7/15 for international students. Application fee: $65. Electronic applications accepted. *Expenses:* Tuition, state resident: full-time $8828; part-time $490 per credit hour. Tuition, nonresident: full-time $22,100; part-time $1228 per credit hour. Required fees: $1118; $57 per semester. Tuition and fees vary according to program. *Financial support:* In 2009–10, 6 research assistantships with full and partial tuition reimbursements (averaging $12,736 per year), 8 teaching assistantships with full and partial tuition reimbursements (averaging $12,350 per year) were awarded. Financial award application deadline: 7/15; financial award applicants required to submit FAFSA. *Faculty research:* Food safety and quality, marine resource utilization, nutrition in underserved populations, eating behavior, lipid metabolism. Total annual research expenditures: $1.5 million. *Unit head:* Dr. Catherine English, Chair, 401-874-5869, Fax: 401-874-5974, E-mail: cathy@uri.edu. *Application contact:* Dr. Linda T. Green, Director of Graduate Studies, 401-874-2905, Fax: 401-874-4561, E-mail: lgreen@uri.edu.

University of Southern Mississippi, Graduate School, College of Health, Department of Community Health Sciences, Hattiesburg, MS 39406-0001. Offers epidemiology and biostatistics (MPH); health education (MPH); health policy/administration (MPH); occupational/environmental health (MPH); public health nutrition (MPH). *Accreditation:* CEPH. Part-time and evening/weekend programs available. *Faculty:* 8 full-time (4 women), 1 part-time/adjunct (0 women). *Students:* 92 full-time (59 women), 20 part-time (14 women); includes 40 minority (36 African Americans, 1 Asian American or Pacific Islander, 3 Hispanic Americans), 13 international. Average age 32. 90 applicants, 73% accepted, 47 enrolled. In 2009, 4 master's awarded. *Degree requirements:* For master's, comprehensive exam, thesis (for some programs). *Entrance requirements:* For master's, GRE General Test, minimum GPA of 2.75 in last 60 hours. Additional exam requirements/recommendations for international students: Required—TOEFL. *Application deadline:* For fall admission, 3/1 for domestic and international students. Applications are processed on a rolling basis. Application fee: $35. *Expenses:* Tuition, state resident: full-time $5096; part-time $284 per hour. Tuition, nonresident: full-time $13,052; part-time $726 per hour. Required fees: $402. Tuition and fees vary according to course level and course load. *Financial support:* In 2009–10, 5 research assistantships with full tuition reimbursements (averaging $7,000 per year), 1 teaching assistantship with full tuition reimbursement (averaging $8,263 per year) were awarded; career-related internships or fieldwork and Federal Work-Study also available. Financial award application deadline: 3/15; financial award applicants required to submit FAFSA. *Faculty research:* Rural health care delivery, school health, nutrition of pregnant teens, risk factor reduction, sexually transmitted diseases. *Unit head:* Dr. James McGuire, Chair, 601-266-5437, Fax: 601-266-5043. *Application contact:* Shonna Breland, Manager of Graduate Admissions, 601-266-6563, Fax: 601-266-5138.

University of Southern Mississippi, Graduate School, College of Health, Department of Nutrition and Food Systems, Hattiesburg, MS 39406-0001. Offers MS, PhD. *Faculty:* 6 full-time (5 women). *Students:* 14 full-time (all women), 31 part-time (29 women); includes 9 minority (8 African Americans, 1 Asian American or Pacific Islander). Average age 30. 23 applicants, 35% accepted, 3 enrolled. In 2009, 15 master's awarded. *Degree requirements:* For master's, comprehensive exam, thesis (for some programs); for doctorate, comprehensive exam, thesis/dissertation. *Application deadline:* For fall admission, 3/1 for domestic and international students. Application fee: $35. *Expenses:* Tuition, state resident: full-time $5096; part-time $284 per hour. Tuition, nonresident: full-time $13,052; part-time $726 per hour. Required fees: $402. Tuition and fees vary according to course level and course load. *Financial support:* In 2009–10, 2 research assistantships with full tuition reimbursements (averaging $12,069 per year), 6 teaching assistantships with full tuition reimbursements (averaging $7,676 per year) were awarded. Financial award applicants required to submit FAFSA. *Unit head:* Dr. Kathleen Yadrick, Chair, 601-266-5377, Fax: 601-266-6343. *Application contact:* Belinda Brock, Manager of Graduate Admissions, 601-266-5377, Fax: 601-266-5138.

The University of Tennessee, Graduate School, College of Education, Health and Human Sciences, Department of Nutrition, Knoxville, TN 37996. Offers nutrition (MS), including nutrition science, public health nutrition; MS/MPH. Part-time programs available. *Degree requirements:* For master's, thesis or alternative. *Entrance requirements:* For master's, GRE General Test, minimum GPA of 2.7. Additional exam requirements/recommendations for international students: Required—TOEFL. Electronic applications accepted. *Expenses:* Tuition, state resident: full-time $6826; part-time $380 per semester hour. Tuition, nonresident: full-time $21,844; part-time $1147 per semester hour. Tuition and fees vary according to program.

The University of Tennessee at Martin, Graduate Programs, College of Agriculture and Applied Sciences, Department of Family and Consumer Sciences, Martin, TN 38238-1000. Offers dietetics (MSFCS); general family and consumer sciences (MSFCS). Part-time programs available. Postbaccalaureate distance learning degree programs offered (minimal on-campus study). *Faculty:* 6. *Students:* 47 (43 women). 5,430 applicants, 1% accepted, 23 enrolled. In 2009, 10 master's awarded. *Degree requirements:* For master's, comprehensive exam, thesis optional. *Entrance requirements:* For master's, GRE General Test, minimum GPA of 2.5. Additional exam requirements/recommendations for international students: Required—TOEFL (minimum score 525 paper-based; 197 computer-based; 71 iBT). *Application deadline:* For fall admission, 8/1 priority date for domestic students, 6/15 priority date for international students; for spring admission, 12/15 priority date for domestic students, 12/1 priority date for international students. Applications are processed on a rolling basis. Application fee: $30 ($130 for international students). Electronic applications accepted. *Expenses:* Tuition, state resident: full-time $6660; part-time $372 per hour. Tuition, nonresident: full-time $18,000; part-time $1005 per hour. *Financial support:* In 2009–10, 3 students received support, including 3 research assistantships with full tuition reimbursements available (averaging $7,234 per year); scholarships/grants and unspecified assistantships also available. Support available to part-time students. Financial award application deadline: 2/15; financial award applicants required to submit FAFSA. *Faculty research:* Children with developmental disabilities, regional food product development and marketing, parent education. *Unit head:* Dr. Lisa LeBleu, Coordinator, 731-881-7116, Fax: 731-881-7106, E-mail: llebleu@utm.edu. *Application contact:* Linda S. Arant, Student Services Specialist, 731-881-7012, Fax: 731-881-7499, E-mail: larant@utm.edu.

The University of Texas at Austin, Graduate School, College of Natural Sciences, School of Human Ecology, Program in Nutritional Sciences, Austin, TX 78712-1111. Offers nutrition (MA); nutritional sciences (PhD). *Degree requirements:* For master's, thesis; for doctorate, thesis/dissertation. *Entrance requirements:* For master's and doctorate, GRE General Test. Additional exam requirements/recommendations for international students: Required—TOEFL. Electronic applications accepted. *Faculty research:* Nutritional biochemistry, nutrient health assessment, obesity, nutrition education, molecular/cellular aspects of nutrient functions.

University of the District of Columbia, College of Arts and Sciences, Department of Biological and Environmental Sciences, Program in Nutrition and Dietetics, Washington, DC 20008-1175. Offers MS. *Degree requirements:* For master's, thesis. *Entrance requirements:* For master's, GRE, 3 letters of recommendation, personal interview. *Application deadline:* For fall admission, 4/15 for domestic students. *Expenses:* Tuition, state resident: full-time $7580. Tuition, nonresident: full-time $14,580. Required fees: $620. *Unit head:* Dr. Freddie Dixon, Chair, 202-274-7401. *Application contact:* Ann Marie Waterman, Associate Vice President of Admission, Recruitment and Financial Aid, 202-274-6069.

University of the Incarnate Word, School of Graduate Studies and Research, H-E-B School of Business and Administration, Programs in Administration, San Antonio, TX 78209-6397. Offers adult education (MAA); applied administration (MAA); communication arts (MAA); healthcare administration (MAA); instructional technology (MAA); international business (Certificate); nutrition (MAA); organizational development (MAA, Certificate); project management (Certificate); sports management (MAA). Part-time and evening/weekend programs available. Postbaccalaureate distance learning degree programs offered (no on-campus study). *Students:* 30 full-time (17 women), 163 part-time (114 women); includes 128 minority (18 African Americans, 3 Asian Americans or Pacific Islanders, 107 Hispanic Americans), 8 international. Average age 35. In 2009, 68 degrees awarded. *Degree requirements:* For master's, capstone. *Entrance requirements:* For master's, GRE, GMAT, undergraduate degree, minimum GPA of 2.5. Additional exam requirements/recommendations for international students: Required—TOEFL (minimum score 560 paper-based; 220 computer-based; 83 iBT). *Application deadline:* Applications are processed on a rolling basis. Application fee: $20. Electronic applications accepted. *Expenses:* Tuition: Full-time $12,150; part-time $675 per credit hour. Required fees: $83 per credit hour. *Financial support:* Federal Work-Study and scholarships/grants available. Financial award applicants required to submit FAFSA. *Unit head:* Dr. Daniel Dominguez, MAA Director, 210-829-3180, Fax: 210-805-3564, E-mail: domingue@uiwtx.edu. *Application contact:* Andrea Cyterski-Acosta, Dean of Enrollment, 210-829-6005, Fax: 210-829-3921, E-mail: admis@uiwtx.edu.

University of the Incarnate Word, School of Graduate Studies and Research, School of Mathematics, Science, and Engineering, Program in Nutrition, San Antonio, TX 78209-6397. Offers administration (MS); medical nutrition therapy (MS); nutrition education and health promotion (MS); nutrition services administration (MS). Part-time and evening/weekend programs available. *Students:* 11 full-time (10 women), 18 part-time (17 women); includes 14 minority (2 African Americans, 12 Hispanic Americans). Average age 27. In 2009, 5 master's awarded. *Degree requirements:* For master's, comprehensive exam, thesis or alternative. *Entrance requirements:* For master's, two letters of recommendation. Additional exam requirements/recommendations for international students: Required—TOEFL (minimum score 560 paper-based; 220 computer-based; 83 iBT). *Application deadline:* Applications are processed on a rolling basis. Application fee: $20. Electronic applications accepted. *Expenses:* Tuition: Full-time $12,150; part-time $675 per credit hour. Required fees: $83 per credit hour. *Financial support:* Federal Work-Study and scholarships/grants available. Financial award applicants required to submit FAFSA. *Faculty research:* Minority nutrition issues, child nutrition, diabetes prevention, food security and hunger, international nutrition. *Unit head:* Dr. Beth Senne-Duff, Associate Professor, 210-829-3165, Fax: 210-829-3153, E-mail: beths@uiwtx.edu. *Application contact:* Andrea Cyterski-Acosta, Dean of Enrollment, 210-829-6005, Fax: 210-829-3921, E-mail: admis@uiwtx.edu.

University of Toronto, School of Graduate Studies, Life Sciences Division, Department of Nutritional Sciences, Toronto, ON M5S 1A1, Canada. Offers M Sc, PhD. Part-time programs available. *Degree requirements:* For master's, thesis, oral thesis defense; for doctorate, comprehensive exam, thesis/dissertation, departmental examination, oral examination. *Entrance requirements:* For master's, minimum B average, background in nutrition or an area of biological or health sciences, 2 letters of reference; for doctorate, minimum B+ average in final 2 years, background in nutrition or an area of biological of health sciences, 2 letters of reference. Additional exam requirements/recommendations for international students: Required—TOEFL (580 paper-based; 237 computer-based), TWE (5), IELTS (7), Michigan English Language Assessment Battery (85), or COPE (4).

University of Utah, Graduate School, College of Health, Division of Nutrition, Salt Lake City, UT 84112. Offers MS. *Accreditation:* ADtA. *Faculty:* 6 full-time (4 women), 2 part-time/adjunct (both women). *Students:* 28 full-time (23 women), 3 part-time (all women); includes 1 minority (Hispanic American), 5 international. Average age 28. 45 applicants, 38% accepted, 17 enrolled. In 2009, 11 master's awarded. *Degree requirements:* For master's, comprehensive exam, thesis. *Entrance requirements:* For master's, GRE General Test, minimum undergraduate GPA of 3.0. Additional exam requirements/recommendations for international students: Required—TOEFL (minimum score 500 paper-based; 173 computer-based). *Application deadline:* For fall admission, 2/3 for domestic and international students. Application fee: $55 ($65 for international students). Electronic applications accepted. *Expenses:* Contact institution. *Financial support:* In 2009–10, 21 students received support, including 3 research assistantships with partial tuition reimbursements available (averaging $5,750 per year), 8 teaching assistantships with partial tuition reimbursements available (averaging $5,750 per year); career-related internships or fieldwork, Federal Work-Study, and institutionally sponsored loans also available. Financial award application deadline: 2/3; financial award applicants required to submit FAFSA. *Faculty research:* Cholesterol metabolism, sport nutrition education, metabolic and critical care, cardiovascular nutrition, wilderness nutrition, pediatric nutrition. Total annual research expenditures: $104,462. *Unit head:* Dr. E. Wayne Askew, Director, 801-581-8240, Fax: 801-585-3874, E-mail: wayne.askew@health.utah.edu. *Application contact:* Jean Zancanella, Academic Adviser, 801-581-5280, Fax: 801-585-3874, E-mail: jean.zancanella@health.utah.edu.

University of Vermont, Graduate College, College of Agriculture and Life Sciences, Department of Nutrition and Food Sciences, Program in Dietetics, Burlington, VT 05405. Offers MSD. *Students:* 12 (all women). 16 applicants, 75% accepted, 5 enrolled. In 2009, 6 master's awarded. *Entrance requirements:* For master's, GRE General Test. Additional exam requirements/recommendations for international students: Required—TOEFL (minimum score 550 paper-based; 213 computer-based; 80 iBT). *Application deadline:* For fall admission, 12/15 priority date for domestic and international students. Application fee: $40. Electronic applications accepted. *Expenses:* Tuition, state resident: part-time $508 per credit hour. Tuition, nonresident: part-time $1281 per credit hour. *Unit head:* Dr. Jane Ross, Director, 802-656-3374. *Application contact:* Amy Nickerson, Coordinator, 802-656-3374.

University of Vermont, Graduate College, College of Agriculture and Life Sciences, Program in Animal, Nutrition and Food Sciences, Burlington, VT 05405. Offers PhD. *Students:* 11 (4 women), 7 international. 21 applicants, 33% accepted, 3 enrolled. In 2009, 1 doctorate awarded. *Degree requirements:* For doctorate, one foreign language, thesis/dissertation. *Entrance requirements:* For doctorate, GRE General Test. Additional exam requirements/recommendations for international students: Required—TOEFL (minimum score 550 paper-based; 213 computer-based; 80 iBT). *Application deadline:* For fall admission, 4/1 priority date for domestic students. Applications are processed on a rolling basis. Application fee: $40. Electronic applications accepted. *Expenses:* Tuition, state resident: part-time $508 per credit hour. Tuition, nonresident: part-time $1281 per credit hour. *Financial support:* Application deadline: 3/1. *Unit head:* Dr. R. K. Johnson, Dean, 802-656-2070. *Application contact:* Dr. David Kerr, Coordinator, 802-656-2070.

University of Washington, Graduate School, School of Public Health, Department of Epidemiology, Interdisciplinary Graduate Program in Nutritional Sciences, Seattle, WA 98195. Offers MPH, MS, PhD. *Accreditation:* ADtA. Part-time programs available. *Students:* 37 full-time (33 women), 10 part-time (all women); includes 8 minority (6 Asian Americans or Pacific Islanders, 2 Hispanic Americans), 3 international. Average age 29. 102 applicants, 26% accepted, 9 enrolled. In 2009, 9 master's, 2 doctorates awarded. Terminal master's awarded for partial completion of doctoral program. *Degree requirements:* For master's, thesis, practicum (MPH); for doctorate, comprehensive exam, thesis/dissertation. *Entrance requirements:* For master's and doctorate, GRE General Test, experience in health sciences (preferred), minimum GPA of 3.0. Additional exam requirements/recommendations for international students: Required—TOEFL (minimum score 580 paper-based; 237 computer-based). *Application deadline:* For fall admission, 2/1 for domestic students, 11/1 for international students. Application fee: $50. *Financial support:* In 2009–10, 19 students received support, including 8 research assistantships with full tuition reimbursements available (averaging $10,000 per year), 2 teaching assistantships with full tuition reimbursements available (averaging $10,000 per year); career-related internships or fieldwork also available. Financial award application deadline: 3/1. *Faculty research:* Lipids, trace elements, nutrition in disease prevention. *Unit head:* Dr. Adam Drewnowski, Chair, 206-543-1065. *Application contact:* Carey Purnell, Graduate Program Assistant, 206-543-1730, Fax: 206-685-1696, E-mail: nutr@u.washington.edu.

University of Wisconsin–Madison, Graduate School, College of Agricultural and Life Sciences, Department of Nutritional Sciences, Madison, WI 53706-1380. Offers MS, PhD. Part-time programs available. Terminal master's awarded for partial completion of doctoral program. *Degree requirements:* For master's, thesis or research report; for doctorate, thesis/dissertation. *Entrance requirements:* For master's and doctorate, GRE General Test. Additional exam requirements/recommendations for international students: Required—TOEFL. Electronic applications accepted. *Expenses:* Tuition, state resident: part-time $594 per credit. Tuition, nonresident: part-time $1504 per credit. Required fees: $65 per credit. Tuition and fees vary according to course load, program and reciprocity agreements. *Faculty research:* Human and animal nutrition, nutrition epidemiology, nutrition education, biochemical and molecular nutrition.

University of Wisconsin–Stevens Point, College of Professional Studies, School of Health Promotion and Human Development, Program in Nutritional Sciences, Stevens Point, WI 54481-3897. Offers MS. Part-time programs available. *Students:* 1 (woman) part-time. *Degree requirements:* For master's, thesis or alternative. *Entrance requirements:* For master's, minimum GPA of 2.75. *Application deadline:* For fall admission, 5/1 priority date for domestic students. Applications are processed on a rolling basis. Application fee: $45. *Expenses:* Tuition, state resident: full-time $7740; part-time $430 per credit hour. Tuition, nonresident: full-time $17,804; part-time $989 per credit hour. Tuition and fees vary according to course load and reciprocity agreements. *Financial support:* Research assistantships, teaching assistantships, career-related internships or fieldwork and Federal Work-Study available. Support available to part-time students. Financial award application deadline: 5/1; financial award applicants required to submit FAFSA. *Unit head:* Dr. Marty Loy, Head, 715-346-2830, Fax: 715-346-2720. *Application contact:* Dr. Jasia Steinmetz, Information Contact, 715-346-2830, Fax: 715-346-2720, E-mail: jsteinme@uwsp.edu.

University of Wisconsin–Stout, Graduate School, College of Human Development, Program in Food and Nutritional Sciences, Menomonie, WI 54751. Offers MS. Part-time programs available. *Degree requirements:* For master's, thesis. *Entrance requirements:* For master's, minimum GPA of 3.0. Additional exam requirements/recommendations for international students: Required—TOEFL (minimum score 500 paper-based; 173 computer-based; 61 iBT). Electronic applications accepted. *Faculty research:* Disease states and nutrition, childhood obesity, nutraceuticals, food safety, nanotechnology.

University of Wyoming, College of Agriculture, Department of Animal Sciences, Program in Food Science and Human Nutrition, Laramie, WY 82070. Offers MS. *Degree requirements:* For master's, thesis. *Entrance requirements:* For master's, GRE General Test, minimum GPA of 3.0. Additional exam requirements/recommendations for international students: Required—TOEFL (minimum score 525 paper-based). Electronic applications accepted. *Faculty research:* Protein and lipid metabolism, food microbiology, food safety, meat science.

Utah State University, School of Graduate Studies, College of Agriculture, Department of Nutrition and Food Sciences, Logan, UT 84322. Offers dietetic administration (MDA); food microbiology and safety (MFMS); nutrition and food sciences (MS, PhD); nutrition science (MS, PhD), including molecular biology. Postbaccalaureate distance learning degree programs

Nutrition

Utah State University (continued)
offered. *Degree requirements:* For master's, thesis; for doctorate, comprehensive exam, thesis/dissertation, teaching experience. *Entrance requirements:* For master's, GRE General Test, minimum GPA of 3.0, course work in chemistry, biochemistry, physics, math, bacteriology, physiology; for doctorate, GRE General Test, minimum GPA of 3.2, course work in chemistry, MS or manuscript in referred journal. Additional exam requirements/recommendations for international students: Required—TOEFL (minimum score 550 paper-based). Electronic applications accepted. *Faculty research:* Mineral balance, meat microbiology and nitrate interactions, milk ultrafiltration, lactic culture, milk coagulation.

Vanderbilt University, School of Nursing, Nashville, TN 37240. Offers adult acute care nurse practitioner (MSN); adult nurse practitioner/cardiovascular disease management and prevention (MSN); adult nurse practitioner/palliative care (MSN); clinical management (clinical nurse leader/specialist) (MSN); emergency nurse practitioner (MSN); family nurse practitioner (MSN); gerontology nurse practitioner (MSN); health systems management (MSN); neonatal nurse practitioner (MSN); nurse midwifery (MSN); nurse midwifery/family nurse practitioner (MSN); nursing informatics (MSN); nursing practice (DNP); nursing science (PhD); nutrition (MS); pediatric acute care nurse practitioner (MSN); pediatric primary care nurse practitioner (MSN); psychiatric-mental health nurse practitioner (MSN); women's health nurse practitioner (MSN), including urogynecology; women's health nurse practitioner/adult nurse practitioner (MSN); MSN/M Div; MSN/MTS. *Accreditation:* ACNM/DOA; NLN (one or more programs are accredited). Part-time programs available. Postbaccalaureate distance learning degree programs offered (minimal on-campus study). *Faculty:* 118 full-time (102 women), 429 part-time/adjunct (309 women). *Students:* 484 full-time (435 women), 319 part-time (284 women); includes 84 minority (55 African Americans, 4 American Indian/Alaska Native, 10 Asian Americans or Pacific Islanders, 15 Hispanic Americans), 16 international. Average age 32. 900 applicants, 65% accepted, 433 enrolled. In 2009, 303 master's, 1 doctorate awarded. *Degree requirements:* For doctorate, comprehensive exam, thesis/dissertation. *Entrance requirements:* For master's, GRE General Test, minimum B average in undergraduate course work, 3 letters of recommendation; for doctorate, GRE General Test, interview, 3 letters of recommendation from doctorally-prepared faculty, MSN, essay. Additional exam requirements/recommendations for international students: Required—TOEFL. *Application deadline:* For fall admission, 12/1 priority date for domestic and international students. Applications are processed on a rolling basis. Application fee: $50. *Expenses:* Contact institution. *Financial support:* In 2009–10, 389 students received support, including 1 research assistantship (averaging $5,000 per year); teaching assistantships, scholarships/grants, health care benefits, and tuition waivers also available. Support available to part-time students. Financial award application deadline: 3/15; financial award applicants required to submit FAFSA. *Faculty research:* Lymphedema, palliative care and bereavement, health services research including workforce, safety and quality of care, gerontology, better birth outcomes including nutrition. Total annual research expenditures: $1.4 million. *Unit head:* Dr. Colleen Conway-Welch, Dean, 615-343-8776, Fax: 615-343-7711, E-mail: colleen.conway-welch@vanderbilt.edu. *Application contact:* Cheryl Feldner, Assistant Director of Admissions, 615-322-3800, Fax: 615-343-0333, E-mail: cheryl.feldner@vanderbilt.edu.

Virginia Polytechnic Institute and State University, Graduate School, College of Agriculture and Life Sciences, Department of Human Nutrition, Foods and Exercise, Blacksburg, VA 24061. Offers MS, PhD. *Faculty:* 23 full-time (16 women). *Students:* 39 full-time (28 women), 5 part-time (3 women); includes 15 minority (8 American Indian/Alaska Native, 6 Asian Americans or Pacific Islanders, 1 Hispanic American), 1 international. Average age 30. 26 applicants, 23% accepted, 6 enrolled. In 2009, 6 master's, 4 doctorates awarded. *Entrance requirements:* For master's and doctorate, GRE, GMAT. Additional exam requirements/recommendations for international students: Required—TOEFL (minimum score 550 paper-based; 213 computer-based). *Application deadline:* For fall admission, 5/15 for international students; for spring admission, 10/15 for international students. Applications are processed on a rolling basis. Application fee: $65. Electronic applications accepted. *Expenses:* Tuition, area resident: Full-time $10,228; part-time $459 per credit hour. Tuition, nonresident: full-time $17,892; part-time $865 per credit hour. Required fees: $1966; $451 per semester. *Financial support:* In 2009–10, 15 research assistantships with full tuition reimbursements (averaging $17,784 per year), 21 teaching assistantships with full tuition reimbursements (averaging $13,683 per year) were awarded; career-related internships or fieldwork, Federal Work-Study, scholarships/grants, and unspecified assistantships also available. Financial award application deadline: 1/15. *Faculty research:* Nutrition and food science research. Total annual research expenditures: $5.7 million. *Unit head:* Dr. Susan M. Hutson, Head, 540-231-4672, Fax: 540-231-3916, E-mail: susanh5@vt.edu. *Application contact:* Sherry Terry, Information Contact, 540-231-5540, Fax: 540-231-3916, E-mail: savillsk@vt.edu.

Washington State University, Graduate School, College of Pharmacy, Department of Nutrition and Dietetics, Program in Human Nutrition, Pullman, WA 99164. Offers MS. *Degree requirements:* For master's, comprehensive exam (for some programs), thesis (for some programs), oral exam, written exam. *Entrance requirements:* For master's, GRE General Test, minimum GPA of 3.0, resume, 3 letters of recommendation, letter of interest. Additional exam requirements/recommendations for international students: Required—TOEFL (minimum score 550 paper-based; 213 computer-based). Electronic applications accepted. *Faculty research:* Nutrition education programs, cultural issues in community nutrition programs.

Washington State University, Graduate School, College of Pharmacy, Department of Nutrition and Dietetics, Program in Nutrition, Pullman, WA 99164. Offers PhD. *Degree requirements:* For doctorate, comprehensive exam, thesis/dissertation, oral exam, written exam. *Entrance requirements:* For doctorate, GRE, minimum GPA of 3.0, resume, 3 letters of recommendation. Additional exam requirements/recommendations for international students: Required—TOEFL (minimum score 550 paper-based; 213 computer-based). Electronic applications accepted. *Faculty research:* Breastfeeding and lactation influence on maternal child wellbeing, sports anemia preschool nutrition.

Wayne State University, College of Liberal Arts and Sciences, Department of Nutrition and Food Science, Detroit, MI 48202. Offers MA, MS, PhD. Terminal master's awarded for partial completion of doctoral program. *Degree requirements:* For master's, thesis (for some programs); for doctorate, thesis/dissertation. *Entrance requirements:* For master's, GRE General Test, minimum GPA of 3.0; for doctorate, GRE General Test, minimum GPA of 3.0; letters of recommendation; personal statement. Additional exam requirements/recommendations for international students: Required—TOEFL (minimum score 550 paper-based; 213 computer-based); Recommended—TWE (minimum score 6). Electronic applications accepted. *Faculty research:* Nutrition, cancer and gene expression, food microbiology and food safety, lipids, lipoprotein and cholesterol metabolism, obesity and diabetes, metabolomics.

West Chester University of Pennsylvania, Office of Graduate Studies, College of Health Sciences, Department of Health, West Chester, PA 19383. Offers emergency preparedness (Certificate); health care administration (Certificate); integrative health (Certificate); public health (MPH), including administration, community, environment, integrative, nutrition; school health (M Ed). *Accreditation:* CEPH. Part-time and evening/weekend programs available. *Students:* 15 full-time (9 women), 128 part-time (91 women); includes 41 minority (34 African Americans, 2 American Indian/Alaska Native, 5 Asian Americans or Pacific Islanders), 22 international. Average age 30. 83 applicants, 88% accepted, 41 enrolled. In 2009, 45 master's, 8 other advanced degrees awarded. *Degree requirements:* For master's, thesis (for some programs). *Entrance requirements:* For master's, one-page statement of career objectives, two letters of reference. Additional exam requirements/recommendations for international students: Required—TOEFL (minimum score 550 paper-based; 213 computer-based; 80 iBT). *Application deadline:* For fall admission, 4/15 priority date for domestic students, 3/15 for international students; for spring admission, 10/15 for domestic students, 9/1 for international students. Applications are processed on a rolling basis. Application fee: $35. Electronic applications accepted. *Expenses:* Tuition, state resident: full-time $6666; part-time $370 per credit. Tuition, nonresident: full-time $10,666; part-time $593 per credit. Required fees: $122.56 per credit. *Financial support:* In 2009–10, 11 research assistantships with full and partial tuition reimbursements (averaging $5,000 per year) were awarded; unspecified assistantships also available. Support available to part-time students. Financial award application deadline: 2/15; financial award applicants required to submit FAFSA. *Faculty research:* HIV/AIDS education, teacher preparation, water quality. *Unit head:* Dr. Roger Mustalish, Chair, 610-436-2931, E-mail: rmustalish@wcupa.edu. *Application contact:* Dr. Bethann Cinelli, Graduate Coordinator, 610-436-2267, E-mail: bcinelli@wcupa.edu.

West Virginia University, Davis College of Agriculture, Forestry and Consumer Sciences, Division of Animal and Nutritional Sciences, Program in Animal and Nutritional Sciences, Morgantown, WV 26506. Offers breeding (MS); food sciences (MS); nutrition (MS); physiology (MS); production management (MS); reproduction (MS). Part-time programs available. *Degree requirements:* For master's, thesis, oral and written exams. *Entrance requirements:* For master's, GRE, minimum GPA of 2.5. Additional exam requirements/recommendations for international students: Required—TOEFL. *Faculty research:* Animal nutrition, reproductive physiology, food science.

Winthrop University, College of Arts and Sciences, Department of Human Nutrition, Rock Hill, SC 29733. Offers MS. Part-time programs available. *Degree requirements:* For master's, thesis optional. *Entrance requirements:* For master's, GRE General Test, PRAXIS, or MAT, interview, minimum GPA of 3.0. Electronic applications accepted.

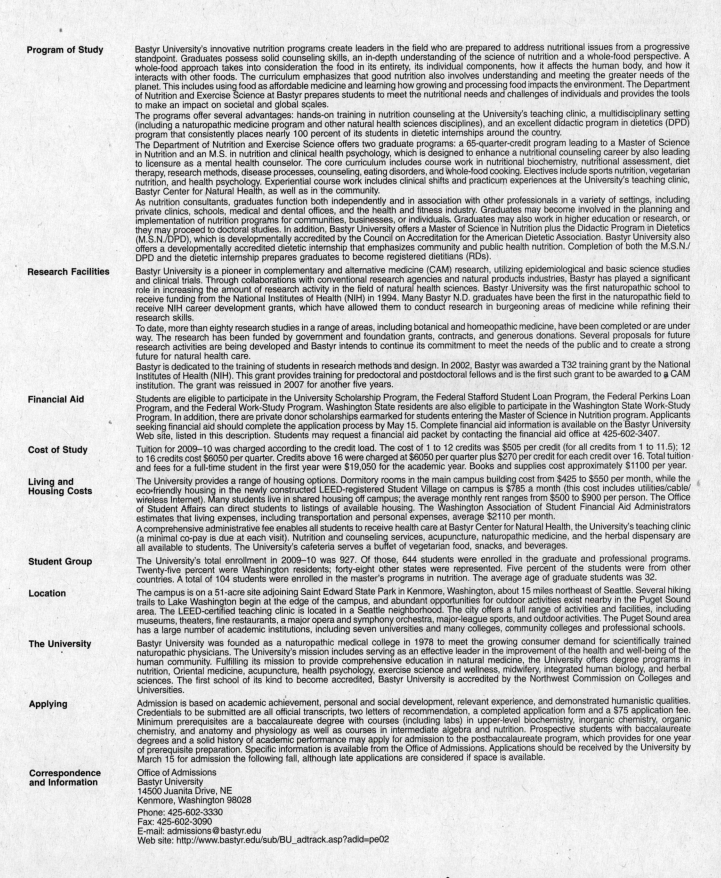

BASTYR UNIVERSITY

Department of Nutrition and Exercise Science

Program of Study

Bastyr University's innovative nutrition programs create leaders in the field who are prepared to address nutritional issues from a progressive standpoint. Graduates possess solid counseling skills, an in-depth understanding of the science of nutrition and a whole-food perspective. A whole-food approach takes into consideration the food in its entirety, its individual components, how it affects the human body, and how it interacts with other foods. The curriculum emphasizes that good nutrition also involves understanding and meeting the greater needs of the planet. This includes using food as affordable medicine and learning how growing and processing food impacts the environment. The Department of Nutrition and Exercise Science at Bastyr prepares students to meet the nutritional needs and challenges of individuals and provides the tools to make an impact on societal and global scales.

The programs offer several advantages: hands-on training in nutrition counseling at the University's teaching clinic, a multidisciplinary setting (including a naturopathic medicine program and other natural health sciences disciplines), and an excellent didactic program in dietetics (DPD) program that consistently places nearly 100 percent of its students in dietetic internships around the country.

The Department of Nutrition and Exercise Science offers two graduate programs: a 65-quarter-credit program leading to a Master of Science in Nutrition and an M.S. in nutrition and clinical health psychology, which is designed to enhance a nutritional counseling career by also leading to licensure as a mental health counselor. The core curriculum includes course work in nutritional biochemistry, nutritional assessment, diet therapy, research methods, disease processes, counseling, eating disorders, and whole-food cooking. Electives include sports nutrition, vegetarian nutrition, and health psychology. Experiential course work includes clinical shifts and practicum experiences at the University's teaching clinic, Bastyr Center for Natural Health, as well as in the community.

As nutrition consultants, graduates function both independently and in association with other professionals in a variety of settings, including private clinics, schools, medical and dental offices, and the health and fitness industry. Graduates may become involved in the planning and implementation of nutrition programs for communities, businesses, or individuals. Graduates may also work in higher education or research, or they may proceed to doctoral studies. In addition, Bastyr University offers a Master of Science in Nutrition plus the Didactic Program in Dietetics (M.S.N./DPD), which is developmentally accredited by the Council on Accreditation for the American Dietetic Association. Bastyr University also offers a developmentally accredited dietetic internship that emphasizes community and public health nutrition. Completion of both the M.S.N./DPD and the dietetic internship prepares graduates to become registered dietitians (RDs).

Research Facilities

Bastyr University is a pioneer in complementary and alternative medicine (CAM) research, utilizing epidemiological and basic science studies and clinical trials. Through collaborations with conventional research agencies and natural products industries, Bastyr has played a significant role in increasing the amount of research activity in the field of natural health sciences. Bastyr University was the first naturopathic school to receive funding from the National Institutes of Health (NIH) in 1994. Many Bastyr N.D. graduates have been the first in the naturopathic field to receive NIH career development grants, which have allowed them to conduct research in burgeoning areas of medicine while refining their research skills.

To date, more than eighty research studies in a range of areas, including botanical and homeopathic medicine, have been completed or are under way. The research has been funded by government and foundation grants, contracts, and generous donations. Several proposals for future research activities are being developed and Bastyr intends to continue its commitment to meet the needs of the public and to create a strong future for natural health care.

Bastyr is dedicated to the training of students in research methods and design. In 2002, Bastyr was awarded a T32 training grant by the National Institutes of Health (NIH). This grant provides training for predoctoral and postdoctoral fellows and is the first such grant to be awarded to a CAM institution. The grant was reissued in 2007 for another five years.

Financial Aid

Students are eligible to participate in the University Scholarship Program, the Federal Stafford Student Loan Program, the Federal Perkins Loan Program, and the Federal Work-Study Program. Washington State residents are also eligible to participate in the Washington State Work-Study Program. In addition, there are private donor scholarships earmarked for students entering the Master of Science in Nutrition program. Applicants seeking financial aid should complete the application process by May 15. Complete financial aid information is available on the Bastyr University Web site, listed in this description. Students may request a financial aid packet by contacting the financial aid office at 425-602-3407.

Cost of Study

Tuition for 2009–10 was charged according to the credit load. The cost of 1 to 12 credits was $505 per credit (for all credits from 1 to 11.5); 12 to 16 credits cost $6050 per quarter. Credits above 16 were charged at $6050 per quarter plus $270 per credit for each credit over 16. Total tuition and fees for a full-time student in the first year were $19,050 for the academic year. Books and supplies cost approximately $1100 per year.

Living and Housing Costs

The University provides a range of housing options. Dormitory rooms in the main campus building cost from $425 to $550 per month, while the eco-friendly housing in the newly constructed LEED-registered Student Village on campus is $785 a month (this cost includes utilities/cable/wireless Internet). Many students live in shared housing off campus; the average monthly rent ranges from $500 to $900 per person. The Office of Student Affairs can direct students to listings of available housing. The Washington Association of Student Financial Aid Administrators estimates that living expenses, including transportation and personal expenses, average $2110 per month.

A comprehensive administrative fee enables all students to receive health care at Bastyr Center for Natural Health, the University's teaching clinic (a minimal co-pay is due at each visit). Nutrition and counseling services, acupuncture, naturopathic medicine, and the herbal dispensary are all available to students. The University's cafeteria serves a buffet of vegetarian food, snacks, and beverages.

Student Group

The University's total enrollment in 2009–10 was 927. Of those, 644 students were enrolled in the graduate and professional programs. Twenty-five percent were Washington residents; forty-eight other states were represented. Five percent of the students were from other countries. A total of 104 students were enrolled in the master's programs in nutrition. The average age of graduate students was 32.

Location

The campus is on a 51-acre site adjoining Saint Edward State Park in Kenmore, Washington, about 15 miles northeast of Seattle. Several hiking trails to Lake Washington begin at the edge of the campus, and abundant opportunities for outdoor activities exist nearby in the Puget Sound area. The LEED-certified teaching clinic is located in a Seattle neighborhood. The city offers a full range of activities and facilities, including museums, theaters, fine restaurants, a major opera and symphony orchestra, major-league sports, and outdoor activities. The Puget Sound area has a large number of academic institutions, including seven universities and many colleges, community colleges and professional schools.

The University

Bastyr University was founded as a naturopathic medical college in 1978 to meet the growing consumer demand for scientifically trained naturopathic physicians. The University's mission includes serving as an effective leader in the improvement of the health and well-being of the human community. Fulfilling its mission to provide comprehensive education in natural medicine, the University offers degree programs in nutrition, Oriental medicine, acupuncture, health psychology, exercise science and wellness, midwifery, integrated human biology, and herbal sciences. The first school of its kind to become accredited, Bastyr University is accredited by the Northwest Commission on Colleges and Universities.

Applying

Admission is based on academic achievement, personal and social development, relevant experience, and demonstrated humanistic qualities. Credentials to be submitted are all official transcripts, two letters of recommendation, a completed application form and a $75 application fee. Minimum prerequisites are a baccalaureate degree with courses (including labs) in upper-level biochemistry, inorganic chemistry, organic chemistry, and anatomy and physiology as well as courses in intermediate algebra and nutrition. Prospective students with baccalaureate degrees and a solid history of academic performance may apply for admission to the postbaccalaureate program, which provides for one year of prerequisite preparation. Specific information is available from the Office of Admissions. Applications should be received by the University by March 15 for admission the following fall, although late applications are considered if space is available.

Correspondence and Information

Office of Admissions
Bastyr University
14500 Juanita Drive, NE
Kenmore, Washington 98028

Phone: 425-602-3330
Fax: 425-602-3090
E-mail: admissions@bastyr.edu
Web site: http://www.bastyr.edu/sub/BU_adtrack.asp?adid=pe02

Bastyr University

THE FACULTY

Jennifer Adler, M.S., Bastyr; CN.
Michelle Babb, M.S., Bastyr; RD.
Debra Boutin, M.S., Case Western Reserve; RD.
Matt Brignall, N.D., Bastyr.
Tess Cabasco-Cebrian, B.S., Washington (Seattle).
Suz Coan, Psy.D.,Pacific; CDP.
Lynelle Golden, Ph.D., Tennessee, Knoxville.
Cristen Harris, Ph.D., Florida International; LD/N, RD.
Alexandra Kazaks, Ph.D., Washington (Seattle); RD.
Elizabeth Kirk, Ph.D., Washington (Seattle); RD.
June Kloubec, Ph.D., Minnesota.
Samer Koutoubi, M.D., Institute of Medicine and Pharmacy (Romania); Ph.D., Florida International.
Cynthia Lair, B.A., Wichita State; CHN.
Naomi Lester, Ph.D., Uniformed Services University of the Health Services.
Buck Levin, Ph.D., North Carolina at Greensboro; RD.
Laura Legel, M.S.Ed., Old Dominion.
Kelly Morrow, M.S., Bastyr; RD, CD.
Tiffany Reiss, Ph.D., Virginia Tech.
Diane Spicer, M.S., Wisconsin.
Sarah Washburn, M.S., Washington (Seattle); CD, RD.

Nutrition students learn cooking techniques in Bastyr's state-of-the-art teaching kitchen.

CASE WESTERN RESERVE UNIVERSITY

Case School of Medicine
Department of Nutrition

Programs of Study	The Department of Nutrition offers programs that span the breadth of the discipline, from applied nutrition and dietetics to basic nutritional sciences. These include the Master of Science in Nutrition Program; the Master of Science in Public Health Nutrition Internship Program, with fieldwork experiences in public health and community-based agencies; and the Coordinated Dietetic Internship/Master's Program, with University Hospitals Case Medical Center and Veterans Affairs Medical Center. The Doctor of Philosophy degree is also offered.
	The master's degree programs require from one to two years of course work, depending upon the student's undergraduate preparation and the specific program. A thesis or nonthesis option may be selected.
	The Ph.D. program emphasizes nutritional biochemistry/metabolism, molecular nutrition, and human nutrition. It builds upon faculty expertise in the Departments of Nutrition, Biochemistry, Molecular Biology, Medicine, and Pediatrics. In recent years, investigators in nutritional biochemistry have used molecular biology techniques to enhance understanding of human metabolism. In the first year, nutrition students join graduate students from the other basic science departments in an integrated course that provides a broad introduction to cellular and molecular biology. The subsequent graduate program includes formal courses in human nutrition and nutritional biochemistry, seminars, and, most importantly, the performance of original research.
Research Facilities	Several well-equipped laboratories are housed in the Case School of Medicine Building. The Department has access to clinical research units at University Hospitals Case Medical Center and Cleveland Clinic Lerner College of Medicine for the conduct of human clinical nutrition and whole-body metabolism studies. The Department has all general equipment necessary for conducting studies in nutritional biochemistry, including three gas chromatographs and mass spectrometers used for human investigation with stable isotopes. Facilities for isolated organ perfusion and a comprehensive organic chemistry laboratory for synthesis of new nutrients are also available.
Financial Aid	The University sponsors a federally funded work-study program as well as loan assistance. Students in the Coordinated Dietetic Internship/Master's Program are paid a stipend by the hospital for the first twelve months of the program. Ph.D. students in nutritional biochemistry or molecular nutrition will receive an annual stipend of $25,000 in 2010–11.
Cost of Study	Tuition for 2010–11 is $1430 per credit hour. It is $17,160 per semester for 12 or more credit hours. Partial-tuition scholarships are available for some master's students. Full-tuition scholarships are provided by the Department for students in the Ph.D. nutritional biochemistry or molecular nutrition program.
Living and Housing Costs	Most graduate students find privately owned apartments near the campus. Costs are below average for large urban areas.
Student Group	The University has 9,228 students, of whom about 5,360 are enrolled in graduate and professional schools. About 305 students attend adjacent institutes of music and art. Approximately 85 graduate students are in residence in the Department.
Location	Cleveland is an industrial and financial center. The city is richly endowed with cultural facilities, nearly all of them located in a single area known as the University Circle. In this area are the University, the Cleveland Orchestra, the Museum of Art, the Museum of Natural History, and several excellent repertory theaters. The city is also the home of the Cleveland Indians and Cavaliers and the Rock and Roll Hall of Fame. The camping, sailing, and skiing areas of Ohio, western Pennsylvania, and western New York are readily accessible.
The University and The Department	The strength of its combined science departments places the University in the top rank of institutions in this country. The Department of Nutrition has a number of associate members in several departments in the Case School of Medicine and in the University and has strong ties with the Departments of Chemistry, Biology, and Biomedical Engineering. A major emphasis is on interdisciplinary training programs in biological and chemical sciences.
Applying	Prerequisites for entrance into the Ph.D. program are organic chemistry, biology, and mathematics through calculus. Applications should be submitted in late autumn or early winter for an anticipated entrance in the following autumn semester. Application forms may be obtained from the Department or online at http://www.applyweb.com/apply/cwrug/menu.html. Ph.D. applicants are required to take the Graduate Record Examinations, including the General Test and one Subject Test.
	Information concerning application and prerequisites for specific master's programs should be obtained directly from the Department.

Correspondence and Information

Graduate Admissions Committee
Department of Nutrition (M.S. or Ph.D.)
Case Western Reserve University
10900 Euclid Avenue
Cleveland, Ohio 44106-4954

Phone: 216-368-2440
E-mail: paw5@cwru.edu
Web site: http://www.cwru.edu/med/nutrition/home.html

Coordinator
Biomedical Science Training Program (Ph.D. only)
Case School of Medicine
WG1
Case Western Reserve University
Cleveland, Ohio 44106-4935
Phone: 216-368-3347

Case Western Reserve University

THE FACULTY AND THEIR RESEARCH

Hope Barkoukis, Associate Professor; Ph.D., Case Western Reserve, 1997. Clinical nutrition, diet and liver cirrhosis.

Henri Brunengraber, Professor and Chairman; M.D., 1968, Ph.D., 1976, Brussels. Metabolic regulation; control of flux through metabolic pathways; design and testing of artificial nutrients; noninvasive probes of liver metabolism; markers of alcoholism; mass spectrometry.

Colleen Croniger, Assistant Professor; Ph.D., Case Western Reserve, 1990. Metabolic regulation of carbohydrate and lipid metabolism using genetically altered animal models.

Paul Ernsberger, Associate Professor; Ph.D., Northwestern, 1984. Genetic obesity and the role of nutrition in cardiovascular disease; novel signaling pathways.

Maria Hatzoglou, Professor; Ph.D., Athens, 1985. Identification of retroviral receptors and their use in gene therapy.

Carolyn Hodges, Instructor; M.S., Case Western Reserve, 2007; RD, LD.

Mary Beth Kavanagh, Senior Instructor; M.S., Case Western Reserve, 1992; RD, LD. Nutritional education for nursing and dentistry; nutrition and the media.

Jane Korsberg, Senior Instructor and Private Practice; M.S., Case Western Reserve, 1977; RD, LD.

Edith Lerner, Associate Professor and Vice-Chairman; Ph.D., Wisconsin, 1971. Assessment of nutritional status during pregnancy; trace-mineral metabolism during pregnancy; nutritional requirements for the preterm infant.

Danny Manor, Associate Professor; Ph.D., Yeshiva (Einstein), 1989. Molecular-level treatment and prevention of cancer.

Isabel Parraga, Associate Professor and Director, M.S. in Public Health Nutrition Internship Program; Ph.D., Case Western Reserve, 1992. Nutritional anthropology; maternal and child nutrition; public health nutrition; child growth and schistosomiasis.

Alison Steiber, Assistant Professor and Director, Coordinated Dietetic Internship/M.S. Degree Program; Ph.D., Michigan State, 2005; RD. General nutrition assessment of patients, with emphasis in chronic renal failure.

James Swain, Assistant Professor and Director, Didactic Program in Dietetics; Ph.D., Iowa State, 2000; RD. Food chemistry; nutrition in management of chronic disease; absorption and efficacy in humans of different forms of iron used in food fortification.

Guofang Zhang, Assistant Professor, Metabolimics Center; Ph.D., Nanjing (China), 2001; Lipid metabolism in the heart.

Secondary Appointments

Catherine Demko, Assistant Professor in Dentistry; Ph.D., Case Western Reserve, 2002.

Saul Genuth, Professor in Medicine; M.D., Western Reserve, 1957. Diabetes mellitus; blood glucose control and complications.

Sharon Groh-Wargo, Assistant Professor in Pediatrics and Neonatal Nutritionist, MetroHealth Medical Center, Cleveland, Ohio; Ph.D.; Case Western Reserve, 2002. Tolerance of a nutrient-enriched post-discharge formula for preterm infants.

Sanjay Gupta, Associate Professor in Urology; Ph.D., Avadh (India), 1992. Mechanisms of prostate carcinogenesis, treatment and prevention of prostate cancer.

Richard Hanson, Professor in Biochemistry; Ph.D., Brown, 1963. Hormonal control of gene expression.

Janos Kerner, Assistant Professor; Ph.D., Hungarian Academy, 1986. Mitochondrial fatty acid oxidation and the regulation of the pathway by a malonyl-CoA.

Douglas Kerr, Associate Professor in Pediatrics; M.D./Ph.D., Western Reserve, 1965. Metabolic disorders in infants.

John Kirwan, Associate Professor in Reproductive Biology; Ph.D., Ball State, 1987. Aging; metabolism; endocrinology.

Laura Nagy, Professor in Pathobiology, Cleveland Clinic, Lerner College of Medicine; Ph.D., Berkeley, 1986. Effects of environmental factors such as diet and drugs on cellular signal transduction mechanisms.

Noa Noy, Professor in Pharmacology; Ph.D., Tel Aviv, 1981. Transcriptional regulations by nuclear hormone receptors.

Adjunct Faculty

Adjunct faculty members provide students with specialized clinical, research, and/or public health fieldwork experiences. Their current job position is listed directly after their name.

Victoria Adeleke, Wake County Human Services WIC Program, Raleigh, North Carolina; M.P.H., North Carolina at Chapel Hill, 1992; RD, LDN.

Phyllis Allen, Office of Public Health, Columbia, South Carolina; M.S., Case Western Reserve, 1989; RD.

Janet Anselmo, Diabetes Self Management Program, Louis Stokes VA Medical Center, Cleveland, Ohio; M.S., Case Western Reserve, 1988; RD, LD.

Anika Avery-Grant, Centers for Dialysis Care, Euclid, Ohio; M.S., Case Western Reserve, 1994; RD, LD.

Cynthia Bayerl, Massachusetts Department of Public Health; M.S., Boston University, 1976; RD, LDN.

Jennifer Bier, MetroHealth Center for Community Health; M.S., Case Western Reserve, 2002; RD, LD.

Mark Bindus, Twinsburg City School District; B.S., Akron, 1993, RD, LD.

Suzanne Bogert, Los Angeles County Department of Public Health, Los Angeles, California; M.S., Case Western Reserve; RD.

Josephine Anne Cialone, North Carolina Division of Maternal and Child Health; M.S., Case Western Reserve, 1980; RD.

Rachel Colchamiro, Massachusetts WIC Nutrition Program; M.S., Berkeley, 1999; RD, LDN.

Cheri Collier, Clement Center, MetroHealth Center for Community Health, Cleveland, Ohio; M.S. Case Western Reserve, 1998; RD, LD.

Janice Davis, Western Reserve Area on Aging, Cleveland, Ohio; M.S., Case Western Reserve, 1986; RD.

Helen Dumski, Diabetes Association of Greater Cleveland; B.S., Ohio State; RD, LD.

Maureen Faron, Hudson City School District, Hudson, Ohio; B.S., Case Western Reserve; RD, LD.

Marcie Fenton, Los Angeles County Department of Public Health, Los Angeles, California; M.S., Case Western Reserve, 1982; RD.

Denise Ferris, West Virginia Office of Nutrition Services; Ph.D., Pittsburgh, 1989; RD.

Karen Fiedler, Adjunct Associate Professor; Ph.D., Tennessee, Knoxville, 1977.

Cynthia Finohr, Orange City School District; B.S., Kent State, 1981; RD, LD.

Michelle Lundon Fox, Abbott Nutrition, Cleveland, Ohio; M.Ed., Vanderbilt; RD, LD.

Lorna Fuller, Sodexho Marriott Services, Huron Hospital; M.S., Kent State, 1995; RD, LD.

Deborah Gammell, MetroHealth Medical Center (WIC), Cleveland, Ohio; M.S., Miami (Ohio), 1980; RD, LD.

Diana Garrison, Regency Hospitals–Cleveland West, Cleveland, Ohio; B.S. Michigan State, 2001; RD, LD.

Brenda Garritson, Baylor University Medical Center, Dallas, Texas; M.S., Texas Woman's, 1993; RD, LD.

Melinda Gedeon, UH Bedford Medical Center; B.S., Ohio State; RD, LD.

Martha Halko, Cuyahoga County Board of Health; M.S., Akron, 2000; RD, LD.

Samia Hamdan, USDA, Food and Nutrition Service, Chicago; M.P.H., Minnesota, Twin Cities, 2003; RD.

Brigette Hires, Ohio Department of Education; Ph.D., Kentucky, 2005; RD.

Karen Horvath, UH Bedford Medical Center; B.S., Akron, 1986; RD, LD.

Claire Hughes, Hawaii State Department of Health; Dr.P.H., Hawaii, 1998; RD.

Lisa Isham, Cuyahoga County Board of Health; M.S., Case Western Reserve, 1997; RD, LD.

Jennifer Kernc, Centers for Dialysis Care, Cleveland, Ohio; B.S., Akron; RD, LD.

Natalia Kliszczuk-Smolio, Mt. Alverna Home, Inc., Parma, Ohio; B.S., Cincinnati, 1982; RD, LD.

Katherine Koch, MetroHealth Center for Community Health, Cleveland, Ohio; M.S., Case Western Reserve, 1988; RD, LD.

Richard Koletsky, Adjunct Assistant Clinical Professor; M.D., Case Western Reserve, 1975.

Jennifer Kravec, MetroHealth Medical Center; B.S., Ohio State, 1997; RD, LD.

Perri Kushan, Menorah Park Center for Senior Living, Beachwood, Ohio; B.S., Akron, 1986; RD, LD.

Lois Lenard, Nutrition and Food Service, Louis Stokes Cleveland VA Medical Center, Cleveland, Ohio; B.S., Kent State, 1974; RD, LD.

Janelle L'Heureux, AIDS Project Los Angeles, Los Angeles,California; M.S., New Haven, Connecticut, 1998; RD.

Patricia Liang-Tong, Native Hawaiian Health Care System; B.S., Hawaii at Manoa, 1998; RD, CDE, CDM, CFPP.

Anita Martin, Duval County Public Health Unit, Jacksonville, Florida; M.P.H., North Carolina at Chapel Hill, 1980; RD, LD.

Lauren Melnick, Expanded Food and Nutrition Education Program, OSU Extension, Cleveland, Ohio; M.S., Case Western Reserve, 2007; RD, LD.

Christine Munoz, Centers for Dialysis Care, Euclid, Ohio; B.S., Bowling Green State, 1995; RD, LD.

Linda Novak-Eedy, Menorah Park Center for Senior Living, Beachwood, Ohio; B.S., Bowling Green State, 1983; RD, LD.

Lisa Ogg, Nutrition Health Professional, Cuyahoga County WIC Program; B.S., Kent State, 1996; RD, LD.

Michelle Ogurwale, MetroHealth Center for Community Health (WIC); M.S., Southern Illinois Carbondale; RD, LD.

Laura Otolski, Food and Friends, Washington, D.C.; M.S., NYU, 2000.

Alison Patrick, Cuyahoga County Board of Health; M.P.H., Ohio State, 2006; RD, LD.

Valerie M. Poirier, Cuyahoga County Board of Health, Cleveland, Ohio; B.S., Kent State, 1983; RD, LD.

Stephen Previs, Ph.D., Merck Research Laboratories, Case Western Reserve, 1997.

Barbara Pryor, Ohio Department of Health; M.S., Ohio State, 1994; RD, LD.

Anne Raguso, Director, Dietetic Internship, VA Medical Center, Cleveland, Ohio; Ph.D., Case Western Reserve, 1985; RD, LD.

Jacqueline Rohr, Parma City School District; B.S., Case Western Reserve, 1973; RD, LD.

Anna Rostafinski, MetroHealth Medical Center (WIC); M.S., Case Western Reserve, 1988; RD, LD.

Jo Ann Ruggeri, CDC at Citiview; B.S., Ohio State, 1966; RD, LD.

Maryanne Salsbury, Cuyahoga County WIC Program, Cleveland, Ohio; B.S., Seton Hill; RD, LD.

Joanne Samuels, Solon City School District; B.S., SUNY, 1992; RD, LD.

Sharon Sass, Arizona Department of Health Services, Bureau of Nutrition and Physical Activity; B.S., Nebraska–Lincoln, 1975; RD.

Najeeba Shine, Cuyahoga County Board of Health; M.S., Case Western Reserve, 1992; RD, LD.

Susan Shubrook, Southwest General Health Center, Middleburg Heights, Ohio; B.S., Rutgers, 1985; RD, LD.

Suzanne Silverstein, Virginia Department of Health; M.A., George Washington, 1999; RD.

Barbara Sipe, Summit County Health District, Ohio; M.A., Kent State, 1979.

Gil Sisneros, California Department of Health Services, Sacramento, California; M.P.H., California State, 1990.

Donna Skoda, Summit County General Health District, Stow, Ohio; M.S., Case Western Reserve, 1980; RD.

Mary Kay Solera, Centers for Disease Control and Prevention, Atlanta, Georgia; M.S., Whitworth, 1988; CHES.

Lura Elizabeth Spinks, Berea City Schools; M.S., Ohio State; RD.

Ann Stahlheber, Cuyahoga County Board of Health, Ohio; M.A., Simmons, 2004; RD, LD, CSN.

Denise Tabar, Olmsted Falls City School District, Ohio; M.S., Kent State, 1982; RD, LD.

Felicia Vatakis, UHCMS Department of Nutrition Services; M.S., NYIT; RD, LD.

Sarah Walden, DaVita Dialysis; M.S., Case Western Reserve, 2002; RD, LD.

Marisa Warrix, Family and Consumer Sciences, Cuyahoga County, Ohio State University Extension; M.A., Kent State, 1991.

Melissa Wilson, Centers for Dialysis Care, Cleveland, Ohio; B.S., Mercyhurst, 1997; RD, LD.

Diane Ohama Yates, Medical Nutritional Representative, Ross Products Division, Abbott Laboratories, Cleveland, Ohio; B.S., Hawaii, 1978; RD, LD.

Wendy Youmans, Davita Dialysis; M.S., Case Western Reserve, 1996; RD, LD.

Sharon Zwick-Hamilton, Harborside Health Care; M.S., Case Western Reserve, 1988; RD, LD, CDE, CSG.

COLUMBIA UNIVERSITY

Institute of Human Nutrition

Programs of Study

The Institute of Human Nutrition offers M.S. and Ph.D. programs in nutrition and nutrition-related sciences. The development of scientific curiosity and acquisition of knowledge and technical competence are primary goals of graduate education. The achievement of these goals is fostered at the Institute of Human Nutrition at Columbia by supervised research, guidance, and collaboration with distinguished laboratories and faculty members in an exciting scholarly and research-oriented environment.

The M.S. program is focused on basic science skills in nutrition. It requires one year of course work and the completion of a master's thesis. Graduates of the M.S. program pursue a variety of career paths including medical and dental school, basic science research or Ph.D. degrees, the health-care industry, clinical research, medical education, health-care communications, and public health. A complete overview is available on the Institute of Human Nutrition Web site at http://www.cumc.columbia.edu/dept/ihn/. A list of recent M.S. thesis topics is also available online at http://www.cumc.columbia.edu/dept/ihn/programs/msthesesbasicscience.html. Additional information about the Ph.D. program is available at: http://www.cumc.columbia.edu/dept/ihn/programs/ihn_programs0003.html.

The Institute also offers an M.S. program that is designed for practicing physicians and health professionals. The program is offered on a full-time or part-time basis and is designed to meet the academic and scheduling needs of a practicing professional.

The M.S. in nutrition requires the completion of 33 credits and can be completed in one year, including summer (full-time). All courses are designed to enhance the students' knowledge of nutrition and are applicable to clinical practice. In addition to core courses, students may choose to focus on and take electives in one of three tracks: basic nutrition science, public health and nutritional epidemiology, or clinical nutrition.

In the first year of doctoral study, the Ph.D. program in nutritional and metabolic biology is typically devoted to acquiring a broad base of scientific knowledge through course work and three research rotations. During the second year, the thesis adviser is chosen, and the student begins research in an area of special interest while taking additional courses, if needed, and completes the qualifying examination. Subsequent years involve the conduct and completion of a dissertation research project, followed by submission and defense of the dissertation. Although M.A. and M.Phil. degrees are awarded during the course of study as requirements are satisfied, only students who wish to obtain the Ph.D. are admitted to this program.

Research Facilities

The administrative offices of the Institute of Human Nutrition, part of the Columbia University Medical Center complex, are located on 168th Street in upper Manhattan. There are extensive research and clinical facilities at the Medical Center. Special facilities available for nutrition research and training include the Arteriosclerosis Research Center, the Herbert Irving Comprehensive Cancer Center, the General Clinical Research Center, the Naomi Berrie Diabetes Center, and the Obesity Research Center, which is located at St. Luke's Roosevelt Hospital Center at 114th Street and Amsterdam Avenue. The Health Sciences Library contains more than 500,000 books and periodicals. It also includes a media center with audiovisual learning aids and computers with word processing, statistical, and other program capabilities for student use.

Financial Aid

Financial aid or loans are available to qualified M.S. students. All students, domestic or international, who are accepted into the Ph.D. program are awarded support that fully provides for the tuition and the medical insurance fees required by the University. These students also receive a stipend for their personal use that commences with registration and normally continues throughout graduate study. This stipend was $30,216 for the 2009–10 school year.

Cost of Study

Full-time tuition for the 2009–10 year was $37,772.

Living and Housing Costs

Housing is provided on the Health Sciences Campus of Columbia University. Accommodations include University Residence Halls, which consist of furnished 2- and 4-person suites, and Institutional Real Estate Apartments, which include studios and one-, two-, and three-bedroom apartments. Membership at the Bard Athletic Club is free to students. It contains a swimming pool, squash courts, a gymnasium, a sauna, and exercise equipment and is accessible to the handicapped. A full-time trainer is on staff. Programs offered include aerobics, weight training, and swimming lessons.

Student Group

There are approximately 70 students in the M.S. and 30 in the Ph.D. programs. There are 349 doctoral students enrolled in the various departments and programs at the Medical Center. Approximately 56 percent of students are women. Students are drawn from all parts of the United States and abroad. The 2009–10 M.S. class included students from Nigeria, Peru, Mexico, Taiwan, Canada, China, and the Netherlands.

Location

The Columbia University Medical Center complex is located at 168th Street and Broadway in upper Manhattan. New York's world-renowned cultural activities are all easily accessible by public transportation, as are sporting events and other recreational opportunities.

The University

Columbia University, a privately supported institution, is one of the world's leading educational, scholarly, and research centers. Founded by charter as King's College in 1754, it is one of the oldest universities in the country.

In addition to the Institute of Human Nutrition, components of the University that are situated on the Health Sciences Campus include the College of Physicians and Surgeons, the School of Nursing, the Mailman School of Public Health, and the School of Dental and Oral Surgery. The Center for Neurobiology and Behavior, the Hughes Institute for Structural Biology, and the Institute for Cancer Genetics are also based on the campus. Classrooms and laboratory facilities for graduate school programs are located in the Julius and Armand Hammer Health Sciences Center, the College of Physicians and Surgeons, the William Black Medical Research Building, the Russ Berrie Pavilion, the Irving Cancer Center Research Building, and the Research Annex of the New York State Psychiatric Institute.

Applying

Scores from either the General Test of the Graduate Record Examinations (GRE), the Medical College Admissions Test (MCAT), or the Dental Admission Test (DAT) are required to apply for the M.S. program. The GRE and an advanced Subject Test are recommended, but not required, for the Ph.D. program. International applicants whose native language is not English are required to take the Test of English as a Foreign Language (TOEFL); applicants must score a 100 or above on the TOEFL to be considered for admission. Completed applications and all supporting materials for fall admission are reviewed on a rolling basis until July for the M.S. program; applications and all supporting materials should be submitted in early December for admission to the Ph.D. program.

Correspondence and Information

For general program information and M.S. program applications:
Sharon R. Akabas, Ph.D.
M.S. Program Adviser
Office of Student Affairs
Columbia University Medical Center
630 West 168th Street
New York, New York 10032
Phone: 212-305-4808
Fax: 212-305-3079
E-mail: nutrition@columbia.edu

For Ph.D. program applications:
Admissions Office
Graduate School of Arts and Sciences
Columbia University Medical Center
701 West 168th Street, Room 406
New York, New York 10032
Phone: 212-305-8058
Fax: 212-305-1031
E-mail: gsasatpands@columbia.edu

For graduate program assistance:
Debra J. Wolgemuth, Ph.D.
Chair, Ph.D. Training Committee
Institute of Human Nutrition
PH 15 East, Room 1512
Columbia University Medical Center
630 West 168th Street
New York, New York 10032
Phone: 212-305-4808
Fax: 212-305-3079
E-mail: nutrition@columbia.edu

Columbia University

THE FACULTY AND THEIR RESEARCH

Domenico Accili, M.D., Professor of Medicine. Insulin resistance; mechanisms of insulin receptor signaling.

Richard J. Baer, Ph.D., Professor of Pathology. Function of the BRCA1 breast cancer susceptibility gene; retinoid signaling in mammary glands.

Jonathan Barasch, M.D., Ph.D., Associate Professor of Medicine and Associate Professor of Anatomy and Cell Biology. Growth factors that induce or repair nephrons; acute renal failure.

William S. Blaner, Ph.D., Professor of Nutritional Sciences. Retinoids and vitamin A metabolism.

Angela M. Christiano, Ph.D., Associate Professor of Dermatology and of Genetics and Development. Genetic basis of skin and hair disorders in humans; basic epidermal biology.

Wendy Chung, M.D., Ph.D., Assistant Professor, Pediatrics and Molecular Genetics. Genetics of human disease (colon and pancreatic cancer).

Jeanine M. D'Armiento, M.D., Ph.D., Assistant Professor of Medicine. Metalloproteases and lung pathophysiology.

Richard J. Deckelbaum, M.D., Chair, Robert R. Williams Professor of Nutrition, Professor of Pediatrics, Professor of Epidemiology, and Director, Institute of Human Nutrition. Lipid-gene-cell interaction; lipid emulsion metabolism; free fatty acids and cell lipid-lipoprotein metabolism.

Bernard F. Erlanger, Ph.D., Professor of Microbiology. Biologically significant receptors: the relationship of their structures to their metabolic and regulatory activities.

W. Anthony Ferrante Jr., M.D., Ph.D., Assistant Professor of Medicine. Mechanisms of obesity-induced complications.

Dympna Gallagher, Ed.D., Assistant Professor of Nutritional Medicine. Energy expenditure and body composition at the organ-tissue level, both cross-sectionally and longitudinally, in growth, aging, and type 2 diabetes.

Anne A. Gershon, M.D., Professor of Pediatrics. Virus infectivity; infant immunity relevant to viral infections; varicella-zoster virus (VZV), the highly contagious etiologic agent of chickenpox (varicella) and shingles (zoster).

Michael D. Gershon, M.D., Professor of Anatomy and Cell Biology. Enteric nervous system.

Henry N. Ginsberg, M.D., Irving Professor of Medicine. Regulation of plasma lipoprotein metabolism; regulation of apoprotein B secretion from hepatocytes; dietary regulation of plasma lipids and lipoproteins.

Ira J. Goldberg, M.D., Dickinson Richards Professor of Medicine. Lipoprotein metabolism; lipolytic enzymes; endothelial cell biology; atherosclerosis.

Maxwell E. Gottesman, M.D., Ph.D., Charles H. Revson Professor of Biochemistry and Molecular Biophysics and Professor of Microbiology. Gene transcription and regulation; cancer; thyroid physiology.

Lloyd A. Greene, Ph.D., Professor of Pathology. Cancer biology; cell specification and differentiation; developmental biology; neural degeneration and repair; signal transduction.

Li-Shin Huang, Ph.D., Research Scientist in Medicine. Molecular genetics of lipoprotein metabolism in humans and induced mutant mouse models.

Gerard Karsenty, M.D., Ph.D., Paul A. Marks Professor of Genetics and Development and Professor of Medicine. Novel physiology of the skeleton.

Sudha Kashyap, M.D., Associate Professor of Clinical Pediatrics. Nutritional support of preterm infants.

Harry R. Kissileff, Ph.D., Associate Professor of Clinical Psychology (Psychiatry). Psychology of eating disorders.

Stavroula Kousteni, Ph.D., Assistant Professor. Molecular and cellular mechanisms controlling bone mass.

Sally Lederman, Ph.D., Special Lecturer, Institute of Human Nutrition. Biological determinants of pregnancy outcome; metabolic adjustments for pregnancy and lactation; psychosocial factors that influence birth weight and course of pregnancy; lactational and gestational nutrient needs and the factors that determine them; energy metabolism and body composition changes during pregnancy and lactation.

Rudolph L. Leibel, M.D., Professor of Pediatrics and of Medicine. Biology of weight regulation and the genetic basis of obesity and diabetes.

Cathy L. Mendelsohn, Ph.D., Assistant Professor of Urology. Retinoids and development of the urogenital tract.

Frederica P. Perera, Dr.P.H., Professor of Public Health (Environmental Sciences). Molecular epidemiology; risk assessment; carcinogenesis.

Francis Xavier Pi-Sunyer, M.D., Professor of Medicine. Carbohydrate and lipid metabolism; obesity; diabetes mellitus; food intake regulation.

Ravichandran Ramasamy, Ph.D., Assistant Professor of Medicine. Carbohydrate metabolism and cardiac function.

Lawrence S. Shapiro, Ph.D., Associate Professor of Biochemistry and Molecular Biophysics. Possible biochemical causes for adult-onset obesity.

Stephen L. Sturley, Ph.D., Associate Professor of Clinical Nutrition. Yeast as a model for extracellular and intracellular sterol transport pathway.

Lori Sussel, Ph.D., Associate Professor of Genetics and Development. Role of transcriptional regulatory factors in specifying the development and differentiation of the pancreatic islet during mouse embryogenesis.

Ira A. Tabas, M.D., Ph.D., Richard J. Stock Professor and Vice-Chairman of Research of Medicine and of Anatomy and Cell Biology. Regulation of intracellular cholesterol esterification (the ACAT reaction) in macrophages; lipoprotein endocytic pathways in macrophages; biochemical consequences of macrophage cholesteryl ester accumulation.

Alan R. Tall, M.D., Tilden Weger Bieler Professor of Medicine. Plasma lipoprotein metabolism; atherosclerosis; protein structure-function and mutagenesis; regulation of gene expression; molecular nutrition.

Timothy C. Wang, M.D., Dorothy L. and Daniel H. Silberberg Professor of Medicine and Chief, Gastroenterology Division. The role of inflammation, cytokines, and growth factors in the development of gastrointestinal cancers.

Sharon L. Wardlaw, M.D., Professor of Medicine, Division of Endocrinology. Neuroendocrine control of pituitary function; hypothalamic regulation of energy homeostasis; neuroendocrine-immune interactions.

Debra J. Wolgemuth, Ph.D., Professor of Genetics and Development and Obstetrics and Gynecology. Physiology processes underlying the progression of meiosis and differentiation of mammalian germ cells to highly specialized cells which support embryonic development.

Section 15
Parasitology

This section contains a directory of institutions offering graduate work in parasitology. Additional information about programs listed in the directory may be obtained by writing directly to the dean of a graduate school or chair of a department at the address given in the directory.

For programs offering related work, see also in this book *Biological and Biomedical Sciences* and *Microbiological Sciences*. In another guide in this series:

Graduate Programs in Business, Education, Health, Information Studies, Law & Social Work
See *Allied Health* and *Public Health*

CONTENTS

Parasitology

Illinois State University, Graduate School, College of Arts and Sciences, Department of Biological Sciences, Normal, IL 61790-2200. Offers animal behavior (MS); bacteriology (MS); biochemistry (MS); biological sciences (MS); biology (PhD); biophysics (MS); biotechnology (MS); botany (MS, PhD); cell biology (MS); conservation biology (MS); developmental biology (MS); ecology (MS, PhD); entomology (MS); evolutionary biology (MS); genetics (MS, PhD); immunology (MS); microbiology (MS, PhD); molecular biology (MS); molecular genetics (MS); neurobiology (MS); neuroscience (MS); parasitology (MS); physiology (MS, PhD); plant biology (MS); plant molecular biology (MS); plant sciences (MS); structural biology (MS); zoology (MS, PhD). Part-time programs available. *Degree requirements:* For master's, thesis or alternative; for doctorate, variable foreign language requirement, thesis/dissertation, 2 terms of residency. *Entrance requirements:* For master's, GRE General Test, minimum GPA of 2.6 in last 60 hours of course work; for doctorate, GRE General Test. *Faculty research:* Redoc balance and drug development in schistosoma mansoni, control of the growth of listeria monocytogenes at low temperature, regulation of cell expansion and microtubule function by SPRI, CRUI: physiology and fitness consequences of different life history phenotypes.

Louisiana State University Health Sciences Center, School of Graduate Studies in New Orleans, Department of Microbiology, Immunology, and Parasitology, New Orleans, LA 70112-1393. Offers microbiology and immunology (MS, PhD); MD/PhD. Terminal master's awarded for partial completion of doctoral program. *Degree requirements:* For master's, comprehensive exam, thesis; for doctorate, comprehensive exam, thesis/dissertation, preliminary exam, qualifying exam. *Entrance requirements:* For master's and doctorate, GRE General Test. Additional exam requirements/recommendations for international students: Required—TOEFL. *Faculty research:* Microbial physiology, animal virology, vaccine development, AIDS drug studies, pathogenic mechanisms, molecular immunology.

McGill University, Faculty of Graduate and Postdoctoral Studies, Faculty of Agricultural and Environmental Sciences, Institute of Parasitology, Montréal, QC H3A 2T5, Canada. Offers biotechnology (M Sc A, Certificate); parasitology (M Sc, PhD).

New York University, School of Medicine, New York, NY 10012-1019. Offers biomedical sciences (PhD), including biomedical imaging, cellular and molecular biology, computational biology, developmental genetics, medical and molecular parasitology, microbiology, molecular oncobiology and immunology, neuroscience and physiology, pathobiology, pharmacology, structural biology; clinical investigation (MS); medicine (MD); MD/MA; MD/MPA; MD/MS; MD/PhD. *Accreditation:* LCME/AMA (one or more programs are accredited). *Faculty:* 1,493 full-time (558 women), 327 part-time/adjunct (122 women). *Students:* 747 full-time (360 women); includes 275 minority (23 African Americans, 5 American Indian/Alaska Native, 199 Asian Americans or Pacific Islanders, 48 Hispanic Americans), 2 international. Average age 24. 7,568 applicants, 7% accepted, 213 enrolled. In 2009, 164 first professional degrees, 13 master's, 50 doctorates awarded. *Degree requirements:* For master's, comprehensive exam, thesis; for doctorate, comprehensive exam, thesis/dissertation. *Entrance requirements:* MCAT. Additional exam requirements/recommendations for international students: Required—TOEFL. *Application deadline:* For fall admission, 10/15 for domestic students; for winter admission, 12/18 for domestic students, 12/15 for international students. Application fee: $100. *Expenses:* Contact institution. *Financial support:* In 2009–10, 524 students received support, including 29 fellowships with full tuition reimbursements available (averaging $31,000 per year), 47 research assistantships with full tuition reimbursements available (averaging $31,000 per year); teaching assistantships, Federal Work-Study, institutionally sponsored loans, and health care benefits also available. Financial award application deadline: 3/1; financial award applicants required to submit FAFSA. *Faculty research:* AIDS, cancer, neuroscience, molecular biology, neuroscience, cell biology and molecular genetics, structural biology, microbial pathogenesis and host defense, pharmacology, molecular oncology and immunology. Total annual research expenditures: $201.1 million. *Unit head:* Dr. Robert Grossman, Dean, 212-263-3269, Fax: 212-263-1828. *Application contact:* Dr. Nancy Genieser, Associate Dean, Admissions, 212-263-5290, Fax: 212-263-0720, E-mail: nancy.genieser@nyumc.org.

New York University, School of Medicine and Graduate School of Arts and Science, Sackler Institute of Graduate Biomedical Sciences, Department of Medical and Molecular Parasitology, New York, NY 10012-1019. Offers PhD, MD/PhD. *Degree requirements:* For doctorate, one foreign language, comprehensive exam, thesis/dissertation, qualifying exam. *Entrance requirements:* For doctorate, GRE General Test. Additional exam requirements/recommendations for international students: Required—TOEFL. *Expenses:* Tuition: Full-time $30,528; part-time $1272 per credit. Required fees: $2177. *Faculty research:* Immunoparasitology, cell biology of parasites, genetics of parasites, mode of action of antiparasitic drugs.

Texas A&M University, College of Veterinary Medicine, Department of Veterinary Pathobiology, College Station, TX 77843. Offers genetics (MS, PhD); veterinary microbiology (MS, PhD); veterinary parasitology (MS); veterinary pathology (MS, PhD). Part-time programs available. Postbaccalaureate distance learning degree programs offered. *Faculty:* 27. *Students:* 31 full-time (20 women), 15 part-time (12 women); includes 6 minority (2 African Americans, 1 Asian American or Pacific Islander, 3 Hispanic Americans), 13 international. Average age 33. In 2009, 1 master's, 4 doctorates awarded. Terminal master's awarded for partial completion of doctoral program. *Degree requirements:* For master's, thesis, seminars; for doctorate, thesis/dissertation, seminars. *Entrance requirements:* For master's and doctorate, GRE General Test, minimum GPA of 3.0 in last 60 hours. Additional exam requirements/recommendations for international students: Required—TOEFL. *Application deadline:* For fall admission, 3/1 priority date for domestic students; for spring admission, 8/1 priority date for domestic students. Applications are processed on a rolling basis. Application fee: $50 ($75 for international students). Electronic applications accepted. *Expenses:* Tuition, state resident: full-time $3991; part-time $221.74 per credit hour. Tuition, nonresident: full-time $9049; part-time $502.74 per credit hour. *Financial support:* In 2009–10, fellowships with partial tuition reimbursements (averaging $16,000 per year), research assistantships with partial tuition reimbursements (averaging $15,400 per year), teaching assistantships with partial tuition reimbursements

(averaging $16,000 per year) were awarded; Federal Work-Study, institutionally sponsored loans, scholarships/grants, traineeships, health care benefits, and unspecified assistantships also available. Support available to part-time students. Financial award applicants required to submit FAFSA. *Faculty research:* Infectious and noninfectious diseases of animals and birds, animal genetics, molecular biology, immunology, virology. *Unit head:* Dr. Fuller Bazer, Interim Head, 979-845-5941, Fax: 979-845-9231, E-mail: fbazer@tamu.edu. *Application contact:* Dr. G. G. Wagner, Graduate Advisor, 979-845-2851, Fax: 979-862-1147, E-mail: gwagner@cvm.tamu.edu.

Tulane University, School of Public Health and Tropical Medicine, Department of Tropical Medicine, New Orleans, LA 70118-5669. Offers clinical tropical medicine and travelers health (Diploma); parasitology (MSPH, PhD); public health and tropical medicine (MPHTM); vector borne infectious diseases (MS, PhD); MD/PhD. MS and PhD offered through the Graduate School. *Degree requirements:* For master's, thesis; for doctorate, comprehensive exam, thesis/dissertation. *Entrance requirements:* For master's, GRE General Test, minimum B average in undergraduate course work; for doctorate, GRE General Test. Additional exam requirements/recommendations for international students: Required—TOEFL.

University of Notre Dame, Graduate School, College of Science, Department of Biological Sciences, Notre Dame, IN 46556. Offers aquatic ecology, evolution and environmental biology (MS, PhD); cellular and molecular biology (MS, PhD); genetics (MS, PhD); physiology (MS, PhD); vector biology and parasitology (MS, PhD). Terminal master's awarded for partial completion of doctoral program. *Degree requirements:* For master's, comprehensive exam, thesis; for doctorate, comprehensive exam, thesis/dissertation, candidacy exam. *Entrance requirements:* For master's and doctorate, GRE General Test. Additional exam requirements/recommendations for international students: Required—TOEFL (minimum score 600 paper-based; 250 computer-based; 80 iBT). Electronic applications accepted. *Faculty research:* Tropical disease, molecular genetics, neurobiology, evolutionary biology, aquatic biology.

University of Pennsylvania, School of Medicine, Biomedical Graduate Studies, Graduate Group in Cell and Molecular Biology, Program in Microbiology, Virology, and Parasitology, Philadelphia, PA 19104. Offers PhD, MD/PhD, VMD/PhD. *Degree requirements:* For doctorate, thesis/dissertation. *Entrance requirements:* For doctorate, GRE General Test, previous course work in science. Additional exam requirements/recommendations for international students: Required—TOEFL. *Application deadline:* For fall admission, 12/8 priority date for domestic and international students. Applications are processed on a rolling basis. Application fee: $70. Electronic applications accepted. *Expenses:* Tuition: Full-time $25,660; part-time $4758 per course. Required fees: $2152; $270 per course. Tuition and fees vary according to course load, degree level and program. *Financial support:* Fellowships, research assistantships, scholarships/grants, traineeships, and unspecified assistantships available. *Unit head:* Dr. Robert Ricciardi, Chair, 215-898-3965. *Application contact:* Anna Kline, Coordinator, 215-898-3918, Fax: 215-573-2104, E-mail: camb@mail.med.upenn.edu.

University of Prince Edward Island, Atlantic Veterinary College, Graduate Program in Veterinary Medicine, Charlottetown, PE C1A 4P3, Canada. Offers anatomy (M Sc, PhD); bacteriology (M Sc, PhD); clinical pharmacology (M Sc, PhD); clinical sciences (M Sc, PhD); epidemiology (M Sc, PhD), including reproduction; fish health (M Sc, PhD); food animal nutrition (M Sc, PhD); immunology (M Sc, PhD); microanatomy (M Sc, PhD); parasitology (M Sc, PhD); pathology (M Sc, PhD); pharmacology (M Sc, PhD); physiology (M Sc, PhD); toxicology (M Sc, PhD); veterinary science (M Vet Sc); virology (M Sc, PhD). Part-time programs available. *Degree requirements:* For master's, thesis; for doctorate, thesis/dissertation. *Entrance requirements:* For master's, DVM, B Sc honors degree, or equivalent; for doctorate, M Sc. Additional exam requirements/recommendations for international students: Required—TOEFL (minimum score 550 paper-based; 213 computer-based; 80 iBT). *Expenses:* Contact institution. *Faculty research:* Animal health management, infectious diseases, fin fish and shellfish health, basic biomedical sciences, ecosystem health.

University of Washington, Graduate School, School of Public Health, Department of Global Health, Graduate Program in Pathobiology, Seattle, WA 98195. Offers PhD. *Students:* 35 full-time (27 women), 3 part-time (all women); includes 5 minority (2 African Americans, 1 Asian American or Pacific Islander, 2 Hispanic Americans), 7 international. Average age 29. 50 applicants, 18% accepted, 5 enrolled. In 2009, 7 doctorates awarded. Terminal master's awarded for partial completion of doctoral program. *Degree requirements:* For doctorate, comprehensive exam, thesis/dissertation. *Entrance requirements:* For doctorate, GRE General Test, minimum GPA of 3.0. Additional exam requirements/recommendations for international students: Required—TOEFL. *Application deadline:* For fall admission, 10/1 for domestic students, 11/1 for international students. Application fee: $50. Electronic applications accepted. *Financial support:* In 2009–10, 34 students received support, including 3 fellowships with full tuition reimbursements available (averaging $27,348 per year), 26 research assistantships with full tuition reimbursements available (averaging $27,348 per year); career-related internships or fieldwork, institutionally sponsored loans, scholarships/grants, traineeships, and unspecified assistantships also available. Financial award application deadline: 12/1; financial award applicants required to submit FAFSA. *Faculty research:* Pathogenesis of chlamydiae, molecular biology of parasites, signal transduction, antigenic analysis, molecular biology of tumor viruses, malaria. *Unit head:* Dr. Andreas Stergachis, Acting Chair, 206-543-8350, Fax: 206-543-3873, E-mail: stergach@u.washington.edu. *Application contact:* Mary Conrad, Manager of Student Services, 206-543-4338, Fax: 206-543-3873, E-mail: pathobio@u.washington.edu.

Yale University, School of Medicine, School of Public Health, Program in Parasitology, New Haven, CT 06520. Offers PhD. *Degree requirements:* For doctorate, comprehensive exam, thesis/dissertation, residency. *Entrance requirements:* For doctorate, GRE General Test. Additional exam requirements/recommendations for international students: Required—TOEFL. Electronic applications accepted. *Faculty research:* Cell biology, vector biology, pathogenesis, immunology, epidemiology.

Section 16
Pathology and Pathobiology

This section contains a directory of institutions offering graduate work in pathology and pathobiology, followed by in-depth entries submitted by institutions that chose to prepare detailed program descriptions. Additional information about programs listed in the directory but not augmented by an in-depth entry may be obtained by writing directly to the dean of a graduate school or chair of a department at the address given in the directory.

For programs offering related work, see also in this book *Anatomy; Biochemistry; Biological and Biomedical Sciences; Cell, Molecular, and Structural Biology; Genetics, Developmental Biology, and Reproductive Biology; Microbiological Sciences; Pharmacology and Toxicology;* and *Physiology.* In another guide in this series:

Graduate Programs in Business, Education, Health, Information Studies, Law & Social Work

See *Allied Health, Public Health,* and *Veterinary Medicine and Sciences*

CONTENTS

Molecular Pathogenesis

Dartmouth College, Graduate Program in Molecular and Cellular Biology, Department of Microbiology and Immunology, Program in Molecular Pathogenesis, Hanover, NH 03755. Offers microbiology and immunology (PhD).

Emory University, Graduate School of Arts and Sciences, Division of Biological and Biomedical Sciences, Program in Immunology and Molecular Pathogenesis, Atlanta, GA 30322-1100. Offers PhD. *Faculty:* 50 full-time (8 women). *Students:* 73 full-time (42 women); includes 19 minority (3 African Americans, 1 American Indian/Alaska Native, 12 Asian Americans or Pacific Islanders, 3 Hispanic Americans), 13 international. Average age 27. 120 applicants, 18% accepted, 9 enrolled. In 2009, 12 doctorates awarded. *Degree requirements:* For doctorate, comprehensive exam, thesis/dissertation. *Entrance requirements:* For doctorate, GRE General Test, minimum GPA of 3.0 in science course work (recommended). Additional exam requirements/recommendations for international students: Required—TOEFL. *Application deadline:* For fall admission, 1/3 for domestic and international students. Application fee: $50. Electronic applications accepted. *Financial support:* In 2009–10, 24 students received support, including 24 fellowships with full tuition reimbursements available (averaging $24,500 per year); institutionally sponsored loans, scholarships/grants, and health care benefits also available. *Faculty research:* Transplantation immunology, autoimmunity, microbial pathogenesis. *Unit head:* Dr. Brian Evavold, Director, 404-727-3393, Fax: 404-727-3659, E-mail: evavold@microbio.emory.edu. *Application contact:* Dr. Joshy Jacob, Recruiter, 404-727-7919, Fax: 404-727-8199, E-mail: jjacob3@emory.edu.

North Dakota State University, College of Graduate and Interdisciplinary Studies, College of Agriculture, Food Systems, and Natural Resources, Department of Veterinary and Microbiological Sciences, Fargo, ND 58108. Offers food safety (MS); microbiology (MS); molecular pathogenesis (PhD). Part-time programs available. *Students:* 4 full-time (all women), 3 part-time (1 woman). *Degree requirements:* For master's, thesis; for doctorate, thesis/dissertation, oral and written preliminary exams. *Entrance requirements:* For master's and doctorate, GRE. Additional exam requirements/recommendations for international students: Required—TOEFL (minimum score 525 paper-based; 197 computer-based; 71 iBT). *Application deadline:* For fall admission, 3/15 priority date for domestic students. Applications are processed on a rolling basis. Application fee: $25. *Financial support:* Fellowships with full tuition reimbursements, research assistantships with full tuition reimbursements, teaching assistantships with full tuition reimbursements, Federal Work-Study and institutionally sponsored loans available. Financial award application deadline: 4/15. *Faculty research:* Bacterial gene regulation, antibiotic resistance, molecular virology, mechanisms of bacterial pathogenesis, immunology of animals. *Unit head:* Dr. Doug Freeman, Head, 701-231-7511, E-mail: douglas.freeman@ndsu.nodak.edu. *Application contact:* Dr. Eugene S. Berry, Associate Professor, 701-231-7520, Fax: 701-231-7514, E-mail: eugene.berry@ndsu.edu.

Texas A&M Health Science Center, Graduate School of Biomedical Sciences, Department of Microbial and Molecular Pathogenesis, College Station, TX 77840. Offers immunology (PhD); microbiology (PhD); molecular biology (PhD); virology (PhD). *Degree requirements:* For doctorate, thesis/dissertation. *Entrance requirements:* For doctorate, GRE General Test, minimum GPA of 3.0. *Faculty research:* Molecular pathogenesis, microbial therapeutics.

University at Albany, State University of New York, School of Public Health, Department of Biomedical Sciences, Program in Molecular Pathogenesis, Albany, NY 12222-0001. Offers MS, PhD. *Degree requirements:* For master's, thesis; for doctorate, thesis/dissertation. *Entrance requirements:* For master's and doctorate, GRE General Test, GRE Subject Test.

University of Chicago, Division of the Biological Sciences, Biomedical Sciences Cluster: Cancer Biology, Immunology, Molecular Metabolism and Nutrition, Pathology, and Microbiology, Department of Pathology, Chicago, IL 60637-1513. Offers molecular pathogenesis and molecular medicine (PhD). *Faculty:* 47 full-time (10 women). *Students:* 30 full-time (13 women); includes 7 minority (1 African American, 5 Asian Americans or Pacific Islanders, 1 Hispanic American). Average age 28. 37 applicants, 22% accepted, 4 enrolled. In 2009, 6 doctorates awarded. *Degree requirements:* For doctorate, thesis/dissertation, ethics class, 2 teaching assistantships. *Entrance requirements:* For doctorate, GRE General Test. Additional exam requirements/recommendations for international students: Required—IELTS (minimum score 7); Recommended—TOEFL (minimum score 600 paper-based; 250 computer-based; 104 iBT). *Application deadline:* For fall admission, 12/1 priority date for domestic and international students. Application fee: $55. Electronic applications accepted. *Financial support:* In 2009–10, 30 students received support, including fellowships with full tuition reimbursements available (averaging $29,781 per year), research assistantships with full tuition reimbursements available (averaging $29,781 per year); institutionally sponsored loans, scholarships/grants, traineeships, and health care benefits also available. Financial award applicants required to submit FAFSA. *Faculty research:* Vascular biology, apolipoproteins, cardiovascular disease, immunopathology. Total annual research expenditures: $18 million. *Unit head:* Dr. Stephen Meredith, Program Director, 773-702-1267, Fax: 773-834-5251. *Application contact:* Kristin Reepmeyer, Administrative Assistant, 773-702-3940, Fax: 773-702-4634, E-mail: reepmeyer@bsd.uchicago.edu.

Washington University in St. Louis, Graduate School of Arts and Sciences, Division of Biology and Biomedical Sciences, Program in Molecular Microbiology and Microbial Pathogenesis, St. Louis, MO 63130-4899. Offers PhD. *Degree requirements:* For doctorate, thesis/dissertation. *Entrance requirements:* For doctorate, GRE General Test, GRE Subject Test. Electronic applications accepted.

Molecular Pathology

Texas Tech University Health Sciences Center, School of Allied Health Sciences, Program in Molecular Pathology, Lubbock, TX 79430. Offers MS. *Accreditation:* NAACLS. *Faculty:* 9 full-time (7 women). *Students:* 20 full-time (8 women), 1 (woman) part-time; includes 10 minority (1 African American, 3 Asian Americans or Pacific Islanders, 6 Hispanic Americans). Average age 23. 48 applicants, 44% accepted, 21 enrolled. In 2009, 17 master's awarded. *Entrance requirements:* Additional exam requirements/recommendations for international students: Required—TOEFL, IELTS. *Application deadline:* For spring admission, 3/1 priority date for domestic students. Application fee: $35. Electronic applications accepted. *Financial support:* Career-related internships or fieldwork, institutionally sponsored loans, and scholarships/grants available. Financial award applicants required to submit FAFSA. *Unit head:* Dr. Hal Larsen, Chair, 806-743-3223, E-mail: hal.larsen@ttuhsc.edu. *Application contact:* Jeri Moravcik, Assistant Director of Admissions and Student Affairs, 806-743-3220, Fax: 806-743-2994, E-mail: jeri.moravcik@ttuhsc.edu.

University of California, San Diego, School of Medicine and Office of Graduate Studies, Molecular Pathology Program, La Jolla, CA 92093. Offers bioinformatics (PhD); cancer biology/oncology (PhD); cardiovascular sciences and disease (PhD); microbiology (PhD); molecular pathology (PhD); neurological disease (PhD); stem cell and developmental biology (PhD); structural biology/drug design (PhD). *Entrance requirements:* For doctorate, GRE General Test, GRE Subject Test. Additional exam requirements/recommendations for international students: Required—TOEFL. Electronic applications accepted.

University of Medicine and Dentistry of New Jersey, Graduate School of Biomedical Sciences, Graduate Programs in Biomedical Sciences–Newark, Program in Molecular Pathology and Immunology, Newark, NJ 07107. Offers PhD. *Students:* 16 full-time (10 women), 3 part-time (1 woman); includes 2 African Americans, 1 Asian American or Pacific Islander, 1 Hispanic American, 10 international. *Entrance requirements:* Additional exam requirements/recommendations for international students: Required—TOEFL. *Application deadline:* For fall admission, 2/1 for domestic students. Applications are processed on a rolling basis. Electronic applications accepted. *Financial support:* Fellowships, research assistantships, Federal Work-Study, institutionally sponsored loans, and tuition waivers (full and partial) available. *Unit head:* Dr. Muriel Lambert, Program Director, 973-972-4405, Fax: 973-972-7293, E-mail: mlambert@umdnj.edu. *Application contact:* Dr. Muriel Lambert, Program Director, 973-972-4405, Fax: 973-972-7293, E-mail: mlambert@umdnj.edu.

University of Medicine and Dentistry of New Jersey, Graduate School of Biomedical Sciences, Graduate Programs in Biomedical Sciences–Stratford, Stratford, NJ 08084-5634. Offers biomedical sciences (MBS, MS); cell and molecular biology (MS, PhD); molecular pathology and immunology (MS); DO/MS; DO/PhD; MS/MPH. *Students:* 79 full-time (43 women), 19 part-time (14 women); includes 44 minority (21 African Americans, 16 Asian Americans or Pacific Islanders, 7 Hispanic Americans), 11 international. Average age 25. 128 applicants, 74% accepted, 64 enrolled. In 2009, 36 master's, 1 doctorate awarded. Terminal master's awarded for partial completion of doctoral program. *Degree requirements:* For master's, thesis (for some programs); for doctorate, thesis/dissertation, qualifying exam. *Entrance requirements:* For master's, GRE General Test, MCAT or DAT; for doctorate, GRE General Test. Additional exam requirements/recommendations for international students: Required—TOEFL. *Application deadline:* For fall admission, 2/1 for domestic students; for spring admission, 11/1 for domestic students. Applications are processed on a rolling basis. Application fee: $40. Electronic applications accepted. *Financial support:* Fellowships, Federal Work-Study available. Financial award application deadline: 5/1. *Unit head:* Dr. Carl E. Hock, Senior Associate Dean, Graduate School, 856-566-6282, Fax: 856-566-6232, E-mail: hock@umdnj.edu. *Application contact:* University Registrar, 973-972-5338.

University of Michigan, Horace H. Rackham School of Graduate Studies, Program in Biomedical Sciences (PIBS), Program in Molecular and Cellular Pathology, Ann Arbor, MI 48109. Offers PhD. *Degree requirements:* For doctorate, thesis/dissertation, oral defense of dissertation, preliminary exam. *Entrance requirements:* For doctorate, GRE General Test, 3 letters of recommendation, research experience. Additional exam requirements/recommendations for international students: Required—TOEFL (minimum score 84 iBT). Electronic applications accepted. *Expenses:* Tuition, state resident: full-time $17,286; part-time $1099 per credit hour. Tuition, nonresident: full-time $34,944; part-time $2080 per credit hour. Required fees: $95 per semester. Tuition and fees vary according to course load, degree level and program. *Faculty research:* Cancer Biology; Stem Cell and Developmental Biology; Immunology and Inflammatory Disease; Neurobiology and Neurologic Disease; Structural Biology; Gene Regulation.

University of Pittsburgh, School of Medicine, Graduate Programs in Medicine, Program in Cellular and Molecular Pathology, Pittsburgh, PA 15260. Offers MS, PhD. *Faculty:* 65 full-time (17 women). *Students:* 39 full-time (23 women); includes 9 minority (3 African Americans, 6 American Indian/Alaska Native), 12 international. Average age 27. 655 applicants, 10% accepted, 20 enrolled. In 2009, 9 doctorates awarded. *Degree requirements:* For doctorate, comprehensive exam, thesis/dissertation. *Entrance requirements:* For doctorate, GRE General Test, GRE Subject Test, minimum QPA of 3.0. Additional exam requirements/recommendations for international students: Required—TOEFL (minimum score 600 paper-based; 250 computer-based; 100 iBT), IELTS (minimum score 7). *Application deadline:* For fall admission, 12/15 priority date for domestic and international students. Application fee: $40. Electronic applications accepted. *Expenses:* Tuition, state resident: full-time $16,402; part-time $665 per credit. Tuition, nonresident: full-time $28,694; part-time $1175 per credit. Required fees: $690; $175 per term. Tuition and fees vary according to program. *Financial support:* In 2009–10, 7 fellowships with full tuition reimbursements (averaging $24,650 per year), 32 research assistantships with full tuition reimbursements (averaging $24,650 per year) were awarded; teaching assistantships with full tuition reimbursements, institutionally sponsored loans, scholarships/grants, traineeships, health care benefits, and unspecified assistantships also available. *Faculty research:* Liver growth and differentiation, pathogenesis of neurodegeneration, cancer research. *Unit head:* Dr. Wendy Mars, Graduate Program Director, 412-648-9690, Fax: 412-648-9846, E-mail: wmars@pitt.edu. *Application contact:* Graduate Studies Administrator, 412-648-8957, Fax: 412-648-1077, E-mail: gradstudies@medschool.pitt.edu.

The University of Texas Health Science Center at Houston, Graduate School of Biomedical Sciences, Program in Molecular Pathology, Houston, TX 77225-0036. Offers MS, PhD, MD/PhD. Terminal master's awarded for partial completion of doctoral program. *Degree requirements:* For master's, thesis; for doctorate, thesis/dissertation. *Entrance requirements:* For master's and doctorate, GRE General Test. Additional exam requirements/recommendations for international students: Required—TOEFL. Electronic applications accepted. *Faculty research:* Infectious disease, carcinogenesis, structural biology, cell biology.

Yale University, School of Medicine and Graduate School of Arts and Sciences, Combined Program in Biological and Biomedical Sciences (BBS), Pharmacological Sciences and Molecular Medicine Track, New Haven, CT 06520. Offers PhD, MD/PhD. *Degree requirements:* For doctorate, thesis/dissertation. *Entrance requirements:* For doctorate, GRE General Test. Additional exam requirements/recommendations for international students: Required—TOEFL. *Application deadline:* For fall admission, 12/6 for domestic and international students. Electronic applications accepted. *Financial support:* Fellowships, research assistantships available. *Unit head:* Dr. Gerry Shadel, Co-Director, 203-785-2475, E-mail: bbs.pharm@yale.edu. *Application contact:* Dr. Gerry Shadel, Co-Director, 203-785-2475, E-mail: bbs.pharm@yale.edu.

Pathobiology

Auburn University, College of Veterinary Medicine and Graduate School, Graduate Programs in Veterinary Medicine, Auburn University, AL 36849. Offers biomedical sciences (MS, PhD), including anatomy, physiology and pharmacology (MS), biomedical sciences (PhD), clinical sciences (MS), large animal surgery and medicine (MS), pathobiology (MS), radiology (MS), small animal surgery and medicine (MS); DVM/MS. Part-time programs available. *Faculty:* 100 full-time (40 women), 5 part-time/adjunct (1 woman). *Students:* 17 full-time (6 women), 51 part-time (35 women); includes 8 minority (2 African Americans, 1 American Indian/Alaska Native, 3 Asian Americans or Pacific Islanders, 2 Hispanic Americans), 22 international. Average age 31. 70 applicants, 34% accepted, 10 enrolled. In 2009, 12 master's, 7 doctorates awarded. *Degree requirements:* For doctorate, thesis/dissertation. *Entrance requirements:* For master's, GRE General Test; for doctorate, GRE General Test, GRE Subject Test. *Application deadline:* For fall admission, 7/7 for domestic students; for spring admission, 11/24 for domestic students. Applications are processed on a rolling basis. Application fee: $50 ($60 for international students). Electronic applications accepted. *Expenses:* Tuition, state resident: full-time $6240. Tuition, nonresident: full-time $18,720. International tuition: $18,938 full-time. Required fees: $492. Tuition and fees vary according to course load, program and reciprocity agreements. *Financial support:* Research assistantships, teaching assistantships, Federal Work-Study available. Support available to part-time students. Financial award application deadline: 3/15; financial award applicants required to submit FAFSA. *Unit head:* Dr. Timothy R. Boosinger, Dean, 334-844-4546. *Application contact:* Dr. George Flowers, Dean of the Graduate School, 334-844-2125.

Brown University, Graduate School, Division of Biology and Medicine, Program in Pathology and Laboratory Medicine, Providence, RI 02912. Offers biology (PhD); cancer biology (PhD); immunology and infection (PhD); medical science (PhD); pathobiology (Sc M); toxicology and environmental pathology (PhD). Terminal master's awarded for partial completion of doctoral program. *Degree requirements:* For doctorate, thesis/dissertation, preliminary exam. *Entrance requirements:* For master's and doctorate, GRE General Test, GRE Subject Test. Additional exam requirements/recommendations for international students: Required—TOEFL. Electronic applications accepted. *Faculty research:* Environmental pathology, carcinogenesis, immunopathology, signal transduction, innate immunity.

Columbia University, College of Physicians and Surgeons, Department of Pathology, New York, NY 10032. Offers pathobiology (M Phil, MA, PhD); MD/PhD. Only candidates for the PhD are admitted. Terminal master's awarded for partial completion of doctoral program. *Degree requirements:* For doctorate, thesis/dissertation. *Entrance requirements:* For master's and doctorate, GRE General Test. Additional exam requirements/recommendations for international students: Required—TOEFL. *Faculty research:* Virology, molecular biology, cell biology, neurobiology, immunology.

Drexel University, College of Medicine, Biomedical Graduate Programs, Interdisciplinary Program in Molecular Pathobiology, Philadelphia, PA 19104-2875. Offers MS, PhD, MD/PhD. *Degree requirements:* For doctorate, comprehensive exam, thesis/dissertation, qualifying exams. *Entrance requirements:* For doctorate, GRE General Test, minimum GPA of 3.0. Additional exam requirements/recommendations for international students: Required—TOEFL. Electronic applications accepted. *Faculty research:* Cell and molecular immunology, tumor immunology, molecular genetics, immunopathology, immunology of aging.

The Johns Hopkins University, School of Medicine, Graduate Programs in Medicine, Department of Pathology, Baltimore, MD 21218-2699. Offers pathobiology (PhD). *Faculty:* 68 full-time (14 women). *Students:* 42 full-time (29 women); includes 5 minority (1 African American, 3 Asian Americans or Pacific Islanders, 1 Hispanic American), 18 international. Average age 29. 124 applicants, 6% accepted, 8 enrolled. In 2009, 4 doctorates awarded. *Degree requirements:* For doctorate, thesis/dissertation, qualifying oral exam. *Entrance requirements:* For doctorate, GRE General Test, previous course work with laboratory in organic and inorganic chemistry, general biology, calculus; interview. Additional exam requirements/recommendations for international students: Required—TOEFL. *Application deadline:* For winter admission, 1/10 for domestic students. Application fee: $85. Electronic applications accepted. *Financial support:* In 2009–10, 42 fellowships with full tuition reimbursements (averaging $26,855 per year) were awarded; scholarships/grants also available. *Faculty research:* Role of mutant proteins in Alzheimer's disease, nuclear protein function in breast and prostate cancer, medically important fungi, glycoproteins in HIV pathogenesis. Total annual research expenditures: $38.6 million. *Unit head:* Dr. J. Brooks Jackson, Chair, 410-955-9790, Fax: 410-955-0394. *Application contact:* Wilhelmena M. Braswell, Senior Academic Program Coordinator, 443-287-3163, Fax: 410-614-3548, E-mail: wbraswel@jhmi.edu.

Kansas State University, College of Veterinary Medicine, Department of Diagnostic Medicine/Pathobiology, Manhattan, KS 66506. Offers biomedical science (MS); diagnostic medicine/pathobiology (PhD). *Faculty:* 22 full-time (4 women), 5 part-time/adjunct (2 women). *Students:* 23 full-time (7 women), 22 part-time (11 women), 8 international. Average age 30.Terminal master's awarded for partial completion of doctoral program. *Degree requirements:* For doctorate, thesis/dissertation. *Entrance requirements:* For master's and doctorate, interviews. Additional exam requirements/recommendations for international students: Required—TOEFL (minimum score 550 paper-based; 213 computer-based). *Application deadline:* For fall admission, 2/1 priority date for domestic and international students; for spring admission, 8/1 priority date for domestic and international students. Applications are processed on a rolling basis. Application fee: $40 ($55 for international students). Electronic applications accepted. *Financial support:* In 2009–10, 26 research assistantships (averaging $14,013 per year) were awarded; teaching assistantships, Federal Work-Study, institutionally sponsored loans, and scholarships/grants also available. Financial award application deadline: 3/1; financial award applicants required to submit FAFSA. *Faculty research:* Infectious disease of animals, food safety and security, epidemiology and public health, toxicology, and pathology. Total annual research expenditures: $2.1 million. *Unit head:* M. M. Chengappa, Head, 785-532-4403, E-mail: chengap@ksu.edu. *Application contact:* T. G. Nagaraja, Director, 785-532-1214, E-mail: tnagaraj@ksu.edu.

Medical University of South Carolina, College of Graduate Studies, Program in Molecular and Cellular Biology and Pathobiology, Charleston, SC 29425. Offers cancer biology (PhD); cardiovascular biology (PhD); cardiovascular imaging (PhD); cell regulation (PhD); craniofacial biology (PhD); genetics and development (PhD); marine biomedicine (PhD); DMD/PhD; MD/PhD. *Faculty:* 137 full-time (33 women). *Students:* 39 full-time (25 women); includes 6 minority (4 African Americans, 1 Asian American or Pacific Islander, 1 Hispanic American), 9 international. Average age 28. In 2009, 16 doctorates awarded. *Degree requirements:* For doctorate, thesis/dissertation, oral and written exams. *Entrance requirements:* For doctorate, GRE General Test, interview, minimum GPA of 3.0. Additional exam requirements/recommendations for international students: Required—TOEFL (minimum score 600 paper-based; 250 computer-based; 100 iBT). *Application deadline:* For fall admission, 1/15 priority date for domestic and international students. Applications are processed on a rolling basis. Application fee: $0 ($85 for international students). Electronic applications accepted. *Financial support:* In 2009–10, 39 students received support, including 39 research assistantships with partial tuition reimbursements available (averaging $23,000 per year); Federal Work-Study and scholarships/grants also available. Support available to part-time students. Financial award application deadline: 3/10; financial award applicants required to submit FAFSA. *Unit head:* Dr. Donald R. Menick, Director, 843-876-5045, Fax: 843-792-6590, E-mail: menickd@musc.edu. *Application contact:* Dr. Cynthia F. Wright, Associate Dean for Admissions and Career Development, 843-792-2564, Fax: 843-792-6590, E-mail: wrightcf@musc.edu.

Michigan State University, College of Veterinary Medicine and The Graduate School, Graduate Programs in Veterinary Medicine, Department of Pathobiology and Diagnostic Investigation, East Lansing, MI 48824. Offers pathology (MS, PhD); pathology–environmental toxicology (PhD). *Faculty:* 22 full-time (8 women), 1 (woman) part-time/adjunct. *Students:* 19 full-time (11 women), 6 part-time (4 women); includes 8 minority (7 African Americans, 1 Asian American or Pacific Islander), 7 international. Average age 31. 6 applicants, 67% accepted. In 2009, 4 doctorates awarded. *Entrance requirements:* Additional exam requirements/recommendations for international students: Required—TOEFL. Electronic applications accepted. *Expenses:* Tuition, state resident: part-time $478.25 per credit hour. Tuition, nonresident: part-time $966.50 per credit hour. Part-time tuition and fees vary according to program. *Financial support:* In 2009–10, 11 research assistantships with tuition reimbursements (averaging $8,442 per year) were awarded. Total annual research expenditures: $2.5 million. *Unit head:* Dr. Laura J. McCutcheon, Chairperson, 517-353-3145, Fax: 517-432-5836, E-mail: mccutc12@msu.edu. *Application contact:* Denise Harrison, Administrative Assistant, 517-432-4685, Fax: 517-432-5836, E-mail: harrison@dcpah.msu.edu.

New York University, School of Medicine, New York, NY 10012-1019. Offers biomedical sciences (PhD), including biomedical imaging, cellular and molecular biology, computational biology, developmental genetics, medical and molecular parasitology, microbiology, molecular oncobiology and immunology, neuroscience and physiology, pathobiology, pharmacology, structural biology; clinical investigation (MS); medicine (MD); MD/MA; MD/MPA; MD/MS; MD/PhD. *Accreditation:* LCME/AMA (one or more programs are accredited). *Faculty:* 1,493 full-time (558 women), 327 part-time/adjunct (122 women). *Students:* 747 full-time (360 women); includes 275 minority (23 African Americans, 5 American Indian/Alaska Native, 199 Asian Americans or Pacific Islanders, 48 Hispanic Americans), 2 international. Average age 24. 7,568 applicants, 7% accepted, 213 enrolled. In 2009, 164 first professional degrees, 13 master's, 50 doctorates awarded. *Degree requirements:* For master's, comprehensive exam, thesis; for doctorate, comprehensive exam, thesis/dissertation. *Entrance requirements:* MCAT. Additional exam requirements/recommendations for international students: Required—TOEFL. *Application deadline:* For fall admission, 10/15 for domestic students; for winter admission, 12/18 for domestic students, 12/15 for international students. Application fee: $100. *Expenses:* Contact institution. *Financial support:* In 2009–10, 524 students received support, including 29 fellowships with full tuition reimbursements available (averaging $31,000 per year), 47 research assistantships with full tuition reimbursements available (averaging $31,000 per year); teaching assistantships, Federal Work-Study, institutionally sponsored loans, and health care benefits also available. Financial award application deadline: 3/1; financial award applicants required to submit FAFSA. *Faculty research:* AIDS, cancer, neuroscience, molecular biology, neuroscience, cell biology and molecular genetics, structural biology, microbial pathogenesis and host defense, pharmacology, molecular oncology and immunology. Total annual research expenditures: $201.1 million. *Unit head:* Dr. Robert Grossman, Dean, 212-263-3269, Fax: 212-263- 1828. *Application contact:* Dr. Nancy Genieser, Associate Dean, Admissions, 212-263-5290, Fax: 212-263-0720, E-mail: nancy.genieser@nyumc.org.

New York University, School of Medicine and Graduate School of Arts and Science, Sackler Institute of Graduate Biomedical Sciences, Program in Pathobiology, New York, NY 10012-1019. Offers PhD. *Expenses:* Tuition: Full-time $30,528; part-time $1272 per credit. Required fees: $2177.

The Ohio State University, College of Medicine, School of Biomedical Science, Department of Pathology, Columbus, OH 43210. Offers experimental pathobiology (MS); pathology assistant (MS); MD/PhD. *Accreditation:* NAACLS. *Degree requirements:* For master's, comprehensive exam (for some programs), thesis. *Entrance requirements:* For master's, GRE General Test. Additional exam requirements/recommendations for international students: Required—TOEFL (minimum score 550 paper-based; 213 computer-based). Electronic applications accepted. *Expenses:* Tuition, state resident: full-time $10,683. Tuition, nonresident: full-time $25,923. Tuition and fees vary according to course load and program. *Faculty research:* Clinical pathology, transplantation pathology, cancer research, neuropathology, vascular pathology.

The Ohio State University, College of Veterinary Medicine, Department of Veterinary Biosciences, Columbus, OH 43210. Offers anatomy and cellular biology (MS, PhD); pathobiology (MS, PhD); pharmacology (MS, PhD); toxicology (MS, PhD); veterinary physiology (MS, PhD). *Faculty:* 45. *Students:* 18 full-time (14 women), 20 part-time (16 women); includes 3 minority (1 African American, 1 Asian American or Pacific Islander, 1 Hispanic American), 16 international. Average age 30. In 2009, 1 master's, 9 doctorates awarded. *Entrance requirements:* For master's and doctorate, GRE General Test. Additional exam requirements/recommendations for international students: Required—TOEFL. *Application deadline:* Applications are processed on a rolling basis. Application fee: $40 ($50 for international students). Electronic applications accepted. *Expenses:* Tuition, state resident: full-time $10,683. Tuition, nonresident: full-time $25,923. Tuition and fees vary according to course load and program. *Faculty research:* Microvasculature, muscle biology, neonatal lung and bone development. *Unit head:* Dr. Michael J. Oglesbee, Graduate Studies Committee Chair, 614-292-5661, Fax: 614-292-6473, E-mail: oglesbee.1@osu.edu. *Application contact:* Graduate Admissions, 614-292-9444, Fax: 614-292-3895, E-mail: domestic.grad@osu.edu.

Penn State University Park, Graduate School, College of Agricultural Sciences, Department of Veterinary and Biomedical Sciences, State College, University Park, PA 16802-1503. Offers pathobiology (PhD).

Purdue University, School of Veterinary Medicine and Graduate School, Graduate Programs in Veterinary Medicine, Department of Comparative Pathobiology, West Lafayette, IN 47907-2027. Offers comparative epidemiology and public health (MS); comparative epidemiology and public heath (PhD); comparative microbiology and immunology (MS, PhD); comparative pathobiology (MS, PhD); interdisciplinary studies (PhD), including microbial pathogenesis, molecular signaling and cancer biology, molecular virology; lab animal medicine (MS); veterinary anatomic pathology (MS); veterinary clinical pathology (MS). *Faculty:* 37 full-time (10 women), 4 part-time/adjunct (2 women). *Students:* 53 full-time (31 women), 2 part-time (1 woman); includes 3 minority (2 African Americans, 1 Hispanic American), 32 international. Average age 35. In 2009, 6 master's, 2 doctorates awarded. Terminal master's awarded for partial completion of doctoral program. *Degree requirements:* For master's, thesis (for some programs); for doctorate, thesis/dissertation. *Entrance requirements:* For master's and doctorate, GRE General Test. Additional exam requirements/recommendations for international students: Required—TOEFL (minimum score 575 paper-based; 232 computer-based), IELTS (minimum score 6.5), TWE (minimum score 4). *Application deadline:* For fall admission, 8/12 for domestic students, 6/15 for international students; for spring admission, 1/12 for domestic students, 10/15 for international students. Application fee: $55. Electronic applications accepted. *Financial support:* Fellowships, research assistantships, teaching assistantships available. Financial award application deadline: 3/1; financial award applicants required to submit FAFSA. *Unit head:* Dr. Suresh Mittal, Interim Head, 765-494-7543. *Application contact:* Denise A. Ottinger, Director, Student Services and Admissions, 765-494-7893, Fax: 765-496-2891, E-mail: vetadmissions@purdue.edu.

Texas A&M University, College of Veterinary Medicine, Department of Veterinary Pathobiology, College Station, TX 77843. Offers genetics (MS, PhD); veterinary microbiology (MS, PhD); veterinary parasitology (MS); veterinary pathology (MS, PhD). Part-time programs available. Postbaccalaureate distance learning degree programs offered. *Faculty:* 27. *Students:* 31 full-time (20 women), 15 part-time (12 women); includes 6 minority (2 African Americans, 1 Asian American or Pacific Islander, 3 Hispanic Americans), 13 international. Average age 33. In 2009, 1 master's, 4 doctorates awarded. Terminal master's awarded for partial completion of doctoral program. *Degree requirements:* For master's, thesis, seminars; for doctorate, thesis/dissertation, seminars. *Entrance requirements:* For master's and doctorate, GRE General Test, minimum GPA of 3.0 in last 60 hours. Additional exam requirements/recommendations for international students: Required—TOEFL. *Application deadline:* For fall admission, 3/1 priority date for domestic students; for spring admission, 8/1 priority date for domestic students. Applications are processed on a rolling basis. Application fee: $50 ($75 for international

Pathobiology

Texas A&M University (continued)

students). Electronic applications accepted. *Expenses:* Tuition, state resident: full-time $3991; part-time $221.74 per credit hour. Tuition, nonresident: full-time $9049; part-time $502.74 per credit hour. *Financial support:* In 2009–10, fellowships with partial tuition reimbursements (averaging $16,000 per year), research assistantships with partial tuition reimbursements (averaging $15,400 per year), teaching assistantships with partial tuition reimbursements (averaging $16,000 per year) were awarded; Federal Work-Study, institutionally sponsored loans, scholarships/grants, traineeships, health care benefits, and unspecified assistantships also available. Support available to part-time students. Financial award applicants required to submit FAFSA. *Faculty research:* Infectious and noninfectious diseases of animals and birds, animal genetics, molecular biology, immunology, virology. *Unit head:* Dr. Fuller Bazer, Interim Head, 979-845-5941, Fax: 979-845-9231, E-mail: fbazer@tamu.edu. *Application contact:* Dr. G. G. Wagner, Graduate Advisor, 979-845-2851, Fax: 979-862-1147, E-mail: gwagner@cvm.tamu.edu.

The University of Arizona, Graduate College, College of Agriculture and Life Sciences, School of Natural Resources, Program in Microbiology and Pathobiology, Tucson, AZ 85721. Offers MS, PhD. *Students:* 42 full-time (23 women), 43 part-time (22 women); includes 2 American Indian/Alaska Native, 2 Asian Americans or Pacific Islanders, 4 Hispanic Americans, 16 international. Average age 31. Terminal master's awarded for partial completion of doctoral program. *Degree requirements:* For master's, thesis; for doctorate, comprehensive exam, thesis/dissertation. *Entrance requirements:* For master's and doctorate, GRE, minimum GPA of 3.0, 3 letters of recommendation, letter of intent. Additional exam requirements/recommendations for international students: Required—TOEFL (minimum score 550 paper-based; 213 computer-based; 80 iBT); Recommended—IELTS (minimum score 7). *Application deadline:* For fall admission, 2/28 for domestic students, 12/1 for international students. Applications are processed on a rolling basis. Application fee: $75. *Expenses:* Tuition, state resident: full-time $9028. Tuition, nonresident: full-time $24,890. *Financial support:* Research assistantships with tuition reimbursements, teaching assistantships with tuition reimbursements, scholarships/grants available. Financial award application deadline: 3/22. *Faculty research:* Antibiotic resistance, molecular pathogenesis of bacteria, food safety, diagnosis of animal disease, parasitology. *Application contact:* Elaine Mattes, 520-621-4466, E-mail: emattes@email.arizona.edu.

University of Cincinnati, Graduate School, College of Medicine, Graduate Programs in Biomedical Sciences, Program in Pathobiology and Molecular Medicine, Cincinnati, OH 45221. Offers pathology (PhD), including anatomic pathology, laboratory medicine, pathobiology and molecular medicine. *Degree requirements:* For doctorate, thesis/dissertation, qualifying exam. *Entrance requirements:* For doctorate, GRE General Test. Additional exam requirements/recommendations for international students: Required—TOEFL (minimum score 620 paper-based; 260 computer-based). Electronic applications accepted. *Faculty research:* Cardiovascular and lipid disorders, digestive and kidney disease, endocrine and metabolic disorders, hematologic and oncogenic, immunology and infectious disease.

University of Connecticut, Graduate School, College of Agriculture and Natural Resources, Department of Pathobiology and Veterinary Science, Storrs, CT 06269. Offers pathobiology (MS, PhD). *Faculty:* 12 full-time (3 women). *Students:* 16 full-time (8 women), 2 part-time (1 woman); includes 2 minority (1 Asian American or Pacific Islander, 1 Hispanic American), 5 international. Average age 31. 14 applicants, 14% accepted, 1 enrolled. In 2009, 2 master's, 2 doctorates awarded. Terminal master's awarded for partial completion of doctoral program. *Degree requirements:* For master's, comprehensive exam; for doctorate, thesis/dissertation. *Entrance requirements:* For master's and doctorate, GRE General Test, GRE Subject Test. Additional exam requirements/recommendations for international students: Required—TOEFL (minimum score 550 paper-based; 213 computer-based). *Application deadline:* For fall admission, 2/1 priority date for domestic and international students; for spring admission, 11/1 for domestic students, 10/1 for international students. Applications are processed on a rolling basis. Application fee: $55. Electronic applications accepted. *Expenses:* Tuition, state resident: full-time $4725; part-time $525 per credit. Tuition, nonresident: full-time $12,267; part-time $1363 per credit. Required fees: $346 per semester. Tuition and fees vary according to course load. *Financial support:* In 2009–10, 13 research assistantships with full tuition reimbursements, 1 teaching assistantship with full tuition reimbursement were awarded; fellowships, Federal Work-Study, scholarships/grants, health care benefits, and unspecified assistantships also available. Financial award application deadline: 2/1; financial award applicants required to submit FAFSA. *Unit head:* Herbert J. Van Kruiningen, Head, 860-486-0837, Fax: 860-486-2794, E-mail: herbert.vankruiningen@uconn.edu. *Application contact:* Steven Geary, Chairperson, 860-486-0835, Fax: 860-486-2794, E-mail: steven.geary@uconn.edu.

University of Illinois at Urbana–Champaign, College of Veterinary Medicine, Department of Pathobiology, Urbana, IL 61802. Offers MS, PhD, DVM/PhD. Part-time programs available. *Faculty:* 21 full-time (6 women). *Students:* 10 full-time (6 women), 5 part-time (1 woman); includes 3 minority (1 African American, 1 Asian American or Pacific Islander, 1 Hispanic American), 6 international. 34 applicants, 21% accepted, 6 enrolled. In 2009, 3 doctorates awarded. Terminal master's awarded for partial completion of doctoral program. *Entrance requirements:* For master's and doctorate, GRE, minimum GPA of 3.0. Additional exam requirements/recommendations for international students: Required—TOEFL (minimum score 590 paper-based; 243 computer-based). *Application deadline:* Applications are processed on a rolling basis. Application fee: $60 ($75 for international students). Electronic applications accepted. *Financial support:* In 2009–10, 3 fellowships, 5 research assistantships, 1 teaching assistantship were awarded; tuition waivers (full and partial) also available. *Faculty research:* Epidemiology, immunology, microbiology, parasitology, clinical pathology. *Unit head:* Daniel L. Rock, Head, 217-333-2449, Fax: 217-244-7421, E-mail: dlrock@illinois.edu. *Application contact:* Paula Moxley, Administrative Aide, 217-244-8924, Fax: 217-244-7421, E-mail: pkm@illinois.edu.

University of Missouri, College of Veterinary Medicine and Graduate School, Graduate Programs in Veterinary Medicine, Department of Veterinary Pathobiology, Columbia, MO 65211. Offers laboratory animal medicine (MS); pathobiology (MS, PhD). *Faculty:* 55 full-time (22 women), 14 part-time/adjunct (5 women). *Students:* 15 full-time (7 women), 30 part-time (18 women); includes 5 minority (1 Asian American or Pacific Islander, 4 Hispanic Americans), 10 international. Average age 30. 13 applicants, 62% accepted, 8 enrolled. In 2009, 1 master's,

2 doctorates awarded. *Degree requirements:* For master's, thesis; for doctorate, 2 foreign languages, thesis/dissertation. *Entrance requirements:* For master's and doctorate, GRE General Test, minimum GPA of 3.0. Additional exam requirements/recommendations for international students: Required—TOEFL (minimum score 500 paper-based; 61 iBT). *Application deadline:* For fall admission, 5/1 for domestic students. Application fee: $45 ($60 for international students). Electronic applications accepted. *Financial support:* Research assistantships with full tuition reimbursements, teaching assistantships with full tuition reimbursements, institutionally sponsored loans available. *Unit head:* Dr. Catherine Vogelweid, Director of Graduate Studies, 573-882-5503, E-mail: vogelweidc@missouri.edu. *Application contact:* Dr. Ronald Terjung, Associate Dean for Research and Postdoctoral Studies, 573-882-2635, E-mail: terjungr@missouri.edu.

University of Southern California, Keck School of Medicine and Graduate School, Graduate Programs in Medicine, Department of Pathology, Los Angeles, CA 90089. Offers experimental and molecular pathology (MS); pathobiology (PhD). *Faculty:* 55 full-time (12 women), 5 part-time/adjunct (1 woman). *Students:* 40 full-time (23 women); includes 19 minority (13 Asian Americans or Pacific Islanders, 6 Hispanic Americans), 10 international. Average age 26. 26 applicants, 38% accepted, 9 enrolled. In 2009, 4 master's, 8 doctorates awarded. *Degree requirements:* For master's, thesis; for doctorate, thesis/dissertation. *Entrance requirements:* For master's, GRE General Test, minimum GPA of 3.0; for doctorate, GRE General Test, minimum GPA of 3.0, BS in natural sciences. Additional exam requirements/recommendations for international students: Required—TOEFL (minimum score 600 paper-based; 250 computer-based; 100 iBT). *Application deadline:* For fall admission, 12/1 priority date for domestic and international students. Application fee: $85. Electronic applications accepted. *Expenses:* Tuition: Full-time $25,980; part-time $1315 per unit. Required fees: $554. One-time fee: $35 full-time. Full-time tuition and fees vary according to degree level and program. *Financial support:* In 2009–10, 27 students received support, including 4 fellowships with tuition reimbursements available (averaging $27,060 per year), 22 research assistantships with tuition reimbursements available (averaging $27,060 per year), 1 teaching assistantship with tuition reimbursement available (averaging $27,060 per year); Federal Work-Study, institutionally sponsored loans, scholarships/grants, health care benefits, and unspecified assistantships also available. Financial award application deadline: 5/1. *Faculty research:* Immunology of lymphomas and leukemias, lung cancer, molecular basis of oncogenesis, central nervous system disease, organic chemical carcinogens and carcinogenic metal salts. *Unit head:* Dr. Michael E. Selsted, Chair, 323-442-1179, Fax: 323-442-3049, E-mail: selsted@usc.edu. *Application contact:* Lisa A. Doumak, Student Services Assistant, 323-442-1168, Fax: 323-442-3049, E-mail: doumak@usc.edu.

University of Toronto, School of Graduate Studies, Life Sciences Division, Department of Laboratory Medicine and Pathobiology, Toronto, ON M5S 1A1, Canada. Offers M Sc, PhD, MD/PhD. *Degree requirements:* For master's, thesis; for doctorate, thesis/dissertation, oral defense of thesis. *Entrance requirements:* For master's, minimum B+ average in final 2 years, research experience, 2 letters of recommendation, resume, interview; for doctorate, minimum A– average, 2 letters of recommendation, research experience, resumé, interview. Additional exam requirements/recommendations for international students: Required—TOEFL (600 paper-based, 250 computer-based), TWE (5) or IELTS (7).

University of Washington, Graduate School, School of Public Health, Department of Global Health, Graduate Program in Pathobiology, Seattle, WA 98195. Offers PhD. *Students:* 35 full-time (27 women), 3 part-time (all women); includes 5 minority (2 African Americans, 1 Asian American or Pacific Islander, 2 Hispanic Americans), 7 international. Average age 29. 50 applicants, 18% accepted, 5 enrolled. In 2009, 7 doctorates awarded. Terminal master's awarded for partial completion of doctoral program. *Degree requirements:* For doctorate, comprehensive exam, thesis/dissertation. *Entrance requirements:* For doctorate, GRE General Test, minimum GPA of 3.0. Additional exam requirements/recommendations for international students: Required—TOEFL. *Application deadline:* For fall admission, 10/1 for domestic students, 11/1 for international students. Application fee: $50. Electronic applications accepted. *Financial support:* In 2009–10, 34 students received support, including 3 fellowships with full tuition reimbursements available (averaging $27,348 per year), 26 research assistantships with full tuition reimbursements available (averaging $27,348 per year); career-related internships or fieldwork, institutionally sponsored loans, scholarships/grants, traineeships, and unspecified assistantships also available. Financial award application deadline: 12/1; financial award applicants required to submit FAFSA. *Faculty research:* Pathogenesis of chlamydiae, molecular biology of parasites, signal transduction, antigenic analysis, molecular biology of tumor viruses, malaria. *Unit head:* Dr. Andreas Stergachis, Acting Chair, 206-543-8350, Fax: 206-543-3873, E-mail: stergach@u.washington.edu. *Application contact:* Mary Conrad, Manager of Student Services, 206-543-4338, Fax: 206-543-3873, E-mail: pathobio@u.washington.edu.

University of Wyoming, College of Agriculture, Department of Veterinary Sciences, Laramie, WY 82070. Offers pathobiology (MS). *Degree requirements:* For master's, thesis. *Entrance requirements:* For master's, GRE General Test, minimum GPA of 3.0. Additional exam requirements/recommendations for international students: Required—TOEFL. *Faculty research:* Infectious diseases, pathology, toxicology, immunology, microbiology.

Wake Forest University, School of Medicine and Graduate School of Arts and Sciences, Graduate Programs in Medicine, Program in Molecular and Cellular Pathobiology, Winston-Salem, NC 27109. Offers MS, PhD, MD/PhD. *Degree requirements:* For master's, thesis; for doctorate, thesis/dissertation. *Entrance requirements:* For master's and doctorate, GRE General Test. Additional exam requirements/recommendations for international students: Required—TOEFL. Electronic applications accepted. *Faculty research:* Atherosclerosis, lipoproteins, arterial wall metabolism.

Yale University, School of Medicine and Graduate School of Arts and Sciences, Combined Program in Biological and Biomedical Sciences (BBS), Pharmacological Sciences and Molecular Medicine Track, New Haven, CT 06520. Offers PhD, MD/PhD. *Degree requirements:* For doctorate, thesis/dissertation. *Entrance requirements:* For doctorate, GRE General Test. Additional exam requirements/recommendations for international students: Required—TOEFL. *Application deadline:* For fall admission, 12/6 for domestic and international students. Electronic applications accepted. *Financial support:* Fellowships, research assistantships available. *Unit head:* Dr. Gerry Shadel, Co-Director, 203-785-2475, E-mail: bbs.pharm@yale.edu. *Application contact:* Dr. Gerry Shadel, Co-Director, 203-785-2475, E-mail: bbs.pharm@yale.edu.

Pathology

Albert Einstein College of Medicine, Sue Golding Graduate Division of Medical Sciences, Department of Pathology, Bronx, NY 10467. Offers PhD, MD/PhD. *Degree requirements:* For doctorate, thesis/dissertation. *Entrance requirements:* For doctorate, GRE General Test. Additional exam requirements/recommendations for international students: Required—TOEFL. *Faculty research:* Clinical and disease-related research at tissue, cellular, and subcellular levels; biochemistry and morphology of enzyme and lysosome disorders.

Baylor College of Medicine, Graduate School of Biomedical Sciences, Program in Developmental Biology, Houston, TX 77030-3498. Offers PhD, MD/PhD. *Faculty:* 52 full-time (16 women). *Students:* 51 full-time (26 women); includes 9 minority (1 American Indian/Alaska Native, 6 Asian Americans or Pacific Islanders, 2 Hispanic Americans), 29 international. Average age 25. In 2009, 4 doctorates awarded. *Degree requirements:* For doctorate, thesis/dissertation, public defense. *Entrance requirements:* For doctorate, GRE General Test, GRE

Subject Test (strongly recommended), minimum GPA of 3.0. Additional exam requirements/recommendations for international students: Required—TOEFL. *Application deadline:* For fall admission, 1/1 priority date for domestic students. Application fee: $0. Electronic applications accepted. *Financial support:* Fellowships, research assistantships, career-related internships or fieldwork, Federal Work-Study, institutionally sponsored loans, health care benefits, tuition waivers (full), and stipends available. *Faculty research:* Molecular and genetic approaches to study pattern formation in Dictyostelium, Drosophila, C.elegans, mouse, Xenopus, and zebrafish; cross-species approach. *Unit head:* Dr. Hugo Bellen, Director, 713-798-6410. *Application contact:* Catherine Tasnier, Graduate Program Administrator, 713-798-6410, Fax: 713-798-5386, E-mail: cat@bcm.edu.

See Close-Up on page 315.

Brown University, Graduate School, Division of Biology and Medicine, Program in Pathology and Laboratory Medicine, Providence, RI 02912. Offers biology (PhD); cancer biology (PhD); immunology and infection (PhD); medical science (PhD); pathobiology (Sc M); toxicology and environmental pathology (PhD). Terminal master's awarded for partial completion of doctoral program. *Degree requirements:* For doctorate, thesis/dissertation, preliminary exam. *Entrance requirements:* For master's and doctorate, GRE General Test, GRE Subject Test. Additional exam requirements/recommendations for international students: Required—TOEFL. Electronic applications accepted. *Faculty research:* Environmental pathology, carcinogenesis, immunopathology, signal transduction, innate immunity.

Case Western Reserve University, School of Medicine and School of Graduate Studies, Graduate Programs in Medicine, Programs in Molecular and Cellular Basis of Disease/Pathology, Cleveland, OH 44106. Offers cancer biology (PhD); cell biology (MS, PhD); immunology (MS, PhD); pathology (MS, PhD); MD/PhD. Terminal master's awarded for partial completion of doctoral program. *Degree requirements:* For master's, thesis; for doctorate, thesis/dissertation. *Entrance requirements:* For master's and doctorate, GRE General Test, GRE Subject Test. Additional exam requirements/recommendations for international students: Required—TOEFL (minimum score 550 paper-based; 213 computer-based). Electronic applications accepted. *Faculty research:* Neurobiology, molecular biology, cancer biology, biomaterials, biocompatibility.

Colorado State University, College of Veterinary Medicine and Biomedical Sciences, Department of Microbiology, Immunology and Pathology, Fort Collins, CO 80523-1619. Offers microbiology (MS, PhD); pathology (PhD). *Faculty:* 43 full-time (18 women), 2 part-time/adjunct (1 woman). *Students:* 51 full-time (43 women), 40 part-time (22 women); includes 8 minority (4 Asian Americans or Pacific Islanders, 4 Hispanic Americans), 9 international. Average age 31. 87 applicants, 14% accepted, 12 enrolled. In 2009, 8 master's, 15 doctorates awarded. *Degree requirements:* For master's, thesis; for doctorate, comprehensive exam, thesis/dissertation. *Entrance requirements:* For master's, GRE General Test, minimum GPA of 3.0, BA/BS in biomedical field, reviewer evaluation forms, resume; for doctorate, GRE General Test, minimum GPA of 3.0, BA/BS in biomedical field, reviewer evaluation forms, resume, statement of interest. Additional exam requirements/recommendations for international students: Required—TOEFL (minimum score 550 paper-based). *Application deadline:* For fall admission, 1/1 priority date for domestic students; for spring admission, 10/1 priority date for domestic students. Applications are processed on a rolling basis. Application fee: $50. Electronic applications accepted. *Expenses:* Tuition, state resident: full-time $6434; part-time $359.10 per credit. Tuition, nonresident: full-time $18,116; part-time $1006.45 per credit. Required fees: $1496; $83 per credit. *Financial support:* In 2009–10, 85 students received support, including 34 fellowships with tuition reimbursements available (averaging $29,724 per year), 45 research assistantships with tuition reimbursements available (averaging $21,337 per year), 6 teaching assistantships with tuition reimbursements available (averaging $12,607 per year); Federal Work-Study, scholarships/grants, traineeships, and unspecified assistantships also available. Financial award applicants required to submit FAFSA. *Faculty research:* Medical and veterinary microbiology, pathology of disease, microbial pathogenesis, industrial and environmental microbiology, vector-borne disease. Total annual research expenditures: $32.6 million. *Unit head:* Dr. Edward A. Hoover, Head, 970-491-7587, Fax: 970-491-0603, E-mail: edward.hoover@colostate.edu. *Application contact:* Marcia Boggs, Graduate Program Coordinator, 970-491-3228, Fax: 970-491-1815, E-mail: marcia.boggs@colostate.edu.

Columbia University, College of Physicians and Surgeons, Department of Pathology, New York, NY 10032. Offers pathobiology (M Phil, MA, PhD); MD/PhD. Only candidates for the PhD are admitted. Terminal master's awarded for partial completion of doctoral program. *Degree requirements:* For doctorate, thesis/dissertation. *Entrance requirements:* For master's and doctorate, GRE General Test. Additional exam requirements/recommendations for international students: Required—TOEFL. *Faculty research:* Virology, molecular biology, cell biology, neurobiology, immunology.

Dalhousie University, Faculty of Graduate Studies and Faculty of Medicine, Graduate Programs in Medicine, Department of Pathology, Halifax, NS B3H 4R2, Canada. Offers M Sc, PhD. *Degree requirements:* For master's, oral defense of thesis. *Entrance requirements:* Additional exam requirements/recommendations for international students: Required—TOEFL, IELTS, 1 of the following 5 approved tests: TOEFL, IELTS, CAEL, CANTEST, Michigan English Language Assessment Battery. Electronic applications accepted. *Faculty research:* Tumor immunology, molecular oncology, clinical chemistry, hematology, molecular genetics/oncology.

Duke University, Graduate School, Department of Pathology, Durham, NC 27710. Offers PhD. *Accreditation:* NAACLS. *Faculty:* 31 full-time. *Students:* 34 full-time (21 women); includes 5 minority (3 African Americans, 1 Asian American or Pacific Islander, 1 Hispanic American), 11 international. 21 applicants, 29% accepted, 5 enrolled. In 2009, 5 doctorates awarded. *Degree requirements:* For doctorate, thesis/dissertation. *Entrance requirements:* For doctorate, GRE General Test, GRE Subject Test (recommended). Additional exam requirements/recommendations for international students: Required—TOEFL (minimum score 550 paper-based; 213 computer-based; 73 iBT), IELTS (minimum score 7). *Application deadline:* For fall admission, 12/8 priority date for domestic and international students. Application fee: $75. Electronic applications accepted. *Financial support:* Fellowships, research assistantships, Federal Work-Study available. Financial award application deadline: 12/31. *Unit head:* Soman Abraham, Director of Graduate Studies, 919-684-9929, Fax: 919-681-8868, E-mail: pamela.harris@duke.edu. *Application contact:* Cynthia Robertson, Associate Dean for Enrollment Services, 919-684-3913, E-mail: grad-admissions@duke.edu.

See Close-Up on page 437.

Duke University, School of Medicine, Pathologists' Assistant Program, Durham, NC 27708-0586. Offers MHS. *Accreditation:* NAACLS. *Faculty:* 42 part-time/adjunct (17 women). *Students:* 16 full-time (14 women). Average age 26. 44 applicants, 18% accepted, 8 enrolled. In 2009, 8 master's awarded. *Degree requirements:* For master's, comprehensive exam. *Entrance requirements:* For master's, GRE. Additional exam requirements/recommendations for international students: Required—TOEFL, IELTS. *Application deadline:* For fall admission, 2/28 priority date for domestic students. Application fee: $55. *Expenses:* Contact institution. *Financial support:* In 2009–10, 15 students received support; fellowships, research assistantships, teaching assistantships, scholarships/grants available. Financial award application deadline: 5/1; financial award applicants required to submit FAFSA. *Unit head:* Dr. Rex C. Bentley, Program Director, 919-684-6423, Fax: 919-681-7799, E-mail: bentl003@mc.duke.edu. *Application contact:* Pamela Vollmer, Associate Director, 919-684-2159, E-mail: vollm003@mc.duke.edu.

East Carolina University, Brody School of Medicine, Department of Pathology, Greenville, NC 27858-4353. Offers PhD. *Degree requirements:* For doctorate, comprehensive exam, thesis/dissertation. *Entrance requirements:* For doctorate, GRE General Test, bachelor's degree in biological chemistry or physical science.

Georgetown University, Graduate School of Arts and Sciences, Programs in Biomedical Sciences, Department of Pathology, Washington, DC 20057. Offers MS, PhD, MD/PhD, MS/PhD. *Degree requirements:* For master's, thesis; for doctorate, comprehensive exam, thesis/dissertation. *Entrance requirements:* For master's and doctorate, GRE General Test. Additional exam requirements/recommendations for international students: Required—TOEFL. *Faculty research:* Virus-induced diabetes, viral oncology, renal pathophysiology.

Harvard University, Graduate School of Arts and Sciences, Division of Medical Sciences, Boston, MA 02115. Offers biological chemistry and molecular pharmacology (PhD); cell biology (PhD); genetics (PhD); microbiology and molecular genetics (PhD); pathology (PhD), including experimental pathology. *Degree requirements:* For doctorate, thesis/dissertation. *Entrance requirements:* For doctorate, GRE General Test, GRE Subject Test. Additional exam requirements/recommendations for international students: Required—TOEFL. *Expenses:* Tuition: Full-time $33,696. Required fees: $1126. Full-time tuition and fees vary according to program.

Indiana University–Purdue University Indianapolis, Indiana University School of Medicine, Department of Pathology and Laboratory Medicine, Indianapolis, IN 46202-2896. Offers MS, PhD, MD/PhD. *Faculty:* 27 full-time (4 women). *Students:* 5 full-time (4 women), 3 part-time (all women). Average age 25. 29 applicants, 17% accepted, 4 enrolled. In 2009, 4 master's awarded. *Degree requirements:* For master's, thesis; for doctorate, thesis/dissertation. *Entrance requirements:* For master's and doctorate, GRE General Test. Additional exam requirements/recommendations for international students: Required—TOEFL. *Application deadline:* For fall admission, 1/15 priority date for domestic students. Applications are processed on a rolling basis. Application fee: $55 ($65 for international students). *Financial support:* In 2009–10, 4 teaching assistantships with full tuition reimbursements (averaging $10,711 per year) were awarded; fellowships, research assistantships with full tuition reimbursements, institutionally sponsored loans also available. Financial award application deadline: 2/1. *Faculty research:* Intestinal microecology and anaerobes, molecular pathogenesis of infectious diseases, AIDS pneumocystis, sports medicine toxicology, neuropathology of aging. *Unit head:* Dr. John Eble, Chairman, 317-274-4806. *Application contact:* Dr. Diane S. Leland, Graduate Adviser, 317-274-0148.

Iowa State University of Science and Technology, College of Veterinary Medicine and Graduate College, Graduate Programs in Veterinary Medicine, Department of Veterinary Pathology, Ames, IA 50011. Offers MS, PhD. *Faculty:* 15 full-time (6 women), 4 part-time/adjunct (0 women). *Students:* 7 full-time (5 women), 4 part-time (1 woman); includes 2 minority (both Hispanic Americans). 2 applicants, 50% accepted, 0 enrolled. In 2009, 1 doctorate awarded. *Degree requirements:* For master's, thesis or alternative; for doctorate, thesis/dissertation. *Entrance requirements:* For master's and doctorate, GRE General Test. Additional exam requirements/recommendations for international students: Required—TOEFL (minimum score 550 paper-based; 79 iBT) or IELTS (minimum score 6.5). *Application deadline:* Applications are processed on a rolling basis. Application fee: $40 ($90 for international students). Electronic applications accepted. *Expenses:* Tuition, state resident: full-time $6716. Tuition, nonresident: full-time $8908. Tuition and fees vary according to course level, course load, program and student level. *Financial support:* In 2009–10, 2 research assistantships with full and partial tuition reimbursements (averaging $21,890 per year) were awarded; teaching assistantships with full and partial tuition reimbursements, scholarships/grants, health care benefits, and unspecified assistantships also available. *Unit head:* Dr. Claire B. Andreasen, Chair, 515-294-0877. *Application contact:* Dr. Claire B. Andreasen, Chair, 515-294-0877.

The Johns Hopkins University, School of Medicine, Graduate Programs in Medicine, Department of Pathology, Baltimore, MD 21218-2699. Offers pathobiology (PhD). *Faculty:* 68 full-time (14 women). *Students:* 42 full-time (29 women); includes 5 minority (1 African American, 3 Asian Americans or Pacific Islanders, 1 Hispanic American), 18 international. Average age 29. 124 applicants, 6% accepted, 8 enrolled. In 2009, 4 doctorates awarded. *Degree requirements:* For doctorate, thesis/dissertation, qualifying oral exam. *Entrance requirements:* For doctorate, GRE General Test, previous course work with laboratory in organic and inorganic chemistry, general biology, calculus; interview. Additional exam requirements/recommendations for international students: Required—TOEFL. *Application deadline:* For winter admission, 1/10 for domestic students. Application fee: $85. Electronic applications accepted. *Financial support:* In 2009–10, 42 fellowships with full tuition reimbursements (averaging $26,855 per year) were awarded; scholarships/grants also available. *Faculty research:* Role of mutant proteins in Alzheimer's disease, nuclear protein function in breast and prostate cancer, medically important fungi, glycoproteins in HIV pathogenesis. Total annual research expenditures: $38.6 million. *Unit head:* Dr. J. Brooks Jackson, Chair, 410-955-9790, Fax: 410-955-0394. *Application contact:* Wilhelmena M. Braswell, Senior Academic Program Coordinator, 443-287-3163, Fax: 410-614-3548, E-mail: wbraswel@jhmi.edu.

Loma Linda University, School of Medicine, Department of Pathology and Human Anatomy, Loma Linda, CA 92350. Offers MS, PhD. Part-time programs available. Terminal master's awarded for partial completion of doctoral program. *Degree requirements:* For master's, thesis; for doctorate, 2 foreign languages, thesis/dissertation. *Entrance requirements:* For master's and doctorate, GRE General Test. Additional exam requirements/recommendations for international students: Required—TOEFL (minimum score 550 paper-based; 213 computer-based). *Faculty research:* Neuroendocrine system, histochemistry and image analysis, effect of age and diabetes on PNS, electron microscopy, histology.

Louisiana State University Health Sciences Center, School of Graduate Studies in New Orleans, Department of Pathology, New Orleans, LA 70112-2223. Offers MS, PhD, MD/PhD. Part-time programs available. *Degree requirements:* For master's, comprehensive exam, thesis; for doctorate, comprehensive exam, thesis/dissertation. *Entrance requirements:* For master's and doctorate, GRE General Test. Additional exam requirements/recommendations for international students: Required—TOEFL. *Faculty research:* Immunohematology, hematology, experimental and epidemiological studies in atherosclerosis, epidemiology of cancer.

McGill University, Faculty of Graduate and Postdoctoral Studies, Faculty of Medicine, Department of Pathology, Montréal, QC H3A 2T5, Canada. Offers M Sc, PhD.

Medical University of South Carolina, College of Graduate Studies, Department of Pathology and Laboratory Medicine, Charleston, SC 29425. Offers MS, PhD, DMD/PhD, MD/PhD. *Faculty:* 14 full-time (5 women), 1 part-time/adjunct (0 women). *Students:* 6 full-time (4 women), 1 (woman) part-time; includes 2 minority (both African Americans). Average age 25. 7 applicants, 29% accepted, 1 enrolled. In 2009, 1 doctorate awarded. Terminal master's awarded for partial completion of doctoral program. *Degree requirements:* For master's, thesis; for doctorate, thesis/dissertation, oral and written exams. *Entrance requirements:* For master's, GRE General Test; for doctorate, GRE General Test, interview, minimum GPA of 3.0. Additional exam requirements/recommendations for international students: Required—TOEFL (minimum score 600 paper-based; 250 computer-based; 100 iBT). *Application deadline:* For fall admission, 1/15 priority date for domestic and international students. Applications are processed on a rolling basis. Application fee: $0 ($85 for international students). Electronic applications accepted. *Financial support:* In 2009–10, 4 research assistantships with partial tuition reimbursements (averaging $23,000 per year) were awarded; Federal Work-Study and scholarships/grants also available. Support available to part-time students. Financial award application deadline: 3/10; financial award applicants required to submit FAFSA. *Faculty research:* Neurobiology of hearing loss; inner ear ion homeostasis; cancer biology, genetics and stem cell biology; cellular defense mechanisms. *Unit head:* Dr. Janice M. Lage, Chair, 843-792-3121, Fax: 843-792-6590, E-mail: lagejm@musc.edu. *Application contact:* Dr. Lisa Cunningham, Assistant Professor and Coordinator of Graduate Studies, 843-792-8324, Fax: 843-792-6590, E-mail: cunninll@musc.edu.

Michigan State University, College of Veterinary Medicine and The Graduate School, Graduate Programs in Veterinary Medicine, Department of Pathobiology and Diagnostic Investigation, East Lansing, MI 48824. Offers pathology (MS, PhD); pathology–environmental toxicology (PhD). *Faculty:* 22 full-time (8 women), 1 (woman) part-time/adjunct. *Students:* 19 full-time (11 women), 6 part-time (4 women); includes 8 minority (7 African Americans, 1 Asian American or Pacific Islander), 7 international. Average age 31. 6 applicants, 67% accepted. In 2009, 4 doctorates awarded. *Entrance requirements:* Additional exam requirements/recommendations for international students: Required—TOEFL. Electronic applications accepted. *Expenses:* Tuition, state resident: part-time $478.25 per credit hour. Tuition, nonresident: part-time $966.50 per credit hour. Part-time tuition and fees vary according to program. *Financial support:* In 2009–10, 11 research assistantships with tuition reimbursements (averaging $8,442 per year) were awarded. Total annual research expenditures: $2.5 million. *Unit head:* Dr. Laura J. McCutcheon, Chairperson, 517-353-3145, Fax: 517-432-5836, E-mail: mccutc12@msu.edu. *Application contact:* Denise Harrison, Administrative Assistant, 517-432-4685, Fax: 517-432-5836, E-mail: harrison@dcpah.msu.edu.

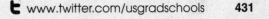

Pathology

New York Medical College, Graduate School of Basic Medical Sciences, Program in Experimental Pathology, Valhalla, NY 10595-1691. Offers MS, PhD, MD/PhD. Part-time and evening/weekend programs available. Terminal master's awarded for partial completion of doctoral program. *Degree requirements:* For master's, thesis; for doctorate, comprehensive exam, thesis/dissertation. *Entrance requirements:* For master's and doctorate, GRE General Test. Additional exam requirements/recommendations for international students: Required—TOEFL. *Expenses:* Tuition: Full-time $18,170; part-time $790 per credit. Required fees: $790 per credit. $20 per semester. One-time fee: $100. Tuition and fees vary according to class time, course level, course load, degree level, program, student level and student's religious affiliation. *Faculty research:* Atherogenesis and endothelial cell biology, immunology and inflammation, tumor biology and metastasis, mechanisms of chemical carcinogens, mechanisms of free radial tissue damage.

North Carolina State University, College of Veterinary Medicine, Program in Comparative Biomedical Sciences, Raleigh, NC 27695. Offers cell biology (MS, PhD); infectious disease (MS, PhD); pathology (MS, PhD); pharmacology (MS, PhD); population medicine (MS, PhD). Part-time programs available. *Degree requirements:* For master's, thesis; for doctorate, thesis/dissertation. *Entrance requirements:* For master's and doctorate, GRE General Test. Additional exam requirements/recommendations for international students: Required—TOEFL (minimum score 550 paper-based; 213 computer-based). Electronic applications accepted. *Expenses:* Contact institution. *Faculty research:* Infectious diseases, cell biology, pharmacology and toxicology, genomics, pathology and population medicine.

North Dakota State University, College of Graduate and Interdisciplinary Studies, College of Agriculture, Food Systems, and Natural Resources, Department of Veterinary and Microbiological Sciences, Fargo, ND 58108. Offers food safety (MS); microbiology (MS); molecular pathogenesis (PhD). Part-time programs available. *Students:* 4 full-time (all women), 3 part-time (1 woman). *Degree requirements:* For master's, thesis; for doctorate, thesis/dissertation, oral and written preliminary exams. *Entrance requirements:* For master's and doctorate, GRE. Additional exam requirements/recommendations for international students: Required—TOEFL (minimum score 525 paper-based; 197 computer-based; 71 iBT). *Application deadline:* For fall admission, 3/15 priority date for domestic students. Applications are processed on a rolling basis. Application fee: $25. *Financial support:* Fellowships with full tuition reimbursements, research assistantships with full tuition reimbursements, teaching assistantships with full tuition reimbursements, Federal Work-Study and institutionally sponsored loans available. Financial award application deadline: 4/15. *Faculty research:* Bacterial gene regulation, antibiotic resistance, molecular virology, mechanisms of bacterial pathogenesis, immunology of animals. *Unit head:* Dr. Doug Freeman, Head, 701-231-7511, E-mail: douglas.freeman@ndsu.nodak.edu. *Application contact:* Dr. Eugene S. Berry, Associate Professor, 701-231-7520, Fax: 701-231-7514, E-mail: eugene.berry@ndsu.edu.

The Ohio State University, College of Medicine, School of Biomedical Science, Department of Pathology, Columbus, OH 43210. Offers experimental pathobiology (MS); pathology assistant (MS); MD/PhD. *Accreditation:* NAACLS. *Degree requirements:* For master's, comprehensive exam (for some programs), thesis. *Entrance requirements:* For master's, GRE General Test. Additional exam requirements/recommendations for international students: Required—TOEFL (minimum score 550 paper-based; 213 computer-based). Electronic applications accepted. *Expenses:* Tuition, state resident: full-time $10,683. Tuition, nonresident: full-time $25,923. Tuition and fees vary according to course load and program. *Faculty research:* Clinical pathology, transplantation pathology, cancer research, neuropathology, vascular pathology.

Purdue University, School of Veterinary Medicine and Graduate School, Graduate Programs in Veterinary Medicine, Department of Comparative Pathobiology, West Lafayette, IN 47907-2027. Offers comparative epidemiology and public health (MS); comparative epidemiology and public heath (PhD); comparative microbiology and immunology (MS, PhD); comparative pathobiology (MS, PhD); interdisciplinary studies (PhD), including microbial pathogenesis, molecular signaling and cancer biology, molecular virology; lab animal medicine (MS); veterinary anatomic pathology (MS); veterinary clinical pathology (MS). *Faculty:* 37 full-time (10 women), 4 part-time/adjunct (2 women). *Students:* 53 full-time (31 women), 2 part-time (1 woman); includes 3 minority (2 African Americans, 1 Hispanic American), 32 international. Average age 35. In 2009, 6 master's, 2 doctorates awarded. Terminal master's awarded for partial completion of doctoral program. *Degree requirements:* For master's, thesis (for some programs); for doctorate, thesis/dissertation. *Entrance requirements:* For master's and doctorate, GRE General Test. Additional exam requirements/recommendations for international students: Required—TOEFL (minimum score 575 paper-based; 232 computer-based), IELTS (minimum score 6.5), TWE (minimum score 4). *Application deadline:* For fall admission, 8/12 for domestic students, 6/15 for international students; for spring admission, 1/12 for domestic students, 10/15 for international students. Application fee: $55. Electronic applications accepted. *Financial support:* Fellowships, research assistantships, teaching assistantships available. Financial award application deadline: 3/1; financial award applicants required to submit FAFSA. *Unit head:* Dr. Suresh Mittal, Interim Head, 765-494-7543. *Application contact:* Denise A. Ottinger, Director, Student Services and Admissions, 765-494-7893, Fax: 765-496-2891, E-mail: vetadmissions@purdue.edu.

Queen's University at Kingston, School of Graduate Studies and Research, Faculty of Health Sciences, Department of Pathology and Molecular Medicine, Kingston, ON K7L 3N6, Canada. Offers M Sc, PhD. Part-time programs available. *Degree requirements:* For master's, thesis; for doctorate, comprehensive exam, thesis/dissertation. *Entrance requirements:* Additional exam requirements/recommendations for international students: Required—TOEFL. *Faculty research:* Immunopathology, cancer biology, immunology and metastases, cell differentiation, blood coagulation.

Quinnipiac University, School of Health Sciences, Program for Pathologists' Assistant, Hamden, CT 06518-1940. Offers MHS. *Accreditation:* NAACLS. *Faculty:* 2 full-time (0 women), 3 part-time/adjunct (1 woman). *Students:* 37 full-time (31 women); includes 5 minority (1 African American, 3 Asian Americans or Pacific Islanders, 1 Hispanic American), 5 international. Average age 27. 109 applicants, 19% accepted, 18 enrolled. In 2009, 18 master's awarded. *Degree requirements:* For master's, residency. *Entrance requirements:* For master's, interview, coursework in biological and health sciences, minimum GPA of 2.8. Additional exam requirements/recommendations for international students: Required—TOEFL (minimum score 575 paper-based; 233 computer-based; 90 iBT), IELTS (minimum score 6.5). *Application deadline:* For fall admission, 12/15 for domestic students. Applications are processed on a rolling basis. Application fee: $45. Electronic applications accepted. *Expenses:* Tuition: Full-time $16,030; part-time $770 per credit. Required fees: $630; $35 per credit. *Financial support:* Career-related internships or fieldwork, tuition waivers (partial), and unspecified assistantships available. Financial award application deadline: 4/15; financial award applicants required to submit FAFSA. *Unit head:* Dr. Kenneth Kaloustian, Director, 203-582-8676, Fax: 203-582-3443, E-mail: ken.kaloustian@quinnipiac.edu. *Application contact:* Kristin Parent, Assistant Director of Graduate Health Sciences Admissions, 800-462-1944, Fax: 203-582-3443, E-mail: kristin.parent@quinnipiac.edu.

Rosalind Franklin University of Medicine and Science, College of Health Professions, Pathologists' Assistant Department, North Chicago, IL 60064-3095. Offers MS. *Faculty:* 5 full-time (2 women), 1 part-time/adjunct (0 women). *Students:* 54 full-time (46 women); includes 15 minority (10 African Americans, 3 Asian Americans or Pacific Islanders, 2 Hispanic Americans). Average age 28. 104 applicants, 38% accepted, 33 enrolled. *Entrance requirements:* For master's, bachelor's degree from an accredited college or university, minimum cumulative GPA of 3.0. Additional exam requirements/recommendations for international students: Required—TOEFL. *Application deadline:* For spring admission, 2/28 for domestic and international students. Applications are processed on a rolling basis. Application fee: $50. *Financial support:* Application deadline: 3/31. *Faculty research:* Adaptation of ACGME/ADASP pathology resident training competencies to pathologists' assistant clinical education, utilization of structural portfolios in pathologists' assistant clinical education. *Unit head:* John Vitale, Acting Chair, 847-578-8638, E-mail: john.vitale@rosalindfranklin.edu. *Application contact:* Melissa Knox, Admissions Officer, 847-578-8772, Fax: 847-775-6559, E-mail: melissa.knox@rosalindfranklin.edu.

Saint Louis University, Graduate School and School of Medicine, Graduate Program in Biomedical Sciences and Graduate School, Department of Pathology, St. Louis, MO 63103-2097. Offers PhD. *Degree requirements:* For doctorate, comprehensive exam, thesis/dissertation, oral and written preliminary exams, oral defense of dissertation. *Entrance requirements:* For doctorate, GRE General Test (GRE Subject Test optional), letters of recommendation, resume, interview. Additional exam requirements/recommendations for international students: Required—TOEFL (minimum score 525 paper-based; 194 computer-based). Electronic applications accepted. *Faculty research:* Cancer research, hepatitis C virology, cell imaging, liver disease.

Stony Brook University, State University of New York, Graduate School, College of Arts and Sciences, Department of Biochemistry and Cell Biology, Molecular and Cellular Biology Program, Stony Brook, NY 11794. Offers biochemistry and molecular biology (PhD); biological sciences (MA); cellular and developmental biology (PhD); immunology and pathology (PhD); molecular and cellular biology (PhD). *Students:* 100 full-time (62 women); includes 8 minority (2 African Americans, 5 Asian Americans or Pacific Islanders, 1 Hispanic American), 60 international. Average age 30. 277 applicants, 15% accepted. In 2009, 15 doctorates awarded. *Degree requirements:* For doctorate, comprehensive exam, thesis/dissertation, teaching experience. *Entrance requirements:* For doctorate, GRE General Test, GRE Subject Test. Additional exam requirements/recommendations for international students: Required—TOEFL. *Application deadline:* For fall admission, 1/15 for domestic students. Application fee: $60. *Expenses:* Tuition, state resident: full-time $8370; part-time $349 per credit. Tuition, nonresident: full-time $13,250; part-time $552 per credit. Required fees: $933. *Financial support:* In 2009–10, 49 research assistantships, 15 teaching assistantships were awarded; fellowships, Federal Work-Study also available. *Unit head:* Prof. Robert Haltiwanger, Chair, 631-632-8560. *Application contact:* Prof. Robert Haltiwanger, Chair, 631-632-8560.

Temple University, Health Sciences Center, School of Medicine and Graduate School, Graduate Programs in Medicine, Department of Pathology and Laboratory Medicine, Philadelphia, PA 19122-6096. Offers PhD. *Degree requirements:* For doctorate, one foreign language, thesis/dissertation, research seminars. *Entrance requirements:* For doctorate, GRE General Test, GRE Subject Test, minimum GPA of 3.0. Additional exam requirements/recommendations for international students: Required—TOEFL (minimum score 550 paper-based; 213 computer-based; 79 iBT). Electronic applications accepted. *Faculty research:* Molecular cloning, cell proliferation, cell cycle regulation, DNA repair, cytogenetics.

Texas A&M University, College of Veterinary Medicine, Department of Veterinary Pathobiology, College Station, TX 77843. Offers genetics (MS, PhD); veterinary microbiology (MS, PhD); veterinary parasitology (MS); veterinary pathology (MS, PhD). Part-time programs available. Postbaccalaureate distance learning degree programs offered. *Faculty:* 27. *Students:* 31 full-time (20 women), 15 part-time (12 women); includes 6 minority (2 African Americans, 1 Asian American or Pacific Islander, 3 Hispanic Americans), 13 international. Average age 33. In 2009, 1 master's, 4 doctorates awarded. Terminal master's awarded for partial completion of doctoral program. *Degree requirements:* For master's, thesis, seminars; for doctorate, thesis/dissertation, seminars. *Entrance requirements:* For master's and doctorate, GRE General Test, minimum GPA of 3.0 in last 60 hours. Additional exam requirements/recommendations for international students: Required—TOEFL. *Application deadline:* For fall admission, 3/1 priority date for domestic students; for spring admission, 8/1 priority date for domestic students. Applications are processed on a rolling basis. Application fee: $50 ($75 for international students). Electronic applications accepted. *Expenses:* Tuition, state resident: full-time $3991; part-time $221.74 per credit hour. Tuition, nonresident: full-time $9049; part-time $502.74 per credit hour. *Financial support:* In 2009–10, fellowships with partial tuition reimbursements (averaging $16,000 per year), research assistantships with partial tuition reimbursements (averaging $15,400 per year), teaching assistantships with partial tuition reimbursements (averaging $16,000 per year) were awarded; Federal Work-Study, institutionally sponsored loans, scholarships/grants, traineeships, health care benefits, and unspecified assistantships also available. Support available to part-time students. Financial award applicants required to submit FAFSA. *Faculty research:* Infectious and noninfectious diseases of animals and birds, animal genetics, molecular biology, immunology, virology. *Unit head:* Dr. Fuller Bazer, Interim Head, 979-845-5941, Fax: 979-845-9231, E-mail: fbazer@tamu.edu. *Application contact:* Dr. G. G. Wagner, Graduate Advisor, 979-845-2851, Fax: 979-862-1147, E-mail: gwagner@cvm.tamu.edu.

Université de Montréal, Faculty of Medicine, Department of Pathology and Cellular Biology, Montréal, QC H3C 3J7, Canada. Offers M Sc, PhD. *Faculty:* 40 full-time (9 women), 2 part-time/adjunct (1 woman). *Students:* 10 full-time (6 women), 24 part-time (15 women). 38 applicants, 16% accepted, 6 enrolled. In 2009, 3 master's, 2 doctorates awarded. Terminal master's awarded for partial completion of doctoral program. *Degree requirements:* For master's, thesis; for doctorate, thesis/dissertation, general exam. *Entrance requirements:* For master's and doctorate, proficiency in French, knowledge of English. *Application deadline:* For fall admission, 2/1 priority date for domestic students; for winter admission, 11/1 priority date for domestic students; for spring admission, 2/1 priority date for domestic students. Application fee: $100. Electronic applications accepted. *Financial support:* Tuition waivers (full) available. *Faculty research:* Immunopathology, cardiovascular pathology, oncogenetics, cellular neurocytology, muscular dystrophy. *Unit head:* Dr. Pierre Drapeau, Director, 514-343-6294, Fax: 514-343-5755, E-mail: p.drapeau@umontreal.ca. *Application contact:* Dr. Nicole Leclerc, Responsible for Graduate Studies, 514-343-5657, Fax: 514-343-5775, E-mail: nicole.leclerc@umontreal.ca.

Université Laval, Faculty of Medicine, Post-Professional Programs in Medical Studies, Québec, QC G1K 7P4, Canada. Offers anatomy–pathology (DESS); anesthesiology (DESS); cardiology (DESS); care of older people (Diploma); clinical research (DESS); community health (DESS); dermatology (DESS); diagnostic radiology (DESS); emergency medicine (Diploma); family medicine (DESS); general surgery (DESS); geriatrics (DESS); hematology (DESS); internal medicine (DESS); maternal and fetal medicine (Diploma); medical biochemistry (DESS); medical microbiology and infectious diseases (DESS); medical oncology (DESS); nephrology (DESS); neurology (DESS); neurosurgery (DESS); obstetrics and gynecology (DESS); ophthalmology (DESS); orthopedic surgery (DESS); oto-rhino-laryngology (DESS); palliative medicine (Diploma); pediatrics (DESS); plastic surgery (DESS); psychiatry (DESS); pulmonary medicine (DESS); radiology–oncology (DESS); thoracic surgery (DESS); urology (DESS). *Degree requirements:* For other advanced degree, comprehensive exam. *Entrance requirements:* For degree, knowledge of French. Electronic applications accepted.

University at Buffalo, the State University of New York, Graduate School, Graduate Programs in Cancer Research and Biomedical Sciences at Roswell Park Cancer Institute, Department of Cancer Pathology and Prevention at Roswell Park Cancer Institute, Buffalo, NY 14260. Offers PhD. *Faculty:* 24 full-time (9 women). *Students:* 10 full-time (5 women); includes 1 minority (African American), 7 international. Average age 25. 14 applicants, 43% accepted, 4 enrolled. In 2009, 2 doctorates awarded. *Degree requirements:* For doctorate, comprehensive exam, thesis/dissertation, dissertation defense, project. *Entrance requirements:* For doctorate, GRE, minimum GPA of 3.0, 3 letters of recommendation. Additional exam requirements/recommendations for international students: Required—TOEFL (minimum score: paper-based 600, computer 250, iBT 100) or IELTS (minimum score 7). *Application deadline:* For fall admission, 2/1 priority date for domestic and international students. Applications are processed on a rolling basis. Application fee: $50. Electronic applications accepted. *Financial support:* In 2009–10, 10 students received support, including 4 fellowships with full tuition reimbursements available (averaging $24,000 per year), 5 research assistantships with full tuition reimbursements available (averaging $24,000 per year); Federal Work-Study and health care benefits also available. Financial award application deadline: 2/1; financial award applicants required to submit FAFSA. *Faculty research:* Molecular pathology of cancer, chemoprevention of cancer, genomic instability, molecular diagnosis and prognosis of cancer, molecular epidemiology.

Total annual research expenditures: $3 million. *Unit head:* Dr. Christine Ambrosone, Chairman, 716-845-3082, Fax: 716-845-8178, E-mail: christine.ambrosone@roswellpark.org. *Application contact:* Craig R. Johnson, Director of Admissions, 716-845-2339, Fax: 716-845-8178, E-mail: craig.johnson@roswellpark.org.

University at Buffalo, the State University of New York, Graduate School, School of Medicine and Biomedical Sciences, Graduate Programs in Medicine and Biomedical Sciences, Department of Pathology and Anatomical Sciences, Buffalo, NY 14260. Offers anatomical sciences (MA, PhD); pathology (MA, PhD). *Faculty:* 13 full-time (2 women), 11 part-time/adjunct (4 women). *Students:* 8 full-time (4 women), 3 part-time (1 woman), 2 international. Average age 29. 19 applicants, 37% accepted. In 2009, 1 master's, 1 doctorate awarded. *Degree requirements:* For master's, thesis; for doctorate, comprehensive exam, thesis/dissertation. *Entrance requirements:* For master's, GRE, MCAT, or DAT, 3 letters of recommendation; for doctorate, GRE, 3 letters of recommendation. Additional exam requirements/recommendations for international students: Required—TOEFL (minimum score 600 paper-based; 250 computer-based; 100 iBT). *Application deadline:* For fall admission, 2/1 priority date for domestic and international students. Application fee: $50. *Financial support:* In 2009–10, 2 students received support, including 1 fellowship with full tuition reimbursement available (averaging $24,000 per year), 1 research assistantship with full tuition reimbursement available (averaging $22,000 per year); health care benefits also available. Financial award application deadline: 2/1. *Faculty research:* Immunopathology-immunobiology, experimental hypertension, neuromuscular disease, molecular pathology, cell motility and cytoskeleton. *Unit head:* Dr. Reid Heffner, Chairman, 716-829-2846, Fax: 716-829-2086, E-mail: rheffner@buffalo.edu. *Application contact:* Dr. Peter Nickerson, Director of Graduate Studies, 716-829-2846.

The University of Alabama at Birmingham, Graduate Programs in Joint Health Sciences, Program in Pathology, Birmingham, AL 35294. Offers PhD. *Degree requirements:* For doctorate, thesis/dissertation. *Entrance requirements:* For doctorate, GRE General Test, interview. Electronic applications accepted.

University of Alberta, Faculty of Medicine and Dentistry and Faculty of Graduate Studies and Research, Graduate Programs in Medicine, Department of Laboratory Medicine and Pathology, Edmonton, AB T6G 2E1, Canada. Offers medical sciences (M Sc, PhD). Part-time programs available. *Faculty:* 8 full-time. *Students:* 8 full-time (4 women), 3 part-time (all women). 25 applicants, 20% accepted. In 2009, 1 master's, 2 doctorates awarded. Terminal master's awarded for partial completion of doctoral program. *Degree requirements:* For master's, thesis; for doctorate, thesis/dissertation, candidacy exam. *Entrance requirements:* For master's and doctorate, 3 letters of recommendation, minimum GPA of 3.0. Additional exam requirements/recommendations for international students: Required—TOEFL. *Application deadline:* For fall admission, 5/15 for international students; for winter admission, 9/15 for international students; for spring admission, 1/15 for international students. Applications are processed on a rolling basis. Application fee: $0. Tuition and fees charges are reported in Canadian dollars. *Expenses:* Tuition, area resident: Full-time $4626 Canadian dollars; part-time $99.72 Canadian dollars per unit. International tuition: $8216 Canadian dollars full-time. Required fees: $3590 Canadian dollars; $99.72 Canadian dollars per unit. $215 Canadian dollars per term. *Financial support:* In 2009–10, 3 fellowships with full tuition reimbursements (averaging $16,000 per year), 6 research assistantships (averaging $12,000 per year), 1 teaching assistantship (averaging $8,000 per year) were awarded; scholarships/grants and unspecified assistantships also available. *Faculty research:* Transplantation, renal pathology, molecular mechanisms of diseases, cryobiology, immunodiagnostics, informatics/cyber medicine, neuroimmunology, microbiology. Total annual research expenditures: $550,000. *Unit head:* Br. John J. O'Connnor. *Application contact:* Dr. Gregory J. Tyrrell, Graduate Coordinator, 780-407-8949, Fax: 780-407-3964, E-mail: g.tyrrell@provlab.ab.ca.

University of Arkansas for Medical Sciences, Graduate School, Graduate Programs in Biomedical Sciences, Department of Pathology, Little Rock, AR 72205-7199. Offers MS. *Faculty:* 15 full-time (3 women). *Degree requirements:* For master's, thesis. *Entrance requirements:* For master's, GRE General Test. Additional exam requirements/recommendations for international students: Required—TOEFL. *Application deadline:* Applications are processed on a rolling basis. Application fee: $0. *Financial support:* Research assistantships available. Support available to part-time students. *Faculty research:* Metastasis of cancer pediatric cancers, oxidative damage of DNA. *Unit head:* Dr. Bruce Smoller, Chairman, 501-686-5170. *Application contact:* Dr. Kathleen D. Eisenach, Information Contact, 501-257-4827, E-mail: eisenachkathleend@uams.edu.

The University of British Columbia, Faculty of Medicine, Department of Pathology and Laboratory Medicine, Vancouver, BC V6T 1Z1, Canada. Offers experimental pathology (M Sc, PhD). *Degree requirements:* For master's, thesis; for doctorate, comprehensive exam, thesis/dissertation, internal oral defense. *Entrance requirements:* For master's, GRE, upper-level course work in biochemistry and physiology; for doctorate, GRE. Additional exam requirements/recommendations for international students: Required—TOEFL (minimum score 570 paper-based; 230 computer-based), GRE Subject Test. Electronic applications accepted. *Faculty research:* Molecular biology of disease processes, cancer, hematopathology, atherosclerosis, pulmonary and cardiovascular pathophysiology.

University of California, Davis, Graduate Studies, Graduate Group in Comparative Pathology, Davis, CA 95616. Offers MS, PhD. *Accreditation:* NAACLS. Terminal master's awarded for partial completion of doctoral program. *Degree requirements:* For master's, comprehensive exam (for some programs), thesis (for some programs); for doctorate, thesis/dissertation. *Entrance requirements:* For master's and doctorate, GRE General Test. Additional exam requirements/recommendations for international students: Required—TOEFL (minimum score 550 paper-based; 213 computer-based). Electronic applications accepted. *Faculty research:* Immunopathology, toxicological and environmental pathology, reproductive pathology, pathology of infectious diseases.

University of California, Los Angeles, David Geffen School of Medicine and Graduate Division, Graduate Programs in Medicine, Program in Experimental Pathology, Los Angeles, CA 90095. Offers MS, PhD. *Degree requirements:* For doctorate, thesis/dissertation, oral and written qualifying exams. *Entrance requirements:* For master's, GRE General Test; for doctorate, GRE General Test, previous course work in physical chemistry and physics.

University of California, Los Angeles, Graduate Division, College of Letters and Science and David Geffen School of Medicine, UCLA ACCESS to Programs in the Molecular, Cellular and Integrative Life Sciences, Los Angeles, CA 90095. Offers biochemistry and molecular biology (PhD); biological chemistry (PhD); cellular and molecular pathology (PhD); human genetics (PhD); microbiology, immunology, and molecular genetics (PhD); molecular biology (PhD); molecular toxicology (PhD); molecular, cellular and integrative physiology (PhD); neurobiology (PhD); oral biology (PhD); physiology (PhD). ACCESS is an umbrella program for first-year coursework in 12 PhD programs. *Students:* 39 full-time (25 women); includes 14 minority (1 African American, 1 American Indian/Alaska Native, 8 Asian Americans or Pacific Islanders, 4 Hispanic Americans), 10 international. Average age 25. 437 applicants, 22% accepted, 30 enrolled. *Degree requirements:* For doctorate, thesis/dissertation, oral and written qualifying exams. *Entrance requirements:* For doctorate, GRE General Test, minimum undergraduate GPA of 3.0. Additional exam requirements/recommendations for international students: Required—TOEFL. *Application deadline:* For fall admission, 12/15 for domestic and international students. Application fee: $70 ($90 for international students). Electronic applications accepted. *Financial support:* In 2009–10, 56 fellowships with full and partial tuition reimbursements, 16 research assistantships with full and partial tuition reimbursements were awarded; teaching assistantships with full and partial tuition reimbursements, Federal Work-Study, institutionally sponsored loans, scholarships/grants, health care benefits, tuition waivers (full and partial), and unspecified assistantships also available. Financial award application deadline: 3/1; financial award applicants required to submit FAFSA. *Faculty research:* Molecular, cellular, and developmental biology; immunology; microbiology; integrative biology. *Unit head:* Dr. Greg I. Payne, Chair, 310-206-3121. *Application contact:* Coordinator, 310-206-3121, Fax: 310-206-5280, E-mail: uclaaccess@mednet.ucla.edu.

See Close-Up on page 239.

University of California, San Francisco, Graduate Division, Biomedical Sciences Graduate Group, San Francisco, CA 94143. Offers anatomy (PhD); endocrinology (PhD); experimental pathology (PhD); physiology (PhD). *Degree requirements:* For doctorate, thesis/dissertation. *Entrance requirements:* For doctorate, GRE General Test.

University of Chicago, Division of the Biological Sciences, Biomedical Sciences Cluster: Cancer Biology, Immunology, Molecular Metabolism and Nutrition, Pathology, and Microbiology, Department of Pathology, Chicago, IL 60637-1513. Offers molecular pathogenesis and molecular medicine (PhD). *Faculty:* 47 full-time (10 women). *Students:* 30 full-time (13 women); includes 7 minority (1 African American, 5 Asian Americans or Pacific Islanders, 1 Hispanic American). Average age 28. 37 applicants, 22% accepted, 4 enrolled. In 2009, 6 doctorates awarded. *Degree requirements:* For doctorate, thesis/dissertation, ethics class, 2 teaching assistantships. *Entrance requirements:* For doctorate, GRE General Test. Additional exam requirements/recommendations for international students: Required—IELTS (minimum score 7); Recommended—TOEFL (minimum score 600 paper-based; 250 computer-based; 104 iBT). *Application deadline:* For fall admission, 12/1 priority date for domestic and international students. Application fee: $55. Electronic applications accepted. *Financial support:* In 2009–10, 30 students received support, including fellowships with full tuition reimbursements available (averaging $29,781 per year), research assistantships with full tuition reimbursements available (averaging $29,781 per year); institutionally sponsored loans, scholarships/grants, traineeships, and health care benefits also available. Financial award applicants required to submit FAFSA. *Faculty research:* Vascular biology, apolipoproteins, cardiovascular disease, immunopathology. Total annual research expenditures: $18 million. *Unit head:* Dr. Stephen Meredith, Program Director, 773-702-1267, Fax: 773-834-5251. *Application contact:* Kristin Reepmeyer, Administrative Assistant, 773-702-3940, Fax: 773-702-4634, E-mail: reepmeyer@bsd.uchicago.edu.

University of Cincinnati, Graduate School, College of Medicine, Graduate Programs in Biomedical Sciences, Program in Pathobiology and Molecular Medicine, Cincinnati, OH 45221. Offers pathology (PhD), including anatomic pathology, laboratory medicine, pathobiology and molecular medicine. *Degree requirements:* For doctorate, thesis/dissertation, qualifying exam. *Entrance requirements:* For doctorate, GRE General Test. Additional exam requirements/recommendations for international students: Required—TOEFL (minimum score 620 paper-based; 260 computer-based). Electronic applications accepted. *Faculty research:* Cardiovascular and lipid disorders, digestive and kidney disease, endocrine and metabolic disorders, hematologic and oncogenic, immunology and infectious disease.

University of Colorado Denver, School of Medicine, Program in Pathology Cancer Biology, Denver, CO 80217-3364. Offers cancer biology (PhD); pathology (PhD). *Students:* 16 full-time (12 women); includes 1 minority (Hispanic American), 1 international. *Degree requirements:* For doctorate, comprehensive exam, thesis/dissertation, 3 laboratory rotations. *Entrance requirements:* For doctorate, GRE General Test, interview, minimum undergraduate GPA of 3.0. Additional exam requirements/recommendations for international students: Required—TOEFL (minimum score 550 paper-based; 213 computer-based). *Application deadline:* For fall admission, 2/1 for domestic students. Application fee: $50. Electronic applications accepted. *Financial support:* Fellowships, research assistantships, teaching assistantships, Federal Work-Study and institutionally sponsored loans available. Support available to part-time students. Financial award application deadline: 3/1; financial award applicants required to submit FAFSA. *Faculty research:* Signal transduction by tyrosine kinases, estrogen and progesterone receptors in breast cancer, mechanism of mitochondrial DNA replication in the mammalian cell. *Unit head:* Dr. Steven Nordeen, Director, 303-724-4301, E-mail: steven.nordeen@ucdenver.edu. *Application contact:* Gary Brown, Program Administrator, 303-724-3700, E-mail: gary.brown@ucdenver.edu.

University of Florida, College of Medicine, Department of Pathology, Immunology and Laboratory Medicine, Gainesville, FL 32611. Offers immunology and molecular pathology (PhD). *Degree requirements:* For doctorate, thesis/dissertation. *Entrance requirements:* For doctorate, GRE General Test, minimum GPA of 3.0. Additional exam requirements/recommendations for international students: Required—TOEFL. Electronic applications accepted. *Faculty research:* Molecular immunology, autoimmunity and transplantation, tumor biology, oncogenic viruses, human immunodeficiency viruses.

University of Georgia, College of Veterinary Medicine and Graduate School, Graduate Programs in Veterinary Medicine, Department of Pathology, Athens, GA 30602. Offers MS, PhD. *Faculty:* 18 full-time (11 women), 5 part-time/adjunct (2 women). *Students:* 15 full-time (7 women), 1 (woman) part-time; includes 1 minority (Hispanic American), 4 international. 20 applicants, 30% accepted, 1 enrolled. In 2009, 4 master's, 2 doctorates awarded. *Degree requirements:* For master's, thesis; for doctorate, one foreign language, thesis/dissertation. *Entrance requirements:* For master's and doctorate, GRE General Test. *Application deadline:* For fall admission, 7/1 priority date for domestic students; for spring admission, 11/15 for domestic students. Application fee: $50. Electronic applications accepted. *Expenses:* Tuition, state resident: full-time $6000; part-time $250 per credit hour. Tuition, nonresident: full-time $20,904; part-time $871 per credit hour. Required fees: $730 per semester. *Financial support:* Fellowships, research assistantships, teaching assistantships, unspecified assistantships available. *Unit head:* Dr. R. Keith Harris, Acting Head, 706-542-5831, Fax: 706-542-5828, E-mail: rkharris@uga.edu. *Application contact:* Dr. Jaroslava Halper, Graduate Coordinator, 706-542-5830, Fax: 706-542-5828, E-mail: jhalper@uga.edu.

University of Guelph, Ontario Veterinary College and Graduate Program Services, Graduate Programs in Veterinary Sciences, Department of Pathobiology, Guelph, ON N1G 2W1, Canada. Offers anatomic pathology (DV Sc, Diploma); clinical pathology (Diploma); comparative pathology (M Sc, PhD); immunology (M Sc, PhD); laboratory animal science (DV Sc); pathology (M Sc, PhD, Diploma); veterinary infectious diseases (M Sc, PhD); zoo animal/wildlife medicine (DV Sc). *Degree requirements:* For master's, thesis; for doctorate, thesis/dissertation. *Entrance requirements:* For master's, DVM with B average or an honours degree in biological sciences; for doctorate, DVM or MSC degree, minimum B+ average. Additional exam requirements/recommendations for international students: Required—TOEFL (minimum score 550 paper-based; 213 computer-based). *Faculty research:* Pathogenesis; diseases of animals, wildlife, fish, and laboratory animals; parasitology; immunology; veterinary infectious diseases; laboratory animal science.

The University of Iowa, Roy J. and Lucille A. Carver College of Medicine and Graduate College, Graduate Programs in Medicine, Department of Pathology, Iowa City, IA 52242-1316. Offers MS. *Faculty:* 26 full-time (6 women). *Students:* 4 full-time (3 women); includes 1 minority (Asian American or Pacific Islander), 1 international. Average age 25. 6 applicants, 33% accepted, 2 enrolled. In 2009, 3 master's awarded. *Degree requirements:* For master's, thesis. *Entrance requirements:* For master's, GRE, minimum GPA of 3.0. Additional exam requirements/recommendations for international students: Required—TOEFL. *Application deadline:* For fall admission, 3/15 priority date for domestic students, 2/15 priority date for international students; for spring admission, 10/15 for domestic students, 9/15 for international students. Applications are processed on a rolling basis. Application fee: $60 ($85 for international students). Electronic applications accepted. *Financial support:* In 2009–10, 4 students received support, including 4 research assistantships with full tuition reimbursements available (averaging $24,250 per year); health care benefits also available. *Faculty research:* Oncology, microbiology, vascular biology, immunology, neuroscience. Total annual research expenditures: $3.5 million. *Unit head:* Dr. Michael Cohen, Head, 319-335-8232, Fax: 319-335-8348, E-mail: michael-cohen@uiowa.edu. *Application contact:* Dr. Thomas J. Waldschmidt, Graduate Program Director, 319-335-8223, E-mail: thomas-waldschmidt@uiowa.edu.

Pathology

The University of Kansas, University of Kansas Medical Center, School of Medicine, Department of Pathology and Laboratory Medicine, Kansas City, KS 66160. Offers MA, PhD, MD/PhD. *Faculty:* 21 full-time, 5 part-time/adjunct. *Students:* 1 (woman) full-time, 7 part-time (3 women), 5 international. Average age 29. Terminal master's awarded for partial completion of doctoral program. *Degree requirements:* For master's, comprehensive exam (for some programs), thesis; for doctorate, comprehensive exam, thesis/dissertation. *Entrance requirements:* For master's, GRE, curriculum vitae, 3 reference letters; for doctorate, GRE, curriculum vitae, statement of research and career interests, official transcripts for all undergraduate and graduate coursework, 3 reference letters. Additional exam requirements/recommendations for international students: Required—TOEFL (preferred) or IELTS. *Application deadline:* For fall admission, 1/15 priority date for domestic and international students. Applications are processed on a rolling basis. Application fee: $60. *Expenses:* Tuition, state resident: full-time $6492; part-time $270.50 per credit hour. Tuition, nonresident: full-time $15,510; part-time $646.25 per credit hour. Required fees: $847; $70.56 per credit hour. Tuition and fees vary according to course load and program. *Financial support:* In 2009–10, 1 fellowship (averaging $24,000 per year), 2 research assistantships (averaging $12,000 per year), 2 teaching assistantships with full and partial tuition reimbursements (averaging $23,000 per year) were awarded; Federal Work-Study, scholarships/grants, traineeships, tuition waivers (full), and unspecified assistantships also available. Financial award application deadline: 3/30; financial award applicants required to submit FAFSA. *Faculty research:* Cancer biology, developmental biology and cell differentiation, stem cell biology, microbial and viral pathogenesis. Total annual research expenditures: $4.6 million. *Unit head:* Marcia Jones, Director of Graduate Studies, 913-588-4876, Fax: 913-588-5242, E-mail: mjones@kumc.edu. *Application contact:* Mayshell-Ann M. Sinclair, Administrative Assistant, 913-588-7390, Fax: 913-588-7073, E-mail: msinclair@kumc.edu.

University of Manitoba, Faculty of Medicine and Faculty of Graduate Studies, Graduate Programs in Medicine, Department of Pathology, Winnipeg, MB R3E 3P5, Canada. Offers M Sc. *Degree requirements:* For master's, thesis. *Entrance requirements:* For master's, B Sc honours degree. Additional exam requirements/recommendations for international students: Required—TOEFL (minimum score 550 paper-based; 213 computer-based; 80 iBT), IELTS (minimum score 6.5). *Faculty research:* Experimental hydrocephalus; brain development; stroke; developmental neurobiology; myelination in Rett Syndrome; glial migration during cortical development; growth factors and breast cancer; transgenic models of breast cancer; molecular genetics and cancer diagnosis; graft-vs-host disease; biology of natural killer cells; transplantation immunology.

University of Maryland, Baltimore, School of Medicine, Department of Pathology, Baltimore, MD 21201. Offers pathologists' assistant (MS). *Accreditation:* NAACLS. Part-time programs available. *Students:* 3 full-time (0 women), 11 part-time (0 women); includes 3 minority (1 African American, 1 Asian American or Pacific Islander, 1 Hispanic American), 1 international. Average age 29. 42 applicants, 36% accepted, 7 enrolled. In 2009, 8 master's awarded. *Entrance requirements:* For master's, GRE General Test, minimum GPA of 3.0. Additional exam requirements/recommendations for international students: Required—TOEFL; Recommended—IELTS. *Application deadline:* For fall admission, 2/1 for domestic and international students. Application fee: $50. Electronic applications accepted. *Expenses:* Contact institution. *Financial support:* Application deadline: 3/1. *Unit head:* Dr. Rudy Castellani, Program Director, 410-328-5555, Fax: 410-706-8414, E-mail: rcastellani@som.umaryland.edu. *Application contact:* Carmen White, Program Coordinator, 410-706-6518, Fax: 410-706-8414, E-mail: cwhite@som.umaryland.edu.

University of Massachusetts Lowell, School of Health and Environment, Department of Clinical Laboratory and Nutritional Sciences, Lowell, MA 01854-2881. Offers clinical laboratory sciences (MS); clinical pathology (Graduate Certificate); nutritional sciences (Graduate Certificate); public health laboratory sciences (Graduate Certificate). *Accreditation:* NAACLS. Part-time programs available. Postbaccalaureate distance learning degree programs offered. *Degree requirements:* For master's, thesis optional. *Entrance requirements:* For master's, GRE General Test, minimum GPA of 3.0, letters of recommendation. *Faculty research:* Cardiovascular disease, lipoprotein metabolism, micronutrient evaluation, alcohol metabolism, mycobacterial drug resistance.

University of Medicine and Dentistry of New Jersey, Graduate School of Biomedical Sciences, Graduate Programs in Biomedical Sciences–Newark, Program in Molecular Pathology and Immunology, Newark, NJ 07107. Offers PhD. *Students:* 16 full-time (10 women), 3 part-time (1 woman); includes 2 African Americans, 1 Asian American or Pacific Islander, 1 Hispanic American, 10 international. *Entrance requirements:* Additional exam requirements/recommendations for international students: Required—TOEFL. *Application deadline:* For fall admission, 2/1 for domestic students. Applications are processed on a rolling basis. Electronic applications accepted. *Financial support:* Fellowships, research assistantships, Federal Work-Study, institutionally sponsored loans, and tuition waivers (full and partial) available. *Unit head:* Dr. Muriel Lambert, Program Director, 973-972-4405, Fax: 973-972-7293, E-mail: mlambert@umdnj.edu. *Application contact:* Dr. Muriel Lambert, Program Director, 973-972-4405, Fax: 973-972-7293, E-mail: mlambert@umdnj.edu.

University of Michigan, Horace H. Rackham School of Graduate Studies, Program in Biomedical Sciences (PIBS), Program in Molecular and Cellular Pathology, Ann Arbor, MI 48109. Offers PhD. *Degree requirements:* For doctorate, thesis/dissertation, oral defense of dissertation, preliminary exam. *Entrance requirements:* For doctorate, GRE General Test, 3 letters of recommendation, research experience. Additional exam requirements/recommendations for international students: Required—TOEFL (minimum score 84 iBT). Electronic applications accepted. *Expenses:* Tuition, state resident: full-time $17,286; part-time $1099 per credit hour. Tuition, nonresident: full-time $34,944; part-time $2080 per credit hour. Required fees: $95 per semester. Tuition and fees vary according to course load, degree level and program. *Faculty research:* Cancer Biology; Stem Cell and Developmental Biology; Immunology and Inflammatory Disease; Neurobiology and Neurologic Disease; Structural Biology; Gene Regulation.

University of Mississippi Medical Center, School of Graduate Studies in the Health Sciences, Department of Pathology, Jackson, MS 39216-4505. Offers MS, PhD, MD/PhD. Terminal master's awarded for partial completion of doctoral program. *Degree requirements:* For master's, thesis; for doctorate, thesis/dissertation, first authored publication in peer-reviewed journal. *Entrance requirements:* For master's, GRE General Test, minimum GPA of 3.0; for doctorate, GRE General Test, GRE Subject Test, minimum GPA of 3.0. *Faculty research:* Effects of rehabilitation therapy on immune system/hypothalamic/pituitary adrenal axis interaction; HLA, GC, CM, KM, and/or genetic factors in the pathogenesis of AIDS; stem cell research; renal disease.

University of Missouri, School of Medicine and Graduate School, Graduate Programs in Medicine, Department of Pathology and Anatomical Sciences, Columbia, MO 65211. Offers MS.

University of Nebraska Medical Center, Graduate Studies, Department of Pathology and Microbiology, Omaha, NE 68198. Offers MS, PhD. Part-time programs available. Terminal master's awarded for partial completion of doctoral program. *Degree requirements:* For master's, comprehensive exam, thesis; for doctorate, comprehensive exam, thesis/dissertation. *Entrance requirements:* For master's, previous course work in biology, chemistry, mathematics, and physics; for doctorate, GRE General Test, previous course work in biology, chemistry, mathematics, and physics. Additional exam requirements/recommendations for international students: Required—TOEFL (minimum score 550 paper-based; 213 computer-based). Electronic applications accepted. *Faculty research:* Carcinogenesis, cancer biology, immunobiology, molecular virology, molecular genetics.

University of New Mexico, School of Medicine, Biomedical Sciences Graduate Program, Albuquerque, NM 87131-5196. Offers biochemistry and molecular biology (MS, PhD); cell

biology and physiology (MS, PhD); molecular genetics and microbiology (MS, PhD); neuroscience (MS, PhD); pathology (MS, PhD); toxicology (MS, PhD). Part-time programs available. Terminal master's awarded for partial completion of doctoral program. *Degree requirements:* For master's, thesis; for doctorate, comprehensive exam, thesis/dissertation. *Entrance requirements:* For master's and doctorate, GRE General Test, minimum undergraduate GPA of 3.0. Additional exam requirements/recommendations for international students: Required—TOEFL. Electronic applications accepted. *Expenses:* Tuition, state resident: full-time $2099; part-time $233.20 per credit hour. Tuition, nonresident: full-time $6650. Required fees: $25 per semester. Tuition and fees vary according to course load, program and reciprocity agreements. *Faculty research:* Signal transduction, infectious disease, biology of cancer, structural biology, neuroscience.

The University of North Carolina at Chapel Hill, School of Medicine and Graduate School, Graduate Programs in Medicine, Department of Pathology and Laboratory Medicine, Chapel Hill, NC 27599. Offers experimental pathology (PhD). *Accreditation:* NAACLS. *Faculty:* 71 full-time (26 women), 5 part-time/adjunct (0 women). *Students:* 24 full-time (15 women); includes 6 minority (3 African Americans, 3 Hispanic Americans), 3 international. Average age 29. In 2009, 7 doctorates awarded. *Degree requirements:* For doctorate, comprehensive exam, thesis/dissertation, oral exam, proposal defense. *Entrance requirements:* For doctorate, GRE General Test. Additional exam requirements/recommendations for international students: Required—TOEFL (minimum score 550 paper-based; 213 computer-based). *Application deadline:* For fall admission, 12/7 priority date for domestic and international students. Applications are processed on a rolling basis. Application fee: $77. Electronic applications accepted. *Financial support:* In 2009–10, 21 students received support, including 12 fellowships with full and partial tuition reimbursements available (averaging $26,000 per year), 9 research assistantships with full and partial tuition reimbursements available (averaging $26,000 per year); Federal Work-Study, institutionally sponsored loans, scholarships/grants, traineeships, tuition waivers (full), and unspecified assistantships also available. Financial award application deadline: 3/1; financial award applicants required to submit FAFSA. *Faculty research:* Carcinogenesis, mutagenesis and cancer biology; molecular biology, genetics and animal models of human disease; cardiovascular biology, hemostasis, and thrombosis; immunology and infectious disease; progenitor cell research. Total annual research expenditures: $11.5 million. *Unit head:* Dr. J. Charles Jennette, Brinkhous Distinguished Professor and Chair, 919-966-4676, Fax: 919-966-6718, E-mail: charles.jennette@pathology.unc.edu. *Application contact:* Dr. William B. Coleman, Professor and Director of Graduate Studies, 919-966-2699, Fax: 919-966-6718, E-mail: william.coleman@pathology.unc.edu.

University of Oklahoma Health Sciences Center, College of Medicine and Graduate College, Graduate Programs in Medicine, Department of Pathology, Oklahoma City, OK 73190. Offers PhD. *Faculty:* 9 full-time (2 women). *Students:* 4 full-time (3 women), 9 part-time (7 women); includes 3 minority (1 American Indian/Alaska Native, 2 Asian Americans or Pacific Islanders), 4 international. Average age 29. 18 applicants, 17% accepted, 3 enrolled. In 2009, 2 doctorates awarded. *Degree requirements:* For doctorate, thesis/dissertation. *Entrance requirements:* For doctorate, GRE General Test, 3 letters of recommendation. Additional exam requirements/recommendations for international students: Required—TOEFL. *Application deadline:* For fall admission, 12/15 for domestic students. Application fee: $50. *Expenses:* Tuition, state resident: full-time $3120; part-time $156 per credit hour. Tuition, nonresident: full-time $11,314; part-time $409.70 per credit hour. Required fees: $1471; $51.20 per credit hour. $223.25 per term. *Financial support:* In 2009–10, 3 research assistantships (averaging $17,000 per year) were awarded; Federal Work-Study, institutionally sponsored loans, and tuition waivers (full) also available. *Faculty research:* Molecular pathology, tissue response in disease, anatomic pathology, immunopathology, histocytochemistry. *Unit head:* Dr. Ann D. Thor, Chair, 405-271-2422, E-mail: ann-thor@ouhsc.edu. *Application contact:* Dr. Yuechueng Liu, Graduate Liaison, 405-271-2422, E-mail: yuechueng-liu@ouhsc.edu.

University of Pittsburgh, School of Medicine, Graduate Programs in Medicine, Program in Cellular and Molecular Pathology, Pittsburgh, PA 15260. Offers MS, PhD. *Faculty:* 65 full-time (17 women). *Students:* 39 full-time (23 women); includes 9 minority (3 African Americans, 6 American Indian/Alaska Native), 12 international. Average age 27. 655 applicants, 10% accepted, 20 enrolled. In 2009, 9 doctorates awarded. *Degree requirements:* For doctorate, comprehensive exam, thesis/dissertation. *Entrance requirements:* For doctorate, GRE General Test, GRE Subject Test, minimum QPA of 3.0. Additional exam requirements/recommendations for international students: Required—TOEFL (minimum score 600 paper-based; 250 computer-based; 100 iBT), IELTS (minimum score 7). *Application deadline:* For fall admission, 12/15 priority date for domestic and international students. Application fee: $40. Electronic applications accepted. *Expenses:* Tuition, state resident: full-time $16,402; part-time $665 per credit. Tuition, nonresident: full-time $28,694; part-time $1175 per credit. Required fees: $690; $175 per term. Tuition and fees vary according to program. *Financial support:* In 2009–10, 7 fellowships with full tuition reimbursements (averaging $24,650 per year), 32 research assistantships with full tuition reimbursements (averaging $24,650 per year) were awarded; teaching assistantships with full tuition reimbursements, institutionally sponsored loans, scholarships/grants, traineeships, health care benefits, and unspecified assistantships also available. *Faculty research:* Liver growth and differentiation, pathogenesis of neurodegeneration, cancer research. *Unit head:* Dr. Wendy Mars, Graduate Program Director, 412-648-9690, Fax: 412-648-9846, E-mail: wmars@pitt.edu. *Application contact:* Graduate Studies Administrator, 412-648-8957, Fax: 412-648-1077, E-mail: gradstudies@medschool.pitt.edu.

University of Prince Edward Island, Atlantic Veterinary College, Graduate Program in Veterinary Medicine, Charlottetown, PE C1A 4P3, Canada. Offers anatomy (M Sc, PhD); bacteriology (M Sc, PhD); clinical pharmacology (M Sc, PhD); clinical sciences (M Sc, PhD); epidemiology (M Sc, PhD), including reproduction; fish health (M Sc, PhD); food animal nutrition (M Sc, PhD); immunology (M Sc, PhD); microanatomy (M Sc, PhD); parasitology (M Sc, PhD); pathology (M Sc, PhD); pharmacology (M Sc, PhD); physiology (M Sc, PhD); toxicology (M Sc, PhD); veterinary science (M Vet Sc); virology (M Sc, PhD). Part-time programs available. *Degree requirements:* For master's, thesis; for doctorate, thesis/dissertation. *Entrance requirements:* For master's, DVM, B Sc honors degree, or equivalent; for doctorate, M Sc. Additional exam requirements/recommendations for international students: Required—TOEFL (minimum score 550 paper-based; 213 computer-based; 80 iBT). *Expenses:* Contact institution. *Faculty research:* Animal health management, infectious diseases, fin fish and shellfish health, basic biomedical sciences, ecosystem health.

University of Rochester, School of Medicine and Dentistry, Graduate Programs in Medicine and Dentistry, Department of Pathology and Laboratory Medicine, Rochester, NY 14627. Offers pathology (MS, PhD). *Degree requirements:* For doctorate, variable foreign language requirement, thesis/dissertation, qualifying exam. *Entrance requirements:* For doctorate, GRE General Test, GRE Subject Test.

University of Saskatchewan, College of Medicine, Department of Pathology, Saskatoon, SK S7N 5A2, Canada. Offers M Sc, PhD. *Degree requirements:* For master's, thesis; for doctorate, thesis/dissertation. *Entrance requirements:* Additional exam requirements/recommendations for international students: Required—TOEFL. Tuition and fees charges are reported in Canadian dollars. *Expenses:* Tuition, area resident: Full-time $3000 Canadian dollars; part-time $500 Canadian dollars per term. Required fees: $700 Canadian dollars; $100 Canadian dollars per term.

University of Saskatchewan, Western College of Veterinary Medicine and College of Graduate Studies and Research, Graduate Programs in Veterinary Medicine, Department of Veterinary Pathology, Saskatoon, SK S7N 5A2, Canada. Offers M.Sc, M Vet Sc, PhD. *Faculty:* 25. *Students:* 14. In 2009, 6 master's awarded. *Degree requirements:* For master's, thesis; for doctorate, comprehensive exam (for some programs), thesis/dissertation. *Entrance requirements:* Additional exam requirements/recommendations for international students: Required—TOEFL, or IELTS (minimum score 6.5). *Application deadline:* For fall admission, 7/1 priority date for domestic students. Applications are processed on a rolling basis. Application fee: $75. Electronic applications accepted. Tuition and fees charges are reported in Canadian dollars. *Expenses:* Tuition, area resident: Full-time $3000 Canadian dollars; part-time $500 Canadian dollars per term. Required fees: $700 Canadian dollars; $100 Canadian dollars per term. *Financial support:* Fellowships, teaching assistantships available. Financial award application deadline: 1/31. *Faculty research:* Thyroid, oncology, immunology/infectious diseases, vaccinology. *Unit head:* Dr. Marion Jackson, Head, 306-966-7332, Fax: 306-966-7439, E-mail: marion.jackson@usask.ca. *Application contact:* Dr. Beverly Kidney, Graduate Chair, 306-966-7304, Fax: 306-966-7439, E-mail: beverly.kidney@usask.ca.

University of Southern California, Keck School of Medicine and Graduate School, Graduate Programs in Medicine, Department of Pathology, Los Angeles, CA 90089. Offers experimental and molecular pathology (MS); pathobiology (PhD). *Faculty:* 55 full-time (12 women), 5 part-time/adjunct (1 woman). *Students:* 40 full-time (23 women); includes 19 minority (13 Asian Americans or Pacific Islanders, 6 Hispanic Americans), 10 international. Average age 26. 26 applicants, 38% accepted, 9 enrolled. In 2009, 4 master's, 8 doctorates awarded. *Degree requirements:* For master's, thesis; for doctorate, thesis/dissertation. *Entrance requirements:* For master's, GRE General Test, minimum GPA of 3.0; for doctorate, GRE General Test, minimum GPA of 3.0, BS in natural sciences. Additional exam requirements/recommendations for international students: Required—TOEFL (minimum score 600 paper-based; 250 computer-based; 100 iBT). *Application deadline:* For fall admission, 12/1 priority date for domestic and international students. Application fee: $85. Electronic applications accepted. *Expenses:* Tuition: Full-time $25,980; part-time $1315 per unit. Required fees: $554. One-time fee: $35 full-time. Full-time tuition and fees vary according to degree level and program. *Financial support:* In 2009–10, 27 students received support, including 4 fellowships with tuition reimbursements available (averaging $27,060 per year), 22 research assistantships with tuition reimbursements available (averaging $27,060 per year), 1 teaching assistantship with tuition reimbursement available (averaging $27,060 per year); Federal Work-Study, institutionally sponsored loans, scholarships/grants, health care benefits, and unspecified assistantships also available. Financial award application deadline: 5/1. *Faculty research:* Immunology of lymphomas and leukemias, lung cancer, molecular basis of oncogenesis, central nervous system disease, organic chemical carcinogens and carcinogenic metal salts. *Unit head:* Dr. Michael E. Selsted, Chair, 323-442-1179, Fax: 323-442-3049, E-mail: selsted@usc.edu. *Application contact:* Lisa A. Doumak, Student Services Assistant, 323-442-1168, Fax: 323-442-3049, E-mail: doumak@usc.edu.

See Display on this page and Close-Up on page 439.

The University of Texas Medical Branch, Graduate School of Biomedical Sciences, Program in Experimental Pathology, Galveston, TX 77555. Offers PhD. *Students:* 27 full-time (16 women); includes 5 minority (2 Asian Americans or Pacific Islanders, 3 Hispanic Americans), 2 international. Average age 29. In 2009, 7 doctorates awarded. *Degree requirements:* For doctorate, thesis/dissertation. *Entrance requirements:* For doctorate, GRE General Test. Additional exam requirements/recommendations for international students: Required—TOEFL (minimum score 550 paper-based; 213 computer-based). *Application deadline:* Applications are processed on a rolling basis. Application fee: $30 ($75 for international students). Electronic applications accepted. *Financial support:* In 2009–10, fellowships (averaging $25,000 per year), research assistantships with full tuition reimbursements (averaging $25,000 per year) were awarded. Financial award applicants required to submit FAFSA. *Unit head:* Dr. Stephen Higgs, Director, 409-747-2426, Fax: 409-747-2437, E-mail: sthiggs@utmb.edu. *Application contact:* Meredith Gardner, Special Programs Coordinator I, 409-772-2521, Fax: 409-747-2400, E-mail: meagardn@utmb.edu.

The University of Toledo, College of Graduate Studies, College of Medicine, Biomedical Science Programs, Program in Pathology, Toledo, OH 43606-3390. Offers anatomic pathology (Certificate); pathology (Certificate). Part-time programs available. *Faculty research:* Cell injury, molecular and clinical molecular carcinogenesis, chemoprevention, hypertension.

University of Utah, School of Medicine and Graduate School, Graduate Programs in Medicine, Department of Pathology, Salt Lake City, UT 84112-1107. Offers experimental pathology (PhD); laboratory medicine and biomedical science (MS). PhD offered after acceptance into the combined Program in Molecular Biology. *Degree requirements:* For doctorate, comprehensive exam, thesis/dissertation. *Entrance requirements:* For doctorate, GRE, minimum GPA of 3.0. *Expenses:* Tuition, state resident: full-time $4004; part-time $1674 per semester. Tuition, nonresident: full-time $14,134; part-time $5915 per semester. Required fees: $324 per semester. Tuition and fees vary according to course load, degree level and program. *Faculty research:* Immunology, cell biology, signal transduction, gene regulation, receptor biology.

University of Vermont, College of Medicine and Graduate College, Graduate Programs in Medicine, Department of Pathology, Burlington, VT 05405. Offers MS, MD/MS. *Students:* 4 (1 woman); includes 1 minority (Asian American or Pacific Islander). 5 applicants, 60% accepted, 0 enrolled. *Degree requirements:* For master's, thesis. *Entrance requirements:* For master's, GRE General Test. Additional exam requirements/recommendations for international students: Required—TOEFL (minimum score 550 paper-based; 213 computer-based; 80 iBT). *Application deadline:* For fall admission, 4/1 priority date for domestic students, 4/1 for international students. Applications are processed on a rolling basis. Application fee: $40. Electronic applications accepted. *Expenses:* Tuition, state resident: part-time $508 per credit hour. Tuition, nonresident: part-time $1281 per credit hour. *Financial support:* Fellowships, research assistantships, traineeships available. Financial award application deadline: 3/1. *Unit head:* Dr. E. Bovill, Chairperson, 802-656-0397. *Application contact:* Dr. S. Huber, Coordinator, 802-656-0397.

University of Virginia, School of Medicine, Program in Experimental Pathology, Charlottesville, VA 22903. Offers PhD. *Students:* 9 full-time (7 women); includes 3 minority (2 African Americans, 1 Asian American or Pacific Islander), 2 international. Average age 26. *Degree requirements:* For doctorate, thesis/dissertation, oral defense of thesis. *Entrance requirements:* For doctorate, GRE General Test; GRE Subject Test (recommended), 2 letters of recommendation. Additional exam requirements/recommendations for international students: Required—TOEFL. *Application deadline:* For fall admission, 1/15 for domestic and international students. *Financial support:* Application deadline: 1/15. *Unit head:* Kevin R. Lynch, Program Director, 434-924-7185, E-mail: molmed@virginia.edu. *Application contact:* Kevin R. Lynch, Program Director, 434-924-7185, E-mail: molmed@virginia.edu.

University of Washington, Graduate School, School of Medicine and Graduate School, Graduate Programs in Medicine, Department of Pathology, Seattle, WA 98195. Offers experimental and molecular pathology (PhD). *Degree requirements:* For doctorate, thesis/dissertation. *Entrance requirements:* For doctorate, GRE General Test. *Faculty research:* Viral oncogenesis, aging, mutagenesis and repair, extracellular matrix biology, vascular biology.

The University of Western Ontario, Faculty of Graduate Studies, Biosciences Division, Department of Pathology, London, ON N6A 5B8, Canada. Offers M Sc, PhD. *Degree requirements:* For master's, thesis; for doctorate, comprehensive exam, thesis/dissertation. *Entrance requirements:* For master's and doctorate, minimum B+ average, honors degree. Additional exam requirements/recommendations for international students: Required—TOEFL. *Faculty research:* Heavy metal toxicology, transplant pathology, immunopathology, immunological cancers, neurochemistry, aging and dementia, cancer pathology.

University of Wisconsin–Madison, School of Medicine and Public Health and Graduate School, Graduate Programs in Medicine, Department of Pathology and Laboratory Medicine, Madison, WI 53706-1380. Offers PhD. *Accreditation:* NAACLS. *Faculty:* 43 full-time (15 women). *Students:* 34 full-time (22 women); includes 2 minority (both African Americans), 7 international. Average age 27. 164 applicants, 10% accepted, 8 enrolled. In 2009, 3 doctorates awarded. *Degree requirements:* For doctorate, thesis/dissertation. *Entrance requirements:* For doctorate, GRE, minimum GPA of 3.0. Additional exam requirements/recommendations for international students: Required—TOEFL (minimum score 580 paper-based; 237 computer-based; 92 iBT). *Application deadline:* For fall admission, 12/15 priority date for domestic and international

Pathology

University of Wisconsin–Madison *(continued)*
students. Applications are processed on a rolling basis. Application fee: $76. Electronic applications accepted. *Expenses:* Tuition, state resident: part-time $594 per credit. Tuition, nonresident: part-time $1504 per credit. Required fees: $65 per credit. Tuition and fees vary according to course load, program and reciprocity agreements. *Financial support:* In 2009–10, 3 students received support, including 1 fellowship with full tuition reimbursement available (averaging $23,500 per year), 4 research assistantships with full tuition reimbursements available (averaging $23,500 per year); health care benefits also available. *Faculty research:* Immunology/immunopathology, cancer biology, neuroscience/neuropathology, growth factor/matrix biology, developmental pathology. *Unit head:* Dr. Michael N. Hart, Chair, 608-265-3735, Fax: 608-265-3301, E-mail: gharvey@facstaff.wisc.edu. *Application contact:* Joanne Thornton, Student Services Coordinator, 608-262-2665, Fax: 608-265-3301, E-mail: gradinfo@pathology.wisc.edu.

See Close-Up on page 441.

Vanderbilt University, Graduate School and School of Medicine, Department of Pathology, Nashville, TN 37240-1001. Offers PhD, MD/PhD. *Faculty:* 74 full-time (29 women). *Students:* 19 full-time (13 women); includes 6 minority (4 African Americans, 1 Asian American or Pacific Islander, 1 Hispanic American), 4 international. Average age 28. In 2009, 5 doctorates awarded. *Degree requirements:* For doctorate, thesis/dissertation, qualifying and final exams. *Entrance requirements:* For doctorate, GRE General Test. Additional exam requirements/recommendations for international students: Required—TOEFL (minimum score 570 paper-based; 230 computer-based; 88 iBT). *Application deadline:* For fall admission, 1/15 for domestic and international students. Application fee: $0. Electronic applications accepted. *Financial support:* Fellowships with full tuition reimbursements, research assistantships with full tuition reimbursements, Federal Work-Study, institutionally sponsored loans, traineeships, health care benefits, and tuition waivers (partial) available. Financial award application deadline: 1/15; financial award applicants required to submit CSS PROFILE or FAFSA. *Faculty research:* Vascular biology and biochemistry, tumor pathology, the immune response, inflammation and repair, the biology of the extracellular matrix in response to disease processes, the pathogenesis of infectious agents, the regulation of gene expression in disease. *Unit head:* Dr. Samuel A. Santoro, Chair, 615-322-2123, Fax: 615-343-7023. *Application contact:* Dr. Sarki Abdulkadir, Director of Graduate Studies, 615-322-2123, Fax: 615-322-0576, E-mail: sarki.abdulkadir@vanderbilt.edu.

Virginia Commonwealth University, Medical College of Virginia-Professional Programs, School of Medicine, School of Medicine Graduate Programs, Department of Pathology, Richmond, VA 23284-9005. Offers MS, PhD, MD/PhD. Part-time programs available. Terminal master's awarded for partial completion of doctoral program. *Degree requirements:* For master's, thesis, comprehensive oral and written exams; for doctorate, thesis/dissertation, comprehensive oral and written exams. *Entrance requirements:* For doctorate, GRE General Test, MCAT. *Faculty research:* Biochemical and clinical applications of enzyme and protein immobilization, clinical enzymology.

Wayne State University, School of Medicine, Graduate Programs in Medicine, Department of Pathology, Detroit, MI 48202. Offers MS, PhD. *Accreditation:* NAACLS. *Degree requirements:* For doctorate, thesis/dissertation. *Entrance requirements:* For doctorate, GRE General Test. Additional exam requirements/recommendations for international students: Required—TOEFL (minimum score 550 paper-based; 213 computer-based); Recommended—TWE (minimum score 6). Electronic applications accepted. *Faculty research:* Cardiovascular physiology, cancer biology, cellular and tissue proteases, cancer chemoprevention, lung development; diabetes.

Yale University, Graduate School of Arts and Sciences, Department of Experimental Pathology, New Haven, CT 06520. Offers MS, PhD. *Degree requirements:* For doctorate, thesis/dissertation, qualifying exam. *Entrance requirements:* For doctorate, GRE General Test.

Yale University, School of Medicine and Graduate School of Arts and Sciences, Combined Program in Biological and Biomedical Sciences (BBS), Pharmacological Sciences and Molecular Medicine Track, New Haven, CT 06520. Offers PhD, MD/PhD. *Degree requirements:* For doctorate, thesis/dissertation. *Entrance requirements:* For doctorate, GRE General Test. Additional exam requirements/recommendations for international students: Required—TOEFL. *Application deadline:* For fall admission, 12/6 for domestic and international students. Electronic applications accepted. *Financial support:* Fellowships, research assistantships available. *Unit head:* Dr. Gerry Shadel, Co-Director, 203-785-2475, E-mail: bbs.pharm@yale.edu. *Application contact:* Dr. Gerry Shadel, Co-Director, 203-785-2475, E-mail: bbs.pharm@yale.edu.

DUKE UNIVERSITY

Department of Pathology

Programs of Study

The Department of Pathology offers the degree of Doctor of Philosophy through the Graduate School of Arts and Sciences. The purpose of the Ph.D. program is to train individuals for careers as independent scientists investigating molecular mechanisms of disease. Flexible programs of training are available to fit individual requirements and goals. The program is open to those holding the B.A. or B.S. degree, as well as to individuals holding the M.S. or the M.D., D.V.M., D.D.S., or other doctoral degree. The Ph.D. program requires a minimum of six semesters of full-time course work and research, plus written and oral preliminary examinations, a dissertation, and a final oral examination. The average time for completion of degree requirements is four to five years. Holders of M.S. or M.D. degrees may obtain one semester of credit by transfer. Summer residence and participation in research programs throughout the course of study are required.

A core program of courses in cell and molecular biology, introductory pathology, and molecular aspects of disease is required. Other course requirements are flexible and depend on the interests and needs of the student. Course work in other departments is encouraged.

Research Facilities

Research laboratories for the Department of Pathology are located primarily in the Medical Sciences Research Building (MSRB), a state-of-the-art research building located adjacent to Duke Hospital. Additional research laboratories are located in the Davison Building of Duke Clinic. Departmental research laboratories are fully equipped with necessary equipment and facilities to carry out research in modern cell and molecular biology, including tissue culture facilities; nucleic and amino acid sequencing; comparative genomic hybridization; flow cytometry; image analysis; immunohistochemistry; analytical and protein chemistry; confocal microscopy; and electron microscopy. Additional resources are available through the Duke University Comprehensive Cancer Center. The Clinical and Anatomic Pathology Laboratories within the Department of Pathology perform approximately 2.3 million laboratory tests, 45,000 cytologic examinations, and 350 autopsies per year, as well as collect and examine 30,000 surgical specimens. Thus, researchers within the Department have ready access to tissue specimens and clinical colleagues. Informatics needs are served by a Departmental library of more than 2,000 volumes, the Duke Medical Center and Duke University libraries, and an extensive Departmental computer network, which is connected via fiber-optic cable to a variety of Duke servers and to the Internet.

Financial Aid

Fellowships are generally available for all accepted students. In 2009–10, fellowships consisted of a stipend of $26,650, plus tuition, fees, and health insurance.

Cost of Study

In 2009–10, annual tuition was $32,340, plus $7950 in registration fees. Additional student fees of $830 per year are required of full-time students. Tuition, fees, and health insurance are paid for fellowship recipients.

Living and Housing Costs

A limited number of on-campus apartments are available to graduate students; however, both furnished and unfurnished apartments can be rented in Durham through private citizens or real estate agencies. Prices vary considerably, and the following are approximations for apartments near the campus: one bedroom, $600 to $700; two bedrooms, $700 to $900. Additional housing information and listings may be obtained from the Office of Housing Management at Duke University.

Student Group

Approximately 3,000 graduate and professional students are enrolled at Duke University, which has a total enrollment of about 9,000. The School of Medicine is an integral part of the University. About 35 graduate students are enrolled in the Department of Pathology.

Location

Durham is a city of nearly 200,000, located in the Piedmont region of North Carolina, with easy access to both seacoast and mountains. It is in the Research Triangle, within 10 to 15 miles of North Carolina State University, the University of North Carolina, and North Carolina Central University, all of which cooperate in teaching and research programs. It is close to a large number of government and private research institutes that enrich the scientific community. Duke University is situated at the southwest fringe of Durham on a tract of about 8,500 acres of rolling, wooded land.

The University

Duke University was founded in 1924. It was developed from Trinity College, a small liberal arts college with a history going back to 1839. From its beginning, Duke has had a substantial endowment, and it carries on a correspondingly ambitious program of research, instruction, and service.

Applying

Students are admitted in the fall. It is mandatory to complete the application process by December 1 for admission the following September. In unusual circumstances, candidates are considered for spring admission; however, it is not possible to grant financial aid to students who are admitted in the spring or summer. Applicants with prior research experience are favored, as are those with good undergraduate backgrounds not only in biology but also in physics, mathematics, and chemistry. Scores on the GRE General Test are required; scores on an appropriate GRE Subject Test are recommended but not required. Students for whom English is not the native language must submit results of the TOEFL. In the case of applicants with advanced degrees (e.g., M.D., D.V.M., D.O., or D.D.S.), the Department may petition the Graduate School to accept scores from other tests, such as the Medical College Admission Test or the Veterinary Aptitude Test, in lieu of the Graduate Record Examinations.

Correspondence and Information

Dr. Soman N. Abraham
Director of Graduate Studies
Department of Pathology
Duke University Medical Center
DUMC 3020
Durham, North Carolina 27710
Phone: 919-684-3630
E-mail: pathgrad@mc.duke.edu
Web site: http://www.pathology.mc.duke.edu

Duke University

THE FACULTY AND THEIR RESEARCH

Experimental pathologists at Duke have their primary focus in the following three areas of research:

Inflammation research is aimed at investigating episodes that occur when white blood cells and their products interact with host cells and tissues, infectious agents, or environmental toxicants. Emphasis is placed on the events that initiate and regulate the inflammatory response and diseases that result from aberrant regulation.

Tumor biology involves analysis of neoplasia at all levels of involvement: molecular, nuclear, cell membrane, intracellular, and matrix. Current research includes the identification and analysis of neoplastic events and the application of novel therapies, including immunotherapy.

Vaccine biology and design seeks to identify vaccine candidates in microbiology categories and to develop efficacious adjuvants and immunization strategies for vaccines against emerging and infectious agents of biowarfare.

Vascular biology seeks to understand processes occurring at the interface between the vessel wall and blood. This includes studies of cell-cell, cell-matrix, and protein-cell interactions, particularly involving receptor-mediated events. Emphasis is also placed on the structure and function of blood proteins involved in these processes.

Inflammation

Soman Abraham, Professor; Ph.D., Newcastle, 1981. Bacterial interactions with inflammatory cells; mast cell biology.
Virginia Byers Kraus, Associate Professor; M.D., 1982, Ph.D., 1993, Duke. Molecular pathogenesis of arthritis and cartilage degradation.
Jeffrey H. Lawson, Associate Professor; M.D., 1991, Ph.D., 1992, Vermont. Vascular surgery.
Salvatore Pizzo, Professor and Department Chairman; M.D./Ph.D., Duke, 1973. Biochemistry of proteinases and proteinase inhibitors.
Greg Sempowski, Associate Professor; Ph.D., Rochester, 1997. Immune reconstitution and response to vaccinia and other infections.
Herman F. Staats, Professor; Ph.D., South Alabama, 1992. Vaccine strategies for mucosal immunity.
Mary E. Sunday, Professor; M.D./Ph.D., Harvard, 1982. Lung developmental biology; neuropeptides as mediators of altered immunity and lung injury.

Tumor Biology

Robin Bachelder, Assistant Professor; Ph.D., Harvard, 1995. Autocrine regulation of breast tumor cell survival and migration.
Darell D. Bigner, Professor; M.D., 1965, Ph.D., 1971, Duke. Neuro-oncology; tumor immunology.
Michael Datto, Assistant Professor; M.D./Ph.D., Duke, 1999. TGF-β signal transduction; emerging techniques in molecular diagnostics.
Gayathri Devi, Assistant Professor; Ph.D., Nebraska Medical Center, 1998. Mechanisms of signaling dysregulation in cancer; genomics; targeted therapeutics.
Stephen Freedland, Associate Professor; M.D., California, Davis, 1997. Effect of diet on prostrate cancer.
Henry S. Friedman, Professor; M.D., SUNY Upstate Medical Center, 1977. Tumor pharmacology; mechanisms of drug resistance.
Laura P. Hale, Research Professor; Ph.D., 1990, M.D., 1991, Duke. Immunopathology of breast cancer; immunotherapy.
Randy L. Jirtle, Professor; Ph.D., Wisconsin, 1976. Liver carcinogenesis; radiation biology; genomic imprinting.
Jeffrey R. Marks, Associate Professor; Ph.D., California, San Diego, 1985. Molecular genetics of breast cancer.
Hai Yan, Associate Professor and Director, Molecular Oncogenomics Laboratory; M.D., Beijing, 1991; Ph.D., Columbia, 1996. Molecular genetics of brain tumors.
Michael R. Zalutsky, Associate Professor; Ph.D., Washington (St. Louis), 1974. Radiation biology; nuclear chemistry.

Vaccine Biology

Soman Abraham, Professor; Ph.D., Newcastle, 1981. Bacterial interactions with inflammatory cells; mast cell biology.
Salvatore Pizzo, Professor and Department Chairman; M.D./Ph.D., Duke, 1973. Biochemistry of proteinases and proteinase inhibitors.
Elizabeth Ramsburg, Assistant Professor; Ph.D., Yale, 2002. Understanding the functional differences between the host immune response to natural infection versus the immune response to vaccination.
John Sampson, Professor; Ph.D., Duke, 1996. Development and application of immunotherapy and drug delivery to benign and malignant tumors of the brain, spinal cord, and meninges.
Herman F. Staats, Professor; Ph.D., South Alabama, 1992. Vaccine strategies for mucosal immunity.

Vascular Biology

Mark W. Dewhirst, Professor; D.V.M., 1975, Ph.D., 1979, Colorado State. Radiation biology; hyperthermia; tumor hypoxia.
Charles S. Greenberg, Professor; M.D., Hahnemann, 1976. Transglutaminase function; angiogenesis.
Maureane R. Hoffman, Professor; M.D./Ph.D., Iowa, 1982. Coagulation; platelet activation.
Thomas L. Ortel, Associate Professor; Ph.D., 1983, M.D., 1985, Indiana. Molecular mechanisms in hemorrhage and thrombosis.
Marilyn J. Telen, Professor; M.D., NYU, 1977. Erythrocyte and tumor adhesion molecules; pathogenesis of sickle cell disease.

Multidisciplinary

Victor Dzau, Chancellor; M.D., McGill, 1972. Identification of novel factor(s) that may aid in protection of myocardium; understanding of signals involved in homing of bone-marrow-derived stem cells to the heart; control of rennin gene expression, and gene therapy for cardiovascular diseases.
Gordon K. Klintworth, Professor; M.D., 1957, Ph.D., 1966, Witwatersrand (South Africa). Ophthalmic pathology and neuropathology.
Christopher Nicchitta, Professor; Ph.D., Pennsylvania, 1983. Protein synthesis, molecular chaperone function, and mRNA localization; tumor biology; tumor immunology; tumor signaling.
Edward Patz, Professor; M.D., Maryland, 1985. Molecular diagnosis.
Alan Proia, Professor; Ph.D., Rockefeller, 1979; M.D., Cornell, 1980. Ophthalmic pathology.
John Shelburne, Professor; Ph.D., 1971, M.D., 1972, Duke. Cell biology; electron microscopy.

UNIVERSITY OF SOUTHERN CALIFORNIA

Department of Pathology
Ph.D. Degree Program in Pathobiology
M.S. Degree Program in Experimental and Molecular Pathology

Programs of Study

The Department of Pathology offers a program leading to the M.S. or Ph.D. degree in pathobiology. The purpose of the program is to educate individuals who are interested in investigating mechanisms of disease and who will pursue careers in research, biotechnology, and teaching. Emphasis is placed on interdisciplinary approaches to the study of human disease. Areas currently under investigation include cellular and molecular biology of cancer, chemical carcinogenesis, virology, stem cell and developmental pathology, liver and pulmonary diseases, environmental pathology, and circulatory, endocrine, and neurodegenerative diseases.

Courses are offered in general pathology, viral oncology, and molecular bases of diseases as well as techniques in experimental pathology. Other graduate courses offered include biochemistry, physiology, histology, and microbiology. A wide range of courses geared to contribute to the individual's educational objectives are available.

The master's program in experimental and molecular pathology offers students the flexibility to prepare for a wide range of careers, including research, teaching, industry, or consulting.

The Ph.D. program in pathobiology may be pursued as part of the M.D./Ph.D. program offered by the University of Southern California (USC). Medical students, residents, and fellows may also apply to this program.

Postdoctoral positions are also available.

Research Facilities

The facilities of the Department include the latest equipment for research in cell biology, biochemistry, and molecular biology. Excellent facilities are also available in the neighboring Kenneth Norris Jr. Cancer Hospital Research Institute, Topping Research Tower, Institute for Genetic Medicine, and Childrens Hospital of Los Angeles. A separate containment level-3 facility is available for studies related to AIDS and human retroviruses and oncogenes. Library services are available at the Health Sciences Campus.

Financial Aid

Research assistantships are available through faculty research grants. Special fellowships are available for qualified students. Most students are financially supported beginning in the second year by their mentors. No financial aid is available for the master's program at this time.

Cost of Study

Research assistantships include tuition. Full tuition for both the M.S. and Ph.D. programs is $32,640 for the 2010–11 academic year, plus mandatory fees of $1833 per year.

Living and Housing Costs

Housing arrangements are the responsibility of the students. Housing costs vary greatly, depending on location and type of accommodations. There are ample housing facilities in the many communities surrounding the medical school.

Student Group

Of the 33,747 students enrolled at the University of Southern California, 16,213 are engaged in graduate or professional study. The student body includes undergraduates from all parts of the United States and many other countries. There are 23 students enrolled in the Ph.D. pathobiology program and 16 enrolled in the M.S. in experimental and molecular pathology program.

Student Outcomes

Job opportunities for graduates are available in academic, hospital, and government institutions and in industry.

Location

The Health Sciences Campus of the University of Southern California is located in the center of Los Angeles, close to other universities and medical schools and within an hour's drive of both beaches and mountains. The city's excellent climate makes it possible to participate the year round in outdoor sports: camping and hiking at nearby mountain parks, skiing during the winter months, and swimming, surfing, and water sports. This exciting seaside city is rich in cultural, athletic, and scholastic opportunities.

The University and The Program

The graduate program in pathobiology is based at the Health Sciences Campus, which is approximately 10 miles from the main University campus. The Health Sciences Campus comprises the School of Medicine, School of Pharmacy, LAC-USC Healthcare Network, Doheny Eye Foundation, Norris Cancer Research Institute, Topping Research Tower, Harlayne J. Norris Research Tower, Institute for Genetic Medicine, and USC University Hospital.

Applying

Admission to the graduate program requires an undergraduate degree in the natural sciences and demonstration of competence and achievement in these studies. Scores on the General Test of the Graduate Record Examinations are required of all students, with a combined score of 1100 or better for the verbal and quantitative sections. The GRE score is preferred over the MCAT score for the master's program; however, only the GRE score is acceptable for the Ph.D. program. A score of 600 or better on the Test of English as a Foreign Language (TOEFL) is required of international applicants. Applicants must have a minimum GPA of 3.0. The deadline for applying to the Ph.D. program is December 1. For the M.S. program, the deadline for applying for fall is July 15, and for the spring semester, it is December 1.

The Ph.D. program is integrated with the Ph.D. Programs in Biomedical and Biological Sciences (PIBBS), an integrated pan–Health Sciences Campus graduate program. For the PIBBS application, students can visit http://www.usc.edu/pibbs for directions on how to apply. For the master's program, students should complete the application form online using the following Web site: http://www.usc.edu/admission/graduate/applyonline/.

Correspondence and Information

Chairman, Graduate Committee
Department of Pathology
School of Medicine
University of Southern California
2011 Zonal Avenue
Los Angeles, California 90089-9092

Phone: 323-442-1168
Fax: 323-442-3049
E-mail: ldoumak@usc.edu
Web site: http://www.usc.edu/medicine/pathology

University of Southern California

THE FACULTY AND THEIR RESEARCH

Thomas C. Chen, Associate Professor and Director, Neuro-Oncology; M.D., California, San Francisco, 1988; Ph.D., USC, 1996. Translational research for brain tumors. *Vaccine* 26:1764, 2008. *Cancer Res.* 67(20):9809, 2007; 10920, 2007. *Mol. Cancer Ther.* 6(4):1262, 2007.

Cheng-Ming Chuong, Professor and Chairman, Graduate Committee; M.D., Taiwan, 1978; Ph.D., Rockefeller, 1983; Academician, Academia Sinica, 2008. Stell cells, regenerative biology, hair engineering, Evo-Devo integument. *Cell Stem Cell* 4:100, 2009. *Proc. Natl. Acad. Sci. U.S.A.* 103:951, 2006. *Science* 305:1465, 2004. *Nature* 451:340, 2008; 438:1026, 2005; 420:308, 2002.

Thomas D. Coates, Professor; M.D., Michigan, 1975. Pathophysiology of vaso-occlusion in sickle cell disease; iron overload and inflammatory damage in chronically transfused sickle cell and thalassemia patients; computer image analysis of biologic systems; role of inflammation in vascular damage in sickle cell disease; abnormal autonomic cardiac response to transient hypoxia in sickle cell anemia. *Blood* 116:537, 2010; 103:1934, 2004; 78:1338, 1991. *Br. J. Haematol.* 141:891, 2008. *Conf. Proc. IEEE Eng. Med. Biol. Soc.* 2008:1996–99, 2008. *J. Cell. Biol.* 117:765, 1992.

Edward D. Crandall, Professor; Ph.D., Northwestern, 1964; M.D., Pennsylvania, 1972. Alveolar epithelial development, growth, differentiation, and pathobiology. *Toxicol. Vitro* 21:1373, 2007. *Am. J. Pathol.* 168:1452, 2006; 166:1321, 2005. *J. Histochem. Cytochem.* 2:759, 2004. *Cell Tissue Res.* 312:313, 2003. *J. Virol.* 75:11747, 2001.

J. A. Louis Dubeau, Professor; M.D., 1979, Ph.D., 1981, McGill. Biology, molecular genetics, and animal modeling of ovarian cancer. *Cancer Res.* 70:221, 2010. *Lancet Oncol.* 9:1191, 2008. *Curr. Biol.* 15:561, 2005.

Alan L. Epstein, Professor; M.D./Ph.D., Stanford, 1978. Monoclonal antibody–based immunotherapy of cancer. *J. Immunology* 185:2273–84, 2010. *J. Immunother.* 31:235, 2008. *Clin. Cancer Res.* 13:4016, 2007; 11:8492, 2005; 11:3084, 2005; 5:51, 1999. *Blood* 101:4853, 2003. *Cancer Res.* 63:8384, 2003.

Parkash Gill, Professor; M.D., Punjabi (India), 1974. Molecular mechanisms of angiogenesis. *Blood,* in press. *Nature,* in press. *Proc. Natl. Acad. Sci. U.S.A.* 94:978, 1997. *N. Engl. J. Med.* 335:1261, 1996.

John Groffen, Professor; Ph.D., Groningen (Netherlands), 1981. Genetics of Ph-positive leukemias and innate immune system regulation. *J. Biol. Chem.* 283:3023, 2008. *Hum. Genet.* 123:321, 2008. *J. Cell. Physiol.* 212:796, 2007. *Leukemia* 21:178, 2007. *Mol. Cell. Biol.* 27:899, 2007. *Cancer Res.* 66:5387, 2006.

Yuan-Ping Han, Assistant Professor; Ph.D., CUNY, Mount Sinai, 1996. Tissue injury, repair, and fibrosis; MMPs. *Am. J. Pathol.* doi:10:2353, September 16, 2010; 176:2447, May 2010; *J. Invest. Dermatol.* 128(9):2344, September 2008. *J. Biol. Chem.* 282(17):12928, April 27, 2007.

Nora Heisterkamp, Professor; Ph.D., Groningen (Netherlands), 1981. Cell biology and innate immunity; signal transduction, drug resistance, and treatment of Bcr-Abl-positive leukemia. *J. Biol. Chem.* 283:3023, 2008. *Hum. Genet.* 123:321, 2008. *Mol. Cancer* 25:67, 2007. *Leukemia* 21:178, 2007. *Mol. Cell. Biol.* 27:899, 2007. *Cancer Res.* 66:5387, 2006. *Blood* 106:1355, 2005.

David R. Hinton, Professor and Vice Chairman, Department of Pathology; M.D., Toronto, 1978. Age-related macular degeneration; retinal pigment epithelium; stem cell therapy for ocular disorders; demyelination. *J. Biol. Chem.* 284:9525–39, 2009. *Blood* 115:3398–406, 2009.

Alan L. Hiti, Professor of Clinical; Ph.D., UCLA, 1981; M.D., Miami (Florida), 1983. Applications of flow cytometry to diagnostic hematopathology and HIV disease.

Florence M. Hofman, Professor and Director, Ph.D. Program; Ph.D., Weizmann (Israel), 1976. Antiangiogenic therapy for primary and metastatic brain tumors; signal transduction mechanisms in tumor-derived vasculature. *Mol. Canc. Ther.* 9:631–41, 2010. *Mol. Canc. Res.* 6(8):1268, 2008. *Am. J. Pathol.* 173(2):575, 2008.

Tingxin Jiang, Assistant Professor; M.D., Shanghai (China), 1978. Tissue engineering of hair formation; reconstitution of feather and hairs. *Int. J. Dev. Biol.* 48:117, 2004. *Development.* 126:4997, 1999.

Emil P. Kartalov, Assistant Professor; Ph.D., Caltech, 2004. Nanotechnology in biology and medicine; focus on elastomer microfluidics in biomedical diagnostics. *Electrophoresis* 29, 2008. *J. Appl. Phys.* 102, 2007; 101, 2007. *Proc. Natl. Acad. Sci. U.S.A.* 103:33, 2006; 100, 2003.

Anthony J. Keyser, Professor of Clinical; Ph.D., Emory, 1976. Connective tissue; clinical pathology; non-mucinous nature of the surface material of the bladder mucosa. *Clin. Biochem.* 30:613, 1997. *Am. J. Med. Sci.* 304:285, 1993.

Yong-Mi Kim, Assistant Professor of Pediatrics and Pathology; M.D./Ph.D., Düsseldorf (Germany), 1998; M.P.H., Harvard, 2003. Leukemia stem cells; survivin and integrins in acute lymphoblastic leukemia; preclinical leukemia models. *Canc. Res.* September 13, 2010 (Epub ahead of print); 70(11):4346, June 1, 2010. *Leukemia* 24(4):813, April 2010; 22(1):66, 2008. *Cancer Cell.* 16(3):232, September 8, 2009.

Krzysztof Kobielak, Assistant Professor of Pathology; M.D., 1996, Ph.D., 1999, Marcinkowski University of Medical Sciences (Poland). Regulation of hair follicle stem cell niche; morphogenesis of skin appendages; skin and hair follicle regeneration. *Proc. Natl. Acad. Sci. U.S.A.* 104:10063, 2007. *J. Cell Biol.* 163:609, 2003.

Robert D. Ladner, Assistant Professor; Ph.D., Rutgers, 1996. Regulation and posttranslational modification of enzymes involved in thymidylate nucleotide metabolism. *Nucleic Acids Res.* 37(1):78, 2009. *Mol. Canc. Therapeut.* 7(9):3029, 2008. *Mol. Pharmacol.* 66:620, 2004. *Pharmacogenetics* 14:319, 2004.

Joseph R. Landolph Jr., Associate Professor; Ph.D., Berkeley, 1976. Molecular biology of neoplastic transformation by carcinogenic Ni^{+2}/Cr^{+6} compounds; differential gene expression in transformed cell lines; oncogene activation/tumor suppressor gene inactivation. *Metal Ions in Biology and Medicine* 10:63, 2008. *Toxicol. Appl. Pharmacol.* 206:138, 2005. *Mol. Cell. Biochem.* 255:203, 2004.

Michael R. Lieber, Professor; Ph.D., 1981, M.D., 1983, Chicago. DNA repair in human cancer, aging, and the immune system. *Cell* 135:1130, 2008; 109:807, 2002; 108:781, 2002. *Mol. Cell* 34:535, 2009; 31:485, 2008; 16:701, 2004; 2:477, 1998. *Mol. Cell. Biol.* 28:50, 2008; 27:5921, 2007. *Nature* 428:88, 2004; 388:495, 1997; 388:492, 1997. *Nat. Immunol.* 4:442, 2003. *Curr. Biol.* 12:397, 2002.

Carol A. Miller, Professor; M.D., Jefferson Medical, 1965. Molecular and cellular basis for degenerative and developmental neurologic diseases. *PLoS ONE* 4(3):e4936, 2009. *Am. J. Path.* 172:6, 2008. *J. Mol. Neurosci.* 25(1):79, 2005. *Mol. Brain Res.* 134:282, 2005. *Proc. Natl. Acad. Sci. U.S.A.* 101(12):4210, 2004; 95:2586, 1998.

Kevin A. Nash, Assistant Professor; Ph.D., Aberdeen (England), 1987. Impact of antibiotics on microbial physiology; molecular basis of drug resistance and drug susceptibility in bacteria, especially *Mycobacterium tuberculosis. J. Antimicrob. Chemother.* 55:170, 2005. *Antimicrob. Agents Chemother.* 47:3053, 2003; 45:1982, 2001; 45:1607, 2001.

André J. Ouellette, Professor, Department of Pathology and Laboratory Medicine; Ph.D., Indiana, 1972. Role of Paneth Cell alpha-defensins in innate mucosal immunity in the lower gastrointestinal tract; structural determinants of alpha-defensin bactericidal activity; mechanisms of pro-alpha-defensin conversion to active forms; Paneth cell homeostasis in health and disease. *J. Biol. Chem.* 284:6826, 2009; 284:27848, 2009. *Infect. Immun.* 77:5035, 2009.

Paul K. Pattengale, Professor; M.D., NYU, 1970. Structure and function of human M-CSF; minimal residual disease in ALL; molecular pathogenesis of lymphoid cell neoplasms (mouse and human). *Am. J. Pathol.* 151:647, 1997. *Blood* 90:2901, 1997. *J. Biol. Chem.* 271:16388, 1996.

Michael F. Press, Professor; Ph.D., 1975, M.D., 1977, Chicago. Pathobiology of breast and gynecologic cancer. *Clin. Cancer Res.* 16:1281, 2010; 14(23):7861, 2008. *Br. J. Canc.* 100(1):89, 2009. *J. Clin. Oncol.,* 27:1323, 2009; 26(34):5544, 2008; 25:118, 2007. *BMC Cancer* 9:43, 2009. *J. Natl. Cancer Inst.* 101:615, 2009. *Drugs* 67:2045, 2007.

Suraiya Rasheed, Professor and Director, Viral Oncology and Proteomics Research; Ph.D., Osmania (India), 1958; Ph.D., London, 1964. Biomarkers and protein-protein interaction pathways in cancer and viral (HIV) diseases (Melanoma/ neuronal stem cells and HIV-associated diseases). *J. Transl. Med.* 7:75, 2009. *PLoS One* 2008. doi: 10.1371. *Cancer Stem Cells, Identification and Targets,* Chapters 1 and 8, John Wiley & Sons Publisher, 2008. *Int. J. Bioinformatics Res. Appl.* 3(4):480, 2007. *Virol. J.* 3:101, 2006. *J. Transl. Med.* 5:14, 2005 (doi: 10.1186/1479-5876-3-14).

Pradip Roy-Burman, Professor; Ph.D., Calcutta, 1963. Modeling human prostate cancer in mice; mechanisms of prostate tumorigenesis and role of cancer stem cells and tissue microenvironment in disease progression. *Cancer Res.* 70:7294, 2010; 68:198, 2008; 67:7525, 2007.

Michael E. Selsted, Professor and Chairman of the Department of Pathology; Ph.D., UCLA, 1980; M.D., UCLA, 1985. Role of host defense peptides in innate immunity and inflammation. *J. Biol. Chem.* 284:5602, 2009. *J. Virol.* 83:11385, 2009. *Science* 286:498, 1999.

Russell P. Sherwin, Professor; M.D., Boston University, 1948. Environmental, occupational, and oncologic pathology; COPD; image analysis; immunopathology. *Mol. Cancer Ther.* 3:499, 2004. *Virchows Arch.* 437:422, 2000; 433:341, 1998. *Inhal. Toxicol.* 9:405, 1997; 7:1183, 1995; 7:1173, 1995.

Darryl Shibata, Professor; M.D., USC, 1983. Molecular clocks; investigating stem cells in human colon by using methylation patterns. *Proc. Natl. Acad. Sci. U.S.A.* 98:10839, 2001.

Michael R. Stallcup, Professor; Ph.D., Berkeley, 1974. Regulation of gene transcription by steroid hormone receptors and transcriptional coactivator proteins. *J. Biol. Chem.* 284:29298, 2009. *Nat. Struct. Mol. Biol.* 15:245, 2008. *Mol. Cell* 31:510, 2008. *J. Biol. Chem.* 281:3389, 2006. *Genes Dev.* 19:1466, 2005. *Proc. Natl. Acad. Sci. U.S.A.* 102:3611, 2005. *Mol. Cell. Biol.* 24:2103, 2004. *Science* 284:2174, 1999.

Bangyan Stiles, Assistant Professor; Ph.D., Texas at Austin, 1998. Regeneration of pancreatic B cells; liver stem cells and liver cancer. *Stem Cell* 2008, in press *Mol. Cell. Biol.* 26:2772, 2006; 25:2498, 2005; 22:3842, 2002. *J. Clin. Invest.* 116:1843, 2006. *Cancer Cell* 8:185, 2005. *Proc. Natl. Acad. Sci. U.S.A.* 101:2081, 2004; 98:10314, 2001.

Clive R. Taylor, Professor; M.B.B.Chir., 1969; D.Phil., 1975, Oxford. Immunohistochemical methods applied to cell identification and tumor diagnosis; immunology of lymphomas and leukemias. *Adv. Pathol. Lab. Med.* 7:59, 1994.

Timothy J. Triche, Professor; M.D./Ph.D., Tulane, 1971. Molecular characterization of chimeric tumor genes, control of gene expression, and relationship to tumor phenotype, biologic aggressiveness, and treatment responsiveness. *Nat. Genet.* 6:146, 1994. *Diagn. Mol. Pathol.* 2:147, 1993. *EMBO J.* 12:4481, 1993.

Prasad Tongaonkar; Assistant Professor of Research, Department of Pathology. Ph.D., University of Medicine and Dentistry of New Jersey, 1999. Expression and biosynthesis of mammalian antimicrobial peptides and their role in innate immnune and inflammatory processes. *J. Biol. Chem.* 284:5602, 2009.

Hide Tsukamoto, Professor; D.V.M., Tokyo, 1975; Ph.D., Kobe (Japan), 1988. Cellular and molecular mechanisms of liver cirrhosis; adipogenic transcriptional programs that are molecular targets for potential treatment of cirrhosis; iron-mediated intracellular signaling for proinflammatory activation of NF-kappaB in macrophages; roles of mesenchyme-epithelial interactions in liver development and regeneration; TLR4-TGFbeta reciprocal interactions in the genesis of liver cancer stem cells. *J. Biol. Chem.* July 27, 2010 (Epub ahead of print); 282:5582, 2007; 280:4959, 2005; 279:11392, 2004; 278:17646, 2003. *Proc. Natl. Acad. Sci. U.S.A.* 106:1548, 2009.

Randall Widelitz, Associate Professor; Ph.D., Arizona, 1986. Growth control in tumorigenesis and embryonic development; focus on roles of sex hormones, adhesion molecules, Wnts, and beta-catenin. *Cell Stem Cell* 4:100, 2009. *Organogenesis* 4:123, 2008. *Am. J. Pathol.* 173:1339, 2008.

Ping Wu, Assistant Professor of Research; Ph.D., Nanjing (China), 1997. Regenerative biology; focus on reptile scale, teeth, and tail regeneration. *Dev. Dyn.* 235:1400, 2006. *Science* 305:1465, 2004. *Int. J. Dev. Biol.* 48:249, 2004.

Jun Xu, M.D., China, 1987; Ph.D., UCLA, 2004. Metabolism in liver function and disease. *Clin. Biochem.* 2010. *Cell Metab.* 5(5):371, 2007. *Diabetes* 55:3429, 2006; 55:3372, 2006. *J. Biol. Chem.* 277(52):50237, 2002.

Dan Hong Zhu, Assistant Professor; M.D., Jiao Tong (China), 1983; Ph.D., USC, 2004. Pathological mechanisms of age-related macular degeneration. Stem cell biology and its application in the treatment of age-related macular degeneration. *Vision Res.* 50(7):643-51, 2010. *J. Biol. Chem.* 281(30):21173-82. 2006. In *Eighth International Conference on the Chemistry and Biology of Mineralized Tissues,* pp. 99–102, eds. W. J. Landis and J. Sodek, University of Toronto Press Inc., Canada, 2005.

UNIVERSITY OF WISCONSIN–MADISON

Department of Pathology and Laboratory Medicine

Program of Study

The Cellular and Molecular Pathology (CMP) graduate training program originated more than fifty years ago as a program focused on general pathology research and education. Through the years, much of the training involved examination of pathological specimens, and graduates were highly valued for their skills by health institutions and industry. Five years ago, the graduate program was restructured to emphasize the pathogenesis of human disease, and the program faculty was expanded. Today, the faculty of the CMP program includes 54 National Institutes of Health/National Science Foundation or similarly funded investigators focusing on research programs in immunology, cancer biology, neuropathology, and signal transduction. These investigators come from twenty different basic science, preclinical, and clinical departments. Of these trainers, 28 hold Ph.D. degrees and 26 hold M.D. or M.D./Ph.D. degrees, and carry out both patient care and basic research. The Department of Pathology serves as a core for the CMP graduate program, integrating these faculty and trainers from across campus into a unified, multidisciplinary graduate training program focused on the pathogenesis of human diseases.

The primary objective of the CMP program is to prepare graduates for productive careers in scientific research and education and to position them to make significant contributions toward the nation's health-related research needs.

The CMP program focuses on the integration of medical knowledge into graduate education, and the Department of Pathology offers a translational bridge between basic and clinical sciences by offering an interdisciplinary curriculum focused on the concepts of human disease pathogenesis and translational research.

Research Facilities

The Department is housed in the Medical School complex at the center of the Madison campus and at the Clinical Sciences Center on the west side of campus. The Department has modern research facilities including centralized support facilities. In addition, the Integrated Microscopy Resource on the Madison campus is a national microscopy center that provides equipment and support for scanning and transmission of electron microscopy and video-enhanced fluorescence microscopy. Extensive library facilities, including Departmental collections, the Medical School Library, and extensive holdings at other science libraries on the Madison campus, are available.

Financial Aid

It is the intention of the program that students receive stipend support during the duration of their graduate study. Support for students is offered through a variety of sources, including Department teaching and research assistantships, research assistantships from individual faculty research grants, project assistantships, fellowships, the thesis adviser's research funds, or other campus sources. In addition, students compete for University fellowships and research assistantships on several training grants on the Madison campus. For the 2010–11 school year, the stipend rate for graduate students in the Department of Pathology and Laboratory Medicine was $24,000, with an increase of approximately 4 percent annually. In addition, assistantship recipients qualify for full remission of nonresident and resident tuition and subsidized enrollment in the Graduate Assistant Health Insurance Program.

Cost of Study

As discussed in the Financial Aid section, students receive stipend support throughout their graduate study. In the fall of 2010, tuition and fees were $5470.72 per semester for Wisconsin residents and $12,554.24 per semester for nonresidents.

Living and Housing Costs

For single graduate students, the University maintains graduate student apartments that offer one- and two-bedroom units; rents range from $785 to $925 per month in 2010–11. University Student Apartments, better known as Eagle Heights, offers one- to three-bedroom unfurnished apartments; rents range from $670 to $1005 per month in 2010–11. There may be a waiting list for the Eagle Heights units, and priority is given to students with dependent children. For more details, students should visit the Division of University Housing Web site at http://www.housing.wisc.edu. Most students live off campus; costs for off-campus housing vary depending on size and location. Additional information about off-campus housing is available at the UW–Madison Campus Information, Assistance, and Orientation Web site at http://www.wisc.edu/cac/housing/.

Student Group

The Madison campus is the flagship of the University of Wisconsin, with an enrollment of more than 40,000 students, including 9,000 graduate students. In the sciences, the graduate students belong to individual department graduate programs or are members of interdepartmental training programs, such as the CMP program.

Student Outcomes

Students in this program have successfully pursued a number of options after obtaining their Ph.D. degrees. They have received postdoctoral training and obtained faculty positions in academic institutions, taken research positions in industry, or continued on to medical school and secured faculty positions in medical institutions.

Location

Madison, recently ranked as one of the top cities of America to live in, is the capital of the state, with a metropolitan population of approximately 215,000. The city, situated on four picturesque lakes, is approximately 150 miles northwest of Chicago. The city and the University offer a wide variety of educational, cultural, and recreational opportunities. Superb facilities are available for summer and winter sports, such as sailing, camping, hiking, ice-skating, skiing, and bicycling.

The University

The University, founded in 1848, is one of the Big Ten schools and has a rich tradition of excellence in research. The University System includes the main campus in Madison plus twelve other comprehensive universities, thirteen freshman/sophomore campuses (UW Colleges), and the UW–Extension Program.

Applying

Applicants should have a bachelor's degree and an undergraduate minimum grade point average of 3.0 (on a 4.0 scale). Applicants should have a strong background in organic and physical chemistry, biochemistry, biology (including genetics), and mathematics through calculus. Completed application forms, Graduate Record Examinations (GRE) scores, transcripts, a resume, statement of purpose, and a minimum of three letters of recommendation are required for an admission decision. The application submission deadline for fall admission is December 15.

Correspondence and Information

CMP Program Coordinator
Department of Pathology
3170-10K/L Medical Foundation Centennial Building
1685 Highland Avenue
University of Wisconsin
Madison, Wisconsin 53705

Phone: 608-262-2665
Fax: 608-265-3301
E-mail: gradinfo@pathology.wisc.edu
Web site: http://www.cmp.wisc.edu

University of Wisconsin–Madison

THE FACULTY AND THEIR RESEARCH

Caroline Alexander, Associate Professor, Oncology. Role of breast stem cells in tumor induction; multiple functions of Wnt signaling in the regulation of mammary epithelial cell growth; changes in tumor susceptibility that are effected by alterations of normal development.

B. Lynn Allen-Hoffmann, Professor, Pathology. Keratinocytes; cancer biology; extracellular matrices.

Craig S. Atwood, Associate Professor, Medicine. Hormonal regulation of aging and neurodegenerative diseases.

Grace Boekhoff-Falk, Associate Professor, Anatomy. Developmental biology; gene expression; hormones; growth and differentiation factors; signal transduction.

Emery H. Bresnick, Professor, Pharmacology. Regulation of transcription, hematopoiesis, and leukemogenesis.

William J. Burlingham, Professor, Surgery. Mechanisms of transplant tolerance and rejection.

Joshua Coon, Assistant Professor, Chemistry. Bioanalytical chemistry; mass spectrometry.

Loren Denlinger, Assistant Professor, Medicine. Host-pathogen interactions; the role of macrophages in immunity to intracellular pathogens.

Arjang Djamali, Assistant Professor, Medicine. The mechanisms of disease progression in kidney disease.

Karen Downs, Professor, Anatomy. Cellular, molecular, and genetic components of differentiation during placental morphogenesis.

Zsuzsa Fabry, Professor, Pathology. Immunopathology; neuroimmunology; multiple sclerosis.

John Fleming, Professor, Neurology. Multiple sclerosis.

Andreas Friedl, Professor, Pathology. Heparan sulfate proteoglycans as modulators of growth factors in human disease; tumor angiogenesis.

Michael Fritsch, Associate Professor, Pathology. Chromatin remodeling during early embryonic stem cell differentiation.

Daniel Greenspan, Professor, Pathology. Extracellular controls of cell behavior.

Anne Griep, Professor, Anatomy. Genetic and molecular regulation of mouse eye development and disease.

Jeff Hardin, Professor, Zoology. Morphogenesis and pattern formation during early development.

Peiman Hematti, Assistant Professor, Medicine. Characterization and study of mesenchymal stromal cells derived from human embryonic stem cells; development of a preclinical rhesus macaque model.

Anna Huttenlocher, Associate Professor, Medical Microbiology and Immunology. Cell migration and chemotaxis; adhesive mechanisms that regulate cell migration; the role of integrin signaling.

Nizar Jarjour, Professor, Medicine. Asthma; circadian rhythm; investigative bronchoscopy.

Juan Jaume, Assistant Professor, Medicine. Endocrine autoimmunity, type 1 diabetes, and thyroid diseases.

Shannon Kenney, Professor, Medicine. Epstein-Barr virus pathogenesis and treatment.

Bruce Klein, Professor, Pediatrics. Microbial immunology and pathogenesis.

Youngsook Lee, Associate Professor, Anatomy. Transcriptional control of cardiovascular development and mechanisms of cardiac-specific gene regulation.

Gary E. Lyons, Associate Professor, Anatomy. Developmental biology of the mammalian cardiovascular system.

James S. Malter, Professor, Pathology. Posttranscriptional gene regulation; cell signaling.

Albee Messing, Professor, Pathobiological Sciences. Transgenic mice; developmental neuropathology; molecular neurobiology.

Deane F. Mosher, Professor, Medicine. Extracellular matrix and cell adhesion.

David O'Connor, Assistant Professor, Pathology. HIV/AIDS pathogenesis.

Julie Olson, Assistant Professor, Neurological Surgery. Role of resident immune cells and infiltrating peripheral immune cells in the response to virus infection in the CNS.

Donna P. Peters, Professor, Pathology. Cell-matrix signaling in the human eye; glaucoma.

Alan Rapraeger, Professor, Pathology. Mechanisms by which the syndecan family of cell-surface receptors regulate cell growth, adhesion, and migration.

Matyas Sandor, Professor, Pathology. Immune responses to infectious disease.

Christine M. Seroogy, Assistant Professor, Pediatrics. Biological role of a novel E3 ubiquitin ligase called GRAIL in T-cell function and hematopoietic tissue development.

John Sheehan, Associate Professor, Medicine. Blood coagulation; intrinsic tenase regulation; coagulation factor IX.

Nader Sheibani, Associate Professor, Ophthalmology and Visual Sciences. Cell adhesion and signaling in vascular cells; diabetic retinopathy.

Igor Slukvin, Assistant Professor, Pathology. Hematopoietic differentiation of human embryonic stem cells; immune-privileged properties of embryonic and fetal tissues.

Paul M. Sondel, Professor, Pediatrics. Immune-mediated recognition and destruction of neoplasms.

Dandan Sun, Professor, Neurosurgery. The role of Na^+, K^+, $2Cl^-$ cotransporter in ion homeostasis and cell volume regulation in the central nervous system.

M. Suresh, Associate Professor, Pathobiological Sciences. Molecular and cellular basis of T-cell memory; $CD8^+$ T-cell responses in chronic viral infections.

Adel Talaat, Assistant Professor, Pathobiological Sciences. Genomic and functional analyses of tuberculosis and paratuberculosis to understand pathogenesis and develop novel vaccines.

David I. Watkins, Professor, Pathology. HIV vaccine development; SIV pathogenesis.

Jon P. Woods, Associate Professor, Medical Microbiology and Immunology. *Histoplasma capsulatum* molecular pathogenesis and host interactions.

Weixiong Zhong, Assistant Professor, Pathology. Redox effects of selenium in human prostate cancer chemoprevention.

Section 17
Pharmacology and Toxicology

This section contains a directory of institutions offering graduate work in pharmacology and toxicology, followed by in-depth entries submitted by institutions that chose to prepare detailed program descriptions. Additional information about programs listed in the directory but not augmented by an in-depth entry may be obtained by writing directly to the dean of a graduate school or chair of a department at the address given in the directory.

For programs offering related work, see also in this book *Biochemistry; Biological and Biomedical Sciences; Cell, Molecular, and Structural Biology; Ecology, Environmental Biology, and Evolutionary Biology; Genetics, Developmental Biology, and Reproductive Biology; Neuroscience and Neurobiology; Nutrition; Pathology and Pathobiology;* and *Physiology.* In the other guides in this series:

Graduate Programs in the Humanities, Arts & Social Sciences
See *Psychology and Counseling*
Graduate Programs in the Physical Sciences, Mathematics, Agricultural Sciences, the Environment & Natural Resources
See *Chemistry* and *Environmental Sciences and Management*
Graduate Programs in Engineering & Applied Sciences
See *Chemical Engineering* and *Civil and Environmental Engineering*
Graduate Programs in Business, Education, Health, Information Studies, Law & Social Work
See *Pharmacy and Pharmaceutical Sciences, Public Health,* and *Veterinary Medicine and Sciences*

CONTENTS

Molecular Pharmacology

Albert Einstein College of Medicine, Sue Golding Graduate Division of Medical Sciences, Division of Biological Sciences, Department of Molecular Pharmacology, Bronx, NY 10461. Offers PhD, MD/PhD. *Degree requirements:* For doctorate, thesis/dissertation. *Entrance requirements:* For doctorate, GRE General Test. Additional exam requirements/recommendations for international students: Required—TOEFL. *Faculty research:* Effects of drugs on macromolecules, enzyme systems, cell morphology and function.

Brown University, Graduate School, Division of Biology and Medicine, Program in Molecular Pharmacology and Physiology, Providence, RI 02912. Offers MA, Sc M, PhD, MD/PhD. *Degree requirements:* For doctorate, thesis/dissertation, preliminary exam. *Entrance requirements:* For master's and doctorate, GRE General Test, GRE Subject Test. Additional exam requirements/recommendations for international students: Required—TOEFL. Electronic applications accepted. *Faculty research:* Structural biology, antiplatelet drugs, nicotinic receptor structure/function.

Dartmouth College, Program in Experimental and Molecular Medicine, Molecular Pharmacology, Toxicology and Experimental Therapeutics Track, Hanover, NH 03755. Offers PhD.

Harvard University, Graduate School of Arts and Sciences, Division of Medical Sciences, Boston, MA 02115. Offers biological chemistry and molecular pharmacology (PhD); cell biology (PhD); genetics (PhD); microbiology and molecular genetics (PhD); pathology (PhD), including experimental pathology. *Degree requirements:* For doctorate, thesis/dissertation. *Entrance requirements:* For doctorate, GRE General Test, GRE Subject Test. Additional exam requirements/recommendations for international students: Required—TOEFL. *Expenses:* Tuition: Full-time $33,696. Required fees: $1126. Full-time tuition and fees vary according to program.

Mayo Graduate School, Graduate Programs in Biomedical Sciences, Program in Molecular Pharmacology and Experimental Therapeutics, Rochester, MN 55905. Offers PhD. *Degree requirements:* For doctorate, oral defense of dissertation, qualifying oral and written exam. *Entrance requirements:* For doctorate, GRE, 1 year of chemistry, biology, calculus, and physics. Additional exam requirements/recommendations for international students: Required—TOEFL. Electronic applications accepted. *Faculty research:* Patch clamping, G-proteins, pharmacogenetics, receptor-induced transcriptional events, cholinesterase biology.

Medical University of South Carolina, College of Graduate Studies, Program in Cell and Molecular Pharmacology and Experimental Therapeutics, Charleston, SC 29425. Offers MS, PhD, DMD/PhD, MD/PhD. *Faculty:* 12 full-time (2 women). *Students:* 2 full-time (both women). Average age 27. 5 applicants, 0% accepted. In 2009, 2 doctorates awarded. Terminal master's awarded for partial completion of doctoral program. *Degree requirements:* For master's, thesis; for doctorate, comprehensive exam, thesis/dissertation, oral and written exams. *Entrance requirements:* For master's, GRE General Test; for doctorate, GRE General Test, interview, minimum GPA of 3.0. Additional exam requirements/recommendations for international students: Required—TOEFL (minimum score 600 paper-based; 250 computer-based; 100 iBT). *Application deadline:* For fall admission, 1/15 priority date for domestic and international students. Applications are processed on a rolling basis. Application fee: $0 ($85 for international students). Electronic applications accepted. *Financial support:* In 2009–10, 2 students received support, including 2 research assistantships with partial tuition reimbursements available (averaging $23,000 per year); Federal Work-Study and scholarships/grants also available. Support available to part-time students. Financial award application deadline: 3/10; financial award applicants required to submit FAFSA. *Faculty research:* Hypertension, kallikrein-kinin, sodium/calcium exchange, receptors and signaling, molecular toxicology. *Unit head:* Dr. Kenneth D. Tew, Chair, 843-792-2514, Fax: 843-792-9588, E-mail: tewk@musc.edu. *Application contact:* Dr. Lauren Ball, Assistant Professor and Co-Director of the Graduate Training Program, 843-792-4513, Fax: 843-792-6590, E-mail: ballle@musc.edu.

New York University, School of Medicine and Graduate School of Arts and Science, Sackler Institute of Graduate Biomedical Sciences, Department of Pharmacology, New York, NY 10012-1019. Offers molecular pharmacology (PhD); MD/PhD. *Degree requirements:* For doctorate, comprehensive exam, thesis/dissertation, qualifying exam. *Entrance requirements:* For doctorate, GRE General Test. Additional exam requirements/recommendations for international students: Required—TOEFL. *Expenses:* Tuition: Full-time $30,528; part-time $1272 per credit. Required fees: $2177. *Faculty research:* Pharmacology and neurobiology, neuropeptides, receptor biochemistry, cytoskeleton, endocrinology.

Purdue University, College of Pharmacy and Pharmacal Sciences and Graduate School, Graduate Programs in Pharmacy and Pharmacal Sciences, Department of Medicinal Chemistry and Molecular Pharmacology, West Lafayette, IN 47907. Offers analytical medicinal chemistry (PhD); computational and biophysical medicinal chemistry (PhD); medicinal and bioorganic chemistry (PhD); medicinal biochemistry and molecular biology (PhD); molecular pharmacology and toxicology (PhD); natural products and pharmacognosy (PhD); nuclear pharmacy (MS); radiopharmaceutical chemistry and nuclear pharmacy (PhD); MS/PhD. Terminal master's awarded for partial completion of doctoral program. *Degree requirements:* For master's, thesis; for doctorate, thesis/dissertation. *Entrance requirements:* For master's, GRE General Test, minimum B average; BS in biology, chemistry, or pharmacy; for doctorate, GRE General Test, minimum B average; BS in biology, chemistry, or pharmacology. Additional exam requirements/recommendations for international students: Required—TOEFL. Electronic applications accepted. *Faculty research:* Drug design and development, cancer research, drug synthesis and analysis, chemical pharmacology, environmental toxicology.

Rosalind Franklin University of Medicine and Science, School of Graduate and Postdoctoral Studies—Interdisciplinary Graduate Program in Biomedical Sciences, Department of Cellular and Molecular Pharmacology, North Chicago, IL 60064-3095. Offers MS, PhD, MD/PhD. Terminal master's awarded for partial completion of doctoral program. *Degree requirements:* For master's, comprehensive exam, thesis; for doctorate, comprehensive exam, thesis/dissertation. *Entrance requirements:* For master's and doctorate, GRE General Test. Additional exam requirements/recommendations for international students: Required—TOEFL, TWE. Electronic applications accepted. *Faculty research:* Control of gene expression in higher organisms, molecular mechanism of action of growth factors and hormones, hormonal regulation in brain neuropsychopharmacology.

Rutgers, The State University of New Jersey, New Brunswick, Graduate School-New Brunswick, Program in Cellular and Molecular Pharmacology, Piscataway, NJ 08854-8097. Offers PhD. *Degree requirements:* For doctorate, thesis/dissertation, qualifying exam. *Entrance requirements:* For doctorate, GRE General Test, GRE Subject Test. Additional exam requirements/recommendations for international students: Required—TOEFL. *Faculty research:* Molecular, cellular, and neuropharmacology; drug metabolism; intracellular signaling systems; protein synthesis and processing; carcinogenesis.

Stanford University, School of Medicine, Graduate Programs in Medicine, Department of Molecular Pharmacology, Stanford, CA 94305-9991. Offers PhD. *Degree requirements:* For doctorate, thesis/dissertation, qualifying examination. *Entrance requirements:* For doctorate, GRE General Test, GRE Subject Test. Additional exam requirements/recommendations for international students: Required—TOEFL. Electronic applications accepted. *Expenses:* Tuition: Full-time $37,380; part-time $2760 per quarter. Required fees: $501. *Faculty research:* Action of such drugs as epinephrine, cell differentiation and development, microsomal enzymes, neuropeptide gene expression.

Thomas Jefferson University, Jefferson College of Graduate Studies, PhD Program in Molecular Pharmacology and Structural Biology, Philadelphia, PA 19107. Offers PhD. *Faculty:* 34 full-time (5 women). *Students:* 14 full-time (7 women); includes 2 minority (both Asian Americans or Pacific Islanders), 3 international. 24 applicants, 25% accepted, 3 enrolled. In 2009, 5 doctorates awarded. *Degree requirements:* For doctorate, comprehensive exam, thesis/dissertation. *Entrance requirements:* For doctorate, GRE General Test, minimum GPA of 3.2. Additional exam requirements/recommendations for international students: Required—TOEFL (minimum score 250 computer-based; 100 iBT) or IELTS. *Application deadline:* For fall admission, 1/15 priority date for domestic and international students. Applications are processed on a rolling basis. Application fee: $50. Electronic applications accepted. *Expenses:* Tuition: Full-time $26,858; part-time $879 per credit. Required fees: $525. *Financial support:* In 2009–10, 14 students received support, including 14 fellowships with full tuition reimbursements available (averaging $52,883 per year); Federal Work-Study, institutionally sponsored loans, scholarships/grants, traineeships, and stipend also available. Support available to part-time students. Financial award application deadline: 5/1; financial award applicants required to submit FAFSA. *Faculty research:* Biochemistry and cell, molecular and structural biology of cell-surface and intracellular receptors, molecular modeling, signal transduction. Total annual research expenditures: $19.2 million. *Unit head:* Dr. Philip Wedegaertner, Program Director, 215-503-3137, Fax: 215-923-2117, E-mail: philip.wedegaertner@mail.tju.edu. *Application contact:* Marc E. Stearns, Director of Admissions, 215-503-0155, Fax: 215-503-9920, E-mail: jcgs-info@jefferson.edu.

See Close-Up on page 467.

University at Buffalo, the State University of New York, Graduate School, Graduate Programs in Cancer Research and Biomedical Sciences at Roswell Park Cancer Institute, Department of Molecular Pharmacology and Cancer Therapeutics at Roswell Park Cancer Institute, Program in Molecular Pharmacology and Cancer Therapeutics, Buffalo, NY 14260. Offers PhD. *Faculty:* 30 full-time (8 women). *Students:* 21 full-time (11 women); includes 11 minority (1 African American, 9 Asian Americans or Pacific Islanders, 1 Hispanic American), 1 international. Average age 26. 26 applicants, 35% accepted, 4 enrolled. In 2009, 1 doctorate awarded. *Degree requirements:* For doctorate, thesis/dissertation, departmental qualifying exam, grant proposal. *Entrance requirements:* For doctorate, GRE General Test (recommended). Additional exam requirements/recommendations for international students: Required—TOEFL; Recommended—TWE. *Application deadline:* For fall admission, 2/1 priority date for domestic students. Applications are processed on a rolling basis. Application fee: $35. Electronic applications accepted. *Financial support:* In 2009–10, 21 students received support, including 6 fellowships with full tuition reimbursements available (averaging $20,772 per year), 15 research assistantships with full tuition reimbursements available (averaging $20,772 per year). *Faculty research:* Molecular pharmacology, cancer cell biology, molecular biology, biochemistry, chemotherapy. Total annual research expenditures: $6.5 million. *Application contact:* Dr. Adam Karpf, Director of Graduate Studies, 716-845-8225, Fax: 716-845-3879, E-mail: adam.karpf@roswellpark.org.

University of Massachusetts Worcester, Graduate School of Biomedical Sciences, Program in Biochemistry and Molecular Pharmacology, Worcester, MA 01655-0115. Offers PhD. *Degree requirements:* For doctorate, comprehensive exam, thesis/dissertation. *Entrance requirements:* For doctorate, GRE General Test. Additional exam requirements/recommendations for international students: Required—TOEFL (minimum score 600 paper-based; 250 computer-based). Electronic applications accepted. *Faculty research:* RNA; molecular, cellular, and regulatory biochemistry; molecular biophysics; chemical biology; structural biology.

University of Medicine and Dentistry of New Jersey, Graduate School of Biomedical Sciences, Graduate Programs in Biomedical Sciences–Piscataway, Program in Cellular and Molecular Pharmacology, Piscataway, NJ 08854-5635. Offers MS, PhD, MD/PhD. *Degree requirements:* For master's, thesis, qualifying exam; for doctorate, thesis/dissertation, qualifying exam. *Entrance requirements:* Additional exam requirements/recommendations for international students: Required—TOEFL. Electronic applications accepted.

University of Nevada, Reno, Graduate School, Interdisciplinary Program in Cellular and Molecular Pharmacology and Physiology, Reno, NV 89557. Offers PhD. *Degree requirements:* For doctorate, one foreign language, thesis/dissertation. *Entrance requirements:* For doctorate, GRE General Test or MCAT, minimum GPA of 3.0. Additional exam requirements/recommendations for international students: Required—TOEFL (minimum score 500 paper-based; 173 computer-based; 61 iBT), IELTS (minimum score 6). Electronic applications accepted. *Faculty research:* Neuropharmacology, toxicology, cardiovascular pharmacology, neuromuscular pharmacology.

University of Pittsburgh, School of Medicine, Graduate Programs in Medicine, Program in Molecular Pharmacology, Pittsburgh, PA 15260. Offers MS, PhD. *Faculty:* 57 full-time (11 women). *Students:* 28 full-time (19 women); includes 2 minority (1 Asian American or Pacific Islander, 1 Hispanic American), 5 international. Average age 27. 655 applicants, 10% accepted, 20 enrolled. In 2009, 9 doctorates awarded. *Degree requirements:* For doctorate, comprehensive exam, thesis/dissertation. *Entrance requirements:* For doctorate, GRE General Test, GRE Subject Test, minimum QPA of 3.0. Additional exam requirements/recommendations for international students: Required—TOEFL (minimum score 600 paper-based; 250 computer-based; 100 iBT), IELTS (minimum score 7). *Application deadline:* For fall admission, 12/15 priority date for domestic and international students. Application fee: $40. Electronic applications accepted. *Expenses:* Tuition, state resident: full-time $16,402; part-time $665 per credit. Tuition, nonresident: full-time $28,694; part-time $1175 per credit. Required fees: $690; $175 per term. Tuition and fees vary according to program. *Financial support:* In 2009–10, 4 fellowships with full tuition reimbursements (averaging $24,650 per year), 24 research assistantships with full tuition reimbursements (averaging $14,650 per year) were awarded; institutionally sponsored loans, scholarships/grants, traineeships, health care benefits, tuition waivers (full), and unspecified assistantships also available. *Faculty research:* Drug discovery, signal transduction, cancer therapeutics, neurophramacology, cardiovascular and renal pharmacology. *Unit head:* Dr. Patrick Pagano, Graduate Program Director, 412-383-6505, Fax: 412-648-9009, E-mail: pagano@pitt.edu. *Application contact:* Graduate Studies Administrator, 412-648-8957, Fax: 412-648-1007, E-mail: gradstudies@medschool.pitt.edu.

University of Southern California, Graduate School, School of Pharmacy, Molecular Pharmacology and Toxicology Program, Los Angeles, CA 90089. Offers pharmacology and pharmaceutical sciences (MS, PhD). *Faculty:* 19 full-time (4 women), 4 part-time/adjunct (2 women). *Students:* 18 full-time (11 women), 1 (woman) part-time; includes 4 minority (1 African American, 2 Asian Americans or Pacific Islanders, 1 Hispanic American), 12 international. 51 applicants. In 2009, 1 master's, 3 doctorates awarded. Terminal master's awarded for partial completion of doctoral program. *Degree requirements:* For master's, thesis; for doctorate, thesis/dissertation, 24 units of formal course work (excluding research and seminar courses). *Entrance requirements:* For master's and doctorate, GRE. Additional exam requirements/recommendations for international students: Required—TOEFL (minimum score 603 paper-based; 250 computer-based; 100 iBT). *Application deadline:* For fall admission, 1/15 for domestic and international students; for spring admission, 10/15 for domestic and international students. Application fee: $75. Electronic applications accepted. *Expenses:* Contact institution. *Financial support:* In 2009–10, 3 fellowships with full tuition reimbursements (averaging $28,656 per year), 11 research assistantships with full tuition reimbursements (averaging $30,144 per year), 13 teaching assistantships with full tuition reimbursements (averaging $29,400 per year) were awarded; health care benefits also available. *Faculty research:* Degenerative diseases, toxicology of drugs. *Unit head:* Dr. Sarah Hamm-Alvarez, Professor/Department Chair, 323-442-3269, E-mail: gongora@usc.edu. *Application contact:* Wade Thompson-Harper, Coordinator of Graduate Affairs, 323-442-1474, E-mail: pharmgrad@usc.edu.

Molecular Toxicology

Massachusetts Institute of Technology, School of Science, Department of Biology, Cambridge, MA 02139-4307. Offers biochemistry (PhD); biological oceanography (PhD); biology (PhD); biophysical chemistry and molecular structure (PhD); cell biology (PhD); computational and systems biology (PhD); developmental biology (PhD); genetics (PhD); immunology (PhD); microbiology (PhD); molecular biology (PhD); neurobiology (PhD). *Faculty:* 54 full-time (14 women). *Students:* 237 full-time (128 women); includes 65 minority (4 African Americans, 2 American Indian/Alaska Native, 33 Asian Americans or Pacific Islanders, 26 Hispanic Americans), 25 international. Average age 26. 645 applicants, 18% accepted, 49 enrolled. In 2009, 41 doctorates awarded. *Degree requirements:* For doctorate, comprehensive exam, thesis/dissertation. *Entrance requirements:* For doctorate, GRE General Test. Additional exam requirements/recommendations for international students: Required—TOEFL (minimum score 577 paper-based; 233 computer-based), IELTS (minimum score 6.5). *Application deadline:* For fall admission, 12/1 for domestic and international students. Application fee: $75. Electronic applications accepted. *Expenses:* Tuition: Full-time $37,510; part-time $585 per unit. Required fees: $272. *Financial support:* In 2009–10, 218 students received support, including 113 fellowships with tuition reimbursements available (averaging $31,816 per year), 109 research assistantships with tuition reimbursements available (averaging $29,254 per year); teaching assistantships with tuition reimbursements available, Federal Work-Study, institutionally sponsored loans, scholarships/grants, traineeships, health care benefits, and unspecified assistantships also available. *Faculty research:* DNA recombination, transcription and gene regulation, signal transduction, cell cycle, neuronal cell fate, replication and repair. Total annual research expenditures: $114 million. *Unit head:* Prof. Chris Kaiser, Head, 617-253-4701, E-mail: mitbio@mit.edu. *Application contact:* Biology Education Office, 617-253-3717, Fax: 617-258-9329, E-mail: gradbio@mit.edu.

New York University, Graduate School of Arts and Science, Department of Environmental Medicine, New York, NY 10012-1019. Offers environmental health sciences (MS, PhD), including biostatistics (PhD), environmental hygiene (MS), epidemiology (PhD), ergonomics and biomechanics (PhD), exposure assessment and health effects (PhD), molecular toxicology/carcinogenesis (PhD), toxicology. Part-time programs available. *Faculty:* 26 full-time (7 women). *Students:* 45 full-time (37 women), 15 part-time (8 women); includes 9 minority (3 African Americans, 3 Asian Americans or Pacific Islanders, 3 Hispanic Americans), 23 international. Average age 31. 60 applicants, 48% accepted, 14 enrolled. In 2009, 11 master's, 10 doctorates awarded. Terminal master's awarded for partial completion of doctoral program. *Degree requirements:* For master's, thesis or alternative; for doctorate, one foreign language, thesis/dissertation, oral and written exams. *Entrance requirements:* For master's and doctorate, GRE General Test, GRE Subject Test, minimum GPA of 3.0; bachelor's degree in biological, physical, or engineering science. Additional exam requirements/recommendations for international students: Required—TOEFL. *Application deadline:* For fall admission, 12/12 for domestic students. Application fee: $90. *Expenses:* Tuition: Full-time $30,528; part-time $1272 per credit. Required fees: $2177. *Financial support:* Fellowships with tuition reimbursements, teaching assistantships with tuition reimbursements, career-related internships or fieldwork, Federal Work-Study, institutionally sponsored loans, and health care benefits available. Financial award application deadline: 12/12; financial award applicants required to submit FAFSA. *Unit head:* Dr. Max Costa, Chair, 845-731-3661, Fax: 845-351-4510, E-mail: ehs@env.med.nyu.edu. *Application contact:* Dr. Jerome J. Solomon, Director of Graduate Studies, 845-731-3661, Fax: 845-351-4510, E-mail: ehs@env.med.nyu.edu.

See Close-Up on page 103.

North Carolina State University, Graduate School, College of Agriculture and Life Sciences and College of Veterinary Medicine, Department of Environmental and Molecular Toxicology, Raleigh, NC 27695. Offers M Tox, MS, PhD. Terminal master's awarded for partial completion of doctoral program. *Degree requirements:* For master's, thesis (for some programs); for doctorate, thesis/dissertation. *Entrance requirements:* For master's and doctorate, GRE General Test, minimum GPA of 3.0. Electronic applications accepted. *Faculty research:* Chemical fate, carcinogenesis, developmental and endocrine toxicity, xenobiotic metabolism, signal transduction.

Oregon State University, Graduate School, College of Agricultural Sciences, Department of Environmental and Molecular Toxicology, Corvallis, OR 97331. Offers toxicology (MS, PhD). *Faculty:* 13 full-time (5 women), 1 part-time/adjunct (0 women). *Students:* 23 full-time (14 women), 2 part-time (1 woman); includes 6 minority (1 African American, 2 American Indian/Alaska Native, 1 Asian American or Pacific Islander, 2 Hispanic Americans), 2 international. Average age 29. In 2009, 5 doctorates awarded. Application fee: $50. *Expenses:* Tuition, state resident: full-time $9774; part-time $362 per credit. Tuition, nonresident: full-time $15,849; part-time $587 per credit. Required fees: $1639. Full-time tuition and fees vary according to course load and program. *Unit head:* Dr. Nancy I. Kerkvliet, Interim Head, 541-737-4387, Fax: 541-737-0497, E-mail: nancy.kerkvliet@oregonstate.edu. *Application contact:* Dr. Stella Coakley, Associate Dean, 541-737-5264, Fax: 541-737-3178, E-mail: stella.coakley@oregonstate.edu.

Penn State Hershey Medical Center, College of Medicine, Graduate School Programs in the Biomedical Sciences, The Huck Institutes of the Life Sciences, Intercollege Graduate Program in Molecular Toxicology, Hershey, PA 17033. Offers MS, PhD, MD/PhD. *Students:* 13 applicants, 8% accepted, 1 enrolled. *Degree requirements:* For doctorate, comprehensive exam, thesis/dissertation. *Entrance requirements:* For doctorate, GRE. Additional exam requirements/recommendations for international students: Required—TOEFL (minimum score 550 paper-based). *Application deadline:* For fall admission, 3/1 priority date for domestic students, 2/1 priority date for international students. Applications are processed on a rolling basis. Application fee: $65. Electronic applications accepted. *Expenses:* Tuition, state resident: part-time $644 per credit. Tuition, nonresident: part-time $1142 per credit. Required fees: $22 per semester. *Financial support:* In 2009–10, research assistantships with full tuition reimbursements (averaging $22,260 per year); fellowships with full tuition reimbursements, career-related internships or fieldwork, scholarships/grants, and unspecified assistantships also available. *Unit head:* Dr. Jung Yun, Head, 717-531-8982, E-mail: grad-hmc@psu.edu. *Application contact:* Kathy Shuey, Administrative Assistant, 717-531-8982, Fax: 717-531-0786, E-mail: grad-hmc@psu.edu.

University of California, Berkeley, Graduate Division, College of Natural Resources, Group in Molecular Toxicology, Berkeley, CA 94720-1500. Offers PhD. *Students:* 11 full-time (7 women). Average age 28. 20 applicants, 1 enrolled. In 2009, 1 doctorate awarded. *Entrance requirements:* For doctorate, GRE General Test, 3 letters of recommendation. *Application deadline:* For fall admission, 12/1 for domestic students. Application fee: $70 ($90 for international students). *Unit head:* Prof. Leonard F. Bjeldanes, Head, 510-643-2863, E-mail: moltox@nature.berkeley.edu. *Application contact:* Information Contact, 510-643-2863, E-mail: moltox@nature.berkeley.edu.

University of California, Los Angeles, Graduate Division, School of Public Health, Department of Environmental Health Sciences, Interdepartmental Program in Molecular Toxicology, Los Angeles, CA 90095. Offers PhD. *Degree requirements:* For doctorate, thesis/dissertation, oral and written qualifying exams. *Entrance requirements:* For doctorate, GRE General Test. Electronic applications accepted.

University of Cincinnati, Graduate School, College of Medicine, Graduate Programs in Biomedical Sciences, Department of Environmental Health, Programs in Environmental Genetics and Molecular Toxicology, Cincinnati, OH 45221. Offers MS, PhD. *Degree requirements:* For doctorate, thesis/dissertation. *Entrance requirements:* For master's, GRE, minimum GPA of 3.0, 3 letters of recommendation. Additional exam requirements/recommendations for international students: Required—TOEFL (minimum score 520 paper-based; 190 computer-based).

Pharmacology

Albany Medical College, Center for Neuropharmacology and Neuroscience, Albany, NY 12208-3479. Offers MS, PhD. *Faculty:* 23 full-time (8 women). *Students:* 18 full-time (7 women); includes 5 minority (2 African Americans, 2 Asian Americans or Pacific Islanders, 1 Hispanic American). Average age 24. 31 applicants, 19% accepted, 6 enrolled. In 2009, 2 master's, 3 doctorates awarded. Terminal master's awarded for partial completion of doctoral program. *Degree requirements:* For master's, thesis; for doctorate, comprehensive exam, thesis/dissertation. *Entrance requirements:* For master's, GRE General Test, all transcripts, letters of recommendation; for doctorate, GRE General Test, letters of recommendation. Additional exam requirements/recommendations for international students: Required—TOEFL. *Application deadline:* For fall admission, 3/15 priority date for domestic and international students. Applications are processed on a rolling basis. Application fee: $0 ($60 for international students). *Expenses:* Tuition: Full-time $18,820. *Financial support:* In 2009–10, 3 fellowships with partial tuition reimbursements (averaging $20,772 per year), 18 research assistantships with full tuition reimbursements (averaging $24,000 per year) were awarded; Federal Work-Study, scholarships/grants, and tuition waivers (full) also available. Financial award applicants required to submit FAFSA. *Faculty research:* Molecular and cellular neuroscience, neuronal development, addiction. *Unit head:* Dr. Stanley D. Glick, Director, 518-262-5303, Fax: 518-262-5799, E-mail: cnninfo@mail.amc.edu. *Application contact:* Dr. Richard Keller, Graduate Director, 518-262-5303, Fax: 518-262-5799, E-mail: cnninfo@mail.amc.edu.

Alliant International University–San Francisco, California School of Professional Psychology, Program in Psychopharmacology, San Francisco, CA 94133-1221. Offers Post-Doctoral MS. Part-time programs available. Postbaccalaureate distance learning degree programs offered. *Entrance requirements:* For master's, doctorate in clinical psychology, minimum GPA of 3.0 in psychology and overall. Additional exam requirements/recommendations for international students: Required—TOEFL. Electronic applications accepted.

American University of Beirut, Graduate Programs, Faculty of Medicine, Beirut, Lebanon. Offers biochemistry (MS); human morphology (MS); medicine (MD); microbiology and immunology (MS); neuroscience (MS); pharmacology and therapeutics (MS); physiology (MS). Part-time programs available. *Degree requirements:* For master's, one foreign language, comprehensive exam, thesis (for some programs). *Entrance requirements:* For MD, MCAT, bachelor's degree; for master's, letter of recommendation. Additional exam requirements/recommendations for international students: Required—TOEFL (minimum score 600 paper-based; 250 computer-based; 100 iBT), IELTS (minimum score 7.5). *Faculty research:* Cancer research, stem cell research, genetic research, neuroscience research, bone research.

Argosy University, Hawai'i, College of Psychology and Behavioral Sciences, Program in Psychopharmacology, Honolulu, HI 96813. Offers MS, Certificate. *Accreditation:* APA.

Auburn University, College of Veterinary Medicine and Graduate School, Graduate Programs in Veterinary Medicine, Auburn University, AL 36849. Offers biomedical sciences (MS, PhD), including anatomy, physiology and pharmacology (MS), biomedical sciences (PhD), clinical sciences (MS), large animal surgery and medicine (MS), pathobiology (MS), radiology (MS), small animal surgery and medicine (MS); DVM/MS. Part-time programs available. *Faculty:* 100 full-time (40 women), 5 part-time/adjunct (1 woman). *Students:* 17 full-time (6 women), 51 part-time (35 women); includes 8 minority (2 African Americans, 1 American Indian/Alaska Native, 3 Asian Americans or Pacific Islanders, 2 Hispanic Americans), 22 international. Average age 31. 70 applicants, 34% accepted, 10 enrolled. In 2009, 12 master's, 7 doctorates awarded. *Degree requirements:* For doctorate, thesis/dissertation. *Entrance requirements:* For master's, GRE General Test; for doctorate, GRE General Test, GRE Subject Test. *Application deadline:* For fall admission, 7/7 for domestic students; for spring admission, 11/24 for domestic students. Applications are processed on a rolling basis. Application fee: $50 ($60 for international students). Electronic applications accepted. *Expenses:* Tuition, state resident: full-time $6240. Tuition, nonresident: full-time $18,720. International tuition: $18,938 full-time. Required fees: $492. Tuition and fees vary according to course load, program and reciprocity agreements. *Financial support:* Research assistantships, teaching assistantships, Federal Work-Study available. Support available to part-time students. Financial award application deadline: 3/15; financial award applicants required to submit FAFSA. *Unit head:* Dr. Timothy R. Boosinger, Dean, 334-844-4546. *Application contact:* Dr. George Flowers, Dean of the Graduate School, 334-844-2125.

Baylor College of Medicine, Graduate School of Biomedical Sciences, Department of Pharmacology, Houston, TX 77030-3498. Offers PhD, MD/PhD. *Faculty:* 16 full-time (1 woman). *Students:* 3 full-time (1 woman); includes 1 minority (African American), 1 international. Average age 21. *Degree requirements:* For doctorate, thesis/dissertation, public defense. *Entrance requirements:* For doctorate, GRE General Test, GRE Subject Test (strongly recommended), minimum GPA of 3.0. Additional exam requirements/recommendations for international students: Required—TOEFL. *Application deadline:* For fall admission, 1/1 priority date for domestic students. Application fee: $0. Electronic applications accepted. *Financial support:* Fellowships, research assistantships with tuition reimbursements, career-related internships or fieldwork, Federal Work-Study, institutionally sponsored loans, health care benefits, and students receive a scholarship unless there are grant funds available to pay tuition available. Financial award applicants required to submit FAFSA. *Faculty research:* Cancer research, neuropharmacology, molecular proteins and U-RNA, gene cleaning, tumor markers. *Unit head:* Dr. P. K. Chan, Director, 713-798-7915, E-mail: pchan@bcm.edu. *Application contact:* Tran Kim, Graduate Program Administrator, 713-798-4457, E-mail: kimt@bcm.edu.

Boston University, School of Medicine, Division of Graduate Medical Sciences, Department of Pharmacology and Experimental Therapeutics, Boston, MA 02118. Offers MA, PhD, MD/PhD. Terminal master's awarded for partial completion of doctoral program. *Degree requirements:* For master's, thesis; for doctorate, thesis/dissertation. *Entrance requirements:* For master's and doctorate, GRE General Test, GRE Subject Test. Additional exam requirements/recommendations for international students: Required—TOEFL. *Application deadline:* For fall admission, 1/15 priority date for domestic students; for spring admission, 10/15 priority date for domestic students. Electronic applications accepted. *Expenses:* Tuition: Full-time $37,910; part-time $1184 per credit hour. Required fees: $386; $40 per semester. Part-time tuition and fees vary according to class time, course level, degree level and program. *Financial support:* In 2009–10, fellowships with tuition reimbursements (averaging $19,000 per year), research assistantships with tuition reimbursements (averaging $19,000 per year) were awarded; Federal

Pharmacology

Boston University (continued)
Work-Study, scholarships/grants, traineeships, tuition waivers, and research stipends also available. *Faculty research:* Molecular pharmacology, neuropharmacology, peptide receptors, psychopharmacology. *Unit head:* Dr. David H. Farb, Chairman, 617-638-4300, Fax: 617-638-4329, E-mail: dfarb@bu.edu. *Application contact:* Dr. Carol T. Walsh, Graduate Director, 617-638-4326, Fax: 617-638-4329, E-mail: ctwalsh@bu.edu.

Case Western Reserve University, School of Medicine and School of Graduate Studies, Graduate Programs in Medicine, Department of Pharmacology, Cleveland, OH 44106. Offers PhD, MD/PhD. Terminal master's awarded for partial completion of doctoral program. *Degree requirements:* For doctorate, comprehensive exam, thesis/dissertation. *Entrance requirements:* For doctorate, GRE General Test, GRE Subject Test, or MCAT. Additional exam requirements/recommendations for international students: Required—TOEFL. Electronic applications accepted. *Faculty research:* Aspects of cellular, molecular, and clinical pharmacology; neuroendocrine pharmacology; drug metabolism.

Columbia University, College of Physicians and Surgeons, Department of Pharmacology, New York, NY 10032. Offers pharmacology (M Phil, MA, PhD); pharmacology-toxicology (M Phil, MA, PhD); MD/PhD. Only candidates for the PhD are admitted. Terminal master's awarded for partial completion of doctoral program. *Degree requirements:* For doctorate, thesis/dissertation. *Entrance requirements:* For master's and doctorate, GRE General Test. Additional exam requirements/recommendations for international students: Required—TOEFL. *Faculty research:* Cardiovascular pharmacology, receptor pharmacology, neuropharmacology, membrane biophysics, eicosanoids.

Cornell University, Graduate School, Graduate Fields of Comparative Biomedical Sciences, Field of Pharmacology, Ithaca, NY 14853-0001. Offers MS, PhD. *Faculty:* 32 full-time (8 women). *Students:* 11 full-time (7 women); includes 3 minority (1 African American, 2 Hispanic Americans), 2 international. Average age 27. 32 applicants. In 2009, 2 doctorates awarded. *Degree requirements:* For master's, thesis; for doctorate, comprehensive exam, thesis/dissertation. *Entrance requirements:* For master's and doctorate, GRE General Test, 3 letters of recommendation. Additional exam requirements/recommendations for international students: Required—TOEFL (minimum score 550 paper-based; 213 computer-based; 77 iBT). *Application deadline:* For fall admission, 12/5 for domestic students. Application fee: $70. Electronic applications accepted. *Expenses:* Tuition: Full-time $29,500. Required fees: $70. Full-time tuition and fees vary according to degree level, program and student level. *Financial support:* In 2009–10, 9 students received support, including 2 fellowships with full tuition reimbursements available, 2 research assistantships with full tuition reimbursements available; teaching assistantships with full tuition reimbursements available, institutionally sponsored loans, scholarships/grants, health care benefits, tuition waivers (full and partial), and unspecified assistantships also available. Financial award applicants required to submit FAFSA. *Faculty research:* Signal transduction, ion channels, calcium signaling, G proteins, cancer cell biology. *Unit head:* Director of Graduate Studies, 607-253-3276, Fax: 607-253-3756. *Application contact:* Graduate Field Assistant, 607-253-3276, Fax: 607-253-3756, E-mail: graduate_edcvm@cornell.edu.

Cornell University, Joan and Sanford I. Weill Medical College and Graduate School of Medical Sciences, Weill Cornell Graduate School of Medical Sciences, Pharmacology Program, New York, NY 10065. Offers MS, PhD. *Faculty:* 31 full-time (6 women). *Students:* 58 full-time (35 women); includes 12 minority (3 African Americans, 8 Asian Americans or Pacific Islanders, 1 Hispanic American), 17 international. 67 applicants, 30% accepted, 7 enrolled. In 2009, 1 master's, 6 doctorates awarded. Terminal master's awarded for partial completion of doctoral program. *Degree requirements:* For master's, comprehensive exam; for doctorate, thesis/dissertation, final exam. *Entrance requirements:* For doctorate, GRE General Test, previous course work in natural and/or health sciences. Additional exam requirements/recommendations for international students: Required—TOEFL. *Application deadline:* For fall admission, 12/1 for domestic students. Application fee: $60. *Expenses:* Tuition: Full-time $44,650. Required fees: $2805. *Financial support:* In 2009–10, 16 fellowships (averaging $20,976 per year) were awarded; scholarships/grants, health care benefits, and stipends (given to all students) also available. *Faculty research:* Modulation of gene expression by drugs, signal transduction, nitric oxide signaling RNA trafficking, neuropharmacology of opiates. *Unit head:* Dr. Geoffrey Abbott, Director, 212-746-6275, E-mail: gwa2001@med.cornell.edu. *Application contact:* Olga Willis, Program Coordinator, 212-746-6250, E-mail: orw2003@med.cornell.edu.

Creighton University, School of Medicine and Graduate School, Graduate Programs in Medicine, Department of Pharmacology, Omaha, NE 68178-0001. Offers pharmaceutical sciences (MS); pharmacology (MS, PhD); Pharm D/MS. Terminal master's awarded for partial completion of doctoral program. *Degree requirements:* For master's, comprehensive exam, thesis; for doctorate, comprehensive exam, thesis/dissertation, oral and written preliminary exams. *Entrance requirements:* For master's and doctorate, GRE General Test, minimum GPA of 3.0, undergraduate degree in sciences. Additional exam requirements/recommendations for international students: Required—TOEFL. Electronic applications accepted. *Expenses:* Tuition: Full-time $11,700; part-time $650 per credit hour. Required fees: $126 per semester. *Faculty research:* Pharmacology secretion, cardiovascular-renal pharmacology, adrenergic receptors, signal transduction, genetic regulation of receptors.

Dalhousie University, Faculty of Graduate Studies and Faculty of Medicine, Graduate Programs in Medicine, Department of Pharmacology, Halifax, NS B3H 4R2, Canada. Offers M Sc, PhD. *Degree requirements:* For master's, thesis; for doctorate, comprehensive exam, thesis/dissertation. *Entrance requirements:* Additional exam requirements/recommendations for international students: Required—TOEFL, IELTS, 1 of the following 5 approved tests: TOEFL, IELTS, CAEL, CANTEST, Michigan English Language Assessment Battery. Electronic applications accepted. *Faculty research:* Electrophysiology and neurochemistry; endocrinology, immunology and cancer research; molecular biology; cardiovascular and autonomic; drug biotransformation and metabolism; ocular pharmacology.

Dartmouth College, Arts and Sciences Graduate Programs, Department of Pharmacology and Toxicology, Hanover, NH 03755. Offers PhD, MD/PhD. *Faculty:* 25 full-time (5 women). *Students:* 17 full-time (8 women); includes 1 minority (African American), 6 international. Average age 28. 1,128 applicants, 2% accepted, 15 enrolled. In 2009, 6 doctorates awarded. *Degree requirements:* For doctorate, thesis/dissertation. *Entrance requirements:* For doctorate, GRE General Test, GRE Subject Test, bachelor's degree in biological, chemical, or physical science. Additional exam requirements/recommendations for international students: Required—TOEFL. *Application deadline:* For fall admission, 1/15 for domestic students. Electronic applications accepted. *Financial support:* In 2009–10, 13 students received support, including fellowships with full tuition reimbursements available (averaging $25,500 per year), research assistantships with full tuition reimbursements available (averaging $25,500 per year), teaching assistantships with tuition reimbursements available (averaging $25,500 per year); institutionally sponsored loans, traineeships, tuition waivers (full and partial), and unspecified assistantships also available. Financial award application deadline: 4/15. *Faculty research:* Molecular biology of carcinogenesis, DNA repair and gene expression, biochemical and environmental toxicology, protein receptor ligand interactions. *Unit head:* Dr. Joyce DeLeo, Chair, 603-650-1667, Fax: 603-650-1129, E-mail: pharmacology.and.toxicology@dartmouth.edu. *Application contact:* Clarissa Kellogg, Academic Assistant, 603-650-1667, Fax: 603-650-1129.

Drexel University, College of Medicine, Biomedical Graduate Programs, Pharmacology and Physiology Program, Philadelphia, PA 19104-2875. Offers MS, PhD, MD/PhD. Part-time programs available. Terminal master's awarded for partial completion of doctoral program. *Degree requirements:* For master's, comprehensive exam; for doctorate, thesis/dissertation, qualifying exam. *Entrance requirements:* For master's, GRE General Test, minimum GPA of 2.75; for doctorate, GRE General Test, minimum GPA of 3.0. Additional exam requirements/recommendations for international students: Required—TOEFL. Electronic applications accepted. *Faculty research:* Cardiovascular pharmacology, drugs of abuse, neurotransmitter mechanisms.

Duke University, Graduate School, Department of Pharmacology and Cancer Biology, Durham, NC 27710. Offers pharmacology (PhD). *Faculty:* 39 full-time. *Students:* 43 full-time (23 women). Average age 23. 78 applicants, 15% accepted, 6 enrolled. In 2009, 9 doctorates awarded. *Degree requirements:* For doctorate, thesis/dissertation. *Entrance requirements:* For doctorate, GRE General Test, minimum GPA of 2.8. Additional exam requirements/recommendations for international students: Required—TOEFL or IELTS (preferred). *Application deadline:* For fall admission, 12/15 priority date for domestic and international students. Application fee: $75. Electronic applications accepted. *Financial support:* In 2009–10, 11 fellowships with tuition reimbursements (averaging $23,000 per year), 8 research assistantships with tuition reimbursements (averaging $25,000 per year), 2 teaching assistantships with tuition reimbursements (averaging $23,000 per year) were awarded; Federal Work-Study, scholarships/grants, traineeships, health care benefits, and unspecified assistantships also available. Financial award application deadline: 12/31. *Faculty research:* Developmental pharmacology, neuropharmacology, molecular pharmacology, toxicology, cell growth. *Unit head:* Dr. Jeffrey Rathmell, Director of Graduate Studies, 919-681-1084, Fax: 919-684-8922, E-mail: jeff.rathmell@duke.edu. *Application contact:* Jamie Baize-Smith, Assistant to Director of Graduate Studies, 919-613-8600, Fax: 919-681-7767, E-mail: baize@duke.edu.

Duquesne University, Mylan School of Pharmacy/Graduate School of Pharmaceutical Sciences, Graduate School of Pharmaceutical Sciences, Program in Pharmacology, Pittsburgh, PA 15282-0001. Offers MS, PhD. *Faculty:* 5 full-time (3 women). *Students:* 14 full-time (10 women), 4 part-time (3 women); includes 1 minority (African American), 7 international. 50 applicants, 10% accepted, 4 enrolled. In 2009, 2 master's, 3 doctorates awarded. *Degree requirements:* For master's, thesis; for doctorate, comprehensive exam, thesis/dissertation. *Entrance requirements:* For master's and doctorate, GRE General Test. Additional exam requirements/recommendations for international students: Required—TOEFL. *Application deadline:* For fall admission, 2/1 priority date for domestic and international students; for spring admission, 10/1 priority date for domestic and international students. Applications are processed on a rolling basis. Application fee: $50. Electronic applications accepted. *Expenses:* Tuition: Part-time $851 per credit. Required fees: $81 per credit. *Financial support:* In 2009–10, 15 students received support, including 14 teaching assistantships with full tuition reimbursements available; research assistantships with full tuition reimbursements available. *Unit head:* Dr. David A. Johnson, Head, 412-396-5952. *Application contact:* Information Contact, 412-396-1172, E-mail: gsps-adm@duq.edu.

East Carolina University, Brody School of Medicine, Department of Pharmacology, Greenville, NC 27858-4353. Offers PhD, MD/PhD. *Degree requirements:* For doctorate, comprehensive exam, thesis/dissertation. *Entrance requirements:* For doctorate, GRE General Test, GRE Subject Test. Additional exam requirements/recommendations for international students: Required—TOEFL. *Faculty research:* GNS/behavioral pharmacology, cardiovascular pharmacology, cell signaling and second messenger, effects of calcium channel blockers.

East Tennessee State University, James H. Quillen College of Medicine, Biomedical Science Graduate Program, Johnson City, TN 37614. Offers anatomy (MS, PhD); biochemistry (MS, PhD); biophysics (MS, PhD); microbiology (MS, PhD); pharmacology (MS, PhD); physiology (MS, PhD). Part-time programs available. Terminal master's awarded for partial completion of doctoral program. *Degree requirements:* For master's, one foreign language, thesis, comprehensive qualifying exam; for doctorate, 2 foreign languages, thesis/dissertation. *Entrance requirements:* For master's, GRE General Test, minimum GPA of 3.0, bachelor's degree in biological or related science; for doctorate, GRE General Test, GRE Subject Test. Additional exam requirements/recommendations for international students: Required—TOEFL (minimum score 550 paper-based; 213 computer-based). *Expenses:* Contact institution.

Emory University, Graduate School of Arts and Sciences, Division of Biological and Biomedical Sciences, Program in Molecular and Systems Pharmacology, Atlanta, GA 30322-1100. Offers PhD. *Faculty:* 46 full-time (8 women). *Students:* 51 full-time (27 women); includes 13 minority (11 African Americans, 2 Asian Americans or Pacific Islanders), 5 international. Average age 27. 75 applicants, 19% accepted, 7 enrolled. In 2009, 7 doctorates awarded. *Degree requirements:* For doctorate, comprehensive exam, thesis/dissertation. *Entrance requirements:* For doctorate, GRE General Test, minimum GPA of 3.0 in science course work (recommended). Additional exam requirements/recommendations for international students: Required—TOEFL. *Application deadline:* For fall admission, 1/3 for domestic and international students. Application fee: $50. Electronic applications accepted. *Financial support:* In 2009–10, 16 students received support, including 16 fellowships with full tuition reimbursements available (averaging $24,500 per year); institutionally sponsored loans, scholarships/grants, and health care benefits also available. *Faculty research:* Transmembrane signaling, neuropharmacology, neurophysiology and neurodegeneration, metabolism and molecular toxicology, cell and developmental biology. *Unit head:* Dr. Edward Morgan, Director, 404-727-5986, Fax: 404-727-0365, E-mail: etmorga@emory.edu. *Application contact:* Dr. Eric Ortlund, Recruiter, 404-727-5014, Fax: 404-727-2738, E-mail: eric.ortlund@emory.edu.

Fairleigh Dickinson University, College at Florham, Silberman College of Business, Program in Pharmaceutical Studies, Madison, NJ 07940-1099. Offers MBA, Certificate. *Students:* 11 full-time (4 women), 26 part-time (13 women), 7 international. Average age 33. 30 applicants, 57% accepted, 4 enrolled. In 2009, 15 master's awarded. *Application deadline:* Applications are processed on a rolling basis. Application fee: $40.

Florida Agricultural and Mechanical University, Division of Graduate Studies, Research, and Continuing Education, College of Pharmacy and Pharmaceutical Sciences, Graduate Programs in Pharmaceutical Sciences, Tallahassee, FL 32307-3200. Offers environmental toxicology (PhD); medicinal chemistry (MS, PhD); pharmaceutics (MS, PhD); pharmacology/toxicology (MS, PhD); pharmacy administration (MS). *Accreditation:* CEPH. *Faculty:* 21 full-time (6 women). *Students:* 438 full-time (296 women), 21 part-time (13 women); includes 417 minority (380 African Americans, 1 American Indian/Alaska Native, 30 Asian Americans or Pacific Islanders, 6 Hispanic Americans), 5 international. In 2009, 4 master's, 7 doctorates awarded. *Degree requirements:* For master's, comprehensive exam, thesis, publishable paper; for doctorate, comprehensive exam, thesis/dissertation, publishable paper. *Entrance requirements:* For master's and doctorate, GRE General Test, minimum GPA of 3.0 in last 60 hours. Additional exam requirements/recommendations for international students: Required—TOEFL. *Application deadline:* For fall admission, 4/1 for domestic students. Application fee: $20. *Financial support:* Fellowships, research assistantships, Federal Work-Study and scholarships/grants available. *Faculty research:* Anticancer agents, anti-inflammatory drugs, chronopharmacology, neuroendocrinology, microbiology. *Unit head:* Dr. Thomas J. Fitzgerald, Chairman, Graduate Committee, 850-599-3301. *Application contact:* Gloria James, Graduate Coordinator, 850-599-3144.

Georgetown University, Graduate School of Arts and Sciences, Programs in Biomedical Sciences, Department of Pharmacology, Washington, DC 20057. Offers MS, PhD, MD/PhD, MS/PhD. *Degree requirements:* For doctorate, comprehensive exam, thesis/dissertation. *Entrance requirements:* For doctorate, GRE General Test, previous course work in biology and chemistry. Additional exam requirements/recommendations for international students: Required—TOEFL. *Faculty research:* Neuropharmacology, techniques in biochemistry and tissue culture.

Howard University, College of Medicine, Department of Pharmacology, Washington, DC 20059-0002. Offers MS, PhD, MD/PhD. Part-time programs available. *Degree requirements:* For master's, comprehensive exam, thesis; for doctorate, one foreign language, comprehensive exam, thesis/dissertation, qualifying exam. *Entrance requirements:* For master's, GRE General Test, minimum GPA of 3.2, BS in chemistry, biology, pharmacy, psychology or related field; for doctorate, GRE General Test, minimum graduate GPA of 3.2. *Faculty research:* Biochemical pharmacology, molecular pharmacology, neuropharmacology, drug metabolism, cancer research.

Idaho State University, Office of Graduate Studies, College of Pharmacy, Department of Biomedical and Pharmaceutical Sciences, Pocatello, ID 83209-8334. Offers biopharmaceutical analysis (PhD); drug delivery (PhD); medicinal chemistry (PhD); pharmaceutical sciences

(MS); pharmacology (PhD). Part-time programs available. *Faculty:* 9 full-time (1 woman). *Students:* 13 full-time (5 women), 7 part-time (3 women); includes 2 minority (both Asian Americans or Pacific Islanders), 14 international. Average age 29. In 2009, 7 master's, 2 doctorates awarded. *Degree requirements:* For master's, one foreign language, comprehensive exam, thesis, thesis research, classes in speech and technical writing; for doctorate, comprehensive exam, thesis/dissertation, written and oral exams, classes in speech and technical writing. *Entrance requirements:* For master's, GRE General Test, minimum GPA of 3.0, 3 letters of recommendation; for doctorate, GRE General Test, BS in pharmacy or related field, minimum GPA of 3.0, 3 letters of recommendation. Additional exam requirements/recommendations for international students: Required—TOEFL (minimum score 550 paper-based; 213 computer-based; 80 iBT). *Application deadline:* For fall admission, 7/1 for domestic students, 6/1 for international students; for spring admission, 12/1 for domestic students, 11/1 for international students. Applications are processed on a rolling basis. Application fee: $55. Electronic applications accepted. *Expenses:* Contact institution. *Financial support:* Research assistantships with full and partial tuition reimbursements, teaching assistantships with full and partial tuition reimbursements, career-related internships or fieldwork, Federal Work-Study, institutionally sponsored loans, scholarships/grants, traineeships, health care benefits, tuition waivers (full and partial), and unspecified assistantships available. Support available to part-time students. Financial award application deadline: 1/1; financial award applicants required to submit FAFSA. *Faculty research:* Metabolic toxicity of heavy metals, neuroendocrine pharmacology, cardiovascular pharmacology, cancer biology, immunopharmacology. *Unit head:* Dr. Timothy Hunt, Chair, 208-282-2682, Fax: 208-282-4305, E-mail: thunt@pharmacy.isu.edu. *Application contact:* Tami Carson, Graduate School Technical Records Specialist, 208-282-2150, Fax: 208-282-4847, E-mail: carstami@isu.edu.

Indiana University–Purdue University Indianapolis, Indiana University School of Medicine, Department of Pharmacology and Toxicology, Indianapolis, IN 46202-2896. Offers pharmacology (MS, PhD); toxicology (MS, PhD); MD/PhD. *Faculty:* 11 full-time (2 women). *Students:* 21 full-time (13 women), 1 part-time (0 women); includes 1 minority (Hispanic American), 10 international. Average age 28. 13 applicants, 38% accepted, 5 enrolled. In 2009, 4 master's, 2 doctorates awarded. Terminal master's awarded for partial completion of doctoral program. *Degree requirements:* For master's, thesis; for doctorate, thesis/dissertation. *Entrance requirements:* For master's and doctorate, GRE General Test, GRE Subject Test, minimum GPA of 3.0. *Application deadline:* For fall admission, 1/15 priority date for domestic students. Applications are processed on a rolling basis. Application fee: $55 ($65 for international students). *Financial support:* In 2009–10, 14 students received support, including 7 teaching assistantships (averaging $20,940 per year); fellowships with partial tuition reimbursements available, research assistantships with partial tuition reimbursements available, Federal Work-Study, institutionally sponsored loans, and tuition waivers (partial) also available. Financial award application deadline: 1/15. *Faculty research:* Neuropharmacology, cardiovascular biopharmacology, chemotherapy, oncogenesis. *Unit head:* Dr. Michael Vasko, Chairman, 317-274-7844, Fax: 317-274-7714. *Application contact:* Director of Graduate Studies, 317-274-1564, Fax: 317-274-7714.

The Johns Hopkins University, School of Medicine, Graduate Programs in Medicine, Department of Pharmacology and Molecular Sciences, Baltimore, MD 21205. Offers PhD. *Faculty:* 42 full-time (8 women). *Students:* 60 full-time (27 women); includes 16 minority (7 African Americans, 8 Asian Americans or Pacific Islanders, 1 Hispanic American), 16 international. 180 applicants, 10% accepted, 9 enrolled. In 2009, 4 doctorates awarded. *Degree requirements:* For doctorate, comprehensive exam, thesis/dissertation, departmental seminar. *Entrance requirements:* For doctorate, GRE General Test. Additional exam requirements/recommendations for international students: Required—TOEFL. *Application deadline:* For fall admission, 1/10 for domestic and international students. Application fee: $85. Electronic applications accepted. *Unit head:* Dr. Philip A. Cole, Chairman, 410-614-0540, Fax: 410-614-7717, E-mail: pcole@jhmi.edu. *Application contact:* Dr. James T. Stivers, Director of Admissions, 410-955-7117, Fax: 410-955-3023, E-mail: jstivers@jhmi.edu.

See Close-Up on page 463.

Kent State University, School of Biomedical Sciences, Program in Pharmacology, Kent, OH 44242-0001. Offers MS, PhD. Offered in cooperation with Northeastern Ohio Universities College of Medicine. Terminal master's awarded for partial completion of doctoral program. *Degree requirements:* For master's, thesis; for doctorate, thesis/dissertation. *Entrance requirements:* For master's and doctorate, GRE General Test, minimum GPA of 3.0, 3 letters of recommendation. Additional exam requirements/recommendations for international students: Required—TOEFL. Electronic applications accepted. *Faculty research:* Neuropharmacology, psychotherapeutics and substance abuse, molecular biology of substance abuse, toxicology.

Loma Linda University, School of Medicine, Department of Physiology/Pharmacology, Loma Linda, CA 92350. Offers MS, PhD. Part-time programs available. *Degree requirements:* For master's, thesis or alternative; for doctorate, 2 foreign languages, thesis/dissertation. *Entrance requirements:* For master's and doctorate, GRE General Test. *Faculty research:* Drug metabolism, biochemical pharmacology, structure and function of cell membranes, neuropharmacology.

Long Island University, Brooklyn Campus, Arnold and Marie Schwartz College of Pharmacy and Health Sciences, Graduate Programs in Pharmacy, Division of Pharmaceutical Sciences, Brooklyn, NY 11201-8423. Offers cosmetic science (MS); industrial pharmacy (MS); pharmaceutics (PhD); pharmacology/toxicology (MS). Part-time and evening/weekend programs available. Terminal master's awarded for partial completion of doctoral program. *Degree requirements:* For master's, thesis optional; for doctorate, thesis/dissertation, candidacy exam. *Entrance requirements:* For master's and doctorate, minimum GPA of 3.0.

Louisiana State University Health Sciences Center, School of Graduate Studies in New Orleans, Department of Pharmacology and Experimental Therapeutics, New Orleans, LA 70112-2223. Offers MS, PhD, MD/PhD. Terminal master's awarded for partial completion of doctoral program. *Degree requirements:* For master's, comprehensive exam, thesis; for doctorate, comprehensive exam, thesis/dissertation. *Entrance requirements:* For master's, GRE; for doctorate, GRE General Test. Additional exam requirements/recommendations for international students: Required—TOEFL. *Faculty research:* Neuropharmacology, gastrointestinal pharmacology, drug metabolism, behavioral pharmacology, cardiovascular pharmacology.

Louisiana State University Health Sciences Center at Shreveport, Department of Pharmacology, Toxicology and Neuroscience, Shreveport, LA 71130-3932. Offers pharmacology (PhD); MD/PhD. Terminal master's awarded for partial completion of doctoral program. *Degree requirements:* For doctorate, thesis/dissertation. *Entrance requirements:* For doctorate, GRE General Test, minimum GPA of 3.0. Additional exam requirements/recommendations for international students: Required—TOEFL. *Faculty research:* Behavioral, cardiovascular, clinical, and gastrointestinal pharmacology; neuropharmacology; psychopharmacology; drug abuse; pharmacokinetics; neuroendocrinology, psychoneuroimmunology, and stress; toxicology.

Loyola University Chicago, Graduate School, Department of Pharmacology and Experimental Therapeutics, Chicago, IL 60626. Offers MS, PhD, MD/PhD. *Faculty:* 9 full-time (3 women), 8 part-time/adjunct (2 women). *Students:* 11 full-time (7 women), 4 international. Average age 27. 42 applicants, 12% accepted, 2 enrolled.Terminal master's awarded for partial completion of doctoral program. *Degree requirements:* For master's, comprehensive exam, thesis; for doctorate, comprehensive exam, thesis/dissertation. *Entrance requirements:* For master's and doctorate, GRE General Test, minimum GPA of 3.0. Additional exam requirements/recommendations for international students: Required—TOEFL. *Application deadline:* For fall admission, 2/1 for domestic and international students. Application fee: $50. Electronic applications accepted. *Expenses:* Tuition: Full-time $14,220; part-time $790 per credit hour. Required fees: $60 per semester hour. Tuition and fees vary according to program. *Financial support:* In 2009–10, 3 fellowships with full tuition reimbursements (averaging $32,165 per year), 15 research assistantships with full tuition reimbursements (averaging $23,000 per year) were awarded; career-related internships or fieldwork and Federal Work-Study also available. Financial award application deadline: 2/1; financial award applicants required to submit FAFSA. *Faculty research:* Neuropharmacology, molecular pharmacology, neuroendocrinology, hematopharmacology, neurodegeneration. *Unit head:* Dr. Tarun Patel, Chair, 708-216-5773, Fax: 708-216-6956. *Application contact:* Dr. Kenneth L. Byron, Graduate Program Director, 708-327-2819, Fax: 708-216-6596, E-mail: kbyron@luc.edu.

Massachusetts College of Pharmacy and Health Sciences, Graduate Studies, Program in Pharmacology, Boston, MA 02115-5896. Offers MS, PhD. *Accreditation:* ACPE (one or more programs are accredited). *Students:* 9 part-time (8 women); includes 1 minority (Asian American or Pacific Islander), 6 international. Average age 29. 29 applicants, 14% accepted, 2 enrolled. Terminal master's awarded for partial completion of doctoral program. *Degree requirements:* For master's, oral defense of thesis; for doctorate, one foreign language, oral defense of dissertation, qualifying exam. *Entrance requirements:* For master's and doctorate, GRE General Test, minimum QPA of 3.0. Additional exam requirements/recommendations for international students: Required—TOEFL (minimum score 550 paper-based; 213 computer-based; 79 iBT). *Application deadline:* For fall admission, 2/1 priority date for domestic students, 1/1 for international students. Application fee: $70. *Expenses:* Tuition: Full-time $28,000; part-time $875 per credit hour. Required fees: $750; $190 per semester. Part-time tuition and fees vary according to course load, campus/location, program and student level. *Financial support:* Fellowships with partial tuition reimbursements, research assistantships with partial tuition reimbursements, teaching assistantships with full tuition reimbursements, tuition waivers (partial) and library assistantships available. Financial award application deadline: 3/15. *Faculty research:* Neuropharmacology, cardiovascular pharmacology, nutritional pharmacology, pulmonary physiology, drug metabolism. *Unit head:* Dr. Dan Kiel, Assistant Professor, 617-732-2975, E-mail: dan.kiel@mcphs.edu. *Application contact:* Tara Hennesey, Coordinator of Graduate Admission, 617-732-2850, E-mail: admissions@mcphs.edu.

McGill University, Faculty of Graduate and Postdoctoral Studies, Faculty of Medicine, Department of Pharmacology and Therapeutics, Montréal, QC H3A 2T5, Canada. Offers M Sc, PhD.

McMaster University, Faculty of Health Sciences and School of Graduate Studies, Program in Medical Sciences, Physiology/Pharmacology Area, Hamilton, ON L8S 4M2, Canada. Offers M Sc, PhD, MD/PhD. *Degree requirements:* For master's, thesis; for doctorate, comprehensive exam, thesis/dissertation. *Entrance requirements:* For master's, honors B Sc, B+ average in related field; for doctorate, M Sc, minimum B+ average, students with proven research experience and an A average may be admitted with a B Sc degree. Additional exam requirements/recommendations for international students: Required—TOEFL (minimum score 580 paper-based; 237 computer-based; 92 iBT).

Medical College of Georgia, School of Graduate Studies, Program in Pharmacology, Augusta, GA 30912. Offers PhD. *Degree requirements:* For doctorate, comprehensive exam, thesis/dissertation. *Entrance requirements:* For doctorate, GRE General Test. Additional exam requirements/recommendations for international students: Required—TOEFL (minimum score 550 paper-based; 213 computer-based; 79 iBT). Electronic applications accepted. Full-time tuition and fees vary according to campus/location, program and student level. *Faculty research:* Protein signaling, neural development, cardiovascular pharmacology, endothelial cell function, neuropharmacology.

Medical College of Wisconsin, Graduate School of Biomedical Sciences, Department of Pharmacology and Toxicology, Milwaukee, WI 53226-0509. Offers PhD, MD/PhD. Terminal master's awarded for partial completion of doctoral program. *Degree requirements:* For doctorate, comprehensive exam, thesis/dissertation, oral and written qualifying exams. *Entrance requirements:* For doctorate, GRE General Test, minimum B average. Additional exam requirements/recommendations for international students: Required—TOEFL. *Faculty research:* Cardiovascular physiology and pharmacology, drugs of abuse, environmental and aquatic toxicology, central nervous system and biochemical pharmacology, signal transduction.

Meharry Medical College, School of Graduate Studies, Program in Biomedical Sciences, Pharmacology Emphasis, Nashville, TN 37208-9989. Offers PhD, MD/PhD. *Degree requirements:* For doctorate, comprehensive exam, thesis/dissertation. *Entrance requirements:* For doctorate, GRE. *Faculty research:* Neuropharmacology, cardiovascular pharmacology, behavioral pharmacology, molecular pharmacology, drug metabolism, anticancer.

Michigan State University, College of Human Medicine and The Graduate School, Graduate Programs in Human Medicine, East Lansing, MI 48824. Offers biochemistry and molecular biology (MS, PhD); epidemiology (MS, PhD); microbiology (MS); microbiology and molecular genetics (PhD); pharmacology and toxicology (MS, PhD); physiology (MS, PhD); public health (MPH). *Students:* 58 full-time (31 women), 31 part-time (25 women); includes 17 minority (7 African Americans, 1 American Indian/Alaska Native, 6 Asian Americans or Pacific Islanders, 3 Hispanic Americans), 22 international. Average age 30. In 2009, 8 master's, 9 doctorates awarded. *Entrance requirements:* Additional exam requirements/recommendations for international students: Required—TOEFL. *Expenses:* Tuition, state resident: part-time $478.25 per credit hour. Tuition, nonresident: part-time $966.50 per credit hour. Part-time tuition and fees vary according to program. *Financial support:* In 2009–10, 17 research assistantships with tuition reimbursements (averaging $7,053 per year), 3 teaching assistantships with tuition reimbursements (averaging $6,607 per year) were awarded. *Unit head:* Margo K. Smith, Director of Graduate Studies, 517-432-5112, E-mail: smithmk@msu.edu. *Application contact:* Margo K. Smith, Director of Graduate Studies, 517-432-5112, E-mail: smithmk@msu.edu.

Michigan State University, College of Osteopathic Medicine and The Graduate School, Graduate Studies in Osteopathic Medicine and Graduate Programs in Human Medicine and Graduate Programs in Veterinary Medicine, Department of Pharmacology and Toxicology, East Lansing, MI 48824. Offers integrative pharmacology (MS); pharmacology and toxicology (MS, PhD); pharmacology and toxicology-environmental toxicology (PhD). *Faculty:* 17 full-time (6 women). *Students:* 21 full-time (10 women), 40 part-time (23 women); includes 7 minority (1 African American, 2 Asian Americans or Pacific Islanders, 4 Hispanic Americans), 11 international. Average age 29. 70 applicants, 27% accepted. In 2009, 1 doctorate awarded. *Entrance requirements:* Additional exam requirements/recommendations for international students: Required—TOEFL (minimum score 600 paper-based; 220 computer-based). *Application deadline:* Applications are processed on a rolling basis. Electronic applications accepted. *Expenses:* Tuition, state resident: part-time $478.25 per credit hour. Tuition, nonresident: part-time $966.50 per credit hour. Part-time tuition and fees vary according to program. *Financial support:* In 2009–10, 11 research assistantships with tuition reimbursements (averaging $7,754 per year) were awarded. Total annual research expenditures: $5.3 million. *Unit head:* Dr. Joseph R. Haywood, Chairperson, 517-353-7145, Fax: 517-353-8915, E-mail: haywoo12@msu.edu. *Application contact:* Diane Hummel, Graduate Secretary, 517-353-9619, Fax: 517-353-8915, E-mail: hummeld@msu.edu.

Michigan State University, College of Veterinary Medicine and The Graduate School, Graduate Programs in Veterinary Medicine, East Lansing, MI 48824. Offers comparative medicine and integrative biology (MS, PhD), including comparative medicine and integrative biology, comparative medicine and integrative biology–environmental toxicology (PhD); food safety and toxicology (MS), including food safety; integrative toxicology (PhD), including animal science–environmental toxicology, biochemistry and molecular biology–environmental toxicology, chemistry–environmental toxicology, crop and soil sciences–environmental toxicology, environmental engineering–environmental toxicology, environmental geosciences–environmental toxicology, fisheries and wildlife–environmental toxicology, food science–environmental toxicology, forestry–environmental toxicology, genetics–environmental toxicology, human nutrition–environmental toxicology, microbiology–environmental toxicology, pharmacology and toxicology–environmental toxicology, zoology–environmental toxicology; large animal clinical sciences (MS, PhD); microbiology and molecular genetics (MS, PhD), including industrial microbiology, microbiology, microbiology and molecular genetics, microbiology–environmental

Pharmacology

Michigan State University (continued)
toxicology (PhD); pathobiology and diagnostic investigation (MS, PhD), including pathology, pathology–environmental toxicology (PhD); pharmacology and toxicology (MS, PhD); pharmacology and toxicology–environmental toxicology (PhD); physiology (MS, PhD); small animal clinical sciences (MS). *Students:* 66 full-time (40 women), 90 part-time (56 women); includes 24 minority (14 African Americans, 6 Asian Americans or Pacific Islanders, 4 Hispanic Americans), 51 international. Average age 33. In 2009, 22 master's, 16 doctorates awarded. *Application deadline:* For fall admission, 12/27 for domestic students. Applications are processed on a rolling basis. Application fee: $50. Electronic applications accepted. *Expenses:* Tuition, state resident: part-time $478.25 per credit hour. Tuition, nonresident: part-time $966.50 per credit hour. Part-time tuition and fees vary according to program. *Financial support:* In 2009–10, 32 research assistantships with tuition reimbursements (averaging $8,131 per year) were awarded. *Faculty research:* Molecular genetics, food safety/toxicology, comparative orthopedics, airway disease, population medicine. *Unit head:* Dr. Susan L. Ewart, Associate Dean for Research and Graduate Studies, 517-432-2388, Fax: 517-432-1037, E-mail: ewart@cvm.msu.edu. *Application contact:* Dr. Susan L. Ewart, Associate Dean for Research and Graduate Studies, 517-432-2388, Fax: 517-432-1037, E-mail: ewart@cvm.msu.edu.

New York Medical College, Graduate School of Basic Medical Sciences, Program in Pharmacology, Valhalla, NY 10595-1691. Offers MS, PhD, MD/PhD. Part-time and evening/weekend programs available. Terminal master's awarded for partial completion of doctoral program. *Degree requirements:* For master's, thesis; for doctorate, comprehensive exam, thesis/dissertation. *Entrance requirements:* For master's and doctorate, GRE General Test. Additional exam requirements/recommendations for international students: Required—TOEFL. *Expenses:* Tuition: Full-time $18,170; part-time $790 per credit. Required fees: $790 per credit. $20 per semester. One-time fee: $100. Tuition and fees vary according to class time, course level, course load, degree level, program, student level and student's religious affiliation. *Faculty research:* Hypertension, neuroendocrine and renal physiology, metabolism of vasoactive peptides, neuroendocrine and hormonal control of circulation.

New York University, School of Medicine, New York, NY 10012-1019. Offers biomedical sciences (PhD), including biomedical imaging, cellular and molecular biology, computational biology, developmental genetics, medical and molecular parasitology, microbiology, molecular oncobiology and immunology, neuroscience and physiology, pathobiology, pharmacology, structural biology; clinical investigation (MS); medicine (MD); MD/MA; MD/MPA; MD/MS; MD/PhD. *Accreditation:* LCME/AMA (one or more programs are accredited). *Faculty:* 1,493 full-time (558 women), 327 part-time/adjunct (122 women). *Students:* 747 full-time (360 women); includes 275 minority (23 African Americans, 5 American Indian/Alaska Native, 199 Asian Americans or Pacific Islanders, 48 Hispanic Americans), 2 international. Average age 24. 7,568 applicants, 7% accepted, 213 enrolled. In 2009, 164 first professional degrees, 13 master's, 50 doctorates awarded. *Degree requirements:* For master's, comprehensive exam, thesis; for doctorate, comprehensive exam, thesis/dissertation. *Entrance requirements:* MCAT. Additional exam requirements/recommendations for international students: Required—TOEFL. *Application deadline:* For fall admission, 10/15 for domestic students; for winter admission, 12/18 for domestic students, 12/15 for international students. Application fee: $100. *Expenses:* Contact institution. *Financial support:* In 2009–10, 524 students received support, including 29 fellowships with full tuition reimbursements available (averaging $31,000 per year), 47 research assistantships with full tuition reimbursements available (averaging $31,000 per year); teaching assistantships, Federal Work-Study, institutionally sponsored loans, and health care benefits also available. Financial award application deadline: 3/1; financial award applicants required to submit FAFSA. *Faculty research:* AIDS, cancer, neuroscience, molecular biology, neuroscience, cell biology and molecular genetics, structural biology, microbial pathogenesis and host defense, pharmacology, molecular oncology and immunology. Total annual research expenditures: $201.1 million. *Unit head:* Dr. Robert Grossman, Dean, 212-263-3269, Fax: 212-263- 1828. *Application contact:* Dr. Nancy Genieser, Associate Dean, Admissions, 212-263-5290, Fax: 212-263-0720, E-mail: nancy.genieser@nyumc.org.

New York University, School of Medicine and Graduate School of Arts and Science, Sackler Institute of Graduate Biomedical Sciences, Department of Pharmacology, New York, NY 10012-1019. Offers molecular pharmacology (PhD); MD/PhD. *Degree requirements:* For doctorate, comprehensive exam, thesis/dissertation, qualifying exam. *Entrance requirements:* For doctorate, GRE General Test. Additional exam requirements/recommendations for international students: Required—TOEFL. *Expenses:* Tuition: Full-time $30,528; part-time $1272 per credit. Required fees: $2177. *Faculty research:* Pharmacology and neurobiology, neuropeptides, receptor biochemistry, cytoskeleton, endocrinology.

North Carolina State University, College of Veterinary Medicine, Program in Comparative Biomedical Sciences, Raleigh, NC 27695. Offers cell biology (MS, PhD); infectious disease (MS, PhD); pathology (MS, PhD); pharmacology (MS, PhD); population medicine (MS, PhD). Part-time programs available. *Degree requirements:* For master's, thesis; for doctorate, thesis/dissertation. *Entrance requirements:* For master's and doctorate, GRE General Test. Additional exam requirements/recommendations for international students: Required—TOEFL (minimum score 550 paper-based; 213 computer-based). Electronic applications accepted. *Expenses:* Contact institution. *Faculty research:* Infectious diseases, cell biology, pharmacology and toxicology, genomics, pathology and population medicine.

Northwestern University, Northwestern University Feinberg School of Medicine and Interdepartmental Programs, Integrated Graduate Programs in the Life Sciences, Chicago, IL 60611. Offers cancer biology (PhD); cell biology (PhD); developmental biology (PhD); evolutionary biology (PhD); immunology and microbial pathogenesis (PhD); molecular biology and genetics (PhD); neurobiology (PhD); pharmacology and toxicology (PhD); structural biology and biochemistry (PhD). *Degree requirements:* For doctorate, comprehensive exam, thesis/dissertation, written and oral qualifying exams. *Entrance requirements:* For doctorate, GRE General Test. Additional exam requirements/recommendations for international students: Required—TOEFL (minimum score 600 paper-based; 250 computer-based). Electronic applications accepted.

Nova Southeastern University, Center for Psychological Studies, Master's Programs in Counseling, Mental Health, School Guidance, and Clinical Pharmacology, Fort Lauderdale, FL 33314-7796. Offers clinical pharmacology (MS); mental health counseling (MS); school guidance and counseling (MS). Part-time and evening/weekend programs available. *Faculty:* 7 full-time (2 women), 27 part-time/adjunct (8 women). *Students:* 270 full-time (238 women), 586 part-time (521 women); includes 417 minority (186 African Americans, 14 Asian Americans or Pacific Islanders, 217 Hispanic Americans), 23 international. 562 applicants, 65% accepted, 262 enrolled. In 2009, 232 master's awarded. *Degree requirements:* For master's, comprehensive exam, 3 practica. *Entrance requirements:* Additional exam requirements/recommendations for international students: Required—TOEFL (minimum score 550 paper-based; 213 computer-based). *Application deadline:* For fall admission, 7/29 for domestic students; for winter admission, 11/29 for domestic students; for spring admission, 3/29 for domestic students. Applications are processed on a rolling basis. Application fee: $50. Electronic applications accepted. *Financial support:* Career-related internships or fieldwork, Federal Work-Study, and institutionally sponsored loans available. Financial award application deadline: 4/1. *Faculty research:* Clinical and child clinical psychology, geriatrics, interpersonal violence. *Unit head:* Karen S. Grosby, Dean, 954-262-5701, Fax: 954-262-3859. *Application contact:* Carlos Perez, Enrollment Management, 954-262-5790, Fax: 954-262-3893, E-mail: cpsinfo@cps.nova.edu.

The Ohio State University, College of Medicine, School of Biomedical Science, Integrated Biomedical Science Graduate Program, Columbus, OH 43210. Offers immunology (PhD); medical genetics (PhD); molecular virology (PhD); pharmacology (PhD). *Degree requirements:* For doctorate, thesis/dissertation. *Entrance requirements:* For doctorate, GRE, GRE Subject Test in biochemistry, cell and molecular biology (recommended for some). Additional exam requirements/recommendations for international students: Required—TOEFL (minimum score 600 paper-based; 250 computer-based). Electronic applications accepted. *Expenses:* Tuition, state resident: full-time $10,683. Tuition, nonresident: full-time $25,923. Tuition and fees vary according to course load and program.

The Ohio State University, College of Medicine, School of Biomedical Science, Program in Pharmacology, Columbus, OH 43210. Offers MS, PhD. *Entrance requirements:* For master's and doctorate, GRE. Additional exam requirements/recommendations for international students: Required—TOEFL (paper-based 550, computer-based 213) or Michigan English Language Assessment Battery (82). Electronic applications accepted. *Expenses:* Tuition, state resident: full-time $10,683. Tuition, nonresident: full-time $25,923. Tuition and fees vary according to course load and program.

The Ohio State University, College of Pharmacy and Graduate School, Graduate Programs in Pharmacy, Division of Pharmacology, Columbus, OH 43210. Offers PhD. *Degree requirements:* For doctorate, thesis/dissertation. *Entrance requirements:* For doctorate, GRE General Test, minimum GPA of 3.0. Additional exam requirements/recommendations for international students: Required—TOEFL (minimum score 600 paper-based; 250 computer-based; 100 iBT). Electronic applications accepted. *Expenses:* Tuition, state resident: full-time $10,683. Tuition, nonresident: full-time $25,923. Tuition and fees vary according to course load and program. *Faculty research:* Neuropharmacology, biochemical pharmacology, toxicology, drug receptor theory, molecular pharmacology.

The Ohio State University, College of Veterinary Medicine, Department of Veterinary Biosciences, Columbus, OH 43210. Offers anatomy and cellular biology (MS, PhD); pathobiology (MS, PhD); pharmacology (MS, PhD); toxicology (MS, PhD); veterinary physiology (MS, PhD). *Faculty:* 45. *Students:* 18 full-time (14 women), 20 part-time (16 women); includes 3 minority (1 African American, 1 Asian American or Pacific Islander, 1 Hispanic American), 16 international. Average age 30. In 2009, 1 master's, 9 doctorates awarded. *Entrance requirements:* For master's and doctorate, GRE General Test. Additional exam requirements/recommendations for international students: Required—TOEFL. *Application deadline:* Applications are processed on a rolling basis. Application fee: $40 ($50 for international students). Electronic applications accepted. *Expenses:* Tuition, state resident: full-time $10,683. Tuition, nonresident: full-time $25,923. Tuition and fees vary according to course load and program. *Faculty research:* Microvasculature, muscle biology, neonatal lung and bone development. *Unit head:* Dr. Michael J. Oglesbee, Graduate Studies Committee Chair, 614-292-5661, Fax: 614-292-6473, E-mail: oglesbee.1@osu.edu. *Application contact:* Graduate Admissions, 614-292-9444, Fax: 614-292-3895, E-mail: domestic.grad@osu.edu.

Oregon Health & Science University, School of Medicine, Graduate Programs in Medicine, Department of Physiology and Pharmacology, Portland, OR 97239-3098. Offers pharmacology (PhD); physiology (PhD). *Degree requirements:* For doctorate, comprehensive exam, thesis/dissertation. *Entrance requirements:* For doctorate, GRE General Test (minimum scores: 500 Verbal/600 Quantitative/4.5 Analytical) or MCAT (for some programs). Additional exam requirements/recommendations for international students: Required—TOEFL. *Application deadline:* For fall admission, 12/1 for domestic students. Electronic applications accepted. Tuition and fees vary according to course level, course load, degree level, program and reciprocity agreements. *Financial support:* PhD students have paid tuition and receive stipends available. *Unit head:* Beth Habecker, PhD, Program Director, 503-494-6252, E-mail: habecker@ohsu.edu. *Application contact:* Julie Mertens, Program Coordinator, 503-494-6252, E-mail: mertens@ohsu.edu.

Penn State Hershey Medical Center, College of Medicine, Graduate School Programs in the Biomedical Sciences, Graduate Program in Pharmacology, Hershey, PA 17033. Offers MS, PhD, MD/PhD, PhD/MBA. *Students:* 419 applicants, 1% accepted, 3 enrolled. Terminal master's awarded for partial completion of doctoral program. *Degree requirements:* For master's, thesis or alternative; for doctorate, comprehensive exam, thesis/dissertation, oral exam. *Entrance requirements:* For master's, GRE General Test; for doctorate, GRE General Test, minimum GPA of 3.0. Additional exam requirements/recommendations for international students: Required—TOEFL (minimum score 550 paper-based; 213 computer-based). *Application deadline:* For fall admission, 1/31 priority date for domestic students, 2/1 priority date for international students. Applications are processed on a rolling basis. Application fee: $65. Electronic applications accepted. *Expenses:* Tuition, state resident: part-time $644 per credit. Tuition, nonresident: part-time $1142 per credit. Required fees: $22 per semester. *Financial support:* In 2009–10, research assistantships with full tuition reimbursements (averaging $22,260 per year); fellowships with full tuition reimbursements, institutionally sponsored loans, scholarships/grants, health care benefits, and unspecified assistantships also available. Financial award applicants required to submit FAFSA. *Faculty research:* Ion pump structure and function, drug development and targeting, mechanisms of drug resistance, neuropharmacology and toxicology, breast cancer, identification of molecular targets for drug development in cancer and cardiovascular and neurological diseases. *Unit head:* Dr. Kent Vrana, Chair, 717-531-8285, Fax: 717-531-5013, E-mail: pharm-grad-hmc@psu.edu. *Application contact:* Elaine Neldigh, Program Secretary, 717-531-8285, Fax: 717-531-5013, E-mail: pharm-grad-hmc@psu.edu.

Purdue University, College of Pharmacy and Pharmacal Sciences and Graduate School, Graduate Programs in Pharmacy and Pharmacal Sciences, Department of Medicinal Chemistry and Molecular Pharmacology, West Lafayette, IN 47907. Offers analytical medicinal chemistry (PhD); computational and biophysical medicinal chemistry (PhD); medicinal and bioorganic chemistry (PhD); medicinal biochemistry and molecular biology (PhD); molecular pharmacology and toxicology (PhD); natural products and pharmacognosy (PhD); nuclear pharmacy (MS); radiopharmaceutical chemistry and nuclear pharmacy (PhD); MS/PhD. Terminal master's awarded for partial completion of doctoral program. *Degree requirements:* For master's, thesis; for doctorate, thesis/dissertation. *Entrance requirements:* For master's, GRE General Test, minimum B average; BS in biology, chemistry, or pharmacy; for doctorate, GRE General Test, minimum B average; BS in biology, chemistry, or pharmacology. Additional exam requirements/recommendations for international students: Required—TOEFL. Electronic applications accepted. *Faculty research:* Drug design and development, cancer research, drug synthesis and analysis, chemical pharmacology, environmental toxicology.

Purdue University, School of Veterinary Medicine and Graduate School, Graduate Programs in Veterinary Medicine, Department of Basic Medical Sciences, West Lafayette, IN 47907. Offers anatomy (MS, PhD); pharmacology (MS, PhD); physiology (MS, PhD). Part-time programs available. *Faculty:* 23 full-time (7 women), 2 part-time/adjunct (1 woman). *Students:* 23 full-time (15 women), 1 (woman) part-time; includes 3 minority (1 African American, 2 Asian Americans or Pacific Islanders), 14 international. Average age 32. 15 applicants, 27% accepted, 4 enrolled. In 2009, 2 master's, 2 doctorates awarded. Terminal master's awarded for partial completion of doctoral program. *Degree requirements:* For master's, thesis; for doctorate, thesis/dissertation. *Entrance requirements:* For master's and doctorate, GRE General Test. Additional exam requirements/recommendations for international students: Required—TOEFL. *Application deadline:* For fall admission, 12/15 priority date for domestic students, 12/15 for international students. Application fee: $55. Electronic applications accepted. *Financial support:* In 2009–10, 14 research assistantships with partial tuition reimbursements (averaging $17,420 per year), 8 teaching assistantships with partial tuition reimbursements (averaging $15,000 per year) were awarded; fellowships with partial tuition reimbursements also available. Financial award application deadline: 3/1; financial award applicants required to submit FAFSA. *Faculty research:* Development and regeneration, tissue injury and shock, biomedical engineering, ovarian function, bone and cartilage biology, cell and molecular biology. *Unit head:* Dr. Laurie A. Jaeger, Head, 765-494-7348, Fax: 765-494-0781, E-mail: ljaeger@purdue.edu. *Application contact:* Dr. Kevin M. Hannon, Chairman, Graduate Committee, 765-494-5949, Fax: 765-494-0781, E-mail: bmsgrad@purdue.edu.

Queen's University at Kingston, School of Graduate Studies and Research, Faculty of Health Sciences, Department of Pharmacology and Toxicology, Kingston, ON K7L 3N6, Canada. Offers M Sc, PhD. *Degree requirements:* For master's, thesis; for doctorate, comprehensive exam, thesis/dissertation. *Entrance requirements:* For master's, minimum 2nd class standing, honors bachelor of science degree (life sciences, health sciences, or equivalent); for doctorate, masters of science degree or outstanding performance in honors bachelor of science program. Additional exam requirements/recommendations for international students: Required—TOEFL (minimum score 600 paper-based; 250 computer-based). Electronic applications accepted. *Faculty research:* Biochemical toxicology, cardiovascular pharmacology and neuropharmacology.

Rush University, Graduate College, Division of Pharmacology, Chicago, IL 60612-3832. Offers clinical research (MS); pharmacology (MS, PhD); MD/PhD. Terminal master's awarded for partial completion of doctoral program. *Degree requirements:* For master's, thesis; for doctorate, thesis/dissertation. *Entrance requirements:* For master's and doctorate, GRE General Test, interview. Additional exam requirements/recommendations for international students: Required—TOEFL (minimum score 550 paper-based; 213 computer-based). *Faculty research:* Dopamine neurobiology and Parkinson's disease; cardiac electrophysiology and clinical pharmacology; neutrophil motility, apoptosis, and adhesion; angiogenesis; pulmonary vascular physiology.

Saint Louis University, Graduate School and School of Medicine, Graduate Program in Biomedical Sciences and Graduate School, Department of Pharmacological and Physiological Science, St. Louis, MO 63103-2097. Offers PhD. *Degree requirements:* For doctorate, comprehensive exam, thesis/dissertation, departmental qualifying exams. *Entrance requirements:* For doctorate, GRE General Test (GRE Subject Test optional), letters of recommendation, resume, interview. Additional exam requirements/recommendations for international students: Required—TOEFL (minimum score 525 paper-based; 194 computer-based). Electronic applications accepted. *Faculty research:* Molecular endocrinology, neuropharmacology, cardiovascular science, drug abuse, neurotransmitter and hormonal signaling mechanisms.

Southern Illinois University Carbondale, Graduate School, Graduate Program in Medicine, Program in Pharmacology, Springfield, IL 62794-9629. Offers MS, PhD. *Degree requirements:* For master's, thesis; for doctorate, thesis/dissertation. *Entrance requirements:* For master's, minimum GPA of 3.0; for doctorate, minimum GPA of 3.25. Additional exam requirements/recommendations for international students: Required—TOEFL. *Faculty research:* Autonomic nervous system pharmacology, biochemical pharmacology, neuropharmacology, toxicology, cardiovascular pharmacology.

State University of New York Upstate Medical University, College of Graduate Studies, Program in Pharmacology, Syracuse, NY 13210-2334. Offers PhD, MD/PhD. *Faculty:* 12 full-time (1 woman), 4 part-time/adjunct (1 woman). *Students:* 16 full-time (5 women); includes 1 minority (Asian American or Pacific Islander), 10 international. In 2009, 8 doctorates awarded. Terminal master's awarded for partial completion of doctoral program. *Degree requirements:* For doctorate, comprehensive exam, thesis/dissertation. *Entrance requirements:* For doctorate, GRE General Test, telephone interview. Additional exam requirements/recommendations for international students: Required—TOEFL. *Application deadline:* Applications are processed on a rolling basis. Application fee: $40. Electronic applications accepted. *Financial support:* In 2009–10, fellowships with tuition reimbursements (averaging $21,514 per year), research assistantships with tuition reimbursements (averaging $21,514 per year) were awarded; Federal Work-Study, institutionally sponsored loans, health care benefits, and unspecified assistantships also available. Financial award application deadline: 4/15; financial award applicants required to submit FAFSA. *Faculty research:* Cancer, disorders of the nervous system, infectious diseases, diabetes/metabolic disorders/cardiovascular diseases. *Unit head:* Dr. Ziwei Huang, Chair, 315-464-5138. *Application contact:* Sandra Tillotson, Coordinator of Graduate Recruitment, 315-464-7655.

See Close-Up on page 465.

Stony Brook University, State University of New York, Stony Brook University Medical Center, School of Medicine and Graduate School, Graduate Programs in Medicine, Department of Pharmacological Sciences, Graduate Program in Molecular and Cellular Pharmacology, Stony Brook, NY 11794. Offers PhD. *Faculty:* 15 full-time (2 women). *Students:* 35 full-time (21 women); includes 12 minority (4 African Americans, 6 Asian Americans or Pacific Islanders, 2 Hispanic Americans), 11 international. Average age 28. 43 applicants, 33% accepted. In 2009, 4 doctorates awarded. *Degree requirements:* For doctorate, thesis/dissertation, departmental qualifying exam. *Entrance requirements:* For doctorate, GRE General Test. Additional exam requirements/recommendations for international students: Required—TOEFL. *Application deadline:* For fall admission, 1/15 priority date for domestic students. Applications are processed on a rolling basis. Application fee: $60. Electronic applications accepted. *Expenses:* Tuition, state resident: full-time $8370; part-time $349 per credit. Tuition, nonresident: full-time $13,250; part-time $552 per credit. Required fees: $933. *Financial support:* Fellowships, research assistantships, teaching assistantships, Federal Work-Study available. Financial award application deadline: 3/15; financial award applicants required to submit FAFSA. *Faculty research:* Toxicology, molecular and cellular biochemistry. Total annual research expenditures: $10.7 million. *Unit head:* Prof. Michael Frohman, Chair, 631-444-3050. *Application contact:* Prof. Michael Frohman, Chair, 631-444-3050.

Temple University, Health Sciences Center, School of Medicine and Graduate School, Graduate Programs in Medicine, Department of Pharmacology, Philadelphia, PA 19122-6096. Offers PhD, MD/PhD. Terminal master's awarded for partial completion of doctoral program. *Degree requirements:* For doctorate, one foreign language, thesis/dissertation, research seminars. *Entrance requirements:* For doctorate, GRE General Test, minimum GPA of 3.0. Additional exam requirements/recommendations for international students: Required—TOEFL (minimum score 620 paper-based; 260 computer-based). Electronic applications accepted. *Faculty research:* Cardiovascular and central nervous systems, biochemical pharmacology.

Temple University, Health Sciences Center, School of Pharmacy, Department of Pharmaceutical Sciences, Program in Pharmacodynamics, Philadelphia, PA 19122-6096. Offers MS, PhD. *Entrance requirements:* For master's, GRE General Test, minimum undergraduate GPA of 3.0; for doctorate, GRE General Test, minimum GPA of 3.0. Additional exam requirements/recommendations for international students: Required—TOEFL (minimum score 550 paper-based; 213 computer-based; 79 iBT). Electronic applications accepted.

Texas Tech University Health Sciences Center, Graduate School of Biomedical Sciences, Department of Pharmacology and Neuroscience, Lubbock, TX 79430. Offers MS, PhD, MD/PhD, MS/PhD. Terminal master's awarded for partial completion of doctoral program. *Degree requirements:* For master's, thesis; for doctorate, thesis/dissertation. *Entrance requirements:* For master's and doctorate, GRE General Test, minimum GPA of 3.0. Additional exam requirements/recommendations for international students: Required—TOEFL. Electronic applications accepted. *Faculty research:* Neuroscience, neuropsychopharmacology, autonomic pharmacology, cardiovascular pharmacology, molecular pharmacology.

Thomas Jefferson University, Jefferson College of Graduate Studies, MS Program in Pharmacology, Philadelphia, PA 19107. Offers MS. Part-time and evening/weekend programs available. *Faculty:* 18 full-time (5 women), 11 part-time/adjunct (4 women). *Students:* 41 part-time (24 women); includes 11 minority (1 African American, 8 Asian Americans or Pacific Islanders, 2 Hispanic Americans), 8 international. 40 applicants, 60% accepted, 22 enrolled. In 2009, 7 master's awarded. *Degree requirements:* For master's, thesis, clerkship. *Entrance requirements:* For master's, GRE General Test or MCAT, minimum GPA of 3.0. Additional exam requirements/recommendations for international students: Required—TOEFL (minimum score 250 computer-based; 100 iBT) or IELTS. *Application deadline:* For fall admission, 3/1 priority date for domestic and international students; for winter admission, 12/1 priority date for domestic students, 6/1 priority date for international students; for spring admission, 4/1 priority date for domestic students. Applications are processed on a rolling basis. Application fee: $50. Electronic applications accepted. *Expenses:* Contact institution. *Financial support:* In 2009–10, 10 students received support. Federal Work-Study and institutionally sponsored loans available. Support available to part-time students. Financial award application deadline: 5/1; financial award applicants required to submit FAFSA. *Unit head:* Dr. Carol L. Beck, Assistant Dean/Director, 215-503-6539, Fax: 215-503-3433, E-mail: carol.beck@jefferson.edu. *Application contact:* Eleanor M. Gorman, Assistant Coordinator, Graduate Center Programs, 215-503-5799, Fax: 215-503-3433, E-mail: eleanor.gorman@jefferson.edu.

See Close-Up on page 159.

Tufts University, Sackler School of Graduate Biomedical Sciences, Program in Pharmacology and Experimental Therapeutics, Medford, MA 02155. Offers PhD. *Faculty:* 16 full-time (6 women). *Students:* 9 full-time (7 women), 3 international. Average age 26. 72 applicants, 8% accepted, 5 enrolled. In 2009, 4 doctorates awarded. *Degree requirements:* For doctorate, thesis/dissertation, qualifying exam. *Entrance requirements:* For doctorate, GRE General Test, 3 letters of reference. Additional exam requirements/recommendations for international students: Required—TOEFL. *Application deadline:* For fall admission, 11/15 for domestic students, 12/15 priority date for international students. Applications are processed on a rolling basis. Application fee: $70. Electronic applications accepted. *Expenses:* Tuition: Full-time $38,096; part-time $3962 per credit. Required fees: $686; $40 per year. Tuition and fees vary according to course level, course load, degree level, program and student level. *Financial support:* In 2009–10, 9 research assistantships with full tuition reimbursements (averaging $28,250 per year) were awarded; scholarships/grants and health care benefits also available. Financial award application deadline: 1/15. *Faculty research:* Biochemical mechanisms of narcotic addiction, clinical psychopharmacology, pharmacokinetics, neurotransmitter receptors, neuropeptides. *Unit head:* Dr. Richard Shader, Director, 617-636-3856, Fax: 617-636-6738. *Application contact:* Kellie Johnston, Associate Director of Admissions, 617-636-6767, Fax: 617-636-0375, E-mail: sackler-school@tufts.edu.

Tulane University, School of Medicine and School of Liberal Arts, Graduate Programs in Biomedical Sciences, Department of Pharmacology, New Orleans, LA 70118-5669. Offers MS, PhD, MD/MS, MD/PhD. MS and PhD offered through the Graduate School. *Degree requirements:* For master's, one foreign language, thesis; for doctorate, 2 foreign languages, thesis/dissertation. *Entrance requirements:* For master's, GRE General Test, minimum B average in undergraduate course work; for doctorate, GRE General Test. Additional exam requirements/recommendations for international students: Required—TOEFL. Electronic applications accepted.

Universidad Central del Caribe, School of Medicine, Program in Biomedical Sciences, Bayamón, PR 00960-6032. Offers anatomy and cell biology (MA, MS); biochemistry (MS); biomedical sciences (MA); microbiology and immunology (MA, MS); pharmacology (MS); physiology (MA, MS).

Université de Montréal, Faculty of Medicine, Department of Pharmacology, Montréal, QC H3C 3J7, Canada. Offers M Sc, PhD. *Faculty:* 30 full-time (9 women), 4 part-time/adjunct (0 women). *Students:* 32 full-time (19 women), 45 part-time (26 women). 57 applicants, 21% accepted, 11 enrolled. In 2009, 12 master's, 2 doctorates awarded. Terminal master's awarded for partial completion of doctoral program. *Degree requirements:* For master's, thesis; for doctorate, thesis/dissertation, general exam. *Entrance requirements:* For master's, proficiency in French, knowledge of English; for doctorate, master's degree, proficiency in French. *Application deadline:* For fall admission, 2/1 priority date for domestic students; for winter admission, 11/1 priority date for domestic students; for spring admission, 2/1 priority date for domestic students. Applications are processed on a rolling basis. Application fee: $100. Electronic applications accepted. *Financial support:* Institutionally sponsored loans available. *Faculty research:* Molecular, clinical, and cardiovascular pharmacology; pharmacokinetics; mechanisms of drug interactions and toxicity; neuropharmacology and receptology. *Unit head:* Dr. Patrick du Souich, Director, 514-343-6334, Fax: 514-343-2359, E-mail: patrick.du.souich@umontreal.ca. *Application contact:* Dr. Rene Cardinal, Graduate Chairman, 514-343-6111 Ext. 3083, Fax: 514-343-2359, E-mail: rene.cardinal@umontreal.ca.

Université de Sherbrooke, Faculty of Medicine and Health Sciences, Graduate Programs in Medicine, Department of Pharmacology, Sherbrooke, QC J1H 5N4, Canada. Offers M Sc, PhD. Terminal master's awarded for partial completion of doctoral program. *Degree requirements:* For master's, thesis; for doctorate, thesis/dissertation. Electronic applications accepted. *Faculty research:* Pharmacology of peptide hormones, pharmacology of lipid mediators, protein-protein interactions, medicinal pharmacology.

University at Buffalo, the State University of New York, Graduate School, School of Medicine and Biomedical Sciences, Graduate Programs in Medicine and Biomedical Sciences, Department of Pharmacology and Toxicology, Buffalo, NY 14260. Offers biochemical pharmacology (MS); pharmacology (MA, PhD); MD/PhD. *Faculty:* 15 full-time (1 woman), 2 part-time/adjunct (0 women). *Students:* 9 full-time (4 women); includes 3 minority (1 African American, 1 Asian American or Pacific Islander, 1 Hispanic American), 2 international. Average age 25. 35 applicants, 20% accepted. In 2009, 3 doctorates awarded. Terminal master's awarded for partial completion of doctoral program. *Degree requirements:* For master's, thesis; for doctorate, thesis/dissertation. *Entrance requirements:* For master's and doctorate, GRE General Test, 3 letters of recommendation. Additional exam requirements/recommendations for international students: Required—TOEFL (minimum score 100 iBT). *Application deadline:* For fall admission, 2/1 priority date for domestic and international students. Applications are processed on a rolling basis. Application fee: $50. Electronic applications accepted. *Financial support:* In 2009–10, 2 fellowships with full tuition reimbursements (averaging $24,000 per year), 12 research assistantships with full tuition reimbursements (averaging $21,000 per year) were awarded; teaching assistantships, Federal Work-Study, scholarships/grants, health care benefits, and unspecified assistantships also available. Financial award application deadline: 2/1; financial award applicants required to submit FAFSA. *Faculty research:* Neuropharmacology, toxicology, signal transduction, molecular pharmacology, behavioral pharmacology. Total annual research expenditures: $1.4 million. *Unit head:* Dr. Margarita Dubocovich, Chairman, 716-829-3048, Fax: 716-829-2801, E-mail: mdubo@buffalo.edu. *Application contact:* Sara S. Goodman, Information Contact, 716-829-2800, Fax: 716-829-2801, E-mail: saragood@buffalo.edu.

The University of Alabama at Birmingham, Graduate Programs in Joint Health Sciences, Program in Pharmacology and Toxicology, Birmingham, AL 35294. Offers PhD. *Degree requirements:* For doctorate, thesis/dissertation. *Entrance requirements:* For doctorate, GRE General Test, interview. Electronic applications accepted. *Expenses:* Contact institution. *Faculty research:* Biochemical pharmacology, neuropharmacology, endocrine pharmacology.

University of Alberta, Faculty of Graduate Studies and Research, Department of Pharmacology, Edmonton, AB T6G 2E1, Canada. Offers M Sc, PhD. *Faculty:* 20 full-time (7 women), 3 part-time/adjunct (0 women). *Students:* 22 full-time (10 women). Average age 26. 19 applicants, 42% accepted. In 2009, 2 master's awarded. Terminal master's awarded for partial completion of doctoral program. *Degree requirements:* For master's, thesis; for doctorate, thesis/dissertation. *Entrance requirements:* For master's, B Sc, minimum GPA of 3.3; for doctorate, M Sc in pharmacology or closely related field, honors B Sc in pharmacology. *Application deadline:* For fall admission, 5/1 priority date for domestic students. Applications are processed on a rolling basis. Tuition and fees charges are reported in Canadian dollars. *Expenses:* Tuition, area resident: Full-time $4626 Canadian dollars; part-time $99.72 Canadian dollars per unit. International tuition: $8216 Canadian dollars full-time. Required fees: $3590 Canadian dollars; $99.72 Canadian dollars per unit. $215 Canadian dollars per term. *Financial support:* In 2009–10, 22 students received support, including 2 research assistantships with partial tuition reimbursements available (averaging $15,428 per year), 2 teaching assistantships with partial tuition reimbursements available (averaging $15,428 per year); scholarships/grants also available. *Faculty research:* Cardiovascular pharmacology, neuropharmacology, cancer pharmacology, molecular pharmacology, toxicology. Total annual research expenditures: $3.6 million. *Unit head:* Dr. Susan P. Dunn, Graduate Coordinator, 780-492-0510, Fax: 780-492-4325. *Application contact:* Information Contact, E-mail: gsec@pmcol.ualberta.ca.

The University of Arizona, Graduate College, College of Pharmacy, Department of Pharmacology and Toxicology, Graduate Program in Medical Pharmacology, Tucson, AZ 85721. Offers medical pharmacology (PhD); perfusion science (MS). *Faculty:* 11 full-time (3 women). *Students:*

Pharmacology

The University of Arizona (continued)

31 full-time (19 women), 1 part-time (0 women); includes 4 minority (1 Asian American or Pacific Islander, 3 Hispanic Americans), 11 international. Average age 28. 40 applicants, 13% accepted, 5 enrolled. In 2009, 7 master's, 4 doctorates awarded. *Degree requirements:* For master's, thesis; for doctorate, comprehensive exam, thesis/dissertation. *Entrance requirements:* For master's, GRE General Test, 3 letters of recommendation; for doctorate, GRE General Test, personal statement, 3 letters of recommendation. Additional exam requirements/recommendations for international students: Required—TOEFL (minimum score 550 paper-based; 213 computer-based; 79 iBT). *Application deadline:* For fall admission, 1/1 for domestic and international students. Applications are processed on a rolling basis. Application fee: $65. Electronic applications accepted. *Expenses:* Tuition, state resident: full-time $9028. Tuition, nonresident: full-time $24,890. *Financial support:* In 2009–10, 17 research assistantships with full tuition reimbursements (averaging $23,929 per year) were awarded; institutionally sponsored loans and tuition waivers (partial) also available. Financial award applicants required to submit FAFSA. *Faculty research:* Immunopharmacology, pharmacogenetics, pharmacogenomics, clinical pharmacology, ocularpharmacology and neuropharmacology. *Unit head:* Dr. I. Glenn Sipes, Head, 520-626-7123, Fax: 520-626-2204, E-mail: sipes@email.arizona.edu. *Application contact:* Trisha Stanley, Coordinator, 520-626-7218, Fax: 520-626-2204, E-mail: stanley@email.arizona.edu.

University of Arkansas for Medical Sciences, Graduate School, Graduate Programs in Biomedical Sciences, Pharmacology Program, Little Rock, AR 72205-7199. Offers MS, PhD, MD/PhD. *Faculty:* 22 full-time (3 women). *Students:* 12 full-time. *Degree requirements:* For master's, thesis; for doctorate, thesis/dissertation. *Entrance requirements:* For master's and doctorate, GRE General Test. Additional exam requirements/recommendations for international students: Required—TOEFL. *Application deadline:* Applications are processed on a rolling basis. Application fee: $0. *Financial support:* In 2009–10, research assistantships with full tuition reimbursements (averaging $24,000 per year); teaching assistantships, stipend and tuition for doctoral students also available. Support available to part-time students. *Faculty research:* Neuroscience, behavior, pharmacokinetics, metabolism. *Unit head:* Dr. Nancy J. Rusch, Chair, 501-686-5510. *Application contact:* Dr. Paul Gottschall, Program Director, 501-686-8655, E-mail: pegottschall@uams.edu.

The University of British Columbia, Faculty of Medicine, Department of Anesthesiology, Pharmacology and Therapeutics, Vancouver, BC V6T 1Z3, Canada. Offers M Sc, PhD. Terminal master's awarded for partial completion of doctoral program. *Degree requirements:* For master's, thesis; for doctorate, comprehensive exam, thesis/dissertation. *Entrance requirements:* For master's, MD or appropriate bachelor's degree; for doctorate, MD or M Sc. Additional exam requirements/recommendations for international students: Required—TOEFL (minimum score 600 paper-based; 250 computer-based; 100 iBT). Electronic applications accepted. *Faculty research:* Cellular, biochemical, autonomic, cardiovascular pharmacology; neuropharmacology and pulmonary pharmacology.

University of California, Davis, Graduate Studies, Graduate Group in Pharmacology and Toxicology, Davis, CA 95616. Offers MS, PhD. Terminal master's awarded for partial completion of doctoral program. *Degree requirements:* For master's, comprehensive exam or thesis; for doctorate, thesis/dissertation, qualifying exam. *Entrance requirements:* For master's and doctorate, GRE General Test, minimum GPA of 3.0, course work in biochemistry and/or physiology. Additional exam requirements/recommendations for international students: Required—TOEFL (minimum score 550 paper-based; 213 computer-based). Electronic applications accepted. *Faculty research:* Respiratory, neurochemical, molecular, genetic, and ecological toxicology.

University of California, Irvine, School of Medicine, Department of Pharmacology, Irvine, CA 92697. Offers pharmacology and toxicology (MS, PhD); MD/PhD. *Students:* 17 full-time (6 women); includes 9 minority (2 African Americans, 3 Asian Americans or Pacific Islanders, 4 Hispanic Americans), 3 international. Average age 29. 28 applicants, 21% accepted, 2 enrolled. In 2009, 1 master's, 4 doctorates awarded. *Degree requirements:* For doctorate, thesis/dissertation. *Entrance requirements:* For master's, GRE, minimum GPA of 3.0; for doctorate, GRE General Test, GRE Subject Test, minimum GPA of 3.0. Additional exam requirements/recommendations for international students: Required—TOEFL (minimum score 550 paper-based; 213 computer-based). *Application deadline:* For fall admission, 1/15 priority date for domestic students, 1/15 for international students. Applications are processed on a rolling basis. Application fee: $70 ($90 for international students). Electronic applications accepted. *Financial support:* Fellowships, research assistantships with full tuition reimbursements, teaching assistantships, institutionally sponsored loans, traineeships, health care benefits, and unspecified assistantships available. Financial award application deadline: 3/1; financial award applicants required to submit FAFSA. *Faculty research:* Mechanisms of action and effects of drugs on the nervous system, behavior, skeletal muscle, heart, and blood vessels; basic processes in the nervous system, skeletal muscle, heart, and blood vessels. *Unit head:* Sue P. Duckles, Interim Chair, 949-824-4265, Fax: 949-824-4855, E-mail: spduckle@uci.edu. *Application contact:* Alice Decker, Administrator, 949-824-8246, Fax: 949-824-4855, E-mail: adecker@uci.edu.

See Display below and Close-Up on page 471.

University of California, Los Angeles, David Geffen School of Medicine and Graduate Division, Graduate Programs in Medicine, Department of Molecular and Medical Pharmacology, Los Angeles, CA 90095. Offers PhD. *Degree requirements:* For doctorate, thesis/dissertation, qualifying exams. *Entrance requirements:* For doctorate, GRE General Test. *Faculty research:* Cardiovascular pharmacology, chemical pharmacology, neuropharmacology, clinical pharmacology, molecular pharmacology.

University of California, San Diego, School of Medicine and Office of Graduate Studies, Graduate Studies in Biomedical Sciences, Department of Pharmacology, La Jolla, CA 92093-0685. Offers PhD. *Degree requirements:* For doctorate, thesis/dissertation, qualifying exam. *Entrance requirements:* For doctorate, GRE General Test. Additional exam requirements/recommendations for international students: Required—TOEFL. Electronic applications accepted. *Faculty research:* Molecular and cellular pharmacology, cell and organ physiology, cellular and molecular biology.

University of California, San Francisco, School of Pharmacy and Graduate Division, Pharmaceutical Sciences and Pharmacogenomics Graduate Group, San Francisco, CA 94158-0775. Offers PhD. *Faculty:* 51 full-time (14 women). *Students:* 43 full-time (22 women); includes 15 minority (14 Asian Americans or Pacific Islanders, 1 Hispanic American). Average age 24. 69 applicants, 23% accepted, 6 enrolled. In 2009, 5 doctorates awarded. *Degree requirements:* For doctorate, comprehensive exam, thesis/dissertation. *Entrance requirements:* For doctorate, GRE General Test, minimum GPA of 3.0. Additional exam requirements/recommendations for international students: Required—TOEFL. *Application deadline:* For fall admission, 12/31 for domestic students. Application fee: $60 ($80 for international students). Electronic applications accepted. *Financial support:* In 2009–10, 4 fellowships with full tuition reimbursements (averaging $27,000 per year), 23 research assistantships with full tuition reimbursements (averaging $27,000 per year), 6 teaching assistantships with full tuition reimbursements (averaging $27,000 per year) were awarded; career-related internships or fieldwork, institutionally sponsored loans, scholarships/grants, traineeships, tuition waivers (full), and unspecified assistantships also available. Financial award application deadline: 4/6. *Faculty research:* Drug development, drug delivery, molecular pharmacology. *Unit head:* Francis

C. Szoka, Program Director, 415-476-3895, Fax: 415-476-0688, E-mail: szoka@cgl.ucsf.edu. *Application contact:* Debbie Acoba-Idlebi, Program Coordinator, 415-476-1947, Fax: 415-476-6022, E-mail: debbie.acoba@ucsf.edu.

University of Chicago, Division of the Biological Sciences, Neuroscience Graduate Programs, Department of Integrative Neuroscience, Chicago, IL 60637-1513. Offers cell physiology (PhD); pharmacological and physiological sciences (PhD). *Faculty:* 8 full-time (all women). *Students:* Average age 30. *Degree requirements:* For doctorate, thesis/dissertation, preliminary exam. *Entrance requirements:* For doctorate, GRE General Test. Additional exam requirements/recommendations for international students: Required—TOEFL. *Application deadline:* For fall admission, 12/28 priority date for domestic and international students. Application fee: $55. Electronic applications accepted. *Financial support:* In 2009–10, fellowships with tuition reimbursements (averaging $26,301 per year), research assistantships with tuition reimbursements (averaging $26,301 per year) were awarded; institutionally sponsored loans, scholarships/grants, traineeships, and health care benefits also available. Financial award applicants required to submit FAFSA. *Faculty research:* Psychopharmacology, neuropharmacology. *Unit head:* Dr. Steven Shevell, Chairman, 773-834-2900, Fax: 773-702-8842, E-mail: shevell@uchicago.edu. *Application contact:* Diane J. Hall, Graduate Administrative Director, 773-702-6371, Fax: 773-702-1216, E-mail: d-hall@uchicago.edu.

University of Cincinnati, Graduate School, College of Medicine, Graduate Programs in Biomedical Sciences, Department of Pharmacology and Cell Biophysics, Cincinnati, OH 45221. Offers cell biophysics (PhD); pharmacology (PhD). *Degree requirements:* For doctorate, thesis/dissertation, qualifying exam. *Entrance requirements:* For doctorate, GRE General Test. Additional exam requirements/recommendations for international students: Required—TOEFL. Electronic applications accepted. *Faculty research:* Lipoprotein research, enzyme regulation, electrophysiology, gene actuation.

University of Colorado Denver, School of Medicine, Program in Pharmacology, Denver, CO 80217-3364. Offers PhD. *Students:* 25 full-time (12 women); includes 5 minority (1 African American, 3 Asian Americans or Pacific Islanders, 1 Hispanic American). In 2009, 9 doctorates awarded. *Degree requirements:* For doctorate, comprehensive exam, thesis/dissertation, major seminar. *Entrance requirements:* For doctorate, GRE General Test. *Application deadline:* For fall admission, 1/15 for domestic students. Application fee: $50. *Financial support:* Fellowships, research assistantships, teaching assistantships, Federal Work-Study, institutionally sponsored loans, and traineeships available. Support available to part-time students. Financial award application deadline: 3/15; financial award applicants required to submit FAFSA. *Faculty research:* Genomics/bioinformatics, cellular biology, drugs of abuse, neuroscience, signal transduction. *Unit head:* Dr. Robert Murphy, Interim Chair, 303-724-3352, Fax: 303-724-3357, E-mail: robert.murphy@ucdenver.edu. *Application contact:* Dr. Robert Murphy, Interim Chair, 303-724-3352, Fax: 303-724-3357, E-mail: robert.murphy@ucdenver.edu.

University of Connecticut, Graduate School, School of Pharmacy, Department of Pharmaceutical Sciences, Graduate Program in Pharmacology and Toxicology, Storrs, CT 06269. Offers pharmacology (MS, PhD); toxicology (MS, PhD). *Faculty:* 12 full-time (1 woman). *Students:* 11 full-time (5 women), 2 part-time (0 women); includes 4 minority (1 African American, 2 Asian Americans or Pacific Islanders, 1 Hispanic American). Average age 29. 48 applicants, 4% accepted, 1 enrolled.Terminal master's awarded for partial completion of doctoral program. *Degree requirements:* For master's, comprehensive exam, thesis; for doctorate, thesis/dissertation. *Entrance requirements:* For master's and doctorate, GRE General Test. Additional exam requirements/recommendations for international students: Required—TOEFL (minimum score 550 paper-based; 213 computer-based). *Application deadline:* For fall admission, 2/1 priority date for domestic and international students; for spring admission, 11/1 for domestic students, 10/1 for international students. Applications are processed on a rolling basis. Application fee: $55. Electronic applications accepted. *Expenses:* Tuition, state resident: full-time $4725; part-time $525 per credit. Tuition, nonresident: full-time $12,267; part-time $1363 per credit. Required fees: $346 per semester. Tuition and fees vary according to course load. *Financial support:* In 2009–10, 5 research assistantships with full tuition reimbursements, 6 teaching assistantships with full tuition reimbursements were awarded; fellowships, career-related internships or fieldwork, Federal Work-Study, scholarships/grants, traineeships, health care benefits, and unspecified assistantships also available. Financial award application deadline: 2/1; financial award applicants required to submit FAFSA. *Unit head:* Robin Bogner, Chairperson, 860-486-2136, Fax: 860-486-4998, E-mail: robin.bogner@uconn.edu. *Application contact:* Leslie Lebel, Administrative Assistant, 860-486-4066, Fax: 860-486-4998, E-mail: leslie.lebel@uconn.edu.

University of Florida, College of Medicine, Department of Pharmacology and Therapeutics, Gainesville, FL 32611. Offers PhD. *Degree requirements:* For doctorate, thesis/dissertation. *Entrance requirements:* For doctorate, GRE General Test, minimum GPA of 3.0. Additional exam requirements/recommendations for international students: Required—TOEFL. Electronic applications accepted. *Faculty research:* Receptor and membrane pharmacology, autonomics, tetralogy, enzymes, opioid peptides.

University of Florida, College of Medicine and Graduate School, Interdisciplinary Program in Biomedical Sciences, Concentration in Physiology and Pharmacology, Gainesville, FL 32611. Offers PhD. *Degree requirements:* For doctorate, thesis/dissertation. *Entrance requirements:* For doctorate, GRE General Test, minimum GPA of 3.0. Electronic applications accepted.

See Close-Up on page 493.

University of Florida, College of Pharmacy and Graduate School, Graduate Programs in Pharmacy, Department of Pharmacodynamics, Gainesville, FL 32611. Offers MSP, PhD, Pharm D/PhD. Part-time programs available. Terminal master's awarded for partial completion of doctoral program. *Degree requirements:* For master's, thesis; for doctorate, thesis/dissertation. *Entrance requirements:* For master's and doctorate, GRE General Test, minimum GPA of 3.0. Additional exam requirements/recommendations for international students: Required—TOEFL. Electronic applications accepted. *Faculty research:* Hypertension, aging, alcoholism, diabetes, toxicology.

University of Georgia, College of Veterinary Medicine and Graduate School, Graduate Programs in Veterinary Medicine, Department of Physiology and Pharmacology, Athens, GA 30602. Offers pharmacology (MS, PhD); physiology (MS, PhD). *Faculty:* 9 full-time (3 women), 1 part-time/adjunct (0 women). *Students:* 10 full-time (6 women), 1 (woman) part-time; includes 3 minority (2 Asian Americans or Pacific Islanders, 1 Hispanic American), 2 international. 18 applicants, 22% accepted, 2 enrolled. In 2009, 1 doctorate awarded. *Degree requirements:* For master's, thesis; for doctorate, one foreign language, thesis/dissertation. *Entrance requirements:* For master's and doctorate, GRE General Test. *Application deadline:* For fall admission, 7/1 priority date for domestic students; for spring admission, 11/15 for domestic students. Application fee: $50. Electronic applications accepted. *Expenses:* Tuition, state resident: full-time $6000; part-time $250 per credit hour. Tuition, nonresident: full-time $20,904; part-time $871 per credit hour. Required fees: $730 per semester. *Financial support:* Fellowships, research assistantships, teaching assistantships, unspecified assistantships available. *Unit head:* Dr. Gaylen L. Edwards, Acting Head, 706-542-5854, Fax: 706-542-3015, E-mail: gedwards@uga.edu. *Application contact:* Dr. Royal A. McGraw, Graduate Coordinator, 706-542-0661, Fax: 706-542-3015, E-mail: mcgraw@uga.edu.

University of Guelph, Ontario Veterinary College and Graduate Program Services, Graduate Programs in Veterinary Sciences, Department of Biomedical Sciences, Guelph, ON N1G 2W1, Canada. Offers morphology (M Sc, DV Sc, PhD); neuroscience (M Sc, DV Sc, PhD); pharmacology (M Sc, DV Sc, PhD); physiology (M Sc, DV Sc, PhD); toxicology (M Sc, DV Sc, PhD). Part-time programs available. *Degree requirements:* For master's, thesis; for doctorate, comprehensive exam, thesis/dissertation. *Entrance requirements:* For master's, honors B Sc, minimum 75% average in last 20 courses; for doctorate, M Sc with thesis from accredited institution. Additional exam requirements/recommendations for international students: Required—TOEFL (minimum score 550 paper-based; 213 computer-based; 89 iBT). Electronic applications accepted. *Faculty research:* Cellular morphology; endocrine, vascular and reproductive physiology; clinical pharmacology; veterinary toxicology; developmental biology, neuroscience.

University of Illinois at Chicago, College of Medicine and Graduate College, Graduate Programs in Medicine, Department of Pharmacology, Chicago, IL 60612. Offers PhD, MD/PhD. *Degree requirements:* For doctorate, thesis/dissertation. *Entrance requirements:* For doctorate, GRE General Test. Additional exam requirements/recommendations for international students: Required—TOEFL. *Faculty research:* Cardiovascular and lung biology, cell signaling, molecular pharmacology of G-proteins, immunopharmcology, molecular and cellular basis of inflammation, neuroscience.

The University of Iowa, Roy J. and Lucille A. Carver College of Medicine and Graduate College, Graduate Programs in Medicine, Department of Pharmacology, Iowa City, IA 52242-1316. Offers MS, PhD. *Faculty:* 11 full-time (1 woman), 10 part-time/adjunct (4 women). *Students:* 23 full-time (9 women); includes 2 minority (1 African American, 1 Hispanic American), 7 international. Average age 28. 33 applicants, 12% accepted, 2 enrolled. In 2009, 1 master's, 5 doctorates awarded. Terminal master's awarded for partial completion of doctoral program. *Degree requirements:* For master's, thesis; for doctorate, comprehensive exam, thesis/dissertation. *Entrance requirements:* For master's, GRE General Test; for doctorate, GRE General Test, minimum GPA of 3.0, undergraduate course work in biochemistry. Additional exam requirements/recommendations for international students: Required—TOEFL (minimum score 600 paper-based; 250 computer-based). *Application deadline:* For fall admission, 2/1 priority date for domestic and international students. Applications are processed on a rolling basis. Application fee: $60 ($85 for international students). Electronic applications accepted. *Financial support:* In 2009–10, 23 research assistantships with full tuition reimbursements (averaging $24,250 per year) were awarded; scholarships/grants, traineeships, and unspecified assistantships also available. *Faculty research:* Cancer and cell cycle, hormones and growth factors, nervous system function and dysfunction, receptors and signal transduction, stroke and hypertension. Total annual research expenditures: $2.7 million. *Unit head:* Dr. Donna L. Hammond, Interim Head, 319-335-7946, Fax: 319-335-8930, E-mail: donna-hammond@uiowa.edu. *Application contact:* Dr. Stefan Strack, Director, Graduate Admissions, 319-384-4439, Fax: 319-335-8930, E-mail: pharmacology-admissions@uiowa.edu.

The University of Kansas, Graduate Studies, School of Pharmacy, Department of Pharmacology and Toxicology, Program in Pharmacology and Toxicology, Lawrence, KS 66045. Offers MS, PhD. *Faculty:* 10 full-time (2 women). *Students:* 11 full-time (10 women), 6 international. Average age 24. 59 applicants, 14% accepted, 4 enrolled. In 2009, 5 master's, 1 doctorate awarded. Terminal master's awarded for partial completion of doctoral program. *Degree requirements:* For master's, comprehensive exam, thesis; for doctorate, comprehensive exam, thesis/dissertation. *Entrance requirements:* For master's, GRE; for doctorate, GRE (minimum score: 600 verbal, 600 quantitative, 4.5 analytic). Additional exam requirements/recommendations for international students: Required—TOEFL (minimum score 600 paper-based; 250 computer-based; 100 iBT). *Application deadline:* For fall admission, 1/15 priority date for domestic students, 2/1 priority date for international students. Applications are processed on a rolling basis. Application fee: $45 ($55 for international students). Electronic applications accepted. *Expenses:* Tuition, state resident: full-time $6492; part-time $270.50 per credit hour. Tuition, nonresident: full-time $15,510; part-time $646.25 per credit hour. Required fees: $847; $70.56 per credit hour. Tuition and fees vary according to course load and program. *Financial support:* Fellowships with full tuition reimbursements, research assistantships with full tuition reimbursements available. *Faculty research:* Neuropharmacology, neurodegeneration. *Unit head:* Dr. Nancy Muma, Chair, 785-864-4001, Fax: 785-864-5219, E-mail: nmuma@ku.edu. *Application contact:* Dr. Rick T. Dobrowsky, Professor/Director of Graduate Studies, 785-864-3531, Fax: 785-864-5219, E-mail: dobrowsky@ku.edu.

The University of Kansas, University of Kansas Medical Center, School of Medicine, Department of Pharmacology, Toxicology and Therapeutics, Kansas City, KS 66160. Offers pharmacology (MS, PhD); toxicology (MS, PhD); MD/MS; MD/PhD. *Faculty:* 27 full-time, 2 part-time/adjunct. *Students:* 1 (woman) full-time, 26 part-time (16 women); includes 1 minority (Hispanic American), 14 international. Average age 28. In 2009, 4 doctorates awarded. Terminal master's awarded for partial completion of doctoral program. *Degree requirements:* For master's, comprehensive exam, thesis; for doctorate, one foreign language, comprehensive exam, thesis/dissertation. *Entrance requirements:* For master's and doctorate, GRE General Test. Additional exam requirements/recommendations for international students: Required—TOEFL. *Application deadline:* For fall admission, 1/15 priority date for domestic students. Applications are processed on a rolling basis. Application fee: $0. Electronic applications accepted. *Expenses:* Tuition, state resident: full-time $6492; part-time $270.50 per credit hour. Tuition, nonresident: full-time $15,510; part-time $646.25 per credit hour. Required fees: $847; $70.56 per credit hour. Tuition and fees vary according to course load and program. *Financial support:* In 2009–10, 26 students received support, including 5 fellowships with full tuition reimbursements available (averaging $24,000 per year), 18 research assistantships with full tuition reimbursements available (averaging $24,000 per year), 3 teaching assistantships with full tuition reimbursements available (averaging $24,000 per year); Federal Work-Study, scholarships/grants, traineeships, and unspecified assistantships also available. Support available to part-time students. Financial award application deadline: 3/30; financial award applicants required to submit FAFSA. *Faculty research:* Liver nuclear receptors, hepatobiliary transporters, pharmacogenomics, estrogen-induced carcinogenesis, neuropharmacology of pain and depression. Total annual research expenditures: $7.4 million. *Unit head:* Dr. Curtis D. Klaassen, Chairman, 913-588-7140, Fax: 913-588-7501, E-mail: cklaasse@kumc.edu. *Application contact:* Dr. Bruno Hagenbuch, Chair, Department Graduate Committee, 913-588-0028, Fax: 913-588-7501, E-mail: bhagenbuch@kumc.edu.

University of Kentucky, Graduate School, Graduate School Programs from the College of Medicine, Program in Molecular and Biomedical Pharmacology, Lexington, KY 40506-0032. Offers pharmacology (PhD); MD/PhD. *Degree requirements:* For doctorate, comprehensive exam, thesis/dissertation. *Entrance requirements:* For doctorate, GRE General Test, minimum undergraduate GPA of 2.75, graduate 3.0. Additional exam requirements/recommendations for international students: Required—TOEFL (minimum score 550 paper-based; 213 computer-based). Electronic applications accepted.

University of Louisville, School of Medicine, Department of Pharmacology and Toxicology, Louisville, KY 40292-0001. Offers MS, PhD, MD/PhD. *Faculty:* 59 full-time (9 women). *Students:* 32 full-time (19 women), 5 part-time (4 women); includes 10 minority (6 African Americans, 3 Asian Americans or Pacific Islanders, 1 Hispanic American), 12 international. Average age 29. 32 applicants, 28% accepted, 6 enrolled. In 2009, 3 master's, 3 doctorates awarded. Terminal master's awarded for partial completion of doctoral program. *Degree requirements:* For master's, thesis; for doctorate, comprehensive exam, thesis/dissertation. *Entrance requirements:* For master's, GRE General Test (minimum score 1000 verbal and quantitative), minimum GPA of 3.0; for doctorate, GRE General Test (Verbal and Quantitative minimum score of 1000), minimum GPA of 3.0. Additional exam requirements/recommendations for international students: Required—TOEFL. *Application deadline:* For fall admission, 1/15 priority date for domestic and international students. Applications are processed on a rolling basis. Application fee: $50. Electronic applications accepted. *Financial support:* In 2009–10, 32 students received support, including 11 fellowships with full tuition reimbursements available (averaging $22,000 per year), 21 research assistantships with full tuition reimbursements available (averaging $22,000 per year). Financial award application deadline: 4/15. *Faculty research:* Molecular pharmacogenetics; epidemiology; functional genomics; genetic predisposition to chemical carcinogenesis and drug toxicity; mechanisms of oxidative stress; alcohol-induced hepatitis, pancreatitis, and hepatocellular carcinoma; molecular and cardiac toxicology; molecular biology and genetics of DNA damage and repair in humans; mechanisms of chemoresistance; arsenic toxicity and cell cycle disruption; molecular pharmacology of novel G protein-coupled receptors. *Unit head:* Dr. David W. Hein, Chair, 502-852-5141, Fax: 502-852-7868, E-mail: dhein@louisville.edu. *Application contact:* Heddy R. Rubin, Information Contact, 502-852-5741, Fax: 502-852-7868, E-mail: hrrubi01@gwise.louisville.edu.

Pharmacology

University of Manitoba, Faculty of Medicine and Faculty of Graduate Studies, Graduate Programs in Medicine, Department of Pharmacology and Therapeutics, Winnipeg, MB R3T 2N2, Canada. Offers M Sc, PhD. Part-time programs available. Terminal master's awarded for partial completion of doctoral program. *Degree requirements:* For master's, thesis; for doctorate, thesis/dissertation. *Entrance requirements:* For master's and doctorate, GRE. Additional exam requirements/recommendations for international students: Required—TOEFL. *Faculty research:* Clinical pharmacology; neuropharmacology; cardiac, hepatic, and renal pharmacology.

University of Maryland, Baltimore, Graduate School, Graduate Program in Life Sciences, Program in Molecular Medicine, Baltimore, MD 21201. Offers cancer biology (PhD); cell and molecular physiology (PhD); human genetics and genomic medicine (PhD); molecular medicine (MS); molecular toxicology and pharmacology (PhD); MD/PhD. *Students:* 61 full-time (37 women), 9 part-time (5 women); includes 19 minority (7 African Americans, 9 Asian Americans or Pacific Islanders, 3 Hispanic Americans), 8 international. Average age 26. 324 applicants, 15% accepted, 20 enrolled. In 2009, 4 master's, 1 doctorate awarded. *Entrance requirements:* Additional exam requirements/recommendations for international students: Required—TOEFL (minimum score 600 paper-based; 100 iBT); Recommended—IELTS (minimum score 7). *Application deadline:* For fall admission, 1/15 for domestic and international students. Application fee: $50. Electronic applications accepted. *Expenses:* Tuition, state resident: full-time $7290; part-time $405 per credit hour. Tuition, nonresident: full-time $12,780; part-time $710 per credit hour. Required fees: $774; $10 per credit hour. $297 per semester. Tuition and fees vary according to course load, degree level and program. *Financial support:* In 2009–10, research assistantships with partial tuition reimbursements (averaging $25,000 per year); fellowships also available. Financial award application deadline: 3/1. *Unit head:* Dr. Dudley Strickland, Director, 410-706-8010, E-mail: dstrickland@som.umaryland.edu. *Application contact:* Sharron Graves, Program Coordinator, 410-706-6044, Fax: 410-706-6040, E-mail: sgraves@som.umaryland.edu.

University of Medicine and Dentistry of New Jersey, Graduate School of Biomedical Sciences, Graduate Programs in Biomedical Sciences–Newark, Department of Pharmacology and Physiology, Newark, NJ 07107. Offers PhD. *Students:* 21 full-time (14 women), 2 part-time (1 woman); includes 7 minority (2 African Americans, 5 Hispanic Americans), 13 international. *Degree requirements:* For doctorate, thesis/dissertation, qualifying exam. *Entrance requirements:* For doctorate, GRE General Test. Additional exam requirements/recommendations for international students: Required—TOEFL. *Application deadline:* For fall admission, 2/1 for domestic students. Applications are processed on a rolling basis. Application fee: $40. Electronic applications accepted. *Financial support:* Fellowships, research assistantships, Federal Work-Study and institutionally sponsored loans available. Financial award application deadline: 5/1. *Unit head:* Dr. Martha Nowycky, Program Director, 973-972-4391, Fax: 973-972-7950, E-mail: martha.nowycky@umdnj.edu. *Application contact:* Dr. Martha Nowycky, Program Director, 973-972-4391, Fax: 973-972-7950, E-mail: martha.nowycky@umdnj.edu.

University of Miami, Graduate School, Miller School of Medicine, Graduate Programs in Medicine, Department of Molecular and Cellular Pharmacology, Coral Gables, FL 33124. Offers PhD, MD/PhD. *Faculty:* 21 full-time (7 women). *Students:* 24 full-time (13 women); includes 1 Asian American or Pacific Islander, 1 Hispanic American, 13 international. Average age 24. In 2009, 7 doctorates awarded. *Degree requirements:* For doctorate, thesis/dissertation, dissertation defense, laboratory rotations, qualifying exam. *Entrance requirements:* For doctorate, GRE General Test. Additional exam requirements/recommendations for international students: Required—TOEFL (minimum score 550 paper-based; 213 computer-based). Application fee: $65. *Financial support:* In 2009–10, 24 students received support, including 24 fellowships (averaging $26,000 per year), research assistantships (averaging $26,000 per year); tuition waivers (full) also available. *Faculty research:* Membrane and cardiovascular pharmacology, muscle contraction, hormone action signal transduction, nuclear transport. *Unit head:* Dr. Charles W. Luetje, Professor and Interim Chairman, 305-243-4458, Fax: 305-243-4555, E-mail: cluetje@med.miami.edu. *Application contact:* Dr. Vladlen Z. Slepak, Director of Graduate Studies, 305-243-3419, Fax: 305-243-3420, E-mail: vslepak@med.miami.edu.

University of Michigan, Horace H. Rackham School of Graduate Studies, Program in Biomedical Sciences (PIBS), Department of Pharmacology, Ann Arbor, MI 48109-5632. Offers PhD. *Degree requirements:* For doctorate, thesis/dissertation, oral preliminary exam, oral defense of dissertation. *Entrance requirements:* For doctorate, GRE General Test, 3 letters of recommendation, research experience. Additional exam requirements/recommendations for international students: Required—TOEFL (minimum score 84 iBT). Electronic applications accepted. *Expenses:* Tuition, state resident: full-time $17,286; part-time $1099 per credit hour. Tuition, nonresident: full-time $34,944; part-time $2080 per credit hour. Required fees: $95 per semester. Tuition and fees vary according to course load, degree level and program. *Faculty research:* Signal transduction, addiction research, cancer pharmacology, drug metabolism and pharmacogenetics.

University of Minnesota, Duluth, Medical School, Program in Pharmacology, Duluth, MN 55812-2496. Offers MS, PhD. Terminal master's awarded for partial completion of doctoral program. *Degree requirements:* For master's, thesis, final oral exam; for doctorate, thesis/dissertation, final oral exam, oral and written preliminary exams. *Entrance requirements:* For master's and doctorate, GRE General Test. Additional exam requirements/recommendations for international students: Required—TOEFL. *Faculty research:* Drug addiction, alcohol and hypertension, neurotransmission, allergic airway disease, auditory neuroscience.

University of Minnesota, Twin Cities Campus, College of Pharmacy and Graduate School, Graduate Programs in Pharmacy, Graduate Program in Social, Administrative and Clinical Pharmacy, Minneapolis, MN 55455-0213. Offers experimental and clinical pharmacology (MS, PhD); social and administrative pharmacy (MS, PhD). *Degree requirements:* For master's, thesis (for some programs); for doctorate, thesis/dissertation. *Entrance requirements:* For master's, GRE General Test, BS in science; for doctorate, GRE General Test. Additional exam requirements/recommendations for international students: Required—TOEFL. *Faculty research:* Pharmaceutical economics, pharmaceutical policy, pharmaceutical social/behavioral sciences.

University of Minnesota, Twin Cities Campus, Medical School, Department of Pharmacology, Minneapolis, MN 55455. Offers MS, PhD. Terminal master's awarded for partial completion of doctoral program. *Degree requirements:* For master's, thesis (for some programs); for doctorate, thesis/dissertation. *Entrance requirements:* For master's and doctorate, GRE General Test. Additional exam requirements/recommendations for international students: Required—TOEFL (minimum score 603 paper-based; 250 computer-based; 100 iBT). Electronic applications accepted. *Faculty research:* Molecular pharmacology, cancer chemotherapy, neuropharmacology, biochemical pharmacology, behavioral pharmacology.

University of Mississippi, Graduate School, School of Pharmacy, Graduate Programs in Pharmacy, Oxford, University, MS 38677. Offers medicinal chemistry (PhD); pharmaceutical sciences (MS); pharmaceutics (PhD); pharmacognosy (PhD); pharmacology (PhD); pharmacy administration (PhD). *Faculty:* 32 full-time (9 women), 8 part-time/adjunct (5 women). *Students:* 84 full-time (37 women), 8 part-time (6 women); includes 6 minority (3 African Americans, 2 Asian Americans or Pacific Islanders, 1 Hispanic American), 64 international. In 2009, 2 master's, 12 doctorates awarded. *Unit head:* Dr. Barbara G. Wells, Dean, 662-915-7265, Fax: 662-915-5704, E-mail: pharmacy@olemiss.edu. *Application contact:* Dr. Christy M. Wyandt, Associate Dean, 662-915-7474, Fax: 662-915-7577, E-mail: cwyandt@olemiss.edu.

University of Mississippi Medical Center, School of Graduate Studies in the Health Sciences, Department of Pharmacology and Toxicology, Jackson, MS 39216-4505. Offers pharmacology (MS, PhD); toxicology (MS, PhD); MD/PhD. Terminal master's awarded for partial completion of doctoral program. *Degree requirements:* For master's, thesis; for doctorate, thesis/dissertation, first authored publication. *Entrance requirements:* For master's and doctorate, GRE General Test, minimum GPA of 3.0. *Faculty research:* Neuropharmacology, environmental toxicology, aging, immunopharmacology, cardiovascular pharmacology.

University of Missouri, School of Medicine and Graduate School, Graduate Programs in Medicine, Department of Medical Pharmacology and Physiology, Columbia, MO 65211. Offers pharmacology (MS, PhD); physiology (MS, PhD). *Degree requirements:* For master's, thesis; for doctorate, thesis/dissertation. *Entrance requirements:* For master's and doctorate, GRE General Test, minimum GPA of 3.0. Additional exam requirements/recommendations for international students: Required—TOEFL (minimum score 500 paper-based; 173 computer-based; 61 iBT). *Faculty research:* Endocrine and metabolic pharmacology, biochemical pharmacology, neuropharmacology, receptors and transmembrane signaling.

University of Nebraska Medical Center, Graduate Studies, Department of Pharmacology and Experimental Neuroscience, Omaha, NE 68198. Offers neuroscience (MS, PhD); pharmacology (MS, PhD). Terminal master's awarded for partial completion of doctoral program. *Degree requirements:* For master's, comprehensive exam, thesis; for doctorate, comprehensive exam, thesis/dissertation. *Entrance requirements:* For master's and doctorate, GRE General Test. Additional exam requirements/recommendations for international students: Required—TOEFL (minimum score 600 paper-based; 250 computer-based). Electronic applications accepted. *Faculty research:* Neuropharmacology, molecular pharmacology, toxicology, molecular biology, neuroscience.

The University of North Carolina at Chapel Hill, School of Medicine and Graduate School, Graduate Programs in Medicine, Department of Pharmacology, Chapel Hill, NC 27599. Offers PhD. *Degree requirements:* For doctorate, comprehensive exam, thesis/dissertation. *Entrance requirements:* For doctorate, GRE General Test, minimum GPA of 3.0. Electronic applications accepted. *Faculty research:* Signal transduction, cell adhesion, receptors, ion channels.

University of North Dakota, School of Medicine and Health Sciences and Graduate School, Graduate Programs in Medicine, Department of Pharmacology, Physiology, and Therapeutics, Grand Forks, ND 58202. Offers pharmacology (MS, PhD); physiology (MS, PhD). *Degree requirements:* For master's, comprehensive exam, thesis; for doctorate, thesis/dissertation, written and oral exams. *Entrance requirements:* For master's, GRE General Test or MCAT, minimum GPA of 3.0; for doctorate, GRE General Test, minimum GPA of 3.5. Additional exam requirements/recommendations for international students: Required—TOEFL (minimum score 550 paper-based; 213 computer-based; 79 iBT), IELTS (minimum score 6.5). Electronic applications accepted.

University of North Texas Health Science Center at Fort Worth, Graduate School of Biomedical Sciences, Fort Worth, TX 76107-2699. Offers anatomy and cell biology (MS, PhD); biochemistry and molecular biology (MS, PhD); biomedical sciences (MS, PhD); biotechnology (MS); forensic genetics (MS); integrative physiology (MS, PhD); medical science (MS); microbiology and immunology (MS, PhD); pharmacology (MS, PhD); science education (MS); DO/MS; DO/PhD. Terminal master's awarded for partial completion of doctoral program. *Degree requirements:* For master's, thesis; for doctorate, thesis/dissertation. *Entrance requirements:* For master's and doctorate, GRE General Test. Additional exam requirements/recommendations for international students: Required—TOEFL. *Expenses:* Contact institution. *Faculty research:* Alzheimer's disease, aging, eye diseases, cancer, cardiovascular disease.

University of Pennsylvania, School of Medicine, Biomedical Graduate Studies, Graduate Group in Pharmacological Sciences, Philadelphia, PA 19104. Offers pharmacology (PhD); MD/PhD; VMD/PhD. *Faculty:* 92. *Students:* 69 full-time (37 women); includes 16 minority (2 African Americans, 1 American Indian/Alaska Native, 10 Asian Americans or Pacific Islanders, 3 Hispanic Americans), 8 international. 100 applicants, 22% accepted, 11 enrolled. In 2009, 11 doctorates awarded. *Degree requirements:* For doctorate, thesis/dissertation. *Entrance requirements:* For doctorate, GRE General Test, previous course work in physical or natural science. Additional exam requirements/recommendations for international students: Required—TOEFL. *Application deadline:* For fall admission, 12/8 priority date for domestic and international students. Applications are processed on a rolling basis. Application fee: $70. Electronic applications accepted. *Expenses:* Tuition: Full-time $25,660; part-time $4758 per course. Required fees: $2152; $270 per course. Tuition and fees vary according to course load, degree level and program. *Financial support:* In 2009–10, 69 students received support; fellowships, research assistantships, scholarships/grants, traineeships, and unspecified assistantships available. *Faculty research:* Properties and regulation of receptors for biogenic amines, molecular aspects of transduction, mechanisms of biosynthesis, biological mechanisms of depression, developmental events in the nervous system. *Unit head:* Dr. Vladimir Muzykantov, Chair, 215-898-9823, E-mail: coord@pharm.med.upenn.edu. *Application contact:* Sarah Squire, Coordinator, 215-898-1790, Fax: 215-573-2236, E-mail: sasquire@mail.med.upenn.edu.

University of Prince Edward Island, Atlantic Veterinary College, Graduate Program in Veterinary Medicine, Charlottetown, PE C1A 4P3, Canada. Offers anatomy (M Sc, PhD); bacteriology (M Sc, PhD); clinical pharmacology (M Sc, PhD); clinical sciences (M Sc, PhD); epidemiology (M Sc, PhD), including reproduction; fish health (M Sc, PhD); food animal nutrition (M Sc, PhD); immunology (M Sc, PhD); microanatomy (M Sc, PhD); parasitology (M Sc, PhD); pathology (M Sc, PhD); pharmacology (M Sc, PhD); physiology (M Sc, PhD); toxicology (M Sc, PhD); veterinary science (M Vet Sc); virology (M Sc, PhD). Part-time programs available. *Degree requirements:* For master's, thesis; for doctorate, thesis/dissertation. *Entrance requirements:* For master's, DVM, B Sc honors degree, or equivalent; for doctorate, M Sc. Additional exam requirements/recommendations for international students: Required—TOEFL (minimum score 550 paper-based; 213 computer-based; 80 iBT). *Expenses:* Contact institution. *Faculty research:* Animal health management, infectious diseases, fin fish and shellfish health, basic biomedical sciences, ecosystem health.

University of Puerto Rico, Medical Sciences Campus, School of Medicine, Division of Graduate Studies, Department of Pharmacology and Toxicology, San Juan, PR 00936-5067. Offers MS, PhD. *Degree requirements:* For master's, one foreign language, thesis; for doctorate, one foreign language, comprehensive exam, thesis/dissertation. *Entrance requirements:* For master's and doctorate, GRE General Test, GRE Subject Test, interview, minimum GPA of 3.0, 3 letters of recommendation. Electronic applications accepted. *Faculty research:* Cardiovascular, central nervous system, and endocrine pharmacology; anti-cancer drugs; sodium pump; mitochondrial DNA repair; Huntington's disease.

University of Rhode Island, Graduate School, College of Pharmacy, Department of Biomedical and Pharmaceutical Sciences, Kingston, RI 02881. Offers medicinal chemistry and pharmacognosy (MS, PhD); pharmaceutics and pharmacokinetics (MS, PhD); pharmacology and toxicology (MS, PhD). Part-time programs available. *Faculty:* 17 full-time (5 women), 1 part-time/adjunct (0 women). *Students:* 33 full-time (16 women), 20 part-time (7 women); includes 12 minority (2 African Americans, 10 Asian Americans or Pacific Islanders), 19 international. In 2009, 6 master's, 6 doctorates awarded. *Entrance requirements:* For master's and doctorate, GRE, 2 letters of recommendation. Additional exam requirements/recommendations for international students: Required—TOEFL (minimum score 550 paper-based; 213 computer-based). Application fee: $65. Electronic applications accepted. *Expenses:* Tuition, state resident: full-time $8828; part-time $490 per credit hour. Tuition, nonresident: full-time $22,100; part-time $1228 per credit hour. Required fees: $1118; $57 per semester. Tuition and fees vary according to program. *Financial support:* In 2009–10, 6 research assistantships with partial tuition reimbursements (averaging $7,119 per year), 12 teaching assistantships with full and partial tuition reimbursements (averaging $10,115 per year) were awarded. Financial award applicants required to submit FAFSA. *Faculty research:* Chemical carcinogenesis with a major emphasis on the structural and synthetic aspects of DNA-adduct formation, drug-drug/herb interaction, drug-genetic interaction, signaling of nuclear receptors, transcriptional regulation, oncogenesis. Total annual research expenditures: $6.2 million. *Unit head:* Dr. Clinton O. Chichester, Chair, 401-874-5034, Fax: 401-874-5787, E-mail: chichester@uri.edu. *Application contact:* Dr. David C. Rowley, Graduate Coordinator, 401-874-9228, Fax: 401-874-2516, E-mail: drowley@uri.edu.

University of Rochester, School of Medicine and Dentistry, Graduate Programs in Medicine and Dentistry, Department of Pharmacology and Physiology, Program in Pharmacology,

Rochester, NY 14627. Offers MS, PhD. Terminal master's awarded for partial completion of doctoral program. *Degree requirements:* For master's, thesis; for doctorate, thesis/dissertation, qualifying exam. *Entrance requirements:* For master's and doctorate, GRE General Test.

University of Saskatchewan, College of Medicine, Department of Pharmacology, Saskatoon, SK S7N 5A2, Canada. Offers M Sc, PhD. *Degree requirements:* For master's, thesis; for doctorate, thesis/dissertation. *Entrance requirements:* Additional exam requirements/recommendations for international students: Required—TOEFL. Tuition and fees charges are reported in Canadian dollars. *Expenses:* Tuition, area resident: Full-time $3000 Canadian dollars; part-time $500 Canadian dollars per term. Required fees: $700 Canadian dollars; $100 Canadian dollars per term. *Faculty research:* Neuropharmacology, mechanisms of action of anticancer drugs, clinical pharmacology, cardiovascular pharmacology, toxicology: alcohol-related changes in fetal brain development.

University of South Alabama, College of Medicine and Graduate School, Program in Basic Medical Sciences, Specialization in Molecular and Cellular Pharmacology, Mobile, AL 36688-0002. Offers PhD. *Degree requirements:* For doctorate, thesis/dissertation. *Entrance requirements:* For doctorate, GRE General Test or MCAT. *Expenses:* Tuition, state resident: part-time $218 per contact hour. Required fees: $1102 per year. *Faculty research:* Cardiovascular, clinical, and molecular pharmacology.

The University of South Dakota, School of Medicine and Health Sciences and Graduate School, Biomedical Sciences Graduate Program, Physiology and Pharmacology Group, Vermillion, SD 57069-2390. Offers MS, PhD. Terminal master's awarded for partial completion of doctoral program. *Degree requirements:* For master's, thesis; for doctorate, comprehensive exam, thesis/dissertation. *Entrance requirements:* For master's and doctorate, GRE General Test, minimum GPA of 3.0. Additional exam requirements/recommendations for international students: Required—TOEFL (minimum score 550 paper-based; 213 computer-based; 80 iBT), IELTS (minimum score 6). Electronic applications accepted. *Expenses:* Contact institution. *Faculty research:* Pulmonary physiology and pharmacology, drug abuse, reproduction, signal transduction, cardiovascular physiology and pharmacology.

The University of Texas Health Science Center at San Antonio, Graduate School of Biomedical Sciences, Department of Pharmacology, San Antonio, TX 78229-3900. Offers PhD. *Faculty:* 30 full-time (7 women). *Students:* 18 full-time (10 women); includes 9 minority (4 Asian Americans or Pacific Islanders, 5 Hispanic Americans), 2 international. Average age 23. In 2009, 2 doctorates awarded. *Degree requirements:* For doctorate, comprehensive exam, thesis/dissertation. *Entrance requirements:* For doctorate, GRE General Test, minimum GPA of 3.0. Additional exam requirements/recommendations for international students: Required—TOEFL (minimum score 560 paper-based; 220 computer-based; 68 iBT). *Application deadline:* For fall admission, 1/15 priority date for domestic and international students. Applications are processed on a rolling basis. Application fee: $0. Electronic applications accepted. *Expenses:* Tuition, state resident: full-time $2832; part-time $118 per credit hour. Tuition, nonresident: full-time $10,896; part-time $454 per credit hour. Required fees: $884 per semester. One-time fee: $70. *Financial support:* In 2009–10, 1 fellowship (averaging $26,000 per year), research assistantships (averaging $26,000 per year), 17 teaching assistantships (averaging $26,000 per year) were awarded; institutionally sponsored loans, scholarships/grants, and health care benefits also available. Financial award application deadline: 4/1; financial award applicants required to submit FAFSA. *Faculty research:* Neuropharmacology, autonomic and endocrine homeostasis, aging, cancer biology. Total annual research expenditures: $11.4 million. *Unit head:* Alan Frazer, Chairman, 210-567-4205, Fax: 210-567-4300, E-mail: frazer@uthscsa.edu. *Application contact:* Emma Carreon, Manager of Academic Programs, 210-567-4220, Fax: 210-567-4303, E-mail: carreoner@uthscsa.edu.

The University of Texas Medical Branch, Graduate School of Biomedical Sciences, Program in Pharmacology and Toxicology, Galveston, TX 77555. Offers pharmacology (MS); pharmacology and toxicology (PhD). *Students:* 10 full-time (2 women); includes 5 minority (2 African Americans, 1 Asian American or Pacific Islander, 2 Hispanic Americans), 2 international. Average age 30. In 2009, 1 master's, 6 doctorates awarded. *Degree requirements:* For master's, thesis or alternative; for doctorate, thesis/dissertation. *Entrance requirements:* For master's and doctorate, GRE General Test. Additional exam requirements/recommendations for international students: Required—TOEFL (minimum score 550 paper-based; 213 computer-based). *Application deadline:* Applications are processed on a rolling basis. Application fee: $30 ($75 for international students). *Financial support:* In 2009–10, fellowships (averaging $25,000 per year), research assistantships with full tuition reimbursements (averaging $25,000 per year) were awarded. Financial award applicants required to submit FAFSA. *Unit head:* Dr. Kenneth M. Johnson, Director, 409-772-1561, Fax: 409-772-9642, E-mail: kmjohnso@utmb.edu. *Application contact:* Penny Welsh, Program Coordinator, 409-772-9626, Fax: 409-747-7050, E-mail: pwelsh@utmb.edu.

University of the Sciences in Philadelphia, College of Graduate Studies, Program in Chemistry, Biochemistry and Pharmacognosy, Philadelphia, PA 19104-4495. Offers biochemistry (MS, PhD); chemistry (MS, PhD); pharmacognosy (MS, PhD). Part-time programs available. *Degree requirements:* For master's, thesis, qualifying exams; for doctorate, comprehensive exam, thesis/dissertation, qualifying exams. *Entrance requirements:* For master's and doctorate, GRE General Test, GRE Subject Test. Additional exam requirements/recommendations for international students: Required—TOEFL, TWE. *Expenses:* Contact institution. *Faculty research:* Organic and medicinal synthesis, mass spectroscopy use in protein analysis, study of analogues of taxol, cholesteryl esters.

University of the Sciences in Philadelphia, College of Graduate Studies, Program in Pharmacology and Toxicology, Philadelphia, PA 19104-4495. Offers pharmacology (MS, PhD); toxicology (MS, PhD). Terminal master's awarded for partial completion of doctoral program. *Degree requirements:* For master's, thesis; for doctorate, comprehensive exam, thesis/dissertation. *Entrance requirements:* For master's and doctorate, GRE General Test. Additional exam requirements/recommendations for international students: Required—TOEFL, TWE. *Expenses:* Contact institution. *Faculty research:* Autonomic, cardiovascular, cellular, and molecular pharmacology; mechanisms of carcinogenesis; drug metabolism.

The University of Toledo, College of Graduate Studies, College of Pharmacy, Program in Pharmaceutical Sciences, Toledo, OH 43606-3390. Offers administrative pharmacy (MSPS); industrial pharmacy (MSPS); pharmacology toxicology (MSPS). *Degree requirements:* For master's, thesis. *Entrance requirements:* For master's, GRE General Test. Additional exam requirements/recommendations for international students: Required—TOEFL (minimum score 550 paper-based; 213 computer-based; 80 iBT). Electronic applications accepted.

University of Toronto, School of Graduate Studies, Life Sciences Division, Department of Pharmacology and Toxicology, Toronto, ON M5S 1A1, Canada. Offers M Sc, PhD. Part-time programs available. *Degree requirements:* For master's, thesis; for doctorate, thesis/dissertation. *Entrance requirements:* For master's, B Sc or equivalent; background in pharmacology, biochemistry, and physiology; minimum B+ earned in at least 4 senior level classes; for doctorate, minimum B+ average.

University of Utah, Graduate School, College of Pharmacy, Department of Pharmacology and Toxicology, Salt Lake City, UT 84112. Offers PhD. *Faculty:* 19 full-time (5 women), 2 part-time/adjunct (0 women). *Students:* 18 full-time (9 women), 3 part-time (2 women); includes 2 minority (both Hispanic Americans), 1 international. Average age 30. 66 applicants, 9% accepted, 3 enrolled. In 2009, 2 doctorates awarded. Terminal master's awarded for partial completion of doctoral program. *Degree requirements:* For doctorate, thesis/dissertation, final exam. *Entrance requirements:* For doctorate, GRE Subject Test, BS in biology, chemistry, pharmacy, or biochemistry. Additional exam requirements/recommendations for international students: Required—TOEFL (minimum score 600 paper-based; 250 computer-based; 100 iBT). *Application deadline:* For fall admission, 1/15 for domestic students, 1/16 for international students. Application fee: $55 ($65 for international students). *Expenses:* Tuition, state resident: full-time $4004; part-time $1674 per semester. Tuition, nonresident: full-time $14,134; part-time $5915 per semester. Required fees: $324 per semester. Tuition and fees vary according to course load, degree level and program. *Financial support:* In 2009–10, 14 students received support, including fellowships with full tuition reimbursements available (averaging $25,000 per year), 14 research assistantships with full tuition reimbursements available (averaging $25,000 per year). *Faculty research:* Neuropharmacology, neurochemistry, biochemistry, molecular pharmacology, analytical chemistry. Total annual research expenditures: $4.3 million. *Unit head:* Dr. William R. Crowley, Chairman, 801-581-6287, Fax: 801-585-5111, E-mail: william.crowley@deans.pharm.utah.edu. *Application contact:* Sheila H. Merrill, Executive Secretary, 801-581-6287, Fax: 801-585-5111, E-mail: sheila.merrill@pharm.utah.edu.

University of Vermont, College of Medicine and Graduate College, Graduate Programs in Medicine, Department of Pharmacology, Burlington, VT 05405. Offers MS, PhD, MD/MS, MD/PhD. *Faculty:* 12 full-time (1 woman). *Students:* 7 (1 woman), 2 international. 17 applicants, 24% accepted, 2 enrolled. In 2009, 1 master's awarded. *Degree requirements:* For master's, thesis; for doctorate, thesis/dissertation. *Entrance requirements:* For master's and doctorate, GRE General Test. Additional exam requirements/recommendations for international students: Required—TOEFL (minimum score 550 paper-based; 213 computer-based; 80 iBT). *Application deadline:* For fall admission, 1/15 priority date for domestic students, 1/15 for international students. Applications are processed on a rolling basis. Application fee: $40. Electronic applications accepted. *Expenses:* Tuition, state resident: part-time $508 per credit hour. Tuition, nonresident: part-time $1281 per credit hour. *Financial support:* Fellowships, research assistantships, teaching assistantships available. Financial award application deadline: 3/1. *Faculty research:* Cardiovascular drugs, anticancer drugs. *Unit head:* Dr. M. Nelson, Chairperson, 802-656-2500. *Application contact:* Dr. Anthony Morielli, Director of Graduate Studies, 802-656-2500.

University of Virginia, School of Medicine, Department of Pharmacology, Charlottesville, VA 22903. Offers PhD, MD/PhD. *Faculty:* 26 full-time (5 women), 2 part-time/adjunct (0 women). *Students:* 14 full-time (9 women); includes 1 minority (Asian American or Pacific Islander), 1 international. Average age 26. In 2009, 3 doctorates awarded. *Degree requirements:* For doctorate, thesis/dissertation. *Entrance requirements:* For doctorate, GRE General Test, GRE Subject Test (recommended), 2 letters of recommendation. Additional exam requirements/recommendations for international students: Required—TOEFL. *Application deadline:* For fall admission, 1/15 for domestic and international students. Applications are processed on a rolling basis. Application fee: $60. Electronic applications accepted. *Financial support:* Fellowships, research assistantships, teaching assistantships available. Financial award applicants required to submit FAFSA. *Unit head:* Dr. Douglas A. Bayliss, Chairman, 434-924-1919, Fax: 434-982-3878. *Application contact:* Dr. Douglas A. Bayliss, Chairman, 434-924-1919, Fax: 434-982-3878.

University of Washington, Graduate School, School of Medicine and Graduate School, Graduate Programs in Medicine, Department of Pharmacology, Seattle, WA 98195. Offers PhD. *Degree requirements:* For doctorate, thesis/dissertation. *Entrance requirements:* For doctorate, GRE General Test, minimum GPA of 3.0. *Faculty research:* Neuroscience, cell physiology, molecular biology, regulation of metabolism, signal transduction.

University of Wisconsin–Madison, School of Medicine and Public Health and Graduate School, Graduate Programs in Medicine, Molecular and Cellular Pharmacology Program, Madison, WI 53706. Offers PhD. *Faculty:* 47 full-time (10 women). *Students:* 46 full-time (26 women); includes 12 minority (1 African American, 8 Asian Americans or Pacific Islanders, 3 Hispanic Americans), 6 international. Average age 26. 115 applicants, 20% accepted, 9 enrolled. In 2009, 4 doctorates awarded. *Degree requirements:* For doctorate, comprehensive exam, thesis/dissertation. *Entrance requirements:* For doctorate, GRE. Additional exam requirements/recommendations for international students: Required—TOEFL (minimum score 550 paper-based; 213 computer-based). *Application deadline:* For fall admission, 12/15 priority date for domestic and international students. Applications are processed on a rolling basis. Application fee: $56. Electronic applications accepted. *Expenses:* Tuition, state resident: part-time $594 per credit. Tuition, nonresident: part-time $1504 per credit. Required fees: $65 per credit. Tuition and fees vary according to course load, program and reciprocity agreements. *Financial support:* In 2009–10, 46 students received support, including 11 fellowships with full tuition reimbursements available (averaging $23,500 per year), 36 research assistantships with full tuition reimbursements available (averaging $23,500 per year), teaching assistantships with full tuition reimbursements available (averaging $23,500 per year); scholarships/grants, traineeships, health care benefits, and unspecified assistantships also available. *Faculty research:* Protein kinases, signaling pathways, neurotransmitters, molecular recognition, receptors and transporters. *Unit head:* Dr. Richard A. Anderson, Director, 608-262-3753, Fax: 608-262-1257, E-mail: raanders@wisc.edu. *Application contact:* Lynn Louise Squire, Student Services Coordinator, 608-262-9826, Fax: 608-262-1257, E-mail: lsquire@wisc.edu.

Vanderbilt University, Graduate School and School of Medicine, Department of Pharmacology, Nashville, TN 37240-1001. Offers PhD, MD/PhD. *Faculty:* 107 full-time (25 women). *Students:* 51 full-time (26 women); includes 6 minority (3 African Americans, 1 American Indian/Alaska Native, 2 Hispanic Americans), 8 international. Average age 29. In 2009, 3 doctorates awarded. *Degree requirements:* For doctorate, comprehensive exam, thesis/dissertation, preliminary, qualifying, and final exams. *Entrance requirements:* For doctorate, GRE General Test, GRE Subject Test (recommended). Additional exam requirements/recommendations for international students: Required—TOEFL (minimum score 570 paper-based; 230 computer-based; 88 iBT). *Application deadline:* For fall admission, 1/15 for domestic and international students. Application fee: $0. Electronic applications accepted. *Financial support:* Fellowships with full tuition reimbursements, research assistantships with full tuition reimbursements, Federal Work-Study, institutionally sponsored loans, scholarships/grants, traineeships, health care benefits, and tuition waivers (partial) available. Financial award application deadline: 1/15; financial award applicants required to submit CSS PROFILE or FAFSA. *Faculty research:* Molecular pharmacology, neuropharmacology, drug disposition and toxicology, genetic mechanics, cell regulation. *Unit head:* Dr. Heidi E. Hamm, Chair, 615-343-3533, Fax: 615-343-1084, E-mail: heidi.hamm@vanderbilt.edu. *Application contact:* Dr. Joey V. Barnett, Director of Graduate Studies, 615-936-1722, Fax: 615-936-3910, E-mail: joey.barnett@vanderbilt.edu.

Virginia Commonwealth University, Medical College of Virginia-Professional Programs, School of Medicine, School of Medicine Graduate Programs, Department of Pharmacology and Toxicology, Richmond, VA 23284-9005. Offers molecular biology and genetics (PhD); neuroscience (PhD); pharmacology (PhD); pharmacology and toxicology (MS); MD/PhD. Terminal master's awarded for partial completion of doctoral program. *Degree requirements:* For master's, thesis; for doctorate, thesis/dissertation, comprehensive oral and written exams. *Entrance requirements:* For master's, DAT, GRE General Test, or MCAT; for doctorate, GRE General Test, MCAT, DAT. *Faculty research:* Drug abuse, drug metabolism, pharmacodynamics, peptide synthesis, receptor mechanisms.

Virginia Commonwealth University, Program in Pre-Medical Basic Health Sciences, Richmond, VA 23284-9005. Offers anatomy (CBHS); biochemistry (CBHS); human genetics (CBHS); microbiology (CBHS); pharmacology (CBHS); physiology (CBHS). *Entrance requirements:* For degree, GRE or MCAT, course work in organic chemistry, minimum undergraduate GPA of 2.8. Additional exam requirements/recommendations for international students: Required—TOEFL (minimum score 600 paper-based).

Wake Forest University, School of Medicine and Graduate School of Arts and Sciences, Graduate Programs in Medicine, Program in Physiology and Pharmacology, Winston-Salem, NC 27109. Offers pharmacology (PhD); physiology (PhD); MD/PhD. *Degree requirements:* For doctorate, thesis/dissertation. *Entrance requirements:* For doctorate, GRE General Test. Additional exam requirements/recommendations for international students: Required—TOEFL. Electronic applications accepted. *Faculty research:* Aging, substance abuse, cardiovascular control, endocrine systems, toxicology.

Pharmacology

Washington State University, Graduate School, College of Pharmacy, Program in Pharmacology and Toxicology, Pullman, WA 99164. Offers MS, PhD. *Faculty:* 19. *Students:* 8 full-time (7 women); includes 3 minority (1 Asian American or Pacific Islander, 2 Hispanic Americans), 3 international. Average age 26. 63 applicants, 11% accepted, 0 enrolled. In 2009, 2 doctorates awarded. *Degree requirements:* For master's, thesis, oral exam; for doctorate, thesis/dissertation, oral exam. *Entrance requirements:* For master's and doctorate, GRE General Test, official transcripts from all undergraduate and graduate schools attended; letter describing research interests, career goals, and research experience. Additional exam requirements/recommendations for international students: Required—TOEFL, IELTS. *Application deadline:* For fall admission, 12/15 for domestic and international students. Applications are processed on a rolling basis. Application fee: $50. Electronic applications accepted. *Financial support:* In 2009–10, 5 fellowships (averaging $6,176 per year), 10 research assistantships with full and partial tuition reimbursements (averaging $14,846 per year), 4 teaching assistantships with full and partial tuition reimbursements (averaging $14,661 per year) were awarded; Federal Work-Study, institutionally sponsored loans, tuition waivers (partial), and staff assistantships, teaching associateships also available. Financial award application deadline: 2/15; financial award applicants required to submit FAFSA. *Faculty research:* Cancer research, immunopharmacology/immunotoxicology, pharmacy, neurobiology/neuropharmacology, toxicology. Total annual research expenditures: $1 million. *Unit head:* Dr. Linda Garrelts MacLean, Chair, 509-335-5545, Fax: 509-335-5902, E-mail: bbr@wsu.edu. *Application contact:* Graduate School Admissions, 800-GRADWSU, Fax: 509-335-1949, E-mail: gradsch@wsu.edu.

Wayne State University, Eugene Applebaum College of Pharmacy and Health Sciences, Department of Pharmacy Practice, Detroit, MI 48202. Offers medicinal chemistry (MS, PhD); pharmaceutical sciences (MS, PhD); pharmaceutics (MS, PhD); pharmacology (MS, PhD); pharmacy (Pharm D). Terminal master's awarded for partial completion of doctoral program. *Degree requirements:* For master's, thesis; for doctorate, thesis/dissertation. *Entrance requirements:* For master's, GRE General Test, minimum GPA of 2.6; for doctorate, GRE General Test, minimum GPA of 3.0. Additional exam requirements/recommendations for international students: Required—TOEFL (minimum score 550 paper-based; 213 computer-based); Recommended—TWE (minimum score 6). Electronic applications accepted. *Faculty research:* Pharmacodynamics and pharmacokinetics of anti-infective agents; efficacy of drug treatments for traumatic head injury and stroke; cultural difference in Arab-Americans related to diabetes treatment and prevention; drug disposition and effect in pediatrics; evaluation of anticoagulation regimens.

Wayne State University, School of Medicine, Graduate Programs in Medicine, Department of Pharmacology, Detroit, MI 48202. Offers MS, PhD. *Degree requirements:* For doctorate, thesis/dissertation. *Entrance requirements:* For master's and doctorate, GRE General Test. Additional exam requirements/recommendations for international students: Required—TOEFL (minimum score 550 paper-based; 213 computer-based); Recommended—TWE (minimum score 6). Electronic applications accepted. *Faculty research:* Molecular and cellular biology of cancer and anti-cancer therapies; molecular and cellular biology of protein trafficking, signal transduction and aging; environmental toxicology and drug metabolism; functional cellular and in vivo imaging; neuroscience.

West Virginia University, School of Medicine, Graduate Programs at the Health Sciences Center, Interdisciplinary Graduate Programs in Biomedical Sciences, Program in Pharmaceutical and Pharmacological Sciences, Morgantown, WV 26506. Offers MS, PhD, MD/PhD. *Degree requirements:* For doctorate, comprehensive exam, thesis/dissertation. *Entrance requirements:* For doctorate, GRE General Test, minimum GPA of 3.0. Additional exam requirements/recommendations for international students: Required—TOEFL. Electronic applications accepted. *Faculty research:* Medicinal chemistry, pharmacokinetics, nano-pharmaceutics, polymer-based drug delivery, molecular therapeutics.

Wright State University, School of Medicine, Program in Pharmacology and Toxicology, Dayton, OH 45435. Offers MS. *Degree requirements:* For master's, thesis optional.

Yale University, School of Medicine and Graduate School of Arts and Sciences, Combined Program in Biological and Biomedical Sciences (BBS), Department of Pharmacology, New Haven, CT 06520. Offers PhD. *Faculty:* 80 full-time (23 women), 2 part-time/adjunct (1 woman). In 2009, 9 doctorates awarded. *Degree requirements:* For doctorate, thesis/dissertation. *Entrance requirements:* For doctorate, GRE General Test. Additional exam requirements/recommendations for international students: Required—TOEFL. *Application deadline:* For fall admission, 1/2 for domestic students. *Expenses:* Contact institution. *Financial support:* Fellowships, research assistantships, teaching assistantships, Federal Work-Study, institutionally sponsored loans, and traineeships available. Support available to part-time students. *Unit head:* Elias Lolis, Director of Graduate Studies and Admissions, 203-785-6233. *Application contact:* Graduate Admissions Office, 203-432-2771.

Yale University, School of Medicine and Graduate School of Arts and Sciences, Combined Program in Biological and Biomedical Sciences (BBS), Pharmacological Sciences and Molecular Medicine Track, New Haven, CT 06520. Offers PhD, MD/PhD. *Degree requirements:* For doctorate, thesis/dissertation. *Entrance requirements:* For doctorate, GRE General Test. Additional exam requirements/recommendations for international students: Required—TOEFL. *Application deadline:* For fall admission, 12/6 for domestic and international students. Electronic applications accepted. *Financial support:* Fellowships, research assistantships available. *Unit head:* Dr. Gerry Shadel, Co-Director, 203-785-2475, E-mail: bbs.pharm@yale.edu. *Application contact:* Dr. Gerry Shadel, Co-Director, 203-785-2475, E-mail: bbs.pharm@yale.edu.

Toxicology

American University, College of Arts and Sciences, Department of Chemistry, Program in Toxicology, Washington, DC 20016-8014. Offers MS, Certificate. Part-time programs available. *Students:* 11 full-time (5 women), 36 part-time (24 women); includes 14 minority (5 African Americans, 5 Asian Americans or Pacific Islanders, 4 Hispanic Americans). Average age 24. In 2009, 1 other advanced degree awarded. *Entrance requirements:* Additional exam requirements/recommendations for international students: Required—TOEFL. *Application deadline:* For fall admission, 2/1 priority date for domestic students; for spring admission, 10/1 priority date for domestic students. Applications are processed on a rolling basis. Application fee: $80. *Expenses:* Tuition: Full-time $22,266; part-time $1237 per credit hour. Required fees: $430. Tuition and fees vary according to program. *Financial support:* Fellowships, research assistantships with full and partial tuition reimbursements, teaching assistantships with full and partial tuition reimbursements, career-related internships or fieldwork and institutionally sponsored loans available. Financial award application deadline: 2/1. *Faculty research:* Carbohydrate chemistry, chromatography, enzyme mechanisms and model systems, environmental analysis with monoclonal antibodies, polymers. *Application contact:* Director, Graduate Admissions.

Brown University, Graduate School, Division of Biology and Medicine, Program in Pathology and Laboratory Medicine, Providence, RI 02912. Offers biology (PhD); cancer biology (PhD); immunology and infection (PhD); medical science (PhD); pathobiology (Sc M); toxicology and environmental pathology (PhD). Terminal master's awarded for partial completion of doctoral program. *Degree requirements:* For doctorate, thesis/dissertation, preliminary exam. *Entrance requirements:* For master's and doctorate, GRE General Test, GRE Subject Test. Additional exam requirements/recommendations for international students: Required—TOEFL. Electronic applications accepted. *Faculty research:* Environmental pathology, carcinogenesis, immunopathology, signal transduction, innate immunity.

Columbia University, College of Physicians and Surgeons, Department of Pharmacology, New York, NY 10032. Offers pharmacology (M Phil, MA, PhD); pharmacology-toxicology (M Phil, MA, PhD); MD/PhD. Only candidates for the PhD are admitted. Terminal master's awarded for partial completion of doctoral program. *Degree requirements:* For doctorate, thesis/dissertation. *Entrance requirements:* For master's and doctorate, GRE General Test. Additional exam requirements/recommendations for international students: Required—TOEFL. *Faculty research:* Cardiovascular pharmacology, receptor pharmacology, neuropharmacology, membrane biophysics, eicosanoids.

Cornell University, Graduate School, Graduate Fields of Agriculture and Life Sciences, Field of Environmental Toxicology, Ithaca, NY 14853-0001. Offers cellular and molecular toxicology (MS, PhD); ecotoxicology and environmental chemistry (MS, PhD); nutritional and food toxicology (MS, PhD); risk assessment, management and public policy (MS, PhD). *Faculty:* 40 full-time (10 women). *Students:* 13 full-time (5 women); includes 1 minority (American Indian/Alaska Native), 5 international. Average age 29. 17 applicants, 0% accepted, 0 enrolled. In 2009, 2 master's, 5 doctorates awarded. *Degree requirements:* For master's, thesis; for doctorate, comprehensive exam, thesis/dissertation. *Entrance requirements:* For master's and doctorate, GRE General Test, GRE Subject Test (biology or chemistry recommended), 2 letters of recommendation. Additional exam requirements/recommendations for international students: Required—TOEFL (minimum score 600 paper-based; 250 computer-based; 77 iBT). *Application deadline:* For fall admission, 1/15 for domestic students. Application fee: $70. Electronic applications accepted. *Expenses:* Tuition: Full-time $29,500. Required fees: $70. Full-time tuition and fees vary according to degree level, program and student level. *Financial support:* Fellowships with full tuition reimbursements, research assistantships with full tuition reimbursements, teaching assistantships with full tuition reimbursements, institutionally sponsored loans, scholarships/grants, health care benefits, tuition waivers (full and partial), and unspecified assistantships available. Financial award applicants required to submit FAFSA. *Faculty research:* Cellular and molecular toxicology, cancer toxicology, bioremediation, ecotoxicology, nutritional and food toxicology, reproductive toxicology. *Unit head:* Director of Graduate Studies, 607-255-8008, Fax: 607-755-0238. *Application contact:* Graduate Field Assistant, 607-255-8008, Fax: 607-255-0238, E-mail: envtox@cornell.edu.

Dartmouth College, Arts and Sciences Graduate Programs, Department of Pharmacology and Toxicology, Hanover, NH 03755. Offers PhD, MD/PhD. *Faculty:* 25 full-time (5 women). *Students:* 17 full-time (8 women); includes 1 minority (African American), 6 international. Average age 28. 1,128 applicants, 2% accepted, 15 enrolled. In 2009, 6 doctorates awarded. *Degree requirements:* For doctorate, thesis/dissertation. *Entrance requirements:* For doctorate, GRE General Test, GRE Subject Test, bachelor's degree in biological, chemical, or physical science. Additional exam requirements/recommendations for international students: Required—TOEFL. *Application deadline:* For fall admission, 1/15 for domestic students. Electronic applications accepted. *Financial support:* In 2009–10, 13 students received support, including fellowships with full tuition reimbursements available (averaging $25,500 per year), research assistantships with full tuition reimbursements available (averaging $25,500 per year), teaching assistantships with tuition reimbursements available (averaging $25,500 per year); institutionally sponsored loans, traineeships, tuition waivers (full and partial), and unspecified assistantships also available. Financial award application deadline: 4/15. *Faculty research:* Molecular biology of carcinogenesis, DNA repair and gene expression, biochemical and environmental toxicology, protein receptor ligand interactions. *Unit head:* Dr. Joyce DeLeo, Chair, 603-650-1667, Fax: 603-650-1129, E-mail: pharmacology.and.toxicology@dartmouth.edu. *Application contact:* Clarissa Kellogg, Academic Assistant, 603-650-1667, Fax: 603-650-1129.

Dartmouth College, Program in Experimental and Molecular Medicine, Molecular Pharmacology, Toxicology and Experimental Therapeutics Track, Hanover, NH 03755. Offers PhD.

Duke University, Graduate School, Integrated Toxicology and Environmental Health Program, Durham, NC 27708. Offers PhD, Certificate. *Faculty:* 36 full-time. *Students:* 5 full-time (4 women). 22 applicants, 27% accepted, 4 enrolled. *Entrance requirements:* For doctorate, GRE General Test, GRE Subject Test (recommended). Additional exam requirements/recommendations for international students: Required—TOEFL (minimum score 550 paper-based; 213 computer-based; 83 iBT), IELTS (minimum score 7). *Application deadline:* For fall admission, 12/8 priority date for domestic and international students. Application fee: $75. Electronic applications accepted. *Financial support:* Fellowships available. Financial award application deadline: 12/31. *Unit head:* Tim Lenoir, Director, 919-668-1952, Fax: 919-668-1799, E-mail: emarion@duke.edu. *Application contact:* Cynthia Robertson, Associate Dean for Enrollment Services, 919-684-3913, E-mail: grad-admissions@duke.edu.

Florida Agricultural and Mechanical University, Division of Graduate Studies, Research, and Continuing Education, College of Pharmacy and Pharmaceutical Sciences, Graduate Programs in Pharmaceutical Sciences, Tallahassee, FL 32307-3200. Offers environmental toxicology (PhD); medicinal chemistry (MS, PhD); pharmaceutics (MS, PhD); pharmacology/toxicology (MS, PhD); pharmacy administration (MS). *Accreditation:* CEPH. *Faculty:* 21 full-time (6 women). *Students:* 438 full-time (296 women), 21 part-time (13 women); includes 417 minority (380 African Americans, 1 American Indian/Alaska Native, 30 Asian Americans or Pacific Islanders, 6 Hispanic Americans), 5 international. In 2009, 4 master's, 7 doctorates awarded. *Degree requirements:* For master's, comprehensive exam, thesis, publishable paper; for doctorate, comprehensive exam, thesis/dissertation, publishable paper. *Entrance requirements:* For master's and doctorate, GRE General Test, minimum GPA of 3.0 in last 60 hours. Additional exam requirements/recommendations for international students: Required—TOEFL. *Application deadline:* For fall admission, 4/1 for domestic students. Application fee: $20. *Financial support:* Fellowships, research assistantships, Federal Work-Study and scholarships/grants available. *Faculty research:* Anticancer agents, anti-inflammatory drugs, chronopharmacology, neuroendocrinology, microbiology. *Unit head:* Dr. Thomas J. Fitzgerald, Chairman, Graduate Committee, 850-599-3301. *Application contact:* Gloria James, Graduate Coordinator, 850-599-3144.

The George Washington University, Columbian College of Arts and Sciences, Department of Forensic Sciences, Washington, DC 20052. Offers crime scene investigation (MFS); forensic chemistry (MFS); forensic molecular biology (MFS); forensic toxicology (MFS); high-technology crime investigation (MFS); security management (MFS). High-technology crime investigation and security management programs offered in Arlington, VA. Part-time and evening/weekend programs available. *Faculty:* 6 full-time (1 woman), 28 part-time/adjunct (5 women). *Students:* 82 full-time (55 women), 54 part-time (35 women); includes 26 minority (12 African Americans, 2 American Indian/Alaska Native, 7 Asian Americans or Pacific Islanders, 5 Hispanic Americans), 10 international. Average age 28. 121 applicants, 81% accepted, 52 enrolled. In 2009, 80 master's awarded. *Degree requirements:* For master's, comprehensive exam. *Entrance requirements:* For master's, GRE General Test, minimum GPA of 3.0. Additional exam requirements/recommendations for international students: Required—TOEFL (minimum score 550 paper-based; 213 computer-based; 80 iBT). *Application deadline:* For fall admission, 1/16 priority date for international students; for spring admission, 10/1 priority date for domestic students, 9/1 priority date for international students. Applications are processed on a rolling basis. Application fee: $60. Electronic applications accepted. *Financial support:* In 2009–10, 19 students received support; fellowships with partial tuition reimbursements available, Federal Work-Study and tuition waivers available. *Unit head:* Dr. Walter F. Rowe, Chair, 202-994-1469, E-mail: wfrowe@gwu.edu. *Application contact:* Dr. Walter F. Rowe, Chair, 202-994-1469, E-mail: wfrowe@gwu.edu.

Indiana University–Purdue University Indianapolis, Indiana University School of Medicine, Department of Pharmacology and Toxicology, Indianapolis, IN 46202-2896. Offers pharmacology (MS, PhD); toxicology (MS, PhD); MD/PhD. *Faculty:* 11 full-time (2 women). *Students:* 21 full-time (13 women), 1 part-time (0 women); includes 1 minority (Hispanic American), 10 international. Average age 28. 13 applicants, 38% accepted, 5 enrolled. In 2009, 4 master's, 2 doctorates awarded. Terminal master's awarded for partial completion of doctoral program. *Degree requirements:* For master's, thesis; for doctorate, thesis/dissertation. *Entrance requirements:* For master's and doctorate, GRE General Test, GRE Subject Test, minimum GPA of 3.0. *Application deadline:* For fall admission, 1/15 priority date for domestic students. Applications are processed on a rolling basis. Application fee: $55 ($65 for international students). *Financial support:* In 2009–10, 14 students received support, including 7 teaching assistantships (averaging $20,940 per year); fellowships with partial tuition reimbursements available, research assistantships with partial tuition reimbursements available, Federal Work-Study, institutionally sponsored loans, and tuition waivers (partial) also available. Financial award application deadline: 1/15. *Faculty research:* Neuropharmacology, cardiovascular biopharmacology, chemotherapy, oncogenesis. *Unit head:* Dr. Michael Vasko, Chairman, 317-274-7844, Fax: 317-274-7714. *Application contact:* Director of Graduate Studies, 317-274-1564, Fax: 317-274-7714.

Iowa State University of Science and Technology, Graduate College, College of Agriculture and College of Liberal Arts and Sciences, Department of Biochemistry, Biophysics, and Molecular Biology, Ames, IA 50011. Offers biochemistry (MS, PhD); biophysics (MS, PhD); genetics (MS, PhD); molecular, cellular, and developmental biology (MS, PhD); toxicology (MS, PhD). *Faculty:* 24 full-time (6 women), 1 (woman) part-time/adjunct. *Students:* 77 full-time (30 women), 3 part-time (2 women); includes 3 minority (1 African American, 1 Asian American or Pacific Islander, 1 Hispanic American), 56 international. 41 applicants, 32% accepted, 13 enrolled. In 2009, 2 master's, 7 doctorates awarded. *Degree requirements:* For master's, thesis; for doctorate, thesis/dissertation. *Entrance requirements:* For master's and doctorate, GRE General Test. Additional exam requirements/recommendations for international students: Required—TOEFL (minimum score 550 paper-based; 79 iBT) or IELTS (minimum score 6.5). *Application deadline:* For fall admission, 1/15 priority date for domestic and international students; for spring admission, 10/15 for domestic and international students. Application fee: $40 ($90 for international students). Electronic applications accepted. *Expenses:* Tuition, state resident: full-time $6716. Tuition, nonresident: full-time $8908. Tuition and fees vary according to course level, course load, program and student level. *Financial support:* In 2009–10, 52 research assistantships with full and partial tuition reimbursements (averaging $18,750 per year) were awarded; teaching assistantships with full and partial tuition reimbursements, scholarships/grants, health care benefits, and unspecified assistantships also available. *Unit head:* Dr. Guru Rao, Interim Chair, 515-294-6116, E-mail: biochem@iastate.edu. *Application contact:* Dr. Reuben Peters, Director of Graduate Education, 515-294-6116, E-mail: biochem@iastate.edu.

See Close-Up on page 155.

Iowa State University of Science and Technology, Graduate College, Interdisciplinary Programs, Program in Toxicology, Ames, IA 50011. Offers MS, PhD. *Students:* 22 full-time (6 women), 1 part-time (0 women); includes 2 minority (both African Americans), 12 international. In 2009, 2 master's, 2 doctorates awarded. *Degree requirements:* For master's, thesis; for doctorate, thesis/dissertation. *Entrance requirements:* For master's and doctorate, GRE General Test. Additional exam requirements/recommendations for international students: Required—TOEFL (minimum score 550 paper-based; 79 iBT) or IELTS (minimum score 6.5). *Application deadline:* For fall admission, 2/1 priority date for domestic and international students. Applications are processed on a rolling basis. Application fee: $40 ($90 for international students). Electronic applications accepted. *Expenses:* Tuition, state resident: full-time $6716. Tuition, nonresident: full-time $8908. Tuition and fees vary according to course level, course load, program and student level. *Financial support:* In 2009–10, 21 research assistantships with full and partial tuition reimbursements (averaging $17,460 per year) were awarded; teaching assistantships with full and partial tuition reimbursements, scholarships/grants, health care benefits, and unspecified assistantships also available. *Unit head:* Dr. Anumantha Kanthasamy, Supervisory Committee Chair, 515-294-7697, Fax: 515-294-6669, E-mail: toxmajor@iastate.edu. *Application contact:* Linda Wild, Information Contact, 800-499-1972, E-mail: toxmajor@iastate.edu.

The Johns Hopkins University, Bloomberg School of Public Health, Department of Environmental Health Sciences, Baltimore, MD 21218-2699. Offers environmental health engineering (PhD); environmental health sciences (MHS, Dr PH); occupational and environmental health (PhD); occupational and environmental hygiene (MHS, MHS); physiology (PhD); toxicology (PhD). Postbaccalaureate distance learning degree programs offered (minimal on-campus study). *Faculty:* 71 full-time (27 women), 58 part-time/adjunct (26 women). *Students:* 65 full-time (43 women), 17 part-time (12 women); includes 22 minority (4 African Americans, 1 American Indian/Alaska Native, 13 Asian Americans or Pacific Islanders, 4 Hispanic Americans), 11 international. Average age 31. 101 applicants, 49% accepted, 31 enrolled. In 2009, 22 master's, 13 doctorates awarded. *Degree requirements:* For master's, essay, presentation; for doctorate, comprehensive exam, thesis/dissertation, 1 year full-time residency, oral and written exams. *Entrance requirements:* For master's, GRE General Test or MCAT, 3 letters of recommendation, transcripts; for doctorate, GRE General Test or MCAT, 3 letters of recommendation. Additional exam requirements/recommendations for international students: Required—TOEFL (minimum score 600 paper-based; 250 computer-based). *Application deadline:* For fall admission, 12/15 priority date for domestic and international students. Applications are processed on a rolling basis. Application fee: $45. Electronic applications accepted. *Financial support:* In 2009–10, 5 fellowships with full tuition reimbursements (averaging $26,500 per year) were awarded; Federal Work-Study, institutionally sponsored loans, scholarships/grants, traineeships, health care benefits, and stipends also available. Support available to part-time students. Financial award application deadline: 3/15; financial award applicants required to submit FAFSA. *Faculty research:* Chemical carcinogenesis/toxicology, lung disease, occupational and environmental health, nuclear imaging, molecular epidemiology. Total annual research expenditures: $23.7 million. *Unit head:* Dr. John Davis Groopman, Chair, 410-955-3720, Fax: 410-955-0617, E-mail: jgroopma@jhsph.edu. *Application contact:* Nina J. Kulacki, Academic Program Manager, 410-955-2212, Fax: 410-955-0617, E-mail: nkulacki@jhsph.edu.

Long Island University, Brooklyn Campus, Arnold and Marie Schwartz College of Pharmacy and Health Sciences, Graduate Programs in Pharmacy, Division of Pharmaceutical Sciences, Brooklyn, NY 11201-8423. Offers cosmetic science (MS); industrial pharmacy (MS); pharmaceutics (PhD); pharmacology/toxicology (MS). Part-time and evening/weekend programs available. Terminal master's awarded for partial completion of doctoral program. *Degree requirements:* For master's, thesis optional; for doctorate, thesis/dissertation, candidacy exam. *Entrance requirements:* For master's and doctorate, minimum GPA of 3.0.

Louisiana State University and Agricultural and Mechanical College, Graduate School, School of the Coast and Environment, Department of Environmental Sciences, Baton Rouge, LA 70803. Offers environmental planning and management (MS); environmental toxicology (MS). *Faculty:* 10 full-time (4 women). *Students:* 21 full-time (13 women), 6 part-time (2 women); includes 4 African Americans, 6 international. Average age 28. 22 applicants, 86% accepted, 12 enrolled. In 2009, 8 master's awarded. *Degree requirements:* For master's, thesis (for some programs). *Entrance requirements:* For master's, GRE General Test, minimum GPA of 3.0. Additional exam requirements/recommendations for international students: Required—TOEFL (minimum score 550 paper-based; 213 computer-based; 79 iBT) or IELTS (minimum score 6.5). *Application deadline:* For fall admission, 1/25 priority date for domestic students, 5/15 for international students; for spring admission, 10/15 for international students. Applications are processed on a rolling basis. Application fee: $50 ($70 for international students). Electronic applications accepted. *Financial support:* In 2009–10, 21 students received support, including 14 research assistantships with full and partial tuition reimbursements available (averaging $13,171 per year), 1 teaching assistantship with full and partial tuition reimbursement available (averaging $15,740 per year); fellowships with full and partial tuition reimbursements available, career-related internships or fieldwork, Federal Work-Study, institutionally sponsored loans, scholarships/grants, health care benefits, and unspecified assistantships also available. Support available to part-time students. Financial award applicants required to submit FAFSA. *Faculty research:* Environmental toxicology, environmental policy and law, microbial ecology, bioremediation, genetic toxicology. Total annual research expenditures: $656,188. *Unit head:* Dr. Nina Lam, Chair, 225-578-3030, Fax: 225-578-4286, E-mail: nlam@lsu.edu. *Application contact:* Charlotte G. St. Romain, Academic Coordinator, 225-578-8522, Fax: 225-578-4286, E-mail: cstrom4@lsu.edu.

Massachusetts Institute of Technology, School of Engineering, Department of Biological Engineering, Cambridge, MA 02139-4307. Offers applied biosciences (PhD, Sc D); bioengineering (PhD, Sc D); biological engineering (PhD, Sc D); biomedical engineering (M Eng); toxicology (SM); SM/MBA. *Faculty:* 18 full-time (2 women). *Students:* 105 full-time (51 women); includes 24 minority (3 African Americans, 16 Asian Americans or Pacific Islanders, 5 Hispanic Americans), 29 international. Average age 26. 371 applicants, 9% accepted, 22 enrolled. In 2009, 5 master's, 20 doctorates awarded. Terminal master's awarded for partial completion of doctoral program. *Degree requirements:* For master's, thesis; for doctorate, comprehensive exam, thesis/dissertation. *Entrance requirements:* For master's and doctorate, GRE General Test. Additional exam requirements/recommendations for international students: Required—TOEFL (minimum score 600 paper-based; 250 computer-based), IELTS (minimum score 7). *Application deadline:* For fall admission, 12/31 for domestic and international students. Application fee: $75. Electronic applications accepted. *Expenses:* Tuition: Full-time $37,510; part-time $585 per unit. Required fees: $272. *Financial support:* In 2009–10, 105 students received support, including 51 fellowships with tuition reimbursements available (averaging $35,187 per year), 49 research assistantships with tuition reimbursements available (averaging $31,622 per year); teaching assistantships with tuition reimbursements available, Federal Work-Study, institutionally sponsored loans, scholarships/grants, traineeships, health care benefits, and unspecified assistantships also available. *Faculty research:* Bioinformatics, computational, systems, and synthetic biology, biological materials, cancer initiation, progression, and therapeutics, genomics, proteomics, glycomics, imaging, transport phenomena, biomolecular and cell engineering, nanoscale engineering of biological systems, neurobiological systems. Total annual research expenditures: $35.2 million. *Unit head:* Prof. Douglas A. Lauffenburger, Head, 617-253-1712, E-mail: be-acad@mit.edu. *Application contact:* Academic Office, 617-253-1712, Fax: 617-258-8676, E-mail: be-acad@mit.edu.

Medical College of Wisconsin, Graduate School of Biomedical Sciences, Department of Pharmacology and Toxicology, Milwaukee, WI 53226-0509. Offers PhD, MD/PhD. Terminal master's awarded for partial completion of doctoral program. *Degree requirements:* For doctorate, comprehensive exam, thesis/dissertation, oral and written qualifying exams. *Entrance requirements:* For doctorate, GRE General Test, minimum B average. Additional exam requirements/recommendations for international students: Required—TOEFL. *Faculty research:* Cardiovascular physiology and pharmacology, drugs of abuse, environmental and aquatic toxicology, central nervous system and biochemical pharmacology, signal transduction.

Medical University of South Carolina, College of Graduate Studies, Department of Pharmaceutical and Biomedical Sciences, Charleston, SC 29425. Offers cell injury and repair (PhD); drug discovery (PhD); medicinal chemistry (PhD); toxicology (PhD); DMD/PhD; MD/PhD; Pharm D/PhD. *Faculty:* 8 full-time (1 woman), 1 part-time/adjunct (0 women). *Students:* 7 full-time (3 women); includes 1 minority (African American), 1 international. Average age 30. In 2009, 2 doctorates awarded. *Degree requirements:* For doctorate, thesis/dissertation, oral and written exams, teaching and research seminar. *Entrance requirements:* For doctorate, GRE General Test, interview, minimum GPA of 3.0. Additional exam requirements/recommendations for international students: Required—TOEFL (minimum score 600 paper-based; 250 computer-based; 100 iBT). *Application deadline:* For fall admission, 1/15 priority date for domestic and international students. Applications are processed on a rolling basis. Application fee: $0 ($85 for international students). Electronic applications accepted. *Financial support:* In 2009–10, 7 students received support, including 7 research assistantships with partial tuition reimbursements available (averaging $23,000 per year); Federal Work-Study and scholarships/grants also available. Support available to part-time students. Financial award application deadline: 3/10; financial award applicants required to submit FAFSA. *Faculty research:* Drug discovery, toxicology, metabolomics, cell stress and injury. *Unit head:* Dr. Rick Schnellmann, Eminent Scholar, Professor and Chair, 843-792-3754, Fax: 843-792-6590, E-mail: schnell@musc.edu. *Application contact:* Dr. Craig C. Beeson, Associate Professor, 843-876-5091, Fax: 843-792-6590, E-mail: beesonc@musc.edu.

Michigan State University, College of Human Medicine and The Graduate School, Graduate Programs in Human Medicine, East Lansing, MI 48824. Offers biochemistry and molecular biology (MS, PhD); epidemiology (MS, PhD); microbiology (MS); microbiology and molecular genetics (PhD); pharmacology and toxicology (MS, PhD); physiology (MS, PhD); public health (MPH). *Students:* 58 full-time (31 women), 31 part-time (25 women); includes 17 minority (7 African Americans, 1 American Indian/Alaska Native, 6 Asian Americans or Pacific Islanders, 3 Hispanic Americans), 22 international. Average age 30. In 2009, 8 master's, 9 doctorates awarded. *Entrance requirements:* Additional exam requirements/recommendations for international students: Required—TOEFL. *Expenses:* Tuition, state resident: part-time $478.25 per credit hour. Tuition, nonresident: part-time $966.50 per credit hour. Part-time tuition and fees vary according to program. *Financial support:* In 2009–10, 17 research assistantships with tuition reimbursements (averaging $7,053 per year), 3 teaching assistantships with tuition reimbursements (averaging $6,607 per year) were awarded. *Unit head:* Margo K. Smith, Director of Graduate Studies, 517-432-5112, E-mail: smithmk@msu.edu. *Application contact:* Margo K. Smith, Director of Graduate Studies, 517-432-5112, E-mail: smithmk@msu.edu.

Michigan State University, College of Osteopathic Medicine and The Graduate School, Graduate Studies in Osteopathic Medicine and Graduate Programs in Human Medicine and Graduate Programs in Veterinary Medicine, Department of Pharmacology and Toxicology, East Lansing, MI 48824. Offers integrative pharmacology (MS); pharmacology and toxicology (MS, PhD); pharmacology and toxicology-environmental toxicology (PhD). *Faculty:* 17 full-time (6 women). *Students:* 21 full-time (10 women), 40 part-time (23 women); includes 7 minority (1 African American, 2 Asian Americans or Pacific Islanders, 4 Hispanic Americans), 11 international. Average age 29. 70 applicants, 27% accepted. In 2009, 1 doctorate awarded. *Entrance requirements:* Additional exam requirements/recommendations for international students: Required—TOEFL (minimum score 600 paper-based; 220 computer-based). *Application deadline:* Applications are processed on a rolling basis. Electronic applications accepted. *Expenses:* Tuition, state resident: part-time $478.25 per credit hour. Tuition, nonresident: part-time $966.50 per credit hour. Part-time tuition and fees vary according to program. *Financial support:* In 2009–10, 11 research assistantships with tuition reimbursements (averaging $7,754 per year) were awarded. Total annual research expenditures: $5.3 million. *Unit head:* Dr. Joseph R. Haywood, Chairperson, 517-353-7145, Fax: 517-353-8915, E-mail: haywoo12@msu.edu. *Application contact:* Diane Hummel, Graduate Secretary, 517-353-9619, Fax: 517-353-8915, E-mail: hummeld@msu.edu.

Michigan State University, College of Veterinary Medicine and The Graduate School, Graduate Programs in Veterinary Medicine, Center for Integrative Toxicology, East Lansing, MI 48824. Offers animal science–environmental toxicology (PhD); biochemistry and molecular biology–environmental toxicology (PhD); chemistry–environmental toxicology (PhD); crop and soil sciences–environmental toxicology (PhD); environmental engineering–environmental toxicology (PhD); environmental geosciences–environmental toxicology (PhD); fisheries and wildlife–

Toxicology

Michigan State University (continued)
environmental toxicology (PhD); food science–environmental toxicology (PhD); forestry–environmental toxicology (PhD); genetics–environmental toxicology (PhD); human nutrition–environmental toxicology (PhD); microbiology–environmental toxicology (PhD); pharmacology and toxicology–environmental toxicology (PhD); zoology–environmental toxicology (PhD). *Faculty:* 44 full-time (8 women). *Students:* 17 full-time (8 women), 8 international. Average age 28. 17 applicants, 0% accepted. In 2009, 11 doctorates awarded. *Entrance requirements:* Additional exam requirements/recommendations for international students: Required—TOEFL (minimum score 550 paper-based; 213 computer-based), Michigan State University ELT (minimum score 85), Michigan English Language Assessment Battery (minimum score 83). *Application deadline:* For fall admission, 12/27 for domestic students. Electronic applications accepted. *Expenses:* Tuition, state resident: part-time $478.25 per credit hour. Tuition, nonresident: part-time $966.50 per credit hour. Part-time tuition and fees vary according to program. *Financial support:* In 2009–10, 10 research assistantships with tuition reimbursements (averaging $7,859 per year) were awarded; career-related internships or fieldwork, Federal Work-Study, scholarships/grants, and unspecified assistantships also available. *Faculty research:* Environmental risk assessment, toxicogenomics, phytoremediation, storage and disposal of hazardous waste, environmental regulation. *Unit head:* Dr. Norbert E. Kaminski, Director, 517-353-3786, Fax: 517-355-4603, E-mail: kamins11@msu.edu. *Application contact:* Amy Swagart, Executive Secretary, 517-353-6469, Fax: 517-355-4603, E-mail: tox@msu.edu.

Michigan State University, College of Veterinary Medicine and The Graduate School, Graduate Programs in Veterinary Medicine and College of Natural Science and Graduate Programs in Human Medicine, Department of Microbiology and Molecular Genetics, East Lansing, MI 48824. Offers industrial microbiology (MS, PhD); microbiology (MS, PhD); microbiology and molecular genetics (MS, PhD); microbiology–environmental toxicology (PhD). *Faculty:* 32 full-time (9 women). *Students:* 50 full-time (22 women), 5 part-time (1 woman); includes 7 minority (2 African Americans, 4 Asian Americans or Pacific Islanders, 1 Hispanic American), 21 international. Average age 27. 104 applicants, 14% accepted. In 2009, 6 master's, 5 doctorates awarded. *Entrance requirements:* For master's, GRE General Test. Additional exam requirements/recommendations for international students: Required—TOEFL (minimum score 550 paper-based; 213 computer-based), Michigan State University ELT (minimum score 85), Michigan English Language Assessment Battery (minimum score 83). Electronic applications accepted. *Expenses:* Tuition, state resident: part-time $478.25 per credit hour. Tuition, nonresident: part-time $966.50 per credit hour. Part-time tuition and fees vary according to program. *Financial support:* In 2009–10, 34 research assistantships with tuition reimbursements (averaging $7,765 per year), 6 teaching assistantships with tuition reimbursements (averaging $7,544 per year) were awarded. Total annual research expenditures: $5.5 million. *Unit head:* Dr. Walter Esselman, Chairperson, 517-884-5292, Fax: 517-353-8957, E-mail: mmgchair@msu.edu. *Application contact:* Suzanne Peacock, Graduate Program Coordinator, 517-884-5287, Fax: 517-353-8957, E-mail: micgrad@msu.edu.

Michigan State University, The Graduate School, College of Agriculture and Natural Resources, Department of Animal Science, East Lansing, MI 48824. Offers animal science (MS, PhD); animal science-environmental toxicology (PhD). *Faculty:* 35 full-time (8 women), 2 part-time/adjunct (both women). *Students:* 35 full-time (21 women), 4 part-time (3 women); includes 2 minority (1 African American, 1 Asian American or Pacific Islander), 12 international. Average age 28. 38 applicants, 34% accepted. In 2009, 3 master's, 4 doctorates awarded. *Entrance requirements:* Additional exam requirements/recommendations for international students: Required—TOEFL (minimum score 550 paper-based; 213 computer-based), Michigan State University ELT (minimum score 85), Michigan English Language Assessment Battery (minimum score 83). *Application deadline:* For fall admission, 12/27 for domestic students. Applications are processed on a rolling basis. Electronic applications accepted. *Expenses:* Tuition, state resident: part-time $478.25 per credit hour. Tuition, nonresident: part-time $966.50 per credit hour. Part-time tuition and fees vary according to program. *Financial support:* In 2009–10, 23 research assistantships with tuition reimbursements (averaging $6,285 per year), 1 teaching assistantship with tuition reimbursement (averaging $6,336 per year) were awarded. Total annual research expenditures: $6.5 million. *Unit head:* Dr. Karen I. Plaut, Chairperson, 517-355-8384, Fax: 517-353-1699, E-mail: kplaut@msu.edu. *Application contact:* Kathleen S. Tatro, Graduate Student Program Secretary, 517-355-8417, Fax: 517-353-1699, E-mail: tatro@msu.edu.

Michigan State University, The Graduate School, College of Agriculture and Natural Resources, Department of Crop and Soil Sciences, East Lansing, MI 48824. Offers crop and soil sciences (MS, PhD); crop and soil sciences-environmental toxicology (PhD); plant breeding and genetics-crop and soil sciences (MS); plant breeding, genetics and biotechnology-crop and soil sciences (PhD). *Faculty:* 27 full-time (6 women). *Students:* 56 full-time (25 women), 5 part-time (0 women); includes 2 minority (1 Asian American or Pacific Islander, 1 Hispanic American), 31 international. Average age 29. 38 applicants, 37% accepted. In 2009, 8 master's, 11 doctorates awarded. *Entrance requirements:* Additional exam requirements/recommendations for international students: Required—TOEFL (minimum score 550 paper-based; 213 computer-based), Michigan State University ELT (minimum score 85), Michigan Michigan English Language Assessment Battery (minimum score 83). *Application deadline:* Applications are processed on a rolling basis. Electronic applications accepted. *Expenses:* Tuition, state resident: part-time $478.25 per credit hour. Tuition, nonresident: part-time $966.50 per credit hour. Part-time tuition and fees vary according to program. *Financial support:* In 2009–10, 45 research assistantships with tuition reimbursements (averaging $6,465 per year), 1 teaching assistantship with tuition reimbursement (averaging $6,053 per year) were awarded. Total annual research expenditures: $6.9 million. *Unit head:* Dr. James J. Kells, Chairperson, 517-355-0271 Ext. 1103, Fax: 517-353-5174, E-mail: kells@msu.edu. *Application contact:* Rita House, Graduate Secretary, 517-355-0271 Ext. 1324, Fax: 517-353-5174, E-mail: house@msu.edu.

Michigan State University, The Graduate School, College of Agriculture and Natural Resources and College of Natural Science, Department of Food Science and Human Nutrition, East Lansing, MI 48824. Offers food science (MS, PhD); food science—environmental toxicology (PhD); human nutrition (MS, PhD); human nutrition-environmental toxicology (PhD). *Faculty:* 23 full-time (10 women). *Students:* 40 full-time (31 women), 2 part-time (1 woman); includes 4 minority (2 African Americans, 1 Asian American or Pacific Islander, 1 Hispanic American), 15 international. Average age 28. 94 applicants, 9% accepted. In 2009, 9 master's, 6 doctorates awarded. *Entrance requirements:* Additional exam requirements/recommendations for international students: Required—TOEFL (minimum score 550 paper-based; 213 computer-based), Michigan State University ELT (minimum score 85), Michigan English Language Assessment Battery (minimum score 83). Electronic applications accepted. *Expenses:* Tuition, state resident: part-time $478.25 per credit hour. Tuition, nonresident: part-time $966.50 per credit hour. Part-time tuition and fees vary according to program. *Financial support:* In 2009–10, 29 research assistantships with tuition reimbursements (averaging $6,399 per year), 2 teaching assistantships with tuition reimbursements (averaging $5,985 per year) were awarded. Total annual research expenditures: $3 million. *Unit head:* Dr. Frederik Derksen, Acting Chairperson, 517-355-8474 Ext. 100, Fax: 517-353-8963, E-mail: derksen@anr.msu.edu. *Application contact:* Deborah Klein, Graduate Secretary, 517-355-8474 Ext. 182, Fax: 517-353-8963, E-mail: kleinde@msu.edu.

Michigan State University, The Graduate School, College of Engineering, Department of Civil and Environmental Engineering, East Lansing, MI 48824. Offers civil engineering (MS, PhD); environmental engineering (MS, PhD); environmental engineering-environmental toxicology (PhD). Part-time programs available. *Faculty:* 21 full-time (3 women). *Students:* 78 full-time (21 women), 19 part-time (6 women); includes 4 minority (2 Asian Americans or Pacific Islanders, 2 Hispanic Americans), 70 international. Average age 28. 130 applicants, 33% accepted. In 2009, 17 master's, 7 doctorates awarded. *Entrance requirements:* Additional exam requirements/recommendations for international students: Required—TOEFL. Electronic applications accepted. *Expenses:* Tuition, state resident: part-time $478.25 per credit hour. Tuition, nonresident: part-time $966.50 per credit hour. Part-time tuition and fees vary according to program. *Financial support:* In 2009–10, 36 research assistantships with tuition reimbursements (averaging $7,704 per year), 22 teaching assistantships with tuition reimbursements (averaging $7,665 per year) were awarded. Total annual research expenditures: $3.4 million. *Unit head:* Dr. Ronald S. Harichandran, Chairperson, 517-355-5107, Fax: 517-432-1827, E-mail: harichan@egr.msu.edu. *Application contact:* Margaret F. Conner, Graduate Secretary, 517-355-5107, Fax: 517-432-1827, E-mail: ceegrad@egr.msu.edu.

Michigan State University, The Graduate School, College of Natural Science and Graduate Programs in Human Medicine and Graduate Studies in Osteopathic Medicine, Department of Biochemistry and Molecular Biology, East Lansing, MI 48824. Offers biochemistry and molecular biology (MS, PhD); biochemistry and molecular biology/environmental toxicology (PhD). *Faculty:* 26 full-time (5 women). *Students:* 64 full-time (26 women); includes 2 minority (1 African American, 1 Asian American or Pacific Islander), 38 international. Average age 27. 111 applicants, 9% accepted. In 2009, 10 doctorates awarded. *Entrance requirements:* Additional exam requirements/recommendations for international students: Required—TOEFL. Electronic applications accepted. *Expenses:* Tuition, state resident: part-time $478.25 per credit hour. Tuition, nonresident: part-time $966.50 per credit hour. Part-time tuition and fees vary according to program. *Financial support:* In 2009–10, 48 research assistantships with tuition reimbursements (averaging $8,017 per year), 3 teaching assistantships with tuition reimbursements (averaging $8,033 per year) were awarded; scholarships/grants and unspecified assistantships also available. Total annual research expenditures: $6.4 million. *Unit head:* Dr. Thomas Sharkey, Chairperson, 517-353-0804, Fax: 517-353-9334, E-mail: tsharkey@msu.edu. *Application contact:* Jessica Lawrence, Graduate Program Secretary, 517-353-0807, Fax: 517-353-9334, E-mail: bmbgrad@cns.msu.edu.

Michigan State University, The Graduate School, College of Natural Science, Department of Chemistry, East Lansing, MI 48824. Offers chemical physics (PhD); chemistry (MS, PhD); chemistry-environmental toxicology (PhD); computational chemistry (MS). *Faculty:* 36 full-time (4 women). *Students:* 193 full-time (86 women), 8 part-time (2 women); includes 9 minority (2 African Americans, 6 Asian Americans or Pacific Islanders, 1 Hispanic American), 104 international. Average age 27. 117 applicants, 53% accepted. In 2009, 8 master's, 49 doctorates awarded. *Entrance requirements:* Additional exam requirements/recommendations for international students: Required—TOEFL. Electronic applications accepted. *Expenses:* Tuition, state resident: part-time $478.25 per credit hour. Tuition, nonresident: part-time $966.50 per credit hour. Part-time tuition and fees vary according to program. *Financial support:* In 2009–10, 49 research assistantships with tuition reimbursements (averaging $7,741 per year), 126 teaching assistantships with tuition reimbursements (averaging $7,635 per year) were awarded. *Faculty research:* Analytical chemistry, inorganic and organic chemistry, nuclear chemistry, physical chemistry, theoretical and computational chemistry. Total annual research expenditures: $5.3 million. *Unit head:* Dr. John L. McCracken, Chairperson, 517-355-9715 Ext. 346, Fax: 517-353-1793, E-mail: chair@chemistry.msu.edu. *Application contact:* Deborah Roper, Graduate Admissions Secretary, 517-355-9715 Ext. 343, Fax: 517-353-1793, E-mail: gradoff@chemistry.msu.edu.

Michigan State University, The Graduate School, College of Natural Science, Department of Geological Sciences, East Lansing, MI 48824. Offers environmental geosciences (MS, PhD); environmental geosciences-environmental toxicology (PhD); geological sciences (MS, PhD). *Faculty:* 12 full-time (2 women). *Students:* 22 full-time (9 women), 1 part-time (0 women), 6 international. Average age 32. 38 applicants, 18% accepted. In 2009, 4 master's, 2 doctorates awarded. *Degree requirements:* For master's, thesis (for those without prior thesis work); for doctorate, thesis/dissertation. *Entrance requirements:* For master's, GRE General Test, minimum GPA of 3.0, course work in geoscience, 3 letters of recommendation; for doctorate, GRE General Test, 3 letters of recommendation. Additional exam requirements/recommendations for international students: Required—TOEFL (minimum score 550 paper-based; 213 computer-based), Michigan State University ELT (minimum score 85), Michigan English Language Assessment Battery (minimum score 83). *Application deadline:* For fall admission, 12/27 priority date for domestic students. Electronic applications accepted. *Expenses:* Tuition, state resident: part-time $478.25 per credit hour. Tuition, nonresident: part-time $966.50 per credit hour. Part-time tuition and fees vary according to program. *Financial support:* In 2009–10, 4 research assistantships with tuition reimbursements (averaging $6,336 per year), 12 teaching assistantships with tuition reimbursements (averaging $6,465 per year) were awarded; Federal Work-Study, scholarships/grants, and unspecified assistantships also available. *Faculty research:* Water in the environment, global and biological change, crystal dynamics. Total annual research expenditures: $607,187. *Unit head:* Dr. Ralph E. Taggart, Chairperson, 517-355-4626, Fax: 517-353-8787, E-mail: taggart@msu.edu. *Application contact:* Jackie Bennett, Graduate Program Secretary, 517-355-4626, Fax: 517-353-8787, E-mail: geosci@msu.edu.

Michigan State University, The Graduate School, College of Natural Science, Program in Genetics, East Lansing, MI 48824. Offers genetics (MS, PhD); genetics–environmental toxicology (PhD). *Faculty:* 111 full-time (33 women), 1 part-time/adjunct (0 women). *Students:* 54 full-time (26 women), 1 part-time (0 women); includes 5 minority (2 African Americans, 1 Asian American or Pacific Islander, 2 Hispanic Americans), 32 international. Average age 28. 41 applicants, 17% accepted. In 2009, 3 master's, 10 doctorates awarded. *Entrance requirements:* Additional exam requirements/recommendations for international students: Required—TOEFL. Electronic applications accepted. *Expenses:* Tuition, state resident: part-time $478.25 per credit hour. Tuition, nonresident: part-time $966.50 per credit hour. Part-time tuition and fees vary according to program. *Financial support:* In 2009–10, 36 research assistantships with tuition reimbursements (averaging $7,896 per year), 8 teaching assistantships with tuition reimbursements (averaging $8,115 per year) were awarded. Total annual research expenditures: $59,433. *Unit head:* Dr. Barbara Sears, Director, 517-353-9845, Fax: 517-355-0112, E-mail: sears@msu.edu. *Application contact:* Jeannine Lee, Graduate Secretary, 517-353-9845, Fax: 517-355-0112, E-mail: genetics@msu.edu.

New York University, Graduate School of Arts and Science, Department of Environmental Medicine, New York, NY 10012-1019. Offers environmental health sciences (MS, PhD), including biostatistics (PhD), environmental hygiene (MS), epidemiology (PhD), ergonomics and biomechanics (PhD), exposure assessment and health effects (PhD), molecular toxicology/carcinogenesis (PhD), toxicology. Part-time programs available. *Faculty:* 26 full-time (7 women). *Students:* 45 full-time (37 women), 15 part-time (8 women); includes 9 minority (3 African Americans, 3 Asian Americans or Pacific Islanders, 3 Hispanic Americans), 23 international. Average age 31. 60 applicants, 48% accepted, 14 enrolled. In 2009, 11 master's, 10 doctorates awarded. Terminal master's awarded for partial completion of doctoral program. *Degree requirements:* For master's, thesis or alternative; for doctorate, one foreign language, thesis/dissertation, oral and written exams. *Entrance requirements:* For master's and doctorate, GRE General Test, GRE Subject Test, minimum GPA of 3.0; bachelor's degree in biological, physical, or engineering science. Additional exam requirements/recommendations for international students: Required—TOEFL. *Application deadline:* For fall admission, 12/12 for domestic students. Application fee: $90. *Expenses:* Tuition: Full-time $30,528; part-time $1272 per credit. Required fees: $2177. *Financial support:* Fellowships with tuition reimbursements, teaching assistantships with tuition reimbursements, career-related internships or fieldwork, Federal Work-Study, institutionally sponsored loans, and health care benefits available. Financial award application deadline: 12/12; financial award applicants required to submit FAFSA. *Unit head:* Dr. Max Costa, Chair, 845-731-3661, Fax: 845-351-4510, E-mail: ehs@env.med.nyu.edu. *Application contact:* Dr. Jerome J. Solomon, Director of Graduate Studies, 845-731-3661, Fax: 845-351-4510, E-mail: ehs@env.med.nyu.edu.

See Close-Up on page 103.

North Carolina State University, Graduate School, College of Agriculture and Life Sciences and College of Veterinary Medicine, Department of Environmental and Molecular Toxicology, Raleigh, NC 27695. Offers M Tox, MS, PhD. Terminal master's awarded for partial completion of doctoral program. *Degree requirements:* For master's, thesis (for some programs); for doctorate, thesis/dissertation. *Entrance requirements:* For master's and doctorate, GRE General Test, minimum GPA of 3.0. Electronic applications accepted. *Faculty research:* Chemical fate, carcinogenesis, developmental and endocrine toxicity, xenobiotic metabolism, signal transduction.

Northwestern University, Northwestern University Feinberg School of Medicine and Interdepartmental Programs, Integrated Graduate Programs in the Life Sciences, Chicago, IL 60611. Offers cancer biology (PhD); cell biology (PhD); developmental biology (PhD); evolutionary biology (PhD); immunology and microbial pathogenesis (PhD); molecular biology and genetics (PhD); neurobiology (PhD); pharmacology and toxicology (PhD); structural biology and biochemistry (PhD). *Degree requirements:* For doctorate, comprehensive exam, thesis/dissertation, written and oral qualifying exams. *Entrance requirements:* For doctorate, GRE General Test. Additional exam requirements/recommendations for international students: Required—TOEFL (minimum score 600 paper-based; 250 computer-based). Electronic applications accepted.

The Ohio State University, College of Veterinary Medicine, Department of Veterinary Biosciences, Columbus, OH 43210. Offers anatomy and cellular biology (MS, PhD); pathobiology (MS, PhD); pharmacology (MS, PhD); toxicology (MS, PhD); veterinary physiology (MS, PhD). *Faculty:* 45. *Students:* 18 full-time (14 women), 20 part-time (16 women); includes 3 minority (1 African American, 1 Asian American or Pacific Islander, 1 Hispanic American), 16 international. Average age 30. In 2009, 1 master's, 9 doctorates awarded. *Entrance requirements:* For master's and doctorate, GRE General Test. Additional exam requirements/recommendations for international students: Required—TOEFL. *Application deadline:* Applications are processed on a rolling basis. Application fee: $40 ($50 for international students). Electronic applications accepted. *Expenses:* Tuition, state resident: full-time $10,683. Tuition, nonresident: full-time $25,923. Tuition and fees vary according to course load and program. *Faculty research:* Microvasculature, muscle biology, neonatal lung and bone development. *Unit head:* Dr. Michael J. Oglesbee, Graduate Studies Committee Chair, 614-292-5661, Fax: 614-292-6473, E-mail: oglesbee.1@osu.edu. *Application contact:* Graduate Admissions, 614-292-9444, Fax: 614-292-3895, E-mail: domestic.grad@osu.edu.

Oklahoma State University Center for Health Sciences, Graduate Program in Forensic Sciences, Tulsa, OK 74107-1898. Offers forensic DNA/molecular biology (MS); forensic examination of questioned documents (MFSA, Certificate); forensic pathology (MS); forensic psychology (MS); forensic sciences (MFSA); forensic toxicology (MS). Part-time and evening/weekend programs available. Postbaccalaureate distance learning degree programs offered (no on-campus study). *Degree requirements:* For master's, comprehensive exam (for some programs), thesis (for some programs). *Entrance requirements:* For master's, MAT (MFSA) or GRE General Test, professional experience (MFSA). Additional exam requirements/recommendations for international students: Required—TOEFL (minimum score 600 paper-based; 250 computer-based), TWE (minimum score 5). *Faculty research:* DNA typing, DNA polymorphism, identification through DNA, disease transmission, forensic dentistry, neurotoxicity of HIV, forensic toxicology method development, toxin detection and characterization.

Oregon State University, Graduate School, College of Agricultural Sciences, Department of Environmental and Molecular Toxicology, Program in Toxicology, Corvallis, OR 97331. Offers MS, PhD. *Students:* 23 full-time (14 women), 2 part-time (1 woman); includes 6 minority (1 African American, 2 American Indian/Alaska Native, 1 Asian American or Pacific Islander, 2 Hispanic Americans), 2 international. Average age 29. In 2009, 5 doctorates awarded. *Degree requirements:* For master's, thesis; for doctorate, thesis/dissertation. *Entrance requirements:* For master's and doctorate, GRE, bachelor's degree in chemistry or biological sciences, minimum GPA of 3.0 in last 90 hours of course work. Additional exam requirements/recommendations for international students: Required—TOEFL. *Application deadline:* For fall admission, 3/1 for domestic students. Applications are processed on a rolling basis. Application fee: $50. *Expenses:* Tuition, state resident: full-time $9774; part-time $362 per credit. Tuition, nonresident: full-time $15,849; part-time $587 per credit. Required fees: $1639. Full-time tuition and fees vary according to course load and program. *Financial support:* Fellowships, research assistantships, Federal Work-Study and institutionally sponsored loans available. Support available to part-time students. Financial award application deadline: 2/1. *Faculty research:* Biochemical mechanisms for toxicology; analytical, comparative, aquatic, and food toxicology; aquaculture of salmonids; immunotoxicology; fish toxicology. *Unit head:* Dr. Robert Tanguay, Director, 541-737-6514, Fax: 541-737-7966, E-mail: robert.tanguay@oregonstate.edu. *Application contact:* Dr. Stella Coakley, Associate Dean, 541-737-5264, Fax: 541-737-3178, E-mail: stella.coakley@oregonstate.edu.

Prairie View A&M University, College of Arts and Sciences, Department of Biology, Prairie View, TX 77446-0519. Offers bio- environmental toxicology (MS); biology (MS). Part-time and evening/weekend programs available. *Faculty:* 5 full-time (2 women). *Students:* 4 full-time (all women), 4 part-time (2 women); all minorities (7 African Americans, 1 Hispanic American). Average age 24. 14 applicants, 86% accepted. In 2009, 8 master's awarded. *Degree requirements:* For master's, comprehensive exam, thesis optional. *Entrance requirements:* For master's, GRE General Test. Additional exam requirements/recommendations for international students: Required—TOEFL. *Application deadline:* For fall admission, 7/1 for domestic and international students; for spring admission, 11/1 for domestic and international students. Applications are processed on a rolling basis. *Expenses:* Tuition, state resident: full-time $2200. Tuition, nonresident: full-time $5600. Required fees: $1720. Tuition and fees vary according to course load. *Financial support:* Federal Work-Study and unspecified assistantships available. Financial award application deadline: 4/1; financial award applicants required to submit FAFSA. *Faculty research:* Geonomics, hypertension, control of gene express, proteins, kigands that interact with hormone receptors, prostate cancer, renin-angiotensin yeast metabolism. *Unit head:* Dr. Harriette Howard-Lee-Block, Head, 936-261-3160, Fax: 936-261-3179, E-mail: hlblock@pvamu.edu. *Application contact:* Dr. Seab A. Smith, Associate Professor, 936-261-3169, Fax: 936-261-3179, E-mail: sasmith@pvamu.edu.

Purdue University, College of Pharmacy and Pharmacal Sciences and Graduate School, Graduate Programs in Pharmacy and Pharmacal Sciences, Department of Medicinal Chemistry and Molecular Pharmacology, West Lafayette, IN 47907. Offers analytical medicinal chemistry (PhD); computational and biophysical medicinal chemistry (PhD); medicinal and bioorganic chemistry (PhD); medicinal biochemistry and molecular biology (PhD); molecular pharmacology and toxicology (PhD); natural products and pharmacognosy (PhD); nuclear pharmacy (MS); radiopharmaceutical chemistry and nuclear pharmacy (PhD); MS/PhD. Terminal master's awarded for partial completion of doctoral program. *Degree requirements:* For master's, thesis; for doctorate, thesis/dissertation. *Entrance requirements:* For master's, GRE General Test, minimum B average; BS in biology, chemistry, or pharmacy; for doctorate, GRE General Test, minimum B average; BS in biology, chemistry, or pharmacology. Additional exam requirements/recommendations for international students: Required—TOEFL. Electronic applications accepted. *Faculty research:* Drug design and development, cancer research, drug synthesis and analysis, chemical pharmacology, environmental toxicology.

Queen's University at Kingston, School of Graduate Studies and Research, Faculty of Health Sciences, Department of Pharmacology and Toxicology, Kingston, ON K7L 3N6, Canada. Offers M Sc, PhD. *Degree requirements:* For master's, thesis; for doctorate, comprehensive exam, thesis/dissertation. *Entrance requirements:* For master's, minimum 2nd class standing, honors bachelor of science degree (life sciences, health sciences, or equivalent); for doctorate, masters of science degree or outstanding performance in honors bachelor of science program. Additional exam requirements/recommendations for international students: Required—TOEFL (minimum score 600 paper-based; 250 computer-based). Electronic applications accepted. *Faculty research:* Biochemical toxicology, cardiovascular pharmacology and neuropharmacology.

Rutgers, The State University of New Jersey, New Brunswick, Graduate School-New Brunswick, Department of Environmental Sciences, Piscataway, NJ 08854-8097. Offers air pollution and resources (MS, PhD); aquatic biology (MS, PhD); aquatic chemistry (MS, PhD); atmospheric science (MS, PhD); chemistry and physics of aerosol and hydrosol systems (MS, PhD); environmental chemistry (MS, PhD); environmental microbiology (MS, PhD); environmental toxicology (PhD); exposure assessment (PhD); fate and effects of pollutants (MS, PhD); pollution prevention and control (MS, PhD); water and wastewater treatment (MS, PhD); water resources (MS, PhD). Terminal master's awarded for partial completion of doctoral program. *Degree requirements:* For master's, comprehensive exam, thesis or alternative, oral final exam; for doctorate, comprehensive exam, thesis/dissertation, thesis defense, qualifying exam. *Entrance requirements:* For master's and doctorate, GRE General Test. Additional exam requirements/recommendations for international students: Required—TOEFL. Electronic applications accepted. *Faculty research:* Biological waste treatment; contaminant fate and transport; air, soil and water quality.

Rutgers, The State University of New Jersey, New Brunswick, Graduate School-New Brunswick, Joint Program in Toxicology, Piscataway, NJ 08854-8097. Offers environmental toxicology (MS, PhD); industrial-occupational toxicology (MS, PhD); nutritional toxicology (MS, PhD); pharmaceutical toxicology (MS, PhD). *Degree requirements:* For master's, thesis; for doctorate, comprehensive exam, thesis/dissertation, qualifying exams (written and oral). *Entrance requirements:* For master's and doctorate, GRE General Test. Additional exam requirements/recommendations for international students: Required—TOEFL. Electronic applications accepted. *Faculty research:* Neurotoxicants, immunotoxicology, carcinogenesis and chemoprevention, molecular toxicology, xenobiotic metabolism.

St. John's University, College of Pharmacy and Allied Health Professions, Graduate Programs in Pharmacy, Program in Toxicology, Queens, NY 11439. Offers MS. Part-time and evening/weekend programs available. *Students:* 17 full-time (13 women), 15 part-time (8 women); includes 16 minority (4 African Americans, 7 Asian Americans or Pacific Islanders, 5 Hispanic Americans), 11 international. Average age 26. 17 applicants, 41% accepted, 6 enrolled. In 2009, 2 master's awarded. *Degree requirements:* For master's, comprehensive exam, thesis optional, one-year residency. *Entrance requirements:* For master's, GRE General Test, minimum GPA of 3.0; 2 letters of recommendation. Additional exam requirements/recommendations for international students: Required—TOEFL (minimum score 500 paper-based; 173 computer-based; 61 iBT), IELTS (minimum score 5.5). *Application deadline:* For fall admission, 3/1 priority date for domestic students, 5/1 priority date for international students; for spring admission, 11/1 priority date for domestic and international students. Applications are processed on a rolling basis. Application fee: $70. Electronic applications accepted. *Expenses:* Contact institution. *Financial support:* Fellowships, research assistantships, career-related internships or fieldwork and scholarships/grants available. Support available to part-time students. Financial award application deadline: 3/1; financial award applicants required to submit FAFSA. *Faculty research:* Neurotoxicology, renal toxicology, toxicology of metals, regulatory toxicology. *Unit head:* Dr. Louis Trombetta, Chair, 718-990-6025, E-mail: trombetl@stjohns.edu. *Application contact:* Kathleen Davis, Director of Graduate Admission, 718-990-2790, Fax: 718-990-5686, E-mail: gradhelp@stjohns.edu.

San Diego State University, Graduate and Research Affairs, College of Health and Human Services, Graduate School of Public Health, San Diego, CA 92182. Offers environmental health (MPH); epidemiology (MPH, PhD), including biostatistics (MPH); global emergency preparedness and response (MS); global health (PhD); health behavior (PhD); health promotion (MPH); health services administration (MPH); toxicology (MS); MPH/MA; MSW/MPH. *Accreditation:* ABET (one or more programs are accredited); CAHME (one or more programs are accredited); CEPH (one or more programs are accredited). Part-time programs available. *Degree requirements:* For master's, comprehensive exam (for some programs), thesis (for some programs); for doctorate, thesis/dissertation. *Entrance requirements:* For master's, GMAT (MPH in health services administration), GRE General Test; for doctorate, GRE General Test. Additional exam requirements/recommendations for international students: Required—TOEFL. *Faculty research:* Evaluation of tobacco, AIDS prevalence and prevention, mammography, infant death project, Alzheimer's in elderly Chinese.

Simon Fraser University, Graduate Studies, Faculty of Science, Department of Biological Sciences, Burnaby, BC V5A 1S6, Canada. Offers biological sciences (M Sc, PhD); environmental toxicology (MET); pest management (MPM). *Degree requirements:* For master's, thesis; for doctorate, thesis/dissertation. *Entrance requirements:* For master's, minimum GPA of 3.0; for doctorate, minimum GPA of 3.5. Additional exam requirements/recommendations for international students: Required—TOEFL or IELTS. Electronic applications accepted. *Faculty research:* Molecular biology, marine biology, ecology, wildlife biology, endocrinology.

Texas A&M University, College of Veterinary Medicine, Department of Veterinary Integrative Biosciences, College Station, TX 77843. Offers epidemiology (MS); food safety/toxicology (MS); veterinary anatomy (MS, PhD); veterinary public health (MS). *Faculty:* 25. *Students:* 34 full-time (22 women), 8 part-time (5 women); includes 2 minority (1 African American, 1 Asian American or Pacific Islander), 20 international. Average age 30. In 2009, 1 master's, 1 doctorate awarded. Terminal master's awarded for partial completion of doctoral program. *Degree requirements:* For master's, comprehensive exam, thesis; for doctorate, comprehensive exam, thesis/dissertation. *Entrance requirements:* For master's and doctorate, GRE General Test, minimum undergraduate GPA of 3.0. Additional exam requirements/recommendations for international students: Required—TOEFL. *Application deadline:* For fall admission, 7/15 priority date for domestic students, 4/1 priority date for international students; for spring admission, 10/1 priority date for domestic students, 9/15 priority date for international students. Applications are processed on a rolling basis. Application fee: $60 ($75 for international students). Electronic applications accepted. *Expenses:* Tuition, state resident: full-time $3991; part-time $221.74 per credit hour. Tuition, nonresident: full-time $9049; part-time $502.74 per credit hour. *Financial support:* In 2009–10, fellowships (averaging $18,000 per year), research assistantships (averaging $15,600 per year), teaching assistantships (averaging $15,600 per year) were awarded; institutionally sponsored loans, unspecified assistantships, and clinical associateships also available. Financial award application deadline: 7/15; financial award applicants required to submit FAFSA. *Faculty research:* Metal toxicology, reproductive biology, genetics of neural development, developmental biology, environmental toxicology. *Unit head:* Dr. E. Tiffany-Castiglioni, Head, 979-862-6559, E-mail: ecastiglioni@cvm.tamu.edu. *Application contact:* Dr. Jane Welsh, Chair, Fax: 979-847-8981, E-mail: jwelsh@cum.tamu.edu.

Texas A&M University, College of Veterinary Medicine, Department of Veterinary Physiology and Pharmacology, College Station, TX 77843. Offers physiology and pharmacology (MS, PhD); toxicology (MS, PhD). *Faculty:* 14. *Students:* 26 full-time (14 women), 3 part-time (2 women); includes 2 minority (1 African American, 1 Asian American or Pacific Islander), 11 international. Average age 30. In 2009, 2 master's, 1 doctorate awarded. *Entrance requirements:* For master's and doctorate, GRE General Test. Additional exam requirements/recommendations for international students: Required—TOEFL. Application fee: $50 ($75 for international students). *Expenses:* Tuition, state resident: full-time $3991; part-time $221.74 per credit hour. Tuition, nonresident: full-time $9049; part-time $502.74 per credit hour. *Financial support:* Fellowships, research assistantships, teaching assistantships available. Financial award application deadline: 4/1; financial award applicants required to submit FAFSA. *Faculty research:* Gamete and embryo physiology, endocrinology, equine laminitis. *Unit head:* Glen Laine, Head, 979-845-7261, E-mail: glaine@tamu.edu. *Application contact:* Graduate Admissions, 979-845-1044, E-mail: admissions@tamu.edu.

Texas Southern University, School of Science and Technology, Program in Environmental Toxicology, Houston, TX 77004-4584. Offers MS, PhD. Part-time programs available. *Students:* 13 full-time (9 women), 20 part-time (12 women); includes 27 minority (25 African Americans, 1 Asian American or Pacific Islander, 1 Hispanic American), 2 international. Average age 35. 9 applicants, 100% accepted, 7 enrolled. In 2009, 1 master's, 10 doctorates awarded. *Degree requirements:* For master's, thesis; for doctorate, thesis/dissertation. *Entrance requirements:* For master's, minimum GPA of 2.75; for doctorate, GRE, minimum GPA of 2.75. *Application deadline:* For fall admission, 7/1 for domestic and international students; for spring admission, 11/1 for domestic and international students. Applications are processed on a rolling basis. Application fee: $35 ($75 for international students). Electronic applications accepted. *Expenses:* Contact institution. *Financial support:* In 2009–10, 2 research assistantships (averaging $4,500

Toxicology

Texas Southern University (continued)
per year), 14 teaching assistantships (averaging $9,607 per year) were awarded; fellowships, institutionally sponsored loans, scholarships/grants, tuition waivers (partial), and unspecified assistantships also available. Financial award application deadline: 5/1; financial award applicants required to submit FAFSA. *Faculty research:* Air quality, water quality, soil remediation, computer modeling. *Unit head:* Dr. Bobby L. Wilson, Professor of Chemistry, 713-313-4259, Fax: 713-313-4217, E-mail: wilson_bl@tsu.edu. *Application contact:* Vera McDaniels, Coordinator, 713-313-4259, Fax: 713-313-4217, E-mail: veramcd@hotmail.com.

Texas Tech University, Graduate School, College of Arts and Sciences, Department of Environmental Toxicology, Lubbock, TX 79409. Offers MS, PhD. Part-time programs available. *Faculty:* 9 full-time (1 woman). *Students:* 47 full-time (24 women), 2 part-time (0 women), 26 international. Average age 28. 48 applicants, 71% accepted, 19 enrolled. In 2009, 5 master's, 6 doctorates awarded. *Degree requirements:* For master's, thesis; for doctorate, thesis/dissertation. *Entrance requirements:* For master's and doctorate, GRE General Test. Additional exam requirements/recommendations for international students: Required—TOEFL (minimum score 550 paper-based; 213 computer-based). *Application deadline:* For fall admission, 3/1 priority date for international students; for spring admission, 11/1 priority date for international students. Applications are processed on a rolling basis. Application fee: $50 ($75 for international students). Electronic applications accepted. *Expenses:* Tuition, state resident: full-time $5100; part-time $213 per credit hour. Tuition, nonresident: full-time $11,748; part-time $490 per credit hour. Required fees: $2298; $50 per credit hour. $555 per semester. *Financial support:* Teaching assistantships with partial tuition reimbursements available. Financial award application deadline: 4/15. *Faculty research:* Terrestrial and aquatic toxicology, biochemical and developmental toxicology, advanced materials, countermeasures to biologic and chemical threats, molecular epidemiology and modeling. Total annual research expenditures: $1.9 million. *Unit head:* Dr. Ronald J. Kendall, Director and Chairman, 806-885-4567, Fax: 806-885-2132, E-mail: ron.kendall@tiehh.ttu.edu. *Application contact:* Dr. Steve Cox, Graduate Program Adviser, 806-885-4567, Fax: 806-885-2132, E-mail: stephen.cox@ttu.edu.

Université de Montréal, Faculty of Medicine, Program in Toxicology and Risk Analysis, Montréal, QC H3C 3J7, Canada. Offers DESS. *Students:* 1 (woman) full-time, 6 part-time (all women). 15 applicants, 0% accepted. In 2009, 8 DESSs awarded. *Application deadline:* For fall admission, 2/1 priority date for domestic students; for winter admission, 11/1 priority date for domestic students; for spring admission, 2/1 priority date for domestic students. Applications are processed on a rolling basis. Application fee: $100. Electronic applications accepted. *Unit head:* Robert Tardif, Director, 514-343-6111 Ext. 1515, Fax: 514-343-2200, E-mail: robert.tardif@umontreal.ca. *Application contact:* Danielle Vinet, Information Contact, 514-343-6134, E-mail: dannielle.vinet@umontreal.ca.

University at Albany, State University of New York, School of Public Health, Department of Environmental Health Sciences, Albany, NY 12222-0001. Offers environmental and analytical chemistry (MS, PhD); environmental and occupational health (MS, PhD); toxicology (MS, PhD). *Degree requirements:* For master's, thesis; for doctorate, comprehensive exam, thesis/dissertation. *Entrance requirements:* For master's and doctorate, GRE General Test, GRE Subject Test, 3 letters of reference. Additional exam requirements/recommendations for international students: Required—TOEFL (minimum score 600 paper-based; 213 computer-based). Electronic applications accepted. *Faculty research:* Xenobiotic metabolism, neurotoxicity of halogenated hydrocarbons, pharmac/toxicogenomics, environmental analytical chemistry.

See Close-Up on page 469.

University at Buffalo, the State University of New York, Graduate School, School of Medicine and Biomedical Sciences, Graduate Programs in Medicine and Biomedical Sciences, Department of Pharmacology and Toxicology, Buffalo, NY 14260. Offers biochemical pharmacology (MS); pharmacology (MA, PhD); MD/PhD. *Faculty:* 15 full-time (1 woman), 2 part-time/adjunct (0 women). *Students:* 9 full-time (4 women); includes 3 minority (1 African American, 1 Asian American or Pacific Islander, 1 Hispanic American), 2 international. Average age 25. 35 applicants, 20% accepted. In 2009, 3 doctorates awarded. Terminal master's awarded for partial completion of doctoral program. *Degree requirements:* For master's, thesis; for doctorate, thesis/dissertation. *Entrance requirements:* For master's and doctorate, GRE General Test, 3 letters of recommendation. Additional exam requirements/recommendations for international students: Required—TOEFL (minimum score 100 iBT). *Application deadline:* For fall admission, 2/1 priority date for domestic and international students. Applications are processed on a rolling basis. Application fee: $50. Electronic applications accepted. *Financial support:* In 2009–10, 2 fellowships with full tuition reimbursements (averaging $24,000 per year), 12 research assistantships with full tuition reimbursements (averaging $21,000 per year) were awarded; teaching assistantships, Federal Work-Study, scholarships/grants, health care benefits, and unspecified assistantships also available. Financial award application deadline: 2/1; financial award applicants required to submit FAFSA. *Faculty research:* Neuropharmacology, toxicology, signal transduction, molecular pharmacology, behavioral pharmacology. Total annual research expenditures: $1.4 million. *Unit head:* Dr. Margarita Dubocovich, Chairman, 716-829-3048, Fax: 716-829-2801, E-mail: mdubo@buffalo.edu. *Application contact:* Sara S. Goodman, Information Contact, 716-829-2800, Fax: 716-829-2801, E-mail: saragood@buffalo.edu.

University of Arkansas for Medical Sciences, Graduate School, Graduate Programs in Biomedical Sciences, Interdisciplinary Toxicology Program, Little Rock, AR 72205-7199. Offers MS, PhD, MD/PhD. *Faculty:* 22 full-time (3 women). *Students:* 7 full-time, 1 part-time. In 2009, 2 doctorates awarded. *Degree requirements:* For master's, thesis; for doctorate, thesis/dissertation. *Entrance requirements:* For master's and doctorate, GRE General Test. Additional exam requirements/recommendations for international students: Required—TOEFL. *Application deadline:* Applications are processed on a rolling basis. Application fee: $0. *Financial support:* In 2009–10, research assistantships with full tuition reimbursements (averaging $24,000 per year); stipend and tuition for doctoral students also available. Support available to part-time students. *Unit head:* Dr. Nancy Rusch, Chair, 501-686-5766, E-mail: jahinson@uams.edu. *Application contact:* Dr. LeeAnn Macmillan-Crow, Program Director, 501-686-5289, E-mail: lmcrow@uams.edu.

University of California, Davis, Graduate Studies, Graduate Group in Pharmacology and Toxicology, Davis, CA 95616. Offers MS, PhD. Terminal master's awarded for partial completion of doctoral program. *Degree requirements:* For master's, comprehensive exam or thesis; for doctorate, thesis/dissertation, qualifying exam. *Entrance requirements:* For master's and doctorate, GRE General Test, minimum GPA of 3.0, course work in biochemistry and/or physiology. Additional exam requirements/recommendations for international students: Required—TOEFL (minimum score 550 paper-based; 213 computer-based). Electronic applications accepted. *Faculty research:* Respiratory, neurochemical, molecular, genetic, and ecological toxicology.

University of California, Irvine, School of Medicine, Department of Pharmacology, Graduate Program in Pharmacology and Toxicology, Irvine, CA 92697. Offers MS, PhD, MD/PhD. *Students:* 17 full-time (6 women); includes 9 minority (2 African Americans, 3 Asian Americans or Pacific Islanders, 4 Hispanic Americans), 3 international. Average age 29. 28 applicants, 21% accepted, 2 enrolled. In 2009, 1 master's, 4 doctorates awarded. *Degree requirements:* For doctorate, thesis/dissertation. *Entrance requirements:* For master's, GRE, minimum GPA of 3.0; for doctorate, GRE General Test, GRE Subject Test, minimum GPA of 3.0. Additional exam requirements/recommendations for international students: Required—TOEFL (minimum score 550 paper-based; 213 computer-based). *Application deadline:* For fall admission, 1/15 priority date for domestic students, 1/15 for international students. Applications are processed on a rolling basis. Application fee: $70 ($90 for international students). Electronic applications accepted. *Financial support:* Fellowships, research assistantships, teaching assistantships, institutionally sponsored loans, traineeships, and unspecified assistantships available. Financial award application deadline: 3/1; financial award applicants required to submit FAFSA. *Unit head:* Sue P. Duckles, Interim Chair, 949-824-4265, Fax: 949-824-4855, E-mail: spduckle@uci.edu. *Application contact:* Alice Decker, Administrator, 949-824-8246, Fax: 949-824-4855, E-mail: adecker@uci.edu.

University of California, Los Angeles, Graduate Division, College of Letters and Science and David Geffen School of Medicine, UCLA ACCESS to Programs in the Molecular, Cellular and Integrative Life Sciences, Los Angeles, CA 90095. Offers biochemistry and molecular biology (PhD); biological chemistry (PhD); cellular and molecular pathology (PhD); human genetics (PhD); microbiology, immunology, and molecular genetics (PhD); molecular biology (PhD); molecular toxicology (PhD); molecular, cellular and integrative physiology (PhD); neurobiology (PhD); oral biology (PhD); physiology (PhD). ACCESS is an umbrella program for first-year coursework in 12 PhD programs. *Students:* 39 full-time (25 women); includes 14 minority (1 African American, 1 American Indian/Alaska Native, 8 Asian Americans or Pacific Islanders, 4 Hispanic Americans), 10 international. Average age 25. 437 applicants, 22% accepted, 30 enrolled. *Degree requirements:* For doctorate, thesis/dissertation, oral and written qualifying exams. *Entrance requirements:* For doctorate, GRE General Test, minimum undergraduate GPA of 3.0. Additional exam requirements/recommendations for international students: Required—TOEFL. *Application deadline:* For fall admission, 12/15 for domestic and international students. Application fee: $70 ($90 for international students). Electronic applications accepted. *Financial support:* In 2009–10, 56 fellowships with full and partial tuition reimbursements, 16 research assistantships with full and partial tuition reimbursements were awarded; teaching assistantships with full and partial tuition reimbursements, Federal Work-Study, institutionally sponsored loans, scholarships/grants, health care benefits, tuition waivers (full and partial), and unspecified assistantships also available. Financial award application deadline: 3/1; financial award applicants required to submit FAFSA. *Faculty research:* Molecular, cellular, and developmental biology; immunology; microbiology; integrative biology. *Unit head:* Dr. Greg I. Payne, Chair, 310-206-3121. *Application contact:* Coordinator, 310-206-3121, Fax: 310-206-5280, E-mail: uclaaccess@mednet.ucla.edu.

See Close-Up on page 239.

University of California, Riverside, Graduate Division, Program in Environmental Toxicology, Riverside, CA 92521-0102. Offers MS, PhD. *Faculty:* 36 full-time (13 women), 1 part-time/adjunct (0 women). *Students:* 23 full-time (14 women); includes 3 minority (all Asian Americans or Pacific Islanders), 11 international. Average age 28. 33 applicants, 45% accepted, 8 enrolled. In 2009, 10 doctorates awarded. Terminal master's awarded for partial completion of doctoral program. *Degree requirements:* For master's, thesis; for doctorate, comprehensive exam, thesis/dissertation, qualifying exams. *Entrance requirements:* For master's and doctorate, GRE General Test, minimum GPA of 3.25. Additional exam requirements/recommendations for international students: Required—TOEFL (minimum score 550 paper-based; 213 computer-based; 80 iBT). *Application deadline:* For fall admission, 1/5 priority date for domestic students, 1/5 for international students; for winter admission, 12/1 for domestic students, 7/1 for international students; for spring admission, 3/1 for domestic students, 10/1 for international students. Applications are processed on a rolling basis. Application fee: $80 ($100 for international students). Electronic applications accepted. *Financial support:* In 2009–10, fellowships with full tuition reimbursements (averaging $16,000 per year), research assistantships with full tuition reimbursements (averaging $18,000 per year), teaching assistantships with full tuition reimbursements (averaging $16,500 per year) were awarded; career-related internships or fieldwork, Federal Work-Study, institutionally sponsored loans, scholarships/grants, health care benefits, tuition waivers (full and partial), and unspecified assistantships also available. Financial award application deadline: 1/5; financial award applicants required to submit FAFSA. *Faculty research:* Cellular/molecular toxicology, atmospheric chemistry, bioremediation, carcinogenesis, mechanism of toxicity. *Unit head:* Dr. Yinsheng Wang, Director, 951-827-2700, Fax: 951-827-5517, E-mail: yinsheng.wang@ucr.edu. *Application contact:* Dawn Huffman Loyola, Graduate Student Affairs Officer, 951-827-4116, Fax: 951-827-5517, E-mail: etox@ucr.edu.

University of California, Santa Cruz, Division of Graduate Studies, Division of Physical and Biological Sciences, Environmental Toxicology Department, Santa Cruz, CA 95064. Offers MS, PhD. *Degree requirements:* For master's, comprehensive exam, thesis; for doctorate, thesis/dissertation, qualifying exams. *Entrance requirements:* For master's and doctorate, GRE.

University of Colorado Denver, School of Pharmacy, Program in Toxicology, Denver, CO 80217-3364. Offers PhD. *Students:* 29 full-time (14 women); includes 1 minority (Hispanic American), 11 international. In 2009, 3 doctorates awarded. *Degree requirements:* For doctorate, comprehensive exam, thesis/dissertation. *Entrance requirements:* For doctorate, GRE General Test, minimum GPA of 3.0, 4 letters of recommendation. Additional exam requirements/recommendations for international students: Required—TOEFL (minimum score 550 paper-based; 213 computer-based). Application fee: $50. *Unit head:* Dr. Vasilis Vasiliou, Director, 303-724-3520, Fax: 303-724-7266, E-mail: vasilis.vasiliou@ucdenver.edu. *Application contact:* Jackie Milowski, Information Contact, 303-724-7263, E-mail: jackie.milowski@ucdenver.edu.

University of Connecticut, Graduate School, School of Pharmacy, Department of Pharmaceutical Sciences, Graduate Program in Pharmacology and Toxicology, Storrs, CT 06269. Offers pharmacology (MS, PhD); toxicology (MS, PhD). *Faculty:* 12 full-time (1 woman). *Students:* 11 full-time (5 women), 2 part-time (0 women); includes 4 minority (1 African American, 2 Asian Americans or Pacific Islanders, 1 Hispanic American). Average age 29. 48 applicants, 4% accepted, 1 enrolled.Terminal master's awarded for partial completion of doctoral program. *Degree requirements:* For master's, comprehensive exam, thesis; for doctorate, thesis/dissertation. *Entrance requirements:* For master's and doctorate, GRE General Test. Additional exam requirements/recommendations for international students: Required—TOEFL (minimum score 550 paper-based; 213 computer-based). *Application deadline:* For fall admission, 2/1 priority date for domestic and international students; for spring admission, 11/1 for domestic students, 10/1 for international students. Applications are processed on a rolling basis. Application fee: $55. Electronic applications accepted. *Expenses:* Tuition, state resident: full-time $4725; part-time $525 per credit. Tuition, nonresident: full-time $12,267; part-time $1363 per credit. Required fees: $346 per semester. Tuition and fees vary according to course load. *Financial support:* In 2009–10, 5 research assistantships with full tuition reimbursements, 6 teaching assistantships with full tuition reimbursements were awarded; fellowships, career-related internships or fieldwork, Federal Work-Study, scholarships/grants, traineeships, health care benefits, and unspecified assistantships also available. Financial award application deadline: 2/1; financial award applicants required to submit FAFSA. *Unit head:* Robin Bogner, Chairperson, 860-486-2136, Fax: 860-486-4998, E-mail: robin.bogner@uconn.edu. *Application contact:* Leslie Lebel, Administrative Assistant, 860-486-4066, Fax: 860-486-4998, E-mail: leslie.lebel@uconn.edu.

University of Florida, College of Pharmacy, Programs in Forensic Science, Gainesville, FL 32611. Offers forensic DNA and serology (MS, Certificate); forensic drug chemistry (MS, Certificate); forensic toxicology (MS, Certificate).

University of Florida, College of Veterinary Medicine, Graduate Program in Veterinary Medical Sciences, Gainesville, FL 32611. Offers forensic toxicology (Certificate); veterinary medical sciences (MS, PhD), including forensic toxicology (MS). Postbaccalaureate distance learning degree programs offered (no on-campus study). Terminal master's awarded for partial completion of doctoral program. *Degree requirements:* For master's, thesis; for doctorate, thesis/dissertation. *Entrance requirements:* For master's and doctorate, GRE General Test, minimum GPA of 3.0. Additional exam requirements/recommendations for international students: Required—TOEFL (minimum score 550 paper-based; 213 computer-based). Electronic applications accepted. *Expenses:* Contact institution.

University of Georgia, College of Veterinary Medicine and Graduate School, Graduate Programs in Veterinary Medicine, Interdisciplinary Graduate Program in Toxicology, Athens, GA 30602. Offers MS, PhD. Postbaccalaureate distance learning degree programs offered (minimal on-campus study). *Faculty:* 9 full-time (3 women), 1 part-time/adjunct (0 women). *Students:* 5 full-time (1 woman), all international. 6 applicants, 67% accepted, 0 enrolled. *Degree requirements:* For master's, thesis; for doctorate, one foreign language, thesis/

dissertation. *Entrance requirements:* For master's and doctorate, GRE General Test. *Application deadline:* For fall admission, 7/1 priority date for domestic students; for spring admission, 11/15 for domestic students. Application fee: $50. Electronic applications accepted. *Expenses:* Tuition, state resident: full-time $6000; part-time $250 per credit hour. Tuition, nonresident: full-time $20,904; part-time $871 per credit hour. Required fees: $730 per semester. *Financial support:* In 2009–10, fellowships with full tuition reimbursements (averaging $14,600 per year), research assistantships with full tuition reimbursements (averaging $16,000 per year) were awarded; scholarships/grants and unspecified assistantships also available. Financial award application deadline: 5/1. *Faculty research:* Neurotoxicology, cell signal modulation, biological toxins, PBPK modeling, environmental risk assessment. Total annual research expenditures: $3 million. *Unit head:* Dr. Jeffrey W. Fisher, Director, 706-542-1001, Fax: 706-542-5285, E-mail: jwfisher@rx.uga.edu. *Application contact:* Dr. Julie A. Coffield, Graduate Coordinator, 706-542-5979, Fax: 706-542-0261, E-mail: coffield@vet.uga.edu.

University of Guelph, Graduate Program Services, Ontario Agricultural College, Department of Environmental Biology, Guelph, ON N1G 2W1, Canada. Offers entomology (M Sc, PhD); environmental microbiology and biotechnology (M Sc, PhD); environmental toxicology (M Sc, PhD); plant and forest systems (M Sc, PhD); plant pathology (M Sc, PhD). Part-time programs available. *Degree requirements:* For master's, thesis; for doctorate, comprehensive exam, thesis/dissertation. *Entrance requirements:* For master's, minimum 75% average during previous 2 years of course work; for doctorate, minimum 75% average. Additional exam requirements/recommendations for international students: Required—TOEFL or IELTS. Electronic applications accepted. *Faculty research:* Entomology, environmental microbiology and biotechnology, environmental toxicology, forest ecology, plant pathology.

University of Guelph, Ontario Veterinary College and Graduate Program Services, Graduate Programs in Veterinary Sciences, Department of Biomedical Sciences, Guelph, ON N1G 2W1, Canada. Offers morphology (M Sc, DV Sc, PhD); neuroscience (M Sc, DV Sc, PhD); pharmacology (M Sc, DV Sc, PhD); physiology (M Sc, DV Sc, PhD); toxicology (M Sc, DV Sc, PhD). Part-time programs available. *Degree requirements:* For master's, thesis; for doctorate, comprehensive exam, thesis/dissertation. *Entrance requirements:* For master's, honors B Sc, minimum 75% average in last 20 courses; for doctorate, M Sc with thesis from accredited institution. Additional exam requirements/recommendations for international students: Required—TOEFL (minimum score 550 paper-based; 213 computer-based; 89 iBT). Electronic applications accepted. *Faculty research:* Cellular morphology; endocrine, vascular and reproductive physiology; clinical pharmacology; veterinary toxicology; developmental biology, neuroscience.

University of Guelph, Ontario Veterinary College, Interdepartmental Program in Toxicology, Guelph, ON N1G 2W1, Canada. Offers M Sc, PhD. Part-time programs available. *Degree requirements:* For master's, thesis (for some programs); for doctorate, comprehensive exam, thesis/dissertation. *Entrance requirements:* For master's, B Sc; for doctorate, M Sc. Additional exam requirements/recommendations for international students: Required—TOEFL (minimum score 550 paper-based; 213 computer-based; 89 iBT).

The University of Iowa, Graduate College, Program in Human Toxicology, Iowa City, IA 52242-1316. Offers MS, PhD. *Degree requirements:* For master's, thesis; for doctorate, comprehensive exam, thesis/dissertation. *Entrance requirements:* For master's and doctorate, GRE General Test, minimum GPA of 3.0. Additional exam requirements/recommendations for international students: Required—TOEFL (minimum score 600 paper-based; 250 computer-based; 100 iBT). Electronic applications accepted.

The University of Kansas, Graduate Studies, School of Pharmacy, Department of Pharmacology and Toxicology, Program in Pharmacology and Toxicology, Lawrence, KS 66045. Offers MS, PhD. *Faculty:* 10 full-time (2 women). *Students:* 11 full-time (10 women), 6 international. Average age 24. 59 applicants, 14% accepted, 4 enrolled. In 2009, 5 master's, 1 doctorate awarded. Terminal master's awarded for partial completion of doctoral program. *Degree requirements:* For master's, comprehensive exam, thesis; for doctorate, comprehensive exam, thesis/dissertation. *Entrance requirements:* For master's, GRE; for doctorate, GRE (minimum score: 600 verbal, 600 quantitative, 4.5 analytic). Additional exam requirements/recommendations for international students: Required—TOEFL (minimum score 600 paper-based; 250 computer-based; 100 iBT). *Application deadline:* For fall admission, 1/15 priority date for domestic students, 2/1 priority date for international students. Applications are processed on a rolling basis. Application fee: $45 ($55 for international students). Electronic applications accepted. *Expenses:* Tuition, state resident: full-time $6492; part-time $270.50 per credit hour. Tuition, nonresident: full-time $15,510; part-time $646.25 per credit hour. Required fees: $847; $70.56 per credit hour. Tuition and fees vary according to course load and program. *Financial support:* Fellowships with full tuition reimbursements, research assistantships with full tuition reimbursements available. *Faculty research:* Neuropharmacology, neurodegeneration. *Unit head:* Dr. Nancy Muma, Chair, 785-864-4001, Fax: 785-864-5219, E-mail: nmuma@ku.edu. *Application contact:* Dr. Rick T. Dobrowsky, Professor/Director of Graduate Studies, 785-864-3531, Fax: 785-864-5219, E-mail: dobrowsky@ku.edu.

The University of Kansas, University of Kansas Medical Center, School of Medicine, Department of Pharmacology, Toxicology and Therapeutics, Kansas City, KS 66160. Offers pharmacology (MS, PhD); toxicology (MS, PhD); MD/MS; MD/PhD. *Faculty:* 27 full-time, 2 part-time/adjunct. *Students:* 1 (woman) full-time, 26 part-time (16 women); includes 1 minority (Hispanic American), 14 international. Average age 28. In 2009, 4 doctorates awarded. Terminal master's awarded for partial completion of doctoral program. *Degree requirements:* For master's, comprehensive exam, thesis; for doctorate, one foreign language, comprehensive exam, thesis/dissertation. *Entrance requirements:* For master's and doctorate, GRE General Test. Additional exam requirements/recommendations for international students: Required—TOEFL. *Application deadline:* For fall admission, 1/15 priority date for domestic students. Applications are processed on a rolling basis. Application fee: $0. Electronic applications accepted. *Expenses:* Tuition, state resident: full-time $6492; part-time $270.50 per credit hour. Tuition, nonresident: full-time $15,510; part-time $646.25 per credit hour. Required fees: $847; $70.56 per credit hour. Tuition and fees vary according to course load and program. *Financial support:* In 2009–10, 26 students received support, including 5 fellowships with full tuition reimbursements available (averaging $24,000 per year), 18 research assistantships with full tuition reimbursements available (averaging $24,000 per year), 3 teaching assistantships with full tuition reimbursements available (averaging $24,000 per year); Federal Work-Study, scholarships/grants, traineeships, and unspecified assistantships also available. Support available to part-time students. Financial award application deadline: 3/30; financial award applicants required to submit FAFSA. *Faculty research:* Liver nuclear receptors, hepatobiliary transporters, pharmacogenomics, estrogen-induced carcinogenesis, neuropharmacology of pain and depression. Total annual research expenditures: $7.4 million. *Unit head:* Dr. Curtis D. Klaassen, Chairman, 913-588-7140, Fax: 913-588-7501, E-mail: cklaasse@kumc.edu. *Application contact:* Dr. Bruno Hagenbuch, Chair, Department Graduate Committee, 913-588-0028, Fax: 913-588-7501, E-mail: bhagenbuch@kumc.edu.

University of Kentucky, Graduate School, Graduate School Programs from the College of Medicine, Program in Toxicology, Lexington, KY 40506-0032. Offers MS, PhD. Terminal master's awarded for partial completion of doctoral program. *Degree requirements:* For master's, comprehensive exam, thesis optional; for doctorate, comprehensive exam, thesis/dissertation. *Entrance requirements:* For master's, GRE General Test, minimum undergraduate GPA of 2.75; for doctorate, GRE General Test, minimum graduate GPA of 3.0. Additional exam requirements/recommendations for international students: Required—TOEFL (minimum score 550 paper-based; 213 computer-based). Electronic applications accepted. *Faculty research:* Chemical carcinogenesis, immunotoxicology, neurotoxicology, metabolism and disposition, gene regulation.

University of Louisville, School of Medicine, Department of Pharmacology and Toxicology, Louisville, KY 40292-0001. Offers MS, PhD, MD/PhD. *Faculty:* 59 full-time (9 women). *Students:* 32 full-time (19 women), 5 part-time (4 women); includes 10 minority (6 African Americans, 3 Asian Americans or Pacific Islanders, 1 Hispanic American), 12 international. Average age 29. 32 applicants, 28% accepted, 6 enrolled. In 2009, 3 master's, 3 doctorates awarded. Terminal master's awarded for partial completion of doctoral program. *Degree requirements:* For master's, thesis; for doctorate, comprehensive exam, thesis/dissertation. *Entrance requirements:* For master's, GRE General Test (minimum score 1000 verbal and quantitative), minimum GPA of 3.0; for doctorate, GRE General Test (Verbal and Quantitative minimum score of 1000), minimum GPA of 3.0. Additional exam requirements/recommendations for international students: Required—TOEFL. *Application deadline:* For fall admission, 1/15 priority date for domestic and international students. Applications are processed on a rolling basis. Application fee: $50. Electronic applications accepted. *Financial support:* In 2009–10, 32 students received support, including 11 fellowships with full tuition reimbursements available (averaging $22,000 per year), 21 research assistantships with full tuition reimbursements available (averaging $22,000 per year). Financial award application deadline: 4/15. *Faculty research:* Molecular pharmacogenetics; epidemiology; functional genomics; genetic predisposition to chemical carcinogenesis and drug toxicity; mechanisms of oxidative stress; alcohol-induced hepatitis, pancreatitis, and hepatocellular carcinoma; molecular and cardiac toxicology; molecular biology and genetics of DNA damage and repair in humans; mechanisms of chemoresistance; arsenic toxicity and cell cycle disruption; molecular pharmacology of novel G protein-coupled receptors. *Unit head:* Dr. David W. Hein, Chair, 502-852-5141, Fax: 502-852-7868, E-mail: dhein@louisville.edu. *Application contact:* Heddy R. Rubin, Information Contact, 502-852-5741, Fax: 502-852-7868, E-mail: hrrubi01@gwise.louisville.edu.

University of Maryland, Baltimore, Graduate School, Graduate Program in Life Sciences, Program in Toxicology, Baltimore, MD 21201. Offers MS, PhD, MD/MS, MD/PhD. Part-time programs available. *Students:* 16 full-time (9 women), 13 part-time (6 women); includes 4 minority (3 Asian Americans or Pacific Islanders, 1 Hispanic American), 6 international. Average age 31. 49 applicants, 31% accepted, 5 enrolled. In 2009, 1 master's, 3 doctorates awarded. *Degree requirements:* For doctorate, comprehensive exam, thesis/dissertation. *Entrance requirements:* For master's and doctorate, GRE General Test, GRE Subject Test, minimum GPA of 3.0. Additional exam requirements/recommendations for international students: Required—TOEFL (minimum score 550 paper-based; 80 iBT); Recommended—IELTS (minimum score 7). *Application deadline:* For fall admission, 2/1 for domestic students, 1/15 for international students. Application fee: $50. Electronic applications accepted. *Expenses:* Tuition, state resident: full-time $7290; part-time $405 per credit hour. Tuition, nonresident: full-time $12,780; part-time $710 per credit hour. Required fees: $774; $10 per credit hour. $297 per semester. Tuition and fees vary according to course load, degree level and program. *Financial support:* In 2009–10, research assistantships with partial tuition reimbursements (averaging $25,000 per year); fellowships also available. Financial award application deadline: 3/1. *Unit head:* Dr. Katherine S. Squibb, Director, 410-706-8196, E-mail: ksquibb@umaryland.edu. *Application contact:* Linda Horne, Program Coordinator, E-mail: lhorne@som.umaryland.edu.

University of Maryland, Baltimore, School of Medicine, Department of Epidemiology and Preventive Medicine, Baltimore, MD 21201. Offers biostatistics (MS); clinical research (MS); epidemiology (PhD); epidemiology and preventive medicine (MPH, MS); gerontology (PhD); human genetics and genomic (MS, PhD); molecular epidemiology (PhD); toxicology (MS, PhD); JD/MS; MD/PhD; MS/PhD. *Accreditation:* CEPH. Part-time programs available. *Students:* 64 full-time (42 women), 60 part-time (40 women); includes 40 minority (17 African Americans, 19 Asian Americans or Pacific Islanders, 4 Hispanic Americans), 16 international. Average age 31. 207 applicants, 48% accepted, 50 enrolled. In 2009, 24 master's, 9 doctorates awarded. *Entrance requirements:* For master's and doctorate, GRE General Test, minimum GPA of 3.0. Additional exam requirements/recommendations for international students: Required—TOEFL; Recommended—IELTS. *Application deadline:* For fall admission, 1/15 for domestic and international students. Application fee: $50. Electronic applications accepted. *Expenses:* Tuition, state resident: full-time $7290; part-time $405 per credit hour. Tuition, nonresident: full-time $12,780; part-time $710 per credit hour. Required fees: $774; $10 per credit hour. $297 per semester. Tuition and fees vary according to course load, degree level and program. *Financial support:* In 2009–10, research assistantships with partial tuition reimbursements (averaging $25,000 per year); fellowships also available. Financial award application deadline: 3/1. *Unit head:* Dr. Patricia Langenberg, Program Director, 410-706-3251, Fax: 410-706-8013. *Application contact:* Rachael Holmes, Academic Coordinator, 410-706-8492, Fax: 410-706-4225, E-mail: rholmes@epi.umaryland.edu.

University of Maryland Eastern Shore, Graduate Programs, Department of Natural Sciences, Program in Toxicology, Princess Anne, MD 21853-1299. Offers MS, PhD.

University of Medicine and Dentistry of New Jersey, Graduate School of Biomedical Sciences, Graduate Programs in Biomedical Sciences–Piscataway, Piscataway, NJ 08854-5635. Offers biochemistry and molecular biology (MS, PhD); biomedical engineering (MS, PhD); cellular and molecular pharmacology (MS, PhD); environmental sciences/exposure assessment (PhD); molecular genetics, microbiology and immunology (MS, PhD); neuroscience (MS, PhD); physiology and integrative biology (MS, PhD); toxicology (PhD); MD/PhD. *Students:* 397 full-time (209 women), 31 part-time (14 women); includes 109 minority (21 African Americans, 1 American Indian/Alaska Native, 58 Asian Americans or Pacific Islanders, 29 Hispanic Americans), 151 international. Average age 28. 1,030 applicants, 15% accepted, 89 enrolled. In 2009, 21 master's, 62 doctorates awarded. Terminal master's awarded for partial completion of doctoral program. *Degree requirements:* For master's, thesis, ethics training; for doctorate, comprehensive exam, thesis/dissertation, ethics training. *Entrance requirements:* For master's and doctorate, GRE General Test. Additional exam requirements/recommendations for international students: Required—TOEFL. *Application deadline:* For fall admission, 1/5 for domestic students. Applications are processed on a rolling basis. Application fee: $65. Electronic applications accepted. *Financial support:* Fellowships, research assistantships, teaching assistantships, career-related internships or fieldwork, Federal Work-Study, traineeships, health care benefits, and unspecified assistantships available. *Unit head:* Dr. Terri Goss Kinzy, Senior Associate Dean, Graduate School, 732-235-5016, Fax: 732-235-4720, E-mail: gsbspisc@umdnj.edu. *Application contact:* Johanna Sierra, University Registrar, 732-235-5016, Fax: 732-235-4720.

University of Michigan, School of Public Health, Department of Environmental Health Sciences, Ann Arbor, MI 48109. Offers environmental health sciences (MS, PhD); environmental quality and health (MPH); human nutrition (MPH); industrial hygiene (MPH, MS); nutritional sciences (MS); occupational and environmental epidemiology (MPH); toxicology (MPH, MS, PhD). *Accreditation:* CEPH (one or more programs are accredited). Part-time programs available. Terminal master's awarded for partial completion of doctoral program. *Degree requirements:* For master's, thesis (for some programs); for doctorate, thesis/dissertation, qualifying exam, oral defense of dissertation, preliminary exam. *Entrance requirements:* For master's and doctorate, GRE General Test and/or MCAT. Additional exam requirements/recommendations for international students: Required—TOEFL (minimum score 560 paper-based; 220 computer-based; 100 iBT). Electronic applications accepted. *Expenses:* Tuition, state resident: full-time $17,286; part-time $1099 per credit hour. Tuition, nonresident: full-time $34,944; part-time $2080 per credit hour. Required fees: $95 per semester. Tuition and fees vary according to course load, degree level and program. *Faculty research:* Toxicology; occupational hygiene; nutrition; environmental exposure sciences; environmental epidemiology.

University of Minnesota, Duluth, Graduate School, Program in Toxicology, Duluth, MN 55812-2496. Offers MS, PhD. *Faculty:* 20 full-time (1 woman), 12 part-time/adjunct (1 woman). *Students:* 7 full-time (3 women); includes 3 Asian Americans or Pacific Islanders, 1 Hispanic American. Average age 35. 13 applicants, 8% accepted, 1 enrolled. In 2009, 1 master's, 1 doctorate awarded. Terminal master's awarded for partial completion of doctoral program. *Degree requirements:* For master's, thesis; for doctorate, comprehensive exam, thesis/dissertation, written and oral preliminary and final exams. *Entrance requirements:* For master's and doctorate, GRE General Test, BS in basic science; full year each of biology, chemistry, and physics; mathematics coursework through calculus. Additional exam requirements/recommendations for international students: Required—TOEFL (minimum score 550 paper-based; 79 iBT). *Application deadline:* For fall admission, 3/15 priority date for domestic and

Toxicology

University of Minnesota, Duluth (continued)
international students. Applications are processed on a rolling basis. Application fee: $75 ($95 for international students). Electronic applications accepted. *Financial support:* In 2009–10, 7 research assistantships with full tuition reimbursements (averaging $17,000 per year) were awarded; institutionally sponsored loans, scholarships/grants, health care benefits, and unspecified assistantships also available. *Faculty research:* Structure activity correlations, neurotoxicity, aquatic toxicology, biochemical mechanisms, immunotoxicology. *Unit head:* Dr. Kendall B. Wallace, Director of Graduate Studies, 218-726-8899, Fax: 218-726-8014, E-mail: kwallace@d.umn.edu. *Application contact:* Cheryl J. Beeman, Director of Graduate Studies Assistant, 218-726-6354, Fax: 218-726-8152, E-mail: toxgrad@d.umn.edu.

University of Minnesota, Duluth, Medical School, Department of Biochemistry, Molecular Biology and Biophysics, Duluth, MN 55812-2496. Offers biochemistry, molecular biology and biophysics (MS); biology and biophysics (PhD); social, administrative, and clinical pharmacy (MS, PhD); toxicology (MS, PhD). *Faculty:* 10 full-time (3 women). *Students:* 16 full-time (5 women); includes 3 minority (all Asian Americans or Pacific Islanders). Average age 29. 7 applicants, 29% accepted, 2 enrolled. In 2009, 1 master's, 1 doctorate awarded. Terminal master's awarded for partial completion of doctoral program. *Degree requirements:* For master's, comprehensive exam, thesis; for doctorate, comprehensive exam, thesis/dissertation. *Entrance requirements:* For master's and doctorate, GRE General Test. Additional exam requirements/recommendations for international students: Required—TOEFL. *Application deadline:* For winter admission, 1/3 for domestic students, 1/2 for international students; for spring admission, 3/15 priority date for domestic and international students. Application fee: $75 ($95 for international students). Electronic applications accepted. *Financial support:* In 2009–10, 8 students received support, including research assistantships with full tuition reimbursements available (averaging $27,300 per year), teaching assistantships with full tuition reimbursements available (averaging $27,300 per year); career-related internships or fieldwork, scholarships/grants, health care benefits, and unspecified assistantships also available. Financial award application deadline: 9/1. *Faculty research:* Intestinal cancer biology; hepatotoxins and mitochondriopathies; toxicology; cell cycle regulation in stem cells; neurobiology of brain development, trace metal function and blood-brain barrier; hibernation biology. Total annual research expenditures: $1.5 million. *Unit head:* Dr. Lester R. Drewes, Professor/Head, 218-726-7925, Fax: 218-726-8014, E-mail: ldrewes@d.umn.edu. *Application contact:* Cheryl Beeman, Administrative Assistant, 218-726-6354, Fax: 218-726-8014, E-mail: ahcd@d.umn.edu.

University of Minnesota, Twin Cities Campus, School of Public Health, Division of Environmental Health Sciences, Area in Environmental Toxicology, Minneapolis, MN 55455-0213. Offers MPH, MS, PhD. *Degree requirements:* For doctorate, thesis/dissertation. *Entrance requirements:* For master's and doctorate, GRE General Test. Electronic applications accepted.

University of Mississippi Medical Center, School of Graduate Studies in the Health Sciences, Department of Pharmacology and Toxicology, Jackson, MS 39216-4505. Offers pharmacology (MS, PhD); toxicology (MS, PhD); MD/PhD. Terminal master's awarded for partial completion of doctoral program. *Degree requirements:* For master's, thesis; for doctorate, thesis/dissertation, first authored publication. *Entrance requirements:* For master's and doctorate, GRE General Test, minimum GPA of 3.0. *Faculty research:* Neuropharmacology, environmental toxicology, aging, immunopharmacology, cardiovascular pharmacology.

The University of Montana, Graduate School, College of Health Professions and Biomedical Sciences, Skaggs School of Pharmacy, Department of Biomedical and Pharmaceutical Sciences, Missoula, MT 59812-0002. Offers biomedical sciences (PhD); neuroscience (MS, PhD); pharmaceutical sciences (MS); toxicology (MS, PhD). *Accreditation:* ACPE. *Degree requirements:* For master's, oral defense of thesis; for doctorate, research dissertation defense. *Entrance requirements:* For master's and doctorate, GRE General Test. Additional exam requirements/recommendations for international students: Required—TOEFL (minimum score 540 paper-based; 210 computer-based). Electronic applications accepted. *Faculty research:* Cardiovascular pharmacology, medicinal chemistry, neurosciences, environmental toxicology, pharmacogenetics, cancer.

University of Nebraska–Lincoln, Graduate College, Interdepartmental Area of Environmental Health, Occupational Health and Toxicology, Lincoln, NE 68588. Offers MS, PhD. *Entrance requirements:* Additional exam requirements/recommendations for international students: Required—TOEFL (minimum score 550 paper-based; 213 computer-based). Electronic applications accepted.

University of Nebraska Medical Center, Graduate Studies, Program in Environmental Health, Occupational Health and Toxicology, Omaha, NE 68198. Offers MS, PhD. Terminal master's awarded for partial completion of doctoral program. *Degree requirements:* For master's, comprehensive exam (for some programs), thesis; for doctorate, comprehensive exam (for some programs), thesis/dissertation. *Entrance requirements:* For master's, GRE General Test, bachelor's degree in chemistry, biology, biochemistry or related area; for doctorate, GRE General Test, BS in chemistry, biology, biochemistry or related area. Additional exam requirements/recommendations for international students: Required—TOEFL (minimum score 550 paper-based; 213 computer-based). Electronic applications accepted. *Faculty research:* Mechanisms of carcinogenesis, alcohol and metal toxicity, DNA damage, human molecular genetics, agrochemicals in soil and water.

University of New Mexico, School of Medicine, Biomedical Sciences Graduate Program, Albuquerque, NM 87131-5196. Offers biochemistry and molecular biology (MS, PhD); cell biology and physiology (MS, PhD); molecular genetics and microbiology (MS, PhD); neuroscience (MS, PhD); pathology (MS, PhD); toxicology (MS, PhD). Part-time programs available. Terminal master's awarded for partial completion of doctoral program. *Degree requirements:* For master's, thesis; for doctorate, comprehensive exam, thesis/dissertation. *Entrance requirements:* For master's and doctorate, GRE General Test, minimum undergraduate GPA of 3.0. Additional exam requirements/recommendations for international students: Required—TOEFL. Electronic applications accepted. *Expenses:* Tuition, state resident: full-time $2099; part-time $233.20 per credit hour. Tuition, nonresident: full-time $6650. Required fees: $25 per semester. Tuition and fees vary according to course load, program and reciprocity agreements. *Faculty research:* Signal transduction, infectious disease, biology of cancer, structural biology, neuroscience.

The University of North Carolina at Chapel Hill, School of Medicine, Curriculum in Toxicology, Chapel Hill, NC 27599. Offers MS, PhD. Terminal master's awarded for partial completion of doctoral program. *Degree requirements:* For master's, comprehensive exam, thesis; for doctorate, comprehensive exam, thesis/dissertation. *Entrance requirements:* For doctorate, GRE General Test. Electronic applications accepted. *Faculty research:* Molecular and cellular toxicology, carcinogenesis, neurotoxicology, pulmonary toxicology, developmental toxicology.

University of Prince Edward Island, Atlantic Veterinary College, Graduate Program in Veterinary Medicine, Charlottetown, PE C1A 4P3, Canada. Offers anatomy (M Sc, PhD); bacteriology (M Sc, PhD); clinical pharmacology (M Sc, PhD); clinical sciences (M Sc, PhD); epidemiology (M Sc, PhD), including reproduction; fish health (M Sc, PhD); food animal nutrition (M Sc, PhD); immunology (M Sc, PhD); microanatomy (M Sc, PhD); parasitology (M Sc, PhD); pathology (M Sc, PhD); pharmacology (M Sc, PhD); physiology (M Sc, PhD); toxicology (M Sc, PhD); veterinary science (M Vet Sc); virology (M Sc, PhD). Part-time programs available. *Degree requirements:* For master's, thesis; for doctorate, thesis/dissertation. *Entrance requirements:* For master's, DVM, B Sc honors degree, or equivalent; for doctorate, M Sc. Additional exam requirements/recommendations for international students: Required—TOEFL (minimum score 550 paper-based; 213 computer-based; 80 iBT). *Expenses:* Contact institution. *Faculty research:* Animal health management, infectious diseases, fin fish and shellfish health, basic biomedical sciences, ecosystem health.

University of Puerto Rico, Medical Sciences Campus, School of Medicine, Division of Graduate Studies, Department of Pharmacology and Toxicology, San Juan, PR 00936-5067. Offers MS, PhD. *Degree requirements:* For master's, one foreign language, thesis; for doctorate, one foreign language, comprehensive exam, thesis/dissertation. *Entrance requirements:* For master's and doctorate, GRE General Test, GRE Subject Test, interview, minimum GPA of 3.0, 3 letters of recommendation. Electronic applications accepted. *Faculty research:* Cardiovascular, central nervous system, and endocrine pharmacology; anti-cancer drugs; sodium pump; mitochondrial DNA repair; Huntington's disease.

University of Rhode Island, Graduate School, College of Pharmacy, Department of Biomedical and Pharmaceutical Sciences, Kingston, RI 02881. Offers medicinal chemistry and pharmacognosy (MS, PhD); pharmaceutics and pharmacokinetics (MS, PhD); pharmacology and toxicology (MS, PhD). Part-time programs available. *Faculty:* 17 full-time (5 women), 1 part-time/adjunct (0 women). *Students:* 33 full-time (16 women), 20 part-time (7 women); includes 12 minority (2 African Americans, 10 Asian Americans or Pacific Islanders), 19 international. In 2009, 6 master's, 6 doctorates awarded. *Entrance requirements:* For master's and doctorate, GRE, 2 letters of recommendation. Additional exam requirements/recommendations for international students: Required—TOEFL (minimum score 550 paper-based; 213 computer-based). Application fee: $65. Electronic applications accepted. *Expenses:* Tuition, state resident: full-time $8828; part-time $490 per credit hour. Tuition, nonresident: full-time $22,100; part-time $1228 per credit hour. Required fees: $1118; $57 per semester. Tuition and fees vary according to program. *Financial support:* In 2009–10, 6 research assistantships with partial tuition reimbursements (averaging $7,119 per year), 12 teaching assistantships with full and partial tuition reimbursements (averaging $10,115 per year) were awarded. Financial award applicants required to submit FAFSA. *Faculty research:* Chemical carcinogenesis with a major emphasis on the structural and synthetic aspects of DNA-adduct formation, drug-drug/herb interaction, drug-genetic interaction, signaling of nuclear receptors, transcriptional regulation, oncogenesis. Total annual research expenditures: $6.2 million. *Unit head:* Dr. Clinton O. Chichester, Chair, 401-874-5034, Fax: 401-874-5787, E-mail: chichester@uri.edu. *Application contact:* Dr. David C. Rowley, Graduate Coordinator, 401-874-9228, Fax: 401-874-2516, E-mail: drowley@uri.edu.

University of Rochester, School of Medicine and Dentistry, Graduate Programs in Medicine and Dentistry, Department of Environmental Medicine, Program in Toxicology, Rochester, NY 14627. Offers MS, PhD. *Degree requirements:* For doctorate, thesis/dissertation, qualifying exam. *Entrance requirements:* For master's and doctorate, GRE General Test.

University of Saskatchewan, College of Graduate Studies and Research, Toxicology Centre, Saskatoon, SK S7N 5A2, Canada. Offers M Sc, PhD, Diploma. *Degree requirements:* For master's, thesis; for doctorate, thesis/dissertation. *Entrance requirements:* Additional exam requirements/recommendations for international students: Required—TOEFL. Tuition and fees charges are reported in Canadian dollars. *Expenses:* Tuition, area resident: Full-time $3000 Canadian dollars; part-time $500 Canadian dollars per term. Required fees: $700 Canadian dollars; $100 Canadian dollars per term.

University of South Alabama, Graduate School, Program in Environmental Toxicology, Mobile, AL 36688-0002. Offers MS. *Entrance requirements:* For master's, GRE. *Expenses:* Tuition, state resident: part-time $218 per contact hour. Required fees: $1102 per year.

University of Southern California, Graduate School, School of Pharmacy, Molecular Pharmacology and Toxicology Program, Los Angeles, CA 90089. Offers pharmacology and pharmaceutical sciences (MS, PhD). *Faculty:* 19 full-time (4 women), 4 part-time/adjunct (2 women). *Students:* 18 full-time (11 women), 1 (woman) part-time; includes 4 minority (1 African American, 2 Asian Americans or Pacific Islanders, 1 Hispanic American), 12 international. 51 applicants. In 2009, 1 master's, 3 doctorates awarded. Terminal master's awarded for partial completion of doctoral program. *Degree requirements:* For master's, thesis; for doctorate, thesis/dissertation, 24 units of formal course work (excluding research and seminar courses). *Entrance requirements:* For master's and doctorate, GRE. Additional exam requirements/recommendations for international students: Required—TOEFL (minimum score 603 paper-based; 250 computer-based; 100 iBT). *Application deadline:* For fall admission, 1/15 for domestic and international students; for spring admission, 10/15 for domestic and international students. Application fee: $75. Electronic applications accepted. *Expenses:* Contact institution. *Financial support:* In 2009–10, 3 fellowships with full tuition reimbursements (averaging $28,656 per year), 11 research assistantships with full tuition reimbursements (averaging $30,144 per year), 13 teaching assistantships with full tuition reimbursements (averaging $29,400 per year) were awarded; health care benefits also available. *Faculty research:* Degenerative diseases, toxicology of drugs. *Unit head:* Dr. Sarah Hamm-Alvarez, Professor/Department Chair, 323-442-3269, E-mail: gongora@usc.edu. *Application contact:* Wade Thompson-Harper, Coordinator of Graduate Affairs, 323-442-1474, E-mail: pharmgrad@usc.edu.

The University of Texas Medical Branch, Graduate School of Biomedical Sciences, Program in Pharmacology and Toxicology, Galveston, TX 77555. Offers pharmacology (MS); pharmacology and toxicology (PhD). *Students:* 10 full-time (2 women); includes 5 minority (2 African Americans, 1 Asian American or Pacific Islander, 2 Hispanic Americans), 2 international. Average age 30. In 2009, 1 master's, 6 doctorates awarded. *Degree requirements:* For master's, thesis or alternative; for doctorate, thesis/dissertation. *Entrance requirements:* For master's and doctorate, GRE General Test. Additional exam requirements/recommendations for international students: Required—TOEFL (minimum score 550 paper-based; 213 computer-based). *Application deadline:* Applications are processed on a rolling basis. Application fee: $30 ($75 for international students). *Financial support:* In 2009–10, fellowships (averaging $25,000 per year), research assistantships with full tuition reimbursements (averaging $25,000 per year) were awarded. Financial award applicants required to submit FAFSA. *Unit head:* Dr. Kenneth M. Johnson, Director, 409-772-1561, Fax: 409-772-9642, E-mail: kmjohnso@utmb.edu. *Application contact:* Penny Welsh, Program Coordinator, 409-772-9626, Fax: 409-747-7050, E-mail: pwelsh@utmb.edu.

University of the Sciences in Philadelphia, College of Graduate Studies, Program in Pharmacology and Toxicology, Philadelphia, PA 19104-4495. Offers pharmacology (MS, PhD); toxicology (MS, PhD). Terminal master's awarded for partial completion of doctoral program. *Degree requirements:* For master's, thesis; for doctorate, comprehensive exam, thesis/dissertation. *Entrance requirements:* For master's and doctorate, GRE General Test. Additional exam requirements/recommendations for international students: Required—TOEFL, TWE. *Expenses:* Contact institution. *Faculty research:* Autonomic, cardiovascular, cellular, and molecular pharmacology; mechanisms of carcinogenesis; drug metabolism.

University of Toronto, School of Graduate Studies, Life Sciences Division, Department of Pharmacology and Toxicology, Toronto, ON M5S 1A1, Canada. Offers M Sc, PhD. Part-time programs available. *Degree requirements:* For master's, thesis; for doctorate, thesis/dissertation. *Entrance requirements:* For master's, B Sc or equivalent; background in pharmacology, biochemistry, and physiology; minimum B+ earned in at least 4 senior level classes; for doctorate, minimum B+ average.

University of Utah, Graduate School, College of Pharmacy, Department of Pharmacology and Toxicology, Salt Lake City, UT 84112. Offers PhD. *Faculty:* 19 full-time (5 women), 2 part-time/adjunct (0 women). *Students:* 18 full-time (9 women), 3 part-time (2 women); includes 2 minority (both Hispanic Americans), 1 international. Average age 30. 66 applicants, 9% accepted, 3 enrolled. In 2009, 2 doctorates awarded. Terminal master's awarded for partial completion of doctoral program. *Degree requirements:* For doctorate, thesis/dissertation, final exam. *Entrance requirements:* For doctorate, GRE Subject Test, BS in biology, chemistry, pharmacy, or biochemistry. Additional exam requirements/recommendations for international students: Required—TOEFL (minimum score 600 paper-based; 250 computer-based; 100 iBT). *Application deadline:* For fall admission, 1/15 for domestic students, 1/16 for international students. Application fee: $55 ($65 for international students). *Expenses:* Tuition, state resident: full-time $4004; part-time $1674 per semester. Tuition, nonresident: full-time $14,134; part-time $5915 per semester. Required fees: $324 per semester. Tuition and fees vary according to course load, degree level and program. *Financial support:* In 2009–10, 14 students received support, including fellowships with full tuition reimbursements available (averaging $25,000 per year), 14 research assistantships with full tuition reimbursements available (averaging $25,000 per year). *Faculty research:* Neuropharmacology, neurochemistry, biochemistry, molecular pharmacology, analytical chemistry. Total annual research expenditures: $4.3 million. *Unit head:* Dr. William R. Crowley, Chairman, 801-581-6287, Fax: 801-585-5111, E-mail: william.crowley@deans.pharm.utah.edu. *Application contact:* Sheila H. Merrill, Executive Secretary, 801-581-6287, Fax: 801-585-5111, E-mail: sheila.merrill@pharm.utah.edu.

University of Washington, Graduate School, School of Public Health, Department of Environmental and Occupational Health Sciences, Seattle, WA 98195. Offers environmental and occupational health (MPH); environmental and occupational hygiene (PhD); environmental health (MS); occupational and environmental exposure sciences (MS); occupational and environmental medicine (MPH); toxicology (MS, PhD). Part-time programs available. *Faculty:* 32 full-time (5 women), 10 part-time/adjunct (4 women). *Students:* 59 full-time (40 women), 11 part-time (4 women); includes 17 minority (2 African Americans, 1 American Indian/Alaska Native, 12 Asian Americans or Pacific Islanders, 2 Hispanic Americans), 5 international. Average age 29. 114 applicants, 31% accepted, 20 enrolled. In 2009, 23 master's, 6 doctorates awarded. Terminal master's awarded for partial completion of doctoral program. *Degree requirements:* For master's, thesis (for some programs), project or portfolio (for some tracks); for doctorate, comprehensive exam, thesis/dissertation. *Entrance requirements:* For master's and doctorate, GRE General Test, minimum GPA of 3.0, prerequisite course work in biology, chemistry, physics, calculus. Additional exam requirements/recommendations for international students: Required—TOEFL (minimum score 580 paper-based; 237 computer-based; 70 iBT). *Application deadline:* For fall admission, 1/1 for domestic students, 11/1 for international students. Application fee: $50. Electronic applications accepted. *Financial support:* In 2009–10, 53 students received support, including 19 fellowships with full tuition reimbursements available (averaging $21,048 per year), 33 research assistantships with full tuition reimbursements available (averaging $21,048 per year), 4 teaching assistantships with full tuition reimbursements available (averaging $21,048 per year); career-related internships or fieldwork, institutionally sponsored loans, traineeships, health care benefits, and unspecified assistantships also available. Financial award application deadline: 1/1. *Faculty research:* Developmental toxicology, biochemical toxicology, exposure assessment, hazardous waste, industrial chemistry. Total annual research expenditures: $14.5 million. *Unit head:* Dr. Rich Fenske, Acting Chair, 206-543-6991. *Application contact:* Rory A. Murphy, Manager, Student Services, 206-543-6991, Fax: 206-543-0477, E-mail: ehgrad@u.washington.edu.

University of Wisconsin–Madison, School of Medicine and Public Health, Molecular and Environmental Toxicology Center, Madison, WI 53706. Offers MS, PhD. *Faculty:* 71 full-time (22 women), 1 part-time/adjunct (0 women). *Students:* 40 full-time (25 women); includes 5 minority (1 American Indian/Alaska Native, 2 Asian Americans or Pacific Islanders, 2 Hispanic Americans), 10 international. Average age 29. 52 applicants, 29% accepted, 6 enrolled. In 2009, 1 master's, 3 doctorates awarded. Terminal master's awarded for partial completion of doctoral program. *Degree requirements:* For master's, thesis; for doctorate, thesis/dissertation. *Entrance requirements:* For master's and doctorate, bachelor's degree in science-related field. Additional exam requirements/recommendations for international students: Required—TOEFL. *Application deadline:* For fall admission, 12/1 priority date for domestic and international students. Application fee: $56. Electronic applications accepted. *Expenses:* Tuition, state resident: part-time $594 per credit. Tuition, nonresident: part-time $1504 per credit. Required fees: $65 per credit. Tuition and fees vary according to course load, program and reciprocity agreements. *Financial support:* In 2009–10, 6 research assistantships with tuition reimbursements (averaging $22,500 per year) were awarded; fellowships with tuition reimbursements, traineeships, health care benefits, and unspecified assistantships also available. *Faculty research:* Toxicology cancer, genetics, cell cycle, xenobotic metabolism. *Unit head:* Dr. Christopher Bradfield, Director, 608-262-2024, E-mail: bradfield@oncology.wisc.edu. *Application contact:* Eileen M. Stevens, Program Administrator, 608-263-4580, Fax: 608-262-5245, E-mail: emstevens@wisc.edu.

Utah State University, School of Graduate Studies, College of Agriculture, Program in Toxicology, Logan, UT 84322. Offers MS, PhD. Terminal master's awarded for partial completion of doctoral program. *Degree requirements:* For master's, thesis; for doctorate, thesis/dissertation. *Entrance requirements:* For master's and doctorate, GRE General Test, minimum GPA of 3.0. Additional exam requirements/recommendations for international students: Required—TOEFL. *Faculty research:* Free-radical mechanisms, toxicity of iron, carcinogenesis of natural compounds, molecular mechanisms of retinoid toxicity, aflatoxins.

Virginia Commonwealth University, Medical College of Virginia-Professional Programs, School of Medicine, School of Medicine Graduate Programs, Department of Pharmacology and Toxicology, Richmond, VA 23284-9005. Offers molecular biology and genetics (PhD);

neuroscience (PhD); pharmacology (PhD); pharmacology and toxicology (MS); MD/PhD. Terminal master's awarded for partial completion of doctoral program. *Degree requirements:* For master's, thesis; for doctorate, thesis/dissertation, comprehensive oral and written exams. *Entrance requirements:* For master's, DAT, GRE General Test, or MCAT; for doctorate, GRE General Test, MCAT, DAT. *Faculty research:* Drug abuse, drug metabolism, pharmacodynamics, peptide synthesis, receptor mechanisms.

Washington State University, Graduate School, College of Pharmacy, Program in Pharmacology and Toxicology, Pullman, WA 99164. Offers MS, PhD. *Faculty:* 19. *Students:* 8 full-time (7 women); includes 3 minority (1 Asian American or Pacific Islander, 2 Hispanic Americans), 3 international. Average age 26. 63 applicants, 11% accepted, 0 enrolled. In 2009, 2 doctorates awarded. *Degree requirements:* For master's, thesis, oral exam; for doctorate, thesis/dissertation, oral exam. *Entrance requirements:* For master's and doctorate, GRE General Test, official transcripts from all undergraduate and graduate schools attended; letter describing research interests, career goals, and research experience. Additional exam requirements/recommendations for international students: Required—TOEFL, IELTS. *Application deadline:* For fall admission, 12/15 for domestic and international students. Applications are processed on a rolling basis. Application fee: $50. Electronic applications accepted. *Financial support:* In 2009–10, 5 fellowships (averaging $6,176 per year), 10 research assistantships with full and partial tuition reimbursements (averaging $14,846 per year), 4 teaching assistantships with full and partial tuition reimbursements (averaging $14,661 per year) were awarded; Federal Work-Study, institutionally sponsored loans, tuition waivers (partial), and staff assistantships, teaching associateships also available. Financial award application deadline: 2/15; financial award applicants required to submit FAFSA. *Faculty research:* Cancer research, immunopharmacology/immunotoxicology, pharmacy, neurobiology/neuropharmacology, toxicology. Total annual research expenditures: $1 million. *Unit head:* Dr. Linda Garrelts MacLean, Chair, 509-335-5545, Fax: 509-335-5902, E-mail: bbr@wsu.edu. *Application contact:* Graduate School Admissions, 800-GRADWSU, Fax: 509-335-1949, E-mail: gradsch@wsu.edu.

Wayne State University, Graduate School, Interdisciplinary Program in Molecular and Cellular Toxicology, Detroit, MI 48201-2427. Offers MS, PhD. *Degree requirements:* For master's, thesis or alternative; for doctorate, thesis/dissertation. *Entrance requirements:* For master's, GRE General Test, GRE Subject Test, personal statement; for doctorate, GRE General Test, GRE Subject Test, minimum GPA of 3.0. Additional exam requirements/recommendations for international students: Required—TOEFL (minimum score 550 paper-based; 213 computer-based); Recommended—TWE (minimum score 6). Electronic applications accepted. *Faculty research:* Molecular and cellular mechanisms of chemically-induced cell injury and death; effect of xenobiotics on cell growth, proliferation, transformation and differentiation; regulation of gene expression; cell signaling; global gene expression profiling.

West Virginia University, Davis College of Agriculture, Forestry and Consumer Sciences, Interdisciplinary Program in Genetics and Developmental Biology, Morgantown, WV 26506. Offers animal breeding (MS, PhD); biochemical and molecular genetics (MS, PhD); cytogenetics (MS, PhD); descriptive embryology (MS, PhD); developmental genetics (MS); experimental morphogenesis/teratology (MS); human genetics (MS, PhD); immunogenetics (MS, PhD); life cycles of animals and plants (MS, PhD); molecular aspects of development (MS, PhD); mutagenesis (MS, PhD); oncology (MS, PhD); plant genetics (MS, PhD); population and quantitative genetics (MS, PhD); regeneration (MS, PhD); teratology (MS, PhD); toxicology (MS, PhD). *Degree requirements:* For master's, thesis; for doctorate, comprehensive exam, thesis/dissertation. *Entrance requirements:* For master's, GRE or MCAT, minimum GPA of 2.75. Additional exam requirements/recommendations for international students: Required—TOEFL.

West Virginia University, School of Pharmacy, Program in Pharmaceutical and Pharmacological Sciences, Morgantown, WV 26506. Offers administrative pharmacy (PhD); behavioral pharmacy (MS, PhD); biopharmaceutics/pharmacokinetics (MS, PhD); industrial pharmacy (MS); medicinal chemistry (MS, PhD); pharmaceutical chemistry (MS, PhD); pharmaceutics (MS, PhD); pharmacology and toxicology (MS); pharmacy (MS); pharmacy administration (MS). Part-time programs available. Terminal master's awarded for partial completion of doctoral program. *Degree requirements:* For master's, thesis; for doctorate, one foreign language, comprehensive exam, thesis/dissertation. *Entrance requirements:* For master's and doctorate, GRE General Test, minimum GPA of 2.75. Additional exam requirements/recommendations for international students: Required—TOEFL; Recommended—TWE. Electronic applications accepted. *Expenses:* Contact institution. *Faculty research:* Pharmaceutics, medicinal chemistry, biopharmaceutics/pharmacokinetics, health outcomes research.

Wright State University, School of Medicine, Program in Pharmacology and Toxicology, Dayton, OH 45435. Offers MS. *Degree requirements:* For master's, thesis optional.

THE JOHNS HOPKINS UNIVERSITY

School of Medicine
Department of Pharmacology and Molecular Sciences

Programs of Study

The Department of Pharmacology and Molecular Sciences offers a multidisciplinary program designed to prepare highly qualified individuals for careers in biomedical research. The focus of this doctoral program is on the molecular interactions of living systems and their application to pharmacology. Within this broad framework, students are encouraged to develop individually tailored programs of study to meet their particular research interests and career objectives.

During their first year, students take courses, participate in individual laboratory research rotations, and choose a research adviser. In the following year, students complete their core courses and examinations, select their focus area of doctoral research, choose a thesis advisory committee, and submit a thesis research proposal. During the remaining two to four years, students focus on their thesis research and take elective courses, many of which are offered by other departments and divisions of the medical institutions.

Graduate studies are offered in the following areas of research: design, synthesis, screening, and biological testing of chemotherapeutic agents and lead compounds; cell-signaling mechanisms; intercellular interactions; molecular and cell biology of cancer; cancer chemoprotection; nerve-cell signaling and neuropharmacology; mass spectrometry; molecular biology and biochemistry of parasites; molecular and cell biology of herpesviruses and retroviruses; neuropharmacology and psychopharmacology; drug and drug-target imaging; drug metabolism and pharmacokinetics; and programmed cell death.

The Department also participates in the Medical Scientist Training Program for M.D./Ph.D. candidates.

Research Facilities

The Department's laboratories provide complete resources for interdisciplinary research in biological chemistry, molecular biology and genetics, virology, cell biology, and chemical biology. These include facilities for chemical synthesis; gas and liquid chromatography; infrared, ultraviolet, and nuclear magnetic resonance spectroscopy; and mass spectrometry. Containment facilities are available for biological and chemical studies. The Department houses the Middle Atlantic Mass Spectrometry Laboratory, and students have access to modern institutional facilities for peptide and oligonucleotide synthesis and sequencing; state-of-the-art microscopy; production and care of transgenic animals; interactive graphics, for use in sequence analysis and molecular modeling; and the extensive clinical facilities of the Division of Clinical Pharmacology.

Financial Aid

Students admitted to the graduate program customarily receive an award that provides a stipend of $27,532 and full payment of tuition, fees, and individual health insurance premiums. These awards are funded by training and research grants from the National Institutes of Health and other funding agencies.

Cost of Study

Tuition, $41,200 in 2010–11, is usually fully covered.

Living and Housing Costs

A limited number of single rooms and apartments are available on campus for approximately $475 per month. Off-campus housing is also available. The University provides free shuttle buses for the many graduate students who live in neighborhoods surrounding the School of Medicine and the University's Homewood campus.

Student Group

There are currently more than 55 graduate students in the Department and about 500 additional Ph.D. candidates at the School of Medicine. In addition, nearly 500 medical students and more than 1,000 students in the School of Hygiene and Public Health share the campus of the Johns Hopkins medical institutions.

Student Outcomes

Graduates typically go on to postdoctoral research fellowships followed by research and teaching careers in academic institutions, government, or industry.

Location

Baltimore is a vibrant waterfront city with a wide variety of recreational, entertainment, and cultural opportunities. From its Inner Harbor attractions to its nightlife in Fells Point, from its museums and galleries to its superb sports stadiums, Baltimore provides all of the amenities of one of America's major metropolises. Among its many cultural attractions are the Baltimore Symphony Orchestra, the Peabody Conservatory, the Baltimore Museum of Art, and the Walters Art Gallery and Center Stage.

The Inner Harbor, with its shops, restaurants, and attractions (including the National Aquarium and Maryland Science Center), brings the Chesapeake Bay into the heart of Baltimore. The city also supports professional teams in major-league baseball (the Orioles), NFL football (the Ravens), and indoor soccer (the Blast). The museums, historic landmarks, and theaters in Washington, D.C., are an hour away. The cultural offerings of Philadelphia and New York are readily accessible by train or car. Year-round opportunities for outdoor recreation are provided by the Chesapeake Bay and Atlantic Ocean, the nearby Maryland countryside, and the mountains and rivers of western Maryland, Pennsylvania, Virginia, and West Virginia.

The School and The Department

The School of Medicine was founded in 1893 as part of Johns Hopkins University, the first American institution to place a primary emphasis on graduate education. The Department, also established in 1893, has served as a model for other pharmacology departments throughout the nation.

Applying

Students are typically admitted in late August, although early arrival for summer research is encouraged. Applicants should have a bachelor's degree from a qualified college or university with a major in any of the biological, chemical, or physical sciences. Entering students are expected to have completed college-level courses in biology, chemistry (inorganic, organic, and physical), calculus, and physics; a strong background in biochemistry is particularly desirable. A completed online application, scores on the Graduate Record Examinations (General Test is required; Subject Test is required for international applicants), at least three letters of recommendation, undergraduate transcript(s), and a statement of interest must be received by the January 10 deadline.

Correspondence and Information

Dr. James T. Stivers
Director of Admissions
Department of Pharmacology and Molecular Sciences
The Johns Hopkins University School of Medicine
725 North Wolfe Street
Baltimore, Maryland 21205
Phone: 410-955-1457
E-mail: jstivers@jhmi.edu
Web site: http://www.hopkinsmedicine.org/pharmacology/

The Johns Hopkins University

THE FACULTY AND THEIR RESEARCH

Richard F. Ambinder, Professor; M.D., 1979, Ph.D., 1989, Johns Hopkins. Virology and human cancer; antiviral therapy; antitumor therapy; lymphoma pathogenesis, prevention, and treatment; immunological approaches to virus-associated malignancies.

L. Mario Amzel, Professor; Ph.D., Buenos Aires, 1968. 3-D structure of proteins: immunoglobulins and other binding proteins; ATP synthase; monoxygenases and dioxygenases quinone reductase.

J. Thomas August, Professor; M.D., Stanford, 1955. Genetic immunotherapy of infectious diseases and cancer by targeting DNA-encoded antigen chimeras to MHC II; MHC II antigen presentation; development of DNA vaccines; immune tolerance.

Namandjé N. Bumpus, Assistant Professor; Ph.D., Michigan, 2008. Role of drug metabolism in non-nucleoside reverse transcriptase inhibitor-mediated toxicity.

Philip A. Cole, Professor and Director; M.D./Ph.D., Johns Hopkins, 1991. Chemical and biochemical approaches in the study of signal transduction, circadian rhythm, and gene regulation.

Robert J. Cotter, Professor; Ph.D., Johns Hopkins, 1972. Development of new analytical techniques and instrumentation for mass spectrometry; applications of mass spectrometry to the structural analysis of peptides, glycopeptides, and glycolipids.

Albena Dinkova-Kostova, Assistant Professor; Ph.D., Washington State, 1996. Protection against cancer: mechanisms and strategies; structure-activity relation of protective agents; inflammation and cancer; skin cancer prevention.

Kelly E. Dooley, Assistant Professor; M.D./Ph.D., Johns Hopkins, 2009. Clinical pharmacology of anti-infective agents; evaluation of new drug regimens for the treatment of tuberculosis and co-treatment of TB and HIV.

Sylvain Doré, Associate Professor; Ph.D., Montreal, 1994. Battling neurodegenerative disorders: stroke, Alzheimer's, and aging.

Charles W. Flexner, Professor; M.D., Johns Hopkins, 1982. Basic and clinical pharmacology of antiretroviral drugs; HIV protease inhibitors and entry inhibitors.

Wade Gibson, Professor; Ph.D., Chicago, 1973. Herpesvirus proteins: studies of their expression, structure, and function using genetic, biochemical, and immunological approaches.

Marc M. Greenberg, Professor; Ph.D., Yale, 1988. Chemical and biochemical approaches to the study of DNA damage and repair, and their applications.

J. Marie Hardwick, Professor; Ph.D., Kansas, 1978. Molecular mechanisms of programmed cell death.

Gary S. Hayward, Professor; Ph.D., Otago (New Zealand), 1972. Pathways of herpesvirus gene regulation and latency; cis-acting DNA elements that modulate gene expression; mechanisms of positive and negative transcriptional regulation; interaction of viral immediate-early transactivators with nuclear domains; molecular piracy by Kaposi's sarcoma herpesvirus.

S. Diane Hayward, Professor; Ph.D., Otago (New Zealand), 1972. Epstein-Barr virus and Kaposi's sarcoma virus; viral latency and tumorigenesis; mechanisms of virus-induced cell proliferation; viral mediated epigenetic modification of cell gene expression; notch and Wnt pathways.

Craig W. Hendrix, Professor and Director, Drug Development Unit; M.D., Georgetown, 1984. Anti-infective drugs; chemoprevention of infectious diseases.

Richard L. Huganir, Professor; Ph.D., Cornell, 1982. Molecular mechanisms in the regulation of synaptic plasticity.

William B. Isaacs, Professor; Ph.D., Johns Hopkins, 1984. Understanding the molecular genetic events responsible for initiation and progression of prostate cancer, with particular interest in inherited susceptibility to prostate cancer.

Kenneth Kinzler, Professor; Ph.D., Johns Hopkins, 1988. Molecular genetics of human cancer.

Jun O. Liu, Professor; Ph.D., MIT, 1990. Chemical biology and molecular biology; use of small molecules as probes to elucidate mechanisms of signal transduction; angiogenesis and cell proliferation.

Caren L. Freel Meyers, Assistant Professor; Ph.D., Rochester, 1999. Organic and medicinal chemistry; chemical biology; drug delivery mechanisms in bacteria; development of antibiotic prodrug strategies; study of bacterial isoprenoid biosynthesis; combinatorial biosynthesis; development of potential therapeutic agents.

William G. Nelson, Professor and Director, Sidney Kimmel Comprehensive Cancer Center; M.D./Ph.D., Johns Hopkins, 1987. Molecular mechanisms of prostatic carcinogenesis; epigenetic alterations in cancer; new approaches to prostate cancer prevention and treatment.

Duojia Pan, Professor; Ph.D., UCLA, 1993. Growth control in normal development and cancer; signal transduction; animal models of cancer.

Paula M. Pitha-Rowe, Professor; Ph.D., Czechoslovak Academy of Sciences, 1964. Effects of viral infection on expression of cellular (cytokines and chemokines and their receptors) and viral (HIV-1, HHV-8) genes; targeted antiviral and anticellular therapy (gene transfer, ribozymes); breast cancer: role of c-erbB-2.

Martin G. Pomper, Professor; M.D./Ph.D., Illinois at Urbana-Champaign, 1990. In vivo molecular and cellular imaging; radiopharmaceutical development; targeted cancer imaging and therapy; functional brain imaging.

Gary H. Posner, Scowe Professor; Ph.D., Harvard, 1968. Organic and medicinal chemistry aimed toward rational design and synthesis of new compounds for effective and safe chemotherapy of malaria and cancer.

Jonathan D. Powell, Associate Professor; M.D./Ph.D., Emory, 1992. Mechanisms of T cell activation and tolerance.

Douglas N. Robinson, Associate Professor; Ph.D., Yale, 1997. Understanding cytokinesis and cell-shape control.

Christopher A. Ross, Professor; M.D./Ph.D., Cornell, 1983. Neuropsychiatric disorders.

Ronald L. Schnaar, Professor; Ph.D., Johns Hopkins, 1976. Cell interactions in the nervous system.

Theresa A. Shapiro, Professor; M.D., Ph.D., 1978, Johns Hopkins. Clinical pharmacology; molecular mechanisms of antiparasitic drug action; effects of topoisomerase inhibitors on DNA of trypanosomes; structure- activity of synthetic antimalarial trioxanes.

Robert F. Siliciano, Professor; M.D./Ph.D., Johns Hopkins, 1983. HIV latency, evolution, and persistence; HIV treatment and drug resistance; pharmacology of HIV drugs.

Solomon H. Snyder, Professor; M.D., Georgetown, 1962. Molecular basis of neural signal transduction.

Simona Stäger, Assistant Professor; D.V.M./Ph.D., Bern (Switzerland), 1997. Immunoparasitology; CD8+ T cells; vaccination; *Leishmania*.

James T. Stivers, Professor; Ph.D., Johns Hopkins, 1993. Structural and chemical biology of uracil metabolism and applications to cancer therapy; innate and adaptive immunity.

Paul Talalay, Professor; M.D., Yale, 1948. Molecular mechanisms in chemical and dietary protection against mutagens and carcinogens.

Sean D. Taverna, Assistant Professor; Ph.D., Virginia, 2004. Histone and chromatin modifications; epigenetics and gene function; identification of histone-binding modules; small-RNA-directed gene silencing.

Craig A. Townsend, Professor; Ph.D., Yale, 1974. Organic and bioorganic chemistry: biosynthesis of natural products and biomimetic synthesis; elucidation of protein function; molecular biology of secondary metabolism and engineering of biosynthetic systems to practical ends; study of the role and inhibition of fatty acid synthesis in human cancer, tuberculosis, and obesity.

Bert Vogelstein, Professor; M.D., Johns Hopkins, 1974. Molecular genetics of human cancer.

Jin Zhang, Associate Professor; Ph.D., Chicago, 2000. Cell signaling; kinases and phosphatases; chemotaxis; live-cell imaging; fluorescent proteins and reporters; chemical biology.

Heng Zhu, Assistant Professor; Ph.D., Clemson, 1999. Signal transduction; protein network; host-pathogen interaction; biomarker identification.

Students accepted into the Pharmacology Graduate Training Program may also carry out thesis research with the following Oncology Center faculty members, who participate in the NCI Anti-Cancer Drug Development Training Program.

Samuel R. Denmeade, Associate Professor; M.D., Columbia, 1989. Targeted therapies for cancer; prodrugs; proteases; peptide libraries.

Robert H. Getzenberg, Professor; Ph.D., Johns Hopkins, 1992. Cancer biomarkers; proteomic analysis of nuclear structure; nanotechnology.

Carol W. Greider, Professor; Ph.D., Berkeley, 1987. Telomerase and telomere length regulation.

Elizabeth M. Jaffee, Professor; M.D., New York Medical College, 1985. Analysis of antitumor immune responses against human tumors; identification of the targets of tumor-specific cytotoxic T cells.

Mark Levis, Associate Professor; M.D./Ph.D., Targeting the FLT3 signaling pathway as a treatment for acute leukemia.

Charles M. Rudin, Professor; M.D./Ph.D., Chicago, 1993. Molecular mechanisms of apoptosis; roles of apoptosis in carcinogenesis and therapeutic resistance; novel therapeutic development in animal models of cancer.

STATE UNIVERSITY OF NEW YORK
UPSTATE MEDICAL UNIVERSITY
Program in Pharmacology

Programs of Study

At SUNY Upstate's College of Graduate Studies, Ph.D. students thrive as they participate in medically relevant research on a campus that is proud of its mentoring and multidisciplinary approach. Students enjoy a student-faculty ratio of nearly 1:1 and publish articles in professional journals during their program.

Students select a department, thesis mentor, and ultimate area of research after their first year, which includes three in-depth laboratory rotations of their choice. All departments support Upstate's four main Research Pillars: cancer; infectious diseases; diabetes, metabolic disorders, and cardiovascular disease; and disorders of the nervous system.

Current research in the Department of Pharmacology focuses on cancer, cell signaling, cardiovascular disease, neurodegeneration, infectious disease, stem cells, and drug discovery. Under the direction of its new chair, the department is also expanding into new research areas—including pharmaceutical discovery and development, cancer pharmacology, and pharmacogenomics.

The significant growth of the department is aligned with the strategic focus on cancer as one of the university's research pillars, and with the development of the new SUNY Upstate Cancer Research Institute, which aims to become a premier cancer research institute in the region.

The department's funding sources include the National Institutes of Health (NIH), the U.S. Department of Defense, and the American Heart Association.

Research Facilities

SUNY Upstate has world-class facilities for faculty members and students. The main core facilities on campus include the Center for Research and Evaluation, Confocal/Two Photon Imaging, Department of Laboratory Animal Resources, DNA Sequencing, Flow Cytometry, Humanized SCID Mouse and Stem Cell Processing, Imaging Research, In Vivo Computed Tomography, Microarray (SUNYMAC), MRI Research, and Proteomics.

SUNY Upstate also maintains a coalition with nearby Cornell University, the University of Rochester Medical Center, and Buffalo's Roswell Park Cancer Institute, which is dedicated to sharing cutting-edge research facilities. There are also full research support services on campus, including laboratory-animal facilities, network access to the SeqWeb suite of software, a computer-age medical library containing more than 183,000 volumes, electronics and machine shops, and photographic and computer services.

SUNY Upstate's growth on the research side is highlighted by a $72 million expansion of its Institute for Human Performance, a high-tech facility housing shared laboratories and core facilities used in basic and clinical research. It also broke ground in 2009 for a dedicated research park facility.

Financial Aid

All accepted Ph.D. students are fully supported throughout their education by full tuition waivers and a stipend ($21,514 per year). Support comes from graduate assistantships, departmental assistantships, and NIH and NSF grants.

Cost of Study

Stipends and full tuition waivers are granted to all students accepted into the Ph.D. program. There is no teaching requirement. Student fees, which include health service, were $552 for the 2009–10 academic year.

Living and Housing Costs

On-campus housing is available in Clark Tower, a ten-story apartment building with attractive, fully furnished standard rooms, studio apartments, and two-bedroom suites. Costs ranged from $4127 (double occupancy) to $8618 (married/family accommodations) for 2009–10. Clark Tower also has study rooms, computer rooms, private and shared kitchens, lounges, a recreation room, laundry, and storage. Clark Tower is next door to the Campus Activities Building, which houses athletic facilities, a bookstore, and snack bar.

Many students rent nearby houses or apartments and bicycle or walk to campus. Syracuse has a low cost of living and abundant affordable housing.

Student Group

There are 124 graduate students in the biomedical sciences (58 percent women; 100 percent full-time) and approximately 600 medical students, 200 nursing students, and 200 students in the health professions enrolled at Upstate Medical University. Twenty-five percent of the graduate students come from Canada, Europe, and Asia. Syracuse University and the SUNY College of Environmental Science are located within a quarter mile of SUNY Upstate, resulting in a population of approximately 23,000 students in the immediate area.

Location

Syracuse is New York's fourth-largest city and is located in the scenic center of the state. A naturally beautiful setting, the area offers excellent hiking, biking, boating, and skiing. Nearby are the Finger Lakes region, the Adirondack and the Catskill Mountains, and Lake Ontario. Syracuse's cultural activities include a professional theater, symphony orchestra and opera company, noted author lecture series, chamber music groups, and several top-notch music festivals (classical, blues, and jazz) as well as art and history museums. The area also offers high-quality family life with many excellent school districts and Upstate's own day care center. Syracuse University's top-level collegiate sporting events are a major recreational activity. Syracuse is easily reached by air, rail, and car.

The University

SUNY Upstate is the only academic medical center in the central New York region and is part of the dynamic University Hill community. In addition to the College of Graduate Studies, SUNY Upstate Medical University includes three other colleges—Medicine, Nursing, and Health Professions—its own University Hospital, and a regional campus in Binghamton, New York. The University is growing with new leadership, degree programs, and further plans for expansion. SUNY Upstate Medical University is close to downtown Syracuse and is adjacent to (but not affiliated with) the campus of Syracuse University. SUNY Upstate's Campus Activities Building houses a swimming pool, sauna, gymnasium, squash courts, handball/paddleball court, weight-lifting area with a Universal Gym and a full Nautilus room, billiards, table tennis, television room, bookstore, snack bar, and lounge. Conference rooms are also available for student use.

Applying

The Admissions Committee for the College of Graduate Studies at SUNY Upstate begins reviewing applications in December prior to entry and continues until all positions are filled, which can be as early as early April. The State University of New York requires a $40 application fee. Competitive applicants must have a bachelor's degree or its equivalent, a minimum 3.0 GPA, and course work that includes biology, calculus, chemistry, and physics. GRE General Test scores are required (combined score 1000 minimum), and scores from the Subject Test in chemistry or biology are recommended. International applicants must provide clear evidence of English proficiency (including speaking) by taking the Test of English as a Foreign Language (TOEFL). Candidates for admission are selected on the basis of their record and qualifications for independent scholarship in a specialized field of study. Selected applicants will be invited to campus to meet with faculty, students and tour lab facilities.

Correspondence and Information

Office of Graduate Studies
State University of New York Upstate Medical University
750 East Adams Street
Syracuse, New York 13210
Phone: 315-464-7655
Fax: 315-464-4544
E-mail: biosci@upstate.edu
Web site: http://www.upstate.edu/grad/

State University of New York Upstate Medical University

THE FACULTY AND THEIR RESEARCH

Eileen A. Friedman, Ph.D., Adjunct Professor. Role of the serine/theonine kinase Mirk/dyrk1B in cancers of the pancreas, ovary, and colon.

George G. Holz, Ph.D., Professor. Molecular pharmacology and physiology of pancreatic beta cells; drug development for the treatment of type 2 diabetes mellitus.

Ying Huang, M.D., Ph.D., Associate Professor. Oncogenic signaling in cellular transformation and apoptosis; tumor suppressor genes.

Ziwei Huang, Ph.D., Professor and Chair. Discovery and mechanism of action of new pharmacological agents for cancer, cardiovascular disease, neurodegeneration, infectious disease, and stem cell–based regenerative medicine.

Grant Kelley, M.D., Associate Professor. Elucidating the regulation of PLC-epsilon and its role in glucose signaling and endothelial cell function in diabetes.

Andrzej Krol, Ph.D., Associate Professor. Molecular and dynamic imaging; image registration and fusion; tomographic reconstruction; ultrafast laser-based X-ray source; brain deformation quantification between mutant and normal mouse.

M. Golam Mohi, Ph.D., Assistant Professor. Molecular mechanism of leukemia; effect of oncogenic mutations in pathogenesis of leukemia, using mouse model.

Arkadii Pertsov, Ph.D., Professor. Biophysical mechanisms of cardiac arrhythmias; fluorescence imaging.

Steven J. Scheinman, M.D., Professor. Molecular genetics of kidney stones.

M. Saeed Sheikh, M.D., Ph.D., Professor. Apoptotic signal transduction and cancer biology.

Edward J. Shillitoe, Ph.D., Professor. Gene therapy for cancer.

Allen E. Silverstone, Ph.D., Professor. How dioxins and estrogens and estrogenic compounds affect the immune system.

Richard D. Veenstra, Ph.D., Professor. Regulation of connexin-specific gap junctions; gap-junction channel biophysics.

Richard J. H. Wojcikiewicz, Ph.D., Professor. Intracellular signaling via $InsP_3$ receptors and the ubiquitin/proteasome pathway.

THOMAS JEFFERSON UNIVERSITY

Jefferson College of Graduate Studies
Kimmel Cancer Center
Department of Biochemistry and Molecular Biology
Program in Molecular Pharmacology and Structural Biology

Programs of Study

This interdepartmental Ph.D. program provides focused training and research experience in molecular pharmacology and structural biology and in the study of drug interactions at the level of the cell and organ. It is designed to provide students with the basis for successful careers as independent scientists and scholars in either the academic or industrial sector. Students entering with a baccalaureate degree take a core biomedical course in the fall semester, incorporating biochemistry, molecular biology, cell biology, and genetics. Advanced courses in pharmacology, biochemistry, cell signaling, and structural biology can be taken in both the first and second years, and the curriculum is flexible to accommodate the individual student's background and interests. All course work is generally completed by the end of the second year. In addition, several weekly public seminar series, frequent laboratory seminars, and invited lectureships form an integral part of the student's education. Current research interests of the faculty members include molecular and cell biology of hormone-receptor interactions, signal transduction across membranes and within cells, membrane trafficking and intracellular organization, cell death and inflammation, signaling pathways in cancer, structural and functional analyses of proteins and nucleic acids, experimental therapeutics and diagnostics, vaccine antigen design, mechanisms of cardiovascular disease, clinical pharmacology and translational medicine, neuropharmacology, and toxicology. The Graduate Program in Molecular Pharmacology and Structural Biology, along with the Programs in Biochemistry and Molecular Biology, Genetics, and Immunology and Microbial Pathogenesis, make up the four Graduate Programs of the Kimmel Cancer Center. Students applying to the Jefferson College of Graduate Studies (JCGS) Flexible Entry Program may perform research rotations or work with faculty members in any of these programs.

Research Facilities

Research laboratories are primarily located in the Department of Biochemistry and Molecular Biology, in the Bluemle Life Sciences Building. In addition to extensive basic equipment and facilities, the program provides access to numerous specialized resources. These include facilities for peptide and oligonucleotide synthesis and sequencing, cell sorting by flow cytometry, protein purification and characterization, proteomics and microarray analysis, and biomolecular imaging. Also available are facilities for transgenic and knockout mouse production, extensive computer facilities, a CD spectrometer, and state-of-the-art X-ray detectors for macromolecular crystallography.

Financial Aid

Financial support is available to full-time Ph.D. students in the form of University fellowships and training grants. In 2010–11, students granted full fellowship support receive funds for payment of tuition and a stipend of $26,300. Also available to students demonstrating financial need are Title IV funds. University loan programs are also available to qualifying students.

Cost of Study

Tuition and fees for 2010–11 full-time Ph.D. students are $28,423 per year.

Living and Housing Costs

Campus housing is available at Thomas Jefferson University; reasonable alternative housing near the University in the Philadelphia area can also be found.

Student Group

The class size in molecular pharmacology and structural biology is expected to be 3 or 4 students per year. Currently, the University enrolls about 2,500 students. The College of Graduate Studies enrolls approximately 630 students, about half of whom are women.

Student Outcomes

Recent Ph.D. graduates have accepted postdoctoral positions in prestigious academic institutions, such as Harvard, Baylor, Johns Hopkins, UC Davis, the University of Texas M. D. Anderson Cancer Center, and the National Institutes of Health, and in industry, including Bristol-Meyers Squibb and Pfizer.

Location

The 13-acre campus of Thomas Jefferson University is located in the historical downtown area of Philadelphia, within walking distance of many places of cultural interest, including concert halls, theaters, museums, art galleries, and historic sites. Numerous intercollegiate and professional athletics events take place nearby. Convenient bus and subway lines connect the University with other local universities and colleges and with several outstanding libraries. The proximity of the New Jersey shore and the Pennsylvania mountains offers year-round recreational opportunities, and New York City and Washington, D.C., are each just a few hours away.

The University

Thomas Jefferson University is an academic health center. It evolved from the Jefferson Medical College, which was founded in 1824. In addition to the medical college, the University includes the College of Graduate Studies, the School of Pharmacy, the School of Health Professions, the School of Nursing, the School of Population Health, the University hospital, and various affiliated hospitals and institutions. Jefferson Alumni Hall houses the TJU Fitness and Recreation Facility, study lounges, a swimming pool, a sauna, a gymnasium, and a handball/squash court.

Applying

The deadline to submit Ph.D. applications and all supporting materials is January 5. Applications received after this date are considered at the discretion of the admissions committee. Scores on the General Test of the Graduate Record Examinations, three letters of recommendation, and academic transcripts are required of all applicants. For those students whose native language is not English, scores on the Test of English as a Foreign Language (TOEFL) are required. Scores on an appropriate Subject Test of the Graduate Record Examinations are recommended. Prospective students are encouraged to visit the Department and discuss the graduate program with members of the faculty.

Correspondence and Information

For applications:
Marc Stearns
Director of Admissions and Recruitment
College of Graduate Studies
Thomas Jefferson University
1020 Locust Street, M-46
Philadelphia, Pennsylvania 19107-6799

Phone: 215-503-4400
Fax: 215-503-3433
E-mail: cgs-info@jefferson.edu
Web site: http://www.jefferson.edu/cgs

For program information:
Joanne Balitzky
Training Programs Coordinator
Kimmel Cancer Center
Thomas Jefferson University
233 South 10th Street, 910 BLSB
Philadelphia, Pennsylvania 19107-5541

Phone: 215-503-6687
Fax: 215-503-0622
E-mail: joanne.balitzky@jefferson.edu
Web site: http://www.jefferson.edu/jcgs/phd/mpsb/

Thomas Jefferson University

THE FACULTY AND THEIR RESEARCH

Emad S. Alnemri, Professor; Ph.D., Temple, 1991. Molecular mechanisms of programmed cell death (apoptosis); pattern recognition receptors and inflammasome activation in innate immune responses to molecular danger signals; role of mitochondria in survival, cell death, and aging.

Andrew E. Aplin, Associate Professor; Ph.D., King's (London), 1996. Targeting mutant BRAF and integrin signaling in melanoma initiation and progression.

Renato Baserga, Professor; M.D., Milan, 1949. Genetic analysis of G1 phase and control of cell proliferation; growth factors and their receptors; apoptosis; anticancer therapy.

Jeffrey L. Benovic, Professor and Chairperson; Ph.D., Duke, 1986. Molecular and regulatory properties of G protein–coupled receptors; role of receptor dysregulation in cancer and neurological disorders.

Wolfgang Bergmeier, Assistant Professor; Ph.D., Witten-Herdecke (Germany), 2001. Adhesion receptors/activation pathways in platelets and neutrophils and their role in health and cardiovascular disease.

George C. Brainard, Professor; Ph.D., Wesleyan, 1973. Photobiology, neuroendocrine, and circadian regulation; control of melatonin in humans; effects of light on physiology, behavior, and cancer progression; use of light as countermeasure in long-duration space flight.

Bruno Calabretta, Professor; M.D., Modena (Italy), 1977; Ph.D., Rome, 1987. Molecular mechanisms of normal hematopoiesis and BCR/ABL-dependent leukemogenesis.

Gino Cingolani, Associate Professor; Ph.D., European Molecular Biology Laboratory (France), 1999. Molecular cell biology of nucleocytoplasmic transport; X-ray crystallography and biophysical analysis of viral DNA-pumping machinery; structure of multisubunit ATP synthases.

Masumi Eto, Associate Professor; Ph.D., Hokkaido (Japan), 1996. Molecular physiology of protein phosphates and cytoskeleton.

John L. Farber, Professor; M.D., California, San Francisco, 1966. Biochemical mechanisms of cell injury in ischemia; biochemical toxicology of liver cell necrosis; biochemical toxicology of activated oxygen; chemical carcinogenesis.

Mark E. Fortini, Associate Professor; Ph.D., Berkeley, 1990. Developmental signaling pathways involved in normal cellular patterning and cancer; proteolytic mechanisms in neurogenesis and neurodegeneration; trafficking and post-translational regulation of cell-surface receptors and ligands.

Jan B. Hoek, Professor; Ph.D., Amsterdam, 1972. Systems biology of intracellular signal transduction networks; deregulation of cytokine and growth factor signaling in the liver associated with chronic alcohol consumption; early signaling responses during liver regeneration; bioenergetics and mitochondrial metabolism and its role in intracellular signaling and apoptosis.

Michael Holinstat, Assistant Professor; Ph.D., Illinois at Chicago, 2004. Regulation of protease-activated receptor (PAR) function in the platelet; signal transduction and regulation of hemostasis and thrombosis in the platelet; regulation of the small GTPase Rap1 in vascular function; regulation of platelet-mediated hemostasis and thrombosis and signal transduction by 12-lipoxygenase; how platelet function regulates the progression of a number of cardiovascular risks such as diabetes and acute coronary syndrome.

Ya-Ming Hou, Professor; Ph.D., Berkeley, 1986. Genetic and biochemical studies of tRNA, including structure and function mechanism of tRNA aminoacylation, maintenance of the tRNA 3′ end, maturation and processing, editing and repair, decoding on the ribosome, and development of bacterial pathogenesis in infectious diseases; targeting tRNAs as strategies against metabolic and neurodegenerative disorders.

James H. Keen, Professor; Ph.D., Cornell, 1976. Molecular mechanisms coupling signal transduction with receptor-mediated endocytosis and exocytosis; membrane transport studied by biochemical, molecular biological, and morphological approaches.

Karen E. Knudsen, Professor; Ph.D., California, San Diego, 1996. Translational prostate cancer research, cell cycle control, hormonal control of gene transcription, chromatin remodeling.

Walter J. Koch, W. W. Smith Professor of Medicine; Ph.D., Cincinnati, 1990. Molecular mechanisms of pathological cardiovascular signaling; novel gene-based therapeutics for congestive heart failure, investigation into organ cross-talk in cardiovascular disease.

Michael Lisanti, Professor; M.D., 1991, Ph.D., 1992, Cornell. Functional role of caveolae and the caveolin genes in normal signal transduction and in a variety of pathogenic disease states, most notably the development of breast and prostate cancers.

Andrea Morrione, Research Associate Professor; Ph.D., Milan, 1992. Characterization of insulin-like growth factor receptor I (IGF-IR) function in bladder cancer initiation and progression; role of the growth factor progranulin (proepithelin) and its receptor in bladder and prostate cancer; characterization of the role of adaptor protein Grb10 in the regulation of IGF-IR ubiquitination, trafficking, and signaling.

Marja T. Nevalainen, Associate Professor; M.D., 1992, Ph.D., 1997, Turku (Finland). Stat transcription factors in prostate cancer.

John M. Pascal, Assistant Professor; Ph.D., Texas at Austin, 2000. Structural biology of DNA replication, repair, and signaling mechanisms; mechanisms of genome maintenance and chromosomal metabolism; biochemical and biophysical studies of nucleic acid enzymes; macromolecular x-ray crystallography.

Richard G. Pestell, Professor; Ph.D., 1991, M.D., 1997, Melbourne (Australia). Molecular mechanisms and gene therapy of breast and prostate cancer; cancer stem cells.

Giovanni M. Pitari, Associate Professor; M.D., 1991, Ph.D., 1997, Catania (Italy). Cyclic GMP signaling pathway, vasodilator-stimulated phosphoprotein (VASP), and matrix metalloproteinase 9 (MMP-9): molecular mechanisms, signaling networks and targeted therapy.

Andrew A. Quong, Associate Professor; Ph.D., California, Irvine, 1991. Clinical proteomics for early detection of breast cancer and prediction of response to therapy; basic mechanisms of tumorigenesis and metastasis; development of new molecular interventions and technologies for clinical diagnostics; systems biology, computational biology, and proteomics; metastatic breast cancer; papillary thyroid cancer.

Natalia A. Riobo, Assistant Professor; Ph.D., Buenos Aires, 2001. Signal transduction mechanisms employed by mammalian hedgehog proteins in cardiomyoctes, endothelium, cancer cells and stromal fibroblasts in the context of cardiovascular regenerative medicine and cancer.

Ulrich Rodeck, Professor; M.D., Germany, 1981. Regulation of epithelial cell survival by the epidermal growth factor receptor; coordinate regulation of cell-cycle progression and cell survival by growth factor– and adhesion-dependent signal transduction; targeted therapies in cancer treatment; mitigation of normal tissue toxicity of cancer therapeutics; genotoxic stress responses of vertebrate organisms using zebrafish embryos.

Michael Root, Assistant Professor; M.D./Ph.D., Harvard, 1997. Structure and function of glycoproteins involved in viral and cell-cell membrane fusion; design of viral entry inhibitors and immunogens for vaccine development; antibody-antigen interactions.

Hallgeir Rui, Professor; M.D., 1987, Ph.D., 1988, Oslo (Norway). Signal transduction and biology of prolactin, growth hormone, and JAK-STAT pathways, with a focus on translational research on drug response prediction in human breast cancer.

Charles P. Scott, Assistant Professor; Ph.D., Pennsylvania, 1997. Combinatorial target and drug discovery; chemical genomics of host-pathogen interactions and cancer.

Federica Sotgia, Assistant Professor; Ph.D., 2001, Genoa (Italy). Role of caveolin-1 in the tumor microenvironment in breast cancer.

Scott A. Waldman, Professor; Ph.D., Thomas Jefferson, 1980; M.D., Stanford, 1987. Molecular mechanisms of signal transduction, with emphasis on receptor-effector coupling and post-receptor signaling mechanisms; molecular mechanisms underlying tissue-specific transcriptional regulation; translation of molecular signaling mechanisms to novel diagnostic and therapeutic approaches to patients with cancer.

Philip B. Wedegaertner, Associate Professor and Program Director; Ph.D., California, San Diego, 1991. Heterotrimeric G-protein, Rho GTPase, and Rho guanine-nucleotide exchange factor (RhoGEF) signaling and cell biology; mechanisms and functions of regulated subcellular localization and trafficking.

Eric Wickstrom, Professor; Ph.D., Berkeley, 1972. Sensing, imaging, regulation, and control of oncogene expression in cells and animal models with nucleic acid derivatives; permanent bonding of drugs to implants.

Edward P. Winter, Associate Professor; SUNY at Stony Brook, 1984. Analysis of meiotic development using molecular genetics in yeast; signal transduction and protein kinases; transcriptional regulation.

UNIVERSITY AT ALBANY, STATE UNIVERSITY OF NEW YORK

School of Public Health
Department of Environmental Health Sciences

Programs of Study

The Department of Environmental Health Sciences at the University at Albany, State University of New York, offers programs leading to the M.S. and Ph.D. degrees, preparing outstanding students for teaching and research careers in academia, public health agencies, and industry. The programs benefit from being based in the Wadsworth Center, the central laboratory complex of the New York State Department of Health. This relationship exposes the student to a range of real-world, scientifically based environmental and public health problems and to an organization with a tradition of high-quality basic research. The Department offers three areas of concentration: environmental health, environmental and analytical chemistry, and toxicology.

Specific areas of research in the toxicology concentration include alterations of immune system function by environmental factors; the function and regulation of phase I and phase II enzymes in estrogen and xenobiotic metabolism in both in vivo and in vitro systems using the tools of cell biology, biochemistry, molecular biology, pharmacogenetics, toxicogenomics, and genetics; neurotoxicity of halogenated hydrocarbons and heavy metals; degradation of halogenated aromatics by anaerobic microorganisms; and detection of pathogenic organisms in water.

Research programs in the environmental and analytical chemistry concentration include laboratory and pilot-scale investigations of photochemical and absorption processes in the aquatic environment, development and application of analytical methods for the detection of inorganic and organic contaminants in environmental media and human tissues, atmospheric processes leading to the development of acid rain, and ozone depletion and smog.

The environmental health concentration focuses on such topics as environmental exposure assessment; air, soil, and water pollution; control of food and waterborne diseases; risk communication, geographic risk analysis, and pest vectors and management.

Research Facilities

The program builds on the resources and state-of-the-art research equipment of the Wadsworth Center. At the Wadsworth Center, faculty and student research is supported by outstanding core facilities in biochemistry, genetics, imaging, immunology, molecular structure, mass spectrometry, and NMR, as well as national centers in biological imaging (NIH/NCRR), genetics (CDC), and nanobiotechnology (NSF). The laboratories provide scientific expertise and analytical support for numerous environmental and public health problems, including the greenhouse effect, acid rain, toxic waste, PCBs in the Hudson River, indoor air pollution, and the combustion of hazardous/municipal waste.

Financial Aid

Graduate assistantships and tuition scholarships are awarded to incoming doctoral students on a competitive basis. Assistantship stipends range from $22,600 to $24,000. Other forms of financial support include research assistantships from faculty research grants.

Cost of Study

Full-time tuition is $4185 per semester for New York State residents and $6625 per semester for out-of-state and international students. University fees are approximately $600 per semester.

Living and Housing Costs

In addition to student residence halls, off-campus apartments are available at rental rates ranging from $600 to $900 per month.

Student Group

Of the 18,000 students at the University at Albany, 4,900 are graduate students who come from all parts of the U.S. and from more than forty other countries.

Location

Albany, the capital of the state of New York, offers a large choice of cultural attractions ranging from music, dance, and theater, to horseracing and sports. In the nearby Adirondack and Catskill Mountains and in the Berkshires, students find an unlimited variety of outdoor activities including hiking, camping, canoeing, skiing, and climbing. Other attractions include Lake George, Saratoga Springs, Tanglewood (in Massachusetts), and the Olympic Sports Complex in Lake Placid. New York City, Boston, Montreal, Vermont, and Atlantic Ocean beaches are all within a few hours' drive. Albany has an airport, bus and train services, and an extensive public transportation system.

The University

The University at Albany is the senior campus and one of four University Centers of the sixty-four-campus State University of New York (SUNY) system. The main campus is housed in a modern complex occupying a 400-acre site at the western edge of Albany.

Applying

College transcripts, Graduate Record Examinations scores on the General Test, three references from persons familiar with the applicant's academic qualifications, a statement of the applicant's educational and professional aims, and a $75 application fee must be submitted to the Office of Graduate Admissions. A GRE Subject Test in biology, physics, biochemistry, or chemistry is recommended. International applicants must submit a minimum TOEFL score of 600. Students applying for the Ph.D. program must submit their application packet to the Office of Graduate Admissions by January 15 to receive full consideration for a graduate assistantship. Students applying for the Master of Science program must submit their application through the Web site at http://www.sophas.org by April 1.

Correspondence and Information

Department of Environmental Health Sciences
Wadsworth Center
University at Albany, State University of New York
P.O. Box 509
Albany, New York 12201-0509
Phone: 518-473-7553
Fax: 518-473-8520
E-mail: ehsdept@wadsworth.org
Web site: http://www.wadsworth.org/sph/ehs

University at Albany, State University of New York

THE FACULTY AND THEIR RESEARCH

David Spink, Chair, Ph.D., Maryland, 1983. Effects of xenobiotics on the metabolism of drugs and steroid hormones.

Katherine T. Alben, Ph.D., Yale, 1976. Chemistry of drinking water; natural and anthropogenic organic compounds in aquatic organisms, rivers, lakes and wetlands.

Kenneth M. Aldous, Ph.D., London, 1970. Instrumental methods of analysis of environmental pollutants; assessment of human exposure to chemicals present in air, water, soil, dust, food or other environmental media via measurement of the chemicals or chemical metabolites present in human specimens, such as blood or urine.

Ilham AlMahamid, Ph.D., Paris, 1990. Radiochemistry; assessment of human exposure to radioactive isotopes in case of nuclear emergency; minimization of radioactive waste toxicity.

Erin M. Bell, Ph.D., North Carolina at Chapel Hill, 2000. Epidemiology of environmental exposures, specifically pesticides; adverse birth outcomes; child development and cancer.

Michael S. Bloom, Ph.D., SUNY at Buffalo, 2004. Effects of environmental exposures, specifically persistent organic pollutants and trace metals, and oxidative stress on human fecundity/fertility (including in vitro fertilization); effects of organic pollutants on human thyroid function; employment of biomarkers for epidemiologic studies.

Ellen Braun-Howland, Ph.D., Rensselaer, 1982. Occurrence and control of pathogens in the environment; molecular detection of environmentally significant organisms.

David Carpenter, M.D., Harvard, 1964. Study of human disease as a result of environmental exposures, especially as a result of PCBs and chlorinated pesticides; use of animal model systems to study mechanisms of toxicity.

Liang T. Chu, Ph.D., Princeton, 1990. Atmospheric chemistry; kinetics and mechanisms of atmospheric reactions; reactions on ice and salt surfaces.

Xinxin Ding, Ph.D., Michigan, 1988. Molecular toxicology; gene regulation, genetic polymorphism, and biological function of cytochrome P-450 monooxygenases; transgenic/knockout mouse models of human diseases.

Vincent A. Dutkiewicz, Ph.D., SUNY at Albany, 1977. Physical and chemical mechanisms of atmospheric sulfur and other environmentally significant pollutants.

David M. Dziewulski, Ph.D., New Hampshire, 1980. Biocorrosion and biofouling in industrial and potable water systems; environmental concentration and isolation methods (polymer partitioning); investigation, detection, and control of legionellae in healthcare settings; investigation of mycobacterial avium complexion potable water systems.

Edward Fitzgerald, Ph.D., Yale, 1982. Environmental epidemiology; exposure assessment; human health effects; PCBs; dioxins.

Jun Gu, Ph.D., Shanghai (China), 1993. The mechanisms of environmental diseases and chemical toxicity.

Bruce Herron, Ph.D., SUNY at Albany, 1999. Functional analysis of the mouse genome; investigation of defects in mammalian organogenesis.

Chia-Swee Hong, Ph.D., CUNY, 1980. Analytical chemistry of environmental pollutants; advanced oxidation technology; UV/TiO2 and Fenton reactions.

Liaquat Husain, Ph.D., Arkansas, 1968. Atmospheric transport of trace chemicals; acid rain.

Robert Jansing, Ph.D., Houston, 1975. Identification of biomarkers of human exposure to environmental chemicals.

Glen D. Johnson, Ph.D., Penn State, 1999. Spatial epidemiology; maternal and child health; built environment and community-level social effects on health.

Kurunthachalam Kannan, Ph.D., Ehime (Japan), 1994. Understanding global distribution; fate and effects of organic pollutants in the environment.

Haider A. Khwaja, Ph.D., New Brunswick (Canada), 1982. Environmental chemistry; inorganic and organic pollutants.

Michael Kitto, Ph.D., Maryland, 1987. Radon in water and air; atmospheric gas and particle pollutants radioactivity.

David Lawrence, Ph.D., Boston College, 1971. Cellular, molecular, and biochemical investigation of the effects of environmental factors on the immune system; regulatory interactions between the nervous and immune systems.

John D. Paccione, Ph.D., Rensselaer, 1993. Use of titanium dioxide and multiphase-flow reactor designs to mineralize organic compounds in potable, recreational, and waste water.

Patrick J. Parsons, Ph.D., London, 1983. Trace-element analysis of biological tissues and fluids; analytical atomic spectrometry.

Ramune Reliene, Ph.D., Zurich, 2001. Gene, environment, and nutrient interactions in the etiology and prevention of cancer.

Richard F. Seegal, Ph.D., Georgia, 1972. Developmental neurotoxicity of PCBs and heavy metals; neuroimmune interactions and Parkinson's disease.

Thomas Semkow, Ph.D., Washington (St. Louis), 1983. Environmental radioactivity; ionizing radiation measurement; mathematical modeling.

Roger Sokol, Ph.D., SUNY at Albany, 1990. Biodegradation of halogenated organic contaminants; control of disinfection byproduct formation in drinking water; aquatic ecology.

Robert Turesky, Ph.D., MIT, 1986. Environmental and molecular epidemiology; assessment of human exposure to toxicants; biochemical toxicology of carcinogenic heterocyclic aromatic amines.

Thomas Wainman, Ph.D., Rutgers, 1999. Research in assessing human exposure to environmental contaminants; utilizing GIS to examine spatial distributions of exposure sources; indoor air pollution.

Ying Wang, Ph.D., SUNY at Albany, 1989. Environmental public health tracking and surveillance; research on identifying environmental and genetic risk factors for major birth defects.

James Webber, Ph.D., SUNY at Albany, 1999. Hazardous microparticles in the environment; analytical electron microscopy.

JoEllen Welsh, Ph.D., Cornell, 1980. Nutrition, nuclear receptors, genomics and chronic disease; interactions between nuclear receptors and environmental factors in cancer development and aging.

Lloyd Wilson, Ph.D., SUNY at Albany, 1995. Evaluation of the fate of environmental contaminants with a focus on understanding potential human exposures.

Qing-Yu Zhang, Ph.D., Michigan, 1989. Intestinal P450 enzymes in drug metabolism and chemical toxicity; regulation and biological functions of tissue-selective drug metabolism enzymes.

Xianliang Zhou, Ph.D., Dalhousie, 1988. Deployment and development of techniques for the measurement of organic and inorganic atmospheric trace species.

Lei Zhu, Ph.D., Columbia, 1991. Kinetics and photochemistry of homogeneous and heterogeneous atmospheric reactions; new technique development; atmospheric application of cavity ring-down spectroscopy and its novel variant; atmospheric application of time-resolved step-scan FT-IR.

Adjunct Faculty

S. Brenner, Ph.D.; L. Kaminsky, Ph.D.; N. Kim, Ph.D.; B. Mayes, Ph.D.; Mary O'Reilly, Ph.D.; B. Pentecost, Ph.D.; J. Silkworth, Ph.D.; K. Swami, Ph.D.; B. Tran, Ph.D.; R. Waniewski, Ph.D.

UNIVERSITY OF CALIFORNIA, IRVINE

School of Medicine
Department of Pharmacology

Program of Study	The Ph.D. program prepares students for careers in academia, research institutions, biotechnology, and the pharmaceutical industry by providing a foundation in all aspects of pharmacology, from molecular mechanisms through behavior. Specific areas of study include molecular and cellular pharmacology, neurosciences, gene regulation, circadian rhythms, epigenetic modifications, neuropharmacology, psychopharmacology, and cardiovascular pharmacology. Emphasis is placed on providing an integrated understanding of drug receptors: their structure, location, and function; molecular aspects of drug action; receptor signaling mechanisms; structure–activity relationships and drug design; and the role of receptors and drugs in development and aging, plasticity, reinforcement and drug abuse, neural disorders, and cardiovascular physiology and disease. Students take three laboratory rotations in the first year, complete the required course work in the first two years, and then take a comprehensive written exam. Students advance to candidacy in their third year by orally defending their research proposal; they generally complete the Ph.D. degree in their fifth year.
Research Facilities	The well-equipped laboratories of the Department of Pharmacology are housed in the Med Surge II Building and the Gillespie Neurosciences Research Facility, located in the School of Medicine adjacent to the main campus. The Science Library and animal-care facility are conveniently located nearby, and a large computing facility is available on the main campus.
Financial Aid	Students who maintain satisfactory academic progress receive full financial support, i.e., tuition, fees, health insurance, and a living stipend ($26,250 for 2009–10). Sources of support include University fellowships and NIH training and research grants.
Cost of Study	The estimated cost of tuition in 2010–11 is $13,415.50 for state residents and $28,517.50 for nonresidents. The tuition levels for 2011–12 have not yet been determined.
Living and Housing Costs	University housing is available, as is off-campus housing in nearby communities. For rates and more information, students should visit the University housing Web site at http://www.housing.uci.edu.
Student Group	The University's total enrollment in fall 2008 was 27,631 students, of whom 4,278 were graduate students. Pharmacology maintains approximately 30 graduate students in its program.
Student Outcomes	Recent graduates of the program are doing postdoctoral research at the University of California, Irvine (UCI); UC Los Angeles (UCLA); UC San Diego (UCSD); UC San Francisco (UCSF); Stanford; Scripps Research Institute; and the National Institute of Mental Health. Other graduates hold faculty positions (tenured or tenure track) at UCI, UCLA, UCSD, Yale, and the Universities of Colorado, Michigan, and Minnesota.
Location	UCI is located 5 miles from the Pacific Ocean and 40 miles south of Los Angeles. The surrounding hills and grazing lands give the campus an open feeling, though an estimated 2 million people live within a 20-mile radius. Concerts, repertory theater, and art galleries are available both on and off campus. Beaches, marinas, ski resorts, and mountain trails are within easy driving distance, and the mild climate permits a wide variety of year-round recreation.
The University	UCI is a young, dynamic campus that has rapidly become a full partner in the region's growing culture and economy. As a major research university, UCI offers excellent opportunities for graduate students in most traditional academic disciplines and in several interdisciplinary programs unique to the campus. Collaborations between departments in the School of Medicine and the School of Biological Sciences enhance the graduate program, providing students with access to all courses and the research expertise of all faculty members. Graduate students have access to the facilities of the entire nine-campus University of California system.
Applying	To be considered for entrance to the program in the fall quarter, students must submit applications no later than December 15 of the preceding calendar year. Applicants are required to submit an official online application, official transcripts, three letters of recommendation, GRE General and Subject test scores in biology or chemistry, and pay the application fee. International students are required to submit TQEFL scores.
Correspondence and Information	Student Affairs Coordinator Department of Pharmacology 360 Med Surge II University of California, Irvine Irvine, California 92697-4625 Phone: 949-824-7651 Fax: 949-824-4855 E-mail: pharm@uci.edu Web site: http://www.pharmsci.uci.edu/

University of California, Irvine

THE FACULTY AND THEIR RESEARCH

Although diverse in their research specialties, the faculty members share a common interest in the molecular basis of drug-receptor interactions. They enjoy international recognition for their contributions to research and service on grant review committees and editorial boards. Graduate students are expected to be active researchers and to publish in major medical and biological journals.

The faculty research programs attract postdoctoral fellows and visiting scientists who provide additional resources for research and training. Strong programs in neuroscience, cell biology, physiology, and molecular biology in other departments of the School of Medicine and the School of Biological Sciences provide students with additional opportunities for interaction. The Department also has affiliations with scientists from other academic institutions and from the growing biopharmaceutical industry in Irvine. The latter especially provides the opportunity to experience pharmacology from a drug discovery standpoint.

Core Faculty

James D. Belluzzi, Adjunct Professor; Ph.D., Chicago, 1970. Brain substrates and pharmacology of reward; characterization of nicotine reinforcement; drug therapies for Parkinson's disease, anxiety, and drug abuse.

Olivier Civelli, Eric and Lila Nelson Professor of Neuropharmacology; Ph.D., Zurich (Switzerland), 1979. Molecular biology of G-protein–coupled receptors; diversity of the dopamine receptors; cloning and analyses of new receptors, in particular orphan receptors (receptors with unknown natural ligand); discovery and characterization of novel neurotransmitters and neuropeptides; determination of the pharmacological, biological, and behavioral activities of the novel neurotransmitters and neuropeptides.

Sue Piper Duckles, Professor and Senior Associate Dean; Ph.D., California, San Francisco, 1973. Pharmacology of blood vessels, regulation of neurotransmitter release, physiology and pharmacology of the autonomic nervous system, unique properties of cerebral circulation, effects of gonadal steroids on vascular function, impact of age on cardiovascular regulation.

Frederick J. Ehlert, Professor; Ph.D., California, Irvine, 1978. Subtypes of muscarinic receptors and their signaling mechanisms in brain, heart, smooth muscle, ocular tissue, and exocine glands; receptor G-protein interactions; interactions between the signaling pathways of specific neurotransmitter receptors; molecular basis of drug selectivity.

Kelvin W. Gee, Professor; Ph.D., California, Davis, 1981. Molecular characterization of a novel receptor site coupled to the GABAA receptor-ion channel complex; discovery of novel ligands that interact with these sites and their potential therapeutic application.

Naoto Hoshi, Assistant Professor; Ph.D., Kanazawa (Japan) 1999. Physiological role and regulation of the M-channel; molecular biology, electrophysiology, live cell FRET imaging.

Diana N. Krause, Adjunct Professor; Ph.D., UCLA, 1977. Characterization of the receptors for the circadian hormone melatonin; pharmacology, localization, and function in the brain and vascular system; vascular effects of estrogen.

Frances M. Leslie, Professor and Acting Dean, Graduate Division; Ph.D., Aberdeen (Scotland), 1977. Cellular and molecular characterization of action of drugs of abuse, with particular reference to morphine and nicotine; analysis of the effects of drug abuse and stress on neural plasticity, particularly during brain development.

Daniele Piomelli, Professor and Louise Turner Arnold Chair in Neurosciences; Ph.D., Columbia, 1987. Various signaling pathways that involve lipids with particular interest in the endogenous cannabinoids; arachidonic acid derivatives that activate cannabinoid (marijuana) receptors in brain and other tissues; biochemical mechanisms involved in the formation and inactivation of these molecules; developing pharmacological tools to interfere with these pathways; wide range of molecular biological, pharmacological, and analytical techniques.

Paolo Sassone-Corsi, Distinguished Professor and Chair; Ph.D., Naples (Italy), 1979. Cellular and molecular pathways regulating gene expression, epigenetic mechanisms, physiological functions, circadian clock, light signaling, metabolism, cancer, and male germ cells.

Qun-Yong Zhou, Professor; Ph.D., Oregon Health and Science, 1992. Physiology and neuropharmacology of prokineticins and prokineticin receptors, circadian rhythms and neurogenesis.

Joint Faculty

Emiliana Borrelli, Professor, Microbiology and Molecular Genetics; Ph.D., Naples (Italy), 1979. Mouse models for the study of brain disorders; dopamine system; molecular basis of addiction and neurodegeneration.

William E. Bunney Jr., Professor, Psychiatry and Human Behavior; M.D., Pennsylvania, 1956. Clinical psychobiological and neuropsychopharmacological studies of manic-depressive illness; schizophrenia and childhood mental illness.

Pietro R. Galassetti, Associate Professor in Residence, Pediatrics; M.D., Rome (Italy), 1986; Ph.D., Vanderbilt, 1998. Physiological and altered adaptive responses to stress in healthy and dysmetabolic children and adults; noninvasive monitoring of metabolic variables through analysis of exhaled gases.

Mahtab Jafari, Assistant Professor and Director of Pharmaceutical Sciences undergraduate program; Pharm.D., California, San Francisco, 1994. Anti-aging effects of botanicals and pharmaceutical compounds; the impact of botanical extracts on mitochondrial bioenergetics, oxidative stress, and other pathways of aging using cell culture and *Drosophila*.

Arthur D. Lander, Professor, Developmental and Cell Biology; M.D., Ph.D., California, San Francisco, 1985. Molecular neurobiology; intracellular and extracellular signaling in the control of axon guidance and cell motility; functions of the extracellular matrix; transgenic animal approaches to neural development and function.

Ellis R. Levin, Professor in Residence, Department of Medicine; M.D., Thomas Jefferson, 1975. Molecular and cellular biology of natriuretic peptides and endothelin and their receptors in the brain and the vasculature; regulation of astrocyte growth by these peptides.

John C. Longhurst, Professor, Department of Medicine; M.D., 1973, Ph.D., 1974, California, Davis. Regulation of the cardiovascular system and the nervous system's role in this regulation.

Z. David Luo, Assistant Professor, Anesthesiology and Preoperative Care; M.D., Guangzhou Medical (China), 1984; Ph.D., SUNY at Buffalo, 1993. Study of gene regulation and signaling pathways in chronic pain processing using animal models and molecular biology techniques.

John F. Marshall, Professor, Neurobiology and Behavior; Ph.D., Pennsylvania, 1973. Recovery of function after brain injury; organization of the basal ganglia motor system; neuronal circuitry of drug craving.

Rainer Reinscheid, Associate Professor, Pharmaceutical Sciences; Ph.D., Center for Molecular Neurobiology (Germany), 1993. Isolation of natural ligands for orphan G-protein-coupled receptors (GPCRs) and their physiological functions; the neurobiology of anxiety and stress behavior; neuropeptides involved in sleep and arousal.

Sandor Szabo, Professor in Residence, Pathology; M.D., Belgrade (Ireland), 1968; Ph.D., Montreal, 1973; Effects of growth factors (e.g., FGF, PDGF) on ulcer healing and prevention.

Section 18
Physiology

This section contains a directory of institutions offering graduate work in physiology, followed by in-depth entries submitted by institutions that chose to prepare detailed program descriptions. Additional information about programs listed in the directory but not augmented by an in-depth entry may be obtained by writing directly to the dean of a graduate school or chair of a department at the address given in the directory.

For programs offering related work, see also all other sections in this book. In the other guides in this series:

Graduate Programs in the Physical Sciences, Mathematics, Agricultural Sciences, the Environment & Natural Resources

See *Agricultural and Food Sciences, Chemistry,* and *Marine Sciences and Oceanography*

Graduate Programs in Engineering & Applied Sciences

See *Agricultural Engineering and Bioengineering, Biomedical Engineering and Biotechnology, Electrical and Computer Engineering,* and *Mechanical Engineering and Mechanics*

Graduate Programs in Business, Education, Health, Information Studies, Law & Social Work

See *Optometry and Vision Sciences, Physical Education and Kinesiology,* and *Veterinary Medicine and Sciences*

CONTENTS

Cardiovascular Sciences

Albany Medical College, Center for Cardiovascular Sciences, Albany, NY 12208-3479. Offers MS, PhD. Part-time programs available. *Faculty:* 18 full-time (3 women). *Students:* 14 full-time (7 women); includes 8 minority (1 African American, 6 Asian Americans or Pacific Islanders, 1 Hispanic American). Average age 25. 8 applicants, 75% accepted, 4 enrolled. In 2009, 4 doctorates awarded. Terminal master's awarded for partial completion of doctoral program. *Degree requirements:* For master's, thesis; for doctorate, comprehensive exam, thesis/dissertation, candidacy exam, written preliminary exam, 1 published paper-peer review. *Entrance requirements:* For master's, GRE General Test, letters of recommendation; for doctorate, GRE General Test, all transcripts, letters of recommendation. Additional exam requirements/recommendations for international students: Required—TOEFL. *Application deadline:* For fall admission, 3/15 priority date for domestic and international students. Applications are processed on a rolling basis. Application fee: $60. *Expenses:* Tuition: Full-time $18,820. *Financial support:* In 2009–10, 11 research assistantships (averaging $24,000 per year) were awarded; Federal Work-Study, scholarships/grants, and tuition waivers (full) also available. Financial award applicants required to submit FAFSA. *Faculty research:* Vascular smooth muscle, endothelial cell biology, molecular and genetic bases underlying cardiac disease, reactive oxygen and nitrogen species biology, fatty acid trafficking and fatty acid mediated transcription control. *Unit head:* Dr. Peter A. Vincent, Graduate Director, 518-262-6296, Fax: 518-262-8101, E-mail: vincenp@mail.amc.edu. *Application contact:* Wendy M. Vienneau, Administrative Coordinator, 518-262-8102, Fax: 518-262-8101, E-mail: hobbw@mail.amc.edu.

Baylor College of Medicine, Graduate School of Biomedical Sciences, Program in Cardiovascular Sciences, Houston, TX 77030-3498. Offers PhD, MD/PhD. *Faculty:* 40 full-time (6 women). *Students:* 12 full-time (3 women); includes 3 minority (2 African Americans, 1 Asian American or Pacific Islander), 3 international. Average age 25. In 2009, 3 doctorates awarded. *Degree requirements:* For doctorate, thesis/dissertation, public defense. *Entrance requirements:* For doctorate, GRE General Test, GRE Subject Test (strongly recommended), minimum GPA of 3.0, strong background in biology and biochemistry. Additional exam requirements/recommendations for international students: Required—TOEFL. *Application deadline:* For fall admission, 1/1 priority date for domestic students. Applications are processed on a rolling basis. Application fee: $0. Electronic applications accepted. *Financial support:* In 2009–10, 12 students received support; fellowships, research assistantships, career-related internships or fieldwork, Federal Work-Study, institutionally sponsored loans, health care benefits, and students receive a scholarship unless there are grant funds available to pay tuition available. Financial award applicants required to submit FAFSA. *Faculty research:* Cell biology of the vascular wall, cell biology of cardiac tissue, biology and models of specific cardiovascular diseases. *Unit head:* Dr. Lloyd Michael, Head, 713-798-6825, Fax: 713-796-0015, E-mail: lmichael@bcm.edu. *Application contact:* Karmen Howard, Graduate Program Administrator, 713-798-4977, Fax: 713-798-0681, E-mail: karmenh@bcm.edu.

Dartmouth College, Program in Experimental and Molecular Medicine, Cardiovascular Diseases Track, Hanover, NH 03755. Offers PhD.

Geneva College, Program in Cardiovascular Science, Beaver Falls, PA 15010-3599. Offers MS. *Faculty:* 9 part-time/adjunct (3 women). *Students:* 4 full-time (0 women). 2 applicants, 100% accepted, 2 enrolled. *Degree requirements:* For master's, RCIS and RCES registry exams. *Entrance requirements:* Additional exam requirements/recommendations for international students: Required—TOEFL. *Application deadline:* Applications are processed on a rolling basis. Electronic applications accepted. *Expenses:* Tuition: Full-time $11,250; part-time $625 per credit. Tuition and fees vary according to program. *Financial support:* Applicants required to submit FAFSA. *Unit head:* Dr. David A. Essig, Coordinator, 724-847-6900, E-mail: dessig@geneva.edu. *Application contact:* Dr. David A. Essig, Coordinator, 724-846-6900, E-mail: dessig@geneva.edu.

Long Island University, C.W. Post Campus, School of Health Professions and Nursing, Department of Biomedical Sciences, Brookville, NY 11548-1300. Offers cardiovascular perfusion (MS); clinical laboratory management (MS); medical biology (MS), including hematology, immunology, medical biology, medical chemistry, medical microbiology. Part-time and evening/weekend programs available. Postbaccalaureate distance learning degree programs offered. *Degree requirements:* For master's, thesis. *Entrance requirements:* For master's, minimum GPA of 2.75 in major. Electronic applications accepted.

Loyola University Chicago, Graduate School, Marcella Niehoff School of Nursing, Acute Care Clinical Nurse Specialist Program, Chicago, IL 60660. Offers acute care clinical nurse specialist (MSN), including cardiovascular health. *Accreditation:* AACN. Part-time and evening/weekend programs available. *Degree requirements:* For master's, comprehensive exam or oral thesis defense. *Entrance requirements:* For master's, BSN, Illinois nursing license, 3 letters of recommendation, 1000 hours experience in acute care before starting clinical. *Application deadline:* Applications are processed on a rolling basis. Electronic applications accepted. *Expenses:* Tuition: Full-time $14,220; part-time $790 per credit hour. Required fees: $60 per semester hour. Tuition and fees vary according to program. *Financial support:* Teaching assistantships, traineeships and unspecified assistantships available. Financial award application deadline: 3/1. *Unit head:* Dr. Judith Jennrich, Associate Professor, 708-216-3813, E-mail: jjrennri@luc.edu. *Application contact:* Dr. Vicki A. Keough, Associate Professor/Master's Program Director, 708-216-3582, Fax: 708-216-9555, E-mail: vkeough@luc.edu.

Loyola University Chicago, Graduate School, Marcella Niehoff School of Nursing, Adult Clinical Nurse Specialist Program, Chicago, IL 60660. Offers adult clinical nurse specialist (MSN, Certificate); cardiovascular health (Certificate); oncology nursing (Certificate). Part-time and evening/weekend programs available. Postbaccalaureate distance learning degree programs offered (minimal on-campus study). In 2009, 1 master's awarded. *Entrance requirements:* For master's, Illinois nursing license, BSN, minimum nursing GPA of 3.0, 3 letters of recommendation, 1,000 hours experience in area of specialty. *Expenses:* Tuition: Full-time $14,220; part-time $790 per credit hour. Required fees: $60 per semester hour. Tuition and fees vary according to program. *Unit head:* Dr. Meg Gulanick, Professor, 708-216-9687, Fax: 708-216-9555, E-mail: mgulani@luc.edu. *Application contact:* Dr. Vicki A. Keough, Associate Professor/Master's Program Director, 708-216-3582, Fax: 708-216-9555, E-mail: vkeough@luc.edu.

McMaster University, Faculty of Health Sciences and School of Graduate Studies, Program in Medical Sciences, Blood and Vascular Area, Hamilton, ON L8S 4M2, Canada. Offers M Sc, PhD, MD/PhD. *Degree requirements:* For master's, thesis; for doctorate, comprehensive exam, thesis/dissertation. *Entrance requirements:* For master's, honors B Sc, B+ average in related field; for doctorate, M Sc, minimum B+ average, students with proven research experience and an A average may be admitted with a B Sc degree. Additional exam requirements/recommendations for international students: Required—TOEFL (minimum score 580 paper-based; 237 computer-based; 92 iBT).

Medical College of Georgia, School of Graduate Studies, Program in Vascular Biology, Augusta, GA 30912. Offers PhD. *Degree requirements:* For doctorate, comprehensive exam, thesis/dissertation. *Entrance requirements:* For doctorate, GRE General Test. Additional exam requirements/recommendations for international students: Required—TOEFL (minimum score 550 paper-based; 213 computer-based; 79 iBT). Electronic applications accepted. Full-time tuition and fees vary according to campus/location, program and student level. *Faculty research:* Hypertension and renal disease, diabetes and obesity, peripheral vascular disease, acute lung injury, signal transduction.

Medical University of South Carolina, College of Graduate Studies, Program in Molecular and Cellular Biology and Pathobiology, Charleston, SC 29425. Offers cancer biology (PhD); cardiovascular biology (PhD); cardiovascular imaging (PhD); cell regulation (PhD); craniofacial biology (PhD); genetics and development (PhD); marine biomedicine (PhD); DMD/PhD; MD/PhD. *Faculty:* 137 full-time (33 women). *Students:* 39 full-time (25 women); includes 6 minority (4 African Americans, 1 Asian American or Pacific Islander, 1 Hispanic American), 9 international. Average age 28. In 2009, 16 doctorates awarded. *Degree requirements:* For doctorate, thesis/dissertation, oral and written exams. *Entrance requirements:* For doctorate, GRE General Test, interview, minimum GPA of 3.0. Additional exam requirements/recommendations for international students: Required—TOEFL (minimum score 600 paper-based; 250 computer-based; 100 iBT). *Application deadline:* For fall admission, 1/15 priority date for domestic and international students. Applications are processed on a rolling basis. Application fee: $0 ($85 for international students). Electronic applications accepted. *Financial support:* In 2009–10, 39 students received support, including 39 research assistantships with partial tuition reimbursements available (averaging $23,000 per year); Federal Work-Study and scholarships/grants also available. Support available to part-time students. Financial award application deadline: 3/10; financial award applicants required to submit FAFSA. *Unit head:* Dr. Donald R. Menick, Director, 843-876-5045, Fax: 843-792-6590, E-mail: menickd@musc.edu. *Application contact:* Dr. Cynthia F. Wright, Associate Dean for Admissions and Career Development, 843-792-2564, Fax: 843-792-6590, E-mail: wrightcf@musc.edu.

Memorial University of Newfoundland, Faculty of Medicine and School of Graduate Studies, Graduate Programs in Medicine, Division of Biomedical Sciences, St. John's, NL A1C 5S7, Canada. Offers cancer (M Sc, PhD); cardiovascular (M Sc, PhD); immunology (M Sc, PhD); neuroscience (M Sc, PhD). Part-time programs available. *Degree requirements:* For master's, thesis; for doctorate, comprehensive exam, thesis/dissertation, oral defense of thesis. *Entrance requirements:* For master's, MD or B Sc; for doctorate, MD or M Sc. Additional exam requirements/recommendations for international students: Required—TOEFL. *Faculty research:* Neuroscience, immunology, cardiovascular, and cancer.

Midwestern University, Glendale Campus, College of Health Sciences, Arizona Campus, Program in Cardiovascular Science, Glendale, AZ 85308. Offers MCVS. *Faculty:* 4 full-time (1 woman). *Students:* 38 full-time (21 women), 2 part-time (both women); includes 7 minority (3 African Americans, 1 Asian American or Pacific Islander, 3 Hispanic Americans), 1 international. Average age 26. 55 applicants, 65% accepted, 24 enrolled. In 2009, 10 master's awarded. Application fee: $50. *Expenses:* Contact institution. *Unit head:* Dr. Jon Austin, Dean, 623-572-3616. *Application contact:* James Walter, Director of Admissions, 888-247-9277, Fax: 623-572-3229, E-mail: admissaz@midwestern.edu.

Milwaukee School of Engineering, Department of Electrical Engineering and Computer Science, Program in Cardiovascular Studies, Milwaukee, WI 53202-3109. Offers MS. *Faculty:* 1 full-time (0 women), 1 part-time/adjunct (0 women). *Students:* 2 full-time (0 women), 3 part-time (2 women). 3 applicants, 67% accepted, 2 enrolled. In 2009, 1 master's awarded. *Application deadline:* Applications are processed on a rolling basis. Application fee: $30. Electronic applications accepted. *Expenses:* Tuition: Part-time $603 per credit. *Financial support:* In 2009–10, 5 students received support. *Unit head:* Dr. Ronald Gerrits, Director, 414-277-7561, Fax: 414-277-7494, E-mail: gerrits@msoe.edu. *Application contact:* David E. Tietyen, Graduate Admissions Director, 800-332-6763, Fax: 414-277-7475, E-mail: wp@msoe.edu.

Milwaukee School of Engineering, Department of Electrical Engineering and Computer Science, Program in Perfusion, Milwaukee, WI 53202-3109. Offers MS. Part-time and evening/weekend programs available. *Faculty:* 1 full-time (0 women), 4 part-time/adjunct (1 woman). *Students:* 10 full-time (2 women); includes 2 minority (both Asian Americans or Pacific Islanders). Average age 33. 31 applicants, 32% accepted, 7 enrolled. In 2009, 1 master's awarded. *Degree requirements:* For master's, comprehensive exam, thesis. *Entrance requirements:* For master's, GRE General Test or GMAT, BS in appropriate discipline, undergraduate work in human physiology or anatomy, 3 letters of recommendation, interview, observation of 2 perfusion cases. Additional exam requirements/recommendations for international students: Required—TOEFL (minimum score 79 iBT). *Application deadline:* Applications are processed on a rolling basis. Application fee: $30. Electronic applications accepted. *Expenses:* Tuition: Part-time $603 per credit. *Financial support:* In 2009–10, 8 students received support. Career-related internships or fieldwork available. Support available to part-time students. Financial award applicants required to submit FAFSA. *Faculty research:* Heart medicine. *Unit head:* Dr. Ronald Gerrits, Director, 414-277-7561, Fax: 414-277-7494, E-mail: gerrits@msoe.edu. *Application contact:* David E. Tietyen, Graduate Admissions Director, 800-332-6763, Fax: 414-277-7475, E-mail: wp@msoe.edu.

The Ohio State University, College of Medicine, School of Allied Medical Professions, Program in Circulation Technology, Columbus, OH 43210. Offers MS. Electronic applications accepted. *Expenses:* Tuition, state resident: full-time $10,683. Tuition, nonresident: full-time $25,923. Tuition and fees vary according to course load and program.

Queen's University at Kingston, School of Graduate Studies and Research, Faculty of Health Sciences, Department of Anatomy and Cell Biology, Kingston, ON K7L 3N6, Canada. Offers biology of reproduction (M Sc, PhD); cancer (M Sc, PhD); cardiovascular pathophysiology (M Sc, PhD); cell and molecular biology (M Sc, PhD); drug metabolism (M Sc, PhD); endocrinology (M Sc, PhD); motor control (M Sc, PhD); neural regeneration (M Sc, PhD); neurophysiology (M Sc, PhD). Part-time programs available. *Degree requirements:* For master's, thesis; for doctorate, one foreign language, comprehensive exam, thesis/dissertation. *Entrance requirements:* Additional exam requirements/recommendations for international students: Required—TOEFL. Electronic applications accepted. *Faculty research:* Human kinetics, neuroscience, reproductive biology, cardiovascular.

Quinnipiac University, School of Health Sciences, Program in Cardiovascular Perfusion, Hamden, CT 06518-1940. Offers MHS. *Faculty:* 1 full-time (0 women), 4 part-time/adjunct (0 women). *Students:* 8 full-time (2 women), 3 part-time (0 women); includes 3 minority (1 African American, 2 Asian Americans or Pacific Islanders), 1 international. Average age 36. 15 applicants, 67% accepted, 8 enrolled. In 2009, 2 master's awarded. *Entrance requirements:* For master's, bachelor's degree in science or health-related discipline from an accredited American or Canadian college or university; 2 years health care work experience; interview. Additional exam requirements/recommendations for international students: Required—TOEFL (minimum score 575 paper-based; 233 computer-based; 90 iBT), IELTS (minimum score 6.5). *Application deadline:* For fall admission, 7/30 priority date for domestic students, 4/30 priority date for international students. Applications are processed on a rolling basis. Application fee: $45. Electronic applications accepted. *Expenses:* Tuition: Full-time $16,030; part-time $770 per credit. Required fees: $630; $35 per credit. *Financial support:* Career-related internships or fieldwork, tuition waivers, and unspecified assistantships available. Financial award application deadline: 4/15; financial award applicants required to submit FAFSA. *Unit head:* Michael Smith, Director, 203-582-3427, Fax: 203-582-8706, E-mail: michael.smith@quinnipiac.edu. *Application contact:* Kristin Parent, Assistant Director of Graduate Health Sciences Admissions, 800-462-1944, Fax: 208-582-3443, E-mail: kristin.parent@quinnipiac.edu.

State University of New York Upstate Medical University, College of Graduate Studies, Major Research Areas of the College of Graduate Studies, Syracuse, NY 13210-2334. *Unit head:* Dr. Steven R. Goodman, Dean, College of Graduate Studies, 315-464-4538. *Application contact:* Sandra Tillotson, Coordinator of Graduate Recruitment, 315-464-7655, Fax: 315-464-4544, E-mail: tillotss@upstate.edu.

Université Laval, Faculty of Medicine, Post-Professional Programs in Medical Studies, Québec, QC G1K 7P4, Canada. Offers anatomy–pathology (DESS); anesthesiology (DESS); cardiology (DESS); care of older people (Diploma); clinical research (DESS); community health (DESS); dermatology (DESS); diagnostic radiology (DESS); emergency medicine (Diploma); family medicine (DESS); general surgery (DESS); geriatrics (DESS); hematology (DESS); internal medicine (DESS); maternal and fetal medicine (Diploma); medical biochemistry (DESS); medical microbiology and infectious diseases (DESS); medical oncology (DESS); nephrology (DESS); neurology (DESS); neurosurgery (DESS); obstetrics and gynecology (DESS);

ophthalmology (DESS); orthopedic surgery (DESS); oto-rhino-laryngology (DESS); palliative medicine (Diploma); pediatrics (DESS); plastic surgery (DESS); psychiatry (DESS); pulmonary medicine (DESS); radiology–oncology (DESS); thoracic surgery (DESS); urology (DESS). *Degree requirements:* For other advanced degree, comprehensive exam. *Entrance requirements:* For degree, knowledge of French. Electronic applications accepted.

University of Calgary, Faculty of Medicine and Faculty of Graduate Studies, Department of Cardiovascular and Respiratory Sciences, Calgary, AB T2N 1N4, Canada. Offers M Sc, PhD. *Degree requirements:* For master's, thesis; for doctorate, thesis/dissertation, candidacy exam. *Entrance requirements:* For master's and doctorate, minimum GPA of 3.2. Additional exam requirements/recommendations for international students: Required—TOEFL (minimum score 600 paper-based; 250 computer-based). Electronic applications accepted. *Faculty research:* Cardiac mechanics, physiology and pharmacology; lung mechanics, physiology and pathophysiology; smooth muscle biochemistry; physiology and pharmacology.

University of California, San Diego, School of Medicine and Office of Graduate Studies, Molecular Pathology Program, La Jolla, CA 92093. Offers bioinformatics (PhD); cancer biology/oncology (PhD); cardiovascular sciences and disease (PhD); microbiology (PhD); molecular pathology (PhD); neurological disease (PhD); stem cell and developmental biology (PhD); structural biology/drug design (PhD). *Entrance requirements:* For doctorate, GRE General Test, GRE Subject Test. Additional exam requirements/recommendations for international students: Required—TOEFL. Electronic applications accepted.

University of Guelph, Ontario Veterinary College and Graduate Program Services, Graduate Programs in Veterinary Sciences, Department of Clinical Studies, Guelph, ON N1G 2W1, Canada. Offers anesthesiology (M Sc, DV Sc); cardiology (DV Sc, Diploma); clinical studies (Diploma); dermatology (M Sc); diagnostic imaging (M Sc, DV Sc); emergency/critical care (M Sc, DV Sc, Diploma); medicine (M Sc, DV Sc); neurology (M Sc, DV Sc); ophthalmology (M Sc, DV Sc); surgery (M Sc, DV Sc). *Degree requirements:* For master's, thesis; for doctorate, comprehensive exam, thesis/dissertation. *Entrance requirements:* Additional exam requirements/recommendations for international students: Required—TOEFL (minimum score 550 paper-based; 213 computer-based), IELTS (minimum score 6.5). Electronic applications accepted. *Faculty research:* Orthopedics, respirology, oncology, exercise physiology, cardiology.

University of Medicine and Dentistry of New Jersey, School of Health Related Professions, Department of Interdisciplinary Studies, Program in Health Sciences, Newark, NJ 07107-1709. Offers cardiopulmonary sciences (PhD); clinical laboratory sciences (PhD); health sciences (MS); interdisciplinary studies (PhD); nutrition (PhD); physical therapy/movement science (PhD). *Degree requirements:* For doctorate, thesis/dissertation. *Entrance requirements:* For doctorate, interview, writing sample. Additional exam requirements/recommendations for international students: Required—TOEFL. Electronic applications accepted.

The University of South Dakota, School of Medicine and Health Sciences and Graduate School, Biomedical Sciences Graduate Program, Cardiovascular Research Program, Vermillion, SD 57069-2390. Offers MS, PhD. Terminal master's awarded for partial completion of doctoral program. *Degree requirements:* For master's, thesis; for doctorate, comprehensive exam, thesis/dissertation. *Entrance requirements:* For master's and doctorate, GRE General Test, minimum GPA of 3.0. Additional exam requirements/recommendations for international students: Required—TOEFL (minimum score 550 paper-based; 213 computer-based; 80 iBT), IELTS (minimum score 6). Electronic applications accepted. *Expenses:* Contact institution. *Faculty research:* Cardiovascular disease.

The University of Toledo, College of Graduate Studies, College of Medicine, Biomedical Science Programs, Program in Cardiovascular and Metabolic Diseases, Toledo, OH 43606-3390. Offers MSBS, PhD.

Molecular Physiology

Baylor College of Medicine, Graduate School of Biomedical Sciences, Department of Molecular Physiology and Biophysics, Houston, TX 77030-3498. Offers PhD, MD/PhD. *Faculty:* 31 full-time (10 women). *Students:* 21 full-time (14 women); includes 2 minority (1 African American, 1 Hispanic American), 12 international. Average age 26. In 2009, 2 doctorates awarded. *Degree requirements:* For doctorate, thesis/dissertation, public defense. *Entrance requirements:* For doctorate, GRE General Test, GRE Subject Test (strongly recommended), minimum GPA of 3.0. Additional exam requirements/recommendations for international students: Required—TOEFL. *Application deadline:* For fall admission, 1/1 priority date for domestic students. Electronic applications accepted. *Financial support:* Fellowships, research assistantships, career-related internships or fieldwork, Federal Work-Study, institutionally sponsored loans, health care benefits, and students receive a scholarship unless there are grant funds available to pay tuition available. Financial award applicants required to submit FAFSA. *Faculty research:* Multi-photon imaging, magnetic resonance imaging (MRI), structure and function of ion channels and transport proteins, signal transduction, synaptic plasticity, cell-cycle control, reactive oxygen species, neurodegenerative diseases and cardiac development. *Unit head:* Dr. Robia Pautler, Director, 713-798-5630, Fax: 713-798-3475. *Application contact:* Cherrie McGlory, Graduate Program Administrator, 713-798-5109, Fax: 713-798-3475, E-mail: molphysgrad@bcm.edu.

Case Western Reserve University, School of Medicine and School of Graduate Studies, Graduate Programs in Medicine, Department of Physiology and Biophysics, Cleveland, OH 44106. Offers cell and molecular physiology (MS); cell physiology (PhD); molecular/cellular biophysics (PhD); physiology and biophysics (PhD); systems physiology (PhD); MD/PhD. Terminal master's awarded for partial completion of doctoral program. *Degree requirements:* For master's, thesis; for doctorate, thesis/dissertation. *Entrance requirements:* For master's, GRE General Test, minimum GPA of 3.28; for doctorate, GRE General Test, minimum GPA of 3.6. Additional exam requirements/recommendations for international students: Required—TOEFL. Electronic applications accepted. *Faculty research:* Cardiovascular physiology, calcium metabolism, epithelial cell biology.

See Close-Up on page 487.

Loyola University Chicago, Graduate School, Program in Cell and Molecular Physiology, Chicago, IL 60660. Offers MS, PhD. MS offered only to students enrolled in a first-professional degree program. *Faculty:* 17 full-time (4 women), 5 part-time/adjunct (1 woman). *Students:* 9 full-time (2 women); includes 1 minority (Asian American or Pacific Islander), 2 international. Average age 28. 13 applicants, 38% accepted, 4 enrolled. In 2009, 1 doctorate awarded. *Degree requirements:* For master's, thesis; for doctorate, comprehensive exam, thesis/dissertation. *Entrance requirements:* For master's, GRE General Test or MCAT; for doctorate, GRE General Test. Additional exam requirements/recommendations for international students: Required—TOEFL. *Application deadline:* For fall admission, 5/15 for domestic and international students. Application fee: $40. Electronic applications accepted. *Expenses:* Tuition: Full-time $14,220; part-time $790 per credit hour. Required fees: $60 per semester hour. Tuition and fees vary according to program. *Financial support:* In 2009–10, 5 fellowships with tuition reimbursements (averaging $23,000 per year), 9 research assistantships with tuition reimbursements (averaging $23,000 per year) were awarded. *Faculty research:* Cardiovascular system—emphasis in neural and metabolic control of circulation, ion channels, excitation contraction coupling, molecular cloning. *Unit head:* Dr. Pieter deTombe, Chair, 708-216-6305, Fax: 708-216-6308, E-mail: pdetombe@lumc.edu. *Application contact:* Dr. Ruben Mestril, Graduate Program Director, 708-327-2395, Fax: 708-216-6308, E-mail: rmestri@lumc.edu.

See Close-Up on page 489.

Rutgers, The State University of New Jersey, New Brunswick, Graduate School-New Brunswick, Program in Endocrinology and Animal Biosciences, Piscataway, NJ 08854-8097. Offers MS, PhD. Terminal master's awarded for partial completion of doctoral program. *Degree requirements:* For master's, thesis; for doctorate, comprehensive exam, thesis/dissertation. *Entrance requirements:* For master's and doctorate, GRE General Test. Additional exam requirements/recommendations for international students: Required—TOEFL. Electronic applications accepted. *Faculty research:* Comparative and behavioral endocrinology, epigenetic regulation of the endocrine system, exercise physiology and immunology, fetal and neonatal developmental programming, mammary gland biology and breast cancer, neuroendocrinology and alcohol studies, reproductive and developmental toxicology.

Stony Brook University, State University of New York, Stony Brook University Medical Center, School of Medicine and Graduate School, Graduate Programs in Medicine, Department of Physiology and Biophysics, Stony Brook, NY 11794. Offers PhD. *Students:* 14 full-time (9 women); includes 3 minority (all Asian Americans or Pacific Islanders), 5 international. Average age 29. 39 applicants, 41% accepted. In 2009, 6 doctorates awarded. *Degree requirements:* For doctorate, comprehensive exam, thesis/dissertation. *Entrance requirements:* For doctorate, GRE General Test, GRE Subject Test, BS in related field, minimum GPA of 3.0. Additional exam requirements/recommendations for international students: Required—TOEFL. *Application deadline:* For fall admission, 1/15 for domestic students. Application fee: $60. *Expenses:* Tuition, state resident: full-time $8370; part-time $349 per credit. Tuition, nonresident: full-time $13,250; part-time $552 per credit. Required fees: $933. *Financial support:* Fellowships, research assistantships, teaching assistantships, Federal Work-Study available. Financial award application deadline: 3/15. *Faculty research:* Cellular electrophysiology, membrane permeation and transport, metabolic endocrinology. Total annual research expenditures: $6 million. *Unit head:* Dr. Peter Brink, Chair, 631-444-2299, Fax: 631-444-3432. *Application contact:* Melanie Bonnette, Graduate Program Administrator, 631-444-2299, Fax: 631-444-3432.

Texas Tech University Health Sciences Center, Graduate School of Biomedical Sciences, Department of Cell Physiology and Molecular Biophysics, Lubbock, TX 79430. Offers MS, PhD, MD/PhD. Terminal master's awarded for partial completion of doctoral program. *Degree requirements:* For master's, thesis; for doctorate, thesis/dissertation. *Entrance requirements:* For master's and doctorate, GRE General Test, minimum GPA of 3.4. Additional exam requirements/recommendations for international students: Required—TOEFL. Electronic applications accepted. *Faculty research:* Cardiovascular physiology, neurophysiology, renal physiology, respiratory physiology.

Thomas Jefferson University, Jefferson College of Graduate Studies, Program in Molecular Physiology and Biophysics, Philadelphia, PA 19107. Offers PhD. *Faculty:* 13 full-time (5 women). *Students:* 2 full-time (1 woman). 4 applicants, 0% accepted, 0 enrolled. *Degree requirements:* For doctorate, comprehensive exam, thesis/dissertation. *Entrance requirements:* For doctorate, GRE General Test, minimum GPA of 3.2. Additional exam requirements/recommendations for international students: Required—TOEFL (minimum score 250 computer-based; 100 iBT). *Application deadline:* For fall admission, 1/15 priority date for domestic and international students. Applications are processed on a rolling basis. Application fee: $50. Electronic applications accepted. *Expenses:* Tuition: Full-time $26,858; part-time $879 per credit. Required fees: $525. *Financial support:* In 2009–10, 2 students received support, including 2 fellowships with full tuition reimbursements available (averaging $52,883 per year); Federal Work-Study, institutionally sponsored loans, scholarships/grants, traineeships, and stipend also available. Support available to part-time students. Financial award application deadline: 5/1; financial award applicants required to submit FAFSA. *Faculty research:* Cardiovascular physiology, smooth muscle physiology, pathophysiology of myocardial ischemia, endothelial cell physiology, molecular biology of ion channel physiology. Total annual research expenditures: $3.2 million. *Unit head:* Dr. Thomas M. Butler, Program Director, 215-503-6583, E-mail: thomas.butler@jefferson.edu. *Application contact:* Marc E. Stearns, Director of Admissions, 215-503-0155, Fax: 215-503-9920, E-mail: jcgs-info@jefferson.edu.

Tufts University, Sackler School of Graduate Biomedical Sciences, Graduate Program in Cellular and Molecular Physiology, Medford, MA 02155. Offers PhD. *Faculty:* 23 full-time (8 women). *Students:* 11 full-time (7 women); includes 1 minority (Asian American or Pacific Islander), 2 international. Average age 28. In 2009, 1 doctorate awarded. *Degree requirements:* For doctorate, thesis/dissertation. *Expenses:* Tuition: Full-time $38,096; part-time $3962 per credit. Required fees: $686; $40 per year. Tuition and fees vary according to course level, course load, degree level, program and student level. *Financial support:* In 2009–10, 11 students received support, including 11 research assistantships with full tuition reimbursements available (averaging $28,250 per year); scholarships/grants, health care benefits, and tuition waivers (full) also available. *Unit head:* Dr. Laura Liscum, Head, 617-636-6945, Fax: 617-636-0445. *Application contact:* Kellie Johnston, Associate Director of Admissions, 617-636-6767, Fax: 617-636-0375, E-mail: sackler-school@tufts.edu.

The University of Alabama at Birmingham, Graduate Programs in Joint Health Sciences, Program in Cellular and Molecular Physiology, Birmingham, AL 35294. Offers PhD.

University of Chicago, Division of the Biological Sciences, Neuroscience Graduate Programs, Chicago, IL 60637-1513. Offers cellular and molecular physiology (PhD); computational neuroscience (PhD); integrative neuroscience (PhD), including cell physiology, pharmacological and physiological sciences; neurobiology (PhD). *Faculty:* 109 full-time (27 women). *Students:* 62 full-time (25 women); includes 13 minority (3 African Americans, 6 Asian Americans or Pacific Islanders, 4 Hispanic Americans), 6 international. Average age 28. 113 applicants, 19% accepted, 10 enrolled. In 2009, 19 doctorates awarded. *Degree requirements:* For doctorate, thesis/dissertation, ethics class, 2 teaching assistantships. *Entrance requirements:* For doctorate, GRE General Test. Additional exam requirements/recommendations for international students: Required—TOEFL (minimum score 600 paper-based; 250 computer-based; 104 iBT), IELTS (minimum score 7). *Application deadline:* For fall admission, 12/1 priority date for domestic and international students. Applications are processed on a rolling basis. Application fee: $55. Electronic applications accepted. *Financial support:* In 2009–10, 62 students received support, including fellowships with tuition reimbursements available (averaging $29,781 per year); research assistantships with full tuition reimbursements available (averaging $29,781 per year); institutionally sponsored loans and scholarships/grants also available. Financial award applicants required to submit FAFSA. *Application contact:* Diane J. Hall, Graduate Administrative Director, 773-702-6371, Fax: 773-702-1216, E-mail: d-hall@uchicago.edu.

University of Chicago, Division of the Biological Sciences, Program in Cellular and Molecular Physiology, Chicago, IL 60637-1513. Offers PhD. *Faculty:* 31 full-time (5 women). *Students:* 6 full-time (3 women); includes 1 minority (Hispanic American). Average age 34. 10 applicants, 20% accepted, 0 enrolled. In 2009, 2 doctorates awarded. *Degree requirements:* For doctorate, thesis/dissertation, ethics class, 2 teaching assistantships. *Entrance requirements:* For doctorate, GRE General Test. Additional exam requirements/recommendations for international students:

Molecular Physiology

University of Chicago (continued)
Required—TOEFL (minimum score 600 paper-based; 250 computer-based; 104 iBT), IELTS (minimum score 7). *Application deadline:* For fall admission, 12/1 priority date for domestic and international students. Application fee: $55. Electronic applications accepted. *Financial support:* In 2009–10, 6 students received support, including fellowships with tuition reimbursements available (averaging $29,781 per year), research assistantships with tuition reimbursements available (averaging $29,781 per year); institutionally sponsored loans, scholarships/grants, traineeships, and health care benefits also available. Financial award applicants required to submit FAFSA. *Faculty research:* Molecular genetics, biochemical biological and physical approaches to cell physiology. *Unit head:* Dr. Eric Beyer, Chairman, 773-834-1498, Fax: 773-702-3774, E-mail: ebeyer@peds.bsd.uchicago.edu. *Application contact:* Diane J. Hall, Graduate Administrative Director, 773-702-6371, Fax: 773-702-1216, E-mail: djh8@uchicago.edu.

University of Illinois at Urbana–Champaign, Graduate College, College of Liberal Arts and Sciences, School of Molecular and Cellular Biology, Department of Molecular and Integrative Physiology, Champaign, IL 61820. Offers MS, PhD. *Faculty:* 12 full-time (4 women). *Students:* 28 full-time (17 women), 3 part-time (1 woman); includes 6 minority (1 African American, 2 Asian Americans or Pacific Islanders, 3 Hispanic Americans), 15 international. In 2009, 4 master's, 3 doctorates awarded. *Entrance requirements:* For master's and doctorate, GRE, minimum GPA of 3.0. Additional exam requirements/recommendations for international students: Required—TOEFL (minimum score 590 paper-based; 243 computer-based). *Application deadline:* Applications are processed on a rolling basis. Application fee: $60 ($75 for international students). Electronic applications accepted. *Financial support:* In 2009–10, 4 fellowships, 22 research assistantships, 18 teaching assistantships were awarded; tuition waivers (full and partial) also available. *Unit head:* Byron Kemper, Head, 217-333-1146, Fax: 217-333-1133, E-mail: byronkem@illinois.edu. *Application contact:* Penny Morman, Office Manager, 217-333-8275, Fax: 217-333-1133, E-mail: morman@illinois.edu.

University of Massachusetts Worcester, Graduate School of Biomedical Sciences, Program in Cellular and Molecular Physiology, Worcester, MA 01655-0115. Offers cellular and molecular physiology (PhD). *Degree requirements:* For doctorate, comprehensive exam, thesis/dissertation. *Entrance requirements:* For doctorate, GRE General Test. Additional exam requirements/recommendations for international students: Required—TOEFL (minimum score 600 paper-based; 250 computer-based). Electronic applications accepted. *Faculty research:* Endocrinology, regulation of cellular and tissue metabolism, electrophysiology, muscle physiology.

The University of North Carolina at Chapel Hill, School of Medicine and Graduate School, Graduate Programs in Medicine, Department of Cell and Molecular Physiology, Chapel Hill, NC 27599. Offers PhD. *Degree requirements:* For doctorate, comprehensive exam, thesis/dissertation. *Entrance requirements:* For doctorate, GRE General Test. Additional exam requirements/recommendations for international students: Required—TOEFL (minimum score 550 paper-based; 213 computer-based). Electronic applications accepted. *Faculty research:* Signal transduction; growth factors; cardiovascular diseases; neurobiology; hormones, receptors, and ion channels.

University of Pittsburgh, School of Medicine, Graduate Programs in Medicine, Program in Cell Biology and Molecular Physiology, Pittsburgh, PA 15260. Offers MS, PhD. *Faculty:* 42 full-time (12 women). *Students:* 16 full-time (9 women); includes 3 minority (1 African American, 2 Asian Americans or Pacific Islanders), 5 international. Average age 27. 655 applicants, 10% accepted. In 2009, 4 doctorates awarded. *Degree requirements:* For doctorate, comprehensive exam, thesis/dissertation. *Entrance requirements:* For doctorate, GRE General Test, GRE Subject Test, minimum QPA of 3.0. Additional exam requirements/recommendations for international students: Required—TOEFL (minimum score 600 paper-based; 250 computer-based; 100 iBT), IELTS (minimum score 7). *Application deadline:* For fall admission, 12/15 priority date for domestic and international students. Application fee: $40. Electronic applications accepted. *Expenses:* Tuition, state resident: full-time $16,402; part-time $665 per credit. Tuition, nonresident: full-time $28,694; part-time $1175 per credit. Required fees: $690; $175 per term. Tuition and fees vary according to program. *Financial support:* In 2009–10, 10 research assistantships with full tuition reimbursements (averaging $24,650 per year), 6 teaching assistantships with full tuition reimbursements (averaging $24,650 per year) were awarded; institutionally sponsored loans, scholarships/grants, traineeships, health care benefits, and unspecified assistantships also available. *Faculty research:* Genetic disorders of ion channels, regulation of gene expression/development, membrane traffic of proteins and lipids, reproductive biology, signal transduction in diabetes and metabolism. *Unit head:* Dr. William H. Walker, Graduate Program Director, 412-641-7672, Fax: 412-641-7676, E-mail: walkerw@pitt.edu. *Application contact:* Graduate Studies Administrator, 412-648-8957, Fax: 412-648-1077, E-mail: gradstudies@medschool.pitt.edu.

University of Vermont, College of Medicine and Graduate College, Graduate Programs in Medicine, Department of Molecular Physiology and Biophysics, Burlington, VT 05405. Offers MS, PhD, MD/MS, MD/PhD. *Students:* 2 (both women), 1 international. 4 applicants, 25% accepted, 0 enrolled. In 2009, 1 master's awarded. *Degree requirements:* For master's, thesis; for doctorate, thesis/dissertation. *Entrance requirements:* For master's and doctorate, GRE General Test. Additional exam requirements/recommendations for international students: Required—TOEFL (minimum score 550 paper-based; 213 computer-based; 80 iBT). *Application deadline:* For fall admission, 4/1 priority date for domestic students, 4/1 for international students. Applications are processed on a rolling basis. Application fee: $40. Electronic applications accepted. *Expenses:* Tuition, state resident: part-time $508 per credit hour. Tuition, nonresident: part-time $1281 per credit hour. *Financial support:* Fellowships, research assistantships, teaching assistantships available. Financial award application deadline: 3/1. *Unit head:* Dr. D. Warshaw, Chairperson, 802-656-2540. *Application contact:* Dr. Terese Ruiz, Coordinator, 802-656-2540.

University of Virginia, School of Medicine, Department of Molecular Physiology and Biological Physics, Charlottesville, VA 22903. Offers biological and physical sciences (MS); physiology (PhD); MD/PhD. *Faculty:* 30 full-time (6 women), 1 part-time/adjunct (0 women). *Students:* 16 full-time (7 women); includes 2 minority (both African Americans). Average age 28. 1 applicant, 100% accepted, 1 enrolled. In 2009, 22 master's, 5 doctorates awarded. *Entrance requirements:* For doctorate, GRE General Test, GRE Subject Test. Additional exam requirements/recommendations for international students: Required—TOEFL. *Application deadline:* For fall admission, 2/15 for domestic and international students. Applications are processed on a rolling basis. Application fee: $60. Electronic applications accepted. *Financial support:* Fellowships, research assistantships, teaching assistantships available. Financial award applicants required to submit FAFSA. *Unit head:* Dr. Mark Yeager, Chair, 434-924-5108, Fax: 434-982-1616, E-mail: my3r@virginia.edu. *Application contact:* Dr. Mark Yeager, Chair, 434-924-5108, Fax: 434-982-1616, E-mail: my3r@virginia.edu.

Vanderbilt University, Graduate School and School of Medicine, Department of Molecular Physiology and Biophysics, Nashville, TN 37240-1001. Offers MS, PhD, MD/PhD. *Faculty:* 80 full-time (22 women). *Students:* 29 full-time (21 women), 1 part-time (0 women); includes 6 minority (3 African Americans, 1 American Indian/Alaska Native, 2 Hispanic Americans), 8 international. Average age 30. In 2009, 1 master's, 6 doctorates awarded. *Degree requirements:* For doctorate, comprehensive exam, thesis/dissertation, preliminary, qualifying, and final exams. *Entrance requirements:* For doctorate, GRE General Test, GRE Subject Test (recommended). Additional exam requirements/recommendations for international students: Required—TOEFL (minimum score 570 paper-based; 230 computer-based; 88 iBT). *Application deadline:* For fall admission, 1/15 for domestic and international students. Application fee: $0. Electronic applications accepted. *Financial support:* Fellowships with full tuition reimbursements, research assistantships with full tuition reimbursements, Federal Work-Study, institutionally sponsored loans, scholarships/grants, traineeships, health care benefits, and tuition waivers (partial) available. Financial award application deadline: 1/15; financial award applicants required to submit CSS PROFILE or FAFSA. *Faculty research:* Biophysics, cell signaling and gene regulation, human genetics, diabetes and obesity, neuroscience. *Unit head:* Roger Cone, Chair, 615-322-7000, Fax: 615-343-0490. *Application contact:* Michelle Grundy, Assistant Director, 800-373-0675, E-mail: michelle.grundy@vanderbilt.edu.

Yale University, Graduate School of Arts and Sciences, Department of Cellular and Molecular Physiology, New Haven, CT 06520. Offers PhD. *Degree requirements:* For doctorate, thesis/dissertation. *Entrance requirements:* For doctorate, GRE General Test, GRE Subject Test.

Physiology

Albert Einstein College of Medicine, Sue Golding Graduate Division of Medical Sciences, Department of Physiology and Biophysics, Bronx, NY 10461. Offers PhD, MD/PhD. *Degree requirements:* For doctorate, thesis/dissertation. *Entrance requirements:* For doctorate, GRE General Test. Additional exam requirements/recommendations for international students: Required—TOEFL. *Faculty research:* Biophysical and biochemical basis of body function at the subcellular, cellular, organ, and whole-body level.

American University of Beirut, Graduate Programs, Faculty of Medicine, Beirut, Lebanon. Offers biochemistry (MS); human morphology (MS); medicine (MD); microbiology and immunology (MS); neuroscience (MS); pharmacology and therapeutics (MS); physiology (MS). Part-time programs available. *Degree requirements:* For master's, one foreign language, comprehensive exam, thesis (for some programs). *Entrance requirements:* For MD, MCAT, bachelor's degree; for master's, letter of recommendation. Additional exam requirements/recommendations for international students: Required—TOEFL (minimum score 600 paper-based; 250 computer-based; 100 iBT), IELTS (minimum score 7.5). *Faculty research:* Cancer research, stem cell research, genetic research, neuroscience research, bone research.

Ball State University, Graduate School, College of Sciences and Humanities, Department of Physiology and Health Science, Program in Physiology, Muncie, IN 47306-1099. Offers MA, MS.

Boston University, College of Health and Rehabilitation Sciences—Sargent College, Department of Health Sciences, Programs in Applied Anatomy and Physiology, Boston, MA 02215. Offers MS, PhD. *Faculty:* 10 full-time (9 women), 5 part-time/adjunct (2 women). *Students:* 4 full-time (2 women), 4 part-time (all women), 1 international. Average age 27. 19 applicants, 63% accepted, 6 enrolled. In 2009, 5 master's, 1 doctorate awarded. Terminal master's awarded for partial completion of doctoral program. *Degree requirements:* For master's, thesis; for doctorate, thesis/dissertation. *Entrance requirements:* For master's, GRE General Test, minimum GPA of 3.0; for doctorate, GRE General Test. Additional exam requirements/recommendations for international students: Required—TOEFL (minimum score 550 paper-based; 84 iBT). *Application deadline:* For fall admission, 1/15 priority date for domestic students; for spring admission, 10/1 for domestic students. Applications are processed on a rolling basis. Application fee: $70. Electronic applications accepted. *Expenses:* Tuition: Full-time $37,910; part-time $1184 per credit hour. Required fees: $386; $40 per semester. Part-time tuition and fees vary according to class time, course level, degree level and program. *Financial support:* In 2009–10, 1 fellowship with partial tuition reimbursement (averaging $21,000 per year), 2 research assistantships (averaging $18,000 per year) were awarded; career-related internships or fieldwork, Federal Work-Study, institutionally sponsored loans, and scholarships/grants also available. Support available to part-time students. Financial award application deadline: 4/15; financial award applicants required to submit FAFSA. *Faculty research:* Skeletal muscle, neural systems, smooth muscle, muscular dystrophy. *Unit head:* Dr. Kathleen Morgan, Chair, 617-353-2717, E-mail: kmorgan@bu.edu. *Application contact:* Sharon Sankey, Director, Student Services, 617-353-2713, Fax: 617-353-7500, E-mail: ssankey@bu.edu.

Brigham Young University, Graduate Studies, College of Life Sciences, Department of Physiology and Developmental Biology, Provo, UT 84602. Offers neuroscience (MS, PhD); physiology and developmental biology (MS, PhD). Part-time programs available. *Faculty:* 19 full-time (0 women). *Students:* 25 full-time (11 women); includes 3 minority (1 American Indian/Alaska Native, 1 Asian American or Pacific Islander, 1 Hispanic American). Average age 30. 14 applicants, 43% accepted, 3 enrolled. In 2009, 3 master's, 3 doctorates awarded. Terminal master's awarded for partial completion of doctoral program. *Degree requirements:* For master's, thesis; for doctorate, thesis/dissertation. *Entrance requirements:* For master's, GRE General Test, minimum GPA of 3.0 during previous 2 years; for doctorate, GRE General Test, minimum GPA of 3.0 overall. Additional exam requirements/recommendations for international students: Required—TOEFL. *Application deadline:* For fall admission, 2/1 priority date for domestic and international students; for winter admission, 9/10 priority date for domestic and international students. Application fee: $50. Electronic applications accepted. *Expenses:* Tuition: Full-time $5580; part-time $301 per credit hour. Tuition and fees vary according to student's religious affiliation. *Financial support:* In 2009–10, 25 students received support, including 1 fellowship with partial tuition reimbursement available (averaging $7,100 per year), 12 research assistantships with full tuition reimbursements available (averaging $15,500 per year), 13 teaching assistantships with partial tuition reimbursements available (averaging $14,900 per year); career-related internships or fieldwork, institutionally sponsored loans, scholarships/grants, tuition waivers (full and partial), unspecified assistantships, and tuition awards also available. Financial award application deadline: 2/1. *Faculty research:* Sex differentiation of the brain, exercise physiology, developmental biology, membrane biophysics, neuroscience. Total annual research expenditures: $848,996. *Unit head:* Dr. William W. Winder, Chair, 801-422-3093, Fax: 801-422-0700, E-mail: william_winder@byu.edu. *Application contact:* Dr. Dixon J. Woodbury, Graduate Coordinator, 801-422-7562, Fax: 801-422-0700, E-mail: dixon_woodbury@byu.edu.

Brown University, Graduate School, Division of Biology and Medicine, Program in Molecular Pharmacology and Physiology, Providence, RI 02912. Offers MA, Sc M, PhD, MD/PhD. *Degree requirements:* For doctorate, thesis/dissertation, preliminary exam. *Entrance requirements:* For master's and doctorate, GRE General Test, GRE Subject Test. Additional exam requirements/recommendations for international students: Required—TOEFL. Electronic applications accepted. *Faculty research:* Structural biology, antiplatelet drugs, nicotinic receptor structure/function.

Case Western Reserve University, School of Medicine and School of Graduate Studies, Graduate Programs in Medicine, Department of Physiology and Biophysics, Cleveland, OH 44106. Offers cell and molecular physiology (MS); cell physiology (PhD); molecular/cellular biophysics (PhD); physiology and biophysics (PhD); systems physiology (PhD); MD/PhD. Terminal master's awarded for partial completion of doctoral program. *Degree requirements:* For master's, thesis; for doctorate, thesis/dissertation. *Entrance requirements:* For master's, GRE General Test, minimum GPA of 3.28; for doctorate, GRE General Test, minimum GPA of 3.6. Additional exam requirements/recommendations for international students: Required—

TOEFL. Electronic applications accepted. *Faculty research:* Cardiovascular physiology, calcium metabolism, epithelial cell biology.

See Close-Up on page 487.

Columbia University, College of Physicians and Surgeons, Department of Physiology and Cellular Biophysics, New York, NY 10032. Offers M Phil, MA, PhD, MD/PhD. Only candidates for the PhD are admitted. Terminal master's awarded for partial completion of doctoral program. *Degree requirements:* For doctorate, thesis/dissertation. *Entrance requirements:* For master's and doctorate, GRE General Test. Additional exam requirements/recommendations for international students: Required—TOEFL. *Faculty research:* Membrane physiology, cellular biology, cardiovascular physiology, neurophysiology.

Cornell University, Graduate School, Graduate Fields of Comparative Biomedical Sciences, Field of Molecular and Integrative Physiology, Ithaca, NY 14853-0001. Offers behavioral physiology (MS, PhD); cardiovascular and respiratory physiology (MS, PhD); endocrinology (MS, PhD); environmental and comparative physiology (MS, PhD); gastrointestinal and metabolic physiology (MS, PhD); membrane and epithelial physiology (MS, PhD); molecular and cellular physiology (MS, PhD); neural and sensory physiology (MS, PhD); physiological genomics (MS, PhD); reproductive physiology (MS, PhD). *Faculty:* 50 full-time (16 women). *Students:* 16 full-time (12 women); includes 2 minority (1 Asian American or Pacific Islander, 1 Hispanic American), 10 international. Average age 29. 9 applicants, 44% accepted, 2 enrolled. In 2009, 1 master's, 5 doctorates awarded. *Degree requirements:* For master's, thesis; for doctorate, comprehensive exam, thesis/dissertation, 1 semester of teaching experience, seminar presentation. *Entrance requirements:* For master's and doctorate, GRE General Test, GRE Subject Test (biochemistry, cell and molecular biology, biology, or chemistry), 2 letters of recommendation. Additional exam requirements/recommendations for international students: Required—TOEFL (minimum score 550 paper-based; 213 computer-based; 77 iBT). *Application deadline:* For fall admission, 12/15 for domestic students. Application fee: $70. Electronic applications accepted. *Expenses:* Tuition: Full-time $29,500. Required fees: $70. Full-time tuition and fees vary according to degree level, program and student level. *Financial support:* In 2009–10, 2 research assistantships with full tuition reimbursements were awarded; fellowships with full tuition reimbursements, teaching assistantships with full tuition reimbursements, institutionally sponsored loans, scholarships/grants, health care benefits, tuition waivers (full and partial), and unspecified assistantships also available. Financial award applicants required to submit FAFSA. *Faculty research:* Endocrinology and reproductive physiology, cardiovascular and respiratory physiology, gastrointestinal and metabolic physiology, molecular and cellular physiology, physiological genomics. *Unit head:* Director of Graduate Studies, 607-253-3276, Fax: 607-253-3756. *Application contact:* Graduate Field Assistant, 607-253-3276, Fax: 607-253-3756, E-mail: graduate_edcvm@cornell.edu.

Cornell University, Joan and Sanford I. Weill Medical College and Graduate School of Medical Sciences, Weill Cornell Graduate School of Medical Sciences, Physiology, Biophysics and Systems Biology Program, New York, NY 10065. Offers MS, PhD. *Faculty:* 33 full-time (9 women). *Students:* 43 full-time (18 women); includes 8 minority (2 African Americans, 5 Asian Americans or Pacific Islanders, 1 Hispanic American), 21 international. Average age 23. 54 applicants, 28% accepted, 5 enrolled. In 2009, 5 doctorates awarded. Terminal master's awarded for partial completion of doctoral program. *Degree requirements:* For master's, comprehensive exam; for doctorate, thesis/dissertation, final exam. *Entrance requirements:* For doctorate, GRE General Test, introductory courses in biology, inorganic and organic chemistry, physics, and mathematics. Additional exam requirements/recommendations for international students: Required—TOEFL. *Application deadline:* For fall admission, 12/1 for domestic students. Application fee: $60. *Expenses:* Tuition: Full-time $44,650. Required fees: $2805. *Financial support:* In 2009–10, 3 fellowships (averaging $27,992 per year) were awarded; scholarships/grants, health care benefits, and stipends (given to all students) also available. *Faculty research:* Receptor mediated regulation of cell function, molecular properties of channels or receptors, bioinformatics, mathematical modeling. *Unit head:* Dr. Emre Aksay, Co-Director, 212-746-6207, E-mail: ema2004@med.cornell.edu. *Application contact:* Audrey Rivera, Program Coordinator, 212-746-6361, E-mail: ajr2004@med.cornell.edu.

Dalhousie University, Faculty of Medicine, Department of Physiology and Biophysics, Halifax, NS B3H 1X5, Canada. Offers M Sc, PhD, M Sc/PhD. *Degree requirements:* For master's, thesis; for doctorate, thesis/dissertation. *Entrance requirements:* For master's and doctorate, GRE Subject Test (for international students). Additional exam requirements/recommendations for international students: Required—TOEFL, IELTS, 1 of the following 5 approved tests: TOEFL, IELTS, CANTEST, CAEL, Michigan English Language Assessment Battery. Electronic applications accepted. *Faculty research:* Computer modeling, reproductive and endocrine physiology, cardiovascular physiology, neurophysiology, membrane biophysics.

Dartmouth College, Arts and Sciences Graduate Programs, Department of Physiology, Lebanon, NH 03756. Offers PhD, MD/PhD. *Faculty:* 25 full-time (4 women). *Students:* 10 full-time (4 women), 6 international. Average age 32. 128 applicants, 19% accepted. In 2009, 3 doctorates awarded. *Degree requirements:* For doctorate, thesis/dissertation. *Entrance requirements:* For doctorate, GRE General Test, GRE Subject Test. Additional exam requirements/recommendations for international students: Required—TOEFL. *Application deadline:* For fall admission, 1/20 for domestic students. Applications are processed on a rolling basis. Application fee: $0. *Financial support:* In 2009–10, 8 students received support, including fellowships with full tuition reimbursements available (averaging $25,500 per year), research assistantships with full tuition reimbursements available (averaging $25,500 per year), teaching assistantships with full tuition reimbursements available (averaging $25,500 per year); institutionally sponsored loans, scholarships/grants, tuition waivers (full and partial), and unspecified assistantships also available. Financial award application deadline: 4/15. *Faculty research:* Respiratory control, endocrinology of reproduction and immunology, regulation of receptors and channels, electrophysiology of membranes, renal function. *Unit head:* Dr. Hermes Yeh, Chair, 603-650-7717, Fax: 603-650-6130. *Application contact:* Dr. Valerie Anne Galton, Coordinator of Graduate Studies, 603-650-7717, Fax: 603-650-6130, E-mail: valerie.a.galton@dartmouth.edu.

East Carolina University, Brody School of Medicine, Department of Physiology, Greenville, NC 27858-4353. Offers PhD. *Degree requirements:* For doctorate, comprehensive exam, thesis/dissertation. *Entrance requirements:* For doctorate, GRE General Test. Additional exam requirements/recommendations for international students: Required—TOEFL. *Faculty research:* Cell and nerve biophysics; neurophysiology; cardiovascular, renal, endocrine, and gastrointestinal physiology; pulmonary/asthma.

Eastern Michigan University, Graduate School, College of Health and Human Services, School of Health Promotion and Human Performance, Programs in Exercise Physiology, Ypsilanti, MI 48197. Offers exercise physiology (MS); sports medicine-biomechanics (MS); sports medicine-corporate adult fitness (MS); sports medicine-exercise physiology (MS). Part-time and evening/weekend programs available. *Students:* 10 full-time (5 women), 32 part-time (10 women); includes 6 minority (2 African Americans, 4 Hispanic Americans), 2 international. Average age 29. In 2009, 12 master's awarded. *Degree requirements:* For master's, comprehensive exam, thesis or 450-hour internship. *Entrance requirements:* Additional exam requirements/recommendations for international students: Required—TOEFL. *Application deadline:* For fall admission, 8/1 for domestic students, 5/1 for international students; for winter admission, 12/1 for domestic students, 10/1 for international students; for spring admission, 3/15 for domestic students, 3/1 for international students. Application fee: $35. Tuition and fees vary according to course level. *Unit head:* Dr. Steve McGregor, Program Coordinator, 734-487-0090, Fax: 734-487-2024, E-mail: stephen.mcgregor@emich.edu. *Application contact:* Dr. Steve McGregor, Program Coordinator, 734-487-0090, Fax: 734-487-2024, E-mail: stephen.mcgregor@emich.edu.

East Tennessee State University, James H. Quillen College of Medicine, Biomedical Science Graduate Program, Johnson City, TN 37614. Offers anatomy (MS, PhD); biochemistry (MS, PhD); biophysics (MS, PhD); microbiology (MS, PhD); pharmacology (MS, PhD); physiology (MS, PhD). Part-time programs available. Terminal master's awarded for partial completion of doctoral program. *Degree requirements:* For master's, one foreign language, thesis, comprehensive qualifying exam; for doctorate, 2 foreign languages, thesis/dissertation. *Entrance requirements:* For master's, GRE General Test, minimum GPA of 3.0, bachelor's degree in biological or related science; for doctorate, GRE General Test, GRE Subject Test. Additional exam requirements/recommendations for international students: Required—TOEFL (minimum score 550 paper-based; 213 computer-based). *Expenses:* Contact institution.

Georgetown University, Graduate School of Arts and Sciences, Programs in Biomedical Sciences, Department of Physiology and Biophysics, Washington, DC 20057. Offers MS, PhD, MD/PhD. *Degree requirements:* For doctorate, thesis/dissertation. *Entrance requirements:* For master's, GRE General Test, MCAT; for doctorate, GRE General Test. Additional exam requirements/recommendations for international students: Required—TOEFL.

Georgia Institute of Technology, Graduate Studies and Research, College of Sciences, School of Applied Physiology, Program in Prosthetics and Orthotics, Atlanta, GA 30332-0001. Offers MS.

Georgia State University, College of Arts and Sciences, Department of Biology, Program in Cellular and Molecular Biology and Physiology, Atlanta, GA 30302-3083. Offers MS, PhD. Part-time programs available. Terminal master's awarded for partial completion of doctoral program. *Degree requirements:* For master's, thesis or alternative; for doctorate, thesis/dissertation, exam. *Entrance requirements:* For master's and doctorate, GRE General Test. Additional exam requirements/recommendations for international students: Required—TOEFL.

Harvard University, Graduate School of Arts and Sciences, Department of Systems Biology, Cambridge, MA 02138. Offers PhD. *Degree requirements:* For doctorate, thesis/dissertation, lab rotation, qualifying examination. *Entrance requirements:* For doctorate, GRE. Additional exam requirements/recommendations for international students: Required—TOEFL. Electronic applications accepted. *Expenses:* Tuition: Full-time $33,696. Required fees: $1126. Full-time tuition and fees vary according to program.

Harvard University, School of Public Health, Department of Environmental Health, Boston, MA 02115-6096. Offers environmental health (MOH, SM, DPH, PhD, SD); occupational health (MOH, SM, DPH, SD); physiology (PhD, SD). Part-time programs available. *Faculty:* 44 full-time (9 women), 22 part-time/adjunct (5 women). *Students:* 85 full-time, 4 part-time; includes 6 minority (all Asian Americans or Pacific Islanders), 42 international. Average age 32. 80 applicants, 48% accepted, 32 enrolled. In 2009, 15 master's, 10 doctorates awarded. *Degree requirements:* For doctorate, thesis/dissertation, qualifying exam. *Entrance requirements:* For master's and doctorate, GRE. Additional exam requirements/recommendations for international students: Required—TOEFL (minimum score 595 paper-based; 240 computer-based; 95 iBT); Recommended—IELTS (minimum score 7). *Application deadline:* For fall admission, 12/15 for domestic and international students. Application fee: $115. Electronic applications accepted. *Expenses:* Tuition: Full-time $33,696. Required fees: $1126. Full-time tuition and fees vary according to program. *Financial support:* Fellowships, research assistantships, teaching assistantships, career-related internships or fieldwork, Federal Work-Study, scholarships/grants, traineeships, tuition waivers (partial), and unspecified assistantships available. Support available to part-time students. Financial award application deadline: 2/8; financial award applicants required to submit FAFSA. *Faculty research:* Industrial hygiene and occupational safety, population genetics, indoor and outdoor air pollution, cell and molecular biology of the lungs, infectious diseases. *Unit head:* Dr. Douglas Dockery, Chairman, 617-432-1270, Fax: 617-432-6913. *Application contact:* Vincent W. James, Director of Admissions, 617-432-1031, Fax: 617-432-7080, E-mail: admisofc@hsph.harvard.edu.

Howard University, Graduate School, Department of Physiology and Biophysics, Washington, DC 20059-0002. Offers biophysics (PhD); physiology (PhD). *Degree requirements:* For doctorate, comprehensive exam, thesis/dissertation. *Entrance requirements:* For doctorate, GRE General Test, minimum B average in field. *Faculty research:* Cardiovascular physiology, pulmonary physiology, renal physiology, neurophysiology, endocrinology.

Illinois State University, Graduate School, College of Arts and Sciences, Department of Biological Sciences, Normal, IL 61790-2200. Offers animal behavior (MS); bacteriology (MS); biochemistry (MS); biological sciences (MS); biology (PhD); biophysics (MS); biotechnology (MS); botany (MS, PhD); cell biology (MS); conservation biology (MS); developmental biology (MS); ecology (MS, PhD); entomology (MS); evolutionary biology (MS); genetics (MS, PhD); immunology (MS); microbiology (MS, PhD); molecular biology (MS); molecular genetics (MS); neurobiology (MS); neuroscience (MS); parasitology (MS); physiology (MS, PhD); plant biology (MS); plant molecular biology (MS); plant sciences (MS); structural biology (MS); zoology (MS, PhD). Part-time programs available. *Degree requirements:* For master's, thesis or alternative; for doctorate, variable foreign language requirement, thesis/dissertation, 2 terms of residency. *Entrance requirements:* For master's, GRE General Test, minimum GPA of 2.6 in last 60 hours of course work; for doctorate, GRE General Test. *Faculty research:* Redoc balance and drug development in schistosoma mansoni, control of the growth of listeria monocytogenes at low temperature, regulation of cell expansion and microtubule function by SPRI, CRUI: physiology and fitness consequences of different life history phenotypes.

Indiana State University, School of Graduate Studies, College of Arts and Sciences, Department of Biology, Terre Haute, IN 47809. Offers ecology (PhD); life sciences (MS); microbiology (PhD); physiology (PhD); science education (MS). *Degree requirements:* For master's, thesis (for some programs); for doctorate, comprehensive exam, thesis/dissertation. *Entrance requirements:* For master's and doctorate, GRE General Test. Electronic applications accepted.

The Johns Hopkins University, Bloomberg School of Public Health, Department of Environmental Health Sciences, Baltimore, MD 21218-2699. Offers environmental health engineering (PhD); environmental health sciences (MHS, Dr PH); occupational and environmental health (PhD); occupational and environmental hygiene (MHS, MHS); physiology (PhD); toxicology (PhD). Postbaccalaureate distance learning degree programs offered (minimal on-campus study). *Faculty:* 71 full-time (27 women), 58 part-time/adjunct (26 women). *Students:* 65 full-time (43 women), 17 part-time (12 women); includes 22 minority (4 African Americans, 1 American Indian/Alaska Native, 13 Asian Americans or Pacific Islanders, 4 Hispanic Americans), 11 international. Average age 31. 101 applicants, 49% accepted, 31 enrolled. In 2009, 22 master's, 13 doctorates awarded. *Degree requirements:* For master's, essay, presentation; for doctorate, comprehensive exam, thesis/dissertation, 1 year full-time residency, oral and written exams. *Entrance requirements:* For master's, GRE General Test or MCAT, 3 letters of recommendation, transcripts; for doctorate, GRE General Test or MCAT, 3 letters of recommendation. Additional exam requirements/recommendations for international students: Required—TOEFL (minimum score 600 paper-based; 250 computer-based). *Application deadline:* For fall admission, 12/15 priority date for domestic and international students. Applications are processed on a rolling basis. Application fee: $45. Electronic applications accepted. *Financial support:* In 2009–10, 5 fellowships with full tuition reimbursements (averaging $26,500 per year) were awarded; Federal Work-Study, institutionally sponsored loans, scholarships/grants, traineeships, health care benefits, and stipends also available. Support available to part-time students. Financial award application deadline: 3/15; financial award applicants required to submit FAFSA. *Faculty research:* Chemical carcinogenesis/toxicology, lung disease, occupational and environmental health, nuclear imaging, molecular epidemiology. Total annual research expenditures: $23.7 million. *Unit head:* Dr. John Davis Groopman, Chair, 410-955-3720, Fax: 410-955-0617, E-mail: jgroopma@jhsph.edu. *Application contact:* Nina J. Kulacki, Academic Program Manager, 410-955-2212, Fax: 410-955-0617, E-mail: nkulacki@jhsph.edu.

The Johns Hopkins University, School of Medicine, Graduate Programs in Medicine, Department of Physiology, Baltimore, MD 21205. Offers cellular and molecular physiology (PhD); physiology (PhD). *Faculty:* 19 full-time (6 women). *Students:* 19 full-time (9 women);

Physiology

The Johns Hopkins University (continued)
includes 3 minority (2 African Americans, 1 Asian American or Pacific Islander), 12 international. Average age 23. 50 applicants, 4% accepted, 2 enrolled. *Degree requirements:* For doctorate, thesis/dissertation, oral and qualifying exams. *Entrance requirements:* For doctorate, GRE General Test, previous course work in biology, calculus, chemistry, and physics. Additional exam requirements/recommendations for international students: Required—TOEFL. *Application deadline:* For fall admission, 1/10 for domestic and international students. Application fee: $85. Electronic applications accepted. *Financial support:* In 2009–10, 2 students received support, including 2 fellowships with full tuition reimbursements available (averaging $26,855 per year), research assistantships with full tuition reimbursements available (averaging $26,855 per year), teaching assistantships with full tuition reimbursements available (averaging $26,855 per year); scholarships/grants, traineeships, tuition waivers (full), unspecified assistantships, and stipends also available. Financial award application deadline: 1/10. *Faculty research:* Membrane biochemistry and biophysics; signal transduction; developmental genetics and physiology; physiology and biochemistry; transporters, carriers, and ion channels. *Unit head:* Dr. William B. Guggino, Director, 410-955-7166, Fax: 410-955-0461. *Application contact:* Madeline J. McLaughlin, Academic Program Manager, 410-955-8333, Fax: 410-955-0461, E-mail: mmclaugh@jhmi.edu.

Kansas State University, College of Veterinary Medicine, Department of Anatomy and Physiology, Manhattan, KS 66506. Offers physiology (PhD). *Faculty:* 14 full-time (4 women), 3 part-time/adjunct (0 women). *Students:* 10 full-time (6 women), 6 international. Average age 32. In 2009, 3 doctorates awarded. Terminal master's awarded for partial completion of doctoral program. *Degree requirements:* For doctorate, one foreign language, thesis/dissertation. *Entrance requirements:* Additional exam requirements/recommendations for international students: Required—TOEFL (minimum score 550 paper-based; 213 computer-based). *Application deadline:* For fall admission, 2/1 priority date for domestic and international students; for spring admission, 8/1 priority date for domestic and international students. Applications are processed on a rolling basis. Application fee: $40 ($55 for international students). Electronic applications accepted. *Financial support:* In 2009–10, 9 research assistantships (averaging $15,107 per year) were awarded; fellowships, teaching assistantships with partial tuition reimbursements, Federal Work-Study, institutionally sponsored loans, and scholarships/grants also available. Financial award application deadline: 3/1. *Faculty research:* Cardiovascular and pulmonary, immunophysiology, neuroscience, pharmacology, epithelial. Total annual research expenditures: $3.3 million. *Unit head:* Frank Blecha, Head, 785-532-2741, Fax: 785-532-4557, E-mail: blecha@vet.ksu.edu. *Application contact:* Bruce Schultz, Director, 785-532-4839, Fax: 785-432-4557, E-mail: bschultz@ksu.edu.

Kent State University, College of Arts and Sciences, Department of Biological Sciences, Program in Physiology, Kent, OH 44242-0001. Offers MS, PhD. *Degree requirements:* For master's, thesis; for doctorate, thesis/dissertation. *Entrance requirements:* For master's, GRE General Test, minimum GPA of 3.0; for doctorate, GRE General Test, minimum GPA of 3.25. Additional exam requirements/recommendations for international students: Required—TOEFL (minimum score 600 paper-based; 257 computer-based).

Kent State University, School of Biomedical Sciences, Program in Physiology, Kent, OH 44242-0001. Offers MS, PhD. *Degree requirements:* For master's, thesis; for doctorate, thesis/dissertation. *Entrance requirements:* For master's and doctorate, GRE General Test, minimum GPA of 3.0, 3 letters of recommendation. Additional exam requirements/recommendations for international students: Required—TOEFL (minimum score 600 paper-based; 287 computer-based). Electronic applications accepted.

Loma Linda University, School of Medicine, Department of Physiology/Pharmacology, Loma Linda, CA 92350. Offers MS, PhD. Part-time programs available. *Degree requirements:* For master's, thesis or alternative; for doctorate, 2 foreign languages, thesis/dissertation. *Entrance requirements:* For master's and doctorate, GRE General Test. *Faculty research:* Drug metabolism, biochemical pharmacology, structure and function of cell membranes, neuropharmacology.

Louisiana State University Health Sciences Center, School of Graduate Studies in New Orleans, Department of Physiology, New Orleans, LA 70112-2223. Offers MS, PhD, MD/PhD. Terminal master's awarded for partial completion of doctoral program. *Degree requirements:* For master's, comprehensive exam, thesis; for doctorate, comprehensive exam, thesis/dissertation. *Entrance requirements:* For master's and doctorate, GRE General Test. Additional exam requirements/recommendations for international students: Required—TOEFL. *Faculty research:* Host defense, lipoprotein metabolism, regulation of cardiopulmonary function, alcohol and drug abuse, cell to cell communication, cytokinesis, physiologic functions of nitric oxide.

Louisiana State University Health Sciences Center at Shreveport, Department of Molecular and Cellular Physiology, Shreveport, LA 71130-3932. Offers physiology (MS, PhD); MD/PhD. *Degree requirements:* For master's, thesis; for doctorate, thesis/dissertation. *Entrance requirements:* For master's and doctorate, GRE General Test. Additional exam requirements/recommendations for international students: Required—TOEFL. *Faculty research:* Cardiovascular, gastrointestinal, renal, and neutrophil function; cellular detoxification systems; hypoxia and mitochondria function.

Marquette University, Graduate School, College of Arts and Sciences, Department of Biology, Milwaukee, WI 53201-1881. Offers cell biology (MS, PhD); developmental biology (MS, PhD); ecology (MS, PhD); endocrinology (MS, PhD); evolutionary biology (MS, PhD); genetics (MS, PhD); microbiology (MS, PhD); molecular biology (MS, PhD); muscle and exercise physiology (MS, PhD); neurobiology (MS, PhD); reproductive physiology (MS, PhD). *Faculty:* 23 full-time (10 women), 1 part-time/adjunct (0 women). *Students:* 23 full-time (13 women), 16 part-time (9 women); includes 1 minority (Asian American or Pacific Islander), 20 international. Average age 25. 95 applicants, 16% accepted, 10 enrolled. In 2009, 3 master's, 5 doctorates awarded. Terminal master's awarded for partial completion of doctoral program. *Degree requirements:* For master's, comprehensive exam, thesis, 1 year of teaching experience or equivalent; for doctorate, thesis/dissertation, 1 year of teaching experience or equivalent, qualifying exam. *Entrance requirements:* For master's and doctorate, GRE General Test, GRE Subject Test. Additional exam requirements/recommendations for international students: Required—TOEFL. Application fee: $40. *Financial support:* In 2009–10, 4 fellowships, 22 teaching assistantships were awarded; research assistantships, Federal Work-Study, institutionally sponsored loans, scholarships/grants, and tuition waivers (full and partial) also available. Support available to part-time students. Financial award application deadline: 2/15. *Faculty research:* Microbial and invertebrate ecology, evolution of gene function, DNA methylation, DNA arrangement. *Unit head:* Dr. Robert Fitts, Chair, 414-288-1748, Fax: 414-288-7357. *Application contact:* Debbie Weaver, Administrative Assistant, 414-288-7355, Fax: 414-288-7357.

McGill University, Faculty of Graduate and Postdoctoral Studies, Faculty of Medicine, Department of Physiology, Montréal, QC H3A 2T5, Canada. Offers M Sc, PhD.

McMaster University, Faculty of Health Sciences and School of Graduate Studies, Program in Medical Sciences, Physiology/Pharmacology Area, Hamilton, ON L8S 4M2, Canada. Offers M Sc, PhD, MD/PhD. *Degree requirements:* For master's, thesis; for doctorate, comprehensive exam, thesis/dissertation. *Entrance requirements:* For master's, honors B Sc, B+ average in related field; for doctorate, M Sc, minimum B+ average, students with proven research experience and an A average may be admitted with a B Sc degree. Additional exam requirements/recommendations for international students: Required—TOEFL (minimum score 580 paper-based; 237 computer-based; 92 iBT).

Medical College of Georgia, School of Graduate Studies, Program in Physiology, Augusta, GA 30912. Offers PhD. *Degree requirements:* For doctorate, comprehensive exam, thesis/dissertation. *Entrance requirements:* For doctorate, GRE General Test. Additional exam requirements/recommendations for international students: Required—TOEFL (minimum score 550 paper-based; 213 computer-based; 79 iBT). Electronic applications accepted. Full-time tuition and fees vary according to campus/location, program and student level. *Faculty research:* Cardiovascular and renal physiology, behavioral neuroscience and genetics, neurophysiology, adrenal steroid endocrinology and genetics, inflammatory mediators and cardiovascular disease, hypertension, diabetes and stroke.

Medical College of Wisconsin, Graduate School of Biomedical Sciences, Department of Physiology, Milwaukee, WI 53226-0509. Offers PhD, MD/PhD. *Degree requirements:* For doctorate, comprehensive exam, thesis/dissertation. *Entrance requirements:* For doctorate, GRE General Test. Additional exam requirements/recommendations for international students: Required—TOEFL. *Faculty research:* Cardiovascular, respiratory, renal, and exercise physiology; mathematical modeling; molecular and cellular biology.

Michigan State University, College of Human Medicine and The Graduate School, Graduate Programs in Human Medicine, East Lansing, MI 48824. Offers biochemistry and molecular biology (MS, PhD); epidemiology (MS, PhD); microbiology (MS); microbiology and molecular genetics (PhD); pharmacology and toxicology (MS, PhD); physiology (MS, PhD); public health (MPH). *Students:* 58 full-time (31 women), 31 part-time (25 women); includes 17 minority (7 African Americans, 1 American Indian/Alaska Native, 6 Asian Americans or Pacific Islanders, 3 Hispanic Americans), 22 international. Average age 30. In 2009, 8 master's, 9 doctorates awarded. *Entrance requirements:* Additional exam requirements/recommendations for international students: Required—TOEFL. *Expenses:* Tuition, state resident: part-time $478.25 per credit hour. Tuition, nonresident: part-time $966.50 per credit hour. Part-time tuition and fees vary according to program. *Financial support:* In 2009–10, 17 research assistantships with tuition reimbursements (averaging $7,053 per year), 3 teaching assistantships with tuition reimbursements (averaging $6,607 per year) were awarded. *Unit head:* Margo K. Smith, Director of Graduate Studies, 517-432-5112, E-mail: smithmk@msu.edu. *Application contact:* Margo K. Smith, Director of Graduate Studies, 517-432-5112, E-mail: smithmk@msu.edu.

Michigan State University, College of Osteopathic Medicine and The Graduate School, Graduate Studies in Osteopathic Medicine, East Lansing, MI 48824. Offers biochemistry and molecular biology (MS, PhD); microbiology (MS); microbiology and molecular genetics (PhD); pharmacology and toxicology (MS, PhD), including integrative pharmacology (MS), pharmacology and toxicology, pharmacology and toxicology-environmental toxicology (PhD); physiology (MS, PhD). *Students:* 6 full-time (1 woman), 39 part-time (22 women); includes 8 minority (2 African Americans, 2 Asian Americans or Pacific Islanders, 4 Hispanic Americans), 3 international. Average age 30. *Expenses:* Tuition, state resident: part-time $478.25 per credit hour. Tuition, nonresident: part-time $966.50 per credit hour. Part-time tuition and fees vary according to program. *Financial support:* In 2009–10, 1 research assistantship with tuition reimbursement (averaging $7,894 per year) was awarded. *Application contact:* Bethany Heinlen, Information Contact, 517-353-7785, Fax: 517-353-9004, E-mail: heinlen@msu.edu.

Michigan State University, College of Veterinary Medicine and The Graduate School, Graduate Programs in Veterinary Medicine, East Lansing, MI 48824. Offers comparative medicine and integrative biology (MS, PhD), including comparative medicine and integrative biology, comparative medicine and integrative biology–environmental toxicology (PhD); food safety and toxicology (MS), including food safety; integrative toxicology (PhD), including animal science–environmental toxicology, biochemistry and molecular biology–environmental toxicology, chemistry–environmental toxicology, crop and soil sciences–environmental toxicology, environmental engineering–environmental toxicology, environmental geosciences–environmental toxicology, fisheries and wildlife–environmental toxicology, food science–environmental toxicology, forestry–environmental toxicology, genetics–environmental toxicology, human nutrition–environmental toxicology, microbiology–environmental toxicology, pharmacology and toxicology–environmental toxicology, zoology–environmental toxicology; large animal clinical sciences (MS, PhD); microbiology and molecular genetics (MS, PhD), including industrial microbiology, microbiology, microbiology and molecular genetics, microbiology–environmental toxicology (PhD); pathobiology and diagnostic investigation (MS, PhD), including pathology, pathology–environmental toxicology (PhD); pharmacology and toxicology (MS, PhD); pharmacology and toxicology–environmental toxicology (PhD); physiology (MS, PhD); small animal clinical sciences (MS). *Students:* 66 full-time (40 women), 90 part-time (56 women); includes 24 minority (14 African Americans, 6 Asian Americans or Pacific Islanders, 4 Hispanic Americans), 51 international. Average age 33. In 2009, 22 master's, 16 doctorates awarded. *Application deadline:* For fall admission, 12/27 for domestic students. Applications are processed on a rolling basis. Application fee: $50. Electronic applications accepted. *Expenses:* Tuition, state resident: part-time $478.25 per credit hour. Tuition, nonresident: part-time $966.50 per credit hour. Part-time tuition and fees vary according to program. *Financial support:* In 2009–10, 32 research assistantships with tuition reimbursements (averaging $8,131 per year) were awarded. *Faculty research:* Molecular genetics, food safety/toxicology, comparative orthopedics, airway disease, population medicine. *Unit head:* Dr. Susan L. Ewart, Associate Dean for Research and Graduate Studies, 517-432-2388, Fax: 517-432-1037, E-mail: ewart@cvm.msu.edu. *Application contact:* Dr. Susan L. Ewart, Associate Dean for Research and Graduate Studies, 517-432-2388, Fax: 517-432-1037, E-mail: ewart@cvm.msu.edu.

Michigan State University, The Graduate School, College of Natural Science and Graduate Programs in Human Medicine and Graduate Studies in Osteopathic Medicine, Department of Physiology, East Lansing, MI 48824. Offers MS, PhD. *Faculty:* 26 full-time (8 women). *Students:* 13 full-time (9 women), 1 part-time (0 women), 7 international. Average age 28. 17 applicants, 6% accepted. In 2009, 1 master's, 2 doctorates awarded. *Entrance requirements:* Additional exam requirements/recommendations for international students: Required—TOEFL (minimum score 600 paper-based; 220 computer-based). Electronic applications accepted. *Expenses:* Tuition, state resident: part-time $478.25 per credit hour. Tuition, nonresident: part-time $966.50 per credit hour. Part-time tuition and fees vary according to program. *Financial support:* In 2009–10, 8 research assistantships with tuition reimbursements (averaging $7,745 per year), 1 teaching assistantship with tuition reimbursement (averaging $7,523 per year) were awarded. Total annual research expenditures: $3.3 million. *Unit head:* Dr. William S. Spielman, Chairperson, 517-355-4539, Fax: 517-432-1967, E-mail: spielman@msu.edu. *Application contact:* Kimberly Crain, Administrative Assistant, 517-884-5075, E-mail: pslgrad@msu.edu.

New York Medical College, Graduate School of Basic Medical Sciences, Program in Physiology, Valhalla, NY 10595-1691. Offers MS, PhD, MD/PhD. Part-time and evening/weekend programs available. Terminal master's awarded for partial completion of doctoral program. *Degree requirements:* For master's, thesis; for doctorate, comprehensive exam, thesis/dissertation. *Entrance requirements:* For master's and doctorate, GRE General Test. Additional exam requirements/recommendations for international students: Required—TOEFL. *Expenses:* Tuition: Full-time $18,170; part-time $790 per credit. Required fees: $790 per credit. $20 per semester. One-time fee: $100. Tuition and fees vary according to class time, course level, course load, degree level, program, student level and student's religious affiliation. *Faculty research:* Cardiovascular physiology, renal physiology, endocrine physiology, neurophysiology, cell biology.

New York University, School of Medicine, New York, NY 10012-1019. Offers biomedical sciences (PhD), including biomedical imaging, cellular and molecular biology, computational biology, developmental genetics, medical and molecular parasitology, microbiology, molecular oncobiology and immunology, neuroscience and physiology, pathobiology, pharmacology, structural biology; clinical investigation (MS); medicine (MD); MD/MA; MD/MPA; MD/MS; MD/PhD. *Accreditation:* LCME/AMA (one or more programs are accredited). *Faculty:* 1,493 full-time (558 women), 327 part-time/adjunct (122 women). *Students:* 747 full-time (360 women); includes 275 minority (23 African Americans, 5 American Indian/Alaska Native, 199 Asian Americans or Pacific Islanders, 48 Hispanic Americans), 2 international. Average age 24. 7,568 applicants, 7% accepted, 213 enrolled. In 2009, 164 first professional degrees, 13 master's, 50 doctorates awarded. *Degree requirements:* For master's, comprehensive exam, thesis; for doctorate, comprehensive exam, thesis/dissertation. *Entrance requirements:* MCAT. Additional exam requirements/recommendations for international students: Required—TOEFL. *Application deadline:* For fall admission, 10/15 for domestic students; for winter admission, 12/18 for domestic students, 12/15 for international students. Application fee: $100. *Expenses:*

Contact institution. *Financial support:* In 2009–10, 524 students received support, including 29 fellowships with full tuition reimbursements available (averaging $31,000 per year), 47 research assistantships with full tuition reimbursements available (averaging $31,000 per year); teaching assistantships, Federal Work-Study, institutionally sponsored loans, and health care benefits also available. Financial award application deadline: 3/1; financial award applicants required to submit FAFSA. *Faculty research:* AIDS, cancer, neuroscience, molecular biology, neuroscience, cell biology and molecular genetics, structural biology, microbial pathogenesis and host defense, pharmacology, molecular oncology and immunology. Total annual research expenditures: $201.1 million. *Unit head:* Dr. Robert Grossman, Dean, 212-263-3269, Fax: 212-263-1828. *Application contact:* Dr. Nancy Genieser, Associate Dean, Admissions, 212-263-5290, Fax: 212-263-0720, E-mail: nancy.genieser@nyumc.org.

New York University, School of Medicine and Graduate School of Arts and Science, Sackler Institute of Graduate Biomedical Sciences, Department of Neuroscience and Physiology, New York, NY 10012-1019. Offers PhD, MD/PhD. *Degree requirements:* For doctorate, one foreign language, comprehensive exam, thesis/dissertation, qualifying exam. *Entrance requirements:* For doctorate, GRE General Test. Additional exam requirements/recommendations for international students: Required—TOEFL. *Expenses:* Tuition: Full-time $30,528; part-time $1272 per credit. Required fees: $2177. *Faculty research:* Synaptic transmission, retinal physiology, signal transduction, CNS intrinsic properties, cerebellar function.

North Carolina State University, Graduate School, College of Agriculture and Life Sciences and College of Veterinary Medicine, Program in Physiology, Raleigh, NC 27695. Offers MP, MS, PhD. *Degree requirements:* For master's, thesis (for some programs); for doctorate, thesis/dissertation. *Entrance requirements:* For master's and doctorate, GRE General Test. Electronic applications accepted. *Faculty research:* Neurophysiology, gastrointestinal physiology, reproductive physiology, environmental/stress physiology, cardiovascular physiology.

Northwestern University, The Graduate School, Judd A. and Marjorie Weinberg College of Arts and Sciences, Department of Neurobiology and Physiology, Evanston, IL 60208. Offers MS. Admissions and degrees offered through The Graduate School. Part-time programs available. *Degree requirements:* For master's, thesis. *Entrance requirements:* For master's, GRE General Test and MCAT (strongly recommended). Additional exam requirements/recommendations for international students: Required—TOEFL. Electronic applications accepted. *Expenses:* Contact institution. *Faculty research:* Sensory neurobiology and neuroendocrinology, reproductive biology, vision physiology and psychophysics, cell and developmental biology.

Nova Scotia Agricultural College, Research and Graduate Studies, Truro, NS B2N 5E3, Canada. Offers agriculture (M Sc), including air quality, animal behavior, animal molecular genetics, animal nutrition, animal technology, aquaculture, botany, crop management, crop physiology, ecology, environmental microbiology, food science, horticulture, nutrient management, pest management, physiology, plant biotechnology, plant pathology, soil chemistry, soil fertility, waste management and composting, water quality. Part-time programs available. *Degree requirements:* For master's, thesis, ATC Exam Teaching Assistantship. *Entrance requirements:* For master's, honors B Sc, minimum GPA of 3.0. Additional exam requirements/recommendations for international students: Required—TOEFL (minimum score 580 paper-based; 237 computer-based; 92 iBT), IELTS, Michigan English Language Assessment Battery, CanTEST, CAEL. *Faculty research:* Bio-product development, organic agriculture, nutrient management, air and water quality, agricultural biotechnology.

The Ohio State University, College of Veterinary Medicine, Department of Veterinary Biosciences, Columbus, OH 43210. Offers anatomy and cellular biology (MS, PhD); pathobiology (MS, PhD); pharmacology (MS, PhD); toxicology (MS, PhD); veterinary physiology (MS, PhD). *Faculty:* 45. *Students:* 18 full-time (14 women), 20 part-time (16 women); includes 3 minority (1 African American, 1 Asian American or Pacific Islander, 1 Hispanic American), 16 international. Average age 30. In 2009, 1 master's, 9 doctorates awarded. *Entrance requirements:* For master's and doctorate, GRE General Test. Additional exam requirements/recommendations for international students: Required—TOEFL. *Application deadline:* Applications are processed on a rolling basis. Application fee: $40 ($50 for international students). Electronic applications accepted. *Expenses:* Tuition, state resident: full-time $10,683. Tuition, nonresident: full-time $25,923. Tuition and fees vary according to course load and program. *Faculty research:* Microvasculature, muscle biology, neonatal lung and bone development. *Unit head:* Dr. Michael J. Oglesbee, Graduate Studies Committee Chair, 614-292-5661, Fax: 614-292-6473, E-mail: oglesbee.1@osu.edu. *Application contact:* Graduate Admissions, 614-292-9444, Fax: 614-292-3895, E-mail: domestic.grad@osu.edu.

Ohio University, Graduate College, College of Arts and Sciences, Department of Biological Sciences, Athens, OH 45701-2979. Offers biological sciences (MS, PhD); cell biology and physiology (MS, PhD); ecology and evolutionary biology (MS, PhD); exercise physiology and muscle biology (MS, PhD); microbiology (MS, PhD); neuroscience (MS, PhD). *Faculty:* 50 full-time (14 women), 6 part-time/adjunct (1 woman). *Students:* 44 full-time (19 women), 8 part-time (3 women); includes 2 minority (1 African American, 1 Hispanic American), 21 international. 95 applicants, 24% accepted, 10 enrolled. In 2009, 4 master's, 9 doctorates awarded. Terminal master's awarded for partial completion of doctoral program. *Degree requirements:* For master's, comprehensive exam, thesis, 1 quarter of teaching experience; for doctorate, comprehensive exam, thesis/dissertation, 2 quarters of teaching experience. *Entrance requirements:* For master's, GRE General Test, names of three faculty members whose research interests most closely match the applicant's interest; for doctorate, GRE General Test, essay concerning prior training, research interest and career goals, plus names of three faculty members whose research interests most closely match the applicant's interest. Additional exam requirements/recommendations for international students: Required—TOEFL (minimum score 620 paper-based; 105 iBT) or IELTS (minimum score 7.5). *Application deadline:* For fall admission, 1/15 for domestic and international students. Application fee: $50 ($55 for international students). Electronic applications accepted. *Expenses:* Tuition, state resident: full-time $7839; part-time $323 per quarter hour. Tuition, nonresident: full-time $15,831; part-time $654 per quarter hour. Required fees: $2931. *Financial support:* In 2009–10, 1 fellowship with full tuition reimbursement (averaging $18,957 per year), 10 research assistantships with full tuition reimbursements (averaging $18,957 per year), 42 teaching assistantships with full tuition reimbursements (averaging $18,957 per year) were awarded; Federal Work-Study and institutionally sponsored loans also available. Financial award application deadline: 1/15. *Faculty research:* Ecology and evolutionary biology, exercise physiology and muscle biology, neurobiology, cell biology, physiology. Total annual research expenditures: $2.8 million. *Unit head:* Dr. Ralph DiCaprio, Chair, 740-593-2290, Fax: 740-593-0300, E-mail: dicaprir@ohio.edu. *Application contact:* Dr. Donald Holzschu, Graduate Chair, 740-593-0425, Fax: 740-593-0300, E-mail: holzschu@ohio.edu.

Oregon Health & Science University, School of Medicine, Graduate Programs in Medicine, Department of Physiology and Pharmacology, Portland, OR 97239-3098. Offers pharmacology (PhD); physiology (PhD). *Degree requirements:* For doctorate, comprehensive exam, thesis/dissertation. *Entrance requirements:* For doctorate, GRE General Test (minimum scores: 500 Verbal/600 Quantitative/4.5 Analytical) or MCAT (for some programs). Additional exam requirements/recommendations for international students: Required—TOEFL. *Application deadline:* For fall admission, 12/1 for domestic students. Electronic applications accepted. Tuition and fees vary according to course level, course load, degree level, program and reciprocity agreements. *Financial support:* PhD students have paid tuition and receive stipends available. *Unit head:* Beth Habecker, PhD, Program Director, 503-494-6252, E-mail: habecker@ohsu.edu. *Application contact:* Julie Mertens, Program Coordinator, 503-494-6252, E-mail: mertens@ohsu.edu.

Penn State Hershey Medical Center, College of Medicine, Graduate School Programs in the Biomedical Sciences, The Huck Institutes of the Life Sciences, Intercollege Graduate Program in Physiology, Hershey, PA 17033. Offers MS, PhD, MD/PhD. *Students:* 40 applicants, 23% accepted, 6 enrolled. In 2009, 2 master's, 4 doctorates awarded. Terminal master's awarded for partial completion of doctoral program. *Degree requirements:* For master's, thesis or

alternative; for doctorate, comprehensive exam, thesis/dissertation, oral exam. *Entrance requirements:* For master's, GRE General Test or MCAT; for doctorate, GRE General Test or MCAT, minimum GPA of 3.0. Additional exam requirements/recommendations for international students: Required—TOEFL (minimum score 500 paper-based; 213 computer-based). *Application deadline:* For fall admission, 1/31 priority date for domestic students, 2/1 priority date for international students. Applications are processed on a rolling basis. Application fee: $65. Electronic applications accepted. *Expenses:* Tuition, state resident: part-time $644 per credit. Tuition, nonresident: part-time $1142 per credit. Required fees: $22 per semester. *Financial support:* In 2009–10, research assistantships with full tuition reimbursements (averaging $22,260 per year); fellowships with full tuition reimbursements, career-related internships or fieldwork, scholarships/grants, traineeships, health care benefits, and unspecified assistantships also available. Financial award applicants required to submit FAFSA. *Faculty research:* Gene expression, diabetes obesity and insulin resistance, DNA repair and carcinogenesis, telomerase cell senescence and cancer, ion channels and cardiovascular function. *Unit head:* Dr. Leonard S. Jefferson, Chair, 717-531-8566, Fax: 717-531-7667, E-mail: physio-grad-hmc@psu.edu. *Application contact:* Lisa Harman, Secretary, 717-531-8566, Fax: 717-531-7667, E-mail: physio-grad-hmc@psu.edu.

Penn State University Park, Graduate School, Intercollege Graduate Programs, Intercollege Graduate Program in Physiology, State College, University Park, PA 16802-1503. Offers MS, PhD. *Unit head:* Dr. Leonard Jefferson, Chair, 717-531-8567, Fax: 814-865-9451. *Application contact:* Dr. Leonard Jefferson, Chair, 717-531-8567, Fax: 814-865-9451.

Purdue University, School of Veterinary Medicine and Graduate School, Graduate Programs in Veterinary Medicine, Department of Basic Medical Sciences, West Lafayette, IN 47907. Offers anatomy (MS, PhD); pharmacology (MS, PhD); physiology (MS, PhD). Part-time programs available. *Faculty:* 23 full-time (7 women), 2 part-time/adjunct (1 woman). *Students:* 23 full-time (15 women), 1 (woman) part-time; includes 3 minority (1 African American, 2 Asian Americans or Pacific Islanders), 14 international. Average age 32. 15 applicants, 27% accepted, 4 enrolled. In 2009, 2 master's, 2 doctorates awarded. Terminal master's awarded for partial completion of doctoral program. *Degree requirements:* For master's, thesis; for doctorate, thesis/dissertation. *Entrance requirements:* For master's and doctorate, GRE General Test. Additional exam requirements/recommendations for international students: Required—TOEFL. *Application deadline:* For fall admission, 12/15 priority date for domestic students, 12/15 for international students. Application fee: $55. Electronic applications accepted. *Financial support:* In 2009–10, 14 research assistantships with partial tuition reimbursements (averaging $17,420 per year), 8 teaching assistantships with partial tuition reimbursements (averaging $15,000 per year) were awarded; fellowships with partial tuition reimbursements also available. Financial award application deadline: 3/1; financial award applicants required to submit FAFSA. *Faculty research:* Development and regeneration, tissue injury and shock, biomedical engineering, ovarian function, bone and cartilage biology, cell and molecular biology. *Unit head:* Dr. Laurie A. Jaeger, Head, 765-494-7348, Fax: 765-494-0781, E-mail: ljaeger@purdue.edu. *Application contact:* Dr. Kevin M. Hannon, Chairman, Graduate Committee, 765-494-5949, Fax: 765-494-0781, E-mail: bmsgrad@purdue.edu.

Queen's University at Kingston, School of Graduate Studies and Research, Faculty of Health Sciences, Department of Physiology, Kingston, ON K7L 3N6, Canada. Offers M Sc, PhD. *Degree requirements:* For master's, thesis; for doctorate, comprehensive exam, thesis/dissertation. *Entrance requirements:* For master's, minimum upper B average. Additional exam requirements/recommendations for international students: Required—TOEFL. *Faculty research:* Cardiovascular and respiratory physiology, exercise, gastrointestinal physiology, neuroscience.

Rosalind Franklin University of Medicine and Science, School of Graduate and Postdoctoral Studies—Interdisciplinary Graduate Program in Biomedical Sciences, Department of Physiology and Biophysics, North Chicago, IL 60064-3095. Offers MS, PhD, MD/PhD. Terminal master's awarded for partial completion of doctoral program. *Degree requirements:* For master's, comprehensive exam, thesis; for doctorate, comprehensive exam, thesis/dissertation. *Entrance requirements:* For master's and doctorate, GRE General Test. Additional exam requirements/recommendations for international students: Required—TOEFL, TWE. *Faculty research:* Membrane transport, mechanisms of cellular regulation, brain metabolism, peptide metabolism.

Rush University, Graduate College, Department of Molecular Biophysics and Physiology, Chicago, IL 60612-3832. Offers physiology (PhD); MD/PhD. *Degree requirements:* For doctorate, thesis/dissertation. *Entrance requirements:* For doctorate, GRE General Test. Additional exam requirements/recommendations for international students: Required—TOEFL. *Faculty research:* Physiological exocytosis, raft formation and growth, voltage-gated proton channels, molecular biophysics and physiology.

Rutgers, The State University of New Jersey, New Brunswick, Graduate School-New Brunswick, Program in Endocrinology and Animal Biosciences, Piscataway, NJ 08854-8097. Offers MS, PhD. Terminal master's awarded for partial completion of doctoral program. *Degree requirements:* For master's, thesis; for doctorate, comprehensive exam, thesis/dissertation. *Entrance requirements:* For master's and doctorate, GRE General Test. Additional exam requirements/recommendations for international students: Required—TOEFL. Electronic applications accepted. *Faculty research:* Comparative and behavioral endocrinology, epigenetic regulation of the endocrine system, exercise physiology and immunology, fetal and neonatal developmental programming, mammary gland biology and breast cancer, neuroendocrinology and alcohol studies, reproductive and developmental toxicology.

Saint Louis University, Graduate School and School of Medicine, Graduate Program in Biomedical Sciences and Graduate School, Department of Pharmacological and Physiological Science, St. Louis, MO 63103-2097. Offers PhD. *Degree requirements:* For doctorate, comprehensive exam, thesis/dissertation, departmental qualifying exams. *Entrance requirements:* For doctorate, GRE General Test (GRE Subject Test optional), letters of recommendation, resume, interview. Additional exam requirements/recommendations for international students: Required—TOEFL (minimum score 525 paper-based; 194 computer-based). Electronic applications accepted. *Faculty research:* Molecular endocrinology, neuropharmacology, cardiovascular science, drug abuse, neurotransmitter and hormonal signaling mechanisms.

Salisbury University, Graduate Division, Program in Applied Health Physiology, Salisbury, MD 21801-6837. Offers MS. Part-time and evening/weekend programs available. *Faculty:* 5 full-time (0 women), 2 part-time/adjunct (0 women). *Students:* 38 full-time (19 women), 11 part-time (4 women); includes 3 minority (2 African Americans, 1 Hispanic American), 7 international. Average age 26. 41 applicants, 73% accepted, 9 enrolled. In 2009, 7 master's awarded. *Degree requirements:* For master's, fieldwork. *Entrance requirements:* For master's, minimum GPA of 2.75, undergraduate course work in anatomy and physiology. Additional exam requirements/recommendations for international students: Required—TOEFL (minimum score 550 paper-based; 213 computer-based). *Application deadline:* For fall admission, 8/1 for domestic students; for spring admission, 1/1 for domestic students. Applications are processed on a rolling basis. Application fee: $45. *Expenses:* Tuition, area resident: Part-time $278 per credit hour. Tuition, state resident: part-time $278 per credit hour. Tuition, nonresident: part-time $574 per credit hour. Required fees: $57 per credit hour. *Financial support:* In 2009–10, 20 students received support. Applicants required to submit FAFSA. *Faculty research:* Body image and self-concept, muscle physiology, pulmonary rehabilitation, non-invasive ventilation. *Unit head:* Dr. Sidney R. Schneider, 410-543-6409, Fax: 410-548-9185, E-mail: srschneider@salisbury.edu. *Application contact:* Dr. Sidney R. Schneider, 410-543-6409, Fax: 410-548-9185, E-mail: srschneider@salisbury.edu.

San Francisco State University, Division of Graduate Studies, College of Science and Engineering, Department of Biology, Program in Physiology and Behavioral Biology, San Francisco, CA 94132-1722. Offers MS.

San Jose State University, Graduate Studies and Research, College of Science, Department of Biological Sciences, San Jose, CA 95192-0001. Offers biological sciences (MA, MS);

Physiology

San Jose State University (continued)
molecular biology and microbiology (MS); organismal biology, conservation and ecology (MS); physiology (MS). Part-time programs available. *Students:* 53 full-time (41 women), 48 part-time (30 women); includes 48 minority (2 African Americans, 1 American Indian/Alaska Native, 36 Asian Americans or Pacific Islanders, 9 Hispanic Americans), 10 international. Average age 30. 158 applicants, 28% accepted, 43 enrolled. In 2009, 36 master's awarded. *Entrance requirements:* For master's, GRE. *Application deadline:* For fall admission, 6/29 for domestic students; for spring admission, 11/30 for domestic students. Applications are processed on a rolling basis. Application fee: $59. Electronic applications accepted. *Financial support:* Teaching assistantships, Federal Work-Study available. Financial award applicants required to submit FAFSA. *Faculty research:* Systemic physiology, molecular genetics, SEM studies, toxicology, large mammal ecology. *Unit head:* Dr. John Boothby, Chair, 408-924-4850, Fax: 408-924-4840, E-mail: jboothby@email.sjsu.edu. *Application contact:* Daniel Holley, Graduate Coordinator, 408-924-4844, E-mail: dholley@email.sjsu.edu.

Southern Illinois University Carbondale, Graduate School, Graduate Program in Medicine, Department of Physiology, Carbondale, IL 62901-4701. Offers MS, PhD. Terminal master's awarded for partial completion of doctoral program. *Degree requirements:* For master's, thesis; for doctorate, thesis/dissertation. *Entrance requirements:* For master's, GRE General Test, minimum GPA of 3.0; for doctorate, GRE General Test, minimum GPA of 3.25. Additional exam requirements/recommendations for international students: Required—TOEFL. *Faculty research:* Hormones, neurotransmitters, cell biology, membrane protein, membranes transport.

Southern Illinois University Carbondale, Graduate School, Graduate Program in Medicine, Program in Molecular, Cellular and Systemic Physiology, Carbondale, IL 62901-4701. Offers MS.

Stanford University, School of Medicine, Graduate Programs in Medicine, Department of Molecular and Cellular Physiology, Stanford, CA 94305-9991. Offers PhD. *Degree requirements:* For doctorate, thesis/dissertation, qualifying exams. *Entrance requirements:* For doctorate, GRE General Test, GRE Subject Test. Additional exam requirements/recommendations for international students: Required—TOEFL. Electronic applications accepted. *Expenses:* Tuition: Full-time $37,380; part-time $2760 per quarter. Required fees: $501. *Faculty research:* Signal transduction, ion channels, intracellular calcium, synaptic transmission.

State University of New York Upstate Medical University, College of Graduate Studies, Program in Physiology, Syracuse, NY 13210-2334. Offers MS, PhD, MD/PhD. *Faculty:* 14 full-time (2 women), 1 part-time/adjunct (0 women). *Students:* 1 full-time (0 women), 1 part-time (0 women). In 2009, 2 master's awarded. Terminal master's awarded for partial completion of doctoral program. *Degree requirements:* For master's, thesis; for doctorate, comprehensive exam, thesis/dissertation. *Entrance requirements:* For master's, GRE General Test, interview; for doctorate, GRE General Test, telephone interview. Additional exam requirements/recommendations for international students: Required—TOEFL. *Application deadline:* Applications are processed on a rolling basis. Application fee: $40. Electronic applications accepted. *Financial support:* In 2009–10, fellowships with tuition reimbursements (averaging $21,514 per year), research assistantships with tuition reimbursements (averaging $21,514 per year) were awarded; Federal Work-Study, institutionally sponsored loans, health care benefits, and unspecified assistantships also available. Financial award application deadline: 4/15; financial award applicants required to submit FAFSA. *Unit head:* Dr. Michael W. Miller, Chairperson, 315-464-4413. *Application contact:* Sandra Tillotson, Coordinator of Graduate Recruitment, 315-464-7655.

See Close-Up on page 393.

Stony Brook University, State University of New York, Stony Brook University Medical Center, School of Medicine and Graduate School, Graduate Programs in Medicine, Department of Physiology and Biophysics, Stony Brook, NY 11794. Offers PhD. *Students:* 14 full-time (9 women); includes 3 minority (all Asian Americans or Pacific Islanders), 5 international. Average age 29. 39 applicants, 41% accepted. In 2009, 6 doctorates awarded. *Degree requirements:* For doctorate, comprehensive exam, thesis/dissertation. *Entrance requirements:* For doctorate, GRE General Test, GRE Subject Test, BS in related field, minimum GPA of 3.0. Additional exam requirements/recommendations for international students: Required—TOEFL. *Application deadline:* For fall admission, 1/15 for domestic students. Application fee: $60. *Expenses:* Tuition, state resident: full-time $8370; part-time $349 per credit. Tuition, nonresident: full-time $13,250; part-time $552 per credit. Required fees: $933. *Financial support:* Fellowships, research assistantships, teaching assistantships, Federal Work-Study available. Financial award application deadline: 3/15. *Faculty research:* Cellular electrophysiology, membrane permeation and transport, metabolic endocrinology. Total annual research expenditures: $6 million. *Unit head:* Dr. Peter Brink, Chair, 631-444-2299, Fax: 631-444-3432. *Application contact:* Melanie Bonnette, Graduate Program Administrator, 631-444-2299, Fax: 631-444-3432.

Teachers College, Columbia University, Graduate Faculty of Education, Department of Biobehavioral Studies, Program in Applied Physiology, New York, NY 10027-6696. Offers Ed M, MA, Ed D.

Teachers College, Columbia University, Graduate Faculty of Education, Department of Health and Behavioral Studies, Program in Applied Physiology Nutrition, New York, NY 10027-6696. Offers Ed M, MA, Ed D.

Temple University, Health Sciences Center, School of Medicine and Graduate School, Graduate Programs in Medicine, Department of Physiology, Philadelphia, PA 19122-6096. Offers PhD, MD/PhD. *Degree requirements:* For doctorate, thesis/dissertation, research seminars. *Entrance requirements:* For doctorate, GRE General Test, minimum GPA of 3.0. Additional exam requirements/recommendations for international students: Required—TOEFL (minimum score 550 paper-based; 213 computer-based; 79 iBT). Electronic applications accepted. *Faculty research:* Pulmonary, microvascular, and molecular physiology; cardiac electrophysiology.

Texas A&M University, College of Veterinary Medicine, Department of Veterinary Physiology and Pharmacology, College Station, TX 77843. Offers physiology and pharmacology (MS, PhD); toxicology (MS, PhD). *Faculty:* 14. *Students:* 26 full-time (14 women), 3 part-time (2 women); includes 2 minority (1 African American, 1 Asian American or Pacific Islander), 11 international. Average age 30. In 2009, 2 master's, 1 doctorate awarded. *Entrance requirements:* For master's and doctorate, GRE General Test. Additional exam requirements/recommendations for international students: Required—TOEFL. Application fee: $50 ($75 for international students). *Expenses:* Tuition, state resident: full-time $3991; part-time $221.74 per credit hour. Tuition, nonresident: full-time $9049; part-time $502.74 per credit hour. *Financial support:* Fellowships, research assistantships, teaching assistantships available. Financial award application deadline: 4/1; financial award applicants required to submit FAFSA. *Faculty research:* Gamete and embryo physiology, endocrinology, equine laminitis. *Unit head:* Glen Laine, Head, 979-845-7261, E-mail: glaine@tamu.edu. *Application contact:* Graduate Admissions, 979-845-1044, E-mail: admissions@tamu.edu.

Tufts University, Sackler School of Graduate Biomedical Sciences, Integrated Studies Program, Medford, MA 02155. Offers PhD. *Students:* 10 full-time (7 women); includes 1 minority (Asian American or Pacific Islander), 2 international. Average age 25. 333 applicants, 6% accepted. *Entrance requirements:* For doctorate, GRE General Test, 3 letters of reference. Additional exam requirements/recommendations for international students: Required—TOEFL. *Application deadline:* For fall admission, 12/15 for domestic and international students. Applications are processed on a rolling basis. Application fee: $70. Electronic applications accepted. *Expenses:* Tuition: Full-time $38,096; part-time $3962 per credit. Required fees: $686; $40 per year. Tuition and fees vary according to course level, course load, degree level, program and student level. *Financial support:* In 2009–10, 10 students received support, including 10 research assistantships with tuition reimbursements available (averaging $28,250 per year); scholarships/grants and health care benefits also available. *Unit head:* Dr. Karina Meiri, Program Director, 617-636-6707, E-mail: james.dice@tufts.edu. *Application contact:* Kellie Johnston, Associate Director of Admissions, 617-636-6767, Fax: 617-636-0375, E-mail: sackler-school@tufts.edu.

Tulane University, School of Medicine and School of Liberal Arts, Graduate Programs in Biomedical Sciences, Department of Physiology, New Orleans, LA 70118-5669. Offers MS, PhD, MD/PhD. MS and PhD offered through the Graduate School. *Degree requirements:* For master's, one foreign language, thesis; for doctorate, 2 foreign languages, thesis/dissertation. *Entrance requirements:* For master's, GRE General Test, minimum B average in undergraduate course work; for doctorate, GRE General Test. Additional exam requirements/recommendations for international students: Required—TOEFL. Electronic applications accepted. *Faculty research:* Renal microcirculation, neurophysiology, NA+ transport, renin/angio tensin system, cell and molecular endocrinology.

Universidad Central del Caribe, School of Medicine, Program in Biomedical Sciences, Bayamón, PR 00960-6032. Offers anatomy and cell biology (MA, MS); biochemistry (MS); biomedical sciences (MA); microbiology and immunology (MA, MS); pharmacology (MS); physiology (MA, MS).

Université de Montréal, Faculty of Medicine, Department of Physiology, Montréal, QC H3C 3J7, Canada. Offers neurological sciences (M Sc, PhD); physiology (M Sc, PhD). *Faculty:* 32 full-time (4 women), 6 part-time/adjunct (1 woman). *Students:* 58 full-time (25 women), 96 part-time (53 women). 23 applicants, 17% accepted, 4 enrolled. In 2009, 25 master's, 8 doctorates awarded. Terminal master's awarded for partial completion of doctoral program. *Degree requirements:* For master's, thesis; for doctorate, thesis/dissertation, general exam. *Entrance requirements:* For master's and doctorate, proficiency in French, knowledge of English. *Application deadline:* For fall admission, 2/1 priority date for domestic students; for winter admission, 11/1 priority date for domestic students; for spring admission, 2/1 priority date for domestic students. Application fee: $100. Electronic applications accepted. *Financial support:* Fellowships, research assistantships available. *Faculty research:* Cardiovascular, neuropeptides, membrane transport and biophysics, signaling pathways. *Unit head:* Allan Smith, Interim Director, 514-343-6347, Fax: 514-343-7072, E-mail: allan.smith@umontreal.ca. *Application contact:* Rejean Couture, Graduate Chairman, 514-343-7060, Fax: 514-343-2111, E-mail: rejean.couture@umontreal.ca.

Université de Sherbrooke, Faculty of Medicine and Health Sciences, Graduate Programs in Medicine, Department of Physiology and Biophysics, Sherbrooke, QC J1H 5N4, Canada. Offers M Sc, PhD. Terminal master's awarded for partial completion of doctoral program. *Degree requirements:* For master's, thesis; for doctorate, thesis/dissertation. Electronic applications accepted. *Faculty research:* Ion channels, neurological basis of pain, insulin resistance, obesity.

Université Laval, Faculty of Medicine, Department of Anatomy and Physiology, Québec, QC G1K 7P4, Canada. Offers M Sc, PhD. Terminal master's awarded for partial completion of doctoral program. *Degree requirements:* For master's, thesis (for some programs); for doctorate, comprehensive exam, thesis/dissertation. Electronic applications accepted.

Université Laval, Faculty of Medicine, Graduate Programs in Medicine, Programs in Physiology-Endocrinology, Québec, QC G1K 7P4, Canada. Offers M Sc, PhD. Terminal master's awarded for partial completion of doctoral program. *Degree requirements:* For master's, thesis; for doctorate, comprehensive exam, thesis/dissertation. Electronic applications accepted.

University at Buffalo, the State University of New York, Graduate School, School of Medicine and Biomedical Sciences, Graduate Programs in Medicine and Biomedical Sciences, Department of Physiology and Biophysics, Buffalo, NY 14260. Offers biophysics (MS, PhD); physiology (MA, PhD). *Faculty:* 24 full-time (4 women), 1 part-time/adjunct (0 women). *Students:* 16 full-time (7 women), 1 (woman) part-time, 7 international. Average age 28. 8 applicants, 75% accepted. In 2009, 2 master's, 2 doctorates awarded. Terminal master's awarded for partial completion of doctoral program. *Degree requirements:* For master's, thesis, oral exam, project; for doctorate, thesis/dissertation, oral and written qualifying exam or 2 research proposals. *Entrance requirements:* For master's and doctorate, GRE General Test. Additional exam requirements/recommendations for international students: Required—TOEFL (minimum score 600 paper-based; 250 computer-based; 100 iBT). *Application deadline:* For fall admission, 2/1 priority date for domestic and international students. Applications are processed on a rolling basis. Application fee: $50. Electronic applications accepted. *Financial support:* In 2009–10, fellowships with tuition reimbursements (averaging $21,000 per year), 17 research assistantships with tuition reimbursements (averaging $21,000 per year) were awarded; Federal Work-Study, institutionally sponsored loans, health care benefits, and unspecified assistantships also available. Financial award application deadline: 2/1; financial award applicants required to submit FAFSA. *Faculty research:* Neurosciences, ion channels, cardiac physiology, renal/epithelial transport, cardiopulmonary exercise. Total annual research expenditures: $5.4 million. *Unit head:* Dr. Harold C. Strauss, Chair, 716-829-2738, Fax: 716-829-2344, E-mail: hstrauss@buffalo.edu. *Application contact:* Dora Horbachevsky, Program Administrator, 716-829-2189, Fax: 716-829-2364, E-mail: dh26@buffalo.edu.

University of Alberta, Faculty of Graduate Studies and Research, Department of Biological Sciences, Edmonton, AB T6G 2E1, Canada. Offers environmental biology and ecology (M Sc, PhD); microbiology and biotechnology (M Sc, PhD); molecular biology and genetics (M Sc, PhD); physiology and cell biology (M Sc, PhD); plant biology (M Sc, PhD); systematics and evolution (M Sc, PhD). *Faculty:* 72 full-time (15 women), 15 part-time/adjunct (4 women). *Students:* 238 full-time (117 women), 32 part-time (15 women), 31 international. 206 applicants, 42% accepted. In 2009, 29 master's, 31 doctorates awarded. Terminal master's awarded for partial completion of doctoral program. *Degree requirements:* For master's, thesis; for doctorate, thesis/dissertation. *Entrance requirements:* Additional exam requirements/recommendations for international students: Required—TOEFL. *Application deadline:* For fall admission, 3/1 priority date for domestic students. Applications are processed on a rolling basis. Application fee: $0. Tuition and fees charges are reported in Canadian dollars. *Expenses:* Tuition, area resident: Full-time $4626 Canadian dollars; part-time $99.72 Canadian dollars per unit. International tuition: $8216 Canadian dollars full-time. Required fees: $3590 Canadian dollars; $99.72 Canadian dollars per unit. $215 Canadian dollars per term. *Financial support:* In 2009–10, 4 research assistantships with partial tuition reimbursements (averaging $12,000 per year), 103 teaching assistantships with partial tuition reimbursements (averaging $12,300 per year) were awarded; career-related internships or fieldwork and scholarships/grants also available. *Unit head:* Laura Frost, Chair, 780-492-1904. *Application contact:* Dr. John P. Chang, Associate Chair for Graduate Studies, 780-492-1257, Fax: 780-492-9457, E-mail: bio.grad.coordinator@ualberta.ca.

University of Alberta, Faculty of Medicine and Dentistry and Faculty of Graduate Studies and Research, Graduate Programs in Medicine, Department of Physiology, Edmonton, AB T6G 2E1, Canada. Offers M Sc, PhD. *Faculty:* 19 full-time (3 women), 9 part-time/adjunct (1 woman). *Students:* 27 full-time (15 women). Average age 25. 123 applicants, 7% accepted, 9 enrolled. In 2009, 2 master's, 4 doctorates awarded. Terminal master's awarded for partial completion of doctoral program. *Degree requirements:* For master's, thesis; for doctorate, thesis/dissertation. *Entrance requirements:* For master's and doctorate, minimum GPA of 3.0. Additional exam requirements/recommendations for international students: Required—TOEFL (minimum score 580 paper-based; 237 computer-based). *Application deadline:* For fall admission, 7/1 priority date for domestic students; for winter admission, 11/1 priority date for domestic students; for spring admission, 3/1 priority date for domestic students. Applications are processed on a rolling basis. Application fee: $0. Electronic applications accepted. Tuition and fees charges are reported in Canadian dollars. *Expenses:* Tuition, area resident: Full-time $4626 Canadian dollars; part-time $99.72 Canadian dollars per unit. International tuition: $8216 Canadian dollars full-time. Required fees: $3590 Canadian dollars; $99.72 Canadian dollars per unit. $215 Canadian dollars per term. *Financial support:* In 2009–10, 5 teaching assistantships (averaging $15,675 per year) were awarded; scholarships/grants also available. *Faculty research:* Membrane transport, cell biology, perinatal endocrinology, neurophysiology, cardiovascular. Total annual research expenditures: $5.5 million. *Unit head:* Dr. Chris I. Cheeseman, Chair, 780-492-2620, Fax: 780-492-8915, E-mail: chris.cheeseman@ualberta.ca. *Application contact:* Dr. Christina G. Benishin, Graduate Studies Coordinator, 780-492-5284, Fax: 780-492-8915, E-mail: christina.benishin@ualberta.ca.

The University of Arizona, Graduate College, Graduate Interdisciplinary Programs, Graduate Interdisciplinary Program in Physiological Sciences, Tucson, AZ 85721. Offers MS, PhD. *Faculty:* 16 full-time (6 women). *Students:* 25 full-time (15 women), 29 part-time (17 women); includes 10 minority (1 African American, 5 Asian Americans or Pacific Islanders, 4 Hispanic Americans), 10 international. Average age 26. 37 applicants, 57% accepted, 19 enrolled. In 2009, 10 master's, 6 doctorates awarded. *Degree requirements:* For doctorate, thesis/dissertation. *Entrance requirements:* For master's, GRE General Test, 3 letters of recommendation, statement of purpose; for doctorate, GRE General Test, 3 letters of recommendation. Additional exam requirements/recommendations for international students: Required—TOEFL (minimum score 600 paper-based). *Application deadline:* For fall admission, 3/15 for domestic and international students. Applications are processed on a rolling basis. Application fee: $65. Electronic applications accepted. *Expenses:* Tuition, state resident: full-time $9028. Tuition, nonresident: full-time $24,890. *Financial support:* In 2009–10, 3 research assistantships with full tuition reimbursements (averaging $20,867 per year), 13 teaching assistantships with full tuition reimbursements (averaging $27,699 per year) were awarded; health care benefits and unspecified assistantships also available. *Faculty research:* Cellular transport and signaling, receptor and messenger modulation, neural interaction and biomechanics, fluid network regulation, environmental adaptation. *Unit head:* Dr. Ronald Lynch, Department Chair, 520-626-2472, E-mail: rlynch@u.arizona.edu. *Application contact:* Holly Lopez, Information Contact, 520-626-2898, Fax: 520-626-2382, E-mail: idp@ccit.arizona.edu.

University of Arkansas for Medical Sciences, Graduate School, Graduate Programs in Biomedical Sciences, Department of Physiology and Biophysics, Little Rock, AR 72205-7199. Offers MS, PhD, MD/PhD. *Faculty:* 20 full-time (4 women), 21 part-time/adjunct (4 women). *Students:* 10 full-time, 3 part-time. In 2009, 1 master's, 4 doctorates awarded. *Degree requirements:* For master's, thesis; for doctorate, thesis/dissertation. *Entrance requirements:* For master's and doctorate, GRE General Test. Additional exam requirements/recommendations for international students: Required—TOEFL. *Application deadline:* For fall admission, 3/15 for domestic and international students. Application fee: $0. *Financial support:* In 2009–10, research assistantships with full tuition reimbursements (averaging $24,000 per year); stipend and tuition for doctoral students also available. Support available to part-time students. *Faculty research:* Gene transcription, protein targeting, membrane biology, cell-cell communication. *Unit head:* Dr. Michael L. Jennings, Chairman, 501-686-5123. *Application contact:* Dr. Richard Kurten, Program Director, 501-686-8269, E-mail: kurtenrichardc@uams.edu.

The University of British Columbia, Faculty of Medicine, Department of Cellular and Physiological Sciences, Division of Physiology, Vancouver, BC V6T 1Z1, Canada. Offers M Sc, PhD. Terminal master's awarded for partial completion of doctoral program. *Degree requirements:* For master's, thesis, oral defense; for doctorate, comprehensive exam, thesis/dissertation, oral defense. *Entrance requirements:* Additional exam requirements/recommendations for international students: Required—TOEFL (minimum score 550 paper-based; 213 computer-based), IELTS (minimum score 6.2). Electronic applications accepted. *Faculty research:* Neurophysiology, gastroenterology, endocrinology, cardiovascular physiology.

University of California, Berkeley, Graduate Division, College of Letters and Science, Group in Endocrinology, Berkeley, CA 94720-1500. Offers MA, PhD. *Faculty:* 13 full-time. *Students:* 13 full-time (8 women). Average age 26. 22 applicants, 4 enrolled. In 2009, 1 master's, 1 doctorate awarded. *Degree requirements:* For doctorate, thesis/dissertation, oral qualifying exam. *Entrance requirements:* For master's, GRE General Test or the equivalent (MCAT), minimum GPA of 3.0, 3 letters of recommendation; for doctorate, GRE General Test or the equivalent (MCAT), minimum GPA of 3.4, 3 letters of recommendation. Additional exam requirements/recommendations for international students: Required—TOEFL. *Application deadline:* For fall admission, 1/15 for domestic students. Application fee: $70 ($90 for international students). *Financial support:* Fellowships, research assistantships, teaching assistantships, unspecified assistantships available. Financial award applicants required to submit FAFSA. *Unit head:* Dr. Gary Firestone, Co-Chair, 510-643-7330, E-mail: ibgradsao@berkeley.edu. *Application contact:* Information Contact, 510-642-7330, Fax: 510-643-6264, E-mail: ibgradso@berkeley.edu.

University of California, Davis, Graduate Studies, Molecular, Cellular and Integrative Physiology Graduate Group, Davis, CA 95616. Offers MS, PhD. *Degree requirements:* For master's, comprehensive exam (for some programs), thesis (for some programs); for doctorate, thesis/dissertation. *Entrance requirements:* For master's and doctorate, GRE General Test. Additional exam requirements/recommendations for international students: Required—TOEFL (minimum score 550 paper-based; 213 computer-based). Electronic applications accepted. *Faculty research:* Systemic physiology, cellular physiology, neurophysiology, cardiovascular physiology, endocrinology.

University of California, Irvine, School of Medicine and School of Biological Sciences, Department of Physiology and Biophysics, Irvine, CA 92697. Offers biological sciences (PhD); MD/PhD. Students apply through the Graduate Program in Molecular Biology, Genetics, and Biochemistry. *Students:* 9 full-time (3 women); includes 3 minority (2 Asian Americans or Pacific Islanders, 1 Hispanic American), 2 international. Average age 27. *Degree requirements:* For doctorate, thesis/dissertation. *Entrance requirements:* For doctorate, GRE General Test, GRE Subject Test, minimum GPA of 3.0. Additional exam requirements/recommendations for international students: Required—TOEFL (minimum score 550 paper-based; 213 computer-based). *Application deadline:* For fall admission, 1/15 priority date for domestic students, 1/15 for international students. Application fee: $70 ($90 for international students). Electronic applications accepted. *Financial support:* Fellowships, research assistantships with full tuition reimbursements, teaching assistantships, institutionally sponsored loans, traineeships, health care benefits, and unspecified assistantships available. Financial award application deadline: 3/1; financial award applicants required to submit FAFSA. *Faculty research:* Membrane physiology, exercise physiology, regulation of hormone biosynthesis and action, endocrinology, ion channels and signal transduction. *Unit head:* Dr. Janos K. Lanyi, Chair, 949-824-7150, Fax: 949-824-8540, E-mail: jklanyi@uci.edu. *Application contact:* Kimberly McKinney, Administrator, 949-824-8145, Fax: 949-824-1965, E-mail: kamckinn@uci.edu.

University of California, Los Angeles, David Geffen School of Medicine and Graduate Division, Graduate Programs in Medicine, Department of Physiology, Los Angeles, CA 90095. Offers PhD. *Degree requirements:* For doctorate, thesis/dissertation, oral and written qualifying exams. *Entrance requirements:* For doctorate, GRE General Test, GRE Subject Test. *Faculty research:* Membrane physiology, cell physiology, muscle physiology, neurophysiology, cardiopulmonary physiology.

University of California, Los Angeles, Graduate Division, College of Letters and Science, Department of Physiological Science, Los Angeles, CA 90095. Offers physiological science (MS). *Students:* 25 full-time (14 women); includes 9 minority (1 African American, 7 Asian Americans or Pacific Islanders, 1 Hispanic American), 3 international. Average age 23. 23 applicants, 57% accepted, 12 enrolled. In 2009, 9 master's awarded. *Degree requirements:* For master's, thesis. *Entrance requirements:* For master's, GRE General Test or MCAT, minimum GPA of 3.0, bachelor's degree in biological or physical sciences. *Application deadline:* For fall admission, 6/30 for domestic and international students. Application fee: $70 ($90 for international students). Electronic applications accepted. *Financial support:* In 2009–10, 7 fellowships with full and partial tuition reimbursements, 10 research assistantships with full and partial tuition reimbursements, 22 teaching assistantships with full and partial tuition reimbursements were awarded; Federal Work-Study, institutionally sponsored loans, scholarships/grants, health care benefits, tuition waivers (full and partial), and unspecified assistantships also available. Financial award applicants required to submit FAFSA. *Faculty research:* Diet and exercise in the prevention and management of degenerative diseases, neuromuscular physiology and plasticity, neural control of movement and homeostasis. *Unit head:* Dr. Arthur Arnold, Chair, 310-825-2169. *Application contact:* Department Office, 310-825-3891, E-mail: mcarr@physci.ucla.edu.

University of California, Los Angeles, Graduate Division, College of Letters and Science and David Geffen School of Medicine, UCLA ACCESS to Programs in the Molecular, Cellular and Integrative Life Sciences, Los Angeles, CA 90095. Offers biochemistry and molecular biology (PhD); biological chemistry (PhD); cellular and molecular pathology (PhD); human genetics (PhD); microbiology, immunology, and molecular genetics (PhD); molecular biology (PhD); molecular toxicology (PhD); molecular, cellular and integrative physiology (PhD); neurobiology (PhD); oral biology (PhD); physiology (PhD). ACCESS is an umbrella program for first-year coursework in 12 PhD programs. *Students:* 39 full-time (25 women); includes 14 minority (1 African American, 1 American Indian/Alaska Native, 8 Asian Americans or Pacific Islanders, 4 Hispanic Americans), 10 international. Average age 25. 437 applicants, 22% accepted, 30 enrolled. *Degree requirements:* For doctorate, thesis/dissertation, oral and written qualifying exams. *Entrance requirements:* For doctorate, GRE General Test, minimum undergraduate GPA of 3.0. Additional exam requirements/recommendations for international students: Required—TOEFL. *Application deadline:* For fall admission, 12/15 for domestic and international students. Application fee: $70 ($90 for international students). Electronic applications accepted. *Financial support:* In 2009–10, 56 fellowships with full and partial tuition reimbursements, 16 research assistantships with full and partial tuition reimbursements were awarded; teaching assistantships with full and partial tuition reimbursements, Federal Work-Study, institutionally sponsored loans, scholarships/grants, health care benefits, tuition waivers (full and partial), and unspecified assistantships also available. Financial award application deadline: 3/1; financial award applicants required to submit FAFSA. *Faculty research:* Molecular, cellular, and developmental biology; immunology; microbiology; integrative biology. *Unit head:* Dr. Greg I. Payne, Chair, 310-206-3121. *Application contact:* Coordinator, 310-206-3121, Fax: 310-206-5280, E-mail: uclaaccess@mednet.ucla.edu.

See Close-Up on page 239.

University of California, San Diego, School of Medicine and Office of Graduate Studies, Graduate Studies in Biomedical Sciences, Physiology Program, La Jolla, CA 92093. Offers PhD. *Degree requirements:* For doctorate, thesis/dissertation, qualifying exam. *Entrance requirements:* For doctorate, GRE General Test. Additional exam requirements/recommendations for international students: Required—TOEFL. Electronic applications accepted. *Faculty research:* Cell and organ physiology, eukaryotic regulatory and molecular biology, molecular and cellular pharmacology.

University of California, San Francisco, Graduate Division, Biomedical Sciences Graduate Group, San Francisco, CA 94143. Offers anatomy (PhD); endocrinology (PhD); experimental pathology (PhD); physiology (PhD). *Degree requirements:* For doctorate, thesis/dissertation. *Entrance requirements:* For doctorate, GRE General Test.

University of Chicago, Division of the Biological Sciences, Neuroscience Graduate Programs, Department of Integrative Neuroscience, Chicago, IL 60637-1513. Offers cell physiology (PhD); pharmacological and physiological sciences (PhD). *Faculty:* 8 full-time (all women). *Students:* Average age 30. *Degree requirements:* For doctorate, thesis/dissertation, preliminary exam. *Entrance requirements:* For doctorate, GRE General Test. Additional exam requirements/recommendations for international students: Required—TOEFL. *Application deadline:* For fall admission, 12/28 priority date for domestic and international students. Application fee: $55. Electronic applications accepted. *Financial support:* In 2009–10, fellowships with tuition reimbursements (averaging $26,301 per year), research assistantships with tuition reimbursements (averaging $26,301 per year) were awarded; institutionally sponsored loans, scholarships/grants, traineeships, and health care benefits also available. Financial award applicants required to submit FAFSA. *Faculty research:* Psychopharmacology, neuropharmacology. *Unit head:* Dr. Steven Shevell, Chairman, 773-834-2900, Fax: 773-702-8842, E-mail: shevell@uchicago.edu. *Application contact:* Diane J. Hall, Graduate Administrative Director, 773-702-6371, Fax: 773-702-1216, E-mail: d-hall@uchicago.edu.

University of Cincinnati, Graduate School, College of Medicine, Graduate Programs in Biomedical Sciences, Department of Molecular and Cellular Physiology, Cincinnati, OH 45221. Offers physiology (PhD). *Degree requirements:* For doctorate, comprehensive exam, thesis/dissertation, publication. *Entrance requirements:* For doctorate, GRE General Test, GRE Subject Test. Additional exam requirements/recommendations for international students: Required—TOEFL (minimum score 560 paper-based; 220 computer-based). Electronic applications accepted. *Faculty research:* Endocrinology, cardiovascular physiology, muscle physiology, neurophysiology, transgenic mouse physiology.

University of Colorado at Boulder, Graduate School, College of Arts and Sciences, Department of Integrative Physiology, Boulder, CO 80309. Offers MS, PhD. *Faculty:* 22 full-time (6 women). *Students:* 50 full-time (18 women), 11 part-time (4 women); includes 4 minority (1 African American, 2 Asian Americans or Pacific Islanders, 1 Hispanic American), 5 international. Average age 27. 67 applicants, 28% accepted, 17 enrolled. In 2009, 19 master's, 5 doctorates awarded. *Degree requirements:* For master's, comprehensive exam, thesis or alternative; for doctorate, thesis/dissertation. *Entrance requirements:* For master's, GRE General Test, minimum undergraduate GPA of 2.75. *Application deadline:* For fall admission, 1/15 priority date for domestic students, 12/15 for international students. Applications are processed on a rolling basis. Application fee: $50 ($60 for international students). *Financial support:* In 2009–10, 24 fellowships (averaging $15,189 per year), 33 research assistantships (averaging $6,975 per year) were awarded. Financial award application deadline: 2/1. *Faculty research:* Integrative or cellular kinesiology. Total annual research expenditures: $8.8 million.

University of Colorado Denver, School of Medicine, Program in Physiology, Denver, CO 80217-3364. Offers PhD. *Students:* 8 full-time (0 women), 4 international. In 2009, 1 doctorate awarded. *Degree requirements:* For doctorate, comprehensive exam, thesis/dissertation. *Entrance requirements:* For doctorate, GRE General Test, 4 letters of recommendation. Additional exam requirements/recommendations for international students: Required—TOEFL (minimum score 550 paper-based; 213 computer-based). *Application deadline:* For fall admission, 1/15 for domestic students. Application fee: $50. *Financial support:* Fellowships, research assistantships, teaching assistantships, Federal Work-Study and institutionally sponsored loans available. Support available to part-time students. Financial award application deadline: 3/15; financial award applicants required to submit FAFSA. *Faculty research:* Nicotonic receptors, immunity, molecular structure, function and regulation of ion channels, calcium influx in the function of cytotoxic T lymphocytes. *Unit head:* Dr. William Betz, Chair, 303-724-4502, E-mail: bill.betz@ucdenver.edu. *Application contact:* Betty McGowan, 303-724-4513, E-mail: becky.mcgowan@ucdenver.edu.

University of Connecticut, Graduate School, College of Liberal Arts and Sciences, Department of Physiology and Neurobiology, Storrs, CT 06269. Offers comparative physiology (MS, PhD); endocrinology (MS, PhD), including comparative physiology (MS), neurobiology (MS); neurobiology (MS, PhD). *Faculty:* 20 full-time (5 women). *Students:* 29 full-time (12 women), 3 part-time (0 women); includes 5 minority (all Asian Americans or Pacific Islanders), 12 international. Average age 28. 46 applicants, 11% accepted, 3 enrolled. In 2009, 5 master's, 2 doctorates awarded. Terminal master's awarded for partial completion of doctoral program. *Degree requirements:* For master's, comprehensive exam; for doctorate, thesis/dissertation. *Entrance requirements:* For master's and doctorate, GRE General Test, GRE Subject Test. Additional exam requirements/recommendations for international students: Required—TOEFL (minimum score 550 paper-based; 213 computer-based). *Application deadline:* For fall admission, 2/1 priority date for domestic and international students; for spring admission, 11/1 for domestic students, 10/1 for international students. Applications are processed on a rolling basis. Application fee: $55. Electronic applications accepted. *Expenses:* Tuition, state resident: full-time $4725;

Physiology

University of Connecticut (continued)
part-time $525 per credit. Tuition, nonresident: full-time $12,267; part-time $1363 per credit. Required fees: $346 per semester. Tuition and fees vary according to course load. *Financial support:* In 2009–10, 12 research assistantships with full tuition reimbursements, 17 teaching assistantships with full tuition reimbursements were awarded; fellowships, Federal Work-Study, scholarships/grants, health care benefits, and unspecified assistantships also available. Financial award application deadline: 2/1. *Unit head:* J. Larry Renfro, Head, 860-486-3285, Fax: 860-486-3303, E-mail: larry.renfro@uconn.edu. *Application contact:* Joseph J. LoTurco, Chairperson, 860-486-3271, Fax: 860-486-3303, E-mail: joseph.loturco@uconn.edu.

See Close-Up on page 491.

University of Delaware, College of Arts and Sciences, Department of Biological Sciences, Newark, DE 19716. Offers biotechnology (MS); cancer biology (MS, PhD); cell and extra-cellular matrix biology (MS, PhD); cell and systems physiology (MS, PhD); developmental biology (MS, PhD); ecology and evolution (MS, PhD); microbiology (MS, PhD); molecular biology and genetics (MS, PhD). Terminal master's awarded for partial completion of doctoral program. *Degree requirements:* For master's, thesis, preliminary exam; for doctorate, comprehensive exam, thesis/dissertation, preliminary exam. *Entrance requirements:* For master's and doctorate, GRE General Test. Additional exam requirements/recommendations for international students: Required—TOEFL (minimum score 600 paper-based; 250 computer-based); Recommended—TWE. Electronic applications accepted. *Faculty research:* Microorganisms, bone, cancer metastasis, developmental biology, cell biology, DNA.

University of Delaware, College of Health Sciences, Department of Health, Nutrition, and Exercise Sciences, Newark, DE 19716. Offers exercise science (MS), including biomechanics, exercise physiology, motor control; health promotion (MS); human nutrition (MS). Part-time programs available. *Degree requirements:* For master's, thesis. *Entrance requirements:* For master's, GRE General Test, interview, minimum GPA of 3.0. Additional exam requirements/recommendations for international students: Required—TOEFL (minimum score 550 paper-based; 213 computer-based). Electronic applications accepted. *Faculty research:* Sport biomechanics, rehabilitation biomechanics, vascular dynamics.

University of Delaware, College of Health Sciences, Department of Kinesiology and Applied Physiology, Newark, DE 19716. Offers MS, PhD.

University of Florida, College of Medicine, Department of Physiology and Functional Genomics, Gainesville, FL 32611. Offers PhD. *Degree requirements:* For doctorate, thesis/dissertation. *Entrance requirements:* For doctorate, GRE General Test, minimum GPA of 3.0. Additional exam requirements/recommendations for international students: Required—TOEFL. Electronic applications accepted. *Faculty research:* Cell and general endocrinology, neuroendocrinology, neurophysiology, respiration, membrane transport and ion channels.

University of Florida, College of Medicine and Graduate School, Interdisciplinary Program in Biomedical Sciences, Concentration in Physiology and Pharmacology, Gainesville, FL 32611. Offers PhD. *Degree requirements:* For doctorate, thesis/dissertation. *Entrance requirements:* For doctorate, GRE General Test, minimum GPA of 3.0. Electronic applications accepted.

See Close-Up on page 493.

University of Florida, Graduate School, College of Health and Human Performance, Department of Applied Physiology and Kinesiology, Gainesville, FL 32611. Offers athletic training/sport medicine (MS, PhD); biomechanics (MS, PhD); clinical exercise physiology (MS); exercise physiology (MS, PhD); health and human performance (PhD); human performance (MS); motor learning/control (MS, PhD); sport and exercise psychology (MS). *Degree requirements:* For doctorate, thesis/dissertation. *Entrance requirements:* For doctorate, GRE General Test. Electronic applications accepted.

University of Georgia, College of Veterinary Medicine and Graduate School, Graduate Programs in Veterinary Medicine, Department of Physiology and Pharmacology, Athens, GA 30602. Offers pharmacology (MS, PhD); physiology (MS, PhD). *Faculty:* 9 full-time (3 women), 1 part-time/adjunct (0 women). *Students:* 10 full-time (6 women), 1 (woman) part-time; includes 3 minority (2 Asian Americans or Pacific Islanders, 1 Hispanic American), 2 international. 18 applicants, 22% accepted, 2 enrolled. In 2009, 1 doctorate awarded. *Degree requirements:* For master's, thesis; for doctorate, one foreign language, thesis/dissertation. *Entrance requirements:* For master's and doctorate, GRE General Test. *Application deadline:* For fall admission, 7/1 priority date for domestic students; for spring admission, 11/15 for domestic students. Application fee: $50. Electronic applications accepted. *Expenses:* Tuition, state resident: full-time $6000; part-time $250 per credit hour. Tuition, nonresident: full-time $20,904; part-time $871 per credit hour. Required fees: $730 per semester. *Financial support:* Fellowships, research assistantships, teaching assistantships, unspecified assistantships available. *Unit head:* Dr. Gaylen L. Edwards, Acting Head, 706-542-5854, Fax: 706-542-3015, E-mail: gedwards@uga.edu. *Application contact:* Dr. Royal A. McGraw, Graduate Coordinator, 706-542-0661, Fax: 706-542-3015, E-mail: mcgraw@uga.edu.

University of Guelph, Ontario Veterinary College and Graduate Program Services, Graduate Programs in Veterinary Sciences, Department of Biomedical Sciences, Guelph, ON N1G 2W1, Canada. Offers morphology (M Sc, DV Sc, PhD); neuroscience (M Sc, DV Sc, PhD); pharmacology (M Sc, DV Sc, PhD); physiology (M Sc, DV Sc, PhD); toxicology (M Sc, DV Sc, PhD). Part-time programs available. *Degree requirements:* For master's, thesis; for doctorate, comprehensive exam, thesis/dissertation. *Entrance requirements:* For master's, honors B Sc, minimum 75% average in last 20 courses; for doctorate, M Sc with thesis from accredited institution. Additional exam requirements/recommendations for international students: Required—TOEFL (minimum score 550 paper-based; 213 computer-based; 89 iBT). Electronic applications accepted. *Faculty research:* Cellular morphology; endocrine, vascular and reproductive physiology; clinical pharmacology; veterinary toxicology; developmental biology, neuroscience.

University of Hawaii at Manoa, John A. Burns School of Medicine, Program in Developmental and Reproductive Biology, Honolulu, HI 96813. Offers MS, PhD. Part-time programs available. *Faculty:* 19 full-time (2 women), 7 part-time/adjunct (4 women). *Students:* 18 full-time (9 women), 8 part-time (3 women); includes 17 minority (all Asian Americans or Pacific Islanders), 2 international. Average age 27. 20 applicants, 70% accepted, 10 enrolled. In 2009, 10 master's awarded. *Degree requirements:* For doctorate, thesis/dissertation. *Entrance requirements:* For doctorate, GRE General Test, GRE Subject Test. Application fee: $50. *Expenses:* Tuition, state resident: full-time $8900; part-time $372 per credit. Tuition, nonresident: full-time $21,400; part-time $898 per credit. Required fees: $207 per semester. *Financial support:* In 2009–10, 1 fellowship (averaging $1,000 per year), 9 research assistantships (averaging $17,109 per year), 3 teaching assistantships (averaging $14,382 per year) were awarded. *Faculty research:* Biology of gametes and fertilization, reproductive endocrinology. Total annual research expenditures: $5.4 million. *Application contact:* Steve Ward, Graduate Chair, 808-956-6598, Fax: 808-956-7316.

University of Illinois at Chicago, College of Medicine and Graduate College, Graduate Programs in Medicine, Department of Physiology and Biophysics, Chicago, IL 60607-7128. Offers MS, PhD. Terminal master's awarded for partial completion of doctoral program. *Degree requirements:* For master's, thesis; for doctorate, thesis/dissertation. *Entrance requirements:* For master's and doctorate, GRE General Test. Additional exam requirements/recommendations for international students: Required—TOEFL. Electronic applications accepted. *Faculty research:* Neuroscience, endocrinology and reproduction, cell physiology, exercise physiology, NMR.

University of Illinois at Urbana–Champaign, Graduate College, College of Liberal Arts and Sciences, School of Integrative Biology, Program in Physiological and Molecular Plant Biology, Champaign, IL 61820. Offers PhD. *Students:* 10 full-time (4 women); includes 1 minority (Hispanic American), 6 international. 2 applicants, 0% accepted. In 2009, 3 doctorates awarded. *Entrance requirements:* For doctorate, GRE, minimum GPA of 3.0. Additional exam requirements/recommendations for international students: Required—TOEFL (minimum score 570 paper-based; 230 computer-based; 89 iBT). *Application deadline:* Applications are processed on a rolling basis. Application fee: $60 ($75 for international students). Electronic applications accepted. *Financial support:* In 2009–10, 1 fellowship, 6 research assistantships, 4 teaching assistantships were awarded; tuition waivers (full and partial) also available. *Unit head:* Stephen Moose, Director, 217-244-6308, Fax: 217-244-1224, E-mail: smoose@illinois.edu. *Application contact:* Carol Hall, Office Manager, 217-333-8208, Fax: 217-244-1224, E-mail: cahall@illinois.edu.

University of Illinois at Urbana–Champaign, Graduate College, College of Liberal Arts and Sciences, School of Molecular and Cellular Biology, Department of Molecular and Integrative Physiology, Champaign, IL 61820. Offers MS, PhD. *Faculty:* 12 full-time (4 women). *Students:* 28 full-time (17 women), 3 part-time (1 woman); includes 6 minority (1 African American, 2 Asian Americans or Pacific Islanders, 3 Hispanic Americans), 15 international. In 2009, 4 master's, 3 doctorates awarded. *Entrance requirements:* For master's and doctorate, GRE, minimum GPA of 3.0. Additional exam requirements/recommendations for international students: Required—TOEFL (minimum score 590 paper-based; 243 computer-based). *Application deadline:* Applications are processed on a rolling basis. Application fee: $60 ($75 for international students). Electronic applications accepted. *Financial support:* In 2009–10, 4 fellowships, 22 research assistantships, 18 teaching assistantships were awarded; tuition waivers (full and partial) also available. *Unit head:* Byron Kemper, Head, 217-333-1146, Fax: 217-333-1133, E-mail: byronkem@illinois.edu. *Application contact:* Penny Morman, Office Manager, 217-333-8275, Fax: 217-333-1133, E-mail: morman@illinois.edu.

The University of Iowa, Roy J. and Lucille A. Carver College of Medicine and Graduate College, Graduate Programs in Medicine, Department of Molecular Physiology and Biophysics, Iowa City, IA 52242-1316. Offers MS, PhD. *Faculty:* 17 full-time (3 women), 16 part-time/adjunct (2 women). *Students:* 20 full-time (6 women); includes 3 minority (all Asian Americans or Pacific Islanders), 3 international. Average age 25. 8 applicants, 100% accepted, 8 enrolled. In 2009, 1 master's, 8 doctorates awarded. Terminal master's awarded for partial completion of doctoral program. *Degree requirements:* For master's, comprehensive exam; for doctorate, comprehensive exam, thesis/dissertation, teaching experience. *Entrance requirements:* For master's, GRE; for doctorate, GRE General Test, minimum GPA of 3.0. Additional exam requirements/recommendations for international students: Required—TOEFL. *Application deadline:* For fall admission, 4/1 for domestic students, 3/1 for international students; for spring admission, 10/1 for domestic students, 9/1 for international students. Applications are processed on a rolling basis. Application fee: $60 ($80 for international students). Electronic applications accepted. *Financial support:* In 2009–10, 4 fellowships with full tuition reimbursements (averaging $24,250 per year), 13 research assistantships with full tuition reimbursements (averaging $24,250 per year) were awarded; traineeships also available. Financial award application deadline: 4/1. *Faculty research:* Cellular and molecular endocrinology, membrane structure and function, cardiac cell electrophysiology, regulation of gene expression, neurophysiology. *Unit head:* Dr. Kevin P. Campbell, Head, 319-335-7800, Fax: 319-335-7330, E-mail: kevin-campbell@uiowa.edu. *Application contact:* Dr. Michael Anderson, Director of Graduate Studies, 319-335-7839, Fax: 319-335-7330, E-mail: michael-g-anderson@uiowa.edu.

The University of Kansas, University of Kansas Medical Center, School of Medicine, Department of Molecular and Integrative Physiology, Kansas City, KS 66160. Offers molecular and integrative physiology (MS, PhD); neuroscience (MS, PhD); MD/PhD. *Faculty:* 32 full-time, 9 part-time/adjunct. *Students:* 1 (woman) full-time, 23 part-time (12 women); includes 2 minority (1 African American, 1 Hispanic American), 12 international. Average age 29. In 2009, 5 doctorates awarded. Terminal master's awarded for partial completion of doctoral program. *Degree requirements:* For master's, thesis; for doctorate, comprehensive exam, thesis/dissertation. *Entrance requirements:* For doctorate, GRE. Additional exam requirements/recommendations for international students: Required—TOEFL. *Application deadline:* For fall admission, 1/15 priority date for domestic and international students. Applications are processed on a rolling basis. Application fee: $10. Electronic applications accepted. *Expenses:* Tuition, state resident: full-time $6492; part-time $270.50 per credit hour. Tuition, nonresident: full-time $15,510; part-time $646.25 per credit hour. Required fees: $847; $70.56 per credit hour. Tuition and fees vary according to course load and program. *Financial support:* Scholarships/grants and unspecified assistantships available. *Faculty research:* Male reproductive physiology and contraception, ovarian development and regulation by pituitary and hypothalamus, neural control of movement and stroke recovery, pulmonary physiology and hypoxia, plasticity of the autonomic nervous system. Total annual research expenditures: $9.5 million. *Unit head:* Dr. Paul D. Cheney, Chairman, 913-588-7400, Fax: 913-588-7430, E-mail: pcheney@kumc.edu. *Application contact:* Dr. Lane K. Christenson, Director of Graduate Studies, 913-588-0420, Fax: 913-588-7180, E-mail: lchristenson@kumc.edu.

University of Kentucky, Graduate School, Graduate School Programs from the College of Medicine, Program in Physiology, Lexington, KY 40506-0032. Offers MS, PhD. *Degree requirements:* For doctorate, comprehensive exam, thesis/dissertation. *Entrance requirements:* For master's, GRE General Test, minimum undergraduate GPA of 2.75; for doctorate, GRE General Test, minimum undergraduate GPA of 2.75, graduate 3.0. Additional exam requirements/recommendations for international students: Required—TOEFL (minimum score 550 paper-based; 213 computer-based). Electronic applications accepted.

University of Louisville, School of Medicine, Department of Physiology and Biophysics, Louisville, KY 40292-0001. Offers MS, PhD, MD/PhD. *Faculty:* 23 full-time (0 women). *Students:* 37 full-time (19 women), 4 part-time (1 woman); includes 8 minority (3 African Americans, 5 Asian Americans or Pacific Islanders), 9 international. Average age 28. 33 applicants, 67% accepted, 19 enrolled. In 2009, 15 master's, 5 doctorates awarded. Terminal master's awarded for partial completion of doctoral program. *Degree requirements:* For master's, thesis; for doctorate, comprehensive exam, thesis/dissertation. *Entrance requirements:* For master's, GRE General Test (minimum score 1000 verbal and quantitative), minimum GPA of 3.0; for doctorate, GRE General Test (Verbal and Quantitative minimum score of 1000), minimum GPA of 3.0. Additional exam requirements/recommendations for international students: Required—TOEFL. *Application deadline:* For fall admission, 1/15 priority date for domestic students. Applications are processed on a rolling basis. Application fee: $50. Electronic applications accepted. *Financial support:* In 2009–10, 24 students received support, including 7 fellowships with full tuition reimbursements available (averaging $22,000 per year), 17 research assistantships with full tuition reimbursements available (averaging $22,000 per year). Financial award application deadline: 4/15. *Faculty research:* Control of microvascular function during normal and disease states; mechanisms of cellular adhesive interactions on endothelial cells lining blood vessels; changes in blood rheological properties and mechanisms associated with increased blood fibrinogen content; role of nutrition in microvascular control mechanisms; mechanism of cardiovascular-renal remodeling in hypertension, diabetes, and heart failure. *Unit head:* Dr. Irving G. Joshua, Chair, 502-852-5371, Fax: 502-852-6239, E-mail: igjosh01@gwise.louisville.edu. *Application contact:* Dr. William Wead, Director of Admissions, 502-852-7571, Fax: 502-852-6849, E-mail: wbwead01@gwise.louisville.edu.

University of Manitoba, Faculty of Medicine and Faculty of Graduate Studies, Graduate Programs in Medicine, Department of Physiology, Winnipeg, MB R3T 2N2, Canada. Offers M Sc, PhD, MD/PhD. Terminal master's awarded for partial completion of doctoral program. *Degree requirements:* For master's, one foreign language, thesis; for doctorate, one foreign language, thesis/dissertation. *Entrance requirements:* For master's, minimum GPA of 3.5; for doctorate, minimum GPA of 3.5, M Sc. *Faculty research:* Cardiovascular research, gene technology, cell biology, neuroscience, respiration.

University of Massachusetts Amherst, Graduate School, Interdisciplinary Programs, Program in Plant Biology, Amherst, MA 01003. Offers biochemistry and metabolism (MS, PhD); cell biology and physiology (MS, PhD); environmental, ecological and integrative (MS, PhD); genetics and evolution (MS, PhD). *Students:* 3 full-time (2 women), 12 part-time (5 women); includes 2 minority (both Asian Americans or Pacific Islanders), 8 international. Average age

27. 32 applicants, 41% accepted, 3 enrolled. In 2009, 3 master's, 1 doctorate awarded. *Degree requirements:* For master's, thesis; for doctorate, 2 foreign languages, comprehensive exam, thesis/dissertation. *Entrance requirements:* For master's and doctorate, GRE General Test. Additional exam requirements/recommendations for international students: Required—TOEFL (minimum score 550 paper-based; 213 computer-based; 80 iBT), IELTS (minimum score 6.5). *Application deadline:* For fall admission, 12/15 for domestic and international students; for spring admission, 10/1 for domestic and international students. Applications are processed on a rolling basis. Application fee: $50 ($65 for international students). Electronic applications accepted. *Expenses:* Tuition, state resident: full-time $2640; part-time $110 per credit. Tuition, nonresident: full-time $9936; part-time $414 per credit. Tuition and fees vary according to course load. *Financial support:* In 2009–10, 11 research assistantships with full tuition reimbursements (averaging $8,884 per year) were awarded; fellowships, teaching assistantships, career-related internships or fieldwork, Federal Work-Study, scholarships/grants, traineeships, health care benefits, tuition waivers (full), and unspecified assistantships also available. Support available to part-time students. Financial award application deadline: 12/15. *Unit head:* Dr. Elsbeth L. Walker, Graduate Program Director, 413-577-3217, Fax: 413-545-3243. *Application contact:* Jean M. Ames, Supervisor of Admissions, 413-545—0722, Fax: 413-577-0010, E-mail: gradadm@grad.umass.edu.

University of Massachusetts Worcester, Graduate School of Biomedical Sciences, Program in Cellular and Molecular Physiology, Worcester, MA 01655-0115. Offers cellular and molecular physiology (PhD). *Degree requirements:* For doctorate, comprehensive exam, thesis/dissertation. *Entrance requirements:* For doctorate, GRE General Test. Additional exam requirements/recommendations for international students: Required—TOEFL (minimum score 600 paper-based; 250 computer-based). Electronic applications accepted. *Faculty research:* Endocrinology, regulation of cellular and tissue metabolism, electrophysiology, muscle physiology.

University of Medicine and Dentistry of New Jersey, Graduate School of Biomedical Sciences, Graduate Programs in Biomedical Sciences–Newark, Department of Pharmacology and Physiology, Newark, NJ 07107. Offers PhD. *Students:* 21 full-time (14 women), 2 part-time (1 woman); includes 7 minority (2 African Americans, 5 Hispanic Americans), 13 international. *Degree requirements:* For doctorate, thesis/dissertation, qualifying exam. *Entrance requirements:* For doctorate, GRE General Test. Additional exam requirements/recommendations for international students: Required—TOEFL. *Application deadline:* For fall admission, 2/1 for domestic students. Applications are processed on a rolling basis. Application fee: $40. Electronic applications accepted. *Financial support:* Fellowships, research assistantships, Federal Work-Study and institutionally sponsored loans available. Financial award application deadline: 5/1. *Unit head:* Dr. Martha Nowycky, Program Director, 973-972-4391, Fax: 973-972-7950, E-mail: martha.nowycky@umdnj.edu. *Application contact:* Dr. Martha Nowycky, Program Director, 973-972-4391, Fax: 973-972-7950, E-mail: martha.nowycky@umdnj.edu.

University of Medicine and Dentistry of New Jersey, Graduate School of Biomedical Sciences, Graduate Programs in Biomedical Sciences–Piscataway, Program in Physiology and Integrative Biology, Piscataway, NJ 08854-5635. Offers MS, PhD, MD/PhD. *Entrance requirements:* Additional exam requirements/recommendations for international students: Required—TOEFL. *Application deadline:* For fall admission, 1/5 for domestic students. Applications are processed on a rolling basis. Application fee: $40. Electronic applications accepted. *Unit head:* Dr. Jiange Ma, Director, 732-235-4494, Fax: 732-235-4483, E-mail: maj2@umdnj.edu. *Application contact:* University Registrar, 973-972-5338.

University of Miami, Graduate School, Miller School of Medicine, Graduate Programs in Medicine, Department of Physiology and Biophysics, Coral Gables, FL 33124. Offers PhD, MD/PhD. *Faculty:* 16 full-time (4 women). *Students:* 8 full-time (7 women); includes 5 Asian Americans or Pacific Islanders. Average age 26. In 2009, 2 doctorates awarded. *Degree requirements:* For doctorate, thesis/dissertation, qualifying exam. *Entrance requirements:* For doctorate, GRE General Test, minimum GPA of 3.0 in sciences. Additional exam requirements/recommendations for international students: Required—TOEFL. *Financial support:* In 2009–10, 8 students received support, including fellowships with full tuition reimbursements available (averaging $25,500 per year); research assistantships, tuition waivers (full) also available. *Faculty research:* Cell and membrane physiology, cell-to-cell communication, molecular neurobiology, neuroimmunology, neural development. *Unit head:* Dr. Karl Magleby, Chairman, 305-243-6821, Fax: 305-243-6898, E-mail: kmagleby@miami.edu. *Application contact:* Dr. David Landowne, Director of Graduate Studies, 305-243-6821, Fax: 305-243-5931, E-mail: dl@miami.edu.

University of Michigan, Horace H. Rackham School of Graduate Studies, Program in Biomedical Sciences (PIBS), Department of Molecular and Integrative Physiology, Ann Arbor, MI 48109. Offers PhD. *Degree requirements:* For doctorate, thesis/dissertation, oral defense of dissertation, preliminary exam. *Entrance requirements:* For doctorate, GRE General Test, 3 letters of recommendation, research experience. Additional exam requirements/recommendations for international students: Required—TOEFL (minimum score 84 iBT), Michigan English Language Assessment Battery or TOEFL. Electronic applications accepted. *Expenses:* Tuition, state resident: full-time $17,286; part-time $1099 per credit hour. Tuition, nonresident: full-time $34,944; part-time $2080 per credit hour. Required fees: $95 per semester. Tuition and fees vary according to course load, degree level and program. *Faculty research:* Ion transport, cardiovascular physiology, gene expression, hormone action, gastrointestinal physiology, endocrinology, muscle, signal transduction.

University of Minnesota, Duluth, Medical School, Graduate Program in Physiology, Duluth, MN 55812-2496. Offers MS, PhD. Terminal master's awarded for partial completion of doctoral program. *Degree requirements:* For master's, thesis; for doctorate, thesis/dissertation. *Entrance requirements:* For master's, GRE or MCAT; for doctorate, GRE or MCAT, 1 year of course work in each calculus, physics, and biology; 2 years of course work in chemistry; minimum GPA of 3.0 in science. Additional exam requirements/recommendations for international students: Required—TOEFL. *Faculty research:* Neural control of posture and locomotion, transport and metabolic phenomena in biological systems, control of organ blood flow, intracellular means of communication.

University of Minnesota, Twin Cities Campus, Graduate School, Department of Integrative Biology and Physiology, Minneapolis, MN 55455-0213. Offers PhD. Part-time programs available. *Degree requirements:* For doctorate, comprehensive exam, thesis/dissertation. *Entrance requirements:* For doctorate, GRE General Test. Electronic applications accepted. *Faculty research:* Cardiovascular physiology.

University of Mississippi Medical Center, School of Graduate Studies in the Health Sciences, Department of Physiology and Biophysics, Jackson, MS 39216-4505. Offers MS, PhD, MD/PhD. *Degree requirements:* For master's, thesis; for doctorate, thesis/dissertation, first authored publication. *Entrance requirements:* For master's and doctorate, GRE General Test, minimum GPA of 3.0. *Faculty research:* Cardiovascular, renal, endocrine, and cellular neurophysiology; molecular physiology.

University of Missouri, School of Medicine and Graduate School, Graduate Programs in Medicine, Department of Medical Pharmacology and Physiology, Columbia, MO 65211. Offers pharmacology (MS, PhD); physiology (MS, PhD). *Degree requirements:* For master's, thesis; for doctorate, thesis/dissertation. *Entrance requirements:* For master's and doctorate, GRE General Test, minimum GPA of 3.0. Additional exam requirements/recommendations for international students: Required—TOEFL (minimum score 500 paper-based; 173 computer-based; 61 iBT). *Faculty research:* Endocrine and metabolic pharmacology, biochemical pharmacology, neuropharmacology, receptors and transmembrane signaling.

University of Missouri–St. Louis, College of Arts and Sciences, Department of Biology, St. Louis, MO 63121. Offers biology (MS, PhD), including animal behavior (MS), biochemistry, biochemistry and biotechnology (MS), biotechnology (MS), conservation biology (MS), development (MS), ecology (MS), environmental studies (PhD), evolution (MS), genetics (MS), molecular biology and biochemistry (PhD), molecular/cellular biology (MS), physiology (MS), plant systematics, population biology (MS), tropical biology (MS); biotechnology (Certificate); tropical biology and conservation (Certificate). Part-time programs available. *Faculty:* 43 full-time (13 women), 2 part-time/adjunct (1 woman). *Students:* 54 full-time (27 women), 79 part-time (43 women); includes 15 minority (6 African Americans, 7 Asian Americans or Pacific Islanders, 2 Hispanic Americans), 47 international. Average age 29. 193 applicants, 44% accepted, 44 enrolled. In 2009, 30 master's, 7 doctorates, 9 other advanced degrees awarded. *Degree requirements:* For master's, thesis or alternative; for doctorate, thesis/dissertation, 1 semester of teaching experience. *Entrance requirements:* For master's, 3 letters of recommendation; for doctorate, GRE General Test, 3 letters of recommendation. Additional exam requirements/recommendations for international students: Required—TOEFL. *Application deadline:* For fall admission, 12/1 priority date for domestic and international students; for spring admission, 10/15 priority date for domestic and international students. Applications are processed on a rolling basis. Application fee: $35 ($40 for international students). Electronic applications accepted. *Expenses:* Tuition, state resident: full-time $5377; part-time $297.70 per credit hour. Tuition, nonresident: full-time $13,882; part-time $771.20 per credit hour. Required fees: $220; $12.20 per credit hour. One-time fee: $12. Tuition and fees vary according to course level, campus/location and program. *Financial support:* In 2009–10, 22 research assistantships with full and partial tuition reimbursements (averaging $16,300 per year), 14 teaching assistantships with full and partial tuition reimbursements (averaging $16,727 per year) were awarded; fellowships with full tuition reimbursements, career-related internships or fieldwork and Federal Work-Study also available. Support available to part-time students. Financial award application deadline: 2/1. *Faculty research:* Molecular biology, microbial genetics, animal behavior, tropical ecology, plant systematics. *Unit head:* Dr. Elizabeth Kellogg, Director of Graduate Studies, 314-516-6200, Fax: 314-516-6233, E-mail: tkellogg@umsl.edu. *Application contact:* 314-516-5458, Fax: 314-516-6996, E-mail: gradadm@umsl.edu.

University of Nebraska Medical Center, Graduate Studies, Department of Cellular and Integrative Physiology, Omaha, NE 68198. Offers physiology (MS, PhD). Terminal master's awarded for partial completion of doctoral program. *Degree requirements:* For master's, comprehensive exam, thesis optional; for doctorate, comprehensive exam, thesis/dissertation, at least one first-author research publication. *Entrance requirements:* For master's and doctorate, GRE General Test or MCAT, course work in biology, chemistry, mathematics, and physics. Additional exam requirements/recommendations for international students: Required—TOEFL (minimum score 600 paper-based; 250 computer-based; 100 iBT). Electronic applications accepted. *Faculty research:* Cardiovascular, renal and visual physiology, neuroscience, reproductive endocrinology.

University of Nevada, Reno, Graduate School, Interdisciplinary Program in Cellular and Molecular Pharmacology and Physiology, Reno, NV 89557. Offers PhD. *Degree requirements:* For doctorate, one foreign language, thesis/dissertation. *Entrance requirements:* For doctorate, GRE General Test or MCAT, minimum GPA of 3.0. Additional exam requirements/recommendations for international students: Required—TOEFL (minimum score 500 paper-based; 173 computer-based; 61 iBT), IELTS (minimum score 6). Electronic applications accepted. *Faculty research:* Neuropharmacology, toxicology, cardiovascular pharmacology, neuromuscular pharmacology.

University of New Mexico, School of Medicine, Biomedical Sciences Graduate Program, Albuquerque, NM 87131-5196. Offers biochemistry and molecular biology (MS, PhD); cell biology and physiology (MS, PhD); molecular genetics and microbiology (MS, PhD); neuroscience (MS, PhD); pathology (MS, PhD); toxicology (MS, PhD). Part-time programs available. Terminal master's awarded for partial completion of doctoral program. *Degree requirements:* For master's, thesis; for doctorate, comprehensive exam, thesis/dissertation. *Entrance requirements:* For master's and doctorate, GRE General Test, minimum undergraduate GPA of 3.0. Additional exam requirements/recommendations for international students: Required—TOEFL. Electronic applications accepted. *Expenses:* Tuition, state resident: full-time $2099; part-time $233.20 per credit hour. Tuition, nonresident: full-time $6650. Required fees: $25 per semester. Tuition and fees vary according to course load, program and reciprocity agreements. *Faculty research:* Signal transduction, infectious disease, biology of cancer, structural biology, neuroscience.

University of North Dakota, School of Medicine and Health Sciences and Graduate School, Graduate Programs in Medicine, Department of Pharmacology, Physiology, and Therapeutics, Grand Forks, ND 58202. Offers pharmacology (MS, PhD); physiology (MS, PhD). *Degree requirements:* For master's, comprehensive exam, thesis; for doctorate, thesis/dissertation, written and oral exams. *Entrance requirements:* For master's, GRE General Test or MCAT, minimum GPA of 3.0; for doctorate, GRE General Test, minimum GPA of 3.5. Additional exam requirements/recommendations for international students: Required—TOEFL (minimum score 550 paper-based; 213 computer-based; 79 iBT), IELTS (minimum score 6.5). Electronic applications accepted.

University of North Texas Health Science Center at Fort Worth, Graduate School of Biomedical Sciences, Fort Worth, TX 76107-2699. Offers anatomy and cell biology (MS, PhD); biochemistry and molecular biology (MS, PhD); biomedical sciences (MS, PhD); biotechnology (MS); forensic genetics (MS); integrative physiology (MS, PhD); medical science (MS); microbiology and immunology (MS, PhD); pharmacology (MS, PhD); science education (MS); DO/MS; DO/PhD. Terminal master's awarded for partial completion of doctoral program. *Degree requirements:* For master's, thesis; for doctorate, thesis/dissertation. *Entrance requirements:* For master's and doctorate, GRE General Test. Additional exam requirements/recommendations for international students: Required—TOEFL. *Expenses:* Contact institution. *Faculty research:* Alzheimer's disease, aging, eye diseases, cancer, cardiovascular disease.

University of Notre Dame, Graduate School, College of Science, Department of Biological Sciences, Notre Dame, IN 46556. Offers aquatic ecology, evolution and environmental biology (MS, PhD); cellular and molecular biology (MS, PhD); genetics (MS, PhD); physiology (MS, PhD); vector biology and parasitology (MS, PhD). Terminal master's awarded for partial completion of doctoral program. *Degree requirements:* For master's, comprehensive exam, thesis; for doctorate, comprehensive exam, thesis/dissertation, candidacy exam. *Entrance requirements:* For master's and doctorate, GRE General Test. Additional exam requirements/recommendations for international students: Required—TOEFL (minimum score 600 paper-based; 250 computer-based; 80 iBT). Electronic applications accepted. *Faculty research:* Tropical disease, molecular genetics, neurobiology, evolutionary biology, aquatic biology.

University of Oklahoma Health Sciences Center, College of Medicine and Graduate College, Graduate Programs in Medicine, Department of Physiology, Oklahoma City, OK 73190. Offers MS, PhD. Part-time programs available. *Faculty:* 5 full-time (0 women). *Students:* 6 full-time (2 women), 3 part-time (2 women), 1 international. Average age 28. 7 applicants, 14% accepted, 1 enrolled. In 2009, 3 doctorates awarded. Terminal master's awarded for partial completion of doctoral program. *Degree requirements:* For master's, thesis (for some programs); for doctorate, thesis/dissertation. *Entrance requirements:* For master's, GRE General Test, statement of career goals, 3 letters of recommendation; for doctorate, GRE General Test, 3 letters of recommendation. Additional exam requirements/recommendations for international students: Required—TOEFL. *Application deadline:* For fall admission, 12/15 for domestic students. Application fee: $25 ($50 for international students). *Expenses:* Tuition, state resident: full-time $3120; part-time $156 per credit hour. Tuition, nonresident: full-time $11,314; part-time $409.70 per credit hour. Required fees: $1471; $51.20 per credit hour. $223.25 per term. *Financial support:* In 2009–10, 4 research assistantships (averaging $18,000 per year) were awarded; fellowships, teaching assistantships, career-related internships or fieldwork also available. *Faculty research:* Cardiopulmonary physiology, neurophysiology, exercise physiology, cell and molecular physiology. *Unit head:* Dr. Robert D. Foreman, Chair, 405-271-2226, E-mail: robert-foreman@ouhsc.edu. *Application contact:* Dr. Bert Mobley, Graduate Liaison, 405-271-2284, Fax: 405-271-3181, E-mail: bert-mobley@ouhsc.edu.

Physiology

University of Oregon, Graduate School, College of Arts and Sciences, Department of Human Physiology, Eugene, OR 97403. Offers MS, PhD. *Degree requirements:* For master's, thesis optional; for doctorate, one foreign language, thesis/dissertation. *Entrance requirements:* For master's, GRE General Test, minimum GPA of 2.75 in undergraduate course work; for doctorate, GRE General Test. *Faculty research:* Balance control, muscle fatigue, lower extremity function, knee control.

University of Pennsylvania, School of Medicine, Biomedical Graduate Studies, Graduate Group in Cell and Molecular Biology, Program in Cell Biology and Physiology, Philadelphia, PA 19104. Offers PhD, MD/PhD, VMD/PhD. *Degree requirements:* For doctorate, thesis/dissertation. *Entrance requirements:* For doctorate, GRE General Test. Additional exam requirements/recommendations for international students: Required—TOEFL. *Application deadline:* For fall admission, 12/8 priority date for domestic students, 12/8 for international students. Applications are processed on a rolling basis. Application fee: $70. Electronic applications accepted. *Expenses:* Tuition: Full-time $25,660; part-time $4758 per course. Required fees: $2152; $270 per course. Tuition and fees vary according to course load, degree level and program. *Financial support:* Fellowships, research assistantships, scholarships/grants, traineeships, and unspecified assistantships available. *Unit head:* Dr. Kevin Koskett, Head. *Application contact:* Kathy O'Connor-Cooley, Coordinator, 215-895-8935, Fax: 215-573-2104, E-mail: camb@mail.med.upenn.edu.

University of Prince Edward Island, Atlantic Veterinary College, Graduate Program in Veterinary Medicine, Charlottetown, PE C1A 4P3, Canada. Offers anatomy (M Sc, PhD); bacteriology (M Sc, PhD); clinical pharmacology (M Sc, PhD); clinical sciences (M Sc, PhD); epidemiology (M Sc, PhD), including reproduction; fish health (M Sc, PhD); food animal nutrition (M Sc, PhD); immunology (M Sc, PhD); microanatomy (M Sc, PhD); parasitology (M Sc, PhD); pathology (M Sc, PhD); pharmacology (M Sc, PhD); physiology (M Sc, PhD); toxicology (M Sc, PhD); veterinary science (M Vet Sc); virology (M Sc, PhD). Part-time programs available. *Degree requirements:* For master's, thesis; for doctorate, thesis/dissertation. *Entrance requirements:* For master's, DVM, B Sc honors degree, or equivalent; for doctorate, M Sc. Additional exam requirements/recommendations for international students: Required—TOEFL (minimum score 550 paper-based; 213 computer-based; 80 iBT). *Expenses:* Contact institution. *Faculty research:* Animal health management, infectious diseases, fin fish and shellfish health, basic biomedical sciences, ecosystem health.

University of Puerto Rico, Medical Sciences Campus, School of Medicine, Division of Graduate Studies, Department of Physiology, San Juan, PR 00936-5067. Offers MS, PhD. Terminal master's awarded for partial completion of doctoral program. *Degree requirements:* For master's, one foreign language, thesis; for doctorate, one foreign language, comprehensive exam, thesis/dissertation. *Entrance requirements:* For master's and doctorate, GRE General Test, GRE Subject Test, interview; course work in biology, chemistry and physics; minimum GPA of 3.0; 3 letters of recommendation. Electronic applications accepted. *Faculty research:* Respiration, neuroendocrinology, cellular and molecular physiology, cardiovascular, exercise physiology and neurobiology.

University of Rochester, School of Medicine and Dentistry, Graduate Programs in Medicine and Dentistry, Department of Pharmacology and Physiology, Program in Physiology, Rochester, NY 14627. Offers MS, PhD. Terminal master's awarded for partial completion of doctoral program. *Degree requirements:* For master's, thesis; for doctorate, thesis/dissertation, qualifying exam. *Entrance requirements:* For master's and doctorate, GRE General Test.

University of Saskatchewan, College of Medicine, Department of Physiology, Saskatoon, SK S7N 5A2, Canada. Offers M Sc, PhD. *Degree requirements:* For master's, thesis; for doctorate, thesis/dissertation. *Entrance requirements:* Additional exam requirements/recommendations for international students: Required—TOEFL. Tuition and fees charges are reported in Canadian dollars. *Expenses:* Tuition, area resident: Full-time $3000 Canadian dollars; part-time $500 Canadian dollars per term. Required fees: $700 Canadian dollars; $100 Canadian dollars per term.

University of Saskatchewan, Western College of Veterinary Medicine and College of Graduate Studies and Research, Graduate Programs in Veterinary Medicine, Department of Veterinary Biomedical Sciences, Saskatoon, SK S7N 5A2, Canada. Offers veterinary anatomy (M Sc); veterinary biomedical sciences (M Vet Sc); veterinary physiological sciences (M Sc, PhD). *Faculty:* 25. *Students:* 35. In 2009, 5 master's awarded. *Degree requirements:* For master's, thesis; for doctorate, comprehensive exam (for some programs), thesis/dissertation. *Entrance requirements:* Additional exam requirements/recommendations for international students: Required—TOEFL (minimum score 80 iBT); Recommended—IELTS (minimum score 6.5). Application fee: $75. Electronic applications accepted. Tuition and fees charges are reported in Canadian dollars. *Expenses:* Tuition, area resident: Full-time $3000 Canadian dollars; part-time $500 Canadian dollars per term. Required fees: $700 Canadian dollars; $100 Canadian dollars per term. *Faculty research:* Toxicology, animal reproduction, pharmacology, chloride channels, pulmonary pathobiology. *Unit head:* Dr. Barry Blakley, Head, 306-966-7350, Fax: 306-966-7376, E-mail: barry.blakley@usask.ca. *Application contact:* Dr. Baljit Singh, Application Contact, 306-966-7400, E-mail: baljit.singh@usask.ca.

University of South Alabama, College of Medicine and Graduate School, Program in Basic Medical Sciences, Specialization in Physiology, Mobile, AL 36688-0002. Offers PhD. *Degree requirements:* For doctorate, thesis/dissertation. *Entrance requirements:* For doctorate, GRE General Test or MCAT. *Expenses:* Tuition, state resident: part-time $218 per contact hour. Required fees: $1102 per year. *Faculty research:* Cardiovascular physiology.

The University of South Dakota, School of Medicine and Health Sciences and Graduate School, Biomedical Sciences Graduate Program, Physiology and Pharmacology Group, Vermillion, SD 57069-2390. Offers MS, PhD. Terminal master's awarded for partial completion of doctoral program. *Degree requirements:* For master's, thesis; for doctorate, comprehensive exam, thesis/dissertation. *Entrance requirements:* For master's and doctorate, GRE General Test, minimum GPA of 3.0. Additional exam requirements/recommendations for international students: Required—TOEFL (minimum score 550 paper-based; 213 computer-based; 80 iBT), IELTS (minimum score 6). Electronic applications accepted. *Expenses:* Contact institution. *Faculty research:* Pulmonary physiology and pharmacology, drug abuse, reproduction, signal transduction, cardiovascular physiology and pharmacology.

University of Southern California, Keck School of Medicine and Graduate School, Graduate Programs in Medicine, Department of Physiology and Biophysics, Los Angeles, CA 90089. Offers MS, PhD, MD/PhD. *Faculty:* 13 full-time (3 women). *Students:* 8 full-time (3 women); includes 1 minority (Asian American or Pacific Islander), 6 international. Average age 28. 11 applicants, 27% accepted, 3 enrolled. In 2009, 2 master's, 2 doctorates awarded. Terminal master's awarded for partial completion of doctoral program. *Degree requirements:* For master's, thesis optional; for doctorate, comprehensive exam, thesis/dissertation. *Entrance requirements:* For master's and doctorate, GRE General Test, minimum GPA of 3.0. Additional exam requirements/recommendations for international students: Required—TOEFL (minimum score 600 paper-based; 250 computer-based; 100 iBT). *Application deadline:* For fall admission, 2/1 priority date for domestic and international students. Application fee: $85. Electronic applications accepted. *Expenses:* Tuition: Full-time $25,980; part-time $1315 per unit. Required fees: $554. One-time fee: $35 full-time. Full-time tuition and fees vary according to degree level and program. *Financial support:* In 2009–10, 1 student received support, including 7 research assistantships with full tuition reimbursements available (averaging $27,060 per year); Federal Work-Study, institutionally sponsored loans, scholarships/grants, traineeships, health care benefits, and unspecified assistantships also available. Financial award application deadline: 5/5. *Faculty research:* Endocrinology and metabolism, neurophysiology, mathematical modeling, cell transport, autoimmunity and cancer immunotherapy. Total annual research expenditures: $4.2 million. *Unit head:* Dr. Richard N. Bergman, Chair, 323-442-1920, Fax: 323-442-1918, E-mail: rbergman@usc.edu. *Application contact:* Elena Camarena, Graduate Coordinator, 323-442-1039, Fax: 323-442-2283, E-mail: physiol@hsc.usc.edu.

The University of Tennessee, Graduate School, College of Agricultural Sciences and Natural Resources, Department of Animal Science, Knoxville, TN 37996. Offers animal anatomy (PhD); breeding (MS, PhD); management (MS, PhD); nutrition (MS, PhD); physiology (MS, PhD). Part-time programs available. *Degree requirements:* For master's, thesis; for doctorate, thesis/dissertation. *Entrance requirements:* For master's and doctorate, GRE General Test, minimum GPA of 2.7. Additional exam requirements/recommendations for international students: Required—TOEFL. Electronic applications accepted. *Expenses:* Tuition, state resident: full-time $6826; part-time $380 per semester hour. Tuition, nonresident: full-time $21,844; part-time $1147 per semester hour. Tuition and fees vary according to program.

The University of Texas Health Science Center at San Antonio, Graduate School of Biomedical Sciences, Department of Physiology, San Antonio, TX 78229-3900. Offers MS, PhD. *Faculty:* 20 full-time (3 women). *Students:* 11 full-time (6 women), 2 part-time (1 woman); includes 1 minority (Asian American or Pacific Islander), 8 international. Average age 25. In 2009, 4 doctorates awarded. *Degree requirements:* For master's, thesis; for doctorate, thesis/dissertation. *Entrance requirements:* For master's, GRE General Test, MAT; for doctorate, GRE General Test. Additional exam requirements/recommendations for international students: Required—TOEFL (minimum score 560 paper-based; 220 computer-based; 68 iBT). *Application deadline:* For fall admission, 1/15 priority date for domestic students, 1/15 for international students. Applications are processed on a rolling basis. Electronic applications accepted. *Expenses:* Tuition, state resident: full-time $2832; part-time $118 per credit hour. Tuition, nonresident: full-time $10,896; part-time $454 per credit hour. Required fees: $884 per semester. One-time fee: $70. *Financial support:* In 2009–10, 13 teaching assistantships (averaging $26,000 per year) were awarded; research assistantships, Federal Work-Study, institutionally sponsored loans, and health care benefits also available. Financial award application deadline: 6/30; financial award applicants required to submit FAFSA. *Faculty research:* Ion channels, cardiovascular function, neuroscience and aging. Total annual research expenditures: $5.8 million. *Unit head:* David Weiss, Professor and Chair, 210-567-4327, Fax: 210-567-4326, E-mail: weissd@uthscsa.edu. *Application contact:* James Nelson, Chairman, Committee on Graduate Studies, 210-567-4324, Fax: 210-567-4410, E-mail: physiologygrad@uthscsa.edu.

The University of Texas Medical Branch, Graduate School of Biomedical Sciences, Program in Cellular Physiology and Molecular Biophysics, Galveston, TX 77555. Offers MS, PhD. *Students:* 3 full-time (0 women), 2 international. Average age 30. In 2009, 3 doctorates awarded. *Degree requirements:* For master's, thesis or alternative; for doctorate, thesis/dissertation. *Entrance requirements:* For master's and doctorate, GRE General Test. Additional exam requirements/recommendations for international students: Required—TOEFL (minimum score 550 paper-based; 213 computer-based). *Application deadline:* Applications are processed on a rolling basis. Application fee: $30 ($75 for international students). Electronic applications accepted. *Financial support:* In 2009–10, fellowships (averaging $25,000 per year), research assistantships with full tuition reimbursements (averaging $25,000 per year) were awarded. Financial award applicants required to submit FAFSA. *Unit head:* Dr. Mark R. Hellmich, Director, 409-772-2124, Fax: 409-762-1826, E-mail: mhellmic@utmb.edu. *Application contact:* Lisa Davis, Coordinator for Special Programs, 409-772-2124, Fax: 409-762-1826, E-mail: limdavis@utmb.edu.

University of Toronto, School of Graduate Studies, Life Sciences Division, Department of Physiology, Toronto, ON M5S 1A1, Canada. Offers M Sc, PhD. *Degree requirements:* For master's, thesis; for doctorate, thesis/dissertation. *Entrance requirements:* For master's and doctorate, minimum B+ average in final year, 2 letters of reference. Additional exam requirements/recommendations for international students: Required—TOEFL (600 paper-based, 250 computer-based), Michigan English Language Assessment Battery (95), IELTS (8) or COPE (5).

University of Utah, School of Medicine and Graduate School, Graduate Programs in Medicine, Department of Physiology, Salt Lake City, UT 84112-1107. Offers PhD. *Degree requirements:* For doctorate, thesis/dissertation, comprehensive qualifying exam, preliminary exam. *Entrance requirements:* For doctorate, GRE General Test, GRE Subject Test, minimum GPA of 3.0. Additional exam requirements/recommendations for international students: Required—TOEFL (minimum score 650 paper-based; 250 computer-based; 100 iBT); Recommended—TWE (minimum score 6). Electronic applications accepted. *Expenses:* Tuition, state resident: full-time $4004; part-time $1674 per semester. Tuition, nonresident: full-time $14,134; part-time $5915 per semester. Required fees: $324 per semester. Tuition and fees vary according to course load, degree level and program. *Faculty research:* Cell neurobiology, chemosensory systems, cardiovascular and kidney physiology, endocrinology.

University of Virginia, School of Medicine, Department of Molecular Physiology and Biological Physics, Program in Physiology, Charlottesville, VA 22903. Offers PhD, MD/PhD. *Students:* 14 full-time (5 women); includes 2 minority (both African Americans). Average age 28. In 2009, 5 doctorates awarded. *Entrance requirements:* For doctorate, GRE General Test, 2 letters of recommendation. Additional exam requirements/recommendations for international students: Required—TOEFL. *Application deadline:* For fall admission, 1/15 for domestic and international students. Applications are processed on a rolling basis. Application fee: $60. Electronic applications accepted. *Financial support:* Fellowships, research assistantships, teaching assistantships available. Financial award applicants required to submit FAFSA. *Unit head:* Dr. Mark Yeager, Chair, 434-924-5108, Fax: 434-982-1616, E-mail: my3r@virginia.edu. *Application contact:* Dr. Mark Yeager, Chair, 434-924-5108, Fax: 434-982-1616, E-mail: my3r@virginia.edu.

University of Washington, Graduate School, School of Medicine and Graduate School, Graduate Programs in Medicine, Department of Physiology and Biophysics, Seattle, WA 98195. Offers PhD. *Degree requirements:* For doctorate, thesis/dissertation. *Entrance requirements:* For doctorate, GRE General Test. Additional exam requirements/recommendations for international students: Required—TOEFL (minimum score 580 paper-based; 237 computer-based; 70 iBT). *Faculty research:* Membrane and cell biophysics, neuroendocrinology, cardiovascular and respiratory physiology, systems neurophysiology and behavior, molecular physiology.

The University of Western Ontario, Faculty of Graduate Studies, Biosciences Division, Department of Physiology and Pharmacology, London, ON N6A 5B8, Canada. Offers M Sc, PhD. *Degree requirements:* For master's, thesis, seminar course; for doctorate, comprehensive exam, thesis/dissertation. *Entrance requirements:* For master's, minimum B average, honors degree; for doctorate, minimum B average, honors degree, M Sc. *Faculty research:* Reproductive and endocrine physiology, neurophysiology, cardiovascular and renal physiology, cell physiology, gastrointestinal and metabolic physiology.

University of Wisconsin–La Crosse, Office of University Graduate Studies, College of Science and Health, Department of Biology, La Crosse, WI 54601-3742. Offers aquatic sciences (MS); biology (MS); cellular and molecular biology (MS); clinical microbiology (MS); microbiology (MS); nurse anesthesia (MS); physiology (MS). Part-time programs available. *Faculty:* 27 full-time (7 women). *Students:* 19 full-time (8 women), 35 part-time (20 women); includes 1 minority (Asian American or Pacific Islander), 2 international. Average age 28. 87 applicants, 32% accepted, 21 enrolled. In 2009, 18 master's awarded. *Degree requirements:* For master's, comprehensive exam, thesis. *Entrance requirements:* For master's, GRE General Test, minimum GPA of 2.85. Additional exam requirements/recommendations for international students: Required—TOEFL (minimum score 550 paper-based; 213 computer-based; 79 iBT). Application fee: $56. Electronic applications accepted. *Financial support:* In 2009–10, 19 research assistantships with partial tuition reimbursements (averaging $10,021 per year) were awarded; career-related internships or fieldwork, Federal Work-Study, health care benefits, unspecified assistantships, and grant-funded positions also available. Support available to part-time students. Financial award application deadline: 3/15; financial award applicants required to submit FAFSA. *Unit head:* Dr. David Howard, Chair, 608-785-6455, E-mail: howard.davi@uwlax.edu. *Application contact:* Kathryn Kiefer, Director of Admissions, 608-785-8939, E-mail: admissions@uwlax.edu.

University of Wisconsin–Madison, School of Medicine and Public Health, Endocrinology-Reproductive Physiology Program, Madison, WI 53706-1380. Offers MS, PhD. Terminal master's awarded for partial completion of doctoral program. *Degree requirements:* For master's, comprehensive exam, thesis, oral defense of thesis; for doctorate, comprehensive exam, thesis/dissertation, oral defense of dissertation. *Entrance requirements:* For master's, GRE, resume, 3 letters of recommendation; for doctorate, GRE, resumé, 3 letters of recommendation. Additional exam requirements/recommendations for international students: Required—TOEFL (minimum score 550 paper-based; 213 computer-based). Electronic applications accepted. *Expenses:* Tuition, state resident: part-time $594 per credit. Tuition, nonresident: part-time $1504 per credit. Required fees: $65 per credit. Tuition and fees vary according to course load, program and reciprocity agreements. *Faculty research:* Ovarian physiology and endocrinology, fertilization and gamete biology, hormone action and cell signaling, placental function and pregnancy, embryo and fetal development.

University of Wisconsin–Madison, School of Medicine and Public Health and Graduate School, Graduate Programs in Medicine, Department of Physiology, Madison, WI 53706-1380. Offers PhD. *Faculty:* 16 full-time (5 women). *Students:* 17 full-time (4 women); includes 10 minority (2 African Americans, 6 Asian Americans or Pacific Islanders, 2 Hispanic Americans). Average age 22. 39 applicants, 8% accepted, 2 enrolled. In 2009, 3 doctorates awarded. *Degree requirements:* For doctorate, thesis/dissertation, written exams. *Entrance requirements:* For doctorate, GRE, minimum GPA of 3.0. Additional exam requirements/recommendations for international students: Required—TOEFL (minimum score 580 paper-based; 237 computer-based). *Application deadline:* For fall admission, 1/15 priority date for domestic and international students. Applications are processed on a rolling basis. Application fee: $45. Electronic applications accepted. *Expenses:* Tuition, state resident: part-time $594 per credit. Tuition, nonresident: part-time $1504 per credit. Required fees: $65 per credit. Tuition and fees vary according to course load, program and reciprocity agreements. *Financial support:* In 2009–10, fellowships with tuition reimbursements (averaging $23,500 per year), research assistantships with tuition reimbursements (averaging $23,500 per year), teaching assistantships with tuition reimbursements (averaging $23,500 per year) were awarded. *Faculty research:* Studies in molecular cellular systems, cardiovascular, neuroscience. *Unit head:* Dr. Donata Oertel, Interim Chair, 608-263-6281, Fax: 608-265-5512, E-mail: oertel@physiology.wisc.edu. *Application contact:* Sue S. Krey, Program Assistant, 608-262-9114, Fax: 608-265-5512, E-mail: krey@physiology.wisc.edu.

University of Wyoming, College of Arts and Sciences, Department of Zoology and Physiology, Laramie, WY 82070. Offers MS, PhD. Part-time programs available. *Degree requirements:* For master's, comprehensive exam (for some programs), thesis; for doctorate, comprehensive exam (for some programs), thesis/dissertation. *Entrance requirements:* For master's and doctorate, GRE General Test, minimum GPA of 3.0. Additional exam requirements/recommendations for international students: Required—TOEFL. Electronic applications accepted. *Faculty research:* Cell biology, ecology/wildlife, organismal physiology, zoology.

Virginia Commonwealth University, Graduate School, School of Allied Health Professions, Department of Physical Therapy, Program in Physiology, Richmond, VA 23284-9005. Offers PhD. *Accreditation:* APTA. *Degree requirements:* For doctorate, thesis/dissertation. *Entrance requirements:* For doctorate, GRE General Test.

Virginia Commonwealth University, Medical College of Virginia-Professional Programs, School of Medicine, School of Medicine Graduate Programs, Department of Physiology, Richmond, VA 23284-9005. Offers neuroscience (PhD); physiology (MS, PhD); MD/PhD. Terminal master's awarded for partial completion of doctoral program. *Degree requirements:* For master's, thesis; for doctorate, thesis/dissertation, comprehensive oral and written exams. *Entrance requirements:* For master's, DAT, GRE General Test, or MCAT; for doctorate, GRE General Test, MCAT, DAT.

Virginia Commonwealth University, Program in Pre-Medical Basic Health Sciences, Richmond, VA 23284-9005. Offers anatomy (CBHS); biochemistry (CBHS); human genetics (CBHS); microbiology (CBHS); pharmacology (CBHS); physiology (CBHS). *Entrance requirements:* For degree, GRE or MCAT, course work in organic chemistry, minimum undergraduate GPA of 2.8. Additional exam requirements/recommendations for international students: Required—TOEFL (minimum score 600 paper-based).

Wake Forest University, School of Medicine and Graduate School of Arts and Sciences, Graduate Programs in Medicine, Program in Physiology and Pharmacology, Winston-Salem, NC 27109. Offers pharmacology (PhD); physiology (PhD); MD/PhD. *Degree requirements:* For doctorate, thesis/dissertation. *Entrance requirements:* For doctorate, GRE General Test. Additional exam requirements/recommendations for international students: Required—TOEFL. Electronic applications accepted. *Faculty research:* Aging, substance abuse, cardiovascular control, endocrine systems, toxicology.

Wayne State University, School of Medicine, Graduate Programs in Medicine, Department of Physiology, Detroit, MI 48202. Offers MS, PhD, MD/PhD. *Degree requirements:* For master's, thesis; for doctorate, thesis/dissertation. *Entrance requirements:* For master's, GRE General Test, GRE Subject Test, minimum GPA of 2.6; for doctorate, GRE General Test, GRE Subject Test, minimum GPA of 3.0. Electronic applications accepted. *Faculty research:* Regulation of brain blood flow, mechanism of hormone action, regulation of pituitary hormone secretion, regulation of cellular membranes, nano biotechnology.

Western Michigan University, Graduate College, College of Education and Human Development, Department of Health, Physical Education and Recreation, Kalamazoo, MI 49008. Offers exercise and sports medicine (MS), including athletic training, exercise physiology; physical education (MA), including coaching sport performance, pedagogy, special physical education, sport management. *Faculty:* 20 full-time (9 women). *Students:* 60 full-time (27 women), 53 part-time (25 women); includes 9 minority (6 African Americans, 2 Asian Americans or Pacific Islanders, 1 Hispanic American), 6 international. 69 applicants, 81% accepted, 21 enrolled. In 2009, 42 master's awarded. *Application deadline:* For fall admission, 2/15 priority date for domestic students. Applications are processed on a rolling basis. Application fee: $25. *Financial support:* Fellowships, research assistantships, teaching assistantships, Federal Work-Study available. Financial award application deadline: 2/15; financial award applicants required to submit FAFSA. *Unit head:* Lee deLisle, Chair, 269-387-2669. *Application contact:* Admissions and Orientation, 269-387-2000, Fax: 269-387-2355.

West Virginia University, Davis College of Agriculture, Forestry and Consumer Sciences, Division of Animal and Nutritional Sciences, Program in Animal and Nutritional Sciences, Morgantown, WV 26506. Offers breeding (MS); food sciences (MS); nutrition (MS); physiology (MS); production management (MS); reproduction (MS). Part-time programs available. *Degree requirements:* For master's, thesis, oral and written exams. *Entrance requirements:* For master's, GRE, minimum GPA of 2.5. Additional exam requirements/recommendations for international students: Required—TOEFL. *Faculty research:* Animal nutrition, reproductive physiology, food science.

West Virginia University, Davis College of Agriculture, Forestry and Consumer Sciences, Interdisciplinary Program in Reproductive Physiology, Morgantown, WV 26506. Offers MS, PhD. Part-time programs available. Terminal master's awarded for partial completion of doctoral program. *Degree requirements:* For master's, thesis; for doctorate, comprehensive exam, thesis/dissertation. *Entrance requirements:* For master's, minimum GPA of 2.75; for doctorate, minimum GPA of 3.0. Additional exam requirements/recommendations for international students: Required—TOEFL. Electronic applications accepted. *Faculty research:* Uterine prostaglandins, luteal function, neural control of luteinizing hormone and follicle-stimulating hormone, follicular development, embryonic and fetal loss.

West Virginia University, School of Medicine, Graduate Programs at the Health Sciences Center, Interdisciplinary Graduate Programs in Biomedical Sciences, Program in Cellular and Integrative Physiology, Morgantown, WV 26506. Offers MS, PhD, MD/PhD. *Degree requirements:* For doctorate, comprehensive exam, thesis/dissertation. *Entrance requirements:* For doctorate, GRE General Test, minimum GPA of 3.0. Additional exam requirements/recommendations for international students: Required—TOEFL. Electronic applications accepted. *Faculty research:* Cell signaling and development of the microvasculature, neural control of reproduction, learning and memory, airway responsiveness and remodeling.

Wright State University, School of Graduate Studies, College of Science and Mathematics, Department of Neuroscience, Cell Biology, and Physiology, Dayton, OH 45435. Offers anatomy (MS); physiology and biophysics (MS). *Degree requirements:* For master's, thesis optional. *Entrance requirements:* Additional exam requirements/recommendations for international students: Required—TOEFL. *Faculty research:* Reproductive cell biology, neurobiology of pain, neurohistochemistry.

Yale University, School of Medicine and Graduate School of Arts and Sciences, Combined Program in Biological and Biomedical Sciences (BBS), Physiology and Integrative Medical Biology Track, New Haven, CT 06520. Offers PhD, MD/PhD. *Entrance requirements:* Additional exam requirements/recommendations for international students: Required—TOEFL. *Application deadline:* For fall admission, 12/6 for domestic and international students. *Unit head:* Dr. Emile Boulpaep, Director of Graduate Studies, 203-785-4041. *Application contact:* Leisa Strohmaier, Graduate Registrar, 203-785-4041, Fax: 203-785-7678, E-mail: physiology@yale.edu.

Youngstown State University, Graduate School, College of Science, Technology, Engineering and Mathematics, Department of Biological Sciences, Youngstown, OH 44555-0001. Offers environmental biology (MS); molecular biology, microbiology, and genetic (MS); physiology and anatomy (MS). Part-time programs available. *Degree requirements:* For master's, comprehensive exam, thesis, oral review. *Entrance requirements:* For master's, GRE General Test, minimum GPA of 2.7. Additional exam requirements/recommendations for international students: Required—TOEFL. *Faculty research:* Cell biology, neurophysiology, molecular biology, neurobiology, gene regulation.

CASE WESTERN RESERVE UNIVERSITY

Case School of Medicine
Department of Physiology and Biophysics

Programs of Study

The Department's Ph.D. training programs in cellular and molecular physiology, structural biology and biophysics, and systems and integrated physiology are tailored to prepare students for successful careers in biomedical, pharmaceutical, and/or industrial research. The Department of Physiology and Biophysics ranks among the best physiology departments in the country. The programs feature individual attention from committed faculty members and are tuition-free. The training programs are designed to provide a mentored training environment that maximizes faculty-student interaction and emphasizes the use of state-of-the art experimental approaches. Prospective students should visit the University's Web sites (http://physiology.cwru.edu or http://biophysics.cwru.edu) for additional information on the Department, individual investigators, and graduate programs.

The Ph.D. program in cellular and molecular physiology embraces investigation that seeks to understand the fundamental organizational and physiological functions of the cell utilizing state-of-the-art scientific methodology and conceptual approaches. The Ph.D. program in structural biology and biophysics emphasizes biophysics and bioengineering concepts and technologies and seeks to develop the students' quantitative skills. The Ph.D. program in systems integrative physiology embraces the concepts of cell and molecular physiology, biochemistry, and allied sciences but seeks to understand the function of the organism at the organ system level. The M.D./Ph.D. program consists of core medical training plus advanced graduate research training, in any of the disciplines outlined above, thereby leading to a combined degree. The Ph.D. for M.D.'s program is specifically designed for individuals who already have an M.D. degree. It can be linked to research-oriented residency programs, such as the clinical investigator pathway, approved by the American Board of Internal Medicine, and other similar programs.

The Master of Science in Medical Physiology program is a 1–3 year post-baccalaureate program designed to prepare students for admission to medical or dental school or careers in the biomedical industry. The Master of Science in Physiology and Biophysics program is designed for staff working at the university, area hospitals, or biotechnology companies that want to expand their critical research knowledge and skills. This program provides an excellent foundation for careers in biomedical professions including academia or industrial research.

Research Facilities

The Department is housed in newly renovated, state-of-the-art laboratory and office space on the fifth and sixth floors of the School of Medicine. These areas were specifically designed to facilitate faculty-student interaction. They are fully equipped with modern research instruments for sophisticated spectroscopic studies, video-enhanced light microscopy with image processing, molecular biology, structural biology, and extensive computer facilities. Interdisciplinary programs with other departments enable students to have access to additional specialized equipment.

Financial Aid

Ph.D. programs are tuition-free and pay a $25,000-per-year cost-of-living stipend that supports student training. Most students qualify for this support. Tuition for the M.S. in Physiology and Biophysics program is usually paid by the students' employer.

Cost of Study

Tuition at Case Western Reserve University Graduate School is approximately $33,000 per year.

Living and Housing Costs

Single rooms are available on campus, and a large variety of off-campus housing is available within 2 miles for married and single students. The cost of living in Cleveland is among the lowest in the United States.

Location

Case Western Reserve University is located 4 miles from downtown Cleveland in University Circle, a 500-acre area containing more than thirty educational, scientific, medical, cultural, and religious institutions. The parklike setting of University Circle contains the world-renowned Cleveland Museum of Art and Severance Hall, home of the famous Cleveland Orchestra. Metropolitan Cleveland has a population of approximately 2 million people and offers a wide array of recreational and cultural activities, including national sports events, theater, ballet, and cinema.

The University and The School

Case Western Reserve University is a private, nonprofit institution created in 1967 by the federation of the adjacent Western Reserve University (founded in 1826) and Case Institute of Technology (founded in 1880). The Case School of Medicine ranks among the top twenty-five schools nationally. It is part of the dynamic and innovative consortium of biomedical research centers that include University hospitals, the MetroHealth Center, and the Cleveland Clinic Foundation. This consortium creates an exceptional array of research and learning opportunities.

Applying

Requirements for admission are an undergraduate degree with a strong background in the natural sciences from an accredited college or university, GRE General Test scores, and three letters of recommendation. Competitive candidates are invited to visit the Department to view the facility and meet the faculty. Applications should be submitted by January 1, but late applications are also considered.

Correspondence and Information

Coordinator, Graduate Degree Programs
Department of Physiology and Biophysics
Case School of Medicine
Case Western Reserve University
Cleveland, Ohio 44106-4970
Phone: 216-368-2084
Fax: 216-368-5586
E-mail: PHOL-INFO@case.edu
Web site: http://physiology.cwru.edu
          http://biophysics.cwru.edu

Case Western Reserve University

THE FACULTY AND THEIR RESEARCH

Mary Barkley, Professor; Ph.D., California, San Diego, 1964. Structure and function of reverse transcriptase.

Venkaiah Betapudi, Assistant Professor; Ph.D., Devi Ahilya University, Indore (India), 1995. Cell cytoskeleton and cancer development; myosin II ubiquitination from basic mechanism to disease development.

Walter Boron, Professor and Chairman; M.D./Ph.D., Washington (St. Louis), 1977. Regulation of intracellular pH; molecular physiology and structural biology of HCO_3 transporters; control of renal proximal-tubule HCO_3 transport; CO_2/HCO_3 receptors; gas channels.

Matthias Buck, Associate Professor; D.Phil., Oxford, 1996. Protein structure and dynamics in transmission of signals in cells.

Cathleen Carlin, Professor; Ph.D., North Carolina at Chapel Hill, 1979. Regulation of ErbB receptor tyrosine kinase membrane protein sorting.

Sudha Chakrapani, Assistant Professor; Ph.D., SUNY at Buffalo, 2004. Understanding atomic level details of ion channel functioning.

Mark Chance, Professor, Department of Physiology and Biophysics; Interim Chair, Department of Genetics; Director, Center for Proteomics and Bioinformatics; and Director, Case Center for Synchrotron Biosciences; Ph.D., Pennsylvania, 1986. Mass spectrometry; structural genomics; macromolecular; colon cancer; diabetes.

Margaret Chandler, Assistant Professor; Ph.D., Kent State, 1998. Myocardial energy metabolism in the pathophysiology of heart failure and diabetes.

Calvin Cotton, Associate Professor; Ph.D., North Carolina at Chapel Hill, 1984. Regulation of ion transport in cells of respiratory, gastrointestinal, and renal epithelia.

Pamela Davis, Professor; Ph.D., 1973, M.D., 1974, Duke. Structure and function of CFTR in cystic fibrosis.

Isabelle Deschenes, Assistant Professor; Ph.D., Laval, 1999. Cellular and molecular mechanisms of cardiac arrhythmias.

Paul DiCorleto, Professor; Ph.D., Cornell, 1978. Regulation of growth factor and leukocyte adhesion molecule genes by the endothelium.

Anthony F. DiMarco, Professor; M.D., Tufts, 1974. Restoration of respiratory muscle function in spinal cord injury.

J. Kevin Donahue, Associate Professor; M.D., Washington (St. Louis), 1992. Cardiac electrophysiology; cardiac arrhythmias.

George Dubyak, Professor; Ph.D., Pennsylvania, 1979. Extracellular ATP release and metabolism in inflammation.

Mark Dunlap, Associate Professor; M.D., Tennessee Health Sciences, 1982. Nicotinic acetylcholine receptors; autonomic nervous system; heart failure; parasympathetic/sympathetic physiology; baroreceptors; reflexes; neurohumoral abnormalities.

Dominique Durand, Professor; Ph.D., Toronto, 1982. Electrical stimulation of neural tissue and biomagnetism.

Thomas Egelhoff, Associate Professor; Ph.D., Stanford, 1987. Signaling pathways that control actin/myosin motility during cell migration in wound healing and cancer.

Steven Fisher, Associate Professor; M.D., Pennsylvania, 1986. Cardiomyocyte apoptosis in heart development.

Joan E. B. Fox, Professor; Ph.D., McMaster, 1979; D.Sc., Southampton (UK), 1993. Molecular basis of integrin-mediated migration in the cardiovascular system.

Harindarpal (Harry) Gill, Assistant Professor; Ph.D., UCLA, 2001. X-ray crystallographic studies on the sodium-bicarbonate cotransporter NBCe1-A.

George Gorodeski, Professor; M.D., Tel Aviv, 1973; Ph.D., Case Western Reserve, 1990. Hormonal regulation of cervical epithelial cell transport.

Brian Hoit, Professor; M.D., Illinois, 1979.

Ulrich Hopfer, Professor; M.D., Göttingen (Germany), 1966; Ph.D., Johns Hopkins, 1970. Cell biology, physiology, and pathology of epithelial transport.

Arie Horowitz, Assistant Professor; Ph.D., Technion (Israel), 1988. Enodothelial cell signaling and motility in angiogenesis; molecular mechanisms of blood vessel sprouting; membrane trafficking.

Philip Howe, Professor; Ph.D., Medical College of Georgia, 1988. TGFβ and Wnt signaling regulation of cell growth and apoptosis.

Faramarz Ismail-Beigi, Professor; M.D., Johns Hopkins, 1966; Ph.D., Berkeley, 1972. Glucose transporter expression and function; control of cardiac bioenergetics.

Mukesh K. Jain, Ellery Sedgwick Jr. Professor and Director, Case Cardiovascular Research Institute; M.D., Buffalo, SUNY, 1991. Transcriptional regulation of cardiovascular cell function.

Stephen Jones, Professor; Ph.D., Cornell, 1980. Voltage-dependent ion channels; mechanisms of channel gating, permeation, and modulation.

Jeffrey Kern, Professor; M.D., Wisconsin–Madison, 1979. Receptor tyrosine kinases, c-erbB-2, lung development, carcinogenesis, JAK-STAT, EGFR.

John P. Kirwan, Associate Professor; Ph.D., Ball State, 1987. Insulin signaling; glucose transport; protein expression, activity, and phosphorylation; intramyocellular lipid content; exercise; low-glycemic diet; body composition.

Joseph LaManna, Professor; Ph.D., Duke, 1975. Control of adaptation to hypoxia and the pathophysiology of stroke; CNS function in cardiac arrest.

Carole Liedtke, Professor; Ph.D., Case Western Reserve, 1980. Regulation of Na-K-2Cl cotransport during fluid and electrolyte balance in epithelia.

Richard Martin, Professor; M.B.B.S., Sydney (Australia), 1970. Respiratory control; lung injury/maturation; airway reactivity; nitric oxide; apnea of prematurity; developmental pulmonology; airway maturation; desaturation; hyperoxia; lung parenchyma; cardiorespiratory monitoring; pulmonary function monitoring; pulse oximetry; multiple intraluminal impedance monitoring; RTPCR; Western blotting; immunohistochemistry; in vivo physiological recording; assays; patch clamping.

Sam Mesiano, Assistant Professor; Ph.D., Monash (Australia), 1988. Hormonal control of human parturition and the interaction of estrogen and progesterone receptors in the control of reproduction.

R. Tyler Miller, Professor; M.D., Case Western Reserve, 1980. The calcium-sensing receptor and G-protein–coupled signaling.

Robert H. Miller, Professor and Vice Dean for Research; Ph.D., UCL, London, 1981. Biology of neural diseases; cellular and molecular control of nervous system glial specification.

Saurav Misra, Assistant Professor; Ph.D., Illinois, 1997. Molecular basis of protein quality control.

Thomas M. Nosek, Professor; Ph.D., Ohio State, 1973. Control of muscle contraction; cellular basis of muscle fatigue.

Mark Parker, Instructor; Ph.D., Bristol (UK), 2000. Causes and consequences of structural and functional diversity among Na+coupled HCO3-transporters.

Rajesh Ramachandran, Assistant Professor; Ph.D., Texas A&M, 2004. Molecular biophysics of membrane remodeling in membrane fusion and fission.

Andrea Romani, Associate Professor; M.D., Siena (Italy), 1984; Ph.D., Turin, 1990. Regulation of transmembrane Mg^{2+} transport and the role of Mg^{2+} transport in metabolism.

David Rosenbaum, Professor; M.D., Illinois at Chicago, 1983. Mechanisms of arrhythmias in myocytes.

William Schilling, Professor; Ph.D., Medical University of South Carolina, 1981. Mammalian TRP channel function; role of Ca^{2+} channels in cell death.

John Sedor, Professor; M.D., Virginia, 1978. Clinical, cellular, and genetic basis of kidney disease.

Daniel I. Simon, Professor; M.D., Harvard, 1987. Inflammation in vascular injury.

Corey Smith, Associate Professor; Ph.D., Colorado Health Sciences Center, 1996. Release of transmitter molecules from adrenal chromaffin cells and the sympathetic stress response.

Julian E. Stelzer, Assistant Professor; Ph.D., Oregon State, 2002. Cellular and molecular mechanisms of cardiac muscle contraction in health and disease.

Kingman P. Strohl, Professor; M.D., Northwestern, 1974. Respiratory physiology and sleep disorders.

Ben W. Strowbridge, Professor; Ph.D., Yale, 1991. Synaptic physiology; hippocampus; modeling; computational neuroscience; olfactory bulb.

Witold Surewicz, Professor; Ph.D., Lodz (Poland), 1982. Structure and function of prion proteins.

Richard Walsh, Professor; M.D., Georgetown, 1972. The heart and cardiovascular disease.

Patrick Wintrode, Assistant Professor; Ph.D., Johns Hopkins, 1997. Hydrogen exchange and mass spectrometry to study protein structure and function.

Xin Yu, Associate Professor; Sc.D., Harvard/MIT, 1996. Magnetic resonance imaging and spectroscopy; cardiac biomechanics of genetically manipulated mice using MRI tagging; systems biology of metabolism; cardiovascular physiology; myocardial structural characterization in diseased hearts using diffusion tensor MRI; cardiac metabolism in diabetic hearts using MRI spectroscopy and systems biology.

Assem Ziady, Assistant Professor; Ph.D., Case Western Reserve, 1999. Cystic fibrosis; proteomic integration of CF and non-CF cells to determine differential protein expression; redox-mediated inflammatory signaling; use of nonviral gene therapy to address defects in CF at the genetic level.

Yuehan Zhou, Instructor; M.D., Third Military Medical University (China), 1984. CO2/HCO3-sensing mechanism in the proximal tubules.

LOYOLA UNIVERSITY CHICAGO

Department of Physiology
Graduate Programs in Cell and Molecular Physiology

Programs of Study

The Department of Physiology offers graduate training programs with primary emphasis in cellular and molecular physiology leading to the Ph.D. and M.S. degrees. The objective of the Ph.D. program is to train independent scientific investigators through the development of their own ideas using state-of-the-art research techniques and instrumentation. The two-year M.S. program may be designed to enhance the expertise and experience of individuals interested in research career paths in academic or industrial settings, enhance the academic qualifications of individuals interested in graduate or professional programs, or provide research training for clinicians interested in academic medicine.

During the four-year Ph.D. program, students take core courses in biochemistry, neurobiology, molecular biology, organ system physiology, and cellular and molecular physiology. Students participate in four research rotations during the first year to introduce the different research lines available in the Department and help define the laboratory where they will conduct their dissertation research.

The Department has strong research programs in excitation-contraction coupling of cardiac and vascular smooth muscle in health and disease, with special reference to the molecular biology, biophysics, and biochemistry of voltage-activated and ligand-activated ion channels as well as contractile protein function. Cardiac electrophysiology, excitation-secretion coupling, and intracellular calcium homeostasis are well-represented areas of research interest. Cell signaling mechanisms involved in the pathophysiology of heart failure and developing septic shock, with special reference to neural-immune interactions, are also important areas of faculty research.

Research Facilities

Each faculty member has a modern, state-of-the-art laboratory, fully equipped to meet research needs. In addition, the Department has the following shared core facilities: radioisotope (liquid scintillation and gamma counting) instrumentation, a machine and electronic shop, histology laboratory, tissue-culture lab, and confocal microscopy lab.

Financial Aid

All Ph.D. graduate students in the Department receive an annual stipend of $25,000. This support is intended to allow the students to devote all of their time to completing the degree; no service is required. Graduate stipends are competitive and carry a waiver of tuition.

Cost of Study

Cost of tuition is fully waived for Ph.D. students receiving support. Tuition cost for M.S. students is $830 per credit hour, which totals $19,920 for the 24 required credits.

Living and Housing Costs

A wide variety of living arrangements can be found within the surrounding suburban communities. A director of housing assists students in locating suitable housing.

Student Group

More than 1,000 students are enrolled in degree programs at the Medical Center. The graduate student body at the Medical Center is approximately 100. In recent years, the graduate enrollment of the Department has ranged from 8 to 15 students.

Location

The Medical Center location on a 73-acre site in Maywood provides the advantages of a suburban environment as well as easy access to the attractions of the Chicago community. The Medical Center campus, adjacent to a forest preserve, includes the large Hines Veterans Hospital and numerous supporting facilities.

The University

Loyola, founded in 1870, was Chicago's first institution of higher learning. It now has four campuses, including the Medical Center. The Medical Center has become one of the top ten academic medical centers in the nation in terms of overall patient volume, trauma, cardiology, cardiac transplants, bypass surgery, neonatology, and other areas. Close research interaction exists between the Cardiovascular Institute, the Neuroscience Institute, and the Burn and Shock Trauma Institute, as well as among several clinical departments.

Applying

Students normally start their graduate training in late July when the fall semester begins. Program prerequisites include one full-year course each in physics, mathematics through calculus, and chemistry through organic chemistry. A fundamental knowledge of biology is desirable but not required. Students are required to submit scores from the GRE General Test.

Loyola University Chicago is an affirmative action agency; applications from members of minority groups and women are encouraged.

Correspondence and Information

Ruben Mestril, Ph.D.
Graduate Program Director
Department of Physiology
Stritch School of Medicine
Loyola University Chicago
2160 South First Avenue
Maywood, Illinois 60153

Phone: 708-327-2395
Fax: 708-216-6308
Web site: http://www.luhs.org/depts/physio/index.html

Loyola University Chicago

THE FACULTY AND THEIR RESEARCH

Pieter P. de Tombe, Professor and Chairman; Ph.D., Calgary. Myofilament length dependent activation. *J. Mol. Cell. Cardiol.* 48(5):851–8, 2010 (with Mateja et al.). Increased crossbridge cycling kinetics after exchange of C-terminal truncated troponin I in skinned rat cardiac muscle. *J. Biol. Chem.* 283(22):15114–21, 2008 (with Tachampa et al.). Approximate model of cooperative activation and crossbridge cycling in cardiac muscle using ordinary differential equations. *Biophys. J.* 95(5):2368–90, 2008 (with Rice et al.). Troponin phosphorylation and myofilament Ca^{2+}-sensitivity in heart failure: Increased or decreased? *J. Mol. Cell. Cardiol.* 45(5):603–7, 2008 (with Marston). Interfilament spacing is preserved during sarcomere length isometric contractions in rat cardiac trabeculae. *Biophys. J.* 92(9):L73–5, 2007 (with Farman et al.).

Samuel Cukierman, Associate Professor; M.D., Ph.D., Rio de Janeiro. Enhancement of proton transfer in ion channels by membrane phosphate headgroups. *J. Phys. Chem. B* 113(19):6725–31, 2009 (with Wyatt and de Godoy). Proton transfer in water wires in proteins: Modulation by local constraint and polarity in gramicidin A channels. *Biophys. J.* 93(5):1571–9, 2007 (with Narayan, Wyatt, and Crumrine). Proton transfer in gramicidin water wires in phospholipid bilayers: Attenuation by phosphoethanolamine. *Biophys. J.* 91(2):580–7, 2006 (with Chernyshev).

Lydia L. DonCarlos, Professor; Ph.D., Kent State. Gonadal steroid hormone effects on early and pubertal brain development; extranuclear steroid receptor regulation in the brain. Pubertal hormones modulate the addition of new cells to sexually dimorphic brain regions. *Nat. Neurosci.* 11(9):995–7, 2008 (with Ahmed et al.). Androgens in health and disease: An overview. *Horm. Behav.* 53(5):589–95, 2008 (with Jordan). Cellular phenotype of androgen receptor-immunoreactive nuclei in the developing and adult rat forebrain. *J. Comp. Neurol.* 492(4):456–68, 2005 (with Lorenz and Garcia-Seguria). Androgen receptor immunoreactivity in forebrain axons and dendrites in the rat. *Endocrinology* 144(8):3632–8, 2003 (with Garcia-Ovejero et al.).

Renzhi Han, Assistant Professor; Ph.D., Western Australia. Molecular mechanisms underlying genetic disorders affecting skeletal muscle and heart. Basal lamina strengthens cell membrane integrity via the laminin G domain-binding motif of α-dystroglycan. *Proc. Natl. Acad. Sci. U.S.A.* 106(31):12573–9, 2009 (with Kanagawa et al.). Dysferlin-mediated membrane repair protects the heart from stress-induced left ventricular injury. *J. Clin. Investig.* 117(7):1805–13, 2007 (with Bansal et al.).

Stephen B. Jones, Professor Emeritus; Ph.D., Missouri–Columbia. Neural-immune interactions, with special reference to mechanisms and consequences of sympathetic activation during injury states. Adrenergic modulation of cytokine release in bone marrow progenitor-derived macrophage following polymicrobial sepsis. *J. Neuroimmunol.* 158(1):50–7, 2005 (with Muthu et al.). Bone marrow norepinephrine mediates development of functionally different macrophages after thermal injury and sepsis. *Ann. Surg.* 240(1):132–41, 2004 (with Cohen et al.). Adrenergic modulation of splenic macrophage cytokine release in polymicrobial sepsis. *Am. J. Physiol. Cell Physiol.* 287:C730–6, 2004 (with Deng et al.).

Richard H. Kennedy, Professor and Senior Associate Dean of Research; Ph.D., Nebraska. Structural and functional cardiac remodeling; role of cytokines in cardiac physiology and pathophysiology. Inhibition of sarcoplasmic reticular function by chronic interleukin-6 exposure via iNOS in adult ventricular myocytes. *J. Physiol.* 566:327–40, 2005 (with Yu, Chen, and Liu). Influence of mast cells on structural and functional manifestations of radiation-induced heart disease. *Cancer Res.* 65:3100–7, 2005 (with Boerma et al.). Protective role of mast cells in homocysteine-induced cardiac remodeling. *Am. J. Physiol.* 288:H2541–5, 2005 (with Joseph et al.).

Stephen L. Lipsius, Professor; Ph.D., SUNY Downstate Medical Center. Cardiac cellular electrophysiology; atrial muscle and atrial pacemaker function; integrin-mediated regulation of beta-adrenergic receptor signaling; remodeling of beta-adrenergic receptor signaling mechanisms in atrial myocytes; regulation of nitric oxide production in cardiomyocytes. Laminin acts via focal adhesion kinase/phosphatidylinositol-3' kinase/protein kinase B to down-regulate β1-adrenergic receptor signaling in cat atrial myocytes. *J. Physiol.* 587(3):541–50, 2009 (with Wang et al).

Mary J. Druse-Manteuffel, Professor; Ph.D., North Carolina at Chapel Hill. Developmental neurochemistry; effects of ethanol on the development of the serotonin system; antiapoptotic effects of serotonin and antioxidants. Effects of ethanol and ipsapirone on the expression of genes encoding anti-apoptotic proteins and an antioxidant enzyme in ethanol-treated neurons. *Brain Res.* 1249:54–60, 2009 (with Lee and Tajuddin). Antioxidants prevent ethanol-associated apoptosis in fetal rhombencephalic neurons. *Brain Res.* 1204:16–23, 2008 (with Antonio). The effects of ethanol and the $serotonin_{1A}$ agonist ipsapirone on the expression of the $serotonin_{1A}$ receptor and several antiapoptotic proteins in fetal rhombencephalic neurons. *Brain Res.* 1092(1):79–86, 2006 (with Tajuddin, Gillespie, and Phong Le).

John A. McNulty, Professor, Vice Chair, and Director, Core Imaging Facility; Ph.D., USC. Neuroendocrinology; neuroimmunomodulation; photoneuroendocrine transduction; computer-aided instruction. Evaluation of computer-aided instruction in a basic science course: A six-year study. *Anat. Sci. Educ.* 2(1):2–8, 2009 (with Sonntag and Sinacore). Characterization of lymphocyte subsets over a 24-hour period in pineal-associated lymphoid tissue (PALT) in the chicken. *BMC Immunol.* 7:1, 2006. (with Mosenson).

Ruben Mestril, Professor; Ph.D., Miami (Florida). Molecular and cellular studies on protective role of heat-shock proteins in cardiomyocytes and skeletal muscle. Overexpression of HSP10 in skeletal muscle of transgenic mice prevents the age-related fall in maximum tetanic force generation and muscle cross-sectional area. *Am. J. Physiol. Regul. Integr. Comp. Physiol.*, 299:R268–76, 2010 (with Kayani et al.). HSP72 protects against obesity-induced insulin resistance. *Proc. Natl. Acad. Sci. U.S.A.* 105(5):1739–44, 2008 (with Chung et al.).

Gregory A. Mignery, Professor; Ph.D., Texas A&M. Molecular and cellular biology of inositol 1,4,5-trisphosphate receptors; structure-function characterization of ligand-gated ion channels; intracellular calcium signaling. The BH4 domain of Bcl-2 inhibits ER calcium release and apoptosis by binding the regulatory and coupling domain of the IP3 receptor. *Proc. Natl. Acad. Sci. U.S.A.* 106(34):14397-402, 2009 (with Rong et al.). Ip_3 receptor-dependent Ca^{2+} release modulates excitation-contraction coupling in rabbit ventricular myocytes. *Am. J. Physiol. Heart Circ. Physiol.* 294(2):H596–604, 2008 (with Domeier et al.). Targeting Bcl-2-IP_3 receptor interaction to reverse Bcl-2's inhibition of apoptotic calcium signals. *Mol. Cell* 31(2):255–65, 2008 (with Rong et al.). Biosensors to measure $InsP_3$ concentration in living cells with spatio-temporal resolution. *J. Biol. Chem.* 281(1):608–16, 2006 (with Remus et al.). Cardiac type 2 inositol 1,4,5-trisphosphate receptor: Interaction and modulation by calcium/calmodulin-dependent protein kinase II. *J. Biol. Chem.* 280(16):15912–20, 2005 (with Bare et al.).

Toni R. Pak, Assistant Professor, Ph.D., Colorado at Boulder. Differential fibroblast growth factor 8 (FGF8)-mediated autoregulation of its cognate receptors, *Fgfr1* and *Fgfr3*, in neuronal cell lines. *PLoS One* 5(4):e10143, 2010 (with Mott, Chung, and Tsai). Binge-pattern alcohol exposure during puberty induces sexually dimorphic changes in genes regulating the HPA axis. *Am. J. Physiol. Endocrinol. Metabol.* 298:E320–8, 2010 (with Przybycien-Szymanska and Rao).

Erika S. Piedras-Rentería, Associate Professor; Ph.D., Illinois at Urbana-Champaign. Voltage-gated calcium-channel function and modulation and channelopathies; calcium-channel function and synaptic activity; modulation of calcium channels by cytoskeletal proteins; molecular biology, electrophysiology, fluorescence, and cell biology techniques. T-type current modulation by the actin-binding protein Kelch-like 1 (KLHL1). *Am. J. Physiol. Cell Physiol.* 298:C1353–62, 2010 (with Aromolaran et al.). Kelch-like 1 protein up-regulates T-type currents by an actin-F dependent increase in α1H channels via the recycling endosome. *Channels* 3(6):1–11, 2009 (with Aromolaran et al.). The Kelch-like protein 1 modulates P/Q-type calcium current density. *Neuroscience* 145(3):841–50, 2007 (with Aromolaran et al.). Altered frequency-dependent inactivation and steady-state inactivation of polyglutamine-expanded $_{1A}$ in SCA6. *Am. J. Physiol. Cell Physiol.* 292(3):C1078–86, 2007 (with Chen). Voltage-gated calcium channels, calcium signaling, and channelopathies. In *Calcium—A Matter of Life or Death,* vol. 41, *New Comprehensive Biochemistry,*pp. 127–66, eds. J. Krebs and M. Michalak. Amsterdam: Elsevier, 2007 (with Barret, Cao, and Tsien).

Seth L. Robia, Assistant Professor; Ph.D., Wisconsin–Madison. Isoform specificity of the Na/K-ATPase association and regulation by phospholemman. *J. Biol. Chem.* 284(39):26749–57, 2009 (with Bossuyt et al.). The E3 ubiquitin ligase atrophin interacting protein 4 binds directly to the chemokine receptor CXCR4 via a novel WW domain-mediated interaction. *Mol. Biol. Cell* 20(5):1324–39, 2009 (with Bhandari and Marchese). Phosphomimetic mutations increase phospholamban oligomerization and alter the structure of its regulatory complex. *J. Biol. Chem.* 283(43):28996–9003, 2008 (with Hou and Kelly). Phospholamban oligomerization, quaternary structure, and SERCA-binding measured by FRET in living cells. *J. Biol. Chem.* 283(18):12202–11, 2008 (with Kelly et al.). Forster transfer recovery reveals that phospholamban exchanges slowly from pentamers but rapidly from the SERCA regulatory complex. *Circ. Res.* 101(11):1123–9, 2007 (with Campbell et al.). Phospholamban pentamer quaternary conformation determined by in-gel fluorescence anisotropy. *Biochemisty* 44(11):4302–11, 2005 (with Flohr and Thomas). Novel determinant of PKC-epsilon anchoring in cardiac myocytes. *Am. J. Physiol. Heart Circ. Physiol.* 289:H1941, 2005 (with Kang and Walker). Localization and kinetics of protein kinase C-epsilon anchoring in cardiac myocytes. *Biophys. J.* 80(5):2140–51, 2001 (with Ghanta, Robu, and Walker).

Sakthivel Sadayappan, Assistant Professor; Ph.D., Madurai Kamaraj (India). Molecular basis of post-translational regulation of cardiac myosin binding protein-C in health and disease. Phosphorylation and function of cardiac myosin binding protein-C in health and disease. *J. Mol. Cell. Cardiol.* 48(5):866–75, 2010 (with Barefield).

Charles L. Webber Jr., Professor; Ph.D., Loyola Chicago. Application of nonlinear dynamics to physiological systems and states; nonlinear classification of sensory-motor reflexes in neuropathies; patterns of atrial fibrillation waves in the human heart. Laminar recurrences, maxline, unstable singularities, and biological dynamics. *Eur. Phys. J. Spec. Tops.* 164(1):55–65, 2008 (with Zbilut). Magnetosensory evoked potentials: Consistent nonlinear phenomena. *Neuroscience Res.* 60(1):95–105, 2008 (with Carrubba et al.). Recurrence quantification analysis of nonlinear dynamical systems. In *Tutorials in Contemporary Nonlinear Methods for the Behavioral Sciences,* chapter 2, pp. 26–94, eds. M. A. Riley, G. Van Orden. Web book: http://www.nsf.gov/sbe/bcs/pac/nmbs/nmbs.pdf, 2005 (with Zbilut)

Robert Wurster, Professor Emeritus; Ph.D., Loyola Chicago. T-type calcium channels and tumor proliferation. *Cell Calcium* 40:253–9, 2006 (with Panner). Activation of various G-protein coupled receptors modulates Ca^{2+} channel current via PTX-sensitive and voltage-dependent pathways in rat intracardiac neurons. *J. Auton. Nerv. Syst.* 76:68–74, 1999 (with Jeong and Ikeda). Proliferation of cultured human astrocytoma cells in response to an oxidant and antioxidant. *J. Neuro-Oncol.* 44:213–21, 1999 (with Arora-Kuruganti and Lucchesi).

Aleksey V. Zima, Assistant Professor, Ph.D., Bogomoletz Institute of Physiology (Ukraine). Termination of cardiac Ca^{2+} sparks: Role of intra-SR $[Ca^{2+}]$, release flux, and intra-SR Ca^{2+} diffusion. *Circ. Res.* 103(8):e105–15, 2008 (with Picht, Bers, and Blatter). Redox regulation of cardiac calcium channels and transporters. *Cardiovasc. Res.* 71(2):310–21, 2006 (with Blatter). Inositol-1,4,5-trisphosphate-dependent Ca^{2+} signaling in cat atrial excitation–contraction coupling and arrhythmias. *J. Physiol.* 555(3):607–15, 2004 (with Blatter).

UNIVERSITY OF CONNECTICUT

College of Liberal Arts and Sciences
Department of Physiology and Neurobiology

Programs of Study

The Department offers course work and research programs leading to M.S. and Ph.D. degrees in physiology and neurobiology with concentration in areas of neurobiology, endocrinology, and comparative physiology. In addition, the Department of Molecular and Cell Biology, the Department of Ecology and Evolutionary Biology, and the Biotechnology Center provide the opportunity for students to obtain a comprehensive background in biological sciences and offer the possibility of collaborative research.

Graduate programs are designed to fit the individual student's background and scientific interests. In the first year, students take two courses on the foundations of physiology and neurobiology. Through the first two years, and occasionally into the third year of training, students select from a number of additional seminars and courses in their area of major interest and related areas. By the end of the first year, the student selects the area of dissertation research, and a committee consisting of a major adviser and 3 associate advisers is formed. Students may begin dissertation research during the first year.

Research Facilities

The Department of Physiology and Neurobiology is located primarily in the new state-of-the-art Pharmacy/Biology Building. The Department houses both shared and individual laboratories for behavioral, cellular, electrophysiological, and molecular research in physiology. The Department also houses the University's electron microscopy facility, which contains equipment for scanning and transmission EM as well as electron probe analysis. Departmental faculty members also utilize the Marine Research Laboratories at Noank and Avery Point, Connecticut.

Financial Aid

Several types of financial support are available to graduate students. Most students are supported either on teaching assistantships or research assistantships from faculty grants. In 2010–11, full-time assistantships (nine months) pay $19,384 for beginning graduate students, $20,396 for those with an M.S. or the equivalent, and $22,676 for those who have passed the Ph.D. general examination. Both half and full graduate assistantships come with a tuition waiver, and students may purchase excellent health-care coverage, heavily subsidized by the University of Connecticut. In addition, the Graduate School provides the Outstanding Scholar Award to as many as 10 incoming Ph.D. candidates during the first year of study. Several additional research fellowships and University fellowships are awarded on a competitive basis. Many labs also provide additional funding for summer research (up to $4000).

Cost of Study

In 2010–11, tuition is $4986 per semester for legal residents of Connecticut and $12,942 per semester for nonresidents, plus fees. Tuition is waived for graduate assistants; however, they pay the full-time University fees of $928 per semester. Tuition is prorated for students registering for fewer than 9 credits per semester. University fees are subject to change without notice.

Living and Housing Costs

Dormitory rooms are available for unmarried graduate students. University-owned and privately owned apartments are available near the campus at moderate rents. Houses and apartments for rent may also be found in the surrounding communities. In 2010–11, the fee for accommodations in graduate residence halls range upward from $3800 per semester; meal plans are separate. Yearly expenses, including books and travel, for a single student living off campus are upward from $19,000.

Student Group

Approximately 16,000 undergraduates and 7,800 graduate students are enrolled at the main campus at Storrs. Seventy-six percent of the undergraduate students and 72 percent of the graduate students are from Connecticut. The rest of the students come from many other states and more than 100 countries. The Department of Physiology and Neurobiology has about 40 graduate students.

Location

The University is located in a scenic countryside setting of small villages, streams, and rolling hills. There is easy access by car and bus to major urban and cultural centers, including Hartford, New Haven, Boston, and New York, and to other educational institutions, such as Yale, Harvard, and MIT. Recreational opportunities include skiing, fishing, sailing, hiking, ice-skating, and athletic events. Cultural opportunities available at the Storrs campus include film series, plays, symphony and chamber music series, public lectures, and art exhibits. A small shopping center is within walking distance of the campus, and several large shopping centers are nearby.

The University

Ranked the top public university in New England for the past eight years, the University of Connecticut stands among the top public institutions in the nation. The University was founded in 1881 and is a state-supported institution. The 1,800-acre main campus at Storrs is the site of vigorous undergraduate and graduate programs in agriculture, liberal arts and sciences, fine arts, engineering, education, business administration, human development and family relations, physical education, pharmacy, nursing, and physical therapy. Extensive cultural and recreational programs and athletic facilities are available.

Applying

For admission to the fall semester, it is suggested that applications be submitted by January 15. To be considered for financial support, students must submit applications by March 15 for admission the following September. U.S. applicants must submit scores on the General Test of the Graduate Record Examinations and must have maintained at least a 3.0 quality point ratio (QPR) for admission as graduate students with regular status. Applications and credentials from international students must be received by March 1 for admission in the fall semester or by October 1 for the spring semester and must include TOEFL scores. The University does not discriminate in admission on the basis of race, gender, age, or national origin. Students can apply online at http://www.grad.uconn.edu/applications.html.

Correspondence and Information

University of Connecticut
Department of Physiology and Neurobiology
Graduate Admissions Committee
Box U-3156
Storrs, Connecticut 06269-3156
Phone: 860-486-3304
Fax: 860-486-3303
E-mail: kathleen.kelleher@uconn.edu
Web site: http://www.pnb.uconn.edu

University of Connecticut

THE FACULTY AND THEIR RESEARCH

Lawrence E. Armstrong, Professor (primary appointment in Kinesiology); Ph.D., Ball State. Research focuses on human physiological responses to exercise, dietary intervention (i.e., caffeine, low-salt diet, glucose-electrolyte solutions, amino acid supplementation), pharmacological agents, heat tolerance, and acclimatization to heat. Laboratory measurements of local sweat production; skin blood flow; and metabolic, ventilatory, cardiovascular, fluid-electrolyte, and strength perturbations are complemented by field observations. This research includes illnesses that arise in association with exercise in hot environments.

Marie E. Cantino, Associate Professor; Ph.D., Washington (Seattle). Research in this laboratory is directed toward understanding the mechanisms of contraction in striated muscle. In particular, the lab is using electron microscopy and biochemical and mechanical assays to study the structure and organization of proteins in the contractile filaments and the mechanisms by which calcium regulates the interactions of these proteins.

William D. Chapple, Professor; Ph.D., Stanford. The interests of the laboratory center on the cellular mechanisms by which arthropods generate and control movement despite varying external forces. The model system is the hermit crab abdomen, which is used to support the animal's shell. To understand the interactions between local and global mechanisms that produce this control, identified motoneurons and interneurons are studied electrophysiologically and their properties are incorporated into a control systems model.

Thomas T. Chen, Professor (primary appointment in Molecular and Cell Biology); Ph.D., Alberta; postdoctoral study at Queen's. Structure, evolution, regulation, and molecular actions of growth hormone and insulin-like growth factor genes; regulation of foreign genes in transgenic fish; development of model transgenic fish.

Joanne Conover, Assistant Professor; Ph.D., Bath (England). Research in the laboratory focuses on neurogenesis and neuronal migration in the adult mouse brain. A combination of techniques including cell culture of neural stem cells, RT-PCR-based gene expression analysis, and examination of mouse genetic models for neurodegenerative diseases aid us in understanding neuronal proliferation, differentiation, and migration in the adult brain.

Joseph F. Crivello, Professor (joint appointment in Marine Sciences); Ph.D., Wisconsin. Research is centered in two areas. One area examines the impact of pollution on marine organisms at a biochemical and genetic level. The other area examines pollution as a selective pressure altering the genetic diversity of marine organisms.

Angel L. de Blas, Professor; Ph.D., Indiana. Research mainly focuses on the brain receptors for the inhibitory transmitter GABA. Studies are being conducted on elucidating the molecular structure of the receptors and the molecular interactions with other proteins that determine the synaptic localization of the GABA receptors. Effects of drugs and aging on GABAergic synaptic transmission are also studied. Techniques include recombinant DNA, monoclonal antibodies, cell culture, and light, electron, and laser confocal microscopy.

Robert V. Gallo, Professor; Ph.D., Purdue. The objective of the research program is to understand the neuroendocrine mechanisms regulating luteinizing hormone release during different physiological conditions. In particular, the research examines the involvement of CNS neurotransmitters and endogenous opioid peptides in this process.

Rahul N. Kanadia, Assistant Professor, Ph.D., Florida. Research is focused on deciphering the role of alternative splicing in neural development. The neural mouse retina is employed as a model system to investigate this question. Various techniques such as in situ hybridizations and molecular biology techniques are used to detect different forms of RNA. Since this is studied in development, live imaging is also used to document changes in splice pattern and its impact on cell fate determination and differentiation.

William J. Kraemer, Professor (primary appointment in Kinesiology); Ph.D., Wyoming. Research focus is directed at the neuroendocrine responses and adaptations with exercise as it relates to target tissues of muscle, bone, and immune cells. Current studies utilize receptor techniques and hormonal immunoassays and bioassays to better understand androgen, adrenal, and pituitary hormone interactions with target cells and their relationship to outcome variables of physiological function and physical performance.

Joseph J. LoTurco, Professor; Ph.D., Stanford. Research in the laboratory focuses on understanding mechanisms that direct development of the neocortex. Currently, a combination of molecular genetics, patch clamp electrophysiology, and cell culture are being used to study the mechanisms that regulate neurogenesis in the cerebral cortex.

Carl M. Maresh, Professor and Director, Human Performance Laboratory (primary appointment in Kinesiology, Department Head); Ph.D., Wyoming. Research focus is directed at the neuroendocrine, body fluid, and substrate responses and adaptations to environmental stress and training in humans. Current projects examine the efficacy of different methods of rehydration, muscle and bone adaptations to physical training in women, and exercise interventions in children at risk for obesity and diabetes.

Andrew Moiseff, Professor; Ph.D., Cornell. The laboratory is interested in the extraction and processing of sensory information by the nervous system. At present, research is concentrated on how the nervous system of the barn owl analyzes interaural time and intensity differences to obtain spatial information. Another line of research is the behavioral analysis of synchronous flashing by fireflies with an aim toward the understanding of the neural mechanisms controlling this communication behavior.

Daniel K. Mulkey, Assistant Professor; Ph.D., Wright State. Research focuses on the cellular and molecular mechanisms by which the brain controls breathing, in particular, understanding the molecular mechanism by which respiratory chemoreceptors sense changes in pH to drive breathing and the cellular mechanisms that modulate activity of these cells. Another interest is the role of nitric oxide on state-dependent modulation of respiratory motor neurons for a better understanding of the mechanisms underlying respiratory control, leading to new therapeutic approaches for the treatment of disorders such as sudden infant death syndrome and sleep apnea. Techniques include cellular electrophysiology in brain slices, cell culture, and single-cell RT-PCR.

Akiko Nishiyama, Associate Professor; M.D., Nippon Medical School; Ph.D., Niigata (Japan). Research focuses on the biology of glial progenitor cells identified by the NG2 proteoglycan in normal and mutant mice and in demyelinating and excitotoxic lesions. Current studies employ immunohistochemical, tissue culture, biochemical, and molecular biological techniques to understand the mechanisms that regulate proliferation and differentiation of these glial cells and to explore their function.

Linda S. Pescatello, Associate Professor and Director, Center for Health Promotion (primary appointment in School of Allied Health); Ph.D., Connecticut. Research focus is on the interaction between the environment, neurohormones, and genetics on the exercise response in order to determine for whom exercise works best as a therapeutic modality. Current projects examine humoral, nutritional, and genetic explanations for postexercise hypotension, the exercise dose response for postexercise hypotension, and the influence of genetics on the muscle strength and hypertrophy response to resistance exercise training.

J. Larry Renfro, Professor and Department Head; Ph.D., Oklahoma. The research program is concerned with the mechanisms and regulation of epithelial transport. Current research deals with transepithelial transport and excretion of sulfate, and phosphate and environmental pollutants in tissues isolated from the urinary systems of a variety of vertebrates, including rats, birds, and fishes. Work has concentrated on ion secretion and its regulation in primary monolayer cultures of renal epithelium and choroid plexus. The laboratory also studies transport by renal tubule brush border and basolateral membrane vesicles.

Daniel Schwartz, Assistant Professor; Ph.D., Harvard. Research is focused on computational and experimental techniques to discover, catalog, and functionally understand short linear protein motifs. Specific projects include: (1) the continued improvement of the motif-x and scan-x web-tools, (2) the development of experimental methodologies to uncover kinase motifs, and (3) the analysis of motif signatures on viral protein primary structure toward the goal of elucidating mechanisms of viral propagation and developing therapeutic agents.

Anastasios Tzingounis, Assistant Professor; Ph.D., Oregon Health & Science. Research in the laboratory concentrates on the cellular and molecular mechanisms that control neuronal excitability in the mammalian brain. To study the molecules and signaling networks that tune the brain's innate ability to prevent epilepsy, a multidisciplinary approach is used that combines molecular and genetic techniques with optical imaging and electrophysiology.

Randall S. Walikonis, Associate Professor; Ph.D., Mayo. Research is directed at studying the postsynaptic signal transduction systems of excitatory synapses. The laboratory uses biochemical and molecular biological techniques to identify proteins associated with NMDA receptors and to determine their specific roles in the function of excitatory synapses. The lab also studies the role of growth factors in modifying excitatory synapses.

Steven A. Zinn, Associate Professor (primary appointment in Animal Science); Ph.D., Michigan State. The laboratory is interested in the somatotropic axis and its influence on growth and lactation. Specifically, the laboratory is investigating the influence of exogenous somatotropin on insulin-like growth factor I and the insulin-like growth factor binding proteins and their role in growth.

Adam Zweifach, Professor (primary appointment in Molecular and Cell Biology); Ph.D., Yale. Signal transduction in immune cells.

UNIVERSITY OF FLORIDA

College of Medicine
Advanced Concentration in Physiology and Pharmacology

Program of Study

The College of Medicine at the University of Florida (UF) offers graduate training in biomedical research leading to a Ph.D. degree through the Interdisciplinary Program (IDP) in Biomedical Sciences. The goal of the Interdisciplinary Program is to prepare students for a diversity of careers in research and teaching in academic and commercial settings. The program provides a modern, comprehensive graduate education in biomedical science while providing both maximum program flexibility and appropriate specialization for graduate students. During the first year of study, incoming graduate students undertake a common, comprehensive interdisciplinary core curriculum of classroom study developed in a cooperative effort by all of the graduate programs in the College of Medicine. In addition, students select from any of the College of Medicine faculty members for participation in several laboratory rotations conducted throughout the first year, concurrent with the core curriculum. By the end of their first year, students select a laboratory in which to conduct their dissertation research; once again, they may choose from any of the graduate faculty members in the College of Medicine. Formal selection of a graduate program and mentor is made after completion of the core curriculum to maximize flexibility and facilitate an informed decision; however, students may make an informal commitment to a program or lab at any time. Ph.D. candidacy is granted after successful completion of course work and defense of a dissertation research proposal. The dissertation research project is overseen by a committee made up of the supervisory faculty member and other members of the graduate faculty. It is anticipated that the student should take four to five years to complete the necessary requirements leading to the Ph.D. degree.

Major research interests in the Advanced Concentration in Physiology and Pharmacology include heart failure and stroke, hypertension and other cardiovascular diseases, cancer biology and treatment, gene therapy, drug development, aging and obesity, pregnancy and fetal development, endocrine systems, the renin-angiotensin system, signal-transduction pathways, vascular biology, ion channels and membrane transport, and toxicology and environmental medicine. Faculty members associated with this advanced program have expertise in a variety of disciplines, including molecular and cellular biology, pharmacology, physiology, neuroscience, and biochemistry, and they bring together unique strengths to provide the students with diverse training.

Research Facilities

The College of Medicine houses state-of-the-art research facilities maintained by the Interdisciplinary Center for Biomedical Research (ICBR), the McKnight Brain Institute, the Clinical Research Center, several other University of Florida Research Centers, and individual research laboratories. Together, these facilities provide services for DNA and protein synthesis and sequencing, hybridoma production, confocal and electron microscopy, NMR spectroscopy, computing and molecular modeling, flow cytometry, transgenic mouse production, and gene therapy vector construction. The University of Florida libraries, including the Health Center library, form the largest information resource system in the state of Florida and support up-to-date computer-based bibliographic retrieval services.

UF's nine libraries offer more than 4 million catalogued volumes and links to full-text articles in more than 34,000 journals. Of national significance are the Baldwin Library of Historical Children's Literature, the Latin American Collection, the Map and Imagery Library, the P. K. Yonge Library of Florida History (preeminent Floridiana collection), the Price Library of Judaica, and holdings on architectural preservation and eighteenth-century American architecture, late nineteenth- and early twentieth-century German state documents, rural sociology of Florida, and tropical and subtropical agriculture.

Financial Aid

Students accepted into the Interdisciplinary Program receive a stipend of $25,750 per annum. Students also receive a waiver that covers tuition.

Cost of Study

Graduate research assistants pay fees of approximately $1400 per year. Books and supplies cost about $1600.

Living and Housing Costs

Married-student housing is available in six apartment villages operated by the University; dormitories for single students are available in limited quantities. The cost of housing for a single graduate student is approximately $5000 per year. Most graduate students live in abundant and comfortable off-campus housing that is near the University; rents vary but are low on a national scale.

Student Group

Enrollment at the University of Florida is both culturally and geographically diverse and numbers about 50,000, including about 10,000 graduate students. There are about 300 graduate students in the College of Medicine.

Location

Situated in north-central Florida, midway between the Atlantic Ocean and the Gulf of Mexico, Gainesville is a nationally recognized academic and research center and was rated the number 1 place to live in the U.S. in a 1995 *Money* magazine survey. There are about 200,000 residents in the Gainesville metropolitan area, excluding University of Florida students. The climate is moderate, permitting outdoor activities year-round. The University and the Gainesville community also host numerous cultural events, including music, dance, theater, lectures, and art exhibits. Many of the men's and women's athletic programs are considered to be in the top 10 programs in the country.

The University and The College

The University of Florida, located on 2,000 acres, is among the nation's leading research universities, as categorized by the Carnegie Commission on Higher Education. UF is a member of the Association of American Universities, the nation's most prestigious higher education organization. UF is also one of the nation's top 3 universities in the breadth of academic programs offered on a single campus. It has twenty colleges and schools and 100 interdisciplinary research and education centers, bureaus, and institutes. The College of Medicine, opened in 1956, has become a nationally recognized leader in medical education and research.

Applying

The Interdisciplinary Program in Biomedical Sciences seeks promising students with undergraduate training in chemistry, biology, psychology, or related disciplines in the life sciences. Applicants are selected on the basis of previous academic work, research experience, GRE General Test scores, letters of recommendation, the personal statement, and a personal interview. Students are admitted for the fall semester, which begins in late August. The application deadline is December 15.

Correspondence and Information

Jeffrey K. Harrison, Ph.D., Co-Director
Department of Pharmacology and Therapeutics
University of Florida College of Medicine
P.O. Box 100267
Gainesville, Florida 32610-0267
Phone: 352-392-3227
Fax: 352-392-3133
E-mail: jharriso@ufl.edu
Web site: http://idp.med.ufl.edu/PPH/

Hideko Kasahara, M.D., Ph.D., Co-Director
Department of Physiology and Functional Genomics
University of Florida College of Medicine
P.O. Box 100274
Gainesville, Florida 32610-0267
Phone: 352-846-1503
Fax: 352-846-0270
E-mail: hkasahar@ufl.edu
Web site: http://physiology.med.ufl.edu/

University of Florida

THE FACULTY AND THEIR RESEARCH

Department of Pharmacology and Therapeutics

Andrew Ahn, Assistant Professor, M.D., Ph.D. Fundamental mechanisms of primary headache disorders such as migraines; action of the anti-migraine drug sumatriptan on modulation of pain-related circuits and behaviors.

Stephen P. Baker, Professor, Thomas Maren Professor of Pharmacology and Therapeutics, and Chair; Ph.D. Structure, activity, and function of G-protein-coupled receptors.

Bradley Fletcher, Assistant Professor; M.D., Ph.D. Identification of oncogenes and anti-apoptotic genes involved in leukemia; generation of novel transposon-based nonviral DNA vectors for gene therapy; gene therapy models of hypertension and hemophilia.

Maria Grant, Professor; M.D. Molecular mechanisms responsible for the development of diabetic retinopathy; roles of growth factors and extracellular matrix in regulation of endothelial cell behavior.

Jeffrey K. Harrison, Associate Professor; Ph.D. Neuroimmunopharmacology; chemokines and chemokine receptors in the central nervous system; hemopoietic- and neurologic-expressed sequence I (Hnl) in nerve regeneration and cancer (glioma).

William R. Kem, Professor; Ph.D. Drug design based on naturally occurring toxins that affect brain nicotinic receptors.

Seong-Hun Kim, Assistant Professor; Ph.D. Molecular pathogenesis of Alzheimer's disease.

Brian K. Law, Assistant Professor; Ph.D. Development of novel anticancer therapeutic strategies that alter cyclin-dependent kinase subunit composition and intracellular localization.

Mary E. Law, Research Professor; Ph.D. Regulation of the cell cycle by NF-KB; identification of novel NF-KB inhibitors.

Allen H. Neims, Professor; M.D., Ph.D. Integrative medicine; spirituality; therapeutics; mind-body medicine.

Roger Papke, Professor; Ph.D. Physiology, pharmacology, and biophysics of neurotransmitter receptors, especially the function of nicotinic acetylcholine receptors in the brain.

Thomas C. Rowe, Associate Professor; Ph.D. Topoisomerases; cancer and microbial chemotherapy; mitochondrial DNA; chromatin structure; malaria, plastid/organellar DNA, and antimalarial drugs.

Philip J. Scarpace, Professor; Ph.D. Mechanisms of impaired leptin signal transduction in the hypothalamus with senescence and obesity; intervention with gene therapy.

Alexandra (Sasha) Shapiro, Assistant Scientist; Ph.D.

Lynn Shaw, Assistant in Pharmacology; Ph.D. Neuronal cytoskeleton intermediate filaments and their associated proteins in the nervous system; protein-signaling modules; computer analysis of protein and nucleic acid sequence.

Kathleen T. Shiverick, Professor; Ph.D. Reproductive and developmental toxicology.

David N. Silverman, Distinguished Professor; Ph.D. Structure-function of efficient enzymes: catalytic mechanisms and inhibition of carbonic anhydrase and superoxide dismutase.

Ferenc Soti, Research Associate; Ph.D. Isolation, structure determination, and organic synthesis and transformation of naturally occurring compounds in plants and marine animals.

Chingkuang K. Tu, Associate Scientist; Ph.D. Mechanisms of human carbonic anhydrase and human superoxide dismutase.

Nihal Tümer, Professor; Ph.D. Regulation of tyrosine hydroxylase expression, age, and stress; aging and catecholamines.

Yi Zhang, Assistant in Pharmacology; Ph.D. Leptin signal transduction in hypothalamus, using aging rat model; mechanisms of leptin resistance and its association with obesity.

Department of Physiology and Functional Genomics

Peter A. V. Anderson, Professor and Scientific Director, Whitney Laboratory; Ph.D. Ion channel physiology, pharmacology, and structure; nervous system evolution; comparative neurobiology.

David Barber, Associate Professor, Ph.D. Molecular mechanisms by which environmental chemicals cause toxicity; acrylamide, heavy metals, nano-materials, and organochlorine pesticides.

Lewis R. Baxter Jr., Professor, M.D. Comparative approach across vertebrate and invertebrate taxa of the basis; presumed evolution of brain mechanisms of complex behaviors; neuropsychiatric disease; gene to biochemistry to nervous system to simple, then complex social behavior.

Chris Baylis, Professor and Director, UF Hypertension Center; Ph.D. Renal and blood pressure control, with emphasis on hemodynamics.

Himangshu S. Bose, Assistant Professor; Ph.D. Protein translocation and cholesterol transport into mitochondria.

George A. Gerencser, Professor; Ph.D. Studies of epithelial transport physiology, in order to elucidate general principles of membrane physiology and gain a deeper understanding of mechanisms responsible for epithelial absorptive and secretory processes.

Pushpa S. Kalra, Professor; Ph.D. Neuroimmunoendocrinology of reproduction; neuropeptidergic regulation of appetite.

Hideko Kasahara, Assistant Professor; M.D., Ph.D. Molecular mechanisms underlying cardiac disease, particularly heart failure and cardiac arrhythmia.

S. Paul Oh, Associate Professor; Ph.D. Genetic and molecular mechanisms for mammalian pattern formation: development of the vascular system, asymmetry of visceral organs along the left-right axis, and vertebral patterning along the anteroposterior axis during mouse development.

Mohan K. Raizada, Professor; Ph.D. Signal transduction mechanism of angiotensin regulation of norepinephrine neuromodulation in the brain; antisense targeting of the renin-angiotensin system in the control of hypertension and other cardiovascular diseases; gene therapy and neurobiology.

Peter P. Sayeski, Associate Professor; Ph.D. Cellular and biochemical mechanisms by which G-protein-coupled receptors activate physiologically important tyrosine kinase signaling pathways.

Deborah A. Scheuer, Associate Professor; Ph.D. Actions of glucocorticoids on neuronal function; neural control of circulation; myocardial ischemia.

Bruce R. Stevens, Professor; Ph.D. Membrane transport of amino acids and organic solutes in cultured brain cells and epithelial cells.

Colin Sumners, Professor; Ph.D. Cellular, molecular, and electrophysiological studies of brain angiotensin receptors.

Glenn Walter, Assistant Professor; Ph.D. Development of technology for the noninvasive monitoring of gene transfer in skeletal and cardiac muscle; bioengineering of skeletal muscle.

Charles E. Wood, Professor and Chair; Ph.D. Fetal neuroendocrine development and cardiovascular physiology.

Section 19
Zoology

This section contains a directory of institutions offering graduate work in zoology, followed by in-depth entries submitted by institutions that chose to prepare detailed program descriptions. Additional information about programs listed in the directory but not augmented by an in-depth entry may be obtained by writing directly to the dean of a graduate school or chair of a department at the address given in the directory.

For programs offering related work, see also in this book *Anatomy; Biochemistry; Biological and Biomedical Sciences; Cell, Molecular, and Structural Biology; Ecology, Environmental Biology, and Evolutionary Biology; Entomology; Genetics, Developmental Biology, and Reproductive Biology; Microbiological Sciences; Neuroscience and Neurobiology; and Physiology*. In the other guides in this series:

Graduate Programs in the Physical Sciences, Mathematics, Agricultural Sciences, the Environment & Natural Resources
See *Agricultural and Food Sciences, Environmental Sciences and Management*, and *Marine Sciences and Oceanography*

Graduate Programs in Engineering & Applied Sciences

See *Agricultural Engineering and Bioengineering* and *Ocean Engineering*

Graduate Programs in Business, Education, Health, Information Studies, Law & Social Work
See *Veterinary Medicine and Sciences*

CONTENTS

Program Directories

Display

Animal Behavior

Bucknell University, Graduate Studies, College of Arts and Sciences, Department of Animal Behavior, Lewisburg, PA 17837. Offers MA, MS. Part-time programs available. *Degree requirements:* For master's, thesis. *Entrance requirements:* For master's, GRE General Test, GRE Subject Test, minimum GPA of 2.8. Additional exam requirements/recommendations for international students: Required—TOEFL (minimum score 550 paper-based; 213 computer-based).

Cornell University, Graduate School, Graduate Fields of Agriculture and Life Sciences, Field of Neurobiology and Behavior, Ithaca, NY 14853-0001. Offers behavioral biology (PhD), including behavioral ecology, chemical ecology, ethology, neuroethology, sociobiology; neurobiology (PhD), including cellular and molecular neurobiology, neuroanatomy, neurochemistry, neuropharmacology, neurophysiology, sensory physiology. *Faculty:* 51 full-time (9 women). *Students:* 36 full-time (15 women); includes 4 minority (1 African American, 1 Asian American or Pacific Islander, 2 Hispanic Americans), 3 international. Average age 29. 44 applicants, 30% accepted, 7 enrolled. In 2009, 8 doctorates awarded. *Degree requirements:* For doctorate, comprehensive exam, thesis/dissertation, 1 year of teaching experience, seminar presentation. *Entrance requirements:* For doctorate, GRE General Test, GRE Subject Test (biology), 3 letters of recommendation. Additional exam requirements/recommendations for international students: Required—TOEFL (minimum score 550 paper-based; 213 computer-based; 77 iBT). *Application deadline:* For fall admission, 12/1 for domestic students. Application fee: $70. Electronic applications accepted. *Expenses:* Tuition: Full-time $29,500. Required fees: $70. Full-time tuition and fees vary according to degree level, program and student level. *Financial support:* In 2009–10, 35 students received support, including 7 fellowships with full tuition reimbursements available; research assistantships with full tuition reimbursements available, teaching assistantships with full tuition reimbursements available, institutionally sponsored loans, scholarships/grants, health care benefits, tuition waivers (full and partial), and unspecified assistantships also available. Financial award applicants required to submit FAFSA. *Faculty research:* Cellular neurobiology and neuropharmacology, integrative neurobiology, social behavior, chemical ecology, neuroethology. *Unit head:* Director of Graduate Studies, 607-254-4340, Fax: 607-254-4340. *Application contact:* Graduate Field Assistant, 607-254-4340, Fax: 607-254-4340, E-mail: nbb_field@cornell.edu.

Emory University, Graduate School of Arts and Sciences, Department of Psychology, Atlanta, GA 30322-1100. Offers clinical psychology (PhD); cognition and development (PhD); neuroscience and animal behavior (PhD). *Accreditation:* APA. *Degree requirements:* For doctorate, comprehensive exam, thesis/dissertation. *Entrance requirements:* For doctorate, GRE General Test, minimum GPA of 3.25. Additional exam requirements/recommendations for international students: Required—TOEFL. Electronic applications accepted. *Faculty research:* Neuroscience and animal behavior; adult and child psychopathology, cognition development assessment.

Illinois State University, Graduate School, College of Arts and Sciences, Department of Biological Sciences, Normal, IL 61790-2200. Offers animal behavior (MS); bacteriology (MS); biochemistry (MS); biological sciences (MS); biology (PhD); biophysics (MS); biotechnology (MS); botany (MS, PhD); cell biology (MS); conservation biology (MS); developmental biology (MS); ecology (MS, PhD); entomology (MS); evolutionary biology (MS); genetics (MS, PhD); immunology (MS); microbiology (MS, PhD); molecular biology (MS); molecular genetics (MS); neurobiology (MS); neuroscience (MS); parasitology (MS); physiology (MS, PhD); plant biology (MS); plant molecular biology (MS); plant sciences (MS); structural biology (MS); zoology (MS, PhD). Part-time programs available. *Degree requirements:* For master's, thesis or alternative; for doctorate, variable foreign language requirement, thesis/dissertation, 2 terms of residency. *Entrance requirements:* For master's, GRE General Test, minimum GPA of 2.6 in last 60 hours of course work; for doctorate, GRE General Test. *Faculty research:* Redoc balance and drug development in schistosoma mansoni, control of the growth of listeria monocytogenes at low temperature, regulation of cell expansion and microtubule function by SPRI, CRUI: physiology and fitness consequences of different life history phenotypes.

University of California, Davis, Graduate Studies, Graduate Group in Animal Behavior, Davis, CA 95616. Offers PhD. *Degree requirements:* For doctorate, thesis/dissertation. *Entrance requirements:* For doctorate, GRE General Test. Additional exam requirements/recommendations for international students: Required—TOEFL (minimum score 550 paper-based; 213 computer-based), IELTS (minimum score 7). Electronic applications accepted. *Faculty research:* Wildlife behavior, conservation biology, companion animal behavior, behavioral endocrinology, animal communication.

University of Colorado at Boulder, Graduate School, College of Arts and Sciences, Department of Ecology and Evolutionary Biology, Boulder, CO 80309. Offers animal behavior (MA); biology (MA, PhD); environmental biology (MA, PhD); evolutionary biology (MA, PhD); neurobiology (MA); population biology (MA); population genetics (PhD). *Faculty:* 32 full-time (10 women). *Students:* 64 full-time (36 women), 15 part-time (9 women); includes 12 minority (1 American Indian/Alaska Native, 3 Asian Americans or Pacific Islanders, 8 Hispanic Americans), 4 international. Average age 29. 145 applicants, 14% accepted, 21 enrolled. In 2009, 9 master's, 6 doctorates awarded. Terminal master's awarded for partial completion of doctoral program. *Degree requirements:* For master's, comprehensive exam, thesis or alternative; for doctorate, comprehensive exam, thesis/dissertation. *Entrance requirements:* For master's, GRE General Test, GRE Subject Test, minimum undergraduate GPA of 3.0; for doctorate, GRE General Test, GRE Subject Test. *Application deadline:* For fall admission, 12/30 priority date for domestic students, 12/1 for international students. Application fee: $50 ($60 for international students). *Financial support:* In 2009–10, 25 fellowships (averaging $17,876 per year), 27 research assistantships (averaging $15,070 per year) were awarded; Federal Work-Study, institutionally sponsored loans, and tuition waivers (full) also available. *Faculty research:* Behavior, ecology, genetics, morphology, endocrinology, physiology, systematics. Total annual research expenditures: $3.1 million.

University of Massachusetts Amherst, Graduate School, Interdisciplinary Programs, Program in Neuroscience and Behavior, Amherst, MA 01003. Offers animal behavior and learning (PhD); molecular and cellular neuroscience (PhD); neural and behavioral development (PhD); neuroendocrinology (PhD); neuroscience and behavior (MS); sensorimotor, cognitive, and computational neuroscience (PhD). *Students:* 28 full-time (19 women); includes 4 minority (1 African American, 2 Asian Americans or Pacific Islanders, 1 Hispanic American), 3 international. Average age 26. 70 applicants, 26% accepted, 5 enrolled. In 2009, 4 master's, 5 doctorates awarded. Terminal master's awarded for partial completion of doctoral program. *Degree requirements:* For master's, thesis or alternative; for doctorate, comprehensive exam, thesis/dissertation. *Entrance requirements:* For master's and doctorate, GRE General Test. Additional exam requirements/recommendations for international students: Required—TOEFL (minimum score 550 paper-based; 213 computer-based; 80 iBT), IELTS (minimum score 6.5). *Application deadline:* For fall admission, 1/2 for domestic and international students. Applications are processed on a rolling basis. Application fee: $50 ($65 for international students). Electronic applications accepted. *Expenses:* Tuition, state resident: full-time $2640; part-time $110 per credit. Tuition, nonresident: full-time $9936; part-time $414 per credit. Tuition and fees vary according to course load. *Financial support:* In 2009–10, 1 fellowship with full tuition reimbursement (averaging $11,144 per year), 3 research assistantships with full tuition reimbursements (averaging $1,477 per year) were awarded; teaching assistantships, career-related internships or fieldwork, Federal Work-Study, scholarships/grants, traineeships, health care benefits, tuition waivers (full), and unspecified assistantships also available. Support available to part-time students. Financial award application deadline: 1/2. *Unit head:* Dr. Elizabeth A. Connor, Graduate Program Director, 413-545-2046, Fax: 413-545-3243. *Application contact:* Jean M. Ames, Supervisor of Admissions, 413-545-0722, Fax: 413-577-0010, E-mail: gradadm@grad.umass.edu.

University of Massachusetts Amherst, Graduate School, Interdisciplinary Programs, Program in Organismic and Evolutionary Biology, Amherst, MA 01003. Offers animal behavior (PhD); ecology (PhD); evolutionary biology (PhD); organismal biology (PhD); organismic and evolutionary biology (MS). Part-time programs available. *Faculty:* 2 full-time (1 woman). *Students:* 33 full-time (21 women), 3 part-time (0 women); includes 2 minority (both Hispanic Americans), 6 international. Average age 27. 53 applicants, 15% accepted, 5 enrolled. In 2009, 2 master's, 4 doctorates awarded. Terminal master's awarded for partial completion of doctoral program. *Degree requirements:* For master's, thesis or alternative; for doctorate, comprehensive exam, thesis/dissertation. *Entrance requirements:* For master's and doctorate, GRE General Test, 3 letters of recommendation. Additional exam requirements/recommendations for international students: Required—TOEFL (minimum score 550 paper-based; 213 computer-based; 80 iBT), IELTS (minimum score 6.5). *Application deadline:* For fall admission, 12/1 for domestic and international students. Applications are processed on a rolling basis. Application fee: $50 ($65 for international students). Electronic applications accepted. *Expenses:* Tuition, state resident: full-time $2640; part-time $110 per credit. Tuition, nonresident: full-time $9936; part-time $414 per credit. Tuition and fees vary according to course load. *Financial support:* Fellowships, research assistantships, teaching assistantships, career-related internships or fieldwork, Federal Work-Study, scholarships/grants, traineeships, health care benefits, tuition waivers (full), and unspecified assistantships available. Support available to part-time students. Financial award application deadline: 12/1. *Unit head:* Dr. Elizabeth M. Jakob, Graduate Program Director, 413-545-0928, Fax: 413-545-3243. *Application contact:* Jean M. Ames, Supervisor of Admissions, 413-545-0722, Fax: 413-577-0010, E-mail: gradadm@grad.umass.edu.

University of Minnesota, Twin Cities Campus, Graduate School, College of Biological Sciences, Department of Ecology, Evolution, and Behavior, Minneapolis, MN 55455-0213. Offers ecology, evolution, and behavior (MS, PhD). Terminal master's awarded for partial completion of doctoral program. *Degree requirements:* For master's, comprehensive exam, thesis or projects; for doctorate, comprehensive exam, thesis/dissertation. *Entrance requirements:* For master's and doctorate, GRE General Test, minimum GPA of 3.0. Additional exam requirements/recommendations for international students: Required—TOEFL (minimum score 550 paper-based; 213 computer-based), Michigan English Language Assessment Battery. Electronic applications accepted. *Faculty research:* Behavioral ecology, community ecology, community genetics, ecosystem and global change, evolution and systematics.

University of Missouri–St. Louis, College of Arts and Sciences, Department of Biology, St. Louis, MO 63121. Offers biology (MS, PhD), including animal behavior (MS), biochemistry, biochemistry and biotechnology (MS), biotechnology (MS), conservation biology (MS), development (MS), ecology (MS), environmental studies (PhD), evolution (MS), genetics (MS), molecular biology and biochemistry (PhD), molecular/cellular biology (MS), physiology (MS), plant systematics, population biology (MS), tropical biology (MS); biotechnology (Certificate); tropical biology and conservation (Certificate). Part-time programs available. *Faculty:* 43 full-time (13 women), 2 part-time/adjunct (1 woman). *Students:* 54 full-time (27 women), 79 part-time (43 women); includes 15 minority (6 African Americans, 7 Asian Americans or Pacific Islanders, 2 Hispanic Americans), 47 international. Average age 29. 193 applicants, 44% accepted, 44 enrolled. In 2009, 30 master's, 7 doctorates, 9 other advanced degrees awarded. *Degree requirements:* For master's, thesis or alternative; for doctorate, thesis/dissertation, 1 semester of teaching experience. *Entrance requirements:* For master's, 3 letters of recommendation; for doctorate, GRE General Test, 3 letters of recommendation. Additional exam requirements/recommendations for international students: Required—TOEFL. *Application deadline:* For fall admission, 12/1 priority date for domestic and international students; for spring admission, 10/15 priority date for domestic and international students. Applications are processed on a rolling basis. Application fee: $35 ($40 for international students). Electronic applications accepted. *Expenses:* Tuition, state resident: full-time $5377; part-time $297.70 per credit hour. Tuition, nonresident: full-time $13,882; part-time $771.20 per credit hour. Required fees: $220; $12.20 per credit hour. One-time fee: $12. Tuition and fees vary according to course level, campus/location and program. *Financial support:* In 2009–10, 22 research assistantships with full and partial tuition reimbursements (averaging $16,300 per year), 14 teaching assistantships with full and partial tuition reimbursements (averaging $16,727 per year) were awarded; fellowships with full tuition reimbursements, career-related internships or fieldwork and Federal Work-Study also available. Support available to part-time students. Financial award application deadline: 2/1. *Faculty research:* Molecular biology, microbial genetics, animal behavior, tropical ecology, plant systematics. *Unit head:* Dr. Elizabeth Kellogg, Director of Graduate Studies, 314-516-6200, Fax: 314-516-6233, E-mail: tkellogg@umsl.edu. *Application contact:* 314-516-5458, Fax: 314-516-6996, E-mail: gradadm@umsl.edu.

The University of Montana, Graduate School, College of Arts and Sciences, Department of Psychology, Missoula, MT 59812-0002. Offers clinical psychology (PhD); experimental psychology (PhD), including animal behavior psychology, developmental psychology; school psychology (MA, PhD, Ed S). *Accreditation:* APA (one or more programs are accredited). Terminal master's awarded for partial completion of doctoral program. *Degree requirements:* For master's, thesis; for doctorate, thesis/dissertation. *Entrance requirements:* For master's, doctorate, and Ed S, GRE General Test. Additional exam requirements/recommendations for international students: Required—TOEFL.

The University of Tennessee, Graduate School, College of Arts and Sciences, Department of Ecology and Evolutionary Biology, Knoxville, TN 37996. Offers behavior (MS, PhD); ecology (MS, PhD); evolutionary biology (MS, PhD). Part-time programs available. *Degree requirements:* For master's, thesis; for doctorate, thesis/dissertation. *Entrance requirements:* For master's and doctorate, GRE General Test, minimum GPA of 2.7. Additional exam requirements/recommendations for international students: Required—TOEFL. Electronic applications accepted. *Expenses:* Tuition, state resident: full-time $6826; part-time $380 per semester hour. Tuition, nonresident: full-time $21,844; part-time $1147 per semester hour. Tuition and fees vary according to program.

The University of Texas at Austin, Graduate School, College of Natural Sciences, School of Biological Sciences, Program in Ecology, Evolution and Behavior, Austin, TX 78712-1111. Offers MA, PhD. *Entrance requirements:* For doctorate, GRE General Test. Additional exam requirements/recommendations for international students: Required—TOEFL. Electronic applications accepted.

University of Washington, Graduate School, College of Arts and Sciences, Department of Psychology, Seattle, WA 98195. Offers animal behavior (PhD); child psychology (PhD); clinical psychology (PhD); cognition and perception (PhD); developmental psychology (PhD); quantitative psychology (PhD); social psychology and personality (PhD). *Accreditation:* APA. *Degree requirements:* For doctorate, thesis/dissertation. *Entrance requirements:* For doctorate, GRE General Test, minimum GPA of 3.0. Electronic applications accepted. *Faculty research:* Addictive behaviors, artificial intelligence, child psychopathology, mechanisms and development of vision, physiology of ingestive behaviors.

Wesleyan University, Graduate Programs, Department of Biology, Middletown, CT 06459. Offers animal behavior (PhD); bioformatics/genomics (PhD); cell biology (PhD); developmental biology (PhD); evolution/ecology (PhD); genetics (PhD); neurobiology (PhD); population biology (PhD). *Faculty:* 13 full-time (4 women). *Students:* 23 full-time (11 women); includes 1 minority (African American), 3 international. Average age 26. 29 applicants, 10% accepted, 2 enrolled. In 2009, 3 doctorates awarded. *Degree requirements:* For doctorate, variable foreign language requirement, thesis/dissertation. *Entrance requirements:* For doctorate, GRE. Additional exam requirements/recommendations for international students: Required—TOEFL. *Application deadline:* For fall admission, 1/15 for domestic and international students. Applications are processed on a rolling basis. Application fee: $0. *Financial support:* In 2009–10, 3 research assistantships with full tuition reimbursements, 19 teaching assistantships with full tuition reimbursements were awarded; stipends also available. Financial award application deadline: 4/15; financial award applicants required to submit FAFSA. *Faculty research:* Microbial population genetics, genetic basis of evolutionary adaptation, genetic regulation of differentiation and pattern formation in *drosophila. Unit head:* Dr. Sonia E. Sultan, Chair/Professor, 860-685-3493, E-mail: jnaegele@wesleyan.edu. *Application contact:* Marjorie Fitzgibbons, Information Contact, 860-685-2140, E-mail: mfitzgibbons@wesleyan.edu.

Zoology

Auburn University, Graduate School, College of Sciences and Mathematics, Department of Biological Sciences, Auburn University, AL 36849. Offers botany (MS, PhD); microbiology (MS, PhD); zoology (MS, PhD). *Faculty:* 33 full-time (8 women), 1 (woman) part-time/adjunct. *Students:* 42 full-time (17 women), 60 part-time (36 women); includes 9 minority (4 African Americans, 1 American Indian/Alaska Native, 3 Asian Americans or Pacific Islanders, 1 Hispanic American), 21 international. Average age 28. 134 applicants, 20% accepted, 18 enrolled. In 2009, 22 master's, 11 doctorates awarded. *Entrance requirements:* For master's and doctorate, GRE General Test. Additional exam requirements/recommendations for international students: Required—TOEFL. *Application deadline:* For fall admission, 7/7 for domestic students; for spring admission, 11/24 for domestic students. Application fee: $50 ($60 for international students). Electronic applications accepted. *Expenses:* Tuition, state resident: full-time $6240. Tuition, nonresident: full-time $18,720. International tuition: $18,938 full-time. Required fees: $492. Tuition and fees vary according to course load, program and reciprocity agreements. *Financial support:* Research assistantships, teaching assistantships available. Financial award applicants required to submit FAFSA. *Unit head:* Dr. James M. Barbaree, Chair, 334-844-1647, Fax: 334-844-1645. *Application contact:* Dr. George Flowers, Dean of the Graduate School, 334-844-2125.

Colorado State University, Graduate School, College of Natural Sciences, Department of Biology, Fort Collins, CO 80523-1878. Offers botany (MS, PhD); zoology (MS, PhD). Post-baccalaureate distance learning degree programs offered (no on-campus study). *Faculty:* 25 full-time (10 women), 1 part-time/adjunct (0 women). *Students:* 31 full-time (15 women), 20 part-time (11 women); includes 4 minority (1 American Indian/Alaska Native, 1 Asian American or Pacific Islander, 2 Hispanic Americans), 7 international. Average age 29. 38 applicants, 26% accepted, 9 enrolled. In 2009, 8 master's, 2 doctorates awarded. Terminal master's awarded for partial completion of doctoral program. *Degree requirements:* For master's, comprehensive exam (for some programs), thesis (for some programs); for doctorate, comprehensive exam, thesis/dissertation. *Entrance requirements:* For master's, GRE General Test, minimum GPA of 3.0; 3 letters of recommendation; for doctorate, GRE General Test, minimum GPA of 3.0; statement of purpose; 2 transcripts; 3 letters of recommendation. Additional exam requirements/recommendations for international students: Required—TOEFL (minimum score 550 paper-based; 213 computer-based; 80 iBT). *Application deadline:* For fall admission, 9/15 priority date for domestic students, 8/15 priority date for international students; for spring admission, 1/15 priority date for domestic and international students. Applications are processed on a rolling basis. Application fee: $50. Electronic applications accepted. *Expenses:* Tuition, state resident: full-time $6434; part-time $359.10 per credit. Tuition, nonresident: full-time $18,116; part-time $1006.45 per credit. Required fees: $1496; $83 per credit. *Financial support:* In 2009–10, 15 fellowships (averaging $26,286 per year), 26 research assistantships with full tuition reimbursements (averaging $11,410 per year), 48 teaching assistantships with full tuition reimbursements (averaging $12,007 per year) were awarded; health care benefits also available. Financial award application deadline: 1/15; financial award applicants required to submit FAFSA. *Faculty research:* Aquatic and terrestrial ecology, cell biology and genetics, plant/animal physiology, developmental biology, evolutionary biology. Total annual research expenditures: $5 million. *Unit head:* Dr. Daniel R. Bush, Chair, 970-491-7013, Fax: 970-491-0649, E-mail: dbush@colostate.edu. *Application contact:* Dorothy Ramirez, Graduate Coordinator, 970-491-1923, Fax: 970-491-0649, E-mail: dorothy.ramirez@colostate.edu.

Cornell University, Graduate School, Graduate Fields of Agriculture and Life Sciences, Field of Zoology, Ithaca, NY 14853-0001. Offers animal cytology (MS, PhD); comparative and functional anatomy (MS, PhD); developmental biology (MS, PhD); ecology (MS, PhD); histology (MS, PhD). *Faculty:* 24 full-time (5 women). *Students:* 4 full-time (all women); includes 1 minority (Hispanic American), 1 international. Average age 34. 7 applicants, 0% accepted, 0 enrolled. *Degree requirements:* For doctorate, comprehensive exam, thesis/dissertation, 2 semesters of teaching experience. *Entrance requirements:* For doctorate, GRE General Test, GRE Subject Test (biology), 2 letters of recommendation. Additional exam requirements/recommendations for international students: Required—TOEFL (minimum score 550 paper-based; 213 computer-based; 77 iBT). *Application deadline:* For fall admission, 2/1 priority date for domestic students. Application fee: $70. Electronic applications accepted. *Expenses:* Tuition: Full-time $29,500. Required fees: $70. Full-time tuition and fees vary according to degree level, program and student level. *Financial support:* In 2009–10, 3 students received support; fellowships with full tuition reimbursements available, research assistantships with full tuition reimbursements available, teaching assistantships with full tuition reimbursements available, institutionally sponsored loans, scholarships/grants, health care benefits, tuition waivers (full and partial), and unspecified assistantships available. Financial award applicants required to submit FAFSA. *Faculty research:* Organismal biology, functional morphology, biomechanics, comparative vertebrate anatomy, comparative invertebrate anatomy, paleontology. *Unit head:* Director of Graduate Studies, 607-253-3276, Fax: 607-253-3756. *Application contact:* Graduate Field Assistant, 607-253-3276, Fax: 607-253-3756, E-mail: graduate_edcvm@cornell.edu.

Emporia State University, School of Graduate Studies, College of Liberal Arts and Sciences, Department of Biological Sciences, Emporia, KS 66801-5087. Offers botany (MS); environmental biology (MS); general biology (MS); microbial and cellular biology (MS); zoology (MS). Part-time programs available. *Faculty:* 13 full-time (3 women). *Students:* 9 full-time (7 women), 17 part-time (11 women); includes 1 minority (African American), 8 international. 22 applicants, 95% accepted, 18 enrolled. In 2009, 24 master's awarded. *Degree requirements:* For master's, comprehensive exam or thesis. *Entrance requirements:* For master's, GRE, appropriate undergraduate degree, interview, letters of reference. Additional exam requirements/recommendations for international students: Required—TOEFL (minimum score 520 paper-based; 133 computer-based; 68 iBT). *Application deadline:* For fall admission, 8/15 priority date for domestic students. Applications are processed on a rolling basis. Application fee: $30 ($75 for international students). Electronic applications accepted. *Expenses:* Tuition, state resident: full-time $4154; part-time $173 per credit hour. Tuition, nonresident: full-time $12,864; part-time $536 per credit hour. Required fees: $948; $58 per credit hour. Tuition and fees vary according to campus/location. *Financial support:* In 2009–10, 7 research assistantships with full tuition reimbursements (averaging $6,876 per year), 10 teaching assistantships with full tuition reimbursements (averaging $7,419 per year) were awarded; career-related internships or fieldwork, Federal Work-Study, institutionally sponsored loans, health care benefits, and unspecified assistantships also available. Financial award application deadline: 3/15; financial award applicants required to submit FAFSA. *Faculty research:* Fisheries, range, and wildlife management; aquatic, plant, grassland, vertebrate, and invertebrate ecology; mammalian and plant systematics, taxonomy, and evolution; immunology, virology, and molecular biology. *Unit head:* Dr. R. Brent Thomas, Interim Chair, 620-341-5311, Fax: 620-341-5608, E-mail: rthomas2@emporia.edu. *Application contact:* Dr. Scott Crupper, Graduate Coordinator, 620-341-5621, Fax: 620-341-5607, E-mail: scrupper@emporia.edu.

Illinois State University, Graduate School, College of Arts and Sciences, Department of Biological Sciences, Normal, IL 61790-2200. Offers animal behavior (MS); bacteriology (MS); biochemistry (MS); biological sciences (MS); biology (PhD); biophysics (MS); biotechnology (MS); botany (MS, PhD); cell biology (MS); conservation biology (MS); developmental biology (MS); ecology (MS, PhD); entomology (MS); evolutionary biology (MS); genetics (MS, PhD); immunology (MS); microbiology (MS, PhD); molecular biology (MS); molecular genetics (MS); neurobiology (MS); neuroscience (MS); parasitology (MS); physiology (MS, PhD); plant biology (MS); plant molecular biology (MS); plant sciences (MS); structural biology (MS); zoology (MS, PhD). Part-time programs available. *Degree requirements:* For master's, thesis or alternative; for doctorate, variable foreign language requirement, thesis/dissertation, 2 terms of residency. *Entrance requirements:* For master's, GRE General Test, minimum GPA of 2.6 in last 60 hours of course work; for doctorate, GRE General Test. *Faculty research:* Redoc balance and drug development in schistosoma mansoni, control of the growth of listeria monocytogenes at low temperature, regulation of cell expansion and microtubule function by SPRI, CRUI: physiology and fitness consequences of different life history phenotypes.

Indiana University Bloomington, University Graduate School, College of Arts and Sciences, Department of Biology, Bloomington, IN 47405. Offers biology teaching (MAT); biotechnology (MA); evolution, ecology, and behavior (MA, PhD); genetics (PhD); microbiology (MA, PhD); molecular, cellular, and developmental biology (PhD); plant sciences (MA, PhD); zoology (MA, PhD). *Faculty:* 58 full-time (15 women), 21 part-time/adjunct (6 women). *Students:* 165 full-time (95 women); includes 14 minority (6 African Americans, 1 American Indian/Alaska Native, 7 Asian Americans or Pacific Islanders), 56 international. Average age 27. 312 applicants, 19% accepted, 24 enrolled. In 2009, 4 master's, 22 doctorates awarded. Terminal master's awarded for partial completion of doctoral program. *Degree requirements:* For master's, thesis, oral defense; for doctorate, thesis/dissertation, oral defense. *Entrance requirements:* For master's and doctorate, GRE General Test. Additional exam requirements/recommendations for international students: Required—TOEFL (minimum score 100 iBT). *Application deadline:* For fall admission, 1/5 priority date for domestic students, 12/1 priority date for international students. Application fee: $55 ($65 for international students). Electronic applications accepted. *Financial support:* In 2009–10, 165 students received support, including 62 fellowships with tuition reimbursements available (averaging $19,484 per year), 27 research assistantships with tuition reimbursements available (averaging $22,605 per year), 76 teaching assistantships with tuition reimbursements available (averaging $20,528 per year); scholarships/grants, traineeships, health care benefits, and unspecified assistantships also available. Financial award application deadline: 1/5. *Faculty research:* Evolution, ecology and behavior; microbiology; molecular biology and genetics; plant biology. *Unit head:* Dr. Roger Innes, Chair, 812-855-2219, Fax: 812-855-6082, E-mail: rinnes@indiana.edu. *Application contact:* Tracey D. Stohr, Graduate Student Recruitment Coordinator, 812-856-6303, Fax: 812-855-6082, E-mail: gradbio@indiana.edu.

Miami University, Graduate School, College of Arts and Science, Department of Zoology, Oxford, OH 45056. Offers biological sciences (MAT); zoology (MS, PhD). Part-time programs available. *Students:* 67 full-time (40 women), 50 part-time (37 women); includes 8 minority (1 African American, 5 Asian Americans or Pacific Islanders, 2 Hispanic Americans), 22 international. *Entrance requirements:* For master's, minimum undergraduate GPA of 3.0 during previous 2 years or 2.75 overall; for doctorate, minimum undergraduate GPA of 2.75, 3.0 graduate. Additional exam requirements/recommendations for international students: Required—TOEFL. Application fee: $50. *Expenses:* Tuition, state resident: full-time $11,280. Tuition, nonresident: full-time $24,912. Required fees: $516. *Financial support:* Fellowships with full tuition reimbursements, research assistantships with full tuition reimbursements, teaching assistantships with full tuition reimbursements, Federal Work-Study, health care benefits, tuition waivers (full), and unspecified assistantships available. Financial award application deadline: 3/1; financial award applicants required to submit FAFSA. *Unit head:* Dr. Douglas Meikle, Chair, 513-529-3103, E-mail: meikled@muohio.edu. *Application contact:* Dr. Paul F. James, Graduate Advisor, 513-529-3129, E-mail: jamespf@muohio.edu.

See Display on page 498.

Michigan State University, The Graduate School, College of Natural Science, Department of Zoology, East Lansing, MI 48824. Offers zoo and aquarium management (MS); zoology (MS, PhD); zoology-environmental toxicology (PhD). *Faculty:* 19 full-time (5 women). *Students:* 53 full-time (28 women), 7 part-time (4 women); includes 6 minority (4 Asian Americans or Pacific Islanders, 2 Hispanic Americans), 7 international. Average age 28. 82 applicants, 15% accepted. In 2009, 5 master's, 5 doctorates awarded. *Entrance requirements:* Additional exam requirements/recommendations for international students: Required—TOEFL. Electronic applications accepted. *Expenses:* Tuition, state resident: part-time $478.25 per credit hour. Tuition, nonresident: part-time $966.50 per credit hour. Part-time tuition and fees vary according to program. *Financial support:* In 2009–10, 13 research assistantships with tuition reimbursements (averaging $7,338 per year), 26 teaching assistantships with tuition reimbursements (averaging $7,366 per year) were awarded. Total annual research expenditures: $1.2 million. *Unit head:* Dr. Fred C. Dyer, Chairperson, 517-353-9864, Fax: 517-432-2789, E-mail: fcdyer@msu.edu. *Application contact:* Lisa Craft, Graduate Secretary, 517-355-4642, Fax: 517-432-2789, E-mail: zoology@msu.edu.

Montana State University, College of Graduate Studies, College of Letters and Science, Department of Ecology, Bozeman, MT 59717. Offers ecological and environmental statistics (MS); ecology and environmental sciences (PhD); fish and wildlife biology (PhD); fish and wildlife management (MS). Part-time programs available. *Faculty:* 12 full-time (2 women), 2 part-time/adjunct (0 women). *Students:* 8 full-time (2 women), 48 part-time (18 women). Average age 31. 18 applicants, 33% accepted, 6 enrolled. In 2009, 6 master's, 7 doctorates awarded. *Degree requirements:* For master's, comprehensive exam, thesis (for some programs); for doctorate, comprehensive exam, thesis/dissertation. *Entrance requirements:* For master's, GRE General Test, letters of recommendation, essay; for doctorate, GRE General Test, letters of recommendation. Additional exam requirements/recommendations for international students: Required—TOEFL (minimum score 550 paper-based; 213 computer-based). *Application deadline:* For fall admission, 7/15 priority date for domestic students, 5/15 priority date for international students; for spring admission, 12/1 priority date for domestic students, 10/1 priority date for international students. Applications are processed on a rolling basis. Application fee: $30. Electronic applications accepted. *Expenses:* Tuition, state resident: full-time $5635; part-time $3492 per year. Tuition, nonresident: full-time $17,212; part-time $7865.10 per year. Required fees: $1441; $153.15 per credit. Tuition and fees vary according to course load and program. *Financial support:* In 2009–10, 2 fellowships with full tuition reimbursements (averaging $17,725 per year), 29 research assistantships with full and partial tuition reimbursements (averaging $19,500 per year), 20 teaching assistantships with full tuition reimbursements (averaging $12,321 per year) were awarded; career-related internships or fieldwork, scholarships/grants, health care benefits, tuition waivers (partial), and unspecified assistantships also available. Support available to part-time students. Financial award application deadline: 3/1; financial award applicants required to submit FAFSA. *Faculty research:* Evolutionary biology, conservation ecology, human impact on ecosystems, biodiversity, applied wildlife and fisheries research, plant and animal community ecology. Total annual research expenditures: $2.6 million. *Unit head:* Dr. David Roberts, Head, 406-994-4548, Fax: 406-994-3190, E-mail:

Zoology

Montana State University (continued)
droberts@montana.edu. *Application contact:* Dr. Carl A. Fox, Vice Provost for Graduate Education, 406-994-4145, Fax: 406-994-7433, E-mail: gradstudy@montana.edu.

North Carolina State University, Graduate School, College of Agriculture and Life Sciences, Department of Zoology, Raleigh, NC 27695. Offers MS, MZS, PhD. Terminal master's awarded for partial completion of doctoral program. *Degree requirements:* For master's, thesis (for some programs), oral exam; for doctorate, thesis/dissertation, oral and written exams. *Entrance requirements:* For master's and doctorate, GRE General Test, minimum GPA of 3.0. Additional exam requirements/recommendations for international students: Required—TOEFL. Electronic applications accepted. *Faculty research:* Acquatic and terrestrial ecology, herpetology, behavioral biology, neurobiology, avian ecology.

North Dakota State University, College of Graduate and Interdisciplinary Studies, College of Science and Mathematics, Department of Biological Sciences, Fargo, ND 58108. Offers biology (MS); botany (MS, PhD); cellular and molecular biology (PhD); environmental and conservation sciences (MS, PhD); genomics (PhD); natural resources management (MS, PhD); zoology (MS, PhD). *Students:* 32 full-time (21 women), 14 part-time (10 women); includes 1 Asian American or Pacific Islander, 14 international. In 2009, 12 master's, 9 doctorates awarded. *Degree requirements:* For master's, thesis; for doctorate, thesis/dissertation. *Entrance requirements:* For master's and doctorate, GRE General Test. Additional exam requirements/recommendations for international students: Required—TOEFL. *Application deadline:* For fall admission, 3/15 priority date for domestic students; for spring admission, 10/30 priority date for domestic students. Applications are processed on a rolling basis. Application fee: $45 ($60 for international students). Electronic applications accepted. *Financial support:* Fellowships with full tuition reimbursements, research assistantships with full tuition reimbursements, teaching assistantships with full tuition reimbursements, career-related internships or fieldwork, Federal Work-Study, institutionally sponsored loans, scholarships/grants, tuition waivers (full), and unspecified assistantships available. Support available to part-time students. Financial award application deadline: 4/15; financial award applicants required to submit FAFSA. *Faculty research:* Comparative endocrinology, physiology, behavioral ecology, plant cell biology, aquatic biology. Total annual research expenditures: $675,000. *Unit head:* Dr. Marinus L. Otte, Head, 701-231-7087, E-mail: marinus.otte@ndsu.edu. *Application contact:* Dr. Marinus L. Otte, Head, 701-231-7087, E-mail: marinus.otte@ndsu.edu.

Oklahoma State University, College of Arts and Sciences, Department of Zoology, Stillwater, OK 74078. Offers zoology (MS, PhD). *Faculty:* 20 full-time (6 women), 3 part-time/adjunct (1 woman). *Students:* 4 full-time (all women), 42 part-time (19 women); includes 5 minority (1 African American, 1 American Indian/Alaska Native, 2 Asian Americans or Pacific Islanders, 1 Hispanic American), 2 international. Average age 29. 27 applicants, 44% accepted, 10 enrolled. In 2009, 2 master's, 5 doctorates awarded. *Degree requirements:* For master's, thesis; for doctorate, comprehensive exam, thesis/dissertation. *Entrance requirements:* For master's and doctorate, GRE General Test. Additional exam requirements/recommendations for international students: Required—TOEFL (minimum score 550 paper-based; 79 iBT). *Application deadline:* For fall admission, 3/1 priority date for international students; for spring admission, 8/1 priority date for international students. Applications are processed on a rolling basis. Application fee: $40 ($75 for international students). Electronic applications accepted. *Expenses:* Tuition, state resident: full-time $3716; part-time $154.85 per credit hour. Tuition, nonresident: full-time $14,448; part-time $602 per credit hour. Required fees: $1772; $73.85 per credit hour. One-time fee: $50. Tuition and fees vary according to course load and campus/location. *Financial support:* In 2009–10, 9 research assistantships (averaging $16,289 per year), 38 teaching assistantships (averaging $16,460 per year) were awarded; career-related internships or fieldwork, Federal Work-Study, scholarships/grants, health care benefits, tuition waivers (partial), and unspecified assistantships also available. Support available to part-time students. Financial award application deadline: 3/1; financial award applicants required to submit FAFSA. *Unit head:* Dr. Loren Smith, Head, 405-744-5555, Fax: 405-744-7824. *Application contact:* Dr. Gordon Emslie, Dean, 405-744-6368, Fax: 405-744-0355, E-mail: grad-i@okstate.edu.

Oregon State University, Graduate School, College of Science, Department of Zoology, Corvallis, OR 97331. Offers MA, MAIS, MS, PhD. *Faculty:* 21 full-time (6 women), 2 part-time/adjunct (1 woman). *Students:* 37 full-time (20 women), 3 part-time (2 women); includes 4 minority (all Asian Americans or Pacific Islanders), 4 international. Average age 29. In 2009, 3 doctorates awarded. Terminal master's awarded for partial completion of doctoral program. *Degree requirements:* For doctorate, thesis/dissertation. *Entrance requirements:* For master's and doctorate, GRE General Test, GRE Subject Test, minimum GPA of 3.0 in last 90 hours. Additional exam requirements/recommendations for international students: Required—TOEFL. *Application deadline:* For fall admission, 1/15 for domestic students. Application fee: $50. *Expenses:* Tuition, state resident: full-time $9774; part-time $362 per credit. Tuition, nonresident: full-time $15,849; part-time $587 per credit. Required fees: $1639. Full-time tuition and fees vary according to course load and program. *Financial support:* Fellowships, research assistantships, teaching assistantships, Federal Work-Study and institutionally sponsored loans available. Support available to part-time students. Financial award application deadline: 2/1. *Faculty research:* Cell and developmental biology, population biology and marine community ecology, behavioral physiology, comparative immunology, plant-herbivore interaction. *Unit head:* Graduate Admissions Coordinator, 541-737-5335, Fax: 541-737-0501, E-mail: zoology@science.oregonstate.edu. *Application contact:* Traci Durrell-Khalife, Graduate Admissions Clerk, 541-737-5335, Fax: 541-737-0501, E-mail: durrellt@science.oregonstate.edu.

Southern Illinois University Carbondale, Graduate School, College of Science, Department of Zoology, Carbondale, IL 62901-4701. Offers MS, PhD. *Degree requirements:* For master's, thesis; for doctorate, thesis/dissertation. *Entrance requirements:* For master's, GRE, minimum GPA of 2.7; for doctorate, GRE, minimum GPA of 3.25. Additional exam requirements/recommendations for international students: Required—TOEFL. *Faculty research:* Ecology, fisheries and wildlife, systematics, behavior, vertebrate and invertebrate biology.

Texas A&M University, College of Science, Department of Biology, College Station, TX 77843. Offers biology (MS, PhD); botany (MS, PhD); microbiology (MS, PhD); molecular and cell biology (PhD); neuroscience (MS, PhD); zoology (MS, PhD). *Faculty:* 37. *Students:* 101 full-time (59 women), 5 part-time (3 women); includes 8 minority (1 African American, 3 Asian Americans or Pacific Islanders, 4 Hispanic Americans), 40 international. Average age 28. In 2009, 9 master's, 5 doctorates awarded. *Degree requirements:* For master's, thesis or alternative; for doctorate, comprehensive exam, thesis/dissertation. *Entrance requirements:* For master's and doctorate, GRE General Test. Additional exam requirements/recommendations for international students: Required—TOEFL. *Application deadline:* For fall admission, 1/15 for domestic students. Applications are processed on a rolling basis. Application fee: $50 ($75 for international students). Electronic applications accepted. *Expenses:* Tuition, state resident: full-time $3991; part-time $221.74 per credit hour. Tuition, nonresident: full-time $9049; part-time $502.74 per credit hour. *Financial support:* Fellowships, research assistantships, teaching assistantships available. Financial award application deadline: 4/1; financial award applicants required to submit FAFSA. *Unit head:* Dr. Jack McMahan, Department Head, 979-845-2301, E-mail: granster@mail.bio.tamu.edu. *Application contact:* Graduate Advisor, 979-845-7755.

Texas Tech University, Graduate School, College of Arts and Sciences, Department of Biological Sciences, Lubbock, TX 79409. Offers biological informatics (MS); biology (MS, PhD); microbiology (MS); zoology (MS, PhD). Part-time programs available. *Faculty:* 31 full-time

(6 women). *Students:* 120 full-time (59 women), 5 part-time (3 women); includes 5 minority (1 Asian American or Pacific Islander, 4 Hispanic Americans), 65 international. Average age 29. 121 applicants, 42% accepted, 24 enrolled. In 2009, 17 master's, 6 doctorates awarded. *Degree requirements:* For master's, thesis or alternative; for doctorate, thesis/dissertation. *Entrance requirements:* For master's and doctorate, GRE General Test. Additional exam requirements/recommendations for international students: Required—TOEFL (minimum score 550 paper-based; 213 computer-based). *Application deadline:* For fall admission, 3/1 priority date for international students; for spring admission, 11/1 priority date for international students. Applications are processed on a rolling basis. Application fee: $50 ($75 for international students). Electronic applications accepted. *Expenses:* Tuition, state resident: full-time $5100; part-time $213 per credit hour. Tuition, nonresident: full-time $11,748; part-time $490 per credit hour. Required fees: $2298; $50 per credit hour. $555 per semester. *Financial support:* In 2009–10, 16 research assistantships with partial tuition reimbursements (averaging $21,854 per year), 11 teaching assistantships with partial tuition reimbursements (averaging $19,985 per year) were awarded; career-related internships or fieldwork, Federal Work-Study, and institutionally sponsored loans also available. Support available to part-time students. Financial award application deadline: 4/15; financial award applicants required to submit FAFSA. *Faculty research:* Biodiversity and evolution, climate change in arid ecosystems, plant biology and biotechnology, animal communication and behavior, zoonotic and emerging diseases. Total annual research expenditures: $2.1 million. *Unit head:* Dr. Llewellyn D. Densmore, Chair, 806-742-2715, Fax: 806-742-2963, E-mail: jlou.densmore@ttu.edu. *Application contact:* Dr. Randall M. Jeter, Graduate Adviser, 806-742-2710 Ext. 223, Fax: 806-742-2963, E-mail: randall.jeter@ttu.edu.

Uniformed Services University of the Health Sciences, School of Medicine, Graduate Programs in the Biomedical Sciences and Public Health, Bethesda, MD 20814. Offers emerging infectious diseases (PhD); medical and clinical psychology (PhD), including clinical psychology, medical and clinical psychology (clinical/dual track), medical and clinical psychology (research track); molecular and cell biology (PhD); neuroscience (PhD); preventive medicine and biometrics (MPH, MSPH, MTMH, Dr PH, PhD), including environmental health science (PhD), medical zoology (PhD), public health (MPH, MSPH, Dr PH), tropical medicine and hygiene (MTMH). *Faculty:* 372 full-time (119 women), 4,044 part-time/adjunct (908 women). *Students:* 176 full-time (96 women); includes 31 minority (6 African Americans, 4 American Indian/Alaska Native, 14 Asian Americans or Pacific Islanders, 7 Hispanic Americans), 11 international. Average age 28. 278 applicants, 20% accepted, 47 enrolled. In 2009, 36 master's, 17 doctorates awarded. Terminal master's awarded for partial completion of doctoral program. *Degree requirements:* For master's, comprehensive exam, thesis or alternative; for doctorate, comprehensive exam, thesis/dissertation, qualifying exam. *Entrance requirements:* For master's, GRE General Test; for doctorate, GRE General Test, minimum GPA of 3.0. Additional exam requirements/recommendations for international students: Required—TOEFL. *Application deadline:* For fall admission, 1/15 priority date for domestic and international students. Applications are processed on a rolling basis. Application fee: $0. Electronic applications accepted. *Financial support:* In 2009–10, fellowships with full tuition reimbursements (averaging $26,000 per year), research assistantships with full tuition reimbursements (averaging $26,000 per year) were awarded; career-related internships or fieldwork, scholarships/grants, health care benefits, and tuition waivers (full) also available. *Unit head:* Dr. Eleanor S. Metcalf, Associate Dean, 301-295-1104, E-mail: emetcalf@usuhs.mil. *Application contact:* Elena Marina Sherman, Graduate Program Coordinator, 301-295-3913, Fax: 301-295-6772, E-mail: elena.sherman@usuhs.mil.

Uniformed Services University of the Health Sciences, School of Medicine, Graduate Programs in the Biomedical Sciences and Public Health, Department of Preventive Medicine and Biometrics, Program in Medical Zoology, Bethesda, MD 20814-4799. Offers PhD. *Faculty:* 43 full-time (14 women), 143 part-time/adjunct (25 women). *Students:* 1 (woman) full-time. Average age 33. 5 applicants, 0% accepted. *Degree requirements:* For doctorate, comprehensive exam, thesis/dissertation, qualifying exam. *Entrance requirements:* For doctorate, GRE General Test, GRE Subject Test, minimum GPA of 3.0, U.S. citizenship. Additional exam requirements/recommendations for international students: Required—TOEFL. *Application deadline:* For fall admission, 1/15 priority date for domestic students. Applications are processed on a rolling basis. Application fee: $0. *Financial support:* In 2009–10, fellowships with full tuition reimbursements (averaging $26,000 per year); scholarships/grants, health care benefits, and tuition waivers (full) also available. *Faculty research:* Epidemiology, biostatistics, tropical public health, parasitology, vector biology. *Unit head:* Dr. David Cruess, Director, 301-295-3465, Fax: 301-295-1933, E-mail: dcruess@usuhs.mil. *Application contact:* Elena Marina Sherman, Graduate Program Coordinator, 301-295-3913, Fax: 301-295-6772, E-mail: elena.sherman@usuhs.mil.

University of Alaska Fairbanks, College of Natural Sciences and Mathematics, Department of Biology and Wildlife, Fairbanks, AK 99775-6100. Offers biological sciences (MS, PhD), including biology, botany, wildlife biology (PhD), zoology; biology (MAT, MS); wildlife biology (MS). Part-time programs available. *Faculty:* 27 full-time (9 women), 2 part-time/adjunct (0 women). *Students:* 95 full-time (61 women), 32 part-time (18 women); includes 13 minority (1 African American, 3 American Indian/Alaska Native, 4 Asian Americans or Pacific Islanders, 5 Hispanic Americans), 9 international. Average age 35. 76 applicants, 32% accepted, 24 enrolled. In 2009, 10 master's, 13 doctorates awarded. *Degree requirements:* For master's, comprehensive exam, thesis, oral exam, oral defense; for doctorate, comprehensive exam, thesis/dissertation, oral exam, oral defense. *Entrance requirements:* For master's and doctorate, GRE General Test, GRE Subject Test (biology). Additional exam requirements/recommendations for international students: Required—TOEFL (minimum score 550 paper-based; 213 computer-based; 80 iBT), TWE. *Application deadline:* For fall admission, 6/1 for domestic students, 3/1 for international students; for spring admission, 10/15 for domestic students, 9/1 for international students. Applications are processed on a rolling basis. Application fee: $60. Electronic applications accepted. *Expenses:* Tuition, state resident: full-time $7584; part-time $316 per credit. Tuition, nonresident: full-time $15,504; part-time $646 per credit. Required fees: $23 per credit. $135 per semester. Tuition and fees vary according to course level, course load and reciprocity agreements. *Financial support:* In 2009–10, 46 research assistantships (averaging $13,543 per year), 24 teaching assistantships (averaging $7,495 per year) were awarded; fellowships, career-related internships or fieldwork, Federal Work-Study, scholarships/grants, health care benefits, and unspecified assistantships also available. Support available to part-time students. Financial award application deadline: 7/1; financial award applicants required to submit FAFSA. *Faculty research:* Plant-herbivore interactions, plant metabolic defenses, insect manufacture of glycerol, ice nucleators, structure and functions of arctic and subarctic freshwater ecosystems. *Unit head:* Dr. Richard E. Boone, Chair, 907-474-7671, Fax: 907-474-6716, E-mail: fybio@uaf.edu. *Application contact:* Dr. Richard E. Boone, Chair, 907-474-7671, Fax: 907-474-6716, E-mail: fybio@uaf.edu.

The University of British Columbia, Faculty of Science, Department of Zoology, Vancouver, BC V6T 1Z1, Canada. Offers M Sc, PhD. *Degree requirements:* For master's, thesis, final defense; for doctorate, comprehensive exam, thesis/dissertation, final defense. *Entrance requirements:* For master's and doctorate, faculty support. Additional exam requirements/recommendations for international students: Required—TOEFL. Electronic applications accepted. *Faculty research:* Cell and developmental biology; community, environmental, and population biology; comparative physiology and biochemistry; fisheries; ecology and evolutionary biology.

University of California, Davis, Graduate Studies, Graduate Group in Avian Sciences, Davis, CA 95616. Offers MS. *Degree requirements:* For master's, comprehensive exam (for some programs), thesis (for some programs). *Entrance requirements:* For master's, GRE General Test, minimum GPA of 3.0. Additional exam requirements/recommendations for international students: Required—TOEFL (minimum score 550 paper-based; 213 computer-based). Electronic applications accepted. *Faculty research:* Reproduction, nutrition, toxicology, food products, ecology of avian species.

University of Chicago, Division of the Biological Sciences, Darwinian Sciences Cluster: Ecological, Integrative and Evolutionary Biology, Department of Organismal Biology and Anatomy, Chicago, IL 60637-1513. Offers functional and evolutionary biology (PhD); organismal biology and anatomy (PhD). *Faculty:* 12 full-time (1 woman), 5 part-time/adjunct (3 women). *Students:* 12 full-time (6 women); includes 1 minority (Hispanic American), 1 international. Average age 27. 14 applicants, 43% accepted, 4 enrolled. In 2009, 2 doctorates awarded. *Degree requirements:* For doctorate, thesis/dissertation, ethics class, 2 teaching assistantships. *Entrance requirements:* For doctorate, GRE General Test. Additional exam requirements/recommendations for international students: Required—TOEFL (minimum score 600 paper-based; 250 computer-based; 104 iBT), IELTS (minimum score 7). *Application deadline:* For fall admission, 12/1 priority date for domestic and international students. Application fee: $55. Electronic applications accepted. *Financial support:* In 2009–10, 12 students received support, including fellowships with tuition reimbursements available (averaging $29,781 per year), research assistantships with tuition reimbursements available (averaging $29,781 per year); institutionally sponsored loans, scholarships/grants, traineeships, and health care benefits also available. Financial award applicants required to submit FAFSA. *Faculty research:* Ecological physiology, evolution of fossil reptiles, vertebrate paleontology. *Unit head:* Dr. Robert Ho, Chairman, 773-834-8423, Fax: 773-702-0037, E-mail: rkh@uchicago.edu. *Application contact:* Jeffrey Heller, Project Assistant III, 773-702-9011, Fax: 773-702-0037, E-mail: jheller@uchicago.edu.

University of Connecticut, Graduate School, College of Liberal Arts and Sciences, Department of Ecology and Evolutionary Biology, Field of Zoology, Storrs, CT 06269. Offers MS, PhD. *Faculty:* 17 full-time (4 women). *Students:* 5 full-time (3 women), 1 international. Average age 34. 8 applicants, 13% accepted, 0 enrolled. In 2009, 1 doctorate awarded. Terminal master's awarded for partial completion of doctoral program. *Degree requirements:* For master's, comprehensive exam; for doctorate, thesis/dissertation. *Entrance requirements:* For master's and doctorate, GRE General Test, GRE Subject Test. Additional exam requirements/recommendations for international students: Required—TOEFL (minimum score 550 paper-based; 213 computer-based). *Application deadline:* For fall admission, 2/1 priority date for domestic students, 2/1 for international students; for spring admission, 11/1 for domestic students, 10/1 for international students. Applications are processed on a rolling basis. Application fee: $55. Electronic applications accepted. *Expenses:* Tuition, state resident: full-time $4725; part-time $525 per credit. Tuition, nonresident: full-time $12,267; part-time $1363 per credit. Required fees: $346 per semester. Tuition and fees vary according to course load. *Financial support:* In 2009–10, 1 research assistantship with full tuition reimbursement, 4 teaching assistantships with full tuition reimbursements were awarded; fellowships, Federal Work-Study, scholarships/grants, health care benefits, and unspecified assistantships also available. Financial award application deadline: 2/1; financial award applicants required to submit FAFSA. *Unit head:* Kentwood Wells, Head, 860-486-4319, Fax: 860-486-6364, E-mail: kentwood.wells@uconn.edu. *Application contact:* Anne St. Onje, Graduate Coordinator, 860-486-4314, Fax: 860-486-3943, E-mail: anne.st_onje@uconn.edu.

University of Florida, Graduate School, College of Liberal Arts and Sciences, Department of Zoology, Gainesville, FL 32611. Offers MS, MST, PhD. *Degree requirements:* For master's, thesis or alternative; for doctorate, one foreign language, thesis/dissertation. *Entrance requirements:* For master's and doctorate, GRE General Test, minimum GPA of 3.0. Electronic applications accepted. *Faculty research:* Behavior, ecology, evolutionary biology, comparative physiology.

University of Guelph, Graduate Program Services, College of Biological Science, Department of Integrative Biology, Botany and Zoology, Guelph, ON N1G 2W1, Canada. Offers botany (M Sc, PhD); zoology (M Sc, PhD). Part-time programs available. *Degree requirements:* For master's, thesis, research proposal; for doctorate, thesis/dissertation, research proposal, qualifying exam. *Entrance requirements:* For master's, minimum B average during previous 2 years of course work. Additional exam requirements/recommendations for international students: Required—TOEFL (minimum score 550 paper-based; 213 computer-based), IELTS (minimum score 6.5). Electronic applications accepted. *Faculty research:* Aquatic science, environmental physiology, parasitology, wildlife biology, management.

University of Hawaii at Manoa, Graduate Division, College of Natural Sciences, Department of Zoology, Honolulu, HI 96822. Offers MS, PhD. Part-time programs available. *Faculty:* 39 full-time (8 women), 7 part-time/adjunct (2 women). *Students:* 93 full-time (48 women), 8 part-time (2 women); includes 22 minority (18 Asian Americans or Pacific Islanders, 4 Hispanic Americans), 8 international. Average age 28. 85 applicants, 34% accepted, 26 enrolled. In 2009, 7 master's, 14 doctorates awarded. *Degree requirements:* For master's, one foreign language, thesis optional; for doctorate, one foreign language, comprehensive exam, thesis/dissertation, seminar. *Entrance requirements:* For master's and doctorate, GRE General Test, GRE Subject Test. Additional exam requirements/recommendations for international students: Required—TOEFL (minimum score 600 paper-based; 250 computer-based; 100 iBT), IELTS (minimum score 7). *Application deadline:* For fall admission, 12/31 for domestic and international students. Applications are processed on a rolling basis. Application fee: $60. *Expenses:* Tuition, state resident: full-time $8900; part-time $372 per credit. Tuition, nonresident: full-time $21,400; part-time $898 per credit. Required fees: $207 per semester. *Financial support:* In 2009–10, 1 student received support, including 10 fellowships (averaging $6,560 per year), 50 research assistantships (averaging $20,734 per year), 24 teaching assistantships (averaging $15,875 per year); tuition waivers (full) also available. Financial award application deadline: 2/1. *Faculty research:* Molecular evolution, reproductive biology, animal behavior, conservation biology, avian biology. Total annual research expenditures: $231,000. *Application contact:* Leslie E. Watling, Graduate Chairperson, 808-956-8617, Fax: 808-956-9812, E-mail: watling@hawaii.edu.

University of Illinois at Urbana–Champaign, Graduate College, College of Liberal Arts and Sciences, School of Integrative Biology, Department of Animal Biology, Champaign, IL 61820. Offers animal biology (ecology, ethology and evolution) (MS, PhD). *Faculty:* 10 full-time (5 women). *Students:* 10 full-time (6 women), 4 part-time (2 women); includes 1 minority (Asian American or Pacific Islander), 3 international. 13 applicants, 15% accepted, 1 enrolled. In 2009, 1 doctorate awarded. *Entrance requirements:* For master's and doctorate, GRE. Additional exam requirements/recommendations for international students: Required—TOEFL (minimum score 570 paper-based; 230 computer-based; 88 iBT). *Application deadline:* Applications are processed on a rolling basis. Application fee: $60 ($75 for international students). Electronic applications accepted. *Financial support:* In 2009–10, 2 fellowships, 3 research assistantships, 11 teaching assistantships were awarded; tuition waivers (full and partial) also available. *Unit head:* Ken Paige, Head, 217-244-6606, Fax: 217-244-4565, E-mail: k-paige@illinois.edu. *Application contact:* Kathy Jennings, Office Support Specialist, 217-333-7801, Fax: 217-244-4565, E-mail: ab@life.uiuc.edu.

University of Maine, Graduate School, College of Natural Sciences, Forestry, and Agriculture, Department of Biological Sciences, Program in Zoology, Orono, ME 04469. Offers MS, PhD. *Faculty:* 15 full-time (4 women). *Students:* 3 full-time (2 women), 1 part-time (0 women). Average age 26. 9 applicants, 0% accepted, 0 enrolled. In 2009, 2 master's, 1 doctorate awarded. Terminal master's awarded for partial completion of doctoral program. *Degree requirements:* For master's, variable foreign language requirement, thesis; for doctorate, one foreign language, thesis/dissertation. *Entrance requirements:* For master's and doctorate, GRE General Test. Additional exam requirements/recommendations for international students: Required—TOEFL. *Application deadline:* For fall admission, 2/1 priority date for domestic students. Applications are processed on a rolling basis. Application fee: $65. Electronic applications accepted. *Financial support:* Career-related internships or fieldwork available. Financial award application deadline: 3/1. *Unit head:* Dr. Stellos Tavantiz, Coordinator, 207-581-2986. *Application contact:* Scott G. Delcourt, Associate Dean of the Graduate School, 207-581-3291, Fax: 207-581-3232, E-mail: graduate@maine.edu.

University of Manitoba, Faculty of Graduate Studies, Faculty of Science, Department of Biological Sciences, Winnipeg, MB R3T 2N2, Canada. Offers botany (M Sc, PhD); ecology (M Sc, PhD); zoology (M Sc, PhD).

Zoology

The University of Montana, Graduate School, College of Arts and Sciences, Division of Biological Sciences, Program in Organismal Biology and Ecology, Missoula, MT 59812-0002. Offers MS, PhD. Terminal master's awarded for partial completion of doctoral program. *Degree requirements:* For master's, one foreign language, thesis; for doctorate, 2 foreign languages, thesis/dissertation. *Entrance requirements:* For master's and doctorate, GRE General Test. *Faculty research:* Conservation biology, ecology and behavior, evolutionary genetics, avian biology.

University of New Hampshire, Graduate School, College of Life Sciences and Agriculture, Department of Biological Sciences, Program in Zoology, Durham, NH 03824. Offers MS, PhD. Part-time programs available. *Faculty:* 25 full-time. *Students:* 16 full-time (9 women), 18 part-time (12 women), 2 international. Average age 31. 18 applicants, 39% accepted, 4 enrolled. In 2009, 6 master's, 1 doctorate awarded. Terminal master's awarded for partial completion of doctoral program. *Degree requirements:* For master's, thesis; for doctorate, one foreign language, thesis/dissertation. *Entrance requirements:* For master's and doctorate, GRE General Test, GRE Subject Test. Additional exam requirements/recommendations for international students: Required—TOEFL (minimum score 550 paper-based; 213 computer-based; 80 iBT). *Application deadline:* For fall admission, 6/1 priority date for domestic students, 4/1 for international students; for spring admission, 12/1 for domestic students. Applications are processed on a rolling basis. Application fee: $65. Electronic applications accepted. *Expenses:* Tuition, state resident: full-time $10,380; part-time $577 per credit hour. Tuition, nonresident: full-time $24,350; part-time $1002 per credit hour. Required fees: $1550; $387.50 per semester. Tuition and fees vary according to course load and program. *Financial support:* In 2009–10, 29 students received support, including 1 fellowship, 11 research assistantships, 14 teaching assistantships; career-related internships or fieldwork, Federal Work-Study, scholarships/grants, and tuition waivers (full and partial) also available. Support available to part-time students. Financial award application deadline: 2/15. *Faculty research:* Behavior development, ecology, endocrinology, fisheries, invertebrates. *Unit head:* Dr. Christopher Neefus, Chairperson, 603-862-2105. *Application contact:* Diane Lavalliere, Administrative Assistant, 603-862-2100, E-mail: zoology.dept@unh.edu.

University of North Dakota, Graduate School, College of Arts and Sciences, Department of Biology, Grand Forks, ND 58202. Offers botany (MS, PhD); ecology (MS, PhD); entomology (MS, PhD); environmental biology (MS, PhD); fisheries/wildlife (MS, PhD); genetics (MS, PhD); zoology (MS, PhD). Terminal master's awarded for partial completion of doctoral program. *Degree requirements:* For master's, thesis, final exam; for doctorate, comprehensive exam, thesis/dissertation, final exam. *Entrance requirements:* For master's, GRE General Test, GRE Subject Test, minimum GPA of 3.0; for doctorate, GRE General Test, GRE Subject Test, minimum GPA of 3.5. Additional exam requirements/recommendations for international students: Required—TOEFL (minimum score 550 paper-based; 213 computer-based; 79 iBT), IELTS (minimum score 6.5). Electronic applications accepted. *Faculty research:* Population biology, wildlife ecology, RNA processing, hormonal control of behavior.

University of Oklahoma, Graduate College, College of Arts and Sciences, Department of Zoology, Norman, OK 73019. Offers cellular and behavioral neurobiology (PhD); ecology and evolutionary biology (PhD); zoology (M Nat Sci, MS, PhD). *Faculty:* 39 full-time (11 women), 3 part-time/adjunct (1 woman). *Students:* 47 full-time (26 women), 4 part-time (1 woman); includes 2 minority (both Asian Americans or Pacific Islanders), 15 international. 18 applicants, 72% accepted, 7 enrolled. In 2009, 6 master's, 5 doctorates awarded. *Degree requirements:* For master's, thesis defense; for doctorate, dissertation defense, general exam. *Entrance requirements:* For master's and doctorate, GRE General Test, GRE Subject Test, 3 letters of recommendation. Additional exam requirements/recommendations for international students: Required—TOEFL (minimum score 550 paper-based; 213 computer-based). *Application deadline:* For fall admission, 12/15 for domestic students, 4/1 for international students; for spring admission, 10/15 for domestic students, 9/1 for international students. Applications are processed on a rolling basis. Application fee: $40 ($90 for international students). Electronic applications accepted. *Expenses:* Tuition, state resident: full-time $3744; part-time $156 per credit hour. Tuition, nonresident: full-time $13,577; part-time $565.70 per credit hour. Required fees: $2415; $90.10 per credit hour. *Financial support:* In 2009–10, 3 fellowships with tuition reimbursements (averaging $4,667 per year), 12 research assistantships with tuition reimbursements (averaging $17,232 per year), 31 teaching assistantships (averaging $14,072 per year) were awarded; scholarships/grants, health care benefits, and unspecified assistantships also available. Financial award applicants required to submit FAFSA. *Faculty research:* Cell signaling, ecology and evolution biology, neurobiology, behavioral ecology, development. Total annual research expenditures: $1.3 million. *Unit head:* Bill Matthews, Chair, 405-325-4821, Fax: 405-325-6202, E-mail: wmatthews@ou.edu. *Application contact:* Dr. Rosemary Knapp, Associate Professor and Director of Graduate Studies, 405-325-4389, Fax: 405-325-6202, E-mail: rknapp@ou.edu.

The University of Western Ontario, Faculty of Graduate Studies, Biosciences Division, Department of Zoology, London, ON N6A 5B8, Canada. Offers M Sc, PhD. *Degree requirements:* For master's, thesis; for doctorate, thesis/dissertation.

University of Wisconsin–Madison, Graduate School, College of Letters and Science, Department of Zoology, Madison, WI 53706-1380. Offers MA, MS, PhD. Part-time programs available. *Degree requirements:* For master's, thesis; for doctorate, one foreign language, thesis/dissertation. *Entrance requirements:* For master's and doctorate, GRE General Test. Additional exam requirements/recommendations for international students: Required—TOEFL. Electronic applications accepted. *Expenses:* Tuition, state resident: part-time $594 per credit. Tuition, nonresident: part-time $1504 per credit. Required fees: $65 per credit. Tuition and fees vary according to course load, program and reciprocity agreements. *Faculty research:* Developmental biology, ecology, neurobiology, aquatic ecology, animal behavior.

University of Wisconsin–Oshkosh, The Office of Graduate Studies, College of Letters and Science, Department of Biology and Microbiology, Oshkosh, WI 54901. Offers biology (MS), including botany, microbiology, zoology. *Degree requirements:* For master's, comprehensive exam, thesis. *Entrance requirements:* For master's, GRE General Test, minimum GPA of 3.0, BS in biology. Additional exam requirements/recommendations for international students: Required—TOEFL (minimum score 550 paper-based; 213 computer-based; 79 iBT). Electronic applications accepted.

University of Wyoming, College of Arts and Sciences, Department of Zoology and Physiology, Laramie, WY 82070. Offers MS, PhD. Part-time programs available. *Degree requirements:* For master's, comprehensive exam (for some programs), thesis; for doctorate, comprehensive exam (for some programs), thesis/dissertation. *Entrance requirements:* For master's and doctorate, GRE General Test, minimum GPA of 3.0. Additional exam requirements/recommendations for international students: Required—TOEFL. Electronic applications accepted. *Faculty research:* Cell biology, ecology/wildlife, organismal physiology, zoology.

Virginia Polytechnic Institute and State University, Graduate School, College of Science, Department of Biological Sciences, Blacksburg, VA 24061. Offers botany (MS, PhD); ecology and evolutionary biology (MS, PhD); genetics and developmental biology (MS, PhD); microbiology (MS, PhD); zoology (MS, PhD). *Faculty:* 42 full-time (11 women). *Students:* 76 full-time (45 women), 5 part-time (1 woman); includes 28 minority (23 American Indian/Alaska Native, 2 Asian Americans or Pacific Islanders, 3 Hispanic Americans). Average age 28. 117 applicants, 15% accepted, 15 enrolled. In 2009, 11 master's, 11 doctorates awarded. *Entrance requirements:* For master's and doctorate, GRE, GMAT. Additional exam requirements/recommendations for international students: Required—TOEFL (minimum score 550 paper-based; 213 computer-based). *Application deadline:* For fall admission, 5/15 for international students; for spring admission, 10/15 for international students. Applications are processed on a rolling basis. Application fee: $65. Electronic applications accepted. *Expenses:* Tuition, area resident: Full-time $10,228; part-time $459 per credit hour. Tuition, nonresident: full-time $17,892; part-time $865 per credit hour. Required fees: $1966; $451 per semester. *Financial support:* In 2009–10, 37 research assistantships with full tuition reimbursements (averaging $17,929 per year), 41 teaching assistantships with full tuition reimbursements (averaging $17,344 per year) were awarded; career-related internships or fieldwork, Federal Work-Study, scholarships/grants, and unspecified assistantships also available. Financial award application deadline: 1/15. *Faculty research:* Freshwater ecology, cell cycle regulation, behavioral ecology, motor proteins. Total annual research expenditures: $4.8 million. *Unit head:* Dr. Bob H. Jones, Dean, 540-231-9514, Fax: 540-231-9307, E-mail: rhjones@vt.edu. *Application contact:* Erik Nilsen, Information Contact, 540-231-5671, Fax: 540-231-9307, E-mail: enilsen@vt.edu.

Washington State University, Graduate School, College of Sciences, School of Biological Sciences, Department of Zoology, Pullman, WA 99164. Offers MS, PhD. *Faculty:* 33. *Students:* 27 full-time (13 women), 1 international. Average age 30. 40 applicants, 20% accepted, 8 enrolled. In 2009, 4 master's, 4 doctorates awarded. *Degree requirements:* For master's, comprehensive exam (for some programs), thesis (for some programs), oral exam; for doctorate, comprehensive exam, thesis/dissertation, oral exam, written exam. *Entrance requirements:* For master's and doctorate, GRE General Test, GRE Subject Test, three letters of recommendation, official transcripts from each university-level school attended, minimum GPA of 3.0. Additional exam requirements/recommendations for international students: Required—TOEFL, IELTS. *Application deadline:* For fall admission, 1/10 priority date for domestic students, 1/10 for international students; for spring admission, 7/1 for domestic and international students. Applications are processed on a rolling basis. Application fee: $50. *Financial support:* In 2009–10, 4 fellowships (averaging $4,500 per year), 3 research assistantships with full and partial tuition reimbursements (averaging $13,917 per year), 21 teaching assistantships with full and partial tuition reimbursements (averaging $13,056 per year) were awarded; Federal Work-Study, institutionally sponsored loans, and tuition waivers (partial) also available. Financial award application deadline: 4/1; financial award applicants required to submit FAFSA. *Unit head:* Dr. Gary H. Thorgaard, Director, 509-335-7438, Fax: 509-335-3184, E-mail: thorglab@wsu.edu. *Application contact:* Graduate School Admissions, 800-GRADWSU, Fax: 509-335-1949, E-mail: gradsch@wsu.edu.

Western Illinois University, School of Graduate Studies, College of Arts and Sciences, Department of Biological Sciences, Macomb, IL 61455-1390. Offers biological sciences (MS); environmental geographic information systems (Certificate); zoo and aquarium studies (Certificate). Part-time programs available. *Students:* 62 full-time (43 women), 28 part-time (17 women); includes 6 minority (2 African Americans, 2 Asian Americans or Pacific Islanders, 2 Hispanic Americans), 10 international. Average age 26. 53 applicants, 72% accepted. In 2009, 25 master's, 15 other advanced degrees awarded. *Degree requirements:* For master's, thesis or alternative. *Entrance requirements:* Additional exam requirements/recommendations for international students: Required—TOEFL (minimum score 550 paper-based; 213 computer-based; 80 iBT). *Application deadline:* Applications are processed on a rolling basis. Application fee: $30. Electronic applications accepted. *Expenses:* Tuition, state resident: full-time $4486; part-time $249.21 per credit hour. Tuition, nonresident: full-time $8972; part-time $498.42 per credit hour. Required fees: $72.62 per credit hour. *Financial support:* In 2009–10, 34 students received support, including 16 research assistantships with full tuition reimbursements available (averaging $7,280 per year), 18 teaching assistantships with full tuition reimbursements available (averaging $8,400 per year). Financial award applicants required to submit FAFSA. *Unit head:* Dr. Michael Romano, Chairperson, 309-298-1546. *Application contact:* Evelyn Hoing, Assistant Director of Graduate Studies, 309-298-1806, Fax: 309-298-2345, E-mail: grad-office@wiu.edu.

APPENDIXES

APPENDIXES

Institutional Changes
Since the 2010 Edition

Following is an alphabetical listing of institutions that have recently closed, merged with other institutions, or changed their names or status. In the case of a name change, the former name appears first, followed by the new name.

Agnes Scott College (Decatur, GA): no longer offers graduate degrees

American Graduate School of International Relations and Diplomacy (Paris, France): name changed to American Graduate School in Paris

Antioch University McGregor (Yellow Springs, OH): name changed to Antioch University Midwest

Arizona State University at the Downtown Phoenix Campus (Phoenix, AZ): will be included with main campus Arizona State University (Tempe, AZ) by request from the institution

Arizona State University at the Polytechnic Campus (Mesa, AZ): will be included with main campus Arizona State University (Tempe, AZ) by request from the institution

Arizona State University at the West campus (Phoenix, AZ): [will be included with main campus Arizona State University (Tempe, AZ) by request from the institution

Arkansas State University (State University, AR): name changed to Arkansas State University–Jonesboro

Asbury College (Wilmore, KY): name changed to Asbury University

Australasian College of Health Sciences (Portland, OR): name changed to American College of Healthcare Sciences

Baker College Center for Graduate Studies (Flint, MI): name changed to Baker College Center for Graduate Studies–Online

Baltimore Hebrew University (Baltimore, MD): now a unit of Towson University (Towson, MD)

Beacon University (Columbus, GA): closed

Belhaven College (Jackson, MS): name changed to Belhaven University

Beth Benjamin Academy of Connecticut (Stamford, CT): no longer offers graduate degrees

Bethel College (McKenzie, TN): name changed to Bethel University

Bridgewater State College (Bridgewater, MA): name changed to Bridgewater State University

British American College London (London, United Kingdom): name changed to Regent's American College London

The Chicago School of Professional Psychology: Downtown Los Angeles Campus (Los Angeles, CA): name changed to The Chicago School of Professional Psychology at Downtown Los Angeles

The Chicago School of Professional Psychology: Grayslake Campus (Grayslake, IL): name changed to The Chicago School of Professional Psychology at Grayslake

The Cleveland Institute of Art (Cleveland, OH): no longer offers graduate degrees

Coleman College (San Diego, CA): name changed to Coleman University

Columbia Union College (Takoma Park, MD): name changed to Washington Adventist University

Dell'Arte School of Physical Theatre (Blue Lake, CA): name changed to Dell'Arte International School of Physical Theatre

DeVry University (San Francisco, CA): closed

Fitchburg State College (Fitchburg, MA): name changed to Fitchburg State University

Framingham State College (Framingham, MA): name changed to Framingham State University

George Meany Center for Labor Studies–The National Labor College (Silver Spring, MD): name changed to National Labor College

Hebrew Theological College (Skokie, IL): no longer offers graduate degrees

International University in Geneva (Geneva, Switzerland): no longer accredited by agency recognized by USDE or CHEA

Joint Military Intelligence College (Washington, DC): name changed to National Defense Intelligence College

Kent State University, Stark Campus (Canton, OH): name changed to Kent State University at Stark

Lancaster Bible College (Lancaster, PA): name changed to Lancaster Bible College & Graduate School

Leadership Institute of Seattle (Kenmore, WA): is now part of Saybrook University (San Francisco, CA)

New England School of Law (Boston, MA): name changed to New England Law-Boston

Otterbein College (Westerville, OH): name changed to Otterbein University

Pepperdine University (Los Angeles, CA): will be included with Pepperdine University (Malibu, CA) by request from the institution

The Protestant Episcopal Theological Seminary in Virginia (Alexandria, VA): name changed to Virginia Theological Seminary

Reinhardt College (Waleska, GA): name changed to Reinhardt University

Robert Morris College (Chicago, IL): name changed to Robert Morris University Illinois

St. Petersburg Theological Seminary (St. Petersburg, FL): no longer accredited by agency recognized by USDE or CHEA

Saybrook Graduate School and Research Center (San Francisco, CA): name changed to Saybrook University

Shorter College (Rome, GA): name changed to Shorter University

Southeastern University (Washington, DC): closed

Southern New England School of Law (North Dartmouth, MA): is now part of University of Massachusetts Dartmouth (North Dartmouth, MA)

Trinity Episcopal School for Ministry (Ambridge, PA): name changed to Trinity School for Ministry

University of Missouri–Columbia (Columbia, MO): name changed to University of Missouri

University of Phoenix–Renton Learning Center (Renton, WA): name changed to University of Phoenix–Western Washington Campus

University of Phoenix–Wisconsin Campus (Brookfield, WI): now listed as University of Phoenix–Madison Campus (Madison, WI)

West Liberty State University (West Liberty, WV): name changed to West Liberty University

World Medicine Institute: College of Acupuncture and Herbal Medicine (Honolulu, HI): name changed to World Medicine Institute of Acupuncture and Herbal Medicine

Abbreviations Used in the Guides

The following list includes abbreviations of degree names used in the profiles in the 2011 edition of the guides. Because some degrees (e.g., Doctor of Education) can be abbreviated in more than one way (e.g., D.Ed. or Ed.D.), and because the abbreviations used in the guides reflect the preferences of the individual colleges and universities, the list may include two or more abbreviations for a single degree.

Degrees

A Mus D	Doctor of Musical Arts
AC	Advanced Certificate
AD	Artist's Diploma Doctor of Arts
ADP	Artist's Diploma
Adv C	Advanced Certificate
Adv M	Advanced Master
AGC	Advanced Graduate Certificate
AGSC	Advanced Graduate Specialist Certificate
ALM	Master of Liberal Arts
AM	Master of Arts
AMBA	Accelerated Master of Business Administration
AMRS	Master of Arts in Religious Studies
APC	Advanced Professional Certificate
App Sc	Applied Scientist
App Sc D	Doctor of Applied Science
Au D	Doctor of Audiology
B Th	Bachelor of Theology
CAES	Certificate of Advanced Educational Specialization
CAGS	Certificate of Advanced Graduate Studies
CAL	Certificate in Applied Linguistics
CALS	Certificate of Advanced Liberal Studies
CAMS	Certificate of Advanced Management Studies
CAPS	Certificate of Advanced Professional Studies
CAS	Certificate of Advanced Studies
CASPA	Certificate of Advanced Study in Public Administration
CASR	Certificate in Advanced Social Research
CATS	Certificate of Achievement in Theological Studies
CBHS	Certificate in Basic Health Sciences
CBS	Graduate Certificate in Biblical Studies
CCJA	Certificate in Criminal Justice Administration
CCSA	Certificate in Catholic School Administration
CCTS	Certificate in Clinical and Translational Science
CE	Civil Engineer
CEM	Certificate of Environmental Management
CET	Certificate in Educational Technologies
CGS	Certificate of Graduate Studies
Ch E	Chemical Engineer

CM	Certificate in Management
CMH	Certificate in Medical Humanities
CMM	Master of Church Ministries
CMS	Certificate in Ministerial Studies
CNM	Certificate in Nonprofit Management
CP	Certificate in Performance
CPASF	Certificate Program for Advanced Study in Finance
CPC	Certificate in Professional Counseling Certificate in Publication and Communication
CPH	Certificate in Public Health
CPM	Certificate in Public Management
CPS	Certificate of Professional Studies
CScD	Doctor of Clinical Science
CSD	Certificate in Spiritual Direction
CSS	Certificate of Special Studies
CTS	Certificate of Theological Studies
CURP	Certificate in Urban and Regional Planning
D Admin	Doctor of Administration
D Arch	Doctor of Architecture
D Com	Doctor of Commerce
D Div	Doctor of Divinity
D Ed	Doctor of Education
D Ed Min	Doctor of Educational Ministry
D Eng	Doctor of Engineering
D Engr	Doctor of Engineering
D Env	Doctor of Environment
D Env M	Doctor of Environmental Management
D Law	Doctor of Law
D Litt	Doctor of Letters
D Med Sc	Doctor of Medical Science
D Min	Doctor of Ministry
D Miss	Doctor of Missiology
D Mus	Doctor of Music
D Mus A	Doctor of Musical Arts
D Phil	Doctor of Philosophy
D Ps	Doctor of Psychology
D Sc	Doctor of Science
D Sc D	Doctor of Science in Dentistry
D Sc IS	Doctor of Science in Information Systems
D Sc PA	Doctor of Science in Physician Assistant Studies
D Th	Doctor of Theology
D Th P	Doctor of Practical Theology
DA	Doctor of Accounting Doctor of Arts
DA Ed	Doctor of Arts in Education

DAH	Doctor of Arts in Humanities
DAOM	Doctorate in Acupuncture and Oriental Medicine
DAST	Diploma of Advanced Studies in Teaching
DBA	Doctor of Business Administration
DBL	Doctor of Business Leadership
DBS	Doctor of Buddhist Studies
DC	Doctor of Chiropractic
DCC	Doctor of Computer Science
DCD	Doctor of Communications Design
DCL	Doctor of Civil Law Doctor of Comparative Law
DCM	Doctor of Church Music
DCN	Doctor of Clinical Nutrition
DCS	Doctor of Computer Science
DDN	Diplôme du Droit Notarial
DDS	Doctor of Dental Surgery
DE	Doctor of Education Doctor of Engineering
DED	Doctor of Economic Development
DEIT	Doctor of Educational Innovation and Technology
DEL	Doctor of Executive Leadership
DEM	Doctor of Educational Ministry
DEPD	Diplôme Études Spécialisées
DES	Doctor of Engineering Science
DESS	Diplôme Études Supérieures Spécialisées
DFA	Doctor of Fine Arts
DGP	Diploma in Graduate and Professional Studies
DH Ed	Doctor of Health Education
DH Sc	Doctor of Health Sciences
DHA	Doctor of Health Administration
DHCE	Doctor of Health Care Ethics
DHL	Doctor of Hebrew Letters Doctor of Hebrew Literature
DHS	Doctor of Health Science Doctor of Human Services
DHSc	Doctor of Health Science
Dip CS	Diploma in Christian Studies
DIT	Doctor of Industrial Technology
DJ Ed	Doctor of Jewish Education
DJS	Doctor of Jewish Studies
DLS	Doctor of Liberal Studies
DM	Doctor of Management Doctor of Music
DMA	Doctor of Musical Arts
DMD	Doctor of Dental Medicine
DME	Doctor of Manufacturing Management Doctor of Music Education
DMEd	Doctor of Music Education
DMFT	Doctor of Marital and Family Therapy
DMH	Doctor of Medical Humanities
DML	Doctor of Modern Languages
DMM	Doctor of Music Ministry
DMP	Doctorate in Medical Physics
DMPNA	Doctor of Management Practice in Nurse Anesthesia
DN Sc	Doctor of Nursing Science
DNAP	Doctor of Nurse Anesthesia Practice
DNP	Doctor of Nursing Practice
DNS	Doctor of Nursing Science
DO	Doctor of Osteopathy
DPA	Doctor of Public Administration
DPC	Doctor of Pastoral Counseling
DPDS	Doctor of Planning and Development Studies
DPH	Doctor of Public Health
DPM	Doctor of Plant Medicine Doctor of Podiatric Medicine
DPPD	Doctor of Policy, Planning, and Development
DPS	Doctor of Professional Studies
DPT	Doctor of Physical Therapy
DPTSc	Doctor of Physical Therapy Science
Dr DES	Doctor of Design
Dr PH	Doctor of Public Health
Dr Sc PT	Doctor of Science in Physical Therapy
DRSc	Doctor of Regulatory Science
DS	Doctor of Science
DS Sc	Doctor of Social Science
DSJS	Doctor of Science in Jewish Studies
DSL	Doctor of Strategic Leadership
DSN	Doctor of Science in Nursing
DSW	Doctor of Social Work
DTL	Doctor of Talmudic Law
DV Sc	Doctor of Veterinary Science
DVM	Doctor of Veterinary Medicine
EAA	Engineer in Aeronautics and Astronautics
ECS	Engineer in Computer Science
Ed D	Doctor of Education
Ed DCT	Doctor of Education in College Teaching
Ed M	Master of Education
Ed S	Specialist in Education
Ed Sp	Specialist in Education
Ed Sp PTE	Specialist in Education in Professional Technical Education
EDM	Executive Doctorate in Management
EDSPC	Education Specialist
EE	Electrical Engineer
EJD	Executive Juris Doctor
EMBA	Executive Master of Business Administration
EMFA	Executive Master of Forensic Accounting

EMHA	Executive Master of Health Administration
EMIB	Executive Master of International Business
EML	Executive Master of Leadership
EMPA	Executive Master of Public Administration Executive Master of Public Affairs
EMS	Executive Master of Science
EMTM	Executive Master of Technology Management
Eng	Engineer
Eng Sc D	Doctor of Engineering Science
Engr	Engineer
Ex Doc	Executive Doctor of Pharmacy
Exec Ed D	Executive Doctor of Education
Exec MBA	Executive Master of Business Administration
Exec MPA	Executive Master of Public Administration
Exec MPH	Executive Master of Public Health
Exec MS	Executive Master of Science
G Dip	Graduate Diploma
GBC	Graduate Business Certificate
GCE	Graduate Certificate in Education
GDM	Graduate Diploma in Management
GDPA	Graduate Diploma in Public Administration
GDRE	Graduate Diploma in Religious Education
GEMBA	Global Executive Master of Business Administration
GEMPA	Gulf Executive Master of Public Administration
GM Acc	Graduate Master of Accountancy
GMBA	Global Master of Business Administration
GPD	Graduate Performance Diploma
GSS	Graduate Special Certificate for Students in Special Situations
IEMBA	International Executive Master of Business Administration
IM Acc	Integrated Master of Accountancy
IMA	Interdisciplinary Master of Arts
IMBA	International Master of Business Administration
IMES	International Masters in Environmental Studies
Ingeniero	Engineer
JCD	Doctor of Canon Law
JCL	Licentiate in Canon Law
JD	Juris Doctor
JSD	Doctor of Juridical Science Doctor of Jurisprudence Doctor of the Science of Law
JSM	Master of Science of Law
L Th	Licenciate in Theology
LL B	Bachelor of Laws
LL CM	Master of Laws in Comparative Law
LL D	Doctor of Laws
LL M	Master of Laws

LL M in Tax	Master of Laws in Taxation
LL M CL	Master of Laws (Common Law)
LL M/MBA	Master of Laws/Master of Business Administration
LL M/MNM	Master of Laws/Master of Nonprofit Management
M Ac	Master of Accountancy Master of Accounting Master of Acupuncture
M Ac OM	Master of Acupuncture and Oriental Medicine
M Acc	Master of Accountancy Master of Accounting
M Acct	Master of Accountancy Master of Accounting
M Accy	Master of Accountancy
M Actg	Master of Accounting
M Acy	Master of Accountancy
M Ad	Master of Administration
M Ad Ed	Master of Adult Education
M Adm	Master of Administration
M Adm Mgt	Master of Administrative Management
M Admin	Master of Administration
M ADU	Master of Architectural Design and Urbanism
M Adv	Master of Advertising
M Aero E	Master of Aerospace Engineering
M AEST	Master of Applied Environmental Science and Technology
M Ag	Master of Agriculture
M Ag Ed	Master of Agricultural Education
M Agr	Master of Agriculture
M Anesth Ed	Master of Anesthesiology Education
M App Comp Sc	Master of Applied Computer Science
M App St	Master of Applied Statistics
M Appl Stat	Master of Applied Statistics
M Aq	Master of Aquaculture
M Ar	Master of Architecture
M Arc	Master of Architecture
M Arch	Master of Architecture
M Arch I	Master of Architecture I
M Arch II	Master of Architecture II
M Arch E	Master of Architectural Engineering
M Arch H	Master of Architectural History
M Bioethics	Master in Bioethics
M Biomath	Master of Biomathematics
M Ch	Master of Chemistry
M Ch E	Master of Chemical Engineering
M Chem	Master of Chemistry
M Cl D	Master of Clinical Dentistry
M Cl Sc	Master of Clinical Science
M Comp E	Master of Computer Engineering
M Comp Sc	Master of Computer Science

M Coun	Master of Counseling
M Dent	Master of Dentistry
M Dent Sc	Master of Dental Sciences
M Des	Master of Design
M Des S	Master of Design Studies
M Div	Master of Divinity
M Ec	Master of Economics
M Econ	Master of Economics
M Ed	Master of Education
M Ed T	Master of Education in Teaching
M En	Master of Engineering
	Master of Environmental Science
M En S	Master of Environmental Sciences
M Eng	Master of Engineering
M Eng Mgt	Master of Engineering Management
M Engr	Master of Engineering
M Env	Master of Environment
M Env Des	Master of Environmental Design
M Env E	Master of Environmental Engineering
M Env Sc	Master of Environmental Science
M Fin	Master of Finance
M Geo E	Master of Geological Engineering
M Geoenv E	Master of Geoenvironmental Engineering
M Geog	Master of Geography
M Hum	Master of Humanities
M Hum Svcs	Master of Human Services
M IBD	Master of Integrated Building Delivery
M IDST	Master's in Interdisciplinary Studies
M Kin	Master of Kinesiology
M Land Arch	Master of Landscape Architecture
M Litt	Master of Letters
M Man	Master of Management
M Mat SE	Master of Material Science and Engineering
M Math	Master of Mathematics
M Med Sc	Master of Medical Science
M Mgmt	Master of Management
M Mgt	Master of Management
M Min	Master of Ministries
M Mtl E	Master of Materials Engineering
M Mu	Master of Music
M Mus	Master of Music
M Mus Ed	Master of Music Education
M Music	Master of Music
M Nat Sci	Master of Natural Science
M Oc E	Master of Oceanographic Engineering
M Pet E	Master of Petroleum Engineering
M Pharm	Master of Pharmacy
M Phil	Master of Philosophy
M Phil F	Master of Philosophical Foundations
M Pl	Master of Planning
M Plan	Master of Planning
M Pol	Master of Political Science
M Pr Met	Master of Professional Meteorology
M Prob S	Master of Probability and Statistics
M Psych	Master of Psychology
M Pub	Master of Publishing
M Rel	Master of Religion
M Sc	Master of Science
M Sc A	Master of Science (Applied)
M Sc AHN	Master of Science in Applied Human Nutrition
M Sc BMC	Master of Science in Biomedical Communications
M Sc CS	Master of Science in Computer Science
M Sc E	Master of Science in Engineering
M Sc Eng	Master of Science in Engineering
M Sc Engr	Master of Science in Engineering
M Sc F	Master of Science in Forestry
M Sc FE	Master of Science in Forest Engineering
M Sc Geogr	Master of Science in Geography
M Sc N	Master of Science in Nursing
M Sc OT	Master of Science in Occupational Therapy
M Sc P	Master of Science in Planning
M Sc Pl	Master of Science in Planning
M Sc PT	Master of Science in Physical Therapy
M Sc T	Master of Science in Teaching
M SEM	Master of Sustainable Environmental Management
M Serv Soc	Master of Social Service
M Soc	Master of Sociology
M Sp Ed	Master of Special Education
M Stat	Master of Statistics
M Sw En	Master of Software Engineering
M Sys Sc	Master of Systems Science
M Tax	Master of Taxation
M Tech	Master of Technology
M Th	Master of Theology
M Tox	Master of Toxicology
M Trans E	Master of Transportation Engineering
M Urb	Master of Urban Planning
M Vet Sc	Master of Veterinary Science
MA	Master of Administration
	Master of Arts
MA Comm	Master of Arts in Communication
MA Ed	Master of Arts in Education
MA Ed Ad	Master of Arts in Educational Administration
MA Ext	Master of Agricultural Extension
MA Islamic	Master of Arts in Islamic Studies

MA Military Studies	Master of Arts in Military Studies
MA Min	Master of Arts in Ministry
MA Miss	Master of Arts in Missiology
MA Past St	Master of Arts in Pastoral Studies
MA Ph	Master of Arts in Philosophy
MA Psych	Master of Arts in Psychology
MA Sc	Master of Applied Science
MA Sp	Master of Arts (Spirituality)
MA Strategic Intelligence	Master of Arts in Strategic Intelligence
MA Th	Master of Arts in Theology
MA-R	Master of Arts (Research)
MAA	Master of Administrative Arts Master of Applied Anthropology Master of Applied Arts Master of Arts in Administration
MAAAP	Master of Arts Administration and Policy
MAAE	Master of Arts in Art Education
MAAT	Master of Arts in Applied Theology Master of Arts in Art Therapy
MAB	Master of Agribusiness
MABC	Master of Arts in Biblical Counseling Master of Arts in Business Communication
MABE	Master of Arts in Bible Exposition
MABL	Master of Arts in Biblical Languages
MABM	Master of Agribusiness Management
MABS	Master of Arts in Biblical Studies
MABT	Master of Arts in Bible Teaching
MAC	Master of Accountancy Master of Accounting Master of Arts in Communication Master of Arts in Counseling
MACC	Master of Arts in Accountancy Master of Arts in Christian Counseling Master of Arts in Clinical Counseling
MACCM	Master of Arts in Church and Community Ministry
MACCT	Master of Accounting
MACE	Master of Arts in Christian Education
MACFM	Master of Arts in Children's and Family Ministry
MACH	Master of Arts in Church History
MACIS	Master of Accounting and Information Systems
MACJ	Master of Arts in Criminal Justice
MACL	Master of Arts in Christian Leadership
MACM	Master of Arts in Christian Ministries Master of Arts in Christian Ministry Master of Arts in Church Music Master of Arts in Counseling Ministries
MACN	Master of Arts in Counseling
MACO	Master of Arts in Counseling
MAcOM	Master of Acupuncture and Oriental Medicine
MACP	Master of Arts in Counseling Psychology
MACS	Master of Arts in Catholic Studies
MACSE	Master of Arts in Christian School Education
MACT	Master of Arts in Christian Thought Master of Arts in Communications and Technology
MAD	Master in Educational Institution Administration Master of Art and Design
MADR	Master of Arts in Dispute Resolution
MADS	Master of Animal and Dairy Science Master of Applied Disability Studies
MAE	Master of Aerospace Engineering Master of Agricultural Economics Master of Agricultural Education Master of Architectural Engineering Master of Art Education Master of Arts in Education Master of Arts in English Master of Automotive Engineering
MAECMS	Master of Aerospace Engineering in Composite Materials and Structures
MAEd	Master of Arts Education
MAEL	Master of Arts in Educational Leadership
MAEM	Master of Arts in Educational Ministries
MAEN	Master of Arts in English
MAEP	Master of Arts in Economic Policy
MAES	Master of Arts in Environmental Sciences
MAESL	Master of Arts in English as a Second Language
MAET	Master of Arts in English Teaching
MAF	Master of Arts in Finance
MAFE	Master of Arts in Financial Economics
MAFLL	Master of Arts in Foreign Language and Literature
MAFM	Master of Accounting and Financial Management
MAFS	Master of Arts in Family Studies
MAG	Master of Applied Geography
MAGU	Master of Urban Analysis and Management
MAH	Master of Arts in Humanities
MAHA	Master of Arts in Humanitarian Assistance Master of Arts in Humanitarian Studies
MAHCM	Master of Arts in Health Care Mission
MAHG	Master of American History and Government
MAHL	Master of Arts in Hebrew Letters
MAHN	Master of Applied Human Nutrition
MAHSR	Master of Applied Health Services Research
MAIA	Master of Arts in International Administration
MAIB	Master of Arts in International Business
MAICS	Master of Arts in Intercultural Studies
MAIDM	Master of Arts in Interior Design and Merchandising
MAIH	Master of Arts in Interdisciplinary Humanities
MAIPCR	Master of Arts in International Peace and Conflict Management
MAIR	Master of Arts in Industrial Relations

MAIS	Master of Arts in Intercultural Studies
	Master of Arts in Interdisciplinary Studies
	Master of Arts in International Studies
MAIT	Master of Administration in Information Technology
	Master of Applied Information Technology
MAJ	Master of Arts in Journalism
MAJ Ed	Master of Arts in Jewish Education
MAJCS	Master of Arts in Jewish Communal Service
MAJE	Master of Arts in Jewish Education
MAJS	Master of Arts in Jewish Studies
MAL	Master in Agricultural Leadership
MALA	Master of Arts in Liberal Arts
MALD	Master of Arts in Law and Diplomacy
MALED	Master of Arts in Literacy Education
MALER	Master of Arts in Labor and Employment Relations
MALM	Master of Applied Leadership and Management
	Master of Arts in Leadership Evangelical Mobilization
MALP	Master of Arts in Language Pedagogy
MALPS	Master of Arts in Liberal and Professional Studies
MALS	Master of Arts in Liberal Studies
MALT	Master of Arts in Learning and Teaching
MAM	Master of Acquisition Management
	Master of Agriculture and Management
	Master of Applied Mathematics
	Master of Arts in Management
	Master of Arts in Ministry
	Master of Arts Management
	Master of Avian Medicine
MAMB	Master of Applied Molecular Biology
MAMC	Master of Arts in Mass Communication
	Master of Arts in Ministry and Culture
	Master of Arts in Ministry for a Multicultural Church
MAME	Master of Arts in Missions/Evangelism
MAMFC	Master of Arts in Marriage and Family Counseling
MAMFCC	Master of Arts in Marriage, Family, and Child Counseling
MAMFT	Master of Arts in Marriage and Family Therapy
MAMM	Master of Arts in Ministry Management
MAMS	Master of Applied Mathematical Sciences
	Master of Arts in Ministerial Studies
	Master of Arts in Ministry and Spirituality
MAMT	Master of Arts in Mathematics Teaching
MAN	Master of Applied Nutrition
MANP	Master of Applied Natural Products
MANT	Master of Arts in New Testament
MAOM	Master of Acupuncture and Oriental Medicine
	Master of Arts in Organizational Management
MAOT	Master of Arts in Old Testament

MAP	Master of Applied Psychology
	Master of Arts in Planning
	Master of Public Administration
	Masters of Psychology
MAP Min	Master of Arts in Pastoral Ministry
MAPA	Master of Arts in Public Administration
MAPC	Master of Arts in Pastoral Counseling
MAPE	Master of Arts in Political Economy
MAPL	Master of Arts in Pastoral Leadership
MAPM	Master of Arts in Pastoral Ministry
	Master of Arts in Pastoral Music
	Master of Arts in Practical Ministry
MAPP	Master of Arts in Public Policy
MAPPS	Master of Arts in Asia Pacific Policy Studies
MAPS	Master of Arts in Pastoral Counseling/Spiritual Formation
	Master of Arts in Pastoral Studies
	Master of Arts in Public Service
MAPT	Master of Practical Theology
MAPW	Master of Arts in Professional Writing
MAR	Master of Arts in Religion
Mar Eng	Marine Engineer
MARC	Master of Arts in Rehabilitation Counseling
MARE	Master of Arts in Religious Education
MARL	Master of Arts in Religious Leadership
MARS	Master of Arts in Religious Studies
MAS	Master of Accounting Science
	Master of Actuarial Science
	Master of Administrative Science
	Master of Advanced Study
	Master of Aeronautical Science
	Master of American Studies
	Master of Applied Science
	Master of Applied Statistics
	Master of Architectural Studies
	Master of Archival Studies
MASA	Master of Advanced Studies in Architecture
MASD	Master of Arts in Spiritual Direction
MASE	Master of Arts in Special Education
MASF	Master of Arts in Spiritual Formation
MASJ	Master of Arts in Systems of Justice
MASL	Master of Arts in School Leadership
MASLA	Master of Advanced Studies in Landscape Architecture
MASM	Master of Aging Services Management
	Master of Arts in Specialized Ministries
MASP	Master of Applied Social Psychology
	Master of Arts in School Psychology
MASPAA	Master of Arts in Sports and Athletic Administration
MASS	Master of Applied Social Science
	Master of Arts in Social Science
MAST	Master of Arts in Science Teaching

MASW	Master of Aboriginal Social Work
MAT	Master of Arts in Teaching
	Master of Arts in Theology
	Master of Athletic Training
	Masters in Administration of Telecommunications
Mat E	Materials Engineer
MATCM	Master of Acupuncture and Traditional Chinese Medicine
MATDE	Master of Arts in Theology, Development, and Evangelism
MATDR	Master of Territorial Management and Regional Development
MATE	Master of Arts for the Teaching of English
MATESL	Master of Arts in Teaching English as a Second Language
MATESOL	Master of Arts in Teaching English to Speakers of Other Languages
MATF	Master of Arts in Teaching English as a Foreign Language/Intercultural Studies
MATFL	Master of Arts in Teaching Foreign Language
MATH	Master of Arts in Therapy
MATI	Master of Administration of Information Technology
MATL	Master of Arts in Teaching of Languages
	Master of Arts in Transformational Leadership
MATM	Master of Arts in Teaching of Mathematics
MATS	Master of Arts in Theological Studies
	Master of Arts in Transforming Spirituality
MATSL	Master of Arts in Teaching a Second Language
MAUA	Master of Arts in Urban Affairs
MAUD	Master of Arts in Urban Design
MAURP	Master of Arts in Urban and Regional Planning
MAW	Master of Arts in Worship
MAWL	Master of Arts in Worship Leadership
MAWSHP	Master of Arts in Worship
MAYM	Master of Arts in Youth Ministry
MB	Master of Bioinformatics
MBA	Master of Business Administration
MBA-EP	Master of Business Administration–Experienced Professionals
MBAA	Master of Business Administration in Aviation
MBAE	Master of Biological and Agricultural Engineering
	Master of Biosystems and Agricultural Engineering
MBAH	Master of Business Administration in Health
MBAi	Master of Business Administration–International
MBAICT	Master of Business Administration in Information and Communication Technology
MBAPA	Master of Business Administration–Physician Assistant
MBATM	Master of Business Administration in Technology Management
MBC	Master of Building Construction

MBE	Master of Bilingual Education
	Master of Bioengineering
	Master of Biological Engineering
	Master of Biomedical Engineering
	Master of Business and Engineering
	Master of Business Economics
	Master of Business Education
MBET	Master of Business, Entrepreneurship and Technology
MBiotech	Master of Biotechnology
MBIT	Master of Business Information Technology
MBL	Master of Business Law
	Master of Business Leadership
MBLE	Master in Business Logistics Engineering
MBMI	Master of Biomedical Imaging and Signals
MBMSE	Master of Business Management and Software Engineering
MBS	Master of Behavioral Science
	Master of Biblical Studies
	Master of Biological Science
	Master of Biomedical Sciences
	Master of Bioscience
	Master of Building Science
MBSI	Master of Business Information Science
MBT	Master of Biblical and Theological Studies
	Master of Biomedical Technology
	Master of Biotechnology
	Master of Business Taxation
MC	Master of Communication
	Master of Counseling
	Master of Cybersecurity
MC Ed	Master of Continuing Education
MC Sc	Master of Computer Science
MCA	Master of Arts in Applied Criminology
	Master of Commercial Aviation
MCAM	Master of Computational and Applied Mathematics
MCC	Master of Computer Science
MCCS	Master of Crop and Soil Sciences
MCD	Master of Communications Disorders
	Master of Community Development
MCE	Master in Electronic Commerce
	Master of Christian Education
	Master of Civil Engineering
	Master of Control Engineering
MCEM	Master of Construction Engineering Management
MCH	Master of Chemical Engineering
MCHE	Master of Chemical Engineering
MCIS	Master of Communication and Information Studies
	Master of Computer and Information Science
	Master of Computer Information Systems
MCIT	Master of Computer and Information Technology
MCJ	Master of Criminal Justice
MCJA	Master of Criminal Justice Administration

MCL	Master in Communication Leadership Master of Canon Law Master of Comparative Law	**MEA**	Master of Educational Administration Master of Engineering Administration
MCM	Master of Christian Ministry Master of Church Music Master of City Management Master of Communication Management Master of Community Medicine Master of Construction Management Master of Contract Management Masters of Corporate Media	**MEAP**	Master of Environmental Administration and Planning
		MEBT	Master in Electronic Business Technologies
		MEC	Master of Electronic Commerce
		MECE	Master of Electrical and Computer Engineering
		Mech E	Mechanical Engineer
		MED	Master of Education of the Deaf
MCMS	Master of Clinical Medical Science	**MEDS**	Master of Environmental Design Studies
MCP	Master in Science Master of City Planning Master of Community Planning Master of Counseling Psychology Master of Cytopathology Practice	**MEE**	Master in Education Master of Electrical Engineering Master of Energy Engineering Master of Environmental Engineering
		MEEM	Master of Environmental Engineering and Management
MCPC	Master of Arts in Chaplaincy and Pastoral Care	**MEENE**	Master of Engineering in Environmental Engineering
MCPD	Master of Community Planning and Development		
MCRP	Master of City and Regional Planning	**MEEP**	Master of Environmental and Energy Policy
MCRS	Master of City and Regional Studies	**MEERM**	Master of Earth and Environmental Resource Management
MCS	Master of Christian Studies Master of Clinical Science Master of Combined Sciences Master of Communication Studies Master of Computer Science Master of Consumer Science	**MEH**	Master in Humanistic Studies Master of Environmental Horticulture
		MEHS	Master of Environmental Health and Safety
		MEIM	Master of Entertainment Industry Management
MCSE	Master of Computer Science and Engineering	**MEL**	Master of Educational Leadership Master of English Literature
MCSL	Master of Catholic School Leadership		
MCSM	Master of Construction Science/Management	**MELP**	Master of Environmental Law and Policy
MCST	Master of Science in Computer Science and Information Technology	**MEM**	Master of Ecosystem Management Master of Electricity Markets Master of Engineering Management Master of Environmental Management Master of Marketing
MCTP	Master of Communication Technology and Policy		
MCTS	Master of Clinical and Translational Science		
MCVS	Master of Cardiovascular Science	**MEME**	Master of Engineering in Manufacturing Engineering Master of Engineering in Mechanical Engineering
MD	Doctor of Medicine		
MDA	Master of Development Administration Master of Dietetic Administration	**MEMS**	Master of Engineering in Manufacturing Systems
		MENG	Master of Arts in English
MDB	Master of Design-Build	**MENVEGR**	Master of Environmental Engineering
MDE	Master of Developmental Economics Master of Distance Education Master of the Education of the Deaf	**MEP**	Master of Engineering Physics
		MEPC	Master of Environmental Pollution Control
MDH	Master of Dental Hygiene	**MEPD**	Master of Education–Professional Development Master of Environmental Planning and Design
MDM	Master of Digital Media		
MDP	Master of Development Practice	**MEPM**	Master of Environmental Protection Management
MDR	Master of Dispute Resolution	**MER**	Master of Employment Relations
MDS	Master of Dental Surgery	**MES**	Master of Education and Science Master of Engineering Science Master of Environmenta and Sustainability Master of Environmental Science Master of Environmental Studies Master of Environmental Systems Master of Special Education
ME	Master of Education Master of Engineering Master of Entrepreneurship Master of Evangelism		
ME Sc	Master of Engineering Science		

MESM	Master of Environmental Science and Management
MET	Master of Education in Teaching
	Master of Educational Technology
	Master of Engineering Technology
	Master of Entertainment Technology
	Master of Environmental Toxicology
Met E	Metallurgical Engineer
METM	Master of Engineering and Technology Management
MF	Master of Finance
	Master of Forestry
MFA	Master of Financial Administration
	Master of Fine Arts
MFAM	Master in Food Animal Medicine
MFAS	Master of Fisheries and Aquatic Science
MFAW	Master of Fine Arts in Writing
MFC	Master of Forest Conservation
MFCS	Master of Family and Consumer Sciences
MFE	Master of Financial Economics
	Master of Financial Engineering
	Master of Forest Engineering
MFG	Master of Functional Genomics
MFHD	Master of Family and Human Development
MFM	Master of Financial Mathematics
MFMS	Masters in Food Microbiology and Safety
MFPE	Master of Food Process Engineering
MFR	Master of Forest Resources
MFRC	Master of Forest Resources and Conservation
MFS	Master of Food Science
	Master of Forensic Sciences
	Master of Forest Science
	Master of Forest Studies
	Master of French Studies
MFSA	Master of Forensic Sciences Administration
MFST	Master of Food Safety and Technology
MFT	Master of Family Therapy
	Master of Food Technology
MFWB	Master of Fishery and Wildlife Biology
MFWCB	Master of Fish, Wildlife and Conservation Biology
MFWS	Master of Fisheries and Wildlife Sciences
MFYCS	Master of Family, Youth and Community Sciences
MG	Master of Genetics
MGA	Master of Governmental Administration
MGD	Master of Graphic Design
MGE	Master of Gas Engineering
	Master of Geotechnical Engineering
MGEM	Master of Global Entrepreneurship and Management
MGH	Master of Geriatric Health
MGIS	Master of Geographic Information Science
	Master of Geographic Information Systems
MGM	Master of Global Management

MGP	Master of Gestion de Projet
MGPS	Master of Global Policy Studies
MGS	Master of Gerontological Studies
	Master of Global Studies
MH	Master of Humanities
MH Ed	Master of Health Education
MH Sc	Master of Health Sciences
MHA	Master of Health Administration
	Master of Healthcare Administration
	Master of Hospital Administration
	Master of Hospitality Administration
MHAD	Master of Health Administration
MHB	Master of Human Behavior
MHCA	Master of Health Care Administration
MHCI	Master of Human-Computer Interaction
MHCL	Master of Health Care Leadership
MHE	Master of Health Education
	Master of Human Ecology
MHE Ed	Master of Home Economics Education
MHEA	Masters of Higher Education Administration
MHHS	Master of Health and Human Services
MHI	Master of Health Informatics
	Master of Healthcare Innovation
MHIIM	Master of Health Informatics and Information Management
MHIS	Master of Health Information Systems
MHK	Master of Human Kinetics
MHL	Master of Hebrew Literature
MHMS	Master of Health Management Systems
MHP	Master of Health Physics
	Master of Heritage Preservation
	Master of Historic Preservation
MHPA	Master of Heath Policy and Administration
MHPE	Master of Health Professions Education
MHR	Master of Human Resources
MHRD	Master in Human Resource Development
MHRIR	Master of Human Resources and Industrial Relations
MHRLR	Master of Human Resources and Labor Relations
MHRM	Master of Human Resources Management
MHS	Master of Health Science
	Master of Health Sciences
	Master of Health Studies
	Master of Hispanic Studies
	Master of Human Services
	Master of Humanistic Studies
MHSA	Master of Health Services Administration
MHSM	Master of Health Sector Management
	Master of Health Systems Management
MI	Master of Instruction
MI Arch	Master of Interior Architecture
MI St	Master of Information Studies

MIA	Master of Interior Architecture
	Master of International Affairs
MIAA	Master of International Affairs and Administration
MIAM	Master of International Agribusiness Management
MIB	Master of International Business
MIBA	Master of International Business Administration
MICM	Master of International Construction Management
MID	Master of Industrial Design
	Master of Industrial Distribution
	Master of Interior Design
	Master of International Development
MIE	Master of Industrial Engineering
MIH	Master of Integrative Health
MIHTM	Master of International Hospitality and Tourism Management
MIJ	Master of International Journalism
MILR	Master of Industrial and Labor Relations
MiM	Master in Management
MIM	Master of Industrial Management
	Master of Information Management
	Master of International Management
MIMLAE	Master of International Management for Latin American Executives
MIMS	Master of Information Management and Systems
	Master of Integrated Manufacturing Systems
MIP	Master of Infrastructure Planning
	Master of Intellectual Property
MIPER	Master of International Political Economy of Resources
MIPP	Master of International Policy and Practice
	Master of International Public Policy
MIPS	Master of International Planning Studies
MIR	Master of Industrial Relations
	Master of International Relations
MIS	Master of Industrial Statistics
	Master of Information Science
	Master of Information Systems
	Master of Integrated Science
	Master of Interdisciplinary Studies
	Master of International Service
	Master of International Studies
MISE	Master of Industrial and Systems Engineering
MISKM	Master of Information Sciences and Knowledge Management
MISM	Master of Information Systems Management
MIT	Master in Teaching
	Master of Industrial Technology
	Master of Information Technology
	Master of Initial Teaching
	Master of International Trade
	Master of Internet Technology
MITA	Master of Information Technology Administration
MITM	Master of International Technology Management
MITO	Master of Industrial Technology and Operations

MJ	Master of Journalism
	Master of Jurisprudence
MJ Ed	Master of Jewish Education
MJA	Master of Justice Administration
MJM	Master of Justice Management
MJS	Master of Judicial Studies
	Master of Juridical Science
MKM	Master of Knowledge Management
ML	Master of Latin
ML Arch	Master of Landscape Architecture
MLA	Master of Landscape Architecture
	Master of Liberal Arts
MLAS	Master of Laboratory Animal Science
	Master of Liberal Arts and Sciences
MLAUD	Master of Landscape Architecture in Urban Development
MLD	Master of Leadership Development
	Master of Leadership Studies
MLE	Master of Applied Linguistics and Exegesis
MLER	Master of Labor and Employment Relations
MLERE	Master of Land Economics and Real Estate
MLHR	Master of Labor and Human Resources
MLI	Master of Legal Institutions
MLI Sc	Master of Library and Information Science
MLIS	Master of Library and Information Science
	Master of Library and Information Studies
MLM	Master of Library Media
MLOS	Masters in Leadership and Organizational Studies
MLRHR	Master of Labor Relations and Human Resources
MLS	Master of Leadership Studies
	Master of Legal Studies
	Master of Liberal Studies
	Master of Library Science
	Master of Life Sciences
MLSP	Master of Law and Social Policy
MLT	Master of Language Technologies
MM	Master of Management
	Master of Ministry
	Master of Missiology
	Master of Music
MM Ed	Master of Music Education
MM Sc	Master of Medical Science
MM St	Master of Museum Studies
MMA	Master of Marine Affairs
	Master of Media Arts
	Master of Musical Arts
MMAE	Master of Mechanical and Aerospace Engineering
MMAS	Master of Military Art and Science
MMB	Master of Microbial Biotechnology
MMBA	Managerial Master of Business Administration
MMC	Master of Manufacturing Competitiveness
	Master of Mass Communications
	Master of Music Conducting

MMCM	Master of Music in Church Music
MMCSS	Masters of Mathematical Computational and Statistical Sciences
MME	Master of Manufacturing Engineering
	Master of Mathematics Education
	Master of Mathematics for Educators
	Master of Mechanical Engineering
	Master of Medical Engineering
	Master of Mining Engineering
	Master of Music Education
MMF	Master of Mathematical Finance
MMFT	Master of Marriage and Family Therapy
MMG	Master of Management
MMH	Master of Management in Hospitality
	Master of Medical Humanities
MMI	Master of Management of Innovation
MMIS	Master of Management Information Systems
MMM	Master of Manufacturing Management
	Master of Marine Management
	Master of Medical Management
MMME	Master of Metallurgical and Materials Engineering
MMP	Master of Management Practice
	Master of Marine Policy
	Master of Medical Physics
	Master of Music Performance
MMPA	Master of Management and Professional Accounting
MMQM	Master of Manufacturing Quality Management
MMR	Master of Marketing Research
MMRM	Master of Marine Resources Management
MMS	Master of Management Science
	Master of Management Studies
	Master of Manufacturing Systems
	Master of Marine Studies
	Master of Materials Science
	Master of Medical Science
	Master of Medieval Studies
	Master of Modern Studies
MMSE	Master of Manufacturing Systems Engineering
MMSM	Master of Music in Sacred Music
MMT	Master in Marketing
	Master of Management
	Master of Music Teaching
	Master of Music Therapy
	Masters in Marketing Technology
MMus	Master of Music
MN	Master of Nursing
	Master of Nutrition
MN NP	Master of Nursing in Nurse Practitioner
MNA	Master of Nonprofit Administration
	Master of Nurse Anesthesia
MNAL	Master of Nonprofit Administration and Leadership
MNAS	Master of Natural and Applied Science
MNCM	Master of Network and Communications Management

MNE	Master of Network Engineering
	Master of Nuclear Engineering
MNL	Master in International Business for Latin America
MNM	Master of Nonprofit Management
MNO	Master of Nonprofit Organization
MNPL	Master of Not-for-Profit Leadership
MNPS	Master of New Professional Studies
MNpS	Master of Nonprofit Studies
MNR	Master of Natural Resources
MNRES	Master of Natural Resources and Environmental Studies
MNRM	Master of Natural Resource Management
MNRS	Master of Natural Resource Stewardship
MNS	Master of Natural Science
MO	Master of Oceanography
MOD	Master of Organizational Development
MOGS	Master of Oil and Gas Studies
MOH	Master of Occupational Health
MOL	Master of Organizational Leadership
MOM	Master of Oriental Medicine
MOR	Master of Operations Research
MOT	Master of Occupational Therapy
MP	Master of Physiology
	Master of Planning
MP Ac	Master of Professional Accountancy
MP Acc	Master of Professional Accountancy
	Master of Professional Accounting
	Master of Public Accounting
MP Aff	Master of Public Affairs
MP Th	Master of Pastoral Theology
MPA	Master of Physician Assistant
	Master of Professional Accountancy
	Master of Professional Accounting
	Master of Public Administration
	Master of Public Affairs
MPAC	Masters in Professional Accounting
MPAID	Master of Public Administration and International Development
MPAP	Master of Physician Assistant Practice
	Master of Public Affairs and Politics
MPAS	Master of Physician Assistant Science
	Master of Physician Assistant Studies
	Master of Public Art Studies
MPC	Master of Pastoral Counseling
	Master of Professional Communication
	Master of Professional Counseling
MPD	Master of Product Development
	Master of Public Diplomacy
MPDS	Master of Planning and Development Studies
MPE	Master of Physical Education
	Master of Power Engineering
MPEM	Master of Project Engineering and Management
MPH	Master of Public Health

MPHE	Master of Public Health Education	**MRS**	Master of Religious Studies
MPHTM	Master of Public Health and Tropical Medicine	**MRSc**	Master of Rehabilitation Science
MPIA	Master of Public and International Affairs	**MS**	Master of Science
	Master Program in International Affairs	**MS Cmp E**	Master of Science in Computer Engineering
MPM	Master of Pastoral Ministry	**MS Kin**	Master of Science in Kinesiology
	Master of Pest Management	**MS Acct**	Master of Science in Accounting
	Master of Policy Management	**MS Accy**	Master of Science in Accountancy
	Master of Practical Ministries	**MS Aero E**	Master of Science in Aerospace Engineering
	Master of Project Management	**MS Ag**	Master of Science in Agriculture
	Master of Public Management	**MS Arch**	Master of Science in Architecture
MPNA	Master of Public and Nonprofit Administration	**MS Arch St**	Master of Science in Architectural Studies
MPOD	Master of Positive Organizational Development	**MS Bio E**	Master of Science in Bioengineering
MPP	Master of Public Policy		Master of Science in Biomedical Engineering
MPPA	Master of Public Policy Administration	**MS Bm E**	Master of Science in Biomedical Engineering
	Master of Public Policy and Administration	**MS Ch E**	Master of Science in Chemical Engineering
MPPAL	Master of Public Policy, Administration and Law	**MS Chem**	Master of Science in Chemistry
MPPM	Master of Public and Private Management	**MS Cp E**	Master of Science in Computer Engineering
	Master of Public Policy and Management	**MS Eco**	Master of Science in Economics
MPPPM	Master of Plant Protection and Pest Management	**MS Econ**	Master of Science in Economics
MPPUP	Master of Public Policy and Urban Planning	**MS Ed**	Master of Science in Education
MPRTM	Master of Parks, Recreation, and Tourism Management	**MS El**	Master of Science in Educational Leadership and Administration
MPS	Master of Pastoral Studies	**MS En E**	Master of Science in Environmental Engineering
	Master of Perfusion Science	**MS Eng**	Master of Science in Engineering
	Master of Planning Studies	**MS Engr**	Master of Science in Engineering
	Master of Political Science	**MS Env E**	Master of Science in Environmental Engineering
	Master of Preservation Studies	**MS Exp Surg**	Master of Science in Experimental Surgery
	Master of Professional Studies	**MS Int A**	Master of Science in International Affairs
	Master of Public Service	**MS Mat E**	Master of Science in Materials Engineering
MPSA	Master of Public Service Administration	**MS Mat SE**	Master of Science in Material Science and Engineering
MPSRE	Master of Professional Studies in Real Estate	**MS Met E**	Master of Science in Metallurgical Engineering
MPT	Master of Pastoral Theology	**MS Metr**	Master of Science in Meteorology
	Master of Physical Therapy	**MS Mgt**	Master of Science in Management
MPVM	Master of Preventive Veterinary Medicine	**MS Min**	Master of Science in Mining
MPW	Master of Professional Writing	**MS Min E**	Master of Science in Mining Engineering
	Master of Public Works	**MS Mt E**	Master of Science in Materials Engineering
MQF	Master of Quantitative Finance	**MS Otal**	Master of Science in Otalrynology
MQM	Master of Quality Management	**MS Pet E**	Master of Science in Petroleum Engineering
MQS	Master of Quality Systems	**MS Phys**	Master of Science in Physics
MR	Master of Recreation	**MS Phys Op**	Master of Science in Physiological Optics
	Master of Retailing	**MS Poly**	Master of Science in Polymers
MRA	Master in Research Administration	**MS Psy**	Master of Science in Psychology
MRC	Master of Rehabilitation Counseling	**MS Pub P**	Master of Science in Public Policy
MRCP	Master of Regional and City Planning	**MS Sc**	Master of Science in Social Science
	Master of Regional and Community Planning	**MS Sp Ed**	Master of Science in Special Education
MRD	Master of Rural Development	**MS Stat**	Master of Science in Statistics
MRE	Master of Religious Education	**MS Surg**	Master of Science in Surgery
MRED	Master of Real Estate Development	**MS Tax**	Master of Science in Taxation
MREM	Master of Resource and Environmental Management		
MRLS	Master of Resources Law Studies		
MRM	Master of Resources Management		
MRP	Master of Regional Planning		

MS Tc E	Master of Science in Telecommunications Engineering
MS-R	Master of Science (Research)
MSA	Master of School Administration
	Master of Science Administration
	Master of Science in Accountancy
	Master of Science in Accounting
	Master of Science in Administration
	Master of Science in Aeronautics
	Master of Science in Agriculture
	Master of Science in Anesthesia
	Master of Science in Architecture
	Master of Science in Aviation
	Master of Sports Administration
MSA Phy	Master of Science in Applied Physics
MSAA	Master of Science in Astronautics and Aeronautics
MSAAE	Master of Science in Aeronautical and Astronautical Engineering
MSABE	Master of Science in Agricultural and Biological Engineering
MSAC	Master of Science in Acupuncture
MSACC	Master of Science in Accounting
MSaCS	Master of Science in Applied Computer Science
MSAE	Master of Science in Aeronautical Engineering
	Master of Science in Aerospace Engineering
	Master of Science in Applied Economics
	Master of Science in Applied Engineering
	Master of Science in Architectural Engineering
	Master of Science in Art Education
MSAL	Master of Sport Administration and Leadership
MSAM	Master of Science in Applied Mathematics
MSANR	Master of Science in Agriculture and Natural Resources Systems Management
MSAPM	Master of Security Analysis and Portfolio Management
MSAS	Master of Science in Applied Statistics
	Master of Science in Architectural Studies
MSAT	Master of Science in Accounting and Taxation
	Master of Science in Advanced Technology
	Master of Science in Athletic Training
MSAUS	Master of Science in Architectural Urban Studies
MSB	Master of Science in Bible
	Master of Science in Business
MSBA	Master of Science in Business Administration
MSBAE	Master of Science in Biological and Agricultural Engineering
	Master of Science in Biosystems and Agricultural Engineering
MSBC	Master of Science in Building Construction
MSBE	Master of Science in Biological Engineering
	Master of Science in Biomedical Engineering
MSBENG	Master of Science in Bioengineering
MSBIT	Master of Science in Business Information Technology
MSBM	Master of Sport Business Management

MSBME	Master of Science in Biomedical Engineering
MSBMS	Master of Science in Basic Medical Science
MSBS	Master of Science in Biomedical Sciences
MSC	Master of Science in Commerce
	Master of Science in Communication
	Master of Science in Computers
	Master of Science in Counseling
	Master of Science in Criminology
MSCA	Master of Science in Construction Administration
MSCC	Master of Science in Christian Counseling
	Master of Science in Community Counseling
MSCD	Master of Science in Communication Disorders
	Master of Science in Community Development
MSCE	Master of Science in Civil Engineering
	Master of Science in Clinical Epidemiology
	Master of Science in Computer Engineering
	Master of Science in Continuing Education
MSCEE	Master of Science in Civil and Environmental Engineering
MSCF	Master of Science in Computational Finance
MSChE	Master of Science in Chemical Engineering
MSCI	Master of Science in Clinical Investigation
	Master of Science in Curriculum and Instruction
MSCIS	Master of Science in Computer and Information Systems
	Master of Science in Computer Information Science
	Master of Science in Computer Information Systems
MSCIT	Master of Science in Computer Information Technology
MSCJ	Master of Science in Criminal Justice
MSCJA	Master of Science in Criminal Justice Administration
MSCJS	Master of Science in Crime and Justice Studies
MSCL	Master of Science in Collaborative Leadership
MSCLS	Master of Science in Clinical Laboratory Studies
MSCM	Master of Science in Conflict Management
	Master of Science in Construction Management
MScM	Master of Science in Management
MSCM	Master of Supply Chain Management
MSCP	Master of Science in Clinical Psychology
	Master of Science in Computer Engineering
	Master of Science in Counseling Psychology
MSCPE	Master of Science in Computer Engineering
MSCPharm	Master of Science in Pharmacy
MSCPI	Master in Strategic Planning for Critical Infrastructures
MSCRP	Master of Science in City and Regional Planning
	Master of Science in Community and Regional Planning
MSCS	Master of Science in Clinical Science
	Master of Science in Computer Science
MSCSD	Master of Science in Communication Sciences and Disorders

MSCSE	Master of Science in Computer Science and Engineering
MSCTE	Master of Science in Career and Technical Education
MSD	Master of Science in Dentistry Master of Science in Design Master of Science in Dietetics
MSDD	Master of Software Design and Development
MSDM	Master of Design Methods
MSDR	Master of Dispute Resolution
MSE	Master of Science Education Master of Science in Economics Master of Science in Education Master of Science in Engineering Master of Science in Engineering Management Master of Software Engineering Master of Special Education Master of Structural Engineering
MSECE	Master of Science in Electrical and Computer Engineering
MSED	Master of Sustainable Economic Development
MSEE	Master of Science in Electrical Engineering Master of Science in Environmental Engineering
MSEH	Master of Science in Environmental Health
MSEL	Master of Science in Educational Leadership Master of Science in Executive Leadership
MSEM	Master of Science in Engineering Management Master of Science in Engineering Mechanics Master of Science in Environmental Management
MSENE	Master of Science in Environmental Engineering
MSEO	Master of Science in Electro-Optics
MSEP	Master of Science in Economic Policy Master of Science in Engineering Physics
MSEPA	Masters of Science in Economics and Policy Analysis
MSES	Master of Science in Embedded Software Engineering Master of Science in Engineering Science Master of Science in Environmental Science Master of Science in Environmental Studies
MSESM	Master of Science in Engineering Science and Mechanics
MSET	Master of Science in Education in Educational Technology Master of Science in Engineering Technology
MSETM	Master of Science in Environmental Technology Management
MSEV	Master of Science in Environmental Engineering
MSEVH	Master of Science in Environmental Health and Safety
MSF	Master of Science in Finance Master of Science in Forestry
MSFA	Master of Science in Financial Analysis
MSFAM	Master of Science in Family Studies
MSFCS	Master of Science in Family and Consumer Science

MSFE	Master of Science in Financial Engineering
MSFOR	Master of Science in Forestry
MSFP	Master of Science in Financial Planning
MSFS	Master of Science in Financial Sciences Master of Science in Forensic Science
MSFSB	Master of Science in Financial Services and Banking
MSFT	Master of Science in Family Therapy
MSGC	Master of Science in Genetic Counseling
MSGL	Master of Science in Global Leadership
MSH	Master of Science in Health Master of Science in Hospice
MSHA	Master of Science in Health Administration
MSHCA	Master of Science in Health Care Administration
MSHCI	Master of Science in Human Computer Interaction
MSHCPM	Master of Science in Health Care Policy and Management
MSHE	Master of Science in Health Education
MSHES	Master of Science in Human Environmental Sciences
MSHFID	Master of Science in Human Factors in Information Design
MSHFS	Master of Science in Human Factors and Systems
MSHI	Master of Science in Health Informatics
MSHP	Master of Science in Health Professions Master of Science in Health Promotion
MSHR	Master of Science in Human Resources
MSHRL	Master of Science in Human Resource Leadership
MSHRM	Master of Science in Human Resource Management
MSHROD	Master of Science in Human Resources and Organizational Development
MSHS	Master of Science in Health Science Master of Science in Health Services Master of Science in Health Systems Master of Science in Homeland Security
MSHT	Master of Science in History of Technology
MSI	Master of Science in Instruction
MSIA	Master of Science in Industrial Administration Master of Science in Information Assurance and Computer Security
MSIB	Master of Science in International Business
MSIDM	Master of Science in Interior Design and Merchandising
MSIDT	Master of Science in Information Design and Technology
MSIE	Master of Science in Industrial Engineering Master of Science in International Economics
MSIEM	Master of Science in Information Engineering and Management
MSIID	Master of Science in Information and Instructional Design

MSIM	Master of Science in Information Management Master of Science in International Management Master of Science in Investment Management		**MSME**	Master of Science in Mathematics Education Master of Science in Mechanical Engineering
MSIMC	Master of Science in Integrated Marketing Communications		**MSMFE**	Master of Science in Manufacturing Engineering
MSIR	Master of Science in Industrial Relations		**MSMFT**	Master of Science in Marriage and Family Therapy
MSIS	Master of Science in Information Science Master of Science in Information Systems Master of Science in Interdisciplinary Studies		**MSMIS**	Master of Science in Management Information Systems
MSISE	Master of Science in Infrastructure Systems Engineering		**MSMIT**	Master of Science in Management and Information Technology
MSISM	Master of Science in Information Systems Management		**MSMM**	Master of Science in Manufacturing Management
			MSMO	Master of Science in Manufacturing Operations
MSISPM	Master of Science in Information Security Policy and Management		**MSMOT**	Master of Science in Management of Technology
			MSMS	Master of Science in Management Science Master of Science in Medical Sciences
MSIST	Master of Science in Information Systems Technology		**MSMSE**	Master of Science in Manufacturing Systems Engineering Master of Science in Material Science and Engineering Master of Science in Mathematics and Science Education
MSIT	Master of Science in Industrial Technology Master of Science in Information Technology Master of Science in Instructional Technology			
MSITM	Master of Science in Information Technology Management		**MSMT**	Master of Science in Management and Technology Master of Science in Medical Technology
MSJ	Master of Science in Journalism Master of Science in Jurisprudence		**MSMus**	Master of Sacred Music
MSJE	Master of Science in Jewish Education		**MSN**	Master of Science in Nursing
MSJFP	Master of Science in Juvenile Forensic Psychology		**MSN-R**	Master of Science in Nursing (Research)
			MSNA	Master of Science in Nurse Anesthesia
MSJJ	Master of Science in Juvenile Justice		**MSNE**	Master of Science in Nuclear Engineering
MSJPS	Master of Science in Justice and Public Safety		**MSNED**	Master of Science in Nurse Education
MSJS	Master of Science in Jewish Studies		**MSNM**	Master of Science in Nonprofit Management
MSK	Master of Science in Kinesiology		**MSNS**	Master of Science in Natural Science Master's of Science in Nutritional Science
MSKM	Master of Science in Knowledge Management			
MSL	Master of School Leadership Master of Science in Leadership Master of Science in Limnology Master of Strategic Leadership Master of Studies in Law		**MSOD**	Master of Science in Organizational Development
			MSOEE	Master of Science in Outdoor and Environmental Education
			MSOES	Master of Science in Occupational Ergonomics and Safety
MSLA	Master of Science in Landscape Architecture Master of Science in Legal Administration		**MSOH**	Master of Science in Occupational Health
MSLD	Master of Science in Land Development		**MSOL**	Master of Science in Organizational Leadership
MSLS	Master of Science in Legal Studies Master of Science in Library Science		**MSOM**	Master of Science in Operations Management Master of Science in Organization and Management Master of Science in Oriental Medicine
MSLSCM	Master of Science in Logistics and Supply Chain Management			
MSLT	Master of Second Language Teaching		**MSOR**	Master of Science in Operations Research
MSM	Master of Sacred Ministry Master of Sacred Music Master of School Mathematics Master of Science in Management Master of Science in Mathematics Master of Science in Organization Management Master of Security Management		**MSOT**	Master of Science in Occupational Technology Master of Science in Occupational Therapy
			MSP	Master of Science in Pharmacy Master of Science in Planning Master of Science in Psychology Master of Speech Pathology
MSMA	Master of Science in Marketing Analysis		**MSPA**	Master of Science in Physician Assistant Master of Science in Professional Accountancy
MSMAE	Master of Science in Materials Engineering			
MSMC	Master of Science in Mass Communications		**MSPAS**	Master of Science in Physician Assistant Studies

MSPC	Master of Science in Professional Communications
	Master of Science in Professional Counseling
MSPE	Master of Science in Petroleum Engineering
MSPG	Master of Science in Psychology
MSPH	Master of Science in Public Health
MSPHR	Master of Science in Pharmacy
MSPM	Master of Science in Professional Management
	Master of Science in Project Management
MSPNGE	Master of Science in Petroleum and Natural Gas Engineering
MSPS	Master of Science in Pharmaceutical Science
	Master of Science in Political Science
	Master of Science in Psychological Services
MSPT	Master of Science in Physical Therapy
MSpVM	Master of Specialized Veterinary Medicine
MSR	Master of Science in Radiology
	Master of Science in Reading
MSRA	Master of Science in Recreation Administration
MSRC	Master of Science in Resource Conservation
MSRE	Master of Science in Real Estate
	Master of Science in Religious Education
MSRED	Master of Science in Real Estate Development
MSRLS	Master of Science in Recreation and Leisure Studies
MSRMP	Master of Science in Radiological Medical Physics
MSRS	Master of Science in Rehabilitation Science
MSS	Master of Science in Software
	Master of Social Science
	Master of Social Services
	Master of Software Systems
	Master of Sports Science
	Master of Strategic Studies
MSSA	Master of Science in Social Administration
MSSCP	Master of Science in Science Content and Process
MSSE	Master of Science in Software Engineering
	Master of Science in Space Education
	Master of Science in Special Education
MSSEM	Master of Science in Systems and Engineering Management
MSSI	Master of Science in Security Informatics
	Master of Science in Strategic Intelligence
MSSL	Master of Science in Strategic Leadership
MSSLP	Master of Science in Speech-Language Pathology
MSSM	Master of Science in Sports Medicine
MSSP	Master of Science in Social Policy
MSSPA	Master of Science in Student Personnel Administration
MSSS	Master of Science in Safety Science
	Master of Science in Systems Science
MSST	Master of Science in Security Technologies
MSSW	Master of Science in Social Work

MSSWE	Master of Science in Software Engineering
MST	Master of Science and Technology
	Master of Science in Taxation
	Master of Science in Teaching
	Master of Science in Technology
	Master of Science in Telecommunications
	Master of Science Teaching
MSTC	Master of Science in Technical Communication
	Master of Science in Telecommunications
MSTCM	Master of Science in Traditional Chinese Medicine
MSTE	Master of Science in Telecommunications Engineering
	Master of Science in Transportation Engineering
MSTM	Master of Science in Technical Management
MSTOM	Master of Science in Traditional Oriental Medicine
MSUD	Master of Science in Urban Design
MSW	Master of Social Work
MSWE	Master of Software Engineering
MSWREE	Master of Science in Water Resources and Environmental Engineering
MSX	Master of Science in Exercise Science
MT	Master of Taxation
	Master of Teaching
	Master of Technology
	Master of Textiles
MTA	Master of Tax Accounting
	Master of Teaching Arts
	Master of Tourism Administration
MTCM	Master of Traditional Chinese Medicine
MTD	Master of Training and Development
MTE	Master in Educational Technology
	Master of Teacher Education
MTESOL	Master in Teaching English to Speakers of Other Languages
MTHM	Master of Tourism and Hospitality Management
MTI	Master of Information Technology
MTIM	Masters of Trust and Investment Management
MTL	Master of Talmudic Law
MTM	Master of Technology Management
	Master of Telecommunications Management
	Master of the Teaching of Mathematics
MTMH	Master of Tropical Medicine and Hygiene
MTOM	Master of Traditional Oriental Medicine
MTP	Master of Transpersonal Psychology
MTPC	Master of Technical and Professional Communication
MTS	Master of Theological Studies
MTSC	Master of Technical and Scientific Communication
MTSE	Master of Telecommunications and Software Engineering
MTT	Master in Technology Management
MTX	Master of Taxation
MUA	Master of Urban Affairs

MUD	Master of Urban Design	**PSM**	Professional Master of Science
MUEP	Master of Urban and Environmental Planning		Professional Science Master's
MUP	Master of Urban Planning	**Psy D**	Doctor of Psychology
MUPDD	Master of Urban Planning, Design, and	**Psy M**	Master of Psychology
	Development	**Psy S**	Specialist in Psychology
MUPP	Master of Urban Planning and Policy	**Psya D**	Doctor of Psychoanalysis
MUPRED	Masters of Urban Planning and Real Estate	**Re Dir**	Director of Recreation
	Development	**Rh D**	Doctor of Rehabilitation
MURP	Master of Urban and Regional Planning	**S Psy S**	Specialist in Psychological Services
	Master of Urban and Rural Planning	**Sc D**	Doctor of Science
MUS	Master of Urban Studies	**Sc M**	Master of Science
MVM	Master of VLSI and microelectronics	**SCCT**	Specialist in Community College Teaching
MVP	Master of Voice Pedagogy	**ScDPT**	Doctor of Physical Therapy Science
MVPH	Master of Veterinary Public Health	**SD**	Doctor of Science
MVS	Master of Visual Studies		Specialist Degree
MWC	Master of Wildlife Conservation	**SJD**	Doctor of Juridical Science
MWE	Master in Welding Engineering	**SLPD**	Doctor of Speech-Language Pathology
MWPS	Master of Wood and Paper Science	**SLS**	Specialist in Library Science
MWR	Master of Water Resources	**SM**	Master of Science
MWS	Master of Women's Studies	**SM Arch S**	Master of Science in Architectural Studies
MZS	Master of Zoological Science	**SM Vis S**	Master of Science in Visual Studies
Nav Arch	Naval Architecture	**SMBT**	Master of Science in Building Technology
Naval E	Naval Engineer	**SP**	Specialist Degree
ND	Doctor of Naturopathic Medicine	**Sp C**	Specialist in Counseling
NE	Nuclear Engineer	**Sp Ed**	Specialist in Education
Nuc E	Nuclear Engineer	**Sp LIS**	Specialist in Library and Information Science
OD	Doctor of Optometry	**SPA**	Specialist in Arts
OTD	Doctor of Occupational Therapy	**SPCM**	Special in Church Music
PBME	Professional Master of Biomedical Engineering	**Spec**	Specialist's Certificate
PD	Professional Diploma	**Spec M**	Specialist in Music
PGC	Post-Graduate Certificate	**SPEM**	Special in Educational Ministries
PGD	Postgraduate Diploma	**SPS**	School Psychology Specialist
Ph L	Licentiate of Philosophy	**Spt**	Specialist Degree
Pharm D	Doctor of Pharmacy	**SPTH**	Special in Theology
PhD	Doctor of Philosophy	**SSP**	Specialist in School Psychology
PhD Otal	Doctor of Philosophy in Otalrynology	**STB**	Bachelor of Sacred Theology
Phd Surg	Doctor of Philosophy in Surgery	**STD**	Doctor of Sacred Theology
PhDEE	Doctor of Philosophy in Electrical Engineering	**STL**	Licentiate of Sacred Theology
PM Sc	Professional Master of Science	**STM**	Master of Sacred Theology
PMBA	Professional Master of Business Administration	**TDPT**	Transitional Doctor of Physical Therapy
PMC	Post Master Certificate	**Th D**	Doctor of Theology
PMD	Post-Master's Diploma	**Th M**	Master of Theology
PMS	Professional Master of Science	**VMD**	Doctor of Veterinary Medicine
	Professional Master's Degree	**WEMBA**	Weekend Executive Master of Business
Post-Doctoral			Administration
MS	Post-Doctoral Master of Science	**XMA**	Executive Master of Arts
PPDPT	Postprofessional Doctor of Physical Therapy	**XMBA**	Executive Master of Business Administration

INDEXES

INDEXES

Close-Ups and Displays

Directories and Subject Areas

Following is an alphabetical listing of directories and subject areas. Also listed are cross-references for subject area names not used in the directory structure of the guides, for example, "Arabic (*see* Near and Middle Eastern Languages)."

Graduate Programs in the Humanities, Arts & Social Sciences

Addictions/Substance Abuse Counseling

Administration (*see* Arts Administration; Public Administration)

African-American Studies

African Languages and Literatures (*see* African Studies)

African Studies

Agribusiness (*see* Agricultural Economics and Agribusiness)

Agricultural Economics and Agribusiness

Alcohol Abuse Counseling (*see* Addictions/Substance Abuse Counseling)

American Indian/Native American Studies

American Studies

Anthropology

Applied Arts and Design—General

Applied Economics

Applied History (*see* Public History)

Applied Social Research

Arabic (*see* Near and Middle Eastern Languages)

Arab Studies (*see* Near and Middle Eastern Studies)

Archaeology

Architectural History

Architecture

Archives Administration (*see* Public History)

Area and Cultural Studies (*see* African-American Studies; African Studies; American Indian/Native American Studies; American Studies; Asian-American Studies; Asian Studies; Canadian Studies; Cultural Studies; East European and Russian Studies; Ethnic Studies; Folklore; Gender Studies; Hispanic Studies; Holocaust Studies; Jewish Studies; Latin American Studies; Near and Middle Eastern Studies; Northern Studies; Pacific Area/Pacific Rim Studies; Western European Studies; Women's Studies)

Art/Fine Arts

Art History

Arts Administration

Arts Journalism

Art Therapy

Asian-American Studies

Asian Languages

Asian Studies

Behavioral Sciences (*see* Psychology)

Bible Studies (*see* Religion; Theology)

Biological Anthropology

Black Studies (*see* African-American Studies)

Broadcasting (*see* Communication; Film, Television, and Video Production)

Broadcast Journalism

Building Science

Canadian Studies

Celtic Languages

Ceramics (*see* Art/Fine Arts)

Child and Family Studies

Child Development

Chinese

Chinese Studies (*see* Asian Languages; Asian Studies)

Christian Studies (*see* Missions and Missiology; Religion; Theology)

Cinema (*see* Film, Television, and Video Production)

City and Regional Planning (*see* Urban and Regional Planning)

Classical Languages and Literatures (*see* Classics)

Classics

Clinical Psychology

Clothing and Textiles

Cognitive Psychology (*see* Psychology—General; Cognitive Sciences)

Cognitive Sciences

Communication—General

Community Affairs (*see* Urban and Regional Planning; Urban Studies)

Community Planning (*see* Architecture; Environmental Design; Urban and Regional Planning; Urban Design; Urban Studies)

Community Psychology (*see* Social Psychology)

Comparative and Interdisciplinary Arts

Comparative Literature

Composition (*see* Music)

Computer Art and Design

Conflict Resolution and Mediation/Peace Studies

Consumer Economics

Corporate and Organizational Communication

Corrections (*see* Criminal Justice and Criminology)

Counseling (*see* Counseling Psychology; Pastoral Ministry and Counseling)

Counseling Psychology

Crafts (*see* Art/Fine Arts)

Creative Arts Therapies (*see* Art Therapy; Therapies—Dance, Drama, and Music)

Criminal Justice and Criminology

Cultural Studies

Dance

Decorative Arts

Demography and Population Studies

Design (*see* Applied Arts and Design; Architecture; Art/Fine Arts; Environmental Design; Graphic Design; Industrial Design; Interior Design; Textile Design; Urban Design)

Developmental Psychology

Diplomacy (*see* International Affairs)

Disability Studies

Drama Therapy (*see* Therapies—Dance, Drama, and Music)

Dramatic Arts (*see* Theater)

Drawing (*see* Art/Fine Arts)

Drug Abuse Counseling (*see* Addictions/Substance Abuse Counseling)

Drug and Alcohol Abuse Counseling (*see* Addictions/Substance Abuse Counseling)

East Asian Studies (*see* Asian Studies)

East European and Russian Studies

Economic Development

Economics

Educational Theater (*see* Theater; Therapies—Dance, Drama, and Music)

Emergency Management

English

Environmental Design

Ethics

Ethnic Studies

Ethnomusicology (*see* Music)

Experimental Psychology

Family and Consumer Sciences—General

Family Studies (*see* Child and Family Studies)

Family Therapy (*see* Child and Family Studies; Clinical Psychology; Counseling Psychology; Marriage and Family Therapy)

Filmmaking (*see* Film, Television, and Video Production)

Film Studies (*see* Film, Television, and Video Production)

Film, Television, and Video Production

Film, Television, and Video Theory and Criticism

Fine Arts (*see* Art/Fine Arts)

Folklore

Foreign Languages (*see* specific language)

Foreign Service (*see* International Affairs; International Development)

Forensic Psychology

Forensic Sciences

Forensics (*see* Speech and Interpersonal Communication)

French

Gender Studies

General Studies (*see* Liberal Studies)

Genetic Counseling

Geographic Information Systems

Geography

German

Gerontology

Graphic Design

Greek (*see* Classics)

Health Communication

Health Psychology

Hebrew (*see* Near and Middle Eastern Languages)

Hebrew Studies (*see* Jewish Studies)

Hispanic Studies

Historic Preservation

History

History of Art (*see* Art History)

History of Medicine

History of Science and Technology

Holocaust and Genocide Studies

Home Economics (*see* Family and Consumer Sciences—General)

Homeland Security

Household Economics, Sciences, and Management (*see* Family and Consumer Sciences—General)

Human Development

Humanities

Illustration

Industrial and Labor Relations

Industrial and Organizational Psychology

Industrial Design

Interdisciplinary Studies

Interior Design

International Affairs

International Development

International Economics

International Service (*see* International Affairs; International Development)

International Trade Policy

Internet and Interactive Multimedia

Interpersonal Communication (*see* Speech and Interpersonal Communication)

Interpretation (*see* Translation and Interpretation)

Islamic Studies (*see* Near and Middle Eastern Studies; Religion)

Italian

Japanese

Japanese Studies (*see* Asian Languages; Asian Studies; Japanese)

Jewelry (*see* Art/Fine Arts)

Jewish Studies

Journalism

Judaic Studies (*see* Jewish Studies; Religion)

Labor Relations (*see* Industrial and Labor Relations)

Landscape Architecture

Latin American Studies

Latin (*see* Classics)

Law Enforcement (*see* Criminal Justice and Criminology)

Liberal Studies

Lighting Design

Linguistics

Literature (*see* Classics; Comparative Literature; specific language)

Marriage and Family Therapy

Mass Communication

Media Studies

Medical Illustration

Medieval and Renaissance Studies

Metalsmithing (*see* Art/Fine Arts)

Middle Eastern Studies (*see* Near and Middle Eastern Studies)

Military and Defense Studies

Mineral Economics

Ministry (*see* Pastoral Ministry and Counseling; Theology)

Missions and Missiology

Motion Pictures (*see* Film, Television, and Video Production)

Museum Studies

Music

Musicology (*see* Music)

Music Therapy (*see* Therapies—Dance, Drama, and Music)

National Security

Native American Studies (*see* American Indian/Native American Studies)

Near and Middle Eastern Languages

Near and Middle Eastern Studies

Near Environment (*see* Family and Consumer Sciences)

Northern Studies

Organizational Psychology (*see* Industrial and Organizational Psychology)

Oriental Languages (*see* Asian Languages)

Oriental Studies (*see* Asian Studies)

Pacific Area/Pacific Rim Studies

Painting (*see* Art/Fine Arts)

Pastoral Ministry and Counseling

Philanthropic Studies

Philosophy

Photography

Playwriting (*see* Theater; Writing)

Policy Studies (*see* Public Policy)

Political Science

Population Studies (*see* Demography and Population Studies)

Portuguese

Printmaking (*see* Art/Fine Arts)

Product Design (*see* Industrial Design)

Psychoanalysis and Psychotherapy

Psychology—General

Public Administration

Public Affairs

Public History

Public Policy

Public Speaking (*see* Mass Communication; Rhetoric; Speech and Interpersonal Communication)

Publishing

Regional Planning (*see* Architecture; Urban and Regional Planning; Urban Design; Urban Studies)

Rehabilitation Counseling

Religion

Renaissance Studies (*see* Medieval and Renaissance Studies)

Rhetoric

Romance Languages

Romance Literatures (*see* Romance Languages)

Rural Planning and Studies

Rural Sociology

Russian

Scandinavian Languages

School Psychology

Sculpture (*see* Art/Fine Arts)

Security Administration (*see* Criminal Justice and Criminology)

Slavic Languages

Slavic Studies (*see* East European and Russian Studies; Slavic Languages)

Social Psychology

Social Sciences

Sociology

Southeast Asian Studies (*see* Asian Studies)

Soviet Studies (*see* East European and Russian Studies; Russian)

Spanish

Speech and Interpersonal Communication

Sport Psychology

Studio Art (*see* Art/Fine Arts)

Substance Abuse Counseling (*see* Addictions/Substance Abuse Counseling)

Survey Methodology

Sustainable Development

Technical Communication

Technical Writing

Telecommunications (*see* Film, Television, and Video Production)

Television (*see* Film, Television, and Video Production)

Textile Design

Textiles (*see* Clothing and Textiles; Textile Design)

Thanatology

Theater

Theater Arts (*see* Theater)

Theology

Therapies—Dance, Drama, and Music

Translation and Interpretation

Transpersonal and Humanistic Psychology

Urban and Regional Planning

Urban Design

Urban Planning (*see* Architecture; Urban and Regional Planning; Urban Design; Urban Studies)

Urban Studies

Video (*see* Film, Television, and Video Production)

Visual Arts (*see* Applied Arts and Design; Art/Fine Arts; Film, Television, and Video Production; Graphic Design; Illustration; Photography)

Western European Studies

Women's Studies

World Wide Web (*see* Internet and Interactive Multimedia)

Writing

Graduate Programs in the Biological Sciences

Anatomy

Animal Behavior

Bacteriology

Behavioral Sciences (*see* Biopsychology; Neuroscience; Zoology)

Biochemistry

Biological and Biomedical Sciences—General

Biological Chemistry (*see* Biochemistry)

Biological Oceanography (*see* Marine Biology)

Biophysics

Biopsychology

Botany

Breeding (*see* Botany; Plant Biology; Genetics)

Cancer Biology/Oncology

Cardiovascular Sciences

Cell Biology

Cellular Physiology (*see* Cell Biology; Physiology)

Computational Biology

Conservation (*see* Conservation Biology; Environmental Biology)

Conservation Biology

Crop Sciences (*see* Botany; Plant Biology)

Cytology (*see* Cell Biology)

Developmental Biology

Dietetics (*see* Nutrition)

Ecology

Embryology (*see* Developmental Biology)

Endocrinology (*see* Physiology)

Entomology

Environmental Biology

Evolutionary Biology

Foods (*see* Nutrition)

Genetics

Genomic Sciences

Histology (*see* Anatomy; Cell Biology)

Human Genetics

Immunology

Infectious Diseases

Laboratory Medicine (*see* Immunology; Microbiology; Pathology)

Life Sciences (*see* Biological and Biomedical Sciences)

Marine Biology

Medical Microbiology

Medical Sciences (*see* Biological and Biomedical Sciences)

Medical Science Training Programs (*see* Biological and Biomedical Sciences)

Microbiology

Molecular Biology

Molecular Biophysics

Molecular Genetics

Molecular Medicine

Molecular Pathogenesis

Molecular Pathology

Molecular Pharmacology

Molecular Physiology

Molecular Toxicology

Neural Sciences (*see* Biopsychology; Neurobiology; Neuroscience)

Neurobiology

Neuroendocrinology (*see* Biopsychology; Neurobiology; Neuroscience; Physiology)

Neuropharmacology (*see* Biopsychology; Neurobiology; Neuroscience; Pharmacology)

Neurophysiology (*see* Biopsychology; Neurobiology; Neuroscience; Physiology)

Neuroscience

Nutrition

Oncology (*see* Cancer Biology/Oncology)

Organismal Biology (*see* Biological and Biomedical Sciences; Zoology)

Parasitology

Pathobiology

Pathology

Pharmacology

Photobiology of Cells and Organelles (*see* Botany; Cell Biology; Plant Biology)

Physiological Optics (*see* Physiology)

Physiology

Plant Biology

Plant Molecular Biology

Plant Pathology

Plant Physiology

Pomology (*see* Botany; Plant Biology)

Psychobiology (*see* Biopsychology)

Psychopharmacology (*see* Biopsychology; Neuroscience; Pharmacology)

Radiation Biology

Reproductive Biology

Sociobiology (*see* Evolutionary Biology)

Structural Biology

Systems Biology

Teratology

Theoretical Biology (*see* Biological and Biomedical Sciences)

Therapeutics (*see* Pharmacology)

Toxicology

Translational Biology

Tropical Medicine (*see* Parasitology)

Virology

Wildlife Biology (*see* Zoology)

Zoology

Graduate Programs in the Physical Sciences, Mathematics, Agricultural Sciences, the Environment & Natural Resources

Acoustics

Agricultural Sciences

Agronomy and Soil Sciences

Analytical Chemistry

Animal Sciences

Applied Mathematics

Applied Physics

Applied Statistics

Aquaculture

Astronomy

Astrophysical Sciences (*see* Astrophysics; Atmospheric Sciences; Meteorology; Planetary and Space Sciences)

Astrophysics

Atmospheric Sciences

Biological Oceanography (*see* Marine Affairs; Marine Sciences; Oceanography)

Biomathematics

Biometry

Biostatistics

Chemical Physics

Chemistry

Computational Sciences

Condensed Matter Physics

Dairy Science (*see* Animal Sciences)

Earth Sciences (*see* Geosciences)

Environmental Management and Policy

Environmental Sciences

Environmental Studies (*see* Environmental Management and Policy)

Experimental Statistics (*see* Statistics)

Fish, Game, and Wildlife Management

Food Science and Technology

Forestry

General Science (*see* specific topics)

Geochemistry

Geodetic Sciences

Geological Engineering (*see* Geology)

Geological Sciences (*see* Geology)

Geology

Geophysical Fluid Dynamics (*see* Geophysics)

Geophysics

Geosciences

Horticulture

Hydrogeology

Hydrology

Inorganic Chemistry

Limnology

Marine Affairs

Marine Geology

Marine Sciences

Marine Studies (*see* Marine Affairs; Marine Geology; Marine Sciences; Oceanography)

Mathematical and Computational Finance

Mathematical Physics

Mathematical Statistics (*see* Applied Statistics; Statistics)

Mathematics

Meteorology

Mineralogy

Natural Resource Management (*see* Environmental Management and Policy; Natural Resources)

Natural Resources

Nuclear Physics (*see* Physics)

Ocean Engineering (*see* Marine Affairs; Marine Geology; Marine Sciences; Oceanography)

Oceanography

Optical Sciences

Optical Technologies (*see* Optical Sciences)

Optics (*see* Applied Physics; Optical Sciences; Physics)

Organic Chemistry

Paleontology

Paper Chemistry (*see* Chemistry)

Photonics

Physical Chemistry

Physics

Planetary and Space Sciences

Plant Sciences

Plasma Physics

Poultry Science (*see* Animal Sciences)

Radiological Physics (*see* Physics)

Range Management (*see* Range Science)

Range Science

Resource Management (*see* Environmental Management and Policy; Natural Resources)

Solid-Earth Sciences (*see* Geosciences)

Space Sciences (*see* Planetary and Space Sciences)

Statistics

Theoretical Chemistry

Theoretical Physics

Viticulture and Enology

Water Resources

Graduate Programs in Engineering & Applied Sciences

Aeronautical Engineering (*see* Aerospace/Aeronautical Engineering)

Aerospace/Aeronautical Engineering

Aerospace Studies (*see* Aerospace/Aeronautical Engineering)

Agricultural Engineering

Applied Mechanics (*see* Mechanics)

Applied Science and Technology

Architectural Engineering

Artificial Intelligence/Robotics

Astronautical Engineering (*see* Aerospace/Aeronautical Engineering)

Automotive Engineering

Aviation

Biochemical Engineering

Bioengineering

Bioinformatics

Biological Engineering (*see* Bioengineering)

Biomedical Engineering

Biosystems Engineering

Biotechnology

Ceramic Engineering (*see* Ceramic Sciences and Engineering)

Ceramic Sciences and Engineering

Ceramics (*see* Ceramic Sciences and Engineering)

Chemical Engineering

Civil Engineering

Computer and Information Systems Security

Computer Engineering

Computer Science

Computing Technology (*see* Computer Science)

Construction Engineering

Construction Management

Database Systems

Electrical Engineering

Electronic Materials

Electronics Engineering (*see* Electrical Engineering)

Energy and Power Engineering

Energy Management and Policy

Engineering and Applied Sciences

Engineering and Public Affairs (*see* Technology and Public Policy)

Engineering and Public Policy (*see* Energy Management and Policy; Technology and Public Policy)

Engineering Design

Engineering Management

Engineering Mechanics (*see* Mechanics)

Engineering Metallurgy (*see* Metallurgical Engineering and Metallurgy)

Engineering Physics

Environmental Design (*see* Environmental Engineering)

Environmental Engineering

Ergonomics and Human Factors

Financial Engineering

Fire Protection Engineering

Food Engineering (*see* Agricultural Engineering)

Game Design and Development

Gas Engineering (*see* Petroleum Engineering)

Geological Engineering

Geophysics Engineering (*see* Geological Engineering)

Geotechnical Engineering

Hazardous Materials Management

Health Informatics

Health Systems (*see* Safety Engineering; Systems Engineering)

Highway Engineering (*see* Transportation and Highway Engineering)

Human-Computer Interaction

Human Factors (*see* Ergonomics and Human Factors)

Hydraulics

Hydrology (*see* Water Resources Engineering)

Industrial Engineering (*see* Industrial/Management Engineering)

Industrial/Management Engineering

Information Science

Internet Engineering

Macromolecular Science (*see* Polymer Science and Engineering)

Management Engineering (*see* Engineering Management; Industrial/Management Engineering)

Management of Technology

Manufacturing Engineering

Marine Engineering (*see* Civil Engineering)

Materials Engineering

Materials Sciences

Mechanical Engineering

Mechanics

Medical Informatics

Metallurgical Engineering and Metallurgy

Metallurgy (*see* Metallurgical Engineering and Metallurgy)

Mineral/Mining Engineering

Nanotechnology

Nuclear Engineering

Ocean Engineering

Operations Research

Paper and Pulp Engineering

Petroleum Engineering

Pharmaceutical Engineering

Plastics Engineering (*see* Polymer Science and Engineering)

Polymer Science and Engineering

Public Policy (*see* Energy Management and Policy; Technology and Public Policy)

Reliability Engineering

Robotics (*see* Artificial Intelligence/Robotics)

Safety Engineering

Software Engineering

Solid-State Sciences (*see* Materials Sciences)

Structural Engineering

Surveying Science and Engineering

Systems Analysis (*see* Systems Engineering)

Systems Engineering

Systems Science

Technology and Public Policy

Telecommunications

Telecommunications Management

Textile Sciences and Engineering

Textiles (*see* Textile Sciences and Engineering)

Transportation and Highway Engineering

Urban Systems Engineering (*see* Systems Engineering)

Waste Management (*see* Hazardous Materials Management)

Water Resources Engineering

Graduate Programs in Business, Education, Health, Information Studies, Law & Social Work

Accounting

Actuarial Science

Acupuncture and Oriental Medicine

Acute Care/Critical Care Nursing

Administration (*see* Business Administration and Management; Educational Administration; Health Services Management and Hospital Administration; Industrial and Manufacturing Management; Nursing and Healthcare Administration; Pharmaceutical Administration; Sports Management)

Adult Education

Adult Nursing

Advanced Practice Nursing (*see* Family Nurse Practitioner Studies)

Advertising and Public Relations

Agricultural Education

Alcohol Abuse Counseling (*see* Counselor Education)

Allied Health—General

Allied Health Professions (*see* Clinical Laboratory Sciences/Medical Technology; Clinical Research; Communication Disorders; Dental Hygiene; Emergency Medical Services; Occupational Therapy; Physical Therapy; Physician Assistant Studies; Rehabilitation Sciences)

Allopathic Medicine

Anesthesiologist Assistant Studies

Art Education

Athletics Administration (*see* Kinesiology and Movement Studies)

Athletic Training and Sports Medicine

Audiology (*see* Communication Disorders)

Aviation Management

Banking (*see* Finance and Banking)

Bioethics

Business Administration and Management—General

Business Education

Child-Care Nursing (*see* Maternal and Child/Neonatal Nursing)

Chiropractic

Clinical Laboratory Sciences/Medical Technology

Clinical Research

Communication Disorders

Community College Education

Community Health

Community Health Nursing

Computer Education

Continuing Education (*see* Adult Education)

Counseling (*see* Counselor Education)

Counselor Education

Curriculum and Instruction

Dental and Oral Surgery (*see* Oral and Dental Sciences)

Dental Assistant Studies (*see* Dental Hygiene)

Dental Hygiene

Dental Services (*see* Dental Hygiene)

Dentistry

Developmental Education

Distance Education Development

Drug Abuse Counseling (*see* Counselor Education)

Early Childhood Education

Educational Leadership and Administration

Educational Measurement and Evaluation

Educational Media/Instructional Technology

Educational Policy

Educational Psychology

Education—General

Education of Students with Severe/Multiple Disabilities

Education of the Blind (*see* Special Education)

Education of the Deaf (*see* Special Education)

Education of the Gifted

Education of the Hearing Impaired (*see* Special Education)

Education of the Learning Disabled (*see* Special Education)

Education of the Mentally Retarded (*see* Special Education)

Education of the Physically Handicapped (*see* Special Education)

Education of the Visually Handicapped (*see* Special Education)

Electronic Commerce

Elementary Education

Emergency Medical Services

English as a Second Language

English Education

Entertainment Management

Entrepreneurship

Environmental and Occupational Health

Environmental Education

Environmental Law

Epidemiology

Exercise and Sports Science

Exercise Physiology (*see* Kinesiology and Movement Studies)

Facilities and Entertainment Management

Family Nurse Practitioner Studies

Finance and Banking

Food Services Management (*see* Hospitality Management)

Foreign Languages Education

Forensic Nursing

Foundations and Philosophy of Education

Gerontological Nursing

Guidance and Counseling (*see* Counselor Education)

Health Education

Health Law

Health Physics/Radiological Health

Health Promotion

Health-Related Professions (*see* individual allied health professions)

Health Services Management and Hospital Administration

Health Services Research

Hearing Sciences (*see* Communication Disorders)

Higher Education

HIV/AIDS Nursing

Home Economics Education

Hospice Nursing

Hospital Administration (*see* Health Services Management and Hospital Administration)

Hospitality Management

Hotel Management (*see* Travel and Tourism)

Human Resources Development

Human Resources Management

Human Services

Industrial Administration (*see* Industrial and Manufacturing Management)

Industrial and Manufacturing Management

Industrial Education (*see* Vocational and Technical Education)

Industrial Hygiene

Information Studies

Instructional Technology (*see* Educational Media/Instructional Technology)

Insurance

International and Comparative Education

International Business

International Commerce (*see* International Business)

International Economics (*see* International Business)

International Health

International Trade (*see* International Business)

Investment and Securities (*see* Business Administration and Management; Finance and Banking; Investment Management)

Investment Management

Junior College Education (*see* Community College Education)

Kinesiology and Movement Studies

Laboratory Medicine (*see* Clinical Laboratory Sciences/Medical Technology)

Law

Legal and Justice Studies

Leisure Services (*see* Recreation and Park Management)

Leisure Studies

Library Science

Logistics

Management (*see* Business Administration and Management)

Management Information Systems

Management Strategy and Policy

Marketing

Marketing Research

Maternal and Child Health

Maternal and Child/Neonatal Nursing

Mathematics Education

Medical Imaging

Medical Nursing (*see* Medical/Surgical Nursing)

Medical Physics

Medical/Surgical Nursing

Medical Technology (*see* Clinical Laboratory Sciences/Medical Technology)

Medicinal and Pharmaceutical Chemistry

Medicinal Chemistry (*see* Medicinal and Pharmaceutical Chemistry)

Medicine (*see* Allopathic Medicine; Naturopathic Medicine; Osteopathic Medicine; Podiatric Medicine)

Middle School Education

Midwifery (*see* Nurse Midwifery)

Movement Studies (*see* Kinesiology and Movement Studies)

Multilingual and Multicultural Education

Museum Education

Music Education

Naturopathic Medicine

Nonprofit Management

Nuclear Medical Technology (*see* Clinical Laboratory Sciences/ Medical Technology)

Nurse Anesthesia

Nurse Midwifery

Nurse Practitioner Studies (*see* Family Nurse Practitioner Studies)

Nursery School Education (*see* Early Childhood Education)

Nursing Administration (*see* Nursing and Healthcare Administration)

Nursing and Healthcare Administration

Nursing Education

Nursing—General

Nursing Informatics

Occupational Education (*see* Vocational and Technical Education)

Occupational Health (*see* Environmental and Occupational Health; Occupational Health Nursing)

Occupational Health Nursing

Occupational Therapy

Oncology Nursing

Optometry

Oral and Dental Sciences

Oral Biology (*see* Oral and Dental Sciences)

Oral Pathology (*see* Oral and Dental Sciences)

Organizational Behavior

Organizational Management

Oriental Medicine and Acupuncture (*see* Acupuncture and Oriental Medicine)

Orthodontics (*see* Oral and Dental Sciences)

Osteopathic Medicine

Parks Administration (*see* Recreation and Park Management)

Pediatric Nursing

Pedontics (*see* Oral and Dental Sciences)

Perfusion

Personnel (*see* Human Resources Development; Human Resources Management; Organizational Behavior; Organizational Management; Student Affairs)

Pharmaceutical Administration

Pharmaceutical Chemistry (*see* Medicinal and Pharmaceutical Chemistry)

Pharmaceutical Sciences

Pharmacy

Philosophy of Education (*see* Foundations and Philosophy of Education)

Physical Education

Physical Therapy

Physician Assistant Studies

Physiological Optics (*see* Vision Sciences)

Podiatric Medicine

Preventive Medicine (*see* Community Health and Public Health)

Project Management

Psychiatric Nursing

Public Health—General

Public Health Nursing (*see* Community Health Nursing)

Public Relations (*see* Advertising and Public Relations)

Quality Management

Quantitative Analysis

Radiological Health (*see* Health Physics/Radiological Health)

Reading Education

Real Estate

Recreation and Park Management

Recreation Therapy (*see* Recreation and Park Management)

Rehabilitation Sciences

Rehabilitation Therapy (*see* Physical Therapy)

Religious Education

Remedial Education (*see* Special Education)

Restaurant Administration (*see* Hospitality Management)

School Nursing

Science Education

Secondary Education

Social Sciences Education

Social Studies Education (*see* Social Sciences Education)

Social Work

Special Education

Speech-Language Pathology and Audiology (*see* Communication Disorders)

Sports Management

Sports Medicine (*see* Athletic Training and Sports Medicine)

Sports Psychology and Sociology (*see* Kinesiology and Movement Studies)

Student Affairs

Substance Abuse Counseling (*see* Counselor Education)

Supply Chain Management

Surgical Nursing (*see* Medical/Surgical Nursing)

Sustainability Management

Systems Management (*see* Management Information Systems)

Taxation

Teacher Education (*see* specific subject areas)

Teaching English as a Second Language (*see* English as a Second Language)

Technical Education (*see* Vocational and Technical Education)

Teratology (*see* Environmental and Occupational Health)

Therapeutics (*see* Pharmaceutical Sciences; Pharmacy)

Transcultural Nursing

Transportation Management

Travel and Tourism

Urban Education

Veterinary Medicine

Veterinary Sciences

Vision Sciences

Vocational and Technical Education

Vocational Counseling (*see* Counselor Education)

Women's Health Nursing

Directories and Subject Areas in This Book

NOTES

NOTES

NOTES

NOTES

NOTES

NOTES

NOTES

NOTES

NOTES

NOTES